MW01492892

PART 4

Student Voices Influencing NSA

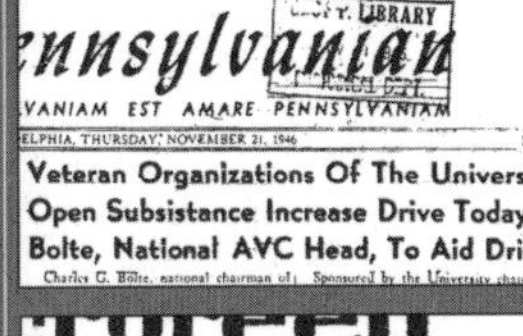
ennsylvanian
VANIAM EST AMARE PENNSYLVANIAM
Veteran Organizations Of The University Open Subsistance Increase Drive Today; Bolte, National AVC Head, To Aid Drive

Agnes Scott N
AGNES SCOTT COLLEGE, WED. FEB. 12, 1947
Christianity Fundamentals Topic of Religious Week
Dr. Miller Leads Dorm Forums; Chapel Topics Student-Suggested

rgreen
ON STATE COLLEGE, PULLMAN, WASHINGTON, FRIDAY, APRIL 12, 1946
REED COLLEGE CONFERENCE FAVORS WORLD GOVERNMENT
Delegates From Northwest Campuses Vote For

and GOLD
NT NEWSPAPER
Students of the University of Colorado
New ASUC Constitution Ratified Despite Greek Combine Opposition
ASUC Commission Holds Final Meeting Of Quarter

NSA's Regions: Creating Intercollegiate Networks

825 Section 1. New England

Alice Brandeis (Gilbert) Popkin, Radcliffe College, p. 825, New England Chair, 1947-48
Curtis Farrar, Yale University, p. 829, 1946 World Student Congress
Shirley Neizer Tyler, Simmons College, p. 832, NSA Exec. Secy., 1950-51
Michael Iovenko, Dartmouth College, p. 841, New England Chair, 1950-51

845 Section 2. Metropolitan New York

Eugene G. Schwartz, City College of N.Y., p. 847, NSA Vice-President, 1948-49
Sheldon Steinhauser, Long Island U., p. 852, Met. NY Chair, 1949-50
Gladys Chang Hardy-Brazil, Sarah Lawrence College, p. 859, Student Body Pres., 1948-49
Walter Wallace, Columbia University, p. 865, Met. NY Chair, 1947-48

867 Section 3. New York State & New Jersey

Leeland Jones, University of Buffalo, p. 875, NSA Treasurer 1947-48
Frank Dowd, U. of Rochester, p. 885, NY State Chair, 1947-48
Thomas Garrity, St. Peter's College, p. 892, New Jersey Chair, 1948-49
John Yewell, Rutgers University, p. 894, New Jersey Chair, 1947-48

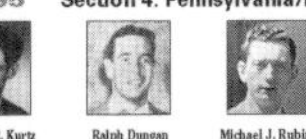

895 Section 4. Pennsylvania/Mid-Atlantic

Kenneth R. Kurtz, Swarthmore College, p. 902, Pennsylvania Chair, 1950-51
Ralph Dungan, St. Joseph's College, p. 909, NSA Vice President, 1947-48
Michael J. Rubino, Catholic University, p. 920, Mason-Dixon Chair., 1948-49
Joseph W. Zebley, U. of Baltimore, p. 921, MD-DE-DC Chair, 1947-48

913 Section 5. The Midwest

Joy Newberger Picus, University of Wisconsin, p. 927, Delegate, 1950 NSA Congress
Richard J. Medalie, Carleton College, p. 935, NSA Vice President, 1949-50
Mary K. Perkins, O.P., Mundelein College, p. 943, NSA Staff Associate, 1949-50
Tesse Hartigan Donnelley, Fontbonne College, p. 951, Missouri Chair, 1949-50

941 Section 6. The South

Richard J. Murphy, U. of North Carolina, p. 973, NSA President, 1951-52
Galen Martin, Berea College, p. 983, KY-TN Chair, 1950-51
John Hunsinger, Georgia Tech, p. 989, NSA delegate, 1951-52
Barefoot Sanders, University of Texas, p. 995, Student Body Pres., 1947

973 Section 7. The Rocky Mountains & Southwest

Leonard Perlmutter, U. of Colorado p. 999, Rocky Mt. Chair, 1947-48
Luis D. Rovira, U. of Colorado, p. 1006, Student Body Pres., 1947-48
Roy Romer, U. of Colorado, p. 1007, Rocky Mt. Chair, 1950-51
Donald A. Martinez, New Mexico Highlands C., p. 1012

989 Section 8. California

Milton Dobkin, U. of Southern Calif., p. 1025, NSA So. CA Chair, 1947-48
Tom Suzuki, L.A. City College, p. 1031, Student Body Pres., 1947-48
Nancy Lee Roth Arnheim, UCLA, p. 1038, NSA Voc Guid Com Chair. '47-48
Sally Holt Smit, U.C. Berkeley, p. 1044, NSA Reg'l. Secy 1947-48

1014 Section 9. The Northwest

William H. Gates, Sr., U. of Washington, p. 1053, Pacific NW Chair, 1949-50
Helen Knudsen Pulsifer, U. of Washington, p. 1053, Pacific NW Secy. 1949-50
Joan Long Lynch, Marylhurst College, p. 1064, Pacific NW Chair, 1951-52
Marvin Jagnels, University of Idaho, p. 1069, Eastern Dist. V.P., 1950-51

Epilogue: What Happened Later

Nixon Urges Students To Take Greater Role In National Affairs

National Student News

Sixty National Unions Join In Program Of International Student Cooperation

USNSA Urges Support Of Integration Efforts In Little Rock Arkansas

SURVIVING ITS BUDGET CRISIS AND THE DRAFT, NSA's move to Philadelphia provided stability and access to support enabling its leaders to develop program and service continuity. The Cold War, McCarthyism, the civil rights movement and internal politics provided major challenges. (Top left: NSA Report to the 11th National Student Congress. Right, above: NSA's *National Student News*, 11/1/57. Below: USNSA Annual Report, 1959-60.)

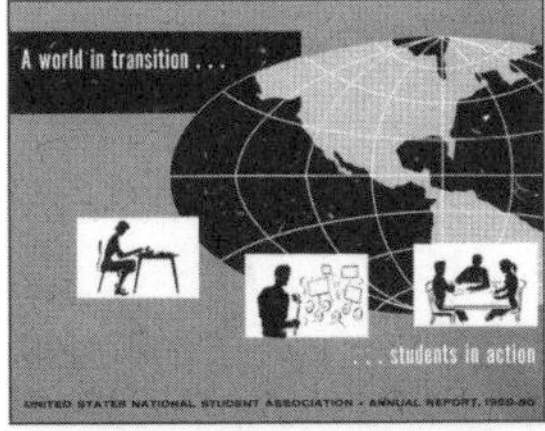

THE NSA CHARTER

APPENDIX

Framing a Comprehensive Vision

CONTENTS

Harvard Crimson
Student Council Backs New N.S.A. Constitution

THE HAWK
Student Council Unanimously Approves NSA Constitution

The Technique
Council Votes to Ratify U.S.N.S.A. Constitution

The Caellian
Assembly Adopts NSA Constitution at First Meeting of the Year

The student leaders who founded the Association were inspired by their traditions and their historic time and place. They expressed that inspiration in the preamble to the NSA Constitution, which begins,

> We, the students of the United States of America desiring to maintain academic freedom and student rights, to stimulate and improve democratic student governments . . .

and concludes,

> . . . and to preserve the interests and integrity of the government and Constitution of the United States of America, do hereby establish this Constitution of the United States National Student Association.

The words in between are a spirited commitment to inclusiveness, international understanding, and the betterment of student life and circumstance.

Pursuing America's Vision

The original NSA Constitution, its supporting policy statements and an overview of its form of organization follow in this Appendix.

In the spirit of that Constitution and its vision, and with the limited financial resources at hand, the founders launched the United States National Student Association.

CONSTITUTIONAL CONVENTION, AUG.30-SEPT.7, 1947 From top: Wisconsin Union; outdoor assem-bly of delegates: Jim Smith (U. of Texas), National Continuations Committee president, addresses the opening session. (Wharton)

RATIFYING THE NSA CONSTITUTION, which included its preamble and Student Bill of Rights, was the action required for affiliation. Above, from top: *Harvard Crimson*, 9/30/47; *The Hawk*, 12/19/47, St. Joseph's College, PA; *The Technique*, 2/14/48, Georgia Tech; *The Caellian*, 10/23/47, New Jersey College for Women.

AMERICAN STUDENTS ORGANIZE

Founding the National Student Association after World War II

An Anthology and Sourcebook

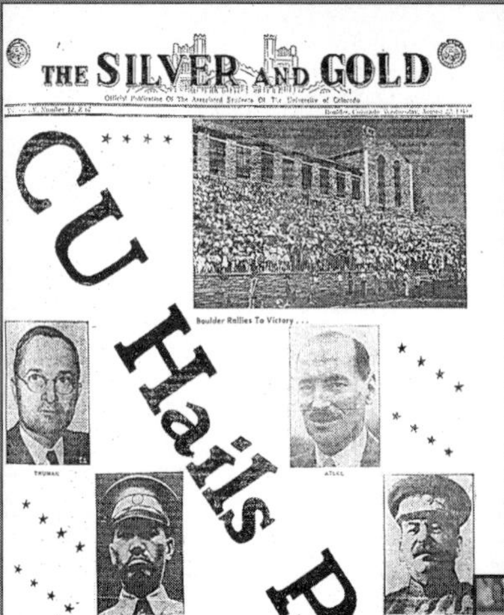

THE SILVER AND GOLD

CU Hails Peace

Boulder Rallies To Victory . . .

CU Holds V-J Convocation . . .

WAR'S END

College newspapers across America celebrate the peace.

(U. of Colorado, *Silver and Gold* 8/22/45)

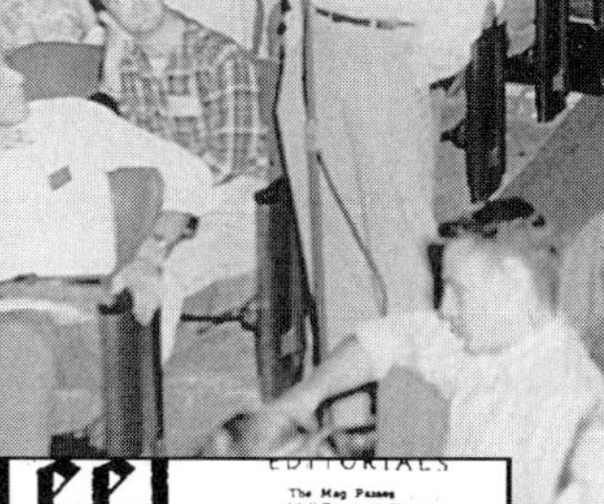

A NEW BEGINNING

Jim Smith, U. of Texas, head of organizing group, addresses the NSA Constitutional Convention at the U. of Wisconsin. (8/47)

Barnard Bulletin

Vol. LII, No. 9 NEW YORK, THURSDAY, OCTOBER 30, 1947

National Student Association Fosters Campus Activities, Foreign Study Plans, Guards Rights

College Plans Special Implementation Committee
TO RATIFY CONSTITUTION, NAME DELEGATES TO NATIONAL CONGRESSES

Women's Colleges Hold Conference

Barnard Plans Activities To Further Aims of NSA
WORK WITH INTERNATIONAL

Daily Tar Heel

CHAPEL HILL, N. C., FRIDAY, MAY 28, 1948

UNC Joins National Students Association

SDA Polls Grads On Negro Question

Davenport Appointed Attorney-General

New Official To Preside Over Council

Amendment Passed To Force Delegation To Ballot as Unit

593 Are Polled; 70 Per Cent Favor Negro Students

THE FORDHAM RAM

NEW YORK, N. Y., MARCH 12, 1948

Elgart to Man Bandstand '49ers' Springtime Prom

Council O.K.'s NSA Constitution

Gallagher's Backing Results in Support For Student Group

Clothing Collection Drive Extended

Kelly Green, Maroon to Mingle In St. Paddy's Day Parade

ORGANIZE

Colleges act on affiliation and newspapers headline issues confronting the new organization.

(Barnard College, *Barnard Bulletin*, 10/30/47; U. of North Carolina, *Daily Tar Heel*, 5/28/48; Fordham University, *The Fordham Ram*, 3/12/48)

Dedication

This book is a work of affectionate celebration.

It is dedicated to the young men and women on U.S. college and university campuses in the years immediately following World War II and to the administrators and faculty who lent them support, who believed that students should participate in self-government, and who joined in efforts to improve American life and to secure world peace.

The foundation of this book is a series of essays written some fifty years later by some of the student leaders of that time. They provide a history of how students, inspired by America's vision, engaged in the quest for a just society and a better world. And how, in so doing, they strengthened their own student governments and the democratic process that protects their liberties.

This book is dedicated also to those of our number who have passed from active life to fond memory.

Finally, those collaborating on this book wish to acknowledge that the book is due in overwhelming measure to the dedicated effort and unflagging vision over nine years of one person, its editor, Eugene G. Schwartz.

❦

"A world where there are differences without hate. . . . This is our desire."
--The USNSA Creed, 1954 (p. 1091)

Contributing Editors and Anthology Project Committee

Sylvia A. Bacon
Vassar College, NY '52
Judge (Ret.), Superior Court, District of Columbia. Judge, Office of Compliance, Distinguished Lecturer, CUA Law School
NSA Vice President, Student Affairs, 1951-52.

Pat Wohlgemuth Blair (Deceased)
Wellesley College, MA '49
International development consultant, writer and editor, Washington, DC.
NSA International Office, Cambridge, MA, 1947-48.

William T. Dentzer, Jr.
Muskingum College, OH '51
Former Chmn. and CEO, The Depository Trust Co.
N.Y. State Superintendent of Banks. Director, USAID Mission to Peru.
NSA President, 1951-52. Asst. Secretary, Cosec, Holland, 1952-53.

Janis Tremper Dowd
Rockford College, IL '48
Former Director, Public Affairs and Community Services, Monroe Community College, NY.
Delegate, Cambridge, England, ISS Conference, 1946. NSA Secretary, 1947-48.

Henry M. Halsted III
Williams College, MA '48
V.P., The Johnson Foundation. V.P., Kansas City Regional Council for Higher Education. V.P., Associated Colleges of the Midwest.
Delegate, NSA Constitutional Convention, 1947.

Richard G. Heggie
University of California, Berkeley '44 & '50
Former Regent, Univ. of Calif. Executive Director, World Affairs Council of Northern CA. Asia Foundation executive.
Vice President, Student Affairs, 1948-49.

Norman L. Holmes
University of Wisconsin '49
Attorney, Washington, DC. Former Counsel, House Banking and Currency Comm. Asst. to V.P. Hubert Humphrey. Gen. Counsel, U.S. AID.
Chair, NSA Wisconsin Region, 1948-49.

Gordon Klopf
Counselor, Student Activities, University of Wisconsin
Member and former Chair, Executive Committee, UN NGOs, New York City. Former Dean and Provost, Bank Street College.
Chairman, NSA National Advisory Council, 1947-50.

Joan Long Lynch
Marylhurst College, OR '52
Homemaker. Former high school counselor, Los Angeles.
NSA Staff Associate, 1950-51. Chair, Pacific Northwest Region, 1951-52.

Martin M. McLaughlin
University of Notre Dame, IN '48
Former V.P., Overseas Development Council. Former Consultant, U.S. Catholic Conference; Center of Concern.
U.S. Delegation, World Student Congress, Prague, 1946.

Robert F. Meagher
City College of New York '49
Attorney, Consultant, Somerville, Mass. Retired Professor of International Law, Fletcher School, Tufts University.
Executive Sec'y., NSA Met. NY Region, 1947-48.

Richard J. Medalie
Carleton College, MN, 1947-49, University of Minnesota '52
Attorney, Wash., DC. Chair Emeritus, Appleseed Foundation.
NSA Vice President, Educational Affairs, 1949-50.

Richard Murphy
University of North Carolina '51
Director of Gov't. Affairs, Unisys, Wash., DC. Assistant Postmaster General. Former V.P., Warner Cable Corp. Director, 1972 Democratic Convention.
NSA President, 1952-53.

Allan W. Ostar
Pennsylvania State University '48
Consultant, Washington, DC.
President Emeritus, American Association of State Colleges and Universities.
NSA Public Relations Director, 1948-49.

Alice Brandeis (Gilbert) Popkin
Radcliffe College '49
Attorney, Chatham, MA. Former Associate Administrator of International Activities, U.S. Environmental Protection Agency.
Chair, NSA Northern New England Region, 1948-49.

Helen Jean Rogers Secondari (Deceased)
Mundelein College, 1947-48. Catholic University '51
Former ABC TV Network documentary producer.
NSA Secretary-Treasurer, 1948-49.

Ralph Lee Smith
Swarthmore College, PA '51
Author. Marketing Consultant, The Connection Newspapers
NSA Public Relations Director, 1949-50.

Robert S. Smith
Yale University '47
Consultant, Wash., DC. Former Ambassador, Ivory Coast. U.S. Delegation to UNESCO. Deputy Assistant Secretary of State.
NSA Vice President, International Affairs, 1947-48.

Royal J. Voegeli (Deceased)
University of Wisconsin '48
Attorney, Washington, DC.
Delegate, Chicago Student Conference, 1946. University of Wisconsin Student Body President, 1947. NSA Observer, IUS and Europe, 1948.

William B. Welsh
Berea College, KY '49
Public Policy Consultant, Falls Church, VA. Admin. Asst., V.P. Hubert Humphrey. Asst. Sec'y., Depts. of HHS, HUD. Legislative Director, AFSCME, AFL-CIO. Admin. Asst., U.S. Senator Philip A. Hart.
NSA President, 1947-48.

Clifton R. Wharton, Jr.
Harvard University '47
Former Deputy Secretary of State. Chairman and CEO, TIAA-CREF. Chancellor, State University of New York. President, Michigan State University.
Secretary, NSO National Continuations Committee, 1946-47.

Mildred Kiefer Wurf
University of California, Berkeley '48
Director of Public Policy, Girls Incorporated. Founding Coordinator, National Collaboration for Youth. President's Council on Youth Opportunities.
Chair, California-Nevada-Hawaii Region, 1947. NSA Asst. Treasurer, 1947-48.

* * *

Eugene G. Schwartz, *Editorial Director and Publisher*
City College of New York '51
President, Consortium House, Publishing Consultants, Malden-on-Hudson, NY. Editor-at-Large, *ForeWord* Magazine.
NSA Vice President, Educational Affairs, 1948-49. NSA Observer, World Student Congress, Prague, 1950.

* * *

Editorial Committee
Sylvia A. Bacon, William T. Dentzer, Jr., Janis Tremper Dowd, Henry M. Halsted III, Richard G. Heggie, Joan Long Lynch, Richard J. Medalie, Allan W. Ostar, Eugene G. Schwartz, Ralph Lee Smith, William B. Welsh, Mildred Kiefer Wurf

Research Contributors
Pat Wohlgemuth Blair, Henry M. Halsted III, Royal J. Voegeli

Finance Committee
Sylvia A. Bacon, William T. Dentzer, Jr., Janis Tremper Dowd, Stanley R. Greenfield, Richard Murphy, Allan W. Ostar, Eveleyn Jones Rich, Clifton Wharton, Jr., Mildred Kiefer Wurf. ***Counsel:*** Richard J. Medalie

AMERICAN STUDENTS ORGANIZE

Founding the National Student Association after World War II

An Anthology and Sourcebook

Eugene G. Schwartz
Editor

Produced by the USNSA Anthology Project

Published by the American Council on Education/Praeger Publishers

Published by the American Council on Education/Praeger Publishers.
Praeger Publishers is an imprint of Greenwood Publishing Group, Inc.

Produced by the USNSA Anthology Project Committee with the cooperation of the USSA Foundation and the NSA Anthology Charitable Trust as fiduciaries. Special thanks to the State Historical Society of Wisconsin and the Hoover Institution for providing generous access to their USNSA archives, and special thanks also for unstinting assistance from the archivists, directors of special collections, reference librarians and library assistants in the colleges and universities listed on pages 1131-1133.

The funding for this project was raised privately by the USNSA Anthology Project, whose generous donors are listed on the last page of this volume, and include the major financial assistance of the following individuals and foundations:
Carnegie Corporation of New York, Charles E. Culpepper Foundation,
Janis Tremper Dowd and Daan Zwick, Bill and Melinda Gates Foundation,
W.K. Kellogg Foundation, Rockefeller Brothers Fund, Bernard and Irene Schwartz Foundation.
The statements and views expressed in this book are those of the authors only.

ISBN 0-275-99100-8

Editor and Publisher: Eugene G. Schwartz
Manuscript acquisition, original overviews and text, album assembly
and director of production: Eugene G. Schwartz
Editorial development consultant: Ralph Lee Smith
Manuscript and content consultants: William T. Dentzer, Jr., Henry Halsted
Manuscript consultant and production editor: Joan Kennedy Taylor
Consulting designer: Don Wright, Broadview Media, Woodstock, New York
Graphics and editorial production coordinator: Shaun Johnston
Permissions and photo acquisition: Gwendolyn Tapper, Shaun Johnston
Index: Kay Schlembach, IndexPro, The Woodlands, Texas
Page production and pre-press by Publishing Synthesis, Ltd., New York City
Director: Otto Barz
Production Manager: George Ernsberger
Copy Editor (first pass, final pass): Nicole Balant
Page Production (Quark): Deborah Constantine
Proofreader: Linda Robinson
Manufactured in the United States of America
by Malloy, Inc., Ann Arbor, Michigan

Set in Adobe Garamond, American Typewriter, Cheltenham Bold, Myriad,
Universe and Universe Extra Bold Extended

PREFACE

They were called the "Greatest Generation" by Tom Brokaw in his best-selling book of that title. Surely part of the greatness came from ordinary women and men rising to meet the challenges in extraordinary times. So it was at the creation of the National Student Association.

For America's college campuses the times were challenging as well. Enrollments were exploding. Returning veterans first questioned and then rejected many of the conventions and constraints of the past. The concept of student self-government was energized and coming alive. One common thread was an awakening of interest in things international. In the early '50s at Shepherd College I joined a handful of other students to form the International Relations Club. We managed to send a letter to all incoming freshmen inviting them to join. Much to our amazement, nearly half said yes. Overnight we had the largest and most engaged student organization on campus.

The founding of the National Student Association was part and parcel of that same era. *American Students Organize* gives voice to many of the ". . . young men and women on U.S. college and university campuses in the years immediately following World War II and to the administrators and faculty who lent them support, who believed that students should participate in self-government, and who joined in efforts to improve American life and to secure world peace."

The excitement of this book is in the many stories it tells, eighty-five separate voices, speaking a half-century later, giving abundant insight and rich detail from a unique era of American history. One senses the shared ideals, visions, and aspirations of the times; the innocence of youth; the excitement of a new and inspired global perspective; an undying belief in democracy and the right to self determination; and the energetic engagement with the timeless struggles played out even today. Most exciting are these eighty-five very special lives and the ways they coalesced in the fifty years that followed to shape the world we know today.

I am pleased to join in the celebration of the publication of *American Students Organize*. For students of higher education, of government and politics, and of international affairs, and for historians and journalists seeking context and perspective, the book is a priceless resource.

Stanley O. Ikenberry
President, American Council on Education, 1996-2001
President, University of Illinois at Urbana-Champaign, 1979-1995

FOREWORD

This book is an anthology of memoirs and documentation about the founding years, 1946-1952, of the United States National Student Association (NSA) and related events. The Association was one of the principal forms that campus activism took and one of the principal channels into which it flowed during the post–World War II years. The book includes a good deal of collateral information on other college and university student organizational activity of the times.

NSA and other intercollegiate groups reflected, organized, and channeled a great reservoir of generosity, international interest, and social concern that were prominent features of the campus world in those years. A number of these concerns, such as challenging racial segregation, democratizing college admissions, strengthening student governments, establishing the concept of student rights, and bringing students to the table of higher education policy making, contributed to pioneering efforts in areas in which American society made far-reaching progress in succeeding years.

Other outcomes included bringing together student body presidents and student newspaper editors at national NSA forums, introducing group dynamics as an alternative to parliamentary procedure, developing a collaboration between student leaders and student personnel administrators, entry of American Catholic colleges into the mainstream of intercollegiate activity, the development of international student travel and foreign student aid, exchange, and technical assistance programs, and participation of U.S. student leaders in international forums during the rapidly evolving Cold War. The organization provided a valuable training ground for a postwar generation of American social, educational, political, and business leadership.

Creating a National Student Organization

In August 1946, a delegation of twenty-five American student leaders attended a World Student Congress in Prague, Czechoslovakia. Several delegates were drawn from student bodies of leading colleges and universities, some represented campus-based religious and social action groups, and some represented student activist and political organizations. The Prague Congress launched an organization called the International Union of Students (IUS), headquartered in Prague. NSA's relations with the IUS are described in a number of essays in this book.

The Americans who attended the Congress were impressed by the fact that the students of many nations, including the countries of both Western and Eastern Europe, the Soviet Union, and the developing regions of Asia, Africa, and Latin America, were represented by delegates from national student groups. The European national student unions were well organized, and all delegates appeared to speak for their country's students. No comparable organization existed in the United States. Although members of the American group spanned the organizational, ideological, and political spectrum, none had the status to "represent" American students or present an "American position" on issues before the World Student Congress.

Challenged by what they had experienced, the returning U.S. attendees convened a National Student Conference at the University of Chicago in December 1946 to consider the creation of an American national student organization that could be the peer and counterpart of such organizations in other nations. Endorsing the idea, the Chicago Conference issued a call for a Constitutional Convention at the University of Wisconsin in September 1947, to create an organization that could speak for American students both nationally and internationally.

The organization, the United States National Student Association, was launched at the Wisconsin convention. Its campus affiliates were student governments rather than individual students or other student organizations.

Choosing the time frame

This book covers the initial cycle of NSA's existence from events in 1945-46 to the American student group's attendance at the Prague Congress, the Chicago Student Conference the following December, the Constitutional Convention at the University of Wisconsin in September of 1947, and events through NSA's Fifth National Student Congress at Indiana University in August 1952.

During this period, NSA's officers traveled to campuses throughout the country (from among the 1,277 four year colleges and universities and 451 junior colleges); hundreds of student governments throughout the nation debated, held elections and referendums, and enacted or rejected affiliation with NSA; the organization established both a national and an international program; and regional organizations and programming were set up from Northern New England to California and from the South to the Northwest.

For four of the organization's first five years, its national offices were at Madison, Wisconsin. In the fifth year, due to financial constraints, the offices were moved to rent-free space at the University of Colorado in Boulder. That year proved, however, that NSA was sufficiently established that it would survive and grow despite a downsized budget, paving the way for its move east the following year to more permanent headquarters in Philadelphia.

The time frame chosen for the core of this work reflects not only the period during which the foundations were laid for NSA's future, but also a distinct phase in the evolution of American college campus culture. During this time, the World War II veterans generation-- widely known also as the "GI Generation"-- made its mark on the undergraduate scene; a number of "un-American" activity investigations on U.S. campuses introduced the era of McCarthyism, and the new challenges of the Korean conflict and the Cold War occupied the attention of student leaders alongside their education and career concerns. The Beat Generation, "flower children," "free speech," conservative and feminist movements, and civil rights revolution were yet to come.

At this writing, there are few contemporary analyses and references to post–World War II college student leadership and activism that address the period covered by this book and its antecedent history. While we have chosen here simply to record our experiences as we can recall and resurrect them, historians may want to reach into them for possible additional insights into the foundations laid immediately after World War II for the character of student leadership and student activism that followed, and for their contributions to American society.

How the book is organized

The core of this book is divided into six parts, plus a Prologue and an Appendix.

The first three parts describe NSA's basic history. The Prologue provides the setting, including a review of prewar and wartime antecedent student organizations. Part 1 provides a year-by-year narrative. Part 2 surveys the Association's domestic activities in areas including student government, student rights, student life, academic freedom, antidiscrimination and civil rights, and cultural programs.

Part 3 focuses on the association's international programs, including student exchange, aid, and travel, relations with the IUS and other groups, and Cold War influences.

Part 4 describes the veterans generation and postwar national student groups that existed alongside NSA and that influenced, and were influenced by, NSA. This section highlights the role of the Student Christian Movement, the Catholic student groups and colleges, and a spectrum of political and social groups, from Federalists to fraternities and from communists to liberals and conservatives. There was a considerable interchange of leadership among the national student groups.

Part 5 describes NSA's presence on the campus and regional levels. It is based on archival research, as well as memoirs and a review of the prolific coverage given NSA by much of the collegiate press of that period. The many efforts to create and build intercollegiate programs, the vigorous battles over NSA membership, and the profiles of some of the early association leaders and educators who supported NSA are covered in this part.

Part 6, the Epilogue, describes the Association's move from Boulder, Colorado, to Philadelphia in late 1952 and reviews some NSA histories written in succeeding years. The appendix reproduces NSA's original constitution and student bill of rights, summarizes its organizational structure, and provides information on the organization's finances.

The authors of the essays

The stories and authors that this book brings together put a human face on NSA and its times. The book's editors have been highly fortunate in being able to reach more than ninety men and women who played roles in NSA and other early postwar student organizations and who agreed either to be interviewed or to write essays describing their roles, their activities, and their recollections. The editors are immensely grateful for their interest in the project and for their generous donations of time, effort, and knowledge. Their first-hand accounts have been supplemented by summaries of their backgrounds, vocations, and attainments.

Neither the authors of the essays nor the editors of the book regard the work as a comprehensive analysis or narrative of the events with which they deal. No person or group can speak for everyone in his or her day or provide a demographically accurate profile of student life. Among other things, organization leadership and membership were often skewed by social class, beliefs, or geography. Many colleges did not encourage student government outreach in those years. Others, particularly professional schools and many Protestant religious schools, did not participate in secular intercollegiate organizations. Also, on any given campus, the student leadership cohort tended to be a small fraction of the student body.

Nonetheless, student leaders and student governments did what they could to both arouse and engage students and to reflect what they thought were their wishes and interests. There can be little doubt that NSA enjoyed a significant reach in the student community among these leaders and student governments. It pursued purposes firmly grounded in America's vision and history and sounded a forward-looking note in keeping with that vision.

NSA reflected the spirit of the "GI Generation." As the *New Mexico Lobo* editorialized in its August 17, 1945 issue, "The returning veterans are going to have an enthusiasm, but it will be for the big things—a peaceful world and the right to live their lives as they want to. They are not going to stand for the regimentations and immaturity so well-established in the college systems of today." And so the organization advocated for "big ideas" in order to achieve those "big things."

How can you use this book?

To help readers find their way, we have provided a comprehensive table of contents, which includes thumbnail biographies of the authors. Each part and section is preceded by a brief overview with both text and graphics describing the contents to follow. People, colleges, newspapers, events, and topics are comprehensively cross-referenced and indexed. A glossary of abbreviations, an almanac, a bibliography, and a listing of archival resources are provided.

These are many stories and not a single narrative, as you will find by examining the Table of Contents. You can start at the beginning or begin reading about any subject anywhere. For example, you might begin with Clif Wharton's account of the 1946 Chicago Conference (Part 1, Section 3), or Janis Tremper Dowd's memoir of her 1946 travels to the International Student Service Conference at Cambridge University in London (Part 1, Section 1), and see where they lead you.

You will find that a tale by and about one person will lead you to other stories and other people, and to events that reflect their time and place in collegiate and American history.

Each part and section begins with an overview summarizing the material that follows, and a table of contents for that section. Reading the overviews provides a summary of the book.

Acknowledgments

We want to acknowledge the efforts and accomplishments of our colleagues and friends, student leaders, and engaged citizens, many of whom have since passed into memory. We hope we have done justice to their recall.

Many acknowledgments and appreciations are owed to organizations, institutions, and individuals that have made this book possible during the more than eight years it has been in the making. We salute them all in the Afterword.

January 2006

CONTENTS IN BRIEF

p. 54

NSFA Withdraws from AYC In Split in Policy, Structure; ASU Raps Coudert Committee

p. 21

p. 135

p. 867

p. 1092

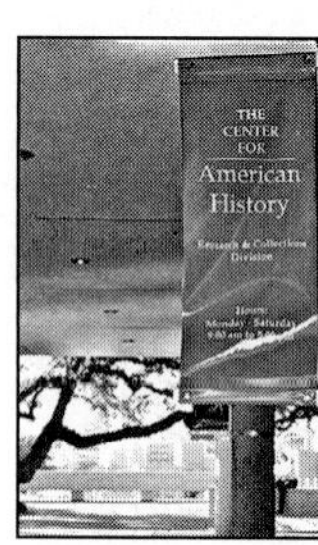

p. 1121

CONTENTS

Editor's note: Numbered articles are principal memoirs or commentaries. Author's or subject's college affiliation, NSA, and student leadership positions are in italics. Career highlights are bracketed in roman type.

p. 4

Cornell Daily Sun
NAZIS ENTER DENMARK; NORWAY DECLARES WAR
Hostilities Started After German Attack
Parent-Teacher Institute Opens; Continues Today
German Troops March Through Copenhagen

p. 5

p. 21

THE SUMMER TEXAN
VICTORY EXTRA
PEACE!!
JAPANESE SURRENDER
University Holiday Wednesday and Thursday
University Shuts Doors To Celebrate Two Days
General MacArthur Commands Jap Homeland, Truman Says

p. 2

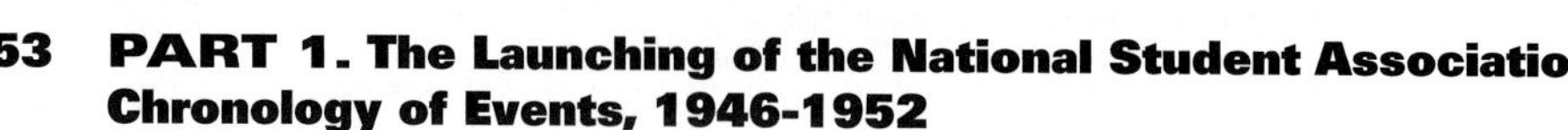

p. 72

p. 82

The Xavier Herald
XAVIER STUDENTS ATTEND CONVENTION IN CHICAGO

p. 109

p. 153

The NSA News
merican Students Organize

p. 163

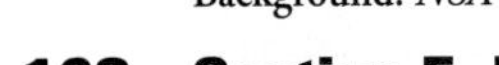

p. 283

p. 312

p. 324

p. 364

p. 366

p. 395

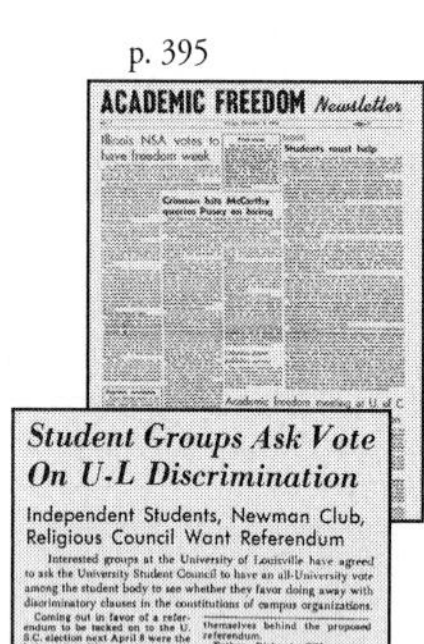

p. 407

p. 421

The Daily Reveille

Inter-Racial Regional Meet Discusses NSO, Calls for Equal Educational Opportunities

Curet Elected Region Prexy

Negroes Desire Better Schools

p. 454

Opportunity NEWS

474 Students Enrolling In 1953, Win $197,000

Two-Way Project Ends First Year

South-Wide Talent Search Underway

p. 465

p. 480

Dean Urges Women Assume Responsibility

Deplores Lack of Interest in Education; Urges Barnard to Meet Teaching Need

p. 490

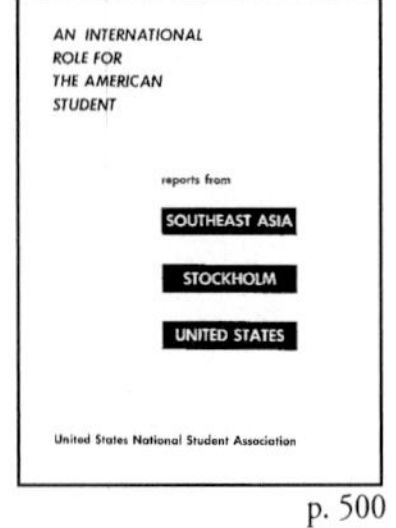

p. 500

p. 501

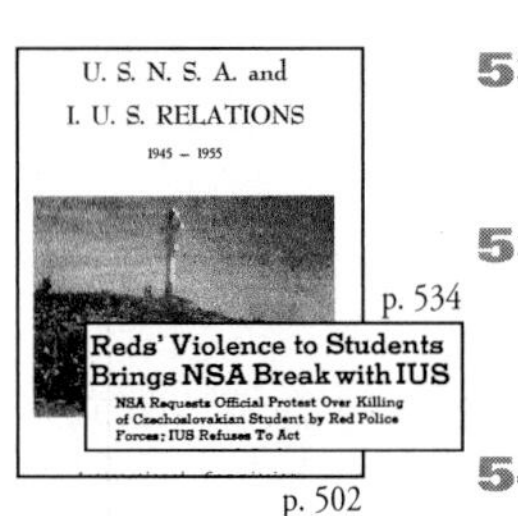

p. 534

p. 502

Conference Plans Secretariat For Worldwide Student Unity

p. 534

NSA Group Establishes International Info Service

p. 580

p. 609

p. 608

Daily Bruin WORLD NEWS PAGE THREE
Bruins assist world students
World Student Service Fund to provide needed clothes, food, medicine for Europeans

p. 612

IDPA BULLETIN
M.I.T. Graduate Off To Ijebu-Igbo

p. 627

Veterans flock to nation's colleges

Carolina Campus Resembles Wartime Boom Town

p. 702

Pennsylvanian

1400 Students Of 900 Schools Attend National Student Assembly In Illinois

Red and Blue Defeat LaSalle 68-56; Carlson Sets New Palestra Record

p. 732

THE HAWK

Nation's Catholic Colleges Moving Into City for NFCCS Convention

Pax Romana Declares Refugee Students Need American Aid Urgently

Clothing Drive

Opens Next Thursday; Federation Celebrating Its Tenth Anniversary

p. 742

The College Fraternity Crisis
By HOWARD WHITMAN

p. 803

p. 824

p. 846

National Student Org Rally Today To State Delegate Rules, Explain Method, Aims Of Group

Wallace, Regional Chairman, Williams To Address Meeting

p. 845

p. 868

p. 867

NY Regional Convention of NSA To Convene Here; 100 Expected

The first convention of the New York Region of NSA will be held at Norton Union this week-end, April 17 and 18, and will be attended by an estimated 75-100 delegates, coming from colleges and universities from all over the state except from the metropolitan New York area.

Among the business scheduled will be a report from the local NSA Committee on the details of the privilege card system in order to acquaint other schools with the ... be considered to fit into the

Revisionists Incorporate Five Articles of NSA Bill of Rights

Decide On This Course at Tuesday Meeting Nine Were Presented for Scrutiny

p. 894

p. 941

p. 935

p. 965

p. 968

p. 987

p. 970

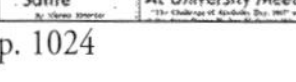
THE DAILY CALIFORNIAN
ASUC Affiliates With NSA; Voted By Executives
Magazine Features Satire
Hap Arnold, Heggie Speak At University Meeting Today
No Financial Obligations To Be Assumed

p. 1024

p. 1052

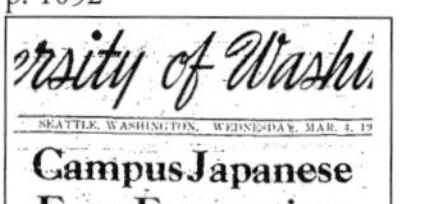
...rsity of Washi...
Campus Japanese Face Evacuation

NSA Plans Purchase Card System For Idaho And WSC
Musicians Return From Conference

p. 1068

p. 1073

p. 1072

p. 1091

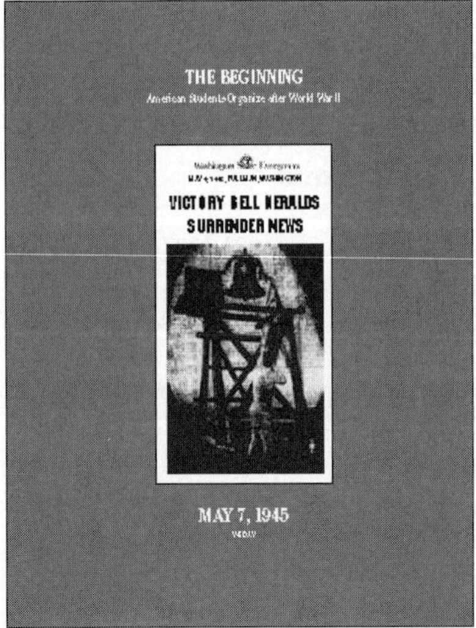
THE BEGINNING
American Students Organize after World War II
VICTORY BELL HERALDS
SURRENDER NEWS
MAY 7, 1945

p. 1104

PROLOGUE TO NSA

Student Organizations Before and During World War II

PROLOGUE TO NSA

Student Organizations Before and During World War II

When U.S. students, invigorated by a wave of war veterans on the G.I. Bill, arrived at college campuses for the 1945-46 school year they marked the end of the war in Europe and in Asia and the beginning of a new era of hope and promise. Many of them pursued a broad agenda for engagement and leadership outside the classroom, based on a vision founded in their American democratic traditions.

Their concerns ranged from raising funds to provide relief for students rebuilding their universities in war-torn Europe and Asia and providing technical assistance personnel to nations emerging out of colonialism in Asia and Africa, to strengthening democratic institutions in the United States by striving to erase racial segregation and discrimination, broadening the opportunities for education, and developing and improving student self-government to which they were firmly committed.

This was an agenda of ambitious challenge for those students who seized it. It harnessed energies put on hold on December 7, 1941, when the bombing of Pearl Harbor focused everyone's attention on wartime needs. It was undertaken with a limited awareness of the earlier college student leadership and organization history that had set the stage for its initiatives in significant ways.

Prewar events and leaders set stage for the formation of NSA

This prologue concerns itself with some of those antecedent circumstances, organizations, and student leaders. Their influence on U.S. college campuses between World War I and World War II set the stage for the founders of the U.S. National Student Association when they attended the World Student Congress in Prague in the summer of 1946. They returned determined to form a new organization that could speak for American students internationally and represent their interests domestically.

In Section 1, historian Miriam Haskell Berlin, a 1946 Prague World Student Congress observer and an early NSA leader, discusses the trends and events that preceded post–World War II U.S. college student government, international relations, and social action. Martin McLaughlin, a member of the U.S. delegation to the 1946 World Student Congress, supplements Berlin's essay in a portion of his doctoral thesis written in 1948, providing a comprehensive profile of student organizations in the United States before the war.

Section 2 describes the prewar National Student Federation of America and American Student Union and the wartime United States Student Assembly. Their activities and concerns presage many of the opportunities and challenges awaiting students after the war.

V·E DAY ANNOUNCED

Last defended Nazi fortress taken by Russians following hard 84-day siege, Reds say

British declare victory in Europe is official statesmen broadcast

SOUTHERN CALIFORNIA DAILY TROJAN

SC celebrates Nazi surrender

V-E day report reveals varied

President in tribute

Trojans shout 'hallelujah'

VICTORY EXTRA

VICTORY EXTRA

PEACE!!

JAPANESE SURRENDER

University Holiday Wednesday and Thursday

University Shuts Doors To Celebrate Two Days

General MacArthur Commands Jap Homeland, Truman Says

ABOVE: From top: *Daily Trojan*, 5/8/45 (U. of Southern California), *Summer Texan*, 8/14/45 (U. of Texas). **BELOW:** *Los Angeles Collegian*, 11/13/45 (LA City College).

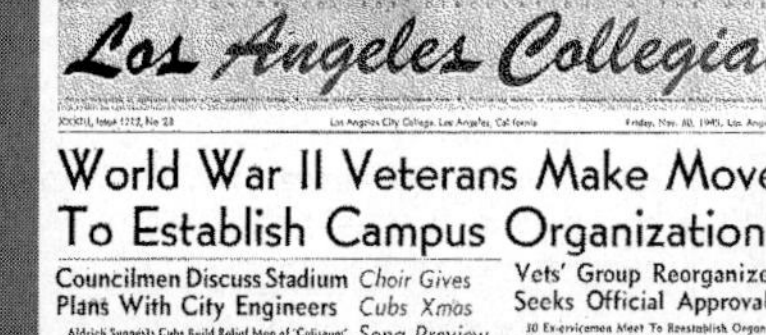

Los Angeles Collegia

World War II Veterans Make Mov

To Establish Campus Organization

Councilmen Discuss Stadium Plans With City Engineers

Choir Gives Cubs Xmas Song Preview

Vets' Group Reorganize Seeks Official Approval

PREVIOUS PAGE: Plenary session, 1946 World Student Congress, Prague, Czechoslovakia (Courtesy Joyce Roberts Harrison)

PROLOGUE TO NSA

SECTION 1

The Setting for Student Organization

CONTENTS

THE VASSAR MISCELLANY NEWS

ASU CONVENTION FORMS POLICIES, ELECTS COUNCIL

OXFORD OATH UPHELD

At the American Student Union's second annual convention which

AGNES SCOTT NEWS

NSFA Considers World Crisis

Delegates Convene During Xmas Holidays

How can U. S. college and university students face the present world crisis?

With this question as their paramount problem, 200 National Student Federation of America delegates from all corners of the nation met at the University of Minnesota to devote a portion of their holiday vacation to a discussion of their mutual problems.

From top: *Vassar Miscellany News*, 1/13/37 (Vassar College, NY), *The Agnes Scott News*, 1/176/40 (Agnes Scott College, GA)

In the following pages, historian Miriam Haskell Berlin, 1946 Prague World Student Congress observer and an early NSA leader, describes the major prewar and wartime student movements of the time. Martin McLaughlin, a member of the U.S. delegation to the 1946 World Student Congress, in a portion of his doctoral thesis written in 1948, supplements Berlin's essay with a comprehensive profile of student organizations in the United States before the war.

The climate for political and social action on U.S. college campuses before World War II was framed by the earlier post–World War I experience. It gave birth in 1920 to European Student Relief, created by the World Student Christian Federation. In 1926, ESR spun off the International Student Service, which, together with Pax Romana, the international Catholic student group, set up World Student Relief in 1940.

The National Student Federation of America, grounded in college student governments, was formed in 1925, and the American Student Union, an individual membership and campus chapter–based organization, was formed in 1935. The Student Christian Movement, the campus YMCAs and YWCAs, founded in the late nineteenth century; the prewar Newman Clubs on secular campuses and the NFCCS at Catholic colleges; and various sectarian groups also provided an outlet for student leadership and a presence and continuity for social action and moral concerns.

Student self-government was achieving greater definition, although college administrations, applying "in loco parentis," maintained strong regulatory oversight.

Peace and isolationist movements attract prewar support

As World War II approached, U.S. pacifist and isolationist voices had joined in the Oxford Peace Pledge movement that opposed U.S. involvement in the global conflict that lay ahead. The Hitler-Stalin pact of 1939 had transformed the American college student left from an antifascist movement to a propeace movement opposing the "capitalist interests" in a Western European defense against Nazi expansion.

Support for U.S. entry into the war and anticommunist voices on campuses were less focused, but found a home in social democratic groups such as the League for Industrial Democracy, in internationalist religious groups, and in outspoken college faculty. Pearl Harbor unified the nation and quieted the antiwar voices, leading to a new U.S. position of global engagement.

American college students went to war. On their return, they elected to pursue peace and justice at home and abroad with renewed commitment. The U.S. National Student Association reflected this resolve.

1937

SEMI-WEEKLY

The Diamondback

TUESDAY EDITION

FOR THE STUDENTS BY THE STUDENTS

Vol. XXIX. University of Maryland, College Park, Md., Tuesday, December 14, 1937. No. 20

Relief Campaign Starts Tomorrow

Students Petition For Extra Holiday

DR. BYRD GETS REQUEST FROM S. G. A., ACTION UNANNOUNCED

As the result of petitions which were circulated among students last week, the Student

Football Squad Celebrates '37 Gridiron Season

Cast For "Night Must Fall" Preps For Performance, January 5, 6, 7, 8

S. G. A. Sends Plea For Aid Of Needy

Md. To Sponsor Coast-to-Coast Radio Program

FULL HOUR'S BROADCAST

ANNUAL FOOD BALL ADDS IMPETUS TO DRIVE TOMORROW

1933

1931

DOROTHEA SHUFORD

A Semi-Monthly Next Issue March 29th

THE HILLTOP

1000 paid subscriptions Circulation of 1917

Published by the Students of Howard University, Washington, D. C.

Vol. I. No. 5 MARCH 15, 1924 25c a Quarter (Students) 5 Cents a Copy

A NEW DAY WANTED

Freedom! Power!! Responsibility!!!

Student Council Presents New Constitution After Fifty-Six Years of Faculty Control

NEW CONSTITUTION OF STUDENT COUNCIL

ON TO NASHVILLE

Students Attend and Stir the College World

1924

1910

1936

FROM THE TOP: *The Diamondback,* 12/14/37, University of Maryland. University of Chicago Peace Strike, 1933-34 (Special Collections, Regenstein Library, U. of Chicago). 1931 May Queen and Head of Student Council, Dorothea Shuford, *The Web*, 6/2/31, Webster College (MO). Captain of Yale football team, 1910, Frederick J. Daly '11 (Manuscripts and Archives, Yale U. Library). *The Hilltop*, Howard U. (DC), 3/15/24. Student Council, Sarah Lawrence College (NY), c. 1936 (Archives of Sarah Lawrence College).

In the Beginning: A Past that Shaped the Present

Some early twentieth-century images provide emblems of campus life in "a past that has shaped the present . . . [and whose] student subcultures, created in particular historic moments, persist over time, [and still], at some level, inform the present"—Helen Lefkowitz Horowitz in *Campus Life* (University of Chicago Press, 1987)

Prewar Student Organization: A High Point of Activism

"The campus of the 1930s was a place of many contradictions. While the colleges and universities had grown substantially in the twenties, administrators continued in their paternalism. . . . The most important issue of the decade was the war-peace question. . . . The 1930s was the high point for student activism. . . ." —Philip G. Altbach in *Student Politics in America* (Transaction Publishers, 1997)

1940

Cornell Daily Sun

ITHACA, N. Y., TUESDAY, APRIL 9, 1940

NAZIS ENTER DENMARK; NORWAY DECLARES WAR

Hostilities Started After German Attack

Parent-Teacher Institute Opens;

German Troops March Through Copenhagen

1940

Vassar Miscellany News

STUDENTS STRIKE FOR PEACE

Carmichael Lauds Achievements of Prof. Washburn

Thousands Strike On Campuses Throughout Country For Peace

PROGRAM FOR PEACE

"'40 Shall Not be '17"

1941

Columbia Spectator

MONDAY, DECEMBER 8, 1941

Japan Declares War on U.S.; Island Possessions Attacked

250 Guests, Students at Social Hour

Speaks at Noon

Action Complete Surprise; Congress Meets Today; Immediate War Proclamation Expected

The Imperial Headquarters of the Japanese Army announced late yesterday afternoon that "a state of war with the United States" exists. This bulletin came shortly after news flashes revealing Japanese air attacks on the Philippine Islands, the Hawaiian Islands, Guam, and Wake Island.

...versity of Wash...

SEATTLE, WASHINGTON, WEDNESDAY, MAR. 4, 1...

Campus Japanese Face Evacuation

When the news came last night that all Japanese, American born and aliens alike, will eventually be evacuated from the Pacific coast area, nearly 200 Japanese students of the University of Washington began to make preparations to leave.

Future orders will be issued that will oust all Japanese and German and Italian aliens from the coastal strip that includes the western half of Washington. The proclamation, issued by General John L. DeWitt, commander of the fourth army, is the drastic answer to the frequent public demands for eviction of all Japanese—citizens and aliens alike—from vital defense areas.

Students Must Leave

Only organized Japanese house on the campus, the Japanese Students' club, began to plan disposal of their clubhouse at 4113 Fifteenth avenue northeast.

1942

1939

Cornell Daily Sun

ITHACA, N. Y., FRIDAY, OCTOBER 6, 1939

Nazis 'Expose' Plot To Destroy U.S. Ship; Hint British Guilty

Navy Sent Aid To Help Vessel, FDR Tells Press

Student Council Votes to Sponsor 'Columbia Hop'

Intramural Dance To Offer Scampole, Rad Severance

Vote Favors Revision Of Neutrality Law; Over 1,750 in Poll

Syracuse Rally To Be Held Tonight For Red Gridmen

Would Fight If U. S. Attacked Voting Reveals

EXTRA!

BULLETIN

Washington Square College *New York University*

Vol. XI, No. 19 SPECIAL ISSUE DECEMBER 18, 1942

Army And Navy Release Overall Program To Gear Nation's Colleges To War Effort

1942

THE HILLTOP

HOWARD UNIVERSITY, WASHINGTON, D.C.

800 Howard Men Answer Selective Draft Call

College Students to Enter Training Camps Next June

1941

Humboldt State College in the Redwood Empire

HUMBOLDT LUMBERJACK, WEDNESDAY, SEPT. 24, 1941

DRAFT CAUSES ENROLLMENT DROP

Play Tryouts To Be Held Monday

Three Join College Faculty

Prue Illingworth To Teach Modern Dance, Sports

Donald Karshner Now Head of Speech, Drama

Former Humboldt Student Becomes HSC Instructor

ENROLLMENT DECREASES 10 PER CENT

Registration has reached a total of 384 students enrolled at Humboldt State for the 1941 fall semester.

WAR AND PEACE

With war in Europe spreading, and the United States not yet engaged, peace movements in the United States that had been vocal on both the left and the right and had unified the policies of the two major national student groups, the National Student Federation of America (p. 22) and the American Student Union (p. 47), began to split them apart.

After Pearl Harbor on December 7, 1941, the nation drew together. Colleges throughout the country mobilized for the war effort as young men enlisted or were drafted into the service, women who could enlisted in the army and navy women's corps, and other women took jobs in war industries.

FROM THE TOP: *Cornell Daily Sun*, 4/9/40 (NY). *Vassar Miscellany News*, 4/17/40 (NY). *Columbia Spectator*, 12/8/41 (NY). *University of Washington Daily*, 3/4/42/. *Cornell Daily Sun*, 10/6/39. *Washington Square College Bulletin*, New York U., 12/18/42. *The Hilltop*, Howard U., 10/41 (DC). *Humboldt Lumberjack*, 9/24/41 (CA).

Reflections on the origins of NSA

1. American Society and American Students: A Historical Perspective

Miriam Haskell Berlin

Smith College. Chair, NSA New England Region, 1947

U.S. Delegation, World Student Congress, Prague, 1946 (Observer Status)

Preamble

This essay seeks to illuminate the historical patterns central to the development of a representative national American student organization after World War II by looking at three issues. First, the idiosyncratic nature of the American college and university system; second, the specific experience of the American Student Union of the 1930s, the largest previous national student organization, whose history is offered here largely for its premonitory value; third, the special problems facing what became the NSA, through the Constitutional Convention in Madison, Wisconsin in September 1947. The objective is to provide an introduction and context for what follows in this volume.

The NSA, conceived on the banks of the Vlatava (Moldau) River in Prague in August 1946 and delivered at its Constitutional Convention a year later, bore the signature of the American social and political landscape of the twenties, thirties, and forties. Nor could it have been otherwise. The American interwar generation, born in the twenties, emerged into consciousness during the Depression. Many participated in World War II, experiencing this tumultuous period in circumstances radically different from the same cohort in Europe, Asia, or Africa.

In most parts of the world, the term *student*, its significance and condition, carried meanings chiefly rooted in class and politics. Not so in America. The U.S. delegation that went to the World Student Congress in Prague in 1946 consisted of a representative from each of ten geographically dispersed universities, and fifteen representatives of what might be called "interest groups."[1] Other nations were represented by national student unions, membership organizations often embracing particular political positions. This was true not only of the USSR and other East Bloc countries, but most Western nations as well. The nature of this and other differences is central to the narrative of our past. It has been said that history and memory are a net with holes, and yet we cling to both to understand what we were and how and why we have become what we are. This essay will try to evoke this past and its impact.

The growth of the American college and university system

The first colleges in the New World reflected "two cardinal principles of English Puritanism . . . not religious tenets but educational ideals: a learned clergy and a lettered people."[2] The charter of William and Mary spoke about a "youth . . . piously educated in good letters and manners."[3] The American college was conceived of as a social investment to produce "masters and servants of society"; seminaries trained the clergy.[4] In these colonies, committed to civilization and culture, confessional groups came together to promote a "safe place where the young would not lose or change faith" and would at the same time develop into educated leaders for business, government, and the professions, as well as religion. The curriculum was usually classical languages, mathematics, and philosophy, all of which could be taught cheaply.

By 1820, 1.5 percent of college-age white males between the ages of 18 and 24 were enrolled in colleges; by 1860, the number was over 3 percent. By 1900, 5 percent of white men and women attended colleges. In England and Germany, the number in the 20-24-year-old cohort who attended colleges amounted to 1 percent.[5]

American higher education was much expanded when the Morrill Land Grant Act of 1862, recognizing the necessity for other kinds of training, made land grants in every state for "agricultural and technical" colleges to educate the sons and daughters of the farmers and merchants. In contrast to the great European research universities, institutions of public learning in the United States were more varied, democratic, populist, and service-oriented. In conjunction with the Agricultural Extension Service, land-grant universities served many elements of the population hardly considered an elite, and opened the way for the proliferation of institutions diverse in origin, intention, character, and quality, public and private, secular and religious. This variety immediately distinguished the American higher education system from any other in the world.

The American student and American society

Characteristics of the American student population differ from generation to generation. According to the 1940 U.S. census, among the 74.8 million Americans twenty-five or older, one-third had gone beyond eighth grade, one-fourth were high school graduates, and one-twentieth had been graduated from a four-year college or university.[6] By 1950, high school graduates had reached 57.4 percent.

A radical change in higher education occurred when the GI Bill, enacted in 1944, provided stipends for education. By 1956, almost half of the veterans had utilized the GI Bill. "Between 1946 and 1956, 2.2 million veterans (97.1 percent of them men) went to college. Another 3.5 million attended technical schools below the college level, and 700,000 received agricultural instruction, at a total cost of $14.5 billion." More than twice as many university degrees were awarded in 1949-50 as in the decade before, four-fifths of them to men.[7]

Thus, the student generation that participated in the birth of NSA reflected social circumstances vastly different from those sponsoring its predecessor in the 1930s. Enormously diverse, with greater opportunity and access to education for parts of the population never before served, the postwar student generation presented needs and demands different from those of earlier groups.

American society of the thirties and forties, in which the founders of NSA grew up, differed profoundly from society today. It was segregated by race, segmented by ethnicity and religion, separated by class. The social order and its images, heroes and heroines, were dominated by WASPS,[8] although the term had not yet been coined. *Saturday Evening Post* stories and movies depicted an America of blond and blue-eyed Anglo-Saxon "Johns" and "Nancys." The immigrant "huddled masses yearning to breathe free" and Negroes (as people of color were then called), Asians, and Jews played only stereotyped roles in the background. Hispanics were rarely even in the picture. The system included restrictive covenants in housing and restricted entry to universities and public accommodations. Clubs limited or excluded membership of Jews, people of color, Asians, and sometimes Catholics, particularly Irish.

Life was local, largely lived on farms or in small towns or small cities. Travel within the country was limited; only the rich went to Europe. Few cities were home to a variety of races. In the 1940s about a million blacks and even more whites migrated to major Northern and Midwestern cities, followed by more than another million blacks in the 1950s.[9] Wartime industrial employment triggered this transformation in the country's demography. The war was also responsible for many other important changes, among them the position of women, black and white, sharply and forever altered by the pressures, imperatives, and demands for labor in factories and workshops.

American student life

The twenties and thirties played a significant role in the narrative of student life. Localism took a particular form in the student subculture of the twenties. The Great Gatsby life of raccoon coats, fraternities, and celebratory football games dominated, lasting well beyond 1929. Lack of interest in the world was notable. Harold Laski, a distinguished professor arriving from the London School of Economics in 1931, was shocked to find little political knowledge and less interest among students. He observed the "indifference of the American undergraduate . . . the idea that citizenship involves on his part an active interest in (political) affairs simply does not occur to him."[10]

In 1925, however, a group called the National Student Federation of America (NSFA) was organized on the West Coast.[11] This group amalgamated with representatives from the World Court Conference, described below, and was officially launched as a national organization at a meeting in Ann Arbor that was attended by representatives from the student governments of 200 colleges and universities. By 1933, 150 student governments had joined, making it the most representative student group of the period, with "representative" denoting the number of enrolled students in the affiliated colleges and universities.

Avoiding political stands, NSFA addressed issues of student government, ways of expediting student travel abroad and receiving foreign students here, and campus-related issues such as honor systems, smoking, freedom of the student press, scholarships, and the role of fraternities and sororities. The organization remained active throughout the Depression, but succumbed to wartime restrictions on travel and merged with the International Student Service in 1942.

As Altbach points out, although it did not "shape the consciousness of its generation, NSFA was the first federation of student governments . . . something of a legitimate voice for American students."[12] Echoes of NSFA are apparent in the form and focus of NSA.

Edward R. Murrow, who became the most celebrated foreign correspondent of World War II, was president of NSFA in the early 1930s.[13] Murrow chided undergraduates for spending so much time on "fraternities, football and fun," and started a radio show at CBS called *University on the Air.* In his last address to the Federation at its convention in Toledo in December 1931, he took the students to task for "their greatest sins: campus consciousness, political apathy and smug complacency."[14] This began to change with the founding of the National Student League in 1931.[15]

Impact of the Depression

The Depression's impact on students was not immediate. The gilded life of undergraduates continued undisturbed until 1932, two years after the collapse of the blue-collar world. Among students on the eve of the Great Depression, 77 percent of women and 54 percent of men were not responsible for any of their own expenses. Many were scarcely concerned about employment after graduation. As Paul Blanshard said in 1926, "a college degree [was regarded] as a backdoor to big business."[16] Membership in the middle class cushioned, for a time, the effects of economic collapse, even as it had created an elitist culture of "drinking, dancing, and dating," free of the "moral policing of college officials."[17] Conservative in politics, oblivious of what was happening around them, these students were ill prepared for downward mobility, the diminution of facilities, and transformed future prospects.

For the more marginal, life quickly became more desperate. Without societal intervention or any kind of safety net, there was no refuge when families fell on hard times. Thousands left school, others continued but lived in conditions of poverty and deep hardship. In time, college life shared the terrible conditions of the general society.

The apolitical attitudes and apathy of the early thirties turned to action as the students reflected a society being galvanized by Franklin D. Roosevelt. This was not immediately apparent. A student straw poll taken before the 1932 elections showed that Hoover outpaced FDR by 49 percent to 31 percent, while Norman Thomas, the Socialist Party candidate, polled 18 percent. At Harvard, Hoover garnered 1,211 votes to FDR's 395; at Columbia, with two-thirds of the students voting, Hoover took 307 votes, FDR 221, and Norman Thomas 421.[18]

As the Depression spread, Democrats and Socialists gained increased student support. In such activities as marshalling student help for miners in Harlan, Kentucky, fighting battles over no-longer-affordable cafeteria food prices, and publishing outspoken criticism of university policies in student newspapers, the organizational skills of the swelling number of socialists and communists among student groups were central to growing awareness and action. Although activists were hardly the majority, student activities in the thirties present a rich, complex and, for the United States, an unusually politicized scene. The wish to play a role in the problems of the larger society stemmed from social and economic conditions and also the frequently radical immigrant backgrounds of students in New York and other major cities across the country, where free higher education extended access.

In various parts of the country students often expressed different, even conflicting, views on political and social issues, particularly on matters of race, but they shared a common problem in the attitudes and actions of university administrations standing in loco parentis. Students had few rights and were generally seen as children to be kept in line. Disagreement with or protest against university policies could lead to serious penalties, summary dismissal, even expulsion. Students were subjected to FBI surveillance whose magnitude is not yet fully known. The FBI compiled 2,000 files on individuals from the University of Chicago alone between the mid-1930s and 1941.[19] Academic freedom and free speech were seen as the rights of professional scholars, not immature students. College officials provided the names of "dissident" students to the FBI. Free speech movements at CCNY and Berkeley in the thirties did much, after great turmoil, to advance the position of the students and their right to express political ideas on campus as well as off.

General characteristics of American student movements

What is notable about the student movements that emerged, both earlier and at this time, is less their differences than their similarities.[20] The consistent pattern of these groups, starting from before World War I, was their orientation to specific issues, not commitment to theories. As we shall see, the American Student Union's embrace of an ideology, a fixed position, in the 1930s, led to its dissolution. Revolution has never been the business of American students; even attacks on the social ills of the American scene in 1968 were never truly systemic. This is not to say that radical voices were absent. Indeed, the pressure of the radical left was often the propelling or clarifying element that forced action.

The most important contribution that students have made to American society was probably in the antiwar and civil rights movements of the sixties.[21] The nonviolent civil rights movement in the South radicalized large numbers of students and brought about fundamental changes, however incomplete, in the social order. Students played a singular role in these developments, fulfilling commitments made by student movements for decades to end racial discrimination and seek equality. But these student movements were an adjunct to the larger movement and not its leaders. This role belonged to the Southern Christian Leadership Conference and Martin Luther King, along with the Student Nonviolent Coordinating Committee and other southern black activists. The same was true of the anti–Vietnam war effort. Students for a Democratic Society spearheaded what became a national movement in the society, in which students played a significant part.

Paradoxically, although the American student body has mostly concerned itself with "local," i.e., specific, student problems such as housing, scholarships, student rights, discrimination, and free speech, major mass student organizations developed from international involvement in response to key problems of foreign policy. Peace and foreign affairs were major interests of both religious and secular student organizations during the early twentieth century. No specific social or political focus drew the concerted attention given to foreign policy. Commitment was sometimes energized by pressing domestic issues such as civil liberties in the 1920s or race issues during the civil rights movement, but peace and antimilitarism, including opposition to ROTC, remained a central commitment, as was demonstrated by the antiwar movement of the 1960s and 1970s.[22]

The National Student Federation of America emerged from a Princeton Conference convened in 1925 to organize support for U.S. participation in the World Court. This group was joined to a west coast group promoting international activities among students. The American Student Union was spawned by the peace movement and antimilitarism expressed by the Oxford Pledge in 1933.[23] NSA was created as a direct response to the formation of the International Union of Students after the postwar birth of the United Nations.[24]

Student religious groups

Religious student organizations were spin-offs from adult organizations, as was also the case with the more radical political groups. This was true as early as the 1830s, when a surge of evangelism in the country stimulated social work and underlined missionary activities. This combination had a long life in various guises.

A student wing of the YMCA was established in 1877 and full-time campus religious workers were appointed. By 1885, the student members in the YM/YWCA reached 10,000.[25] In the 1920s, unprecedented numbers of students were involved in Christian groups with social concerns. In fact, the religious student movement was stronger in the twenties than at any other time—not surprising, given religion's centrality in American life (Altbach, p. 48).

Although the Christian student movement as a whole was not radical, some members were strongly socially committed. In 1927, for example, at a meeting of the National Conference of the Student Christian Movement (YMCA and YWCA affiliates), 2,500 expressed opposition to the profit motive as anti-Christian. Their activities in bringing students into factories and urban slums were seminal for social action programs developed later. Denominational groups in the black colleges demonstrated the influence of this earlier incipient action in their work in the 1950s civil rights movement.[26]

For Catholics, the 1920s was a period of relative dormancy. After World War II, Catholics increasingly challenged the dominant role of the Protestant denominations in the area of social action, offering a rather more conservative posture.[27]

The legacy of nearly a century of student activism included a primary commitment to peace, and an awareness of the need for social service and social work. A specific political dimension was not central to this stance, though many committed socialists and political figures such as Norman Thomas, A. J. Muste, Paul Douglas, and John Dewey spent formative years in the Christian student movement. The social activism of a Dorothy Day was to emerge later.

Organizations of the Depression era

The National Student League

The first student organization committed exclusively to student interests and concerns, and intent on radicalizing the campus, was the National Student League (NSL), founded in 1931 by various left-oriented groups in metropolitan New York. This was the organizational beginning of student activism in the Depression era. Led by a diverse coalition of "communists, socialist liberals, pacifists and Trotskyites," the group challenged the collegiate culture of the past and urged students to "identify with the working class rather than the upper class, to value racial and ethnic diversity, instead of exclusivity, and to work for progressive social change."[28] Inclusion of communists was a novelty, as the Communist Party had hitherto shunned the campus as too bourgeois for attention. Outstanding political skills, and views widely shared by others rapidly gave them an important place. The social historian Theodore Draper states that, though the NSL was born with a "revolutionary temperament," it represented the views of a wide membership.[29]

Throughout the early thirties, the NSL and the Student League for Industrial Democracy (SLID), the student arm of the League for Industrial Democracy, squabbled about ideas and politics, sometimes joining together to promote policies or programs, and sometimes not.

The American Student Union

During the Christmas holiday of 1935, "all interested students" from NSL, SLID, and NSFA were invited to meet and create a new group to cope with domestic issues and the deteriorating national and international situation. Their meeting place at Columbus, Ohio, had to be shifted from the University to the downtown premises of the YMCA at the last minute, either because of fuel shortages or the accusations of the Hearst press that the students were communists. This meeting created the American Student Union.

ASU's domestic platform achieved consensus on educational opportunity and economic security for students, racial and religious equality, support for the labor movement, and the right of teachers and students to free expression.[30] These positions had already been charted in the previous evocations of the student movement.

Peace advocacy before World War II

Foreign policy issues proved more contentious and divisive. Mirroring the Oxford Pledge of February 9, 1933, when, by a vote of 275 to 173, the Oxford Union adopted a motion that "this House will in no circumstance fight for King and country,"[31] students in the 1930s expressed deep concern for peace in a number of ways. Anti-ROTC agitation was pervasive and took many different forms. Several polls taken in mid-decade found that 39 percent of the students surveyed would not participate in any hostilities, and 33 percent would fight only if the United States were invaded.[32] This position reflected deep disillusionment with the Wilsonian idealists, opposition to war profiteering, militarism in education, and the kinds of intolerance, bigotry, and repression generated at home by World War I. As Altbach points out, the emphasis of student activities in the thirties on foreign affairs, during a period of such enormous domestic crisis, indicates the "middle class nature of the student movement in general and of the student population as a whole."[33]

Still, as events ensued, tensions escalated between the focus on economic/social disintegration, given the New Deal efforts to solve domestic problems, and the tragedy unfolding abroad. Pressures on neutrality increased: Hitler's rise to power in 1933, Italy's invasion of Abyssinia in 1935, the Spanish Civil War in 1936-39, Germany's and Italy's support for Franco, Germany's increasingly virulent anti-Jewish policies, the invasion of Austria in 1938, of Czechoslovakia in 1939,[34] Japan's spreading war in China, Soviet invasion of Finland in 1939 . . . in short, World War II.

Given this increasingly catastrophic scenario, conflicts erupted between the pacifist socialists and Trotskyites and the growing support for collective security embraced by liberals and communists, the antiwar strikes of the early thirties culminated in that of 1936 in which 500,000 students participated, almost "half the national undergraduate population...rallying against both war and compulsory ROTC."[35] This seeming unity of purpose masked increasing division. The Spanish Civil War became the fault line on which the American Student Union would crack. Isolationism could no longer compel the loyalty of students. In 1937, the ASU rejected the Oxford Pledge and the neutrality position of the U.S. government in favor of "aiding those nations which are attacked."[36]

This resolution did not, of course, end the tensions and problems. If the Spanish Civil War was the bellwether for a more realistic assessment of the U.S. position in the world of the late thirties, the Nazi-Soviet Pact of August 1939 sounded ASU's death knell. Communists were among the major figures who had pressed for collective security and played a positive role in educating and organizing within the student movement.[37] When these persons, following the Communist Party, supported the Soviet alliance with Hitler, they were seen as betraying the movement. The American Student Union did not survive the war.[38]

This ideological division left a bitter memory of anguish and manipulation. Much of this generation lost its idealism, too many lost their lives. Given this past, it is not surprising that the proclivities of American students, like the larger culture of which they are a part, remained steadfastly pragmatic, hostile to ideological or even philosophical systems. If pragmatism is taken to be the "doctrine that estimates any assertion solely by its practical bearing on human interests" (Shorter Oxford English Dictionary), we will see that this was to become a positive contribution of the Americans in the international arena.

The postwar setting for NSA

The invitation to participate in the World Student Congress in August 1946 interested a wide spectrum of American students.[39] Our position in the world had changed radically after the war. Alone among the advanced industrial and democratic nations, the United States emerged from the conflict not only physically intact, but enormously transformed in economic and physical power. Our sense of responsibility for leadership in maintaining the peace had developed commensurately.

On March 5, 1946, less than a year after the cessation of hostilities and the founding meeting of the United Nations, Winston Churchill delivered a speech at Fulton, Missouri, that set forth the premise of the Cold War.[40] The swift deterioration of a sense of common purpose, even amity, with our former ally the USSR was crystallized in the phrase *Cold War,* symbolized by the "iron curtain." The simultaneous emergence of the United Nations, so carefully constructed to become the mediator, peacekeeper, and innovator in international affairs, seemed a contradiction, indeed.

The postwar student movement emerged from this context and these attitudes. The language of discourse revealed the polarization. The Jesuit scholar Father John Courtney Murray published an article in the April 13, 1946, issue of the Catholic magazine *America* urging Catholic youth, hitherto passive in student affairs, to participate in the world student movement. "The problem," Father Murray stated, "is how Catholic youth can be put on the move, in the international field, in a solidly organized movement, with a truly conquering spirit, that will carry through a positive program and also combat communist influence." He suggested that "a group of twelve students be selected, carefully and intensively trained, and sent over to the Prague meeting of the International Student Federation [The International Union of Students] in August with the quite sober and entirely feasible intent of 'taking it over.' They could do it, they would not be without allies among European Catholic students."[41]

Despite the growing triumphalism and intensifying political divisions in American public discourse, the American student delegates at Prague consistently demonstrated their pragmatic tradition in insisting on democratic procedures for nominations, elections, and the articulation of policies on specific issues of interest to students everywhere. Although they were not always successful, they presented a stark contrast to the prevailing ideological uses of inflated, meaningless, pompous, and Manichean rhetoric by communist delegates. Unwillingness to define *fascism,* in preference to using it as a pejorative for opposing political positions, and a mantra-like repetition of a commitment to "unity" without defining it and without acknowledging differing views—these features of traditional communist discourse dominated all discussion.[42]

NSA and the formation of the IUS

This meeting created the International Union of Students (IUS), with a Czech president and vice presidents from the United States and the USSR. The American vice president was William Ellis, from Harvard and the YMCA. His deputy was Jim Smith, from the University of Texas. Their presence in Prague, affirmed by NSA's Constitutional Convention in August 1947, assured the continued articulation of American democratic values in this international organization, and heroic efforts to implement them.

Ellis's and Smith's tenure at Prague lasted less than a year. On Friday, February 19, 1948, after a coup carried out by communist action committees in Prague, President Benes acceded to the demands of Minister Gottwald, leader of the Communist Party, that Gottwald be named to form a new government immediately, rather than waiting for spring elections when it was anticipated that the communists would lose their controlling position. Czech students, who had erupted into the streets to protest, were dispersed and crushed.

Bill Ellis was in Switzerland, recovering from illness, when these events occurred. Jim Smith was in Prague. Ellis wrote a letter of resignation as IUS vice president, protesting the "action and inaction" of the IUS during the coup with respect to student rights. In a letter of February 28, Smith called on the IUS to support free speech and the right of assembly for students, protest the arrest of students, demand fair public trials for those in custody, protest the dissolution of the Czech National Union of Students, which had taken place as part of the coup, and protest the expulsion of students and professors from Charles University in Prague. This was followed by a letter from Ellis to IUS, attacking the violations of basic rights and the "brutal and undemocratic treatment of Czech students by their government." Both resigned.[43]

Building an American student unity

Building American student unity among the conflicting messages symbolized by the United Nations and the Iron Curtain on the one hand and the widely differing political views of American students on the other was no small task. All the elements sketched out here have a role. Motivated by hopes for connection to the wider world, NSA's original organizers were often faced by college presidents and student councils fearful of any such links, lest they be duped or contaminated by wily political enemies who ostensibly existed everywhere.[44] It is difficult to reconstruct the mindset of this period, which judged any alternative political ideas in the context of conspiracy and the feared omnipotence and omnipresence of an unscrupulous political "other." The fifties brought these views to the surface and bred deep distrust in American political and social life for ideas, political action, and even unusual views on any question. The shorthand description is, of course, McCarthyism; the basis was great fear and the legacy, distrust.

Historians of the student movement have tended to divide students and student groups into radical, liberal, and conservative factions. These are not wholly inaccurate labels, but they are unsatisfactory. The crosscurrents of commitment and interest are too complex for such classification, as they are with most large and diverse groups.

Part of the difficulty with previous movements, including ASU, lay in the degree of control that adult groups, including the Communist Party, maintained over their student offspring. Such control or linkage in policy matters continued through the American Youth for Democracy, formerly the Young Communist League, and the Catholic student organizations.[45]

In a letter published in the June 1, 1947, issue of *Newman News*, for instance, Archbishop Richard J. Cushing, Chairman of the Youth Department of the National Catholic Welfare Conference, said, "I am sure that authorities of our colleges and universities will exercise a sympathetic and prudent interest in the relationship of their students to a student movement beyond the jurisdiction of the Church . . . beyond . . . the Chicago meeting [the National Student Conference, December 1946], any further activities or alliances of our student groups must be subject to the direction of institutional authorities and subject to final review by the hierarchy." Even where such fears existed, many students made their determinations independently. A thicket of competing interests existed for each person to cut through, to make individual assessments of their various constituencies and their own beliefs.

Some radicals and some conservatives are immediately recognizable, but to have the great undistributed middle lumped as liberals makes no sense. That is the good fortune of a relatively untidy political system, and it was evident all through NSA's growing pains, particularly in framing civil rights planks at conventions. Those who embraced the broadest coverage were constrained by the desire, indeed necessity, to keep the southern whites in the organization. Many southern white leaders were in advance of their constituencies and acknowledged the crucial importance of direct contact between blacks and whites, often meeting as equals for the first time in the regional gatherings of the incipient NSA. To keep such a process alive meant moderating, to some degree, the language of the equal rights plank to mollify traditional white southerners. Is this liberalism? Is it trimming? Is it wisdom with a sense of reality, and a balancing act between the desired and the achievable?[46]

These questions cannot be easily answered. We are as our choices and history have made us. Diversity characterizes our culture and our educational system. But this diversity takes different forms in each generation. What constitutes radicalism or conservatism changes with each historical era. The concepts are fluid, but the procedures and principles of action of primary concern to students remain constant. The centrality of student interests, unfettered by any external pressures, remains imperative for the well-being of the student movement. Student aims and objectives resonate from the U.S. Constitution and its Bill of Rights.[47]

Student cohorts by definition enjoy a short time span, and their accomplishments reflect the values, passions, and concerns of the contemporaneous world. The glory is in the doing. The NSA emerged with a distinct profile, but, like all movements, its lineage is traceable, rooted in the past.

Miriam Haskell Berlin has been an Assistant Professor at Wellesley College, a lecturer at Harvard University, and a lecturer in the National Faculty Teaching Institutes. She holds a B.A. from Smith College and an M.A. and Ph.D. from Radcliffe College.

END NOTES

[1] An international student gathering in November 1945 in Prague called for a multination student congress for the summer of 1946, to create an organization that became the International Union of Students. A similar plan had emerged from a meeting held a few weeks earlier by the British National Union of Students. A twelve-nation preparatory committee was set up to allocate delegation numbers for participating nations. The United States and USSR were given twenty-five delegates each, with other countries' numbers running down a sliding scale. An ad hoc American committee of youth organizations chose the universities and the groups: four delegates each from the National Intercollegiate Christian Council and the National Catholic Youth Council; one each from the Student World Federalists, American Unitarian Youth, U.S. Student Assembly, American Youth for Democracy (formerly the Young Communist League), the Association of Interns and Medical Students, and Youthbuilders, Inc.; one student each from Harvard, Hunter, Texas, Pennsylvania, Wayne, Chicago, UCLA, North Carolina, Fisk, and Wisconsin (Peter T. Jones, *Relations of USNSA and IUS, 1945-1955*, Cambridge, MA: International Commission, UNSA, 1955). For further IUS background, see page 538. See Tibbetts, page 68.

[2] Morison in Rudolph, F., *American College and University: A History.* Athens: U. of Georgia Press, 1962, p. 6.

[3] Ibid.

[4] Rudolph, pp. 58-59.

[5] Robert L. Church, "Collegiate Education," in *American Encyclopedia of Social History*, Vol. 3, 1993, p. 2521.

[6] Patterson, James T., *Grand Expectations. The United States, 1945-1974*, New York and Oxford: Oxford University Press, 1996, p. 67.

[7] Patterson, p. 68.

[8] White Anglo Saxon Protestants.

[9] Patterson, pp. 18-19.

[10] Cohen, Robert, *When the Old Left Was Young: Student Radicals and America's First Mass Student Movement, 1929-1941.* New York and Oxford: Oxford Univ. Press, 1993, p. 8.

[11] See Kerr, p. 22.

[12] Altbach, Phillip, *Student Politics in America: An Historical Analysis.* New York: McGraw-Hill, 1974, p. 41.

[13] See Murrow, p. 26.

[14] Cohen, p. 7. See background on NSFA, p. 22, and Murrow, p. 26. See also Stanley Greenfield's visit with Murrow in 1947, p. 56.

[15] Ibid., p. 22.

[16] Ibid., p. 8.

[17] Ibid., p. 14.

[18] Ibid., pp. 75-76.

[19] Ibid., p. 99.

[20] See McLaughlin, "Prewar Student Activism," p. 15.

[21] Altbach, p. 194.

[22] Earlier efforts to address civil rights on campuses and by NSA in the years just after World War II are described by Janet Brown in her essay on page 375.

[23] See "American Student Union," p. 47.

[24] See Blair, p. 538.

[25] Altbach, p. 14.

[26] See Part 2, Section 3, "The South, Civil Rights, and Segregation," pp. 425, 433, 445.

[27] See discussions of the role of the Catholic schools and student groups and the Student Christian Movement in Dungan, p. 909, Des Marais, p. 734, Miller, p. 717, and Purkaple, p. 685.

[28] Cohen, p. 22.

[29] Ibid., p. 39.

[30] Ibid., p. 141.

[31] Ibid., p. 79.

[32] Altbach, p. 63.

[33] Ibid., pp. 64-65.

[34] *Editor's Note:* The 1939 invasion of Czechoslovakia led to the killing on November 17, 1939 of 147 Czech students by Nazis when they occupied the country and closed the universities. The event was subsequently marked each year by International Students Day. See p. 580.

[35] Cohen, p. 152.

[36] See Ostar, p. 209, and Miller, p. 718.

[37] Cohen, p. 174. An unusual element in this unfolding tale was Eleanor Roosevelt's developing interest in the student movement. Meeting a number of student leaders, including Joseph Lash, president of the ASU and later chronicler of the Roosevelts' lives, at the August 1939 Youth Congress, Mrs. Roosevelt acted as the eyes and ears of the president, apprising him of student attitudes and positions in this period of national crisis. Lash resigned from the ASU in 1940 after it had been effectively taken over by the communists. See Munts, p. 40. Joseph Lash, p. 42.

[38] See Munts, p. 35.

[39] See Part 1, Section 1, p. 68.

[40] See Part 3, Section 2, NSA in the Cold War, p. 533.

[41] *America*, April 13, 1946, Vol. 75, 28-29. See p. 739 for complete text of Murray's article.

[42] See Meyer, p. 143, Farber, p. 592, West, p. 556, Ellis, p. 107, Birenbaum, p. 584, Cater, p. 536.

[43] Data from Peter Jones, *Relations of USNSA and IUS*, pp. 20-26. See also Blair, digest of Jones report, p. 538, and Break with IUS: Bill Ellis and Jim Smith Resign, p. 188.

[44] See Welsh, p. 168, Detroit Economic Club, p. 191, Dobkin, p. 1026, Sanders, p. 995, LSU, p. 454.

[45] *Editor's note:* On the matter of adult relations, see also Jonas, p. 771, on the Student Federalists, Reisen, p. 781, on the SDA, Wurf, p. 178, and McLaughlin, p. 819, both on the Catholic Caucus.

[46]See Statement of southern Delegates, report of the NSA Constitutional Convention, p. 1113.

[47] See "NSA Constitution and Student Bill of Rights," p. 1108.

PICTURE CREDITS: *Then:* c. 1945. *Now:* c. 2000 (*Both, author*)

MIRIAM HASKELL BERLIN

Professional Summary: In more than three decades of teaching undergraduates, and more recently in adult degree programs, I have worked in a variety of culture areas (Western Europe, Russia and Soviet, Islamic and Middle East) and in a number of interdisciplinary contexts (regional studies, history and literature, peasant societies, theory and institutional development, modernization) and a core curriculum for the Radcliffe Seminars, involving an interdisciplinary approach to the evolution of western culture taught over a span of three years.

Education: B.A. History, Smith College, Magna cum laude, History prize, Phi Beta Kappa. M.A. Radcliffe College, Regional Studies, USSR. Ph.D. Radcliffe College. Thesis in Russian History.

Teaching Experience: Harvard University, Extension School. Lecturer in History, 1986-present; Radcliffe Seminars, 1974-1988. Lecturer, Semester at Sea, 1994. Lecturer, History and Modern Culture, Harvard University, Slavic Department, Social Studies. Lecturer, 1981-1984, University of Puget Sound. Visiting Lecturer, Islamic Culture, 1984, Wellesley College. Assistant Professor, Lecturer in Russian, European, and Middle Eastern History, 1958-1975, Harvard University. Teaching Fellow and Instructor in Social Studies and General Education, 1951-1956; Associate, Davis Center for Russian Studies, Harvard University.

Consulting: National Faculty. Lecturer in Humanities, Teaching Institutes, Long Beach, CA, 1996. Delta Academy, Tulane, 1994. Pennsylvania Academy, State College, PA, 1993; Delta Academy, University of Mississippi, 1992; San Rafael, CA, 1987; Guildford College, Greensboro, NC, 1980; Rockville Center, Long Island, NY, 1978; Gary, Indiana, 1978; Consortium of Springfield Colleges, Humanities Program, Springfield, MA. Lecturer and facilitator, 1986, Lilly Foundation, Indianapolis, IN, University/School Linkage Project. Project judge.

Background and family: I was born in 1926 and grew up in Brookline, MA. I went to Brookline High School. I married Gerald A. Berlin. We have 3 children and 5 grandchildren.

Perspectives on U.S. Student Life and Movements

Editor's note: This Anthology does not aspire to provide either a political or a cultural viewpoint characterizing student life and politics during the period it covers. However, for the reader inclined to explore the subject further, the two contemporary works of scholarship excerpted below can provide comprehensive starting points.

Undergraduate Cultures

Excerpt from the Preface to *Campus Life: Undergraduate Cultures from the End of the Eighteenth Century to the Present,* by Helen Lefkowitz Horowitz. The University of Chicago Press, Chicago, 1987.

This is a book about college students and their lives on campus. It attempts to describe the variety of ways that undergraduates have defined themselves, viewed their professors and fellow collegians, formed associations, and created systems of meaning and codes of behavior....

Since the late nineteenth century the American reading public has had an intense curiosity about college life, fed by magazine articles and books on college customs. In the 1920s the deeds of flaming college youth, seemingly squandering their opportunities, alternately frightened and titillated an older generation and led to a minor genre of college fiction. The political and cultural radicalism of some American college students in the 1960s grabbed headlines and occasioned a vast literature. More quietly, psychologists and sociologists have been researching and writing about undergraduates since the early twentieth century, focusing especially on student values.

* * *

This book offers a new synthesis and a new perspective. Critical to my understanding of undergraduates and their lives on campus are three elements. The first is that college students in the past, as in the present, are not all alike....

The second element is that the past has shaped the present. Not just in the usual sense that all children have parents or all events have causes, but in the sharper, more direct sense that some students in the past created undergraduate subcultures that have been passed down to successive generations and that continue to shape how students work and play in college.

The third is that as America has changed, so too have the institutions of higher education been changing in the last century....

* * *

Differences between present and past are immense. In the 1980s over 7 million young people attend college or university full-time. This constitutes roughly half of American youth between the ages of eighteen and twenty-one, in contrast to an estimated 2 percent in the early 1800s who went to college. The college population of 1800 was white and male and largely of British descent; today slightly more women than men attend college, and the ethnic mix on campus mirrors, with the significant distortion of the under representation of blacks and Hispanics, that of the population. College has always served disproportionately the privileged, but the field of privilege has widened to include greater reaches of the middle and working classes.

Moreover, intrinsically connected to the broadening and deepening of the student body is the basic change in the relation of the college to the society. In a largely agrarian and mercantile society, college served as one of many competing routes to adulthood. In our industrial, bureaucratic one, it has become the pre-eminent channel for those who aspire to gain or keep middle-class status.... Today college graduation has become the necessary prerequisite to professional school. As American society has become transformed in the last two centuries, so has the purpose and function of its institutions of higher education.

Two hundred years ago the college taught a prescribed curriculum to all who entered. Now students choose among a vast array of programs, the less technical of which offer a wide range of electives. Then each class recited together each day. Today's students—depending upon their particular majors and preferences—attend lectures, participate in discussion classes, take labs and studios, work on independent studies, and enter internships. The notion of a prescribed body of knowledge that all educated men must know has moved to the background, while to the foreground has come a commitment to inquiry, to teaching male and female students how to ask questions and to undertake the appropriate research to find answers. Initially the route to the acquisition of the culture of a gentleman or to ministerial training, the undergraduate course has become the standard rite of passage for youth, adapting to meet their highly divergent needs.

Student Politics in America

Excerpt from the 1974 edition Introduction to *Student Politics in America: A Historical Analysis,* by Philip G. Altbach. Transaction Publishers, New Brunswick, New Jersey, 1997.

This volume considers student political and social activism in the United States from 1900 to 1960. It focuses on those periods during which students were most heavily committed to politics, notably the thirties, the late fifties, and the early sixties. The study is largely historical in nature and traces the development of student organizations and assesses their impact on universities and on society....

Within the framework of this study of student organizations and movements, this study concentrates on the actions, values, and ideologies of the organized student movements.[1] ... Focusing on this type of history, however, is problematic because of the lack of continuity. While some student groups, especially those linked to and financed by adult organizations, have been long-lived, most have been unstable. As a result, it is important to focus both on specific student groups and also continuing themes evident in American student activism. For example, the criticisms of society and the university raised by both religious and political student organizations in the late 1920s are important in understanding the more programmatic and active decade of the thirties. The concerns of the Student Peace Union in the late 1950s are reflected, to some extent, in the resurgence of the antiwar movement and the Students for a Democratic Society (SDS) in the sixties.

The organized student movement represented only a small fraction of the student population. For the most part, American students have not been notably radical or opposed to the status quo. In the midst of the turmoil of the past decade [the 1960s], it has often been forgotten that most students have few quarrels with the Establishment and that a powerful student movement has rarely existed on the campuses. Despite the fact that student activism has never represented the opinions of a majority of the student population, nor has even a significant minority of the students participated in activist campaigns, student activism does represent something of the "tip of the iceberg" of American student discontent. The level of discontent can be broadly measured by the success of activist organizations in mobilizing support on the campus.... It is important to keep in mind that student activist organizations and movements represent a constituency substantially larger than its own numbers would indicate. Throughout the period under discussion here, student groups with only a small membership were able to mobilize widespread support for particular causes.

[1] The problem of obtaining adequate data for this study has been a serious one. Student organizations have left fewer records than, for example, labor unions or political parties. Many groups are very short-lived, and much campus protest has been of a local nature. Further, there has in general been more adequate coverage of liberal and radical groups in the literature, in part because such groups had a greater historical sense.

Some thirty organizations could be enumerated

PREWAR STUDENT ACTIVISM: A PROFILE

Martin McLaughlin
University of Notre Dame
Member, U.S. Delegation to the 1946 World Student Congress

Editor's note: This essay originally appeared as a portion of Chapter II in Political Processes in American National Student Organizations, *by Martin McLaughlin, his doctoral dissertation submitted to Notre Dame University, April 1948. McLaughlin provides a useful profile of the major prewar college student organizations and their origins, benefitting from his own status as an undergraduate student before the war and as an undergraduate and graduate student after the war. Author's biography, p. 86.*

It is within this impermanent, intense, youthful, but relatively stable social milieu that the existing national student organizations in the United States operate. Some thirty of them could be enumerated in this country at the present time; they fall into several distinguishable categories:

(a) *Sectarian:* Most prominent among these are the National Federation of Catholic College Students, the Newman Club Federation, the National Intercollegiate Christian Council, the B'nai B'rith Hillel Foundations, and the student division of such sectarian youth groups—e.g., Methodist Youth League, American Unitarian Youth, etc.[1]; there is also the worldwide Student Christian Movement, numbering many United States affiliates, which first took root here in 1858.[2]

(b) *Political:* Under this heading can be listed the Student League for Industrial Democracy (primarily an educational organization at the present time), Students for Democratic Action (college division of Americans for Democratic Action), the new Students for Wallace, and the intercollegiate and student divisions of the Young People's Socialist League, Young Progressive Citizens of America, American Youth for Democracy, etc.[3] A special case is the American Veterans Committee[4]—founded mainly by students and very active in colleges and universities.

(c) *Professional:* Best known group of this type is the Association of Internes and Medical Students.

(d) *Service:* Groups falling into this category are rarely controlled by students; since they exist mainly for relief and exchange purposes—which functions often require expert administrators—their directors are usually adult youth workers: e.g., World Student Service Fund and the American Committee for International Student Service.[5]

(e) *Social:* Here we include the Greek-letter fraternities and sororities which are national in scope.

(f) *General:* The United States National Student Association is currently the only completely student-controlled organization explicitly and politically devoted to serving the needs of students.[6]

* * *

The National Student Federation of America

In contrast to the Student Christian movements, which had been in existence for over two hundred years and in the United States for ninety,[7] these general associations of students did not appear on the scene until the founding of the National Student Federation of America in 1925 at a conference at Princeton University.[8] Representatives of two hundred and forty-five colleges and universities established the Federation as a national intercollegiate student government association. The unit of organization was the student governing body in the affiliated college. The Federation's first convention listed the main purposes:

> to achieve a spirit of cooperation among the students of the United States; to develop an intelligent student opinion on questions of national and international importance; to foster understanding among the students of the world in the furtherance of an enduring peace. In working for these ends the Federation acts independently of any political party or religious sect.[9]

The annual Christmas congress was to be the occasion for thorough discussion of student problems, adoption of stands on these and on national issues, and election of the national officers whose duties for the ensuing year would be to carry out the agreed policies.[10] For the first three years the Federation concentrated on the tasks of strengthening itself, building up a student public opinion behind it, and securing affiliates among the nation's colleges and universities. Then it expanded to other functions—travel and exchange; publications; the conducting of surveys and polls on such questions as part-time work by students, the Prohibition Law, the Oxford antiwar Pledge; participation in international conferences; and stimulation of open-forum-type discussions in member colleges. Although accused from time to time of being "radical," it remained the "approved" student organization of national scope.

Until 1932 this organization occupied the national student scene alone. But forces were already at work to produce a rival destined to crowd it into the background, so far as political interest was concerned.

As early as 1905 Upton Sinclair, Jack London, Clarence Darrow, and others had established an Intercollegiate Socialist Society to create students of socialism, they said, not to produce socialists. The post–World War I world produced a new Intercollegiate Liberal League, its successor, with "a curious admixture of doctrine...an extravagant projection of Wilson's heralded vision, blended with the inspiration occasioned by the end of Tsarist darkness."[11] The group expanded rapidly, merged in 1922 with the National Student Committee for the Limitation of Armaments, and began to issue *The New Student*[12]—a journal which continued for six years to be the most influential student periodical in the country.[13] Over this period, however, the vitality of the movement was sapped by a decreasing membership; and in 1928 the remnant ceased to publish *The New Student* and joined the League for Industrial Democracy under the title of Student League for Industrial Democracy.

The National Student League

Three years later, in 1931, the Communist wing of this organization seceded and set itself up as the National Student League, devoted to student needs and to "student participation in the revolutionary movement against capitalism." Its purposes were listed in official documents which contained such statements of policy as the following: "To give active support to militant organizations of workers and farmers...[and]...to oppose all preparations against the Soviet Union, whose policy arises from the new social order it is developing."[14]

The publicity attendant upon the "student invasion" of the Harlan County (Kentucky) coal fields in March, 1932,[15] launched the League on its short but spectacular career; and during the next three years it was the center of many a battle on campus and off. Its members vociferously adopted the Oxford Pledge,[16] condemned the Reserve Officers Training Corps,[17] promoted antiwar strikes, and periodically protested suspensions, expulsion, hirings, and firings of teachers and students from New

York City to Los Angeles. It was frequently and violently attacked in newspapers and public addresses as being the student section of the Communist Party.[18]

The American Student Union

Ever since the split in 1931 the National Student League and the Student League for Industrial Democracy had been quarreling about ideology, but engaging in such joint activities as the various protests and peace strikes; during the period of 1934-35 there had also been considerable defection from the National Student Federation of America by more or less radical elements who could not, nevertheless, quite bring themselves to join either of the other two organizations. To meet this situation the Student League for Industrial Democracy and the National Student League held a joint meeting for all interested students on the premises of the Young Men's Christian Association in Columbus, Ohio, during the 1935 Christmas holidays.[19] Four hundred and fifty student delegates from two hundred colleges established the constitution of a new organization and accepted its program. This was the beginning of the American Student Union.

The original executive committee of the Union consisted of eleven Socialists, nine Communists, and ten unaffiliated "liberals." The program, however, was completely non-Marxist and contained four major points—the alliance of the American Student Union with labor, freedom of expression in classrooms and student publications, opposition to "militarism in education," and condemnation of discrimination because of race or creed.

Like its rival, the National Student Federation, the Union lent itself rather easily to the control of the small group which did in fact direct it for approximately four years.[20] . . . The highest governing body was the annual convention, whose main duties in actual practice were to debate broad issues and to elect the National Executive Committee. In the hands of this committee the constitution itself concentrated the powers of making policy between conventions, setting the time, date, and representation for conventions, coopting members, cooperating with other organizations, issuing charters and special memberships, and determining the personnel of the Administrative Staff. This last body, consisting of those executive members and field secretaries who "find it possible to attend meetings," worked to carry out policies (and set them) between the semiannual meetings of the Executive Committee.[21]

It was the political policies of this small group that brought the Union most into the limelight and eventually led to the minority control which destroyed it. These policies grew out of that section of the original platform which dealt with peace: peace in 1936 meant the Oxford anti-war Pledge; in 1937, collective security and the League of Nations; in 1938, the lifting of the arms embargo on Spain; in 1939, remaining aloof from the "imperialist" war and condoning the Soviet invasion of Finland.

This final shift and other events of the year 1939 deprived the organization of its most capable and influential leaders and started it on the final road to disintegration. In January, 1940, Joseph P. Lash, General Secretary for four years, "separated from his former associates because he had become convinced that their beliefs were not compatible with the preservation of the American way of life."[22] What had apparently convinced him was the persistent refusal of the Union's Madison convention of 1939 to brand the Soviet invasion of Finland an act of aggression.[23]

At the same time a few hundred miles away, in Minneapolis, the National Student Federation of America, perennial foe of the Union, was holding its fifteenth annual convention. Direction had for years rested within a small group of fraternity leaders, and by this time it was less conservative than the general membership—due to the continuous arguments with the American Student Union; in view of the controversy over the war, however, the convention adopted a series of anti-war and isolationist resolutions.

The New Jersey Conference

For one more year the Federation and the Union went their respective ways quietly and separately. The former was conservative and isolationist, the latter left-wing and also isolationist. In November, 1940, a newcomer to the United States scene, the American Committee for International Student Service, which had been cooperating with the National Student Federation for several months, engaged Lash as its General Secretary.[24] This action transferred the former ruling group of the American Student Union to the new organization and marked the beginning of an attempt to establish a student movement to counter the Union by combining the International Student Service's American membership with the Federation.

The junction was to have been accomplished at a joint convention of the two organizations at New Jersey College for Women in December, 1940. Delegates were greeted the first day by a message from President Roosevelt which stated in part that "every student must be a volunteer in the intellectual and spiritual struggle to preserve freedom for mankind."[25] But although the Federation withdrew from the American Youth Congress—in which it had been an active, middle-of-the-road member—still, in spite of this Administration support, it did not endorse the newly formed Student League for Progressive Action, nor did it merge with the American Committee for International Student Service.

The net result of the Conference was the loss by "the Young Communist League of its initiative in the American youth movement for the first time in six years";[26] but still the proposed affiliation of the non-communist general student organizations—although desired and worked for by the leaders—did not materialize. The American Committee for International Student Service had committed itself to more extended action, and the National Student Federation of America had come back into the foreground of the national student scene; but their merger did not take place until almost a year later.

During 1941 the Federation managed to hold its membership steady and followed in general the New Deal policy line; but the American Student Union's seventh annual convention, coming immediately after another complete reversal of policy in December, 1941, found the Union's ranks sadly depleted.[27] Having pledged its services unqualifiedly to the Administration in the war "against fascism and aggression," the convention adjourned; it was the last national meeting of the American Student Union and the end of a political history. The real leaders, who had originally built up the organization and crystallized and probably enforced their opinion, found themselves suddenly in a weak minority situation. By trying to find compromises with the Communist minority in the Executive Committee, they had gradually lost their moderate followers. When the break came in 1939, the original leaders were forced to resign because of lack of any backing; this left the organization almost completely in Communist hands and ultimately (in 1941 as we have seen) destroyed it. It is a pattern not unfamiliar.

The International Student Assembly

The entry of the United States into the war brought most of the student leaders into the armed forces; no large-scale continuous action was possible, particularly during the early days and the mobilization period. Note should be taken, however, of the International Student Assembly, sponsored by the American Committee of International Student Service, which brought together delegates, many of them in uniform, from fifty-three nations, in Washington, D.C., in September, 1942.[28] President Roosevelt received them at the White House and delivered a major address, broadcast in thirty-two languages, hailing the Assembly and calling upon the students to play their role in the future of the world. And again a small group consisting of Joseph P. Lash (on furlough from the Army), Molly Yard (his former colleague in the American Student Union), and Mrs. Elliot Pratt (chairman of the Assembly and *ex officio* member of all its committees, Lash's successor as General Secretary) exercised unofficial, but actual control over the officially elected directorate.[29]

This Assembly, judged from its list of speakers—which included labor-union officials, educators, Associate Justice Jackson of the Supreme Court, and many officers of the administration—possessed a quasi-official character; governments of the United Nations took an almost official part in its work and showed great interest in the postwar reconstruction plans, both cultural and material. The active cooperation of Mrs. Roosevelt lent it Administration sanction in this country, and it was mainly through her efforts that this distinguished array of speakers was assembled.

The most heated battle on the convention floor resulted in perpetuating the Assembly's presiding committee as a Permanent Committee for the International Student Assembly to continue the work of the Assembly and plan for a postwar meeting of students in connection with the Peace Conference.[30] This result was what had been sought by the controlling group; but it was achieved over great opposition by such devious parliamentary activity that it aroused great resentment. During a national caucus the American delegation established a continuations committee for the United States—again with the support of the controlling group.[31]

The United States Student Assembly

While the International Student Assembly proceeded on its international business, the Continuations Committee in succeeding months made plans for the establishment of the United States Student Assembly—which was to be the American affiliate of the international body. The constitutional convention of the United States Student Assembly was held in May, 1943, and was marked by a strong and almost open move by the Young Communist League to gain control through a new tactic, by deluging it "with delegate applications from law, medical, and dental schools whose students have never been a part of undergraduate organizations."[32] These applications were rejected on the ground that "the undergraduate setup of USSA precludes the membership of graduate professional students who have traditionally had organizations of their own."[33]

Two major attempts by Communists to gain control were defeated, as vigorous debate marked their efforts; the Constitution explicitly excluded Communists and Fascists and stated rather that the Assembly was "a confederation of autonomous democratic student groups, organized democratically, and bound together by the common belief that democracy is the only just society."[34] It was political primarily; its activities continued for approximately four more years—celebration of International Students' Day, support for student relief drives, and representation in the American delegation to the World Student Congress which took place in Prague, Czechoslovakia, in August, 1946.[35] In 1947 it merged with the Union for Democratic Action to form the Students for Democratic Action.

Preparations for the National Student Association

On this troubled scene, in 1947, came the National Student Association. The story behind the Constitutional Convention at Madison, Wisconsin, in September, 1947, begins at the World Student Congress at Prague, Czechoslovakia, in August, 1946.[36] That Congress had been conceived at a previous international student celebration in the same city in November, 1945; a twelve-nation International Preparatory Committee of student leaders did the planning. . . .[37]

What impressed the twenty-five members of the American delegation most, however, was the fact that national student organizations in other countries had a strength, a recognition, and an effectiveness far beyond anything yet seen in the United States. They became convinced that American college students would never be able to make the weight of their opinions and ideas felt in international student affairs—especially in the new International Union of Students, established at the Prague Congress—until some similar organization, of a representative character, existed in this country. The Chicago Student Conference of December, 1946, was the direct result of this conviction.[38] Out of it came the National Continuations Committee whose work was the preparation of the constitutional convention of the new United States National Student Association.

END NOTES

1 *Editor's note:* For more on the Protestant and Catholic Student groups, see pp. 688, 732, and 741.

2 C. P. Shedd, *Two Centuries of Student Christian Movements*, 94; Although religious student society records exist from American college records as early as 1706, it was not until the establishment of the University of Virginia's Young Men's Christian Association chapter on October 12, 1858, that a formal beginning of a student Christian movement was made in the United States.

3 See Reisin, pp. 781 and 787, Keating, p. 811.

4 See Bellush, p. 708.

5 See ISS, p. 50, WSSF, p. 622.

6 This characteristic has been one of the most bitterly debated matters since the beginning of the Association: what precisely is the distinction between the partisan political activity in which the Association cannot engage and the nonpartisan student activity which it must perform.

7 C. P. Sheed, *loc. cit.*

8 *New York Times,* December 13-14, 1925 (except where otherwise noted, the historical material contained in this chapter is adapted from the files of the New York Times, covering the twenty-year period from 1925 to 1945).

9 *Fifteen Years of Student Leadership,* National Student Federation of America brochure, 4. (Quotation is from the Constitution of the Federation.)

10 *Ibid.,* 3.

11 J. A. Wechsler, *Revolt on the Campus,* 26.

12 Not to be confused with American Youth for Democracy's publication, recently begun, of the same name.

13 J. A. Wechsler, *op. cit.,* 27.

14 *New York Times,* January 14, 1934.

15 At the height of the Kentucky mining disturbances an expedition of some forty students, arranged by the National Student League, the Workers' International Relief, and the Social Problems Club of Columbia University, left New York City after a mass meeting at the University, to study actual conditions in the mines. After a series of sensational adventures, including search by armed Bell County (Kentucky) deputies, arrest and harangue in a county court room by the County Attorney, expulsion and threats of lynching, and fruitless protests to the governors of Tennessee and Kentucky, the travel-weary group arrived in Washington, D.C., to confer with Senators Costigan and Cutting, sponsors of a bill calling for investigation of the Harlan County mining operations.

16 A pledge taken by a group of students at Oxford University, England, declaring that they would not participate in any war waged for any purpose by the British Empire. It became popular among pacifist students in the United States between wars.

17 These protests continued in crescendo for several years—until the passage of an act of Congress rendering ROTC noncompulsory. They were directed mainly against the Supreme Court's opinion in the Hamilton case: Several students at the University of California (Berkeley), Methodist by religion, had refused because of their religion to take

military training and had been dismissed from the university. Their appeal for reinstatement on the ground that California's action violated the liberty guaranteed under the Fourteenth Amendment was denied by the Court: "California has not drafted them or called them to attend the University. They are seeking education offered by the state and at the same time insisting that they be excluded from the prescribed course solely upon grounds of their religious beliefs and conscientious objections to war, preparation for war, and military education. . . . Viewed in the light of our decisions, that proposition must at once be put aside as untenable (citation of United States v Schwimmer, United States v MacIntosh, Pearson v Coale) . . . Plainly there is no ground for the contention that the regents' order, requiring able-bodied male students under the age of twenty-four as a condition of their enrollment to take the prescribed instruction in military science and tactics, transgresses any constitutional right asserted by these appellants." (Hamilton et al. v Regents of the University of California, 293 U.S. 245 (1934)).

[18] An interesting and significant contrast between the Federation and the League was provided by the annual conventions of the two organizations held concurrently but separately in Washington, D.C., at the end of 1933. On December 28 of that year both groups quite coincidentally visited the White House; the Federation's delegates presented roses to Mrs. Roosevelt; the League's envoys presented to the President's secretary a 5,000-signature petition asking for the abolition cf the Reserve Officers Training Corps!

[19] Barred from the Ohio State University grounds at the last moment because of either (a) the fuel shortage or (b) the Hearst papers' charges of communism, the sessions had to be moved to downtown Columbus.

[20] Its major constitutional provisions established individual membership of high-school or college students, faculty, and alumni; at least ten members were required to form a chapter and apply for an official charter; district, state, and regional divisions could be made at the discretion of the national office.

[21] *Constitution* (in American Student Union *High-School Handbook*, pp. 21-25).

[22] *New York Times,* January 17, 1942.

[23] The convention's equally persistent and sweeping condemnation of the "war-mongering" Roosevelt Administration, which Lash supported, also indicated that his group could no longer control the Union in the face of Communist strength.

[24] B. Minton, "The Plot against the Youth," *New Masses*, December 1940.

[25] *New York Times,* December 27, 1940. The American Student Union was holding its annual congress in nearby New York City—condemning aid to Britain, and calling for an alliance of China, Russia and the United States to preserve the peace. Many delegates also attended the New Jersey Conference, obtained the floor with difficulty, and denounced the proposed merger; the credentials committee of the Conference alleged that the Union had attempted to pack the meetings with their own members.

[26] R. G. Spivack, "Youth Reorganizes," *Nation*, January 18, 1941.

[27] The membership had been falling off ever since the withdrawal of the moderates at the 1939 convention; at its beginning the Union numbered perhaps 6,000 students (according to its General Secretary); by 1938 it had 20,000 in 130 colleges and 100 high schools; in 1940, from a membership which had shrunk to less than 2,000—mostly centered around New York City—the delegates to the New York convention numbered 355, from 79 colleges and 41 high schools in 25 states; in 1941 there were 230 delegates from 25 high schools and colleges in only 15 states.

[28] *International Student Assembly,* 5.

[29] Report of the International Student Assembly [sic], 9.

[30] *Ibid.,* 72.

[31] *Ibid.*, 84.

[32] *New York Times*, May 7, 1943.

[33] *Ibid.*

[34] *Ibid.*

[35] *Statistics,* World Student Congress.

[36] Fuller treatment appears in the brochure *Operation University*, edited by Henry W. Briefs and the author, and published by the National Catholic Youth Council, 1947. *Editor's note:* See Kirchner, p. 76.

[37] See Tibbetts, p. 68, and Bellush, p. 73.

[38] "Conference in Chicago," *America,* March 29, 1947, contains a more detailed account of this meeting.

PROLOGUE TO NSA

SECTION 2

Prewar and Wartime Predecessors

CONTENTS

Edward R. Murrow
Washington State College, p.26
Pres., NSFA, 1930-33

Joseph P. Lash
City College of New York, p.42
Natl. Sec., ASU, 1935-39

Mary Lou Rogers
Swarthmore College, p.34
Pres., USSA, 1943-44

This section provides an overview of the major players and issues in domestic and international U.S. student intercollegiate affairs just before World War II.These are the stories of the National Student Federation of America (NSFA) and Washington State College's Edward R. Murrow, its most prominent leader; of the United States Student Assembly (USSA) and of Swarthmore College's Mary Lou Rogers, who was its first President in 1943; and of CCNY and Columbia University's Joseph P. Lash, charismatic national student leader of the American Student Union (ASU) and the center-left.

Dean Marguerite Kehr, who was an adviser to both NSFA and NSA, tells the story of NSFA, which was formed in 1925. Its member colleges were represented by student governments, and it developed campus, national, and international programs similar to those that would be formed by NSA after the war. USSA was based on campus chapters and individual student memberships, and focused on public policy and student economic and social issues. It was formed two years after the ASU (also a campus chapter-based organization) was split when its choice to follow a Communist pro-Soviet "party line" led Joe Lash to quit as Executive Secretary and First Lady Eleanor Roosevelt to withdraw her support.

The stories highlight both their contrasting missions and their active engagement in international affairs. This latter engagement was colored at every level by wars in Europe and Asia threatening to become global, and by the complex ideological, political, and national security interests which fueled the struggles for organizational power and for the control of policy agendas throughout the country, including in student organizations. These struggles involved a small number of highly organized communist and Marxist students and their sympathizers, pacifists, isolationists, and anticommunist liberals and social democrats.

The International Student Service provides an interim safety net

The infrastructure role of the International Student Service (described in Janis Tremper Dowd's Part 1 essay) is highlighted here. ISS was an outgrowth in the 1920s of the World Student Christian Federation. The newly opened ISS New York City office in 1941 provided a haven for Joe Lash, who became its Executive Secretary. It refocused the support of Mrs. Roosevelt's continuing interest as a mentor of U.S. youth and student organizations and service agencies, and provided continuity for a global noncommunist, secular U.S. presence on the international student relief scene after World War II.

These precursors of postwar intercollegiate student organizations remained almost dormant until war's end in 1945, and were largely unknown to the student leaders who founded the U.S. National Student Association in 1946-47.

1931-1944

Student Organization before the End of World War II

During the 1930s through the early forties, student governments, the Student Christian Movement, Catholic and Jewish organizations, and the social fraternities maintained a stable presence. National debates and demonstrations were dominated by issues of war and peace, the economy, and the ideological struggle between communism, socialism, capitalism, and fascism. No stable national student organization devoted to public policy survived the war. This section traces these organizations through the NSFA, ASU, and USSA. The USSA, in collaboration with the ISS and YWCA/YMCA, provided support for the small group of student leaders in 1945 who organized the U.S. delegation to the 1946 World Student Congress, which led to formation of the U.S. National Student Association in 1947.

1937

Welcome A.S.U. Delegates

The Vassar Miscellany News

Published Semi-Weekly

VOL. XXII. Poughkeepsie, New York, Monday, December 27, 1937

AMERICAN STUDENTS UNION BRINGS 600 TO VASSAR

JOSEPH P. LASH

Executive Secretary of the A.S.U.

GEORGE WATT GIVES BANNER TO F.U.S.S.

Vermont Meets California to Plan Year's Prog at Annual Convent

MacCRACKEN SPEA

Education in Democ Subject of Discussi

With delegates pouring in all over the country, the V A.S.U. prepared to play host the third annual convention American Student Union. Se hundred delegates are expec have arrived by tonight and tal of about 600 will be on tomorrow morning when E tive Secretary Joseph P. bangs the gavel.

The delegates from New and surrounding districts been arriving by busloads and loads all afternoon. Besides ter delegates, many ...

4

A. S. U. FORMED BY NAT'L CONVENTION AT COLUMBUS, OHIO

Students From 113 Schools Send Delegates To Meetings On Dec. 28-29

UNITED MOVEMENT

Strives For Betterment Of Economic Position Of Students In School

With 427 delegates representing students in every section of the country, the American Student Union was formed at a convention held in the Y. W. C. A. at Columbus, Ohio, on December 28 and 29. In spite of a heavy snowstorm, 113 schools sent representatives—76 colleges and universities and 37 high schools.

This new organization—the American Student Union—is a broad united student movement against war and Fascism. Its program states that it strives for the betterment of the economic position of students in school and their right to a job when graduated. It fights against racial, religious, and political discrimination and defends academic freedom. Its main point stresses the students' fight against war and supports the Oxford Pledge.

N. S. L., S. L. I. D. Represented

1936

3

W. S. C. N. Y. U.

Bulletin

NEW YORK UNIVERSITY, MONDAY, FEBRUARY 26, 1940 No. 23

Inter-Faith Religion-in-Life Week Begins Today; JCF, Newman Club, Christian Association Hold Forums and Seminars to Discuss Problems

Schedule of Events for Week

MONDAY

Prominant Speakers Will Lecture on Youth, Education, Economics, and Labor in Religion

By WILLIAM BLANCK

Religious programs planned by the three faiths, outside speakers presenting their views on religious and ethical problems in the classroom, and the Day Org's keynote program will form the basis for the observance of Religion-in-Life Week beginning today. For the next five days, religion will become a major part of the curriculum throughout the entire University.

Speaks On China

Six seminars on subjects of special interest to students will meet every afternoon, Monday through Thursday. Each will be conducted by an expert in his particular field: T. Z. Koo, formerly an official in the Chinese Government; the Rev. A. J. Muste, Director of the Labor Temple Church; and

6

1940

THE L.I.D. IN ACTION

The Campus

The Industrial Front

The Picket Line

The Platform

The Radio

The City Chapters

Publications

Poster printed for West Virginia workers by L.I.D.

What the League for Industrial Democracy thinks, discusses, debates and does in these critical days.

LEAGUE FOR INDUSTRIAL DEMOCRACY

1

1931

5

MRS. ROOSEVELT HEARS STUDENT LEADER TESTIFY

Sits With Dies Committee as Joseph Lash Calls One Group Communist.

WAS SOCIALIST TILL 1937

Witness Says Fear of Fascism Prompted Formation of the Student Union.

WASHINGTON, Dec. 1 (A. P.).—Mrs. Franklin D. Roosevelt today made her third visit to the Dies committee to hear testimony by leaders of American youth organizations. She said she joined the committee spectators again especially to hear Joseph Lash, executive secretary of the American Students Union.

"I thought I'd like to hear what he had to say," Mrs. Roosevelt smiled to reporters as she took her seat among a group of young men and women on the front row.

She showed up at the hearing in the House Office Building for the first time yesterday morning and returned again in the afternoon when the American Youth Congress had its hearing. Asked today how she thought the Youth Congress leaders had acquitted themselves, Mrs. Roosevelt thought for a second and then said:

"Well, don't you think I'd better leave that to your judgment rather than mine?"

Youth Leader Takes Stand.

When Mr. Lash took the stand, Mrs. Roosevelt moved from the front row of spectators to the end of the committee table—the same place she occupied yesterday when the Youth Congress leaders were on the stand. The Student Union is an affiliate of the Youth Congress.

Sitting beside Mr. Lash at the table was Agnes Reynolds, a tall brown-eyed girl who is the college secretary of the Student Union.

Under questioning by J. B. Matthews, committee investigator, Mr. Lash testified—while Mrs. Roosevelt listened intently—that he joined the Socialist party in 1929 and resigned in 1937 shortly after returning from the Spanish war. Asked his reasons for quitting, he said:

1939

2

STUDENT REVIEW

Official Organ National Student League

KENTUCKY MAKES RADICALS

☆

COLUMBIA UNIVERSITY STRIKES

☆

PROF. CARVER SURVIVES HIS REVOLUTION

☆

"1919", A REVIEW

MAY, 1932

10c

(1) *League for Industrial Democracy*, c. 1931. (2) *Student Review*, National Student League, May 1932. (3) Johns Hopkins *Newsletter* (MD), 1/16/36. (4) *Vassar Miscellany News* (NY), 12/27/37. (5) *New York Sun*, 12/1/39. (6) *Bulletin*, New York University, 2/26/40. (7) *Bulletin*, 1/6/41. (8) Ad from *The Princeton Bulletin* (NJ), 1/16/44. (9) ISS, *Vassar Miscellany News*, 12/31/41. (10) *The Targum*, Rutgers U. (NJ), 12/11/40. (11) *The New York Times*, 5/10/43. (12) *Simmons News*, Simmons College (MA), 10/5/44. (13) *The Daily Princetonian*, 9/15/37. (14) *The Agnes Scott News* (GA), 1/17/40. (15) Federalist photo, courtesy, Gil Jonas. (16) Harvard photo from Report to the Third Annual Convention, ASU, 1937.

NSFA Withdraws from AYC In Split in Policy, Structure; ASU Raps Coudert Committee

"Cease War Drive Abolish Inequality" DemandsConvention

When the American Student Union assembled for its sixth annual convention during Christmas Week, 11 regular delegates from WSC attended. There were present at this time more than 400 delegates representing various educational institutions from various parts of the country. A "Charter of Students Rights and Responsibilities" formulated at the convention will form the basis of American Student Union activity during 1941.

Affirms Neutrality Stand

The charter affirms the ASU stand for neutrality in the European war, aid to China and an embargo on Japan, and the adoption of a far-reaching program to "preserve the American educational system from the present war drive," it was stated. As a part of its campaign around said charter which, among other things, calls for an end to discrimination in

Columbia Law School Sets Application Deadline

The Columbia Office of Admissions announces that candidates for admission to the Columbia Law School must submit their applications not later than February 15, and that it is desirable to apply in January. Interested seniors should write to the Office of University Admissions, Columbia University, for the proper forms.

Youth Groups Hear Leaders at Convention

Held by Youth Committee Against War; LaFollette, Wheeler, Thomas Speak

Various student organizations in the United States, the Progressive Student League, the Student Service, the Young People's S League, and the League for Ind Democracy held a convention

Federation Also Refuses to Join Forces with ISS

Disagreement on foreign policies and organization structure led the National Student Federation of America to withdraw from the American Youth Congress last Monday at the close of the four-day conference of the Federation at the New Jersey College for Women. The delegates of the NSFA, representing over a hundred college student councils, voted to withdraw 87 to 24.

Refuses ISS

The NSFA also refused to affiliate with the International Student Service, one of the sponsors of the conference. The ISS, which has had the

1941

7

8

ACTUAL PICTURES OF THE

INVASION

of

EUROPE

WILL BE SHOWN AT THE

Playhouse & Garden

Sunday, Monday, Tuesday, Wednesday

1944

9

Students Discuss Their Role In Pan-Americanism At Yale ISS Conference

Announcement that Japan had attacked Honolulu and Manila brought to a dramatic close the International Student Service Conference on *The Role of the University in Hemispheric Solidarity* at Yale University this past weekend. "Now the moment has come when we're going to test the spirit of this meeting" stated Professor Samuel

And prominent author, Dr. Carlos Concha, Minister Plenipotentiary

At the plenary session on Saturday afternoon, speakers presented the background of hemispheric solidarity, stressing the difficulties which confront permanent relations between the two Americas. Discounting economics as the sole basis of men's actions, Dr. Duggan pointed out the climatic influence on Latin America, its aristocratically organized civilization, and its religious and social variances with the United States.

The keynote of Dr. Concha's address was the danger of journalistic misrepresentation of the Latin American countries. John Gunther, in his latest best-seller *Inside Latin America*, and colorful p... using as his tw... mation the lead... party and a mu... in Fortune mag... ample of misre... Hollywood ver... two-Americas. Professor F...

1941

10

The Targum

New Group Seeks To Abolish Interfraternity Council

Committee Probes Bleacher Crash

Wesley Mitchell To Give Lecture Before Students

No Desire For US Participation In War, Says Irish Student

'House Presidents Club' Holds Two Sessions

Pledged To Revitalize Greek Situation

Petition Council For Vigilantes

Junior Honorary Group Asks For Formation Of Sophomore Society

16

HARVARD STUDENTS STRIKE FOR PEAC

1937

The Simmons News

SIMMONS COLLEGE, BOSTON, MASS., THURSDAY, OCTOBER 5, 1944

...leanor Roosevelt Speaks Oct. 27

Fall Stop Singing Starts This Week

President's Wife is to be Guest of USSA at Assembly

...homores Hear ...ident Beatley

1944

12

College Undergraduate Council Concerned With Diverse Problems of Student Life

The Undergraduate Council at Princeton is a representative body of students which is concerned with problems of student life not directly under the aegis of the college administration. It acts as an intermediary between the 2200 undergraduates and University authorities.

Until two years ago this body was not fully representative of every phase of student life. It was then composed of the three Senior Class officers, the President and Vice-President by popular vote elects its representative to the Council. In this way every undergraduate feels represented on the body, not only by his class officers but also by the member from the particular extra-curricular group to which he may belong.

The questions which come before the Undergraduate Council at its monthly meetings are ones which particularly concern students, their relations to the Faculty, problems of student discipline at dances, etc. An ex-

13

1937

15

STUDENT UNIT BARS REDS AND FASCISTS

Newly Formed Assembly Puts Ban Into Its Constitution After a Lively Fight

PROGRAM OFFERED TO U. S.

Free Trade, a Second Front and End of Insecurity Are Among the Demands

Communist undergraduate organizations in the colleges of this country—and Fascist organizations, if any should present themselves—were barred from membership in the newly organized United States Student Assembly by the constitution it adopted here yesterday at the Y. W. C. A., 610 Lexington Avenue, at the close of a heated three day's session.

Although the constitution defines the United States Student Assembly as "a confederation of autonomous democratic student groups, organized democratically and bound together by the common belief that democracy is the only just society," the Communists

11

1943

NSFA Considers World Crisis

Delegates Convene During Xmas Holidays

How can U. S. college and university students face the present world crisis?

With this question as their paramount problem, 200 National Student Federation of America delegates from all corners of the nation met at the University of Minnesota to devote a portion of their holiday vacation to a discussion of their mutual problems.

Relegating to second place such usual NSFA convention topics as the honor system and campus election problems, the delegates set to work to reconcile their divergent viewpoints on how to keep America out of war.

Support Neutrality

Resolutions passed only after stormy debate called upon the

1940

14

Tom Hughes, left (Carleton College, MN; see. p. 637), newly elected President, meets with Board of Representatives at Student Federalist convention in Chicago, September 30, 1944.

(Gil Jonas)

1944

Founded to fulfill the need for a national student organization

1. The National Student Federation of America (1925-1941)

Marguerite Kehr

Dean of Women, Bloomsburg State Teachers College, Pennsylvania
NSFA Board of Advisers, 1938-1941. NSA National Advisory Council, 1954-1958

"When the college students of America gathered together in 1947 to found the U.S. National Student Association, they had no knowledge of the National Student Federation of America."

Editor's note: This article first appeared in NSA's Student Government Bulletin, *April 1954.*

The National Student Federation of America [NSFA] was founded in 1925 following a conference at Princeton University, called for the purpose of having representative college students consider whether the United States should enter the World Court. This was a hotly debated issue at the time. Delegates assembled from some 245 colleges and universities. At this conference some Vassar College students who had attended an International Student Confederation (Confederation Internationale des Etudiants) meeting at Copenhagen emphasized the need for a national student organization in the U.S.A., and the first steps were taken toward this end. Student government organizations were to be the voting units and the organization would function through national officers and representatives of seven regions. Officers and regional representatives were to form a National Executive Committee which could function between the annual congresses.

NSFA builds an international program

In its early days, the work of the organization was carried on entirely through student efforts without a national office and without adequate finances. In 1928, with the aid of the National Union of Students of England and Wales, a small office was established in New York, primarily to handle student travel to Europe. But soon the activities of this office increased. That same year, the World Student Union amalgamated with the Federation. In addition, international intercollegiate debates were inaugurated, which continued without interruption through the years until the onset of World War II ended the activities of NSFA.

As its member colleges realized the advantage of a central clearinghouse for information, an entirely new group of services was undertaken in answer to the demands made upon the national office. These included surveys, research studies, weekly news releases, and a series of educational radio broadcasts over nationwide networks. Each year following the first conference at Princeton, national congresses were held in addition to local regional meetings. Each congress saw new members and new ideas on interracial cooperation, academic freedom, and training for citizenship included in the program. To stabilize the Federation's work, there was created a national Board of Advisers, chosen from the field of education.

NSFA expands links to ISS and launches the Public Affairs Council, 1933-37

Sensing the need for a medium of student expression, NSFA undertook in 1933 publication of a magazine, *The National Student Mirror*, which for three years was outstanding in its field. The year 1934 saw the federation's initiation of a movement which established the National Institute of Public Affairs. At the time of the economic depression, NSFA participated in conferences ultimately leading to the creation of the National Youth Administration, which brought federal aid to college and high school students and to unemployed youth. Since the student refugee problem was becoming serious in 1935, the federation merged its efforts with those of the International Student Service, later broadening its scope to include other groups concerned with student relief.

With increasing interest in national and international problems, the number of student open forums on college campuses grew, and NSFA was called upon to aid in the establishment of additional discussion groups, as well as in the distribution of bibliographical and other helpful data. Realizing that its efforts were overlapping those of the Intercollegiate Council on Public Affairs, the latter organization was merged with the Federation, and from this sprang the NSFA Public Affairs Council, with prominent national figures in that field as advisers. In June 1938, a Student Government Conference was held in Washington, sponsored jointly by the Federation and the U.S. Office of Education, to lay a firm foundation for a philosophy of student government and student citizenship training. In 1939, to increase its educational research facilities and its services to student groups, the national office was moved to Washington, D.C.

NSFA sets up a national clearinghouse on student government, 1938-39

A summary of the 1938-39 activities is typical of the later years of NSFA.

On the campus, the Federation acted as a clearinghouse for student information on student government problems and related fields; issued a weekly *NSFA Reporter,* which contained information about contemporary college happenings and NSFA activities; aided in the development of college open forums to stimulate interest in current worldwide problems by issuing bibliographies, by radio broadcasts, and by actual direction of the establishment of forums; undertook special studies, such as the Survey on Women's Social Regulations; sponsored short speaking tours for the president of NSFA, who visited over 40 member colleges that year; and developed new organizational patterns, which helped greatly in Federation work. Among these improvements was the enlisting of a group of Permanent Friends of NSFA, made up of administrators and faculty representatives from the member colleges.

Nationally, NSFA initiated the Washington Student Government Conference, held under the joint auspices of the U.S. Office of Education and the Federation. College administrators and NSFA officers spent two days in studying the meanings and scope of student government. The published findings of that conference have been of great value toward student progress in self-government, and also toward better student-faculty-administration relationships.

At the annual Christmas Congress at Purdue University, some 200 student leaders gathered to discuss problems and aspects of campus government. A series of eight regional student conferences gave opportunity for more detailed discussion of college life.

Collaboration with other student groups

The Federation participated in the programs of various national organizations with which it was affiliated. NSFA was represented on the steering committee of the National Peace Conference, on the membership and legislative committees of the United Student Peace Committee, and on the cabinet of the American Youth Congress.

NSFA helped to raise funds for nonpartisan aid to victims of the war and to student refugees. The Federation cooperated with the Far Eastern Student Service Fund, the International Committee to Aid Spanish Students, the Intercollegiate Committee to Aid Student Refugees, and the International Student Service.

In cooperation with a number of prominent Americans, the federation sponsored the "Redeclaration of American Faith" calling on young student citizens to rededicate themselves to American ideals of democratic government.

Internationally, NSFA participated in international conferences, including the World Youth Congress at Vassar College in August 1938, and helped with preparations for the Inter-American Student Congress, which was held in Cuba, in December of 1939.

NSFA promotes student travel and exchange

The Federation arranged the exchange of debate teams with various countries. . . .

In order to promote student travel, NSFA, in cooperation with other educational organizations, arranged a series of student tours. . . .

The federation distributed to hundreds of American student travelers the International Student Identity Card, enabling them to obtain substantial price reductions while abroad, and the *Handbook of Student Travel,* containing valuable data on all European countries.

Copies of the *NSFA Reporter* were sent abroad in exchange for literature from foreign student groups. An interesting exchange of college papers between American institutions and those in South Africa was effected.

This summary of activities shows that primary emphasis was placed by NSFA upon assistance to college student governments in the affairs and problems of the campus, such as student-faculty relations, point systems, curriculum, the honor system, and the extracurricular program.

NSFA assists student governments on campus and nationally

But NSFA also fully realized that student interests necessarily extended beyond the campus. Certain things desired by students could be accomplished only through concerted action on a national basis. Such problems as student employment, world peace, and academic freedom are issues larger than the campus, but part of it.

Any stands upon such issues, however, were taken by

NSFA only when its members were relatively unified in their point of view. Federation resolutions therefore indicated a widespread agreement among representative student leaders. All NSFA policies were democratically determined by discussion and vote of delegates at the annual congresses. The national office was charged with bringing resolutions to the attention of those affected and with carrying on programs formulated at the Congress. The Federation also asked its member student governments to cooperate in making Congress action effective on their campuses.

NSFA takes position on national issues of concern to students

NSFA also felt that American student interests and problems had a relation to those of students of other countries and that it was important for college students of the world to know each other.

All this was in accordance with the original statement of the purpose of NSFA in its constitution, which was never modified. According to this statement, NSFA was organized:

> to achieve a spirit of cooperation among the students of the United States; to develop an intelligent student opinion on questions of national and international importance; to foster understanding among the students of the world in the furtherance of an enduring peace. In working for these ends the Federation acts independently of any political party or religious sect.

Along with other youth organizations, NSFA was sometimes called radical. This was balanced by other criticisms of the organization as too reactionary. As a matter of fact, "middle-of-the-road" would be the best description of the policies and activities of NSFA.

As the entrance of the United States into World War II approached, NSFA began to suffer from lack of manpower and lack of funds. The last annual Congress to be called was to have been held at the University of Minnesota, at Christmastime 1941, but it was canceled by the travel restrictions imposed by the Office of Defense Transportation. The New York office soon had to be closed, and NSFA thus gradually disappeared from the wartime college scene.[1]

NSA founded with no knowledge of the prewar NSFA

When the college students of America, almost all of them veterans of World War II, gathered together in 1947 to found the United States National Student Association [USNSA] they had no knowledge of the National Student Federation of America. It is an illuminating demonstration of the need for a national student organization, that USNSA independently developed a program of activities almost parallel to that of NSFA.

EDITOR'S NOTE

[1] Philip G. Altbach writes in *Student Politics in America*:

> The NSFA's importance as a national student organization came at the end of the 1930s and the early 1940s, when the radical student movement collapsed following the Nazi-Soviet pact and some formerly activist students joined the NSFA in a more active but anticommunist program. At this time, the NSFA merged with the International Student Service. The 1940 convention of the NSFA reflected this trend. With the coming of the war, however, the NSFA became mainly concerned with student service activities and support for the American war effort.
>
> The NSFA survived because it served a stable element of the American student community: college student governments, which were regularly in need of services such as speakers, publications, and travel bureaus. Its radical political stance was a temporary response to the leftward trend of the campus at the time, and probably reflected its constituency. For the most part, NSFA affiliates engaged in traditional student government educational and service activities, and its leadership was far from being committed social activists. The revival of the NSFA's importance at the end of the decade was due more to the collapse of other elements of the student movement than to the vitality of the NSFA itself. (New York: McGraw-Hill, 1974; reprint, New Brunswick, NJ: Transaction Publishers, p. 86)

PICTURE CREDIT: *Bloomsburg Press*, 3/14/75 (Bloomsburg University Archives).

"When we have any troubles, she is the one to whom we turn"

2. Marguerite Kehr, Adviser to Generations of Students

Dean of Women, Bloomsburg State Teachers College, Pennsylvania
NSFA Board of Advisers, 1938-1941. NSA Advisory Council, 1954-1958

Editor's note: Marguerite Kehr was one of a legion of deans, presidents, and student advisers who served as mentors, role models, and friends in need for generations of students and student leaders. The constitution adopted by NSA in 1947 provided for an advisory council that would establish an active relationship between the organization and the educators with whom they wished to collaborate and on whose advice and support they wanted to draw. Part 5 of this Anthology commemorates a number of these mentors from various regions, most of whom served on the NSA National Advisory Council.

A Strong Advocate of Participation in Student Government

Excerpt from "Dean Kehr Retires," Bloomsburg State Teachers College Alumni Quarterly, *June, 1953.*

To all of the women students who have lived in Waller Hall Dormitory during the past twenty-five years and to countless others, Bloomsburg means Dr. Kehr, and Dr. Kehr means Bloomsburg. She has made a strong impression on all those who have worked with her.

Realizing that leadership is gained largely through participation in activities outside the classroom, Dean Kehr has been a strong advocate of participation in student government and all other campus activities and has encouraged students to assume duties and accept responsibilities. She was able to draw out the students' potential abilities because of their love and respect for her. As one student expressed it recently, "When we have any troubles, she is the one to whom we turn."

Dr. Kehr was honored by faculty at a dinner held Tuesday, May 12, at the Eagles' Home in Berwick. On that occasion, she was presented with a string of pearls and a book containing autographs of all the members of the staff.

She was also honored by the student body at the Honor Assembly held Wednesday, May 20. She was at that time presented with a Wedgewood tea set as a gift from the students and received a standing ovation from them. As far as our recollection goes, this was the first time that a retiring faculty member has been so honored,

The Student Council has recommended that the Ward Loan Fund be renamed the "Kehr-Ward Loan Fund" and that the fund be increased in amount. By means of this augmented loan fund, the name of Dean Kehr will be cemented as a friend of youth . . . at the Bloomsburg State Teachers College.

PICTURE CREDIT: 1934 (Bloomsburg University Archives).

Dr. Kehr was honored at the National Association of Deans of Women held recently at the Conrad Hilton Hotel in Chicago. Miss Kehr was presented a citation as a tribute to her long years of distinguished leadership to young women.

At the Chicago convention, she was seated at the speaker's table and presented orchid corsages by the national group as well as the Pennsylvania organization. Featured speaker at the testimonial dinner held in the Grand Ballroom of the Conrad Hilton was Miss Dorothy Stratton, National Executive Secretary, Girl Scouts of America, New York City.

Dean Kehr Has Retired After 25 Years Here

From the Bloomsburg *[Pennsylvania]* Press, *July 1, 1953*

With a service of twenty-five years and outstanding contributions to student life at the Bloomsburg State Teachers College, Dr. Marguerite W. Kehr has retired as dean of women.

Dr. Kehr was appointed dean of women at Bloomsburg in 1927, coming here from Lake Forest College in Illinois, where she served as dean of women and assistant professor of education from 1921 to 1927.

She is a graduate of the University of Tennessee and holds a Master of Arts Degree in Philosophy and Psychology from Wellesley. She received the Degree of Doctor of Philosophy in 1920 from Cornell University. Her teaching career covers classroom teaching at Knoxville, Tenn., High School; the University of Tennessee; Wellesley College; and Bryn Mawr College. During World War I, she served as secretary to the Army representative on the Priorities Commission of the War Industries Board, and from 1920 to 1921 she was secretary to an engineering firm in Washington, D.C. She also held an assignment as editorial assistant in Junior Red Cross publications in Washington, D.C.

Dr. Kehr was active in the National Association of Deans of Women, serving as publicity chairman for two terms, and in the affairs of the Pennsylvania Association of Deans of Women. She served one term as president of that organization, another term as vice president, and as chairman of a number of important committees.

She was also active in the organization of the Bloomsburg Branch of the American Association of University Women, serving two terms as president and a number of terms as chairman of the education, legislative and international relations committees.

Active in the formation of the Pennsylvania Association of College Students, Dean Kehr was also active as a member of the National Student Federation of America.

At a time of national economic decline, NSFA provided a forum for shaping public policy and a foundation for a pioneering career in broadcast journalism

3. Edward R. Murrow: From Student Leader of the 1930s to Leading Journalist

President, Student Government, Western Washington State College 1929
President, NSFA, 1930-31

The 1930 NSFA Atlanta Convention: "The first time Negro students ever came in the front door."

Excerpts from Chapter IV, Prime Time: The Life of Edward R. Murrow, *by Alexander Kendrick. Copyright © 1969 by Alexander Kendrick. By permission of Little, Brown and Company.*

Banks were closing throughout the United States, the stock market had touched new lows, wheat, cotton and corn prices were dropping and unemployment was rising when, just out of college, Ed Murrow came to New York in June 1930 as president of the National Student Federation of America. He had assets of forty dollars and a few debts. His job was an unpaid one but it carried a living allowance of twenty-five dollars a week, and he had decided to continue with it full-time because, for one thing, there were not too many other jobs available, as the depression began to settle in, and because he hoped it would lead to something broader in what he now accepted as his chosen field of "education."

As he noted later, he had embarked on two of the best years of his life. The federation, an organization of student body officers, was less than five years old, an outgrowth of the Intercollegiate World Court Congress which had met at Princeton in December 1925—the following month the United States refused to join the court except on its own unacceptable terms—and it was vague about its objectives, except that American students, like students in other countries, should "get together," both nationally and internationally. In 1927 it had actually sent four groups of fourteen American students each as a "delegation" to the Soviet Union for travel and study.

From a one-room basement office on midtown Madison Avenue, opposite the baronial bulk of the Pierpont Morgan library, the president of the federation busied himself with cheap tours to Europe for American undergraduates, and with visits to the United States by debating teams from Oxford and Cambridge.

That summer he received in New York fourteen foreign students from Britain, Austria, Italy, Sweden, Switzerland, Poland and South Africa, and saw them off on a three weeks' tour of America. He himself then embarked for a similar tour of Europe, working his way over as a sort of shipboard monitor. On this, his first trip abroad, he lived in youth hostels and visited student organizations in Britain, France, Germany, Holland and Belgium.

The purpose of the journey was to attend a congress of the Confederation Internationale des Etudiants, in Brussels, and the purpose of those who sent him was to demonstrate to European students that American students were not as feckless and frivolous as they seemed to believe. Ed Murrow was their case in point.

At the New York office, when he arrived there, Murrow had found, acting as secretary, Chester S. Williams, a thoughtful young Minnesotan, made more so by suffering from poliomyelitis. Just graduated from the University of California, Williams had helped elect Murrow to the NSFA presidency six months before, at the annual convention, at Stanford University. He had heard the representative from Washington State College make a speech deploring exactly what Europeans felt about American students, that they were "too provincial, overly concerned with fraternities, football and fun, and too unconcerned with the wider world." Murrow wanted the federation to change that, and Chet Williams wanted to help him.

* * *

Murrow speaks to international student conference

When he got to the conference he made a speech calling for the admission of German students to the international organization, because the sins of their fathers in the First World War could not be attributed to them. The European students were enthusiastic about Murrow, but less so about taking in the Germans. The motion was defeated, and the American declined the presidency. . . .

For Murrow his trip to Europe was the beginning of an ever-widening circle of acquaintanceship on the Continent, and an ever-present awareness of European political problems.

The NSFA was part of an international students' confederation which represented nearly forty countries. The English and Americans, less "political" than the Continentals, were more interested in cheap travel, cultural exchange, and the desire to "avoid war" by strengthening ties among youth. But at student congresses held in Prague, Rome, Budapest, and now Brussels, the young of the new nations that had emerged from the war were taking themselves as seriously as their elders at Geneva.

Some delegations were led by government youth functionaries professing to be students. European students were older than the Americans, and fervently nationalistic. . . .

Despite the frictions generated by the rival nationalisms in the international student movement, it was the hope of many, especially the Anglo-Saxons, that these could be counteracted by emphasizing peace, cooperation, and understanding, even to the extent of what later came to be called appeasement. In England the student movement played a major role in creating the Peace Oath mood which held the country before Munich.

Murrow, aged twenty-two, thoroughly enjoyed his first trip abroad. . . . After only a few weeks in Europe he came back much older and wiser, he thought.

He and Chet Williams found a one-room apartment together, in an old brownstone house around the corner from the office, and set up light housekeeping. Their combined income was $150 a month, of which $45 went for the rent.They played poker to decide who went down three flights for milk on cold mornings . . .

Their principal charge was to raise funds for the student cause, and Murrow visited many colleges and universities and made earnest speeches about Europe and education. . . .

CBS University of the Air: Murrow's first radio venture

The two young men also engaged in radio to advance and advertise the student movement. Williams had persuaded the Columbia Broadcasting System to put on a weekly program, called University of the Air, over thirty stations, and Murrow joined him in getting speakers for it, from college campuses and public life.

It was Murrow's first radio venture. Among those he persuaded to broadcast were Rabindranath Tagore, the Indian poet, and Albert Einstein, the latter from dockside as he arrived in New York by ship. . . .

* * *

The NSFA convention at the end of that year, when he was reelected president, was held at Atlanta. It is still remembered in that city as the first of its kind to be racially integrated there, or as a headwaiter recalled thirty years later, "the first time Negro students ever came in the front door of the Biltmore—and no trouble!"

The integration, though only a partial one, was managed by Murrow. He persuaded the Southern white delegates not to walk out, lest they besmirch the federation name "in the *New York Times*," and he reminded the hotel that its convention contract compelled it to accommodate "all delegates," for it had never dreamed that some of the delegates could be black. There were a dozen of them, and they actually dined at the Atlanta Biltmore in 1930. The hotel refused to serve them directly, as a violation of the custom of the country, but agreed to let them sit at the table while the white students were served. The latter then passed their plates to the Negroes. The Negro waiters thought it all rollicking.

The Atlanta convention voted to end any bar to NSFA membership by reason of color or race

The shoestring financing of the student federation came from the dues of its members in four hundred colleges, but guidance and advice came from the Institute of International Education, which was part of the Carnegie Endowment. The institute's director, Dr. Stephen Duggan, an internationally known educator with a spruce goatee, believed that "education is the only certain road to the attainment of world peace."[1]. . .

The Duggan-Murrow friendship would last twenty years, until the educator's death, and would lead the younger man into the broader endeavor he envisioned.

* * *

1931 summer travel across eastern and central Europe

Again in the summer of 1931 he worked his way to Europe, and this time he drove with two others from Paris across central and eastern Europe to Bucharest. There Crown Prince Carol had just become king, and the international students' confederation was holding its congress.

The depression had begun to grip the Old World also. The Credit-Anstalt had failed in Vienna, Britain was leaving the gold standard, and the Smoot-Hawley high tariff in America was definitely reducing European trade. Even more threatening was the political uncertainty growing out of the economic [situation]. A Fascist coup was attempted in Austria, and Adolf Hitler formed an alliance with the old German Nationalists led by the businessman [Alfred] Hugenberg. In Asia overt aggression was beginning, with the Japanese move into Manchuria.

Ed Murrow at twenty-three, a long way from Beaver, Washington, was receiving his political education early and at first hand. In this respect he was regarded by the European students he met as quite untypical of American students, though few of them had met very many American students as yet. The depression and the worsening political situation kept student exchange at a minimum.

* * *

Economizing had become a national necessity. Britain's departure from the gold standard brought fears the United States might follow suit, and when the Bank of United States failed in New York that winter—many believed, because of its name, that this private institution was operated by the Government—it touched off something of a panic, as assets were liquidated, loans called, and collateral stocks and bonds sold off. Theaters were blacked out on Broadway and taxis stopped running. Unemployment reached the eight-million mark, affecting a quarter of the nation's families.[2]

In this economic decline, radio came into its own as a form of entertainment and communication, helping alleviate the depressed frame of mind which accompanied the depressed state of business.

On the flight line for a simulated atomic bomb run, c. 1953

Radio was the universal solvent, a forum, schoolroom, music hall, convalescent ward, companion and soothsayer. . . .

The national habit of regular mass radio listening, formed during the depression, would remain until television replaced it, and when times improved, offered the largest and most susceptible market of consumers in the history of buying and selling. Radio in the Thirties was not only the "poor man's theater," but, as the CBS vice president, Paul Kesten, remarked, "the only form of advertising that runs like a train, that people wait for, that becomes an event or institution in their lives."

At the student federation's convention, held in Toledo that year, [Murrow] again rebuked American students for their "political apathy and complacency," and declared conformism to be "an opiate to intellect." He called for "radical" individualism, though, as he explained, he was not avowing any particular radical cause.

* * *

NSFA split on issues of pacifism

The convention's major debate was on military training in colleges. The issue split the membership, many of whom saw military training as making war more acceptable, and the federation finally voted to oppose compulsory training, a kind of rebuke to its president who, after all, had been a cadet colonel himself and firmly believed in ROTC. By 1933, however, with Hitler come to power, the federation would have second thoughts and vote its endorsement of ROTC, while at the same time withdrawing from the International Confederation of Students as "too nationalistic."

After two years as president of the National Student Federation—which would eventually founder between pacifism and "patriotism" with the coming of the Second World War—Murrow "retired" and was elected an honorary director.

Murrow joins the IIE staff as assistant director

He was planning to take a course in educational administration, the "deans' course," at Teachers College, but instead stepped into another job, this one with a salary attached. Dr. Duggan, director of the Institute of International Education and the student federation's paternal adviser, had passed sixty, but instead of contemplating retirement was looking for an assistant. Both Murrow and Chet Williams applied for the post, the latter at Murrow's suggestion. Murrow was chosen, while Williams went back to the West Coast, then joined the United States Office of Education.

* * *

As for international education, which was the institute's reason for existence, that was suffering from politics as well as economics. Adolf Hitler ruled in Germany. The Burning of the Books had taken place, and the great exodus of European scholarship had begun. Every ship brought new refugees. Part of Murrow's job was to arrange radio broadcasts and other appearances by scholars, poets and educators—American as well as refugee European—and he served as intermediary between the radio networks and the educational world, in which he had become widely acquainted.[3]

PICTURE CREDITS: All photos from *Prime Time: The Life of Edward R. Murrow,* by Alexander Kendrick. Copyright © by Alexander Kendrick (by permission of Little, Brown and Company, Inc.)

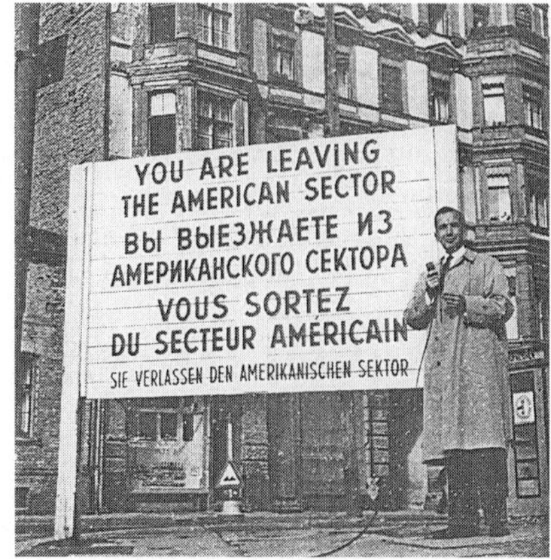

On assignment in divided Berlin, 1953

EDITOR'S NOTES

[1] Stephen Duggan's son, Lawrence Duggan, followed him as director of the Institute of International Education (IIE) and served on the National Advisory Board of NSA in 1947-48. IIE played a central role in international student educational exchange after the war. As did the NSFA, NSA maintained an active liaison with the IIE in developing its own travel and exchange programs. See pp. 654 and 693.

[2] Kendrick writes further, on p. 118,

> During the 1932-1933 term, a third of a million children were out of school for lack of funds, and thus of teachers. Nearly two million people were "on the road" in America, including the "Okies." The Bonus Marchers had descended on Washington and finally been routed by the Army chief of staff, General MacArthur, and his aide, Major Eisenhower. Back in Murrow's home state of Washington wooden nickels were issued by several communities, as a form of scrip, and the city of Seattle had gone over to widespread barter. The unemployed cut unsalable timber for fuel, dug unsalable potatoes, picked unsalable fruit and caught unsalable fish all of which they exchanged for the services of doctors, barbers, carpenters and cobblers.

[3] See Stanley Greenfield's 1947 Murrow interview, p. 156.

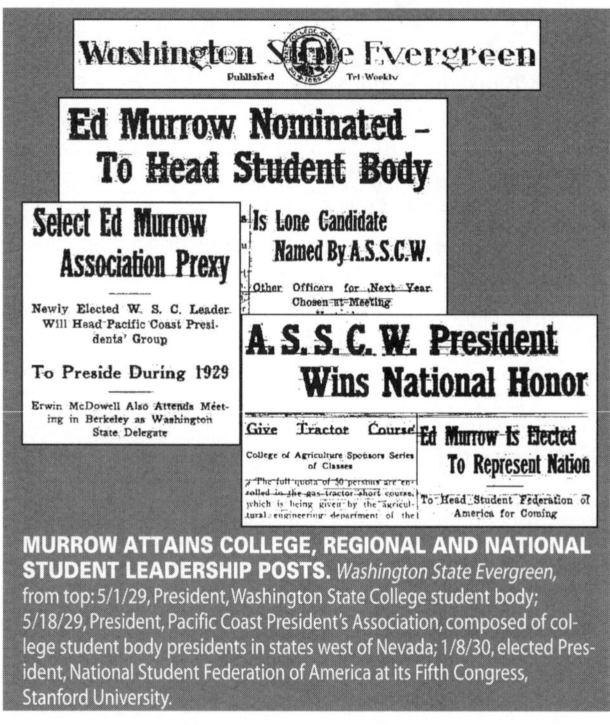

Washington State Evergreen
Published Tri-Weekly

Ed Murrow Nominated – To Head Student Body

Select Ed Murrow Association Prexy

Newly Elected W. S. C. Leader Will Head Pacific Coast Presidents' Group

To Preside During 1929

Erwin McDowell Also Attends Meeting in Berkeley as Washington State Delegate

Is Lone Candidate Named By A.S.S.C.W.

Other Officers for Next Year Chosen at Meeting

A. S. S. C. W. President Wins National Honor

Give Tractor Course

College of Agriculture Sponsors Series of Classes

The full quota of 50 persons are enrolled in the gas tractor short course, which is being given by the agricultural engineering department of the

Ed Murrow Is Elected To Represent Nation

To Head Student Federation of America for Coming

MURROW ATTAINS COLLEGE, REGIONAL AND NATIONAL STUDENT LEADERSHIP POSTS. *Washington State Evergreen,* from top: 5/1/29, President, Washington State College student body; 5/18/29, President, Pacific Coast President's Association, composed of college student body presidents in states west of Nevada; 1/8/30, elected President, National Student Federation of America at its Fifth Congress, Stanford University.

"If You Have the Time—Jump in with Both Feet"

Give Your Best and Grow

Editor's note: Ed Murrow believed that a student should bring maximum effort to whatever his choice of activity and study. "Step into the game and play it hard," he advised freshmen, below, as he did ("jump in") in the title above. He also advocated for recognition in successfully working to restore the College's Crimson Circle honorary service society. He displayed these attributes of intense engagement and recognition for achievement throughout his life. Below, are shown some of Murrow's own engagements in student life through vignettes taken from the college's 1927-1930 editions of The Chinook *yearbook.*

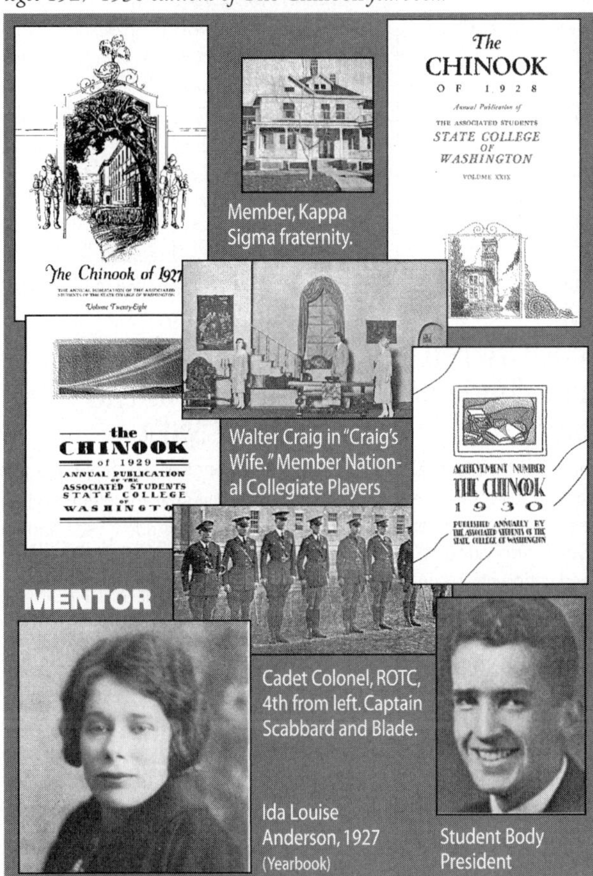

Member, Kappa Sigma fraternity.

Walter Craig in "Craig's Wife." Member National Collegiate Players

MENTOR

Cadet Colonel, ROTC, 4th from left. Captain Scabbard and Blade.

Ida Louise Anderson, 1927 (Yearbook)

Student Body President

Learn How We Govern Ourselves

(Murrow's welcome to the freshman class. Washington State Evergreen, *9/16/29.)*

It is indeed a pleasure to welcome the largest freshman class in the history of the State College of Washington. Your presence here is a tribute to the ever growing popularity and prestige of this institution and you are to be congratulated on your choice of this school for your alma mater.

We who have been here two or three years are proud of our school, we have observed its steady progress and have endeavored to do our part. Whether or not that progress continues depends largely on you. Step into the game and play it hard, whether your efforts be along scholastic, athletic or extra-curricular activities. Give your best for a better State College of Washington. The opportunity is here for this freshman class to render great and lasting service to the college—it depends on your spirit and the way you fall into the steps just what the results will be. Remember that a college is made up of more than fine gymnasiums, a field house and beautiful campus.

Don't forget that you are a member of the Associated students of the State College of Washington and entitled to all the privileges of that organization. Attend the meetings, express your views and learn the system by which we govern ourselves.—ED MURROW, President, A.S.S.C.W.

The Power of a Teacher

Ida Louise Anderson inspired Murrow throughout his career. Born in Morganton, Tennessee, on November 6, 1900, and stricken by polio as a child, she became physically handicapped. In 1924, after receiving an undergraduate degree in speech from the State College of Washington, Anderson began a sixteen-year teaching career in the school's Department of Speech. Her career ended in 1939, when the lingering effects of polio forced her to retire. She died on 16 September 1941 and was buried in Colfax, Washington.

Ida Lou Anderson was one of the State College's most respected instructors with a powerful mind and character that reached well beyond the classroom. She pioneered the field of radio broadcasting. One of Anderson's earliest and most impressive students was Edward R. Murrow.

Biographer Norman Finklestein, interviewed on the power of teachers (www.jfklibrary.org), tells of Murrow's pleading to enroll in her class, "She was the toughest teacher he would ever meet. But she began to see that there was something in this young man, some hidden talent. She invited him over to her house, gave him books to read and they discussed Greek poetry... When, finally, he becomes the great Edward R. Murrow and delivers the famous broadcasts from London during the blitz, it was Ida Lou Anderson who would write him frequent letters, making suggestions as to his diction. She was the one who told him, When you introduce the program, and you say, 'This is London,"why not put a little pause after the word 'this' and put that inflection in.' So that it came out 'THIS ... is London,' which became not only his trademark, but the trademark for CBS to this very day: "THIS ... is CBS."

Attending her classes, Murrow wrote in a Eulogy after Anderson died, was a "rare privilege" like "having had an altogether unique and lasting ex-perience ...in the presence of one who was, in the true sense of the word, greater than anyone we had met or were likely to meet."
(Adapted. WSU Archives and Special Collections and JFK Library postings, 2002)

EDWARD R. MURROW

Edward [Egbert] Roscoe Murrow was born to Roscoe and Ethel Murrow on April 25, 1908, near Greensboro, North Carolina, the youngest of three boys. The family moved to Blanchard, Washington when Murrow was five. Murrow attended Washington State College in Pullman, graduating in 1930. He was president of the National Student Federation of America from 1929 to 1932 and assistant director of the Institute of International Education from 1932 to 1935. In 1934 he married Janet Brewster. Their son, Charles Casey, was born in 1945, Murrow worked for CBS from 1935 until 1961 as war correspondent in London, 1939 to 1945, vice president, director of public affairs, 1945 to 1947, and news analyst and host for the television programs "Person to Person," "See It Now," and "Small World" during the 1950s. He was on the CBS board of directors from 1949 to 1955. In 1961, he was appointed director of the United States Information Agency (USIA), serving until 1964. He died April 27, 1965.
(Adapted from WSU Archives posting, 2002. Photo, c. 1950, from Kendrick, op. cit.)

NSFA, 1925-1941: For Student Governments

"A Student Venture in Practical Idealism"

Editor's note: Defining itself as "an organization of the student councils of American colleges and universities," NSFA's broad-ranging domestic and international travel service programs foreshadowed those of the U.S. National Student Association after World War II. Its membership of 250 at its peak was a much larger percentage of the prewar institutional base than NSA reached in its early years with memberships of 250-350. On the other hand, NSFA seemed to have a wider base of southern members but virtually no Catholic college members. It operated with a small full-time staff in its New York office, actively supervised by its elected officers and board. In 1939 its national office moved to Washington.

In the mid-thirties, NSFA began to concern itself with public policy and "war and peace" issues, and, along with numerous left and liberal secular, ethnic, labor, and Christian youth and student groups, joined the American Youth Congress. Formed in 1934, AYC concerned itself with the economic issues arising out of the Depression, and with discrimination and equal opportunity in education and employment. In 1940 NSFA withdrew from AYC, which was following the Communist line.

Despite financial problems and preoccupation with the war in Europe, NSFA maintained its independence through 1941, when it finally merged with the newly formed American Committee for the International Student Service, whose General Secretary was Joseph Lash, the former National Secretary of the American Student Union. ISS thus provided a "holding space" for anticommunist liberal and centrist student leaders until the United States Student Assembly was formed in 1943. It wasn't until after the war that another student government association—NSA—could be formed. (See Miriam Haskell Berlin, Martin McLaughlin, and Mary Lou Rogers Munts in this book's Prologue.)

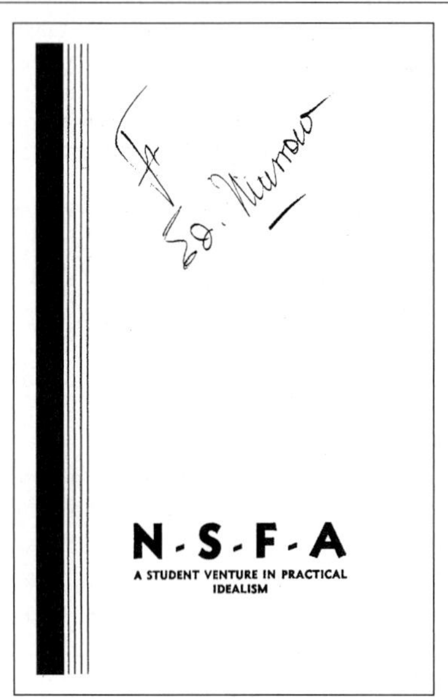

Statement of Purpose

From the 1931 brochure, above

- We would achieve a spirit of co-operation among the students of the United States to give consideration to questions affecting students' interests.
- We would develop an intelligent student opinion on questions of national and international importance.
- We would foster understanding among students of the world in the furtherance of enduring peace.
- In working towards these ends the Federation acts independently of any political party or religious creed.

The Maryland Diamondback, 1/9/33

NSFA Report and Recommendations Offered by Ralph Williams, Student Government Chief

One of the principal purposes of the National Student Federation of America is to promote an increasing interest on the part of the younger generation in cultural fields and in the vital problems of national life. The Federation has recognized a dangerous nonchalance of American youth towards matters of intellectual achievement, politics and governmental management,

Six efficient advertising channels are being employed by the organization to bring student affairs before the students themselves: broadcasts over the Columbia network featuring the messages of prominent men on pertinent subjects; foreign debating teams that have been in this country for the past eight years as well as American teams abroad . . . ; the Federation also maintains an active information bureau, a weekly news release for campus newspapers, and a magazine, the Student Mirror. . . .

The University of Maryland is not a member of the Federation and paid the penalty of being excluded from the competition with American University to extending an invitation to the group for the 1933 convention. . . .

* * *

The Congress was held in New Orleans with some two hundred delegates attending and 125 colleges being represented. The business sessions lasted long past the time scheduled for adjournment and the interest manifested in the problems of student government indicated very clearly that the delegates had one idea in mind—the solution of the problems and the best possible remedies suggested. . . .

The Agonistic, Agnes Scott College, 1/11/33

A.S. Delegates attend Congress of NSFA

Margaret Kelley and Charlotte Reid represented Agnes Scott College at the eighth annual congress of the National Student Federation of America. . . . Margaret said, "Throughout the discussions I felt deeply the seriousness of the students concerning the present economic crisis of the world, and I gained much from the foreign students in their meeting of this problem." In the discussion of the relationship between the students and the faculty of the college, Margaret stated that ours seemed very much more advanced. . . . She added that only nine colleges felt that the Honor System was successful.

The Maryland Diamondback, 1/8/34

NSFA Convention

The recent convention of the National Student Federation of America, held in Washington under the auspices of American University, gives rise to the belief that, until certain conditions within the organization are remedied, it would be unwise and unnecessary for the University of Maryland to become affiliated with the federation as a voting member.

The Diamondback is inclined to agree with Vice President Fred Cutting, official S.G.A. delegate . . . in the statement that the Federation "must come down to earth" before it can accomplish anything. . . . Until the NSFA can bring itself to consideration of local problems and reserve such discussions as that concerned with "the cooperation of American and Pan-

American students" until a later date, nothing of real value to the institutions represented can come of the conventions.

The problem of racial segregation was brought violently to the to the fore in the waning hours of the conclave when a small group of Negro representatives appeared at social functions and were requested to leave by members of Southern delegations. Prior to that episode, colored students had participated in most of the group sessions, and the undercurrent of feeling reached a point where open clashes between the Southerners and the Negroes were barely averted....

Under these circumstances, it seems that the only logical way for the Federation officials to avoid such unpleasant occurrences is to organize into two federations with joint officers. Problems which confront the Negro student are far different from those facing the white student. The two should not be intermingled....

Campus News, New Jersey College for Women, 1/16/37

NSFA Decides Compulsory Chapel Disintegrates Full Religious Life

That the present system of compulsory, college-sponsored chapel service tends to detract from the full religious life on the college campus was decided by the annual congress of the N.S.F.A. on the recommendation of the commission on religion, of which Margaret Lamont '38, chairman of the religious activities committee, was a member.... [C]ollege(s) should hold a simple Sunday service conducted in a dignified and worshipful manner on a purely voluntary basis of attendance.

In order to coordinate and integrate the religious life of the campus through cooperation with local churches, the YMCA, YMHA, YWCA, YWHA, Newman Clubs and similar organizations, the NSFA recommends the establishment of a Board of Religion, composed of faculty and students....

The Agonistic, Agnes Scott College, 1/18/39

Two Delegates Give Reports

Mary Ellen Whittles and Henrietta Thompson returned full of ideas for the New Year from the N.S.F.A. convention held December 27-31 at Purdue University, Lafayette, Indiana....

The theme of the program was "Student Leadership in Community Life." In connection with this theme, some of the many topics they discussed were problems of student organization, problems of discipline, and problems connected with the athletic programs of their schools and curriculum....

In an open letter to the N.S.F.A. convention, President Roosevelt said, "It is my faith that you, with a high appreciation of the essential nobility of the individual as your guide in the management of men, will not only maintain and preserve our democratic heritage in the years to come, but will enrich and extend it in ways that can be only dimly foreseen."

The Agonistic, Agnes Scott College, 1/17/40

NSFA Considers World Crisis

How can U.S. college and university students face the present world crisis?

With this question as their paramount problem, 200 National Student Federation of America delegates from all corners of the nation met at the University of Minnesota....

Relegating to second place such usual NSFA convention topics as the honor system

EXCERPTS APPEAR IN THIS ALBUM from *The Diamondback,* 1933, '34, (University of Maryland); *The Agonistic,* 1933, '39, '40 (Agnes Scott College, GA); *The Targum,* 1941 (Rutgers University, NJ); *Campus News,* 1937 (New Jersey College for Women); and *Bulletin,* 1941 (Washington Square College, New York University)

1925--1940

"Fifteen Years of Student Leadership"

1940 NSFA information brochure

THE NSFA IN 1940

President

Mary Jeanne McKay
Florida State College for Women

Vice Presidents

William Aycock, North Carolina State
John Darnell, Fresno State College

Board of Advisers

Dr. Donald J. Cowling, *Chairman*
Dr. Stephen Duggan
Dr. Frank P. Graham
Dr. George F. Zook
John A. Lang
Dr. Homer P. Rainey
Dr. James Shotwell
Dr. Abrose Suhrie
Thomas Fair Neblett
Dean Sarah Blanding
Dr. Walter Van Kirk
Dr. John W. Studebaker

Public Affairs Council

Charles A. Beard
Wiliam T. Stone
Mordecai Johnson
Francis P. Miller
Felix Morley
Charles W. Pipkin
Charles W. Taussig
Stephen Duggan, Jr.
Waldo Stephens
Jean Preston Tilt

Executive Committee

Herbert Fishburn .... Purdue University
Herbert Futrell .... Fresno State College
David Hitchcock .... U. of Wyoming
John Ivey .... Alabama Polytechnic Institute
Jim Joyner .... U. of North Carolina
Blanche Kirsch .... Brooklyn College
Arthur Northwood, Jr. ...... Princeton University
Steve O'Connell .... U. of Florida
Ralph Reilly .... Purdue University
James Robb .... St. Cloud State Teachers
Elizabeth Robertson . Texas State Coll. for Women
Helen Webb .... MacMurray College
Al Werner .... Springfield College
Mary Ellen Whetsel .... Agnes Scott College

and campus problems, the delegates set to work on how to reconcile their divergent viewpoints on how to keep America out of war.

Support Neutrality

Resolutions passed only after stormy debate called upon the United States to strengthen neutrality legislation by withholding war materials and economic and financial aid from warring nations.

Most hectic parliamentary struggle of the session was precipitated by a resolution calling upon colleges and universities to divide all student offices into major and minor classifications and to remunerate those students holding major offices.....

son their votes were taken away from them. The Youth Committee also claimed, in a resolution, that the International Student Services was an administration front, since it supported the Student Training Camps, the administration's defense program, and the administration's foreign policy. They were condemned as being unprogressive.....

Washington Square College, New York University, *Bulletin*, January 6, 1941

NSFA Withdraws from AYC in Split in Policy, Structure; ASU Raps Coudert Committee

Federation Also Refuses to Join Forces with ISS

Disagreement on foreign policies and organizational structure led the National Student Federation of America to withdraw from the American Youth Congress[1] last Monday at the close of the four-day conference of the Federation at the New Jersey College for Women. The delegates of the NSFA, representing over a hundred college student councils, voted to withdraw 87 to 24.

Refuses ISS

The NSFA also refused to affiliate with the International Student Service, one of the sponsors of the conference. The ISS, which has had the interest of Mrs. Roosevelt[2] since her disagreement with the Youth Congress policies, had offered a $3,000 a year grant to the NSFA if it would join. The practically impoverished Federation voted against affiliation 69 to 52.

Marjorie Jonas, president of the LOW, one of the NYU delegates to the conference, abstained from voting on the question of withdrawal from the Youth Congress, but voted for affiliation with the ISS. Frank Grace, the Student Council representative at the conference, voted to leave the Congress.

Spurn Financial Aid

The biggest bar to joining the ISS seemed to be the "altruism" in the offer of financial aid. One of the objections offered to continuing membership in the Youth Congress was the source of its money, and the difficulty the NSFA would have in sustaining itself if it didn't withdraw from the AYC.

The resolution for withdrawal, as it was finally adopted by the delegates, covered the beginnings of the Congress, the cooperation which had been evidenced in the past, and then continued: "But whereas the NSFA believes now that the American Youth Congress is not a representative organization, that its structure and condition is at present such that it cannot regain its usefulness, that the AYC cannot even further those particular aims that the NSFA may agree with."

Policy schism

Two of the resolutions voted on reveal the schism in the policies of the AYC and the NSFA. A resolution to uphold the Selective Service Act was adopted, and a resolution advocating sending food and supplies to European countries that have been made the victims of war was defeated.

The mention of "structure" in the resolution for withdrawal is emblematic of the continued association of the Young Communists League with the AYC. Also the AYC position on foreign policies of the government is contrary to the sentiments expressed in the action on the resolutions dealing with selective service and with American aid to war-torn countries.

The only large organization still connected with the Youth Congress that has not been accused of being a communist front is the Y.W.C.A.

Youth Groups Hear Leaders at Convention:

Held by Youth Committee Against War; LaFollette, Wheeler, Thomas Speak

Various student organizations in the United States, the Progressive Student League, the Student Youth Service, the Young People's Socialist League, and the League for Industrial Democracy, held a convention recently under the suspices of the Youth Committee Against War, in Madison, Wisconsin. The convention was initially to be held in the Congregational Church. But, at the last moment they were refused that hall.

The speakers at the convention included Senator Burton K. Wheeler, who spoke from Washington by special telephone, Bob LaFollette, the former boy wonder, Mr. Eccles, mayor of Madison, and Norman Thomas, socialist candidate for President.

At one point the proceedings were interrupted by some who were described as "Communists." The Youth Committee Against War claimed that they had at no time had any affiliation with these "Communists" and for that reason their votes were taken away from them.

Cease War Drive, Abolish Inequality, Demands Convention

When the American Student Union assembled for its sixth annual convention during Christmas week, 11 regular delegates from WSC [Washington Square College] attended. There were present at this time more than 400 delegates representing various institutions from various parts of the country. A "Charter of Student Rights and Responsibilities" formulated at the convention will form the basis of American Student Union activity during 1941.

Affirms Neutrality Stand

The charter affirms the ASU stand for neutrality in the European war,[3] aid to China and an embargo on Japan, and the adoption of a far-reaching program to "preserve the American educational system from the present war drive," it was stated. As part of its campaign around said charter which, among other things calls for an end to discrimination in academic life and for complete freedom of student organization, the ASU plans to give "all possible support" to the campaign currently waged by the NYU Committee for student equality appropos to the demand that Jim Coward, colored basketball player, be given a place on the NYU team....

In regard to the recent subpoenaing of 30 New York students by the Rapp-Coudert legislative committee, delegates declared that this new charter "will give a sharp answer to those who would intimidate American students into supporting the Roosevelt war drive."

END NOTES

[1] See Munts p. 35.

[2] See p. 40.

[3] *Editor's note:* In 1939 Hitler and Stalin signed a non-aggression pact, Germany invaded Poland, and Britain and France declared war on Germany.

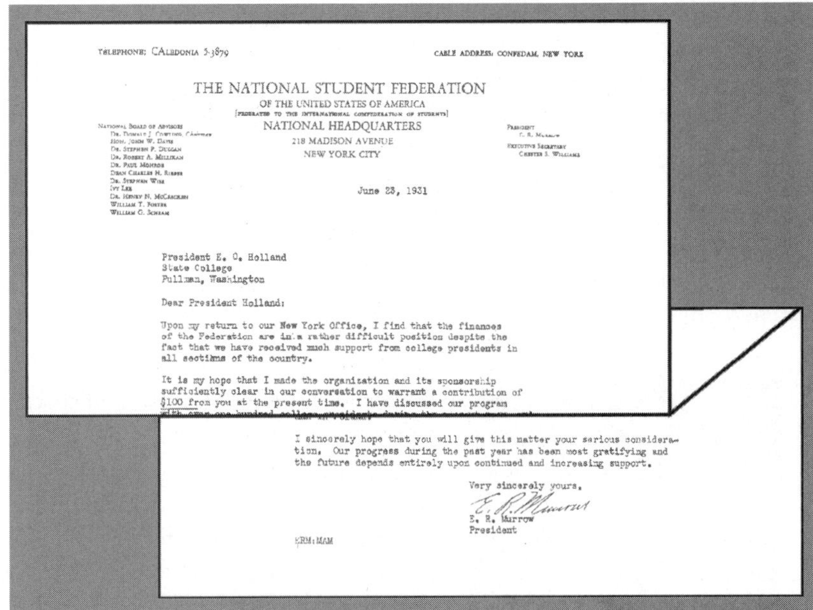

TELEPHONE: CALEDONIA 5-3879

CABLE ADDRESS: CONFEDAM, NEW YORK

THE NATIONAL STUDENT FEDERATION
OF THE UNITED STATES OF AMERICA
[FEDERATED TO THE INTERNATIONAL CONFEDERATION OF STUDENTS]
NATIONAL HEADQUARTERS
218 MADISON AVENUE
NEW YORK CITY

NATIONAL BOARD OF ADVISORS
DR. DONALD J. COWLING, CHAIRMAN
HON. JOHN W. DAVIS
DR. STEPHEN P. DUGGAN
DR. ROBERT A. MILLIKAN
DR. PAUL MONROE
DEAN CHARLES H. RIEBER
DR. STEPHEN WISE
IVY LEE
DR. HENRY N. MACCRACKEN
WILLIAM T. FOSTER
WILLIAM G. SCHRAM

PRESIDENT
E. R. MURROW
EXECUTIVE SECRETARY
CHESTER S. WILLIAMS

June 23, 1931

President E. O. Holland
State College
Pullman, Washington

Dear President Holland:

Upon my return to our New York Office, I find that the finances of the Federation are in a rather difficult position despite the fact that we have received much support from college presidents in all sections of the country.

It is my hope that I made the organization and its sponsorship sufficiently clear in our conversation to warrant a contribution of $100 from you at the present time. I have discussed our program

I sincerely hope that you will give this matter your serious consideration. Our progress during the past year has been most gratifying and the future depends entirely upon continued and increasing support.

Very sincerely yours,

E. R. Murrow
President

ERM:MAM

HOPE FOR "A CONTRIBUTION OF $100." Edward R. Murrow, NSFA president, writes his alma mater college president, E. O. Holland, at Washington State College in Pullman on June 23, 1931, for a $100 contribution. He notes also that he will be sailing in July to England, and then to Gemany and Poland, where he will be fulfilling speaking engagements, and to Bucharest (Rumania) for an international meeting.

Rutgers University, New Brunswick, N.J. *The Targum,* January 11, 1941

University Represented at National Youth Conclaves

One Finds Possible Good in German Victory; Several Attend Conference of ISS, NSFA at NJC; One Delegate Brands ISS Procedure "Undemocratic"

By George Gilbert

Seven Rutgers students were present while some of the country's major youth opinions were formulated at three national conventions held in Washington and New Brunswick during the Christmas vacation.

International Relations Clubs

Howard J. Crosby, Alfred V. Sloane and Douglas F. Bushnell, all '41, and Warren Freedman '43 were at the annual History and International Relations Clubs convention in Washington when students representing colleges throughout the country declared at panel discussions that "a possible German victory might not lead to world destruction, but instead to an eventual peaceful 'United States of Europe.'"

The convention opinioned that although a British victory would be preferable, the advantages to a German victory might be a complete European anschluss of all the powers to form a united confederation of states that would eventually overthrow Hitler and pave the way for peace in Europe.

"Well-Informed Delegates"

According to Crosby, the students at the convention, all of them "well-informed, liberal and intelligently acquainted with current world situations," resolved that the ideal United States of Europe would call for a scheme of complete cooperative industry. The heavy industries and public utilities should be owned by the states, and the rest should be operated on a cooperative basis, such as in Sweden.

NSFA Congress

Charles H. Prout '41 represented the Student Council at the National Student Federation of America congress held at NJC [New Jersey College for Women] jointly with the International Student Service, and featuring Mrs. Franklin D. Roosevelt as guest speaker. The NSFA, composed of delegates from student councils of nation-wide colleges to discuss problems of student government, resolved that it would withdraw all affiliations with the American Youth Congress because that organization is "dominated by Communist groups" and voted strongly for more aid to Britain.

International Student Service

Samuel D. Zagoria and Herbert Gersten, both '41, attended the International Student Service. Zagoria also found many of the students well-informed and liberal, but criticized the organization of the convention for fostering undemocratic procedures.

He said, "Evidently Joe Lash, an official of the ISS, wanted pro-Roosevelt comment, because he did his best to prevent any anti-administration talk, and worked to organize a new student organization alliance with NSFA which would be for aid to Britain, as opposed to the American Student Union stand of no aid to Britain. That he failed in this attempt is a credit to the clear thinking of the NSFA delegates."

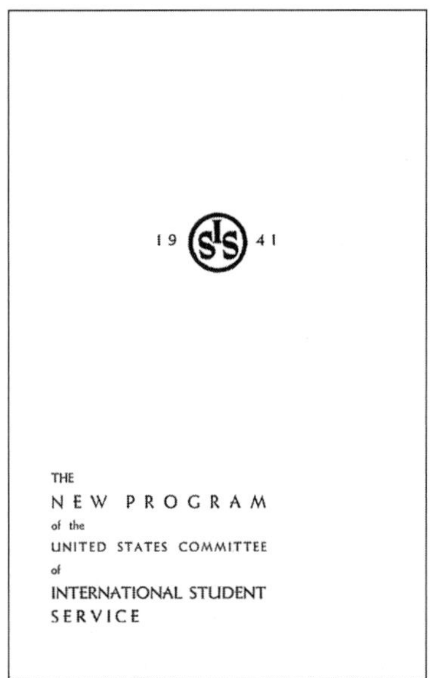

A STUDENT GOVERNMENT DEPARTMENT

From the 1941 ISS brochure shown above

ISS believes that the field of student self government and the training in democracy that it may provide is relatively unexplored and undeveloped. For this reason ISS is desirous of establishing a Student Government Department. Possibilities so provided will furnish the opportunity for new and more fruitful relationships between faculties and student bodies.

An attempt to form an affiliation of some kind with the National Student Federation of America is in progress. Affiliation is naturally conditioned on the approval of NSFA. ISS has no desire to duplicate work already being done.

Sources: NSFA documents in this album are from the Archives, Washington State University.

A prewar teenage activist leads a wartime student movement

4. Origins of the United States Student Assembly (1943-1947)

Mary Lou Rogers Munts
Swarthmore College, 1941-44
First President, United States Student Assembly and International Student Assembly, 1943-44

I grew up in the Chicago area, initially in Whiting, Indiana, where my father worked in the research laboratory of the Standard Oil Company of Indiana (now BP-Amoco), eventually becoming its director of research. My father, a southern Democrat, encouraged my early interest in politics. Being a Democrat was a matter of family pride, as my Kentucky grandmother bragged that she had even voted for Al Smith. By 1932, when I was eight, Roosevelt was my political idol.

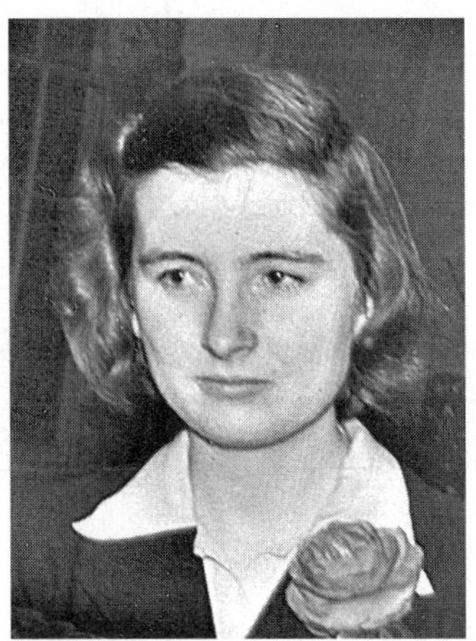

Living in the Depression years left a lasting impression on me. Whiting was less severely affected, being a company town of Standard Oil, but unemployment devastated the nearby steel towns of East Chicago, Indiana Harbor, and Gary. I was deeply shocked by the poverty of homes I visited at Christmas with canned goods and toys from my church. My developing social conscience was also piqued because I sensed how unjust it was that I got more attention from a teacher than a child of immigrant parents who started school speaking little English.

Moving to Chicago and growing political interests

In 1937 our family moved to Chicago to give me the challenge of the University of Chicago High School (the lab school). My interest in politics became more intense. Our lively Hyde Park neighborhood elected Paul Douglas, a university professor, to the City Council, where he became the lone reformer. Because he had a cabin at the Indiana dunes, as we did, I took a strong personal interest in his career, which culminated in his election to the U.S. Senate in 1948.

I showed my political pragmatism early by being the sole volunteer willing to debate in my social studies class for the reelection of Mayor Kelly, despite his being the boss of the corrupt machine. My best argument was that the Republican candidate would throw great numbers of people off the welfare rolls, a talking point I picked up from the director of a Chicago neighborhood house, as it appealed to my sympathy for the underdog.

As the war in Europe loomed, my passions were aroused by the isolationist-interventionist debate, which split the University of Chicago community. Robert Hutchins, the president of the university, and a leader of the America First Committee, was squared off against Quincy Wright, a political science professor, a leader of the William Allen White Committee to Defend America by Aiding the Allies. The raging controversy about Lend-Lease hit home when the League of Women Voters, in which my mother was active, supported the legislation. To my great consternation, my father, disillusioned by World War I, was an isolationist, opposing both Roosevelt's bid for a third term and Lend-Lease. The family dinner table saw heated debates between us which strengthened both my Democratic and interventionist allegiance and my ability to defend my views.

Entering Swarthmore in 1941

As a freshman, I could not have found a better hall assignment to further my activism. A neighboring group of junior women, leaders in the Swarthmore Student Union (SSU), took me under their wing and soon had me involved up to my ears. Part of my training was sitting at the feet of my mentors to learn the dramatic history of the SSU and the American Student Union (ASU). The Nazi-Soviet pact had led many ASU leaders in other colleges to follow a series of gyrations as the "party line" changed. After a convention at Madison, WI, in December 1939,[1] it became clear that the communists had gained the majority, and chapters like ours resigned in protest.

Our independent chapter then played an important role in trying to rebuild a noncommunist student movement. Our SSU and the Harvard Liberal Union, also a former ASU chapter, took the lead with similar former ASU chapters at

Radcliffe and Mount Holyoke to form the Student League for Progressive Action (SLPA) at a meeting jointly sponsored by International Student Service and the National Student Federation of America in December 1940.[2]

Although I was told about the SLPA by my Swarthmore mentors, there was little evidence of its development, as it lacked money and staff. However, the SSU and the Harvard Liberal Union continued to maintain very close ties until its leadership was absorbed by the war. Some of its leaders stayed in touch and attended the United States Student Assembly (USSA) convention in May 1943 in uniform. The formation of USSA was the fruition of the dream that the Swarthmore SSU and Harvard Liberal Union leaders had for SLPA—to initiate a noncommunist liberal student movement. My choice as president of USSA probably owed something to the strong role Swarthmore had played after the demise of the ASU in keeping this dream alive.

At the end of my freshman year (1942) I was astonished to be selected to attend the second (and last) Leadership Training Institute sponsored by International Student Service (ISS) at Campobello Island in the Roosevelt home. I had been recommended by my SSU mentors to Joe Lash, ISS general secretary, for selection and found myself the only freshman among a group of student council presidents and college newspaper editors.[3]

By the time the institute took place, Joe Lash had entered the army and Molly Yard took his place as director of the student program. I soon found a friend in Molly, who had gone to Swarthmore. My admiration knew no bounds as I learned that she had led the efforts to abolish sororities at the college in the early thirties. I was thrilled when I learned that Molly had just moved to Philadelphia, which led her to play a continuing role as a mentor for me. (Molly became a dear friend for life, with whom I shared many a discussion about her distinguished career as a leader in Democratic politics in Pennsylvania, in Americans for Democratic Action, and as president of the National Organization for Women.)

The perils of the 1930s United Front

Molly recounted for me a great deal of the history of the ASU and the American Youth Congress (AYC), the organization that Mrs. Roosevelt befriended and that ultimately betrayed her loyalty and caused her bitter disillusionment. Molly, along with Joe Lash and many other young socialists, joined the United Front of the thirties; this led to a close working relationship over a broad political spectrum, which included a strong communist element both in the ASU and in the AYC. Joe Lash served as general secretary and Molly Yard as treasurer, organizational secretary, and, finally, chairman of ASU.

The Nazi-Soviet Pact in August 1939 was the seminal event that revealed the extent to which communists had gotten themselves in key positions in the leadership of both organizations, leading to the groups' destruction. It was Molly's tutelage about these events, together with that of my Swarthmore mentors, that made me so wary of a repeat performance in the United States Student Assembly that I was to chair.

(Later, as executive secretary of the Swarthmore Student Union, I saw the residue of the communist taint that lingered from our group having once been affiliated with the ASU. I was sought out by FBI investigators wishing to know whether candidates for officers training school had been members of the ASU, despite the fact that our own chapter had never been under communist leadership. I quickly got rid of our old membership lists, as it was clear to me that FBI agents could not be educated about the history of the student movement.)

Leadership role of Joseph P. Lash

Joe Lash did not take his ouster from his leadership role in the American Student Union lightly and looked for a way to continue his commitment to a noncommunist student movement. The vehicle for his leadership became International Student Service. This organization had a long history of international work, which became curtailed when the war began, except for work with refugees. It became an opportune time for work in the United States to be expanded, and the United States Committee of ISS under the leadership of its chairman, Alvin Johnson, hired Joseph Lash as general secretary.[4]

Mrs. Roosevelt became a member of the National Committee in July 1940, and of its Executive Committee in April 1941. She provided great assistance to the new program of activity begun under the leadership of Lash. Trude Pratt, vice-chairman of the Executive Committee, also played an important role. (Trude Pratt became a very close friend of Mrs. Roosevelt and later married Joe Lash.)

Lash began an imaginative series of student conferences with the help of Louise Morley, conference secretary. He also initiated an excellent magazine, *Threshold*, edited by Irwin Ross. Molly Yard became director of the Washington Student Service Bureau to provide a resource for students seeking knowledge of government and to organize conferences of students and faculty.

Although the major emphasis of ISS was on student education and leadership training, Lash gave important assistance to the rebuilding of a noncommunist student movement. Joe Lash pursued an alliance with the National Student Federation of America (NSFA), the national body of student council representatives. The two organizations jointly sponsored a conference in December 1940. It was at this conference that the Student League for Progressive Action was launched, with our Swarthmore SSU as one of the key actors.

The convention of NSFA subsequently debated whether to affiliate with ISS, which had offered to give staff and financial support. To the disappointment of ISS, NSFA decided not to affiliate. It was not until a year later that Joe Lash announced a pooling of the efforts of the two organizations. This was just as the war began, and soon thereafter the ISS program begun by Lash was terminated, after he entered the army. The demise of NSFA as a viable organization during the war years left a vacuum that was not filled until the formation of the National Student Association.

An important legacy of Joe Lash was his training of a new sophisticated cadre of liberal student leadership. In both the summers of 1941 and 1942 he organized a five-week leadership-training institute at Campobello Island. Mrs. Roosevelt lent the family homes for these institutes, where outstanding academic and governmental leaders participated. It was heady wine for students like myself, who had the opportunity to sit on the floor to have a bull session with Mrs. Roosevelt.

I have felt it important to highlight briefly the remarkable accomplishments of Joe Lash during his two brief years at ISS because his shadow loomed so large in my life and that of many others in the student movement, to which he gave such devotion. Although Joe selected me to attend the Campobello institute in 1942, he had already left for the service by the time it took place. I did not have the pleasure of meeting him until his wedding to Trude Pratt in November 1944.

The International Student Assembly

The most ambitious project organized by Lash was the International Student Assembly held in September 1942. It drew almost four hundred students from fifty countries, an amazing achievement in wartime. Many delegates were in uniform. The most notable was Ludmilla Pavlichenko, a Russian woman sniper alleged to have killed 309 persons. There were also delegates representing anti-Nazi and antifascist groups from enemy countries.[5]

The assembly heard from a distinguished group of speakers, including Supreme Court Justice Robert Jackson; Mrs. Roosevelt; Walter Nash, Minister of New Zealand; Dr. Hu Shih, retiring ambassador of China; and Count Sforza, of the Free Italy Movement. The high point of the convention was an address by President Roosevelt, which was broadcast to thirty-one countries around the world. The assembly acted to form a permanent organization, the International Student Assembly (ISA), and a caucus of the American delegates agreed to form a United States Student Assembly (USSA), to be fleshed out at a future convention.

By the time the assembly met, Joe Lash had entered the service. He only returned on furlough to attend the ISA meeting. The loss of the dynamic leadership of Joe Lash left a serious gap for the future of ISA and USSA. With his departure, the work he had started at ISS was terminated and USSA had to find its own way. Only Joe Lash could have balanced the continuation of the work of ISS with the development of USSA and ISA as viable organizations. Without his help and vision, USSA had a more difficult struggle.

I have always regretted that I missed the wonderful experience of the International Student Assembly. Many Leadership Institute participants went directly to the Washington meeting from Campobello, but, unhappily, I had a commitment to a family reunion. However, my friends persuaded me that I must accept Mrs. Roosevelt's invitation for us to stay overnight at her New York apartment on my way to Chicago. With my luggage checked through, I was flattered to accept Mrs. R.'s loan of her spacious nightgown!

Becoming the first USSA (and ISA) president

It was with great eagerness that I looked forward to attending the USSA Convention in May 1943 in New York City. A small staff for USSA was established from persons who had worked under Joe Lash at ISS. Irene Murray, who had been on the staff at Campobello in 1942, became general secretary. Florence Yard, sister of Molly Yard and later married to pollster Lou Harris, was office manager. Bill Leuchtenburg, later to become a prominent historian of modem American politics, was hired as conference secretary to work on organizing the convention.

Molly Yard was asked to participate in the convention because of her long experience in the student movement, and was named chair of the Nominating Committee. I was named chair of the Credentials Committee because I had the trust of the conference organizers vis-à-vis a possible communist threat to dominate the convention.

It had become apparent that the young communists were sending in a flood of applications from numerous postgraduate organizations in the New York area. Our Credentials Committee met this problem by limiting the scope of the organization to undergraduate colleges. This decision created a furor, which hit the media, leading Mrs. Roosevelt and James Carey, secretary-treasurer of the AFL-CIO, who had both had bitter experience with communist takeovers, to come to our defense in their speeches to the convention.[6] The convention went on to take formal action to bar communist affiliates from membership in USSA.

While I was going through the travails of the Credentials Committee, the Nominating Committee was meeting under Molly's leadership. I was bowled over to learn that I had been elected president just before it was announced. Not only did I become president of USSA but also of the International Student Assembly (ISA). As chair of the ISA executive committee, my duties were quickly dispatched. I called a meeting, and the two members available to attend were a Russian representative selected by the Soviet government and a Chinese representative selected by the Chiang Kai-shek government. I quickly saw that our little group could not make beautiful music together and that the ability to build a democratic international student organization was nil in wartime. I called no further meetings.

However, an ISA existence was maintained and could be a useful tool. As ISA president I lent our name to sponsor a rally at Hunter College in August 1944 to honor the memory of anti-Nazi students killed in an uprising in Munich. I was inspired to do this by Anna Caples Frank, who was executive secretary of American Friends of German Freedom, a difficult cause to champion during the war. Anna scored a coup in getting Jan Masaryk, Czech ambassador, to join other distinguished speakers to honor the Munich students and to laud the efforts of students in all the resistance movements in fascist-dominated Europe.

(Anna Frank, who was married to the German resistance leader Paul Hagen [his pseudonym], became a lifelong friend. This selfless woman later served most of her career as the chief fund raiser for the NAACP Legal Defense Fund. She later married James Loeb, formerly executive director of Americans for Democratic Action.)

It was enough at age nineteen to feel the responsibility as USSA president to revive a national student movement in wartime, a daunting task. Even what direction the organization should take was problematic. For me there was no question that it should be a liberal political organization like my own SSU. We headed in this general direction, although chapter affiliates might be groups such as political forums on campuses with a less activist tradition. As I look back, I have wondered what the vision of Joe Lash had been for USSA. If the president had been one of the many student council presidents at the convention, it is even possible the organization might have headed toward an organization of student body leaders similar to the National Student Association organized after the war.[7]

Building a new organization

Our task was to try to build a new organization from scratch, getting affiliates from existing organizations like the SSU, and creating new chapters on other campuses. Bill Leuchtenburg became our first field secretary,[8] and Irene Murray quit as general secretary to join her husband in the service. I spent the summer doing my best to direct the office at 8 West 40th Street in New York City, until we hired Margot Haas as our executive secretary.

It was a relief to start my junior year at Swarthmore as just a volunteer and part-time worrier. Money problems began when International Student Service stopped bankrolling the USSA. Fund raising was to become the Achilles heel of the organization, despite the continued generous help of Mrs. Roosevelt, assisted by her friend Trude Pratt. I went up many weekends to New York for fund-raising events and for executive committee meetings of USSA.[9]

I also was involved in strategy and in organizing efforts. I made a train stopover in Ohio more than once to visit Antioch and Denison groups about potential USSA affiliation. I visited campuses in the Philadelphia area and attended the national convention of the student branch of the National Association for the Advancement of Colored People at Lincoln University to seek student affiliates at black colleges. (Here I met Patricia Roberts [Harris], a Howard delegate and later a member of President Jimmy Carter's cabinet. She was to become one of my closest friends, and never stopped goading me to achieve the vision she conceived of me when we first met at the conference.)

I also took an interest in the role young communists tried to play in the mainstream student movement. I went to observe the last convention of the Young Communist League when it dissolved and reconstituted itself as American Youth for Democracy (AYD). This rebirth was later denied by AYD leaders, so my eyewitness observation was of considerable value in debates on this issue.[10]

However, in the middle of my senior year I made the agonizing decision to resign as president when I found I could not give my whole heart to two causes. I had taken a semester leave of absence from Swarthmore to run the student campaign of our political science professor, Vernon O'Rourke. It was to be my best campaign until I ran my own, almost thirty years later. O'Rourke, off on a naval destroyer, finally learned that he had lost narrowly, although running 20,000 votes ahead of Roosevelt through the split-ticket efforts of our student canvassers.

At the USSA convention in May 1944, the fledgling organization had 150 delegates from thirty-one colleges and universities, and I was elected its president. Alice Horton [Tibbetts], of Wellesley College, succeeded me as president after my resignation in fall 1944, and by the May 1946 convention, 300 delegates from seventy-five colleges and universities attended.[11] (Alice and I first became friends at the University of Chicago High School, before we linked up again in USSA. Our friendship was later happily renewed when our husbands both took positions at the School for Workers at the University of Wisconsin-Madison in 1953.)

It was painful to leave the presidency of USSA when I was so worried about its viability. I had already begun to talk with Jim Loeb, then the director of the Union for Democratic Action (UDA), about our becoming its student affiliate. After UDA recast itself as Americans for Democratic Action in March 1947, USSA became the nucleus to form its student organization, in 1947.[12] Bill Leuchtenburg became its executive secretary.

The war in Europe intervenes

After the O'Rourke election, I returned to Chicago, fully expecting to go back to Swarthmore in January and to resume some role in USSA. Instead, soon after my return I was devastated to learn of the death of a very dear friend in action in France. I did not know how to grieve, but I did know how to chastise myself about the marvelous time being a woman had permitted me to have at home while Harvey died in France. I decided not to go back to Swarthmore in January and instead to take a job in a tank plant. In April the war in Europe was over, our plant closed, and I became an organizer of Montgomery Ward office workers for the United Retail, Wholesale and Department Store Employees–CIO.

When the war ended in August, I knew that it was time for me to get back to the unfinished business of college. I could not face going back to Swarthmore with my baggage of overinvolvement in the student movement and neglect of my studies. Instead, I transferred to the University of Chicago.

At Chicago I rejected various overtures to get involved in liberal student activities because I was determined to prove to myself that I could do well academically, as contrasted with my Swarthmore career, during which I majored in extracurricular activities. I was also quite aware that the time of leadership for women had passed, as men returned to campus. This was witnessed by the fact that the American Veterans Committee became the big liberal organization on campus.[13] But, most important, my interests had shifted to the world outside as I pursued study in labor economics and followed closely such developments as the rise of Walter Reuther in the United Automobile Workers Union.

I received my master's degree in economics in 1947, taking my Ph.D. preliminary examinations as an alternative to writing a master's thesis. I had achieved my ambition to be a good student at Chicago, and to my surprise was elected to Phi Beta Kappa. It was not until much later that I thought about the fact that I had received no encouragement to get a Ph.D.—not from the faculty, my parents, or others. My own thoughts, like those of so many women of my age, were turned toward marriage. Ray Munts and I tied the knot just as I finished my degree.[14] Then we honeymooned for a year in Paris, where Ray finished his master's degree in political science and I worked in the Treasury Department at the American embassy.

SDA Includes Wellesley USSA Representatives

USSA Transforms itself into the SDA

From *The Wellesley College News*, February 27, 1947

Michal Ernst Feder '47 and two other official delegates from the Wellesley USSA will go to Washington to attend the first national convention of the newly formed Students for Democratic Action to be held March 28-30. At this initial meeting, the group will set up a program and organization for independent liberal college students throughout the country.

SDA, an outgrowth of the United States Student Assembly, is setting up the new organization in conformity with the principles of Americans for Democratic Action, which is headed by Co-Chairmen Leon Henderson and Wilson Wyatt. Serving in her capacity as national president of the USSA, Michal Feder attended the organizational meeting of ADA, which was held In Washington January 4, and she will also serve as president of SDA.

Mike reported that the tentative plans for the coming convention include students' visits with their local congressmen, a speech by Franklin D. Roosevelt, Jr., and a tea to be given by Mrs. Franklin Roosevelt. She said that she hoped that "a number of interested Wellesley students would come along as unofficial observers."

"Both ADA and SDA are pledged to its policy of expanding the nation's program of social legislation, protecting civil liberties, urging increased support for the UN, and extending the Four Freedoms to all peoples of the world," Mike said. "Both organizations reject alliance with totalitarian groups—either communist or fascist—or their sympathizers."

Mike wished to make it clear that the SDA will maintain the same independent structure it now has under USSA, and will continue to hold annual conventions to elect officers and adopt its own program. Individual chapters will maintain their autonomy, and are free to vote on the adoption of the name of the new organization.

Mary Lou Munts is co-chair of Wisconsin Common Cause. She served in the Wisconsin Assembly for 12 years, and was the first woman member and then chair of the Public Service Commission.

END NOTES

[1] The attack of the USSR on Finland in November 1939 led to the final schism within the ASU, when it became completely apparent that the communists had gained control of the organization. Delegates at the Madison convention voted overwhelmingly, 322 to 49, to reject the condemnation of the Soviet invasion of Finland. Joe Lash, general secretary of the ASU and Molly Yard, its chairman, did not run for reelection at the convention.

[2] This event is reported fully in the *New York Times*, 12/28/40 ("Students Line Up for Policy Battle") and 12/19/40 ("New Youth Group for Aid to Britain").

[3] An insight into my selection to attend Campobello came when I worked for USSA the summer of 1943. I found a letter in the Swarthmore file to Joe Lash from one of my junior year mentors that explained that, as "one person has gone into the Army" and another "has gone into the Navy," a freshman, "Mary Lou Rogers, although a little wet behind the ears, was the best person available." This letter was illustrative of the unexpected gift of leadership opportunities that I and many other women received during the war years, although I did not understand its true significance then. *Editor's note:* A front page report on ISS in the 11/15/41 issue of the *Vassar Miscellany News* notes that a "Student Leadership Institute at Campobello Island last summer and the various summer work camps such as Highlander Folk School, Grafton and Green Farms give the student practical experience in democratic living and point the way towards what constructive efforts can be made in a war-torn world." See USSA Album in this section.

[4] See International Student Service, pp. 50, 56, 60, and 66.

[5] In October 1999, Allan Ostar wrote me:

> in 1942 when I was a delegate from Pennsylvania to the International Student Assembly held in Washington, DC, I was a freshman at Penn State. I was selected by the Penn State Christian Association to be a delegate because I was one of the few students at that isolated university interested in international affairs and one of the few students who was a professed liberal. As I recall, Joe Lash was very much involved as was Mrs. R. A number of us were housed in private residences. Several of us stayed in the home of Ernest K. Lindley who was head of Newsweek's Washington bureau. One thing I do remember clearly is that one of the delegates from the Soviet Union was Lt. Ludmilla Pavlichenko who had quite a reputation as a sniper. We were encouraged to arrange for her to speak at our campuses. I had her come to Penn State where I was co-chairman of Russian War Relief. We sold pins in the shape of a bear to raise money. (See Ostar, p. 209.)

[6] *Editor's note:* This concern by student leaders over probable communist takeover strategies found its echo during the formation of the U.S. delegation to the World Student Congress in 1946 and in organizing conventions for the National Student Association in 1946 and 1947 (see Part 1, Sections 1, 2, and 3).

[7] At a lunch in May 2000 I met with Bill Leuchtenburg, conference secretary for the USSA convention, who said that he was under the impression then that it had always been intended for USSA to be a liberal political group. So whatever may have been Joe Lash's own original vision, certainly people working on the convention and then elected to leadership had that view.

[8] See William Leuchtenburg, *Editor's note*, p. 50.

[9] *Editor's note:* The problem of adequately funding national intercollegiate student organizations comes up again dramatically in the early years of NSA. See Dungan, p. 175, Tyler, p. 279, Dentzer, p. 299, Brown, p. 384, Murphy, p. 1075, and Keating, p. 814. Also see p. 1119 in the Appendix.

[10] See Reisin, AYD, p. 787.

[11] *Editor's note:* In 1946 Alice Horton (Tibbetts) became executive secretary of the American Preparatory Committee, which organized the U.S. delegation to the World Student Congress in Prague that summer. See Tibbetts, p. 68.

[12] See sidebar re the founding of Students for Democratic Action, p. 38. See also Reisin, p. 781.

[13] See The Veterans, p. 697.

[14] See Mildred Wurf and Janis Dowd, "Women in NSA's Early Years," p. 489.

PICTURE CREDITS: *Then:* 1942. *Now:* 75th birthday, 1999 (*Both, author*)

MARY LOU (ROGERS) MUNTS

Education: Swarthmore College, 1941-44; University of Chicago, M.A. in Economics, 1947, Phi Beta Kappa; University of Wisconsin Law School, J.D., 1976.

Highlights: Mary Lou Rogers was born in Chicago, IL, on August 21, 1924. She attended Swarthmore College, where her passion for politics began. She quit college in her senior year to run the student campaign for a Swarthmore professor running for Congress. She later transferred to the University of Chicago, where she received her master's degree in economics and married a fellow student, Ray Munts, in 1947.

The Munts's early years were spent in Paris and Wilkes-Barre, PA, where Lisa and Roger were born. They came to Madison in the mid-fifties, where Polly arrived. In her "spare time" Mary Lou threw herself into the exciting efforts to build a new Democratic Party. The family then spent ten years in Bethesda, MD. Here Andrew completed the Munts family. Mary Lou's activist side was expressed in pioneering work in civil rights to pass a public accommodations law and to found a fair housing organization.

In 1966 the Munts family returned to Madison. The death of their son Roger, a year later, affected Mary Lou profoundly. Struggling to come back to life, she entered law school in 1970 and then ran successfully for the Assembly in 1972. Mary Lou became a legislative legend as she shepherded through one piece of legislation after another. She ended her legislative career as the first woman co-chair of the Joint Finance Committee and then was appointed the first woman member of the Public Service Commission and later its chair.

A year after her retirement in 1991, Mary Lou was devastated by Ray's death. Her recovery was assisted by her three children and seven grandchildren and by her passions for gardening and travel. She also pursued her interests in political and energy issues by joining the national boards of the Energy Foundation and of Common Cause. Currently she co-chairs Wisconsin Common Cause and is a founding member of Madison's award winning Monona Terrace Community and Convention Center.

Mary Lou Munts addressing the State of Wisconsin Assembly in 1975. (Legislative photo)

"A beacon for my generation"

5. A Tribute to Eleanor Roosevelt

Member, NSA Advisory Council, 1951-1959

Editor's Note: Written by Mary Lou Rogers Munts for the Eleanor Roosevelt Celebration of the Democratic Party of Wisconsin on October 11, 1999, in Milwaukee. Tipper Gore was the honored guest and Mary Lou was one of four Wisconsin women political leaders honored for their contributions.

There is no woman, living or dead, whom I admire more. I was lucky to be one of the legions of young people of my generation to whom she reached out.

In the summer of 1942, after my freshman year at Swarthmore, I was selected by Joe Lash to attend a Leadership Training Institute at Campobello in the Roosevelt summer home. A high point of our five weeks was Mrs. Roosevelt's stay with us for several days. My most vivid memory is of all of us sitting on the floor with her in the dim kerosene light. We could ask her anything we wanted to, and I can assure you we did!

We also went in a large boat over to Maine to visit a project of the National Youth Administration, in which she took a great interest. What an inspiration for me it was to see this interracial group at a time when I was deeply involved in trying to get the first African-American student admitted to Swarthmore.

After Campobello was over, Mrs. R., as we called her among ourselves, invited several of us to spend the night at her apartment on Washington Square in New York City. My other friends were on their way to a conference in Washington and I to my home in Chicago. Since my luggage had gone on ahead, Mrs. R. loaned me a nightgown, which delighted me by its generous fit on my then very slim figure.

Later, I became the first president of United States Student Assembly, later to become the student wing of Americans for Democratic Action. Mrs. Roosevelt came to our organizing convention to give encouragement and then became our most important angel to raise funds. Asking her help became hard for me to the point of embarrassment because I knew how many good causes depended on her.

It was much easier to ask her to come to our college to speak, which she did with such generosity for student groups. The day of the speech she asked me whether I would like to ride around with her to visit various settings related to the war effort. Of course I was thrilled to have such a good reason to cut classes. I saw what her column, "My Day," was really like as her long steps literally kept me on the run.

I am forever grateful to have had the opportunity to know Mrs. Roosevelt briefly in my student days. Today it is hard to believe how bitter and how powerful were her enemies as she fought tirelessly for equality for minorities and women, and, of course, for the Democratic Party. For my generation she was a beacon who by her example made us feel that victory could be snatched from defeat if we just worked hard enough.

Eleanor Roosevelt, First Lady of the United States from 1932 to 1945 and later U.S. Delegate to the United Nations General Assembly, encouraged the development of national youth and student organizations in the United States both before and after World War II. She lent her support to the American Student Union in the thirties, withdrawing after ASU supported the Hitler-Stalin pact in 1939.

She was a sponsor of the International Student Service when it opened U.S. offices in New York in 1940. From 1951 to 1959 she was a member of the NSA National Advisory Council. Mrs. Roosevelt spoke before and met frequently with student groups and leaders. She met Joseph Lash, ASU Executive Secretary, in 1939 and they became close friends. In 1947, at a five-week Encampment for Citizenship, she met Allard Lowenstein, later to become NSA President in 1950-51, and they developed a lasting friendship. In the early forties, she sponsored leadership training institutes at the Roosevelt summer home in Campobello, Maine, such as the one mentioned in this article.

Editor

Mrs. Roosevelt and Mary Lou Rogers, 1943 U.S. Student Assembly President, in 1942. (Photo from Mary Lou Munts)

"...The ideal Democracy is the system of government in which every individual accepts personal responsibility with courage to think things out for himself"

—Eleanor Roosevelt
August 1952

MRS. ROOSEVELT TALKS

(STORY ON PAGE 2)

The Hilltop

HOWARD UNIVERSITY

New Projects For Chemistry and Zoology Dep'ts

PRESIDENT JOHNSON ATTENDS CONFERENCE IN FRANCE

Senator Douglass Lectured Here

Mrs. Eleanor Roosevelt
America's First Lady

Photos (counterclockwise): Mrs Roosevelt with Austrian students at a Twin Lakes, CT, garden party (*The Lakeville Journal* 8/28/52); Delivering a keynote at the 11th National Student Congress in August 1958 at Ohio Wesleyan University; Appearance at Howard University (*Hilltop* 1/25/51); At a later reception: (?) Winegar, Daniel Idzik (U. of Buffalo), *NSA Exec. VP, 1957*, James T. Harris, *NSA President, 1948-49*, (?) Jacobs, Ray Farabee (U. of Texas), *NSA President 1957-58.*

PICTURE CREDITS: Roosevelt and Munts (*Munts*). Roosevelt and students, *The Lakeville Journal,* 8/8/52, with permission. Roosevelt speaks, *The Hilltop*, Howard U., Washington, DC, 1/25/51, with permission. Roosevelt addressing NSA and meeting with leaders (*SHSW*).

The Legacy of Franklin Roosevelt

For most of the veterans college generation, Roosevelt was the only president they knew when they were growing up. For all of that generation, he was remembered as their wartime president. His death on April 12, 1945 was headlined by college dailies across the country (Left: 4/13/45 editions of the California Bruin, UCLA, *and* New York University Bulletin*). As Doris Kearns Goodwin observes about Roosevelt in* No Ordinary Time*:* Franklin and Eleanor Roosevelt: The Home Front in World War II*: "Through four years of war, despite strikes and riots, overcrowding and confusion, profiteering, black markets, prejudice, and racism, he kept the American people united in a single cause." In a letter to Joe Lash, National Secretary of the American Student Union, Roosevelt wrote on 12/18/37, "The schools of our country, especially the colleges and universities, are expressions of democracy's interest in youth."*

CALIFORNIA BRUIN

U C L A

Nation Mourns Roosevelt

President Succumbs on Eve of German Collapse

Americans Smash on to Berlin

Campus Receives News with Incredulity, Grief

Truman Takes Oath of Office, Vows Victory

Parley Plans Unchanged by F.D.R.'s Death

Bulletin

NYU Students Organize Tribute To Franklin Roosevelt's Memory

Vets Council Plans VE-Day Anniversary

Memorial Service To Honor Him

Will Gather At Noon Today To Hold Service Commemorating Death

Break U.S., Spanish Ties, AVC Says

Franklin Delano Roosevelt

To Us . . . The Torch

[Editorial, *Temple University News*, p. 1, Monday, April 16, 1945.]

President Roosevelt was buried yesterday.

With him, it is true, were buried the smile, the voice, the personality that led us so close to victory. But his courage of spirit lives on. It is a challenge to us—to the youth of America—to fulfill his dreams for the future peace and security of our nation.

We cannot express adequately the grief we feel on this occasion. We knew no other President. We knew no greater friend. . . . .

President Roosevelt said in his first inaugural address that we need fear only fear itself. We cling to those words now when we see fear for the future gripping the hearts of a stunned America. . . .

The San Francisco Conference will be held in a few days. President Roosevelt won't be there—but every one of us knows that his plans, his blueprint of future policies will be a guiding force. We must fulfill his aims.

We accept the challenge.

American Student Union advocate of a popular front peace movement, he concluded in 1941 that communists were "unreliable allies in the march toward a more democratic America and a better world."

6. Joseph P. Lash: Leader of the Student Movement on the Left

Communist support for the 1939 Nazi-Soviet pact within the 20,000 member ASU undid Lash's efforts. Supported by Eleanor Roosevelt, he organized the International Student Assembly in 1942

Excerpts from Chapter 9, When the Old Left Was Young: Student Radicals and America's First Mass Student Movement, 1929-1941, *by Robert Cohen, copyright 1993 by Robert Cohen. Used by permission of Oxford University Press, Inc.*

Editor's note: Although he followed Edward R. Murrow by almost ten years, Joseph P. Lash was of the same era, historically, as a national student leader on the U.S. college scene in the 1930s. Together, they epitomize the two main strands of student activism of the period—that of the student government and service program–based representative assembly of the National Student Federation of America, and that of the membership and campus chapter–based public policy and political action organization, the American Student Union, which Lash led.

Each was a charismatic leader and each had to deal with the same overarching issues that captured the passions of student activists at the time, and that influenced the course of their own lives: (1) the threat of war and the isolationist Peace Movement and interventionist student factions active on campuses and (2) the well-organized communist and pro-Soviet student factions, which attempted to influence and control the agendas of the major U.S. student and youth organizations.

Lash figured importantly in the life of Eleanor Roosevelt during this period. The following is from pp. 122-124, No Ordinary Time: Franklin and Eleanor Roosevelt: The Home Front in World War II, *by Doris Kearns Goodwin:*

> An intense, moody intellectual with brown eyes and black hair, Lash had been swept up by the revolutionary fervor of the 1930s. While still at City College, he had joined the Socialist Party. After receiving a graduate degree in English at Columbia, he had served as national secretary of the American Student Union, a militant popular-front organization committed to radical change in the economic and social order.
>
> Eleanor first met the young student leader in November 1939, when he was called upon to testify before the House Un-American Activities Committee. "It was a confusing time for Joe," his college friend Lewis Feuer recalled. On the one hand, he was still committed to the radical program of change which united liberals, socialists, and communists in the popular front. But with the signing of the Nazi-Soviet pact, which gave Hitler a green light to invade Poland, he had lost his fervor for the popular front and had become increasingly disenchanted with his communist colleagues in the American Student Union, who were, he believed, mindlessly following the Soviet line in calling for an isolationist policy at home. The conflict in loyalties and the ideological crosscurrents revealed in his statement to the committee struck a responsive chord in Eleanor, who sat through the entire proceedings to assure the young people of her moral support. When the testimony was completed, she invited Lash and five of his friends back to the White House for dinner. . . .
>
> After dinner, Eleanor and Joe sat together on the porch in the gathering dark and talked till midnight. Had Joe been close to his father? Eleanor wanted to know. The answer was no. His parents were Russian Jews who had ended up in New York City, in a small grocery store in Morningside Heights which kept them so busy that there was little time for family life. Joe was only nine when his father died. She talked with him about philosophy and his plans for the future. She gave him advice. Here was a perceptive and intelligent young man . . . easy and pleasant to talk [to], a sympathetic soul. . . .*

The epigram with Joseph P. Lash's photo in the CCNY 1931 yearbook reads, "... a muse of fire, that would ascend the brightest heaven of invention!"

As Goodwin noted earlier, this event "marked the beginning of her intimate friendship with Joe Lash, a friendship that would endure to the end of her life."

Robert Cohen, in the digest that follows from pages 282-321 of When the Old Left Was Young, *traces the climactic years of Lash's leadership of the American Student Union after the Hitler-Stalin nonaggression pact of 1939 and the brief period during which Lash served as executive secretary of the International Student Service, from 1941 until he entered the army in 1943. Cohen shows how the struggle for control between students of the noncommunist and Communist left, and Lash's efforts to overcome the communist agenda in the ASU that caused him to abandon his belief that alliances with communists were possible, influenced the attitudes of the noncommunist left after the War. In this anthology, the echoes of that prewar experience can be found in failed American student efforts after the war to cooperate with the Soviet bloc and the communist-dominated International Union of Students. The experience also served to help marginalize any possible influence the communist and pro-Soviet left might have sought within the new U.S. National Student Association.*

At first glance it might seem that because of the student political environment in 1939 Lash and his allies in the ASU leadership should have found it easy to turn back the communist challenge. After all, the vast majority of the ASU's 20,000 members were not communists, and that majority had solidly backed the foreign policy positions that Lash was seeking to defend against the communists. Moreover, the Nazi-Soviet Pact was extremely unpopular both on campus and off, leaving the communists in the very difficult position of having to explain why after years of promoting anti-fascism they were now forsaking it for isolationism. This would hardly seem an opportune moment for communists to mount a successful challenge to the ASU's experienced and popular noncommunist leadership.

Lash works to overcome communist control of the ASU

But these factors favoring the ASU's noncommunists were more than offset by the communists' organizational advantages. The communists were the only faction within the ASU which in the fall of 1939 had a tight national political network in place. This network of campus YCL [Young Communist League] units was by mid-September 1939 already coordinating a national effort to reverse the ASU's foreign policies and drive noncommunists out of the leadership of the student movement. This gave the communists a big headstart over their noncommunist rivals in the ASU, who had to try to create their own national network almost overnight to compete with the communists at the upcoming ASU convention over the Christmas break. Lash worked frantically, attempting to assemble this network, but it was, as he explained to a friend in late September, a formidable task: "I am leading a one man struggle to galvanize the ASU into action. . . . I have never written so many letters—exhorting. demanding, threatening, philosophising—but I feel that the time spent is worth it, for a false move now and the ASU is finished. . . .

* * *

Having been frequently redbaited himself, Lash could not rid himself of the idea that a direct public attack on communist ASUers would smack of demagoguery and political persecution. Lash was especially sensitive to this problem because at the very moment he was preparing for his showdown with communist ASUers, the nation's most prominent redbaiting group, the House Un-American Activities Committee, was on the offensive against both the ASU and the entire student movement. The Committee, headed by Texas Congressman Martin Dies, threatened throughout the fall of 1939 to probe the ASU's communist connections, and would subpoena ASU leaders—including Lash—before the end of the year.

Like most ASUers, Lash viewed the work of Dies' committee as part of a rightwing assault on both the American Left and liberalism. He therefore avoided public discussion of his battle against communist domination in the ASU so as not to aid that committee. A Lash diary entry in the late fall of 1939 confirms that these congressional anticommunists were simply making it more difficult for communist domination to be battled in the ASU.

* * *

The 1939 Armistice Day demonstrations

The battle between the ASU's communist and noncommunist leaders began to heat up as the ASU national office prepared for campus Armistice Day demonstrations. These were scheduled to be the first major anti-war protests of the fall 1939 semester. The literature that the ASU national office began preparing for these protests was strongly antifascist. As part of this mobilization effort, Lash, on September 25, sent an open letter to President Roosevelt, endorsing his attempt to revise the Neutrality Act. The letter also condemned isolationism and stressed "that a victory for Hitler will menace our security, our well being, our democratic institutions." Though this letter was consistent with ASU policy, as set in the ASU's Fall Planning Conference and last convention, it elicited an angry response from communist leaders in the ASU. On the day that Lash wrote the FDR letter, Bert Witt, the ASU's most vocal communist leader, personally rebuked Lash over the contents of the letter. Witt argued that the letter ran contrary to the current sentiment of the ASU National Executive Committee and warned that if Lash sent out the letter the committee might force him to [sic] "issue [a] retraction."

Less than a week after this angry confrontation, Lash's letter to FDR became the focus of a stormy meeting of the ASU National Executive Committee. Witt told his fellow committee members that Lash's letter distorted both the international situation and ASU policy. Witt found especially objectionable the portion of Lash's letter which stated that "the victory of Hitlerism in Europe . . . would have disastrous effects on American democratic institutions." Witt argued that this was "not a correct analysis" because "the defeat of Hitler does not necessarily mean the defeat of Chamberlain and Daladier, nor does aid to Daladier defeat Hitler, as was implied in the letter." Witt charged that the entire idea of revising the Neutrality Act to aid France and Britain, which Lash so strongly urged in the letter, was misguided and inconsistent with the ASU's peace policy . . . arguing that Britain and France were as imperialist as Germany and just as much a danger to peace.

The noncommunists at the meeting quickly and forcefully repudiated the communist line. Agnes Reynolds pointed out the inconsistency between what the communists were saying now and the antifascist foreign policies that they (and the rest of the ASU) supported in the past. "We have always said that equating British imperialism with German fascism is an aid to appeasement and this is still true." Molly Yard told the communists that their new line would prove unpopular on campus and that the ASU would lose all credibility with students if it adopted that line. Yard warned "those wanting to change the ASU position" that though

> there is confusion on the campus about peace . . . the feeling on the whole is that the situation is the same today as it was a few weeks ago. Poland has been invaded, and England and France are defending Poland. We still stand for aid to victims of aggression and their allies. If we deny this, students will say the ASU is communist-dominated and is doing this only because of the Soviet Union. . . . We must remember that to most people there is a distinction between Chamberlain and Hitler.

* * *

Mrs. Roosevelt supports student leaders subpoenaed by Dies Committee

Mrs. Roosevelt had proven an especially valuable ally to the Youth Congress and the ASU when those organizations came under attack by the Dies Committee in the fall of 1939. The First Lady loathed the Dies Committee and what she termed its "Gestapo methods." The committee had recklessly redbaited hundreds of innocent individuals—engaging in trial by headline and refusing to accord most of the accused any opportunity to respond to the charges. . . .

The First Lady used her syndicated newspaper column and her personal prestige to fend off Dies' attack on the youth leaders in the fall of 1939. Her column praised the Youth Congress and ASU. She further demonstrated her solidarity with the subpoenaed youth leaders by accompanying them to the Dies Committee hearing and inviting them to the White House. Mrs. Roosevelt spoke to the press about the value of political tolerance and suggested that rather than seeking to ban radicalism, the nation should concern itself with eliminating the social problems that bred radicalism. . . .

Mrs. Roosevelt's defense of these young activists had been based not only upon political principle, but also personal friendship. Having cooperated with the Youth Congress on behalf of several causes—especially on their common goal of expanded federal aid to needy youth—the First Lady had befriended that organization's national leaders. She trusted them. Some of those leaders, however, would prove unworthy of that trust. The Youth Congress officers who were either in or close to the Communist Party hid their Party ties from Mrs. Roosevelt.

* * *

College isolationism dominates antiwar movement

The persistence of collegiate isolationism was a product of both fear and disillusionment. The fear was, of course, fear of war—fueled by the Nazi military advances and a sinking feeling that the United States was moving inexorably toward war. Several sources contributed to the disillusionment. Disdain for World War I remained strong among undergraduates. A poll of Columbia students in the spring of 1940 revealed that by an almost five to one margin they saw United States entry into war in 1917 as "the result of propaganda and selfish interests"; and most thought that if the United States went to war again its motivation would be equally sordid. By 1940, moreover, new sources of disillusionment had been added to this old one. The Allies had stood by while Spain fell to fascism; Chamberlain had bowed to Hitler at Munich; the Soviets, who had championed an international movement for collective security against fascism had abandoned that cause by signing their pact with Hitler. All of this left a vocal segment of the student population feeling cynical about the Allies and their antifascist slogans.

* * *

Before the fall semester of 1940 was over, however, isolationist students would have more to contend with than middle-aged critics. The isolationist monopoly on student organizing came to an end. Inspired by England's courage in the Battle of Britain and worried by the fall of France, interventionist students on scores of campuses began to organize. Joseph Lash, who participated in this anti-isolationist resurgence, saw it as "a heartening sign" that the "condition of shell shock or paralysis among liberal young people" that had lasted for "a long time after the Nazi-Soviet Pact" was finally ending. As Lash's words suggest, the timing of this anti-isolationist resurgence was in part linked to organizational factors. Lash and other foes of isolationism had been tied down the previous year first by the futile battle to free the ASU and Youth Congress of communist domination, and then by the demoralization and disorganization which followed the failure of those efforts. Now, however, with their own organizations, they were able to focus on the task of influencing the campuses.

International events also made the fall of 1940 a good moment for such an anti-isolationist offensive. The German conquests the previous spring had demonstrated that America could no longer hope that a stalemate in Europe would curb Nazi aggression. And the Battle of Britain, waged over the summer, had suggested that with the English determined to fight on, it might be possible for the United States—through aid to Britain—to play a role in stopping Hitler without actually entering the war. This was the time of Winston Churchill's stirring calls for an unending fight against Hitler; and simultaneously came Edward R. Murrow's moving radio broadcasts from London documenting the brutal Nazi bombings of civilians. Such events enabled student foes of isolationism to reconstruct some of the antifascist idealism which had been so powerful and appealing to collegians during the Popular Front era.

* * *

Interventionist faculty dispute student isolationism

The fall of 1940 also witnessed a continuation of the clashes between isolationist students and their interventionist elders. The opening salvo came just as classes began with the appearance of "Where Do You Stand? An Open Letter to American Undergraduates," in *Atlantic Monthly*, in which Yale Professor Arnold Whitridge accused isolationist students of "hysterical timidity." The Yale professor's article quickly drew a polemical response, "We Stand Here," by Kingman Brewster and Harvard Crimson editor Spencer Klaw, which also appeared in the *Atlantic*. Brewster and Klaw held that it was unfair for interventionists to single collegians out for special condemnation when a majority of all Americans opposed war; they offered the standard America First arguments that the United States was not ready for a European war and that such a crusade would constitute "a transoceanic war of aggression with no end in sight"—which would scuttle "democracy and freedom" in America. Americans must "take our stand here on this side of the Atlantic . . . because at least it offers a chance for the maintenance of all the things we care about in America, while war abroad would mean their certain extinction."

At Harvard this intergenerational clash moved from polemic to theater. For almost a year Harvard's isolationist students had been feuding with President James Conant, one of the nation's most vocal interventionists. The *Harvard Crimson* found it appalling that Conant's agitation was helping to bring America closer to a war which "may soon send to destruction the lives" of his own students.

Lash moves base from ASU to ISS

Lacking any central organization like the old ASU to mobilize anti-isolationist sentiment, a variety of different student groups emerged over the fall semester. By December, twenty college chapters of William Allen White's Committee to Defend America by Aiding the Allies were functioning. Agnes Reynolds, a former ASU leader, presided over the creation of Student Defenders of Democracy, a group urging war preparations and aid to Britain. This group attracted endorsements from student leaders on more than 100 campuses. Joseph Lash took over the leadership of the International Student Service (ISS), and converted it from a refugee aid group into an aid the Allies organization. The ISS managed to sponsor some high profile events for the interventionist cause, thanks in part to the fundraising, contacts, and sponsorship of Eleanor Roosevelt, who was by now a good friend of Lash's. The ISS also attracted the National Student Federation, the organization of American student governments, as an affiliate, after the NSF broke with the isolationist and communist-dominated American Youth Congress.

* * *

After the U.S. entered the war, former peace protesters often became soldiers, sailors, and pilots. Neal Anderson Scott, the commencement day orator who preached the isolationist gospel to his graduating class at Davidson College in 1940, died in battle as a navy ensign in the Pacific War less than two years later. There were many like Scott. Few students who had been peace activists during the Depression decade became conscientious objectors during the war. . . .

No student peace movement could have survived in a nation as threatened by war and fascism as America became during the early 1940s. In retrospect, then, it was not the movement's collapse but rather the way that it collapsed that was so memorable. . . . In these campus conflicts of the late 1930s and early 1940s one hears early expression of the bitter debates and restrictive philosophies that would yield so much political bloodletting and repression in Cold War America. Liberals, who had entered the Popular Front era of the student movement willing to work with communists, came away from the post–Nazi-Soviet Pact period embittered; they began to articulate an anti-communist language of exclusion.

Fundamental to this exclusionary mind-set was the notion that communists represented not a normal political party, but rather a conspiratorial group.

* * *

Lash stresses need for a noncommunist leadership

This shift toward exclusion was illustrated most dramatically in the case of Joseph Lash. As late as November 1939, when the ASU's internal communist-noncommunist struggle was escalating, Lash had stood for an inclusive student movement. Called before the red-probing Dies Committee, Lash praised communists for helping to build the student movement and defended their right to participate in the ASU—arguing that a democratic organization must be open to all. In the midst of his hearing before the Dies Committee, Lash ridiculed the red hunters, bursting into song: "If you see an un-American lurking far or near just alkalize with Martin Dies and he will disappear." Yet within two years Lash abandoned the principles which had led him to advocate an inclusive ASU and was defending an exclusive ISS.

As ISS General Secretary, Lash opposed the admission of communists into the organization. Nor would he allow ISS cooperation with the communists, even after the German invasion of Russia when the communists' new interventionist position placed them in agreement with ISS foreign policy. Explaining this position in 1941, Lash cited his experience in the Youth Congress and ASU. The "inescapable conclusion from the events of the past two years" was that communists were "unreliable allies in the march towards a more democratic America and a better world." The communists "paraded as liberals" and anti-fascists, then as "isolationists," leaving noncommunists who had worked with them wondering why "the slogans and loyalties of one month became the anathemas and heresies of the next." Lash observed that the communist slogans used for public consumption, whether interventionist or isolationist, masked their true goal of serving Soviet foreign policy interests. . . ."In the ISS Lash would stress the need to develop a noncommunist student leadership, capable of preventing communists from controlling campus politics. "Joe taught me," recalled former ISS member Louis Harris, "how to out-think, out-maneuver and to out-sit the communists whom we were struggling against in the student movement."

* * *

The bitterness and exclusionary politics which grew out of the campus battles of the Depression era endured even into the 1960s. They shaped the way that leading liberal anticommunist alumni of the old student movement initially responded to the new generation of student rebels who had begun to protest the Vietnam War. . . .

They were the aftermath of the student movement of the Depression era—a movement which in its heyday had promoted political tolerance, but which died in a fit of intolerance.

PICTURE CREDITS: *Then:* Archives of the City College of New York. *Now:* Courtesy Trude Pratt Lash (Thomas Victor)

JOSEPH P. LASH

Born in New York City in 1909, Lash attended De Witt Clinton High School in the Bronx. He graduated City College of New York in 1931 and received his Master's Degree from Columbia University in 1932. He was secretary of the Student League for Industrial Democracy before becoming Executive Secretary of the American Student Union in 1935. He traveled to Spain during the Spanish Civil War and served in the U.S. Army during World War II in the Pacific. He joined the New York Post *in 1950 as UN correspondent and became Assistant Editorial Page Editor in 1962, working with the Editor, James Wechsler, who had been ASU Director of Publications. Lash left his position in 1966 to write the definitive biography of Eleanor Roosevelt at the request of her family. He was author of* Eleanor Roosevelt: A Friend's Memoir *and* Dag Hammarskjold: Custodian of the Brushfire Peace. *In 1977 he was named to the first Samuel Eliot Morison Award for his work* Roosevelt and Churchill, 1939-41: The Partnership That Saved the West. *Lash married Trude Pratt in 1944. They had one son. Lash died in Key West in 1987.*

The Campus: A Fortress of Democracy

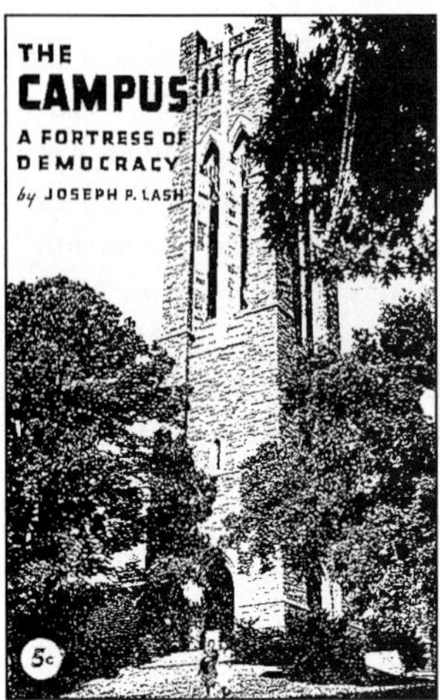

Joseph P. Lash
National Secretary,
American Student Union,
1937

Editor's note: These excerpts, from the 48-page report prepared for the Third Annual Convention of the American Student Union at Vassar College in 1937, stress the Depression-era and prewar issues which faced college students at the time and which fueled the agenda of the student movement on the left.

It used to be said that College and school, instead of being windows through which the student looked out upon the world with sharpened eyes, were really feudal walls that shut him off from the world. If the depression and the distant threat of war sapped the barriers between school and society, the development of the last few months have not only breached those barriers, but engulfed the campus with a plenitude of problems. Students once were smug; they were indifferent; they made a pose of their cynicism. Today they are worried; they throng the lecture room searching for answers; they even look into their textbooks to see whether past generations had similar difficulties.

We shall not try to enumerate all the historical forces that have caused this profound change in the temper of the student body. Two, however, are basic: the formation of the Rome-Berlin-Tokyo alliance for war and fascism, and the economic recession. The wars this unholy alliance already have inspired in Spain and China have made world enslavement, world war, world catastrophe, no longer academic matters, remote in space and history, but immediate and urgent, threatening our very lives. It is as if a plague that had been raging in distant parts of the globe suddenly descended upon this campus. The consolidation of the war alliance has transferred the problem of war front the headlines into our lives....

* * *

That is the reason for this, the largest convention in the history of the progressive student movement. That is why greater throngs than ever before are turning out to the local meetings of the American Student Union. That is what accounts for the emphasis on social action in the Y's. That is the explanation of the growth of the Catholic Student Peace Federation. The campus is actively searching for leadership. It gives the American Student Union great pleasure that at the present moment hundreds of other students are meeting to consider similar problems. We extend our most cordial salutations to the magnificent assembly of the Student Christian Movement being held in Ohio. We hope that the National Student Federation, meeting in New Mexico, the Wesley Foundation's meeting in St. Louis, and the American Medical Students Association in Chicago will arrive at decisions fruitful to our generation. All these organizations are the foundation of the broad progressive front that has been forged on the campus in recent years, a solidarity which obtains its most concrete expression in the United Student Peace Committee. To the latter we pledge our continued support and loyalty.

* * *

The American Student Union believes, and the campus *believes*, that world war can still be prevented. All our efforts are bent toward averting the outbreak of that holocaust which spells the end of human civilization. We will not despair of peace. Our convictions, all our actions are motivated by the sincere and passionate aspiration to defend the peace we have and to help bring peace to the peoples that have been plunged into war by fascist aggression.

* * *

All our lives we have been brought up to venerate the symbols of humanity and civilization, from the time we learned the story of William Tell to the time we plumbed the deeper problems of mankind and the universe with Plato and Aristotle. But the truths these men have uttered, the values they represent, today are challenged. The old order cannot pay more than lip-service to human values and to truth because truth is on our side, not on that of privilege and the vested interests. That is why we grow. That is why those who were brought up in the traditions of honesty and equality and justice throng our movement. Our belief in these values is our salvation.

Vassar Miscellany
12/27/37

AMERICAN STUDENTS UNION BRINGS 600 TO VASSAR

Vermont Meets California to Plan Year's Program at Annual Convention

MacCRACKEN SPEAKS

Education in Democracy Subject of Discussion

...elegates pouring in from ... the country, the Vassar ...repared to play hostess to ... annual convention of the ...n Student Union. Several ... delegates are expected to ...ived by tonight and a to-...out 600 will be on hand ...y morning when Execu-

Times Wide World

ATTENDING AMERICAN STUDENT UNION MEETING AT VASSAR

Joseph P. Lash, executive secretary of the group; Molly Yard, organization secretary, and Britt... Harris, member of the national committee on arrangements, during a conference at Poughkeepsie yesterda...

New York Times
12/28/37

MOLLY YARD (Swarthmore College) was organization secretary and treasurer of the ASU. In later years she became head of the National Organization for Women. Here she is shown at a 1992 Campobello (ME) reunion (See Munts, p. 35; also Yard in 1937, album, p. 901).

(Document source: Archives of the City College of New York. Photo of Molly Yard, courtesy Mary Lou Munts)

ASU, 1935-1941: The Peace Movement

"For the betterment of the economic position of students in school"

Editor's Note: Founded by the competing communist (National Student League) and anticommunist (Student League for Industrial Democracy) Marxist organizations, the ASU extended its reach to depression era liberal students concerned about economic issues as well as segregation and discrimination barriers and the overarching issue of war and peace.

The brief but dramatic history of this organization is reviewed in Section 1 of this Prologue by Miriam Berlin and by Martin McLaughlin and presented in detail in Cohen's When the Old Left Was Young *and Altbach's* Student Politics in America. *A determined effort by American communists to manage the national agenda of political and social action, in an era of the "United Front," was played out during the 1930s. Mainstream student, youth, religious, and labor groups had joined with the American Youth Congress, legitimized by the support it received from Eleanor Roosevelt and the president, in an effort to do something about a world which seemed to be careening out of control around them.*

The opposition from the right in those years tended to be argued on grounds of patriotism or conspiracy (see LID piece below), without the intellectual and moral distinctions between communists and noncommunists that students themselves appeared able to make.

Student activism in the first half of the twentieth century seems to have been largely defined by the left. As Altbach notes also, "it has often been forgotten that most [U.S.] students have few quarrels with the establishment and that a powerful student movement has rarely existed on campuses. . . . The organized student movement represented only a small fraction of the population."

Johns Hopkins Newsletter, Baltimore, 1/10/36

ASU Formed by National Convention at Columbus, Ohio

With 427 delegates representing students in every section of the country, the American Student Union was formed at a convention held in the Y.W.C.A. at Columbus, Ohio, on December 28 and 29. In spite of a heavy snowstorm, 113 schools sent representatives—76 colleges and universities and 37 high schools.

The new organization—The American Student Union—is a broad united student movement against war and Fascism. Its program states that it strives for the betterment of the economic position of students in school and their right to a job when graduated. It fights against racial, religious, and political discrimination and defends academic freedom. Its main point stresses the students' fight against war and supports the Oxford Pledge.

NSL, LID Represented

One hundred and forty-one delegates were representatives from N.S.L. chapters; 116 were members of the Student League for Industrial Democracy, while the remainder were students unaffiliated with these two organizations. Among the latter were delegates from twenty college student councils, many school newspapers and clubs composed of R.O.T.C. officers....

The Vassar Miscellany News, Poughkeepsie, 4/24/37

Vassar Joins in Nation Wide Strike with Large Peace Demonstration

Over a thousand students and faculty members heralded together the Vassar Peace Strike of 1937 with a triumphant march from the Soap Palace in main to Students' on Thursday morning....

On past Strong and Lathrop they marched in groups of six or seven with the faculty and several Poughkeepsie ministers at the head. Bold, alliterative printed posters, carried by girls from all the campus organizations, proclaimed "Careers not Conscription," "Sanity not Slaughter," "Scholarships not Battleships," "Pax Vobiscum," and on the teachers' Union placard, "Workers of the World, Unite for Peace." In Students' where Dean C. Mildred Thompson presided, the peace strikers filled the main floor, with others listening from the balcony.

After Sally Jenkins, President of Students', had read the new revised Peace Call, Erika Mann, the daughter of the German writer Thomas Mann, described the preparations for war that were being carried on in Nazi Germany, and stressed the urgent need for peace....

Johns Hopkins Newsletter, Baltimore, 1/11/38

Hopkins ASU Delegate Attends Convention at Vassar

Vote is 4 to 1 Against Oxford Pledge, As Collective Security is Sustained; Program Adopted by 625 Delegates Advocates Withdrawal of Forces Abroad.

Reflecting the change in public opinion that accompanied President Roosevelt's famed Chicago speech regarding America's standpoint in world affairs, the American student Union voted an overwhelming 4 to 1 in favor of adoption of a program of collective security....

At the convention in a brilliant burst of oratory, Joseph Lash, national executive secretary, voiced the opinion of the vast majority of delegates when he cried, "We consider it (the Oxford Pledge) not only valueless in the present circumstances, but actually a deterrent in the campaign for peace. Our concern is to keep America out of war...."

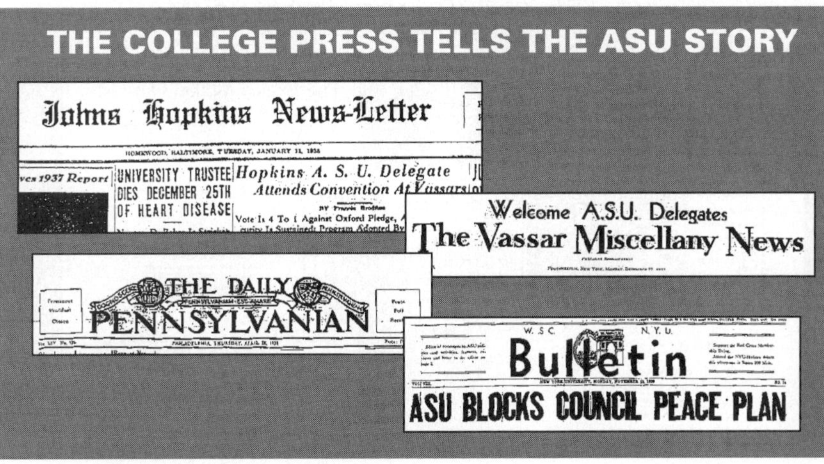
THE COLLEGE PRESS TELLS THE ASU STORY

Johns Hopkins News-Letter

UNIVERSITY TRUSTEE DIES DECEMBER 25TH OF HEART DISEASE

Hopkins A. S. U. Delegate Attends Convention At Vassar

Vote Is 4 To 1 Against Oxford Pledge

Welcome A.S.U. Delegates

The Vassar Miscellany News

THE DAILY PENNSYLVANIAN

W. S. C. N. Y. U. Bulletin

ASU BLOCKS COUNCIL PEACE PLAN

Excerpts appear in this album from *Johns Hopkins News-Letter*, 1936, '38 (MD), *The Vassar Miscellany News*, 1937, '40 (NY), *The Daily Pennsylvanian*, 1939, '41 (University of Pennsylvania), *W.S.C.-N.Y.U. Bulletin*, 1939 (Washington Square College, NYU), and *The Daily Texan*, 1935 (University of Texas)

The Daily Pennsylvanian, Philadelphia 10/13/39

Students Favor Cash and Carry Neutrality; Differ on Willingness to Fight for Country

Campus opinion leans toward the cash-and-carry plan, and a faith in President Roosevelt to keep us permanently neutral from the now raging world war.

Overwhelmingly, students believe that Germany's economic system will crack under the war strain and the allies will emerge victorious. The moment the United States entered the struggle, 30% would volunteer immediately. But 40% would wait until they were drafted before they would take up arms.

The figures computed from the results of the Daily Pennsylvanian poll conducted yesterday represent the opinions of one thousand university men in the fraternity, dormitory and commuter groups.

24% won't fight

Surprise of the poll was the discovery that 24% of the undergraduates, one out of every four, claim they would refuse to arms if the United States went to war. Some, to be sure, qualified this declaration by adding, "if on European battlefields"....

W.S.C.–N.Y.U. Bulletin, New York University 11/13/39

ASU Blocks Council Peace Plan

Prevents Condemnation of "All New War Aggressors"

Students carrying signs reading "Condemn all Aggressors—Stalin As Well As Hitler" and "Against the Commu-Nazis" were mobbed by members of the ASU Friday and their placards destroyed when they attempted to introduce into the ASU Peace Demonstration a shade of opinion not included in its program.

Later Friday afternoon Jack Cottin, former president who resigned recently, said he "deplored" the action of the ASU and declared that it no longer represented liberal student opinion....

The Vassar Miscellany News, Poughkeespsie, 4/17/40

Students Strike for Peace

"'40 Shall Not Be '17"

Slogans, strikes and demonstrations will be the order of the day on college campuses throughout the country today....

The demand for peace is characteristically dramatized on every campus: Bennington has a modern dance group to express anti-war sentiments. Peace-minded intellectuals will meet on the library steps at Harvard for a discussion led by foreign student members of the A.S.U.

"This is Europe's War"

The peace sentiment flowering this week in college newspapers' editorials is epitomized in the underlined words of *The Dartmouth* last week, "Europe's War." The Wisconsin's *Daily Cardinal,* pursuing the same line of thought, finds that "there is less reason for this event to move us in the direction of war than for almost any other that has so far occurred."...

The Daily Pennsylvanian, Philadelphia 12/8/41

University Votes for Nazi War if Need for Hitler's Defeat In Intercollegiate Survey

As the Axis struck at America's Far Eastern outposts, the University completed her first intercollegiate survey, voting sixty-five percent that it was more important that Germany be defeated than that we stay out of the war. Today that percentage would very probably be increased....

The survey was held under the supervision of Dr. George Gallup in conjunction with universities and colleges throughout the nation.

League for Industrial Democracy—Precursor of the ASU

Editor's Note: In the excerpt on the next page from the February 19, 1935, issue of the Daily Texan, *the program and history of the LID are described.*

The National Student League, the Communist wing, split from the LID in 1931, to become "the prime organizer of the radical student movement."

As McLaughlin points out earlier, the NSL and LID competed ideologically but collaborated in many aspects of political action, including the founding of the ASU.

"Industrial democracy"—socialism—had a continuing attraction for generations of student leaders on the left. Its principal spokesman, Norman Thomas, who several times ran as presidential candidate of the Socialist Party, is listed as one of the Executive Directors of the LID in 1932.

As exemplified by the Johns Hopkins Newsletter *headline of 1/11/38, Thomas often appeared as a featured speaker on college campuses both before and after the war.*

Socialism and communism were lumped together politically, and fears of subversion and for "the destruction of the United States government" energized private groups such as the Washington, D.C.-based National Republic (and, later in NSA's time, the Detroit Economic Club).

In a 10/1/32 letter to a University of Texas alumnus donor, Walter B. Steele, General Manager of National Republic, wrote, "Our organization has made intensive study of the radical question since 1916. We have kept 'eternal vigilance', never failing to note when a step was made. . . .

"Radical dupes attempt to have one laughed out of the picture as a 'nut' if he shows any concern. . . . A few thousand of us have become hardened to this and have continued on as the shock troops of Americanism. . . ."

SOCIALISM SEEN AS THREAT Norman Thomas, leader of the U.S. Socialist Party, was a frequent speaker on American college campuses in the 1930s and 40s (*Johns Hopkins News letter,* January 11, 1938). Thomas is one of the Executive Directors of the League for Industrial Democracy listed in its 1931-32 organizing brochure (below), whose formation of campus chapters and call for "Solidarity Forever" is emblematic of "The Enemy Within Our Gates" (below), against which the Washington, D.C.-based National Republic declared "eternal vigilance."

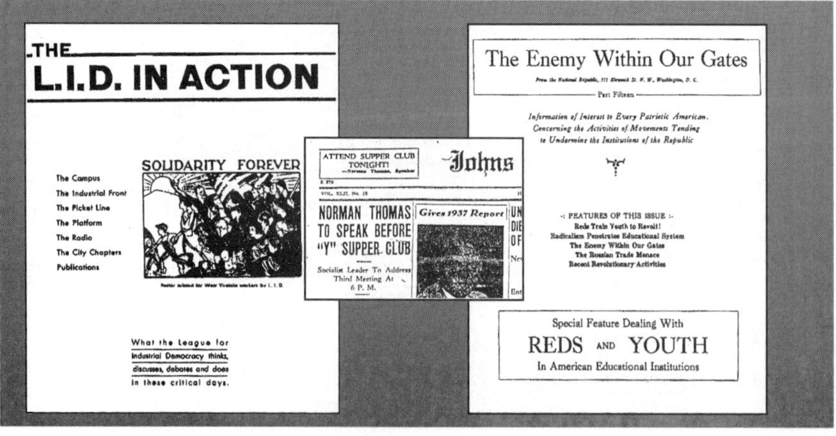

From *The Daily Texan* 2/19/35

L.I.D. Chapter to Organize Thursday

A local chapter of the League for Industrial Democracy will be organized on the University campus Thursday night following a meeting of the Public Affairs Federation in the Y.M.C.A. at 7:30 o'clock, Ray Thurston announced Monday. . . .

The League, Thurston said, pledges itself to a program of education for a new social order based on production for use and not for profit . . . opposition to international war, war preparations and propaganda; the elimination of the R.O.T.C. on campuses; the maintenance of academic freedom. . . .

Started in 1905

The history of the Student L.I.D. dates from 1905 when a call signed by Clarence Darrow, Jack London, Upton Sinclair, William English Walling and others was issued for the formation of an Intercollegiate Socialist Society whose primary object "was to create students of socialism, not to produce socialists." . . .

Most of the chapters were disbanded during the war [World War I], since the draft turned the colleges into military campus and the Socialists refused to support the war.

After the end of the war chapters were again organized, Thurston said, but students desired a more inclusive name than "socialist" . . . thus, "the League for Industrial Democracy was formed."

The president of the L.I.D. at present is Robert Lovett; the treasurer, Stuart Chase; executive directors, Harry W. Laidler and Norman Thomas.

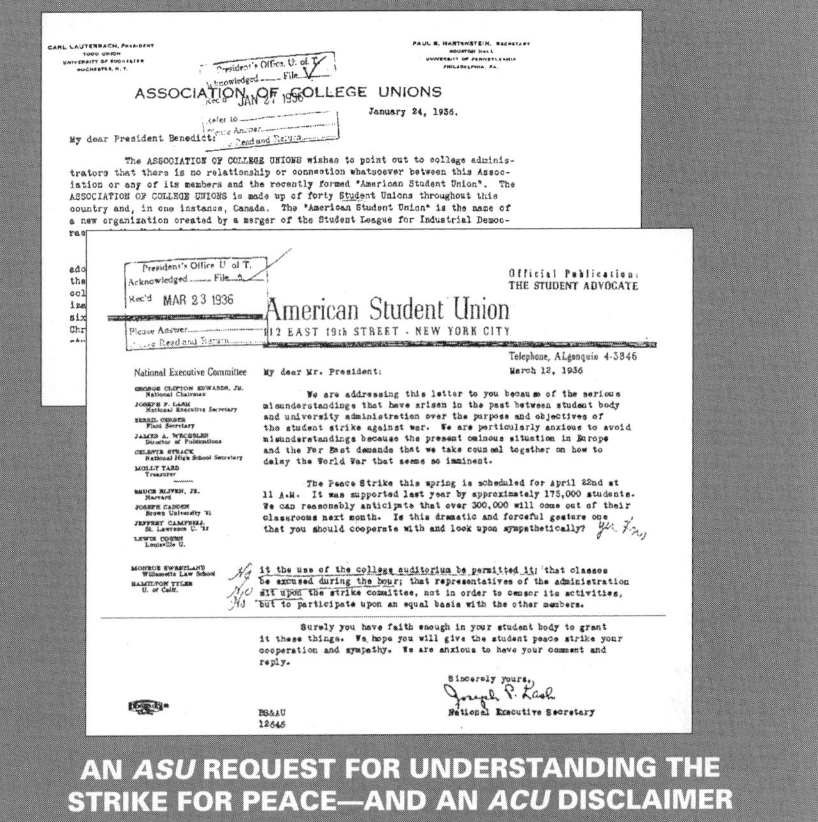

CARL LAUTENBACH, PRESIDENT
TODD UNION
UNIVERSITY OF ROCHESTER
ROCHESTER, N. Y.

PAUL B. HARTENSTEIN, SECRETARY
HOUSTON HALL
UNIVERSITY OF PENNSYLVANIA
PHILADELPHIA, PA.

President's Office, U. of T.
Acknowledged ____ File ✓
Rec'd JAN 27 1936
Refer to ____
Please Answer ____
Read and Return ____

ASSOCIATION OF COLLEGE UNIONS

January 24, 1936.

My dear President Benedict:

The ASSOCIATION OF COLLEGE UNIONS wishes to point out to college administrators that there is no relationship or connection whatsoever between this Association or any of its members and the recently formed "American Student Union". The ASSOCIATION OF COLLEGE UNIONS is made up of forty Student Unions throughout this country and, in one instance, Canada. The "American Student Union" is the name of a new organization created by a merger of the Student League for Industrial Democ-rac[...]

President's Office U. of T.
Acknowledged ____ File ____
Rec'd MAR 23 1936
Please Answer ____
Read and Return ____

Official Publication:
THE STUDENT ADVOCATE

American Student Union
112 EAST 19th STREET · NEW YORK CITY

Telephone, ALgonquin 4-3846

National Executive Committee
GEORGE CLIFTON EDWARDS, JR., National Chairman
JOSEPH P. LASH, National Executive Secretary
SERRIL GERBER, Field Secretary
JAMES A. WECHSLER, Director of Publications
CELESTE STRACK, National High School Secretary
MOLLY YARD, Treasurer
BRUCE BLIVEN, JR., Harvard
JOSEPH CADDEN, Brown University '31
JEFFREY CAMPBELL, St. Lawrence U. '32
LEWIS COHEN, Louisville U.
MONROE SWEETLAND, Willamette Law School
HAMILTON TYLER, U. of Calif.

March 12, 1936

My dear Mr. President:

We are addressing this letter to you because of the serious misunderstandings that have arisen in the past between student body and university administration over the purpose and objectives of the student strike against war. We are particularly anxious to avoid misunderstandings because the present ominous situation in Europe and the Far East demands that we take counsel together on how to delay the World War that seems so imminent.

The Peace Strike this spring is scheduled for April 22nd at 11 A.M. It was supported last year by approximately 175,000 students. We can reasonably anticipate that over 300,000 will come out of their classrooms next month. Is this dramatic and forceful gesture one that you should cooperate with and look upon sympathetically? Yes & No

No — it the use of the college auditorium be permitted it; that classes
No — be excused during the hour; that representatives of the administration
No — sit upon the strike committee, not in order to censor its activities, but to participate upon an equal basis with the other members.

Surely you have faith enough in your student body to grant it these things. We hope you will give the student peace strike your cooperation and sympathy. We are anxious to have your comment and reply.

Sincerely yours,
Joseph P. Lash
National Executive Secretary

BS&AU
12646

AN *ASU* REQUEST FOR UNDERSTANDING THE STRIKE FOR PEACE—AND AN *ACU* DISCLAIMER

(Bottom letter) In preparation for the 1936 peace strike, just four months after the ASU was formed, ASU National Executive Secretary Joseph Lash writes college presidents on March 12, 1936, that, "we are particularly anxious to avoid misunderstandings because the present ominous situation in Europe and the Far East demands that we take counsel together on how to delay the World War that seems so imminent." Lash then asks, referring to the 300,000 students expected to participate nationally, "Is this dramatic and forceful gesture one that you should cooperate with and look upon sympathetically?" There is no record of a response by the University of Texas President's Office, but a notation in the margin reads "Yes and No," while requests for use of the auditorium, time off for students, and cooperation of the faculty show notations of "No" in each case.

(Top letter) Earlier, on January 24, Paul B. Hartenstein, Secretary of the 40-member Association of College Unions (the organization of campus Student Union buildings and services), headquartered at the University of Pennsylvania, wrote college presidents that it had "no connection whatsoever" with the new ASU and that "despite a personal pleas that they chose another name made before the six hundred delegates at their convention . . . they officially adopted the name 'American Student Union.'"

Mr. Hartenstein's request that "administrative action" be taken to prohibit use of the name on campuses that had traditional Student Unions appears to have gone unanswered to President Benedict's file, as did Lash's.

Poster printed for West Virginia workers by L. I. D

The Campus Goes to Nearby Towns to Arrange Meetings

"THE CAMPUS GOES TO TOWN" LID 1931-32 organizing brochure promotes the role of students: "Here is a poster advertising a meeting of workers of Lewiston, Maine, organized by Bates College members of L.I.D.," and "On the campuses of 141 colleges and univesities, student members of L.I.D. are working in close contact with local labor bodies, raising funds and food for strikers, fighting the sinister Reserve Officers Training Corps with its emotional drive for the next war, speaking at forums and out on street corners for a new social order, mobilizing student sentiment for social justice."

ISS/ISA/USSA, 1941-1946: Transition

Editor's Note: For different reasons that have been previously noted, the ASU and the NSFA ceased functioning in 1941. Also, the war in Europe and ultimately the Japanese attack on Pearl Harbor rendered moot the public policy agendas that had stirred both organizations. As many of their student leaders went off to military service, sufficient funding for the paid staffs that provided administrative continuity was no longer forthcoming from dues and donations.

A new generation of activist student leaders was incubating, seeking a vehicle for public policy engagement. For several years the U.S. office of the International Student Service sponsored programs and events that provided a bridge to the formation of the United States Student Assembly (USSA) in 1943. In September 1942, ISS sponsored a founding meeting of delegates from 53 nations for the International Student Assembly. At that meeting, plans were launched for USSA to be established as the American affiliate.

As then Swarthmore undergraduate Mary Lou Rogers [Munts], its first president, notes in her memoir earlier, it was debatable whether it could have chosen to emulate NSFA and lay the foundations for the postwar organization that became NSA. The second President of USSA, Alice Horton [Tibbetts] of Wellesley, tells in Part 1 of this book how, working with the YWCA staff, she organized the U.S. delegation to the 1946 World Student Congress in Prague. On their return, they called the Chicago Student Conference which led to the formation of NSA.

USSA leaders and members were most interested in political and social action, and their liberal political roots led, ultimately, to the formation of Students for Democratic Action (SDA) in the spring of 1947.

As noted in many of the memoirs in this book, USSA and then SDA leaders joined with the Student Christian and Catholic student movement leaders, the student Federalists and other national student groups to provide leadership in NSA during its formative years.

USSA Organizes

"...democracy is the only just society."

Excerpts from *The New York Times,* Monday, May 10, 1948

Student Unit Bars Reds and Fascists

Free Trade, a Second Front and End of Insecurity Are Among the Demands

Communist undergraduate organizations in the colleges of this country—and Fascist organizations, if any should present themselves—were barred from membership in the newly organized United States Student Assembly by the constitution it adopted yesterday at the Y.W.C.A., 610 Lexington Avenue, at the close of a heated three days' session.

Although the constitution defines the United States Student Assembly as "a confederation of autonomous democratic student groups organized democratically and bound together by the common belief that democracy is the only just society," the Communists wanted to get in, and they made no secret of it.

Eighteen Who Quit Return to Vote

The eighteen delegates who walked out the day before, when Mrs. Franklin D. Roosevelt denounced the Young Communist League, returned to vote for the amendment [introduced by Lawrence Harris of CCNY] that would have let in the Communists among the believers in democracy....

The anti-Communlst forces were led by Irwin Ross, editor of Threshold, the Student Assembly publication. He reviewed the mercurial foreign policy of the Young Communist League "which changed according to the Moscow weather at any moment"....

Out of the resolutions committee came a program of foreign and domestic policy for the United States that disposed in forthright undergraduate fashion of most of the major issues now confronting the world....

For four hours, while the organization launched itself as the American branch of the International Students Assembly, the air was full of debating fury ... and appeals to the floor from rulings of the chairman, Stanley Cleveland of Princeton.

Mary Lou Rogers of Swarthmore College, who was elected president without oppositlon, said in her Inaugural address: "We intend to make the college student a force in the country."

Editor's note: The article also reported that William Leuchtenburg of Cornell University "introduced an amendment in opposition to the Young Communist League." Leuchtenburg became the first executive secretary of the newly formed Students for Democractic Action in March 1947 and attended the NSA Constitutional Convention. He became a noted historian and Roosevelt scholar and is William Rand Kenan, Jr., Professor of History at the University of North Carolina.

Vassar Miscellany News, 11/15/41

ISS Stimulates Student Interest and Activity

The basic aims of ISS are: (1) to help students towards a fuller comprehension of the origins and meaning of American democracy; (2) to promote closer cooperation between faculty and students in the solution of these problems and other problems concerning the American campus; (3) to develop international cooperation among students and scholars; and (4) to succor the student victims of oppression and disaster.

ISS is not a membership group, but consists of an executive committee and staff. It was founded in 1921 to help students in war-torn Europe, and today one of its main activities is to help student refugees, with scholarships and placement in American colleges.

Threshold, the new ISS magazine, culls the literary creations of people on campuses all over the country and attempts to point the way towards a realization of a true democracy through clarifying the issues involved.

Student Leadership Institute, initiated at Campobello Island last summer, and the various summer work camps such as Highlander Folk School, Grafton and Green Farms give the student practical experience in democratic living and point the way towards what constructive efforts can be made in a war-torn world.

The newly innovated Washington Bureau is an attempt to make Washington educationally available to the student by offering the opportunity to study—at first hand—the operations of the Federal government.

Middlebury Campus, May 2, 1946

Seven Students Represent Midd at USSA Convention

A total of seven men and women represented the Middlebury chapter of the United States Student Assembly at their fourth annual conference held April 26, 27 and 28 at the New School for Social Research at 66 West 12th Street, New York City.

On Friday evening, Mrs. Eleanor Roosevelt, the United States representative to the United Nations Organization, spoke to the conference on "UNO Working." She gave an inside picture of the U.N. Assembly meeting in London.... She strongly criticized the unwelcoming attitude of the American People towards the U.N.... [this attitude is] the strongest reason for the UN's presence in this country.

The next speaker was Dr. Channing Tobias, outstanding expert on race relations, and Senior Secretary of the Y.M.C.A. He pointed out that the discrimination in our own country is embarrassing to us in our foreign policy....

At 8:00 P.M. the delegates met at the home of Alice Horton, the USSA delegate to London and Prague youth conferences, to lay plans for the coming conference at Prague this summer. USSA will send one delegate, chosen from chapter nominations...."

Wellesley College News, May 9, 1946

USSA Works For Progress

Michal Ernst Feder, National President

The position of all student organizations is this year complicated by the necessity of reorientation. New groups have formed during the war years and with the coming of peace. The revived activity of students in Europe, the obviously critical state of affairs abroad and reconversion at home present undergraduates in American colleges with a challenging opportunity to make themselves and their views felt as never before.

This will be a mighty year for organization and for action. The congressional elections, the meetings of the United Nations in the United States, the continuing need for relief abroad and other concrete issues should stimulate ... programs on many campuses.

The return of travel to a more or less peacetime status will mean more conferences, action weekends, educational gatherings....

Progressive Organization

U.S.S.A. is a progressive organization of college and high school students. It is not controlled by any group or political party but receives advice from its consultant organizations (American Civil Liberties Union, Union for Democratic Action, etc.). The national office, located in New York. publishes "USSA IN ACTION." It also sends out projects or suggestions for programs at regular intervals on topics such as UNNRRA, The Atom Bomb, The Full Employment Bill, the FEPC, FOOD, International Students Day....

"We intend to make the college student a force in this country"

Mary Lou Rogers, Swarthmore College

THE COLLEGE PRESS TELLS THE USSA STORY

1/23/47

[WELL]ESLEY COLLEGE NEWS, JANUARY 23, 1947

• Coffee Sales Soar As Exams Close In

Michal Feder, USSA President, Attends Conference in Washington

"I believe that this organization will prove to be the rallying point for American liberals," declared Michal Ernst Feder '47, speaking of the newly formed Americans for Democratic Action. Acting in her capacity as national president of the United States Student Assembly, a progressive organization of college hourly caucuses in various corners of the room." She also remarked that the entire assembly was extremely impressed when Franklin Delano Roosevelt Jr. and Eleanor Roosevelt walked into the meeting. "The two of them made a striking and interesting couple."

5/1/46

Wellesley College News

Van Doren Will Speak At Harvard

"Body Politic" Reappears for Junior Prom

Alice Horton '45 Returning May 8

Mark Van Doren

Alice Horton '45

Societies Invite Sophs, Juniors

5/2/46

MIDDLEBURY CAMPUS

MIDDLEBURY CAMPUS, MIDDLEBURY, VT., NOVEMBER 29, 1946

Seven Students Represent Midd at USSA Convention

A total of seven men and women represented the Middlebury chapter of the United States Student Assembly at their fourth annual conference held April 26, 27, and 28 at the New School for Social Research at 66 West 12th Street, New York City.

The delegates were: Donald Gilmore '47, recently elected to the executive committee as a regional representative for the coming year, William Gilbert '49, Larzar Ziff '48, Joanne E. Buckeridge '47, Joan L. Biggs '48, Ruth C. Murphy '48, and Jean N. Rapaport '48. Mary H. Albertson '46 attended the conference as a member of the national organization of USSA, but she did not go as a voting delegate.

Mrs. Roosevelt Speaks

On Friday evening, Mrs. Eleanor Roosevelt, the United States representative to the United Nations Organization, spoke to the conference on "UNO Working." She gave an inside picture of the UN assembly meeting in London. Mrs. Roosevelt pointed out that the assembly intended to do no more than organize the machinery for UN and elect the officers; therefore, when so many issues confronted the assembly at one time, We cannot have peace if we continue with self interest and a blind inability to see another person's point of view, we need understanding of the backgrounds of other peoples. Mrs. Roosevelt does see one bright sign in the fact that nations are not neglecting to discuss the highly difficult matters which they refused to face after the last war. Mrs. Roosevelt concluded by emphasizing the importance of backing the UN as an effective predecessor of a future world government.

Mr. James Loeb, Jr., Speaks

On Saturday morning, Mr. James Loeb, Jr., the National Director of the Union for Democratic Action, spoke on "Political Action for Working Peace." Mr. Loeb stressed the dire need of obtaining a good vote to secure a more active congress next fall.

Mr. Anthony Wayne Smith

Mr. Anthony Wayne Smith, assistant director of the Industrial Union Councils, C. I. O., spoke about "Labor Working for Peace." He represented labor as standing for a world control of atomic energy and the strengthening of the UN.

(Continued on page 6)

Vassar Miscellany News

5/19/43

SLA Votes To Affiliate With USSA

The Vassar Student Liberal Association has by a unanimous vote become affiliated with the United States Student Assembly. Although its name and its autonomous plan of action will be kept, it will work next year in close cooperation with the national program of the USSA.

The USSA conference held in New York last weekend was described by Betty Uchitelle, president of the SLA and delegate at the conference. Miss Uchitelle outlined the national program of the USSA as adopted at the conference. Mary Coker, vice-president, read the Constitution of the USSA.

Programs Similar

SLA members felt that the program, which includes the support of the NRPB Report, anti-poll tax legislation, and endorsement of the President's seven-point program of economic stabilization; and recommendation of a United Nations

5/10/44

Mrs. Roosevelt Advises USSA

First Lady, Third Party Leader, B. Fine Address USSA

"The older people don't know the answers to the problems of the future any better than the younger people," declared Mrs. Roosevelt speaking after Sunday luncheon to the second annual convention of the United States Student Assembly held in New York last

4/28/43

Leuctenberg Traces U.S. Youth Movement

"Individuals are ineffective, but a united, well organized youth group can certainly be of consequence," said Bill Leuctenberg, campus affairs secretary of the U. S. Student Assembly, in his talk Monday on "The Need of a New National Youth Movement" given under the auspices of the SLA.

The U. S. Student Assembly was formed at an International Student Assembly held last September. "This organization should be more successful than its predecessors," said Mr. Leuctenberg, "because of its international ties, its financial security, and its support by colleges all over the country including many never before interested in student movements."

Tracing the development of youth movements in America, Mr. Leuctanberg said that the Y.M.C.A. and Y.W.C.A. had really been the first, but they were not political organizations. After a period of disinterest, Jack London and others tried to organize groups to ...

STUDENT LEADERS PROVIDE A WARTIME BRIDGE. The news excerpts appearing in this album highlight some of the network of New England college student leaders who provided the wartime bridge to NSA from 1943 to 1947. The May 10, 1943, edition of the *New York Times* reported the 1943 election of Swarthmore College's Mary Lou Rogers (now Munts) as the first president of USSA (see her essay in this section). She was followed as USSA president by Wellesley's Alice Horton (now Tibbetts), whose return from her summer 1945 trip as USSA delegate to the International Youth Conference in London was reported in the May 1, 1946, issue of the *Wellesley College News*. As a consequence of that trip Horton undertook to form the U.S. delegation to the summer 1946 World Student Congress (see her essay in Part 1, Section 1). The planned attendance of Wellesley's Michal Feder at the April 1947 meeting at which USSA voted to transform into the Students for Democratic Action (SDA) is reported in the January 23, 1947, issue of the *News*. Middlebury College, represented at the 1946 USSA convention (*Middlebury Campus*, May 2, 1946), heard Smith College's Miriam Haskell (now Berlin) report on the Prague Congress U.S. delegation, which Alice Horton (now Tibbetts) organized (see p. 68). Berlin described plans for the December 1946 Chicago Student Conference at which a new national student organization (later to become the NSA) was to be discussed (*Middlebury Campus*, November 29, 1946) (see her essay in Part 1, Section 2).

1945

World War II ends and United Nations is born

Animal Farm published and *Carousel* opens on Broadway

Roosevelt, Stalin, and Churchill set guidelines for war's end at Yalta. President Roosevelt dies and Harry Truman succeeds him. San Francisco Conference adopts United Nations Charter and League of Nations holds final meeting. Hitler commits suicide and Mussolini is killed by Partisans. War ends in Europe with VE Day on May 8. U.S. drops atomic bombs on Hiroshima and Nagasaki on August 6 and 9. War's end with VJ Day in the Pacific on August 14. Nobel prize to Fleming, Flory, and Chain for discovery of penicillin. Shintoism abolished in Japan. Nobel prize for literature to Chilean poet Gabriela Mistral. American novelist Theodore Dreiser dies. Frank Lloyd Wright submits design for Guggenheim Museum. Billy Wilder's film *The Lost Weekend* and Serge Eisenstein's *Ivan the Terrible* screened and Benjamin Britten's opera *Peter Grimes* opens. Empire State Building struck at 78-79th floors, July 28, by a B-25 bomber. Detroit defeats Chicago in the World Series.

Source: Adapted from citations in Bernard Grun, *The Timetables of History* (Simon and Schuster, 1991)

Thursday, February 8, 1945
EDUCATION FOR PEACE
—Jean Nol Kemper, '48

Student Life, Washington U. in St. Louis, 2/8/45

PART 1

The Launching of the National Student Association: Chronology of Events, 1946-1952

Program cover of the World Student Congress

Program cover of the NSA Constitutional Convention

PART 1

The Launching of NSA: Chronology of Events

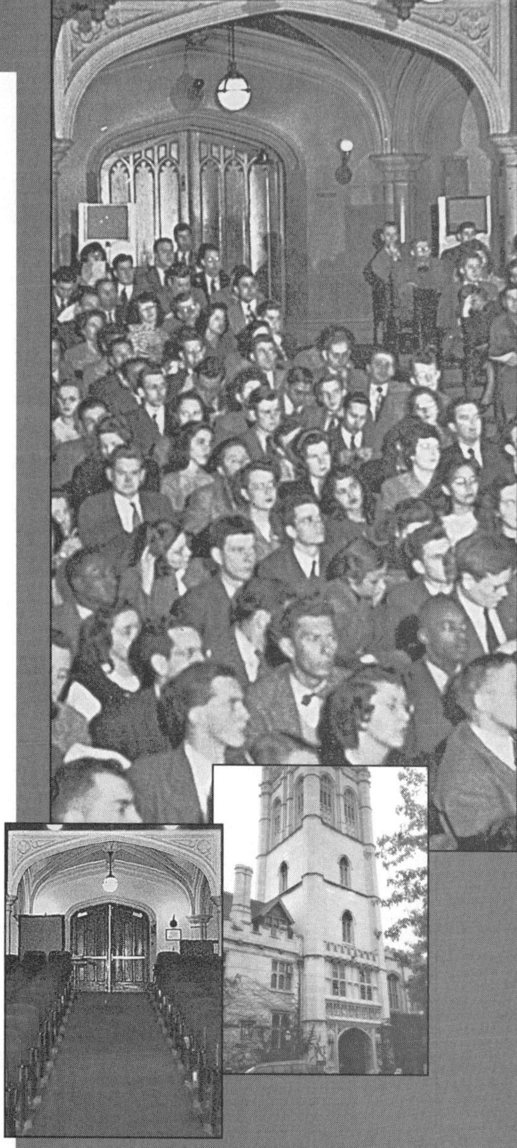

Top: December, 1946. Chicago Student Conference plenary session in the University of Chicago's Reynolds Club auditorium. **Bottom:** the Reynolds Club and auditorium 52 years later in 1998.

NSA's founding years were bracketed by two hot wars—World War II and Korea. They were dramatically shaped by the impact of the Cold War on its international programs, of the "Red Scare" attacks at home on academic freedom and of the practice of segregation on academic and social life.

These years were energized by the impact on undergraduate life of an informed and purposeful generation of veterans and of a responsive cohort of non-veteran fellow students. They were nurtured by a generation of college presidents, deans, and student personnel administrators who saw in the Association an opportunity to endow students with greater opportunities for personal growth and development as well as to channel their engagement in issues of concern to the larger community.

These challenges and opportunities were played out at the Association's founding and annual student conferences, as well as in its regional organizations and campus level outreach.

In Part 1, NSA founders and leaders take us through the chronology of events from 1946-52 which began with the World Student Congress in Prague in August 1946 and led to the Chicago Student Conference in December. There, more than 700 delegates and observers from 307 colleges and universities and 28 national student organizations decided to form a representative national student organization, and laid the groundwork for its Constitutional Convention in September, 1947.

Building a representative national student organization

NSA modeled its constitution after the U.S. Constitution, and built its membership on student governments to assure that it would be truly representative of the students it sought to represent.

It expected to operate under the management of a full-time, annually elected student staff, implementing policies and programs adopted at its annual congress and supported by its member student bodies and in their autonomous regional groupings.

Each of the nine sections in this part provides a selection of first-hand memoirs of former students who played central roles as officers and leaders of the association in building the organization during those years, as well as background documentation and complete rosters of the national leaders and the attending member colleges at the Congresses.

SECTION 1

London, 1945-46, and Preparations for Prague, 1946

CONTENTS

See the Old World in a New Way
NBBS
RAPENBURG 6 · LEIDEN · NETHERLANDS

NBBS (The Netherlands Office for Foreign Student Relations)—a Dutch student voluntary organization—was NSA's principal partner from 1948 in providing transportation for thousands of U.S. students traveling to Europe and beyond after the war. (p.654)

When Janis Tremper (now Dowd) represented Rockford College (IL) at the twentieth annual International Student Service (ISS) Conference at Cambridge University in July 1946, she was one of thousands of American students traveling to Europe, Asia, Africa, and Latin America after the war. ISS had just resumed its international student exchange and service programs after wartime interruption. Janis Tremper Dowd's introductory memoir highlights how ISS provided a medium for students to meet and collaborate with their counterparts from many nations.

During the war, the ISS administered World Student Relief, an agency that it co-founded with the World Student Christian Federation and Pax Romana, the Catholic international student organization. The broad support the ISS U.S. affiliate, the World Student Service Fund, received on U.S. campuses is recalled in Part 3, Section 4.

Observers from the organizing committee of the first World Student Congress, called to form a new International Union of Students (IUS) in Prague the following month, attended the ISS conference. A twenty-five-member U.S. student delegation was meeting in New York at the same time to prepare for the Prague event. These preparations are described in this Section.

A year earlier, also in London, Alice Horton (now Tibbetts; Wellesley '45), President of the United States Student Assembly (USSA), represented that organization at the World Youth Congress. It was there that she learned of plans to form IUS the following summer. Her subsequent travels with a group of Americans, including Muriel Jacobson of the YWCA, through war-ravaged cities of the USSR, reinforced her determination that the United States be represented at the 1946 Congress. Jacobson writes of the challenges to U.S. students in Europe in Part 4, Section 2.

U.S. students form a delegation to go to Prague

Alice Horton Tibbetts and Jewel Lubin Bellush (University of Wisconsin '46) describe how they organized the U.S. delegation. Excerpts from the diary Tibbetts kept on her USSR trip are also provided.

Edward Kirchner (Ohio State '35), representing Pax Romana, describes how the Catholic students on the U.S. delegation were trained to stand up effectively to experienced Communist delegates.

Background materials are published here for the first time in rare excerpts from the State Department files of the U.S. Embassy in Czechoslovakia. They include a moving appeal by University of North Carolina delegate Jimmy Wallace to President Truman requesting travel visas for Russian students to visit the U.S. The U.S. was not yet ready, the State Department replied.

The International Student Service Conferences

Born of the first European Student Relief committee, which was created after World War I in 1920 by the World Student Christian Federation, ISS became an autonomous organization in 1926. In 1940 ISS, the WSCF, and Pax Romana (the international Catholic student movement) together set up World Student Relief, the administration of which was entrusted to the ISS.

As a service organization, ISS did not have a formal membership. It was governed by an international assembly whose delegates were selected by its sponsors to be broadly representative of the student communities in the countries it served around the world. Its purpose was to provide relief, student exchange programs, and research and international conferences concerning student and higher education needs and interests. Its General Secretariat was headquartered in Geneva. Andre de Blonay was its Executive Director in 1946.

In April 1946, the Assembly met for the first time since 1939. It initiated preparations for a reorganization, to adapt to postwar conditions and to provide for broader participation. Its presence in the United States after the war was manifested through the World Student Service Fund, the leading student international relief fund-raising agency on college campuses. (The ISS and its significant role in prewar and postwar U.S. student leadership history and the role of the WSSF are reviewed in Part 3, Section 4.)

Janis Tremper's memorable and influential experience at the 1946 Cambridge ISS conference was replicated for many students in the postwar years. The first three major ISS postwar conferences, held in August each year, were at Combleaux, France (1945), Cambridge, England (1946), and Aarhus, Denmark (1947). American students were well represented at all of them. Scores of students from campuses throughout the country took part in its conferences and programs, returning to report on and share their experiences with fellow students. Many NSA leaders acquired useful global insights and developed lasting international friendships as a result.

(Portions of this account were adapted from a 1946 ISS brochure distributed by the Student Service of America, 2 West 45th Street, New York, NY)

THROUGH THE WAR AND THE ROAD TO PEACE were the themes of the 1946 (Cambridge) and 1947 (Aarhus) conferences. ISS also reports on its first Southeast Asian Regional Conference, which delegates from Burma, India, and Indonesia attended. Those from Ceylon, Siam, Malaya, and Viet Nam were unable to attend due to the unsettled conditions in the region.

ISS to Hold Annual Meet in New York

150 Students to Meet At Wells College July 25

Plans have been announced for the fourth post-war conference of International Student service which will be held at Wells College, New York, from July 25 to August 3.

This will be the first ISS conference to be held in this country since the war. The conference theme will be "Role of the free university in training leadership for social development."

In 1946 the conference was held at Cambridge University, England, in 1947 at Aarhus University, Denmark, and in 1948 at Combloux, France.

The conference is expected to bring ISS representatives from the 25 countries where national committees for ISS carry out the work of this organization.

Approximately 150 students and professors from many countries, including China, South East Asia, Eastern Europe and North America are expected. Seventy-five of the students will come from abroad, while the remaining 75 will be selected from the United States and Canada from applications submitted to the

To better acquaint students of the U. S. with the objects and principles of International Student Service, we reproduce here the official statement of principles which guides ISS:

"International Student Service shall have for its object to encourage and support all efforts on the part of students, professors and others to better the material conditions of life, and to develop the cultural means of action inside

FIVE GERMAN YOUTH LEADERS, sent by the National Social Welfare assembly on a study trip to America, are shown here as they visited the University of Wisconsin campus. They conferred with NSA national executives while in Madison. From left to right they are: Gertrude Klaussen, Munich; Max Moser, Stuttgart; Elisabeth Stein, Wuerttemberg; Brigitte Fenner, Wellburg, and Berthold Glugher, Oberlraken.

Plan Orientation For Students On Volendam

Orientation and recreation programs are being planned for the 1,800 students traveling to Europe on the Volendam, a student-ship released by the Dutch Ministry of Shipping to the Dutch Office for Foreign Student Relations (NBBS).

NBBS with the assistance of NSA International commission is preparing the program designed to help prepare the students for their European summer experiences.

A staff of 35 students and instructors from Europe and America will be used. Four American lecturers and discussion leaders will join two Holland instructors, one French and one Danish discussion leader.

1

2

3

4

5

6

THE 1949 ISS WELLS COLLEGE CONFERENCE: NSA News reported in its May 1949 issue that the July 25, 1947, meeting at Wells College was the first to be held in the United States since the war. "The conference theme will be 'The role of the free university in training leadership for social development.' Attending will be ISS representatives from the 25 countries where national committees for ISS carry out the work of the organization." The program included discussions of the theme of "background and trends in university education in China, Southeast Asia, Eastern Europe, North America and Western Europe . . . current conceptions of the role of the university," including "speeches by Catholic and Protestant educators," and the work of the ISS and World Student Relief. "The ISS Assembly, which sets the policy and program for its work . . . will meet immediately after the conference." (1) Clara Shapiro and Dick Thomas of WSSF. (2) Leaders of ISS including Douglas Aitkin, Secretary General (2d right), and Paul Bouchet (2d left). (3) Bill Ellis on right (Harvard, former NICC delegate and U.S. Vice President of the IUS.) (4) From left: Bill Allaway (U. of Illinois, 1948-49 Illinois Regional International Affairs V.P.), Bush Olmstead. (5) From left: 1948-49 NSA officers Dick Heggie (U.C. Berkeley, V.P. Student Affairs) and Rob West (Yale, V. P. International Affairs). (6) Foreground, from left: Ted Harris (La Salle College, 1948-49 NSA President), Bob Smith (Yale, 1947-48 NSA International Vice President); on right, Aitkin. (Photos from Bill Allaway).

Congressus Studiosorum Orbis Terrarum

Prague 1946

Malcolm Adiseshiah

To the World Student Congress at Prague, which began on August 17th 1946, came by land, sea and air more than 300 student delegates mandated by 2,700,000 students from 40 countries of Europe, Asia, North and South America, Africa and Australasia.

The Summer Meetings of the W. S. C. F.

The General Committee of the World's Student Christian Federation

A. J. Coleman

The General Committee of the World's Student Christian Federation, which is its governing body, was held at the Chateau de Bossey, near Geneva, from August 10th to August 20th. It was, perhaps, the most representative committee

World Union of Jewish Students

François Brunschwig

The first post-war Congress of the World Union of Jewish Students took place at Uriage-les-Bains, near Grenoble, on September 1st to 5th. Delegates from the following countries were present :

Belgium — Italy
Bulgaria — Palestine

The Pax Romana Congress

Gérard Pelletier

Pax Romana, international secretariat of Catholic university students, held its XXth Congress in Fribourg, Switzerland, in the first days of September. Last in the long series of international gatherings which took place this summer, both the Pax Romana Study Week and Congress were attended by a very large and representative group. Delegations from 41 different nations participated and 22 new federations affiliated.

First, in Estavayer-le-Lac, a small, mediæval town on the Lake of Neuchatel,

A Message from W.S.R.

The following letter is being sent from Geneva to W.S.R. friends who were in Europe this summer. Its contents are self-explanatory. It is signed by the secretaries of the three constituent bodies of W.S.R., André de Blonay, the Abbé Gremaud and

The Annual Conference of I.S.S.

Margaret McClumpha

The Twentieth Annual Conference of I.S.S. was held at Girton College, Cambridge, England from July 22nd to 29th, 1946. Nearly

I. S. S. BULLETIN

SEPTEMBER 1946

CONTENTS

ORGAN OF INTERNATIONAL STUDENT SERVICE

PUBLISHED AT 13, RUE CALVIN, GENEVA, SWITZERLAND

Relief

Continuing the work of relief which it has conducted since 1920, ISS has, since 1939, through the European Student Relief Fund, and since 1943, through World Student Relief, undertaken a large-scale relief action for

Student victims of the war

Ruins of Warsaw University.

Books - Study Materials - Medical Supplies Foods - Scholarships

have been given to thousand of

PRISONERS OF WAR • REFUGEES • INTERNEES STUDENTS OF THE OCCUPIED COUNTRIES

Today WSR continues its action; its efforts are now chiefly concentrated on Eastern Europe and the Far East :

$1,500,000 were spent in 1945-1946
$2,125,000 are needed this year

ISS needs your support • Help it to act!

Research and Information

To make students aware of their rights and their responsibilities.

To make available to them material for comparison with universities abroad.

Through its cooperating committees, ISS receives and distributes information and documents throughout the world.

Current inquiries :

European universities during the war.
University reform.
The condition of students after the war.

Subscribe to

"UNIVERSITÉ 46"

International Review of ISS

$1 a year

AN INFORMATIVE REVIEW
A CONSTRUCTIVE REVIEW
A FIGHTING REVIEW

International Education

CONFERENCES
INTERNATIONAL STUDENT EXCHANGES
enable students to realise the psychology, problems, and conditions of other countries.

The **COMBLOUX CONFERENCE** (July 1945) was the first international student meeting since 1939.

With the **CAMBRIDGE CONFERENCE** (July 1946) ISS takes its place in the post-war world.

STUDY TOURS in Europe are organised in August 1946 for 60 overseas students.

At the Combloux Conference.

INTERNATIONAL STUDENT CENTRES

organised by ISS and WSR

help students to regain their health,
are an experiment in community life,
create favourable conditions for study,
are centres of international living.

COMBLOUX (France) — ASHTON HAYES (England)
ROCCA DI PAPA (Italy) — SHAPINGPA (China)

Soon in AUSTRIA, in CZECHOSLOVAKIA, in GREECE, in HUNGARY

RUINS OF WARSAW UNIVERSITY

AT THE COMBLOUX CONFERENCE

AN ARRAY OF KEY CONFERENCES IN THE SUMMER OF 1946 are reported in the 9/46 ISS Bulletin. "For the first time since the war, students have been able to meet again in large numbers . . . to draw up their future programmes on the basis of these contacts," Margaret McClumpha, Editor, wrote. Focusing on budget needs of 21 million Swiss francs for World Student Relief (WSR), she continued, "The relief needs of the world are large and more urgent for this year because we are entering new areas hitherto untouched in Eastern Europe and Asia. It is up to you, our friends in the universities of the world, to reach this goal, and overtop it if possible." The issue also featured an article on the ISS study tours by Janis Tremper (now Dowd), of Rockford College, IL, who became NSA's first Secretary in 1947-48 (see her essay in this section).

ISS PROGRAMS FOR 1946-47 covering "Relief, International Education, Research" are described in the brochure above. "Continuing the work of relief which it has conducted since 1920, ISS has, since 1939, through the European Student Relief Fund, and since 1943, through World Student Relief undertaken a large scale relief action for student victims of the war. . . . Books—Study Materials—Medical Supplies—Foods—Scholarships—have been given to thousands of prisoners of war, refugees, internees, students of the occupied countries. Today WSR continues its action; its efforts are now chiefly concentrated on Eastern Europe and the Far East. $1,500,000 were spent in 1945-46. $2,125,000 are needed this year." Headquartered in Geneva, Switzerland, the brochure is distributed by "Student Service of America, Inc., 2 West 45th Street, New York 19, N.Y."

Colleges Send Students to ISS Conferences

Smith College SCAN, MA 4/9/46

SMITH COLLEGE SCAN ASSOCIATED NEWS

Board Chooses ISS Delegates

Two Juniors, One Sophomore Selected By Joint Group; Attend London Meeting

SPEAK FRENCH

Allison Butler, 1947, Marguerite Peet, 1947, and Miriam Haskell, 1948, have been chosen to go to Europe this summer as the delegates of International Students' Service. The students were chosen by members of the administration and a student board from a slate of nine names which had been drawn up.

All three students speak French, have had experience in leading discussion groups and meetings, and are interested in international affairs. They were chosen on the basis of these requirements.

The Caellian, New Jersey College for Women 6/12/46

The Caellian

PUBLISHED BY THE STUDENTS AT NEW JERSEY COLLEGE FOR WOMEN, NEW BRUNSWICK, N. J.

Bernice Roessler '47 To Act As Delegate To ISS Conference

Bernice Roessler '47, president of G.A., will leave in July for Cambridge, England, where she will attend a week's conference sponsored by the International Student Service organization.

Girton College will be the "melting pot" for 25 delegates from America and representatives from 20 other countries, who will take up the conference theme "New Patterns of University Community." As part of the theme, examples of student life in various countries will be given and the future activities of the I.S.S. will be discussed under the topic of "Man in Modern Society."

In order to become acquainted with conditions in Europe, delegates will make a three week educational tour of the continent, each one choosing the country he most prefers to visit.

Bernice who, while at Girton and on the continent, will live at one of the student centers, was selected to make the trip by the Student Service of America, Inc., United States committee of the I.S.S. A Rutgers student also will attend the conference.

The Campus, Sarah Lawrence College, NY 1/11/47

THE CAMPUS

of SARAH LAWRENCE COLLEGE, Bronxville, New York

Martha Rockwell Relates Experiences While Touring With ISS In Czechoslovakia Last Summer

Martha Rockwell spoke last Wednesday night in MacCracken living-room about the International Students Service and her trip abroad last summer under its auspices. The purpose of the ISS, which has its headquarters in Geneva, is to send students abroad to learn about foreign countries and promote international understanding. Last year an important result of the trip was the raising of relief supplies which was more easily accomplished by first hand informa-

three groups. After five days in London and a night in Paris, Martha went to Czechoslovakia with her group to work in camps. This plan was not very successful because the people treated them more like tourists and they were not able to see what student life was like since the schools were not in session. However, Martha said that she went to a harvest festival which was "wonderful fun" and they did do things other

Mills College Weekly, CA 10/3/47

Mills College Weekly

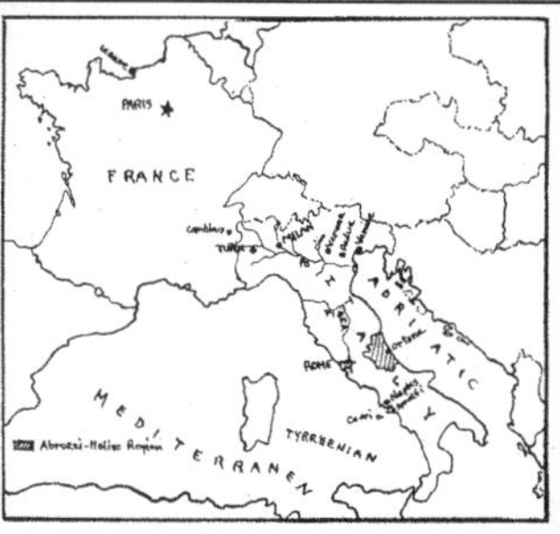

Lorrie Eisenberg Reports On International Student Service Tour of Italy This Summer

International Student Service, an organization concerned with student relief, cultural exchange, and international student forums, sponsored in the summer of 1947 an international student conference held at Arhus, Denmark, and study tours through various European countries. Lorrie Eisenberg was appointed by Executive Board to represent Mills College on the ISS tour through Italy. The map indicates the cities through which the ten students traveled. Not indicated are Perugia, Pisa, and Florence, which were visited by seven members of the group while the rest of th students spent nine days in Ortona and the Abruzzi region. The following is the

During the ten-day voyage the chow line and the dining table were to prove one of the main places for meeting people and exchanging ideas.

There were about forty student groups on board, comprising approximately 700 students, faculty members, and a few commercial passengers. The Orientation program was planned by members of the American Friends Service Committee, and the days were soon taken up with language classes, lectures and discussions, group meetings, movies, folk dancing and singing, skit nights, and concerts. The ship was a floating university with all the formality of the classroom gone.

The Emory Wheel, Emory University, GA 4/10/47

THE EMORY WHEEL

NO. 22. Emory University, Ga. April

Emory One of 15 Universities to Send Student Representative to Denmark

Emory will be one of 15 American universities to send a delegate to the International Student Service Conference in Denmark this summer. Applications from members of the student body for the post are now being accepted.

In addition to the conference, study tours will be made of Poland, Czechoslovakia and Italy. The purpose of these tours is to acquaint student leaders with conditions and problems facing the educational institutions and people of these countries.

The Emory representative will be chosen for interest in and knowledge of international problems, educational research work, and cultural exchange between peoples of the nations. Advanced undergraduate students or graduate students are especially requested to apply.

The representative should plan to return to the Emory campus for the 1947-48 season, at which time he will relate his experience to campus groups in this area. Knowledge of European languages will be helpful. Applications should be filed with Al Foster, Box 447, before Friday, April 18. A committee from the student council and a faculty member will make the selection.

During World War II the International Student Service provided relief for foreign students in the form of books, medical supplies, food, study material and scholarships. At that time the organization was represented in this country by the World Student Service Fund. The ISS is composed of both students and faculty members who are active in student relief, educational research, and international education.

It has been estimated that the total cost will be approximately $1000. Investigations are now in progress to raise money but nothing definite has yet been decided.

LaSalle Collegian, PA 1/27/50

COLLEGIAN AWARD TO MORLEY CASSIDY — La Salle COLLEGIAN — FROSH ELECTIONS CONTINUE TODAY

Harris Represents ISS At Meeting In Paris

The International Student Service was represented by its American Senior Secretary, Ted Harris '48, at a recent meeting in Paris of the United Educational Service Cooperative Organization.

Harris, along with the representatives of twenty other organizations, reviewed the work the UNESCO has been doing in connection with its youth and student activities. Several of the UNESCO departments gave reports, concernng their

Temple University News, PA 5/2/47

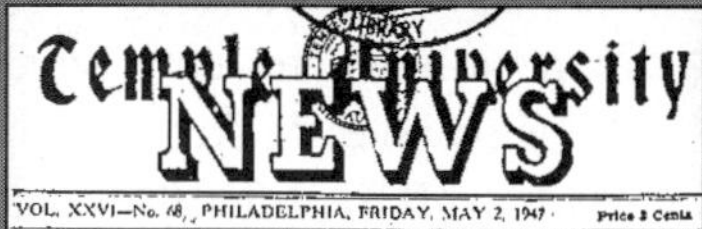

VOL. XXVI—No. 68, PHILADELPHIA, FRIDAY, MAY 2, 1947 Price 3 Cents

Teachers College Sophomore Named Temple ISS Delegate

Lawrence Levan Chosen for Summer Sessions In Four European Countries

Lawrence R. Levan, Teachers '49, has been designated Temple representative at the International Student Service conference to be held in Europe this summer.

A combined student-faculty committee selected Levan on Tuesday as the local delegate to attend sessions in Denmark, Holland, France and Italy. He will leave about June 21, and return shortly before the fall semester.

Dr. Frederick H. Lund, professor of psychology, will attend the meeting in Denmark, while Levan expects to tour Italy. In this way Temple will get double representation and a first hand opportunity to contact students in both northern and southern Europe.

The 45 American delegates plan to meet in Chamonix, near Mont Blanc, France, in September. Tentative schedule includes a visit

Mitten Hall Will Feature CPA Forum

Practitioners to Speak To Accounting Students

The fourth of the Philadelphia Accounting Forums, sponsored by the Philadelphia chapter of the Pennsylvania Institute of Certified

THE INTERNATIONAL STUDENT SERVICE, with a prewar global network in place, provided immediate postwar opportunities for U.S. students to meet counterparts primarily in Europe, but also in Asia, Africa, and South America. Following its formation in 1947, NSA provided global U.S. student representation at international conferences and to other national student unions (see Part 3).

The odyssey of a student from a small midwestern college

1. From Cambridge, England, to Chicago and Madison, 1946-1948

Janis Tremper Dowd

Rockford College, Illinois. NSA National Secretary, 1947-48

A personal prologue

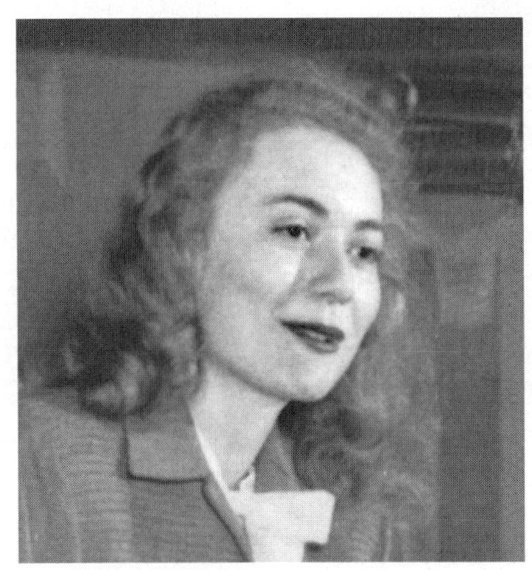

Mary Ashby Cheek, former president of Rockford College, had been active in international education before World War II and was a member of the U.S. National Advisory Committee of International Student Service (ISS). Because of her interests, Rockford was invited to be one of twenty-one colleges to send a delegate to the twentieth annual ISS Conference at Cambridge University in 1946. It was my good fortune to be that delegate.[1]

Rockford was a small liberal arts college for women, about ninety miles northwest of Chicago. Jane Addams was our most illustrious graduate and our model. I was a member of the centennial graduating class of 1947, a philosophy major, former president of my class and of the International Relations Club, and, in 1946, the new president of the student government. Financial help from family, friends, faculty, alumnae, and some campus clubs enabled me to go.

These recollections draw on a diary I kept during that lively time. In the same box in my crowded attic I found a few of the reports I wrote and material relating to the ISS Conference activities. There are also notes about discussions of ISS relationships with the proposed International Union of Students (IUS) and with the U.S. national student organization to be formed. The box yielded a few letters and reports describing the National Student Conference in Chicago in December 1946, our preparation of a draft constitution in the months immediately following, and the NSA Constitutional Convention. My files are thin for our first year in office, so I am delighted that Bill Welsh and Mildred Kiefer Wurf will also be writing about that year.

The U.S. delegation to the ISS conference

The twenty-six ISS delegates who assembled in New York in July 1946 represented Brooklyn, Bryn Mawr, Columbia, Harvard, Haverford, Hood, Hunter, Mount Holyoke, New Jersey College for Women, Rutgers, Sarah Lawrence, Smith, Swarthmore, Wellesley, Wilson, Yale, Hollins, Spelman, Sweet Briar, Mills, Occidental, and the University of Oregon. Rockford was the only Midwestern college. Like many Midwestern girls, I felt that the center of culture and sophistication was surely in the East.

More than half the colleges in this list were women's colleges. In this respect, our delegation differed from all others at the conference. Two-thirds of our group were women, while only a fifth of all other student delegates were women. The one-to-four ratio held for all the representatives of other national and international organizations attending the conference.[2]

This trip was already full of firsts for me—first flight, first visit to New York, first great adventure on my own. Most of the men in our group were World War II veterans. During the war, I had worked during several summers as a skilled riveter, assembler, and drill press operator in a small factory owned by a family friend, making hand-held generators for the Signal Corps. Like many other students, I held a variety of part-time jobs in college, including switchboard operator, waitress, tutor, and, for a short, lucrative period, palmist. Still, I felt very young and inexperienced.

The schedule and learning about the ISS

The U.S. delegates were scheduled to attend the Cambridge conference, at Girton College, July 22-29, then to participate in one of four European study tours. We would reconvene in Geneva on August 22 for meetings with ISS officers and then go to the international student center at Combloux, in the French Alps.

Shipping difficulties delayed our departure from New York for several days. We used this time to meet at the Institute for International Education[3] for briefings on the urgent needs of student victims of war—students of the occupied countries, prisoners, internees, refugees. We also learned more about ISS—that it was a service, not a membership, organization, proud of its inclusion of "every religious tendency and all the various currents of political and social democracy." I later learned that this "positive neutrality" was seen as "reactionary" by students who pressed for political advocacy. The ISS emphasis on service contrasted with the focus of the proposed IUS.

Aboard the *SS Brazil* and previewing the issues

Feeling acutely what I saw as the provincialism of my home state of Indiana, where I had been surrounded by conservative Republicans skeptical of organized labor and world politics, I was eager to have discussions with the crew, and was pleased to be invited to a union meeting the night we sailed. I still have a copy of the Constitution of the National Maritime Union that they gave me. Several days later the captain announced that students were not to mix with the crew.

The theme of the ISS conference was "The University Community in a Changing Society," to be examined in four commissions. Because we would be four days late arriving, we organized discussions on board on each of the topics. When we arrived, we were ready with our recommendations on each topic. The ISS Assembly adopted them with only a few changes.[4]

We also tried to prepare ourselves for the political and social questions we anticipated: what *is* U.S. foreign policy and how do we feel about it; elements of strength and weakness in American democracy; purpose and value of student government; student participation in international affairs. We were advised not to proceed from the view that we, from our largesse, would generously bestow aid on "them." We were warned that we would very likely encounter the same antagonistic feeling that a Russian might experience at that time in the United States.

These shipboard discussions soon became popular, and many of the other passengers came to listen and contribute. One was Opal Thomas, a Rockford alumna who was then chief technical adviser to the head of the UN Economic Reconstruction Commission. I was proud that this graduate of my college was doing important and interesting work.

There were also endless informal conversations and other diversions. My diary records discussions with a Czech theologian, then at Princeton, of Whitehead's theory of immortality and the narrowness of French existentialism. Another entry notes that a French hairdresser asked me to model an elaborate fleur-de-lys hairdo, intending to promote his shipboard business. Quite a range!

The 20th Annual ISS conference and the German relief dilemma

Getting to Cambridge was difficult for many of those who attended. In 1946, there were often visa complications, transportation problems, and a general lack of funds. Despite these obstacles, the conference was attended by almost 200 delegates and observers, representing more than twenty-five countries and all five continents. Poland, Greece, and Hungary each had one delegate, but the Soviet Union had none.[5]

There were two delegates, a French and a British student, from the International Preparatory Commission for the forthcoming World Student Congress at Prague in August. ISS had decided both to increase student participation and to invite these representatives to participate in the ISS Assembly.

The urgent message of the conference was the immediate need for material relief in India, Burma, China, and Eastern Europe and the importance of bringing these students into the international university community. This was regarded as the only way to avert division of the student world into isolated political and geographic blocs.

The agenda notwithstanding, the big question of the Cambridge conference, aid for Germany, had been saved for our arrival. ISS, the World Student Christian Federation, (WSCF), and Pax Romana had formed World Student Relief in 1940, the administration of which was entrusted to ISS. The U.S. section of WSCF included the National Intercollegiate Christian Council, the Student Volunteer Movement, the Interseminary Movement, and the University Commission of the Council of Church Boards of Education. Pax Romana was the international secretariat of Catholic University students.[6]

Roughly, those speaking for the occupied countries wanted to send only "intellectual relief"—books and study materials—to German students, while the majority of American and British students, with some other delegates, believed that material relief also should be sent.

On the last day, a French student spoke:

> France knows the suffering of the millions the Nazis crushed, and that they are still suffering. We have so little to give now. We must give first to our allies who have been opposed. Give the Germans books and pens and papers, but the need of the Germans has been for one year only, while the need of others, whom the Germans crushed, has been for seven.

Danish, Czech, and Canadian delegates spoke in support of the French position. Then the head of the American delegation spoke: "How can we hope to educate a starving country? In a Christian world of brotherly love, we cannot say we will feed *these* people and let *those* people starve."

A compromise was reached: to begin a program of intellectual relief at once and to send a commission to Germany to report on the need for material aid and the practical possibility of sending it. That denouement seemed to me to portend what postwar relations between the United States and Europe might be: America supplying the dollars and intending to call the shots.[7]

The ISS conference concluded with a list of resolutions to be considered at the September ISS Assembly.

Some personal notes contrasting the United States and other delegations

My diary includes many references to long and lively conversations and to dancing and tea. Despite the imposition of bread rationing on the day the conference began, Girton College managed to provide ample cakes at teatime.

The two groups at the conference who impressed me as most articulate were the Marxists and the Catholic activists. They both appeared to have a formula that allowed them to know their position on an issue promptly and with assurance. They could spring quickly to their feet in every debate. I envied that. Then I began to see that, knowing clearly their own perspective, they could ignore the particular circumstances of the issues. It was only gradually that I began to recognize their underlying views. By the end of the conference I began to hear these delegates as Marxists or Catholics, only secondarily as students.

Almost all the foreign delegates appeared to me to be more mature than we were. They had more knowledge of language, literature, and political issues. Since so many of our delegation were undergraduate women whose education had not been interrupted by war, we were among the youngest. Because we had not been touched by the civilian losses or the damage to our land, these differences in experience made us seem even more naive. We worked hard to reach positions on issues, to learn, listen, understand, and be responsible. The reaction from other delegates was often a mix of curiosity and interest, but sometimes, I felt, disdain and resentment.

What concerned me most was that we in the U.S. delegation might not recognize the political implications of a resolution. Our response in meetings was slower and less confident, yet we were drawn to action and wanted change from the way the world had been. Many of us lacked the political experience of some who were so articulate and persuasive. I did not want to have someone telling us how to respond, but I did wish there were more time for us to consider the issues and come to our own decisions.

It seemed evident in these discussions that students forced to maturity by their experience of war felt their universities had failed either to prepare students or, as some felt, to play a constructive role themselves to avert the catastrophe of the war. Dutch students had said of the Dutch universities, "They have withdrawn into a vague, colorless neutrality."

For some students, this fostered a decision to be more involved in revitalizing the university, so it would, as a French

As listed in the conference report

U.S. Delegates to the XXTH Annual ISS Conference

Cambridge, England, July 22-29th, 1946

ABERNETHY Bradford	Student Counsellor, Rutgers University
ANDERSON Leila	General Secretary YWCA
BOSWORTH Eleanor	Student at Sweet Briar University
BRETTAUER A.B.	Observer
BUTLER Allison	Student at Smith College
CLARKE Jr. A. William	Student at Swarthmore College
CONDICT Avis	Student at Wilson University
DAVIS Anne	Student at Mount Holyoke College
DECOU Elisabeth	Student at University of Oregon
DOERR Wallace	Student at Yale University
ELLIS William	Student at Harvard University
FAIRGRAVES Robert	Regional Secretary WSSF
FISHWICK Manetto	Student at Hollins University
GLASSE James	Student at Occidental College, Los Angeles, California
HASKELL Miriam	Student at Smith College
HOGAN V.P.	Observer
JANNEY Frederick	Student at Yale University
JANNEY Mary	Ditto
JUNKER Curtis	United Movement of the Churches Youth and the Canterbury Group
JOHNSON David	Student at Haverford University
KASS Enid	Student at Hunter College
KINMAN Mary	Student at Hood College
KIRCHNER Edward	Director of Pax Romana, in USA
KIRCHNER Mrs.	
KITCHEN J. William	Executive Secretary World Student Service Fund
MAHLER Doris	Student at Brooklyn University
MOREHOUSE Nancy	Student at Bryn Mawr University
NICHOLSON Mary	Student at Mills College, Oakland, California
PICKARD Joy	Smith College
ROCKWELL Martha	Student at Lawrence University
ROESSLER Bernice	Student at New Jersey College for Women
ROSS Mary	Student at Wellesley College
THOMAS Winburn	Delegate of United Student Christian Council
TRUSLOW Walter	Student at Columbia University
TREMPER Janis	Student at Rockford College
WILSON Howard	(speaker) Deputy Executive Secretary UNESCO
YATES Clara	Student at Spelman College, Atlanta, Georgia
YEWELL John	Student at Rutgers University

student said, "stand at the center of the nation." For other students, it meant a determination to be involved in national policy as well. For almost all, it meant a greater sense of personal responsibility.

"Stronger than treaties: students united," a phrase that became the theme of ISS in the United States, expressed the hope, if not the fact. We heard the message of European students, counting on our help to send relief. Our response was, "We are convinced that solidarity is not a vain word."

Study tours and war-ravaged areas

After a few days in London and Paris, the Canadian and U.S. students separated into four groups for three-week study tours of Holland and Belgium, France, Czechoslovakia, or Italy. Each tour group lived in student centers, visited ravaged areas, and saw some of the efforts to rebuild.

My group, which toured France, began at Cité Universitaire and the University of Paris. In Normandy, we visited some of the battlegrounds of 1944 and saw some of the enormous destruction. Students at the University of Caen described the bombardment by the armies of the Allies on July 7, 1944: "Everything went up in flames." They had lost the university library and its 300,000 volumes, the city library with 350,000 books, and all material and scientific equipment. Only one-fourth of the city remained more or less intact.

Bombing from June 6 to August 15, when the Germans had evacuated and the last German shell had been fired, had left 40,000 homeless. We were in awe of the courage and resourcefulness the students had shown fighting fires, aiding the homeless, organizing a "Student Mutual Aid." I left the group briefly to visit the U.S. military cemetery near Caen, with its enormous fields of crosses, where a close friend was buried. From Caen we went to Grenoble, where we learned more about the formation of the Maquis and the French Resistance. The terrible devastation moved me deeply.

Châlets des Etudiants, Combloux, and the needs for recovery

The Canadian and American students from the four tours met briefly in Geneva with the international staff of ISS and then went to the Châlets des Etudiants at Combloux, near Grenoble. The Châlet, with a magnificent view of Mont Blanc, had opened in May 1945 to serve fifty students who "are physically and mentally worn out by their work in the Resistance or their experiences as deportees or prisoners." Students stayed from one to three months.

In addition to medical care, the center was designed

> To give students who had been living in hiding or leading an abnormal existence as outlaws, prisoners of the Gestapo, or deportees, an opportunity to recover from the terrible ordeals to which they have been subjected and to readapt themselves to normal conditions of life. The purpose is to make the center a true retreat where students can enjoy real liberty amid surroundings calculated to restore confidence and strength.

Sadly, but understandably, there was little interaction between our group and those in residence at the Châlet. The contrast between the material and psychological suffering of many of these students and our own security and well-being impelled me to much deeper personal reflection.

The U.S. and Canadian students reported on each of the study tours. We were predictably enthusiastic about our contacts with other students and felt new awareness of the need for aid. We also discussed what we should do to implement our decisions made at Cambridge. Beyond the ISS-specific plans, we wanted to build the student community in the United States, and develop a American counterpart to the national student unions of other countries.

Return to Geneva and looking ahead

During these discussions, I was chosen by the U.S. and Canadian students to return to Geneva to represent them in developing plans for the revitalization of ISS in North America. This decision was not made without dissent. One of my new friends, a Marxist from India, urged me not to go, arguing that a strong U.S. ISS would encourage U.S. students to feel that they could spurn cooperation with the emerging IUS. "All European students are hoping you won't play the dummy part. It would be a political betrayal," he said. I responded that I would do my best to see that ISS did not become a reactionary haven interested only in opposing IUS. What a grand illusion of the part I might play!

The trick now was to get me across the border from France without a Swiss visa, for mine had expired with my earlier visit. It was Sunday. It was decided that I would travel with Andre deBlonay, the Swiss general secretary of ISS, and Maurice Didier, French member of the ISS staff and director of the Châlets des Etudiants. We would cross just as the border closed at night. The taxi ride down the mountain was beautiful, the excitement terrific. The twinkling lights of the villages down the mountainside added a fairytale touch. Whatever Andre said to the border guard was sufficient to extend the protection of his diplomatic passport to get me through.

But we had not anticipated the crowds in Geneva, where I had no reservation. This was the occasion of Churchill's first visit since before the war and, more important, the first international horse show. We finally found a small hotel willing to let me sleep on a couch in an elaborately decorated party room filled with gilded flowers in gilded vases atop a gilded piano.

During this week in Geneva, I met a few women who were working for units of the League of Nations. They were eager to talk with the ISS staff, and I could watch and listen. They were attractive and bright. I felt they were here by choice, not because they had no alternatives. I knew that many women were lonely during and just after the war. These women seemed so, too. But what I responded to more was their fading vitality. I recalled the very few women I had met on the trip, working in Europe with international agencies. None was married. I had just turned twenty-one. My observations here seemed to reinforce the view from home, and my worst fears, that the option for women was either career or marriage (and promised happiness), but not both.

The ISS observers to the World Student Congress in Prague returned while I was in Geneva, enthusiastic about the possibility of close cooperation with the International Union of Students that had been launched by the Congress. But when I rejoined the U.S. students in Paris, I heard a different view. Mimi Haskell and Enid Kass, who also had gone to Prague, expressed more reservations and had more questions. The American students who had attended the Congress were in agreement that the United States needed a national student organization to represent U.S. students nationally and internationally, which could serve as a forum for working out issues and relationships with IUS.[8]

Rockford and a return to controversy

I returned to Rockford College, and very shortly faced a group of students who were influenced by the isolationist views of Col. Robert McCormick's *Chicago Tribune*. They began an effort to impeach me as president of student government because of my involvement in international activities. After some lively meetings, I won a vote of confidence with a good majority.

During the next several months I wrote and talked often in the community about the ISS Conference. While I was speaking at International House at the University of Chicago, I learned of preparations for the Chicago Student Conference to be held in December, at which plans for a national student organization would be considered. I soon received an announcement of this meeting through the student government. I attended the conference eagerly.

The Staff Committee following the Chicago Student Conference

That dramatic Conference in Chicago is described in other essays in this book. The conference created a National Continuations Committee (NCC) to make preparations for a constitutional convention for the proposed new organization, which would be held at the University of Wisconsin the following September. A committee of four was selected to draft a constitution and prepare for a constitutional convention.

Tom Farr of the University of Chicago, Bill McDermed of DePaul University, Al Houghton of the University of Wisconsin, and I were elected for this job. Roy Voegeli, also from the University of Wisconsin, soon replaced Al. Bill McDermed recalls that he had come to the Chicago conference because he had complained to his dean about the issue of paternalism and was told to get involved. "DePaul *appointed* people, they didn't elect them!" he said. Veteran students such as Bill found this campus paternalism intolerable; it inspired NSA's mission to assure the autonomy of student government. Bill found himself deeply interested and involved.

From January until June, we met almost every weekend, often beginning on Friday evening and working through a good part of Sunday. This excerpt from an article I wrote for the Rockford *Vanguard* describes one of our committee sessions and a visit by Jim Smith, of the University of Texas, who had been elected president of the NCC:

> It was almost midnight and the night watchman came for the second time to tell us we MUST leave. Jim Smith, who had flown in that morning from Texas, asked for just five minutes more to finish up one issue. The old man relented.
>
> For twelve hours that Sunday seven earnest students wrestled with their task. Freezing in the unheated room at International House and working constantly, we were tired. But we had progressed. The first section of the constitution for the National Student Organization would be complete when we settled this point.
>
> Jim said, "We have avoided being too specific all along the line, and that's good. But on THIS point we MUST list some of the main considerations, because everyone at the conference will have a different opinion. We must say, 'To secure

Janis Tremper, having served on the Staff Committee which helped draft the proposed Constitution for the new organization, explains the document to a group of delegates at the NSA Constitutional Convention in September of 1947 at the University of Wisconsin.
(State Historical Society of Wisconsin)

academic freedom for faculty, including specifically: freedom for research, the right to teach the results of this research, and to act as citizens of the community.'"

Tom, our self-appointed stylist, warned that here we were going to fall into the very pit that we had been consciously avoiding, unless we said simply "To support academic freedom." Anyhow, the wording was poor.

Bill, the theorist of the group, agreed with the wisdom of the technique heretofore. Nevertheless, if we couldn't say exactly what we meant on this point, an issue that is really one of our basic drives in forming the whole organization, all of our time and energy would be wasted.

Wrestling with this kind of discussion of every point we plugged along, issue after issue. We were excited about our goal, and we worked hard.

Money and time were both tight in this final term of my senior year. We were very frugal, but the meetings meant new expenses and added pressures on time. My solution on one occasion was to hitch a ride to the committee meeting with the two philosophy professors from the University of Chicago who were returning from being my honors examiners.

Russ Austin, of the University of Chicago, who had been chairman of the U.S. delegation to Prague and was elected vice chairman of the National Continuations Committee, usually worked with us and was an effective facilitator. When Jim Smith, NCC president, arrived from the University of Texas, he joined us. Although major directions had been identified at the Chicago Conference, we were essentially creating the document out of whole cloth. All the big issues had to be worked through, including involvement of national student organizations, number of representatives and number of votes per college, and a student bill of rights.

The NCC also operated with inadequate funding.[9] Jim Smith made urgent pleas to the regional organizations to send their dues as soon as possible so that the NCC could continue to operate.

After I graduated in June, I worked with Jim and Russ in Chicago and in Madison to help with arrangements for the constitutional convention. This was another labor-intensive period. Roy Voegeli's essay in the following section describes the enormous volunteer effort that managed to accomplish a virtually impossible task. It seemed almost miraculous that we were able to greet more than seven hundred arriving delegates, arrange for their housing, find meeting places, and supply them with drafts of the constitution and other documents.

The first year and the joy of building on shared beliefs

I was surprised and pleased to be elected the first NSA secretary. The first slate of officers reflected the desired balance with respect to size and type of college, geography, religious affiliation, race, and gender: Bill Welsh, president, from Berea College; Ralph Dungan, vice president for student affairs, from St. Joseph's College in Philadelphia; Bob Smith, vice president for international affairs, from Yale; and Leland Jones, treasurer, from University of Buffalo.

I must admit that I had a moment of self-doubt, wondering if I had been chosen because the slate needed a woman and because the position of secretary was the traditional female slot.[10] And having been elected, I soon learned another political reality when various groups, generally on the left, came to press a position, announcing that "*they* got me elected."

Just after the delegates left, Lee Jones told us that he would have to return to Buffalo and could not serve.[11] Mildred Kiefer, from the University of California at Berkeley, saved us by stepping in to become acting treasurer, and so much more. Essays by Bill, Bob, and Mildred in this book describe the ensuing year in Madison, when we worked so hard together. I feel a great bond of affection for my remarkable friends. It was a strenuous year and a wonderful experience.

By the end of that fascinating first year of NSA I had learned a little about political issues and a lot about the joy of working with others for shared beliefs. We focused on what brought us together, not on what separated us. That was the strength of our small group of officers and those who worked with us. It was also the strength of NSA.

Janis Tremper Dowd was Director of Community Services and Public Affairs at Monroe Community College, NY. She has been a homemaker and an active volunteer at Lincoln University, PA, and in Rochester, NY.

END NOTES

[1] See International Student Service, p. 50, and p. 56.

[2] See p. 62 for complete list of U.S. delegates.

[3] See IIE, p. 693.

[4] I have a copy of the "American Delegation's Report on Reorganization of ISS and Its Relationships," but this is undated and may be the work of the two U.S. members of the ISS Assembly, who were nonstudents. The summary report of the conference does not indicate who sponsored particular proposals. With those caveats, I think it is safe to say that the U.S. recommendations included: That ISS (a) take positive action in all situations that threaten the academic, political, social, or religious freedoms of students and faculty everywhere; (b) provide facilities for the exchange of students on an international scale; (c) increase the number of student cultural cen-

ters; (d) increase general student participation in the planning and execution of the program of the ISS. The conference recommendation was "not less than 50% of the Assembly members should be students or student representatives" ("student representative: preferably a student who is nominated by a student organization").

[5] From one ISS publication of about that time: ISS has committees or corresponding members in:

Australia	Czechoslovakia	Egypt	Italy	Sweden
Austria	Denmark	Great Britain	Norway	Switzerland
Belgium	Eire	Holland	New Zealand	United States
Canada	Finland	Hungary	The Philippines	Yugoslavia
China	France	India	South Africa	

Another list included Palestine and mentioned contact with an organization of Arab students based in London.

[6] See background on the World Student Christian Federation, p. 732, and Pax Romana, p. 741.

[7] NSA later furnished participants for several postwar student seminars in Germany designed to help reintegrate German students into the world community. See Perkins, p. 603, Halsted, p. 679.

[8] I cannot report very much on this series of meetings. My diary entries refer to meetings we held to discuss programs to be developed, but my notes are vague on details, with one exception. I pressed for ISS-IUS cooperation and noted the skepticism of some, particularly the general secretary of the World Student Christian Association, who were older and more experienced in organizational politics. The official ISS observers to IUS returned to Geneva at this time, very enthusiastic about the Prague conference and also strongly encouraging cooperation. I find a later reference in my diary to my report on our proposals to the U.S. students in Paris as we waited for our transportation home to be arranged: "Mimi Haskell and Enid Kass had just arrived from Prague, so the first half hour was spent on their report (see Berlin (Haskell), p. 87, and Kass, p. 94 ff). Finally read our program, and the discussion took on the problem of IUS-ISS relationship . . . what need for ISS, fear of IUS, fear of competiton, etc." The diary notes are more detailed about good dinners.

[9] Inadequate funding dogged the NSA staffs continuously during the organization's formative years. See Appendix, Organization and Finance, p. 1119.

[10] Selection of candidates and nomination of officers during the early years appear to have arisen out of informal leadership networking and caucusing shortly before and at each of the annual conventions. Some of these are recalled by anthology authors Bill Welsh, Dick Heggie, Gene Schwartz, Joan Lynch, and Bill Dentzer in Part I.

[11] An interview with Lee Jones on page 869 describes some of his personal history and student leadership experiences at the University of Buffalo.

PICTURE CREDITS: *Then:* Constitutional Convention, September 1947 (NSA Photo. *SHSW*). *Now:* Rochester, NY, 1998 (*Schwartz*).

JANIS TREMPER DOWD

Early Years: Born 1925; raised in Fort Wayne, Indiana; and attended South Side High School, Fort Wayne.

College: Rockford College, A.B., honors in philosophy, 1947. Boston University, A.M. in philosophy, 1949.

Additional graduate studies in philosophy, University of Rochester and Cornell University.

Career and community highlights: I taught philosophy at the University of Rochester until 1955, when family responsibilities grew. For the next twenty years I was a homemaker and active volunteer in Rochester and at Lincoln University, PA, where we spent the 1960s. Community activities included organizing a junior high school for the Rochester school district, community-based planning for human service agencies, the Rochester Women's Foundation and many other programs to assist women, and, in Pennsylvania, a planning school for local elected officials, a watershed association, and sheltered workshops. From 1975 to 1989 I was Director of Community Services and Public Affairs at Monroe Community College.

Family: I was married to Frank J. Dowd from 1949 to 1986. We had three children: Judith, who died in 1964; Laura; and Allan. Frank was involved with early NSA activities from the Chicago conference until 1948. He chaired the New York State Region. Frank retired as Vice President for Student Affairs of the University of Rochester and died in 1997. I have been married to Daan Zwick since 1988.

The ISS in the United States

Excerpt from 2pp bulletin, "Programme of Action for 1946-1947," ISS General Secretariat, Geneva, Switzerland. (Source: Janis Dowd papers. See also Lash and Munts, Prologue, Sec. 2.)

The story of ISS in the UNITED STATES is a long and somewhat complicated one. At the beginning of the war, following the participation of representative American delegations to our last prewar Conferences, the American committee of ISS was well established and was developing an interesting programme of work. From 1939 to 1942, conferences were organized with great success and this phase came to its climax with the organization of the international student assembly held in Washington in 1942, with the support of Mrs. Roosevelt and of the American Government.

Following this conference, some difficulties arose within the ISS committee, as a result of which activities had to be very much curtailed.

The responsibilities of representing ISS interests in the United States remained, from that date onwards, with a body called Student Service of America. This body was chaired by Professor Harry Gideonse; it decided that it would not endeavour to display any real activity as long as the war lasted.

Following the General Secretary's visit to the United States in the fall of 1945, Student Service of America has shown new life, mainly on the initiative of Dr. Alfred Cohn. Its main activity during recent months has been the preparation of a delegation for the 20th Annual Conference. Some 20 students will attend it on its behalf and it is hoped that these students, once returned to the United States, will contribute sponsoring to [sic] ISS in their colleges.

CHOSEN FOR CONFERENCE—Miss Janis Tremper, above, 1115 Nuttman Avenue, daughter of Mr. and Mrs. Allen J. Tremper, Sr., will leave Fort Wayne by air today for New York where she will sail for Europe to participate in conferences of the International Student Service. She will return in early September.—Staff Photo.

Janis Tremper Off To World Student Parley In Europe

Today a dream comes true for a Fort Wayne girl just turned 21. with the majority coming from the East and West coasts. Miss Trem-

Janis Tremper Elected To NSA Office

Miss Janis Tremper, 1947 Rockford College graduate and daughter of Mr. and Mrs. Allan Tremper of 1115 Nuttman Avenue, was elected secretary of the United States National Student Association yesterday at Madison, Wis.

Convention delegates, representing 370 colleges and universities, adopted a 12-point "student bill of rights," declaring it the right of every student to have a college education. The newly-formed organization will wind up its constitution program today.

The NSA is dedicated to developing democratic student self-government, securing equal educational rights for all students, fostering better educational standards and methods, improving students' welfare and promoting international understanding.

Miss Tremper was graduated with honors in philosophy from Rockford College, Rockford, Ill., in June. She is also a South Side High School graduate and recently has been working on the Student Continuation Committee, a non-political organization with headquarters

ELEMENTS OF AN ODYSSEY

Janis Tremper (Dowd) was selected by Rockford College (IL), to attend the 20th annual conference of the International Student Service (ISS) at Girton College, Cambridge, England, in July of 1946—the first ISS conference since World War II (Fort Wayne *Journal Gazette*, July 7, 1946). That started her odyssey, which led to her election as Secretary on the first year's national staff of NSA (*Journal Gazette*, 1947. See Pt. 1, Sec. 4) Tremper writes in this essay of her summer's work during the war as a riveter and drill press operator for which she collected the "diploma" shown.

ELECTRIC MOTORS AND SPECIALTIES CO.

AWARDS THIS

DIPLOMA

(MAGNET COME LOUD) TO

FOR UNEXCELLED SKILL AS

GENERATOR - GETTER - TOGETHER

WE HEREBY SET OUR SEAL

WAYNE MORRILL

..... HIS MARK..

EDW. J. SCHAEFER

... HIS MARK...

UNIVERSITIES RESPOND TO WAR, DEBATE ROLE IN ITS AFTERMATH

(Excerpt from a March 1948 issue of NSA News *by Janis Tremper. She deals with the concepts of education and reviews a pamphlet published by the Student Christian Movement of Great Britain. NSA opened a forum for student leaders to join the dialog with educators in an exploration of the university's purpose.*

Probably at no other time has there been so much debate on the role of the university. During the war there were two major trends to this discussion. In the occupied countries, students and professors, joining together in the resistance movements, were developing plans for the reform of the post-war university.

In Great Britain and the U.S. the universities were called on to produce skilled technicians as their contribution to the war effort. Post-war developments in the university world have emphasized the necessity for a reevaluation of the functions of the university in modern education and as a unit of the total community.

The Student Christian Movement in Great Britain joined in this discussion. . . . "The Foundations of a Free University," by Dorothy M. Emmet, University of Manchester, is an attempt to analyse the function of the university as it maintains its autonomy and at the same time serves the community. Because of the tradition common to the universities both of Great Britain and of the U.S., this analysis applies closely to our own problems. . . .

The major question discussed is whether the "impartiality" of the university, as we understand it, is sufficiently positive to motivate the university to fulfill its function in the demands of society.

This function Miss Emmett describes briefly as "that of preserving, interpreting and passing on our cultural heritages in the arts and sciences, of fostering original work, and of turning out a succession of people with trained minds, free minds, and a sense of responsibility." . . .

Building a representative student voice

2. Organizing the U.S. Delegation to Prague

Alice Horton Tibbetts

Wellesley College '45

Executive Secretary, American Preparatory Committee, 1946

President, United States Student Assembly, 1945

During the war years at Wellesley I became active in Forum, our current affairs organization. Through this affiliation I became involved with United States Student Assembly, a liberal student political group, which had chapters on many campuses. This organization had emerged after the split and demise of the American Student Union, which had been strong in the late 1930s. During my senior year, in 1945, I became president of the organization. I followed the reign of Mary Lou Rogers of Swarthmore (who had been a high school friend in Chicago and who later, after marrying Ray Munts, moved to Madison, Wisconsin, and became prominent in Wisconsin politics).[1]

The 1945 World Youth Conference

My sudden (or so it seemed at the time) interest in current affairs and the idea of "making the world a better place" came from a stimulating history teacher, Hubert Wilson. I was lucky enough to take a class with him in American history at a Vermont boarding school that I attended while my parents were abroad for a year.

My dad was a minister interested in social action, and my mother was active in Christian education, where she worked hard to instill in young people a sense of social and individual responsibility. I suspect that the atmosphere at home was such that when I encountered these ideas away from home, I was very receptive. I remember that year as one of real awakening.

In late summer 1945 USSA looked for a delegate to go to the World Youth Conference in London. I qualified, volunteered, raised money for the trip, joined other delegates on the *Queen Mary* (still equipped as a troop ship), talked, argued politics, danced, ate, and finally arrived in London for the conference. Several of us, including Muriel Jacobson of the YWCA student division, went on from London to a preliminary Prague student conference designed to make preparations for the organization of the International Union of Students, which would be held in the summer of 1946.[2] Our participation there was minimal since, having been delayed in London by bad weather, we reached Prague only for the final two days of the conference. From Prague, several of us, including Muriel, went on to a visit to the Soviet Union, at the invitation of the London Soviet delegation.

These events, of course, were eye-openers for our group of American young people. We knew of the devastation and the hardships of those who experienced the war on their own soil. But now we had a chance to see the bombed-out parts of London and the destroyed cities of the Soviet Union and to talk to people in these countries about their experiences and their losses.[3]

Returning from Europe and starting the APC

I returned to the States in early February 1946. Those of us who had been to Prague felt that it was important for the United States to have student representation at the Prague Student Conference that would be held the following summer. An American Preparatory Committee for the Prague Student Conference was formed[4] and seems to have consisted of representatives from the Student YM/YWCA, B'nai Brith, United States Student Assembly, American Youth for Democracy, Student Federalists, and the Association of Internes and Medical Students.[5] I was able to start right in on the job of recruiting a delegation for the Prague conference. I was given office space at 8 West 40th Street, the office of United States Student Assembly, and I had a place to live in New York City. This last was a real consideration, for the housing situation at that time was very tight. My dad had a rent-controlled apartment on Riverside Drive, large enough so that we often had it filled with temporary guests. Both my father and brother remarked at the time that when they came home, they were never sure who might be occupying their beds.

One of the first jobs was to establish the authenticity of the American Preparatory Committee. This was done by getting sponsors, prominent people who would be willing to have their names put on our letterhead. There were some sponsors we could count on. Mrs. Roosevelt always lent her name to good causes, and there were certain senators and congressmen such as Claude Pepper from Florida and Helen Gahagan Douglas of California who needed only a phone call or letter for permission to use their names. One had to be careful not to use names of people who lent their support to communist-front groups. Mildred McAfee, former captain of the Waves and president of Wellesley College, had recently become my stepmother. Although it was not her style to lend her name to liberal "good cause" organizations, she obligingly let me use hers on the letterhead, and this helped us in obtaining other "respectable" names. I notice that we also obtained the names of the presidents of Smith, Brooklyn College, Queens College, and the University of Toledo.[6] I haven't the remotest memory of what our connection could have been with the University of Toledo. Someone must have known someone.

Importance of a credible and representative delegation

The left-wing nature of the international sponsors of the Prague conference was known.[7] Yet it seemed very important that we cooperate with the Soviets for the sake of future stability and peace. We acknowledged their tremendous sacrifices made during the war, their crucial role in winning the war, but we did not want to be co-opted by left-wing undemocratic forces. We had support from the National Intercollegiate Christian Council (YM/YWCA) and worked hard to persuade the National Catholic Youth Council to send delegates to the Conference. Each was allotted four places on the delegation. I have no memory of how that figure was decided upon, but I am sure we felt that their presence would lend stability and legitimacy to the group going to Prague. Their presence on many campuses would also help make the delegation more representative. I don't remember how we decided which colleges and universities should send delegates, but it was probably a combination of a desire to represent different parts of the country and of finding schools that were willing, interested, and able to find a good, representative campus delegate.

I was new at administrative work and at first figured that this would be a necessary, but not enjoyable, job. However, I remember realizing part-way into the project that I anticipated with great pleasure coming into the office each day. What would be in the mail? What college had agreed to send a representative? Any news from Prague?[8] What travel plans were developing? Were the passports going to come in time? How were the plans shaping up for the preliminary delegates' conference in New York? It was a time of great optimism. The war was over, international cooperation was essential, and students and student organizations were eager to further the cause.

Jewel Lubin, a graduate student at Columbia, had come to help on the Preparatory Committee sometime during that winter. She had heard about what we were doing and offered her services. How welcome they were! She and I did the day-to-day work of letter writing and phoning. As we developed plans for the delegation, it became evident that this group of twenty-five needed an executive secretary to accompany it. She was chosen to go.

On the way—Almost without mishap!

Various crises developed but were solved in one way or another. The one I remember most vividly (probably because my own carelessness was responsible for it) had to do with the passports, which had finally arrived. I had them in my purse while enjoying a warm early summer evening on the grass in Riverside Park with my boyfriend at the time (and he is still around fifty-two years later). When the time came to call it an evening and collect our things, we found that my purse was gone—stolen! And the delegation was due to leave for Prague in a few days! Frantic phone calls were made the next day to Mrs. Shipley, the strong-willed lady who ran the passport division of the State Department. She was a formidable personality and one whom many feared, but she came through for us.[9] Perhaps our letterhead sponsors helped. The passports were reissued, arrived in New York City in time, and the delegation was able to board the ship to take them across the Atlantic.

We were proud of the delegation that had emerged after months of hard work. Its members were bright, representative, idealistic, energetic, ready and eager to do what was necessary to function as an efficient group and to represent American students properly.[10]

I saw them off, cleaned up our temporary office on West 40th Street, and went to New Hampshire to climb mountains.

Aftermath—an American student voice

I remember receiving interesting newsy reports of the Conference from Jewel. Unfortunately, I don't have copies of them. The International Union of Students (IUS) was finally organized at Prague amid much political maneuvering (detailed

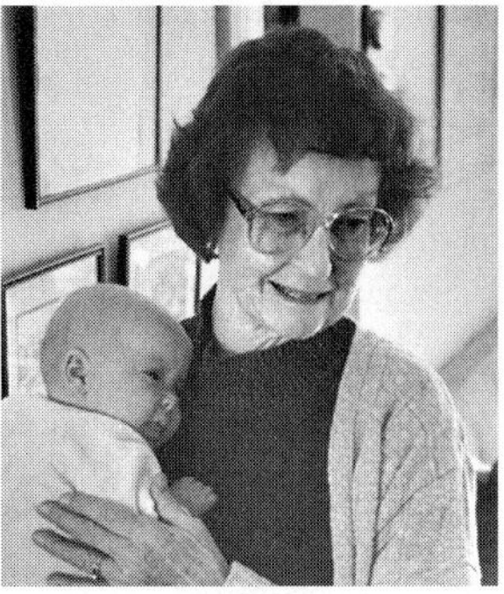

Alice Horton Tibbetts obtained a Masters in Education while raising four children and a foster child. She taught elementary school for twenty years in Madison, Wisconsin.

elsewhere in these essays). It was evident that a nation-wide student organization was needed that could be a U.S. voice in dealing with the IUS. It was also clear that this student organization must be nonpolitical and that it must deal exclusively with student affairs. It must be an organization that could not be labeled as a front group or as liberal or conservative. Just where the division was between student affairs and political affairs would still need to be determined. This was not always easy, as delegates to the Chicago and Wisconsin conferences found out later.

The delegation returned from Prague, and somehow the Chicago conference was organized. I don't remember that I was involved, and I cannot remember who took the primary responsibility. I studied Russian that fall and winter at Columbia, got engaged, and left student affairs to others.

END NOTES

[1] See Munts essay, p. 34.

[2] I first met Muriel Jacobson on the way to the Youth Festival. We got to know each other pretty well—although she was older than I. We roomed together, my diary tells me, during our brief time in Prague. We were the main connection between USSA and NICC, the student division of the YW and YMCA.

[3] *Editor's note:* Alice Tibbetts wrote up extensive notes about her travels. Excerpts from some of those notes appear in the box on p. 71.

[4] I don't remember exactly how the APC was formed. Muriel Jacobson, I am pretty sure, came back to the States the same time that I did. In my diary, I did record that she flew with me (and others) from Moscow to London, and there we waited to get a ship back—we traveled on the *Joseph P. Nicolet*, a liberty ship, and I think she was on it with me. To speculate: we probably got together after being in NYC for a while to catch our respective breaths and called a meeting of representatives from organizations that had been represented at the World Youth Conference and perhaps some others. The APC was formed from representatives of the groups that agreed to participate. I offered to do the work, and the USSA agreed to supply office space.

[5] Although I do not have a first-hand recollection of the APC's membership, it was composed of these groups, according to an article in the *Wellesley College News*, May 22, 1946.

[6] *Wellesley College News,* November 21, 1946, p. 7.

[7] How was the left-wing nature of the Prague sponsors known? I do not know. We did, though. People and organizations had reputations—and were known as "legitimate" or "front" groups. The "front" groups were cordial to Communists; the "legitimate" groups were not. During our USSR trip, I had become a good friend of Mollie Lieber—a Communist from AYD—and was friendly with other representatives of front groups. I used to be impatient with people who would not work with them at all—who would refuse to be on committees with them. My theory was that as long as your goals were the same, you worked together—and when the goals became different, you separated. USSA was suspicious of this position—they thought that if you cooperated, you would soon be "taken over by the commies"—and then your cause would be lost.

I was aware of the fact that if the APC or our delegation to Prague had representatives of too many front groups, this would lessen the interest of "legitimate" groups. We wanted the Catholics to join us. This would make us (the APC) more "legitimate." I would speculate that Muriel and the powers that were at NICC helped get their cooperation. Also, it seems that there were influential Catholics who realized that we in the United States had to cooperate with the Soviets if there was to be peace in the postwar world. This is borne out in some of the letters I have seen that the editors of this anthology acquired from the NCYC archives at Catholic University. The Catholics always kept their guard up, though—and were sometimes as difficult to work with as the Communists.

[8] I have no recollection of how we kept in touch with Prague, but a copy of a June 4, 1946, letter from Muriel to the World Student Relief office in Geneva (in the Yale Divinity and NSA archives) implies that it was not without problems and that the YWCA, through World Student Relief, was a channel of communication. She, incidentally, gave us a lot of moral support at this time, I am sure, but she also was very busy with other YM/YW student affairs at her office.

[9] *Editor's note:* The formidable Mrs. Shipley was a well-known figure among international travelers of the time. She figured in another chapter of our history when, in 1950, the IUS World Student Congress NSA observer team had their passports lifted by the FBI after returning from Prague, and efforts were made for their return. See Schwartz, p. 217.

[10] *Editor's note:* The makeup of the delegation, their experiences and reports of its members are treated in detail elsewhere in this work. See especially Part 1, Section 1.

PICTURE CREDITS: *Then:* 1947. *Now:* c. 1997 (*Both, author*).

ALICE HORTON TIBBETTS

I was born in 1924. Our family lived in Middleton, CT, then Brookline, MA, where my dad, Douglas Horton, was a minister to Congregational churches. He later became active and influential in church ecumenical endeavors. School years were spent in Chicago's South Side, where I attended public school and then the University of Chicago Elementary School and High School (now called the Lab School). In 1938, when my parents spent a year abroad visiting missions, I attended the Putney School in Vermont. I finished my last two years of high school there before attending Wellesley College, majoring in political science, and graduating in June 1945. In August of that year, Mildred McAfee, President of Wellesley College, became a part of the family.

The following fall and winter I traveled through Europe, as a delegate of the United States Student Assembly to the International Youth Conference in London and to the International Student Congress in Prague, and later had a six-week tour of the Soviet Union as a guest of the Anti-Fascist Youth Committee and the Soviet Government. On my return I helped to organize the U.S. delegation to the 1946 World Student Congress.

In 1947 I married Norris Tibbetts. We lived briefly in Allentown, PA, and then for five years in Danville, VA, where Norris was educational director for the Textile Worker's Union.

After a bad strike, we moved north to Madison, WI, where Norris worked for many years with the University Extension School for Workers. Madison was a good place to bring up four children. I obtained a Master's in Education at the University of Wisconsin and taught at a nearby elementary school for twenty years, starting when our youngest child was in fifth grade.

Life since retirement has consisted of summers in New Hampshire with siblings and their families in nearby cottages, Elderhostels, bluegrass music (we play mandolin, bass, and guitar), meals on wheels, tutoring, book clubs, church activities, and an increasing number of doctors' appointments.

"We were horrified at the devastation"

Travels through the USSR after the War

"They found a place amidst the ruins and got the university functioning. . . . Many students and teachers died of hunger."

Alice Horton Tibbetts
Wellesley College '45
Executive Secretary, American Preparatory Committee, 1946
President, United States Student Assembly, 1945

Editor's Note: Before NSA organized its large-scale student travel programs in 1947, thousands of U.S. students had already found their way to all parts of Europe and the rest of the world after war's end in 1945. Their impressions, along with the memories of American student veterans, energized much of the postwar efforts for world student relief, as well as NSA's determination to take part actively in helping to build an international student community. They also inspired the efforts that led American students to go to the Prague World Student Congress in summer 1946 and, later, to form the U.S. National Student Association.

Following are some extracts describing Alice Horton Tibbett's journeys through Russia, as recorded in her diaries at the time:[1]

Wednesday, September 12, 1945: Minsk

We were awakened at 8:00 A.M. by our host. I screwed up my courage and washed my face in the icy water brought to us. We were driven to the government house and for the first time saw the city by daylight. We were horrified at the devastation, block upon block of ruined houses, completely vacant lots at the center of the city. Eighty percent of the city had been destroyed. We were thankful that we had had any kind of a place to sleep.

* * *

We had a little time before our plane left, and so sat talking to a Mrs. Platner who had had breakfast with us. She was a teacher of English at Minsk University and the wife of a Jewish writer. We asked her to tell us about what she had done during the war.

When the Germans were approaching Minsk in June of 1941, she had left the city just two days before the last people were able to leave. She knew only too well what happened to those left behind who had any Jewish connections. She walked out of the city, there being no other mode of transportation, walked until she came to a station where she was able to get on a railroad car. She made her way to a collective farm to the east and found her place there as a worker and a teacher of German. That was a hard winter. The snow came in September. The next summer she went to work in a city hospital as a nurse. Later she found that she was needed as a librarian. In July of 1944 the Germans left Minsk, and she returned in September of that year. She came back to find that she had been fortunate to have left the city. The Jews of the city had been herded into a Ghetto, and the horrible conditions under which they were forced to live were revealed by the diary of one of the women who had survived. She described the terrible [day of] November 7, when 30,000 Jews had been killed on the one day.

Mrs. Platner did not waste time mourning over a city which was 80 percent destroyed, but set about to put things right again. The members of the Minsk University who were straggling into the city got together and began to work in a ruined city without food, water, or electricity. They tried to get in touch with their former staff, paid them a salary, gave them clothes which they received from the government or from foreign relief agencies such as the Red Cross. They found a place amid the ruins and got the university functioning, at first in a small way, slowly restoring it to its former size. The classes now are being conducted in the schools, since the White Russian universities were completely demolished.

We felt strangely humble before Mrs. Platner. She had relatives in New York, and we offered to take back a letter or present to them for her, but she said she was not allowed to do this. Our efforts to be helpful fell a little flat, for this was a woman who obviously did not need help.

We bade her a fond farewell, and boarded the plane at about 10:30 A.M. and three hours later landed thirty kilometers outside Moscow.

Thursday, December 27, 1945: Leningrad

We then went to visit the Leningrad University, where we were immediately captivated by the director, Alexander Vasnesenski. He had a round, jolly face and thick white hair. He told us proudly that this was the university where Lenin passed his exams in law. The university was closed many times by the Czarist government before the revolution because of the revolutionary activity of the students.

The story Professor Vasnesenski told of the students and teachers during the siege was one of the most moving I have ever heard. The fall of 1941, when the Germans were approaching, was a tense and difficult time, but students enrolled in the university that September, anyhow. That winter was one of the hardest, since they had no heat, no light, no water, and very little food. Practically all the men had gone to the front and the girls who did not go to the front behaved heroically, extinguishing incendiary bombs, organizing fire brigades, carrying water from the river, fetching wood from the forests. They helped take care of the wounded. The professor remembered some of his girl students holding wooden torches when an emergency operation had to be performed on a wounded soldier. One incident the professor remembered most vividly was that of a bomb falling on the student hostel. Fifty students were killed and sixty injured. One girl lay for four days under the wreckage on the bodies of her friends. When they finally got her out, she refused to go to a hospital.

Many students and teachers died of hunger. The professor remembered one morning when he counted thirteen corpses in the university yard. There was no one to carry them to the churches or graveyards. One of the hardest things to do, he said, was to try and persuade the populace not to eat their daily ration all at once, but to divide it instead into three portions. Some of the students were evacuated over the ice-road, and when they were out of the danger zone, they would be given rations for several days. Sometimes they simply did not have the will power to hold off on the food and ate it all at once. In one group, many died from doing this, for their emaciated bodies could not take it.

Thursday, January 16, 1946: Stalingrad

Up at 6:30 A.M. to catch a plane to Stalingrad. Incredibly enough, no one was sick on the plane, although we definitely were not feeling at our best after the party on the night before. We flew over the highest Caucasus, beautiful and rugged snow-capped peaks, at 15,000 feet. It was a most unpleasant feeling to have to take deep breaths while we were at that height to make sure we could still breathe.

At 2:00 P.M. we landed on an icy field, which made a terrible noise as we hit it. I looked quickly out the window to make sure that both wings weren't crackng off. We were greeted with the news that the other three members of the delegation who had been delayed traveling from London to Moscow had finally arrived at Moscow and were to arrive In Stalingrad in fifteen minutes. We had been waiting for them to join us for three weeks. Sure enough, in the third plane that taxied up, there they were. We were so busy relating experiences in the bus into town that we almost missed looking out of the window to see a completely destroyed city. We had seen other destroyed cities in our travels, but never anything like this. There was simply nothing standing. Ninety-eight percent of the city was gone. We couldn't imagine where we would sleep, but amidst the ruins in the middle of the city, there seemed to be one building intact, and there we stayed for three nights. There was no hot water or central heating, but again we had been given accommodations much better than those of the general populace.

We walked around the town after dinner by moonlight; it was an eerie experience. The moonlight shining on the lone walls that had managed to withstand the bombardment, on the piles of rubble, and into the huge bomb pits made it seem a city in which ghosts alone could be at home. I saw a few lights here and there and realized that people were living in basements or in parts of buildings that they had been able to fix up to be livable. We saw the "bargain basement" where General Von Paulus and his staff had been captured. The basement was the only part of the building not completely in ruins. We saw what used to be the busy center of town, now like a vacant lot, looking all the more vacant because there the rubble had been cleared away. Our hosts pointed out a ruined Lutheran church, which the Germans had used for a horse stable. Life in Stalingrad seemed a little less gay and carefree than it had been in Georgia [in the Caucasus], I thought to myself, as I dozed off to sleep that night.

END NOTE

[1] See Henry Halsted's 1948 account of his return to Munich after the war, p. 682.

1

2

4

Wellesley College News

Alice Horton '45 Returning May 8

Delegate to International Student Conference Will Describe Europe Trip

Alice Horton, an active member of the class of 1945, and daughter of Dr. Douglas Horton, will speak on the subject of her recent travel through Europe, Wednesday, May 8, at 8:45, in Pendleton Hall. A reception will be held before the lecture at one of the society houses where all those who are interested, may talk with Alice about her experiences during her extensive trip.

Alice was a delegate of the United States Student Assembly to the International Youth Conference in London, where the rights and needs of youth today

Alice Horton '45

3

SUMMER AND WINTER OF 1945

From top left: **THE LONDON WORLD YOUTH CONFERENCE** set the stage for formation of the World Federation of Democractic Youth (WFDY) the following year. Alice Horton represented the United States Student Assembly. Photo (1) shows Meyer Bass, Muriel Jacobson (National Student YWCA), and Gloster Current (NAACP). **TRAVELS THROUGH RUSSIA.** (2) Moscow, 12/45 (l to r) Ann Postina (Universalist Youth Fellowship), Ernesto Madero (Spanish Embassy), Horton, Mollie Lieber (AYD). Bottom: (3) (l to r) Joe Engel (Young People's League of United Synagogues), Olivia Stokes (Baptist students), Ann Postina (Universalist Youth Fellowship), Mollie Lieber (American Youth for Democracy), Jacobson, Horton, Doris Senk (AYF World), Larry Day (Washington Federation of Churches). Top right: (4) The 5/1/46 issue of the *Wellesley College News* announces Horton's appearance at the college.

(Photos courtesy Alice Horton Tibbetts)

West Meets East and I Get to See Europe

3. How the Prague Delegation Was Chosen

Jewel Lubin Bellush
University of Wisconsin, '46
Secretary, U.S. Delegation to the World Student Congress

I begin the saga with the best the heavens accord me in memory about the preparation of the delegation with Alice Horton all through spring 1946 until the end of the Prague conference at the end of August, when delegates returned to the United States or to places in Europe and when I accepted with other students from other countries the invitation to Yugoslavia. I wanted very much to get behind the Iron Curtain to see for myself, and this was a chance in a lifetime.

I had been an active student all my life, from high school on into college. I was always interested in student affairs and was very political. I took part in election campaigns, worked for peace until World War II made me its strong supporter, and was active in war relief efforts.

I graduated in January 1946 from the University of Wisconsin and came back home to New York to enroll at Columbia University, majoring in history and political science. Somewhere, I read about Alice Horton having gone to the Soviet Union the year before (1945) and that she was working on plans for sending students to the World Student Congress in Prague, in August 1946. I called her and offered my services—and we went to work together.

How the U.S. delegates were selected

As I recall it, basically Alice Horton and I made the decisions on selection of delegates, as we really did not have a committee that was involved in this. At first, we ran the operation from her father's home on Riverside Drive—then from a 40th Street office.[1] For the selection of delegates we had two categories:

- Organized youth groups like the YM and YWCA, the Catholic youth organization, the young doctor's group (AIMS), the American Youth for Democracy (AYD) which was a kind of leftover from the war of what remained of the left), and other religious and political student groups. I do remember that we decided that the YM and YWCA were most helpful and useful in getting us started for delegates.
- Individual students to be chosen from select campuses. Here we sort of divided the country into geographical areas and chose one campus from each. If one did not respond, we turned to another college in that region. We contacted student governments and left it up to them entirely to choose the student and provide the money.

I want to underscore the fact that this was, for its time, a very representative group of young people. It was a mixture—and that was the overall reality of U.S. campus life: a few students were politically more aware; most were simply interested and dedicated students, typically active in student government and student newspapers; one, AYD, was an organization I considered "left," pro–Soviet Union. The several Catholics were more conservative. It was a delegation for its time, very reflective of students' thinking. I recall that Joseph Malik from the University of Texas was most helpful to me, assisting with the technical parts of the conference, setting up caucus meetings, and so forth.

A wonder: Getting twenty-five typical Americans to Prague

There was a lot of clerical work to do—passports, arranging travel (we went by boat, pretty slow in those days and cheap, because we were set up in a kind of big barracks with other students). That it all came to pass is a wonder when I think back. I had no thought of going. I had no money or any idea of how it would be possible, but I was determined that we have a broadly representative group of our student bodies spread over America. I was politically aware, and knew that we had a diverse population in the United States. We had no thought to further any particular point of view. We wanted it to be "representative"—and that wasn't so easy at all.[2]

Of course it was not completely cohesive. It could not be if it was to be representative. There was no party line. The twenty-five delegates, selected independently by various organizations and campus groups, were rather typical Americans who, however, served as the student activists in a wide range of organizations. I really enjoyed some whom I remember well, like Doug Cater of Harvard; Russell Austin from the University of Chicago; Bill Ellis, an NICC delegate from Harvard; Enid Kass of Hunter—to name a few.

It is not now clear to me how I came to go and who made this decision. But it was obvious that with twenty-five in a delegation, they needed assistance in their travels and related matters across the Continent—and then in Prague with arrangements for registering at the congress, their meetings, places to stay, and record keeping. So, as something of a shock, the job came to me; some money was found to help, and I raised the rest from family and friends.

The boat ride took about nine to ten days I think. On board I found Rabbi Wise, well known in the Jewish world, and I asked him to give a lecture on the war and its impact on the Jewish people and on the postwar recovery—which he did. I made all the travel arrangements—just learned how on the job! When we arrived in Europe, we went by train, of course. Accommodations in Prague were sparse—typical student dorms. The food was pretty poor because it was just after the war.

Western delegates meet the Eastern bloc

Many students came to the Congress from around the world, from England to India and beyond. Being held in Prague 1946, it was obvious we were near the Soviet bloc. A large element of the conference was communist-influenced, but there was a sizable Western, democratic group from England and France, who often spoke up at meetings. Josef Grohman was the chair, a leader of the Young Communist League of Czechoslovakia. Personally, I disliked the Soviet representatives. They were much older, and really did not appear to be "students." They were, of course, of one voice, always. I did not like the way they acted. They brought lots of food and vodka and had many parties at a time when we in Prague were eating very minimal food. The year 1946 was close to the end of the war and things were still grim. All the Eastern Bloc acted as a bloc. The U.S. agenda items as I recall did deal with issues of concern to our students who were active at the time: peace, pro–United Nations, against racial discrimination, and support for the four freedoms overall. School issues of concern included a free student press, strengthening student self-government, and student influence on curriculum development.[3]

Thinking back on the political environment at the time, the Cold War was actually on the way, even during World War II. We in the United States were never quite relaxed with Soviet power and its spread through Eastern Europe. However, Czechoslovakia at the time had a coalition government, which included Communists, Democratic Socialists, and two other parties. When the Soviet troops marched in years later and destroyed it, it was sad indeed! The youth movement even at that time, however, was controlled by the Communists, and they ran the conference.

Reception at the embassy and then home to start the NSA

Our students, as I mentioned previously, were not as savvy, but they weren't taken in by the communist influences.[4] Our delegation was very pro–United Nations and wanted to have students collaborate across country lines. They were anxious to work together for peace and for the items on a student agenda The U.S. embassy, under Ambassador Laurence Steinhardt, was very suspicious, if not negative, toward this conference.[5] I made contact with the embassy as soon as we arrived—we were anxious to meet with the "powers that be." I also urged the embassy to host a reception on behalf of the American students. This took a lot of back and forth, but finally they did run a reception (for two students per delegation, because there were, I believe, over three hundred students at the conference).

At the end of the conference, the American students met and agreed to further organize a U.S. students' association on a national scale when they returned. That was my last contact with them. I then joined about eighteen students from other countries, accepting the invitation from Yugoslavia to work on a Youth Railroad (Omladinska Pruga).

Jewel Lubin Bellush, right, is Chair of U.S./Israel Women to Women, was Professor of Political Science at Hunter College, and is presently Professor Emerita. She is shown here in 1999 with Alice Horton Tibbetts (see p. 68).

EDITOR'S NOTES

[1] The May 6, 1946, issue of *The Middlebury Campus*, Middlebury, VT, reporting on the fourth annual conference of the United States Student Assembly, held April 26, 27, and 28 at the New School for Social Research, notes that on Saturday, "At 8:00 P.M. the delegates met at the home of Alice Horton, the USSA delegate to [the] London and Prague youth conferences, to lay plans for the coming conference at Prague this summer. USSA will send one delegate, chosen from chapter nominations." Alice Horton writes that she has no recollection of this event, nor that "we ever worked out of our Riverside Drive apartment," but "I do remember the USSA office at 8 West 40th Street very well." See Tibbetts (Horton), p. 68.

[2] A digest of State Department correspondence with Alice Horton and of internal memoranda, on p. 104, is instructive. It reveals the seemingly cooperative but cautious public posture of the department and the suspicions and concerns about communist influence voiced internally. At one point, a note was hand-written on a May 7, 1946, office memorandum, reading, "I suggest we do nothing more on this matter at present because we should not be placed in a position of sponsoring an affair which might not be approved by the Passport Division."

[3] See "Tentative Program of the American Delegation to the International Student Conference at Prague," p. 80.

[4] In his essay on p. 76, Edward Kirchner describes the training the Catholic delegation received prior to going to Prague.

[5] See p. 99 for a digest of embassy records. In his report to the State Department dated August 30, 1946, Ambassador Steinhardt writes: "The American Institute of Czechoslovakia held a tea dance on the arrival of the American delegation to enable them to make the acquaintance of various Czechoslovak students, and toward the end of the conference the American Ambassador held a reception for the members of the American delegation and leading members of the other students' delegations."

"By and large, the members of the American delegation constituted an able group whose influence was considerable in the Conference, although it was somewhat hampered by great difference of opinion within the delegation. In this connection, it is worth mentioning that two or three members of the American delegation were either Communist Party members, or communist in sympathy, and in addition, a great majority of the American delegates was of the opinion that it would be most unwise to introduce any resolutions that might offend the sensibilities of the U.S.S.R. delegation or those from other countries in Eastern Europe."

PICTURE CREDITS: *Then:* Prague, 1946 (*Author*). *Now:* 1999 (*Schwartz*).

JEWEL LUBIN BELLUSH

Early years: I was born May 20, 1924, in New York City and went to Tilden High School in Brooklyn.

Education: I received my B.A. from the University of Wisconsin in 1946, majoring in American Institutions. Attending Columbia University, I received an M.A. in American History in 1948 and a Ph.D. in American Government in 1959.

Professional experience: 1983: Fulbright Professor, University of Haifa; 1976-78: Director, Women's Center for Community Leadership, Hunter College, New York; 1971-72: Staff Director, Mayor Lindsay's Commission on State-City Relations; 1970-71: Guest Professor, University of Utrecht, Netherlands, Institute of Political Sociology; 1959-60: Assistant Director, Governor Brown's Commission on Metropolitan Area Problems, State of California; 1947-1959: Professor of Political Science, Hunter College, presently Professor Emeritus.

From 1947 to the present I have been a consultant to campaigns for local, state, and national office. My responsibilities have included: director, operations; coalition building among labor unions, Jewish and women's organizations; speakers bureau; training for political action in primary and election campaigns; campaign organization; lobbying; and active participant in feminist movement.

Publications and affiliations: Coauthor, *Union Power and New York* (Praeger Publishers, 1984); *Subsidizing Campaigns: Dangers to the Democratic Process*, in collaboration with William Boyd (Center for Policy through Participation. Hunter, 1974). *Mayor-Board-Council: The Real World of New York City Government* (Citizens Union, April 1973); *Race and Politics in New York City*, in collaboration with Stephen David (Praeger Publishers, 1971); *Urban Renewal: People, Politics and Planning*, in collaboration with Murray Hausknecht (Anchor Books, 1967). Affilliations include: Chair, U.S./Israel Women to Women; Governing Council and Commission on Women's Equality, American Jewish Congress; Executive Board, Long Island Congress.

Family: Married, two children, two grandchildren.

JEWEL BELLUSH GOES TO PRAGUE: FIRST STOP ON THE WAY TO BELGRADE

DELEGATES ARRIVE AND PREPARE. *Clockwise from left:* Joseph Malik (U. of Texas), Bellush, Frank Meyers (U. of Penna.), Otik ____ (Czech student); Bellush (center) with National Intercollegiate Christian Council delegates Winburn Thomas (YMCA staff) and Joyce Roberts (Pembroke College, RI). Bellush (left) and Alice Horton flank Yugoslav student Branimir Jankovitch. (Photos: Bellush, Roberts, Bellush).

The World Student Congress in Prague, 1946

4. Preparing the Catholic Delegation

Edward J. Kirchner
Ohio State University
Pax Romana. U.S. Delegation, World Student Congress, Prague, 1946

I was born on a large farm in Pittsfield, Massachussetts. In those days, my "school bus" was Muggins, a pony who cooperated by always needing help when my teacher gave me an assignment that I could not, or would not, fulfill. I graduated in spite of Muggins and went on to Ohio State University, from which I received my bachelor's degree in 1935. At Ohio State, I had been a member of a Catholic fraternity. In 1937, this fraternity sent me to a congress of Pax Romana, the international Catholic student organization.

I kept in touch with national student federations in many parts of the world. Contact with Europe was, of course, eliminated except for neutral Spain, where Joaquin Ruiz-Giminez, my successor in the Pax Romana presidency, lived. Occasional contacts with individual students included Polish refugees who had found their way to London and had established a federation-in-exile. This stimulated the creation of a series of such federations, which continued in existence until East and Central Europe were finally liberated.

Pax Romana before and during World War II

With war clouds gathering in Europe, Pope Pius XI advised Pax Romana to build strength outside Europe. I was elected International President of Pax Romana[1] and was assigned the task of organizing a world congress. This Congress was convened in Washington, D.C., in 1939. It was in session and I was presiding when Hitler's troops invaded Poland and World War II broke out. In the spirit of reconciliation in which Pax Romana was established after World War I, the Polish students asked me to bring them together with the German students as well as with the French and British, which I did.

After the difficult and heartbreaking task of securing safe passage home for the European students whose countries were at war (some never returned to their families), I established the organization's wartime secretariat in Washington. Although the central office was in Switzerland, it could not function freely because neutral Switzerland was surrounded on all sides by nations at war.

Meanwhile, I had been doing graduate work at Catholic University. When the United States entered the war, I joined the navy. Fortunately, I was stationed at the Naval Ordnance Laboratory in Washington throughout the war and could devote my evenings to Pax Romana. With help from other students (one of whom I later married), I ran the movement from an office in Washington. I served in the navy during the war as Personnel Officer of the Laboratory, with all its secret work. My greatest contribution to Allied victory was that I persuaded Albert Einstein to accept a position at the "Lab."

The 1945 revival of the international student movement

With the end of the war in sight in 1945, students from the allied countries began activities to revive the international student movement. In November, the British National Union of Students convened a meeting in London for this purpose. I was one of 150 students who attended. The meeting provided a wonderful opportunity to contact student leaders. I met member of Allied student groups, including many of Pax Romana's federations-in-exile.

A number of students who attended this meeting then went to Prague to attend a meeting, arranged by students at the University of Prague, of persons interested in creating an international student organization. This meeting approved plans for a World Student Congress, to be held in Prague in August 1946. It was envisioned that this congress would create and launch the new organization.

The orientation of many attendees at the London meeting was left wing, and Communist presence among the planners at Prague was strong. Though the convention was convened by the students of Prague, it was clear to all but the most naive that the Russians were really in charge.

Planning for the 1946 Prague Congress

The plans for the Prague Congress nevertheless stirred excitement among noncommunist persons and groups in many nations. Among those who reacted with great interest was Father John Courtney Murray, S.J., who was also Ecclesiastical Assistant of Pax Romana. In an article in the Catholic publication *America*, April 13, 1946, Father Murray proposed that Catholic students be included in the U.S. delegation to the Prague Congress. "In general," he wrote, "the problem is how Catholic youth can be put on the move, in the international field, in a solidly organized movement, with a truly conquering spirit, that will carry through a positive program and also combat communistic influence." He proposed that the Catholic delegation be trained for its important and challenging task before it journeyed to Prague. His proposal received immediate strong support from the Catholic hierarchy.[2]

The Prague planners specified that the U.S. and Russian delegations could each consist of twenty-five persons, and an ad hoc U.S. committee assigned four of the American slots to the National Catholic Youth Council. Father Murray selected Martin McLaughlin and Vince Hogan of Notre Dame, Henry (Hank) Briefs of Georgetown, and myself for the task. Father Murray arranged that we would receive several days of orientation and training at an estate on the Hudson River. Though he was basically a theologian, he also lived in the world and had contacts in many fields. He was able to provide knowledgeable persons to provide the training.

I was also asked to help secure reliable students for some of the national student delegations going to the Congress. My advisers and I, and especially John Courtney Murray, S.J., secured delegates from Canada and some European nations to join their delegations.

That summer, Father Murray married my fiancée Louisa and me, and we honeymooned for several days at the Hudson estate before the others arrived and the training sessions began. Ruth Fischer, who had been the secretary general of the Communist Party in Germany and was now a strong anti-communist, was our chief instructor. In an amusing touch, while she was holding forth one night on the ways of the "evil empire," the lights went out! We continued to learn how to fight evil by the spooky shadows of candlelight.

Training the Catholic delegation

Ruth asked to see the program of the upcoming sessions. When she scanned it, she spotted what she identified as a typical trick. The Russian delegation was scheduled to throw a banquet the night before important elections were to take place. There would be a long series of vodka toasts to Stalin and his associates. Then Americans and others would be toasted. Of course, it would be rude to refuse to toast. But Russians, she said, served their vodka in tiny, jigger-size glasses that can be carefully concealed in the hand and then discreetly emptied into a well-placed receptacle, such as a nearby plant. By merely touching the glass to their lips, they could survive numberless toasts. She also warned about filling the stomach with cheeses and fats. The Russians and their allies, she said, were likely to have two teams, one to drink and carouse, another to go to bed and be ready early the next morning to deal with important politics and cast votes.

Non-Russian delegations would no doubt include many communists or fellow travelers, some simply naive, and others well prepared and equipped. These persons, she said, could generally be identified. They were likely to be dedicated and hard-working, scrupulously attending all sessions, laboring late into the evenings, and starting again early in the morning.

Pax Romana has branches in many countries. We made early contact with Pax Romana in Canada and encouraged them to include knowledgeable persons in the Canadian delegation. After the training session, Louisa and I went to the long-postponed Pax Romana Congress in Spain, which had originally been scheduled to take place in 1939. From there we went to a series of youth and student meetings, including sessions of the International Student Service (ISS), which met in England.[3] At all of these meetings, I tried to locate knowledgeable noncommunist students who would be going to Prague. As a result, a small network was developed in other student delegations.

Successful participation recognized

When we arrived in Prague, we learned how knowledgeable Ruth Fischer had been. The importance of the American delegation was evident from the beginning. We were seated in the first row in the auditorium. The Russians sat immediately behind us, enabling them to keep a close eye on all that we did. We spotted dedicated, hard-working students, and assumed that they had strong, behind-the-scenes influence. We managed to cope with the vodka toasts and were present and ready for the elections the next morning.

Our successful participation was recognized. At the end of the Congress, the leader of the Russian delegation said to me: "Who are you? You are obviously either a former Communist or you have been trained by them." It would be hard to imagine a higher compliment!

When the international work came to an end in Prague, I did not return to the United States and, consequently, did not participate in the founding of the National Student Association. I went to Fribourg, Switzerland, the headquarters of

Edward J. Kirchner, shown here with his wife, Louisa, worked for the U.S. State Department and held various positions with Pax Romana. He holds a B.A. from Ohio State University.

Pax Romana, the International Movement of Catholic Students, where I opened its Relief Department.

Working with postwar refugees and student relief

From Prague, I went to Fribourg, Switzerland, to rejoin Louisa and to set up Pax Romana's relief department. From this neutral land, we were able to provide relief to students in the war-torn countries. Later, I became director of a resettlement camp in Munich, Germany, run under the auspices of the UN International Relief Organization (IRO).

Refugees from many nations came to the camp to prepare for resettlement in free lands. No preceding director had lasted for more than a few months, principally because those arriving for resettlement came from many nations and ethnic groups, many of whom were historical enemies. No fewer than eighty-one ethnic groups were represented in the camp. Czechs hated Slovaks; Hungarians hated Romanians; Poles hated Ukrainians; and so on. It was like a little Bosnia. However, thanks to the Pax Romana international network, I was able to survive as director until IRO had completed its task.

END NOTES

[1] See background on Pax Romana, p. 741.

[2] See "Operation University" by J. C. Murray, p. 739.

[3] See International Student Service background, pp. 50, 56.

PICTURE CREDITS: *Then:* Salamanca, June 1946. *Now:* c. 1997 (*Both, author*).

EDWARD J. KIRCHNER

I was born in Pittsfield, MA. Following my student days at Ohio State University, my graduation in 1935, and my service in Pax Romana (detailed in my essay for this book), I joined the U.S. State Department and took up life in the United States. In 1956, when Hungary rebelled against the occupying Russians, I again became active in student relief, but this time with no organization to back or help me. I set up an office in New York with some dedicated Hungarians, and we found scholarships or jobs for those who had fled from Hungary. Louisa and our three children, ranging from a few months to nine years old, and I picketed the United Nations to urge support of our work.

In 1960, Louisa, two of our children, and I traveled to Soviet-controlled Yugoslavia, Hungary, Czechoslovakia, and Poland. Later, when the Soviet Empire eventually fell apart and these lands were liberated, Louisa and I went on a triumphal tour of Hungary, Romania, Ukraine, Lithuania, and Latvia. Wherever we went, people from Pax Romana welcomed us and told us tales of the courageous and often tragic experiences of these people during the years of Russian domination.

Louisa and I were decorated by the Holy See for our work among postwar refugees. I became a Knight of St. Sylvester and she received the only decoration given to women (that was before Beijing). I later became a Knight of St. Gregory for my social work in the Diocese of Bridgeport, Connecticut. I am also a Knight, and Louisa a Lady, of the Holy Sepulchre.

After Louisa and I had retired, Pax Romana's International Catholic Movement for Intellectual and Cultural Affairs held a World Assembly in Dobogoko, Hungary, outside Budapest. We attended. To our surprise, we were greeted by representatives of the president of Hungary and given honors and thanks for our work for Hungarians.

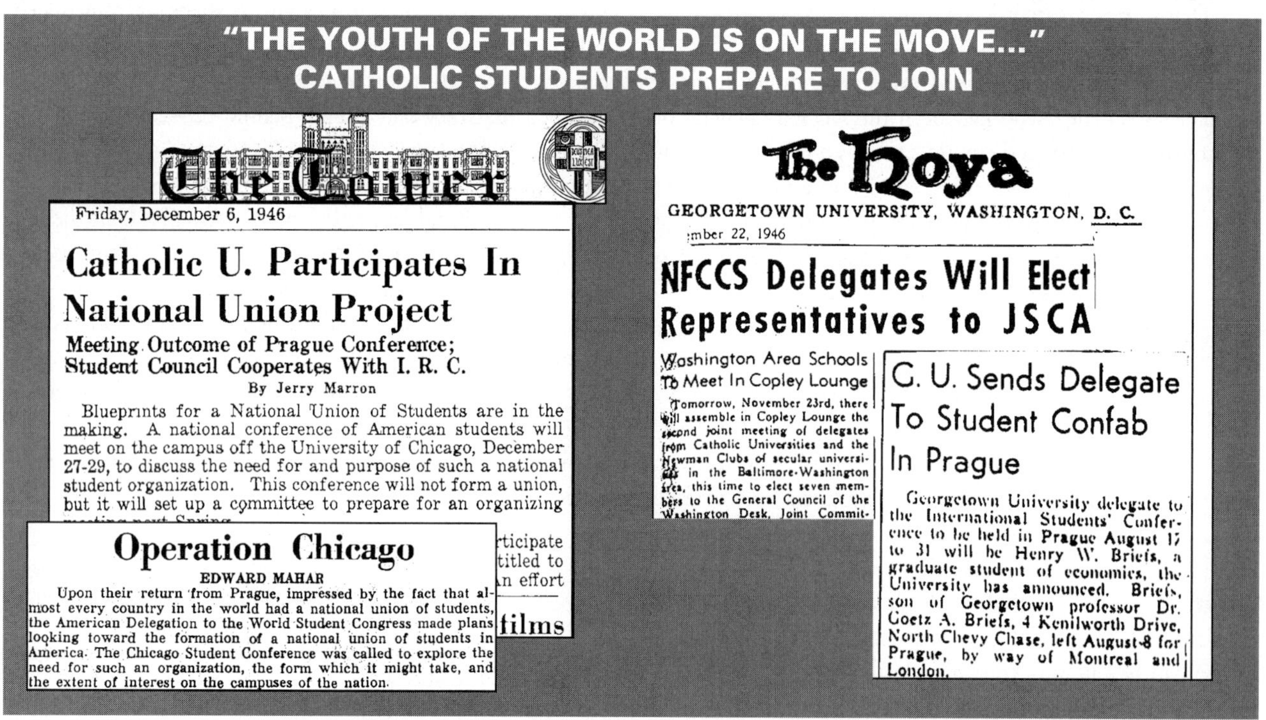

"THE YOUTH OF THE WORLD IS ON THE MOVE..."
CATHOLIC STUDENTS PREPARE TO JOIN

The Tower

Friday, December 6, 1946

Catholic U. Participates In National Union Project

Meeting Outcome of Prague Conference; Student Council Cooperates With I. R. C.

By Jerry Marron

Blueprints for a National Union of Students are in the making. A national conference of American students will meet on the campus off the University of Chicago, December 27-29, to discuss the need for and purpose of such a national student organization. This conference will not form a union, but it will set up a committee to prepare for an organizing

Operation Chicago

EDWARD MAHAR

Upon their return from Prague, impressed by the fact that almost every country in the world had a national union of students, the American Delegation to the World Student Congress made plans looking toward the formation of a national union of students in America. The Chicago Student Conference was called to explore the need for such an organization, the form which it might take, and the extent of interest on the campuses of the nation.

The Hoya

GEORGETOWN UNIVERSITY, WASHINGTON, D. C.

mber 22, 1946

NFCCS Delegates Will Elect Representatives to JSCA

Washington Area Schools To Meet In Copley Lounge

Tomorrow, November 23rd, there will assemble in Copley Lounge the second joint meeting of delegates from Catholic Universities and the Newman Clubs of secular universities in the Baltimore-Washington area, this time to elect seven members to the General Council of the Washington Desk, Joint Commit-

G. U. Sends Delegate To Student Confab In Prague

Georgetown University delegate to the International Students' Conference to be held in Prague August 17 to 31 will be Henry W. Briefs, a graduate student of economics, the University has announced. Briefs, son of Georgetown professor Dr. Goetz A. Briefs, 4 Kenilworth Drive, North Chevy Chase, left August 8 for Prague, by way of Montreal and London.

"OPERATION UNIVERSITY," an article by John Courtney Murray in *America* magazine (9/14/46. See full article in Part 4, Section 2), called Catholic college students to action, and major universities responded (above, 1946 and 1947 student newspapers at Catholic and Georgetown Universities). They formed a Joint Committee for Student Action (JCSA), bringing together the National Federation of Catholic College Students (NFCCS) and the Newman Club Federation to coordinate their activities (see Des Marais, Part 4, Section 2).

The Programme: The tasks of student youth in the postwar world

Call to the World Student Congress and the American Delegation Agenda

There can be no meaningful peace until the four freedoms are realized: freedom from fear, freedom from want, freedom of speech, and freedom of religion

Call to the Congress

The International Preparatory Committee, representing 12 nations, is responsible for setting up the World Student Congress at Prague to establish a representative international students organization. "This is an important step in establishing stable and lasting peace, in promoting friendship among all peoples and in defending the rights and interests of students." An American national Student Preparatory Committee will select delegates to attend this important meeting. Bring this information before your Student Council. Write to the national headquarters of your student organization or to the American Preparatory Committee, Room 911, 8 West 40th Street, New York, New York, for further information.

THE PROGRAMME

The programme of the World Student Congress will be divided into 3 parts:

I. The tasks of student youth in the postwar world
II. Creation of a new world organization of students
III. Organization and coordination of student activities

The Congress will be a working congress. It has two main aims:

1. To set up a new international student organization
2. To decide the policies of this body for the succeeding year.

First Week

Saturday, August 17

A manifestation in favor of establishing a new world students organization

Title: "The Students Work for a Better World."

Monday morning

Plenary session and report of the Preparatory Committee

Wednesday

Commission 1. "Tasks of student youth in the elimination of Fascism."

Commission 2. "The tasks of student youth in reconstruction."

Commission 3. "The tasks of student youth for peace and a better world."

Thursday

Plenary session: "Creation of a new world organization of students."

Friday

Plenary session: election of officers. A general session for suggestions.

Saturday Morning

Open meeting to celebrate birth of new organization. Carnival procession through the streets of Prague on carts, lorries and on foot and masquerade ball in the evening.

Second Week

Sunday

Picnic in the country

Monday–Tuesday

Six commissions working on specific problems:

1. Intellectual cooperation: education, science, culture and interrelations of the faculty commissions.
2. Student exchange and travel.
3. Press and publications, films, books, periodicals, etc.
4. Student relief.
5. Sport.
6. Living conditions and the health of students, e.g., scholarships, cost of education, examination of income groups of students.

Wednesday–Friday

Reports of the commissions and meetings of the faculty commissions.

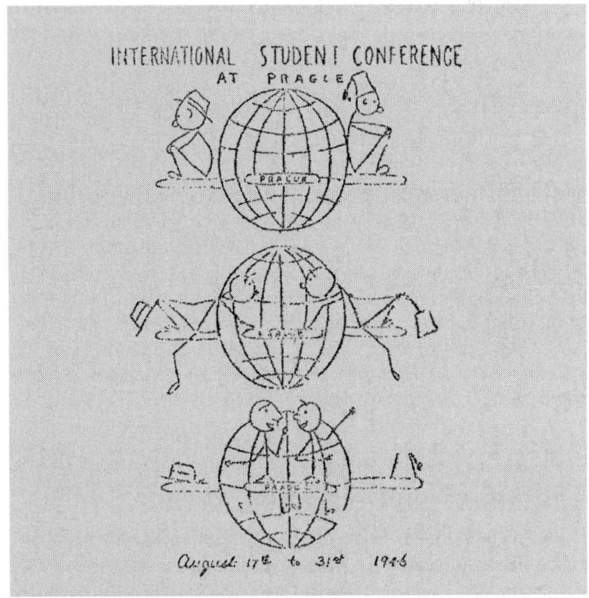

"THE UNITED STATES RALLIES TO THE CALL." The American Preparatory Committee announces its intention to organize a U.S. delegation.

Friday Afternoon

Plenary session: passing of reports and presentation of Congress resolutions

Saturday, August 31

Closing session: speech of new president, public announcement of resolutions.
Evening: each delegation is asked to prepare in advance a song or a short performance

Sunday

Afternoon: garden party in one of the gardens in Prague.
Evening: farewell party.

Monday

Departure of delegates wishing to visit parts of Czechoslovakia, Yugoslavia, France, USSR, etc.

Editor's Note: This presentation is an abbreviation of the original two-page announcement.

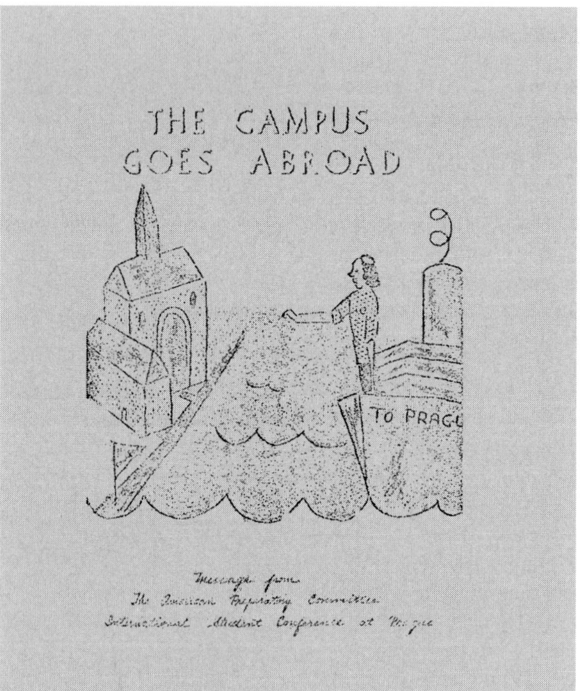

ADDRESSED TO CAMPUS LEADERS at the ten colleges selected to choose representatives to the U.S. delegation, the notice illustrated above stated that 500 foreign students met with the newly liberated Czechs November 17, 1945, in Prague "to commemorate International Students Day, a commemoration of those Czech students who in 1939 were massacred by the Nazis." This meeting issued a call to students throughout the world for a conference at which a permanent international students organization could be formed.... "Students must use their special skills to build understanding between nations, so necessary for peace. This conference will provide the opportunity...."

The American Delegation Agenda

I. The American student delegation to the International Student Conference at Prague stands on the following basic principles as necessary for insuring peace, security, and freedom in the years to come. The members of the American delegation pledge to utilize their abilities as students to work to see that these principles are realized.

A. We give wholehearted support to the United Nations. Cooperation of Great Britain, the Soviet Union and the United States must be restored and extended through the United Nations machinery. We will work to strengthen the charter of the United Nations so that it can be an organ which can better study, understand, and resolve international conflict. We must guard against use of the Security Council for mere diplomatic maneuvering.

B. We realize that there can be no meaningful peace until the four freedoms are realized: freedom from fear, freedom from want (the right to gainful and satisfying employment with adequate wages, good housing, adequate nutrition, medical care, ample rest, and recreation), freedom of speech, and freedom of religion.

C. We consider that all people must be accorded their full rights of citizenship without discriminatory restrictions on account of race, color, creed, sex, national origin, or political belief.

D. We believe that all peoples should have the right to determine their own destiny and support the efforts of all colonial peoples to form governments of their own choosing.

II. The American delegation is particularly interested in seeing these principles implemented throughout the student world.

A. Students must get to know and understand students of other countries. To this end we favor:

1. Cleansing the curricula of primary, secondary and higher educational institutions of material which encourages popular prejudices. Inclusion of a course of basic anthropology in primary and secondary schools would help in eliminating race prejudice. History books of all schools should not be allowed to misrepresent races or peoples.
2. Increased dissemination of information on student activities in other countries.
3. Properly executed student exchange programs with appropriate follow-up.

B. We favor extension of educational benefits to all. Secondary schooling should be free and compulsory. Higher education should be available to all who have the ability to learn. The United States G.I. Bill of Rights is a step in this direction.

C. We believe in both professorial and student academic freedom. Professors must be free to teach and conduct research as they see fit. Students must be free to express themselves. They must be free to indulge in political activity, to form democratic student councils, and to have a voice in the curriculum of their university.

D. We encourage students to take seriously their responsibilities as citizens, to vote, and to participate in local and national affairs.

E. We strongly condemn any kind of discrimination because of race, religion, economic status, either against students entering institutions of higher education or during their course there.

F. We stand for effective democratic reeducation in former enemy countries.

G. In order to attract individuals of the highest calibre to the staffs of educational institutions, adequate pay and security must be provided for teaching personnel.

H. Immediate relief in the way of food, medical and educational supplies must be made available to countries devastated by the war, so that students in these countries can carry on their work.

I. We support the efforts of colonial peoples to extend their educational opportunities, and to educate themselves in their own culture and language.

Document source: American Preparatory Committee announcements, Center for American History, University of Texas at Austin.

SECTION 2

The World Student Congress, Prague, 1946

CONTENTS

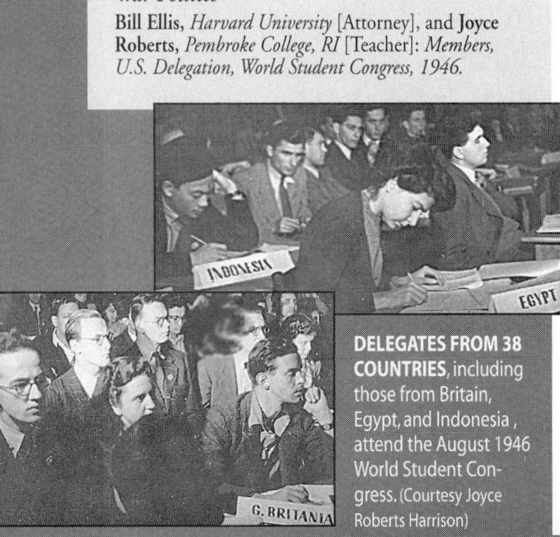

DELEGATES FROM 38 COUNTRIES, including those from Britain, Egypt, and Indonesia, attend the August 1946 World Student Congress. (Courtesy Joyce Roberts Harrison)

The call to the World Student Congress announced to the world that the event would be "an important step in establishing stable and lasting peace, in promoting friendship among all peoples and in defending the rights and interests of students."

"Hopes were high at the Congress," Miriam Haskell Berlin (Smith College '48), an observer at the meeting, writes in this section, as she describes the road back to the U.S. and her efforts to "spread the word" in the four months preceding December 1946 during which the delegation organized the Chicago Student Conference (see below).

Martin McLaughlin, a Notre Dame Ph.D. in 1948, a U.S. delegate at the meeting, traveled widely and wrote extensively about the Congress and the new organization in media reaching Catholic students and colleges. His memoir describes the keen interest shown by Church leaders and Catholic student groups in taking part in postwar student events that were not specifically Catholic.

A collection of excerpts from delegate reports published by student newspapers at Harvard University, Hunter College, and the Universities of Chicago, North Carolina, Pennsylvania, and Texas bring the events in Prague to life with the immediacy of the times. An album of photographs and documents captures some of the "old world" postwar mid-twentieth century flavor of the global events taking place in those years. They were retrieved from boxes located in the attics and basements in the homes of former delegates that survived the fifty-five years that have since passed.

Also presented are recollections about delegation leader and American Veterans Committee activist Russell Austin (University of Chicago) and delegates Douglass Cater (Harvard University), later an assistant to President Johnson and President of Washington College, and Jimmy Wallace (University of North Carolina), later the Mayor of Chapel Hill, NC, whose appeal to President Truman to ease restrictions on Soviet student travel to the U.S. appears in this section.

Cold War dashes hopes for East-West collaboration

Despite the good will and yearning to build "bridges of understanding," the emerging Cold War eventually dashed the hopes of U.S. students for collaboration with Soviet and Eastern European students. A foretaste is painstakingly set forth in excerpts from the report on the Congress itself, prepared by Joyce Roberts, now Harrison (Pembroke College, RI '47), and William Ellis (Harvard University) who represented the National Intercollegiate Christian Council (NICC) of the YM and YWCA's at the Prague Congress.

The events described in this section inspired the returning U.S. delegation to call for a Student Conference at Chicago in December 1946. More than 700 delegates and observers at this conference decided to form a U.S. national student organization, referred to as the National Student Organization (NSO), which became the NSA in September 1947.

WORLD STUDENT NEWS

BULLETIN OF THE INTERNATIONAL PREPARATORY COMMITTEE

Prague August 15, 1946

CONGRESSUS STUDIOSORUM ORBIS TERRARUM · PRAGAE 1946 ·

17.-31. VIII. 1946 PRAHA-ČSR

WORLD STUDENTS CONGRESS
CONGRÈS MONDIAL DES ÉTUDIANTS
МЕЖДУНАРОДНЫЙ СТУДЕНЧЕСКИЙ СЪЕЗД В ПРАГЕ
CONGRESO MUNDIAL DE LOS ESTUDIANTES
SVĚTOVÝ SJEZD STUDENTSTVA

VIGNETTES OF THE 1946 WORLD STUDENT CONGRESS

MORE THAN 350 STUDENTS FROM 38 COUNTRIES were warmly welcomed in a colorful ceremony at the Masaryk Kolej ornate House of Arts and Music. The ten days of meetings and festive programs in Prague were set in a background, as Jimmy Wallace of the University of North Carolina reported, of "great insecurity" for many delegates coming from countries that heavily controlled freedom of speech and movement. Douglass Cater of Harvard wrote later of "the irrepressible optimism of European students" and "an almost fanatic determination that [the Congress] should not fail."

SCENES OF THE CONGRESS: Top left, view of the dais at a general session; left, delegates mingle at a picnic; below, arriving at Masaryk Kolej and assembled at one of the sessions.

(Photos courtesy Libby Cater Hallaby and Jewel Lubin Bellush. WSC announcement, top, courtesy Joyce Roberts Harrison)

U.S. DELEGATES: Below: (1) Jewel Lubin (U. Wisc.), delegation secretary and Douglass Cater (Harvard), 3rd and 4th from left, with Czech students in Masaryk Kolej dormitory, which had been raided in 1939 by Germans and in 1947 by Communists. Middle: (2) Bill Ellis (National Intercollegiate Christian Council; Harvard), far right, who later became American Vice President of the International Union of Students and resigned in 1948 as a protest against the Communist coup (Sections 2 and 3); 2d from right at table, Charles Proctor (Fisk). Top right: (3) U.S. delegates at Congress session: Douglass Cater (Harvard), foreground. To his rear right, Bill Ellis, Curt Farrar (United World Federalists; Yale). Bottom right, Martin McLaughlin (National Catholic Youth Conference; Notre Dame).

3

2

1

EASTERN EUROPEAN DELEGATES: (1) Soviet Union, (2) Romania, (3) Bulgaria. U.S. efforts through the yet to be formed National Student Association to bridge the Cold War gap with Eastern European students lasted until 1951, when the Association endorsed formation of a non-Communist international student alternative, Cosec (Part 3, Section 2). This effort formed a large part of NSA's international relations story in its early years.

3

1

2

The events of 1946 opened up a broader world

1. The Prague Conference and the Beginnings of NSA, 1946

Martin M. McLaughlin
University of Notre Dame, Indiana
U.S. Delegation, World Student Congress, Prague, 1946

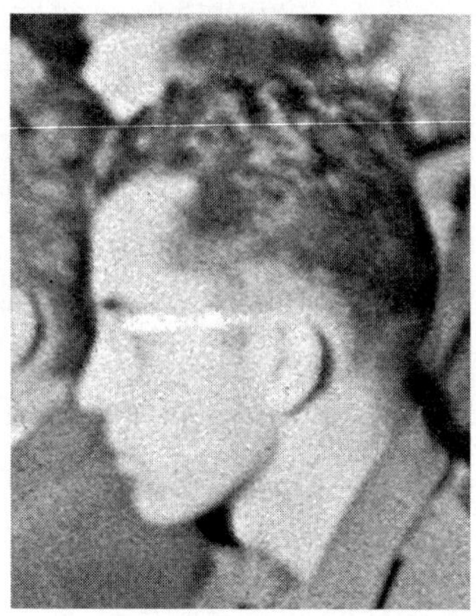

Of the many strands that made up the fabric of the U.S. National Student Association (NSA), I am familiar mainly with what might be called the Prague Connection: the World Student Congress of 1946, which established the International Union of Students (IUS); some of the events leading up to it; and its influence on the beginnings of NSA. The story suffers from my fading memory of what took place a half-century ago and from the fact that I was only one of the twenty-five students who made up the U.S. delegation to the 1946 Congress. My account also reflects some information that we did not have at the time, as well as the questionable clarity of twenty-twenty hindsight.[1]

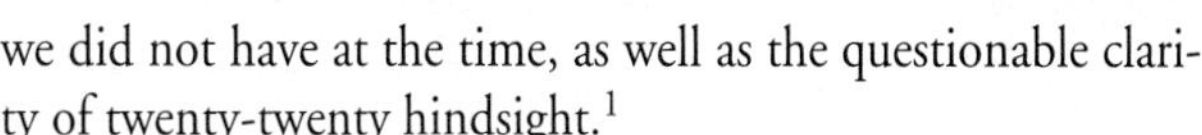

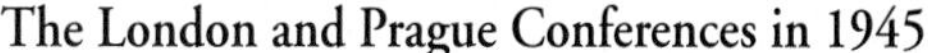

The London and Prague Conferences in 1945

With the defeat of Nazi Germany clearly in sight in the early months of 1945, the British National Union of Students brought together about two dozen students from Allied countries to plan a meeting in London in November, for the purpose of reviving the international student movement, which had lapsed during the war. About 150 students from nearly forty countries, including exile groups, participated. The participants in this meeting drafted a constitution for a new international student organization.

Afterward, several of the attendees traveled to Prague, where the Czech Student Union, with support from its just-restored government, had organized a meeting with a similar purpose. At this meeting, it was agreed that the founding meeting of a new international student organization should take place in Prague in August 1946. A twelve-nation International Preparatory Committee, with strong communist leadership, looked forward to adding the new organization to a coordinated communist network that already included the World Federation of Democratic Youth, the Women's International Democratic Federation, the World Federation of Trade Unions, and others.[2]

The U.S. delegation to the 1946 Congress

The International Preparatory Committee determined the size of country delegations to the forthcoming conference. The Soviet Union and the United States were allotted twenty-five delegates each, with other countries being assigned smaller numbers on a sliding scale. A self-selected, informal American preparatory committee further determined that existing U.S. student organizations would provide fifteen of the twenty-five delegates and persons elected on specified college campuses would round out the total. Of the fifteen organizational delegates, four chosen by the National Council of Churches would represent Protestant groups, four chosen by the Youth Division of the National Catholic Welfare Conference would represent Catholic groups, and the remaining seven would be chosen from other national student and youth organizations.

The resulting delegation was as follows: Leila Anderson (National Intercollegiate Christian Council/YWCA); William Ellis (NICC/YMCA); Hoyt Palmer (NICC/YMCA); Joyce Roberts (NICC/YWCA); Edward Kirchner (National Catholic Youth Council); Henry Briefs (National Catholic Youth Council); Vincent Hogan (National Catholic Youth Council); Martin McLaughlin (National Catholic Youth Council); Jean Casson (American Unitarian Youth); John C. Farrar (Student Federalists); Lada Hulka (U.S. Student Assembly); Bernard Lown (Association of Interns and Medical Students); Lee Marsh (American Youth for Democracy); Walter Wallace (Youthbuilders); Winburn Thomas (Student Volunteer Movement); Douglass Cater (Harvard University); Enid Kass (Hunter College); Joseph Malik (University of Texas); Frank Mayers (University of Pennsylvania); Warren Rovetch (Wayne University); Russell Austin (University of Chicago); William Stout (Win the Peace Committee, University of California at LosAngeles); James Wallace (University of North Carolina); Charles Proctor (Fisk University); and Albert Houghton (University of Wisconsin).

This group was diverse and fairly representative, but hardly harmonious; politically, it stretched from moderate to communist. It is doubtful that many of the delegates were aware of the full history of events preceding the selection of the delegation. Certainly the Catholics, of whom I was one, were not.[3]

Catholic student participation

Catholic interest stemmed from an article written by the distinguished Catholic theologian John Courtney Murray S.J. [1904-1967],[4] which appeared in the Jesuit magazine *America* in April 1946. Murray believed that the Prague Congress, though intended as a communist propaganda event, offered Catholic students the opportunity to participate more fully in events and matters not specifically Catholic, and at the same time to help block communist domination of an important sector of society—universities—and a crucial segment of future leadership—students. This perception was reflected in events at Prague and afterward.

Murray's article, perhaps unexpectedly, got quick results from the leadership of the U.S. Church—strong support, including funds, for U.S. Catholic students to participate in the delegation, attend the conference, and play a role in future national and international student activity. Although Murray may have intended to select the participating students from Jesuit colleges on the East Coast, a letter from Vince Hogan, a friend of mine at Notre Dame, prompted him to cast the net somewhat more widely. Hogan wrote that he would be in Europe that summer working on his doctoral dissertation and would be glad to add Prague to his itinerary. Murray accepted the offer and asked Hogan if he had a friend at Notre Dame who would also like to participate. I was the friend.

In the end, about a dozen Catholics took part in a rather intense "training" program provided by Murray and by Catholic activists and communist defectors. Seven of us went to Europe that summer, four to Prague and three to Catholic events in the United Kingdom, Switzerland, and France. The four for Prague—Henry Briefs of Georgetown University, Edward Kirchner[5] of the international Catholic student organization Pax Romana, Vince Hogan, and I—joined the larger U.S. delegation for much of its preparatory meeting in New York City, the boat-and-train trip to Prague, and the conference itself.

The Prague Congress and the establishment of IUS

The Prague Congress created and launched the International Union of Students (IUS). The Czech government of Klement Gottwald, the only Communist premier ever elected anywhere in a free election (he got forty percent of the vote in a three-way race), made strenuous and successful efforts to orchestrate the meeting as an event that would arouse the enthusiasm of the participants and fulfill the purposes of the organizers. The conference was dominated by the Communists. Their leaders were elected to most of the offices, and their agenda[6] was, in the main, adopted.

Parliamentary procedure was generally followed at the Congress. However, there were shortcomings. Secret ballots were not permitted. Serious debates were sometimes interrupted for "antifascist" demonstrations or "pilgrimages" to the sites of fascist massacres. The agenda was occasionally changed without notice, especially if a Communist dignitary appeared to address the students.

However, it was still the early postwar era of good feeling. The war had just ended. The Soviets had been in it longer than the United States, had suffered more, and were perceived by many to have contributed more to the victory. They boasted of their achievements and power and were geographically closer to Prague than the United States. There was considerable ambivalence about Western colonial powers and "capitalists." Many students from non-Communist countries or organizations were reluctant to be seen as supporters of fascism by opposing Communist initiatives.

Subsequent developments in the United States

The judgments and views of the members of the U.S. delegation varied widely, but they were united on one thing. In the absence of a U.S. national student organization comparable to those of other nations represented at Prague, there was no way for U.S. students to participate effectively in the new IUS. This conviction, however, was accompanied by an equally strong belief that the twenty-five members of the delegation were not an adequately representative sample of U.S. student opinion on the question of establishing a national union or what its structure, programs, and activities should be.

The delegation determined to convene a meeting that would be broadly representative of U.S. students, to provide a more valid indicator of student sentiment on whether to cre-

Martin M. McLaughlin has been Vice President of the Overseas Development Council and a Consultant with the U.S. Catholic Conference Center of Concern.

ate such an organization and, if sentiment was favorable, to take the first steps toward launching it. The conference was scheduled to take place at the University of Chicago during the 1946 Christmas holidays.[7]

The Catholic participants in the Prague preparations had created a Joint Committee for Student Action (JCSA), representing the two national Catholic student groups, the National Federation of Catholic College Students (NFCCS) and the Newman Club Federation. JCSA spent a good part of the fall and early winter urging Catholic colleges and universities to send delegates to Chicago and persuading Newman Clubs at non-Catholic institutions to participate in campus elections for delegates to the Chicago event. The efforts reflected the view that refusal of Catholic students to participate in previous national student groups had, in several cases, helped open the way for control by communists.[8]

The Chicago Conference, intense and exhausting though it may have been, was nevertheless a pleasant surprise and a successful enterprise. It was controlled entirely by students rather than by the professional youth leaders who had often dominated previous organizations. The approach to problems was businesslike and rarely emotional. Hard-line partisan politics was largely excluded. Generally constructive attitudes marked the discussion of even such controversial issues as racial equality and nondiscrimination (it was, after all, only 1946). The delegates overwhelmingly supported the creation of a national student organization and elected a Continuations Committee, composed only of campus-based, rather than organizational, representatives, to prepare and organize a constitutional convention at the University of Wisconsin the following September, which would create the U.S. National Student Association. I continued to be active in NSA preparations at Notre Dame and became a delegate to the Madison convention at which NSA was officially created.[9]

For me, as a product of many years of Catholic education who had spent his life up to that time (except the four very concentrated war years) in a very Catholic environment, the events of 1946 in New York, Europe, and Chicago opened a broader world. Though these events may fade in memory, I doubt that I'll ever forget the essentials; and I will always be grateful for the possibilities they opened up.

END NOTES

[1] See Albums and Background in this section.

[2] See p. 538, for a digest of the founding of the IUS and relations with NSA.

[3] See Tibbetts, p. 68, and Bellush, p. 73, for information on the Prague delegation selection.

[4] See reproduction of this article on p. 739 as well as additional Operation University references in the index.

[5] See Kirchner essay, p. 76.

[6] Some of the main elements of their agenda, with a 1946 communist tilt, were antifascism and democracy, anticolonialism, appeal to youth, appeal to the underprivileged, peace, and an antinuclear program.

[7] See Wharton, p. 112.

[8] See Des Marais, p. 734.

[9] See Wharton, p. 144.

PICTURE CREDITS: *Then:* At World Student Congress, August 1946, Prague, Czechoslovakia (*Author*). *Now:* c. 1999 (*Schwartz*).

Martin McLaughlin of Notre Dame was one of four delegation members representing the National Catholic Youth Conference. He wrote and spoke extensively about his experiences there and at the Chicago Student Conference. Portions of the doctoral thesis he wrote on the formation of NSA are reproduced in this Anthology (See Prologue and Part 4). He is shown above at a World Student Congress plenary session, second row, second from right.

(Photo courtesy Jewel Bellush)

POLITICAL PROCESSES IN AMERICAN NATIONAL STUDENT ORGANIZATIONS

Dissertation Submitted to the Graduate School of the University of Notre Dame in Partial Fulfillment of the Requirements for the Degree of Doctor of Philosophy

BY

MARTIN M. MCLAUGHLIN, M.A.

NOTRE DAME, INDIANA
APRIL, 1948

AMERICA DECEMBER 14, 1946
Student congress at Prague
Martin M. McLaughlin

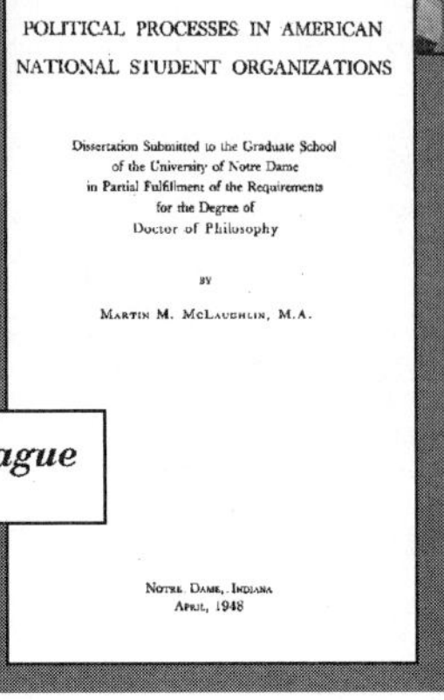

MARTIN M. MCLAUGHLIN

Early Background: Born June 23, 1918. Grew up in Portland, Oregon; attended Catholic grammar school and Columbia Preparatory School.

Military Service and Education: University of Portland (Oregon), B.A., 1938. U.S. Army Air Corps. Drafted in 1942, while doing graduate work at the University of Notre Dame. Spent the war years in India, and was discharged as a captain in March 1946. University of Notre Dame: returned to Notre Dame, received Ph.D. in political science in 1948. Thesis, entitled *Political Processes in American National Student Organizations,* discusses the structure and initial congresses of NSA, analyzing them as exercises in political process. It describes various factions and how the organization built its checks and balances.

Career: Taught at DePaul University, Chicago, 1949-1951. Worked for U.S. government for twenty-six years, 1951-1973 (plus military service). State Department and Agency for International Development (AID). Overseas Development Council, 1974-1983 (retired as Vice President). Consultant, U.S. Catholic Conference, 1983-1993. Currently volunteer, Center of Concern.

Family: Married to Patricia Ollivier. Seven children and eight grandchildren.

The challenge of communicating a new idea

2. A Prague to Madison Journal

Miriam Haskell Berlin

Smith College. U.S. Delegation, World Student Congress, Prague, 1946 (Observer Status)
Chair, NSA Northern New England Region, 1947-48

Selection as a delegate to the ISS

In spring 1946, my sophomore year at Smith College, a committee of faculty and students chose three undergraduates as the college's delegates to the first postwar meeting of the International Student Service (ISS), to be held at Cambridge University in England. I was chosen as one of the three. ISS was an organization of faculty and students founded after World War I to aid the university community.[1]

I was jubilant to be going to Europe, my lifelong dream. Then came the blow. The college discovered that it could send only two representatives, so the junior member was to be dropped. The other two students were older and had proven themselves as scholars and citizens, one as the incoming head of student government, the other on the judicial board.

The student body, however, made other judgments; a swell of protest arose, arguing that these two reflected only one dimension of college life, not the whole. Both science majors, they had made their mark in student government, but did not necessarily speak for those with other interests and concerns, whose views and attitudes should be represented. My interest in languages, history, and politics made me the focus and symbol of the protest. After long negotiations, one of the elder "stateswomen" was dropped and I was reinstated.

The dean of the college, Hallie Flanagan Davis, called me in to underscore the importance of the events. A recognized and seasoned contributor to the life of the college had been replaced by someone younger, unproven, unknown. My responsibility was great—to the college, to the students who had banded together to widen the scope of the delegation, and to the displaced young woman. For me, this context was exaltation and responsibility in equal measure.

Extraordinary experiences at Cambridge and afterward

When I arrived at Cambridge University, extraordinary experiences began immediately, and continued. There were French students who gobbled up the sugar cakes at tea, so starved were they for something sweet. Some forearms bore concentration camp numbers—scarcely known about in 1946 America. There were tales of the occupation, of underground activities, of lost families. There were the bombed-out buildings, first in London and later as the train crossed three military zones from Paris to Prague. There were the heaps of rubble that had been major cities, such as Nuremberg and Stuttgart, and there were the wasted, haunted faces of Germans standing by the railroad. These images have never left my mind. Part of my story lies simply in being female, American, and a Jew. Had the fates so decreed, any of us could have been one of them. All that became part of the legacy of this journey.

Each delegate to the conference was to choose a country to travel in for a month after the meetings. As I was fluent in French and greatly interested in French literature and culture, I planned to go to France. However, the liveliest, most interesting, and most powerful personalities from every delegation, including the U.S. group, were going to attend the World Student Congress scheduled to be held in Prague in August. Many urged me to come, even though I was not an official delegate. I agreed and changed my plans in order to go to Czechoslovakia. I was carrying newspaper credentials issued to me by the *Boston Globe*, and in Prague, was accredited to the Congress as a nonvoting observer. The American delegation treated me as one of them, and that is how the twenty-five-member U.S. delegation became, for nonofficial purposes, twenty-six.[2]

American students inspired to form a national organization

Hopes were high at the congress. Organizing an international body of students that included the Soviets, binding the student community together despite evident and growing differences on issues of great significance, addressing common problems—for us the value of this effort was enhanced by the fact that the United Nations was established in the same year.

To my regret, my recollections of the congress proceedings are not nearly as detailed as I would wish. In addition to speaking French, I had a rudimentary knowledge of Russian, so that the reach of my acquaintance was wide. Not being responsible for voting gave me freedom to roam, talk, and explore, in a way not always available to the official delegation members. The friendships that evolved from these encounters, a few lasting even to the present, contributed to my sense of obligation. We felt we owed a debt to all these students for our good fortune as Americans spared the suffering and pain of the war years and their scars. This feeling of debt further fueled my passionate involvement in the plans to create a U.S. national student organization made by the U.S. delegation after the congress, and in the organizing efforts later.

Issues raised by our experience at the Prague Congress and their significance for an American student union were discussed on the long shipboard journey home. Meeting students from varied national political and cultural contexts had stimulated and compelled us to look at the disarray of our own student bodies, each centered on a specific agenda and none embracing or even imagining some unity fashioned from our various purposes. Imagining is, of course, the first step.

It was evident from the makeup of the American delegation, itself reflecting the society, that it would not be possible to create an organization with a political objective. For some this disappointment would never be alleviated. Most realized, however, that student life generated enough important problems to more than justify an organization's existence.

Issues to be faced by an American student organization

Central was racial discrimination, the scourge of our social order, resulting in inequality, lack of rights and dignity, and a divided society. Persisting from the 1930s were paternalistic attitudes of university administrations toward students, which were particularly inappropriate for the new student population that included returning veterans, married students, and older students with adult responsibilities. This greatly expanded population also presented a whole panoply of problems and needs to the university world in areas that included housing, health care, counseling, and child care.

We also felt a strong obligation to create programs to compensate for American students' geographical isolation. We believed that the rich and illuminating interpersonal and intercultural experiences that we had enjoyed at the conferences should be made available to all U.S. students at reasonable cost. Travel offered the way for us to grow out of our parochialism, widen our vision, and play an effective international role.

Americans habitually give voice to new needs. Despite the contentious history of past student organizations, little known to most of us in 1946, we wanted to do what de Tocqueville had noted as an outstanding American characteristic, to come together to accomplish our specific ends.

Spreading the word about the new organization

Responsibilities for spreading the word were assigned, and a Continuations Committee was established. I do not remember precisely when (in fall 1946, after contacting student governments in many New England institutions) I was elected Chair of the New England Region. But it came to pass (certainly by the time of the Chicago Student Conference in December), and I have vivid memories of endless telephone calls in the dormitory hall, nights with little sleep, and struggles to keep up with the Honors Program and the requirements of my generous scholarship at Smith. I visited many colleges by bus and train, through snowstorms and cold weather, to preach a new gospel of local, national, and international American student responsibility.

The immediate task was to persuade as many institutions as possible to send delegates to a constitutional convention in Madison, Wisconsin, in the summer of 1947. A meeting had taken place in Chicago over the 1946 Christmas holidays to discuss the proposed organization and the concerns and attitudes of student bodies and administrations. Most of the attendees were enthusiastic; a few were fearful of joining any group that might possibly have any connection with Communists; some were just wary; some opposed involvement in any activity that lay beyond campus control.

One episode bears retelling. The attitude of paternalism toward students was exemplified by the reaction of Mildred McAfee Horton, president of Wellesley College. The Wellesley delegate to the New England regional meetings informed me that Dr. Horton would not sanction spending student council funds to send a representative to the constitutional convention because the organization, yet unborn, was an unknown entity. I wrote a stinging letter suggesting that Wellesley's justified pride in its international connections and position (its students had included Madame Chiang Kai-Shek and Mrs. Pandit, sister of Jawaharlal Nehru) carried obligations and responsibilities. Of course, the incipient organization could not be known, but only active participation in its development would assure that it might be worthy of commitment. The upshot was positive; the college sent delegates. However, this was the beginning of the Cold War era, and such attitudes of suspicion reflected concern about the political direction of both the nascent student association and the international body that had spawned it.

The challenge of communicating a new idea

The task of developing a rhetoric to stimulate a sense of responsible citizenship on an international scale, of kindling imaginations to envision wider possibilities, and of doing the actual work of creating an American student association had an enormous impact on my life then and my future career in college teaching. It was an apprenticeship in communication to ensure that what a wide variety of students heard had some relationship to what I was trying to say. And, of course, the politics, both seen and not seen but felt, were of the greatest importance.

Outstanding in my memory and, for me, symbolic of the profound complexities of our task in the United States of the 1940s was the all-night session of the Constitutional Committee, made up of the regional chairmen and the national officers of the Coordinating Committee, at which we hammered out the plank on civil rights. My two constituencies, the New England Region, of which I was chair, and Smith College, for which I was a delegate, stood for the most liberal, open, all-encompassing statement that it was possible to create. Not all the southern regions and delegates shared this approach, however.

In the wee hours of the morning, Gillis Long, Student Council president at Louisiana State University, described the months it had taken him to find a venue in the state where Negro and white students from the different institutions could meet together.[3] He said that, when the delegates finally gathered in the basement of the First Presbyterian Church in Baton Rouge, the white students were overwhelmed by the intelligence, wit, and power of the Negro delegates. They had never before encountered black people of their own intellectual and educational level. With tears in his eyes, he begged us to write a civil rights plank sufficiently elastic to permit Southern white students to remain in the organization so that they could, and would, continue to experience these encounters. When I returned to Smith College to report to the student body, there was a profound silence as I told this story.[4]

Soon after the Madison Convention, my official association with NSA ended. I continue to feel that participating in this enterprise from its beginnings was a rare privilege indeed.

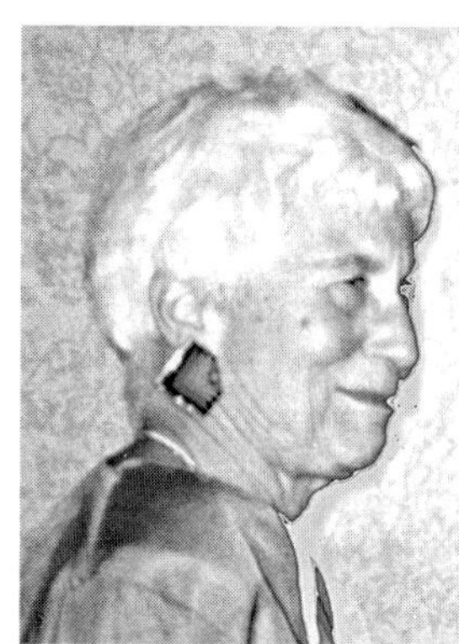

Miriam Haskell Berlin has been an assistant professor at Wellesley College, a lecturer at Harvard University, and a lecturer in the National Faculty Teaching Institutes. She holds a B.A. from Smith College and an M.A. and Ph.D. from Radcliffe College/Harvard University.

(See p. 13 for an extended biography.)

END NOTES

[1] See pp. 50, 56 for background on the ISS.
[2] See p. 73 for background on the U.S. delegation to the World Student Congress.
[3] See the story of the subsequently failed affiliation campaign at LSU on p. 454.
[4] See pp. 146, 1113. See also n. 22, p. 415.

PICTURE CREDITS: *Then:* 1946 Chicago Student Conference (A.L. Cohen, Chicago). *Now:* 1997, Madison, WI (*Both, Schwartz*).

World Student Congress Inspires Launch of U.S. Student Organization

DELEGATES RETURNING FROM PRAGUE BECAME EVANGELISTS. Upon her return, Mimi Haskell toured New England colleges, reporting on the World Student Congress and spreading the word about the upcoming Chicago Student Conference. *The Middlebury Campus* (11/29/46) reports on her forthcoming visit and on the outcome (12/5/46). Smith College's *SCAN* (1/14/47) devoted half its front page to reports by Allison Butler, Natalie Zemon, and Haskell about the Chicago Conference (see Section 3). Foreshadowing the recurring pressures on the new organization to resist Communist influence and debate over the influence of Catholic Colleges entering the new organization, controversy over the selection of delegates to Chicago had already broken out at Smith College and was reported in the *Wellesley College News* (1/23/47).

MIDDLEBURY CAMPUS

VOL. XLIII — MIDDLEBURY CAMPUS, MIDDLEBURY, VT., NOVEMBER 29, 1946 — NO. 27

Smith Speaker to Explain Plan of U.S. Student Union

M. Haskell to Ask Midd's Affiliation With Nat'l Group

Local Fraternity Will Nationalize; To Become ATO

Paul Robeson, Renowned Bass-Baritone, To Sing Dec. 4 At High School Gym

Final Rushing Plans Revised For Neutrals

Versatile Actor To Appear Here For First Time

Member of P.B.K., Holds Degrees Of 5 Colleges

CAMPUS, MIDDLEBURY, VT., DECEMBER 5, 1946

Miriam Haskell Of Smith College Discusses I.S.U.

SMITH COLLEGE SCAN ASSOCIATED NEWS

Smith Delegates And Observer Discuss National Student Conference In Chicago

The Chicago Student Conference of December 28-30, at which Smith was represented by Allison Butler, 1947, and Miriam Haskell, 1948, has resolved to establish a National Student Organization. A National Continuations Committee has been set up to draft a tentative constitution and to call a constitutional convention later this year. Miriam Haskell was elected chairman of the Massachusetts regional committee and is therefore a member of its executive committee.

Wellesley College News

NSO Causes Controversy at Smith Over AYD and Catholic Groups

Nomination of Delegate Arouses Fear of Control By Communists And Student Religious Organizations

The recent election of delegates to the National Student Organization Conference in Chicago at Smith College caused a campus-wide controversy over the place of the American Youth for Democracy and Catholic student groups on campus. Delegates to the Conference believe this is indicative of the type of problems student organizations will have to ... fortunate that some members of the college saw fit to introduce issues into this election in a way not basically in accord with democratic ideals," the editorial stated.

Protests Many

Letters stating all sides of the issue came in, many from people not connected with either group but protesting the "nice propaganda writing" used by these

11/29/46

12/5/46

1/14/47

1/23/47

Prepares the Way for U.S. Cooperation with the IUS

3. Russell Austin: U.S. Delegation Leader

Editor's note: Russell Austin is remembered as a reserved and confident presence who left little in the way of a written record about himself. However, he played a key role in the formative year of NSA's history, heading the U.S. delegation to the World Student Congress and organizing NSA's Constitutional Convention.

The Chicago Maroon, October 11, 1946

Letter from Prague

By Russell Austin

The opening session of the congress was held on August 18 with several members of the Czech government present, including Prime Minister Gottwald. The meetings were held in the Masaryk hostel, a huge building, one of 25 in Prague owned and operated by the Czech Students' Union.

The U.S. delegation did a very good job at this congress. Almost every report and clause in the constitution has our mark on it. Our delegation was about the best prepared of all that came.

There was no lack of democracy and no insidious influences from the left. We were all interested in how the Russian delegation would behave. In general it was very quiet. It did not vote as a block. The delegates spoke rarely—and only when a major point was in question.

My impression was that they acted in a very democratic manner. The meetings were rather slow because everything had to be translated into four languages.

Lending importance to U.S. student life

Our delegation is very interested in forming a national students' organization in the U.S., since seeing those in Europe, and the power and prestige they possess and the importance they give to the student in the life of his country.

We hope to hold a preparatory conference during Christmas vacation this year at the University of Chicago if possible. We hope to draw about 300 representatives from such groups as the AYD, Youthbuilders, student councils, student newspapers.

As for social life, a ball was held for us the first evening. There was also a reception at the Ministry of Foreign Affairs. Everyone met Mr. Gottwald and stood around eating and chatting. There were receptions by the French and Polish embassies—the usual stuff. Lots of wine, brandy and food. I tried the vodka, Russian style, drinking no water. It didn't work well.

Be seeing you. . . .

The Chicago Maroon, Friday, Nov. 1, 1946

Russ Austin Back from Prague Meet

Tells of Experiences as U.S. Delegate to International Student Conference

By Barbara Kohn

"Three hundred and fifty delegates from youth organizations of 40 countries founded the International Union of Students at the World Student Congress held in Prague, Czechoslovakia, August 17, August 31," reports Russ Austin, U. of C. delegate to the World

The Chicago Maroon

Austin Heads US Prague Group

INFLATIONARY TREND IN FOOD PRICES REPORTED BY OFFICIALS

American Delegation Leaves for London; Complete Report on Conference Activities

"Set It in Troy" Opens Wednesday At Reynolds Club

London-bound . . .

Russ Austin

Friday, August 6, 1946

By Dick Pelz

Russell Austin, University of Chicago delegate to the International Student Conference in Prague, has been elected chairman of the 25-man American delegation and is now en route to London, according to reports received this week by Inter-Org.

The Conference, scheduled for August 17th to August 31st, was planned during a meeting in Prague last November of 500 students representing 51 nations.

Austin, chairman of the campus chapter of the American Veterans Committee and former combat infantryman in Italy, was elected a member of the American delegation by a campus-wide vote last May. Part of his expenses have been contributed by Inter-Org. from the proceeds of a Tag Day held at the time of the voting; an equal portion was contributed by the University, and it is hoped that all or most of the remainder will be raised at a C-Dance on August 17 to be sponsored by Interfraternity Council.[1]

Student Congress. Austin, a member of AVC who was elected delegate by the student body last spring, has just returned to the campus from the Congress and from an extensive tour of Europe.

"The most important tangible results of the Congress are the adoption of a program and a constitution for IUS," Austin explained. "The intangible results are harder to state," he added, "but they are no less real. They include the spirit of friendliness and understanding that developed at the Congress between delegates from different countries."

Three-point IUS program

The program of the IUS consists of three points: the elimination of all remnants of fascism in schools, textbooks, etc.: relief and rehabilitation for students in war-torn countries to bring about full reconstruction of student life, and the exchange between countries of students, professors, books, or anything that will lead to a broader knowledge and understanding of students' cultural heritage. A resolution was passed urging the affiliation in a consultative status of IUS with the United Nations Education, Science, and Cultural Organization. Action upon this resolution is awaited by UNESCO.

The constitution provides for the establishment of an executive committee, each member of which is to represent a different country, and for a council to meet twice yearly. The council, on which all countries have representatives according to size, will carry on the business of IUS between meetings of the Congress. The Congress is scheduled to meet every three years in Prague. Joseph Grohman of Czechoslovakia was elected president, and Thomas Madden of England, secretary of IUS. The constitution states as IUS's aim the attainment of greater educational opportunities for a greater number of people in all countries.

IUS will strengthen cooperation

"IUS is a non-political organization," explained Austin, "but it may indirectly affect the political developments by strengthening understanding and cooperation between peoples of different countries. The agenda was prepared by the International Preparatory committee which met in November 1945 in Paris to prepare for the World Student Congress. It was adopted by the Congress with a few amendments," he added.

"Language was a major problem. Everything said had to be translated into five languages, and this slowed up the pace of the Congress considerably."

When asked what reception the delegates received in Prague. Austin, tall, self-confident, matter-of-fact, became very enthusiastic. "We received a wonderful reception," he explained. "The Czech government welcomed us and threw parties for us, and the Czech Student Union, to which all Czech student organizations are affiliated, housed us in one of their hostels where the meetings were held and where the delegates ate."

Austin traveled throughout Europe

On his way to Prague, Austin visited London and Paris. After the completion of the Congress, he traveled through Hungary, visited Budapest, and spent some time in Yugoslavia. Here he and several of the delegates who had traveled to Yugoslavia with him had the opportunity to work on the "youth railway."

"I will explain what the 'Youth railway' is. Yugoslavia has been greatly devasted by war. Members of the Yugoslav youth movement volunteered to construct a 50-mile stretch of railway connecting an undeveloped part of the country, which is rich in coal, with the outside world. They do not get paid for their work. They do common labor. And we worked with them for three days," Austin added.

After their return from the Congress, the U.S. delegation unanimously voted to issue a call to all student organizations in the United States to send delegates to a meeting to lay plans for the formation of a national U.S. student organization. A three-day meeting is being planned during the Christmas vacations at which 300 delegates are expected.[2]

END NOTES

[1] The September 23, 1946, issue of *The Chicago Maroon* reported: "Austin, chairman of the campus AVC and former combat infantry man in Italy, was elected a member of the American delegation by the campus last May. At that time the Inter-Organizational Council sponsored the student election of candidates to the convention. Austin was supported by AVC, the Negro Student Club, Anti-Discrimination Club, World Federalists and other liberal clubs on campus, during the election. Austin's expenses were raised by the I-O Council during a tag day and an All Campus dance, plus an equal amount given by the University."

[2] *Editor's note:* As it developed, 672 delegates from over three hundred colleges attended. Another commentary about Austin written about him in the August 1947 issue of Isaac Don Levine's *Plain Talk* about the up-coming constitutional convention, states:

> Most prominent among the leaders of the left-wing forces is Russell Austin, vice-president of the NSO National Continuations Committee, who opposed the resolution against communism in the Chicago American Veterans Committee. Thirty-three years old, he is still active in student affairs, despite the fact that many delegates will have only half his years. Austin hides a definite political viewpoint behind ostentatious sincerity and impartiality; the target of concerted right wing and liberal attacks, he is expected to decline any nomination in favor of someone of his own choice.

PICTURE CREDITS: *Then:* 1946 (*Chicago Maroon*).

RUSSELL AUSTIN

Russell Austin left little behind from which we can create a narrative of his life preceding and following his leadership of the U.S. delegation to the World Student Congress in 1946. This brief outline is based on inquiries conducted by Royal Voegeli. Austin was born on February 18, 1913, in Wisconsin. He graduated from Wayland Academy, Beaver Dam, Wisconsin, 1931.

He attended the University of Chicago from 1938 to June 1942, and from fall 1946 until summer 1947. He served as a combat infantryman with the U.S. Army in Italy in World War II.

His mother, Elsa Morse, resided in Milwaukee, Wisconsin, in 1947. In August 1941, he changed his name from Russell Austin Morse to Russell Austin. Wayland Academy records show him as deceased, but have no date of death.

4. Jimmy Wallace and Douglass Cater: From Prague to Lifetimes of Leadership

Jimmy Wallace (University of North Carolina) and Douglass Cater (Harvard University) were both young men of the South, both born in 1923. They came together on the U.S. delegation to the World Student Congress in August of 1946, helped organize and attended the Chicago Student Conference that December, collaborated in the experience, and, upon their return, applied their positive outlook and gifts of leadership and rhetoric to separate and distinctive lifetime careers.

When they returned from Prague, each reported to his campus on the experience (see "Prague Delegation," p. 94. See also Cater, "Collapse of Youth's One World," p. 535, and Wallace, "Letter to the President," p. 105). It was a time when hopes for peace following World War II were being threatened by the incipient Cold War. But as with many college students at the time, they would not be discouraged.

In the Harvard Crimson *on 10/21/46, Cater wrote:*

> All over Europe, in the embassies, in the military posts and in the news bureaus, there are Americans who have given up any hope of peace.
>
> But the students who were at Prague have not resigned themselves so easily. Americans, British, Russians, and Yugoslavs alike pledged support to the United Nations. For the one delegation that walked out [the Dutch] there were thirty-seven who remained, actively working to further the cause of peace.

In the Daily Tar Heel, *the same week (also on 10/21/46), Wallace wrote:*

> After looking at all the conflicts in the world, dragging them out into the light of day where they appear with such clarity that they threaten to overwhelm us, what conclusions can be drawn?
>
> Probably it would be more logical to give up in despair. But in the matter of international relations, logic is not given a place of prominence. All is illogical; so peacemakers continue their weary task. I would like to see a world government....The conflicting nationalisms must permit themselves to be somewhat absorbed and subordinated.

Cater pursued a career as a journalist, as a staff member with the Johnson administration, and, from 1970, as an educator, until his retirement as president of Washington College. Cater died in 1995 at age seventy-two.

Jimmy Wallace served on various Chapel Hill, North Carolina, town committees, eventually becoming mayor. He died in 1991 at age sixty-eight.

Portions of eulogies for Cater and Wallace, which tell something of their lives and the difference they made in society, follow.

Jimmy Wallace was informed by his determination to guide change within constructive channels

Jimmy Wallace entered the University of North Carolina in the fall of 1940, and so began a fifty-one-year-long love affair. For all but three of those fifty-one years, Jimmy was also a resident of the town of Chapel Hill, and he nurtured a lasting affection for this community as it grew from a quiet village into a bustling little city.

Jimmy served the university directly as an undergraduate active in the campus affairs of his day, as director of Graham Memorial during his graduate student period, and in many informal ways in after years. The Town claimed his services for nearly twenty years as a member of the Planning Board, member of the Board of Alderman and the Town Council, and mayor.

Jimmy's contributions were honored by the University with its Distinguished Alumnus Award in 1972 and by the community with the Chamber of Commerce's Town and Gown Award in 1983.

Jimmy's views of both Town and University were informed by his extraordinary foresight—his capacity to comprehend the long-range tendency of things—and by his determination to guide change within constructive channels. He understood the interdependency of University and Town, and he encouraged cooperation between them.

Jimmy knew the futility of trying by direct or indirect means to freeze either the university or the town in some fancied (and often romantically misperceived) state and keep it there, unchanging, forever. To him, the goal was to plan for and accommodate growth constructively, minimizing the loss of some of those amenities associated with smallness.

Above left: Jimmy Wallace and UNC leaders in early 1952 (l. to r. Jane Jenkins, Wallace, Ann Mackie, Cam Studs, Dick Murphy). Right: Jimmy Wallace remained rooted in Chapel Hill, becoming its mayor, and active in civic affairs for his lifetime.

For example, Jimmy's efforts ensured that when the community water system was sold by the university in the 1970s, its control remained chiefly in hands responsive to the needs of Chapel Hill and the university. A few years later, in 1987, when some in the community stridently objected to the early version of the university's land use plan, Jimmy took the lead, with Chancellor Christopher C. Fordham III, in creating a temporary joint Town-University Committee that proposed a set of accommodations that both town and university could accept.

In many such instances with which Jimmy had no publicly known connection, he was able to play an ameliorating role because he was trusted by university and town leaders alike. And he played that role not out of concern for personal credit, or desire to impose his way and will on others, but because he understood so well and cared so deeply about his University and his Town.

—*Adapted from a memorial delivered in Gerrard Hall by John A. Sanders on 12/8/91*

Doug Cater had the enormous patience it takes to achieve anything important in a democracy

Silas Douglass Cater, Jr., was born on August 24, 1923, in Montgomery, Alabama, which he readily identified as the birthplace of the Confederacy. His father, a lawyer, served as a state senator and as the Montgomery City Clerk. Doug grew up with a Southerner's love for politics, but he never crossed the line to elective office. He said the *genus politicus* was an endangered species.

When he was eleven, rheumatic fever laid him on his back for a year. At Harvard, he was the editorial chairman of the daily *Crimson,* a member of the Signet, and the Class Orator. During World War II, Doug worked for the OSS as a Russian specialist; he said afterwards he found the work so dull that he decided always to be a generalist.

Starting in 1950, Doug spent fourteen years reporting, chiefly inside the Beltway, as the Washington editor and later the national editor for *The Reporter.* He wrote a book, *The Fourth Branch of Government,* criticizing Washington's daily correspondents. In the time of Senator Joseph McCarthy, Doug dared to point out that the elusive journalistic goal of objective reporting resulted in printing what the paranoid senator said simply because he had said it—even if it was false. The press, Doug wrote, needed to do better.

In spring of 1964, Lyndon Johnson made him a Special Assistant to the President. At first, Doug floated with no fixed assignment, but he soon was influencing policy in the areas that mattered most to him—education, health care, and broadcasting. He liked to say he became the "midwife" of the Public Broadcasting System. On Election Day, 1964, he wrote a one-page memo that is credited with persuading Johnson that he wanted to become "The Education President." Playing a part in erecting the Great Society, Doug would smile and call himself a "back room presidential deputy," and he relished the role.

In 1968, after LBJ and he left the White House, Doug wrote a political novel called *Dana: The Irrelevant Man* and tried to help make a successful presidential candidate out of Hubert Humphrey. When that campaign failed, Doug was appointed Regents Professor at the University of California. In 1970 he became a senior fellow and trustee of the Aspen Institute for Humanistic Studies and created a communications program for the institute. In time he convinced Robert O. Anderson, the oil man and chairman of the Aspen Institute, to buy the *Observer,* England's oldest newspaper, out from under Rupert Murdoch; and Doug and Libby, his wife, spent three delightful years in London—Doug as vice chairman of the newspaper.

Finally, Doug served eight years as president of Washington College in Chestertown on the Eastern Shore of Maryland. He set out to change things. One of his prime targets was to encourage students to develop and debate their own ideas and values as they mature toward citizenship. He urged them to "cultivate thinking as something more than a spectator sport."

Doug wrote five books on politics, the press, and education, He received seven honorary degrees and both a Guggenheim and an Eisenhower Fellowship. He taught at Princeton, Wesleyan, the University of California, and Stanford, and he was a visiting fellow at the Brookings Institution and the first President's Scholar at the University of Alabama.

Doug was helped always by Libby's charm and vitality. She was welcoming, strong, and bright. Libby was also a native of Alabama; they had met in Washington when she was the chief assistant to the congressman from Birmingham. They were married for forty-five years and had two sons and two daughters.

Although he could be blunt and outspoken, Doug worked from within the Establishment; he was not a revolutionary. He was known for his impatience, but he had the enormous patience that it takes to achieve anything important in a democracy.

—*Adapted from a Century Association memorial by J. Robert Moskin on 2/9/98*

Above left: Douglass Cater with a U.S. embassy official in Prague, 1946. Right: Special Assistant to the President, with President Lyndon B. Johnson in 1967. Cater later became President of Washington College in Maryland.

PICTURE CREDITS: Wallace and group, 1952, University of North Carolina (*Murphy*); at piano, c. 1970s (?) (*Class of 1944 Memorial Services Program*). Cater, 1946, and with President Johnson, 1967 (*Yoichi Okamoto, courtesy Libby Cater Hallaby*).

A PRAGUE DELEGATION JOURNAL: COLLEGE PRESS REPORTS

We met on a sweltering day in early July . . . detailed proposals were worked out. One night, over several glasses of very good vodka . . . the opposition was scuttled.

Editor's note: These selections are based largely on excerpts prepared and organized by Pat Wohlgemuth Blair (see p. 538). Unless otherwise noted, photographs are from collections furnished by Libby Cater Halaby and Jewel Lubin Bellush. For additional first-hand Prague delegation reports see also Ellis and Roberts, p. 106, Kirschner, p. 76, Bellush, p. 73, Cater, p. 535, McLaughlin, p. 84.

PREPARATIONS IN NEW YORK CITY

Take Food to Student Conference

STUDENT REPRESENTATIVES of U. S. colleges and national groups who leave today on S.S. Brazil to attend international student conference in Prague. (L. to r.) Jewel Lubin, 9324 Av. B, Brooklyn, executive secretary of delegation; Russell Austin, U. of Chicago, delegation chairman; Enid Kass, 1543 Jessup Av., The Bronx, Hunter College, and Charles Proctor, St. Louis, vice chairman, representing Fisk College. Delegates will present CARE food remittances to hosts, Union of Czechoslovak Students.

CITY GREETS DELEGATES TO WORLD STUDENT CONCLAVE

Albert Houghton (right), University of Wisconsin, accepts scroll from William Mishkin, vice-chairman of N. Y. Youth Council, on behalf of U. S. delegation to the International Student Conference in Prague, August 13-31. Hotel Diplomat reception was planned by American Preparatory Committee to give group its instructions. Others are, l. to r.: Walter Wallace, Youth Builders; Charles Proctor, Fisk University; Alice Horton, chairman of APC, and Jewell Lubin, delegation's executive secretary.

(Mirror Photo)

From top: *New York Post* 7/1/46, *New York Daily Mirror* 7/10//46

The preliminaries

***Douglass Cater* (Harvard University)**

University students will have a chance to air their views on the much discussed International Union of Students Thursday evening at 7:30 o'clock in Phillips Brooks House.

Under the direction of the Harvard Liberal Union, the discussion has been planned with the approval of the Student Council, and is open to all members of the University....

Results of the discussion will be sent to S. Douglass Cater, Jr., '46, American Delegation representative from the University and New England, who is now on his way to Prague for the conference. Cater sent the policy and committee reports to [Edric A.] Weld ['46] with the request that the recommendations and expressions of opinion representative of the Harvard student body be determined and relayed to him (*"Students to Meet Thursday to Debate Prague Proposals," Harvard Crimson,* July 30, 1946, p. 1).

***Russell Austin* (University of Chicago)**

Russell Austin, University of Chicago delegate to the International Student Conference in Prague, [is] chairman of the campus chapter of the American Veterans Committee and former combat infantryman in Italy. [He] was elected a member of the American delegation by a campus-wide vote last May. Part of his expenses have been contributed by Inter-Prog. from the proceeds of a Tag Day held at the time of the voting; an equal portion was contributed by the University, and it is hoped that all or most of the remainder will be raised at a C-dance on August 17 to be sponsored by Inter-Fraternity Council (*"Austin Heads US Prague Group"* by Dick Pelz, *Chicago Maroon,* August 2, 1946, p. 1).

***Enid Kass* (Hunter College)**

Enid Kass, lower junior English major, was elected Hunter representative to the London and Prague Youth conference, to be held this summer. As a result of the May 8 re-election, Miss Kass received 1,045 votes; her opponent, Sylvia Kimmelman, received 600 votes; and three votes were invalid, making a total of 1,648 votes cast. $1,000 will be needed to finance both trips. Only $200 has been raised so far... (*"Choose Enid Kass to Attend European Youth Conference," Hunter Bulletin,* May 14, 1946).

***Frank K. Mayers* (University of Pennsylvania)**

Eleven nominations for a delegate to the World Student conference in Prague, Czechoslovakia have been filed at the Office of Student Affairs. The nominees will be voted on by the entire University student body next Monday, June 10...(June 5, 1946). Frank K. Mayers, Wharton '47, was elected as the University's representative to the forthcoming Prague meeting by a plurality of 540 votes. A total of 1,846 votes were cast in Monday's election....The elected representative has been active in undergraduate campus activities, which include beside being his fraternity president (Phi Gamma Delta), participation in Mask and Wig, member of the Sphinx Senior Society, a Phi Kappa Beta and a member of the Christian Association (*"Mayers is Elected Prague Delegate," The Pennsylvanian,* June 12, 1946, p. 1)

Mission to Prague

The task to be faced at Prague is immense, and it will require the energies and abilities of representatives who are well-schooled, deeply interested and thoroughly able in the fields of current affairs and student welfare. The University is not allocating $700 to send someone on a joyride to Europe for his summer vacation. Pennsylvania's representative will have to show his mettle and abilities when working in close cooperation with some of the outstanding student leaders in the world—men and women who have more on the ball than the ability to win a popularity contest.

—Editorial in *The Pennsylvanian*,
University of Pennsylvania,
June 5, 1946, p. 2

***Joe Malik* (University of Texas)**

The University Students' Association has selected Joe Malik, graduate student in education and a member of the University staff, as a delegate to the conference.... Approximately $850 is needed to cover the delegate's expenses.... So far, only $210 [eventually $750] in donations...has been received.... [In the end], Joe put up his own money and started by automobile ... for New York. (*"Malik to be Delegate to Prague,"* by Faye Loyd, *Daily Texan,* June 11, 1946, and, *"Short of Funds, Joe Malik Begins Trip to Prague,"* by Laurie Belzung, *Daily Texan,* June 14 1946).

***Jimmy Wallace* (University of North Carolina)**

Jimmy Wallace will represent the University of North Carolina at the International Student conference this August. The UNC Preparatory Committee, representing the overwhelming majority of student organizations here, elected him after a two and a half hour session in which three candidates were thoroughly questioned and their qualifications discussed (*"Jimmy Wallace Chosen Prague Delegate,"* by Dick Koral, *Daily Tar Heel,* May 31, 1946, p. 1).

Preparations and Briefings

Douglass Cater

Once [the delegates] assembled, the American Preparatory Commission ... was formally dissolved. We were left to work out our own programs....

[We met] on a sweltering day in early July ... in New York City ... one short week before sailing to work out a program representative of American student opinion. A week of bombastic sessions lasting late into the nights proved that this was no easy assignment.

I had felt some misgivings beforehand that this delegation might be stacked with one political faction or another. It was relieving to find that there was a great diversity of opinion among us, but no hard division into cliques. In everlasting tribute to our sanctity, not even the Hearst newspapers found a use to smear on the old familiar label. In fact, news coverage of the New York sessions was thorough and accurate.

We did not shy away from an attempt to define students' interest in the world outside the ivory tower. In fact, the resolutions we adopted were quite prominent in Prague, whole sections being incorporated into the final report of the Congress. But we gave emphasis ... to the proposed International Union of Students that we wished to establish. Detailed proposals were worked out ... during those wearisome 12-hour sessions (*"New York Session of Delegation to Prague,"* by Douglass Cater, *Harvard Crimson,* October 7, 1946. First of a series of reports to the *Crimson* on the Prague Conference).

COLLEGES SELECT DELEGATES, RECEIVE REPORTS ON OUTCOMES

Each of the ten colleges represented on the 25 member delegation held campus debates and selected their delegates by student government votes or referendums. The delegates returned and prepared series reports published in the college press and discussed in campus forums. (*Hunter Bulletin* 5/14/46, 10/15/46, *Harvard Crimson* 7/30/46, 10/7/46, *Texan* 6/11/46, 9/24/46, *Pennsylvanian* 5/29/46, 11/8/46)

HUNTER BULLETIN Tuesday, October 15, 1946

Enid Kass Tells of Voyage To Europe on "S.S. Brazil"

by Enid Kass

"A dream come true?" It was a dream with a purpose and a beautiful goal. What young person hasn't hankered to get to a new country, meet other young people who speak a different language and do things in a different way—and yet have the most basic problems and ideals in common.

Last summer this gal's dream got elected to reality, representing Hunter College at international conferences held at Cambridge, England and at Prague, Czechoslovakia.

With two suitcases of soap, Chiclets, Kleenex, and much advice, I boarded the "SS Brazil," sailing July 16. There were eighteen girls crowded into a state room built originally for two.

Every day all the fellows and girls ...

...TER BULLETIN

...ORK, N. Y., TUESDAY, MAY 14, 1946

Choose Enid Kass to Attend European Youth Conference

ENID KASS

The Harv...

VOL. CXVI No. 37.

Students to Meet Thursday To Debate Prague Proposals

Revival of O.P.A. Inspires Merchants to "Wait and See"

As OPA officials swing back into action, preparing revised price lists, merchants in the Square hold tight on their bulging price lines, waiting ...

Liberal Union Holds Session At PBH to Learn College Opinion Toward IUS Policies

University students will have a chance to air their views on the much discussed International Union of Students ...

New York Session of Delegation to Prague Created Orderly Program

Last May, after a College-wide referendum, a committee of the Student Council voted to send Douglass Cater '46, then Editorial Chairman of the CRIMSON, as the Harvard (and New England) delegate to an international conference of students to be held in Prague, Czechoslovakia. Cater returned to Cambridge last week and has prepared a report to the student body on the results of the Conference. This is the first section of that report.

By Douglass Cater

On a sweltering day in early July, 25 students from colleges all over the country met in New York City. As the American delegation to the International Students Congress taking place in Prague during the latter part of August, this group had allotted itself one short week before sailing to work out a program

THE DAILY TEXAN

US Delegates to International Concave Plan for National Union, Reports Malik

Editor's Note: The following is the last of a series concerning preparation, the first meeting, and future plans of the World Student Congress that met in Prague, Czechoslovakia, August 17-31.

By LAURIE BELZUNG

With a successful conclusion to organization of the world's first International Student Union, the twenty-five United States delegates to the Prague congress have returned with plans to organize a national representation for the students at home.

The University's delegate, Joe Malik, a graduate student in education and a member of the fac-

Official Notices

Scholarships Open To Latin-Americans

October 4 Last Chance For Blanket Tax Photos

As Top Notch Minds Gathered—

Students World-Over Organize

By LAURIE BELZUNG

NEW WIGGERS SHOW TO OPEN NOV. 22

The Pennsylvanian

COGNOSCERE PENNSYLVANIAM EST AMARE PENNSYLVANIAM

Students Will Elect Delegates To Prague International Conference

Undergraduate or graduate students who wish to represent the University in the Interna- ... graduate Council and Women's Student Government Associa- ...

THE DAILY PENNSYLVANIAN

Mayers Concludes Report; U. S. Group Organizes

Conclusions

The Prague Congress set out to do two things—to establish a world students organization and formulate a policy for it to follow. These aims were accomplished with remarkable efficiency. The International Union of Students is now a reality. However, the International Union of Students is not an end in itself. It is only hoped that through this means, progress can be made toward the ultimate goal of international understanding and cooperation. The success of the International Union of Students, depends on the support which it receives from national student groups. It can do nothing in itself. Its func-

First Impressions

Douglass Cater

Half the delegates left New York on July 16 aboard the *SS Brazil*, while the rest followed ten days later on the George Washington.... As we neared the continent of Europe, a certain tension settled over us all. We felt keenly the gulf... between American and European students and wondered rather fearfully whether it could ever be bridged.

The American delegation was first to arrive in Prague. For more than a week we had the indescribable thrill of watching more than 300 delegates from 38 countries gather at the Congress; of awakening one morning to find Moslems bowed down toward Mecca on the lawn outside; of brushing past kilted Scots in the packed dining hall; of looking on while Yugoslavs chanted defiant partisan songs and wound slowly about in their lock-step snake dance....

The irrepressible optimism of European students came as a surprise to most of the Americans.... Certainly, we had not hoped for such boundless energy from Joseph Roger, [who had been with] the French underground....Today, still carrying [a Nazi] bullet somewhere in his head, he is back at the Sorbonne, leading the French student movement.... One did not have to look far to find the pale, undernourished look of an ex-occupant of the German concentration camp. Two Czech students bore the unmistakable hack of the tubercular victim.... But little mention was made of past suffering....There seemed to be an almost fanatical determination that [the Congress] should not fail.

...It is difficult to comprehend the immensity of the language bamier until you butt your head against it.... [and encounter] the irritating tedium of endless translations....All the spontaneous speeches from the floor—those which had not been pre-translated and mimeographed—had to be repeated in English, French, Russian and Spanish by the student interpreters.... But language difficulties were not the only barriers. Evidence that hate and mistrust were still rampant in a world not yet at peace began to crop up before the Congress began....Two complete delegations of ten each arrived from Italy, both claiming to represent the Italian student body.... Indian students arrived in three separate delegations;... before the second week was over, the Moslems had moved to a corner of the hall and were sitting under the banner of the independent, if not yet existent, state of Pakistan (*"New York Session," Harvard Crimson*, Oct. 7, 1946, and *"Russian, French, Moslem Students," Harvard Crimson*, Oct. 9, 1946, p. 1).

Joe Malik

The American delegation...made short wave broadcasts to the world, held press interviews and traveled around the country.... Malik was very impressed with the number of unusually good minds that were present at the conference. None were prejudiced and all realized that to succeed they had to have the cooperation of all there. Most of the delegates...could speak two or three languages.... (Malik can speak Russian and Czech and has some knowledge of Spanish.) (*"Students World-Over Organize,"* by Laurie Belzung, *Daily Texan*, Sept. 24, 1946, p. 1. Second in a series of three articles based on interviews with Joe Malik).

Russell Austin

As for social life, a ball was held for us [and a reception at the] Ministry of Foreign Affairs.... There were receptions at the French and Polish embassies....The Russian and American delegates threw a party...lots of wine, brandy and food....I tried the vodka Russian style, drinking it with water. It didn't work very well (*"Letter from Prague,"* by Russell Austin, *Chicago Maroon*, Oct. 11, 1946. Last in a series of letters from Russell Austin to the *Maroon*).

AT THE WORLD STUDENT CONGRESS

From top: Delegation's dormitory at Charles University. Joseph Grohman of Czechoslovakia, later elected President of the IUS, addresses the Congress.

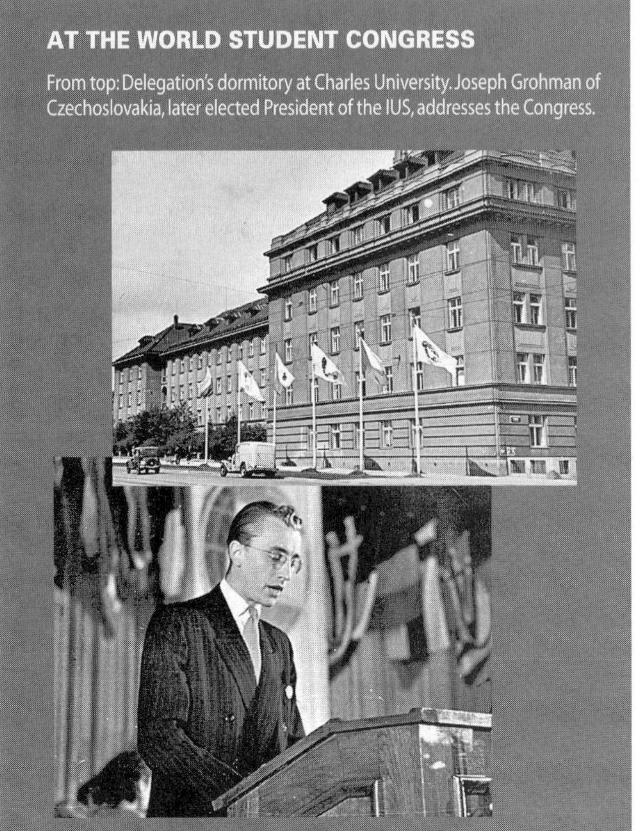

Politics

Russell Austin

There was no lack of democracy and no insidious influences from the left ...The Russian ... delegates spoke rarely and only when a major point was in question. My impression was that they acted in a very democratic manner...("Letter from Prague," by Russell Austin, *Chicago Maroon*, Oct. 11, 1946).

Jimmy Wallace

It is necessary to sketch a little background before one can understand the reasons for some of the actions of delegations.... For example on August 26, just 4 days prior to the end of the congress, a law was passed in Egypt which made it a crime for any student in Egypt to participate in a student congress without first obtaining permission from the government.... The Greek students were not allowed to leave Greece.... Several students who were being hunted as subversive agents by... Franco's Gestapo in Spain turned up in Prague ("Actual Congress Was Divided in Two Well-Defined Parts," *Daily Tar Heel*, Oct. 16, 1946).

Student Issues

Douglass Cater

During two weeks of daily sessions, often stretching into the early morning hours, the delegates ... mapped out a set of resolutions, framed a constitution, and outlined the work for a permanent international student organization. No simple task.... Section by section it was argued out on the floor of the Congress in free debate. This was a tiresome process, but it was deemed necessary in order to secure a democratic constitution which all the delegates could support.

The Constitution, as adopted, provides for a permanent student organization in which democratic and representative student organizations from every nation may participate. Once every three years a Congress will be held which will decide the future policies of the IUS. In the interim, it will be governed by a Council...of delegates from every member country. But the driving force of the organization will be the 17-man executive committee . . . (*"Conscientious Attitude, Tremendous Effort Highlight Work of Delegates,"* by Douglass Cater, *Harvard Crimson,* Oct. 17, 1946, p. 1).

Jimmy Wallace
Many students at the conference were willing to go along with the idea that the IUS should be an autonomous associate member of the [communistic] WFDY, but that it should not be mentioned in the constitution. Since the Communists wanted the item left in the constitution, an issue was thereby made. . . . This argument came very close to wrecking the conference. . . . One night, over several glasses of very good vodka, a certain member of the American delegation and the head of the Russian delegation reached an agreement . . . that we would remove the mention of the WFDY from the Constitution and place it in the bylaws as an appendix to the constitution. . . . It was done. The opposition was scuttled (*"Smear Tactics Were Common at Conference,"* by Jimmy Wallace, *Daily Tar Heel,* Oct. 29, 1946. Part of a series of reports by Wallace on the Prague Conference).

Aftermath

Joe Malik
. . . of the 53 nations represented at Prague, only India and the United States did not have a national student union back home ("U.S. Delegates . . . Plan for National Union," by Laurie Belzung, *Daily Texan,* Oct. 26, 1946. Last of a series based on interviews with Jimmy Wallace).

***Curt Farrar* (Yale University)**
On the day the Students Congress held its final sessions . . . [we] sat in a room in the Masarykova Studenski Kolej in Prague and talked about plans for the Chicago Student Conference (*"What About IUS?"* by John Curtis Farrar, *Student Progressive,* Sept. 1947).

Russell Austin
The U.S. delegation unanimously voted to issue a call to all student organizations in the United States...to send delegates to a meeting to lay plans for the formation of a national US student organization. . . . A three-day meeting is being planned during the Christmas vacations at which 300 delegates are expected. (*"Russ Austin Back from Prague Meet,"* by Barbara Kohn, *Chicago Maroon,* Nov. 8, 1946, p. 1).

Joe Malik
In the meantime . . . a committee chosen from the twenty-five delegates to Prague will be preparing a draft constitution ("US Delegates . . . Plan for National Union," by Laurie Belzung, *Daily Texan,* Oct. 26, 1946).

Frank Mayers
The Prague Congress set out to do two things—to establish a world students organization and formulate a policy for it to follow. These aims were accomplished with remarkable efficiency. . . . It is impossible at this early date to draw definite conclusions regarding the results of the Prague Congress. It can be said that the Congress was carried out in the spirit of true democracy with no attempts at guidance or domination by either Eastern or Western blocks. (*"Mayers Concludes Report; U.S. Group Organizes," The Pennsylvanian,* Nov. 8, 1946, p. 2. Conclusion to a series of reports by Frank Mayers).

U.S. DELEGATES GO TO THE 1946 WORLD STUDENT CONGRESS

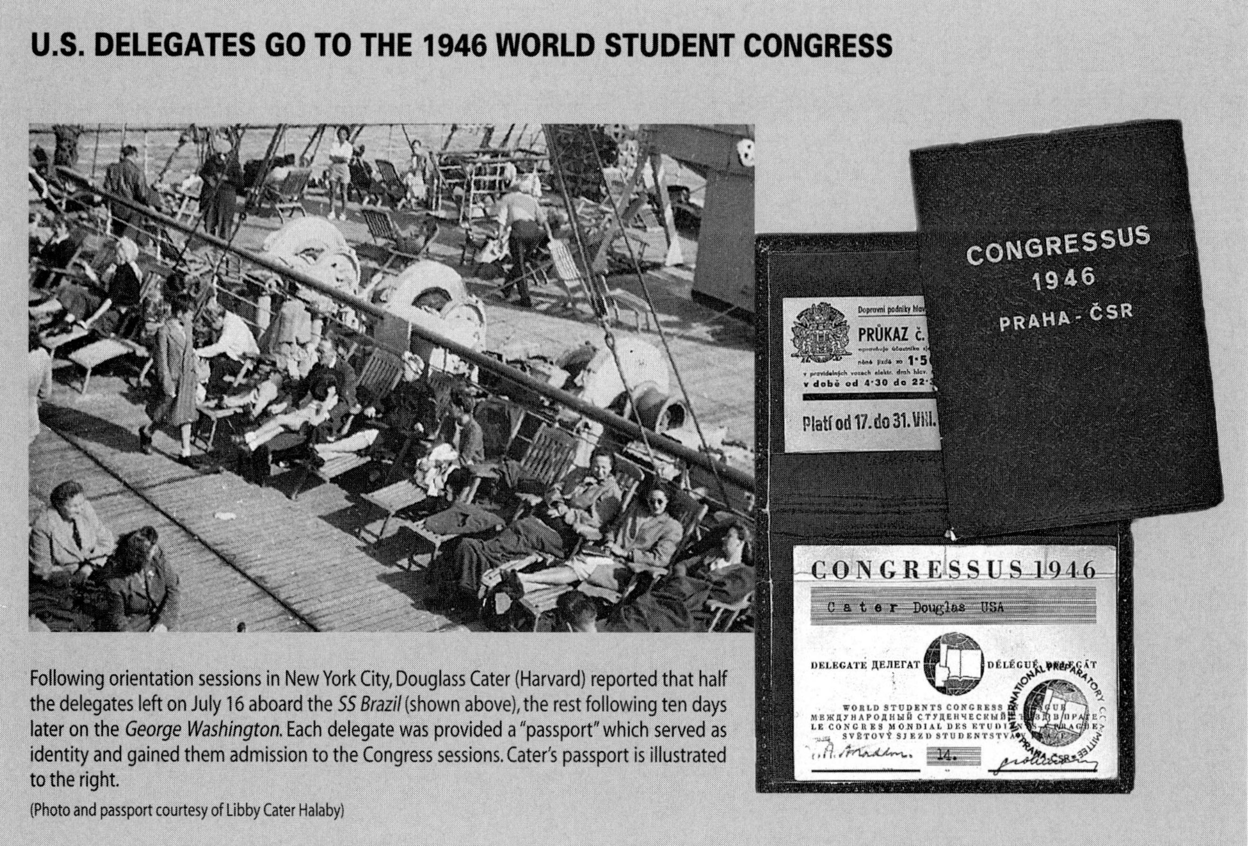

Following orientation sessions in New York City, Douglass Cater (Harvard) reported that half the delegates left on July 16 aboard the *SS Brazil* (shown above), the rest following ten days later on the *George Washington.* Each delegate was provided a "passport" which served as identity and gained them admission to the Congress sessions. Cater's passport is illustrated to the right.

(Photo and passport courtesy of Libby Cater Halaby)

JOE MALIK GETS TO PRAGUE FROM TEXAS ON A SHOESTRING

Hitching a ride to New York . . . and lifting the curfew for a benefit dance

Students Asked to Contribute Funds

Malik to Be Delegate to Prague

Short of Funds, Joe Malik Begins Trip to Prague

THE SUMMER TEXAN

Malik Leaves U.S. For Conference

6 New Appointees Named to Assembly

'No Degree, No Job' Nonsense, He says

American Preparatory Committee

INTERNATIONAL STUDENT CONFERENCE AT PRAGUE

8 WEST 40th STREET, ROOM 912

New York 18, N. Y.

LAckawanna 4-2555

June 7,1946

Mr. Jim Smith
President of the Student Body
University of Texas
Austin, Texas

Dear Mr. Smith:

Received your telegram this morning awarding to Joe Malik the position of delegate from the University of Texas. However, I am sorry to inform you that no observers will be allowed to go to Prague. This ruling was layed down by the International Preparatory Committee due to inadequate housing and food. Over 400 delegates will bethere. The United States has been assigned a delegation of 25. Observers and visitors have been omitted from representation.

STUDENTS' ASSOCIATION
THE UNIVERSITY OF TEXAS
AUSTIN

PRESIDENT'S OFFICE, U of T
Rec'd JUL 10 1946

July 9, 1946

Dr. T. S. Painter, President
The University of Texas
Main Building 101

Subject: Expense Fund Account

Dear Dr. Painter:

Mr. Sparenberg advises me that the account which you authorized is momentarily in somewhat of a predicament. We have authorization to deposit funds in the account but no authorization for making withdrawals.

This oversight is a result of my own ignorance with regard to University financial practices. On the advice of Mr. Sparenberg I am requesting that you authorize a method of withdrawal from the account on the submission of vouchers signed by myself. This procedure will enable us to dispatch funds to our delegate as his need for them arises.

We have now received a total of some $230 for the fund. Of this amount $150 was given directly to our delegate prior to his departure. It was not deposited in the account set up because of the withdrawal difficulties mentioned above.

Thank you for your very kind cooperation in this matter.

Sincerely,

Jim Smith, President
Students' Association
The University of Texas

En Route To Student Meeting In Prague

These American college students, en route to a student meeting in Prague, Czechoslovakia, chat aboard the U. S. Line's liner Brazil at New York City, yesterday, prior to sailing. Left to right, are: Joyce Roberts, Danielson, Conn., representing the student group of the Young Women's Christian Association; Joe Malik, Placedo, Texas, representing Texas University; and Jewel Lubin, New York City, executive secretary of the delegation. The three students, accompanied by seven others, each carried 25 pounds of foodstuffs for Prague collegians. (AP Photo)

ITEMIZED STATEMENT BY JOE MALIK, THE UNIVERSITY OF TEXAS STUDENT REPRESENTATIVE TO THE INTERNATIONAL STUDENT CONFERENCE IN PRAGUE, CZECHOSLOVAKIA.

TO PRAGUE:
Expense to New York, plus passport, visas, and vaccinations.......$ 72.80
Stay in New York (one week) Room and Board.......28.00
Registration at Ne...
Communication for ...
Food sent to Czech...
Boat fare to South...
Train to London...
Stay in London...
Ticket to Paris...
Stay in Paris 6 da...
Ticket Paris to Pr...
Food taken on trip...
Travelers cheques...
TOTAL...

AT PRAGUE:
Stay at Prague (be...
Registration fee a...
Stay in Prague (du...
Ticket to Paris (p...
Stay in Paris...
Cablegrams...
Ticket to St. Nazaire (Port of debark).......16.00
Tips on both boat trips.......38.00
Boat ticket New York.......172.00
Plane home.......79.00
Express.......8.00
Baggage to Paris by plane (excess).......11.00
TOTAL.......$564.00

Total money received by Joe Malik:

Cash.......$150.00
Wire.......500.00
TOTAL.......650.00

Expenses:

To Prague.......$512.55
At Prague and trip home.......564.00
TOTAL.......$1,076.55

Total Expenses.......$1,076.55
Cash received by Joe Malik.......650.00
Balance owed to Joe Malik.......$ 426.55

Joe Malik

MALIK'S JOURNEY *The Daily Texan* followed Malik's travels and his reports on his return from June through November of 1946. Jim Smith, President of the Student Assembly at Texas, set up an Expense Fund Account after receiving confirmation from the American Preparatory Committee on 6/7/46 of Malik's appointment to the delegation—discovering to his chagrin that only deposits to the account had been authorized. Unable to raise the $1,076 needed in advance, Malik picked up "a ride to New York City with Miss Lucille Moseley, an Austin musician who is traveling to New York," *The Texan* reported. After he laid out the $426.55 shortfall himself, the Students Assembly sponsored a benefit dance on his return (also intended to raise funds for their delegation to the Chicago Student Conference). Jim Smith, in a letter to faculty requesting the event be announced in class, wrote that students would be interested to know that "Late permission has been granted by the Dean of Women to all girls attending the dance, allowing them to stay out until 1:45. . . . Girls will be admitted into their residence after the normal time of 12:45 only upon presentation of their ticket stubs from the dance."

(Credits: Correspondence from the Center for American History, University of Texas at Austin. Newsphoto from Jewel Bellush. Source unknown).

The U.S. Government and the Delegation

May 28 "It is our belief that we should take no active part in encouraging this Conference . . ."
Division of International Exchange of Persons, U.S. State Dept

June 6 "We are all agreed that world peace will only result from world cooperation . . ."
Alice M. Horton, Executive Secretary, American Preparatory Committee, International Student Conference at Prague

August 7 "It is particularly gratifying to know that these young people have studied problems facing the post-war world . . ."
Division of Public Liaison, U.S. State Department

United States Student Assembly with the International Student Assembly

26 March, 1946

Dr. Raymond Swimmeret
Chief, Division of Cultural Cooperation
Department of State
Washington, D.C.

. . . An international Student Conference is to be held in Prague this Summer from August 17th to 31st. . . . A preparatory Committee has been organized in this country. . . . Consequently, I as executive secretary of this committee will be making an application to the State Department for passports to Czechoslovakia for about twenty-five students sometime early in June. I wonder if you have any suggestions on steps I should take before making formal applications.

Sincerely yours,
Alice M. Horton
(Note: Similar letters sent April 8, 1946, asking for appointments, to John S. Dickey, Director, Public Affairs, Department of State; Mr. John Studebaker, Commissioner, U.S. Office of Education)

April 11, 1946
Miss Alice Horton
Executive Secretary
American Preparatory Committee
International Student Conference at Prague
8 West 40th Street, Room 912
New York 18, New York

. . . Your communication to Commissioner Studebaker of April 8, and the reply of the Commissioner's secretary to you have just reached my desk.

I shall be happy to meet with you as suggested by the Commissioner's secretary . . .

Very sincerely yours,
George J. Kabat
Acting Chief
European Educational Relations Section
Division of International Educational Relations

FEDERAL SECURITY AGENCY, U.S. OFFICE OF EDUCATION, Washington, D.C.

April 11, 1946

Mr. Harry H. Pierson
Division of Cultural Cooperation
Department of State. . .

. . . I am enclosing a copy of a letter addressed to Dr. Studebaker and a reply by his secretary and my reply to Miss Horton.

As I am leaving for Chicago on the afternoon of the 16th . . . I have written that I would be able to meet with her on Tuesday morning.

I would appreciate it very much if you or a member of your staff could sit in on this conference. . . .

Sincerely yours,
George J. Kabat
Acting Chief, European Educational Relations Section
Division of International Relations

INTERNATIONAL PREPARATORY COMMITTEE, C/O NATIONAL UNION OF CZECHOSLOVAK STUDENTS, PRAHA II

PRAHA, April 16, 1946

To the Ministry of Foreign Affairs
of the United States of America
Washington, D.C.

Dear Sirs,

The Students International Preparatory Committee was set up at the time of the World Student Congress in Prague, in November, 1945...Student representatives of the following countries have worked or are entitled to work on this Committee:

The United States of America, Great Britain, USSR, France, China, South America, Dominions, India, Yugoslavia, Czechoslovakia, Belgium and Denmark

In calling the Congress to Prague this summer, the Preparatory Committee finds itself in serious financial difficulties. . . .

We therefore appeal to you by all means in your power to assist in the birth of the future representative body of the students of the world. We have already received promises of assistance from several European governments.

We are in touch with the following student organizations in your country which will call together a nationally representative delegation:

National Intercollegiate Christian Council, Students YWCA-YMCA
National Students Federation of America, 1410 H Street, Washington, D.C.
American Youth for Organization for a Free World, 144 Bleecker Street, New York 12
American Youth for Democracy, Intercollegiate Division, 150 Nassau Street, New York, N.Y.

If our first request cannot be met, we would ask you to assist these students financially and materially (by the issue of passports, visas, etc.). To be present in full strength at your Congress. . . .

For and on behalf of the IPC.

Thomas A. Madden	John Grohman
Chairman of the 3rd Session	Head of the Secretariat

In reply refer to the IEP

My dear Miss Horton,

. . . Your letter of March 26 to Dr. Zwimmer and April 8, 1946 to Mr. Dickey have been referred to me for reply.

The main problems involved in this undertaking are transportation and passports and I understand from our conversation when you were here that you are working on these matters.

I shall bring your letter to the attention of interested persons in the Department.

Harry H. Pierson
Acting Assistant Chief
Division of International Exchange of Persons

May 4, 1946

Mr. Eugene Anderson
Cultural Division
U.S. Department of State

I am writing Mrs. Shipley [of the Passport Division] informing her that we will be wanting passports for twenty-five student delegates to this conference early in June. The delegates will probably leave early in July. . . .

Sincerely yours,
Alice Horton,
Executive Secretary

OFFICE MEMORANDUM, UNITED STATES GOVERNMENT

To: Harry H. Pierson, IEP Date: May 7, 1946
From: Clifton R. Read, ADENOPATHY

When you have read this note on International Student Conference at Prague, August 17th to 31st. Will you pass it on to Kurt London who will want to keep in touch with it.

[handwritten note on above]

I suggest we do nothing more on this matter at present because we should not be placed in a position of sponsoring an affair which might not be approved by the Passport Division.

—O.C. [O. J. Caldwell]

May 28, 1946

To: [ADENOPATHY]
FROM: IEP - HHPierson
[SUBJECT:] International Student Conference at Prague

I am attaching a copy of letter to Miss Alice Horton of the American Preparatory Committed, International Student Conference at Prague.

It is our belief that we should take no active part in encouraging this Conference because of the critical situation regarding food, transportation and lodging in Europe.

American Preparatory Committee,
INTERNATIONAL STUDENT CONFERENCE AT PRAGUE

June 6, 1946

Hon. Spruille Braden
Department of State
Washington, D.C.

Dear Secretary Braden:

On July 9, twenty-five students from all sections of the country will assemble in New York. . . .
. . . We feel that you would be especially qualified to speak to those attending to stress the significance of this, the first International Student Conference to be held since the war. . . .
We hope to hear from you soon that you will be able to speak at the meeting. . . .

Sincerely yours,
Alice Horton

Executive Secretary
June 12, 1946
Dear Miss Horton,

I greatly appreciate your courtesy in inviting me to participate in this meeting, but my schedule for the next two months is extremely full, and I regret, therefore, that it will not be possible for me to accept. . . .

Sincerely yours,
Spruille Braden

June 18, 1946
[TO:} HRW, PJC
[FROM:] HHP
[SUBJECT:] Miss Alice Horton and the coming International Student Conference in Prague

The following information is submitted by Mr. Caldwell:*

1. Alice Horton is a member of . . . [the] American Student Assembly. This is almost certainly a Communist front. . . .
2. The American Student Assembly (it changes its name occasionally) called this conference under the sponsorship of the Czechoslovakian Minister of Education.
3. This Minister is a Communist.
4. It is proposed at Prague to form a permanent world-wide student organization. The chance this might offer for Communist penetration is obvious.

Editor's note: *This memorandum illustrates the misinformation by which some State Department officials were evidently guided. It is inaccurate on its face. The International Student Conference was called by the World Student Congress in Prague in November 1945 and not by any U.S. organization then or later. The American Preparatory Committee was hosted initially by the United States Student Assembly, not called into being by it. The USSA never changed its name. By the time this memorandum was written, the Committee's affiliated organizations and individual sponsors included a diverse spectrum of student groups and civic leaders, most of whom were in the mainstream (such as the National Intercollegiate Christian Council and the National Catholic Youth Conference). See box, p. 103.*

Moreover, the anticommunist position of the USSA was well documented, as evidenced by the headline in the New York Times *of May 10, 1943, reporting on the USSA's formation, which read, "STUDENT UNIT BARS REDS AND FASCISTS. Newly Planned Assembly Puts Ban into Its Constitution after a Lively Fight" (see USSA Album, Prologue, Section 2).*

In the climate of the times, government officials and many others seemed unable to make the distinctions that differentiated the anticommunist and noncommunist student internationalists, pacifists, Federalists, and various social democratic factions on the liberal left, from the fellow-traveling, pro-Soviet, and overtly or secretly enrolled Marxist/communist students—the latter comprising a cadre relatively small in number.

At the same time, the Marxist/communist strategy, as documented in many forums, did seek to co-opt these noncommunist and anticommunist groups by promoting the adoption of their pro-Soviet political agenda through an appeal to liberal-left idealism, tolerance, or political naivete. It was also true, as subsequent events revealed (see IUS/NSA Relations, p. 538), that the Communists were already intent on controlling the forthcoming World Student Congress and eventually took complete control of the International Union of Students.

With a more informed and nuanced frame of reference, however, the writer's fourth point could have reached a different conclusion: namely, an observation about the value of having the Americans at the conference. That conclusion was reached by most of the other organizations which participated. In particular it prompted the Catholic student participation, which was guided by the strategy outlined in Operation University (see p. 739). It is also supported by Ambassador Steinhardt's own September 16, 1946, report on the U.S. student participation in the World Student Congress ("an able group, whose influence was considerable"), which is excerpted in this series of documents. Unfortunately, as this chronology reveals, the State Department felt it had to distance itself from any but minimal pro forma support to the delegation.

See also Munts (Rogers) on the founding of the USSA, p. 34; Tibbetts (Horton), p. 68, and Bellush (Lubin), p. 73, on the organization of the American delegation; and American Student Union, p. 47.

This kind of "red scare" or "red-baiting" harmed not only those who were so maligned, sometimes publicly, sometimes in secret, but also the bonds of trust, civility, and justice that are so important to a free exchange and exploration of ideas on the college campus. NSA's national student congresses later took a position in this issue, and its national officers were outspoken. See NSA presidents Dentzer, p. 310, and Murphy, p. 1080. Also see Brown on student rights and academic freedom, p. 375.

UNRESTRICTED June 13, 1946
No. 760

To the Officer in Charge of the American Mission, Praha

The Acting Secretary of State refers to the International Student Conference which is scheduled to be held in Prague in August of the current year. Miss Alice Horton, who is acting as executive for the American delegation has been in frequent contact with the Department. While it is not possible for the Department to take any official cognizance of this conference or to support it [in] any way, it is suggested that the Officer in Charge, in his discretion, might assist the American delegation in whatever way may seem desirable. It is understood that there will be twenty-five students in the American delegation representing many different political groups.

The Acting Secretary of State understands that this conference is being sponsored by the Minister of Education of Czechoslovakia. The Department will welcome any information on this conference which may be provided by the Officer in Charge.

IEP:OJCaldwell:rep 6/25/46

July 26, 1946

President Harry S. Truman
The White House
Washington, D.C.

The twenty-five delegates from this country to the International Student Conference at Prague are now on their way to Europe. We feel that you will be interested in the conduct of the student conference and in the results which will be forthcoming.

I am enclosing a list of the delegates, with the schools and organizations which they represent, and a copy of the program adopted by the delegates in conference before they sailed.

Sincerely yours,
Alice Horton,
Executive Secretary

DEPARTMENT OF STATE,
INCOMING TELEGRAM, SECRET

FROM: Paris
TO: Secretary of State
NO: 3158, August 7, 6 p.m.

The principal seat of the International Student Union is in Prague and its French section, the National Student Union, is not particularly important. Available information indicates that it is directed by Communists and fellow travelers. The International Student Union is affiliated with the World Federation of Democratic Youth which regards it with favor. . . .

The Secretary General of the National Student Union in France, E. Lebert, is a Communist, according to a well informed source, and its president, Pierre Trogvat [sic], is known to be a fellow traveler.

Sent Berlin 289, repeated Dept 3158, Prague 104.
CAFFERY

My dear Miss Horton:

I have received, by reference from the White House, your letter of July 26, 1946. . . .

You are assured that this expression of the views of the delegation has been read with interest by the officers of the Department. It is particularly gratifying to know that these young people have studied problems facing the post-war world and are keenly aware of the necessity for interest in and support of the United Nations. Students such as these can make an extremely valuable contribution to public understanding of the principles of international peace and security on which the Charter is based.

Thank you for your courtesy in making this information available to the Government.

Sincerely yours,
For the Acting Secretary of State
Francis H. Russell
Chief
Division of Public Liaison

THE FOREIGN SERVICE OF THE UNITED STATES OF AMERICA

UNRESTRICTED — American Embassy, Praha
No. 1219 — August 30, 1946

SUBJECT: Summary of the Political Events for the Week August 14 through August 20, 1946

The Honorable
The Secretary of State
Washington, D.C.
Sir:

In continuation of my despatch no. 1208 of August 26, 1946, I have the honor to transmit a summary of political events in Czechoslovakia for the week of August 14 through August 20, 1946 . . .

Respectfully yours,
Laurence A. Steinhart

* * *

Opening of the Student Congress

The first plenary session of the World Student Congress was opened on August 19, with delegations from forty-one countries participating.

CONFIDENTIAL — American Embassy, Praha
No. 1284 — September 16, 1946

I have the honor to refer to the Department's instruction no. 760, dated July 13, 1946, concerning the International Student Conference held at Praha from August 15 to August 29, 1946, and to report that the Conference resulted in the establishment of an International Union of Students with permanent headquarters at Praha.

[*Editor's note:* There followed 5 legal-size pages summarizing the events, the participants and the outcomes, along with an analysis of the political affiliations of the 17 members of the Executive Committee.]

According to the best information available concerning these individuals, the Communists have a clear majority both in the entire Executive Committee (11 or 12 out of 17), and the seven officers who carry on the "practical activities" of the IUS (4 out of 7). Mr. Grohman of Czechoslovakia and Mr. Sheljepin of the U.S.S.R. are both communists, while Mr. Trouvat of France is believed to be a Marxist with anarchistic tendencies and Mr. Madden of Great Britain is known as a "fellow traveler," noted as much for his praise of Communism as for his criticism of the Government of his own country. Mr. Au of China and Mr. Meerts of Belgium are both Catholic and, together with Mr. Ellis [of the U.S.], are firm believers in democracy. Among the ten ordinary members of the Executive Committee, Mr. Tomovic of Yugoslavia is a Communist; Mr. Acebez of the "Republic of Spain" is a Marxist and probably a Communist; Mr. MacLean of Canada is a Communist; Mr. Salvador of Mexico is understood to be a Communist; Mr. Shevcov of the Ukraine S.S.R. is a Communist; Mr. Ghali of Egypt is understood to be a Communist; Mr. Chattopadhya of India is understood to be a Communist; Mr. Wroblewski of Poland is a Communist; Mr. Sommerfelt of Norway and Mr. Vasquez of Cuba are both non-Communist. . . .

As of special interest to the Department, the American member of the Executive Committee, Mr. Ellis, is at present a student at Harvard University and came to the Conference as a representative of the YMCA students. He is a Negro. His present plans are to go to the United States at the end of September and to return to Praha in January or February of 1946, where he intends to take special courses in English at the Charles University which are planned by the Czechoslovak Ministry of Education expressly for the members of the Executive Committee.

The American Institute of Czechoslovakia held a tea dance on the arrival of the American delegation to enable them to make the acquaintance of various Czechoslovak students, and toward the end of the Conference the American Ambassador held a reception for the members of the American delegation and leading members of the other students' delegations.

By and large the members of the American delegation constituted an able group whose influence was considerable in the Conference, although it was somewhat hampered by great difference of opinion within the delegation. In this connection, it is worth mentioning that two or three members of the American delegation were either Communist Party members, or Communist in sympathy, and in addition, the great majority of the American delegates was of the opinion that it would be most unwise to introduce any resolutions which might offend the sensibilities of the U.S.S.R. delegation or those from other countries in Eastern Europe.

Respectfully yours,
Laurence A. Steinhardt

UNRESTRICTED
AMERICAN EMBASSY
No. 1729 Prague, January 15, 1947

. . . We have been approached by the editors of "World Student News," a monthly published by the International Union of Students, with a request that we supply material on American students for this publication.
The monthly appears in five languages: English, French, Russian, Spanish and Czech, in about 100,000 copies and is distributed throughout the world. In U.S.A. through member organization of the I.U.S. An English copy is attached.
. . . We would appreciate your consideration of the matter, which, in our opinion, is not without importance.

Respectfully yours,
Laurence A. Steinhardt

The American Preparatory Committee

Affiliated Organizations

Association of Internes and Medical Students
B'nai B'rith Hillel Foundation
Intercollegiate Division
American Youth for Democracy
National Intercollegiate Christian Council
Student Federalists
United States Student Assembly
University Section, National Catholic Youth Council
Youth Builders

Sponsors

Sen. George D. Aiken
Paul Klapper
Queens College
Dean Harriet M. Allyn
Mt. Holyoke College
Pres. Herbert Davis
Smith College
Rep. Helen Gahagan Douglas
Rep. Albert J. Engel
Pres. Harry D. Gideonse
Brooklyn College
Pres. Mildred McAfee Horton
Wellesley College
Pres. Bryn Hovde
New School for Social Research
Prof. Charles S. Johnson
Fisk University
Anna M. Kross
City Magistrate
Prof. Kirtley P. Mather
Harvard University
Pres. Philip C. Nash
University of Texas
Sen. Claude Pepper
Sen. Leverett Saltonstall
Mark Starr
Education Director, I.L.G.W.U
Frank L. Weil
Jewish Welfare Board
Dr. Stephen S. Wise
Amer. Jewish Congress

The American Delegation

Organization	Delegate
National Intercollegiate Christian Council	
YWCA	Leila Anderson
YWCA	Joyce Roberts
YMCA	William Ellis
YMCA	Hoyt Palmer
University Section, National Catholic Youth Council	
	Henry Briefs
	Edward Kirchner
	Vincent Hogan
	Martin McLaughlin
American Youth for Democracy	Lee Marsh
Association of Internes and Medical Students	
	Bernard Lown
Student Federalists	Curtis Farrar
Student Volunteer Movement	Winburn Thomas
Unitarian Youth, Student Section	Jean Casson
United States Student Assembly	Lada Hulka
Youthbuilders	Walter Wallace
University of Chicago	Russell Austin
Fisk University	Charles Proctor
Harvard University	Douglass Cater
Hunter College	Enid Kass
University of North Carolina	James Wallace
University of Pennsylvania	Frank Mayers
University of Texas	Joseph Malik, Jr.
University of California at Los Angeles—	
Win the Peace Committee	William Stout
Wayne University	Warren Rovetch
University of Wisconsin	Albert Houghton
Executive Secretary to the Delegation	
	Jewel Lubin

Before e-mails and satellites, snail-mail and telegrams reveal

STUDENTS HOPEFUL AND STATE DEPARTMENT NOT SO SURE

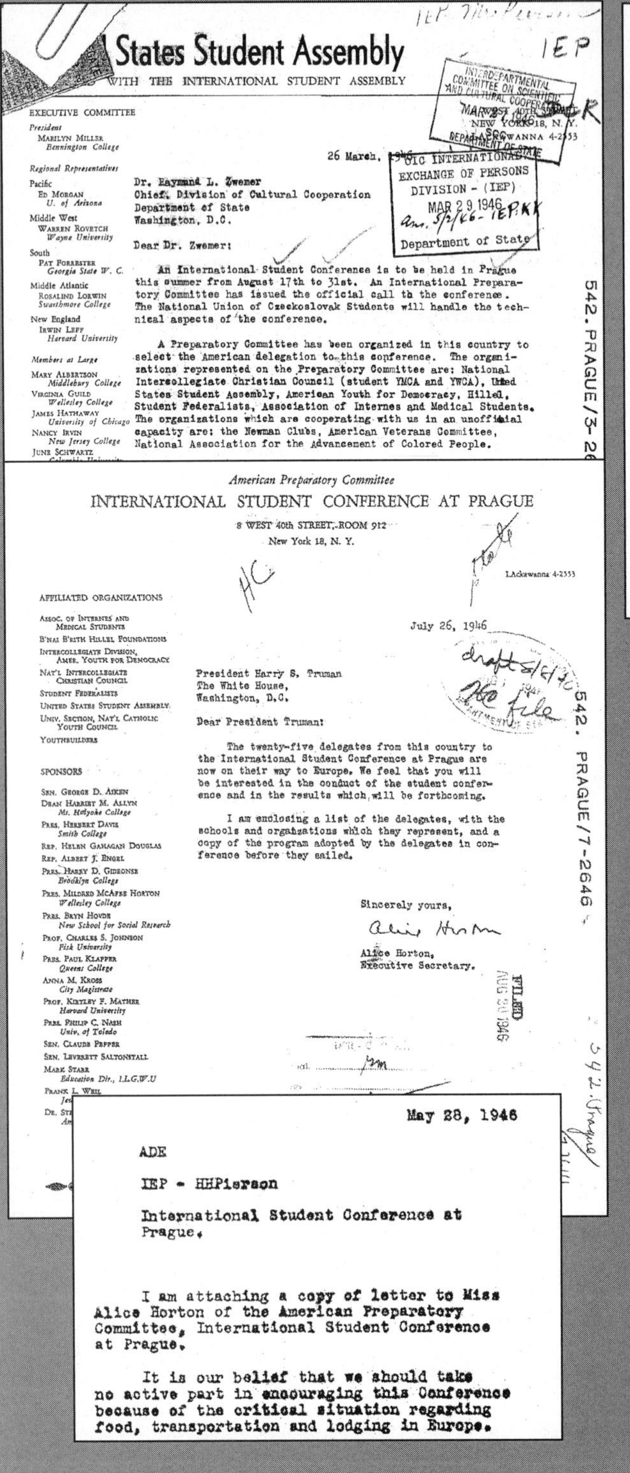

States Student Assembly

WITH THE INTERNATIONAL STUDENT ASSEMBLY

8 WEST 40TH STREET, NEW YORK 18, N. Y. LACKAWANNA 4-2353

EXECUTIVE COMMITTEE

President
MARILYN MILLER, *Bennington College*

Regional Representatives
Pacific: ED MORGAN, *U. of Arizona*
Middle West: WARREN ROVETCH, *Wayne University*
South: PAT FORRESTER, *Georgia State W. C.*
Middle Atlantic: ROSALIND LORWIN, *Swarthmore College*
New England: IRWIN LEFF, *Harvard University*

Members at Large
MARY ALBERTSON, *Middlebury College*
VIRGINIA GUILD, *Wellesley College*
JAMES HATHAWAY, *University of Chicago*
NANCY IRVIN, *New Jersey College*
JUNE SCHWARTZ

26 March, 1946

Dr. Raymond L. Zwemer
Chief, Division of Cultural Cooperation
Department of State
Washington, D.C.

Dear Dr. Zwemer:

An International Student Conference is to be held in Prague this summer from August 17th to 31st. An International Preparatory Committee has issued the official call to the conference. The National Union of Czeckoslovak Students will handle the technical aspects of the conference.

A Preparatory Committee has been organized in this country to select the American delegation to this conference. The organizations represented on the Preparatory Committee are: National Intercollegiate Christian Council (student YMCA and YWCA), United States Student Assembly, American Youth for Democracy, Hillel, Student Federalists, Association of Internes and Medical Students. The organizations which are cooperating with us in an unofficial capacity are: the Newman Clubs, American Veterans Committee, National Association for the Advancement of Colored People.

INTERDEPARTMENTAL COMMITTEE ON SCIENTIFIC AND CULTURAL COOPERATION MAR 2? 1946 SCC DEPARTMENT OF STATE

OIC INTERNATIONAL EXCHANGE OF PERSONS DIVISION - (IEP) MAR 29 1946 Department of State

542.PRAGUE/3-26

American Preparatory Committee

INTERNATIONAL STUDENT CONFERENCE AT PRAGUE

8 WEST 40th STREET, ROOM 912
New York 18, N. Y.

LAckawanna 4-2353

AFFILIATED ORGANIZATIONS

ASSOC. OF INTERNES AND MEDICAL STUDENTS
B'NAI B'RITH HILLEL FOUNDATIONS
INTERCOLLEGIATE DIVISION, AMER. YOUTH FOR DEMOCRACY
NAT'L INTERCOLLEGIATE CHRISTIAN COUNCIL
STUDENT FEDERALISTS
UNITED STATES STUDENT ASSEMBLY
UNIV. SECTION, NAT'L CATHOLIC YOUTH COUNCIL
YOUTHBUILDERS

SPONSORS

SEN. GEORGE D. AIKEN
DEAN HARRIET M. ALLYN, *Mt. Holyoke College*
PRES. HERBERT DAVIS, *Smith College*
REP. HELEN GAHAGAN DOUGLAS
REP. ALBERT J. ENGEL
PRES. HARRY D. GIDEONSE, *Brooklyn College*
PRES. MILDRED MCAFEE HORTON, *Wellesley College*
PRES. BRYN HOVDE, *New School for Social Research*
PROF. CHARLES S. JOHNSON, *Fisk University*
PRES. PAUL KLAPPER, *Queens College*
ANNA M. KROSS, *City Magistrate*
PROF. KIRTLEY F. MATHER, *Harvard University*
PRES. PHILIP C. NASH, *Univ. of Toledo*
SEN. CLAUDE PEPPER
SEN. LEVERETT SALTONSTALL
MARK STARR, *Education Dir., I.L.G.W.U*
FRANK L. WEIL
DR. ST…

July 26, 1946

President Harry S. Truman
The White House,
Washington, D.C.

Dear President Truman:

The twenty-five delegates from this country to the International Student Conference at Prague are now on their way to Europe. We feel that you will be interested in the conduct of the student conference and in the results which will be forthcoming.

I am enclosing a list of the delegates, with the schools and organizations which they represent, and a copy of the program adopted by the delegates in conference before they sailed.

Sincerely yours,

Alice Horton

Alice Horton,
Executive Secretary.

FILED AUG 30 1946

542.PRAGUE/7-2646

May 28, 1946

ADE

IEP - HHPierson

International Student Conference at Prague.

I am attaching a copy of letter to Miss Alice Horton of the American Preparatory Committee, International Student Conference at Prague.

It is our belief that we should take no active part in encouraging this Conference because of the critical situation regarding food, transportation and lodging in Europe.

My dear Miss Horton:

Thank you for your letter of April 25, 1946, with which you enclosed a press release and a tentative agenda of the International Student Conference to take place in Prague this summer. I have read these with interest. Your letter of March 26 to Dr. Zwemer and April 8, 1946, to Mr. Dickey have been referred to me for reply.

The main problems involved in this undertaking are transportation and passports and I understand from our conversation when you were here that you are working on these matters.

I shall be glad to bring your letter to the attention of interested persons in the Department.

Sincerely yours,

Harry H. Pierson
Acting Assistant Chief
Division of International
Exchange of Persons

Miss Alice Horton,
Executive Secretary,
American Preparatory Committee,
International Student Conference at Prague,
8 West Fortieth Street, Room 912,
New York 18, New York.

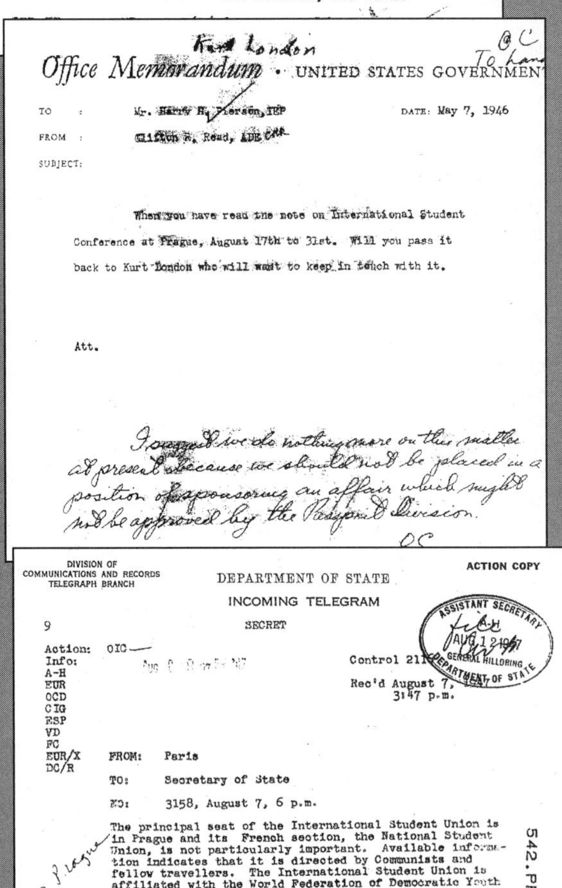

Office Memorandum • UNITED STATES GOVERNMENT

TO : Mr. Harry H. Pierson, IEP

DATE: May 7, 1946

FROM : Clifton R. Read, ADE

SUBJECT:

When you have read the note on International Student Conference at Prague, August 17th to 31st. Will you pass it back to Kurt London who will want to keep in touch with it.

Att.

I suggest we do nothing more on this matter at present because we should not be placed in a position of sponsoring an affair which might not be approved by the Regional Division.

DIVISION OF COMMUNICATIONS AND RECORDS TELEGRAPH BRANCH

DEPARTMENT OF STATE

ACTION COPY

INCOMING TELEGRAM

9

SECRET

Action: OIC
Info: A-H, EUR, OCD, CIG, ESP, VD, FC, EUR/X, DC/R

Control 2117
Rec'd August 7, 3:47 p.m.

FROM: Paris
TO: Secretary of State
NO: 3158, August 7, 6 p.m.

The principal seat of the International Student Union is in Prague and its French section, the National Student Union, is not particularly important. Available information indicates that it is directed by Communists and fellow travellers. The International Student Union is affiliated with the World Federation of Democratic Youth which regards it with favor. Your 322, August 5, repeated to Dept as 1875.

The Secretary General of the National Student Union in France, E. Lebert, is a Communist, according to a well informed source, and its president, Pierre Trogvat, is known to be a fellow traveller.

Sent Berlin 289, repeated Dept 3158, Prague 104.

CAFFERY

542.PRAGUE/8-747

A CONTRAST IN VISIONS is shown in this selection of a few of the notes reproduced in the previous pages between the serious and hopeful intent of the American student group in Alice Horton's letters of 3/26/46 and 7/26/46, the State Department's internal procedural worries about involving itself, and its greater political worries about Communist influence.

Jimmy Wallace and the President

Jimmy Wallace of the University of North Carolina writes the President from Prague about good relations with other nations and about inviting Russian students to the United States

Trida Jana Opletala 38
Prague II, Czechoslovakia
August 17, 1946

Harry S. Truman
President of the United States
Washington, D.C.

Dear Mr. President:

The purpose of this letter is to make a single observation, an observation which is bound up with several facts pertaining to the same thing. That thing is good international relations between the United States and other nations, particularly between the United States and Russia.

I am one of twenty-five American delegates now attending the International Students Conference at Prague. This conference has been given little publicity in the United States, but here in Czechoslovakia it is a very important thing. Delegates are here from over 50 nations representing every major political and religious viewpoint in the world today. The American delegation is largely liberal or middle-of-the-road politically speaking. We have extremes, yes, but the great majority of the delegation is very American in its approach to political problems and their solution.

This delegation is unofficial. That is, we do not represent or speak for, in any sense of the word, the American government. But, even in our unofficial capacity, what we say and do here is vitally important, because to everyone else we are more than a representative group of students. We are representative Americans as well. We realize this point of view and try to act accordingly. We realize that such international conferences as this will do much to promote world peace. We realize that if students cannot agree, there is little hope for governments to agree.

Last year, the Russians invited the American delegation to Russia, at government expense. This the Americans did. They came back from the trip with much more information than they had before. This year, we have asked the Russians for an invitation again. Perhaps we will get it and perhaps we won't. Our purpose is to go and observe with our own eyes what goes on the other side of the Iron Curtain. To observe, to criticize, to report [our] own observations, are our purposes. However, it has filtered back to us that the Russian students can't understand how it is that they invite us to come to Russia, and we do not invite them to come to the United States. They do not understand when we tell them that we are not representing the government, and that at present the government does not have funds for such purposes. We, of course, would be glad to have them see our country; perhaps they might learn something.

We have also received invitations from Czechoslovakia, Yugoslavia, and Albania. We will probably receive more. We cannot extend any at all.

I think that it is a great shame that these students who will be people of importance in the future should leave here with such a misconception of our own country and our hospitality. I realize that you too probably feel the same way. I realize that there is pending legislation which would appropriate funds for the State Department which would be used for this purpose. But, unfortunately, the need is a present one, since the Congress here adjourns on August 31.

I have written this letter in the hope:

1. that something might be arranged for these people at present:
2. that attention might be directed to preparing for such instances in the future.

Surely your desk is cluttered up every day with thousands of requests from people and governments all over the world. I hesitated to write this letter, realizing that you were very busy and that perhaps, after all, it was a small matter, but then I decided to do it in the hope that something could be done to enable us in some small way to show our appreciation and cooperation to the other nations represented here. With kindest regards, I remain cordially yours,

Jimmy Wallace
University of North Carolina Delegate to the International Students Conference at Prague.

P.S. I might also add that I have been asked upon the part of the Carolina Political Union to convey the regards of its members. If you will recall, we presented you from our speaker's platform in Chapel Hill, N.C. in 1941.

The Government responds:

My dear Mr. Wallace:

The receipt is acknowledged, by reference from the White House, of your letter of August 17, 1946, to President Truman. . . .

As you are aware, the people of the United States have contributed and are contributing a major proportion of the funds and the material for relief and reconstruction in many parts of the world, including the Soviet Union. These contributions are the largest made by any people in history for such purposes, and I am sure the majority of the American people consider the money well spent. However, Congress to date has not authorized any programs or appropriated any money for student exchanges with countries of the Eastern Hemisphere. Thus it is impossible at present for the United States to invite students to come to this country. Should legislation requested by the Department be passed by Congress, it is possible that the Department will also ask for an appropriation to promote student exchanges with the countries of Europe, Asia and Africa.

You may be interested to know that efforts have been made by the Department to encourage, on a private basis, the exchange of students between Soviet and American universities. Up to this point it has been impossible to initiate such exchanges because the Soviet Government has not indicated any desire to permit such exchanges to take place strictly on the basis of scholastic ability.

Your interest in the development of international understanding is to be commended. I regret that it is not possible to assist you in this matter.

Sincerely yours,
Harry H. Pierson, Acting Chief
Division of International Exchange of Persons

In international cooperation the lack of the same background and tradition continually causes problems to arise. They must be faced.

Learning the Art of Cold War Politics

Report on the World Student Congress at Prague, 1946, delivered in fall 1946 to the National Intercollegiate Christian Council

William Ellis, *Harvard University,* and
Joyce Roberts, *Pembroke College, RI, National Intercollegiate Christian Council*
Members of the U.S. Delegation

Background

In London, March 1945, an international students' meeting was held, out of which a committee of seven nationalities was set up including Canada, China, France, Great Britain, USA, USSR, and Yugoslavia empowered to call a conference which would establish an International Students' organization. Because of the difficulties of calling such a conference, two days were set aside at the World Youth Conference in London, November 1945, for the purposes of exchanging ideas and reporting. It was at this meeting of 57 nations that the International Preparatory Committee was set up, whose job it would be to prepare a fully representative conference in summer 1946.

The principle "that the elections should be on the basis of countries, representing on a small scale the great variety of conditions and opinions of students all over the world" was agreed upon. The following were the twelve countries represented with the number of votes allocated for each: China, 3; India, 3; Latin America, 3; USA, 3; USSR, 3; France, 2; Great Britain, 2; Australia, 1; Belgium, 1; Czechoslovakia, 1; Denmark, 1; Yugoslavia, 1.

The first meeting of the IPC was held after the Prague Congress 1945. (This Congress was a meeting of students from 51 countries gathered to celebrate International Students' Day—an occasion of remembrance and resolve and an opportunity for the exchange of information and expression of opinion on student problems.) The Czech Union of Students was asked to serve as a technical bureau because the seat of the committee was to be in Prague. It was decided to finance the work of the IPC by a levy of ten shillings per 1000 organized students. This money was used for the running of the secretariat of the IPC, and the small sum that remained after costs were covered forms the nucleus of the property of the IUS.

* * *

[The IPC] was also instructed to work in close cooperation with the WFDY so that the IPC should study together with the council of the WFDY the methods of affiliation and bring this information to the 1946 conference. At the Prague Congress in 1945, the IPC was also mandated to establish close contact with World Student Relief to give them every possible assistance for their post-war program of relief, and to try to find ways for the coordination of WSR and the future IUS.

The IPC has met at four different times—the first after the Congress in November, in January, in April, and then again in August. Each of the last two sessions covered a period of at least two weeks. At all meetings at least one half of the number of countries represented and two-thirds of the individual delegates have been present. At the last important session, all but one nation was able to be present.

* * *

The draft constitution was drawn up at the April meeting and sent to all delegates for their consideration before the Congress. All delegates were asked to send suggestions as to the tasks for the commissions and subjects that should be considered—to send also material for the use of the commissions.

The Congress fees were as follows: cost of accommodations and food for two weeks—$45; congress delegates fee—$15 per member. Delegates were asked to pay for some of the entertainment and excursions, and in this way the Congress was able to cover their expenses.

We feel that special note should be taken of the work of the National Union of Czech Students for the Congress and of the work of the Secretariat. Over one hundred students worked in all departments of the Secretariat, the Press department, the Entertainment section, and the Reception and Housing Bureaus. Working brigades of students spent the few weeks before the conference repainting, furnishing, decorating, and preparing Masaryk College, where we were housed. Another group of students worked in the Arts faculty and Carnival procession.

* * *

Relationships

The IPC established contact with UNESCO. It will be the Commission on Intellectual Cooperation under Mr. Ellis's direction which will have the opportunity of debating the nature of our future representation in an advisory capacity to this international organization.

A small group of the IPC contacted the World Federation of Trade Unions and discussed the importance of cooperation in the future on the problem of students organized in some countries within the Trade Union movement.

A representative of the World Federation of Democratic Women was also at the Congress.

At the various meetings of the IPC a representative of the WFDY was present in the spring of 1964 and full discussions took place con-

Bill Ellis (Harvard) and Joyce Roberts (Pembroke College, RI), representing the YM and YWCA on the U.S. delegation to the World Student Congress. Seated just behind and to the right of Ellis is Walter Wallace (Columbia), representing Youthbuilders.

cerning the relationship of the two organizations. Henry Jones, vice president of WFDY, was present at the Congress.

Contact had also been established with ISS, WSR, WSCF, Pax Romana, and the World Union of Jewish Students; and representatives from the first four were at the Congress.[1]

* * *

The American Preparatory Committee

When the American delegation returned to New York from Russia, they formed under the leadership of Alice Horton an American Preparatory Committee. It was the task of this committee to choose a strong delegation representative of American students in order to attend the International Congress of Students in Prague.[2]

In view of the very little time left to this committee, we feel that the American delegation was one truly representative of this country's students. The three major religions, the races, and the regional areas of the American woman and man student reflected different shades of student opinion. The other ten delegates were chosen from ten major colleges of the country.

The American Delegation

However, representative as the delegation was, we feel that the attention of all should be called to four delegates who were not students, namely, Mr. Thomas, Mr. Palmer, Mr. Kirchner, and Miss Anderson.[3] As well equipped as these people were in student problems, their function in a wholly student assembly could be merely advisory, for they themselves seemed to sense the difference of years. The result was that in purely American delegation meetings, their experience was important, but on the floor of the assembly and the different committees, they were reluctant to speak.

We call this to the attention of the NICC so that they will realize that adults acting in a purely student capacity will be handicapped always in their participation. Therefore, as grateful as we are to the valuable experience and advice of the above delegates, it would appear wise in the future rather to choose exceptionally good student delegates who are well briefed in order to have greater direct expression of student opinion.

The fact that this delegation was representative is important, for its opinions and decisions must reflect the desires and hopes of American students. Moreover, this representative character is the badge of its authority when it speaks to American students in the future.[4]

* * *

Defining the term "left wing" as being left of a purely laissez-faire society without controls and right of a socialistic society, one might describe the entire delegation as being of the left wing. However, two of the delegation were, in our opinion, either avowed Communists or of communistic leanings. The rest of the delegation agreed almost unanimously on the American program with one other exception. When it came to a question of communism the Catholic delegates displayed an uncompromising hostility, whereas most delegates were determined to be firm in their beliefs but cooperate with all nations wherever possible.[5]

The Delegation Platform

The platform of the delegation was not in any way inconsistent with, nor unlike, the Report of the NICC's Commission on Community Responsibility. The delegation strongly supported the United Nations and advocated a strong atomic control commission, which should be exempt from the veto of the Security Council. It opposed fascism, which it defined, and advocated freedom and dissemination of all material and extension of educational privileges to all. Specific proposals were expounded for the economic betterment of the peoples of the world and the right of self-determination of colonial peoples.

In the realm of student exchange, the delegation stressed the tremendous potentialities involved in cooperation with UNESCO, especially in fostering student exchange. The NICC's suggestion on farm and industrial projects such as are found at Hartford, Conn., were enlarged to an international scope—including such ideas as TVA, British Land Army, and United Nations. Support was given to WSR and WSSF as the relief organizations of the IUS. Finally, recommendations were made for the extension of education and academic freedom in educational institutions.

* * *

The International Student Conference

On the 18th of August, 1946, 299 delegates from 38 different countries and representing two and a half million students assembled for the opening of the New International Union of Students. Prime Minister Gottwald, other dignitaries, and 12 student representatives expressed a desire for international cooperation and peace. The assembly was a magnificent affair and lent the correct tone of internationalism to the beginning of the Congress.

* * *

Defining Democracy and Fascism

Before discussing the composite resolutions, it is necessary to point out two important facts which may have greater importance in the future, First, it was extremely difficult to obtain a definition of the terms "democracy" and "fascism." The American delegation—especially Mr. Brief[s] and Mr. McLaughlin—succeeded in defining fascism in the resolutions of the first commission. This definition can be found in the recommendations following the composite resolutions. However, the difficulty involved in accomplishing this task gives an inkling as to the problems common to international cooperation today.

The terms "democracy" and "fascism" either mean some things slightly different from the American definition or they are terms which call forth an emotional reaction. In so far as definitions differ, there is hope for eventual common understanding. Whether individualism, civil rights, and personal freedom are as closely associated with democracy in the Eastern part of Europe as economic opportunity is dubious. Still, there is no reason for too great alarm.

* * *

Still, if there is, as years pass, a steadfast refusal to define fascism more willingly, there is a danger which we can not afford to overlook. Whenever a student experiences an emotion similar to that associated with fascism, there may be the tendency to denounce the new experience as fascistic. Thus, mere political opposition in these terms may be labeled fascistic. In our opinion, this hesitancy to define terms concretely may for the time being be attributed to an emotional intensity which we should hope will decrease as the years pass. However, if the process continues, we will probably discover that the antifascists have become fascists. We express this idea, not to alarm any people or to present an unduly pessimistic outlook, but because in our determination to make the IUS a success we must consider all eventualities.

Mr. Vasquez of the Cuban delegation encountered the same type of difficulty in presenting a resolution on imperialism. He later informed us in private conversation that this opposition was in direct contrast to the willingness of the November conference to denounce imperialism. The reasons for this shift in sentiment may probably be found in the swift changing foreign policy of certain nations.

It is this type of problem that confronted us at Prague and will continue to do so as long as we cooperate internationally. Yet it is far better to understand these problems and to acknowledge their existence, for in international cooperation, the lack of the same background and traditions continually causes such problems to arise. They must be faced.

* * *

Selecting the Council and Executive Committee

On August 28, 1946, the council, whose members were chosen by the delegations themselves, met to elect the President, Secretary and other members of the Executive Committee. After discussing the merits of Joseph Grohman and Thomas Madden, the council elected Grohman to the presidency and Madden to the Secretary's position. The list is as follows:

Mr. Grohman	*Chairman*	Czechoslovakia
Mr. Trouvat	*Vice Chairman*	France
Mr. Au Sik-Ling	*Vice Chairman*	China
Mr. Ellis	*Vice Chairman*	USA
Mr. Sheljepin	*Vice Chairman*	USSR
Mr. Madden	*Secretary*	England
Mr. Meerts	*Treasurer*	Belgium
Mr. Acebez A.		Spain
Mr. Wroblewski		Poland
Mr. Ghali G.		Egypt
Mr. Tomovic R.		Yugoslavia
Mr. Sommerfelt		Norway
Mr. Chattopadhya		India A.I.S.F.
Mr. MacLean		Canada
Mr. Salvador		Mexico
Mr. Vasquez A.		Cuba
Mr. Shevcov		Ukraine

Before the elections took place a request was made for the secret ballot. At first, there was opposition, but the request carried.

* * *

When the election of the Executive [Committee] members was made known, it must be said that some delegates had slips of paper with a list of names. Apparently, those that they had on the list were elected. The basis for this statement is that when the decision to vote secretly was made known, two friends saw the word passed to change some of the names. In an open ballot, some, to show that they were above party lines, would have voted for members not believing as they do, but in a secret ballot this was unnecessary. Thus, some of the names were changed. This undoubtedly proves that some had organized before the elections, but this is merely smart political strategy, which In the future need not be limited to just a few.

* * *

Analyzing this Executive Committee, one would say that the Chinese, Belgian, Norwegian, and American delegates were not of communistic leanings. The Cuban delegate is a Marxist, but a very good, trustworthy man. The other delegates are either very favorable to communists or unknown quantities. Also, it is quite noticeable that the Executive Committee has no women. The only explanation for this is that, with the exception of Miss Roberts, it cannot honestly be maintained that any woman showed the type of ability that would have warranted a position of this type—very unfortunate.

This analysis presents a very unfavorable report, but again it is best to report all and know the worst. We still feel that the IUS can be a success.[6]

END NOTES

[1] See Part IV, Sections 2 and 3, for descriptions of these wartime and postwar international student relief and exchange organizations.

[2] See Tibbetts (Horton), p. 68, and Bellush (Lubin), p. 73.

[3] Editor's note: The non-students were staff members Winburn Thomas of the Student Volunteer Movement, Hoyt Palmer and Leila Anderson of the NICC, and Edward Kirschner of Pax Romana, with the NCYC delegation.

[4] *Editor's note:* The original report contained a complete list of the delegation. See p. 103 for the list.

[5] See Kirchner, p. 76, and J. C. Murray, "Operation University," p. 739.

[6] See p. 159 for a biography of Bill Ellis.

PICTURE CREDITS: *Then:* Ellis and Roberts. *Now:* Roberts and son (*Both, courtesy Joyce Roberts Harrison*).

Joyce Roberts Harrison is shown here with her son, Scott Harrison, after they had returned from a trip to Prague in 1996.

JOYCE ROBERTS HARRISON

Early years: Born in 1926, I grew up in Danielson, CT, a small textile manufacturing town, where I attended public schools.

College years: I attended Pembroke College, RI, graduating in 1946 with a BA in Sociology. Active in the Student Christian Movement on campus and in New England, I was a National Intercollegiate Christian Council delegate to the WSCF meeting in Bossey and the IUS meeting in Prague during the summer of 1946. That fall, I traveled four months for the National Student YWCA to college campuses to share with students our summer experiences. In 1948, I received my MA in Christian education from Union Theological Seminary and Columbia University. I earned an additional 30 credits beyond Masters in Education at Southern Connecticut State University and the University of Connecticut.

Career highlights: For twenty-three years in North Haven, I taught elementary school in all K-6 grades. In 1971, two teachers and I received approval to set up an "Integrated Day" pilot project—a personalized learning educational alternative environment where a student could make many decisions about what he learns. Enrollment was strictly voluntary, and it is still operating thirty years later as a K-6 alternative. In 1991, I retired from teaching and spent the last ten years traveling to Asia, Europe, and South America and *much* time baby-sitting for my grandchildren.

Family: In 1948 I married Robert Harrison, who was then working for Yale Student Health as a psychiatric social worker. We have three children and three grandchildren.

SECTION 3

The 1946 Chicago Student Conference

CONTENTS

The Xavier Herald

"ALL-CATHOLIC"—FOURTEEN YEARS—1932-1946

XAVIER UNIVERSITY, NEW ORLEANS, LA., JANUARY, 1947

XAVIER STUDENTS ATTEND CONVENTION IN CHICAGO

University Displays Interest In Expanding International Education

Xavier's Stand

...ve Students From Xavier ...tend Regional Conference

Scholarly Attitude Seen At Xavier

Industrial Arts Meets Need

ANCHORING NSA IN THE DEEP SOUTH from its inception, co-ed Xavier University in New Orleans, the only all-black Catholic school in the nation, sends six reps to Chicago (*Xavier Herald*, Jan., 1947) (see Pt. 2, S. 3).

In four short months following their return from Prague (without the benefit of computer, fax, or Xerox), the U.S. delegation organized the December 1946 Chicago Student Conference. It was attended by over 727 delegates and observers from 307 colleges and universities and 28 national student organizations. They came by bus, train, and carpool. Its purpose was to lay the groundwork for a new representative national student organization.

Alice Horton, Jewel Lubin, and Muriel Jacobson, who, as described in Section 1, spearheaded the American Preparatory Committee, were once more travelling through Europe, and the torch was passed to the Chicago Student Conference Preparatory Committee, headed by Russell Austin and located at the University of Chicago.

In his memoir, Clif Wharton, a Harvard University delegate who later became National Continuations Committee Secretary, provides a narrative of the hopeful and controversial setting for the conference. Delegates debated issues concerning the form of the organization and its positions on academic freedom, student rights, segregation and discrimination, and international relations.

Wharton reports the passionate debates of Southern and Northern college students confronting the issue of racial segregation and socially separate colleges and how best to work towards their elimination at a time when it was standard practice in Southern states.

Plans laid for constitutional convention

The conference created a National Continuations Committee (NCC) to prepare for a constitutional convention the following September. The high hopes for this new organization in creating a national student voice are typified in the digest of articles written by student leaders Mildred Kiefer (U.C. Berkeley), Royal Voegeli (University of Wisconsin), and Ralph Dungan (St. Joseph's College, Philadelphia).

Jim Smith (University of Texas), the NCC president, makes the case for grounding the new organization on strong student governments. John Simons (Fordham University), treasurer of the NCC, was an eloquent spokesman, inspiring conference delegates in debate as well as evangelizing for the new organization in national publications.

Bill Ellis of Harvard, serving as American vice president of the Prague-based International Union of Students (IUS), also representing the National Intercollegiate Christian Council, reported hopefully, but guardedly, on the prospects for American affiliation with the IUS through the soon to be formed National Student Organization.

Chicago Sets a Postwar Student Agenda

"THE DESIRE TO CREATE THE NEW ORGANIZATION WAS STRONG," Clif Wharton writes in the pages following. "Nevertheless a certain anxiety permeated the meeting, largely because it was the first time many of the delegates participated in a national meeting of college students." Delegates from 307 colleges and universities attended one of four panels in which recommendations were voted out concerning organization, structure, student needs and international affairs, and purposes and programs (left, delegates vote at a panel session).

ELECTED TO HEAD A CONTINUATIONS COMMITTEE to oversee drafting a proposed constitution and to organize a constiututional convention for the coming summer (Pt. 1, S. 4): The committee, from left: Russell Austin (U. of Chicago), Vice President, James Smith (U. of Texas), President, John Simons (Fordham U.), Treasurer, Clifton Wharton (Harvard), Secretary.

College Press Follows the Issues Closely

The Chicago Maroon

THE UNIVERSITY OF CHICAGO, MONDAY, DECEMBER 2, 1946

Editorial

en Letter To Pres. Colwell:

Harper Lights

'No Comment On Blackout'

Many Schools Attend Student Conference To Convene At UC

Vassar Miscellany News

Chicago Conference Of U.S. Students Lays Groundwork For First National Student Organization In This Country

STANFORD DAILY

International Affairs to Take Part in Creation of NSO

Needs and responsibilities of American students in international affairs, as well as campus and national affairs, will form part of the future

Highlighted by the college press across the country. From top: *The Chicago Maroon*, 12/2/46, the host college; *Vassar Miscellany News*, 1/15/47, NY; *Stanford Daily*, 1/14/47, CA.

Significance Observed

The Michigan Daily

WALKOUT WARNED:

Student Conference Splits On Racial Discrimination

By TOM WALSH

ELECTION PREPARATION:

NSO Week To Be Observed By Informational Rally Here

FINAL DECISION DELAYED:

Student Conference Divided over IUS

By TOM WALSH

NSO FORUM:

American Student Ignorant Of Own Educational System

The American student knows less and cares less about his educational system than any other student in the world, James Smith, president of the continuations committee of the National Student Organizations, said last night.

PAGE TWO

Chicago Student Politics

Issues were covered by the U. of Michigan *Michigan Daily* as did many college newspapers around the country. The as yet to be formed NSA was still known as NSO (National Student Organization). The paper also reported campus-wide events designed to inform and involve students about the NSO. (from left: 1/8/47, 1/10/47, 1/14/47, 4/29/47, 5/2/47).

Issues Raised

Students Bring Hope and Purpose to Conference

AN END AND A BEGINNING

The Chicago Conference has come and gone. Large representation from the colleges in the New England area has borne witness to the fact that the effort of Smith in arousing interest in the conference had not been in vain. Three days of hard work in a spirit of compromise and unity have laid the basis for a National Student Organization which can become a strong and constructive force in the student life of America.

While we may be content with the successful character of this initial meeting, and while we can applaud the attitude of the delegates who consistently placed the interest of the student community as a whole above regional and personal considerations, we cannot consider the conference as a climax. It is rather the start of a gigantic task, a task which will absorb the energies of every student in Smith College and in the United States at large.

Smith's Leading Role

In the plans for NSO Smith has thus far played a leading role. We have had the good fortune to be especially well informed about the work of the IUS and ISS meetings in Europe last summer. Now one of our delegates to Chicago has been elected to the national executive committee as chairman of the Massachusetts region. This participation in the main organization places upon us an added responsibility which cannot be shirked in the time to come.

Editorial appearing in the Smith College *SCAN*, 11/14/47

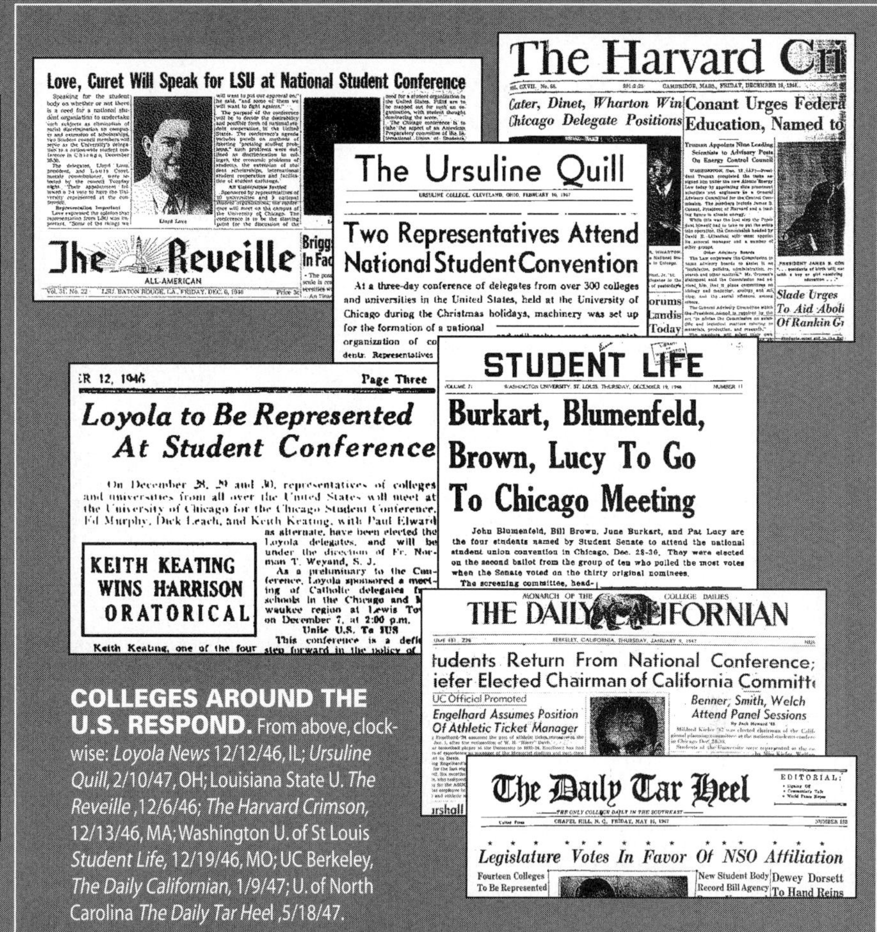

Love, Curet Will Speak for LSU at National Student Conference

The Reveille

The Harvard Crimson

Cater, Dinet, Wharton Win Chicago Delegate Positions

Conant Urges Federal Education, Named to

The Ursuline Quill

Two Representatives Attend National Student Convention

At a three-day conference of delegates from over 300 colleges and universities in the United States, held at the University of Chicago during the Christmas holidays, machinery was set up for the formation of a national organization of co... Representatives

Loyola to Be Represented At Student Conference

On December 28, 29 and 30, representatives of colleges and universities from all over the United States will meet at the University of Chicago for the Chicago Student Conference. Ed Murphy, Dick Leach, and Keith Keating, with Paul Elward as alternate, have been elected the Loyola delegates, and will be under the direction of Fr. Norman T. Weyand, S. J.

KEITH KEATING WINS HARRISON ORATORICAL

STUDENT LIFE

Burkart, Blumenfeld, Brown, Lucy To Go To Chicago Meeting

John Blumenfeld, Bill Brown, June Burkart, and Pat Lucy are the four students named by Student Senate to attend the national student union convention in Chicago, Dec. 28-30. They were elected on the second ballot from the group of ten who polled the most votes when the Senate voted on the thirty original nominees.

THE DAILY CALIFORNIAN

Students Return From National Conference; Kiefer Elected Chairman of California Committee

Engelhard Assumes Position Of Athletic Ticket Manager

Benner, Smith, Welch Attend Panel Sessions

The Daily Tar Heel

Legislature Votes In Favor Of NSO Affiliation

COLLEGES AROUND THE U.S. RESPOND. From above, clockwise: *Loyola News* 12/12/46, IL; *Ursuline Quill*, 2/10/47, OH; Louisiana State U. *The Reveille*, 12/6/46; *The Harvard Crimson*, 12/13/46, MA; Washington U. of St Louis *Student Life*, 12/19/46, MO; UC Berkeley, *The Daily Californian*, 1/9/47; U. of North Carolina *The Daily Tar Heel*, 5/18/47.

. . . and Find the Need for a New Organization

The Chicago Student Conference finds that there does exist in the United States a definite need for the formation of an NSO; and that this proposed organization should be founded on the common needs and desires of all American students; that these needs and desires are clearly defined by the concern of the student for peace, democracy and the strengthening of international friendships . . . that racial and religious prejudice, bigotry and discrimination be totally disavowed by this NSO. . .

From the "Reports of the Chicago Student Conference, December 28 to 30, 1946"

REPORTS OF THE
CHICAGO STUDENT CONFERENCE
DECEMBER 28 TO 30, 1946

HELD AT THE
UNIVERSITY OF CHICAGO
CHICAGO, ILLINOIS

The National Continuations Committee

1. The Chicago Student Conference

Clifton R. Wharton, Jr.
Harvard University
Secretary, National Continuations Committee, 1946-47

Editor's note: This essay has been adpated from "Black Pioneer: A Personal History. Part Three: The College Years," an extended autobiographical reference which, at this writing (2002), is being completed by the author and is intended for deposit and access to researchers and others with his archives at Michigan State University. The author is also preparing a standard autobiography for future trade publication.

My involvement in the founding of the U.S. National Student Association resulted from my background and interest in international affairs. My father served in the Foreign Service for forty years and was the first Black to become a career ambassador, when he was posted to Rumania (1958-1961) and Norway (1961-64). I was majoring in U.S. diplomatic history at Harvard in 1946, expecting to follow in my father's footsteps. I had joined the Student Council Committee on International Student Activities and had become a member of the World Relatedness Commission of the New England Student Christian Movement, the regional organization of the National YMCA/YWCA.

William S. Ellis, my college roommate, graduated in June 1946 and was selected by the National Intercollegiate Christian Council (YMCA/YWCA) as a delegate to the August 1946 meeting of the World Student Congress in Prague, Czechoslovakia, which established the International Union of Students (IUS). Bill was elected vice chairman of IUS and returned to America in October to prepare for his permanent residence abroad.

Call for a national student conference

Americans attending the Congress were surprised to find that the United States was the only major country that did not have a national student organization. The delegation returned home committed to establishing such an institution, although a previous attempt had failed.[1] Representing nine sponsoring U.S. organizations, the twenty-five delegates formed a committee to sponsor a national student conference to be held in Chicago.

The call for the conference stated:

> The experiences of the past summer in Europe among students of many nations have brought home to the committee the fact that a new segment of society is emerging—a group with recognizable characteristics of its own which often transcend national differences. Having recognized the existence of this INTERNATIONAL STUDENT COMMUNITY, we are further drawn to the conviction that each individual has a responsibility to this community of his fellow students—not only on the international, but also on a national and a local plane.
>
> One way in which this responsibility of the American student can be realized is by the establishment of a non-partisan organization, representative of all students of the United States, democratic in principle and practice, and devoted to the needs and problems of students.

The call was sent out to about nine hundred U.S. colleges and universities, public and private, to participate in a National Student Conference with a threefold purpose:

> 1. Hear a report on the international student scene, with special reference to the World Student Congress at Prague;
> 2. Discuss the need for and character of a national student organization in the United States; and
> 3. Establish, if so decided by the conference, a national preparatory committee to make specific plans for such an organization.

The conference was to be held at the University of Chicago at the end of December. Each college was asked to hold campus-wide delegate elections, with the number of delegates based on undergraduate enrollment. In addition, a number of student organizations were asked to participate, including the National Intercollegiate Christian Council (YMCA-YWCA), Students for Democratic Action, the National Federation of Catholic College Students, the Young Communist League, Student World Federalists, and the Newman Club Federation.[2]

Bill Ellis's story of his experience in Prague and the prospect of this new national student organization intrigued me greatly. Although I was busy working on my senior honors thesis and preparing for graduate school, I decided to run for one of the three undergraduate Harvard delegate positions.

Harvard appointed a four-person nominating committee to screen some twenty suggested candidates. I was somewhat taken aback when I learned that one of the other candidates had developed a campaign team and had enlisted Bobby Kennedy, Class of '48, as one of his key advisers. Although none of Joseph P. Kennedy's sons had yet moved onto the political scene, the Kennedy name had considerable political magic, largely because of Bobby's maternal grandfather, John Francis "Honey Fitz" Fitzgerald, the legendary mayor of Boston. I was undaunted, however, because I thought that I had a "secret weapon": I had been an announcer on the Harvard student radio station, WHCN, for several years, and consequently my name was fairly well known across the campus.

Selection of Harvard delegates

After interviews on December 9, the nominating committee chose a slate of ten, including me, to run for the three undergraduate slots. After a round-table discussion on the Harvard Crimson [radio] Network (welcome to my parlor!), the election was held. The three winners were Douglass Cater '46, who had been a member of the delegation to Prague; Eugene A. Dinet '44; and me. A fourth delegate, Andrew Rice, was selected to represent graduate students.

Soon after the election, I was asked by Harold Ingalls of the National Intercollegiate Christian Council (NICC) to serve as one of their four delegates, the other three being Bill Ellis, Joyce Roberts, and Muriel Jacobson. I explained that I was already going as a Harvard delegate, but he strongly urged me to represent the NICC as well. I reluctantly accepted the dual role.

Next, a "communist" controversy erupted. Ten days before the Chicago meeting, William Yandell Elliott, professor of government at Harvard, gave an interview to the *Harvard Crimson*[3] in which he warned that student delegates to Chicago should "keep a sharp lookout for Communist control bids." He blasted IUS as an organization "beyond doubt in the hands of Russian-oriented leaders who will render it a Soviet propaganda arm" and called for the American students to "pull up stakes" and get out of the organization. On the basis of information provided to him by Prague delegates from Georgetown University, Elliott stated that the seventeen-person IUS executive committee was weighted three to one in favor of the communist bloc and had only one American representative, Bill Ellis. He also stated that the impetus for the IUS conference came from the World Federation for Democratic Youth, a parent body of American Youth for Democracy (AYD),[4] "which is widely considered the successor to the Young Communist League." In the context of the emerging Cold War tensions and a growing anticommunist political mood in America, the reaction was not surprising. Yet to come were Winston Churchill's "Iron Curtain" speech in Missouri, charges of communist influence in the U.S. government, conviction of Alger Hiss for spying, the Korean War, and Senator Joe McCarthy's witch-hunt.

The bombshell produced an immediate reaction from Doug Cater, who condemned Elliott for relying on only one source of information and not checking with other American students who had attended the meeting. With regard to the forthcoming National Student Conference in Chicago, Cater stated, "Our paramount effort has been to make certain that delegates to the Chicago Conference be elected by their student bodies, and not by non-representative campus organizations." Cater saved his most scornful jibe for Elliott's charge that the U.S. delegates to Prague had been naive. "If we are so naive that we must fail every time we come up against representatives from Communist countries," Cater's statement said, "then let us withdraw from the IUS and the United Nations and send the first bomb on its merry way."

The National Student Conference

The National Student Conference, which convened in Chicago on December 28-30, 1946, was my first experience with national student politics. Held in the Reynolds Club auditorium on the University of Chicago campus, the conference was attended by 672 student delegates and observers, representing over three hundred colleges and universities. In addition, there were 55 delegates and observers from twenty-eight student organizations.[5]

The opening speaker on Saturday was Professor R. P. McKeon, dean of humanities at the University of Chicago. Russell Austin from the University of Chicago and the Young Socialist League, who had chaired the U.S. delegation to Prague and had served as chairman of the Chicago Conference Convening Committee, gave the keynote address. Three plenary sessions, one each day, were chaired by Cater, Ellis, and James Wallace from the University of North Carolina.

Four panels were organized. Panel 1, chaired by Russ Austin, dealt with the organizational structure and duties of a "National Continuations Committee," which would carry forward the recommendations of the Chicago meeting. This panel presented the formal resolution to create a U.S. national student organization that later was adopted by the plenary session.

Panel 2, chaired by Douglass Cater, prepared recommendations on the new organization's structure, including an executive committee and its powers and limitations, judiciary and advisory councils, membership requirements, relationship to member institutions, and finances. Panel 3, chaired by Al Houghton, was devoted to student needs and responsibilities in international affairs. Panel 4, chaired by Walter Wallace, drafted the preamble, aims, and activities of the proposed organization.

The desire to create the new organization was strong. Nevertheless, a certain anxiety permeated the meeting, largely because it was the first time that many of the delegates had participated in a national meeting of college students. The few delegates who obviously knew what they were doing and did most of the talking (and leading) were those who had attended the IUS meeting in Prague. Many represented student organizations, and therefore were seen somewhat suspiciously as "professional student leaders." (Despite my dual role as an elected Harvard delegate and a delegate from the NICC, I was viewed by most conferees as a delegate from Harvard.)

Added to this mix was the underlying national mood regarding communism, the escalating Cold War tensions with the Soviet Union and its satellites, and growing distrust of the U.S. left. These sentiments most often were reflected in tension between the students representing Catholic organizations and those whose political views were to the left.[6]

The situation was further complicated by the shortness of the Conference. Because of time constraints, only Panel 1's report was voted upon (and accepted, with amendments). The other three panel reports were passed on to the National Continuations Committee, with partial amendments to Panel 4's report.

There was clear willingness to work toward compromise on difficult or thorny issues, sometimes even with a bit of humor. In the midst of a tense discussion in which tempers flared, the parliamentarian from North Carolina broke the ice with this calm statement: "Mr. Chairman, I suggest we divide this conference into those with drawls, and those without."

Behind the scenes, certain student organizations, particularly the more radical left-wing groups, sought to dominate the agenda and alter the proposed call for a founding convention. I quickly learned their major technique: push for all-night sessions so that the quorum numbers would gradually diminish while their own ranks held firm. In this fashion they hoped to outwait and outvote the moderates.

One night the discussion dragged on until nearly 4:00 A.M. and the participants were virtually out on their feet. Seemingly at an impasse, we took a break and went into the coffee room, where there happened to be a piano. I sat down and began to play some songs, which drew others around to sing. This reduced the tension and renewed our energy. When we went back into session, the desired motion was passed.

Another effective tactic for dealing with the leftist ploy was introduced by several of those, like Curt Farrar, who had encountered the same phenomenon at Prague. It was a system of "rotating naps," in which we would doze in shifts while maintaining our presence. Similarly, attempts by our opponents to use alcohol, especially vodka, to lessen our ranks were skillfully avoided.

Unresolved issues

Four issues were not successfully resolved at the conference. The first dealt with membership and the participation of student organizations. There was a substantial preference that members should be students representing campuses, rather than those representing single-issue or special interest student organizations. A plan offered by the University of Texas advocated total exclusion of organizations, arguing that students were already represented by their campus-elected delegates. A temporary solution was to allow student organizations to have 10 percent of the places on the National Continuations Committee, leaving the final resolution of the issue until it could be taken up again at the founding convention.

A second issue concerned affiliation of the proposed organization with the IUS. Two reports presented to Panel 3 differed somewhat on the degree of communist influence in the IUS, with the Catholic delegate stating that twelve of the seventeen members of the IUS executive committee were communists and the Protestant delegate stating that there were eight. Yet the importance of affiliation was recognized, acknowledging that a U.S. national student organization should assume an international role. Far more concern was expressed over terms of affiliation that might subsume U.S. national views to those of IUS's majority representation. Panel 3 recommended against immediate affiliation and asked for further study of how it might be achieved while protecting the independence of the U.S. organization. In effect, this issue was also postponed until the founding convention.

The third issue was whether the organization should take political positions on student-related issues, and the effect of partisan political positions on the membership. Strikingly, the conference revealed what Marty McLaughlin called a strong "studential" nature. The delegates, McLaughlin stated, behaved, not as politicians, but as students interested in student concerns. Therefore, the majority were not interested in partisan politics.

The fourth issue dealt with racial equality and discrimination. This issue proved to be so contentious that it almost prevented the proposed organization from being formed. While everyone appeared to agree with the principle of racial equality, controversy centered on what that meant in terms of action.

It must be remembered that the racial climate of the time was much more virulent than it is today. Poll taxes and "Jim

Crow" segregation laws were still in force in the South. It would be 1954 before the Supreme Court ordered an end to the "separate but equal" doctrine in public schools, and another two years before the Rev. Martin Luther King, Jr., won the Montgomery, Alabama, boycott that empowered Blacks to sit at the front of the bus. The first major civil rights legislation was not passed until 1964. In 1946, racial discrimination was still a massive cancer in much of America.

Panel 4, which dealt with this topic, proposed that, upon returning to their campuses, the students work for the repeal of state laws that prohibit interracial meetings, thereby adversely affecting NSA regional meetings.[7] White students from the South angrily asserted that, while they accepted the principle of racial equality, taking back such a "Yankee-drafted" statement would work against the attainment of the goal. They stated that they must be allowed to work out more realistic solutions that recognized and accommodated individual local situations.[8]

I offered a compromise, proposing to shift the language, which had been introduced by southern Negro students and to which Southern white students objected, into the bylaws of the constitution. This involved a twofold approach. The first step was to strengthen the equal rights section of the preamble by stating "that racial and religious bigotry and discrimination be totally disavowed by this National Student Organization" and to insert seven specific action steps under the third stated organizational "aim," which was, "To secure for all people equal rights and possibility of primary, secondary, and higher education regardless of sex, race, religion, economic circumstance, social standing, or political convictions."[9] Several key leaders of the larger student delegations were contacted to push the compromise forward. Allan Ostar of Penn State was particularly helpful as a "floor manager." The compromise passed, again as a temporary measure. It was clear that the issue would have to be revisited at the founding convention.[10]

Many suggestions and proposals were made for activities that might be undertaken by the proposed organization, including: a national student employment bureau; an information bureau on extracurricular activities; aid to counter the current student housing shortage, especially for married students; and a clearinghouse for student international activities.

The National Continuations Committee

Among the leaders at Chicago who had attended the IUS meeting in Prague were Bill Ellis, Wally Wallace, Curt Farrar, and Doug Cater. Cater was probably the most colorful and effective performer. I had not seen him in action before and was most impressed. He would stand at the very back of the auditorium, wait until the right strategic moment, and then raise his deeply accented Montgomery, Alabama, voice: "Mr. Speakahh, Mr. Speakahh." When all heads had turned to see who was interrupting the session, he would dramatically stride down the aisle repeating "Mr. Speakahh" along the way. By the time he got to the microphone he had the entire audience transfixed and proceeded to give a marvelous speech in stentorian southern tones.

The National Continuations Committee was formed, and was assigned the tasks of working on preparations for the

THE NATIONAL CONTINUATIONS COMMITTEE

National Officers

James Smith, President (University of Texas)
Russell Austin, Vice President (University of Chicago)
John Simons, Treasurer (Fordham University)
Clifton Wharton, Secretary (Harvard)

Regional Chairmen

Miriam "Mimi" Haskell, Massachusetts
John F. Yewell,* New Jersey
Jack Minkoff, New York (Upstate)
Emmet D. Hurley (Joseph Zebley), Maryland-Delaware-D.C.
Mildred Kiefer, California
Phil Des Marais, Minnesota
Howard Bowles (Bill Welsh), Tennessee-Kentucky
Ralph A. Dungan , Pennsylvania
Paul F. Kirk, Illinois
Patricia Groom, Kansas-Missouri
Frances Rollins (Tom Walsh), Michigan
Walter Wallace (Eugene Schwartz), New York (Metropolitan)
Norm Israel, Oregon-Washington
John P. Hunter (Roy Voegeli), Wisconsin
Robert S. Smith (Curtis Farrar), Connecticut-Rhode Island
Lynn Derrick,* Maine-Vermont
Eugene Berman, Nebraska-North and South Dakota
Albert P. Foster, Alabama-Georgia
Lloyd Love, Arkansas-Mississippi-Louisiana
Jerry Goodman,* Colorado-New Mexico
Arizona-Utah-Nevada (no delegates at Chicago)
Manuel Alvarez,* Florida
Wally Cook, Indiana
Montana-Wyoming-Utah (no delegates at Chicago)
R. J. O'Brien,* Iowa
Dick Bredenberg,* New Hampshire
William H. Miller and Charles Wallace (cochair), North and South Carolina
Earl Wood, Virginia–West Virginia
Leo E. Rattay, Ohio
John Wilson, Texas-Oklahoma

Organizational Representatives

John Burns, Newman Club Federation
Joyce Roberts, National Intercollegiate Christian Council (NICC)
Don Willner, Students for Democratic Action (SDA)

Note: The names in parentheses are those who either later became chairpersons or who served as their designees at committee meetings. Asterisks (*) indicate temporary chairpersons.

founding convention and drafting a proposed constitution. The committee consisted of four national officers, thirty regional chairpersons, and three organizational representatives. Although Doug Cater was a logical choice for president, he withdrew his name from consideration, and Jim Smith from the University of Texas was elected. Smith was a mature, calming voice of reason during the meetings, and was an obvious future leader. Russell Austin was chosen vice president, and John Simons of Fordham University was elected treasurer. I was elected secretary.

A committee was organized to prepare a draft constitution. Its members were: Al Houghton, University of Wisconsin; Thomas Farr, University of Chicago; Janis Tremper, Rockford College; and William McDermed, DePaul University.

The end of the Chicago conference was marked by a renewal of the "communist-domination" issue. During the meeting, we had learned that the sessions were being secretly observed by the FBI, largely because of its concern that the organization might be an offshoot of the IUS. The Harvard delegation wondered whether Professor Elliott had precipitated the surveillance, using his extensive Washington connections. The issue was exacerbated by the fact that the only national press coverage was a picture of the elected officers on the front page of the *Daily Worker*, the official publication of the Communist Party. When my father, then U.S. Consul to the Azores, heard about this, his apoplectic outburst could be heard all the way across the Atlantic. He told me in no uncertain terms to resign my position, which I refused to do. I tried to explain to him that this was truly an independent student organization, that I could not help it if a tiny minority of the members were avowed communists, and that the participants overwhelmingly came from middle America. He was not convinced, but a father's influence on a twenty-year-old is naturally weak.

The period from January to August 1947 was devoted to drafting the proposed constitution and promoting, through regional meetings and newsletters, wide participation in the forthcoming convention.[11] The first draft of the constitution was discussed by the National Continuations Committee at its March 1-3 meeting. The draft was then sent to the thirty regional committees for discussion and suggested changes. In August 25-30, the NCC executive committee met to consider the regional reactions and develop the final draft.

At the meeting, the committee also thrashed out a variety of issues ranging from credentialing to institutional eligibility. Does a graduate school count as a separate institution—Harvard College and Harvard Graduate and Professional? Should Hunter College be considered one or two entities because it conducted both day and evening sessions? Meanwhile, by July 15, some 316 colleges and universities had submitted credentials and an intention to send delegates.

In July, word came that Bill Ellis had been stricken with paratyphoid on a visit to Florence, Italy, and had returned to Prague for rest and recuperation. He nevertheless sent a report strongly endorsing affiliation of the national student organization with IUS.[12]

A minor controversy arose over whether the NCC should support U.S. student participation in the World Youth Festival, sponsored by the World Federation of Democratic Youth, to be held in Prague from July 20 to August 17. Several students who had participated in the Chicago Conference organized a U.S. World Youth Festival Committee, but there was resistance within the NCC over formal participation. The concern related to doubts about the political bias of the sponsors and participants. Although no formal support was given, several NCC leaders did attend.

Clifton R. Wharton was Deputy Secretary of State, Chairman and CEO of Teachers Insurance Annuity Association and College Retirement Equities Fund (TIAA-CREF), Chancellor of the State University of New York, and President of Michigan State University.

END NOTES

1 For a description of these early attempts, see Martin M. McLaughlin, "Prewar Student Activisim," p. 15.

2 See p. 103 for a complete list of the national student organizations represented in Chicago.

3 "Elliott asks wariness of communists at Chicago; student conference must fight minority 'capturing' tactics, seek democratic principles; flays liberals' naivete; International Student Union is under Russian domination, he claims; points to past," *Harvard Crimson*, December 19, 1946.

4 Editor's note: Although the 12/19/46 edition of the *Harvard Crimson* cites Elliott as stating that the WFDY is the "parent body" of the AYD, this was a loose use of the term, since the AYD was formed in New York City in October 1943 as a direct outgrowth of the Young Communist League, and the World Federation of Democratic Youth, a Communist-dominated organization, was formed in November of 1945 in London. See Reisin, p. 787, and AYD, p. 795.

5 There were 500 voting delegates—474 students and 26 organizational representatives (National Continuations Committee, "Reports to the Chicago Student Conference December 28 to 30, 1946, held at the University of Chicago, Chicago, Illinois," printed pamphlet, n.d., p. 23). Other sources gave slightly different numbers. McLaughlin says that there were

> 475 student delegates from 295 colleges and universities...nineteen national student organizations were represented, and there were between 150 and 200 official observers. This total of almost 700 was 50 percent over the expectations and caused the preparatory committee some last-minute (but welcome) headaches. [Martin McLaughlin, "Conference in Chicago," *America*, Vol. 26, No. 26 [March 29, 1947]: 711)

[6] "Participation by Catholic students . . . to a large extent . . . was prompted in this particular instance by the conviction that if Catholics did not take some interest in this national student conference, the affair would be dominated by communists; it was anticipated that there would be a subtle but strong bid for control by these subversive elements. No doubt the possibility of creating another front to replace the defunct American Student Union . . . was the incentive behind the hard work and zeal displayed by the American Youth for Democracy and similar organizations." Martin McLaughlin, "Conference in Chicago," *America*, 26, no 26 [March 29, 1947]: 713).

[7] The proposed resolution read as follows:

> Whereas it is an aim of the NSO [National Student Organization] to extirpate discrimination in education, and whereas the state laws of some southern areas prohibit interracial meetings, and whereas it is likely that the NSO will involve regional organizations which must meet regionally, Resolve that a specific aim of the NSO be to take every means within its power to effect the repeal of such state legislation. (Undated copies in Chicago conference files, CRWJr. Archives)

[8] This issue bedeviled subsequent affiliation campaigns on southern campuses after the Constitutional Convention. See pp. 454, 995 for reports of the failed affiliation referendum contests at Louisiana State University and at the University of Texas in February of 1948.

[9] The relevant suggested two activities were as follows:

> Urge schools and colleges to help students appreciate the varied racial and cultural backgrounds which enrich our nation. We suggest the fulfillment of this objective by enrolling and employing faculty members of various religious and cultural backgrounds.
>
> Investigate the extent of quota systems, segregation in student dormitories, discriminatory student employment, student dining halls, and segregation in student hospitals; and subsequently inform our student membership of findings. (Undated copies in Chicago conference files, CRWJr. Archives)

See also n. 22, p. 415.

[10] The conference's mimeographed daily newsletter, The Chronicle, reported a telling racial incident on the day of the debate:

> Four Negro delegates entered the Tropical Hut, a local [Chicago] eatery on East 57th Street at 4:30 P.M. Sunday. About three-fourths of the tables and booths were empty. The manager would not allow them to sit down. When asked point blank if he was refusing them service, the manager said, "Yes." Two white delegates in the place picked up their coats and walked out without eating. (*Chronicle,* 1, no. 2 [December 29, 1946]: 1)

[11] For example, several regional groups were formed. The Harvard-Radcliffe group held a special meeting on March 27, called "Needed World Student Co-operation." The Massachusetts Regional Committee held a conference at Smith College on February 15-16. The North Dakota/South Dakota/Nebraska Regional Committee held a meeting at Augustana College on May 10-11 and issued a regular "Informational Newsletter." One of the more innovative efforts was Berea College's printed newspaper, called *The Wallpaper* (see pp. 172, 987).

[12] Ellis later resigned his position as IUS vice president, returned to the United States, graduated from Harvard Law School, and became a highly successful lawyer. For the circumstances that caused Ellis to resign, see William B. Welsh's essay, p. 170. See also p. 188 for excerpts from Ellis's resignation letter.

PICTURE CREDITS: *Then:* announcer for the *Harvard Crimson* Network (WHCN), 1944 or 1945. *Now:* Deputy Secretary of State, U.S. Dept. of State, 1993. (*Both, author*).

CLIFTON R. WHARTON

Early years and education: I was born in Boston in 1926, the son of a career diplomat, and spent six years of my childhood in the Canary Islands, Spain, where I became fluent in Spanish. My father served in the U.S. Foreign Service for 40 years and was the first Black to be named a career ambassador. I attended Boston Latin School, America's first public school, and at age sixteen entered Harvard University, where I received a B.A. in history in 1947. After graduating from Harvard, I became the first Black to be admitted to, and graduate from, the Johns Hopkins School of Advanced International Studies and the first to receive a doctorate in economics from the University of Chicago.

Career Highlights: For twenty-two years I worked with the Rockefeller philanthropic interests in foreign economic development in Latin America and Southeast Asia. In 1970 I was elected president of Michigan State University, thereby becoming the first Black to head a predominantly white major university in the United States. In 1978, I became Chancellor of the State University of New York System with sixty-four campuses, and subsequently pioneered as the first Black to become Chairman and CEO of a Fortune 100 company when, in 1987, I was chosen to head the Teachers Insurance Annuity Association and College Retirement Equities Fund (TIAA-CREF), the world's largest pension fund (with $250 billion in assets). In 1993, I served briefly as Deputy Secretary of State in the Bill Clinton Administration. I have been a director of ten major corporations and served six U.S. presidents in various capacities. I was chairman of the Rockefeller Foundation, deputy chairman of the Federal Reserve Bank of New York, and a trustee of many nonprofit organizations.

Publications: I have written extensively on the problems of development. I am editor of the book *Subsistence Agriculture and Economic Development* (1969) and coauthor, with Rev. Theodore M. Hesburgh and Dr. James Miller, of *Patterns for Lifelong Learning* (1973). I have been a contributor to many professional journals.

Awards: I have won numerous awards, including Boston Latin School "Man of the Year" (1970) and the Alumni Medal, University of Chicago (1980). I have received sixty-one honorary degrees from such institutions as the University of Michigan, the Johns Hopkins University, City College of New York, Georgetown University, Columbia University, Amherst College, the University of Vermont, Colgate University, Michigan State University, University of Notre Dame, Tuskegee University, Washington University, and Harvard University.

Other Government Service: In 1976, I was appointed by President Gerald Ford to be the first chairman of the Board for International Food and Agricultural Development, AID, U.S. Department of State, and re-appointed chairman by President Jimmy Carter in 1980, serving until 1983.

Family: I am married to the former Dolores Duncan of New York City. Mrs. Wharton is Chairman and CEO of The Fund for Corporate Initiatives, Inc., a nonprofit organization which she founded devoted to strengthening the role of minorities and women in the corporate world. She serves on three corporate boards of directors, Kellogg Company, COMSAT and Gannett Co., Inc., and was a director of Phillips Petroleum Company for seventeen years. We have two sons, Bruce and the late Clifton III.

CONTINUATION COMMITTEE (NCC) CHARTS NSO COURSE

CHICAGO CONFERENCE LAYS GROUNDWORK FOR NEW ORGANIZATION The *Harvard Crimson* reports in its 1/7/47 issue [The future "NSA" was still known by the formative acronym "NSO," for National Student Organization]. Clif Wharton, one of four Harvard delegates, was elected Secretary of the NCC and seated front row left in the photo of a Committee meeting below. Balance of row: Russell Austin (Chicago), Vice President, Jack Minkoff (Cornell), NY State Regional Chair, Walter Wallace (Columbia), Met NY Regional Chair. To rear right of Minkoff, Mimi Haskell (Smith), Massachusetts Regional Chair; to her rear right, Ralph Dungan (St. Joseph's, PA), Pennsylvania Regional Chair.

(Photos: *Al Cohen*, Chicago. Schwartz)

ard Crimson

ASS., TUESDAY, JANUARY 7, 1947. PRICE FIVE CENTS.

Delegates at Chicago Term Conference 'Representative'

Windy City Conference Attains Main Aims in Vacation-Time Panels; Wharton Gets Office

EASY COMPROMISES FOUND

Delegates' Report Asks Further Participation by University In NSO Summer Program

Five hundred students from 350 colleges throughout the nation attended the long heralded Chicago Student Conference and in three days of meetings beginning on December 28 set up executive committees and made tentative declarations to lay the groundwork for the proposed National Student Organization scheduled to be organized next June.

In their report to the Student Council and the University, the four delegates from Harvard stressed the representative character of the conference and the success of the group in restricting its field of work and thereby getting a maximum of work done. They emphasized that no final resolutions or decisions were adopted but merely recommendations to a Continuations Committee and to next summer's Constitutional Congress.

Held in the Reynolds Club Auditorium in Chicago, the conference was the result of a call sent out this fall by the delegates to the International Student Union in Prague last summer to mobilize American student opinion for participation in world-wide groups.

Grill Reopened, Is Heavy Demand

g houses in the University found a new competitor last n the Eliot Grill, opened for t time since ante-bellum days, staff or four which manned r eating emporium was still ing why a veteran-riddled col- is drinking as much milk to- it did cokes in the pre-war

175 hungry patrons jammed le cafeteria in Eliot's base- the rush hours from 9 to o'clock closing time, taking a from their studies to have to eat. Hot dogs were their order from a menu which in- about ten different sand- candy, cigarettes, and ... beverages.

Radio Peeves Soap Operas, y Announcers

eras, singing commercials, hill- e, and "too much talking" will average undergraduate turn for his amusement according ation obtained by the Crimson in its recent college-wide radio oll.

ion to the standard set of ever handfull of misogynists listed nouncers as number one com- n the credit side, more than se polled cited classical music avorite evening program type, lar music running second

Percent Have Radios

Mountaineer Duo Join Ronne Jaunt To Antarctic Pole

Two undergraduate members of the Mountaineering Club have decided to drop their books for a while and accept the invitation of the Ronne Expedition to spend 14 months in the frozen wastes of Antarctica.

William Latady, special student and president of the Club, has already left Cambridge and is heading for Beaumont, Texas, where the expedition will set sail on January 16. Latady is taking the frigid trip in the capacity of aerial photographer, while his colleague, Robert H. T. Dodson '47, a former vice-president of the mountaineers, will be the trip's geologist.

Sponsored by four private scientific societies, with some backing from the Navy, the expedition has no relation to the Byrd outfit which is already digging in to the the snowfields. Commander Finn Ronne, for whom the trip is named, will lead his group on their various scientific quests to Palmerland, an area of the Antarctic lying directly south of Cape Horn.

Geological, geographical, and astronomical research are the principal purposes of the trip. The expedition will live in ... ents and igloos in their base camp and will make a trip to the pole itself during their stay.

NATIONAL CONSTITUTION DRAFTED BY NCC

Students INTERNATIONAL ACTIVITIES Bulletin

Vol. I, No. 2 — Published for the National Continuations Committee of the Chicago Students Conference by the International Activities Committee of the Harvard Student Council — April 15, 1947

Campuses Rally for Overseas Relief

Five Sections Proposed for NSO in U. S.

With the drafting of a United States National Student Organization constitution this month, plans are going rapidly ahead for assembling a nation-wide convention in the late summer, at which the proposed union is expected to be officially formed.

In an effort to "get down on paper" the ideas expressed at the ...

Money-Raising Campaigns Reported Leading Drives For Foreign Student Aid

Early replies to the questionnaire on campus international activities, published in the March Bulletin, reveal continued emphasis on money-raising drives among over-all campaigns for student relief abroad. Colleges throughout the country are topping last year's records in contributions to the World Student Service Fund while many schools report additional book and clothing collections.

In addition to relief and reconstruction activities, increasing numbers of universities are ex- ...

Travel Problem Restricts Year's ...

Students INTERNATIONAL ACTIVITIES Bulletin

VOL. I, NO. 1 — Published for the National Continuations Committee of the Chicago Students Conference by the International Activities Committee of the Harvard Student Council — MARCH 1, 1947

Food and Clothing Drives Lead Campus Campaigns To Help Rehabilitation

Varied activities of campus groups interested in international student organization have been reported recently to the National Continuations Committee. Such activities range from food and clothing drives, to sizeable contributions for direct relief abroad, collections of scientific equipment and books, and the setting up of student exchange scholarships.

So far, the University of Wisconsin, Mt. Holyoke, Swarthmore, Rutgers University, Smith, Harvard, and Colgate have been heard from. Student bodies have been urged by the committee to report any similar activities to the Bulletin.

Excerpts from some of these reports follow:

University of Wisconsin

A student contribution of $5,000 to the World Student Service Fund launched the University of Wisconsin's activities at Madison last fall. Specific relief projects are underway in both the French and German departments. The French department has adopted the elementary school of Bliesbruck in Alsace-Lorraine, while the German Club sponsors a monthly package to students in Vienna. Through a speakers' bureau, foreign students at the university reach citizens in all parts of the state.

Mt. Holyoke College

At Mt. Holyoke College, South Hadley, Mass., 13 foreign students ...

Plans for New Student Group Set at Chicago

To lay groundwork for formation of a permanent national students organization in America, delegates from over 300 colleges and universities representing 42 states met in Chicago from Dec. 28 to Dec. 30, 1946, and set up a National Continuations Committee to carry out its program and prepare for a subsequent conference this summer.

The Chicago Conference, in four panel discussion groups, considered aims and purposes of the proposed union, international student activities, and general organizational detail. As a result, a clearing house of information on student exchange, travel, relief, and rehabilitation was set up, and possibilities of affiliation with the International Union of Students were discussed. ...

Jim Smith was elected president of the National Continuations Committee at the Chicago Students Conference.

New Aid Sought As World Relief Needs Increase

"Students of American universities send greetings—and food, clothing, and equipment—to their fellow students in Europe and Asia." This is the theme of all-campus relief drives in hundreds of American colleges and universities from which aid is flowing to war-devastated educational institutions overseas.

Bulletin Makes Its Debut To Exchange Information On Study, Travel and Relief

Providing information on student exchange, travel, relief, and rehabilitation to American colleges and universities, the Students International Activities Bulletin begins monthly publication today, as a project of the clearing house set up by the National Continuations Committee after the National Students Conference in Chicago last December.

New Legislation Assists Study in Colleges Abroad

The G.I. Bill and the newly passed Fulbright Act are today working hand in hand with foreign universities to promote international student exchange.

Despite overwhelming difficulties, universities abroad have opened their doors to American students, who under educational benefits of the G. I. Bill, may now study overseas as well as at home. By next year, the Fulbright Act will add to these provisions by releasing funds of accumulated foreign credit to finance student exchange programs. In addition, a system has been set up by the Convention for Promotion of Inter-American Cultural Relations providing for the exchange of two students annually between the United States and certain other American republics. ...

The Bulletin will include latest data available from European countries on needs for assistance from American students, as well as opportunities abroad for education and travel in connection with rehabilitation. It will also attempt to facilitate co-ordination of relief efforts of students throughout America, by the exchange of information at regular intervals.

Questionnaire Included

A direct result of the conference held at the University of Chicago last December, the Bulletin is being published in accordance with recommendations of the International Activities Panel for formation of the clearing house to gather and distribute information concerning the committee's activities.

In an effort to simplify presentation of data from American schools, a questionnaire is being included in this issue of the Bulletin (see page 2), to which local students activities chairmen are asked to reply. ...

OVERSEAS RELIEF AND REHABILITATION AID TO STUDENTS was an initial focus of NCC promotional efforts while it was preparing a draft constitution for the proposed new organization. Two issues of the *Student International Activities Bulletin* were produced for the NCC by the International Activities Committee of the Harvard Student Council (see Fisher, Part 2, Section 1). In the photo below, Middle Atlantic area regional chairs hold an informal caucus at Chicago. From left to right: Ralph Dungan, Pennsylvania (St. Joseph's College, Philadelphia), John Yewell, New Jersey (Rutgers University), Emmet D. Hurley (Georgetown University) Maryland, Delaware, DC, Jack Minkoff (Cornell), NY State, and Walter Wallace (Columbia), Metropolitan NY.

"Strong, democratic student governments will be the backbone of the NSO"

2. Perspectives on the New Organization

Jim Smith
University of Texas
President, National Continuations Committee, 1946-47

"The success of organizations is dependent on the attitude of their members rather than the statements of their constitution. . . . I do not believe that the organization will be controlled by any faction."

Editor's note: Jim Smith, a popular and eloquent student leader at the University of Texas, brought his leadership qualities to the Chicago Student Conference. He was elected President of the National Continuations Committee and entrusted with being the first such postwar leader with a mandate to speak in behalf of American students.

Jim resigned his position as student body president and came to Chicago in February of 1946 to work full time to bring the organization into being. It was not until 1967 that he returned to the university to receive his degrees in economics in 1970 and 1971, after having gone to work in a steel mill and building a career on the staff of the United Steel Workers of America.

Jim was able to electrify a large audience and engage intimately with small groups. Most importantly, he had the patience to deal with the mundane building blocks of organization to build successful action programs and reach strategic goals.

Later, when he went to Prague in 1948 to replace the ailing Bill Ellis as IUS vice president and then resigned in protest, he laid out a vigorous political testament and challenge to American students to build a strong program of social justice and civil rights.[1]

As President of the precursor to NSA, he laid the groundwork for the future association and became its face and voice in the college community. It was uncharted territory. How far should the leader of a nonpolitical, nonpartisan student organization reach in using the bully pulpit? The following pages provide a few examples of the ways in which he tested and gave voice to the organization's purposes.

A Report to the Dean

Editor's note: This letter, excerpted, was written to Dean Arno Nowotny of the University of Texas just after Smith's election in Chicago as President of the National Continuations Committee. In it he demonstrated his understanding that the first priority was to build a sound organizational foundation for the new organization.

STUDENTS' ASSOCIATION
THE UNIVERSITY OF TEXAS, AUSTIN

January 5, 1947

Dear Dean Nowotny,

Before I say anything else I wish to thank you from the very bottom of my heart for all the things you did to make our trip to Chicago possible. The financial problems you ironed out, the advice you gave on the mechanics of fund-raising and money handling, your constructive ideas in the first meeting of our delegation, and your attitude throughout, were the basic reasons for the success of our delegation at the Conference.

You will receive complete reports on the Conference from George [Nokes], as Delegation Chairman. This letter includes my personal opinions regarding specific matters on which I want you to have the fullest information. . . .

The matters to which I refer are, to be specific, the various attempts to influence the recent Conference along non-student interests, the possibilities of future control of the permanent organization to divert it into political or other narrow channels, and my own plans, with regard to the latter. . . .

In my opinion the Communist students came to the Conference with the principal objective of supporting anything which they would term progressive.[2] The Catholics came, I believe, to oppose strongly any attempts at leftist domination, and to promote their own specific views with regard to the IUS. . . .

In view of the fact that the deepest loyalties of each group arise out of philosophical, political, or religious creeds, the above paragraph cannot be considered as a criticism of either group. It is a statement of facts which must be taken into consideration.

The number of Communist Party card holders at the Conference was impossible to determine, nor is it particularly significant. It was very small, I am sure. . . .

The Catholic students immediately envisioned in the proposals of the Texas delegation a plan for the permanent organizational structure which fitted their aims closely. Two significant features of the "Texas Plan" were carefully designed to eliminate the future possibility that the organization might be controlled by a small group, whose principal aims were other than student welfare, pure and simple.[3]

The radical students and others opposed the "Texas Plan," partially because it had Catholic and other support which the radicals considered to be non-progressive, and partially because they looked on the "Texas Plan" as offering the opportunity for faculty control of the organization, apparently....

Because I have learned that the success of organizations is dependent on the attitudes of their members rather than the statements of their constitutions, I was discouraged about the Conference until the closing hours of the last day. I feared that there was and would be too little agreement on common aims and methods, too much confusion about aims and methods among the non-partisan delegates, and too much factionalism among the various partisans (of whom I have mentioned only two groups).[4]

As the Conference progressed, however, both principal factions began to decide that if a permanent organization is to be formed, their participation in it will be only on a basis of common interest in student needs and student welfare, without regard for political and religious dogmas. Simultaneously the non-partisan and relatively uninformed delegates began to unite on a common program of student unity on specific student problems. On the last afternoon the issue of racial prejudice was injected into the plenary session. It was at that time that a true spirit of "compromise for the sake of unity" was molded. The willingness of the Negro delegates to sacrifice certain class interests, at least to a degree, in order to obtain the participation of Southern students in the temporary and future permanent organizations, was the greatest single contribution to the success of the conference.[5]

At that time I decided that there is an opportunity to build a national association of students, along the general lines of the Bar Association, the American Medical Association, or the AAUP. Because of that decision I agreed to requests that I be a candidate for the presidency of the temporary Continuations committee which will function until the Constitutional Convention. My election I attribute to the general appeal of the "Texas Plan" and the effectiveness of our delegation in convincing the various delegates of its merits.

I was opposed by most of the radicals, and supported by the Catholics. The latter group particularly feared the election of any of the twenty-five Prague Delegates, I gathered, and desired a chief executive who they were convinced would be impartial. The radicals probably doubted my impartiality, and favored the University of Chicago delegate to Prague, Russell Austin. I do not believe that he is strongly influenced by either faction. He was unanimously elected vice-president.[6]

John Simons, a Catholic leader from Fordham, is our treasurer, and Cliff Wharton, a brilliant Negro student at Harvard, is secretary. Wharton is a YMCA man, and fully as neutral as either Austin or myself from my brief observation.

I do not believe that the permanent organization will be controlled by any faction. It will be progressive, undoubtedly, but it will be progressive in the field of student needs and student welfare rather than partisan political or religious fields.

To quote from Harold Laski, its aims and activities will be designed "to make the path of learning an easier one," rather than "to promote a body of specific political doctrine in which its members are interested." So long as all the various sections of the country are represented in its congresses, and so long as none of the views held by large groups of students are suppressed in its deliberations, there need be no fear that the organization will be diverted from its original purpose.

The administrations of the various colleges and universities can guarantee that the above two conditions of permanent non-partisanship will exist, if they choose to do so. It is particularly important, in my mind, that the Western and Southern students not be prevented by administration actions from enjoying the fullest participation in the organization.[7] If their respective points of view are deprived of fair proportional representation in the policy-forming body of the organization by administration fears or administrative lethargy the organization will not be soundly based as a *national* student organization, both national in scope and national in representation. I am counting on your assistance in this particular matter.

... I shall do everything in my power to see that the constitution is written with the aim of perpetuation of a united student front on the general problems facing students *in their functions and activities as students*....I shall do everything I can to obtain the best possible public relations for the embryonic organization, which means among other things the elimination of the possibility that we may be successfully "Red-baited."

Your friend,
Jim Smith

As president of the NCC, I have no authority to take action on this matter of a "Red Hunt"

A Message To Michigan Region Delegates

You have it in your power to establish a pattern of intelligent, effective, student opposition to coercive tactics by those who refuse to recognize student rights....It is, therefore, imperative that you act wisely.

NATIONAL CONTINUATIONS COMMITTEE
OF THE CHICAGO STUDENT CONFERENCE
Reynolds Club Room 302, University of Chicago,
5706 University Avenue, Chicago 37, Illinois

February 7, 1947

ATTENTION: All Michigan Delegates or Observers to the Chicago Student Conference.

Dear Delegate or Observer:

This letter is to call your attention to three facts which may or may not be related in your minds. First, as most of you know, seven students of Michigan State College, Lansing, were recently placed on "indefinite disciplinary probation" by their Dean. The Chicago papers are extremely hazy on the exact reason for this action, but it appears to have resulted from either their distribution of pro-FEPC material or from their membership in an unrecognized chapter of AYD, or both. Almost simultaneously, according to the Chicago papers, a state-wide "Red Hunt" was begun in your state.

Second, Panel IV of the Chicago Student Conference adopted the following statement among its recommendations regarding the aims of the prospective NSO.

"To encourage student-faculty cooperation on student problems and the extension of democratic student-controlled student government and establish the independence and freedom from censorship of student organizations and publications." (From the Reports of the Chicago Student Conference, Panel IV, Sec. I, Par. 5.)

Third, the Michigan Regional Committee of the NCC of the Chicago Student Conference, of which you are a member, is meeting some time in February, I assume....

... As President of the NCC, I have no authority to take action on this matter of a "Red Hunt" in the Michigan schools. Neither do I have authority or inclination to request or recommend any specific action on your part. I'm not in a position to know the facts of the matter, and cannot express an opinion without such knowledge. Furthermore, as those of you who observed the Conference debates will clearly recognize, I am not, personally, a particularly ardent admirer of the AYD organization....

I do wish to outline the course of action I would take if I were dealing with such a situation in my home state of Texas:

First, I would observe carefully all administrative activities of my own campus bearing on this subject, carefully attempting to distinguish between investigative, coercive, and directly suppressive activities,

Second, I would bring the problem up for discussion at the Regional Committee meeting in my state, giving a full report of my observations from my own campus.

Third, I would attempt to devise some effective plan to be adopted by my Regional Committee for student action on the matter. Such a plan would, in my mind, have to recognize the right of the State to investigate its educational system for any purpose. However, the plan would envision student resistance to all coercive or suppressive acts which directly deny the freedom of expression to which every student of whatever political viewpoint is entitled, by virtue of his citizenship in the United States of America. It would have to be a plan for action on a state-wide level, unifying the sentiment of all students, of whatever political conviction, to resist suppression of student rights.

When the NSO is established, investigation of student suppression and resistance against student suppression will certainly be one phase of its broad program. The NSO will, I am sure, recognize that suppression of students whose political convictions may be extremely leftist can easily lead to suppression of students for reasons not concerned with political characteristics at all,

You have it in your power to establish a pattern of intelligent, effective, student opposition to the coercive tactics employed by those who refuse to recognize student rights. Future policies and methods of the NSO may easily be affected by the decisions you make. It is, therefore, imperative that you act wisely if the facts of the case as you observe them require action. It is equally imperative that your action, if action is taken, be effective action.

With the sincerest hope that I have not unduly intruded myself into the affairs of the State of Michigan and its students, but with the realization that the private affairs of Michigan students may easily become public affairs of students everywhere, I am

Sincerely yours,

Jim Smith
President, NCC

Suddenly it boiled up....You are the elected leader of those students. If you will not lead them in the cause of world understanding and world peace, who will?

The March, 1947 Executive Committee Faces a Decision

[Letter from Jim Smith to Kathleen Bland, postmarked 3/14/47]

301 Reynolds Club
Chicago 37, Ill

Hello, Darling,

This letter is long overdue, I know. I had the executive committee meeting's decisions to execute for 18 hours daily since March 3.[8]...

* * *

Dates were set for Sept. 1-15 [for the Constitutional Convention], not to last less than eight days. U. of Wisconsin selected as site. Other decisions more or less trivial, with one exception. The question as to whether the six Americans elected last summer to the International Union of Students Council (despite the fact of not formal participation of U.S. students in the IUS) should be sent back.

The six include one avowed Communist, one fellow traveller, one very official and very articulate spokesman for the Vatican from Notre Dame, and three New Dealers.[9]

Exec committee members from Virginia, Pennsylvania and Minnesota have mandates from their regional conferences against endorsement of, or financial aid to, their return. The Catholics and Southerners were obviously opposed.

Should we send the Americans back to Prague?

A Harvard man framed a resolution which specifically disclaimed financial responsibility of the NCC to [sic] their return, but endorsed the principle of their return as unofficial representatives of American student opinion. Only four committee members spoke for it, the stony faces turned to them were audible indications of reaction, hysterical anti-Communism cleverly converted into anti-internationalism....It looked like a passionless meeting of the America First Committee.

When they were all through it was 11:00 Sunday night, and the question was called. I asked their tolerance of a statement of my own opinion on the matter. They raised no objection. Wasn't I generally following the conservative line? What could I do but join the chorus?

I rose and moved to the side of the room while they chatted with one another about regional activities, and [I] spoke a few halting sentences. They continued to chat. Suddenly, darling, it boiled up, and I was chewing nails with each word—

> I hope that those of you who do not care to listen to my remarks are so blindly biased that you will go right on and vote your religious and sectional prejudices without regard to my remarks, so that it won't matter whether you hear me or not, I whispered.

They sat up straight, many of their faces turned white, they hadn't heard such plain talk for two days of circumlocution.

I talked about the atomic bomb, about the future leaders of their nations.

Then I talked, for fifty minutes. I talked about the atomic bomb. I talked about American foreign policy, present and future. I talked about the leaders of the IUS, who are the future leaders of their nations.

I talked about the responsibilities of leadership and the difference between the functions of a voting machine and the functions of the leader:

> If your region voted against this idea, then your responsibility as of now is to go work to improve the attitudes of your region. You not only owe that responsibility to your nation and the peoples of all other nations, you owe it to the students and future citizens of your region, and to yourself. You are the elected leader of those students. If you will not lead them in the cause of world understanding and world peace, who will? Col. McCormick? William Randolph Hearst?

And on and on.

The vote was unanimous for the resolution, and many were the promises of assistance in raising the funds on a tacit and voluntary bases. And so they proved that they were not blinded, but merely misguided, and they put another little bolster under my faith in the eventual ability of the people to judge between right and wrong.

END NOTES

[1] See Marsh, p. 149.

[2] See Murray, "Operation University," p. 739.

[3] See Bill Ellis and the NICC, p. 158.

[4] See McLaughlin, "Factions in NSA," p. 818.

[5] See Wharton, p. 115 and Simons, p. 126.

[6] See Austin, p. 90.

[7] *Editor's note:* Smith was correctly anticipating the concerns and resistance of many cautious and conservative administrations. There are several instances cited in this anthology as examples of administration concerns and intervention. See Shaffer, p. 326; Klopf, p. 336; President's veto of USC (p. 1026) and of Georgetown (p. 738) affiliation. See also administration correspondance, pp. 193, 933, 942, 1030, 1070.

[8] Eighteen members of the twenty-nine-member Executive Committee, plus Smith and Rusell Austin, were reported present in the minutes.

[9] Peter T. Jones in "USNSA and IUS Relations, 1945-1955" (Cambridge, MA: International Commission USNSA, 1955) writes, "The Americans chose Lee Marsh (American Youth for Democracy), Walter Wallace (Youth Builders), James Wallace (North Carolina), William Ellis (National Intercollegiate Christian Council), Douglass Cater (Harvard), and Martin McLaughlin (National Catholic Youth Council)." According to the minutes of the IUS Council meeting, July 31-August 11, 1947, five American members attended. They were "Callan, D.; Cater, Douglass; Wallace, Walter; Cassidy, Sally; Fisher, Frank." An observer, "Wainfield," from the Association of Internes and Medical Students, was also listed.

PICTURE CREDITS: *Then:* 1946 Chicago Student Conference (*A.L. Cohen,* Chicago. Schwartz). *Now:* Special Edition, *Steelabor,* April 12, 1990, United Steel Workers of America (Courtesy, Michael Smith).

Houston

HOUSTON, TEXAS, THURSDAY, MAY 2,

STUDENT PRESIDENT — A graduate of Lamar High School and former Rice Intitute student, Jim Smith, 3031 Albans road, has been elected president of the University of Texas student body. Jim is a member of the Unversity YMCA, Tejas Club and Rainey for Governor Club. He is the nephew of Miss Alta Smith, Lanier school teacher.

SMITH'S SUPPPORT FOR DR. HOMER RAINEY is reported in this notice by way of his membership in the Rainey for Governor Club. Dr. Rainey was the popular U. of Texas President fired by the Trustees in 1944 in a widely publicized academic freedom conflict. Losing the brutally fought race for governor, Rainey went on to become President of Stephens College, MO, and served on the NSA National Advisory Committee in its first year, 1948-49. (*Houston Post* 5/2/46)

KATHLEEN BLAND, left, to whom Jim Smith writes on this page and whom he married in 1947, is shown here with Janis Tremper, later elected NSA's first national Secretary, at one of Madison's lakes during the Constitutional Convention. (Courtesy Roy Voegeli)

James Wesley Smith: From Student Leader to Labor Leader

Jim Smith was born in 1924 in Fairmont, West Virginia, to a family with nineteenth-century roots in West Virginia and Indiana. Jim's natural mother died when he was two. He was raised by his Aunt Alta in Houston. She taught eighth-grade math and was a fixture in Houston teacher groups. He attended Rice University from 1941 to 1942, and the University of Texas, Austin, where he was president of the student body, from 1944 to 1946, returning later to receive his B.A. degree in economics in 1967, then a earned a Master's and completed doctoral studies in economics from the University of Houston in 1970. His son, Michael, writes:

"After his student days, my father's life was dedicated to the Labor Movement. It was a cause to which he was totally committed, and was to occupy him for virtually his entire working career. Jim saw unions as a vehicle for social justice, uplifting the dignity of workers and helping to cure specific problems of poverty, bigotry, and ignorance. He was acutely aware of using 'this brief time we have on God's Earth' to make the world a better place. Through the economic power of the Union, he found an instrument for good that allowed him to realize his aims, serving as a change agent on a larger stage.

"Jim worked part-time for the Texas CIO during college, and sought a staff job upon his return from Prague in 1948. But certain labor leaders were suspicious of his middle class origins and college training. Another problem may have been his success in getting elected as University of Texas student body president, perhaps even his NSA service abroad.

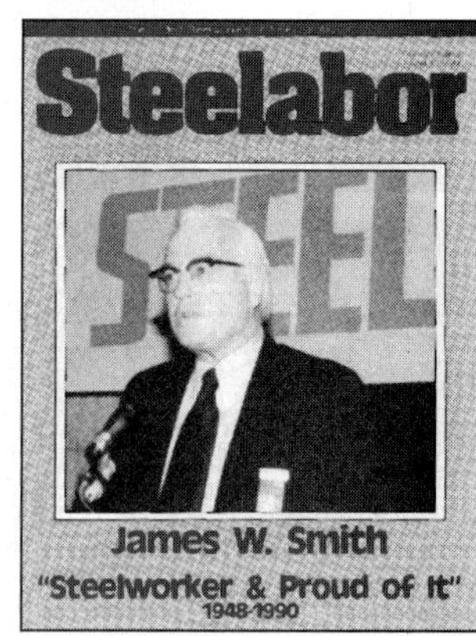

"Denied in his first job bid with the Steelworkers, Jim went to work as a welder in a pipe mill. He ran for office in his local union, rising to president in 1951. Not until 1953 did he receive an offer to join the Steelworkers as a staff representative. That began a thirty-nine-year relationship that asked and received his best work.

"Jim's union service was evenly split between Texas (1953-1967) and Pittsburgh (1971-1990). In between he went back to school. He ultimately served four USWA presidents as research director and principal economist. The heart of the job, however, was negotiating collective bargaining agreements with steelmakers, and in this Jim excelled. At his retirement dinner, one colleague remarked, 'I always thought there were two Jim Smiths, one who slept while the other sat at the bargaining table.'

"Jim married Kathleen Bland in 1947, and they had three sons. Widowed in 1986, he later married Anna Batchler. Jim Smith died August 16, 1995 from complications of a brain tumor."

THE DAILY TEXAN

The First College Daily In The South

Vol. 48 — Price Five Cents — AUSTIN, TEXAS, TUESDAY, JANUARY 7, 1947 — Eight Pages Today

Jim Smith Elected National Student President

Educators Enter Instructional Aid

Pre-registrants Pay Fees This Week

By BEN HARTLEY

Shivering Texans Ramrod Chicago Meet

Will Resign UT Post To Form New Group

By FAYE LOYD
Texan Associate Editor

Student President Jim Smith will this week step down from his unexpired term as top executive of the University student body to accept the presidency of a new nationwide student organization that embodies more than three-hundred colleges and universities over the United States.

He was elected to the post by a large majority during the Christmas holidays at the Chicago Student Conference which met in that city December 28-30 for the purpose of taking preliminary steps toward the formation of a national organization of American students.

John Wilson, Arts and Sciences assemblyman was chosen chairman of the Texas-Oklahoma region. Smith and Wilson were attending the conference as members of The University of Texas delegation.

He has announced that he will officially resign as president of the Students' Association Thursday. He will leave for Chicago, where the organization's central offices are temporarily located, immediately after the close of the present semester and resume work started toward the formation of a permanent student organization.

There he will head the National ...

HOWARD D. McELROY
He takes over . . .

JIM SMITH
. . . as he moves up

Report from Chicago, Part III:

'Texas Plan' Widely Accepted

(Editor's Note: This is the third in a series of articles to be published by The Daily Texan explaining the organizational features, aims, and proposed activities of the new national association of American students, which was formed at the Chicago Student Conference December 28-30. The preceding articles have been concerned with the background and history of the Conference itself, and with the reasons such an organization was formed and the activities it shall pursue.)

By FAYE LOYD and JIM SMITH

With a review of the background and motivating forces behind the Chicago Student Conference and a listing and discussion of its objectives and activities already con- ... to function. The outline of the Texas Plan is briefly:

The organization would consist of ALL college and university student bodies in the United States who subscribed to the principles and objectives of the Association and who wished to affiliate. Membership would require a ratification of the Constitution of the Association by a majority vote of the student body petitioning for membership prior to affiliation. ALL delegates from that student body at national or regional meetings would be elected by majority vote of their respective student bodies.

The organization would be subdivided into a number of geographic regions in an attempt to group together those states where ... provision would guarantee that the organization remain strictly "student" in character, and eliminate the possibility of the organization falling into the hands of "professional students" or political organizations, etc.

The officers would have specified duties and would be duly elected. They would be allowed to withdraw from school for the term of their office.

An executive committee, made up of regional representatives, would assist the officers in performance of executive functions of the national organization.

The Texas Plan also provides for a judicial body that would try cases of impeachment of officers and review decisions of the legislative ... lative action, on contention that such action was contrary to the Constitution of the Association. The judicial body would consist of students elected by the national legislature of the association together with a minority of faculty members elected by the administration of member colleges and universities.

In addition to the executive, judicial, and legislative bodies, there would be a series of permanent commissions to gather facts and make recommendations on specific student problems. These would include, for example, commissions on: student health, student housing, student recreation, exchange scholarships, discrimination in educational opportunity, student gov- ...

WHEN SMITH WAS ELECTED NICC PRESIDENT (*The Daily Texan* 1/7/47 above) he had to resign the student body presidency to devote full time to the task of preparing for the Constitutional Convention at which the new organization in which he so passionately believed would be launched. The Texas delegation to the Chicago Student Conference presented a plan for the structure of the new organization (*The Daily Texan*, 1/16/47 above), which formed the framework for its eventual student government membership base, regional organization and national commission structure. In particular, officers would have to be students and could not serve more than one term, and membership in NSA would require a majority vote in a student referendum. However, their recommendation for a judiciary of eected students was not adopted. Ironically, affiliation of Texas with NSA was turned down by a heavy margin in a hard-fought referendum in February 1948 (see Barefoot Sanders, Pt. 5, S. 6). By 1958, Texas had joined.

(Document and clipping source: Archives, Center for American Democracy, University of Texas at Austin)

The main purpose of the NSO is to represent all the students, not just the perpetual joiners.

3. John Simons: An Eloquent Advocate

At that crucial point, with the fate of the NSA hanging in the balance, John Simons took the floor.

Editor's note: The following column, written by John Simons, appeared in the August 23, 1947, issue of the New Leader. *Simons was elected treasurer of the National Continuations Committee following the Chicago Student Conference in 1946. He will also be remembered in NSA's later history as executive director of the Foundation of Youth and Student Affairs, which served as a major conduit for covert U.S. government funding of NSA's international programs from the 1950s through 1967 (See Welsh et al., p. 565).*

Simons' importance to the period of NSA's story covered in this anthology is his early leadership and advocacy for NSA as one of the spokespeople in the Catholic college student movement. Fordham was an active and supportive member of the Metropolitan New York region of NSA. Its membership in NSA helped provide grounding for the college's introduction of a student government for the first time, in 1948 (see pp. 866, 891).

Simons argues for inclusiveness and warns, paradoxically, of potential difficulties that including communist students might pose in attaining that goal. His concerns appear throughout this history in various forms as the new organization grappled with the applications of student rights, academic freedom, and international relations to campus-level associations with Communists.

He called for an organization that would "become an integral part of the education system, and . . . perform an important function by becoming the severest critic of that system." In doing that, "It must attract rather than repulse the rest of the campus, including the football player and the fraternity man."

At least three of those football players appear in this book (see Barefoot Sanders, U. of Texas, p. 995, John Hunsinger, Georgia Tech, p. 989, and Lee Jones, U. of Buffalo, p. 869). As regards fraternities, NSA became actively engaged in efforts to remove discriminatory fraternity admissions practices while maintaining a relationship with the fraternity community. Many fraternity leaders opposed NSA membership, while others became regional and national leaders in the organization (see the units on fraternities, p. 398 and p. 743).

The Catholic colleges Simons encouraged to participate actively in NSA provided key leadership for the organization (see Dungan, p. 909, Donnelley, p. 951, Lynch, p. 493, DesMarais, p. 734).

From The New Leader, 8/23/47

Need for a National Student Group

John Simons

Fordham Law School

Treasurer, National Continuations Committee, 1946-47

The American student movement has been many things in its short history, but it has never included an organization which will represent *all* the students of *all* the campuses. On August 31st, at the University of Wisconsin, nearly 1,000 delegates from more than 350 colleges and student organizations will meet to complete just such an organization. Known as the National Student Organization, it was conceived by the American delegation to the first Prague convention of the International Union of Students, and was launched at a Chicago meeting in December, 1946.

NSO needs to bring in students of all faiths and politics

This new organization represents the opening of a new and hopeful chapter in the development of the American student movement. The new development is best characterized by the wholehearted participation of the National Federation of Catholic College Students and the Federation of Newman Clubs of America, who are joining other students of other faiths and other political philosophies for the first time in their ten years of existence. For the main purpose of the NSO is to represent *all* the students and not merely the perpetual joiners, to establish a campus community and not merely to mobilize only one sector of the national campus, to represent the students who, in deep aversion to politics, have heretofore retreated into seclusion. In doing that the NSO will be making a large contribution to the student movement and to the very development of our democracy, and will be filling a great need. But in order to do that successfully, it must not ignore or go beyond the restrictions which are a natural consequence of its aims.

Total membership of the student organizations which sent representatives to the Chicago meeting where the NSO was formally launched totaled 495,000. The total campus population was 2,000,000. Obviously only one-fourth of the nation's campus has been attracted by the existing student organizations. Yet the other three-fourths certainly have interests in student issues, and a majority of them would like to join with other students in some form of an organization. Those figures seem to show that political-action organizations have not won very wide support on the campus. This is underscored by the fact that of the 495,000, non-political organizations accounted for 420,000.

Can conflicting ideologies work together?

To represent the other 1,500,000 is the chief aim of the NSO. But the 495,000 are obviously the leaders in campus politics and off-the-campus activities. To bring all these sectors of the student body together will involve the joint participation of Communists, liberals, conservatives, Protestants, Jews, Catholics, Socialists and others. *Thus, the basic question which the Wisconsin convention must answer is whether or not conflicting ideologies can work together with any degree of effectiveness.*

That is the question which must be answered. The attacks upon academic freedom, the outrageous quota systems, the rise in tuition costs, the outdated curricula, are immediate problems which all students must face and solve. Moreover, they are problems which can be solved best with the broadest participation of those immediately concerned—the students themselves.

* * *

But experience has shown conclusively the impossibility of working with Communists. Even sincere students devoted to high ideals are made to serve the partisan purposes of the Communist Party and of Soviet Russia if they join Communist-led organizations. Their minds become afflicted with the poison of totalitarianism and its contempt for democratic procedures. They inject extraneous issues into student struggles. They are loyal only to Communism and in the final analysis, to Soviet Russia. Every attempt in the past to unite the student movement has been wrecked by the Communists.

In the NSO are representatives of the American Youth for Democracy, the Young Progressive Citizens of America, and the Council of Student Clubs of the Communist Party. Can these representatives work harmoniously with the National Federation of Catholic College Students, the Federation of Newman Clubs of America, the United World Federalists, the Students for Democratic Action and the YMCAs? The difficulties are great, but it is hoped that an explosion can be averted. The reason that unity did not work before was that it was unity for action on issues which evoked conflicting and irreconcilable approaches from diverse groups. Now the test will come—will Communists cooperate on a broad non-controversial program?

One of the questions to be decided at the convention is whether organizations shall be represented as such in the NSO. I am opposed to this since it might give the Communists—and others—double representation—as delegates from campuses and delegates from organizations. The official recognition of Communist-led groups as bona fide student organizations would strengthen their position. The solution is to leave the election of delegates and officers to each particular college.

We live in a democratic society. As students we face the same Communist threat that confronts society generally, and must solve the problem democratically. A constitutional provision against participation of Communists in the NSO would not keep them from infiltrating the organization, just as they infiltrated unions with such constitutional barriers. They cannot be defeated by administrative fiat from above. It is up to the students on each campus to expose them when they run for office.

If Communists are elected, the NSO as a national body cannot refuse to recognize them as representatives of the students who voted for them. But the damage they can do will be narrowed by confining NSO activities to that common area of agreement which is represented by student issues which concern students *as students.* Academic standards, policies of discrimination, unrealistic and outmoded curricula, underpaid and poorly trained faculties, an inadequate educational system—those are points of common agreement, those are foci upon which all 2,000,000 students can come together to act as one.

NSO activities should be confined to areas of common agreement

That is the specific need which is the main *raison d'être* of the NSO, and it is only by adhering closely to that need that it can adequately function. The NSO must not become the sounding board for any special interest group or for any special ideology. It must attract rather than repulse the rest of the campus, including the football player and fraternity man. If it can do that it can become an integral part of the educational system, and it can perform an important function by becoming the severest critic of that system. And finally, by injecting an awareness of the importance and responsibilities of citizenship, the NSO will become a boon to democracy.

Austria's Student Union has just withdrawn from the International Union of Students because it is led by Communists and is not primarily devoted to student welfare or educational reform, but essentially political in character. The Austrian students made affiliation conditional upon full autonomy and action restricted to student problems. Our NSO has proposed similar conditions. In view of the experience of the Austrian Student Union, it is unlikely that the American organization will be able to affilliate with the IUS.

The issues involved at the forthcoming convention are complicated ones of methods of proportional representation, relations with existing student organizations and adoption of a program. But if the student delegates will keep in mind the underlying purpose of the NSO and the restrictions thereby placed upon it, and if they will also maintain an awareness and maturity which will prevent domination by any special interest group, the NSO will be a success and the campus will be grateful.

[The following is the original author identificaton that appeared in the *New Leader*]

The author of this article is national treasurer of the National Continuations Committee of the NSO and former vice president of the National Federation of Catholic College Students. He is a law student at Fordham University. He has had a lot of experience fighting the Communists in the student movement.

From the Fordham Ram, *10/3/47*

A Speech at a Crucial Point

By Joe Valerio

"The opening session of the plenary convention almost became the last," said Warren Gallagher '48, who, along with Thomas Gassert, '49, comprised Fordham College's delegation to the National Students Association's Convention at the University of Wisconsin, early last month. "You see," Gallagher continued, "the preamble to the NSA constitution called for the complete elimination of racial discrimination in all member colleges. Naturally this point evoked a howl of protest from the Southern delegates. At that crucial point, with the fate of the NSA hanging in the balance, John Simons, Fordham Law School, took the floor," Gallagher said. In a speech that served as the keynote of the entire convention, Simons pointed out the need of trust among the delegates as being the only way to realize the ideals and the aspirations of youth. "Fordham can be proud of that speech," he said, "It was great."[1]

With that crisis passed, the convention went on to approve the remainder of the preamble, which provides for functional student governments, the preservation of student rights, and complete academic freedom.

END NOTE

[1] See Wharton, p. 146, for more on this event. See also n. 22, p. 415.

PICTURE CREDIT: Constitutional Convention, September 1947, Madison, WI (*Welsh*).

NATIONAL CONTINUATIONS COMMITTEE (NCC) MEMBERS from right, Clif Wharton (Harvard), Secretary, and Russ Austin (U. of Chicago), Vice President, meet with John Simons, Treasurer, Al Houghton (U. of Wisconsin), NCC Staff Committee, and, standing, Emil Drobac, U. of Wisconsin delegate. (SHSW)

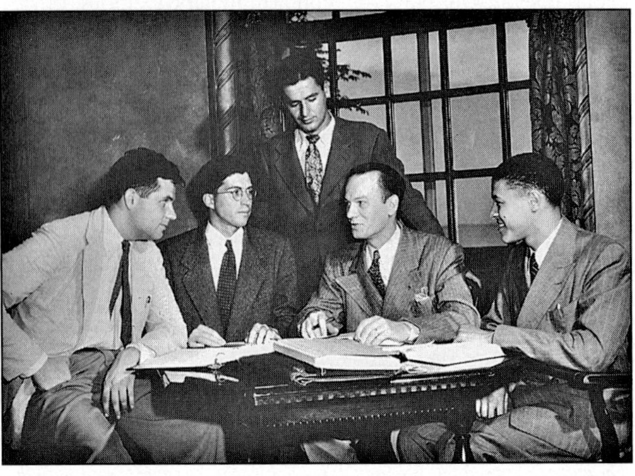

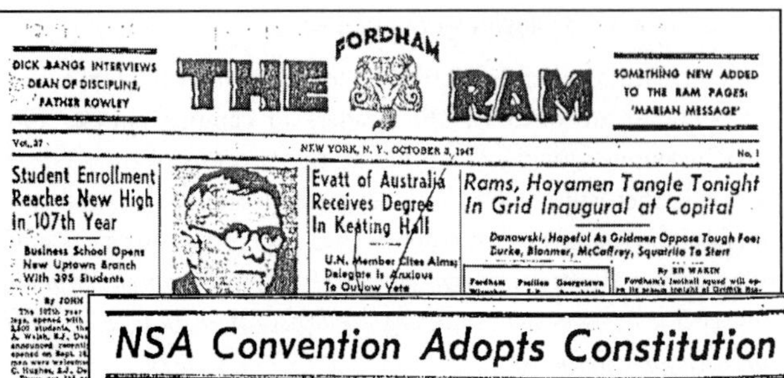

DICK BANGS INTERVIEWS DEAN OF DISCIPLINE, FATHER ROWLEY

FORDHAM THE RAM

SOMETHING NEW ADDED TO THE RAM PAGES: 'MARIAN MESSAGE'

Vol. 37 NEW YORK, N. Y., OCTOBER 3, 1947 No. 1

Student Enrollment Reaches New High In 107th Year

Business School Opens New Uptown Branch With 395 Students

Evatt of Australia Receives Degree In Keating Hall

U.N. Member Cites Aims; Delegate Is Anxious To Outlaw Veto

Rams, Hoyamen Tangle Tonight In Grid Inaugural at Capital

Danowski, Hopeful As Gridmen Oppose Tough Foe; Burke, Blonmer, McCaffrey, Squatrito To Start

NSA Convention Adopts Constitution

By JOE VALERIO

"The opening session of the plenary convention almost became the last," said Warren Gallagher, '48, who along with Thomas Gassert, '49, comprised Fordham College's delegation to the National Students Association's Convention at the University of Wisconsin, early last month.

"You see," Gallagher continued ...

With that crisis passed the convention went on to approve the remainder of the preamble which provides for functional student governments, the preservation of student rights, and complete academic freedom.

"The only other issue that caused any trouble was the matter of affiliation with the International Union of Students," Gallagher said. "Because of the left wing tenden- ...

Right now we're busy here in the city trying to organize regional and campus participation in the projects of the NSA," Gallagher continued. "Operating from Manhattanville College, the regional board under Walter Wallace, of Columbia, has already plunged into another controversy," he said.

The issue involved is the Schultz Amendment in the charter of the N. Y. Board of Higher Education, ...

RESPONSIBILITY IS NOT RADICALISM

In the past few months, many pastors have bemoaned the fact that there are so few Catholic college graduates taking a full share in the activities of their parishes. The pastors feel that there is an appalling lack of courageous leadership among these graduates, many of whom, they believe, have failed to develop properly as Catholic members of society. But why should this be so, after being exposed to a Catholic education? In a recent issue of "America," several reasons for this condition were put forth by Martin M. McLaughlin, a student at Notre Dame.

How can we become leaders, he asks, when we are not trained to leadership, when, on the contrary, college officials assume that everything must be done for their students? Some educators have the idea that students are completely passive in school, that they are in college only to receive, not to give anything except their respectful attention. Too often, McLaughlin says, the initiative of the students is stymied or completely squelched by an administration jealous of its own authority, or fearful of student "radicalism."

A person must be trained to become a chemist or a teacher, so why not to become a leader in parish activities? This training can only come about if the college authorities are willing to give their students some measure of responsibility. Students should be delegated responsibility which is real, and not fictitious. They should be encouraged to make decisions for the students in their particular club or organization.

It is heartening to notice the large amount of responsibility which has been given to Fordham students in the past in such activities as the Mimes and Mummers, the Harvester Club, and The Monthly. Only last month, Warren Gallagher and Thomas Gassert were sent to the University of Wisconsin as Fordham College's delegates to the National Students' Association conference. While there, they acted entirely according to their own discretion, and, from the results, did a fine job as our representatives. This only proves that students can be relied upon, and need not be led by the hand. If a policy of giving students responsibility is continued and expanded, then perhaps our pastors will not much longer be distressed by a lack of leadership in our college graduates.

THE SIMONS "CRUCIAL POINT" SPEECH at the Constitutional Convention in September 1947 was reported in the Fordham Ram (above) and is excerpted in the adjacent column. On the same page is an editorial which in a gentle way refers to the movement among many Catholic colleges at the time towards relaxation of supervision and greater student self-government and reliance (see Part 6, Dungan, DiLegge, Mother O'Byrne).

JOHN SIMONS

Born in Elizabeth, NJ, in 1920. He attended St. Benedict's Preparatory School in Newark, NJ, and graduated from Seton Hall University, South Orange, NJ, in 1942. After service in the U.S. Army, he entered Fordham Law School. In 1947, he took a position as Executive Secretary of the National Federation of Catholic College Students (NFCCS) and elected not to complete his law degree. He moved to the staff of World University Service in Geneva and in 1951 became Executive Director of the Foundation for Youth and Student Affairs. After serving as Director of University Relations in the Peace Corps from 1961 to 65, he joined Fordham University as Assistant Director for Foundation Relations. From there he took a position as Director for Foundation Relations at St. Elizabeth's Hospital in Elizabeth, NJ, until his retirement.

(Biography furnished by Philip Des Marais)

Strong, democratic student governments...will be the backbone of NSO

A Call for a Strong Student Body

Jim Smith
University of Texas
President, National Continuations Committee, 1946-47
From the Chicago Maroon, *April 11, 1947*

By distributing information on such solutions of student problems as [the formation for the first time of a student government at the University of Chicago],[1] the NSO[2] will assist students in solving similar problems or dealing with similar situations on their respective Campuses. To prepare and distribute information on steps being taken to deal with campus problems, the NSO will organize a series of student commissions on the national level.

These campus committees should be established by the student government on each campus. The student government will have the responsibility of selecting delegates to national and regional conferences of the NSO. This responsibility may be discharged by direct selection of such delegates by the student government, or by student body election of such delegates.

Responsibility Great

Thus we see that student governments will have two important functions to perform in the NSO. First, the student governments will organize campus commissions to carry out investigations of student problems of interest to the NSO and to carry on the work of alleviating these problems with the assistance of the NSO, and second, the student governments will be responsible for the selection of qualified, representative delegates to national and regional conferences of the NSO, to ensure that the decisions of the NSO will be representative of the opinions, needs, and interests of the students of the United States.

Only a strong student government will be able to perform the first of these functions. Only a democratically representative student government can perform the second. Students at the University of Chicago and every other campus in the nation must therefore shoulder the responsibility of building strong and democratic student governments, if the NSO, an organization of great potential benefit to American students and the society in which they live, is to succeed.

Strong, democratic, student governments at the University of Chicago and hundreds of other college and university campuses over the nation will be the backbone of the National Students Organization. Just as a student body obtains a voice in the conduct of the affairs of its college or university through the formation of a student government, the students of the nation may look forward to obtaining a voice in the formulation of state and national educational policies through the formation of NSO. This article is an attempt to illustrate this basic concept of the relationship between student governments and the NSO.

There will be no "local chapters" of the National Student Organization, similar to the local chapters of national fraternal, political, or religious organizations. The NSO will be a campus-wide as well as nation-wide organization, representing the needs and interests of all students. Since the only campus-wide agency on each campus is the student government, that agency has naturally been selected to serve as the connecting link between the individual student and the national and regional organizations of the NSO.

Act on Student Problems

The NSO will render its greatest service, aside from providing a medium of contact and cultural exchange with foreign students, by compiling and distributing information on specific student problems and by conducting regional and national student conferences on these problems. Among the problems mentioned by the Chicago Student Conference, which established the framework of the NSO, are:

1. The inadequate social and cultural life on most campuses,
2. The lack of sufficient vocational information and guidance for undergraduates,
3. Lack of an extensive program of public and private scholarships for would-be students who cannot afford the expense of an education,
4. The problems of discrimination in undergraduate and professional educational opportunity,
5. Inadequate health and housing facilities for students,
6. Outmoded undergraduate curricula, and
7. Problems of weak or undemocratic student government systems.

Campus Action Taken

At the University of Texas the student government conducted an exhaustive survey of the student medical facilities. A report was prepared and presented to the Board of Regents of the University, with the result that the Board shifted its plans for University expansion and gave priority to the erection of a new sixty-bed hospital on campus. At the Universities of Washington and California, student cooperative units operate central kitchens that solved the problem of good, inexpensive meals for large groups of students.

END NOTES

[1] The April 11, 1947, issue of the *Chicago Maroon* reported, "Student governments have been the center for election of delegates and discussion of local NSO plans....At the University of Chicago no student government has yet been formed. Unless the election of April 18 [to approve a student government] receives active student support, it seems unlikely that University of Chicago students will play a leading part in the National Student Organization."

[2] Prior to the Constitutional Convention in September 1947, the pending association was known as the National Student Organization (NSO).

Student leaders express visions before the 1947 Constitutional Convention

High Hopes and Expectations

If in these, their college years they had received encouragement... our culture might now have undreamed of riches

Excerpts from The Student Progressive (Harvard *Liberal Union, Sept. 1947)*

What the NSA Can Do1[1]

- **Provide a channel for students around the world to reach American students**
- **Provide the stimulus for intercollegiate experiences in the arts to enrich our culture**

Mildred Kiefer
University of California
California Regional NSO Chairman

What NSO can do is not to be reviewed but to be built. NSO must provide a channel through which the rest of the world's students can reach the previously inaccessible American students. NSO must stimulate and organize inter- and intranational student travel and idea exchange. NSO must bring to totally self-centered student bodies the realization that they are part of the student movement. These are some of the things which NSO can do, but I imagine that the others [in this special issue of the *Progressive*] have to discuss these paramount tasks.

In the hope of pointing [in] a direction we usually ignore I will risk seeming academic or pedantic and consider the field of the arts.

Fostering arts programs will fulfill aspirations and enrich our culture.

It has always seemed that there is little opportunity offered to creative artistic ability in the American college world. As a result, our culture has suffered an irreplaceable loss. Too often we meet people who know they could paint, or who have undesigned buildings stirring in their souls. Now they are completely occupied earning a living. Yet there was a time in their lives when their full energies, not just their Sunday afternoons, could be devoted to activities of their own choosing, even to creative art. If in these, their college years, they had received encouragement, if the spirit of competition or at least the possibility of recognition and valid criticism had been offered them, our culture might now have undreamed-of riches. Our society might also have fewer neurotic personalities.

Create intercultural bridges and understanding through the arts

These are big things and possibly too generalized to seem real, but there are specific contributions art can make. A greater understanding and appreciation of minority groups, national, racial, and religious, through their folk arts can do much to relieve group inferiority and superiority complexes—the devil currently besetting our United States.

What NSO can do is to provide the stimulus and the pattern for establishing regional, national, and even intraregional competitions, institutes, and compilations of student effort in music composition and performance, painting, sculpture, architectural design, dance, literature, and dramatic production for stage and radio. Traveling exhibits would be made up. One of the great benefits would be to bring this cultural expression to the small college where academic instruction might not be provided in all fields of art. And if this touring art could be developed to a national scale we might work out such healthy exchanges of ideas as, for instance, the bringing of California architecture to the Midwest and the mountain ballads of the South to New England.

Providing help to grow a society that will last as long as art does

In suggesting all this I do not mean to sound like a revivalist for the most oppressive type of women's club, where a very cultured, arty outlook is tied like a paper bag over what was once an expression of individuality. I do believe, however, that if we produce a reading and writing public we have necessarily produced a thinking public, and if we produce an artistically creative and appreciative society we may find that we have grown ourselves a society which will last as long as art does.

* * *

- **Provide unified action carrying out our student government programs for students**
- **Avoid becoming ideological and partisan**

Royal J. Voegeli
University of Wisconsin
President of the Student Board
and Acting Member of the NCC Staff

The successful formation of the National Student Association will mean the fruition of a long time dream among forward-looking students all over the nation. Particularly auspicious is the timing of the constitutional convention at the threshold of a post-war era in which higher education has assumed unprecedented importance.

Working through the commission system on the campus, regional, and national levels, the NSA can efficiently make comprehensive studies of student problems, make available statistics and information through a central channel, and take unified action in carrying out programs decided upon by students.

Lend support to student government, welfare, and educational opportunity

Specifically, the NSA will find tremendous need for work in the field of student government, both establishing new setups and bolstering existing ones; stimulating better student publications; promoting campus recreational and cultural centers; providing for the exchange of art exhibits, arranging for lowcost concert and lecture tours; removing economic, racial, and religious barriers to educational opportunity; procuring scholarships for study both in this country and abroad; arranging student tours in foreign countries and encouraging foreign students to visit and study in the United States; promoting exchange professorships; and in general fostering closer understanding among college students both in this country and abroad.

This list by no means exhausts the possibilities for constructive endeavor by the NSA. Any and all legitimate student interests can be served in a unique way through an association such as this, authorized and supported by the official student governing bodies of institutions in all parts of the country.

Reinforce existing campus activity on a broader scale

Of course, many of these student programs are already being carried on in varying ways and with varying degrees of success on individual campuses; the national body will coordinate and stimulate these efforts, and will go further in accomplishments on a broader and far more efficient scale than has heretofore been possible.

It does not take a great stretch of the imagination to realize this. Since time immemorial man has united smaller units into larger to achieve greater efficiency and increase the sphere of his activity to better his welfare. Certainly students, as one of the most progressive elements of society, should not be an exception to this movement.

In general, NSA's work lies in such fields as are outlined above. Any effort to change it into an ideological propaganda organ can only lead to the defeat of its own purpose. But, If devoted to the real needs of students, NSA can introduce a new era in student welfare.

What Liberties on the Campus?

- **Student rights and academic freedom can be defined and defended**

- **The idea of contract between students and administration**

Ralph Dungan
St. Joseph's College
Chairman, Pennsylvania NSO Region

The following is offered in an attempt to lay down some basic concepts which, it is hoped, will aid in the discussion of student rights and the academic freedom proper to students.

It is quite evident that a student possesses all of the rights, and corresponding responsibilities, of every other member of a free society. In addition he has rights peculiar to his particular state in life. Generally these rights due to a student, because he is a student, are alienable rights, i.e., may be transferred or renounced. Among these might be included the right to organize, to publish newspapers, and to participate in campus political activity.

The concept of the "contract" and the concept of "right"

However, in a discussion of student rights there is still another concept which must not be overlooked: that is the idea of a contract. The contract of which we speak is that which exists between student and administrator and which is so often the root of any difficulty that exists. Too often the student is ignorant of the existence, either actually or tacitly, of any such contract. But just as it is essential for a teacher to be fully aware of the nature of the contract that he makes with the college or university, so also is it essential for the student to be advised.

Uniting the concept of the right with that of the contract, it is not difficult to ascertain where the controversy arises, for there will be as many opinions as there are different contracts. These might range from a religious seminary where virtually all alienable rights are surrendered, to a liberal institution in which there is no limitation.

Concepts applied to academic freedom

The question of academic freedom for students may be disposed of in the same manner which has been applied above. It is felt that a rather fair and complete definition of academic freedom was presented in the Bylaws of the constitution as drawn up by the National Continuations Committee. In accord with the idea of a contract, the third paragraph of this definition specifically mentions that both student and teacher be advised of the limitations the institution places on its personnel in order to fulfill its educational aims and purposes. In connection with a discussion of freedom it might be well to bear in mind that it is not the same as license.

The NSO can do much in this field, especially in the protection of rights where they have been abridged. However, the method it adopts in handling such a situation must be just, intelligent, and non-dictatorial. The spirit of cooperation and unity which should be characteristic of the educational community must pervade any action that is undertaken.

Application of sound principles will make for a successful convention

American students, therefore, will do credit to themselves and a free educational system, if they study this and similar issues with wisdom and tolerance, taking into consideration the characters of their several institutions as influenced by tradition, educational custom and socio-religious forces. Understanding, coupled with objective thinking based on sound principle, are the elements which will lend themselves to the culmination of a successful convention.

END NOTE

[1] Note: During the spring of 1947, prior to the formation of NSA at the Constitutional Convention, the as-yet-unformed organization was referred to as the NSO (National Student Organization).

PICTURE CREDITS: Wurf: NSA offices, Madison, WI (*Schwartz*). Voegeli, 1947 (*Voegeli*). Dunga: Constitutional Convention, September 1947, Madison, WI (*Welsh*).

International relations begin long before one graduates from college.

Bill Ellis: American Vice President in Prague

A Report on the International Union of Students

Can American students defy traditional modes of thought and unite with students of the rest of the world? Can the IUS overcome the challenge of maintaining inclusiveness?

Editor's note: Bill Ellis (Harvard University) was elected as the American Vice President of IUS at the World Student Congress, August 1946. He was one of the four representatives of the National Intercollegiate Christian Council. At the Chicago Student Conference, delegates "unanimously endorsed" him as "interim representative" for the United States[1] and allocated $600 "toward the cost of his passage back to Prague" in January.

Following is a portion of his report of the March 1947 IUS Executive Committee Meeting. It reflects his continuing commitment to make the relationship work and to address programs and issues on the merits. As he notes, American students preparing for the NSA Constitutional Convention that summer would be considering affiliation as the cornerstone of their postwar international engagement, overriding traditional suspicions of collaboration with communists. The report also reveals the profound seeds of ideological and Cold War conflict that were to overtake all else in the ensuing months.

In September 1947, American students will be faced with a tremendous decision, the first of its kind in their history. It will be necessary to decide at this time whether the American Union [the forthcoming NSA] can defy all traditional modes of thought and with courage unite itself with students of the rest of the world. It will be necessary to decide whether American students mean by international cooperation just their country working through *the* United Nations, *or* whether they mean the fullest cooperation of all segments of society with similar groups in other countries. It will be necessary for American students to realize that Europe and Asia mean not simply English, Russian, and Chinese peoples, but also aged civilizations which in their differences have given each segment of their society—even students—an outlook which varies greatly. Will American students accept the challenge this fall by affiliating to the IUS?

* * *

The Executive Committee Meeting

After the recent three months in the United States, I was not prepared for the problems which I faced at the Executive Committee Meeting. Before, I with many others had explained and stressed the potential importance of the IUS in the student world. Also there had been the necessity to attempt to rectify the impression which some had that this organization was a political one controlled by one group. Actually, when I arrived in Prague the problem was not ideological, but practical—in fact, too practical. The questions were, firstly, how to make the IUS administratively and financially a success, and secondly, how to include all student groups with their varied characters. When Josa [Grohman, the President] and Tom [Madden], the Executive Secretary, spoke, they enumerated the practical problems of the IUS. We needed personnel and Executive members or deputies to organize and run departments. Member organizations had to pay their fees. Also, there was the ever-present problem of how to continue the student character of the IUS and yet produce work of professional competency.

* * *

The role of IUS in Asia

After careful consideration of the role of the IUS in Asia and [a possible] conference, we decided to do three things. First, the IUS would plan a conference in South East Asia, probably after the AISC'S conference. There was no desire to compete with the AISC, but when one considers that the ISS and WFDY are planning conferences here, it is necessary that the IUS study more closely the relations which it wishes to have with Asia and how to realize these relations. Secondly, Mr. Tomovic, executive Committee member from Yugoslavia, who is on the WFDY's commission to India, was to be requested to attempt to bring all the three Indian organizations together, AISC, AISF, and the All Indian Moslem League.[2] He was instructed also not to make use of the AISF in India lest it cause even greater friction between the other organizations. Thirdly, he was to visit as many countries in Asia as possible in order to widen IUS contacts—if possible with [the Indian delegate] Mr. Chattopadhya. In other words, Mr. Tomovic would take advantage of the AISF in all Asiatic countries except India.

At this point, I requested that Mr. Tomovic should be instructed that since the IUS represented many points of view, he should visit all student organizations in the countries he visited. I did this, not because I distrusted Mr. Tomovic, for I know him personally to be very honest and sincere, but in order to insist on representation of all groups from Asia. It was agreed.

Americans not represented on Indian commission

This particular session irritated me very much, for I know that regardless of how honest Mr. Tomovic is, he will unconsciously slant his report to the IUS. Since there is no American student on this Indian commission, there will be no report from anyone with a background different from that of Mr. Tomovic. The censure for this omission must fall squarely on those American youth groups who were offered an opportunity to send an American on this commission and failed. The results are that there is no one else to present his report to the IUS or to return to the United States and describe Indian youth and students.[3]

When American students affiliate to the IUS they must realize that affiliation means full participation. You must be prepared to send on different commissions your representative who will report to the IUS and you. This is absolutely essential both for the IUS and the development of international consciousness among American students.

Note: From the Council this summer, there will probably come a decision to send two commissions to Greece and Germany. I request that some of the American Council members or other delegated students be prepared to accept positions on these commissions. I regard this request as one of the utmost importance. Also I hope these students will be able to speak another language besides English.

Vietnam consideration highlights inclusiveness obstacles

From India, we moved to Vietnam. It was in this discussion that one saw the real obstacles involved in making the IUS world-embracing. Yet in this all-inclusiveness lies the success of the organization which supported the students in their fight for freedom. Mr. Trouvat of France and Mr. Sadar of France wrestled over the resolution for one hour trying to reword the text so that it would express the original idea and yet not offend the French or dissatisfy the students of India or Vietnam.

It was this incident which reaffirmed my belief that the more inclusive the IUS membership becomes, the greater will be the obstacles in working together. Yet, in this all inclusiveness lies the success of the organization, for there is less possibility of either the right or left wings among the students exerting undue control. This problem of true and genuine world representation is the key to IUS success but also its greatest challenge.

* * *

Student life means taking a role in society

Overemphasis on the practical work must not be so stressed that one loses sight of other factors—the difference in the character of the student organizations of the world. The national unions of the Scandinavian countries, England, and France are more mature and aggressive than American student organizations; the student unions of the colonial countries like Vietnam, India, and Burma more radical—not that they are naturally radical, but rather because the national problem of independence is so vital that it affects every group in society. For example, disagree as the Indian students do among themselves, they are united on the question of India's independence. Thus, student life does mean for these students taking a very pronounced role in society.

This difference means, therefore, that American students cannot, even if they try, place the IUS in a vacuum in which political questions will not rise in some form or other. This is inevitable, due to the role of the students in their countries and also to the very interrelatedness of modern life itself. One can only maintain that there are certain rights which must underlie every university which seeks for the truth. These principles must be upheld, fought for, and defended wherever threatened, for they are fundamental to world understanding and peace.

At the World Student Congress, these principles were in general terms an opposition to fascism and a belief in democracy. The crisis came not in the presentation of the principles, but in the attempts of some to define these terms. Certainly, agreement on the term *democracy* between Russians, Cubans, Americans, English, Indians, etc., is going to be very difficult to reach. I personally feel that if the United Nations were compelled to define some of the abstract terms in its Constitution, there would be disagreement also. This should not surprise anyone, but rather be recognized as an inevitable problem in all international cooperation.[4]

Ellis advocates for affiliation with the IUS

I present these views not because the IUS is a political organization, for it certainly is not. It is a world student organization which will engage in practical student work. However, at times a defense of the principles which must underlie the University in society do necessitate a certain stand which touches on politics. When this occurs, as it has with the Egyptian students, one must face the challenge. To fail in this will mean the complete emasculation of the sources of strength of the University and the IUS.

I sincerely hope that American students affiliate to the IUS. I believe that international cooperation begins long before one has graduated from college. I believe that it is necessary to introduce all segments of our society to an appreciation of the problems in international work. I believe that students should develop a habitual outlook which extends beyond San Francisco and New York to the farthest parts of the world. I believe that students should develop this international frame of mind by practical work in an international organization like the IUS. I believe that as future leaders American students owe this mental development and practical work to themselves. I believe that the IUS can offer all this to American students.

Finally, I wish to express my satisfaction with the developments in the IUS Secretariat since my arrival in Prague. The tasks before us are difficult, but the idealism and determination of all are strong. With confidence in the IUS, we here in Prague await the decision of American students.

Respectfully presented
William S. Ellis
Vice-President

EDITOR'S NOTES

[1] See "Bill Ellis and the NICC," p. 158.

[2] *Editor's note:* AISC was the noncommunist All India Student Congress and AISF, The communist All India Student Federation. Melvin Conant on p. 81 of his 7/29/51 "Report on Southeast and Southern Asia" (NSA Archive, SHSW) discusses these groups in detail.

[3] In this event can be found the origins of NSA's interest in making contact with, and learning about, the student organizations in Asia and elsewhere in the Third World. An organized program of international teams was mounted by 1949-50 International Vice President Erskine Childers in summer 1950 (see p. 609).

[4] The significance of differences between the way the terms "opposition to fascism" and "belief in democracy" were defined lies in the context of the postwar anticolonial movement in Asia, the Middle East, and Africa and the ideological contest between the communist forces and the Western democracies. These conflicts, which had been resolved by the end of the twentieth century, were on center stage after World War II. Almost all the countries outside Western Europe and the Americas, Australia, New Zealand, and Japan were under totalitarian or colonial rule. Bill Ellis here defines the dilemma confronting American students who tried to maintain on the international scene their traditions of an open society, in which voluntary student and civic organizations were expected to be "nonpartisan" or "nonpolitical."

(For Ellis bio and photo, see pp. 158-59)

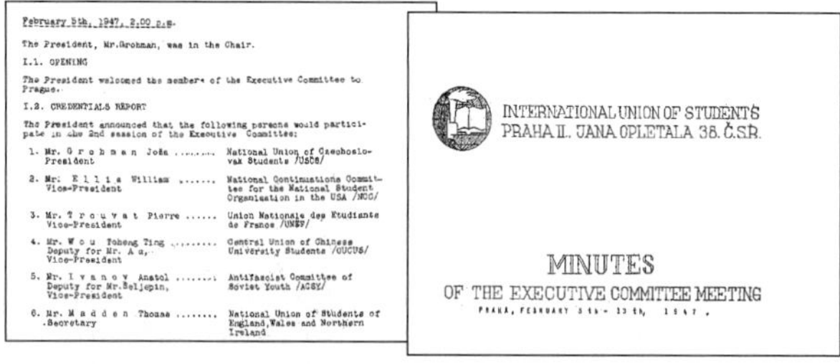

February 5th, 1947, 2.00 p.m.

The President, Mr. Grohman, was in the Chair.

I.1. OPENING

The President welcomed the members of the Executive Committee to Prague.

I.2. CREDENTIALS REPORT

The President announced that the following persons would participate in the 2nd session of the Executive Committee:

1. Mr. G r o h m a n Joža .... President — National Union of Czechoslovak Students /USCS/
2. Mr. E l l i s William .... Vice-President — National Continuations Committee for the National Student Organization in the USA /NCC/
3. Mr. T r o u v a t Pierre ...... Vice-President — Union Nationale des Etudiants de France /UNEF/
4. Mr. W o u Tcheng Ting .... Deputy for Mr. A u, Vice-President — Central Union of Chinese University Students /CUCUS/
5. Mr. I v a n o v Anatol .... Deputy for Mr. Seljepin, Vice-President — Antifascist Committee of Soviet Youth /ACSY/
6. Mr. M a d d e n Thomas .... Secretary — National Union of Students of England, Wales and Northern Ireland

INTERNATIONAL UNION OF STUDENTS
PRAHA II. JANA OPLETALA 38. Č.S.R.

MINUTES
OF THE EXECUTIVE COMMITTEE MEETING
PRAHA, FEBRUARY 5th - 13th, 1947.

MINUTES OF IUS EXECUTIVE COMMITTEE, Feb. 5-13, 1947. The IUS followed formal protocols, listing officers first. Mr. William Ellis, Vice President (National Continuations Committee for the National Student Organization in the USA/NCC), is listed second after Mr. Joza Grohman, President (National Union of Czechoslovak Students/USCS), and before Mr. Pierre Trouvat, Vice President (Union Nationale des Etudiants de France). (Source: Hoover Institution)

The 1946-47 National Continuations Committee

NATIONAL OFFICERS

President
Jim Smith, *University of Texas*

Vice President
Russell Austin, *University of Chicago*

Secretary
Clifton R. Wharton, *Harvard University*

Treasurer
John Simons, *Fordham University*

STAFF COMMITTEE MEMBERS

William McDermed, *DePaul University, Illinois*
Al Houghton, *University of Wisconsin*

Tom Farr, *University of Chicago;*
Janis Tremper, *Rockford College, Illinois*

CHAIRMEN OF THE REGIONAL COMMITTEES AND MEMBERS OF THE NATIONAL EXECUTIVE COMMITTEE

Alabama & Georgia
Temporary Chairman
Albert P. Foster
Emory University

Arkansas, Miss., La.
Permanent Chairman
Lloyd Love
Louisiana State University

California
Permanent Chairman
Mildred Kiefer
University of California

Colorado & New Mexico
Temporary Chairman
Jerry Goodman
University of Colorado

Connecticut & R.I.
Robert Smith
Yale University

Florida
Temporary Chairman
Manuel Alvarez
University of Tampa

Illinois
Permanent Chairman
Paul F. Kirk
De Paul University

Indiana
Permanent Chairman
Wally Cook
Purdue University

Iowa
Temporary Chairman
R. J. O'Brien
Grinnell College

Kansas & Missouri
Permanent Chairman
Patricia Groom
Maryville College

Maine and Vermont
Temporary Chairman
Peter S. Mallett
University of Vermont

Md., Del., DC
Permanent Chairman
Emmit D. Hurley
Georgetown University

Massachusetts
Permanent Chairman
Miriam B. Haskell
Smith College

Metropolitan New York
Permanent Chairman
Walter Wallace
Columbia University

Michigan
Permanent Chairman
Frances Rollins
Marygrove College

Minnesota
Permanent Chairman
Philip Des Marais
University of Minnesota

New Hampshire
Temporary Chairman
Dick Bredenberg
Dartmouth College

New Jersey
Temporary Chairman
John P. Yewell
Rutgers University

New York State
Permanent Chairman
Jack Minkoff
Cornell University

North & South Carolina
Co-Chairmen
W. H. Miller
University of North Carolina
Charles Wallace
A&T College

N. & S. Dakota, Nebraska
Temporary Chairman
Eugene Berman
University of Nebraska

Ohio
Permanent Chairman
Leo E. Rattay
Cleveland College

Oregon-Washington
John Elwood
Lewis and Clark College

Pennsylvania
Permanent Chairman
Ralph A. Dungan
St. Joseph's College

Tennessee & Kentucky
Temporary Chairman
Howard Bowles
University of Kentucky

Texas & Oklahoma
Permanent Chairman
John Wilson
University of Texas

Virginia & W. Va.
A. B. McCullock
Virginia Polytechnic Institute

Wisconsin
Permanent Chairman
John P. Hunter
University of Wisconsin

ORGANIZATIONAL MEMBERS OF THE NEC

See p. 1126 for list of organizations attending the Chicago Student Conference

Joyce Roberts
National Intercollegiate Christian Council

Don Willner
United States Student Assembly

John Burns
Newman Club Federation

Note: As listed in the Reports of the Chicago Student Conference published by the National Continuations Committee.

Roster of Colleges—Chicago Student Conference

Alabama–Georgia
Birmingham Southern College
Emory University
Georgia State College
Morehouse College
Tuskegee Institute
University of Alabama
University of Georgia

Arkansas–Louisiana–Mississippi
Blue Mountain College
College of the Ozarks
Jackson College
La. State Univ. Law School
Mississippi State College
Southeastern Louisiana Inst.
Tulane University
Ursuline College
Xavier University

California
College of the Pacific
Fresno State College
Immaculate Heart College
Marymount College
Mills College
Mount St. Mary's College
San Jose State College
Scripps College
Stanford University
University of California, Berkeley
University of California at Los Angeles
University of Southern California

Colorado–N. Mexico
Colorado College
New Mexico Highlands University
University of Colorado

Connecticut–Rhode Island
Bryant College
Connecticut College for Women
Hillyer Junior College
Teachers College of Connecticut
Trinity College
University of Connecticut–Storrs
Yale University

Florida
University of Tampa

Illinois
Aurora College
Barat College of the Sacred Heart
Blackburn College
Chicago Teachers College
College of St. Francis
DePaul University
Elmhurst College
Herzl Junior College
Illinois Institute of Technology
Illinois College
Illinois State Normal Univ.
Institute of Design
Lake Forest College
LeClerc College
Loyola University
MacMurray College
Mt. St. Scholastica College
Mundelein College
National College of Education
North Central College
Roosevelt College
Rosary College
Rockford College
St. Xavier College
University of Chicago
University of Illinois
Wheaton College
Wright Junior College
Observers
Northwestern University

Indiana
DePauw University
Earlham College
Huntington College
Indiana State Teachers College
Marian College
Purdue University
St. Joseph's College
St. Mary's College, Notre Dame
Tri-State College
University of Notre Dame
Observers
Marian College
Saint Mary-of-the-Woods College

Iowa
Clarke College
Drake University
Grinnell College
Loras College
Mt. St. Clare College
Parson's College
University of Dubuque
Observers
University of Iowa

Kansas–Missouri
College of Emporia
College of St. Theresa
Fontbonne College
Kansas State College, Manhattan
Kansas State College, Ft. Hays
Lincoln University
Maryville College
Missouri School of Music
Mt. St. Scholastica College
Ottawa University
St. Benedict's College
The St. Mary College
St. Louis University
University of Kansas City
Washington University
Webster College
Observers
St. Benedicts College

Maine-Vermont
Bangor Theological Seminary
Bennington College
Bowdoin College
Colby College
Lyndon Normal School
Middlebury College
University of Vermont

Massachusetts
American International College
Amherst College
Assumption College
Boston College
Boston University
Boston Univ. Medical School
Clark University
Emanuel College
Framingham State Teachers College
Garland School
Harvard University
Harvard Divinity School
Jackson College
Massachusetts Institute of Technology
Mount Holyoke College
Mass. State College
Mt. St. Mary College
Northeastern University
Radcliffe College
Regis College
Simmons College
Smith College
Springfield YMCA College
Suffolk University
Wellesley College
Wheaton College
Williams College

Maryland–Delaware–DC
Catholic University of America
College of Notre Dame of Maryland
Coppin Teachers College
Dunbarton College of Holy Cross
Georgetown University
Goucher College
Hood College
Howard University
Immaculata Jr. College
Johns Hopkins University
Johns Hopkins Univ. Medical School
Loyola College
Morgan State College
Mt. St. Agnes College
Princess Anne College
St. Joseph's College
Trinity College
University of Baltimore

Metropolitan New York
Adelphi College
CCNY Business Day
CCNY Business Evening
CCNY Main Day
CCNY Main Evening
College of New Rochelle
Columbia University
Fordham University
Fordham School of Education
Good Counsel College
Hunter College-Day
Hunter College-Evening
Juilliard School of Music
Long Island University
Manhattan College
Manhattanville College of the Sacred Heart
New York University–School of Education
New York University–University Heights
New York University—Washington Square
Pratt Institute
Queens College
School for Teachers & Higher Jewish Education, JPFO, IWO
Sarah Lawrence College
Observers
Hunter College–Veterans Session

Michigan
Aquinas College
Hillsdale College
Marygrove College
Mercy College
Nazareth College
Olivet College
Siena Heights College
University of Detroit
University of Michigan
Wayne University
Western Michigan College
Observers
Michigan State College

Minnesota
Augsburg College & Theological Seminary
College of St. Scholastica
College of St. Theresa
College of St. Teresa
College of St. Thomas
Concordia College
Gustavus Adolphus College
Macalester College
St. John's University
St. Mary's College
St. Olaf College
University of Minnesota

Montana-Wyoming-Idaho
University of Wyoming

New Hampshire
Dartmouth College

New Jersey
Caldwell College
College of St. Elizabeth
New Jersey College for Women
New Jersey State Teachers College–Montclair
New Jersey State Teachers College
Paterson
Rutgers University–Newark
Rutgers University–New Brunswick
St. Peter's College

New York State
Alfred University
Bard College
College of New Rochelle
College of St. Rose
Cornell University
Good Counsel College
Hamilton College
Nazareth College
Russell Sage College
St. Lawrence University
Skidmore College
University of Rochester
Vassar College
William Smith College
Observers
Eastman School of Music

North and South Carolina
Ag & Tech College of NC
Allen University
Guildford College
Johnson C. Smith University
Limestone College
North Carolina State College
State A &M College
University of North Carolina

North Dakota, South Dakota, Nebraska
Dana College
Duchesne College
No. Dakota Ag. College
University of Nebraska
University of South Dakota

Ohio
Capital University
Cleveland College of Western Reserve University
College of Mt. St. Joseph
College of Wooster
Fenn College
John Carroll University
Kenyon College
Lake Erie College
Mary Manse College
Miami University
Notre Dame College
Oberlin College
Ohio State University
Ohio University
Otterbein College
Ursuline College
University of Akron
Western Reserve University
Wilberforce University
Youngstown College
University of Dayton
Observers
Notre Dame College
Western College

Oregon-Washington
Lewis and Clark College
State College of Washington
University of Washington
Observers
Reed College

Pennsylvania
Albright College
Beaver College
Bryn Mawr College
Gettysburg College
Haverford College
Immaculata College
Lafayette College
La Salle College
Lehigh University
Lincoln University
Marywood College
Mercyhurst College
Mount Mercy College
Pennsylvania State College
Rosemont College
St. Joseph's College
Seton Hill College
Bloomsburg
Swarthmore College
Temple University
University of Pennsylvania
Villanova College
Westminster College
Wilson College
Observers
Bucknell University
Seton Hill College

Tennessee-Kentucky
Kentucky State College
King College
Nazareth College
University of Kentucky
Ursuline College
Villa Madonna College

Texas-Oklahoma
Panhandle A&M College
Southern Methodist University
Trinity University
University of Texas

Virginia–West Virginia
Hampton Institute
Marshall College
Randolph Macon Women's College
Sweet Briar College
Virginia Polytech Institute
West Virginia Institute of Tech.
William & Mary College, Richmond

Wisconsin
Carroll College
Marquette University
Milwaukee Downer College
Mount Mary College
University of Wisconsin
University of Wisconsin-Milwaukee

Source: "List of Delegates and Observers Attending the Chicago Student Conference (Dec. 28-30, 1946). Alphabetically According to Region." Mimeographed (SHSW)

Birth of The United Nations and the Iron Curtain
The Iceman Cometh and *Annie Get Your Gun* open on Broadway

The U.S. tests an atomic bomb at Bikini Atoll. The UN holds its first session in London, Churchill gives his "Iron Curtain" speech in Fulton, MO, and the Nuremberg Tribunal sentences Ribbentrop, Goering, and ten other Nazi leaders to death. Congress overturns President Truman's veto of the Taft-Hartley Act restricting the rights of labor unions. The xerographic process is invented. Eugene O'Neill's *Iceman Cometh* and Arthur Miller's *All My Sons* open on Broadway. Robert Penn Warren's *All The King's Men*, John Gunther's *Inside USA*, and Dr. Spock's *Baby and Child Care* are published. W.C. Fields dies and William Wyler's *Best Years of Our Lives* opens. The Salzburg Festival reopens for the first time after the war. Menotti's opera *The Medium* is first performed on NBC. *Brigadoon* and *Annie Get Your Gun* first appear. Hit songs are "How Are Things in Gloccamorra," "Zipadee-Doo-Dah," "Shoofly Pie and Apple Pan Dowdy." Alabama wins the Rose Bowl against Southern California and St. Louis defeats Boston in the World Series. The U.S. population is 140 million and the population of China is 455 million.

1946

Source: Adapted from citations in Bernard Grun, *The Timetables of History* (Simon and Schuster, 1991)

The Highlands' Candle

Weekly Publication of the Associated Students of Highlands University

Vol. XXI — Las Vegas, New Mexico, January 17, 1947 — No. 12

CHICAGO DELEGATES ENDORSE N. S. O.

Feature By Jack Wharton
PROJECT PLANS EXPANSION MOVE IN ARTS, CRAFTS

ANNUAL PICTURES MUST BE TAKEN IN NEXT 2 WEEKS
To Be Taken at De Castro's
Cost Is $1.25
Time Will Not Be Extended

HIGH I. Q. AT NEVADA U. REVEALED
Report By Dr. Irwin
Test Measures Ability To Think
LOW GRADE STUDENTS TURNED AWAY

VETS DON'T USE RULE BREAKING MUCH RED TAPE
Certificate Should Be Obtained Before Changing Schools

Mexico's Famed Picture Star To Appear Tonight

ALL-SCHOOL ICE SKATING TOMORROW
Beta Chi's In Charge

REPORT ON CHICAGO CONFERENCE

A STURDY NSA OUTPOST IN NORTHEAST NEW MEXICO, sixty miles from Santa Fe and 350 miles from Denver, in the center of the Rocky Mountain NSA region, Highlands University was the only New Mexico member. The *Highlands Candle* in its 1/17/47 issue (above) greeted Chicago editorially for accomplishing its "primary aim," to call a "Constitutional Convention to establish a permanent [NSO] in the United States", for which, it noted, "there is a terrific amount of interest." At the same time, its news report stated that, "The conference itself was awkwardly handled," with delegates having to go through "a number of maneuvers" to find the conference location, and "the only schools who had any idea as to what to expect, were those who sent delegates to . . . [The World Student Congress] last year." Conclusion by the editors: "Our student body and student government are to be commended for sending delegates to the conference. . . . Every facility of our school must be used in organizing the New Mexico half of the New Mexico-Colorado Region. . . we have a chance to lead. . . we have the initiative" (see Pt. 5, S. 7). Left, delegates to the Chicago Student Conference assembled in Reynolds auditorium at the U. of Chicago (*A.L. Cohen, Chicago.* Schwartz)

SECTION 4

The 1947 Constitutional Convention

CONTENTS

In just eight months, the four National Continuations Committee officers led by its President, Jim Smith (University of Texas), and thirty regional chairs, four staff committee members drafting a constitution in Chicago, and scores of volunteers organized a Constitutional Convention at the University of Wisconsin on August 30, 1947. It was attended by some 700 delegates representing 350 colleges and universities, as well as by observers from the major national student organizations who had been present at Chicago, three of whose number had seats on the Continuations Committee.

Karl Meyer (University of Wisconsin), editor of the *Wisconsin Daily Cardinal* (later to become a journalist, author, and member of the *New York Times* Editorial Board), presents an overview of 1947 and the hopes and challenges confronting students of the early postwar world.

Clif Wharton (Harvard University), Secretary of the NCC (later in life to become President of Michigan State University and Chancellor of the State University of New York), picks up the dramatic narrative he began in Section 3 and recreates the high points of the nine-day event.

He describes the major decisions: to be exclusively a student government-based organization with no individual or national organization membership; to set the terms for opening negotiations with the International Union of Students, which was increasingly seen as being under Soviet control; to resolve issues concerning the Association's stand on academic freedom and the newly adopted Student Bill of Rights; and—the source of the most intense debate—to arrive at a declaration in opposition to segregation while retaining southern college membership.

Royal Voegeli, then University of Wisconsin student body president, recalls the politics of winning over an administration at first skeptical of the meeting to enthusiastic sponsorship of the convention.

Enlisting the media and visiting Ed Murrow

Stanley Greenfield (Johns Hopkins University, MD) describes his strategy of gaining access to and recognition by the major media—which at that time were limited to print and radio—and the major higher education organizations. He reports an engaging vignette of his interview with Ed Murrow, by then a renowned radio journalist, who had been President of the National Student Federation of America sixteen years earlier.

The election of Bill Welsh (Berea College, KY) as the association's first president, and the year that followed, is detailed by Welsh in the next Section. In Europe, Bill Ellis, American Vice President of the IUS, is taken ill and replaced by Jim Smith.

The high hopes for that year are summed up in a *Mademoiselle* magazine "campus report" which declares, "if Midwestern college support is indicative of the Nation, NSA not only can consolidate student opinion and effort into a vital working force, but can easily become the seed of a collegiate United Nations."

OFFICIAL CALL which drew 350 colleges to NSA's founding convention.

A National Voice for American Students is Born

Columbia Daily Spectator Founded 1877

NSO—Student Voice

Four months ago, at the University of Chicago, 700 observers representing 800,000 students in 300 colleges and universities in the United States, overwhelmingly passed a motion to establish a National Student Organization. The gears started turning from that day on. A continuations committee was elected to draw up a draft constitution for the approval of the members. A staff committee was appointed to pave the way for a massive, all-inclusive, constitutional convention. Publicity staffs were selected to keep the colleges in constant touch with the progress of these groups.

The draft constitution was completed this month and colleges all over the continent are receiving copies. The staff committee having made tentative arrangements for a convention at the University of Wisconsin sometime between September 1 and 15, is extending invitations to hundreds of colleges and universities.

It would seem that for the first time in history, American students will have some instrument for expressing their thoughts, revealing their needs, and satisfying their legitimate requests. With the adoption of the constitution this September 3,000,000 students will be allied in the attempt to better the educational conditions in this country.

On a regional basis, the NSO is preparing to press for equality of education in the South. Already, regional committees elected at the Chicago conference have arranged interracial meetings. In Kentucky, the NSO is ready to challenge the state law prohibiting such meetings.

On the national level, the NSO plans to investigate and improve the academic, cultural, social and physical conditions of campus life.

On the international level, the NSO hopes to gain a seat on the United Nations Educational, Scientific, and Cultural Organization. (See page 1).

On all levels, it looks as if a fine beginning has been made. The continued success of the whole organization depends upon the sustained interest of the students on every campus in the nation.

1947

"IT LOOKS AS IF A FINE BEGINNING HAS BEEN MADE," *The Columbia Spectator* wrote on 4/22/47 (left) as colleges around the country began to debate "Yes" or "No" to affiliation (Los Angeles City College *Collegian* 5/28/48). 700 delegates from 350 colleges gathered at the University of Wisconsin to hammer out a constitution. Photos from top left: (1) "Welcome Delegates" banner outside Student Union, (2) Delegates awaiting session outside Wisconsin Union, (3) Conference break. From left: Curtis Farrar (Yale U.), Merrill Freed (U. of Chicago), Bill Welsh (Berea C., KY), Bob Smith (Yale U.), (4) Plenary session in Union Theater, (5) Jim Smith (U. of Texas), President of National Continuations Committee, addressing Plenary Session. From right, Royal Voegeli, President of WI student body and Edwin R. Fred, U. of WI President.

We, the students of the United States of America, desiring to maintain academic freedom and student rights, to stimulate and improve democratic student governments . . . to foster the recognition of the rights and responsibilities of students to the school, the community, humanity and God, and to preserve the interests and integrity of the government and Constitution of the United States of America, do hereby establish the Constitution of the United States National Student Association.

From the Constitution of the USNSA, adopted at its Constitutional Convention, August 30-September 7, 1947

UNITED STATES
NATIONAL
STUDENT
ASSOCIATION

•
•
•

1947-1948
MADISON, WISCONSIN
CONSTITUTIONAL CONVENTION

Colleges Follow Convention Outcomes

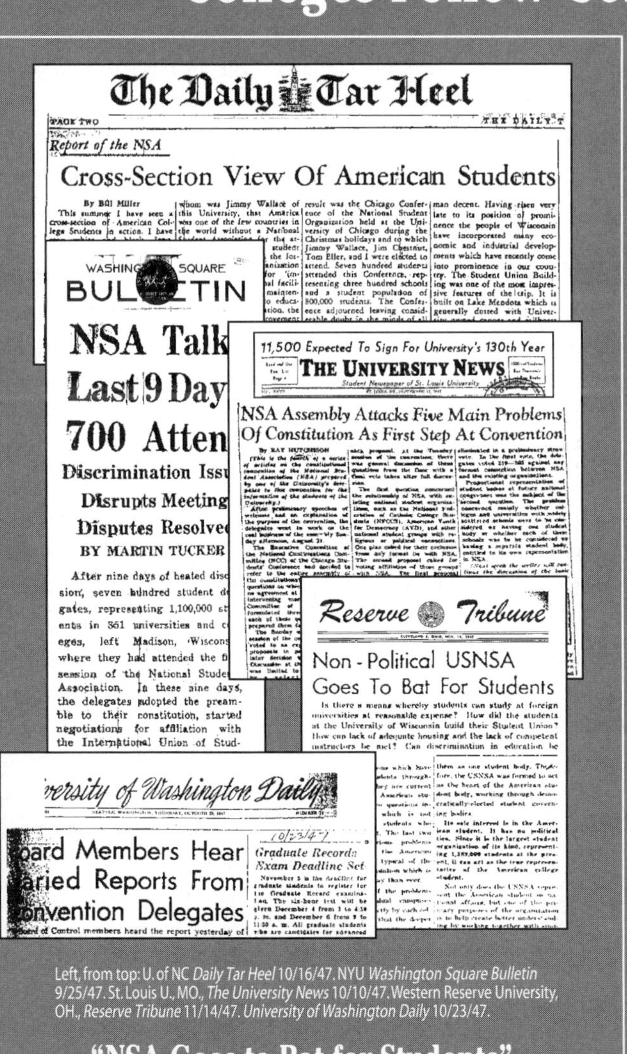

The Daily Tar Heel

PAGE TWO

Report of the NSA

Cross-Section View Of American Students

By Bill Miller

This summer I have seen a cross-section of American College Students in action. I have ...

... whom was Jimmy Wallace of this University, that America was one of the few countries in the world without a National ...

... result was the Chicago Conference of the National Student Organization held at the University of Chicago during the Christmas holidays and to which Jimmy Wallace, Jim Chestnut, Tom Eller, and I were elected to attend. Seven hundred students attended this Conference, representing three hundred schools and a student population of 800,000 students. The Conference adjourned leaving considerable doubt in the minds of all ...

... man decent. Having risen very late to its position of prominence the people of Wisconsin have incorporated many economic and industrial developments which have recently come into prominence in our country. The Student Union Building was one of the most impressive features of the trip. It is built on Lake Mendota which is generally dotted with Univer- ...

WASHINGTON SQUARE BULLETIN

NSA Talk[s] Last 9 Day[s]

700 Atten[d]

Discrimination Issu[e] Disrupts Meeting

Disputes Resolve[d]

BY MARTIN TUCKER

After nine days of heated disc[us]sion, seven hundred student de[le]gates, representing 1,100,000 st[ud]ents in 351 universities and c[oll]eges, left Madison, Wiscons[in] where they had attended the fi[rst] session of the National Stude[nt] Association. In these nine days, the delegates adopted the preamble to their constitution, started negotiations for affiliation with the International Union of Stud- ...

11,500 Expected To Sign For University's 130th Year

THE UNIVERSITY NEWS

Student Newspaper of St. Louis University

NSA Assembly Attacks Five Main Problems Of Constitution As First Step At Convention

By RAY HUTCHISON

Reserve Tribune

Non - Political USNSA Goes To Bat For Students

Is there a means whereby students can study at foreign universities at reasonable expense? How did the students at the University of Wisconsin build their Student Union? How can lack of adequate housing and the lack of competent instructors be met? Can discrimination in education be ...

... them as one student body. Therefore, the USNSA was formed to act as the heart of the American student body, working through democratically-elected student governing bodies.

Its sole interest is in the American student. It has no political ties. Since it is the largest student organization of its kind, representing 1,189,000 students at the present, it can act as the true representative of the American college student.

Not only does the USNSA represent the American student in national affairs, but one of the primary purposes of the organization is to help create better understanding by working together with stu- ...

[Uni]versity of Washington Daily

[B]oard Members Hear [V]aried Reports From [C]onvention Delegates

[B]oard of Control members heard the report yesterday of ...

Graduate Records Exam Deadline Set

November 5 is the deadline for graduate students to register for the Graduate Record examination. The six-hour test will be given December 4 from 1 to 4:30 p. m. and December 6 from 9 to 11:30 a. m. All graduate students who are candidates for advanced ...

Left, from top: U. of NC *Daily Tar Heel* 10/16/47. NYU *Washington Square Bulletin* 9/25/47. St. Louis U., MO., *The University News* 10/10/47. Western Reserve University, OH., *Reserve Tribune* 11/14/47. *University of Washington Daily* 10/23/47.

"NSA Goes to Bat for Students"

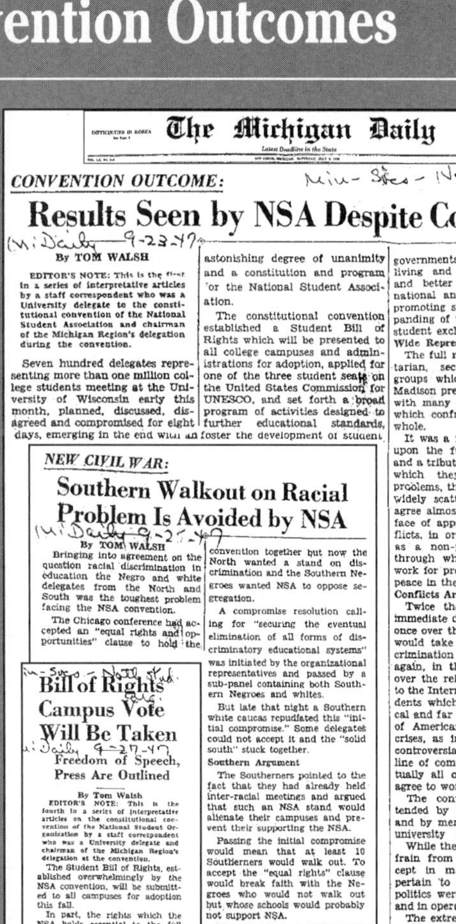

The Michigan Daily

Latest Deadline in the State

CONVENTION OUTCOME:

Results Seen by NSA Despite Conflicts

By TOM WALSH

EDITOR'S NOTE: This is the first in a series of interpretative articles by a staff correspondent who was a University delegate to the constitutional convention of the National Student Association and chairman of the Michigan Region's delegation during the convention.

Seven hundred delegates representing more than one million college students meeting at the University of Wisconsin early this month, planned, discussed, disagreed and compromised for eight days, emerging in the end with an astonishing degree of unanimity and a constitution and program for the National Student Association.

The constitutional convention established a Student Bill of Rights which will be presented to all college campuses and administrations for adoption, applied for one of the three student seats on the United States Commission for UNESCO, and set forth a broad program of activities designed to further educational standards, foster the development of student governments, improve students' living and studying conditions, and better inform students on national and world problems by promoting student travel and expanding of two-way international student exchange.

Wide Representation

The full range of political, sectarian, sectional, and racial groups which were on hand at Madison presented the convention with many of the basic problems which confront the nation as a whole.

It was a favorable commentary upon the future of our country and a tribute to the sincerity with which they approached those problems, that delegates from 350 widely scattered campuses could agree almost unanimously, in the face of apparently insoluble conflicts, in order to form the NSA as a non-partisan organization through which all students can work for progress in America and peace in the world.

Conflicts Arise

Twice the convention was in immediate danger of breaking up, once over the stand that the NSA would take regarding racial discrimination in education and, again, in the international field, over the relationship of the NSA to the International Union of Students which is admittedly political and far to the left of the bulk of American students. In these crises, as in a number of other controversial measures, the fine line of compromise at which virtually all of the delegates could agree to work together was found.

The convention was well attended by the educational press and by members of a number of university administrations.

While the NSA is pledged to refrain from political activity except in matters which directly pertain to students, intra-mural politics were very much in order and in operation.

The extremes of both the right and left were exceedingly active but the NSA succeeded in following a middle-of-the-road policy representative of the bulk of American students.

Tomorrow: The International Union of Students

NEW CIVIL WAR:

Southern Walkout on Racial Problem Is Avoided by NSA

By TOM WALSH

Bringing into agreement on the question racial discrimination in education the Negro and white delegates from the North and South was the toughest problem facing the NSA convention.

The Chicago conference had accepted an "equal rights and opportunities" clause to hold the convention together but now the North wanted a stand on discrimination and the Southern Negroes wanted NSA to oppose segregation.

A compromise resolution calling for "securing the eventual elimination of all forms of discriminatory educational systems" was initiated by the organizational representatives and passed by a sub-panel containing both Southern Negroes and whites.

But late that night a Southern white caucas repudiated this "initial compromise." Some delegates could not accept it and the "solid south" stuck together.

Southern Argument

The Southerners pointed to the fact that they had already held inter-racial meetings and argued that such an NSA stand would alienate their campuses and prevent their supporting the NSA.

Passing the initial compromise would mean that at least 10 Southerners would walk out. To accept the "equal rights" clause would break faith with the Negroes who would not walk out but whose schools would probably not support NSA.

The executive committee met all night, finally sent two Negroes and two whites out to find a compromise, unanimously adopted their suggestion and had it placed on the agenda ahead of the other alternatives.

Bill of Rights Campus Vote Will Be Taken

Freedom of Speech, Press Are Outlined

By Tom Walsh

EDITOR'S NOTE: This is the fourth in a series of interpretative articles on the constitutional convention of the National Student Organization by a staff correspondent who was a University delegate and chairman of the Michigan Region's delegation at the convention.

The Student Bill of Rights, established overwhelmingly by the NSA convention, will be submitted to all campuses for adoption this fall.

In part, the rights which the NSA holds essential to the full development of the student as an individual and to the fulfillment of his responsibilities as a citizen are:

Above, from top: *Michigan Daily* 9/23/47, 9/25/47, 9/27/47

"Astonishing Degree of Unanimity"

Present at the Creation

1. NSA and the Postwar World in 1947

Karl E. Meyer

Chair, University of Wisconsin Delegation, 1951

Reporter, Wisconsin Daily Cardinal, 1947; Editor, 1949-50

Here speaks a grizzled journalist, never mind how old, who is looking back with awe and incredulity at his own young self, his country, and its universities fifty years ago.

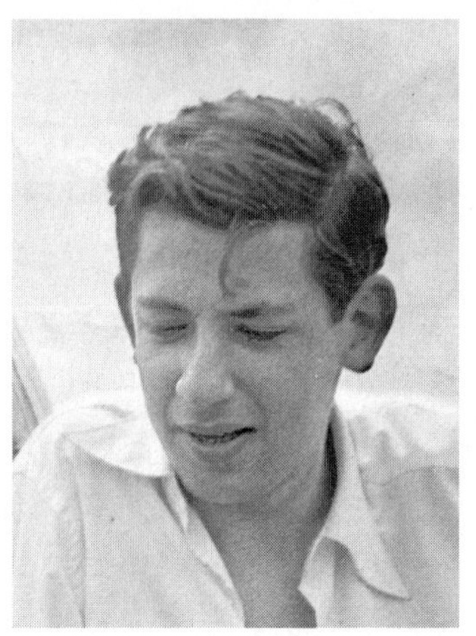

It is September, 1947. I was an entering freshman at the University of Wisconsin, with one great goal in mind: to become the editor of the student newspaper, *The Daily Cardinal.* To that end, I sought out John T. McNelly, a former editor and dapper dresser with prematurely silver hair, who was then doing a turn at the university's information office.

"Your timing is excellent," I recall his saying. "You can just catch the last day of the founding convention of a new national student association. We're helping with press relations, since we expect the new officers to make their headquarters here in Madison."

So prompted, my young self headed to the Memorial Union Theater overlooking Lake Mendota, just in time to share the euphoria attending the creation of the National Student Association. There I had my first glimpse of NSA's (to me) impossibly self-assured leaders, notably Bill Welsh from Berea College in Kentucky; who had been eloquently nominated by Clif Wharton, a black student from Harvard; Ralph Dungan from St. Joseph College, who seemed serenely confident where he and the world would be heading; and Janis Tremper from Rockford College, who was impressive and articulate.[1] I came to know others on the team, and their successors, since the *Cardinal* offices were practically next door to the frugal and flyblown former elementary school on Park Street where NSA made its headquarters for five years.

The early postwar years

Surely it is not solely nostalgia that persuades me that those were good years to be young in America. We had just won a global conflict against two truly evil empires, and after five wartime years the economy was like a stoked boiler bursting with steam. In 1947, the United States produced half the world's manufactures, 57 percent of its steel, 43 percent of its electricity, and 62 percent of its oil. The average American enjoyed an income fifteen times greater than the average foreigner, a hard-to-believe disparity due in good part to the ocean ramparts that spared America from invasion, occupation, and/or bombardment during the war.

True, the war cost 300,000 American lives and affected everything from the workplace to the nursery (soon to be crowded by baby boomers, whose sheer numbers took nearly everybody, especially demographers, by surprise). But immediately at war's end, despite casualties, the air reverberated with energy and optimism. The dominant mood was captured in the Hollywood film "The Best Years of Our Lives," the story of three returning veterans, which won nine Oscars in 1946.

In colleges, 1947 was the Year of the Veteran. More than 12 million veterans took advantage of the G.I. Bill, at a total expenditure of $3.7 billion by 1949, indisputably the most fruitful federal investment in higher education since the Morrill Land Grant Act of 1862. I had come of draft age after the war was over, but most of my male friends at the University were older and had served abroad. Of the record 18,600 students registering at Wisconsin that fall, perhaps a third were veterans who qualified for free tuition, textbooks, and a monthly stipend. This affected the flavor of campus life—less rah-rah, married students crammed in improvised trailer camps, a chain of quonset huts stretching from State Street to the Ag Campus, and not least, more sophistication about sex, liquor, and politics.

The political tone was initially fixed by the left-of-center American Veterans Committee (AVC), and the calendar was crowded with an alphabet soup of diverse student groups—AYD, SDA, NAACP, YCL, SLID—plus Young Republicans, Democrats, Socialists, and, in 1948, Progressives. For the politically inclined, there was ample fodder for debate.[2] The wartime consensus had cracked in the 1946 midterm vote (known as the "meat-shortage" election), which returned Republicans to power on Capitol Hill for the first time since the coming of the Depression.

New faces included Senator Joseph R. McCarthy of Wisconsin and two promising novices, Congressmen Richard M. Nixon and John F. Kennedy. A defiant President Truman ignored suggestions, from Senator J.W. Fulbright of Arkansas among others, that he resign, and moved vigorously in a liberal direction at home, favoring national health insurance, more aid to farmers and schools, Federal housing programs. He vetoed (though he was overridden by the 80th Congress) the punitive Taft-Hartley labor law and the repressive McCarran Immigration Act.

Civil rights

Most memorably, Truman seized the civil rights nettle. He appointed a commission whose 1947 report, *To Secure These Rights*, urged passage of fair employment and right-to-vote measures. Within a year, he issued the landmark executive order that desegregated the armed forces. It is hard nowadays to imagine how radical these steps seemed to many in a country of 140 million whose 14 million Negroes were generally treated as low-caste inferiors. Down south, three of four black Americans lived below the poverty line, in a region where everything was segregated— schools, churches, parks, beaches, buses, waiting rooms, hotels, restaurants, and cinemas. Similar Jim Crow rules applied to the nation's capital, where, until 1944, no black journalist had ever attended a presidential press conference and where the color bar was not broken in the Senate press gallery until 1947.[3]

The north was less blatant in its practices but hardly more liberal. In Westport, Connecticut, where my father was editing a country weekly in 1942, a troupe of black actors could not find a hotel in Fairfield County that would put them up. Yet African Americans were conscripted to fight for democracy. This indefensible contradiction energized the NAACP, whose membership jumped from 50,000 to 450,000 during the war. It prodded President Truman and shamed even the timid overlords of baseball, "the national pastime." In 1947, the Brooklyn Dodgers signed Jackie Robinson, ending segregation in the major leagues. The team went on to win the pennant, though losing to the Yankees in the World Series, a drama that overlapped with the founding of NSA.

One may reasonably say that the national student civil rights movement had its start in Madison in 1947. NSA leadership was multiracial from the beginning. Lee Jones from the University of Buffalo, an African American, was nominated by the Atlanta-Georgia region and elected treasurer in 1947. When Ted Harris from LaSalle College, also African American, became NSA's second president, it was evident that the student debate on civil rights was mainly over pace and tactics, not principles.[4] There was a similar broad consensus on the need for unfettered academic freedom and a "student bill of rights."

The international scene

There was markedly less agreement on international student matters. NSA owed its origin to the August 1946 World Student Congress in Prague that established the International Union of Students. America's twenty-five delegates, representing nine sponsoring organizations, were embarrassed to discover that they spoke for the only sizable Western country lacking a national student organization.[5] A summons followed to a national conference at Chicago in December to repair the omission, opening the way to the NSA's founding convention in Madison.

But the postwar world pivoted 180 degrees during 1946-48. The new United Nations and its Charter, chiefly Washington's creations, crystallized hopes for genuine collective security enforced by the wartime "Big Five," the United States, USSR, Britain, France, and China. Reality intruded in a series of hard bumps. Stalin's violations of his promises at Yalta to hold free elections in Soviet-occupied Poland, Hungary, Bulgaria, and Romania prompted Churchill, in a speech at Fulton, Missouri, in March 1946, to decry the "iron curtain" falling across Europe. By then, George Kennan had sent his epochal "long telegram" from Moscow, urging collective containment of Soviet expansion.

In March 1947, after the British notified Washington that they were pulling out of Greece and Turkey, Truman persuaded Congress to vote $700 million to fill the vacuum. In May, there followed Secretary of State Marshall's call at Harvard to Europeans, West and East, to devise a recovery plan, an invitation initially accepted by Czechoslovakia as well as victors and vanquished in Western Europe. When Stalin rebuffed the Marshall Plan, five decades of Cold War commenced, with the division of Germany, the Communist takeover in Prague, the formation of NATO and the Warsaw Pact, Mao's victory in China, and the announcement in September 1949 that the Soviet Union had detonated an atomic bomb, ending America's four-year nuclear monopoly. Debates over the rapidly growing East-West confrontation were reflected in the 1948 presidential election, in which Henry Wallace, as Progressive candidate, blamed Truman for the ice-cap hardening around the globe.

A number of essays in this book describe the twists and turns of the argument within NSA over its response to the swiftly changing international scene. A majority view emerged that East-West confrontation had undermined, probably mortally, any hopes for working with the Prague-based IUS, which was quickly turning into a communist front. But this was by no means the only view. I remember a standing-room-only AVC meeting at Science Hall on the Madison campus, at which Al Houghton, one of NSA's founders,[6] denounced the Communist coup in Prague, although his wife Jennie, a graduate student, chaired the local AYD chapter, which took a very different view. I also recall another NSA founder, John Patrick Hunter from West Virginia, leading Veterans Against MacArthur during the 1948 Wisconsin primary; he staged a mock "I-have-returned" landing on the shores of Lake Mendota.

NSA's ambitious, global international program placed considerable strain on its limited financial resources. In the years after both NSA's national offices and the author left Madison, some of NSA's officers felt it right to accept secret funding from the Central Intelligence Agency. It has to be said that the revelation in the press in 1967 of the secret funding produced surprise and shock, since NSA stood for openness. Yet I can understand the pressures brought on NSA as it coped with its precarious finances.

In retrospect, one does wonder if a well-directed, sustained effort might have produced the needed funds to secure permanent, stable, and open funding for the NSA international program. Given the enthusiasm, energy, and lack of cynicism of the NSA officers I knew in those early years, I think it might have been possible.[7]

NSA and the "Red Scare"

During the five-year period covered by this book, NSA's national and regional officers and its campus affiliates were frequently called upon to combat and refute accusations of communist sympathy or affiliation, arising from the growing postwar tide of anticommunism in America. Suspicions and fears of alleged communist activities and influence were fanned by investigations by the House Un-American Activities Committee, the espionage trial of Alger Hiss in 1948, and the coming of the "McCarthy Era," launched by Wisconsin Senator Joseph McCarthy with his 1950 allegations that the State Department was riddled with communists.

Some of the essays in this book document a virtually constant stream of McCarthy-style attacks and insinuations against NSA. At the national and regional levels and on campuses, NSA was obliged to devote major amounts of time to responding to these attacks and refuting them. An afternote to this essay provided by the book's editors lists a number of these attacks. It is good to be able to report that, while making heavy demands on NSA's energies, the anticommunist sniping did little actual harm. Throughout the period, NSA maintained a 250-300 student government membership, embracing about a million of the 2.3 million students then enrolled in college, with a broad base among public, private, Protestant, and Catholic institutions and representing all areas of the country.

The "process" approach

A major characteristic of the ethos of the veterans' era, which found expression in NSA, was a non-confrontational, "process" approach to policymaking and problem solving. In the field of civil rights, NAACP followed this approach, seeking to achieve equity through the judicial and legislative process. Similarly, student leaders participating in NSA sought to break down segregation barriers and erase the impulse to discriminate by non-confrontational methods, including education, sponsoring of human relations programs, and working for progress through gradualism and compromise. This approach contrasts sharply with the confrontational approach that was increasingly adopted by students and activists in the sixties and later.[8]

Avoidance of confrontation and search for workable processes were equally evident in NSA's approach to the issues that were created in international student affairs by the swift coming of the Cold War. NSA's first four international vice presidents, Bob Smith, Rob West, Erskine Childers, and Herb Eisenberg, believed that dialogue and efforts to arrive at mutual understanding between East and West offered hope for surmounting Cold War and superpower tensions, at least in some areas and on some levels. As a consequence, although NSA remained wary and kept institutional ties with IUS at arm's length, it discouraged the creation of competitive programs and organizational arrangements. In 1950-51, NSA president Al Lowenstein gave voice to a more aggressive alternative approach that involved building structural arrangements and programs among NSA and the student unions of non-Communist countries. This approach was carried forward by NSA's 1951-52 president, Bill Dentzer, and his international vice president, Avrea Ingram.

The *Svalbard* and me

In 1949, I became editor of *The Cardinal*, and along with my successor, Jack Zeldes, sailed on the *Volendam* to see Europe on $5 a day—which was actually possible, thanks to cheap meals provided by cooperating student groups. The trip went so well that in 1950, along with another undergraduate, Herbert Haessler, a good photographer, we offered ourselves as a team willing to edit *The Dam Daily*, the shipboard paper during the ten-day voyage, and to publicize the NSA tour program in exchange for free passage. A deal was struck, but we were asked to undertake a related chore gratis, which was to publicize the departure from New York of a second student ship, the *M.S. Svalbard*, which had been chartered by NSA in Norway. Herb and I duly churned out daily releases from NSA's offices in the Woodstock Hotel on West 43d Street, a block from the *New York Times*.

On departure day, as we were preparing for the dockside press conference, Mildred Kiefer came running towards us, all but shouting, "Herb! Karl! Cancel the press conference, call up all the papers and tell them not to come. The ship is not sailing!"

It appeared, as we were breathlessly informed, that the U.S. Coast Guard had determined that the *M.S. Svalbard* was not safe and seaworthy. Some 1,200 students and their families were at the dock when Rob West tried his best to explain what happened and to promise that everything possible would be done to find alternative transportation. This was at the end of June, a dead news time, and the forlorn students made the front pages of every New York newspaper.[9]

Later, back at the Woodstock, Haessler and I were approached by Laurie Johnston, the *New York Times* reporter covering our plight. She said that she might be able to help, since the paper's ship editor, then an important post, had a White House military contact and would call immediately to see what might be done—provided, of course, that the *Times* was given the news first and exclusively. The call was made; and the situation was saved when President Truman immediately released a military transport, the *General Ballou*, to transport the beached students to Europe.[10]

NSA and its times

NSA reflected and embodied the special idealism of the youth world of its times. The Cold War abroad and racial segregation and the "Red Scare" at home were hurdles to be surmounted on the way to the attainment of the postwar college generation's goals. These issues, however, were not the basic reason for NSA's creation or for the immense grass-roots support that the new organization received. These stemmed from shared intentions and values, extending far beyond the organization's politically inclined leaders and reaching broadly into this student generation.

College students saw the victory of World War II as a gateway through which to channel energies for the betterment of society, and to utilize America's democratic ideals as working tools for the betterment of life on the campus and in the community. The postwar college generation also believed that it had an obligation to contribute to the reconstruction of war-torn nations, and to help developing countries—at that time mostly colonial—to achieve the economic and political freedoms that were enjoyed in the developed democracies. NSA represented a vision and a belief that a student-based and student-run national organization could unify American students in a common commitment to these ideas and make a practical contribution to their achievement.

All of us who were present at this particular creation have every reason to look back in wonder, gratitude, and celebration.

Editor's Note: *To assist those with an interest in the matter, the book's editors have identified a number of anticommunist attacks, warnings, and/or insinuations that are noted in essays and sidebars in this book. These references illustrate an important feature of life in the United States in the years immediately following World War II, which affected virtually all civic efforts and activities.*

- *Clif Wharton, Secretary of the National Continuations Committee, notes Harvard professor William Yandell Elliott's 1946 warning to the Chicago Conference delegates that they be "on the lookout" for Communist control efforts relating to their discussions about opening up a dialog with the communist-bloc-dominated International Union of Students (IUS) (see p. 113).*
- *In February 1947, the National Continuations Committee was drawn into a controversy at Michigan State University over what Jim Smith, NCC President, quoted Chicago newspapers as characterizing as a statewide "Red Hunt" (see p. 120).*
- *Barefoot Saunders, University of Texas delegate to the NSA Constitutional Convention and subsequently student body president, notes that in 1948, the University of Texas student body voted not to join NSA after a vigorously fought campaign in which NSA's interest in the IUS was the issue. A similar battle took place in the same month at Louisiana State University where Gillis Long, also an NSA delegate and student body president, led a losing campaign against a strong "Red Scare" opposition. Both student newspapers,* The Daily Texan *and the* LSU Reveille *supported affiliation (see p. 995, p. 455).*
- *In 1947-48, NSA President Bill Welsh and his staff were required to deal continuously with the letter-writing campaigns of Allan B. Crow, President of the business-supported Economic Club of Detroit. Crow communicated with college administrations throughout the country, challenging the integrity of NSA's platform and implying a communist-tinged agenda (see p. 191).*
- *Alexander Pope, Chairman of the NSA Illinois Region, describes the impact of Congressman Velde's May 1951 charge that the Illinois Region was under control of "powerful elements of the Illinois Communist Party" (see p. 390).*
- *An article in the January 14, 1951, issue of the Interfraternity Research and Advisory Council Bulletin described the "Red influence" in NSA. Bill Dentzer, 1951-52 NSA President, wrote a half-page editorial in the May 1952* NSA News, *rebutting the article, which he termed a "vicious smear" (see p. 310).*
- *Students for America, formed in 1952 in California, undertook a direct and vigorous campaign in its publications challenging NSA as "an insidious left wing pressure group" (see p. 805).*

Karl E. Meyer has been on the Editorial Board of the New York Times *and served as London and New York Bureau Chief for the* Washington Post. *He is currently editor of the* World Policy Journal *at New School University. He has written or edited nine books including* Fulbright of Arkansas *(1963) and* Pundits, Poets and Wits *(1990) and is co-author with his wife, Shareen Blair Brysac, of* Tournament of Shadows: The Great Game and the Race for Empire in Asia *(1999).*

END NOTES

[1] See essays by Welsh (p. 164), Wharton (p. 112, p. 144), Tremper (p. 60), and Dungan (p. 174).

[2] A guide to organizational acronyms appears on p. 1126. See also p. 149, "Other Voices Speak on NSA's Formation."

[3] See Welsh, p. 170.

[4] It should be noted that the twenty-five-member U.S. delegation to the World Student Congress in Prague in 1946 included three blacks, Bill Ellis, Charles Proctor, and Wally Wallace. At the National Student Conference in Chicago in December 1946, Clifton Wharton was elected Secretary of the National Continuations Committee and Walter Wallace was elected Chairperson of the Metropolitan New York Region. Ted Perry of Temple University was elected NSA Vice President for Student Life on the 1949-50 national staff, and Shirley Neizer of Simmons College was elected Executive Secretary on the 1950-51 national staff. Meanwhile, black and white NSA college delegations and observers were meeting together at NSA regional meetings in North Carolina, Georgia, and Louisiana in the late 1940s and early 1950s, piercing the wall of segregation at significant personal risk.

[5] See Part 1, Section 1, "London, Prague and Chicago: 1946," p. 55.

[6] Al Houghton was elected at the Chicago student Conference in December of 1946 to be one of four National Continuations Committee staff members.

[7] *Editor's note:* See Welsh et al., on covert U.S. Government funding, p. 565. It consists of a report on research to identify any CIA-related or other covert funding of international programs that may have occurred during the time period covered by this book. It also addresses the sustained period of such funding, which took place from 1952 to 1967.

[8] See Brown, "Student Rights, Academic Freedom, and NSA," p. 375, and Part 2, Section 3, "The South, Civil Rights and Segregation," p. 419.

[9] *Editor's note:* The "*Svalbard* Incident" first broke in the New York press on June 23, 1950. On June 25, it began to share national headlines with the North Korean invasion of South Korea.

[10] For more on the *Svalbard* incident and related events, see Part 3, Section 5, "Student Travel and Exchange," p. 639.

PICTURE CREDITS: *Then:* On a European tour, 1950 (Herbert Hessler Photo. *Schwartz*). *Now:* c. 2000 (*Author*).

KARL E. MEYER

Early years: I was born in Madison, WI, raised in New York City, and went to Elizabeth Irwin High School in New York. My parents were from Wisconsin and New York.

Education: B.A. (History), University of Wisconsin; Master of Public Affairs, Woodrow Wilson School of Public and International Affairs, Princeton University; Ph.D. (Politics), Princeton University.

Career Highlights: Editor, *World Policy Journal* (World Policy Institute, New School University). Member, Editorial Board, the *New York Times* (1979-98), senior writer on foreign affairs. Presently contributing editor to *Arts and Ideas.* Senior Reuter Fellow, Green College, Oxford University (1996-97). Resident Fellow, Wissenschaftskolleg zu Berlin (Institute of Advanced Studies, Berlin) (1994-95). Correspondent in Residence, Fletcher School, Tufts University (1979-80); visiting professor, Yale University (1984, 1988). McGraw Professor of Writing, Princeton University, (1993-94). Television columnist, contributing editor, *The Saturday Review* (1975-79). Reporter, editorial writer, London Bureau Chief, New York Bureau Chief, *The Washington Post* (1956-71). American correspondent, *The New Statesman* of London (1962-65). Contributing editor, *Archaeology* magazine (1998 —).

Publications: *The Dust of Empire,* Public Affairs, 2003. *Tournament of Shadows: The Great Game and the Race for Empire in Central* Asia (with Shareen Blair Brysac*)*, Counterpoint, 1999. *Pundits, Poets and Wits: An Omnibus of American Newspaper Columns*, Oxford University Press, 1990. *The Art Museum: Power, Money, Ethics*, Morrow, 1978. Twentieth Century Fund study. *Teotihuacan,* Newsweek Books, 1975. *The Plundered Past,* Atheneum, 1973. Serialized in the *New Yorker. The Pleasures of Archaeology,* Atheneum, 1970. *Fulbright of Arkansas,* Robert Luce, Washington D.C., 1963. Preface by Walter Lippmann. *The Cuban Invasion* (with Tad Szulc), Praeger, 1962. Ballantine Paperback. *The New America,* Basic Books, 1961.

Associations: Fellow, Davenport College, Yale; Society of Fellows of New York University; member of the Council on Foreign Relations and the Century Association.

Family: Married to Shareen Blair Brysac.

ON THE ROAD TO EUROPE
U. of Wisconsin's Karl Meyer (below) and photographer Herb Haessler, editors of the *Volendam*'s shipboard daily (far right) with Helen Bryan, NSA's travel program director in Europe, 1950. (Herbert Haessler photo. Karl Meyer). Near right, Meyer and the Paris Edition, *Herald Tribune* (NSA Travel Brochure).

1949-50 *Daily Cardinal* Editor Highlights Student and Global Issues

The Daily Cardinal, September 27, 1949
Karl Meyer tells . . .

A Story of Slavs, Semantics, and Wisconsin

NEWS ITEM: At the University of Illinois, two new course offerings have been announced, Russian and Semantics.

THERE'S A MORAL to this story—the two must be studied together. This was brought sharply home to a gathering of Wisconsin daily newspaper editors last weekend by a man who knows—because his job is to sort out the semantics from Slavic in a United Nations subcommission.

The man was Carroll Binder, now editorial editor of the *Minneapolis Tribune* and a veteran foreign correspondent. He is the American representative on the subcommission on freedom of information. And his story is one of patient untangling of words and meanings.

* * *

THE RUSSIANS WANT a "responsible" press. And what does responsible mean? It means that the press must not be allowed to print "untruths" about any government and it means there must be control to prevent just that occurrence.

The United States wants a "free" press. And, what does this mean to the Russians? Why, you blockheads, a free press means freedom to be irresponsible and print lies about the true democratic governments in Eastern Europe.

It is no wonder that other nations are sucked into the confusion. On the world political scene words are tossed with [the] abandon of a child tossing bird feed to the pigeons.

But the pigeons in this case are the people of the world. And to the illiterate, the hungry and unemployed, those words have a music. "Peace, Land and Bread" were the slogans of the Russian revolution and people fought and died for those words.

* * *

ON THE *SS VOLENDAM* THIS SUMMER, I had another chance to catch a glimpse of this confusion. The ship was a student ship and on it were 15 delegates to the World Youth and Student Festival, a leftist sideshow staged in Budapest.

On the return to the United States, the leaders of this group presented a report to the students on the festival. In the course of the discussions it developed that the American delegation to this world festival painted the United states as a vast slum with veterans drawing "meager allowances" and the majority walking the streets "unemployed and looking for jobs."

Several students asked if the delegates told the other countries that they represented all of American thought. "No", the delegation leader retorted, "we emphasized that we represented only progressive American youth."

And what was his definition of "progressive"? After stumbling around hopelessly for a phrase, the youth festival delegate replied that "everyone knows what we mean."

But everyone didn't, and subsequent discussion did nothing to clear the muddied verbal waters.

* * *

TODAY, it is more and more imperative that college students know something about semantics. The college student and especially the budding journalist must be familiar with the "loaded" words that change color in hopping from ideology to ideology.

He must recognize these words in context and know the real intent behind them. He must develop a discipline for demanding definitions and probing for hidden meanings.

Which brings us to the university. A glance through the timetable shows that only one fairly technical course in the subject is offered: English 123—"History of the English Language." The other courses are in philosophy and deal with symbolic logic—again on a technical level.

The university should offer a popularized and introductory course in semantics—and perhaps in the case of journalism students, make it compulsory. In today's nightmare of ideological press agentry, that "continual and fearless sifting and winnowing"* is largely a matter of semantics.

**Editor's note: This quote is excerpted from the University's motto (see Voegeli, p. 152). The point of this article is brought home sharply by Bill Ellis in his report with Joyce Roberts to the NICC on the World Student Congress (p. 106). There he discusses the problems raised by differing definitions between Eastern European and Western student delegates of terms such as "democracy" and "fascism."*

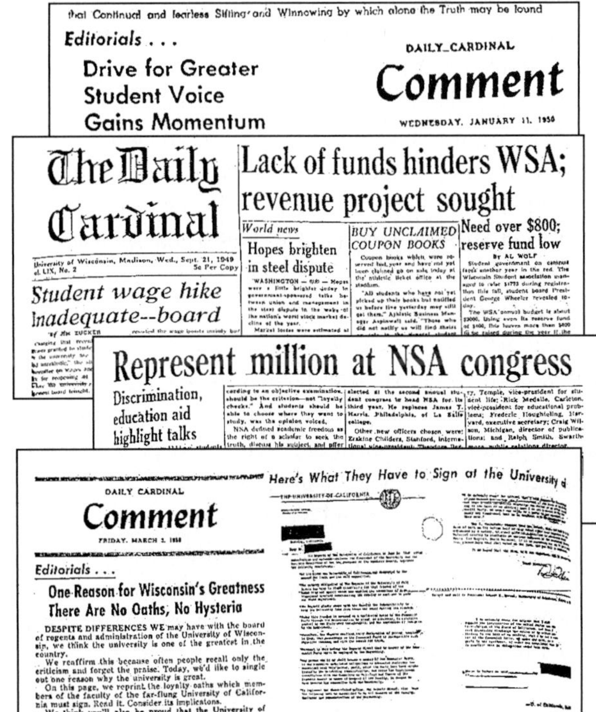

that Continual and fearless Sifting and Winnowing by which alone the Truth may be found

Editorials . . .

Drive for Greater Student Voice Gains Momentum

DAILY CARDINAL Comment

WEDNESDAY, JANUARY 11, 1950

The Daily Cardinal

Lack of funds hinders WSA; revenue project sought

World news

Hopes brighten in steel dispute

BUY UNCLAIMED COUPON BOOKS

Need over $800; reserve fund low

Student wage hike inadequate--board

Represent million at NSA congress

Discrimination, education aid highlight talks

Here's What They Have to Sign at the University of California

DAILY CARDINAL Comment

Editorials . . .

One Reason for Wisconsin's Greatness
There Are No Oaths, No Hysteria

DESPITE DIFFERENCES WE may have with the board of regents and administration of the University of Wisconsin, we think the university is one of the greatest in the country.

We reaffirm this because often people recall only the criticism and forget the praise. Today, we'd like to single out one reason why the university is great.

On this page, we reprint the loyalty oaths which members of the faculty of the far-flung University of California must sign. Read it. Consider its implications.

We think you'll also be proud that the University of

HEADLINES from the *Daily Cardinal* highlight some of the issues capturing attention during Karl Meyer's year as Editor. Student government (WSA, Wisconsin Student Association) support (9/29/49) and a "greater student voice" in policy-making (1/11/50) were also a cornerstone of NSA's goals. Its Second Annual Congress (see Pt. 1, S. 6) is reported on 9/15/49. Commenting on the loyalty oaths required of the University of California faculty (see Pt. 5, S. 8), the *Cardinal* (3/3/50) wrote to its readers, "you'll be proud that the University of Wisconsin has refused to bow under the weight of unreasonable hysteria and compromise its cherished academic freedom."

The founding of the U.S. National Student Association

2. The 1947 Constitutional Convention

Clifton R. Wharton, Jr.
Harvard University
Secretary, National Continuations Committee, 1946-47

Editor's note: This essay has been adapted from "Black Pioneer: A Personal History. Part Three: The College Years," an extended autobiographical reference which, at this writing (2002), is being completed by the author and is intended for deposit and access to researchers and others with his archives at Michigan State University. The author is also preparing a standard autobiography for future trade publication.

The convention that founded the U.S. National Student Association was held at the Madison campus of the University of Wisconsin from August 30 through September 7, 1947.[1] A more beautiful site could not have been chosen, and the conference had the locale and setting of heartland America. The convention was attended by about seven-hundred delegates representing 351 colleges and universities.[2]

The opening ceremonies on Saturday were impressive. President Harry Truman sent greetings. Dr. Homer P. Rainey, president of Stephens College, was the keynote speaker.[3] He advocated that universities should educate youth to think in world terms and that students should "slough off the protective shell of 'ivory towers of learning' and mix in with the realistic, hard-bitten world of politics, economics, and conflicting ideologies." He counseled our organization to avoid partisan politics. His concluding remarks deplored cynical attitudes toward politics and politicians and stressed the need for a rebirth of patriotism and statesmanship.

As secretary, I was responsible for delegation seat assignments. From the stage, I could identify the delegation when a person rose to speak, which was to prove an advantage later in my various lobbying strategies on the floor.

I was amazed to see how accurately the delegations seemed to reflect regional geographic characteristics. Some of this was undoubtedly due to the fact that a large proportion of the delegates were from state universities, which tend to have predominantly local student bodies. Many delegates from California looked just like they were supposed to look—blond, blue-eyed, well tanned. Those from New York sounded like New Yorkers. Even the delegates' attitudes and humor reflected their regional roots. The "Mainiacs" (from Maine) had a dry wit; the Midwesterners were direct. There also was a fairly heavy representation of veterans of the armed forces, giving the deliberations a more mature cast.

The question of whether student organizations should be part of the proposed NSA arose early. It was clear to me that the college-based delegates were deeply suspicious of the motivation and role of the outside student organizations. As the debate proceeded, strong feelings surfaced and the tension made the atmosphere quite electric. Part of the difficulty was that most of the elected delegates were new to each other and could not tell whether they were outnumbered by the organizational delegates who had been permitted to attend. When the question was called, the convention rejected all membership by student organizations. With the pro-organization resolution resoundingly defeated, there was a collective sigh of relief throughout the hall. The campus-elected delegates now knew that they really had the necessary clout and were in charge.[4]

New York was split into Upstate and Downstate (New York City) delegations. During the early votes, I noticed that the New York City delegations had adopted a Unit Rule, by which all of the delegation votes were cast in favor of the majority position, regardless of any internal split. This meant that no minority views, no matter how substantial, were reflected on the convention floor. As recorder of the votes, I could tell from my vantage point on the stage that this procedure was causing strong negative reactions among the other delegations when, on roll call, the New Yorkers always cast "fifty-four votes for and zero votes against." After this happened several times, I tried a bit of humor to break the habit. In the back of the auditorium I found an old prop box that contained a bullwhip. I coiled up the whip, concealed it under my jacket, then put it on the shelf under the podium. On the next roll call, when the New York delegation announced their unit rule vote, I reached under the podium, pulled out the bullwhip, and snapped it across the stage with a loud crack. This produced gales of laughter, and thereafter a somewhat embarrassed New York delegation avoided any more unit rule votes.

At another tense moment, I tried to help the delegates unwind by taking them on a "Lion Hunt," which I had previously introduced at the Chicago meeting. This involved my sitting in a straight-backed chair on center stage and leading the audience through the steps of an imaginary hunt. They were to repeat my words and mimic my motions as we climbed a tree, crossed a swamp, parted the grass, and took other elaborate steps to try to find the elusive lion. Upon sighting the ferocious lion, they were to flee in terror by repeating the entire process, only in reverse and at high speed. The ensuing laughter suggested there was nothing better to relieve tension than a lion hunt.[5]

In addition to the issue of membership by student organizations, other matters that temporized at the Chicago meeting also threatened to derail the Madison proceedings. One issue was whether the new student organization should participate in direct political activities. Those in favor of political involvement argued that this was a central feature of national student unions and organizations around the globe, and that only through political activities could the broader interests of students be advanced and protected. The counter position was advanced by those who were concerned about the politicization of the student organization along ideological lines between the left and the right or partisan maneuvering on the Democratic or Republican spectrum. There was also concern over the possible political orientation of future leaders of the organization and whether, between annual meetings, they might adopt political positions with which the broader group might disagree. It was decided that the constitution would expressly prohibit the NSA from engaging in direct political activities. This action further disenchanted a number of student organizations, weakening their likely support for the organization in the future.

Affiliation with IUS

The issue of affiliation with the International Union of Students (IUS) once again drew fire. The need for U.S. students to be involved internationally was generally accepted, but there was concern that NSA might become a minority within an organization dominated by the Soviet Union and by leftist students with a political agenda that a large majority of U.S. students could not accept.

WHARTON'S "LION HUNT"

"I'm going on a lion hunt!" I announce, stomping my feet to simulate walking, while slapping my open palms on my thighs in a synchronous walking motion.

The audience responds, "I'm going on a lion hunt," while they rhythmically slap their thighs and move their feet in unison.

"Have to find a lion."

"Have to find a lion," they echo.

"Have my trusty rifle." (I grab my imaginary rifle, waving it in the air).

"Have my trusty rifle." The slapping of thighs and stomping of feet continue.

"Must climb that tree."

"Must climb that tree," they parrot. (I then simulate climbing the tree while the audience imitates the climbing motion.)

"Can't see any lions," I chant, while holding my hand above my eyebrows and peering left and right.

"Can't see any lions," they intone.

Clif Wharton leading the "Lion Hunt" at a convention plenary session, Aug. 30-Sept. 7, 1947 (Wharton)

Then I pretend to climb down the tree, which the audience copies.

"Must cross the swamp."

"Must cross the swamp," they mimic, while I pull at my feet as though they are stuck in mud.

Then we go back to the regular rhythmic thigh slapping and foot stomping.

"Must cross the bridge." (Now I pound my chest with both fists doubled up, causing loud thumps, while my feet continue stomping.)

"Must cross the bridge," they repeat.

"Going through the brush." (My outstretched arms move in a parting motion, going through imaginary brush.)

"Going through the brush."

The audience and I continue slapping our thighs and stomping our feet.

"Very deep grass."

"Very deep grass."

"Must move slowly."

"Must move slowly."

Now we switch to very quiet thigh-slapping rhythms and tiptoeing. I stop suddenly, leaning forward even farther in my seat.

"What are those eyes?"

"What are those eyes?"

"It must be a lion."

"It must be a lion."

"Let's get out of here!"

"Let's get out of here!"

At high speed, everyone must do exactly, in reverse sequence, what was originally done—tiptoeing, grass and brush parting, bridge and swamp crossing, tree peering and rifle waving!

The international panel captured these concerns in its report:

1. We recognize that the majority of the present leadership of IUS and many of the member organizations of IUS are far to the left of American students and that within that majority, Communists exercise influence far out of proportion to the Communists within the world student community.

2. The IUS has tended to lay greater stress upon political activities and expression of opinion than is customary or desirable in student organizations in the United States, which are avowedly non-partisan and non-sectarian. . . .

4. As a member of IUS, the NSA will have both to exercise the strictest constant care to avoid the abuse of its prestige and backing for activities contrary to or outside its scope and program. . . .[6]

Nevertheless, the panel argued cogently for the positive benefits of seeking better mutual understanding to reduce tensions, the possibility (shown by events to be naive) of opportunities to modify and even change the organization's extreme orientation, and the practical value of "student exchanges, international tours, student relief, faculty conferences and exchanges, joint projects and exchanges on art, drama, dance, science, etc."

The solution proposed by the panel was to negotiate an "Agreement on Affiliation," which stipulated the political and administrative autonomy of NSA within IUS. "No decision of the IUS which may be specifically repudiated by the NSA shall bind or shall be published as representing the opinions of American students," the proposed agreement stated. Also specified were the right to append a minority report to any publication with whose views NSA disagreed and the fact that "on the national level, the NSA shall have complete administrative autonomy."

The final provision was that any affiliation agreement negotiated with IUS must be ratified by the individual U.S. campuses. The conditions set forth were that at least half of the member colleges, representing two-thirds of the member students, had to endorse the agreement. This was approved by a vote of 304 to 211. The provision to refer to the individual campuses was also approved, 297 to 245. NSA was now ready to establish a delicate, wary relationship with IUS.

The race relations compromise

A fourth major issue was the "American dilemma" of race. Attendees at the convention included a substantial number of delegates from both predominantly Black colleges and white Southern universities. The Southern Negro students spearheaded an effort to introduce a variety of constitutional amendments dealing with racism and discrimination in higher education. They were joined by the liberal white students, particularly those from the extreme left, such as the Young Communist League (YCL). In the plenary sessions of the Madison conference, the YCL became virtually the joint voice on the issues of racism and discrimination.

I was chairman of the Educational Opportunities Panel, where the issue first came to a head. Because of my leadership position, some of the Southern Negroes sought my support and assistance. I told them that in my judgment, they were being exploited by the YCL, which really did not care about the issue and merely sought to destroy the student organization before it was even born. I felt that the YCL's position reflected a level of expedient hypocrisy and that it really did not reflect a genuine commitment to the cause of racial justice. The Southern Negro student leadership disagreed, and felt that I was a traitor to their goals. Meanwhile, a group of Southern white students strongly objected to introducing the issue into the proposed constitution at all, and at one point threatened to walk out of the convention. This would have made it less than a truly national organization. As the debate proceeded, emotions escalated and became intense, with verbal brickbats thrown back and forth.

Soon the opposing groups had locked themselves into rigid positions and could see no way to resolve their differences. The situation was explosive, and the future of NSA was threatened. At the Chicago meeting, we had strengthened the section of the preamble dealing with issues of equal rights. Now the conflict was over implementation—how the necessary steps might be taken and/or mandated at the national and regional levels. The Southern white delegates did not want their regional autonomy impaired with a by-law on the elimination of discrimination, while the Negro delegates and others wanted NSA to act, and not leave the issue solely to local or regional initiatives.

On the afternoon of September 4, after seventy-two hours of turbulent and intense debate in panels, committees, and corridors, the issue reached a climax. At an earlier all-night meeting of the Steering Committee, Jim Smith had led the development of an eleventh-hour compromise that brought together the key leaders on both sides.

The compromise involved modifying the two sections of the by-laws that I had helped develop at Chicago. When this issue came to the floor for final debate, Bill Welsh, the plenary chairman, called upon Jim Smith to present the compromise proposal. John Simons, treasurer of the NCC, then spoke eloquently in support of the compromise. But once again the issue boiled over into a steady, two-hour harangue from both sides. Dissatisfaction was concentrated on the implementation by-law, which called for action to work toward eliminating discrimination on the regional level only. The by-law read, ". . . it shall be the policy of the United States National Student Association that each region undertake such action as is necessary within its own area." After a series of proposed amendments from the floor modifying this section, Jim Smith presented a proposal combining the best points of the original amendment offered by Janis Tremper. The key was adding a phrase that NSA would "take action on national, regional, and campus levels...with regard to the legal limitations involved."[7]

When it became clear that we had the votes to pass the compromise, the leader of the YCL got up and spoke in favor of it. I turned to look at the Southern Negro student leadership, who were aghast and felt totally betrayed. They had expected YCL to argue against the proposed compromise and in favor of their position. I felt deeply saddened by their feeling of dismay and betrayal.

The final vote approving the compromise was greeted by a burst of applause from all the delegates in Union Hall. As a University of Wisconsin press release put it: "Antagonisms and regional suspicions were forgotten as the students celebrated the settlement of the knottiest problem before the convention. The Southern-Yankee conflict was whiffed away completely when the large New York delegation broke into the singing of 'Dixie.'"[8]

Choosing the new leadership

The final major action of the convention was to choose the National Student Association's first leaders, who would be critical to the future of the fledgling organization. Several of us felt that the best person to be the first president was Bill Welsh, a twenty-three-year-old senior majoring in history at Berea College in Kentucky. During the constitutional convention, Welsh and I were roommates, and I came to know and respect him. Bill was a three-year veteran of the army infantry, and therefore older and more mature than the traditional student. There was no question about his commitment to social issues, including those relating to racism and discrimination, even though he came from the border state of Kentucky. The fact that he was from Kentucky made him acceptable to the Southern student groups, and among the Northern students his social commitment and political acumen gave him great cachet, while genuine leadership qualities made him a strong choice among many students. In delivering the nominating speech from the convention floor, I spared none of the usual nomination hyperbole:

> [Welsh] has the ability of leadership. His is the leadership that we need in this coming year. His is the leadership which will keep our not-too-distant goals in view while emphasizing and stressing those immediate objectives which will lead to those ends. His is the leadership which will pour every last ounce of energy into the effort to lay firm foundations for the USNSA which we have started here. . . .
>
> We have made an organization with all its instruments, but we will need more than a hard, efficient approach. We need a man who will pour and mold his very soul into the organization. It needs but the breath of life-dealing air breathed into its nostrils.
>
> I give you a man who will give that breath and who will lead that living form in its first momentous steps.
>
> I give you the man who will take my dream and your dream and treat it tenderly.
>
> I give you a man who also shares that dream.
>
> I give you—Bill Welsh!

I believed that we had the votes to elect Bill over the opposing candidate, William M. Birenbaum, an air force veteran who was a law student and speech instructor at the University of Chicago.[9] However, just in case, in structuring the debate sequence, we left open the third seconding speech. This would put us in a position, if there seemed to be any contrary groundswell, to block any attempt to stampede the convention against Welsh. My nominating speech was followed by our two preselected seconders, keeping the third speech in reserve. However, I was furious when a student rose and said that, since we had not used the third seconding speech, she would speak in favor of Welsh. This upset our careful strategy and left us vulnerable. But luck was with us, and a stampede did not develop.

Welsh won, 321 to 244. Ralph Dungan, from St. Joseph's College in Philadelphia, was elected vice president for domestic affairs (301 to 255), defeating Royal Voegeli, the head of student government at the University of Wisconsin. Robert S. Smith of Yale ran uncontested for vice president for international affairs and was elected by acclimation. Lee Jones, a Negro who was head of the student body at the University of Buffalo and a varsity football player, was unopposed for treasurer. It is worth noting that Jones was nominated by the Alabama-Georgia region and seconded by John Clampett, a white student from the University of North Carolina. Janis Tremper, a graduate of Rockford College, defeated Jane Wilder of UCLA [University of California at Los Angeles] for secretary. (Wally Wallace from Columbia University withdrew.)

Clifton R. Wharton, Jr., was U.S. Deputy Secretary of State, Chairman and CEO of Teachers Insurance Annuity Association and College Retirement Equities Fund (TIAA-CREF), Chancellor of the State University of New York, and President of Michigan State University.
(See p. 117 for extended biography.)

KEY LEADERSHIP IN NSA'S FORMATION was provided by Harvard students who appear elsewhere in this work, including Doug Cater (Prague delegation), Bill Ellis (NICC representative and U.S. Vice President of IUS), Clif Wharton (NCC Secretary), Andrew Rice and Frank Fisher (Harvard International Commission), and Alice Gilbert, Radcliffe (New England regional chair). Shown standing above and to the left are Gilbert and Wharton at a New England regional caucus. Seated at far left is Henry Halsted, Williams College.

The delegates' experience of politics, from drafting legislation to negotiating its passage, was both invigorating and educational. It is little wonder that most of the delegates seemed to operate on a constant "high" during the convention. Perhaps most significant, the experience of involvement in national student politics at Chicago and Madison proved to be an early seedbed for many of the participants, who subsequently achieved positions of major leadership in higher education, government and foreign affairs, and business. NSA was a great crucible.

When I learned that *Newsweek's* September 22, 1947, issue carried a lengthy, well-written article on the convention, including a photo of Bill Welsh, I knew that our struggle to establish a representative, independent U.S. national student organization had succeeded. The foundations had been laid for a vigorous and permanent life.

END NOTES

[1] Finding a site was difficult. In a recent conversation, I learned from Gordon Klopf, who was then assistant dean of students at the University of Wisconsin, that most universities were leery of hosting the convention. He and Roy Voegeli were the key persons who persuaded the University of Wisconsin leadership to extend the invitation (see Voegeli, p. 150).

[2] It should be noted that, although press releases stated that 700 were in attendance, plenary session votes never exceeded 581.

[3] The press reported that Rainey, the former president of the University of Texas, had been "ousted from his Lone Star State post for his alleged liberal views" (Sterling Sorenson, "NSA Delegates Urged to Enter Politics, 'Think in World Terms,'" *The Capitol*, August 31, 1947) (see Smith, p. 122).

[4] In recent correspondence, Curt Farrar accurately observed that the "main motivation [for the exclusion of student organizations] was to ensure against the possibility that communist control would be extended through a multiplicity of student organizations" (letters, Curtis Farrar to author, February 19, 1997) (see Farrar, p. 829).

[5] Lee Jones, of the University of Buffalo and NSA treasurer in 1947-48, attended the 1950 Michigan congress of NSA where he led the delegates once more in "Wharton's Lion Hunt" (see "Life Goes to a Collegiate Convention," p. 295). Joy (Newberger) Picus (University of Wisconsin delegate in 1950), in her essay on p. 928, recalls how, many years later, as a Los Angeles City Councilwoman on a safari in Africa, she found herself reaching back into memory to recall the "Lion Hunt." Herb Eisenberg (MIT), NSA 1950-51 International Vice President, recalls using it at several international meetings (p. 520).

[6] "Statement to American Students," draft adopted by the International Activities Panel and approved by the convention, September 3, 1947 (NSA Madison Conference Files, CRWJr. Archives).

[7] The full text read:

> I. To secure and maintain equal rights for all people and to secure equal opportunities for education at all levels regardless of race, sex, national origin, creed and political belief or economic circumstances; especially by securing the eventual elimination of all forms of discriminatory educational systems anywhere in the United States, since the United States National Student Association is opposed in principle to such systems.
>
> II. The United States National Student Association encourages wide investigation and discussion of the problems of inequality which exists throughout the United States in order to secure their elimination. However, in view of the complex nature of the problem, with its diversity throughout the entire United States, and the limitations imposed by present state rights, statutes and laws, it shall be the policy of the United States National Student Association to take action on national, regional, and campus levels through the corresponding organization of NSA to implement its stated principles, with regard to the legal limitations involved. (NSA Madison conference files, CRWJr. Archives)

[8] University of Wisconsin News Service, September 5, 1947.

[9] Birenbaum became a member of the NSA Advisory Board in 1949 and enjoyed a distinguished career as an educator (see p. 581).

PICTURE CREDITS: *Then:* Chicago Student Conference, Dec. 1946. *Now:* Chairman and CEO, TIAA-CREF (*Both, author*).

The Harvard Crimson

VOL. CXIX, No. 53 CAMBRIDGE, MASS., FRIDAY, NOVEMBER 21, 1947. PRICE FIVE CENTS.

College Votes for N.S.A. Affiliation; Student Ballot Shows 1382 Majority

THE WHY AND THE WHEREFORE

Excerpts from Harvard Crimson *editorial, November 19, 1947*

Question number one: Why vote for an organization that is going to serve as a nation-wide megaphone for radical minorities? Answer: vote for it because it will not be political. It cannot be....No religious or political organizations will receive representation in NSA....

Question number two: Why vote for a theoretical set-up—political or nonpolitical—that will affect nobody but its delegates? Answer: vote for NSA because it may well become the first student organization in the history of the United states that will touch the majority of individual students....

Question number three: What good is there to an organization that has been speechifying for a year while getting at none of its objectives? Answer: On the national level, NSA's main work will be done through its regional offices. On the international level, objectives have been approached....

Question number four: Who pays for NSA? Answer: you do—to the extent of allowing the Student Council to utilize about one twenty-fifth of whatever you donated to the Council fund ...

Put it all together, and you have something that costs each individual little and that might become America's first vital national student organization. In the creation of NSA, Harvard delegates have been notable for their leadership. At this point it would neither be consistent nor sensible to fail to support NSA.

THE *CRIMSON* EDITORIAL above sums up the arguments just prior to the student body vote on affiliation, 1957-575.

OTHER VOICES SPEAK ON NSA'S FORMATION

The Intercollegian, November, 1947 (National Intercollegiate Christian Council)

In a new way, the Protestant student movement—by far the largest organized intercollegiate force-takes its place in an overall student picture. A notable fact at the NSA organization was the Roman Catholic solidarity backed up with a letter by Archbishop Cushing In *Newman Club News* which demands complete clearance by the Church hierarchy of any action by Roman Catholic students. This unity of purpose was influential, of course, in minimizing Communist effectiveness—such as that which "took over" previous national student organizations. As NSA may itself soon be related to IUS, this may again become an issue. Criticism of the new Roman Catholic "bloc" process drew the logical reply that Protestants too are free to organize just as tightly. Shall we?

We may have played too long in a league where ours was the only team!

Jesuit Educational Quarterly, January 1948

With the N.S.A. still in the formative state,

Catholic students have the opportunity to help chart its path along the proper course.

They have the opportunity to advance from the isolationism of which they have been justly accused to a position of responsibility in national student affairs, a position of responsible leadership. If in the future it should become apparent that the N.S.A. is falling into Communist or other dangerous hands, that will be the time to withdraw.

—Norman Weyand, SJ

Political Affairs, October 1947 (Council of Student Clubs, Communist Party)

It begins life with a democratic Constitution, a good program, and a representative and liberal group of officers. These are real and important accomplishments.

....On the other hand, the American student, if he is not to fight but half a battle, must soon learn that the most important issues—of peace or war, of economic security or crisis, of democracy or fascism—face him as well as other Americans, and call for action in the political arena.

What happens on the campus, among the rank and file of the student body, will thus determine the future of N.S.A.

As they move ahead, seeing the issues more clearly, resolving their confusions, so will the N.S.A. advance—in program, in understanding, in activity.

—Marvin Shaw

Survey Graphic, December 1948 ("The Magazine of Social Interpretation")

The key to NSA's longevity will probably in the long run remain with its ability to widen interest in its programs among students across the land. Unlike European student movements, the organization will probably have no political significance. And if it sticks to its constitution, it won't try to have, except for issues in which students are directly concerned.

But many college administrators are looking to it hopefully to bring a long needed vitality to American student life.

. . . the consensus of those who have viewed NSA from close range seems to be that the scales are tipped in its favor by the earnestness and maturity of most of the students who have thus far participated in it.

—Kathryn Close

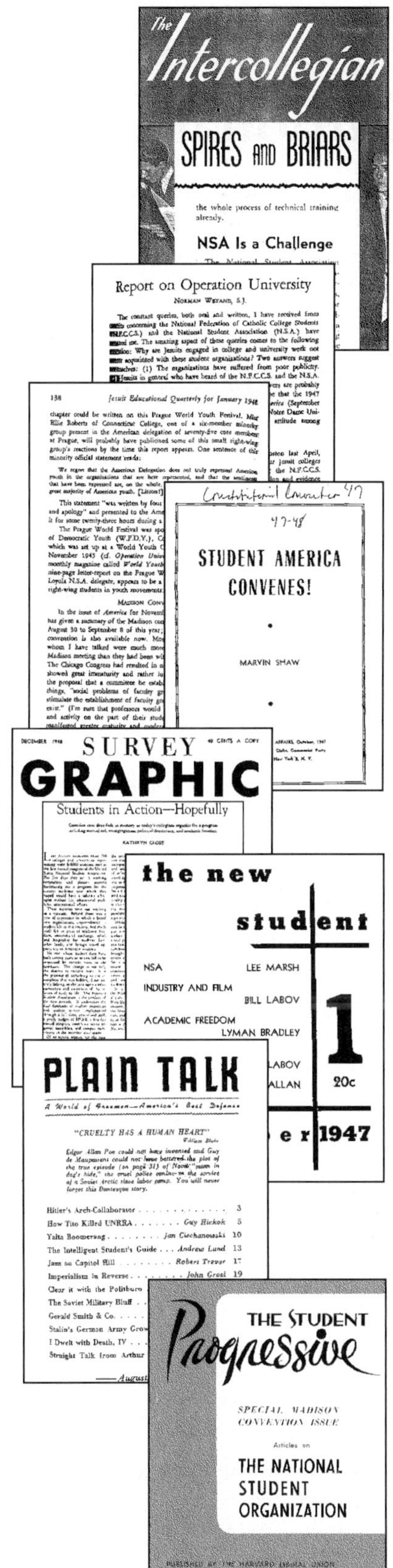

The New Student, December, 1947 (Intercollegiate Division, American Youth for Democracy).

Reactionary reports on the Madison convention have stressed red-baiting.

The beginning, middle and end of these "analyses" are concerned with Communism. They assert the convention was a success because the "reds" were unable to achieve immediate affiliation to the IUS, were kicked out of the NSA through the rejection of formal cooperation with national student organizations, were not elected to national office, and were defeated in their "attempt" to break up the convention in the fight against segregation! ....

The AYD is proud of its constructive part in the formation of the NSA and of the American student body which has responded so overwhelmingly to the formation of an all-student organization. We wish the NSA the best of success.

—Lee Marsh

Plain Talk, August 1947 (Isaac Don Levine, Editor)

Important to the whole picture has been the emergence of a third group—non-Communist liberal students,

Affiliated with no particular organization and fearful of politics along sectarian lines. Though this group was not at all organized in Chicago, its mere existence served to put others on their guard and prevented both the Catholics and the left-wingers from taking any extreme positions. The liberal group has since become aware of its own importance and has been girding its loins for the coming convention.

—Andrew Lund (anonymous)

The Student Progressive, September 1947 (The Harvard Liberal Union)

The NSA most decidely should not become a group with a viewpoint. Instead of uniting fewer students around a broad area of agreement, NSA should unite all students behind a narrow area of agreement. A group with a viewpoint stresses the role students as citizens, the NSA stresses students as students.

The NSA must not become a sounding board for a philosophy;

it must remain a place in which students with differing philosophies can meet together on common problems and common needs.

—Don S. Willner, National Chairman, SDA.

Doubts overcome—The university collaborates

3. Organizing the NSA Constitutional Convention

Royal J. Voegeli
University of Wisconsin
Delegate, Chicago Student Conference, 1946

The request that I write my recollections about NSA and how the NSA Constitutional Convention came to be held at the University of Wisconsin has given me a wonderful opportunity to relive a time that now seems very distant.

I have read several accounts written by other NSAers of the great expectations for a better world that were so much a part of our thinking at the time. It was indeed a time of great hope. World War II was over, and there was comparative prosperity at home. Everything seemed possible, especially for the hundreds of thousands of veterans who had swarmed to the colleges and universities under the GI Bill of Rights, bringing with them a maturity and sense of purpose that were transforming American campuses.

By late 1946 and 1947, however, tensions abroad were mounting and anticommunist rhetoric at home was beginning to have an impact. Eventually, the rhetoric would escalate into McCarthyism, but even then, it was something that could not be safely ignored.

All these hopes, expectations, and cross-currents played their part in shaping the formation of NSA and its early history, including the decision by the University of Wisconsin to extend an invitation to hold the NSA Constitutional Convention on its campus. The decision represented a triumph of the best influences at work at the time and of the nature and character of the university itself and of its regents and administrators, particularly its president, Dr. Edwin B. Fred. The invitation reflected the university's traditional willingness to hold itself out as a haven of liberalism and academic freedom.

My part of the story began when I returned to the university for the fall semester in 1946 after a two and a half years' absence in the navy. I was a first-year law student and immediately become involved in student government activities. In December, I was elected as a delegate to the pre-NSA National Student Congress in Chicago.

Drafting the NSA constitution

At the congress, the decision was made to form a U.S. National Student Association to bring to college students the benefit of regional and national cooperation on educational problems and programs and provide responsible U.S. student representation in the increasingly important sphere of international student activities. A Continuations Committee was elected and charged with the task of drafting a constitution and calling a constitutional convention. One of the four persons elected to the committee was Al Houghton, a fellow delegate from the University of Wisconsin.

Almost immediately after his election, Houghton began to question whether he should have agreed to have his name placed in nomination. He was concerned that he would not be able to devote adequate time to the committee's tasks. On the train trip back to Madison, he suggested that I take his place. I readily agreed and, in early January 1947, began the first of many weekend trips to Chicago to work on the draft constitution with Janis Tremper, Jim Smith, Russ Austin, and others.

It was also in early January 1947 that I was appointed as one of two legislative clerks of the Wisconsin State Legislature. Among law students, the clerkships were coveted appointments. The work was part time and paid the astronomical sum of $240 a month at a time when the GI Bill paid only $75 a month. More important, it was an opportunity to work closely with state legislators and the governor's office. It also put me in close contact with the legislative sessions and with the press that covered state politics.

In March I ran for, and won, a seat on the University of Wisconsin Student Board, and the board had then elected me its president. I now had close contacts with the university administration as well as the state legislature and the press.

Finding a convention site

By mid-April, we were approaching the end of our task in Chicago. The draft constitution was nearly finished, and we began to focus on the task of finding a place to hold the convention. It was assumed that the site would be centrally located, which meant the Midwest. We also knew that, because of the large number of expected attendees, it would have to be a large college or university. We had to recognize that, given the emerging political climate, there were colleges and universities that would not be willing to risk allowing this new, untried organization to hold its constitutional convention on their campuses. It was clear to me that there was one university that was big, centrally located, and would, I was sure, have the courage to say yes—that was my own University of Wisconsin.

I do not recall the exact sequence of my early efforts, but I am sure that the first person I would have talked to would have been Dr. Fred. I had known of him for many years and greatly admired him. Before becoming president, he had been with the College of Agriculture, and he knew my father, a prominent Green County farmer who had frequent contact with, and great respect for, the "Ag School." The first telephone call I made from the Student Board office in the Memorial Union after being elected president had been to Dr. Fred. After congratulating me, he said, "If you're free, come by to see me," and within a few minutes I was in his office in Bascom Hall having the first of many talks with him.

Dr. Fred believed in a strong, independent role for students in university affairs, and he made that clear on many occasions, both by word and deed. Two weeks after I became president, Dr. Fred asked whether I would appear and testify before the joint finance committee of the state legislature, which was considering the university budget. True to form, he made no attempt to suggest what I should say, nor did he even ask in advance about what I was going to say.

For my part, whether dealing with Dr. Fred or others in the administration, I always made it clear that the Student Board, which represented the student body as a whole, would always guard its independent role and voice in university affairs but would never abuse that independence. We would do our best to act responsibly and with the over-all best interests of both the students and the university in mind.

To use the finance committee's budget hearing as an example, my testimony strongly endorsed the university's position. The April 3 issue of the *Daily Cardinal* said:

> Speaking before the committee and 40 spectators, which included Pres. E. B. Fred, members of the Board of Regents and deans of many university schools...the budget hearing was brought to a dramatic close yesterday as Royal Voegeli, Student Board president, called on the committee to keep faith with the student body by passing the budget as recommended by the regents and the governor.[1]

By the time consideration of a site for the NSA convention began in mid-April, I had also developed excellent ties to Frank Holt, director of the Department of Public Service, and to LeRoy Luberg, assistant vice president for academic affairs. I am sure, therefore, that they would have been high on my list of people that I felt would view the idea favorably. I also recall talking to several of the key legislators to give them an alert on what might be in the offing.

In addition I contacted both of the Madison newspapers, the *Wisconsin State Journal* and, with the help of John P. Hunter, the *Capitol Times*. John, who was NSA Wisconsin regional chairman and associate editor of the *Daily Cardinal,* had close ties to the *Times*. (He later became associate editor of the *Times* and a well-known political columnist.)[2] Both newspapers took a favorable view of having the convention held at the university. The *Journal* asked me to write an article on the convention, which it printed on the editorial page as "The Guest Editorial," together with a picture and a favorable companion "Profile" article.

Political concerns

As I made my rounds of visits and telephone calls, the question that was foremost in the minds of those I contacted, whether explicitly asked or not, was "What will be the political orientation of this organization?" Many already knew that the organization had its genesis in the Prague meeting, followed by the meeting in Chicago. Given the political climate and the growing concern of some about "left-wing takeovers," I did not treat those concerns lightly. Fortunately, it was comparatively easy to lay out the future with relative certainty and to list the milestones by which the organization's political character would become known.

Most important would be the constitutional convention's decision on whether NSA membership would be limited to student governments, or whether members would include student organizations, ranging from the YMCA and YWCA to the left-wing American Youth for Democracy. If membership were limited to student governments, NSA would reflect mainstream values of American students. If organizations could join, it was still a virtual certainty that NSA would emerge from the convention as a mainstream organization, but its long-term future would be much less certain as, in time, dedicated and disciplined organization members could exert an influence far beyond their numerical strength.

It was therefore comparatively easy to put concerns about the NSA's political orientation in perspective. Nevertheless, some concerns were voiced about the wisdom of inviting this untried, and basically unknown, organization to hold its founding convention on campus. Skeptical parties included several members of the university's Administrative Committee. Fortunately, there were not many of them, nor were they very influential. In the end, the prevailing view was that, in keeping with the university's long tradition of liberalism, the invitation should be extended and the convention allowed to take place on the campus.

Preparing for the convention

After the invitation had been extended, the Student Board and the university were faced with the task of organizing the event, which, it was estimated, would bring as many as eight hundred delegates to the campus. The *Daily Cardinal* for August 13, 1947, carried a story under the headline, "Badger Hosts Make Plans for NSA Meet—Student Board, U. Officials, Memorial Union Cooperate." The story read in part:

> With an idealistic light burning deep within them, a group of Wisconsin students under the leadership of Student Board members are throwing themselves into the job of laying the foundation for the constitutional convention of the National Student Association on this campus from Aug. 30 to Sept. 7.
>
> About 50 meeting rooms must be reserved, the meetings must be correlated and the function of each made explicit in a directory; special trains, traffic problems, news service, housing, recreation, and dining facilities must be arranged for; and delegates from all over the country must be registered, identified, and accommodated with special information.
>
> This is the job of the Wisconsin Student Board, which is receiving full cooperation from the national office of NSA, university officials, the Wisconsin Union, and a large number of far-sighted student volunteers.

The key words in the article are *idealistic* and *far-sighted.* Both accurately describe the student volunteers, who devoted countless hours to working on the preparations. Students and university officials both believed that we were preparing for an important, and even historic, event, and we did everything possible to anticipate and prepare for every contingency.

At the convention

At the convention, the university's greetings to the delegates, as published in the convention program, read in part:

> The University of Wisconsin is a fitting site for the Constitutional Convention of the National Student Association because, in addition to a beautiful and spacious campus ideal for such a large gathering, this fourth largest university in the nation is blessed with a distinguished tradition of liberalism. This liberal spirit is manifested in encouragement of progressive thought and teaching, of academic freedom, and of an unusually large area of free expression and action by students....
>
> The spirit at the University is probably best conveyed in a noble statement by the Board of Regents in 1894, and now recognized by all as the University Creed: "Whatever may be the limitations which trammel inquiry elsewhere, we believe the great State University of Wisconsin should ever encourage that continual and fearless sifting and winnowing by which alone the truth can be found."

Those words reflected the early and unswerving support of Dr. Fred,[3] Frank Holt, and many others. In his greetings in the convention program, Dr. Fred said, "We have very high regard for student leadership on this campus." I knew from my many dealings with him that he meant it. Frank Holt reflected the university creed perfectly by telling the delegates at the opening session that colleges and universities should teach students "not what to think, but how to think." In my own words of greeting, I expressed my sense of indebtedness to the university by saying, "The forward-looking University of Wisconsin officials who have done so much to make this gathering possible deserve special thanks from all the delegates."

The constitutional convention was successful beyond anyone's expectation. Over seven hundred delegates attended, representing over a million students and nearly four hundred colleges and universities. President Truman sent a message of greeting. The plenary sessions reflected a maturity and political sophistication that drew rave comments from the press and virtually every observer. The outcome was particularly impressive in view of some of the serious, and potentially divisive, issues that the delegates had to resolve.

High on the list of important questions was NSA's relationship with the communist-dominated International Union of Students (IUS). The delegates voted to seek affiliation, but only under conditions that would assure NSA's basic autonomy. Another was the emotion-laden issue of racial segregation and discrimination in education. This issue truly tested the ability of the delegates to reach accord without tearing the organization apart. The resolution adopted by the convention represented one of the first successful national efforts to address the issue and to reach a positive accord.

Although it was expected to be a major issue, the question of NSA membership was easily resolved by an overwhelming vote in favor of limiting it to student governments.

For me, one of the most satisfying votes of the convention was the decision to locate NSA's headquarters in Madison. I think that all the delegates developed an appreciation for the beauty of the campus (and the unheard-of freedom of having beer served in the student union building). I think that they also came to know that Wisconsin stood for the kind of academic freedom that is the mark of a truly great university. They saw Madison and the university as the right home for their newly created, and already much respected, U.S. National Student Association. For our part, we were very happy to have them.

In Retrospect

The facts that the university invited NSA's founding convention to its campus and that I had a part in bringing it about were then, and still are, a matter of great pride to me.

Now, fifty years later, I look back on NSA's beginning days with undiminished enthusiasm. The organization that we created has endured through various times and in various forms and has done itself much credit. From its ranks have come outstanding leaders in many fields. Hopefully, that will all continue for another fifty years and even beyond.

Royal J. Voegeli was an attorney in private practice in Wisconsin and Washington, D.C., and served on the legal staff of the U.S. Nuclear Regulatory Commission.

END NOTES

[1] An interesting side note: the total budget request for the entire university for that fiscal year was $9.7 million.

[2] In 1999, Hunter was recognized as one of the 21 Wisconsin "People Who Shaped Our Lives from 1900 to 2000." See Hunter, p. 932.

[3] I later had cause to be grateful to Dr. Fred for yet another reason. When my term as president of the Student Board ended in March, 1948, Dr. Fred appointed me as the student representative on the Faculty Court of Appeals, the highest appointive position available to a student.

PICTURE CREDITS: *Then:* c. 1947. *Now:* c. 1998 (*Both, author*).

ROYAL J. VOEGELI

I was born in Monticello, Green County, Wisconsin, on January 16, 1926. I was raised in Green County, attended Monticello High School, and entered the University of Wisconsin in 1943.

I joined the navy in 1944, and was assigned to the Naval Reserve Officers' Training Corps (NROTC) at the University of Minnesota. I received a B.S. from the University of Minnesota in May 1946 and was commissioned an ensign. I returned to the University of Wisconsin in the fall 1946, and received my LL.B (J.D.) in 1950.

At Wisconsin, I became active in student government and, in March 1947, was elected president of the Student Board. I had been a delegate to the pre-NSA Chicago Convention and, as president of the Student Board, was active in bringing the NSA Constitutional Convention to Madison.

Later, I acted as personal representative of NSA President Bill Welsh at an international youth conference in London and at the Council Meeting of the International Union of Students (IUS) in Paris, both in summer 1948. While a law student, I was also a legislative clerk for the Wisconsin State Legislature and was appointed by Dr. Edwin Fred, president of the University, as student representative on the Faculty Court of Appeals.

I began my legal career in 1950, practicing law in Wisconsin. In 1951, I took a two-year leave of absence to work with the U.S. Central Intelligence Agency in Europe. In 1953, I returned to Wisconsin. In 1957 I went to Washington, D.C., as a litigation attorney for the U.S. Department of Justice. I later joined the Washington office of the law firm of Fulbright, Crooker, Freeman, Bates & Jaworski. In 1974, I joined the legal staff of the newly created U.S. Nuclear Regulatory Commission, from which I retired in 1993.

I now pursue my favorite interests, which are sailing, hiking, skiing, writing, music, painting, and traveling.

Editor's note: Roy Voegeli was actively engaged in the development of this anthology as a member of its project committee. He passed away in February 2001, while on vacation traveling in Egypt. This essay and biography, as well as his essay on p. 545, both written for this anthology, were completed in 1999.

ADMINISTRATION SUPPORT for NSA's convention at Wisconsin was provided by LeRoy Luberg, left, assistant vice president for academic affairs, here cited by Voegeli and J. Kenneth Little, Director of Student Personnel Services (see Klopft, Pt. 2, S. 1). (Photo from Joy Picus)

APPEARING AT A PLENARY SESSION, Roy Voegeli, then student body president at the U. of Wisconsin and a convention host, is joined by Janis Tremper (Rockford College, IL), later elected 1947-48 NSA national secretary.

National Student Assn. Organizes on Campus

1,000 Students From All Regions Meet For 10-Day Conference Here

By BOB SOLLEN

This is the first of four articles dealing with the National Student association which was organized on the campus between Aug. 31 and Sept. 7.

Seven hundred students responded and set up a national continuations committee to write a proposed constitution and document of purposes. These were to be presented for revision and approval at the

attractiveness. National off be located in the Union.

Keynote speaker for the tion was Dr. Homer P. Rai mer president of the Univ Texas and now head of college, Missouri. Rainey for his fight for academic at Texas and his subsequ missal because of his stand

The convention also hear

Student Organizations Defeated In Bid for Voice, Vote Privilege

By BOB SOLLEN

This is the second in a series of four articles dealing with the National Student association which was organized on this campus between Aug. 31 and Sept. 7.

Although a number of national student groups were represented at the recent constitutional convention of the National Student association, they will no longer have voice or vote in the organization.

Segregation, Discrimination Were Explosive Issues at NSA Assembly

This is the third in a series of four articles dealing with the National Student association which was organized on this campus between Aug. 31 and Sept. 7.

By BOB SOLLEN

for handling the problem in Southern and non-Southern institutions. One report asked that all federal aids to non-Southern non-sectarian schools be cut off if discrimination is practiced in those institutions.

It appeared obvious to the Sout

Bitter Fight Raged Against NSA Affiliation With Pink-Tinted International Student Union

This is the last in a series of articles dealing with the National Student association (NSA) which was organized on this campus between Aug. 31 and Sept. 7.

By BOB SOLLEN

Long before the opening of the recent constitutional convention of NSA, it was evident that the ques-

that NSA should wait a year to establish itself in the United States before joining international groups. They opposed the left-wing influence of IUS, the financial cost, and possible unfavorable publicity for NSA.

Douglas Cater, Harvard, who headed the American delegation at the recent Prague meeting, advocated

that "although at present there are fundamental differences between the NSA on the one hand and the IUS and some of its member-organizations on the other hand, (the panel) recommends affiliation as soon as possible with the IUS," subject to reservations which would prevent NSA from being bound by political actions taken by the international

CAMPUS, CITY, STATE NEWSPAPERS WELCOMED NSA TO WISCONSIN

On this page are 8/47 and 9/47 headlines (above) from the student newspaper, *The Daily Cardinal*, and a feature on Royal Voegeli from the *Wisconsin State Journal.* NSA's convention and choice of Madison for its national headquarters were also featured prominently by the *Capitol Times* (see p. 164), and the *Milwaukee Journal* (see p. 228). Madison-based papers provided key early leadership for NSA. John Hunter of the *Times* (see p. 932) and Bob Smollen (above by-lines) of the *Cardinal* were, successively, Executive Editors of *NSA News* during its first year. Karl Meyer, later editor of the *Cardinal*, became active in NSA programs concerned with civil liberties issues (see p. 476 n. 5). As a consequence of being launched and maintaining its headquarters in Wisconsin for the first four years, the State Historical Society of Wisconsin has incorporated the association's story as part of Wisconsin history and maintains a formal USNSA/USSA archive to which the research material and records of this anthology are being contributed.

Sunday, Aug. 24, 1947

The Guest Editorial

Student Rule, National Scale

By ROYAL VOEGELI
(President of Wisconsin Student Assn.)

The Profile

Voegeli Can See Better U.S. Citizens in Student Group

By REX KARNEY
(State Journal Staff Writer)

A SLENDER, 21 - YEAR - OLD youngster named Royal Voegeli is worried that the world is going to hell in a hurry, and he is interested in doing something about it.

Which makes him a bit different from most citizens his own age, and a great deal different from those who are older but who lack his enthusiasm.

Voegeli, a second-year law student at the University of Wisconsin, is the son of Mr. and Mrs. Jacob Voegeli, who operate a Brown Swiss dairy farm near Monticello in rich Green county. He is the third of four children, a young man who was graduated from Monticello high school, won a Bachelor of Science degree at Minnesota while a navy trainee, but who came to his own state university to study law because **"Minnesota is just a brain fatory—at Wisconsin the faculty, students, and the administration are more alive."**

Voegeli admits he has "always been interested in government and politics," and his record seems to bear that out. In 1946 he ran for the university student board, which is the student governing body, and was elected. The out-going and in-coming boards selected him as the new chairman, which he admits is an every day and three nights-a-week job."

* * *

The student board, he explains, is "the community government of 20,000 students." It runs its own courts, handles orientation work for new students, works on university public relations, promotes a speakers' bureau, and even dispatches "lobbyists" to the state capitol. Last legislative session Voegeli and other student representatives tried to convince lawmakers that compulsory ROTC training isn't necessary. They "didn't get very far."

* * *

VOEGELI IS INTERESTED IN THE National Student Assn. because **"It's pretty much like my own brainchild,"** he says.

"Last summer I had an idea of my own to promote a national and international student organization," Voegeli explains.

"It would have been like a little United Nations. Students in universities all over the world could have elected their own governing bodies, and then would have elected delegates to a world student congress. **My idea was to have this world-wide student group discuss the same issues that are discussed at Lake Success.** The diplomats would have had a chance to learn rather accurately what the youth of the world is thinking about. **It is easier for us younger people to leave behind the prejudices that many times trouble the older diplomats."**

Europe, however, has had such organized student groups for many years, and last year American students were invited to participate in an international student gathering, sponsored by Czech and English student, at Prague. Later, the National Student Assn. was organized at Chicago by 25 American students who had attended the Prague gathering.

"About the only similarity between the present organization and the idea I had is the international aspect," Voegeli explains.

* * *

"I WANTED THIS NEW ORGANIzation to worry about political issues. The National Student Assn. will stick strictly to student problems, however."

The founders of the NSA, apparently, felt that if the national organization and the international student gathering permitted debates and actions on international politics, the entire structure might soon become nothing but a sounding board for left-wing political philosophies.

"The way the thing is set up now," Voegeli points out, **"it is hard for the Leftists to take over because neither the NSA nor the international meeting are things that just anyone can join.** The various delegates must be elected by their student bodies. They represent student governments. The NSA is not a Frankenstein that cannot be controlled."

* * *

YOUNG VOEGELI IS SOLD ON THE idea of students governing themselves through their own elected representatives. He insists the student governing system at the University of Wisconsin, for example, is a **"swell laboratory for democracy—a place where we try to get students interested in their own government."**

He points out that "too many older citizens aren't much interested in their government," and they **"have a tendency to sneer at what they call politics."** He argues that university students who learn the importance and mechanics of good government will make better citizens later.

Mr. Voegeli's point seems to be well taken.

Wisconsin State Journal 8/24/47, with permission.

Changing the Course of a Lifetime

4. Publicizing the New Organization

Stanley R. Greenfield
Johns Hopkins University
Publicity Liaison, National Continuations Committee

In January 22, 1946, I wrote a letter to Jim Smith, president of the National Continuations Committee. I had attended the National Student Conference in Chicago in December 1946, representing the Johns Hopkins University. In reviewing the plans for the proposed National Student Organization (NSO), which had been made at the Chicago Conference, I had come to believe that a major area was not being addressed. Jim, Russ Austin, and Clif Wharton were, as might be expected, dealing with matters of organization, structure, and on-campus activity. I called the matter not being addressed "PA"—for perception and acceptance. It seemed important to consider other "publics," as the public relations practitioners (since renamed directors of communications) referred to them: the media, government, and the education community.

I volunteered to undertake a program to reach these groups. I was then in my senior year at Johns Hopkins. When I returned from navy service in 1945, I decided to change my undergraduate major, dropping physics in favor of a liberal arts degree. My schedule consisted primarily of junior-level liberal arts courses, which I did not find taxing. Hopkins had a liberal policy on class attendance. In addition, my father agreed to cover expenses.

My targets

My targets were clear. In the media they were the *New York Times*, *Time*, *Newsweek*, the Associated Press; in government, the U.S. Department of State and the U.S. Office of Education; in education, the Institute of International Education, the American Association of University Professors, the American Association of University Women, the Carnegie Endowment, et al.

Another key target emerged. I learned that the newly established United States National Commission for UNESCO, under the direction of Dr. Milton Eisenhower, was to choose three youth organizations for membership during the first week of September, just a few days after the NSO constitutional convention in Madison. I wanted one of those places for our not-as-yet-established organization. I identified key members of the commission, and then, with a mandate from Jim, I set to work on all my tasks.

Why the new group was different

Prior to the establishment of NSA, student activity on matters dealing with educational policy, government support, segregation, or international affairs had been carried out by groups with particular interests, whose membership reflected specific objectives. They were not structured to be representative, and indeed they were not. The most active and vocal groups were affiliated, openly or covertly, with the left or the extreme right. As a result, a new national student group would be viewed with suspicion, especially if it sprang from the meeting in Prague that created the International Union of Students, which was widely regarded as dominated by student groups from Communist countries.

Central to overcoming such suspicions and to building acceptance was to make it clear that, in accordance with decisions made at the Chicago conference, the new organization would have no campus chapters or individual members. College or university membership would be only by action of the duly constituted student governments, and delegates to the organization's meetings would be elected by procedures determined by the student governments. This structure proved to be acceptable.

Initial appointments

My first appointment was with Benjamin Fine, education editor of the *New York Times* for more than thirty years. He was very positive and "bought in."

At the U.S. Department of State, I met with Lyman Bryson, counselor of the department. A veteran diplomat, he asked all the right questions, and I conclude that I must have given many correct answers. His particular interests were in international student activities. He also wanted to know about Jim, Russ, and Cliff and about the structure of the proposed organization.

I first learned from Lyman Bryson about the National Student Federation of America, which was formed in the early 1920s.[1] Bryson had been an adviser to that organization, and he suggested that I look up Edward R. Murrow, who had been its president in 1931.[2]

Edward R. Murrow

The only time Murrow could meet with me was for a brief chat in Columbus, Ohio, where he was to speak at the annual conference of the Institute of International Education by radio at the University of Ohio. We met in his hotel room, and most of our conversation took place while he was shaving (it was a large bathroom). Murrow shaved with care, talking all the while. For those who may be interested, the trademark highly starched, pointed collars on the Murrow white shirts were detachable.

It was encouraging to know that Murrow had begun his career in the student movement of his day. His message was that the time was right and our structure sound. He attributed much that had happened in his career to his early student leadership activities. I could not know at that time how history would repeat itself with many of my NSA colleagues.

Continued favorable reception

Academic freedom for faculty was a burning issue in 1946. My reception by Ralph Himstead, general secretary of the American Association of University Professors, and by Kathryn McHale, general director of the American Association of University Women, was supportive. Laurence Duggan, president of the Institute of International Education, who had decades of experience in dealing with student groups around the world, immediately recognized the potential international significance of what we proposed to do. He was subsequently a speaker at the NSA Constitutional Convention and a member of the NSA Advisory Committee in 1947-48.[3]

The possibility of responsible student activity on matters of race led to an uplifting meeting with Dr. Mordecai Johnson, president of Howard University.

And so it went for four exhilarating months prior to the meeting in Madison.

University of Wisconsin help at the convention

For the convention, the University of Wisconsin News Bureau assigned an able, amiable member of its staff, John McNally, to work with me. The news bureau provided typewriters, mimeograph machines, and telephones.

John and I would do a wrap-up release each day, frequently posting it well after midnight. Often we finished off with a dip in Lake Mendota.

Two immediate results of this work were a major article, including a picture of NSA President Bill Welsh in *Newsweek*, and selection of the newly constituted NSA for one of the three youth organization memberships on the United States National Commission for UNESCO. The latter came just ten days after the Madison meeting. This UNESCO affiliation provided a solid base for NSA's initial international activities.

A personal note

This six-month activity changed the course of my life. My work with NSA was probably a factor in my admission to the Harvard Business School, Class of 1949.

The experience led to a career in publishing and information. While it has been largely in the for-profit sector, I have also published biographical directories with the United Nations and the national AFL-CIO.

Between 1975 and 1979, when diplomatic relations between the People's Republic of China and the United States were established, a small company of mine was the sole American representative of the China National Publications Import Corporation of the People's Republic of China for the acquisition of all scientific and technical bibliographic materials from the United States. This service was performed with the cooperation of the U.S. Departments of State and Commerce.

In 1984, via an FOI [Freedom of Information Act] request, I had received a copy of files maintained on Stanley R. Greenfield by various federal government agencies. At that time I had some concern about heavily blacked-out portions. The willingness of State and Commerce to cooperate with me in the acquisition and transshipment of books, conference proceedings, patents, databases, juridical materials, and government documents (unclassified and declassified) for the People's Republic of China was reassuring.

My current activities are still publishing related but now involve the Internet, the ultimate international medium.

Remembering Jim Smith

No communications program, to use current terminology,

Stanley R. Greenfield served for many years as senior vice president with the Ziff-Davis Publishing Company. Later, he founded Nicholas Publishing Company, a reference publisher. He also served as president and publisher of Playbill, *the Broadway theater program, and was founding publisher of* The Corporate Board, the Journal of Corporate Governance.

can be any better than the client organization and its principals. What made my activities effective was the structure of NSA and the caliber of the NCC officers. What kind of persons were these? The incident I now recount is indicative.

On a business trip to Austin, Texas, in 1951, I arranged to meet for a drink with Jim Smith, president of the National Continuations Committee and former president of the student body of the University of Texas at Austin, its largest campus. Kathie Bland Smith, his wife, was with him. Kathie's mother had been dean of women at the Austin campus.

When we met, Jim was wearing a workingman's lumber jacket and carrying a lunch pail. Puzzled, I asked him about his dress. He said that he was on his way to the A. O. Smith plant, where he worked on the night shift.

Still more puzzled, I asked what he was doing on the night shift at A. O. Smith. Jim said that he hoped to work in the United Steel Workers union [USW], and the only way he could do that was to start on the shop floor.

And Jim succeeded. He became president of the local, ran statewide actions for the Steel Workers, and subsequently joined the Washington, D.C., staff of Leonard Abel, national president of USW, where he helped to direct the activities of this giant player in the American economic and social scene. He ultimately became USW's chief economist.[4]

It has been said that there is no free lunch. That is essentially true, but so is the converse. One gets from life in proportion to one's input. The nature and direction of my life were due, in no small part, to my days with NCC and my NSA colleagues, including Rob West, Ted Harris, Doug Cater, and Jim Smith.

END NOTES

[1] See background on the National Student Federation of America, pp. 22, 30.

[2] See Murrow, p. 26.

[3] See IIE, p. 693.

[4] See p. 119 for more on the role of Jim Smith as chairman of the National Continuations Committee.

PICTURE CREDITS: *Then:* NSA, International Office, Cambridge, MA, 1948 (*West*). *Now:* 1997, 50th National Student Congress, Madison, WI (*Pope*).

STANLEY R. GREENFIELD

Early years: Born March 5, 1925. Attended Abraham Lincoln High School, Brooklyn, NY.

Education: B.A. Physics, Johns Hopkins University, 1947. M.B.A. with Distinction, Harvard University Business School, 1949.

Career: I spent much of my career with Ziff-Davis Publishing Company, a leading publisher of consumer special-interest magazines. When Bill Ziff took over the company in 1955, I was the first executive he hired. I served for many years as senior vice president.

I left Ziff-Davis to found Nicholas Publishing Company. At Nicholas, I created, edited, and produced seven directories, including two American Library Association "Outstanding Reference Book of the Year" designees. The first of these, the *National Directory of Addresses and Telephone Numbers* (first edition, Bantam Books, 1975) was the first hard-copy national telephone directory. More than a million copies of its annual editions have been sold. Other reference works were produced in cooperation with the United Nations and the AFL-CIO.

During the period 1975-79, Nicholas Publishing Company was sole representative of the People's Republic of China for the acquisition of all scientific and technical bibliographic materials from the United States, including serials, monographs, indexing and abstracting services, patents, U.S. government documents, juridical materials, and commercial databases. This function was performed with the concurrence of the Departments of State and Commerce during this period prior to the establishment of diplomatic relations between the two nations.

I also served as president and publisher of *Playbill,* the Broadway theater magazine, and was founding publisher of *The Corporate Board, the Journal of Corporate Governance.* In 1982, I inaugurated the first course in the New York City area on the Information Industry, at New York University.

Family: Betty F. Greenfield, my wife of forty-four years, was a delegate from Wellesley College to the NSA Annual Convention in 1948. She received an M.P.A. from Harvard University's Kennedy School of Government in 1985. We live in the Riverdale section of New York City. We have three children and four grandchildren. All of us live within twenty minutes of each other, which we consider to be one of our greatest blessings in a society where almost everything except family turns out to be transitory.

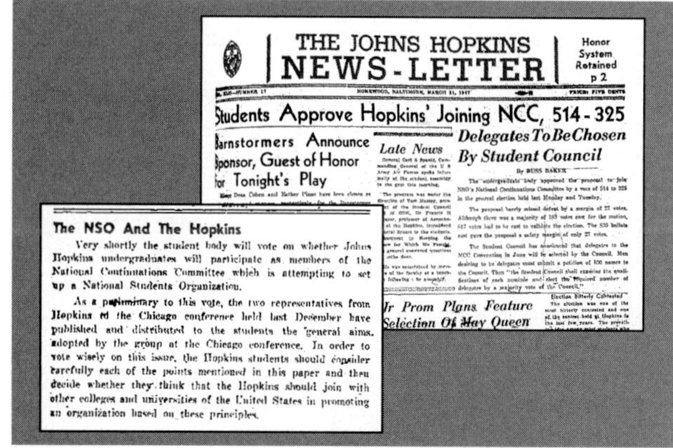

THE JOHNS HOPKINS NEWS-LETTER

Honor System Retained p 2

PRICE: FIVE CENTS

Students Approve Hopkins' Joining NCC, 514 - 325

Barnstormers Announce Sponsor, Guest of Honor For Tonight's Play

Late News

Delegates To Be Chosen By Student Council

By RUSS BAKER

The undergraduate body approved the proposal to join NSO's National Continuations Committee by a vote of 514 to 325 in the general election held last Monday and Tuesday.

The proposal barely missed defeat by a margin of 27 votes. Although there was a majority of 189 votes cast for the motion, 617 votes had to be cast to validate the election. The 839 ballots cast gave the proposal a safety margin of only 27 votes.

The Student Council has announced that delegates to the NCC Convention in June will be selected by the Council. Men desiring to be delegates must submit a petition of 100 names to the Council. Then "the Student Council shall examine the qualifications of each nominee and elect the required number of delegates by a majority vote of the Council."

Jr Prom Plans Feature Selection Of May Queen

Election Bitterly Contested

The NSO And The Hopkins

Very shortly the student body will vote on whether Johns Hopkins undergraduates will participate as members of the National Continuations Committee which is attempting to set up a National Students Organization.

As a preliminary to this vote, the two representatives from Hopkins to the Chicago conference held last December have published and distributed to the students the general aims adopted by the group at the Chicago conference. In order to vote wisely on this issue, the Hopkins students should consider carefully each of the points mentioned in this paper and then decide whether they think that the Hopkins should join with other colleges and universities of the United States in promoting an organization based on these principles.

"ONE OF THE MOST BITTERLY CONTESTED" ELECTIONS, according to the *Johns Hopkins News-Letter* of 3/31/47, "and one of the zaniest . . . in the last few years. The prevailing idea among most students who voted against NSO was that they were voting against some kind of leftist organization.

"As one man jammed his ballot into the box last Monday, he muttered to a friend, 'There's one vote against the Young Communist League.'" The *News-Letter* reported, "Stan Greenfield and Hank Bobrow, protagonists of NSO, spent two days in an effort to get out the necessary majority vote."

Editorializing earlier on 2/21/47 about "The NSO and the Hopkins," the paper reviewed the pros and cons and observed, "Nevertheless all the preliminary signs point to a progressive organization that will be in a position to promote the welfare of students in general and the college student in particular. A truly representative organization of college students could be an extremely influential group in the United States. However, the group denies having any political aims; its only aims are those which will improve the status of students."

Ellis, taken ill, appoints Jim Smith his proxy at the recommendation of NSA, and the NICC raises concerns that its interests may not be taken into account.

Bill Ellis and the National Intercollegiate Christian Council

Should the YMCA decide not to participate, it is open if Ellis would be asked to stay.

Editor's Note: Bill Ellis was elected in August 1946 as the American vice president of the International Union of Students, and later as a member of the Secretariat, a full-time post at the Prague, Czechoslovakia, headquarters. At the time he was representing the student YMCA on the National Intercollegiate Christian Council, which initiated negotiations for membership in the IUS. The Chicago Student Conference and, later, the NSA Constitutional Convention endorsed Ellis as the representative for U.S. students. Ellis then became ill and chose Jim Smith as his proxy. The complications of the situation, preceding their decision to resign their positions in March 1948 (see p. 188), are traced in the excerpts below.

AN OPEN QUESTION

Excerpts from a letter by Edwin Espy, executive secretary of the YMCA National Student Council, written to Herbert P. Landsdale, Jr., December 6, 1946

The Student YMCA was officially represented by two delegates at the meeting in Prague in August which organized the International Union of Students. These two delegates were: William Ellis, graduate student at Harvard, and Hoyt Palmer, Preparatory School Secretary for the National Student Committee.

At Prague it was clear that left-wing elements there, specifically Communist groups including the delegations from Russia and Russian-dominated countries, held a dominant position.On the other hand, the delegations from the Western countries represented fairly good cross-sections of their genuine youth organizations and were able to exercise a balancing influence on the deliberations of the Congress. However, the persons elected to the Executive Committee, which will handle the affairs for the IUS between its biennial meetings, were about two-thirds Communists.

Bill Ellis, who is a thoughtful and committed Christian, was elected as one of the International Vice-Presidents of the IUS and has also been invited to return to Prague as a member of the Secretariat for a period of probably two or three years. This he has agreed to do and [he] will go to Prague in January. In this capacity he will not officially represent the student YMCA but the total IUS. Should the student YMCA decide not to participate, it is an open quuestion whether Ellis would be requested to continue in the official position as Vice-President and member of the staff.

NSA APPOINTS SMITH AS ELLIS PROXY

Excerpts from October 13, 1947, document, "To Whom It May Concern," from William Welsh, President, USNSA

...At the Chicago Student Conference, the NCC was instructed to contribute $600 toward the cost of Bill's passage back to Prague to take up his duties as a Vice-President, representing United States students....

In Panel III of the Constitutional Convention, the following recommendation was accepted:

> a. That the USNSA express a vote of confidence in the work of Mr. Bill Ellis as Vice-President of the IUS to date; and that Bill Ellis be unanimously endorsed as the interim representative of the USNSA pending the mission of the negotiating delegation to Prague next summer.

Mr. Ellis requested the executive committee of the USNSA to select a person that he could appoint as a personal proxy because of his ill health. In the Executive Committee meeting of September 8, "Doug Cater recommended that Jim Smith be sent as the personal proxy for Bill Ellis, Vice-President of the IUS, leaving about the middle of October for Prague. J. Smith was accepted as proxy for Bill Ellis by acclamation."

Therefore, Jim Smith, as personal proxy for Bill Ellis, is considered by the USNSA to be the interim representative of the USNSA....

NICC RAISES CONCERNS OVER PROXY

Excerpts from a three-page letter of October 28, 1947, from Ernest M. Howell, co-chairman, National Intercollegiate Christian Council

All of us of NICC have heard with great misgiving and sympathy the reports of your Ill health, and we send our sincere best wishes for a speedy recovery....

I have been Informed by Bob Smith that prior to the Madison, Wisconsin, Congress this summer you had requested that the NSA make suggestions to you of a suitable proxy to represent you in the capacity of American Vice-President of the IUS. As a result of this request it has been widely reported by NSA officers and delegates that Jim Smith, former President of the National Continuations Committee of the NSA from the University of Texas, will. soon depart for Prague to act as proxy for you in the IUS.

When I learned this recently I was naturally concerned, and immediately consulted Bob Smith,[1] who has his office here at Harvard, to clarify the problems I felt such action would pose for NICC by learning from him the facts of the situation....

...The NICC has traditionally been extremely careful as to the persons selected to represent and speak for it on every occasion, and it therefore seems to be sound organizational policy to bring the matter to your attention, just as I recently presented it to Bob Smith. Bob and I agree, I believe, according to the precedent in selecting proxies this summer by other delegates, and according to the resolution of the executive committee of the NCC, in which the NICC was included, that you have the final decision to make as to selection of a proxy.

I would hope however, that in making your decision, if such is to be made as reported here, you might choose some person thoroughly aware of both NICC and NSA policies, views and organizational procedures. . . .

ELLIS TAKEN ILL

Excerpts from a November 7, 1947, letter "To Friends of Bill Ellis," from Harold B. Ingalls, Program Secretary, National Student Council, YMCA

When word of Bill's serious illness reached us, many friends wanted to help. We did not have adequate information, but now have received it and pass it on to you.

Last spring Bill was taken ill while in Rome, but recovered sufficiently to return to Prague in the summer. In the late summer he again was invalided and in very bad condition. The newspaper PM had sent a small quantity of streptomycin to Prague for another patient and Bill was given the few grams that were left. PM printed the story, and we had our first word of his serious condition. Betty Johns[2] got Boston Red Cross to rush 12 grams [of streptomycin]. . . .

As soon as Bill can be moved to the better climate of Switzerland, he will be; then he will come back to the U.S. when sufficiently recovered. The I.U.S. and Y.M.C.A. friends in Prague are cooperating in doing all that can be done for Bill. . . .

THE CAMPUS MIRROR,
Spelman College, Atlanta, Georgia,
Jan–Feb. 1948

BILL ELLIS FUND

It was this past November that the officers of the National YMCA and the United Student Christian Council (USCC) circulated letters seeking aid for Bill Ellis.

Bill's name should be a familiar one to this college generation. He is one of the many graduates of whom Harvard is justly proud. In 1946-47 he was the N.I.C.C. vice-chairman. In addition, he was elected as an officer to the International Union of Students, which has its headquarters in Prague. There he ably represented you, the Americana Christian students, in a worthy and secular organization.

A letter from Harold B. Ingalls reads in part:

"Last spring Bill was taken ill while in Rome but recovered sufficiently to return to Prague in the summer. In the late summer he again was invalided and in very bad condition. The newspaper PM had sent a small quantity of streptomycin to Prague for another patient and Bill was given the few grams that were left." Other aid was got for Bill through the Red Cross and his Alma Mater. He needs one grain of streptomycin a day to recover enough to be moved to Geneva and later to be brought home.

Here is our opportunity to make a Christian contribution to a fellow student, a member of a great movement, and a friend. The Spelman Y.W.C.A. cabinet members are contributing individually.

Watch the bulletin boards for additional information.

END NOTES

[1] Bob Smith was NSA international vice president. See Smith, p. 504.

[2] Betty Johns was director, New England Region, National YWCA.

PICTURE CREDITS: *Then:* November, 1949, Intercollegian (Schwartz).

THE NICC AND NSA AT MADISON

Editor's note: Leaders of the NICC were concerned that NSA's autonomy not be compromised by the influence of any other national student organizations—the key factions being the Communists and their followers and the Catholics. As it turned out, the Catholic student groups were equally concerned. The issue came to a head in the vote not to include national student organization representation in NSA's membership (see Wharton, this section). *This concern is expressed in the following excerpt from a memorandum dated August 15, 1947, addressed to "Regional and Local NICC Staff" from Harold B. Ingalls, Acting Executive Secretary, and in the 9/3/47 telegram draft (below) from Hoyt Palmer, NICC staff delegate at the Convention, reporting the defeat of national organization membership to staffer Muriel Jacobson.*

Word has come that delegations representing Protestant groups at the National Student Organization Constitutional Convention . . . . are lagging badly. Along with this comes news of full interest and heavy enrollment from Catholic colleges and Catholic groups generally (see Pt. 5, S. 2). They are to be commended for their interest. However, inasmuch as the organization of the NSO and its policies will be formulated at Wisconsin, the more balance there is there, the better. Therefore, it is a concern at headquarters as to whether sufficient interest is being shown by the members of our group, inasmuch as it has been our policy from the first to encourage cooperation with the NSO in every way and at [NICC] Assembly it was so voted.

Other factors enter in. Joyce Roberts is very busy with summer plans . . . and Bill Ellis was taken ill on a journey to Italy and has been in serious condition. . . . Therefore we have been deprived of the leadership that these two students, who have represented us from the first with NSO, would be able to give.

It is suggested that those who are in a position to encourage attendence at Madison do whatever they can to get registrations completed and the persons ready to go.

Document Source: Stephen Schodde, from Hoyt Palmer file.

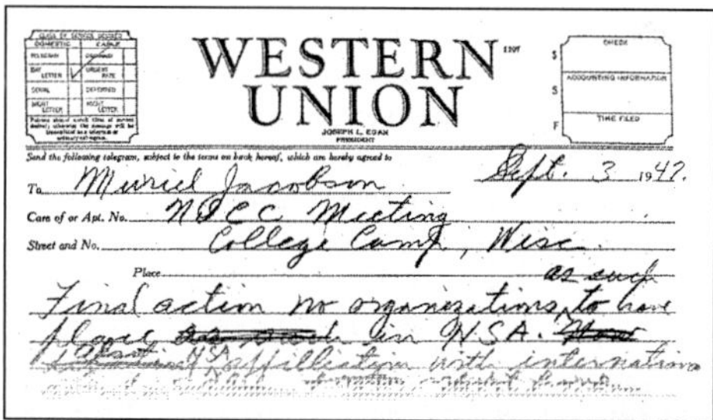

WESTERN UNION

Send the following telegram, subject to the terms on back hereof, which are hereby agreed to

To Muriel Jacobson Sept. 3 1947.

Care of or Apt. No. NICC Meeting

Street and No. College Camp, Wisc.

Place

Final action no organizations to have place in NSA.

NATIONAL ORGANIZATION MEMBERSHIP IN NSA VOTED DOWN Draft of NICC delegate Hoyt Palmer's wire to NICC staffer Muriel Jacobson reporting victory, limiting NSA membership to student governments.

WILLIAM S. ELLIS

Born: March 8, 1923, Somerville, Massachusetts

Education: Harvard University (A.B.), Harvard University (LL.B.)

Career highlights: Attorney: Forsythe, Holbrook, Patton, Bovone & Ellis, New York City

Awarded: Doc. Humane Lett., Augustana College, 1969; LL.D., Carthage College, 1969. Assistant U.S. Attorney, Southern District of New York, Criminal and Civil Divisions, 1955-60. Deputy Assistant Counsel, New York State Commission on Investigation, 1960-61. Member: Association of the Bar of the City of New York; New York State and American Bar Associations.

Campus correspondence

NSA domestic and international goals win wide approval

CEDRIC PARKER

Recognition comes to NSA with the award of one of three youth seats on UNESCO National Commission. NSA's Janis Tremper tells panel

TALKING TO COLLEGE STUDENTS AFTER THE NSA CONSTITUTIONAL CONVENTION

Mademoiselle, which covered the college scene regularly, reported "If Midwestern college support is indicative of the nation, NSA ... can consolidate student opinion and effort into a vital working force."

Biggest, most stimulating topic of conversation (next to football, naturally) on my fall tour to eight Midwestern colleges was the new National Student Association. Everywhere—in bull sessions, casually in between classes and at club meetings—students' conversation turned from Chappuis, next week's games and Homecoming to enthusiastic discussion of NSA's goals.

These goals, as clearly set forth in the NSA constitution, are both international and domestic in scope. Key objectives in their program of international cooperation are: encouraging and facilitating international exchange of students; supporting a student ship program; negotiating for student work passages with maritime unions; sponsoring a World Student Service Fund. At home, NSA is working for student self-governments, efficient student employment plans, improved student-faculty relations and equal rights and privileges in education for all.

The idea for NSA evolved in 1946 when twenty-five delegates to the Prague World Student Congress saw the progress being made by national student groups from almost every country in the world, except the U.S.A. Groundwork for an American national organization was laid in Chicago twelve months ago, and the constitution was adopted in September 1947 at Wisconsin by 760 delegates from forty-six states.

Delegates representing 1,100,000 students came and worked in sessions from two to seventy-two continuous hours in order to frame a constitution that would compromise none of their basic ideals and that would be acceptable to colleges in all parts of our nation. Heated arguments were terminated with rational, objective discussions which brought unity where there might have been chaos and subsequent dissolution of the conference.

The three most turbulent issues were resolved as delegates voted: (1) to make surveys of racial discrimination on national, regional and campus levels and to take action against unfair practices "with due regard to the legal limitations involved"; (2) to negotiate affiliation with International Union of Students at Prague, reserving NSA political autonomy; (3) to allow representation at annual NSA congresses only to officially constituted student-governing bodies.

NSA plans to organize regional and national collegiate cultural exhibitions through which the outstanding work of our nation's youth can be recognized. This can prevent a repetition of America's dismal showing at the 1947 Prague World Youth Festival. There, the Russians sent brilliant exhibits and performers, consequently won most of the awards. The United States was represented by a disunified group who squabbled among themselves, presented a spur-of-the-moment exhibit emphasizing unemployment and lynching and squandered the opportunity of a lifetime to impress thirteen thousand students from fifty nations with America's political democracy, high standards of living and cultural progress.

NSA's future rests at the polls of 351 colleges, which will vote on affiliation this year. If Midwestern college support is indicative of the nation, NSA not only can consolidate student opinion and effort into a vital working force, but can easily become the seed of a collegiate United Nations. BETTY CLAIRE SCHMID, CAMPUS REPORTER

The spirit's willing but the flesh is weak, after a seventy-two-hour session at the Wisconsin convention

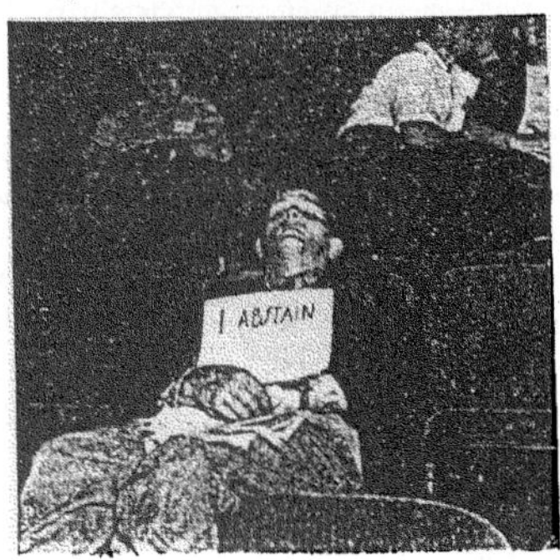

PAUL C. JOHNSON

Roster of Colleges 1947 Constitutional Convention

Compiled from the Convention Program and 1948 Staff List

Alabama–Georgia
Agnes Scott College
Alabama State Teachers College
Emory University
University of Alabama

Arizona-Utah-Nevada
Arizona State College

Ark.–La.–Miss.
Arkansas State Teachers College
College of the Sacred Heart
College of the Ozarks
Louisiana State University
St. Mary's Dominican College
Sophie Newcomb Memorial College
Southeastern Louisiana College
Southwestern Louisiana Institute
Southern University A&M
University of Mississippi
Xavier University

Colorado–N. Mexico
Colorado College
New Mexico Highlands University
University of Colorado
University of Wyoming

California
California College of Arts and Crafts
College of the Holy Names
College of the Pacific
Fresno State College
George Pepperdine College
Immaculate Heart College
Loyola University of Los Angeles
Mills College
Mount St. Mary's College
Sacramento College
San Jose State College
Stanford University
University of Santa Clara
University of California, Berkeley
University of California at Los Angeles
University of Southern California

Connecticut–Rhode Island
Albertus Magnus College
Brown University
Connecticut College for Women
Hillyer Junior College
New Haven YMCA Junior College
Pembroke College
R.I. College of Education
St. Joseph College
Trinity College
University of Connecticut
Yale College
Yale Divinity School
Yale Graduate College

Florida
Barry College
University of Tampa

Illinois
Augustana College
Aurora College
Barat College of the Sacred Heart
Bradley University
Chicago Medical School
Chicago Teachers College
College of St. Francis
DePaul University
George Williams College
Illinois Institute of Technology
Institute of Design
John R. Knox College
LeClerc College
Loyola University
Mundelein College
National College of Education
Northwestern University
North Park College
Rockford College
Roosevelt College
Rosary College
St. Xavier College
University of Chicago
University of Illinois
University of Illinois Medical School
Wright Junior College

Indiana
Anderson College & Theological Seminary
Evansville College
Indiana State Teachers College
Indiana Technical College
Marian College
Notre Dame University
Purdue University
St. Joseph's College
St. Mary of the Woods College
St. Mary's College

Iowa
Clarke College
Grinnell College
State University of Iowa
University of Dubuque

Kansas–Missouri
College of St. Theresa
Fontbonne College
Kansas State College
Maryville College
Missouri School of Mines & Metallurgy
Mt. St. Scholastica College
Park College
Rockhurst College
Stephens College
Washington University
Webster College
William Wood College

Maine–Vermont
Bates College
Bennington College
Bowdoin College
Middlebury College
University of Vermont

Massachusetts
American International College
Amherst College
Assumption College
Boston College
Boston University
Boston Univ. Medical School
Clark University
Emanuel College
Framingham State Teachers College
Garland School
Harvard University
Harvard Divinity School
Harvard Graduate School
Holy Cross College
Jackson College
Massachusetts Institute of Technology
Massachusetts State College
Mount Holyoke College
Mt. St. Mary College
Northeastern University
Radcliffe College
Regis College
Simmons College
Smith College
Springfield College
Suffolk University
University of Massachusetts
Wellesley College
Wheaton College
Williams College

Maryland–Delaware–D.C.
American University
Catholic University of America
College of Notre Dame of Maryland
Dunbarton College of Holy Cross
Georgetown University
Goucher College
Hood College
Howard University
Immaculata Jr. College
Johns Hopkins University
Johns Hopkins University School of Medicine
Loyola College
Mt. St. Agnes College
Princess Anne College
St. Joseph's College
Trinity College
University of Baltimore
Western Maryland College

Metropolitan New York
Barnard College
Brooklyn College
Brooklyn College Evening
CCNY–Business Day
CCNY–Business Evening
CCNY–Main Day
CCNY–Main Evening
College of Mt. St. Vincent
College of New Rochelle
Columbia University
Cooper Union School of Arts & Engineering–Day
Fordham University
Hunter College-Day
Hunter College-Evening
Juilliard School of Music
Long Island University
Manhattan College
Manhattanville College of the Sacred Heart
Marymount College
New York University-School of Education
New York U–University Heights
New York U–Washington Square
Pratt Institute
Queens College
St. Francis College

Michigan
Aquinas College
Hillsdale College
Marygrove College
Michigan State College
Nazareth College
Siena Heights College
University of Detroit
University of Michigan
Wayne University

Minnesota
Augsburg College
Carleton College
College of St. Catherine
College of St. Theresa
College of St. Thomas
Concordia College
Hamline University
Macalester College
St. Cloud State Teachers College
St. John's University
St. Mary's College
St. Olaf College
University of Minnesota

Montana–Wyoming–Idaho
North Idaho Junior College
University of Idaho
University of Wyoming

New Hampshire
Colby Junior College
Dartmouth College
Mt. St. Mary's College
Rivier College

New Jersey
Bloomfield College and Seminary
College of St. Elizabeth
Monmouth Junior College
Montclair State Teachers College
Mount St. Scholastica College
New Jersey College for Women
New Jersey State Teachers College
Rutgers University
Stevens Institute of Technology
St. Peter's College

New York State
Adelphi College
Alfred University
Bard College
Bennett Junior College
Clarkson College of Technology
College of Mt. St. Vincent
College of New Rochelle
College of St. Rose
Cornell University
D'Youville College
Eastman School of Music
Good Counsel College
Hamilton College
Nazareth College
New York State College of Forestry
Rochester Institute of Technology
Russell Sage College
Sarah Lawrence College
St. Bonaventure College
St. Lawrence University
Skidmore College
University of Buffalo
U of Rochester–Men's College
U of Rochester–College for Women
U of Rochester–School of Nursing
Vassar College
William Smith College

N. Carolina–S. Carolina
East Carolina Teachers College
Johnson C. Smith University
North Carolina State College
North Carolina Teachers College
University of North Carolina

N. Dakota–S. Dakota–Nebraska
Dana College
Doane College
N. Dakota Ag. College
University of Nebraska

Ohio
Antioch College
Ashland College
Capital University
College of Mt. St. Joseph
College of Wooster
Denison University
Fenn College
Flora Stone Mather College
Hiram College
John Carroll University
Kenyon College
Lake Erie College
Mary Manse College
Miami University
Notre Dame College
Oberlin College
Ohio State University
Ohio University
Ohio Wesleyan University
Otterbein College
Our Lady of Cincinnati College
University of Akron
University of Dayton
University of Toledo
Ursuline College
Western Reserve University–Cleveland College
Wittenberg College
Xavier University
Youngstown College

Oregon–Washington
Holy Names College
Lewis and Clark College
Central Washington College
Reed College
Seattle College
State College of Washington
University of Washington

Pennsylvania
Albright College
Bryn Mawr College
Bucknell University
Carnegie Institute of Technology
Chestnut Hill College
College of Misercordia
Duquesne University
Gettysburg College
Immaculata College
La Salle College
Martin College
Mercyhurst College
Mount Mercy College
Pennsylvania State College
Rittenhouse College
Rosemont College
St. Francis College
St. Joseph's College
Seton Hill College
Sproul College
State Teachers College
Swarthmore College
Temple University
Thiel College
University of Pennsylvania
Villanova College
Wilson College
Women's Medical Coll. of Penna.

Tennessee–Kentucky
Berea College
Nazareth College
Peabody College for Teachers
Southwestern at Memphis
University of Kentucky
Ursuline College

Texas–Oklahoma
Our Lady of the Lake College
Rice Institute
Southern Methodist University
Sam Houston College
S.F. Austin College
Southern Methodist University
Texas A&M
Texas State College for Women
University of Houston
University of Tulsa
University of Texas

Virginia–West Virginia
Ferrum Junior College
Glenville State College
Hollins College
Lynchburg College
Marquette University
Marshall College
Randolph Macon Women's College
Sweet Briar College
Virginia Polytechnic Institute
Virginia State College
West Virginia Institute of Tech.

Wisconsin
Beloit College
Carroll College
Lacrosse State Teachers College
Marquette University
Milton College
Milwaukee State Teachers College
Mount Mary College
Pioneer State Teachers College
St. Norbert College
University of Wisconsin
University of Wisconsin–Milwaukee

The Marshall Plan is launched and India is declared independent
A Streetcar Named Desire opens, and Jackie Robinson breaks the color barrier

General George C. Marshall is appointed secretary of state by President Harry Truman and calls for a European recovery plan (which became known as the Marshall Plan) for rebuilding Europe's shattered landscapes and economies. The British plan to divide Palestine, rejected by both Jews and Arabs, is supported by a United Nations call for partition. The nation of India is proclaimed independent, and in one of the most massive population transfers in human history is partitioned into India and Pakistan. Pandit Nehru becomes Prime Minister of India. The Eastern bloc of nations and the Soviet Union establish the Cominform at the Warsaw Conference. Albert Camus's *The Plague* is published, as is Anne Frank's *Diary*. Tennessee Williams's *A Streetcar Named Desire* opens. *The Dead Sea Scrolls* are discovered in Wadi Qumran. The classic movies *Monsieur Verdoux* and *Gentleman's Agreement* open. Henry Ford dies. Jackie Robinson joins the Brooklyn Dodgers, becomes the first black player in major league baseball. Illinois wins the Rose Bowl over UCLA, and New York wins the World Series four-to-three over Brooklyn.

Source: Adapted from citations in Bernard Grun, *The Timetables of History* (Simon and Schuster, 1991)

N.S.A. Comes Up Shouting

Something new has been added to the national college scene—a student government organization which is definitely on the rise. Such things have been before, but this has important differences

By E. HOYT PALMER

ANYONE PRESENT at the National Student Association constitutional convention at Madison in Wisconsin last September, recognized in that event two outstanding qualities. One was *the determination to be all-inclusive.* The other was *the tendency to thrash out issues,* never letting go of important things until effective ways of working toward the accepted goals had been found.

As to all-inclusiveness, there is one important element which should be mentioned. The Catholic groups, including not only representatives from the Newman clubs in non-Catholic colleges, but also delegations from all-Catholic colleges as well, were present and in force. This inclusiveness has never existed before in national student affairs—and it is a good omen for the future importance of NSA that it represents this important segment of American college life along with all the rest.

As to the determination to work out difficult issues, a case in point is the struggle over the question of racial equality. Central was the principle of local autonomy. All of the typically diverse American elements were in evidence. There were the Northerners who wanted to make race a sectional issue; but, more important, there were the Northerners who saw it as a truly national problem. There were the Negroes who were willing to accept compromises disastrous in the end to their own interests; but, more important, there were Negroes who saw that, while compromise was essential for progress, the way the compromises were effected was important too. There were Southern white students who reflected the all-out prejudices of some of their colleges; but, more important, there were Southerners who saw this problem realistically and, knowing that progress had to be made, used sanity in judging the steps which could be taken effectively now. As a result, the subpanel and the steering committee sat in long hard sessions that twice lasted throughout the night. Compromise after compromise! Finally, when it seemed impossible to reach an effective settlement, an agreement was found which was acceptable to the leaders on both sides. When the matter came to the floor of the plenary session, an amazing and heartening discussion took place. The issues were clearly stated. Unreasonable statements were avoided. Finally Jim Smith—retiring president of the *ad interim* organization, a Texan and a representative of the liberal Southern white position—made a slight additional move in favor of national responsibility. It passed with a big majority. Much joy, much unanimity of feeling and much satisfaction that they had gotten over a tough spot well. They had!

Leadership Is Up-and-Coming

Speaking of personalities, perhaps we should pick up on a few others that showed potent leadership. The gavel for the plenary session mentioned above had been handed to Bill Welsh, of Berea. Immediately, he was accepted by the group as an outstanding member of the organization—and was later elected President for the coming year.

In the discussion on racial equality, two Negroes, both closely related to our Student Christian Movement, gave important leadership. One was Cliff Wharton of Harvard, who also was on the organizational committee. The other was Jim Jordan of the University of Pittsburgh, who was in Oslo last summer and was at Madison as an NICC representative.

The vice-president for international affairs is Bob Smith of Yale, who had attended the Prague Council meeting of the IUS. His leadership in the international affairs panel showed him to be a person of tremendous capacity and excellent outlook.

The vice-president for national activities, Ralph Dungan of St. Joseph's College, Philadelphia, Pa., was nominated by Curtis Farrar, a prominent Student Federalist. He is a person who inspires confidence.

For secretary, they chose Janis Tremper, honor student of Rockford College, Rockford, Illinois, who has been active in ISS and WSSF and traveled in Europe with a student group the summer of '46.

For treasurer, Leeland Jones, Jr., of Buffalo University was named—a Negro nominated by the NAACP delegate. He was elected by acclamation.

The selection of such persons—all eager and all very sincere—makes one realize that this group of students means business and has terrific vitality.

THE INTERCOLLEGIAN

Excerpted from the November, 1947 issue of *Intercollegian* (the National Intercollegiate Christian Council). Hoyt Palmer was a YMCA staff delegate to Prague.

SECTION 5

NSA's First Year, 1947-48

CONTENTS

NSA's first national staff confronted formidable challenges of organization, the need to lay the foundations for its domestic and international programs, and the promotion of student government affiliations to the new organization. These latter efforts were challenged by Allan Crow, President of the Economic Club of Detroit, which he directed at college presidents and deans throughout the country, to undermine the association by questioning its capacity to manage itself and to overcome communist efforts at infiltration.

William Welsh (Berea College, KY), NSA's first president, an impressive and inspirational leader (and a future Assistant Secretary in the Departments of HUD and HHS), and Ralph Dungan (St. Joseph College, Philadelphia), Vice President for Domestic Affairs (later a White House official and Chancellor of Higher Education in New Jersey), traveled to Detroit where they debated directly with Allen Crow at a meeting of the Economic Club. The visions for strong and democratic student governments laid out there by Welsh are presented vividly in his memoir, his letter to his then fiancée, and his address to the twenty-first annual meeting of the American College Personnel Association.

Mildred Kiefer (Wurf) (University of California, Berkeley) took over the full time job as Treasurer in Madison since Leeland Jones (University of Buffalo), elected to that position, returned to his family in Buffalo (where he later became President of the Common Council). Jones's recollections appear in Part 5. Wurf, who became public policy director for Girls, Inc., describes the intensely personal adventure NSA provided as she took her journeys cross-country and to Europe while the Association was growing.

Ralph Dungan presents candid recollections of the limitations as well as the potentials of student interest in the new organization which he encountered while "going out on the road" on a shoestring.

NSA responds to the Communist coup in Czechoslovakia

The shock of the Communist coup in Czechoslovakia in February 1948 and the brutal treatment of some students and professors found NSA at a crossroads in its consideration of affiliation with an International Union of Students that refused to criticize any of the events. Welsh and his staff—with subsequent widespread support nationally—responded promptly in support of the decision by Jim Smith and Bill Ellis to resign from IUS, risking the uncertainties of whether they were constitutionally authorized to do so. Excerpts from the Ellis and Smith resignation letters voice thoughtfully the complexities and disappointments of the emerging Cold War challenges.

By the time of the first Congress in August of 1948, close to 300 colleges had joined the Association, and the staff delivered a vibrant organization to their successors.

The NSA News
Official Publication of the United States National Student Association
Vol. 1, No. 1 — Madison, Wisconsin — October, 1947

American Students Organize

Antioch College First to Complete NSA Affiliation

750 U.S. Students Meet to Create National Group

Regions Report NSA Activities Coast to Coast

Student Gov't Authority

Delegates Select

THE FIRST ISSUE OF *NSA NEWS*, with Wisconsin's John Hunter (Pt. 5, S. 5) as founding editor, proclaimed NSA's organizing goals to student leaders and educators throughout the country.

1947-1948 ALBUM

Clockwise from top, left: Ralph Dungan (St. Joseph's C., PA), VP National Affairs; Robert S. Smith (Yale U.), VP International Affairs; Leeland Jones, Jr. (U. of Buffalo), Treasurer; Janis Tremper (Rockford C., IL), Secretary; William Welsh (Berea C., KY), President.

Building a Lasting Foundation

NSA welcomed by both the state and local press in Wisconsin. Clockwise from top left: *Capitol Times* (9/7/47). Bill Welsh featured in the Office of Education publication *Higher Education* (11/1/48) and a year earlier in *Newsweek* (9/22/47). Setting the agenda and building membership were first priorities. *NSA News* highlights segregation (3/48) and international (4/48) issues. U. of Baltimore *Baloo* highlights NSA (1/30/48) To the left and below, vigorously debated affiliation contests and rejections are headlined in the college press (*Daily Bruin*, UCLA 11/13/47; *Daily Pennsylvanian*, U. of PA, 12/16/47); Smith College *SCAN*, 10/24/47; *Technique*, Georgia Tech, 2/14/48; *Student Life*, Washington U., St. Louis, 10/17/47; *Princetonian*; 4/12/48. *Daily Trojan*, USC; U. of Kentucky as reported in U. of Louisville *Cardinal*, 3/3/48).

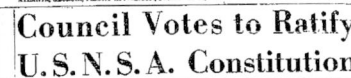

Successes

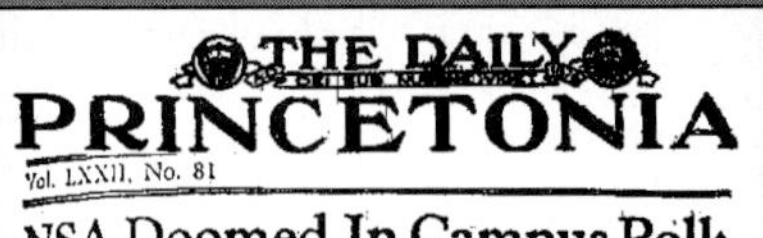

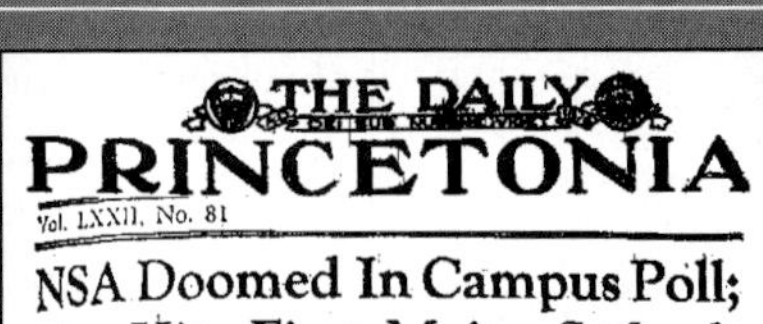

Setbacks

From the Constitutional Convention through the First Congress

1. Launching the NSA

William B. Welsh
Berea College
President, NSA, 1947-48

Madison, Wisconsin, was steaming in August 1947, and I was just off a bus from Berea, Kentucky. The executive committee of the National Continuations Committee from the Chicago convention was meeting at the new air-conditioned University of Wisconsin Memorial Union. I slipped into a vacant seat and was acknowledged by Jim Smith as the new chairman from the National Continuation Committee's Kentucky-Tennessee Region. Within a few moments I sensed an interest in the table location I had chosen. Little did I know that placing myself beside Ralph Dungan from St. Joseph College sent a signal to this politically "wired" committee.

At the end of the first day's meeting, a line formed for dorm room assignments. Clif Wharton from Harvard and I were standing together so I asked him if we might room together—another signal, and a fortuitous one, for it was Clif who subsequently nominated me for the presidency of NSA. For the next week, the eighteen-hour days proved to be a total immersion in national student politics and personalities, as the NCC's Executive Committee of regional chairs and officers argued and voted on the final draft constitution and bylaws to be recommended to the convention.[1]

Background: Berea College

To this day, students at Berea College pay minimal tuition and are largely selected from the Appalachian Mountain region. The college has a unique labor program designed to reduce college costs and give students work experience. At critical times in its history, Berea stood at the center of the struggle for equality in education for both black and white students. Prior to the Civil War, abolitionists from Ohio established a school and church that were open to both races. Land and support came from Kentucky abolitionist Cassius Clay as well as northern missionary groups. Harassed and closed during the Civil War, the school was reopened in 1865. Its students now included black Civil War veterans and their families.

Berea continued as an integrated institution until it lost its legal challenge to Kentucky's segregation statutes in a 1903 U.S. Supreme Court decision. Black students were welcomed back into classes in the 1950s. When I attended Berea, it was an all-white school with a unique history in the struggle for racial equality and a continuing commitment to provide education to students from the poverty-stricken counties of Appalachia. This heritage had seeped into my family and my life.

Both my parents were employed by Berea, my father as assistant dean of labor and my mother as superintendent of the dining halls. Both had graduated from Berea and then continued with employment at the college. To be employed by Berea was akin to missionary work, not in the context of the physical surroundings or student body, but in terms of salary and commitment. From the primary grades on, I was in the college's school system. I knew all the presidents, faculty, deans, and administrators and, for better or worse, they knew me.

I had volunteered for the army in my sophomore year and returned to campus in spring 1946, after three years' service in Europe. Berea was restructuring its student government, and I took an active role in drafting its constitution. Student rights, participation in student disciplinary decisions, and acceptance of joint responsibility for academic and campus conduct were all redefined for the postwar era.

The new student government charter was comprehensive, democratic, and ground-breaking. In retrospect, I can see that this was, in large measure, due to my ability to communicate with the deans and administration with the confidence of one raised in the college community. My comfort level in communicating with college presidents and administrators and my understanding of their world proved to be valuable preparation for NSA leadership. I never felt overwhelmed in the hundreds of meetings that we held with college officials during the year as we campaigned for acceptance and ratification of the NSA Constitution.

An NCC-sponsored regional meeting

Temporary chairs of the thirty geographical regions in which the National Continuations Committee planned to carry out its work of fostering campus interest in the creation of the proposed student organization had been selected at regional caucuses at the December 1946 Chicago convention (see Wharton, p.000). These temporary regional chairs continued until they were ratified at regional meetings held in spring 1947. In addition to the regional chairs, the four national NCC officers and three representatives of existing student organizations (Students for Democratic Action, the Newman Club Federation, and the National Intercollegiate Christian Conference) constituted the NCC's Executive Committee.

In March, Berea's student association received an invitation to send a delegate to a regional meeting to discuss the formation of a new national student organization. The weekend meeting was to be held at the University of Kentucky in Lexington. The invitation was signed by Howard Bowles, chairman of the Kentucky-Tennessee Region of the NCC. I knew Bowles as a classmate in the Berea College Academy in 1941 but had not seen him since.

The Berea student government selected me for the Lexington meeting. I believed that the experience of negotiating the new student charter at Berea would be of interest to other campuses, and I expected to share this experience.

Berea was one of a dozen institutions represented at the meeting. All were private religious or non-denominational schools except the host university. Bowles was a good debater with a powerful voice, who patterned his speeches after Kentucky political orators. His keynote to the two dozen attendees was a call to arms to go to Madison and save the new national student organization (NSO) from being overtaken by the international communist student movement. What a waste, I thought, as I listened to the harangue. I had no intention of staying for the Sunday session. Before leaving, I spoke of more important agendas for students than merely fighting to overcome communist infiltration. I told the delegates that if this was what going to Madison was about, they could count Berea out.

Back in Berea, I called for a date on Sunday and came home that evening to a long-distance call from a delegate from Ursuline, a women's college in Louisville. She told me the group had selected me as the Kentucky-Tennessee regional chairman to represent them at the constitutional convention of the NSO. They had agreed with my speech and would help raise the funds to send me to Madison.

So it was that a student from Berea College was sitting in Madison, injected into the issues of educational opportunity, campus democracy and student rights, international student cooperation, and political control of the new organization.

Issues at the constitutional convention

At Madison, the NCC Executive Committee was finalizing its work on issues raised by the regional organizations, which concerned key organizational questions relating to the draft constitution. There were many questions.

A representation system split between existing national youth and student organizations and campus student governments, advocated by some, seemed to me to be imbalanced and potentially too remote from students.

Some delegations from large universities with multiple campuses sought representation for each university unit.[2]

On international affiliations, my inclination was to go slow until we had a viable, recognized national organization.

I believed that the organization's officers should be students carrying full executive responsibility, with annual terms of office. NSA, I believed, should avoid a permanent officer cadre. I wanted the least possible buffer between the current generation of students and their organization.

I argued for a ratification process of the new NSA constitution that required an affirmative vote by a majority of the student bodies or their student governments in attendance at Madison. Sadly, this requirement, which was adopted, consumed the major portion of the time and energy of the NSA national office during the first year. A full-blown national campaign was required to achieve ratification.

I was chosen to chair the convention's final plenary debate on the constitutional provisions and by-laws stating NSA's policy in opposition to educational discrimination and supporting equal educational opportunity. Tension and dissent arose over the drafts of these provisions, and this last session came at the end of many hours of drafting, redrafting, and caucusing.

The nation had yet to confront the facts and disgrace of segregated education, which became a top issue on the national agenda during the coming decade of legal challenges. At the convention, regional and political factions were prepared to split NSA over the issue, or at least to force walkouts and boycotts. Just a year later, at the Democratic National Convention, the party was split by such a walkout by the Dixiecrats. We faced a plenary session in which the political left was not satisfied, and some delegates from the South made it clear that any statement would result in their inability to gain affiliation. Delegates from Southern black colleges were equally adamant and determined that the convention take an unequivocal stand against segregation in institutions of higher education.

The compromise that turned the key in the lock was a recognition of the necessity for regional approaches to working toward the goal of equal access to educational opportunities. When the proposed compromise language was presented to the plenary session by Clif Wharton, there remained significant factions prepared for a volatile debate. As chairman, I had arranged to recognize a limited number of sequenced speakers at the six floor microphones, and then to quickly recognize a motion for the previous question. I do not recall all the speakers. Douglass Cater from Harvard spoke in his soft southern voice in support of the proposed provisions. The last speaker was the delegate from the student branch of the National Association for the Advancement of Colored People (NAACP), who was positioned at one of the balcony microphones. The delegates fell silent as the voice from the balcony said that this was the time to support the proposed by-law and constitutional commitment to equal educational opportunities. The previous question was moved, and the motion was passed to commit NSA to equal access to educational opportunity regardless of race.

A short time later, in fall 1947, President Truman's Commission on Higher Education and the President's Committee on Civil Rights both issued their reports. These were the first federal reports to condemn segregation in higher education and call for the repeal of segregation statutes where they existed in seventeen states and the District of Columbia.

The Commission on Higher Education urged that:

> educators support in their respective States the passage of carefully drawn legislation to make equally applicable in all institutions of higher education the removal of arbitrary discriminatory practices in carrying out of admission policies.

Approaching the attack on segregation on a state-by-state basis was similar to the NSA compromise, although the NSA constitution and by-laws did not specifically mention the repeal of segregated admission policies [see the text of the NSA statements in the appendix, pp. 1110, 1113, 1115]. The Commission's stand was featured in the *NSA News* and proved helpful in consolidating support for NSA's policies.

Elected as first president

Early in the morning of the scheduled election for the permanent NSA officers, I was asleep in a top dorm bunk when several delegates came into the room and shook me awake, saying I should run for president. Clif Wharton was in the group. I believe this was a slate prepared by Students for Democratic Action (SDA) delegates, but the planners of the slate were never clear to me. SDA was the student arm of the Americans for Democratic Action, a recently formed organization of liberals whose purposes included creating an alternative to the Wallace Progressive movement.[3]

I reluctantly agreed to run, giving little thought to the consequences for my college degree, which had already been interrupted by military service, and the impact on my fiancée, Jean Justice, who was returning to Berea for her last semester. (Upon being elected I wired Jean and said "nothing has changed." In her frequent recounting of this family story, Jean tells of her instant reaction: "What do you mean 'nothing has changed'?")

The slate was formed without my input. The nominees came from diverse educational institutions, representing Catholic colleges, nondenominational private colleges, and public universities. They reflected a cross-section of the convention delegates. However, the slate also reflected some less desirable societal conventions. In particular, the secretary nominee was the only female, and no college west of the Mississippi was represented.

Clif Wharton delivered a speech worthy of a national political convention for my nomination (see Wharton essay, p. 147). I was elected president, with Ralph A. Dungan from St. Joseph's College in Pennsylvania as domestic affairs vice president, Robert S. Smith of Harvard as international affairs vice president, Lee Jones of the University of Buffalo as treasurer, and Janis Tremper of Rockford College in Illinois as secretary.

These newly elected officers were left in Madison after the convention, sans bank account, housing, office, or equipment, but with a charge to convince 182 colleges and universities to ratify the proposed NSA constitution and send dues! Bob Smith determined that the international office would be located in Cambridge, Massachusetts.

A first priority was to assemble a coherent text of the convention's actions on the organization's constitution and by-laws and prepare it for printing and mailing. Most of the editing took place in the cafeteria in the University of Wisconsin's Memorial Union, as the juke box endlessly played the hit "Near You."

NSA's first office was a rented classroom in a former elementary school next to the university, at 304 North Park Street (the school had at least one famous graduate, Thornton Wilder). Military surplus desks and typewriters were purchased. Support from the university's administration was crucial. Gordon Klopf from the Student Personnel Offices was the principal university liaison to NSA. Dean of Women Helen White and her assistant, Emily Chervinek, gave welcome counsel. Emily even loaned her small apartment and its all-important kitchen halfway through the year.

Royal Voegeli, president of the University of Wisconsin student board, provided much-needed counsel and, at times, material support. Many student volunteers helped with mimeographing, addressing, mailing, and morale raising. The first few dues checks were cause for great celebration.

Treasurer Lee Jones had to return to his family in Buffalo, so Mildred Kiefer, a delegate from Berkeley, was selected as acting treasurer. Mildred quickly became the ultimate repository of campus intelligence, reading every college newspaper mailed to Madison. Her memos summarizing and interpreting campus climate and personalities were essential for those of us who were traveling, and saved us many missteps. Mildred could interpret life and campus politics of large state universities—a new world to all the other officers. She also knew how to organize an office. Moreover, Mildred also added a much-valued West Coast perspective to our "east of the Mississippi" staff.

John P. Hunter, editor of the Wisconsin *Daily Cardinal,* took over the task of editing and publishing the *NSA News*, with the first issue being mailed by October. For me, Hunter became a crucial source of background and guidance for judging campus organizations, leaders, and volunteers. Through his willingness to share insights, I avoided political pitfalls that might have seriously distracted the staff during those early months.

Political climate and outside pressures

The classroom office was barely organized and the phone installed when a call came from Allen B. Crow, president of the Detroit Economic Club (DEC). This was the first of frequent inquiries and demands for information on how the organization was progressing, how we planned to carry out the mandates of the convention, and how we were going to keep the communist-dominated IUS from taking over NSA and infiltrating America's campuses.

We had received several calls from Crow when Gordon Klopf arrived in the office in mid-September with a mimeographed, legal-size, six-page communication signed by Crow on Detroit Economic Club letterhead.[4] It was addressed to the dean of students, University of Wisconsin. The covering letter told of NSA's origins within the U.S. delegation to Prague and the Chicago and Madison conventions. There followed several pages, in a question-and-answer format, outlining why NSA might become the conduit for communists to influence the college students of the nation. Crow, who knew more about NSA's history than 99 percent of college deans, mailed his memo to every campus ahead of our mailing of the NSA Constitution to the delegates and student governments. It was clear to Crow that only the naive could believe American students were capable of playing in the big leagues of the world student movement. He urged all deans to issue an alert on their campuses to this imminent threat of subversion.

The nation was in the early years of the witch-hunts and anticommunist hysteria. The Republican-controlled Eightieth Congress had been underway since January 1947, with the Senate Internal Security Committee and the House Un-American Activities Committee (HUAC) sitting in full investigatory regalia. In October 1947, HUAC held hearings that resulted in the blacklisting of dozens of Hollywood writers, actors, and producers. Richard Nixon had defeated Congressman Jerry Voorhees in 1946 and was in the House of Representatives. After defeating Bob LaFollette, Joseph McCarthy began serving his first term in the U.S. Senate.

After innumerable long and intense phone conversations, I finally told Crow that I wanted to come to Detroit and set the record straight. Ralph Dungan and I soon received invitations to address a section of the DEC. I arrived a day early, and Crow met me in his Chrysler at the airport. On the drive into Detroit, he asked about my father's position as dean of labor at Berea College. I explained the Berea student labor program, and the specter of a union leader's son was removed.

That evening we ate dinner at a Grosse Point country club and stayed at Crow's antiques-filled home. The last time I had taken a bath in a tub with marble and gold fixtures had been during the postwar occupation, in an Austrian hunting lodge once commandeered by Nazi Field Marshall Herman Goering.

Displayed on a long conference table at the DEC's office were several large scrapbooks of clippings, copies of most of the documents produced at the Chicago and Madison conventions, and reports from local contacts on NSA activities at many campuses. There were special reports written by observers at Chicago and Madison, naming delegates and detailing convention debates. The clippings, reports, and files were more comprehensive and current than any files in the schoolroom at Madison.[5]

The display included a transcript of a talk given before the DEC by Warren Rovetch, the Wayne University delegate to the IUS Congress in Prague. Rovetch had been invited to Yugoslavia after the IUS Congress, and, when he returned to the United States, had been invited to share with the DEC his impressions of Prague and his visit with Yugoslav Marshall Tito. The first page of the stenographic transcript of his talk read something like this: "You guys would really like to talk with Marshall Tito. . . . He is a real fellow and showed me a very good time in Yugoslavia. . . . We don't understand him here in this country."

My speech to the assembled Michigan educators and other Detroit Economic Club invitees contained a simple message. NSA was going to be no stronger than the individual campus student leaders and student governments who voted to join. The question was not whether joining NSA would create a conduit for infiltration by communists, but whether there existed confidence and trust in campus leaders to deal with the challenges of postwar America and the postwar world, including negotiations for acceptable and democratic terms for any IUS affiliation. I described the constitutional structure of the NSA, the requirement for annual election of officers, and the absence of any permanent executive secretariat. Dungan and I answered questions and reiterated the limited and sequenced approach being taken before deciding on any formal relationship with the IUS. We carried the day. While Crow's memo continued to impact decisions on many campuses, it was easier to rebut it by reporting that we had confronted Crow and successfully held our ground.

I believe Crow told me his son was an FBI agent, but I never learned whether any of Crow's interests in NSA were piqued through his son. My own sense is that the speech by Rovetch set off the interest and subsequent investigations.

Organizing for ratifying the NSA constitution

Ralph, Janis, Mildred, and I traveled to campuses for meetings with student leaders, deans, and, at times, an entire student body. The eighteen regional organizations headed by the members of the Executive Committee played a central role in obtaining campus support for ratification. It was this regional structure, along with the requirement of an affirmative ratification vote on the 182 campuses, that launched NSA as a viable and sustainable national organization.

The West and the Northeast had strong regional organizations, as did Pennsylvania, Illinois, and Wisconsin. We concentrated on the regions with limited representation or wavering leadership. I went south and, at Ralph's urging, accepted invitations to a few Catholic women's colleges. These latter visits, which involved talking to several hundred young women and their college administrators and teachers, were new and intimidating experiences for me, but the Catholic women's colleges that joined provided strong and continuing leadership to NSA.

In the South, the campus atmosphere ranged from cool to outright hostile. Arriving at the University of Georgia, I contacted the office of the dean of students and was told I was unwelcome at the university and was not to come on the campus or meet with any students. Allen Crow's missive had arrived.

A poignant vignette occurred at Southeastern Louisiana State Teachers College in Alexandria, Louisiana. Before meeting with a small group of students, our local contact invited me into his bedroom at his boarding house. He drew the shades and reached for a copy of the *New Republic* under his mattress. He said he had read it and what did I think of it? Something more than Allen B. Crow pervaded the climate on this campus.

At Louisiana State University (LSU), Madison delegate Gillis Long, later a leader in the U.S. House of Representatives, hosted my visit and exuded that genetic Long charm. While LSU did not vote to affiliate, the climate was full of southern courtesy and football.

Antioch College was the first to affiliate with NSA, not an unusual circumstance for this pioneer in education. Mundelein in Chicago was the second, followed by the University of Baltimore. By November, twenty additional schools had ratified—UC/Berkeley, UCLA, Stanford, Chicago, Wisconsin, Michigan, NYU, Carnegie Institute, Our Lady of Cincinnati, Austin Peay in Tennessee, Smith, Rutgers, Connecticut College for Women, St. Olaf, Haverford, LeClerc, New Jersey College for Women, College of St. Theresa, Bloomsburg State in Pennsylvania, and Rockford College. The dues for member schools with enrollments over ten thousand students were $369, so there was a cheer as well as a sigh of relief whenever these large checks arrived at Park Street.

I married Jean Justice in January 1948. She came to the snows of Madison and found a paying job, which was assurance to all the officers that at least we would still eat when the dues receipts dropped off.

Government recognition

The staff, and certainly most delegates, wanted a national organization focused on domestic issues of educational opportunity and meaningful student participation in educational decisions, although international ties were also important. However, it was evident, not only from A. B. Crow's attack, but from the growing national paranoia about communism, that NSA needed a strong signal of recognition and acceptance from the federal government—if not an explicit endorsement, at least an implied acceptance.

President Truman had sent a letter to the delegates at the Madison convention, and Dr. R. Johnson from the U. S. Office of Education had addressed a plenary session. But the first direct action that could be exploited was a mid-September invitation from the U.S. National Commission for UNESCO for NSA to be one of three youth and student groups to sit on the commission. Our efforts to secure this appointment had begun before the Madison Convention, and when the invitation came, it could not have been more timely. We used the UNESCO Commission appointment to say, "You can't believe the U.S. State Department would have permitted NSA to hold one of the seats if they believed that an international communist student organization was dictating its policies."

Subsequently, meetings were held with the U.S. commissioner of education, and a favorable article appeared in a bulletin from the Office of Education. The National Education Association's Office of Higher Education was supportive, and NSA officers were invited to speak at several national educational conferences.

On one trip to Washington, D.C., with Mildred Kiefer, we stayed at the Willard Hotel and called Clif Wharton to join us for lunch. Clif was attending the Johns Hopkins School of Advanced International Studies. Fortunately, the segregation practices of Washington restaurants didn't prevent us from having a good lunch, but on my return to the Willard, there was a call from the assistant manager who asked if the man who had met me was a Negro. I said I didn't know. He stated that he would not be allowed back in the lobby, and that if I wanted to invite him to meet me in my room, he would have to use the freight elevator. Fifty years later I recall this racial affront every time I go into one of the Pennsylvania Avenue hotels.

The Prague coup and the crisis in NSA-IUS relations

Detailed information on events relating to the proposed affiliation of NSA with IUS is provided elsewhere in this volume by Bob Smith and others.[6] Bob, who was based in Cambridge, recalls that he, Clif Wharton, and I visited with State Department officials on the trip previously described. There ensued a rigorous interrogation about the possible IUS affiliation and our abilities as students to play on the international stage. While I do not recall this meeting, I accede to Bob Smith's memory.

Jim Smith had gone to IUS headquarters in Prague as an interim replacement for Bill Ellis, who was recuperating from illness in Switzerland. Ellis had been selected at the 1946 Prague Congress as IUS vice president. Smith carried the first information from the NSA Constitutional Convention on what were tough and precise terms for any NSA-IUS negotiations that might be undertaken following the 1948 NSA Congress.

The February 1948 communist coup in Czechoslovakia involved an assault on the democratic Czech government, the University of Prague, and Czech students. Ellis responded with a wire to the NSA office, calling on NSA to break all ties with the IUS. I confirmed his response, and announced my action within twenty-four hours of receiving the cable.

Others writing the history of these events have assumed that my quick response was a result of the meeting with State Department officials described in this volume. Perhaps this is correct. However, there was another reason for this personal decision. I had traveled in Europe during winter and spring 1938 with an aunt and uncle just returned from Nanking, China, with the Japanese invasion fresh in their experience. I spent a month in Munich. Toward the end of that visit, troops began to pass daily under my window, and I leaned out to take pictures of the horse-drawn artillery, infantry, and supply wagons. We left early on the morning of March 12 for Salzburg, Austria. By eight o'clock we had crossed the Austrian border. From the windows of the train we saw German soldiers and Nazi flags in every town and at every stop. At Salzburg our plans were quickly changed and we left for Zurich.

Witnessing this *anschluss* and knowing of the ensuing tragedies were certainly factors in my decision that NSA must take quick, decisive action to break contact with IUS and condemn its support of the coup. Clearly, delay and debate over severance with IUS would not have served the embryo organization.

The NSA statement was carried in the *New York Times* and received wide notice. Despite questions of whether I had the authority to take this action without consultation with the NSA Executive Committee, I am sure it was the correct action for NSA, as well as for the Prague student martyrs.

In April, the Executive Committee confirmed my actions by a vote of twenty-to-one. The committee authorized an observer team to travel to Prague during the summer and report to the first annual NSA congress in September.

The minutes of the committee's meeting show the dilemma that the organization faced in desiring to establish continuing contacts with other national student assemblies and international student organizations outside IUS. They also reflect an early report from the Dutch Union of Students seeking an alternative international student assembly and an intense debate over the instructions and parameters governing the NSA international team's 1948 summer mission.

After receiving this team's report the first congress voted to support the steps taken in breaking negotiations but also authorized observers to attend future IUS meetings.[7]

First congress and initiatives mark NSA's success

The First National Congress was held in Madison late in summer 1948. More than a sufficient number of colleges had ratified the constitution and were paying dues. The books were balanced, and a new organization had been launched.

The program for the congress contained a "Staff Statement" outlining the officers' views on organizational principles and programs. Here, more clearly than in any other document, the first group of staff officers summarized the experience of long days and nights of discussion, redefinition, consultation, and travel. This work reflects personal respect for each point of view that marked a year without factionalism or personality conflict. Could a different group of officers from different backgrounds have launched a successful National Student Association? Perhaps, but they might have fumbled during that first cold winter in Madison—and in any event, they would never have had as much fun. Issues of the monthly *NSA News* for the first year leading up to the 1948 congress reflect a sweep of interests and activities that challenged student governments and campus leaders. The subjects covered included:

1. Student foreign travel and exchange programs to Europe—surely the most successful programs for NSA and many member schools: the NSA publication, *Study, Travel and Work Abroad—Summer 1948* was a best-seller. The demand for summer student travel accommodations brought two U.S. merchant marine surplus troop ships back into trans-Atlantic service.[8]

2. Foreign student activities, the IUS controversy, overseas educational programs, other national student unions, and relief programs for students in ravaged postwar countries: These subjects accounted for almost half the stories.

3. Academic freedom controversies: The stories described reports of students and faculty expelled for disallowed political activity, as anticommunist hysteria swept many campuses. NSA provided guidance to student governments in dealing with the Student Bill of Rights that was included in the NSA Constitution. Several regions formed committees to confront campus attacks on freedom of political expression.[9]

4. NSA participated in a ten-school conference, in Oklahoma, on methods for overcoming segregation in higher education.

5. Lobbying was done by the New York region for a state university system, and the New Jersey delegation worked for the establishment of state medical and dental colleges.

6. The *NSA News* coverage of the report of the President's Commission on Higher Education, entitled *Higher Education for Democracy,* emphasized the report's attack on racial discrimination and the need to overcome economic barriers.

7. An interracial regional NSA meeting was held at Emory University in Atlanta. The meeting was identified as only the second interracial meeting ever held on that campus.

8. Exploration was carried out by the Pennsylvania region on ways to integrate qualified Negro teachers into the Pennsylvania school systems and to remove indicators of racial and religious affiliation from college applications.

9. Reports were issued by many student governments on efforts to clarify with their college administration more precise ways for delegating authority for the assumption of student responsibility over disciplinary activities and other aspects of campus life. The NSA publication, *Student Leadership and Government in Higher Education,* by Ralph Dungan, was distributed in January 1948, and focused on these issues.[10]

Personal impact and growth

What did I gain from my NSA experience? First and foremost, I gained the ability to evaluate individuals, groups, and political situations on the basis of contacts and experiences with people of diverse backgrounds in all regions of the nation. My NSA experience also provided me with a sense of accomplishment and a feeling of assurance that I could successfully accomplish virtually any task that I was assigned or that I assigned myself, especially when working with a high-quality team of colleagues.

NSA prepared me for a career in public and political service with men and women who made extraordinary and lasting contributions to the nation: Senator Herbert H. Lehman, Democratic National Committee Chairman Paul Butler, Senator Philip A. Hart, Vice President Hubert H. Humphrey, Health and Human Services Secretary Patricia Roberts Harris, and American Federation of State, County and Municipal Employees (AFSCME) President Jerry Wurf.

William Welsh is a Public Policy Consultant in Falls Church, VA. He was administrative assistant to Vice President Hubert Humphrey: asst. sec'y., Depts. of HHS and HUD; legislative director, AFSCME, AFL-CIO; and administrative assistant to U.S. Senator Philip A. Hart.

END NOTES

[1] See p. 1108 for the original NSA Constitution and by-laws.

[2] See note 3 in Birenbaum, who chaired the congress's constitution committee, p. 589. Martin McLaughlin, secretary to the committee, comments extensively on this issue.

[3] The noted historian William E. Leuchtenburg, who was executive secretary of Students for Democratic Action at the time, attended the congress as an official observer and recalls taking part in late-night slate-making sessions among some of the other national organization representatives who were there (11/3/98 letter to Leuchtenburg from the Anthology editor).

[4] The Crow communication is reproduced on p. 191.

[5] A careful search of the Economic Club archives at the Detroit Public Library turned up no correspondence or NSA files.

[6] A digest of IUS/NSA relations also appears on p. 538.

[7] See p 534 for the text of this resolution and p. 540 for related background material.

[8] NSA's travel program became a major undertaking for the association and is described fully in Part 3, Sec. 5, p. 639.

[9] See Janet Brown's essay, p. 375, for a review of NSA's continuing involvement in student rights and academic freedom issues on the national and regional levels.

[10] NSA's student government programs are discussed further in Gordon Klopf's essay on p. 331 in Part 2. See also p. 185 for excerpts from my article, "Democracy through Student Government," which appeared in the April 1948 issue of *Educational and Psychological Measurement.*

PICTURE CREDITS: *Then:* NSA Constitutional Convention, August 1947, Madison, WI (*Schwartz*). *Now:* 1991 (Martha Stewart. *Author*).

UP FROM KENTUCKY TO BUILD A NATIONAL ORGANIZATION

THE NEW STAFF Clockwise from upper left: (1) Janis Tremper (Rockford), NSA Secretary, Roy Voegeli, U. Wisconsin student body President, and Bill Welsh (SHSW) .(2) Lee Jones (U. of Buffalo), 2d from left, before election as NSA Treasurer. From left: Mimi Haskell (Smith, Northern New England regional co-chair), Jones, John Simons (NCC Treasurer, Fordham), Harvey Weisberg (U. Michigan, Co-chair MI region). Right rear is Jim Smith, NCC President (Photo, Wharton). (3) Bill Welsh and Jean Welsh at NSA birthday party; (4)Wisconsin State Fair, Fall 1947, from left: Bob Smith (Yale, International Affairs VP), Jean and Bill Welsh, Janis Tremper, Ralph Dungan (St. Joseph's, National Affairs VP). (Photos, Welsh)

BEREA COLLEGE's *The Wallpaper* gave early support to NSA. From top: 9/20/47, 9/27/47. In May of 1947, *The Wallpaper* printed a special 2-page broadside edition for the National Continuations Committee. It included announcement of Welsh's election as KY-TN regional chair, an article by Bob Smith of Yale, then Chair of the CT-RI region, and a speech by Charles Boggs, a junior at U. of KY who had worked as a traveling secretary for the World Student Service Fund. Poll Results (3/13/48) for affiliation: 572 in favor and 60 opposed.

WILLIAM B. WELSH

Early years: Born 1924 in Munfordville, KY, and graduated from the Berea Academy. I enrolled in Berea College and enlisted into service from 1943 to 1946 in the U.S. Army Infantry, serving in the European Theater.

Career highlights: After serving as NSA president during 1947-48, in fall 1948 I returned to Berea College and graduated in 1949. That summer I was accepted as a fellow in the Southern Regional Training Program for Public Administration, a joint program of the Universities of Alabama, Tennessee, and Kentucky (UK), leading to a masters' degree at UK. This program was an early effort by the Rockefeller Foundation to improve the quality of public service in Southern state governments. For me this included an internship with the Alabama State Planning Board in Tuscaloosa in summer 1949, for which I was assigned to monitor the Alabama State Senate, where Doug Cater's father was a fixture and George Wallace was beginning his career.

After this Southern exposure, I accepted a fellowship at the Maxwell School at Syracuse University. I had completed the exams and class work for a doctorate in political science and was teaching when Dean Finley Crawford urged me to interview for a position with Senator Herbert H. Lehman. The senator's interview consisted of two questions: Did I support the United Nations, and would I find his strong positions on civil rights uncomfortable? As a result of giving the correct answers, I was launched on a thirty-five-year Washington career.

These years included two stints at the Democratic National Committee, first as the research director in 1957-58 and then as executive director in 1969-1971. From 1959 to 1966 I was privileged to be the administrative assistant to one of the twentieth century's most humane and beloved senators, Philip A. Hart of Michigan.

Next came a tour with Vice President Hubert H. Humphrey as his administration assistant. I stayed with him through the trials of the 1968 election campaign.

In 1972, at AFSCME, the largest public employee union in the AFL–CIO, I was the director of governmental affairs, and remained there until Secretary Patricia Roberts Harris asked me to come to Housing and Urban Development (HUD) as the assistant secretary for legislation and intergovernmental affairs. When President Jimmy Carter moved Secretary Harris to the Department of Health and Human Services (HHS), she took me along, again as assistant secretary. Following the Carter administration, Congressman Bill Ford of Michigan appointed me as staff director of the U.S. House of Representatives Post Office and Civil Service Committee where I served during the ninety-seventh Congress. Then I went back to AFSCME as legislative director under its new president, Gerry McEntee, and then into a "private" life of teaching and consulting after 1988.

Family: I am married to Jean Justice. We have three children, Charles Welsh, William Welsh, and Mary J. Walsh, and two grandchildren, Benjamin Welsh and Andrew Stroud Welsh.

It couldn't happen anywhere in the world, darling, except in America

There Is a System in the World by Which Each Man Is Given a Fair Chance to Be Heard

I had read about it in the books—now I believe in it—I am a part of it

William B. Welsh
Berea College. President, NSA, 1947-48

Editor's Note: On September 16, 1947, a little more than a week after Bill Welsh was elected president of NSA, he found himself facing an even greater challenge—convincing the woman with whom he passionately wanted to share the rest of his life that she should join him (with no notice in advance) in putting the rest of their lives on hold for a year.

Young men and women—just married, about to or soon to graduate—recruited to run for office in late-night caucuses and elected one or two days later—had to write home to stunned sweethearts, mothers, and fathers and persuade them to welcome and support a year of comparative poverty in pursuit of a cause that they were hearing about, to all intents, for the first time. In this excerpt from a letter found by his wife, Jeanie, more than fifty years later while sorting through old papers, Bill expresses the passion, commitment, and vision that animated the student leaders of that time who chose to seize the moment.

Jeanie, I feel that there is something here bigger than both of us, but that it is going to take tremendous sacrifice from both of us together to whip it. If you could have only seen the spirit of leadership, and desire of building something that each student in the U.S. could work through—to bring about better world understanding, better opportunities for education, the end of educational discrimination; then you would realize the terrific responsibility that these kids place on me—why they chose me I don't know—perhaps it was because I wasn't linked to any party-line, or didn't represent any special group that was trying to gain prestige for itself, but anyway I have the job.

The whole business is not so fantastic as it may sound—there were mature thinking people here, who grasped the problem at hand and wanted to do something about it. They felt that by having an organization that already represents 1,100,000 American students, and may grow to 2,000,000, an organization that could speak for them, and would help them solve their local campus problems more readily, then they would be able to tackle problems that faced everybody in the world today.

A thrilling experience in democracy

Don't think I am talking and thinking in the clouds, for in many ways I'm a skeptic, but take just one thing that happened here: There was a very strongly organized group of students and leaders from the Communist Party here; they had to take the floor with everybody else, and lay their problems and ideas out in the open where they had to be democratically defended—something I dare say has not ever happened so openly in America before. What Happened? Every time, through plain democratic process, their ideas and plans were discussed, analyzed and *defeated*—they were not defeated by police methods, or by red-baiting, they were openly defeated by discussion and fair play. It was a thrilling experience.

Another thing—We had a terrific fight over the By-Laws in the Constitution about the eventual elimination of discrimination of Negroes in southern schools. Many of the delegates from the South swore they would walk out if it were even mentioned in the whole Constitution. What Happened? The whole problem was brought to the floor for open discussion by the seven hundred delegates—everybody presented their views, all sides were heard, and when the vote came it was unanimous to include in the Constitution that the NSA would work for the eventual elimination of discriminatory practices in all forms of education. The fellows from the Southern schools were willing to take that back and sell it to their schools! You should have heard the cheering and excitment, when this kind of compromise was reached.[1]

A matter of building trust

I'm not a person who believes in flag waving, Jeanie, but there was something really fundamental here at the convention—People came distrusting each other, afraid of new ideas, but after eight days they realized that there is a system in the world by which each man is given a fair chance to be heard, where each man can work for his own ideas without being scoffed at, and then when the final decision is made, a compromise can be reached that will be fair to everyone, so that he can go back and really work under it. It couldn't happen anywhere else in the world, darling, except in America—Jews, Catholics, Communists, pinks, middle of the road, and conservative and backward South, all came together, were respected as man to man, and were able to lay their ideas on the table for a scientifically democratic balancing. I have a faith now that I never had before—oh yes, I had read about it in the books, heard the commencement speakers hit the high spots; but now I believe in it—I am part of it.

I want you to be part of it with me—part of a fight that is going to last all our lives—that will have to be taught to our children, and that [we] will have to live with all our neighbors—something I want to teach to my history classes....That is why I want you to understand—this specific problem of our immediate life this next year can be solved....I'm asking you now Jeanie to understand—to build this thing with me...and to be my wife.

[Epilogue: Jean Justice married Bill Welsh in January 1948 and joined him in Madison, Wisconsin, that month].

END NOTE

[1] See Statement of Southern Delegates, p. 1113, University of Texas and Louisiana State University affiliation contests, pp. 995, 454, Welsh, p. 166, and Wharton, p. 146.

Questions of motive, organization, personality, and politics

2. The Ups and Downs of Getting NSA Organized

Ralph A. Dungan
St. Joseph's College, Philadelphia
NSA Vice President, Domestic Affairs, 1947-48

It is hard for me looking back to see any big domestic issue that was impelling college students or institutions to join in this movement in 1946 other than a bunch of guys getting together in Chicago and bang, the thing gets its own momentum.

What you really had was a confluence of the new international outlook spawned by the war, by certain organizations like the United World Federalists (UWF), and by postwar idealism. The focus seemed to be entirely on that world outlook—that internationalist outlook—rather than a preoccupation with changing institutional structures or with putting new structures in place in higher education like student government or faculty rating. Those were not big underlying issues. They were issues that came along.

The academic freedom/student rights issue came up early on. There was always a celebrated case somewhere. I remember very well when the National Continuations Committee (NCC) issued a resolution at one of the national executive committee meetings concerning the banning of the American Youth for Democracy at Olivet College. But I think if faced with the issue, while most of the colleges and student leaders responded that way, I just don't think it was an issue that was high in the minds of most collegians that I knew, including the larger institutions in Pennsylvania.

NSA raised issues many students hadn't thought about

To the extent that issues like student rights and academic freedom were issues for students, it was usually a minority, of which I certainly would have been a part had it been an issue on my campus. A lot of that was brand new stuff and part of the NSA experience for me, and for many of my colleagues. Our eyes were opened up to many issues like that that we never would have experienced in our own environments.

I don't think that was just Catholic students, I think it went for the run of secular or remotely religious places that Pennsylvania had oodles of—Muhlenberg, Lehigh, Lafayette—although a college like Swarthmore would have been the exception.

NSA was not always a popular institution as far as the average student experience was concerned—we were not a student movement. Many were skeptical. And of course many of the larger universities were either fraternity or athletics dominated. Certainly Penn (the University of Pennsylvania) was. And you can generalize about that—the University of Texas being jock oriented and fraternity dominated, as you could Wisconsin.

The issues that NSA did concern itself with were significant enough to be concerned with—discrimination, academic freedom, world peace, international student dialogue—there was no doubt of that, but did it really matter? In retrospect? Possibly. It's hard to say. In those days it mattered because we were all keyed to the Cold War, but as I look back on some aspects of the Cold War—maybe a lot of those tensions weren't real but were manufactured, either by the Soviets or by us.

Did it matter whether students were given a greater voice? What would have happened had the students not been given a greater voice? Yet something did happen that mattered. There was no doubt about that.

The state of student governments

The state of student governments, as I found them nationally, was pretty highly developed in the larger state universities, particularly in the West. Berkeley was terribly sophisticated. Ted Harris used to swoon when Mildred would tell us stories about how that student government ran.

It was fairly typical for fraternities to dominate student government on large campuses after the war. But not at a place like Temple, as far as I know. But certainly Penn was dominated by the large fraternities.

If I had to generalize I would have to say that student governments were weak, somewhat dependent on the administration's goodwill, and vehicles for the advancement of big men on the campus. They were not really terribly aggressive in their efforts on behalf of students. On my own campus opposition to student government was rather intense: "Why do we need a student government? What's the matter, everything's all right."

It was seldom a debate on concepts of representative student government and whether it can have any influence on what goes on around here. For one thing, they didn't believe in that in a Jesuit institution.

Slate making and choosing leaders in NSA

The last thing in the world I had in mind in Madison was to run for anything—except perhaps to run after a train or a bus to get back to Philadelphia. But I became part of a slate-making process. Even though the decision was made to exclude national organizations in the membership, that slate-making process was designed to ensure that their influence didn't get exerted by individuals indirectly. So it had to be individuals who were really not tarred by any brush. It had to be a balanced ticket.

I have no doubt that the Catholic groups came together and said, boy, we're going to get one of those spots. And I'll bet Bill Welsh came off Jim Smith,[1] somehow—not necessarily directly but indirectly. And I think there was a group of leaders, such as Doug Cater and Curt Farrar,[2] who came together to settle on a "balanced" slate. And each of these people on the slate, in addition to being Negroes or women, also had to have some trust within the group that they were supposed to represent. It is really amazing how that process worked. We probably couldn't have done it better if we'd had some clever chap sitting back there masterminding the whole thing.

At the end of my term, I was not directly involved in putting together a slate, but I was on the periphery. I remember when Helen Jean Rogers[3] came to me teary eyed, could she do this? I was flabbergasted because I thought of her as a youngster who ran a mimeograph machine. A good person, but I didn't think of her then as an officer. And also I was sensitive to her and her background, so I remember that as being a very emotional discussion.

I think Bill Welsh must have had an appeal—people turned to him so instinctively. He had that charm about him that was so innocent, and they would just turn to him as being "Mr. Wise Man." He came there as a total unknown. I would guess he was chosen primarily because he was a Berea College, Kentucky, type. While they didn't want a Deep Southerner, they wanted someone who was on the border.

I don't think there was any definite plan at the time—but I don't know because I wasn't part of it if there was. What made it work? It could be just the intrinsic quality of the people who tended to get involved and then, however you mixed them and pulled them out of the hat, you got people who will work together effectively. Although, in the case of Bob Kelly,[4] that apparently wasn't the case. And I gather Al Lowenstein had an analogous set of problems during his year, and there was a staff split on policy with Herb Eisenberg, his International Vice President.[5]

I was a junior when I was elected and when I went back I thought, "What the hell are you doing?" But I just got struck like everybody else—you owe it to your fellow students and so forth. It was really a romantic tour—having the nerve to start the damn thing in the first place.

Although I had already made a personal decision while I was in the military to pursue a career in public service because I felt it was important, I had nothing like this in mind.

Organizing NSA on a shoestring

Our first year in Madison was concerned with organizing, paying the bills, and feeding ourselves. It was that elemental. And it meant going out on the road making speeches, trying to get colleges to join. Each of us went to a different part of the country.

The big debate was whether there was enough money to get us out to somewhere in the West. We didn't have the bus fare. My tendency to pick up people along the road was born of those early NSA days out on the road. I'll never forget hitchhiking back from Milwaukee in a snowstorm because I couldn't afford a bus. I sat out there on that snowy highway freezing my ears off and swore that, if I was ever in a position and had an automobile, I would never let anyone stand alone on the side of the road. To this day, although I don't do it universally, more often than not I stop.

There wasn't much time available for us to hustle for money. None of us had any of that kind of experience in those days for you to do that. Millie was the most sophisticated about that kind of thing, but we all had to acquire the expertise.[6]

Bill and I rented a room together over on the east side of Madison until his wife, Jeannie, came. We slept in an old army bunk bed. I'll never forget it. It was crummy.

There was a lovely woman in Madison, the assistant dean of women, Emily Chervinik, who was just wonderful to us. Professor Helen C. White was also good to us and, of course, Gordon Klopf, then a student affairs office staff member. I think Emily lent us an apartment right on the alley above Rennebom's drug store and coffee shop there. I remember cooking in that place. Jeannie didn't know anything about cooking yet. Ahhh, she was wonderful.

I covered mostly the Midwest, mainly because of financial constraints. Bill and I did go over to Detroit because

Alan Crow, president of the Detroit Economic Club, was trying to lay the communist thing on us. We had to address the Club and we stayed at Crow's house.[7] I wouldn't say we convinced them, but we certainly convinced them that we weren't the devils that Crow was portraying. When Bill Welsh stood up, how could anyone call him a communist? I have a positive memory of that trip, and we were kind of pleased with ourselves.

The International Office

One thing I was unhappy about was the location of the International Office in Cambridge. It had a certain logic, but from an organizational point of view it reflected the attitude of the eastern Cambridge people—the folks in the Midwest didn't know anything about international affairs. I don't think it was a good idea. We had really no control of their operation.[8]

The lasting relationships

The warmth, fraternal feelings, and relationships that I formed then have lasted until this day—Bill and Jeannie Welsh; Millie Kiefer (Wurf) and later her husband, Jerry Wurf; Janis Tremper (Dowd)—all of that crew. And my old, dear friend Jim Dougherty, not specifically in the NSA but in the context of college life.

Our NSA staff relationship during that first year in Madison was a really intimate one. Perhaps that was true of every year, but I think our year was particularly so because of the economic pressures on us. We were new and very aware of the responsibility we had to get this thing going. It threw us into a more intimate contact. I think that although it was an age when we were beginning to build mature adult relationships, there was also something unique about the circumstances.

It was a great, great, great time.

PICTURE CREDITS: *Then:* NSA Constitutional Convention, August 1947, Madison, WI (*Schwartz*). *Now:* 2001, St. John, Barbados (*Author*)

Ralph Dungan was chancellor for higher education in the state of New Jersey. Earlier he was special assistant to Presidents John Kennedy and Lyndon Johnson and also served as ambassador to Chile. He currently lives and maintains a small farm in St. John, Barbados.

END NOTES

[1] Jim Smith, of the University of Texas, was elected in Chicago in December 1946 as the President of the National Continuations Committee. Bill Welsh, delegate to the August 1947 Constitutional Convention from Berea College, Kentucky, was elected NSA's first president.

[2] Cater was the Harvard University student on the twenty-five member summer 1946 U.S. delegation to the International Student Congress in Prague. Farrar, a student at Yale, was the United World Federalist representative on the delegation.

[3] Rogers, from Mundelein College in Chicago, was elected secretary-treasurer at the First National Student Congress in Madison for the year 1948-49.

[4] Bob Kelly, of St. Peter's College in Newark, New Jersey, was elected president for 1949-1950 at the 1949 Third National Student Congress at the University of Illinois.

[5] Al Lowenstein, University of North Carolina, was elected 1949-1950 NSA president by the Third National Student Congress at the University of Michigan. Herb Eisenberg, MIT, was elected international vice president at the same time. See also Lynch, p. 271, and Eisenberg, p. 522.

[6] Mildred Kiefer, University of California at Berkeley, was appointed acting treasurer in Madison for 1947-48, replacing Lee Jones, who had been elected by the Constitutional Convention. Because of a family obligation, Lee had to return to the University of Buffalo, from which he continued to retain his office. See Kiefer Wurf, p. 178, and Jones, p. 869.

[7] See Welsh, p. 168, and Economic Club of Detroit, p. 191.

[8] See Robert Smith, p. 504, Frank Fisher, p. 511, and Helen Bryan Garland, p. 641.

James Dougherty Elected National Prexy of NFCCS

Catholic College Delegates Select St. Joseph's Freshman at Toledo Congress

James E. Dougherty, freshman student at the College, was elected president of the National Federation of Catholic College Students during the Federation's Fourth Congress held at Toledo, Ohio, on April 18-20. The Congress, attended by over 500 delegates representing 135 Catholic Colleges throughout the country, also selected Thomas Harper of La Salle College, Philadelphia, as one of the three vice-presidents to assist Dougherty in his work.

This marks the second time within the present school year that Dougherty has been honored with important posts in ... national collegiate organizations, having been ...

THE HAWK

Vol. XVIII, No. 1 — St. Joseph's College, Phila. 31, Pa. — October 3, 1947

Dungan Receives Vice-Presidency of N. S. A.; Will Head Domestic Activities Commission

... efforts of its student representa... St. Joseph's College is rapidly ... intercollegiate student activities. ... college prominence in this field ... the position of vice-president in ... American campuses and bettering educational opportunities throughout the country.

Commissions Established

To carry out its programs, two commissions were established for the purpose of coordinating activity and disseminating information. One commission deals with international student activities while the other concerns itself with domestic educational affairs. It is this latter commission of which Dungan in his vice-presidential role, is chairman.

WISCONSIN BOUND

Vol. XVI, No. 4 — St. Joseph's College, Philadelphia 31, Pa. — January 24, 1947

National Conference Names Dungan State Chairman of Regional NCC

Treasurer's Post Goes to James E. Dougherty '50, During Chicago Meeting of National Student Conference

At the National Student Conference which opened on the University of Chicago campus December 28, Ralph Dungan, '49, was elected chairman of the newly organized Pennsylvania Region of the National Continuation Committee, and James E. Dougherty, '50, was named Regional Treasurer. Dungan's position as State Chairman automatically makes him a member of the National Executive Committee in the recently formed student union.

STATE CHAIRMAN

Ralph Dungan, '49

December 19, 1947

Student Council Unanimously Approves NSA Constitution

The Student Council formally accepted and ratified the Constitution of the United States National Student Association, Friday, Dec. 13.

The Council voted unanimously to approve the Constitution following a report read by Benjamin T. Britt, '49, chairman of the Constitutional Review Committee. The committee, composed of Council President John

NATIONAL LEADERSHIP IN BOTH NSA AND THE NFCCS (National Federation of Catholic College Students) was provided by St. Joseph's College when Ralph Dungan and Jim Dougherty were elevated to state and then national office simultaneously (*The Hawk* 1/24/47, 5/9/47, 10/3/47). As Dungan notes in his piece in Pt. 5, S. 4, "we sort of divided the turf," working closely together to encourage students to engage in events beyond their immediate campus concerns. St. Joseph's College was among the 60 to 70 Catholic colleges which became active members of NSA during its founding years (see Des Marais, Pt. 4, S. 2).

National Student News

National Comment

By Ralph Dungan

Chairmanter of a serious teacher shortage looms ominously over U.S. education. Absorbed with the crass materialism of the day, legislators and public alike are responsible for the situation.

As students we have not forgotten the tragedy, called education, in a one room schoolhouse. We have seen the social stigma attached to the teacher who cannot provide adequately for his family's needs. On the other hand we know how desperately the nation needs men and women who are trained in the art of teaching and who can guide and inspire our youth with the real ideals of democracy.

The situation will not change basically until the teaching profession is returned to the level of other professional workers. Students in our universities are prone to say, "Yes, I'd like to teach, but . . ." Then a variety of reasons come forth, from a) the acceptance of a position in a society which is untenable, to 2) my salary would be less than a Chicago street cleaner.

We who are destined to step into the classroom must not be deterred in this hour of need. But more important those of us who will go into ...

Sub-Commission Work to Be Done By Local Groups

Opportunities to serve as national sub-commissions are available, Ralph Dungan emphasized at the December executive meeting.

Write to the national affairs commission, 304 Park st., Madison 5, Wis., for assignment.

lowing projects:

Student cultural welfare (Art, music, drama and dance, lecture).
Student orientation programs.
Student unions.
Student employment.
Vocational information and guidance.
Student housing.
Student publications.
Student health and recreation.
Student co-operatives.
Discrimination in Southern States
Discrimination in non-Southern states.
Graduate study.

Privilege Card System Adopted

Adoption of the three month plan to begin in February and a pilot project for the privilege card plan were the major financial decisions of the Executive Committee meet-

... establishing the privilege card system will be on NSA Bulletin available to every area. The advantages of reductions in the price of clothing, transportation, entertainment, and sundries should be a nation-wide boon to students hard-pressed by the high cost of living. Details of the plan are available through the University of Buffalo.

Executive Committee Backs Michigan Plan For 1949 Culturale

Full support of the Michigan region plan for a 1949 Culturale has been voted by the executive committee and California has been urged to proceed with plans for FIESTA in '50.

The Michigan proposal would locate the Culturale in Metropolitan Detroit, using facilities of the area as well as the University of Michigan and Wayne university.

Five thousand foreign students in addition to American students can be accommodated in hotels of Detroit.

The 1949 NSA congress would climax the program. Sole sponsor of Culturale would be USNSA, though other student organizations would be invited to participate.

Coastal regions will be asked to serve as hospitality centers for incoming foreign students, and all regions will contribute to the program.

Advance ground-work was done by the Michigan region by sending Carl Weideman, University of Detroit, and Al Schaffer, Wayne University, to New York and Washington in December.

Having received favorable response from Detroit industrial, labor, church and civic groups, they approached the U. S. state depart- ... gan representatives contacted. Indications are that these groups would support the program.

Student Government Explained In Booklet

RALPH DUNGAN

"Student Leadership ... ment in Higher Education ... let by Ralph Dungan and ... Klopf, fellow at the University Wisconsin, is being distributed by NSA to student government leaders from coast to coast.

Searching for solid material the general question of the functi... of student government, Ralph ... covered the "appalling lack of stud... on the question." Scattered information was available in other co... texts, and in theses. The atten... to correlate all this and to provide a reference list for further research produced this NSA publication.

The first section of the booklet deals with the personality traits of the current "wheel" on campus as determined in case studies throughout the country.

The application of the principle of leadership by these people to the problems of a college commu...

NSA Staff Bulletin Pushes Increased Vet Subsistence

The NSA staff has issued bulletins to student government leaders ... cordance with the resolution passed by the constitutional convention in September.

Wisconsin Region Plans State Wide Culturale In August

The Wisconsin regional commission for international activities, headed by Lynn Giese of the University of Wisconsin, has planned several projects for its first year.

It has enlisted the aid of WSSF, ISS, International relations clubs and more than 325 foreign students in the region.

The following projects have been planned: 1) Distributing World Student News throughout the region; 2) Encouraging lectures, films, courses, and books to promote international understanding 3) A state-wide culturale for Aug. 8 to Sept. 8 to depict the culture and life of college students, emphasizing the international aspects; 4) Eliminating ...

Kits On Student Leadership Open Monthly Projects

Initiating the program of monthly national NSA projects is the student government kit now being distributed to all schools represented at Madison.

Prepared by Ralph Dungan, the kit consists of two copies of the ...

Two Officers Attend Meeting of American College Association

Student Bill of Rights Reaffirmed For Application to Campus Issues

In light of recent instances involving student rights at the University of Wisconsin, University of Michigan, Columbia, Brooklyn, Hunter and various campuses of CCNY, NSA re-affirms the stand taken by the Constitutional Convention in adopting the Student Bill of Rights and its implementation.

The basis of NSA action nationally, regionally, and locally is the Bill of Rights stated in By Law III of the USNSA Constitution. To make these principles apply directly and effectively, they must be considered by the students, faculty, and admin-...

"OUR EYES WERE OPENED TO MANY ISSUES," Dungan writes, and his job in the first year, it turned out, was to launch programs on all of them. In the page above from the January 1948 issue of *NSA News* are reported publication of a new student leadership booklet (see Klopf, p. 331), advocacy for veterans subsistence, regional culturales, adoption of the student Bill of Rights on various campuses, laying the groundwork for the student discount purchase card system, attendance at a college administrators' conference, and the outline of the Subcommission system by means of which program responsibilities were parceled out to volunteer campuses.

RALPH A. DUNGAN

Early years: I was born April 22, 1923, in Philadelphia, Pa., to Elsie (Callaway) and Ralph A. Dungan. My mother was a nurse and my father an attorney at law. Mother was descended from English-Alsatian mid-nineteenth century immigrants. My paternal family was well established in colonial Philadelphia.

Education: Elementary education in parochial schools, in Phila.; secondary education, St. Joseph's Preparatory School (Jesuit), Phila. Drexel Univ. (evening), chemical engineering. B.S. Political Science, St. Joseph's College 1950. MPA, Woodrow Wilson School, Princeton Univ., 1952.

Military: Enlisted U.S. Navy V-5 (aviation cadet), July 1942. Called to active duty Nov. 1942; commissioned ensign, Jan. 1944; assigned as flight instructor at Olathe, Kansas, and Ottumwa, Iowa. Assigned to Pensacola, Florida, June 1945 for advanced training. Discharged December 1945.

Career highlights: During my undergraduate years I worked one summer with Labor's League for Political Education, the AFL's (premerger) political action department. As a graduate student (1951) I was employed as a summer intern with the U.S. Budget Bureau, to which I returned as a regular employee upon graduation in 1952. I served in the Legislative Reference and International divisions and as Assistant to the director. I left the Budget Bureau in Nov.–Dec. 1957 to join the then three-person staff of Senator John F. Kennedy (JFK) as legislative assistant and subsequently to the Labor Subcommittee of the Senate Labor and Public Welfare Committee.

In spring 1960 I joined the JFK presidential campaign staff and subsequently the White House staff in January 1961. After the assassination, I remained on the White House staff at President Lyndon Johnson's request. I was appointed ambassador to Chile in December 1963 where I served until 1967. In mid-1967 Governor Richard Hughes of New Jersey appointed me as chancellor of higher education, a newly created post designed to coordinate the development and growth of higher education in the state. After ten years of service, I declined the offer of a third term and returned to Washington as U.S. director of the Inter-American Bank, where I served until retirement in 1981. Following a one-year stint with the Caribbean Development Bank, I served as the director of the Eastern Caribbean office of the International Executive Service Corps for eight years.

Family: Until her death in 1987, I was married to Mary T. Rowley. We had seven children. I remarried in 1988 to Judith H. E. Briggs. I have seven grandchildren.

Travels through 1946-1950

3. From Berkeley to the World at Large

Mildred Kiefer Wurf
University of California, Berkeley.
NSA Acting Treasurer, 1947-48.
Chair, California-Nevada-Hawaii Region, 1946-47

In other pages of this book, events of the first five years of the U.S. National Student Association are told from many points of view. My point of view at the time was that of a twenty-year-old, unaffiliated liberal from Berkeley moving Back East, across the Mississippi to Wisconsin, and meeting and entering the larger world of public affairs. I've never left that larger world. I have enjoyed it hugely, and I am enormously grateful for having been part of the founding of NSA. Happily, I can say that many of my best friends today are people whom I met through that experience.

Here are glimpses of those formative years.

Berkeley

The Associated Students of the University of California (ASUC) is the student government at Berkeley. In 1946, I chaired Welfare Council, the activist arm of official student affairs, and so sat ex officio on the ASUC Board. That meant I brought issues to ASUC meetings—a move to raise the minimum wage for student employees to $1 (literally laughable, but we got sixty-five cents), a proposal to test cases of racial discrimination in hiring. I rarely won the battles that I started, but everyone realized that I was both serious and sincere in my quests.

Until my involvement with NSA, I did not know that it was unusual for a student government to tackle such matters. The ASUC owned the football stadium, which meant that we took in gate receipts and employed over 100 people—including, in my day, the football coach. Similar patterns existed in big state universities west of the Rockies, but apparently not on the eastern side.

When an invitation to the Chicago meeting arrived and I brought it to the attention of the ASUC president, he kindly said, "That's the kind of thing you'd like, and you deserve something once in a while." So our delegation was formed and I was on it.

Shortly after my credentials were sent in, I received a letter urging me, as a Catholic student, to contact the priest at the Newman Club on campus to discuss the importance of the coming meeting from a Catholic point of view! This was astounding. I had never met the priest, was uncertain in my faith, had attended only public schools, and certainly did not participate in the ASUC as a Catholic. I identified myself as female, young, white, and from San Francisco (also tall). My conversation with the Father was as astounding as the letter. As he knew few facts about the situation, he suggested I follow the lead offered by Catholic students, who would be organized by the time of the meeting and would contact me. I confessed uncertainty about my faith but certainty that I would represent the ASUC and the West, but not the Church, in Chicago.[1]

Chicago—Well, getting to Chicago

The sensible thing seemed to be to fly. This, my first plane trip, was on a DC-4 through heavy winter turbulence, with a routine stop in Denver for refueling. While we waited in the terminal, my seatmate—a swashbuckler who had lost a leg in some adventure, founded Trader Vic's restaurants, and was quite famous in the Bay Area, persuaded me that I was sufficiently brave and strong to get back on the plane. I did so, secretly determined to take the train home. Two nights and three days of coach train travel from Chicago to San Francisco, however, made me a confirmed, if initially edgy, airline passenger for life.

Chicago

First off, there was the snow, and it was cold, and it didn't look a bit like Berkeley. And the proceedings in the meetings seemed now and then to be conducted in a foreign language. Delegate after delegate from the core schools (I viewed them all as from Back East) spoke of the intricacies and the importance of the relationships between the IUS, WFDY, SDA, WSSF, UWF, AIMS, and so on.[2] I got the picture but not the meaning. Feeling frustrated, intrepid, and foolish, I rose to a point of order during an obviously important discussion. My request was simple. Would everyone who had used an acronym please write it on a bit of paper along with the full name? At the close of the meeting, I would wait in the back of the hall and collect these nuggets. I assumed I could figure out their importance if I could just get the names straight. Probably red-faced, I sat down, sensing the exasperation of the platform people at this evidence of the ignorance with which they were confronted.

Today, I might have guessed what would happen, or even planned it. When I stood in the back of the hall, probably a third of the delegates joined me and asked if they could have the names, too. Thus are political activists born. Looking over the voluminous materials our editor has dug up, I was delighted to discover that the 1949 Congress Workbook had a glossary of fifty-six acronyms, even more than I had gathered in Chicago!

Somehow or other, I was elected chair of the California-Nevada-Hawaii Region. However, during my tenure, there was never a member school from Nevada or Hawaii.[3]

Between Chicago and Madison

As regional chair, I convened a meeting of California schools, ranging from the School of Arts and Crafts to the University of Southern California (USC) and the University of California at Los Angeles (UCLA). Most participants were men who were veterans and who were two or three years older than the women. However, the scarcity of men on campus other than armed forces trainees meant that women enjoyed much greater leadership opportunities than they did before or after that immediate postwar period.

I learned, a bit to my surprise, that most of the California delegation felt as strongly as I did that ending racism was our most important mission. I think we called it ending segregation, and we focused on racially integrating our student bodies. Looking back, I believe that our fervor came from our common experience of witnessing the evacuation of the Japanese from California when we were all in high school. One day we saw signs posted on telephone poles, saying that all persons of Japanese ancestry should report on a certain date to a racetrack called Tanforan (in the case of my neighborhood). When we got to school, we asked our Japanese classmates, "Why would they want you to go to a racetrack—Tanforan?" What did this mean? None of us knew, but we all knew it wasn't good. I suspect it colored all of our thinking. It certainly affected the intensity of my feeling about racial discrimination. Ah, that's the right phrase!

As regional chair, I served on the national executive committee, and sat through marathon meetings at which we hammered out our purpose, structure, and positions. During one torturous meeting, southern representatives tearfully and honestly explained that interracial meetings were illegal in their communities. They had managed to hold some, but pleaded with us not to move too fast. The phrase "all deliberate speed" had not yet been invented. My temper rose. Finally, however, I saw that we must compromise to keep moving forward. I insisted that southern students must understand that we were compromising also—that we were giving way on our deepest beliefs in accepting a go-more-slowly approach. As I write, I can still feel the strength of my feelings at that meeting.[4]

One of the peripheral experiences involved going out to get a burger in Chicago. A dozen or so of us joined forces, inviting everyone standing around to come along. Ted Harris, who was to become the second NSA president, patiently tried to explain that he wasn't coming because, as a Negro, he wouldn't be served. We wouldn't hear of it. We gathered him up and went in a neighborhood joint. Sure enough, the waiter came over and said he couldn't serve us. We asked why. He explained. We said we intended to stay and be served. I guess we represented sufficient trade and seemed to be from the University of Chicago. In any event, we were given the dimmest table in the back and essentially asked to put Ted in the most obscure corner. It was hardly worthy of being called a sit-in, but it was apparently a pioneering event in that pub.[5]

Another exchange illustrates the different perceptions and lack of common understanding that we all had to overcome. As we talked about our regional meetings, I spoke to Jim Smith, the chair, who was student body president at the University of Texas and a most impressive person. I told him that one of our regional delegates was so delighted to be part of this effort to connect with the rest of the world, particularly the communist student unions, that he had started studying Russian to be able to read Marx in the original! Missing the joke altogether, Jim told me carefully that *Das Kapital* was actually written in German. I was mortified. Did he think me that ignorant, or did he just think all blonde women were dumb?

Madison

I decided to go to summer session at the University of Wisconsin in Madison, both to help set up the Congress and to see what this fabled institution of liberal thought was all about. It came as a shock to be told earnestly over a beer by my companion that although his folks were prejudiced against Catholics, he was not. I also overheard the distinctly pejorative descriptions of girls from New York City coming to "summer camp" at Madison. I quickly revised my expectations of this liberal bastion in the Midwest.

My offer to help organize the convention was immediately accepted by the student council. In those days, few students had cars or gas money, and fewer had airfare. Large numbers, perhaps hundreds, would therefore be arriving on the few daily buses and trains that came to Madison from Chicago. As I pondered the puzzle of how to register and house them, the experience of registering at Berkeley, with its long "rat mazes," came to mind. In the event, we organized systems, dredged up volunteers, and registered hundreds of arriving students in reasonable fashion. At least, I have no memory of disaster.

Then the convention started, with its hectic, thrilling, absorbing days and nights of debate, contention, struggle, and lion hunts—all described in other places in this book.

One memory captures our condition. While preparing to participate on a panel at a local radio station, I struggled to print my name on a card for the moderator but giggled a little shamefacedly as the pencil kept sliding from my fingers. I was so tired I couldn't hold a pencil. In those days, when the issues and the work were urgent, we worked through the nights. One result was that, by the end of the convention, reasoned civil debate occurred only by chance.

When NSA's first set of officers was elected, everyone assumed they would simply stay on in Madison. However, Lee Jones, the elected treasurer, was a veteran of the armed forces, as were most male delegates and all the male officers. He had a family, and law school to attend, in Buffalo, and had to return.[6] So I was asked to be "assistant treasurer," and accepted. My mother and my boyfriend in the Bay Area both thought that I had taken leave of my senses. Subsequently, each arrived in Madison (at different times during the year), to find out why I was staying Back East and what my intentions might be.

Setting up the office

We set up the office at 304 N. Park, in an abandoned schoolhouse. Our space had a warehouse aspect, with the high ceilings required before air conditioning. Bill Welsh, Ralph Dungan, Janis Tremper, and I moved in. Bob Smith, who had been elected international vice president, was in the midst of his doctoral studies at Harvard and made a plausible case for setting up his office in Cambridge. The international office remained there for several years, which, I believe, ultimately turned out to be a serious mistake.

Fortunately, the Madison staff members did not have much feeling of hierarchy, since it would have been difficult to determine which was the premier space in the one large, ramshackle room in which we worked. Somewhere we got old desks, an Elliott addressograph, a mimeograph machine, and a few typewriters, and we were in business.

My clearest recollection of this start-up is Bill saying to me that my first job was to create a mailing list. I was comfortable enough by that time to ask, "What is a mailing list?" I not only created a mailing list, but also set up our bookkeeping, with the help of the Office of the Student Financial Adviser at the university. In addition, I was appointed assistant editor of the *NSA News,* having been high school editor and on the *Daily Cal* staff. I also served as "utility person," which was a good description of my position. We soon acquired loyal volunteers from the university, some of whom are friends to this day.

I gained bookkeeping skills from experience, lugging the ledgers over to Mr. Hilsenhoff[7] every month to make sure that everything was in order. There wasn't much money to account for, just what came in from dues of member schools, but we were meticulous. The records for September 1947 through July 1948 show income of $20,940.01. With this sum, it was barely possible to operate the organization, even with our salaries pegged at $166 per month. We soon found that it wasn't possible to live independently, pay rent, buy food, do laundry, and buy a newspaper, so our existence become an early version of communal living, supplemented by invitations to dinner from faculty and staff at the university. I particularly recall the generosity of Emily Chervinik of the Dean's Office.

But we managed. Ralph was a good cook. We piled our laundry together for trips to the laundromat. Jan and I shared a room, as did Ralph and Bill. Bill married his fiancée, Jeanie, over the Christmas holidays. She moved to Madison and got a job with a normal salary and regular hours, as well as achieving what could be called adjunct staff status.

To me, the cold and snow were astonishing. I thought I had a winter coat, I had never heard of stadium boots, and, with a straight face, I turned down an invitation to a football

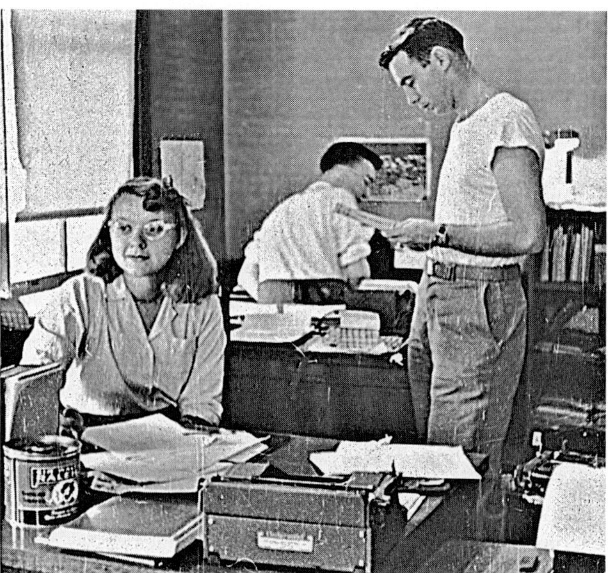

"SOMEWHERE WE GOT OLD DESKS," Mildred Wurf writes. Staff settled in to the large empty schoolroom in an abandoned schoolhouse just off the University campus. Shown here, in addition to the desks, are Wurf, Ralph Dungan, standing, and Bill Welsh to the rear. (Photo, Welsh)

game because I didn't like the sun in my eyes for so long. (At Berkeley, students sat on the sunny side of the stadium for home games and did card tricks, so my football viewing ended early in my freshman year. My boyfriend, a medical student in San Fransisco, used my tickets, which were free as an ASUC benefit for most of my college years.)

We all traveled to colleges and universities, urging them to affiliate. I made the western circuit from Los Angeles to Berkeley, up to Oregon, and then on to Seattle, Spokane, Pullman, Moscow, and Walla Walla. Thus did I learn of the "Inland Empire of Eastern Washington and Southern Idaho," where I encountered Empire Airlines billboards proclaiming hot meals, stewardesses, and other amenities. A close inspection revealed an asterisk and a footnote, "We wish we had them too. But for now we are providing pioneer service to the Inland Empire." The solo pilot opened the door of the cockpit to offer us sandwiches from a pile of brown paper bags stacked behind his seat! I had traveled a long way from that first, 1946 flight!

But I had not traveled so far that I even considered joining Ralph when he suggested that perhaps the least expensive way to get to the University of Nebraska was to rent a plane and fly it! I couldn't envision this; I asked him how he would find Nebraska from up there. We had all become so comfortable with one another that I had completely forgotten that Ralph had been a navy flight instructor. He reminded me of it, but it didn't change my mind one bit.

We continued to enroll member schools, began putting out the *NSA News* on a regular basis, and, with the help of our volunteers, had the national office up and running within months. The time was punctuated by exhausting Executive Committee meetings, intense confrontations such as Bill and Ralph's experience with the Economic Club of Detroit,[8] and a memorable trip to Washington, D.C.

For reasons that I have now forgotten, Bill and I went to Washington, D.C., where our expenses must have been paid because we stayed at the Willard Hotel—definitely not on the NSA budget plan! Clif Wharton was then a student at the Johns Hopkins School of Advanced International Studies, and Bill suggested that the three of us have dinner. Where we ate in segregated Washington I don't recall, but I vividly remember that when Bill and I came back to the lobby, the assistant manager approached us and asked Bill to step into the office. Perhaps Bill's Southern antennae went up, because I distinctly recall that his border state accent intensified. His suspicions were correct. The manager wished to advise him that if his friend was a Negro, he could not come in the front door, but was welcome to come in the back door and go directly onto the back elevator up to Bill's room. The difficulty was that the management was not sure whether Clif was or was not "colored," perhaps due to his sophisticated, easy manner or his light skin.

Not only was I shocked, I was genuinely perplexed. The whole race thing had seemed to be about color and visible difference of appearance, but if they couldn't tell by looking, then what was it about? I think this must have been the naïveté of the westerner, for there was only one black student in my junior high school in San Francisco and only one in high school, each an outstanding musician and prominent member of the student body.

The second-year staff arrives

As the year progressed, we began preparations for the 1948 congress. After returning to Berkeley in the summer for a final course and graduation, I came back for the congress. The new officers seemed a more diverse group than we had been. Ted Harris, our new president, was black, and had a wife and children. Dick Heggie, from Berkeley, was also married. Gene Schwartz, from "Met NY," arrived at the congress in a double-breasted pin-striped suit and painted tie, carrying a bulging briefcase. Helen Jean Rogers was our first officer from a "Catholic girls' school." Rob West from Yale headed the international office, now assumed to be situated in Cambridge.

I stayed on to help orient the new group and discovered that the most challenging task was to find housing for Ted and his family. Although Madison had recently been declared an "All-American City" by *Life* magazine, it was not so hospitable to a black family with small children. I told Ted that if he kept chickens, he would be a candidate for the world's worst housing problem. He replied that he thought his present status gained him rank. The help of a local Catholic priest proved invaluable, and the Harrises were housed.[9]

One episode still gives me a sense of how different our backgrounds and expectations were within the group and, by extension, within the organization. Dick had a car, a first, and we decided to celebrate by going to dinner in a country restaurant. Six of us piled in and set off on an early wintry night. True Californian that Dick is, he found the snow and ice daunting. We went into a skid that seemed to bring the highway patrol in a trice. We all piled out of the car. Ted, who was certain that a black man in this situation was going to make it worse for everyone, immediately started looking to see if there was a bus stop along the road so that he could feasibly claim to have been standing there waiting for a bus. Gene, at that time an engineer to his finger tips, began studying the skid marks, estimating velocity and trying to determine if the accident had been avoidable. Dick complained to the officers that the car in front, into which we had slammed, had no tail light, and therefore the occurrence was not Dick's fault. Dick's wife, Bea, kept assuring Dick that it was not his fault, that no one was hurt, and that the car could be repaired. I stood quietly and observed. Erskine Childers, a born diplomat and negotiator, who would succeed Rob West as international vice president, said to a patrol officer: "I say, we have two ladies in the group. May they sit in your vehicle, and do you have a spot of brandy, as they may be a bit shook up?" Bea and I were astonished to be snug and warm, with a spot of brandy, in a matter of moments, while the paperwork and reporting were completed.

Cambridge

I left Madison in midyear to work with Rob in the Cambridge office. Within two years of my intimidating experience in Chicago, I was working in Harvard Square and my friends came mainly from Ivy League and Seven Sisters schools. With Jan Tremper, now a graduate student at Boston University, and Florence Volk, a friend of Helen Bryan's from Sarah Lawrence, I shared a house in Jamaica Plain—a real house with a center hall, double drawing rooms, dining room, and three upstairs bedrooms. It was in terrible disrepair and the heating bill was astounding. But this wonderful place became a center of social life for NSA delegates, volunteers, Dutch Union of Students travelers, and other friends. It was exuberant enough that the police appeared at our door one day to inquire what we did, given the number of out-of-state cars that came and went each weekend.[10]

As usual, there was little money, so I worked mornings at the State Biologic Lab in Jamaica Plain as editorial assistant on the *Journal of Immunology, Virus Research and Experimental Chemotherapy*. I had probably never heard of a virus before I took the job. I remember straightening out the punctuation and grammar of an article on the superiority of ground-up mosquito stomachs for a particular experiment. At some point, I did realize that, hidden in the complex of polysyllabic words, were such interesting matters as a political argument over expanding the testing of chemical and biological substances as weapons. But it took the wonderful editor, Dr. Geoffrey Edsall, to help me recognize this.

The trip to New York from Boston

As a result of my student activities, I was asked to serve on a national committee of the YWCA. I explained to a fellow worker at the lab that I would be away for a day, to attend a meeting in New York. She was dumbfounded. How would I get there? How would I get back? She had been to New York City on her wedding trip, but didn't expect to go there again in the foreseeable future. Her response made me see how far my life had moved out of the ordinary path. In those days, only 32.6 percent of Americans graduated from high school only, and 5.4 percent from college. The figures for women were 34.3 percent and 4.6 percent.[11] The notion that college was for everyone and that the government had responsibilities in this regard were unthinkable.

Quebec

In the afternoons, I went to the office in Cambridge, where I spent most of my time organizing NSA's first European student tour—a summer in England, France, and the Netherlands, arranged in cooperation with the student unions of those countries. I was going on the tour. I went ahead to Quebec, the point of embarkation for the converted troopship *Volendam* which was to take us to Europe, to handle the registration and other aspects of this pioneering program.

While on the pier, I leaned against a newly painted fire plug, smearing red paint on my skirt. Since we had fewer clothes than a student today might have, it was essential that my skirt be cleaned so that I could wear it while traveling. I finally found a dry cleaner and went in to ask for one-day service. I was astonished when he replied in French. Not only did we face differences of politics, experiences, religion, race, and gender as we created a national student organization, but regional and geographic differences were also very great in the days before television, jet planes, faxes, and e-mail. As a graduate of Berkeley, I was somewhat knowledgeable about what we now call the Pacific Rim countries, completely clear about the Gold Rush and Comstock Lode, a little weak on the Civil War, and utterly ignorant that there was such a thing as French-speaking Canada.

The Atlantic

On the *Volendam*, I made another great self-discovery: I don't get seasick, and I love standing at the prow of a ship with the wind and waves whipping about. I found it impossible to sleep below, where the bunks were stacked four-high. Working on the daily ship's paper, I realized that the brig, which was our newsroom, had double-decker, instead of four-decker, bunks and that the room could be entered at night through the window. For a day or two I had a single, and then others crept in. I don't think I ever saw them in

Mildred Kiefer Wurf was director of the Washington Office and director of public policy for Girls Incorporated (formerly Girls Clubs of America). She holds an A.B. from the University of California.

daylight, since we each crawled off to our official places below-decks before dawn. Not that anyone was sleeping much in any case.

Europe

That summer was wonderful—traveling with one of the first postwar student tour groups, consisting of American students from all over the country, to places none of us had ever seen except in pictures of the war's ravages. Our student guides were great.[12]

I agreed to spend the next summer in Paris, staffing an NSA office there. My big problems were dealing with the French telephone system with my one year of college French and driving around L'Etoile at rush hour. The student who had left the car in my care explained that it did not go into reverse, a feature that was only one of its difficulties.

The real difficulty of the summer was the *Svalbard* incident, discussed in other essays.[13] When the students arrived in Europe aboard the *General Ballou*, we had no idea how they were going to get back. The Korean War had broken out, and all ships that could have been made available by the government were under the auspices of the military. Needless to say, ingenuity, perseverance, and luck saved us.

Probably my most indelible impression of those two summers in Europe was a night spent in Aachen. I attended a seminar that NSA and the Swedish National Union of Students had brought together, which was attended by Swedish, German, and American students. There I met Olof Palme. After hours of talking about his days at Kenyon College, what was new on Broadway, what we were reading, and so on, he steered me to a bombed-out section of town. For the rest of the night, we walked through ruins of houses, with Olof pointing out where the living room, kitchen, and bedrooms must have been. Blocks and blocks of such rubble were visible in the eerie moonlight. It brought home to me the meaning of "wartorn Europe" as nothing else had.[14]

New York

Whether I was ahead of my time or following the path of least resistance, I decided to go on to graduate school at Columbia, where I was startled to discover that the tuition was roughly ten times that at Berkeley. My experience of an excellent state university ran up against the realities of private education. A phone call home to borrow half the money, a student loan taken for the other half, and four part-time jobs saw me through.

I lived in the East and had friends from all over New England. I thought of my direct involvement with NSA as over. I had met far too many "professional students" in educational organizations and student unions of other countries, and I had no desire to earn that designation. However, the NSA experience had meant so much to me, and I expected to be supportive. To my surprise, the records collected for this anthology include a substantial report from an evaluation committee that I cochaired in the early 1950s. It was a large and complicated committee and must have involved hours and hours of work, but I have little recollection of it all, except that the cochair was Stanley Greenfield, who was at the start of his career in New York.[15]

Stanley had come across the river from Harvard Business School to Cambridge one day to volunteer as a public relations officer for the nascent student organization.[16] None of us had seen that need, but we recognized the enormous value of his work once he had undertaken it. Our friendship continues to this day, although our paths cross infrequently. It is typical of the bonds that grew between many of us fifty years ago.

My life was changed by my NSA days, I was changed, and I have never regretted a day of it.

END NOTES

[1] The story of Catholic college participation in NSA is told in an essay by Philip Des Marais, and in related documents, on p. 734.

[2] A complete list of abbreviations and their definitions appears on p. 1126.

[3] A list of colleges of the Chicago Student Conference appears on p. 132.

[4] Affiliation with NSA was later vigorously contested at many of the California campuses. See p. 1023.

[5] *Editor's note:* Numerous experiences of discrimination in restaurants and public places in NSA's early years are reported by writers in this book. Typical of the learning experience this offered to white students and how it fueled their outrage is the incident, similar to the writer's, reported by Norman Francis of Xavier University, New Orleans, on p. 433.

[6] See the interview with Lee Jones on p. 869.

[7] Ray Hilsenhoff was the university's student financial adviser.

[8] See Bill Welsh, p. 168, for the story of the efforts of Allen B. Crow of the Economic Club of Detroit to persuade college administrators throughout the country to question NSA affiliation.

[9] *Editor's note:* This experience in Madison was repeated in the following years in efforts to find housing for Ted Perry, vice president for student affairs in 1948-49 (see Kelly, p. 244), and Shirley Neizer, executive secretary, 1949-1950.

[10] Helen Bryan worked in the Cambridge office from 1948 to 1950. See her essay on p. 641.

[11] For the year 1947. In 1998, 82.8 percent of the population had completed high school, and 24.4 percent had four or more years of college. For women, it was 82.9 percent and 22.4 percent, respectively. Source: *Statistical Abstract of the United States, 1999.*

[12] See the story of NSA's travel program and the student ships on p. 639. See also Dutch student representative Jos Vos's essay on p. 651.

[13] See Robert F. Meagher, p. 665.

[14] Janis Tremper [Dowd], p. 63, Alice Horton Tibbets, p. 71, Mary Kay Perkins, p. 604, and Henry Halsted (p. 679) report similar experiences.

[15] See Appendix, p. 1120, "Organization and Finance Review Commission." Also, p. 242 in the essay on the 1949-1950 year.

[16] See "Publicizing the New Organization" by Stanley Greenfield, p. 155.

MONARCH OF THE COLLEGE DAILIES

THE DAILY CALIFORNIAN

VOLUME 131 Z28 BERKELEY, CALIFORNIA, THURSDAY, JANUARY 9, 1947

Students Return From National Conference; Kiefer Elected Chairman of California Committee

ASUC Official

Engelhard ... Of Athlet...

Benner, Smith, Welch Attend Panel Sessions

By Jack Howard '48

Mildred Kiefer '47 was elected chairman of the California regional planning committee at the national students conference in Chicago Dec. 28-30.

VOLUME 133 Z28 BERKELEY, CALIFORNIA, FRIDAY, AUGUST 29, 1947 NUMBER 10

Student Conventions

Constitution Top Issue At NSO Convention

UCSCA Plays Host At Co-op Conference

THURSDAY, FEBRUARY 19, 1948

Kiefer Named to Editorial Post On National NSA News

Volume 134 Z28 BERKELEY, CALIFORNIA, WEDNESDAY, NOVEMBER 12, 1947 NUMBER 41

ASUC Affiliates With NSA; Voted By Executives

Pelly Soars

Magazine Features Satire

Hap Arnold, Heggie Speak At University Meeting Today

No Financial Obligations To Be Assumed

THE NSA NEWS

The opinions expressed in signed columns on this and other pages do not necessarily reflect the views of the NSA News. All articles may be reprinted provided credit is given.

Offices: United States National Student Association, 304 N. Park St., Madison 5, Wis.

Editorial Board: Bill Welsh, NSA president; Ralph Dungan, vice-president; Bob Smith, vice-president; Janis Tremper, secretary; Eleanor Jones, treasurer.

EXECUTIVE EDITOR ROBERT H. SOLLEN
ASSOCIATE EDITOR MILDRED KIEFER

"THUS ARE POLITICAL ACTIVISTS BORN," Wurf recalls of her experience at the December 1946 Chicago Student Conference. Her election as California regional Chair is reported in the 1/9/47 issue of the *Daily Californian*, which provided reporting on the new organization's development (8/29/47) and UC Berkeley's affiliation (11/12/47). Wurf (then Kiefer) was already in Madison working on staff as Assistant Treasurer and later as Associate Editor of *NSA News* (reported in the 2/19/48 *Californian*).

PICTURE CREDITS: *Then:* NSA Office, Madison, WI, 1947. *Now:* Washington, DC, 1999 (*Both, author*).

MILDRED KIEFER WURF

Early years and Education: Born in 1926. Attended Lowell High School in San Francisco, CA.

A.B., University of California at Berkeley. Graduate year, Columbia University, School of Public Law and Government.

Career: 1990-present. Girls Incorporated (Formerly Girls Clubs of America). Director of public policy and senior adviser. Appointed to Government Relations Committee of Independent Sector. Chair, Washington Support Group, National Collaboration for Youth. Vice president, National Youth Employment Coalition. 1986-1996. Affinity Group Marketing, Inc. Labor program manager. 1979-1986. Girls Clubs of America (CGA). Director, Washington Office. 1974-79. National Collaboration for Youth. Founding coordinator. This organization now has twenty-seven national organization members, including all major youth-serving organizations. 1970-74. Consultant. Transportation Institute. National Board YMCA. Girls Clubs of America. 1967-1970. President's Council on Youth Opportunity. Senior staff member.

1959-1966. American Travel Association. Labor program coordinator.

1952-59. American Federation of State, County and Municipal Employees, AFL-CIO. Director of education.

Past Appointments: U.S. Department of Labor, Citizen Review Commission, Comprehensive Youth Employment Commission. U.S. Department of Commerce. U.S. Travel Service Advisory Committee. Represented the nonprofit sector. National Commission on Youth, I/D/E/A, Kettering Foundation.

Volunteer Activities: Past chair, Board of Directors, Center for Youth Services. Past vice chair, Board of Directors, National Committee for Citizens in Education. Chair, Futures Committee. Board member, Fund for an OPEN Society (a nonprofit mortgage fund to decrease housing segregation). Trustee, Jerry Wurf Memorial Fund. Liaison to Kennedy School of Government. Past board member, Sutton Towers Condominium Association. Member, Board Committee, Living Stage.

Family: Married to Jerry Wurf, 1960. Two children: Nicholas and Abigail.

Address delivered to the American College Personnel Association

Democracy through Student Government

An excellent way of developing potential leadership

William B. Welsh
Berea College, Kentucky
President, U. S. National Student Association, 1947-48

Editor's Note: This is a talk delivered at the Twenty-first Annual Meeting of the American College Personnel Association in Chicago, IL, March 29-April 1, 1948. It is reprinted from Educational and Psychological Measurement, Vol. 8, No. 3, Autumn 1948. Establishing and strengthening the legitimacy and value of student governments as a partner to college administrators and faculty was a primary goal for the association, on which its effectiveness would rest. NSA officers sought out opportunities to speak before the conferences and write for the journals of the major higher-education professional associations. Their objective, as in this talk by Bill Welsh, was to provide a balanced rationale for the possibilities, as well as the limits, of what student governments could be expected to do. A by-product was to provide "intellectual ammunition" that could support efforts of the new generation of college personnel administrators, who were encouraging greater student involvement in university governance. See Part 2, Section 1, p. 334.

I should like to share with you some of the observations that I have made in the last few months while working on the Staff of the National Student Association. One of the important things on which I have been assembling data is—how well [are] the teaching and practicing of democracy being carried out in our colleges and universities? It has been both encouraging and discouraging at times to get into bull sessions with student leaders from many different types of colleges and to find out what they are really thinking.

We all know that within a university community there are usually three general divisions of personnel directly concerned with the educational process—the administration, the faculty and the student body. It is true that over a period of many years the administration and faculty have been able to develop fairly logical and workable means of coordinating their activities, and the structures by which this can be done fairly easily have been set up. At least it appears this way to the students. But the third group, the student body, has generally been the last group to attempt to coordinate and organize its activities. In fact it would be safe to say that in the majority of cases this has only been going on in the last thirty years, and then with varying degrees of success.

At first glance it might seem that the physical problems of organizing this transient group, which has spent little if any time in the specialized field of higher education, would be insurmountable. However, I believe that surprising results have been obtained in the past, and especially are being brought about in the years since the war.

Attitudes toward student government

Let us call this organized student group that we shall be discussing the student government, and see in what light it is looked upon by the members of the three large divisions on the campus. I have found while talking with faculty members and administrators that some of them hopefully look for some ideal system of student government which can take off their hands the red tape and confusion of student activities. Others of this group seem to think the student government is a fine place to put a great deal of the responsibility for the disciplinary problems that arise on the campus. Others feel that it is dangerous to give students too direct a way to express their opinions and that the student's only role in college is the attending of classes and the passing of exams. And then there is the group who do believe that work in student government is an excellent way of developing potential leadership and understanding of organizational problems, but I'm afraid the group that looks upon student government as a place to encourage an understanding of the real meaning of living within a democratic society is all too small.

I've also talked with a great number of students and am sorry to say the general attitude seems to be even more discouraging. All too often I've heard such comments as, "Oh, that's just an outfit for the big-wheels to get their name in the paper" or "It's only good to run a dance, but it never does anything for me." Sometimes the students even feel that the real reason for student government is to put up a front for the administration and that really the dean holds a veto over any worthwhile project that might be undertaken.

Of course the whole purpose of outlining these observations for you is to bring out what NSA feels is the real purpose in having a student government. The long range purpose should be almost self-evident: it is to provide students with a practical education in democratic self-government. It is in effect an insurance policy for a nation that prides itself on the capacity of its people to govern themselves. We feel that in any discussion of this matter student government should be regarded primarily as a learning process in which the lesson taught through actual practice is the hard and tiring way of an ordered democratic society. We recognize that democracy is probably the most difficult form of government and system of ordering a society ever conceived by man, but that it is the only successful one in which the individual is given a full opportunity for intellectual and moral growth and in which he may use his full capacity to contribute to the common good. And within this context we feel student government has an important role to play. As the report by the Harvard committee on *General Education in a Free Society* expresses it:

> Student government is valuable in shaping the quality of later citizenship. It is only when the student faces the actual difficulties of governing by democracy that he begins to appreciate the complexity of a free society. To learn to resist pressure, to discover the power of a minority, to have free speech used against one, to prescribe rules and then to abide by them is training of the first order.

This then is what students may learn if they have the opportunity of participating in student government activities.

The functions of student government

The student government itself, like any government, has two major functions—to serve the people it is made up of, and to represent them democratically to the other groups with which those people must work and live. Now to discover whether or not student governments really have the chance to do these things, and the opportunity to learn those things listed by the Harvard Committee, some system of evaluation should be developed. The individual college should be able to evaluate the workings of democracy within itself, and then the level of evaluation of democracy should be brought down to the individual student. We must have the tools for analysis within the reach of the campus. It is very commendable to talk of saving the remnants of democracy on the international scene, or in Washington. But the evaluation of what I am looking for must not begin there. It must start within the fraternity house and in the Union building. There must be some new sort of checklist or criteria of action by which every student can evaluate his participation in the democracy of the campus.

It will do little good for NSA to tell a student government where it is making mistakes or for us to write an editorial in the *NSA News* about the undemocratic student government at a specific school. It will do little good for members of the student government to call the members of the student body apathetic or to criticize the members for taking little interest. Each individual student government must work out for itself the techniques of making democracy a learning process, and each student must be urged to participate and then to evaluate his own part.

I would further like to see some method of evaluating democracy not only within the student government, but within the whole educational community. I'm afraid too often it is the bad example set by the faculty and administration of a college that puts our students on the wrong track when they form a student government. It is much easier to sit behind a shiny desk and say to a group of students that this can be done and that can't. It's easier for the president of the student government to run his affairs with a yes or no answer, but we would all cry loudly if this were the method used in our local or national governments. It is always harder to reach agreement through the free exchange of ideas and by majority decision.

Need for criteria to judge democracy

I hope that from this group will come the suggestion to each of your student groups that they wind up their activities this year with an overall evaluation of how well they were able to use the democratic process in their work this past year. Before they can do this, of course, they will have to evolve some sort of criteria to judge the democracy of their work. I hope that many of them will take the time to do this. The results of this should certainly be kept for the new members the following year, so that they may see the strong and weak points of their predecessors. Then each of us in our work with student governments should stop and take a look around. Do we feel that discipline is the prime objective of our work with student activities? Are we afraid of making a mistake by letting the student government stumble slowly along in the democratic process?

The example that each person in the field sets in his own practices will be a determining factor in how student groups function. Let's not wave the American flag and think it is grand to give lip service to democracy, but rather let us think out how we can put democracy to practice within our own spheres of influence, and make it live and grow. If democracy fails within the educational circles of America, I hate to think how miserably it will fail in the city, state and national spheres.

Perhaps I have painted a rather bleak scene. For a minute I would like to think of the reasons I believe the university community is an ideal place for even the transient group of students to learn the workings of democracy. Here the student has an opportunity to deal with problems within his own scope without too much outside interference, and in areas where mistakes can be accepted. Too often it is because of fear of public opinion against the university that sufficient areas of defined authority are not turned over to students—and because mistakes might be made. I feel that one of our first jobs is to inform the public that student government is a learning process, and is an accepted part of each university system. Also, working in a student government gives the students a chance to see that the solution to organizational problems does not lie in merely writing a beautiful constitution. I don't know how many times this year I have heard that some student government is rewriting its constitution. I wish I could call out to all of them not to get jammed-up in words, but to put their efforts into making what they have work.

Mistakes in defining student government authority

Let us look briefly at some of the specific mistakes that are being made today in this field.

1. I feel that there has been a failure to outline clearly the areas of authority in which a student government may work. I realize that in every instance this authority will properly come from the administration of the university, but it must be clearly outlined and understood, and it must be complete. The advisors that work with student government should realize this and constantly be on guard to see that they do not try to pressure decisions in the areas in which authority has been clearly delegated.

2. Highly organized campuses, especially those with independent and fraternity groups, are prone to take the politics of student government as something that can be kicked around for excitement. This talking and playing politics for politics' sake is often exciting, but if that is the end, it is usually the end of functional student government.

3. Many of the larger university student governments find their meetings almost completely dominated by consideration of athletics. In some cases this has been carried to the extreme and resulted in the complete neglect of broader considerations of student welfare.

4. One of the worst faults that I have run into is the student government's accepting the responsibility for a conglomeration of disciplinary powers over student behavior. I am sure that wherever discipline is the stated or actual prime purpose of having a student government, the student government is not very effective in that field or any other. Too often I have found that rules and regulations are left unexplained to new generations of students, and the only people who know that discipline is in the hands of the student government are the administration and a few of the student council members themselves. Disciplinary functions of student government should be taken on only as the whole student body is willing to accept the responsibility. The ideal situation might be for a set of jurisdictional by-laws that required re-acceptance each spring by the student body. This would always keep the responsibility before the changing student body, and give the student council a vote of confidence in this very important field. A group that starts its existence with an imposing list of jurisdictional or disciplinary powers won't have a very long life. It will soon find that it is losing the respect of both the administration and the student body as it finds it can not use police powers wise-

ly. If it becomes clear that one or two disciplinary powers are being handled effectively by the student government, an additional power might be added each year until a workable list is obtained. The key to the ideal situation, however, is to have the whole student body accept the responsibility, and not just to have the executive body of the student government act as a policing agency.

Where student government functions successfully

Now let us consider where student government does function successfully, and in what areas constructive projects that are beneficial to the campus are being carried out.

1. The coordination of campus social activities, and their expansion until every student has an opportunity to participate, [have] been the concern of many student governments. Several have expanded intramural sports.

2. Some student governments have surveyed housing facilities in the surrounding community, and checked up on local restaurants to see that they are keeping high health standards.

3. Many of the student governments have taken on the project of running a campus community chest and consolidating all of the varied relief and welfare drives into this one campaign.

4. There has been increasing interest in the problem of constructive student evaluation of teachers, and several student governments have taken the lead in coordinating this project with faculty groups.

5. At one school the student government has been instrumental in obtaining a place for at least one student representative on every university committee, thus tying in more closely the loose ends of the educational community.

NSA's role in this broad picture of student government is primarily to make more effective the work of the student body in the university community, and to act as their representative and consultant in national and international educational, and governmental groups.

The role of NSA

One of our first jobs on the national scene this year was to compile material and information on the actual structure and functioning of student government. We have published a booklet on *Student Government and Leadership in Higher Education*[1]—and along with it sent plans for student government clinics that can be held by interested groups on a single campus, and by several schools in a region. A survey of 360 colleges is being completed to show the functioning and structure of student government in all types and sizes of colleges and universities in the United States....

Some of our most immediately successful work has been done in the field of international student activities....

* * *

We hope that through NSA we can help individual students to look beyond their classrooms, and to encourage them to help themselves with their educational problems. NSA itself is a learning process and will never reach any ultimate goal in itself, but it will make the job easier for its member student governments and will provide them with channels through which their activities can be expanded into the regional and national scene. It is with this in mind that students from all types of colleges are willing to cooperate and to work with each other in the National Student Association.

END NOTES

[1] See Klopf, p. 331.

PICTURE CREDIT: NSA offices, Madison, WI, 1947 (*SHSW*).

Bill Welsh at the national offices of NSA in 1947.

A PRACTICAL EDUCATION IN SELF-GOVERNMENT

12/12/46

THE LOYOLA NEWS

STUDENT UNION ON WAY

Next Semester To See Formation of Union

NEWS CAMPAIGN STIRS FACULTY TO ACTION ON IMPORTANT ISSUE

4/18/47

Cornell Daily Sun

Action by Student Council Approves New Constitution

Texas City Evacuates; Shifting Winds, Blazes Menace Ravaged Town

K ADAMS CAPTURES PRESIDENCY

Phil Palmer Named Vice-Prexy; Jimmie Kaldal, Jim Beardsley Are

4/15/48

BOB PADGETT WINS

Southern California Daily Trojan

Non-Orgs Push in First Student Body President in 27 Years

Seawanhaka

8/29/49

Polk Plaque Awarded To Joseph Callahan; Met News Men Honored

Elections Declared Void as Dean Hits Poor Student Vote

Last Term's Officers to Govern Pending Outcome of Oct. Returns

9/22/49

Student government as front-page news shown in various contexts. From the top: Loyola U., Chicago, 12/12/46, reports on the drive to bring its separate college student councils into a university-wide Student Union. Cornell U., 4/18/47, Student Council approves a new constitution which requires ratification by the student body. U. of Washington receives voting machine tally announcing election of Brock Adams—a future U.S. Senator. U. of Southern California (9/29/49) learns that it has elected its first non-fraternity student body President in 27 years. Long Island University election outcome is voided by Dean due to poor turnout. (See Pt. 2, S. 1 for Morehouse College *Maroon Tiger* columnist's commentary on the Welsh speech.)

Ellis: "I resign my position in protest of your refusal to condemn the brutal and undemocratic treatment of Czechoslovak students."

NSA Breaks with IUS over Prague Repression

IUS: "The new developments among students are paralleled among the whole people."

Editor's Note: The NSA News, *on page 1 of its March 1948 issue, reported: "On February 25 at least one student was reported killed and several wounded when police fired on 1,500 students marching to ask President Benes not to install the new government." The failure of the IUS Executive Committee to act on a series of resolutions protesting this event, which were introduced by Jim Smith (U. of Texas), the proxy for Bill Ellis (Harvard), American vice president, who was recuperating from an illness in Switzerland, led to their resignations and the ultimate suspension of further negotiations by NSA for membership in the IUS. See Blair, "NSA's Relations with the International Union of Students." p.000.*

Excerpts from four-page letter received at the NSA National Office, Madison, Wisconsin, March 11, 1948

Bill Ellis Letter of Resignation

For the American students the principle is the decisive factor, not the politics.

Mr. Grohman, President of the IUS
Mr. Madden, Secretary of the IUS

Gentlemen:

I, the American Vice-President of the IUS, resign my position in protest of your refusal to condemn the brutal and undemocratic treatment of Czechoslovak students by their government during the week of February 22, 1948. I refuse to be a partner to your dastardly non-action, your past omissions, or your future political machinations. By your non-action, you have betrayed the trust and principles of all freedom-loving students. You have betrayed the very tradition of November 17th, which was yours to cherish and defend. You are no longer worthy of that tradition.

* * *

Recalling the 1939 Nazi closing of the University

November 17th gripped the imagination of the students and peoples of the world because it was a dramatic revelation of these two facts [the importance of democratic rights and role of Nazism in their suppression].[1] On this day, it was from the professors and students, armed only in their belief in democracy and truth, that there came the first resistance against the spirit of Hitlerism. There came from the centers of learning the most effective opposition to German might when all other forces were dispersed and helpless. The Nazi answer was the execution of the student leaders of the Czech National Union, the closing of the universities and imprisonment in concentration camps of 2,000 students and professors. Is it any wonder that the students of the world could bequeath to the International Union of Students no greater treasure than the tradition of November 17th as a symbol of their ideals?

During the two years of the IUS existence, many of us have attempted to live and act according to this symbol, Nov. 17th. We have supported the rights of students and protested many incidents where such rights were violated. We protested the arrest and illegal banishment of the Greek students in March 1947, by their government, the killing and arrest of Egyptian students in 1946 by the police force, and the suppression of students' rights and academic freedom by the Kuomintang government.

Today, we have before us a similar violation of students' democratic rights in Prague, Czechoslovakia. When Mr. Klement Gottwald addressed his followers in Wenceslas Square during the week of Feb. 22, a demonstration of students began a march to Hradcany Palace to proclaim to President Benes their allegiance to the principles of Masaryck.[2] This demonstration was fired on and clubbed with rifle butts by the security police. Since then, students have been illegally arrested, student groups seized by the action committees, the National Union dissolved, professors and students who were alleged reactionaries thrown out of the universities, and faculty buildings violated.

For me, these actions assume a peculiar importance and significance to November 17, 1939....

These charges being true, Mr. [Jim] Smith, the deputy in Prague to the American Vice-President, felt compelled to submit five resolutions of protest to the IUS secretariat. You refused to take action.

The IUS put politics above principle

The reason for this refusal is obvious. All the protests heretofore issued by the IUS had two common factors. In each case the students were oppressed by the right-wing forces. However, in the case of the Czechs, the students were persecuted by a left-wing police force. The second common factor was the suppression of democratic rights. For the American students, the principle is the decisive factor, not the politics. Thus, the fact that you have refused to support Mr. Smith's resolutions, which he was honor-bound to present, means that you have acted in the past only because principle and politics coincided. Today, that is not possible. You have shown your colors.

* * *

Because so many other student organizations in other countries believe in the same principles as American students, simple withdrawal of organizations in my country is not sufficient. It is necessary that all freedom-loving student organizations proclaim their spiritual and moral unity with the actions of Czech students and their opposition to the undemocratic forces which persecuted them by no other act than disaffiliation from the IUS.

Therefore, I call on the national unions of countries such as England, France, the Scandinavian countries, Cuba, South America, and Canada to disaffiliate from the IUS. By this action at least, we can show our unity and faith in our principles. Gentlemen, I regret that for us this is a parting of the ways, the end of a great hope. The responsibility for this separation lies with you, not with me or American students.

I am,
/s/ William Ellis
Former Vice President

Excerpts from a thirteen-page letter detailing the background to the IUS and the events in Prague, sent to Bill Ellis and to Bill Welsh, March 6, 1948.

Jim Smith Explains Resignation but Also Charts a Course for American Students to "Put Their Own House in Order"

For the American students with whom you and I are concerned... the problem is what they can do, not what others can do.

Dear Bill,

In this letter I will attempt to give you a full report on the recent developments in Czech student life, which you asked me for, of the IUS reaction to these developments, and an explanation of my resignation. As you will recall I sent you a telegram Saturday night, Feb. 28, notifying you of my resignation. On Sunday morning you called from Leysin and we discussed the matter on the telephone. Following our discussion you sent your telegram of resignation to the IUS, which was received Monday. On Wednesday, I received a telegram from Bill Welsh, president of USNSA, confirming the position we had taken. I also received a telegram from Dr. Bernard Lown, of the AIMS,[3] notifying me that he wanted a full report on the whole matter, and that until such a report was received, AIMS would take no action....

* * *

Resignation is not an act of submission to isolationism or extreme conservatism

My resignation is not and must not be considered to be an act of submission to the forces of isolationism and extreme conservatism which are attempting to influence American student thought today. Although I myself will no longer be associated with the United States student movement, I believe that all American students who have stood for the principles on which you and I stand have definite tasks before them.

Primarily, their task is to put their own house in order. By that I mean that they must actively and vigorously translate the principles of NSA into a program of action at the regional and local level. Those Southern students who have not yet fought with some success for equal educational opportunities regardless of race cannot criticize the IUS for failing to fight for equal educational opportunities for Czech students regardless of political belief. Those students who have not yet fought vigorously against the banning of leftist political organizations from their campuses and for the unqualified principle [of academic freedom] cannot criticize the IUS for failing to fight for academic freedom in the Czech universities. Those American students who have not yet protested the murder and imprisonment of students in Spain, Greece, and China will have no right whatsoever to criticize the IUS for failing to protest the arrest of Prague students, and the shooting, whether accidental or otherwise, of one of them.

When the American students have built an organization that fights for students' rights and educational opportunities for all students in all countries regardless of race, religion, or political belief, then let them look at the IUS. When they are prepared to expose and attack the undemocratic effects of imperialism and fascism on student life as vigorously as they are now prepared to expose and attack the undemocratic practices of Communism such as are described in this report, then let them give instruction to the IUS. By that time the international tension may have resolved itself. Stranger things have happened. And, by that time the IUS may be prepared to stand without qualifications on those principles which you and I have believed and still believe were the principles on which it was created by the World Student Congress.

Because of your influence in American student life, I ask you to call upon American students to work in this way towards the goal of a democratic and unified world student community.

In spite of disappointment, peace can be built, if we work for it

In spite of the disappointing experiences which you and I have had in our experiment in international cooperation, I still do not believe the inevitability of a third world war. I not only still have hope for peace, I still think that peace can be built, if we are all willing to work for it. And I am absolutely convinced that if American students will go to work now to "put their house in order" they will thereby be working for peace in the most effective way open to them at the present time.

I need not add to you, Bill, that I fully realize that a great deal of work must be done by the students of Russian and Eastern European universities before we may be assured of a peaceful world. The events of the past two weeks have strongly impressed this fact on my mind. For the American students with whom you and I are concerned, however, the problem is what they can do, not what others can do. I hope you will give them my message.

Sincerely yours,
Jim Smith

Excerpts from a two-page memorandum to the National Executive Committee

NSA's Staff Supports Ellis and Smith and Confronts Its Own Constitutional Challenge

It was clear that something pretty serious had taken place in Prague

USNSA
304 North Park
Madison 5, Wis.
March 27, 1948

In a recent secretarial letter, we asked you for your opinions on the NSA-IUS situation and the action taken by the NSA Staff Committee, as indicated in the press release of March 2, 1948. The replies we have received are such as to indicate a desire for knowing the reasoning on which we based our action. Since this matter will be under discussion at the forthcoming Exec. Committee meeting, we feel that you should know in advance our thinking on the matter, in order that discussion may start on some common ground.[4]

* * *

In the pressure of the moment the Staff did overstep its prerogatives. Terminating the official relationship which has existed was sound insofar as the resignation of our interim representatives made this relationship impossible. But when we stated that "the negotiating team will not go abroad this summer," we were announcing a policy which was clearly the prerogative of the Executive Committee in accordance with the Affiliation Agreement. This Agreement states: This Congress therefore authorizes the Executive Committee of USNSA to undertake negotiations with the IUS and to guarantee maximum American participation in that organization during the coming year (including preparation and sending of an American delegation to the IUS Council meeting during the summer of 1948). In its review at the April meeting the Executive Committee should be the body to decide what action on negotiations is to be taken.[5]

(Signed)
Bill Welsh
Ralph Dungan
Bob Smith
Janice Tremper

The IUS Responds to the Resignations and Criticisms

Late in March the IUS issued a report defending its refusal to protest the treatment of students and professors by the Communists on the grounds that: the parade had been organized by National Socialists who were collaborators, and in defiance of city laws against such demonstrations; that the jailed students would be given fair trials according to Czech judicial procedure; and that the Action Committees were doing no more than applying those principles which had already been adopted by the students themselves, but which had never been put into practice. It also stated that officers of the Czech NUS had, before the coup, been charged with manipulation of elections and malfeasance of funds and stated "the IUS cannot demand the reinstatement of people against whom serious charges have been made both by the IUS and the law of the land." It also denied that Action Committee dismissals of students and professors had been based on political belief. The twenty-four-page report concluded:

> The Secretariat does not consider that the taking up of a partisan position is implied by its failure to support the resolutions of Mr. Smith. Indeed had those resolutions been supported, it would have been a much more positive indication that the IUS had set itself in opposition to the events which have recently taken place in the life of the people of Czechoslovakia.... The previous undemocratic character of the Czech NUS was related to a situation existing in the country, and similarly, the new developments among the students are paralleled by new changes among the whole people. (Jones, p.27)

EDITOR'S NOTES

[1] Ellis wrote that the two important facts are "Democratic rights mean free speech, free assembly, academic freedom and freedom from arrest without warrant" and that "the true significance of Nazism was never so clearly revealed as in the closing of the universities and the persecution of professors and students whose only crime was devotion to the spirit of truth."

[2] Chief founder and first president (1919-1935) of Czechoslovakia.

[3] The Association of Internes and Medical Students (AIMS) was also an American member organization of the IUS.

[4] *Editor's note:* The staff outlined nine points and laid out the chronology of events, the importance of both Jim Smith and Bill Ellis having joined in the action to resign, and that "It was clear that something pretty serious had taken place in Prague in IUS to warrant the action Jim had taken and recommend [sic] that we take." They laid out the legal considerations and the notification procedures—Ellis having also notified the other IUS members, the NICC, AYD, and AIMS. They underlined that in their announcement they had made clear that "the officers of the NSA" believed that the resignations precluded any further affiliation efforts and that the matter would be reviewed by the National Executive Committee in April.

[5] The April meeting of the National Executive Committee endorsed the staff action but also voted to send a fact-finding delegation to Prague that summer to report back to the First Congress at Madison that August. Its members were William Birenbaum (University of Chicago), Robert L. West (Yale), and Larry Jaffa (Yale Divinity School). See Welsh, p. 170, Blair, p. 541, and Birenbaum, pp. 583, 586. Bill Welsh also appointed two representatives, Royal Voegeli and Norman Holmes, to represent NSA at the IUS Council meeting in September. See Voegeli, p. 545, and Holmes, p. 551.

IUS Fails To Protest Murders

US Delegates Cut Ties With Prague IUS Conference

Jim Smith and Bill Ellis, American delegates to the International Union of Students at Prague,

Regional NSA Group Hits Move to Cut IUS Relations

A vehement protest against the recent resolution by the National Student Association's staff committee to sever relations with the International Union of Students was registered last night by Lawrence M. Jaffa 2D, chairman of the NSA's Northern New England Regional Division, and a member of the four-man board appointed in December to consider NSA-IUS affiliation.

The staff committee's resolution came early this month, following the resignation of two American students on the IUS executive committee at Prague, who stated that suppression of Non-Communist student activity by the newly established Czech régime made further cooperation impossible.

Jaffa's statement agreed with the staff committee's censure of the IUS for not protesting the suppression of student demonstrations in Prague at the time of the Communist coup, but questioned the right of the group to make such a move.

Commenting on reasons for his protest, Jaffa pointed out that when affiliation with IUS was first considered by the NSA last September, "it was known that the IUS leadership was, at least, pro-Soviet and, probably, Communist-dominated.

"The recent tragic events in Czechoslovakia have only proved definitely what we assumed then. Nevertheless, we still feel that if representative American students are to meet with students of other nations, we must continue to seek whatever opportunity the IUS affords to spread understanding and cooperation in the educational world."

Few Men Go to Post in College's Big Prize Derbies

Sarah Lawrence Approves Motion Urging NSA's Participation In IUS Activities

Recommends Further Student Effort For World Cooperation

By Ann Roller

duct. One student was shot in the leg. The IUS did not take any action: it was due to this lack of

Czech Crisis Forces NSA To Pull From IUS; Charges Inaction By Group

MADISON, Wis. (Special) — Two interim representives of the National Student Association to the International Union of Students in Europe have resigned their positions as a result of the failure of the IUS secretariat to condemn the action of the present Czechoslovakian government with regard to the treatment of students in Prague.

The NSA Staff has confirmed the position taken by its representatives in condemning the action of the IUS secretar-

Election For NU Board To Board Tomorrow

University of Buffalo students will elect a Board of Managers of Norton Union on Tuesday, March 16 and Wednesday, March 17. The polls will be open from 9:30 to 4:30 each day.

The Schools of Arts and Sciences and Business Administration each will elect two men and two women represent-

The NSA News

Official Publication of the United States National Student Association

Madison, Wisconsin — March, 1948

US Student Voice Heard at UNESCO

American college students were represented at the fourth meeting of the U. S. national commission for UNESCO in Washington in February by two executive officers of NSA.

Bob Smith, vice-president in charge of international activities, represented the association at the conference and was accompanied by Ralph Dungan, vice-president

Seven Educators Accept Advisory Council Positions

Seven nationally recognized ex-

Staff Supports Smith, Ellis On Repudiation of IUS

Representatives Resign as Abuse Of Prague Students Is Unprotested

The NSA News

Official Publication of the United States National Student Association

Madison, Wisconsin — March, 1948

Executive Body Ends IUS Talks

Madison Is Site For '48 Congress

The first annual Congress of NSA will be held on the campus of the University of Wisconsin in Madison, it was agreed at the Executive Committee meeting in Chicago last week.

Madison was also the site of the constitutional convention of the association last summer.

Staff Plans Executive Convo Agenda

Votes to Suspend Affiliation Deal By 21-3 Ballot

The Executive Committee of NSA voted 21 to 3 to suspend negotiations for affiliation with the IUS.

Welsh Advocates

"FOR US THIS IS . . . THE END OF A GREAT HOPE." Bill Ellis's closing words spoke for the deep disappointment shared by the many U.S. students who had worked in these early years of the Cold War to find a way to maintain a connection with students in the Communist world. The repression of students and faculty in Czechoslovakia, and the NSA reponse was reported in *NSA News* (3/48 and 4/48 above) and widely in the college student press (left, clockwise from top: 3/2/48 *Columbia Spectator*, 3/13/48 *Harvard Crimson*, 12/15/48 Sarah Lawrence *Campus*, 3/15/48 U. of Buffalo *Argus*).

College presidents and deans throughout the United States are asked, "Just who is going to run it?"

The Economic Club of Detroit Challenges NSA

Is affiliation with the IUS a "blank check" to deliver the colleges to the Communists?
The NSA Staff responds: "The USNSA will not be a haven for subversive groups"

Excerpts from "Challenging Questions Which Have Been Thrust upon Our Colleges & Universities," by Allen B. Crow, President, Economic Club of Detroit, October 1, 1947

Editor's note: Throughout the history of college student organizations there have been private individuals and organizations that have undertaken roles as watchdogs or advocates to assure that these groups would not be subverted by unsavory or alien ideologies. One such prewar group, noted in Section 1 of the Prologue, was the National Republic (p. 48). When NSA was formed, the same task was undertaken by the Economic Club of Detroit, led by its president, Allen B. Crow.

Crow prepared a detailed, eight-page Q&A in Socratic form (portions of which are reproduced here), raising questions about NSA's organizational, financial, and political viability. It was mailed to college administrators throughout the country in October 1947, just following the NSA Constitutional Convention.

Crow's action had a significant negative affect on NSA's organizing effort. In his essay in this section, Bill Welsh describes the staff response (a portion of which is reproduced here) and his and Ralph Dungan's appearances before the group in Detroit.[1]

CHALLENGING QUESTIONS WHICH HAVE BEEN THRUST UPON OUR COLLEGES AND UNIVERSITIES BY THE ORGANIZING CONVENTION OF THE UNITED STATES NATIONAL STUDENT ASSOCIATION

Recently held at Madison, Wisconsin, August 30 to September 9, 1947

[Questions I and II concerned the method and conduct of NSA Constitution ratification.]

III. SHOULD THE CONSTITUTION AND BY-LAWS OF THE NSA BE RATIFIED?

A. YES

1. Because it provides an instrument through which all the students who are now enrolled in the colleges and universities of the United States may actively participate in the processes of democratic self-government thereby becoming currently informed and technically trained, in practical methods, whereby they may more largely assume their own responsibilities of citizenship on the campus, as well as in the national and international affairs of the United States and other nations of the world.

B. NO

1. Because it provides a vehicle through which the Communist controlled International Union of Students, the World Federation of Democratic Youth, the World Youth Congress and affilliated national and international bodies having their headquarters for the most part in Prague, Czechoslovakia, may convert every college and university in the United States into an incubator where Communists may hatch among both students and faculty their totalitarian ideas and may establish favorable contacts for their fellow travelers to infiltrate and to further promote their already well advanced program for world domination.

IV. SHOULD THE BUDGET OF THE NSA BE APPROVED AND THE ASSESSMENT PAID WHICH HAS BEEN LEVIED AGAINST EACH PARTICIPATING COLLEGE OR UNIVERSITY?

A. YES

1. Subversive influences are already well organized and at work within many of our colleges and universities throughout the United States. Probably the best way to fight Communism is to bring it out into the open where all of our people will be able to learn of the scope of its program and may observe both the personnel and methods of its operations.

2. Although it is not possible at this time to ascertain the full extent of either the ultimate income or of the expenses of NSA, the only way to launch this program undoubtedly would be to proceed upon the basis of the figures which the recent Organizing Convention at Madison and the Executive Committee have adopted.

B. NO

1. Unless the NSA becomes incorporated whereby any financial liabilities to be assumed by each of its participating member institutions will be specifically limited...each member institution may be liable for any and all debts of the organization as a whole.[2]

2. The experience of the officers of the NSA and the supervision which is provided in its Constitution and By-Laws do not justify the placing of large sums of money in the hands of its officers and committeemen who may thereby be encouraged to malfeasance or misfeasance in the handling of such funds.

V. SHOULD THE RECOMMENDATIONS OF THE THREE PANELS OR COMMISSIONS BE RATIFIED?

A. The Panel or Commission on ACADEMIC FREEDOM

1. YES

Our colleges have no right, particularly if they are tax-supported institutions, to rule any individual or group off the campus who is eligible to seek election and to hold office under our form of government.

2. NO

This section is designed to throw the support of the entire NSA to the American Youth for Democracy and other Communist and subversive groups in their efforts to promote their activities on and off the campus without the interference or supervision from the administrative authorities of our American colleges and universities.

C. The Panel or Commission on RACIAL DISCRIMINATION

1. YES

a) Our Declaration of Independence sets forth, "We hold these truths to be self-evident, that all men are created equal, that they are endowed by their Creator with certain unalienable rights, that among these are life, liberty and the pursuit of happiness."

b) The Constitution of the United States guarantees that, "Congress shall (a) make no law respecting an establishment of religion, or prohibiting the free exercise thereof; or abridging the freedom of speech, or of the press; or the right of the people peaceably to assemble, and to petition the Government for a redress of grievances."

2. NO

(a) This section is the result of agitation by Communists to gain favor with Negro, Jewish and other racial, industrial and social groups here in the United States, as they have for years in almost every other country around the world, by promoting strife and confusion, to serve their own ends. Ample evidence of this is found in the case of the movement which was started by them to establish a Negro Soviet Republic in certain of our Southern states as well as the revolutions they have launched to stir up the natives under the slogans "White supremacy is a thing of the past" and "Henceforth the world will be ruled by the colored races," in other parts of the world.

C. [sic]The Panel or Commission on the AFFILIATION WITH THE INTERNATIONAL UNION OF STUDENTS WITH HEADQUARTERS AT PRAGUE, CZECHOSLOVAKIA.

1. YES

(a) The proposals for affiliation with the IUS are so limited as to the time and extent to which they may become operative, that the NSA may become an agency whereby the leaven of democracy may begin to work behind the Iron Curtain among the youth of all the colleges and universities, who are the hope of the world.

2. NO

(a) The Netherlands, New Zealand, Switzerland, and Austrian delegations already have all withdrawn from the IUS after repeated efforts to cooperate because they have found it entirely under Communist control.

(b) The language of the Constitution and By-Laws as well as the Reports of the Commissions of the NSA is so ambiguous that the full scope of their impact and implications upon the established policies and traditions of our American educational institutions will probably be discovered only after they have been put to the acid test of experience in operation and after the Communists have gained their objectives through infiltrating their totalitarian ideas more completely among the colleges and universities throughout the United States.

(c) The fact that the permanent headquarters of the IUS has been established in Prague, Czechoslovakia, and that its activities have been largely supported and subsidized by the Czech government and their undisclosed sources assures us that the IUS is under Communist domination.

* * *

(g) How can an unbiased and fair report be given to the next convention of the NSA concerning the objectives, policies and program of the IUS, if the four or more who are to be appointed on the Investigating Committee on the IUS which was provided by the recent Organizing Convention of the NSA are already pledged to full participation by the NSA with the IUS?

(h) What are Jim Smith, former Chairman of the Interim Committee of the NSA, and his wife going to do for the IUS in Prague, Czechoslovakia, between now and the next meeting of the United States National Student Congress and why were they selected for this job?

VI. SHOULD NOT THESE OTHER PROBLEMS WHICH WILL BE INVOLVED IN SUPERVISING THE ADMINISTRATION OF THE NSA BY ITS OFFICERS AND EXECUTIVE COMMITTEE BE TAKEN INTO CONSIDERATION BY ALL THE COLLEGES AND UNIVERSITIES OF THE UNITED STATES BEFORE THEY RATIFY THE CONSTITUTION AND BY-LAWS OF THE UNITED STATES NSA?

A. The National Headquarters of the NSA has been established by the Convention at Madison, Wisconsin. It subsequently has been reported, however, that the employed officers of the NSA including its President, Vice President on Domestic Affairs, and its Secretary are to operate out of Chicago, its Treasurer out of Buffalo, and its Vice President in Charge of International Affairs out of Harvard.[3] If this is to be the case, where and in whose name are all funds of the NSA to be deposited and who is to be authorized to sign all the checks withdrawing any money from the Treasury of the NSA?

B. Upon whose specific written approval and authorization will all bills of the NSA be paid?

C. Are the Treasurer and all other officers to serve under bonds? If so, just what will the bonds cover and in what amount?

D. Whose responsibility is it to see that all income and expenditures will be handled strictly in accordance with sound business principles and the budget which was adopted at the Organizing Convention recently held at Madison, Wisconsin?

[Items E-G deal with additional issues of accountability. H asks if "there is to be a National Publication" to keep members informed. I-J questions U.S. distribution of the IUS publication *World Student News*.]

K. Is the National Student Association designed to provide an instrument for mass thinking, crowd psychology, group pressures and political manipulations at the expense of independent and creative thinking as a basis for group cooperation which is the main function of education?

L. Considering the rivalry which has already developed among certain groups for representation and control in both the NSA and the IUS, is there not a probability that these organizations will inject elements of discord and strife rather than encourage the pursuit of culture and cooperation in the attainment of our highest ideals of American citizenship among the student bodies, the faculties and the administrative boards of our institutions of higher education?

With both the Communist and the Catholic groups so well organized and articulate in both the NSA and the IUS, what steps should other groups take to secure and maintain similar representation as well as a proper balance of power?

M. The NSA in its Constitution and By-Laws and in all its other declarations places the emphasis entirely upon the rights and privileges of those who are now enjoying the benefits of our institutions of higher education. It has made no reference whatever to the responsibilities and duties which these same students should assume by way of cooperation either while in school or following graduation....

* * *

[Item N concerns screening of students for study-abroad programs.]

O. Has not the U.S. NSA already been used to propagandize and to bring pressure whereby the students of our American colleges and universities, in accordance with the pattern which has been established in socialized European countries, will look increasingly to various agencies of our own government to pay for their tuition and living expenses....

This point of view constitutes quite a recent and a radical departure from our fundamental conception that it is the primary responsibility of each American to pay his own way and to provide for the advancement of himself and his family....

P. Since the following four items heretofore have been considered to be of paramount importance in the time available to the students of our American colleges and universities—

1. From their own earnings or from the gifts of parents or others, to provide sufficient income to COVER THEIR LIVING AND OTHER EXPENSES while in college.

2. THE ATTAINMENT OF PASSING GRADES OR BETTER, to insure final graduation with the other members of their class.

3. Participation on the campus in such EXTRA-CURIRICULAR ACTIVITIES as have been approved and recognized as most worthwhile by the entire student body, as well as by the college and university authorities.

4. The pursuit and ultimate capture of a mate for MARRIAGE.

—just how is the above sequence in priority now to be changed so that our students will be able adequately to take care of all the affairs and interests of the U.S. National Student Association and the International Union of Students, within their already crowded schedules and without unduly sacrificing the other main educational objectives for which they have come to college?

[Items: Q, R, and S delve into greater detail on matters concerning linkage of NSA with domestic and international Communist influence. T asks, IS NOT THE AFFILIATION OF THE UNITED STATES NSA WITH THE IUS JUST ANOTHER GAME OF GIVE-AND-TAKE, WITH US HERE IN THE UNITED STATES BEING GULLIBLE AS USUAL, BY DOING ALL THE GIVING AND THE COMMUNISTS AS IN THE PAST SMART ENOUGH TO DO ALL THE TAKING?]

U. Are you among the rapidly increasing number of our citizens, on the campuses of our American colleges and universities, as well as off the campus, who are becoming very much interested in ascertaining **WHO ARE THE INDIVIDUALS, ORGANIZATIONS AND GOVERNMENTS THAT HAVE BEEN PROVIDING UP TO THIS TIME THE FINANCIAL SUPPORT** TO COVER ALL THE COSTS OF THE EXPANDING PROGRAMS OF THE INTERNATIONAL UNION OF STUDENTS, WORLD FEDERATION OF DEMOCRATIC YOUTH, WORLD YOUTH CONGRESS, WORLD STUDENT NEWS, AMERICAN YOUTH FOR DEMOCRACY AND THE NATIONAL STUDENT ASSOCIATION, THROUGHOUT THE UNITED STATES AS WELL AS ABROAD?

The above "CHALLENGING QUESTIONS" are respectfully submitted personally, as a basis for further investigation and study by students, faculties, officers, administrative boards, alumni, taxpayers, benefactors, parents and any others who are concerned in promoting the best interests of our American educational institutions and of their personnel.

Allen B. Crow
President
The Economic Club of Detroit
920 Detroit Free Press Building
Detroit 26, Michigan
October 1, 1947

EDITOR'S NOTES

[1] Correspondence the editors found in college archives corroborates its behind-the-scenes impact and how seriously it was taken by administrators. One such exchange is cited below. (*Source:* University of Chicago Library.)

THE UNIVERSITY OF CHICAGO

October 4, 1947

To: Mr. E. C. Colwell, Central Administration

Fr: Robert M. Strozier, Dean of Students

I should like to arrange a conference with you and Mr. Harrison for Mr. Bergstresser and me to discuss with you the National Student Association. We have made no commitment about payment of dues from the University of Chicago to this organization, although we think the document circulated by the Economic Club of Detroit is only in part true.

THE UNIVERSITY OF CHICAGO

October 25, 1947

To: Mr. E.C. Colwell,

Mr. R.W. Harrison, Central Administration

Fr: Robert M. Strozier, Dean of Students

Last Christmas, Mr. Bergstresser and I aided a mid-western committee of students in calling a National Student Organizational meeting at the University of Chicago. We were well impressed by the organization and their Continuation Committee was furnished office space in the Reynolds Club during the spring.

During the summer a constitutional meeting was held at. . . the University of Wisconsin. . . . [We] have kept in close touch with this organization to assure ourselves that it was not politically flavored and that it was truly representative of all of the colleges and universities throughout the United States.

Recently a document concerning this organization has been circulated by Allen B. Crow, President of the Economic Club of Detroit, which I understand is an important club of financiers in that city....[We] will, of course, continue to keep our ear to the ground, but I felt you both should be informed about an issue which might become controversial on a somewhat larger scale.

THE UNIVERSITY OF CHICAGO

October 30, 1947

To: Mr. Robert M. Strozier

Fr: E.C. Colwell

Re: National Student Association

Thank you for sending me the NSA Questionnaire. It brings one question to my mind—whether the University of Chicago should pay fees to an organization such as this.

[2] The 1966 "USNSA Codification of Policy" records the following resolution on incorporation adopted by the nineteenth National Student Congress in 1966:

> WHEREAS, the United States National Student Association has been incorporated as a District of Columbia not for profit corporation; and
>
> WHEREAS, the Constitution and By-Laws and Rules of USNSA, an incorporated association, have been adopted collectively as the interim By-Laws of the corporation until the first meeting of the members;
>
> NOW, THEREFORE, the members of USNSA at their first meeting hereby resolve:
>
> That the Constitution and By-Laws and all Rules enacted in accordance therewith which heretofore have served as the Constitution, By-Laws and Rules of USNSA, an unincorporated association, and which have been adopted as the Interim By-Laws of USNSA, a not for profit corporation, collectively shall constitute and hereby are adopted as the permanent By-Laws of said corporation.

[3] In point of fact the headquarters was established in Madison as intended, while the international office was opened in Cambridge, MA. Lee Jones, elected treasurer, returned to Buffalo as his base, while Mildred Kiefer was appointed assistant treasurer to supervise daily operations in Madison (Wurf, p. 180).

NSA STAFF Responds

Late in October of 1947, NSA's staff circulated a statement to the National Executive Committee and others. Excerpts from an undated copy appear here. (See also Bill Welsh's narrative on the Economic Club of Detroit, p. 168.)

STATEMENT CONCERNING THE HISTORY AND PRESENT STATUS OF THE RELATIONSHIP BETWEEN THE USNSA AND MR. ALLEN B. CROW, PRESIDENT OF THE ECONOMIC CLUB OF DETROIT.

From the beginning of the development of the USNSA, Mr. Crow has shown intense interest in the student movement and especially as it has developed in the United States. Throughout the past year he has accumulated much material relating to the Chicago Student Conference, the National Continuations Committee, the Madison Constitutional Convention, the USNSA, and groups and individuals who have been associated with the aforementioned. Mr. Crow corresponded with educators, businessmen, newspapers, etc. regarding the proposed National Student Association. He corresponded and spoke with members and representatives of the National Continuations Committee relative to the issues and programs of the Constitutional Convention.

Because of the interest shown by Mr. Crow, Bill Welsh, NSA President, in a letter to Mr. Crow immediately after the Convention (Sept. 11) explained briefly the decision of the Convention regarding IUS. He also volunteered to present further information at any time. As a result of this letter Bill Welsh, Ralph Dungan, NSA Vice-president, and Harvey Weisberg, Michigan Regional Chairman, were invited to speak on Oct. 7 to the Industry and Education Cooperation Section of the Economic Club of Detroit.

The three topics of discussion were:

(1) Should the Constitution adopted at this NSA Convention be ratified by all the colleges and universities of the United States?

(2) What does the NSA propose to do

(a) about Academic Freedom?

(b) about Racial Discrimination?

(3) Should the NSA join the International Union of Students, which has headquarters at Prague, Czechoslovakia?

On Oct. 1, 1947, Mr. Crow personally published a list of questions with possible answers on two sides. The intent of these questions was to provide "a basis of further investigation and study by students, faculties, officers, administrative boards, alumni, taxpayers, benefactors, parents and any others who are concerned in protecting the best interests of our American educational institutions and their personnel."

We understand that these letters have been given rather wide national circulation and we feel that members of the Executive Committee and others who are vitally concerned should know our reactions to them.

Fourteen additional points of discussion were included in a letter of Oct. 14 from Mr. Crow to Bill Welsh. These 14 points pertain to the possible affiliation of the USNSA with the IUS. Comments on these 14 points are also included in the following statement.

Because so many of the questions raised by Mr. Crow . . . highlight discussions of the Constitutional Convention, it might be valuable to restate the factual material on these points in such a way that this resume may be permanently included with your reference files.

* * *

[Editor's note: Following the foregoing, the staff then provided two pages of response and discussion of the issues raised by Allen Crow, citing NSA's Constitution and By-Laws, which appear here in the Appendix along with digests of the policy reports coming out of the Constitutional Convention. The staff noted that "The responsibility of students to their country and their community is one of the underlying principles on which were based the USNSA Constitution, By-Laws, resolutions, and many discussions of the Constitutional Convention." Preceding a clarification of the nature of NSA's interest in IUS, the staff noted, "The USNSA has been obliged since its inception to lay much greater stress on the question of affiliation with IUS than is warranted by its relation to the total program of NSA." The staff statement closed with the following paragraph.]

We are sincerely anxious to receive questions and comments on our organization when it is apparent that they are meant to be constructive in their approach. Therefore we encourage everyone who may be interested in our work to write to us. We appreciate the help and extend our thanks to those many educators, students, and businessmen who have been honest and sincere in their efforts to aid us in forming this new organization. We are hopeful that we shall be able to fulfill the trust that they have placed in us.

Americanism Called Only Aim of New Student Group

DET. NEWS 10-8-47

THE NEWLY-ORGANIZED National Student Association has taken no stand on any "ism" except Americanism, its president declared here Tuesday.

Speaking before the industry and education co-operation section of the Economic Club, William Welsh, of Berea College, its head, said that NSA is "truly American in action." Stress will be on American ideals and fostering academic freedom and race and religious tolerance, he continued.

Welsh, Harvey Welsberg, of College, Philadelphia, emphasized that the NSA has not yet affiliated with the acknowledgedly Red-dominated International Union of Students at Prague.

Four negotiating members will be selected to go to Prague next summer, Dungan explained. They will be given training first. No affiliation can take place, he added, for a year or more and then only by a two-thirds vote.

Meanwhile, he continued, the NSA will work with the International Union of Students on a co-operating basis." Such co-operation, he assured, would be on an educational nonpolitical level.

As for the possibility of Communists working into the NSA convention, the speakers asserted that could only come about if a Communist student were selected by a college student council or a campus vote.

Weisberg told the audience that many of the rights given Americans under the Bill of Rights are incorporated in the constitution of NSA, which is to be ratified by member student bodies within nine months.

NSA Campaign at Radcliffe to Begin

"International Students Day" on November 17 will mark the beginning of a week-long drive to win Radcliffe ratification of the new National Student Association's Constitution, delegates to Sunday's Barnard conference of women's college NSA leaders have announced.

Sussanne Ehrenthell '48 and Alice Gilbert '49 told the eight-school meeting that they already have a group of 46 working for NSA projects here. On the basis of this they advocated the superimposing of NSA activities on the student government structure through the creation of another vice-presidency.

Bombshell at the Barnard sessions was the warning of Communists sent to college presidents and newspapers by one Allan Crow.

All-Campus Rally To Be Held by NSA

In an effort to acquaint students with the aims, organization and activities of the National Student Association, an all campus NSA rally will be held at 8:30 p.m. tomorrow at Rackham Lecture Hall.

William Welsh, national president of the association, will open the rally with a plea for ratification of the new NSA constitution. Written early this fall by student delegates to a convention held at the University of Wiscon-

NSA relationships with the International Union of Students, a topic which provoked heated discussion at the convention, will be outlined by Ralph A. Dungan, vice-president in charge of National Affairs, from St. Joseph's College, Philadelphia.

Harvey Weisberg, president of the Student Legislature, will clarify NSA policies regarding racial discrimination, in education, and academic freedom.

Chairman of the rally will be Erich A. Walter, director of the Office of Student Affairs.

The three speakers appeared yesterday at a luncheon sponsored by the Economic Club of Detroit where Tom King, Men's Advisor at Michigan State College told the group that NSA potential- that the recent convention "was ities were surprisingly great and the most democratic group of its kind" he had seen.

NSA-IUS Bond Explained by Dungan, Welsh

Officers Define Aims Of National Group

The National Student Association is no rabble rousing, flag waving or "radical liberal" organization, Ralph Dungan, national vice-president of NSA told a student audience last night at the Rackham lecture hall.

CONFRONTING CRITICS AT THEIR OWN TABLE. Bill Welsh and Ralph Dungan's visit to Detroit was widely reported in the region (*Detroit News* 10/8/47, top left), and on the nearby U. of Michigan campus in Ann Arbor (*Michigan Daily*, 10/8 and 10/10/47). The impact of the letters sent by the Club to college presidents around the country was felt on a number of campuses (see preceding Background piece) and was illustrated by the 10/14/47 *Harvard Crimson* notice of the Radcliffe NSA affiliation campaign and the "Bombshell" impact of the Crow letter at a conference of 46 women's college NSA leaders held at Barnard College.

(Clippings courtesy Bentley Historical Library, U. of Michigan)

Staff, Advisers, Regional Chairs

1947-48 National Organization

As listed in the Program, the Report of the Constitutional Convention and the Staff Report to the 1948 Congress
A list of colleges attending the Constitutional Convention appears at the close of Section 4.

NATIONAL OFFICERS

President
William B. Welsh, Berea College, Kentucky

Vice President, National Student Affairs
Ralph Dungan, St. Joseph's College, Pennsylvania

Vice President, International Student Affairs
Robert S. Smith, Yale University

Secretary
Janis C. Tremper, Rockford College, Illinois

Treasurer
Leeland N. Jones, Jr., University of Buffalo

Assistant Treasurer
Mildred Kiefer, University of California, Berkeley

Acting *NSA News* Editor
Robert Smollen, University of Wisconsin

REGIONAL REPRESENTATIVES AND MEMBERS OF THE NATIONAL EXECUTIVE COMMITTEE

(From the "Report of the Constitutional Convention." Revisions to the committee in Spring 1948 are in parentheses.)

Ark., N.Mex., So. Colo.
Jack Wharton
New Mexico Highlands University (N/A)

Connecticut, Rhode Island
Robert L. West
Yale University

Calif., Nev., Hawaii
Richard Heggie
University of California, Berkeley
Dick Hough
University of California, Los Angeles
(Jack Knox,
Occidental College)

Georgia, Alabama, Florida
C. Ray Martin
University of Alabama
(Al Newton
Georgia Institute of Technology)

Great Northwest
Norm Israel
University of Washington

Illinois
Samuel Golden
University of Chicago
Brian J. Buckley
Loyola University

Indiana
Dennis Trueblood
Indiana State Teachers College

Iowa
Terrence J. Rooney
University of Dubuque
(Beverly Bond
Grinnell College)

Kentucky, Tennessee
Rosemary Herre
Ursuline College
(James Harpster
Christian Brothers College)

La., Miss., Ark.
Lloyd G. Teekell
Louisiana State University

Md., Del., D.C.
Joseph Zebley
University of Baltimore

Me., N.H, Vt., Mass. (Northern New England)
Lawrence Jaffa
Harvard Divinity School
Mimi Haskell
Smith College
(William Tracy
Springfield College)

Minnesota
Norris Erdal
St. Olaf College

Metropolitan New York
Walter Wallace
Columbia University
Eugene Schwartz
City College of New York

Michigan
Harvey J. Weisberg
University of Michigan
Carl Weideman, Jr.
University of Michigan

Mo., Nebr., Kans.
Pat Groom
Maryville College

New Jersey
John Yewell
Rutgers University

New York State
Frank Dowd
University of Rochester

North Dakota, South Dakota
Gloria Crews
North Dakota Agricultural College

Ohio
James L. Gallagher
John Carroll University
Leslie Forney
Ohio State University

Pennsylvania
James T. Harris
LaSalle College
Robert Troxell
Pennsylvania State College
(William Heckler
Temple University)

Texas, Okla.
Leo S. Goodman
University of Texas
(Dick Brickley
Texas Christian University)

Utah, Wyo., No. Colo. (Rocky Mountain)
Len Perlmutter
University of Colorado
(I. John Olsen
Colorado A&M)

Va., W.Va., N.Car., S.Car.
Herman Baker
University of North Carolina
Leon C. Thompson
Virginia State College

Wisconsin
George Capwell
Pioneer State Teachers College
(Lynn Giese
University of Wisconsin)

NATIONAL ADVISORY COUNCIL

R. O. Johnson
Assistant Director, Project for Adult Negro Education, U.S. Office of Education

Lawrence Duggan
Director, Institute of International Education

Rev. Vincent J. Flynn
President, College of St. Thomas, Minnesota

Dean Newhouse
Dean of Students, University of Washington

Helen White
Professor of English, University of Wisconsin

Homer Rainey
President, Stephens College, Missouri

Gordon Klopf
Student Personnel Director, University of Wisconsin

Monroe E. Deutsch
University of California, Berkeley

1948

The Berlin Airlift is launched and State of Israel is formed *South Pacific* opens and Joe Louis retires

Mahatma Gandhi is assassinated and Klement Gottwald is elected president of Czechoslovakia after a coup d'état by the Communists. Chiang Kai-shek is reelected president of China, and the Jewish state of Israel comes into existence. The Berlin Airlift begins in response to the Soviet blockade of Berlin. Harry S. Truman is elected for a full term after filling out Franklin Roosevelt's fourth term after the latter's death in 1945. Thomas Merton's *Seven-Storey Mountain*, Alan Payton's *Cry the Beloved Country*, Norman Mailer's *The Naked and the Dead,* and James Michener's *South Pacific* are published. Tennessee Williams's *Summer and Smoke* appears. During the year, 135 million paperbacks sold, marking a resurgence of book publishing. Film classics appear: *The Red Shoes*, *Oliver Twist*, *The Naked City*, *Bicycle Thief.* Cole Porter's *Kiss Me Kate* opens in New York City. High on the charts are "All I Want for Christmas Is My Two Front Teeth" and "Buttons and Bows." The Porsche 356 is introduced in Germany by Frederick Porsche. The 200-inch Mt. Palomar telescope is dedicated. Babe Ruth dies, and Joe Louis retires. The Selective Service Act provides for a continuing military draft, which will last until 1973. Citation wins the Triple Crown. Michigan trounces Southern California, 49-0. Cleveland wins the World Series 4-2 over Boston.

Source: Adapted from citations in Bernard Grun, *The Timetables of History* (Simon and Schuster, 1991)

USNSA OPERATING STATEMENT,
(Til May 1948) Fiscal year to date

Income	
Membership dues	15,212.00
Donations	100.00
Publication Sales	680.61
Advertising	89.98
Sale of mailing list	24.00
Harvard I.A.C.	24.56
Cambridge receipts	24.16
Travel pool	4.50
Total Income	15.647.28

Expenses	
Salaries - Officers	7,202.00
Secretary	645.29
Secretarial help	317.23
Rent	495.00
Travel	1,621.17
Office supplies	781.96
Postage	1,218.43
Telephone and telegraph	388.46
Printing and pictures	2,118.63
Magzines and subscriptions	55.55
Clipping services	45.45
NCC Expenses	492.46
Moving and transportation	25.85
Bank service charge	23.66
Publications purchased	50.45
Rent of meeting room	40.00
Canada - US Fund	41.39
Conference registration	24.30
Accounting services	60 00
Total expenses	16,159.8
Net loss	512.5

USNSA BUDGET FOR THE YEAR 1947-1948 (adopted by the Consitutional Convention 9-7-47, and revised by NEC 12-27-27)

Budget Item	CC	NEC Revison
Officers salaries	$12,000	11,000
Secretarial help	8,500	4,400
Office rental	2,400	1,400
Travel	5,000	5,000
Postage	500	2,450
Telephone-telegraph	600	1,150
Printing	3,000	5,000
Office equipment	1,944	3,044
Magazines and periodicals	200	200
Press clipping service	200	200
Miscellaneous	500	1,000
Total	$34,844	$36,844

INVENTORY OF USNSA OFFICE EQUIPMENT

6 desks and chairs

5 typewriters

1 electric mimeograph machine

1 wire recorder

1 hand addressograph and file

2 steel filing cases

1 adding machine

6 desk lamps

3 metal wastepaper cans

BUDGETING NSA'S MILESTONES: 1947-48

Membership dues were the principal source of revenue to support a modest budget that relied on considerable unpaid effort from among student volunteers nationally and from student government infrastructures locally. For a budget of $36,000—of which one-third was for $2,000/yr full-time officer's salaries—300 member colleges would have to pay an average of $120/yr each in dues out of an annual range of from $20 (under 300 students) to $240 (over 10,000 students). Staff relied on assistance from the University of Wisconsin's student financial adviser's office for its accounting. Budgets and dues structure were adopted by the National Student Congress and monitored by the National Executive Committee, which consisted of the heads of NSA's 25 regions.

(Document sources: SHSW archives, Sylvia Bacon. Reproduced here are portions of mimeographed NEC and Congress reports).

SECTION 6

NSA's Second Year, 1948-49

CONTENTS

The great NSA affiliation battles on the major university campuses had been fought during the previous year—some won (Yale, Stanford, Wisconsin, UCLA, U. of Washington) and some lost (Indiana U., LSU, U. of Texas, U. of New Mexico), some adopted handily (Harvard, Columbia, U. of Michigan, U. of Wisconsin, U. of Louisville), and some vetoed by administrations (Georgetown, USC). When the new staff arrived there were close to 300 member colleges, an active but uneven regional structure, marginal cash flow, and increasing visibility in the higher education community. Their challenge, described by Dick Heggie (UC Berkeley), 1948-49 Vice President for Student Affairs, was to continue to build the organization and the foundations for its national and international programs.

The Catholic colleges affiliated in good numbers, and one of their leaders, Ted Harris (LaSalle College, Pennsylvania) was elected President. Heggie, later to pursue a career in international relations, recalls how the group of six young people who had not earlier known each other came together, organized their programs and, like the staffs before and after them, forged lifetime bonds of friendship.

Ted Harris advanced the Association's vision of building strong student government—emphasizing responsibilities along with rights—articulated in his address to the Association of American Colleges.

Foundations laid for extensive array of domestic programs

Heggie describes the foundations laid for the organization's cultural programs, purchase card discount program, human relations and student leadership training sessions, as well as the system of "subcommissions" that enabled campus student leaders to undertake responsibility for specific projects (e.g., the Symphony Forum at San Francisco State, Student Government Survey, College of New Rochelle). Helen Jean Rogers (Mundelein College, Chicago), National Secretary, kept a weekly newsletter going, as had her predecessor Janis Tremper.

Allan Ostar (Pennsylvania State College), NSA Public Relations Director, describes the development of *NSA News* as a national intercollegiate newspaper. Later to become President of the Association of State Colleges and Universities, Ostar looks back on his World War II infantry experience and his lifetime in higher education.

Gene Schwartz (City College of New York), Vice President for Educational Affairs, recalls growing up in New York City during the Depression years, and the optimism and the spirit of the times after the war — the pervading belief that students could help build a better world. Schwartz also recalls how far they had yet to go when restaurant service in Cleveland was refused to NSA President Ted Harris and his colleagues, because Harris was black.

Three vignettes of officer travels to colleges around the country provide anecdotes on the varied receptions and challenges the fledgling organization faced on different campuses and in different regions.

The First Congress, with the theme, "The Student in the University Community," drew 550 delegates and observers from 295 colleges.

INCOMING AND OUTGOING NSA PRESIDENTS Ted Harris (LaSalle College, PA) and Bill Welsh (Berea College, KY) pass the baton at the end of NSA's first Congress in 1948. (SHSW)

1948-1949 ALBUM

Summer Edition
Daily Cardinal
Complete Campus Coverage
University of Wisconsin, Madison, Thursday, August 19, 1948 Free Copy

...gins Today
...nds; NSA Congress Opens Monday

NATIONAL STUDENT ASSOCIATION

National Student Congress

AUG. 23 - 28

University of Wisconsin at Madison

. . .

Security Council Recalled To Avert New Palestine War

From left: University of Wisconsin Campus; NSA Announcement (SHSW); *Daily Cardinal* 8/19/48; Congress Plenary Session (SHSW), staff photo (*Hugh R. Wallin*, Schwartz); Helen Jean Rogers, NSA Secretary-Treasurer, at NSA offices (Heggie).

SECOND YEAR NATIONAL STAFF Clockwise from top, left: Eugene G. Schwartz (CCNY), V.P. Educational Problems; Robert L. West (Yale U.), V.P. International Affairs; Richard G. Heggie (UC Berkeley), V.P. Student Life; Allan W. Ostar (Penn State), Public Relations Director; James T. Harris, Jr. (LaSalle C., PA), President; Helen Jean Rogers (Mundelein C., IL), Secretary-Treasurer.

Consolidating Membership

THE FIRST CONGRESS opened NSA's second year, electing a staff (above right) headed by James T. Harris, Jr. (La Salle College, seated center), whose task was to consolidate the gains made by Bill Welsh and his staff.

Exec Committee Hits Fear, Hysteria As Dangers to Academic Freedom

The NSA News
Official Publication of the United States National Student Association
MADISON, WISCONSIN, APRIL, 1949

Opposes Firing on Basis Of Political Affiliations

Congress Features Student Gov't Training Program

NEC Gets the 'Beat Look'

Harris Answers Charge Of Unconstitutionality

Vol. II, No. 2 MADISON, WISCONSIN, NOVEMBER, 1948

NSA to Place DP Students

50 Colleges Adopt Purchase Card Plan

Groups Establish Secretariat

Area Committees Increased to Six

An Experiment

To Students Of the World

MADISON, WISCONSIN, MARCH, 1949

...SA Calls for Civilian G.I. Bill

Minnesota Art Exhibit Goes on Tour

Need and Ability Criteria for Aid

...Committee ...Evaluate NSA ...Ohio Meeting

Clinics Study Student Government

Spring Programs
Regions Sponsor Culturales

Regional Program Use Many New Techniques

By HELEN JEAN ROGERS

N.Y. State Festival Features 'Joe College'

...NNER Holds Mammoth Fete

Minn. Publishes Literary Magazine

Policies and programs were featured in *NSA News* (above,, 4/49, 11/48 headlining WWII Displaced Persons program, 3/49, 5/49)

National and International Affairs

Columbia Daily Spect...
FOUNDED 1877
MONDAY, NOVEMBER 22, 1948

NSA to Institute Purchase Cards

Schools Will Name All CUSC Proxies

Barnard Gals Give Carnival For Stude Pals

Tar Heel

Regional NSA Convention Opens On Campus Today

Registration Begins at 2; Meet Tonight

Representation From 15 Schools

March 25, 1949 TEMPLE UNIVERSITY NEWS

NSA Sets Up Clinic For Race Relations

1949's Best Books

UCLA Daily Bruin

NSA Holds Regional Meeting Here

Sixty Delegates Discuss Interests

McHenry, Childers Open NSA Regional Convention

THE DAILY ILLINI

NSA Establishes Travel Bureau On Campus

NSA to Convene at Emory; Will Discuss Plans, Problems

By Bill Shepherd

Wooster Voice

NSA Art Exhibit Opens January 15

Under the auspices of the National Student Association, a student art exhibit will be displayed in lower Kauke beginning January 15. The show will continue until January 22 and will consist of the work of American college students.

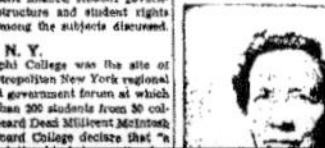

Local officers and volunteers brought NSA's reach to a wider range of students and student leaders. (From top: *Columbia Spectator* 11/22/48; U. of North Carolina, *Daily Tar Heel* 2/19/49; *Temple University News* 3/25/49; UCLA Daily Bruin, 5/9/49; U. of Illinois, *Daily Illini* 3/1/49; *Emory Wheel* 2/11/49; *Wooster Voice*, 1/13/49, Ohio)

Regional and Local Programming

Laying the groundwork for national and regional programming

1. From Madison to Urbana

Richard G. Heggie
University of California, Berkeley
NSA Vice President for Student Affairs, 1948-49

The bat swooped down from the high ceiling, seemingly intent on disrupting Helen Jean's hair and maybe more. She let out a shriek: "Get that thing away from me!" Whether deterred by such a formidable foe, or following its normal instinct to avoid humankind, the bat swerved at the last minute and retreated to the dark recesses above. The rest of us—Gene, Allan, Ted, and I—had adopted a determined antibat stance but probably did little to affect the outcome.

What were we doing here? What was I doing late at night in a virtually abandoned old schoolhouse in Madison, Wisconsin, a couple of thousand miles from home?

What indeed? The answer: this was the headquarters of the National Student Association, and the others and I had been elected full-time officers to lead the association during the 1948-49 year. My election to the position of vice president for student life had not been the result of a carefully plotted political campaign. I seemed to have arrived almost by sheer chance.

My years at Berkeley

I had grown up in Berkeley, California, the second son of parents who had separately emigrated from Scotland. I attended Berkeley schools, including the University of California, which has continued to figure prominently in my life. During the latter part of World War II, I served as an officer aboard a navy destroyer escort, returning to the university after the war's end to study for a master's degree in international relations.

During my years at Cal, I was appointed to various councils and boards but had never run for student government office. Nonetheless, when the Executive Committee of the Associated Students of the University of California (ASUC) announced it would send a representative to a conference of the International Student Service (ISS) to be held in summer 1947 in Aarhus, Denmark,[1] I applied and was selected.

The conference was to focus on problems of postwar reconstruction and student relief. The meeting would be followed by a study tour. ASUC was to meet half the costs, a sophomore women's honor society had agreed to cover 25 percent, and I was to provide the remainder.

In addition to appreciating my academic background, the committee was apparently intrigued by my being both a member of the Big C Society and president of the Symphony Forum. Whatever the reasons for its choice, my life was permanently changed. Part of the package: I would be one of the ASUC delegates to the Constitutional Convention of the U.S. National Student Association in Madison.

En route to Europe aboard a converted army transport, the *Marine Tiger*, I was thrown together with some forty-two students representing American colleges and universities, including Doug Cater and Frank Fisher from Harvard and Bob Smith from Yale.[2] For some reason, Smith College had four representatives. I, for one, had no complaint about that.

Traveling together was both an educational experience and a pleasant social one. To prepare ourselves for the forthcoming conference, we spent most of the daylight hours in seminars, usually conducted by Cater and Smith. Thus, we were well prepared to deal with the issues—once we had made our own way to Aarhaus via Paris! During the conference, we listened to a plethora of speakers and argued at length about what should be done. We also consumed a lot of food and drink, sang college songs, and enjoyed what I can only term male-female discourse. My most vivid recollections are of after-hours conviviality. There were many choruses of "Gaudeamus Igitur," punctuated by beer and schnapps. I'll never forget the sight and sound of Chuku Nwapa, a leading African, perambulating down the hall of the dormitory area at 4:00 A.M., chanting African love songs.

The IUS Council in 1947

After the ISS conference, the American delegation broke up into study groups to explore conditions in various countries. I selected the Czechoslovakia study tour, a fortunate choice because it enabled me to attend the World Youth Festival and to be an observer at the council meeting of the International Union of Students. I knew that the question of affiliation with IUS was to be an important issue at the NSA convention.

Attendance at the festival left a deep impression on me. After a performance by a Yugoslav folk group in the large outdoor auditorium provided for the festival, the crowd erupted with a Gatling-gun fusillade of sound: "Tito, Tito, Tito. . . ." This went on and on, increasing in emotional fervor and ending only after the great wave of shouting people had belched forth from the theater. Even more disturbing was the rumbling, mortar-like chant the next night following a presentation by a professional Soviet dance troupe: "Sta-lin, Sta-lin, Sta-lin," and the mass demonstration that followed. I had grown up listening on the radio to the frightening "Sieg Heils" of crowds around Adolf Hitler, and these outbursts were too close to the mark.

At the IUS Council meeting, the proceedings were more subdued, but nonetheless troubling. Although Doug Cater, the usual spokesman for the American delegation, was free to speak, Tom Madden, the British chairman, clearly favored representatives from the communist bloc. Most of these delegates took their cue from the Soviet delegation. For example, when an important issue was being discussed, the Mongolian delegate always consulted with the Soviet leader, Aleksandr Shelepin, before speaking or casting his vote.[3] The whole process caused me to question whether NSA could benefit from affiliation with IUS.

The NSA Constitutional Convention

Bob Smith and Doug Cater returned to the United States early to be at the opening of the NSA convention. Three of us—Frank Fisher, John Elwood, and I—completed the program and planned to arrive in Madison a day late. However, because of problems with flight scheduling, we arrived three days after the convention started, when many of the major issues were bubbling at full heat. Among these was the IUS question.

I was immediately subjected to a barrage of questions from members of the California delegation, who mistakenly regarded me as an authority on IUS.[4] If nothing else, this caused me to think more deeply about where I stood. In the end, I came down on the side of seeking a measured affiliation, provided that certain conditions were met, and cooperating with IUS on nonpolitical projects if these could be arranged. My objective was to maintain contact with Eastern European students without becoming involved in IUS political maneuvers. This position was supported by most of the California delegation. (The following year, following the communist coup in Czechoslovakia [February 1948], we unanimously endorsed the staff's action in suspending negotiations with IUS.)

The California delegation paid me back by electing me as chair of the California-Nevada-Hawaii Region. In fact, we had no delegates from Nevada and Hawaii, but the title had a certain resonance. I spent the next year balancing my effort to complete a master's degree with organizing the region. With the help of other officers, especially the secretary, Sally Holt,[5] also from Cal, we garnered between fifteen and eighteen member schools, depending on who was counting. Our principal opposition came from Father Raymundus Feely, S.J., of the University of San Francisco, and Pat Hillings, a University of Southern California delegate to the convention. Hillings's warning to me: he and his friends would be watching us closely and would smash NSA if he didn't like what we were doing. Years later, he was elected a congressman from Richard Nixon's district and became nationally influential in the Republican Party.[6]

Father Feely seemed convinced that, at best, we were dupes of the communists. Fortunately, most of the Catholic schools in the region didn't agree and took an active part in the organization. Among the leaders was Gene Tighe of Loyola University, who later became a Lieutenant General and director of the U.S. Defense Intelligence Agency.

Participation in the constitutional convention and, subsequently, the National Executive Committee had an unexpected influence on my political sophistication. Because I had grown up in a community with relatively tolerant religious attitudes, I was not psychologically prepared to deal with the political schisms among Protestants, Catholics, and Jews that were evident further east. These differences had an impact on the course of events.

The 1948 First National Student Congress

The constitutional convention had taken up several matters that it had not fully resolved. These included relationships with the IUS, how to deal with segregation, and the Student Bill of Rights. These became priority issues a year later, at the First Congress. Once again, delegates caucused in smoke-filled rooms into the wee hours, but could not bridge all the differences. The lines were drawn between an activist group, which wanted to deal strongly and immediately with matters of discrimination and to push hard to implement the Bill of Rights, and a group that believed NSA should move more slowly and wanted to add a section on responsibilities to the Bill of Rights. As at the constitutional convention, compromises were reached, but there were a number of minority reports. The Bill of Rights was referred to the Student Life Commission for further study. On IUS there was greater agreement, though some delegates criticized the staff for taking preemptive action in ending negotiations, while others objected to any form of cooperation.

The congress also adopted a program to provide services to students and student governments at the local level, but there was too little discussion of how this could be implemented. The politically tinged subjects were more exciting, after all.

For those of us directly involved, the most intriguing part of the congress was the maneuvering involved in the election of officers. Various names for the office of president were bandied about including, most prominently, Ted Harris, an African American from LaSalle College in Pennsylvania. Rob West of Yale appeared to have the inside track for international vice president, but a number of delegates, particularly from Catholic schools, mistrusted him. Someone suggested that I run for the post, but, though the idea was intriguing, I believed Rob to be more qualified. Moreover, this appeared to be a political tactic to undermine our international policies.

Dan Pulsifer, a delegate from the University of Washington,[7] urged me to run for president. This was ludicrous on its face: I had never led a student government and was ill-prepared to run NSA. Moreover, my primary interests were international. However, ego being what it is, and after a strong push from the California delegation, I eventually agreed to have my name put forward.

In order to gain more exposure, it was important that I chair a plenary session, where I could showcase my talents. I soon found that this was like throwing David into the lion's den, except that in this case, David got eaten. But I did learn something about politics.

During the election session, I was nominated by Jack Knox, student body president of Occidental College in California, whose stirring speech gave promise of a future political career. And in fact, he became speaker pro tem of the California State Assembly. His speech was followed by another stirring nominating speech on behalf of Ted Harris, who had a strong base of support among the Catholic school delegates. From the applause that followed, it was clear that my chances were zilch. At that point, I was approached by an emissary who proposed that I withdraw so Harris could be nominated by acclamation and that I accept instead the position of vice president, student life. For reasons that I still cannot explain, I accepted, and that was that. It was a good move.

The national staff in Madison

That was why, a few months later, I was fending off bats at 304 North Park Street in Madison. My fellow bat-eers were: Ted Harris; Eugene Schwartz, vice president for educational problems, from City College of New York; Rob West; Helen Jean Rogers, secretary-treasurer, from Mundelein College in Chicago; and Allan Ostar, public relations director, from Penn State. I must also mention Mildred Kiefer, a fellow Californian, who loyally consented to stay on as acting treasurer for several months to help us adjust to our new responsibilities and to hold our hands when the need arose.[8] We faced a formidable challenge: to continue the momentum established by an exceptionally competent first-year staff.

We were a diverse group. What we had in common was our ideals. We were convinced of the perfectibility of mankind, and we were sure that, at least in our little corner, we could help. Working together with this talented group was certainly a high point in my life.

As I've implied, the office at 304 North Park Street was not a luxury accommodation. The building was dreary, and one could imagine cobwebs arching down from the ceiling, seeking to grab the humans below in their sticky fingers. We never did discern where the bats resided. Like all self-respecting bats, they folded up their tents and disappeared when morning dawned. Nonetheless, this was home, and we quickly filled up vacant spaces with the detritus of our ponderings.

There were other tenants, but the only one I recall was the man responsible for the Madison draft board. Since all of us except Helen Jean had already served in the military, we got along with him very well. He shared with us innumerable ideas on how to deal with the building's idiosyncrasies and the landlord's "thriftiness." Accordingly, by the end of November we were able to convince said landlord—the City of Madison—to wash our office walls and apply some much-needed paint. Lo! They were not dirty gray at all. We ended up with a white ceiling and cream-colored walls. Even the bats were happy.

There were other concerns. It soon became clear that we could not survive unless something was done to organize our office clutter. We quickly learned that when we had a physical problem, there was only one person who could solve it: Super Schwartz! Thanks to Gene's carpentry skills, our office was soon garnished with a phalanx of seven-foot shelves.

Day in and day out, we spent long hours in this "home," hammering away at our typewriters, steeping ourselves in mimeograph ink, sorting, stacking, filing, mailing. It was all done to communicate to our constituents, who paid our bills and expected us to do something that would validate their memberships. We were expected to develop projects and services that would benefit students at the local level.

Implementing the NSA program

We approached the challenge in two ways. First, we used our positions as "bully pulpits" to advance NSA's ideological agenda. We scattered across the nation, visiting campuses, NSA regional meetings, and regional and national conferences of educational organizations. We wrote editorials for the *NSA News*, dispatched periodic bulletins to our members, and engaged in voluminous correspondence promoting NSA's precepts. We made speeches to whatever groups would listen. When it was available, we would use radio.

Our other principal method of meeting our challenge was to set up a large network of subcommissions to take on project responsibilities. Our subcommissions proliferated like rabbits, poking their noses into every facet of educational life. You want to advance academic freedom? We had a subcommission. You want to study honor systems? We had a subcommission. You want to develop a roster of summer work opportunities abroad? We had a subcommission. Student government finance, discrimination, student unions, university placement of displaced persons, symphony forums—all were under subcommissions reporting to one or the other of our national officers.

Each subcommission was the responsibility of an NSA committee or student government at a particular campus, which had volunteered, or been dragooned, for the task. Some were charged with conducting surveys and distributing the results, others with collecting and analyzing information from existing sources, still others with organizing a project and putting it into action. We in the national office were there to provide advice, coordination, and promotion, presumably with the help of the regional organizations.[9]

One of our biggest problems was, and is, not unfamiliar to politicians on the larger scene: how to develop a program that would satisfy populations in all parts of the country. Students from City College of New York had quite a different set of priorities than those at Mount St. Mary's in Los Angeles, and both of these viewpoints differed from those at Louisiana State University. In the late 1940s, populations were not as mobile as they became in later decades, and attitudes tended to be more parochial. As a result, while we totally eschewed the forked tongue, we did find ourselves mellowing the message to fit the audience. Nowhere was this more evident than in our efforts to deal with the major political issues that confronted the organization: racial discrimination, academic freedom, student rights, and relations with IUS.

The IUS issue

Our major chore with regard to IUS was to explain why it made sense to deal with the organization at all. Although Rob West maintained an arms-length contact, there were already stirrings that we should be seeking another, less-politicized mechanism for multinational contacts with students.

An off-the-record event that stands out in my memory was a semiclandestine meeting of national student organization leaders attending the 1949 ISS conference at Wells College.[10] This unofficial meeting sprang from a common frustration about the difficulty of working with IUS. I do not recall who organized it—I believe that it was chaired by Rob West—but we gathered around a quiet lake within walking distance of the conference site. Among those present were heads of national student unions of Scandinavia, the Low Countries, Great Britain, France, and, I believe, Italy, as well Ravindra Varma, president of the All-Indian Student Congress. After each had expressed his concerns, we discussed what we should do. Someone suggested that we consider a permanent mechanism to coordinate contacts and assist in the development of joint projects. Although no action was taken, the leaders agreed to consult further. A few years later, the Coordinating Secretariat of National Student Unions was established in Leiden.[11]

Student rights and academic freedom

On the student rights issue, we made little progress. During the year, through the *NSA News* and in the regions, various proposals were made to modify or strengthen the Student Bill of Rights. There was sufficient disagreement at the second national congress to prevent a consensus for change from being reached. A Bill of Responsibilities would not be added until years later.[12]

The meaning of academic freedom occupied much of our attention throughout the course of our term. This was a time of growing sensitivity to the possibility of communist influence in education. Professors and instructors on several campuses had been suspended or fined for holding Marxist views. NSA had taken an unequivocal stand that faculty should be judged by what they taught and not by their personal beliefs. This was similar to the stand taken by the American Association of University Professors.

The staff involved itself in a number of specific cases, including Olivet College, the University of Washington, Michigan State, and Oregon State, writing to the administrators to urge adherence to this standard.[13] While most of our member student governments supported our policy in principle, a large number did not in practice, whether for ideological reasons or for fear of being branded locally as "Red." On some nonmember campuses, our stand impeded our membership recruitment efforts.[14]

Opposing discrimination and furthering human relations

Of all the issues we addressed, discrimination against minorities was the most important and, in some areas of the country, the most controversial. The constitutional convention had called for "the eventual elimination of all forms of discriminatory practices anywhere in the U.S." Led by our resident workaholic, Gene Schwartz, we chose to carry this a step forward. Shortly after taking office, Gene established a Subcommission on Educational Practices and Human Relations, which he challenged to approach discrimination as a national problem. In an *NSA News* editorial, he wrote:

> We must ask ourselves whether or not the practices of educational institutions, be they quota systems, exclusions, or segregation, defeat the essential purpose of education in a democracy. We must ask ourselves: Does this practice violate the inherent dignity of the individual?

He went on to stress that "NSA is a national student organization, and not a treaty between the geographical sections of the U.S."

This stand and the various activities that it spawned did not make our forays into the South any easier.[15] My new wife and I made an effort to recruit new members on a swing through the Southwestern and Southern states on our way back to Wisconsin from our November wedding in California. We had little success. Among those student governments that were willing to listen, there were several that seemed to agree that segregation was wrong. But few were willing to commit themselves to membership in a national organization identified with locally unpopular views, particularly when the other benefits seemed to be obscure. And for some, the issue was preempted. Barefoot Sanders, the president of the University of Texas student body, favored affiliation but was not able to win student body support.[16]

On a trip to other Southern states, Helen Jean noted that most of the student leaders whom she met were opposed to discrimination, but they did not think that the average student on their campuses agreed with them.

Nevertheless, the national office carried out an active antidiscrimination campaign, sponsoring the establishment of subcommission units in various parts of the country, and promoting regional conferences on human rights by supplying local leaders with information kits, speakers, and other assistance. Fostering discussion undoubtedly brought about some progress. The April Executive Committee meeting after the second congress voted to urge fraternities to eliminate discriminatory clauses in their charters and by-laws. Not an earth-shaking stand, but it was the first time that NSA had come to grips with the actual structure of American apartheid. Most student leaders began to focus on the issue, and an environment was created that made it easier to take strong action later. Yet the fact remained: we were not able or willing to attack the problem as forcefully as we might have preferred.

Although these major policy areas were what attracted the most attention, pro and con, to NSA, it was the meat-and-potatoes projects that would undergird the interest of student governments.

A barrage of project ideas flowed from the Madison headquarters, some stemming from the congress, some from the regions and individual schools, and some from our own heads. The results were uneven.

International travel and Purchase Card programs

Among the most successful projects was the international travel and work-study program. The project included a publication on summer study and work opportunities abroad, exchanges with other national student organizations, study tours, and heavy involvement in arranging low-cost student travel, particularly on the so-called student ships, the converted troop carriers *Marine Tiger* and *Marine Jumper*. Hundreds of students benefited from these programs.[17]

The most ambitious domestic program was the Purchase Card System, which had been proposed by the First Student Congress but came to maturity under the guidance of Gene Schwartz. The idea was to obtain discounts for card-carrying students at retail stores throughout the country. Gene prepared a detailed manual on how to set up and carry out such a program locally, and he generated a torrent of sustaining documents meticulously labeled "Administrative Bulletin #1," "Administrative Bulletin #2," and so on all the way to #10.

My fondest memory of Gene is of his struggling with a grumpy old mimeograph machine, coaxing it to churn out dozens of pages without splattering ink over himself and everyone else within reach. He had some success. By May, seventy colleges were participating in the Purchase Card program, and over 230 merchants in fifteen cities were offering 5 percent to 30 percent discounts on a variety of goods.[18]

Student government and leadership

The improvement of student governments and student leadership was at the core of my own responsibilities. Across the country, there was a wide variety of student governments, some with major responsibilities and others that were student governments in name only. The Associated Students at the University of California, Berkeley (ASUC), was one of the most advanced, having responsibilities that included athletics, the student union, and a student cooperative bookstore. I drew heavily from this example and from ASUC personnel in preparing articles and establishing subcommissions. However, most schools were much smaller and had different sets of problems, so I depended to a large degree on information from NSA surveys.

The results of one such survey, undertaken by the previous NSA administration, had produced a wealth of data on student government, which was analyzed and distributed by the New York Metropolitan Region. I was never able to find an NSA affiliate to analyze the returns of another survey on student government finance, and I suspect that the returns were gathered up by the bats and made into nests long ago.

The surveys, however, proved useful in the preparation of a new booklet on student government and leadership. During the year, we circulated a substantial amount of material on these subjects, but there were many gaps in our coverage. I devoted much effort to expanding the excellent but short monograph jointly written by Ralph Dungan, NSA vice president for student affairs on the 1947-48 staff, and Dr. Gordon Klopf, chair of our board of advisers. This emerged as *Student Leadership and Government in Higher Education, Revised*, after much work and much pressure from my non-procrastinating colleagues.[19]

If the level of participation in training sessions is an indicator, NSA had some success in enhancing the capabilities of would-be student leaders. During the year, our staff took an active part in several regional and national meetings on improving student governments and developing leadership, including, most notably, the Lake Forest Conference, which was cosponsored with the National Conference of Christians and Jews. An important feature of the second national congress was a student government training program.

Looking back on these efforts, I realize that so many of them were rooted in our conviction that student institutions were perfectible. Yet sometimes, developments move in the opposite direction. One of my principal models, the student government at Berkeley, no longer controls, or even has any say in, athletics, and recently lost authority over the student store.

Cultural affairs and the arts

In the cultural field, we had some limited, and perhaps temporary, success. One project I promoted was the Symphony Forum, a mechanism for building interest in music by enabling students to obtain concert season tickets at a drastically reduced price. It was adopted by schools in several cities beyond San Francisco, where it had begun. This was largely due to dedicated promotion by Paul Denise, the subcommission chair from San Francisco State University. I do not know whether it continued outside California.

Some cultural projects attracted the interest of smaller member schools. A modestly successful student art tour was carried out under the auspices of a subcommission at Mundelein College, and the groundwork was laid for a literary magazine.[20]

Despite these efforts, it is clear that we had a major problem tapping into the felt needs of students nationwide. Most students were apathetic about student government and how it works and should work. Sports, sex, and studies were the principal preoccupations of the majority.

NSA News, public relations, and membership building

We pressed on in our efforts to generate greater participation. Our principal means of publicizing our projects was the monthly *NSA News*, which was distributed to campuses in proportion to their membership dues. Under Allan Ostar's direction and editorial acumen, it was transformed from a house organ into an all-encompassing periodical reporting on student and educational news from around the country. Partly to solidify NSA's reputation among campus newspapers, Allan involved himself in subcommissions on the student press and organized a college newspaper conference at the second congress.

Our public relations efforts netted one big coup. We were invited to talk about student concerns and the NSA program in five coast-to-coast CBS network radio programs hosted by CBS's star commentator, Quincy Howe. Ted Harris; Bill Welsh; Bob Smith; Jane Fouracre, who was chair of the Pennsylvania Region; and I took part. I would like to think that these broadcasts improved and expanded NSA's image.

Financial problem and challenges

Whatever the public might think, we couldn't speak for students if we didn't have a substantial number of members. Moreover, we needed their money to survive! Hoping to overcome resistance based on cost, the first congress reduced annual dues by 20 percent. By dint of hard slogging, we were able to increase membership to 306 schools by the end of the academic year. The organization's financial condition was nevertheless shaky. We concluded early on that we should seek funding from other sources, particularly foundations.[21]

We thought that we had a chance. NSA was receiving wider recognition in educational circles. We were invited to be an associate member of the American Council on Education, and we had an important presence on the U.S. National Commission for UNESCO, with Bob Smith elevated to the Executive Committee and Rob West a member. Our enhanced status helped us in dealing with university administrations and other institutions but did not contribute to our exchequer.

During one eastern swing, I sounded out a few of the New York foundations, including the Rockefeller Foundation. Although I received figurative pats on the head, neither this nor efforts by other officers ever produced a dime. We were just a bit naive in our understanding of how foundations work.

We had good relations with the U.S. Office of Education but were strongly against seeking or receiving government help even if it were proffered, which it wasn't. Although the Purchase Card System produced a few dollars through the sale of discount cards, the amounts were negligible. This was even more true of receipts from publication sales.

What money did come in was managed by Helen Jean. At the outset she struggled a bit—she had no previous experience with accounts—but with the experienced help of Mildred Kiefer and the advice of her father, she quickly became a pro. In her role as secretary, she maintained regular contact with the regional officers, chiefly through a chatty newsletter, which brought the recipients up-to-date on developments in the national office and enjoined them to move foreward on various programs and commitments (e.g., send money!). Helen Jean also did much more than her title implied. She instigated our weighty discussions of such questions as the meaning of free will and whether it was appropriate to accept death if one had not attained a state of grace. St. Thomas Aquinas became a regular protagonist. With her energy, her intelligence, and her sense of humor she was a tremendous asset for NSA.

Ted Harris, staff relations, and managing the office

Ted Harris presided over both our philosophical and our official discourse. He was the one who had to deal with our idiosyncrasies, moderate far-out points of view, and insure that we stayed on course. His thoughtful presence was a good balance for all of us, and his usually quiet leadership was a stabilizing force.[22]

Ted chose to lead by Socratic method rather than by authoritarian technique and, thus, was able to generate an atmosphere that welcomed free expression from our own somewhat disparate group. The end result: a strong feeling of unity and commitment to a common purpose.

Although relationships in the office were generally warm, it was inevitable that working and playing together so closely would produce occasional tension. The miracle was that there was so little. In fact, the biggest irritation arose from a misunderstanding between our office in Madison and Rob West in Cambridge. At Rob's insistence, the International Commission, which had been moved from Cambridge to Madison after the first congress, soon returned to Cambridge. Rob argued that most of our international work was directed toward Europe. It therefore made sense to be on the East Coast. It also made sense, he said, because many of the organizations with which we worked internationally were headquartered in New York and Washington, D.C. Cambridge was also the location of a group at MIT that was heavily involved in organizing student travel.

Rob was highly intelligent. He was also usually convinced that his course was the only correct one and did not require approval of a group far removed from the scene of his activities. I do not recall the specific incident that triggered the dispute; the issue was one of his taking action on what we regarded as a policy matter without seeking our support. There was a hot exchange of letters, but the tension soon cooled, and all was peaceful by the time I visited Rob in New England a few months later.

There were other players in and around the Madison office. Anne Harris, Ted's wife, was a gracious hostess for some of our informal gatherings. One of my most compelling memories is of a holiday stroll in a local park with Jane Boutwell, one of our Wisconsin friends, walking alongside Ted and carrying Ted and Anne's baby. The intense and disapproving stares cast our way underlined the task we faced even in "liberal" Madison.

My wife, Bea, cooked an occasional meal for the staff and, until she took a job at the university, worked part-time in the office. (She told me that she would never work for me again!) As I recall, we consumed immense mounds of spaghetti, only too rarely punctuated by an inexpensive pork loin. The Wisconsin Student Union was our principal outside mess. Once in awhile, when we really wanted to live it up, we repaired to the Italian Village and its flashy red-and-white tablecloths.

During the year, we had the equivalent of one full-time clerk-typist working in the office, and during the last months we had a part-time Purchase Card System secretary. However, we performed most of the clerical work ourselves, albeit with a notable lack of efficiency.

We were fortunate to have access to an outstanding group of educators on our National Advisory Council. We benefited not only from their knowledge and good judgment but also from their willingness to go to bat for the organization at educational conferences and in articles.

BEA HEGGIE joined Dick Heggie in Madison after their November wedding—bringing to three out of five the number married on the Madison staff (Harris and Ostar were the other two. Schwartz and Rogers were available, and West was exploring global horizons in Cambridge). Above left: Bea is helping in the shipping area of NSA's cavernous schoolhouse office (Heggie). Right: Bea and Dick at the close of the 2d Congress at the U. of Illinois in September 1948 (Allaway).

The adviser closest to us and most prolific in his writings about NSA was Gordon Klopf, student activities counselor at the University of Wisconsin. Gordon became a friend as well as a valued counselor, and helped us over many rough spots. His style was not very subtle. When he wanted to put a point across, he would preface his comment with, "Don't you think...?" Well, usually we didn't, or at least not up to that point! His methods became a source of merriment among the staff, but he caused us to listen, and we often accepted his views. In addition to the new edition of *Student Leadership and Government in Higher Education*, previously described, we published his short monograph, *Developing Group Leadership*.

Looking back

As we approached the end of our year, we realized only too well that we had fallen far short of the objectives we had set for ourselves after the first congress. In our final issue of *NSA News*, Ted wrote that we had failed to translate the goals and functions of the association into easily understood language. Moreover, we had not been able to spend enough time in personal contact with the regional officers, who should have been the key to carrying out our programs and interpreting them for local campus use. Although we recognized that not everything could be done from Madison, we had not been able to provide the wherewithal to decentralize our efforts—for example, through the hiring of regional field officers.

As I review our work from the vantage point of fifty years, I also appreciate the truth that was so evident to our advisers. We had tried to do too much, too fast, and we spread ourselves too thinly across a vast landscape of programs and projects. Our incentive was simple: we had so little time. This points up the weakness of all student-run programs. Student leaders won't be students very long. Often, by the time that they learn to lead, they are "outta here." The pressure to accomplish something in the available time is intense.

What we did accomplish should not be discounted. I believe that we provided a responsible voice for students and stimulated many campus leaders to think more deeply about the major problems confronting education and our nation. This was our most important legacy.

As the time drew near for the second congress, to be held at the University of Illinois in Urbana, we began to think about future leadership for the organization. One respected regional leader who seemed to be interested in the presidency was Harvey Weisberg of the University of Michigan. Robert Kelly, chair of the New Jersey Region, was being promoted by delegates from Catholic schools. He was both bright and vocal.

The members of our staff, Catholic and non-Catholic alike, were concerned that Kelly might be too inflexible on many important issues. At the congress, without taking an open position against Kelly, we did some soundings to determine if Weisberg had the necessary backing to win. It soon became clear that he did not, so we considered promoting an alternative. Gene Schwartz then tossed his hat into the ring. In the end, Louise Miller and Phil Des Marais[23] of the Minnesota delegation organized the Catholic caucus so well that Kelly won handily.[24]

Our departure from Madison was not without sadness. We had completed a year with some wonderful people who would remain lifelong friends. For many years I was a terrible correspondent and did not communicate often with my former colleagues. However, when my work took me to the East Coast, I usually enjoyed a meal or stayed with one or another of them. Gene, Helen Jean, Allen, and Ted all visited us in California. Rob, Ted, and Helen Jean are gone now, but all remain in my heart.

Did the NSA experience have an impact on my later life? No question. Without my NSA background, I probably would not have been offered my initial position on the World Affairs Council of Northern California. The responsibilities included organizing a student branch. And I certainly would not have been hired later at the Asia Foundation as a student affairs specialist, which launched me onto a quite different path. I soon moved beyond the student designation and served as an officer of the foundation in Japan, Pakistan, Sri Lanka, and India. I worked for the foundation for nineteen years. I then returned to the World Affairs Council as executive director, from which position I retired twelve and a half years later.

The skills that I haltingly developed in NSA contributed to my ability to assist and lead the many educational, governmental, and other nonprofit organizations with which I have been involved. These activities included serving as a regent of the University of California. Perhaps I would have developed these skills anyway, but not under such interesting and challenging circumstances.

Richard G. Heggie was an executive of the Asia Foundation, executive director of the World Affairs Council of Northern California, a regent of the University of California, and the first mayor of the city of Orinda, California.

In sum, I am grateful for my association with NSA and with the people who were involved in it. My life has been enriched. I can think of no better tribute than the 1949 appraisal of the late Harold Taylor, president of Sarah Lawrence College: "The NSA is strong, good, liberal, responsible, and full of new ideas—some of which may curl the hair of the academic profession!"

Amen to that.

END NOTES

[1] See pp. 50, 56, and Dowd, p. 60 for background on the International Student Service.

[2] See Fisher, p. 511, Robert Smith, p. 504, and Cater, p. 92.

[3] It was stretching a bit to call Shelepin a student. He was clearly beyond usual student age. Some years later, he became head of the Soviet KGB.

[4] The California group had gained notoriety at the convention by tossing oranges during the opening plenary session. Mainly, they tossed them up in the air or to each other, not at people. That variation was reserved for football games. Few of the Northern California delegation knew an orange tree from a peach tree, but in the interest of North-South solidarity they went along. However, I made clear that I was not an orange thrower.

[5] See Sally (Holt) Smit's reflections, p. 1044.

[6] A vigorous NSA affiliation battle later took place at USC. See pp. 1026, 1030.

[7] Dan Pulsifer was later elected chair of the Pacific Northwest Region. See the interview with Helen Pulsifer and Bill Gates, Sr., p. 1053.

[8] See Mildred (Kiefer) Wurf's essay, p. 178.

[9] Among the subcommissions were: Honor Systems, New Jersey College for Women; Student Opinion Research, Wellesley College, Mass.; Foreign Correspondence, University of Illinois (Philip Stoddard, Chair); Symphony Forum, San Francisco State University (Paul Denise, Chair); Academic Freedom, Stanford University (Erskine Childers, Chair); Art Exhibit, Mundelein College, Chicago; Electoral Procedures; Vocational Guidance and Scholarship Opportunity; and six area subcommisions on Human Relations and Educational Practices, based around the country.

[10] See Wells College meeting pictorial, p. 57.

[11] See background on Cosec, Dentzer, p. 301.

[12] See the Janet Brown essay, p. 378.

[13] See Pulsifer and Gates on University of Washington, p. 1053, and Alex Pope on the University of Chicago, p. 390.

[14] A resolution adopted by the National Executive Committee on April 3, 1949, by a vote of 22-0 with 1 abstention, stated that it "opposes with grave concern the present tendency in the educational community toward the long established principles of academic freedom because of hysterical emergency circumstances," and goes on to cite principles of academic freedom as laid out by the AAUP. It then appealed to "the university community of the United States of America: To refute and quell the rising tide of fear, rumor, suspicion and misinformation concerning alleged subversion in the education community." This resolution, although widely supported, also caused considerable controversy. On record were at least two identical protests from student governments (University of Santa Clara, California, and Chestnut Hill College, Philadelphia) "denouncing" the NEC on the grounds of reaching beyond its authority in taking an "unconstitutional action."

[15] See Heggie, Rogers, and Schwartz, p. 225.

[16] Barefoot Sanders became a distinguished federal judge. See his comments, p. 995. A vigorous affiliation contest was waged at Louisiana State University at the same time, in February 1948. See p. 454.

[17] See the unit on student travel and the student ships, p. 639.

[18] See the album unit on the Purchase Card System, p. 366.

[19] See the essay by Gordon Klopf, p. 331.

[20] *Editor's note*: The art exhibit program went on national tour for several years (see p. 369 and Perkins, p. 944). *Essai*, NSA's literary magazine, was published in a fall and spring edition in 1949-1950 (see Cashen, p. 362).

[21] See Appendix, "Organization and Finance," p. 1119.

[22] See Harris, p. 219.

[23] See Philip Des Marais' essay, p. 734.

[24] *Editor's note*: There are various versions of this story. See Schwartz, p. 236, Kelly album, p. 257, and Donnelly, p. 952.

PICTURE CREDITS: *Then:* 1948, Madison, WI (NSA Photo. *Schwartz*). *Now:* c.2000 (*Author*).

HT THE DAILY CALIFORNIAN FRIDAY, SEPTEMBER 10, 1948

ick Heggie Elected NSA ational First Vice President

legates to the first student con- of NSA elected Dick Heggie, e University, national vice pres- in charge of student govern- and student life.

ggie has been associated with since it was constituted at Mad- Wis. in 1947. At that time he named provisional chairman of California-Nevada region.

the regional constitutional con- ion two months later, Heggie re-elected permanent senior co- rman of the region. In that ca- y, he spoke to educators and ent bodies all over the state in ffort to explain aims and pur- of NSA, and recruit member ols for this region.

is the case with all national of- of NSA, Heggie will take up ear's residence at Madison, the iation's headquarters.

her national officers elected by congress are: Ted Harris, of La university, Philadelphia, pres- t; Robert West, Harvard, vice dent in charge of international activities; Gene Schwartz, CCNY, vice president in charge of education and educational problems.

Helen Jean Rogers, Mundelaine college, was elected secretary-treasurer of the organization.

Regional officers, elected at a regional caucus during the convention, are: Erskine Childers, Stanford, senior co-chairman; Jack Knox, Occidental college, co-chairman (re-elected); Steve Lagudis, Fresno state college, chairman of national committee; Lois Keister, Stanford, secretary; Gloria Padilla, Mt. St. Mary's, treasurer; Gene Tighe of Loyola and Jim Goodwin and Gary Goldsmith, U.C., reps-at-large.

Report From NSA Convention

Delegates Resolve Major Issues

By Verne Stadtman

Two major problems occupied more than 700 delegates during the closing days of NSA's first Student Congress at Madison, Wis.

First, there was ned for a definite policy in international student relations.

International Union of Students, an issue since last March, when the NSA Staff committee voted to discontinue negotiations for IUS affiliation, clouded all congressional deliberations for several days.

INTERNATIONAL SITUATION

A panel on the international student situation was heard early in the convention, Walter Wallace, asked to speak two days later.

Finally, the matter was brought to the floor. Two decisions followed: the action of the staff committee in breaking off negotiations for IUS affiliation

The follo ed: "The U congress do the formati students o union of st

The gen favor coope tain cultur ects, withou

It must that details

the convention was a decision with regard to a national policy. NSA's first congress had to decide which student problems needed attention first.

European Trip FRIDAY, APRIL 25, 1947

Richard Heggie Chosen To Represent NSO Abroad

Richard G. Heggie was selected yesterday to represent the University chapter of NSO in Europe. The selection was made by a board composed of members from both the ASUC and NSO.

Heggie is a graduate student majoring in international relations who listed travels in England, Scotland, Ireland, the Netherlands, Belgium and France as part of his background in the field.

Heggie will leave on the first lap of his trip to Europe on June 15. He will upon arrival either attend an international conference of students in Denmark or make a tour of one of the European countries.

Heggie's activities at the University include membership in Big "C" society, Athletic council, University and San Francisco Symphony forums and class councils.

NSA'S ROLE ON CAMPUS AND GLOBALLY was a focus of the *Daily Californian's* coverage. Heggie along with Mildred Kiefer earlier (see previous section) became key leaders in the region and nationally. The paper reports on his 1947 travel to the ISS conference in Denmark (4/25/47) and his election as Vice President (9/10/48). *Californian* night editor Verne Stadtman, who had also been a delegate, provided a series of in depth reports on the Association (see also next page).

"NSA'S GREATEST CONTRIBUTION: PRODUCING OPPORTUNITIES FOR STUDENTS TO ACCEPT RESPONSIBILITY"

Daily Californian Editorial Page TUESDAY, SEPTEMBER 28, 1948

Student Brotherhood

NSA Role Is Misunderstood

By Verne Stadtman

(This is the first in a series of articles explaining the functions, processes, organization and activities of the National Student association. In addition to his duties as a Daily Californian night editor, Stadtman recently attended the First National Student Congress at Madison, Wis., as a delegate from the University. The views expressed in these articles are his own and do not necessarily coincide with the views of the NSA).

The National Student association is as important to us as the ASUC, yet there is probably no organization quite so misunderstood by the average University student.

Despite the fact that ASUC has been an affiliate of NSA for almost a year, the mention of it still brings out the question, "Just what is NSA?"

To cut it down to a cold, hard statement, NSA is a "national association of student bodies." But NSA is much more than that.

STUDENT COUNCILS

More generally, NSA is an association of students themselves, represented on national and regional levels through their student councils and organized under impetus of common problems and interests.

As the national staff committee of NSA puts it, the function of a university is, "the preserving, fostering and passing-on of our cultural heritage, the stimulation of original work and research, and the training of free minds with a sense of responsibility *to society.*"

It is the latter function of the university with which NSA is most concerned. Sense of responsibility hardly can be taught in textbooks or lecture rooms. Responsibility is something that is learned by the act of assuming it, not by reading about it.

ACCEPT RESPONSIBILITY

The university student then, it is believed, should accept responsibility for (1) his own welfare and (2) finding opportunities to contribute to the welfare of the national and international student community. And NSA's greatest contribution is in producing opportunities for students to accept responsibility.

At many universities, students have already started to accept responsibility for their own welfare. This start has been made through student governments already established, those in the process of establishment and those in the process of reorganization so that more responsibilities can be shouldered.

"NSA is dedicated to the idea of student government. As a representative national organization, NSA naturally relies upon representative student governments to maintain that status.

CONSTRUCTIVE PROJECTS

Some of NSA's most constructive projects have been those dealing with organization and perfection of student governments. Acting as a clearing house for information on the subject of student government, NSA has made many contributions in that field—and ultimately to the cause of increased student responsibility for their own welfare.

The National Student Association's national and international activities have aroused interest not only from students, but also from the U.S. state department, the U.S. commission for UNESCO and the commission on student exchange set up under the Fullbright act.

Students of one religion, political thought or social interest have organized on the national, even international, level before. But never before have students recognized the even broader bond of studenthood itself irrespective of religious, political, racial or social considerations.

As a result, students at one university need no longer rely entirely upon its own intellectual resources when a knotty problem develops. Responsibility of the student broadens to include every problem which he faces in common with fellow students wherever an NSA campus exists.

But more than that, international activities of NSA extends our responsibilities even further. NSA is a sponsor of the World Student Service Fund, which contributes financial aid to both poorly equipped universities and hungry, or physically deficient students all over the world.

FOREIGN STUDY

Through foreign travel and study projects, NSA also promotes intellectual exchange between students of this country and students abroad. Person to person exchange of ideas is quite a contribution to world understanding. In this way, then, students of this country are also free to accept some real measure of responsibility for peace.

So the best answer for "What is NSA?" seems to be that it is a national association of students—including every student on the University campus who holds an ASUC card.

As to the question, "What does NSA do?," the best answer seems to be, that NSA, through its projects, opens the way for students to accept responsibility not only for their own welfare, but for the welfare of studenthood throughout the world.

RICHARD G. HEGGIE

Early Background and Military Service: Born in Oakland, California, in 1923. Raised in Berkeley, California. Served as a navy officer in World War II aboard a destroyer escort in the Pacific Theater.

Education: B.A., General Curriculum, University of California. M.A., International Relations, University of California.

Career: Following completion of my term as NSA vice president for student affairs, I joined the staff of the World Affairs Council of Northern California, in San Francisco. A few years later I transferred to the Asia Foundation, also headquartered in San Francisco. I served with the Asia Foundation for nineteen years, supervising its educational support programs in Japan, Pakistan, Ceylon (now Sri Lanka), and India.

Two years after returning to the foundation's head office in the United States in 1968, I was appointed executive director of the World Affairs Council and held that post until my retirement in 1983. During this period I served two terms as president of the National Council of Community World Affairs Organizations.

Both before and after my retirement, I have been active in many local, state, and regional organizations and institutions. I was the first mayor of the city of Orinda, having been elected to the city council at the time of Orinda's incorporation in 1985. I served on the council for two four-year terms, a period that included a second one-year term as mayor. I was named Orinda Citizen of the Year in 1993.

I also served as president of the East Bay Division of the League of California Cities and was vice chairman of the state league's Public Safety Committee and of its Committee on Growth Management and Regional Issues. I was a member of the Contra Costa Transportation Authority and was chairman of the City-County Relations Committee and Fiscal Unity Committee appointed by the Contra Costa County Mayors' Conference.

Continuing my involvement in higher education, I have been president of the University of California Alumni Association and served for two years as a regent of the University. Also at the university, I am a member of the Executive Committee of the Center for Slavic and East European Studies at Berkeley, a board member of International House, and chair of the War Classes 50th Anniversary Gift Campaign. I am a Berkeley fellow and was awarded the California Alumni citation and the Wheeler Oak Award.

Other associations include the Japan Society of Northern California, the International Diplomacy Council, the Society for Asian Art, and the San Francisco Committee on Foreign Relations, all of which I have served as president, and the East Bay Community Foundation, the Oakland Museum of California Foundation, and the Golden Gate Chapter of Red Cross, as a trustee. I have been a partner in Freemark Abbey Winery, am a Chevalier of the Order of St. John, and was decorated by the government of Belgium.

Family: My wife, Beatrice, and I celebrated our fiftieth wedding anniversary in 1999. She has been active as a docent for the hearing-impaired at the Oakland Museum of California. We have three daughters: Karen, a lawyer; Jennifer, an executive search specialist; and Deborah, a clinical psychologist and HMO executive; we also have two granddaughters.

A Social Conscience Shaped by Family, Wartime, and Campus Experience

2. NSA: Gateway to 50 Years in Higher Education

Allan W. Ostar
Pennsylvania State College[1]
NSA National Public Relations Director, 1948-49

When Ted Harris called me at my parents' home in East Orange, New Jersey, right after the first NSA Congress in 1948, little did I realize that—as it would for many others—NSA would profoundly change the course of my life.

I had returned from that Congress to prepare for my graduate studies in psychology at Penn State. Ted had just been elected president at the Congress. He wanted me to become NSA's first national public relations director, which meant taking a year off to join the rest of the national staff in Madison, Wisconsin.

I don't know who or what prompted Ted to call me, or why he thought I might be interested. True, I had played a relatively active role in supporting the establishment of NSA, both as editor of the Penn State *Daily Collegian* and as a delegate from Penn State to the 1947 Constitutional Convention and to the First Congress.

Perhaps he knew from Clif Wharton[2] and others who observed, based on the positions I took or supported at the various sessions, that I was aligned with neither of those groups of delegates who were identified as the "right" or the "left." It made sense that the person responsible for NSA's publications and public relations journalistically should be viewed as politically neutral.

I had associated myself with the political center that included delegates who were encouraged by campus YMCAs to become active in NSA. We were determined to resist any effort by right-wing or left-wing factions to gain control of the new organization. We felt that the best way for NSA to have credibility nationally, internationally, and on campus was to be rooted in duly elected student governments.

A family example of courage and loyalty to democratic values

So what was there in my background and sense of values that would prompt me suddenly to decide to take a year out of my life to do what I could to help this fledgling national organization of students—especially as I already had taken more than three years out of my life to serve in the U.S. Army during World War II?

It began by growing up in a family of immigrants who'd had the courage at the turn of the twentieth century to leave an uncertain existence in Eastern Europe for an even more uncertain future in a new country—learning a new language and struggling to make a living.

My father was a talented musician who strongly supported the Musicians' Union. But even with the help of the union it was difficult to earn a decent living as a musician. So, while still a teenager he joined the U.S. Army as a bandsman. He was not yet fluent in English, but he was a fast learner and read everything he could get his hands on. He was proud to be an American and to serve his new country before, during, and after World War I.

Certainly I was influenced by his patriotic fervor and his devotion to his adopted country, which continued even after he left the Army with many years of service. I was influenced also by his strong commitment to democratic values and his abhorrence of bigotry and discrimination. I remember, for example, his revulsion when the Ku Klux Klan burned a cross in front of the Catholic Church in the small town in New Jersey where we were living.

Depression era stimulates interest in world events

During the latter stages of the Great Depression we moved to a blue-collar neighborhood in Philadelphia where I attended a large urban all-boys public high school. I had both black and white friends and I began to be troubled by reports of racial discrimination and lynchings in the South.

With the encouragement of superb teachers in high school and a "leftist" cousin, I also began developing an interest in world events. The Spanish civil war and the rise of fascism were of particular concern to me in high school. I helped raise money for Spanish war relief and for the Abraham Lincoln Brigade—which was composed of Americans who volunteered to fight against fascist forces in Spain.

My interest in world affairs carried forward when I went to Penn State in 1942 and became cochairman of the campus Russian war relief drive. This included bringing to the campus Lt. Ludmilla Pavlichenko to speak. She was a famed sniper in the Red Army.[3]

Penn State is located in an isolated section of central Pennsylvania. There was much less interest in international issues than at urban and Ivy League universities. I became active in the Penn State Christian Association (PSCA) because it was the focal point for student concerns about world affairs and social issues. For example, the organization had been a long-time sponsor of Lingnan University in China.

In 1942 Penn State was invited to send one of two delegates from Pennsylvania to a meeting of the International Student Assembly in Washington, D.C. I was selected by PSCA to be the Penn State delegate. There were two delegates from every state plus student delegates from throughout the world. I believe the prime mover for the meeting was Joseph P. Lash, acting on behalf of the Roosevelt administration.[4] It was at this meeting that I met Lt. Ludmilla Pavlichenko. She was touring the United States in support of Russian War Relief.

The principal purpose of the meeting was to mobilize college students from throughout the world—including those in the German-occupied countries—to encourage and assist underground efforts. One of the subcommittees worked on plans to smuggle duplicating equipment and supplies to antifascist underground student organizations.

Desire to defeat fascism prompts army enlistment

Participating in this meeting further strengthened my desire to play whatever role I could to help defeat fascism. So when I returned to Penn State after the meeting I signed up for the Enlisted Reserve Corps. I did not want to wait to be drafted; the purpose of the Corps was to allow college students to remain in school until they were needed. In March 1943 I went into active duty and was sent to Camp Crowder, Missouri, for basic training and for training as a radio operator in the Army Signal Corps.

Then the Army decided it would need college-educated specialists and sent everyone who scored high on the Army General Classification Test off to college in a program called the Army Specialized Training Program (ASTP). I really did not want to go back to college, but in the Army you aren't given a choice. I was sent to Regis College, which was contracted by the University of Denver to teach engineering—a field in which I had no interest or aptitude.

The best thing about that experience was the opportunity to be taught by Jesuit professors who were among the best teachers I have ever had—before or since. They also made themselves available for off-duty bull sessions where we discussed philosophy and religion. I learned that it is very hard to win an argument with a Jesuit.

I also developed a healthy respect for and a better knowledge of Catholicism. This came in very handy during the NSA national meetings and especially in the bull sessions we had when I was a member of the NSA national staff in 1948-49. Two of the national officers on our staff, President Ted Harris and Secretary-Treasurer Helen Jean Rogers, were Catholic.

As casualties began to mount in the Pacific, and after D-Day in Europe, the Army decided that it needed infantrymen more than college educated specialists. It shut down ASTP and sent us, along with Air Force trainees and technicians, administrative Officer Candidate School cadets, and other highly trained specialists from noncombat units off to infantry units or as replacements for depleted infantry divisions.

Combat furnishes front-row seat to horrors of war

I was assigned to the 42nd Infantry (Rainbow) Division at Camp Gruber, Oklahoma. Because of the increasingly desperate need for more troops in Europe, our three infantry regiments were sent ahead of our artillery and other support units. We were shipped directly to Marseilles, France, and then north into combat just in time to engage in the last major German offensive in the Alsace and during one of the severest winters Europe had ever experienced.

As a combat infantryman I had a front-row seat where I could witness the horrors of war—the death and wounding of both friend and foe, refugees whose homes and families had been destroyed, towns and cities reduced to rubble. And, worst of all, to see and experience the smell of a concentration camp when my division liberated Dachau.

I was determined to do whatever I could after the war to contribute to efforts that would help eliminate future wars, yet knowing full well that we have a long way to go before we reach the level of civilized behavior that will achieve that goal. But we will never reach that goal unless we try.

I mention this wartime experience because of the profound effect it had on my choice of goals and activities throughout the rest of my life. It will also explain in part why I decided to become part of the development of NSA as an organization established to advance social justice and democratic values at home and abroad, and to promote international understanding and education as a means for achieving lasting peace.

NSA also helped me decide on a career that turned out to be both personally and professionally rewarding. My year as the organization's director of public relations opened opportunities that otherwise would not have been available to me.

Journalism and social action

On reflection, joining the NSA staff was a logical progression from my activities as a student at Penn State. As a freshman in 1942 I began work as a reporter on *The Daily Collegian.*

After the war I returned to Penn State on the GI Bill and continued my work on the newspaper. I found it more satisfying than my academic studies in psychology, although I did manage to keep up my grades and meet the requirements for acceptance into the graduate program. I also became somewhat active in the campus chapter of the American Veterans Committee (AVC) which was much more liberal than the American Legion or the Veterans of Foreign Wars. I found appealing the AVC slogan "Citizens First, Veterans Second," or something like that.[5]

The greatest thrill of my life up to that point was when, at the end of my junior year, I was selected to be the editor in chief, much to the consternation of the School of Journalism. It had always been assumed that the editor would be a journalism major. Publishing a newspaper five days a week, training and managing a large staff, and being accountable for a substantial budget was an awesome responsibility for a full-time student. Ordinarily it would take years after graduation from college to gain that kind of experience. But it certainly came in handy when I became director of public relations for NSA a year later.

Being editor also gave me the opportunity to support Penn State's active involvement in NSA and to be selected as one of the delegates to its constitutional convention and the first congress. It also gave me the opportunity to support several social issues. One was to urge the establishment of a cooperative bookstore on campus like the one I had seen at the University of Wisconsin during the NSA meeting in Madison. The commercial interests in downtown State College, however, succeeded in convincing the Penn State Board of Trustees that a coop would be unfair competition.

But we were successful in forcing the local barbershops to serve our Negro students. (That is what African Americans were called in 1947). The barbers insisted that they did not know how to cut Negro hair, but after some of our veterans who had cut hair in the service opened a free service in one of the dormitories and the campus Council on Racial Equality (CORE) organized a boycott, the downtown barbers backed down, though not without some ugly incidents.

Bucking segregation in athletics and the Cotton Bowl

A major issue involved an invitation for Penn State's undefeated football team to play Southern Methodist University in the Cotton Bowl in Dallas, on New Year's Day 1948. Penn State had two Negro players on its team. The Cotton Bowl committee informed Penn State that the two players would have to stay home since football was not integrated in the South. As editor of the newspaper and as a student member of the Athletic Advisory Board I insisted that we should not accept the invitation unless the entire team could go. With support for our position from student leaders and the president of Southern Methodist, the Cotton Bowl committee backed down, and for the first time black players and white players competed together in Texas. (The final score was 13-13.) Doak Walker, SMU's All-American tailback, went out of his way to be gracious to our two black players.

The story didn't end there. The hotels in Dallas were segregated; we were told our two black players would have to stay in a hotel for blacks. Again we insisted that the team had to stay together. The result was that the team had to stay in barracks at a naval air base on the outskirts of Dallas instead of a luxury hotel. That did not make me very popular with some members of the team.

Building a national student newspaper for NSA

As noted above, shortly after I returned home at the conclusion of the NSA Congress in Madison, Ted Harris called to ask me to become NSA's first national public relations director. I quickly decided to accept and to postpone my graduate studies for a year. It was one of the best decisions I ever made. It changed the course of my life and opened up a whole new career path, one that I never knew existed—one that has been enormously satisfying and rewarding.

Whatever success I have achieved over the past 50 years I owe principally to my wife Bobbie, to NSA, and to Professor Scott Cutlip. Cutlip was in charge of public relations for the University of Wisconsin when NSA was based in Madison. He became my mentor, my friend, and later my major professor when he persuaded me to stay on in Madison after my year with NSA to do

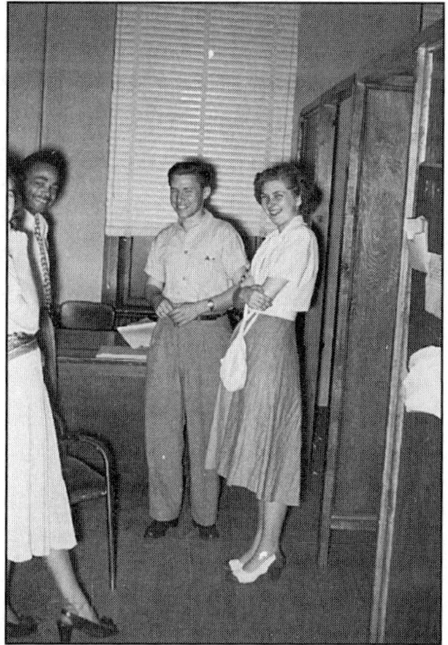

BOBBIE OSTAR joined Allan in Madison after their marriage. Here they are shown in the famous high-ceilinged NSA schoolroom office, with Ted Harris and a bit of Bea Heggie on the left. (Heggie)

graduate work there in mass communications instead of returning to Penn State. Apparently he was impressed by my public relations work with NSA and steered me toward a career in public relations for higher education.

NSA gave me a great opportunity to remake the *NSA News,* which began mainly as a house organ, into a national student newspaper. I had tremendous help from Karl Meyer, editor of the University of Wisconsin student newspaper, and Jane Boutwell, a Wisconsin student whose father was publisher of *Scholastic* magazine. Both became distinguished journalists and writers. Karl went on to become an editorial writer for the *New York Times.* He received national recognition when, as a reporter for the *Washington Post,* he traveled into the mountains in Cuba to get an exclusive interview with the leader of the guerrilla movement—Fidel Castro.[6] Jane went on to head the USIA office in Trieste and later became a columnist for the *New Yorker.* Jane's father was a strong supporter of NSA and helped open doors for me with the New York–based national media.

The *NSA News* was a total team effort by the national officers. I would scan upwards of a hundred college student newspapers for each issue. Each member was expected to write articles, and then after the paper was printed to work all night to prepare bundles for mailing to the member institutions. We had high-level volunteer help from people like Roy Voegeli and Norm Holmes, student government leaders at the University. We reached a circulation of 13,000 copies. The paper received national recognition from the wire services and newspaper and broadcasting media as a reliable source of information about student issues in the United States. It also helped establish NSA as the authentic voice of American college students.

NSA gets major national press coverage

My work on behalf of NSA also gave me valuable public relations experience by enabling me to develop programs on student issues for the CBS radio network[7] featuring the NSA national officers and to establish productive relationships with such publications as the *New York Times*[8] and *TIME* and *LIFE* magazines. Those contacts proved to be extremely helpful in gaining national coverage of the 1949 NSA Congress held at the University of Illinois. An effort to cultivate the media in Chicago paid off when the Chicago *Sun Times* assigned a reporter and a photographer to cover the entire congress. The reporter filed positive stories daily about the congress which were picked up by the wire services. We also had a reporter and photographer from *LIFE,* as well as local radio and newspaper coverage.

We received accolades from the public relations director of the University of Illinois as well as from the media who covered the congress for the professional quality of our press room operations. Here we had highly competent volunteers such as Ralph Smith and Ken Kurtz from Swarthmore and Craig Wilson from the *Michigan Daily.*

Experience provides career impetus

Among the many other valuable experiences gained during my year with NSA was the opportunity to be a panelist, along with the other officers, at the annual meeting of the American Council on Education, the principal national organization of institutions of higher education represented by their presidents. To my knowledge this was the first time students were invited to participate in the deliberations of the council. I believe NSA is the only student organization offered membership in the council, which gave it national legitimacy in the higher education establishment.

Another extremely valuable experience that benefited me throughout my professional career was the training in group dynamics facilitated by Gordon Klopf and provided to the NSA staff by the National Conference of Christians and Jews.[9]

Best of all were the close personal relationships with my fellow national staff members. I learned a great deal from our lengthy discussions covering a wide range of political, social, and philosophical issues. It is not often that one can be engaged round the clock over a period of a year with so extraordinarily talented and diverse a group.

Clearly, my year with NSA gave me the impetus to pursue a fifty-year-long career in higher education with the opportunity to advance the commitment by NSA to international education and to access, equity, and quality. A highlight was my involvement in the development and passage of the Higher Education Act of 1965, the first major federal legislation since the GI Bill to provide significant student financial assistance. It was designed to achieve President Lyndon Johnson's goal that "no student should be denied a college education because of lack of funds." The prime mover was another former NSAer—Douglass Cater[10]—who was President Johnson's education aide.

Many former NSAers became involved in development and implementation of national and international public policy initiatives that could be traced back to NSA's own public policy agenda. I am proud to be one of them.

Allan W. Ostar is President Emeritus of the American Association of State Colleges and Universities (AASCU), a national organization of 400 public four-year institutions. He served as head of AASCU for 26 years until his retirement. Since 1991 he has been a senior consultant with the Academic Search Consultation Service, assisting higher education institutions in their selection of presidents, chancellors, and chief academic officers.

END NOTES

[1] Pennsylvania State College became Pennsylvania State University in 1953.

[2] *Editor's note:* See Ostar as a "floor manager," Wharton, p. 115.

[3] See Mary Lou Munts, p. 36, who also writes of this experience.

[4] *Editor's note:* Roosevelt withdrew her support and Lash resigned from the American Student Union in 1939 as a result of its takeover by communists and fellow travelers. See Munts, p. 35, and Lash, p. 42, for background on prewar student organizations and the role of Mrs. Roosevelt in student affairs. Mrs. Roosevelt served on the NSA National Advisory Council from 1951 to 1958.

[5] See more on the American Veterans Committee, Bellush, p. 708.

[6] See Meyer, p. 138.

[7] In a letter dated September 12, 1949, from the Columbia Broadcasting System, Dwight Cook wrote to Ostar, "CBS has done two very fine programs with the National Student Association—YOU AND THE CAMPUS and THE PEOPLE'S PLATFORM "Who Owes Me a Job?...In the hundreds of national organizations in the country with whom I have come in contact over the years, I have found very few public relations men in the country who combine your ability to map out the right kind of material both for yourself and an organization like CBS."

[8] *Editor's note:* As an example of the outcomes for Ostar's thorough PR efforts in behalf of NSA, see sidebar below, right, with *New York Times* editorial written by Leonard Buder of the Education News Department on August 23, 1949. Buder sent Ostar a copy of the editorial with a congratulatory note.

[9] See Klopf, pp. 333, 335.

[10] See Cater, p. 92. As a student at Harvard, Cater was one of the original 25 American delegates to the Prague World Student Congress in 1946.

PICTURE CREDITS: *Then:* 1948, Madison, WI (NSA Photo. *Schwartz*). *Now:* c. 2000 (*Schwartz*).

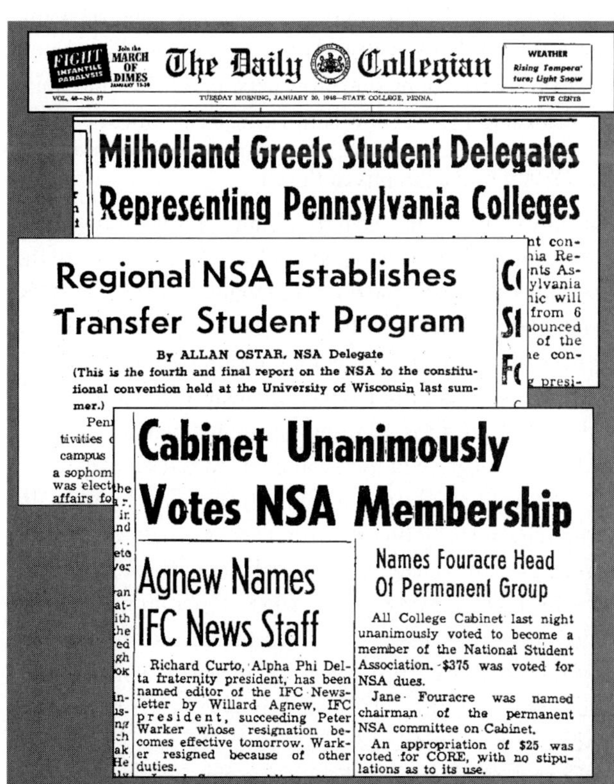

FIGHT INFANTILE PARALYSIS — Join the MARCH OF DIMES JANUARY 15-30

The Daily Collegian

WEATHER: Rising Temperature; Light Snow

VOL. 48—No. 57 TUESDAY MORNING, JANUARY 20, 1948—STATE COLLEGE, PENNA. FIVE CENTS

Milholland Greets Student Delegates Representing Pennsylvania Colleges

Regional NSA Establishes Transfer Student Program

By ALLAN OSTAR, NSA Delegate

(This is the fourth and final report on the NSA to the constitutional convention held at the University of Wisconsin last summer.)

Cabinet Unanimously Votes NSA Membership

Agnew Names IFC News Staff

Richard Curto, Alpha Phi Delta fraternity president, has been named editor of the IFC Newsletter by Willard Agnew, IFC president, succeeding Peter Warker whose resignation becomes effective tomorrow. Warker resigned because of other duties.

Names Fouracre Head Of Permanent Group

All College Cabinet last night unanimously voted to become a member of the National Student Association. $375 was voted for NSA dues.

Jane Fouracre was named chairman of the permanent NSA committee on Cabinet.

An appropriation of $25 was voted for CORE, with no stipulations as to its use.

ALLAN W. OSTAR

Early Background: Born in New Jersey. Graduated from Philadelphia's Northeast High School in 1942.

College Education and Military Service: Ostar did undergraduate and graduate work in psychology at Penn State and postgraduate work in mass communications at the University of Wisconsin. After serving as a combat infantryman with two Bronze Stars for valor with the 42nd Division in Europe during World War II, he returned to Penn State on the G.I. Bill. He left Penn State to become the first national public relations director of the U.S. National Student Association based in Madison.

Career: President Emeritus of the American Association of State Colleges and Universities (AASCU), a Washington, DC–based national organization of 400 public four-year institutions. He served as head of the organization for 26 years until his retirement in 1991. Since 1991 he has been a senior consultant with the Academic Search Consultation Service, assisting higher education institutions in their searches and selection of presidents, chancellors, and chief academic officers. Ostar also is an adjunct professor of higher education at Penn State University and held a similar position at the University of Arizona. Currently he is a member of the Penn State Libraries Development Board and the Advisory Board of Bowie State University in Maryland.

He has served on numerous education advisory boards and commissions. Before becoming head of AASCU in 1965, he was Director of the Joint Office of Institutional Research in Washington for seven years while on leave from the University of Wisconsin to serve members of the National Association of State Universities and Land-Grant Colleges. At Wisconsin he was a member of the faculty, an administrator in the University Extension Division, and Director of Communications Services. In the early 1950s he was on the staff of the Commonwealth Fund concerned with the improvement of medical education and international exchange.

Recognition and Awards: *Change* magazine included Ostar among the 44 most influential leaders in American higher education. He has been awarded honorary doctoral degrees from 27 U.S. universities and from Kyung Hee University in Korea for his national and international contributions to higher education. He is listed in *Who's Who in the World* and *Who's Who in America* and is co-author of *Colleges and Universities for Change.*

Family: He is married to the former Roberta Hutchison. They have three married children and six grandchildren.

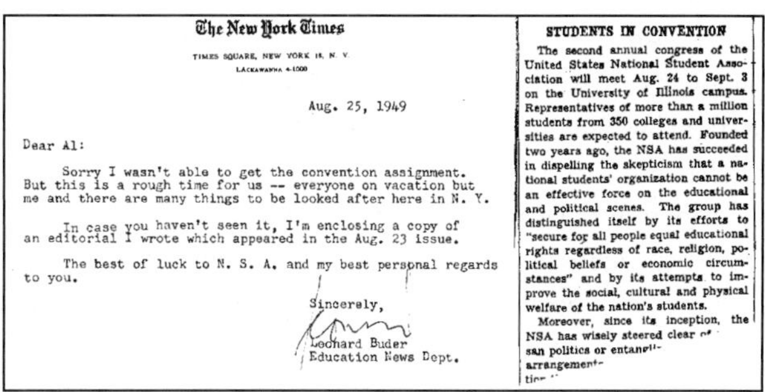

The New York Times

TIMES SQUARE, NEW YORK 18, N. Y.
LACKAWANNA 4-1000

Aug. 25, 1949

Dear Al:

Sorry I wasn't able to get the convention assignment. But this is a rough time for us -- everyone on vacation but me and there are many things to be looked after here in N. Y.

In case you haven't seen it, I'm enclosing a copy of an editorial I wrote which appeared in the Aug. 23 issue.

The best of luck to N. S. A. and my best personal regards to you.

Sincerely,

Leonard Buder
Education News Dept.

STUDENTS IN CONVENTION

The second annual congress of the United States National Student Association will meet Aug. 24 to Sept. 3 on the University of Illinois campus. Representatives of more than a million students from 350 colleges and universities are expected to attend. Founded two years ago, the NSA has succeeded in dispelling the skepticism that a national students' organization cannot be an effective force on the educational and political scenes. The group has distinguished itself by its efforts to "secure for all people equal educational rights regardless of race, religion, political beliefs or economic circumstances" and by its attempts to improve the social, cultural and physical welfare of the nation's students.

Moreover, since its inception, the NSA has wisely steered clear of [illegible]san politics or entan[illegible] arrangement[illegible]

AN IMPORTANT ROLE IN INTERNATIONAL ACTIVITIES for NSA at Penn State was predicted by Alan Ostar, also editor of the paper, in his 1/20/48 delegate report in the *Collegian,* the last of a series. The *Collegian* provided ongoing coverage to NSA (Top left: Penn's hosting of 175 delegates from 90 colleges, 12/10/47. Bottom: 3/12/48, Penn State joins NSA.) Recognition by mainstream press was important to NSA. To right is 8/25/49 letter from *NY Times* Education Editor Leonard Buder and clip of an editorial praising NSA's accomplishments in its first two years.

"The Brotherhood of Man"

Back to College after the War

Eugene G. Schwartz
City College of New York
NSA Vice President for Educational Problems, 1948-49

A glance fifty years into the past can sharpen the focus of blurry images as well as blur what at one time seemed so well defined. Some events from my years with the National Student Association seem almost as sharp today as when they occurred. Others emerge only after rummaging through long-forgotten papers.

What was it like to be in college then? What were the circumstances that drew me into this unique moment in U.S. student history? Here is what springs to life for me.

When I returned, in April 1946, from twenty-eight months of military service in the United States, the Philippines, and the postwar occupation of Japan,[1] I was eager to get on with my life, and yet was uneasy about the choices I had made when I entered the City College of New York (CCNY) in 1943. During the four years that followed my return, the birth of NSA drew me into an experience that forever changed my life. It liberated me from my presumed career choice in civil engineering, which, by the time I got my degree, no longer seemed to be relevant to my interests.[2]

The GI Bill made it possible for middle- and working-class young men, and some women, to break away from both their provincial roots and their economic imperatives, and to so broaden their outlooks and careers that they energized America as never before. I believe that it is not possible to overemphasize how this process accelerated the erosion of the barriers of race, class, region, ethnicity, religion, and gender that stood in the way of attaining the equal opportunity that the American system promised, and that it fulfilled, even with its inequities, to a greater extent than any other society. This was the process that most energized me.

A nation with a conscience

The America I returned to after the war was a nation with a newly awakened conscience, ready to expand the horizons it had already reached. This conscience had been stirred by the horrors and tragedies experienced in Europe and Asia during the war. It was prodded by the injustice and brutality wreaked by the Axis war machines in the cause of racial superiority. There appeared to be nothing but opportunity ahead. The ideals of the nation's founders never seemed more capable of fulfillment, and of extension to all who had previously been left out. At least, in retrospect, that was how I saw it.

I became involved in student government and veterans' activities on the campus. I attended the Chicago Student Conference in winter 1946, and joined delegates from colleges around the country who voted to form the U.S. National Student Association at the constitutional convention in Madison, Wisconsin, in September 1947.[3] NSA was the first postwar national U.S. student public policy organization, unaffiliated with sectarian or political movements, attempting to reflect the idealism of the nation as expressed in the Declaration of Independence and the Constitution.[4] And NSA furnished a venue through which America's globally conscious student generation of the time could lend its zeal to postwar efforts to secure a permanent peace.

CCNY: A vibrant campus in the city

The City College I returned to in summer 1946 was exuberantly connected to the world around it. It was the pride of the city, with a national reputation for tough academic standards. Its open-air Lewisohn Stadium was host to packed audiences for the prewar twenty-five-cent-admission New York Philharmonic summer concerts. The nationally renowned CCNY basketball team filled Madison Square Garden and had not yet fallen from grace in the 1950 point-spread scandal.

The college was also a center of political ferment. Its cluster of stately Gothic structures was located on Manhattan's St. Nicholas Heights, next to Harlem, which had erupted into angry street riots in 1943. On campus, Italian-Americans debated Italy's postwar future and its powerful Communist Party, Irish-Americans debated Northern Ireland's separation from the Irish Republic, Eastern European Jewish-Americans argued about support for Zionism in Israel, and everyone joined the rising tide of protest against the legal support of discrimination and segregation through the "separate but equal" doctrine and the enforcement of restrictive housing covenants. New York State was dismantling its one-year residency requirement for welfare, and the great migration of Puerto Ricans looking for new opportunities was just beginning to fill Manhattan's East Harlem. Their increasing presence intensified campus debates among their statehood, commonwealth, and independence movements.[5]

In some ways, the headline-grabbing political demonstrations and protest rallies were at odds with the academic and professional goals of many students. The engineering school was one of the best in the country, but students grumbled at the employment difficulties they felt the radical political scene on the campus created for them. Nonetheless, the mood on campus was energetic, hopeful, and vibrant. Old Abe Lincoln's nose, on a bronze bust then mounted before the Main Building, where the student council met weekly in the evenings, was shinier than ever, polished by generations of students for good luck.

Students in postwar New York

As was true in most of the country, New York City's economy was bustling. There was a rising tide of job opportunity in the entertainment, cultural, financial, fashion, advertising, and publishing industries, which radiated energy and kept the pulse of the city throbbing. Students coming on foot, by bus, and by subway to this commuter day-and-night school filled its classes, preparing to join this economy.

We also took time to enjoy the city's vibrant entertainment and cultural diversity. We went to Yankee Stadium in the Bronx, the Polo Grounds in Manhattan, and Ebbets Field in Brooklyn to watch the Yankees, Giants, and Dodgers. In the summer, we traveled to Coney Island and rode the Steeplechase and Cyclone. We downed those great hot dogs at the original Nathan's, which had not yet become a national chain of fast-food stands. Frank Sinatra was singing at the Paramount.

We took our dates to the Starlight Roof and went dancing at Roseland. Greenwich Village, a Mecca for artists, writers, and performers, was a nickel subway ride away. We went there for cappuccino or for a candlelit meal in Little Italy. Further downtown was Chinatown, with its chow mein and dim sum. There were summer concerts in the bandshell on the mall in Central Park, and skating in the parks in the winter. The whole city was our campus.

The Depression years

College students of the late 1940s experienced the Depression as schoolchildren and the war as teenagers. These immense events shaped our outlook.

I came from what we used to call a working-class family. I was born in Manhattan and raised in the East Bronx by my working mother. My mother was a garment worker and my father, who left us when I was an infant and who worked out of Providence, Rhode Island, was a wholesale grocery salesman.

Our neighborhood was one of the many Eastern European Jewish immigrant communities in New York City. At this time, the Bronx was still partially undeveloped, and there was a good deal of open space. We lived near Bronx Park, in a five-story walk-up brick apartment building complex with ivy-covered Tudor facades and gardens, creating a country-like setting.

We were separated by elevated subway tracks from a thriving Italian-American community to our east. During the Depression, some immigrant Italian-Americans occupied vacant lots, cultivating vegetable gardens on them. They lived in corrugated shacks, some on our side of the tracks. We were able to watch them from our apartment windows. Later, they invested their earnings in two-family attached homes, which many of their descendants occupy to this day.

Vendors delivered produce to the neighborhoods in horse-drawn wagons. Used-clothes peddlers walked through the apartment courtyards hawking, "I cash clothes." Knife and scissor sharpeners came by with their grinding wheels strapped to their backs, attracting apartment dwellers down to the streets to renew their cutlery. On weekends you could have your picture taken by a Kodak box camera and developed on the spot for a nickel. All of this was a part of life in the Bronx before the war.

And yes, people really sold apples and pencils on downtown corners.

Culture shock in the army

Until my service in the army field artillery, I had never been west or south of New Jersey or north of the Canadian border. When I was a boy, a subway trip from the Bronx to Brooklyn was considered a major excursion. Basic training took me to Fort Benning, Georgia; Fort Bragg, North Carolina; Fort Leonard Wood, Missouri; and Camp Gruber, Oklahoma. We debarked for the Philippines from Fort Ord, California.

If you've seen Neil Simon's *Biloxi Blues*, Eugene in the play might have been me in many respects, keeping a journal of his experiences, excited by the adventure of it all. I took my leaves in small Southern towns, where I met people who were unconditionally patriotic and supportive of the troops; had never seen a New Yorker, let alone a Jew, before; and generally took me for an "Eye-talian." It was culture shock all around. But it broadened my outlook in a way that would not have been otherwise possible in those days without television and easy access to travel.

Prejudices amidst liberties

World War II–era America was still wearing the mantle of its traditional prejudices amidst its liberties. American Jews knew that there were hotels to which they could not go, clubs they could not join, and neighborhoods in which they were not welcome. Restrictive residential covenants continued to be enforced until the 1960s, when the Supreme Court ruled them unconstitutional.[6]

During the war, the armed services laid the groundwork for dismantling this system of religious and ethnic apartheid by throwing us all together and forcing people to discover one another while they were still young enough to take a second look. After the war, the movement toward national racial desegregation began to gain momentum when President Harry Truman ordered the desegregation of the army.

While the army expanded my relations with other Americans, my service in the Philippines and Japan filled me with curiosity about these cultures. What struck me almost immediately about the families I met in both countries was their inherent kindness, their instinctive sense of manners and propriety, and their respect for elders. In shameful contrast, many GIs looked at these strangers as something less than human, referring to them as "Geeks" and "Gooks." These expressions of contempt distressed me. As a boy, I had listened on the radio to both Adolf Hitler and Father Coughlin (the latter a bigoted preacher of the 1930s) fulminating against Jews, and such prejudice sent a chill up my bones.

NSA: An instrument of unity

These experiences fostered my enthusiasm for the promise of uniting the country and the world in an inclusive sense of community and connection. I was drawn to the proposed NSA as a means for achieving that unity. My enthusiasm turned to organizational efforts. I was intrigued by the challenge of developing structures that would make it possible for a representative organization to have its policies initiated locally, debated regionally, and settled at annual national conventions. I spent many hours poring over college population statistics and delegate and organization schemes on which we could base our proposed new constitution.

After the Chicago conference, as we got into the organizing year under Jim Smith and his team, I began to meet students from other New York City colleges in our metropolitan region, which was then headed by Walter Wallace, now a sociology professor at Princeton. I remember Walter as an astute and articulate spokesperson and a role model for the emerging new presence of black Americans in college affairs. Until NSA, even though I grew up in New York City, I had known only one African American personally. He worked as a superintendent in the apartment building I lived in. The army was still segregated.

NSA also built a bridge for me to the Catholic college students who became active in the association. Until then, my experience with Catholic young people was largely defined by the Italian-American neighborhood adjacent to the community where we lived. We boys met in not-so-friendly combat from time to time in the vacant lots in the area. Their church, shrines, and clergy were a complete mystery to me.

Next door to CCNY was the walled and park-like Manhattanville College campus.[7] This Catholic college volunteered a room for our regional headquarters. As regional secretary, I spent a lot of time there and soon became acquainted with a number of the sisters. As with the folks in those small Southern towns who had never met a Jew, I had never previously met a Catholic nun. I shared the sense of unease of many non-Catholics toward these white capped women in black flowing robes. Contact and conversations then, and in later years, humanized these ladies for me as real people in a special vocation.[8] They were enthusiastic and interested in our work. That experience, and contact with students from other Catholic schools through NSA, enabled me to understand the religious principles that shaped their moral and political views and to feel comfortable in their company.

Dominant themes and interests

Dominant themes of interest and debate in NSA's early years included: postwar international relations among student and youth groups, with initial emphasis on relationships with the Communist-dominated International Union of Students (IUS), which had been created in 1946; problems of racial

CONSTITUTIONAL CONVENTION in 1947 brings together Metropolitan NY regional and outgoing NCC and incoming NSA national officers. From left: John Simons (Fordham U.), Treasurer, NCC; Jim Smith (U. of Texas), President, NCC; Bill Welsh (Berea C.), NSA President; Alan Aaronson, CCNY School of Business delegate; Walter Wallace (Columbia U.), Pres., Met. NY Region; Ralph Dungan (St. Joseph's C.), NSA National Affairs V.P.; Gene Schwartz (CCNY), V.P., Met. NY Region. (Welsh)

discrimination and racial equality; and religious, political, and regional factional influences within the Association.

On the international front, our hopes that we could work with the Marxist-driven international student movement were soon to be disabused. My naïve assumption that Marxism was a benevolent vision equal to others led me to write an editorial in *NSA News* for the 1949 Brotherhood Week observance, entitled, "Christ, Marx and Brotherhood." In it I equated Jefferson's political democracy with Marx's economic utopia. The resolution, I suggested, might be found in the teachings of Christ, Moses, and "eastern doctrines"—in the "Brotherhood of Man." "Through education and its institutions," I wrote, "the Brotherhood of Man must all the more be taught. These are challenges to NSA."

This was, and is, a benevolent thought. I wish, however, that my engineer's understanding of metaphysics and politics had been a lot more rigorous! I later learned that the free-will thinking of many Christian philosophers and Marx's historical determinism are wide of each other's mark and that the politics of civil society are a lot more complex than simple goodwill can manage.

On racial discrimination, we revisited the Civil War and refought the North-South civil rights issue on our own stage. We determined that discrimination against black Americans was a blight that we would work vigorously to erase.[9]

In the area of group interests, two widely differing factions of special importance were: the radical and communist youth movement, which wanted to capture the voice of U.S. students through its front organizations; and the Catholic student movement, which was entering for the first time into the arena of national student affairs and was concerned about the impact of secularism, the influence of communism, and garnering support for federal aid for such items as religious school construction and busing.[10]

Veterans brought back with them a maturity that enlarged their interests and served as an antidote to efforts at factional control.

The women on campus, who were perhaps three to five years younger than the male veterans, were also expressing themselves professionally, intellectually, and politically. However, it was still a "man's world," and it took another ten to twenty years for women's rights to become a major social and educational issue.[11]

Other major issues dealt with by NSA included: academic freedom and student rights; the powers of student governments on campus to influence college policy without faculty or administration censorship; and methods of rating the teaching effectiveness of faculty.

Overriding individual issues was the thrill of the process itself. Through NSA, we were developing a forum for dealing with basic issues of educational development and governance and creating an opportunity for students to have a voice in shaping the postwar world.

IUS wasn't interested in our views

In 1950, Rob West of Yale, Bill Holbrook of the University of Minnesota, and I were selected as NSA delegate-observers to the World Student Congress in Prague, sponsored by IUS. Along with the British, Scottish, and some six other observer groups, we were the only delegates among the thousands in the meeting hall who were not controlled by, or sympathetic to, the communist cause. The constraints placed upon us left little doubt that they were not interested in our views.

My efforts to present and distribute a paper explaining the U.S. education system and our traditions of local control and public support were defeated when the paper got "lost" somewhere in the Congress mimeograph room (no Xeroxes in those days) and never appeared. We served as convenient bullying targets for daily demonstrations against U.S. "imperialism" and involvement in the Korean War.[12] The atmosphere in Prague, as a city in a newly converted Soviet satellite, was eerie. The young people who came up to us to whisper words of determination to recapture their freedom left me both inspired and chilled.

On our return to the United States, where Senator Joe McCarthy and the House Un-American Activities Committee were beginning to terrorize anyone who didn't knuckle down and swear fidelity to their inquisition, my passport for our State Department-approved trip was lifted by the FBI, and it took me six months and a meeting with Mrs. Shipley, the widely feared director of the Passport Office, to get it back. I must have had some file!

The civil rights front

On the civil rights front, two NSA-related experiences with prejudice and hostility that touched me personally come to mind. Such incidents taught me how strong and principled Americans can be when challenged, while small numbers of the discontented can set the tone and the rules.

I frequently traveled with Ted Harris, our African-American NSA president from LaSalle College in Philadelphia. Ted was a sophisticated and well-grounded student of international affairs who was witty, articulate, well spoken, and proud of his Christian Brothers training. I had little grounding in the humanities and was still wet behind the ears. We became great friends and had some hilarious times together. Although it was not unusual for us to encounter curious stares in public places when we were together, we avoided confrontational situations.

Nonetheless, on one of our trips in 1949, we went into a coffeeshop for lunch in Cleveland, Ohio, and we were asked to leave because there was "no service for your kind." It was an infuriating experience of humiliation and helplessness.

The other incident occurred in Madison at the time of the 1948 congress. I was with a group of City College students who had stopped in at a local beer place. We had heard that a group of toughs had come down from Milwaukee to get the "New York Jews." We inadvertently advertised by wearing our prominent CCNY monograms on our sweatshirts. Sure enough, they found us. We fled epithets and threats in a swift chase back to the campus. As we were nearing exhaustion, who should we come upon rounding the corner of one of the campus buildings but Dick Heggie, leading a group of the California delegation to our rescue!

So there you have it—some early postwar "intercollegiate sport," which was both frightening and inspiring at the same time. These experiences lent very personal meaning to our efforts to break down the barriers of prejudice.

Toward a brighter world

NSA changed my life for the better. It enabled me to develop an informed respect for the strengths and diversity of our nation and its people. It connected me profoundly to our philosophical and historic roots. It also gave me some of my dearest lifetime friends, with whom I served on the national staff. None of us knew each other before we met in Madison in 1948.[13] United in our purposes and basic goodwill, we put our shoulders to the wheel, aiming toward a brighter world. Looking back, I can still see the tracks.

Eugene G. Schwartz is a publishing and business consultant and editor-at-large for ForeWord Magazine, *and has served as a production executive for several major publishers. After completing graduate course work at NYU in 1953, he worked as a union organizer and was in the printing business. He holds a B.S. in civil engineering from the City College of New York.* *(See p. 247 for extended bio.)*

END NOTES

[1] I was in Eighth Army field artillery, poised for an invasion of Japan, from which we were thankfully spared by the dropping of the atom bomb in 1945 and the armistice that followed. The horror of Hiroshima and Nagasaki at that time was a frightening climax to all of the brutality and horrors that brought us there.

[2] I must acknowledge Dr. John J. Theobold, then Dean of Engineering at CCNY, and Dr. James Peace, dean of students. Both these men fostered a level of support and openness that helped guide many of us through the adjustments to campus life and activity. They typified the commitment to, and engagement in, the educational process of college administrators who believed in their students. Dr. Theobold, in particular, exerted a strong influence on my ultimate decision to complete my engineering degree after returning from Madison in 1949. He later became superintendent of schools and then president of Queens College in New York City.

[3] There were two delegates from City College at Chicago and Madison, both named Schwartz but not related to each other. The other one, from the School of Business and Civic Administration, was Bernard Schwartz, now chairman and CEO of the Loral Corporation (see p. 857). Altogether, the four separate CCNY Uptown and Downtown day and evening sessions were represented by seventeen voting delegates at the constitutional convention.

[4] NSA's founders drew considerably on the U.S. Constitution and the notions of federalism in the development of the NSA constitution. Martin McLaughlin demonstrated this in considerable detail in his thesis, "*Political Processes in American National Student Organizations*" (Notre Dame, Indiana, April 1948).

[5] Academic freedom at the University of Puerto Rico became one of the major issues that occupied my attention later, as NSA's educational vice president in 1948-49. The NSA Executive Committee took a position opposing what it believed to be the stifling of dissent at the university. See Brown, p. 379.

[6] The de facto observance of restrictive covenants lasted well after the Supreme Court decision. When I moved to Del Mar, California, in January 1969, it had only been a year or so since UC San Diego, which was trying to recruit a world-class faculty, got the local real estate community to start selling properties in La Jolla to Jews.

[7] See Schwartz, p. 850. Mother Eleanor O'Byrne, then president of Manhattanville, became a member of NSA's national advisory committee from 1954 to 1958 (p. 862). A year or two after I graduated, Manhattanville relocated to Purchase, New York, and sold its thirty-acre campus to the city of New York for CCNY expansion.

[8] In preparation for this book, I spent a marvelous summer weekend in Bend, Oregon, visiting with and interviewing Sister Mary Kay Perkins, O.P., whom I hadn't seen since fifty years earlier when she attended the Illinois Convention as a delegate from Mundelein College. Perkins has devoted a lifetime as a teacher through her order and is now the diocesan superintendent of schools in western Oregon (see Perkins, p. 943).

[9] See Wharton, pp. 114, 146.

[10] See Part 4, "Student Voices Influencing NSA," p. 695.

[11] Four of the national staffs of five or six elected officers during NSA's first five years included a woman. Three of the elected women held the position of national secretary: Janis Tremper [Dowd], Rockford College (1947-1948), Helen Jean Rogers [Secondari], Mundelein College, IL, (1948-1949), and Shirley Neizer [Tyler], Simmons College, MA (1950-1951). Sylvia Bacon, Vassar College, NY, who later became a federal judge, was elected vice president for student affairs, 1951-52. The exception was the 1949-1950 staff, which included an appointed woman, Mary Kay Perkins of Mundelein College, as staff associate. In 1950-51 Joan Long [Lynch] of Marylhurst College, OR, was also appointed as a staff associate. See *The Impact of Women and Women's Leadership on the National Student Association and the United States Student Association (1946-1994),* by Sandy England (Indiana University, 1994). This unpublished thesis by the 1994-96 USSA Midwest Field Organizer offers an interesting historical perspective on women's issues in NSA. See also, Part 2, Sec. 5, "Women and NSA," p. 489.

[12] See West , p. 556, and Holbrook, p. 559.

[13] Dick Heggie describes our year together in his essay on p. 199.

PICTURE CREDITS: *Then:* On furlough, U.S. Army, 1944. *Now:* Bearsville, NY, 1998 (Both, Schwartz).

We are in the middle of a social revolution every bit as significant as many of the great revolutions in our history

4. Ted Harris: In Search of Truth and Justice

La Salle College, Philadelphia
Pennsylvania Regional Chairman, 1947-48. NSA President, 1948-49

Editor's note: When Ted Harris was elected Pennsylvania regional chairman in 1947, the La Salle Collegian *wrote (11/26/47, p. 4) that "on seeing Ted Harris at a meeting you would have immediately said to yourself, 'Here is a powerful speaker, here is a brilliant leader of men,' and above all, 'here is a gentleman.'" Harris, an African American from an urban Catholic college, from the outside was seen to break trails when he was elected to NSA's presidency in its second year. Within NSA, however, he seemed the obvious choice on the metrits when Bill Birenbaum of the University of Chicago withdrew his own name and made the nominating speech for Harris (see Birenbaum, Part 2, Sec. 3). During his NSA tenure as a national spokesman Harris advocated building effective student governments and the national organization to represent them. As he moved into a career with international organizations concerned with student relief and world affairs, he turned his voice to building bridges between races and religions, particularly for interracial justice within the Catholic church, and for helping the disadvantaged in the inner cities. This and the following unit provide excerpts from some of his speeches and albums of some of his NSA and career highlights.*

On Building a National Student Organization

Excerpts from President's Report to the National Executive Committee, April 1, 1949, Cleveland College, Ohio

It is probably best to start with first things and discuss administration and finances. The most outstanding fact about this area of concern has been that we have operated at about three times the level that was contemplated. . . . Coordination and system at the Staff level has for most part been rather frustrating, . . . it is virtually impossible to devise a system that will work when five people are attempting to do the work of at least ten. . . . I do not think that it is either fair or wise to depend on this type of sacrifice for the perpetuation of the Association, and I recommend to your earnest attention the suggestions that will be offered later at this meeting for helping next year's operations.

A word about projects—still another sense of frustration creeps upon us when we realize that the term "projects" has only a paper significance for us—no matter how concrete we like to think the projects that we are working on or with. We can only provide the ideas, information, direction, and in some cases funds, by which regional or campus groups actually implement a program. We have to depend on self-sacrifice of the regional officers to investigate the particular needs of their regions and campuses and adapt the NSA program to those needs. . . .

Looking for signs of life

For all these reasons, it is with anxious eyes that we scan the college press for any sign of life in what often seems to be a dead foetus. This is why we line up in the mornings to read the dribbles of information that accidentally find their way into the office; it's why we drop our chins, and tongues, and pant when we find that some school that we are visiting actually has an active effective NSA program.

News like the Minnesota Civil Rights program and Art Tour gives Schwartz new spurts of creative genius which he lavishes in art work for the secretarial letters and in building shelves for the only office in the U.S. that has an intercom system with carrier pigeons. The California Region's Operation Amigos gives Dick [Heggie] the charge that enables him to give his best for his newest commission activity which he will describe only if coaxed. New England's Human Rights Commission, Kentucky Tennessee's radio programs and art tours and other similar programs let us know that our information, direction, and leadership—national and region as well as campus—is taking root. We need a lot more of this type of encouragement.

Policies: The policy decisions of the last Congress—scant though they were—have provided a framework within which we have been able to find avenues for implementation for almost twenty-four hours per day. . . .

* * *

Coming to grips with need for clear policies

Now, because students, as well as others in the community, are beginning to look for a clear statement of position of the USNSA in certain areas which are considered fundamental to student interests and which are now so much the concern of the public in general, as well as the educational world, the NSA will have to concern itself with these questions in an organized and concentrated manner.

We have found it necessary to avoid—in many cases—coming to grips with certain of our perennial problems because we lack a clear policy. Such things as segregation, a permanent or more permanent policy in international activities with respect to the International Union of Students, academic freedom—or more specifically the issue of Communist students or professors teaching or studying on public college or university campuses, the [Student] Bill of Rights, a clarification of certain ambiguously worded statements, etc. In many of these areas, the Staff has not generally felt that we had the authority to interpret the policies of our Association to the degree that it would be necessary to clearly answer these questions. . . .

* * *

I believe that one reason why much of the drive and enthusiasm that motivated our founders is lost is because there are not enough of us who are capable of transmitting a respect for the fundamental values of NSA. Too often we depend on the specific "services" of the Association to "sell" NSA to specific groups of students.

Trips to Europe, 20% discounts on a suitcase, or traveling drama groups are not enough to keep NSA alive for any length of time, nor for that matter to justify our existence at all. As leaders we must focus our minds on the fact that whether by accident or design, NSA is a medium through which the whole pattern of American higher education may be affected, expanded, and improved; a medium through which American students may cooperatively add to the economic, social, and cultural welfare of the student everywhere. We must keep in sight the community of faculty, students, and administration which is ideal in securing these objectives, and this vision must be beamed to enough students to maintain an intellectual, spiritual, and moral direction to all our activities. A reading of our preamble makes this patently clear—without these directives, we are floundering around in a sea of meaningless activities.

Universities: Eradicating Ignorance, Providing Leadership

Following are excerpts from the Keynote Address by James T. Harris, Jr., Administrator, USNSA Foreign Student Leadership Project, to the 8th National Student Congress at the University of Minnesota, August 21, 1955.

The university must provide the opportunity for the eradication of all forms of ignorance. Putting it more positively, there must be an environment where the search for truth can be intensive, continuous, and unfettered.

It does not seem to me that the university is justified in firing or hiring on the basis of types, groups, or classes rather than individual competence. If this be an infinitely more difficult and painful task and admits of no pat formulas or solutions, then let me say that I know of no institution better equipped to assume it. It would appear that misconceptions of the needs of national security have warped enough of our free institutions and ideas of justice. It is time that a halt be called in the universities. We must continue to have more love for freedom than hatred for communism or any other "ism." We must continue to believe that we have not reached the state in America where we must choose between using undemocratic means to fight an alien and detested ideology and national collapse. We must continue to believe that one of our most valuable assets in the titanic struggle between ideologies is the loyalty of free minds.

It is a matter of some considerable concern that the two-thirds of the world which (at least by American usage) can be classified as "colored" is watching us with a mixed attitude of disappointment, hope, frustration, contempt, and anxiety with respect to our racial attitudes as manifested here at home.

In some six years of travel and study in about twenty-four different countries, I have observed that democracy is by no means accepted, even in principle, as the way of life. . . . In many, if not most of these countries, the articulate segment of the population happens to be the university students. These are the young men and women with whom USNSA is in contact in more than fifty nations of the world. More than three-quarters of these nations are those which we have come to refer to by the noncommittal designation of "growth potential areas." . . . USNSA has won the friendship of the representative student groups in all of these countries to an extent which no other agency, private or governmental, ever has. Why is this so? I believe it is because these young men and women look to their relationship with USNSA and the hundreds of thousands of students it represents as a source of genuine and disinterested friendship. They believe we are sincerely interested in understanding their aspirations and their needs.

Is this just so much idealistic chatter? Perhaps, but you may be no less inclined to believe it when you realize that students with whom USNSA has had intimate and friendly contact during the past seven years are now, for example: secretary to the prime minister of an important European nation; consular officials in several diplomatic establishments; policy-making foreign affairs appointees or civil servants; professors and teachers; and important municipal and provincial officers.

If one of our objectives is to create the student ties today which will serve us as citizens and statesmen tomorrow, it would appear that, in many cases, tomorrow is already today.

Racism as Sin

Excerpts from a news story on August 22, 1969, in the Philadelphia Bulletin *by Betty Medsger, of the* Bulletin *staff.*

Los Angeles—Roman Catholic Church authorities should make racism as serious an offense as missing Mass on Sunday or committing adultery, according to the executive director of the National Catholic Conference for Interracial Justice [NCCIJ].

James T. Harris, Jr., of Chicago, who is black, said here last night in the opening address to a four day meeting of the NCCIJ that the organization would press for such an interpretation of Church law.

* * *

"By whatever name—domestic Marshall Plan, reparations, compensatory capital development, freedom budget—the central theme is clear," said Harris.

"That theme," he said, is "the need for a massive input into our domestic social program.". . .

More Social Action

Harris called for a major shift in the church's use of its resources.

"We do not want to see more cathedrals, and hardly more churches, built before a substantially improved effort of social action has come about," he said.

Speaking of the role of layman and priest, Harris said:

"We will not accept any longer the arrangement of priorities and roles within the church which involves us in alms-giving, but excludes most of us in discussions on how money is used.

"We want a piece of the action."

Questions independent education systems

Harris said the NCCIJ calls on the church to "profess a de-investment in real estate in our cities and a re-investment in the real state of the human being who lives in the city."

He said the NCCIJ also "will cause to be questioned" the use of Roman Catholic resources "to support an independent education system."

The Catholic educational system, said Harris, "in many cases deprives the larger public community of the concern and involvement of Catholic people in the public educational system which must serve the needs of the vast majority of the poor. . . .

"We have not said there is no place for a parochial school system," said Harris. "We have said we question its present scope, purpose and effectiveness, and the drain it causes on scarce resources."

PICTURE CREDITS: *Then:* 1948, Madison, WI (NSA Photo, *Schwartz*). *Now:* c. 1989 (James T. Harris, Jr., Memorial Service program, October 26, 1989. *Courtesy, ____ Sims*).

Ted Harris was widely traveled throughout Europe, the middle East, Africa and in India and Pakistan in non-government agency service and was Executive Director of the national Catholic Council for Interracial Justice.

JAMES THEODORE (TED) HARRIS

Adapted from the October 31, 1989 memorial service program, St. Madeline Sophie Church, Philadelphia, with additional career highlights added.

Early years and military. Ted was born July 11, 1923, in Philadelphia, Pennsylvania to James T. and Alice Heiskell Harris. He grew up in Germantown and attended Northeast Catholic High School. Ted served honorably in the Second World War with the Army Engineers, attaining the rank of Sergeant Major.

Education. He graduated from La Salle College with a Bachelors degree in Economics and received the John McShain Award for the student with high academic rating who "had done the most for the public welfare of the college." He went to Princeton University where he received his Masters in Public Affairs from the Woodrow Wilson School. He was a John Hay Whitney Fellow at Princeton. He received an Honorary Doctorate of Laws in 1964 from La Salle College. Ted was president of the National Student Association from 1948 to 1949. He attended the University of Geneva, Switzerland, in 1950 where he obtained distinction as a French/English interpreter. In 1951 he received honors in the African Middle East Affairs program at the University of Cairo, Egypt.

Career highlights. Ted's career included the James J. Hoey Award, with Sargent Shriver, given to the two Catholic laymen who had done most to promote interracial justice.

He was Senior Secretary of the International Student Service in 1949, later Associate General Secretary of the World University Service, Assistant Director of the American Society for African Culture, director of the Ford Foundation Foreign Student Leadership Project in 1955, later a director of its Overseas Development Program for the Middle East and Africa. He was Vice President of the African-American Institute, and in 1969 became Executive Director of the National Catholic Conference for Interracial Justice.

In 1965 he was appointed by President Lyndon B. Johnson to the official delegation to Africa with Under Secretary Katzenbach and visited heads of state in 12 African countries.

Ted was fluent in French, Arabic, and Italian. He traveled to over 55 countries in Europe, Africa, and the Middle East and to India and Pakistan. He lived with his family in several of them.

Family. Ted was married to Anna Louise Dow on June 28, 1947, in Philadelphia. They have four children: Karen Harris Hill, James T. Harris III, Portia Lynn Harris Benson, and Aida Louise Harris. In addition to his wife and children, when he died on October 26, 1989, he was survived also by five grandchildren, two brothers, two sisters, a multitude of nieces and nephews, and an aunt and an uncle. Ted had a brilliant mind and a marvelous sense of humor. He was an avid collector of art. He enjoyed music, both classical and contemporary. He played both piano and organ. He was a devoted father and husband.

Harris and the Issue of Racial Justice

Harris Speaks on Race Issue

By PETE GARITO

To solve today's racial issue, C. Theodore Harris, in his lecture, "The Race Question and the Christian Conscience," on Wednesday, October 2, indicated that a synthesis of the formation of a true conscience and the action prompted by that conscience is necessary.

The distinguished Negro alumnus of the Class of 1948 pointed out the deficiency of conscience of black and white as the cause of the present situation; proposed methods for the shaping of a Christian conscience; and explained the action already taken by a few springing from that conscience.

For the barriers between the black and the white to come down, a more vital connection among men living as Americans, as Catholics, and as social beings, must be instilled. Mr. Harris continued to say that if the conscience of the present is based on the Philosophy and Theology of the past, it has got to be changed and conform to the times.

Theodore Harris

2

3

Philadelphian Heads Catholic Racial Group

JAN 19 1969

James T. Harris, Jr., a Philadelphia-born Roman Catholic, has been named executive director of the National Catholic Conference for Interracial Justice.

Since 1966 Harris has been vice president of the African American Institute in New York City.

He describes the Roman Catholic Church as "one of the most important reservoirs of human resources in this country.

"It also," he adds, "is one of the largest areas of entrenched prejudices. I'd like to have a hand in turning this around."

The Chicago-based Conference for Interracial Justice operates programs in housing,

Ted Harris focused his talents on the issue of racial justice after an earlier career in international relations emphasizing African and Middle Eastern affairs. (1) In an early speech to an NAACP Youth Conference, Harris focused on NSA human relations programs (*NSA News* 11/48). (2) In 1963 (*La Salle Collegian* 10/11/63) he addressed the issue as a matter of Christian conscience. (3) In 1968, as Executive Director of the National Catholic Conference on Interracial Justice, he moved to a frontal assault on "the priorities and roles within the church". (*Philadelphia Bulletin* 1/19/69)

Ted Harris Speaks To NAACP Delegates

1

The program of the United States National Student Association in the field of human relations was enthusiastically received by delegates to the 10th Annual Youth Conference of the National Association for the Advancement of Colored People, in St. Louis on November 12.

Ted Harris NSA president in ad-

Address delivered to the Association of American Colleges

Scholarship and Citizenship

Students in too many cases have not been prepared to assume responsibility.

James T. Harris, Jr.
La Salle College, Pennsylvania
President, 1948-49

Editor's Note: Reprinted from the Association of American Colleges Bulletin, *Volume 35, Number 1, March 1949, pages 56-61. In a counterpoint to the perspective advanced by Bill Welsh in his address to the American College Personnel Association in 1948 (see p.000), Ted Harris continues the theme of tying NSA's success to success in strengthening the role and partnership of student government with the administration. In addition, now midway into the association's second year, he is able to lay out both successes and some of the obstacles that the association faced, including faculty and administration resistance, financial limitations, and the "national environment of near hysteria," referring to what was then known as the "Red Scare."*

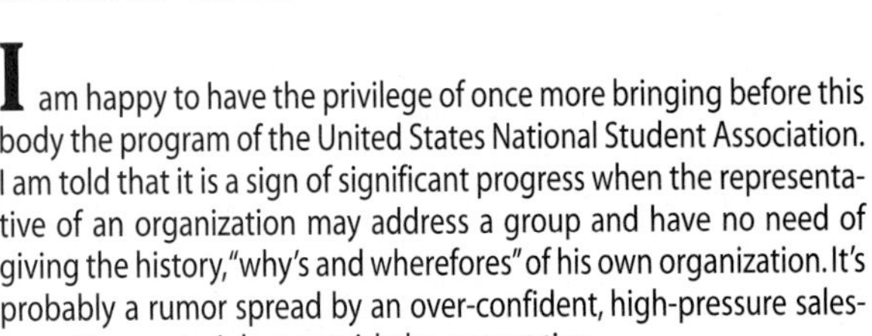

I am happy to have the privilege of once more bringing before this body the program of the United States National Student Association. I am told that it is a sign of significant progress when the representative of an organization may address a group and have no need of giving the history,"why's and wherefores" of his own organization. It's probably a rumor spread by an over-confident, high-pressure salesman. At any rate, I dare not risk the assumption.

Last, year when my predecessor, Mr. Bill Welsh, spoke to you, the NSA had just embarked upon its program of establishing and improving student government, developing international friendship and understanding among students, arousing interest in the curricula and extracurricular pursuits, that enable the integration on the campus which is forced upon the student after graduation.

NSA's need to crystallize a unity of purpose

The Chicago student conference and the initial enthusiasm which it engendered was still a substantial factor in whatever success could be claimed at that time. In the ensuing months, the association has had to rely increasingly on the specific services that it could render to the student bodies comprising its membership. We have every reason to believe that the services of the association such as the regional leadership conferences, student government clinics, human relations conferences, the Purchase Card System, foreign study-travel tours and summer study projects for foreign students in the United States have justified the support of the 278 colleges and universities which now make up our membership. Time does not permit a detailed description of these projects but such information can be obtained from the campus NSA personnel or the National office.[1]

All the huge organizational problems of finance, members and of administrating a national organization, although not completely solved, have met with a degree of success that portends ultimate achievement of our goal. The more subtle difficulties, such as crystallizing a unity of purpose in the minds of students, as well as devising means of achieving this purpose, are still in the early stages of development. It is conceivable, however, that in the general concern—and I humbly suggest confusion—in the whole educational world concerning values and objectives in education there is a limit to the measure of success we can anticipate.

Where do we go from here?

The question that I would like to speak of at this point is "Where do we go from here?" With your permission I would like to outline briefly and frankly what I consider to be the major areas of concern for the association if it is to realize its vast potential and become a tremendous instrument of good in American higher education.

1. We must double our efforts to reach elusive Joe and Betty average who are not interested in the discussion and conference groups which, whatever their value, have no direct appeal to them. Projects and programs must be developed which encourage the participation of more than the so-called leaders on the campus. The Purchase Card System, a plan whereby students receive discounts from local merchants, has done much thus far to realize this goal.[2] We recognize, nevertheless, that this is not an ideal solution and are developing a cooperative plan which we believe to be a more wholesome approach to the student economic problem.

2. We must remove from student government the stigma attached to it by faculty and administrative personnel who view it as an annoyance at best, and often as an instrument for the benefit of a few campus "wheels," and also the stigma attached by students who view the local student government as a sham, a mouthpiece for the faculty and/or administration, or a self-perpetuating clique. This, of course, means we must remove the substantial elements of truth in all these views. To do this effectively on a national level, we believe that it is necessary to get together representatives of all three groups—faculty, administration, and students—to realistically analyze the so-called student government; to discover how thoughtful and responsible students may help determine policies of the university that may result in a more valuable educational experience as well as regulate and create solely student activities.

Student government role needs discussion

The specific problems that might very well be discussed by such a group are germane to the function and effectiveness of the National Student Association as well as the student governments on campus. Some of them are:

1. What are the sources of authority of student governments?
2. What are the obligations of students to the legal authority for their delegated powers?
3. If the student government has legal authority, what is its obligation to the university?
4. What are the best means of financing student governing units?

5. What techniques may be employed to provide mature and experienced leadership?

6. How can student governments achieve continuity of personnel and policy?`

7. What are the justifiable limitations of student political activity?

8. How can the purpose and functions of all parts of the university community be fully appreciated by the whole community?

As I have indicated, the answers to these questions, particularly the last four, are of vital concern to the NSA, and I venture to say, to most of you here.

NSA's efforts show varying degrees of success

Our own attempts to solve these problems on a national and local level have been characterized with varying degrees of mature deliberation and judgment and, therefore, with varying degrees of success.

We have inspired the establishment of student governments and suggested procedures and methods that appear to have improved others.

Our "Student Bill of Rights," though possibly extravagant in some of its claims, has awakened the interest of many students, professors, and administrators in this field. Discussion and evaluation of these "rights" is being encouraged and we feel that what finally evolves may be a generally acceptable standard for the activities of students in the university community.[3]

The financial structure of the Association, though at first quite wobbly and the occasion of grave concern—especially for the national officers who had to pitch pennies to see who got dessert—is now more stable, and we believe we have devised means of establishing ourselves on a sound and permanent financial base. Some of our experiences will be valuable for many student governments having the same problem.

The national and regional offices of the Association have provided adequate opportunities for leadership. The fortuitous selections of original officers have set precedents which, in the main, are being followed despite the increasing number of younger students who hold office. This has undoubtedly been as much the result of the leadership training programs and other projects of the Association as it has been the personal interest of outgoing officers in those who follow.

Environment of hysteria clouds "clear path"

Our activity in the political sphere has been almost inconsequential. First, because, of constitutional limitations, we are prohibited from acting in partisan political spheres or where the best interests of the welfare and good name of the association militate against it. Secondly, because in the present national environment of near hysteria and confusion of people and parties with issues, it has been impossible for the association to define a clear path for itself. It is interesting to note, in this respect, that the questions concerning academic freedom that have been referred to us have invariably been political. As the attention of the academic and non-academic community is drawn to political freedoms and the alleged abridgments thereof, it is highly likely that as a representative organization, we will have to concern ourselves more with this type of activity. It would be valuable if the group that I have suggested would concern themselves with the question of separating political liberty from political license as it pertains to the university

This outline of the problems as well as our attempts to answer them indicate the critical areas in which there appears to be conflicting interests or insufficient information and training. There would seem to be merit in the plant [sic] to call together from all over the country the administrators, faculty personnel, and students to determine some courses of action that would lead to the solution of some of these difficulties.

Lest it be assumed that this is to impose some sort of national pattern on college campuses, I would like to emphasize the fact that the basic and fundamental conflicts regarding the role of the student on the campus make for strife and confusion rather than diversity which is admittedly desirable for a democratic educational system.

3. The third goal toward which we must direct our efforts is that of providing ever greater opportunity for students to assume responsibility for their academic, economic, and social welfare. We are also aware of the necessity of developing those qualities and providing that training which will enable students to effectively discharge the responsibility delegated to them. Questions of academic freedom, racial discrimination, student welfare, and "student rights" melt into insignificance before the patently clear fact that students in too many cases have not been prepared to assume responsibility because of lack of experience and training. This, I believe, has been a failure of higher education. It would appear that the curriculum must be adjusted to provide training and experience for students to discuss, evaluate, judge, and act as mature citizens.

Student involvement needs faculty and administration support

4. The last area of concern is directly related to my present sphere at this meeting. The vicious circle of "wait and see what they do" around to "See, we told you they can't do it" must be broken somewhere. As in any community enterprise, the effectiveness of its program depends largely on the interest and active support of all the parties. If students are to make a worthy contribution to the educational process while they are yet students, the other parts of the community must first of all be receptive to the idea. Moreover, every opportunity must be created for independent student judgment and action consistent with the democratic process. This, of course, means that room must be left for trial and error.

Without the vision and foresight, the assistance and advice of faculty and administration in colleges and universities throughout the United States, the NSA would still be a dream. Without the continued cooperation and expanded efforts of these and more faculty and administrative persons the realization of our ultimate hopes will fall short of the ideal. As we have struggled in our growth with the disruptive forces of youthful impetuousness, special interests, student apathy, suspicion, and hostility, we have emerged stronger and more confident, though more keenly aware of our limitations. We invite your analysis of our program and criticisms of our methods and objectives. We recommend to your immediate attention the NSA groups on your campuses in the knowledge that your active interest will increase the total sense of responsibility. The cooperative spirit that may be thus enhanced will in itself be a partial realization of our objectives....

Scholars, citizens emerge from well-integrated college career

We believe that an alert and informed student body will be invaluable in developing the university atmosphere which is conducive to a high calibre of scholarship even as an alert and informed citizenry is conducive to a high calibre of citizenship.

The NSA will continue its efforts to assist in the development of students who through a well-integrated college career may emerge scholars and citizens.

END NOTES

[1] See Parts 2 and 3.

[2] See p. 366.

[3] See Brown, p. 375.

PICTURE CREDIT: *Then:* Addressing the 8th National Student Congress, August 1955, University of Minnesota (SHSW).

BALANCING SCHOLARSHIP, LEADERSHIP, AND CAREER

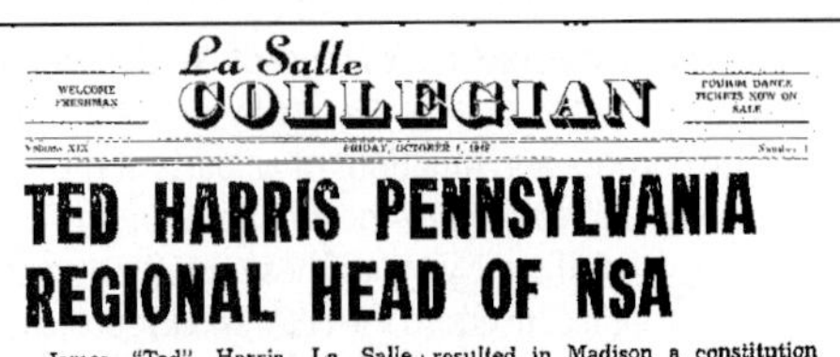

La Salle COLLEGIAN

WELCOME FRESHMAN

FOURUM DANCE TICKETS NOW ON SALE

TED HARRIS PENNSYLVANIA REGIONAL HEAD OF NSA

James "Ted" Harris, La Salle College pre-law student, returned from the National Student Association convention held in Madison, Wisconsin, from August 30 to September 7 as chairman of the Pennsylvania Region of the organization.

With Ted and the thre

resulted in Madison a constitution for national representation and a program of activities to organize member student government, to increase cooperation between American college students and those

Ted Harris Is Elected National Head Of NSA

In a dramatic session at Madison, Wisconsin, on August 28, James "Ted" Harris was elected National President of the National Student Association.

...arris, who graduated from La ... last June, was not a candi... until an hour before the no...ation speeches began. His ...ed was placed in nomination in ... unprecedented maneuver when ...ph Beerbalm, a leading candi... from the University of Chica... withdrew his own name and

Temple University NEWS

NSA President Honored; 110 Delegates at Banquet

One hundred ten delegates attended the National Student Association banquet in Mitten Hall Saturday night, when James "Ted" Harris, president of NSA, was honored.

The group was welcomed by University Vice-President William W. Tomlinson. Brother George Thomas, Dean of Freshmen at LaSalle College, next introduced Ted Harris, who told ... The organizational program of the National Conference of Christians and Jews was explained by Chaplain Kiemel, who is director of the organization. The banquet was climaxed with singing by Joy Gains, who was accompanied by Phoebe Caldwell. Joseph

American Student No. 1

James T. (Ted) Harris '48, who recently ended his term as president of the National Student Association, will sail from New York on Friday, October 7, to assume the position of American Senior Secretary of

been gained by the organization as the representative of the American student.

Harris' headquarters in Europe will be Geneva, Switzerland. His principal duties will be to arrange international conferences, travel, and study for American students. He will also arrange for tours and study in America for foreign students. The ISS also provides relief service for foreign students and is planning a project to send American students to Europe for the summer to help in the reconstruction of devastated areas.

Harris will remain in Europe for at least two years. His family will join him in Geneva later this year. Following this two year period with

TIMES—PHILADELPHIA, FRIDAY, SI

Appointed To Geneva Post

Brother G. Paul, F.S.C., president of La Salle College, Philadelphia, congratulates honor graduate James T. Harris upon his appointment as American senior secretary to the International Student Service at Geneva, Switzerland. Harris was the first Negro to be so honored, and was graduated with honors from La Salle in 1948

OCT 1 1949

GRADUATE OF LA SALLE HONORED

James T. Harris Selected American. Senior Secretary of Students' Service, Geneva

James T. Harris, winner of the John McShain prize in 1948 which is awarded annually to the La Salle student who, in the opinion of the faculty, has done the most for the welfare of La Salle, has been appointed American senior secretary of the International Students' Service in Geneva, Switzerland.

Harris, who just finished a term as president of the 300 college member National Student Association,

American students sent abroad on cultural studies, an increase in relief collections, the establishment of human relations institutes in five critical areas, the establishment of the purchase card system under which 60,000 students received discount benefits, and the establishment of a legislative committee in Washington to search out and advise both educators and students of pending legislation that would affect them.

In addition to the duties already outlined for him, Harris hopes to accomplish his own three point program, which is: 1, develop a stronger working group in the US for greater support of the ISS; 2, through ISS assistance, help develop better methods of research and research techniques and make this information more available internationally; 3, to affect a closer relation between the students in

Former Student Named to High Office in WUS

Ted Harris '48 has been appointed Associate General Secretary of the World University Service, a newly-formed international university organization with headquarters in Geneva, Switzerland. WUS combines the former activities of International Student Service and World Student Relief.

Before receiving his new assignment, Harris was American Senior Secretary of the ISS. Along with his duties as General Secretary, he will conduct the conferences, seminars and other educational projects of the association.

Harris has been prominent in national and international student activities since his graduation from La Salle in June, 1948. He was elected president of the NSA that summer and the following year was appointed to the position with ISS.

TED HARRIS LEADING NSA (From top) Addressing the Pennsylvania Region as its Chairman at Penn State, June 1948 (Ostar), National Executive Committee Meeting, Cleveland College, April 1949 (Schwartz). Mike Rubino (Mason-Dixon Regional Chair) and Mary Colfer (Catholic U.) are in rear (Schwartz). NSA 2d Birthday, Second Congress at U. of Illinois. Dick Heggie, V.P., and Helen Jean Rogers, Sec'y.-Treas., look on (SHSW). Harris in an expansive mood at home in Madison, WI (Heggie). Harris at the Madison, WI, national offices (Heggie).

BUILDING EXPERTISE IN PUBLIC POLICY Harris moved from campus, regional, and national NSA positions to staff assignments with the International Student Service and then the World University Service while at the same time completing his undergraduate degree at La Salle and his graduate degree at the Woodrow Wilson School. (From top) *La Salle Collegian* 10/21/47 and 10/1/48. *Temple University News* 2/25/49. *Collegian* 9/30/49. *Main Line (?) Times* c. 10/1/49. *La Salle Collegian* 2/14/51.

The regional organizations are struggling along on a day-to-day basis.

Reports from the Precincts

Student government leaders are eager to take on new responsibilities.

Editor's note: Each year, NSA national officers conducted organizing and liaison trips around the country, meeting with regional and campus leaders and administrators and addressing student governments and student assemblies. Without the benefit of professional or field staff (the latter was initiated in the 1950s), these travels brought the first postwar truly national year-round "third-party" student government voice onto the American college campus and into its councils. Staff correspondence and reports document the periodic considerations and reconsiderations—often passionate and dramatiic —of NSA membership as student leadership posts changed hands from year to year. These reports also reveal, in the candid comments of their authors, the difficulties in building widespread student participation in NSA programs that its leaders faced. The reports, adapted from those appearing in NSA News *in spring 1949, reflect the diversity of circumstance and interests that NSA sought to address.*

Louisiana: not promising; Texas: hopeful

Southwest and Eastern Outlook

On the way: Philadelphia Music Festival, New England Culturale

Richard G. Heggie
University of California, Berkeley
NSA Vice President, Student Affairs, 1948-49

In a land that is such a fertile breeding ground for both young steers and young politicians, it is surprising that NSA has not had more success. From the vast expanses of Texas, through such free-thinking Texans as Jim Smith, president of the National Continuations Committee, sprang many of the conceptions and ideas that gave NSA its form and direction.

Actually the decline of Texan influence since the Constitutional Convention has resulted as in other parts of the South from the conscious efforts of a few people to destroy the NSA through the presentation of a distorted picture of its program. Their initial success in Texas has been largely the result of the national political environment.[1]

Happily there are some Texas schools which have never discussed NSA at any length so that there is hope of an unprejudiced approach from the students attending these schools. Among them are Texas Tech, Baylor University, the University of Houston, Texas State University, and Rice Institute. The race question, though important to the Texas student leaders, did not appear to be the prime factor of consideration....

[At the University of Texas] Barefoot Sanders, the Student Association president, who is still remembered by feminine delegates to the Constitutional Convention, is guiding the smooth-running operations of the Student Association. It is a pity that this great university is not a member of NSA; its open-mindedness far exceeds that of most northern institutions.

Hope for Texas lies in Houston

The greatest hope for a Texas expansion of the NSA lies [in Houston] ... a large student population [is] anxious to demonstrate civic and educational accomplishments to the rest of the country. The student referendum on NSA to be held at the University of Houston ... may set the pace for the city and the state.

The situation in Louisiana is still not too promising. Though here again many student leaders are favorable to NSA, the effects of the race issue have slowed or prevented affiliations. The presence of such institutions as Loyola University is a spark of hope for the future, however, for they are dedicated to raising the level of inter-group relations. The Negro students, who have thus far carried the load in the area, are doing a valiant job against the tremendous odds.

It is the formation of such groups as the proposed Louisiana student government federation which is presenting the most direct threat to NSA in the South.

—*NSA News* 1/49

* * *

An active West Virginia College Federation

After a brief stopover in Madison ... I journeyed to the Semi-annual Convention of the West Virginia College Federation, to present NSA to the assembled delegates.

This federation was very active in the field of student government before the war and has recently been reorganized. Tom Crossan, the 1948-1949 president ... has foreseen the desirability of making the Federation part of a larger entity, i.e., NSA. The main obstacle to this consolidation appears to be a financial one, but at least some of the schools appear to be making headway in overcoming it.

Dr. Stewart Smith of the host school, Marshall College, represents the type of college president which others should emulate in their rela-

HEGGIE, ROGERS, AND SCHWARTZ WITH 1948-1949 & 1949-1950 NSA NATIONAL STAFFS: Assembled in national office at 304 North Park in Madison, Wisconsin. L. to r., standing: Craig Wilson (U. Michigan), '49-50 *NSA News* Editor; Robert A. Kelly (St. Peter's, NJ), '49-50 President; Eugene G. Schwartz, '48-49 V.P. Educational Problems; Helen Jean Rogers (Mundelein, Chicago), '48-49 Secretary-Treasurer; Charlotte Allen and Phillip Stoddard (both U. Illinois, Illinois Regional International Commission); Richard J. Medalie (Carleton, MN), '49-50 V.P. Educational Problems; Allan Ostar (Penn State), '48-49 Public Relations Director; Ted Perry (Temple U., Philadelphia), '49-50 V.P. Student Life; Beatrice Heggie (U. California, Berkeley). Kneeling: James T. Harris, Jr. (La Salle, Philadelphia), '48-49 President; Richard G. Heggie (U. California, Berkeley), '48-49 V.P. *Student Life.*

tions with students. For one year Dr. Smith served as faculty advisor to the Marshall student council.

A resurgence of the traditional American town meeting

Though most college presidents, including Dr. Smith, could not for long spare the time in such activity, they can remain in touch with the student body and maintain an interest in its doings. The great distance between faculty and students existent in our larger institutions it too often widened by faculty "white-towerism."...

In the discussions the students demonstrated both vigor and confidence in themselves. The "spirit of democracy" that is so much discussed but so little practiced in the world today was very much in evidence. To me such local and state conferences represent a resurgence of the traditional American town meeting. With proper leadership they can be turned in the future to the accomplishment of practical projects of the NSA variety.

—*NSA News* 4/49

* * *

Culturales in Philadelphia and New England, Purchase Card System (PCS)

A day at Virginia State College was truly a fine experience. The student government leaders there are eager to take on new responsibilities. Both Mike Rubino [Mason-Dixon] and Tom Garrity [Met. New York] report their regions have almost ceased project work and are now settling down to orientation for the Congress.[2] The Pennsylvania people held their big Music Festival in Philadelphia, April 22 and 23.[3] The show was a tremendous success artistically, with talented musical groups from all parts of the state giving great performances, but a disappointment financially. It is a pity more Philadelphians weren't aware of this biggest entertainment value in town ... the committee has established the foundation for a worthy Pennsylvania tradition.

NNER [Northern New England Region] had its own culturale which, though on a smaller scale than the Philadelphia affair, came out a good deal better financially. NNER, in fact, seems to be booming in all directions, bringing in new schools by the half dozen.[4]

The big topic in SNER [Southern New England Region] these days is the tremendous success of PCS in New Haven. Under the chairmanship of Rusty Wirth, who is a born salesman, the Yale Committee lined up the best men's stores in town and sold 1,500 cards all in the first three weeks of operation.

Symphony Forum, Student Government Clinic

Developments at the SNER assembly, held in Providence April 30 and May 1, indicate that one of the big issues at the National Congress will be the NEC's stand on academic freedom.[5]

During my visit to Chicago and Boston I contacted the managers of the respective symphony orchestras of these cities with a view toward getting something going on the Symphony Forum ... progress has been disappointing. Plans must be made now for the fall season.

The New England Student Government Clinic held at the University of Connecticut (Storrs) May 7 and 8 was fairly successful ... but was not too well attended. Ben Labaree of Yale and Pug Greenberg of Mt. Holyoke, however, did a swell job of planning and organizing the sessions.

Needed: some "traditional American huckstering"

From the response that has been indicated to all the programs that have been going on in the East, it can only be concluded that in most cases student governments and the responsible NSA Committees are not ... making the projects attractive to their students.

Each activity like the Music Festival, the Symphony Forum, PCS, and the student government clinic does have interest for particular groups of students if the trouble is taken to set up the project properly and then to sell it in the traditional American huckstering manner.

—*NSA News* 5/49

HEGGIE VISITS THE NORTHWEST

A University of Washington stopover provided the opportunity once again to meet Dan Pulsifer, the regional chairman ... doing a bangup job organizing a growing region, but is still hampered by the great distances ... I was privileged to speak to the Organizations Assembly at the University before meeting with the non-member schools in the Seattle area. It was apparent that both member and non-member student bodies still did not understand the relationship of NSA to the local student government.... The most successful meeting of the trip was held at Reed College in Portland, Ore. The Reed College Congress delegate, Bette Jane Warnock, organized a full day's conference which was attended by eight schools in the Portland area ... The day was topped off by a dinner at the University of Portland ... the first time the Portland student councils had met together.

—*NSA News* 4/49

Students in the South are very eager to work with their fellow collegians.

'Way Down South

Responsible leaders, convinced of the need for change, face violent public opposition.

Helen Jean Rogers
Mundelein College
NSA Secretary-Treasurer, 1948-49

Unfortunately, students in the South have to a large extent remained aloof from inter-regional activities of a religious, political, or educational nature. For example, in the National Student Association with a membership of nearly three hundred schools there are only twenty-five which are in the South.

This condition of separation exists primarily, I think, because public opinion in the South fearing social change seeks to resist it by isolating the area from the rest of the country....

Because of this isolation students in other parts of the country, knowing little about southern collegians, look upon them with sentiments ranging from mild curiosity to real disdain.

During [my] tour of the South, I addressed student governments of thirty-five colleges and met with representatives of seventy other southern schools in conventions and conferences. By meeting and working with these people I have changed some of my ideas about southern student life that were based on misconceptions shared, I believe, by many other northern collegians. Some of these misconceptions which seem to me to be most prevalent are:

1. Southern schools have poor student activities programs.

On the contrary, a large number of the schools I visited have effective student government with comprehensive programs and wide areas of authority. Nearly all of them have honor systems of which the southern students are particularly proud. At University of North Carolina there are no campus police or proctors during exams. All through the South the code of personal honor is emphasized in every field of college life and disciplinary actions including recommendations for expulsion are handled by student committees.

2. Southern schools participate in no intercollegiate activities.

This is, again, untrue. Southern schools have developed strong intercollegiate programs. There is a southern women's student government association and a similar organization for student leaders of large universities. There are southern forensic groups, religious organization and social leagues.

In addition there are federations of student governments in several states.... Unfortunately these organizations are either exclusively for white students or for negroes and although some efforts have been made to bring the two groups together for meetings there has been little success thus far.

3. Students in the South do not wish to know or work with students in other parts of the country.

This is probably the most unfortunate misconception of all. Students in the South are very eager to work with their fellow collegians throughout the nation.

They feel that they have a great deal to contribute to an organization such as NSA and they want to participate fully. They have a strong sense of regional pride and a feeling that the rest of the country looks down upon them.

As one student government president said to me, "...I attended the last national congress and was ashamed at the lack of southern participation."

—*NSA News* 3/49

Editor's Note: Helen Jean Rogers' report on segregation and possibilities for change, not reproduced here, appears in the 4/49 issue of NSA News.

Nine northern regions with two-thirds of NSA's membership

Strongholds of NSA

With few exceptions regions are, at best, struggling on a day-to-day basis.

Eugene G. Schwartz
City College of New York
Vice President, Educational Problems, 1948-49

My recent organizational tour took me through nine regions which together contain two-thirds of NSA's student membership and more than 175 of its member colleges.[5]

While these regions might truly be called the "strongholds of NSA," even the briefest of discussions with the more than three score regional officers I spoke to will reveal that with few notable exceptions, the regional organizations in these areas are at best struggling along on a day-to-day basis.

Regional officers lack funds and resources

Regional officers from Northern New England to Minnesota share equivalent burdens. They bear the brunt of the intercollegiate responsibilities of NSA in the project and activity field. At the same time they are almost without funds ... in many cases in the red ... and subsist on the labors of two or three earnest people and the secretarial help of a small girls' college in the vicinity of the regional chairman. This is a picture of the typical "stronghold of the NSA."

As one regional officer in Mason-Dixon put it, "NSA is 75 percent Staff Committee nationally, 0 percent region, and 25 percent college locality."

[Almost unanimously], regional chairmen spoken to believed that several organizational needs will have to be [satisfied] before their regions could adequately fulfill their functions. First, some means of raising funds for the support of at least a part-time, if not full-time, regional officer is necessary.

Hopes for revenues from regional events

Some regions, such as Northern New England, Met. N.Y., N.Y. State, Michigan, Illinois, Pennsylvania, and Mason-Dixon can look forward to the somewhat tenuous possibility of substantial assistance from the Purchase Card System operating in their metropolitan areas.

A few of them, such as Pennsylvania and Met. N.Y., are planning extensive intercollegiate cultural programs. These displays of student talent which can draw large audiences are also potential fund raisers.

The second suggestion made is that the position of traveling secretary on the national level be created. A year and a half of experience reveals that that the U.S. mails are not the most dependable means of keeping a massive organization such as NSA intact. National and regional projects need to be tied together through personal contact.

Regions such as Met. N.Y. and Northern New England are still beset by unhealthy struggles of factionalism. In the Met. N.Y. Region this condition has almost brought regional activity to a halt.

Colleges in the outlying areas of New York State, Pennsylvania, Northern New England, and Wisconsin are becoming restive at the inability of their regions to draw them together. Groups such as Mason-Dixon, Illinois, and Met. N.Y. still depend to a great degree on the work of a few.

All of the regions suffer from poor public relations, with the notable exceptions of New Jersey and Michigan.

Programs developed in NNER, Minnesota, New Jersey, and Pennsylvania are to be commended, while Mason-Dixon, mainly through the efforts of one school, is to be praised for having shouldered the burden of three national sub-commissions.

—*NSA News* 2/49

EDITOR'S NOTES

1 See University of Texas affiliation contest, p. 995.
2 See Rubino, p. 920, and Metropolitan New York Region, p. 845.
3 See Albums, pp. 325, 368, and Pennsylvania Region, p. 916.
4 See New England Region, p. 823.
5 See Brown on NSA and Academic Freedom, p. 375.

BUILDING REGIONAL ORGANIZATION

NSA NEWS November, 1948

NSA Officers Tour Nation

Schwartz Attends Michigan Assembly

Eugene Schwartz, vice-president on Educational Problems, recently attended the La Crosse (Wisconsin) student problems conference where

Heggie Addresses College Conference

Vice-president Dick Heggie, who spoke on student work in the UNESCO field, represented NSA at the semi-annual conference of the

Ted Harris Speaks To NAACP Delegates

The program of the United States National Student Association in the field of human relations was enthusiastically received by delegates

NSA N

NEWS FROM THE REGIONS

Region Debaters Consider British Medicine Plan

The Second Annual Collegiate Debate Tournament sponsored by NSA's New Jersey Region will be held at St. Peter's College on Feb. 12.

NANCY YERGES, OHIO REGIONAL CHAIRMAN, AND DICK PETERS, Ohio Wesleyan University student body president (seated at desk), talk with representatives of non-member schools at the Ohio Region Assembly held at Ohio State University, December 4-5. Delegates from 28 colleges and universities mapped plans for foreign student hospitality programs, PSC activity and human relations projects.

Regions Schedule Winter Assemblies

PLANNING A CONCRETE PROGRAM for 1949 will be the major task of the delegates attending the many regional conventions to be held in the near future.

Ky-Tenn Holds Leadership Clinic

Met New York Plan Trip to Puerto Rico

Illinois Acts To Lower Fares

California Plans Student Exhibit

REGIONAL FOCUS in the early years was on how NSA could build the organization, create additional opportunities for leadership, draw on existing college campus infrastructure and provide incentives for volunteer energies without a paid field staff. *NSA News* (11/48, 1/49 editions above) supported that effort in its reporting. 28 Ohio region colleges attended the 12/48 regional assembly shown in the photo.

7 Sunday, September 19, 1948 THE MILWAUKEE JOURNAL Sunday, September 19, 1948 7

A senior at Alfred (N. Y.) university, Ingram Paperny, New York, represented the training division of a United Nations department.

Smiling Preston Hodges, 20, of Petersburg, Va., is a senior at Sweet Briar (Va.) college. She hopes to continue her studies in Europe after graduation.

The ambition of Martin Wolfs[illegible]n, 21, of Springfield, Ohio, a junior at Wittenberg college, Springfield, is to [illegible] a health and physical education tea[illegible]cher.

From Shanghai, Gladys Chang, 19, came to Sarah Lawrence college, Bronxville, N. Y. She is president of the college student body.

Some day Margaret Sellers, 20, of Brookline, Mass., intends to teach English literature and history. She is a senior at Regis college at Weston, Mass.

Joan Rader, 20, senior at Western State college, Pullman, Wash., grew up on a 6,500 acre ranch near Walla Walla; now wants to travel in China.

The World May Need Reforming, but NSA Tackles Its Own Field

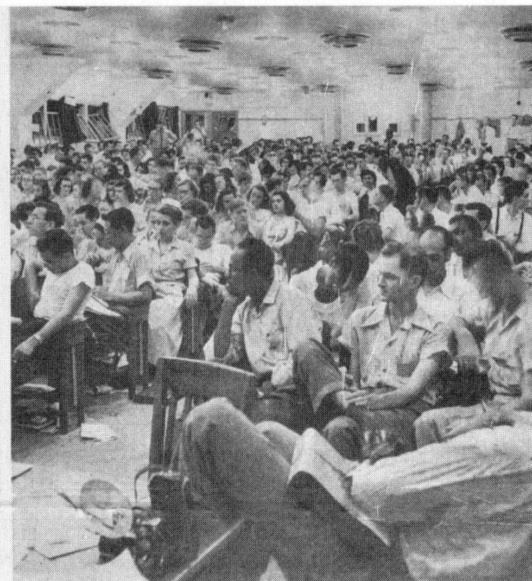

The impulse when our vital youth gets together usually is to start out rec[illegible]ing the world. There are few who will disagree with the need, but the United States National Student association had its own problems to solve first and pr[illegible]ty generally stuck to them at its first congress, held last month at the Uni[illegible]rsity of Wisconsin in Madison. National headquarters are in Madison. Around [illegible],00[illegible] [illegible]erious students representing 270 universities and colleges met for five days. They held general meetings and dozens of seminars. They lived in university do[illegible]rmitories. The social program was kept at a minimum. When the congress was [illegible]er, NSA had refused to join the International Union of Students because it was felt that the international group was Communist dominated and affiliation would contribute nothing to international understanding. NSA is only a year old, but already takes pride in its accomplishments. It has resisted pressure and continues nonpartisan. It is looking into student government and is doing something about it on campuses where it is not too democratic. It has cast a critical eye on student guidance services and expects to do something about them. Its funds have enabled 150 students to tour Europe. With college pennants creating atmosphere, a view of the platform at a session is shown above at the left. The speaker is Norris Erdal, Minneapolis, University of Minnesota, who is Minnesota region chairman. Others are Don Bercey (left), 1301 E. Lake Bluff blvd., University of Wisconsin, and John Marcham, Ithaca, N. Y., Cornell university. The other view shows a general session of the congress, meeting in one of the buildings on the campus. The portraits on these pages are of delegates. —Journal Staff Photos by Angus McDougall

A composer and conductor who has worked for Fred Waring, Charles Warner, 28, studies at the Eastman School of Music, Rochester, N. Y.

FIRST NATIONAL STUDENT CONGRESS. The *Milwaukee Journal,* after interviewing student delegates from all over the United States, reported that "NSA is only a year old, but already takes pride in its accomplishments. It has resisted pressure and continues [to be] nonpartisan."

WHAT THEY DID LATER. Anthology editors contacted college archives and alumni associations to learn more about the later lives of the delegates pictured in the *Milwaukee Journal* article. As has been the case in many instances, tracking down many of the students of our era is often impossible, without a networking connection, despite the cooperation of archive and alumni officials, as well as the use of internet searches. Following are some of the traces we picked up, clockwise from lower left:

Joan Rader Wilson (Western Washington State College), now living in British Columbia, traveled with her mining engineer/geologist husband throughout the Hudson Bay, raising two sons and working with Eskimos and Indians. **Gladys Chang Hardy-Brazil** (Sarah Lawrence C., NY) initially pursued radio and documentary reporting/writing interests, later becoming a Massachusetts and Federal government education and a Ford Foundation executive and a consultant to a wide reach of agencies. Married, widowed and remarried she has two children and three grandsons (see Hardy-Brazil, Pt. 5, S. 2). **Margaret Sellers Fitzpatrick** (St. Regis, MA) went on an NSA-sponsored tour to an English work camp, sailing in 1949 on the *Volendam* (see Pt. 3, S. 5). She taught English, raised three children, and is now involved in reading literacy programs in Toledo, Ohio. **William Allaway** (U. of Illinois) was active in Illinois region inter-

7 Sunday, September 19, 1948 THE MILWAUKEE JOURNAL Sunday, September 19, 1948 7

Just back from a work camp in Holland, Bill Allway, 24, of Downers Grove, Ill., a senior at Illinois, was about the tallest delegate—6 feet 5.

After getting a master's degree in chemistry, Jean Pew, 20, of Los Angeles will teach. She's a senior at Immaculate Heart college, Los Angeles.

Wilberforce Jones, 23, of Nashville, Tenn., a senior at Roosevelt college in Chicago, intends to be a speech correction teacher after graduation.

A senior at California, Joanne Cardiff, 21, of Pasadena, hopes to work for the state department after graduation in political science.

A student in chemistry, John P. Silsby, 22, of Smyrna Beach, Fla., is a senior at Rochester (N. Y.) Institute of Technology. He will seek his master's.

The week of the convention found both temperature and humidity high, so some astute delegates decided the best listening to sessions was from outside the lecture hall where the congress held its meetings.

Problems were discussed informally by James Garst (left), Beverly Hills, Calif., UCLA; Richard Mould, Reading, Pa., Lehigh university; Nancy Roth, Los Angeles, and [illegible] Barbara Finch, Los Angeles, both UCLA.

An aspiring fashion designer, Mary Elizabeth Schmidt, 21, of Cincinnati, Ohio, represented the College of Mount St. Joseph, Cincinnati. She's a senior.

A number of foreign students attended the NSA congress, including (left to right) Philippe Troller, 20, of Roubaix France; Louis de Monspey, 21, of Beaulon-Allier, France; Renee Cantrel, 21, of Paris, France; Trygve Mjoset, 25, of Oslo, Norway, and Nikolaus Voegeli, 21, of Glarus, Switzerland.

That big hat says, "west" and Robert Lord, 23, a law student at Stephen Austin State college, Nacogdoches, Tex.; is from Hemphill, Tex.

national programs, became founding Director of the University of California Education Abroad program and pursued a lifetime career devoted to international exchange working with many agencies and universities (see Allaway, Pt. 3, S. 4). **Joann Cardiff Dickenson DePuy** (U. of California, Berkeley) created two businesses: Wine Tours International, Inc. and Tennis Limited, as well as three children. She has organized hundreds of tennis and wine tours throughout the world, and currently lives with her husband on a knoll in an agricultural preserve in Napa Valley. **James Garst** (UCLA) became City Editor of the UCLA Bruin and was a member of NSA's summer of 1950 International Team (see Pt. 3, S. 3), visiting and developing liaison with the Scandinavian countries. **Nancy Roth Arnheim** (UCLA) headed NSA's first 1948 vocational guidance survey, attended the 1949 Washington Student Citizenship Seminar, went on an NSA student tour in the summer of 1950, sailing on a replacement ship after the Coast Guard failed to certify the original ship (see Pt. 3, S. 6) and returned to a career in high school and adult education personnel and counseling. She raised two children and, retired, is active as President of the Friendship Force of Los Angeles (see Arnheim, Pt. 5, S. 8).

Staff, Advisers, Regional Chairs, Colleges

1948-49 National Organization

(as presented in the First National Student Congress report)

NATIONAL OFFICERS

President
James T. Harris, Jr., La Salle College, Pennsylvania

Vice President, Student Life
Richard G. Heggie, University of California

Vice President, Educational Problems
Eugene G. Schwartz, City College of New York

Vice President, International Affairs
Robert L. West, Yale University

Secretary-Treasurer
Helen Jean Rogers, Mundelein College, Illinois

Public Relations Director
Allan W. Ostar, Pennsylvania State College

REGIONAL REPRESENTATIVES

Ariz., New Mex., So. Colorado
Winfield Meadows
N. Mex. Highlands University

California, Nev., Hawaii
Erskine Childers
Stanford University
Jack Knox
Occidental College

Dakotas
Harold Burnett
Dakota Wesleyan University

Georgia, Ala., Fla.
Al Newton
Georgia Tech

Great Northwest
Dan Pulsifer
University of Washington

Illinois
Mary Jo Domino
Rockford College

Indiana
Mary Jane Porter
Marian College

Iowa
Dale S. Bingham
University of Iowa

Ky., Tenn.
Robert E. Delahanty
University of Louisville

La., Miss., Ark.
Harry T. Alexander
Xavier University

Md., Del., D.C.
Michael J. Rubino
Catholic University

Michigan
Harvey L. Weisberg
University of Michigan
Joe Hansknecht
Aquinas College

Minnesota
Ed. Miller
Hamline University

Mo., Kan., Nebr.
Peggy Mason
Webster College

New Jersey
Robert Kelly
St. Peter's College

New York Metropolitan
Tom Garrity
City College of N.Y.

New York State
Albert A. Szymanski
University of Buffalo

Northern New England
Alice Gilbert
Radcliffe College
Frederic D. Houghteling
Harvard University

Ohio
Nancy Yerges
Ohio State University
Walter Grosjean
Wooster College

Pennsylvania
Harry Brown
Penn. State College
Wm. Heckler
Temple University

Rocky Mountains
I. John Olson
Colorado A. and M.

So. New England
Chris M. Parrs
University of Bridgeport

Virginia, Carolina
Jess Dedmond
University of North Carolina

Wisconsin
F. Frederick Stender
University of Wisconsin

NATIONAL ADVISORY COUNCIL

Dr. Everett Moore Baker
Dean of Students, Massachusetts Institute of Technology

Dr. Monroe E. Deutsch
Provost Emeritus, University of California

Laurence Duggan
Director, Institute of International Education

Father Vincent J. Flynn
President, College of St. Thomas

Dr. R. O. Johnson
Assistant Director, Project for Adult Education of Negroes, U. S. Office of Education

Gordon Klopf
Student Activities Counselor, University of Wisconsin

Dean Newhouse
Director of Student Affairs, University of Washington

Dr. Homer Rainey
President, Stephens College

Dr. Helen C. White
Professor of English, University of Wisconsin

1948-49 Roster of Colleges First National Student Congress

Arizona–N. Mexico–So. Colorado Region
New Mexico Highlands University

California-Nevada-Hawaii Region
California School of Arts and Crafts
College of Holy Names
College of Notre Dame
Fresno State College
Immaculate Heart College
Loyola University
Marin College
Mills College
Mount St. Mary's College
Occidental College
San Francisco State College
Stanford University
University of California, Berkeley
University of California at Los Angeles
University of Santa Clara
Observers
George Pepperdine College
Los Angeles City College

Dakota Region
Dakota Wesleyan University
Observers
Northern State Teachers College, SD

Georgia-Alabama-Florida Region
Barry College for Women
Emory University
Georgia School of Technology
Morehouse College
Alabama State Teachers College
Observers
Tuskegee Institute
University of Alabama

Great Northwest Region
Reed College
State College of Washington
University of Washington

Illinois Region
Aurora College
Barat College of the Sacred Heart
Chicago Teachers College
De Paul University
Evansville College
Illinois State College
Knox College
Mundelein College
National College of Education
North Central College
Northern Illinois State Teachers College
Roosevelt College
Rosary College
Rockford College
St. Procopius College
Observers
College of St. Francis
De Paul University
Illinois Wesleyan University
James Millikan University
Loyola University
Northwestern University

Indiana Region
Franklin College
Indiana State Teachers College
Indiana Technical College
Marian College
Saint Mary-of-the-Woods College
St. Mary's College
Observers
Earlham College
Parson College
Purdue University
St. Francis College

Iowa Region
Clark College
Grinnell College
Marycrest College
University of Iowa
Observers
Wartburg College

Kentucky-Tennessee Region
Christian Brothers Junior College
King College
Nazareth College
Southwestern at Memphis
University of Louisville
Ursuline College
Observers
Berea College
Tennessee Polytechnic Institute

Louisiana-Arkansas-Mississippi Region
Arkansas A. M. & N.
Southern University & A. & M. College
University of Arkansas
Xavier University
Observers
Louisiana State University
Northwestern State College, Louisiana
Southeastern Louisiana College
Southwestern Louisiana College

Maryland-Delaware-D.C. Region
Catholic University of America
College of Notre Dame of Maryland
Dunbarton College of Holy Cross
Hood College
Loyola College
Mt. St. Agnes College
Trinity College
University of Baltimore
Observers
St. Joseph's College
University of Maryland

Michigan Region
Aquinas College
Central Michigan College of Education
Highland Park Junior College
Hillsdale College
Marygrove College
Mercy College
Michigan College of Mining
Siena Heights College
University of Detroit
University of Michigan
Wayne University
Observers
Michigan State College

Minnesota Region
Augsburg College and Theological Seminary
Carleton College
College of St. Benedict
College of St. Teresa
College of St. Thomas
Concordia College
Hamline College
Macalester College
St. Cloud State Teachers College
St. John's University
St. Olaf College

Missouri-Kansas-Nebraska Region
Doane College
Pontbonne College
Kansas State College
Kansas State Teachers College
Le Clerc College
Marymount College
Maryville College
Mt. St. Scholastica College
Webster College
William Woods College
Observers
University of Kansas

New Jersey Region
College of St. Elizabeth
Monmouth Jr. College
New Jersey College for Women
New Jersey State Teachers College–Montclair
New Jersey State Teachers College–Paterson
Rutgers University-Newark
Rutgers University-New Brunswick
St. Peter's College
St. Peter's School of Business

New York Metropolitan Region
Adelphi College
CCNY Business Day
CCNY Business Evening
CCNY Main Day
CCNY Main Evening
College of New Rochelle
Columbia University
Fordham College
Fordham School of Education
Good Counsel College
Hunter College-Day
Hunter College-Evening
Juilliard School of Music
Long Island University
Manhattan College
Manhattanville College of the Sacred Heart
New York University–School of Education
New York University–University Heights
New York University–Washington Square
Pratt Institute
Queens College
Sarah Lawrence College

New York State Region
Alfred University
Bard College
College of St. Rose
Cornell University
D'Youville College
Eastman School of Music
LeMoyne College
New York School of Applied Arts and Sciences
Niagara University
Rochester Institute of Technology
Russell Sage College
St. Bonaventure College
St. Lawrence University
Siena College
Skidmore College
University of Buffalo
University of Rochester College for Women
University of Rochester College for Men
University of Rochester School of Nursing
Vassar College
William Smith College
Observers
Nazareth College
Syracuse University

Northern New England Region
American International College
Bates College
Bennington College
Bowdoin College
Colby Jr. College
Emmanuel College
Garland School
Harvard College
Harvard Divinity School
Massachusetts Institute of Technology
Mount Holyoke College
Mt. St. Mary College
Radcliffe College
Regis College
Simmons College
Smith College
Springfield YMCA College
Wellesley College
Wheaton College
Williams College
Observers
College of the Holy Cross
Harvard Graduate School
University of Massachusetts
Women's College of Middlebury, VT

Ohio Region
Antioch College
Ashland College
Case Institute of Technology
Cleveland College of Western Reserve University
College of Mt. St. Joseph
College of Wooster
Flora Stone Mather College
Hiram College
John Carroll University
Muskingum College
Notre Dame College
Oberlin College
Ohio State University
Ohio Wesleyan College
Otterbein College
Our Lady of Cincinnati
Ursuline College
University of Akron
Youngstown College
Observers
Capital University
Denison University
Lake Erie College
Miami University
Ohio University
Wittenberg College

Pennsylvania Region
Albright College
Allegheny College
Beaver College
Bryn Mawr College
Bucknell University
Chestnut Hill College
Immaculata College
La Salle College
Lehigh University
Martin College
Mercyhurst College
Mount Mercy College
Pennsylvania State College
Rittenhouse College
Rosemont College
St. Francis College
St. Joseph's College
Seton Hill College
State Teachers College, Bloomsburg
Swarthmore College
Temple University
Thiel College
University of Pennsylvania
Wilson College
Observers
St. Vincent College

Rocky Mountain Region
Colorado A. & M.
Colorado College
Loretto Heights College
Regis College
Regis College-Downtown
University of Colorado

Southern New England Region
Albertus Magnus College
Connecticut College for Women
New Haven YMCA Junior College
Pembroke College
St. Joseph's College
Teachers College of Connecticut
Trinity College
University of Bridgeport
University of Connecticut–Fort Trumbull
University of Connecticut–Storrs
Wesleyan University
Yale Divinity School
Yale University–Undergraduate
Observers
University of Connecticut

Texas-Oklahoma Region
Our Lady of the Lake
Stephen F. Austin State Teachers College
University of Tulsa
Observers
University of Oklahoma

Virginia-Carolina Region
Lynchburg College
Randolph-Macon Women's College
Sweet Briar College
University of North Carolina
Virginia State College
Observers
Johnson C. Smith University
North Carolina State College
West Virginia Institute of Technology
West Virginia Wesleyan College

Wisconsin Region
Beloit College
Carroll College
La Crosse State Teachers College
Marquette University
Mount Mary College
St. Norbert College
University of Wisconsin
University of Wisconsin–Milwaukee Extension
Observers
Milwaukee State Teachers College

The People's Republic of China is formed and apartheid introduced in South Africa

1984 is published and *Death of a Salesman* opens

The Chinese Civil War pushes Chiang Kai-shek to the island of Formosa, and the Communist People's Republic is proclaimed under Mao Tse-tung with Chou En-lai as premier. The North Atlantic Treaty Organization is formed. Britain recognizes the independence of the Republic of Eire. The Vietnam state is established in Saigon after the French are defeated. Holland transfers sovereignty to Indonesia. The communist Democratic Republic is established in East Germany. Apartheid is introduced in South Africa. The Berlin Airlift ends, after 277,264 flights. Eleven U.S. communists are found guilty of conspiracy to overthrow the U.S. government. George Orwell's *1984* and T.S. Eliot's *The Cocktail Party* are published. Arthur Miller's *Death of a Salesman* and Carson McCullers's *A Member of the Wedding* open. Classic films include *The Third Man* and *Les Enfants Terribles*. Rodgers and Hammerstein's *South Pacific* and Leonard Bernstein's *Age of Anxiety* are performed. High on the charts are "Bali Hai," "I'm in Love with a Wonderful Guy," "Riders in the Sky," and "Rudolph the Red-Nosed Reindeer." Northwestern defeats California 20-14 at the Rose Bowl, and New York defeats Brooklyn 4-1 in the World Series.

Source: Adapted from citations in Bernard Grun, *The Timetables of History* (Simon and Schuster, 1991)

BUDGETING NSA'S MILESTONES: 1948-1949

USNSA BUDGET FØR YEAR 1948-1949:

Furniture	1,010
Insurance	40
Salaries	14,000
Rent	1,500
Travel	2,500
Office supplies	1,200
Postage	1,400
Telephone	600
Printing	2,200
Magazines	m 60
Clipping service	90
Misc.	700
	25,300

ANTICIPATED INCOME:

Cach on had	4,000
Dues	20,000
Publications	1,000
Misc.	50
Advertising	100
	25,478

INCOME AND EXPENSES FROM SEPT. 30, 1948 TO June 30, 1949

Income:	
Membership dues	20,945.00
Stu. Ldrshp & Gov't.	97.03
WST Abroad	688.53
Program and RRport	290.06
NSA NEWS	169.05
USNSA Constitution	33.80
Faculty Rating	10.83
Personall & Guidance	2.55
Developing Group Leadership	97.42
Art Exhibit	126.78
Advertising	2.50
Job Opps. Booklet	16.39
Mailing list	5.00
PCS	59.68
Total Income	$22,544.6

Expenses	
Officer's salaries	10,121.28
Secretarial wages	2,091.34
Rent	1,250.00
Travel	3,348.09
Office supplies	b1,718.02
Postage	2,662.52
Telegraph - telephome	925.30
Printing	3,639.02
Engravings	183.83
Magazine subscriptions	76.32
Clipping service	142.56
Misc. - Depreciation	293.47
Insurance	18.18
Auditing	100.00
Storage exhibits	60.00
other	387.49
Tr-Nation Tour film	252.25
Total Expense	27,269.67
Net loss	4,725.05

Note: the statement does not include from PCS or the NSA tour program.

COMING OFF A FRUGAL FIRST YEAR, the budget was reduced to $25,000, of which $14,000 included full-time officer salaries of $2,000/yr. In its June 30 accounting the staff reported a revenue shortfall of $3,000 and over budget of about $1,800 on expenses—due almost entirely to printing costs. Staff expected to close the deficit gap with revenues from the travel program and from its share of Purchase Card sales. (Document sources: SHSW archives, Sylvia Bacon. Reproduced here are portions of mimeographed NEC and Congress reports.)

SECTION 7

NSA's Third Year, 1949-1950

CONTENTS

With a solid base of some three hundred college members, the Association's Second Annual Congress (heralding its third year), at the University of Illinois, was notable for the breadth of programming it undertook and its confidence that it could be achieved. Harold Taylor, President of Sarah Lawrence College, keynoted the theme "The World and the American Student" (See excerpts, p. 888) to 800 delegates and observers from 312 colleges.

Bob Kelly (St. Peter's College, NJ) was elected president. He brought to his position polished communications skills as a parliamentarian, speaker, and debater which found warm receptions as he traveled the country. He often appeared before student bodies on campuses in the South and elsewhere that were suspicious of NSA's willingness to consider working with the Communist controlled International Union of Students, and at Catholic schools newly introduced to the concept of student rights. Those skills stood the future Korean War veteran in good stead later, at law school and as a partner in a major Wall Street law firm.

The broad, ambitious sweep of NSA's program that year, culminating in the appointment by Kelly of an organization review commission to report to the next congress, is presented by Gene Schwartz, the previous year's vice president for educational affairs and the candidate defeated by Kelly, with whom Kelly developed a trusting and warm relationship.

Unlike the staff comity of the first two years, tensions developed between Kelly and the rest of the staff. These are referred to tangentially in the memoir by *NSA News* Editor Craig Wilson (U. of Michigan), the piece by Vice President for Educational Affairs Rick Medalie (Carleton College, MN) on the educational program in Part 2, and in the memoir of Staff Secretary Mary Kay Perkins (Mundelein College, Chicago) in Part 5.

Student travel crisis and Korean War frame the summer of 1950

The groundwork for the international student travel program laid by prior International Vice Presidents Robert Smith (Yale) and Robert West (Yale) was carried forward by Erskine Childers (Stanford University) when about 13 percent of all U.S. students going abroad in summer 1950 were handled by NSA out of its Cambridge office. Detailed more completely and dramatically in Part 3 of this book, the Coast Guard's refusal to allow an NSA-chartered ship to sail and the problems resulting from this and the rapid growth of the program had resulted in serious financial consequences as well as organizational repercussions.

In contrast, Childers was able to launch a substantial global "international team," which represented NSA in Europe, Africa, and Asia. Craig Wilson relates the strange way in which covert funding found its way to NSA and made sending the team possible. Later, in Part 3, aspects are revisited of the stormy conclusion of that year's international program, occasioned by the U.S. entry into the Korean War and the experience and report of NSA's observer team to the IUS Congress that summer.

NSA's INCOMING PRESIDENT, Bob Kelly (St. Peter's College, NJ) presiding over a plenary session at the University of Illinois before his election.

1949-1950

ALBUM

second
NATIONAL STUDENT CONGRESS
UNIVERSITY OF ILLINOIS
Aug. 24 to Sept. 3
UNITED STATES NATIONAL STUDENT ASSOCIATION

THE DAILY ILLINI

Serving Illini for Over Three-Quarters of a Century

URBANA-CHAMPAIGN, THURSDAY, SEPTEMBER 15, 1949 — FIVE CEN

National Student Association Holds 2nd Congress at UI

The University was host for 10 days this summer to over 600 delegates of the National Student association meeting from Aug. 24 to Sept. 3 for its second annual congress.

Headquarters were set up in the Illini Union with plenary sessions held in the Auditorium and caucus meetings in Gregory and Lincoln halls.

NSA is requesting a ban on discrimination in new campus organizations including fraternities and sororities and an education program to eliminate discrimination in existing groups. It also seeks a "practical" program with the International Union of Students, said to be controlled by Communist students in Eastern Europe.

Political Firing Condemned

Firing of teachers because of ... filiations also ... the delegates ... and univer- ... the United ... was apparent ... y affair with ... control of the ... shown from

private schools could get along on endowments and grants since they already are wealthier generally than public schools.

Formal action was taken to urge limitation on federal grants and scholarships in that aid should not be discriminatory and "where segregation exists in the primary and secondary levels, scholarships in higher education should first be divided in proportion to racial groups within the population." Merit and need should be the criterion, NSA decided.

NSA also called for legislation against schools refusing admission to students because of race, religion, sex, national origin, political beliefs, and economic circumstances. Delegates approved the "Michigan plan" whereby new campus organizations are denied approval if discriminatory clauses are in their constitutions.

IF, Panhel Changes Urged

National Interfraternity council and the Panhellenic council were urged to eliminate discriminatory clauses within member social sorority and fraternity groups.

Keynote speaker of the congress

SCHOOL AND SOCIETY

I. L. KANDEL, Editor — L. REMMY BEYER, Managing Editor

A REPORT ON THE 1949 NATIONAL STUDENT ASSOCIATION CONGRESS

MARION LYNCH
Director of Social Action, Marygrove College
and
GORDON KLOPF
Chairman, Advisory Council, National Student Association; Counselor of Student Activities, The University of Wisconsin

U. of Illinois 9/15/49 issue of *Daily Illini*, above, reports NSA Congress. Above left, NSA brochure announcing the Congress.

Christians on campus mav know NICC, USCC, WSCF and WSSF—

The Intercollegian

Now Know NSA

By RALPH LEE SMITH

These three initials—NSA— keep turning up. If a student is interested in student government work, he is referred to NSA's literature, or to an NSA Intercollegiate Student Government Clinic. If he finds the cost of living high in the local college ... gram, the disorganized USA delegation found itself the victim of an unremitting offensive launched by well-briefed delegations from communist countries. Small Western European countries, which had looked to the United States students ... draft NSA busy and s Th with must

Only Intercollegiate Newspaper

The NSA News

Offical Publication of the United States National Student Association

National Office, 304 N. Park St., Madison 5, Wis. Cable: NAYSTUD

Vol. III, No. 1 — Madison, Wisconsin, October, 1949 — Price 5 Cents

300 Schools Attend Congress

Crack-Down By VA May Restrict Vets

Official Report To Be Ready

1950 THIRD NATIONAL STUDENT CONGRESS UNITED STATES NATIONAL STUDENT ASSOCIATION

A NEW NATIONAL STAFF: Above, from left, standing: Erskine Childers (Stanford U., CA), V.P. International Affairs, Ted Perry (Temple U., PA), V.P. Student Life, Rick Medalie (Carleton C, MN), VP Educational Problems; Seated: Bob Kelly (St. Peter's C, NJ), President; Robert Delahanty (U. of Louisville), Executive Secretary. A year later (right), Kelly (top) and Childers (bottom) address the Third Congress at the U. of Michigan. Below: Perry (center) with NCCJ officials and other NSA staff.

Extending NSA Programs

Moving into its third year with a broadening national and international array of programs and no revenue growth, managing the operation, coordinating the regions, and traveling to campuses and conferences around the country kept staff in Madison and Cambridge fully occupied. The association continued to attract professional media attention, and *School and Society* published the second of its annual reviews of NSA's conventions.

The NSA News

Official Publication of the United States National Student Association

Vol. III, No. 3 — Madison, Wisconsin, December, 1949 — Price 10 Cents

Foreign Travel Summer Programs Set Up

Sea, Air Voyages To Be Scheduled For 800 Students

With low-cost ocean transportation ... plans have been completed for nine NSA ...

NSA, WSSF Plan India Seminar

NSA's International Commission is cooperating with World Student Service Fund (WSSF) and International Student Service (ISS) on a seminar in India and Pakistan this summer.

A group of ten faculty men and carefully-selected students will fly

Loos-Leaflet 1

PCS Cards Save Student Money

Missouri Region Confers With Officials On Campaign for College Bus Passes

Officers of the Missouri Region of NSA met with the St. Louis Public Service Co., on the college-level bus pass the Region is asking in the St. Louis area.

No decision satisfactory to the region was made.

The region is still working towards its goal of 50,000 signatures on a petition calling for the pass.

Attending the meeting were Mary Therese Hartigan, regional chairman; Ed Farmer, chairman of the Bus Pass drive, and regional pr director; and John W. Dameron, executive assistant of the public service co.

According to Farmer, the argument went this way:

Company: College students need not be subsidized. The company is losing money on present high school passes. Everyone wants passes.

NSA: Higher education is more and more becoming a necessity.

Company: Students should acquire a college education of their own.

NSA: Although a grade and high school education is all that is re-

Loyalty Oath Controversy Nears Close

By LOUIS BELL
(Daily Californian)
(Special to the NSA News)

BERKELEY, CALIF.—The Uni-

Cultural Vagabond:

64 NSA Schools To View Art Tour

BASCOM BILL FEATURED:

Human Relations Booklet Published by NSA

A comprehensive handbook for campus human relations programs is now available through the NSA publications bureau.

The 32-page printed booklet is entitled, "Human Relations in the Educational Community." The authors are NSA veep Richard J. Medalie; and chairman of the NSA advisory counsel, Gordon Klopf, student activities counselor, University of Wisconsin.

Harrison, University of Wisconsin. Bascom Bill won the initial approval of the Ohio NSA Region:

"Bascom Bill, a fictional character who reads the book over your shoulder, is really the spirit of the individual student on campus. Bill relieves the book of any tendencies to be stuffy and illustrates the aims of NSA," the Ohio Regional Bulletin commented.

A selection of headlines out of *NSA News* in its 12/49 issue (above) tracks events and programs. Affiliated colleges gave NSA front page and featured coverage.

SCOTT NEWS, DECATUR, GA., Wednesday, Oct. 5, 1949

Delegates Report on Activities At NSA's Congress in Urbana

ASHLAND COLLEGIAN

New N.S.A. Prexy

Californian

OF THE COLLEGE DAILIES

California, Friday, Sept. 9, 1949 — No. 12

The Urbana congress

Rights bill unchanged — By Bob Lehne

U.C. delegates speak up against discrimination — By Arnt Froshaug

Urbana keynoter belittles Red scare

URBANA, Illinois, Aug. 25—"Students are not being corrupted by communism," President Harold ... attitude towards the student and an ignorance of the real situation in which students learn in college." ... student is suspicious ... and all people who ...

Travel and Study in Mexico Offered In NSA's 'Operation Amigos' Program

"Operation Amigos," a program of student study and travel in Mexico this summer, has been added to the National Student Association's summer program for 1949.

NSA is also conducting 10 study-tours and five work camps in Europe, and a seminar in

'Campus Quiz,' Franklin Talk On WXPN Tonight

Ted Perry On Tour For NSA

SQUARE BULLETIN

Pollock To Choose As Topic Of Talk

COMMUNISTS NOT FI... TO TEACH, CHASE SA...

Second NSA Congress Takes Stand On Academic Freedom, Discrimination

By STAN COOPERMAN

From top: *Agnes Scott News* 10/5/49; *Ashland Collegian* 10/7/49, OH; *Daily Californian* 9/9/49, UCLA; *Daily Pennsylvanian*, 4/7/49; *Temple University News* 12/7/49, PA; *Square Bulletin* 10/25/49, NYU.

International Travel, Human Relations, Academic Freedom, Student Services

The year of reconsideration and consolidation

1. From Urbana to Ann Arbor

Eugene G. Schwartz
City College of New York
NSA Vice President for Educational Problems, 1948-49

What a difference a year made! When I joined the nearly seven hundred delegates,[1] alternates and observers representing three hundred colleges on the broad expanse of the University of Illinois campus in Urbana from August 24 to September 3, 1949, NSA had acquired a history, with the 1946 Chicago conference and two summer congresses behind it. In the life cycle of a college student, it was enough to create a cohort of "elder" statesmen and stateswomen.

Ahead of us was a year during which NSA expanded its international outreach in student travel and global representation; gave shape to ongoing programs in the fields of human relations training, student government services, student rights and academic freedom, and segregation and quota systems; and established itself as a credible voice in local, regional, and national educational policy forums. In this year, NSA also undertook a massive review of its organization and programs with the help of its "elders."

All of this can be seen now in retrospect. At the time, some of NSA's leaders were expressing considerable doubt among themselves about the organization's ability to survive its internal leadership conflicts, financial limitations, lack of infrastructure, and student indifference, reflected, among other things, by a significant decline in NSA membership. As the chair of one of the Midwest regions wrote me at the time, "I am convinced that if we are to thwart the rumor that NSA will die, it is imperative that we start working in the regions." However, these concerns did not dampen our enthusiasm, our commitment to the vision that had brought the organization into being, or our belief that we could make it work.

Changing of the guard

Two of us who came to Urbana had been long-distance collaborators in setting up the national Purchase Card System during the past year. At the congress, we would find ourselves in an unexpected, dramatic contest for the NSA presidency. The soon-to-be rivals were Bob Kelly, a twenty-year-old senior history major at St. Peter's College in Jersey City, New Jersey, and myself, a twenty-five-year-old senior civil engineering major from City College of New York, across the Hudson River. Each of us was enrolled in an urban "day-hop" campus and was accustomed to a college experience in which home was the dorm and a working "mom" was the house manager. Each of us had been a regional chairman—I, in 1947-48, of the feisty Metropolitan New York Region, with its twenty-eight factionally split campuses within subway-shot of each other, and Bob, in 1948-49, of the more genteel, consensus-building New Jersey Region, with its ten member campuses spread throughout the state.[2]

As I see it now, the contests for national office were shaped by the desire for "balance" by region, religion, gender, and race. They were also shaped by the interests of two major factions. One faction, which included many Catholic, small-town, and Southern college delegates, sought to assure that the staff did not lean too heavily to the left or harbor "communist" sympathies. The other faction, which included many delegates from small liberal arts, public, and nondenominational Northern and Western institutions, did not wish the staff to be accountable to an external influence promoting an orthodox, morality-based agenda—the Joint Committee for Student Action (JCSA), formed by the National Federation of Catholic College Students (NFCCS) and the Newman Club Federation.[3] Bob and I became instruments of this conflict.

Writing home to my "Mom" on August 18, 1949, about the forthcoming convention arrangements, I reported,

> Yesterday we started work on getting things set up for the congress and so far all is going well. The university has done a tremendous job in helping us out, and all the facilities are at our disposal. We have large, roomy offices in the union building with ample space for all of the work that needs to be done. The staff itself has a private office, in addition to the rooms we will have in the union. The latter, by the way, with all hotel services, is being given to us free of charge, the money coming from the university president's fund. That's one example of the fine help we're getting.

In the same letter I mentioned the four national radio broadcasts that would be originated by NBC, CBS, and ABC at the congress during the coming week. I predicted a busy congress. I have a clear recollection of the fine work done by the Illinois host committee—particularly Bill Allaway; Phil Stoddard, who was student body president; and Char Allen—which enabled a complex event to take place on a smooth schedule.[4]

On August 31, midway in the congress, I wrote again to "Dear Mom":

> We're swinging into the "last lap" of the Congress and two of the major resolutions on policy have already been adopted. NSA's attitude towards fraternity discrimination took some four hours of plenary sessions and several all night committee meetings to adopt.[5] The second, which called for retaining the association's present policy towards cooperating with the International Union of Students, was carried in a dramatic 205 to 177 roll call vote by regions.

Originally, our teller's count on the roll call was 201 to 197, a rather close margin, and the four members of the staff on the stage, Ted, Helen Jean, Rob, and myself threw in our four votes with the majority, which was heart-warming. Later it was discovered that the teller's count was in error by 20 votes.

Then the "bombshell":

> Now comes an item which I find it very difficult to explain.... It is being urged that I be a candidate for President of NSA. This comes from all the members of the staff and a number of National Executive Committee people who closeted me this evening and threw out the bombshell. I told them it was impossible for me to consider it, but they asked that I at least think out the possibility before finally declining. There is an extreme lack of confidence at the Congress in...the candidate [whom] I am supporting, and the possibility looms that he may be defeated by several much less able candidates whose more dynamic performance at this convention has won the support of many delegates. This group feels that I am the only one who can be elected who would have the complete confidence of the entire association here assembled, and they seem to feel that I will be able to make a valuable contribution to NSA.

Clearly, I was smitten with temptation, but I nonetheless expressed indifference to my mother and gave her veto power by return wire. She left it up to me, as did my father.

The Second Congress elections

So, having declared myself (and gone back on my word to a student whom I had ardently encouraged to run), I enlisted the acceptance-speech coaching of my good Met New York friend Tom Callahan of St. Francis in Brooklyn, who became NSA's first Travel Office director in New York in 1952.[6] I don't have a copy of the speech, nor do I recall anything of it but the first phrase, which was, "We are gathered here today . . . ," and Tom's advice that I raise and open my arms in an embracing gesture to launch that auspicious opening.

Meantime, there were other forces at work.[7]

Here is how the October 6, 1949, edition of the St. Peter's College student newspaper, *Pauw Wow,* reported it:

> When Bob Kelly was first nominated as a presidential candidate, he refused the nomination and, in turn, nominated Eugene Schwartz of CCNY, last year's national vice president. But Bob's efforts were to no avail. Many of the delegates were familiar with Bob's ability and personality, which he demonstrated as Acting Chairman of the Congress as well as in his chairmanship of two previous Plenary Sessions. They knew the man they wanted.
>
> After several anxious moments and almost against his own feelings, Bob consented, in deference to those who sought his nomination....On the second ballot, Bob was elected handily over the man he himself had nominated.

On the first pass Bob received 184 votes, I got 121, Alex Pope (U. of Chicago), 49, and Harvey Weisberg (U. of Michigan), 44. On the second round, 18 fewer votes were cast, and Kelly won 203 to 177.

My retrospective view is that there were good reasons for the outcome. I was a fan of Bob's in many ways, and felt that he brought the leadership energy and focus to the job that it needed. During his year as president, it developed that his management style and temperament were out of step with those of his staff colleagues, as is noted by Craig Wilson in his essay in this book. This created a sad and poignant experience for the staff. However, despite the serious staff division, there remained a broad consensus on policy issues. Helen Jean Rogers wrote me from the Chicago National Executive Committee (NEC) meeting in December of that year that Kelly had "really a united staff against him." From my perspective, I remained an admirer and booster of Bob as a brilliant parliamentarian and an effective spokesman for NSA and was heartbroken over the staff dissension. Yet, historically, a look at the national organization's favorable public posture and the clarity with which its agenda was presented at NEC meetings and to the Michigan Congress reflects both Kelly's positive leadership contribution to NSA as well as the initiatives taken by the other officers to carry out their programs.

The business of selecting candidates for office at those early NSA conventions was a matter of situational ethics and tactics, despite whatever advance planning might have been attempted to develop nominees. With the diffuse method of delegate selection and the one-year term limits on which NSA's structure was built, it was almost impossible to manage a slate in advance of the congress.

Rick Medalie, a premed junior at Carleton College, MN, whom I was encouraging to replace me as educational problems vice president, recalled in a recent interview with Ralph Lee Smith and me:

> This was my sophomore year at college. . . . I was involved in the Carleton NSA Committee as a freshman and also ran the Student Project for Amity Among Nations ("SPAN") office in Minneapolis in the summer of '48. I had no concept whatsoever that I would become an NSA national officer. I had no pretensions to it nor interest in that regard. My intention was that this was an extracurricular activity. I had a feeling that my parents were negatively inclined toward it, and when it suddenly came up at the Congress I fought against it, as you may recall. I was really beaten over the head by a variety of people, including Gene. So I worked out a quid pro quo with Gene and said, OK, I'll run. But if I'm elected, you'll have to promise me that you're going to come home with me to Minneapolis as a buffer for my parents.

After Rick's election, with nominal opposition and no recorded vote, I did go home with him to do the buffering job.

Twenty-year-old Irish-born Erskine Childers, cochair of the California region and a Stanford junior international relations major, was elected vice president for international affairs, by a vote of 212-124, over the more conservative University of Minnesota candidate, Bill Holbrook. Bill, together with Rob West and myself, were later selected by Bob Kelly and the staff to form the observer team to the IUS World Student Congress in Prague in summer 1950.[8]

Ted Perry, a twenty-five-year-old accounting senior at Temple, was elected vice president for student life. An African American, he was the first student to be appointed to the board of directors of the Philadelphia branch of the National Association for the Advancement of Colored People (NAACP).[9]

Bob Delahanty, a twenty-six-year-old civil engineering graduate of the University of Louisville, was appointed by Kelly as executive secretary, to hold the position for six months, then to be replaced by Harvard prelaw senior Fred Houghteling, who was elected the second time around out of a field of four, without a recorded vote. Fred's election was the first attempt to create a staff position with staggered terms that would carry over from one administration to the next.

NEWLY ELECTED STAFF From left: Fred Houghteling (Harvard U.), Secretary; Rick Medalie (Carleton C., MN), V.P. Educational Problems; Bob Kelly (St. Peter's C., NJ), President; Erskine Childers (Stanford U., CA), V.P. International Affairs; Ted Perry (Temple U., PA), V.P. Student Life. *(2nd Congress Report)*

The National Executive Committee named Ralph Lee Smith, age twenty-one, a Swarthmore College, PA, junior, as public relations director.[10] Craig Wilson, twenty-two, a journalism senior at the University of Michigan, was named publications director and editor of the *NSA News.*[11]

A few weeks into the school year, Mary Kay Perkins of Mundelein College in Chicago was hired as a full-time staff associate to manage the Madison office. The Illinois Region contributed two key people to energize the national organization that year. Mary Jo Domino, chair of the Illinois Region, wrote me when she learned Mary Kay was resigning her upstate Illinois Regional post, "We'll never be able to get anyone in as Cultural Chair with the energy and ideas of Mary Kay." In addition, as noted elsewhere, Charlotte Allen (U. of Illinois) in charge of the region's mock UNESCO conference, signed on to work in the Cambridge office for the year.

The Second Congress program

A daunting array of issues and events confronted the congress, at which Kelly demonstrated his parliamentary prowess. In the mimeographed publication, *The Daily Bull,* which was circulated to delegates, Allan Ostar, outgoing (public relations) Director, reported that there had been scheduled 294 round table sessions, 192 regional caucuses, 62 commission and plenary sessions, and 168 committee meetings. Out of these sessions came a program and an agenda for the coming year. Highlights included:

Student Government and Student Life

- Strengthening the role and effectiveness of programs in the areas of student governments in student affairs.
- Promoting the faculty rating and student leadership programs.
- Mounting an effective cultural affairs program in music, literature, and the arts, including *Essai* magazine and the Symphony Forum.

Student Rights and Discrimination

- Addressing threats to academic freedom and adding responsibilities to the Student Bill of Rights. "After prolonged discussion," it was resolved that "All consideration of the Student Bill of Rights is referred to a National Subcomission on Student Rights," to report back to the next congress.

- Reaffirming NSA's opposition to "unfair educational practices" of discrimination in admissions. In its resolution, NSA reflected the mores of the time by exempting from its definition of "unfair" practices" admissions requirements of "non-coeducational" schools, inquiries about religion by denominational schools, residential priorities set by public institutions, and "sex quota systems" in teachers' colleges so that "a sufficient number of teachers of each sex are educated."[12]
- Expanding the human relations programs by drawing colleges into programs for the elimination of prejudice and discrimination. Urging student governments to work for the elimination of discriminatory membership clauses and practices in fraternities and sororities at the campus level.

Economic Benefits

- Enlarging and institutionalizing the Purchase Card System (PCS), "one of the Association's most attractive and popular programs," and other student economic benefit programs. PCS, renamed Student Discount Service, rose to bring in close to 8 percent of NSA's operating budget in later years.
- Activating NSA's legislative program and "removing the stigma which many students unfortunately attach to political activity." The program included support for federal scholarships and fellowship grants, because "the decision as to who should go to college is at present influenced far too much by economic considerations. . . . Where segregation exists in the primary and secondary level of education in a state, scholarships given should first be divided in proportion to racial groups in the total population of that state."

International Programs

- Institutionalizing NSA's international programs in the areas of international exchange, relief and reconstruction, UNESCO membership, and IUS relations. Reaffirming support for the Word Student Service Fund.
- Laying out the requirements for a "truly representative international organization of world students" to embody geographic, political, racial, and religious inclusiveness. The congress stated that "the IUS does not at present incorporate the characteristics" of such an organization.

Organization

- Strengthening provisions for the travel pool, which equalized delegate travel costs to national conventions by a formula that related assessments and rebates to travel distance.
- Assessing NSA's future organization and financial stability.

The "group dynamics" process

Some issues were passionately debated and closely decided. These included fraternity discrimination, IUS relations, adding responsibilities to the Student Bill of Rights, and federal aid. NSA had nevertheless shown in its first two years that it could manage a program by national and regional consensus, while fending off divisive attacks at the campus level. These issues included alleged communist influence, antisegregation policies, and the organization's international outlook.

Commenting on the actions of the congress in the October 1949 issue of *NSA News*, Kelly wrote, "It was a tribute to the democratic processes followed that delegates of varying religious, political, social and educational backgrounds, having in common scarcely more than their humanity and vocations as students, could not only discuss, but resolve their differences on most major points."

A process called "group dynamics," involving listening and consensus building, played a major role in bringing about this outcome. Group dynamics, one of the threads running through NSA's management culture, had been introduced to the national officers by Wisconsin's Gordon Klopf, then the chair of the National Advisory Committee.[13] It was alien to the kind of adversarial parliamentary procedure practiced in many student councils, where argument and debate amounted to a field sport with a life of its own. This was especially true at CCNY, where I had received my basic training in rhetorical combat. I recall Mildred Kiefer's astonishment at the parliamentary parrying when I brought her to her first CCNY (Uptown Day) student council meeting. Tom Garrity (CCNY Uptown Evening) reports a similar reaction from Al Lowenstein on the occasion of his visit to the Evening Session's council. We learned to apply group dynamics in NSA meetings.

Kelly comments in the same editorial, "It is not possible for one individual to comprehend, much less describe, this group method in its entirety, but it is possible to note its most salient features. Briefly the attitude of the Congress was one of confidence, conciliation and desire for action."

This "desire for action" was reflected in a broadranging effort during the Kelly year to implement a host of policies and programs. Operating with what I would call "collaborative autonomy," each officer managed his own programs with considerable independence, consulting with the others for advice and coordination of scheduling and use of resources. The international office in Cambridge continued on its own course, reporting primarily to the National Executive Committee and to the annual congresses rather than to the Madison staff.[14]

Ted Perry and the student affairs program

Ted, the oldest member of the staff, was much beloved as a sweet and moderating temperament, with an infectious and effervescent chuckle that drew you to him. Under his guidance, a number of programs were carried out:

- More than sixty-four colleges took part in the annual NSA Art Tour, which was coordinated by Mary Kay Perkins and Lucille Crews at Mundelein College until Mary Kay joined the staff.
- A forty-page pilot issue of *Essai,* NSA's national literary magazine, was distributed at the congress and was deemed a success. St. Theresa and St. Mary's Colleges in the Minnesota Region united to produce the magazine during the year. A twenty-four-page second issue in "large magazine" format was published in the spring, with a thirty-five-cent cover price.
- Ted was especially enthusiastic about the Symphony Forum, a project designed to promote interest in symphonic music by involving college students in orientation programs with, and attendance at, concerts of their local symphony orchestras. During 1949-1950, the program was administered at San Francisco State College by Paul Denise, working with the San Francisco Symphony. During the year, Symphony Forum programs were also launched in Washington, D.C.; Boston; Chicago; Indianapolis; Buffalo; and Seattle.
- Student government clinics provided forums for local student leaders to exchange information and attend workshops concerned with campus issues. At a clinic organized by Columbia University in the Metropolitan New York Region, Ted appeared along with college administrators from the region. Sheldon Steinhauser (NYU), president of the region, typified those chairs at the time who successfully activated the subcomission system in their regions. I recall meeting and working with Shelley several times after returning from Madison. He was an energetic, focused leader.[15]

Academic freedom issues were dominated by the continuing controversy over efforts by the University of California Board of Regents to impose a loyalty oath requirement on faculty and by similar issues raised in the U.S. Congress. Rick Medalie, writing in *NSA News,* called attention to the "dangerous loyalty requirements" that were being advocated for National Science Foundation legislation.[16]

Rick Medalie and the educational affairs program

Rick's major areas of activity were: managing the human relations workshop and publications program; monitoring race relations and discrimination issues; managing the Purchase Card System; and updating and promoting the faculty-rating system and student involvement in setting educational standards.[17] The next year's education vice president, Herb Goldsmith of the University of Wisconsin, was appointed chair of a subcommission on the evaluation of higher education.

A measure of NSA's success in gaining consideration of student rating of faculty was publication in the January 1950 issue of *Phi Beta Kappan* of Rick's article, "Grading the Teachers."[18]

Discrimination in the selection of members of fraternities and sororities was a major issue at the time. Exclusion on the basis of economic and social class, race, religion, and/or ethnicity was deeply rooted in the fraternity tradition. As Bob Delahanty wrote in the December *NSA News*:

> Most fraternities were established some time ago and reflect the thinking of that generation.... By observing my own fraternity at school (University of Louisville) and at two national conventions, I came to the not-so-astounding conclusion that it was not the students who were vehement in their opposition to the removal of discriminatory clauses, but the alumni and national officers.[19]

Rick and Gordon Klopf jointly authored a thirty-two-page handbook for campus human relations programs, entitled *Human Relations in the Educational Community.* Publication was made possible by a grant from the National Conference of Christians and Jews (NCCJ).[20]

Rick deals in greater depth with his experiences in his essay in Part 2.

Although we only had one-year terms, it was possible, through maintaining contact in subsequent years, to see the outcomes of programs launched or enhanced during one's term in office, as well as to furnish some continuity of memory and experience. At least it was that way for me. To see in Rick, Ted, and Bob's hands the flowering of programs I had been a part of was a real reward for the effort. And to see now that these, in turn, were the outcome of a vision first articulated at the Chicago Student Conference in 1946 is deeply satisfying.

The purchase card system

The idea for the purchase card system (PCS) student discount plan first emerged at the constitutional convention in 1947 and was piloted at the University of Buffalo by Lee Jones.[21] A successful outcome there led to a national launch during my vice presidency.[22] Kelly, when chair of the New Jersey Region, was an enthusiastic PCS booster there and continued to support it during his presidency.

By midyear in our term, more than 50,000 cards had been distributed to PCS systems in twenty-five areas throughout the country and 7,500 had been sold. They cost the student $1, and brought discounts of 5 to 25 percent on merchandise sold by cooperating merchants. Student governments retained 70 percent of the receipts from card sales. Ten percent went to the region, and 20 percent went to the national office. Looking back at the detailed regulations and procedures we put into place—without the aid of an attorney!— most of which I had personally drafted the year before, I marvel at the bureaucratic impulse that reached its flower in this program and passed muster with so many students. "The application is filled out on PCS Form E-2, and authorization is granted on PCS Form E-1," Craig Wilson reported with a straight face in his "Loos-Leaflet" promoting the program.

PCS was well received by most local merchants. It was also the subject of controversy and opposed by others (the Emory University NSA committee, for example, was unable to persuade local merchants to join). In a Seattle, WA, survey conducted by NSA committeeman Dan Pulsifer, 50 percent of the thirty-eight merchants contacted in their University of Washington area favored the idea; 18 percent had no opinion. Shelly Steinhauser, Met NY Region president, reported that more than 120 stores had contracted into the system by December, including the Vim stores, a major chain at the time.

While the purchase card system never achieved significant critical mass nationally, it continued to be a key feature of appeal in many campus NSA affiliation campaigns (for example, San Francisco State, UCLA, Columbia) and continued to attract successive generations of local NSA leaders to try and make it work.

As it turned out, the purchase card system, which became known as the student discount system, remained a functioning program at least well into the late 1950s or early 1960s.

Erskine Childers and the international program

Erskine was a charismatic, articulate, and energetic internationalist, whom I counted as a dear friend. He had high visibility within the organization, which was enhanced to a degree by the colorful history of his family in Irish politics.[23]

Low-cost student summer tours to Europe, operated under Erskine's direction from the Cambridge office, were among NSA's most popular programs. By December, the *NSA News* reported that plans were in place for more than eight hundred students to travel abroad, by sea and by air, in nine NSA foreign travel programs, six foreign work camps, and two foreign study programs. Prices ranged from $340 to $625. They were kept at that level with the aid of cooperative arrangements with national student unions in Western and Eastern Europe and the Middle East. The third edition of *Work, Study, Travel Abroad*, a forty-page compendium of information on student travel programs and travel information (fifty cents cover price, twenty-five cents to member schools) continued to be NSA's best-selling publication.

As is described by Bob Meagher and Helen Bryan Garland in their essays in Part 3, the 1949-1950 program achieved sudden notoriety when the Coast Guard refused to allow entry into New York harbor of one of the student ships, the *Svaalbard*. This was also the source of a substantial financial deficit, whose impact carried over into the Lowenstein (1950-51) and Dentzer (1951-52) administrations.

During the summer, thirteen NSA observers and representatives were sent on various missions to Europe, and one each was sent to Southeast Asia and the West Indies. Commissioned with detailed instructions and limitations, a team of ambassadors was appointed by the staff to visit and report on the student unions and student life. They were:

British Isles—Billie Wright, Fisk University
Scandinavia—James Garst, UCLA
Benelux and Germany—Claude Salomon, Colorado A&M
Italy and Switzerland—Hector Corral, Loyola of Los Angeles
Yugoslavia and Austria—Gerald Maryanov, Columbia University
Middle East—William Polk, Harvard
Africa—William Strassburg, Ohio Wesleyan
Southeast Asia—James Grant, Harvard
West Indies—Fred Flach, Cornell

Maryanov's assignment was diverted to the task of opening a Paris office for NSA, and he didn't make the trip to Yugoslavia and Austria. The trip to Yugoslavia was subsequently undertaken by Frank Fisher of Harvard (see his essay in Part 3).Grant and Flach were technically not part of the team, which included, in addition to those listed here, an executive group consisting of Erskine Childers, Bill Ellis, Bill Holbrook, Rob West, and myself.

The structure and report of the team were carefully documented in a written instrument ("Confidential—for team members and staff only") and an "NUS Liaison Representative Fact Sheet" ("Keep a daily diary noting the places and persons visited, materials gathered and your personal observations"). An overall team report and individual country reports were presented to the 1950 congress in Michigan.[24]

NSA was represented at the third meeting of the Council of the International Union of Students, held at Sofia, Bulgaria, in September, by its observer, Pat Baker (Baker was a graduate of Chicago Teachers College who had attended the constitutional convention and was working for UNESCO that summer). Also present was Halsted Holman, the delegate from the Association of Internes and Medical Students (AIMS), who was elected to the American vice presidency of IUS. Reflecting the left-leaning activist position of AIMS, his statement to the IUS was reported in *NSA News* as "emphasizing barriers to democratic education [in the United States] through economic restrictions, racial discrimination and segregation...and devotion of United States economic energies to military preparations." The depiction of the United States as a "threat to world peace" was a major theme of leftist and pro-Soviet students of the time.

Rob West served as NSA representative on the U.S. Commission for UNESCO. A major NSA interest was UNESCO's programs for postwar overseas student relief.

Rob, Bill Holbrook, and I were selected by the staff to represent NSA as observers to the IUS World Student Congress in summer 1950.[25] Rob headed the delegation. I recall a "team executive meeting" at a Paris café, with Jay Maryanov, Bob Smith, and Ted Harris joining Erskine, Rob, Bill, and me.[26] Having never been to Europe before and anticipating the week in Prague soon to follow, I experienced this as a moment of rare adventure. When we learned that only three of us would be granted visas for Prague, Erskine withdrew, allowing Rob, Bill, and me to go. You can imagine the sense of unfolding mystery I felt as we flew through the clouds and fog over the Swiss Alps on our way "through the Iron Curtain" to the Czech capital.[27]

These activities made the international program one of the crowning jewels of the 1949-1950 year. Such forays out into the postwar world must be counted as one of NSA's signal contributions to broadening the perspectives of our generation of civic leaders and activists.

Ralph Lee Smith and Craig Wilson, public relations and publications

Both Ralph Lee Smith, public relations director, and Craig Wilson, *NSA News* editor, have written essays for this volume.[28] NSA enjoyed the benefit of journalistic skills that contributed to nine issues of *NSA News*, a wide range of student government and international reference materials, and the publication of articles about NSA under Ralph's and other bylines in national magazines. These publications form a valuable record of the programs initiated by NSA, as does the reportage that appeared in hundreds of college student newspapers. These materials, providing documentation of events and of the way in which we and other students saw the issues at the time, have constituted a valuable resource for this book.

Ralph determined early on that it was not practical for him to maintain a full-time presence at the national office, so he returned to finish school at Swarthmore, doing the job from the campus.

Craig is remembered by his contemporaries for his unstinting energy at work, as well as his insistence on commanding the territory embraced by publication of the *NSA News*. In an organization that relied on self-starters and personal initiative, this proved to be of immense value. It was also a source of occasional friction.

Erskine Childers, in Cambridge, engaged in a running dispute with the Madison office over what he felt was the need for "channeling of all international copy" appearing in *NSA News* through the international office. In a letter from Childers to Ralph Smith written March 10, 1950, Childers dwells at length on his concerns, citing an ad carried for what he felt was an unreliable travel agency and a sympathetic story in the February 1950 issue of *NSA News* about the Central Union of Ukrainian Students, which Childers characterized as a "highly questionable refugee organization." Craig Wilson wrote to me recently (July 12, 1998), "I don't recall any controversy over the acceptability of advertising. In those days, publications accepted advertising from all comers."

Recruiting and maintaining membership

As was the case during the first two years, the national staff spent much of its time on membership recruitment and retention. Bob Kelly characterized the challenge in a December 31, 1949, communication to the Executive Committee:

> Though we have achieved the substance of unity, we are confronted with an association that is radically unbalanced. We are geographically centered in the Middle Atlantic area and the Midwest. Except for the Virginia-Carolina region, and despite tremendous efforts by regional personnel, the South remains unorganized. Some of our member schools are despairing of an extra-national program because there are no member schools near them.[29]

Kelly's travel schedule for recruitment and membership included the following:

October—Chicago, Indianapolis, Dayton, Cincinnati
November—D.C., New York, New Jersey, New England
December—Missouri, Minnesota
February—Minnesota, North Dakota, Colorado, Texas, Louisiana, Arkansas, Missouri, Illinois
March—The "Southeast"

Disaffiliations and nonrenewals plagued the organization. Although more than six hundred delegates attended the Michigan Congress, membership had fallen during the year from 280 colleges and universities to 205.[30]

Gordon Klopf and the National Advisory Committee

Gordon Klopf, chair of the Advisory Committee, circulated a periodic newsletter to the thirteen members, among whom were Harold Taylor, president of Sarah Lawrence College; Frank P. Graham, chancellor emeritus of the University of North Carolina; the Very Rev. Vincent J. Flynn, president of the American Association of Colleges; Ted Harris, immediate past president of NSA, and Bill Birenbaum, 1947 University of Chicago delegate, then on the staff of the university's dean of students.[31]

In his December report, Klopf noted that "NSA now represents the American student on a number of very important national committees and commissions, and has been asked to attend conferences to represent the American student. Reports are that the officers are doing an excellent job at these conferences."

He also wrote that "the problem of finance still remains an important one....Another problem is that of organization of the local campus. NSA is not set up as a separate organization or commission on each campus." He urged committee members to write the national staff "concerning problems of local and regional NSA organization."

Responding to Gordon's inquiry, Francis J. Brown, then staff associate with the American Council on Education, observed, "I am personally of the opinion that some relaxation of the insistence that officers be students on leave for one year is necessary. There are very few Bob Kellys, to cite one illustration, and when found, the Association should retain his leadership in my judgement for two years."

Addressing staff tendencies to load up the mails, he said, "In some areas there is again too much mimeographed material being sent to the campuses and the region."

Bob Kelly and the organizational study

The organization problems described by Gordon were important. However, NSA possessed an extended network of locally based volunteers, commissions and subcommissions, regional officers and regional commissions, and connections throughout the education community. While it had little physical property or cash in hand, it had commitment and vision, enormous resiliency, and access to "mimeograph machine power" in the hands of enthusiasts from Seattle to Atlanta.

A number of NSA leaders believed that the organization was undergoing a crisis of purpose and structure. On a more intimate, staff level, reports from visitors to the Madison office and from staff members themselves, both at the time and in retrospect today, tell of a serious rift between Kelly and his associates, which was centered around his leadership and management style (see Craig Wilson's essay following). It is a conflict to which Kelly seemed oblivious, as I have no recollection nor mention in any of my correspondence or his that he himself ever raised the subject.

In response to looming financial and structural stresses, the Executive Committee, at its March meeting, authorized the staff to appoint a committee to conduct a broad-based study of NSA. The full name was the NSA Special Advisory Committee on Organizational Affairs (SACOA). Members included Janis Dowd, Bill Ellis, Ralph Dungan, Rob West, Elmer Brock, Alice Gilbert, Shirley Neizer, Jay Maryanov, John Yewell, Ralph Smith, Ken Kurtz, Walter Wallace, Helen Jean Rogers, and Frank Fisher.

Bob Kelly described the committee's assignment in a May 9, 1950, letter to Mike DiLegge, then a Fordham University delegate to the Met New York region. Laying out Mike's charter as head of the Administration and Finance Group within the study, Bob described the purpose as "to re-evaluate the National Student Association in all phases of its organization and program, making recommendations for improvements through the staff to the forthcoming Congress."

Bob referred to the committee as "the Schwartzers" because he asked me to head the study and recruit the committee's members. The study was subsequently headed by Mildred Kiefer and Stanley Greenfield, who agreed to take over when I found the task interfering with my work in graduate school at night and my job by day.

Bob provided us with a list of "suggestive" issues to address, including such questions as:

- Should the national office be moved and united with the international office?
- What should be the president's executive and operating authority?
- What should the functions of the National Congress be, and how should it be organized?
- How should the regions be organized?
- Should there be an office of treasurer?

Among other things, conducting such a study opened the question of whether the organization should be run entirely by students contemporaneous to their times, or partially or wholly by a professional staff.

In the introduction to its report, the Committee stated that

"It accepted the mandate of the NEC only after long and careful deliberation. We realized that the establishment of the Committee might set a dangerous precedent with one of NSA's firmest traditions—that policy considerations must be completely determined by student representatives."

While loyalty to NSA and a strong desire to help won the participation of forty present and former NSA leaders, not everyone was prepared to breach the wall. In a March 20, 1950, letter declining my invitation, Clif Wharton, 1946-47 NCC Secretary, wrote:

> Twenty-five...are former officers, either national or regional. Regardless of their deep interest in NSA and their present status of students or non-students, I do not feel that they can be validly considered in the same category of responsive representatives of student campuses who have been duly elected.

On the first weekend in April, an organizing meeting was held at Sarah Lawrence College. On April 9, 1950, I wrote a letter to Mary Jo Domino, then chair of the Illinois region, that reflected not only my conviction at the time, but also, I see now, my passionate feeling of attachment to the organization:

> It is my general feeling that to "save NSA" the student leadership of today will be making a grave error if they fall back on the "concrete project" approach. . . . If effective leadership cannot be found, if proper organizational techniques cannot be exploited to still awaken among college students an awareness of their social responsibility, then I say let's stop kidding ourselves and change the prospectus to that of an "intercollegiate service organization"...better the loss of a few schools—or all schools—than the self delusion of thinking we now work for the translation of the NSA preamble into reality.

By May 29, Mildred Kiefer was able to circulate draft reports from each of the subcommittees for final review by the drafting committee, and then by the full committee "when it considers the report at our meeting this weekend." There was no grass growing here. "Please come prepared to work hard and consistently . . . [and] also to finish together in a *blaze of glory*," she wrote.

In a concise, double-spaced, eleven-page synthesis of the subcommittee reports, the committee report dealt with three themes:[32]

1. Basic assumptions that define the nature of NSA, emphasizing that "the unit of structure of NSA is the individual student body."
2. General considerations dealing with program techniques, emphasizing that NSA programs "must be severely delimited to three or four major objectives at any one time."
3. Structural and administrative considerations, including the recommendation that the national offices be relocated in the East.

Some thirty-five pages of subcommittee detail accompanied the report. Much of it was included in the working papers submitted to the Michigan congress.

The Michigan congress

Decisions relating to the Michigan congress in August were made at the March Executive Committee meeting in Madison. In its report, the staff recapitulated the main policy and organizational statements at the Chicago Student Conference, the Constitutional Convention, and the first Congress. In many respects, the forthcoming congress was to be a stock-taking event. The congress attained higher-than-anticipated visibility because of the *Svaalbard* incident, the reports of the international team, and the decision of *LIFE* magazine to do a three-page photo essay on the congress (See "Life Goes to a Student Convention," in this section).

The staff prepared reports in four areas, Student Affairs, Educational Affairs, International Affairs, and Organizational Affairs, with recommendations dealing with twenty-one topical subcommission areas. Despite the Organization Affairs Committee's call for focus on broad substantive themes, the Michigan congress (and all the congresses that followed, it appears) continued to engage itself in a multitude of program objectives.

Some of the issues and proposals presented by the staff to the congress dealt with the following topics.

Student Government and Student Life

"The inadequacy of present student health programs" and whether NSA should engage itself in the issue.

The need for oversight in governance of athletic recruiting, academic standards, and financial aid.

Continuation of NSA's literary magazine, art tour, and Symphony Forum programs.

Attention to issues concerning campus student political parties, methods of polling, and student government administration.

The need for a "more comprehensive and stimulating program" in the field of educational affairs, extending beyond the successful faculty-rating system introduced by NSA.

Student Rights, Academic Freedom, and Discrimination

Perfection of the language in the Student Bill of Rights and addition of a statement of responsibilities.

Continued engagement in issues affecting academic freedom.

Continued engagement in national and regional human relations programs and advocacy efforts against "unfair educational practices" (discrimination). Collaboration with National Conference of Christian and Jews and National Scholarship Service for Negro Students.

Economic Benefits

Support for programs of federal scholarships and aid to education.

Consideration of the future of the Purchase Card System.

International Programs

Continued engagement in campus relief efforts, including support for WSSF and UNESCO relief activities.

Maintaining the current policy of opposition to membership in IUS.

Organization

Reviewing the major recommendations of the Organizational Affairs Committee.

Reviewing the obstacles to publication of *Fortnightly*, a proposed national college newspaper supplement recommended by the College Press Conference at the second congress.

Consideration of a recommendation of the Advisory Committee chair that NSA form joint college staff-student commissions to advise in all areas of NSA programs.

Joan Long Lynch deals with the outcome of these proposals and the major events of the third congress in her essay.[33]

The personal touch

My year as educational problems vice president in 1948-49 had shaken up my life in ways I couldn't have imagined when I took leave of City College for Madison in summer 1948. In August, I returned to help set up the convention after taking three weeks off in July to complete a summer surveying course in Van Cortlandt Park, the Bronx, which I needed in order to complete my degree. John J. Theobold, dean of engineering, who later became New York City superintendent of schools, had persuaded me to finish my fourth year, rather than changing to a major in political science and heading toward what I imagined would be a calm and bucolic academic life between the shores of Madison's two lakes.

The letters that Bob and I wrote to our "Moms" during that period (which they lovingly saved and passed on to us) reveal in a highly personal way one of the greatest contributions that NSA made to its generation of student leaders. Young people brought up in geographic, ethnic, social, economic, and culturally diverse pockets of American society, who were still provincially separated, as Dick Heggie notes in his essay, were given a crash course in the strengths of their shared heritage. This came about by exposure to, and interaction, with this diversity. We dealt with the conflicts and opportunities that arose in our efforts to perfect the society we inherited, and we experienced the novelty of each other's company, families, and campuses.

Writing home to "Mom, Dad, Joan and Pat" about the forthcoming Executive Committee meeting in December 1949, Kelly reports:

> Our mimeograph has been grinding away at voluminous reports for the NEC meeting on the 26th. Thank heaven, it will be over in time for us to enjoy some sort of rest on New Year's Eve. We have secured the entire Kappa Sigma fraternity house for the meeting. It is a magnificent place overlooking the lake, with 32 rooms and two plush living rooms. In short, we shall meet in high style and in an ultra-collegiate atmosphere. It will be nice to be within a frat for a while. That is a part of college that I have never known and really should.

In contrast, Bob Kelly writes on October 3:

> As I have already written, the laundry service we have discovered is excellent and cheap...even mends socks for homeless bachelors. And speaking of homeless bachelors, I may as well be frank on our housing setup. Everyone is placed comfortably in private homes except Ted Perry and myself. There are six of us and we split up into groups of two. Believe me, we have advertised and pounded doorbells, but there is something about a Negro that seems to scare people away from renting. Ted is a Negro and I have no intention of either (1) leaving him alone, or (2) subjecting him to further icy stares when we look over rooms. That, and that only, is why we were unable to rent a house. So it looks like the Y for us until next August. Frankly, I like it. It is as good as a hotel.

In retrospect, I marvel at how naturally it seemed to come to us that we should take a year out of an intended career path, spend it in close quarters with people whom, in most cases, we had never met before, move out onto the national scene to "make a difference," and then expect to pick up the threads and proceed with our lives as before.

Here is Bob, writing on October 22 about one of the half-dozen or more extended trips that he and other staff members took during the year:

> Hello again. You nearly got this letter from Sheboygan, but I mislaid the manuscript on the bus. Yours truly was the keynote speaker at the Wisconsin High School Student Council Convention on October 20th and now all you have to do is "just mention my name in Sheboygan." My speech was very well received and in the course of my bus-ride, I went further North than I had ever gone before.
>
> The mother of Marlin Smith, one of our Minnesota regional officers, put me up for the night, and as a result the trip was very pleasant. In the next month or so, I will not only travel East, but also to Missouri and Minnesota. Minnesota invited me to come on November 26th and 27th and I will speak at the University of Missouri on December 2nd, and in St. Louis on the 3rd. The American Council on Education meeting will take place on November 3rd in the Edgewater Hotel in Chicago....[Jawaharlal] Nehru of India will be speaking at the university the next day [November 4] and we have been invited to a banquet in his honor.

Summing up: Faith in the future on a shoe string

The story of NSA's third year exposes both the virtues and flaws of the organization. On a practical level, it reveals how sensitive NSA's fortunes were to the personalities and energies of its elected leaders. The split between Bob Kelly and his fellow officers seriously damaged the esprit of the national office and of many regional NEC members. Yet such was the openness of structure that the programs and initiatives cited in this memoir nonetheless proceeded apace in the hands of their stewards.

NSA's vital organizing force rested on an unconditional faith in volunteerism and individual initiative. It was guided by the broad principles and vision reflected in its constitution and its vigorously debated policy initiatives. We complained about apathy and about spreading ourselves too thin—and any management consultant or rational political operative could easily have blown holes in the whole schema—but we truly believed in the value of our purposes and that we could do it all.

At the Michigan congress, impressively informed and detailed reports on the world student scene were submitted by the international team, shepherded by Erskine Childers and backed up by his predecessors, Bob Smith and Rob West.

Bob Kelly's "Schwartzers" came up with a model plan for procedure and focus. When it was delivered into the hands of a new cohort at the Michigan congress, it was received respectfully. Mildred Kiefer and Stanley Greenfield voiced the committee's conclusions and recommendations carefully. Bob Kelly intoned their import in his staff report. However, the congress then enthusiastically took over the wheel and determined to test things out all over again on its own. It cut annual dues by another 30 percent, to a range of $20 (schools under three hundred students) to $150 (those over ten thousand)!

Can any one person or faction be credited with having set this course, or as being responsible for the unreality of NSA's financial underpinnings? The minutes of the congress attach names to the policies that were proposed and the programs that were executed. However, these initiatives seem to have been largely supported by everyone significantly involved. There were too many moving points of light for any one beacon to crowd them off the stage at any moment in time.

NSA's staying power established

NSA depended almost completely on the de facto leadership that emerged in its more consistently committed regions, including New England, New York, Wisconsin, Pennsylvania, Minnesota, Michigan, Illinois, the Northwest, California, Missouri, Virginia-Carolinas, and Mason-Dixon. These regions, in turn, relied on a core group of regional officers, and several campuses with strong NSA support within their student governments and administrations. An example: in a letter from Helen Jean Rogers in October 1949, after reporting on a visit by Bob Delahanty, the incoming executive secretary, who "seems to feel that things are going pretty well despite minor personality problems [in the national office] and even a few rather major ones," she notes that "Bob reported that a meeting at Chapel Hill was very well attended and gives indications of a good year for the Virginia Carolina Region. Ben Jones predicts that the membership of the region will be doubled this year."

With this infrastructure, we had launched a national and global advocacy, programming, and service organization with no money in the bank, no business plan, and no source of assured funding outside a modest dues structure and a congress travel pool equalization fund. Foundation support was not forthcoming in those early years. An examination of the few national operating budgets and financial reports that we have been able to recover shows them ranging from $36,000 in 1947-48 down to $22,000 in 1951-52 during the first five years, with full-time staff salaries at a maximum of about $2,000 per year.

Mike Di Legge recalls a trip to the Cambridge office to review the accounting systems there and the concern at the time over the need for a system that could pass audit muster when required. As he noted in a letter to Helen Jean Rogers, "Administration and Finance is not a subject which lends itself to metaphysical speculation." The association's momentum overrode these limitations, and NSA's founders and leaders believed the obstacles could be overcome.

Lessons learned

This year of reconsideration and consolidation established NSA's staying power through the determination of its leaders, past and future, to let its survival rest in the hands of the student governments to whom it would have to prove itself and who would have to renew its franchise each year, and to the new crop of leaders who were ready each year to exercise their franchise.

Student leaders such as Bob Kelly (who was yet to become a Korean War veteran) emerged with the talent, insight, and skill to take on national or regional responsibilities and then apply the experience to creative careers without becoming "professional students."

NSA's structural ambiguity on the campus level (should it be "part of student government," a separate committee, or simply vested in the student government), although frustrating at the time to the organization-minded among us, was probably one of the reasons why it was able to replenish itself and find its way each year.

I believe that the odyssey through NSA taken by the authors of this book, and numerous others, exemplifies the

Eugene G. Schwartz is a publishing and business consultant and Editor-at-Large for ForeWord Magazine *and has served as a production executive for several major publishers. After completing graduate course work at NYU in 1953, he worked as a union organizer and was in the printing business. He holds a B.S. in civil engineering from the City College of New York. (See p. 247 for extended biography)*

wide reach that was possible to us in that world after World War II. We young men and women who came out of the war, both veterans and not, and who, in many cases, were about to enter into another war in Korea used that interim period to affirm to the rest of the country and the world our idealism, commitment, optimism, and faith in the system.

END NOTES

[1] An 8/29/49 unpublished tally by staff shows 674 delegates, alternates, and observers.

[2] See Schwartz, p. 847, and Kelly/Garrity album, p. 892.

[3] See Philip Des Marais essay, p. 734.

[4] Bill Allaway, p. 613, and Phil Stoddard, p. 655, have contributed to this volume. Char Allen was an unsuccessful candidate for the new post of NSA executive secretary, after I had resigned it shortly after accepting it following the congress. She graduated in 1951 and went to Cambridge, MA, where she worked for a year in the International office. (See p. 658, on her reporting in the *Champagne News Gazette* from her travels abroad.)

[5] NSA urged student governments to initiate changes in discriminatory membership requirements by social and professional organizations and "encourage[d]" the National Interfraternity and National Panhellenic Conferences "to urge the elimination of any discriminatory clauses within its member social sorority and/or fraternity groups."

[6] In 1952 I was in the groom's party at Tom Callahan's marriage to Virginia Gardner, whom he had met while she was chair of the Wisconsin Region.

[7] Tess Donnelly, then a Fontbonne College, Missouri, delegate, reveals what to me is a touching recollection of one of the sidelights to the event in her essay on p. 952. Clearly, Kelly's nomination was carefully floor-managed by the Catholic school caucus. Mine was promoted assiduously by my staff colleagues. See also the Dick Heggie essay, p. 206.

[8] See West, p. 556, and Holbrook, p. 559.

[9] See NSA and the NAACP, p. 452.

[10] See Ralph Smith's essay on p. 899.

[11] See Craig Wilson's essay on p. 248.

[12] In its resolution, NSA reflected the mores of the time by exempting from its definition of "unfair" practices" admissions requirements of "non-coeducational" schools, inquiries about religion by denominational schools, residential priorities set by public institutions, and "sex quota systems" in teachers' colleges so that "a sufficient number of teachers of each sex are educated."

[13] See the Gordon Klopf essay, pp. 333, 335.

[14] It is interesting to note how, during the following year, Allard Lowenstein, as president, took an aggressive and participatory role in aspects of the international program (Lynch, p. 301) that had not been the case with NSA's national office since the days of the National Continuations Committee and Bill Welsh's endorsement of Jim Smith's resignation from the IUS in 1947 (pp. 170, 189).

[15] See Steinhauser, p. 853.

[16] See Brown, p. 381, on NSA and academic freedom.

[17] See Medalie and the NSA educational affairs programs, p. 347.

[18] See the essay on faculty rating, p. 360.

[19] See Delahanty, p. 410, NSA and the fraternities, p. 398, and Lee, "Fraternities without Brotherhood," p. 745.

[20] See Klopf, p. 334.

[21] See Lee Jones's interview, p. 869, Medalie, p. 348, and PCS album, p. 366.

[22] See the Richard Heggie essay, p. 203.

[23] See Childers, p. 517.

[24] Copies of these documents can be found in both the Wisconsin Historical Society and Hoover Institute NSA archives. See also p. 609.

[25] See footnote 8, also Joan Long Lynch, p. 269.

[26] See photo, p. 506.

[27] Funding for our travel expenses as well as for those of the other team "ambassadors" evidently came from the money raised by Fred Houghteling, as described in Craig Wilson's essay, p. 249. Whether this was CIA or State Department sourced remains unclear, but it was not revealed by Fred until 1967 (see the report on covert U.S. funding, p. 565). I was not aware of this until three years ago, when I started on this book project. Ironically, as I described in my Section 6 essay (p. 217), the FBI—apparently with its own agenda—lifted our passports when Rob, Bill, and I returned from Prague. It took me six months to get mine back. Rob West and I prepared an article on the experience, which was published in the March 15, 1951, issue of the U.S. Office of Education's *Higher Education.*

[28] See Smith, p. 897, and Wilson, p. 248.

[29] At the time of the Michigan congress, NSA listed twenty-one member colleges in the traditional Southern states.

[30] Each year, NSA published a list of member schools, along with observers, attending the national congresses. Gordon Klopf, Dennis Trueblood, Bob Sollen, and other administrator authors also cited membership and attendance at various congresses in their annual reports, which were published in *School and Society* for each of the years covered by this volume. This combined historical record shows the following college attendance counts: Chicago (12/46), 393 plus 28 national student organizations; Madison 1 (8/47), 351; and the following membership counts at convention time: Madison 2 (8/48), 251 and 44 observers; Illinois (8/49), 280 plus 32 observers; Michigan (8/50), 205 plus 27 observers; Minnesota (8/51), 225; and Indiana (8/52), 275.

[31] A complete list of the Advisory Board membership can be found in the Appendix, p. 1123. Bill Birenbaum followed a career in higher education, which led to several college presidencies, including that of Antioch College, before he retired. See also Gordon Klopf's essay, p. 239.

[32] See p. 1120 for a summary of its recommendations.

[33] See Lynch, p. 267.

PICTURE CREDITS: *Then:* 1948, Madison, WI (NSA Photo). *Now:* 1998 (*Both, author*).

CONGRESS ARRANGEMENTS COMMITTEE, University of Illinois. From left: Martha Innis, William Allaway, Charlotte Allen, Phillip Stoddard.

UNITED STATES NATIONAL STUDENT ASSOCIATION

The Daily Bull

Vol. I No. 6 August 30, 19

OF THE SECOND NATIONAL STUDENT CONGRESS

"A DELEGATE'S DAY" by Ronnie Macht

THE LIGHTER SIDE OF CONVENTIONEERING

Editor's note: Intense debates and long hours characterized the annual gatherings of NSA. However, programs also allowed free time for social events and networking. The congresses took place on major university campuses, such as Illinois, Wisconsin, Michigan, and Minnesota, where ample dormitory, social, and recreational facilities were available to delegates. The daily news bulletins produced at each Congress in the then universal form of instant print—the mimeograph—provided news, information, and humor. The cartoons at the left and the quotations below are from the Second Congress "Daily Bull," *published by the NSA staff:*

From the Bull Pen (Thursday 8/30/49)

Just out of curiosity, one of us in the Bull Pen counted the number of meetings. Here are the results: Number of round tables, 42; total number of meetings, 722; number of guest speakers,32.

A breakdown of sessions shows: Round table sessions, 294; Regional caucuses, 192; commission and plenary sessions, 62; committee meetings, 168; NEC [National Executive Committee] meetings, 6. No wonder we're all so busy!

* * *

Colorado, Michigan Top in Art Exhibit (Tuesday 8/23)

Two students from Colorado and one from Michigan came out on top in the second annual National Student Art Exhibit, sponsored by the USNSA. . . .

Chief cultural attraction at the Congress, the 131-entry exhibit is on display in the second floor ballroom of the Illini Union until September 30.

* * *

Notes from the Steering Committee (Wednesday 8/24)

A musical note was added both nights when Dick Heggie, student life vice president, Ben Labaree, S New England, and Charlotte Allen, U of Ill. joined voices. International flavor was injected Tuesday by Ravindra Varma, president of the India National Union of Students, and Paul Bouchet, French vice-president.

EUGENE G. SCHWARTZ

Early Years, Education, and Military Service: Born in New York City in 1925. Lived for two years on a farm in New Brunswick, NJ. Grew up in the Bronx. Attended Public Schools 96 and 89, and Townsend Harris and Christopher Columbus High Schools in New York City. U.S. Army Field Artillery, 1943-46. Served in the Philippines and Japan. Bachelor of Civil Engineering, City College of New York, 1951. Completed course work towards a masters degree in Public Administration, New York University, 1951-52.

Career: Held public relations positions with United World Federalists, National Scholarship Service, and Fund for Negro Students (1950-51). Business agent, New York City District Council #37, American Federation of State, County and Municipal Employees (1952-54). Printing industry sales and management, 1954-1966. Publishing industry, New York 1966-69: production manager, Monarch Press; director of production, Random House. Publishing industry, California (1969-1980): Production manager, CRM Books/Psychology Today; Vice President, Production and Operations, Goodyear/Prentice-Hall; Publisher, Whole Classroom Publishing Group; editor-at-large, *ForeWord Magazine,* 1998 to date. Publishing and Business Consultant, Del Mar, California (1981-1992); Bearsville and Malden-on-Hudson, NY (1992 to date).

Civic: Columnist for the Del Mar *Surfcomber* and North County *Blade/Citizen* (San Diego), 1982-1992. Served on local zoning and cable committees in Del Mar, CA, and Woodstock, NY.

Memberships: Bookbuilders West, Bookbuilders of Boston, Bookbinders Guild of NY, Authors Guild, American Printing History Association. Founding president of Southern California Bookbuilders (1971) and San Diego Publishers Group (1981). Member and former treasurer (1990-94), Publishers Marketing Association.

Interests: Amateur violist. Music, writing, reading, movies, swimming, public policy, news junky, education, communities, and civil society.

Family: Parents (both of whom had read Shakespeare and Mark Twain in Russian by the age of sixteen), Edward Schwartz, a grocery worker, and Bella Dovbish, a garment worker, emigrated from the Ukraine before the Russian Revolution and met in New York City. Half-sister Ruth Snyder and half-brother Sholom Schwartz. Married the late Betty Freedman, with whom I have a son, Joseph, and a daughter, Alexandra. Three grandchildren, Ben, Willa and Layla. Remarried Caroline Epstein. Divorced twice.

Building a national newspaper amidst office conflicts

2. Random Notes of the *NSA News* Editor

Craig Wilson
University of Michigan.
NSA News Editor, 1949-50

I was born on July 20, 1927, so I had just turned twenty-two when I became an NSA staffer. Most of the other staffers were either my age or a year older. Several of us had been in the service during World War II, mostly toward the end, and with little or no combat experience. I am sure that at least some of the first NSA leaders were older, having served several years in the war, with various degrees of experience in combat and having held leadership responsibilities. Many of these NSAers were mature beyond their years. But that was a temporary situation. Our staff was transitional to a younger, less mature leadership.

I served on active duty with the navy for less than a year, beginning in August 1945. I managed to squeeze three years of academic credit at the University of Michigan out of the GI Bill before my benefits were exhausted.

Part I: Reminiscences of Madison

In 1949, I learned from a copy of the *NSA News* that was floating around the office of the *Michigan Daily* that NSA was looking for a director of publications. In summer 1949, I hitchhiked to the University of Illinois at Champaign-Urbana, in time for the opening of the Second Student Congress. I went to the press room, which had been abandoned for the moment, and started to answer the phone. Allan Ostar, NSA's outgoing public relations director, came in briefly while I was phoning copy to a rewrite man at the *Chicago Tribune*. By the end of the congress I had been offered the job at $35 a week. I could save money on that, I said to myself. And I did.

Most NSAers had exceptional leadership qualifications, but my resume was sparse. I could run a Linotype, compose pages, and operate a Gordon job press. On campus, I was a stringer for the *Detroit Free Press*. I knew about as much about world affairs as that hillbilly cartoon character "L'il Abner."

I learned just recently that two of NSA's major concerns in selecting a nonprofessional, all-student, all-new staff for the third operating year were, would Bob Kelly be a capable leader, and could a national organization with this kind of administrative setup survive, endure, grow, and mature?

Bob Kelly

Despite his education, intelligence, and charisma, Kelly was unable to see himself as an administrative leader as well as a spokesman for the student movement. When he wasn't traveling from campus to campus giving talks (which were always well received), he was squirreled away in his private office with the door shut, composing speeches, writing and phoning, and listening to his phonograph playing orchestral music.

When pressed, he would emerge reluctantly and help with mailings. But he would rarely enter the conversational banter that livened these occasions. Many of us got fairly adept at collating reports from accordion-expandable racks, whamming in the staples, and folding and stuffing the papers into college-bound envelopes.

In an effort to develop office continuity, the idea of staggered terms began. Bob Delehanty was executive secretary the first semester, Fred Houghteling the second. The executive secretary should have been the president's right-hand person in the office, but very quickly Kelly had a falling out with Delehanty and would no longer speak to him. This even extended to the few social occasions to which the staff was invited.

At one event, we all played charades. We had to assume roles and answer questions in character. The person who was "it" had to determine who each person was and the overall premise, such as, "We are all movie stars." Kelly was fairly good at this when his turn came up. But he would not ask Delehanty any questions. When it came down to it, someone asked him whether he was going to guess who Delehanty was. Kelly refused, and abruptly left the party.

The staff and the office

Despite Bob Kelly's detachment, the rest of us had each other and got along well, more or less as coequals. Neither Delehanty nor Houghteling had any specific experience in being an executive secretary, and neither had any clerical supervisory skills. Both were wonderful guys, and I enjoyed their company, companionship, and cooperation. Rick Medalie, Ted Perry, and I participated in Delehanty's wedding to Dolores Sheslo.[1]

I can't remember who suggested it, perhaps Kelly or Delehanty, but early on we hired Mary Kay Perkins of Mundelein College in Chicago as staff secretary. Mary Kay was not a student leader, as was Helen Jean Rogers of the previous staff. She was simply a very friendly, very helpful person who enabled all of us to work with a fair degree of harmony. If anyone made up for the lack of administrative leadership and dysfunction, that person was Mary Kay, with her gentle affection for all of us.[2]

About the best thing I can say about the old Draper public school building at 304 N. Park Street, where we had our office, was that I could cut through an alley across the street and get in the back door of the Wisconsin *Daily Cardinal*, where the *NSA News* was printed. Most helpful at the *Cardinal* was Jim Zucker, who was a surprise drop-in at the Fiftieth Anniversary Reunion at Madison in 1997. The previous staff's offices had been on the second floor, which was hotter than the first floor and involved climbing steps. We were on the first floor, in a small area with rickety partitions. I suggested some ideas to make it workable.

In Madison, I ate in a Chinese restaurant for the first time. Most of us dined together, but rarely with Kelly. After labeling and bundling the *NSA News* or collating, stapling, folding, stuffing, and labeling one of Ted's or Rick's monster mailings, we would drive to the "Uptown," an all-night eatery. Most of us were saving as much money as we could and so ate lightly. Fred Houghteling usually had a cheese omelet, and sometimes he went the limit and added hash browns.

At first I lived alone in a sleeping room off some woman's kitchen. I bought a bicycle to get to my room. I often stayed much later than the others so I could use a typewriter. Usually I was so tired, I would try to read in bed and would fall asleep with the light on. When the census taker came one morning, I was too exhausted to get up. The person shouted a few questions through the kitchen door and let it go at that. The landlady was delighted when I told her that I was moving in with Fred Houghteling, as it saved her money on her electric bill.

Our University of Wisconsin (UW) adviser was the patient, diplomatic Gordon Klopf, whom we called "Gorklop." He could pull campus strings when we needed help. He arranged a room for Ted Perry in a UW men's dorm, since it was unlikely that he could find a room in lily-white Madison.[3]

The Lowenstein staff, September-November 1950

My term was to run to the start of the second semester of the 1950-51 school year, at which time I would return to the University of Michigan to complete my journalism degree. However, I soon realized that my worth as a transitional person was practically nil. Mary Kay Perkins had stayed over, which was good. The new president, Al Lowenstein, although more gracious and communicative than Kelly, was even more enamored of speaking on campuses and attending conferences. This may have been necessary for both of them to do, considering the problems of survival and transition facing NSA. But in Draper School, their absences created confusion and leadership vacuums.

I found that, instead of having the freedom to get out press releases, lay out pages for the *NSA News*, and do other work as director of publications, all my activities had to be supervised, minute by minute, by the deputy leader, Elmer Brock.[4] Although he was a dedicated and spirited student leader, Brock seemed to know little about public relations and publications. Most of my time was taken up checking back with him as to whether this or that detail was acceptable. My opportunities to do anything productive were circumscribed. I felt that what I was doing was no longer worth $35 a week. Also, I had learned about as much as I could in the job.

I did not see the need to make an issue of all this, as I doubted that anything would change. So I typed a letter of resignation [probably October or November], slipped it into a pile of work in my "in" basket, and caught a bus to Chicago. From the train station, I phoned the office and told Mary Kay where to find my letter. She cried when she read it, but my mind was made up.

Finishing my degree

Back in Ann Arbor, I got a job driving Yellow Cab No. 31, for a few bucks more than I had made at NSA. Starting in January, I attended classes on Mondays, Wednesdays, and Fridays. I drove the cab from 6 P.M. to 6 A.M. six nights a week, and slept during the day on Tuesdays, Thursdays, and Saturdays.

About 1 A.M. one night, I was in my cab when a guy in a leather jacket approached and got in. It was Elmer Brock! He asked how I was doing. I told him that I was doing fine and taking my last three courses. No, I wasn't mad at him or anyone else. Leaving quietly just seemed like the best thing to do.

Part II: A remarkable trip

In 1950, Erskine Childers, NSA's international vice president, wanted to send twelve U.S. students abroad as representatives of and ambassadors for NSA. This would cost about a thousand dollars per student. NSA had barely enough money to keep the lights lit in Draper School. The organization was just a pipe dream, I figured.

Sometimes I skipped office conferences. I could get more done by using the time to write press releases and get out the *NSA News*. However, Kelly made it clear that on this occasion he wanted everyone to attend. As we lounged in some old, dirty wicker chairs, Fred Houghteling announced that he had found a way to get the $12,000.

"My father [who was a Washington attorney] has friends who are interested in our plans," he said. "We need to make a formal presentation to a couple of key people. One is in Chicago. The other is in Wilmington, Delaware."

Fred said that he would have to do this himself, but that he would need another NSA national officer present to back him up and fill in the details in case he overlooked anything. Who could the staff spare? Who could be the most convincing? I was chosen. After all, I had convinced NSA to hire me in the first place! Fred and I threw a couple of suitcases in the trunk of "Matilda," his old, gray Chevrolet sedan.

Off to Chicago and Washington, D.C.

The Chicago contact turned out to be an attorney with a fancy office in the Loop. He had decorated the place with displays of University of Wisconsin "Badger" memorabilia. He listened attentively to Fred for a few minutes. He commended us for our good intentions. Then he began reminiscing about the good times he had had canoeing with his girl friends on Lake Mendota. We got no commitment at all.

"I think we just wasted a couple of hours," I told Fred.

That night, old gray Matilda rolled swiftly eastward on U.S. 30 across Ohio, small town after small town, each with its single traffic light; solitary, concrete-block gas station; and lonely, all-night diner (usually economically described in neon with the three-letter word "EAT").

In Washington, I lunched on the back patio with Fred's mother, who was described in that day's *Washington Post* society column as "the stunning Mrs. Houghteling." Fred had disappeared for a few hours, so I was left to cope with a glass-topped table and finger bowls.

We reached Wilmington very late one afternoon. From a smelly, cramped, pebble-finish metal phone booth, I called the office of the attorney we were to meet. He was just leaving, but a secretary gave me intricate directions to his home in a hilly suburb without street lights, about fifteen miles out. Despite the blackness of the night and the vagueness of the road signs, I steered us directly to a winding lane that took us, past vast lawns, to the correct mansion. Since the Chicago meeting had been so inconclusive, we agreed that this time I would do the talking, with Fred as the backup. After all, a kid who could sell *Liberty* magazine door-to-door at age nine in 1936 must have some powers of persuasion.

I talked about winning friends in the uncertain postwar world. I mentioned how the International Union of Students, an organization with member schools in the communist-dominated nations, was sending students everywhere, promoting the vague notion of "peace." As free and independent students, we should be out there too, espousing freedom, real democracy, and international friendship among all peoples.

Our host broke in. "Why are you telling ME all this?"

Fred offered the specifics that I had overlooked: "The National Student Association needs $12,000 to send twelve students abroad as friendly ambassadors to students overseas. We were hoping that you could provide some funds for this purpose."

Our Wilmington contact said he would "take the matter under advisement." That was a new phrase to me at the time.

"As long as you boys are here, would you like to see my place? I've just finished a barn out back for my sons. They are about your age."

He opened a door in a huge outbuilding and snapped on the lights. We were standing in a fully equipped gymnasium with a side lounge, plush sofas, and a wet bar. Overhead was a loft with two double beds, huge closets, and lavatories marked "his" and "hers."

"C'mon, see this," he said, leading the way into the men's lavatory. He pulled the curtain on the shower stall. The floor of the stall was covered with a lumpy pink foam mat. The top of each lump was decorated with a round, dark red spot that I quickly recognized as an areola.

I never got the conversation back to NSA's money problem. My presentation had fizzled worse than Fred's. Fred consoled me as he steered Matilda toward New York City.

"You did fine," he said.

Much to my surprise, the hoped-for $12,000 did turn up, and our twelve student ambassadors left from Europe, Africa, and Asia, some by ship, some by air. When they returned in the fall, they brought glowing reports of making good friends everywhere overseas. But many of them predicted that political and economic events in Asia would soon overtake and overshadow affairs in Europe.

"The rest of the story"

In 1967, *Ramparts* magazine broke its expose. NSA was being subsidized by the Central Intelligence Agency.[5] The story stated that the CIA had been quietly slipping funds to NSA since 1950. I wrote a sidebar for the *Akron Beacon Journal*, where I worked, that was headlined, "If CIA Financed Student Group, It's News to Me, BJ Staffer says."

In the intervening years, Fred graduated from Harvard Law School, worked as an attorney in Chicago, then got a job with the Civil Aeronautics Board in Washington. I sent him a clipping of my sidebar, and he phoned a few days later.

"Your story needs clarifying," he said. "Our trip to Chicago and Wilmington was a piece of a charade. I played my part. You played yours. The difference was that I was in on the secret and you were not."

He told me that a good friend from Washington had turned up in Madison while NSA was looking for ways to finance its student ambassadors.

> We went for a ride out near the Madison airport. We stopped and two men got in the car. They told me that the government was interested in NSA and its problem. About time, I suggested. However, they would have to administer an oath under the Official Secrets Act before they could say more. Would I agree? Yes, I would.
>
> We get out of the car in a lonely field far from everything. I take the oath. Then the revelation: the State Department wants the delegation to go. The CIA, blessed with unaudited pockets, will supply the money. Any objection? No.
>
> A few days later, I get my orders. Visit X and Y. Make a pitch. Take someone with you. The money will arrive thereafter.
>
> A few days later, I announce at the NSA office that I, through my valuable family connections, have a couple of hot prospects. Joy at Draper School. Houghteling and Wilson dispatched to make the sale.

Obviously, my L'il Abner naivete helped make the charade work.

Fred Houghteling died in 1986. I have no names, addresses, or phone numbers for either of the lawyers who played their parts in the 1950 solicitation.

Since work started on this book, former NSA leaders have used the Freedom of Information Act to verify my report via government records. Thinking back on it all now, I feel that this secret CIA subsidy and all the others that followed had a profound effect on NSA.

Craig Wilson was a reporter and feature writer for the Akron Beacon Journal. *He holds a B.A. from the University of Michigan.*

END NOTES

[1] See Delahanty and Sheslo, p. 410.

[2] See Mary Kay Perkins, p. 945.

[3] See the reference to this housing problem in Bob Kelly's correspondence, p. 244.

[4] See Brock, p. 358.

[5] See "Covert U.S. Government Funding of NSA International Programs," p. 565.

PICTURE CREDITS: *Then:* c. 1949 (*SWHS*). *Now:* 2001 (*Author*).

CRAIG WILSON

Early Background and Military Service: I was born July 20, 1927, in Detroit, Michigan, served in the U.S. Navy at the end of World War II, and was graduated with a B.A. in journalism from the University of Michigan in 1951.

Career: My career at the *Akron Beacon Journal* began June 14, 1951. I was a reporter-photographer in Ravenna, Cuyahoga Falls, and Barberton. In the metro department, I was night-beat reporter, religion writer, and sub on the cop beat and obit desk. After that, I spent almost five years reorganizing the morgue as chief librarian. I was Action Line director from 1967 to 1985. From then on, I was a feature writer, copy editor, and compiler of entertainment items, until I retired after 40 years, 5 months, and 1 day, on November 15, 1991.

Activities: Since then, I continued as a freelance writer, public speaker, and historical actor, bringing back from 1892 the character of Sam Lane, early Akron newspaperman, Gold Rush adventurer, sheriff, mayor, temperance lecturer, and historian. I also bring back to life the poet Clement Moore, author of "The Night before Christmas." I retired, in December 1998, from public speaking and historical acting, but continue work as a freelance writer.

Family: I was married August 27, 1955, to the former Ella Mae Leonard. We had two daughters, Dawn Wilson (Harper) of Fort Wayne, Indiana, and Andrea Korow, Grand Junction, Colorado. Ella died July 21, 1992, of lung cancer and a brain tumor, a victim of cigarettes. I married Elizabeth Bendall on May 21, 1993.

FREDERICK DELANO HOUGHTELING

Editor's note: Craig Wilson writes of his "adventure" and lifetime friendship with Fred Houghteling (Harvard), an active New England NSA leader in its founding years (Pt. 5, S. 1). He was elected at the Second Congress as the first "cross-over" Executive Secretary, intended to provide continuity between consecutive staffs, by taking office in February of the school year (Bob Delahanty [U. of Louisville] was appointed to the first Sept.-Feb. half-year term). His summary bio follows:

Born 1927 in Chicago. Graduated Phillips Exeter Academy, 1944. U.S. Marine Corps, 1944-46.Harvard BA 1951, LLB 1954. Practiced law in Chicago 1954-1963. Office of General Council, CAB, Washington, DC 1963-67. 1967-68 Assist. Div. Chief. 1968-1970 Associate General Counsel. Assistant to Joseph Minette, 1970.

He was married to Penelope Bou Knight; they had a son and a daughter. Houghteling died in 1986.

(See also photos, pp. 237, 453, 866, 1089.)

NSA is in a state of stability, of growing unity and yet unbalance in its totality

3. Bob Kelly: A Priceless Experience

If student government has any reason to exist, then that reason is NSA's as its community

St. Peter's College, New Jersey
NSA President, 1949-1950

Editor's note: Bob Kelly was widely admired in NSA as an impressive speaker, logician, and parliamentarian. While active as a student, he sharpened these skills as a national leader, devoting his energies to building the association. After graduating and serving as an advisor for several years to the leaders who followed, he left the public stage, devoting his future years to family, community, and a career in corporate law, becoming a partner at one of New York's prestigious law firms. He was sociable, attractive, and engaging in the exercise of his ceremonial NSA duties, but at home base he preferred a solitary work environment and a disciplined routine. Kelly brought a clear sense of purpose to his assignment, one in which he believed and from which flowed his priorities. In his report to the National Executive Committee, from which excerpts follow, he addressed the organization's problems and shortcomings while articulating its vision and inspiring his listeners to continue striving for its attainment.

In contrast, in his correspondence with his parents and two sisters, portions of which his widow Marie Kelly generously provided to us, Kelly intimately reveals how he viewed the "first time" personal experience as NSA President: his wonder at its novelty, his obligation to the routine, his perspective on it as a job to be done, his appreciation of its benefits—large and small—and his wry sense of humor.

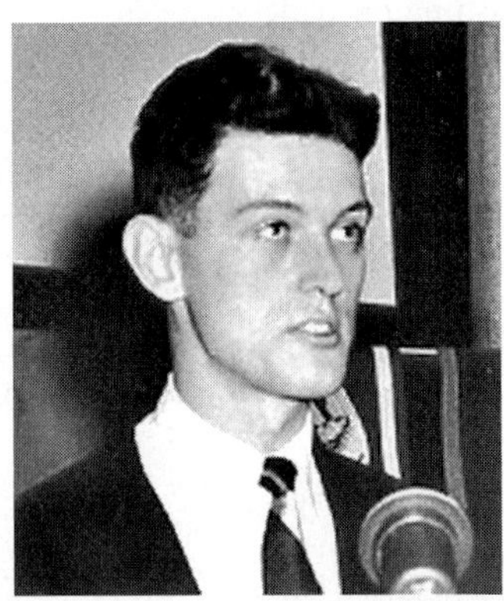

Our Grandest Function—Unifying the American Student Community

Excerpts from President's Report, National Executive Committee 21/31/49, University of Wisconsin.

We have few traditions which have had the opportunity to become venerable in our short existence, but I think there is one regularly recurring event which deserves the epithet "quaint," if no other, and that is the semi-annual meditation of the President before the National Executive Committee on the affairs of NSA. In times past, someone with a penchant for dry stereotypes has designated this phenomenon a "Report" and as such you find it here. I hope you will not be deceived, however. Reports, in the true sense of that much abused word, come from people who act on specific mandates, and in NSA this means our Vice Presidents, our Executive Secretary and our Regional Organizations. From the president there can come no more than a set of speculations, for he has no specific mandates. To the President there is left that baffling, tortuous, always unrewarding yet vitally important important task of evaluation. . . .

What is the state of the National Student Association, then? It is one of stability, of growing unity and yet of unbalance in its totality. . . .When I say I believe that NSA is stable . . . [I mean] that NSA has established itself as a functioning part of the educational community and that as such it has invariably been recognized in academic circles. . . . [For example] a recent conference on the education of college teachers heard discussions of our Faculty Rating System and a scheduled address on the subject. . . .

Strengths and weaknesses

There has not been a single college in all my travels where I have not encountered greater support among the faculty and administrative personnel for the basic ideals and immediate project objectives of NSA than among the student body. Sometimes I think that had we one tenth the support among students that we have among faculty and administrators nothing in this world could hold us back. But still, in the face of this semi-apathy among our constituents, I nonetheless feel that the Association is characterized by a substantial unity, which prior to the Congress was more theoretical than real. . . .[I say this] because the tensions of some time, dating in many cases back to the Chicago Student Conference, have largely disappeared as delegates and colleges have learned through working and thinking together that even if they no longer find themselves in agreement on every point, at least they understand the reasons for opposing stands and respect the sincerity of those who uphold them. . . .

Though we have achieved the substance of unity, we are confronted with an Association that is radically unbalanced. We are geographically centered in the Middle Atlantic Area and the Midwest. Except for the Virginia-Carolina Region, and despite tremendous efforts by regional personnel, the South remains unorganized. Some of our member schools are despairing of an extra-national program because there are no other member schools near them. . . .

* * *

Let me summarize for you. What are our purposes? Read our Preamble. You will find them stated there as succinctly as they will ever be. How do we implement them? Scan the Congress Reports, the workshops of your assemblies and the activities of campus delegates. But remember both [purposes and implementation]are essential to the stability, the unity, the balance and thus the total effectiveness of the Association.

* * *

To conclude my remarks, I should like to express something that is probably more fit for a *News* editorial but nonetheless something I would like to discuss with you personally. And this is the "Why" of NSA as I see it. I think there are three of them, and that if they and others are not kept always in mind, NSA is going to be a great magnificent superstructure resting upon sand or at best, on soft clay, to tumble down with a great clatter with the first ill wind, as so many of our predecessors have done.

Three reasons for NSA's existence

Why does NSA exist? . . . Why does campus student government exist? . . . Precisely for this reason: to represent all students on campus and to do for them who are its constituents and source of authority many of the things they cannot do for themselves. In short, a student government's competence begins where the competence of the individual student ends. . . .

Now, let us proceed logically from that premise. If we do, eventually we shall find a point where the student government cannot competently provide for itself and the students it represents what it needs, requires or wants. . . . Thus, if student government has any basic reason for its existence, if student government should exist, the National Student Association should, and may I add, must also, if we are reasonable.

Now what is the other reason? The society in which we live is a society that is becoming more and more complex. It is a society which, since it is becoming complex, is dividing into its component elements and therefore tensions are created. . . . This is a reason for NSA—to unite the student community, all those who have the explicit purpose of learning, so that it can work fortuitously with the other elements of the overall educational community. . . .

What is a third reason for NSA? To supplement the formal education of the classroom. Education, I think, seeks to train the whole man to the limit of his capacities. If education should do that, it has got to do more than merely train a man's mind. Man is not only an intellectual being, he is a social being and as such must live with other men. . . .

What is the role of the National Student Association in this facet of education? The role of NSA is to bring together the students of the college community, who are after all to be the leaders of the next generation, and show them that regardless of the fact that they may have only two things in common—their humanity and their vocation as students—they still have common problems and common aspirations which can be achieved only by common efforts and common deliberation.

To me this is our grandest function and our most compelling justfication—unifying the American student community. We alone can do it for we alone encompass, even imperfectly, our total milieu.

I Am Enjoying the Job Immensely

Excerpts from Bob Kelly's letters to his parents and sisters, written during his year as NSA President.

September 10, 1949

Dear Mom, Dad, Pat and Joan:

I have been very busy but I am enjoying the job immensely. We have four paid employees in addition to the five Staff members and some volunteer workers. It is as a result very flattering for me to preside over the entire works—you must agree it is rather nice to begin my first full time job as the head man. . . .

We have moved our offices to a new location within 304 North Park. Our quarters are somewhat larger (particularly my room) and much more functional. Here is the floor plan:

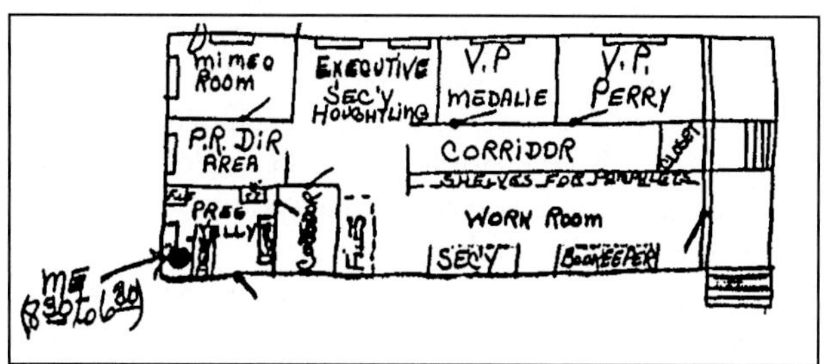

What do you think of it? We are stuck in only one way. The building in which we are located is an old and somewhat disreputable school house vintage 1890 and while it is sturdy and safe, does not exactly impress anyone. By the way, we have been frustrated in our effort to get a furnished house and as a result, the University Housing Bureau will help us obtain small apartments so that we will be permanently settled early this week. The rent will be about $30 per month, with no extras.

October 24, 1949

Dear Joan:

Frankly, I'm in an epistolatory rut. My letters are down to a science. I have about six forms drawn up which will take care of 80% of my incoming mail . . . everything from a request for tour information to a plea to endorse a student strike. . . . They [the form letters] are peppered with clichés like: "Thanks ever so much for your letter of ___, however"; "Due to our somewhat limited office force, we regret___"; "We note with great interest the formulation of___"; "If ever I can be of any service, do not hesitate to call on me."

But there is a lighter side to all this. The job is a wonderful experience in the art of meeting people and gaining poise such as cannot be gained from a book or by being instructed. It is very broadening too, just to know how other people think and act in various parts of the country, in places where there are no Catholics, foreigners or sewage facilities. The surprise of my life was when I discovered that the natives of Bloomington, Ind. spoke with thick Southern drawls. No, I would not change this job for the world. . . .

October 31, 1949

Dear Mom, Dad, Joan and Pat,

. . . The next two days will be very busy. This evening I will address the Student Board on Campus Chests. Tomorrow I have an NCCJ conference in Milwaukee and dinner engagement with the

Director. That evening we will drive to Chicago for the ACE-B'nai B'rith meeting on the 3rd from which I must hasten back to interview Nehru. Busy Little Bee, ain't I. All this makes being NSA President so fascinating.

Just moving in the same circle with these people is a priceless experience. I am learning now the poise and social polish necessary to life in the legal world I am soon to enter, without my livelihood depending on an absence of mistakes. Frankly, the job is worth ten thousand dollars and three years of my life.

For the rest, it is rather a stiff grind from the point of view of hours expended, but it is such an expenditure that I do not mind it a bit. And then there is the traveling around which while inconvenient in the extreme, is quite broadening. . . .

. . . after my next letter . . .I will be on tour en route home. You can throw Nehru, ACE, NCCJ, the University and the Swiss Plan all in a scale and they wouldn't even budge 'home' were it on the other end of the balance.

December 16, 1949

Dear Mom, Dad, Joan and Pat,

The lake is frozen now and with the temperature hovering around 15 degrees should it ever precipitate we will have snow and I my first white Christmas. . . .

Sunday we are to have a very unique treat. The Memorial Bell tower . . . is going to give a concert of Christmas carols at 7:45 P.M. The setting is magnificent. The tower is situated on Black Hawk point overlooking the lake and in among acres and acres of trees that have remained untouched since the Indians were here except for the site of the Tower. All that is needed to make it heavenly would be a light powdery snowfall. . . .

Advocating for NSA in the West

"A brilliant speaker . . . given a standing ovation," Daily Trojan *3/17/50 reporting Kelly's address.*

Senate Hears NSA Leader Deny Red Ties

Robert Kelly, president of the National Student association, told the ASSC Senate Friday that the NSA is neither Communist-dominated, controlled, nor backed.

NSA has been screened by the FBI and by educational groups of which it is a member, Kelly said. "There is a possibility of Communist infiltration, but there is that possibility in every American organization todap. We do not intend to make martyrs of the Communists by kicking them out," he said.

Kelly pointed to the association's stand toward affiliation with the International Union of Students as indicative of NSA policy. By a unanimous vote the NSA Congress unanimously reaffirmed its previous decision to refuse affiliation with IUS, which has been called a Communist front organization.

A brilliant speaker, Kelly gave a 45-minute talk built around three questions—What is NSA? What does it stand for? What has it done?

Taking the title National Students association, Kelly first defined the word "association" and

ROBERT KELLY
Tells of NSA

told of the organization's membership and powers.

Southern California **Daily Trojan**

association's meetings.

GIVE OVATION

In answer to a question on the difference between being a member or an observer of NSA, Kelly told the senators that it was the difference between being a part of NSA or being on the outside of it. NSA is a year-round organization, he said. A school that is not a member of NSA may only send observers to the meetings and cannot actually participate in the organization's program, Kelly said.

Kelly was given a standing ovation by the senate before he left to attend a reception at Los Angeles City college.

The senate adopted Bob Reynold's election report by common consent. Also approved were Bob Padgett's appointments to the committee that will present the "race and descent" report to the administration. Mrs. June Tapp, Jack Shaeffer, Maury Avins, and two members from the Council on Religion will form the committee.

CALIFORNIA, OREGON, WASHINGTON, AND IDAHO provided a western reach at major state universities, as well as among Catholic colleges and key private campuses. Nonetheless, there were strong voices of skepticism ("What will it do for us?") and opposition ("It will be a magnet for Communist infiltration") which NSA officers encountered and responded to on their travels. In some cases affiliation battles seesawed back and forth for years. USC was one such instance, while across town at LACC (Los Angeles Collegian 3/20/50) NSA enjoyed firm support (See Dobkin and Suzuki, Part 5, Sec. 8.)

Los Angeles Collegian

Kelly Speaks At Luncheon

Robert Kelly, United States National Student Association president, will be introduced by Harry W. Flannery, former news commentator, at a luncheon-reception given in his honor today at 1 p.m. in Newman Hall.

Spending two days in Los Angeles while on a good will tour, Kelly will be guest of the N.S.A. Southern District of California-Nevada-Hawaii region.

Kelly Meets Leaders

Kelly's itinerary includes confering with regional leaders and speaking before the University of Southern California, Los Angeles State College of Applied Arts and Sciences, and the International Affairs Conference at Occidental College.

A talk on N.S.A.'s aims, purposes, and programs, will be given by Kelly Friday at U.S.C., a non-member school. The same talk will be given before State College, also a non-member school, Friday at 3 p.m.

GREAT NORTHWEST REGION welcomed Kelly on March 14, 1950 at Marylhurst College, Oregon. From the left: Richard Pizzo, student government president, U. of Portland. Eileen Kruegel, student government president, Marylhurst College, Joan Long, NSA Chair, Marylhurst College, Bob Kelly, NSA President (Courtesy Joan Long Lynch)

Presidential address to the 1950 Third National Student Congress

A New Student Body Takes Up An Awesome Task

In this spirit will we bring new vigor to the heritage of the twenty-five students in 1946

Robert A. Kelly
St. Peter's College, New Jersey
NSA President, 1949-1950

Editor's notes: In these excerpts from Bob Kelly's presidential address to the Third Congress, his rhetorical rejection of the "myth" of the twenty-five students who went to Prague sets the stage for a review of the intervening challenges to the association, as a consequence of which he looks to the future and calls on the delegates to "take the heritage of the twenty-five students in 1946 and give to it a new green vigor, born of the changes in student life during the past four years but reposing solidly on the perennial desire for the solution of common problems through common discussion, common deliberation, and common action."

In his message to last year's annual Congress, my predecessor made reference to the fact that he no longer found it necessary to recapitulate the well-nigh Homeric legend of the twenty-five American students who journeyed to Prague in 1946 and thus gave impetus to the founding of the United States National Student Association.... Indeed, may I repeat it with greater emphasis, even if the reasons for the re-utterance are vastly different from those originally prompting the statement.

Last year the content of the Prague legend was tiresome; this year it is obsolete.

The year 1946 closed on an America done with the horror of world conflict and preparing for a generation of growth and tranquility. It reveled in the abundance of a bountiful land and made ready to share its prosperity with those nations blighted by a decade of strife and decline.

* * *

World conflict returns after postwar optimism

The four brief years since then—a college generation, if you will—has watched the slackening and final death of this postwar optimism. It has seen a world conflict in microcosm return to the headlines, and the flow of goods abroad include more and more weapons needed for the defense of helpless democracies. The plans of the brave new world have been consigned to libraries and reference files while the nation rose to the challenge of aggression and garbed its strength in armor.

In education, the bulk of the veterans moved on to rear their families and careers beyond the campus and a new student body took up the awesome task of continuing their internationalism, social consciousness and extra-curricular achievements in the face of a deepening world crisis. Educators wondered, and still wonder, if they were equal to it as indeed did the newcomers themselves. Some of the old apathy and provincialism returned, and their elimination was not being made easier now that every rifle volley on a Korean hillside had its faint but distracting echo in an American lecture hall....

A new context: Once buoyant, now cautious, retrenching and uneasy

Yes, the context of the Prague legend bares little resemblance to the context of the Michigan Congress. Then, the circumstances surrounding student life were buoyant, expansive and conducive to reciprocal international fellowship. Student leadership was tested, experienced and foresighted. Now, student life has as its most descriptive adjectives: cautious, retrenching and uneasy. Unyielding partisanship on the international student scene finds continued cooperative efforts made difficult or in some quarters rebuffed completely.

Too many of the newer student leaders on our campuses are superficial in their attitude toward activities, unimaginative in their concept of education, and completely lacking in the realization that a national and world community of students does exist, ready to assist, and be assisted by, all its component parts....

A challenge to effect a transition from past to present

The particular challenge to this present Congress lies...in its responsibility to effect a transition from the conditions of the immediate past to those of the present....

Because of the great significance attached to your deliberations then, as your chief executive by terms of our constitution, I am taking this opportunity to present for your consideration several recommendations in the various spheres of NSA activity. It is my hope that you will find them useful in your evaluation of the issues confronting American students today.

Student Bill of Rights little understood

By far the most resolved upon, talked about, and as you would expect, least understood question which may come before you will be the Student Bill of Rights.[1] In it, NSA has attempted to define the desireable and necessary status of students in our nation's colleges and universities. Some of the present provisions of the Bill and its lack of philosophical foundation have been criticized by administrators and students themselves. Two successive Congresses, regional assemblies and a special subcommission in the Rocky Mountain Region have had the matter under study for some time and in consequence, you will not lack for recommended courses of action.

I would add to these but little. My suggestions would be merely that in your shaping of the final statement, you bear in mind the concept of a unified educational community whose three elements—faculty, students, and administrators—are interrelated both in their prerogatives and in their obligations to each other and to the general public; and that you consider as a primary objective of all elements in the educational community to be the disinterested pursuit of truth with the end of increasing knowledge, developing the whole human personality and promoting the common good of our society.

As a corollary of this reasoning I would conclude that if the statement you adopt is to have deep and abiding meaning, it must be more than the isolated pronouncement of a single element of education. To insure the general recognition and application of its provisions, the Congress would do well, I believe, to submit the result of its deliberations in this field to the American Council of Education through whose good offices a conference of our entire community could be convoked—at which the document submitted by NSA might be adopted as an article of educational policy in much the same manner and with perhaps the same binding character as was the AAUP {American Association of University Professors] statement on academic freedom....

Student life issues: Student unions, cultural programs, economic welfare

Also in the field of student affairs, may I commend to your attention the problem of college union–student government relationships. Most disturbing in the past has been the tendency of one to invade the province and functions of the other and to carry on an almost internecine warfare in campus activities. I suggest that a formula for establishing the legislative supremacy of student government and preserving the business-like management of the college union be devised by the Congress with particular attention to said procedures now in operation at the University of Washington.

* * *

You would do well also, I believe, to evaluate the present cultural program of the association with a view to extending it to all phases of student artistic endeavors. It should be our object to serve as the connecting link between the professional cultural groups of our nation and the student artist so that each may have easy and mutually beneficial access to the other.[2]

* * *

In the field of educational affairs, it is my hope that you will devote much of your efforts to a consideration of the Association's role in prompting the economic welfare of students.... Time should be given over to discussion of the cooperative movement which NSA officers in this field have always regarded as the long-range solution to student economic problems.... I urge your support of the $100 million federal scholarship program fashioned by the American Council on Education.

* * *

In the broader aspects of education, I respectfully suggest that the Educational Affairs Commission and the Congress, itself, earnestly consider the impact of the present world crisis on the student; that it investigate means by which American students can assist their government and the United Nations in their efforts to repel aggression and reestablish peace.... [and] that it accept an invitation to participate in the forthcoming definitive ACE–Defense Department Conference on the subject.

* * *

Internationally: A "manifest obligation" for new global relationships

In your international deliberations, you will doubtless be confronted with the problem of our relationship to our fellow national unions of students throughout the world. . . . As the representatives of the American student community, you speak for the largest and most fortunately endowed segment of the world student movement, yet its most provincial and least organized as well.... It is my hope that you will give particular attention to the student communities of Africa, Eastern Europe, the Near East, Southeast Asia and Japan, with whom there has been lamentably little contact since the beginning of our international program and from most of whom concrete overtures of cooperation and liaison have been received.

These areas of the student movement, together with the Latin American [student organizations] hold the key to any constructive and expanded international policy which NSA can devise....This Association, I believe, would shirk its manifest obligation to students here and abroad if it does not set forth a detailed program of cooperation....

With regard to organic relations with an international student organization *[i.e., the IUS—ed.]*, I am waiting ... for the report of the NSA representatives who have spent the summer in conversations with student leaders and who have attended [international] meetings, including the World Student Congress....

I also commend to your deliberation the work of UNESCO and its work to construct the bulwarks of peace in the minds of men.

The "sheer importance" of organizational affairs

Dramatic as these aspects of our Commission activity may be, however, they defer to general organizational affairs for sheer importance to the continued effectiveness of NSA. The decisive battles of this Association, strange as it may seem, are fought as often with a budget, a mimeograph, a well-drafted form and a structural chart as they are with rhetoric, substitute motions and General Robert's guide for the bedevilled. More retreats, indeed, have been occasioned in NSA by shadowy lines of communication than by a hundred unproductive regional assemblies. It is my hope, therefore, that you will consider with more than external attention our general mechanics, our finance and levels of administration.[4] Particularly I urge you to diligently consider three things: campus, region, staff.

And so, I am led back inevitably—as are all other things in NSA—to the Congress. It would be an understatement to say that the nine days ahead will mean a great deal to the Association; they will mean everything to it. It will be you, the elected representatives of our member student bodies, and you alone, who will cast the precise meaning of these days of deliberations.

A tongue-in-cheek guide to making the most of a Congress

Oh, to be sure, there may very well be pressure—group caucuses, self-appointed slatemakers and all the other claptrap which habitually attaches itself to assemblies of this kind. You will find zealots with a favorite cause who will neither rest nor be satisfied until they have molded NSA to the image and likeness of their ideal group.

There will be some who find not the substance but the technique of deliberation alone worth their strife and who enmesh themselves in parliamentary and extra-parliamentary mechanics simply to gain experience for a budding political career back home. Others will view the entire proceedings as far beyond their powers of comprehension and will therefore strive with all their power to learn as little as possible about anything at all. Still others will diligently implement a social program of their own, converting their stay here into a continuous date or beer-bust built upon the representative resources of our entire student community.

...And the additional inspired options for service

But for every one of these, there are happily many others who are here to speak for their student bodies and participate fully in, the direction of NSA affairs on their behalf. These are the representatives whose concept of the student community encompasses the purpose of creating, through the instrumentality of student activities, an atmosphere in which students can become factors in the shaping of education, can assist one another in the realization of personal happiness and thus attain, even if only in microcosm, a society wherein individual self-expression and service to God and fellow man [are] facilitated.

These are the representatives who know that no caucus or group of slatemakers can prevail against their desires and the voting cards they will raise in this assembly hall. These are the representatives who will, in concert even if at times in disagreement, take the heritage of the twenty-five students in 1946 and give to it a new green vigor, born of the changes in student life during the past four years but reposing solidly on the perennial desire for the solution of common problems through common discussion, common deliberation, and common action.

In this spirit, may the Third National Student Congress perform its appointed tasks. In this spirit, will its service to the total community of students here and the world over be fruitful and enduring.

ROBERT A. KELLY

Robert Allan Kelly graduated from St. Peter's College in Jersey City, New Jersey, in 1951 and from Harvard Law School in 1954. He served in the U.S. Army Counterintelligence Corps stationed in Germany from 1954 to 1956. He was a member of the New York and New Jersey Bar Associations and was a partner at the New York law firm of Dewey, Ballantine, et al., retiring in 1985. His specialty was corporation law. Bob Kelly served as a trustee of the Summit, NJ Taxpayer's Association. He was a speaker at many communion breakfasts and civic associations. In 1959 he was president of the St. Peter's College (Jersey City) Alumni Association. He was married to Marie Becker Kelly, and they had three children; Irene Kelly, M.D., of Monterrey, CA; Mrs. Mary Fran Faraji of Basking Ridge, NJ; and John Kelly of Boston. He had two sisters, Joan Crosbie and Patricia Clark, and four grandchildren. Bob Kelly passed away on January 29, 1996.

Robert Kelly N.S.A. National President Draft-Elected Over Man He Nominated

When the St. Peter's seniors returned this fall for their last year, one well known face was missing. Robert A. Kelly was not with them. This past August, at its National Congress, Bob had been elected President of the National Student Association. Consequently, he had to withdraw from school to devote himself entirely to this important, national organization. But these few sentences hide much of the drama that surrounded the election.

In late August, more than 500 delegates, representing almost a million students, assembled on the campus of the University of Illinois for the Second National Congress of the N. S. A. The highlight of the congress was the election of national officers.

When Bob Kelly was first nominated as a presidential candidate, he

LEFT TO RIGHT: Rev. Fr. Phillip X. Walsh, S.J.; Mayor John V. Kenney; Bob Kelly; Fr. Gerard Murphy, S.J.

Robert A. Kelly practiced corporate law as a partner in the New York law firm of Dewey, Ballantine, et al., until his retirement in 1985. He served in the U.S. Army Counter Intelligence Corps in Germany from 1954 to 1955.

END NOTES

[1] See Student Bill of Rights, p. 1110, and Brown, p. 378.

[2] See Medalie, p. 352.

[3] This reference is to the second IUS World Student Congress, which had three NSA observers. See West, p. 556, and Holbrook, p. 559.

[4] See Schwartz, p. 242

PICTURE CREDITS: *Then:* c. April 2, 1949, NSA National Executive Committee meeting (*Schwartz*). *Now:* c. 1990 (*Courtesy, Marie Kelly*).

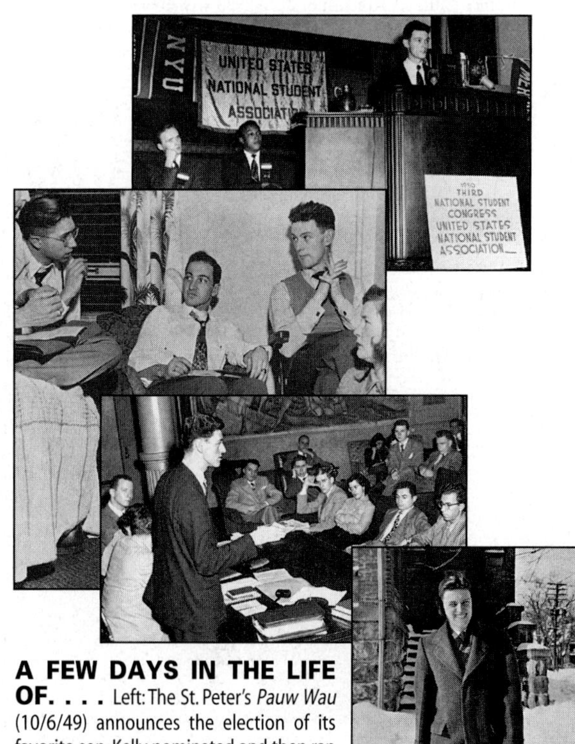

A FEW DAYS IN THE LIFE OF. . . . Left: The St. Peter's *Pauw Wau* (10/6/49) announces the election of its favorite son. Kelly nominated and then ran against Gene Schwartz, CCNY (see Schwartz, Sec. 6). From top: Kelly addresses the 1950 3d Congress at the U. of Michigan. Seated are V.P.'s Erskine Childers (Stanford, International Affairs) and Ted Perry (Temple, Student Affairs). At a 1949 caucus with Michigan regional chair Harvey Weisberg (U. Michigan), left, and Helen Jean Rogers, Mundelein College, Chicago, right. Addressing the Metropolitan N.Y. Region in New York City, 1949. Sheldon Steinhauser, LIU, regional chair, is to the left, rear. Revisiting the national office at 304 N. Park in Madison, 12/51. (Credits, in order: Courtesy St. Peter's College Archives. Marie Kelly. Schwartz. SHSW. Joan Long Lynch)

Actions you have taken demonstrate your determination to keep democracy flourishing

A Message from President Truman

The White House
Washington

1950

August 23,1950

Dear Mr. Kelly,

It is a genuine pleasure for me to extend warm greetings to the U.S. National Student Association on the occasion of its Third Annual Congress.

The fact that you are assembling for a frank and open discussion is in itself one of the demonstrations of democracy. As American students seeking answers to your problems, you are free from controls of any kind—an opportunity that has been lost in too many countries in the world. In your deliberations, you live under no fear or threat compelling the acceptance of pre-determined dogmas handed down by the State. Especially in these days we are gaining a new appreciation of these freedoms and are determined to defend them against enemies at home and abroad.

I am personally gratified by the wise and forthright positions your organization has taken in support of a Federal program of scholarships and loans as a means of broadening educational opportunities. These and other actions you have taken demonstrate your determination to keep democracy flourishing in our higher institutions.

If the NSA were only a laboratory in which students learn the ways of democracy, it would justify itself, but the fact that it promises to give active leadership to college and university youth in America and abroad leads me to hope that your Third Annual Congress will give comfort and encouragement to the friends of democracy everywhere.

Very sincerely yours,

Harry S. Truman

1951

The Cornell Daily Sun

ITHACA, N.Y., WEDNESDAY, APRIL 11, 1951

Truman Ousts MacArthur

Press Protests Plans to Defer Able Students

TRUMAN REMOVES UN COMMANDER

HARRY S. TRUMAN — GEN. DOUGLAS MacARTHUR

General Ridgway to Succeed As UN Supreme Commander

House Cuts UMT To Authorization

SC Funds Committee Slashes Appropriation

1950 President Truman and General Douglas MacArthur meet for the first time on Wake Island, October 14, 1950. Source: Truman Library.

1948

Yale News

TRUMAN VICTORY LOOMS!

Nation Amazed At Unexpected Election Trend; Democrats Seize Control Of Senate And House

Chester Bowles Defeats Shannon In State

Student Organizations Mourn, Celebrate Balloting Returns

HARRY S. TRUMAN was President from April 12, 1945 (when he succeeded Franklin D. Roosevelt) to January 20, 1953, after losing the 1952 election to General Dwight D. Eisenhower (*Yale Daily News* 11/3/48, as reproduced in the Yale Class of '49 Yearbook). He was President throughout the formative years of NSA. It was Truman's choice to drop the A-Bomb shortly after his inauguration that helped bring WWII to a close. The Truman Doctrine limiting Soviet expansion and the U.S. entry into the Korean conflct set the direction of U.S. foreign policy for decades to come. His most direct boost to NSA's fortunes came in June, 1950, when he made available a student ship for NSA student tour travelers to replace the one which the Coast Guard had declared unsafe (Pt. 3, S. 5). He is shown above at his first meeting with General Douglas MacArthur on Wake Island, October 14, 1950. MacArthur was dismissed by Truman on April 11, 1951 for "being unable to give his full support" to UN and US policies in Korea (*Cornell Daily Sun*, 4/11/51.)

Concord visits the NSA Congress

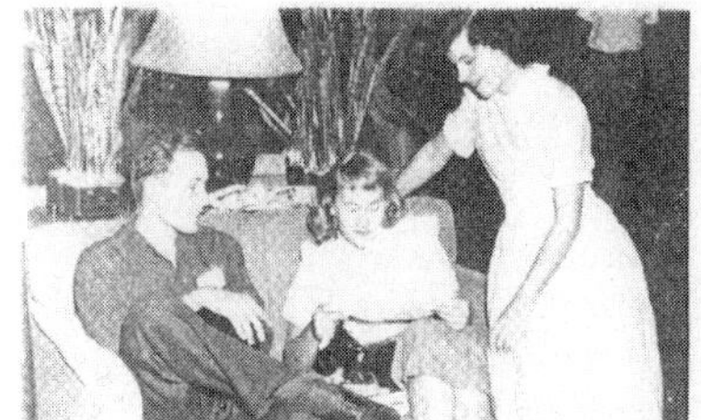

1. Orientation

4. National Executive Committee

2. Commission

CONCORD VISITS NSA CONGRESS. These pictures present a graphic view of how 800 delegates worked at Second Annual NSA Congress Aug. 23-Sept. 3 at the University of Illinois.

Credit lines for pictures are gratefully given to Nick Kondak, Wayne University, Detroit; Mel Larson, Chicago "Sun-Times"; and Joe Walski, De Paul University, Chicago.

5. Floor Tension

3. Plenary

6. Recreation

CONCORD MAGAZINE REPORTS ON NSA'S SECOND CONGRESS. *Concord Magazine* attended the Congress and devoted much of its October (in which these photos appeared) and November 1949 issues to the event. Then in its third year, *Concord* had been founded and operated by Catholic college students working and living together as a community in the Chicago area. The magazine invited and published analysis and news articles from a variety of student leaders on student affairs and their role in society. Martin McLaughlin (Notre Dame), active in the formation of NSA (See Part 1, Sec. 2), in an e-mail to the editor on 4/14/02 wrote, "My recollection is that [*Concord*] was launched in 1947 or 1948 by the U.S. Young Christian Students (YCS), an affiliate of the European (French) Jeunesse Etudiant Chretien (JEC), an international Catholic action group similar to others among workers (Young Christian Workers), farmers, families, etc. The movement began in the United States before World War II, and was looked at somewhat askance by the more "official" Catholic organizations, such as the National Federation of Catholic College students (NFCCS) and Pax Romana. My wife, Paddy, and I were both members—in fact, national officers. Several of us started the magazine *Concord* as a way to get some of our ideas into circulation. Its final editor was Vincent Giese who died about a year ago. I think the magazine lasted about three years—that is, until Vince went into the seminary and it ran out of money with no organization to support it." (See also Pat Groom, p. 954.)

Leadership in Action

I

THE United States National Student Association is the most healthy democratic organization in America. I say this after observing for ten days the Second National Student Congress at the University of Illinois where some 800 representatives from 300 colleges and universities worked out policy and program for the coming year.

I say this despite the criticism which will be levelled at the Congress for arguing too much over policy and too little over program. I say this despite the criticism that plenary sessions were nothing but parliamentary dialogues. I say this despite the fact that some of the resolutions passed may not be well-received when the delegates report back to their student bodies this month. I say it because no one can honestly view the Congress in full perspective and not say it.

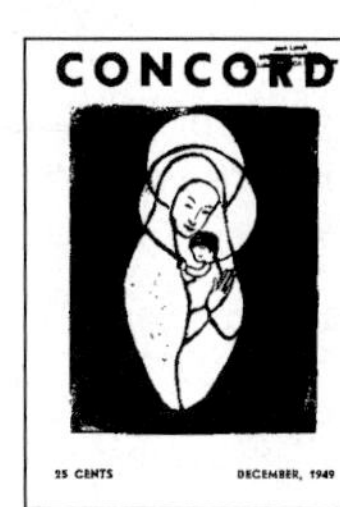

Editor's note: The interest of Protestant and Catholic student organizations in NSA and the energy they brought to its leadership ranks are documented throughout this Anthology and specifically addressed in Part 4, Section 2. Intercollegian, *the official publication of the National YM and YWCA's National Intercollegiate Christian Council (NICC), also covered NSA regularly during this period.*

Staff, Advisers, Regional Chairs, Colleges

1949-1950 National Organization

(As presented in the Second National Student Congress Report)

NATIONAL OFFICERS

President
Robert A. Kelly, St. Peter's College, New Jersey

Vice President, Student Life
Theodore Perry, Temple University, Pennsylvania

Vice President, Educational Problems
Richard J. Medalie, Carleton College, Minnesota

Vice President, International Affairs
Erskine B. Childers, Stanford University

Executive Secretary
Robert E. Delahanty, University of Louisville
Frederick D. Houghteling, Harvard College
(second half of year)

Public Relations Director
Ralph L. Smith, Swarthmore College, Pennsylvania

Director of Publications
Craig H. Wilson, University of Michigan

REGIONAL REPRESENTATIVES TO THE NATIONAL EXECUTIVE COMMITTEE

California, Nev., Hawaii
Dick Kelton
Stanford University
K. Wallace Longshore
Los Angeles City College

Georgia, Ala., Fla.
Roy Wiggins
Emory University

Great Northwest
William Gates
University of Washington

Illinois
Mary Jo Domino
Rockford College

Indiana
Emil Tesdsari
State Teachers College

Iowa
Richard Dice
Iowa State University

Kansas, Nebraska
Joan DeWoody
Mt. St. Scholastica College

Ky., Tenn.
Samuel T. Stumbo
University of Louisville

Mason-Dixon
Richard Cadigan
Loyola College

Michigan
Duane Johnson,
Wayne University
Joan Mauer
Marygrove College

Minnesota
Robert Treanor
College of St. Thomas

Missouri
Mary Terese Hartigan
Fontbonne College

New Jersey
Ariel M. Landy
Rutgers University

New York Metropolitan
Shelly Steinhauser
Long Island University
Joseph Clancy
City College Main Day

New York State
Robert Powell
Niagara University

Northern New England
Robert Stern
Harvard College
Fred Houghteling
Harvard College

Ohio
Philip J. Hart
Antioch College

Pennsylvania
Elmer Brock
LaSalle College

Rocky Mountains
Frank Krasovec
University of Colorado

So. New England
David Zimmer
University of Bridgeport

Virginia, Carolinas
Ben M. Jones
University of North Carolina

West Virginia
Bob Swartzel
Concord College

Wisconsin
Winston McDaniel (temp.)
University of Wisconsin

Unorganized Areas (incl. Ark., La., Okla., Tex.)
Robert E. Lord
Stephen F. Austin State College, Texas

NATIONAL ADVISORY COUNCIL

Gordon Klopf (Chairman)
Student Personnel Advisor, University of Wisconsin

William Birenbaum
Office of the Dean of Students, University of Chicago

Monroe E. Deutsch
Provost-Emeritus, University of California

Very Rev. Vincent J. Flynn
President, College of St. Thomas

Frank Graham
President Emeritus, University of North Carolina

James T. Harris, Jr.
President, 1948-49, NSA

R. O. Johnson
Professor of Education, Atlanta University

Millicent MacIntosh
Dean, Barnard College

Mrs. Carl Meineke
Dean, Colby Junior College

Dean Newhouse
Dean of Students, Case Institute of Technology

Donald Shank
Director, Institute for International Education

Harold Taylor
President, Sarah Lawrence College

Helen C. White
U.S. National Commission for UNESCO

1949-1950 Roster of Colleges: Second National Student Congress

(Institutions in italics attended with visitor status)

California-Nevada-Hawaii
California School of Arts and Crafts
College of Holy Names
College of Notre Dame
College of Osteopathic Physicians and Surgeons
Fresno State College
Immaculate Heart College
Los Angeles City College
Loyola University
Marymount College
Mills College
Mount St. Mary's College
Occidental College
San Francisco State College
Stanford University
St. Mary's College
University of California, Berkeley
University of California at Los Angeles
University of Santa Clara
Los Angeles City College
George Pepperdine University

Georgia-Alabama-Florida
Agnes Scott College
Alabama State Teachers College
Barry College for Women
Emory University
Georgia School of Technology
Morehouse College
University of Miami
Tuskegee Institute
University of Alabama

Great Northwest
Eastern College of Education
Lewis and Clark College
Marylhurst College
Reed College
State College of Washington
University of Idaho
University of Washington

Illinois
Aurora College
Barat College of the Sacred Heart
Chicago Teachers College
De Paul University
Institute of Design
Knox College
Loyola University
Mundelein College
North Central College
Northern Illinois State Teachers College
Rockford College
Roosevelt College
Rosary College
St. Francis College
St. Procopius College
St. Xavier College
University of Chicago
University of Illinois
College of St. Francis
Illinois Wesleyan University
James Millikan University
Northwestern University
Parson College
Purdue University

Indiana
Franklin College
Indiana State Teachers College
Indiana Technical College
Manchester College
Marian College
Saint Mary-of-the-Woods College
St. Mary's College
Earlham College

Iowa
Clark College
Grinnell College
Loras College
Marycrest College
Parsons College
University of Iowa
Wartburg College

Kansas, Nebraska
Dana College
Doane College
Kansas State Teachers College
Marymount College
Mt. St. Scholastica College
University of Kansas

Kentucky, Tennessee
Berea College
Christian Brothers Jr. College
Fisk University
King College
Nazareth College
Southwestern at Memphis
University of Kentucky
University of Louisville
Ursuline College
Tennessee Polytechnic Institute

Mason-Dixon
Catholic University of America
College of Notre Dame
Dunbarton College of Holy Cross
Hood College
Loyola College
Morgan State College
Mt. St. Agnes College
Trinity College
University of Baltimore
Howard University
St. Joseph's College
University of Maryland

Michigan
Aquinas College
Central Michigan College of Education
Detroit College of Law
Highland Park Junior College
Hillsdale College
Marygrove College
Mercy College
Michigan College of Mining
Nazareth College
Siena Heights College
University of Detroit
University of Michigan
Wayne University
Western Michigan College
Michigan State College

Minnesota
Augsburg College
Carleton College
College of St. Benedict
College of St. Teresa
College of St. Thomas
Concordia College
Hamline College
Macalester College
St. Cloud State Teachers College
St. John's University
St. Mary's College
St. Olaf College
University of Minnesota

Missouri
College of St. Theresa
Fontbonne College
Maryville College
St. Louis University
Washington University
Webster College
William Woods College

New Jersey
College of St. Elizabeth
Monmouth Jr. College
New Jersey College for Women
New Jersey State Teachers College–Montclair
New Jersey State Teachers College–Paterson
Rutgers University at Newark
Rutgers University at New Brunswick
St. Peter's College
St. Peter's School of Business

New York Metropolitan
Adelphi College
Brooklyn College
CCNY Business Day
CCNY Business Evening
CCNY Main Day
CCNY Main Evening
College of New Rochelle
Columbia University
Fordham College
Fordham School of Education
Good Counsel College
Hunter College–Day
Hunter College–Evening
Iona College
Juilliard School of Music
Long Island University
Manhattan College
Manhattanville College
Marymount College
New York University, Education
New York University, University Heights
New York University, Washington Square
New York University, Commerce
Notre Dame College
Pratt Institute
Queens College
Sarah Lawrence College
St. Francis College
St. John's University
Vassar College

New York State
Alfred University
Bard College
Canisius College
Clarkson College
College of St. Rose
Cornell University
D'Youville College
Eastman School of Music
LeMoyne College
New York State Institute of Applied Arts
New York State Teachers College–Buffalo
Niagara University
Rochester Institute of Technology
Russell Sage College
St. Bonaventure College
St. Lawrence University
Siena College
Skidmore College
University of Buffalo
University of Rochester–Men
University of Rochester–Women
University of Rochester–Nursing
William Smith College
Syracuse University

Northern New England
American International College
Bates College
Bennington College
Boston College
Boston College in Town
Boston University
Bowdoin College
Colby Jr. College
Emerson College
Emmanuel College
Framingham State Teachers College
Garland School
Harvard College
Harvard Divinity School
Harvard Graduate School
Massachusetts Institute of Technology
Mount Holyoke College
Mt. St. Mary College
Radcliffe College
Regis College
Simmons College
Smith College
Springfield YMCA College
Tufts-Jackson College
Wellesley College
Wheaton College
Williams College
Women's College of Middlebury
Worcester Junior College
College of the Holy Cross
University of Massachusetts

Ohio
Antioch College
Ashland College
Cleveland College
College of Mt. St. Joseph
College of Wooster
Flora Stone Mather College
Hiram College
John Carroll University
Muskingum College
Notre Dame College
Ohio State University
Ohio Wesleyan College
Our Lady of Cincinnati
Ursuline College
Youngstown College
Capital University
Denison University
Lake Erie College
Miami University
Ohio University
Wittenberg College

Pennsylvania
Albright College
Allegheny College
Beaver College
Bloomsburg State Teachers College
Bryn Mawr College
Bucknell University
Chestnut Hill College
Immaculata College
La Salle College
Lehigh University
Mercyhurst College
Mount Mercy College
Pennsylvania State College
Rosemont College
Seton Hill College
St. Francis College
St. Joseph College
St. Vincent College
Swarthmore College
Temple University
Thiel College
University of Pennsylvania
Wilson College

Rocky Mountain
Colorado A. & M. College
Colorado College
Colorado State College of Education
Loretto Heights College
Regis College,
Regis College–Downtown
University of Colorado

Southern New England
Albertus Magnus College
Connecticut College for Women
New Haven YMCA Jr. College
Pembroke College
St. Joseph's College
Teachers College of Connecticut
Trinity College
University of Bridgeport
University of Connecticut–Storrs
University of Connecticut–Fort Trumbull
Yale University
Yale Divinity School
University of Connecticut–Hartford

Virginia, Carolinas
Hollins College
Johnson C. Smith University
Lynchburg College
Mary Washingtion College
North Carolina State A. & E.
Randolph-Macon Women's College
Sweet Briar College
University of North Carolina
Virginia State College
Women's College of Duke University
Johnson C. Smith University
North Carolina State College
Suffolk University

West Virginia
Bethany College
Concord College
West Virginia State College
West Virginia Wesleyan University
Beckley College
Marshall College
West Virginia Institute of Technology

Wisconsin
Beloit College
Carroll College
Milwaukee State Teachers College
Mount Mary College
St. Norbert College
University of Wisconsin
University of Wisconsin–Milwaukee

Unorganized Areas
Arkansas A. M. & N.
Jackson College
Our Lady of the Lake College
Southern University
Stephen F. Austin State Teachers College
University of Arkansas
University of Tulsa
Xavier University
Northern State Teachers College
New Mexico Highlands University
Louisiana State University
Northwestern State College
Southeastern Louisiana College
Southwestern Louisiana College
University of Oklahoma

McCarthyism and the Korean War
Cool Jazz and *Guys and Dolls*

China's forces occupy Tibet. Senator Joseph McCarthy unleashes the era of "McCarthyism." Riots occur in Johannesburg, South Africa, against apartheid. North Korea invades South Korea on June 25 and captures Seoul. General Douglas MacArthur is appointed commander of UN forces in Korea. A State of Emergency is declared in the United States. Chinese forces cross the 38th parallel. The United States recognizes Vietnam, supplies arms, and sends a military mission. Dr. Ralph Bunche wins the Nobel Peace Prize. The Anti-Communist Alien Registration Act is passed by Congress. An assassination attempt is made against President Truman by Puerto Rican nationalists. Thor Heyerdahl's *Kon Tiki* and John Hersey's *The Wall* are published. Cultural icons die: George Bernard Shaw, Edgar Rice Burroughs (*Tarzan*), Edna St. Vincent Millay, Edgar Lee Masters, Al Jolson, and Carl Van Doren. National Council of Churches in Christ formed. Film classics include: *La Ronde*, *Sunset Boulevard*, *Rashomon*, and *All About Eve*. Cool jazz develops from bebop. *Guys and Dolls* opens. High on the charts are "A Bushel and a Peck," "Goodnight, Irene," and "Tzena, Tzena, Tzena, Tzena." Antihistamines introduced into the market. World population is 2.3 billion and the U.S. population is 150.7 million. 1.5 million TV sets are in use—reaches 15 million in 1951. Ohio State defeats California 17-14 in the Rose Bowl. New York shuts out Philadelphia 4-0 in the World Series.

Source: Adapted from citations in Bernard Grun, *The Timetables of History* (Simon and Schuster, 1991)

BUDGETING NSA'S MILESTONES: 1949-50

UNITED STATES NATIONAL STUDENT ASSOCIATION
FINANCIAL OPERATING STATEMENT
(National Office)
1 September 1949 - 30 September 1950

INCOME:		Actual	Budget
National dues		19,800.75	20,000.00
Purchase Card System - income	2380.75		
expense	-352.00	2,528.75	3,000.00
Publications Bureau - income	3277.73		
expense	-1067.27	2,210.46	1,500.00*
International Office - receipts from	3460.00		2,000.00*
disbursements to	-912.82	2,547.18	8,500.00
1950 Congress Net Proceeds - income	2281.65		
expense	-80.38	2,201.27	-
Miscellaneous Income		88.12	-
TOTAL INCOME		29,376.53	35,000.00

EXPENDITURE:		Actual	Budget
Salaries - Officers	11737.73		15,000.00
Secretarial	1796.95		3,600.00
Employer's SS Tax	142.08	13,676.76	
Rent		1,625.00	1,500.00
Travel		1,522.42	6,000.00
Office Supplies - expense	1534.10		
reimbursement	-62.72	1,471.38	1,500.00
Postage & Mailing - expense	2490.85		
reimbursement	-88.42	2,402.43	1,800.00
Telephone & Telegraph - expense	1131.47		
reimbursement	-252.50	877.97	900.00
Printing		712.10	
NSA NEWS Net Expense - expense	2081.47		3,000.00*
advertising	-327.57	1,753.90	
Promotional Publications		1,835.14	
Public Relations Expense		88.00	-
Furniture & Equipment - depreciation	537.18		
maintainance	47.95	585.13	500.00
Subscriptions, Literature, & Meetings		137.23	
NEC & Staff Meetings		64.89	
Insurance		118.40	
ESSAI - expense	648.54		
income	-346.50	302.04	1,200.00
Art Tour - expense	127.30		
income	-95.00	32.30	
Miscellaneous Commission & Subcommission expense		218.88	
Miscellaneous Expense		578.60	
TOTAL EXPENDITURE		28,002.57	35,000.00
NET OPERATING PROFIT, FISCAL 1949-50		1,373.96	

* The Budget specified Income of 1,500.00 from the Publications Bureau and 2,000.00 from NEWS Advertising. It allocated to Printing Expense, lumping together publications, NEWS, and office printing, the sum of 3,000.00. This then looked toward a net income from all printing-publishing operations of 500.00. In actuality, these operations showed a net expense of 2,390.68.

YEAR THREE CAME IN UNDER BUDGET, BUT

. . . showing $28,000 in expenditures and $29,376 in receipts against a $35,000 budget. Savings were realized in salaries and travel expense. What was not shown—nor known at reporting time—was the later $25,000 loss reported by NSA's travel program that summer (see Lynch, Sec. 8 ff)—a program bedeviled by a Coast Guard decision holding up certification of NSA's chartered student ship the *Svaalbard* and briefly stranding 550 students in New York City (See Garland and Meagher, Pt. 3, S. 5). The impact of this loss was felt for the next two years, leading to the Association's move to Boulder, CO, and reduction in full-time staff in 1951-52 (Pt. 1, S. 9), its move to Philadelphia in 1953 (see Pt. 6, S. 1), and the opening of an independently managed travel office in New York City (Pt. 3, S. 5). (Document sources: SHSW archives, Sylvia Bacon. Reproduced here are portions of mimeographed NEC and Congress reports.)

SECTION 8

NSA's Fourth Year, 1950-51

CONTENTS

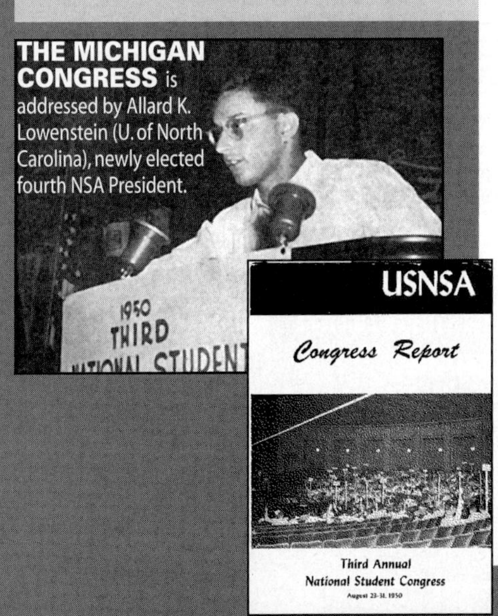

THE MICHIGAN CONGRESS is addressed by Allard K. Lowenstein (U. of North Carolina), newly elected fourth NSA President.

The NSA staff that was elected at the Michigan Congress, headed by Allard K. Lowenstein (University of North Carolina), entered a year when most undergraduate veterans on the GI Bill had left the campus and moved on to work and family or graduate school. The theme of the Congress was "The Role of the Student in the Educational Community."

The Korean War loomed over the Congress agenda, and over the report of the dramatic experiences of Robert L. West, NSA's 1948-49 International Vice President and NSA observer team member at the International Union of Students (IUS)–sponsored Second World Student Congress in Prague. The memorable speech that he delivered in Prague appears in Part 3.

Lowenstein, a popular and charismatic spellbinder, who later attained national prominence as a Congressman and leader of the "Dump Johnson" movement during the Vietnam War, changed the course of the association's policy toward the IUS in his controversial speech delivered in Stockholm that December (detailed in Part 3), criticizing Soviet imperialism and proposing more effective collaboration among noncommunist national student unions.

What had been tensions of management style among the prior year's staff were exacerbated by policy and program differences among the new staff. These are reported as part of the overview of that year presented by Joan Long Lynch (Marylhurst College, OR), 1950-51 Staff Associate, as well as in the recollections of Shirley Neizer Tyler (Simmons College, MA), Executive Secretary.

Leadership role among NSA's staff is debated

Both writers discuss how, on opposite sides of the issue, Elmer Brock (LaSalle College), Vice President for Student Life, and Herb Goldsmith (University of Wisconsin), Vice President for Educational Affairs, voiced the split over the meaning of NSA's recently adopted policy that among its elected officers the president was "the first among equals." Until that year the elected officers largely maintained autonomy in their respective program areas and reached consensus through collaborative relationship. Both Lynch, in her memoir in this section, and International Vice President Herb Eisenberg (Massachusetts Institute of Technology), in his memoir in Part 3, report how this balance was strained, if not ruptured, in the articulation of NSA's "foreign policy." Nonetheless, Lowenstein voiced a passionate vision for his generation that "we shall learn to build better bridges . . . and to live with one another." His presidential speech to the Michigan Congress is presented here.

LIFE magazine, in its picture story of the convention, highlighted the appearance of Cornell student Robert Fogel (later a Nobel Laureate in Economics) as representative of the communist-oriented Labor Youth League, who was given floor time to present his argument against U.S. engagement in the Korean War, which appears in this section.

Attendance at the Congress included 780 delegates and observers from 232 colleges and also 100 administrators and press.

1950-1951 ALBUM

The Michigan Daily

Latest Deadline in the State

'U' WILL BE HOST:

Annual NSA Congress To Arrive Next Week

...third annual National Student Congress will bring more ...300 college and university ...ts and edu... campus fr... nd the U... are hosts ... is sponso... al Student...

...ELCOME ... was exte... stein, chai... ittee of St... sions of th... o Universit... administ...

and a faculty representative will welcome the delegates to the Congress.

Student Mobilization Urged By Speakers At U-M Parley

Rapid mobilization of American students for war and peace was urged today by three student leaders attending the third annual National Student Congress on the campus.

Bob Treanor of St. Thomas Col...

problems ranging from academic freedom to how to meet the high cost of living.

The three student talks were given at 12:45 this afternoon on a National Broadcasting Co. nation-wide radio hookup.

Students Urged To Fight For Intellectual Freedom

The kind of intellectual freedom needed in American colleges extends far beyond bookiearning, the third annual National Student Congress was told last night at its opening meeting on the campus.

Dr. Ralph E. Himstead of Wash...

groups.

Welcoming talks at last night's opening session were given by Dean of Students Erich A. Walter and Prof. Preston W. Slosson.

The students this morning divided into committees to begin consideration of specific problems such as...

(Angell Hall, University of Michigan)

Third Annual National Student Congre...

Aug. 23-31, University of Michigan
Ann Arbor, Michigan

"The Role of the Student in the Educational Community"

The Cold War and Korea

Wars, cold and hot, captured headlines and attention, as NSA moved into its fourth year with a strong sense of its role "as the voice for American students" (Lowenstein) but "drastically underfunded" as programs became "more numerous and complex" (Lynch). The third Congress was welcomed to Ann Arbor (above) by the *Michigan Daily* (8/13/50) and the *Ann Arbor News* (8/26, 8/27/50). Photos above. Left: Jack Shaffer, USC observer, wife and child. From top right: (1) Elmer Brock (La Salle C, PA), V.P. Student Life; Gordon Klopf (U. WI), Chairman, National Advisory Council; Allard K. Lowenstein (U. of NC), President; Herbert B. Goldsmith (U. of WI), V.P. Educational Problems. (2) From left: Shirley Neizer (Simmons C, MA), Executive Secretary, Merrill Freed (U. of Chicago), Chair, Illinois Region; Joan Long (Marylhurst C, OR), Staff Associate, (3) Left: Herbert W. Eisenberg (MIT), V.P. International Affairs with Paulo Martins, President of the Brazilian National Union of Students.

World Student Congress

THE National Student Association is now in the process of forming a delegation to the second World Student Congress to be held in Prague this summer.

This congress, sponsored by the Inter...

exhausted our postwar dreams of full employment smashed. To the ever louder demand of our youth for jobs, all Wall Street can answer is "Join the Army."

A report of this festival elicites an an...

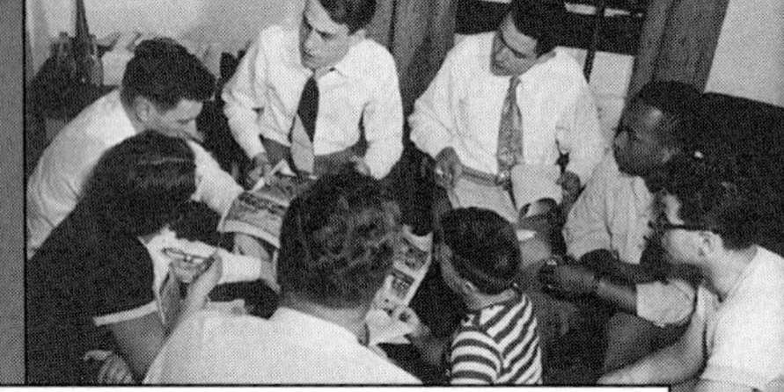

U-M Parley Hears How Reds Rigged World Student Meet

An eyewitness report of the Com... rupted sessions, the U. S. students...

BUILD NSA

The NSA News

United States National Student Association

VOL. IV, NO. 3 DECEMBER, 1950

19 Student Unions Hold Conference at Stockholm

Leaders of 19 national student unions will meet at Stockholm, Sweden, this month to discuss proposed multi-lateral working arrangements between their organizations.

Sponsored by the Swedish union of students, the meeting will convene Dec. 17-21. NSA's voting delegate will be represented by its President, Al Lowenstein. NSA's "Veep" for international affairs, Herb Eisenberg, may also participate in the discussions as a technical advisor.

The purpose of the meeting is in line with...

THE IUS HELD ITS SECOND CONGRESS in Prague. NSA sent three observers. Middle photo: Robert West (Yale, Pt. 2, S. 2) addresses the Congress. Bottom photo: Gene Schwartz (CCNY) and Bill Holbrook (U. Minn), 3d and 4th from right, deliver report to NSA staff. (Clips: *Mich Daily* 6/2150, *Ann Arbor News* 8/28/50). Bottom: Alternate conference to IUS called for Stockholm.

World's Students Divide

TEMPLE UNIVERSITY NEWS

Local Great Debate

Students from 9 Colleges Attend NSA's Weekend Peace Program

Delegates from nine colleges attended an NSA sponsored intercollegiate student conference "By What Means Peace" at the University Friday, Saturday and Sunday.

University of Pennsylvania, Swarthmore, City College of New York, Cheyney, Antioch, Brooklyn, Lincoln and Fordham as well as the University, sent representatives.

Francis Russell, State Department official, addresses delegates to the "What Means Peace" student conference at the University during the weekend.

NEW YORK Tribune Late City Edition

FRIDAY, JUNE 23, 1950

Picture of Dejection

550 Are Stranded, Student Tour Ship Held as 'Fire Trap'

SUNDAY, JUNE 2...

Korea Reds Open Attack On South Korea, War On; U. S. Takes Case to U. N.

Cabinet Falls In France on Pay Rise Issue

Bidault's Regime Loses by 122 Votes

Tuesday Afternoon, October 31, 1950 THE TECHNIQUE, ATLANTA,

Third Student Congress Discusses Korean Battle

NSA Delegates Meet Behind Iron Curtain For World Congress

LA SALLE COLLEGIAN Wednesday, October 4, 1950

NSA Backs U.N. Korean Stand; Federal Aid To Education

NSA Congress Considers Aggression, Academic Freedom, Discrimination

Ann Arbor, Mich... campus problems fo... more than 300 Ameri... the Third Annual N... here.

'Loyalty Oaths' in Universities Denounced at NSA Convention

SQUARE BULLETIN

Published By The Students Of Washington Square College, New York University

MONDAY, SEPTEMBER 18, 1950

Third National Student Congress Supports UN Resolutions On Korea

6,000 STUDENTS ENROLL

The Detroit Free Press

BRITISH LAND IN KOREA

STRANDED STUDENTS SHARE HEADLINES. Clips, right, from top: *New York Herald Tribune* 6/23/50, 6/25/50 ("Korea Reds"). See "Student Ships" Pt. 2, S. 5. *Temple University News* 5/9/51. *The Technique* 10/17/50, GA Tech, *La Salle Collegian*, 10/4/50, PA, NYU, *Square Bulletin* 9/18/50 ("Aggression") 10/13/550, *Columbia Spectator* ("Loyalty Oaths") 10/2/50. Photo: Unidentified delegate at NSA 3d Congress (SHSW).

A Renewed "Hot War" Focus

The fourth year, 1950-51

1. From Ann Arbor to Minneapolis

Joan Long Lynch
Marylhurst College, Oregon
NSA National Staff Associate, 1950-51. Chair, Pacific Northwest Region, 1951-52

The year 1950-51 was a difficult one for NSA. The Korean War began in June of 1950; with it ended the hopeful post–World War II era in which the association was born. The international crisis and its effect on organizational programs, policy, and personnel coincided with the need for the NSA to reevaluate its operations. The association had grown in size and complexity, but its managerial and financial systems had not kept pace. The vitality of the organization was being sapped internally at the same time that it was being acknowledged by the educational and cultural community of the country as an authentic and effective voice for American students.

Korea and the Cold War

Following the outbreak of hostilities in South Korea, Congress voted to extend the Selective Service Act. Once again, college students faced the prospect of military service and of personal plans being postponed. To seek or not to seek educational deferments became a preoccupation for many. Several delegates to the Michigan congress received draft notices while they were in Ann Arbor, and the newly appointed treasurer of the association served in office only one week before resigning to return to school because his number had been called. The draft status of newly elected President Allard K. "Al" Lowenstein was an ongoing source of anxiety during most of his year in office.[1]

As the bulk of World War II servicemen and women who had taken advantage of the educational benefits of the GI Bill moved from the campuses into careers and family life, enrollment pressures eased and the average age of the student population lowered. Proposals to adopt some form of Universal Military Training (UMT) increased. NSA did not yet have a position on UMT, but public policy leaders turned to the association for student opinion on the question.[2]

In February 1950, U.S. Senator Joseph McCarthy began his infamous campaign of charges of treason in high places. He dominated the headlines for months. The publicity he gained encouraged others to emulate him, exacerbating the climate of fear and suspicion abroad in the land. Along with other segments of the educational community, USNSA experienced an attack from one of these headline seekers during the 1950-51 term.[3]

Several states had already adopted requirements that public employees, including college and university professors at state institutions, sign loyalty oaths or face dismissal. Six members of the California State College system who refused to sign were fired in 1950. Threats to free speech and free association on college campuses increased; the loyalty of persons with differing social or political views was questioned. NSA participants at the American Association for the United Nations meeting in Chicago in early 1951 were publicly called Communists by a representative of the National Pan-Hellenic Association who disagreed with NSA's stand on racial and religious discrimination.[4]

The Korean War presaged the end of NSA's attempt to find comity with the International Union of Students (IUS). The Third National Student Congress convened in Ann Arbor as the Second World Student Congress was meeting in Prague. There, delegates from North Korea dressed in military garb were hailed as heroes and paraded about the hall while the Americans were vilified as warmongers.[5] The delegates in Michigan awaited the return of the three-man NSA delegation to the world student congress, whose report and recommendation would guide decisions on future relations with the IUS. Even before their return, however, there seemed little doubt that NSA had reached the end of the line in its attempts to influence that international body. Several proposals for an alternative to the IUS were already floating around as the congress began.

Existing internal problems

When Robert (Bob) Kelly determined that there were significant problems interfering with the effective operations of NSA early in his 1949-1950 term as president, he appointed a committee to study the problem. Eugene Schwartz has covered the Special Advisory Committee on Organizational Reform (SACOA [sic]) in detail in his account of that year.[6] The report of the committee was ready for delegates to the 1950 congress. The report addressed many problem areas, but failed to confront the most critical need of the organization: adequate financing.

The association was drastically underfunded in 1950. The cost of operations had long since outstripped membership dues, the principal source of revenue. In 1949-1950 they were insufficient to finance day-to-day operations. Even so, there was strong sentiment for a further dues reduction. Bob Kelly, himself, was in favor of the move because he believed it would stimulate membership.[7]

Fund-raising for programs and projects was pursued without coordination or control or appropriate accounting. (There had evidently been no thought of hiring a professional fund-raiser for the organization.) USNSA was not incorporated as a nonprofit organization. Money raised for association projects from donors who wanted a tax benefit had to be given to other organizations, who in turn passed it on to NSA. It was not a good arrangement. The lack of corporate status also exposed individual officers to unlimited personal liability for debts or other liabilities of the organization.[8]

As NSA's programs became more numerous and complex, the internal systems and procedures of earlier days were outgrown. The mechanics of day-to-day management, including financial control and reporting, no longer served the organization well. Executive power was decentralized; the president had responsibility without authority. Each staff member pursued his or her own projects. In the absence of harmonious staff relations, neither coordination nor accountability was assured.

Relations between the increasingly autonomous International Commission in Cambridge and its travel office in New York and the National Office in Madison suffered from the geographic distance separating them. More important was the lack of timely or complete communication among them. Financial reporting and oversight were inadequate. Sentiment for consolidating the offices was strong as a cost-saving measure as well as a way to bring the domestic and international arms of the association closer together.

The international travel program had become an urgent source of concern. It was operated by the international vice president, rather than by an experienced travel business professional. NSA's foray into the ship-chartering business earlier in summer 1950 was a near disaster. The episode, which came to be known as the "*Svalbard-Ballou* Affair," exposed the association to unquantified financial consequences as the Congress convened.[9] These problems—internal, national, and international—faced the delegates to the Michigan congress and the organization as it entered a new year.

The Michigan congress—New faces of 1950

I signed in for the precongress National Executive Committee meeting of the Third National Student Congress at the University of Michigan in Ann Arbor as chair of the Great Northwest Region. I felt almost like a veteran NSAer, although my experience with the association was not that extensive. As a delegate from Marylhurst College, I had represented my small, suburban, Portland, Oregon, Catholic women's college at the Second National Student Congress at Urbana. Our 1949 delegation of seventeen from six institutions in the four-state region (Washington, Oregon, Idaho, and Montana) was led by Bill Gates from the University of Washington.[10] I was elected as southern vice president of the region in December, and at the spring 1950 regional meeting was chosen to succeed Bill.[11] And so I found myself, a lightly seasoned veteran, at the Ann Arbor gathering.

There were approximately 750 persons registered for the congress, including delegates and alternates from some 350 member schools, observers from nonmember schools, faculty members, and guests.[12] The majority of delegates at the Michigan congress were new to the association or had at least not attended the Illinois congress, as a comparison of rosters for the two events reveals. In my delegation, only 2 of the 10 of us were returnees; in the California delegation, 32 of 33 members were new; in Illinois it was 29 of 37; and in Pennsylvania, 23 of 25. The Metropolitan New York delegation was a little better off, but of their 63 delegates, only 19 had prior congress exposure. Members of the National Executive Committee (NEC) were the most experienced: 24 of the 27 had attended at least one prior congress, and several had been around since the constitutional convention in 1947.

Youthful optimism confronting the ugly reality of a badly divided world: this was the context in which the Congress opened. The atmosphere was different than it had been at Urbana; less carefree, somewhat anxious and uneasy. I don't remember as much late-night singing on the lawn as we had done in 1949. Among other recollections from the congress, two stand out:

Representatives from a number of other student organizations were also in attendance: the United World Federalists, the Newman Club, Students for Democratic Action, and so forth. Some had set up information tables in the lobby, where their literature was available for the taking. Among them was the Labor Youth League (LYL), a very left-wing organization. From the LYL table came a continual flow of mimeoed bulletins to delegates, urging support for, or opposition to, various issues being discussed in the commissions. They were harshly critical of U.S. foreign and domestic policy and of American political leadership. They also criticized proposed NSA resolutions on student rights, federal aid to education, and relations with the IUS. Their most interesting missive was one under the name of "Challenge." It featured a bold headline: "Prevent World War III—No Guns, No Planes, No U.S. Lives for Wall Street's War against Korea." It carried a photograph of John Foster Dulles and a group of unidentified men, several in military uniform, purporting to show ". . . Dulles . . . peering at North Korean territory with some of his stooges . . . five days before Wall Street's war of intervention against Korea unfolded!" There was no ambiguity in the LYL's message.[13]

When a resolution supporting President Truman's action of sending American troops to support the United Nations in Korea was placed on the congress's agenda, an LYL member asked to be allowed to speak in opposition to the proposal, although he was only a visitor to the congress. The NEC debated the merits of granting the request through several late-night closed sessions and finally arrived at a strategy that required the full cooperation of the delegates.[14] In my diary I found a cryptic note for that day; it read: "Intrigue. Intrigue. Intrigue."

For the next day, another note in the diary read: "F.B.I. Mr. Case." A delegate from the Mason-Dixon Region and I were approached by a gentleman unknown to either of us. He asked us to have lunch with him and we accepted. Over a pleasant meal of Lake Superior whitefish at a restaurant somewhere in Ann Arbor, he identified himself as an agent of the Federal Bureau of Investigation. He asked us to assist him in identifying communists or other suspicious individuals at the congress. Neither of us knew any, although the LYL people certainly represented a very left-wing point of view. We told him we couldn't be much help, thanked him for lunch, and heard no more from him. We presumed he had observed the LYL activity himself. (I hypothesized that he may have approached me because I had a low-level security clearance due to my work as a summer hire at the Hanford Atomic Energy installation, as a clerk-typist. My home was there, in Richland, Washington, where my father was employed on the project. The FBI was as much a part of that landscape as were sagebrush and sand.) It was a surprise to find, forty-nine years later, the agent's name on the roster of registered visitors to the congress, without identification of his organization.[15]

Student and educational affairs

Among the numerous legislative actions of the congress, the delegates supported a broad program of federal aid to education, including scholarships and grants to students on the basis of qualification and need, as well as funds for operating expenses, new buildings, and other capital projects. They also endorsed financial aid for graduate study. The delegates reaffirmed their opposition to segregation and discrimination and encouraged support for efforts to eliminate these practices and the laws that perpetuated them. They adopted the resolution in support of the principle of academic freedom, noting that "violations of and threats to academic freedom...have been intensified during the last few months as an immediate consequence of the increasing international tension." The resolution declared that the hiring, firing, and placing on tenure of professors should be on the basis of professional competence, not on the basis of political, religious, or social criteria; that standards for judging professional competence should be determined solely by the university community; and that loyalty oaths (i.e., oaths above and beyond constitutional allegiance) were destructive to academic freedom and constituted an ethical breach of a professor's constitutional rights.[16]

Revisions of the National Purchase Card System and the association's travel pool were approved. (The travel pool formula was revised; however, a large number of schools failed to contribute their assessments, negating the effectiveness of the program in 1950).[17] Proposed changes to the Student Bill of Rights were hotly debated on a level that would have made philosophy professors proud of their students.[18] In the end, the revisions only clarified and regrouped the rights, while maintaining substantially the same basic statement of ideal conditions in student-faculty-administration relations.[19]

Organizational affairs

In his opening address to the delegates at the beginning of the 1950 congress, President Robert A. Kelly implored them to understand that nothing they would consider would be as important to the future of NSA as legislation related to the finances, operations, and administration of the organization.[20]

I don't believe most of those listening to his speech had a clue as to what he was really saying. Delegates new to the association, as well as others like me, had minimal contact with the National Office. Few of us knew anything about problems within the staff or that the organization's management structure no longer served the association well.

The congress (and the NEC in its postcongress meeting) adopted many recommendations for institutional charge, most having come from the SACOA group, including the consolidation of the National and International Offices in Madison, Wisconsin, and the creation of the Offices of Treasurer and Travel Director, both to be appointed by the NEC. The duties of the public relations and publications directors were combined, and the position was made appointive. Along with the personnel changes, delegates voted for discontinuing the *NSA News* as it was currently constituted and for the development of a new medium of mass communication for both member and nonmember schools.[21] The congress urged the reorganization and strengthening of regional components of the organization, and the NEC directed the staff to emphasize and support regional activity in the coming year.

The delegates adopted several resolutions that, taken together, shifted the focus of the organization's activities. They called for a deemphasis on programs and, at the local, regional, and national levels, emphasis instead on the importance of the organization as a responsible voice for American students in the educational and cultural community. They included as part of a resolution elsewhere that "USNSA shall take a stand on all issues which directly affect students as students." The staff was directed to evaluate and prioritize existing programs and to discontinue those that did not materially contribute to the revised objectives of the organization.

Difficulties interpreting the congress's intent

It is possible to say that once again the delegates did not understand the impact of what they had done. Despite the refocus, the congress approved the initiation of a great many new programs. The interpretation of the intent of the congress in this shift of focus gave rise to a number of staff conflicts during the 1950-51 year. For example, at a number of conferences on mobilization NSA representatives were asked to give student opinion on the merits of some sort of program of Universal Military Training (UMT). The organization had no stand on the issue. Could a staff member say anything? Could he express his personal opinion? Al Lowenstein responded to questions about UMT at meetings in New York and in North Carolina. In both cases he told the audience that he could only express his own opinion, since his organization had not taken a stand on the issue. Several members of the staff, in New York at the time, confronted Al about his response to the question. When a story about the North Carolina meeting, misquoting him, was picked up on the news service wires, it caused another furor in the staff.[22]

Lines of staff authority remain contentious

The two most important pieces of administrative legislation at the Congress were the adoption of a resolution on "Authority within the Staff" and the reduction of membership dues. The first *increased* the shared executive authority of the staff, emphasizing joint staff responsibility for the implementation of NSA programs. Further, it was decided that the staff, by majority vote, should "supervise and direct" all the activities of each of its members and employees. The president should be the chief spokesman to those outside the organization, but within the staff the president's role was to be limited to that of "first among equals," with administrative and executive powers "subject to the direction of the Staff." This was Bob Kelly's worst nightmare come true! It compounded the ineffective governance formula, which had troubled him during his term in office. The resolution on staff function did nothing to assure accountability of individual members of the staff, nor give the president the power to act as an executive when needed.[23] It was the underlying cause of the conflict that came to characterize the performance of the National Staff during the 1950-51 year.[24]

There was popular support for reducing membership dues, and it was believed that by eliminating programs, combining offices, selling rather than giving away NSA publications, and so on, significant economies could be realized. But the delegates had no information on which to make that decision. The 30 percent cut in dues that they approved was made in the absence of a current financial report. Few knew that the income from dues at the 1949-1950 year level was insufficient to operate the organization, nor did they know that an attempt to reduce the operational deficit was the motivation for the ship-chartering venture.

According to Erskine Childers, the international vice president in 1949-1950, the association budget for that year included as income an amount to be generated from the traditional international work, study, and travel programs. Early in 1950 Erskine realized that the estimate of the profit from the programs was too high. However, the travel industry predicted that 1950 would be a big year for foreign travel. Erskine came to believe there was a good prospect of sizable profit to be made by chartering a ship to carry students to Europe; this would be more than enough to make up for the shortfall. A decision to pursue the plan was made. But unfortunately, the venture was not a success.[25] The NEC heard rumors of problems on the horizon from the affair; there might be a debt of five thousand dollars. Information on the extent of the damage was not forthcoming during the 1950 congress, and the delegates were not apprised of the situation at all.

The financial crisis that resulted from the cut in income, combined with the debt from the travel fiasco, affected every aspect of the association during the 1950-51 year.

International relations—New directions

Gordon Klopf, chairman of the National Advisory Committee, in his report on the 1950 congress in the educational journal *School and Society*, noted that fewer delegates participated in the deliberations of the International Commission than in prior years.[26] The new generation of delegates seemed more interested in student and educational affairs and programs that would benefit their individual campuses, despite their ratification of the proposal to change the focus of the organization from generating programs to representing student opinion. However, as in prior congresses, it was still the international agenda that provoked the most discussion, received the most publicity, and generated the most excitement.

The resolution supporting the United Nations in Korea (see pp. 266-67) received national press coverage, including a spread in *LIFE* magazine.[27] The strategy that the NEC devised to avert a potentially explosive situation worked perfectly: namely, to accommodate the Fogel speech—but with absolutely no reaction by the delegates. When Elmer Paul Brock, chairman of the Pennsylvania delegation, moved, on behalf of the NEC, that the rules be suspended to allow Robert Fogel of the Labor Youth League to speak, Roy Romer of the Rocky Mountain Region seconded him. The resolution was adopted unanimously. Fogel's inflammatory speech attacking U.S. foreign policy and opposing NSA support of the UN action was met by absolute silence on the part of the delegates. *LIFE* captured the moment in a photograph of Fogel at the microphone while the NEC floor managers, Elmer and Roy, sat feigning sleep. At the conclusion of the speech, the presiding officer called for the orders of the day and moved on to the next order of business, just as planned.[28]

Earlier in summer 1950 a group of NSA representatives, "The NSA European Team," visited student organizations and educational institutions in many countries. The twelve team members were originally chosen to attend the IUS congress at Prague and to survey student conditions abroad. When the number of NSA delegates (and necessary visas from the Czechoslovakian government) was cut to three by the IUS, the decision was made to go ahead with the group's travels but to emphasize other objectives. They were to present students and officials in target countries with an accurate picture of life in the United States and of the American educational system, to gauge the reactions of national unions of students to NSA international policies (specifically, the resolutions of the Second National Student Congress concerning international relationships) and to gather information that might lead to practical activities of cooperation. Team members also were to be "on the lookout for student and educational problems common to many countries, on which exchange of information or concerted action could be a useful function of an international organization." Each team member was to prepare a report on his or her visits, including the contacts made, materials gathered, and impressions.[29]

Funding the international team

The project was funded by grants from two anonymous sources, facilitated by Fred Houghteling, according to a recent account by Craig Wilson.[30] Participants included the three World Student Congress delegates—former NSA vice presidents Gene Schwartz and Rob West and Bill Holbrook from the University of Minnesota—and Billie Wright of Fisk University, James Garst of UCLA, William Kennedy of Georgia Tech, Hector Corral of Loyola of L.A., Claude Salomon of Colorado A&M, Jay Maryanov of Columbia, William Polk of Harvard, William Strasburg of Ohio Wesleyan, and Frederic Flack of Cornell. James Grant of Harvard made a tour of countries in Southeast Asia at the same time. Later in 1950, Melvin Conant, also of Harvard, made another trip to Southeast Asia to visit countries that Grant had missed. These reports provided valuable information about world student conditions and organizations for the association as it began to formulate a new international policy.[31]

On their return from the IUS meeting in Prague, the report of the NSA delegates confirmed the belief that the international organization continued to promote a partisan political agenda incompatible with the belief of American students and contrary to the stated aims and principles of the international organization itself. The congress again affirmed that NSA could not consider affiliation with the IUS, but would send observers to the next IUS council meeting. The delegates adopted a resolution articulating the necessary characteristics of a representative international organization, agreed to cooperate in multilateral working arrangements for programs of international study, travel, student exchange, and so on, and authorized consultation with other national student unions around the world to determine if the basis existed for formation of an international student organization—one open to, and enjoying, the support of students not only from Europe, but from Asia, Latin America, the Middle East, and Africa as well.[32]

Unfinished business of the congress

Leftover items from the commissions at the 1950 congress that were not considered by the full assembly due to lack of time were given to the NEC for consideration at their post-congress meeting. A few dealt with minor policy matters. Most, however, were desirable programs, which the NEC endorsed without recognition that funding them would be difficult or impossible or would conflict with the decision to refocus the energies of the association.

New leadership at mid-century and Al Lowenstein

The congress elected a talented, experienced, and interesting group of individuals to lead the organization in 1950. It included: Allard K. Lowenstein (University of North Carolina), age 21, President; Elmer Paul Brock (LaSalle College, PA), 25, Vice President for Student Affairs; Herbert Goldsmith (University of Wisconsin), 23, Vice President for Educational Affairs, and Herbert Eisenberg (MIT), 24, Vice President

International Affairs. Shirley Neizer (Simmons College, MA), 21, was elected as Executive Secretary to succeed Frederic D. Houghteling (Harvard), 23, later in the year. Craig Wilson (University of Michigan) had served as Publications Director in the previous administration and was appointed to the newly combined position, which now included public relations. Winston Martin, from the University of Missouri, was appointed the first Treasurer of the association but left office after only one week. His office was assumed by Fred Houghteling (Harvard University) when Shirley Neizer (Simmons College) took over the position of Executive Secretary in November. I was hired by Al Lowenstein as staff associate.

Allard K. Lowenstein

Allard K. Lowenstein, known as "Al," graduated from the University of North Carolina (UNC), where he was an active participant in student government as well as in the North Carolina State Student Legislature. Al had been around the association from its very earliest days, even before the first Prague meeting.[33] He represented UNC at the 1947 Constitutional Convention and two subsequent congresses. Well known and respected for his vision and leadership skills, Al was drafted to run for the presidency in 1950. He was a charismatic leader and a dynamic and articulate spokesman for the association. He had a wealth of political experience, in on-campus student organizations, with other groups like the United World Federalists and the Students for Democratic Action, and in national party politics. Al had an amazing network of friends and acquaintances from all over the country. (During these years he slept on many of their couches.)[34] He knew his way around Washington from the time he had spent on the Capitol Hill staff of U.S. Senator Frank Graham of North Carolina. His interest in international affairs was longstanding, and he was impatient with the years wasted in efforts to forge a workable relationship with the IUS.

Al believed the time had come for NSA to pursue a more proactive foreign policy and was enthusiastic about the stand the congress had taken relative to a new international initiative. He also believed that his constitutional role as spokesman for the organization authorized him to speak on international as well as domestic issues. In prior years, NSA's international activities were principally the province of the international vice president. Thus it is not surprising that Al's determination to lead the association into a new international era brought him into conflict with new international vice president Herb Eisenberg.[35]

For Al, as for many others, NSA was a launching pad into public service. His year as president of the association marked the beginning of his public life and what was to be a high-profile career in leadership and service to the country. He maintained close connections with NSA and its successor organization for many years, and he used that relationship as a base from which to encourage countless thousands of students to get involved in the great causes of our times.

Elmer Brock and Herb Goldsmith

Elmer Paul Brock, from La Salle College in Philadelphia, was a veteran of the U.S. navy and the oldest member of the new officer team. He had also attended the 1947 Constitutional Convention as a representative of Rittenhouse College in Philadelphia, an institution founded to accommodate returning servicemen and -women. He represented, first, Rittenhouse at the second and third congresses, and then LaSalle College, and was on the NEC during the Michigan meeting. Elmer was active in student government on both campuses and had served as a member of the Pennsylvania Governor's Advisory Committee on Children and Youth. He was a strong advocate for the full participation of students in the governance of the educational community.

Herbert B. Goldsmith graduated from the University of Wisconsin with a degree in education. He served as chair of a NSA National Subcommission on Evaluation of Higher Education and was the regional educational affairs commission chairman as well. Herb's interest in educational affairs was developed at the university, where he was chairman of both the Student-Faculty Conference Committee on Educational Affairs and the Academic Affairs Committee of the student government, as well as a member of the Committee to Study Discriminatory Practice. He also held membership in several campus honorary organizations. Herb was the only married staff member; he and his fiancée, Lynn, were married in fall 1950.

Herbert Eisenberg and Shirley Neizer

Herbert Eisenberg, a senior in architecture at the Massachusetts Institute of Technology, was also a veteran. His involvement in international affairs began at MIT, where he served as chairman of the Foreign Student Summer Project, which the institute sponsored. He also was chair of two NSA subcommissions on international activities at MIT as well as the NSA committee there. He chaired the Central Committee for the United States of the International Association for the Exchange of Students for Technical Experience. His experience in international student exchange programs gave him a strong background for his role as International Vice President.[36]

Shirley Neizer graduated from Simmons College in Boston with a degree in social science in 1950. She had served NSA at all levels. During her college career she represented Simmons at the first and second congresses and was an NEC member at the Michigan gathering. Shirley sat on the Special

Advisory Committee on Organizational Affairs studying the International Commission functions. An active member of the Simmons student government, she held elective office and other important positions, including heading the leadership training program for student government. She also served the Northern New England Region on several committees. Shirley was the first African-American woman to hold national office in the association.[37]

Fred Houghteling and Craig Wilson

The two holdovers from the previous staff were Frederick Delano Houghteling and Craig Wilson. Fred, a prelaw senior at Harvard College, was a former Marine and scion of a famous family. The term of the executive secretary was changed in 1949 to January-December in hope that this would improve continuity between the outgoing and incoming national staffs. Fred was to serve until December 1950. However, by October his health became a problem, and he left the position in November (but stayed on in Madison until the end of December). Fred had been active in NSA affairs since the constitutional convention, where he represented Harvard. He served as NEC representative from the Northern New England Region, as well as regional treasurer. He was on the Harvard Student Council and chaired its Extra-Curricular Activities Committee. He participated in the Harvard Debate Council and the Harvard Democratic Club and was on the national board of the Student Federalists and the Students for Democratic Action.

Craig Wilson was also a veteran, enrolled at the University of Michigan, where he was a journalism major. He served as director of publications under Bob Kelly, and then stayed on to assume the dual role of publications and public relations director. Craig decided to leave NSA in November 1950 to earn more money so he could return to Michigan.[38]

My role was staff associate, a position that had no formal job description (or typing test, thank God!) but consisted of clerical and secretarial duties. It was sometimes ambiguous, (e.g., I was asked to represent the two delegates from the California, Nevada, Hawaii Region at the December 1950 NEC meeting). Holding their two proxy votes, I was Miss California for one short week.[39]

The national office

Fred and Craig met me at the train on my arrival in Madison in mid-September 1950 and took me to the old Draper School at 304 N. Park Street. The memory of the smell of the place lingers still; it was of the oily sweeping compound used by decades of janitors to clean the wooden floors, which made the building a real firetrap! My first order of business was to find someplace to live. I hoped to find a place that Shirley and I could share, but as others before had learned, Madison was not the enlightened city I thought it was. The hunt proved fruitless, so I became the fourth girl sharing upstairs rooms in a house on North Pinckney Street, several doors away from Lake Mendota. (When Shirley arrived, she found a room in a house owned by two elderly ladies.)[40] My place served as guest quarters for a steady stream of NSA women visitors. We had a fully equipped kitchen and I was a fairly competent cook, so it was also where we could get together for a meal. My Scandinavian Lutheran roommates were intrigued by the NSA people, who seemed so different from themselves. The situation could have provided commentator Garrison Keillor with the plots for several reports from "Lake Woebegon." The landlord and his wife, an elderly couple who ice-danced, would have fit right into his accounts.

Madison was a lovely city in 1950, although the layout of the main streets radiating from the square surrounding the state capitol was confusing to one accustomed to the rectilinear grid of Western towns. The vivid autumn colors were a beguiling prelude to what turned out to be a dreadfully cold winter. What had been a delightful walk to the office through fallen leaves became a frigid ordeal when the temperature fell to thirty below for days on end.

In early October, part of the International Office moved to Madison. Herb Eisenberg drove out, towing a rented trailer full of files from the Cambridge office, accompanied by Mary Saunders, his secretary, and Charlotte Agnew, a volunteer. The Cambridge activities did not cease when Herb left; James Grant and others there continued the work of the European team. Herb split his time between the two locations. To accommodate the additional people, it was decided to relocate our office upstairs, where there was more room. Alterations were made in the space, creating new offices and workrooms. Much of the carpentry was done by staff members, aided by volunteers. Rob West came into town to talk about UNESCO but willingly picked up a hammer to help, commenting that he wasn't very skilled but he was willing.[41]

Craig stayed on staff long enough to prepare the report of the Third Congress and a first issue of a new type of *NSA News* before resigning. Attempts to hire his replacement were unsuccessful, so for the rest of the year the public relations and publications duties were taken on by members of the University of Wisconsin student newspaper *The Daily Cardinal*. Staffers Jim Zucker, Jerrold Schecter, and Karl Meyer[42] provided valuable journalistic services to the organization throughout the year.

Staff's differences and Al's office on wheels

Differences of opinion on how the new staff should function surfaced at its very first meeting in Ann Arbor, increased with time, and were never resolved. As a result, the group had difficulty in arriving at agreement on even trivial issues. Right or wrong, Al Lowenstein decided that it was futile to spend his time in continual infighting in Madison when the urgent business of the USNSA was to increase the membership, influence, and visibility of the organization. He delegated his limited executive powers to Elmer Brock; commissioned me (and Shirley when she arrived in November) to keep him informed about the day-to-day happenings in the office, then spent most of the year on the road. He returned to Madison from time to time to catch up with correspondence and to plan the itinerary for his next trips.

Communicating with him was often frustrating; mail was forwarded to him but sometimes went awry as his itinerary changed. He rarely knew where he would be staying, so tracking him down was always a challenge. His maroon Studebaker convertible was his office on wheels and often his sleeping quarters as he moved about the country. He kept abreast of developments in the organization by mail and telephone.[43]

Al cared little for the ceremonial prerogatives of his office but did feel a deep sense of responsibility for the organization. He worried about the financial straits it was in, but was determined that there be no loss of momentum in its mission of service to American students. He believed that if he stayed in Madison he would become a captive of his colleagues, so he stayed away.

Follow the money—the Travel Office travails

The most pressing issue in the office was to get an accurate picture of the association's financial status. The books in the Madison office were in complete disarray, and there were questions about those in Cambridge as well. There was no suggestion of malfeasance or misappropriations of funds; rather it appeared to be a case of inadequate systems for keeping track of income from a variety of sources, inept bookkeeping, incomplete records, and failure to issue reports in a timely manner. Herb Goldsmith located a student from the School of Commerce at the University of Wisconsin who took on the job of setting up a new accounting system. He, in turn, found a student to serve as a part-time bookkeeper, but warned that it would take several months to pull the figures together. It was a frustrating task for both of them. When they finished in February 1951 they concluded that the books could not be audited since so many records were missing.[44]

In early October after the S.S. *Ballou* returned from Europe with the last of the student tourists, we learned that the rumor about a large loss from the travel program was true; the amount was much greater than previously believed. It looked as if it would be in excess of $20,000, which was more than our income for the year! Money was owed to our partners in the travel business, the national student unions of France, Britain, and Holland. They did not press us for immediate repayment but made it clear that they expected us to continue in the travel business in the summer of 1951 or they would do so. Some members of the National Advisory Committee, and others, believed that we shouldn't be in the travel business at all, but now we had to make the best of it.

Thomas Callahan, an NSAer from New York (St. Francis College) came to Madison on his way to Iowa one day in November. He was then working for the National Scholarship and Service Fund for Negro Students. When he left the next day he did so as NSA's new travel director.[45] Although Tom lacked experience in the travel business, he was able to get the program back on track. By the end of his second year the debt from the 1950 operation was wiped out. Ted Perry, NSA student affairs vice president in 1949, joined Tom as bookkeeper in the Travel Office in the Woodstock Hotel in New York City. For the 1951 season NSA engaged passage on the Holland-American Line ship the *Volendam,* as it had done in prior years.[46]

National staff in dire financial straits

Before the whole picture was fully developed, it was clear the association was in a very dangerous financial situation. Reasonable estimates of future income were bleak; there would not be enough money to make it through the year. It was necessary to cut spending everywhere. The office was again reconfigured, and the additional space rented in September was relinquished. Program and publication spending were curtailed, and economies of every kind were imposed. The NEC wrestled with the problem at its December meeting but was unable to provide any solution to it other than to endorse a proposal for the regions to help pay the cost of travel of national staff members to regional assemblies.[47] Those regions that had funds available did so. The Northern New England Region even made an interest-free loan to the National Office. The staff cut their salaries to $28 a week and encouraged members to take unpaid "vacations" when possible. Occasionally, paydays were delayed. A proposal was made to cut the staff and have some of the members return to their campuses, but the idea was rejected. Several of us took jobs at Paisan's Restaurant, across the street from the office, where we waited on tables in exchange for meals. Elmer gave up his room and moved into the office, where he slept on the couch, keeping company with the mice.

Anxiety about money persisted until the end of the year. It affected every aspect of activity of the association, not only programs and personnel. Our inability to provide member schools with full financial statements was a source of concern for all of us. Several schools dropped their membership in

NSA because of the missing information—or used it as the reason to do so. The University of Washington, among others, was very vocal in its demand for a full accounting. When it was not forthcoming it withdrew from the association and encouraged others on the West Coast and elsewhere to do so as well.[48]

The elected officers were personally liable for the debts of the organization, and the jeopardy in which they found themselves was alarming. Through the good offices of Gordon Klopf at the university, we began working with the LaFollette legal firm in Madison for incorporation of the organization. The matter was complicated because the Travel Office operated in New York and so had to be handled separately from the association itself. In my diary there is a note about the first meeting of Educational Enterprises, Inc., the corporate name chosen for the association. (Attempts to find these records have been unsuccessful.)[49]

The Stockholm Conference

A conference to explore the sentiment for a new avenue of international cooperation was called by the Scandinavian student unions for late December 1950. Groundwork for the conference was prepared prior to fall 1950. Al Lowenstein discussed it with his Canadian counterpart when he visited the annual meeting of the Canadian Union of Students in early October. He told the NSA staff he planned to attend the meeting well before the invitation from the Scandinavians arrived. When it became clear that NSA could not afford to send two people to the conference, Al arranged to borrow the money for his trip from his parents.[50] Herb's expenses were paid by NSA. Al was the delegate, as were his counterpart presidents of other national student unions. Herb was either the alternate or the "expert." Herb believed that the purpose of the conference was technical, that it had been called only to explore programs of international cooperation. He prepared a proposal for a "Students' Mutual Assistance Program" (SMAP), which was well received by the Stockholm delegates. USNSA was designated as the coordinating body for the program.[51] Al saw the conference as the opportunity to begin planning for a new vehicle for international student cooperation (in line with the resolution adopted by the NSA delegates in Ann Arbor).

In a speech at the conference, Al condemned the IUS, particularly its subservience to the Soviets, its manipulation of national student unions, and its campaign of domination of the world student community. He advocated the establishment of "a continuing committee, responsible to a future conference, to investigate the need and desirability, the financial possibility and the structural form of a new international union." At the same time he went on record in opposition to the formation of a new organization at that time, saying:

> We are opposed to setting up a new union here, because first we must know that a basis exists in South East Asia and that adequate financing is available. We will never know these things until we create the committees to investigate and report back. We are further opposed to setting up a new union here because we are representatives of only 21 nations; and it is our conviction that it would be a major fallacy to have any part in the creation of a western union.

Al endorsed the establishment of meaningful technical programs by the Stockholm group, but reminded the audience that "political" decisions would have a significant impact on carrying them out.[52]

There were protests about the political tone of his speech from some delegates and an official expression of regret was made part of the record of the meeting. (In a letter written after his speech, Al told NSA staff members that some of those who voted to censure him told him privately that they agreed with him.)

Herb Eisenberg was outraged. He believed that the avenues of exchange and cooperation among students should be kept free from the power struggle between the world powers. The disagreement between the pair was never resolved and became one more area of controversy within the staff.[53] The National Executive Committee endorsed Al's position at their December meeting. They also approved participation at a second conference, similar to, but more broadly representative than, the Stockholm meeting. Several regions took on projects related to preparation for that conference.[54]

I have come to believe that Al's speech was probably more calculated than it appeared at the time. As the president of USNSA, he was able to say forthrightly what many of his international colleagues could not; he did not have to face a large left-wing faction in his organization at home, as many of them did, nor were the Soviets sitting on our doorstep. He could afford to be the point man and get the real issues out in the open. At the same time, he appreciated the concerns of students in former colonial states who did not want to get drawn into the East-West struggle but who did need assistance. It was perhaps not "diplomatic," but he did represent the views of American students as expressed by them in Ann Arbor. The Stockholm conference marked the beginning of a new era in international student relations.

A busy year despite the turmoil

Despite the problems caused by the budget crisis, the work of the association went on. Staff members attended regional assemblies in all parts of the country during the course of the year, and Al visited hundreds of member and nonmember schools. An impressive number and variety of national meetings and conferences of educational, cultural, and governmental groups had NSA officers as participants, from the inauguration of the president of the College of Idaho in Caldwell to the celebrity-laden *Philadelphia Bulletin* Forum.

Educational affairs

Herb Goldsmith acted for the association, in cooperation with the American Council on Education, in sponsoring a conference on Human Relations in Higher Education. He took a leadership role in preparing educational program materials on manpower problems and the national emergency for campus and regional use. Herb also obtained a grant from the National Council of Christians and Jews for a campus-based human relations program for students. He brought order to the Student Discount Service[55] and organized the travel pool for the 1951 congress.

Student affairs

Elmer Brock represented the association at the White House Mid-Century Conference on Children and Youth, the American College Personnel Association, and the National Association of Deans of Men. He produced program materials for use on campus, including a handbook on parliamentary law and the *Student Government Newsletter.* To promote better understanding between NSA and member campuses, Elmer organized the Student Body Presidents' Seminar which was held as part of the 1951 National Student Congress.[56] When Al was away from the office, Elmer was his designated representative. Unfortunately, however, it was a position for which he was not temperamentally well suited. In March he made good on a threat to resign, but was persuaded to return and stayed on until the end of the year.[57]

International affairs

While the Stockholm conference held center stage in the international arena during the year, there were other activities as well. Arnie Weiss of the University of Wisconsin coordinated a campus-based international program. NSA participation on the U.S. Commission for UNESCO continued, with Rob West as the representative. Tom Garrity, from St. Peter's, New Jersey, and CCNY, was the permanent representative to the Executive Committee of the World Student Service Fund (WSSF) and chair of the NSA delegation. In December 1950 a confusing issue regarding WSSF aid money already budgeted for China arose after Chinese military forces joined those of North Korea. NSA opposed sending the money as long as there were Chinese military forces in the field aiding the North Koreans and also because there was no guarantee that the funds could get to the students for whom they were intended. (The position was ultimately endorsed by the WSSF Executive Committee.)[58] Herb Eisenberg attended the World University Service meeting in Geneva prior to going to Stockholm. In July he and Helen Jean Rogers, former NSA secretary, attended the Brazilian National Union of Students Congress in Rio de Janeiro. Helen Jean stayed on in South America, visiting other countries on behalf of the association.[59] The German Seminar, funded by the Rockefeller Foundation, had a delegation selected by NSA.[60] A similar seminar to be held in the Far East was also planned. The grant to fund it was not received by the association until June, however, too late for the project to proceed in the summer of 1951.[61]

Organizational affairs

Shirley Neizer kept the daily office business moving forward and coordinated official business with Al Lowenstein on his travels. She became the de facto financial officer, working closely with the UW students as they attempted to straighten out the books. She worried constantly about how to pay the bills. Shirley also represented the association at regional assemblies and national meetings of educational groups. She initiated a *Secretarial Newsletter* to keep NEC members informed about current developments in the national office. When it became apparent that the association needed to pursue incorporation, Shirley handled the interchanges with counsel from the La Follette law firm.[62]

In addition to the volunteer journalists from Wisconsin, a number of other NSAers spent time in Madison helping out. Their extra hands and good spirits were particularly appreciated at mass-mailing times. They mimeographed, stapled, collated, and carried heavy bags to the post office. Ben Jones from North Carolina, Phil Berry and Leonard Wilcox from the University of Michigan, and Merrill Freed from the University of Chicago were a few who pitched in. Merrill spent part of summer 1951 in Madison helping to prepare materials for the 1951 congress and pulling together the comprehensive overview of the year's events in the precongress *NSA News.*

NSA under attack

On May 15, 1951, the Illinois Region of USNSA and the delegations from the University of Chicago and Roosevelt College were attacked on the floor of the U.S. House of Representatives by Harold Velde, a Republican congressman from downstate Illinois. Velde asserted that "communist elements" had gained control of these groups. His accusation was picked up and carried on the Associated Press wire service.

The charges stemmed from resolutions adopted at the Illinois NSA regional meeting urging repeal of the federal subversives control act (the McCarran Act)[63] and opposing the Broyles-Young bill in the Illinois Legislature, which required loyalty oaths for teachers. Even though Congressman Velde said there was "little evidence of Communist control over NSA on the national level," he asserted that the Chicago and Roosevelt delegations, in sponsoring the "pro-Communist resolutions, were actually not so much interested in preserving academic freedoms as they were in following the communist party line" and that the two delegations had "through the usual communist technique of 'divide and conquer' gained control of the offices and policies of the Illinois Regional Chapter of NSA."[64] In reponse to the charges, Al Lowenstein issued a strongly worded statement in support of the Illinois Region and the two delegations that were under fire. It said in part, "The National Student Association has just undergone its first attack from McCarthyism.[65] It is too soon to know what the effect of the attack will be. The important thing is that it has been made, with the usual use of half-truths, misinformation and scurrilous insinuation." He expressed his confidence in the delegates from the two institutions, "who need no testimony from me or from anyone else to establish their loyalty and devotion to America and to freedom." He went on to say, "I happen to be very well acquainted with this year's University of Chicago delegates...[who] have done an outstanding job of defeating, by democratic means, the very left-wing elements on their campus which Congressman Velde now accuses them of representing."

We contacted NSA alumni in Washington, including Helen Jean Rogers and Robert Treanor, former chairman of the Minnesota Region (then an aide to Minnesota Congressman Eugene McCarthy), and asked them to visit Velde and talk to him about his misrepresentations of the facts in the case. They met with him several times, but he was unmoved by their evidence or that of other congressmen and public figures who spoke out in support of the maligned students.[66] The Velde affair was NSA's official baptism into the community of victims of the reckless, self-promoting "Red-hunters" of the McCarthy era.[67]

Preparations for the Minnesota congress

The University of Minnesota's bid to host the congress in 1951 was accepted by the delegates at the Urbana congress. Planning for the meeting started in late 1950, with Paul Moe from Minnesota as chair of the arrangements committee. At their December 1950 meeting, the NEC selected "The Role of the Student in the World Community" as the theme for the 1951 Congress. The wish list for keynote speaker included Eleanor Roosevelt, Dr. Ralph Bunche, Dr. Robert M. Hutchins, and Dr. Frank Graham.[68]

There would again be many new, inexperienced delegates attending the congress. The staff and the NEC encouraged regional organizations to establish precongress training programs for their member schools. There was a consensus that inexperienced delegates would benefit from orientation to the organization's structure and operations, the issues that would be discussed, and the parliamentary procedures that would be used.

It was anticipated that international relations would be a hot agenda item again, following upon the Stockholm meeting, as were the issues that had caused the 1950-51 staff so much grief: money and organization management. Alternative proposals for remedying the latter problem were advanced by national staff members. They now all agreed upon on the need for a strong executive. However, one group believed that it should be the executive secretary, with the president serving as a traveling public relations person and unpaid vice presidents staying on their campuses. The other group advocated the position that the president be the strong executive, with an appointed executive secretary responsible to him, and that the vice presidents should be two rather than three, one for internal and the other for external affairs. Both groups agreed on the need for a public relations person and a bookkeeper. The ultimate decision made by the delegates to the Minnesota congress for a full-time president, an appointed full-time executive secretary, and three vice presidents, who would remain on their campuses, was strongly influenced by the association's fragile financial situation.[69]

I was assigned the responsibility for the Minnesota Congress Secretariat, but when I was elected as chairman of the Great Northwest Region for the 1951-52 year, the situation became complicated. I needed to be available for the NEC meetings during the congress. All the arrangements had been made well in advance because I wanted to take summer classes at the university. I enlisted the assistance of Don Lynch, already a management expert and then the Student Body President at the Illinois Institute of Technology, who was an observer at the 1949 and 1950 congresses, to serve in my stead, although he was from a nonmember school. He was also, by summer 1951, my unofficial fiancé. Don, with friend Walter Kaiser, also from IIT; Gene McLoon, from LaSalle in Philadelphia; and Cliff Sheets, from Wayne State University in Detroit, kept the Congress in motion and in paper. Don and I were married (not in Bloomington) the following summer, on the day the Indiana Congress opened.

Was it all worth it?

Despite the disappointments and unhappy times that were part of my year with the national staff, I would do it again tomorrow. There were many more good days than bad—more stimulating conversations, exhilarating adventures, opportunities for personal and intellectual growth than I could ever have had at school. It was a life-transforming experience. I met my husband of forty-nine years there, and set aside plans to become a dean of women for marriage and family. As we traveled from coast to coast in our life in the consulting and aerospace businesses, we had NSA friends wherever we went. (Three of our children have NSA godparents.) My exposure to the collegiate world helped me with two jobs. The first was with the Atomic Energy Commission, where research grants in health, physics, and biology were administered. I could tell my boss the location of every college and university. The second was as a high school college counselor; although a number of years had passed, I still knew where the schools were.

Did the organization help to change the world as I believed it would in 1950? I'd vote yes, but not in a grand, earth-shaking manner. Instead, in giving thousands of students, like and unlike ourselves, the opportunity to come together, to learn about and to work with one another for worthwhile societal goals that we might not have thought much about otherwise, NSA made a difference. Our struggle in 1950-51 to keep the Association alive was important. We helped it survive so that it could continue to provide students who followed us with those same opportunities.

Joan Long Lynch was Director of College Admissions Counseling for Immaculate Heart High School, Los Angeles, California. She holds a B.A. from Marylhurst College.

END NOTES

Note regarding source documents: Letters and documents referenced by the author that do not appear in this anthology are being deposited by the author with the Lowenstein Papers at the University of North Carolina archives at Chapel Hill.

[1] *Editor's note:* NSA continued to have difficulties retaining its male officers throughout the period of the Korean conflict. See Murphy (1952-53), p. 1076. Lowenstein's draft status was also of concern to the U.S. government. See "Covert Funding of NSA International Programs," p. 569.

[2] *Editor's note:* See background on the evolution of NSA's position on the draft and UMT, p. 370.

[3] See Pope, p. 390.

[4] Meeting of the American Association for the United Nations in Chicago, February 25-27, 1951; Al Lowenstein and Phyllis Berezny, delegates; Merrill Freed and Joan Long, alternates. See also "The Pan-Hellenic Conference and NSA," p. 408, and Brown, p. 378.

[5] Report to NEC, Third National Student Congress, from Gene Schwartz and Bill Holbrook; handwritten notes of Joan Long; also official report to delegates. See also Holbrook, p. 559, and Schwartz, p. 217.

[6] Eugene Schwartz's essay on 1949-1950 deals comprehensively with the work of the committee. See p. 242.

[7] *Editor's note:* See "Organization and Finance," p. 1119, and Tyler, p. 279. Typical annual budgets adopted for the early years, cited at the close of Pt. 1, Secs. 5-9 and Pt. 6, Sec. 1, which were expected to pay for the full-time staff salaries of five to seven people, plus office expense (exclusive of international programs) were:

1947-48	$36,884	1950-51	26,500
1948-49	25,300	1951-52	21,009
1949-50	28,002		

[8] *Editor's note:* Records of correspondence leading to tax exemption for contributions initiated with the Internal Revenue Service by NSA's attorneys in January 1948 are contained in the Wisconsin Historical Society archives. The application was denied in 1950. An August 31, 1949, letter from the deputy commissioner asks among other questions, "Whether you have actually been made a member of, or have you renewed negotiations with the International Union of Students." A five-page letter dated March 3, 1954, from LaFollette, Sinykin and Doyle, NSA's previous Wisconsin attorneys, to Covington and Burling, NSA's new Washington, D.C., attorneys, concludes with the statement, "If the desired ruling is refused, it will not be for lack of skill on the part of your firm." On April 20, 1954, NSA received its exemption under then section 101(6), "beginning with October 1, 1952, as it is shown that since that time you have been operating exclusively for educational purposes." No record of NSA's incorporation existed as of 1966, the effective date of Shodde's study on NSA. However, the 1948-1966 Codification of NSA Policy states that NSA was incorporated in the District of Columbia at the time of the Eighteenth National Congress in 1965.

An interesting sidelight to this problem appears in the critique of NSA circulated by the Economic Club of Detroit (ECD) in October 1947. At the time the club expressed concern over the implications for liability by "member institutions" in the absence of incorporation. As history attests, there is no record of contingent liabilities ever having been pursued. Ironically, the ECD was also concerned about the "placing of large sums of money in the hands of [NSA] officers or committeemen." See Economic Club of Detroit, p. 191.

[9] Erskine Childers's report to the NEC, August 1951. See Meagher, "The *Svalbard* and the *Ballou*," p. 665.

[10] See Gates and Pulsifer, p. 1053.

[11] See Lynch, "The Great Northwest Region," p. 1064.

[12] "USNSA Congress Report, Third Annual National Student Congress, August 23-31, 1951."

[13] *Challenge*, published by the National Organizing Conference for a Labor Youth League, 799 Broadway, New York 3, N.Y., undated. See also Fogel, p. 289, and Labor Youth League, pp. 790, 796.

[14] See Eisenberg, p. 521.

[15] Joan Long diary and Roster of Delegates to Third National Student Congress.

[16] Minutes of the Third Annual National Student Congress, University of Michigan, Ann Arbor, August 30, 1950.

[17] *Editor's note:* The travel pool was introduced in 1947 to mitigate the costs of travel to NSA congresses for delegates traveling long distances, by providing rebates based on payments made into the pool by the schools on behalf of their delegates traveling shorter distances.

[18] See Brown, p. 381, Klopf, p. 332, n. 13, p. 340, Dungan, p. 129.

[19] *Editor's note:* In Stephen Schodde's unpublished 1965 Columbia Teachers College doctoral thesis (see Bibliography), he meticulously traces the evolution of the Student Bill of Rights, both in the way in which the rights are expressed and in the addition of responsibilities.

[20] Robert A. Kelly, address to delegates at Third National Student Congress, August 23, 1950. See p. 255.

[21] *Editor's note:* For insights on the publishing history of *NSA News,* see the essays by two of its editors in this book, Ostar, p. 211, and Wilson, p. 248. See also Wurf, p. 180, and Background note, p. 293.

[22] Letter, Joan Long to Al Lowenstein, October 19, 1950. A collection of letters between Joan Long and Al Lowenstein from this period will be made part of the Lowenstein collection at the University of North Carolina Library.

[23] Minutes of the Third Annual National Student Congress, University of Michigan, Ann Arbor; "Authority within the Staff," August 29, 1950.

[24] *Editor's note:* On the staff authority issue, see Eisenberg, p. 521, Tyler, p. 280, Brown, p. 384, Medalie, p. 353.

[25] See Garland on Childers, p. 643.

[26] Gordon Klopf and Dennis Trueblood, "A Report on the 1950 National Student Association Congress," *School and Society,* November 25, 1950, pp. 339-41 (The Society for the Advancement of Education, Inc., Lancaster, PA).

[27] "*Life* Goes to a Collegiate Convention," *Life* magazine, September 24, 1950. See p. 294.

[28] Minutes of the Third Annual National Student Congress, University of Michigan, Ann Arbor, August 30, 1950. *Editor's note:* Robert Fogel in later years received a Nobel Prize for economics. For excerpts from his statement to the Congress, see Fogel, p. 289.

[29] "Instrument—NSA European Team, Summer, 1950," NSA Staff Committee (undated). See p. 610.

[30] Craig Wilson account, p. 249. See also Gordon Klopf's July 8, 1950, letter to the National Advisory Committee. *Editor's note:* The editors of this anthology have prepared a review, "Covert U.S. Government Funding for NSA's International Programs." Funding was begun in an organized fashion by the CIA in late 1951. The true source of the funding sought by Houghteling was not revealed until 1967. See p. 565.

[31] *Editor's note:* A set of these reports, contributed by Frank Fisher, will be deposited in the Wisconsin Historical Society archives.

[32] Minutes of the Third Annual National Student Congress, University of Michigan, Ann Arbor, August 30, 1950.

[33] William H. Chafe, *Never Stop Running; Allard Lowenstein and the Struggle to Save American Liberalism* (New York: Basic Books, 1953), pp. 92-93. See also Douglass Hunt, p. 972, and numerous recollections of Lowenstein in this work, cited in the index.

[34] *Editor's note:* See recollections of Lowenstein by Hunt et al., p. 283, Francis, p. 434, Hunsinger, p. 991, Kurtz, p. 908, and Murphy, p. 976. Also Frank Graham, p. 979.

[35] See Eisenberg, p. 520.

[36] See Eisenberg, pp. 526, 635.

[37] See (Neizer) Tyler, pp. 279 and 458.

[38] See Craig Wilson, p. 248, Houghteling, p. 251.

[39] NEC Minutes, December 27-31, 1950, Madison, Wisconsin.

[40] For story of Cambridge office, see Smith, p. 505, Fisher, p. 511, Garland, p. 641.

[41] *Editor's note:* Robert L. West was 1948-49 NSA international vice president. See West, pp. 515, 528, and p. 556.

[42] See Karl Meyer, p. 138.

[43] Lowenstein/Long correspondence.

[44] *Editor's note:* I have conducted extensive searches for NSA financial records in various archives. Until the year 1950-51, the first for which complete form 101(6) returns were submitted to the IRS, (of which there are copies in the Wisconsin Historical Society archives), NSA's financial reports were typewritten statements prepared by the staff each year, generally requiring no more than two pages. These budgets for annual national association expenses, of between $20,000 and $36,000 (including salaries and exclusive of travel programs) are presented in detail at the close of Sections 4-9 in this Part, and of Section 1, Part 6; also surveyed in the Appendix, p. 1119. See end note 8, above. Both Mildred Wurf in 1947 (p. 180) and Shirley Neizer in 1950 (p. 279) make reference to bookkeeping services and advice from the University of Wisconsin. However, no journals or ledgers appear to have been preserved.

[45] Long letters to Lowenstein, February 1, 1950, and February 2, 1950. See Callahan, p. 673.

[46] See the William Dentzer essay on the 1951-52 year, p. 299. See also "Life Aboard the Ships," p. 669, and Callahan, p. 673.

[47] NEC Minutes, December 27-31, 1950, Madison, Wisconsin.

[48] "Veep Reports on Confab," Marylhurst College *Tower,* February 27, 1951; see also Joan Long, letter to Paul Pitner, chair CA-NV-HI Region, February 8, 1951.

[49] See note, p. 676, for incorporation of travel office.

[50] Long letter to Lowenstein, November 14, 1950.

[51] NEC Minutes, December 27-31, 1950, Madison, Wisconsin; see also the Herbert Eisenberg essay on the International Program, 1950-1951, p. 522, and SMAP, pp. 526, 635.

[52] Allard Lowenstein's speech in Stockholm (see p. 562); see also letter from Lowenstein to Long, Neizer, and Brock, December 16, 1950, and Lowenstein, letter to the NEC, written on December 7, 1950.

[53] *Editor's note.* Eisenberg elaborates on his own position in his memoir on p. 522.

[54] NEC Minutes, December 27-31, 1950, Madison, Wisconsin.

[55] *Editor's note:* The early beginnings of the Purchase Card System (renamed the Student Discount System in 1950), are described in Heggie, p. 203; Schwartz, p. 239; Medalie, pp. 348, 366; and Jones, p. 869.

[56] *Editor's note:* The student body president's conference became an annual event. It was accompanied by an annual college newspaper editor's conference, which was initiated by Student Affairs Vice President Sylvia Bacon at the 1952 Indiana University Fifth National Student Congress. See p. 477.

[57] Brock wired Lowenstein on March 17, 1951, announcing his resignation.

[58] Report on WSSF Executive Committee Meeting, Thomas Garrity; NEC Minutes, December 1950.

[59] See (Rogers) Secondari, p. 597. See also Farber, p. 606, on the 1952 Inter-American (Rio) Conference.

[60] See Perkins, p. 603, and Halsted, p. 679.

[61] On June 11, 1950, Brock told Lowenstein by telephone that a letter from James Grant reported that NSA had received a $10,000 grant for a Southeast Asia Seminar. In the Chafe biography of Lowenstein, *Never Stop Running* (see end note 32), there is an account of this affair, in which Paul Pitner, from the University of California at Berkeley and chair of the California, Nevada, Hawaii Region, solicited the money from the Committee for a Free Asia. See Chafe, p. 103.

[62] See (Neizer) Tyler, p. 279.

[63] See Pope, p. 390.

[64] Associated Press account of Velde statement, Washington, May 15; see also "NSA Head Denies 'Reds' in Ill. Region," *The Daily Cardinal,* University of Wisconsin, May 17, 1951.

[65] *Editor's note:* See Dentzer on McCarthyism, p. 310.

[66] Joan Long/Robert Treanor correspondence re: the Velde matter, May 1951.

[67] *Editor's note:* Alex Pope writes in detail about the Velde incident on p. 390. Lowenstein's statement about the irony of Velde's criticisms calls to mind the critique by the Economic Club of Detroit in 1947 (p. 191) and the internal State Department "communist front" charge against the United States Student Assembly in the summer of 1946 (see p. 101).

[68] NEC Minutes, December 27-31, 1950, Madison, Wisconsin.

[69] Joan Long, letter to Paul Pitner, July 31, 1951.

PICTURE CREDITS: *Then:* Marylhurst College senior photo, 1952. *Now:* October 1996 (*Both, author*).

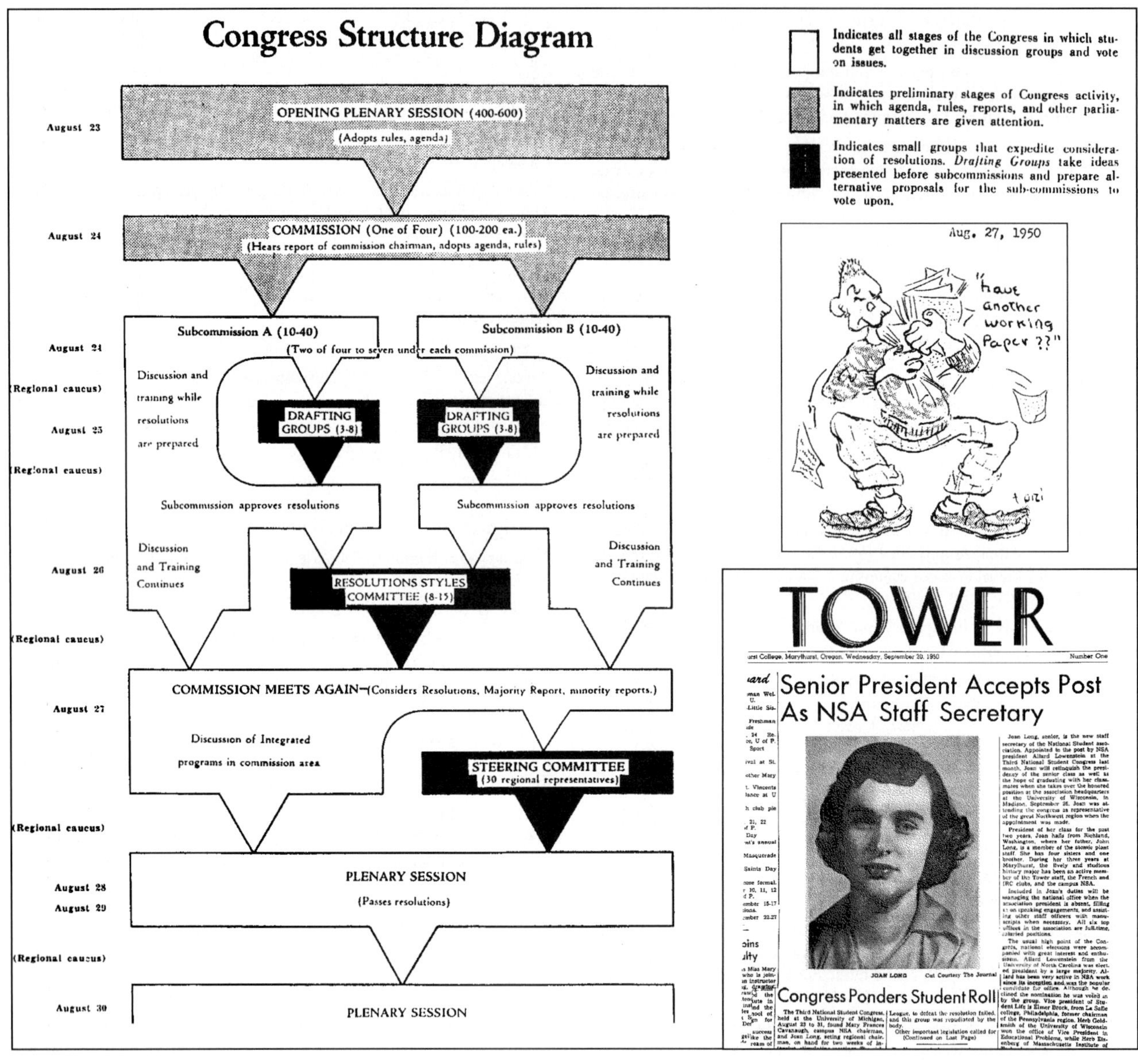

TOWER

Marylhurst College, Marylhurst, Oregon, Wednesday, September 20, 1950 — Number One

Senior President Accepts Post As NSA Staff Secretary

JOAN LONG — Cut Courtesy The Journal

Joan Long, senior, is the new staff secretary of the National Student association. Appointed to the post by NSA president Allard Lowenstein at the Third National Student Congress last month, Joan will relinquish the presidency of the senior class as well as the hope of graduating with her classmates when she takes over the honored position at the association headquarters at the University of Wisconsin, in Madison, September 26. Joan was attending the congress as representative of the great Northwest region when the appointment was made.

President of her class for the past two years, Joan hails from Richland, Washington, where her father, John Long, is a member of the atomic plant staff. She has four sisters and one brother. During her three years at Marylhurst, the lively and studious history major has been an active member of the Tower staff, the French and IRC clubs, and the campus NSA.

Included in Joan's duties will be managing the national office when the association president is absent, filling in on speaking engagements, and assisting other staff officers with manuscripts when necessary. All six top offices in the association are full-time, salaried positions.

The usual high point of the Congress, national elections were accompanied with great interest and enthusiasm. Allard Lowenstein from the University of North Carolina was elected president by a large majority. Allard has been very active in NSA work since its inception and was the popular candidate for office. Although he declined the nomination he was voted in by the group. Vice president of Student Life is Elmer Brock, from La Salle college, Philadelphia, former chairman of the Pennsylvania region. Herb Goldsmith of the University of Wisconsin won the office of Vice President in Educational Problems, while Herb Eisenberg of Massachusetts Institute of

Congress Ponders Student Roll

The Third National Student Congress, held at the University of Michigan, August 23 to 31, found Mary Frances Cavanaugh, campus NSA chairman, and Joan Long, acting regional chairman, on hand for two weeks of in-

League, to defeat the resolution failed, and this group was repudiated by the body.

Other important legislation called for

(Continued on Last Page)

ROADMAP TO MAKING THE MOST OF IT For nine days, delegates will be spending time in hundreds of commissions, subcommissions, workshops, and caucuses in addition to eight special conferences on leadership, student government officers, college press, junior colleges, teachers colleges, and others. (Diagram from Congress brochure. Cartoon from daily bulletin to delegates).

JOAN LONG'S APPOINTMENT is announced in the 9/22/50 issue of the *Marylhurst Tower*, Marylhurst College, OR.

JOAN LONG LYNCH

Education: B.A., history, Marylhurst College, Marylhurst, Oregon. Kappa Gamma Phi.

Career: 1992-present. Retired. 1989-1992, principal, Lynch Clark Associates. Educational Consultants. 1986-89, Immaculate Heart High School, Los Angeles, CA, director, college admissions counseling. 1985-86, Providence High School, Burbank, CA, director, college admissions counseling. 1983-85, construction superintendent and clerk of the works, Major House Remodel and Landscape Project. 1978-1983, Immaculate Heart High School, director, college admissions counseling. 1977-78, Angeles Girl Scout Council, fund development director. 1972-77, Immaculate Heart High School, Development Office and New Programs. 1952-53, University of Chicago School of Education, secretary, Office of Committee on Human Development.

Professional Activities: Western Association of College Admissions Counselors, National Association of College Admissions Counselors; Los Angeles Area Independent Secondary School Counselors.

Volunteer Activities: Angeles Girl Scout Council; League of Women Voters; United Way of Los Angeles; Los Feliz Oaks Homeowners Association.

Family: Married 1952-present, to Donald J. Lynch, B.S., J.D. Parent of ten children, ages 35 to 48. Grandparent of twelve.

Reflections on a divided staff in 1950-1951

2. A View from the NSA National Office

Shirley Neizer Tyler
Simmons College, Massachusetts
NSA Executive Secretary, 1950-51

The positive attitude and relative cohesiveness of our international staff, as evidenced in the Cambridge, Massachusetts, office, did not prepare me for the atmosphere that greeted my arrival late in the fall of 1950 at the National Office in Madison. Only the air of the winter that followed, one of the coldest in memory, was frostier. The staff, though highly dedicated to NSA's mission, was divided in ways that affected our work throughout the year. Fortunately, commitment to NSA's mission made it possible for the president and vice presidents to accomplish most of their goals.

Arriving for a staff changeover

Joan Long Lynch's report on our 1950-51 term of office and Herb Eisenberg's reflections about international affairs give very good overviews of our year. Al Lowenstein's decision to bring Joan to Madison, Wisconsin, as staff associate was an important one. By the time I arrived, she had begun to bring order to the office operations. She had good typing and organizational skills, which were essential to our operation. Between the two of us, we managed to cover the offices of staff associate, executive secretary, treasurer (after Fred Houghteling's departure), and public relations director.

I am not sure why Al asked me to come to Madison several months before Fred Houghteling's term expired. I have great respect for the Fred Houghteling I knew in the New England Region and the National Office. During the brief time between my arrival and Fred's departure, I felt he was uncomfortable with the environment in the Madison office. After he left, Fred's contact with our staff ended.

Craig Wilson, public relations director, was still at the office when I arrived. Disillusioned by the lack of unity within the staff, he left before the end of his term. In my judgment, Craig's public relations skills and his institutional memory had been important to the health of the association. Al made the decision not to replace him due to funding problems.

Fortunately, three University of Wisconsin students helped fill the void in public relations. They were Karl Meyer, Jim Zucker, and Jerrold (Jerry) Schecter. I started a series of newsletters to the Executive Committee, with Joan's assistance. Our goal was to circulate positive information about the association, with the hope that the news would filter down to the individual member campuses in each region. Staff attendance at several regional meetings and Al's campus visits also helped.

Reduced salaries and limited staff

In its wisdom, the Executive Committee had reduced dues during its precongress meeting.[1] To stay afloat, the staff reduced our weekly salaries to a net after taxes of a barely subsistence level of $28.02! While the treasurer and public relations positions remained vacant, we did manage to recruit a paid bookkeeper as advised by a professor from the University of Wisconsin's business school. Besides accounting advice, our adviser recommended incorporating the association.[2] Upgrading bookkeeping procedures took the remainder of the year. Although we believe the incorporation papers were filed, there are apparently no records verifying incorporation in the state of Wisconsin in 1951.[3]

Student volunteers also assisted us in the National Office. Merrill Freed came from the University of Chicago. Ben Jones visited from the University of North Carolina. There were also others. Each, in his or her way, was invaluable.

We escaped the twelve- to eighteen-hour days two or three times and drove to Chicago. Tess Hartigan housed Joan and me. She and the Young Christian Workers were an intelligent, enthusiastic group of young women—a lively change of pace from Wisconsin. And then there were the jazz clubs we visited once or twice. At that time, outside New Orleans, there was probably no better place in the country to hear great classical jazz than Chicago.

The many students with whom we worked during the year included people like Alex Pope and Frank Logan of the University of Chicago. They provided stimulating conversation, which helped us recharge. They were gifted, creative thinkers, able to take courageous stands on controversial issues on campus. They also generally had great senses of humor.

The U.S. government visits

Several times, while working in Madison, representatives from the U.S. government visited me. As I remember it, their identification indicated a link to the U.S. State Department. They checked on our contacts with the various international unions of students and the publications we were receiving. Since this kind of communication was almost nonexistent, at least in the Madison office, the visits seemed nonproductive and eventually stopped.

Staff dynamics

In the office at 304 North Park Street, Elmer Brock, vice president for student affairs, and Herb Goldsmith, vice president of education affairs, were philosophically worlds apart. When in Madison, Herb Eisenberg often disagreed with Elmer as well. While I managed to work reasonably well with all the staff, my relationship with Elmer was not as smooth as I would have liked. Herb Goldsmith did a great deal to promote USNSA's relationship with other educational organizations. The effectiveness of his work with the American Council on Education opened a number of doors on college campuses. People responded well to Herb's compassionate approach to issues.

Fred Houghteling, Herb Eisenberg, and I came from the Northern New England region. I enjoyed working with Herb. Like the Massachusetts Institute of Technology (MIT) volunteers who worked with the Cambridge office, Herb was professional in his approach to his work with the association. He was also a realist in his approach to international affairs.

Three men stand out in my mind as primary advisers to our national office and executive committee. Dr. Gordon Klopf, Wisconsin's assistant dean of students, kept a door open for our staff. He was always available when we needed advice—a discerning listener and a friend. Another was Dr. William Birenbaum of the University of Chicago. A third was Dr. Dennis Trueblood of the Southern Illinois University staff.[4]

Al Lowenstein's leadership in the national office

In the minds of many people, Al Lowenstein was a charismatic leader. In that role, he stayed on the road most of the year, leaving a leadership void in the national office. For example, while the telephone expense incurred as a result of this travel sometimes ran to $300 or $350 per month—excessive in those days—staff salaries were drastically reduced. As executive secretary, I had hoped Al would provide more leadership in directly addressing our financial needs.

Although many hailed Al's work in the field, I would also like to have seen more concrete evidence of the long-term effects of his travels—on programs as they related to improving student government and student welfare, and particularly on growth in membership.

One major concern of mine was reaching the racially segregated Southern colleges and universities, both white and black. The association had much to offer both, and we had much to learn from them as well.

Another of my concerns was the role Al assumed in international affairs, which was Herb Eisenberg's area of expertise. It added to staff tension. Herb Goldsmith and I generally were in agreement with Herb Eisenberg. Elmer generally agreed with Al. Having spent time in the International Office, I felt that Al did not completely take into account the subtleties involved in our work with some of the international groups, including the unions of students. As Herb Eisenberg's report indicates, Al's actions eventually led to his censure by the IUS.[5] This was felt by many to have been an avoidable embarrassment for USNSA. My personal feeling was that the matter could have been handled more diplomatically. Again—different philosophies about strategy.

I believe the 1950 congress report articulates the responsibilities of each officer in a report by a special committee, a subgroup on finance which was led by Michael DiLegge. In my judgment, Al interpreted his role as Chairperson differently from that recommended by the committee. In effect, this negated some of the committee's work. For better or worse, this is often what happens when strong people stay true to their convictions.[6]

News notes on the lighter side of office life

Despite the aforementioned differences among us, there was an affable side to the office experience. Looking back into files, I found in my *Secretarial Newsletter* of November 14, 1950, the following cheerful announcement of my arrival, and some office anecdotes that reflect some of that spirit:

> Dear Regional Chairman:
>
> I know that you must be surprised to find a letter from the Executive Secretary two months before she was to go into office. In case you haven't heard, the draft caught up with NSA, and Win Martin is back in Missouri finishing out the term so that he can graduate before going into the service. Fred has been made treasurer and I am here making a vain attempt to fill his shoes...that's a big order.
>
> There have been lots of other changes in office personnel. We now have a bookkeeper, and an analysis of office procedure beginning with the bookkeeping system is underway. Roy Anderson and Jim Crosser, the accountant, are both students from the University of Wisconsin. . . . Tom Callahan has resigned from his position with the National Scholarship Service and Fund for Negro Students to run the travel bureau, and Charlotte Agnew, who has worked on the travel program

before will assist him....Andy Ter Har and Tom Herbschleb of NBBS [the Dutch national student union] are here to work on the travel program, and in another week Jos Vos[7] also of the NBBS will be with us to begin work on the Work-Study-Travel Program.[8] When the international commission moved, they really moved!

* * *

Joan and I are nothing but office widows. No sooner does one staff member get back than another leaves. It's like trying to keep track of loose jumping beans. The Herbs and Al are on the road at present writing. Fred is leaving tomorrow. Elmer will be leaving next week. If we're lucky, we'll have the honor of Mr. Lowenstein's company for a few days next week . . . the life of a woman in NSA!!!

As you know, Al has been touring schools on the East Coast, and will go to Missouri, Iowa and Minnesota during this next week. He has been doing a wonderful job visiting both member and nonmember schools and representing the Association at meetings and conferences.

* * *

December is coming soon and Joan and I are going to try our wings. She goes to the Mid-Western Conference on Student Government for Small You Know Whats,[9] to be held at Mt. St. Mary in Milwaukee, while I head South for a visit to the Indiana Regional Assembly. Craig and Fred will have a fine time—they'll have complete control of staff decisions for three days. We'll probably come back to find ourselves impeached.

By the way, have you heard the latest? Last year when Bob Delahanty wrote his first letter, the office had just been moved down from upstairs. I came out here to find that we have moved up from downstairs and have greatly expanded. There are two offices now—one for the executives and one for the administrators. Craig, Fred and I have barricaded ourselves with worktables and office machines so that the philosophers on the other side of the hall find themselves defeated before they enter. Psychologically it's wonderful, and besides they trip over our defenses as they come in.

The 1951 Congress at Minnesota

The University of Minnesota was a very warm host for the 1951 convention—from the snowy winter day when I first met with their staff to begin planning through to the final session in August.

If my memory is correct, we had many more representatives attending the Congress than we originally projected.[10] Given our inability to communicate regularly with our membership due to lack of money, this was a tribute to the work of past administrations; to Vice Presidents Elmer Brock, Herb Goldsmith, and Herb Eisenberg; to our executive committee; and to Al Lowenstein's work on the road.[11]

The support by Staff Associate Joan Long and our volunteers was invaluable. Carl Rowan's reports in the *Minneapolis Tribune* gave us an avenue for national coverage of the congress, another step in the right direction.[12]

Madison is a beautiful state capital, with its four lakes and lively university life. I was sorry when time came to leave early that fall. I am sure the new USNSA staff members, Bill Dentzer and Marian Andert, found Boulder, Colorado, as welcoming as Madison and the University of Wisconsin had been for the staffs preceding them.

Shirley Neizer Tyler recently retired as Head of School, Grace Episcopal School, in Alexandria, Virginia.

END NOTES

[1] See p. 266.

[2] See n. 8, p. 276.

[3] *Editor's note:* In 1950 NSA was granted exemption from taxes by the IRS as a nonprofit, unincorporated, voluntary association. NSA's travel program, Educational Travel, Inc. (launched in 1948), was incorporated in 1954. Documentation to establish NSA's corporate status will probably emerge in the years following the time frame covered by this work.

[4] See essays by Klopf, p. 329, and Birenbaum, p. 581. See p. 345 for background on Trueblood.

[5] See Eisenberg, p. 522. Also, see Lynch, p. 273.

[6] *Editor's note:* Al Lowenstein is extensively referenced in this work. Shirley Tyler's reflections add another useful dimension to the picture that can be drawn of his remarkable and complex presence on the student scene. See the index for other citations.

[7] See Vos, p. 651.

[8] *Editor's note:* In an effort to improve communication and coordination, the International Office, under international vice president Herbert Eisenberg (MIT), was moved to Madison from Cambridge, Mass., where it had been since NSA was founded in 1947. During the following year, when NSA moved its headquarters to Boulder, Colorado, for the year, the office was moved back to Cambridge. At that time, Avrea Ingram (Harvard) had been elected international Vice President. (See Ingram, p. 575.)

[9] Catholic women's colleges were affectionately referred to as "Small You Know Whats." See Lynch., p. 493.

[10] Five hundred delegates and observers from 225 colleges were in attendance, in addition to sixty-nine participants at the First Annual Student Body President's Conference.

[11] The work of Elmer Brock is cited on p. 358; also p. 595. See Eisenberg, p. 520.

[12] The late Carl Rowan was one of the first African-Americans to be employed by a major city newspaper. He later became a highly respected author, nationally syndicated journalist, and TV network panelist.

PICTURE CREDITS: *Then:* 1950 (Simmons News, 10/8/50). *Now:* 1996 (*Author*).

WELCOME BACK

The Simmons News

SUPPORT STU-G

VOL. XXVIII SIMMONS COLLEGE, BOSTON, MASS., THURSDAY, OCTOBER 5, 1950 No. 1

FORMER NSA HEAD GAINS POST

Thirty-One Simmons Students Qualify For Academy This Fall

Thirty-one juniors and seniors have qualified for membership in Academy this fall, on the basis of their scholastic averages over the past two years, Anne Newton, president, announced this week.

NSA Congress Elects Shirley Neizer, '50 To Office Of National Executive Secretary

Shirley Neizer, '50, was elected national executive secretary of the U. S. National Student Association at the Third Annual Congress at the University of Michigan August 23-31. She was one of two New Englanders to be chosen for a top office in the student organization.

Shirley Neizer
Elected NSA Secretary

Miss Neizer's term of office becomes effective in January and will continue for one year. Since her duties will require full-time attention, she will give up her position on the executive training squad in Gilchrist's personnel department. As executive secretary she will be in charge of office duties at NSA headquarters in Madison, Wis., will serve as a liaison between the regional and national offices and will be responsible for all physical arrangements for next year's congress.

Miss Neizer was vice-chairman, then chairman of the Simmons NSA Committee, a member of the Student Council, YWCA and PCA. The recipient of the first Robert C. Rankin award, she was selected by the Student Council as "the girl who best displays the qualities of friendliness and understanding and interest in her fellow men so richly evident in Dr. Rankin's own life."

She was selected by the Northern New England region executive board to attend the Congress as a representative on the National Executive Committee in place of the treasurer, who was unable to attend.

Step-Sing Features Rose Presentations

THE SIMMONS NEWS • Thursday, November 2, 1950

NSA AND THE BIG PICTURE

Al Lowenstein, the new NSA national president, spoke informally the other night in Cambridge as a part of his New England tour. What he said is not just important to the several dozen people who happened to be at Phillips Brooks House, but to anyone who has ever asked the question, "Why NSA?"

It is not enough to say that we, as students, need an organization to represent us. This suggests that we have an organization for organization's sake. And particularly at this time this answer is neither true nor satisfactory

First, Lowenstein emphasized the obligation of the American student to assume his proper place in world society. In a united body, he is better able to present his ideas of freedom in serious competition with other ideologies. He must not only say that these are the truths for which he stands, but he must go out into areas where Communist ideas are sympathetically received because they apparently represent a sincere interest of a partisan group in the welfare, for example, of colonial students. Once he is able to meet these students—in work camps, in conferences, in informal talks—he can prove the interest of the free world in helping peoples whose choice of the way they will live still hangs in the balance. This is certainly a part of preventing world conflict at its very roots, and has become an imminent duty of the NSA.

What duty does the Association have to the American student himself? The duty of maintaining the freedoms which both member and non-member schools wish to preserve, and of spreading the fact that all students have the common denominator of free thinking no matter how different their beliefs may be. People who do not think alike have a responsibility to themselves to preserve a democratic system in which they may at least hear conflicting viewpoints, turn them over, reject some and accept others and emerge thoughtful. Lowenstein himself cited the influence of NSA meetings themselves upon solidly Southern schools which might never have stopped to hear the case for racial and religious equality in education had some detached organization pleaded it.

What effects does NSA have in the outside world? The skeptical have suggested that it is all very well to organize and present student opinion, but who will listen? The American Council on Education has. In recent discussions in Washington, the ACE heard national NSA leaders' opinions on pertinent, close-to-home issues like the peacetime draft. Out of these suggestions came the ultimate decision that draft exemptions to students would be granted, temporarily at least, on the basis of scholastic standing. This exemption basis may not be practical nor fair over a long stretch of time, and if students feel the need for a change, their leaders will be able to say so for them.

NSA's incidental services—student tours, the new Student Discount Service—are only sidelines in its overall work area. Its resposibilities and its capabilities are what actually matter, and are worth the moral and financial support of member schools like Simmons and the schools who have still to learn that this is their voice.

SHIRLEY NEIZER TYLER

Early years and education: I was born in Philadelphia, Penn., in 1929 and grew up in Salem, Mass. I attended Salem Classical and High School. In 1950 I received my B.S. in pre-professional studies at Simmons College in Boston and in summer 1953 attended the University of Virginia. Since 1969 I have attended numerous workshops and institutes concerned with early childhood education, elementary education, and school administration.

Career Highlights: Following my service in 1950 as executive secretary of NSA, I taught for a year in Arlington, Va., and in 1953-54 joined the National Scholarship Service and Fund for Negro Students (NSSFNS) in New York City as staff and public relations associate, (about which I have written some recollections in Part 2 of this anthology). After starting a family, I returned to teaching in 1969 at the Grace Episcopal School in Alexandria, Va., retiring as head of school in 1998.

Volunteer service: From 1973 to 1982 I served on the Alexandria City School Board, including two years each as chair and vice chair. During this period we desegregated schools, built a new school, dealt with the end of a school population explosion and the decline that followed, closed schools, and transferred our newest building to northern Virginia's burgeoning community college. Those were busy times as we established a magnet school and tried to stay ahead of Federal Title IX and Special Education regulations. From 1968 until the present I have served on a number of boards and committees, including: Northern Virginia Family Service, Alexandria Clinic, Mid-Atlantic Episcopal Schools Association, PTA, Civic Association, Alexandria Hospital Corporation, and several Alexandria Hospital committees. Among awards I have received are those from the NAACP, Northern Virginia Urban League, Alexandria Chamber of Commerce, and Grace Episcopal Church (the Rector's Cross).

Family: I have two children and a daughter-in-law. Most recently my son has been consulting with groups on issues related to education. My daughter is a senior architect in the Washington, D.C., division of a nationally prominent architectural firm and an associate professor of architecture and design. Each has two daughters, all of whom appear to be following in the footsteps of their activist parents and grandparents.

Let right be done. . . . He longed for the day of man's humanity to man

3. Allard K. Lowenstein: A Legacy

University of North Carolina
NSA President, 1950-51

Editor's note: Al Lowenstein was, arguably, NSA's most omnipresent and enduring charismatic leader. As many of the memoirs in this book reveal, his public persona and leadership are recalled with a mixture of both affection and undiluted admiration, on the one hand, and his energy and manner with incredulity and bemusement, on the other. Whatever one's recall, viewed through the lens of history today, Lowenstein's passions and causes stand as a mirror of much of the spirit that animated his generation of leaders in NSA. Lowenstein was shot and killed by a former friend and associate on March 14, 1980. Five weeks later, a memorial service was held at the University of North Carolina. Following are recollections voiced at the service by three of his student leader contemporaries: James C. Wallace, John Sanders and Douglass Hunt—all of whom appear elsewhere in this anthology.

JUNE 1945

James C. Wallace
Former Mayor of Chapel Hill, NC
UNC Delegate to the 1946 World Student Congress

It was late in June, and the hour was late—not far from midnight—and the year was 1945. The University had begun its summer session and the new students were ending their first day in Chapel Hill. Douglass Hunt and I were having a conversation in number 4 Steele Dormitory, going over the events of the day, ranging all the way from campus politics to the coming end of World War II. Everyone's door was open, mine included, because it was hot, so I happened to be looking out the door and saw Al as he was coming down the stairs. In one hand he held a small clock. He headed toward the water fountain (there were no fountains on the other floors) and he had a drink of water. Then he appeared in the doorway and asked for the time. Once that information was provided, we introduced ourselves around and he came in and pulled up an extra chair. From our vantage point of over five extra years he appeared very young—a little past sixteen, he used to say, and I noticed how slender he seemed.

The newest Freshman had arrived at the University. He had heard of Frank Porter Graham. He had read about him in the New York papers. For Al, it was Dr. Frank who had put the University on the map and here he was. And on the very first night he had sat down with two Southerners who happened to be friends of this same man and who shared many of his ideas. I did not realize at the time the vast unlikelihood of the event, nor even at this moment can I understand why I remember it in such detail. We talked until four o'clock about the emerging state of Israel, about civil rights in the South, and about what the world would be like after the war.

After the marathon conversation had ended, Al went back upstairs and I walked with Douglass past the Old Well and we paused at the northeast corner of Old West. One of us said it, and the other agreed, that we had just met an extraordinary person about whom we would hear more. He went on to his room on Rosemary Street and I returned to Steele and shut the door. It had gotten cooler.

Nearly thirty-five years were to pass—it will be thirty-five years in a little over two months—and we never managed to have another conversation quite like that one. We promised ourselves year in and year out, but always there was something that intervened. The nearest thing to it occurred one night in 1949, when Al and I were sitting just beneath the Wright Memorial at Kill Devil Hills. He was then an advisor to Senator Frank Graham. The issue of civil rights, the prospect of Southern filibuster, and whether Frank Graham should vote for cloture. But during most of the years the talks came on the run, none alike, always something new.

"May I speak to Al, please?"

The hint of a forthcoming visit was usually given by the ring of the telephone. In the younger years a voice would ask, "May I speak to Al, please?" Later it was "May I speak to Professor Lowenstein?" And then it became "Congressman Lowenstein" and then "Ambassador Lowenstein." I learned to interpret this crackling of the ether as the years passed and came to understand that Al was on his way, had been detained, and would arrive eventually. We made the necessary preparations—a list of the calls, a supply of fruits and juices to be consumed while he returned the calls and made others to yet farther courses of his itinerary, and a bed for a ten-minute nap. After his departure the phone would ring for another day or two, as a few stragglers would try to catch up with him, and then it would stop. Throughout it all, whenever I said, "I'm sorry, but he isn't here," there was a moment of shocked silence as if someone were thinking, "But he *has* to be there," followed by a "Thank you," and a name and number if he called.

But I shall remember him as he was at the moment of our first meeting, as he was embarking upon the many quests that would lead him around the world. The symbolism of the water fountain and the clock remains with me. He tried to slake the thirst of much of humankind for decency and self-respect and most of all for freedom. And always in his efforts was the press of time, the remorseless ticking away of opportunity to do another good thing and to do it now. Wherever he went, one could sense the rising of the wind that would bring change and the flowing of rivers that would bring life and hope. Now his causes belong to others—to the thousands who knew him and drew their inspirations from him, to the many more who were touched by his examples and to all of us who are in his debt because he passed our way. May the earth rest lightly upon him.

MAN OF COMPASSION

John Sanders
Former Vice President, University of North Carolina
UNC Student Body President. NSA Delegate, 1950-51

Al Lowenstein came here in June of 1945, drawn by his deep regard for President Frank Graham. He quickly became enmeshed in student activities ranging from wrestling to the Glee Club, but focussing chiefly on student politics, broadly interpreted.

He was a member of the committee which drafted the first Student Constitution in 1945-46; served two terms in the Student Legislature and one term on the Student Council; was a member, Vice President, and President of the Dialectic Senate; represented this campus three times in the State Student Legislature and twice at National Student Association Congresses; was a writer and ultimately Associate Editor of the *Daily Tar Heel;* ran unsuccessfully for Vice President of the Student Body in 1949; and headed student orientation that fall.

In these activities, Al was always a significant participant. Of all the vast number of people who knew him on this campus, few were neutral about him: They admired him (though not many shared all of his political views) or they detested him, but all respected his energy, his eloquence, and his sincerity of purpose. He heightened our concerns for social justice, especially in relations between blacks and whites, at a time when too few of us felt deeply about such matters. Paradoxically—or so it might seem to those who did not know Al's manifold dimensions—he introduced many of us to the unending delights of Gilbert and Sullivan operettas.

After graduation in 1949, Al worked in Dr. Graham's Senate office for a year. Then followed a year's term as President of the National Student Association (1950-51), a law degree from Yale in 1954, two years in the Army (1955-56), a year as a graduate student here in the late 1950s, service as an adviser to Senator Hubert Humphrey (1959), a teaching and administrative role at Stanford University in the early 1960s, a couple of years of teaching at North Carolina State University at Raleigh, and teaching assignments at several other universities in the 1960s and 1970s.

Throughout much of the 1960s, Al spent a great deal of time in the deep South, organizing and leading freedom marches and other efforts to change the racially repressive practices and institutions of the region. He married in 1966, and his three children carry the names of his heroes and heroines. He served a term in Congress (1969-71) and tried several times without success to return to that body. He was national Chairman of Americans for Democratic Action (1971-73) and a member of the Democratic National Committee for several years in the 1970s. Every national political campaign found him passionately engaged. I doubt that there was a national political convention of either major party from 1948 forward at which he was not present, sometimes as a Democratic convention delegate.

His most notable public offices were those of Alternate Representative to the United Nations and United States Representative to the United Nations Human Rights Commission and Trusteeship Council in 1977-78.

But to catalog Al Lowenstein's myriad activities on this campus and afterward says too little about the character and purposes of this man whom we remember in love today.

Al had more compassion for other people than anyone of my generation whom I have known. This compassion extended not only to those of his own kind or class or nation, but to all people, everywhere. He was deeply concerned with how people lived, and especially with the state of their political freedom.

Al believed with Thomas Paine that "those who expect to reap the blessings of freedom must, like men, undergo the fatigue of supporting it."

On battlelines from Mississippi to Rhodesia

And so he was found on battlelines from Mississippi to Rhodesia. By action and exhortation, he sought to change unacceptable political and social institutions and conditions, and to do so in ways that would produce civil and constructive results. He was able to enlist thousands of others in the causes that moved him. And like Frank Graham, he had an extraordinary capacity to claim and hold the affectionate support of many people who often disagreed with both his principles and their application.

Al never wholly accepted anyone else's analyses of society's problems or their solutions for those problems. He devised his own, and they suited neither his opponents nor those creatures of passionately held doctrine with whom he was often allied.

Al had a unique capacity to draw people to him, to make them know that he cared about them, and to cause them to care deeply about him. And it was fascinating to see him work the same magic on my generation's children that he had worked on those of us who were his contemporaries.

Al Lowenstein enriched his time and this planet in ways few will ever fully comprehend. His was a superb example of the difference one person can make, acting without the advantage of high office or large fortune, but with great strength of character, intelligence, compassion, purposefulness, hard work, good humor, and determination to better the lot of mankind everywhere.

LET RIGHT BE DONE

(Excerpts)

Douglass Hunt
Former Vice President Finance, Columbia University
UNC Delegate to the 1945 San Francisco Conference

In English law there once existed a remedy called a Petition of Right. By it a subject could have redress for a wrong done by the King or his ministers. When such a petition was endorsed by the Attorney-General, he wrote upon it: "Let right be done."

I think of Al as Counselor on most of the significant Petitions of Right in my time. In a sense, the theme of his life was, Let Right be Done.

I count myself blessed to have learned his worth early and not to have had cause to doubt him in thirty-five years since.

Soon after his arrival at Carolina we served together on the committee that drafted the first constitution of the student body. He understood the need for a constitution, but he was also deeply concerned about anti-Semitism in fraternities and sororities: he liked neither those that excluded Jews nor those, formed in response, that included only Jews. We agreed on that. What should we do first? One afternoon on the steps of South Building we agreed that we must win the constitution before we could tackle the issue of bias in the fraternities. The incident was a model for many later in his life: he never forsook a battle on principle, but he might delay one if he saw another more important to fight first.

Over the years since he was thought of by some who did not understand him well as shifting too quickly among positions and programs. He was, in fact, utterly steadfast in all his ultimate concerns. Thus, he was an enemy to Fascism in Spain when he was a boy, and, when he was a man, his trips to Spain to work with the Underground continued until the Franco Regime was no more. But he avoided all his life the trap of persisting in an activity when the reason for it had vanished. On all the main themes of his concern, he continued to work by undertaking those new activities that could bring nearer an end to man's inhumanity to man.

A restless, ceaselessly energetic, varied and useful life

Indeed, if one looks for the skein of meaning that bound together his restless, ceaselessly energetic, varied, and useful life, it is to be found in love and hatred: love for persons and hatred for the wrongs they do each other. He longed for the day of man's humanity to man. More, much more, than most of us, he spent his life to bring us all nearer that day....

Ringing in my brain since his death are his last reported words: "Help me!" It strikes to the heart that those are the words to which he responded most quickly all his life. We would not do justice to his memory if we could not resolve to find better ways to respond to that cry in our time.

Most of us here are more concerned to observe the protocols and proprieties of the world than Al was. But he observed them insofar as they were part of the system that made possible orderly and fair decisions directed to the ends of justice and mercy....

We need to find ways to place at the heart of every institution a means to put right the wrongs done by our imperfect human instrumentalities. Al's work in the world was to do just that. If we would serve his ideals best, we should make it our business during the rest of our lives—as opportunities come to us—to provide in the whizzing, shiny, perfectly conceived contraptions of our limping institutions a way to deal with human cries for help. In honor of our friend and what he loved on earth, in the interest of all humankind, we should continue his noble work and so Let Right be Done.

ALLARD K. LOWENSTEIN

Born in Newark, N.J., in 1929 and graduated from Horace Mann School in 1945. BA University North Carolina, 1949. LLB Yale, 1954. [See tributes above for career highlights.] Three children. Assassinated March 14, 1980. Buried in Arlington National Cemetery, Va.

PICTURE CREDITS: *Lowenstein:* Appearing at the 1950 National Student Congress at the U. of Michigan (*LIFE Magazine,* September 18, 1950. With permission). *Wallace, Sanders and Hunt:* c. 1946 (From *The Story of Student Government at the University of North Carolina, Chapel Hill* by Albert Coates and Gladys Hill Coates. Professor Emeritus Fund, 1985.) *Lowenstein in the 60s:* Lowenstein Papers, Southern Historical Collection, Library of the University of North Carolina at Chapel Hill.

Excerpts from the President's Message and Report following the 1950 Congress

We Shall Learn to Build Better Bridges and to Live with One Another

A generation born into uncertain and confusing times....
We will not have time to improve this society unless we protect it.

Allard K. Lowenstein
University of North Carolina
NSA President, 1950-51

Editor's note: Al Lowenstein assumed the presidency a little over two months after the United States sent troops to Korea in response to the North Korean invasion of the South. By this time, most of the World War II veterans had moved on from the undergraduate scene and a new generation of "veterans-to-be" dominated the campus scene. They, along with their co-ed counterparts, were surrounded by the fury of the Cold War, on the one hand, and "McCarthyism" and various state committee anticommunist campus investigations. Reflecting the anxieties and the passions of that year, Lowenstein's presidential address turns to overarching themes of the importance of learning and education in dealing with the tensions and conflicts of the time.

We are a generation which, to say the least, was born into uncertain and confusing times. We find ourselves benefiting as promised from almost unimaginable technological and scientific achievements, but the unparalleled happiness and security which were supposed to accompany these wonders still elude us. We are trained to be very competent engineers and filing clerks and filling station attendants and lawyers. We have learned to harness electricity, to smash the atom, to construct mechanisms which make it possible to go almost anywhere in almost no time.

We have learned systems for computing mathematical formulae so involved that our ancestors would not even have conceived of the formulae. We have learned how to construct buildings so the sunlight can enter more readily, and how to put on advertising campaigns that will make us believe that nicotine is good for our lungs. We have learned to have laws so intricate that only the most expertly trained can begin to cope even with everyday situations.

Progress and advances meaningful only as they fulfill human aspirations

We regard these achievements as manifestations of and aids to progress, made possible by advances in knowledge through the centuries. But for "progress" to be progress, it must aim toward something; and in the general perspective afforded by time, our advances in knowledge, and the achievements they have made possible, seem useful and meaningful only as continuing expressions of the uphill struggle of human beings in their quest for the opportunity to live decently, and with dignity, in peace.

Likewise changes over the years in institutions of government can be adjudged "advances" only as they may help to fulfill the overall aspirations of the human race. We build bridges so people can cross rivers with greater ease and comfort; we enact laws so people can be assured of equitable justice; we build power plants to make heat and light available more cheaply to more people so they may be warmer and more comfortable. We seek to govern ourselves democratically because it is our faith that democracy is that means of government which makes these aspirations most easily attainable.

We have not been learning enough of the right things fast enough

Our technical knowledge defies comparison—and so [do] the uncertainty and confusion of the times. It sometimes seems that we have learned all there is to know about life except how to live in the dignity and peace toward which both our yearning and our learning have so long been directed; that we do not know how to give direction to our know-how; that we have not been learning enough of the right things fast enough to keep up with, and make fruitful, the things which we have been learning which are in themselves neither right nor wrong.

The fact of war in Korea hung over the Third Congress

Hanging over the Third Annual Congress of the United States National Student Association was the stark fact of war in Korea, and the consequently intensified grim uncertainty which has enshrouded the future of this generation through its school years.

The unprecedented impermanence and insecurity which characterize this age of tension and upheaval might have been expected to have stultifying and demoralizing effects on young people. It is good news that, to the contrary, greater unity of purpose and deeper understanding of the qualities indispensable to a useful education seem to be resulting in the student community.

The principles and promise which heretofore have made it possible to look to the future with something approaching placidity now face an ominous menace. Almost everything seems uncertain and almost everyone unsettled....

We seem even to understand now that we will not have long to improve this society unless we protect it, and that we cannot long protect it except as we improve it. We would protect it by striving for the world-wide triumph of those forces which, while not insuring a brave new world for all, would at least give us more time. And we would improve it by...utilizing those values which would put our specialized and technical competence to work as weapons for the bettering and ...enriching of lives of human beings everywhere.

A striking unity in the face of new dangers and opportunities

Perhaps it is this awakening to danger and to opportunity which explains the rather striking unanimity of purpose and of determination that was apparent throughout the Congress.

It came as a sharp jolt to some to find that there were delegates to the Congress whose attendance had to be cut short so they could enter into active duty with the armed forces; and to realize with each newscast that again Americans—this time of our age—were being called on to enter the front lines of a struggle in a far-off place. But there was full comprehension that involved in the outcome in that far-off place were the hopes and plans of every one of the students represented by the one thousand who had come together from every sort of background and from every corner of the country; and from this comprehension welled an awakened realization of the common goals and shared heritage of Americans and of all free men. And notably absent from the 1950 Congress were the suspicion and mistrust which in past years had caused bitterness and threats of schisms.

NSA's survival a tribute to deeper understanding of our purposes

That the idea of NSA is here to stay, and that it has managed to grow progressively stronger and more effective despite the flux of the world about it, must be a source of astonishment to those who have known of the apathy and disunity that characterize American student history.

Perhaps we had to have our focus sharpened by tragedy and our hopes suspended by doubts before we could adequately appreciate that it has been more than futile to continue deepening our technical know-how without learning to use it to help us live together.... [E]ducation, to be a meaningful process, must make more attainable the fulfillment of the higher aspirations of the human race;...[b]eing educated for democracy means learning more than how to be competent engineers or filling-station attendants or lawyers. Today it means learning to stand with one another and with our teachers and families as bastions for preserving and strengthening the roots of liberty and the heritage of respect for individual worth....

And this in turn means a willingness to give our all in the struggle to gain mastery over the immediate threat to our lives, as well as to all the gains of the ages, whose machine-guns spit murderous fire in unarmed places in Asia, whose distortions spread disastrous disunity in underprivileged areas across the globe, and whose allies within our gates seek personal power in the backwash of a contrived confusion and hysteria.

Education's most urgent aspect: The application of wisdom to understanding differences

We can live adequately and rather happily for a long time without the discovery of further scientific wonders, though there is no reason why we should do so. But we can no longer neglect the most practical, and currently most urgent, aspect of education—the inculcation of the ethical fibre, the spiritual qualities, the patience, and the wisdom by which differences between men can be made instruments of understanding and aspects of the strength of a free people. We know that in the absence of such education and understanding, these differences are not neutral in their effect on society. They become the cause of discord, of misunderstanding, and of hate.

We may even know enough now not to continue to surrender the word "practical" to the exclusive use of the visionaries who think men can live by machine alone. Students in the United States still want good school buildings, higher salaries for their teachers, competent instruction in their technical courses; for these are necessary aspects, like power plants and bridges, of a more comfortable and a fuller life. But the Congress this summer seemed to reflect that we are also now aware...that there is another part of an adequate education not so simple to name nor so easy to find or preserve.

Education for freedom will help fulfill the hopes of mankind

We have come to know, or so it seemed this summer, that education for freedom and progress must yield the warmth of mutual respect and of devotion to honor; must instil patience for human frailty and concern for the well-being of others; must convey understanding of the obligations of individual responsibility in the community; must encourage wide discussion of honest convictions; and must value courage in the free expression of independent thought.

It is not too late to change what it is that has made modern man so obsolete in the face of his modernness. [T]he American student seems ready to make his stand. He seems better prepared than ever to seek the furtherance of those long-neglected values in our training which we know are indispensable if the hopes and prayers of humankind are ultimately to be fulfilled.

We cannot but have the faith of those who seek to do right and who know the love of the Lord for His creatures that it is not too late; and we cannot but find it reassuring to realize that when it seems most possible that time is running out, American students are not.

NSA dedicated again to unifying hearts and lifting spirits

In an hour when our Nation, our futures, and all we hold dearest in our lives are in great peril, we would again dedicate the National Student Association to unifying the hearts and lifting the spirits of all men who love freedom. As the voice of American students, we are determined to do our utmost to help beat back the forces which pervert the cherished dreams and prey on the honest fears of decent men, in their efforts to forge the weapons with which they would destroy all that is most worth preserving in life.

And we are equally determined, as we strive to do our part in meeting the immediate challenge, to further in our learning and in our living what we know to be the aspirations of men of good will always, and the values of worth in all times. We shall learn to build better bridges and to do better research, but we shall also learn to value varying viewpoints and to live with one another.

It is in this spirit and with this faith that the United States National Student Association, in uncertain and confusing times, sets out to serve the educational community and the Nation.

Allard K. Lowenstein was a member of Congress from New York in 1969-1971, national chairman of the Americans for Democratic Action, and U.S. representative to the United Nations Human Rights Commission and Trusteeship Council. He was also a prominent civil rights leader. Lowenstein was shot and killed in March 1980.

PICTURE CREDITS: *Then:* Fifth National Student Congress, Indiana U., 1952. *Now:* c. 1960s (Lowenstein Papers, Southern Historical Collection, Library of the University of North Carolina at Chapel Hill).

LOWENSTEIN ON THE STUMP FOR NSA, SECURITY AND DEMOCRACY

The Cornell Daily Sun 10/27/50

The Cornell Daily — ITHACA, N.Y., FRIDAY, OCTOBER 27, 1950

NSA PRESIDENT ADDRESSES COUNCIL

AL LOWENSTEIN, president of the National Student Association as he spoke last night before Council. To Lowenstein's left is Jack Vinson '51, Council president; to his right, Harry Coyle '53, first vice-president.

SC Hears Lowenstein Describe Role of NSA

"National Student Association is the only accepted and invited voice of American students today and as such is here to stay," Al Lowenstein, NSA president, told Student Council last night in the Willard Straight Rehearsal Room.

Lowenstein, a graduate of the University of North Carolina, expressed the belief that the current period of mobilization may last at least for 20 years and in such a situation students of the nation must have a central agency through which to voice opinions both on domestic and international affairs.

(Cornell is not a member of NSA, which claims representation of 300 colleges and universities. Last spring Council withdrew membership on the grounds that NSA did not offer anything to the campus.)

Emphasizing the role of NSA abroad, Lowenstein pointed out that the International Union of Students which met in Prague for the first time in 1948 and which represents 5,000,000 students, both from behind and without the Iron Curtain, has sent out textbooks and other aid to students in Africa and Southeast Asia. "Only the Communists have gone to the students, the future leaders in any nation," Lowenstein declared.

On the domestic level, Lowenstein indicated NSA as voicing student opinion in regard to such issues as draft policies and acceleration of academic programs.

So far NSA has set up student tours at lowest rates and has sent teams into areas such as Indonesia to lay groundwork for aiding students. At Prague this summer, Lowenstein stated, NSA members could for the first time say that they represented American students and that other delegates at the conference who purported to do so actually did not.

"If it does not seem worth the two-and-a-half to three cents per student necessary to belong to NSA and to have their voice heard," Lowenstein declared, "then I submit that the other things we can do are relatively

Continued from Page 1

ity to as many students as wish to discuss what will be affecting them for the next 20 years," Lowenstein continued.

Through NSA a network of students discussing domestic and international affairs can be built, a network of understanding which is the result of working together in the democratic way, Lowenstein said. "NSA offers priceless opportunity to make one's opinions known through discussion on the campus, regional, and national levels."

U. of NC *Daily Tar Heel* 11/18/50

Tar Heel — WEATHER Partly cloudy and [illegible]

UMT For Security, Says NSA Prexy

A spokesman of some 1,000,000 American students called yesterday for universal military service and said students must take a leading role in fighting Communism.

Allard Lowenstein, President of the National Students Association which includes some 325 American colleges and universities, said the United States must work out a draft program "to keep the armed forces of the nation strong without impairing for a long period of time the training of leadership in all fields of public service.

"We must work out a formula which provides a certain amount of security for students unless total mobilization becomes necessary," the 22-year-old Carolina graduate and former aide to Sen. Frank Graham (D-NC) said.

"I am in favor of a national service plan whereby each male spends two years in military service at the end of his undergraduate college days or at the age of 18 if he does not go to college."

Lowenstein represented the NSA as the only student organization in the American Council of Education when it was asked to make draft deferment recommendations to Selective Service Director Louis B. Hershey.

He will go to Stockholm, Sweden, next month to discuss a fight against communism with leaders of student organizations in other free countries.

"Students must assume the obligation of stopping communism in areas of the world where they alone can best reach out to other students with the truth about democracy in the face of Communist distortions and lies," he said.

This was particularly true, he said of colonial areas where students hold a position of importance.

U. of Rochester College for Women *Tower Times* 11/3/50

The College for Women TOWER TIMES University of Rochester

NSA Helps To Combat Communism Menace Says Lowenstein

In his speech last Friday evening in Cutler Union, Al Lowenstein told why NSA is important in the world crisis of today. Working on the premise that Communism presents the greatest menace in history, Al suggested how students can help fight this menace.

Communism works in those areas of the world where there are few students with influence. Thus, the areas that have the worst educational facilities and the least freedom of thought are easy prey to Communist propaganda. If these students are not reached now by democratic peoples, they will not be people on whom we can depend for leadership during the next twenty years.

There are two levels on which we can work to remedy this world situation: the international and national. On the international level we must present democracy to peoples across the globe who are being perverted by Communism. This can be done by sending NSA there, by discovering the state of mind and the needs of the people.

On the national level, we must maintain freedom of opinion and thought. This can be done on campus by stimulating intergroup and inter-campus discussions, by working for intellectual as well as racial and social coordination, and by striving to increase the number of NSA member schools.

LOWENSTEIN IN MADISON, 1951, after his term came to a close. From far left: Joan Long (Lynch) and Jean Sarvonat, President of the French Union of Students and Lowenstein, right. (Photos, Lynch)

Letter appearing in New Foundations *November 1950*

NSA Has Departed from Its Founding Principles of Peace and Internationalism

"The NSA leadership worked diligently to concoct a tissue of lies" about the IUS.

Robert Fogel
Cornell University '48, Columbia University '60
Labor Youth League Observer, 1950 NSA National Student Congress

Dear Editor:

As you know, the United States National Student Association was founded in 1947 on the initiative of 25 American students who were delegates to the first World Student Congress of the International Union of Students (I.U.S.).

Just a few weeks ago the N.S.A. held its third annual Congress and showed how far it had departed from the principles of peace and internationalism on which it was founded.

In the first few hours after the Congress was opened it became clear that the prime airn of the leadership of this meeting was to tie the N.S.A. as completely as possible to the foreign policy of our State Department.

Thus the N.S.A. leadership worked diligently to concoct a tissue of lies "proving" to the delegates why, in the interests of "peace" and "internationalism" (sic!), it was necessary to break *ALL* relationships with the I.U.S. (the mother of the N.S.A.) which unites almost 90% of the students in Higher Education outside of the United States—over 6,000,000 students in 71 countries of the World.

Imagine the gall of these N.S.A. leaders when they told the delegates that the I.U.S. (which is twice as large today as it was in 1947 when the first N.S.A. Congress called it "the most widely representative student organization in the world") is unrepresentative of the international student community, one-sided and partisan.

This same leadership which continuously professed its devotion to the cause of peace did everything possible to avoid answering the question of how American students can contribute to bringing about an immediate peaceful solution to the war in Korea. Instead it supported the intervention of our troops in Korea.

Like our State Department representatives in the U.N. they fell into turmoil whenever a delegate put forward a real peace proposal. Thus when a Yale Divinity student introduced a resolution for world disarmament he was called out of order and voted down. And when the leader of the Wisconsin delegation introduced a resolution to withhold aid from oppressive governments like the Bao Dai government in Viet Nam his resolution was amended into its opposite and he was forced to withdraw it.

Of course such a Congress could not be expected to be a fighter for students' rights on any front.

Quite the contrary, the intention of the leadership was to wipe out the N.S.A.'s Bill of Rights and pave the way for the new attacks on academic freedom that the men of the monopolies who dominate our colleges have up their sleeves.

This move, however, was defeated. It is a tribute to the few liberal students who were at the Congress that the Bill of Rights was upheld. For they led a militant and forthright struggle for its principles.

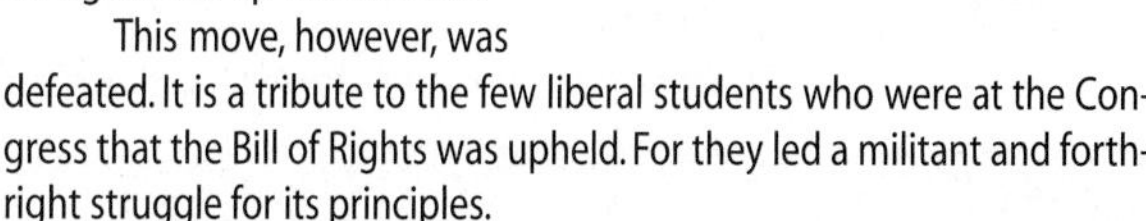

These liberals also won a strong resolution defending the rights of Communists to teach and attacking the system of loyalty oaths.

But they were not able to uphold a resolution against the use of Federal funds for schools that discriminate against Negroes and they were blocked in their efforts for a resolution against the Mundt Bill and other police state legislation.

On the question of Negro rights the N.S.A. leadership showed itself to be completely bankrupt. Their attitude was exemplified by the report of the President which while it touched on almost every other issue did not once discuss, mention or even allude to the struggles of Negro students and white students against jim crow in education.

In my opinion this Congress showed that the N.S.A. in its higher levels is a reactionary and dangerous organization. For while it professes its devotion to peace it tries to lead students down the road to war and reaction.

Progressive students must begin to pay more attention to the N.S.A., which by and large is the most formidable enemy of the true interests of American students.

At the same time it must be said that this Congress despite all that was wrong with it reflected the fact that the mass of American students do stand for peace and democracy.

Throughout the Congress the leadership was forced to mouth its devotion to the cause of peace and had to make serious concessions to the demands of the few liberal delegates at the Congress for the defense of academic freedom, in order to cover over the reactionary nature of its program which otherwise would be completely and immediately rejected by the various student bodies.

They were forced to allow a representative of the LYL [Labor Youth League] to speak because of the basically democratic spirit of the mass of students on Campus.

Sincerely yours,
Robert Fogel

[To the Anthology reader: The following is the original Editor's Note as it appeared in New Foundations, *November 1950.]*

Editor's Note: The writer of this letter was the representative of the Labor Youth League to the Third Annual N.S.A. Congress. At the Congress, he asked for and was given the floor after 2 days of heated debate. For ten minutes he spoke about the facts behind the Korean war and asked the N.S.A. to come forward with some kind of program which would solve the Korean war peacefully, which would prevent the campuses from being militarized, and which would stop the war hysteria from stifling academic freedom on the campuses.

Dr. Robert W. Fogel is Director, Center for Population Economics, Graduate School of Business, and member of the Economics Department at the University of Chicago. He was president-elect of the American Economics Association in 1997 and received the 1993 Nobel Prize in Economic Sciences with Douglas C. North.

PICTURE CREDITS: *Then:* Appearing at the 1950 National Student Congress at the U. of Michigan (*LIFE Magazine,* September 18, 1950. With permission). *Now:* c. 2000 (*Courtesy, Center for Population Economics, University of Chicago School of Business*).

Editor's note: Due to the Cold War and the war in Korea, when Robert Fogel appeared before the NSA Congress, both he and the Congress faced a climate especially hostile to Marxist and Communist views. It could be irreparably damaging to any student, faculty member, or organization to be accused of such sympathies. But not for all who stood out in the open, as Fogel's subsequent career demonstrates (For more on the "Red Scare," see Economic Club of Detroit, p. 191, Dentzer, p. 311, Brown, p. 385, and Murphy, p. 1080. See also p. 48, p. 141, and Munger, p. 805). For more on Communist and socialist voices see Prologue and Part 4, Sec. 4.

ROBERT W. FOGEL

Early years: Born in New York City, July 1, 1926, and graduated from Stuyvesant High School in 1944.

Education: A.B., Cornell University, 1948. A.M., Columbia University, 1960. Ph.D., Johns Hopkins University, 1963. DSc. (honorary), University of Rochester.

Academic Appointments: Instructor, Johns Hopkins University, 1958-59; Assistant Professor, University of Rochester, 1960-64; Associate Professor, 1964-65 Professor, University of Chicago, 1965-1975; Professor, University of Rochester (Autumn semester), 1968-1975; Professor, Harvard University, 1975-1981; Professor, University of Chicago, 1981-present.

Other career highlights: Numerous professional appointments, honors, and awards, including the Nobel Prize in Economics, 1993. Appearances at lectures to faculty seminars and colloquia throughout the United States, Europe, Canada, Argentina, Australia, Japan, Korea, and the Middle East. Numerous books and papers published, including *The Union Pacific Railroad* (Johns Hopkins, 1960), *Railroads and American Growth* (Johns Hopkins, 1964), [jointly with S. L. Engerman] *Time on the Cross: The Economics of Negro Slavery* (Little, Brown, 1974), *The Fourth Great Awakening: The Political Realignment of the 1990s and the Fate of Egalitarianism* (Univ. of Chicago Press, 1999).

Family: Married, 2 children.

ADVOCATING FOR SOCIALISM "AND/OR" COMMUNISM

'Capitalism Curbs Political Liberty' Erber Asserts in Address to SLID

"Full political liberty, as we understand it, is incompatible with the existence of capitalism," declared Ernest Erber, national director of the Workers Party, speaking on "Socialism or Chaos" before the Student League for Industrial Democracy last night. The United States cannot exist in a half-state of political democracy and economic autocracy".

Former member of the Socialist party, Erber participated in the

prevalent business boom, "a... dercurrent of insecurity exi... the business world, which r... the lack of capitalistic conf... that the free enterprise s... will remain a movi...

Emphasizing soc... alternative to su... chaos, Erber stress... ance of an econom... economic democr... planning. Such an ... problem would be ...

Cornell Daily Sun

Left, from top: *Cornell Daily Sun* 3/29/47, 3/7/47,5/22/47. Bottom right, 11/17/51

FRIDAY, MARCH 7, 1947

Marxist Group Introduces Courses, Re-elects Fogel as Spring Leader

Fogel, Roche Debate Desirability of Communism in US; Argue on Captialist Inequities, Loss of Personal Rights

Robert Fogel '48, arguing from a standpoint of economic inequities under the capitalist system and John Roche, Grad, basing his opposing views on the loss of individual freedom debated the desirability of Communism in America last night.

Addressing the last meeting of the Marxist Discussion Group Fogel, president of the organization, declared that "while we have tremendous resources, our present society is so constructed that we have lavishness for a few and discrimination, poverty and war for the many.

Quoting from Lenin he pointed out that there is no conflict between Communism and Socialism in the classical sense. The Communists in this country and in most countries throughout the world are actually working for socialism, he said.

"Today they (the Communists) fight for anything that will help the majority of the people." Citing the Communist Party stand in favor of such legislation as the housing and national health bills, Fogel declared, "Anything that aids the majority of the people brings the country that much closer to Socialism."

Maintaining that the present economic system does not provide for the economic and social needs of the people and generates racial inequality he cited the widespread sub-standard living conditions and the relatively low wage schedule and high death rate of American Negroes especially in the South.

Deploring the use of "barbaric expedients," John Roche, president of the Student League for Industrial Democracy, said that he was in favor of eliminated the class system but that a government dominated by the Communists "would establish a despotism which would make the present capitalistic system, with its admitted inequalities, seem like Utopia. In the name of classless society the Communists would enslave the people they came to liberate."

Claiming a basic dichotomy between promise and reality in the Soviet Union he described the gradual replacement of workers' committees by "bolshevik bureaucrats" in the factories after the revolution with a subsequent loss of individual freedom. "Today a worker who leaves his job can be imprisoned for from two to four months," he said.

Referring to the 100-1 ration of pay rates between officers and enlisted men in the Soviet army, Roche quoted George Orwell as saying, "In Russia all men are equal but some men are more equal than others."

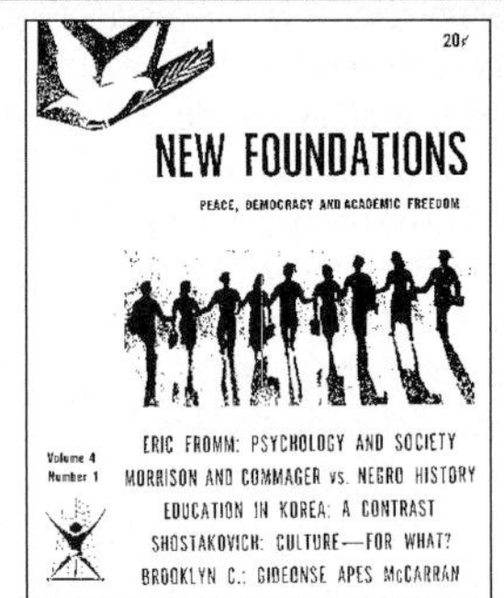

new foundations

THE EARTH SHALL RISE ON NEW FOUNDATIONS

Excerpt from the masthead page of the November 1950 issue of *New Foundations*:

"We declare that we are partisan. As students, we take our stand with the American working class which is the decisive force in the fight for peace, democracy and Socialism, and with its great ally, the Negro people.

Thus we present Marxist theory in the hope that it will enrich the content of campus activity.

The editors want NEW FOUNDATIONS to be the fighting voice of American students.

Cornell Daily Sun 11/17/51

Advocating Overthrow of U.S. Basis for Faculty Dismissal

Staff, Advisers, Regional Chairs, Colleges

1950-51 National Organization

(As presented in the Report of the Third National Student Congress)

NATIONAL OFFICERS

President
Allard K. Lowenstein, *University of North Carolina*

Vice President, Student Life
Elmer Paul Brock, *La Salle College, Pennsylvania*

Vice President, Educational Problems
Herbert B. Goldsmith, *University of Wisconsin*

Vice President, International Affairs
Herbert W. Eisenberg, *Massachusetts Institute of Technology*

Executive Secretary
Shirley V. Neizer, *Simmons College, Massachusetts*

Treasurer
Frederick D. Houghteling, *Harvard University*

Director of Publications
Craig H. Wilson, *University of Michigan*

Staff Associate
Joan Long, *Marylhurst College, Oregon*

REGIONAL REPRESENTATIVES TO THE NATIONAL EXECUTIVE COMMITTEE

California, Nev., Hawaii
Paul Pitner
University of California–Berkeley
Lewis E. Arnold
Univesity of California–Berkeley

Georgia, Ala., Fla.
Stuart McDonald III
University of Miami

Great Northwest
James Seelig
Eastern Wash. College of Ed.

Illinois
Merrill Freed
University of Chicago

Indiana
Phyllis Berezny
St. Mary's College

Iowa, Nebraska
Ross A. Williams, Jr.
University of Iowa

Kentucky, Tennessee
Galen Martin
Berea College

Mason-Dixon
Agnes M. Downey
Dunbarton College, DC

Michigan
Duane Johnson,
Wayne University
Leonard Wilcox
University of Michigan

Minnesota
Wayne Dauba
Gustavus Adolphus College

Missouri, Kansas
Jean Anderson
Fontbonne College

New Jersey
Rosemary Honecker
New Jersey College for Women

Metropolitan New York
Norton Garfinkle
Columbia University
John J. McCullough, Jr.
Fordham University–Education

New York State
Richard Appel
University of Rochester

Northern New England
Michael Iovenko
Dartmouth College
John R. Fox
University of Massachusetts

Ohio
William T. Dentzer
Muskingum College

Pennsylvania
Kenneth R. Kurtz
Swarthmore College

Rocky Mountains
Roy Romer
University of Colorado

Southern New England
Stanford Summers
Yale Divinity School

Virginia, Carolinas
Richard Murphy
University of North Carolina

Wisconsin
Virginia Gardiner
Mount Mary College

NATIONAL ADVISORY COUNCIL

Gordon Klopf (Chairman)
Student Personnel Advisor, University of Wisconsin

William Birenbaum
Office of the Dean of Students, University of Chicago

Monroe E. Deutsch
Provost-Emeritus, University of California

Very Rev. Vincent J. Flynn
President, College of St. Thomas, Minnesota

Frank Graham
President Emeritus, University of North Carolina

Kenneth Holland
Director, Institute for International Education

Charles S. Johnson
President, Fisk University

Robert A. Kelly
NSA President 1949-1950

Mrs. Carl Meineke
Dean, Colby Junior College

Dean Newhouse
Dean of Students, Case Institute of Technology

1950-51 Roster of Colleges
Third National Student Congress

(Institutions in italics attended with visitor status.)

California-Nevada-Hawaii
California School of Arts and Crafts
College of Holy Names
College of Osteopathic Physicians and Surgeons
Los Angeles City College
Mills College
Mount St. Mary's College
University of California, Berkeley
University of California at Los Angeles
University of Santa Clara
Modesto Junior College
University of Southern California

Georgia-Alabama-Florida
Agnes Scott College
Barry College for Women
Georgia School of Technology
Morehouse College
University of Miami
Alabama College
University of Alabama

Great Northwest
Eastern Wash. College of Education
Marylhurst College
Washington State College
University of Idaho
University of Washington

Gulf Coast
Arkansas A.M. & N. College
Southeastern Louisiana College
Southern University, La.
University of Tulsa
Xavier University
Northwestern State College, La.
University of Oklahoma

Illinois
Aurora College
Bradley University
Chicago Teachers College
College of St. Francis
De Paul University
Institute of Design
Lake Forest College
Loyola University
Mundelein College
North Central College
Rockford College
Roosevelt College
Rosary College
University of Chicago
University of Illinois
Concordia Teachers College
Illinois Institute of Technology
Morton Junior College

Indiana
Saint Mary of the Woods College
St. Mary's College
Indiana University
Purdue University

Iowa, Nebraska
Clark College
Grinnell College
Marycrest College
University of Iowa

Kentucky, Tennessee
Berea College
Fisk University
Tusculum College
University of Louisville

Mason-Dixon
College of Notre Dame
Dunbarton College of Holy Cross
Hood College
Howard University
Loyola College
Mt. St. Agnes College
Trinity College
University of Baltimore
Georgetown University
University of Maryland

Michigan
Central Michigan College
Marygrove College
Mercy College
Michigan College of Mining
Michigan State Normal
Nazareth College
University of Detroit
University of Michigan
Wayne University
Highland Park Junior College

Minnesota
Augsburg College
Carleton College
College of St. Benedict
College of St. Teresa
College of St. Thomas
Concordia College
Gustavus Adolphus College
Hamline College
Macalester College
St. Cloud State Teachers College
St. John's University
St. Olaf College
University of Minnesota

Missouri, Kansas
Fontbonne College
Kansas State Teachers College
Maryville College
Mt. St. Scholastica College
University of Missouri
Washington University
Webster College
Dana College
College of Emporia
Friends University
Kansas Wesleyan College

New Jersey
College of St. Elizabeth
New Jersey College for Women
Rutgers University
St. Peter's College

New York Metropolitan
CCNY, Business Day
CCNY, Business Evening
CCNY, Main Day
CCNY, Main Evening
College of New Rochelle
Columbia University
Fordham College
Fordham University
Good Counsel College
Hunter College, Day
Hunter College, Evening
Iona College
Manhattan College
Manhattanville College
New York University, Commerce
New York University, Education
New York University, Heights
New York University, Wash. Square
Pratt Institute
Queens College
Sarah Lawrence College
University College of St. John
Vassar College

New York State
Buffalo Tech
Buffalo State Teachers College
Canisius College
College of St. Rose
Cornell University
D'Youville College
Eastman School of Music
Fredonia State Teachers College
Hobart College
LeMoyne College
Niagara University
Rochester Institute of Technology
Russell Sage College
St. Bonaventure College
Siena College
Skidmore College
Syracuse University
University of Buffalo
University of Rochester–Men
University of Rochester–Women
University of Rochester–Nursing
William Smith College
Nazareth College

Northern New England
American International College
Bennington College
Boston University
Dartmouth College
Emerson College
Emmanuel College
Framingham State Teachers College
Garland School
Harvard College
Harvard Graduate School, Arts and Sciences
Keene Teachers College
Massachusetts Institute of Technology
Mount Holyoke College
Mt. St. Mary College
Newton College of the Sacred Heart
Radcliffe College
Regis College
Simmons College
Smith College
Springfield College
University of Massachusetts
Wellesley College
Wheaton College

Ohio
Antioch College
College of Wooster
Fenn College
John Carroll University
Muskingum College
Ohio Wesleyan College
Ursuline College
Youngstown College
Baldwin-Wallace College
Ohio State University

Pennsylvania
Beaver College
Bloomsburg State Teachers College
Bryn Mawr College
La Salle College
Lehigh University
Mercyhurst College
Mount Mercy College
Muhlenberg College
Pennsylvania College for Women
St. Joseph College
St. Vincent College
Swarthmore College
Temple University
Thiel College
University of Pennsylvania
Wilson College
University of Pittsburgh
University of Scranton

Rocky Mountain
Colorado A. & M. College
Colorado College
Colorado State College of Education
Highlands University
Loretto Heights College
Regis College
Trinidad State Jr. College
University of Colorado
University of Utah

Southern New England
Albertus Magnus College
Connecticut College for Women
St. Joseph's College
University of Bridgeport
Yale University
Yale Divinity School

Virginia, Carolinas
Duke University
Johnson C. Smith University
North Carolina State A. & E.
Sweet Briar College
University of North Carolina
Virginia State College
Clemson A. & M. College
Duke University
Greensboro College

West Virginia
West Virginia Wesleyan
Beckley College
Marshall College
West Virginia Institute of Technology

Wisconsin
Carroll College
Milwaukee State Teachers College
Mount Mary College
Stout Institute
University of Wisconsin
Milwaukee Downer College

MacArthur relieved of command, Rosenbergs sentenced to death *Catcher in the Rye* published and *The King and I* opens

North Korean and U.N. forces seesaw in battles at the 38th Parallel. Truman relieves General MacArthur of his Far East command. King Abdullah of Jordan is assassinated in Jerusalem. A U.S. peace treaty with Japan is signed in San Francisco. Peron is reelected president of Argentina. The Twenty-second Amendment to the Constitution is adopted, providing for a two-term maximum for the presidency. Julius and Ethel Rosenberg are sentenced to death for espionage against the United States. J.D. Salinger's *Catcher in the Rye,* Herman Wouk's *The Caine Mutiny,* and James Jones's *From Here to Eternity* are published. Film classics include: *African Queen, Miracle in Milan,* and *An American in Paris.* Rodgers and Hammerstein's *The King and I* opens on Broadway. High on the charts: "Hello Young Lovers," "Getting to Know You," "Shrimp Boat," and "Come On-a My House." Color TV is first introduced in the United States. The N.Y. Giants beat the Yankees 4–2 in the World Series, and Michigan defeats California 14–6 in the Rose Bowl.

Source: Adapted from citations in Bernard Grun, *The Timetables of History* (Simon and Schuster, 1991)

BUDGETING NSA'S MILESTONES: 1950-51

UNITED STATES NATIONAL STUDENT ASSOCIATION

Proposed Budget, Fiscal 1951

	This Year to Date Oct - Dec	Remainder of Year Jan - Sep	Total for Fiscal 1950-51	Last Year Fiscal 1949-50	This Year Present Scale
INCOME:					
National Dues	7,000.00	7,500.00	14,500.00	19.800.00	14,500.00
Student Discount Service	200.00	200.00	400.00	2.525.00	400.00
Publications Bureau	300.00	1,200.00	1,500.00	2,200.00	1,500.00
International	2,000.00	-	2,000.00	2,550.00	2,000.00
Congress Net Proceeds	-	2,500.00	2,500.00	2,200.00	2,500.00
Miscellaneous Income	-	100.00	100.00	100.00	100.00
TOTAL INCOME	9,500.00	11,500.00	21,000.00	29,375.00	21,000.00
EXPENDITURE:					
Salaries, Officers*	4,500.00	5,400.00	9,900.00	11,875.00	14,000.00
Salaries, Secretarial*	2,000.00	-	2,000.00	1,800.00	8,000.00
Rent	690.00	1,125.00	1,815.00	1,625.00	2,760.00
Travel	1,300.00	800.00	2,100.00	1,525.00	3,000.00
Office Supplies	650.00	800.00	1,450.00	1,475.00	2,000.00
Postage & Mailing	800.00	1,400.00	2,200.00	2,400.00	2,600.00
Telephone & Telegraph	1,400.00	600.00	2,000.00	875.00	3,[illegible]00.00
Printing	300.00	300.00	600.00	700.00	800.00
NSA NEWS	400.00	-	400.00	1,750.00	1,100.00
Promotional Pubs. & PR	700.00	400.00	1,100.00	1,925.00	1,500.00
Depreciation & Maintenance	400.00	300.00	700.00	600.00	700.00
Subscr.,Lit., & Meetings	50.00	150.00	200.00	200.00	240.00
Insurance	100.00	-	100.00	125.00	100.00
Commissions & Subcomms.	335.00	100.00	435.00	550.00	500.00
Miscellaneous	275.00	125.00	400.00	575.00	500.00
New Furniture & Equip.**	1,100.00	-	1,100.00	375.00	1,200.00
TOTAL EXPENDITURE	15,000.00	11,500.00	26,500.00	28,375.00	42,000.00
SURPLUS/DEFICIT	- 5,500.00	0.00	- 5,500.00	- 1,000.00	-21,000.00

* Salaries. Currently, the Staff consists of 7 officers full-time, and 2 full-time and 4 half-time secretarial & technical workers. Full-time salary is at the rate of $2000 per annum. Total salaries for a year on the present scale, therefore, would be about $22,000. Full-time workers are the President, 3 VPs, Exec.Secy, Treasurer, PRDirector, and 2 Staff Associates. Half-time are International Education Director, acting Publications Secretary, bookkeeper, and stenographer. Note that the Travel Director has been omitted, as his salary id to come from a travel program subsidy.

The proposed retrenchment would reduce the Staff to 5½ -- President, 3 VPs, Executive Secretary, and half-time Treasurer. No new PRDirector would be appointed except on an unpaid basis; and all paid secretarial help would be dispensed with. Moreover, the salary rate would be reduced to $1600.00 per annum. Further, during the summer Staff members would be given vacations without pay, during which they could work or gp back to school, totalling about 9 man-months. This would bring salaries for the rest of the year down to atotal of only $5400.

** New Furniture and Equipment is not actually an item of expense, since it increases Assets. The real expense for furniture and equipment falls under Depreciation.

BUDGETING FOR FISCAL AUSTERITY was introduced, as noted by both Joan Lynch and Shirley Neizer in this section. With a staff of seven full-time officers and two full- and four part-time office help, salaries were cut to $28 weekly and paid help eliminated in December. Although three one-page issues of *NSA News* were produced, using varitype, the paper was abandoned for the year. The new travel department was expected to be self-sustaining. The summer travel deficit of $22,000–25,000 would be paid off through the travel program over several years with the cooperation of the European student union creditors. (Document sources: SHSW archives, Sylvia Bacon. Reproduced here are portions of mimeographed NEC and Congress reports).

EDITOR'S NOTE RE *NSA NEWS* Efforts were made by the Anthology Project to assemble a complete set of the newspaper published by NSA during its first five years. Most but not all issues could be acquired for Volumes I-IV. Printed on unsized newsprint, they have become brittle and yellowed (this is true, incidentally, of many of the college papers of that period, now deteriorating in cloth binders in various college archives). As best as can be determined, following is the publication history:

Spring 1947. Two issues (March 1 and April 15), of the *International Activities Bulletin* published by the Harvard International Commission for the NICC. Each issue was 2 pages, 17″ × 22″.
1947-48. Vol. I, 7 issues October through May, mostly 4 pages, some 8 pages. All issues in the first five years were 11″ × 17″.
1948-49. Vol. II, 8 issues October through May, mostly 8 pages.
1949-1950. Vol. III, 8 issues October through May, 8 and 12 pages.
1950-51. Special 12-page 8/51 convention issue in pre- and post-convention editions with article changes on page 1 and page 10. *Vol. IV.* 3 issues Oct.-Dec., 1950. 1 page.
1951-52. Vol. "Fifth Year," November, March, and May, 4 pp. each.

PRETENDING TO SWIM across the ocean, delegates mimic motions of leader who relieved the monotony of the meetings by getting them to act out a song describing a lion hunt in the African jungle.

SHOWING THEIR STRENGTH, students follow their leader (back to camera) as he demonstrates his

Life Goes to a Collegiate Convention

STUDENTS DEBATE WORLD PROBLEMS IN ATMOSPHERE OF CAMPUS FUN

Last month on the campus of the University of Michigan 750 college students came together in what looked like the combination of a state legislature in session and Saturday night at a fraternity house. The National Student Association, an organization of U.S. college students founded in 1947, was holding its third annual convention. The 750 delegates, representing the student bodies of 350 U.S. schools, were on hand to settle the world's problems and, between the debates, to have some fun.

For a week the N.S.A. delegates made political deals over bottles of beer, worried about Communism and sang songs. They passed a resolution opposing loyalty oaths for professors on the grounds that the oaths fail to trap real subversives and have been used to oust innocent people. As a demonstration of open-mindedness they also listened to a Communist explanation of the war in Korea (*opposite page*). But before they adjourned they voted complete approval of U.N. action in Korea and celebrated with a song their final break with the International Union of Students, a Communist-led organization with headquarters in Czechoslovakia, with which N.S.A. has unsuccessfully tried to cooperate. One verse of the song, sung to the tune of a union song called *Joe Hill:*

"I dreamt I was in Prague last night;
Joe Stalin was there, too.
Says I, 'But Joe, you'll have to go.
N.S.A. won't play with you.'"

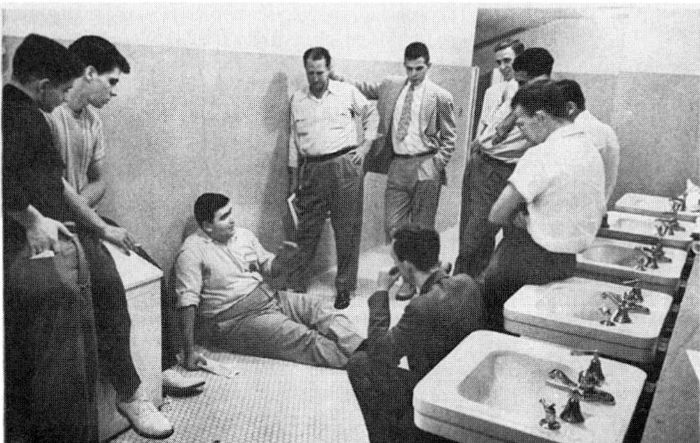

IN MEN'S ROOM, delegates listen as Aram Goshgarian of the University of Miami explains political maneuver to get Al Lowenstein of North Carolina U. (*picture at right*) to run for president of the N.S.A.

RELUCTANT CANDIDATE Lowenstein tries to decline the job so he can study. He was elected anyway.

muscles and brags about his bravery. The leader is Leeland Jones, a graduate of University of Buffalo.

LOOKING FOR LION, the students and Jones continue to flaunt their bravery. In the final verse Jones "sees" a lion and runs from the stage, shivering with fright while the strident audience roars with laughter.

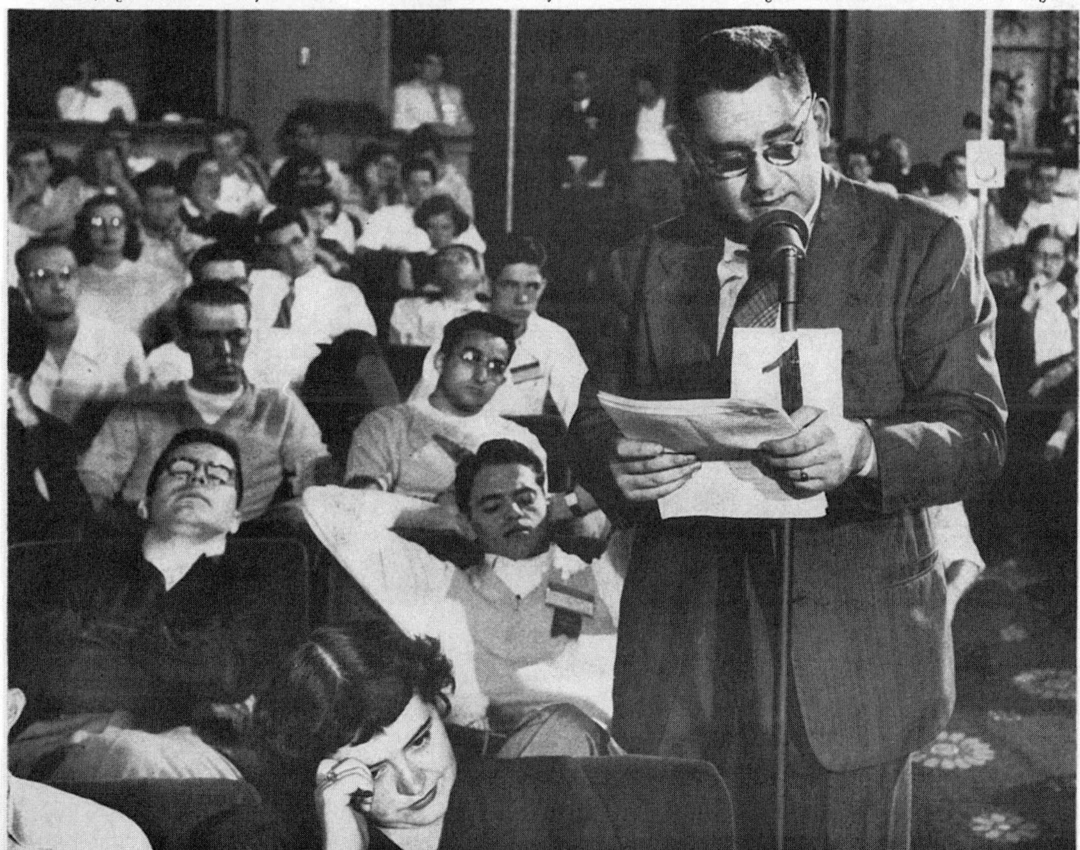

COMMUNIST EXPLANATION of Korean war is read to delegates by Robert Fogel of the Communist-front Labor Youth League. He said war was begun by the South Koreans and that the U.S. is oppressing colored people of Asia. The students let him talk but were plainly bored and unimpressed by his argument.

Collegiate Convention CONTINUED

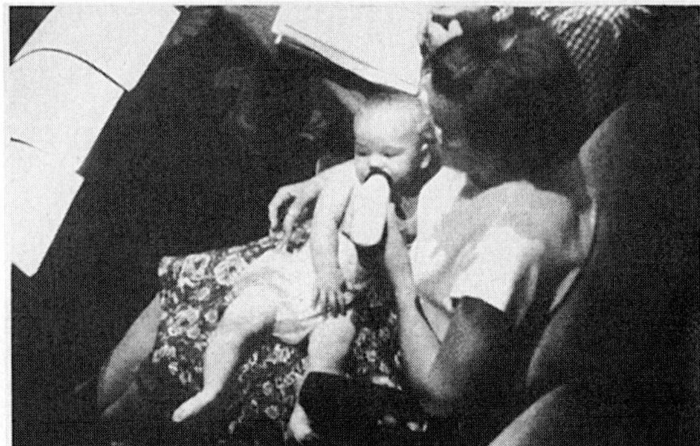

DELEGATE'S SON, 6-month-old Bill Shaffer, drinks from bottle held by mother, who accompanied her husband from University of Southern California.

PROPAGANDISTS from California invade meeting hall in shorts and bright shirts to distribute tourist pamphlets and sing songs in praise of their state.

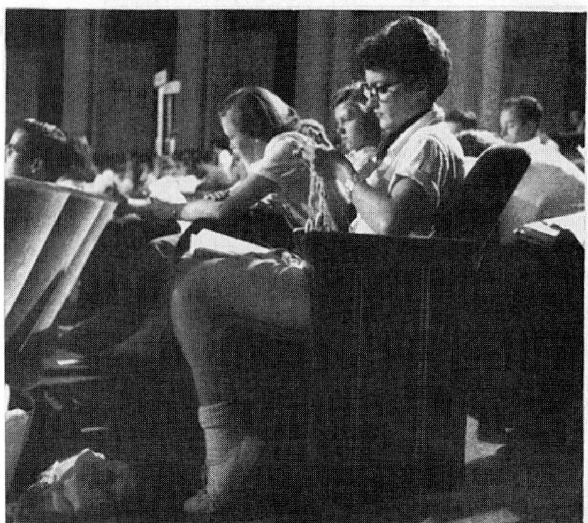

PREOCCUPIED DELEGATE, Ellen Englert of Boston's Newton College of the Sacred Heart, counts stitches during discussion of convention expenses.

Collegiate Convention CONTINUED

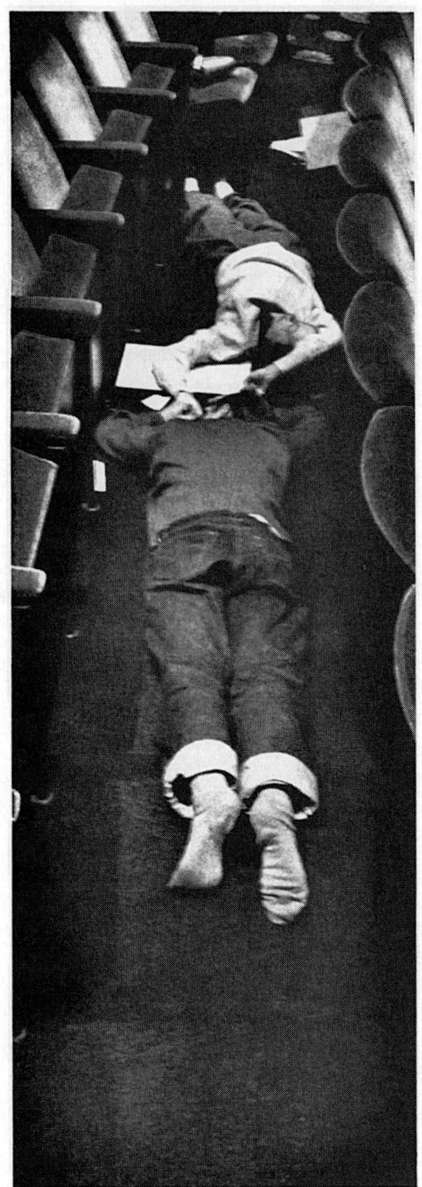

TIRED PAIR, Earl Wilson of Los Angeles City College and Goldie Bernstein of Temple University, who had been up all night at meetings, hold hands and nap between seats waiting for delegates to show up for morning session.

THIRD NATIONAL STUDENT CONGRESS. *LIFE* magazine's September 18, 1950, issue covered the NSA Congress held two months after the United States entered the Korean conflict, an event which dominated the Congress international agenda. Leeland Jones, then a University of Buffalo graduate and NSA's first elected treasurer (1947-48) helped break tension by leading a plenary session in the "Going on a Lion Hunt" change. It was first introduced at an earlier 1947 Constitutional Convention marathon session by Clifton Wharton, Harvard delegate and National Continuations Committee Secretary.

While *LIFE*'s coverage of the NSA convention was a major promotional boost, not all the students who were there appreciated the focus on the Lion Hunt, tired delegates, and the Labor Youth League speaker. At the close of a lengthy review, Nancy Dean '52, a Congress delegate, writing in the 10/18/50 *Vassar Miscellany News* summed up those feelings. "We had gone to the Congress because we enjoyed it. No one forced us. We were not being martyrs by any means, nor were we being spectators at a Derby Day picnic. My request [is that] newspapers and periodicals emphasize less sensationalism and more accuracy."

SECTION 9

NSA's Fifth Year, 1951-52

CONTENTS

With determined leadership provided by newly elected 1951-52 NSA president Bill Dentzer (Muskingum College, OH), the NSA staff loaded a truck and moved their offices to the campus of the University of Colorado. The student government there had offered free space to the financially ailing organization whose presence "on a national scale," paradoxically, had "begun to have a say in academic and administration matters," as *Mademoiselle* magazine reported.

He was assisted by Marion Andert (University of Minnesota), the only other full-time national staff member, with the remaining staff working from their campuses and from the International Office at Harvard. Dentzer, who in later life held senior government and business positions, describes how they set about to rebuild, on a $9,000 budget, the declining membership and repair NSA's vanishing treasury—reduced by lower annual dues and the deficit from the 1950 summer travel program. Dues had been reduced from the original range of $25 to $369, based on college enrollment, to from $20 to $150.

In this task, member colleges and their regional groups continued to help build on NSA's student government, human relations, and intercollegiate cultural programs, turning out larger numbers of colleges at its events than appeared on its membership rolls, and fueling its summer travel programs operated by its then newly incorporated travel office in New York City (See Part 3) headed by Thomas Callahan (St. Francis College, New York).

Groundwork laid for new international group

Dentzer and Avrea Ingram (Georgia Tech and Harvard), international vice president, joined at the January 1952 Edinburgh International Conference with student leaders of twenty-four European and other nations to launch the Coordinating Secretariat of National Unions of Students (Cosec), as the democratic noncommunist alternative to the Communist-front IUS.

Dentzer also describes preparations for the 1952 Congress at Indiana University for which Sylvia Bacon (Vassar College, NY), Student Affairs Vice President, organized the first of NSA's groundbreaking College Newspaper Editors' Conferences (See Part 2, Section 4), at which campus freedom of the press was a central theme. The Congress keynote, "Education and Freedom," was delivered to 500 delegates and observers from 225 colleges by University of Pennsylvania President and former Minnesota Governor, Harold Stassen.

Ken Kurtz (Swarthmore College, PA), who was a candidate for the NSA presidency, recalls his view of the politics of the Minnesota Congreess.

At this time, also, McCarthyism, known as the "Red Scare," had been roiling the nation. Drawing on the spirit of NSA's commitment to academic freedom, Dentzer articulated the perils of indiscriminate anticommunism in an *NSA News* editorial.

CONVENING IN MINNESOTA, William T. Dentzer, NSA's fifth president, addresses the Fourth National Student Congress as the U.S. enters the Korean war.

Youth Will Solve World Crisis, Says Stassen

The N S A News

SPECIAL POST-CONGRESS EDITION — August, 1951

Korean Conflict Creates Uncertainty, Fear Among U.S. Students; Freedom Threatened

CONGRESS ELECTS THESE STUDENTS TO LEAD USNSA THROUGH COMING YEAR

New Generation Assumes Leadership As Veterans Leave Campus

600 Delegates Legislate in Minneapolis

By GENE McLOONE

Minnesota Daily

Summer Session Issue

The University of Minnesota, Tuesday, Aug. 21, 1951

NSA Congress Convenes Here

Over 400 representatives from 185 colleges and universities in the United States convened here yesterday for the fourth annual congress of the National Student association.

The delegates met last night to hear a talk by former Gov. Harold Stassen and to adopt rules and an agenda for the 10-day congress. Today the congress will meet in the Museum of Natural History auditorium to hear a panel discussion of NSA's program and purposes.

Observers say that the most important issue before the congress may be the organization of NSA's national office. This has thus far been a major issue in meetings of the national executive committee, composed of regional presidents.

The executive committee had been accepting placidly the reports of the national vice-president until late afternoon on Saturday. At that time Shirley Neizer, national executive secretary, presented a financial report. It included a nine-month expense of over $2750 for telephone and telegraph.

The report set off a storm of criticism. The executive committee met until early Sunday morning. Two sub-committees were elected, one to consider next year's budget and one to consider the problem of financial control of the national office.

NSA's public relations staff indicates that other issues will include policy resolutions on loyalty oaths, universal military training, deferment of college students, dis-

What Is NSA?

The National Student association is an organization of college and university students represented through their individual student governments. The organization is run entirely by students elected at each year's national congress.

NSA was founded in 1946 by a group of 25 students who, returning from the World Student congress in Prague, Czechoslovakia, felt the need for an organization to represent American college and university students. The association now parallels many of the

1951-1952 Album

4TH NATIONAL STUDENT CONGRESS in the *Minnesota Daily* (8/28/51). Clockwise from immediately above: Marty Budin, CCNY delegate (*Minnesota Daily*); VA-Carolinas delegate; Delegates at Pioneer Hall Residence (Both Haessler Photos. SHSW). Keynote Speaker Harold Stassen, President U. of PA, and outgoing NSA President Al Lowenstein (*Minnesota Daily*).

MOVING TO COLORADO, to save money and rebuild, a new staff takes charge: from left: Avrea Ingram (Georgia Tech/Harvard), V.P. International Affairs; Sylvia Bacon (Vassar C., NY), V.P. Student Affairs; William Dentzer (Muskingum C., OH), President; John Haley (Emory U. GA), V.P. Student Gov't; Rollo O'Hare (Wayne U. Law, MI), V.P. Educational Affairs). (*NSA News* 8/51)

Staying the Course

NSA Moves National Offices To Boulder; Headquarters Represent 195 Colleges

National Student association headquarters will be moved to the University in about two weeks from the previous capitol site at the University of Wisconsin in Madison, Wis., John Warren, campus president of NSA, announced yesterday.

A University delegation bid for the capitol at the National Student congress held at the University of Minnesota Aug. 20 to

time in the office assisted by some part-time secretarial help from this area.

The Coloradan will move to the north garret of Memorial, Warren explained. Their new premises will include part of Independent Student association's room and part of the north balcony, which will be enclosed.

Warren stated that the new national capitol will be "a great help to the University and an honor, as it does represent over 600,000 students."

The Cornell Daily Sun

ITHACA, N.Y., TUESDAY, OCTOBER 9, 1951

National NSA Leader To Speak Before S.C.

National Student Association President Bill Dentzer will speak at the invitation of Student Council in the Willard Straight Rehearsal Room at 7:30 p.m. today, as two weeks' discussion and debate on rejoining NSA draws to a close.

XAVIER UNIVERSITY,

N. S. A. President Visits University

William T. Dentzer, president of the National Student Association, visited Xavier March 17 on a tour of schools. Ronald Rousseve, chairman of the NSA Gulf Coast Region, welcomed Mr. Dentzer to the university.

Dentzer was elected to the presidency of the NSA at the 4th annual NSA Congress held at Minneapolis, last summer. He represented the Ohio Region at the Congress and served as a member of the National Executive Committee, the interim executive body of NSA. A native of Rochester, Pennsylvania, Dentzer is now associated with the national offices of the NSA at Boulder, Colorado.

Following his election as president, Dentzer said, "I will do all in my power to work for the development of the moral student com-

The Carletonian

Number 10 — Carleton College, Northfield, Minnesota — Saturday, December 1, 1951

NSA PRESIDENT SPEAKS

Minnesota Regional Assembly Convenes On Carleton Campus

Eighty Students Represent Eleven Colleges At Three-Day Convention

REGIS HERALD

Council Leader Stresses Government Policy As Seen in Minnesota Student Conference

Caellian

AT NEW JERSEY COLLEGE FOR WOMEN, NEW BRUNSWICK, N.J.

THURSDAY, NOVEMBER 8, 1951

NSA Begins Conference Plans; Names 'Leadership' As Theme

Provost Gross, Harold Stassen Possible Speakers; All Schools in New Jersey Invited to Attend

THE EMORY WHEEL

"The South's Most Independent College Newspaper"

NSA—Students United

Among other pertinent items in its long comprehensive report on the status of the American university system today, the current issue of the New Republic has a section devoted to the National Student association. Since the NSA's news headquarters will soon be situated in Atlanta, Emory students have an especial interest in the values and policies of that student group.

The article points out that the NSA is one of the strongest attempts to date to date to organize college students throughout the country. Previously, problems facing students had been dealt with on a local or regional basis.

It should be obvious that with the emergence of such national issues as universal military service and loyalty oaths, these problems can no longer be handled effectively on the local level. A strong national organization is needed; and if NSA is the answer, Emory will be in a key position to provide the leadership requisite to any group desirous of shaping national policies.

Building Regional Organizations

Facing "The Red Scare"

THE CARDINAL

UNIVERSITY OF LOUISVILLE'S OFFICIAL WEEKLY PUBLICATION

"McCarthyism" Is Condemned By National Student Group

The fourth annual conference of the National Student Association was held at the University of Minnesota, from August 17-29 of this year. The two delegates from Louisville were Bill Burbank, USC President, and Don McIntosh, Co-chairman of the NSA Commission of the USC.

More than 500 delegates from over 200 colleges and universities attended the conference, representing more than 670,000 students. Dr. Harold Stassen delivered the keynote address. Many students representing students in Europe and South American countries also attended.

The accomplishments of this conference were: 1. Passed a resolution in favor of Universal Military Training. 2. Formulated a "Student Bill of Right," in which they affirmed that qualified students have a right to get an education. 3. Endorsed the use of the "Honor system." 4. Recommended that college athletics be decommercialized and returned to the students. 5. Reaffirmed NSA's stand on academic freedom, urging that no teacher be dismissed without knowing the charges and having a chance to defend him self. 6. Condemned "McCarthyism," which was characterized by guilt by association and unproven scattershot charges. 7. Urged the passage of a new G.I. Bill for the Korean Emergency. 8. Decided to continue its boycott of the Communist dominated International Union of Students.

Mary Bennet of Nazareth College was elected president of the

CREDITS. Above: U. of Louisville *Cardinal* 10/4/51; Below: The *NSA News*, Special Post Congress Edition 8/52; Cover, NSA's annual travel information booklet, 1951. Left, from top down: U. of Colorado *The Silver and Gold* 9/21/51; Xavier U, LA, *Xavier Herald* 3/52; *Cornell Daily Sun* 10/9/51; NY; Carleton C., MN, *The Carletonian* 12/1/51; Regis C., MA, *Regis Herald* 10/15/51; Emory U., GA, *The Emory Wheel* 11/1/51; NJ College for Women, *The Caellian*, 11/8/51.

work
study
travel
ABROAD
. . . 1952
U. S. National Student Association

THE NSA NEWS

Experience, Better Planning Result In Smooth, Balanced European Tour

The Travel Program Grows

Surviving budget woes and moving the national office

1. From Minneapolis to Bloomington

William T. Dentzer, Jr.
Muskingum College, Ohio
NSA President, 1951-52

I was elected President of NSA at the Fourth National Student Congress at the University of Minnesota on August 29, 1951, my twenty-second birthday. Elected with me as vice presidents were Sylvia Bacon (Vassar College, NY), student affairs; Rollo O'Hare (Wayne State University, MI), educational affairs; Avrea Ingram (Harvard University, MA), international affairs; and John Haley (Emory University, GA), student government, a new vice presidency created at that congress.

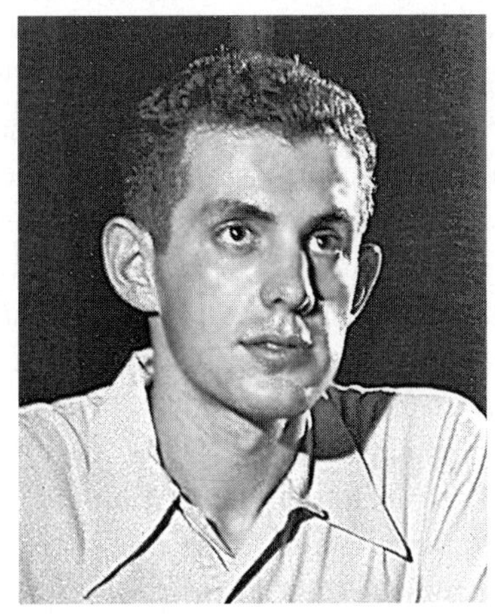

Background

I attended the First NSA Congress at the University of Wisconsin in 1948, as an alternate delegate, just prior to my sophomore year at Muskingum College. The following summer I remained longer in my summer job to earn more money to return to college, and so missed the second congress. I made the third congress at the University of Michigan two years later as an upcoming senior and president of the student government.

Because serendipitous dormitory room assignments at the Michigan Congress made Al Lowenstein a roommate of my fellow delegate from Muskingum, I came to know Al there. Charismatic and a spellbinding speaker, he was a dynamic, sensitive, humorous, and moralistic person, with a relentless commitment to the cause of human freedom and social justice. On the eve of his election as NSA president, Al urged me to run for an NSA vice presidency. I declined, because I savored the prospect of my senior college year and the opportunity to become better acquainted with Celia Hill, the Muskingum coed I had begun dating and would later marry.

In the academic year that followed, I was chairman of the Ohio Region, and thus a member of the NSA National Executive Committee (NEC). I saw Al at the NEC and during stops that he made at Muskingum during his travels. In spring 1951, he began to urge me to run as his successor, primarily to carry on his campaign to build a free world alternative to the Communist-front International Union of Students (IUS). Toward the end of the fourth congress, in late August, I postponed my plans for graduate school and agreed to run. The future of Al's campaign for an alternative to IUS was in doubt, and another NEC member whom Al also had urged to run proved even more reluctant than I to do so. I was elected because I was Al's candidate and would continue his international policy. I won by a vote of 153 to 138 over Ken Kurtz from Swarthmore, who was supported by those opposed to Al and that policy. And so a delegate from a small Midwestern college, hailing from the small town of Rochester, PA, became head of NSA for a year in which the association was forced to contract and move its national office in order to survive.

Moving the national office to Boulder

Due largely to earlier financial losses in NSA's student travel program, the fourth congress decided to move the national office from Madison to rent-free space in the student union at the University of Colorado in Boulder. The offer of free space by the student government was the only hard offer that NSA had in hand. Finances dictated that the downsized office staff would consist only of me and Marion Andert, elected at the postcongress NEC meeting as executive secretary.

Marion's post was a new position intended to provide some continuity to NSA staffs, which turned over each year. She had occupied a similar post in the National Newman Club Federation. Marion had the necessary office management skills and the driving commitment of a Catholic nun, which she almost had become. Our annual budget was only about $9,000. The Colorado student government promised volunteer help for project research, production of mailings, and other tasks.[1]

September was spent in Madison preparing for the move and outlining the year's program by a decentralized staff, most of whom barely knew each other. Sylvia, Rollo, and John returned, respectively, to their studies at Vassar, Wayne, and Emory (Sylvia later became a widely respected federal judge). Avrea, who had been doing graduate work at Harvard after graduating from Georgia Tech, headed the International Office, which was housed at Harvard. Early in the morning of October 1, Marion, Elmer Paul Brock, and I arrived in Boulder with the contents of the Madison office, in a two-ton truck that we had driven straight from Madison.

The 1951-52 program year: setting priorities

The postcongress NEC meeting agreed that I should spend most of my time out of the office, seeking new NSA members, speaking at member campuses and NSA regional meetings, representing the association to other organizations, fund-raising, and leading NSA's international program. The itineraries that I sent home to my parents during the year (and fortunately kept by them) show that I spent about 75 percent of my time on the road, traveling and speaking. Marion, in Boulder, facilitated contact among NSA members and staff and handled requests for information and program data. Provisions were made for the usual post-Christmas NEC meeting and for fall and spring meetings of the National Interim Committee, a newly created committee drawn from the NEC; its purpose was to bring the geographically disbursed staff together periodically and address any new policy questions. Despite the slim resources, our goal was to survive and grow during what we hoped would be a one-year stay in Boulder.

My early mailings to member schools described our program for the year and included a list of matters that the staff would address. I identified NSA with the following goals:

- To help student governments become more meaningful to their student bodies, both by making them better able to provide services and by encouraging them to address important campus problems such as parochialism, apathy, and honor systems—issues in what I sometimes referred to as "the moral community."
- To represent American student opinion as formulated at the congresses on national issues affecting students such as universal military training, the GI Bill, federal scholarships, and commercialization of intercollegiate athletics.
- To combat racial discrimination in higher education and campus organizations.
- To uphold academic freedom, and to combat McCarthyism and other threats to the free exchange of ideas.
- To foster the creation of a noncommunist international student group that would be prodemocratic, and in consequence antitotalitarian and anticommunist, and that would reach out to students in the Third World.

These goals formed the core of "the speech"—the message that I carried to both member and nonmember student governments. In addition to retaining and building NSA's membership, my purpose was to lift their sights higher than what I described as "little more than those of closed groups arguing over dances and May Queens." As my experience with local student legislatures deepened, I often began inviting my listeners to agree that, given their current agenda, "student government is no damn good."

Reaching student governments; exposure to broader visions

I spoke to student governments in most of the forty-eight states, sometimes making three speeches in a single day. In my low-cost, frenetic travels, I often slept on buses, dormitory couches, and living room floors. Part of my $2,000 salary paid for some of the expenses. When back in Boulder, I slept in a spare bedroom at the rectory of a nearby Catholic church, thanks to arrangements made by Marion to aid an impoverished Protestant and a blessed student organization. In the summer weeks leading up to the Fifth NSA Congress, my new bride, Celia, and I shared a house with the newly married Roy and Bea Romer. As chairman of the Rocky Mountain Region the previous year, Roy had been an NEC member and had then moved on to law school. Some thirty years later, he fulfilled his aspiration of that summer by becoming governor of Colorado.

In these early years, NSA leaders often held differing views regarding the desirable major thrust of the association's activities. One group stressed concrete programs for students and student governments, such as the Purchase Card System. Others saw NSA's principal task as leading students to loftier levels of action in such areas as opposition to racial discrimination and the assertion of student rights. Al Lowenstein once said that if NSA stood only for concrete programs, it should fly a flag emblazoned with a cement mixer! Like most others, I believed that NSA should pursue both thrusts—to help member schools with practical programs of their choosing in order to meet their needs and keep them in NSA, and to raise their vision. One problem was that ever-changing student governments, while elected by and representative of their students, were imperfect vehicles through which to transmit practical programs to their student bodies.

Where local programs were desired, NSA congress workshops offered participants mines of information and many follow-up leads on numerous topics. However, it was the exposure of student leaders to broader visions and encounters with other able student leaders in exploring those visions that helped them see the greater value of NSA. These intangible rewards explain why many congress delegates subsequently said that they benefited greatly from the congress but found it difficult to bring that benefit back to the campus. They had been inspired by words that challenged them toward higher visions,[2] but then fell swiftly from the mountaintop back to prosaic campus life.

Educational issues and racial discrimination

NSA, representing about three hundred student governments serving some 800,000 students, was regarded as the most representative voice of American college students. Whether we or any other single organization influenced the outcome of any national policy affecting higher education is another matter. Rather, the value of NSA's addressing such issues was largely internal—as a national forum where representative student leaders could debate, refine, and express their views and foster consideration of these issues on many campuses.

However, in the area of racial discrimination in higher education, NSA's impact was real. The association provided a stimulus on a number of campuses for antidiscrimination initiatives and for the larger desegregation efforts that followed. In the South, some NSA regional meetings were among the first that brought students from black and white colleges together in integrated gatherings.[3] A number of student leaders returned from NSA congresses inspired, for the first time, to address racial discrimination in fraternities, sororities, and elsewhere on campus.

Racial discrimination was not subtle in those days. In my travels to the South to expand NSA membership, I was persistently assaulted with visual evidence of Jim Crow practices, which showed how much America would have to change to meet NSA's goal of total colorblindness. I left one meeting with a student government in Louisiana so enraged that I sat in the rear of a bus until its driver convinced me that the bus would not move until I did. In more rational moments, I used NSA's anti-IUS stance and the moral foundation of NSA's opposition to racial discrimination to blunt the hard core of opposition at Southern universities.

An alternative to IUS

Al Lowenstein had given a speech at the Stockholm Conference of Western national student unions in December 1950 in which he called for steps toward the formation of a new international student organization to oppose the IUS.[4] His unvarnished attack on what he referred to as the Soviet imperialism behind world Communism and the IUS caused the conference formally to censure the speech because of its political nature; in fact, most conferees privately shared this view, as I was to learn later. Al's speech caused great controversy within the association leading up to the fourth congress and deepened the division among that year's elected national officers.

An important issue at that congress, at which I was elected, was the position that NSA should adopt at the next International Student Conference (ISC), scheduled to take place in Edinburgh in January 1952. The second ISC was designed to be a follow-up to the Stockholm meeting. Various of Al's opponents argued that he was highly impolitic to employ strong anticommunist language; that a solely Western student union was undesirable; and/or that NSA should not abandon efforts to develop a peace-enhancing dialogue with the IUS and communist bloc students. Personal animosities between several national officers exacerbated the shades of policy differences between the warring camps.

The Resolutions adopted at the Congress:

- were critical of the IUS;
- opposed formation of a "Western Union of Students"; and
- opposed the creation of any new framework for international student cooperation that could not enjoy the support of students in the less-developed world.

This left substantial leeway to the new officers if they could agree on a course of action. Moreover, that congress had made it clear that among NSA officers, the president was no longer the first among equals, but NSA's chief officer and spokesman.[5]

After talking with foreign national student union leaders early in my presidency, it was clear to me that a noncommunist alternative to the IUS could be formed only by avoiding public anticommunist rhetoric such as Lowenstein had used at Stockholm. Such language created problems for student unions in the Third World and for key Western national student leaders. While the latter opposed the IUS, their memberships included sizable left-wing contingents. They also wished to avoid jeopardizing the hope that a new organization could reach students unions in Asia, Africa, Latin America, and the Middle East.

International Vice President Avrea Ingram and I had been elected as representing opposing camps. He was the candidate of NSA's international establishment, centered at Harvard and opposed to Lowenstein. I had publicly opposed his election. However, as we came to know each other during the autumn, we found ourselves sharing similar views on strategy and tactics and became close friends.

At Edinburgh, Avrea and I worked with national student union leaders from twenty-four other countries to establish the International Student Conference as an annual event and to create its Coordinating Secretariat of National Unions of Students (Cosec). Key players in addition to Avrea and me included: Fred Jarvis and John Thompson, respectively current and past presidents of the National Union of Students of England, Wales, and Northern Ireland; Olof Palme, president of the Swedish National Union of Students (who later became prime minister of Sweden); and the presidents of the national unions of students of the Netherlands and France. We all saw the IUS as an unreformable tool of the Communist Party of the Soviet Union and a barrier to practical, nonpartisan cooperation with student unions in the Third World.

Together, we sought to form an alternative to the IUS with fewer organizational trappings and more limited powers, thereby making it less vulnerable to political attack from the left. It was agreed that the secretariat of the new organization would be located in Leiden, the Netherlands. The Secretariat, Cosec, would carry out the program adopted by the ISC, under the oversight of a Supervision Committee elected by the conference. NSA and the four other national student unions cited previously were elected to the five-member Supervision Committee.

Five months later, at a meeting of the Supervision Committee in June, Jarl Traneus, a former president of the Swedish union, was elected secretary of Cosec. The committee also agreed that I would become assistant secretary upon completion of my NSA presidency, thereby providing Cosec with a two-member staff. I received word of my election just prior to Celia and my wedding in Indiana on June 15, at which Al Lowenstein was one of our ushers. Once again my plans for graduate school were postponed.

The Fifth NSA Congress at Indiana University

The Fifth NSA Congress was held at the University of Indiana, August 18-27, 1952. Its theme was "The Student and the Crisis in Education," which reflected our view of the current state of higher education and our role in its future. We sought to use a November 1951 *Time* magazine cover story on the "Silent Generation" to challenge our member students to action that would nurture a "significant generation."

The Congress was preceded by the Second Annual Student Body Presidents Conference. This gathering was an effort to involve more student government presidents in NSA and to prevent local "NSA Committees" from implementing well-intentioned but ineffective agendas somewhat removed from their student governments. The First College Newspaper Editors Conference was held at the same time, to provide these opinion leaders with information on NSA goals and programs.[6] Both conferences helped NSA gain support from key campus leaders and were continued in later years.

The tone of the fifth congress differed from that of its predecessor. The staff was unified. NSA had survived a downsized year and had achieved membership gains, notably in the South, that more than offset losses.[7] The congress warmly endorsed the work of the Edinburgh Conference, issued a detailed critique of IUS partisan political activity, and overwhelmingly rejected sending an NSA delegation to an IUS "unity" meeting scheduled to take place in Bucharest shortly after the congress.

Toward the end of the congress, a number of us prevailed on Dick Murphy from the University of North Carolina to run for president and on Avrea Ingram to run again for international vice president. Both were easily elected. Dick later became a long-time senior officer of the Democratic National Committee and was an assistant postmaster general in the administrations of Presidents John Kennedy and Lyndon Johnson.

With the association still operating on a shoestring budget, the Congress approved moving the national office from Boulder to Philadelphia, where another offer of rent-free space would put the full-time national staff, now increased from two to three, on the East Coast, where the bulk of representational activity was required.

CIA contact with NSA

After the congress, Celia and I prepared to leave for Holland and Cosec. Accounts by others notwithstanding, it was then that I was contacted by the CIA. I was informed that the funds obtained from several sources during my presidency for foreign travel by NSA representatives were CIA funds, which had been covertly channeled through these sources. I also was invited to consult with CIA representatives about future funding for NSA and for Cosec's plans. Later, I was able to learn beyond any shadow of a doubt that it was in the latter part of 1951, during my term of office, that the CIA began its sustained financial support for NSA's international program.[8] The immediate impetus for this involvement was the Berlin Youth Festival in summer 1951, which was sponsored by the IUS and its sister front organization, the World Federation of Democratic Youth.

Personal reflections

My NSA experience decisively influenced my life. It deepened my appreciation for the values of individual freedom, democracy, and social justice inculcated in me by my parents; my sense of Christian values; and my understanding of why America had fought World War II. NSA inserted me into the public square. It introduced me to a number of outstanding young people who shared similar values, many of whom became life-long friends. It directed me into international activity, which became my vocation until age forty, when the assassinations of Martin Luther King, Jr., and Robert Kennedy shifted my vocational focus from international to domestic economic and social problems.

More specifically, it was Ralph Dungan, a member of NSA's first staff and a special assistant to President Kennedy,[9] who in April 1961 named me to the President's Foreign Aid Task Force, which created the Agency for International Development (AID). After three years as director of the AID Mission to Peru and eight months as deputy U.S. ambassador to the Organization of American States in Washington,D.C., I was brought to New York in 1969 by Eugene R. Black, former president of the World Bank and a member of a commission appointed by President Kennedy, of which I had been executive secretary in 1962-63. That led to my appointment as banking commissioner in New York by Governor Nelson Rockefeller. In 1972, I became founding chairman and CEO of the Depository Trust Company, a national clearinghouse for the settlement of U.S. securities transactions.

This checkered and challenging career grew out of personal associations and interests established in my NSA years.

William T. Dentzer, Jr., was director of the U.S. AID Mission to Peru, New York State Superintendent of Banks, and chairman and CEO of the Depository Trust Company. He holds a B.A. from Muskingum College.

END NOTES

1 *Editor's note:* Despite extensive efforts, the Anthology Project has been unable to trace Marion Andert's later career.

2 See Harold Taylor, p. 888.

3 *Editor's note:* Among such regional meetings were those held in 1947 at the University of Texas, Austin (March, Texas-Oklahoma); Emory University, Atlanta (November, Ga.-Ala.-Fla.); Lynchburg College, Virginia (December,Va.-W.Va.-Carolinas), Southwestern at Memphis (November, Ky.-Tenn.) and in 1948 at Louisiana State University (LSU)—although the latter meetings took place only after a vigorous referendum campaign at LSU, which gained nearly two-to-one approval from the students to hold an interracial meeting (see p. 454). The YM-YWCA and National Federation of Catholic College Students, as well as other religious college student groups, were holding interracial intercollegiate meetings regularly in those years. All of these meetings (except that at LSU) were held without overt publicity. College newspaper articles reporting the meetings did not call attention to their interracial character. See Francis, p. 433, Peoples, p. 425, Proctor, p. 969, Murphy, p.975.

4 See the excerpts from Lowenstein's ISC Stockholm address, p.562.

5 The issue of staff authority was first raised at the third Congress in 1950, see p. 268.

6 See "NSA and the College Press," p. 477.

7 *Editor's note*: Membership as reflected in the annual congress reports shows total college affiliation as having grown from the 1951 low point of 225 at Minnesota to 275 at the 1952 congress at Indiana. Membership in the fourteen traditional Southern states rose from 20 to 29. For the total period of this book, the figures are:

	Total	South	
1946	307	39	Chicago Conference
1947	351	44	Constitutional Conv., Wisconsin
1948	295	35	First Congress, Wisconsin
1949	312	34	Second Congress, Illinois
1950	232	29	Third Congress, Michigan
1951	225	20	Fourth Congress, Minnesota
1952	275	29	Fifth Congress, Indiana

8 *Editor's note:* See "Covert U.S. Government Funding of NSA International Programs," p. 565.

9 See Dungan, pp. 174 and 909.

PICTURE CREDITS: *Then:* Fourth National Student Congress, August, U. of Minnesota,1951. *Now:* 1994 (*Both, author*).

WILLIAM T. DENTZER, JR.

Background: I was born August 29, 1929, in Rochester, Penn., and graduated in 1951 from Muskingum College in Ohio. After serving as president of the National Student Association in 1951-52, I spent a year in Europe establishing the Coordinating Secretariat of National Unions of Students. Thereafter, I attended law school at Yale University and the University of Pennsylvania. I then entered the U.S. Army in 1954 and worked at the Central Intelligence Agency.

Later Career: I joined the Agency for International Development (AID) in 1961, serving as special assistant to the agency's first two directors and to the U.S. coordinator of the Alliance for Progress. In 1963, I was executive secretary of a commission named by President Kennedy and headed by General Lucius Clay to review the U.S. foreign economic assistance program. From 1965 to mid-1968, I was director of the AID mission in Lima, Peru. Upon returning to Washington, D.C., I was deputy representative, with the rank of ambassador, to the Organization of American States and the Inter-American Committee of the Alliance for Progress.

I moved to New York early in 1969 to be executive director of the New York State Council of Economic Advisors and was appointed by Governor Rockefeller in April 1970 as New York state superintendent of banks. In 1972 I became founding chairman and CEO of the Depository Trust Company (DTC), a post held until my retirement in 1994. The DTC is the national clearinghouse for the settlement and custody of trades in corporate and municipal securities.

Family and Interests: My wife, Celia, and I live in Larchmont, New York, and have five grown children. I am a member of the boards of Muskingum College, the Larchmont Public Library, the Custodial Trust Company, the Bretton Woods Committee, and other nonprofit groups. I am an elder and former president of the Board of Trustees of the Larchmont Avenue Presbyterian Church.

The SILVER and GOLD

AN INDEPENDENT NEWSPAPER

Official Publication of the Associated Students of the University of Colorado

Fifty-Eighth Year — Boulder, Colorado, Friday, September 21, 1951 — Vol. LXII No. 160, Z69

Frosh Registration Sets New Record

The largest freshmen class in University history will conclude new student week activities Saturday with a pre-game pep rally and pep club seats for the football game.

The 1,750 freshmen will receive their final orientation and learn school yells at an all-school rally on the quadrangle tonight. At this time they will become acquainted with University traditions.

New Band Performs

... that new student week has served to successfully launch the freshmen on their new careers.

NSA Moves National Offices To Boulder; Headquarters Represent 195 Colleges

National Student association headquarters will be moved to the University in about two weeks from the previous capitol site at the University of Wisconsin in Madison, Wis., John Warren, campus president of NSA, announced yesterday.

A University delegation bid for the capitol at the National Student congress held at the University of Minnesota Aug. 20 to 29. Attending the fourth national convention were 600 students representing over 195 colleges and universities across the country.

Warren said NSA President Bill Dentzer and Executive Secretary Marion Andert will move into the old Coloradan office, Memorial 12, as soon as the equipment arrives from Madison. Both will spend full time in the office assisted by some part-time secretarial help from this area.

The Coloradan will move to the north garret of Memorial, Warren explained. Their new premises will include part of Independent Student association's room and part of the north balcony, which will be enclosed.

Warren stated that the new national capitol will be "a great help to the University and an honor, as it does represent over 600,000 students."

Center Of Administration

All administration between national headquarters and any of 195 member schools will come to or leave Boulder, he said. Considerable international correspondence is also expected.

The University delegation to the congress outbid teams representing the University of Chicago, Illinois, Wisconsin, Miami, Georgia Tech, New York Metropolitan area, and Cleveland. Cost estimations for the Boulder site ran substantially lower on almost every item.

Nine Convention Delegates

Delegates to the convention were ...

Boulder, Colorado, Thursday, September 27, 1951 — Vol. LXI, No. 1

Dentzer, Newly Elected National NSA Head From Ohio, Directs Business From Memorial Offices After October

William T. Dentzer, newly elected president of National Student association, will arrive in Boulder about Oct. 20 or 21 to set up the new national headquarters.

John Warren, campus president of the NSA, said the new office facilities will be ready for him at that time.

Eric Erickson, student union commissioner, reported that remodeling would have to be done on the north balcony of Memorial building before the Coloradan would vacate their office, which is intended for NSA.

Past Regional Chairman

Dentzer, 22, was an Ohio regional chairman before being elected at the fourth National Student congress. He was graduated from Muskigum college, New Concord, Ohio, and intended to enter the Woodrow Wilson school of international relations at Princeton university this fall.

Other national officers will remain in their areas and correspond with Dentzer here at the capitol. They are:

National Officer List

Sylvia Bacon, junior at Vassar college, vice-president of student affairs; Rollo O'Hare, senior at Wayne university Law school, vice president of educational affairs; Avera Ingram, graduate student at George Tech and Harvard university, vice-president of international affairs; and John Haley, senior at Emory university, vice-president of student government.

Marion Andert, former executive secretary of the National Newman Club federation, was appointed executive secretary of NSA. She will be employed in the headquarters here until January 1953.

PICTURED ABOVE in their new national headquarters in Memorial building, are NSA's President Bill Dentzer and Executive Secretary Marion Andert. The national site was recently moved from University of Wisconsin in Madison, Wis., to Boulder. Miss Andert and Dentzer were, in their own words, overwhelmed by the beauty of this part of the country and gratified by the friendliness of the University students.

Boulder, Colorado, Tuesday, January 15, 1952

Dentzer Visits Europe, Rio Before Returning To States

Bill Dentzer, president of NSA, is completing a tour in Europe before attending the first Inter-American Student congress from Jan. 15 to 22 in Rio De Janeiro.

Dentzer began his tour by attending the Second International Student conference in Edinburgh, Scotland. Cooperation among the non-communist students of the world was discussed at the conference held Jan. 3 to 8.

Avrea Ingram, international vice-president, accompanied Dentzer. The conference was attended by delegates from all over the world.

Promotes Understanding

Dentzer is continuing his tour in Europe so that he can contact student leaders to promote better understanding and cooperation between students of America and European countries.

The NSA president will meet other delegates in Rio De Janeiro on Jan. 15 and will attend the first meeting of the Inter-American Student congress. Other delegates will include Ingram, Godfrey de Castro and Helen Jean Rogers, NSA executive secretary in 1948-49.

Purpose of the congress is to aid the growth of understanding and assistance between the students of the Americas by work in solving common problems.

And Still Another Meet

Dentzer will return to the United States on Jan. 24 and will attend the American Council on Education on Jan. 25 and 26 in Washington, D.C.

After the Washington conference Dentzer will attend the third UNESCO conference which will be held at Hunter college. NSA will be in charge of workshops on college organizations at this conference.

Dentzer will return to Boulder on Feb. 4 before attending more conferences throughout the country during February.

NSA IN BOULDER. U. of Colorado welcomed NSA to campus and the *Silver and Gold* provided extensive coverage throughout the year.

"FREEDOM ISN'T SOMETHING TO BE STORED AWAY. IT HAS TO BE EARNED EVERY DAY"

MUSKINGUM COLLEGE, located in New Concord in Eastern Ohio, about 50 miles West of Wheeling, WVA, was first chartered in 1837, became coeducational in 1854, and came under the jurisdiction of the United Presbyterian Church in 1877. By merger with Ohio Central College, Warren G. Harding, 29th President of the United States (1921-23), became its most famous alumnus. Bill Dentzer, who put the college on the map in the student government world, provided advice to incoming students in its 1950-51 handbook (right). His election to NSA was featured in the 10/27/51 issue of the *Muskingum College Bulletin*. The *Bulletin* cover shows a portion of the Muskingum campus. In photo right from left: Dr. Robert N. Montgomery, college President, Dick Ferguson, NSA Ohio regional chair, and Bill Dentzer. (Photos Courtesy Muskingum College Library)

Greetings by President Student Council

Muskingum is one of the few colleges in America that can look back on the development of student participation in extra-curricular activities and see this activity progress to a point near its fruition.

Many years ago, certain "liberals" conceived the cock-eyed notion that students were capable of setting some of their own regulations, under proper supervision, of course. Their more conservative brethren on college administrations saw this as one more opportunity to keep students out of trouble by letting them do a little harmless work under the complete domination of the college officials.

As time passed, the concept grew more prevalent that students had the ability to analyze their problems and perhaps determine a desirable course of action to satisfy their needs. This concept reasoned that by allowing students to do this, they could gain experience and confidence in the representative democracy in which they were being fitted to live.

At Muskingum, we have moved beyond even this stage. We have reached the realization that students as well as faculty and members of the administration must work together in solving mutual problems, making a more effective educational community, and building a basis of democratic human relationships.

Students are granted the privilege of having the opportunity to live up to their rights as individuals. But each privilege carries with it a responsibility.

Each of us must realize that if he is to have the privilege of acting as an individual, he must take the responsibility of intelligent investigation and effective democratic action. Freedom isn't something to be stored away. It has to be earned every day, else it becomes meaningless and is soon lost. We must realize our responsibility, for if we do not, we do not deserve the privilege of a student voice in campus affairs.

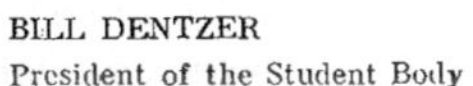

BILL DENTZER
President of the Student Body

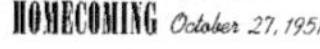

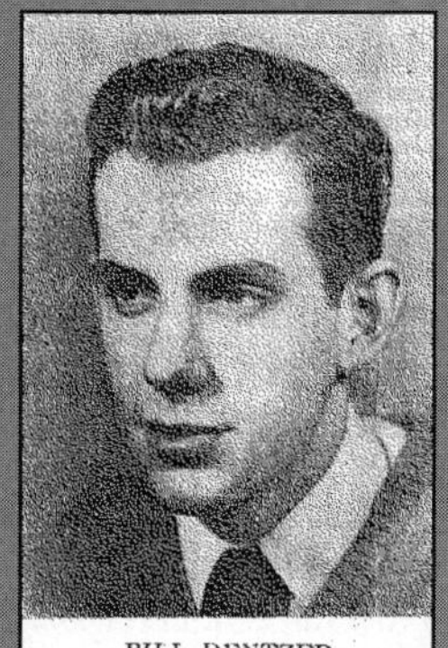

BILL DENTZER
President Student Council

Muskingum Man Heads National Students Association This Year

Left to right: Dr. Robert N. Montgomery, Dick Ferguson, regional chairman NSA; William Dentzer, president of the National Student Association.

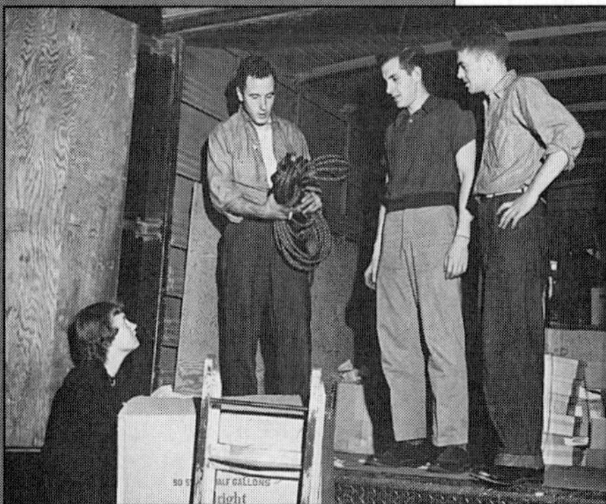

DENTZER MOVES NSA TO BOULDER. October: Loading the truck in Madison, WI from left are: Marion Andert, Executive Secretary, Joe Rodgers (Illinois Institute of Technology), Bill Dentzer, and Navy Radioman-2d Class Elmer Brock (former 1950-51 NSA Educational Affairs V.P.). Andert, Dentzer and Brock drove out to Boulder afterwards.

BUILDING THE NSA. Photos from left above: 1) Post-Congress 1951. Elmer Brock (La Salle C.), 1950-51 NSA VP Educational Problems, James Zucker (U. of WI), acting PR Director, Al Lowenstein (U. of NC), 1950-51 NSA President, Bill Dentzer; 2) Spring 1952 Bill Dentzer at Marylhurst C., OR, with students; 3) August 1952. Dentzer, left, with Ted Harris (1948-49 NSA President) and Al Lowenstein at the Indiana Fifth National Student Congress. (Photos 1,2: Lynch. Photo 3: WSHS)

From small college idealism to big convention politics

2. Candid Reflections of a Candidate

Kenneth R. Kurtz
Swarthmore College, Pennsylvania
Chair, Pennsylvania Region, 1950-51

Editor's note: This essay has been prepared by the editors from transcripts of an interview conducted with Ken Kurtz in Lexington, Kentucky, in October 1998, with the addition of material researched in Pennsylvania regional college newspapers and USNSA archives.

I knew that I had lost the election as NSA president—by seven votes, the closest in NSA history—even before the official results were announced. The winner, Bill Dentzer, was sitting only a few rows behind me in the hall. I don't think Bill knew he had won, but I had been keeping my own tally as the regions reported, and my system showed I had lost. I got up and went over to Bill, sticking out my hand, and offered him congratulations as the new president. He looked surprised,[1] but just then the official results were announced from the rostrum and he smiled as the hall erupted in a noisy reaction.

Why had Bill won? Maybe, more to the point, why had I lost?

A contrast in candidate support

We both came from small schools, so there was no obvious big school–small school split. That had often been rumored in NSA, but I had seldom seen evidence of it. If there were geographic favorites, I don't remember them. Most regions reported a split vote, but then most NSA regions were split—between liberal and conservative students, between public and private schools, between religious and non-religious schools—and even between coed and noncoed colleges. Most regions had a mix of these elements and it showed in their split votes.

It was rumored I was the more liberal of the two candidates. Probably true. It was rumored some Catholic schools were supporting Bill as a result. Probably true. It was rumored some of the Deep South schools, especially the state universities, wouldn't vote for me because of my feelings on integration. (If so, they got a Tartar in Bill, who supported the civil rights movement also.) Having presided over the Pennsylvania Region, with its heavy contingent of "small you-know-whats," many of which strongly supported me and "spread the good word" about me to other Catholic schools, I was pleased to see the vote I got in many areas where these schools were important. ("Small you-know-whats" were small Catholic girls schools, and there was a blue zillion of them in NSA.[2] They did the work. They were in the trenches. They could be counted on wherever NSA had a project, as I learned early in the Pennsylvania Region of NSA, or PRUSNSA.)

Still, there was no denying Catholic influence since the early days of Chicago and Madison. Catholic students and their advisers had played a major role in creating NSA and deserved a lot of credit from the rest of us.[3] Many of our student meetings turned into philosophical bull sessions, discussing religion and everything from civil rights to Cold War relations. While the viewpoint from the Catholic schools was not monolithic, even from the small you-know-whats, there did tend to be differences between them and people of my own backoround—WASP, small town, a student at a coed liberal arts school. NSA was unparalleled as a forum, a meeting point, a bull session for these types of discussions. We may not have settled anything, we may not have convinced anyone, but boy—did we discuss!

"Liberals" versus "conservatives"

And so I may have been labeled, probably accurately, as someone out of step with the mainstream of more conservative delegates, whether conservative for religious, social, economic, or other reasons.

I well remember one Met New York regional meeting during the Congress I attended. A fellow Swarthmorean and I, while at the 1949 Illinois National Congress, started dating two fellow delegates from the Midwest.

My date was a tall brunette from a "small you-know-what" near Chicago. Ralph's date was a short blonde with an Irish name from a Lutheran school in Minnesota—not too well known within NSA. Because Swarthmore was considered "simpatico" with the liberal part of the Met New York delegation, the two of us were invited to attend a secret strategy conference. We had never been invited to such a gathering, a type unheard of at our small Quaker school. So we went and took our dates with us.

It was a short caucus. Soon after we entered, discussion seemed to trail off and the meeting adjourned. The motion to do so was made by a skinny guy from City College of New York (CCNY). We were disappointed not to have had a greater opportunity to hear the debate over issues to come up on the floor the next day, but were assured we had just come too late. My date straightened us out. The skinny guy had recognized her as from a Catholic school and spread the word, and the liberal caucus had assumed she was a "spy" and cleared out. (The Met NY conservative caucus, heavily attended by Catholic school delegates, was also meeting that night.) Naive me! But that was my upbringing and my Swarthmore education. You took people as they were, and always thought the best of them until proven otherwise.

Swarthmore also cost me the election

Following the nominating speeches in the presidential election, the regions huddled around the hall, and when the roll call began, each reported its votes between Bill and myself. When the Pennsylvania Region was called, I had arranged for the vice chairman to report our vote. I already knew it was split. We voted by secret ballot, but I had already learned that the two Swarthmore delegates, officers of our student council, had been talking against my candidacy and would presumably vote against me. Neither of them ever talked to me, during the convention or since, even though I knew both of them fairly well. For whatever reasons, they opposed my candidacy. When word of this reached me, carried by friendly delegates from "small you-know-whats," they were surprised at my seeming calm. I simply told them that at Swarthmore we voted our consciences, and if theirs led them to vote against me, that was the way it was.

Transparency in voting

This was a time of the "unit rule" in the two major national political party conventions, a pernicious rule whereby the entire state's vote would be cast for the one candidate who won a majority of the delegation. Some NSA delegates supported a "unit rule" for NSA, but we adopted a completely democratic approach and cast our region's vote just as it was.

Now, some Dentzer supporters wanted the full convention to know I was not going to get a unanimous vote of the region I chaired. (I never thought I would. Ours was too diverse a region, and I had also screwed up some things during my chairmanship, which was well known.) But some people apparently felt they could influence the regions that hadn't yet voted by making public what anyone who knew PRUSNSA already knew—that we voted as we wished. They also wanted to make known that my own school's delegation was going to vote against me.

Someone got to the floor to ask that, alone of all the regions, the Pennsylvania region "be polled"—shades of the Mississippi delegation at the 1948 Democratic National Convention. This had never been proposed at any previous NSA meeting. The chair, Al Lowenstein, I think, seemed unsure if this could be done. (It couldn't under NSA procedure or Robert's Rules.) While the request was being decided, I asked for the floor on a point of personal privilege and was recognized.

I told the convention, as objectively as I could, that as a past convention parliamentarian, such a request was out of order. But I went on to tell those who didn't understand the request what was behind it: "I will not get a solid vote from the Pennsylvania delegation." I told them:

> We don't operate that way. We vote, each of us as we see fit, and that includes the delegates from my own school. I have not asked them to support me because I am a Swarthmore student. I have not asked anyone in Pennsylvania to vote for me because I am from this region. There is no need to have an unnecessary floor fight over parliamentary procedure because what these people seek to tell the rest of you is that PRUSNSA is split. We are. We always have been. We always will be. We are students who vote not by blocs but by consciences.

At least that's what I tried to tell them. It was true and I hope, clear. The polling of our delegation request was denied. The voting continued. I lost.

Al Lowenstein's controversial influence

Two other factors may have caused this. I can prove neither, but here they are.

That summer, in 1951, Al Lowenstein was ending the most contentious year as president that NSA had ever seen.[4] I believe he viewed the convention as an opportunity to vindicate his policies of the past year. I didn't. I did my poli-sci major darnedest to separate the man from the policy. Sometimes I agreed with Al. Often I did not. I spoke to the policy, not *ad hominem.* My views were well known. I don't think Bill's were that well known.

Al introduced Cold War politics to NSA. Many of us opposed splitting the international student movement, as our elders and nations were doing on their level. We were not ignorant, but wished to try harder to avoid that split. Many of us felt that Al wrapped himself in the flag at every opportunity. He was certainly a powerful speechmaker. He led the conservative group, and I suspect he tarred me, since I opposed his foreign policy views, as "that commie sympathizer," "that liberal from Swarthmore." No one ever specifically told me that such a talk was made against me, but several people have indicated that they feel it was.[5]

So Al, and more particularly Al's supporters, felt Bill was more sympathetic to their man than I was. I'm sure Bill got Al's and his followers' support, and that more than anything probably cost me the election.

Putting to rest suspicions of CIA influence

Years later, when "the skunk was on the table," when *Ramparts* magazine revealed the role the CIA had played within NSA—it was rumored the CIA had taken an even earlier role than has been substantiated, by supporting Dentzer. These rumors get a little credence because of Bill's later work for U.S. government agencies with CIA connections. However, Bill has denied that the CIA relationship with NSA began during his tenure as president, and I believe him.

Further, I have a hard time understanding how the CIA would exert any influence in our election. Would they call some student aside and threaten the loss of some U.S. grant if he or she didn't vote for Bill? Would they say "No federal job for you if you support Kurtz?" Highly dubious. Highly.

Had any outside agency, especially a governmental agency, tried to pressure me on a matter of principle, I would have told them where to go. I would hope most NSA delegates would have done the same. I don't believe it ever happened.

So Bill Dentzer was elected, along with a good staff of veeps (vice presidents) and others. Most of his staff were long-standing friends of mine, people I supported, people whose views were very much in accord with mine as to NSA and its future. Bill had a good year. His major accomplishment was healing the breach that Al had created and restoring the NSA national office as an effective body.

As it happened. I attended the NSA conference the next year, when Bill's term was ending. I heard his speech about the need for compassion, for understanding, for acceptance of all the different social, ethnic, religious, racial, cultural, and political views within NSA, for—as he put it—the need for "love" among us all. I couldn't have put it better myself: indeed I doubt that I could have put it half as well as he did.

Compliments to the winner for a job well done

When that session was over, I went up to Bill and congratulated him on his talk. I had been in graduate school for the past year and largely "out of the loop." But I had kept track of how NSA had fared in a general way. I felt that he had healed many of the rifts of the previous year and had done a good job as president.

And I told him so. I told him, as things had worked out, I felt he had made a better president than I would have. I meant it then. I mean it now.

Ken Kurtz has been a radio and TV broadcast journalist since 1955, working with stations in Augusta, GA, Charleston, SC, Wayne, IN, Greensboro, NC, and Lexington, KY. He currently hosts public affairs and news shows for Kentucky PBS.

END NOTES

1 I had been active in NSA longer, and was probably better known.

2 *Editor's note:* Out of an estimated 200 U.S. Catholic colleges at the time, Catholic college membership ranged from early high totals of 75 down to 65 out of from over 300 down to 250 members of NSA during its first five years—about 25 percent of its institutional membership. About 60 to 70 percent of the Catholic membership were small women's colleges, thus tilting the student body populations represented by these colleges to probably under 100,000, or less than 10 percent of the average more than 1,000,000 college students represented by NSA during the period 1947-1952. These figures are based on the editor's tally of membership lists appearing in the rosters of this volume. See also Des Marais, p. 734, Dungan, p. 909, and roster, "The Catholic Colleges," p. 914.

3 See Des Marais essay, p. 734, on the Catholic colleges and NSA.

4 *Editor's note:* See p. 283 for a recollection of Al Lowenstein, NSA's fourth president, and p. 562 for Lowenstein's Stockholm speech presenting his views on IUS and the Cold War. Lowenstein's presidency and influence are also discussed by Joan Lynch, p. 270, Shirley Neizer, p. 280, Bill Dentzer, p. 299, and Herb Eisenberg, p. 522. Lowenstein's influence in the University of North Carolina, the Carolinas-Virginia region, and the national scene also is mentioned in a number of other essays, as noted in the index. See especially Murphy, p. 976, and Hunsinger, p. 990.

5 *Editor's note*: It is useful to note that Ken Kurtz's use of the term "conservative" in this essay is a distinction made within the "liberal" camp, of which Lowenstein, an active Students for Democratic Action (SDA) member, would consider himself a part.

PICTURE CREDITS: *Then:* c. 1951, Swarthmore College Yearbook (Swarthmore Archives). *Now:* c.2001 (Author).

KENNETH R. KURTZ

Early years. Born Weston, WV, December 25, 1929. Graduated from Weston High School.

Education and military. AB, political science, Swarthmore College; attended Columbia University Graduate School, 1951-53. U.S. Army Signal Corps, Ft. Gordon, GA, 1953-55.

Career highlights. Broadcast journalist: 1955-present, includes News Director of radio stations in Augusta, GA, Columbia, SC, Charleston, WV, and TV stations in Charleston, Fort Wayne, IN, Greensboro, NC, and Lexington, KY. "Retired" work includes hosting public affairs and news shows for Kentucky Education TV (KET), the statewide PBS network.

Family: Married Juanita (Jonny) Frye. Three daughters, Jeannie, Elizabeth, Margaret.

KEN KURTZ: YOUTH OF OTHER NATIONS HAVE MORE POLITICAL POWER

Vassar Miscellany News 12/5/51

K. Kurtz Discusses Role Of US's Youth

Youth's place in United States foreign policy was the subject under consideration at a meeting of Public Discussion Dec. 3. Leading the discussion was Mr. Ken Kurtz, graduate student in political science at Columbia. Mr. Kurtz is a member of NSA and the United World Federalists.

Role of Youth

Mr. Kurtz showed that the young peopel, whom he defined as those under thirty years of age, in other countries, play a much more important role in the government and policies of their country than do the young people of the United States. One reason for this is that there is so much illiteracy in some countries that a minority of young people, who are the literate segment of the country, can dominate the illiterate majority. Another reason is that new states which have been forming, need new people to form their government, to give technical assistance, to be teachers, and to do other jobs of importance. These new nations are calling on their young people to fill these needs. The youth groups of other nations also have more power than those in the United States, and they have more political power. Mr. Kurtz gave numerous examples showing to what a great extent foreign nations are influenced by their youth.

Contact

Because of the great power that they have, it is necessary to establish friendship with them. Mr. Kurtz stressed the fact that young people from the United States make very good ambassadors to the young people of foreign countries. American students find a ready audience abroad that is eager to learn about democracy and America. Mr. Kurtz also recommended the exchanging of students and correspondence with students of foreign countries. International student relief is another way to show good will. This consists of raising money to help students abroad with their studies, to help them buy books and necessary supplies.

TIME MAGAZINE, 1951: U.S. YOUTH IS NOWHERE NEAR THE ROSTRUM

Agnes Scott News 11/7/51

TIME Appraises U. S. Youth, Reports on 'Silent Generation'

(Released by TIME Magazine, New York)

In the November 5th issue, TIME analyzes American youth in a provocative report titled "Portrait of the Younger Generation."

This is the first nation-wide appraisal of what this younger generation is thinking and saying about itself, its country and its future. An exclusive survey by TIME correspondents gathered opinions from every section of the country. Across the U. S. they observed and questioned the younger generation as well as its teachers and guardians. TIME's working definition of the younger generation is age 18 to 28.

This article is of such scope that it will be of unprecedented interest not only to the younger generation itself but to older generations, educators, parents — everyone. It discusses what this younger generation thinks about religion, sex, government, war, marriage, jobs, ambition and many other subjects.

In general, TIME reports that American youth is silent, fatalistic, security-minded, conservative, grave, morally confused, tolerant of almost anything and blaming no one for its troubles.

Girls Want a Career —

"American young women are, in many ways, the generation's most serious problem," reports TIME. "Large numbers of them feel that a home and children alone would be a fate worse than death and invade the big cities in search of a career. There is every evidence that women have not been made happy by their ascent to power (equality with men)," says this report. "They are dressed to kill in femininity. The bosom is back; hair is longer again." The consensus now is that the career girl has retreated to the point where she would like, if possible, to have marriage AND a career.

'Silent Generation'

"The most startling fact about the younger generation is its silence," says TIME. "With some rare exceptions, youth is nowhere near the rostrum. It has been called the 'silent generation.' But what does the silence mean? What, if anything, does it hide? . . . they do not speak out for anything." Professors find that they "cannot get a rise out of the docile note-takers in their classes."

This generation does not blame anyone for the state of their world, not on parents, politicians, cartels, etc. The fact of this world is war, uncertainty, the need for work, courage, sacrifice. Nobody likes that fact. But youth does not blame that fact on its parents dropping the ball. In real life, youth seems to know people always drop the ball. Youth today has little cynicism because it never hoped for much."

TIME'S "SILENT GENERATION" In November 1951 *Time Magazine* published an in-depth survey of American youth in which the term "Silent Generation" originated. It was widely discussed and quoted at the time and still is. *Time* promoted the publication in advance, issuing releases that were sent to all colleges, reprinted in the *Agnes Scott News* 11/7/51 (above), as well as placing ads in the press (right: from U. of Colorado Archives). It is presented here alongside Ken Kurtz's discussion of U.S. youth at the top of the page as well as in parallel with the NSA story.

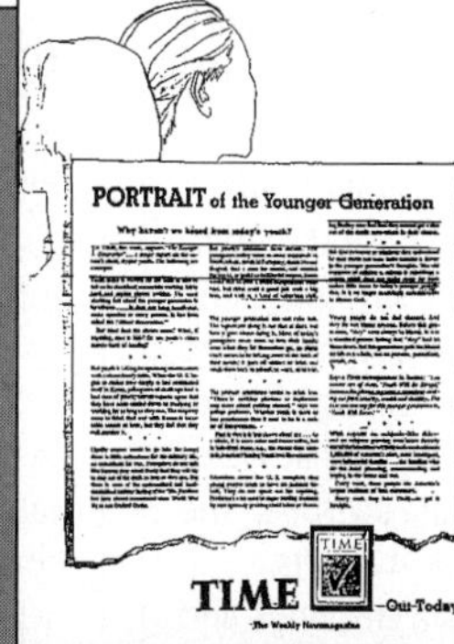

MINNESOTA CONGRESS SECRETARIAT STAFF

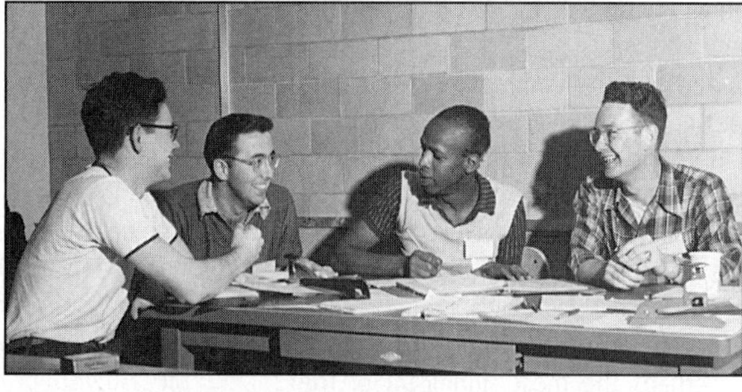

TAKING CARE OF BUSINESS: from left: Gene McLoon (La Salle College, Philadelphia, PA), Don Lynch (Illinois Institute of Technology, Chicago), Clifford Sheets (Wayne State U., Detroit, MI), Walter Kaiser (Illinois Institute of Technology). (Joan Lynch)

The smearing of innocent men and the driving from public life of honorable persons

The Challenge and the Test of McCarthyism

William T. Dentzer, Jr.
Muskingum College, Ohio
NSA President, 1951-52

Editor's note: This editorial is adapted from one which appeared in the March 1952 issue of NSA News. *Bill Dentzer presided over NSA's most vulnerable year of survival, during which, as he reports in his essay, full-time staff was reduced to two and the association moved from Madison to Boulder. Despite these constraints, Dentzer maintained a full calendar of organization efforts while also producing three issues of a revived* NSA News *(whose publication the Congress had suspended the previous year). The association used the* NSA News *to continue to promote its programs, as well as to provide a national voice for its affiliates as they contended with anticommunist crusades and collateral attacks on the association. In this editorial, Dentzer states the equal importance of upholding basic freedoms while being vigilant against communism. This editorial, along with others, illustrates the determination with which NSA held to the principles of its constitution and the readiness of its leaders to stand publicly in its defense.*

According to the results of the Associated College Press national poll of student opinion, taken recently throughout the nation and shown [here], it seems that more than half of the American college students are where they are because of the desire to get a good job, while the desire to gain more knowledge is secondary. This in itself is a sad commentary on the students of the United States.

And yet, the commentary would be sadder if the national student community closed its eyes to the outbursts of hysteria around the country. For it would be a sign that we lack faith in ourselves as people, and worse, faith in the strength that is our freedom, our sense of fair play and our heritage of respect for differing opinions.

Perhaps the most significant of the recent outbursts was leveled at Sarah Lawrence College in Bronxville, N.Y., where Dr. Harold Taylor of the NSA National Advisory Council is president of what is generally recognized as one of the outstanding educational institutions in the United States.

The great significance of events there was not only the ridiculousness of the charges made and the vicious manner in which they were passed, but the failure of the student community to take the responsibility of defending their college against false accusations.

More than ever, the words spoken last year by former President Allard K. Lowenstein at the *Philadelphia Bulletin* Forum need to be heard:

> If we are not against communism just because it is fashionable to be against communism in America, we shall have to know what it is we are against and why. And then we will know why we cannot tolerate the most obnoxious of the practices we have just said we are against, even when these practices are committed in the name of fighting against communism.

In the struggle of promise and accusation, our behaving like the communists we denounce strengthens us not one bit. Quite the opposite; it gives supporting evidence of what we have been declaring are communist lies about how we live.

If American students and the American people are to have any chance of success in the struggle to save [a] great section of this planet from falling prey to the siren song of a little group of evil men bent on ruling the world, they shall have to stand with equal strength and courage for the things which they hold dearest. They will have to understand and proclaim that the dismissal of men accused of no crimes is not anti-communism but communism, that the smearing of innocent men and the driving from public life of honorable persons who dare to speak the truth is a vital concern of free students.

McCarthyism presents a challenge and a test: If we do not combat this kind of lie with a vigor equal to that with which we combat Red lies, we are on the way to losing not only the right to win but the very possibility of winning. It is not as though the choice of whether or not to tolerate McCarthyism is difficult. To tolerate McCarthyism is precisely to weaken ourselves in the global struggle against tyranny. The way to answer the communist promises of more freedom for the people of the world is to show that we will not abandon piece by piece our cherished freedoms to anyone who yells the magic words, "I hate Communists."

I think it was Sinclair Lewis who said, "if fascism ever comes to the United States it will come in the name of anti-fascism." Surely the last two years have made it clear that if communism ever comes to the United States it will come "cloaked and daggered" in the guise of anti-communism, proclaiming national unity, wrapped in flag-waving Americanism.

Someone has been kind enough to remind us that Abraham Lincoln once said: "If this nation is ever destroyed, it will not be from without, but from within."

THE POLL

College students from all parts of the country were asked to pick either one or two choices which came closest to their reasons for attending college. The results:

1. A good job after college	53%
2. Desire for more knowledge	36%
3. To find a mate	2%
4. It was "the thing to do"	3%
5. The parents wished it	4%
6. None of these	2%

* * * *

In the same poll students were asked to rate the education they have received so far in college. Here are the results:

1. Excellent	17%
2. Good	57%
3. Fair	23%
4. Poor	2%
5. No opinion	1%

American Legion Attacks Sarah Lawrence College

Mark Emond

(Excerpts from an article in NSA News, *May 1952)*

Whittaker Chambers and Louis Budenz testified on Aug. 16, 1951, that Joseph Barnes, teacher at Sarah Lawrence college, was a Communist. Budenz said Barnes was known to him as a Communist, and Chambers said the teacher had been a member of an underground unit.

The Americanism committee of the Westchester county American Legion heard the report on April 9, 1952, as testimony which had been given before the senate sub committee on internal security. Their immediate action was to demand dismissal of Barnes.

THE NEW YORK TIMES observed that Sarah Lawrence was "again under fire." The college had had two previous scrapes with the American Legion. The Legion claimed that the newspapers were hanging up a "paper curtain concealing the facts of our dispute with Sarah Lawrence college."

The disputes started in October, 1951, when the Legion read in the American Legion magazine an article by Louis Budenz which attempted to throw suspicion of "harboring subversives" on 15 colleges and universities, among them Harvard, Cornell, Amherst, Columbia, Pittsburgh, New York University, California, Chicago and Sarah Lawrence.

* * *

The barbed inquiry came to Sarah Lawrence from Donald E. Woodhull on November 23, 1951, after the meeting with the board of trustees had not satisfied the Americanism committee. He wrote:

> As commander of the Leonard Morange post of the American Legion, Bronxville, I ask you, as president of Sarah Lawrence college, to write to me just as soon as you can an unequivocal answer to the following two very simple questions:
>
> 1. At the present time has Sarah Lawrence college on its faculty any known Communist party members or sympathizers?
>
> 2. At the present time would Sarah Lawrence College tolerate on its faculty any known Communist party member or sympathizer?
>
> THIS IS A CLEAR-CUT LETTER and I seek to get a clear-cut "yes" or "no" to the two simple questions above, and I am not interested in any qualifications whatsoever.
>
> If I do not get such a clear-cut answer, I believe that the situation should have the fullest publicity.

* * *

THE AMERICAN LEGION criticized Harold Taylor, president of Sarah Lawrence, for having described Barnes as "a valuable addition to our faculty." When Barnes offered to resign from the faculty, according to the Legion, Taylor rejected the resignation.

In February, a plea for a Congressional investigation was made by Rabbi Benjamin Schultz of New York, Coordinator of the Joint Committee Against Communism in New York, who wired his request to John S. Wood, Chairman of the House Un-American Activities committee in Washington. No investigation followed.

Sarah Lawrence college throughout the disputes had been an eloquent spokesman of its cause. Though it and other institutions will probably be attacked again, the principles it advanced in answer to the Legion cannot be ignored or forgotten.

PRESIDENT TAYLOR and the board of trustees wrote:

> It is an essential part of good educational policy that a college ask for no orthodoxy in its teachers as to religion, politics, or philosophical theory. If it were otherwise, teaching would be done not by the faculty but by the governing board of the institution.
>
> The teacher would be a mouthpiece for the preconceived philosophy of the institution rather than a seeker for the truth about problems in his field of learning.
>
> It is in this refusal to exact an oath or to cross-examine the teacher as to political belief or to spy upon his political activities that the educator differs from the outsider who wishes to investigate college faculties. The latter fails to understand the necessity that the teacher be free to have and to express his own ideas, and that the teacher is not a person hired to follow certain rules and to advocate certain economic or political dogmas.

THE STUDENT NEWSPAPER at Sarah Lawrence reports in its 1/30/52 and 2/13/52 issues on the local American Legion chapter's challenge to the College. NSA strongly endorsed the principles of Academic Freedom as defined by the Association of American University Professors in NSA's Student Bill of Rights (see Appendix). In his editorial on the previous page, Bill Dentzer identifies McCarthyism as a threat to Academic Freedom.

THE CAMPUS

BRONXVILLE, NEW YORK, WEDNESDAY, JANUARY 30, 1952 Yearly Rate $4.00

Board Releases Policy Statement To Meet Attacks On Academic Freedom

Moral Indignation Of Faculty And Students Rises As Sarah Lawrence Is Attacked; American Legion Branch Submits 14 Questions

During the past two months the College has been attacked by various sources which have, in different ways, questioned Sarah Lawrence policy on academic freedom.

These have been a part of the malicious and unfounded attacks education has been meeting throughout the country. The moral indignation of Sarah Lawrence faculty and students, and of others who believe in freedom in education, continues to rise as more pressure is placed on this and other public and private institutions by demands of irresponsible and uninformed individuals to bar certain speakers from the campuses, to screen text books, to impose loyalty oaths and to investigate faculty mem-

Scarsdale, Englewood, Pasedena and elsewhere.

The November issue of American Legion Magazine carried an article about higher education in America written by Louis Budens, ex-communist. Sarah Lawrence was mentioned along with Harvard, Cornell, Amherst, M.I.T., Columbia, Pittsburgh, California and Chicago with the implication that all these institutions of higher education are encouraging subversion.

Allen Zoll, who has been linked to anti-semitic and pro-fascist activities for years, has just published an attack on women's colleges including, Wellesley, Smith and Sarah Lawrence as places where subversives are harbored.

The most recent attack on Sarah Lawrence has come from the

Board of Trustees, authorized by the Executive Committee, released to the American Legion and to the Press as well as to the students, faculty and Alumnae Council of Sarah Lawrence a letter summarizing the situation and stating the Board's policy on attacks from outside sources.

A widespread response from parents, alumnae, educators, Westchester citizens and students from other colleges has expressed admiration for the courageous stand the Board of Trustees has taken on the matter of these attacks.

The policy as stated in the above mentioned release is as follows:

"An educational institution must teach its students to think for themselves by giving them the knowledge on which to base judgments. The teaching faculty of Sarah Lawrence College is responsible for the development in students of intellectual indepen-

SARAH LAWRENCE COLLEGE, BRONXVILLE, NEW YORK, WEDNESDAY, FEBRUARY 13,

Student Council Affirms Faith In Principles of Academic Freedom as 175 Villagers Protest Legion Tactics

Hohly Declares SLC Principles Unassailable

"Only good can come out of any further investigation of the college because I feel that the basic principles for which the college stands, as set forth in the statement of the board of trustees, is unassailable," declared the Rev. Harold F. Hohly in an interview at Christ Church, Saturday. The citizens who signed the petition protesting the American Legion attack on Sarah Lawrence College were "rejecting

Signers Of Petition Challenge Right To Investigate

For several months community opposition to the American Legion's attack on Sarah Lawrence was silent, but with the Rev. Harold F. Hohly's public condemnation of Legion tactics, the flood gates were opened and local citizens rose in protest against what they considered the tyranny of the obsessed few.

One hundred and seventy-five

27 Representatives Of Student Body Pass Statement

The Student Council of Sarah Lawrence announced its affirmation of faith in the principles of academic freedom upheld by the faculty, administration and the Board of Trustees with the passage of a policy statement at last week's regular Thursday meeting.

"Council drafted this statement," said Glenna Brodsky, President of the Student Council, "because we believe that students are most

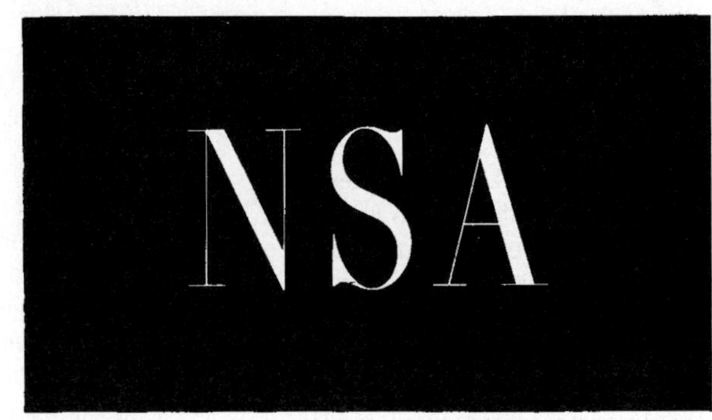

College Board Department

By Barbara Witten

A coed at N.Y.U. hops the rush-hour subway to her evening class in accounting. Her counterpart at Vassar walks across campus to an afternoon child-study conference. An Antioch student, eight times during her stay at college, puts away her physics texts, packs her clothes and leaves school for a co-op job. Each girl lives a separate, isolated life from the others—sings her own school songs, roots for a different football or chess team, hands over to the bursar a different sum of money for tuition. Do they have in common anything more than their mutual concern over finals and the right date for Saturday night?

A good deal more, say the coeds who help pay their college's membership dues in the National Student Association. Students everywhere want to be responsible for their own actions. They hope to be taught by capable, inspiring professors. They need job counseling and they worry over the high cost of college. By banding together and exchanging information, students learn from each other how to set up a strong, democratic student government, how to tell the college administration what they think of their professors, how to run a career conference or a secondhand bookstore.

Some schools have little to learn, a lot to give in the way of practical ideas and suggestions. They join NSA because they believe it's their job to help other students strengthen their means to an education. And because they want to have a say in the national policies of an organization that represents over 650,000 students. Through NSA they work for academic freedom, help give qualified people of all races and creeds a chance to go to college.

NSA schools band together for another reason. They feel that students can do as much—and in some ways more—for international understanding as any other nongovernmental group. Many are free to travel, work or study abroad three months of the year if the cost is within their reach. They can send textbooks, clothing and information to colleges in Asia, Europe and Africa, send their leaders to discuss educational aims and student problems with the future teachers and government officials of the tinderbox spots of the world.

For a little over four years now, NSA-ers have worked toward these aims. Member schools elect or appoint delegates to the annual ten-day Congress to talk out and vote in National policies and elect the National officers. A president, on a year's leave from undergraduate or graduate study, four vice-presidents and an executive secretary administer NSA's programs, send information to regional and campus groups, make arrangements for the next Congress, run the mimeographing machines and the finances. Regional representatives meet between congresses and make policy decisions. On member campuses, an NSA chairman shuttles information from the regional or National to campus groups, attends regional meetings, directs some projects, suggests others.

How much each college helps itself through NSA depends in great part on whether it elects or appoints an active, alert NSA chairman. The campus chairman's job is to know what problems his school has and what it needs to solve them. He may write to the National for some of its thirty-odd how-to publications; he must listen, ask questions and bring back from meetings new ideas his college can use.

Schools with poor or nonexistent student governments have learned the most from NSA. Delegates to the 1947 National [Continued on page 153]

FOURTH NATIONAL STUDENT CONGRESS AT MINNESOTA. *Mademoiselle*, which reported on NSA's founding in 1947, revisited the Association in a comprehensive review of its accomplishments, positions on issues, leadership problems, strengths and weaknesses, noting that observers "who watch students in action at their Congress know they accomplish more than they think they do, that they work with judgment and maturity not often matched by their elders."

Ivy League, aggie school, small college, large u.:
special and different? Yes . . .
but all with problems and goals that every student shares

A delegate to the National Student Congress at the University of Minnesota waits for recognition from the Chair during debate on Universal Military Training. Students from schools in her region and adult observers look on

WALLACE KAMAN, BLACK STAR

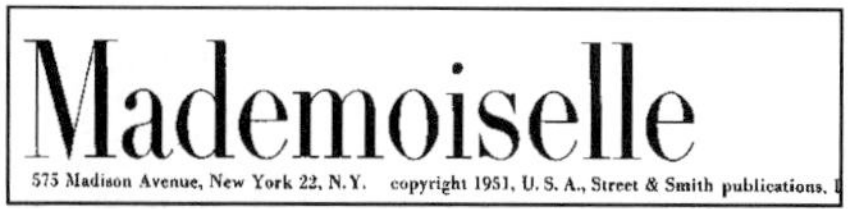

Mademoiselle
575 Madison Avenue, New York 22, N.Y. copyright 1951, U. S. A., Street & Smith publications,

Student Congress from the U. of Bridgeport, for example, brought back to campus plans for setting up Bridgeport's student government. Using NSA's files of student government associations, Muskigum College in Ohio revised its own s. g. constitution, organization and meeting procedures. But even schools with strong student governments learn from NSA. New Jersey College for Women's NSA stirred up interest in its government association by holding a pre-election town meeting on aims and issues. With NSA material, Berea College in Kentucky held a leadership conference, and Ursuline College in Cleveland gives its student leaders a noncredit course on parliamentary procedure.

Though anxious to have a say in how late they'll stay out at night, whether or not they'll keep cars on campus and what rules should govern college extracurricular groups, students leave most academic matters to their teachers and to the administration. The one big exception is faculty evaluation. With help from NSA, students at the U. of Michigan, Stout Institute, Marygrove, the U. of Miami, to name a few, have all graded their profs. Some campus NSA's have brought in honor systems. Grinnell's NSA suggested the idea, put it to a vote and lost. In the process, though, students took a look at what their school was trying to do and examined their own educational aims.

On a national scale, NSA has begun to have a say in academic and administration matters. The U.S. Office of Education and the State Department consult their officers on matters related to students. NSA joined the American Council on Education, has a representative on all committees concerned with student problems, and twice this year NSA officers spoke at Council meetings, told educators what they thought about acceleration and Universal Military Training.

Though many of its members expected NSA to be political—but nonpartisan—it sits on the fence in all but a few important controversial educational problems. It favors a system of Federal scholarship and fellowship aid. And students at the third Congress declared that "the hiring, firing and placing on tenure of academic personnel should be on the basis of professional competence and not on the basis of political, religious or social criteria. Standards for judging professional competence should be determined and maintained solely by the university community.... Interests providing financial support... should not have the power of infringing upon such academic freedom."

The association as a whole takes no formal stand on segregated schooling but NSA works hard to improve opportunities for Negroes to go to college. It is one of the sponsors of the National Scholarship Service and Fund for Negro Students; with four other organizations it held a seminar for students on discrimination in higher education. Some Northern schools wish it would do more; many Southern schools have never joined NSA because they feel it does too much. Perhaps its major accomplishment is bringing Negro and white students from all over the country to its Congress, where they sit down together and learn to know each other in committee meetings or at lunch.

To help fight the high cost of college, NSA worked out its Student Discount Service. Member schools send to the National for an outline of the plan and identification cards for its students, arrange with local merchants to sell goods to card bearers 10 to 20 per cent off. The plan won't work in many college communities. Merchants who are the college's sole resource for Kleenex or loafers often would lose money by giving a discount, gain no new customers in return. Some schools run it successfully: the U. of Miami, St. Catherine's, Mount St. Mary's, Wayne, Reed, Simmons, City College of New York.

Of all its activities, NSA's international programs have been the most successful. Each year it publishes a booklet listing opportunities in foreign study, work and travel, in one year sent abroad over eight hundred students through its own travel and study groups at a cost of less than seven hundred dollars apiece. NSA has a seat on UNESCO's national commission. It sponsors with other organizations the World Student Service Fund, through which U.S. students send books, clothing and money to colleges abroad and to the National Council for Placement of DP Students.

For the past two summers, student leaders from this country met with German student leaders to discuss educational aims and problems. The Rockefeller Foundation provided funds for these NSA-sponsored seminars in Germany.

The summer following the invasion of Korea, three NSA-ers attended, as nonmembers observers, the Prague meeting of the International Union of Students. There, with observers from a dozen or so nonmember Western nations, they sat tight-lipped while delegates of the Communist-dominated IUS staged a demonstration against the Western "imperialists," carried to the platform the "hero" of the day, a young North Korean delegate in a lieutenant colonel's uniform. After the demonstration the NSA team met with Western-nation observers and planned their strategy. For the rest of the meeting, their speeches were calm, careful answers to the Communist charges and their own objections to IUS—that the Communist bloc was using it for political ends rather than for doing what they could for student welfare. The Western observers won a small but important victory. Delegates from Asian and African countries took the NSA team aside and told them they'd gained new understanding of Western aims and objectives.

Until students of Asia and Africa join with them, student unions of North Atlantic Treaty nations won't start a new international student organization. Meantime, they met in Stockholm to talk over what they could do to help themselves and set up a plan for giving assistance and exchanging information with unions in undeveloped countries. To find out how U.S. students can work with students of Asia, Africa and South America, NSA teams traveled these areas and talked with student leaders.

In spite of its accomplishments, NSA is still far from being a full-grown movement of American students. At present, it represents only about one-fourth of the students in the country and some of its members are inactive or half-hearted.

Many schools stay out of NSA because of the cost. Though dues are prorated and the fee per student is low, the U. of Miami's ten thousand students, for example, spend around three thousand dollars a year for campus NSA projects, dues and the cost of sending delegates to the national Congress and to regional meetings. Miami thinks NSA is worth it, but many schools would expect good-sized, concrete returns on their money in the form of campus benefits. Others feel they can work out their own problems by themselves, see no reason to join NSA just to take part in its national and international projects.

NSA members are its own worst critics. They are easily discouraged by their organization's inefficiency or a fence-sitting stand it takes, by apathy or student isolationism back home on campus. NSA has internal problems too. Because they stay in office only a year—hardly enough time for even trained administrators to learn to be useful—students who run the National are often inefficient, always harried. In turn, poor leadership on some campuses and apathy on others hamper the National. One regional officer figures that the efficiency of the whole organization would double if each NSA chairman on each campus would only answer his mail!

Observers, however, who watch students in action at their Congress know they accomplish more than they think they do, that they work with judgment and maturity not often matched by their elders. Men and women from colleges of every size, kind and purpose sit down together for ten days to mull over academic freedom, how they can help the students of Asia, whether or not to take a stand on Universal Military Training. They debate among themselves, listen critically to what their fellow-delegates have to say, vote in policies and elect officers carefully and with intelligence. Through the Congress alone, through the experience it gives students in democratic leadership and action, NSA performs a valuable and successful function.

American people abroad...can do a tremendous amount of good for the free world

Student Programs for International Understanding

William T. Dentzer, Jr.
Muskingum College, Ohio
NSA President, 1951-52

Editor's Note: This article originally appeared in NSA's Student Government Bulletin and Report, *February 1953.*

It seems that the role of higher education in affecting international understanding generally has been overlooked, though people inside and outside of it have paid it periodic lip-service. It is encouraging to see real progress being made now. But if the role of higher education in this whole picture has been overlooked, how much more has the role of students been neglected! Soviet Russia surely hasn't overlooked the importance of students and student activities, and Hitler also realized their importance.

Student organizations across the world are doing a great deal which affects "international understanding." The Communist-dominated International Union of Students, professing to represent 5,000,000 students in 60 countries, has a tremendous program of activity. The IUS Secretariat in Prague, supported by the Iron Curtain governments, sends voluminous color-illustrated publications in many languages all over the world. This is the organization which was one of the sponsors of the East Berlin Peace Festival last summer, a gigantic rally attended by more than 20,000 young people from many countries. The Kremlin realizes the importance of capturing the minds of tomorrow and uses the IUS very effectively toward this end.

Almost every country in the world has a national union of students, their own counterpart of our U.S. National Student Association. Unlike the five-year-old USNSA, these national unions are often twenty years old and are well-established on the national scene.

Importance of student activity in underdeveloped areas

Student activity in the underdeveloped areas is especially important. Two out of the last three of Burma's prime ministers were students either during or immediately before the Second World War. All of the graduates of the Law School in Indo-China last June were judges by September. In the revolution preceding the latest one in Bolivia, the students hung the president of the Republic from a lamppost. I could tell you still more about other interesting student activities as we learned of them from South American students at the First Inter-American Student Congress, held this past January in Rio de Janeiro.

Illiteracy is high—90 percent often—in these areas. What students think there is important, for they make up a large portion of the literate population, and the literate groups lead the illiterate. It is because of this that our thoughts on international relations must not be only in terms of *now*, but also in terms of *tomorrow*. Tomorrow's international relationships are often made today; this, I think, should emphasize the importance of international student relations.

There is one more point which should be stressed before dealing with the problem of coordinating programs for international understanding. That is this: that voluntary groups in the United States often can do perhaps even more than the Department of State in effecting good international relations and friendliness toward the United States. The efforts of the Department abroad often are labeled as "government propaganda," but American people abroad acting as just plain persons who honestly are interested in peace, liberty, and democracy, and in helping foreign groups, can do a tremendous amount of good for the free world as they operate free from the label of "agent of the State Department."

I cannot begin to cover my subject in this short space of time, but I will sketch briefly (1) what NSA is doing internationally, (2) where the need for coordination of programs seems to be, and (3) what the most effective means of cooperation may be.

The international program of the National Student Association has expanded enormously this year and promises to expand even more next year.

NSA builds a global program

Perhaps the most outstanding part of the program lies in its cooperation with the International Coordinating Secretariat, established this past January in Edinburgh, Scotland, for the purpose of coordinating and assisting the programs of non-Communist national student unions in their operation. The Edinburgh conference itself was a big achievement. There, representatives of more than a million students, including delegates from Indonesia, Brazil, Iraq, Israel, Malaya, the Union of South Africa, Australia, Canada, the United States, Yugoslavia, and all of Western Europe, took a significant step forward in the field of international student activities in establishing the Secretariat.[1]

NSA also took part this January in the First Inter-American Student Congress, which marked the first time in history that the national student unions in most of the countries of the Americas had sent representatives to discuss common problems and possibilities for joint action. Though much anti–United States feeling was prevalent, the NSA representatives ultimately were well received. A Pan-American Student Bureau was formed as a result of the meeting to facilitate the exchange of persons and information. This is the beginning of a vast new field of closer cooperation among the students of the Americas.[2]

The National Student Association also has been active in sponsoring seminars in various areas of the world. This summer, for the third consecutive year, NSA will sponsor the International European Student Seminar, which brings together student leaders from the United States and Western European countries for a six-week session in Germany.[3] We are also in the process of exploring the possibility of a student seminar in Southeast Asia, and an NSA representative is now in that area. Next year may see NSA sponsorship of a similar seminar in the Middle East; difficulties this year made this impossible.

Working through the Harvard University Student Council, the *NSA International Student Information Service* is going out regularly to Southeast Asia and the Middle East as a technical publication on student activities and programs. Another bulletin, *La Vida Estudiantil (Student Life)* is a publication in Spanish by the NSA International News Center at Georgia Institute of Technology.[4] This newspaper, sent to Latin-American university student governments, is aimed at explaining American college life and activities by students.

Students Mutual Assistance Program

Potentially the most important of its international activities is NSA's work on the Students Mutual Assistance Program. This program, worked in conjunction with other Western European student unions, is fundamentally "Point Four" on the student level. Its purpose is to send technical information and technical teams of students experienced in such fields as engineering, medicine, social work, administration, agriculture, etc., to underdeveloped areas as advisers to student unions and student governments.[5]

NSA also operates the lowest-cost travel program in the United States as a service to the student community, providing opportunities to "Work, Travel, and Study Abroad" at prices within the reach of students. Each summer, more than 400 college students take advantage of this operation, which is run on a technical basis by full-time professional employees.[6]

There are many other international programs operated by NSA, too numerous to mention, including sending student teams to Latin-American universities, having representatives in Yugoslavia, Mexico, and at the UNESCO meeting in Paris, and running a "Pen Pals" center at Wayne University.

The association also has a representative on the U.S. National Commission for UNESCO, is a member of the Young Adult Council which is the American affiliate of the World Assembly of Youth,[7] sponsors the World Student Service Fund[8] along with several other groups, and is assisting a new group called International Development Placement Association,[9] a student group whose aim is to place young United States teachers in African schools for short-term service.

Foreign student exchange programs

NSA recently has become especially active in the field of international educational exchange.

It is evident that, for many years, foreign students have been coming to the United States with a language barrier, a difficulty in "conceptualizing," and many other handicaps, only to become engrossed in a four-year study of physics, chemistry, or engineering which keeps them from becoming fully acquainted with the educational community....

NSA has asked the Department of State and other agencies to consider a general type of plan whereby *student leaders* in foreign countries would be brought over to the United States for a period of about one year only. They would be placed under the charge of the student government at a college and the dean of students or foreign student adviser, who together would work out a program which would enable them to study, not any particular technical subject, but instead, the way we Americans live in our own sometimes crazy fashion.

* * *

The Department of State is often rather justly criticized for the lack of an "educational approach," though there are many indications that this is becoming a thing of the past.

This new approach is being tried on a pilot basis for the coming year. If it works, it will be spread no doubt to other countries and on an increased basis. The Institute of International Education also has given NSA the opportunity to select several incoming foreign students for such a program, while we are working directly with the Indian government on an exchange program in the Middle West.

With this emphasis on educational exchange, we are trying to impress on local student governments across the nation the importance of seeing that programs are worked out on campus to make those foreign students already on campus feel more welcome as our friends and more a part of the campus community. NSA emphasized this strongly when it was one of the leaders in bringing displaced persons to American campuses, and it is emphasizing it again. It is a real pity that so large a number of foreign students leave the United States with a feeling of some sort of disappointment, largely because of our own default of responsibility.[10]

* * *

Need for cooperation among various organizations

This much seems certain. An exchange center, a clearinghouse of information on the activities of organizations in this field of international cultural exchange, is needed badly. Such an agency could serve as a reference point for those organizations interested in this field. On the basis of information provided, various organizations could comment on and help improve the work of other groups in given areas; could provide certain contacts, for example, in geographical areas in which both are operating; and in general, work out bilateral or multilateral approaches on the basis of information on each other's work. Of course, this would be on a purely voluntary basis.

Cooperation is possible and is needed on a national level. But the information must be made available. The American Council on Education [ACE] has a Canada–United States Committee on Education. It could be that the ACE would want to use the week-end exchange programs working now between Canadian and United States universities in part of the work of this committee. Cooperation between the Institute of Student Personnel Services in Japan—which, incidentally, is doing tremendous work—and NSA with its contacts with Japanese student groups, can help the work of both. There can be cooperation on NSA programs in the Middle East and Southeast Asia, as is evident from the previous speakers' statements. On many cases, we can work together on certain legislative matters, for example, the amendment of certain provisions of the McCarran Act.

Some cooperation can take place also on the local level as members and member groups of organizations are informed by their national offices of the possibility for cooperation with the local groups of other organizations in the same vicinity.

It will be a big job to get something like this under way and keep it going. Unlike the Soviets, we cannot regiment any group nor force it to do what it may not particularly care to take the trouble to do. But I think all of us clearly see the real need for something to be accomplished soon. True, there will be difficulties, technical and otherwise, in bringing it to fruition. The important thing is that the need is clear and that the will is there; the way must surely follow.

END NOTES

1 See Dentzer, p. 301
Almanac, p. 1129.

2 See Farber, p. 606.

3 See Perkins, p. 603.

4 See Hunsinger, p. 990.

5 See SMAP, pp. 526, 635.

6 See Callahan, p. 673.

7 See WAY, p. 778.

8 See WSSF, p. 622.

9 See IDPA, p. 627.

10 See CRF, p. 688.

DENTZER: "THE NEED IS CLEAR. . .THE WILL IS THERE . . .THE WAY MUST SURELY FOLLOW"

USNSA Delegates Attend Congress At Rio

Three NSA Representatives Visit Celebration In Mexico

Three representatives of NSA attended the celebration of the 400th anniversary of the National Autonomous university of Mexico as guests of the Federation Estudiantil Universitaria (Mexico University Student Federation) in Mexico City, September 21-30.

Helen Jean Rogers, Claude Salomon, graduate of Colorado A&M, and John Langley, of the University of Texas, represented U. S. students at the celebration.

They presented a plaque to the were discussed, and the NFCUS conference voted to investigate the possibility of using the NSA Travel bureau as the channel for their students' summer trips abroad.

M. Jean de Margerie of Laval was elected President and will attend the Fifth Annual NSA Congress in August of 1952. Sydney L. Wax, University of Toronto, was elected International Activities chairman.

First Inter-American Meeting Of Students Aims For Better Hemisphere Relations

Delegates from the United States National Student association will represent American students at the First Inter-American Student Congress, to be held in Rio de Janeiro sometime in January or. February.

This Pan-American Student congress was called by the Unaio Nacional Dos Estudantes (National Union of Students of Brazil) and is the first of its kind in the history of student relations in the western hemisphere.

National unions of students from every country in the Americas are expected to send representatives to be addressed by the president of the Republic of Brazil and other outstanding figures.

The USNSA delegates include William Dentzer, president of the association; Avrea Ingram, international vice-president; Godfrey university and presently at Harvard law school, and Helen Jean Rogers, NSA executive secretary in 1948-49. At present Miss Rogers is in Rio as NSA's representative to the congress organization committee.

NSA Offers Stimulating Summer Travel

Prices Of Tours Range From $525 To $750

By ESTEE GORDON

NSA summer travel programs are well-known for providing the lowest cost opportunities for students to travel in Europe.

This in itself fits in with the aims of a student-serving organization. But, addition, the particular programs that NSA organizes are geared "to promote international understanding and fellowship."

THE TRAVEL PROGRAM enables people to meet in an atmosphere of friendship and good will, to travel together and live together in the intimate enclosure of a small group.

The travel program is a completely student-run operation on both sides of the Atlantic. The various national unions of students handle the arrangements in their individual countries and provide invaluable contacts both with students and with government leaders, outstanding educators, etc.

The direct and close cooperation el by rail, bus, boat and plane through Denmark, Sweden, Norway and Finland visiting Olso, Copenhagen, Stockholm, Malmo, Trondheim, Uppsala, Gripsholm, Jyvaskyla, Lahti, Helsinki and Abo. The trip will end with a week in Paris with excursions to nearby places of interest. The program lasts 45 days, costs $700, and sails on the SS Zuiderkruis.

IBERIAN TOUR

The first program in Spain and Portugal ever sponsored by NSA, this tour was organized by the Office du Tourisme Universitaire of France. Cities that will be visited there include Madrid, Toledo, Cordoba, Grenada, Seville, Mafra, Estoril, Caldas de Rainha, Nazare, Tomar, Salamanca, Valladolid, Valencia, Burgos, Vitoria, San Sabastian and Biarritz. In addition, the group will also travel extensively in Holland and Spain. This program casts $870 and sails

Trips Cover West Europe, Scandanavia

European Plane Tours Cater To Americans

NSA Sends 60 To UNESCO, Emphasizes World Awareness

The National Students association was represented by 60 student delegates at the Third National conference for the United Nations Educational, Scientific and Cultural organization held recently at Hunter college in New York City. The theme of the conference, sponsored by the United States Nation commission for UNESCO, was "The Citizen and the United Nations."

More than two thousand delegates from organizations and institutions of learning all over the United States met Jan. 27-31 to and travel and should investigate existing legislation designed to limit such activity.

4. ADDITIONAL emphasis should be placed on the exchange of foreign students for study in the United States, particular care being taken to promote association of these students with American students, as opposed to their segregation into isolated groups.

5. Greater use should be made of the abundance of foreign speakers available from consulates, diplomatic missions and the United Nations.

The final recommendation of the College Youth group concerned the atmosphere of fear and intimidation found in many college communities today.

IT READ: "In order to promote UNESCO activities on the college

German Seminar Now In Progress

NSA Receives $10,000 Grant to Run Similar Seminar In Southeast Asia

NSA's seminar score was one down and one to go as the fourth annual Congress began in Minneapolis.

At Seeshaupt auf Starnberger See in Bavaria, eight U.S. students chosen by NSA were discussing the importance of student self-government in a democratic education with some 30 students from the nations of western Europe largely Germany.

National Students Association Joins WAY; Prepares Way For Student Cooperation

NSA became associated with the World Assembly of Youth in December, 1951, when NSA's National executive committee voted to join the Young Adult council.

WAY was created at a conference held in London in 1948 by representatives of youth organizations from all over the world. Its objectives are:

1. To provide a channel through which the solidarity of world youth could be expressed;

2. To establish the Universal Declaration of Human Rights as the frame of reference for all young people and youth organizations;

3. To give real meaning to the principle that the desires, problems and concerns of any one social, economic, political or geographic grouping are the desires, problems and concerns of all.

tory. Soon after the London meeting, a Secretariat was set up in Brussels which guides the implementation of WAY's broad program.

WAY's members now number 42 national committees in North America, Asia, Africa, the Middle East and Europe. With help from WAY, these committees are steadily growing in program and representatives and other national committees are in the process of formation.

DEPENDENT OR COLONIAL countries are eligible to full and equal status in WAY and comprise half of the membership. More than half of the members are from so-colled underdeveloped countries. This structure is reflected in WAY's program which gives much emphasis to overcoming social and economic problems in underdeveloped areas.

Latin Americans Receive News Of American Colleges From INC

Long before Aug. 28, 1951, the day on which the USNSA congress passed its official resolution stating the establishment of an International News center, the plans for such news center were being completed in Atlanta, Ga.

Thus the International News center was established in Atlanta, Ga. The officials of the International News center are members of the NSA schools in the Atlanta area. The four schools are Agnes Scott college (private women's nonsectarian college), Morehouse college (privately controlled college for Negroes), Emory university (private Methodist church-controlled university), and Georgia Institute of Technology (a technical university supported by the state).

Conference Plans Secretariat For Worldwide Student Unity

Delegates from 23 countries voted unanimously at the Edinburgh International Student conference Jan. 3-10 to create a Coordinating Secretariat to strengthen international student cooperation.

The Secretariat would promote cooperation through coordination of the work of national student

Resolving not to form a western union of students, the conference ensured that the Secretariat would not have executive powers or extensive scope, stating:

"The Secretariat shall be the administrative agency to ensure the implementation of the decisions of the International Student con-

Meeting in the cold Scottish winter at the University of Edinburgh and the Grosvenor hotel, where the conference participants were housed, the conferees also voted to place the calling of the next International Student conference in the hands of the NSA and the Swiss national union.

NSA NEWS covers the growing international outreach of NSA. From top: Rio, Mexico, both 11/51. Summer Travel, UNESCO, WAY, INC, Secretariat, all 3/52.

Staff, Advisers, Regional Chairs, Colleges

1951-52 National Organization

(As presented in the Fifth National Student Congress Directory)

NATIONAL OFFICERS

President
William T. Dentzer, Muskingum College, Ohio

Vice President, Student Affairs
Sylvia Bacon, Vassar College

Vice President, Educational Affairs
Rollo O'Hare, Wayne University, Michigan

Vice President, Student Government
John Haley, Emory University, Georgia

Vice President, International Affairs
Avrea Ingram, Harvard University

Executive Secretary
Marion Andert, University of Minnesota

REGIONAL REPRESENTATIVES TO THE NATIONAL EXECUTIVE COMMITTEE

(Compiled from 1951 Congress Directory and 1951-52 NSA letterhead.)

California, Nev., Hawaii
Peggy Bradish
Mt. St. Mary's College

Georgia, Ala., Fla.
William Kennedy
Georgia Inst. of Tech.

Great Northwest
Joan Long
Marylhurst College

Gulf Coast
Ronald Rousseve
Xavier University

Illinois
Manfred Brust
University of Illinois

Iowa-Nebraska
Patricia Donohue
Clarke College

Kentucky, Tenn.
Daniel C. MacIntosh
University of Louisville.

Mason-Dixon
Eileen O'Connell
Trinity College

Michigan
Leonard Wilcox
University of Michigan
Sheldon Otis
Wayne University

Minnesota
James N. Grathwol
College of St. Thomas

Missouri-Kansas
James Swafford
Central Missouri St. College

New Jersey
Walter J. Palasits
St. Peter's College

New England
Janet Welsh
Smith College
John Fox
University of Massachusetts

Metropolitan New York
James Murphy
Manhattan College
Anthony Peluso
Manhattan College

New York State
William Dewey
Niagara University

Ohio, Indiana
Richard Ferguson
Muskingum College

Pennsylvania
William Klisanan
Pennsylvania State College
Marie Minnick
University of Pennsylvania

Rocky Mountain
Patrick Eagan
Regis College

Virginia, Carolinas
Barry Farber
University of North Carolina

Wisconsin
Ann Doyle
Mount Mary College

NATIONAL ADVISORY COUNCIL

Dennis L. Trueblood, Chairman
Student Activities Counselor, Indiana University

William B. Birenbaum,
Director of Student Activities, University of Chicago

Very Rev. Vincent J. Flynn
President, College of St. Thomas

Frank P. Graham
United Nations Mediator

Kenneth Holland
Director, Institute of International Education

Althea Kratz Hottel
Dean of Women, University of Pennsylvania

Charles S. Johnson
President, Fisk University

Gordon J. Klopf
Dean of Students, Buffalo State College

Allard K. Lowenstein
1950-51 President, NSA

Mrs. Carl W. Meinecke,
Dean, Colby Junior College

Eleanor Roosevelt
U.S. Representative, UN General Assembly

Harold Stassen
President, University of Pennsylvania

Harold Taylor
President, Sarah Lawrence College

1951-52 Roster of Colleges
Fourth National Student Congress

(Institutions in italics attended with visitor status.)

California-Nevada-Hawaii
California School of Arts and Crafts
College of Holy Names
Immaculate Heart College
Los Angeles City College
Loyola University
Mills College
Mount St. Mary's College
University of California, Berkeley
University of California at Los Angeles

Georgia-Alabama-Florida
Agnes Scott College
Emory University
Georgia School of Technology
Morehouse College
University of Miami

Great Northwest
Eastern Washington College of Education
Washington State College
University of Idaho

Gulf Coast
Arkansas A.M.&N. College
Our Lady of the Lake
Southern Univ., LA
Xavier University

Illinois
De Paul University
Mundelein College
North Central College
Rockford College
Roosevelt College
Rosary College
University of Chicago
University of Illinois
Wheaton College

Iowa, Nebraska
Clark College
Grinnell College
State University of Iowa
Wartburg College

Kentucky, Tennessee
Berea College
East Tennessee State College
Fisk University
University of Louisville

Mason-Dixon
Catholic University of America
College of Notre Dame
Dunbarton College
Hood College
Howard University
Loyola College
Trinity College
University of Baltimore

Michigan
Central Michigan College of Education
Marygrove College
Siena Heights College
University of Detroit
University of Michigan
Wayne University

Minnesota
Augsburg College
Carleton College
College of St. Benedict
College of St. Catherine
College of St. Teresa
College of St. Thomas
Concordia College
Gustavus Adolphus College
Hamline College
Macalester College
St. John's University
St. Olaf College
University of Minnesota

Missouri-Kansas
College of Emporia
Fontbonne College
Kansas Wesleyan University
Mt. St. Scholastica College
Pittsburg State College
University of Missouri
Webster College

Metropolitan New York
CCNY, Business Day
CCNY, Business Evening
CCNY, Main Day
CCNY, Main Evening
College of New Rochelle
Fordham College
Fordham Univ. School of Education
Good Counsel College
Hunter College, Day
Hunter College, Evening
Iona College
Manhattan College
Manhattanville College
Marymount College
New York University, Education
New York University, University Heights
New York University, Washington Square
Queens College
Sarah Lawrence College
Vassar College

New Jersey
College of St. Elizabeth
New Jersey College for Women
Rutgers University

New York State
D'Youville College
Eastman School of Music
LeMoyne College
Niagara University
Rosary Hill College
St. Bonaventure College
Siena College
Skidmore College
State U. of NY, Inst. App. Arts & Sci., Buffalo
University of Buffalo
University of Rochester–Women
University of Rochester–Nursing
William Smith College
Nazareth College
State U. of N.Y.–Geneseo

Northern New England
American International College
Bennington College
Boston College
Boston University
Dartmouth College
Emmanuel College
Framingham State Teachers College
Garland School
Harvard College
Harvard Graduate School
Massachusetts Institute of Technology
Mount Holyoke College
Mt. St. Mary College
Newton College of the Sacred Heart
Radcliffe College
Regis College
Simmons College
Smith College
University of Vermont
Wellesley College
Wheaton College

Ohio-Indiana
Baldwin-Wallace College
Cleveland College
College of Mt. St. Joseph
College of Wooster
Flora Stone Mather College
Hiram College
John Carroll University
Muskingum College
Notre Dame College
Ohio State University
Ohio Wesleyan College
Our Lady of Cincinnati
Saint Mary of the Woods College
Ursuline College
Youngstown College
Capital University
Denison University
Indiana Central College
Indiana University
Lake Erie College
Miami University
Ohio University
Purdue University
Wittenberg College

Pennsylvania
Albright College
Bryn Mawr College
Chestnut Hill College
Lehigh University
Mercyhurst College
Mount Mercy College
Pennsylvania College for Women
Pennsylvania State College
Seton Hill College
St. Vincent College
Swarthmore College
Temple University
University of Pennsylvania
University of Scranton
Marywood College
University of PIttsburgh

Rocky Mountain
College of Idaho
Colorado A. & M. College
Colorado College
Colorado State College of Education
Colorado Women's College
Highlands University
Mesa College
Trinidad State Jr. College
University of Colorado
University of Denver
University of Utah

Southern New England
St. Joseph's College
University of Bridgeport
Yale University

Virginia, Carolinas
Duke University
Randolph-Macon Women's College
Sweet Briar College
University of North Carolina
Virginia State College
Women's College of Duke University
Clemson A.&M. College
Duke University
Greensboro College

West Virginia
West Virginia Wesleyan
Beckley College
Marshall College
West Virginia Institute of Technology

Wisconsin
Mount Mary College
Stout Institute
University of Wisconsin
Milwaukee Downer College

First Hydrogen Bomb Exploded and Queen Elizabeth II Crowned Ellison's *Invisible Man* Published and *High Noon* opens

Dwight Eisenhower elected President of the United States, defeating Adlai Stevenson. Egypt erupts in anti-British riots, King Farouk abdicates, General Mohammed Naguib seizes power. 16,000 people escape from East to West Berlin during month of August. Albert Schweitzer wins Nobel Peace Prize. Labor leaders Philip Murray and William Green die. "Waiting for Godot" opens. Peale's "Power of Positive Thinking," Ferber's "Giant," and Hemingway's "Old Man and the Sea" published. John Dewey dies. The films "Limelight" and "Moulin Rouge" open. "I Saw Mommy Kissing Santa Claus" and "Your Cheatin' Heart" are on the charts. Nobel Prize to Selman Waxman for discovery of streptomycin. Rocky Marciano wins world heavyweight boxing championship. Illinois defeats Stanford in the Rose Bowl, 40-7. New York Yankees win World Series against Brooklyn Dodgers, 4-3.

Source: Adapted from citations in Bernard Grun, *The Timetables of History* (Simon and Schuster, 1991

BUDGETING NSA'S MILESTONES: 1951-52

Proposed Budget, 1951-1952

INCOME		
Dues from member schools		$10,000
Payment for services to INC		700
		$10,7000
Receivables	$ 300	
Less: Payables	2,025	
	$1,725	1,725
EXPENDITURES		$ 8,975
Salaries		
President		$ 2,000
Executive Secretary		2,800
Travel by President		800
Telephone and Telegraph		200
Rent		00
Insurance		85
Legal Fees		100
Dues to Educational Associations		105
Subscriptions to Educational Magazines		65
Clipping Service		90
Printing		730
Office Supplies and Mailings		
Advisory Amounts		
Mailing	440	
Stencils	80	
Office Supplies	980	
	1,500	Control Amount 1,500
Expenses of National Commissions		500
		$8,975

COMMISSION ON NATIONAL FINANCE

The Congress observes that the USNSA is faced with a limited budget for the ensuing fiscal year, that grants and gifts have been singularly lacking, that inefficiency and overlapping of authority in the national structure have led to unnecessary expenditures, that the absence of stringent control has contributed to overall inefficiency and caused a dearth of operating records, in particular that the lack of financial records has impaired the operation of a number of commissions at this Congress.

The commission believes that the USNSA cannot function properly during the coming year without the fulltime services of the president.

The commission urges that the Congress budget a salary for a full-time president.

Minority Report

Add article III D 5 "which must provide an item for stenographic assistance to the Executive Secretary.

United States National Student Association
Statement of Receipts and Disbursements for the period
October 1, 1951 through July 31, 1952

NATIONAL OFFICE FUNDS

Balance beginning of period		$ 834.01
Receipts:		
Dues received from member schools	$ 10,463.00	
General Publications	895.99	
Transferred from Congress Fund	2,308.35	
Contributions	230.00	
Edinburgh Account	84.64	
Travel Services	2,000.00	
Speaking services	100.00	
Refunds:	92.34	
Educational Projects Inc.-- Fee	177.78	
Transfer from Educational Projects Inc.	3,900.00	
International Commission Administration Fee	165.00	
Miscellaneous items	673.55	
Sale of furniture	122.00	
Gross Receipts		21,262.65
Total Cash Handled		22,096.66
Disbursements :		
Salaries	4,904.99	
Postage and Express	1,699.84	
Travel	2,428.96	
Mimeograph supplies	2,401.92	
Telephone and Telegraph	592.46	
Deposits with the U. of Colorado	50.00	
Business office charge, legal, accounting	2226.41	
Dues and Subscriptions	135.95	
Printing	1.569.09	
Refunds	242.01	
Commission operation expenses	291.51	
Back Taxes and penalties	2,834.08	
International Affairs Commission Administration	400.00	
Transfer to Congress Fund	503.35	
Repair travel Department Loan	1,013.60	
Theft of receipts	69.10	
National convention registration fees and exhibits.	46.66	
City of Madison : rent with facilities.	82.10	
Cash short (as compared with list of dues)	408.00	
Miscellaneous small items	1,110 .01	
Total Disbursements		21,009.44
Cash Balance : July 31, 1952		$ 1,087.22

STAFF BEGAN THE YEAR WITH AN $8,975 BUDGET (exclusive of its travel office) with which to continue to build NSA'S franchise and find other revenue sources. The move to Boulder provided free rent and office services. By fiscal year's end CPA Vinton S. Curry (842 Grant Place, Boulder, CO) reported dues, receipts, and salaries almost exactly as budgeted, and revenue increases that enabled a $1,000 surplus after $21,000 spent. The 5th Congress was launched at Indiana. NSA maintained its presence in Europe and Latin America and laid the foundation for a move to Philadelphia the next year (Pt. 6, S. 1). (Document sources: SHSW archives, Sylvia Bacon. Reproduced here are portions of mimeographed NEC and Congress reports.)

PART 2

Domestic Programs: Toward Equal Rights and Opportunities

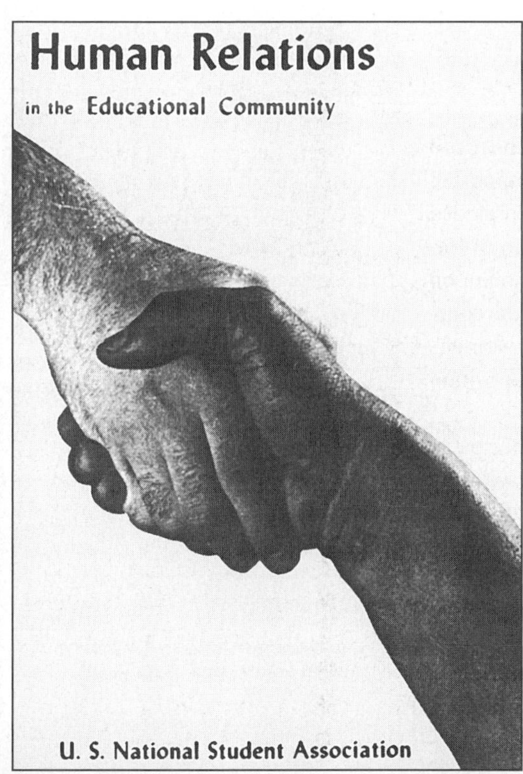

SON, WISCONSIN, JANUARY, 1949 — Price 5 Cents

NEC Adopts Legislative Goals; Urges Federal Aid Support

Asks U.S. to Aid Private Colleges

Travel Booklet

Study, Travel, Work Abroad, Summer 1949, a booklet contain-

NSA Backs Bills Vital to Students

Exec Committee Takes Action In Academic Freedom Cases

Both Parties At Fault In Puerto Rican Riots

A National Executive Committee (NEC) decision that both adminis-

No Just Reason Found To Dismiss Olivet Prof

NSA last week requested President Aubrey L. Ashby and the

NSA Seeks to Improve Civil Rights on Campus

A subcommission on Academic Freedom designed to strengthen

Six Pages Today — No. 95

Highest Court Orders OU to Admit Negro

WASHINGTON, Jan. 12—(AP)—The Supreme Court held Monday that Negroes are entitled not only to receive in state insitutions any sort of educational training that whites can get in such schools, but also to get it as quickly as any other group.

Strict application of the order would give the state of Oklahoma just three days to admit a Negro girl, Ada Lois Sipuel, to the law school at the all white University of Oklahoma, or set up separate and equal facilities for her.

A new semester in which white students can enter begins January 15. There is no Oklahoma state law school for Negroes now. The applicant already has been waiting two years while the case was in litigation.

Sweatt's Lawyers Silent on OU Case

PART 2

Domestic Programs: Toward Equal Rights and Opportunities

College enrollments more than doubled in the school years following VE and VJ Days in 1945. Much of that growth was fueled by veteran students and the GI Bill as well as by other student aid programs that broadened the economic and social base of the college student body population.

As noted here by Robert Shaffer, dean of students at Indiana University 1955-1969 and an NSA adviser 1960-65, NSA was a reflection as well as an instrument in the "rapid changes that occurred throughout higher education immediately following World War II."

The memoirs and essays in this part describe the Association's ambitious efforts to initiate student life and student government service and leadership programs, and its efforts to engage—in a "non-partisan" manner—in the key academic, political, and social action issues that affected student life in the nation as a whole.

These issues included racial segregation, ethnic discrimination, economic limits on educational opportunity, student rights and academic freedom, faculty loyalty oaths, student organization restrictions based on presumed or actual communist influence, direct student involvement in the development of curriculum programs and assessment of faculty, and strengthening of autonomy in student government and management of the college press.

New horizons for student governments

Of particular interest were new techniques of managing meetings and decision-making that NSA introduced, networks the Association opened in support of the growing desegregation movement, and the avenues of experiment it provided for students in the many Catholic colleges whose religious orders and administrators believed the time had come to introduce more active student government on their own campuses and encourage their students to relate to the rest of the collegiate world. Contrariwise, the Association reflected a climate in which women's issues were not on the agenda, and was slow to move from pro-forma opposition to fraternity "Aryanism" to more active engagement in the 1950s.

What made it all possible, despite financial limitations, were reliance by its founders on a decentralized volunteer regional and campus structure, with the limited but important continuity and leadership training it provided, and a national system of appointing region- and campus-based "commissions" under the aegis of the national vice presidents. These commissions, with varying degrees of accomplishment, depended for success entirely on the initiatives of the volunteer student chairs and members. (See also Part 5 on the regions.)

THE NSA NEWS December, 1948

NSA Launches Human Relations Program to Combat Prejudice

More Schools Join NSA

Leadership Camp Requests Student-FacultyCommittee

Bob Delahanty, Bill Rummage Report; Bill Welsh, NSA President, Is Camp Guest

THE RAM

Students Ratify New Constitution

Debaters Win 5th Straight

Council Approves Set Of Election By-Laws

Students Examine Failures Of the Educational Process

STUDENT GOVERNMENT AND LEADERSHIP INITIATIVES. From top: *NSA News*, December, 1948. Bill Welsh and Bob Delahanty pictured at U. of Louisville leadership conference, *Cardinal*, 10/1/48. Fordham U. *The Ram* 3/24/49. NSA News 5/49. (Cartoon by Harrison from U. of Wisconsin *Daily Cardinal*.)

PREVIOUS PAGE. Left. Cover, "Human Relatrions in the Educational Community," Medalie and Klopf, NSA, 1950. Right: Top and center, *NSA News*, January, 1949. Bottom: *Daily Texan*, January, 1948.

PART 2. DOMESTIC PROGRAMS

SECTION 1

Student Government, Student Life, and Educational Affairs

CONTENTS

In their review of NSA's campus presence, Robert Shaffer, former Indiana University dean of students and NSA Advisory Council member, and Gordon Klopf, first chair of the NSA Advisory Council, informal headquarters staff counselor, and on the University of Wisconsin student affairs staff at the time, illustrate the importance of NSA's choice to provide for a National Advisory Council of educators, as well as to seek collaboration with the major higher education associations.

NSA's status as the only student association member of the American Council on Education was an important measure of its acceptance. In their memoirs, Gordon Klopf and Richard Medalie (Carleton College, MN), 1949-1950 NSA Educational Affairs Vice President (later to represent NSA abroad and to build a career as an attorney), detail the groundwork NSA laid in building student leadership training, group dynamics, human relations, and student government publication workshop programs. As a complement to its programs against discrimination and segregation, on which it worked with the National Conference of Christians and Jews (NCCJ) and other groups, NSA introduced student government leaders to pioneering alternatives to the win-lose parliamentary methods of managing meetings and decision making. These methods, known as "group dynamics," focused on the need for people to listen to one another and to seek consensus to achieve intergroup understanding.

NSA attempts broad range of student life programs

Carol O'Brien Cashen (College of St. Theresa, MN), editor of *Essai*, NSA's literary magazine, provides some reflections on her experiences. Rick Medalie's memoir, along with an extended album, recreates the campus and regional presence, successes, and failures of student life initiatives such as the Purchase Card discount system, Faculty Rating Program, National Art Exhibit tours, regional "culturales," and human relations workshops.

The activities of three outstanding NSA leaders are also described in this section: Dennis Trueblood (Indiana State Teachers College), who won the affection and regard of his peers as a student leader and later as an administrator; Elmer Paul Brock (La Salle College, PA), 1950-51 NSA Vice President for Educational Affairs (later a Deputy Assistant Postmaster General), and Ted Perry (Temple University), 1949-1950 vice president for student affairs, who later became a staff member for the NCCJ and NAACP.

Student Government and Leadership

NSA REGIONS sponsored workshops at various times of the year. Photos, left: WI students in 1949 at Kohler Corporation Conference Center, WI, and right, Green Lake, WI (Joy Picus). Top: *The Carletonian*, Carleton C., MN 1/21/50. Cartoon: 8/25/48 NSA Congress Bulletin (Western Reserve U. Archives)

Leadership Workshops

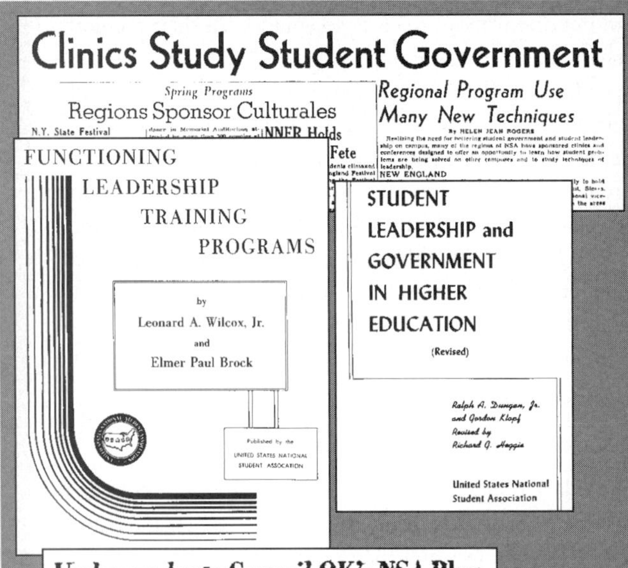

PROGRAM PUBLICATIONS and surveys published each year as guides to campuses and regions. From top: *NSA News* 5/49. NSA leadership publications, left c.1952. Right, 1948. "Evaluating," U. PA, *Daily Pennsylvanian* 10/17/49. "Strengthen," Western Reserve U., *The Reserve Tribune*, 1/9/48.

Training Programs

Page 2 LA SALLE COLLEGIAN November 7, 1947

Student Government

What Are The Purposes of Student Government?

The purposes of student government are: 1. To place in the hands of the students themselves control over their own activities, in accordance with a grant of power made by the faculty. 2. To train leaders. 3. To foster better faculty student relations.

Then the Powers of Student Government are Delegated?

Most certainly. The college is a legal entity with financial responsibility. Any power of a student government must be delegated by the college to the student body.

What Kind of Powers are Delegated to a Student Gov't.?

Powers delegated to student governments vary with different colleges. However, powers commonly found in student governments are the following:

1. The coordination of student club and society activities, e.g. resolving calendar conflicts.
2. The organization and management of various campus activities, e.g. traditional dances.
3. The right to represent the student body at national and international student gatherings.
4. The power to start new services to solve campus problems, e.g. book exchanges.
5. Disciplinary powers.

How Can a Student Government be Initiated?

Class officers of the student body can decide to draw up a constitution outlining the powers that the administration of their college wishes to delegate to the student body. Then this constitution must be ratified by the student body.

Is Student Government a Right, Privilege, or Responsibility?

More than a right or a privilege, student government is a RESPONSIBILITY of the individual student. It is his duty to see that student government works for the good of himself and his fellow student.

What things can Guarantee a Successful Student Gov't.?

1. An interested and informed student body which recognizes its responsibilities toward student government.
2. Competent and wide awake student government officers who work for the common good of the student body.
3. A clearly written definition of student government powers.
4. A school administration that wishes to see student government function properly.

STUDENT GOVERNMENT was central to NSA programming and base of membership. Top: La Salle C., PA, *Collegian* 11/7/47 promotes discussion. Shown here is the 1948 Student Government Association at Indiana State Teachers College (now Indiana State U.), "launched in fall of 1946 as democratic self government attempts to establish itself at Indiana State" (*ISTC Yearbook.* ISU Archives) (see Trueblood, ff.).

The Role of Student Government

STUDENT GOVERNMENT

The general purpose of student government is to aid in developing the society of any educational institution so that it may better

1. *Aid in the self-education of each student through his student government.*
2. *Awaken the student to his rights, responsibilities, and his common interest with the rest of the college or university community.*
3. *Coordinate all faculty and student activities toward a common goal.*

Panel on Student Government,
NSA Constitutional Convention, 9/47

Intercollegiate Cultural Programs

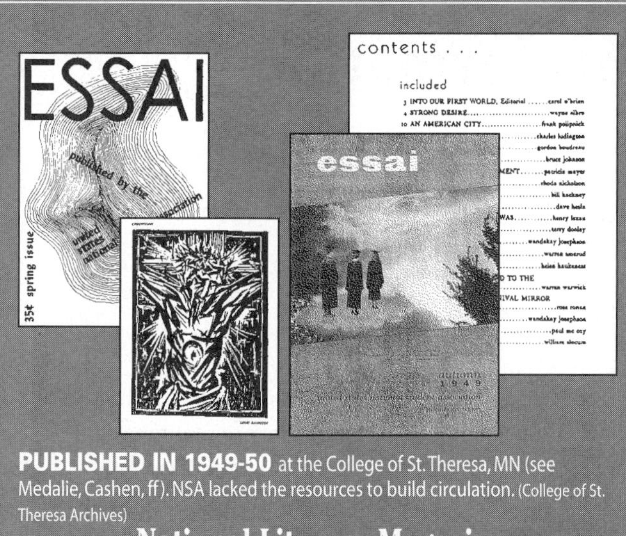

ESSAI

published by the united states national student association

35¢ spring issue

essai

autumn 1949

contents . . .

included

3 INTO OUR FIRST WORLD, Editorial ...... carol o'brien

4 STRONG DESIRE ...... wayne albee

10 AN AMERICAN CITY ...... frank pasipnick

PUBLISHED IN 1949-50 at the College of St. Theresa, MN (see Medalie, Cashen, ff). NSA lacked the resources to build circulation. (College of St. Theresa Archives)

National Literary Magazine

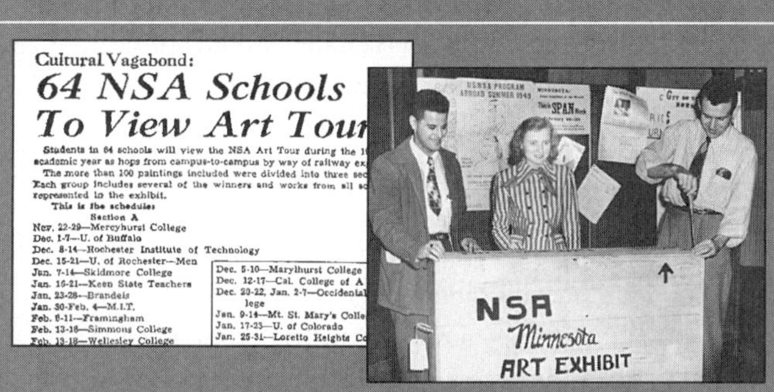

Cultural Vagabond:

64 NSA Schools To View Art Tour

Students in 64 schools will view the NSA Art Tour during the academic year as hops from campus-to-campus by way of railway ex... The more than 100 paintings included were divided into three sec... Each group includes several of the winners and works from all sc... represented in the exhibit.

This is the schedule:

Section A

Nov. 22-29—Mercyhurst College
Dec. 1-7—U. of Buffalo
Dec. 8-14—Rochester Institute of Technology
Dec. 15-21—U. of Rochester—Men
Jan. 7-14—Skidmore College
Jan. 15-21—Keen State Teachers
Jan. 23-28—Brandeis
Jan. 30-Feb. 4—M.I.T.
Feb. 6-11—Framingham
Feb. 13-18—Simmons College
Feb. 13-19—Wellesley College

Dec. 5-10—Marylhurst College
Dec. 12-17—Cal. College of A...
Dec. 20-22, Jan. 2-7—Occidental College
Jan. 9-16—Mt. St. Mary's College
Jan. 17-23—U. of Colorado
Jan. 25-31—Loretto Heights College

SHOWN AT EACH CONGRESS, launched in 1948, exhibits were circulated each school year by a campus subcommisslon (Album, ff). Left: *NSA News* 12/3/49. Photo L to R, Rick Medalie, Harriet Tyson, Dick Newman, Carleton College, MN (SHSW).

National Traveling Art Exhibit

NSA Culturale

an Intercollegiate MUSIC FESTIVAL

Vocal Soloists • Glee Clubs • Choirs
Instrumental Soloists
Instrumental Ensembles
Folk Dances of various countries
Modern Dancing • Interpretive Dancing

Albright, Allegheny, Beaver, Bloomsburg, College Misericordia, Chestnut Hill, Franklin & Marshall, King's College, La Salle, Lehigh, Rosemont, St. Joseph's, St. Vincent's, Swarthmore, Temple, University of Pennsylvania

at THE MET THEATRE
BROAD & POPLAR STREETS

on FRIDAY, APRIL 22 – 8:15 P. M.

United States National Student Organization

Metropolitan Regional Organization

Presents

ITS FIRST INTERCOLLEGIATE CONCERT

Friday, March 19, 1948—8:00 P. M.

Hunter College Assembly Hall
69th Street and Park Avenue, New York City

Program Director and Stage Manager
NATHAN KROMAN
Juilliard School of Music

Chairman, Music Committee
ARNOLD BROWN

Chairman, Cultural Activities Commission
KATHRYN M. SHAKER
College of Mount Saint Vincent

Thousands to Attend Culturale

REGIONAL NEWS

Michigan Sets Two Statewide Student Meetings

Illinois To Oppose Broyles Bills In Legislature

Northern New England Holds Human Relations Institute

FROM SAN FRANCISCO TO ATLANTA, NSA metropolitan area members organized performance arts events with varying degrees of success (Medalie, Album, ff). From top left, handbill, Philadelphia Culturale, 4/49. Program, Met. NY First Regional Concert 3/29/48. *NSA News*, 3/49.

Intercollegiate Culturales

Pocket Book Initiatives

Purchase Card System

An intercollegiate plan to reduce the student's cost of living.

UNITED STATES NATIONAL STUDENT ASSN.

The SILVER and GOLD

NSA, Chamber Plan Meeting To Revamp Discount System

MATHER RECORD

NSA Offers Cut Prices To Students

Notions of the Americans . .
Inge Skanning of Denmark

The Harv...

NSA Group Meets on 'Purchase Card' Plan

NSA's FIRST MAJOR "PRACTICAL PROGRAM," tested in Buffalo in 1947-48, the discount card system (Album, ff) was launched the following year and came and went in many urban areas for the next twenty years, providing a popular and controversial voluntary initiative. From top left 1948-49 brochure. Photo: U. of Wisconsin Quonset hut, 1949 (SHSW). *Silver and Gold* U. of Colo. 1/25/49, Flora Stone Mather College, *The Mather Record* 12/14/49. *The Harvard Crimson* 12/4/49.

Purchase Card Discount System

...ISON, WISCONSIN, JANUARY, 1949 Price 5 Cents

NEC Adopts Legislative Goals; Urges Federal Aid Support

Asks U.S. to Aid Private Colleges

Travel Booklet

NSA Backs Bills Vital to Students

Universal Military Training Proposal Hotly Contended As Student-Faculty Teams Wage Debate in Barnes Hall

NSA Discusses DP Students And Federal Aid to Education

Programs of action of such diverse interests of college and university students as federal aid to education, placement of DP students in American colleges, discrimination in education, and violations of academic freedom were outlined by the National Executive Committee of the United States National Student Association ...

NSA RELIED ON INFORMATION SERVICES to regions and campuses to advance legislative goals in its first five years (Album,ff). From top *NSA News* 1/49. Cornell *Daily Sun* 1/20/48. *The Technique* 1/25/49, Georgia Tech.

Legislative Action

NSA in retrospect: a dean's view

1. The Postwar Transformation of Student Life

Robert H. Shaffer
Assistant Dean of Students, Indiana University, 1952. NSA National Advisor, 1960-65.
Dean of Students, Indiana University, 1955-1969
Professor Emeritus, Schools of Education and Business, Indiana University

From the perspective of a student affairs administrator, the USNSA attempted to introduce content, maturity, and breadth to typically insular, self-centered student governments specifically, and to student activities in general. Such an emphasis should have been universally welcomed in academia. It was not. Often, its efforts were misinterpreted and even resented. It was all too easy for many academics, traditional student leaders, and conservative politicians to attribute NSA organizers' efforts to outside agitators, communists looking for a foothold on campuses, or just plain troublemakers.

Protecting students from the worldwide communist threat was felt by many administrators and student leaders to have a high priority—a higher priority than reforming the university or its student government. Strong student unions, such as existed in some countries, were often viewed as a challenge to the integrity and autonomy of the university, not as a welcome reform to involve students more in their education. International organizations composed of national student unions, whether based in Prague or in Leiden, were equally suspect and feared because of their alleged foreign influences. The International Union of Students and the World Federation of Democratic Youth were viewed as providing pulpits to dangerous elements and were not welcomed on most campuses.

Prewar attitudes toward student activities

In fact, most college and university campuses prior to World War II were isolated islands in a fast-changing world. Their traditional approach to student development, student activities, and even undergraduate education was that they were preparing their students for later adult life in the larger society. Colleges were expected to control students' behavior in order that they could be educated in the classroom. Students were viewed by most professors, administrators, trustees, and the general public as practicing leadership skills and human relationships preparatory to assuming active societal roles after they had graduated.

For student government to be legitimate, its concerns should be campus centered. While students were judged worthy of representation on committees and university bodies, such agencies were expected to be firmly under the control of the faculty and administration. The student role was advisory only. Students were viewed as worthy of having input into rules and regulations, but final decisions were to be made by the institution—meaning faculty, administrators, and trustees. Student governing groups and associations were required to have a faculty or staff adviser before they could be recognized by the dean's office. Nonrecognized groups were usually denied the privileges of using university facilities, even meeting rooms in the student union or in residence halls. Such a view of the campus and its students resulted in tidy enclaves and focused educational efforts not to be disturbed by challenging, shocking, or improper influences. This relationship was verbalized in nearly all student handbooks by such statements as "Students enrolling at —— college or university voluntarily place themselves under the rules and regulations published in this handbook." Students were often required to sign a statement that they had read the handbook and agreed to abide by it. Such an historically entrenched concept of higher education was based on the doctrine of "in loco parentis"—acting in place of the parents. By definition it was protective, controlling, supervisory, and authoritarian. Although it was difficult to perceive immediately, this traditional orientation changed abruptly and substantially within a few fast-moving and, often, traumatic years.

The rapid postwar transformation of student life

Many factors contributed to the rapid changes which occurred throughout higher education immediately following World War

II. While it is dangerous to generalize too broadly, if the USNSA did not actually bring these changes about, it certainly reflected and reinforced what was happening. The war and its aftermath were the equivalent of an academic atomic bomb, which drastically reshaped higher education and student affairs.

The GI Bill, which paid the educational expenses of over 2,230,000 veterans, introduced higher education to many individuals who otherwise would not even have thought of attending college. While far from angelic in their behavior, the onslaught of veterans introduced seriousness of purpose, career-dominated educational goals, and a broad view of life in general. These views had generally been lacking in traditional campus life, with its rules regarding housing, scheduling of social events, and dress codes, which usually required coat and tie for men and heels and hose for women at evening meals. Often the regulations focused on women students, such as having closing hours in women's residences, sign-out requirements if they were going to leave over a weekend, limits on the number of dates an undergraduate woman could have in a week, and a limitation of days on which social events could be held. It was often stated that colleges "controlled the men through the regulations for women." It was generally thought that if women had to be in their residences by 10:30 P.M. during the week and 12:00 P.M. on Fridays and Saturdays, the men would go home and study.

The fact that such an approach was blatantly discriminatory was not even considered until some enterprising students raised the issue years later. For example, a typical rule declared that undergraduate single women under the age of twenty-five had to live in approved women's housing. The stated intent was to preserve apartments for married students. However, the origin predated the avalanche of married students that hit campuses immediately after the war. One can easily imagine the difficulty a dean had in trying to explain to a group of former army nurses why they had to live in supervised women's housing even though men did not. On most campuses that dilemma was solved by classifying women veterans as married students. In retrospect, is it any wonder that parietal rules (regarding residences within a college) were major agenda items for USNSA conferences and campus activism?

Student rights and civil rights issues emerge

Eventually, of course, nearly all such rules, and even the parental approach, broke down in the face of successful legal challenges that established that students had the rights of citizens and did not lose those rights simply by enrolling in a college or university. The concept that students were entitled to legal due process, for example, was often viewed as a slap in the face to most student affairs administrators. After all, the demand seemed to imply that they were not fair and just. Even deans and faculty members, who were generrally sympathetic to greater and more responsible student involvement, felt threatened by legal procedures based upon an adversarial rather than a collegial approach to student relations. The USNSA's "Bill of Student Rights" led the way and for many years increased the blood pressure of most deans. It finally evolved into the "Statement of Student Rights and Responsibilities," which was approved by, among others, the National Association of Student Personnel Administrators.[1]

The extension of constitutional rights and protections, particularly in the 1960s, sent the campus a second major shockwave that forever prevented higher education from returning to its controlling, prescribing, limited concept of student life. There was no longer a question of only discussing civil rights in the South; it became a question of involvement and participation. Civil rights marches to the South led to demonstrations at home regarding racial and sexual discrimination, questionable educational policies, and custodial student regulations. Rules regarding dress codes, specific hours for women but not for men, and required residence for some students in campus housing all proved to be not only untenable, but illegal as well.

In the political arena, rules such as "Students will not use campus facilities to plan off-campus illegal events" were patently illogical when challenging racial segregation and limitations on freedom of assembly and speech. USNSA led the national movement for students to be appointed as full members on boards of trustees, faculty councils, and related governing bodies.[2] When told that the law did not provide for such membership, the response was logical and representative of the new era: "Then change the law." In short, the college campus became married to society-at-large, with all its problems, concerns, issues, and political development.

Political activism on campus—Left and right

The third major event that forever changed student life was the eighteen-year-old majority and resultant adult status, including the right to vote. Obviously, if there were hundreds of voters on a campus, political parties would find, and appeal to, them through a variety of channels. Students had been involved for many years, particularly in presidential campaigns, in supporting political parties and candidates. However, they were usually regarded as merely helpers, not as integral participants in the political process. The eighteen-year-old vote was the culmination of many years of political activism on campuses. The force that finally brought the vote in 1971 was probably the drafting of so many young men in three wars—World War II, Korea, and then Vietnam. With the vote, no longer were "Young Republicans," "Young Democrats," and "Young Socialists" composed of students just preparing for participation in "adult" politics; they became part of the political process. Senator Barry Goldwater's calling on so many young campus supporters to be campaign workers now led to young people on campuses becoming delegates, candidates, and officeholders.[3] The political reality sealed forever the adult status of college students.

The experience of the Indiana University (IU) student government in considering and rejecting membership in the USNSA reflected the generally conservative political tradition of the Midwest. The question was considered many times over a period of ten or twelve years, only to be rejected even in 1952, when the Fifth National USNSA Congress[4] was held on the campus, although both the student government adviser, Dennis Trueblood, and I, then assistant dean of students for activities, recommended membership. However, higher administrators were opposed to membership. Most students were simply apathetic. Others felt membership was too expensive for the benefits received. Still others felt that the USNSA program was a radical influence that was alien to the IU campus, with its heavy influence on athletics, social life, and a conservative political outlook.

From "college kid" to responsible adult

Unfortunately, many college students and organizations attempting to appeal to them still face major challenges in involving large numbers of students in substantial issues. Many students, many faculty, and much of the public do not understand what has happened. To this day, students often prefer the privileged, protected life of traditional college life. An observer need only witness the hi-jinks associated with spring break, campus elections, and some campus activities to realize the truth of the old adage of "kids will be kids." Much of the public questions why colleges don't supervise their students more closely. Over their cocktails, many off-campus adults still wonder why colleges and universities don't stop "all that drinking" or why they "permit" such outlandish behavior. Many college students themselves are still questioning if they want to exchange their perceived special status before the law and in public judgment for the awesome responsibilities of adults in a society that is often ambiguous and contradictory in its expectations.

Robert H. Shaffer is professor emeritus in the Schools of Education and of Business at Indiana University, where has held a number of positions since joining the faculty in 1941. He was assistant dean of students in 1952 when NSA held its fifth congress at Indiana.

The change in concept from "college kid" to responsible adult was led in a large part by USNSA—a change so monumental that it is still in process fifty years later. The challenge is great and much still needs to be done

END NOTES

[1] *Editor's note:* See p. 1110 for the original Bill of Student Rights adopted at the NSA Constitutional Convention in August 1947. See also the discussion of student rights in the Janet Brown essay, p. 375. Stephen Schodde, in the doctoral thesis cited in Klopf, fn 1, p. 339, traces in detail the reactions to the bill in its original form and its transformation to a bill of rights and responsibilities. NSA Vice President Sylvia Bacon initiated, at the fifth congress, at Indiana University, the process that resulted in the enumeration by the sixth congress of seven responsibilities regarding learning, respecting the rights of others, and complying with college regulations.

[2] *Editor's note:* NSA became the first national student constituent member of the American Council on Education and the National Education Association. On August 19, 1951, the Thirty-Seventh Annual Convention of the American Association of University Professors adopted a resolution stating that it "welcomes the developing program of the National Student Association for making an informed student opinion effective in American higher education and for extending the influence of free education to the other parts of the world." In April 1953, after several years of study, the USNSA Liaison Committees of three major professional organizations reported that "In the opinion of your committees it is the most representative of such organizations in the American scene." The organizations were the National Association of Woman Deans and Counsellors, American College Personnel Association, and National Association of Student Personnel Administrators.

[3] *Editor's note:* Conservative student involvement in the years leading up to the 1964 Goldwater campaign echoed the widespread campus support on the left for Henry Wallace in his failed 1948 campaign, after he left the Truman administration. See Part 4, pp. 804, 796.

[4] See p. 1079.

PICTURE CREDITS: *Then:* c. 1969. *Now:* May, 1999 (*Both, author*).

ROBERT H. SHAFFER

Early background: Born in Delphi, IN. Attended Mishawaka High School in Mishawaka, IN.

Education: A.B., DePauw University. M.A., Teachers College, Columbia University. Ph.D., New York University. Honorary LL.D., DePauw University, 1976. LL.D., Indiana University, 1985.

Career: Currently professor emeritus at Indiana University, he has held a number of positions at that institution since joining its faculty in 1941. He was assistant dean of students in 1952, when NSA held its fifth congress at Indiana.

These included service as dean of students and chairman of the Departments of Student Personnel Administration and of Higher Education.

He has received recognition and awards for his writings and service in the field of student affairs from various associations, including the American College Personnel Association, the National Association of Student Personnel Administrators, the National Campus Activities Association, the National Interfraternity Conference, the Association of Fraternity Advisors, and the Fraternity Executives Association.

He was a member of the USNSA National Advisory Council from 1959 to 1966 and attended a number of NSA national congresses in the 1950s and 1960s.

Recollections of a student personnel adviser in the early years of NSA

2. As Memory Speaks

Gordon John Klopf

Assistant Dean, University of Wisconsin. NSA Advisory Council, 1948-53; first Chair, 1949-51; NSA Advisory Board, 1954-58
Dean Emeritus, Bank Street College of Education
Chair, UNICEF NGO Working Group on Education; Chair, UN NGO International Year of the Older Person, 1999

This brief commentary is being called *As Memory Speaks* because I am reporting about people and happenings as they have come to mind. I did go through some old papers and pamphlets, and one of my doctoral students at Teachers College, Columbia University, Stephen Schodde, did an excellent thesis on NSA, if the reader wants a full history.[1]

As I observe the student scene today I'm pleased to see some new approaches in higher education. Included is the development of an increased literature and study on teaching and learning. The new journal *On Campus*, published by the American College Personnel Association, focuses on institutions seeing themselves as learning communities with collaborative ways of teaching. We also have the development of campus centers for improving instruction at a number of institutions including consultations, seminars, and publications. There are twenty centers and programs in the state of Georgia alone. In a recent *Chronicle of Higher Education* issue, a Princeton professor cites twelve books that she found provided guidance for college teaching.[2]

On Campus also reflects a new literature on student leadership and activities, both on campus and in the civil society. There is also a new series of books and studies aimed at strengthening student participation, again in both the civil and campus society. An illustration of student participation today is reflected in a recent happening near where I live on the Columbia University Campus called "Take Back the Night," a demonstration and speak-out for survivors of domestic and sexual abuse, which is seen as a highly powerful and touching experience, a real civil concern.

NSA's goal to strengthen student participation

These teaching and student concerns today have some parallels in the years following World War II, when the National Student Association was formed. At its constitutional convention in Madison, Wisconsin, in early September 1947, NSA voiced the following vision for student engagement in the teaching and learning process:

> The commission of the USNSA on Student Government and Student Government Functions shall work from certain fundamental premises. The first of these is that one of the principal purposes of the new organization will be to strengthen student government systems. If the new organization succeeds in developing strong and functional student governments throughout American colleges and universities, it will help to provide the mechanism through which American students can receive a real education in democracy.
>
> Student governments provide the opportunity for student leader and ordinary student alike to obtain badly needed practice in such citizenship activities as intelligent voting, parliamentary procedure, responsible representation of public opinion, intelligent leadership of public action, advocacy, analysis of community problems and solution of those problems.
>
> The general purpose of student government is to aid in developing the society of any educational institution so that it may better
>
> 1. Aid in the self-education of each student through his student government.
> 2. Awaken the student to his rights, responsibilities, and his common interest with the rest of the college or university community.
> 3. Coordinate all faculty and student activities toward a common goal.
>
> Control of the Student Society is exercised not for its own sake, but only to implement the desired transformation of the whole society of any educational institution. Any control which does not further such a transformation is unnecessary and undesirable, regardless of who imposes it.

The report goes on to say, "It is a primary aim of the USNSA to develop a campus community spirit based upon student, faculty and administration understanding and friendship." (*Report of the Constitutional Convention*, p. 20)

This vision, my own career interests, and the happy circumstance of my presence at the University of Wisconsin during NSA's formative years opened up for me a rewarding collaboration with NSA's student leadership and with college personnel administrators around the country.

I think the professional personnel movement today may be ahead of the faculty. The *On Campus* magazine and the whole focus on improving instruction was student motivated, but now it's perhaps more faculty motivated.

Working with the NSA Leadership

I have served the association in several ways. I was chair of the first Advisory Council for about three years. I served as a personal and professional informal adviser to some of the officers and general leadership from the very beginning of the association's residence in Madison.[3]

I also did advising on NSA organizational matters and worked extensively with the staff and others on many program ideas, materials, and conferences. I saw the NSA and the structure with which I was involved as what some would call a learning organization, focusing on generative learning, which involves creating as well as adapting. We were creating concepts as well as our actual capability to strengthen the role of the student on the American campus.

As I look back, I now believe we needed to work harder at our own leadership competencies, which might have started with a more defined vision of what was needed. We worked too much on the role of campus leadership and not enough on a vision of regional and national leadership.

The process sometimes failed in relationship to the NSA leadership team itself, even as those leaders applied it to their student government and human relations programming. While the first two staffs were quite collegial, in retrospect, I should have been stronger there, almost more dogmatic. With the conflicted 1949-1950 staff, I should have said, "Now let's sit down and deal with these serious internal staff conflicts."[4]

Many of the NSA leaders became very close as participants. It was almost an academy of friendships. The leaders developed a strong bonding, which has survived fifty years. Some of the NSA family saw me as kind of an "uncle" figure. I was a student affairs staff member at the University of Wisconsin and was responsible for student organizations but was only a few years older than many of the NSA leaders. In this role I worked closely with the national officers in Madison, Wisconsin, during NSA's first three years.

I recall well one situation counseling with two officers lying in the grass on the edge of a cornfield on a Midwestern campus where a major meeting was being held. The outcome of many tears and discussions was a relationship that had great meaning for them both, personally and professionally. Differences of faith, geography, and life-style were overcome in what became one of the great friendships in the history of the association.

The "uncle" was becoming a cook and also one with friends with apartments for entertaining NSA staff. One, Emily Chervinek, the assistant dean of women, had a fine apartment right across from the NSA office (which was in an old school).

The student union, which had good food, was a block and a half from the NSA office, and my office was on the top of Bascom Hill, also about a block from the NSA office area. We had a great many meals together discussing organizational issues as well as broader social and political concerns and personal career goals. There was a lot of discussion on regional and campus matters. The regional concept was new then and still isn't very strong. Even in Morningside Heights, where I now live, among the institutions up there there isn't much bonding or cooperation. And that's certainly true with so many of the campus student leaders, who didn't have a tradition of their institution working with other institutions.

The role of regions and other issues that engaged the staff

Although individual regions (such as California, Metropolitan New York, Wisconsin, New England, and Kentucky-Tennessee, for example) would undertake projects from year to year, they were seldom sustained over a period of years. As a common denominator, regions seemed to furnish training for national leaders, sponsor regional conferences and meetings on such matters as student government, human relations, academic freedom and international travel, and furnish a caucus to support candidates out of their regions at national conventions.

Other matters that occupied our attention at the time on an organizational level included NSA's financial needs and how to build membership. We also had discussions about race and ethnicity. Women's issues were coming up, though still below the surface, because we were involving women in the political leadership. We had some strong women leaders in NSA active on every level as national and regional officers. Among those who come to mind are Miriam Haskell, Smith College; Janis Tremper, Rockford College; Mildred Kiefer, UC Berkeley; Helen Jean Rogers, Mundelein College; Cynthia Courtney, Dunbarton College; Jane Wilder, UCLA; Mary Jo Domino, Rockford College; Tesse Hartigan, Fontbonne College; Alice Gilbert, Radcliffe College; Joan Long, Marylhurst College; Shirley Neizer, Simmons College; Constance Curry, Agnes Scott College; and Sylvia Bacon, Vassar College.

And, of course, among women advisers close at hand in Madison in addition to Emily Chervenick was Helen C. White, professor of English and a member of the Advisory Council.

If you took a look at the population that came to the conferences, there was a high percentage of women.[5] At the time, issues of harassment or career were not on the agenda. Nor were any resolutions offered at congresses, to my recollection, on women's issues during those first five years. But women were coming to meetings and speaking as women and people tried to get them involved as women. And we didn't deal with women's issues as much as we dealt with women's participation in the activities of the moment.

Examining the role of student government

The development of the National Student Association came at a particular time in higher education in the United States, one of excitement and new activity. Students were back from service in World War II and were concerned with their futures and those of the people of the world. What role could students serve to strengthen their own education and to provide a meaningful life for the diverse population of America?

One answer was to look at academic programs and their evaluation, and to get students to take part in their development. When I became dean of students at the State University College at Buffalo in 1951-52, we had students on all the academic committees—not just sports or the arts. That's what stood for student representation in government, not student government. The president of the college, Harvey Rice, was very supportive of the students participating in the governance of the college. Prior to my Buffalo assignment, incidentally, in July 1950 I went to Japan for the American Council on Education. In this postwar period we were helping the Japanese develop participatory student life. I worked with student personnel offices at all the campuses in the country. Every campus had a participant in a three-month institute. The institutes were at Tokyo University, Kyushu University, and Kyoto University. The council published a study on this whole program.[6]

Buffalo was the home campus for Lee Jones, NSA national treasurer from 1947 to 1948, and it remained an active member of NSA in the New York State Region during that period. Jones was the second of a series of African-American national officers during that era.[7] Academic programs were being strengthened to serve the more mature student, and college student personnel workers were becoming fully professional student group advisers. The student life program was being seen as a fertile place for the development of future leaders. Students looked at the world as if it could become otherwise. They were more reflective, more intentional—to be learning meant to be involved in a quest.

Part of the professionalization was to permit the students to develop fully through experience. The adviser perceived the student as learning about leadership through participation. Prior to the clarification of the role of the student organization adviser, advisers were simply good people who helped the student organization do things properly for the college, or helped get chaperones. One major assignment on campuses at that time was that the adviser had to chaperone all the social events. That was the case until the adviser and personnel worker became more professionally recognized in the role of group adviser.

At Madison, I always had a good secretary and at least two other staff people. One took care of fraternities and one took care of all events that had to be covered with a faculty member. And if there were one hundred events on a weekend—whether you were having a controversial speaker or running a dance—there had to be a faculty person at each one.

Developing student leadership

We did an institute every summer at the University of Wisconsin in those years, in which some NSA leaders were involved; it was an institute for personnel workers. In my position in the personnel program at Wisconsin, I would bring together several hundred people every summer for a workshop for both high school and college personnel workers, mostly in relationship to student counseling.

Whenever there was a meeting, we tried to have an NSA speaker. Deans of women were very helpful. In point of fact, they were more helpful than the deans of men in the inclusion of students and programming and training activities.

I myself was completing my doctorate in education with a focus on student personnel work, and was a great believer in the potential for personal growth through participation in student activities on campus. The profession had developed what was called "The Student Personnel Point of View," which was well stated in a booklet of the same title published in 1937 by the American Council on Education. The publication appeared to bring a surge of interest and support for strength in student leadership and student organizations on the campus.

One feature of these early efforts was my collaboration with Ralph Dungan (St. Joseph's College, Philadelphia), the 1947-48 NSA vice president for national student affairs, when we authored and published the first edition of NSA's *Student Government and Leadership in Higher Education,* which was kept in print and updated by successive NSA vice presidents for decades. It was a historical document—adressing the topic in its way for the first time in student life history.[8]

NSA's unique contribution to the student government scene was its commitment to the group process as a supplement to parliamentary procedure and the classical rules of debate. In the Foreword to the book, the NSA staff declares:

> Two facts have motivated the writing of this booklet. First, the U. S. National Student Association believes that understanding the group process and the relation of the individual to it, is essential to the social and political health of the country. The USNSA also believes that student government is one of the most effective means of educating for democratic citizenship. Second, the USNSA has a strong desire to further the establishment and strengthening of student government because it is a direct means by which students can contribute their full share to the community of which they are a part.

Bringing students "to the table"

It is useful also to recall the Detroit Economic Club questionnaire, which Bill Welsh has written about elsewhere in this book,[9] that went out during the first year of NSA to all of the college presidents and to refresh our memories of the kind of attack that NSA was under by some of the conservative business forces and what the various professional deans had to take into account when they were furthering the idea that administrations should collaborate with NSA. They had to contend with a significant external force that was questioning whether NSA was politically legitimate.

And academically—for example, take a student at age nineteen or twenty, say he or she is a beginning student at Latin, does he or she have an equal say as to what's to be in the course alongside the professor of Latin? I believe a student's right and responsibility is to respect the contribution of both the student and the teacher. And if you're a historian or linguist, you most likely know more than I, the student, know. And my role is to learn from you and question you, challenge you even. But in the role of professor I have to see myself as more knowing.

During the early years of NSA, the single most important way in which NSA attempted to bring students to the table on the matter of teaching was through the faculty rating system. Now I differ with that professionally. As it works, if I'm teaching a course for the final session, students turn in a rating form without some discussion about it. I would much rather have a discussion, and that the faculty member be open and able to listen and comment. If the student has a recommendation, let's talk about it rather than just check yes or no. That's that student's perception. I'm more for exploring and discussing rather than checklists or short answers.

I sort of stood at arm's length from the faculty evaluation program with NSA at the time. I want to know why you say you didn't like the course. What could I have done to make it more meaningful to you?[10]

The NSA leadership and the students they represented had a sober earnestness and awareness of the relationship of the academic to life. They saw themselves, not as intellectual children, but as individuals sharing in the responsibility of their own education. They also needed the freedom to move toward their own political and social maturity. Harold Taylor, president of Sarah Lawrence College,[11] who was a mentor for many students, believed they were responsible persons in American life. Administrators in some institutions would let me know that they were a bit wary of their students being a part of alliances outside of their own student governing boards and constituencies.[12]

The concept of student rights and role of mentoring

The whole area of student rights—of student participation in the development of academic life, of student participation in governing—could lead to a kind of resentment by the faculty person with the legal power who had to share that power with students. This adjustment was very hard for some administrators in those years.[13]

As I attended academic meetings, and particularly personnel meetings, I found that the concept of a student as totally independent or having rights separate from their student status bothered some personnel workers. And their presidents and their academic deans would hold the personnel worker responsible for these students taking part in activities where they saw themselves as socially, politically, and academically separate from the faculty member.

We should have built a seminar or conference or two around the whole role of each person in the academic picture to work out relationship roles and defined roles. What is the student role? What is the academic role? The professor and the dean? Because the professors and deans would have differences, too. And then you began with the board of overseers, or the board of trustees, or the board of regents who at Wisconsin defined the liberal social atmosphere at the institution—where you could drink beer, or have communist speakers on the campus at student events and activities. That was cleared by the Board of Regents at the University of Wisconsin. So I guess now as I look back, we should have worked harder at an academic fellowship of what I call a learning community. Each working on our role and how we could work together and on what.

The word "mentoring" was not used commonly in the years I was associated with NSA, but the process was certainly taking place. I observed it in the leader-leader, student-student relationships rather than between faculty and students. I had little opportunity to observe students with their faculty but heard them quote their campus faculty idols. For example the influence of Frank Graham, president of the University of North Carolina, on Al Lowenstein was very clear. The strong student leaders on a campus or in the regional or national organization would have their small follower groups and be quoted extensively.

Al Lowenstein, NSA president in 1950-51, had a cluster of believers wherever he went, both men and women, who would believe in him and support him. Now, I had less understanding of Bob Kelly, who preceded Al as president, but from what I've read now by people who have made comments about him then, he must have had follower groups, people who believed in him. He was reported to be a very effective public speaker in behalf of NSA, and received high marks as an NSA spokesman from some college administrators.

Human relations and group dynamics

What I brought to the association in terms of program was due to a long history of participation in groups and community and educational settings.

From early childhood on I was a great believer in the group. It flowed from my family experience and tradition. I endeavored to enable the NSA leadership to strengthen democratic processes and leadership in the various social settings in which students participated—both on the campus and in regional and national activities.

NSA brought a new focus to the vision of the college as community, with student government seen as student participation in college government. In addition to their own councils and activities this meant taking part in educational policy-making groups and structures in which students had a role and a meaningful place.

NSA was seeking to change the historic notion that while the faculty community and the student community had complementary roles, participation in government was not the student's place. The student was there to learn.[14]

One of the main very early events that gave a new focus and content to leadership and the way groups functioned was participation in the Lake Forest Conference, a week-long training session sponsored by the National Conference of Christians and Jews and NSA. The organization had very forward-looking leadership in Chicago and Milwaukee who worked with a planning committee for national leadership conferences for the Association on the Lake Forest College campus. I attended them and served as Dean of the second session. We all learned much from Arthur Shedlin, a consultant from the University of Chicago.

Although the conference objectives were quite traditional in sought-for outcomes, the experience brought a new awareness of group dynamics and processes to the participants. They became very aware of their individual roles and the movement and behavior of the group. They analyzed their group processes as well as their topics. Not all the officers participated in the conference, but those who did will say even today that this was a major leadership experience of their whole life. As an experience it represented what leadership in education can and should be. These conferences were held for three years, in 1948, 1949, and 1950, just prior to the annual meeting, and some of the processes were used for the opening group sessions of the association's congress. One of the students who attended recently wrote how the processes that were studied and practiced at Lake Forest have been a key part of ways of working in group settings all through her professional and political life.

The 1948 Lake Forest Conference

With the support of the NCCJ, Shedlin's was a major contribution to the thinking of NSA leaders who were experiencing their first exposure to this new approach to group dynamics, and who furnished a real test of its efficacy. This is an excerpt from a commentary on the first (1948) conference:

> The first Lake Forest Conference was held in June of 1948 at Lake Forest College in Illinois. The conference was originally conceived by a committee consisting of staff members from the National Conference of Christians and Jews, college faculty and administrators, and the student officers of the National Student Association meeting in Chicago in December of 1947.
>
> Professor Arthur Shedlin, then Dean of Students at University College, University of Chicago, was selected as the dean for the conference. Dean Shedlin was appointed because of his interest and experimental work with a psychological approach to group leadership. Having experimented with satisfactory results with the client-centered approach to psychotherapy he applied similar principles to group procedures. He was particularly known for his investigations with "social climate" and has been concerned with the need for recognition by the leader of attitudes and feelings as expressed by the members of his group. Shedlin sees as one of the primary functions of the leader that of communicating an atmosphere of democratic unity in the group. The leader is non-judgmental and attempts to establish an atmosphere of permissiveness and warmth. This kind of atmosphere emphasizes the tendency for the individuals to be self-sufficient, and to accept responsibility and independence.
>
> The group leaders met for two days with Arthur Shedlin and achieved not only a group spirit among themselves but gained insights into the philosophy of group leadership techniques and skills for working with their groups.
>
> The sixty young people who attended the conference had what was to many of them an almost spiritual experience. They left the campus of Lake Forest College with the feeling that the most satisfying human relations are those in which there is a sincere respect for others with sharing and a warm give and take in the business of living together.[15]

We brought students from around the country to these meetings if they were in a leadership position in NSA. And they played a leadership role in the beginning of the congress.

I encouraged their involvement because I had been working with the NCCJ person from the Milwaukee office in my role as student activities adviser at Wisconsin. He wanted to be involved with fraternities and that whole scene.[16] So I had worked with him. We talked about NSA, and I asked, "What about helping us?" He had all these ideas. I had also met Arthur Shedlin of the Chicago office. Arthur Shedlin was a jewel, very smart, the students loved him; he was very believing in them. If you had a session with him you'd get captivated. He wanted everything to be more group responsible. He was at the height of the group process movement theorists.

There was another set of meetings for the University of Wisconsin held at a conference center in Green Lake and at the Kohler Corporation. Those conferences used the Lake Forest model, which involved extensive discussion and looking at how we were functioning as a group of people. You looked at content and you looked at process. Content could have been student faculty evaluations. Process was how were we handling this? Who was the leader? How do we share leadership? How do we move ahead on the agenda? How do we clarify?

Development of human relations programming

As an expression of NSA's commitment to Human Relations programming, I coauthored a booklet with Rick Medalie, NSA's 1949-1950 educational affairs vice president, *Human Relations in the Educational Community.* We quoted President Harry Truman when he said, "The challenge of the twentieth century is the challenge of human relations, and not of impersonal natural forces."

In its Preface we wrote:

> There are four main goals to be achieved in the production, distribution and use of this booklet:
>
> 1. To develop a growing realization on the part of the campus community of the problems of human relations in areas including campus organizations administration—faculty-student relations, admissions requirements, teaching and curriculum, campus-town relations, and living units.
>
> 2. To clarify the potentialities of democratic human relations when campus groups work together.
>
> 3. To expand the understanding of interpersonal and intergroup tensions and prejudices and their attendant dangers.
>
> 4. To develop ways of reducing tensions and minimizing prejudice among students and campus groups.
>
> This booklet is focussed for long-term programming designed to improve human relations in the educational community. The direction and motivation of the human relations program for American colleges and universities is being developed on the national level by the National Conference of Christians and Jews (NCCJ) and the U.S. National Student Association (NSA).

If interpreting NSA to the higher education community was a role that some of us accepted, I also had a second role that was exciting to me, that of my contribution to the ideas and concepts which the association promoted in its program and direction.[17]

As I've noted, with several of the officers I shared the production of a number of publications on student government, leadership, and human relations. The focus of the governing role of the student was not just on student activities but on students' real participation in campus decision making. Although student leadership conferences continue to be held on many campuses and in many states and regions, the participation of students in the real governing of institutions may not be as common as was hoped for in the 1950s.

I am still quite familiar with the literature in student life and have talked with individuals who know higher education. The general feeling is that there is little student involvement in institutional committees but that students are being invited to serve on major governing boards and committees in an increasing number.

The NSA Advisory Council

I became an adviser in 1947-48 and first chair of the NSA Advisory Council in 1948-49. The council was a group of faculty and administrators invited to serve in an advisory role by the association. The group never met as a body but members were in communication by letter and telephone. I developed a newsletter, which went out several times a year to the council and to others who asked to be on the mailing list.[18] We had no budget, and the University of Wisconsin paid for the mailing and duplicating as well as any small travel I might do. The leadership of NSA and the American higher education community always seemed most appreciative of the information we provided. I am sure that some critics would like to have seen a more controlling council with some final decision-making powers and veto rights. We were there to support, to counsel, to believe, to care and enable, and to build together. Some thought we were too positive about the association, too trusting.

Along with another member of the council, I would publish in one of the educational journals, *School and Society*, an annual review of the association. *School and Society* covered the association's history each year, at least through 1952. William Birenbaum (University of Chicago) and Dennis Trueblood (Indiana University) collaborated on the 1951 report. Dennis Trueblood collaborated with me on the 1950 and 1952 reports. Marion Lynch (Marygrove College) joined me on the 1949 report. The first two years were handled independently in one article by Robert Sollen of the University of Wisconsin.[19]

INTRODUCING GROUP DYNAMICS TO STUDENT LEADERS

Gordon Klopf writes: One of the main very early events that gave a new focus and content to leadership and the way groups functioned was participation in the Lake Forest Conference, a week long training session sponsored by the National Conference of Christians and Jews and NSA. . . . Although the Conference objectives were quite traditional in sought-for outcomes, the experience brought a new awareness of group dynamics and processes to the participants. They became very aware of their individual roles and the movement and behavior of the group. They analyzed their group processes as well as their topics. Not all the officers participated in the Conference, but those that did will say even today that this was a major leadership experience of their whole life.

These conferences were held for three years, in 1948, '49 and '50, just prior to the annual meeting, and some of the processes were used for the opening group sessions of the Association's Congress.

Begin Planning Lake Forest Meet

Plans for the 1950 Lake Forest (Ill.) Conference—which is setting the style for student leadership meetings—are being made by NSA and the National Conference of Christians and Jews.

Meeting at University of Wisconsin, representatives of both groups have agreed to a June Conference and plan for more than 100 students, faculty members and educators to attend the five-day meeting.

* * *

THE CONFERENCE SEEKS to develop democratic procedures for campus groups and activities.

It emphasizes the immediate problems of the participants in connection with student government, as well as human relations in residential, fraternity, political and religious groups.

Stress is placed on consideration of the campus as a community of students, faculty and administration, and the surrounding city or town. Attention is also given to the development of the students as a citizen of the local, national, and international scene.

Initial contact to campuses on attending the Conference will be made by March 1, according to NSA veep Ted Perry, who is co-chairman of the Lake Forest Committee.

NSA News 2/50

ARTHUR SHEDLIN, above, of the Chicago NCCJ office and also Dean of Students at University College, U. of Chicago. Klopf writes, he "was a jewel, very smart, the students loved him; he was very believing in them. If you had a session with him you'd get captivated. He wanted everything to be more group responsible. He was at the height of the group process movement theorists." (Klopf)

GORDON KLOPF, left, with Lake Forest faculty. Klopf writes, "NSA brought a new focus to the vision of the college as community, with student government seen as student participation in college government. In addition to their own councils and activities this meant taking part in educational policy making groups and structures in which students had a role and a meaningful place." (Klopf)

1950 CONFERENCE PLANNING COMMITTEE, above, from left: Earl S. Kelp, Midwest educational director of NCCJ and co-Chair of the Committee; James D. Nobel, Cleveland area director of NCCJ; Dolores Sheslo, Rockford College, IL, NSA human relations program midwest director; Ted Perry (Temple U.), co-Chair and NSA student affairs V.P.; Robert Delahanty (U. of Louisville), NSA Executive Secretary; Gordon Klopf, U. of Wisconsin student activities counselor and NSA Advisory Committee chair; Maurice H. Terry, WI NCCJ regional director, and Richard Medalie, NSA V.P. Educational Problems. (Schwartz)

1948 CONFERENCE STUDENT PARTICIPANTS. Top row, left: Norman Holmes, U. of WI NSA Committee; right: Janis Dowd, NSA National Secretary. 2d row right: Ralph Dungan, NSA V.P. domestic affairs. (*Ward McMasters.* Klopf)

In August 1949, I wrote for *School and Society*, in "The College Administrator Looks at the National Student Association":

> That the National Student Association has been well received and has an important contribution to make to higher education is the opinion of a majority of college presidents and deans expressed in a recent survey made by several members of the Advisory Council of the Association. Harold Taylor, President of Sarah Lawrence College, sums up the attitude of many of the college administrators queried when he says that he believes "the National Student Association is one of the most important developments in the field of higher education that has occurred during the last ten years."

In August 1951, Dennis Trueblood and I collaborated in another evaluation in which we began:

> Since the Chicago Student Conference of 1946, the United States National Student Association has come to be accepted as a part of the American College scene. Five years ago it was just an idea in the minds of some 600 students; now, the evolution of this organization has become an important chapter in the history of higher education in America. . . .
>
> The concept of the educational community composed of students, administrators and faculty working together with all aspects of higher education has been developed and implemented by the National Student Association in all of its programs and conferences. Student government is no longer thought of as such, but as the role of the student in the government and the development of higher education.

We then concluded with a cautionary note:

> It is most evident that with a change in the experience and maturity since the founding of NSA, an organization that was keyed to a student with strong social concerns needs to take a look at its functioning in a community of students quite different. . . . [S]tudents see NSA as meaningful to them through concrete projects such as cultural exchanges, publications, the discount service, student government conferences, etc. The emphasis given to the role NSA plays as the representative voice of the American student in the nation and the world is important as well. . . .
>
> As students face a world in crisis, an organization which is keyed to developing social, economic and political awareness and understanding in the educational community and the world needs to play a greater role than ever. . . . Whether or not [NSA] will meet the continuing needs of the educational community will depend upon the interest of and support of faculty, administrators, and students as well as organizations and federal agencies.

The turbulent times of the Cold War abroad and the Red scare at home created a rocky environment for the young organization. The support of the Advisory Council and the network of college administrators, presidents, and deans, whether public, private, or parochial, were crucial to the organization's ability to make its case on college campuses and to win the support of student governments wanting to affiliate.

Dennis Trueblood

I mentioned Dennis Trueblood as a collaborator. He was more than that at the time—an emerging leader who enjoyed great trust and admiration in NSA circles. His untimely death at the age of thirty-eight deprived us of a true leader.[20]

Dennis was a student at Indiana State University, who became an NSA delegate and Indiana Regional chair. Upon graduating he continued a career in student personnel work. Dennis was very committed to the role of students in higher education, and he studied, wrote, and spoke on the subject. He was very earnest, very sincere, radical in a very quiet way. He wouldn't be perceived as radical, but his ideas were certainly new and radical.

He truly believed in all that NSA stood for. And his dedication was considered by some at the time to be radical and certainly on the forefront. Because he was so committed and so sincere, he developed a tremendous respect from the more senior deans of men and deans of women. He was a very young man. When he came into prominence and student personnel work in his mid- to late twenties, he was invited to move from Indiana University—where he did his doctorate and worked on the staff under the Dean of Students, Robert Shaffer—to Southern Illinois University at Carbondale.

He invited me to come there to be a coprofessor with him, and I was going to get a full professorship. He was so highly respected there that they gave him this opportunity to bring somebody, and I was the first one he chose. We were, in some ways, much alike. He was perhaps less adventuresome and less dramatic, very hard-working, very diligent, very honest, very straightforward, no gossip, straight all-around person. And his death in 1964 was a real shock. Although people knew he was ill, they didn't expect him to die.

The people at Indiana, and Bob Shaffer, deeply respected him. Most everybody felt this way about him. In a way he lived the student personnel movements. And we had a very good relationship.

College administration supporters and Advisory Council Members

In reviewing the early history of NSA, a tribute has to be given to individuals in higher education and various association and government offices who supported the organization in its early years. Associations of student personnel officers, deans of students, deans of women, deans of men, and other administrative units and faculty invited NSA leadership to speak at their area and national meetings.

During NSA's fifth year, a study was undertaken by the NSA Liaison Committee of the National Association of Deans of Women, National Association of Student Personnel Administrators, and American College Personnel Association. Its purpose was to "audit" the organization's legitimacy in the face of various criticisms and questions raised regarding its finances, politics, and representative character.[21]

On April 1, 1953, the Liaison Committee issued a favorable report, which began by stating, "NSA is the most representative national student organization in the United States."

Among other things, it noted:

1. NSA "is not now, nor does it appear to be in danger of becoming communist or leftist dominated."
2. "As a young and growing organization, NSA has not yet achieved a secure financial basis."
3. "NSA is now in accord with the principles of academic freedom as expressed by the American Association of University Professors."
4. "The purposes and the program of NSA . . . deserve the support and counsel of student personnel workers in the colleges and universities of this country."

Many, as organizations and as individuals, could be very supportive. Robert Strozier, dean of students at the University of Chicago, was one of these early supporters.

The individual who was most instrumental with building support with the administrative group was the student personnel officer at the University of Washington at Seattle, Dean Newhouse. He died shortly after he went to Case Western Reserve in Ohio. He was a very great friend of the association.

He carried on frequent correspondence with me. It was through communications that he had many enquiries from other deans. Dean (that was his first name) Newhouse was a trusted, sort of middle-of-the-road guy.[22]

Others included E. G. Williamson of the University of Minnesota, Robert Shaffer of the University of Indiana, and Christine Conaway, along with Deans of Women Kathryn Hopwood of Ohio State and Miriam Sheldon at the University of Illinois. E. B. Fred, president of the University of Wisconsin, with the counsel of Roy Voegeli, then the student body president, arranged for the association to use the Wisconsin campus for the constitutional convention and the first congress (see Pt. 1, S. 4).

A network of support

This network of support was extremely important in the early survival and acceptance of NSA as various college administrations were deciding whether to encourage or discourage their student governments or their student personnel people to work with the organization.[23]

The Very Rev. Vincent Flynn, president of the College of St. Thomas, was a very supportive member of the Advisory Council, who served to interpret the association to institutions in Catholic higher education. He served on the council from 1948 through 1953. He was followed, during 1953-1960, by a series of distinguished Catholic college educators, including Reverend Celestine Steiner, S.J., president, University of Detroit; Mother Eleanor O'Byrne, president, Manhattanville College of the Sacred Heart; and Reverend T. M. Hesburgh, president, University of Notre Dame.

J. Kenneth Little, vice president at Wisconsin, and his staff provided much support.[24] This would be both in the use of the university for the constitutional convention and in responding to inquiries. And once we decided to make Madison our headquarters, they lent support to us by way of my mentoring with the staff.

Dennis Trueblood (NSA Advisory Council chair in 1951-52) and William Birenbaum (NSA Advisory Council chair in 1952-53 and then director of student activities at the University of Chicago) were students when they first became involved, but as they moved into administrative and teaching positions, they became real strengths for the association.

I've already written about Dennis Trueblood. Bill Birenbaum had been a student and NSA delegate from the University of Chicago. He moved quickly from student status into the student personnel and higher education world. He appeared regularly as a speaker and resource person at NSA conventions. Among other positions, he was dean of the New School and president of Staten Island Community College. He was also president of Antioch College for fifteen years.

There were a number of college administrators on the upper level, people like Harold Taylor (president, Sarah Lawrence College) and Frank Graham (president, University of North Carolina), who spoke to and for the organization. And then, on the beginning levels, there were people who were junior personnel coming up who lent their names, who showed up at events and lent a presence of the administrative side of the college community, which NSA was interested in being connected to.

Emily Chervenik, assistant dean of women at Wisconsin, gave much professional and personal counsel as well as physical nourishment. Eleanor Roosevelt was a strong supporter of the association and very close to some of the officers, most notably Al Lowenstein.

Helen White, a famous professor of English at the University of Wisconsin, was always available for discussion and had her own contacts in the academic world as well as that of the Catholic Church. She also represented women in higher education and used her contacts to build an appreciation of the association with other notable women in education.

Other educators and public figures who served on the NSA Advisory Council during the first five years and lent support to the organization during those early years included Millicent McIntosh (Dean, Barnard College), Kenneth Holland (Director, Institute of International Education), Harold Stassen (President, University of Pennsylvania), Althea Kratz-Hottle (Dean of Women, University of Pennsylvania), Homer Rainey (President, Stephens College), Monroe Deutsch (Provost-emeritus, University of California), Charles S. Johnson (President, Fisk University), and Everett Moore Baker (Dean of Students at Massachusetts Institute of Technology) an early NSA booster, who was killed in a plane accident after his first year of service.

A significant affiliation for NSA was its standing as the only student organization that was a constituent member of the American Council on Education (ACE), whose membership embraced all of the major professional educational organizations and colleges and universities. Francis Brown, ACE staff associate, was a strong supporter of NSA, as was George F. Zook, the ACE president.

The questions of discrimination

The organization was strongly opposed to racial segregation and served, through its activities and publications, as a positive force on the question of race. The early southern delegates had the complex task of evolving working processes to integrate all races in their local communities that would be consonant with what NSA said in speeches, meetings, and in print. As a staff member at the University of Wisconsin, a politically and socially liberal institution, I appreciated the overt and underlying support that this background gave me in working with some of the decisive integration issues.

This was a very tough issue for NSA staff members as well. It was often very hard on these people because, as I have read in some of their correspondence, landing in a town on their many organizing tours, African-American members of staff couldn't get a room or service in a restaurant.

During the first four years, there were four black members of staff who had to get housing in Wisconsin. Lee Jones, 1947-48 treasurer, went back to Buffalo, so it was not an issue, but it was for Ted Harris (president, 1948-49) and his family, for Ted Perry the next year (vice president, 1949-1950), and then for Shirley Neizer (executive secretary, 1950-51). Although we had a very good housing office, which was under Dr. Ken Little—and as I recall, they worked at it too—getting housing for them with other staff members was a problem, even in liberal Madison, Wisconsin.

I am sure my professional colleagues in the student affairs area had their share of concerns as they listened to their students who had returned from an NSA meeting where they had been involved in the more inclusive thinking on integration on their campuses. They had to face both local cultural and legal patterns of discrimination. Confronting issues that the association raised on a student Bill of Rights and on academic freedom was not always appreciated by the American higher education leadership.

The issue of gender discrimination existed in elected and appointed positions at the state, regional, and national levels, but was not openly discussed. Although women were very active on committees and in believing in and supporting NSA, the gender issue was just beginning to be faced.

NSA had a large number of women delegates and a significant number served as regional chairpersons. Women were elected to one of the five or six elected national staff positions during four of the first five years. Yet the issues facing women—sexual, career, employment, appointment, inheritance—all those issues were just beginning to be touched, although they had not yet emerged on NSA's national congress agendas.

The areas in which I served the least were the international student issues and programs. I was asked to be in charge of one of the student ships, but was intent on finishing my thesis and remained in Madison. I had some concern at times about the efficient handling of the finances of the student tours, but in the long run they did very well.

In the Foreword to a book of mine on college student government, Samuel Gould, the former president of Antioch College, stated that we cannot champion one of the most important ingredients of democracy, such as creative leadership, without offering students practical opportunities to develop such an attribute. NSA did provide opportunities for students to serve in real leadership roles on the American campus. The positions the former leadership of NSA has held on the major national and regional political and social scenes testify to the rewards these experiences gave this leadership group.

A personal perspective

Looking back at the early influences in my life that led to the vocation I chose, I must pay tribute to my family experience, which furnished a foundation on which I built my life's work.

I came from a family of very strong women. They were active in their religious groups as speakers, as trainers, and as supporters in the Protestant church. I had one aunt who supported a missionary in Japan, and when I went to Japan I visited with this missionary and her project, which was to work with the women and children deserted by American servicemen. She wasn't reading the Bible and holding a candle as a church missionary. She was providing vocational training and career counseling for these deserted women, mothers of servicemen's children, so that they could make a living and raise their children.

My father was a socialist politician in Milwaukee, which was in quite a socialist state. When my father died, my mother developed a new self. She became the book editor of a newsletter for older people.

I have a younger brother who has published many books in the areas of writing, speaking, and communications. He is a great communications person between all the Pacific Basin countries on the rim of the Pacific Ocean. He's been chairman of the Department of Communications at the University of Hawaii and then, when he retired, taught at the University of West Virginia.

I have an older brother who was a very fine doctor, and who died a year and a half or two ago. He had three daughters and a son. The son is one of the heads of the Arizona Heart Institute in Phoenix. His grandchildren are doing well.

My father's father was born in Two Rivers, Wisconsin, which was up in the middle part of the state. The family were great cheese makers. My mother's father had a cheese factory in the Milwaukee area. They had owned farmland, and my mother's family also built a lot of roads in Milwaukee.

They came over from Europe in the early 1800s, and they came to Wisconsin because of the great dairy industry there.

The civil society and the learning community

My family and personal history has given me a rich and broad experience in the civil society, with its focus on community and human relationships. We now, however, not only have to continue building a sense of community between students and faculty/administration, but we have to deal with the new technologies that see learning as gaining information.

The introduction to a recent study of the American Association of University Women sees education as a "knowledge industry." I see education as happening in learning communities: the concept is that the college is a learning community, not only serving as a source of information, but as a setting in which to learn from one another, students and faculty, and members of the working society—for developing competencies that are refined and strengthened throughout one's life.[25]

As we all function more fully in the civil society of the world, I see the strengthening of relationships and a sense of community being even more important for us. Information and knowledge can provide a base, but becoming competent to build a better world involves opportunities for individuals at all ages to be able to function more effectively as human beings in a wide range of roles and settings.

I have been a lifelong learner. The importance of becoming more competent came from the great women in my family and from some of the men who truly saw themselves as learners. They were pioneers. I owe them much.

So, as a result, building on this tradition, for me the whole experience has been a learning one, beginning conceptually with the study of group dynamics and leadership on the American campus and moving towards being more generative in the civil and professional society.

We not only adapted a body of knowledge from the social scientists but created and added to it. NSA activities taught me a great deal both for my institutional and professional leadership roles and for application to the local, national, and international levels of the civil society.

I must say that for myself, *I am here* because *they were there.*

Gordon Klopf is dean emeritus of the Bank Street College of Education. He has served as chair of the United Nations NGO Executive Committee and chair of the UN NGO International Year of the Older Person. He was NSA's first Advisory Council chair.

END NOTES

[1] Schodde, Stephen Clements, *Certain Foci of the United States National Student Association, and Their Implications for Student Personnel Administrators* (unpublished doctoral thesis, Teachers College, Columbia University. 1965). A complete copy, with the permission of the author, has been made and will reside in the USNSA/USSA archives at both the Wisconsin Historical Society and the Hoover Institution. This document is more than just an excellent professional thesis—it's a very readable document. If a student is interested in the area of the history of student life, it will prove helpful and resourceful, taking NSA from 1946 through to the year 1965 and covering topics such as: "Origins, Structure, Finances and Selected Programs," "NSA, Academic Freedom and Student Rights," "NSA and Desegregation," "NSA and the Campus," and "Trends and Implications." Appendices cover a complete roster of national officers, advisory board and advisory council members, and a bibliography. Schodde, who had been director of Student Development Services at Drake University, Iowa, retired in 1996 at sixty-one as Dean of Students.

[2] Elaine Showalter, "The Risk of Good Teaching: How 1 Professor and 9 TA's Plunged into Pedagogy." *Chronicle of Higher Education,* Vol. 45, No. 44, p. 85.

[3] I served with NSA in various advisory capacities from 1947 through 1958. I was chair of the Advisory Board in 1949-1950, 1950-51, and again in 1954-55.

[4] See Wilson, p. 248.

[5] See Sandy England, *The Impact of Women in Leadership on the National Student Association and the United States Student Association, 1946-1994.* Sub-

mitted to Indiana University as a master's degree thesis. England was Midwest Field Organizer for USSA, 1994-96. Copies of the document may be available from USSA and will be in the archives at Wisconsin and Hoover.

[6] Wesley P. Lloyd, *Student Personnel Services in Japan* (American Council on Education, Washington, D.C., 1957).

[7] See Wharton, p. 112, and Jones, p. 869. African Americans elected to national office during that period were: Clifton Wharton (Harvard), Secretary, NICC, 1946-47; Lee Jones (U. of Buffalo), Treasurer, 1948-49; James T. Harris, Jr. (LaSalle), President, 1948-49; Ted Perry (Temple), Vice President, Student Affairs, 1949-1950; and Shirley Neizer (Simmons), Executive Secretary, 1950-51. On the National Executive Committee were Ted Harris (LaSalle) and Leon C. Thompson (Va. State College) in 1947-48; Harry Alexander (Xavier), Chair, La.-Miss.-Ark., in 1948-49; Dolores Cooper and Ronald Rousseve (both of Xavier), who split the 1950-51 year; and Ronald Rousseve (Xavier), Chair, La.-Miss.-Ark.,1951-52.

[8] In 1960, I prepared a revised and enlarged edition of *Student Government and Leadership in Higher Education*. It was published by Harper and Brothers as *College Student Government*. The book places NSA's emergence after World War II in its historical context:

> Some form of student government has been apparent in American colleges since the late 1700's when William and Mary College organized a student governing body. With the founding of the University of Virginia, Jefferson recommended a modified plan of student discipline, and since that time many other institutions have claimed that American student government was founded on its campus. Although early attempts were fraught with failure, the seeds were sown.
>
> Jefferson's ideas of student government were advanced and his main thesis was that it should provide training in citizenship. Experiments were tried along these lines by Trinity, Yale, Oberlin, and Union colleges. During the period following 1870, many more attempts were made, including those at the universities of Illinois, South Carolina, and Amherst, to provide student government of some type. Not a few failed because they leaned too far to the extremes. On the one hand the system has failed because a large amount of power was given to students with little faculty or administration guidance and the students were unable to handle the powers. On the other hand too little power was given or too close supervision was maintained, leading to student government in name only.
>
> The National Self-Government Committee, Inc., an organization led by Richard Welling, wielded some influence in higher education in the development of concepts of student government in the 1920's and 1930's. The National Student Federation of the United States of America (sic), a loosely knit federation of student governments functioning during the thirties, met annually and discussed the organization and principles of student government.
>
> Basically the first half of the twentieth century saw student government evolve on most American campuses, but its function has been chiefly that of supervision of student social activities. The Intercollegiate Association of Women Students has done much to stimulate interest in women's student government. With the organization of the National Student Association in 1946, student government was given a tremendous impetus. The mature veteran students were interested in having a voice in the governing of their affairs and student governing groups flourished.
>
> As a result of this great upsurge of interest in student government, the exploration of the student's role in the government of the college initiated several studies in the ensuing ten years. The National Student Association has distributed a series of mimeographed pamphlets concerning student government and leadership. A summary of some loosely structured questionnaires on student leaders, *Student Government, Student Leaders and the American College*, edited by E. Friedson, was also published by the association in I955. Another document which deals with some original material and some of the observations in the Friedson study, *The Student's Role in College Policy Making*, by H. Lunn, was issued by the American Council on Education in 1957. The Bureau of Publications of Teachers College, Columbia University, published *Student Participation in College Administration*, by Francis Falvey, in 1954.

[9] See Welsh, p. 168, and Economic Club of Detroit, p. 191.

[10] *Editor's note:* See samples of the Faculty Rating forms and excerpts from Rick Medalie's Faculty Rating System article in the *Phi Beta Kappan* of January 1950, on p. 361.

[11] *Editor's note:* Harold Taylor delivered the keynote address to the 1949 Second National Student Congress at the University of Illlinois in Urbana. See Taylor, p. 888.

[12] A variant of this attitude was expressed by the director of student life at a smaller New York City college who wrote me in 1952 that while "I am in favor of the National Student Association and what I know of its major objectives. . . [o]ur representatives feel swallowed up in what they describe as [the region's] politics and big time operations. Our group is far more conservative. . . . However they see the value of their own point of view being presented."

[13] A letter to me in January 1949 from a Midwestern university dean illustrates the hurdle NSA sought to overcome. He writes:

> The crux of the problem probably lies in the Bill of Rights which, as you know, is a very poorly drawn document. Administrators, including ours, are not going to accept it in its present form. For N.S.A. committees and student leaders to agitate for campus changes in which they are personally interested, using the Bill of Rights as their standard of reference, leads to nothing but unnecessary conflict and friction and is likely ultimately to lead to the tossing out by many of our universities of the N.S.A. You are probably familiar with the article by President Fitzpatrick, of Mount Mary College, which appeared in *School and Society* for August 14, 1948. While I do not agree with those criticisms in their entirety, it does indicate the attitude of many administrators toward the present document and points up the necessity for serious revision. It is in this type of work that the advisory group can be especially helpful. There is also a strong feeling that there is too much emphasis upon Rights, and too little emphasis on upon the Responsibilities which are a correlative of Rights.

[14] See Shaffer, p. 326.

[15] This discussion appears in the introduction to the second conference report, *1949 College Conference, Lake Forest, Illinois.*

[16] That was the time when Jewish students weren't allowed in many fraternities. It was a big issue at Madison, and a major concern for the National Conference of Christians and Jews.

[17] In a note sent to me recently, Eugene Schwartz summarizes it briefly when he says, "It has become clear to me that you were the inspiration and guiding light—the godfather of NSA's programming and promotion of student government, leadership, group dynamics, and human relations."

[18] Copies of these newsletters are in the NSA/USSA Collection at the Wisconsin Historical Society.

[19] See bibliography for complete citations.

[20] See Shaffer, p. 326, and the Trueblood retrospective, p. 345.

[21] See Shaffer, n. 2, p. 328.

[22] An example of the confidence Dean Newhouse enjoyed (see p. 1070) is found in an exchange of correspondence he shared with me late in 1948 between himself and the student affairs personnel at a Michigan University. An open conflict had been brewing between some members of the student government and their NSA delegation. It had the appearances of a power struggle, and Dean Newhouse was asked for his views on NSA's credibility. Commenting in a December, 1948, letter to me, he wrote:

> it is very possible that NSA delegates will be rebellious minorities on their own campuses where student government doesn't have established autonomy. Such rebellion will be good in many respects and may turn into constructive and successful leadership, but it may also cause some institutions to decide that NSA is a source of difficulty and insist it be avoided. Such thinking takes me back to my original thinking about NSA which is that it cannot exist except on the basis of sound local student government, and that therefore it is absolutely necessary that NSA consider the encouragement and development of sound student government local campuses as its primary function.

[23] *Editor's note:* Two examples of the powerful influence of college administrators on NSA campus acceptance were recalled during researches for this book. In April 1948, Fred D. Fagg, president of the University of Southern California, vetoed the Student Senate vote to affiliate with NSA (see Dobkin, p. 1026). In March 1951, Very Rev. Hunter Guthrie, S.J., President of Georgetown University, made the decision in response to a student recommendation to join NSA that "we will not seek membership in the National Student Association" (see album, p. 738).

[24] *Editor's note:* Dick Heggie, NSA 1948-49 vice president, interviewed Dr. Little at the age of ninety-one in September 1996 at his home in Walnut Creek, CA. Heggie writes that Dr. Little said:

> The University was very concerned about its public image. The issue of holding the Constitutional Convention on University premises came up. A few persons worried whether the Convention would become a vehicle for radical demonstrations or student confrontations. Gordon Klopf was asked to verify that the Convention proceedings would be consistent with University principles. . . . With Little's support, the University agreed to host the convention.

In a letter to this editor on October 21, 1996, Dr. Little wrote ,"I remember with satisfaction my joining with Gordon Klopf in finding a way for the University of Wisconsin to sponsor the meeting of the USNSA on the Wisconsin campus."

[25] Reviewing the studies on the college student of the 1990s gives a picture of a student waiting to make the world a better place. Jeannette Cureton and Arthur Levine, in their study of student life today, also see students as more conciliatory. Their volume, *When Hope and Fear Collide,* published by Jossey-Bass in 1998, is very positive about the role of the American student in our society. Other volumes which support strong programs for students with a real focus on relationships, community, and leadership, include:

Clement, Linda M. *Effective Leadership in Student Services.* Jossey-Bass, 1992. 248 pp.

Komives, Susan, Lucas, Nance, and McMahon. *Exploring Leadership.* Jossey-Bass. San Francisco, 1998. 347 pp.

Kuh, George, Schuh, John, and Whidt, E. J. *Involving Colleges.* Jossey-Bass. San Francisco. 453 pp.

Little, Priscilla. *Gaining a Foothold.* AAUW, 1989. 100 pp.

Roberts, Dennis. *Designing Campus Activities to Foster a Sense of Community.* 1989. 94 pp.

PICTURE CREDITS: *Then:* La Crosse State Teachers College Workshop, Winter, 1948 (*La Cross Tribune* photo). *Now:* Honorary degree ceremony, Bank Street College, NY, 1998 (*Schwartz*).

THE RELATIONSHIP OF STUDENTS, FACULTIES, AND ADMINISTRATIONS

It is a primary aim of the USNSA to develop a campus community spirit based upon student, faculty, and administration understanding and friendship. This can be accomplished by periodic meetings within an institution of representatives from student, faculty, and administrative groups, meeting to discuss problems that jointly affect the life of the community. Regional meetings along these same lines should also be held. The orientation program for students should include information on the specific methods used on the campus to further this community development. The Constitution of the student governing body should clearly define the authority delegated to it, and a clear channel should be established through which suggestions may flow from each group. It is further suggested that encouragement within an institution of student, faculty, and administration participation in such activities as sports, dramatics, music, dances, and receptions will do much to encourage understanding and cooperation.

Panel on Student Government, NSA Constitutional Convention, 9/47

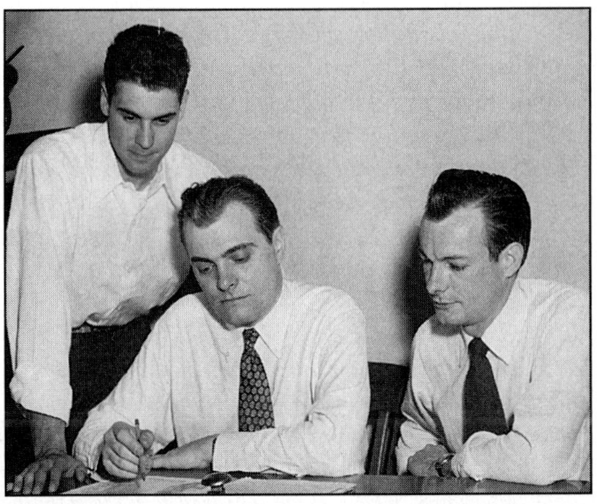

GORDON KLOPF AND STUDENTS at the University of Wisconsin. Klopf championed a collaborative relationship between student government and administration. In his 1960 work *College Student Government* (Harper and Brothers), an expanded treatment of NSA's *Student Leadership and Government in Higher Education,* first published in 1948, Klopf writes (p. 73), "... the experiences students have in student government and student activities should be considered a part of the educational program of an institution. It cannot be assumed that just engaging in group activities automatically results in educational and meaningful experiences. Students need help in attaining the values that can accrue from group activities. This professional assistance is the responsibility administratively of the personnel program and responsibility, as well, of all of the faculty and administration." (Photo: *George E. Stewart,* Klopf)

STUDENT APATHY

Student apathy is an overall self-centered approach to the role of the student (as related to the institution, the community, and the nation) which leads to a pronounced lack of interest in the affairs of the students, organizations, activities, and elections.

The USNSA Commission shall investigate the causes of student apathy, temporary and permanent, all of which are manifestations of a self-centered attitude. Among the causes to be investigated are: the inactivity of the student governments themselves; changes of values brought on by the war and varied technological developments; veteran and non-veteran groupings; over-crowded institutions and communities; commuting students; improper financial controls of student government expenditures; that kind of supervision by faculty-administration groups which deprives students of much initiative; high pressuring which intimidates faculty groups into silence, and deprives the students of faculty advice and experience; and lack of adequate social opportunities and functions.

Panel on Student Government, NSA Constitutional Convention, 9/47

GORDON JOHN KLOPF

Early years: Born 1917 in Milwaukee, WI, and graduated from the Dover Street School, where I had an early interest in drama and theater.

Education: I entered the University of Wisconsin majoring in speech, first at the Milwaukee extension campus and then at Madison. I received my B.S. in Speech and English Education in 1939, and Master of Philosophy in Education degree in 1941; and in 1950 a Ph.D. in Education—all from Wisconsin.

Career highlights: From 1939 to 1941 I was an English and Language Arts teacher in the Burlington public schools, Burlington, Wisconsin. After serving from 1941 to 1947 as a Speech Instructor and Counselor of Men's Activities at Wayne State University in Detroit, I returned to the University of Wisconsin as a Graduate Fellow in 1947-48, moving on to Coordinator of Student Activities and then Assistant Dean from 1948 to 1950—also the period when I first served as an adviser to NSA staff and as its first National Advisory Council chair,

In July of 1950 I accepted an assignment for a year as an educational specialist for the U.S. Department of State, working in Tokyo, Japan, with the Japanese Ministry of Education. In September of 1951 I became dean of students and professor of education at the State University of New York, where I served until January of 1959. In the Spring of 1954 I accepted a brief State Department assignment as an educational specialist in Japan and India, returning the following autumn. I left Buffalo in 1959 to Teachers College, Columbia University, New York, as Associate Professor of Education. In 1964 I joined the Bank Street College of Education as Associate to the President and Counselor Education Program Chairman. I became Dean of the Faculties in 1966 and then Provost and Dean in 1969, serving in that capacity until my retirement in 1980 as Dean Emeritus. Since 1961 I have accepted numerous consulting assignments with the U.S. Office of Education and other government agencies, and state and local education departments including Texas, New York, Illinois, Ohio, Louisiana, Delaware, Colorado, Kansas and Hawaii, and abroad in Puerto Rico, Iran, and Venezuela.

Until this day I have been active in non-government activities with the United Nations, having served as Chairperson of the U.S. UNICEF Working Committee for the International Year of the Child in 1979, Member of the Board and Chairperson of the U.S. Committee for UNICEF, Chair of the UNICEF Working Group in Education, and Chair of the UN NGO International Year of the Older Person, 1999.

Additionally I have served in various capacities as board member, program committee and/or panel chair for professional groups such as the Association for Supervision and Curriculum Development, Urban League of New York, American College Personnel Association, American Personnel and Guidance Association, New York State Deans Association, and Board of Directors, Brooklyn Children's Museum.

I have also authored and co-authored numerous articles, publications, and books in the fields of counseling and guidance, teacher education, student government and leadership, and the practice of education.

In 1998, I received an honorary doctorate from the Bank Street College of Education.

Family: Two brothers, three grandnieces, and a grandnephew.

Editor's Note: Gordon Klopf was an encouraging and affectionate presence and friend throughout the early years I was associated with NSA. Many of the writers in this book recall the significance of his influence in guiding our attention to the importance of empathetic listening and communication in the process of human interaction. It seemed a role flowing easily from his nature to provide a mentoring presence in every circumstance. When we launched the Anthology project he provided active support and advice in its early stages, keeping things on an upbeat plane with a constant flow of ideas and an irrepressably impish sense of humor. We rekindled a strong bond of comradeship—a relationship which I treasure highly.

The qualities Gordon brought as an adviser to the early leadership of NSA were being celebrated forty and fifty years later by his students at the Bank Street College of Education. On the occasion of Gordon's 85th birthday in 2002, Tom Roderick, a former student, wrote of him in verse, "T'was a boy from green Wisconsin/ a shoot from a progresssive tree, A child full of wonder/ born with a motive—to set the world free! . . . He came from a line of thinkers/ who liked to tinker with the status quo . . . and became a bold exponent/ of that vital life component—justice!"

On April 18, 1986, the Bank Street College of Education sponsored "A Celebration to Honor Gordon Klopf, His Life and Work." In a profile for the occasion Deborah Stone, one of his students, wrote, "Students coming into his classroom sense immediately that he takes them seriously. It is clear that Gordon assumes that everyone has a life story of tremendous importance, whose telling will lead to understanding." In many ways that is what this book is about. —Eugene G. Schwartz

WORKSHOP AT LACROSSE STATE TEACHERS COLLEGE, WI, with students and faculty in 1948. Center seated, Gordon Klopf. Third from right, Eugene G. Schwartz (CCNY), NSA 1948-49 Vice President for Educational Problems. (*La Crosse Tribune* photo. Schwartz)

BY GORDON KLOPF
VISITING PROFESSOR OF EDUCATION
TEACHERS COLLEGE
COLUMBIA UNIVERSITY

COLLEGE STUDENT GOVERNMENT

Foreword by Samuel B. Gould
former President, Antioch College
and Chancellor,
University of California,
Santa Barbara

Harper & Brothers, New York

"ITS EVERY PAGE . . . PROCLAIMS that until we begin offering the college students the opportunities and responsibilities of adulthood they will continue to be children," wrote Samuel B. Gould, Chancellor, U. of California, Santa Barbara, in his foreword to Klopf's book (see above). He continued, "The truly vital lesson we all must learn is that of faith in the present generation of youth."

Clinics Study Student Government

NSA News, March 1949

Regional Program Use Many New Techniques

By HELEN JEAN ROGERS

Realizing the need for bettering student government and student leadership on campus, many of the regions of NSA have sponsored clinics and conferences designed to offer an opportunity to learn how student problems are being solved on other campuses and to study techniques of leadership.

NEW ENGLAND

Northern and Southern New England joined together recently to hold a student government clinic at the University of Connecticut, Storrs. The delegates heard an address by Richard Heggie, NSA national vice-president, and participated in small discussion groups in which the areas of student finance, student government structure and student rights were among the subjects discussed.

MILLICENT CAREY McINTOSH

MET. N. Y.

Adelphi College was the site of the Metropolitan New York regional student government forum at which more than 200 students from 30 colleges heard Dean Millicent McIntosh of Barnard College declare that "a close relationship between the faculty and students in a college is one of the most important elements in making education effective."

Following this address the representatives participated in group discussions of the topics, "How can the student government best take part in curriculum reform?", "How can student extra-curricular activities best be directed?", "What are the powers of the student government?", "How can the student government best function?", "How can the student government develop leadership within its school?", and "How can cooperation be developed between the student government and the faculty?"

Al Luca, president of the Student Council of New York University at University Heights, addressed the group at the close of the session, asserting "power and responsibility invariably go together in student government; a disproportion of power or responsibility has the definite effect of lessening the quality of student government." The results of the conference will be published shortly in booklet form, it was announced by Jacki Guest of Adelphi College, general chairman of the forum.

NEW JERSEY

A distinctive innovation in the area of student government conferences has been initiated by the New Jersey region. Each month a member school in the area plays host to other New Jersey schools for a forum presented on some area of student government concern. Dinner and informal recreation usually followed the discussions. Forums have considered scope of student government, student government organization, and student rights.

KENTUCKY-TENNESSEE

Concentrating on developing the "know-how" necessary for competent campus leadership, the Kentucky-Tennessee region held a two-day leadership conference at Berea College, Kentucky, during the winter. Following an address by Ted Harris, president of NSA, the group explored the problems of leadership and considered ways of training new student officers in methods of conducting meetings, parliamentary procedure, duties of various officers and other needed information. Bill Welsh, former president of NSA, headed the leadership workshop and the whole conference was under the direction of Bob Delahanty, University of Louisville, chairman of the Kentucky-Tennessee region.

PENNSYLVANIA

Bryn Mawr College has been the headquarters of the Pennsylvania effort toward the improvement of student government. At this college the regional student government clinic is located, which keeps on file pertinent information about student government and assists campuses in solving problems. The clinic, in addition to filling requests for help that come into the office, also sends out questionnaires in the area to obtain more information and suggests programs that will be of benefit to all the student governments.

MICHIGAN

Substituting a socio-drama and buzz session for the usual keynote speaker, the Michigan region initiated a new technique for NSA leadership conferences.

The socio-drama was presented at the first session by four players—representing faculty, student leader administration and "ordinary" student—each of whom was interviewed asked to point out the problems as he sees them in the student government area. The purpose of the drama is to have each participant speak freely in presenting his point of view, thus bringing out questions

view, thus bringing out questions that might not come up during workshop sessions, and also orientating the audience toward thinking in terms of the problems for the workshop discussions.

After the drama the group divided into small buzz sessions of four to six persons. In the buzz sessions specific problems are brought forth, then presented to the general session for inclusion on the agenda of the workshops. The buzz sessions are designed to give the delegates a feeling that they are establishing the scope of the conference.

Prior to the conference the group leaders and recordeas met to hold training sessions. Resource persons who assisted the groups in solving problems also attended the pre-conference sessions. In the workshops students discussed the four areas of "the student body and the student leaders," "student-faculty relations," "student administration relations," and "student government and the student body."

Other regions have presented some type of student government conferences including Indjana, Virginia - Carolina, Georgia - Alabama-Florida, and Ohio. The latter three held student government meetings in connection with regional conventions while Indiana held two student government clinics, one at Purdue University in the fall and the second a spring meeting at Indiana State Teachers' College at Terre Haute.

NSA News, May 1949

Student Government, Leadership Conferences Receive Wide Acclaim

Biggest news of the month on the student government front has been the tremendous growth of Student Government Clinics and Leadership Conferences all over the nation.

Both the UNIVERSITY OF WISCONSIN and the Michigan Region of NSA are holding large scale meetings during the last week in March to improve the procedures of student government and to train those students aspiring to positions of responsibility.

The Michigan meeting, specifically oriented toward the latter objective, will be held in Ann Arbor March 25-28. Students and faculty members from all Michigan colleges and universities have been invited to attend.

ST. MARY'S COLLEGE of Winona, Minnesota, played host to an "extremely successful" student government workshop in which most of the colleges in the central Midwest took part. Delegates who attended report that everyone left with the feeling that much had been accomplished in all areas from Student Government Structure to Finance. An official summation of the proceedings will be available for distribution in the near future.

Recognizing the need for a permanent regional agency to carry out exchange of information on student government procedures, several areas have established district committees of student government representatives which are able to meet at frequent intervals.

The Greater Boston Student Government Association, one of the more recent of these agencies, reports that its winter meeting, held at BABSON INSTITUTE, Feb. 26, was very successful. Information which is being compiled concerning hotels and orchestras in and around Boston will be condensed in the form of a complete Boston social schedule before the end of the school year, it was stated.

Many schools have set up campus leadership training programs in order to insure continuous education for would-be activity leaders.

WASHINGTON STATE COLLEGE student government has just concluded the Spring session of its leadership course which included such subjects as "How to conduct a meeting effectively," "Financial procedures," "How to get a job done—planning the program and delegating responsibility," and "Minutes and record-keeping." Though each section was directed toward a special interest group, many students from the campus-at-large attended the session.

While the leadership course is now a traditional part of Washington State's student activity, at COLORADO COLLEGE it is a comparatively new experience.

CC's first all-college student leadership conference was held Sunday, Feb. 27, for the purpose of bringing about closer cooperation among the branches of the college family as well as of helping the individual student leader. Much of the discussion related to the role of each student in his student government and in the public relations of his college.

"NSA WAS SEEKING TO CHANGE THE HISTORIC NOTION that participation in [college] government was not the student's place," Klopf writes on p. 333. NSA's program of student government clinics was at the core of its efforts to provide college students with new techniques and effective tools for self-government.

Group Dynamics: NSA Introduces Alternative to "Robert's Rules"

The Columbia University Student Council
Wing B- University Hall Annex

Columbia University — New York 27, N. Y.

1949 - 1950
Chalmers F. Frazer, *Chairman*
Daniel J. Ehrlich, *Vice-chairman*
Ann Hicks, *Secretary*
Gibson Gray, *Treasurer*

UNiversity 4-3200
Extension 856
Executive Secretary
Betty Ann Sagle

November 21, 1949

Mr. Michael DeLegge
3216 Kosouth Avenue
Bronx, New York

Dear Michael:

This is a formal invitation to you to be the panel leader on the panel on Student Apathy at the Student Government Clinic and Forum to be held at Columbia University on December 10.

A training session for panel leaders is planned for Friday, November 25 at 7 p.m. in the Columbia University Student Council office.

Please let us hear from you as soon as possible.

Sincerely yours,
Dick Ajalat
Dick Ajalat, Chairman
External Affairs Committee
Columbia University Student Council

On December 10, the Columbia University Student Council and the USNSA N.Y. Metropolitan region are sponsoring a Student Government Clinic and Forum. The members of your student government are invited. The clinic will take place in the auditorium of Casa Italiana on Columbia campus (see enclosed map.) The agenda is as follows:

10:00-11:00 Registration
11:00 - 12 Opening Session
12:00 - 1:30 Luncheon
1:30 - 4:15 Divide into panels
4:15 - 5:00 Intermission, Afternoon refreshments
5:00 - 6:00 Report from Panel Leaders

The Panels are as follows:

1. Machinery of Student Government: Discussion of the student government constitution, its form, scope, and revision; electoral procedure: discussion of the nomination, election system, and system of representation. Committees: what committees are necessary, how they are set up and business carried on.
2. Operation of Student Government: Training of leadership, finances of the student government and the relationship to other campus activities; discussion of proper financing and budgeting.
3. a) Student Government Function: Services to the student; organizing of clubs; judiciary systems; honor systems; student courts; setting up committees on sports, dances, etc.
   b) Responsibility of the Student Government: in areas such as discrimination, academic freedom and orientation programs.
4. Student Apathy: Stimulation of student interest in student organizations, elections, special projects, etc.
5. Publications: how information is gotten, how personnel is obtained and tr[...] how publicity is assimilated.

NSA BULLETIN
FIRST ANNUAL CONGRESS
Executive Committee Authorization
Vol. 11, Number 3, NSA Congress Bulletin
August 25, 1948--Wednesday
WORKSHOP ONCE*OVER

RESOURCE PERSONNEL PRESS CONFERENCE
MINUTES

Milwaukee Sentinel's
Ed Canare--I have here a copy of the "NSA Congressional Record" issued by National Students for Wallace which says that "in most of yesterday's workshops the question became how to discuss a discussion". What is your reaction to statement?

Dr. Mable R. Walter-Nat. Director American Red Cross College Activities:
I disagree heartily. There has been no waste of time at all. I've been to three workshops and the students are doing a magnificent job. They stepped in and worked out their own problems without adult supervision, asking only technical advice from resource personnel. They convey a great breadth of understanding. ...The first day is one of exploration and lays the groundwork for positive planning. The method is a time-consuming one and might give an initial feeling of frustration with students new to the idea, but leads to a feeling of group satisfaction, each individual having contributed to the discussion.

Joe Miller, Congress Pulic Relations Dir:
Would you all say that the non-directive technique then seems to be the best method of discussion for the NSA to use?

Frank Sulewski, Mid-West Reg. Socy., WSSF:
If the degree of individual participation in discussion is any criteria of success, and I think it is...You certainly have success here. The method allows for greater group cohesion, common understanding on projects, and outlaws arbitrary rules"

NON*DIRECTIVE CHAIRMEN
Resolved — Call the Question — Motion Defeated

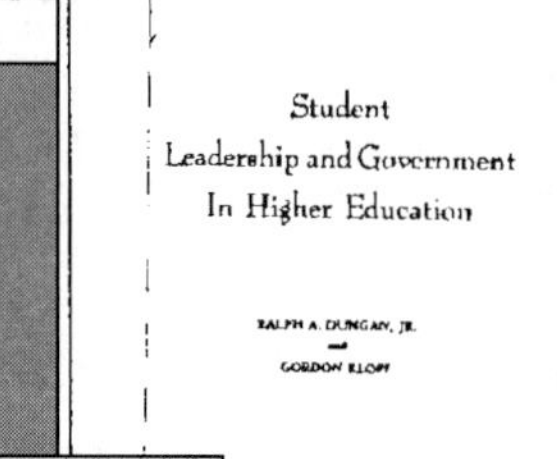

Midwest College Student Conference

A pioneering job is being undertaken in this conference for college students. The emphasis will be upon the attitudes and techniques of democratic group methods.

Leadership will probably spell the difference between a cooperating world and a pile of rubble. Leadership is fundamental on the campus as well as in other areas of community living. Clarification of the principles of effective leadership and understanding guidance can be achieved by the members of this conference, so too can an increased knowledge of human relations and group dynamics. The accomplishment of these purposes will mean hard work and intense cooperation.

JUNE 20 - 25, 1948

Lake Forest, Illinois

Sponsored by

The National Conference of Christian and Jews
203 North Wabash Avenue
Chicago 1, Illinois

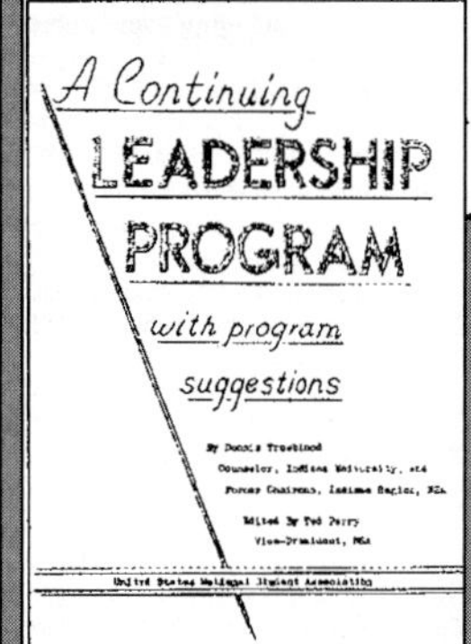

"AN ORGANIZATION NEEDS TO OBSERVE ITS OWN FUNCTIONING as a group before it can go far" ("Student Leadership and Government in Higher Education"). Introduction of group process observation and evaluation was a basic element in the leadership training programs developed by NSA—working collaboratively with a new generation of student personnel administrators interested in enhancing the student leadership and government experience as a learning instrument. On this page, examples of its use in 1948-49 regional programs and (above) at the 1948 Congress. See also p. 335.On the left, key NSA manuals of the time.

(Berea College Archives; Michael DiLegge)

"No student organization can flourish on the American college campus as an effective and vibrant organization without the support of the educator"

3. Dennis Trueblood: From Student Leader to Leading Personnel Administrator

Indiana State Teachers College (Indiana State University)
Chair, Indiana Region, 1947-48; NSA Advisory Council, 1951-53. Chair, 1951-52

Editor's Note: Dennis Trueblood was a popular regional leader in the founding years of NSA who worked closely with Gordon Klopf in laying the groundwork together with NSA's national officers for its leadership training programs. He was among several early NSA leaders who pursued student personnel work as a career (See William Birenbaum, Pt. 3, S. 3, University of Chicago, who also became a member and Chair of the NAC). His untimely death at the age of 38 cut short a promising career.

NSA, the Voice of the American College Student

Excerpts from NSA Advisor Newsletter, *undated, c.1952*

It is as the student voice of America that USNSA has its most direct contact with educators and government officials of the nation. It is this function which has served to motivate the development of strong individual leaders within NSA. Essentially, the leadership flow of NSA has been from individual campus student government to regional NSA affairs, to national student services affairs, to interest in the voice function of the Association. The expression of the student-voice-of-America-function of NSA has manifested itself in numerous ways. . . .

* * *

Nationally and internationally, NSA policy is implemented by NSA representatives attending numerous conferences. At these conferences, NSA representatives are asked to speak for the American college student. NSA qualifies as the most representative American student organization since its membership of about 300 colleges and universities represent about 800,000 college students. During its brief five years of existence NSA representatives have appeared at many international conferences and have conferred with other students in almost every corner of the earth—Africa, Southeast Asia, Europe, South America, the Middle East and North America. NSA has been and is being accepted as the voice of the American college student, nationally and internationally

The voice of the American college student function of NSA raises many questions to the educator. Will NSA continue to be accepted as the voice of the American college student? If so, what role should the educator play in encouraging the development of a "voice" which includes not 800,000 students but all American college students? Do non-member schools have an obligation to investigate, more energetically, affiliation with NSA? Does the educator, particularly the college student personnel worker, need to re-examine his position toward the organization of students to express their opinions on issues which affect their education? Do we as educators really believe that every individual, student or otherwise, should be stimulated to think and express himself on those issues fundamental to the American Way of Life? If so, do we believe that NSA should be stimulated to growth, or shall the passive attitude which appears to be a prevalent attitude today, continue to prevail?

These are all intriguing questions. The answers are fundamental, in my opinion, as to the path which NSA shall travel in the following years. The educator's answers are of vital importance to NSA because no student organization can flourish on the American college campus as an effective and vibrant organization without the support of the educator.

Why Leadership Training?

Excerpts from Aids in Building Leadership Programs, *by Dr. Dennis L. Trueblood (USNSA, 1954)*

To develop campus leaders who will use their knowledge in later life as community citizens and to develop in the non-participating student a desire to participate in community affairs after graduation from college, is a primary problem in educational circles today. That there is a single solution is doubtful. Rather, it would appear that the problem is of a multi-solution nature. Any effort in the total area of developing campus and community leadership is a start, and a necessary one, until all social institutions involved in the training for citizenship and perpetuation of our democratic way of life are able to combine their efforts toward a total program.

"Thirty years ago the great danger to the American way of life was inner dissension. Today it is complacency. We now realize that we may not pursue social re-education in too leisurely a fashion. In many parts of the world, and in some circles among ourselves, democracy is under attack, or the concept has been tortured out of all resemblance to its original meaning. There is urgent need, therefore, for further experimentation and, especially, for a rapid diffusion of proved methods of community self-study and of deliberative group discussion." These words of [Bruno] Lasker [*Democracy through Discussion*, H.W. Wilson, 1949] are the keynote words to an attempt to interject into the campus scene a number of activities to develop more and better leadership.

* * *

There is evidence to support the belief that higher education is assuming a greater responsibility for forwarding the progress of the present-day society. The rise of the state university, the development of the student personnel movement, the setting up of curricular concentrations such as the Institute of Citizenship at Kansas State University, and the creation of the general college and the junior college are evidences of this trend. Still more responsibility can be accepted.

The rise of the United States National Student Association following World War II and the subsequent re-emphasis of student government as an integral part of higher education are the most recent developments. It is the National Leadership Training Program of USNSA which next promises to further develop the universities' responsibility for training more and better leaders. The National Leadership Training Program will serve as a stimulus for the conscious development of more and better leaders and citizens from present day college students.

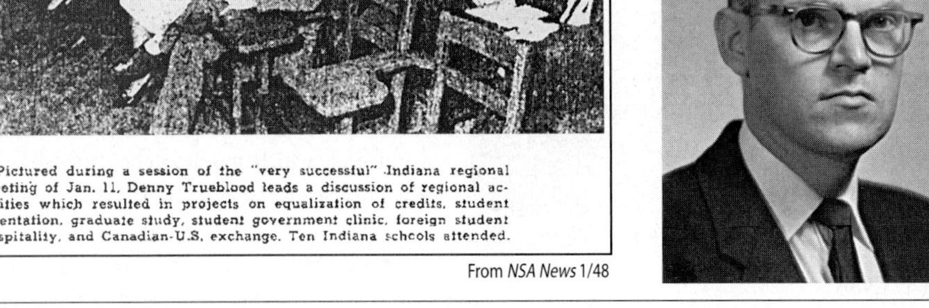

Indiana Discusses Regional Activities

Pictured during a session of the "very successful" Indiana regional meeting of Jan. 11, Denny Trueblood leads a discussion of regional activities which resulted in projects on equalization of credits, student orientation, graduate study, student government clinic, foreign student hospitality, and Canadian-U.S. exchange. Ten Indiana schools attended.

From *NSA News* 1/48

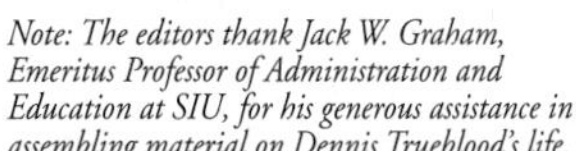

Dennis Trueblood was Chair of the Department of Guidance at Southern Illinois University. He was President of the American College Personnel Association in 1963, before his untimely death in 1964.

Note: The editors thank Jack W. Graham, Emeritus Professor of Administration and Education at SIU, for his generous assistance in assembling material on Dennis Trueblood's life.

DENNIS LEE TRUEBLOOD, SR., 1926-1964

Dennis Trueblood was born April 12, 1925, in rural Vigo County near Prairie Creek, Indiana, and graduated from Honey Creek High School in 1943 at Terre Haute. The following is excerpted from a biographical note prepared for the Anthology by Jack W. Graham, Emeritus Professor of Administration and Higher Education, Southern Illinois University at Carbondale:

Dr. Trueblood earned his B.S. degree from Indiana State University in 1948. He received his MBA and Ph.D. Degrees from Indiana University in 1949 and 1954 respectively. He was an outstanding student at Indiana University and started his prolific record of scholarly publications while in graduate school. His interest in students, the profession of college student personnel work, and his involvement in the National Student Association began during his undergraduate years. He demonstrated his keen ability to work with people in a personable and effective manner as a student and later as a student personnel administrator and as a university professor.

Dr. Trueblood came to Southern Illinois University in December of 1957 from the New York office of the National Conference of Christians and Jews. Prior to that time he served as Director of Financial Aid at the U. of Kansas (1954-56). He was a member of both the Departments of Guidance and of Higher Education, and later became Chair of the Department of Guidance in 1963.

Professor Trueblood guided and molded the Graduate Programs in Higher Education at Southern Illinois University. He was elected President of the American College Personnel Association in 1963. This was a high honor bestowed by his professional colleagues. He was unable to complete his term of office due to his untimely death in 1964 following open heart surgery. His premature death at the age of 38 cut short a most promising professional career.

Dr. Trueblood was ahead of his time in writing clearly of the important task of including all students from all minorities as well as women in the varied academic and out of class activities of the collegiate scene. He wrote over 50 articles for professional journals and related publications in the area of higher education: These were directed to students, professional staff, and to scholars in higher education. One chapter in the monograph "College Student Personnel Work in the Years Ahead" proved to be most accurate and an important part of the monograph series published by the American College Personnel Association.

Dennis Trueblood was a respected scholar, teacher, and administrator. He provided leadership for the early development of the National Student Association. He was a strong proponent of the civil rights of all students and the development of programs providing access to higher education to all students through a combination of clear rules of non-discrimination and providing services that facilitated the learning process. This also included improving financial aid and providing a caring attitude on the part of the academic community that encouraged the recruitment of minorities and support for their continued attendance and the completion of their degrees. He demonstrated his concern for assisting minorities by his consultation with admission's staff and those involved in student work and financial assistance. He recruited minority students and women as graduate students in the College Student Personnel program.

He married Dorothy Drown in 1952. She completed a master's degree at Indiana University in Food and Nutrition. She passed away in 1989.They have two children, Dennis Lee, Jr., and Zoe Annette.

PICTURE CREDITS: *Then:* Indiana State Teachers College "Sycamore Yearbook," 1947-48 (*Jack W. Graham*). *Now:* c. 1960, Southern Illinois University (SIU Photo Service, *Jack W. Graham*).

Establishing a campus presence

4. NSA's Educational Affairs and Student Life Programs

Richard J. Medalie
Carleton College, Minnesota
NSA Vice President, Educational Affairs, 1949-50

I first became active in NSA at Carleton College and in the Minnesota region the year before I was elected to the vice presidency. Because of an interest in world affairs, I had become involved with the United World Federalists[1] on campus, as well as with SPAN—the Student Project for Amity among Nations—an intercollegiate program of work and study abroad. I was campus chairman in 1947-48, and statewide orientation chair in 1948-49.

One of Carleton NSA's major projects, which received national prominence, was an NSA art exhibit, which was sent to many NSA colleges throughout the country, and ended up at the 1949 NSA Congress at the University of Illinois.

I had also become very deeply involved in the politics of NSA. Minnesota was one of the major conservative regions—as conservatism went in those days—the major issue being our active opposition to any relationship with the International Union of Students (IUS). We had been very close to the Maryland-D.C.-Virginia and the Carolina regions because Phil DesMarais, who became executive director of the Catholic students' Joint Committee for Student Action[2] had originally been a student at the University of Minnesota and Chair of the Minnesota Region. He then went to Georgetown University in Washington. So we played a very active role with respect to the IUS issue. Although the knock-down, drag-out fight over IUS happened the year before, we undertook the cleanup operation at the 1949 convention.

I tell the story about my Carleton College and Minnesota Region experience elsewhere in this book (see Part 5). In this part, I review the domestic programs of NSA in which I became involved, and which led to my election as vice president for educational affairs in 1949-50, during Bob Kelly's presidency.

NSA voices a view of education

Our staff report to the Third National Congress at Michigan in August 1950 sketched out the ambitious program NSA had embraced. In educational affairs, NSA articulated the view so widely accepted today that the formal educational process did not begin and end at the classroom door. In addition, our staff had presided over the year in which most of the World War II veteran population moved on to graduate school or out into the work force.

In my congress report, I wrote:

> Even as we enter another period of national crisis, the postwar generation of student veterans are leaving the campuses and giving up their control of student and college community life. Their replacements are no less ambitious, but are younger and possess a narrower range of experience. They are to assume, without ceremony and without careful preparation, traditions and responsibilities of which they are unaware....
>
> It is our duty to consolidate and protect the gains of the post-war years by insuring that its technology and its ideas are effectively transferred to the new student leaders and to the functioning student governments....
>
> We face at this Congress...the equally difficult job of interpreting a new concept of education for student governments, students, student leaders, faculty and administrators. This new concept departs widely from the traditional definition and practice, for it recognizes from the start that students experience, learn and develop outside the four walls of the classroom and that extra-curricular experience should in some purposeful way be integrated with, and related to, the formal curriculum.[3]

Each of us vice presidents was considered to head a commission. Mine was on educational affairs, and covered the following subcommission areas:

- Education: evaluation of curriculum and instruction, academic freedom.
- Human Relations: Brotherhood Week, the Human Relations Handbook, National Scholarship Service and Fund for Negro Students, unfair educational practices.

- Economics of Education: federal scholarships, federal aid.
- Student Economic Welfare: vocational guidance and job opportunities, student cooperatives, the NSA Purchase Card System.
- Legislative Activity: legislative newsletter, federal aid, the draft and universal military training.

Janet Welsh Brown deals extensively with NSA's program in the areas of academic freedom and student rights elsewhere in this anthology.[4] The focus here will be on the other programs in which I was engaged.

Faculty Rating

Faculty Rating was a program initiated by the First Congress in 1948, which took hold in various forms on many campuses. Gene Schwartz prepared the first edition of the NSA Faculty Rating booklet. The first-year response by student governments was good, and faculty groups began to consider it seriously. We continued the program. Craig Wilson and I worked on an update of the first edition of the NSA booklet. We sent out a presentation to all the campuses. As a result of the popularity and widespread interest in the program, I was invited to write an article on Faculty Rating for the *Phi Delta Kappan* journal, portions of which appear in the resource unit of this section. I also made a presentation on Faculty Rating at a major conference on higher education sponsored by the American Council on Education (ACE) in early 1950.

On a number of occasions during my travels, I met and talked with administrators about the rating program. Whenever I went out into the field, I would also meet with student body presidents, explaining the program and encouraging them to utilize it.

In its second year, the February 1949 issue of *NSA News* reported student evaluation of faculty programs being implemented at colleges and universities, such as the University of Michigan, Albright College (PA), Brooklyn College, Loyola (IL), University of Idaho, Illinois Institute of Technology, New York University (Heights), and Penn State.

In the January 1949 issue of the *Journal of Higher Education*, its editor, R. H. Eckelberry, wrote in a lengthy editorial praising the program that "The United States National Student Association is to be congratulated on having undertaken as one of its major projects, the improvement of instruction in colleges and universities through rating by students of instructors and courses."

Ralph Dungan, NSA's first vice president for national student affairs in 1947-48, who developed the original faculty-rating bulletin, recalls in a recent interview for this book that one of the reasons Faculty Rating was popular was that veteran students were not afraid to challenge the system and to expect effective teacher performance in the classroom. Often the veterans were the same age as some of the instructors.

We also recognized that there were limitations to this kind of an evaluation and that, as I wrote, "a rating form that required a technical knowledge of teaching methods and procedures would defeat the whole purpose of the system," but by making the sheets available to the teacher, it would help him or her "recognize and correct flaws in instructional techniques."

Legislative activity: federal aid and universal military training

Most of our effort in this area went into producing a legislative newsletter. NSA had not yet mobilized aggressive lobbying efforts. As I wrote in our report to the Congress:

> The problem of NSA's participating in legislative or political activity has been a continual source of difficulty ever since the founding of NSA. The NSA constitution specifically forbids NSA "on all levels from taking part in partisan political and sectarian religious activities...." It has been the custom, however, for NSA to participate in that type of political activity that affects "students as students."

Federal aid to education was one of our legislative agendas, however, and we tried to organize the students in support of it. In the December 1949 issue of *NSA News*, I wrote that "The educational world should have student ideas on educational legislation in order that the bills drafted be of the type that best suits the student needs." I noted that we would be presenting our ideas at an American Council on Education (ACE) conference that month at which ACE would be drawing up provisions for a federal scholarship bill.

Subsequently, NSA congresses took positions on the draft, universal military training, and educational deferments. United States involvement in Korea in summer 1950 brought military service to the fore as a concern on all college campuses. NSA had already begun to concern itself in 1948 with the issue of "compulsory military training" when it appointed Philip John Hart of Antioch College (later to become a senator from the state of Michigan) to chair a committee to do a national campus survey and develop a national information program on the issue. The August 1952 NSA Congress supported selective service, opposed universal military training, and supported student deferments "until graduation."

The NSA Purchase Card/Student Discount Service

The Purchase Card System (renamed in 1950-51 as the Student Discount Service) was another major NSA program.[5] Although it was very popular with campus NSA committees and student governments, it was also highly controversial and of uneven success throughout the more than twenty years and various permutations in which it survived.[6] It was developed as a way to save students money by getting local merchants to offer them purchase discounts. Originally, the student bought the card for a dollar; the money would go primarily to the student government, with 10 percent to the region and 20 percent to the NSA office. Local purchase card committees recruited the merchants and signed them up, using contract forms furnished by NSA. (After the PCS reorganization in 1950-51, the card was given to students free of charge.)

The Purchase Card System (PCS) was first introduced as the New Jersey Plan at the 1947 congress, which handed it over to the University of Buffalo to implement in a pilot project in Spring 1948. Under the energetic leadership of Lee Jones, then NSA treasurer, some 1,500 students, five Buffalo area colleges, and more than twenty-five merchants took part. The result was a recommendation to the first congress, at Madison in 1948, to launch the national program.

As originally designed, the program called for local organization on a campus and regional basis, and top down administration through the national office. This generated considerable paper work and a flurry of bulletins and forms issued by Gene Schwartz, the 1948-49 educational problems vice president, to get the program off the ground.

Bob Kelly, who had developed the system for Newark, NJ, when he was the New Jersey Regional chair, was a big supporter of the program. In the December 1949 issue of *NSA News*, Craig Wilson prepared a special eight-page insert promoting the program.

In September, I announced in the PCS Bulletin that "PCS is in full swing again! The new cards were finished a few days ago....50,000 were printed. We expect to sell 10,000 cards during the months of October and November. Already 4,000 cards have been sent to Chicago, 5,000 to Detroit, 6,000 to Boston and 1,500 to New Jersey."

In December, I was able to report another 30,000 cards back to press, with news such as "63 stores have been contracted in the Greater Boston area alone. Word has just come from Met. N.Y. that a tremendous publicity drive is under way—500 merchants in New York is Met's minimum goal." Of the 19 area and one college committees we listed, 15 were active from Newark to Detroit to Louisville to Los Angeles.

Merchants received the local organizing efforts with mixed response. It was resisted and opposed in some areas.[7] But PCS, in our eyes, was a noble cause. In an editorial in the October 1949 issue of *NSA News,* I wrote:

> PCS reports have come to the national office that anonymous literature is being sent out to various retail merchant associations "exposing" PCS as a proprietary and unfair business practice. Never has such information been so fallacious! . . . Not only does PCS serve the student, but local businesses cooperating with the system find substantial increases in their sales more than offsetting the discounts offered. . . . PCS offers that opportunity for the community to help itself by broadening the educational opportunity for the many who will later make material contributions to the nation's progress.

In point of fact, PCS never returned revenues to NSA more than a fraction of the value to students of the cards that had been distributed, although in 1949-1950 dollars it contributed nearly 10 percent of our operating revenues: $2,525 out of the total $29,375 in revenues (against expenses of $28,375—which paid for a full- and part-time staff of seven). Many felt that it was a distraction from the primary purposes of NSA as an advocate and voice for student interests.

The Special Advisory Committee on Organizational Affairs that we chartered in spring 1949, consisting of over forty former NSA national and regional officers, in their report to the congress said of the Purchase Card System:

> This project is an end, not a means toward achieving a major objective. . . . Since the alleviation of the student's economic burden is accomplished to a very small degree, the project takes more of the time of the responsible officer than is justified. A de-emphasis of PCS is necessary, and due to the very great financial liabilities involved. . . . [T]he only course of action would seem to be dropping of the Purchase Card System as a national program.

In response to this recommendation, the Third Congress at Michigan renamed the program and recast it to one of locally based administration, with no fee for the card, while the national office furnished legal and paperwork services. Thus, the 1950-51 *SDS Handbook* observed about the program:

> On the primary level of value, the NSA was conspicuously successful: students were cooperating to reduce their cost of living. But the Purchase Card System had a baneful influence on the other programs and purposes of the Association. Student governments and NSA Committees, long accustomed to the philosophy that their only meaningful function was to provide material services for students, found their way to NSA via the restrictive pathway of this economic program. If the PCS cards did not come in on time, if a local program that was hopefully begun petered out—NSA was declared at fault, labeled valueless. Student leaders with a strange, almost perverted, logic found in the Purchase Card System all the raw material to credit or discredit the Association.

In this same manual, the new Student Discount Service (SDS) card was reproduced over a heading which read: "THIS CARD IS NOW HELD BY OVER 100,000 STUDENTS IN FORTY COLLEGE COMMUNITIES."

Vocational guidance and job opportunities, student co-ops

NSA had formally committed itself from its founding to a concern over student economic welfare. In the early years, we focused on information services.

The 1947-48 staff published a booklet by Emily Chervenic, assistant dean at the University of Wisconsin, entitled *Planning a Job Opportunities Conference.* During my year, the NSA Vocational Guidance Subcommission, under the chairmanship of Beverly Nemer at UCLA, continued the expansion of its vocational library and information service started the previous year. As I reported to the Michigan congress, "The work of the commission was hampered by a lack of skill and lack of workers as well as money." This subcommission recommended that it be disbanded and that "similar organizations be set up on each campus."

NSA had also endorsed and cooperated with the North American Student Cooperative League in disseminating information about co-ops. We recommended, and the Michigan Congress approved, establishment of formal ties with the league for the exchange of delegates at their conventions and for cooperation in programs of student cooperatives, such as campus co-op stores, book stores, and housing and eating co-ops. During my term I assembled and edited an NSA publication, *Campus Co-ops.*

Human Relations

Human relations was a very key program during our year. Gordon Klopf and I wrote a booklet, *Human Relations in the Educational Community.* The cover (illustrated on p. 321) shows the arms of Ted Perry and me shaking hands—the joining of colors, black and white.

The scope of the program is suggested by the chapter titles and some of the topics treated: "The Philosophy of Good Human Relations" (principles and personal characteristics), "Human Relations in the Campus Group" (group processes and leadership), "The Campus Conference" (subject, process, evaluation), "Initiating the Campus Human Relations Program" (setting up a committee, conducting an audit), "A Continuing Human Relations Program" (curriculum, student government, residential groups, fraternities and sororities, religious and political groups), and "Communicating the Idea of Human Relations" (publications, radio, social events, convocations, panels, visual aids, special weeks).

In collaboration with the National Conference of Christians and Jews (NCCJ), we organized a number of conferences around the country. A so-called auditor would analyze the student dynamics and how people acted and reacted to each other. Dealing with substance at the conferences was really the means by which students from diverse backgrounds would get to interact and build harmonious relations with each other.

Students from all over the country participated in an annual NCCJ/NSA Lake Forest, Illinois, conference. We broke down into different work groups, each with group leaders and auditors. The National Student Congresses began to use the technique as well. The Congress was broken down into various sessions relating to specific issues of the NSA, and each session would always have the "auditor" in it. At the end of the session, the auditor would analyze how individuals in the group operated with each other. The concept was to make decisions by consensus, especially in the smaller committees. As an alternative to rhetoric and debate, it was founded on the idea that, if people only knew each other, and how they thought, they could find some common ground.

What was most interesting was that, when a human relations approach began, born from the actual experience of discrimination, it branched out. First, it dealt with how to get the different races to listen to one another, and then it shifted to procedural tools by means of which people can live together.

Human Relations was a central theme in NSA's efforts to address the problems of discrimination. It was one shared widely in the college community. In 1951, the American Council on Education sponsored a National Student Conference on Human Relations in Higher Education in cooperation with NSA, along with the Anti-Defamation League, NAACP, National Federation of Catholic College Students (NFCCS), Newman Club Federation, YMCA, and YWCA. NSA Vice President Herb Goldsmith was on the steering committee for the conference.

National Scholarship Service and Fund for Negro Students (NSSFNS)

NSSFNS was a non-profit agency formed in the late forties to help locate and then financially assist academically qualified Negro students (the accepted terminology in those years before "Black" and then "African American" became accepted). It enjoyed the endorsement of hundreds of college presidents around the country and was partially a response to the desire of many Northern and Western colleges to integrate their campuses and the lack of any infrastructure through which to do so.

The agency invited NSA to become a sponsor and created two positions on its board for NSA, which were initially filled by Eugene Schwartz, my predecessor, and myself. At the Michigan congress we recommended, and the congress formally approved, sponsorship. Dr. Kenneth Clark, one of its board members, was a sociologist whose work became one of the cornerstone rationales used by the Supreme Court in *Brown v. Board of Education.*[8]

Discrimination in education and campus social organizations

From its inception, NSA opposed discrimination in all of its forms. It was a position that set NSA apart as a "mainstream" student government affiliated organization, given that virtually all Southern college campuses, many fraternities and sororities, and all of the major athletic conferences continued to practice overt segregation and discrimination after World War II and well into the 1950s.[9]

In November 1949, I represented NSA at the Conference on Discrimination in College Admissions, sponsored by the American Council on Education and the Anti-Defamation League. As the December issue of *NSA News* reported, it was "the first national attempt of college and university officials to examine and eventually eliminate discrimination on any grounds other than ability and moral character." Issues considered, in addition to admissions criteria, included "restricted curricula, inadequate educational facilities, limited financial resources of applicants [and] geographic barriers."

The following April, I also attended the first follow-up regional conference, held in Washington with educators and students from colleges and universities in Maryland, Virginia, Delaware, and Washington, DC. The Mason-Dixon region was represented by its energetic chair, Gloria Abiouness of Dunbarton College.

The Illinois NSA Congress in 1949, at which I was elected, adopted a sweeping resolution which went to the heart of social organization practices and read, in part:

> Whereas, USNSA has stated that its ultimate policy is to work for the elimination of discrimination in higher education, and
>
> Whereas, USNSA recognizes that various stages of progress have been reached in the attainment of this ultimate goal, and
>
> Whereas, USNSA recognizes that the chief responsibility for the elimination of discriminatory practices rests with the campus community, and
>
> Whereas USNSA recognizes that a policy of encouragement and cooperation is necessary for the progressive elimination of discrimination,
>
> Therefore be it resolved that student governments be urged to cooperate with the local chapters of social and professional organizations of their campuses directed toward…eliminating clauses of a discriminatory nature….
>
> Be it resolved that the USNSA encourage the National Interfraternity and the National Pan Hellenic Conferences to urge the elimination of any discriminatory clauses within its member sorority and fraternity groups.[10]

After adopting another resolution expressing deep regret concerning discrimination against NSA delegates which occurred during the convention at a local restaurant, and a determination to correct it, NSA adopted a strong unfair educational practices resolution. Its main features, after allowing for consideration of denominational school purposes, gender-specific colleges and gender quotas in teachers colleges, proclaimed as unfair practices:

1. Denial or limitation of admission because of race, religion, sex, national or economic circumstance.
2. To make any oral or written inquiry prior to admission regarding the foregoing.
3. To discriminate in the use of its facilities.
4. "To establish, announce or follow a policy of denying or limiting through the device of a quota system or otherwise, admission of students or use of facilities because of race, religion, sex, national or economic circumstance."
5. To penalize any person for opposing these practices or having testified or assisted in proceedings in opposition to them.

It is interesting to observe how strongly we fought to eliminate the practices of applying racial and religious quota systems in admissions, as well as recording racial information on student records—practices that are currently supported by student groups as a means of assuring inclusiveness.

In her essay in this anthology, Janet Welsh Brown offers an overview of NSA's involvement in issues of discrimination and segregation.

Ted Perry and NSA's Student Affairs Programs

I remember Ted Perry as one of the most decent human beings I've ever come across. He was a wonderful and very competent person, who came from Temple University in Philadelphia, where he had been a leader in the Pennsylvania Region. While I don't recall the specific things he did in carrying out his program goals because we went about our own areas quite independently, I recall the great enthusiasm and energy he brought to his work as vice president for student affairs.

Ted's jurisdiction covered the following subcommission areas:

Welfare (health, athletics, recreation);
Social Activities (campus social calendars, National Collegiate Dance Bureau);
Cultural Activities (Symphony Forum, National Student Art Tour, national student literary magazine, *Essai*);
Film Groups (student film societies);
Student Government (administration and techniques, relationship to campus organizations); and
Student Rights (Student Bill of Rights).

In his report to the Michigan Congress, Ted underscored the importance he attached to what we used to call "practical programs" when he wrote:

> Although the writer is convinced that the academic courses required by institutions of higher learning are an integral—if not the most important—contribution to this process, he does, nevertheless, feel that it is of the utmost importance that subject matter be balanced by practical application or implementation. To do this is the function of the co-curricular program. Whether courses be in the social sciences, humanities, natural sciences, or other fields, and whether the co-curricular activities be in the form of social events, religious activities, student government, or welfare work—if designed to develop the student both as an individual and as an integral part of society—the activity or course can be justified, because it is contributing to the formation of a potentially responsible citizen.
>
> Recently, in a survey on the values of a college education, conducted by the American Association of University Women, many of the persons questioned indicated that there is a need for a greater degree of realism on the part of college students and recent college graduates. In observing the functioning of the United States National Student Association during the past few years, the writer would point out that in his opinion this is one of the major handicaps facing the Association. Although there is no intrinsic evil in a moderate degree of idealism, unless it is counteracted by concrete programs—geared to meet the realities of our environment—the end result is a learned misfit, unable to cope with the upheavals of a largely dynamic society.

Ted produced a comprehensive, fifty-page manual, *Student Government—Administration and Techniques,* and actively promoted NSA's student government information programs. He also tracked the work of the Student Bill of Rights Subcommission headed by Oliver Holtzmann at Colorado A&M College.

NSA's Student Government program is addressed in some detail in Gordon Klopf's essay and Ralph Dungan's piece elsewhere in this anthology. Janet Brown also reviews the Student Bill of Rights.

NSA's venture into national programs in the arts

The year 1949-1950 was probably the one time in which the goal of advancing an intercollegiate cultural program on the national level showed promise of viability. As with other "practical programs" in NSA's early years, they were difficult to sustain with only a small full-time national staff. Looking back at their reception, as illustrated by the news clippings and documents in the later Scrapbook section, it seems remarkable now that NSA was able to accomplish as much as it did, coordinated entirely through volunteer committees on campuses throughout the country.

The Symphony Forum

The highly successful and popular San Francisco Symphony Forum was first initiated by students at the University of California in 1938. It was revived after the war with the enthusiastic support of Howard Skinner, the manager of the orchestra, and more than twenty colleges and universities in the Bay area. It was presented to the NSA congress in 1948 by the California Region, where it was adopted as a part of the Student Life Program.

Students organized to create local campus committees to stimulate interest, and to offer discounted season-ticket sales. The Symphony Orchestra management provided meeting space and pre-program meetings with musicians, critics, and other commentators.

The NSA program was chaired by Paul Denise at San Francisco State College. A list of 125 orchestras and their managers throughout the country was circulated to member colleges. In his July 1950 report, Denise reported the following level of activity:

1. Active forum areas: Chicago, Washington, D.C., Cincinnati, Indianapolis, Buffalo, Seattle, and, formerly, Boston.
2. Negotiation Areas: Philadelphia, Portland, Minneapolis/St.Paul.
3. Interest Areas: Rochester, Los Angeles, Baltimore.
4. Dormant areas: Pittsburgh, Cleveland, Boston.

NSA developed detailed organizing and promotional aids for the program. There were high hopes for the program, cited in our Congress report as "one of NSA's highest priority 'up and coming' projects."

Adjuncts to the Forum were a series of student music and performance arts events called Culturales, sponsored in a number of regions, including Philadelphia, Metropolitan New York, the Twin Cities, Denver, and Atlanta.[11] Some of the Forum, Music, and Culturale programs are illustrated in the Scrapbook section.

National Student Art Tour

The first National Student Art Exhibit and Art Tour was launched by National Affairs Vice President Ralph Dungan in 1948. It was supervised by a committee at Mundelein College in Chicago, headed by Margaret Leipsiger and Helen Jean Rogers (elected that summer as NSA secretary-treasurer). It was exhibited at the first congress in Madison. It consisted of one hundred paintings from thirty-seven colleges and universities, and went on tour the next year to over forty-five campuses. NSA also sent thirty prints of the exhibit to the IUS sponsored Exhibition of Arts and Crafts, held in Prague in November of 1948.

Mundelein's Lucille Crews and Mary Kay Perkins (who shortly joined us in Madison as Staff Associate) organized the 1949-1950 exhibit. As Ted Perry reported to the 1950 congress:

> During the past year, the National Student Art Tour, composed of one hundred thirty-one mats from student artists located in forty colleges and universities throughout the country, was viewed by students in more than sixty-five colleges and universities. The tour was divided into three sections with an equal number of mats included in each section, to insure its distribution to the largest possible number of schools.
>
> Although faced with a number of administrative problems in scheduling and timing the arrival dates of the tour...it is a justifiable project since it is financially independent, and, much more important, designed to implement the cultural objectives of the Association. Preparation has been made to exhibit entries submitted for the 1950-51 National Student Art Tour at the Third National Student Congress [1950]. The Commission has contacted the American Federation of Arts in an attempt to secure judges for the exhibit.

Essai, the national literary magazine

During the course of the 1949-1950 academic year, the first and only two issues of this well-executed publication were published—Autumn and Spring. The publication was launched by a subcommission at the College of Saint Theresa in Winona, Minnesota, under the chairmanship of Carol O'Brien, who was also the editor. (A brief memoir by Carol appears in this section.)[12] With a cover price of 25 cents, approximately 1,500 copies of the first issue were sold nationally.

Perry reported that "approximately 20% of the NSA committees" cooperated in appointing an *Essai* representative on campus. In addition "one representative from each region . . . was to be selected as a member of an editorial board." For the spring issue, the price was raised to 35 cents, with a 10 cent commission on each magazine sold. More than three-hundred manuscripts had been received for publication.

NSA News in April 1950 reported that the second issue had been distributed on more than 50 campuses. Its twenty-four pages contained essays, fiction, and poetry from students at the University of Wisconsin, Muskingum College (OH), Beaver College (PA), Clarke College (IA), Lewis and Clark College (OR), Southwestern College (KY), Dana College (NE), College of the Sacred Heart (CT), St. Francis College (NY), St. Peter's College (NJ), Randolph Macon College (VA), Grinnell College (IA), and College of St. Theresa (MN).

"*Essai* has been most favorably received on the whole," Perry noted, but the project illustrated the formidable barrier of lack of financial resources posed for this kind of program as "attempts to obtain non-NSA financial support, from foundations, for example, proved fruitless." Intended as a quarterly, only two issues were published that year.

On being a vice president

NSA vice presidents were both spokespersons and program managers. There was always a tension between the two roles. In an *NSA News* editorial of April 1950, "The High Purpose of NSA Should Be Kept in Mind," I addressed this issue:

> The aim of NSA is to contribute to the education goal of providing the "knowledge and incentive" for the achievement of a society in which everyone may work and live together in the highest degree of happiness.
>
> This statement seems to me to be the best expression of the purpose of NSA.
>
> Each of us working in NSA should at all times be able to keep before him a high purpose toward which he strives.
>
> The degree to which this vision leaves us in our daily lives . . . to this degree will the quality and the substance of our efforts deteriorate. [Yet] . . . many of us had come to accept the need for practical projects, not in their true perspective but as ends in themselves. . . . It has thus become increasingly important to hold ever present in the minds of those in the student community that the practical programs should never be detached from the raison d'être—the basic policies—of NSA.

The national staff: an epilogue

Looking back at that year, we made our limited budgets and resources stretch a long way. Things were not as bad as they were for some of the subsequent national staffs because we did have some money in our account. Our salaries were $2,000 a year; toward the end, we started cutting down, but $2,000 went a long way in those days.

Alan Ostar stayed on in Madison and was our link to the previous year. Periodically he'd have us over to a nice meal, as opposed to what we were used to eating. Ted Perry and I lived together in a room in a house in Madison and became great friends.

Bob Delahanty (University of Louisville), former chair of the Kentucky-Tennessee Region, was there as executive secretary for the first half of the year. He was replaced by Fred Houghteling (Harvard), who came in February to start the practice of staggered terms for that position. Mary Kay Perkins of Mundelein arrived shortly thereafter as office assistant.

Ralph Smith, who was elected as public relations director, stayed for a few months and decided to complete his term while finishing his degree at Swarthmore. Craig Wilson of the University of Michigan was hired as editor of *NSA News* and joined us full time.

Volunteers came in from the University of Wisconsin from time to time to help out with mailings—especially with the *NSA News*—which was the bane of our existence every month.

The office was big and drafty. We all had our own work spaces. Bob Kelly, the president, had a separate smaller office. He rarely socialized with us and liked to work alone, often staying late into the evening. He was a terrific spokesman and a wonderful speaker who would spend most of his time out of the office rousing the troops. Craig Wilson and Gene Schwartz in their essays refer in greater detail to our often difficult staff relations.[13]

The rest of us cooperated with each other and worked together as a team. We would get together and throw ideas off of each other as we were formulating our plans.

The tremendous strain we were all under ultimately had the effect after my term of office of my withdrawing for a couple of years from any relationship with NSA. It was only later, teaming up with old friends again or people whom I did know, and as one of NSA's delegates to the Dubrovnik Conference between the Western Unions of Students and the member Unions of the IUS, that I became involved again in the mid-1950s as the NSA representative on the student ships.

When I went to college, I was energized by the many veterans on the campus. Becoming involved with NSA was one of the great experiences in my life. It opened my vision from a very limited, small-town, middle-class environment to one of unlimited opportunity and diversity.

Richard J. Medalie is in law practice in Washington, DC, and is counsel to the New York law firm of Brock Partners. He is also chair of the Appleseed Foundation in Washington, a national nonprofit corporation, the goal of which is to organize statewide, systemic public interest law centers throughout the country.

END NOTES

[1] Carleton contributed two national leaders to the Student Federalists, Tom Hughes, who became national president in 1944, and Bill Friedlander, who became a national board member. See the Jonas essay on the Student Federalists, p. 761.

[2] See Des Marais, p. 734.

[3] This and other quotations are from the 1950 *Staff Report to the Michigan Congress.*

[4] See Brown, p. 375.

[5] The Purchase Card System received a good deal of college newspaper coverage in areas where it was introduced. See Album, p. 366.

[6] The report of the Twenty-first Congress in 1967 lists, as one of NSA's ongoing student services, the American Discount Card.

[7] See Album, p. 367. A headline in the April 14, 1949, issue of the *Michigan Daily* reads, "NSA Impossible: Merchant Opposes Purchase System." In the October 5, 1950, issue of the *Emory Wheel* (Georgia), under the headline, "NSA Cards Sales Said Failure in Emory Area," Bob Flournoy, PCS ticket sales chairman, is reported to have "attributed the failure to the fact that the merchants, especially in the Village, have a virtual monopoly anyway and the plan would not help them."

[8] Richard Plaut, executive director of NSSFNS, initiated the practice, in 1949-50, of recruiting former NSA officers and leaders to join his counseling and field staff for a year after their graduation. Among those who did so were Gene Schwartz, Shirley Neizer, Ken Kurtz, and Tom Callahan. Both Gene and then Ken also edited the NSSFNS newsletter, *Opportunity News.* See (Neizer) Tyler on NSSFNS, p. 458.

[9] See Wilcox, "NSA and Fraternity and Sorority Discrimination," p. 398, and Lee, "Fraternities without Brotherhood," p. 745.

[10] The enforcement among fraternities and sororities of a white "Aryan" membership policy (detailed by Alfred McClung Lee in his landmark 1955 book, *Fraternities without Brotherhood,* see p. 745), either by open constitutional provisions, or in practice, remained widespread after World War II. It was being widely attacked by local campus groups, as well as in national policy statements and pressure from groups such as the National Conference of Christians and Jews and the Anti-Defamation League. This movement, the positions of the National Interfraternity Council and the Pan-Hellenic Council regarding the issue as well as NSA's active role during the post-war years, is detailed on pp. 398-409.

[11] On April 10, 1949, a variety show was presented in Denver that included performance pieces by students at the University of Colorado, Colorado State College of Education, Colorado College, Colorado College for Women, Regis College, Pueblo Junior College, Trinidad State Junior College, Weber Junior College (Utah), and Idaho State College. The Pennsylvania Region's April 22-23, 1949, Culturale in Philadelphia, at the Met Theater, featured groups from Albright College, Allegheny College, Beaver College, Bloomsburg College, College of Misericordia, Chestnut Hill College, Franklin and Marshall College, King's College, La Salle College, Lehigh University, Rosemont College, St. Joseph's College, St. Vincent's College, Swarthmore College, Temple University, and the University of Pennsylvania.

[12] See Carol O'Brien Cashen, p. 362.

[13] See Schwartz, pp. 236, 244, and Wilson, p. 248.

PICTURE CREDITS: *Then:* First National Student Congress, August, 1948 (NSA Photo, SHSW). *Now:* Feb., 1997, Washington, DC (*Schwartz*).

Saturday, September 24, 1949

THE CARLETONIAN

Volume 69, Number 1 — Carleton College, Northfield, Minnesota — Saturday, September 24, 1949

Medalie Accepts NSA Veep Post

NATIONAL Student Association annual congress at the University of Illinois elected Carleton delegate Rick Medalie to the office of vice president in charge of educational problems. Since this is a full time position, Rick will not return to classes here this year.

More than 800 delegates from 300 colleges and universities met for 10 days and nights trading ideas and learning about situations which their fellow students face. They met both in informal round tables and larger commissions besides the plenary sessions.

Bill Holmquist, Marlin Smith and Ruth Connolly were also Carleton delegates to the convention.

The congress went on record for legislation against schools with discriminatory entrance requirements, endorsed federal [illegible]ships and federal grants with merits and needs as criteria.

ADVOCATING FOR STUDENT INTERESTS IN EDUCATION

Educational Problem - - - For U.S. Congress

"Inadequacy of family income is one of the primary factors limiting the opportunity of American youth to enter college."

"The decision as to who should go to college is at present influenced far too much by economic circumstances."

"Seven out of ten persons having college abilities never finish an undergraduate course of studies because of low parental income."

"A total of 73.7% of all children in this country under 18 years of age are members of families whose income is wholly insufficient to carry the costs of higher education."

* * * *

These are the sordid facts of the American educational picture today.

National action is necessary to meet this national need. And the people of the United States are ready for such action, according to the results of the surveys taken by the American Council on Education, the New York Times, and Fortune. There is overwhelming agreement among the American people that a program of federal scholarships and fellowships is needed. The time for federal action is here.

In the proposals for federal scholarships, there are several important criteria that should be taken into consideration:

1 The student receiving the grant should be allowed to attend the institution of his choice and study the subject of his choice. Above all, there should be no possibility of federal control or pressure on the student or institution.

2 The allocation of funds for scholarships should follow the basic formula of half being allocated on the basis of college-age population and half on the annual number of high school graduates as was suggested by the President's Commission on Higher Education.

3 At the same time, however, the distribution of federal funds must provide against discrimination on the basis of race, sex, religion, color, national origin or political belief. In the seventeen states where segregation exists, applicants should compete for scholarships only within their particular racial groups.

4 Student ability should be the chief criterion of eligibility with no arbitrary ceiling of parental income or financial ability used to eliminate any applicant.

5 At the same time the basic grant should be between $500 and $1,000 a year in order to give sufficient aid to the college student.

6 Heavy emphasis should be placed on adequate guidance procedures. So large an undertaking justifies the outlay of a percentage of the funds for the development of better counseling and guidance services. In the long run, then, federal funds being spent would be more efficiently distributed as a result of such an allocation for counseling and guidance.

A program of federal scholarships and fellowships is the desparate need of the educational community. The decision is up to the 81st Congress. "The time is ripe; the plans are ready; the cost is reasonable; the need is clear."

Richard J. Medalie
Vice President

Teachers Hear NSA Veep on Faculty Rating

Faculty evaluation by students themselves came in for consideration by educators facing the problem of preparing college teachers for their profession.

More than 175 officials of public and private institutions, meeting in Chicago, heard NSA veep Richard Medalie, outline NSA's program of rating college teachers.

* * *

MEDALIE—FIRST STUDENT to address such a group — explained three phases of evaluation: 1. students answering specific categorical questions concerning professors, 2. departmental committees considering the same questions, and 3. casual reports of course "popularity" with students.

Dr. George F. Zook, president of the American Council on Education, —sponsors of the conference with the U.S. Office of Education—said a "reformation" of teacher calibre may be effected in five years.

Objective: Less specialization in one subject and practical apprenticeship in teaching or in some other occupation, actual training in teaching methods.

Both from *NSA News*, January, 1950

RICHARD J. MEDALIE

Early Background: Born in Duluth, Minnesota, in 1929. Raised in Chisholm, Minnesota. Graduated Chisholm High School in 1947.

Education: Following two years at Carleton College and my year as an NSA Vice President, I changed my major to Soviet and East European Studies and completed my B.A., summa cum laude, in 1952 at the University of Minnesota (Phi Beta Kappa; Phi Alpha Theta); University of London School of Slavonic and East European Studies, certificate, 1953 (Fulbright Scholar); Harvard Graduate School of Arts and Sciences, A.M., 1955 (Russian Research Center Junior Fellow, 1953-54; Ford Fellow, 1954-55); Harvard Law School, J.D., cum laude, 1958 (case editor, Harvard Law Review)

Career: While pursuing my various college degrees, I became active in international student affairs. In summer 1956, I was the NSA delegate to the Conference on Cooperation (with the IUS) in Dubrovnik, Yugoslavia. I took part in the Moscow Youth Festival in summer 1957, and was a participant in the first U.S.-USSR Student Exchange in the summer of 1958.* In summer 1959, I was a participant in the Vienna Youth Festival as well as a member of the Executive Committee of the antifestival organization.

Following my graduation from Harvard Law School in 1958, I worked during 1958-59 as a law clerk to U.S. Court of Appeals Judge George T. Washington of the D.C. Circuit, and then research assistant to Chief Judge David L. Bazelon. In 1960-1962, I served as assistant to the solicitor general of the United States (J. Lee Rankin and Archibald Cox).

In 1962, I joined Kaye, Scholer, Fierman, Hays & Handler in New York City as an associate, returning to Washington, DC, in 1965 as deputy director of the Ford Foundation Institute of Criminal Law and Procedure at the Georgetown University Law Center until 1968. I was also an adjunct professor of administrative and criminal law at the Georgetown University Law Center from 1967 through 1970.

In subsequent years, I became active in domestic and international arbitration, serving as a member of American Arbitration Association panels and American Bar Association sections, as well as authoring, coauthoring, and editing books and articles on the subject.

At present, I am in law practice in Washington, DC, and am counsel to the New York law firm of Brock Partners, specializing in corporate and commercial litigation and arbitration and estate planning. I am also chair of the Appleseed Foundation, in Washington, DC, a national nonprofit corporation, the goal of which is to organize statewide, systemic public interest law centers throughout the country. To date, Appleseed has established eighteen such centers.

I hold bar memberships in the District of Columbia, New York, the U.S. Supreme Court, and various other federal courts.

Family: I married Susan D. Abrams in 1960. We have two children, Samuel David and Daniel Alexander, and twin grandchildren, Clara Sophie and Benjamin Ari.

**Note:* See Halsted on the 1958 US-USSR exchange group, p. 681.

The struggle for principle can create "restrictions which gradually . . . destroy the principle"

5. Ted Perry: Democracy Requires Participation

Ted Perry
Temple University, Pennsylvania
NSA Vice President, Student Affairs, 1949-50

Editor's note: Ted Perry graduated from Temple University with a degree in Accounting in 1951. He served on the staff of NSA's Travel Bureau when Tom Callahan was its director (see p. 673) and then on staff with the NCCJ and NAACP. He was one of NSA's most beloved and popular regional and national officers. The editors have been unable to learn of his later career and family history. Excerpted below are three editorials Perry wrote for NSA News *in 1949.*

So, John Was a Real Credit to His Race

"John Doe, junior at Democracy College, became the first 'Negro,' in the history of this age-old and ivy-clad institution to be elected to the position of Senior Class President! Besides being a great credit to his race, John is regarded very highly by his associates and others at Democracy College."

So what!

In criticizing this type of publicity, certain questions must be asked:

1. Is this type of news story generally used for every student, i.e., does every release contain the racial, religious, or national origin of the celebrity involved?

2. Is the group desirous of clearing itself of guilt by showing the world that it not only accepts other groups, but, also, "Negroes?"

3. Are there separate qualifications which "Negroes" must meet in order to become a member of the so-called exclusive group?

4. Should individuals be adjudged "a credit to" particular religious or ethnological groups as compared to humanity as a whole? . . .

Of course you will be told . . . this is the type of thing the American public wants.

Well, what's wrong with this? The old cliche, "Which came first, the chicken or the egg?" can apply very well in this situation. . . . I am forced to conclude that "news-value" stories can still retain their significance without resorting to the branding or labeling of the "subject."

Idealism, some will charge? How many times in the midst of abstract, philosophical discussions do we state that our "Christian" and "democratic" principles would prevent us from judging individuals on any criteria—except as a man, created and dignified in the likeness of the Almighty? But in reality—almost unconsciously—upon hearing the name of an individual's being elected or appointed to a position of responsibility, our conditioned minds wander to such questions as:

"Is he a Negro, Catholic, or a Jew?" "What kind of implications will arise if a member of a particular group gets the position?"

Ability, capacity and other traits, generally looked upon as those necessary for success, are completely divorced until these "artificial" curiosities are satisfied. . . . "Democracy" requires a further step—participation—participation in the expounding of and living up to the ideals which make democracy a living experience. (*NSA News* 10/49)

The Oath Makers

During the past few years, students, as well as faculty and administrative personnel, have been faced with the humiliation from a postwar rash of loyalty oaths and other infringements of academic freedom and tenure—dangerous weapons in the hands of persons frightened by ideas. Unfortunately, oath-makers have forgotten a basic requisite of competent instruction—a full, frank and free relationship between teacher and student, with no ideological holds barred.

The requiring of loyalty oaths for teachers or students is a violation of free thought and an important factor in creating that atmosphere of intimidation which would throttle all academic progress. . . . What are we as students to do about this? If we accept the theory that truth is the result of free inquiry, and agree that freedom of inquiry is an inalienable right, then how can we justifiably accept as truths any of the utterances from those who are bound by oath to disseminate only a particular philosophical ideology, the violation of which would render undue hardships?

Many times, in the struggle to substantiate principles we are apt to allow the fight to become obscured by eventual restrictions which gradually tend to destroy the principle. (*NSA News* 11/49)

Campus Political Parties, Good—But

Campus political parties—are they an aid or hindrance to effective student government?

Campus political parties can be a very effective means of inspiring greater election participation. The evils that exist in campus political parties—bitter competition, lack of leadership training, social separation instead of separation based on issues, fraud—are direct faults, in the majority of cases, of the student government.

It may be argued that because student government has no real responsibility, these evils cannot be averted. If this is the case, campuses in this predicament should avoid using the political party system.

When student responsibility does become real, elections tend to become more than popularity contests for offices which have no duties and dubious honors; participation by the whole student body is forced by the strongest authority available—public opinion of their own age group through duly elected representatives, elected on the basis of political differences on real campus and student issues.

In order for student government to be an effective agency in university administration, it must have the support of the whole campus and should be truly representative and not a tool of small cliques. . . . Political parties must be molded around specific campus issues as well as principles of action. Social stratification in forming political parties is the most effective way of destroying the concept of democratic government. (*NSA News* 11/49)

PICTURE CREDITS: *Then:* NCCJ planning session, 1948, Madison, WI (NSA Photo. *Gordon Klopf*).

September 29, 1950 TEMPLE UNIVERSITY NEWS

Personalities That Glitter

Ted Perry Relaxes Here; Toured Nation Last Summer

By MARTIN SALDITCH

After travelling 3,500 miles, visiting 200 colleges and meeting 2,000 people, Ted Perry is taking a rest. That is, if attending Temple is considered a rest.

The recently-retired NSA national vice-president, glad to be back after a hectic but exciting 12-month leave of absence, is completing his last term at Teachers College.

"The past year was worth more to me than my entire education up to that point," says Ted. "I feel a little lost with my slower-paced life now. I'm not used to having my evenings free."

Ted was elected to one of the five full-time NSA posts during the 1949 convention in Illinois. Working from the national office in Madison, Wisconsin, he was responsible for programming and implementing NSA policy in the fields of student government, health, athletics, social activities and academic freedom.

He wrote and edited numerous books, pamphlets and letters, addressed students and faculty members in more than 200 colleges and universities in 12 states; and served as NSA delegate on various panels and organizations.

It was while working on these groups that Ted got a chance to rub elbows with such people as President Harry Truman, Vice-President Alvan Barkley, Mrs. Eleanor Roosevelt, newscaster Edward R. Murrow, and former Secretary of Labor Frances Perkins.

Ted was invited to a tea at the White House together with other members of a Conference on Citizenship which was meeting in the nation's capitol. After the tea, the President took the delegates into the White House garden, climbed on a bench, and made a short speech.

At a dinner for the United Nations National Committee, also in Washington, Ted had brief conversations with the "Veep" and Mrs. Roosevelt. Ted reports the former First Lady "is very easy to talk to. She has a warm personality, and always a smile.

Ted spent much of his time on extended tours of college campuses for the purpose of organizing NSA units at non-member schools, and to aid existing groups with the pro- ~~blems which constantly arise with-~~ in their units.

He spoke before university audiences, in Iowa, Illinois, Missouri, Wisconsin, Arkansas, Ohio, Pennsylvania, New York, Massachusetts Rhode Island, Conneticut and Michigan. From Harvard to Columbia, and Yale to Purdue, Ted emphasized the importance of student participation in university affairs.

TED PERRY
. . . back home

The vice president pointed out the advantages of joining NSA, the only national student government organization of college students. Ted took his mission seriously. "If student government fails, NSA fails," he declared "NSA is built on the premise that student government can succeed."

Ted reports that the administration-student government relationship at Temple is tops compared to the situations he found on many other campuses.

"We're really fortunate to have one of the best student governments I have seen," he said. "As a matter of fact, Temple rates high everywhere I've been. It's academic reputation is very good, and I have met many grads in top positions in the colleges I visited."

Ted built an impressive record in extra-curricular activities prior to his election as NSA vice-president of the Student Senate, chairman of the Philadelphia area NSA, and president of the Business Education Department Club. He was a member of the A Capella Choir, the Sword Society, and Kappa Phi Kappa.

Now he is attending Temple at night and is student-teaching at Bok vocational school during the day, instructing classes in bookkeeping, advertising, English, typing and machine calculating.

"Teaching is what is keeping me from going berserk right now," says Ted, referring to his much slower tempo now. "Working with kids is a good adjustive device. And like the job of NSA vice-president, it is also a challenge."

December 7, 1949

Ted Perry On Tour For NSA

Ted Perry

During December students in four states will hear Ted Perry, Teachers '50, vice-president of the U. S. National Student Association, speak on "The Role of NSA in the Student Community."

Perry, who is majoring in accounting, is vice-president for student government and student life and was elected to the post at the August NSA Congress. Previously, he was chairman of the Eastern Pennsylvania Sub-region of NSA, and was the first student to hold a high position in the National Association for the Advancement of Colored People, when he was named a member of the Philadelphia board of the NAACP.

Perry, who started his tour Monday when he attended a general meeting of the students in the Cleveland area, will speak at St. Vincent's College and Franklin and Marshall College today.

Temple University NEWS

Vol. XXVII—No. 32 PHILADELPHIA, MONDAY, DECEMBER 15, 1947 Price, 3 Cents

THE *TEMPLE UNIVERSITY NEWS* covered NSA news extensively. After Ted Perry graduated, he worked for the NAACP and, when NSA opened its travel office in New York, he joined Tom Callahan, travel director as Educational Travel, Inc., accountant. Anthology editors have made efforts to trace his subsequent careeer, but have been unsuccessful.

There is really nothing we cannot achieve so long as the belief is deep enough and the will is strong enough.

6. Elmer Brock: "A Kind and Noble Spirit"

Rittenhouse College, 1947-48; LaSalle College, 1949-50, Philadelphia
Pennsylvania Regional Chair, 1949-50. NSA Vice President, Student Affairs, 1950-51

Editor's note: Joan Lynch, an NSA Staff Associate who served with Elmer Brock, recalls him in this brief memoir, which captures some of the intensity of commitment with which he applied himself to his vision of the campus community. In the 1950 staff Congress report he envisioned that "Through our common efforts to achieve common objectives we will develop the desire to learn, to teach, to serve and to progress."

A portion of an article that appeared in Good Housekeeping *magazine in November 1964 cites a letter from Brock to President Kennedy which provided the title for this testimonial and is reproduced at the end.*

The Passionate Idealist

Elmer Paul Brock was a native of Philadelphia. A veteran of the U.S. Navy, he attended Rittenhouse College in Philadelphia upon his release from the service. After two years at Rittenhouse, during which he represented the College at the Constitutional Convention of USNSA in 1947, he transferred to LaSalle College, Philadelphia. During his years at LaSalle, from which he graduated with a degree in political science in 1950, he served as chairman of the NSA Pennsylvania Region and attended the Second and Third Congresses of NSA. He was active in student affairs on both campuses, and also served as a member of the Governor's Advisory Committee on Children and Youth.

Always the passionate idealist, Elmer truly believed in the principles and promise of NSA. As Vice-President for Student Affairs he worked hard to promote the values in which he believed. A "community" model of campus governance in which students, faculty and administrators would all be represented was one of his pet projects. He was frustrated in his pursuit of this and of other initiatives because of the Association's shaky finances and the distractions of internal staff conflicts.

Elmer Paul was recalled to the U.S. Navy in the summer of 1951, after his year on the national staff. He was stationed in Japan with the Seventh Fleet Staff as a Radioman. During his stay in Japan he became involved with the student movement there, much to the consternation of his superiors, who regarded his activities as suspect. He was transferred to a "non-sensitive" job with the Shore Patrol which did not involve security information, and became the subject of a loyalty investigation. The investigation determined that he was not "disloyal" to the government of the United States, but he was cautioned about any further work with Japanese students. A psychologist involved in the "investigation" concluded that Elmer was perfectly normal, but was "obsessed with student organizations." Elmer proved him right; he chose to ignore the advice of the Navy superiors and continued to assist in the organization of a representative, democratically controlled student association in that country.

Following his release from the Navy he returned to Philadelphia, where he served on the administrative staff at Harcum Junior College, then as Educational Director of Public Television Station WHYY. In 1955, he married Adoria Smetana (an NSAer from Mt. Mercy College in Pittsburgh, who was Student Government Vice President in the Pennsylvania–West Virginia Region in 1953-54).

Elmer and Adoria moved to Wilmington, Delaware, where he worked for the National Conference of Christians and Jews. He signed on for the John F. Kennedy presidential campaign, and following the election took a position in the United States Post Office as Deputy Assistant Postmaster General for Personnel.

Elmer Paul and Adoria had five sons: Stephen, Francis, Peter, Vincent and John, who, tragically, were not to know their father well, for Elmer Paul died of lung cancer on March 19, 1963, at the age of 38. He was buried at Arlington National Cemetery. A moving eulogy to his memory was published in *Good Housekeeping* magazine in November of 1963, immediately prior to the assassination of President Kennedy, whom he had so proudly served.

Joan Lynch, *Marylhurst College, OR*
NSA Staff Associate, 1950-51

Elmer Brock, 1950-51 VP Student Affairs (left) and other NSA leaders discuss student liberties with Dr. Patrick Malin (second from left), President of the American Civil Liberties Union, after his speech at the 12/50 regional assembly. To right of Dr. Malin: Ted Perry, Temple senior, 1949-50 VP Student Affairs (p. 356) ; Ken Kurtz, Swarthmore senior, President of the Pennsylvania Region (p.902); Brother George Thomas, La Salle College, Dean of Freshmen and Chair, Regional Advisory Board (*La Salle Collegian* 1/4/51 [Photo by *Kane*])

"Yours Is the True Courage"

Editor's note: In the November 1964 issue of Good Housekeeping, *an article by Charles U. Daly began: "Two months before he died, a man named Elmer Paul Brock wrote a remarkable letter to President Kennedy. That letter and how it came to be written [are] is a remarkable testament to them both." The article tells how Brock, shortly before he died, was invited to the White House for lunch and, without knowing in advance, met briefly with the president, whom he "admired so much." As a consequence he wrote a letter to the president, which is reproduced below:*

POST OFFICE DEPARTMENT
ASSISTANT POSTMASTER GENERAL
BUREAU OF PERSONNEL
WASHINGTON 25, D.C.

January 23, 1963

The President
The White House
Washington 25, D.C.

Dear Mr. President:

I am most grateful for your kindness in taking a moment to say "hello" and to allow me to have my picture taken with you. Often I ask, "What shall I leave my sons?" A room full of books, a philosophy of life, the Faith of their father, the hopes and aspirations of their country. If I should lose my battle with cancer, I can now add to that treasure a brief moment of history. (I hope you don't mind my enclosing a picture of them—the eldest is six and the youngest is nine months.)

You mentioned something about my courage: Mr. President, I face only one crisis and it is something over which I have no power of decision. But you, sir, face new and continuing crises, day after day; upon you depends much of what happens to the free society and much of what happens to mankind. Your ability to face each day with its many harrassments, its unending challenges—yours is the true courage

Socrates, standing before his jury of more than 500, said, "A man who is good for anything ought not to calculate the chance of living or dying." Finally, it is important to only a few that I should live; it is extremely important to your children and mine—to future generations—that you should prevail.

I am pleased to serve your administration, for you lead your people wisely. I am honored to serve you, for yours is a kind and noble spirit. May the road rise with you; may the wind always be at your back; and may you one day rest in the hand of the Lord.

With warm personal regards, and a sense of deep gratitude.

Elmer Paul Brock
Deputy Assistant Postmaster General

From the La Salle Collegian, *November 28, 1949*

Brock To Attend NEC Meeting At Madison

Elmer P. Brock '50, president of the Pennsylvania Region of the National Student Association, will attend the National Executive Committee meeting of NSA starting December 26, at Madison, Wis.

Brock will be representing the region which has twenty-four member colleges and universities.

The NEC will formulate plans for the National Congress to be held next summer and will review national organization and administration, and regional organization and administration.

Brock plans to leave for the NEC meeting as soon as he and Ted Perry, national vice-president in charge of student life, investigate "alleged violations of student rights at New York University."

He plans to spend the time before the NEC meeting helping the National Staff.

As president of the Pennsylvania Region, Brock is chairman of the plenary sessions of the regional convention being held at Albright College, Reading, Pa., today, tomorrow and Sunday.

We Must Forever be Radical

Excerpt from Student Affairs *report to the 1951 Congress*

Now, more than ever, the Association must provide great leadership. Inter-Collegiate Athletics is stripped of its cleanliness with the recent expose, of the numerous "fixes"—then, an I.A. Association bans T.V. showing of its games because it "cuts into the cash receipts." Our educational institutions [practice] "Momism" [over] a student for four years and then expect a matured person to come forth. Our "bastions of freedom"—those institutions dedicated to the search for truth wherever it may lead—are fast becoming the "bastions of the status quo."

NSA can not remain static. We must forever be radical. We must fight as much against McCarthyism as Communism; we must be willing to defend Student Rights as we are willing to defend the nation's Bill of Rights; we must be a manifestation of that revolutionary spirit which enabled our forefathers to declare:

"We hold these truths to be self-evident, that all men are created equal, that they are endowed by their Creator with certain unalienable rights, that among these are Life, Liberty, and the pursuit of Happiness."

During these times when "dissent" is equated with "Communism" and "liberalism with "subversive-ism"—we who have received the treasures of the Paines, Jeffersons, Lincolns—we must be willing to stand the test of our times. . . .

As ever, Elmer

Elmer Brock (right) with President John F. Kennedy at the White House in January, 1963, several months before Brock died of lung cancer.

PICTURE CREDITS: *Top of previous page:* U.S. Navy c. 1951-52 (Courtesy, Joan Lynch). *Right:* White House photo, 1963 (Courtesy Adoria Brock Frei)

The National Student Association Program

Grading the Teachers

Richard J. Medalie
Carleton College, Minnesota
NSA Vice President, Educational Affairs, 1949-50

Excerpts from The Phi Delta Kappan, *January 1950*

"He's a good man, but can't put it across.""He's rough on exams and grades, but he gives you a chance to get something out of the course."

How often have you heard such remarks from students in college? These informal conclusions will often have a lasting affect upon a given course or instructor. In recent years it has become evident that organized and cooperatively sponsored systems of faculty rating or student evaluation of instruction can do a great deal to provide a useful outlet for students to offer constructive criticisms and suggestions and to help improve the quality of instruction in the various courses of instruction. . . .

In September 1947, the student delegates to the constitutional convention of the United States National Student Association recognized the need of developing a program of faculty rating and student evaluation of instruction in the colleges and universities throughout the country. These representatives of more than three hundred colleges and universities believed that such a program would provide the student with an opportunity to contribute to the general welfare of the educational community. During the first year of the association's existence, various experimental faculty rating systems were tried. On the basis of these, a file of resource material on the evaluation of instruction was acquired which facilitated the preparation of a reference booklet. It has proved valuable as a guide for the analysis of instruction in our campus committees. . . .

In view of the limitations of student evaluation and the questions raised as to the student ability to make a keen analysis of instruction, the NSA has tried to develop faculty rating forms that would not involve knowledge beyond that of the student. A rating form that required a technical knowledge of teaching methods and procedures would defeat the whole purpose of the system. NSA worked out general rating sheets that would be available to the teacher (and ultimately to the student) in helping him recognize and correct flaws in his instructional technique. For illustrative purposes some of the forms used are pictured with this article.

It is to be noted that the rating form should not be looked upon as the only criterion for the evaluation of the instructor. The rating system as developed by the National Student Association is intended to be used by the teacher for his own benefit. What use is made beyond this point is a matter for the discretion of the college.

In using the rating, the questionnaires are generally distributed by the instructor or a committee authorized by him. In some classes the forms have been mailed directly to the student in order that he would feel free to state his candid opinion. No matter how that form is distributed, there are assurances that no identification is possible and that each individual knows the importance of critical, serious analysis.

Students and faculty alike have praised the value of student evaluation of instruction in a number of educational institutions. At the University of Michigan, 50,000 forms were returned, rating the 400 faculty members of the Literature, Science, and Arts College in the fall of 1948.

The project tested three different kinds of opinion. In addition to the standard forms distributed, each of the several departments created a committee of three members to observe teaching methods in each class surveyed. These teams filled out the same forms used by the students and, when compared with the survey, disclosed a marked similarity of teaching methods. The third source used was of a casual nature. Faculty advisors in several departments turned in reports on courses continually asked for or avoided by students as an indication of the teaching ability of the instructor in charge.

The Brooklyn College survey covered some 7,000 students, about 90% of the student body. The more than 30,000 forms returned analyzed 400 instructors in all departments.

In addition, a detailed analysis of the status, grade-level, and extra-curricular activity of the student replying was made and compared with the returns. The rating system used was developed and tabulated by the Social Research Office of the Department of Sociology at Rutgers University, through a grant from the Carnegie Corporation of New York.

At the University of Buffalo, the rating system used was unique in that the final results were made available to all students. The system used at Buffalo has two purposes: to aid students in selecting instructors and to aid instructors in improving teaching methods. By publishing results and selected comments concerning each instructor, the University students felt able to accomplish their first objective.

Other institutions at which student evaluation of faculty is being or has been conducted include Albright (Pa.), Loyola (Ill.), University of Idaho, University of Illinois, University of Minnesota, Virginia State and Webster (Mo.).

Despite the success of faculty rating systems throughout the country, it has been the feeling of the National Student Association that the program to date is not enough.

One of the greatest weaknesses in the program has been the failure to promote direct student action and interest in the further analysis of the curriculum and educational process. To further develop the program of faculty rating in order to be all inclusive, NSA is now encouraging the various campuses to undertake critical surveys of the educational process. Coincident with that encouragement, NSA is now preparing to offer concrete aids in terms of approach, analysis and organization in order that the program may be carried out in the best possible manner.

In perspective, the plan will be to study the trends in higher education and the curriculum reforms in the various educational institutions in the country, evolve programs to stimulate the student to take a more active interest in his education: to question, to analyze and to take stock of his education, and to "re-examine the objectives and the methods . . . of higher education in the light of the social role it has to play."

The program shall be based on the valuable research in education done last year by the Harvard Student Council as evidenced in the report, "Harvard Education, 1948."

Thus, as can be seen, the whole program of NSA in the field of faculty rating, evaluation of instruction, and evaluation of education itself has been based upon the realization that "we students must consider critically the way in which we are being educated, and the things we want to gain from our education. It is for us to change the general attitude from one of indifference to one of active participation.... Only through the interaction with men about us, faculty and fellow students, can we achieve the true intellectual individuality of educated men" (Harvard Student Council, *Harvard Education, 1948,* p. 64).

FACULTY RATING SHEET NO. 1

Instructor .... Dept. & Course ....

Do not indicate at any place on this blank your name. The results of this sheet will be used to improve the quality of instruction. It is important that you fill the sheet out with care. Place a check (✔) in the box which you think most accurately describes the quality of your instructor.

A—Excellent
B—Above average
C—Average
D—Below average
E—Failing

I Evaluation of the instructor:	A	B	C	D	E
1. Knowledge of his subject					
2. Ability to arouse interest in the subject					
3. Adequacy of organization and preparation					
4. Integration of subject with other areas of study					
5. Willingness to assist students through consultation					
6. Method of presentation					
7. Openmindedness to controversial issues					
8. Your interest in further courses from this instructor					
9. Awareness of and use of current developments in his field					
10. Considering everything evaluate this teacher's fitness to teach this course					

II. Evaluation of the course:	A	B	C	D	E
1. Value of class meeting to you					
2. Aptness of description of course and prerequisites in catalog					
3. Correlation of quizzes, lectures, labs, etc.					
4. Fairness of questions in exams					
5. Value of textbook					
6. Your interest in further courses in this Dept.					

Please indicate the number of hours per week that you spend on this course outside of class. .... hrs.
Please add any other comments on the course or the instructor on the reverse side of this sheet.

FACULTY RATING SHEET NO. 2

Instructor .... Course ....

A—Too much.
B—Not enough.
C—Enough to be satisfactory.
D—So as to be excellent.

	A	B	C	D
1. Does instructor stick closely to subject matter of course?				
2. How much current material is presented?				
3. Does the instructor use illustrations and examples to clarify lectures?				
4. How much of your time do the assignments take?				
5. Does the instructor encourage students to ask questions?				
6. Does he welcome class discussion and encourage students to voice opinions?				
7. Does he encourage independent thought?				
8. In determining grades how much weight does he place on: (a) tests				
(b) problems, reports and recitations				
(c) final exams				
9. Are his test questions clear?				
10. How much of the material covered in tests has been treated in lectures and reading assignments?				
11. Does he return test papers promptly?				
12. Does he go over exams when he returns them?				
13. Is his presentation of class material well organized?				
14. Is he interested in the subject?				
15. Is his voice clear and understandable?				

SUM TOTAL OF TRAITS ANSWER yes or no	Yes	No
16. Does his teaching inspire you to work hard?		
17. Does he command your respect so that you would not think of cheating in his class?		
18. Is he impartial in his treatment of students?		
19. Would you advise another student to schedule this instructor?		

20. Of all the instructors you have had where would you place this one?
upper third ( ) middle third ( ) lower third ( )

Please make any additional comment on the reverse side of this sheet.

FACULTY RATING SHEET NO. 3

Department ____ Course ____ Instructor ____

Do not put your name anywhere on this sheet. Place a check in the area on each line that you think indicates the degree to which your instructor fulfills the statement.

1. Organization of course material
   well organized — loosely organized — confusing
2. Content of lecture
   interesting — mildly interesting — dull
3. Recitations
   encourages questions — answers questions when asked — ignores questions
4. Discussion
   encourages original thinking — demands only memory work
5. Lab work
   completed within period — requires outside work
6. Assignments
   reasonable — occasionally too long — too long
7. Examinations
   returned and explained — returned only — not returned
8. Content of exams
   reasonable selection of material — exams composed of minor details
9. Partiality
   impartial — easily 'apple-polished'
10. Mastery of subject matter
    adequate knowledge of subject — limited knowledge — inadequate knowledge
11. Presentation of current material
    frequently — occasionally — never
12. English
    encourages use of good English — no attention to proper usage
13. Appearance
    neat — poorly groomed
14. Attitude toward student
    considerate — occasional cutting remarks — sarcastic
15. Cooperation
    cooperative — indifferent — antagonistic
16. Instructor-Student relationship
    maintains desirable relationship — unpleasantly personal
17. Voice
    understandable in all parts of the room — hard to understand
18. Sense of humor
    excellent sense of humor — no sense of humor
19. Value of course
    unusually valuable to students — fails to meet student needs
20. Stimulation of intellectual curiosity
    creates interest — destroys interest

Please add any additional comments below.

Nº 29011 Nº 29011

NORTH CAROLINA STATE COLLEGE STUDENT REACTION SHEET

In order to help maintain high standards of instruction at North Carolina State College, the Council of the Campus Government and Honor System requests you to rate your instructor in terms of the qualities listed below. Make your rating conscientiously and individually.

Instructor's Name .... Fr........ So. ...... Jr........ Sr......... Gr........ Class
Time Class Taught .... Expected Course Grade A......B......C..... D......F......
Course Number........................ Lec....... Lab...... Curriculum ....

Do not mark in above blocks.

Black in only one square under each title:

I. Knowledge of Subject:
☐ Well versed in subject and its application ☐ Knows subject but not practical applications ☐ Knows only what's in textbook ☐ Poor knowledge of subject and its applications

II. Organization and Presentation of the Course:
☐ Well organized and presented ☐ Well organized but poorly presented ☐ Fair organization and presentation ☐ Poorly organized and presentation lacks continuity

III. Quizzes:
☐ Are unfair ☐ Are too easy ☐ Are fair but difficult ☐ Are fair but not too difficult

IV. Grading:
☐ Unfair in grading ☐ Grading consistent with associates in same course ☐ Grading inconsistent with associates in same course ☐ Fair in grading

V. Ability to Teach:
☐ Arouses interest and stimulates thinking ☐ Puts the subject across ☐ Good teacher but often gets sidetracked ☐ Lacks ability to teach

VI. Interest in Teaching:
☐ Lacks interest in teaching ☐ Indifferent attitude toward teaching ☐ Interested in teaching ☐ Enthusiastically interested in teaching

VII. Approachability outside class:
☐ Encourages students to seek outside help ☐ Will make appointments if asked ☐ Avoids outside consultations ☐ Refuses to give outside help

VIII. Discipline in class:
☐ Class noisy and often disrupted ☐ Many interruptions to restore order ☐ Class order kept by force ☐ Inspires order in class

IX. Appearance:
☐ Dresses neatly and appropriately ☐ Fairly neat ☐ Sometimes untidy in dress ☐ Slovenly in appearance and dress

X. Distracting mannerisms:
☐ (none) ☐ (some) ☐ (many)

List distracting mannerisms—if any ____

XI. In your opinion the teacher being rated is
☐ (excellent) ☐ (good) ☐ (fair) ☐ (poor)

XII. Is this an elective or required course?
☐ ☐

XIII. Do you think this course will be of value to you?
☐ (yes) ☐ (no) ☐ (doubtful)

XIV. Were the prerequisites necessary for this course?
☐ (yes) ☐ (no) ☐ (doubtful)

(Use the other side of the sheet for any remarks you wish to make)

Above is shown in slightly reduced size a faculty rating sheet as it was actually used. It is expected that suggestions from the N. S. A. for faculty rating sheets would be adapted for use in any particular institution in conferences including representatives from the students, the faculty, and the administration.

Early lifetime lessons with NSA in Minnesota

7. Creating *Essai* Magazine

Carol O'Brien Cashen
College of St. Theresa, Minnesota
Editor, Essai, *1949-1950*

I was fortunate to live less than fifty miles from the University of Wisconsin during summer 1949, and therefore made many trips to the NSA office in Madison, where I found willing listeners and lots of support in our discussions about goals of NSA in general and *Essai*, in particular. How idealistic we were then!

Since I am an Adjunct English Professor at Macomb Community College, I can look at our ambitious writing project of so many years ago with perhaps more critical eyes, but certainly with much nostalgia.

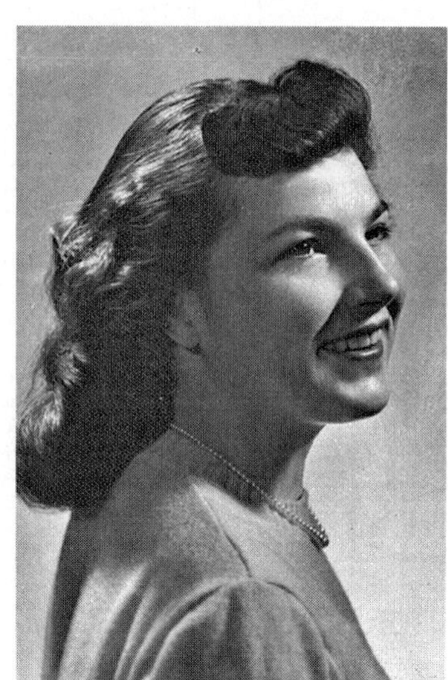

Bringing *Essai* into being

Thinking of the two years I was involved with NSA brings back to my mind the warmth of companionship and general excitement of being involved in something with nobility of purpose and a scope far beyond our own small part of the world at that time. As far as *Essai* was concerned, I remember that despite the crowded circumstances and smoke-filled atmosphere of the tiny "upper room" I was assigned at the College of St. Theresa (smoking was discouraged at CST, so only in the "attic" were we allowed to smoke), I spent many hours reading over the wonderful literary selections sent to me for publication. That alone was gratifying to an English/Latin major and aspiring poet! I had good assistance from those campus persons from the various districts of NSA, who promoted the literary magazine and gathered the manuscripts to be submitted.[1]

Without computers and with little money for much long-distance discussion, a lot of letter writing and note sending went on between CST and the various agents, and good friendships were formed. Besides these general impressions, however, there are two quite poignant memories I would like to recount that give, perhaps, an interesting portrait of the mores of the times.

Early lessons on parliamentary procedure

Several of us from CST attended the conference of 1949 at Champagne/Urbana. I remember being utterly fascinated by the refinements of parliamentary procedure I observed (from the "inside"), which were employed at the convention, at least with one particular issue being hotly debated at the time. It is a bit ironic that I cannot even remember that burning issue. On the first evening, our Minnesota delegates had a somewhat secluded meeting, which did not start until after ten. Because I was staying in a women's dorm, it was an absolute rule that one must be in one's room by nine o'clock, at which time the outer doors were duly locked. Because I was determined not to miss such a deliciously enticing meeting (and because I was particularly interested in a young man named John Garney) I made plans to get out, and then reenter surreptiously, by arranging with one of my friends in the dorm to creep out in the hall after midnight and wedge a board in the door.

At the meeting I was intrigued with the elaborate plan of "stacking" the mikes the next day so as to assure our talking the delegation to death and then bringing forth an amendment to the aforementioned issue on the agenda, with tactics to ram it through. What a lesson in democratic manipulation! I was one of the ten or so assigned to a particular mike. I presume members from a few other delegations were in agreement with us and were part of the same plan. At any rate, I crept back to the dorm in the wee hours of the morning, at fever pitch with anticipation and just plain exhilaration at the prospect of participating in real policy making in an organized way. Luckily, I found my way across the campus without getting lost or being seen at that forbidden hour, and found the vital board properly in place. When the convention agenda began and our issue came on the floor the next morning, sure enough we all eagerly pushed our way into line at the mikes, and after considerable argumentation, we won the day! I learned a lot from that convention—not only about effective action in a parliamentary situation, but also about how to organize and how to elicit the interest of others in one's own prime objective. (I married a Circuit Court judge in Macomb County, and sometimes when working on his campaigns, recalled those early days of neophyte political activity.)[2]

Social reality challenges idealism

The other memory is just a brief, bittersweet comment on the social reality of the time, in that I found an instance of real friendship in the face of a rather bewildering (at the time) barrier. One of the young men officers of the NSA was an African American, Ted Perry from Temple.[3] He was especially helpful to me with my *Essai* project, and I liked him a lot. I had never been around any prejudice against African Americans, and felt none. Of course, at the Madison central office we all worked together as friends and I don't think anyone even thought about it. On this particular occasion, there was a plan for a couple of NSA officers, of which Ted was one, to go to Macalaster College in the Twin Cities, along with myself and several other Minnesota delegates, to speak to the student body about NSA. We gave our speeches, answered questions, and then planned to socialize a bit with the students.

There was a band that came in, and dancing began. I had been going to meet a boyfriend of mine from Saint Thomas who was coming over to the dance to get me, but in the interim, Ted asked me to dance. We had danced before in Madison, and it seemed to me a natural thing to do with a friend. As we began to dance, smiles turned to frowns on the faces around us and many of the dancers moved off the floor. Ted apologized quietly to me for the embarrassment; I was absolutely furious at such treatment of my friend, much more than for myself (remember, I was idealistic), and if I had not cared about his feelings, I would have danced all evening with him just "to show 'em"!

Ted's good sense prevailed: we sat down, and the officers left shortly thereafter. My boyfriend, who had arrived at the end of the incident, did not appreciate my exhibition and declined to take me home. I can still remember the emotion of those few minutes. I was not so naive as not to know that prejudice existed, but I guess one does not truly understand its impact until one feels it personally. I remember afterward being grateful that, at least in my experience, NSA was a place where young people could work together with a sense of comradeship, unhampered by consideration of differing backgrounds.

END NOTES

[1] See Medalie, p. 353.

[2] See Donnelly, p. 951, for a similar experience.

[3] See Ted Perry, p. 356.

PICTURE CREDITS: *Then:* c. 1949. *Now:* Sept., 2000 (*Both, author*).

Carol O'Brien Cashen is an Adjunct English Professor at Macomb College in Warren, Michigan, currently on leave. She is the mother of seven children, and has twenty grandchildren.

CAROL O'BRIEN CASHEN

I was born Carol M. O'Brien in Portage, Wisconsin, in 1928. I attended the College of St. Theresa, Minnesota, and received a Bachelor's degree in Latin and English, 1950. In 1976 I received my Master's in English from Saginaw University.

I taught Latin at Mercy High School in Detroit from 1950 to 1953. I was married to Raymond R. Cashen in 1951, and subsequently had seven children—great kids. My husband used to say, "Not a ringer in the bunch." One of the girls is a surgeon, the other a high school English teacher. Among the five boys, I have two lawyers, a Colonel in the Air Force, a land developer in Phoenix and a superintendent at the Sterling Ford Plant. I have 20 grandchildren.

My husband became a circuit judge in 1966. I went back to teaching in 1969, and am now Adjunct English Professor at Macomb College in Warren, Michigan. I was a Girl Scout trainer for the Otsikita Council, a School Board member for four years, and taught in a ten-year pilot program in Kettering-sponsored individually guided education. My interests are golf, genealogy, and writing poetry.

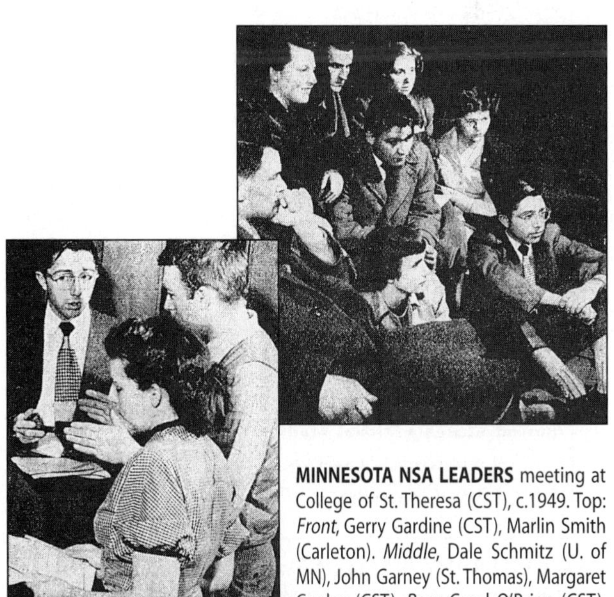

MINNESOTA NSA LEADERS meeting at College of St. Theresa (CST), c.1949. Top: *Front,* Gerry Gardine (CST), Marlin Smith (Carleton). *Middle,* Dale Schmitz (U. of MN), John Garney (St. Thomas), Margaret Conley (CST). *Rear,* Carol O'Brien (CST), Don Dowling (St. Thomas), Margaret Manahan (CST). Photo left: Marlin Smith, National Affairs Chmn, MN Region; Dave Birt (U. of MN), Carol O'Brien (CST). (Photo clips from Carol Cashen)

Essai Literary Magazine

essai

In this first *Essai*, the policy has been that of selecting for publication one contribution (as a rule) from each member-school in the Minnesota Region of USNSA. Hereafter, the staff will judge manuscripts according to their merits in respect to all the other material submitted, in order to assure the high literary quality which will result from competition and to stimulate a spirit of unity. In some instances, material was accepted which had previously been printed in local campus magazines. The lateness of preparation for the project necessitated this procedure for the introductory number; but in the future, *Essai* will include only unpublished poetry, short stories, and essays. Notes about the contributors in this issue include information given in response to a questionnaire sent out from the editorial office. More complete and pertinent introductions may be presented with a revised questionnaire and fuller cooperation from writers whose work appears.

Students on all campuses belonging to USNSA are encouraged to begin writing now for the next issue. Each member-college may submit three manuscripts — a short story, an essay, and a poem — to be selected by the head of the English department; these choices should represent the best the college has to offer in literature. They will be less smooth, perhaps, but more fresh in technique, and they will be more challenging in form and ideas, than the achievements of the professional magazine world. *Essai* strives, by moving away from the mediocre, to help fill a cultural need in the student milieu and to serve as an outlet for creative talent. This magazine, on a national scale, will not only provide an organ through which students of America can unite their voices and make them heard, but will tend to bring the local divisions of USNSA into closer concord. The first issue of the national magazine will appear in December.

EDITORIAL BOARD MEMBERS:

Northern New England and Southern New England—Miss Ildiko de Papp, Wellesley College, Wellesley 81, Massachusetts;

Metropolitan New York — Joseph Fioravanti, Saint Francis College, Brooklyn, New York;

New York State, New Jersey and Pennsylvania — Thomas Dowgin, c/o NSA Committee, Fordham University, 302 Broadway, New York, New York;

Georgia, Florida, Alabama, Kentucky-Tennessee, Virginia, Carolinas, West Virginia and Mason-Dixon—Miss Georgeanna Meuthe, Randolph Macon Women's College, Danville, Virginia;

Illinois, Indiana, Michigan, Ohio, and Wisconsin—Miss Helen Carney, 1603 Allport Street, Chicago 8, Illinois;

Iowa, Kansas-Nebraska, Minnesota, Missouri and Unorganized Areas—Peter Teisberg, Concordia College, Moorhead, Minnesota;

California, Nevada, Hawaii, Great Northwest and Rocky Mountain — Varley McBeth, 2333 Eighth Street, Berkeley, California.

essai

EDITOR . . . . carol o'brien
ASSISTANT EDITOR . . . . rose ronan
BUSINESS MANAGER . . . . veronica le compte
PUBLICITY MANAGER . . . . norma iversen
EDITORIAL ASSISTANTS . . . . margaret o'hara
patricia murphy
eleanore krage

published by the
united states national student association
autumn, 1949
twenty-five cents

contents . . .

included

COLLEGE OF THE SACRED HEART

summer river

• *MIRIAM HAYES*

There are horses in water.
Necks arching, curved.
The ripples curve outwards, but not these alone.
There is a circling half-sound of horses drinking,
Of water falling on rounded stone.
Even our thinking turns in a circle,
Tips on, rounds off, comes and is gone.

Here, oh here,
In this circumscribed cool silence
Many circles meet and disappear.
Even the trees arch.
Everything flexes.

The sky is a curving.
The world is a sphere.

18 —

NSA's LITERARY MAGAZINE was well-received but lacked the funding and management needed to build circulation (see p. 353).

The editors are indebted to Sister Margaret Style, Archivist of the former College of St. Theresa, for lending copies of *Essai*.

CRUCIFIXION

LOUIS SALOUTOS

MOUNT SAINT AGNES COLLEGE • ANN COMBER

Eliot and the Practical Cats

pussy cats . . .

DURING the course of his essay on Kipling's work, T. S. Eliot differentiates between poetry and verse in such a sentence as "Kipling's verse reaches from time to time the intensity of poetry." From this quotation can be derived the attitude of Eliot towards poetry and verse. If verse becomes intense, it becomes poetry: but this im-

doing, exposes the foibles and follies of man. The Gumbie Cat's name is Jennyanydots. She is a perfect any Jenny or Jennyanydots because, by cooking nightly for the mice

SOUTHWESTERN COLLEGE

reveille - -

a poem in dramatic form

• MARK ALEXANDER HARRIS

Wine so scarlet with prophet's blood, now dead,
Drink this cup with impure lips of passion.

DANA COLLEGE

• HERBERT A. HJORTSVANG

revelation

AS he waited for the ringing of rusted bells to announce the morning rest period for the employeees of Blyth Chemical Company, Will Hayden was on edge with nervous fear. He felt like a hunted mouse with the cat ready to pounce on him at any moment. Looking up at the electric clock, he became more tense. In a moment it would be ten o'clock, and the rest period would be at hand.

When the harsh clamor of the bells died away, he noted the dying machinery noise and the fading laughter of the

cool, damp concrete. When he dared to look up, she had gone.

"Fellow, what did you do to that poor girl? You sure scared her out of here!"

"Yeah, never saw any guy do that to her before. The way you blushed she must'a thought you wuz a Indian!"

Will straightened up, turned and rushed to the small cubicle balance room, slamming the door. The assistants came a moment too late. Finding their pounding and taunts had no effect, they went out to the yard back of

BEAVER COLLEGE

internal hell

• MARY REAVES

ELYSE hurried through the Metro. They stopped running at one and it was almost that now. If she didn't make it, she'd have to walk. And it was so dark; Paris was so dark. The Metro was so dark with all its little passageways and queer little gates that opened and closed without one touching them. She felt as if she were an animal in a maze and some unseen person were watching her every move, opening the gates for her, laughing as she scurried nervously through the twisting tunnels.

when she got home he'd be there laughing and joking with Sevren. Elyse liked to sit on the other couch and pretend she was reading, only she'd be listening to him. Garya was so vivacious, so excitable. He talked too fast and exploded so easily. And yet always the humor and tenderness from within him broke through his agitated voice and softened it to a lullaby. Sevren often mimicked Garya for Elyse when they were alone. The way he always stood in fifth position and talked with his head tilted to one side. And his hands, the hands of Shelley. Sevren didn't really appreciate him. Didn't see how fine

'Essai' Plans Quarterly In January

"Essai"—NSA's national literary magazine—will become a regular quarterly beginning in January.

Carol M. O'Brien, St. Theresa College, Minn., will be editor and Daniel A. McCarthy, St. Mary's College, Minn., will be business manager.

• • •

A PILOT EDITION for autumn 1949 appeared at the recent NSA Congress and won enthusiastic support from delegates.

Distribution of the 40-page magazine is through the NSA campus committees, which sell them directly to students at 25 cents each.

Students from every NSA member school may submit manuscripts for publication through the English departments of their schools.

From *NSA News* 10/49

Second 'ESSAI' Is Published

The second issue of NSA's literary magazine ESSAI, has been published and distributed on more than 50 campuses through NSA committees.

The spring edition, 24 pages at large-magazine size, is selling for 35c per copy. Order: publications bureau, NSA, 304 N. Park St., Madison 5, Wis.

• • •

The magazine features essays, fiction, and poetry from students at the following institutions:

University of Wisconsin, Muskingum College, Beaver College, Clarke College, Mt. St. Agnes College (2), Lewis and Clark College, Southwestern College, Dana College, College of the Sacred Heart, St. Francis College, St. Peter's College, Randolph-Macon College, Grinnell College, and College of St. Teresa.

The magazine is edited by a national sub-commission, headed by Carol O'Brien, College of St. Teresa.

From *NSA News* 4/50

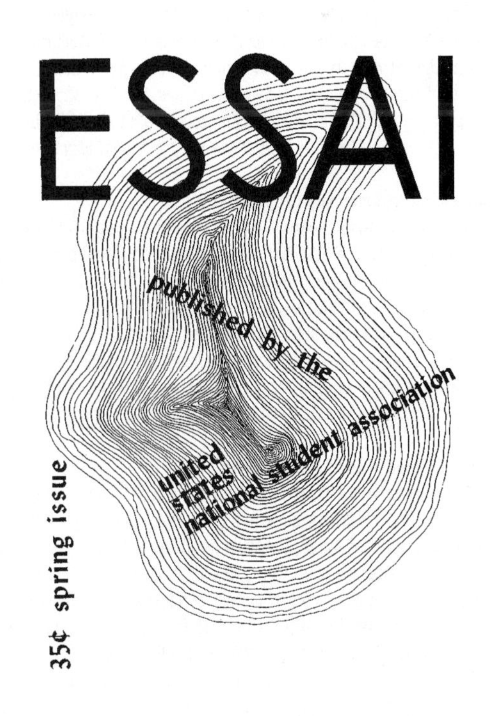

The Purchase Card (PCS) and Student Discount (SDS) Systems

Loos-Leaflet 1

SAVING DOLLARS—A University of Wisconsin co-ed surveys a newly-painted announcement of the arrival of the Purchase Card System at Wisconsin. An annex to the main library, the quonset huts are the Badger schools, top advertising medium.

* * * * *

PCS Cards Save Student Money

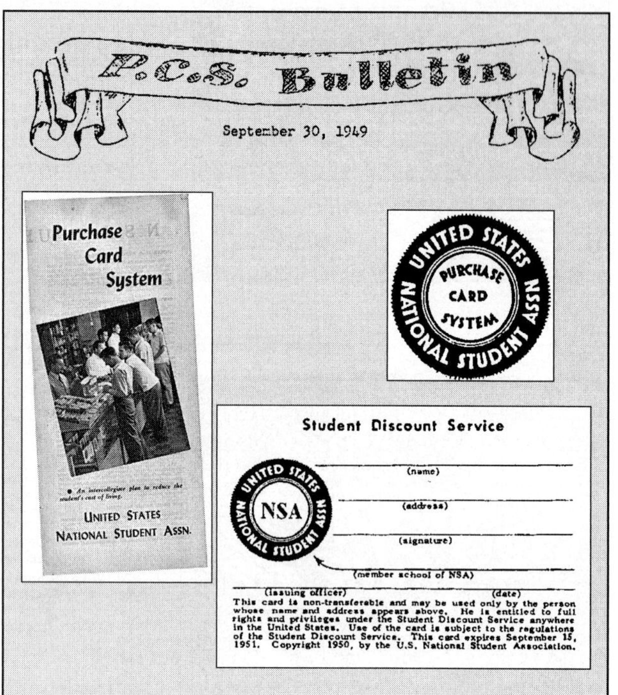

Student Discount Service

(name)

(address)

(signature)

(member school of NSA)

(issuing officer) (date)

This card is non-transferable and may be used only by the person whose name and address appears above. He is entitled to full rights and privileges under the Student Discount Service anywhere in the United States. Use of the card is subject to the regulations of the Student Discount Service. This card expires September 15, 1951. Copyright 1950, by the U.S. National Student Association.

FIRST INTRODUCED IN 1947 as the "New Jersey Plan," it was tested out with 1500 students and 25 merchants by the U. of Buffalo under the leadership of Lee Jones, NSA's first national Treasurer (Pt. 5, S. 3). By 1950-51, renamed as the Student Discount System, it claimed use by 100,000 students in 40 communities (see Medalie, this Sec.). Above, *NSA News* 12/49. Right, from top, 1949; mimeograph bulletin masthead; PCS information brochure, merchant window sticker emblem. 1951, SDS student membership card.

A PROGRAM THAT WOULDN'T GO AWAY

1948: Purchase Card System encouraged

The purchase card system is designed to obtain, through community level organization of NSA Area Committees, purchase discounts at local business concerns for students at member NSA colleges. The cards, which will be issued by the national office to area committees and sold by the member college, will entitle the student holder to guaranteed discounts at any cooperating enterprise throughout the nation. In addition, he will receive a subscription to NSA News. Coordinated through the National Commission on Educational Problems, NSA encourages the adoption of this plan, where feasible, throughout the nation, as a part of its program for the improvement of student welfare.

September, 1948, Report of the First National Student Congress

1950: Commission recommends dropping PCS

This project is an end, not a means toward achieving a major objective . . .of minor importance, since the alleviation of the students' economic burden is accomplished to a very small degree, the project takes more of the time of the responsible officer than is justified. A de-emphasis of PCS is necessary, and, due to the very great financial liabilities involved, the relegation of the project to a sub-commission seems out of the question. The only course of action would seem to be the dropping of the Purchase Card System as a national program.

June, 1950, Report, NSA Special Commission on Organization Affairs

1959: Student Discount Service explained

The Student Discount Service was born as the Purchase Card System almost at the very inception of USNSA back in 1947. The leadership of the newly-formed Association and of student governments at the time was composed mainly of veterans returned from World War II. A great many students were married and the vast majority were acutely concerned with their economic welfare. They realized that, if solutions to their financial problems were to be found, they would be principally responsible for finding them.

The Purchase Card System was thought of as a means of reducing the students cost of living, Agreements were negotiated with merchants to enable college students at member schools to get discounts at participating stores. For this privilege students paid one dollar for a PCS card. One of the first publications on the subject has this comment, "NSA does not look upon the PCS as the best solution to the problem... It is offered rather as an immediate and practical method for reducing the overall 'student cost of education.'"

The first full year of operation for PCS ended in December, 1948, with 30 stores participating in the New Jersey region, four in Minneapolis, and contracts negotiated with merchants in Chicago, Boston, Detroit, and Philadelphia, bringing PCS benefits to potentally more than 175,000 member school students.

The *PCS Bulletin* of December 1949, announced that the 50,000th PCS card had just been sent out and that 30,000 more cards were being printed for the 17 states from Massachusetts to California which had a functioning PCS program. The organization of the program also included 24 areas with area chairmen and committees. The methods of operation were similar to those of the SDS program. In later years the name of the program was changed to the Student Discount Service, in order to have a name which more accurately described the program. The operation of the SDS program has been at various times under the control of the Ed Affairs, National Affairs, and Student Affairs Vice Presidents. In recent years the program has been somewhat de-emphasized and the number of participating schools has steadily declined.

1959 NSA Student Discount Service information booklet

There is a tremendous lack of continuity from one student generation to another . . . Students [on 32 campuses surveyed] have never heard of the program not because it had never existed or been discussed . . . but because it had never been brought to their attention by their predecessors.

1959 SDS Survey

1963: Special Programs of NSA

The Student Discount Service program was established to aid student governments in augmenting the economic welfare of their students. Through the USNSA program, students on member campuses have achieved substantial savings.

1963 USNSA Report

• BUY • A ROSE TODAY

ARGUS — THE UNIVERSITY OF BUFFALO

• BUY • NSA CARDS

VOL. I. MAY 3, 1948 BUFFALO, NEW YORK No. 19

Henry Wallace Accused Of Racial Discrimination In Commerce Dep't

Protest Made By Negro Farmers In The South Was "Repeatedly Brought To Wallace's Attention."

BY MARTY FRIED

UB Radio Playhouse To Conduct Poll

162 Class Officer Candidates Compete In Wednesday Elections

YOUR NSA CARDS ARE GOOD AT THESE STORES

Mary Burns Tea Room, 3604 Main St.
Sample Shop, 1631 Hertel Ave., 10%.
Record Rack, 1313 Jefferson Ave., 10%.
Dick Fisher's Athletic Goods, 699 Main St., 20%.
North Park Cleaners, 3333 Bailey Ave., 15 and 25%.
Florette Flower Shop, 3236 Main St., 15%.
Park Lane, 33 Gates Circle, 10%, Two persons per card.
Club Moonglo, Michigan and William Sts., No minimum week days.
Sheral Furniture & Appliance Co., 3016-22 Main St., Furniture, 15 to 20%; appliances 10%.
Kuehner Leather Goods, 693 Main St., 20%.
Bidwell Garage, 947 Elmwood Ave., 640 Linden Ave., 15% for Repair Work.
E. & H. Motor Service, 950 Fillmore Ave., 15% for Repair Work.
The Tire Shop, 1548 Main St., 20%.
Caruso Shoe Repair Shop, 2825 Delaware, 15%.
Riviera Restaurant, 454 Pearl St., 10%. Two persons per card.
The Trailer Headquarters, 3618 Delaware, Kenmore, $100 discount.
American Auto Parts, 554 Genesee St., 25%.

PLAZA MEN'S SHOP (Opposite U. of B.—UN 4643)
SLACKS
GABARDINES
GLEN PLAIDS
COVERTS
HOUNDS TOOTH
SPORT JACKETS
CORDUROY JACKETS
U. S. N. S. A. CARDS HONORED HERE

NORTH BUFFALO'S MOST COMPLETE SPORTING GOODS STORE
20% Discount Given With N.S.A. Cards
STEERINGS SPORT GOODS 1504 HERTEL

BRAD MENIG MOBILGAS STATION
MAIN and WINSPEAR
N.S.A. Discount Cards Honored on gas (2c per gallon)
ALSO — DISCOUNT ON TIRES BATTERIES AND ACCESSORIES

NSA Plans Purchase Card System For Idaho And WSC

According to Bob Dahlstrom, NSA president, the Idaho NSA group is now working to obtain the cooperation of Moscow merchants for a purchase card system. Plans for instituting such a system came from the national NSA office.

This purchase card system would allow a 10 per cent discount to students possessing a card for all purchases. Arrangements would be made with merchants to issue purchase cards to all University of Idaho students.

Joint System With WSC

Because Moscow and Pullman are so small, the Washington State college NSA board is attempting

Musicians Return From Conference

Professors Hall Macklin, Kermit Hosch, and Glen Lockery returned Sunday from the Northwest regional conference of the Music Educator's association, held in Portland.

Thirty-five alumni of the Uni-

The Loyola News

Students Will Save Cash In NSA Discount Plan

Fr. Hussey to Say Faculty Mass Oct. 31

THE CARDINAL

NSA Purchase Card System Discussed For Louisville Use

To Cast

Diamondback

SGA Schedules

Terp Gridmen Star On Stage Tomorrow

Capitol Theater Holds Night For Footballers

NSA Purchase Cards Yeild Price Cuts

Student Members Get Discounts From Merchants

Columbia Spectator

NSA to Institute ... McMillin Assembly

NSA to Institute Purchase Cards

Schools Will Name All CUSC Proxies

Barnard Gals Give Carnival

The SILVER and GOLD

AN INDEPENDENT NEWSPAPER

NSA, Chamber Plan Meeting To Revamp Discount System

NSA officials and the chamber of commerce are working out difficulties today which arose in the application of the Student Discount service in Boulder, Campus NSA Chief George Christiansen said today.

Professor Testifies At Washington Hearing

THE MATHER RECORD

NSA Offers Cut Prices To Students

You are a member of Mather's NSA. What is it? It is the National Student Association, "an organization of college student bodies, represented through their student governments." It began because of the need for a representative intercollegiate organization to serve not only the American student community, but also to promote student interests.

Although NSA has not been active on Mather campus, it will be in the future, for several projects have been initiated at the NSA Cleveland area meetings. One of these is the Purchase Card System upon which action has already begun.

"The purchase card, sold by a member NSA college to any of its students for one dollar, will

THE EMORY WHEEL FRIDAY EDITION

NSA Cards Sales Said Failure In Emory Area

Sale of National Student association cards on the Emory campus was a complete flop last year, Bob Flournoy, ticket sales chairman, said this week.

Flournoy also reported that many tickets and some money still had not been collected from last year's sales.

NSA conducts the ticket selling drive. Last year the drive was started during the Spring quarter by the Student council.

Student council members and Intrafraternity council members sold the tickets this year and Flournoy said letters and editorials in The Wheel had not succeeded in bringing in

La Salle COLLEGIAN

FRIDAY, MARCH 25, 1949

(Photo by Kane)

Five promoters of the Purchase Card System prepare for last Tuesday's "Don't Be a Sucker" campaign. In front row, left to right, are William Breeze, William Sweet and Quentin Mecke; in the rear, Edward Chesnes and Walter Toth. They hold a few of the 1000 lolly-pops which were distributed.

Purchase Cards On Sale; 200 Stores Cooperating

The Purchase Card System started operations on the campus yesterday, offering discounts for student buyers in more than 200 Philadelphia retail stores.

16 Men To Attend NSA Convention

Mills College Weekly

NSA NEWS . . .

PURCHASE CARDS ENDORSED HERE

Results of the NSA Purchase Card Plan questionnaire, which was distributed in the halls just prior to Christmas vacation, showed almost unanimous enthusiasm for the plan on this campus. Although it would seem that some students have no great need for the reductions which are to be obtained by the system, few objections to its establishment were voiced. Any information as to the actual operation of the plan in the Bay Area is, as yet, indefinite. However, further information will be made available in future issues of the *Weekly*.

On the NSA national scene this organization is backing "Brotherhood Week." All regions and colleges are urged by the National Executive Committee of NSA to adopt programs in keeping with "Brotherhood Week," February

INTRODUCTION OF PCS as a local program was followed closely by college press around the country. Top left, U. of Buffalo, NY, announces stores: *Argus,* 5/3/48, "Plaza," 3/11/49, "Steerings," 5/5/50; "Mobilgas," 2/29/52. Left, above. *La Salle Collegian,* PA, 11/28/48, masthead, 3/25/49. *Mills College Weekly,* CA, 2/18/49. Top, right, clockwise: U. of Idaho, *Idaho Argonaut,* 4/8/49; *The Loyola News,* Chicago, 10/28/48; U. of Louisville, KY, *The Cardinal,* 2/25/49, masthead, 3/25/49; U. of Maryland, *Diamondback,* 10/11/49; Columbia U., NY, *Spectator,* 11/22/48; U. of Colorado, *Silver and Gold,* 6/5/51, masthead, 12/6/50; Flora Stone Mather C., Cleveland, *The Mather Record,* 12/14/49; Emory College, GA, *The Emory Wheel,* 10/5/50, masthead 4/13/51.

PCS—A mixed blessing

On the primary level of value, the NSA [PCS] was conspicuously successful —students were cooperating to reduce their costs of living. But the Purchase Card System had a baneful influenece on the other programs and purposes of the association. Student governments and NSA committees, long accustomed to the philosophy that their only meaningful function was to provide material services for students, found their way to NSA via the restrictive pathway of this economic program. If the PCS cards did not come in on time, if a local program that was hopefully begun petered out—NSA was declared at fault, labeled valueless. Student leaders with a strange almost perverted logic found in the Purchase Card System all the raw material needed to credit or discredit the Association.

As a consequence, at the Third Student Congress [1950], a subcommission was given the task of correcting PCS's administrative and ideological malfunctionings . . . the desire to secure additional revenue, and the urgency to construct, at least, one program that would provide the material returns so important to student governments were primary. . . . An examination of the Purchase Card System's two years of operating experience revealed its narrow idea base, its administrative inflexibility, its predictable limitations and marked it for renovation.

1950-51 SDS Handbook, USNSA

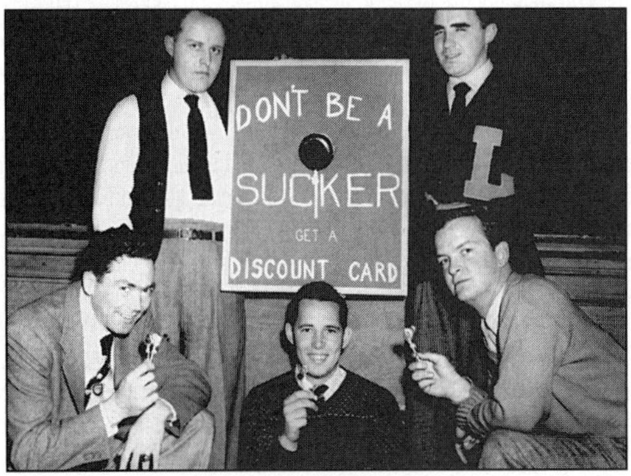

STUDENTS AT LA SALLE COLLEGE, Philadelphia, help launch 11/48 PCS drive (see column left above).

Publications and the Arts

1946 Chicago Student Conference: Goals and Implementation

I. Aims. It shall be the aim of the NSO ....

7. To foster student cultural activities; to secure the widest possible publication of advances of knowledge. In the pure, natural, industrial, and social sciences, and the fine arts, and methods of circulation of these publications which would make available to all students the fullest information regarding such new developments.

II. Activities

To implement the aims outlined in the previous section, it is recommended to the NCC, by Panel IV, that the following activities be considered in preparing a draft platform.

The NSO shall: . . .

11. Distribute to its members and to the faculties, especially of schools not having student governments, information on the histories and principles of organization as they function in student governments in other colleges throughout the U.S.
12. Have its own periodicals and publications which shall be distributed to its members.
13. Function as a national clearing-house, catalog, and republication center for local and regional student publications and for material pertinent to student problems and issues.
14. Sponsor national radio forums on specific interests or problems of students.
15. Advocate the wide circulation of student contributions to American culture through:
    A. Nationwide student exchange and festivals in drama, poetry, publications, magazines, bands, glee clubs, etc.
    B. Rotating student art exhibits, and glee clubs, etc.
    C. Sponsoring national student conferences for student groups with special interest in various fields, i.e., law, history, philosophy, etc.
16. Advocate that the NSO establish a press association of its own.
17. In addition, we recommend that the NCC investigate the possibility of cooperation with the American Association of Collegiate Press and the Intercollegiate Broadcasting System.

December, 1946, Reports of the Chicago Student Conference

1948 Constitutional Convention Framework

The USNSA recognizes culture as a social manifestation, differing in form and substance in various environments. The cultural base is not a static element but, when properly nourished, one that can develop and enhance the social progress of our nation. In light of this the USNSA will help to achieve the best possible opportunities for the cultural development of all American college and university students. Also it will attempt to serve the American campus by adopting a program that will present the creative efforts of the students to the American public and peoples of the world and at the same time bring to the campuses the best of all cultures of the world.

The first object in setting up a program along these lines is to obtain the widest possible student participation in a general cultural program, both as audience and producer. The work and program of American and foreign students should be made available to every campus, through exhibits of art schools, tours of theatre and dance groups, exchange of musical groups. Professional groups should be encouraged to take their concerts, exhibits, lectures and plays to as many campuses as possible. Audio-visual programs should be made available to all schools to study the cultures of all peoples.

The USNSA should conduct a series of competitions for all students to encompass the fields of all arts and sciences. The possibility of an annual cultural festival should be carefully studied, and participation in international cultural festivals should be encouraged. It is felt that this is one of the important methods through which understanding of all peoples can be facilitated.

September, 1948, Report of the First National Student Congress

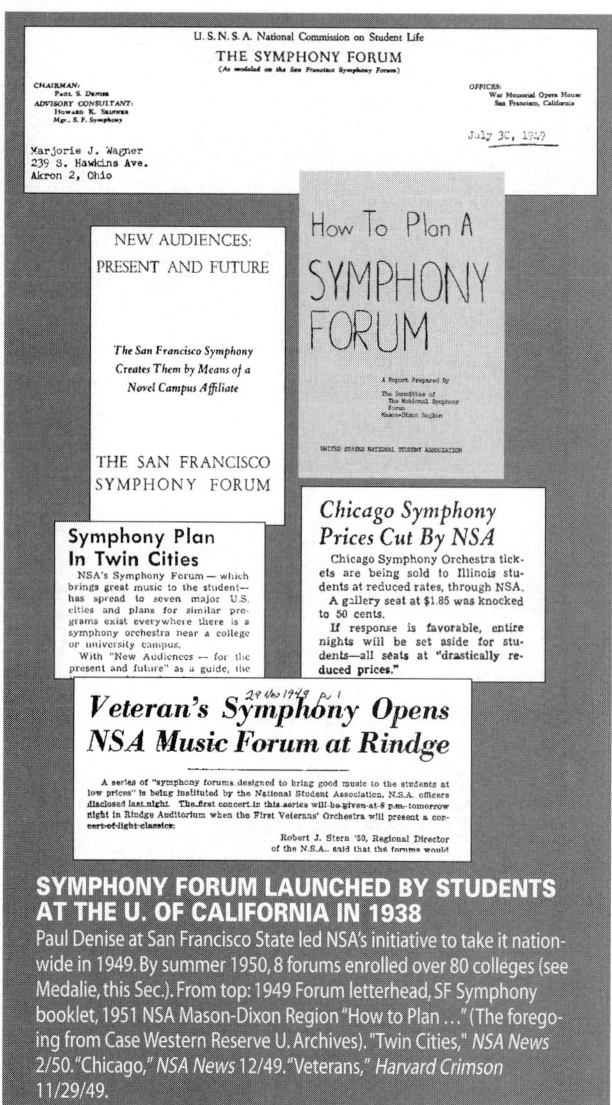

U. S. N. S. A. National Commission on Student Life

THE SYMPHONY FORUM

(As modeled on the San Francisco Symphony Forum)

CHAIRMAN: Paul S. Denise
ADVISORY CONSULTANT: Howard K. Skinner, Mgr., S. F. Symphony

OFFICES: War Memorial Opera House, San Francisco, California

July 30, 1949

Marjorie J. Wagner
239 S. Hawkins Ave.
Akron 2, Ohio

NEW AUDIENCES: PRESENT AND FUTURE

The San Francisco Symphony Creates Them by Means of a Novel Campus Affiliate

THE SAN FRANCISCO SYMPHONY FORUM

How To Plan A SYMPHONY FORUM

A Report Prepared By The Committee of The National Symphony Forum Mason-Dixon Region

UNITED STATES NATIONAL STUDENT ASSOCIATION

Symphony Plan In Twin Cities

NSA's Symphony Forum — which brings great music to the student— has spread to seven major U.S. cities and plans for similar programs exist everywhere there is a symphony orchestra near a college or university campus.

With "New Audiences — for the present and future" as a guide, the

Chicago Symphony Prices Cut By NSA

Chicago Symphony Orchestra tickets are being sold to Illinois students at reduced rates, through NSA.

A gallery seat at $1.85 was knocked to 50 cents.

If response is favorable, entire nights will be set aside for students—all seats at "drastically reduced prices."

29 Nov 1949 p. 1

Veteran's Symphony Opens NSA Music Forum at Rindge

A series of "symphony forums designed to bring good music to the students at low prices" is being instituted by the National Student Association, N.S.A. officers disclosed last night. The first concert in this series will be given at 8 p.m. tomorrow night in Rindge Auditorium when the First Veterans' Orchestra will present a concert of light classics.

Robert J. Stern '50, Regional Director of the N.S.A., said that the forums would

SYMPHONY FORUM LAUNCHED BY STUDENTS AT THE U. OF CALIFORNIA IN 1938

Paul Denise at San Francisco State led NSA's initiative to take it nationwide in 1949. By summer 1950, 8 forums enrolled over 80 colleges (see Medalie, this Sec.). From top: 1949 Forum letterhead, SF Symphony booklet, 1951 NSA Mason-Dixon Region "How to Plan . . ." (The foregoing from Case Western Reserve U. Archives). "Twin Cities," *NSA News* 2/50. "Chicago," *NSA News* 12/49. "Veterans," *Harvard Crimson* 11/29/49.

Mills to Be In N.S.A. Concert

By Carol Gurian

There is something new and completely different in music for the Bay area. The Mills College Chorus and the male choirs of five other schools in the Bay area are collaborating on a program of music to be presented in the San Francisco War Memorial Opera House Thursday night, April 15. The other schools participating in this program are the University of San Francisco, Santa Clara, Cal, Stanford and St. Mary's. This is the first program of its kind to be given and promises to be a very interesting and successful innovation.

The National Students' Asociation is sponsoring the program for the benefit of the World Student Service

MIDDLEBURY CAMPUS

Brooks, C. Paterson to Speak At Conference | New Enrollment Lists 20 Students Formerly at Midd | Art Mooney And Band To Play For Carnival

Middlebury Chosen For NSA Culturale

Middlebury College has been selected by the National Student Association as

CULTURALE music festival in 49

NATIONAL STUDENT'S ASSOCIATION PENNSYLVANIA REGION

INTERCOLLEGIATE PERFORMANCE EVENTS

were first intiated in Philadelphia, Denver, New England, NY City, San Francisco. *Mills College Weekly* 3/5/48, CA. *Middlebury Campus*, 2/12/48, VT. Letterhead, PA Region, 1949 Culturale. (See also p. 956 for efforts in Nebraska and Michigan.)

THE NSA NEWS

Traveling Student Art

NSA ART TOUR—Mary Kay Perkins (left) and Lucille Crews plan the second year of Mundelein College's NSA art tour. They are inspecting a water color by Joan Fritchie, Mundelein. More than 75 schools are expected to exhibit art work.

Town Meeting Will Wind Up

The world tour of "America's Town Meeting of the Air" will end in Washington, D. C., Oct. 18.

"Report to the People" will be the topic of the last broadcast, from 8:30 to 9:30 p.m., EST.

The broadcast will be from the auditorium of the Department of In-

NSA Plans Student Art To Again 'Hit the Road'

Students will again view the art work of their contemporaries.

More than 50 schools have signed up to receive the Mundelein College-operated NSA Art Tour, and the total is expected to mount above

pointed secretary to the Madison national office.)

The Art Exhibit, which was originally shown at the recent NSA Congress, will be divided into two 60-works sections, which will circulate throu... States

AR... will ... and a... be di... to M...

64 Schools NAS Art Tour

(Continued from page 1)

Mar. 27-Apr. 1—Duke University
Apr. 3-8—Emory
Apr. 10-15—W. Va. Wesleyan
Apr. 16-June 6—Michigan Region

Section C

Nov. 22-29—S.F. Austin S.T.C.
Dec. 1-9—U. of Tulsa
Dec. 12-17—Northern S.T.C.
Dec. 19-24—(Art Tour available for schools in the vicinity of Northern S.T.C. or Carleton.)
Jan. 9-14—Carleton College
Jan. 16-21—Hamline University
Jan. 23-28—Marycrest College
Jan. 30-Feb. 4—Clarke College
Feb. 6-11—Webster College
Feb. 14-20—Paterson S.T.C.
Feb. 22-27—N.J.C. for Women
Mar. 1-6—Muhlenberg College
Mar. 8-13—St. Joseph, Philadelphia
Mar. 15-20—Immaculata College

—Harvey Samuels, Rochester Inst. of Tech.

TIME OUT FOR ART—Students attending an NSA luncheon at Rochester Institute of Technology take time out to review the second annual NSA Art Tour, which is visiting more than 100 college and university campuses during the 1949-50 school year. Left to right: William Nowson, Brockport State Teachers College; Claudia Symonds, Rochester Institute of Technology; Jean Lane, Nazareth College; and Dick Appel, University of Rochester.

Caellian

Weekend NSA Conference Here; Consid...

NSA Member Schools Exhibit Art in Beehive

The NSA Art Exhibit, which began its six-day stay on the NJC campus Tuesday, will be on view in the Beehive until April 24.

Two award-winning paintings are included among the 28 student original works. First place honors were given to "The Street" by Charles

Wooster Voice

NSA Art Exhibit Opens January 15

Under the auspices of the National Student Association, a student art exhibit will be displayed in lower Kauke beginning January 15. The show will continue until January 22 and will consist of the work of American college students.

Included in the exhibit will be forty-eight of the paintings of the NSA collection now touring European ... ject

EXHIBITS MANAGED AT MUNDELEIN COLLEGE, Chicago. Far left, *NSA News* 10/49 (see Perkins, Pt. 5, S. 5). Photo, *NSA News* 2/50. NJC for Women *Caelian* 4/20/50, Masthead 11/3/49. C. of Wooster, *Wooster Voice* 1/13/49.

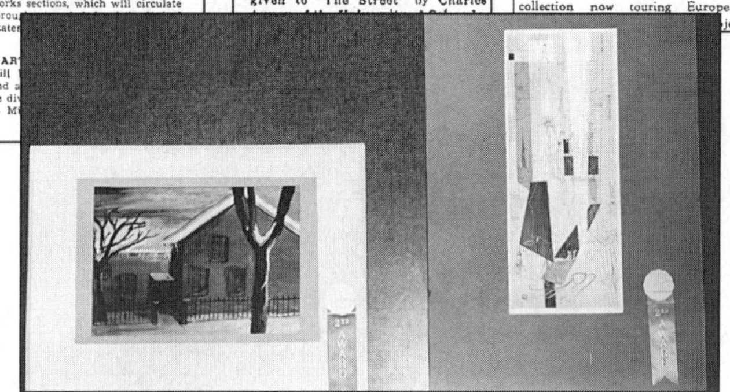

LAUNCHED IN 1948, NSA Art Exhibit shown at each National Congress and then sent on the road. Above, students assemble exhibit in 1948 (SHSW).

Right, National Student Art Exhibit Catalog, 1948-49, prepared by the 1947-48 NSA staff, with 122 artists from 37 colleges (Archives, Case Western Reserve University).

PUBLICATIONS CATALOG

(TEMPORARY)
OCTOBER, 1952

United States National Student Association
13th & Sansom Sts., Philadelphia 7, Pa.

PUBLICATIONS ON STUDENT GOVERNMENT

Reg. NSA

A Call to Order, (Guide to Parliamentary Procedure), Brock, (Revised) 1952, 16pp. Simplified handbook on parliamentary procedure for student governments and campus organizations; designed to introduce the student to the accepted rules of order and to provide a handy reference and supplement to Robert's Rules .... .50 .25

Student Government—Administration and Techniques, Perry, 1950, 55pp. (Mim.) Discusses purpose, administration, and activities of student governments; includes many sample forms frequently used by student governments .... .40 .20

Student Leadership and Government in Higher Education, Dungan, Klopf, and Heggie, 1949, 36pp. Consideration of student leadership, and a formulation of the aims and purposes of student governments .... .50 .25

A Continuing Leadership Program, Trueblood and Perry, 1950, 19pp. (Mim.) Specific programming for leadership training as well as techniques, organization, and use of the group method. .... .40 .20

Student Bill of Rights (Statement and Commentary), Bacon, 1951, 8pp. (Mim.) Document adopted by the Fourth National Student Congress .... .20 .10

Faculty Rating, Goldsmith, 1951, 12pp. (Mim.) An inter-collegiate program for evaluation of faculty instruction, student participation, and course content-method; includes sample rating sheets .... .40 .20

Freshman Orientation, New Meaning, Brock, 1951, 9pp. (Mim.) An evaluation of orientation programs with suggestions for a new approach; emphasizes the role of the student and faculty; outline for a year-around program .... .20 .10

Honor System in Higher Education, Sanders and Brock, 1951, 35pp. (Mim.) Discussion of the objectives and essentials of an Honor System; includes full reports of the survey conducted among USNSA member schools; provides information for establishing an Honor System .... .40 .20

PUBLICATIONS ON INTERNATIONAL AFFAIRS

Reg. NSA

Work, Study, Travel Abroad, Travel Department, USNSA, 1952, 48pp. A comprehensive outline of summer educational travel opportunities for American students .... .50 .25

An International Role for the American Student, Staff, 1951, 23pp. A comprehensive explanation of the role of the American student in world affairs; contains reports from the meeting of world student leaders from twenty-one countries in Stockholm in December, 1950; contains reports on the international program of NSA; practical cooperation with other national unions of students is discussed together with technical student assistance programs in underdeveloped areas .... .50 .25

International Student Conference in Stockholm, Swedish National Union of Students, 1951, 12pp. (Mim). Detailed report of the meeting of leaders of twenty-one national student unions to discuss areas of practical cooperation and technical assistance programs in under-developed areas .... .40 .20

PUBLICATIONS ON HUMAN RELATIONS

Human Relations and the Educational Community, Medalie and Klopf, 1950, 33pp. Programming designed to improve human relations in the educational community; an examination of the problems of inter-personal and inter-group tensions with the end of reducing these prejudices and clarifying the principles of democratic human relations .... .50 .25

Michigan Attitudes Survey, Michigan Daily, University of Michigan, 1949, 4pp. A statistical analysis of student attitudes toward minority groups **Free on request.**

PUBLICATIONS ON USNSA ORGANIZATION

NSA — Citizenship, Scholarship, Fellowship, Staff, (Revised) 1952 10pp. folder. Explains organization purposes, and policies of USNSA. AVAILABLE AFTER DECEMBER 1, 1952 .... .02 .02

USNSA CONSTITUTION, (Revised) 1952. Includes constitutional amendments adopted by Fifth National Student Congress. AVAILABLE AFTER DECEMBER 1, 1952 .... .20 .10

Reg. NSA

SDS Handbook, Goldsmith, 1950, (Mim.) Programmatical report on the operations of the Student Discount Service operated by USNSA. Provides detailed information for establishment of an SDS committee and local operation .... .40 .20

Student Body Presidents Conference, Second Annual Meeting Report and Directory, August 1952, Indiana University. Compiled in October issue: **Student Government Bulletin and Report** .... .35 .20

PROGRAMMATIC AIDS

Carleton DP Plan, Carleton College, 1949, 3pp. (Mim.) Report on the college plan for foreign and displaced students to attend American institutions of higher learning. **Free upon request.**

Colorado DP Plan, National Sub-Commission on Displaced Persons (University of Colorado), 1949, 5pp. (Mim.) Report on the USNSA study conducted on placing of displaced students on American campuses. **Free upon request.**

Bowdoin Plan, Bowdoin College, 1948, 8pp. (Mim.) Explains the plan whereby fraternities contribute to international understanding by providing housing for foreign students. **Free upon request.**

Colorado Graduate Travel Savings Plan, University of Colorado, 1950, 2pp. (Mim.) Explains a college plan for student financing of foreign and domestic travel and study. **Free upon request.**

NSA CATALOG of publications (excerpts), 10/52. An expanded publication program was launched in 1952-53. (See Album, p. 1100.)

NSA's Positions on Legislative Advocacy, Federal Aid to Education, Universal Military Training

Editor's note: During NSA's formative years, NSA Congresses and national staffs took great pains to avoid engaging in any form of political action that would extend the organization in areas beyond its immediate organizing, student and civil rights, student government, educational and international affairs programs. Much of this constraint was the result of the diversity of its membership among public and private, religious and sectarian, and liberal and conservative college campuses. It also reflected the association's limited financial and personnel resources available to mount any national campaign,its view that legislative action also had a strong educational purpose, and its intention to rely heavily on regional initiatives. Nonetheless, its leaders recognized that in order to establish itself as a "voice for the American college student" NSA needed to address the broad national issues which affected student welfare. The two most dominant issues at the time were federal aid to education and universal military training and the draft. Following are short summaries of the evolution of NSA's approach to these issues and how it balanced its various interests:

LEGISLATIVE ACTIVITY POLICIES

Basic Policy By-Law (1947 Policy)

One of two proposed by-laws the Constitutional Convention did not have time to act upon, this By-Law was adopted by a vote of 19 in favor, 8 against, and 2 abstentions by the National Executive Committee on December 28, 1947.

Since this organization cannot achieve its objectives or maintain the active support of all college and university students if its influence should be diverted into partisan, sectarian, or other narrow channels, be it resolved that the NSA shall have as its objectives only those which contribute to the enhancement of the welfare of students and facilitate student contributions to international understanding and good will; and shall specificallv refrain from becoming involved in partisan political affairs, sectarian religious considerations, or similar matters which do not directly affect students in their functions and activities as students, with the single exception that the NSA shall stand unalterably opposed to any political doctrine which would stifle free and democratic education in the United States.

The foregoing resolution repeats in exact words the policy statement recommended by Panel IV at the Chicago Student Conference, December 28-30, 1946 (p. 21, Reports of the Chicago Student Conference).

Regional Implementation (1952 policy)

The [NSA]Congress observes that certain of USNSA's legislative policies are intended to be carried out on the regional level; the Congress further observes that the regions have frequently neglected to carry out these programs. The Congress directs that the Vice-President for Educational Affairs can, in the event that a region is not, in his opinion, making a reasonable effort to implement such programs, appoint a person from the region, whose duty it shall be to carry out the implementation of the program in question.

National Implementation (1953 Policy)

Fact: There is at present no effective mechanism established for the purpose of implementing legislative policy established by the National Student Congress.

Principle: The successful implementation of USNSA's national legislative program depends upon effective action at regional and local levels.

Action: We therefore direct that the national legislative clearing house be continued. The Vice-President for Educational Affairs shall determine the location of this clearing house. It is recommended that it be located in or near Washington, D.C.

The functions of the clearing house shall be:

a. To collect and disseminate information on legislative matters ...

b. To inform the national office of all hearings on legislative matters affecting students and ....

c. To urge positive action [nationally, and in the regions and on campuses] on specific legislation when so directed by the Educational Affairs Vice-President in accordance with USNSA policy....

FEDERAL AID TO EDUCATION POLICY

NSA's early federal aid policy was comprehensive in its expectations for federal financial support. However, it also reflected two of the highly charged agendas within the organization at the time: the pressing needs of the Catholic and private colleges for expansion of their physical plant in response to the surge in postwar enrollments, and the push for equality in the allocation of funds to the then segregated colleges in the South.

The Third National Student Congress at the University of Michigan stated that it "affirms the position on Federal Aid to Higher Education as contained in the NEC resolution of December 1948." This latter resolution endorsed the goals of the President's Commission on Higher Education which stated that at no level should "a qualified individual in any part of the country encounter an insuperable barrier to the attainment of the kind of education suited to his aptitudes and interests." The resolution then enumerated various specific goals, criteria and programs for federal and federal scholarships. Among them:

"Because the balance between public and private institutions is one of the primary values of our educational system, NSA recommends that, in addition to these proposals of the President's Commission, legislation be drafted to extend federal aid to all institutions, regardless of the source of institutional control, for capital outlay on the basis of federal allotment to the state concerned, provided that no funds shall be appropriated for that (sic) personnel, and those services or facilities exclusively and specifically devoted to sectarian religious purposes.

"Federal support for the general support of higher education should clearly recognize the full powers of the states to administer and control their own educational programs, provided that the same amount is spent on college education for any student by the state in publicly controlled institutions."

The complete policy statement will be found on pages 17-19, of NSA's "Education Affairs 1953 Codification".

Chicago Student Conference (December 28-30,1946)

It shall be the aim of the NSO....

4. To secure for all students an extensive system of governmental and private aid In obtaining scholarships, family allowances, the provision of textbooks and supplies, and all other means to assure their Independence wherever necessary.

Constitutional Convention (August 30-September 7, 1947)

Panel II endorsed the principle of granting federal, state, and local aid to higher education. The following implementation was proposed for the USNSA:

The NSA advocates a program of federal aid to the individual student who is scholastically qualified but financially unable to secure a higher education, aid which will be granted without regard to race, religion, sex, or political belief; support increase in GI subsistence in proportion to the family unit; encourage increased private contributions to scholarship and loan funds by organizations as well as individuals; encourage individual colleges and universities to adopt more liberal scholarship policies; work to prevent the increase of educational fees, and ask that, when such increases are necessary, the administration discuss the problem with the local student government, especially with regard to those students for whom the raising of fees will be a hardship; encourage other legislative programs designed to alleviate economic barriers to education.

The Panel also recommends further consideration of the Privilege Card Plan and, in cooperation with the North American Student Cooperative League, investigation of the problems and promotion of student cooperatives.

NSA & UNIVERSAL MILITARY TRAINING
1948-No Comment. 1951-For. 1952-Against

UMT became an issue of high priority as a result of the Korean War outbreak in June of 1950. The NSA News in its Special Post Congress Edition for the 1951 Fourth National Student Congress at the University of Minnesota in August reported, "After heated debate, the delegates passed a resolution, 138-103, in favor of Universal Military Training at this time. A minority report against UMT was also filed."

*The minutes of that Congress currently available are missing the complete record of the vote and the resolution adopted. Dennis Trueblood and Bill Birenbaum in their report on the Fourth National Student Congress (*School and Society *12/14/51) stated:*

With many students awaiting the call of their draft-boards, the students emphasized the primary importance of the Universal Military Training issue in higher education. After thoroughly considering the implications of military training, the Congress defeated a resolution condemning UMT and approved, instead, a statement ackowledging the necessity of some form of universal military training in the present world situation. A slogan advanced by some of the proponents of the approved statement caught the fancy of the delegates, and became a rallying cry for some of the later actions of the Congress. The slogan was: "None are so blind as those who refuse to see."

*The Summary Minutes of the August 26, 1952, afternoon session of the Fifth Annual National Student Congress at the University of Indiana reports the following resolution opposing UMT adopted by a vote of 149 in favor, 91 opposed, and 8 abstentions.**

The Congress recognizes the need for security and believes our manpower needs can be served adequately solely by a professionally trained nucleus of enlisted personnel which can institute immediate mobilization upon incidence of aggression or a dangerous threat to our security. The Congress further believes that the establishment of a program of Universal Military Training is not in the best interests or tradition of our country because it institutionalizes military service as part of American life. The Congress recommends that our manpower needs be met by an equitable and consistent program of selective service, so long as a state of national emergency exists.

Students Vote Down UMT

Slightly more than two-thirds of our student body have gone on record as being opposed to Universal Military Training! This fact was brought to light by a student opinion poll held in chapel last week under the sponsorship of the National Student Association. Despite lingering wisps of tear gas, Sophomore, Junior and Senior classes entered chapel to hear Mr. Halliday and Mr. Chittum, both members of our faculty, present the issues involved in peacetime conscription.

College of Wooster, OH, *Wooster Voice* 1/23/48

*The 1952 resolution continued to remain as NSA policy at least through 1956, when it appears in the 1956 Codification of NSA Policy. The resolution was introduced by Charles Aswad, Harpur College, who was Chairman of the Educational Affairs Commission and of the New York State Region.

USNSA BULLETIN
MADISON 5, WISCONSIN

304 North Park St. December 18, 1947

UNIVERSAL MILITARY TRAINING INFORMATION KIT

Prepared, by the staff of the U.S.N.S.A.

One of the bills on the agenda of the 80th Congress when it reconvenes in January 1948, will be H.R.4278, a house bill which grew out of the Report of the President's Advisory Commission on Universal Military Training, May 29, 1947. In short, the bill provides that all men upon reaching the age of 18 must spend twelve months in the Armed Forces.

The staff of the USNSA has read college newspapers from all parts of the United States, and has talked extensively with various student leaders acquainted with the local and national scene. The result of this research has been rather shocking. Very little information has been made available to the individual student concerning the arguments pro and con on the question, should the United States adopt a system of Universal Military Training. Many students are of voting age and should be informed citizens, others will be directly effected by the passage of such a bill, and all are concerned with the security of the United States. . . . The National office of the USNSA has prepared the enclosed material and obtained the booklets for your student government, so that adequate information is now available to the students of America.

The United States National Student Association is not taking a stand for or against Universal Military Training.

Student Poll Shows Campus Favors Compulsory Training

City College Thinks Plan Necessary for Security, Men, Veterans Show Larger Percentage in Favor

That City College thinks compulsory military training has some place in post-war America was revealed by a student poll conducted on campus.

A majority declared that military training is necessary for national security, though a much smaller percentage was inclined to suggest other advantages to the plan. In general, men showed a larger percentage in favor than the women veterans were more inclined to favor it than non-veterans

Los Angeles City College, *Los Angeles Collegian* 10/31/47

UMT Opposition Includes MSM National Seceretary

A national youth committee to fight the adoption of universal military training was announced this week with William Luechtenburg, Executive Secretary of the student division of Americans for Democratic Action, as its National Chairman. The group, which includes members of Catholic, Protestant, and secular youth groups, has affiliated with the National Council Against Conscription and will serve as its Youth Division.

The youth group claimed that every important student or youth organization which has considered universal military training has come out in opposition to it. Among the groups opposed, it listed the National Conference of Methodist Youth, the student divisions of the Y.M.C.A. and Y.W.C.A., Students for Democratic Action, the Student League for Industrial Democracy, and the Westminister Fellowship, which is the national youth organization of the Presbyterian Church.

METHODIST STUDENT MOVEMENT joins opposition to UMT (Milsap College, MS, *Purple and White*, 4/11/47).

Students Introduce Faculty Rating Systems

SEATTLE, WASHINGTON

[N]SA Regional Conference [D]iscusses Intercollegiate [A]ctivity, Course Evaluation

Intercollegiate activities and evaluation of education were [fea]tured in discussions before the NSA Northwest Regional [conference] held here over the weekend.

UCLA *Daily Bruin*

NSA Sponsors Prof Evaluation In 47 Classes

Forty-seven classes, selected at random, are being given an opportunity by NSA during the next three days to air their opinions of present teaching methods at UCLA.

Under the sponsorship of the NSA Curricular problems committee, a "Survey of Student Opinion

Students Want Faculty Evaluation; Poll Reveals

[TH]E CARDINAL
[U]NIVERSITY OF LOUISVILLE'S OFFICIAL WEEKLY PUBLICATION

Faculty Rating System Begins At Speed School

Students Evaluate Teachers At Brooklyn College, Rutgers

Should Students Rate The Faculty? 'Yes' And 'No' Say Guest Editors

Pro:

By Larry Travis

God knows, even if nobody else does, that students have to endure a lot of poor teachers in this school.

And teachers have to endure a lot of poor students.

By grades and by teachers' criticisms students are told whether and how they should improve as students.

But they never get a chance to tell teachers where they have failed and how they could have done a better job of teaching.

A letter on this page from Mrs. Dora Polk

Con:

By Dora Beale Polk

A questionnaire aimed at getting student evaluation (A, B, C, D, or F) of professors is nothing more than a mechanistic system which may conceal the truth and lead to abuse.

Such a system may have been designed

Silver & Gold

Editor Congratulates NSA

Faculty Ratings Praised

(The following is an editorial reprinted from the January 1949 issue of the JOURNAL OF HIGHER EDUCATION.)

THE UNITED STATES NATIONAL Student Association is to be congratulated on having undertaken as one of its major projects the improvement of instruction in colleges and universities through rating by students of instructors and courses. The practice of such rating is not new; it has existed sporadically for a long time. Many instructors individually have developed more or less elaborate plans which they ask their students to use in evaluating the courses they give. In some institutions, students rate all teachers, or all who wish to be rated.

The Association is working for the extension and improvement of this practice. It has requested its representatives on each campus to take steps to initiate a faculty-rating system, through a student-faculty committee if practicable; and, if not, through the appropriate administrative officer. It has developed five rating forms which differ in various ways, but which are similar in that each provides scales on which the student can rate his instructor on a number of characteristics. The ratings are to be anonymous.

THE ASSOCIATION INSISTS UPON the importance of "unity of purpose of the teacher and student" if a course is to be effective. It believes that proper use of a rating blank can promote such unity. In answer to the argument that students are not mature enough to evaluate their teachers, it contends that "the maturity required to fill out the faculty-evaluation form is no greater than that required to carry on functions of everyday college life." It points out that rating by students is not to be regarded as the only, or even the chief, means for the evaluation of teachers. It is one means by which the teacher can be helped to improve his teaching.

In this argument, the Association is on firm ground. Rating of instructors by students, particularly rating of those who wish it, can contribute substantially to the improvement of instruction. No one in his senses would maintain that such ratings should be taken at face value, and other criteria disregarded. Students are immature as compared with their instructors and are not infallible in their judgments of what is best for them. On the other hand, every teacher needs to see himself as others see him—a most difficult task—and use the knowledge so gained to improve his work. Rating by students is an important source of such knowledge. In short, it is not true in educational matters that the customer is always right, but it is true that he should always be consulted and that serious consideration should always be given to what he has to say.

SO WE WISH THE National Student Association every success in carrying out its project. But we hope that it will modify its plan by including in it another, and quite different, method of instructor- and course-evaluation. This is the method of group judgment, based on group discussion. The method works in this way. At an appropriate time, the instructor announces that he is asking the class to devote one or two periods at the close of the term to an evaluation of the course. He asks the class to elect from its own members a chairman and a secretary for the evaluation. He outlines the duties of these two officers, emphasizes the importance of selecting persons who have the proper qualifications, and presides at their election. He requests the most searching evaluation.

On the day or days of the evaluation, the teacher is absent; hence every member of the class can speak with complete freedom.

ON THE BASIS OF LIMITED but highly favorable experience with this method, the writer can affirm that it has important advantages. It differs from the use of a rating blank in much the same way that the work of a deliberative assembly differs from the procedure involved in conducting a referendum or opinion poll. It calls for give-and-take discussion, which gets at matters that would not be reached by other methods. It is likely to lead to conclusions that no individual student would have reached without the stimulus of group discussion. It provides a highly educative experience for those who participate; indeed, students in classes where this practice has been followed have sometimes said that the evaluation session was the best class period of the entire quarter.

THIS METHOD IS NOT A CURE-ALL, nor is it foolproof. As with any rating plan, much depends upon the teacher's genuine desire for searching criticism and his ability to convince the class that the judgments it expresses will be given serious consideration. Much depends also upon the choice of a chairman who is a good group leader. But the method has great possibilities and deserves to be widely used. Hence we hope that the NSA will promote it, as well as the use of rating blanks.

—R. H. ECKELBERRY, Editor

NSA News 2/49

UNITY OF TEACHER AND STUDENT AIMS was NSA's goal in developing and promoting the Faculty Rating System, one of its enduring and popular programs in its early years. Highly controversial, it also enjoyed considerable support from educators who, as suggested by R.H. Eckelberry (excerpted above), were interested in engaging students in the process of improving the quality of instruction. Left, from top: U. of Washington, *Washington Daily*, 12/6/49; UCLA, *Daily Bruin*, 1/5/49; College for Men, U. of Rochester, NY, *The Campus*, 3/7/47; U. of Louisville, *The Cardinal*, 3/3/50; Williams C., *Williams Record*, 9/25/48; U. of Colorado, *Silver & Gold*, 5/16/50.

SECTION 2

Student Rights, Discrimination, and Academic Freedom

CONTENTS

Michigan State College Expels Member of AYD

Ohio State U Disowns Wallaceites

Harvard Crimson, 5/27/49

Poll Reveals College Students Object to Quota Requirements

Columbia Daily Spectator, 2/17/50

Compulsory loyalty oaths hit by NSA Regional assembly

U.C. Berkeley, *Daily Californian*, 10/25/49

The memoirs and essays in this section provide a snapshot of some of the ferment which unsettled many of the nation's campuses as traditional prejudices, restraints on free speech and association, and regulation of student life were challenged by students.

Janet Welsh Brown (Smith College), 1951-52 New England Regional Chair and 1952-53 Vice President for Student Affairs, opens with a survey of the scope, strengths, and weaknesses of NSA's engagement in student rights and academic freedom issues, noting how in this area its lack of professional full-time staff limited its ability to provide effective independent investigatory depth of field to back up its advocacy.

Alexander Pope (University of Chicago), 1950-51 Illinois Regional Chair, recalls his university's and regional organization's resistence to state and federal Un-American Activity legislative investigations. Such investigations and attacks occurred throughout the country.

NSA: Fraternities and Discrimination

During its cautiously evolving early relationship with the national fraternity leadership, NSA became more assertive in attacking traditional fraternity exclusionary practices. This issue is explored here and in greater depth in Part 4. At the same time, NSA sought a productive relationship with what was then an important source of opposition to NSA affiliation on the campus level. Leonard Wilcox (Phi Kappa Tau, U. of Michigan), Michigan Region Chair in 1950-51 and NSA National Affairs Vice President in 1952-53, looks back on this period.

While Protestant and Catholic student organizations played a significant role in the organization and development of NSA (see Parts 1 and 4), the Jewish student interest, which also embraced establishing a Jewish homeland after the war as well as civil rights, was largely expressed in anti-discrimination agendas of the Anti-Defamation League and the National Conference of Christians and Jews (NCCJ), with which NSA actively collaborated. In this section the role of the Hillel Foundation is recalled by Leonard Jick (Washington University in St. Louis), first president of his campus chapter. In NSA's early years, Muslim, Buddhist, and other major religions outside the Judeo-Christian tradition did not appear to have a significant national student organization presence.

Declaration of Rights Essential to Students

BY-LAW III. BILL OF RIGHTS

In order to preserve and extend these conditions indispensable to the full achievement of educational objectives, and with full cognizance of the responsibilities and obligations which ensue from any assertion of fundamental rights, the National Student Association holds the following rights essential to the full development of the student as an individual and to the fulfillment of his responsibilities as a citizen:

1. The right of every student to a college education.

2. The right to conduct research freely and to publish, discuss, and exchange any findings or recommendations, whether individually or in association with local, national, or international groups.

3. The right of students to a clear and concise statement, before entering college, of their contractual rights, obligations, and responsibilities pertaining to educational and cxtra-curricular activities.

4. The right of every student to exercise his full rights as a citizen in forming and participating in local, national, or international organizations for intellectual, religious, social, political, economic or cultural purposes, and to publish and distribute their views.

5. The right of recognized student organizations to use the institution's name subject to its regulations with respect to off-campus activities.

6. The right of students and recognized student organizations to use campus facilities, provided the facilities are used for the purpose contracted, subject only to such regulations as are required for scheduling meeting times and places.

7. The right to invite and hear speakers of their choice on subjects of their choice.

8. The right of students to engage freely in off-campus activities, provided they do not claim to represent the institution, exercising their rights as citizens of community, state, and nation.

9. The right to establish and issue regular publications free of any censorship or other pressure aimed at controlling editorial policy, with the free selection and removal of editorial staffs reserved solely to the organizations sponsoring these publications.

10. The right to establish democratic student governments with adequate democratic safeguards against abuse of their powers.

11. The right to petition through proper channels for changes in curriculum or professors.

12. The right of equal opportunity to enjoy these rights without regard to race, color, sex, national origin, religious creed, or political beliefs.

From USNSA Constitution, September, 1947.

Exec Committee Hits Fear, Hysteria As Dangers to Academic Freedom

Opposes Firing on Basis Of Political Affiliations

(See editorials, page 2; text of statement, page 3)

NSA's national executive committee concluded its three-day meeting at Cleveland College on April 3 by passing a statement for student rights and academic freedom which took a firm stand against the practice of dismissing college professors for membership in an association or organization without reference to their teaching ability.

At the same time, the committee, composed of the chairmen of NSA's 27 regions throughout the country, empowered its national staff to investigate the dismissal and placing on probation of University of Washington professors and the firing of a professor at Oregon State College.

The national staff was also authorized to conduct an investigation of the expulsion of James Zarichny from Michigan State College. The investigation will begin at such time that the staff receives a petition signed by 500 Michigan State College students.

In discussing its stand on academic freedom, the committee stated that

* * *

Harris Answers Charge Of Unconstitutionality

The National Executive Committee's action in passing its "Statement of Academic Freedom and Student Rights" was fully in accordance with NSA's Constitution which authorized the NEC to supervise the execution of policies established by the Congress, according to Ted Harris, president of NSA.

The University News

Academic Freedom No Pretext To Teach Systems Destructive Of All Freedom, President States

1500 Fill Gym

The Campus

Undergraduate Newspaper of The City College

NEW YORK, THURSDAY, OCTOBER 23, 1947 — By U-Card Only

ce
uys:
r '11'

College Administration to Fight Bill Barring Red Groups Here;

COLLEGE ADMINISTRATIONS DIVIDED on whether and how to place limits on what ideological affiliations are allowed for teachers in the classroom and speakers and groups on campus. From top: *NSA News* 4/49; St. Louis University, *University News* 9/30/49; City College of New York, *The Campus* 10/23/47.

The impact of staff politics on NSA politics

1. Student Rights, Academic Freedom, and NSA

Janet Welsh Brown
Smith College, Massachusetts. Chair, New England Region, 1951-52
NSA Vice President, Student Affairs, 1952-53

Academic freedom was already a well established concept by the time the National Student Association was founded, but student rights were more recently asserted and little known. Both were controversial.

In the catechism of academia, the intellectual freedom of the faculty (who were the strongest power on campus in those days) was the first commandment. Indeed, faculty tenure was considered essential, not just to provide economic security for what was then an underpaid profession, but also as the absolute necessary protection for faculty in their teaching of controversial issues, their research questioning established theories, and their private political and religious beliefs. Though sometimes honored more in the breach than in fact, the principle of academic freedom was the cornerstone of the university foundation. Few openly questioned the principle, though legislators, trustees, and significant financial benefactors of particular institutions sometimes disagreed with faculty in what was included in the concept and who deserved protection.

The new concept of student rights

Student rights, on the other hand, were scarcely heard of before the post–World War II period and the founding of NSA. Even among students and rare faculty or administrative advocates of student rights, there were continuing arguments about which rights were important. Some would be easily satisfied with a student role in rule making about campus life—about dormitory hours and other regulations of student life by institutions, in loco parentis, and the campus system of judgments and punishments made when infractions were committed. For some, focus was on the right of the elected student government to represent the collective will of the student body. Others asserted a role for students in shaping the curriculum—and it must have been the rare faculty member who did not feel threatened by such a usurpation of what most faculties considered their primary responsibility. (One college president said the new student organization's Bill of Rights implied "incompetence in administration and faculty" and that students were being "exploited."[1]) Still others were concerned most about the freedom of students to control their own publications.

Equal rights to higher education, without regard to "sex, race, religion, political belief or economic circumstance," were asserted in the preamble to the NSA Constitution drafted by the National Continuations Committee in spring 1947 and voted on in August 1947 by the founding National Student Congress at Madison. By-laws I and II, adopted at the same time, declared that NSA would seek equal opportunities for education, especially by securing the eventual elimination of all forms of "discriminatory educational systems"—and sought to encourage NSA-wide investigation, discussion, and action on problems of inequality. Then the longer By-law III spelled out a student Bill of Rights and criteria for their application, declared the organization to be in favor of the principles of academic freedom as espoused by the American Association of University Professors (AAUP), and called for NSA investigations of alleged violations.[2]

The twelve rights enunciated there were meant to protect student activities on campus and students' rights to full citizens' rights off campus. Indeed, they added up to a clear responsibility of students to contribute to the improvement of their educational institutions and the world: they called on students to lead American society in the postwar period. The NSA founders were, even in the postwar period of enthusiasm for democracy and U.S. world leadership, far ahead of their time and, indeed, of many of their peers.[3] And the principles of racial equality, academic freedom, and student rights were embraced unanimously and unconditionally by the elected student delegates at the founding Madison Convention. Those were heady times on college and university campuses, when the overcrowded institutions were, though we did not recognize it at the time, on the cusp of revolutionary changes in higher education.

All of these "rights" were resisted on many campuses in 1947, but it was the assertion of wider civil and political rights—the rights of students as citizens—that provoked the widest comment and resistance, from both inside and outside the academic institutions. Student concerns about discrimination on the basis of religion or race drew attention wherever asserted, as did student activists who asserted their right to bring political debate to their campuses.

The values of a wartime generation

All of these rights reflected the values of a generation that grew up in wartime and became imbued with a sense of personal and collective responsibility for protecting and expanding democracy. They were influenced also by the participation in NSA of mature veterans, seasoned adults who came to campus after often extensive military service. Students, at least that portion of them who were vocal and visible, were imbued by a liberalism that was idealistic, international, and often integrationist.

The values of NSA founders may also have been, in part, the legacy of the prewar student movement, where both of the dominant competing factions—the communist-inspired youth organizations and the Christian youth organizations, both Catholic and Protestant—opposed fascism and racial discrimination and promoted democracy, freedom, and individual rights. An important factor for the California delegation to the founding Convention was their horrifying recollection of the forced evacuation and internment of Japanese Americans during the war and their determination that the freedoms of American citizens should never again be so compromised.

Also clear to many of the delegates at Chicago and Madison was the fact that academic freedom and student rights were already under attack in 1947 in some parts of the country. California already had its blacklisted "Hollywood Ten" in the movie business and a loyalty oath required of all state employees, including university faculty. The state legislatures in Texas and Michigan had passed laws intended to ferret out communists. When Harry Gideonse took on the Presidency of Brooklyn College in the early 1940s, he accepted the charge to "clean out the communists" from the faculty. On many campuses, politicians were not allowed to speak. Originally, such prohibitions were probably an effort to keep state politics out of the public universities, but by 1947 they meant that any controversial visitor (to the University of California–Berkeley) had to be cleared by the Dean of Students at Berkeley. Indeed, the 1947 editor of the student paper, Jack Howard, was summoned to President Sproul's office because he resisted an Administration order not to print an ad for a local communist club meeting. Mildred Kiefer Wurf says that for the California and maybe other western delegations at the Madison Congress these academic-freedom and student-rights issues were of greater interest than the international issues, which to them seemed more remote.[4]

NSA's national student affairs agenda

In the early years the NSA Vice President (VP) for National Student Affairs (later called the Vice President for Student Life and the Vice President for Educational Problems) had broad responsibilities beyond the issues of race, academic freedom, and student rights covered in this chapter. Throughout the first five years, there was an ongoing competition for the VP's attention between the practical issues directly affecting students (housing, health services, financial issues, campus cultural and social life, and later the issues of athletics and federal aid to education) and the national issues—considered more political—such as Universal Military Training and even the Korean War and nuclear weaponry, on which delegates were periodically asked to take a stand.

Educational issues (curriculum reform and student participation in education decisions) were split off in 1948 and assigned to a separate Vice President for Educational Problems. Student governments, which, after the departure of the veterans from the NSA leadership, successfully demanded an increasing share of help and services, acquired their own Vice President in 1951. By 1951, when Sylvia Bacon took over, the agenda of the VP for Student Affairs was highly political and controversial, and she reports that the responsibility of dealing with visiting student art exhibits became a burden. By 1952, when I took office, student rights and academic freedom took up most of my time, and in later years when I explained my own role to others, I came to refer to myself as the "VP for Academic Freedom and Student Rights."

The national student agenda was also changed by the politics and temper of the nation over those five years. As the vets disappeared from campus, NSA domestic issues (both campus and national) ascended in importance—and controversy—and student interest in the international faded a bit. The NSA International Program would probably have receded to a much more modest part of the total had it not been for the secret financial support from the government.[5] As the Cold War intensified, so did the hysteria that became known as McCarthyism. In early 1952, President Bill Dentzer wrote a long editorial in the *NSA News* decrying the harmful effects of McCarthyism on U.S. campuses.[6] As time went on, the NSA's cardinal principles of racial equality, academic freedom, and student rights were attacked more and more frequently, and more vehemently, by increasingly hostile and powerful enemies.

In specific examples discussed in the remaining pages of this essay, I have dealt briefly also with the issues of equal rights and discrimination in higher education. Elsewhere in this book others recall their personal experience with civil rights, but the issue is pertinent here also, for in the NSA Constitution, the right of *all* to equal educational opportunity in institutions free of bias is asserted as the first right, on which all the other rights depend. The other respect in which equal rights comes together with academic freedom and student rights is in the opposition facing all three. Students advocating any of these rights were lumped together by NSA's detractors: an integrationist was automatically seen as a communist, as was any student who defended the right to hear a controversial speaker on campus.

Over the five years covered in this book, these brave principles of academic freedom, student rights, and racial equality were repeatedly tested. All were eroded, some more quickly than others, and some more seriously than others. On academic freedom and student rights in particular, it became increasingly difficult to defend the principles that were adopted in 1946 and 1947 without serious objection.

1. Racial equality

Race, not surprisingly, evoked the first challenge. At Madison (1947), there was a debate—and the first compromise. No delegate openly questioned the principle and goal of racial equality, but the issue for delegates from the few white southern institutions present[7] was how to reconcile the NSA principles with state laws requiring segregation. And how were we to recruit other southern schools, a task already identified as necessary if the NSA was to be a geographically *national* organization? In the Madison debate, the purists who insisted that the principle of equality was indivisible and absolute lost to a majority who were themselves perhaps more comfortable with the idea that integration should be gradual; and thus the key word "eventual" was inserted before "goal."[8]

Though many of us northern liberals thought at the time that racial discrimination was a southern phenomenon, others knew better and educated the rest with their recognition of discriminatory practices on our own campuses—in admissions, housing, athletics, and in most of campus life. NSA responded by asking all colleges to eliminate racial and religious references on admissions applications and asserting that colleges should withdraw from athletic associations that discriminated and remove restrictive clauses from all campus organizations.[9] Unequal opportunity for higher education was recognized by NSA in its 1950 affiliation with the National Scholarship Service Fund for Negro Students (NSSFNS).[10]

During NSA's first five years, the intention and goal of racial equality remained intact. The early leadership included Negro students in high, visible office. Clif Wharton, representing the Harvard student government at Chicago and Madison, was elected Secretary of the National Continuations Committee and was one of the small group of insiders on the larger committee who drafted the constitution and bylaws, programmed the Madison founding Congress, and—Solomon-like—selected the "balanced" slate that became NSA's first officers (one Southerner, one Catholic, one woman from the Midwest, one Negro, one Ivy-Leaguer). In each of the first four years, a Negro was elected to national office. Lee Jones (Buffalo) was elected Treasurer in 1947. In 1948-49, Ted Harris from LaSalle served as President. In 1949-1950, Ted Perry, from Temple University, was elected Vice President. Shirley Neizer from Simmons College was Secretary in 1950-51. Although Negro students were but thinly represented among the delegates, their election to high office was an important symbol, and newspaper photos of the officers helped spread the word that the principle of racial equality reigned in national student life—at least until 1951.

Early integration efforts by NSA

Giving meaning to the principle of racial equality within NSA programs and activities, however, was a more difficult task.[11] The claim has been made that NSA southern regional meetings marked the first integrated student meetings in the South. While I do not think that is true—some of the 1930s left-wing student organizations and the progressive Christian youth associations such as the Ys had integrated meetings in North Carolina and elsewhere in the 1920s and 1930s—there is no doubt that NSA meetings greatly added to the number of such contacts and increased their legitimacy.[12] NSA Secretary Helen Jean Rogers, back from a visit to southern campuses, reported in April 1949 that the vast majority of students and student leaders with whom she had talked were opposed to discrimination on their campuses.[13] Specific efforts to integrate campus life were inspired and supported by NSA policy. Indeed, it is my recollection that southern white students at the annual Congresses saw NSA policy on racial equality as a lever they could use to press for change on their own campuses.

By the second year of operation, the NSA office was responding to requests from campuses and regional groups for information on "human relations," the new euphemism applied to issues of race and religion. And in early 1949 the staff published a guide to planning campus human-relations programs that led to the creation of HR committees on several campuses. At the 1949 Congress, delegates resolved to "acknowledge and combat discrimination" and created a national subcommission on Human Relations and Educational Practices, whose job it was to collect information and combat prejudice and discrimination. The New England region organized a five-state institute, and Wayne University students created a Human Rights Clinic.[14]

In 1951, responding to a proposal that NSA investigate whether the American Fencing League discriminated on the basis of race, the National Executive Committee (NEC), acting on behalf of the organization between annual Congresses, for the first time took on athletics—which would be a major university issue a decade later. It passed a resolution asking for an inquiry into possible discrimination against any group by fencing and "other athletic and recreational organizations." I wonder if any of us at the time knew how intense the coming struggles with the National Collegiate Athletic Association would be.

When six Negro students, admitted to the University of North Carolina graduate school in 1951 under threat of federal court action,[15] tried to claim seats at the football stadium in the regular (white) student section on the 15-yard line instead of the commercial Negro section in the end zone, they were thrown out. The incident, orchestrated as a test, sparked strong student protest. The university Administration, while making clear that student government and other student groups had no say in policy, nevertheless met with thirteen student groups, and caved in on the issue. NSA principles were cited in the arguments, especially by the student government, which asserted that students must be consulted about such policies.[16]

NSA confronts fraternity discrimination

Efforts to remove restrictive clauses governing fraternities was another area where the NSA policies were used to justify initiatives on individual campuses.[17] Indeed, the NSA depended on member schools and regions to implement NSA programs and policies. A 1949 NSA Congressional resolution "urged" the independent Interfraternity Council and the Pan-Hellenic Council to eliminate discriminatory membership clauses from their constitutions, but the only way NSA could pressure the fraternities and sororities was by asking NSA member student governments to prohibit recognition of new campus groups that discriminated in any way. That same year, Phi Epsilon Phi, a Jewish fraternity at the University of Connecticut, pledged a Negro student, in keeping with action called for at NSA Congresses, and was suspended by its national organization after losing an appeal to the national organization. It received support of the City College of New York (CCNY) chapter, which promised also to disaffiliate if the penalties against the Connecticut chapter were upheld.

A Cornell delegate to the 1951 National Interfraternity Council, backed by representatives from five other northeastern schools, took the lead in urging the Council to "eliminate selective membership restrictions" from the members' constitutions. But back on the Cornell campus, the fraternities were exempted from the purview of a student committee on discrimination created to examine problems at the university. Student legislators at Michigan and Rutgers led similar attempts to purge discriminatory practices in their fraternities and sororities. At UCLA and Wisconsin, students went so far as to demand that their universities control discrimination in off-campus housing as well.[18] Students on many other campuses tried—and failed—to get sufficient votes to end discrimination, but had significant public debate on the issue in the process.

How effective was NSA in promoting racial equality? One cannot measure with the sparse evidence available the separate and collective efforts made on the campus, regional, and national levels, but one is tempted to answer, "Not much." But at that time, not much equality was being achieved in any walk of life, except for some important constitutional cases moving slowly through the federal courts. NSA did help focus national and local attention on the issue, did help make some progress on some campuses, and did subsequently feed some of its activists into the civil rights movement, where students were very effective indeed.

2. Student rights

While opposition to the principle of racial equality was never openly challenged in NSA, the concept of students' rights came under regular and increasingly strong attack over the first five years of NSA—from within and without the organization. The most fundamental of student rights—the expectation that every institution of higher education should have an elected student government, independent of faculty and administration, and the more general concept that students had something to say about all matters that affected them, including the content of the education they received—grew in strength during those first five years. Popular widespread acceptance of these rights can truly be said to be one of NSA's certain achievements.

It was when the specific political rights of students enumerated in the NSA Bill of Rights were insisted on—the rights to have their own organizations, to invite to campus speakers of choice, to publish their own newspapers—that students on some campuses got in trouble. Abrogation of those rights and demands that they be limited—most often by administrators, but also by trustees and state legislators and sometimes by students—became more frequent and more brazen as anticommunist fervor grew across the nation. Numerous cases were brought to the attention of the NSA, specifically to the regions or to the Vice Presidents for Student Life or Student Affairs. And at each National Congress, doubters challenged the Bill of Rights itself.

NSA's first student rights challenges

Student organizations were having trouble on campus even as the Continuations Committee was putting NSA together. In early 1947 at Michigan State, seven students were placed on indefinite probation for distributing on campus materials supporting the Fair Employment Practices Commission. It was probably not the materials that drew the Dean's punishment so much as it was the allegation that the students were members of an unrecognized chapter of American Youth for Democracy (AYD), an extreme left-wing organization.[19] Writing admittedly without NSA constitutional authority, Continuations Committee President Jim Smith quoted the NSA Chicago convention with regard to freedom of student organizations and publications and advised NSA student participants on all Michigan campuses on this opportunity to "establish a pattern of intelligent, effective student opposition to the coercive tactics" in this "Red Hunt" in the Michigan schools. For the elected founding leader of the new student organization-in-the-making, Michigan presented a civil liberties challenge by denying every student's political rights as a citizen.[20]

In December 1947, the University of Wisconsin Administrative Committee ruled against an AYD request to have Gerhard Eisler, a communist activist then under indictment for contempt of Congress, speak on campus. Roy Voegeli, then student-body president, writing about the incident in 1998, recalls his shock at this breach of the campus group's right to hear a speaker of its choice. He is still especially proud of the letter of protest he sent to the university administration, which reads in part:

"If a man, by law, has the right to speak and appear before assembled groups, students should be allowed to hear him." "The student body should be fully informed as to just who this man is, and what his record is, so that any student who hears him knows exactly what manner of person he is, and can judge what he says accordingly; but under no circumstances do I think that such considerations (i.e., moral implications) are valid grounds for refusing a student group the right to hear him." "A university and its student body must be absolutely free to study any problem and be allowed to hear all sides of that problem. To do any other would be to violate the fundamental purpose of this, or any, university. . . . Whatever may be gained in the short-run by deviating from this premise can in no way compensate for the over-all loss which any institution suffers by following such a course."

Roy concludes that this was Wisconsin's only, but still regrettable, denial of the students' right to hear a speaker of their choice.[21]

One of the earliest cases, a 1948 University of Puerto Rico student protest over arbitrary administration actions that led to violence and disruption of classes, illustrates the approach taken by NSA in these cases. The National Executive Committee (NEC) found great confusion that could only be corrected by the formation of a student government and observation of student rights. But it also condemned student disruption of academic life and called for conciliatory faculty-student cooperation to solve the University's problems. Recommendations were to be sent to both the Chancellor and the students, and NSA offered help. In response to another inquiry from CCNY, NSA President Ted Harris, on behalf of officers that year, denied also that student rights included a right to strike.[22] NSA leaders clearly intended the process to be conciliatory and cooperative, not confrontational.

In one of many abrogations of student rights and academic freedom at Brooklyn College, President Harry Gideonse ruled in May 1949 that there would be no student elections that year and announced that a (faculty-appointed) faculty-student committee would rewrite the constitution of the student government.[23] Students were seething about this affront and appealed to the NSA Region, but in this as in other cases, Gideonse prevailed.

Illinois region attacked in Congress

In Illinois, the NSA Region tackled proposed legislation that threatened the rights of both students and faculty. They agreed to send a representative to lobby against the Broyles bills and urged student governments in the region also to take action against this legislation, which would make it a felony for anyone to subscribe to communism or attend meetings of communist or communist-front organizations.[24] NSA opposition to the legislation (part of which was eventually passed, but vetoed by Governor Adlai Stevenson on the grounds that it was unconstitutional) earned the Region—and the University of Chicago and Roosevelt College in particular—a vitriolic attack by Congressman Harold H. Velde (R.-Ill.), then Chair of the House Un-American Activities Committee, who charged on the floor of the House that NSA was a bunch of communists.

Alexander Pope, as Regional Chair, responded to Velde in a well-reasoned letter, moderate in tone, asked for a retraction, and got nowhere.[25] Subsequent attempts (two visits to Velde in Washington by NSA regulars) met with absolutely no success. The delegation reported back to NSA that when they disagreed with Velde and argued successfully on any point, the Congressman fell back on charges that they were either illogical or communist sympathizers. Helen Jean Rogers, a former NSA officer then at graduate school at Catholic University, was at one of those sessions. Herself a firm anticommunist, she found the experience frightening. None of the students, she said, had ever been that close to McCarthyism before, and they now realized how dangerous it was.[26]

By 1950, assaults on student freedoms by the U.S. Congress and state legislatures were so widespread that the annual NSA Congress went on record condemning "restrictions on the rights of political association [that] impair the freedom which is necessary in the educational community," and urged that NSA regions take this stand to state legislatures, the American Council on Education (ACE), and other educational associations.

Control of political speakers at colleges

One issue that showed up early in NSA experience was the university administration control of "political" speakers exercised on many campuses. Coming from Smith, an eastern liberal arts college where classroom discussions of Marxist theory were followed by late-night dormitory debates on the practical implications of Leninism under Stalin, I was shocked by such arbitrary administration prohibitions of selected speakers, and am still surprised today when I realize how widespread the practice was. Increasingly, it was speakers who were thought to be communists or sympathizers who were banned or disinvited.

The problems were mostly at big public universities, and some—but not all—Catholic colleges, where outside speakers were chosen with care, usually under the close supervision of faculty or deans. Even on those campuses that were thought of elsewhere around the country as liberal bastions of the eastern seaboard, there were always individual professors and administrators who feared infiltration of the campuses by "subversive" elements. Harvard Political Science Professor William Yandell Elliot was one who did not hide his hostility to NSA regional and international efforts, and his accusations of NSA leaders later showed up in FBI files.[27] I recall feeling insulted by the implication that we students would somehow be poisoned by exposure to views other than our own. Indeed, one of the liveliest evenings I remember on the Smith campus was an agile and intense debate between two Yale students, Bill Buckley (*God and Man at Yale* was his then current youthful accomplishment) and former NSA President Al Lowenstein.

But elsewhere around the country, controversial speakers were fewer and often screened. In 1948, students at Wayne State University sought NSA help in overcoming a ban on political activity and discussion.[28] In 1951, at the request of the Region, NSA protested a trustees' gag rule at Ohio State University that denied even a Quaker pacifist the right to speak. In a conciliatory move meant to mollify outraged students, the university promised that only speakers "disloyal to the United States" would be banned![29] Caught in this kind of regulation at UC Berkeley, students had to get the Dean's approval to invite inveterate anticommunist Socialist Party leader Norman Thomas. Pete Seeger was banned from *singing* on the Brooklyn College campus from the early 1950s until 1962, when President Gideonse left the college.

In 1952-53, the University of Washington banned "political" speakers—not just candidates for political office, but anyone the administration deemed "political." Outraged students, including NSA representatives, and pressure from the Region managed eventually to get the rule rescinded.[30] Much later, in the early 1960s, Stanford still had such a ban, presumably to protect the formative minds of their young innocents from issues not germane to higher education. In the atmosphere of growing national hysteria about communism, assertion of administrative control over political speech—even when overturned, as at the University of Washington—undoubtedly had a chilling effect on student activism and open debate and contributed to what NSA called, in the theme of its 1952 meeting, the "national educational crisis," that is, student apathy and withdrawal from participation in public issues.

Student newspapers and political speakers

Campus newspapers also came under assault. Some of the cases NSA got drawn into seem almost unbelievable today. In 1950, the Michigan State College paper was suspended because an article criticized an American Legion–sponsored "Boys' State" for its "militaristic methods," and in particular for staging a mock trial (of an alleged communist) that the paper thought made a mockery of American justice.

More serious was the Brooklyn College case that broke in spring 1950. At the college, famous by that time for violations of student rights and academic freedom, *The Vanguard* was suspended and the editor fired. The paper's staff selected as successor a junior sports editor who had no political reputation or affiliations, and the suspension was lifted after the new editor agreed to a "dual editorial" policy, wherein any issue discussed would be approached in two editorials, one pro and one con.

The new editor, Bill Taylor, now a nationally known civil rights lawyer, lasted less than four months in the job. He was charged with tampering with an editorial (he says it was edited, as was all nonstaff writers' work) and shortening it (he says it was shorter to begin with). The complaining student was considered a tool of the administration, "a Quisling," Bill says. An inactive faculty-student committee was hastily reactivated and revoked the paper's charter. (A new paper with different staff was chartered shortly thereafter.) When the editors and staff returned to their office right after the meeting, the janitor was already clearing it out—on the order of the college president. Bill and others were disciplined—and banned from nomination to *Who's Who in American Colleges and Universities*. Fifteen years later, Bill's nomination as Staff Director of the U.S. Civil Rights Commission was held up because there was derogatory information in his FBI file about his *Vanguard* days, supplied by a Brooklyn College faculty "advisor."[31] The NSA Region, brought into the case by Brooklyn students, called for reinstatement of *The Vanguard* and acquiesced to the dual editorial policy, provided it was administered by students.[32]

The university administration's firing of the editor and suspension of *The Maroon* at the University of Chicago in 1951were handled much more professionally by NSA. That summer, while editor Alan Kimmel was in Europe attending a communist-sponsored youth rally, he was fired by the Dean of Students. The Student Government took the case to the NSA, and Vice President Sylvia Bacon directed the investigation, which led to a finding by the NEC that the firing was a "violation of a basic student right" and unwarranted, despite a "serious abuse" of editorial responsibility. The NEC resolution also chided the University of Chicago student government for its failure "to provide adequate democratic safeguards" that would assure "the newspaper's ultimate responsibility to the university community."[33] The paper was reinstated, but not the editor. This procedurally impeccable, politically adroit outcome was aided by the election to student government of a coalition of mostly leftist, but anticommunist, groups and by the belief of most of those contesting the Dean's action that most Chicago University students were happy to see Kimmel go.

There were a few clear victories. In February 1949, the University of Michigan Regents rescinded a ban on political speakers on campus that they had imposed the year before. The action resulted from a ten-month battle by both students and faculty against the ban. Similarly, in early 1949, Oklahoma students claimed victory in a legislative fight against a bill that would have required both students and faculty to sign noncommunist affidavits or face harsh penalties. They succeeded in getting the state Senate to modify the measure, passing a watered-down oath of loyalty to the U.S. government.[34]

Defense of the Student Bill of Rights

In addition to the individual cases of student rights violations that NSA was trying to deal with, the NSA Student Bill of Rights was itself challenged, and defended, at every national Congress. As early as the Second Congress in 1949, the officers ("staff") recommended that it be reviewed and be paired with a Bill of Responsibilities. They further suggested that it was properly a policy, not a bylaw. That was seen by the beleaguered Congress liberals as a threat, an effort to whittle down and weaken the rights under fire, and though many realized that the wording did need to be refined to clear up ambiguities, they resisted any change—and prevailed.

Despite the atmosphere of fear that was engulfing the country, a year later the Third Congress, after impassioned and confusing debate, again voted to retain the Bill of Rights without change. But at the Fourth Congress in 1951, a revised Bill of Rights was finally passed. The language was refined and the rights spelled out with greater care, and the new formulation took into consideration the variety of higher-education institutions—without diluting the basic rights. These were, in the words of the preamble, the guarantees "to preserve and extend the conditions indispensable to the full achievement of the objectives of the educational community and with full cognizance of the responsibilities and obligations which ensue from any assertion of fundamental rights." That was my first Congress. Every revision was debated with passion, and some changes were made on the floor. I was impressed with the high level of debate on principles and specifics, and with the rhetorical and parliamentary skill of my fellow students. The final document passed by a vote of 243 to 17. We had endorsed "the free market of ideas" in the face of growing McCarthyism. (I must have participated in that and other debates because I was elected Chair of the New England Region at the close of the Congress.) In 1954, the Congress passed a comparable bill of student responsibilities.[35]

The Congress called also for an awareness campaign, including a national conference (which was never held), incorporation of the Bill of Rights into student government constitutions, and development of procedures for investigation into alleged violations. The latter task fell to the new Vice President of Student Affairs, Sylvia Bacon, who, despite being relegated back to Vassar (there were only two full-time, paid officers that year) and to her course work, set an example of how to conduct an investigation. Her lawyerly investigation of the University of Chicago *Maroon* case presaged the judicial temperament she later exhibited on the bench.

3. Academic Freedom

In retrospect, I would say there was a steady and severe erosion of academic freedom during the first five years of NSA, despite the fact that the organization maintained its support for unqualified academic freedom through multiple challenges. Most NSA actions on academic freedom were taken at the regional level, and some regions were clearly more active than others. In the early years, loyalty oaths were the problem. California's was perhaps the first, and certainly the most famous. At UC Berkeley (UCB), six faculty members refused to sign, and they had the vocal support of students in 1946. By 1950, students figured that forty-eight courses had been canceled due to the departure of faculty who refused to sign and were fired, or left. In 1951, at the request of the Berkeley student government, NSA's Executive Committee commended UCB President Sproul and the minority (ten out of twenty-two) of trustees who fought the oath. For some NSA critics, that position was just another truncheon with which to beat on the Association.

By 1951, loyalty oaths had become what the *NSA News* called a "fad."[36] Maryland, Oklahoma, Colorado, New Hampshire, Washington, New York, and New Jersey all had imposed such requirements. Students fought similar legislation in Massachusetts, Illinois, Wisconsin, Minnesota, and Pennsylvania. Though some statutes, such as New York's Feinberg Law, were eventually struck down by the Supreme Court, others passed court tests or, when they failed to, were replaced with language more precise, and constitutional, as in California's case. Educators and students argued back, and sometimes prevailed. In Texas, for instance, the University President and trustees, cheered on by students, politely refused, in the name of academic freedom, demands to fire a particularly popular professor.

Academic Freedom cases at NSA

NSA was asked to investigate specific violations. In 1948, the National Executive Committee (NEC), which was composed of the officers and the regional chairs and enabled by the NSA constitution to act on behalf of the organization between congresses, ruled on a case brought to NSA by student petition from Olivet College, a venerable small institution where a professor of twelve years had been dismissed for reasons unknown. The NEC finding that there had been a "breach of normal academic practice" was couched in moderate terms that argued the need for good student-faculty-administration cooperation and the assumptions of academic freedom. It asked the college administration to provide the professor with reasons for dismissal and opportunity for a full hearing. But it also chided the students for boycotting class. In those days, NSA did not support direct action of any kind by students.[37]

Two 1949 cases on the West Coast also involved the arbitrary dismissal of established professors. The NSA decided in a University of Washington case to use the findings being collected by the American Association of University Professors, but to investigate another case, at Oregon State College. The NEC also asked the Sub-commission on Academic Freedom "to objectively review every supposed violation on U.S. campuses, whether appealed to NSA or not" and to survey deans of students on the state of academic freedom and student rights on the nation's campuses.[38] When the Congress met in 1951, at least three such surveys had been made. The *Harvard Crimson* found thirty-five cases of alleged abridgment of academic freedom and student rights in thirty-seven institutions surveyed in seventeen states. Eleven of these were interference with the educational freedom of student papers. The *New York Times* survey (May 10, 1951), interviewing students, faculty, and administrators on 72 campuses, found "a subtle, creeping paralysis of thought and speech, and not many overt instances of violations" but "considerable evidence of self-censorship." The *Times* found the "pressure generated by Senator Joseph McCarthy" an "important contributing factor." Fear pervaded many campuses.

NSA leaders noted that, despite the many violations on campuses, NSA had not once that year been asked to investigate, and suggested procedural changes that would allow NSA itself to initiate such investigations when students were afraid to bring a complaint.[39] And indeed only students at resolutely independent institutions came forward that year. The University of Minnesota student government requested an investigation of the dismissal of a professor. In a slightly different case, at the behest of Harvard students, the NEC asked the Defense Department (which controlled civilian access to occupied Japan) to make public the reasons why Professor John Fairbanks, recipient of Social Science Research Council and Guggenheim grants and on leave from Harvard, was prevented from going to Japan for research—or to grant him a visa.[40]

At the time, there was a steady barrage of attacks on NSA for its stand on these issues and its international activism. A 1951 national sorority magazine charged NSA with "A Communist Conspiracy." The Young Republicans compiled "evidence" of the same in a detailed report. Local American Legion posts hammered away for years at colleges like Sarah Lawrence. And of course, the U.S. Congress was busy holding hearings "investigating" faculty members and student organizations. A 1953 endorsement by three national associations of deans and other higher education professionals comforted the staff and strengthened NSA's sense of legitimacy, but probably did not have any effect on the attackers, who charged that the whole academic establishment was infiltrated by "Reds."[41]

Resource limits impede action

Each year at the NSA Congress, the principles and policies on academic freedom came under attack also from some student delegates. Their primary objection was that the existing (AAUP/NSA) policy provided safe harbor for communist professors whom they charged were, ipso facto, unfit to teach.

Every year the majority of delegates argued back that faculty must be judged only by their competence in the classroom and their research in their field, not by past or current political affiliations. As in the ongoing argument on student rights, the overwhelming majority annually re-affirmed national student support of academic freedom. In doing so, NSA compiled a record as a staunch defender of liberty, one of a core of beleaguered organizations that clung to traditional American values during one of the most alarming periods in U.S. twentieth-century history.

I think one has to conclude in retrospect that NSA never had the resources, human or financial, to conduct a really thorough investigation—though perhaps Sylvia Bacon's term was the exception. In 1948 and 1950 the NEC spelled out some rules to go by, and in 1952 the Congress promulgated a quite good set of procedures. It improved on earlier versions by making it possible for NSA to initiate investigations under certain circumstances if students at the offending university were afraid to do so, and it opened the process also to administrators and faculty. The rules required, as had earlier ones, that NSA make no pronouncements on a case until the investigation was complete and action was taken. Either the Vice President for Student Affairs or the Vice President for Educational Affairs was to chair the inquiry, and the regions had a role, but only the Congress or NEC could actually decide that a violation had occurred and suggest remedies. Again, recognizing NSA's limitations, the 1952 resolution advised, as did earlier ones (1948), cooperation with the AAUP or American Civil Liberties Union (ACLU) on investigation whenever possible.

These were good guidelines, but the resources mostly just were not in place. Timeliness was often lost in the face of many other demands on officers. At least one case, that of NYU Professor Bradley, who was fired in 1948 after being found guilty of contempt of the House Un-American Activities Committee, got lost for a year when the Vice President, looking into the validity of the case, had difficulty getting information and referred it to the regional office, where it apparently got buried.

Most of the Vice Presidents, myself included, did not have the skills to conduct a proper inquiry. Nor did we have the time (as full-time students and national officers) or the money to travel to the site to do so. Inevitably, we fell back on the regions and the very students who had brought the charge to NSA in the first place. Under such circumstances, being able to consult with the AAUP and ACLU and share information and conclusions reached by these organizations was a great relief. In fact, in my term I found relations with these organizations very supportive. Visits to their offices in Washington and New York, respectively, and participation in their board and committee meetings, where the NSA representative was welcomed as a full and equal participant, were very reassuring—reminding us that NSA was not alone and had committed allies. These organizations, with their resources, made me feel it was possible to do this impossible job. Besides, NSA was saved by the fact that most of the student-rights and academic-freedom violations that came to our attention were so transparent and so gross as to require relatively little dependence on the fine art of investigation.

NSA's impact on academic freedom

How much difference did NSA make on the issues of academic freedom and student rights? NSA's investigations, reports and recommendations, and just the attention drawn to situations and recommendations, surely helped in some individual cases. However, the burden of the task was borne, not so much by the national organization, NEC, and officers, but by the regions and by the students on the campuses where the violations took place. In the last analysis, those closest to the scene did most of the work, and when those students were intimidated and fearful of taking action—as they increasingly were over the five years in question—the abrogations went unchallenged. At institutions where the administration was a determined agent of anticommunism, with powerful political backers, as at Brooklyn College where the president was appointed with Mayor LaGuardia's directions to clean up "the Little Red Schoolhouse," NSA and afflicted students could do little more than publicize the breach of rights and freedoms.

There were numerous institutions where the president and trustees stood firmly behind student rights and academic freedom. My impression is that they were mostly at private colleges and universities that did not have to face state legislators and politically appointed trustees and regents. They did not flinch, at least in public, before attacks by the local Legion vigilantes or vociferous wealthy alumnae, although I know some colleges lost alumnae contributions in the process.

But the national climate was hostile to rights and freedoms, and for advocates like NSA, there wasn't a whole lot of support out there, except in a few organizations. Correspondence between Gordon Klopf (student activities counselor at Wisconsin, chair of NSA's Advisory Board and a strong supporter of NSA) and his colleagues during the formative NSA years shows how numerous the doubts were—even among faculty and administrators who supported the NSA—especially with regard to the Student Bill of Rights. Some complained only that it was poorly drafted. Others charged that small groups of NSAers on campus were using the Bill of Rights to pursue their own interests or to "dominate" the student government. One charged that NEC could not possibly be "representative" if it endorsed the California students' opposition to loyalty oaths; others attacked the organization as dangerous.

In the broadest sense, NSA made a big contribution to protecting student rights and academic freedom. The organization did not buckle under to the harsh criticism from powerful adversaries. The NSA Congresses never gave in on the basic principles, and a lot of students were educated in the process. The students pursued their ideals with steady, rational argument. They debated and reaffirmed the principles each year. In doing so, they presented an admirable model. It is too bad the "adult" institutions in society did not have such public debate.

NSA politics and the issues

Sometimes tasks set at the national level for the member schools and officers were quite unrealistic, in view of the lack of resources with which to do them. Budget allocations for 1952-53, for instance, were $18,000 for domestic programs and running the national office, $25,000 for the international program and office, and—providing the grants we hoped for came through—$17,000 for "educational projects," which were all international. The annual Congress ($7,000) and the Travel Program ($180,000) were both expected to be self-supporting.[42] Although student interest in the international issues was clearly waning by comparison with the first three years, as measured by the amount of time devoted to the issues at annual Congresses and NEC meetings, the international program had 70 percent of the budget. I remember being jealous of International Vice President Avrea Ingram's financial support that just seemed to flow effortlessly to his program and was puzzled by its source—but I approved of the international program and I admired Avrea.[43]

A scholarship student who worked 25 to 30 hours a week at a variety of campus jobs, I had no money in the bank. My older sister, who had just graduated from college and was working at her first job, loaned me the money for postage, long-distance calls, and transportation to meetings and conferences. After two years working with NSA, I owed her $900, which at the time was the equivalent of one-and-a-half years' tuition.

Staff organization and politics

The officers' jobs were made even more difficult by the fact that half of them, starting in the 1951-52 term, would serve from their campuses, while going to school full time. In 1951, because of the financial crisis in the Lowenstein presidency (in large part due to chaos in the travel program the previous year),[44] only the President and the International Affairs Vice President would serve full time, along with a newly appointed Executive Secretary in the national office. The Vice Presidents for Student Affairs and Education and the newly created Vice President for Student Government (split off from Student Affairs, against the better judgment of some, including the new Vice President for Student Affairs, Sylvia Bacon) were to return to their campuses and their studies. Without budgets and support from the national office, now moved even further away from Madison, to Denver, the vice presidents operated under a severe handicap. It is something of a miracle that they did get to NEC meetings and regional meetings and represented NSA as well as they did before the American Council on Education (ACE), AAUP, NSSFNS and other national organizations.

Because officers from 1951 on were separated from their colleagues and did not live and work around the clock together, we did not experience the bonding with fellow staff and volunteers nor develop the life-long friendships that Mildred Kiefer Wurf and others have written of elsewhere in this volume. My own relationships within the organization were intense ones, chosen largely on the basis of political alignments around issues. I remember vividly the people I quickly came to admire at NSA Congresses and at NEC and regional meetings. Although I saw them only for brief periods at great intervals, trusting their values, I would have trusted them with my life. There were the Metropolitan New York and Pennsylvania progressives who stuck by liberal principles through thick and thin, including some Catholic radicals the like of whom I had never met before and who did not fit my stereotype of Catholics who took orders from the Pope. There were the internationalists from Harvard and MIT who supported Avrea Ingram so steadily and who, with others from the New England region, organized an extraordinary regional conference on poverty and economic development in 1953. And the whole University of Chicago crowd with their consummate political and parliamentary skills.

I am still in touch with a few of these people, but there are today no close relationships. When I left abruptly for Asia at the end of my term, I effectively lost touch with NSA. And being a woman was part of it. There was sexism, though I did not recognize it as such at the time.

There was another subtle political change taking place at the same time that made the vice presidents' jobs harder—and for some of us, more frustrating. Through Ted Harris's presidency the officers were called—and indeed thought of themselves as—"staff" who served the member schools. They made all important decisions together. That continued to be the case in 1949-1950 for the rest of the officers, though President Kelly's aloof manner set him apart from his colleagues. In 1950-51, Lowenstein openly asserted the primacy of his office. He made it an issue and sought from the Michigan Congress a resolution that designated the president as the first among equals and chief spokesman for the organization—while holding him responsible to the NEC and Congress and giving the staff, by majority, supervision of individual officers. That year, Lowenstein made the major decisions, especially in the international arena, without consulting his colleagues. Indeed, the stand he took at the Stockholm Conference defied the policy approved by the 1950 NSA Congress and a strategy worked out by all the democratic student unions meeting there, for which the Conference voted to censure him. Alas, for those of us trying to write the history of the organization, Al also made the decision not to publish the *NSA News* in 1950-51.[45]

Lowenstein's style and policies sparked resentment at the 1951 Congress, sharper partisan differences, and close political votes. But Al was a superb, persuasive orator who cast an admiring spell over delegates, even among those of us who disagreed with him on issues. This subtle shift of power was a decision the importance of which I did not fully understand at the time, having little notion then of the importance of structure to power in organizational politics. In a reflection of a widening split among NSA delegates, the elections that year were hotly contested. Al's candidate, Bill Dentzer, defeated the more liberal Ken Kurtz, Pennsylvania Region Chair, but Avrea Ingram won the international slot over Lowenstein's nominee, Helen Jean Rogers, who was immensely popular with delegates but whose status as a non-delegate made her eligibility questionable—as Lowenstein must have known.

Lowenstein's own fervent anticommunist orientation and the growing national phenomenon of McCarthyism were having an effect on NSA. Although there had always been some political divisions in the organization—clearly manifest in the annual debates on academic freedom and student rights as well as international policy—the split now widened further. The center of the organization was pulling slowly to the right, and those of us on the left were hanging on tenaciously.

The split was fully apparent to me at NEC meetings and at the 1951 and 1952 Congresses. Indeed, I have always thought of NSA as a very *political* organization. But in 1952, the division was not allowed to affect the elections. We reverted to the earlier model of a politically and geographically balanced slate. (There had been no African American among the officers since the 1950-51 staff.) Maneuvering ahead of time in consultation with liberal and conservative caucuses resulted in an uncontested slate. I was first approached by Al Lowenstein—and flattered, I must admit, although I did not approve of much that he represented and was suspicious of his hanging around NSA a year after he had left office[46]—then by President Bill Dentzer, who said Richard Murphy had agreed to run for President. I consulted my own allies, and it seemed like a good deal. The next day the slated nominees sailed through unopposed until the very last office, when the delegates, in revolt at the now obvious fait accompli, challenged Manfred Brust's nomination for V.P. of Educational Affairs, although he had less to say than any of us about the slate. I was embarrassed, even ashamed, to have been part of what looked to many like manipulation from behind the scenes.[47]

But looking back at the result, I understand now that the conservative forces (centrist, really—we were all liberals) had outsmarted us—whether they had meant to or not. The Congress had created a new Vice President for National Affairs and elected Leonard Wilcox, Michigan University student body president and a friend of Dick Murphy's, who would run the new leadership-training program, in effect reducing the role of the Vice President for Student Government and of the other Vice Presidents, who were now on the third rung down on the ladder of officer hierarchy. Murphy, Wilcox, and Avrea Ingram, the legatees of the Lowenstein-Dentzer regimes, would work full time, with real, though modest, budgets and offices. The so-called liberal caucus nominees, Steve Voykovich (Student Government), Manny Brust (Educational Affairs), and I (Student Affairs) returned to campus with no money and no released time.

"Communists" or "true patriots"?

Being financially strapped did not bother me as much as the assaults on academic freedom and student rights and the attacks from right-wing politicians, the FBI, and the press on the "communist" NSA. The earliest charge against NSA that I have come across is one made in Minnesota in early 1948 by a Senator Ball, who said NSA was a communist youth group "or one which will eventually fall into communist dominated leadership."[48] At the same time, ironically, the International Union of Students was attacking NSA as "war-mongering, imperialist agents of undemocratic government." I felt personally responsible for fighting off such attacks, and completely unequipped to do so. In my mind, in defending NSA and the principles of academic freedom, student rights, and racial equality, NSA leaders were just defending the essentials of democracy. We thought ourselves worldly in our understanding of the threats to democracy of the international communist movement, and patriotic in our defense of freedom of speech and association. Having some understanding of the Communist Front strategy of the 1930s, I never believed that American institutions—student or otherwise—could be infiltrated or taken over by communists, so long as vigorous open debate about public issues continued. I was disbelieving, and not a little frightened, that Congressmen and FBI officials would question the loyalty of Americans who claimed constitutional rights for ourselves and others. In my mind, we were the true patriots, and our accusers, the threat to democracy.

But I did feel outnumbered and inadequate to the task of defending academic freedom and student rights—harassed, even, by the House Un-American Activities Committee and the FBI. The national atmosphere was increasingly hostile. The FBI onslaught was largely responsible for my not recognizing at the time the soon obvious source of money flowing to NSA international programs. I did not know much about government intelligence agencies until the following year—they were not included in my International Relations curriculum. It was inconceivable to me that one federal agency might be funding NSA while another was harassing it.[49] A year later, when traveling in India and Pakistan with the Canadian World University Service and living in Burma under the Fulbright program, I became acquainted with the kind of programs the CIA funded and the agents through whom they worked (including student/youth organizations such as the World Assembly of Youth). When I learned how the CIA worked through its own "front" organizations, it dawned on me that the money for the NSA international program must also have come from the CIA.

I have never forgiven the NSA colleagues who got us into, and kept secret from our constituency, the NSA/CIA collusion. Nor have I forgiven myself for not acting on my suspicions of John Simons,[50] the Youth and Student Foundation officer, benefactor of the international program, who was allowed to sit in on our NEC meetings as early as December 1951 and take notes on our most sensitive of discussions. When we took a break, I recall raising the inappropriateness of his participation with the NEC chair, who must have been Dentzer at the time, but when he responded that he could not ask Simons to leave because of the foundation's support of NSA, I did not press the issue. I cannot think of anything worse that could have happened to NSA than this clandestine affair with the CIA. American students had founded a real democratic national student organization, consciously and deliberately independent of the U.S. government, in contrast to the Soviet model. And then we allowed the government to buy us off. This well-kept secret was inimical to NSA's standing as an independent student organization and made a mockery of students' high ideals and hard work.[51]

Conclusions

As my year in office fled by, I felt more and more beleaguered. All of us were affected by the attacks. And in defense of NSA and our own loyalty, our own language and positions were subtly changed. We noncommunists came to protest more and more often that we were anticommunists, too. The anticommunist dogma of the day crept into our own speech, and into all of NSA. But we never gave up the principles of academic freedom and student rights, and we continued to fight back, even though I knew in my heart that the job I was doing was inadequate to the task and that we continued to lose ground. We took seriously our responsibility to students, to academia, and to the nation. And I am sure that my report and recommendations to the Sixth Congress, long since lost somewhere in the national office, were full of energy and hope for improvement if we would just hang in there and do the right thing!

Even while overwhelmed by NSA responsibilities, I appreciated the experience. I was learning every day from this whole new world of students of every persuasion, from institutions of every kind. For me, this was the beginning of a life-long interest in higher education. NSA also fine-tuned my political antennae and sharpened my political acumen. I never mastered the parliamentary skills that some colleagues wielded, but I learned how to build coalitions and alliances, to recognize leadership, the importance of organizational structure and strength of constitutional principles; and how to compromise—and then build on the compromise. And as one who had never before been west of the Hudson River, I learned to travel—the beginning of a life-long addiction.

But it was the training on the substantive issues from which I benefited most. NSA reinforced my beliefs in freedom, democracy, and equality and strengthened my confidence in young people in general and students in particular. That was education that served me well when teaching in the 1960s at Howard University and the University of the District of Columbia. There I took another turn at defending student rights and academic freedom—which led me quite naturally into the civil rights movement, and then to the peace movement and the women's movement. NSA provided me, as it did others, with fundamental education on the issues of our generation—except for women's issues, which did not surface at all in my time at NSA. Nor did I miss them, because I was not yet a feminist. But as I reviewed all the documents and clips in preparation for writing this piece, I realize how male-dominated the NSA culture was, despite the many able women who participated in it. But that's another story. . . .

Janet Welsh Brown was a senior associate (later fellow) at the World Resources Institute from 1985 to 2000. She was executive director of the Environmental Defense Fund from 1979 to 1984. Earlier, she taught political science at Sarah Lawrence College, Howard University, and the University of the District of Columbia.

END NOTES

[1] Quoted in Gordon Klopf, "The College Administrator Looks at the National Student Association," *School and Society*, 70, no. 1810 (August 27, 1949).

[2] See NSA Statement on Academic Freedom and Student Bill of Rights, pp. 388, 1110.

[3] See Jim Smith, p. 127, and Bill Welsh, p. 185.

[4] See Mildred Wurf, p. 179.

[5] See p. 565 for a discussion of CIA covert funding of NSA international programs.

[6] *NSA News*, May 1952.

[7] There were 48 colleges from the 14 Southern states of the 351 represented at the Constitutional convention in 1947. Only 18 of the 295 total were in attendance at the first Congress in 1948. By 1950 this number had grown to 28 out of 232 colleges. In 1957 there were 71 Southern colleges out of close to 400 in NSA. The attendance of historically Black colleges is estimated at 7 in 1947, and 12 in 1957. See also p. 440; p. 451; Pt. 2, Sec. 3; and Pt. 5, Sec. 6.

[8] See Clif Wharton's discussion of this event on p. 146. See also n. 22, p. 415

[9] NSA National Executive Committee (NEC) Minutes, December 1949.

[10] See p. 458 for the story of NSSFNS.

[11] Although most NSA initiatives about race in its early years appear to have been efforts on individual campuses or regional educational efforts, the organization did occasionally support national efforts, such as the unsuccessful 1949 congressional attempt to end racial discrimination in Washington, D.C. (*NSA News*, April 1949). See also Curry, p. 444.

[12] See Peoples, p. 425; Francis, p. 433, p. 438; Proctor, p. 969; Murphy, p. 975.

[13] *NSA News* (April 1946), and Jim Smith, in a letter, "Hello Darling," March 14, 1947 (see p. 121), attributed similar attitudes to southern white students. See also "NSO Regions in South Aid Race Relations," *Columbia Daily Spectator*, April 24, 1947.

[14] See Gordon Klopf, p. 333.

[15] The Supreme Court had earlier ruled that the Universities of Texas and Oklahoma must admit Negro students to their law schools or provide separate but truly equal programs for them, and it was apparent in which direction the Court was headed.

[16] *NSA News*, November 1952.

[17] See "NSA and Fraternity-Sorority Discrimination", p. 398; Lee, "Fraternities without Brotherhood," excerpts, p. 745.

[18] *NSA News*, May 1949. [19] See AYD, p. 794.

[20] Jim Smith, Memo to All Michigan Delegates and Observers to the Chicago Student Conference, February 7, 1947.

[21] Royal Voegeli, Letter to Gene Schwartz, August 28, 1998.

[22] NEC Minutes, December 1948.

[23] Hal Orbach (CCNY), Letter to AL Lowenstein, May 20, 1949.

[24] *NSA News,* March 1949.

[25] See Alexander Pope, p. 390.

[26] Helen Jean Rogers, Memorandum to USNSA Staff, May 22, 1951. See also note 4, p. 435.

[27] See p. 569.

[28] NEC Minutes, December 1948.

[29] *NSA News*, November 1951.

[30] See William Gates, Sr., and Helen Pulsifer, p. 1053, also Album, p. 1061.

[31] Interview, Bill Taylor, Washington, D.C., July 1998.

[32] *NSA News*, August 1951.

[33] *NSA News*, March 1952. It was practice at some institutions large and small, in those these years, for the editor of the student newspaper to be elected by the student government (occasionally the student body), or appointed by a joint faculty-student committee. See the report on NSA's first annual college newspaper editor's conference at Indiana University in 1952 organized by Sylvia Bacon, p. 471.

[34] *NSA News*, March 1949.

[35] See Stephen Clements Schodde, *Certain Foci of the United States National Student Association and Their Implications for Student Personnel Administrators,* unpublished 1965 doctoral thesis at Columbia University Teachers College.

[36] *NSA News*, August 1951.

[37] Richard Heggie, Memorandum to Student Government Presidents et al., and NEC minutes, December 1948.

[38] NSA, *Report to the Second National Student Congress*, 1949.

[39] *NSA News*, August 1951. [40] *NSA News*, March 1952.

[41] See Klopf, p. 337.

[42] Edward R. Garvey, *History and Development of USNSA* (Philadelphia, USNSA), 1963.

[43] See Avrea Ingram, p. 575.

[44] See NSA Travel Program, p. 673.

[45] William Chafe, *Never Stop Running; Allard Lowenstein and the Struggle to Save American Liberalism* (Princeton, N.J.: Princeton University Press, 1998), p. 104.

[46] We had a song we sang late in the evening to the tune of Joe Hill: "I dreamt I saw Lowenstein last night, alive as you and me, But Al, I said, you're one year gone, I never died, said he . . . ."

[47] See Donnelly, p. 951, who writes about a similar experience.

[48] *NSA News*, March 1948.

[49] One of the NSA colleagues I interviewed while working on this piece, a man who subsequently worked for the CIA, mused about the difference between the FBI and the CIA in the 1950s. His explanation of the federal schizophrenia with respect to NSA was that the FBI was anticommunist, conservative, and antidemocratic, whereas the CIA was anticommunist, liberal, and prodemocracy. See also p. 567, note 5.

[50] See p. 124. [51] See p. 566.

PICTURE CREDITS: *Then:* Dec., 1952, Wayne State U., Detroit, NEC meeting (NSA photo). N*ow:* Sept., 1998, Washington, DC (*Schwartz*).

JANET WELSH BROWN

I grew up in the Boston area, one of three children. Our parents, though only high school graduates, had high aspirations for their kids. A year and a half in South and Southeast Asia after college (Smith '53) and travel in Africa changed my life. I returned to graduate school at Yale (MA '55) and then at NYU, while teaching for two years at Sarah Lawrence College. I married and came to Washington in 1958, where I enrolled at the American University. Six years, three kids, and a Ph.D. later, I went back to work, teaching political science and international relations at Howard University and then at the University of the District of Columbia.

In 1973 I left academia for the American Association for the Advancement of Science, where I developed a program to promote the status of women, minorities, and disabled persons in science. Finding the not-for-profit world an effective platform from which to work on national policy, I moved in 1979 to be Executive Director of the Environmental Defense Fund, and five years later to the World Resources Institute (WRI), a policy research institute, where I worked primarily on development issues and international environmental politics. Though mostly retired these days, I remain a visiting fellow at WRI. I am still married to the same man, who from the beginning encouraged me to have a career and shared family responsibilities.

WEDNESDAY, MAY 25, 1949. THE HARVARD CRIMSON PAGE THREE

Academic Freedom---Crimson Report

U of Washington Leads List Of Faculty Dismissal Cases

By JOHN G. SIMON, BURTON S. GLINN, and DAVID E. LILIENTHAL, JR.

Six weeks ago, the authors of this article set out to conduct a survey of the problems of academic freedom. Some 42 days wiser, we now realize that what follows is not a survey but only a healthy glance. For every case reported here, we have heard of another, but have had insufficient material for publication. For every one of those in turn, there were probably many others of which we never heard. Even had every infraction been uncovered, every firing been exposed, the picture would still be incomplete. There is no way to tabulate the men who were never hired or the promotions that were never made.

But even in this "glance," we have found that since the end of World War II, 39 professors have been dismissed or placed on probation, or have resigned; and that there has been legislation in 30 states affecting countless thousands of students and faculty members. We have discovered a total of 40 instances involving professors, students, visiting speakers, and legislative actions, spread over 19 states and the District of Columbia.

In gathering this material, we have done our best to contact all the principals concerned. When this was not possible, we have printed public statements made on both sides of the issue and have refrained from any interpretation.

The articles are arranged so that today's installment will cover the cases of professors and instructors who have been fired or suspended, or whose positions have been endangered by their political beliefs. In the next two days, we will take up legislative activities in various states and also abrogations, both confirmed and alleged, of student rights.

NSA ALIGNS WITH AAUP ON ACADEMIC FREEDOM

The USNSA is in accord with the principles of academic freedom as expressed by the American Association of University Professors, in Vol. 32 #4 *AAUP Bul.* Concerning academic freedom we believe that:

1. The teacher is entitled to freedom of research, and in the publication of the results is subject only to the limitations imposed by the performance of his other academic duties; but research for pecuniary return should be based upon an understanding with the institution.
2. The teacher is entitled to freedom in the classroom in discussing his subject, but he should not introduce into his teaching controversial matter which has no relation to his subject.
3. The teacher has the right to join organizations whether religious, political, or social, provided that these organizations are not illegal under the civil statutes, without being discriminated against through economic, social, or political pressures because of such activity.
4. When the teacher speaks or writes as a citizen outside the campus he should be free from institutional censorship or discipline.
5. The basis for employment of faculty shall be only their ability to fulfill the requirements of the position.

From By-Law 3, NSA Constitution, 1947

The University of Washington has over 18,000 students enrolled and attending classes on its Seattle campus. It turns out excellent crews and better than average football teams. Howie Odell, formerly of Yale, coaches the latter. The "U," as it is called by Washingtonians, is pretty typical of large state universities throughout the country. It is, also typically, extremely sensitive to the state legislature and that body's tugs on the purse strings.

In 1948, the legislature's un-American Affairs Committee, under the chairmanship of Albert F. Canwell, turned its full attention to "subversive" activities on the U of W campus. Canwell, a photographer before his election, said, "the last hope of freedom rests with us." One month later, Canwell outlined his method of nourishing that last hope. "Counsel (for the defendants) . . . may not make objections, cross examine or make speeches."

Canwell imported the same group of witnesses that had been used at almost all other investigations of un-American activities. These witnesses included J. B. Matthews, former investigator for the Dies Committee, a Hearst journalist and the list of "reformed Communists" such as Benjamin Gitlow and George Hewitt. During the course of the committee hearings not only were members of the Washington faculty accused but such other figures as J. Robert Oppenheimer of the Princeton Institute of advanced study, Arthur M. Schlesinger Jr. '38, of Harvard, and General Dwight D. Eisenhower, were mentioned as men who "fronted" for Communists.

Canwell himself defined Communists in a public statement: "If a person says that in this country Negroes are discriminated against and that there is inequality of wealth there is every reason to believe that person is a Communist."

Reaction Develops

At the time that Canwell was conducting the investigation at the University, public reaction against his methods began to form. Educators and even other legislators complained of the inability of the accused to defend themselves. J. Alfred Schweppe, former dean of the University law school and a past president of the Washington bar, complained that the Canwell Committee itself was "un-American." One of the professors accused of being a Communist, Herbert Phillips, was prevented from replying to the "are you now or have you ever been a member of the Communist Party?" question with anything but a yes or no answer when his replies were cut off by the repeated banging of the Canwell gavel. Canwell himself admitted that the gavel was used to "terminate those typical speeches."

In the last elections Canwell and three of the members of his committee were defeated. But on their way out they made several recommendations. They asked that the committee be continued with enlarged powers; that it screen the textbooks used in the schools in the State of Washington; and that a person affiliated with three or more "Communist front organizations" be labelled a Communist without recourse to slander or libel action. "Affiliation with recognized Communist front organizations should place the burden of proof as to loyalty on the individual so affiliated," the committee stated.

While the committee was investigating the University, the administration took a friendly attitude toward Canwell's efforts. Professors were requested to cooperate in every way possible with the committee, and the administration went so far as to ask that no faculty member criticize the committee. When well was running for reelection he used testimonials from the president of the Board of Regents and also from President Raymond B. Allen of the University as campaign material. In February of 1949, Allen endorsed the work of the committee and thanked Canwell for his "unfailing courtesy and integrity with all your dealings with the University."

On September 8, 1948, as a result of the findings and publicity of the Canwell committee, the University Faculty Committee on Tenure and Academic Freedom served complaints made by the administration against six faculty members. These men were Ralph H. Gundlach, associate professor of Psychology, Herbert T. Phillips, assistant professor of Philosophy, Joseph Butterworth, associate professor of English, Harold Eby and Garland Ethel of the department of English, and Melville Jacobs of the department of Anthropology.

The faculty committee conducted its hearings for almost two months and at the conclusion in December of 1948 it recommended that of the six men only Gundlach be dismissed. The report was given to President Allen on January 7 and to the Regents the next day. On January 17, Allen submitted an analysis of the Committee's report and recommended that three men be fired. The Board of Regents finally changed all but one of the committee's findings. This was almost without precedent, the faculty committee's recommendation being considered final.

On January 22, the Regents met for three hours. When they walked out of the meeting, Gundlach, Phillips and Butterworth were un-

FACULTY FIRINGS AT THE UNIVERSITY OF WASHINGTON received widespread national attention at the time. See Gates and Pulsifer, Pt. 5, S. 9.

WEDNESDAY, MAY 25, 1949. THE HARVARD CRIMS

Olivet Spawns Rebel School

Six Fired, Twelve Instructors Quit

Olivet College, Olivet, Michigan, was founded 109 years ago by Father Shipherd, a revivalist minister who had helped found Oberlin College, and who told his followers, "Be not conformed to this world" and "Dare to do what we acknowledge to be right."

Professor Akeley's contention. At that time, nothing was proven which was detrimental to Professor Akeley's reputation."

Throughout the month of November, the faculty continued to press for hearings on the Akeley case and for a comprehensive tenure system. But a statement of Ashby's to the Detroit alumni on December 9 diverted attention to another issue.

Referring to the Student Action Committee pickets, Ashby remarked, "Ninety percent of the student picket line were of a certain race and from a certain section of the country." Six days later Ashby told a student protest meeting that he had not meant to deprecate any one race, and that he still believed in Olivet's traditional non-discriminatory policy.

"Olivet Policy"

Communist Grad Student Freistadt Fired from UNC Teaching Position

Two weeks ago, Hans Freistadt was just another one of hundreds of graduate students doing research in nuclear physics. Upon the recommendation of the National Research Council, he had received a $1,600 government fellowship.

Then on May 12, Congressman W. Sterling Cole of New York charged that Freistadt was a Communist. Called before a congressional committee, Freistadt admitted the charge. The Atomic Energy Commission explained that there was no "loyalty check" of fellowship applicants unless restricted data were involved.

THE HARVARD CRIMSON

Academic Freedom—A Crimson Report

Syracuse Fires Student Jailed For 'Disorderly' Rally Speech

The history of the Young Progressives of America chapter at Syracuse University, New York, has been stormy. The Syracuse Daily Orange, the undergraduate paper, has called Y.P.A. "a political thorn in the administration's side." Y.P.A. has also had conflicts with officials of the university town.

On March 8, 1949, the Young Progressives staged a demonstration in protest of the city's decision to revoke a permission for a speech by O. John Rogge, former U. S. Assistant Attorney-General, in a high-school auditorium.

During the protest rally, which took place on a street corner, a student named Irving Feiner addressed the crowd for around ten minutes. He was then arrested on the charge of "disorderly conduct."

Feiner's trial began on May 6. The policemen who arrested him testified that Feiner had called the Syracuse mayor a "champagne-sipping bum."

C.C.N.Y. Drops 2 Y.P.A. Units for Rules Infractions

Young Progressives of America chapters at both the uptown and downtown branches of City College of New York

PAGE FOUR THE HARVARD CRIMSON FRIDAY, MAY 27, 1949.

Academic Freedom—A Crimson Report

Michigan State College Expels Member of AYD

Zarichny First Put on Disciplinary Probation for Two Year Period

In December, 1948, James Zarichny was expelled from Michigan State College. Officially, the reason for the expulsion was "violation of the terms of disciplinary probation."

Zarichny had passed out American Youth for Democracy leaflets at an official campus rally on January 28, 1947, to support the Fair Employment Practices Commission Bill. The rally was backed by 12 college organizations. However, the A.Y.D. was not one of them, as it had not been accorded official recognition. It was operating as an off-campus group.

All known members of the A.Y.D. were placed on probation for distributing the leaflets. College president John A. Hannah informed Zarichny in a letter dated February 6, 1947: "The terms of this probation means that you will not participate in any extracurricular activities . . . If you participate in any activities of the A.Y.D. organization, so long as it remains an unrecognized student organization, you will have automatically suspended yourself and will no longer be a student of this college.

"I am sure that you understand that this action is based solely on your continued participation in the A.Y.D. after it had been refused recognition by the student council. Any political beliefs you may hold play no part in this action."

JAMES ZARICHNY, student at Michigan State College, who was expelled in December, 1948, after being on probation for two years. A few months before, Zarichny was convicted of contempt of the legislature.

Other College

Dean S. E. Crowe spoke to Zarichny in the spring of 1947 about the "advisability of your making arrangements to continue your college work at some other institution." He wrote to him in July: "I think that this advice should be carried out." Zarichny, however, did return to Michigan State that fall.

Ohio State U Disowns Wallaceites

Another left-wing student organization lost official college standing a little more than a week ago when Ohio State University withdrew recognition from the campus Students for Wallace. The controversy arose over the appearance of an unapproved speaker at a meeting of the Wallaceites.

O.S.U. has a ban against political speakers appearing on the campus. As a result all speakers must be approved by the University before they address a college group.

Business Meeting

For some time the O.S.U. Students for Wallace had been attempting to have the speaker ban lifted. On May 10 they scheduled a regular business meeting to be held on the campus. They were given permission by the administration to hold the meeting. There was no mention made by the Wallace group of the possibility of a speaker attending.

At the meeting, unknown to University officials, Herbert Phillips, the fired faculty member of the University of Washington and an avowed Communist, spoke to the group.

Professor Robert C. Elliott of the O.S.U. English Department, faculty advisor to the Wallaceites, had urged the members not to have Phillips speak. When Phillips appeared at the meeting Elliott resigned from his advisory position with the Wallace organization.

On May 18, the University's Council on Student Affairs announced that recognition had been withdrawn from the Students for Wallace organization. Mrs. Christine Y. Conaway, secretary of the Council, indicated that the move had been taken because Phillips had not been approved and had appeared against the advice of the faculty advisor.

The loss of recognition means that the Wallaceites will no longer have official standing in the university. They will not be able to meet in campus buildings or otherwise use campus facilities.

A Mistake

Roy Kauffman, president of the Students for Wallace, said that the organization had made a mistake in having Dr. Phillips speak without proper authorization. However he maintained that the real reason for the Council's action was the politics of the Wallaceites, particularly their stand against the speaker ban.

An observer at Ohio State told the CRIMSON that Phillips was brought in deliberately to force the administration's hand on the issue of political speakers. He remarked that it was a bad time to try to change University policy because the state legislature is now discussing the O.S.U. budget.

Student Group's Magazine Barred By UNH Officials

In January, 1948, a faculty committee at the University of New Hampshire ban-

HYD Publication Refused Harvard Name Last Year

When the Harvard Youth for Democracy, an "autonomous affiliate" of the American Youth for Democracy, was

Wayne University Ousts 'Politically Controlled' AYD

There are many instances throughout the country where left-wing student organizations have been banned. The American Youth for Democracy is the most frequently mentioned of these groups. The following statement was sent to the CRIMSON by the administration of Wayne University in reply to an inquiry on the occasion in April, 1947, when the A.Y.D. was barred at Wayne:

"Wayne University chapter of the American Youth for Democracy was banned April 8, 1947, following receipt by Wayne President David D. Henry of a letter from the United States Department of Justice supporting J. Edgar Hoover's assertion before the congressional Committee on un-American Activities that the A.Y.D. was a Communist front and that A.Y.D. groups 'could be termed Communist youth recruiting centers.'

No Disassociation

"The local chapter was first asked to disassociate itself voluntarily from the

FRIDAY, MAY 27, 1949. THE HARVARD CRIMSON PAGE THREE

Academic Freedom—A Crimson Report

'Radical' Students Face Pressures on Campus

A.Y.D. Banned at Queens; O'Dwyer Accused Of Interfering in Selection of President

By JOHN G. SIMON, BURTON S. GLINN and DAVID E. LILIENTHAL, JR.

Copyright 1949 by the Editors of THE HARVARD CRIMSON

This is the third and last article in a series surveying the condition of academic freedom in American universities. In the two preceding articles we reported on pressures exerted on faculty members because of their political beliefs; on attempts of state legislatures to supervise education; and on cases where college administrations have denied outside speakers the opportunity to address campus meetings.

Today's article will deal with instances where students or student groups have charged they have been subjected to pressure because of their political opinions or activities. Two other cases which do not fall into these categories appear on page five.

For the past three months, the position of the president of Queens College, New York,

America and the Students for Democratic Action.

The storm blew over for the time being. In October, however, it sprang up again. Henry E. Schultz, a Queens member of the Board of Higher Education, proposed an amendment to the Board's by-laws that would bar "subversive" groups from all city college campuses.

Eighteen out of 20 college administrators and faculty representatives testified against it. Lenz, student dean at Queens, opposed the amendment strongly.

"As one who would have to administer it," he said, "I must state unequivocally that this amendment will be of no use to me. It offers

Lysenko Theory Sets Off West Coast Imbroglio

Washington

(Continued from page three.)

of these men by placing them on probation. There has never been any adequate definition of the terms of this probation. Any one of the three will presumably think a long time before he advances any political opinion or indulges in any political activity that might displease the Board of Regents while he is still on probation.

ment of "a standard of political orthodoxy . . . the next step may be whether a belief in Catholicism or the single tax are acceptable. Both of these are doctrines of considerable rigidity and both have been at times highly unpopular."

The Connecticut Valley Educators have attacked the Washington decisions as "establishing the principle that an instructor may be dismissed solely upon the basis of his political beliefs without regard to academic performance or qualifications . . . the continuation of this

Baxter Backs Up Williams Teacher

"Like most if not all of my other colleagues on the Williams faculty," Williams College President James Phinney Baxter, 3rd, wrote in an article for his school's May, 1949, Alumni Review number, "I support the Marshall Plan, the Atlantic Pact, and the furnishing of

Strand, Spitzer Clash At Oregon

August Leroy Strand is the president of Oregon State College in Corvallis, Oregon. He is an entomologist with some pretty definite ideas about "party liners" and their rights to teach. On January 14, 1949 Strand notified L. R. LaVallee, assistant professor of Economics, that

you have been reading too much communist propaganda that has appeared under the guise of the Progressive Party." In another letter Strand put "Communist organization apologists for the Soviet Union, officials of the Progressive party, and many other fellow travellers" in the same category.

Closing his statement to the faculty, Strand said, "Many men in Soviet Russia have died in concentration camps, or by other means, because they would not accept the untruths which Ralph Spitzer has chosen to espouse . . . Dialectical materialism! A better name would be dialectical murder. The case is closed so far as I am concerned."

Both Spitzer and LaVallee are appealing to the American Association of University Professors.

THE *HARVARD CRIMSON* prepared an extensive review of academic freedom and student rights cases in its May 25 and 27, 1949 issues. A portion of its lead article, along with a selection of headlines, are excerpted here. Below right is a page 1 feature from the San Francisco State College *Golden Gater* 5/18/50.

employed. Eby, Ethel, and Jacobs were on two year probation. Nobody has gone so far as to define probation, but Professor Ethel said, "whatever they require of me I intend to comply."

Through the overwhelming minutiae of these reports and through the technicalities of interpretation of the tenure code, some facts can be readily spelled out. The most important of these is that the three dismissed professors lost their jobs because of political activity. This activity was membership in, or, in Gundlach's case, sympathy with, the Communist Party. Likewise, it is certain that the three men on probation are in this unenviable position because of their former affiliation with the Communist Party.

Throughout the testimony much was made of the answers of the various defendants to the question posed by Dr. Allen as to membership in the Communist Party. No one on the committee ever challenged Dr. Allen's right to ask this question.

It is impossible to evaluate completely the effect of the action of the Board of Regents on the University. But already eminent men have refused appointment to the University. Thomas Cook, a conservative historian, has resigned because of the firings. A letter signed by 430 leading educators and scholars was sent to the Board of Regents claiming that its action was tantamount to the establishment of "a standard of political orthodoxy . . . the next step may be whether a belief in Catholicism or the single tax are acceptable. Both of these are doctrines of considerable rigidity and both have been at times highly unpopular."

Golden Gater

SAN FRANCISCO STATE COLLEGE

Vol. 51, No. 13 San Francisco, California Thursday, May 18, 1950

What Is Academic Freedom?

Last Monday was set as the deadline by the University of California Board of Regents for signing of the compromise loyalty oath which has been accepted by the Senate Academic employees. We present here the statement issued by the opposing group, the Non Senate Academic employees.—The Editors.

What is a university? A university is an assemblage of searchers whose function it is to seek and disseminate truth. All recorded history shows that judgments of men are never final. Truths must be continually re-examined and reformulated in an ever-changing world. The world has progressed only because people have honestly questioned accepted theories in the light of new experience.

RESPONSIBILITY OF EDUCATORS

The fight for broader educational opportunity and academic freedom is a basic part of the fight for extension of democratic rights. The purpose of education is to provide all people with the knowledge they need to develop their great potentialities and to live as thinking free men. It is the duty and responsibility of educators and of all citizens to insure that this liberating force of education is not misused and distorted. Education which forbids questioning of accepted ideas produces meek followers rather than independent and critical citizens.

Academic freedom means freedom of teachers and students to examine all theories in the light of facts with complete assurance that no particular ideas are politically required or politically forbidden. A political test for academic employment forbids by decree the reaching of certain conclusions and threatens all who question, all who doubt, with loss of their jobs. History shows that forbidding of certain ideas is only the first step toward forbidding all but one set of ideas.

FACULTY ACCEPTS CONTROLS

The controls now being imposed on our University stem from a small group of political appointees more keenly aware of their interests in the world of affairs than of the purpose for which a university exists. The faculty have accepted these controls as a condition of their own employment. In so doing they have agreed to restrict their effort to seek and to teach truth, in direct contradiction to their social obligations. To the detriment of the welfare of the people of this state, the Regents are now deciding questions of academic and education policy.

EDUCATION IN JEOPARDY

No University is an island complete unto itself. Not only are all the universities threatened by the loss of freedom at one, but the entire educational system of our nation is placed in jeopardy. To make men slaves, tyrants must first enslave their schools.

We fought this danger at the University of California. Despite present defeats, we pledge to keep fighting until the University of California is again a free university. We call on all friends of freedom to join their efforts to ours, by recognizing and defeating the invasion of their own campuses, and, by defending and aiding the intended victims of the political purges at the University of California.—

The Steering Committee of the Non-Senate Academic Employees, University of California, Berkeley, California.

Standing up to state and federal legislative committees

2. Un-American Activity Searches Hit the Illinois Region

Alexander Pope
University of Chicago
Chair, Illinois Region, 1950-51

The Student Government (SG) at the University of Chicago came into existence almost at the same time as the National Student Association. Its first full year of operation was the 1947-48 academic year. SG representatives were elected from the College, the graduate divisions and the professional schools of the University, in proportion to their respective student enrollments.[1]

As a representative from the College, I spent most of that year representing a minority viewpoint in the Student Government. The majority of the representatives believed in an activist left/radical role for SG, with numerous debates and resolutions on many of the major national and international political issues of the day. (Even during that period, it should be noted, there was no question of communist domination of SG. For example, a resolution condemning the suppression of academic freedom at the University of Prague after the Communist take-over in Czechoslovakia was passed overwhelmingly.)[2]

Believing that the Student Government should focus primarily on student welfare and take positions only on those political issues of direct relevance to students, I found myself on the short end of the great majority of the actions taken by SG that year. I was, nevertheless, able to get elected as an NSA delegate at the end of the year and attended the second Madison Convention in the summer of 1948.

Organizing the Independent Students League

Arriving early on campus in fall 1948, I felt that my views were more representative of general campus opinion at the University of Chicago than those of the previous year's SG members. I worked with Matt Holden,[3] a personal friend and fellow political activist, to organize our own student political party to be ready for the fall Student Government elections. The name we chose, the Independent Students League (ISL), continued for many years to be a presence in student politics at Chicago.

We did not fully realize before the votes were counted what a sympathetic chord we would strike with our fellow students. The ISL fielded seventy-four candidates (all we could drum up) for the eighty-four Student Government seats. All but one of them were elected. After a year on the back benches, I was then the almost unanimous choice for President of SG in 1948-49 and was also again an NSA delegate to the Champaign-Urbana (University of Illinois) Convention in the summer of 1949.

From being largely a left-wing debating society, the UC Student Government became focused primarily on pocketbook issues for students and on representing the student viewpoint in negotiations with the University over the administration of student affairs. We generally adopted a liberal Democratic position on the political issues we felt were of particular concern to students. (Personally, I spent so much time working on the Harry Truman campaign in October 1948 that I had to study around the clock after the election to be able to pass my fall quarter courses.)

Political Conflict on *The Maroon*

Interestingly, an analogous scene was being played out almost simultaneously on *The Maroon*, the campus newspaper, which elected its editor by vote of the staff. As described by David Broder,[4] a leftist faction and a centrist group were both recruiting people to work on the paper in spring 1948 in anticipation of an upcoming election for editor. The first group was seeking to make the *Maroon* a voice for leftist sentiments on national issues, while the second group argued that the paper should focus on campus events and controversies.

Neither David Canter, the leftist candidate, nor Broder, the middle-of-the-road choice, was able to win the required 60 percent majority. It was agreed, instead, to split the editorship. Canter would be the editor during the 1948 summer and autumn quarters, with Broder taking over in winter and spring 1949. As it turned out, Canter contracted tuberculosis during the summer, requiring Broder to serve as editor for most of the year. But that was not before Canter had put out one issue with the memorable headline: "CP [Communist Party] INDICTMENT STIRS UC PROTEST."

The State Broyles Commission comes up against Chancellor Hutchins

Parenthetically, toward the end of my term as Student Government President, the University was investigated by the State Seditious Activity Investigation Commission. (The Commission was, as I recall, upset by the Springfield lobbying by University students against a package of antisubversive bills introduced in the legislature by Senator Paul Broyles, later the Chairman of the Commission.) The Commission held hearings in Springfield on April 21-23, 1949, with Chancellor Robert M. Hutchins as the first witness. The testimony of Chancellor Hutchins was so devastating to the Commission interrogator, J. B. Matthews of House Un-American Activities Committee (HUAC) fame, that, despite two additional days of testimony, the Commission was never really able to develop its anticommunist theme to any extent and nothing came of the hearings. Along with a large group of other UC students, I attended the Springfield hearings, wearing my only suit in case I had to be called to show what clean-cut young Americans the University was turning out. (An account of this incident, entitled "The Great Investigation," is included in the NSA Archive at the State Historical Society of Wisconsin, in Madison.)

The following academic year, 1949-1950, the ISL continued its political domination on campus, and my close friend Frank Logan[5] was elected President of the Student Government. Starting law school drastically cut down the level of my participation, and leadership passed to Frank, Sandy Levin (now a Michigan Congressman), Roger Woodworth,[6] and other ISL activists. In 1950-51, my second year in law school, I did find time to be the Illinois Regional Chair of NSA. However, that was not a particularly onerous chore since most NSA activity was at the campus and national/international levels, with state activity largely confined to a few sparsely attended meetings and modest interim contact among the officers. At the April 1951 annual meeting, we did pass five resolutions (largely following previously established policy) opposing some of the McCarthyist legislation then pending in the Illinois Legislature as inconsistent with our view of academic freedom.

The Illinois Region enters the fray and Bradley University withdraws from NSA

As my term was ending in spring 1951, those resolutions suddenly caused a flare-up in the type of extreme anticommunist activity that was then unfortunately so prevalent. A student at Bradley University in Peoria, Warren Reynolds, had attended the Illinois Regional NSA Convention and was upset over the five resolutions that we had passed. Using the resolutions as a basis, Reynolds generated an effort to disaffiliate Bradley from the NSA. A student election to decide the issue was scheduled for May 18 on the Bradley campus. Three days before the election, the Congressman from Peoria, Representative Harold Velde, a HUAC member, made a statement on the floor of the House of Representatives attacking the Illinois Region of NSA as being communist-dominated.[7] HUAC files, according to Velde, showed that communists and communist sympathizers were in control of "many student organizations" on the University of Chicago and Roosevelt College campuses and, in particular, the Chicago and Roosevelt NSA chapters. That control, according to Velde, had enabled those communists and sympathizers to gain "control of the officers and policies of the Illinois Regional Chapter of NSA." Obviously, the floor statement was timed to be used in the Bradley election (and the Bradley students did dutifully vote to disaffiliate from NSA, by a vote of 265 to 87 out of a student body of 3,000). The statement was also, presumably, intended to generate publicity for the Congressman, which it did, appearing, among other places, on the front page of the *Chicago Tribune*.

Velde effort expires after vigorous response

Needless to say, everyone involved in the Illinois Regional Chapter of NSA was amazed and outraged by these ridiculous

Congressman Harold Velde eventually recognized NSA's legitimacy in his appearance on the College News Conference with host Ruth Geri Hagy (see Part 6) in January, 1953. Standing from left: Elmer Brock, NSA Vice President, Student Affairs, 1950-51; Robert A. Kelly, NSA President, 1949-1950; Tesse Hardigan (Donnelley), Missouri regional Chair, 1949-1950; and Allard K. Lowenstein, NSA President, 1950-51.

(Courtesy, Tesse Donnelley)

accusations. Having led the charge in forestalling a pale version of exactly what Congressman Velde claimed to fear (although, as pointed out above, there was never any real question of "communist domination"), the extreme irony of his false statements left me angry, and also very frustrated by our inability to make any effective response. Helen Jean Rogers[8] and other NSAers did call on Velde on two occasions, but without satisfaction. He was clever enough not to repeat his slanderous statements off the floor, where they would not have been privileged and could have given us grounds for a defamation suit. I wrote a detailed letter to Velde pointing out the complete falsity of his charges, and got back a weasely, unapologetic reply. (Copies of the *Congressional Record*, my letter, Velde's letter and correspondence and memos from Rogers summarizing her contacts with the Congressman are available in the NSA Archive. The Archive also contains copies of letters condemning Velde's charges from then Senator Paul Douglas and Congressman Sidney Yates.)

There the matter essentially ended. Velde achieved his little success in assisting, perhaps crucially, in the Bradley disaffiliation and getting some momentary publicity. His irresponsible statements had, fortunately, no other tangible impact on NSA activities (to the best of my knowledge).

(That spring, Senator Broyles again introduced his antisubversive bills. In 1949, there had been an independently formed All-Campus Committee Opposing the Broyles Bills and the Broyles Investigation [of which I was a board member] to oppose that year's bills. A second All-Campus Committee was formed in 1951 [called the All-Campus Civil Liberties Committee], this time under the aegis of the Student Government, with SG President Roger Woodworth as its Chairman.[9] There was a third repeat performance in 1953, with Matt Dillon, former ISL President, being the Chairman of the third ACCLC. To the best of my knowledge, none of Senator Broyles's proposals was ever enacted into law. Governor Adlai Stevenson had promised to veto the substance of the original set as unconstitutional.)

Postscript

I should add that this was not the only problem I had with the anticommunist zealots of the McCarthy era. On two occasions, I did not get federal positions because of the length of time the federal government's security procedures took to obtain the necessary clearances for me. One was in 1952, when I applied for a Judge Advocate General (JAG) commission at the time of my military service, and the other was in the 1960s, when a State Department friend wanted me for a temporary assignment in Washington requiring a high-level clearance.

More ironic was a strange (and disturbing) event during my Army service in 1953. As a PFC at Fort Leonard Wood in Missouri, I was an Information and Education instructor, a job that required a low-level clearance because our unit was also responsible for filing G-2 reports for the Division (a meaningless function on a training base—there never was any substance to our reports on the "intelligence" status of the Division). While the regular G-2 officer was on leave, a young fill-in Lieutenant revoked my clearance because, as he told my commanding officer, I belonged to so many political organizations (about whose actual purposes and activities he probably did not have a clue). Knowing that I was a lawyer and might create some static, the Lieutenant arranged to have me immediately (that same day) shipped off the base (to Korea). I did complain about this treatment, but a colonel in the Inspector General's office refused to review my security file to determine whether there was any rational basis for the revocation of my clearance. (He appeared to me to be overwhelmed at the prospect of becoming involved in any way in a "security" problem.)

The ironic result was that in Korea, where the Army had more urgent functions to perform, I was assigned the job of Eighth Army News Analyst, a position that involved constant exposure to all sorts of important confidential information. No one in Seoul ever appeared to have the slightest concern about my loyalty or fitness to handle highly secret information.

I later obtained copies of the bulk of my security file pursuant to the Freedom of Information Act. The contents certainly confirmed the Seoul judgment as to my character and fitness. The garbage in the file is truly amazing[10]—and especially depressing when you consider the huge expense that must have been incurred in collecting the great quantity of useless material the file contains.

Alexander Pope was Executive Director of the California Citizens Budget Commission. A former practising attorney, he has also served as Los Angeles County Assessor and Legislative Secretary to California Governor Edmund G. Brown, Sr.

END NOTES

[1] See Birenbaum, p.581, Smith, p. 127.

[2] See Ellis/Smith, p. 188.

[3] Today, Professor Matthew Holden, Jr. was the Henry L. and Grace M. Doherty Professor of Government and Foreign Affairs at the University of Virginia and a past President of the American Political Science Association.

[4] Now the *Washington Post's* Pulitzer Prize–winning political reporter and columnist.

[5] Now retired, Frank was for several years the Chair of the Executive Committee of Milbank, Tweed, Hadley & McCoy, a prestigious New York law firm, and played a key role in the secret financial arrangements that led to the release of the Americans held hostage in Iran during the Jimmy Carter administration.

[6] A long-time political staff member in Boston and Washington, D.C., Roger was serving with Senate Minority Leader Brian P. Lees in the Massachusetts Legislature when he was fatally injured in a bus accident, in November 1999. In the past he was a Policy Assistant to Senator Edward W. Brooke, Special Assistant to HHS Secretary Margaret M. Heckler, and head of the Office of Elder Affairs for Massachusetts Governor William Weld.

[7] I believe Congressman Velde had a son at Bradley at the time, which probably explains why he knew about the student election.

[8] Sadly, Helen Jean Rogers Secondari passed away in March 1998 in Washington, D.C., after a distinguished career as a producer of radio and television documentaries. Helen Jean had served as the national Secretary-Treasurer of NSA. See Secondari, pp. 597, 599.

[9] A sidelight on the tenor of those times: The student group that went to Springfield from the University to oppose the Broyles legislation that year was racially mixed. When they went to a coffee shop across the street from the State Capitol, they were refused service and so sat in for two hours in protest. In a letter to me, Roger Woodworth recalled that episode and wrote about his effective testimony in Springfield as coming from

> fortuitously, a Republican and a veteran, dressed in an elegant borrowed suit. [Dan Rostenkowski, of later congressional fame, was a member of that legislature.]
>
> "After the proceedings, the thirty- or forty-member U of C delegation repaired to a nearby restaurant to celebrate with food and drink. Several members of the delegation were African-Americans. After twenty or twenty-five minutes, it slowly dawned on the delegation that Mr. James Crow was in command of the restaurant serving policy. Nonetheless, every member of the campus delegation sat silently for almost two hours in the hope that civility would be met with civility.
>
> But in the city where Lincoln practiced law—where he served in the House of Representatives—where he launched his campaign for the Presidency—the color curtain remained drawn and shuttered. So the U of Cers returned to campus, their innocence about race shattered forever.

Editor's note: Roger Woodworth graduated from Suffolk School of Law in 1957 and began his career on the Republican State Committee in Massachusetts.He later became an assistant attorney general for the State of Massachusetts. Struck by a bus in November of 1999, he died of complications at the age of 72 in April, 2000.

[10] An equally disturbing sidelight on the tenor of the times: One of the items in my security file was a detailed summary (apparently made from a hidden microphone someone had on their person) of remarks critical of HUAC that I had made in a *private* meeting in a friend's home. I was asked to justify those remarks sentence by sentence in my FBI interview for the State Department clearance.

PICTURE CREDITS: *Then:* March, 1958 (*Flynt Studio, Los Angeles*). *Now:* 1999, Mt. St. Gorgonio, So. Cal. (Author).

ALEXANDER H. POPE

Early background and military service: Born June 4, 1929, New York City. Attended public grammar schools in New Jersey and Illinois, and North Shore Country Day School, Winnetka, Illinois (Junior and Senior High School). United States Army (1952-54) (Service at Ft. Leonard Wood, MO, and as the 8th Army News Analyst in Korea).

Education: University of Chicago, A.B. 1948 (Political Science), J.D. 1952 (Law) (Phi Beta Kappa, Coif, Student Government President, Managing Editor of Law Review).

Public Service: Executive Director, California Citizens Budget Commission (1997-2001). Los Angeles County Assessor (1978-1987). Consultant to the Governor on Implementation of the McCone Commission Report on the Watts Riots (1966). Legislative Secretary to Governor of California (1959-1961).

Law practice. Of Counsel, Seyfarth, Shaw, Fairweather & Geraldson (Los Angeles) 1993-96. Partner, Barash & Hill (Los Angeles) 1989-1993. Partner, Mayer, Brown & Platt (Los Angeles) 1987-88. Partner, Fine & Pope (Los Angeles) 1957-77. Partner, Shadle, Kennedy & Pope (Los Angeles) 1956. Associate, Law Offices of David Ziskind (Los Angeles) 1955. Law Clerk, Illinois Appellate Court (Justice Ulysses S. Schwartz) 1951-52.

Policy-making Commissions: Los Angeles Board of Airport Commissioners (1973-78) (President 1975-76). California Highway Commissioner (1966-1970). I have served in various capacities with a number of civic groups including the California Citizens Budget Commission, Los Angeles Theatre Center, International Association of Assessing Officers (Metropolitan Jurisdiction Council President 1983), University of Chicago Club of Greater Los Angeles.

Political: Candidate for State Board of Equalization, 4th District (1986), and for Los Angeles County Board of Supervisors, 4th District (1984).

International Travel: During the past fifty years I have traveled each year, visiting nations throughout Europe, Africa, Asia, and Australia, North and South America.

Family: Married to Katherine Pope. By previous marriages: I have three children and two grandchildren; Kate has five children and seven grandchildren.

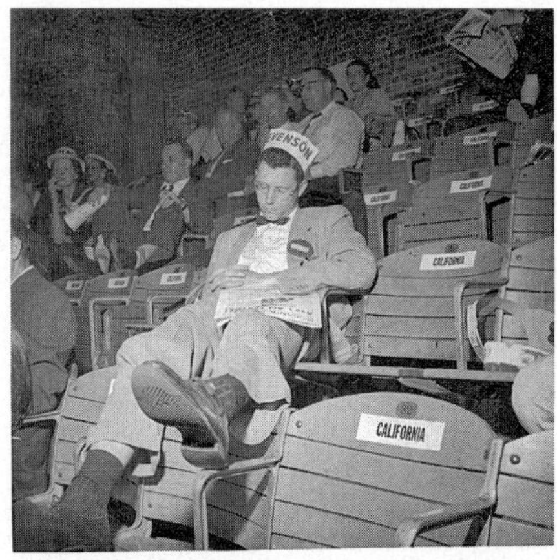

Alexander Pope is uncertain whether this shows him as a national officer for Volunteers for Stevenson at the 1952 Democratic Party Convention, or alternate delegate at the 1956 Convention. What is certain is the state of terminal exhaustion. (Courtesy, author)

Students and Faculty Confront Communist Issue

Editor's Note: As can be seen throughout this book not all colleges responded in the same way, nor did all state legislatures, to the "Red Scare" or "Communist threat." Nonetheless, the issue was kept alive by various efforts to ban left-wing student organizations (such as the AYD or YPCA) and speakers known to have or suspected of Communist taint, to require faculty to sign oaths of allegiance, and to subpoena faculty, students and administration to appear at high-profile legislative hearings on subversive activity. Among U.S. students before, during and after World War II, there were many student leaders who understood the danger to democratic institutions posed by the global Communist apparatus, and who also saw the damage being done those institutions by indiscriminate "Red Scare" investigations and initiatives. These balancing considerations appear throughout this volume, and especially in Janet Brown's essay in this section, the story of NSA's initial efforts to deal with the International Union of Students (Prologue and Part 1), and in Part 4: Bernard Bellush on the American Veterans Committee, Phillip Des Marais on Operation University, Seymour Reisin on the American Youth for Democracy.

1946-53

vard Crimson

GE, MASS., FRIDAY, OCTOBER 4, 1946. PRICE FIVE CENTS.

Communist-Led Bloc Beaten as HLU Cleans House, Votes New Executives

Hotels Announce Few Rooms Left

Falangist Emissary Gets Cold Shouldered by AYD Members

Liberal Union Stages Surprise Coup to Oust Alleged Reds In Heated Four-Hour Session

Tulane Hullabaloo

Vol. XLII NEW ORLEANS, LA., THURSDAY, MARCH 13, 1947 Z-258 No. 23

Marine Corps Offers Officer Training Plan

Communism Threatens World, Fortas Warns In Address

The Loyola News

Chamberlin Next to

SPEAK ON COMMUNIST ACTION

LAW SCHOOL AIDED BY HON.

Fr. Hussey, S.J., Speaks at Dinner

LECTURE NEXT WEDNESDAY ON COMMUNISM IN RUSSIA, ORIENT

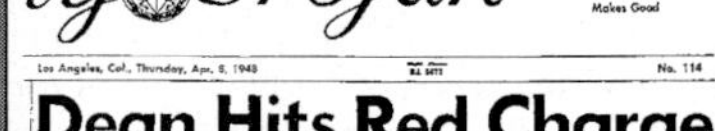

ly Trojan

PAGE THREE

Predecessor Thinks Dean Makes Good

Los Angeles, Cal., Thursday, Apr. 8, 1948 No. 114

Dean Hits Red Charge

LAS Lecturer Discusses US

IR Lays Plans To Fete Noted

Warren Doubts Militant Communists on Campus

nian

LLEGE DAILIES

3, 1949 No. 31

Compulsory loyalty oaths hit by NSA Regional assembly

The Simmons News

CHRISTMAS CARDS

FOR THE D P FUND

FACULTY ADOPTS RESOLUTION

DEAN HAVICE WILL SPEAK AT THANKSGIVING SERVICE

Review's Fall Issue Dedicated To Frosh Goes On Sale Soon

Stand Taken On Loyalty Oath Controversy In Recent Vote

Audience Gives Approval To Anti-Red Arguments

By JOE OGLESBY

Two law students defeated two English majors in a debate at the Student Union Building on Monday on the question of whether or not the Communist Party in America should be outlawed.

Tom Nicholas and Tim Bornstein, arguing in the affirmative, received 37 votes on a show of

Outlaw Reds, Say U of L Students

U of L students voted to outlaw the Communist Party in the United States in a mock election held by the Political Arena Wed-

HILL TOP

VOL. 35, NO. 6 HOWARD UNIVERSITY, WASHINGTON, D. C. FEBRUARY 18, 1953.

McCARRAN EYES H. U. REDS

Senator Turns on HU "Subversives"; Howard University on His List

1947

The Daily Reveille

ALL-AMERICAN

[Excerpts]

Communism's Antidote in the U.S.

What must America do about Communism?

The question is a compelling one, and fully as far-reaching as any ever posed. It has become at least a part of the framework (a very substantial part) of the nation's foreign policy. It is weaving itself into the pattern of domestic activity.

* * *

If actually there exists a movement which infiltrates itself into our system in such a way that the system itself is endangered, it cannot be ignored. The phrase "fifth column" is still too keenly and too bitterly remembered to permit passive acceptance of national death.

Equally as dangerous, however, is the line of action proposed by those who would outlaw the Communist Party. For the product of any labor will not be satisfactory if it is accomplished with tools which themselves oppose the reason for that labor. We have gone too far with our program of "freedom" to begin now to curtail the activity of minority groups with whom we disagree.

* * *

Communism's strength lies always in the prevalence of unrest and discontent. Hunger and unemployment and maltreatment are its most forceful weapons. And there lies America's responsibility if it is serious in its desire to eliminate communism: the responsibility of removing its breeding grounds—not by acting in violation of the spirit which has moulded our system, but by making democracy work.

1952

Los Angeles Loyolan

AN OFFICIAL STUDENT NEWSPAPER

EDITORIAL: [Excerpts]

Academic Freedom?

Academic freedom, as stated by Friedrich Paulsen, professor of moral philosophy at Berlin at the turn of the century, means that "no thought can be commanded or forbidden to the academic teacher or his students." "The fear that unlimited academic freedom opens the door to serious error should not in the least deter us from it," says Adolph Harnack, another of the famous German "liberal" thinkers.

Destruction of Faith

The primary result of adherence to that principle was the destruction of all Christian faith in hundreds of thousands of young people educated in Germany. American universities and colleges quickly swallowed the hook and engaged in a mad scramble to fill up their faculties with exponents of the theories of Paulsen and Harnack and other liberal thinkers. Today we are beginning to see the many ramifications and results of this apparently "democratic" principle.

* * *

Academic freedom has its points, but freedom must not be understood as the right to do as you please. Freedom is the right to do what you OUGHT to do.

BOB KRIBS

1948-53

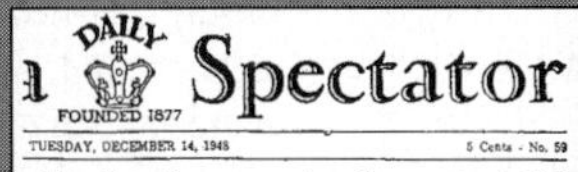

Daily Spectator

FOUNDED 1877

TUESDAY, DECEMBER 14, 1948 5 Cents - No. 59

Fight Looms in Local AVC Group on Communist Issues

FOUNDED 1877

MONDAY, MARCH 28, 1949 No. 106

CUSC Refuses to Allow Hall To Address Marxist Society

FOUNDED 1877

WEDNESDAY, NOVEMBER 22, 1950 No. 27

Hutchins Warns of Crushing Free Thought in Universities

Brr! It's Cold Outside

Chicago Head Hits

Republicans Stage blic Rally of Year

Link Nine Professors To Communist Fronts

COLUMBIA SPECTATOR

Congress Red Inquiry May Reach Columbia But Nothing Definite Is Set

EACH YEAR the same controversies arose on different campuses as illustrated by the clippings above: **Speakers at campus forums—both invited and banned:** Abe Fortas, *Tulane Hullabaloo* 3/13/47, LA; William Henry Chamberlin, Loyola U., Chicago, *Loyolan* 3/18/48; Gus Hall, indicted Communist Party leader, Columbia U., *Columbia Spectator* 3/28/49; Robert M. Hutchins, *Spectator,* 11/22/50. **Battles for control of student organizations:** Harvard Liberal Union, *Harvard Crimson* 10/4/46; American Veterans Committee, *Spectator,* 12/14/48. **Legislative questioning of professor/student affiliations:** U. of Southern California, *Trojan,* 4/8/48; Columbia U., *Spectator,* "Nine Professors" 10/9/52, "Red Inquiry," 1/9/53; Howard U., DC *Hilltop* 2/18/53. **Student and faculty opinion resolutions/polls:** U. California, Berkeley, *Daily Californian* 10/25/49, "loyalty oaths"; Simmons College, MA, *Simmons News* 11/16/50; U. of Louisville *Cardinal,* 11/19/50 "Anti-Red Arguments." Louisiana State University. **Editorials**: Excerpt from Louisiana State University *Daily Reveille* 4/?/47 sees "making democracy work as the antidote to Communism." Excerpt from Loyola University *Los Angeles Loyolan* 5/27/52 discusses the obligations as well as rights of academic freedom. See also note 4, p. 435.

ACADEMIC FREEDOM *Newsletter*

No. 1 Chicago, December 2, 1953

Illinois NSA votes to have freedom week

An academic freedom subcommission was established by the Illinois region schools of the US National Student Association, at the regional meeting held November 20 - 22 at Roosevelt College and the University of Chicago.

As one of its main functions, the subcommission has been directed to sponsor, in cooperation with USNSA, an academic freedom week. The purpose of the academic freedom week as stated in the unanimously passed resolutions will be to serve to educate and inform the member campuses of the problems concerning academic freedom.

Establish newsletter

A newsletter will be distributed in the Illinois region to further the exchange of information relating to problems of academic freedom within the region.

The resolution also enumerated a broad set of principles defining the basis of educational rights and setting forth the criteria which are necessary to secure these rights.

Hit inquiries

The recent Congressional investigations in the education field were characterized by the NSA group as creating widespread and increasing fear among educators, who are subjected to irresponsible and unjustified criticism arising from the inquiries. It was stated that freedom of thought requires an atmosphere free from intimidation."

Uphold Constitutional rights

The NSA region declared that "academic competence should be the only criterion for the hiring and continued employment of teachers. Refusing to testify before investigating bodies on the basis of the First or Fifth Amendment is a constitutional right, the exercise of which is not relevant to classroom competence and does not constitute a valid basis for dismissal.

The NSA resolution also declared that "Legislative investigations into the beliefs and associations of teachers in a university have resulted in great harm to intellectual and academic freedom."

Reprints available

Persons desiring reprints of the Academic Freedom Newsletter should submit their requests as soon as possible. Reprints are available in bulk quantities at nominal cost.

First Issue

This is the first issue of the newsletter instituted by the Academic Freedom Conference held at the Univ. of Chicago last June. It has been printed with the cooperation of the Chicago MAROON. The center spread appeared as a supplement to the MAROON issue of November 20. The contents were prepared by members of the Student Committee on Academic Freedom, a student organization at the Univ. of Chicago.

Crimson hits McCarthy queries Pusey on hiring

The Harvard **Crimson** issued a challenge of "put up or shut up" to Senator Joseph McCarthy in answer to his charges, published on Nov. 5, that Harvard students are being exposed to "communist teachers and party philosophy."

The **Crimson** declared, in an editorial on Nov. 8, that it knew of "no faculty member who acted as if he were under Communist domination" and called on McCarthy to "actually name the professor or professors."

The major part of the statement, however, was sent in a telegram to Nathan M. Pusey, new president of Harvard asking his attitude "toward returning teachers who refuse to state whether they are Communists." McCarthy referred especially to Wendell H. Furry, Harvard professor of physics, who, McCarthy claimed, refused to testify before the Senate Internal Security Committee.

Furry used 5th Amendment

Summoned last November in connection with security leaks in the Army radar program at Fort Monmouth, N. J., Furry testified that he was not at that time a Communist but he sought the protection of the Fifth Amendment when asked about party membership before March 1, 1951.

In May he was put on 3-year probation by The Harvard Corporation for "grave misconduct" in having belonged to the Communist Party nine years before.

Furry was retained on the faculty because "he had not given a Communist slant to teaching, nor had he sought to influence the political thinking of students."

To the inference that Furry was unfit to teach, Frankel answered that Furry had testified that he was not a member of the Communist party after March 1, 1953, and he had not indoctrinated students in Communist philosophy.

Pusey answers McCarthy

"My information," Pusey wired McCarthy in return, "is that Furry has never given secret material to unauthorized persons or sought to indoctrinate his students."

His refusal to testify before the McCarthy committee on the basis of possible self-incrimination could not be regarded as "a confession of guilt." Harvard would always hold a position "unalterably opposed to communism," Pusey added.

McCarthy charges: 'soft-head'

McCarthy's retort followed. "Even the most soft-headed and fuzzy-minded cannot help but realize that a witness' refusal to answer on the ground that his answer would tend to incriminate him is the most postive proof obtainable that the witness is a Communist. You and The Harvard Corporation can of course continue to keep Fifth Amendment Communists teaching the sons and daughters of America."

Columbia paper publishes survey

The Columbia Spectator, the Student newspaper at Columbia University, has announced that it will publish its second annual academic freedom supplement early in December.

Editorial

Students must help

There should be no need to convince the reader of this newsletter that a threat to academic freedom exists. This freedom; which is the basis of our educational system and of our cultural and intellectual heritage and development, is being faced with increasing pressures for conformity.

It is encouraging that some students are beginning to oppose this trend to conformity. Various student groups have collected information, made statements of principle, held conferences, and lobbied against legislation adverse to academic freedom. Many religious groups have published strong declarations on academic freedom.

But many students fail to act even though they acknowledge the ned for action. We think this state exisis, first, because they feel that they alone cannot achieve any worthwhile results, and second, because it is often the case that well intentioned people "just don't get around to starting something." We should like to quote Confuscius' maxim that "It is better to light even one small candle than to sit and curse the darkness."

But we are not so sure that the candle needs to be small. In addition to the activities mentioned above, there have been student academic freedom conferences in New York, at the Univ. of Wisconsin, and at the Univ. of Chicago in which students resolved to support principles and a program of action similar to those on the last page of this newsletter. There should be no shortage of manpower if we can only reach all these people.

From these conferences and from personal contacts we know that the nucleus of an active group exists. Our first aim must be to increase the number of interested students who keep in touch with us, to reach student organizations who will work with us, and to give the new people the spark that sets off the actions they desired but never performed.

We must show these people that they are not isolated, but that their problems are shared by students all over. Finally we want to help coordinate the programs of groups which are already active, so as to promote efficiency, and to enable cooperative projects to be carried out on a scale impossible for single groups working alone.

How can we get started? We have learned from experience that one cannot just express fine ambitions and expect people to come flocking to carry them out. There is only one way in which our group can achieve its aims. This is the hard, unglamorous job of gradually increasing the number of supporters, following up every lead we get to people who might be sympathetic, and begging these people to do something now.

We can say no more about the dangers students face and the ned for action. We have been expressive — now we must be effective. And the only way in which we can be effective is if you help us by sending us information about what is going on in your campus or community and volunteer to give us your support, even if only in some small way. This is the way in which you can show us if you think we are planning something worthwhile, and can help us do it successfully.

What you can do to help

1. Keep us informed about individuals and/or organizations interested in receiving our literature, or who might be of assistance in the defense of academic freedom.

2. **One of our functions is to serve as a clearing house for information which could be used for our plans and publications and for the coordination of student action. In order to accomplish this, we need the active participation of as many persons as possible in gathering information about academic freedom from campus newspapers, circulars or any other sources.**

3. Submit ideas for forthcoming newsletters. This issue was compiled by the Chicago group alone; we were unable to include a summary of what all schools are doing, because information was so incomplete. We would like to include reports on student activities throughout the country, but this is impossible unless we're kept well informed.

4. **We need money to carry out any effective program. Do you know of persons or groups who could contribute, even a small amount? If our readers were to contribute —if only in stamps—the cost of mailing the newsletter could be met.**

5. If you can volunteer to assist us, please let us know. Aid might take the form of writing, suggestion of ideas for the defense of academic freedom, soliciting funds, locating interested persons, etc.

Please address replies to:
Student Committee on Academic Freedom
Reynolds Club
The University of Chicago
Chicago 37, Ill.

Academic freedom meeting at U. of C. hits investigations, plans student action

"The only reasonable and logical procedure which will safeguard the integrity of the teaching profession is an insistance that the individual teacher be judged by his professional peers for his professional competence and his personal integrity," declared H. H. Wilson, associate professor of politics at Princeton University, in the keynote address before the student academic freedom conference sponsored by the All Campus Civil Liberties Committee of the University of Chicago.

Wilson, who outlined the various pressures for conformity in education and the need and basis for granting full academic rights to persons of even the most radical views, spoke on June 14 before student delegates and observers from fifteen colleges, mainly in the midwest area.

Two other prominent educators, Howard K. Beale, professor of history at the University of Wisconsin and John J. DeBoer, professor of education at the University of Illinois, addressed the conference. Beale presented an extensive background of past attacks on education and also emphasized the need of allowing teachers to be free to hold any political view. DeBoer spoke on the possibilities for practical action in defense of academic freedom.

Conference had six workshops

The conference itself was divided into six workshops. Three in which the various threats to academic freedom were discussed were the workshops on the "Rights of Teachers," the "Rights of Students" and the "Implications of Investigations." The remaining three workshops were devoted to specific methods of meeting the present attacks on academic integrity. Resolutions were prepared in the workshops and then discussed in plenary sessions.

Delegates score investigations

Taking cognizance of the Congressional probes of education the delegates declared:

"The Congressional investigation of the political beliefs and affiliations of a teacher in itself should not be taken as casting doubt on the teacher's professional competence. . . . The use of the Fifth Amendment or any other Constitutional privilege in no way reflects the lack of professional competence . . . ; nor does it place upon the teacher the burden of proving his qualifications."

A wide range was covered by the student resolutions. They reaffirmed the various rights of students as citizens, and stated in part: "A university exists to educate its students—to help them develop their critical facilities. . . . As students we feel that the pressure towards indoctrination and the existence of fear within the classroom are destroying the basis of genuine education."

Plan inter-campus action

The workshop which considered specific methods for meeting attack on academic rights, made plans for organizing various inter-campus projects and enlisting support of student, community, and national organizations.

It was voted to petition the National Students Association to call a national conference on academic freedom and monthly academic freedom newsletter was established. A continuations committee of one representative from each attending school was set up by the conference.

Peter H. Greene, who had been chairman of the ACCLC conference committee and Derek Staats from Northwestern University were elected temporary co-chairmen of the continuations group. Richard Ward of the University of Chicago was appointed editor of the newsletter.

DURING THE HEIGHT OF THE MCCARTHY ERA, and following state and federal legislative inquiries into Illinois colleges, the NSA Illinois Region established an academic freedom subcommission in December of 1953, headquartered at the University of Chicago. Its mission was to focus attention on academic freedom issues and provide a national information service.

Aligned with the Association of American University Professors (AAUP)

NSA's Academic Freedom Policies

Stephen Clements Schodde
Teachers College, Columbia University, 1965

This is an excerpt from Stephen Schodde's 1965 thesis for his Degree of Doctor of Education at Teachers College, Columbia University.[1] *See pp. 809-810 for author photo and biography.*

Closely allied with the development of an NSA position on student rights were the Association's statements on academic freedom. This concept was being defined by the students at the same time as student rights and responsibilities but was perceived first as a right belonging to professors only. Early resolutions clearly cast the student in the role of defender of the teacher's freedom. Gradually the conception of academic freedom was broadened by the students to include freedom for their own activities in their role as students.

It was also seen that such concepts as a free student press, free speech, and the right to hear speakers on all sides of controversial questions and due process in the event of violation of university regulations must apply to students. Further, the time-honored doctrine of *in loco parentis* was inherently in conflict, in the student's view, with student academic freedom.

The resolution on academic freedom at the constitutional convention was linked with the student bill of rights but applied solely to teachers. Briefly, it called for freedom of research, freedom in class discussion (with the proviso that the professor should not introduce controversial subject matter which has no relation to the subject), and the right to join any organization not illegal under civil statutes, without facing reprisals because of such membership. Teachers speaking and writing as citizens should also be free of institutional restrictions and ability should be the sole basis for employment.

A few minor qualifications were added as follows:

Limitations of academic freedom because of the avowed purpose of the institution should be clearly stated in writing at the time of appointment. Since ... his profession and institution may be judged by his utterances ... at all times he should be accurate, exercise appropriate restraint and make every effort to indicate that he is not an institutional spokesman.

A procedure for investigating violations of either the bill of rights or academic freedom was established consisting of a preliminary investigation conducted by a national staff committee at the request of the college administration, student government, or a student petition. The National Executive Committee could then take action regarding publication of any report if it was deemed necessary.[2]

Fifth National Student Congress amplifies NSA position

Such was the state of affairs until the Fifth Congress [Indiana University, August, 1952] when the student delegates began to amplify and broaden their position on academic freedom in response to McCarthyism. At that time resolutions not passed by the plenary session could be referred for action to the National Executive Committee meeting in post-Congress session. The post-Congress National Executive Committee meeting after the Fifth Congress acted on a resolution which took a strong position on academic freedom. in this case the concern was the academic freedom of the teacher and what offset his membership in alleged subversive organizations would have on his status as a teacher. A liberal interpretation of the rights of the teacher is evident in the resolution along with concern over various state legislation calling for restrictive loyalty oaths or conditions of employment:

> The Congress observes that a growing number of states impose oaths and conditions of employment upon teachers, which do not allow them to belong to organizations defined by legislatures or administrations as subversive.
>
> The Congress believes that the teacher has the right to join any organization not illegal under civil statutes, without being discriminated against through economic, racial, or political pressures because of such membership except in those cases where, because of the avowed purpose of the institution a limitation of academic freedom is clearly stated in writing at the time of the appointment.

In this statement the students were saying, or at least the National Executive Committee was saying since the regular Congress had adjourned, that teachers should not be restricted in organizations they might join, at least not restricted by legislation and administration. If they were, any restriction would be put in writing before the teacher committed himself to the institution. The resolution continued:

> The Congress directs that:
>
> (1) The Student Affairs Vice-President immediately have sent to the body of each state legislature a copy of USNSA basic policy declarations.
>
> (2) The Student Affairs Vice-President use his discretion to arrange to send a Student Affairs second letter addressed to the body of each state legislature which has passed or in considering legislation in conflict with basic policy and USNSA Congress legislation to the State Legislature in question shall be pointed out [sic].
>
> (3) The Student Affairs Vice-President arrange to have the letters of section 2 sent at his earliest convenience, but the first attention go to the Broyles bills in Illinois, the Levering Act in California, the Feinberg Act in New York, the Peckam Bill in Pennsylvania, and the Ober Bill in Maryland.
>
> (4) Both letters referred to above include a statement that USNSA is a federation of autonomous student governments representing whatever the current number of student members may be.[3]

The resolution carried fifteen in favor, none against, and two abstentions. It represented a strong first stop in the Association's reaction to legislative pressure against teachers. It indicated an identification with the teacher and an idealistic, libertarian point of view in regard to teachers' academic freedom.

At the same post-Congress meeting, the National Executive Committee endorsed the work of the American Association of University Professors and directed the national staff "to give full support and publicity to this group's efforts."[4] In further discussion of how academic freedom violations should be reported, the same National Executive Committee voted to amend and tighten the procedure of reporting alleged violations of academic freedom. The original resolution began:

> The Congress observes that news of violations of academic freedom is often tardy and incomplete.
>
> The Congress believes that violations of academic freedom on one campus are harmful and are therefore of direct concern to all students.
>
> The Congress enacts the following procedure in order that Information regarding alleged violations of USNSA's basic policy

on academic freedom and student rights be quickly communicated to American students.

Who could report a violation was spelled out:

1. The president of the student body of the institution concerned;
2. Any accredited persons representing the school concerned in the NSA region [sic];
3. The editor of the campus newspaper;
4. Petition signed by 20 per cent or 200 members of the student body, whichever is the lesser figure;
5. A member of the faculty or administration.

The resolution went on to describe how the National Vice President could request 500-word statements from the parties involved and publish the statements through a college press service. An escape clause stated in effect that in exceptional cases the Vice-President could use his discretion to rule the alleged violation not subject to the provision of the resolution.

After discussion, the National Executive Committee tightened the procedures to read:

1. A majority of the student government of the institution concerned;
2. A majority of the NSA delegation representing the school concerned in the region;
3. A majority of the editorial board of the campus newspaper;
4. A petition signed by 20 per cent or 200 members of student body, whichever is the lesser figure;
5. Any accredited representative of the administration of the school concerned;
6. Any five accredited members of the faculty of the school concerned.[5]

These amendments which were passed would obviously have the effect of making it more difficult to present frivolous or specious complaints to the NSA. It may also be a source of some delight to college administrators that the word of one administrator (see five above) was the equivalent of five faculty members (see six above).

Policy statements adopted by NEC in behalf of the Congress

It is also important to note here that a relatively small group of NSA regional chairmen, not more than nineteen or twenty, were deciding on policy statements which, although identified as National Executive Committee resolutions, in effect, by the educational world and the public at large, would be seen as representing the voice of the student congress. There was no effective check on possible abuses of this executive prerogative. The National Executive Committee was simply a smaller group of students taking up unfinished business of the Congress and acting upon it. This practice of referral was ended at the Sixteenth Congress. Currently [1965], the methods for reporting and acting on alleged violations of the student bill of rights or the basic policy declaration on academic freedom are defined in By-Law ten of the NSA Constitution entitled "Procedure for Enforcement of Basic Policy Declarations." These procedures depart somewhat from earlier efforts both in technical details and in greater attention given to due process. An inquiry can be requested by any of the following means:

a. A majority vote of the appropriate student legislative authority of the school involved.

b. A petition of inquiry signed by not less than 30 members or 15 percent of the student body, whichever is the greater figure.

c. A majority of the membership of the regional executive committee of the region in question.

d. The administration of the school involved.

The provision, as defined in item c, for the regional executive committee to act might be important if the local student government officials feared administrative reprisals should student government request an inquiry.

Except in those cases where legislation is mandated by the Congress, final decision to accept requests for inquiry rents jointly with the NSA President and the Chairman of the National Supervisory Board. These two people, together with the chairman of the region, can appoint a three-man board of inquiry. The committee is to visit the school in question and:

> confer with all parties to the dispute, discuss the matter with the administration of the school in preparing their report [sic]. The function of the board of inquiry shall be that of obtaining information pertinent to the charge and to make recommendations for legislative and executive action to the National Supervisory Board and the National Student Congress with provisions for minority reports.

Another important provision was that "all parties to the dispute shall be afforded the opportunity of appending statements to the final report."

On completion of the inquiry copies of the final report "will be distributed to the committees of the American Association of University Professors, the United States Student Press Association . . . the National Supervisory Board, and the Congress for the purpose of taking such action as they feel appropriate."[6] This constitutes the enforcement provision of the by-law.

Student personnel administrators should note the possible link between a student investigation and the American Association of University Professors and no mention of a student personnel association. This may be another example of students perceiving their rights being better protected by their professors than student personnel administrators.[7]

EDITOR'S NOTES

[1] Schodde, Stephen Clements, *Certain Foci of the United States National Student Association, and Their Implications for Student Personnel Administrators.* Teachers College, Columbia University, 1965.

[2] United States National Student Association, *Report of the Constitutional Convention* (Philadelphia: The Association, 1947), p. 16.

[3] United States National Student Association, Summary Minutes of the Post-Fifth Congress National Executive Committee (Philadelphia: The Association, 1952), pp. 17-18.

[4] Ibid., p. 24.

[5] *Editor's note:* See Brown, Pt. 6, S. 2.

[6] United States National Student Association, Codification of Policy: Seventeenth National Student Congress (Philadelphia: The Association, 1965), pp. 19-20.

[7] *Editor's note:* After tracing the evolution of NSA's original 1947 academic freedom by-laws, Schodde returns to the Ninth Student Congress (1956) at which NSA addressed "An important defense against the false principle of guilt by association and the protection of an individual's right to use of the fifth amendment without creating an unfavorable presumption of guilt . . . ," adopting a special resolution on academic freedom. At that Congress NSA also "broadened its attack on restrictions regulating student activity," extending the reach of academic freedom for the first time to explicitly include students as well as faculty.

Opposed to discrimination in social organizations, NSA balances advocacy with dialogue

3. NSA and Fraternity-Sorority Discrimination

Recollections today and excerpts from a November 5, 1952, memorandum

Leonard A. Wilcox, Jr.

Phi Kappa Tau, University of Michigan. President, Student Legislature, 1951-52. Michigan Regional Chair, 1951-52. NSA Vice President, National Affairs, 1952-53

Editor's note: During its formative years, NSA, as an association built on student governments, sought to couple its opposition to discrimination and segregation with a desire to bring into its orbit the colleges and social organizations that were the mainstream of its practice—which included, at the time, almost all U.S. college campuses, but most especially those in southern and border states, the elite colleges, and the major social and professional fraternities and sororities across the nation.

Many forces were at work among political, social action, and ethnic organizations to batter away at these practices, largely through legislative, judicial, and educational means. The more direct confrontations of the civil rights movement in the late 1950s and 1960s were yet to occur.

NSA played an important role in its early years, providing legitimacy to antidiscriminatory advocacy among student government and organization leaders and building bridges to the fraternity and sorority infrastructure.

In this unit, NSA 1952-53 National Affairs Vice President Leonard A. Wilcox, Jr., looks back on that period. His memoir is followed by a background piece in which a series of extracts from earlier and later correspondence and documents illuminate the organizational relationships at the time, as well as the offense taken over NSA's pronouncements within national fraternity/sorority leadership.

Included in the background piece is a 1952 memorandum prepared by Wilcox that states NSA's policy positions toward fraternity discrimination as well as the efforts of its leadership to maintain a collaborative relationship with the fraternity community.

Social fraternities and sororities on American college campuses enjoyed substantial growth and expansion in the period following the end of World War II. Returning veterans had boosted college enrollments, and wartime limitations on construction had left many schools with inadequate student housing. Dormitories were crowded and student services often lacking. Fraternities and sororities offered more comfortable space, better food, and greater social activities, which accommodated the growing student bodies. Especially on the larger university campuses, with their impersonal character, the fraternity and sorority houses offered smaller, more attractive group living arrangements.

The rituals and practices of fraternities and sororities, as well as membership policies, had been established over many years, with some reaching back into the prior century. Racial, religious, and national origin restrictions were almost universally found in the governing documents of these groups. But post–World War II student generations, first the veterans and then the younger nonveterans who followed them onto the campuses, began questioning whether these discriminatory practices really belonged as a part of American higher education.

There existed a generational gap in this situation, with older alumni seeing nothing wrong with membership restrictions while younger undergraduates, particularly in more progressive areas of the country and on more liberal campuses, did not favor their perpetuation.

The United States National Student Association (NSA) had addressed this subject early on at National Student Congresses and declared its policy to be one of seeking the elimination of discriminatory practices on campuses, leaving to each member school and its student government how best to achieve the goal. This approach was in keeping with the concept of NSA as a federation of student governing bodies with each member school retaining its autonomy.

Joining a fraternity and facing up to discriminatory issues

In fall 1948, I ventured upon this scene as an eighteen-year-old nonveteran, entering the University of Michigan as a freshman. The Ann Arbor campus had grown at that time to a student body of over 30,000. Within a few weeks, I joined the Phi Kappa Tau fraternity, and the following fall moved into the chapter house, where I lived for three years. I found this group of men congenial and I established close friendships, many of which have lasted right up to the present day. Our chapter comprised men of various points of view on issues, but among most there was a recognition that the discriminatory character of our membership policy was outdated and incompatible with the aims of present-day higher education.

Meanwhile, I had been elected to the Student Legislature, the all-campus student government body. It had already taken a policy position against the discriminatory practices of campus organizations and continued to do so throughout my undergraduate years. A fraternity brother and veteran, Quentin Nesbitt (who would later serve as president of the Student Legislature), and I were sent, in summer 1949, as delegates from our chapter to the Phi Kappa Tau national convention, held in Excelsior Springs, Missouri. I recall that the issue of discriminatory membership policy never reached the convention floor, although we and several other chapter representatives made efforts to get it there. Only one national officer of the fraternity, chaplain Reverend Spottswood, supported our position and encouraged us to continue efforts to have the discriminatory clause removed from the organization's constitution.

During the remainder of my undergraduate years at Michigan, I served one year as fraternity chapter president and continued as an elected member of the Student Legislature, serving as president during 1951-52. Our student government fully supported an end to the discriminatory membership policies of fraternities and sororities; the university's student-faculty Committee on Student Affairs, on which the Student Legislature held two seats, would not, however, consider withdrawing recognition from the groups.

At the Fifth National Student Congress, held at Indiana University in August 1952, I was elected vice president for national affairs, a newly created full-time position, and served under the able leadership of President Richard J. Murphy, a graduate of the University of North Carolina. One of my first assignments from Dick was to go to the national office in Boulder, Colorado, and prepare it for moving to its new location in Philadelphia. The trip out to Boulder was by car, with Sylvia Bacon (who owned it) and myself as drivers and executive secretary Marion Andert as a passenger. The beauty of the Rocky Mountain range could not be denied, but the location of the national office was simply too remote as a practical matter.

Dealing with Pan-Hellenic hostility to NSA policy

While in Colorado I visited several member and prospective-member schools as Dick and I had agreed was important for a national officer to do. I addressed student body assemblies at smaller campuses such as Loretto Heights and student government bodies at larger institutions such as the University of Colorado. Opportunity was also afforded to meet with administrators and deans of students. I well remember calling on the dean of women at the University of Colorado. I had been cautioned by the student government president that she was a national Pan-Hellenic leader who had a negative view of NSA and its stand against the discriminatory practices of fraternities and sororities. It was my first experience as a representative of NSA to encounter such hostility to our organization, and in particular such opposition to the position on this issue taken by NSA. The dean expressed surprise that I was a fraternity member; I assured her that many who participated in NSA at all levels were fraternity and sorority people like myself. At the close of our talk together, she complimented me on being on time for our meeting—something she said that Allard Lowenstein had never done!

Relocation of the national office to Philadelphia was accomplished in October 1952. Soon thereafter I was contacted by Jerry Fox at the University of California at Los Angeles (UCLA). He had encountered a growing negative attitude toward NSA on his campus and turned to me for help in countering the onslaught. In particular, as I recall, he was facing opposition to continued affiliation of his school because of a perceived anti-fraternity bias on the part of NSA. In an effort to support him in meeting this challenge, I sent him a memorandum on November 5, 1952 (which is reproduced in conjunction with this article), in which I outlined the policies adopted by NSA with respect to discrimination in campus organizations, including fraternities and sororities, but stressed the autonomy of the member schools in determining how to implement these policies.

Confronting negative attitudes at the National Interfraternity Conference

At about this time I met Dr. Clyde S. Johnson, executive secretary of Phi Kappa Sigma fraternity and a member of the Executive Committee of the National Interfraternity Conference (NIC). His fraternity's national office was located in Philadelphia. He respected the work of NSA and the importance of the role it played on American campuses. At his suggestion I made arrangements to attend the forthcoming annual meeting of the NIC at the Waldorf-Astoria Hotel in New York City on the Thanksgiving holiday weekend in November 1952. He thought I might be able to dispel some of the negative attitude toward NSA in the NIC. As his guest I had the opportunity of meeting many of those in attendance and talking informally about NSA and my experiences with it. I was not on the speaking program, but as I left the meeting I felt it had been a worthwhile effort.

Unbeknownst to me, on the following day after I had returned to Philadelphia, the NIC was addressed by Bob Munger, organizer of Students for America. In what had become a standard charge, he asserted that NSA was an insidious left-wing pressure group and was anti-fraternity in its opposition to discriminatory clauses. It was clear to me that he and his organization were responsible for the pressure being felt on Southern California campuses to disaffiliate from NSA or to reject joining the organization as a new member school, and he was seeking fraternity and sorority support in this effort. The request for help we had received the prior month from Jerry Fox at UCLA in dealing with the unfounded claim that NSA affiliation required member schools to withdraw recognition from organizations with discriminatory clauses was now more understandable.

It was at this point in time that my tenure as a national officer came to an end. The Korean War was still in progress, and my student deferment was cancelled because, as a full-time NSA staff member, I was no longer attending college and thus eligible for deferment from the draft. Dick Murphy strove to persuade Selective Service to allow me to complete my term, but to no avail. I applied and was accepted for the navy's officer candidate school, leaving the national office early in 1953. My position on the NSA staff was filled by the appointment of my longtime friend and associate at the University of Michigan, Philip C. Berry, who more than capably served out my term.

"These [discriminatory] clauses must ultimately go"

That summer, at the Sixth National Student Congress, James M. Edwards, Student Senate president at the University of Illinois, was elected to succeed Dick Murphy as NSA president. Jim was a member of Beta Theta Pi fraternity. He shared with me the conviction that NSA needed to tell its story to the National Interfraternity Conference to offset the negative attitudes being engendered by Bob Munger. Like myself, Jim was not given a speaking opportunity at the NIC annual meeting, held in Cincinnati, Ohio, in November 1953. But he was introduced as a guest and made the most of the opportunity to informally talk with both alumni and undergraduates in attendance. In a report he later submitted to the national office in Philadelphia, he said, "The biggest misgivings about NSA, of course, are because of the stands which have been taken on discriminatory clauses." He then observed, "But, they are all defensive on this point, recognizing down deep, I think, that these clauses must ultimately go."

NSA never waivered from its opposition to all forms of racial discrimination during the years that I was involved with it. Fraternities and sororities were not singled out for their practices in this regard. They were, however, the most prominent campus groups practicing discrimination. To bring about an end to it, NSA sought, as I have described in this article, to encourage the groups themselves to eliminate the practice and, at the same time urged student governments to cooperate with them in achieving an end to restrictive membership policies. It was believed that progress would be made by taking this approach. I thought then, and I still do today, that because the principle involved was right, reasonable minds would prevail in the academic community if you just kept working at it.

Leonard A. Wilcox, Jr., has practiced law in Detroit, Michigan, since 1958. A retired Naval Reserve Captain, he now resides with his wife in Ft. Lauderdale, Florida.

PICTURE CREDITS: *Then:* 1951, U. Michigan Yearbook. *Now:* 2001 (*Courtesy, author*).

WILCOX ON NSA IN 1952

A Defense of NSA

Mi Daily 12-9-52

(EDITOR'S NOTE: The following article is a discussion of the functions of the National Student Association. Mr. Wilcox, '52, last year's SL president, is now NSA vice-president for national affairs.)

By LEONARD WILCOX

PHILADELPHIA—A recent issue of "The American Student," official publication of Students for America, sharply criticizes the United States National Student Association as "the most dangerous of all the left-wing political pressure groups now operating on American campuses."

The condemnation continues with the charges that USNSA "milks about $37,790 a year from students who are ignorant of its existence; wants to eliminate fraternities which do not conform to its desires; advocates letting Communists teach; and refuses

* * * *

USNSA does not want to eliminate fraternities that do not conform to its wishes. Many leaders in student government and in USNSA are fraternity presidents and members. The issue here is whether fraternities should maintain discriminatory structures in their constitutions while being recognized on the campus. This is a highly controversial issue among fraternity people themselves. USNSA by its constitution can only recommend; it has no power to coerce or demand conformity; a school can take or leave any policy or program recommendation of the Association.

USNSA recommends that an educational program be developed on campuses toward the goal of eventual elimination of discriminatory clauses where student governments favor such a program. USNSA recommends that campus organizations be given a period of time in which to effect removal of clauses from their constitutions or face loss of recognition. This latter policy is recommended for the consideration of student governments where the climate of student-faculty-administration opinion is ready for such a step. These controversial policy recommendations are intended for the use of student governments that desire to put them to use.

"USNSA CAN ONLY RECOMMEND; it has no power to coerce or demand conformity," Wilcox wrote in a comprehensive review of NSA policies, responding to the 1951-52 attack on NSA by the Students for America (see p. 404, 805) in which it charged NSA as a "dangerous ... left wing pressure group," that would "eliminate fraternities which do not conform to its desires."

"The issue," Wilcox wrote, "is whether fraternities should maintain discriminatory strctures ... while being recognized on campus."

(*Michigan Daily, 12/9/52*)

LEONARD A. WILCOX, JR.

Early Years: Born July 12, 1930, in Detroit, MI. Attended Detroit public schools and graduated from Redford High School in June 1948.

Education and NSA: A.B. University of Michigan, 1952. M.A. Tulane University, 1956. J.D. University of Michigan, 1958. President Student Legislature, 1951-52. Delegate to Third, Fourth and Fifth National Student Congresses, 1950-52. Chair, NSA Michigan Region, 1951-52. Chair, NSA National Executive Committee and National Interim Committee, 1951-52. Vice President for National Affairs, NSA, 1952-53.

Career Highlights: Attorney admitted to practice in Michigan since 1958. Retired Captain, United States Naval Reserve.

Family: Married 46 years to the former Betty Barrett Dougherty; three children, five grandchildren. Current residence in Ft. Lauderdale, FL.

"I believe that all these men would be interested in knowing just what your organization is"

NSA and the National Interfraternity Conference (NIC)

The Evolution of NSA's Relations with National Fraternities

Editor's note: From its inception, eliminating the practices of racial segregation and of discrimination on account of color or national origin was one of the paramount goals of the Association. However, as has been noted in the reports in this anthology on the 1946 Chicago Student Conference and the 1947 Constitutional Convention, the desire to retain a Southern college membership led to hard-fought compromises in the statement of those objectives (see Part 1, Sections 3, 4, and 5) as expressed in By-Laws I and II of its Constitution, "to secure and maintain equal rights for all people, and to secure equal opportunities for education at all levels regardless of race, national origin, sex, creed and political belief or economic circumstances." There was no mention at that time of discrimination in campus social organizations. (See Appendix: The NSA Charter.)

The Association's early efforts in this area were to focus on developing human relations programs designed to confront the issues of attitude and behavior (see Section 1, this part). By 1949, however, at the Second National Student Congress at the University of Illinois, NSA addressed discrimination in campus organizations directly in a set of resolutions which recognized "that the chief responsibility for the elimination of discriminatory practices resides within the campus community and that a policy of encouragement and cooperation is necessary for the progressive elimination of discrimination."

It also urged "all national professional, honorary, social and service organizations to take action to eliminate any discriminatory clauses in charters and constitutions of, and discriminatory practices in, their member societies" while recognizing that "groups established by religious organizations for specifically avowed religious purposes may require the conformity of their members to their particular principles and practices."

Early NSA-NIC Contacts

Editor's note: Two letters from NIC chairmen to NSA's first two presidents indicate the early mutual interest of NIC and NSA in each other.

September 29, 1947

William Welsh, Esq., President
National Student Association
Union Memorial Building
University of Wisconsin
Madison, Wisconsin

Dear Mr. Welsh,

As you may already know, the National Interfraternity Conference is deeply interested in the work of your new organization. One of our committee members attended your recent meeting at Madison and last week I had the pleasure of having a long talk with Mr. Greenfield, who gave me a very interesting report on the history, background, and future plans of the organization.

The next plenary session of our Conference will be held at the Hotel Commodore in New York on the Friday and Saturday morning after Thanksgiving, i.e., November 28th and 29th. The Conference is normally attended by some 250 to 300 delegates from the fifty-nine fraternities comprising the Conference and about 75 to 100 college presidents and deans from all over the United States. This year we are also re-instituting the undergraduate section, which probably will be attended by from fifty to one hundred undergraduate representatives of the various interfraternity councils throughout the country.

I believe that all these men would be interested in knowing just what your organization is, what it is doing, and what it plans to do to further the cause of American college education. As I explained to Mr. Greenfield, our time at the Conference is very much limited, inasmuch as the work for the entire year has to be crowded into three sessions of from two to three hours each. Nevertheless I regard the work of your organization as being of sufficient importance to set aside fifteen or twenty minutes somewhere in our program for you if you would be interested in addressing one of our sessions. I cannot yet suggest a definite time but it might be at the Friday luncheon when the entire group will be together or early Friday afternoon or perhaps Saturday morning.

I understand from Mr. Greenfield that your association is keenly interested in getting before the public and particularly those organizations that are interested in college and university work the story of what you are and what you are doing, and he felt that there was a strong probability that you might arrange to be with us at our session.

Will you be good enough to let me know whether you care to come and whether you think it will be possible for you to do so.

Very truly yours,
David A. Embury, Chairman

November 17, 1948

Mr. James T. Harris, Jr.
304 North Park Street
Madison 5, Wisconsin

Dear Mr. Harris:

Mr. Embury, former Chairman of the Interfraternity Conference, has forwarded your letter to me. I note that you desire to have your representative speak to the undergraduate session of the Conference.

The Undergraduate Conference is in charge of Mr. Wilbur Walden, 225 Lafayette St., New York, whose telephone number is Canal 68128. I am forwarding your letter to Mr. Walden with a copy of my reply.

Yours most sincerely,
Gilbert W. Mead
Chairman

From *NSA News,* February 1949

NSA to Study Fraternity Bias

Fraternities and sororities will be the latest groups brought into the NSA Human Relations program under a new project directed toward the combating of racial and religious prejudice within fraternal organizations.

This project will utilize student governments and interested fraternity members to bring to the attention of local interfraternity councils educative methods of reducing prejudicial attitudes and to aid in the initiation of such methods on each campus.

Largely based on the work of the Fraternity Inter-Racial Relations Committee of the University of Wisconsin, the program will involve four types of action: the distribution of pamphlets and other printed material pertinent of the subject, the engagement of prominent speakers to address the whole campus on racial issues, the provision of group moderators for house discussions inspired by the inter-racial committee, and the organization of exchange social functions between racial and religious groups.

Though the project will be a part of the work undertaken by the Human Relations sub-commission, a decision of the National Executive Committee in December placed it under the direct administration of the National Commission on Student Life.

From the *Middlebury Campus,* December 1, 1949

NIC Urges Fraternities to Remove Restrictions

The National Interfraternity Conference, meeting in Washington, D.C., on November 26, recommended the elimination of restrictive membership provisions, completely reversing its former stand that this controversial issue was not proper for consideration by the organization. This action, which was forced into the open by undergraduate fraternity leaders from New England and the Middle West, could affect membership patterns in approximately 2,700 fraternity chapters throughout the United States. The question was one which had interested many college officers and fraternity men, both undergraduates and alumni, it was emphasized.

The statement was approved without discussion by an outstanding vote of 36 to 3 by the resolution committee with 19 of the 58 member fraternities abstaining from the vote. A more forcefully worded resolution which sought to "repeal and abolish" [any] by-law or constitutional provision that discriminates "against any college student because of his religion, color or creed" was not adopted by the delegates.

The resolution as adopted reads as follows:

(1) It recognizes that many member fraternities have had and now have restrictive provisions.

(2) It recognizes that the question is of concern to many interested parties.

(3) It calls these facts to the attention of all member fraternities, appreciating that membership is an individual fraternity responsibility.

(4) It recommends that member fraternities that do have selective membership provisions consider this question in the light of prevailing conditions and take such steps as they may elect to eliminate such selectivity provisions.

Although undergraduates and college administrators are invited to attend the meetings of the National Interfraternity Conference only the official fraternity representatives hold the power to vote, to present motions or resolutions.

NSA Responds to Appeal for Help from UCLA Coordinator in 1952

Editor's note: In October 1952, Leonard Wilcox, NSA's vice president for national affairs, received a request from Jerry Fox, the UCLA NSA coordinator, to provide some ammunition to counter a claim being made by some fraternity leaders that affiliation with the organization would require the college to withdraw recognition from organizations with discriminatory clauses (see Wilcox, this section).

Below are excerpts from a memorandum Wilcox sent to Fox in response to his request.

TO: Jerry Fox, USNSA Coordinator
University of California at Los Angeles

FROM: L. A. Wilcox, Jr.
Vice-President for National Affairs

DATE: November 5, 1952
SUBJECT: USNSA-Fraternity Relationships

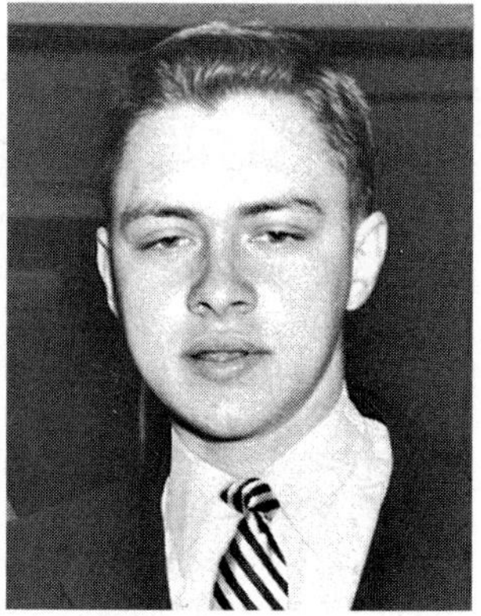
Leonard Wilcox

ACTIONS REQUIRED OF A STUDENT GOVERNMENT IN AFFILIATING WITH USNSA

"(2) Recognition of the Basic Policy Declarations and policies of USNSA as policies of the national and regional organization although not necessarily those of the affiliating school, student government, or administration."

It is important to note here that the policies of USNSA, while representing the consensus of delegates attending the most recent USNSA Congress and constituting recommendations to the member schools, are not binding upon the member schools in any manner whatsoever. A member school may choose to subscribe to those policies in which it strongly believes while it may refuse to enact certain other policy recommendations of the national association. The school in affiliating with USNSA enjoys complete autonomy and does not place itself in the position of being coerced or otherwise pressured by the national association to enact any policies or projects which it does not give its wholehearted support to by its own action.

POLICIES OF USNSA RE FRATERNITIES WITH REGARD TO DISCRIMINATION

"The USNSA encourages wide investigation and discussion of the problems of segregation and discrimination which exist throughout the United States in order to help to secure their elimination. However, in view of the complex nature of the problem, with its diversity throughout the United States, and the limitations imposed by present state statutes and laws, it shall be the policy of USNSA to support and stimulate legislative and legal action on the national, state, and local levels to seek the elimination of statutes and laws which are used to perpetuate discrimination and/or segregation." (Basic Policy Declaration II)

"**Fact:** Various stages of progress have been reached in the elimination of discrimination in higher education; Declaration: USNSA recognizes that the chief responsibility for the elimination of discriminatory practices resides within the campus community and that a policy of encouragement and cooperation is necessary for the progressive elimination of discrimination." (Congress, 1949)

"**Declaration:** Student Governments should cooperate with local chapters of social and professional organizations of their campuses directly toward the purposes of eliminating clauses of a discriminatory nature in their constitution and charters and of practices antagonistic to the best interests of minority groups." (Congress, 1949)

"**Declaration:** USNSA urges member student bodies, wherever feasible and consonant with state law, to initiate through their student governments proposals for changes in regulations which would prohibit the recognition of any student organization which by statements within its constitution discriminates against groups or individuals on the basis of race, color, creed, or national origin." (Congress, 1949)

"**Action:** The National Commission on Student Affairs shall assist such agencies as campus fraternities and sororities on discrimination problems and also establish a group familiar with issues involved to recommend methods of implementing USNSA policies." (NEC, December 1948)

"**Declaration:** USNSA encourages the National Interfraternity and the Panhellenic Conference to urge the elimination of any discriminatory clauses within their member social groups." (Congress, 1949)

"**Declaration:** USNSA urges that student governments working in cooperation with campus organizations meet periodically to determine the degree of progress made in the elimination of discrimination; the student governments and these organizations should then jointly determine what further programs should be followed."

"**Declaration:** USNSA urges its member student governments to set a deadline by which time campus organizations whose constitutions contain discriminatory clauses must remove these clauses or be denied further recognition by the University unless they can show evidence that removal can be secured in the foreseeable future."

It is important to note from the above summary of existing USNSA policies that:

(1) A member student government may take one of four directions in dealing with the subject of discrimination practiced by fraternities and sororities:

(a) Student government may set a deadline for removal of discriminatory clauses.

(b) Student government may deny recognition to new groups seeking recognition that have such clauses.

(c) Student government may work together with other directly affected student organizations to plan a joint educational program in human relations that can be evaluated periodically.

(d) Student government may choose to forego any action in this area, <u>for the above policies are those of the national and regional USNSA and are not binding on the local campus</u>.

"**Declaration:** USNSA commends the many campus chapters of fraternities and sororities which have instituted the "Help Week" programs as a significant contribution to constructive student activity." (NEC, December 1951)

It is important to remember always that USNSA is much more than one particular area of policy. Whether a person agrees or disagrees with the existing USNSA policies on discrimination in fraternities and sororities, the activities of USNSA in student government information and programs, international activities aimed at assisting democratic student organizations throughout the world, and in putting forward student views on national issues of direct concern to us in education is sufficient reason to enthusiastically support the Association.

Many fraternity and sorority members have been national, regional, and local campus leaders in USNSA. Last year, John Haley, Vice-President for Student Government Commission, USNSA, was a member of Sigma Chi at Emory University, Atlanta, Ga. This year, two members of the national staff are fraternity members: Leonard Wilcox, member of Phi Kappa Tau at the University of Michigan, and Avrea Ingram, Vice-President for International Affairs, Sigma Alpha Epsilon at Georgia Tech.

Regional Chairmen this year include: Jim Young (Ohio-Indiana), member of Sigma Alpha Epsilon at Ohio Wesleyan University; Dave Jones (Kentucky-Tennessee), Lambda Chi Alpha at University of Louisville; Fran DeLucia (Pennsylvania), member of Pi Lambda Phi at Temple University; Larry Buttenweiser (Illinois), member of Phi Kappa Psi at University of Chicago; Ken Barton (Virginia-Carolina), member of Chi Psi at University of North Carolina. Some of the women officers associated with sororities include the Secretaries of the Kentucky-Tennessee and Michigan regions, members of Pi Beta Phi and Chi Omega, respectively. This is only a partial list of the fraternity people involved in the Association, but it should give some indication of their interest and support on many campuses.

The most important thing which fraternity people can derive from participation in USNSA activities is the opportunity to discuss their fraternity system with students from all parts of the United States. There is much beneficial in the fraternity system, much more exists in sound fraternity life than emphasis on discriminatory practices which need to be pointed out to critical students who do not understand the total system. Fraternity members have the opportunity through USNSA to educate student leaders from all parts of the nation that fraternities have a positive and beneficial contribution to make to campus life, and that their members are vigorous, active, and able people devoted to building the best in higher education.

Robert Munger Attacks NSA at the NIC 1952 Undergraduate Conference

Editor's note: Robert Munger, a Los Angeles City College atudent who founded Students for MacArthur and then Students for America, was an outspoken opponent of NSA, devoting much of his efforts in 1952 and 1953 to attacking the organization as "the most dangerous of the many left wing groups on campus" (see "Robert Munger and Students for America," in Part 4, Section 3). Munger was invited to address the Undergraduate Conference of the NIC on Saturday morning, November 29, 1952, at the Waldorf Astoria Hotel in New York City. His topic was "The Students' Answer to Communism."

Robert W. Beyers, Editor-in-Chief of the Cornell Daily Sun *was a member of the Cornell delegation. Following is the text of two brief notes he sent Dick Murphy, NSA's President, and a letter he later arranged to have sent to the NIC by the Cornell delegates to the conference. (See also Beyers, p. 480.)*

The Cornell Daily Sun
Incorporated 1905
Cornell University
109 East State Street
Ithaca, New York

30 November 1952

Dick:

Thought this little item might be of interest to you. Munger appeared before the Undergraduate and Graduate Con-ferences of the National Interfraternity Conference in New York last weekend. Much floor discussion ensued at the Undergraduate Conference, unanimously opposed to the remarks made concerning NSA. Interesting to note that he slams ACLU trial lawyers on page three, endorses book of Morris Ernst on page one. Munger refused to answer questions concerning financing of organization, indicated that most of it came through interested adults outside the group (he acknowledged members received more propaganda than dues should cover). "We have no foreign policy" was his reply to question on point four in editorial stand page two . . . etc, etc. More info if you'd like it later.

Bob Beyers
Editor

The Cornell Daily Sun

3 December 1952

Dick:

Additional poop on Munger:

Maintained Commies and Socialists had "crept into control" of student govt. and press on many campuses, said frats should go all out to prevent this. Noted growth of ogn. [organization] membership (SFA) from 8 to 2,000 within first year—has chapters on 80 campuses, or claims to. Appeal to frats very similar to that in The S [Sun], quite warped as you can see—his was NOT received with enthusiasm. Delegates from Penn and Penn State were leaders against him on the floor, if I recall rightly. Did NOT actually call NSA communist or front group, DID everything short of this—indicated his group should thrive as opposition to socialistic ideas of groups like SDA, NSA, etc. That's about it—no time to interview him or ask more detailed questions, unfortunately, for he was "one of those busy people" at the convention, agitating everywhere throughout Saturday, esp. among adults I would suppose. More appreciation for his views there.

Bob Beyers

Bob

Editor's note: On February 26, 1953 Bob Beyers wrote Marian Andert, NSA executive secretary, "Attached please find a copy of a letter being sent by Cornell delegates to the national Interfraternity Conference . . . please feel free to call on us for any support we can furnish you, for your task does not end and your crisis seems continual." The letter follows.

FIRST DRAFT COPY

Mr. C. R. Yeager, Chairman
National Interfraternity Conference
Attleboro, Massachusetts

Dear Sir,

As undergraduate delegates to the National Interfraternity conference this year we wish to state disagreement with the views expressed by Robert Munger, president of Students for America, concerning the United States National Student Association.

As students at a university which has been affiliated with the Association for the past three years, we do not believe that NSA has at any time appeared to be "an insidious leftist pressure group" as charged by Mr. Munger in his publication, The American Student.

As fraternity leaders we have at no time found our own self-government impaired by any of the Association's policies or activities, contrary to the implications of Mr. Munger's address to the undergraduate conference.

We do not feel the extremely emotional character of Mr. Munger's address was in keeping with the high calibre of the remainder of the conference, nor do we believe the political implications of his speech were particularly relevent to the fraternity system.

Robert F. Munger

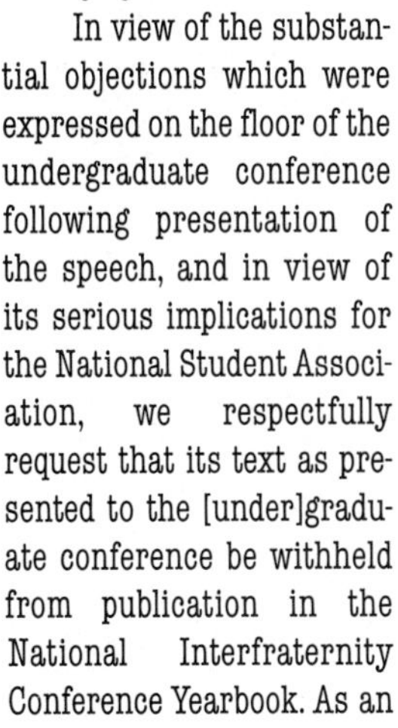
In view of the substantial objections which were expressed on the floor of the undergraduate conference following presentation of the speech, and in view of its serious implications for the National Student Association, we respectfully request that its text as presented to the [under]graduate conference be withheld from publication in the National Interfraternity Conference Yearbook. As an alternative we would recommend that the Association be given an adequate opportunity to reply to Mr. Munger's charges in the same issue.

Sincerely,

Jim Edwards Repairs the Damage in 1953

Editor's note: In 1953, Jim Edwards attended the NIC Conference. The exchange of correspondence and his handwritten notes for his conference report follow.

Hilton Hotel
Fort Worth, Texas

Oct. 29, 1953

Mr. Jas. M. Edwards, Pres.
U.S. National Students Assn.
1234 Gimbel Bldg Ninth & Chestnut
Philadelphia 7, Pa.

Dear Jim,

Your letter, asking about arranging to have an NSA speaker at the 1953 meeting of N.I.C., reached me here at Fort Worth.

The person to whom to write about this is Mr. C. Robt. Yeager, Chairman of N.I.C., c/o L.G. Balfour Co., Attleboro, Mass.

I can tell you, however, that the chances are slight. The program for the Nov. NIC meeting at Cincinnati is already tight and was made up some weeks ago. Announcement of speakers, etc. has already been made. Mr. Yeager, however, may be able to work something out for the Ntl. Undergraduate Conference ses-sion. In any event, I am sure he will give your proposal courte-ous consideration and do what he can.

Yours Sincerely.
Horace Nichols [?]

INTERFRATERNITY COUNCIL
University of Illinois
157 Administration Building
Urbana, Illinois

November 2, 1953

Mr. Horace G. Nichol, President
National Interfraternity Conference
271 Madison Avenue
New York, New York

Dear Sir:

Once again we are anticipating the coming National Interfraternity Conference, whose yearly occurrence has become an integral part of our standard operating procedure. We recognize in the Conference an opportunity to present our views and profit by those of others.

It has come to our attention that a unique organization, The National Student Association, is doing a great deal of constructive, unsung work for students, unsung at least in terms of praise. Apparently, certain uninformed persons have openly stated their misbeliefs and misunderstandings concerning the work of NSA.

The president of NSA, James Edwards, an alumnus of the University of Illinois and Beta Theta Pi fraternity, has contacted us expressing his wish to present the positive side of his organization to a representative group such as undergraduate NIC and in that way clear up any misconceptions or questions that have arisen on this subject. We have become acquainted with Jim both through Council work and through his having been president of our Student Senate last year, and we feel that both he and his organization are qualified for presentation to the coming Conference.

We will appreciate any attention you are able to give to this matter. Thank you.

Sincerely,
John Thompson, President
Interfraternity Council

Jim Edwards Report on the 1953 Meeting of the National Interfraternity Conference

Bob Munger spoke at the 1952 meeting in New York and increased suspicions in regard to NSA. His presentation received mixed reactions but the conference regretted having him there and did not ask him back.

I was very cordially received by all, with some suspicious attitude present at first. It was thoroughly demonstrated that even the oldest and most reactionary of the alumni can be persuaded that NSA is indeed a confederation and is not and cannot be out to wreck fraternities. I was introduced to the body as a "guest."

The biggest misgivings about NSA, of course, are because of the stands which have been taken on discriminatory clauses. But they are all defensive on this point, recognizing down deep, I think, that these clauses must ultimately go. A resolution passed at the 1949 meeting, in fact, urged the removal of discriminatory clauses. The most deep-rooted conviction is that the fraternity should be autonomous in setting up membership requirements, including those based upon race.

Following are listed the major contacts which I have with high-placed fraternity persons.

Jim Edwards

Phi Kappa Sigma—Dr. Clyde S. Johnson, Exec. Sec., member of NIC executive committee
Sigma Alpha Epsilon—Fred H. Turner, Dean of Students, U. of Illinois, former national president of ΣAE.
Sigma Chi—Warren Renshaw, Executive Sec., formerly at Illinois
John Neal Campbell, past National President
Alpha Tau Omega—Stuart Daniels, Exec. Sec., old friend in Champaign
Bob Simons, Daniel's asst., old friend in Champaign
Tau Kappa Epsilon—Vernon Hampton, secretary, asst. dean of men at Illinois
Beta Theta Pi—A. J. G. Priest, National President
Edward Brown, member of NIC executive committee
Ralph Fey, executive secretary

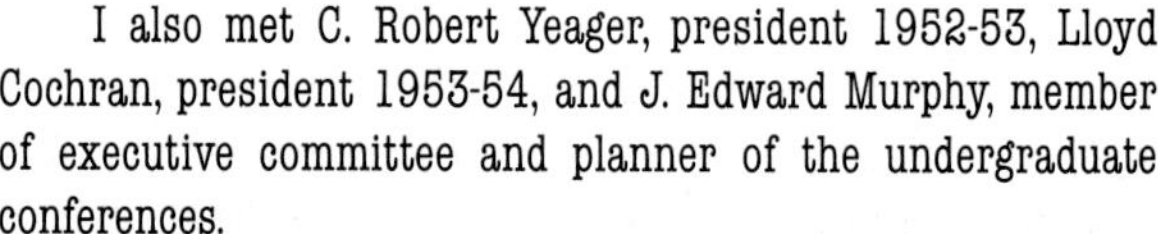

I also met C. Robert Yeager, president 1952-53, Lloyd Cochran, president 1953-54, and J. Edward Murphy, member of executive committee and planner of the undergraduate conferences.

The NIC is run by a small group of old-timers and the undergraduates have no independent organization and no voice in this one.

The functioning group is the executive committee which meets monthly in New York.

PICTURE CREDITS. Bob Beyers, 1953 *Cornellian* (Cornell U. Library). Jim Edwards: c. 1953. *Student Government Bulletin*, 10th Annual National Student Congress, 8/57. Robert Munger: L.A. City College *Collegian* 5/1/51. Leonard Wilcox: 1951 U. of Michigan Yearbook.

NSA JOINS POSTWAR EFFORTS TO DISMANTLE FRATERNITY DISCRIMINATION

University of California, Berkeley, 9/9/49

U.C. delegates speak up against discrimination

By Arnt Froshaug

The University's delegation made its presence felt — particularly on the question of racial discrimination—at the National Student Association congress, which ended last Sunday.

This was the opinion of three delegates—ASUC President Danny Coelho, ASUC vice president Edie McEwing and Paul Pitner—who arrived home from Urbana, Ill., Tuesday. (Other delegates are expected back by the end of the week.)

In the racial discrimination debate, Coelho, delegate Harry Keaton and Miss McEwing proposed a "California plan."

This plan would have provided for "the mandatory exclusion of any fraternity or other organization which would retain its (discriminatory) clauses five years after the adoption of the charter." (It was exceeded in broadness by only the Amherst plan which called for a two year time limit.)

According to Coelho, a four-step program which urges each college or university to begin participation at the level best suited to its local conditions was finally adopted.

The steps are: 1) an educational campaign, 2) campus groups like Executive committee refusing charters to new groups with restrictive covenants in their constitutions, 3) working on local organizations (with no national affiliations) to eliminate restrictive covenants on threat of withdrawal of recognition and 4) persuading local chapters of national organizations to press the national organization for removal of the restrictive covenants.

University of Louisville, KY, 3/25/49

Student Groups Ask Vote On U-L Discrimination

Independent Students, Newman Club, Religious Council Want Referendum

Interested groups at the University of Louisville have agreed to ask the University Student Council to have an all-University vote among the student body to see whether they favor doing away with discriminatory clauses in the constitutions of campus organizations.

Coming out in favor of a referendum to be tacked on to the U. S.C. election next April 8 were the Independent Women, three members of the executive board of the Free Lancers, the Newman Club, the executive board of the Religious Council, and the President of the Kentucky-Tennessee region of the National Student Association.

The statement from the independent men and women came at a joint meeting held Wednesday night in the Woman's Building.

Independent Women President, Harriet Korphage said, "It should interest everybody on campus. You get the same question in the social science classes. And it's the democratic thing to do."

The three members of the executive board of the Free Lancers said they couldn't talk for the rest of their membership who weren't there, but they themselves were in favor of the proposal.

Louis Hecht, President of the Newman Club announced that his membership had definitely placed themselves behind the proposed referendum.

Father Richard O'Hare, moderator of the Newman Club, said in a letter to The Cardinal:

"We, as Catholics, are committed to many principles, not the least of which is the principle of the equality of all men together with the inherent dignity of man himself.

"Because of this conviction, we the members of the Newman Club must stand against any and all discrimination of our fellow men wherever and however it raises its ugly head.

"Unchristian Mode of Behavior"

"Restriction naturally sets groups apart, and in effect, creates circles within circles. It is a contributory ingredient of unrest and the lack of solidarity among us as a nation. Besides, it is a most unchristian mode of behavior."

Saul Loeb, President of the University Religious Council stated that the executive board of the Religious Council is definitely behind the referendum proposal.

Bob Delahanty, President of the Kentucky-Tennessee region of the National Student Association placed himself and his organization directly behind the move. He declared that the N.S.A. policies are directly in accord with the resolution.

Gene Schwartz, official of the N.S.A. in Madison, Wisconsin, wired the University that among the many U. S. colleges and universities which have restricted discrimination are Columbia, City College of New York, University of Washington, Amherst, Swarthmore, Connecticut University and the University of New Mexico.

Washington University in St. Louis, 11/25/47

Hilltop IFC Selects Seven Reps. to Nat'l Undergraduate IFC

The first post-war meeting of the National Undergraduate Interfraternity Council will be held in conjunction with the Nationl Interfraternity Conference in New York City on November 28-29. Representing W. U. will be Dean Don Fischer of the Engineering school, and six members of the campus IFC.

The undergraduate delegates will confer with representatives from other schools concerning problems of overcrowding, rushing, and providing fraternal connections for all students interested. A school session for undergrads will be held to familiarize them with the problems and techniques of the national chapters. The convention will feature speakers Lyman Bryson, public relations counselor for CBS; William Welsh, president of NSA; and Clyde Johnson, assistant dean of men at UCLA.

59 FRATS TO ATTEND

Dean Fischer will be the W. U. representative to the National Interfraternity Conference, which will be attended by delegates from 59 national fraternities

NSA RAISES THE ISSUE ON ALL LEVELS. Its first president, Bill Welsh, addresses the November, 1947 National Interfraternity Conference as reported in *Student Life*, Washington U. in St. Louis, 11/25/47 (Left) (See NIC letter to Welsh, earlier). U. of California, Berkeley, *Daily Californian*, 9/9/49 reports on resolutions for elimination of restrictive covenants in social organization constitutions adopted at the Second National Student Congress (Above left). One of the delegates was Danny Coelho, ASUC student body president. Bob Delahanty, Kentucky-Tennessee NSA Regional Chair, lends NSA's support to a U. of Louisville student body vote to do away with discriminatory clauses in the constitutions of campus organizations. Reported in *The Cardinal*, 3/25/49 (above right).
Excerpt below, U. of Colorado *Silver and Gold*, 10/19/49, evaluates NSA policy as a guideline for University policy.

University of Colorado, 10/19/49

THE SILVER AND GOLD

Editorial And Opinion

Page 2 — Wednesday, October 19, 1949

Coping Constructively With Discrimination

The stand taken by delegates to the Second National Student congress on discriminatory clauses in the constitutions and charters of campus social organizations is feeble, but not futile.

At least it is a step in the right direction. At most it can provide only a flimsy foundation, one that should have been laid many years ago, for attacking an unhealthy condition which time and perseverance will have to rectify.

Nevertheless, the congress cannot be criticized adversely for taking a weak stand on such a far-reaching issue. Rather, it should be commended for not attaching a highly restrictive clause setting a definite time limit after which discriminatory clauses must either be abolished or the organization itself is abolished.

The congress used foresight.

It foresaw the possible disintegration of generally accepted social systems on member campuses, in many cases, if a definite short-range time limit were established.

It foresaw the varying degrees of difficulty in fighting discrimination from one section of the United States to the next, from one school to the next in the same section, and even from one organization to the next in the same school.

It foresaw the need for action on more than just a campus level, realizing that discriminatory clauses for the most part will have to be removed through the national structures of fraternal organizations.

In general, it foresaw the futility of a time limit—especially a short-range time limit. Coming down to a campus level, the question arises as to whether or not ASUC commission will spawn the same foresight in handling the same problem.

The NSA congress approach, although somewhat weak, should be adopted for its merits as a constructive, sound, and sane basis for executing policy. An evolutionary method, it calls for the establishment of a joint student-faculty-administration board on each campus to meet regularly and hear progress reports by representatives from each social organization having discriminatory clauses in its charter or constitution.

Whether or not organizations would be permitted to continue under University charter would depend not only on actual progress toward removal of the clauses on a national level, but also on sincere attempts at progress. Only if the board decided the organization had ceased to strive for equal membership opportunities would the University be obligated to withdraw the group's charter.

Let's hope ASUC foresees the futility of the time-limit proposal and chooses the constructive course for coping with discrimination. des

"And remember that the first objective of totalitarianism is the destruction of the right to choose one's associates."

The Pan-Hellenic Conference and NSA

Editor's note: Fraternities and sororities, through their national organizations and conferences, fought vigorously against efforts on various campuses to eliminate discriminatory practices, which they saw as a violation of private rights of association. Following is a "Letter to Pan-Hellenic Councils" circulated to sororities from the National Pan-Hellenic Council in 1950-51, now in the NSA archives at the State Historical Society of Wisconsin. It attempts to discredit the organization in a manner described by Alfred McClung Lee in Fraternities Without Brotherhood *(Boston: The Beacon Press, 1955); see excerpts in Section 4, Part 4. He writes on page 4, "For a while certain fraternity leaders experimented with a 'red scare' technique to counteract widespread opposition to self-segregative practices. . . in general, responsible leaders, whether committed to discrimination or not, have not stooped to such propagandistic name-calling."*

Letter to Pan-Hellenic Councils

National Pan-Hellenic Council, 1950-51

The NSA has announced a "double-edged program" on so-called discrimination by publishing what colleges have done about it and by a nation wide survey on the matter. The coercive spirit of this attempt at a mass youth group recalls the role of mass youth groups in the development of totalitarian systems in Europe. Consequently it is important to know something about NSA.

It is the result of American delegates sent by various groups to the World Student Congress in Prague in 1946. At that meeting the International Union of Students was formed which is communist controlled according to the NSA News. This inspired some of the American delegates to form a national student movement in our country. This was accomplished in 1947 and the official name is United States National Student Association, abbreviated to NSA. Among its purposes are:

1. To speak for the American student locally, nationally and internationally.
2. Complete integration with campus government organizations and considerable regimentation.
3. Rating faculty members, evaluation of curriculum, and concern with administrative phases.
4. Rights of student to participate in "local, national and international organizations for intellectual, religious, social, political, economic or cultural purposes and to publish and distribute their views."

In spite of this emphasis on rights NSA denies the right to groups to choose their friends. Their most publicized purpose is to end any discrimination in the choice of friends. Also, its confused idea of rights is illustrated in its condemnation of the loyalty oaths required in Naval Reserve training at Harvard and the University of North Carolina. Its blatant spirit is shown in talks by officers on such themes as "Challenging Questions Which Have Been Thrust Upon Our Colleges and Universities by the Organizing Convention of the United States National Student Association."

At a Pennsylvania Assembly of NSA, 11 out of 12 faculty guests thought it over-organized, which was a polite form of evaluation. Three hundred and fifty-one colleges were represented at the 1947 meeting but about 300 were represented at its 1949 meeting. Some campuses have joined NSA with one fourth of the students voting. Probably not 2% of a faculty knows NSA thoroughly and probably not 10% of a student body knows what it is.

NSA will send a full delegation to the meeting of IUS in Europe this year to answer attacks of that communist controlled group; although it is already established that no one influences carefully indoctrinated communists.

It is important that members whose fathers or brothers are lawyers discuss with them "rights" as contained in the Bill of Rights in the Constitution of the United States and also discuss with father or brother lawyers the authority that resides in administrative authorities under charters of institutions.

Such discussions contribute to your maturity and understanding of your responsibilities as an educated citizen. It is not maturity to attempt on a campus, violations of personal rights. And remember that the first objective of totalitarianism is the destruction of the right to choose one's associates.

A Dean of Women Responds to an Inquiry

Editor's note: Following is an excerpt from an April 20, 1958, letter by Hugh Ellis, a University of Wyoming student member of Sigma Nu Fraternity, and a reporter for the student newspaper, addressed to Christine Y. Conaway, dean of women at Ohio State University, and an excerpt from her April 25, 1958, reply.

Dear Miss Conaway:

A statement attributed to you appeared in a brochure published by the National Students Association. Your highly complimentary statement coupled with the fact that you are president of the National Conference of Fraternities and Sororities is an inconsistency to this whole NSA issue as we understand it. If you could set us straight on this, we would greatly appreciate it.

The Student Senate of the Associated Students of the University of Wyoming recently appropriated $300 to send a student observer to the national convention of NSA at Ohio Wesleyan this summer. The vote, however, was only 9-7 with eight senators abstaining. Most of the opposing votes and abstentions were registered by senators who are fraternity men or sorority women. They were swayed, in my opinion, by remarks made to the committee-of-the-whole by a woman who identified herself as

Hugh Ellis
University of Wyoming
Branding Iron reporter

Faith Luther, traveling secretary for Alpha Chi Omega—one of the sororities represented on the Wyoming campus. Miss Luther cited what she termed the "official view" of the National Panhellenic Council. She said that National Panhell opposes NSA because NSA "recommends the complete elimination of discriminatory clauses from the constitutions of fraternal organizations."

Tom Dawson, a senator from Wyoming's college of arts and sciences and also the campus's most outspoken advocate of NSA, rebutted Miss Luther by reading from an NSA committee report which was in direct contrast to what Miss Luther had said. Dawson also read the official recommendations of the National Interfraternity Conference which whole-heartedly endorses NSA. Still, Wyoming fraternity men are undecided about NSA, probably because NIC is not so militant in forcing its views on member fraternities and chapters as is National Panhell. So, to clear up a few matters of local importance, we would like to draw upon your experience. . . .

Yours very truly

Hugh Ellis
Branding Iron Senate Reporter

"[NSA] has stimulated considerable interest among the students for a more worthwhile program of student government."

Dear Mr. Ellis:

We have been a member of NSA for some time and we feel that it has stimulated considerable interest among the students for a more worthwhile program of student government. It has taken it away from the emphasis on some of the immediate "activities" areas and put it in the broader university emphasis. For example, a committee on human relations was formed some two years ago to follow through on the report from the USNSA Congress the summer before on human relations. In this NSA report, called the Model Educational Practices Standards, the different areas of the university community had been studied with regard to discrimination. For an entire year, a group of faculty and students studied the NSA report and tried to relate it to our university. We didn't follow it precisely by areas but tried to develop it as it fit our campus. The enclosed report is the outgrowth of this local committee. Our Student Senate has established committees comparable to the areas of NSA such as educational affairs, student affairs, etc., and has attempted to inspire interest among the student body in these areas.

National Panhellenic Council has not recognized NSA in any way. In fact, they have almost agitated against it. NSA has invited their representatives to the NSA Congress for several years now so that NPC could see them in action, but there does seem to have been a misunderstanding. As I have attended a number of NSA Congresses, I have noticed that a great many of the students are members of fraternities and sororities. To me, there is no conflict between the two. NSA has wanted individuals to be judged on their merit rather than as groups. They have not waged an all-out war on sororities and fraternities, in my estimation. The majority of the officers of NSA with whom I have worked have been members of fraternities and sororities. We have felt no pressure here at all as to a need to eliminate clauses but have been free to discuss the problems and work out a solution locally.

Christine Y. Conaway
Ohio State University
Dean of Women

Christine Y. Conaway
Ohio State University

Editor's note: On September 21, 1964, Stephen C. Schodde, then a doctoral student at Teachers College, Columbia University, wrote Elizabeth Dyer, chairman of the National Panhellenic [sic] *Conference, asking for information about the Council's "experiences with and feelings about NSA." On October 6, 1964, Ms. Dyer responded as follows:*

Dear Mr. Schodde:

Your letter of September 21 has come, asking for information about United States National Student Association.

National Panhellenic Conference, as far as I know, has no file on this organization and has taken no stand for or against it.

National Panhellenic Conference is a federation of National Women's Fraternities, each of which is autonomous. N.P.C. does not poll its members, in an effort to obtain information concerning private affairs of the member fraternities, or pass resolutions or rules, or suggest policies that infringe upon the basic rights and privileges of individual organizations within the Panhellenic Conference.

I am not familiar with articles which appear in other sorority magazines. N.P.C. has no material on the subject for distribution. We have no permanent office and, therefore, we do not accumulate material for distribution. Our officers change every two years.

I am sure you will be able to obtain all the information you need to complete your study.

Sincerely yours,
Elizabeth Dyer, Chairman

Editor's note: In his 1955 book on fraternities, Alfred McClung Lee writes on page 6, "... the National Panhellenic [sic] *Conference of thirty-two women's social fraternities, rarely refers to such matters [discrimination] in its official minutes. Very quietly—and, in all but one case, without written statements of policy—sororities segregate themselves even more effectively than fraternities do."*

PICTURE CREDITS: Hugh Ellis, 1959 Yearbook (U. of Wyoming American Heritage Center). Christine Conaway, 1959 (Ohio State U. Library).

Temple University News 10/11/46 (Excerpted)

Sorority Life Asset, Says Dean to Pan-Hel

Miss Osgood Presents Rushing, Eligibility Rules at Convocation

"Belonging to a sorority is a great addition to your college life and helps to round out your college experiences," Miss Margaret L. Osgood, assistant dean of students, said in the main address of the Pan-Hellenic Association convocation Monday afternoon in Thatcher Hall.

Speaking to about 100 Freshman women, Miss Osgood, who is also Pan-Hellenic adviser, enumerated the sorority rushing rules and the eligibility requirements for sorority membership. In addition to having completed 15 semester hours, undergraduate women must obtain a 2.0 rating, the equivalent of a "C" average, before they can be considered for a sorority, she said.

While emphasizing that it is not necessary to become a sorority member in order to be active in campus organizations, Miss Osgood pointed out that "Sorority membership and the friends you make will be of help later in life."

A voice for interracial justice

4. Robert Delahanty: In Defense of Rights

University of Louisville
Kentucky-Tennessee Regional Chair, 1948–49. NSA Executive Secretary, 1949 (Half Term)

Editor's note: Bob Delahanty was an early NSA leader in the Kentucky-Tennessee region who was a strong advocate for effective student government and a champion of student rights. Both as a student and in his legal career he was an outspoken voice for interracial justice as well as a moderate conciliator in the Louisville community. He was elected to be the first holder of the position of Executive Secretary of the Association.

Dolores Sheslo Delahanty, Bob's wife, provided these summaries of some of the cases Bob Delehanty handled as an attorney and a member of the Kentucky Civil Liberties Union before becoming a judge. Dolores Delahanty has been a civic leader in Jefferson County and is currently a county Commissioner. She was a Rockford College, IL, NSA delegate and 1949-50 Midwest director of NSA's human relations program. (See photos pp. 335, 590.)

Fraternity Rights

From NSA News *11/49*

The basis of the fraternity system in our colleges is the right of its members to select those students who they are to be most closely associated with throughout their college life.

However, this premise is violated by precedent or written restriction in the constitution or ritual of most of the fraternal organizations. This contradiction in one of the basic principles is of deep concern to all students.

Before condemning members of fraternities you must consider who set this precedent or wrote these clauses. Most fraternities were established some time ago and as a consequence reflect the thinking of that generation.

By observing my own fraternity at school and at two national conventions, I came to the not so astounding conclusion that it was not the students who were vehement in their opposition to the removal of discriminatory clauses but the alumni and national officers. This is not an exception to the rule, as I have found this is the case in most all fraternities with which I have contact.

There is a sincere effort on the part of many fraternity members to seek complete recognition and trust to follow their basic right to pledge students to their organization without restriction. The progress is evident in the large number of fraternal orders that have given them this trust and recognition in the past several years.

Let's make this a cooperative effort and give fraternities and their members all the aid that is possible in this all-important problem.

Open Housing Demonstrations, April 1967–March 1969

As a member of the KCLU legal panel, Bob was one of three attorneys who represented hundreds of demonstrators. The three were Neville Tucker, an African-American attorney who later became the first Black elected Police Court Judge. Neville appointed Bob as one of his Trial Commissioners in Police Court and this led to Bob's judicial career. Bob was the only one of the three who came out of the civil rights movement with a political career, although he was labeled as a "communist" or "commy sympathizer" during the McCarthy era, and some conservatives continued to do so during some of his judicial campaigns.

Not only did Bob represent the demonstrators pro bono, he lost his major client at the time, a Savings and Loan Association, because Bob personally joined in some of the demonstrations. His picture along with hundreds of others was published in the *Courier Journal* sitting in the intersection of 4th and Broadway. The President of the S and L saw the picture printed on the front page and immediately fired him. Needless to say this caused an economic hardship on us with five young children.

A complaint was filed in the US District Court alleging "the plaintiffs are subject to and threatened with prosecution for 'engaging in protest activities against racial discrimination in the sale and rental of housing' and have been arrested during a series of peaceful protest demonstrations."

The bottom line is that the open housing demonstrations finally resulted in a victory. A fair housing ordinance was passed by the City of Louisville, barring discrimination based on race.

Muldraugh Coffee House Case: November 1969

Muldraugh was a small rural community in the shadow of Fort Knox. A group of antiwar activists opened a coffee house frequented by the military from Ft. Knox. Three attorneys, Bob Delahanty, Stuart Lyons, and Bill Allison represented the Youth Development Corp. which ran the coffee house.

The sentiment of the populace of the community was expressed by the prosecuting attorney JR Watts, "Communistic people have got hold of the place and are agitating against the capitalistic system." According to the *New York Times,* "Some here say the 'Communists' have infiltrated the Fort Knox command. This belief stems from the decision of Maj. General James W. Sutherland Jr., the base commander, to follow as far as possible a 'hands off' policy toward the dissenters under recent Army guidelines designed to avoid embarrassing military confrontations in the courts with uniformed militants. Such incidents occurred earlier this year in Fort Jackson, S.C. Officers at Fort Jackson seemed delighted, however, that Muldraugh's civilians are fighting the coffee house. There has been 'some army cooperation' with local authorities, a base spokesman said, but Chief Ridenour (Muldraugh Chief of Police) maintains that it has been 'not enough.'"

At a grand jury hearing four of the coffee house defendants invoked the fifth amendment and were jailed without bond for contempt of court. The contempt was appealed to the Court of Appeals. The *New York Times* quoted Bob as saying, "At the hearing in Frankfort today, Mr. Delahanty argued that the county was 'using the grand jury for the suppression of dissent.' The only disturbance related to the coffee house, he (Delahanty) said, was in the middle of the night when vandals threw two fire bombs at it." The Court of Appeals declared that the bond for contempt was excessive and the defendants were released and a $500 bond was set. The coffee house remained open for a period of time during the height of the antiwar movement as a citadel for military personnel to "discuss" current social issues, peaceful persuasion, association with others, dissemination of literature and similarly constitutionally protected activity.

From *Cardinal* 9/48, U. of Louisville

BILL WELSH, former head of the National Student association, left, and Bob Delahanty, President of the University Student Council, lead a discussion on student government at the annual Leadership Camp. Bob is also president of the Kentucky Tennessee Region.

Leadership Camp Requests Student-Faculty Committee

Bob Delahanty, Bill Rummage Report; Bill Welsh, NSA President, Is Camp Guest

Robert Delahanty was Chief District Court Judge in Jefferson County, Kentucky.

ROBERT E. DELAHANTY
1923-1993

Early years. Born: April 4, 1923, Louisville, Kentucky. Graduated from DuPont Manual High School, June 1940.

Military and education. US Air Force, 1942–43. Disabled veteran, lost hearing in right ear. Bachelor of Civil Engineering (BCE), Speed Scientific School, University of Louisville, Louisville, KY, 1948. Juris Doctor, School of Law, George Washington University, Washington DC, 1954.

Student activities. President Theta Tau Engineering Fraternity, 1946. President University of Louisville Student Government, 1947-48. President KY/Tenn. Region NSA, 1948-49. Executive Secretary NSA, 1949. Director, Foreign Student Tour of USA, Summer of 1950, Cambridge, MA.

Career highlights. Defense Attorney, Civil Rights and Criminal Law, Member of the Lawyers Panel, ACLU Kentucky, 1952–1978. Judge Pro Tem, Louisville Police Court 1974–1978. Chief District Court Judge 1978–1980. Key architect of the implementation of the Unified State Court system in Jefferson County, Kentucky, 1978. Led effort to abolish Bail Bond System and the implementation of Pre-Release Program in Jefferson District Court, 1978. Retired from the Judiciary in 1988.

Family. Parents: Elizabeth Harrison Delahanty, Richard J. Delahanty. Youngest of three children. Married to Dolores Sheslo Delahanty, June 1950. Five children: Judge Sean Delahanty, Judge Kevin Delahanty, Tim, Shannon, and Terence Delahanty.

PICTURE CREDITS. *Then:* 1949 (NSA Staff Photo,SHSW). *Now:* c. 1990 (Dolores Delahanty).

Jewish students focus on concentration camp survivors, Zionism, and civil rights

5. The Transformation of Washington University and the Arrival of Hillel

Leon A. Jick
Washington University, St. Louis
President, Washington University Hillel Foundation, 1946-47

Editor's note: While the national Protestant and Catholic student organizations were actively involved in the founding of NSA (see Part 4), as were various political and social action groups, the Jewish student community did not take part in NSA as an organized force. Their organization agenda, as described here by Leon Jick, was largely pursued outside NSA. However, NSA worked closely with the Jewish Anti-Defamation League, the National Conference of Christian and Jews, and the Youth Division of the NAACP on fraternity discrimination, admissions quotas, and racial discrimination issues, with which Jewish students were very much concerned. For the foregoing reasons, the story of Hillel is included in this section.

It is appropriate to note at the time of this writing that there were no U.S. national Muslim student groups active on the college scene after World War II of which NSA was aware. In the December, 1954, issue of the USNSA News *bulletin (successor to* NSA News*), NSA announced "Arabs Plan Campus Talks," a speaker service inaugurated in 1952. "The organizaiton of Arab students in the USA is one of seven foreign student groups in the United States with which USNSA cooperates in programs designed to further mutual understanding among students."*

In spring 1941, as graduation from Soldan High School approached, the principal, H. P. Stellwagen, nominated two students for scholarship to Ivy League Colleges—William Landau to Harvard and me to Yale. We were both rejected because, we were informed, no Jews were accepted. A third student, Bruce Dunbar, who was not "tainted," was accepted to Columbia University. As a result, I stayed home and entered Washington University. I was "rushed" by the Kappa Alpha fraternity until they discovered my religious background, after which they were not heard from again.[1] There were three Jewish fraternities on campus, at least one of which expressed an interest in me, which I did not reciprocate.

At that time, Washington University was a provincial, primarily commuter institution located on the city limits trolley line in the outskirts of St. Louis. If any political activity stirred the campus, it was not evident to me. The school, like all public and private educational institutions in the border city of St. Louis, did not admit "Negro" students. After Pearl Harbor, I do recall the arrival of a few Japanese American students displaced from the West Coast. Their presence did not elicit significant comment or response.[2]

In October 1942, I turned eighteen, and the following month, news confirming the mass murder of European Jewry was published. I enlisted in the Air Force, determined to participate in the war against Hitler. Ironically, as a result, I spent the war years in a series of technical schools, while my friends who waited to be drafted ended up in the infantry in Europe. The war ended when I was about to embark for the invasion of Japan.

It is unlikely that the news of my imminent arrival contributed to the Japanese decision to surrender.

Veterans return to the campus

In the spring of 1946 I returned to a changed university in a changed America. In April 1945, Arthur Holly Compton, a distinguished scientist and Nobel Laureate from the University of Chicago, had become chancellor.[3] He represented the escalation of image and aspiration of the university. The campus was overrun with returning veterans taking advantage of the G.I. Bill of Rights.[4] The student newspaper described:

> an awakening campus. . . . time was that a study-minded student could wander into Ridgley Library . . . and find himself surrounded by vast empty space . . . But times have changed! During a typical Monday, Tuesday, or any other weekday hour ye olde library is as popular a hangout as the Q-X itself. Can it be that married veterans have orders from the home front to finish their lessons before leaving campus? Or have courses been made so difficult that college is no longer a place to loaf on father's money?[5]

Many of the veterans came from distant and disparate communities. By 1947, "twenty-one foreign countries and all but two states" were represented in the enrollment of students.[6] Some came from families which had been too poor to send them to college before the war. One classmate had worked for a number of years as a letter carrier. All were older, more experienced, more worldly, more serious than the students I had known previously. Many were filled with zeal for the prospect of building a better world, and the university fostered their enthusiasm. In November 1946, Chancellor Compton was appointed one of five U.S. delegates to the Paris Conference of the United Nations Educational, Scientific, and Cultural Organization (UNESCO). Compton stated "his conviction that the United Nations can be the means of preventing future wars."[7] Clearly, the campus was a forum for addressing the important issues of the day.

Founding of the American Veterans Committee

In October 1944, a group of veterans at the university had organized a Veterans Association, and in November 1945 the group became a post of the American Legion.[8] This affiliation did not satisfy many of the veterans who followed. In February 1946, a chapter of the American Veterans Committee was established.[9] The AVC was intended to be a "non-veterans' veterans' organization," that is to say, an organization devoted to a broad agenda of social reform, and not merely to narrowly defined veterans' issues. In the words of its acting chairman: "The days of the university as an ivory tower secluded from the world has ended. . . . Veterans must not only be good students. They must take an active progressive role in the community to insure lasting peace, full employment, decent adequate housing, and the good things in life for all. They must do this as a part of the community, not as a high powered pressure group engineering a grab for themselves."[10] I returned to the campus in February in time to become a founding member of the AVC chapter.[11] In April, Chancellor Compton agreed to become its faculty advisor.[12]

After a few heady months of activity, which included a controversial invasion of a rally by the racist Gerald L. K. Smith,[13] the AVC was rocked by controversy over communist infiltration, and the Washington University chapter withdrew from the St. Louis area council.[14]

Hillel chapter established

At the very same time, another organization established its presence on campus. Hillel, the national Jewish student organization sponsored by the B'nai B'rith Fraternal Order, had been established at the University of Illinois in 1923. Prior to the war, twenty foundations had been established, almost all at state universities, where the prevailing motivation was to establish "a home away from home." The postwar increase in student enrollment and the intensification of Jewish consciousness and assertiveness resulted in the rapid expansion of Hillel chapters on campuses across the country. By 1946, twenty new chapters had been established, one of which was on the campus of Washington University.

On November 14, 1946, the newly established Hillel Foundation held its first organizational meeting.[15] A dynamic young rabbi, Robert P. Jacobs, had arrived on campus and inaugurated Hillel as "a self-governing body to provide for religious, cultural, social, community welfare, inter-faith and personal counseling needs" for Jewish students. I was elected president by a steering committee of student representatives.[16] The first responsibility involved the distinctly unintellectual task of cleaning and decorating the house near the campus that had been purchased for Hillel. As a result of diligent and devoted student input and output, the house was ready for use on February 1, 1947.[17]

Prior to the opening of the house, a crowd of 650 students turned out for an inaugural meeting held at a nearby temple. Committee chairs presented reports, and a newspaper, *Hilltop Hillel,* made its first appearance.[18] The Jewish presence on campus was not only increased, it was energized. Hillel soon became a beehive of religious, cultural, and social activity. Interfaith contacts with other campus religious organizations were inaugurated. Lecturers and cultural events were brought to the campus. While the primary focus of Hillel was religious and social, it also served as a locus for political action, especially on the question of the survivors of the concentration camps who remained in displaced-persons camps in Europe, the issue of Zionism, and the problem of civil rights.

Hillel rallies for displaced persons and a Jewish national homeland

In 1946, the joint Anglo-American Commission of Enquiry Regarding Problems of European Jewry and Palestine issued its report unanimously recommending the admission of 100,000 displaced persons to Palestine. President Harry Truman accepted the report, but British Foreign Secretary Ernest Bevin rejected it. On Friday, February 28, 1947, the Zionist Committee of Hillel sponsored an all-campus rally, at which the speaker was Aharon Engel, a member of Haganah, "the Jewish underground resistance group." In accordance with the terminology of those days, Engel was described as "a Palestinian." Two faculty members spoke, and *Student Life* quoted me as saying that "we as informed American youth must demand a firm stand on policy which all American presidents since Woodrow Wilson have maintained: a Jewish national homeland in Palestine." Regarding Bevin's rejection of Truman's proposal, I was further quoted as saying: "we must not allow American policy to become a tail to the British kite." In conjunction with the rally, the "Hillel Zionist committee conducted a campaign in the quadrangle to urge students to inform their senators and representatives by postcard and telegram of their support of the Zionist issues."[19] This activity marked a breakthrough in the willingness of Jewish students to present a Jewish issue to the campus community.

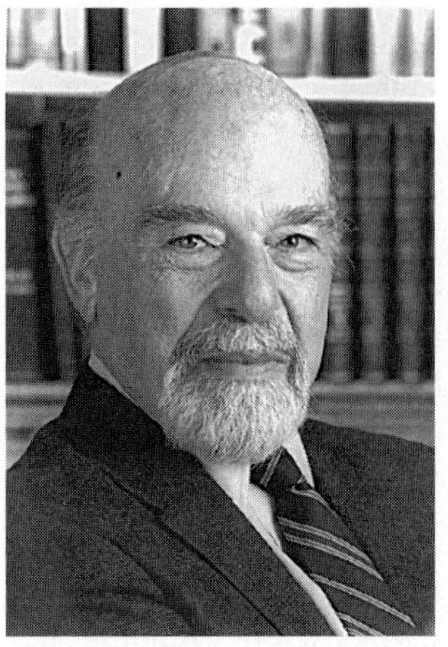

Leon Jick is Professor Emeritus at Brandeis University, where he serced for twenty-five years as Professor of American Jewish Studies and for six years as Chairman of the Department of Near Eastern and Judaic Studies. A widely traveled lecturer, from 1945 to 1966 he served as a Rabbi with congregations in Boston and Mount Vernon, NY.

Hillel also joins in interracial efforts and opposition to segregation

The question of Palestine and the resettlement of Jewish refugees was not the only issue which engaged the attention and enlisted the support of Hillel and its members. Washington University was still an all-white institution, and agitation for breaking the racial barrier was growing. In spring 1946, nine campus organizations had approved a resolution favoring the admission of "Negroes." Petitions were circulated to "consolidate opinion on campus."[20] Thereafter, an Interracial Committee was formed to continue pressure on the issue.[21] Hillel members, myself among them, were among the leaders of this endeavor. The committee sponsored numerous forums and met with Chancellor Compton to urge his support. At that time, the issue of desegregation was still so controversial that the infant National Student Organization (not yet "NSA") was unable to pass a resolution opposing segregation.[22] However, Compton was sympathetic, and it was clear that a change was in the works. In 1947, "Negro" graduate students were admitted to the School of Social Work, and in 1949 they were admitted to "graduate schools of all divisions."[23]

After graduation

After graduating in 1947, I went to live on a kibbutz in the newly established state of Israel, spending a few months en route working in a displaced-persons camp near Marseilles, France, on the way. Returning to the United States in 1950, I entered Rabbinical school and, after ordination, spent twelve years as a congregational rabbi. The influence of Rabbi Robert Jacob and my experience in Hillel were crucial to leading me to this career. During these years, I was actively engaged in the civil rights struggle and even spent a night in jail in St. Augustine, Florida, while demonstrating in support

Rabbi Jacobs Opens First Hillel Meeting

The newly established Hillel Foundation at Washington University, which is sponsored by B'nai B'rith, the international Jewish fraternal order, held its first organizational meeting last night at United Hebrew Temple. Rabbi Robert P. Jacobs, director of the foundation, opened the meeting which was held to acquaint the students with the program and work of the all-student off-campus organization. The election of the group's officers also took place.

Rabbi Jacobs came to St. Louis at the suggestion of Dr. Abram L. Sachar, a graduate of Washington University in 1920, who is national director of the B'nai B'rith Hillel Foundation. Chancellor Arthur H. Compton soon after extended a welcome to Hillel and with the fullest permission to function within the provisions of the charter of the University, the Hillel Foundation began its organizational work. This unit is one of 150 now established at campuses throughout this country, Canada, and Cuba.

OFF-CAMPUS GROUP

Rabbi Jacobs, in acknowledging the greetings of the administration of the University, declared in part, "Hillel is the result of student experience at campuses where Jewish students need a self-governing body to provide for religious, cultural, social, community-welfare, inter-faith, and personal counselling needs. Since the charter of the University pro-

Rabbi Robert P. Jacobs, who recently arrived in St. Louis as the director of the newly-established Hillel Foundation.

STUDENT LIFE

VOLUME 71 WASHINGTON UNIVERSITY, ST. LOUIS, THURSDAY, NOVEMBER 14, 1946 NUMBER 7

650 Turn Out Sunday For Hillel Gathering

Approximately 650 people turned out for the first social meeting of Hillel, Jewish students' organization sponsored by B'nai Brith, at Temple Israel Sunday evening. The chairman of the program committee, Alvin Mellman, presided over the meeting. Leon Jick, president of the organization, gave a welcome speech, and each ofthe committee chairmen gave short reports on what had been accomplished and what was hoped would be accomplished in the future.

"Hilltop Hillel", the organization's newspaper, made its first appearance last week.

In addition to Jick, Hillel officers are Eugene Sacks, vice-pres.; Sid Hurwitz, treas.; Don Kramer, head of the House Committee; Charles Hartmann, Constitution Committee chairman; Sonia Bushkin, Social Committee chairman, and Betty Kerman, editor of publications.

Jick Chosen Hillel Head

Leon Jick, senior in the college of Liberal Arts, was elected president of Hillel, Jewish students' organization, at the last meeting.

A steering committee composed of all chapter officers and committee chairmen has been formed and has begun operations The purpose of the steering committee is to coordinate the activities of the organization.

THE LATEST OF 150 HILLEL CHAPTERS, the international Jewish fraternal order, is launched in 1947 at Washington University in St. Louis. Leon Jick is its first President. National Hillel had an observer at the Chicago Student Conference in 1946. From left, *Student Life* 11/14/46, 1/16/47, 1/23/47 of Martin Luther King, Jr.'s campaign to integrate public facilities there.

Eventually, I returned to the university campus as a member of the faculty of Brandeis University where, in the late 1960's, I encountered another period of student activism. But that is a tale for another time.

END NOTES

[1] *Editor's note:* See Alfred McClung Lee, "Fraternities without Brotherhood," p. 745.

[2] *Editor's note:* See Suzuki, p. 1031, Wurf, p. 179, and Miller, p. 720, on Japanese-American students during and after World War II.

[3] *Student Life,* April 19, 1945. *Editor's note: Student Life,* the student newspaper, was "published Weekly under the direction of the Faculty Committee on Student Publications" and produced by a Board of student editors.

[4] See "The Veterans," Part 4, Section 1.

[5] *Student Life,* April 4, 1946, p. 2.

[6] Ibid., February 14, 1947. [7] Ibid., November 16, 1946.

[8] Ibid., October 13, 1944, November 1, 1945.

[9] Ibid., February 28, 1946. [10] Ibid.

[11] See Bellush, "American Veterans Committee," p. 708.

[12] *Student Life,* April 4, 1946. [13] *Ibid.*

[14] Ibid., January 22, 1947. [15] Ibid., November 14, 1946.

[16] Ibid., December 19, 1946. [17] Ibid.

[18] Ibid., January 16, 1947. [19] Ibid., February 27, 1947.

[20] Ibid., May 9, 1946. [21] Ibid., January 9, 1947.

[22] *Ibid. Editor's note:* In a particularly vivid report by-lined by Bill Toulouse, he describes the effort to adopt a statement of policy on discrimination at the December 1946 Chicago Student Conference (see also Berlin, p. 89 on the same event). Toulouse writes on page 1 of *Student Life*:

> Verbal fireworks flared brightly when racial questions worked their way into the final session of the national student conference at the University of Chicago, Dec. 30. For three and one-half hours eloquent, keen-minded students, both Negro and white, blasted all sides of adopted "equal rights" resolutions.
>
> The fiery debate was centered around section 15 of a resolution made the night before by one of four panel groups. It stated that the proposed National Student Organization should fight for the repeal of any state legislation prohibiting interracial meetings and all other state legislation interfering with the equal rights of students.
>
> When the meeting had been called to order earlier in the afternoon, the only business left on the agenda from two previous days was the election of national officers. However, before election proceedings could be inaugurated four delegates were on their feet asking recognition from the chair. Recognition of the first representative was like touching a match to a long, fast-burning fuse. The racial question immediately took the floor and threatened to blow the convention wide open.
>
> Three unsuccessful attempts were made by the chairman to table the controversial issue until the spring convention, but a strong bloc formed by six southern states refused to let the issue ride.
>
> "As much an we desire to see NSO formed," a Georgia spokesman said, "our delegation cannot go back to the south following this meeting and say we are going to fight state legislation. . . . we would be laughed off the campus. I move that section 15 be stricken out. . . . if it isn't, the southern states will not be permitted to return to the constitutional convention this spring."
>
> In rapid-fire order students jumped to their feet to argue for or against the measure, sometimes shouting loudly, sometimes arguing irrelevant points and all angles of the race problem. Even the convention chairman was attacked by one delegate for being out of order in his remarks.
>
> A vote by the 371 delegates present on one compromise proposal indicated an almost perfect split in opinion.
>
> After remaining in session for a heated hour and forty-five minutes past scheduled adjournment, the necessary majority favored removal of Section 15 from the resolution—and the delegation got down to the election of officers, "the only business on the agenda."

NSA at its Constitutional Convention in September 1947 pledged "to secure and maintain equal rights" by "securing the eventual elimination of all forms of discriminatory educational systems anywhere in the United States, since the United States National Student Association is opposed in principal to such systems." (See NSA Constitution, By-Laws 1 and 2, p. 1110, and Statement of Southern Delegates, p. 1113. See also Clif Wharton, p. 114, and Janet Brown, p. 377.

[23] *Student Life,* December 12, 1947; March 22, 1949.

PICTURE CREDITS: *Then:* 1943. Home on furlough in Forest Park, St. Louis *Now:* 1998 (*Courtesy author*).

LEON A. JICK

Education: A native of St. Louis, Professor Jick is a graduate of Washington University and holds Bachelor's and Master's degrees from Hebrew Union College in Cincinnati and a Ph.D. in American and Jewish History from Columbia University.

Military and Postwar Service: During World War II Professor Jick served for three years in the Army Air Force. Following the war, he worked in a displaced persons camp near Marseilles, France. Arriving in Israel in 1948 shortly after the establishment of the state, he participated in the establishment of Kibbutz Gesher Haziv in Western Galilee. Later, he taught at the Bet Berl Institute in Kfar Saba.

Career Highlights: Leon A. Jick is Professor Emeritus at Brandeis University, where he served for twenty-five years as the Helen and Irving Schneider Professor of American Jewish Studies and for six years as Chairman of the Department of Near Eastern and Judaic Studies. During this time he also served for three years as Dean of the College of Arts and Sciences and Associate Dean of Faculty. He has been a visiting professor at the Hebrew University in Jerusalem and at the University of Wisconsin in Madison, Wisconsin, and is a regular participant in the seminars on "Facing History and Ourselves."

In 1969, he organized the Colloquium of University Professors of Judaica, which led to the founding of the Association for Jewish Studies, the organization of professors of Judaica in American universities. He also served for two years as the first president of the Association.

From 1954 to 1957 he was Assistant Rabbi at Temple Israel, Boston, and then served, until 1966, as Rabbi of the Free Synagogue of Westchester in Mt. Vernon, New York. During these years Professor Jick was active in a multitude of communal endeavors. He was also active in the civil rights movement and has been involved in a variety of causes devoted to peace and social justice.

He has served as consultant to the U.S. Holocaust Memorial Council. He has served on numerous boards and commissions, including as a member of the Board of Trustees of the Boston Hebrew College, the Commission on Education of the Council of Federations and Welfare Funds, the Board of Trustees and the Academic Advisory Council of the American Jewish Historical Society, the World Union for Progressive Judiaism, and the Association of Reform Zionists of America (ARZA). He is co-chair of the Reform Zionist Think Tank of ARZA.

A widely traveled lecturer, Professor Jick has written extensively on Judaism and Jewish history.

Family: He and his wife are the parents of four sons and grandparents of six grandchildren. They live in Chestnut Hill, Massachusetts.

Programs to eliminate discrimination were often coordinated with the American Council on Education as well as the National Conference of Christians and Jews and the B'ni B'rith Anti-Defamation League

Human Relations in Higher Education

Editors note: In the late 1940s and 1950s NSA adopted the strategy prevailing in the higher education community that dealt with discriminatory practices in admissions, student organization, financial support, and facilities through targeted educational efforts on the campus, regional, and national levels to achieve change. These programs were developed collaboratively by the major higher education professional organizations as well as religious, civic, and student organizations concerned with the issue.

The American Council on Education (ACE) provided leadership and coordination in the organization of periodic events that brought together the interested parties to furnish resources and impetus to their antidiscrimination and human relations programs.

NSA worked closely with the ACE (becoming its only national student organization member), broadening outreach in the student government community.

On March 29-31, 1951, the ACE sponsored a National Student Conference on Human Relations in Higher Education (of which NSA was one of several cosponsors) which included 231 students representing 95 colleges in 27 states. Excerpted here are portions of the report that reflect how the problems of discrimination were being addressed through human relations programs, an approach embraced by NSA.

Excerpts from
HUMAN RELATIONS IN HIGHER EDUCATION

A Report of a National Student Conference Held at Earlham College, March 29-31, 1951
Edited by Francis J. Brown and Richard B. Anliot
American Council on Education Studies (1951)

PREFACE

THE NATIONAL STUDENT CONFERENCE on Human Relations, reported in this publication, differed from the earlier conference of administrative officers of colleges and universities (see *Discriminations in College Admissions,* report of a conference held November 4-5, 1949) in that it included problems of campus life. The 231 students in attendance, representing 95 colleges and universities in 27 states, sought to come to grips with the day-to-day problems involved in the complex pattern of human relations on the campus. The recommendations approved by the conference as a whole or by the sections may not be equally acceptable in all institutions of higher education, but they indicate a striving for means through which democracy may be a living reality for college students.

It is hoped that these recommendations may be the basis for discussion among college groups, students, faculty, and administrations, in order that they may have value far beyond the experience of those who participated in drafting them.

ARTHUR S. ADAMS
July 31, 1951

BACKGROUND AND ORGANIZATION OF THE CONFERENCE

IN 1948 THE AMERICAN COUNCIL ON EDUCATION conducted an extensive study on discriminations in college admissions under the direction of its Committee on Discriminations in Higher Education. In order to disseminate the results of this research and to consider its implications for colleges and universities, the Committee on Discriminations sponsored, with the Anti-Defamation League of B'nai B'rith cooperating, a national conference of educators on discriminations in college admissions.

One of the recommendations of the earlier conference was that a series of regional conferences be arranged. Therefore, the committee has cosponsored, with regional committees of educators, regional conferences on this same problem. The first was of 85 educators and students from 28 institutions in Virginia, Maryland, Delaware, and the District of Columbia. The Midwest Educators Conference on Discrimination in Higher Education was a meeting of 198 educators from 75 institutions in Indiana, Michigan, Illinois, and Wisconsin. The Mountain States Regional Conference on Discriminations in Higher Education was attended by 80 administrators, faculty members, and students of 14 colleges and universities in Colorado, New Mexico, Utah, and Wyoming.

The committee also sponsored the National Student Conference on Human Relations in Higher Education, of which this is the report. The conference was convened by the committee with the cooperation of the Anti-Defamation League of B'nai B'rith, National Association for the Advancement of Colored People, National Federation of Catholic College Students, Newman Club Federation, United States National Student Association, Young Men's Christian Association (Student Division), and Young Women's Christian Association (Student Division).

Invitations were sent to the presidents of all accredited colleges and universities. The institutions which indicated an interest in being represented were sent registration material. Total attendance at the conference was 265, including resource persons and staff members. There were 231 students representing 95 colleges and universities in 27 states, widely distributed geographically. The student delegates participated in the conference as authorized representatives of their institutions. Each institution was represented by a number of voting delegates in proportion to its enrollment.

The purpose of this conference of students was to discuss how to encourage and promote the equalization and expansion of opportunties for all persons to share in the experience of higher education without any restriction beyond that of individual capacity.

The conference made possible, without any restriction, a thorough consideration not only of policies toward which the student representatives believed institutions should strive, but also of ways by which campus groups might effectively work for their implementation. It also provided an opportunity for an informed discussion of areas of campus life other than admissions in which discriminations sometimes occur, namely, student organizations, economic aid to students, housing and eating facilities, athletics, recreation and health, teacher employment, and curricula.

The delegates expressed the hope that the conference recommendations would be translated into functioning policies on campuses. They also hoped that the recommendations might prove useful to campus, state, regional, or national meetings of educators and students as possible agenda for discussion and for further implementation as is deemed advisable.

RECOMMENDATIONS OF THE CONFERENCE
Student Organizations

Social, honorary, and professional fraternities and sororities; other student organizations

1. Preamble

The problems of discrimination and prejudice in student organizations are not isolated problems, but are aspects of the broader problems of interpersonal and intergroup relations. Any student organization creates poor human relations when: (a) It contributes to tension and antagonism between itself and other student organizations through its development of exclusiveness; (b) It places such high value on prestige and status that it emphasizes inequality rather than equality between men, resulting in disharmony and tensions in interpersonal relations; (c) Its values become distorted to the extent that it places a high premium on the symbols of power and prestige, such as high economic status, class, race, or appearance, and thereby loses sight of the essential human values involved in respect for individual worth and dignity; (d) Its members become so devoted to the aims and ideals of the organization that they lose sight of and become detached from the functions and aims of the educational institution.

The following principles are essential in developing good human relations in student organizations:

a) The purposes and aims of any student group should be consistent with and in keeping with the philosophy, aims, and functions of higher education in our democratic society.
b) A student organization should offer its members a democratic and permissive atmosphere in which they can develop their own unique personalities by expressing themselves creatively and through mutual association with others in the group.
c) A student organization should foster good interpersonal relations, based on respect, understanding, and trust, within the group and between its members and other persons outside the group.
d) A student organization should strive to develop unity and a well feeling among its members, but it should not become exclusive and divisive in human affairs; rather, it should emphasize those qualities, goals, and aspirations common to all humanity; it should seek to create cooperation with groups and individuals rather than antagonism and aloofness; it should strive to be inclusive rather than exclusive.

2. Restrictive Clauses

This conference opposes membership clauses that restrict membership on the basis of race, color, religion, or national origin in student organizations in institutions of higher education. This shall not prevent church-related groups from requiring their members to accept certain religious tenets.

The conference recommends that the bodies having authority to recognize student organizations on the several campuses adopt the policy of setting a definite terminal date of not later than October 1956, by which student organizations which restrict membership on the basis of race, religion, or national origin should remove such restrictive membership clauses. On their failure to do so, official campus recognition should be withdrawn, unless it is shown that the organization is trying to get rid of its discriminating clauses, in which case the organization should be granted one year's extension of recognition by the student council. We commend the following colleges and universities for adopting a similar policy: Arizona State College, University of Washington, Syracuse University, Rutgers University, Brooklyn College, University of Connecticut, Columbia University, Harvard University, University of Houston, New York University, University of Toledo, Middlebury College, University of Minnesota, University of Chicago, University of Michigan, Michigan State College, and others.

3. Gentlemen's Agreements

This conference urges all student organizations in institutions of higher education to eliminate tacit or gentlemen's agreements restricting membership in these organizations.

4. Encouraging Groups Working against Discrimination

This conference recommends that administrations and student governments in institutions of higher education encourage democratic groups working for the betterment of human relations and for the removal of discriminatory practices.

REPORTS OF DISCUSSION GROUPS
Student Organizations

1. Restrictive Clauses

We recommend that on each campus the student council and/or the administration establish, if needed, a committee on human relations which would have the following responsibilities:

a) To implement the recommendations of this conference.
b) To develop a program of education concerning discriminations in human relations for student leaders, freshmen, and other key groups. Such a program might use such educational media as: (1) movies, (2) lectures, (3) reading lists, (4) student newspapers and bulletin boards, and (5) informal intergroup association in athletics, recreation, co-ops, work projects, and discussions.
c) To keep the campus aware of problems of human relations in the community.
d) To propose appropriate legislation to the group empowered to take such action in this area of student life.
e) To continue the educational program after the legislation has been passed.

2. Gentlemen's Agreements

a) The members of this conference are urged to work individually within their own groups to encourage membership policies which are based on individual merit rather than race, color, religion, creed, or national origin.
b) Groups are urged to establish committees to appraise their own membership practices in the light of democratic principles.
c) Groups are urged to provide intercultural experience for their members, such as financially supporting foreign students, and having exchange dinners and cooperative work projects with minority group members.

3. Encouraging Groups Working against Discrimination

a) Groups working against discrimination are urged to work cooperatively with college administrations, especially in the initial stages of their programs. Groups should give careful thought to the procedure and consequences of their work, winning new friends to the project rather than creating unnecessary antagonism.
b) Groups are urged to participate in intercultural programs with community groups, such as the YMCA, YWCA, and NAACP.
c) Questions on the objectivity of the teacher in developing human relations might be incorporated in student evaluations of faculty members, since faculty members need to be educated, too, concerning good human relations.
d) Such groups are urged to obtain strong faculty advisers.

Human Relations Programs Attack Discrimination

NSA News 12/49

Educators Survey Bias in Enrollment

The Chicago Conference of Educators on "Discrimination in College Admissions" marked a turning point in the history of higher education, according to Dr. Andrew C. Ivy, vice-president in charge of professional schools of the University of Illinois.

The Chicago Conference under the sponsorship of the American Council on Education held on Nov. 4 and 5 was the first national attempt of college and university officials to examine and to eventually eliminate discrimination on any grounds other than ability and moral character.

• • •

ONE HUNDRED LEADING educators attended the conference. The four workng areas of the conference dealt with the specific areas of admission procedures in undergraduate schools, admission procedures in graduate and professional schools, regional problems, and economic problems affecting discrimination.

For the first time in American education, programs for the institution of correctibe measures in educational policies in regard to discrimination were planned out by a national conference of educators. Plans for further conferences of this type for other educational groups were planned. In these meetings, the "how" of curbing discrimination will be more thoroughly discussed and program developed to take immediate and long range action steps.

Ten overall questions on the overall problems of barriers to higher education were raised by Prof. Floyd W. Reeves, University of Chicago, chairman of the council's committee on discriminations in college admissions.

• • •

THEY INCLUDED restricted curricula and inadequate educational facilities, limited financial resources of applicants, geographic barriers, difference among youth in their desire for higher education, the extent to which college admission techniques lend themselves to discriminatory practices, applicant's sex, race, religion, and national origin, and "the relationship between the types of control of higher institutions and the (admission) policies and practices of such institutions."

NSA News 10/49

Need Human Relations Group Seen

A definite need exists for a national Human Relations Institute for the college campus level.

That is the opinion of Richar J. Medalie, NSA vice-president for educational problems.

• • •

"THE INSTITUTE would be a catalyst for projects of other organizations to improve relations between persons of difference, racial religious and ethnic backgrounds," he commented.

Typical Institute projects would include:

1. Community educational programs in the promotion of the UN Declaration on Human Rights.

2. Campus inter-group co-operatives and living houses.

3. Surveys on campus or community human relations attitudes and levels of prejudice.

4. Re-orientation of appropriate curricula for the promotion of better inter-group understanding and the inclusion of human relations in college courses.

5. Establishing openings on faculty and in student groups for minority group members not presently represented or admitted.

6. Solving specific instances of community or campus discrimination or inter-racial, inter-faith tension.

7. Educational program conducted by and for fraternities and sororities on campuses.

8. Establishing speaker bureaus and information centers on human relations problems.

9. Sponsorship of intercollegiate and campus human relations conference, programs and get-togethers.

A PROGRAM

HUMAN RELATIONS & EDUCATIONAL PRACTI[CES]

TABLE OF CONTENTS

****

UNITED STATES NATIONAL STUDENT ASSOCIATION

Left: NSA 12/48 Program Guide. Right: "Human Relations," published Spring 1950 (Medalie)

Carleton Heads NSA Human Relations Work

CARLETON has been designated as the western area headquarters of the NSA Educational Practices and Human Relations subcommission.

The encouragement of colleges to set up committees similar to the campus bureau of the Carleton Civil Rights committee is the purpose of the headquarters. Stimulation of campus discussions of the civil rights issue and letter writing campaigns to influence legislation will be tried.

Work on elimination of segregation and discrimination in social life, athletics and living groups will be undertaken from both the student and administrative angle by suggesting constructive programs to meet such problems.

Co-chairmen of the subcommission are Rick Medalie and Marlin Smith. John Rosenheim is executive secretary and Roger Knapp, corresponding secretary. The western area includes Colorado, Iowa, Kansas, Minnesota, Missouri, Nebraska, North Dakota, South Dakota and Wyoming.

Carleton C, MN *Carletonian* 2/5/49

Human Relations, DP's, Festival, Set Up As NSA Projects

A Human Relations Institute that will bring together prominent speakers to discuss the economic, geographic, legislative, and racial barriers to improved human relations in our country is to be held at Boston University. The conference, to be held on March 12 and 13, was announced at the NSA Regional Assembly held at the University of Massachusetts over the week-end.

Among the personalities who have already consented to attend are Dr. Conant of Harvard University, Dr. Taylor of Sarah Lawrence College, and Ted Harris, president of the USNSA. The Institute is being cosponsored by the NSA and the National Conference of Christians and Jews.

Plans for a Boston Area festival, as yet incomplete, call for choral singing, plays, and an art exhibit to be held at Regis and Emerson Colleges April 22 and 23, and a concluding barn dance April 23.

MIT, MA *The Tech* 2/49

The Wayne University Committees

NATIONAL STUDENT ASSOCIATION And INTERCULTURAL RELATIONS

UNIVERSITY

CLINIC ON HUMAN RELATIONS

Detroit, Michigan

May

". . . to guarantee to all people . . equal rights . . . for primary, secondary and higher education re[gardless of] race, religion, political belief or economic circums[tances]

Workshop program, Wayne University 4/29-5/1/49

Working within the framework of the group dynamics technique, particularly from the question of discrimination against Negro students, the Clinic participants will formulate their concepts in this area of human relations through panel and general meetings. In the early stages of the Clinic the activity will be conducted in the panel sessions. Each panel will be constructed around an area in which discrimination has occurred — e.g., restaurants social activities, admissions to colleges or universities. The various areas of discrimination will be presented by an actual case or cases of discrimination against Negro students in campus communities throughout Michigan, Illinois, Indiana, Ohio and Wisconsin.

FROM PANEL TO PLENARY

The conclusions of the panels will be integrated into one report which will be presented to the entire membership. After this report has been delivered, administrative representatives from two schools, located in the region from which students are being invited will present their concept of the areas in "which students can act" to combat discrimination. Proceeding from this, the participants, through series of general meetings, will emerge with their goals for action and education in the field of human relations, using as frame of reference the purposes of the students in the panels, and the statements of administrative representatives.

AREAS FOR ACTION

HOW CAN STUDENTS ACTING IN AND THROUGH THE STUDENT COMMUNITY COMBAT DISCRIMINATION

NSA President .... *Ted Harris*
Chairman of Clinic .... *Eugene Schwartz, NSA Vice-Preident*
Panel Leaders .... *Students from campuses in Ohio, Indiana, Illinois, and Michigan*
Faculty Director .... *Dr. Lloyd C. Cook, Wayne University*

BASCOM BILL FEATURED:

Human-Relations Booklet Published by NSA

A comprehensive handbook for campus human relations programs is now available through the NSA publications bureau.

The 32-page printed booklet is entitled, "Human Relations in the Educational Community." The authors are NSA veep Richard J. Medalie; and chairman of the NSA advisory counsel, Gordon Klopf, student activities counselor, University of Wisconsin.

• • •

PUBLICATION OF THE booklet was made possible by a grant from the National Conference of Christians and Jews (NCCJ).

The booklet covers the philosophy of good human relations, application of principles to the campus, and details of human relations conferences and audits.

The booklet also introduces "Bascom Bill," (left) creation of Randy Harrison, University of Wisconsin. Bascom Bill won the initial approval of the Ohio NSA Region:

"Bascom Bill, a fictional character who reads the book over your shoulder, is really the spirit of the individual student on campus. Bill relieves the book of any tendencies to be stuffy and illustrates the aims of NSA," the Ohio Regional Bulletin commented.

• • •

THE BOOKLET INCLUDES an extensive list of books related to human relations activities and organizations engaged in human relations projects.

Copies of the booklet are available from the publications bureau, NSA, 304 N. Park St., Madison 5, Wis., at 25 cents to students, faculty and administration of NSA schools and 50 cents to all other persons.

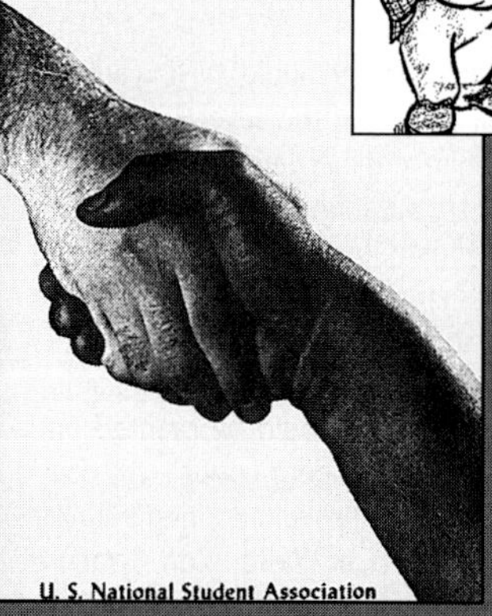

THE AMERICAN COUNCIL ON EDUCATION INITIATIVE in November 1949 (Top of page, left) provided higher education administrator support and professional resources which NSA was able to adapt and use in its campus and regional programming. National Affairs and Educational Vice Presidents Ralph Dungan (47-48), Gene Schwartz(48-49), Rick Medalie (49-50) and Herb Goldsmith (50-51) laid the groundwork for these programs.

(Documents, Berea College Archives)

SECTION 3 The South, Civil Rights, and Segregation

CONTENTS

There was no more perplexing and painful an issue confronting NSA than segregation in Southern and many Northern colleges, and the refusal of service to African Americans in restaurants, hotels, and other public places in both the North and the South.

The memoirs in this section provide the remarkable first-hand experiences of two Black college Presidents, John Peoples (Jackson State College for Negro Teachers—now Jackson State University, Mississippi) and Norman Francis (Xavier University, New Orleans), who, when students, were NSA delegates from their colleges. They discuss their experiences growing up in small Southern towns, and how the bonds of family and community nurtured their determination to overcome the barriers of discrimination.

From their experience, we learn that NSA was one of the channels that provided opportunities for Black and white students to become acquainted with each other in ways not otherwise possible at the time. Many of the essays in this volume include recollections by white student leaders who, for the first time in social as well as formal occasions, were witness to the degrading practices of Black exclusion.

Barry Farber (University of North Carolina), later to become a radio talk show host, tells of one of the numerous initiatives taken by white students at the time in support of the small number of Black students beginning to enter previously all-white campuses.

NSA's anti-segregation and civil rights initiatives

Constance Curry (Agnes Scott College, GA), 1952-53 Chair of the NSA Great Southern Region, who later became a civil rights attorney, takes us forward to the sixties as she traces NSA's role, along with many other student organizations, in helping to lay the groundwork for the civil rights movement.

Working quietly behind the scenes, the National Scholarship Service and Fund for Negro Students (NSSFNS), formed in 1947 by Felice N. Schwartz, a former NAACP staff member, provided small sums of seed money to supplement scholarships offered by Northern colleges seeking to bring academically promising African Americans to their campuses for the first time. NSSFNS was endorsed by NSA, which had a place on its board. Dick Plaut, its executive director, recruited staff members each year from among NSA national staff alumni. Shirley Neizer Tyler (Simmons College), 1950-51 NSA Executive Secretary, later a church school head, was one of those staff members and tells the NSSFNS story. Dean Harry J. Carman of Columbia University was Chairman of the Board. He is profiled in Part 5. Evelyn Jones Rich (Bryn Mawr), later an educational administrator, provides a personal memoir on the NSSFNS experience.

Students Target Segregation, Race Relations, Quotas

1946-1950

Sweatt, Denied Entrance, Has No Plans, Wanted UT 'Quality'

Lawyers Present Brief To U.S. Supreme Court On Sweatt Controversy

NEGRO CHALLENGES STATE'S RIGHT TO SEGREGATE RACES

In The
Supreme Court of the United States
October Term, 1949
No. 44.
HEMAN MARION SWEATT, Petitioner,
v.
THEOPHILUS SHICKEL PAINTER, ET AL.
On a Writ of Certiorari to the Supreme Court of the State of Texas.

Through the Courts

1950

U. OF MD. RULED TO ADMIT NEGRO

The Diamondback

State's Highest Court Overrules Rejection Of Esther McCready

Poll Reveals College Students Object to Quota Requirements

American college students were declared to be overwhelmingly ... ing admission, according ... tion employed by the

U of L to Admit Negroes To Some Schools This Fall, All Schools In '51

PHILADELPHIA, WEDNESDAY, OCTOBER 18, 1950

'RACE' REMOVED FROM FORMS

EDITORIALS

End of a Controversy

Red Cross Statement Ends Bloodmobile Issue

The Daily Tar Heel

HAYES RULES NEGROES CAN'T ENROLL

In Racial Practice

1948-49

Integrated Southern Area YMCA, YWCA Conference Held At Berea

By Lorenzo Gunn, YMCA Delegate

Brotherhood Week: 'Pattern for Peace'

The stresses and strains within our nation and the impact of

NFCCS Interracial Commission To Sponsor Oratorical Contest

Winner Will Compete in Region Contest March 13

New Orleans to Observe Interracial Day, March 13

With Student Outreach

1948

NAACP On Campus Strives To Erase Racial Prejudice

The National Association for the Advancement of Colored People has been sponsoring a membership drive on campus for its recently organized Youth Council Chapter at the University of Buffalo.

When the NAACP was organized, its primary purpose was to combat the forces of segregation and

1951

Drive Benefits Negro Schools & Scholarships

Solicitation for the Term Drive began last Wednesday. This year the campaign receipts will be divided equally between two organizations — the United Negro College Fund and the National Scholarship Service and Fund for Negro Students.

With Campus Drives

ELIMINATION OF SEGREGATED EDUCATION, RACIAL SCREENING AND QUOTAS became a national agenda in support of which a broad spectrum of religious, civil rights, higher education and student groups joined. During its early years NSA collaborated actively with many of them (see appendix for abbreviations): notably, the NAACP, NCCJ, NICC, NFCCS, ACLU, NSSFNS and the American Council on Education.

Left from the top: *Daily Texan*, 3/19/46; Berea College, KY *Wallpaper*, 2/6/50; Cover page, respondent's brief, Heman Sweatt photo, both Center for American Studies, U. of Texas Archives; *Maroon Tiger*, 10/48, Morehouse C., Atlanta; Los Angeles City College *Collegian*, 2/17/48, Xavier C., *LA Record*, 2/49. Right from the top: U. of MD *Diamondback*, 4/18/50; Columbia U. *Spectator*, 2/17/50; U. of Louisville *Cardinal*, 4/28/50; Temple U. 10/18/50; U. of NC *Tar Heel*, 10/18/50; U. of Buffalo *Bee*, 4/23/48; *Barnard Bulletin*, 11/19/51.

1947

Wednesday, December 10, 1947 — VASSAR MISCELLANY NEWS

The Vassar Miscellany News 12/10/47

40 Colleges Attack Prejudice On Campus

Lindeman Stresses Student Task In Overcoming Racial Prejudice

Dr. Edouard Lindeman, noted educator, Professor at the New York School for Social Research, in his speech opening the SCED conference at Princeton stressed the responsibility of students in overcoming prejudice on the college campus. He said that the students, the main force behind campus life must make the initial effort to overcome the stigma of discrimination too often reflected by them. He emphasized that by doing this job well, the student could ...vidual's racial and religious background, but pointed out that the problem does not end there. He stressed the importance of working with high schools in encouraging members of minority groups to apply. However, he pointed out that of eighty private schools in New York City only four do not use discriminatory methods.

Problems of Insecurity

Two problems of insecurity face

What We Can Do . . .

Suggested means of encouraging Negroes to apply for admission at Colleges and Universities (SCED Race-Relations Conference):

1. Letter-writing; contacting off-campus groups and organizations that might be of some assistants;
2. Working through Student Councils;
3. Advertising in Negro periodicals and other sources;
4. Making availability of opportunities known to Negroes through the College Scholarship Fund for Negroes and like agencies;
5. Encouraging the hiring of Negro faculty members;
6. "Living" democracy on the college campuses;
7. The elimination of fraternities and sororities;
8. Increased Negro participation in extra-curricular activities in those schools in which they are now enrolled;
9. The inception of inter-racial fraternities;
10. Encourage high schools to tackle the problem.

The basic problem is to get the minority groups into the colleges.

SCED Meeting Organizes For Concrete Action

by Virginia Lewisohn '49

Action was the keynote of the SCED conference at Princeton last weekend. From Dr. Lindeman's fiery opening speech through the carefully planned panels and business meeting, to Rustin and Cantril's brilliant closing speeches, the Conference was filled with an enthusiastic spirit ...

Through Action Programs

The awakening of a southern black student

1. Toward a New Era of Freedom

John A. Peoples
President, Student Body, Jackson State College, Mississippi, 1948-49
Delegate, NSA Second National Student Congress, 1949

Author's note: Portions of this essay have been adapted from my book, To Survive and Thrive: The Quest for a True University, *published in 1995 by Town Square Books, Inc., Jackson, Mississippi.*

Jackson State College was established by the American Baptist Home Mission Society in 1877. The explicit and implicit purpose of this institution was to provide for the education, under free conditions, of that group of American citizens which was previously held in bondage.

In my inaugural address as the sixth President of Jackson State, nearly 91 years later in 1968, I set forth the manifesto that Jackson was "to be an incubator for the pursuit of knowledge, truth and freedom. Let it thus be understood that a good teacher at Jackson State College cannot be a peaceful man. He must be a man at war against the forces of ignorance, and tyranny of the mind, and spirit."

This was an expression of my resolve to lead Jackson State College into a new era of *freedom—freedom of the mind and spirit*—for the students, the faculty, and the alumni. I took the helm of this college that had been repressed by the scourge of racism. By the grace of God, for the seventeen years of my Presidency, it was my quest to advance it far beyond the narrow mindsets of its governing board upward toward the level of a bona-fide comprehensive university.

That quest was the centerpiece of a lifetime, the course of which was set by my family and early childhood in the small town of Starkville, Mississippi, and by my experiences in the segregated United States Marine Corps. It attained focus when, as an undergraduate at Jackson State, I was inspired by the mentoring of its then great President, Jacob Reddix. There I also developed my leadership skills and broadened my horizons through student government, Student Christian Movement and National Student Association experiences.

At the beginning of my presidency in March 1967, it had been twenty years, September 1947, since I first set foot on the campus of Jackson College for Negro Teachers, as it was then named. Two months earlier, in July, I had been discharged from the Marine Corps with grandiose plans to attend MIT or Cal Tech, majoring in engineering. Despite the fact that I had graduated number two in my high school class, both colleges advised me to apply later when I had strengthened my academic background. To matriculate in engineering, they required high school preparation of four years of rigorous mathematics, one year of physics, one year of chemistry and one year of a foreign language, along with other courses in English and social studies.

Preparing for a career in education

I had taken every course offered at the segregated Oktibbeha County Training High School in Starkville, Mississippi, with one exception. Girls only took home economics, while boys took agricultural shop. Yet I had only one and one half years of mathematics, consisting of two semesters of algebra and one semester of plane geometry. In science, I had the only course the school offered, two semesters of biology with no laboratory. There were no courses offered in foreign languages and only the bare minimums in English and social studies.

So, on advice of my high school Principal, I went to Jackson State with the original intention to take courses requisite to transferring to a school of engineering after, at most, two years. After I enrolled at Jackson State and was allowed to take mathematics with the sophomores, and after I made straight "A's" the first quarter, I was still planning to transfer to an engineering school, until I found that engineers were being laid off all over the country due to the end of World War II. In fact, many engineers were seeking jobs as mathematics and science teachers in high schools. Thus, it seemed a timely choice to remain at Jackson State with plans to be a mathematics teacher.

During my three years of study for the Bachelor's degree, I was "Mr. Everything" at Jackson State: student government president for two consecutive years, football star, track star, and straight "A" student. The time spent there as a student had been the happiest period in my life.

I finished Jackson State in three years, number one in my class, in May 1950. I went on to the University of Chicago to earn the Master of Arts Degree in mathematics education in 1951 (and, in December of 1961, my Ph.D.), and I took a position with the Gary, Indiana, public school system in September 1951. Now, after seven years as a teacher and six years as a principal, I was going back to Jackson State as its first vice president, thinking about the road I traveled to get here.

High school in Starkville and thoughts about civil rights

In 1943, I was in the eleventh grade at Oktibbeha County Training School in Starkville, Mississippi. In many areas of Mississippi, high schools for blacks were called "training schools." This was based upon the racist assumption that blacks could not be truly educated, but could only be trained like animals. I did not realize the term "training" was demeaning until I was inducted into the Marine Corps and found that my high school's name caused some to think that I had been in a reform school.

I was a good student, and I had a close relationship with all of my teachers and especially with the Principal, Mr. Childs Henderson, or Professor Henderson as we all called him. It was customary to give all black male teachers the title of "professor," regardless of their educational level. This made it possible for whites to refer to black male educators as "Professor" rather than Mister. Black female teachers were called by their first names, or "Auntie," if they were elderly. This was true even at the college level where whites would rather give black teachers the title of "Professor" or even "Doctor" than to give them the courtesy title of "Mister" or "Mrs."

Professor Henderson was also the mathematics and civics teacher, two of my favorite subjects. "Professor Henderson," I said one day in our civics class, "I have been reading the U.S. Constitution in the back of our textbook. Does it really mean what it says? Are we really free? Why don't we Negroes vote? Why can the white folks lynch us and not go to jail?"

"Now, John Arthur, things are going to get better. Some of our people are just not ready to vote. They need more education."

"But, Professor Henderson, if we are not really free, then this civics textbook is not telling the truth."

I can say one thing about Professor Henderson, he certainly emphasized patriotism. We learned all of the patriotic songs and anthems. We also learned "Lift Every Voice and Sing," but we were not taught that it was a protest song. We studied history in the mode of the traditional textbooks of the day, but there was never any emphasis on civil rights. This was understandable because Professor Henderson was under the same harsh racial restrictions as were all of the other black educators of that time. There was no other way for him or any other teacher to maintain their jobs or even keep alive during those times.

Although this was not the first time I had thought about civil rights and freedom, it was the period during which my ideas were coming into focus. When I was a child, my mother, Mrs. Maggie Peoples, regularly bought copies of *The Chicago Defender* or *The Pittsburgh Courier.* These two black newspapers would carry news about black lynching and would editorialize about the constitutional rights of African Americans. I began to read these papers with more interest during the latter part of my high school days. I also began to notice the extreme contrast between the white and the black high schools.

Contrasts between white and black schools

The high school for whites, Starkville High School, with its beautiful brick structure, was well equipped. I knew about the equipment because my great-uncle, Tony Manuel, worked there as a janitor and would tell me about the fine things in the school.

The school for African Americans, Oktibbeha County Training School (now Henderson Middle School), had a rotting frame structure and was totally bereft of instructional equipment. The library, if it could be called that, was literally in a closet, with a small set of hand-me-down books from the white school. God bless Mrs. Sadie Weir, who doubled as an English teacher and librarian. She not only encouraged us to read books, she also made us learn the Dewey Decimal System for the classification of library books. A few of the graduates of Oktibbeha County Training School did fairly well in life. However, whatever they learned at Oktibbeha County Training School was because of the dedicated teachers who gave their all, in spite of the deplorable, inadequate conditions at the school.

I did not realize that the school was as inadequate as it really was, for I had nothing with which to contrast it. My first occasion to compare came when Professor Henderson got a call from the county superintendent asking if he had anybody at the school whom he could recommend to take the Army Specialized Training or the Navy V-12 Examination. These examinations were designed to select gifted high school students for direct admission to Officer Training School. Professor Henderson recommended me. This was in 1943. I was sixteen years old and a junior in high school.

The tests were given in Starkville at Mississippi State A&M College, now Mississippi State University, in one of the classroom buildings. In one room were about forty white high school boys taking the test, and in an adjacent room was

I, one black boy. I did the best I could, but I had not been taught the mathematics, physics, chemistry, and language skills required to pass that test. I realized just how unprepared I was when I received the letter, which said, "I regret to inform you that your score on the examination was not sufficiently high for your selection at this time . . . Best of success in your military career."

Frankly, I was proud of that letter, even though I didn't pass the examination. I became determined to learn much more than what was being taught in that black high school in Starkville. I also became more aware of the gross unfairness of the educational setup in the state. I had never seen a college other than Mississippi State. From that time, in my mind, Mississippi State University symbolized the racism in higher education that existed in the state.

I vowed that the next time I took a standardized test, I would be ready. I bought a new *Webster's Dictionary* and started to read it page by page, trying to build my vocabulary. I didn't think that it mattered that I was learning words completely out of context. As I began to use my growing vocabulary, one of my female high school mates said, "Junior Peoples, why are you using so many big words, and why do they all begin with A?"

I didn't think it was funny then, because I was serious about supplementing my meager high school education. This was truly the real beginning of my high school education because, from this time on, I "chewed and digested" every book I read.

The United States Marine Corps

I was drafted into the segregated U.S. Marine Corps (USMC) on December 29, 1944, and stationed at Montford Point, Camp Lejeune, North Carolina, the recruiting unit for training black Marines. I arrived there on New Year's Day 1945, with several other black recruits.

Black marines were not commissioned. They could only go as high as sergeant major. I was selected to attend noncommissioned officers (NCO) school so I went to NCO school and was assigned to be a drill instructor. I had the dubious honor of being the drill instructor for the last all-black platoon trained at Montford Point and in the USMC, which completed its training on January 25, 1946. Since I didn't have enough GI Bill time to finish college, I reenlisted for two more years and was selected, along with ten other African-American marines, to attend radio technician's school at Camp Pendleton, California (two of us, Clarence Lusby and myself, were being trained to establish a school to teach electronics to blacks).

As it turned out, the USMC went back on the deal to set up the school. While they were trying to figure out what to do next, an All Navy Letter of Instruction (ALNAV) came out and was posted on the bulletin board:

> All Negro Marines except those who are cooks, bakers or stewards are hereby authorized to be discharged without regard to the number of discharge points earned, between the dates of June 15 and July 15, 1947, for the convenience of the government.

This was an amazing document. It was designed, in effect, to reduce all the African Americans in the Marine Corps to servants for white marines. There were some black marines who wanted to remain in the service, particularly those who were high-ranking NCOs receiving good pay. "We got to fight this thing, man. We can't let them kick us out because we are black," they were saying at a barracks meeting of about fifty black marines one night.

I had already become known as someone willing to speak my mind. Everyone was waiting to see what I was going to say. "This order is pure racism," I said, "and of course it should be fought. But we black marines do not have the clout to carry out this fight. I can tell you now, this fight must be taken to an arena larger than Montfort Point or the U.S. Marine Corps. The black press or the NAACP would be the appropriate agencies to take up the fight, and I am sure there are men among you to carry the request for help to such agencies."

I had been in the U.S. Marine Corps for two years, six months and four days. I was about to be honorably discharged "for the convenience of the government." I had enough GI bill time for four years of college and more. The many racial encounters I had experienced in the corps (detailed in my book, *To Survive and Thrive)* had not made me bitter. They only made me more determined to be an opponent, if not an actual fighter, against racism—and to do so in the arena of the life I was about to build for myself.

While in the service I matured, and found first of all that I was able to compete with people from all over the country. Mississippi had a bad reputation. People thought we didn't even wear shoes. They called us the "Bilbo's boys" (after Senator Theodore Bilbo). Blacks from other Southern states, like Tennessee or Carolina, also thought Mississippi was the worst place in the world.

Racism in Mississippi

Having completed my education to the doctorate and spent thirteen years as a teacher and principal in Gary, Indiana, I was invited to return to Mississippi as Vice President of Jackson State. All of our Gary friends thought I was foolhardy, if not insane, when I told them of my decision to move back to Mississippi to assume the vice presidency of historically black Jackson State College. Unquestionably, they had good reason to think that way. The racial situation in Mississippi was horrendous, to say the least. Black churches and homes were being burned and bombed by segregationist extremists. African Americans and liberal-thinking whites were being beaten, jailed and even killed for exercising or advocating the most basic civil rights. The much publicized murders of the three civil rights workers in Philadelphia, Mississippi, had not been solved. Hundreds of "freedom riders" were descending on the state to join the cause of civil rights for black citizens. Civil rights advocate Medgar Evers had been murdered by a Klansman. The state was looked upon as the worst place in America for African Americans to live.

And Jackson, Mississippi, was a racist city in the most racist state of the nation. No, I was not bereft of my senses. I had for a long time given thought to going back to Mississippi to be a part of the effort to bring progressive change to that state. Several of the heroes in that bloody struggle were my contemporaries. I had not personally known Medgar Evers or Charles Evers, but the records show they both were Alcorn College students when I was a student at Jackson State, and that we even played on the highly competitive football teams during the period 1947-1950.

I realized that much of my undergraduate experience at Jackson State had prepared me for this mission I was about to undertake.

Student government at Jackson State

I ran for student government president the third quarter of my Freshman year in 1947-48, and I became President my Sophomore year and Junior year (I finished Jackson in three years because I went to school in two summers, taking a full load). The authority of student government was more or less limited by the President, because there was no institutionalized authority.

While I was President of the student government association, I did a few things to make it more independent. I rewrote the constitution requiring that one had to be an upcoming senior to be President. I tried to liberate the student newspaper (which was really controlled by the President, who appointed the faculty sponsor of the newspaper), although I didn't quite succeed. When I came back and became President of the college, I gave the student government significant freedom.

The influence of President Reddix

The most important friend I had at Jackson State College was President Jacob L. Reddix, the one who influenced me to return to Mississippi with his optimism about the future of the state. His mentoring campaign had begun as early as my Sophomore year at Jackson State, at which time I was student government president.

Two particular situations are worth noting. In the fall of 1948, Jackson College had provided football scholarships for the first time. They were tuition, room and board scholarships for the fall quarter only. President Reddix had mandated that the World War II veteran athletes were not entitled to the scholarships since they received tuition and subsistence checks from the Veterans Administration. Since I was the student government president, I was delegated to see the President and petition for consideration.

I can recall my nervousness as the time approached to see President Reddix. After all, I was only a Sophomore and, at that time, not even considered a first-string football player. Yet I was going to see the exalted man who headed this institution.

After a short wait, I was admitted to the President's office and invited by him to sit down in front of his massive executive desk. He was forceful but kind in telling me that the veterans were much better situated financially than the other players and thus did not need the college scholarships.

I could not counter this argument. But I told him that almost all of the veterans on the football team were needy and from poor homes. Many were married, and it seemed unfair that they should be penalized for having served their country.

President Reddix said he was truly impressed by such a good argument from a student, and he would give it further thought. The next day, Coach T. B. Ellis announced that the World War II veteran football players would receive work-aid scholarships along with the other players.

The second occasion on which President Reddix gave me special attention was one year later, in the fall quarter of 1949. By that time, I had become a BMOC ("Big Man on Campus"). I had been elected to a second term as student body president, I was a straight-A student, and was considered to be quite a good football player in the position of offensive end. In almost every game I was making one or more touchdowns. In the previous year, 1948, Dillard University had been a powerhouse in the South Central Athletic Conference (SCAC) and had beaten us severely in Jackson. This year, we had a very good team, and we went on to defeat Dillard by forty-six to six.

The Monday following that football game, as I was leaving a class at Johnson Hall, I met President Reddix in front of the building. He greeted me warmly and began to talk about the Dillard game. The President then proceeded to question me about my career plans. I told him about my plans to become a mathematics teacher. He thought this was fine for a beginning, but he felt I was administrative material. "If you are an administrator," he said, "you'll have mathematicians working for you."

On subsequent occasions, he was to be more specific about this advice, to the extent of suggesting that I think of one day returning to Jackson College as president when he retired. Our discussions in this vein extended over a thirteen-year period, to the time when I decided to return to Mississippi, in 1964.

The YMCA and YWCA and interracial change

During 1948-1950, I had been one of the activists in a sub-rosa interracial movement for educational change consisting of college students from Jackson College, Mississippi State University, and the University of Mississippi. We were members of the YWCAs and YMCAs of our respective schools. We first met in summer 1948 at the Southern Regional Christian Conference at Berea College in Kentucky.[1] We later had meetings at Jackson State and Mississippi State and pledged to work in our state for racial justice through education.

When I came back I wrote an article in the student newspaper about this. The paper was suppressed, however. It could not be publicized that I attended this interracial meeting because of the segregationist political atmosphere of the state.

I took the initiative to call a Mississippi caucus while we were at Berea College. Subsequently, that next year we met at Jackson State with students and faculty sponsors from Ole Miss and Mississippi State. Things were going fine in the meeting until we had to eat somewhere and were told that we could not go through the line at the cafeteria. The Dean came down to the dormitory lounge and said, "We really can't let you do that because it could cause problems for the President if we allow the whites and blacks to eat together in the cafeteria." The white kids said, "That's okay, we'll go out and get something and come back to the meeting."

This was a follow-up to our meeting in Kentucky and our desire to follow up and see what we could do. The YWCA sponsors were also trying to be a little more liberal. Mississippi State is in my hometown in Starkville, so we met in the YMCA up there. Once, when I went in through the front door, somebody thought I was one of the people working there. That was a memorable experience for me.[2]

NSA, Aaron Henry, and a window on the world

It was during my second year as student body president, in 1949, that I went to the NSA Congress at the University of Illinois in Urbana.[3] I had learned about NSA through the mail. I may not have known at the time that we were represented at the Chicago Student Conference in December of 1946 by Ethel L. Nichols, as I learned from looking at the delegate lists recently. Apparently, there had been no follow-up from the 1946 conference attendance by Miss Nichols.

I was able to go to meetings like that because we weren't regulated at that time and the authorities didn't pay any attention to us. The President would have been censured by the State College Board if they had known he was sending kids to an interracial meeting. It was OK as long as it wasn't publicized.

Aaron Henry, the world-renowned freedom fighter, was the student government president at Xavier University of New Orleans when I was student body president at Jackson State in 1949. Aaron and I first met at that NSA conference in summer 1949. At this meeting we two native Mississippi black college students found how terribly backward our state was, in education as well as racial progress. We pledged ourselves to remain in our state after graduation so as to do our part in effecting change. We also met at the NSA regional meeting in New Orleans at which Aaron Henry was one of the leaders.[4]

While I took a detour to Gary, Indiana, to initiate my career as an educator, Aaron Henry had indeed gone back to his hometown of Clarksdale, Mississippi, where he established a pharmacy and continued the fight for freedom.

When I came back to Jackson, we renewed our acquaintance. We were on many platforms at various meetings together. Whenever he was on the platform, he would bring up the NSA meeting. We would talk about how backward our state was then and how our eyes were opened. We had seen those young men, black and white, together. We had marveled at how those young black men from the North were as able as the white college students in making floor speeches. We had seen the students from California in interracial dancing. They were all good friends, and it was no big deal. Aaron and I realized that we were way behind and had so much to do to catch up. We always brought up that Aaron and I went way back to the University of Illinois—to the NSA meeting where we became friends and our eyes were opened.

Jackson State was totally isolated racially, as were many of the state institutions in the Deep South. Although I had been in the Marine Corps, I had not connected with college people.

Dr. John A. Peoples, Jr., was President of Jackson State University from 1967 to 1984. Earlier, after serving thirteen years in the public school system of Gary, Indiana, he was Professor of Mathematics and Vice President at the university from 1964 to 1967.

One big issue at the NSA meetings was fraternities and integration. In the discussions about these matters, we blacks had to be defended by white kids who would get up and make these sustained eloquent speeches in favor of integration. Here we were, the ones suffering it, yet we couldn't make those kinds of speeches. No doubt about it, those Northern students were far ahead of us in vocabulary and in confidence.

When I came back to Jackson, I can recall being toned down in writing essays when one teacher said: "Now, Mr. Peoples, if you were at the University of Wisconsin, this would be appropriate. But this is too wordy. You're using too many big words. You need to tone it down."

We had very few international programs. Historically, Jackson State had a connection with Liberia, which came about because an alumnus by the name of Jones had been a missionary over there. Because of that connection, there were some people in Liberia who were sending students back to Jackson State. At that time, there were two students from Liberia at Jackson State. President Reddix was invited to go over there on a tour paid for by some foundation. Beyond that specific case, there was no international movement at Jackson State at that time.

Epilogue

Initially in this article, I quoted from my inaugural speech, entitled *You Shall Know the Truth*. This is a direct quote from the Holy Bible (John 8:32), "Ye shall know the truth and the truth shall make you free." This bit of scripture encapsulates all that I have striven for.

I further delineated that theme in the speech, foretelling "This truth will engender in men a determination to fight for freedom, and the ability to win freedom. Indeed, this knowledge of the truth will produce in men such desire, appreciation and dedication to freedom that, if necessary, they will die for the cause of it."

END NOTES

[1] *Editor's note:* Berea College furnished significant leadership for NSA and other intercollegiate events at the time, as well as being active in the NSA Kentucky-Tennessee Region. See Welsh, pp. 165, 172, and Martin, pp. 983, 987.

[2] *Editor's note:* Both the YWCA and YMCA, separately and through the National Intercollegiate Christian Council, were early leaders in sponsoring interracial meetings on U.S. campuses both before the war and during the period covered by this book. They were also instrumental in the formation of NSA. See Miller, pp. 721, 733, Ellis, p. 159, Purkaple, p.685.

[3] On the 1949 NSA Second National Student Congress, see Schwartz, p. 285, also Heggie, p. 206.

[4] See Aaron Henry, p. 456.

PICTURE CREDITS: *Then:* 1961, Ph.D. ceremony, U. of Chicago. *Now:* November 1984, President, Jackson State University.

The Killings at Jackson State

John A. Peoples
Jackson State College, Mississippi

Author's note: When I entered Jackson State as a student, veterans had just been relieved of the poll tax requirements that still were in force for everyone else. We were required to sit in the back of the bus and in the front of the trains, where most of the smoke and soot were deposited. We occasionally resisted with minor symbolic acts of defiance. Twenty years later, a new generation of black students had grown up unfettered by any reticence. Following are excerpts from my book, To Survive and Thrive.

The student freedom movement at Jackson State College was well in progress when I arrived in September 1964 as vice president. There had been student protests on campus since the advent of the sixties. As a matter of fact, Jackson State College's protests were very much part of a nationwide movement for black civil rights. In the fight for civil rights, black students made excellent shock troops since they had less to lose than their more conservative elders who risked economic penalties if they got identified as radicals in civil rights.

When I became president of Jackson State I did not know when or in what manner the struggle would take place. The students took their struggle beyond the bounds of the campus in the May 1967 riot against the Jackson police. It was in this initial disturbance that I first perceived the deep-seated anger in the students who had suffered racial discrimination and suppression. When the white policemen invaded the campus and fired shotguns and teargas at students who were doing no more than peacefully protesting, all the repressed anger, rage and aggression came forth. The students stoned the cars of any white persons who drove down Lynch Street (named for John R. Lynch, the black U.S. Congressman from Mississippi during the Reconstruction Era). This May 1967 disturbance was the one in which Benjamin Brown, a non-student, was killed at Lynch and Rose Streets.

The Jackson State students vented their rage again in April 1968, the night Dr. Martin Luther King, Jr., was killed. The students besieged Lynch Street, stoning any whites who drove through, As in previous incidents, the Jackson police, led by "Thompson's Tank," came down Lynch Street firing teargas and bird shot. Luckily, no one was killed in that incident.

Again in April 1969, some Jackson State male students who had gotten into a fight with some street boys down at Lynch and Rose were chased back onto campus. The Thompson's Tank corps appeared and put down the riot with teargas and bird shot. There were no fatalities.

On May 4, 1970, at Kent State University, anti-war protests had resulted in four students being killed and nine wounded by Ohio National Guardsmen. The students at Jackson State held a rally on campus on May 7, to protest the Kent State killings. On Wednesday evening, May 13, 1970, as I walked out the front door of the campus union, a group of female students approached me rapidly. Their eyes showed fearful excitement. "President Peoples, those boys up there are throwing rocks at passing cars," the first girl shouted, pointing toward Alexander Hall.

Then I heard it. Thud! Crash! Bang! Screech! Rocks and bricks were breaking the windows and windshields of any cars carrying white persons or even fair-skinned African Americans. Lynch Street, a major thoroughfare dividing the campus, was crowded with screaming, yelling, cursing students, and all so suddenly.

My first thought was to wade into the crowd, which would have been fruitless. So I crossed Lynch Street to the president's home and called Sgt. M. R. Stringer, the ranking security officer. He was already in the streets trying to restore order: "Dr. Peoples, it looks pretty bad. I've never seen the students so mad before."

This was the beginning of the first night of what was to become a two-day period of student riots and police mayhem, which resulted in the mobilization of the National Guard, the placing of the Mississippi Highway Patrol on standby and the spray shootings of the Women's dormitory where some of the demonstrators had gathered that night.

At about 2:00 A.M. I called all of the hospitals and the police station and received the tragic news about the dead and wounded. About an hour later, I returned to Alexander Hall yard with the report of dead and wounded. I called off the wounded first. Then I called off the dead, of whom there were two, Philip Gibbs and James Green.

Because of the chaos on campus, we had to close the college that week and not have a formal commencement. At the beginning of the summer session in June, the students came back and wanted to resume their protest in the streets. I cautioned them that the cops would not hesitate to shoot them again. So I invited them to join me in the football field, and I would lead the protest.

That evening at 7:00 P.M., Alumni Field was filled to its capacity with three thousand students. The students cheered me as I stood before them. There was an air of expectancy. I don't recall the speech I gave. I know, however, I spoke in the vernacular of a black freedom fighter in such terms as these: "My fellow lovers of Jackson State, we are here tonight to mourn the deaths of two young black brothers, Philip Gibbs and James Green, and to protest the maiming of fourteen others of our beloved young men and women."

I concluded with a vow:

> We shall never forget what happened on that fatal night. We shall dedicate our hearts, our souls, our minds, and all our efforts to making Jackson State College the great university it is destined to be. Hate can't stop us, racism can't stop us, and murdering bullets did not and will not stop us—so help us God.

My students gave me a thunderous ovation with the clenched-fist salute of a revolutionary. I raised my open hand in acknowledgment. I could never bring myself to the clenched-fist salute. I guess I had too much of the U.S. Marines in me.[1]

END NOTE

[1] *Editor's note:* Clifton Wharton, then President of Michigan State University (MSU), writes in his own autobiography:

> May 16. The next day, Saturday, came word of the deaths of two students at Jackson State College, an historically Black college in Mississippi, followed by word of a similar tragedy in Georgia. I was especially shocked, because the Jackson State College president, John Peoples, had visited our campus where his brilliant daughter had enrolled as a National Merit Scholar. I called on him immediately to express my condolences and to offer any help that we might provide. . . .
>
> These deaths provoked further protests on several campuses. To prevent it from contributing to escalation at MSU, I ordered all flags on the campus to fly at half-mast for five days as a "mark of concern and respect." I added, "The latest loss of life at Jackson State is another shocking reminder of the terrible price of uncontrolled emotions and rash actions." Other campuses in Michigan and in the country also flew their flags at half-mast.

See also Wharton, p. 112 and p. 144.

Jackson College As We See It

I had little regard for the schools of Mississippi until I heard of Jackson College, where a program of functional education was being implemented. I decided to make an investigation; however, I had no intention to matriculate. My intention went awry, for after I came here, I was indoctrined with the philosophy and later I became thoroughly imbued with this education for life adjustment.

Since being at Jackson College I have found media for development in several aspects; namely, the physical, intellectual, moral, and social aspects.

John A. Peoples, Jr.

The Blue and White Flash, 2/50

VALEDICTORIAN

JOHN ARTHUR PEOPLES

The Blue and White Flash

JACKSON COLLEGE, JACKSON, MISSISSIPPI, MAY, 1950

Valedictorian of the Class of 1950 and President of the Student Council for two consecutive years, John A. Peoples, Jr. is one of the Seniors who will be greatly missed at Jackson College.

Mr. Peoples, an ex-Marine Sergeant, is leaving an admirable record behind him. He is an active Y.M.C.A. worker, a verteran end on the College Tigers football team, and a 3-letter track man. He served creditably on the Student Council, and along the lines of scholarship he has completed four years of college work in three four years of college work in three years time and has easily gained the coveted place of highest ranking student scholastically from among a class of over 100 students. He is a charter member of Alpha Kappa Mu Honor Society and was president of the local chapter this year. He is also a member of the Omega Psi Phi Fraternity, Inc.

On June 26, 1950, John Peoples will enter the University of Chicago to pursue study toward a Master's degree in mathematics. His place will be hard to fill.

JOHN A. PEOPLES, JR.

Early Background and Influences: I was born and grew up in Starkville, Mississippi. I was the only child of John and Maggie Peoples, but I had an extended family of cousins who were like brothers and sisters.

My father worked as a waiter in a café, downtown. It was called Peoples café. It belonged to a man by the name of Mumaduke. Dad also had his own café and he ran a dance hall. So we were not poor as compared to other persons. We had our own home and owned rental property.

My dad wanted me to come and take over the business he had. But Momma always said, I guess you're going to be some kind of a professor or something because you always want to read. A lot of the neighboring women worked in white people's homes, as cooks and maids, and they would always bring me all kinds of discarded, throwaway books or magazines to read. So I would read and read.

I learned to read before I started school, when I was about three, because my mother used to help my dad's baby sister, and I'd be watching her. When I got to school, I could read the whole primary book. The teacher couldn't believe it. She would cover the pictures and see if it were really true that could I read the book.

My mother, Maggie, had finished, I think, sixth grade. But she saw something in me, so she would encourage me to read. So she provided those books. My nickname became "Professor," or "Fess."

Then when I started school, I was known as a bright kid, a smart boy in the class. And if there was any kind of a program or a long part to remember in a play, I was given that because I also had a good memory. By the time I got into high school, I was one of the best kids in mathematics or science. But I didn't know about the world outside until I took the Navy V-12 program test in 1943 at Mississippi State. I tell that story and what happened later in this essay.

Education and Military Experience. After graduating high school second in my class, I was drafted into the U.S. Marine Corps, serving for two and a half years and attaining the rank of Sergeant. I served as a drill instructor for Black Marines at Camp Lejeune, North Carolina, during World War II, and subsequently served as a radio technician at Camp Pendleton, California.

After my discharge, I entered Jackson State University where I earned the Bachelor's degree in Mathematics. I was on the varsity football and track team, and elected President of the Student Government Association. After graduating number one in my class in 1950, I attended the University of Chicago, where I earned my M.A. and Ph.D. degrees.

Career Highlights: Following thirteen years as a teacher and school administrator in the public school system of Gary, Indiana, I joined Jackson State University as a Professor of Mathematics and Vice President. I served as President of the university from 1967 to 1984. During my tenure, enrollment grew from 2,200 to 7,800, and the academic program developed from a teacher education baccalaureate program to a five-school professional program going up to the doctoral level.

During my tenure, Jackson State experienced four consecutive years of student upheavals. A reflection of the dramatic years of the Black Student Revolution, the most tragic year came in 1970 when, on May 14, city and state law officers fired on students in a women's dormitory, killing two students and wounding twenty-two. I also played an active role in the landmark Mississippi desegregation suit in 1974. Both these critical events are treated in my 1995 book, *To Survive and Thrive.*

I have been active in the academic world, serving on boards and commissions of virtually all of the major national and southern regional associations. I was the first African American to serve as Chairman of the Board of the American Council on Education.

I have also served on numerous community boards and councils. I am a member of the Omega Psi Phi and Sigma Pi Phi fraternities. I have been elected to the Jackson State University Hall of Fame and the Southwestern Athletic Conference Hall of Fame. In 1993, I received the National Black College Hall of Fame Lifetime Achievement Award.

Family: I married the former Mary E. Galloway. We have two children, Kathleen Peoples-Sedlak, Ph.D., a clinical psychologist, and Mark A. Peoples, Esq., an attorney.

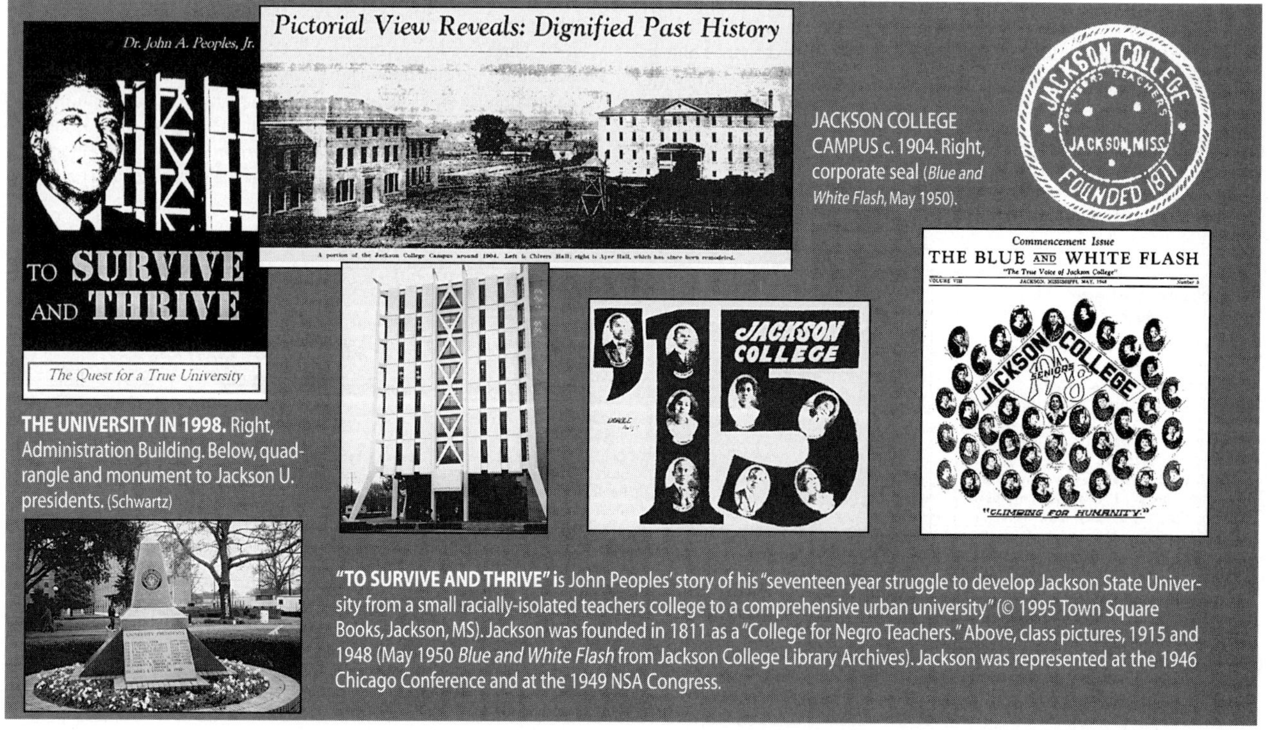

JACKSON COLLEGE CAMPUS c. 1904. Right, corporate seal (*Blue and White Flash*, May 1950).

THE UNIVERSITY IN 1998. Right, Administration Building. Below, quadrangle and monument to Jackson U. presidents. (Schwartz)

"TO SURVIVE AND THRIVE" is John Peoples' story of his "seventeen year struggle to develop Jackson State University from a small racially-isolated teachers college to a comprehensive urban university" (© 1995 Town Square Books, Jackson, MS). Jackson was founded in 1811 as a "College for Negro Teachers." Above, class pictures, 1915 and 1948 (May 1950 *Blue and White Flash* from Jackson College Library Archives). Jackson was represented at the 1946 Chicago Conference and at the 1949 NSA Congress.

Establishing beachheads before the civil rights movement

2. Leadership in a Southern Black Catholic College

Norman Francis
Xavier University, Louisiana
Delegate, NSA Third National Student Congress, 1950
President, NFCCS Southeastern Region, 1951

Xavier University of Louisiana occupied a unique place among Catholic colleges in the forties and fifties. It was black, it was coeducational, it was in the Deep South, and it was cosmopolitan. While recently recognized on the national scene, it had almost been a well-kept secret for many years. Throughout those years Xavier was a ground-breaking force in many ways, furnishing authentic, well-educated and well-rounded black leadership in Deep South student, educational, and civic organizations and helping pave the way for the civil rights movement within and outside of the Catholic Church.

During my student years, I was a participant and witness in particular to our role as a Southern black college anchor for the National Federation of Catholic College Students (NFCCS) as well as for the National Student Association. Xavier maintained active membership, lent prestige and recognition to student participation in regional and national NSA and NFCCS programs, and furnished outstanding leaders to both organizations.

In this memoir, I want to try and bring alive some of the background that nurtured our unique college community and some of the events of that energetic and purposeful post-war period.

The founding of Xavier in 1925

Our founder, Katharine Drexel, was a great visionary. Not only did she open an uptown New Orleans university in 1925 for young blacks to get a Catholic liberal arts education equal to that which was offered at all-white Loyola, but she opened Xavier's college of pharmacy because Loyola had a college of pharmacy that did not admit blacks. The irony is that today Xavier has the only college of pharmacy left in the city of New Orleans. Loyola left pharmacy. Tulane left pharmacy. And now about 20 percent of our college of pharmacy is white. (The total pharmacy enrollment is 500, and the total for the university, primarily in the arts and sciences, is about 3,800.)

When our foundress left our original uptown New Orleans campus in 1932 and bought our current campus, what they didn't sell her is the land that fronts on Carollton Avenue, the major thoroughfare bounding the campus and a canal that runs alongside it. About 75,000 cars now pass there each week, and if you keep going, you'll hit Loyola and Tulane. Yet, the only way you could get to us four years ago, until we acquired that strip, was to come off the two small bridges crossing the canal.

But the point is that her act was dramatic. She was breaking ground in the culture to open a Catholic college for blacks. *Time* magazine, in 1932, had an article about this white nun opening this Catholic college, and the locals were upset because she was spending all of that money to educate blacks when she should be giving it to the poor.

To underscore her intent, she purposely had the original main building designed in the limestone "Ivy League" mode so that when you drive by, it looks exactly like Tulane. She was saying to the South and to the New Orleanians, you may not know what I'm going to do inside, but you'll know from the outside that I'm investing in the best possible kind of a building, which will last forever. So that if a beautiful building marks a good school such as Tulane, I'm going to have the same kind of building marking Xavier.

Developing fortitude through segregation and speaking French

I was born in 1931, and I grew up in a segregated town, Lafayette, Louisiana, where everybody said you were inferior. But your parents were able, as the best psychologists in the world, to say no, don't let that faze you, because you're better than that. In fact, you're as good as anybody else. And they were able to do that when everything around you was saying something different. It's like keep your eyes on the prize. How do you do that? I still have no answer, except that for those of us who grew up in the Judeo-Christian and Catholic background, I say to people, it is because God gave us more faith than other people—to believe in what we were being told and be encouraged to be educated.

Most of my early life was in the segregated South. I went to a segregated Catholic elementary school, as well as a Catholic high school. The city of Lafayette was a typical small country town. But there was something very unusual about it, in that both whites and blacks spoke a common language. It wasn't English—it was French. There was a bond somehow in this French language that was different from what I suspect lots of other cities faced, although the rules of segregation were quite clear, as clear as they were in any other places. We followed them rather strictly, and they were strictly enforced. Everybody knew what his or her place was, whether they were black or white.

We had the same separate bus station and separate railroad station facilities. Blacks sat in the back of the bus if you were traveling on Greyhound or Trailways. And, conversely, blacks sat in the forward railroad cars. I remember the railroad travel fondly, as everyone does. These were all coal-burning steam engines, and the windows of these cars were not in any way as sealed, as we would have it today. Blacks rode in either the first or second cars behind the mail car, where the coaches were always sooty and dirty. The further back you got, of course, the cleaner they were.

Nurturing confident youth

What has been amazing is how the parents and the grandparents of black children, my age and even older, grew up in this segregated South and did not come out of it being bitter and angry to the extent that they lost their minds or worse. The incredible thing, as I noted earlier, is what great psychologists or great communicators those parents were, to be able to raise their children in a culture that said you were supposed to be inferior and that you could not enjoy some of the nicer things of life in the cities that you grew up in.

Even in your churches—and I grew up in the Catholic church, where you would think things would have been different—they were no different than any other on the political side. If you went to Mass and you were not in your "black church," and you happened to go to one that was a "white church," you sat in the last two rows of the church. At the time for Communion, you were the last ones to receive it. Having seen this day in and day out, in the normal process you would expect a person to come out of that totally and mentally devastated. However, the vast majority of us did not—I'd say better than 90 percent of us did not.

The other world of the blacks in the North

It's interesting for those of us who are Southerners to note another side of this issue that's important. Many Northern blacks looked down on Southerners in general, and black Southerners in particular. For those of us who were Southern blacks, we had withstood the humiliations and the contempt of whites, but we were in no way going to take that from Northern blacks. We reminded Northern blacks, not only that we were as good as they if not better, but that they had no right to feel any degree of arrogance because they, too, were living in a segregated world. They just didn't know it.

If you look at some of those blacks who succeeded in great measure in the North, they have Southern roots. They came North with a feeling that they were not going to be distracted by what people thought about them, and that they were going to rise above that. Now, some will say, that's the same as saying that you're not going to rock the boat. As I said, there are two ways to approach things. Sometimes you get people's attention by doing something dramatic, other times you wage a subtle guerrilla warfare. You don't let them think that you are disturbed about it, because if you do you lose your sense of balance, you lose your sense of logic and everything else. I think that was part of what Southern blacks came to appreciate.

Never lose your balance

So, how did these families pass this attitude on to their children? They never lost their balance. As an example, I had children who grew up in the same system, although updated to 1958-59, after I came back from the service. I remember specifically with one of my sons, rather frequently we passed a theater that was being built in New Orleans—and he would say to me as a young child, what are they doing? I'd say, they're building a theater. He said, are we going to go to that theater? I'd say, yes, when they finish it.

And they did finish it, but this was roughly 1960. The public accommodations changes, even in New Orleans, didn't take place until 1964-65. We could not go to that theater. When he asked me, well, the theater is built, when are we going to go? I said, when we get an invitation. I faced the same questions that my parents had to answer for me, but in a different light, because my son did not see the same degree of segregation that I saw. But what answers could I give him?

I remember distinctly that when the Civil Rights Act was passed, public accommodations were opened. I was not in the city. I called my son's mother and said, tell Michael we got an invitation. And he asked his mother, where from? And I said, the President of the United States.

That's a way of showing how all of us grew up and yet did not lose our balance.

Touches of relationship

When I came to New Orleans in 1948, I had come from a totally segregated system. Of course, Xavier was historically and predominantly black. But the difference was that Xavier had a vast majority of white teachers at the time. So for the first time, I was being taught by a sizable number of white teachers. This is not to say that I had not been taught by white professionals earlier. The priests in my hometown were white. So, as a boy I took Theology, or Religion if you will, and I served Mass with priests who were white. But aside from that experience, this was my only contact with whites in a professional way.

I could pause and say, though, that there were other integrating experiences in my hometown. They are ironies that people who did not live in the South could not fully appreciate. In fact, some of us lived in integrated neighborhoods. We were all poor—black and white. And down the block I played with a young white friend whose family was just three doors away from us, and they were very poor.

I'll never forget as a 6-year-old one day watching my father and the black men in the block cooperatively building a box. I asked my mother, what were they doing building a box? It was a pine box. She said oh, you know, your little friend down the street? I said, yes. His father died and his mother did not have the money to bury his father. So here were black men building a pine box as a coffin for a white neighbor in a segregated South. The point I'm making is that we had touches of relationships, but those relationships were restricted and limited.

The makeup of Xavier after the war

When I came to Xavier the new dimension was the number of white teachers along with black teachers and black students. I came into a different world because this place was like a United Nations. We had every color, every race, every creed.

We blacks were being educated by an integrated, multiracial, multiethnic faculty. So you lost color. You concentrated on that which you were learning, and you were being fortified by what you were going to have to do. You were being treated as a human being capable of learning whatever you had to learn. So it was dramatic in a way—because here color wasn't a problem, and yet when we literally walked across this canal and caught the bus, we went immediately into another world. Because we took the sign and moved it back and forth (symbolically—every bus had a movable sign designating the row separating the races).

When we rode the bus downtown, everything was segregated. So, we had to compartmentalize our life. We were totally American and a child of God on campus, and when we went outside, still being the same, we lived in another world that said we were not.

The veteran influence

Even more different, and very interesting, was the fact that we had former servicemen enrolled—perhaps the highest number of servicemen to ever enter college—just about the time that I entered as an 18-year-old. They were men who had served in the war, mature, they knew what they wanted. Some were married.

The veterans' presence was good for us as 18-year-olds. I think my education was greatly enhanced outside the classroom because of these men. They knew when to study, when to play, and they were quite focused. As I have looked back at this, they had just served their country, but they had come back to a segregated South. In 1948-49 and for some years after, you still sat in the balconies at the movies, you still rode behind the screen in the bus, and you still had white and black water fountains and the like.

Though they did not openly protest at the time—we had protests later, with the civil rights movement—you could tell that there was a maturity and a distaste for what it was they were experiencing, after having fought for their country and having seen their friends and even relatives die. So while they were focused on getting an education and getting a fresh degree, they had not abandoned their social conscience. And many of them joined organizations that were quietly starting the desegregation process, or moving toward an integrated process.

The Southern Parish Project creates a stir

I remember working as a Freshman in 1949, with several of them who had volunteered to help Father Joseph Fichter, S.J., who was writing a sociological study on Catholic parishes in New Orleans, segregated Catholic parishes. It was called the Southern Parish Project. It was funded by the Ford Foundation. He had the money to do three volumes. And we did the grunt work. We visited churches, asked questions, and gathered information. That was interesting for me, coming from a Catholic background and knowing white churches, to be questioning pastors and parishioners.

As it turned out, after Father Fichter wrote his first book, it was banned in the Archdiocese by the then Archbishop Francis Rummel. Father Fichter did not write the other two volumes. In fact, he left at some point and filled a chair at Harvard. But prior to his leaving I think he already had determined as a sociologist that the Catholic Church and some of its practices had to be exposed and changed. So that was the reason for his book. But after that book was banned, it galvanized more and more of us who were in school to work for social justice.

In about 1950, Father Fichter and his comrade, Father Twomey, decided to bring together white and black Catholic leaders at what I remember to be the Catholic Committee of the South. Those men and women were made up largely of Loyola and Xavier faculty members and staff people, and a few others in the Archdiocese. As I look back at it now, they did not have the force of either political or money power, but they had the force of their moral convictions to identify ways and means to integrate aspects of the Catholic Archdiocese and agencies. Most of these men and women were not from the South, although some were. If I had to speculate, it was probably fifty-fifty. But there were many from the North, because the faculty members at Xavier in those early days came from the North and the East—particularly white faculty members. And there were black faculty members as well; not that many, but some. They joined the group.

Integrating Loyola University

One special task they took on, and I'm positive it was encouraged by Father Fichter and Father Twomey, was, how do we integrate Loyola University? This was 1950. As I understand it, they identified several Xavier students who would make good candidates for the Loyola law school. The first person who was encouraged in this strategy to apply was Harry Alexander—he later became a federal judge in Washington, D.C. His father was a shoemaker in this city, and he was a Xavier Senior. He applied and was turned down. The second one, in 1951, was Richard Gumbel (father of Bryant and Greg Gumbel). He applied, and he was turned down. Those two men, both servicemen, then went straight to Georgetown, and both became lawyers.

The third try was in 1952; that was my class, and I was the candidate. The clock stopped on me, and I was accepted. So, after three years of negotiating, I applied and was admitted to Loyola law school. And this leads into my recollections of some of the student activity at the time.

When I went to Loyola, being the first black at that law school, when I answered questions on philosophy, my classmates wondered where I learned that much philosophy. Well, I may have been in a student body that was historically and predominantly black, but I was with a faculty offering a traditional Catholic education which was strong in liberal arts, which covered the length and breadth of what it is that you're supposed to learn in liberal education. There were eighteen hours of theology, twenty hours of philosophy, foreign language, drama, opera.

So I had a traditional Catholic education, but I was living in a segregated world, in a cocoon, so to speak. What drove us here at Xavier was getting out of the cocoon to another level, where we were eventually one day going to be leaders in that world. We wanted to associate with students who hopefully had some of the same views we had, but even if they did not, we might educate them to what worlds we were living in and who we were. I'm sure that in some ways we did.

We also seek to educate others about us and make a revolution

NSA and NFCCS were vehicles to meet other students in general, and to meet white students in particular. When we joined NFCCS, it started to be seen by white Southerners in the same way as white Southerners saw NSA. White Southerners put the communist tag on NSA because NSA was asking and doing the kind of things that were not acceptable, namely, having young college students—black and white—meeting together, socializing together, talking about important issues, about things that weren't right.

So they thought we were going to start talking about overthrowing the government. Well, yes, in a way. We were going to be talking about overthrowing certain aspects of the way we were living. But the fact is that we were already meeting in NFCCS locally in what was called the Southern Educational Interracial Committee. So we had Loyola and Xavier students meeting together. Then we brought all of the Catholic colleges together. Xavier was the only black college in the group.

One of my best white friends, who became a well-known public figure in New Orleans, will say that he got his Civil Rights education going to law school with me. We met when he was an undergraduate at Loyola and we traveled on the same bus upstate. When we who were black planned a trip, we planned where we could eat and use the bathroom. And whites would say, wait a minute, why are we going to stop here? They never thought that there were no places along the way where we could go in to use the restroom or to buy a

Mother M. Agatha, Xavier U. President, meets with students in 1950. From left: Jonas E. Mason, Norman C. Francis, Zirl Palmer, Richard Gumbel (elected as National Treasurer, NFCSS) and Darrel Jameson (Courtesy Norman Francis).

hamburger. So we used to say that when blacks travel in the South, they have to be great demographers in order to know where they could stop. He'd tell you today that he learned that traveling with me.

Learning that segregation cuts both ways

So what we did in NFCCS and NSA was to educate a cadre of young white college students as to what race relations was really all about. But something else very important was happening. We were showing to our white friends that while the segregation laws of the state were written to keep us out of certain places, the knife cut both ways. Those laws were also telling them whom they could choose as friends.

This became dramatically clear when I was in law school. We were studying in the office of one of my young law school classmates. We were on about the fourteenth floor of this huge building in downtown New Orleans and we took a break. They said, time to eat. And I said, bring me a hamburger and a root beer, and some fries. They were putting on their coats and they said, who do you think you are? I said, just bring me a root beer and that's it. But they answered, we're not bringing you anything. If you're too lazy to go with us you're not going to eat.

They said, you come with us if you want to eat. I said okay, I'll come with you. We went down to Canal Street, went in to the restaurant, and the waitress came and said, we can't serve him. They said (and here you have students whose fathers were mayors and public officials—they were the political figures at Loyola), what do you mean you can't serve him? And it struck home. I said, I told you. But you wanted me to come. They said, you get the manager, lady. And they told the manager, you're going to serve him tonight. That was the greatest example of their being told that the law cut both ways.

I had already accepted the fact that I wasn't going to be putting myself in a position where somebody was going to refuse to serve me. I was in law school. That was what my duty was that year. It would be later, after I got my degree, that I took up the challenge. Meanwhile, they learned. And that stuck. The first thing my white friend did when he became a City Councilman (at twenty-six years of age) was to put through an ordinance to eliminate all city laws that discriminated because of race. He was one man in the Louisiana legislature voting against every segregation law in the sixties when Jimmy Davis was governor. The point I'm making is that I can trace all of these experiences back to my student days. And then you tie in the NSA experience, which helped us broaden our horizons, and you know the experience broadened NSA as well.

My friend Moon Landrieu became the Mayor of New Orleans, and later U.S. Secretary of Housing and Urban Development. He literally changed race relations in New Orleans single-handedly.

The Southern Interracial Committee.

Early during my years at Xavier in 1949, we started a companion student group to the Catholic Committee of the South. In order to have a natural sort of way to do this, both Loyola and Xavier took on memberships in the National Federation of Catholic College Students. Our region was the Southeast Region, and I remember the name of the group was the Interracial Committee of the Southeast Region of the NFCCS. It started with Xavier and Loyola. And it expanded later, within the year that I was there, to what was then Ursuline College and Dominican College—two all-female schools—and Sacred Heart College at Grand Coteau.

In the second semester of my first year, I participated in the NFCCS regional essay contest. Each member institution had someone write and give an inspiring talk on the bad effects of segregation or some similar topic. It was held, not in New Orleans, but in Southwest Louisiana, just 20 miles from Lafayette. This again was a way of bringing black and white students together. Of course, there were no blacks at any other schools, so Xavier had to furnish all the black students. And there you had, in a way for the first time in our area, black and white students addressing the issue that was so volatile in the South, segregation, and discussing what could and should be done about it.

We were meeting together, which was something that just wasn't done. We were traveling together to places, that wasn't done. We were eating together, that wasn't done. These things were against the law. But we were doing this, again, with the support of the Catholic Committee of the South, the lay people as well as Father Fichter and Father Twomey. It was my first occasion then to meet Moon Landrieu, who, as noted, was later a classmate of mine in law school and a prominent public figure in New Orleans. I met him as an undergraduate because he was taking sociology with Father Fichter. Father Fichter taught sociology to Freshman and Sophomores, and as I look back at it, all of the young politicians who were "open-minded," or what people called liberals, all came out of Father Fichter's sociology class.

Xavier, NSA, NFCCS, and the "Red Scare"

I was President of my class for four years, and I sat on the student council the entire time. I chaired the council in my fourth year. That's how I got involved with NFCCS and NSA. I attended the National Student Congress at the University of Michigan in summer 1950.

On the regional level, I became a delegate to the NFCCS in 1949, and to NSA in 1950. I was preceded by a number of outstanding Xavier delegates. Our first delegation head was Harry Alexander, who, as I mentioned earlier, went on to become a federal judge. It was Harry's letter to LSU in March of 1947 requesting Xavier representation at the first La-Ark-Miss Regional Meeting following the Chicago Student Conference that led to the area's first integrated student government meeting that spring, as well as to a vigorously contested referendum (which preceded the meeting) favoring an interracial meeting on the LSU campus.[1] Harry was also later elected Regional Chairman.

During 1949-1950 Aaron Henry was Chairman of our Student Activities Committee, and he headed our delegation at the Illinois Convention of NSA in the summer of 1949. Although not a Catholic, he was president of his Junior and Senior classes and President of the Xavier Student Body in his Senior year, in 1950. Aaron went on to become a state legislator, a nationally renowned leader in the Mississippi civil rights movement and head of the state National Association for the Advancement of Colored People (NAACP) in 1960.[2]

A number of us who represented NFCCS in the national organization also were representatives to NSA. Richard Gumbel, who was denied admission to Loyola in New Orleans and so went on to Georgetown, gave great leadership in NFCCS. I think he was the first black national officer at NFCCS when he was elected Treasurer in 1950. He was an ex-serviceman and very mature. I traveled with him on a number of occasions to the national meetings. It was his involvement in the national NFCCS that helped us and inspired us to belong to NSA.

By 1950, when I was active in NSA, no white Catholic or private colleges in the Louisiana Region belonged to NSA.[3] Tulane did not belong to NSA. I think some students there wanted to join. However, they ran into all kinds of problems. As I recall, they participated in some local meetings, but it was during that time that NSA in particular was labeled by some in the South as a communist organization. The worst thing you could do at that time was to call somebody a communist.[4]

NSA had such a "bad name" as being a communist organization on some campuses, that Tulane wouldn't touch it. Loyola wouldn't touch it. And there even was some hesitancy at Xavier behind the scenes, except that we were now into the national student movement with NFCCS and felt there was no reason why we couldn't be in NSA. We figured we were strong enough, and I guess, now that I look back at some of this, I think what moved us forward was that the people who were calling us communist were the same people who were what I called conservative or segregationists. So, I believed, simply, if they are against this, therefore, this must be good for us. Also, we didn't think anybody should tell us what we could or could not do at an institution. But Tulane and Loyola wouldn't touch membership.

The 1950 Michigan NSA Congress

I attended my first NSA convention at the University of Michigan in 1950, when Al Lowenstein was elected President. We were holding the election of the President in Rackham Auditorium. We couldn't agree on a candidate, so a compromise candidate was offered. It was Al Lowenstein of the University of North Carolina. He wasn't even in the room. He was out playing tennis. I was one of the four people who left the auditorium to get him off the tennis court to tell him we had just elected him President of NSA. Al was like so many of NSA's alumni, who were all leaders in their respective schools and went on to become leaders nationally. For me, as a Southern black person, that experience was a memorable one, broadening my view of what the range of student issues was nationally, and especially how issues of race fit into that national agenda.

More particularly, I found that the places we traveled to in the North were not that much different than the South, except that they didn't have "no colored wanted" signs on the bathrooms or at the bars and other places. But the feeling that you got, for those of us who were black, was that you weren't welcome.

As a pointed example, I recall an incident the following year, during the 1951 NFCCS convention in St. Paul, Minnesota (which was happening at the same time as NSA's University of Minnesota Congress). About five of us went into a nice local neighborhood tavern. I was the only black in the group. We went to the bar and we each ordered a beer. One of my white colleagues noticed that we weren't being served. He reminded the bartender that we had ordered five beers, and the man finally brought them. We drank the beers, and when he collected the glasses, he threw mine in the trash can.

That was a striking reminder to me that our problems were not just Southern problems, they were national problems. It was the hypocrisy that struck me, the old saying that "we in the South had a cold and were trying to treat it." Other parts of the country had a cold and didn't know or were ignoring it. Our NSA and NFCCS experiences taught us that.

Allard Lowenstein

NSA also forged my association with Al Lowenstein, who went on to great prominence. Al wrote the powerful and widely acclaimed 1962 book *Brutal Mandate*, about his experiences with apartheid in South Africa. Tragically, he was killed by a distraught acquaintance in 1980. Al became an outspoken leader after the 1967 NSA Congress, inspiring the nationwide "Dump Johnson" movement in the Democratic

Party. Earlier, he mobilized his extensive network of former and current NSA leaders and activists in courageous support of the 1964 Mississippi Freedom Summer.[5]

I remember fondly that when he'd come to New Orleans, he'd always come and see me. Back when I was in law school, we would ride behind the screen in the bus and the bus driver would constantly say to him, you can't ride back there. And Al would just say, I ride where I want to ride. And he'd always be sitting behind the colored screen on the New Orleans buses. He was a great NSA President and student leader.

An arena for leadership training.

The South had a lot of fine public leaders who got their basic training in NSA and NFCCS, where they broadened their view of what was to be important to them in leadership, not just for Southern people, but what was a broader view nationally. Moon Landrieu was a typical example of that. Another one was Pascal Calogero, who is currently Chief Justice of the State Supreme Court for Louisiana. Others out of Xavier include Maurice Fykes, Clifford Lemelle, Harry Alexander, Aaron Henry, Richard Gumbel, Aloha Collins, Ann Darensbourg, Noel Gray, Charles Bell, Dolores Cooper, Wilbert Sykes, and Ronald Rousseve.

For myself, it proved an invaluable experience, which helped to shape the directions I took in life and in my career. After forty-two years in higher education administration for African Americans, including thirty-three years as the President of Xavier University, I had the privilege of serving thousands of Xavier graduates who today are championing the causes NSA envisioned for America. These African Americans serve in virtually every professional field, including leadership positions as mayors, legislators, federal and state judges and attorneys, university professors and presidents, ambassadors, teachers, U.S. cabinet secretaries, and religious professionals.

My NSA "pebble experience" dropped in the 1950 waters has produced many human ripples for furthering civic and educational rights in this democratic society.

Since 1968, Norman C. Francis has been President of Xavier University in New Orleans, the only U.S. Catholic university with a predominantly black enrollment. He is Chairman of the Board for the Southern Education Foundation in Atlanta, and has served as President of the American Association of Higher Education and as Chairman of the Board of the Educational Testing Service.

END NOTES

1 *Editor's note:* According to the March 19, 1947, issue of LSU's *Daily Reveille,* the LSU Student Council, which was to be host to simultaneous meetings of the NSO (as it was known in spring 1947) regional organizing meeting and the Conference of Southern and Southwestern Colleges, voted to exclude delegates from Negro colleges. Lloyd Love, student body president, is quoted as saying, "I do not think it is wise to have an inter-racial conference at this time." The reaction to this from the student body was so negative, with angry letters to the editor filling the paper's editorial pages, that the Council ran a campus-wide referendum, which resulted in a 2,491–1,359 vote in favor of holding an interracial meeting. (See p. 454.)

Determined to avoid an on-campus integrated event, the Council decided to hold two meetings, with the NSO regional meeting held at the First Presbyterian Church, off-campus. According to the April 27, 1947, issue of the *Daily Reveille,* Negro delegates from six colleges were in attendance, along with an unspecified number of the delegates from the sixteen white colleges attending the Southern regional meeting.

Although the meeting was not reported in the *Xavier Herald,* a citation appears in the annual 1947 Report of the President of Xavier University, after a note that Charles Bell and Harry Alexander had represented the university at the first regional conference of the National Student Association, which met in Baton Rouge, April 19. "At first there was objection to having colored students at this meeting. However, some of the students at Louisiana State University openly protested against this in their school newspaper and they finally won out; the colored students were permitted to attend and were well received." (See p. 437.)

The following year, there was a bitterly fought "Red Scare" affiliation battle at LSU, during which the campaign in favor of joining was led by Gillis Long, who later became a Louisiana Congressman. He had attended the Constitutional Convention of NSA and was then the student body president. In the end, LSU students voted 1,302 to 620 against affiliation. The February 19, 1948, issue of the *Daily Reveille* reported, "The NSA amendment was the highlight of yesterday's election. Red-painted hammers and sickles with 'NSA' painted under them decorated campus sidewalks yesterday. On several of the polling places were red painted signs urging voters: 'Send Our Students to Moscow: Vote for NSA,' and 'Uncle Joe Says Vote 'Yes' on NSA.'" (See p. 455.)

The paper itself was also a strong supporter of NSA, and had editorialized a few days earlier that "When you vote Thursday on the NSA issue consider well the opportunity which the national group affords our own campus. With it LSU students can go forward. . . . Let's pool our efforts and profit from the NSA."

2 See Aaron Henry, p. 456. See also John Peoples, p. 425. Peoples, who later became President of Jackson State College, met Aaron Henry at the 1949 NSA convention, where they formed a lifetime friendship.

3 During the years 1946-1952, Xavier attended all of the NSA Congresses and maintained its membership. Following is the record of Louisiana membership and Congress attendance during that period (the 1946 Chicago Conference and 1947 Constitutional Convention were not membership events): Louisiana State University (1946, 1947, 1948 observer); Southeast Louisiana (1946, 1947, 1948, 1950, 1952 observer); Southwest Louisiana (1946, 1947, 1948); Southern University (1947, 1948, 1950, 1951, 1952); Tulane (1946); Xavier University (1946-1952).

4 *Editor's note:* The January 16, 1947, issue of the *Tulane Hullaballoo* reports, following the Chicago Student Conference:

> Tulane's student body president Dick Page returned to New Orleans last week unimpressed. "Because of the fact that the proposed organization is indefinite as to scope and purpose, I do not think it will benefit Tulane until it is better organized and has proved its worth."

That Tulane was also in the thick of the "Red Scare" is evidenced by some of the college newspaper editorials of the time:

In a December 1948 editorial, the *Hullabaloo* noted that a recent House Un-American Activities Committee list of communist-sponsored American schools thankfully did not include Tulane. However, it noted, "this recent list post-dates by four months a statement by one committee member, F. Edward Hebert of Louisiana, that 'there are more Communists who infest that place (Tulane) than Americans.'" The editorial then proceeds to debunk the Congressman and question why he didn't offer "one scrap of proof," suggesting that he had "gone overboard." In an editorial on November 6, 1947, the paper takes on critics who "laud freedom of speech for themselves," but had "set up a howl" that permitting "a speech by Henry Agard Wallace means that Tulane has become a bee-hive of Communism." On May 6, 1948, the newspaper was still addressing the issue. It editorialized, "Saturday was a Red-letter day in Birmingham. The local gestapo arrested Senator Glen Taylor, D. Idaho, the Wallace vice-presidential candidate, because he tried to use the 'Negro' entrance of a building in which he was to address the Southern Negro Youth Congress."

5 See William H. Chafe's biography of Al Lowenstein, *Never Stop Running* (New York: Basic Books, 1993).

PICTURE CREDITS: *Then:* c. 1950, Xavier. *Now:* c. 1998, President, Xavier University (both, courtesy author).

NORMAN C. FRANCIS

Early Background and Military Service. Dr. Francis was born in Lafayette, Louisiana, where he attended Catholic elementary and high schools. He served in the Third Armored Division of the U.S. Army from 1955 to 1957.

Education. Bachelor of Arts, 1952, Xavier University of Louisiana, New Orleans, LA. Doctor of Jurisprudence, 1955, Loyola University Law School, New Orleans, LA.

Career. During his thirty-one year tenure as President of the nation's only predominantly Black Catholic college, since 1968, the University has more than tripled its enrollment, broadened its curriculum, and expanded its campus.

Dr. Francis served in an advisory role to four presidential administrations—including the historic National Commission on Excellence in Education, whose findings, published in the work *A Nation at Risk,* created a sense of urgency for bringing about educational reform in the nation's school system. He has served as Chairman of the Member President's Council for the United Negro College Fund, President of the American Association of Higher Education, Chairman of the Board of the Southern Association of Colleges and Schools, and as Chairman of the Board of the Educational Testing Service.

He has provided leadership for civil rights, educational, civic, and religious organizations throughout his career. He serves as Chairman of the Board for the Southern Education Foundation in Atlanta. He is a member of the National Advisory Committee on Institutional Quality and Integrity, the National Science Foundation 2000 Advisory Committee, and a number of boards, including the Carnegie Foundation for the Advancement of Teaching, the National Foundation for Improvement in Education (NFIE), and the American Council on Education. He is a Fellow of the American Academy of Arts and Sciences (Cambridge, MA). He holds honorary degrees from twenty-five institutions of higher education.

In New Orleans, he serves as Chairman of the Board of Liberty Bank and Trust, and is a member of several boards including Bank One, the Greater New Orleans Foundation, the Foundation for the Mid-South, and the Advisory Board of *The Times-Picayune* Publishing Co. He is a member of the Business Council of New Orleans and other local organizations.

After becoming, in 1955, the first Black to receive a law degree from Loyola University, and then completing military service in 1957, Dr. Francis returned to Xavier. There he held the positions of Dean of Men, Director of Student Personnel Service, Assistant to the President for Student Affairs, Assistant to the President in Charge of Development, and, in 1967, Executive Vice President. He became Xavier's first lay, male, and Black head in 1968. Its previous Presidents were Sisters of the Blessed Sacrament, its founding order.

Family. Married forty-five years to Blanche Macdonald Francis. He is the father of six children and grandfather of eight.

The Xavier Herald

"ALL-CATHOLIC"—FOURTEEN YEARS—1932-1946

VOL. XXII XAVIER UNIVERSITY, NEW ORLEANS, LA., JANUARY, 1947 No. 3

XAVIER STUDENTS ATTEND CONVENTION IN CHICAGO

Xavier University was well represented at the National Students Conference in Chicago. Shown in the picture above are the delegates and observers. Left to right, they are: Howard Mason, '48; Maurice Fykes, '48; Charles Thibodeaux, '47; Noel Gray, '47; Sandra Smithson, '49, and Clarence Jupiter, '49. Miss Smithson had a place of vantage in the press gallery, as reporter for the Xavier Herald.

University Displays Interest In Expanding International Education

Fully bent on keeping abreast with the progressive march of modern education, Xavier, upon invitation, sent six representatives—two delegates and four observers—to the National Student Convention held at the University of Chicago, December 28-30.

Ernest Charles Thibodeaux and Noel Gray, seniors in the School of Liberal Arts, were the delegates chosen by the senior class to represent Xavier University at the Chicago Convention. The junior class elected as observers: Maurice Fykes, Science, and Howard Mason, Physical Education as their representatives; the sophomore class, Saundra Smithson, Liberal Arts, and Clyde Jupiter, Science.

These students were selected on a basis of possessing a well founded general knowledge of international affairs, an objective interest in students and student problems, general skill in carrying parliamentary discussions, and a firm desire for preserving world peace.

Xavier's Stand

The convention represents the initial attempt at an exclusive student union in the United States. The need for a National Student Organization was clearly seen when this country alone, of all the major powers, did not have a unified representation at the International Union of Students Convention held at Prague, Czechoslovakia, last year.

...ve Students From Xavier ...tend Regional Conference

Scholarly Attitude Seen At Xavier

"Did you take your history exam yet?"—

Xavier Herald 11/49

Xavier Delegates Relate NSA Convention Activities

The four students who represented Xavier at the National Student Association convention this summer gave a brief outline of their experiences and activities at the regular weekly assembly Nov. 16.

The convention, held on the University of Illinois campus Aug. 23 to Sept. 3, was attended by John L. Finley, Donald F. Barry, Dolores J. Cooper and Aaron E. Henry.

After opening remarks by Sister Mary Frances, dean of the University, the delegates, introduced by Henry, addressed the student body. The origin, meaning, aims and this

Xavier Herald 3/52

N. S. A. President Visits University

William T. Dentzer, president of the National Student Association, visited Xavier March 17 on a tour of schools. Ronald Rousseve, chairman of the NSA Gulf Coast Region, welcomed Mr. Dentzer to the university.

Following his election as president, Dentzer said, "I will do all in my power to work for the development of the moral student community." Mr. Rousseve spoke highly of the association president, terming him "a mature student, possessed of quiet ways and a simple dignity.

XAVIER SENT DELEGATES to NSA congresses each year from 1946 through 1952, and provided active regional leadership. Delegates to Chicago pictured above include Howard Mason, Maurice Fykes, Charles Thirodeaux, Noel Gray, Sandra Smithson and Clarence Jupiter. Right, Harry Alexander was regional chair in 1948-49. Ronald Rousseve served as regional chair in 1951-52. Ann Darensbourg was senior Xavier delegate in 1950 and 1951.

Harry Alexander

Ronald Rousseve

Ann Darensbourg

NSA and NFCCS: A Tale of Two Associations (1947-1951)

Excerpts from the corporate minutes and annual Report of the President, Mother M. Agatha, Xavier University.

1947

NATIONAL CONFERENCE, NATIONAL STUDENT ASSOCIATION

Xavier University was among the institutions of higher learning represented at the first regional conference of the National Student Association, which met in Baton Rouge, Louisiana, April 19th. Mr. Julian A. Parker of the faculty attended as an observer; also Mr. Noel Gray, '47. The student delegates were Charles Bell and Harry Alexander. This regional meeting was an outgrowth of the Chicago meeting held last December, at which Xavier was represented.

At first there was objection to having colored students at this regional meeting. However some of the students at Louisiana State University openly protested against this in their school paper, and they finally won out; the colored delegates were permitted to attend and were well received.

At the meeting of the National Student Association held in Wisconsin, early in September, Clifford LeMelle and Harry Alexander represented the students at Xavier. Xavier was one of the two Catholic colleges to send delegates from the Louisiana, Mississippi and Arkansas region. Mr. Robert Smith Shea attended the meeting as a delegate of Xavier University.

1948

INTERRACIAL INSTITUTE

Sister M. Gonzaga and Mother M. David attended a series of weekly interracial institute meetings held at the Y.W.C.A., New Orleans. The meetings were attended by one hundred delegates, representing public white and colored schools, Catholic white and colored schools, Dillard University, Loyola University, Tulane University and Xavier University. Dr. Glock of Tulane University was Chairman of the Institute. The meetings were held weekly from the latter part of 1947 through March 1948. At one meeting, Mother M. David presented a paper entitled, "What Does the Curriculum of the School Contribute to Good Interracial Relations?" As a result of the Institute, it is believed that the delegates became more conscious of the problem of interracial relations and will undoubtedly carry on in their classrooms and schools a campaign for better race relations.

NATIONAL STUDENT ASSOCIATION

At the annual meeting of the National Student Association, held at the University of Wisconsin, Mr. Harry Alexander, Chairman of the Committee on Student Activities at Xavier, was elected Provisional Regional Chairman of the Louisiana, Mississippi, Arkansas region, a newly formed national student group.

1950

NFCCS

Mr. Richard Gumbel was elected National Treasurer of the National Federation of Catholic College Students at a meeting in Pittsburgh during the week of April 10th.

INTERRACIAL DAY

The Interracial Commission of the Southeastern Region of the N.F.C.C.S. held its second annual Catholic Interracial Day at the College of the Sacred Heart, Grand Coteau, Louisiana, on Sunday, March 12, 1950, at 11:00 a.m. Guest Speakers were Mr. Clarence A. Laws, of The Louisiana Weekly, and Mr. John J. McCann, Attorney, at the Student Forum in the afternoon, over which Aaron E. Henry of Xavier presided. Winners of the College Speech Contests at Ursuline, Xavier, Sacred Heart, Loyola, and Dominican spoke on "Prejudice, The Crucifixion of the Mystical Body." Norman Francis, Xavier sophomore, was declared the winner, and Reverend Jules B. Jeanmard, D.D., Bishop of Lafayette, presented the trophy. Sister M. Gonzaga and Sister Marie Barat, several lay faculty, and 50 students attended. The Commission held regular meetings during the year at Xavier and Loyola, alternating each month.

NATIONAL STUDENT ASSOCIATION

The Third Annual National Student Association Congress met at the University of Michigan, Ann Arbor, Michigan, August 23 to 31, 1950. It was attended by more than 750 delegates and observers representing some 354 schools. Xavier's delegates were Dolores Cooper and Norman Francis; and observers Ann M. Darensbourg and Ronald Rousseve. Dolores Cooper was appointed subcomission leader. Mr. Francis and Mr. Rousseve served on the Constitution Revision Committee, and Miss Darensbourg as secretary of the N.E.C. for two days. Miss Cooper was chosen as Parliamentarian for Commission I. She was also offered the position as national staff worker in the national office, but declined. The theme of the Congress was "The Role of the Student in the Educational Community." Mr. Ronald Rousseve and Dolores Cooper were selected regional chairman and secretary, respectively.

On April 27, the president of the NSA, Robert A. Kelly, student at St. Peter's College. New Jersey, stopped at Xavier on a tour to confer with N.S.A. members. The students of the Committee on Student Activities met Mr. Kelly and showed him around the campus, after which he remained for dinner in the Dining Hall.

1951

NATIONAL STUDENT ASSOCIATION

Two delegates from Xavier—Ronald Rousseve and Anne Marie Darensbourg, juniors—together with two student observers—Aloha Collins and Wilbert Sykes—attended the 4th Annual National Student Association Congress held in August at the University of Minnesota. The Congress theme was "The Role of the Student in the World Community." Mr. Rousseve, in a report of the delegates at a general Xavier assembly, presented the highlights of the congress, which featured an address by Dr. Harold Stassen, former governor of Minnesota who is now president of the University of Pennsylvania.

NFCCS ANNUAL CONGRESS

The College of St. Thomas, St. Paul, Minnesota, was the scene of the Eighth National Congress of the National Federation of Catholic College Students August 26 through September 1, 1951. Mr. Norman Francis, Education senior who had been recently elected President of the Southeastern Region of the NFCCS, Mr. Charles Allain, and Mr. Edmund Broussard attended the Congress. "The Catholic College Student and the Parish," was the theme of the Congress, offering a challenge to the students in a field yet untried as an NFCCS activity. Highlights of the Congress were addresses by the Most Rev. James J. Byrne, S.T.D, Auxiliary Bishop of St. Paul; Very Rev. Vincent J. Flynn, president of the College of St. Thomas; Very Rev. Ignatius Smith, O.P., dean of the School of Philosophy at the Catholic University of America; and Monsignor Joseph E. Schieder, national director of the NFCCS.

To each generation there is given a great decision.

THE CATHOLIC COMMITTEE OF THE SOUTH (1940s-1950s)

"It involves the fundamental rights of men"

Excerpts from an undated booklet published by The Catholic Committee of the South, Rock Hill, South Carolina, used by the Commission on Human Rights in New Orleans in the 1940s and 1950s.

Fried chicken, yams and cornbread; cotton, textiles, tobacco, poverty; progressive thinking, reaction, statesmanship, demagoguery—a thousand words, a thousand phrases, fiery speeches, graphs, charts; hundreds of books and articles, the work of serious minded men who have analyzed the South, have all painted a varicolored picture.

Years ago some Catholic Bishops, priests, and laymen saw this picture with its moral, religious and cultural implications. They formed the Catholic Committee of the South to study the situation.

The Catholic Committee of the South is a regional organization. It studies the problems prevalent in the States of Alabama, Florida, Georgia, Kentucky, Louisiana, Mississippi, North Carolina, South Carolina, Virginia, and the District of Columbia. Studying these problems in the light of the Sacred Scriptures and of the teachings of the Church; applying the principles found therein to the problem, the Committee strives to develop this most vital section of the country.

The Committee was conceived by a group of Southern bishops, clergy and laity who were attending a meeting called by the Social Action Department of the National Catholic Welfare Conference in Cleveland, Ohio, in 1939. The South was even then the maternity ward of the nation, accounting for one-third of the annual national population increase. Looking into the future, one could foresee vast throngs of new Americans infected with ideas and ideals contrary to Christian principles and effectively depriving them of their birthright as children of God and citizens of a Christian democracy. Many of the best minds of the nation recognized the impending danger of this situation, and this small group of Southern Catholics saw it as a challenge for the Church in the South.

Although these Southerners realized that no parish, diocese or region is an island unto itself, they recognized the fact that the Southeastern Region of the United States did have numerous problems peculiar to itself and morally dangerous both for itself and for the nation in general. There was an obvious need for some kind of effective Christian action on a regional basis, This thinking led to the organization of the Catholic Committee of the South at a convention called in Atlanta, Georgia, under the sponsorship of the Southern Bishops in 1940.

YOUTH

The Department of Youth has perhaps the most important program of all—to devise and implement techniques for training the Catholic youth of today's South for leadership in the South of tomorrow. This department employs every available means to present the youth of the region with the challenge of the South and to stimulate them to accept the challenge.

THE SPIRIT OF THE COMMITTEE

This is the Catholic Committee of the South, but it is even more than this. It is a spirit, too; it is dedicated love and willing sacrifice on the part of its active participants. It is no mere idealistic dream. It is Catholic Action in a pitched battle against forces of evil. It is bishops, priests, religious and laity struggling together against tremendous odds to improve social conditions and relationships in the South as an important necessary step towards making the South Christian. The fruits of their labors are encouragingly evident, but their chief concern is to give unselfishly to the building of a Christian heritage for successive generations.

To each generation there is given a great decision. A previous generation made a political decision, it won independence. Another generation made a social decision, another an economic decision.

Our Generation faces a decision. That is social, religious and cultural. It involves the fundamental rights of men, with implications that are national and international. We Catholics face a decision in the South. We believe in the full Life of the Mystical Body of Christ. It is our answer to the present crisis. The Committee strives for a full use of the Life of Christ. You can work with it. It is your generation.

7927-A ST. CHARLES AVE. NEW ORLEANS 18, LA.

The Catholic Committee of the South

PHILIP S. OGILVIE
EXECUTIVE SECRETARY

7927-A ST. CHARLES AVE. NEW ORLEANS 18, LA.

August 17, 1950

The Registrar
Xavier University
New Orleans, Louisiana

Dear Sir:

I have received recently a letter from Mr. Thomas Callahan, Student Councelor of the National Scholarship Service and Fund for Negro Students, 31 W. 110 St., N. Y., 26, N. Y., in which he requested information concerning which private and particularly Catholic High Schools are exclusively for Negroes. He has requested that I refer his inquiry to some person who might be in a position to give him this information. I shall deeply appreciate it if you will have one of your secretaries take care of this matter, or if you will refer it to someone who will have the information available. I regret that my own busy schedule of the moment will not permit me enough time in New Orleans to gather this information or call on you personally.

Thank you for what ever attention you can give this matter.

Sincerely yours in Christ,

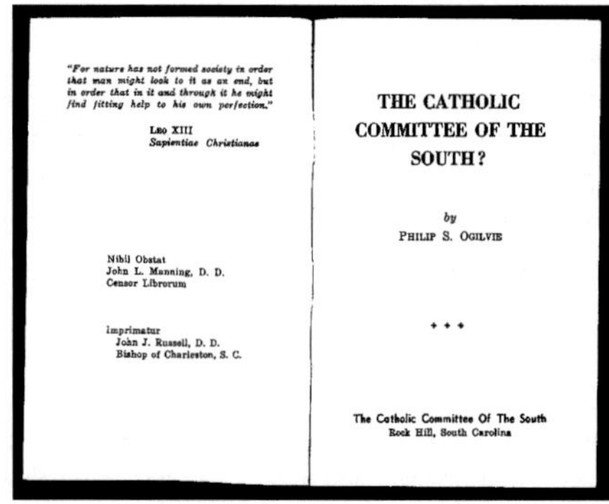

"For nature has not formed society in order that man might look to it as an end, but in order that in it and through it he might find fitting help to his own perfection."

Leo XIII
Sapientiae Christianae

Nihil Obstat
John L. Manning, D. D.
Censor Librorum

Imprimatur
John J. Russell, D. D.
Bishop of Charleston, S. C.

THE CATHOLIC COMMITTEE OF THE SOUTH?

by
PHILIP S. OGILVIE

\+ + +

The Catholic Committee Of The South
Rock Hill, South Carolina

NEW CONNECTIONS WERE BEING FORMED for the advancement of racial justice. At left is a letter to Xavier from Phillip S. Ogilvie, Executive Secretary of the Catholic Committee referencing an inquiry from Thomas Callahan (later to become NSA Travel Director) in behalf of the National Scholarship Service and Fund for Negro Students (see Tyler, this section). Above, the title page of the booklet excerpted on this page.

XAVIER UNIVERSITY AND THE COMMISSION ON HUMAN RIGHTS (1950-1952)

Excerpts from an undated memorandum in the Xavier University archives, probably originating between 1950 and 1952.

Does the Commission take part in any extra-Catholic interracial activity?

A. The Commission supports all movements which honestly seek to end obvious injustices towards Negroes; either by mutual action or through expressed approval, it cooperates with other agencies and groups working in the field of human relations. To be more definite, the Commission has actively taken a stand on such questions as police brutality towards Negroes, the discriminatory policies of New Orleans newspapers, segregation in the Municipal auditorium, and the segregated and discriminatory pattern now in force in New Orleans' public schools.

Is it true that the membership rolls are dominated by "Northern whites" who are not fully cognizant of affairs as they stand in the South in regards to racial matters and who are, therefore, hasty, rash and imprudent in their judgments ?

A. There are 60 white members on the rolls; of this total 45—or 75%—are bona fide Southerners by birth.

Is it not true that faculty members from Xavier University dominate the membership of the Commission both in numbers and influence?

A. Of a total membership of more than 100, there are but 10 Xavier faculty members, less than 10% of the total. But 3 members of the Xavier faculty hold posts involving the determination of Commission policy. . . .

Has the Commission on Human Rights actually accomplished anything?
A. Actual direct accomplishments of the Commission:

1. Public appearances of an interracial group at Mass and Holy Communion have made a profound impression.

2. The public meeting arranged by this Commission, together with the Students' Interracial Group, in honor of Bishop Kiwanuka at Holy Name Auditorium saw a non-segregated Audience in that hall for the first time.

3. An interracial experiment in the Institute of Industrial Relations at Loyola University was only undertaken by the Institute's director, Father Louis Twomey, after he had received assurances of the Commission's support. The Institute is now progressing favorably along interracial lines. . . .

8. Cooperation and support of Catholic Interracial Day sponsored by the student groups in New Orleans. . . .

10. The very existence of the Commission—THE FIRST CATHOLIC INTERRACIAL GROUP IN THE DEEP SOUTH—is in itself a great achievement.

11. The great increase in membership over a period of less than two years without any membership drive of any kind is an indication of the growing interest in our ideals.

A final word: The Commission is being talked about! Its weight is being felt. The greatest set-back we could possibly suffer is to be ignored, and that is not happening.

Three of the program planners of the Annual Interracial Day at Loyola (left to right): Norman Francis, Father J. H. Fichter, S. J., and Thomas Tirney, Southeastern regional publicity chairman (*Xavier Herald*, February 1951).

NORMAN FRANCIS
. . . *regional prexy*

Norman Francis Elected Regional NFCCS President

Norman Francis, education senior, from Xavier University, was elected president of the Regional Council of the National Federation of Catholic College Students this past summer at an NFCCS meeting at Xavier.

He succeeds Harold Lamy of Loyola who was elected to the treasurer's position.

Other new officers include Miss Claire Barker, Grand Coteau, vice-president; Miss Sue Fucich, Dominican, recording secretary; Miss Joan Barrios, Ursuline, corresponding secretary, and Lamy, Loyola, treasurer.

The meeting was opened with a prayer by Father F. O'Flynn, S.J., dean of Loyola University and closed by Father E. Bergen, S.J., dean of men, Loyola.

Xavierite Richard Gumbel Is Named to NFCCS Post

Richard Gumbel was elected national treasurer of the National Federation of Catholic College Students at its recent meeting in Pittsburgh, Sister Mary Frances, dean, announced.

The business administration major, who has long been active in the work of the Interracial and International Relations commissions of the Federation, attended the meeting along with Doris Walker, Norman Francis and Larry Brown.

Other officers elected at the national meeting are: president, Louis Manderino of St. Vincent's college, Latrobe, Pa.; vice president, Charles Starrs, Niagara university, Niagara, N.Y.; second vice president, Ray

RICHARD GUMBEL
National Treasurer

(1951 Yearbook. Xavier Archives)

XAVIER STUDENTS PROVIDED LEADERSHIP to the Catholic student movement's interracial programs. Left, Norman Francis (*Xavier Herald* 10/51). Right, Richard Gumbel (*Herald* 5/50) who had also been student body president.

NSA participation would be hard to prove. It would, however, be impossible to deny

3. Desegregating Kenan Stadium in Chapel Hill

Barry Farber
University of North Carolina
Chair, NSA Virginia-Carolinas Region, 1951-52

There were no black students at the University of North Carolina in 1951. That was not considered outrageous, even by us NSA "liberals." (Were we liberals? Great question. We opposed racial injustice, but the notion of organizing a campaign to have blacks admitted to the university never occurred to any of us. It would have been regarded by us as an absurdity; an absurdity akin to flying down to the Amazon and getting our heads shrunk.) Looking back I marvel at the strangeness of our thinking. Racial segregation to us was evil, but our all-white University of North Carolina was "normal." I'd love to know right now what I would have said if somebody had asked me in 1951, "Why don't you rise up against an all-white, segregated university?" Nobody ever did. We weren't wimps. We preached against segregation. We sought out venues where we could (shockingly to our nonactivist friends) associate with blacks. We never, however, got together and said, "Hey. This system down here has got to go!"

Until the Kenan Stadium incident.

We were much more assertive in our opposition to dictatorships. Had the year been 1941 I'm sure we would have done all we could to oppose the Nazi dictator. It was, however, 1951, and the malevolent and malignant dictatorship of that day was communism, and we opposed it. (That was not a universal emotion throughout all of NSA. Historians should seek out NSA veterans of downtown Chicago!)[1]

First Negro students admitted to law school in 1952

In 1951 the University of North Carolina made precisely the kind of history you might expect from the University of North Carolina. They hauled off and admitted five black graduate students (We liberals called them "Negroes"), becoming thereby the first state university in the south to admit black students without a court order.

We of NSA were thrilled. I'm still thrilled. I just wish they had been admitted to the "real" university. They were not. They were admitted to grad school; the Law School. Never mind. We could face down our other southern brothers and claim bragging rights to being the first to "do right" about race.

Chancellor Robert House, the venerable hands-on manager of the university, did something, which today would be seen as breathtaking. Then it merely seemed wrong.

He summoned the five black law students into his office and said something like:

> Boys, we're proud to have you. We're going to do wonderful things together. We're going to set an example for the whole South. You and we both have taken a giant step and the world's already better for it.
>
> There's one little housekeeping detail, however, we'd like to take care of right here at the outset to make sure nothing mars or impedes our progress.

All students were automatically issued passbooks that entitled them to sit in the student section of home football games in Kenan Stadium. But Chancellor House asked the five black students to surrender their passbooks and accept tickets instead to Section K.

Chancellor House was laboring under the establishment wisdom that feared the mix of football Saturday, fraternity men with their dates, beer-wine-whiskey, gridiron tension—and blacks—just might be a little too combustible. Section K, thought Chancellor House, could save us all.

Seats offered in jim-crow section of stadium

Section K was the jim-crow section of the stadium, where the local blacks from Chapel Hill and vicinity could sit. Section K was not only in the end zone. It was in a far corner of the end-zone, split off from the rest of the end zone by a passageway, through which the football players ran out onto the field from the field house. For some reason I can't remember, I sat in the end zone across that passageway from Section K one time. You'd have needed a transistor radio to learn what *sport* they were playing out there, much less what was going on.

The black students said, "Nothing doing." They weren't going merely for the "touchdown" of university admission. They were going for the extra point of full university citizenship![2]

And so were we.

To claim NSA valor in the ensuing encounter seems fatuous over half a century later. At no point did we NSAers on campus seek to put our fingerprints on the fight. We established no paper trail to prove our participation in the glory that followed. But it can be claimed without fear of rebuttal that every single NSA activist on campus was instinctively wedded to the position that there must be no "second-class students!"

We no more needed a paper trail than a new mother needs proof that she welcomed the opportunity to nurse her baby. We were in NSA precisely in hopes of fighting fights like that one.

As NSA's regional chairman, I was invited to join a delegation of about thirty-five student organizations that rose up and demanded that the new black students be allowed to sit with us at home football games. We were grudgingly granted an audience with Chancellor House in his office. He was arrogant, but eloquent. The representative of one of the religious groups on campus opened our entreaty by saying:

> Chancellor House, our Bible as well as our Constitution tell us it's wrong to discriminate against anyone because of his race and we students demand our new Negro classmates be allowed to keep their student passbooks and sit among us in Kenan Stadium like any other student of any other color.

"That's not without its poetic value," said Chancellor House,

> but I have responsibilities you students can't even begin to fathom and I will stand with you in any house of worship in the land and debate with you the theology and the practicality that underlies our handling of this transition in the prudent manner your administration has chosen.

The student representing the debating society rose to protest the fact that students were not consulted before the administration moved to repossess the passbooks of the new black students.

"Not only were you not consulted," said a steely Chancellor House. "You were not considered!"

Shamefully, as one who always viewed political correctness as only a half step preferable to outright evil, I smiled inwardly at Chancellor House's Mussolini-like putdown of our juvenile foray into civil rights. Proudly, though, my admiration for his slashing domination of that little meeting did not diminish or deflect my opposition to his dictate.

Organization of athletes drawn into protest

Clout unrecognized is clout wasted. One of the members of our defeated and deflated delegation pointed out to me that, in addition to being NSA regional chairman, I was also vice president of the Monogram Club, the organization of the athletes themselves who, in effect, held a moral franchise over Kenan Stadium and every other athletic venue in Chapel Hill.

"Why don't you try to get the Monogram Club to pass a resolution against the denial of student passbooks to the new Negroes?" asked he.

It was a great question and a great concept.

The two campus organizations that counted far more than all the dozens of others were, of course, the Monogram Club and the Student Legislature: the elected representatives of the student body. The Student Legislature was due to meet the following night to take a stand. They could support the administration, denounce the administration, or ignore the whole thing. There was voluble campus support for each of those possibilities.

I was merely vice president of the Monogram Club. The president, football player Dick Bestwick, had already told me he had to be elsewhere during our meeting the following evening and he asked me to preside. The Student Legislature was to meet and take up the issue about the same time our Monogram Club was set to meet.

The problem was, it wasn't really a Monogram Club meeting that night. It was to be a party; a beer party with dates in attendance and no club business to be transacted.

I asked Dick if he'd mind if I interrupted the meeting just long enough to present the issue and take a vote. He agreed.

Many times at many meetings over the years it's been my duty to rise, clink a glass with a fork, and make some announcement. I doubt that I'll ever have occasion to stage an interruption more monumental than this one! Here were gathered the jocks of the usually triumphant University of North Carolina teams hoisting beer mugs in the presence of the fairest of their female classmates in the year 1951.

"Excuse me," I began. I then reviewed the situation regarding the new black students and the injustice of their being denied by our university administration the right to sit in the student section of home football games. I pointed out that the Student Legislature was meeting that very evening to take a position and that position could very well be influenced by a strong resolution by the Monogram Club demanding that there should "be no second-class students at the University of North Carolina."

Today such a move would be a given in any student context. You'd get nothing but annoyance for interrupting anything as important as a beer party for such a moral cliche.

This, however, was 1951. Never will I forget the discomfort and, yes, the fear, of those beautiful southern girls of 1951 standing there in the Monogram clubhouse thinking there'd be nothing but beer and giggles with high-profile jocks and all of a sudden having the party interrupted with all sorts of subversive talk about Negroes and justice and integrating the stadium and defying the university administration.

Journalism student from Virginia Frank Alston grabbed a pen and pad and instantly ad-libbed a Jefferson-worthy document demanding the administration reverse itself and return the inserted passbooks to the "Negroes" so they could sit alongside the rest of us in Kenan Stadium.

The resolution passed unanimously.

Truth be told, early in the day we had buttonholed members whom we figured would be friendly toward such an effort. Ronnie Basescu, a member of the swimming team, cared nothing about the normal meetings of the Monogram Club or about beer parties. He was a New Yorker who'd heard we were going to take a stand against segregation and came specifically to lend his vote to the resolution. The vote, however, did not need what our foes called "northern agitators." The University of North Carolina student body was, by law, 90 percent North Carolinian. And so were those voting unanimously against jim-crow as members of the Monogram Club that night.

A race across the campus to the Legislature

I grabbed our resolution and raced across campus to the chamber where the Student Legislature was meeting. The trapeze timing was pure Hollywood. When I arrived on the floor with the Monogram Club's resolution scrolled up in my hand and tried to hand it off to one of the members we knew was on our side, the segregationist members of the Legislature saw through the whole plan.

There were angry shouts of "Point of order!" accompanied by vehement demands that I be ejected forthwith and not permitted to pass any document to any member of the Legislature in any manner for any reason.

There followed a procedural vote on that; and it was determined that there was no stricture, structure, rule, or precedent prohibiting a non-member of the Student Legislature from handing a note to a member during a business session. I think the member's name that was pre-selected to take the hand-off, provided we could swing the Monogram Club vote, was Ed Stevens. If I'm wrong, I apologize. If I'm correct, I want to honor him forever.

The member read our Monogram Club resolution with just the right dramatic cadence and emphasis. A roar went up. The segregationist bloc dissolved like an Alka-Seltzer tablet under Niagara Falls.

You didn't monkey around with the will of athletes in that part of the South.

The next day the student newspaper, the *Daily Tar Heel,* played the story big time. Later that day the administration capitulated. The demand for the black students to relinquish their student passbooks was rescinded.

The embittered segregationists told each other that once the broader rank and file of the Monogram Club realized their good name had been manipulated they would eject me from the club. They did not. Instead, they then elected me president.

And Kenan Stadium—student section and all—has been happily and peacefully integrated ever since.

NSA "cadre" went dorm to dorm to line up votes

Was this specifically an NSA triumph?

Call it any way you will.

As stated, we kept no paper trail, so NSA participation in that effort would be hard to prove. It would, however, be impossible to deny.

Football is a conspiracy. Basketball is natural and organic.

In football there's a secret meeting before every offensive play called a "huddle." The quarterback lets the other ten players know exactly what he wants them to do.

In basketball it's a lot more fluid. Without specific prearrangement, a player may pass to another player, who, rhythmically and automatically, knows to pass the ball back to one of his teammates racing down-court.

I never had to call a huddle and instruct my NSA teammates on campus to go dorm to dorm and make sure every decent-minded member of the Monogram Club made sure to attend that crucial meeting that night.

My entire NSA activist cadre, however, knew what was at stake, and it just sort of worked out that way.[3]

And the University of North Carolina has been great at basketball ever since.

Barry Farber is a national sydicated talk radio host. He has edited a daily newspaper, been a foreign correspondent and writes a nationally syndicated general interest newspaper column. He speaks sixteen languages. (See p. 596 for an extended biography.)

END NOTES

[1] This is a reference to the violence which accompanied the National Democratic Convention in 1968.

[2] *Editor's note:* University of North Carolina's *Daily Tar Heel* reported, on September 27, 1951:

> James R. Walker, Jr., Negro senior in the School of Law, this week returned to the University administration the football tickets he had been issued at registration in place of the athletic passbook normally issued students. . . . He said, "I feel that I am part of the student body and I want to cheer and express school spirit as part of the student body. Not be set apart down behind the goal post in an undignified and humiliating manner as proposed by the administration." In explaining the situation, Chancellor R. B. House said. "There is a distinction between education services and social recognition. By law Negroes are entitled to dormitory rooms and a section has been reserved for them in Steele Dormitory."
>
> They are also entitled to use the University dining room—Lenoir Hall. The Athletic Association handles the sales and seating in Kenan Stadium, he pointed out, and the Association is not considered an educational service.

The next day, on September 28, the *Tar Heel* headlined, "UNC Policy Hit by Bowers. Segregation of Walker to Bring Suit by NAACP." It reported, "Henry Bowers, president of the student body, yesterday challenged the right of the University Administration to place Negro students in the colored section of the football stadium." The article explained that "The University was ordered to admit Negroes to the Law School last spring by the United States Fourth Circuit Court of Appeals. At about the same time the trustees voted to admit Negroes in cases where separate facilities are not provided by the State, 'Without regard to race, creed or color.' "

[3] *Editor's note:* Commenting further on the Kenan Stadium event, Dick Murphy (later to become NSA National President, in 1952-1953) wrote, on August 17, 1998,

> The key organizers of the 35 groups that called on Chancellor House were virtually all NSAers: Henry Bowers, student body President (and my roommate); Jimmy Wallace, one of the original delegates at Prague; Ken Barton, NSA delegate; and myself, then serving as [NSA's] NIC [National Interim Committee] Chairman. . . . this started as a secret project of the Golden Fleece, the honorary society on campus. Barry played a critical role, as he describes. . . . I was appointed (by President Bowers) to act as floor leader for the resolutions condemning the administration's actions.

An editorial in the October 5, 1951, *Tar Heel* noted:

> Tuesday night we heard two speeches—both so excellent that we wish every student could have heard them. . . . Speech of the evening was made by Dick Murphy, newly appointed SP [Student Party] legislator, but an old hand in campus politics. Always a powerful, and sometimes vehement orator, Murphy alone made the issue clear. . . . "A student's right has been abridged," he said. "If this is allowed to go unquestioned (the rights of) every member of the student community are in danger."

Coincidentally, Barry Farber, a regular columnist for the *Tar Heel*, was writing alongside this editorial about the NSA Congress in Minneapolis that past August and quoting one of the three Brazilian student representatives who had come there as observers. Farber wrote:

> These Brazilian boys were amazed that American students have been slow to organize and show a little backbone. In other parts of the world the title of "Students" rank right up there with "Doctor" and "Lawyer," Amado told me. "For too long students of America have been patted on the head and told to run along. If you ever hope to win the recognition of your people and your government you've got to build a powerful national students' organization."

PICTURE CREDITS: *Then:* c. 1953-54, College News Conference (Courtesy Richard Murphy). *Now:* c. 1990s (both, courtesy author).

Editorial, *The Daily Tar Heel*, 10/5/51

Reason Speaks

Tuesday night we heard two speeches—both so excellent that we wish every student could have heard them.

The student legislature debated a resolution opposed to segregation in seating of Negro students in Kenan Stadium. Vice-president Bunny Davis commended the legislators on their orderly debate. They should also be complimented on the logic and calm with which it was conducted, on both sides.

Speech of the evening was made by Dick Murphy, newly-appointed SP legislator, but old hand in campus politics. Always a powerful, and sometimes a vehement, orator, Murphy alone made the issue clear.

He began by saying that the question was not one of liberalism versus conservatism. "A student's right has been abridged," he said. "If this is allowed to go unquestioned, (the rights of) every student here and every member of the student community are in danger."

Murphy pointed out that the current seating policy is discriminatory toward certain students because of the color of their skin, and that membership in an organization would be an equally valid basis for discrimination.

"I am thinking of fraternities," he said, adding that it might as well be members of a certin religion or discussion group. The true issue, he said, was found in the fact that the administration has set up two clasess of students. "There ought to be only one class student on this campus—first class."

He also asserted that the morality of the propaganda warfare program was at stake, asking how this nation could honestly maintain a program designed to teach the principles of democracy to the world, two thirds of it colored, if citizens hesitated to fight for those same principles wthin the nation.

The magnificent Murphy also managed to sidetrack for a time on the principles of representative government, in answer to an argument propounded by another legislator. All this in about 10 or 15 minutes.

The Daily Tar Heel

VOLUME LX — FRIDAY, SEPTEMBER 28, 1951 — CHAPEL HILL, N. C. — NUMBER 8

UNC Policy Hit By Bowers

'Georgia Next' Rally Tonite With No Butts About It!

Pool Tables! At WC

Segregation Of Walker To Bring Suit By NAACP

By O. Mac White

Henry Bowers, president of the student body, yesterday challenged the right of the University Administration to place Negro students in the colored section of the football stadium.

This challenge came on the heels of the National Association for the Advancement of Colored Persons' decision to

, 1951 — CHAPEL HILL, N. C. — NUMBER 14

Resolutions Are Presented To House In Informal Segregation Discussion

Town Meeting Helps People

After a two-hour informal conference with Chancellor R. B. House yesterday, a delegation representing various student organizations left South Building with a realization of the University's position as to Negro segregation, and with a determination to continue its efforts for "a more wholesome policy" on the matter.

House made it clear to the delegation that the students

Y, OCTOBER 16, 1951 — CHAPEL HILL, N. C. — NUMBER 23

Students To Attend Games; Deny Gentleman's Agreement With House

The five Negro law students said yesterday that they plan to attend football games and indicated that they had not said they would follow Chancellor House's suggestion that they observe segregation at Kenan Stadium.

"The impression conveying the idea that we made a deal with the Chancellor whereby he would give us the tickets and we wouldn't attend the games was erroneous," J. Kenneth Lee, asserted, speaking for the five students.

Lee was referring to remarks in a letter to the students signed by the Chancellor when he issued passbooks for the games last Fri-

Phi To Hear

Five Negroes Send Telegram To Gov. Scott

All five Negro law students here have wired Gov. Kerr Scott to get a legal opinion on the University's policy of segregation in the cheering section during football games at Kenan Stadium.

The students asked Scott to re-

NO GENTLEMEN'S AGREEMENT to accommodate social discrimination in public seating at football games. Five newly admitted UNC law students break barriers in 1951 with the support of the student body. From the top, U. of North Carolina *Daily Tar Heel* 9/28/51, 10/5/51, 10/16/51, 10/7/51.

Footnotes to the origins of the SNCC and the Southern Project

4. NSA's Southern Civil Rights Initiatives

Constance Curry
Agnes Scott College, Georgia
Delegate, NSA Congress at the University of Indiana, 1952
Chair, Great Southern Region, 1953–54

Editor's Note: This memoir was adapted by the author from her chapter in Deep in Our Hearts: Nine White Women in the Freedom Movement.

I was born on July 19, 1933, in Paterson, New Jersey, to parents who had immigrated from Belfast, Northern Ireland. We moved to North Carolina when I was in the third grade, and I have always considered myself a Southerner. This in spite of the fact that a boy in the fourth grade knocked me down on the playground after I told him not to call the woman server in the cafeteria a "nigger"—that she was just as good as his mother. I was Southern, and feisty Irish, too.

The 1952 Indiana Congress

Probably the most enlightening and broadening experience of my teenage life was attendance at the United States National Student Association Congress at the University of Indiana in the summer of 1952. I had just finished my freshman year at Agnes Scott College, a small Presbyterian woman's college in Decatur, Georgia. I must admit that my entry into the NSA world was not from the noblest of motives.

In 1951, in the fall quarter of my freshman year, a handsome, blond young man named Pete Dunlap came from Georgia Tech to see if any Agnes Scott students might be interested in working on a student news service. It was to be called the International News Service (INS),[1] and would exchange information and ideas about college and university life in the United States and abroad. If we were interested, we would go to Georgia Tech[2] for regular meetings to discuss the plans and program. "Great way to meet interesting men," I thought. I had not had much fun at the fraternity parties at Georgia Tech and Emory University, when we "Scotties" were piled into buses to meet the rushees.

As it turned out, the INS meetings were interesting—as were the men. I found out that INS was sponsored by NSA. I read some NSA material they gave us, including the preamble of the NSA constitution. A primary goal of NSA, the preamble stated, was to guarantee "to all people, because of their inherent dignity as individuals, equal rights and possibilities for primary, secondary and higher education, regardless of sex, race, religion, political belief or economic circumstances."

In the spring of my freshman year, Pete Dunlap asked if anyone at our INS meeting wanted to represent us at the National Student Congress to be held at the University of Indiana in Bloomington. I immediately raised my hand. I later discovered that the Agnes Scott student government had joined NSA early on, and was one of the few white member schools in the Deep South. I remember some vague talk about NSA being a "commie front," especially because of its early pro-integration resolutions and support of academic freedom, but who cared?[3] In any event, I was elected a delegate from Agnes Scott to the 1952 Indiana Congress.

The Congress was a gathering of 500 student leaders, interesting young people, and the men—oh brave new world! They were smart, they talked fast, they were funny, and they cared—such passion in the debates on universal military training, the eighteen-year-old vote, nuclear disarmament, and other issues. I can still call their names, and remember wondering how I could have so many instant crushes in one ten-day period. This euphoria was enhanced by the flattering attention that the men paid to an eighteen-year-old woman from the South. They delighted in my Southern accent, and were somewhat surprised to find my interest in the issues as passionate as theirs.

Chairperson of the Great Southern Region

The structure of NSA called for regional groupings of member college student governments. The regions, chaired by students elected at the national Congress, were to carry on NSA activities and hold related conferences during the academic year. In August 1953, I was elected chair of the Great Southern Region, which stretched eastward from Texas through Arkansas, Oklahoma, Louisiana, Mississippi, Alabama, and

Florida, to Georgia. Geographically, it was the largest NSA region, but it had the fewest member schools. Suspect to many white Southern colleges since its inception, NSA lost some members, including Georgia Tech and Emory, after the 1954 Supreme Court decision declaring "separate but equal" public schools unconstitutional.

NSA remained firm in its stand for integration, and it became necessary to lump our few members in the deep South into one huge region. I believe that Agnes Scott was the only white Southern member school in the region for some time. Morehouse, Clark, Arkansas A.M.&N. and several black colleges in New Orleans remained faithful members.

Undaunted by the challenge, I was thrilled to be chair of the region, and labored into the night in my little "office" in the basement of "Main," our central campus building. It was a janitor's closet, provided by the dean's office at my insistence on having some sort of office space. The room, which was lit by a bulb that hung on a cord from the ceiling, held two cardboard file boxes, a small table, and a chair.

A regional meeting and segregation

By late fall of 1953, I had been able to organize a regional meeting. Segregation was still the law, and the Luckie Street YMCA in downtown Atlanta was the only place that would risk giving us a room for an integrated meeting. If I were to pinpoint the moment when the consequences of racial segregation really hit me personally, it would be the lunch hour at that Saturday meeting.

It was against the law for blacks and whites to eat together, so the YMCA could not permit a lunch gathering. I knew some of the black delegates from previous meetings. When noon came—I can see still see and feel it clearly—the black delegates walked down the steps of the Y and headed toward Auburn Avenue to the black restaurants, and the rest of us walked down the steps and headed in the other direction. I couldn't eat with my friends and knew then that segregation took away *my* personal freedom as surely as if I were bound by invisible chains.[4]

In February 1996, I was reminded dramatically of that Atlanta meeting. I was in New York on a book-signing tour and had lunch with Babatunde Olatunji, whom I had not seen in forty-two years. Baba is an internationally known musician and drummer. When I first met him, he was a Nigerian exchange student at Morehouse College, sponsored by the Rotary Club. He had been elected student body president of Morehouse, an unusual achievement for a foreign student at that time. Baba was part of the group who walked the other way for lunch.

Later that year, we both attended the 1953 NSA Congress at Ohio State. Back in Atlanta, we had some "undercover" meetings with our few interested colleagues. We had strong feelings for each other, but after graduation went our separate ways. We never forgot each other, and the night in New York, after our lunch together, I cried over the memories evoked by the reunion with Baba—of our clear-eyed beliefs and our optimism that we could change things.

NSA activities in 1954-55

For years, nothing could stop me from making the NSA Congresses. In the summer of 1954, I was on an Experiment in International Living[5] program and was about to fly from Paris to Ireland to visit my relatives for the first time. Instead, I ended up in a Paris hospital for an emergency appendectomy. As soon as I was released, I flew back to the United States to make the Congress at the University of Wisconsin. In his usual supportive style, my father met my plane in New York, got me through customs in a hurry, warned me about adhesions, and put me on the plane to Madison. I don't think my mother and father ever really understood what "NSA" was. They just knew that I loved the meetings and all the activities, and that was enough for them.

Unable to cut the cord, I represented NSA at an international meeting in Alsace-Lorraine in 1955 during my Fulbright year in France. In the Summer of 1956, I came back to the NSA Congress as translator for a French student delegation. That Fall, I enrolled in graduate school at Columbia University, and continued to see Cynthia Courtney[6] and other NSA friends.

The Collegiate Council for the United Nations

In the Fall of 1957, I succeeded Al Lowenstein, 1950-1951 NSA President, as national field secretary for the Collegiate Council for the United Nations (CCUN).[7] Al had been at most of the NSA Congresses of my era, and we were friends. He was close to Eleanor Roosevelt,[8] who had helped found the American Association for the United Nations, and she had asked him to help recruit colleges for CCUN, the Association's youth branch.

Al served for several years as CCUN national field secretary, then called me one day in Greensboro in the late summer of 1957, and asked me to come to New York for an interview to succeed him. I was chosen, and traveled for CCUN for the next two years, using many of my NSA contacts. I recruited colleges to join CCUN, organized Model United Nations meetings, and tried to combat anti-UN feeling that pervaded some parts of the country. My work took me to campuses in thirty-six states, including many all-black institutions.

I have a clear memory of a dance that was held at Arkansas A.M.&N., a black university in Pine Bluff,

Arkansas, after an afternoon meeting. I stood—the only white person to be seen—talking to a history professor, watching the lights and the dancing couples, listening to the music, and wondering if anyone would ask me to dance. I had a fleeting thought: "What am I doing here?" But by 1960, my experiences with NSA and CCUN had paved the way for work in the civil rights movement. I was used to being the only one, or one of few, white women in a room, at a meeting or social event.

The NSA Southern Student Human Relations Seminars

During my CCUN years, I knew of the work that NSA was doing in the South. Ray Farabee, from the University of Texas, was elected NSA President in 1957. He strongly believed that many Southern white college students were different from their parents and that, with exposure to another set of values and encouragement from sympathetic forces, they could be rallied to support the tides of social change. He also believed that black students were as isolated and as fearful of integration as many whites. He wanted to bring black and white students together to study the forces in the South that underlay its contradictory and oppressive social and political structures.

Ray assembled a star-studded regional advisory committee of Southern professors, ministers, activists, newspaper editors, and civil rights leaders, and submitted a proposal to the Marshall Field Foundation, which was interested in work in the South. In 1958, the Foundation gave NSA a $10,000 grant to fund the first Southern Student Human Relations Seminar (SSHRS). In the program, eighteen students from black and white colleges throughout the South were chosen and then brought together in early August for three weeks of intensive study of human relations in the South, in a curriculum that included Southern history, religion, economics, culture and other subjects. Experts were brought in to lecture, and books and papers were assigned.

At the end of the Seminar, the students attended the NSA Congress, which provided exposure to the ideas of many young people, and direct association with students from other parts of the country and from other nations. Participants better understood the insularity of ideas in the "closed society" they inhabited, and felt a little less isolated in their wish to change that segregated world.

Convinced of the program's value, the Field Foundation funded a second seminar in 1959. In its renewal application for a third seminar in 1960, NSA also asked for funding to start a full-time program based in Atlanta. Field responded positively, providing one-year funding for the NSA Southern Student Human Relations Project, known as the Southern Project. I came back South as its first director.

The Southern Project

I convened the initial meeting of the Project's extraordinary Southern Advisory Committee, which included many persons whom I knew from my years of southern NSA work—representatives from the National Council of Churches, Anti-Defamation League, American Friends Service Committee, Southern Regional Council, Southeastern Regional NAACP, Community Church of Chapel Hill, University of Louisville Women's College, University of North Carolina, Loyola University, Morehouse College, Atlanta University and the editor of the Atlanta newspaper. The listing reflects the quality of leadership and diversity of agencies that worked with NSA from 1956 on, to establish a different framework for southern students.

Don Hoffman, NSA President and Curtis Gans, National Affairs Vice-President, were also at the meeting. Although new NSA officers were elected each year at the Congress, I received unswerving support from all the administrations during my four years with the Southern Project.

The first advisory group suggested that we continue with the annual summer seminars and organize smaller integrated workshops and conferences across the South, while establishing a network of like-minded students and faculty. Advisory Committee members put me in touch with their contacts from the past seminars' work. With broad goals and lots of encouragement, I was ready to go.

The sit-ins

Everything changed within five weeks. On February 1, 1960, I was in Greensboro to visit my sister Eileen when the sit-in movement started—right when I was driving down one of the city's main streets. My car radio carried the voice of a news announcer, reporting with some wonderment that four black students from the Greensboro A&T College had just been arrested for sitting at the segregated lunch counter at the downtown Woolworth's store and refusing to leave. I had never dreamed of such a thing, although my neighbor was convinced until the day she died that I was behind the sit-ins. I was the only person she knew who had been involved in "interracial things." I was in town, and, as she told me, "I can put two and two together."

The sit-in movement spread like wildfire during the spring of 1960, and my office began to report what was happening. In March we launched a newsletter listing the places where demonstrations were occurring, how many arrests were made, and what help was needed. NSA quickly passed this information on to a national student network, and the chain reaction of northern student support and demonstrations led to many of our breakthroughs. Several variety store chains desegregated their lunch counters, partially in response to national picket lines and demonstrations.

By June over 70,000 Southern college students, mostly black, were involved in demonstrations. For the first time, U.S. students seized the chance to participate in direct action to bring about social change. It was an exciting time, and the direction of my project soon changed drastically. My activities included witnessing demonstrations, sit-ins, and marches, and providing information to groups who wanted to help, and to the media. Julian Bond subsequently reminded me that he had a key to our office, and used to come in at all hours of the night to use our mimeograph machine to run off copies of the Student Nonviolent Coordinating Committee (SNCC) newsletter, *The Student Voice*, press releases, and fund-raising letters.

I don't think I ever even wondered if the Field Foundation would mind if we took this new direction. Maxwell Hahn, the Foundation's director, never questioned NSA or me, either in the beginning months, or later when we were actually paying SNCC phone bills and other bills.

The Student Nonviolent Coordinating Committee (SNCC)

I went to the organizational meeting of the Student Nonviolent Coordinating Committee (SNCC) at Shaw University in Raleigh, N.C., during Easter weekend of 1960. My recollection of such details as where I stayed and where we ate, are now vague. What I do recall seems like a view through a kaleidoscope, with images of young black students getting up and speaking passionately and eloquently about what had already taken place in their towns or on their campuses, or what they were planning to do in this new fight for freedom. I remember Reverend James Lawson and his call for nonviolence as the credo of the movement; seeing and hearing Dr. Martin Luther King, Jr., for the first time; and being inspired by Ella Baker's now-famous speech, in which she laid out the challenge that the fight and the struggle was for "more than a hamburger."

Following the conference, SNCC representatives from the most active colleges met in Atlanta. The SNCC executive committee chose Ella Baker and me as adult advisors. I was the first white woman on the Committee.

The 1960 NSA Southern Seminar

In the spring of 1960, through SNCC, I came to know Chuck McDew, a sit-in leader at black South Carolina State in Orangeburg. That summer, he came to our first NSA Southern Seminar, along with an outspoken, irreverent, brilliant young man, Bill Caldwell from Loyola University; Sandra Cason (Casey Hayden) from the University of Texas, and representatives from thirteen other Southern campuses. Reverend Will Campbell, from my Advisory Committee, agreed to serve as consultant to the Seminar and helped me select the group, which assembled at the University of Minnesota on August 3.

The seminar was memorable for me, both because it was my first one and because that year was so pivotal for the civil rights movement. The participants were in an emotional maelstrom most of the time. For some, additional turmoil was produced by another new type of experience. In 1960, a white Southern co-ed proceeded to fall in love with Chuck McDew. Similar things happened at all of the seminars. For most of the participants, it was the first time to be part, of or witness, personal interracial relationships.

"The Display of a Feather"

The ending of the seminars was always the hardest. The intensity of the three weeks bound us all together and changed us irrevocably.

On the last day of the Minnesota seminar, Will Campbell told us goodbye in a memorable farewell that was later published as "The Display of a Feather." Will's tale described a primitive savage returning from battle who stooped and picked up a feather, not because it had value but because it spoke to his deepest feelings. He soon realized that its beauty manifested itself only if he shared it with others. "With this feather," Will said, "civilization began and human relations began." Human relations is still the display of a feather—"the effort to say there is some other way—that it doesn't have to be this way—that the time is out of joint." The effort to create a better way unites beauty with truth, justice and love. "In this moment of farewell," he concluded, "I say that your heart will not rest till it finds rest in personal involvement."

The panel on sit-ins at the 1960 NSA Convention

During the National Congress at the University of Minnesota that followed the seminar, Casey Hayden from the seminar was on a plenary session panel. The night before, representatives of the Student Nonviolent Coordinating Committee made a presentation to the Congress on the sit-ins and civil disobedience, and asked for NSA's support. The panel was hastily assembled to meet demands by white Southern students to respond to the SNCC presentation. When NSA officers sought my advice, I recommended Casey as a panelist.

The panel consisted of three white Southern male students and Casey. All of the men spoke against the sit-ins as "being violations of the law, involving private property and legal rights of businessmen." But Casey's presentation in favor of the sit-ins created a sensation, both at the Congress and in the media.

The *Minneapolis Tribune* carried the story with a headline reading, "White Coed Backs Sit-ins, Gets Ovation." The lead sentence read, "A beautiful University of Texas coed with honey blond hair and a southern voice so soft it would not startle a boll weevil made a statement of ethical principles on the Negro sit-in movement Thursday."

Part of her speech was quoted:

> I cannot speak for the sit-ins or for white southerners. I consider this problem to be an ethical one for which there can be only a personal decision. On this question, I hope we do not lose its essential simplicity because of its complexities. The simplicity is this: when an individual human being has been denied by the attitudes of his community the exercise of his rights as a human being, has he the right to peaceably protest? The answer to this simple question can only be yes.

My scalp tingles as I hear again the thunder of the standing ovation and see the eyes filled with tears. Following the panel, the Congress, by a large majority, passed a resolution endorsing the sit-ins and promising support for the movement on the national and local campus levels. There is no doubt that Casey's presentation was a personal turning point for many of the white delegates, and a decisive moment in the history of NSA's civil rights activism. By my suggesting her as a panelist and by what she said, Casey and I, two Southern women, helped solidify NSA support for civil disobedience and the freedom movement.

In December of that year, seminar participant Valerie Brown, then editor of a campus publication at Texas Christian University, sent me a copy of their fall issue. It carried a reprint of a letter written by Chuck McDew to Valerie in October, on brown paper towels—all he could find to write on in the Orangeburg jail. The letter read in part:

> Hi Val, . . . Please excuse my stationery. I was arrested over an hour ago along with three other students. We sat down at the S. H. Kress & Co. lunch counter and asked to be served. . . . I can hear singing outside. They are singing "We Shall Overcome" and it sounds so wonderful that I kind of want to cry. Dot, the girl in the next cell, can see them and there are nearly four hundred students outside . . . all singing. Now they are singing the "Star Spangled Banner" and I feel a kind of bitter sick feeling deep inside. I know that those singing as well as we who are in here believe that "we shall overcome and the truth will make us free" and I'm trying so very, very hard to believe too that this is "the home of the brave and the free." I keep asking myself, how brave are the people who put me here? . . .
>
> . . . Let me be me, Charles Frederick McDew, man, student, lover of life. I don't want to be that nigger with no personality, no being, just a dark blob. I want to be me with the color that I love, with my eyes, my body, my dreams and aspirations. I'd better close now. It has been a very trying day and we have trial in the morning. Pray for us, Val; pray for us all.
>
> Chuck, or as the fellows in this cell call me,
>
> 24771.

When I came back from the seminar and the Congress, I found that my belongings had been moved lock, stock and barrel to another apartment. One of my roommates had invited a black student working with SNCC to the apartment, and the landlady had given notice to be "out by sunset" that day.

In an issue of a Georgia segregationist paper, the NSA Southern Project address and phone number was listed under "Atlanta Mixing Organizations," and my assistant and I were cited as two white women working for "mixing the races." That same summer, my red and white Kharmann Ghia, my first car and my pride and joy, was spray-painted with blue KKK signs and circles. We received threatening phone calls, and a friend told us that we were under surveillance by the Georgia Bureau of Investigation.

Three more seminars

The Southern Project sponsored three more summer seminars. By the end of the 1964 gathering, I had been present at eight NSA Congresses—do I hold the record? Seminar participants continued to go back and "find their place in the struggle":

> —Bob Zellner of Alabama became the first white person on the SNCC field staff.
>
> —Joe Louis Smith was expelled from Southern University in Baton Rouge for his civil rights activities.
>
> —Miles Lovelace of the University of Mississippi wrote an article on the shame of the riots there in 1962.
>
> —Joan Browning, who attended the third seminar, was one of the white women jailed in Albany after the freedom ride from Atlanta.

They, along with the sixty-odd other southern students, black and white, who participated in the four seminars between 1960 and 1964, heard Will Campbell's same farewell and challenge. Will named us "The Order of the Variegated Feather." NSA officers asked Will to speak at the 1962 Congress. Like Casey, he received a standing ovation.

Continuing the work

Building on the seminar contacts and the work that the students did when they returned to campus, I stayed in touch with all of them, ever trying to broaden the circle of young people who were tired of living in their segregated world. Working to implement NSA's pledge to support the movement, NSA national officers pushed for involvement in voter registration, as part of a broader effort to engage civil rights workers in voting rights work. Foundation money was given to support the Voter Education Project, based in Atlanta. In 1962, NSA helped to sponsor a Voter Registration training program in Raleigh, which helped to lay the groundwork for SNCC's future work.

In 1963, the Southern Project helped to pay travel expenses for black student leaders to attend a Civil Rights

Leadership Conference in Nashville. Later on, I was at the meeting that led to the formation of the Southern Student Organizing Committee, a group of southern white students working in white communities.

My Southern Project Advisory Committee fully supported the movement, my membership on the SNCC executive committee, and virtually everything I did. They supported my assistance to SNCC, and my observing and reporting on direct action, demonstrations, arrests, and trials. However, they made it clear that my personal role did not include direct action, being arrested, or going to jail. They held me to the original idea of the project as a vehicle for building communication between and among Southern white and black students. I was, and am, deeply grateful for the acceptance of my role by my friends in the movement, at a time when "putting your body on the line" was often the test of one's commitment.

Years later, Julian Bond, describing my work, wrote, "Connie was a bridge between the overwhelming number of black sit-in students and white students who were predisposed to join with us. And she got us into the NSA network. It was an invaluable resource for recruiting money and political support; provided the basis later for Friends of SNCC groups on college campuses. She publicized the sit-in movement within the NSA network, interpreted it, and created an audience for us that might not have been there." These were pretty heady times for a first-generation-Irish, Southern young woman.

A memento

One of my favorite keepsakes from that era is a large, framed plaque sent to me by a friend in New York after the CIA/NSA connection had been revealed.[9] I had once told her about my being named in the book *Outstanding Young Women in America*. She also knew our constant battle against the charges of communism that were aimed at groups working for integration. The plaque was to "Constance Curry, Outstanding Young Dupe of America." It was in recognition of my being "duped" simultaneously by both the right and the left. I will always treasure it.

Constance Curry is an attorney who was Director, Office of Human Services in Atlanta from 1975 to 1990. Earlier she was Southern Field Representative of the American Friends Service Committee and Director of NSA's Southern Student Human Relations project. She is author of the prize-winning book Silver Rights, *and of* Aaron Henry: The Fire Ever Burning; *and contributor to* Deep in Our Hearts: Nine White Women in the Freedom Movement. *She has just completed a book with Mrs. Winson Hudson, Mississippi civil rights leader.*

END NOTES

[1] See "Information Exchange," p. 581, Hunsinger, p. 990 and end note 5, p. 991.

[2] See Hunsinger on Georgia Tech, p. 989.

[3] See Brown, p. 385,

[4] *Editor's note::* A version of this kind of experience was recalled by many NSA leaders of that era. See Francis, p. 433, Schwartz, p. 217, Kelly letter, p. 244, Cashen, p. 363, Lynch, p. 271, Welsh, p. 170.

[5] See Halsted, p. 683.

[6] See Cynthia Courtney, p. 921.

[7] See Al Lowenstein, p. 283.

[8] See Eleanor Roosevelt, p. 40.

[9] See Welsh et al., p. 565.

PICTURE CREDITS: *Then:* 1955, Agnes Scott graduation photo. *Now:* c. 2000 (Both, courtesy author).

CONSTANCE WINIFRED CURRY

Early Background. Born July 19, 1933, in Paterson, New Jersey, to parents who had immigrated from Belfast, Northern Ireland.

Education. Woodrow Wilson College of Law, Degree of Juris Doctor, March 1984. Columbia University Graduate School, Pol. Sci., 1956–1957. University of Bordeaux, France, Fulbright, 1955–1956. Agnes Scott College, Decatur, Georgia, B.A. History, 1955, Phi Beta Kappa, Summa Cum Laude.

Career Highlights. 1990 to present: Completed writing book on Aaron Henry, Mississippi civil rights leader (*Aaron Henry: The Fire Ever Burning,* University Press of Mississippi, 2000). Previous book, *Silver Rights*, published by Algonquin Books, October 1, 1995, paperback, Harcourt Brace. Winner, 1996 Lillian Smith Award for nonfiction; Finalist for 1996 Robert F. Kennedy Book Award; 1996 *New York Times* summer recommended reading; 1996—Named for Outstanding Book on the subject of Human Rights in North America by the Gustavus Myers Center for the Study of Human Rights in North America.

1975-1990: Director, Office of Human Services, Mayor's appointment in City of Atlanta Government; 1964-1975: Southern Field Representative, American Friends Service Committee, Atlanta, Georgia. Established and maintained contacts to facilitate school desegregation, voter registration, and economic development; 1960-1964: Director, Southern Student Human Relations Proiect of U. S. National Student Association, Atlanta, Georgia. Developed and administered program for black and white college students to communicate and organize. Served as advisor on executive committee of Student Nonviolent Coordinating Committee (SNCC), during campus-based years; 1957-1959: National Field Representative, Collegiate Council for United Nations, New York City.

Affiliations. Board, Georgia Advocacy; Member, Southern Regional Council, Atlanta, GA; 1993, 1994, and 1995 Jury to select winners of Lillian Smith Book Award in Southern fiction and nonfiction. Certified Mediator, Georgia office of Alternative Dispute Resolution and Justice Center of Atlanta.

CONNIE CURRY: FROM STUDENT LEADER TO CHAMPION FOR CIVIL RIGHTS

11/11/53 (Excerpted)

Curry Answers Accusations Against Students' Association

By Connie Curry

Is the National Student Association really worth something to the colleges and universities in the United States? This seems to be the basic question from which scepticism, suspicions, accusations, and arguments have grown, especially in this section of the country in the past two years. If each student could know the facts concerning this question, I am sure that he would acknowledge its many benefits and wholeheartedly support the NSA.

NSA is generally accepted as an organization of college student governments whose aim is to "serve the educational community," on a regional, national and international level. Few people deny NSA's success in the international field. Dean Houston of the University of Colorado has expressed it by saying, "through student tours and contacts with student groups in other countries NSA in encouraging the growth of a healthy feeling of cooperation among students throughout the world."

Most of the arguments against the association, however, have arisen on the campus and national level.

* * *

NSA has been censured many times because it claims to represent the student opinion in the United States when only a little over one third of the student population is members. NSA really makes no such claim — its voice is accepted because it is the ONLY union of students in the United States and therefore the most representative group. However, it has not been the singularity of the Association but rather, to quote Miss Blanding, president of Vassar college, "the workmanlike fashion" in which it was organized and the "real maturity of judgment" that its members have shown thus far that have given NSA the privilege to send the only permanent student delegate to the UNESCO Commission of the United Nations and have caused the present National President of NSA to be a committee member of the American Council on Education. * * *

Another favorite point of opposition is that the Association is communist or leftist dominated. This, to me, is the weakest argument of any, and those who support it speak solely from lack of knowledge. * * *

Also, a recent report from an investigation by the National Association of Deans of Women, the National Association of Student Personnel Administrators, and the American College Personnel association states that "NSA has spearheaded and led the mobilization of the unions of students of the free worlds in combatting the propaganda and distortion of truth fostered by the Communist International Union of Students."

Many student-government leaders are sceptical about NSA because of several political stands and resolutions that delegates have made at past Congresses. In our world today and especially on the college level, it is practically impossible for a student to close his mind to such issues as federal aid to education, FEPC, the Taft-Hartley, etc.

Emory university has recently withdrawn from NSA partly on the basis that they have received too few benefits from it. The answer to this can be found here on our own campus. We have travel tours, a new voting system, leadership training conferences, and many other programs, but we also have had active NSA campus chairmen, and we have sent delegates to the National and Regional meetings. In other words — without a doubt, your campus will get from NSA exactly what you put into it.

2/10/54 (Excerpted)

The Agnes Scott News

VOL. XXXIX — Agnes Scott College, Decatur, Ga., Wednesday, February 10, 1954 — Number 10

Administration Names Curry For International Experiment

By Ann Allred

Connie Curry has been selected by the Agnes Scott administration to participate in the 1954 Experiment in International Living. During each of the past five years, one outstanding member of the junior class has received this opportunity through funds provided by an anonymous friend of the college.

The Experiment in International Living, sponsored by the Putney Institute of Putney, Vt., enables students to gain personal insight by living with an average family in any one of the 27 foreign countries. Free choice is given the student in selecting a country.

* * *

A leaflet published by the Putney Institute states that "the Experiment is more interested in the quality than the quantity of its membership. In considering applicants preference is given to those who have genuine interest in making a personal contribution to international understanding, demonstrated ability to get along well with others, special achievement in personal interests or hobbies, outstanding record in extra-curricular activities, experience in camping and roughing it out-of-doors, academic standing in the top half of their class."

CONNIE CURRY

Connie has fulfilled several of these requirements through her experience with NSA. She first became seriously interested in international relations while working with students not only from the United States but also from all over the world in various NSA conferences. In the summer of 1952, Connie represented Agnes Scott at the National Student Congress in Bloomington, Ind. Last summer, she attended the Student Congress in Columbus, O.

As chairman of ASC Lower House, Connie is automatically campus NSA chairman. Elected chairman for the Great Southern Region by the 1953 Congress, Connie met in Chicago this past Christmas holiday 18 other regional chairmen.

Connie will sail from New York on June 15, and plans to fly back on August 22 in time for the 1954 Conference in Ames, Iowa.

AS A STUDENT LEADER, Connie Curry was at the1952 and 1953 NSA Congresses, and was elected Chair of the Great Southern Region in 1953. The strong NSA presence in Atlanta had been weakened by the withdrawal of Emory in favor of the new Southern Universities Student Government Association and is one of the reasons for the article, far left (See also Pt. 5, S. 6). The Experiment in International Living was one of the major exchange program sponsors at the time. See the story of the Experiment in Pt. 3, S. 6.

WRITING THE STORY

DEVOTING MOST OF A LIFETIME to the freedom struggle in the South, Connie Curry was of a generation of "young white women who came of age in the era of the civil rights movement, participated actively in that movement and were, in many ways transformed by it," according to Barbara Ransby, Assistant Professor of African American Studies and History at the University of Michigan, in her introduction to *Deep in Our Hearts*. It is one of three books already published at this writing in which Connie applies her narrative skills and personal experience to telling the story of some of the people, black and white, privileged and out of poverty, whose lives were enriched by their commitment to racial equality and justice.

Above, *Silver Rights* (Harcourt Brace and Company, © 1995 Constance Curry), *Deep in Our Hearts* (U. of Georgia Press © 2000), *Aaron Henry* (U. Press of Mississippi, © 2000).

NSA's Positions on Equal Opportunity and on Opposition to Segregation and Quota Systems

Editor's note: NSA's goals were to provide a forum from which it could advocate and advance on behalf of U.S. students the unconditional cause of equal opportunity and the elimination of segregation, and at the same time make membership in NSA politically feasible for as many of the white Southern colleges governed by segregation laws and regional practices as possible.

In addition to Janet Brown's earlier essay in this part, the dramatic efforts made at early Congresses to attain this goal are described in Part 1, Sections 3 and 4, by Clif Wharton, and by a number of other writers in this volume.

During its first five years, and before the more activist era described by Connie Curry in her memoir in this Section, NSA relied heavily on educational, interracial and facilititative efforts through regional and campus programming. The policy guidance which governed these activities are highlighted below:

NSA's Basic Policy Declarations on discimination as adopted by its 1947 Constitutional Convention

BY-LAW I

The USNSA will seek to secure and maintain equal rights for all people, and secure equal opportunities for education at all levels regardless of race, national origin, sex, creed, and political belief or economic circumstances; especially by securing the eventual elimination of all forms of discriminatory educational systems anywhere in the United States, since the United States National Student Association is opposed in principle to such systems.

BY-LAW II

The United States National Student Association encourages wide investigation and discussion of the problems of inequality which exist throughout the United States, in order to secure their elimination. However, in view of the complex nature of the problem, with its diversity throughout the United States, and the limitations imposed by present state rights, statutes, and laws, it shall be the policy of the United States National Student Association to take action on the national, regional, and campus levels through the corresponding organization of the USNSA to implement its stated principles, with regard to the legal limitations involved.

Declaration of Unfair Educational Practices as adopted by the 1949 Second National Student Congress

Principle. The function of an education is to develop the fullest potentialities of every individual and to prepare him for responsible citizenship.

No potentially useful servant of society should be denied access to educational opportunity. Character and academic standing are the only two valid considerations determining admission to an educational institution

Declaration. It shall be an unfair educational practice to:

a) deny or limit the admission of, or otherswise discriminate against any person seeking admission as a student to such institutions because of his race, religion, sex, national origin, political belief, or economic circumstance.
b) make or cause to be made any oral or written inquiry prior to admission concerning race, religion, sex, national origin, political belief, or economic circumstance.
c) discriminate in the use of its facilities against any student because of race, religion, sex, national origin, political belief, or economic circumstance.
d) establish, announce or follow a policy of limiting through the device of a quota system or otherwise admission of students or use of facilities because of of race, religion, sex, national origin, political belief, or economic circumstance.
e) penalize any person because he has opposed any action forbidden by this section or because he has testified, participated in or assisted in any proceedings under any law relating to discrimination in educational institutions. However, the following shall not be considered guilty of unfair educational practice:
    a) denominational schools which require applications from a particular faith.
    b) non-coeducational schools which discriminate against the opposite sex.
    c) teachers colleges which maintain a sex quota, provided the quota is designed to prepare a sufficient number of teachers of each sex.
    d) state and municipally supported institutions which give preference to students from within their own areas, so long as they do not discriminate because of race, religion, sex, national origin, political belief, or economic circumstance.

Action. NSA regions shall support legislation to eliminate unfair educational practices in accordance with the limitations imposed by the Constitution and By Laws of NSA. (Congress, 1949).

Restatement of policy in 1955: "USNSA stands for immediate steps toward integration in higher education."

Following the Supreme Court decisions on school segregation in 1954-1955, NSA's 1955 8th National Student Congress adopted a lengthy and detailed statement of principle and rationale and a detailed action plan which replaced earlier resolutions (see above and Section 2). While continuing to rely heavily on educational programs (integration seminars, human relations workshops) and regional solutions, NSA embraced more legislative activity and restated the following unconditional commitment:

The USNSA reaffirms its acknowledgement of the concept of equality of opportunity for all people and remains unalterably opposed to all forms of discrimination in education which are based on race, religion or national origins. To realize the objectives set forth in the preceding statement of principles, we of the USNSA pledge ourselves to the education of the university and college community of which we are a part concerning the problem of integration and its possible solutions. This program will necessarily encompass action on the national, regional, and local levels toward the ultimate achievement of integration. USNSA stands for immediate steps toward desegregation in higher education....

The National Association for the Advancement of Colored People (NAACP) and post-war campus initiatives

The NAACP and NSA: Human Relations and Civil Rights

Editor's note: The Youth Division of the NAACP maintained a liaison with NSA beginning with its presence at the Chicago Student Conference in 1946. NSA's national leadership, strongly committed to desegregation and to integration, originally showed their support of the NAACP's efforts through mutual appearances at each other's conventions and in informal information sharing. When the first NAACP Youth Secretary to work with NSA, Ruby Hurley, left her position after her appearance at the NSA 1950 Congress, the groundwork had been laid for a good working relationship on civil rights issues which her successor, Herbert Wright built on during the following years. NSA's interest in integration culminated in NSA's 1958 Southern Student Human Relations Project and its involvement in the formation of the Student Non-Violent Coordinating Committee (SNCC) in 1960 after the Greensboro sit-ins (see Curry, p. 446).

NAACP Launches Interracial Harmony Initiative on Campuses

October 19, 1946
Letter from Felice N. Schwartz,, NAACP Director of Education
To: Student Governments throughout the U.S.

President of Student Government
University of Texas, Austin 12, Texas

Dear Friend:

You have a great responsibility. You have been chosen by your fellow students to lead them, the future leaders of our country. The influence of college graduates on the thought and action of the American people is vast and unquestionable - for our society is coming more and more to respect the qualities and qualifications with which higher education endows the individual. You have an opportunity to help make your college a truly democratic institution. You can thereby do your part to create a situation that will equip your fellow students to put American ideals into practice when they take their places as citizens and leaders in our country.

I'm sure that I don't have to point out to you the correlation between interracial harmony and peace in the world, and especially in our country, today. But even those who have the will to extend the rights enjoyed by white, Protestant, third generation Americans to all Americans, often sit back in seeming complacency because they cannot find their individual roles in the cooperative job of achieving our professed ideals.

The National Association for the Advancement of Colored People offers you its guidance and help. We will send you suggestions about what you can do and advice about exactly how these things can be done. The job can be accomplished whether or not you have colored students on campus.

If you have an interracial group in your college, please give this letter to the student at its head. If you have no such group then call together a few students whom you think are interested in working for better interracial understanding, or have another student call this group together. If the head of this group (even if it consists of only two or three) will write to me, I will contact him/her immediately.

Let's pool our resources and our ideals and work together for peace, and happiness.

Thank you for your cooperation.

Editor's note: In 1947, the writer, Felice N. Schwartz, recruited a group of educators and launched the College Scholarship Service which became the National Scholarship Service and Fund for Negro Students (see Tyler, p. 458).

Document sources: Schwartz letter above, Center for American History, University of Texas at Austin. NSA/NAACP correspondence: Library of Congress, NAACP Papers; State Historical Society of Wisconsin.

NSA Appears at NAACP Conventions

November 2, 1948
Letter to Allan W. Ostar, NSA Public Relations Director
From Ruby Hurley, NAACP Youth Secretary

Although our program is almost completely arranged, if Mr. Harris can come to St. Louis, we shall be very happy to find some place on the program where he can tell the delegates about the National Student Association, and how we in the NAACP can help.

October 2, 1949
Letter to Ted Perry, NSA Vice President, Student Life
From Ruby Hurley, NAACP Youth Secretary

Congratulations on your election to the National Vice-Presidency of NSA. Your public relations man sent us your picture and biographical sketch which I have given to the Crisis for publication. You have my best wishes for much success in this year's work with NSA.

February 27, 1952
Letter to William Dentzer, NSA President
From Herbert L. Wright, NAACP Youth Secretary

I wish to express my deep gratitude and thanks to you for giving me the opportunity to attend the Rio Congress *[see pp. 606, 608]*. . . .We wish to commend NSA for its action in passing a resolution condemning the wanton and malicious Christmas night bomb slaying of Harry and Harriet Moore. My only regret about our activities at Rio is that we didn't present the matter before the First Inter-American Congress of Students. I could certainly realize the issues involved, yet I feel that a resolution from that body or any other international organization would greatly aid us in this fight against the entrenched forces of bigotry and reaction.

June 30, 1960
Letter to Donald Hoffman, NSA President
From Herbert L. Wright, NAACP Youth Secretary

It is with great personal pleasure that I write this letter to commend you on your very outstanding presentation before delegates attending our recent 51st Annual Convention at St. Paul, Minnesota.

Your obvious sincerity, depth of understanding, and forensic talents combined to make yours one of the most talked about presentations at the convention. The entire national staff joins with me in saying, "congratulations for a difficult task well performed."

Collaboration on Student Rights Issues

June 26, 1953
Letter to Herbert W. Wright, NAACP Youth Secretary cc: Richard Murphy
From J.V. Berreman, Faculty Advisor, NAACP, University of Oregon

Thank you for your letters regarding our success in obtaining recognition of the college chapter of NAACP on this campus. We share with you a high degree of satisfaction in winning this recognition and wish to thank you for your assistance.

We have discussed the advisability of continuing the fight by appealing to the National Students Association, and we are of the opinion that no purpose will be served by doing so under present circumstances. We secured reversal of the committee's decision by an appeal to the faculty and students, and we had overwhelming support of both groups. . . .

July 6, 1953
Letter to: Mr. Herbert Wright, NAACP Youth Secretary
From: Richard Murphy, NSA President

I was very much distressed to learn of the situation which exists on the University of Oregon campus re: The National Association for the Advancement of Colored People. . . . Since Oregon is not a member school . . .we have no power or authority in the case; however . . . I would appreciate your sending on to me any further information . . . am sure, too, that the Congress would be interested in learning the facts on the situation. . . . *[see Murphy, p. 1075]*

NAACP at 1950 NSA Congress Featured in Negro Press

Race, War Hot Issues At Student Meet

Youths Will Fight Bias In Schools

By LLOYD DAVIS

ANN ARBOR, Mich. — With the Korean crisis, racial discrimination in education and the renewed attacks upon student academic freedom as the issues, 1,000 members of the National Student Association were in session here last week evaluating the position of America's 2,000,000 students in regard to the pressing problems of the day.

Three hundred and fifty colleges and universities from North and South, Catholic and non-Catholic institutions have announced NSA's intention to fight Jim Crow and race bias in every phase of student life, including student admission policies, student housing, student organizations and town-school relationships.

NAACP Youth Sec'y Present

Among the participants formulating NSA policy at its third annual congress, in the battle to bring democratic living to the American campus, is Ruby Hurley, national youth secretary of the NAACP.

Meet On Michigan Campus

The eight day meeting of the NSA on the campus of the University of Michigan has been broken down into four categories. The break down takes in student affairs, educational affairs, international affairs and organizational problems.

Delegates are discussing such matters as student government, human relations, international relationships, legislative activity, constitution and finances.

So-called hot issues at this year's Congress center around the issue of American action in Korea. Left wing student leaders are attempting to give the impression

STUDENTS' CONGRESS—Student leaders attending third annual congress of National Students Association, in Ann Arbor, Mich., discuss telegram from President Harry S. Truman to the organization's meeting. Representatives of one and one half million students attend congress to tackle problems of human relations, education affairs and international student relations. Left to right, Ted Perry, NSA vice president; Erskine Childers, NSA vice president of international affairs; Mary Kay Perkins, NSA national staff secretary; Ruby Hurley, youth secretary, national NAACP; Lloyd Davis, national vice president, Students for Democratic Action.

criminatory issues in their charters or constitutions.

The Michigan plan was adopted by both the Student Legislature and the school administration.

Present leadership of the NSA includes Robert A. Kelly, president; Theodore Perry, vice president in charge of student life; Richard J. Medalie, vice president in charge of educational problems; Erskine B. Childers, vice president in charge of international affairs, and Frederic D. Houghteling, executive secretary.

Members of the advisory council are Very Rev. Vincent J. Flynn, president of the American Association of Colleges; James T. Harris, Jr., past president of NSA, and Helen C. White, United States National Commission of UNESCO.

Dr. Lore Rose David Joins Wilberforce U.

WILBERFORCE, Ohio — Dr. Lore Rose David, a brilliant biologist and zoologist who received her doctor of philosophy degree from the University of Berlin in 1931 and has done extensive research work in her field of specialization, will join the Wilberforce university faculty in September as head of the department of biology. The announcement was made this week by Dr. Charles L. Hill, president of the institution.

Named College Director

ALBANY, Ga.— Julius A. Lockett, formerly with the business department, Albany State college, will be director of the Columbus branch of the Albany State college, it has been announced by Dr. Aaron Brown, president of the in-

STUDENTS RELAX—Student leaders attending the National Student Congress take time out to relax. Representatives of one and a half million students attending the congress to discuss problems of human relations, educational affairs and international student relations are, left to right, Frederick Houghteling, NSA executive secretary; Ruby Hurley, national youth secretary of the NAACP; Mary K. Perkins, NSA national staff secretary; Lloyd Davis, national vice president of Students for Democratic Action, and Ted Perry, NSA national vice president.

Collegians Assail Discrimination

Perry Pleads for 'Brotherhood' Before Nat'l Student Congress

By LLOYD DAVIS

ANN HARBOR, Mich. — A Negro student, Theodore Perry, vice president of the National Students Association, opened the third annual National Students Congress here last week with a stirring plea for an international crusade of students for "Intellectual Freedom and Universal Brotherhood.

One thousand delegates from 350 colleges and universities in the United States called for cooperation between U. S. students and students of Africa and the Far East.

Speaking for a million and a half American students, representatives to the eight day congress of the NSA greeted the personal message from President Truman, who called the conference a "demonstration of democracy" and cheered with approval the announcement by Robert A. Kelly, president of the National Students Association, that the organization will "assist their government in its effort to repel agression and re-establish peace in the world".

DISCUSS RELATIONS

Meeting Aug. 23, 31, NSA student leaders discussed the problems of student government, human relations, international student affairs and educational problems.

Delegates called for an end to race bias in programs and activities of institutions of higher learning, including such areas as admission policies, student organizations, living facilities and town-campus relationships.

Dr. Ralph E. Himstead, general secretary of the American Association of University Professors young people to have the guts to make democracy work within the greatest nation in the world.

Observers from Germany, Holland, and Yugoslavia, joined with U. S. student leaders from the Red Cross, Anti-Defamation League, NAACP Youth Council, Catholic Welfare Conference, National Conference of Christians and Jews, Nat'l Federation of Catholic College students, Newman Club Federation of Catholic College students, Nat'l Scholarship Service and Fund for Negro students, Students for Democratic Action, youth section of Americans for Democratic Action, United World Federalists Student Division, and the World Student Service Fund, in the deliberations intended to extend the influence of NSA in the field of higher education.

DIFFICULT PROBLEM

A difficult problem which faced NSA delegates was the discrimination practiced by most of the fraternities and sororities on the nation's campuses.

The National Inter-Fraternity Conference has called upon local units to remove race bias clauses from their charters and constitution. The problem seems to be that of forcing local groups to carry out the recommendations of the national organizations.

Leaders of these fraternities and sororities are opposed to any rapid action in doing away with discrimination in their organizations. Considerable support has been announced for the "Michigan Plan" adopted by the student legislature of the University of Michigan, requesting that the administration prohibit the recognition of previously unrecognized student organizations which have discriminatory issues in their charters or constitutions.

The Michigan plan was adopted by both the student legislature and the school administration.

"There exists in colleges, universities and professional schools throughout the nation, policies which discriminate against members of minority groups by means of quota systems and exclusion in all forms. . . apathy and indifference on the part of the majority of students . . . should be overcome."

Editor's note: This declaration was embodied in a resolution prepared for the Congress, but which did not reach the plenary session. It was adopted by the post-1950 Congress Executive Committee updating its Human Relations program. The focus at the convention on fraternity discrimination reported on this page was already embodied in established NSA policy and human relations programs (see fraternity discrimination, p. 398, human relations programs, p. 416, and NSA policies, p. 451).

Sources this page: 9/2/50 top, unidentified, and 9/2/50 left, from *The Courier*, city unidentified, and below the *Shreveport Sun*, 9/9/50 (Library of Congress, NAACP papers).

Youth Seretary for NAACP Attends National Student Congress

ANN ARBOR, Michigan—Mrs. Ruby Hurley, youth secretary of the National Association for the Advancement of Colored People, is serving as a resource person in campus race relations at the Third National Student Congress of the United States National Student Association being held here, August 23-31.

The USNSA is an organization of college student bodies, represented through their student government, created to promote the interests and welfare of the American student community. The present conference of the organization is discussing recommendations that the group adopt a cooperative working arrangement with the youth division of the NAACP.

Mrs. Hurley will supply information on the education of and discrimination against Negro students on American campuses, and the progress made in the elimination of this discrimination.

Louisiana State University: Divided on Race, Reds and NSA

Council Rules Out Negro Representation At College Conference Here in April

After a brief discussion and no vote, the Student Council last night decided to exclude delegates of Negro colleges from attending the Conference of Southern and Southwestern Colleges to be held here April 17-19.

"I do not think it is wise to have an inter-racial conference at this time," Lloyd Love, student body president, said.

In a letter addressed to Love, Xavier College, New Orleans, requested permission to send representatives to the conference in order to participate in the discussion of establishing a National Student Organization.

The National Student Organization, which would include Negroes and whites, was first proposed at the Chicago Student Conference in December where Xavier College was represented. It is also listed on the April conference agenda.

Love said that he would write a letter to the college stating that because the conference is an outgrowth of the one held in Tulsa, Okla., last spring, Xavier College would not be represented.

The council set a tentative agenda for the April conference, consisting of two main panel discussions. Drafting of

Xavier Representation Will Go To Student Vote

The Daily Reveille

Lloyd Love Says Poll Decision May Not Settle Invite Question

Because of the wide expression of student opinion concerning the exclusion of Xavier Col- ... on my own hook," the student body president said. "It will be just an opinion vote to be made

Long, Representation Issue Win

★ ★ ★ ★ ★ ★ ★ ★ ★ ★ ★

Council Rejects Negro Vote, Passes Alternate Inter-Racial Meet

★ ★ ★ ★

Opinion Poll Draws 2 to 1 'Yes'; Dual Conferences Scheduled

Expressing an opinion that was almost 2-1 affirmative, ... The Student Council voted 7-5 last night to exclude representatives from Negro schools from

★ ★

Teekell Wins; 3,987 Establish Record Vote

Louis Curet

★ ★ ★ ★

Inter-Racial Conference Opens In Presbyterian Church at 9

Delegates from Louisiana, Mississippi and Arkansas already assembled for the Southern and Southwestern con-

The Daily Reveille

Vol. 51, No. 75 LSU, BATON ROUGE, LA., SATURDAY, APRIL 19, 1947 Price 3c

Conference OK's Segregated Equality; Third Panel Disagrees on NSO Purposes

Minor crises were solved by compromise when the Conference of Southern and Southwestern colleges disagreed on proposed purposes of the National Student Organization yesterday.

Meeting in plenary session, panel no. 3 began the afternoon discussion with a reading of the NSO Constituton.

Louis Curet, elected permanent panel chairman, had read only through section C under the head "Purposes" when a protest was voiced.

John L. McClellan, Jr., University of Arkansas, objected to the provision, protesting that a clause including the words "political beliefs" might conflict with the Arkansas state law against communism.

By Pat O'Bryan

Climaxing an afternoon of heated discussion, the Conference of Southern and Southwestern colleges passed without a dissenting vote a resolution approving legislative programs to institute an equal system of educational appropriation for both white and Negro schools.

Four delegates did not vote.

The resolution reads: "Be it resolved that this conference of Southern and Southwestern colleges and universities go on record as approving a legislative program, in the several states represented, to institute an equal system of educational appropriation based on apportionment according to population of the several races, in seg-

Students May Give To Disaster Fund

Students who desire to contribute to the Texas City Disaster Fund may mail donations to Mayor Powers Migglabo-

A TALE OF TWO CONFERENCES AND TWO UNIVERSITIES. After the 12/46 Chicago Student Conference, the La.-Ark.-Miss. region of the new NSO scheduled an organizing meeting for 4/47 at LSU to coincide with the meeting of the Southern and Southwest Student Government Association. The LSU Student Council, as host, decided to limit the meeting to white-only colleges, as in the past. Xavier University wrote that as an NSA member it expected to be invited. Put to referendum, LSU students voted 2-1 in favor of an interracial meeting. The Council decided to run two meetings, with the interracial NSO meeting held off campus at the Presbyterian Church (*The Daily Reveille* 2/47, 3/22/47, 3/26/47, 4/22/47).

[See end note 1, p. 435.]

The Daily Reveille

Vol. 51, No. 76 LSU, BATON ROUGE, LA., TUESDAY, APRIL 22, 1947 Price 3c

Inter-Racial Regional Meet Discusses NSO, Calls for Equal Educational Opportunities

★ ★

Curet Elected Region Prexy

Louis Curet, president of the College of Arts and Sciences and student council morale commissioner, was elected president of the Louisiana-Arkansas-Mississippi Region of the National Student Organization at an all-day conference in the First Presbyterian Church Saturday.

Both Curet and Gillis Long, student body president-elect were nominated for the office. On the strength of his familiarity with the NSO, C uret was chosen.

Long was named vice-president, but in a precedent-setting move he requested permission to refuse the office in order that a Negro delegate might be chosen. Lucius J. Barker , Southern University sophomore, was elected vice-president.

Declaring that the president and secretary should be from the same university, the conference voted without a dissenting vote to authorize Curet to appoint a secretary-treasurer.

Lloyd Love, who was elected president of the region at the Chicago organization conference, informed delegates that his studies in law school made it necessary to resign from the presidency.

Delegates to the National Student Association meeting in the Baton Rouge First Presbyterian Church passed resollutions, offered one amendment to the proposed constitution, and elected permanent officers during the course of their all-day session.

Negro delegates from six colleges in Louisiana, Arkansas and Mississippi were in attendance.

Love Discusses NSO

Lloyd Love, student body president, occupied the chairman's seat. He opened the conference by outlining the history of the National Student Organization.

Louis Curet, LSU, informed delegates of progress that had been made toward a constitutional convention.

In the morning session, delegates voted unanimously to insert as the first purpose of the organization: "To promote and perpetuate democratic ideas throughout the United States and the rest of the world."

Arkansas Objects

The resolution followed objections by John L. McClellan, University of Arkansas, that a resolution containing the words "political beliefs" might conflict with Arkansas law forbidding the activities of communists.

Racial relations did not enter into the conference until McClellan attempted to introduce a resolution approving an equal system of education in segregated schools.

Harry Alexander, Xavier University, promptly secured recognition: "Regardless of what our personal beliefs are, we've got to face facts," he said in protesting against the term "segregation."

Not Progressed

McClellan replied that he did not think that his college had made sufficient progress to consider non-segregation.

"Segregation brings about discrimination," Alexander declared. "If you look at separate education facilities you will find that

See NEGROES DESIRE, Page 2

All-White Clause Passed In Final Conference Meet

In the closing minutes of the Southern and Southwestern Student Government Conference Saturday afternoon, delegates voted 21-6 to exclude all but white students from its organization.

The proposal was made by Chandler Clover of Louisiana College, as an amendment to the Articles of Organization which had previously been accepted by Panel 3.

LSU was named host school for the 1948 meeting of the Southern and Southwestern Student Government Conference at the final meeting of the organization Saturday.

Lloyd Love, president of the LSU student body, called the final session of the Southern and Southwestern Conference together at 4:10 p.m. to review the accomplishments of the conference, the reading of resolutions from Panels 1 and 2.

Race Reappears

In reviewing the proceedings of the Conference, the acceptance of Articles of Organization was discussed. Chandler Clover of Louisiana College asked if any provision had been made for the exclusion of Negro delegates.

Tulsa's Neil Morgan, at request of the chair, explained what had

See DELEGATES COME, Page 2

★ ★

Panel Three Debates Race

With the question of an inter-racial conference dominating discussion, Panel 3 of the Southern and Southwestern Conference held its last meeting Saturday afternoon.

Acting as chairman for Louis Curet, Bruce Beard of LSU presided over the first part of the meeting and introduced the subject. He explained that an inter-racial conference would be impractical in the South when social functions were involved and that social functions were an important part of a student government conference.

Not Relative

Neil Morgan, delegate from Tulsa, did not see that social entertainment was particularly relative to such a conference and said he considered the matter one

See DELEGATES, Page 3

Negroes Desire Better Schools

(Continued from Page 1)

they are not equal." He maintained that the conference should not go on record as favoring segregation.

Silas M. Hunt, Arkansas A. M. and N. College, told the conference, "Arkansas has one Negro school, 7-9 for whites. If the proportion is 3-1, will the state give to Negroes in proportion?"

Negroes Want Education

Delivering an impassioned plea, Noel Gray, Xavier, said, "All my race wants now is education. Some of the Negro schools are not up to the white schools. I want schools comparable to LSU and when we get them, you can build a wall around LSU."

After further discussion, McClellan withdrew his resolution. Following a recess for lunch, a joint resolution approved by both whites and Negroes was adopted.

Calls for Equal Education

Citing the need of rectifying an existing inequity, the resolution called for "ample funds for instituting a program to provide adequate and equitable educational opportunities, standards and facilities regardless of race, color, creed, sex, or religion."

Postponed until a future meeting when delegates will be expected to poll their respective schools for a definite opinion, was a motion for accepting or rejecting affiliation with the National organization.

(Excerpted)

"YOU CAN BUILD A WALL AROUND LSU" after we get "comparable schools," Noel Gray of Xavier U. told delegates. "All my race wants now is education."

APRIL 1947: "TO PROMOTE AND PERPETUATE DEMOCRATIC IDEAS"

Louisiana State University: Lloyd Love, Louis Curet, Gillis Long

Xavier University: Harry Alexander, Noel Gray

THE DILEMMA OF SOUTHERN STUDENTS IN 1947—BLACK AND WHITE: White delegates representing 29 southwest colleges moved off campus to meet for one day on April 19 with delegates of 6 Negro colleges in the La.-Ark.-Miss. region for what Lloyd Love, student body president, stated was "the first interracial conference in Baton Rouge." Louis Curet of LSU was elected the new NSO region's President, and Gillis Long withdrew as Vice President in favor of Southern University Negro delegate Lucius J. Barker. "Cooperation Was the Watchword" headlined the LSU *Reveille* the next day. "Negro groups … could not go on record favoring segregation," it reported. "A white delegate could not go back to his college and report that he had agreed to non-segregation." Chandler Clover, delegate from Louisiana College, and Harry Alexander, Xavier delegate, drew up a compromise measure that might well stand as a creed for race relations on both sides, deploring "the lack of present facilities for Negro education," and calling for the "appropriation of ample funds." The same white delegates earlier, after affirming Southern Conference all-white membership, recommended that NSA include in its statement of purposes that it "should promote and perpetuate democratic ideas throughout the United States and the rest of the world." (*Reveille* 4/19/47)

(Continued from Page 1)

taken place. The question had been brought up and voted down, he said; as being a matter to be left to the discretion of the host school.

"I think that some stipulation should be made to exclude Negro delegates," Clover said.

School Says No

During the discussion that followed Clover said, "I particularly asked the officials of my school about this matter and I know that Louisiana College could not enter into any conference which included Negro delegates."

A delegate from Texas Tech said that when he came to the conference he was not prepared to discuss race so thoroughly. "That's all we talk about—race. I came here to find out something about student government.

"We've been all over these Articles of Organization and have decided that the host school could make the choice of delegates. Why don't we elect the host school, hear the panel reports and then I can leave and you can talk about race all you want to."

Must Know

The Louisiana College delegate replied that he must know whether or not Negro deegates would be included as that would determine his school's remaining a part of the organization.

Delegates from Mississippi voiced a similar opinion. "We can't just shove this off from year to year. We must know now."

A delegate from Arkansas said he did not think the students at his school would be willing to send delegates to an interracial meet.

Doesn't Know

To this another Arkansas delegate said, "I doubt if you know what the students at your school would want. I don't. We've never voted on this thing as LSU has and I think it would be better if we went back and got a vote there before we decide anything like this. I shall refuse to vote on such a proposal."

A motion was made by Clover to ammend the Articles by stipulating that the conference would be composed exclusively of white delegates. Delegates from Oklahoma objected that such an amendment would discriminate against Indian students in their school, as well as chinese and other non-white races.

* * *

Delegates from Louisiana and Mississippi reiterated that they would have to withdraw from the conference unless the provision was made and a vote was called.

The conference voted 21-6 to pass the ammendment to exclude all but white delegates from the organization.

(Excerpted)

February, 1948: "Send Our Students to Moscow: Vote for NSA"

40 Per Cent Student Vote To Be Required For NSA

NSA -- The Real Opportunity

In just five days from today, students will be called upon to vote on whether LSU joins the National Student Association, an organization founded in 1946 and for which a constitution was written last August.

Failure for this University to become affiliated with NSA is for LSU to refuse to go forward in a program of better understanding among students all over the nation, realizing that the race problems throughout the United States cannot be solved in a day or in a year. The organization, because it is made up of broad-minded students from all parts of the country, admits that each race problem must be carefully handled because of the many factors involved.

When you vote Thursday on the NSA issue, consider well the opportunity which the national group affords our own campus. With it, LSU students can go forward. Without it, we admit we had rather not discuss anything with anybody.

Let's pool our efforts and profit from the NSA.

★ ★ ★ ★ ★

NSA Fails to Get 40 Per Cent Vote;

LSU Votes 'No' to NSA Affiliation by 2 to 1 Vote

By L. Gibbs Adams

LSU students yesterday defeated by a 2 to 1 vote the proposed amendment to the Student Constitution that this University become affiliated with the National Student Association. The three other amendments passed.

Of the 1,922 voting in yesterday's special election, 1,302 voted against the NSA proposal and 620 voted for it.

In an election here December 18, 913 students supported the proposal that LSU join the organization while 617 voted against it. Since the Student Council had passed a motion requiring that 40 per cent of the student body vote in the election before joining the association, the 17.73 per cent of the students casting ballots was not enough.

The NSA amendment was the highlight of yesterday's election. Red-painted hammers and sickles with "NSA" painted under them decorated campus sidewalks yesterday. On several of the polling places were red-painted signs urging voters: "Send Our Students to Moscow; Vote for NSA" and "Uncle Joe Says Vote 'Yes' on NSA."

The only autonomous school on the campus favoring the proposal was the School of Music which cast 30 ballots for NSA affiliation and 15 against.

Affiliation With NSA Is Urged by Long, Teekell and Other Student Body Leaders

By Dorothy Harrell

Advocating that LSU join the National Student Association, Student Body President Gillis Long and Vice-President Lloyd Teekell spoke last night in Parker Auditorium to approximately 20 students who braved the bad weather and passed up more amusing activities to learn something about the organization at the YWCA meeting.

Long stressed the fact that the organization is not communistic. He said that delegates to the congress are selected in a democratic way from colleges. Red-tinged groups which sent representatives to the congress last summer tried to have delegates chosen from organizations as well as educational institutions. They were voted down by other members who did not want to have double representation, Long said.

Both Teekell and Long said that LSU should take the lead in the South by adopting the NSA Constitution and becoming a member. They expressed the opinion that other universities, and colleges of this area would then join.

Long said, "The organization is a good thing; it is a step forward. To me, the question seems to be not whether we can afford to join, but whether we can afford not to join. Let's not wait

THE NEXT SPRING IN 1948 the tide of anticommunism was running strong, linked ideologically to "racial mixing." Despite the vigorous support of student leaders returning from the Constitutional Convention and editorially from the student newspaper, "obvious to the point of absolute clarity," it was not to be. Gillis Long had urged "Let the South take the lead for awhile." (See Pt. 5, S. 6). NSA affiliation was defeated 2-1 as described in the article above.

(*Reveille* 12/12/47, 12/17/47, 12/19/47, 2/19/48) [See end note 1, p. 435]

From Sharecropper's Son and Student Leader at Xavier University to "Conservative Militant"

5. Aaron Henry: Confronting White Supremacy in Mississippi

Excerpts from the book Aaron Henry: The Fire Ever Burning *(University Press of Mississippi, 2000) by Aaron Henry with Constance Curry, Agnes Scott College, Georgia, NSA's Great Southern Region Chair, 1952-53.*[1]

From Connie Curry[2]*:* Although Aaron Henry (1922-1997) was one of the nation's major grassroots fighters in the freedom movement on local, state and national levels, his name has not yet been accorded its full recognition. Long before many of his contemporaries, he was a civil rights activist, but he preferred to stay out of the limelight. A certified pharmacist and owner of Fourth Street Drug store in Clarksdale, he considered himself a down-home businessman who must not leave Mississippi.

He was a key figure in bringing Head Start and improved housing, employment, and health services to his state, but his tact and his quiet diplomacy garnered him less attention than more radical protesters received.

Leading the Mississippi NAACP

Born in the age of segregation in the Mississippi Delta, the son of a sharecropper, he became state President of the NAACP in 1959. He spearheaded the formation of the Mississippi Freedom Democratic Party and the Council of Federated Organizations (COFO). Some activists criticized him for urging protesters to take the middle ground between the NAACP's conservative position and SNCC's militant activism. Facing recurring death threats, thirty-three jailings, and Klan bombings of his home and drugstore, Henry remained stalwart and courageous. (*From jacket copy*)

Henry at Xavier University

From Aaron Henry[3]*:* Before going into the service, I had been saving my money to go to Alcorn A&M at Lorman, Mississippi, but when I returned I had decided to go to pharmacy school. I was eligible for the GI bill of rights, and I decided to enroll in the pharmacy school at Xavier University in New Orleans. I started in the fall of 1946, and my first revelation was that I had not learned much at the agricultural high school. What chemistry I had learned was of little value, and I had to begin all over. I had enough money from the GI bill—a lifesaver because I didn't have to work. I had to study so much, I could never have held down a job on the side. I was too busy with my studies to take an active role in the New Orleans NAACP, but I was elated in 1947 when I read that a motion had been filed in the courts to abolish segregation in public schools. I was not very optimistic about the success of the suit, and I was content to live for a while with things as they were and work the best I could for my individual improvement.

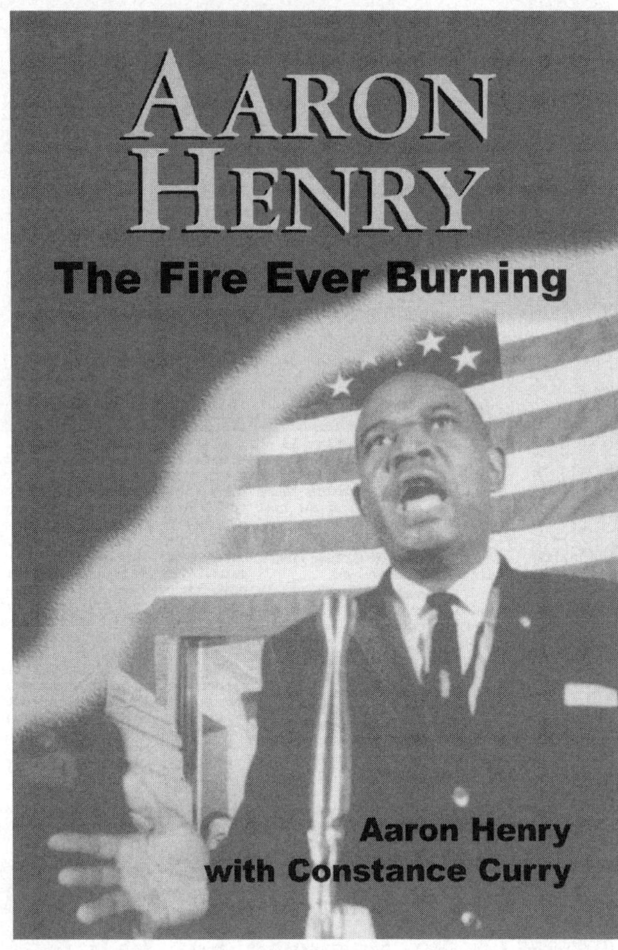

Book jacket, *The Fire Ever Burning*, University Press of Mississippi, 2000.

Henry and NSA

Some of us from Xavier did stay in contact with the few right-minded white students from Tulane and Loyola, mostly through the United States National Student Association (NSA). NSA was a national confederation of student governments founded in 1947 by returning veterans, and I even went as a delegate from Xavier to one of the very early national congresses in the Midwest. That is where I met Al Lowenstein, who later helped us with 1964 Freedom Summer.[4]

END NOTES

[1] See Curry, p. 444.

[2] From jacket copy.

[3] Page 65.

[4] See Francis, p. 434, and Peoples, p. 425.

The Xavier Herald

Xavier Delegates Relate NSA Convention Activities

The four students who represented Xavier at the National Student Association convention this summer gave a brief outline of their experiences and activities at the regular weekly assembly Nov. 16.

The convention, held on the University of Illinois campus Aug. 23 to Sept. 3, was attended by John L. Finley, Donald F. Barry, Dolores J. Cooper and Aaron E. Henry.

After opening remarks by Sister Mary Frances, dean of the University, the delegates, introduced by Henry, addressed the student body. The origin, meaning, aims and this year's NSA activities were told.

AARON HENRY AS STUDENT LEADER. Henry was Chairman of the Committee on Student Activities at Xavier University and is shown in the July 1950 issue of the *Xavier Herald* greeting Robert A. Kelly, President of NSA, during his visit to the University. The November 1949 issue of the *Herald* writes about Henry's report to the student body about his attendance at the NSA Second National Student Congress at the University of Illinois that summer. (See Part 1, Sec. 7, p. 233.)

He Went on to Change Mississippi History

(*Adapted from the Introduction to* The Fire Ever Burning *by John Dittmer of DePauw University*)

Aaron Henry was among the last of that generation of Black leaders who came out of World War II dedicated to cracking open Mississippi's closed society. . .

An NAACP activist who became state president in 1959, Henry exhibited a commendable independence. . . Henry faced down death threats, spent time in jail, and survived Klan bombings. All these qualities came together in his leadership of the Clarksdale boycott and direct action campaign in the early 1960s. . . .

During the spring of 1963 black Clarksdale was subjected to an unprecedented reign of terror. In early March someone broke out the front windows in Henry's pharmacy, and on Good Friday two white men firebombed the Henrys' home. . . .

A "Freedom Vote" was held in November of 1963, a mock election designed to prove that blacks would vote if given the opportunity. Henry was the candidate for governor. . . . More than 80,000 blacks cast their ballots, in the face of white harassment and violence . . . . The "Freedom Summer" of 1964 brought national and international attention to the Magnolia State. . . . At the Democratic National Convention at Atlantic City Henry headed the Mississippi Freedom Democratic Party delegation that was challenging the seating of the white Mississippi segregationists. . . .

In the late sixties Henry was part of a coalition that successfully challenged the re-licensing of Jackson's major television station, WLBT, which had a long history of anti-black programming and policy. He was the key figure in building an interracial state Democratic party in the late 1970s, and served as party co-chair. In 1979 he won election to the state legislature, a position he held until 1995. . . . In the twilight of his career, as age and infirmity began to take their toll, Aaron Henry remained the dedicated activist, taking to the streets one final time to lead a demonstration against a state-sponsored plan to close two of the state's historically black colleges. Henry died in 1997, a "giant" in the eyes of the movement.

AFTER HIS GRADUATION, AARON HENRY WENT TO WORK AS A PHARMACIST in his hometown of Clarksdale. Shown above, left, is Henry's pharmacy, a center for movement gatherings. He was an NAACP activist who became state President in 1969. Center above is Henry (third from left standing) at a late 50s NAACP strategy meeting. During the 1964 campaign for voting rights, three young civil rights activists were murdered. Large posters are displayed (right) of Andrew Goodman, James Chaney and Mickey Schwerner in Henry's Fourth Street Drug Store. Henry had recruited Goodman at Queens College, NY, and brought the body back to his family.

(Caption adapted and photos from *The Fire Ever Burning*)

The National Scholarship Service and Fund for Negro Students (NSSFNS)

6. Building a Foundation for College Campus Integration

Shirley Neizer Tyler

Simmons College, Massachusetts. NSA Executive Secretary, 1950-51
NSSFNS Staff Associate, 1953-54

The years immediately following World War II were exciting times, both on and off campus, as students and recent graduates sought concrete resolution of issues confronting them and the nation. The presence of the older veterans brought a level of maturity, which influenced those of us who were younger. The U.S. National Student Association (USNSA) was but one of the organizations founded in that period which had a major impact on the lives of American students.

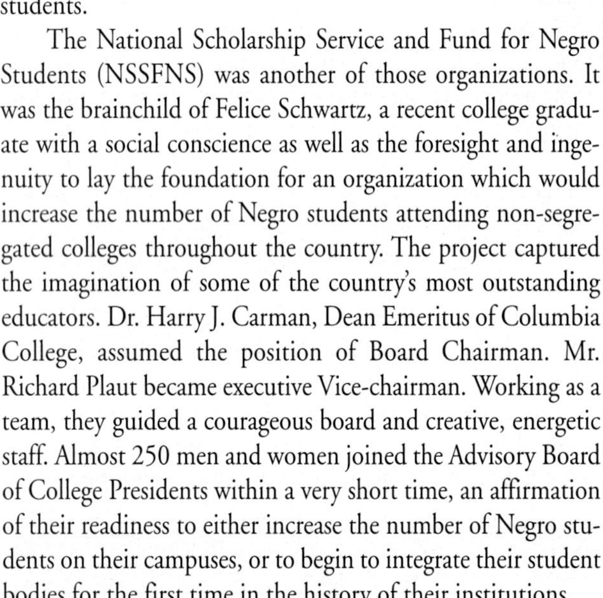

The National Scholarship Service and Fund for Negro Students (NSSFNS) was another of those organizations. It was the brainchild of Felice Schwartz, a recent college graduate with a social conscience as well as the foresight and ingenuity to lay the foundation for an organization which would increase the number of Negro students attending non-segregated colleges throughout the country. The project captured the imagination of some of the country's most outstanding educators. Dr. Harry J. Carman, Dean Emeritus of Columbia College, assumed the position of Board Chairman. Mr. Richard Plaut became executive Vice-chairman. Working as a team, they guided a courageous board and creative, energetic staff. Almost 250 men and women joined the Advisory Board of College Presidents within a very short time, an affirmation of their readiness to either increase the number of Negro students on their campuses, or to begin to integrate their student bodies for the first time in the history of their institutions.

NSSFNS was charged with counseling high school students about the opportunities for admission and financial aid at nonsegregated colleges. Counseling was done primarily by mail. Twice a year, staff associates traveled to colleges in the East and Midwest which had accepted students referred by NSSFNS and talked to enrollees about their experiences. They also oriented non-participating colleges and universities on NSSFNS goals and programs.

At least three NSAers preceded me on the staff. They were Tom Callahan, former travel director for NSA; Eugene Schwartz, past Vice President; and Kenneth Kurtz, a former member of the Executive Board. By 1953, when I arrived in New York City, the previous staffs had institutionalized the counseling process. It flowed reasonably well, with substantive results. The same was true of the supplementary scholarship program ($400 per student). This was used for books and miscellaneous expenses. For some students, it was the difference between the affordability of higher education, and not attending college at all.

Challenges traveling in the field

Mt. Holyoke College alumna Nancy Crosier and I were privileged to serve the year that NSSFNS instituted the Two-Way Integration Project, led by Dr. Paul F. Lawrence and Mr. Donald Wyatt. These administrators were on leave from Howard and Fisk Universities, respectively. They visited seventy-five Negro high schools in forty-five southern communities several times during the year. They identified schools with high caliber educational programs as well as students with the ability and discipline to succeed in highly competitive academic programs. When the men returned to our Manhattan office, they shared their experiences and insight. Nancy and I received invaluable in-service training during staff meetings and casual conversations. This was an unplanned benefit.

In 1953, sixty-five NSSFNS counselees who had overcome the obstacles of a segregated education had been admitted to nonsegregated institutions. In addition, some white students were admitted to predominately Negro colleges. Overall, 91 percent (842) of NSSFNS student applicants had been admitted to 280 interracial colleges.

Nancy shared counseling and staff associate responsibilities with me. She was assigned to travel to colleges in New England, New York State and the City of Philadelphia. My assignments included the rest of Pennsylvania and the Midwest—Ohio, Indiana, Illinois, Wisconsin, Minnesota, and

Iowa. Attendance at several NSA Congresses held at major universities, visits to colleges while on staff for the NSA office in Madison, Wisconsin, and my personal contacts made me feel at home in our nation's heartland. Since I am an African-American, challenges were inevitable.

Once, after making and confirming my reservation at a hotel in the middle of Illinois, I was refused accommodations. The white businessmen in line behind me had no reservations, but they were given rooms! I spent the night in the basement room of a Knox College dorm counselor who was away for the evening.

Another time, a hotel in Pennsylvania was in the process of refusing me a room. I knew the governor was staying at the hotel. Casual mention of this fact was made to those at the desk with a hint that either my organization or I might contact the governor in the morning. The decision not to honor my reservation was suddenly reversed!

I learned as I traveled about the many ways our students and our program had enriched college communities. Knowing about NSSFNS's successes made racism easier to cope with while on the road.

Visiting students on campus

My reception at most campuses, including Knox, was a positive one—warm, welcoming and caring. Administrators' experiences with students referred by NSSFNS had generally been positive. They were pleased to find that there were Negro high schools in the still segregated South which were producing students with strong academic backgrounds and the ability to compete with students from the North. While at college, these students faced racism on and off campus daily. The obstacles and frustrations they overcame made the majority of them stronger. We should salute these pioneers.

When my schedule allowed, I met with students we had referred. One, Milton Pharr, a student from North Carolina, was a freshman at DePauw University in Indiana. He had a four-year scholarship. He appeared to have adapted well at this nonsegregated college that reportedly had welcomed Dr. George Washington Carver on staff years before.

Another was Evelyn Jones, who told reporters that hard work and good fortune had brought her to Bryn Mawr College. Besides taking advantage of its exceptional academic opportunities, she was active in student government. She also became a regional officer for NSA. Evelyn and Joyce Mitchell, another Negro student on campus, and the Bryn Mawr administration all had very positive feelings about the work of the USNSA and NSSFNS.

One of my many unique experiences occurred on a visit to Blackburn College, a small school in Carbondale, Illinois. When I arrived by train, just before dawn, a town man was literally putting out the town's gas lights. The students did most of the work on the campus. Some students appeared to lack training in social amenities, but these young adults built and maintained their dorms and school facilities. They learned many life skills along with their college education.

Later, when I was leaving and waiting for the train, a man ambled up to me, and asked, "Be's you an Injun?" I was amused, I must say. Knowing he would probably not understand what I wanted to answer, I said simply, "Yes, I am part Indian," which is true. He walked off, still perplexed.

NSA promoted college campus chest support for NSSFNS

NSSFNS received financial support from campus chests throughout the country, the Ford Foundation, other non-profit organizations and corporate groups. Campus chests were the college equivalent of the nation-wide community chests, the forerunners of the United Way. NSA strongly endorsed campus chest support for NSSFNS.[1] The NSSFNS staff reciprocated by producing a booklet to help student leaders adapt better professional fundraising strategies with the goal of increasing contributions.

NSSFNS lives on in the lives of participants

The experience with NSSFNS was an eye opener for me. Growing up in New England where the Ivy League and Seven Sister colleges were the standard for judging the quality of higher education, I began my field work in the Midwest with a bias. My attitude changed as I traveled, and learned more about the offerings within the Big Ten universities as well as the high-quality programs at a number of the smaller colleges—Oberlin, Carleton, Case Institute, Western Reserve, Knox, Ripon, Denison, Kenyon, Lehigh, etc. To this day, I continue to promote schools in the Midwest and Pennsylvania.

While the NSSFNS no longer exists, its story goes on in the lives of the people who participated in its program. Perhaps one day, someone will research the long-term effect of the interracial experiences of the students—educational, economic, and social. Did those students who were the first among black or white students on their campuses have positive experiences, or was life, at least initially, traumatic? Did they eventually integrate socially? Would they do it again?

The NSSFNS Board

In reflection, Leonard Wilcox and Richard (Dick) Murphy, NSA representatives on the 1952-1953 NSSFNS Board, and Eugene Schwartz and Rick Medalie, who preceded them, must have had fascinating experiences at board meetings. Among the outstanding leaders were Time Life's publisher, Henry Luce; Dr. Robert C. Weaver, Director of the John Hay

Whitney Foundations Opportunity Fellowship; Dr. Channing H. Tobias, director of the Phelps Stokes Foundation; and Dr. Carman.

Making history

The NSSFNS Manhattan office was in the same building with Dr. Kenneth Clark, the renowned African-American psychologist. During baseball season, Dick Plaut would disappear to an upper floor where either Dr. Clark or the Lincoln School (another tenant in our building) had a radio. Our staff suspected that there also was an early television set available. While NSSFNS was making history on college campuses, Jackie Robinson, Willie Mays and other players were making baseball history. Mr. Plaut and Dr. Clark were among their biggest fans.

Little did we know that Dr. Clark had also been making history as he worked on the research supporting the monumental 1954 Supreme Court *Brown vs. the Board of Education* decision to desegregate America's public schools. In many ways, 1954 was a momentous year.

Shirley Neizer Tyler recently retired as Head of School, Grace Episcopal School, in Alexandria, Virginia. (See p. 282 for extended biography.)

END NOTE

[1] *Editor's note:* From the time NSA endorsed NSSFNS in 1950, it encouraged NSSFNS support through Campus Chests (see p. 612). NSA's only other Campus Chest fund-raising endorsement at the time was its strong support of the World Student Service Fund, which was granted when the association was formed in 1947.

PICTURE CREDITS: *Then:* 1950 (*NSA Third National Student Congress Report*). *Now:* 1996 (Courtesy author).

NSSFNS: INCREASING NEGRO ATTENDANCE AT NON-SEGREGATED COLLEGES

Opportunity NEWS IN INTERRACIAL COLLEGES

Published by: NATIONAL SCHOLARSHIP SERVICE AND FUND FOR NEGRO STUDENTS

VOL. 4, No. 1 — 31 WEST 110TH STREET, NEW YORK CITY — OCTOBER, 1953

TWO LATEST ADDITIONS to the NSSFNS staff are associates in research and public relations, Nancy M. Crozier and Shirley V. Neizer.

NANCY M. CROSIER

Miss Crozier is a 1953 graduate of Mount Holyoke College, where she served as Student Government President. She is, incidentally, the third ex-student body president to serve on the NSSFNS staff.

Visiting northeastern colleges, universities, preparatory, and high schools, Miss Crozier's fall field trip, from October 1 through November 15, will take her through New England, upstate New York, northern New Jersey and the Philadelphia area.

SHIRLEY V. NEIZER

A former Executive Secretary of the U.S. National Student Association, as well as a teacher in the Arlington, Va., high-school system, Miss Neizer was graduated from Simmons College in 1950. Her field trip, also extending from October 1 to November 15, will cover central and western Pennsylvania, Michigan, Wisconsin, Minnesota, Illinois, Indiana, and Ohio.

* * *

The New York Times, March 6, 1950

DISCUSSING SCHOLARSHIP FUND FOR NEGRO STUDENTS

Dean Harry J. Carman of Columbia College, seated, who heads the drive, talking to trustees yesterday. They are, left to right, Frank T. Simpson, Executive Secretary, Connecticut State Inter-Racial Commission; Margaret Halsey, author; Dr. Robert C. Weaver, John Hay Whitney Foundation; Mrs. Nathan Straus, and Felice N. Schwartz, and Richard L. Plaut, Executive Directors of the fund.

The National Scholarship Service and Fund for Negro Students, 31 West 110th Street, has established a supplementary fund to augment inadequate scholarships won by Negro students at inter-racial colleges and universities, it was announced yesterday.

Dean Harry J. Carman of Columbia College, chairman of the service's board, explained that many such students were unable to attend colleges because their scholarships were insufficient. "It will take an average of $250 a year to supplement a scholarship, or $1,000 for four years," he said. "The fund hopes in its first year to supplement at least twenty scholarships."

"I believe that it was the residential campus experience that shaped the life I would live from then on"

7. Revolutionary NSSFNS

Evelyn Jones Rich
Bryn Mawr College, PA, NSSFNS Scholar, 1950-54

Revolutionary ideas sometimes play out quietly. Yet their power resonates in many corners and their influence is often felt for generations. So it is with the idea of the National Scholarship Service and Fund for Negro Students.

I was an NSSFNS scholar at Bryn Mawr from 1950–1954. On the cusp of my 50th reunion, I reminisce about that defining experience.

What is it that I gained and what role did NSSFNS play?

NSSFNS provided counseling for students which focused on interracial colleges and supplementary scholarship aid. Imagine the years immediately following WWII—fought to insure the survival of "freedom" under siege by Nazi oppression. The expansion of educational opportunity to "Negroes" represented a natural response.

I remember meeting Annie Lee Broughton, Bryn Mawr's Director of Admissions, who first told me about NSSFNS when I went for my admissions visit and interview. Bryn Mawr was among the women's "Ivy League" colleges participating in the project.

The NSSFNS grant of $400 supplemented several other scholarships. Renewed each year, this supplementary grant enabled me to live as a resident student on the campus for four years. I continue to believe that it was the residential campus experience which shaped the life I would live from then on!

There, I made great and lasting friendships. I met young women who introduced me to the destructive aspects of religious and social class conflict. They taught me how both work, and why! They also taught me about loyalty and commitment. Many of them remain my friends today.

Learning how to value and pursue excellence

At Bryn Mawr, I learned how to value and pursue excellence. I understood for the first time how little I knew—how much I would never know. I also learned how to write simply and well, how to research topics effectively, and the value of oral sources. I learned how to be relentless in my search for truth and I learned that pursuit of it would be a life-long quest. I also learned how to be a presence. In retrospect, it is amusing but at the time I resented the posture classes, the swimming tests, the endless teas and occasional sherry parties and the often strange food. Exposure to all these experiences has served me well in later life.

There, I also learned to appreciate diversity. So far as I know, I was one of the first Negro students at Bryn Mawr and the first student of color to be in residence for the entire undergraduate experience. At the same time, however, the campus had its share of "public school" girls, girls from rural settings, holocaust survivors, young women from Europe, Asia, the Caribbean and even North Africa. I sought them out and compared experiences. Simultaneously, I played pinochle with the "Negro" maids and porters in their quarters and taught them bridge. We silently acknowledged that we were together for the long haul.

An equally important part of that on-campus experience was participation in extracurricular activities. I joined Students for Democratic Action (SDA) my first day and added a host of other organizations to the list including The Bryn Mawr League and the Self-Government Association. I became active in regional student organizations and attended student government meetings in the metropolitan Philadelphia area, traveling as far as Columbus, Ohio, for a National Student Association (NSA) convention in 1953.

For a working-class girl from Philadelphia, this was big-time stuff and I loved it! I learned how to be an effective organizer, agitator and advocate, how to design and produce leaflets, meet across the table with opponents and press my point of view in the face of adversity.

A campus rallies to the struggle for equality

Perhaps the most important experience came from the Bryn Mawr administration, when it placed the resources of the College behind me to support my demand for access to a local restaurant which refused to serve me and my ("Negro") date. Arguing that it did not serve "Negroes" in groups, the restaurant ultimately backed down in the face of a threatened college lawsuit. In the interim an entire campus rallied to the struggle to reaffirm equality for all students as the president and faculty stood their ground. These years and experiences were interspersed with visits from NSSFNS staff including Ken Kurtz and Shirley Neizer. Other NSSFNS scholars—Joyce Mitchell, Joyce Greene and Camilla Tatum—joined me in subsequent years. There were informal meetings with NSSFNS scholars at other colleges—Jewel Taylor and Lois Dickson—and visits to NSSFNS headquarters in New York. I remember several encounters with Executive Director Richard Plaut at 31 West 110th Street, arguing the case for residence on these integrated campuses which played host to increasing numbers of "minority" students. He treated me like a grown-up. I like to think I acted like one!

Years later, there were meetings with other NSSFNS officials like Ken Clark and Don Wyatt.* When I identified myself as a

NSSFNS scholar, there was an immediate bond and a recognition of the common task we continued to address.

The enduring legacy of lessons learned in the larger arena

None of this rejects the academic rigor I learned to appreciate as a student. Yet, a half-century later, I know deep down inside that the most powerful lessons came after class and the enduring legacy of lessons learned in that larger arena has shaped my persona. NSSFNS made all that possible and I am very grateful.

In many senses I am a quiet revolutionary. Today, I see myself as an activist and advocate on the side of right and justice. It is a continuing struggle waged in various arenas—educational, social, political and economic. It is my life's work and I know full well that skills identified, developed, and nurtured at Bryn Mawr help me play my small part.

Evelyn Jones Rich is currently President of Rich Solutions, a consulting firm focusing on issues affecting students in public elementary and secondary schools, and public policy issues affecting the elderly. She has served as a teacher, principal and dean in the public schools and colleges of New York City. She is actively involved in a range of public policy and education organizations.

**Editor's note:* Board Member Kenneth Clark and Donald Wyatt, project administrator, on leave from Fisk University.

EVELYN JONES RICH

Early Years: Born 1933 in Philadelphia. Attended Roxborough High School.

Education: Columbia University, Ph.D. African History and Education, 1978; Hunter College, City University of New York, M.A. Social Studies, 1965. Bryn Mawr College, A.B. Political Science, 1954. New York University, Graduate School of Business, Careers in Business Certificate, 1978.

Career highlights: 1996 to date: Executive Director, Shelley & Donald Rubin Foundation. A small, family foundation funding innovative projects: health care, at-risk children and families, ethnic and cultural diversity, the environment and Himalayan art. 1993 to date: President, Rich Solutions. A consulting firm: access, equity and instructional issues affecting students in elementary and secondary schools as well as public policy issues affecting the elderly. 1985-1992: Associate Dean, Division of Programs in Education, Hunter College, City University of New York; Dean and Director of Admissions, Hunter College Campus Schools; Coordinator of research; supervisor of elementary and secondary school principals; monitor of personnel & budget.1980-85: Principal, Andrew Jackson High School. 1962-1980: New York City Board of Education. Classroom teacher of social studies (1962-1972) Executive Assistant to the Superintendent (1978-1980). 1972-76: Director, School Services Division, African American Institute.

Other Activities: Member, Professional Standards & Practices Board in Teaching, NYS Board of Regents; Secretary, Americans for Democratic Action; Chair, Education Committee, New York City Americans for Democratic Action Board of Directors, National Association on Drug Abuse Problems; Co-Chair, Lincoln House Outreach; Member, African Studies Association; Educational Priorities Panel, National Alliance of Black School Educators.

Family: Married to Marvin Rich.

Opportunity NEWS IN INTERRACIAL COLLEGES

Opportunity News, the NSSFNS Newsletter, January 1953.

A NEGRO AT BRYN MAWR

BY EVELYN JONES

I WAS STILL ALIVE when it happened! All of my life I had been searching for it, telling myself that some day, even if I didn't live that long, this ideal of mine, and of all free men, would actually exist, would not be just a few words, some faith, embedded in the Constitution of a great nation and not extending far beyond that in actual practice

I mean this living in an environment with no inter-racial friction—where I would be judged and respected as an individual with a contribution to make—and not as a Negro.

But it did happen! I am at Bryn Mawr because of hard work and good fortune and because I saw this challenge—this opportunity to be an individual—to work, to play, and to live for the first time in my life as I wanted to and to be rewarded on the merits of my achievements alone.

School Not Without Problems

Certainly at Bryn Mawr there are problems. With so many diverse groups, with such different backgrounds and objectives, there must be! But they are not racial problems. In this educational community where the individual is accepted at face value, the problem is rather one of getting recognition as an individual in the community—but this is not difficult for the student who wants this type of recognition and is willing to work for it.

I cannot say that everyone at Bryn Mawr shares my views. Even here, there may be some students who regard Joyce Mitchell and myself, not as individuals but as representatives of the Negro race, and perhaps even non-typical representatives at that! Freedom of participation for everyone, however, in all extra-curricular activities is typical of Bryn Mawr's attitude of judgment and evaluation of the individual, rather than by group stereotypes. If there are students or even faculty and administration at Bryn Mawr who emphasize the latter, they are few in number and their attitude is lost in the majority point of view.

Dormitory Life Important

Dormitory life has contributed materially in helping to realize this need to be accepted as an individual. My life in the residence halls has been a rich, happy, and beneficial part of my college career. I cherish friendships with girls who, I am sure, were not accustomed to accept Negroes as equals at home.

I fully realize, of course, that I cannot live here forever. Outside the college campus, the sharp prick of inter-racial tension and inequality still exist. My whole association with Bryn Mawr, nevertheless, has stimulated my belief that some day people everywhere will be able to live harmoniously.

Perhaps her motto "veritatem delixi" best illustrates Bryn Mawr's attitude. She accepts the concept that "all men are created equal" and this choice leaves no room for racial friction.

Evelyn Jones, now in her junior year at Bryn Mawr, is a NSSFNS counselee and winner of both Bryn Mawr and NSSFNS scholarships. She is active in student government, and a regional officer of the U.S. National Student Association.

NSSFNS/NSA HIGHLIGHTS (1947-1954)

COLLEGE SCHOLARSHIP FUND
FOR NEGRO STUDENTS

360 West 122nd Street New York, 27, N.Y.

June 19, 1947

We are writing to you on behalf of a group of educators interested in increasing educational opportunities for Negro youth. We have come together in the form of a provisional committee because of a common belief that a disproportionately large number of highly qualified Negro students are being prevented by financial reasons from attending our colleges and universities. We have reason to believe that if we are able to secure the moral support of a group of leaders in American higher education, we shall be in a position to meet this financial need in cases of a substantial number of outstanding Negro candidates for college and university educations.

The general purpose of our Fund is to advise Negro students of scholarships already available to them and, through public subscription of funds, to create additional scholarships for Negro students at accredited non-segregated colleges and universities....

The presidents of many of the country's major institutions of higher learning are being invited to serve the Fund in an advisory capacity as members of its Advisory Board of College Presidents....

Sincerely,
Henry P. Van Dusen Harry J. Carman

Provisional Advisory Board of College Presidents:

Paul Klapper	Eleanor M. O'Byrne
Norman Angell	George N. Schuster
Robert C. Clothier	Harold Taylor
Byrn J. Hovde	Henry P. Van Dusen

Provisional Executive Committee

Harry J. Carman	James H. Robinson
Chairman	*Treasurer*

Note: See 10/19/46 letter from Felice N. Schwartz, founder of NSSFNS, p. 452.

NSA 1950 Congress Support for NSSFNS

Fact: Economic conditions exist which prevent Negro students from obtaining a college education.
Principle: The congress reaffirms NSA's belief that because of the inherent dignity of people as individuals, equal rights and possibilities for higher education should be guaranteed.
Action:

1. The Congress directs that the USNSA becomes a permanent sponsor of NSSFNS.
2. The Congress urges member schools to develop a program of support for the NSSFNS, including such activities as:

a. The allocation of a percentage of Campus Chest collections or the holding of special fund raising drives;
b. The compiling of a list of available scholarships to forward to NSSFNS;
c. To aid in the dissemination of the "NSSFNS information" to high schools and prospective applicants;
d. The initiation of a letter-writing program to prospective Negro students, the purpose being to encourage their applying and to acquaint them with the organization and the activities of the campus Community;
e. The encouragement of campus organizations interested in the field of human relations to establish a direct working relationship with NSSFNS.

Note: Each year from 1950-51 on, an NSA officer served on the NSSFNS Board of Directors. Four former NSA leaders served on the NSSFNS staff during 1951-1954 after their terms of office and graduation.

CHAIRMAN'S REPORT

National Scholarship Service and Fund For
Negro Students
31 West 110th Street, New York 26 ENright 9-6868

October, 1952

THE PIONEER "TWO-WAY INTEGRATION PROJECT," designed to take advantage of newly opened opportunities for inter-racial education in colleges and universities in the southern states, has moved forward rapidly since it was first discussed last year at this time....

With the aid of staff members from the National Association for the Advancement of Colored People, and the Young Women's Christian Associations, as well as our own staff, 70 southern colleges have been visited in order to determine their attitudes about admission and scholarship aid to students of all races. Returns have shown, as anticipated, that many schools were ready and willing to break down the segregation barriers; some had already done so. Our next step is clear: to act as the catalytic agent in bringing together these colleges and students wishing to available themselves of these opportunities, just as we have been doing in the northern states.

* * *

Fifteen to twenty formerly all white schools and six to eight formerly all-Negro schools have agreed to participate.... Providing the necessary financing is available, the first year's goal provides for 150 students, Negro and white, from North and South, to go to colleges, predominantly of the other race, in both North and South.... A part of the project's total needs has already been granted by one foundation, and consideration of the balance needed is now before other interested groups.

CHAIRMAN'S REPORT

October 1953

For the college year beginning in September, 1953, 474 of our college candidates, 47% more than in the preceding year, were admitted to 224 inter-racial colleges with the aid of 207 scholarships totalling $197,301 in value, an increase of 106% over last year, giving the agency by far the most successful year in its existence....

Of this accepted group, 156 students came from the 17 southern states and District of Columbia, where educational segregation still exists on the secondary school level. Of these, 60 were awarded $40,619 worth of college scholarships by inter-racial colleges and other sources.

Fifteen Negroes and four white students are entering 11 newly inter-racial southern colleges, predominantly of the other race, under the "two-way integration" project with the help of $5,344 worth of college and other scholarships, supplemented by $6,525 from our "two-way integration" fund.

* * *

Preparatory Schools:

This year a total of 11 students were accepted and granted a total of $10,025 worth of scholarships by the Abbot Academy, Buxton Academy, Groton School, The Gunnery, Loomis, Mt. Hermon School for Boys, Northfield School for Girls, Phillips Academy at Andover, Slovak Girls Academy, and Taft, Westminster, Westover and Windsor Mountain Schools.

The Gunnery, Loomis, Taft and Westminster accepted their first Negro students for enrollment this year as a result of our preparatory school program.

* * *

Southern Project:

In the spring of 1953, the Agency received a grant of $170,000 from the Fund for the Advancement of Education of the Ford Foundation, for a two-year talent search and study project in the southern states....

Approximately 75 high schools in some 45 cities will be visited four times each during the school year by the co-directors of the southern field services, Dr. Paul F. Lawrence and Mr. Donald W. Wyatt, on leave from Howard and Fisk Universities, respectively....

UNITED STATES NATIONAL STUDENT ASSOCIATION NEWS, NOVEMBER, 1954

NSSFNS HEARS LONGSHORE

Plans to strengthen campus-support for the National Scholarship Service and the Fund for Negro Students (NSSFNS) at USNSA member schools were outlined by the National Affairs Vice-President K. Wallace Longshore at a meeting of the NSSFNS Board of Directors in New York this month.

In accord with resolutions passed at the Seventh National Congress, Longshore indicated that USNSA support would be given the national information program of NSSFNS among college students and that member schools would be encouraged to expand their support of NSSFNS through campus chest drives.

Highlight of the meeting was publication of a report on the NSSFNS "talent search" program, which seeks to broaden opportunities for higher education among qualified Negro students.

NSA News, April 1950

Vol. III, No. 7

NSA Given Seats On Agency for Negro Students

NSA has been granted two seats on the Board of Directors of the tional Scholarship Service and and for Negro Students (NSSFNS). Appointed to fill the positions were veep Richard J. Medalie and former national staff member Eugene Schwartz.

* * *

THE SCHOLARSHIP FUND contacts negro students and advises them of opportunities that exist for study in interracial colleges and universities.

Information supplied by the Scholarship Fund includes listings of scholarships at interracial schools, and the where and when of applying for them. The Fund also supplements existing scholarships that are not sufficient for Negro students.

According to the Fund, Negroes total less than 1 percent of the enrollment in non-segregated colleges, although they represent 10 per cent of the nation's population.

It points out that more than $11 million in scholarships are available each year without racial strings attached.

A TWO-PHASE PROGRAM OF cooperation has been planned between NSA and the Fund according to Medalie.

NSA will aid in securing and maintaining liaison between the Fund and campus groups conducting Campus Chest or other fund drives. A survey of the situation has already been made by the NSA national staff, and and another will be conducted at the third annual National Student Congress, which will be held Aug. 23-31, at the University of Michigan, Ann Arbor, Michigan.

NSA and the Fund will also cooperate to the eventual goal of publishing a comprehensive listing of all scholarships available in the United States. However, no immediate action will be possible Medalie said.

In addition to the board of directors, the Fund has an advisory board of more than 150 presidents of American colleges and universities.

NSA LENT ITS SUPPORT TO NSSFNS in 1950, when the agency had just begun to expand its program nationally. NSA helped NSSFNS reach and gain the support of college campus chest fund drives throughout the country. It also provided a student voice on the NSSFNS board, as successive NSA educational program vice-presidents were selected to serve. In addition, as Shirley Neizer Tyler recounts in this section, a number of former NSA officers joined the NSSFNS staff for one-year stints—traveling around the country recruiting campus chest support and visiting and counseling with NSSFNS placements. Among them were Gene Schwartz (CCNY, NSA VP 1948-49), Ken Kurtz (Swarthmore, PA regional Chair, 1949-50), and Tom Callahan (St. Francis, later to become NSA's Travel Director). Both Schwartz and Kurtz, successively, also edited the NSSFNS Newsletter, *Opportunity News*.

Felice N. Schwartz and Richard L. Plaut

Felice N. Schwartz

Richard L. Plaut

The vision and the mission that Felice Schwartz and Richard L. (Dick) Plaut shared and which shaped the students whom NSSFNS served over the past half-century is very much alive to-day. Although Schwartz and Plaut have passed on, they left a wonderful legacy of service and commitment among NSSFNS alumni.

NSSFNS today, based in Atlanta, Georgia and now known as the National Scholarship Service, has transformed its mission to serve all disadvantaged students without regard to age, race, ethnicity and cultural background.

The "old" NSSFNS, that I knew, granted students supplementary scholarship aid at interracial colleges. Founded by Felice N. Schwartz, an activist student at Smith College, in the years immediately following World War II, NSSFNS attracted gifted and talented "Negro" students from all economic classes who qualified for admission and scholarship aid from the College itself.

Tony Schwartz, Felice Schwartz' son, described his mother as passionate about civil rights and both unable and unwilling to accept women's prescribed roles, incredibly creative and a pragmatist who was ahead of her time. Felice Schwartz subsequently founded Catalyst in 1962. Catalyst, a national organization, was dedicated to help women choose and advance careers in varying roles in major U.S. corporations including Board membership.

Felice Schwartz died in 1996 but her legacy of example and commitment survive, serving as a beacon to all feminists.Her husband, Irving, a scientist, educator and physician, still shares his memories of her as he shared her time and energy with the causes she held dear. She is also survived by a daughter, Cassie Schwartz Arnold, and another son, James, also a recognized scientist and writer. She is remembered by her family, all of whom I recently spoke with, as a pioneer - out there living her principles and setting examples.

Dick Plaut, who was the administrator responsible for day-to-day operations, died in 1973 .His son and namesake described him as a true believer, totally committed to his work. Felice Schwartz had brought Plaut into NSSFNS at its founding.A Williams College graduate, Plaut never doubted that "Negro" students could succeed in the most rigorous academic environments.He saw himself as an enabler and, according to his son, always insisted that his own role was negligible.

Plaut is remembered by Gene Schwartz, the first of a line of former NSA staff members who worked for a year for NSSFS, as a warm-hearted mentor. His wife, Aileen, then the editor of Vogue magazine, provided "merciless blue pencil guidance," in the editing of *Opportunity News*, the NSSFNS newsletter.

More than a half-century later, those of us who benefited from the NSSFNS' mission and its work acknowledge that the debt we owe to these forward-looking individuals is monumental. But, we also know that the struggle for full equality of educational opportunity continues.

Evelyn Jones Rich

Opportunity NEWS IN INTERRACIAL COLLEGES

Published by: NATIONAL SCHOLARSHIP SERVICE AND FUND FOR NEGRO STUDENTS

VOL. 4, No. 1 31 WEST 110TH STREET, NEW YORK CITY OCTOBER, 1953

474 Students Enrolling In 1953, Win $197,000

THE MORE THAN 900 STUDENTS counselled and referred for admission to interracial colleges by NSSFNS, for September, 1953, set a new high-water mark for success in gaining acceptances and scholarship awards at 224 institutions.

Highlights of their achievements, as reported by Dr. Harry J. Carman, NSSFNS Chairman, in his annual October report, show the following pattern for the 615 students who have to date advised the agency of their results:

1. Of 500 who completed their applications, 474 (a 47% increase over last year), or 95% of the applicants, were accepted at 224 interracial colleges.

2. Of these students, 165 (40% more than last year) were awarded 214 scholarships totaling $197,301 in value, a rise of 106% over last year's total, at 147 colleges.

3. Of the 474 accepted, 156 students came from the 17 Southern states and the District of Columbia, where educational segregation still exists on the secondary school level. Sixty of them were awarded $48,619 worth of scholarships.

Enter New Interracial Colleges

4. Fifteen Negro and four white students are entering 11 newly interracial southern colleges, predominantly of the other race, under the NSSFNS new "two-way integration" project. They will be helped by $5,344 worth of college and other scholarships, supplemented by $6,525 from the NSSFNS "two-way integration" fund.

5. A total of 72 students were granted $23,860 in direct awards from NSSFNS supplementary scholarship funds.

(*Continued on Page 2*)

South-Wide Talent Search Underway

FOR THE FIRST TIME, an extensive south-wide talent search will be conducted on a planned and controlled basis among Negro high-school seniors with the ability to qualify for college admission and scholarship assistance.

Financed by a two-year grant of $170,000 from the Fund for the Advancement of Education of the Ford Foundation, the new "southern project" will include three major activities:

To Discover Able Seniors

First, it aims to discover those Negro high-school seniors able and qualified to apply for college admission and scholarship assistance.

Those wishing to attend interracial colleges will then be given full counselling and information to aid in their selection of colleges; in addition, they will be guided through the necessary steps of filing applications, taking CEEB and other entrance tests, and in the determination of their financial needs.

Secondly, three demonstration projects

(*Continued on Page 2*)

'Two-Way' Project Ends First Year

THE PIONEER PROJECT in "two-way integration" during its first year brought about the referral of 263 Negro and white students to 13 colleges, predominantly of the other race. Nineteen of the students (15 Negro and 4 white) not only went through with their applications but were accepted and awarded scholarship aid by 11 colleges, thus qualifying them for supplementary assistance from NSSFNS.

Considering the unusual nature of the program—to accelerate integrated education at private undergraduate southern colleges which formerly maintained racial barriers, and where changes were entirely voluntary—this year's experience, although falling short of the original numerical goal, indicates that the results should be cumulative from year to year.

Need for Better Recruitment

One of the main obstacles to be overcome, before a large number are admitted through the project, is the development of sounder techniques of recruitment, particularly of white students. More readiness was shown by both Negro and white colleges to accept qualified students of the

(*Continued on Page 3*)

AMONG TOP AWARD WINNERS from the Southern States: JORETHA LANGLEY — Graduate of the C. A. Johnson High School, Columbia, S. C., and an "A" student, she was admitted to Wilson College, Pa., with a scholarship from the college supplemented by NSSFNS. DAVID RAY — A Dunbar High School graduate of Washington, D. C. Entering Bates College, Vt., he was a top science student, active in student government. David was also a Bates and NSSFNS scholarship winner.

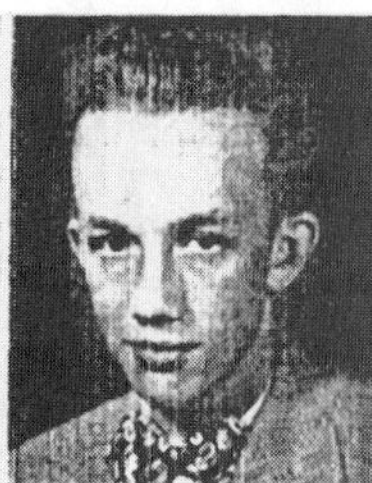

TWO OF THE 19 PIONEERS in the first year of the "two-way" integration project. RONALD A. DAVIDSON — The first Negro admitted to the Georgetown School of Foreign Service, he was graduated from Fordham Preparatory School, N. Y., where he was active in student congress and the track team. JOHN R. ANDRESS — One of four white students admitted to predominantly Negro colleges, he will enter Lincoln University, Pa. He is an honor graduate of Oxford High School, Pa.

Report Shows Record Placements, Awards

(*Continued from Page 1*)

The year's activities have been enriched by a larger number of students being reached by NSSFNS services in the areas where they are most needed.

Students from the South, the region of poorest educational opportunity, composed about 1/3 of the total served. Increased funds have made it possible to greatly expand NSSFNS field services and supplementary scholarship awards in the South.

The most significant result of these expanding services over the past five years is the demonstration to high schools, preparatory schools, and colleges that it is not enough to accept a policy of non-segregation or non-discrimination, but that Negro students must be more adequately prepared and stimulated to take advantage of that policy.

It has been shown time and again that without the benefit of sufficient and constructive guidance and assistance, colleges will continue to receive applications from many Negro students who are inadequately prepared to meet their academic standards; and, from those able to qualify, a large number will be financially unable to enter college without supplementary aid.

Problem of Recruitment in the Southern States

In the southern states, particularly, it has been necessary to conduct a "fine tooth-comb" operation in order to discover a significant number of students with adequate secondary school preparation to do creditable work in the keenly competitive colleges.

The stepped-up field program among the southern high schools, described elsewhere in this issue, is designed to awaken both teachers and students to available opportunities, and to ensure in time that promising Negro students will carry the minimum curriculum to qualify them for admission to first-rate colleges.

Finally, NSSFNS has given a great deal of attention to the social and intellectual challenge facing the individual students who may be pioneering at one of the colleges or preparatory schools admitting Negro students for the first time under NSSFNS auspices. Both our most heartening, and most frustrating experiences occur in this area. On the one hand, the successful placement of students who grow and move forward in their new interracial environment, and on the other, the many who must be told that they are inadequately prepared to enter the colleges of their choice.

The agency is guided in its program by the conviction that the role of education in raising the status of Negro Americans, by enabling them to realize their full potential as individuals and as citizens, is perhaps the principal factor in the elimination of racial segregation and discrimination.

ALLEN WILLIAMS — Admitted to Harvard with a very large award, supplemented by NSSFNS. A graduate of Howard High School, Wilmington, Del., he was an all-around athlete and student leader. CLARICE DIBBLE — Of Tuskegee Institute, Alabama, she is a graduate of the Northfield School for Girls. Ranking in the top fourth of her class, she was admitted to Sarah Lawrence College, N. Y., with both college and NSSFNS awards.

It is this conviction that continues to encourage the National Scholarship Service and Fund for Negro Students in its efforts to broaden opportunities for Negro students for higher education in an interracial environment.

Ford Fund Aids South-Wide Talent Search

(*Continued from Page 1*)

will be undertaken in order to develop and test methods of enlisting the active and effective participation of local community groups and committees in a continuing local talent search program —more thoroughly than could be done by staff representatives working alone.

DR. PAUL F. LAWRENCE

Finally, the project is to provide accurate information about the number of Negro students qualified for higher education, the quality of their preparation, and the extent of their financial need.

MR. DONALD W. WYATT

To be carried out mainly by means of an extensive field program, the project will be under the general direction of Richard L. Plaut, NSSFNS Executive Vice Chairman, and under the immediate supervision of its two co-directors of southern field services, Dr. Paul F. Lawrence and Mr. Donald Wyatt, on leaves of absence from Howard and Fisk Universities, respectively. Their program calls for field visits to 75 selected high schools in some 45 cities four times each during the school year.

Two-Way Integration

(*Continued from Page 1*)

other race than was shown by qualified students to apply to these colleges.

The most effective media of recruitment were the churches, which so far have been the most productive source of white student applications. The Department of Racial and Cultural Relations of the National Council of Churches of Christ in the U.S.A. and their constituent bodies have been most cooperative and helpful in this activity.

The "two-way integration" project was begun last year with the aid of a grant from the New York Foundation, together with some unexpended reserve funds from the previous year.

JOAN E. COLE — First Negro woman student to enter St. John's College, Md., she is graduate of Paul L. Dunbar High School in Baltimore. Miss Cole received top State Senatorial and NSSFNS awards. BARBARA JEANNE LEECE — Graduate of New Hope High School, W. Va., she will enter West Virginia Wesleyan with NSSFNS award. Active in school affairs, she served on orchestra, school paper, and student government.

According to Harry J. Carman, NSSFNS Board Chairman, "this project, still in its infancy, will be of great importance in the extension of equality of opportunity in higher education."

The program is being evaluated from time to time by a special advisory committee. Its members include representatives of the colleges taking part in the program, experts in intercultural education, and representatives of student organizations.

Negro College Press: Voice of Hope, Irony, Anger

Maroon Tiger

Founded In 1898 — Voice of the Students

Vol. 49, No. 4 — MOREHOUSE COLLEGE, ATLANTA, GA. — February, 1948

CIVIL RIGHTS CONFAB STEERING COMMITTEE—Planners for the "All-University Student Study Conference on Civil Rights" at Atlanta University are student and faculty members of Atlanta University and affiliated colleges. Shown discussing the conference program are (seated left to right) Miss Marymal Morgan, Spelman; Robert Threatt, Morris Brown; Miss June Blanchard, Clark; Robert E. Johnson, public relations chairman, Morehouse; Miss Billie M. Jones, Atlanta University; Dr. Mozelle Hill and Prof. Walter R. Chivers, faculty chairman and co-chairman, Atlanta University and Morehouse. Standing, left to right, are Anderson O. Phillips, Atlanta University; Dr. Ira DeA. Reid, special adviser, Atlanta University; John D. Reid, student co-chairman, Atlanta University; Miss Pearl Smith, Moris Brown; A. Calvin Crowder, Atlanta University; Miss Mildred Brummell, Atlanta University; Joseph T. Brook and James Herndon, Morehouse. (Photo by Bowens)

Students Spearhead Civil Rights Confab at A. U.

This is a big country. It harbors a lot of people. And it harbors a lot of prejudices.

When they have endured long enough, most of us incline to take them for granted. It's not so much an affirmative feeling on our part, a conscious rejection of their consideration, a wilful determination to be indifferent about them. We just don't think about them.

But these are trying days. President Truman's Civil Rights declaration has pit the forces of light against the forces of darkness. We can't escape it.

Hence, the students and faculty members of Atlanta University and affiliated colleges formulated an "All-University Student Study Conference on Civil Rights".

DEFINES PURPOSE

Having formulated plans for a series of meetings on the campus, students were given copies of the report of the President's Committee on Civil Rights to find out what is in the report and how it affects the South; to find out how short we in the South are away from the goals and to work out techniques, strategies and methods of achieving "These Rights."

Freedom---It's Wonderful

By John Edwards

A lynching, a riot, a Ku Klux Klan . . . but we're for freedom man to man. The way of life which we live . . . keeps not from us the power to give . . . advise and support to others who . . . strive for that which is their due.

Our own we keep in hopeless plight . . . there's second-class citizens because that's right. . . . To others, though across the sea, . . . we'd gladly grant their liberty. . . . Nothing wrong with the gospel we preach . . . or the racial supremacy that we teach. . . . If some black ni - - er wants to object . . . just hang a rope around his neck.

Let all men know, for it's a fact . . . that freedom you can have, unless you are black. . . . Ho Protestant, Catholic, Negro, Jew. . . . Say to Germany that "we're for you." . . . Fret not if this freedom is not thine. . . . Just place your name on the dotted line.

But always remember to stay in your place . . . unless you belong to the master race. . . . If you'll just behave as you've been told . . . maybe some day you'll get a Freedom Scroll.

THE ANGER AND ENERGY which exploded during the February, 1960 Greensboro sit-ins, described by Connie Curry in this section, and which galvanized black students—"by June over 70,000 Southern college students, mostly black, were involved in demonstrations"—was always expressed in the Negro college press. On this page are some of those expressions as they appeared in the press of three Negro college NSA members during the period covered by this Anthology (Left, both from Morehouse College, GA *Maroon Tiger,* February, 1948. Right, top two, Howard University, DC *Hilltop*, 4/15/48. Bottom, Jackson State College, MS *Blue and White Flash*, 12/46 (see Peoples, this section).

Hilltop

VOL. XXV No. 10 — HOWARD UNIVERSITY, WASHINGTON, D. C. — THURSDAY, APRIL 15, 1948

LISNER BARS H. U. STUDENTS

Democracy in America may not be dead, but if the goings-on at Lisner Auditorium are any indication, it is definitely in its death throes. Last Thursday night, when most people were busy delving into the superstitions and tomfoolery of Hallowe'en, four Howardites met up with a more realistic brand of American "custom." In attempting to view a performance by Miss Ingrid Bergman in the much-touted "Joan of Lorraine," Jean Drew, Hermán Gibson, William Gardner and Aileen Clarke presented their tickets at the door of the auditorium. At least, they tried to present said tickets. The doorman immediately barred the way, and, on the flimsy excuse of "community policy," refused to allow the group to enter.

The group tried in vain to see the manager of the auditorium in order to get a clear-cut statement of this vague "policy" of the Washington community, but he proved to be the little man nobody could find. While the flashbulbs exploded, the interested spectators cast curious glances at the obviously discomfited officials. Probably the most composed group was the student delegation.

* * *

This marked the second time that such a performance was played in the lobby of Lisner. The audience may not have been an appreciative one, nor the protagonists wise in the way of drama, but each of those present felt that some far-reaching event had just occurred, as, in the shadow of the Nation's Capitol, one more blow was struck for American fascism.

Excerpted

ON CIVIL DISOBEDIENCE

Conclusion of remarks by A. Phillip Randolph, national treasurer of the committee against jim crow in the military service and training and President of the Brotherhood of Sleeping Car Porters, AFL, prepared for delivery before the Senate Armed Services Committee, March 31, 1948, as quoted in The Hilltop, *4/15/48.*

Since the military, with their Southern biases, intend to take over America and institute total encampment of the populace along jim crow lines, Negroes will resist with the power of nonviolence, with the weapons of moral principles, with the good will weapons of the spirit—yes with the weapons that brought freedom to India. I feel morally obligated to disturb and to keep disturbed the conscience of jimcrow America. In resisting the insult of jimcrowism to the soul of black America, we are helping to save the soul of America. And let me add that I am opposed to Russian totalitarian communism and all its works. I consider it a menace to freedom. I stand by democracy as expressing the Judaeo-Christian ethic. But democracy and Christianity must be boldly and courageously applied for all men regardless of race, creed or country.

We shall wage a relentless warfare against jimcrow without hate or revenge for the moral and spiritual progress and safety of our country, world peace and freedom. Finally, let me say that Negroes are just sick and tired of being pushed around, and we just don't propose to take it, and we do not care what happens.

Jackson, Mississippi, December, 1946

THE BLUE AND WHITE FLASH

"The True Voice of Jackson College"

College Represented at Youth Congress

George Swan '47

The Southern Youth Congress met one thousand strong in Columbia, South Carolina, October 18-20.

George W. Swan, Jr., a senior, represented Jackson College at the Congress. Another senior, Estemore A. Wolfe, attended the meet as a representative of the AVC.

The Southern Youth met in solemn session—Militant, courageous Negro youth of the South. Youth—which must and will be served. Youth—dedicated to the struggle for freedom. Youth—determined to achieve that freedom in its lifetime.

The U.S. Negro Colleges in 1948

Source: Richard H. Ostheimer, State College for Teachers, Albany, N.Y., *The Organization of Higher Education in the United States, 1948-1949.* Columbia University Press, New York, 1951. Colleges preceded by an * were members/observers of NSA for one or more Congresses, 1946-1952.

UNIVERSITIES

Public, Federal, Negro, both Men and Women

DISTRICT OF COLUMBIA
*Howard University, Washington (46, 47, 49)

SEPARATE LIBERAL ARTS COLLEGES

A. Complex

Public, State, Negro, both Men and Women

MISSOURI
*Lincoln University, Jefferson City and St. Louis (46, 52)

Private, Protestant, Negro, both Men and Women

GEORGIA
*Atlanta University Affiliated System (Atlanta University, Clark, Morehouse, Morris Brown, and Spelman Colleges), Atlanta (Morehouse: 46, 48, 49, 50, 51)

Private, Roman Catholic, Negro, both Men and Women

LOUISIANA
*Xavier University, New Orleans (46, 47, 48, 49, 50, 51, 52)

B. Others

Public, State, Negro, both Men and Women

MARYLAND
Morgan State College, Baltimore

NORTH CAROLINA
North Carolina College at Durham, Durham

Private, Protestant, Negro, both Men and Women

ALABAMA
Miles College, Birmingham
Talladega College, Talladega

GEORGIA
Paine College, Augusta

LOUISIANA
Dillard University, New Orleans (52)

MISSISSIPPI
Tougaloo College, Tougaloo

NORTH CAROLINA
*Johnson C. Smith University, Charlotte (47, 49, 50)
Livingstone College, Salisbury
Saint Augustine's College, Raleigh
Shaw University, Raleigh

SOUTH CAROLINA
Allen University, Columbia
Benedict College, Columbia
Claflin College, Orangeburg

TENNESSEE
*Fisk University, Nashville (50, 51, 52)
Knoxville University, Knoxville
Lane College, Jackson
LeMoyne College, Memphis

TEXAS
Bishop College, Marshall
Samuel Huston College, Austin
Texas College, Tyler
Tillotson College, Austin
Wiley College, Marshall

VIRGINIA
Virginia Union University, Richmond

Private, Protestant, Negro, Men

PENNSYLVANIA
*Lincoln University, Lincoln University (46)

Private, Protestant, Negro, Women

NORTH CAROLINA
Bennett College, Greensboro

SEPARATE PROFESSIONAL SCHOOLS

A. Teachers Colleges

Public, Municipal, Negro, both Men and Women

DISTRICT OF COLUMBIA
Miner Teachers College, Washington

MISSOURI
Stowe Teachers College (includes Junior College), St. Louis

Public, State, Negro, both Men and Women

ALABAMA
*Alabama State Teachers College, Montgomery (47, 48)

GEORGIA
Albany State College, Albany

MISSISSIPPI
*Jackson College for Negro Teachers, Cheyney (46, 49)

NORTH CAROLINA
Elizabeth City State Teachers College, Elizabeth City
Fayetteville State Teachers College, Fayetteville
Winston-Salem Teachers College, Winston-Salem

OHIO
College of Education and Industrial Arts, Wilberforce

PENNSYLVANIA
Cheyney Training School for Teachers, Cheyney

WEST VIRGINIA
Bluefield State College, Bluefield

Private, Protestant, Negro, both Men and Women

FLORIDA
Bethune-Cookman College, Daytona Beach

B. General Professional Training Schools

Public, State, Negro, both Men and Women

ALABAMA
Alabama Agricultural and Mechanical Institute, Normal

DELAWARE
Delaware State College, Dover

FLORIDA
Florida Agricultural and Mechanical College, Tallahassee

GEORGIA
Fort Valley State College, Fort Valley
Georgia State College, Savannah

KENTUCKY
*Kentucky State College, Frankfort (46)

LOUISIANA
*Southern University and Agricultural and Mechanical College, Baton Rouge (46, 47)

MISSISSIPPI
Alcorn Agricultural and Mechanical College, Alcorn

NORTH CAROLINA
Agricultural and Technical College of North Carolina, Greensboro

OKLAHOMA
Langston University, Langston

SOUTH CAROLINA
South Carolina State Agricultural and Mechanical College (State Colored Normal, Industrial, Agric., and Mech. College of South Carolina), Orangeburg

TENNESSEE
Tennessee Agricultural and Industrial State College, Nashville

TEXAS
Prairie View Agricultural and Mechanical College of Texas, Prairie View

VIRGINIA
Virginia State College (includes Norfolk Division), Petersburg

WEST VIRGINIA
West Virginia State College, Institute

Private, Nonsectarian, Negro, both Men and Women

ALABAMA
*Tuskegee Institute, Tuskegee Institute (46, 49)

FLORIDA
Florida Normal and Industrial College, St. Augustine

VIRGINIA
Hampton Institute, Hampton

C. Protestant Theological Seminaries

Private, Protestant, Negro, both Men and Women

GEORGIA
Gammon Theological Seminary, Atlanta

D. Medical Schools

Private, Protestant, Negro, both Men and Women

TENNESSEE
Meharry Medical College, Nashville

SEPARATE JUNIOR COLLEGES

Public, Municipal, Negro, both Men and Women

ARKANSAS
Dunbar Junior College, Little Rock

MISSOURI
Lincoln Junior College, Kansas City

Private, Nonsectarian, Negro, both Men and Women

SOUTH CAROLINA
Bettis Academy, Trenton

Private, Protestant, Negro, both Men and Women

ALABAMA
Oakwood College, Huntsville
Stillman College, Tuscaloosa

ARKANSAS
Shorter College, North Little Rock

FLORIDA
Edward Waters College, Jacksonville

MISSISSIPPI
Okolona College, Okolona
Southern Christian Institute, Edwards

NORTH CAROLINA
Immanuel Lutheran College, Greensboro

SOUTH CAROLINA
Clinton Normal and Industrial College, Rock Hill
Friendship College, Rock Hill
Voorhees School and Junior College, Denmark

TENNESSEE
Morristown Normal and Industrial College, Morristown
Swift Memorial Junior College, Rogersville

TEXAS
Butler College, Tyler
Mary Allen College, Crockett

PART 2. DOMESTIC PROGRAMS

SECTION 4

NSA and the College Press

CONTENTS

1/17/47

The Hoya
GEORGETOWN UNIVERSITY, WASHINGTON, D. C.
VOL. XXVIII January 17, 1947 NO. 10

Chicago Student Conference

At eight in the evening, December 27, 1946, the first of 475 delegates and 195 observers from 295 college campuses in 47 states began to pour into the large auditorium of the Reynolds Club at the University of Chicago. They represented universities from New England and Florida, from California and Mississippi; they were negro and white, Jew and gentile, Catholic and Communist, Yankee and Rebel. They had, however, one thing in common, an intense belief in the need for

10/3/47

The Diamondback

Our Problem

Should We Join National Association?

11/11/47

California Daily Bruin

STUDENT LEADERS GIVE VIEWS ON NSA RATIFICATION

Hough Says: 'Definitely' Koenig Says: 'Yes' In Favor, BUT...'

5/5/51

The Carletonian — Saturday, May 5, 1951

NSA Committee Asks, "Is It Worth Keeping?"

(This is the second in a series of articles written by members of NSA to acquaint the Carleton students with the organization and

10/26/51

Tower Times
The College for Women University of Rochester

NSA Set-Up Depicted

AUTHORITY AND ORGANIZATION OF N.S.A.
Prince Street Campus
elects through S A
N S A representative
delegates to.
DISTRICT CONFERENCE
1. Elect District officers
REGIONAL CONFERENCE
1. Regional constitution
NATIONAL CONGRESS

10/11/52 The Michigan Daily

INTERNATIONAL IN SCOPE: Mich-Soc- NSD

NSA Represents 750,000 Students

Mi Daily 10-11-52

In August 1952, just prior to the Fifth National Student Congress at Indiana University, NSA hosted its first annual College Newspaper Editors Conference. The five-day event was attended by editors of fifty college newspapers. The conference was organized by Sylvia Bacon, NSA Vice President for Student Affairs, and Robert Brunsell, Editor of the *Minnesota Daily* and Chairman of NSA's College Press Subcommision. A central issue concerned press and editorial independence as highlighted by controversies at the University of Chicago, Michigan State, Radcliffe, Brooklyn College, and Brown University—some of which are referenced in this section.

The conference covered all aspects of newspaper management. Brunsell's report on the college press is excerpted, as are Sylvia Bacon's remarks to the congress on issues concerning student rights, academic freedom, and student affairs. The results of an NSA survey, as well as of the UCLA 1951-52 college newspaper survey, present a snapshot of student newspaper editorial control, management, frequency, circulation, and staff organization.

NSA widely reported in the college press

The formation and early years of NSA were covered widely in the newspapers of those colleges that attended its congresses or regional events and those that considered affiliation. This coverage was of great benefit to NSA's organizing efforts. Editorial comment was generally vigorous and supportive—although not always so—and sometimes ran contrary to student opinion, both for and against. Not infrequently, a given year's editorial staff ignored NSA completely.

The heavy GI Bill veterans' presence on campus also prompted considerable coverage of housing and tuition issues. The formative years of the United Nations, the emerging cold war, issues of academic freedom and anticommunist fears—"the Red Scare"—all received coverage. NSA's engagement in international student relations, its active program of student travel and exchange, and its various domestic programs were also reported on campuses with an NSA presence.

The interest of college newspaper people in NSA was also manifested in the numbers who became NSA delegates as well as staff members including Allan Ostar (Penn State's *Daily Collegian*), Karl Meyer and John Hunter (Wisconsin's *The Daily Cardinal*), Craig Wilson (*The Michigan Daily*), Bob Beyers (Cornell *Daily Sun*), Len Perlmutter (Colorado's *Blue and Gold*), and Donald Martinez (New Mexico *Highlands Candle*), all of whom appear elsewhere in this Anthology.

College newspapers also mirrored student life in its light-hearted as well as academic and political aspects. The section closes with an album of headlines and clippings reflecting some of the campus highlights and high-jinks as viewed in the college press: sports, holidays, special events, April Fool's days, homecoming, rush weeks, and the enticing cigarette advertising that helped support the papers.

KEEPING STUDENTS INFORMED AND RAISING QUESTIONS. From top: Georgetown U., UCLA, U. of Maryland, Carleton C., MN, College for Women, U. of Rochester, U. of Michigan.

National Themes Link College Press and NSA Interests

THE STANFORD DAILY

WILL NATION'S CAMPUSES BE UNITED?

Toyon Men Challenge Search

'Y' Delegates Explain New 'I' Institute

Colleges Will Debate Joining Student Group

1/20/47

DUNBARTON DIAL

The NSA And You!

By Mary Catharine Ostmann

In these awful days when discord, ignorance and misunderstanding are running rampant among the peoples of the globe, it is heartening to attend a gathering of young people whose homes are thousands of miles apart, and whose ideas are separated by an ... is the National Student Association means simply this: that matters · Absolute Truth and basic tenets we not up for study at Wisconsin; at so, for the time being, diametrical opposed ideologies were not in co flict. What was before the body f

10/47

The Williams Record

North Adams, Massachusetts — Williamstown, Massachusetts

VOL. LXI — OCTOBER 29, 1947 — No. 8

Vote Yes

10/29/47

Page 2 — 1-16-48

Ashland Collegian

Official Student Publication of Ashland College

Published semi-monthly during the school year by the students of Ashland College at the Brethren Publishing Company, Ashland, Ohio. Entered as Second Class Matter at Ashland, Ohio, Postoffice. Subscription price $1.00 per year payable in advance. Single copies, five cents each. Advertising rates on application. Office: Room 8 F. Editor .... Dick Topper

1/16/48

THE TECHNIQUE

A Great Opportunity

Georgia Tech is now a member student body of the United States National Student Association.

The Student Council, by its action of ratifying the NSA Constitution last Tues-

2/14/48

Page Two — Wednesday, Feb. 18, 1948 — Daily Trojan

Southern California DAILY TROJAN

★ **We Say Affiliate**

Tonight the ASSC senate will debate the ratification of the constitution of the National Student association and may vote on SC's affiliation.

It is the considered opinion of this paper that the senate should not hesitate to affiliate with NSA.

We know that there are a few reasons why we should not attach ourselves to this, the first widespread move to unite and channel the effort of the nation's great body of students. We do not think they are valid reasons.

The NSA may find the first few years ... universities and colleges in this area had approved NSA, was actually based on something a good deal more sinister than the reasons presented, namely, fear of Communist influence through possible NSA affiliation with the International Union of Students in Prague.

But to explain again that this affiliation is nothing more than an exchange of services would be to labor the point needlessly. Are we to crawl within our shells and refuse to recognize the rest of the world, simply because we do not like

2/18/48

STUDENT LIFE, PAGE 4

STUDENT LIFE

WASHINGTON — Founded 1878 — UNIVERSITY

Action Needed On NSA

As Mark Twain would say it, the report of the death of National Student Association has been greatly exaggerated. Eighteen months old, the student group has already demonstrated a maturity of purpose greater than its youth would indicate.

1/14/49

THURSDAY, OCTOBER 6, 1949 — p. 3

NSA On Trial

The National Student Association is beginning the new academic season with a heavy schedule of projects that were hatched or discussed at its convention in Urbana, Illinois this summer. The Harvard chapter, which belongs to the Boston area of the New England Region of the NSA, is supposed to perform a dual function. Primarily it is part of

10/6/49

Page 4 — THE DIAMONDBACK

Editorials

No Dramatics At NSA Defeat

THE NSA ISSUE that was such a big bombshell on the floor of the Executive Council last year was up again Thursday night.

Time plays strange tricks.

ALL EIGHT MEMBERS of the committee and many members of SGA attended the Mason-Dixon Regional Congress held here last week. They knew what they were voting about.

3/3/50

WHEEL EDITORIALS—

Ideals Are at Stake In Fight Over NSA

Emory's Student council is at present confronted with a predicament that has all the earmarks of a full-blown ethical dilemma. There is a miniature clash between idealism and expediency involved in the situation, although the

1/15/53

Hundreds Still AWOL:

'NSA News' Scans 227 Newspapers

The NSA News now scans college newspapers

Recent additions are:

ARKANSAS—Oracle, Henderson College; Arkansas Traveler, U. of Arkansas.

AUSTRALIA—Farrago, U. of Melbourne.

CALIFORNIA—Cougar's Claws, Lassen J. C.; Collegian, Los Angeles College; View, Mt. St. Mary's College; Collegian, Modesto J. C.

CANADA — Carleton, Carleton College, ...

MARYLAND—Greyhound, Loyola College.

MASSACHUSETTS—News, Radcliffe College; Collegian, University of Massachusetts; Record, Williams College.

MICHIGAN—Clamor, Flint J. C.; Jaycee Journal, Gogebic J. C.; News, Northern College.

MISSISSIPPI—Spectator, Mississippi State College for Women.

MISSOURI—Teresan, College of St. Teresa; Web, Webster College.

NEBRASKA — Creightonian, Creighton University; Nebraskan, University of Nebraska.

NEVADA—Sage Brush, University of Nevada.

NEW HAMPSHIRE — Kearsarge Beacon, Colby J. C.

NEW JERSEY — Minuteman, Bloomfield College; Outlook, Monmouth J. C.; Observer, Newark College of Rutgers; Caellian, New Jersey College for Women; News, Rider College; State, Stevens Institute of Technology; Pauw Wow, St. Peter's College; Gazette, Upsala College.

NEW YORK — Anodyne, General View; Columbia University; Curved Horn, Fordham; ... Long Island University;

College Newspaper Exchange

The following 157 college newspapers have been reviewed for this issue:

ARIZONA: Arizona Wildcat. ARKANSAS: Arka Tech (Ark. Poly.); College Chatter (Little Rock J. C.). CALIFORNIA: Chaffey United Press; Cougar's Claws (Lassen Coll.); Daily Bruin (UCLA); Daily Californian; Koranette (Grant Tech.); Loyolan; Mills College Weekly; Occidental; Pacific Weekly (COP); Spartan Daily (San Jose State); Student Life (Pomona Coll.). COLORADO: Miner (Col. State Coll. of Ed.); Tiger (Col. Coll.). CONNECTICUT: Conn. Campus; Scribe (U. of Bridgeport); Silver Bern (Albertus Magnus). FLORIDA: Florida Alligator. GEORGIA: Red and Black (U. of Georgia); Technique (Ga. Tech.). IDAHO: Idaho Argonaut ... Francis Coll.); Knox Student; Loyola News; ... News (Ill. Tech.); Tempo (Chicago Teachers); ... ford Coll.); Wright Coll. News; Xavierite ... man (Ind. State Teachers); Oak Leaves ... Purdue Exponent; Purdue Independent; ... (Morningside Coll.); Courier (Clarke Coll.); ... Collegian (Asbury Coll.); Wallpaper (Berea ... U.); U-Topia (Ursuline Coll). MAINE: ... Columns (Coll. of Notre Dame). MASSACHU... Coll.); Mt. Holyoke News; Regis Herald; ... field Student; Tomahawk (Holy Cross U.); ... national U.). MICHIGAN: Adrian Coll. ... (Flint J. C.); Hillsdale Collegian; Michi... (Highland Park J. C.); Technonian ... Western Herald (Western Mich. Coll. of ... tonian; College Chronicle (St. Cloud State ... (Macalaster Coll.); Manitou Messenger ... (East Central J. C.). MISSOURI: ... Kaimin. NEW HAMPSHIRE: Dartmouth; ... shire. NEW JERSEY: Bloomfield Minute ... Pauw Wow (St. Peter's Coll.); Maroon ... clarion (MSTC); Observer (Newark U.) ... U.). NEW MEXICO: Highlands Candle ... (U. of Buffalo); Bardian; Campus (CCNY) ... (Fordham School of Ed.); Main Events ... Index; Observation Post (CCNY); Report... News; St. John's News; Ticker (CCNY); ... Vassar Miscellany News. NORTH CAROLI... DAKOTA: Spectrum (N. D. St. Coll.); ... vance (Hiram Coll.); Antioch Record; ... (Youngstown Coll.); Kent Stater; ... Stone Mather Coll); Oberlin Review; ... OREGON: Pioneer Log (Lewis and Clark ... and White (Lehigh U.); Bucknellian; ... Hawk (St. Joseph's Coll.); La Salle Coll... Coll.); Penn State Daily Collegian; ... Billboard. SOUTH DAKOTA: Exponent ... ton Springs Coll.); Mirror (Augustana ... Orange and White (U. of Tenn.); Tech ... VERMONT: Beacon (Bennington Coll.); ... Bullet (Mary Washington Coll.). WASHIN... State Evergreen; Whitworthian. WEST VIRGINIA: Mercury (Glenville St. Coll.); Pharos (W. Va. Wesleyan; Tech Collegian (W. Va. Tech.). WISCONSIN: Badger Record (U. of W.—Milwaukee Extension); Daily Cardinal (U. of Wisconsin); Roundtable (Beloit Coll.).

NSA NEWS — November, 1948

Politics Stir Campus Debates

Editorials Express Varied Attitudes

Editorial comment in the college press covered a wide range of attitudes toward the national elections.

The Caellian, of New Jersey College for women, echoing the sentiments of many other papers, called upon its students to assume "the obligation to be acquainted with events on a national and international level. Although all of us can't vote," they say, "we can read the newspapers."

Reflecting the traditional pre-election appeals to get out the vote, some papers chose attractive editorial titles to gain reader attention. They ranged from the studied "Vote Sagely" of Tempo (Chicago Teachers) to "Put Your Finger in the Pie" of the Pony Express (Sacramento College), and "That Day" Daily Collegian (Penn State). The Loyolan (Loyola, Calif.) created no problems for the reader by simply titling its editorial "Election Day—1948."

With many papers tired by Nov. 2, ...

Review of College Newspapers IndicatesLivelyStudentInterest

By EUGENE SCHWARTZ

With many college papers featuring political forums on their editorial pages, and the intense political pre-election discussion on most campuses, one might question the truth of the contention that the college student is not preparing to meet the responsibilities of citizenship.

The Long Island University Seawanka writes editorially, "Welcome, Political Clubs", in response to the ...

Savants Analyze Polling Results

College professors ... selves analyzing the national elections ... were finally in.

Dr. Stuart C. Dodd ... the Washington Pu... oratory, stated that ... in polling techniques ... necessary." Neverth... they would gain ... had lost in the ... cated that some ... told pollsters they ... Republican "becau... the greatest presti...

In the opinion o... Madow, statisticia... of North Carolina ...

Borrowed Comment

NSA in the College Press

NO AXE-GRINDING

NSA ISN'T GOING to be an axe-grinding organization tearing about the nation and excoriating through press and forum the actions of college administrations when they are not favorable to student interests. The NSA will work by investigation, persuasion, and enlightenment of student bodies on matters of their vital concern. It will serve as a vast storehouse of information on academic freedom, student rights, educational standards, teaching methods and student social, economic, and cultural welfare. The NSA is becoming the unified voice of American college students. — Howard Woodham in the Technique, Georgia Tech.

• • •

FROM THE STUDENTS

SCOFFERS HAVE RETURNED from organizational meetings on both national and regional levels to sing the praises of the NSA. Above all, this one thing is certain, this is a movement that comes not from a higher authority but from students themselves.—The Record, St. John's university, Collegeville, Minn.

• • •

NO RAH-RAH OUTFIT

A LUSTY INFANT in September, 1947, the U. S. National Student association is demonstrating that it does not intend to grow up as a "rah-rah" outfit. Its publications reflect an awareness of the seriousness of being a student and a lively interest in worth-while problems. The NSA NEWS . . . includes thoughtful discussions of university problems.—School and Society, Feb. 28.

• • •

WHAT'S IN IT FOR ME?

OF COURSE most students at once ask—"What's in NSA for me?" The answer is the improvement of college social life, attention to the problem of discrimination, establishment of faculty-student committees on curricular reform, orientation courses for freshmen, part-time employment service, and a host of other advantages.

Cultural exchange will be established between colleges here in this country and students abroad. World-wide travel and study will be greatly facilitated. It is in this exchange of information and the gathering of new ideas that the greatest advantage of NSA lies.—The Bowdoin Orient, Bowdoin college, Brunswick, Me.

From top: *NSA News* 12/49, 5/49, 11/48, 3/48.

NSA'S APPEARANCE IN 1947 aroused interest at colleges across the country, and provided college editors with local news and national themes. At the same time, NSA's leaders recognized the importance of the college press as a mirror of student interests and as a voice through which students could be reached. In its early years, *NSA News* reviewed college papers from throughout the country. Limited in staff and resources, and unable to organize a base for national advertising, its potential for developing an intercollegiate paper could not be realized (See Ostar, Pt. 1, S6, Wilson Pt. I, S. 7). However, NSA did establish a relationship with the college press, launching in 1952 its annual College Editors Conference at the Fifth National Student Congress at Indiana U.

NSA's fortunes were followed by college editors. From the top: Stanford's *Daily* voices the hopes of the 1946 Chicago Student Conference (Pt. 1, S. 3). Dunbarton's *Dial*, DC: Catholic college students balance issues of faith and politics with a "heterogeneous assortment of minds." (Pt. 4, S. 1)

The Williams Record, MA, *Ashland Collegian*, OH, Georgia Tech *Technique*, and USC *Trojan* all voice the benefits of pending or accomplished affiliation. "A huge step towards student rights," says the *Collegian.* Facing strong opposition the Trojan asked in 1948, "Are we to crawl within our shells and refuse to recognize the rest of the world?" (USC's President eventually vetoed the student council decision to affiliate, (Pt. 5, S. 8). Washington University's *Student Life*, MO, complimenting the Student Senate, wrote, in 1949, "the time for caution has ended. NSA has proved itself."

Harvard's *Crimson*, noting "promising" projects, challenged its campus NSA committee to prove "if such activities are worth an expenditure of $1,300." After three years of contentious affiliation battles (Pt. 5, S. 4), U. of Maryland's *Diamondback* complimented its student government (SGA) for "reaching its decision calmly" not to affiliate because NSA "could not offer the University any more than the SGA." In1953, the Wheel urged Emory in Atlanta not to withdraw,and asked the council to pledge its "intention of rejoining the national group just as soon as her sister universities of the South find the political climate in NSA more to their liking."

The best newspaper is the one most free to tell the truth.

1. A Report on the College Press, 1952

Robert Brunsell

University of Minnesota. Editor, Minnesota Daily, *1951-52*
Chairman, NSA, College Press Subcommission, 1951-52

Reproduced from A Report on the College Press, *published in 1952 by NSA.*

The Problem

Last fall at the University of Chicago, an action taken by Dean of Students, Robert M. Strozier, drew nationwide attention to the problem of the college press. At that time, Dean Strozier removed Alan Kimmel as editor of the Chicago *Maroon* after he used his title as editor to sponsor a communist youth rally in East Berlin.

This action seemed to be an outright violation of press freedom; actually, its roots ran deep into the problem of press responsibility. The *Maroon* had been widely criticized for failing to show any sense of responsibility toward the University community.

The executive committee of the National Student Association, in a resolution adopted at its December 1951 meeting, criticized the method of action taken by Dean Strozier. It also "regretted" that Chicago's student government had not taken steps to insure "adequate safeguards for the conduct of the *Maroon.*"

In point five of its *Maroon* case opinion, the committee said:

> This problem of the responsibility and relationship of the campus press to the student body, the student government, and the administration is not unique at Chicago, but exists universally. Attention should be paid to it by all student governments. To aid in definition and solution of the problem, NSA has created the national subcommission on the college press, one of whose duties is to examine the question.

By direction of the national executive committee, the national subcommission on press and public relations here presents its brief study of the relationship between the college press and its campus.

This report also includes some recommendations concerning press-campus relationships. These recommendations represent the thinking of leaders in publications and student government at the University of Minnesota. They are based on limited research and are not to be taken as a solution to the problem, but rather as a guide.

College Press Aims

This committee asserts that the two major aims of the college press are to provide a newspaper for the college community, and to provide a training ground for journalism and good citizenship. The press ought to maintain relationships with students, student government, and college administration which will further these major aims.

Furthering the Goals

The best newspaper is the one most free to tell the truth, the one which informs without prejudice or ax-grinding, the one which allows varying points of view to be expressed. Similarly, the best training ground for citizenship is the college press which is free to make decisions and to make mistakes. This committee does not feel that responsibility can be taught out of a book.

On any college campus there are forces which work against the college press's two major aims. Often the press is censored by the administration for publishing the facts or viewpoints embarrassing to the college. Sometimes student government exerts pressure, or outright force, to prevent the press from being critical of its activities. Sometimes the editorial staff of the paper itself distorts the truth or in other ways fails to provide an adequate newspaper for the campus.

A recent survey by Carl Conner, graduate student at the University of Minnesota, shows that the college press is widely censored. (Some exact figures are included in an appendix to this study.) Conner found that most of censorship was exercised on editorials dealing with administration policies; budgets; finance; and state legislature; campus conditions; the food situation; and liquor.

Methods of censorship varied, the survey shows. Favorite techniques of the administration were to put a blue pencil right to the copy before it was published, and to call editors on the carpet after publication. But students themselves were found to be just as notorious for withholding news from the press.

Methods of selecting college editors frequently encourage bias and censorship. On larger papers the editors usually are picked by a publication board, composed merely of faculty or administrators, or by the outgoing editorial staff. Neither method provides for responsibility to the community as a whole.

Some Principles

Administrators often will argue that censorship is necessary to protect the long-range interests of the college from irresponsibility in the college press. This idea of responsibility to the college was incorporated in a "publication code" recently adopted at Michigan State University:

> It (the code) will serve as a guide in helping students determine publication's policies where there may appear to be a conflict between their editorial desires and the long-range interests of the college. It will take no responsibility from the student editors, but is intended to impress upon them their obligation to consider interests of their college, just as professional editors consider the interests of the community.

To this, the editor of the *Quill*, professional journalism magazine, commented:

> I can conceive of situations in which students' "editorial desires" might legitimately conflict with what a faculty member would consider the "long-range interest of the college." And while a professional editor certainly considers the interests of the community, his idea of what needs to be printed to further those interests often annoys large sections of the citizenry who wants things to be left alone.
>
> . . . More often college administrators who believe deeply in student freedom of expression, even when it hurts, are the captives of their trustees and alumni.

The *Quill* editorial concludes that:

> a campus editor should be let alone as much as possible, for his own good as well as that of his student readers. Certainly, he will make mistakes. If they are too frequent or too serious, he must pay the penalty. That is the way free newspapermen work in the world beyond the campus. How better can he learn to be a free newspaperman himself?

This committee believes that an honest presentation of facts and varying viewpoints can never conflict with the long-range interests of a college devoted to high educational and democratic ideals.

Insuring an Honest Press

What protection can a reader have against distortions of truth by small segments of the campus population, including the editorial staff itself? When a reader loses confidence in a professional newspaper, he can cancel his subscription. But on the college campus the press usually holds a monopoly on distribution of news. (A notable exception was the existence, until February 1952, of two competing student newspapers at Smith College, Mass. The papers merged this year because the campus couldn't support both of them.) Some college papers have a system of required subscriptions. The reader's only insurance of an acceptable campus paper is through legal control.

This committee favors the board of publications as the best means of control. The function of such a board should not be to censor the college press, but rather to protect it from censorship. The board should have the power to select a competent editor, to make recommendations about editorial policy, and to remove an editor who has shown bias or incompetence.

A publication board also should act as a liaison group between the campus population and the editorial staff. Board members should be active critics, always careful to see that student, faculty, and administration complaints come to the editor's attention. They should not, however, exercise day-to-day control over editorial policy. To do so would be to destroy the value of a student newspaper as a training ground for active responsibility.

Membership of the publications board should include representatives of major segments of the campus population. Students elected directly by the student body should hold a strong majority on the board. Students, taken as a whole, have fewer axes to grind and will not be prone to censor the press. (It is suggested that, where subscription to the newspaper is voluntary, only subscribers be allowed to elect representatives to the board.) Faculty and administration also should be represented. These members will perform the extra function of giving experience and continuity, but they should never outnumber the student members, who represent the largest segment of the campus population.

Bob Brunsell putting the finishing touches on an editorial for the *Minnesota Daily*. According to the *Gopher* (1952 Yearbook), the Daily "had an income of approximately $120,000, 138 deadlines to meet, and a circulation given out officially as 21,960." (Courtesy, University of Minnesota Archives)

A publications board should not be tied to student government, but should stand as a separate body. A publications board does place a protection between the press and administration. Once the machinery has been established administrators must operate through it. The board absorbs pressures ordinarily directed at the editor.

About Journalistic Quality

Students who complain about their college press usually do not attack its honesty, but they frequently complain that its coverage is poor, or that it is colorless. And they are frequently right.

Students, while they may be mature enough to express opinions editorially, are not necessarily qualified to publish a smooth, professional newspaper. This committee believes that if it is worthwhile to maintain a college newspaper as an educational experience it is also worthwhile to employ a trained journalist as newspaper advisor. Where the college has no journalism school, this journalist can teach courses in addition to his advisory duties.

The presence of a professional journalist not only would improve the quality of the college press, but would ease the tension between student editors and faculty members who, for lack of other authority on the subject, consider themselves qualified to pass judgment on the student newspaper.

No Final Answer

There is no cure-all for the problem of a distorted college press. From his survey, Carl Conner concludes that "censorship of the college press is here to stay. Even though the 'blue pencil' disappears, it seems reasonable to say that a great deal of news suppression would still exist."

But by protecting the college editor from pressure, by protecting the reader from an incompetent editor, and by stimulating a desire for free expression on the campus, even when it hurts, student leaders can help to correct the undemocratic position of today's college press.

ROBERT BRUNSELL

Note re career highlights: The editors regret that we have been unable to find additional information about Robert Brunsell following his college years.

PICTURE CREDIT: *Then: Minnesota* alumni magazine, May-June, 1951, v. 50, nos. 9-10 (University of Minnesota Library).

APPENDIX

The following information was gathered in a poll of college editors attending a convention of the Association Collegiate Press in October 1951. It is emphasized that the sample in this survey was extremely small and the results therefore are not accurately representative.

Sixty-three college newspapers were included in this survey.

BREAKDOWN:

State College	26	Weeklies	31
Private colleges	19	Semi-weeklies	11
Denominational	14	Dailies	10
Others	4	Others	11

SELECTION OF EDITORS:

Weeklies:		*Dailies:*	
Publications boards	38.7%	Publication boards	60.0%
Outgoing staffs	29.0	Outgoing Staffs	30.0
Popular election	6.4	Other methods	10.0
Administration	9.7		
Other methods	16.1	*Others:*	
Semi-weeklies:		Publications boards	27.3%
Popular election	18.2%	Outgoing staffs	18.2
Publication boards	45.5	Popular election	27.3
Outgoing staffs	36.4	Other methods*	27.3

*This included selection by the administration.

DETERMINATION OF POLICY

Weeklies:		*Dailies:*	
Editor and staff	29.0%	Editor and staff	20.0%
Editor	38.7	Editor	20.0
Editorial board	25.8	Editorial board	30.0
Others	6.5	Others and combinations	30.0
Semi-weeklies:		*Others:*	
Editor and staff	54.5%	Editor and staff	27.3%
Editorial board	27.3	Editor	45.5
Administration	9.1	Editorial board	9.1
Combinations	9.1	Administration	18.2

LIMITATIONS

The percentages given below include those answering "yes" or "occasionally" to the questions.

1. Does the faculty advisor, any member of the administration, or staff of the college censor material for publication?

Denom.	35.7%	Private	31.6%	State	33.6
Weeklies	29.0%	Semi-weeklies	27.3	Dailies	0.0
Others	81.8%				

2. Does the faculty advisor, any member of the administration, or staff of the college exert pressure on members of the staff after publication?

Denom.	57.1%	Private	26.3%	State	38.4
Weeklies	35.5%	Semi-weeklies	45.5	Dailies	50.0
Others	27.2%				

3. Have students or student organizations withheld news?

Denom.	50.0%	Private	68.4%	State	53.8
Weeklies	61.3%	Semi-weeklies	27.3	Dailies	60.0
Others	54.5%				

4. Does the administration or any member of the college staff withhold news, to your knowledge?

Denom.	57.1%	Private	52.4%	State	50.0
Weeklies	51.7%	Semi-weeklies	36.4	Dailies	70.0
Others	54.6%				

5. Do you feel free to publish anything (short of libel, indecent material, etc.) in the student newspaper?

Denom.	57.1%	Private	89.4%	State	80.7
Weeklies	74.2%	Semi-weeklies	81.8	Dailies	90.0
Others	54.5%				

It is not correct that we [students] are a fearful group of jellyfish.

2. Sylvia Bacon: I Tell Them about NSA

"It is a voice not bound by fears and conformities"

Sylvia A. Bacon,
Vassar College
Vice President of Student Affairs, NSA, 1951-52

Editor's note: Sylvia Bacon organized NSA's first annual pre-Congress College Editors Conference. A champion for student rights, Bacon worked with Robert Brunsell, editor of the Minnesota Daily, *to bring college editors together to consider pressures on the college press by college administrations and others. Following are edited excerpts from Bacon's report to the Fourth National Student Congress at the University of Minnesota from the minutes of the Plenary Session on August 19, 1952. In it she voices her vision for the role of the Association in meeting the challenges ahead, as well as reflections on the constraints of NSA's limited resources as she experienced them.*

I'm so glad that you are all here. I know that this is an awfully simple statement to begin a report to the Congress with. But you see, all year I have been talking to groups of adults and to some of your regions, saying: " You know the cliches of my generation. I belong to that group typified as the silent, fearful group of jellyfish." Then I tell them that this is not correct. I tell them about NSA. It is the best evidence I know. It is the evidence of students speaking as a coordinated voice nationally on Universal Military Training, Intercollegiate Athletics, discrimination, educational opportunity. It is an international voice. It is a voice not bound by fears and conformities. But sometimes I have felt like a lone voice.

Regrettably in this year the pressures which would make our generation silent and fearful have grown stronger. Don't be insulted if I ask you whether you have succumbed? You see, I have read *God and Man at Yale*;[1] I have heard some say that NSA must only be an informational clearinghouse; and I have seen efforts to block the Association's abilities to speak on legislative matters pertaining to the educational community. . . .

Student Affairs Commission: developing student potential

It has been my belief during the past year that the National Student Association has had an increasingly important role to play in the development of student potentialities at a time when some have viewed with alarm decreasing enrollments, irresponsible action on the part of students, and growing apathy. The importance of this role, as shown in the Student Affairs Commission, rests on these assumptions:

1. There are three parts to the educational community: Faculty, Students, and Administration. One taken alone cannot build the best educational community.
2. In order to take part in the educational community there are certain requisites for a student affairs program:
   (a) development of the student's abilities, including extra-curricular leadership, new educational opportunities, and inter-cultural credit courses.
   (b) eradication of student weaknesses: one is not externally strong without internal strength—we must therefore rid ourselves of such debilitating factors as athletic scandals, apathy, and discriminatory inequality.
   (c) development of cooperation in the educational community through a clear definition of our rights and responsibilities.

With this point of view, I took the mandates of the last Congress and implemented them. Now with a confidence in a 1952 Republican victory that is second only to my confidence in the growth and expansion of the student affairs program, let's look at its varied categories:

Student Bill of Rights: Clarity of concept, effectiveness of action

First you gave me a *Student Bill of Rights* to implement. While it is not in my estimation a clear cut document that is perfected, it holds within it great potentiality. I have operated on the assumption of Thomas Paine that responsibility is inherent in rights. We have used an approach of calmly and quietly going into each case of violation of student rights. Such cases have included: (1) Brooklyn College; (2) the University of Chicago's suspension of the *Maroon*; (3) the suspension and expulsion of Mrs. Lorraine Faxon Meisner from Wayne University; (4) the Ohio State University "Gag Rule"; and (5) the censorship invoked on the *Daily Cal* of the University of California at Berkeley.

At the December National Executive Committee Meeting, a revised implementation procedure was formulated. The Congress should now make a clearer delineation of the areas outlined. The student bill of rights does not represent a battle with the administration but an area for cooperation. Special conferences of the entire educational community and more regional conferences on student rights and responsibilities would produce greater clarity of concept and effectiveness of action.[2]

The range of student affairs projects

Next you gave me a resolution on Inter-Collegiate Athletics. The National Subcommission on Inter-Collegiate Athletics established at Wayne University under the chairmanship of Sheldon Otis very ably broke ground on this project. It is now up to the Congress to pass a program demanding student representation on athletic boards. A complete analysis of athletic scholarship policies should be a definite objective in the subcommission's on-going program.

Then you told me about Art Tours. The response from the regions was scant. Eight Regions held Art Tours. The prize-winning exhibits of three of these Regions are now on display at the Congress. With careful planning and administration the National Art Tour could be restored. *Essai*, the intercollegiate quarterly magazine, should also be put back into circulation. A more vigorous implementation of symphony forums rounds out the cultural programming upon which both the national and regional level should place greater emphasis.[3]

Lastly you demanded information on health insurance. The subcommission established on health insurance did not develop the program demanded in this area; therefore, further investigation will be necessary next year.

* * *

Relations with Fraternities and Sororities

Two major interests developed in this area: 1) rush systems—the deferred vs. the established mode and 2) discrimination which still exists in fraternity/sorority admission policies. A superficial survey of rush systems now in effect was secured through the cooperation of member schools and the Inter-Fraternity Council (which is currently conducting a more thorough study). Cornell University, University of Michigan and Rutgers conducted studies on alleged discriminatory practices in this particular area.[4]

College Press Subcommission

The College Press Subcommission established at the University of Minnesota under the chairmanship of Bob Brunsell was largely the result of our investigation on the MAROON case. Compilation of a report and formulation of the pre-Congress editors' conference were the chief achievements of the subcommision. Fifty-two editors attended the conference which soon revealed that the needs of the heterogeneous groups were not being met. The editors joined unanimously in demands for another conference carefully tailored to meet the distinctive needs of the college press based on their operations—e.g., a daily like the *Minnesota Daily* is faced with far different problems than a bi-weekly like the *Rocky Mountain Collegian*. The editors also expressed enthusiasm for regional conferences styled on the national pattern and the issuance of an American [publication] parallel to the European Student Union.

* * *

Lastly, today, I shall report to you on various organizational relationships and attempt to evaluate them in terms of my year's experience.

The American Civil Liberties Union

Here is an organization with which we must maintain liaison.[5] Not only can it be of valuable assistance in the area of Academic Freedom and Student Rights, but it is a superior training ground in judicious thinking. . . .

* * *

A year of tumult and frustration

These comments on our programs portray little of what I have felt or known this past year.

It has been a year of tumult and frustration. It has been one which has sometimes made me wonder if I really knew what I was doing one night in a very late caucus. That night over a year ago, I was scared. I've been scared all year . . . afraid of failing something I believed in very deeply and somewhat unsure as the first woman that has tried to do this job.

Today, though, I would be failing you if I didn't give my views of the Association as a whole and my recommendations in terms of last year's experience. Therefore, I say to you: a vice president located on the campus can do very little more than hold the line on already established programs. For me to have tried to establish a program like the intercollegiate wire service would have been impossible because local commitments, studies, theses, etc., made keeping abreast of the daily mails difficult enough.

If this system is established, your commission programs will be sporadically and superficially implemented. Under this scheme the real progress of the Association rests on one man's shoulders. This year you may say "Thank God that Bill's [Dentzer] were broad. . . ." His ability permits me to say NSA has had a year of progress. Last year you constitutionally placed a tremendous burden on the president. One which should not in my estimation be borne all alone.

A strong domestic program needed

Let me illustrate. I was lonely, very lonely at Vassar because I had no one with whom to share my problems, no one to aid in examining my programs. You know the tale of two heads being better than one. There must be more than one officer in the national office for this reason—and [for] yet another, more important one.

Unless the Association develops a strong domestic program we may as well forget its existence. I impress upon your minds that our sole power stems from your student governments. I impress upon you that these student governments have great and pressing needs. Today, your Association must be in a position to supply them. In

Sylvia Bacon retired as a judge in the District of Columbia. She is currently teaching at the law schools of Catholic University and Georgetown University

the domestic programming for the student governments, you need officers approaching a professional understanding of student activities just as in the international program you need a man trained and experienced in international student relations.

For the operation of such a domestic program, furthermore, you cannot rely on membership dues alone. There must be additional monies available. I believe that we can sell as projects some of our domestic activities, such as the *American Student Mirror*, an inter-collegiate news service, a national health insurance, and an extensive cultural program.

It is courage that counts

. . . Add these general recommendations to my specific calls for legislation. Fulfill them with stout hearts and we will know that if success is never final, failure is never fatal. It is courage that counts. Courage to face the needs of the Association and place its needs above your own political aggrandizement either here in this Congress or home on your campus. Courage to speak in areas where many more mature individuals now fear to speak.

END NOTES

[1] See Buckley, p. 797, excerpted from *God and Man at Yale*.

[2] See Janet Brown on student rights and NSA, p. 375.

[3] See Cashen on *Essai*, p. 362, and Albums, pp. 364 and 368.

[4] See NSA and the fraternities, p. 398, and excerpt from Lee, *Fraternities without Brotherhood*, p. 745.

[5] *Editor's note:* In a letter to Patrick Malin, Executive Director of the American Civil Liberties Union, dated 9/30/51, Sylvia Bacon, newly elected NSA Vice-President, Student Affairs, wrote that NSA at its Fourth National Student Congress at the University of Minnesota "voted in favor of accepting representation in your organization." She served as the Association's representative on its Academic Freedom Committee. During the 1962-53 year, Karl Meyer (See p. 138), then a graduate student at Princeton, represented NSA, reporting to Janet Welsh, that year's Student Affairs VP. Welsh writes that, given NSA's limited resources to investigate academic freedom cases, "being able to consult with the AAUP or ACLU . . . was a great relief." (See p. 383). Meyer's membership on the committee was at a time when the ACLU was riven by an internal debate as to whether it should permit exceptions to "the traditional view" that Professors cannot be fired for refusing to answer questions about possible Communist Party membership. Malin had suggested in pubilc statements that the ACLU might not protest such an act in certain circumstances. Meyer wrote Welsh on 12/10/52 that "outside teacher organizations (the NEA, AFT) were bringing pressure to bear on committee members to shift to a new position on CP members. AAUP, NSA and ACLU are the three major groups still holding to the traditional view." (correspondence and documents detailing the events of this period are in the Anthology Project archives). NSA continued a cooperative relationship with the ACLU for some time thereafter.

PICTURE CREDITS: *Then:* 1951 staff photo, 4th National Student Congress, University of Minnesota (SHSW). *Now:* October, 1997, Washington, DC (Schwartz).

SYLVIA BACON

Early years: Born July 9, 1931, in Watertown, SD. Attended Watertown High School.

Education: A.B., Vassar College, NY, 1952. Cert., London School of Economics, 1953; L.L.B., Harvard University, 1956; L.L.M., Georgetown Law Center, 1959.

Career highlights: Law Clerk, U.S. District Ct. Judge Burnita Shelton Matthews 1956-57. Asst. U.S. Atty., Washington, DC, 1957-1965; Associate Director, President's Commission on Crime in Washington, DC, 1965-67; Trial attorney, U.S. Dept. of Justice, 1967-68; Exec. Asst., U.S. Atty., DC, 1968-1970. Judge, Washington, DC Superior Court, 1970-1991; Adjunct Professor, Georgetown Law Ctr., 1963-1970; Catholic University Law School, 1992-present; Board of Directors, American Bar Association, 1988-1991.

SYLVIA BACON: "IT REQUIRES AN ORGANIZATION OF INDIVIDUALS TO EXERT AN EFFECTIVE FORCE."

Vassar Miscellany News

Bacon Receives Rotary Club's Fellowship; Plans To Gain Master's Degree In London

Sylvia Bacon, a senior at Vassar College, has been awarded a fellowship by Rotary International for advanced study abroad in 1952-53. She is one of 109 outstanding students from 34 countries to receive this award.

Rotary Fellows are chosen from candidates endorsed by the Rotary Clubs in their home towns. Candidates must be between 20 and 28 years of age. They must have a college or university degree, a record of high scholastic standing, and a thorough knowledge of the language of the country in which they propose to study. They must have the ability to make friends easily, be internationally minded, and possess an instinct for leadership. Rotary Fellowships are granted without regard to race, creed or citizenship.

Miss Bacon, a native of Watertown, South Dakota, plans to use her fellowship for study at the London School of Economics, where she will work for a Masters Degree in Economics. She is an Economics major at Vassar and will complete her college course in three years instead of the customary four, having taken summer courses at the Universities of Portland, Oregon, and Arizona. A Vice-President of Student Affairs of the U.S. National Students Association, Miss Bacon is also vice-chairman of the collegiate division of the New York State Young Republicans. Last October she participated as a speaker at the "New York Herald Tribune" Forum. At Vassar she served as advertising manager for the "Vassar Chronicle," station manager of the radio workshop, and business manager for the Polit Association. She was elected Senator of the Class of 1953 to the Student Legislative Assembly. **After her year abroad Miss Bacon plans to enter Harvard or Yale Law School.**

2/27/52

S. Bacon Discusses Plans And Policies Of N.S.A. Platform

by Sylvia Bacon '53

(Ed. Note: *This is the first in a series of articles designed to clarify those policies upon which Vassar acted at the national convention of the NSA.*)

"In a democratic society there is much that the individual can do to make that democracy meaningful, but it requires an **organization of individuals to exert an effective force.**" With this in mind representatives of 356 American colleges and universities gathered in Michigan this summer. It was the third annual convention of the United States National Students Association and Vassar was there to participate in the formulation of the policies to which it now adheres.

* * *

Throughout the coming months Vassar delegates will participate in an amplification of policies and further clarification of them at regional meetings with the Metropolitan New York area. Action on Academic Freedom, Bill of Rights, IUS and other issues will in turn be placed before the Vassar student body through the newspapers.

10/4/50 (Excerpts)

Wednesday, October 17, 1951

N.S.A. Embarks On Vital Action

by Sylvia Bacon '53

American orators have long extolled the virtues of the "grass roots" in the growth of a democracy. Likewise the National Student Association might well eulogize its campus groups who continue to be the driving force in all student reforms. In light of this, the current NSA programming is emphasizing campus action.

During the past year campuses throughout the country embarked on outstanding projects which indicate the strength of the organization as a whole.

* * *

Plans for Vassar

For the coming year the local committee envisions several programs which will be directed primarily toward the improvement of the existing campus situation. The local NSA is examining past procedures for choosing conference delegates and attempting to draw up a proposal which will give Vassar the advantage that is to be derived from inter-collegiate meetings.

(Excerpts)

The college newspaper editor: Like a man at the circus with his head in the lion's mouth

The 1952 College Newspaper Editors Conference

Excerpts from a resolution adopted by the College Newspaper Editors Conference at the 1952 NSA National Student Congress.

College Press Associations and NSA's Student News Service

Collegiate press association education programs

Resolved: that the USNSA, recognizing the need for better communications among members of the college press and for improved standards of performance in the college press, urge the existing collegiate press associations to do all they can in expanding their communications facilities, with the object being more complete and efficient collegiate news coverage; and that USNSA urge these collegiate press associations to emphasize their journalism education programs by means of instruction manuals and clinics and short courses, affording small college newspapers the opportunity to learn basic journalism. The three collegiate press services are: the Associated Collegiate Press, Intercollegiate Press, and Columbia Student Press Association.

National Subcommission on Press and Publc Relations

On a national level, the Conference recommends that USNSA maintain its National Subcommission on the Press and Public Relations, including representatives of both large and small college newspapers on an advisory basis. This National Subcommission would be responsible for investigation of available newspaper training manuals, both from college dailies and press associations, and for their preparation if necessary. These shall be designed to aid editors of smaller college newspapers in teaching their staffs headline writing, copy editing, news writing and other fundamentals of journalism too often overlooked by college newspapers throughout the country.

Regional information centers

On a regional level, it is recommended that USNSA urge each region to designate a member school as a regional information center for press activities. These regional centers, with the help of other papers in the region, would be responsible for administering a program similar to that of the National Subcommission. They would be responsible for obtaining immediate news coverage in any case of importance to the college press. Wherever possible, news reports would be requested from the college newspaper on the campus involved. These reports would be credited only to the newspaper responsible for their preparation and would in no way supplant an official USNSA investigation of any such incident.

NSA's Student News Service

Believing that the opportunity of college newspaper editors to inform themselves and their readers of significant news events in the educational community outside their immediate campus is now inadequately fulfilled, the 1952 College Press Conference recommends that the Student News Service of NSA assume responsibility for the collection, and republication of news on student government from American college newspapers for national and international distribution to student groups. When funds become available, the conference recommends that the Student News Service publish an American Student Mirror for distribution to NSA member student bodies, to individual publications through subscription, and to similar news services in other areas of the world on an exchange basis.[1]

END NOTE

[1] *Editor's note:* The concept of issuing a national publication of some kind had been considered several years earlier by NSA. In a February 2002 note to the editor of this Anthology, Craig Wilson, editor of *NSA News* in 1949-50, writes:

> One unique thing I tried to do was set up a national fortnightly tabloid magazine that could be inserted into college newspapers under NSA auspices. I had some talks with Reuben Donnelly, a very large Illinois magazine printer. The firm was very interested in getting the business. The publication would have been formatted like *Parade* magazine, but with some intellectual stuff to go with the mass-appeal entertainment copy and art.
>
> I sent a preliminary proposal to student newspapers on NSA campuses. The response was mildly favorable, but noncommital. One newspaper was smart enough to note that it had an exclusive contract for all national advertising with a New York ad agency. When I checked, I found that this ad group had practically every college newspaper in the country bound hand and foot with its contract. All the campus newspapers got out of it was a few Camels advertisements. No one at that time realized the potential of the student consumer market. I got the bad news about April 1950 and estimated that NSA, with its very limited funds, would not want to get into an expensive legal battle to free the newspapers from these contracts. So the idea died right there.

Allan Ostar also discusses the concept of *NSA News* as a national newspaper in Pt. 1, S6. A listing of the editions of *NSA News* published from 1947 through 1952-53 is on page 293. Doubts about the value of *NSA News* were voiced in the following resolution to discontinue publication adopted by the 1950 Post-Congress Executive Committee.

> THE CONGRESS OBSERVES that the *NSA News* has proved highly unsatisfactory on both the editorial and financial levels as a medium of mass communication with the student bodies of NSA member colleges and non-member colleges.
>
> THE CONGRESS DIRECTS that the *NSA News* be discontinued as soon as a new medium of mass communication is established.

In another resolution re-stating NSA policy the Congress said, "We recommend that the re-direction of *NSA News* policy in such a manner that it will appeal more directly to the average student, and if it should prove impossible to do this, the alternative publication of a weekly news sheet to be read primarily by the average student."

The 1950-51 staff implemented this policy in three 1-page tabloid size issues—October, November, and December. Craig Wilson resigned the staff in November (See Willson Pt. 1, S7), and publication was suspended until the special 12 page broadside edition produced by Merrill Freed for the 1951 Congress at Minnesota. Bill Dentzer revived three issues of a tabloid size version for 1951-52, once again providing NSA leaders and student governments a journalistic accounting of events.

In retrospect, NSA tried to combine three disparate applications: a house organ for leadership and affiliates, an intercollegiate national newspaper, and a popular news sheet for the general student. Only the "house organ" format seems to have worked.

Conference Directory, August 14-17, 1952

An * following the name of the school indicates NSA members

COLLEGE	NEWSPAPER	CIRCULATION	EDITOR
Agnes Scott College*	*Agnes Scott News*	Weekly	Curry, Connie
Alabama College	*The Alabamian*	Semimonthly; 1500	Buckner, Willodean
Albertus Magnus*	*Silver Horn*	Bimonthly; 650	Donnelly, Eileen Mary
Antioch College*	*Antiochian/Daily Record*	Bimonthly/Daily	Kagan, Stan
Brescia College	*The Brescia Broadcast*	Quarterly; 500	Edge, Mary Christine
CCNY Bus. Day*	*The Ticker*	Weekly; 3500	Bernstein, Ira J.
Central Washington College*	*Campus Crier*	Weekly; 1500	Aum, Richard A.
College Board Editor	*Mademoiselle*	Monthly	Little, Marybeth
Colorado A&M*	*Rocky Mountain Collegian*	Weekly; 4000	Abrahamson, Frank
Columbia College	*Post Script*	Bimonthly; 500	Hatchett, Ann
Cornell U.*	*Cornell Daily Sun*	Daily; 4000	Looby, Stuart H.
			Beyers, Robert W.
Florence S.Q.C.	*Flora-Ala*	Weekly	Jones, Mary Magdalene
Fordham College*	*The Ram*	Weekly; 3500	Freeman, Jacob A.
Fort Smith Junior College	*Lion's Roar*	Biweekly; 350-500	Wakefield, Mary
Free University of Berlin	*Colloquium, European Student's Mirror*		Hess, Otto H.
Ga. Tech*	*Technique*	Semiweekly; 5000	Leverette, Russ
Greenville College	*The Papyrus*	Bimonthly; 6700	Stimer, Loraine
Hood College*	*Blue and Gray*	Weekly; 700	Endres, Charlotte L.
Hunter College*	*The Hunter Arrow*	Weekly; 6000	O'Neill, Maureen
Marymount*	*Cormont*	Bimonthly; 3000	Ruggero, Vina
			Scervini, Ursula
Millsaps College	*Purple and White*	Weekly; 650	Cavett, Van
Mount Holyoke*	*Mt. Holyoke News*	Weekly; 850	D'Oench, Gloria
Mount Mary College*	*Times*	Monthly	Balistrin, Catherine
NYU Heights*	*Heights Daily News*	Daily; 2500	Goodman, Harold
NYU School of Commerce	*Commerce Bulletin*	Weekly; 6000	Pascal, John R.
Rollins College	*Sandspur*	Weekly; 1000 plus	Puiger, Daniel
Roosevelt*	*Torch*	27 issues/year; 4000	Shanfield, Morris
Rosary College*	*The Rosarian*	Monthly; 1000	Jarvis, Ann
Rosary*	*Rosarian*	Monthly; 900	Minehan, Barbara
S.D. School of Mines*	*South Dakota Tech*	Bimonthly; 650	Morris, Robert C.
Skidmore College*	*Skidmore News*	Weekly; 1000 plus	Sprague, Sally
Smith*	*The Sophian*	Biweekly; 1500	Damon, Marcia
State Teachers College	*Keystone*	Triweekly; 1800	Konhaus, Janet
Sweet Briar*	*Sweet Briar News*	Weekly; 800	Hamilburg, Janet I.
U. of Baltimore*	*Baloo*	Weekly; 1000	Stansbury, Ruth Ellen
U. of Louisville*	*The Cardinal*	Weekly	Shelton, Judy
U. of Michigan*	*Michigan Daily*	Daily; 6000	Young, M. Crawford
U. of North Carolina*	*Daily Tar Heel*	Daily; 6000	Raff, Joe
U. of California, Berkeley*	*Daily Californian*	Daily; 27,500	Scharinghausen, Charles T.
			Dugas, David
U. of Colorado*	*Silver and Gold*	Daily; 3500	Shaw, Hank
University of Detroit*	*The Varsity News*	Biweekly; 8000	Biro, Emery
			Cooper, Janet C.
U. of Dubuque	*Cue*	Semiweekly; 700	Coppage, George
U. of Louisville*	*Cardinal*	Weekly; 4000	Bornstein, Tim
Wellesley College*	*Wellesley College News*	Weekly	Powers, Barbara
Western Ill. State	*Western Courier*	Weekly; 2000 plus	Cramm, Joetta M.
Westminster College	*The Holcad*	Weekly; 1500	Carnahan, Joan
Wheaton College*	*Wheaton News*	Weekly; 800	Keegan, Patricia

UCLA 1951-52 College Newspaper Survey

School	Paper	Enrollment	Circulation	Days Issued	Size	Editor-in-Chief	Managing Editor	Sports Editor	Bus. Mgr. or Adv. Dir.	Circulation Mgr.
Baylor	*Lariat*	4,100	3,500	T-F	Tabloid	$50.00		$25.00	$100.00	$.50/hr.
Butler	*Collegiate*	3,800	2,800	Not stated	Tabloid	100.00s	$100.00s		200.00s	
California	*Californian*	17,017	14,000	M-F	Tabloid	75.00	60.00	40.00	75.00	
Colorado	*Silver & Gold*	7,000	6,000	T-F	Tabloid	60.00	48.00	2@28.00	48.00	40.00
Columbia	*Spectator*	38,000	15,000	M-F	Tabloid	Profit-sharing plan for editorial and business staffs (50% of any profit divided equally)				
Dartmouth	*Dartmouth*	2,800	1,950	M-Sat.	Tab (6 col.)	Profit-sharing plan, not to exceed 5% per individual				
Harvard	*Crimson*	10,000	Not stat.	M-Sat.	Standard	Profit-sharing plan (approx. half net income divided in February each yr.)				
Illinois	*Illini*	15,500	4,400	T-Sat.	Standard	25.00		15.00	25.00	25.00
Indiana	*Ind. Student*	10,000	3,500	T-Sat.	Standard		Profit-sharing plan for key editorial & business staff members. Most of staff works for credit.			
Iowa	*Iowan*	7,400	6,300	T-Sat.	Standard	85.00	40.00	25.00	125.00	145.00 (Dir.) 120.00(City)
Iowa State	*Iowa State*	7,550	4,700	T-Sat.	Tabloid	60.00	40.00	25.00	60.00	
Kansas	*Kansan*	5,700	5,500	M-F	Tabloid	No salaries or stipends paid				
Kansas State	*Collegian*	4,947	5,500	M-F	Tabloid	60.00			60.00	
Kent State	*Stater*	4,300	3,500	T-F	Tabloid	4.00d			Local 10% Natl.–2%	
Michigan	*Michigan Daily*	16,000	5,900	T-Sun.	Standard		41.00	33.00	41.00	30.00 Asst-33.00
Michigan State	*State News*	13,091	10,700	M-F	Standard	20.00	15.00	10.00	20.00	12.00 Asst.–7.00
Missouri	*Missourian*	8,200	3,400	M-Sat.	Not stated	Varies depending upon conditions—no amount stated				
Montana State U.	*Kaimin*	2,250	2,400	T-F	Tabloid	60.00			45.00	1.75
Nebraska	*Nebraskan*	6,500	5,500	M-F	Standard	87.50	2@55.00	55.00	85.00	80.00
New York U. Of Arts & Sciences	*Heights Daily News*	2,500	3,000	M-F	Tabloid					
Northwestern	*Northwestern*	6,000	5,000	T-F	Tabloid	50.00	21.85	21.85	50.00	
North Carolina	*Tar Heel*	5,379	5,500	T-Sun.	Tabloid	7.50	16.00	10.00	Natl.–5% Local–7%	75.00
Ohio State	*Lantern*	16,500	4,000	M-F	Tabloid	50.00	25.00		Percentage	Percentage
Oregon State	*Barometer*	5,000	4,500	T-Sat.	Standard	60.00	15.00	10.00	60.00	5.00
Pennsylvania	*Pennsylvanian*	15,000	4,000	M-F	Tabloid	No salaries. Bonuses when paper makes money and they seem warranted				
Penn State	*Collegian*	10,500	7,000	T-Sat.	Tabloid	*	48.00	36.00	81.00	2@15.00
Purdue	*Exponent*	9,500	3,000	T-Sat.	Standard	No salaries paid to editorial or business staffs				
San Jose State	*Spartan*	6,200	5,000	M-F	Tabloid	No salaries or commissions paid—staff works for college credit				
So. California	*Trojan*	13,500	6,000	M-F	Standard	600.00a	405.00a	20.00	64.50 plus 15%	
Stanford	*Stan. Daily*	7,500	7,500	M-F	Standard	60.00	40.00		75.00	$350 a yr. bonus
Syracuse	*Orange*	9,500	10,000	M-Sat.	Standard	25.00	16.00	16.00	3% of all plus 5% own accts	10.00
Texas	*Texan*	12,824	9,000	T-F	Standard	80.00	75.00	25.00	Full time; sal. & comm.	
Texas State (Women)	*Lass-O*	1,800	1,800	T-F	Tabloid	50.00			50.00	
UCLA	*Bruin*	12,882	9,000	M-F	Tabloid	50.00	40.00	30.00	5% all local; 15% owns Ls; 5% net natl.	15.00
Utah	*Chronicle*	6,900	3,700	M-F	Tabloid	3.50		1.00	3.50	1.25
Washington	*Wash. Daily*	14,000	12,500	T-F	Standard	75.00			75.00	
Washington State	*Evergreen*	4,800	5,000	T-F	Tabloid	60.00			60.00	5.00 Asst-2.00
West Virginia	*Athenaeum*	4,200	4,800	T-Sat.	Tabloid	150.00	150.00	25.00	250.00	
Wayne	*Detroit Collegian*	19,584	7,500	M-F	Tabloid	40.00	25.00	12.50	Not stated	
Wisconsin	*Cardinal*	13,000	3,780	M-Sat.	Tabloid	50.00			50.00	70.00 Asst. 60.00
Yale	*Daily News*	4,753	2,800	M-Sat.	Tabloid	Paid, but amounts not stated				

Note: Unless otherwise listed, all compensation is on a monthly basis. s=semester; d=daily; q=quarterly; a=annually

*$90.00 qtr. plus 50% of net profit at the end of the yr.

Nearly all of them became, even under Chicago's tough standards, good newspapermen

The College Newspaper Editor

Campus Editor as Professional

Excerpt from The Quill: A Magazine for Writers and Editors, *Vol. 37, No. 3, March 1949*

I doubt if many able newspaper editors really ever held the college applicant in the contempt of legend. I got my first newspaper job that way in 1920. The editor of one of my hometown newspapers hired me, sight unseen, mostly because he knew I had edited a college newspaper. Perhaps he was ahead of his time, in theory if not in practice as far as my particular talents were concerned. But practically all the men with whom I had worked on that campus paper got newspaper jobs, too—and still have them.

Fifteen years later, I saw a time when one could fire a single shot, blindfolded, in a highly regarded Chicago newsroom and hardly miss an ex-editor of a campus paper, from the *Harvard Crimson* to the *Daily Nebraskan*. Editors of the *Illini* and the *Michigan Daily* came to us practically in procession. Some stayed to become foreign correspondents or departmental editors. Others turned to magazines or public relations. Nearly all of them became, even by Chicago's tough standards, good newspapermen.

If there ever was a school of thought that rejected the college editor as a prospective reporter, it was probably due to an impression that campus papers were badly written and irresponsibly edited by young fire eaters who would be difficult to handle. Actually most campus publications were reasonably well done even three or four decades ago. They have become much better. Today's big campus dailies are frequently not only impressive in content and format but biggish business as well.

In two highly readable articles in recent issues of the *Editor & Publisher*, Dwight Bentel estimated that advertisers spend more than $1,000,000 a year in forty-one college dailies alone. And at that, he felt that advertisers considerably underbuy a good medium. A survey showed that co-eds on one West Coast campus—it was in California of course—spend $103,000 a year on sweaters alone!

But lineage is not the only problem connected with college journalism. Bentel found a real headache was the degree of control, if any, that should be exercised over undergraduate journalists. How is a faculty to teach democracy and practice censorship? Conceding that good college newspapers are a force for campus leadership and public good will, he also pointed out that some undergraduate editors can "make more errors of fact and judgment in a single four-page issue than a professional editor ever dreamed of after a midnight snack."

I agree. I know that as an undergraduate I wrote more than one blistering editorial strictly from personal prejudice. But I paid for my fun. I was allowed to graduate, after a final bout of senior editing, principally because it seemed easier to get rid of me by natural causes than to precipitate another campus uproar. And I was lucky. Two of my contemporaries in the editorial chair were rusticated (mine was a college with a fine classical nicety about such things).

My two pals were suspended from college for good causes, although they no longer seem important. My immediate successor had especially bad luck. He left ivied halls hurriedly not only because of what he had printed (which was plenty) but because of what he told the world he intended to print next. He is still printing things many editors dare not. He also owns one of the better weeklies and has been president of his state press association.

In short, we were sounders-off and so, I suspect, are many campus editors. Which may be another way of saying that we disliked many things we found around us and were inclined to do something about them in black and white. As undergraduates we may have been neither wise nor skilled in our editorial approach but we tried. I find a capacity for indignation and action in local affairs no very great handicap in a prospective newspaperman.

Carl R. Kesler

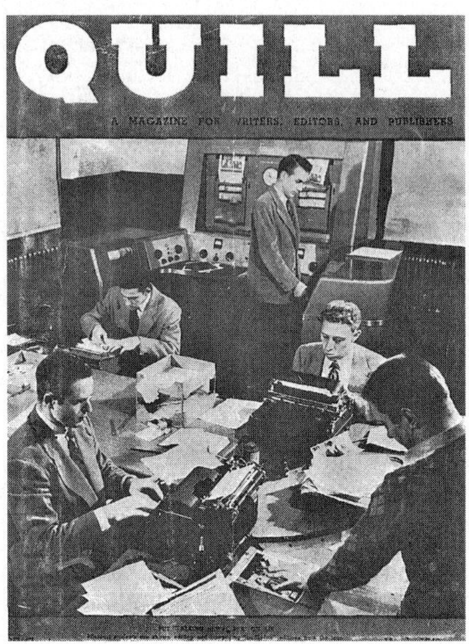

University of Missouri School of Journalism in 1949
(Cover, *Quill*, March, 1949, Sigma Delta Chi)

Concept of a College Editor

Bob Beyers
Editor-in-Chief, Cornell *Daily Sun*, 1952-53

Excerpt from NSA's Student Government Bulletin, *Vol. 3, No. 3, December 1954.*

Today's campus editor faces a three-fold challenge: he is at once a reporter, educator and critic of his college community. If he's not, he should be.

Basically, of course, the editor's primary concern still lies in securing complete, accurate reporting on all those events which directly affect his audience.

Today, however, this traditional function stands vastly magnified in comparison with yesteryear. Not only must the campus editor take into account the whole realm of activities occurring on his campus, but he must also find the time and space necessary to report those news events occurring in the outside news world which, in time, will make their influence felt in every college community.

Meeting enlarged responsibilities

There are many ways in which this expanded demand can be met. One of the most common is use of a national wire service, a practice inaugurated on a few campuses prior to World War I, now followed in most large college dailies.

Another answer, common to papers at large and small schools alike, is the use of interviews with persons on campus to tell a world story in local terms. Foreign students, guest speakers, and delegates to national conventions are three of the favorite vehicles for bringing these messages to the campus community.

Still further means of meeting this obligation exist in such national services as the Associated Collegiate Press, the Columbia Scholastic Press Association, and Intercollegiate Press. These have shown increasing popularity with editors at smaller schools.

Expansion of newspaper exchanges and the introduction of press clippings columns based on these exchanges reflect a fourth way in which the campus press has endeavored to fulfill its primary function as a purveyor of news.

Improving existing services

The existence of these new services and techniques, however, does not necessarily mean they are adequate to meet the needs of a top-flight campus editor. Each can be improved by him to enrich the content of his newspaper.

Material received over the wires, for instance, must be scrupulously edited and sharply condensed to meet space limitations, even on the largest dailies. The major press associations do not, as a general rule, provide enough detail and background material on major issues affecting students to permit a thorough-going presentation in the campus press; this material must be sought aggressively from campus and national news sources, or adapted from information through such channels as our Association.

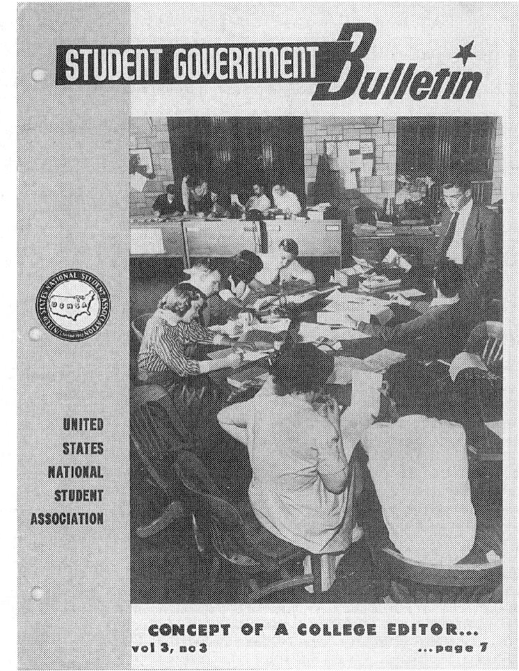

Michigan Daily newsroom in 1954
(Cover, *Student Government Bulletin*, NSA, December 1954)

Failure of the campus press to furnish complete, reliable information on such issues as ROTC [Reserve Officers' Training Corps] loyalty oath requirements, Selective Service provisions, tax changes, student exchange programs, etc., can result in much unwarranted confusion and concern among its audience. Consistently good coverage, on the other hand, can gain broader readership and respect of the student newspaper, notably from faculty and administrators.

BOB BEYERS

Bob directed the Stanford News Service from September 1961 to January 1990, when he took early retirement. He also served as information officer of the Faculty Senate from its creation in 1968 to 1990.

Bob graduated from Cranbrook School in Bloomfield Hills, Mich., in 1949, where he was associate editor of *The Crane*, a weekly student newspaper. One of its writers was Daniel Ellsberg, a Pepsi Cola scholar in the Pepsi generation.

Bob was editor-in-chief of *The Cornell Daily Sun* in 1952-53, which provided the model for *The Stanford Daily's* reorganization in the early 1970s. While at the Sun, Bob and John Naisbitt edited the *National Academic Freedom Newsletter*, covering the campus impact of the McCarthy hearings. Naisbitt later wrote the best selling book, *Megatrends*. In 1953-54, Bob worked as a reporter on the Marshall, Texas, *News Messenger*, a small daily whose staff included Bill Moyers, now of PBS fame.

After a brief stint in advertising with Procter & Gamble, Bob became public information director for the U.S. National Student Association in 1954-55, never realizing it was partially funded by CIA.[1] Bob also was student anchor for the ABC network TV show, "College News Conference."[2] During 1956-57, Bob edited *The Reporter*, a tri-community weekly near Ann Arbor, Mich. Later, Bob joined his first wife, Alice, at the University of Michigan News Service.

In June 1964, Bob volunteered with the Mississippi Freedom Summer, serving as coordinator of police and media relations for the Council of Federated Organizations (SNCC, CORE, SCLC and NAACP). In 1966, he and several Stanford colleagues created *The Stanford Observer* newspaper, and in 1968 *Campus Report* (subsequently retitled *Stanford Report*).

In 1974, Bob was recruited to the board of Editorial Projects in Education, creators of *The Chronicle of Higher Education*. He was one of three persons who conceived of *Education Week*, America's newspaper of record for K-12 education. Bob served as EPE board chairman from 1986 to 1997. EPE launched *Teacher* magazine (nine issues per year, circulation 130,000). Its revolutionary premise: to treat teachers as though they were intelligent adults.

After leaving Stanford, Bob became an associate editor at Pacific News Service in San Francisco, a news agency giving public voice to those at the edges of society. He helped launch *Youth Outlook*, a Bay Area newspaper for high school youth. Since the early 1960s, Bob has served as an information consultant for about two dozen colleges, universities, foundations and government agencies, most recently the Hewlett Foundation, Carnegie Foundation for the Advancement of Teaching, and the National Center for Public Policy and Higher Education.

Since 1986, he has helped his second wife, Charlotte, president of Peregrine Productions, produce 10 documentary films on AIDS, crack, homeless teens, drug-resistant TB, hiring the handicapped, and health care choices for arthritis and back pain. He has three children by his first marriage, she four by her first marriage. Combined, they now have 13 grandchildren.

1. See Welsh et al., Pt. 3, S2. 2. See Pt. 6, S1.

PICTURE CREDIT: Beyers: 1953 *Cornellian* (Cornell U. Library)

*The college newspaper editor: like a "man at the circus with his head in the lion's mouth"**

College Newspapers in the Crossfire

WEDNESDAY, JUNE 20, 1951. THE HARVARD CRIMSON PAGE THREE

Many Colleges Place Limits on Student Press

Administrators Scrutinize Policies, Discipline Editors, Take Control

By Douglas M. Fouquet, Andrew E. Norman and William M. Simmons

Suspensions of student publications, combined with a series of punishments of individual writers and editors, are marring the concept of a free press in the nation's colleges. According to a CRIMSON survey completed this week, an increasingly large number of university administrators are today disciplining newspapers, magazines, and individual students for "objectionable" articles and for editorial policies.

The CRIMSON check reveals at least 11 main cases during the past two terms in which student editorial freedom has been abridged. Four of the cases involve disagreements with the administration over general editorial policy; three other cases resulted from university dislike of specifice articles; two more arose out of charges of "bad taste" in humorous parodies; one was concerned with advertising policy, and one other involved reporting of a news story.

In every instance responsibility for what appeared in the publications passed from student editors to college administrators. In several of the cases, reported below, college administrators were able to assume this responsibility by directly suspending the newspapers or magazines through their power of charter or financial subsidation; in other instances, officials exerted influence by disciplining individuals or by stopping circulation of certain editions.

when its advisor resigned, but it published twice last fall under a new agree-

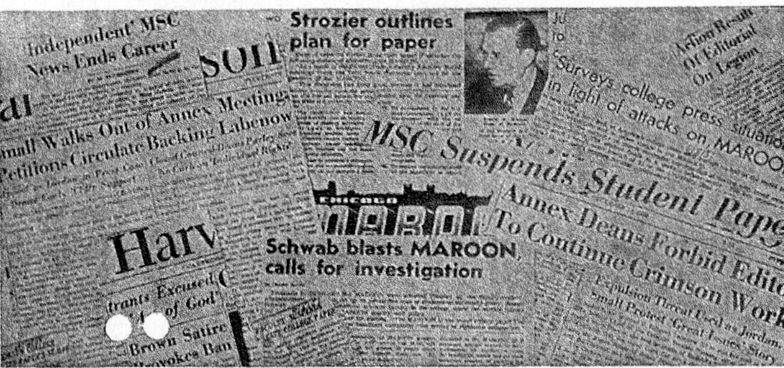

Legion "Boys' State" last June brought a summer's suspension of the Michigan State News. The News had called the Legion's mock trial of Communists "an experimemt shot with narrow principles,

In December, R. Deborah Labenow '51 was forbidden to continue as the CRIMSON'S Radcliffe Bureau Chief because she had written a story "not in the best interests of Radcliffe" and which contained some

for either the CRIMSON or the Press Board, President Jordan this spring named a six-member committee to "review the appointment, functioning, and responsibility of the Radcliffe Press Board."

"MARRING THE CONCEPT OF A FREE PRESS IN THE NATION'S COLLEGES"— *Harvard Crimson* editors reviewed 11 main cases in 1950 and 1951 in which "writers and editors were disciplined for 'objectionable' articles and for editorial policies."

WANTED . . .

3-14

A FACULTY MEMBER TO DEFEND THE DAILY CALIFORNIAN ADVISORY BOARD

At a Forum on

"The Daily Californian Advisory Board —An Aftermath of the Loyalty Oath"

WEDNESDAY, MARCH 19, – 4:00 P.M.

PLACE TO BE ANNOUNCED

ACADEMIC FREEDOM AND STUDENTS RIGHTS COUNCIL WELFARE BOARD

Call THornwall 3-7521

"THE COLLEGE EDITOR IS SUBJECT TO EVERY KIND OF PRESSURE." Alva Senzak, retiring editor of the *Daily Californian,* is quoted in *Editor and Publisher* (2/16/52). Above, the *Daily Californian* (3/14/52) looks for faculty support in an upcoming debate.

Right: San Fransisco State College *Golden Gater* 3/17/50

Page 2 THE GOLDEN GATER

What Is Happening to Freedom of the Collegiate Press?

UCLA Daily Bruin and San Diego State Aztec Newspapers Made Political Footballs; San Jose State Student Intimidated

(Over the past several months a series of calamities seem to have overtaken the collegiate newspapers in this state. Our interests originally stemmed from the threat which was held out to this paper, but was fortunately settled in an amicable way. Freedom of the press is vital on the college campus as well as off of the college campus. This whole subject of press freedom will be brought to the attention of the students whenever it appears, since, as far as can be determined, there is a dangerous trend developing which threatens the whole concept of democracy on the college level . . . rd.)

UCLA CENSORSHIP

The story of the UCLA Daily Bruin is one which might hint of the passing of free editorial expression from the campus scene. Today the Bruin is neither able freely to appoint its own editorial staff, nor does the paper enjoy editorial expression without the threat of censorship from a supervisory publications board.

Originally, the pub board was an advisory body offering technical advice to student publications, but a new constitution gave the board the power to examine editorials prior to publication and to forbid that they be published.

Bruin editor Jim Garst protested strongly, claiming that "a body of appointed students not representative of the student body should not be given the power of pre-publication censorship."

On the question of editorial appointments, Milton E. Hahn, Dean of Students, instructed the student executive council that the long standing single slate method of appointments was forbidden. Only a plural slate which offered a choice of several candidates would be acceptable. This was the first time, according to Garst, that the administration had acted to forbid student government legislation.

Carried to an extreme, the Bruin would have to recommend its four best people for editor. With the appointment of one candidate, the remaining nominees would be without editorial positions. Also, as the voting representative of the publications board on the student executive council, editor Garst is required to vote as the majority of the board vote.

SAN JOSE STATE FORCED APOLOGY

Recently a San Jose State college student, Raymond Frost, submitted two letters to the Letters to the Editor column of the Spartan Daily in which he took some healthy swipes at a member of the faculty. Shortly after the publication of the first two letters, a third one appeared which was an abject apology to the instructor for the writing of the first two.

The original letter was written in sympathy with a student who was told by the instructor to "go stick your head out the window and take a deep breath," in answer to a question he put to the instructor during the course of the lecture.

In his third letter, which was an apology for the first two, student Frost stated, "For all the discourteous statements and inferences in these two articles, I apologize. I am deeply sorry all this has happened." An investigation by members of the Spartan Daily at first brought a "no comment" statement from both the instructor in question, Dr. Leo C. May and Raymond Frost. Dr. May also asserted that nothing more about this "had better go in the paper," while Frost refused "in absence of a statement by Dr. May."

By the end of the week Frost had changed his mind and charged that instructor May had used "grade pressure" in forcing him to write a letter of retraction for the Spartan Daily. Said Frost, "the letter appearing over my signature in Thursday's Daily was dictated by Dr. May." He further stated that the instructor had threatened to expel him from class with an FW (withdrawal-failure).

Later Dr. May called the Daily office and made the following statement:

"I have requested that the college Fairness committee investigate this affair. Mr. Robinson assured me that the group will conduct an investigation . . ."

Mr. Elmo Robinson, chairman of the Fairness committee could not be reached for comment.

SAN DIEGO STATE APPOINTED EDITOR

Bypassing a recommendation of the public relations committee the San Diego state student council appointed Frank Reynolds as editor of the college newspaper Aztec last January.

The appointment came after John Curley raised the cry for "new blood" after veteran staff members Jim Abarr and Nathan Terrill were nominated for the post by the public relations committee. While Abarr had three years Aztec experience behind him and Terrill two years the newly appointed editor had but a brief experience as an advertising assistant on the paper.

Commenting in a front page editorial outgoing editor John N. Macdonald stated, "It is too bad that the editorship must be decided by people who apparently know little of the situation. Maybe it's best that we leave the drama positions and speech team appointments up to this body also. After all they handle the money for those two groups also."

In an interview the new editor revealed that he did not believe a college paper should do any "crusading," or engage in writing editorials of an "argumentative" nature. Mr. Reynolds felt that in the past the Aztec had not presented both sides of controversial issues. On the question of staff appointments he stated there would be "some revisions. Some of my personal friends will get some vacant positions." The outgoing editor did not disclose the existence of any vacancies at this time.

A signed editorial also stated that "the man chosen was waived by neither the Aztec editor nor the journalism advisor, thus setting up a clear-cut and direct violation of the A. S. constitution."

Shortly afterwards student councilman Jim Boggus moved that the Aztec be instructed to publish a retraction of the charges that the council had violated the associated students constitution in actions regarding the appointment of the editor. The council passed the motion.

Speaking for the Aztec staff, Ed Stone said that the charges were made by editorial writers chastening the council's alleged "moral violation" of the constitution. "Anyhow," said Stone, "it is not the policy of any paper to retract its editorials."

By last month everything had become quiet on the San Diego Aztec once more with the appointment of councilman Bill Scarborough as interim editor of the paper. After several weeks he resigned and recommended the once-refused Jim Abarr for the editorship which was confirmed by a student council vote of 11 to 6.

What happened to Frank Reynolds was not disclosed by the San Diego State Aztec.

An Editorial

Other college publications have their periods of tribulation also. San Jose State, UCLA and San Diego State have just blossomed out with censorship, editorial and/or personnel problems.

A classic example of student government interference can be seen in the case of "The Aztec," San Diego State's campus newspaper. There the student council appointed an editor whose opening statement was: "I do not think a college paper should do any crusading . . ." No more 'argumentative' editorials would appear in the campus publication.

And it is this statement, we believe, that indicates the basis of the trouble that is often associated with the college press. News dissemination, editorial comment, crusading or what-have-you should be no different from that of the commercial press. On a college campus, it is particularly important that certain issues which concern the outside press should also concern the college newspaper. It should not class itself as being in a different field of endeavor. Once the college newspaper does limit itself, then it becomes static.

*Title quote: Dwight Bentel in "College Press Freedom Merits Editor Support," *Editor and Publisher,* 2/16/52

NSA Cites Student Bill of Rights in Support of College Press

University of Pennsylvania, 11/11/48

Pennsylvanian

PHILADELPHIA, THURSDAY, NOVEMBER 11, 1948 No. 34

Disciplinary Committee Refuses To Lessen Editor's Punishment

Three Senior Editors Resign In Protest; Board Seeks Student Representation

By Herbert A. Fogel
For the Senior Board

The University Committee on Discipline will neither commute nor lessen the sentence given to William J. Lowney, Col. '50, who was suspended from the University for one week and placed on conduct probation for an article that appeared in the Nov. 3 issue of the *Daily Pennsylvanian*.

Barnard Bulletin, NY, 3/24/52 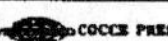 PRICE 10 CENTS

NSA Investigates Suspension Of Brooklyn College Paper

A committee of five has been appointed by the Metropolitan New York Regional Council of National Student Association to investigate and collect data on the suspension of the Brooklyn College newspaper, "Vanguard." The NSA committee will present its information to student executive bodies so that these governments can consider the question: "Was the suspension of Vanguard a violation of the Student Bill of Rights and of academic freedom?"

Brooklyn College's Faculty-Student Committee on Publication voted on October 9 to suspend Vanguard for an alleged violation of the college ruling that equally strong "pro and con" editorials be presented on all controversial topics considered editorially.

Hilltop — Howard University

Howard U., DC, *Hilltop* 2/14/51

WASHINGTON, D. C. FEBRUARY 14, 1951

Council Threatens To Suspend Cite "Poor Journalistic Principles"

H. U.'s SHARP SWIM SHARKS

Columnist Accused Of Libel

by Art Peters

The student Council last week threatened to suspend publication of the Hilltop. Reasons given for the threatened suspension were: "That there is a complete absence of a definite policy and a marked lack of adherence to basic journalistic principles." Additional reasons given for suspension of the campus publication were that many of the opinions of the writers "are not representative of student opinion."

BULLETIN!!

As the Hilltop went to press, it was reported that Charles Epps, Student Council president and Vassal Marcus, Hilltop editor "had come to an agreement." What the agreement was was not stated.

See Editorial, page 2 and Jimmie Lee's Letter to Charles Epps, page

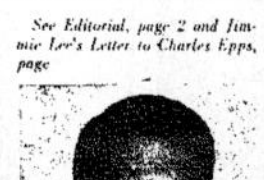

Fordham U., NY, *Ram* 4/3/52

Campus Press Censorship Frowned on at NSA Forum

A unanimous vote of support was given by representatives of more than twenty metropolitan college newspapers at the First Metropolitan Intercollegiate Press Conference held on March 22 at Fordham University to a resolution which said in part that Catholic college administrations should advise, but not censor campus publications on matters not affecting faith and morals.

The resolution was first passed unanimously by a special committee of Catholic college editors, which met under the leadership of John Leahy to study what was termed "the peculiar position of Catholic college publications" in regard to Administration censorship and control.

The committee acknowledged the right of the Administration to "retain direct control on matters of faith and morals," and the "effect of the newspaper upon the general reputation of the school . . ." But, the resolution stated, this effect is secondary in importance to the real purpose of the newspaper, that of serving the interest of the student body.

"As a means of practically implementing" these principles, the resolution went on to state, "we suggest that each school honestly study the feasibility of placing financial control of and the responsibility for the newspaper in the hands of the students."

U. of Colorado *Silver and Gold*, 2/14/52

Regents Take Over Rights Of 'Californian's' Editorials

(Editor's note: The following material was taken from an article by Dwight Bentel in the Feb. 2 edition of EDITOR AND PUBLISHER, a magazine whose readers are almost all in the publishing field.)

"Forty years of editorial independence ended last week for the Daily Californian, University of California student newspaper.

"The University's regents directed that an advisory board be created to oversee the Californian's policies and conduct.

Actual Censorship?

"Observers disagreed as to whether this meant actual censorship—and both regents and the University's president, Dr. Robert Gordon Sproul, denied such intentions. But at least the Californian, which has one of the top circulations among college dailies—16,600—had lost its autonomy."

The Associated Collegiate Press, the largest collegiate press organization in the country, rated the Daily Californian as the best newspaper in the United States during the second semester 1950-51.

Bentel continues: "The action was a consequence of two articles favorably presenting life behind the Iron curtain as seen by two students who traveled in Russia last summer. At a meeting of the regents, clippings of the two stories were displayed and President Sproul was instructed to report on the Californian at the next meeting. Decision to create an advisory board resulted.

No Charge of Communism

"No one accused the Californian of communist tendencies, nor any member of its staff of pro-communist leaning. Dr. Sproul told the regents, 'There was some indication that a disproportionate amount of space was given to some minority groups—but youth has a traditional sympathy for minority groups.

" 'There are no real panaceas for the traditional excesses in student journalism,' he said, but even if mistakes are made I am sure there are no Communists or Communist sympathizers on the Daily Californian.'

"The Californian's offense consisted specifically of publishing 2 articles representing view-points of student non-staff members. One, an interview, quoted Miss Brunette Reid as saying the Russian people deny existence of slave labor camps. She said she was selected to visit Russia as a guest of USSR because 'they wanted us to bring back a true picture of the Soviet Union and its people.'

"The other, a contribution by Robert Blauner, described the Berlin festival in East Berlin. He wrote that "we saw many reports of the Berlin Festival in the U.S. papers that were just downrig' lies."

Bentel concluded: "Printing of student contributions in the letter-to-the-editor column, whatever the viewpoint, has been a long-time policy of the Californian. Presumably this policy now will be changed."

Barnard Bulletin, NY, 10/26/50

NSA Defends Ousted Editor Of 'Maroon'

The National Student Association declared that the removal of Alan Kimmel as editor of the Chicago "Maroon" violated "a basic student right," at its National Executive meeting last December, according to the March issue of "The NSA News." The action of Robert Strozier, Dean of Students at Chicago, was unwarranted, NSA said, despite Kimmel's "serious abuse" of editorial responsibility.

Kimmel was dismissed from his position for his "action in sponsoring and attending the East Berlin Youth Festival," which, according to Dean Strozier, "demonstrated his lack of qualification to edit a free and independent newspaper." The "Maroon" was suspended until its staff elected a new editor.

The NSA Executive Committee also criticized the failure of the University of Chicago student government to "provide adequate democratic safeguards for the conduct of the 'Maroon' in line with the realization of a collegiate newspaper's ultimate responsibility to the university community."

Stating that, "this problem of the responsibility and relationship of the campus press to the student body, the student government and the administration is not unique at Chicago but exists universally," the Executive Committee recommended the study of this relationship to all student governments and to its national subcommission on the college press.

WHAT IS THE RESPONSIBILITY OF THE STUDENT PRESS TO THE COMMUNITY? NSA's Executive Committee raises that question in its resolution on the Chicago *Maroon* case (above). The NSA Subcommission on Press and Public Relations responds in its "Report on the College Press" in this section. All of the incidents on this page are the result of conflicting views as to the nature of that responsibility. (Clippings are excerpted.)

College Press Celebrates and Lampoons Campus Life

THE DAILY PRINCETONIAN

Recipe: 17 Clubs, '561 Girls; Result . . .

PARTIES BEGIN TONIGHT

SWARM OF BEAUTIES COME FOR THREE-DAY SPREE

UNDERGRADUATES' CONVERTIBLES WILL CROWD CAMPUS

1946

the Hunter HARROWED

2000 Arrested in Sing 'Fix'; Rehearse in County Jail

'New Ideas' Chairman Speaks At Openings

Cafeteria Food Peril

1949

I Was A Coffee Dancer

By Shur Mauledover, Bassar '0

THE BARELY NEWS

Published Yearly by the Barnard Bulletin

Any References Purely Coincidental

NOO YOKE, TUESDAY, APRIL 1, 1952

GAMES TO SOPHS

1952

1951

The Highlands CANDLE

CO EDS DIG TUNNEL TO LUNA

BST Boys Return From Chicago in Style

OBITUARY

Obtain Funds For Frat House

Cornell Daily Sun

ITHACA, N.Y., SATURDAY, MAY 13, 1950

CORNELL SECEDES! GAINS AUTONOMY! HITLER LEADS SECESSION MOVEMENT AS WSGA DECLARES ITSELF DICTATOR

Hitler, Ex-Teacher of English, Accepts Recognition from UN

1950

DOUGHERTY SKIPS PAX ROMANA; ON WILD SPREE ALONG RIVIERA

THE HAWK

Teams Up with Red Delegates In Squandering NFCCS Funds

Soph Left Official Portfolio at Home But Carried Suntan Lotion with Him; Sends Post Card to Student Council as Cover-up for Fraudulent Trip Overseas; Due Back Here on April 11

Clinton Fails to Show Up; Senior B...

1948

The BEE

POLICE GAZETTE ISSUE

BUFFALO, N.Y., FRIDAY, NOVEMBER 22, 1946

PEM DANCE-PAGE 3

Caught in the Web

WSC NEWS SENSE

NEW YORK UNIVERSITY, THURSDAY, APRIL 1, 1943

BABIES TO TAKE OVER NYU

MAJOR SHAKE-UP PUTS MINORS ON TOP!

Chancellors—Old and New

Baby Chase Receives Keys of the College

EXTRA

VACATION CANCELLED

EXTRA

REGENTS ANNOUNCE DRASTIC DECISION

Washington State Evergreen

STUDENTS STRIKE AS ORDER RESCINDS SPRING VACATION

1943

1947

1946

dance notes

1950

From top: Hunter C., NY, *Hunter Arrow*, 4/1/49; *Barnard Bulletin*, 4/1/52; St. Joseph C., PA, *The Hawk*, 4/1/48; Webster College, MO, *The Web*, 10/1/48. Left: U. of Buffalo, *The Bee*, 11/22/46; Below: "dance notes," Sarah Lawrence C., NY, *The Campus*, 1/22/50.

ATHLETIC RIVALRIES, HOMECOMING, APRIL FOOLS, HOLIDAYS, SPECIAL EVENTS. All inspired eye-catching headlines and graphics. Many papers seasoned their pages with spot illustrations. They enlivened the campus scene. Cigarette ads were a major source of revenue. Examples of all of the foregoing emerged during the college newspaper research for this volume.

From top: Princeton U., 5/17/46; Highlands C., NM, 4/1/51; Cornell U., 11/13/50; Washington Square C., NYU, Bulletin 4/1/43; Washington State C., 4/1/47.

April 1 and Other Foolishness

"Traditional Classics"

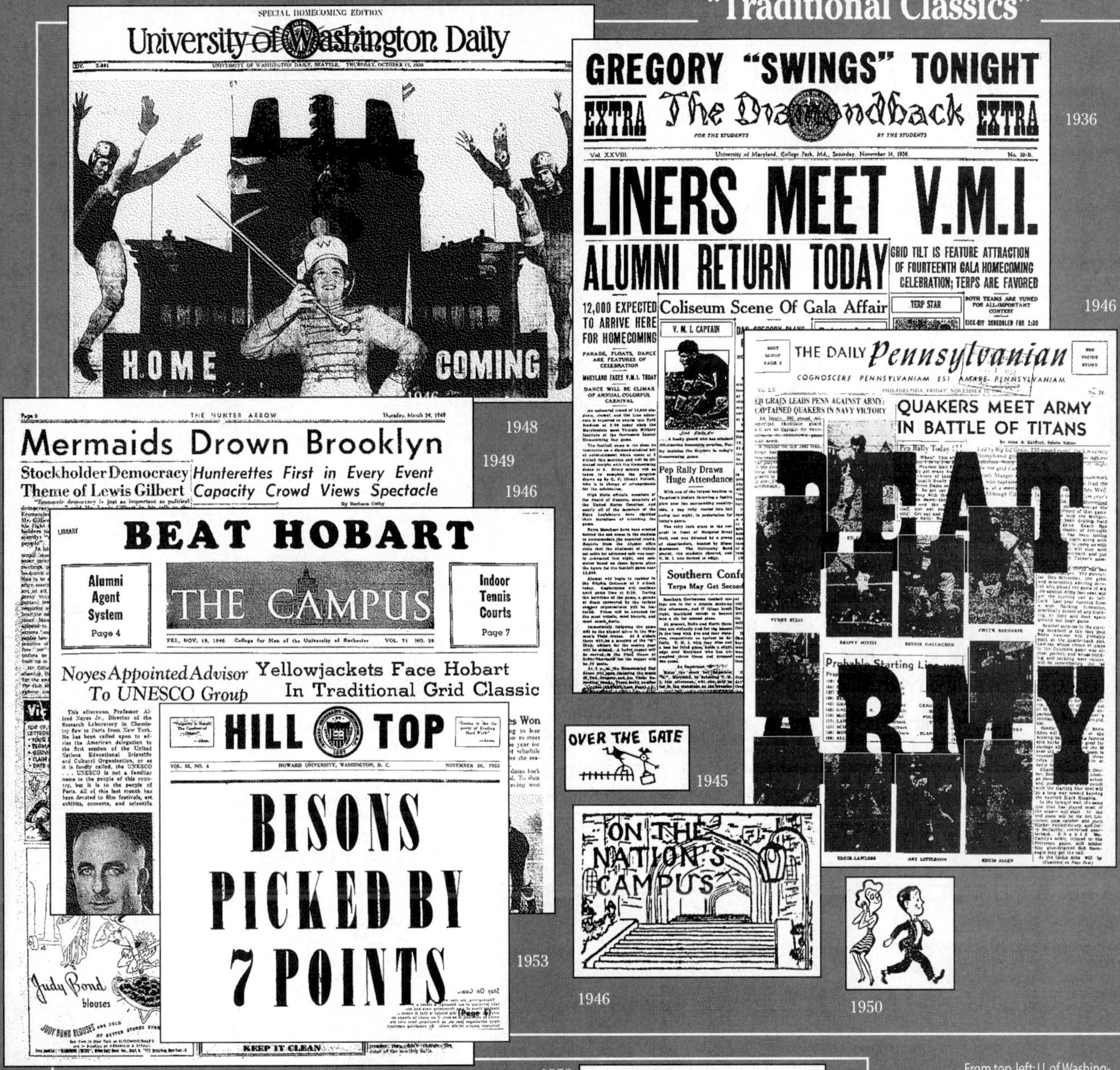

SPECIAL HOMECOMING EDITION

University of Washington Daily

HOME COMING

1946

THE HUNTER ARROW

Mermaids Drown Brooklyn

Stockholder Democracy Theme of Lewis Gilbert

Hunterettes First in Every Event Capacity Crowd Views Spectacle

1948

1949

1946

BEAT HOBART

Alumni Agent System Page 4

THE CAMPUS

Indoor Tennis Courts Page 7

Noyes Appointed Advisor To UNESCO Group

Yellowjackets Face Hobart In Traditional Grid Classic

HILL TOP

BISONS PICKED BY 7 POINTS

1953

GREGORY "SWINGS" TONIGHT

EXTRA The Diamondback EXTRA

1936

LINERS MEET V.M.I.

ALUMNI RETURN TODAY

GRID TILT IS FEATURE ATTRACTION OF FOURTEENTH GALA HOMECOMING CELEBRATION; TERPS ARE FAVORED

12,000 EXPECTED TO ARRIVE HERE FOR HOMECOMING

Coliseum Scene Of Gala Affair

Pep Rally Draws Huge Attendance

1946

THE DAILY Pennsylvanian

QUAKERS MEET ARMY IN BATTLE OF TITANS

BEAT ARMY

OVER THE GATE

1945

ON THE NATION'S CAMPUS

1946

1950

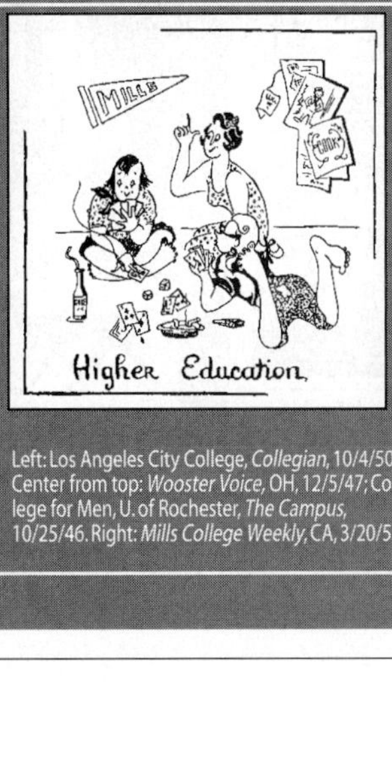

From top, left: U. of Washington, 10/1/38; Hunter C., NY, *Hunter Arrow*, 3/24/49; College for Men, U. of Rochester, NY, *The Campus*, 11/15/46; Howard U., *Hilltop*, 11/26/52. From top, right: U. of Maryland, *Diamondback*, 11/14/36; U. of Pennsylvania, 11/15/46; "Over the Gate," Sarah Lawrence C., NY, *The Campus*, 10/14/45; "Nation's Campus," *The Daily Princetonian*, 1/3/46. Couple, Los Angeles City College, *Collegian*, 11/20/50.

A Touch of Humor

1950

1952

1946

1947

Left: Los Angeles City College, *Collegian*, 10/4/50. Center from top: *Wooster Voice*, OH, 12/5/47; College for Men, U. of Rochester, *The Campus*, 10/25/46. Right: *Mills College Weekly*, CA, 3/20/52.

Athletic Festivities

1935

10 Pages UNIVERSITY SPORTS NEWS Thanksgiving EXTRA

Complete Reports of University Sports

BILLS OUT TO MUZZLE BEARS

Kloepper Shines As St. Louis Whips De Paul, 6-0

Wild Passing Attack Shown By Chicagoans In Tight Game

THEY Don't Want A Slice, But WANT A Chunk Of Mister BEAR Whom The Bills Will MEAT

Elevens Clash In Annual Tilt Tomorrow At Francis Field

1946

WE BEAT 'EM California Daily Bruin WE BEAT 'EM

University of California at Los Angeles

ROSE BOWL BOUND!

Bruins outmud Trojans, 13-6, in bowl clincher

1952

BEAT GEORGIA!

THE Technique

GEORGIA INSTITUTE OF TECHNOLOGY, ATLANTA, GEORGIA, TUESDAY, NOVEMBER 25, 1952

Big Bonfire, Pep Rally Scheduled for Tonight

Bowl-Bound Jackets Prepare for Bulldogs

Dodd Seeks Fifth Win Over Georgia's Butts

Will Be Available In '53 Fall Quarter

From top: St. Louis U. *University News*, 11/27/35; UCLA, 11/25/46; Georgia Tech, 11/25/52.

1950

Welcome Mat Out

HOMECOMING BEGINS TONIGHT; GRADS RETURN FOR FESTIVITIES

Temple University NEWS

Owls Duel for Old Shoe

Temple U. 11/10/50

1946

University Open House . . . Rifle Match . . . Football Halftime Festivities . . . Alumni Mixer . . . Dancing

THE Diamondback

STUDENT PAPER OF THE UNIVERSITY OF MARYLAND

MARYLAND PLAYS HOST TO ALUMNI

Little Man, Big Job

Festivities Open With Registration Tomorrow At 8 a. m.

U. of Maryland 11/8/46

ART INTERLUDE

1950

Playmakers' 'Saint Joan' Opens Tonight;

1947

1939

1940

Top left: Sarah Lawrence C., NY, *The Campus*, 4/26/50; Above: U. of North Carolina, *Daily Tar Heel*, 10/29/47; Right, from top: *Daily Princetonian*, 10/10/39; *Daily Pennsylvanian*, 12/13/40.

Holidays: Reverent and Light

THE UNIVERSITY NEWS

Student Newspaper of St. Louis University

Fashion Parade—1945

Stix Shows Newest In Suit Styles

EASTER

THE CAMPUS

Harold Taylor Foils Gunmen

Boston Reviews Of "The Lady's Not For Burning"

EXTRA!

1950

For Victory... Buy U.S. DEFENSE BONDS STAMPS

1942

1948

SMITH COLLEGE SCAN ASSOCIATED NEWS

2200 SMITH GIRLS DISAPPEAR; COLLEGE FEARS FOUL PLAY

IS THERE A KLEPTO IN THE HOUSE?

Police Drag Lake; Faculty Rout Joe's

SANTA STUCK; FUN DELAYED

Admiral Byrd Takes Poll From Students; College Is Wrong Even In Arctic Regions

Merry Christmas

Smith College 12/17/48

1942

Campus Mirror

Published During the College Year by the Students of Spelman College, Atlanta, Georgia

VOL. XIX NOVEMBER, 1942 NO. 2

Paul Robeson Speaks at Atlanta University

Spelman College Represented at N.A.A.C.P. Conference

The call to the fourth Annual Student Conference of the N.A.A.C.P. was answered by two hundred or more students and young people from various parts of the country. The conference which assembled to deliberate on "War and Post-War Problems for Negro Youth" met at Clark College from October 30 to November 1.

All of us desire a better world which can be realized only by adequate planning during the present struggle. With this thought well in mind, the delegates fortunate enough to attend the November N.A.A.C.P. conference, delved wholeheartedly into the various panel discussions and activities of the conference. There were five panels concerned with: (1) Post-War problems for Negro youth; (2) Negro Youth and the franchise, (3) Minority strategy in war time, (4) Negro Youth and civil liberties, (5) Negro youth and jobs.

From these panels came one tangible result of the conference . . . that of drawing up a charter called "The Demands of Negro Youth." This charter will furnish the basis for the year's work in the youth chapters of the N.A.A.C.P.

The students alone, however, could not have made a success of the conference.

Above, from left: St. Louis U., 11/23/45; Sarah Lawrence C., NY, *The Campus* 11/1/50; "Bonds," *The Simmons News*, MA, 4/16/42. Right: Spelman College, GA, *Campus Mirror*, 11/42. Below: Xavier U., LA, *Xavier Herald*, 12/46.

The Xavier Hera[ld]

"ALL-CATHOLIC"—FOURTEEN YEARS—1932-1946

XAVIER UNIVERSITY, NEW ORLEANS, LA., DECEMBER, 1946

The N.A.A.C.P. Holds Eighth Youth Conference In The Crescent City

". . . and Peace on Earth to Men of Good Will"

May the brightness that emanates from the Divine Babe, light up your heart and home

Program In Democracy Presented By Students

1946

1947

Mills College Weekly

Hall Election Results Given

Student Body Ratifies NSA, Hears Eisenberg at Assembly Monday

FOR STUDENTS OF THE WORLD

THANKSGIVING

1950

Above: Mills College, 11/28/47. Right: Los Angeles City College *Collegian*, 11/20/50.

1947

No double talk from Old Gold... our single aim is Pleasure

1948

PROVE CAMEL MILDNESS IN YOUR 'T-ZONE'!

NO THROAT IRRITATION due to smoking CAMELS!

MORE DOCTORS SMOKE CAMELS THAN ANY OTHER CIGARETTE

1946

TRIPLE SMOKING PLEASURE

ALWAYS MILDER

BETTER TASTING

COOLER SMOKING

THEY SATISFY

Always Buy CHESTERFIELD

1948

Let's Get together

PHILIP MORRIS is so much better to smoke!

CALL FOR PHILIP MORRIS

TRY A PACK... TODAY

From left, top: UCLA, *Daily Bruin*, 5/14/47; 11/24/48. From left, bottom: Washington U., St. Louis, *Student Life*, 12/12/46; UCLA, *Daily Bruin*, 4/26/48.

The "Joy" of Smoking

College Editors Look at Student Government

Excerpt from NSA's Student Government Bulletin and Report, *Vol. 1, No. 5, February 1953*

Ann Jarvis

Editor, 1953, The Rosarian, *Rosary College, Lake Forest, IL*

We at Rosary like to think of ourselves as forming an educational community. Very honestly our work is education, strictly academic. Yet there is peace and order to be kept, future leaders to be trained and student opinion to be voiced. That's where the Rosary College Student Cooperative Government Association comes in.

I am the editor of *The Rosarian*, monthly publication of our Catholic liberal arts college, and I know the Student Government best from my dealings with it. Broadly I would say the Student Council's job in our community is to foster in the students certain religious, intellectual, social and cultural ideals, to stimulate intelligent thinking on and discussion of college problems, to act as liaison between students and faculty and to advance the students' interests in other educational institutions and with the public in general.

Actually we're very proud of our Student Government and its operation here at Rosary. Some weaknesses are apparent, but its successes have been most evident in the practical order. In May 1951, the constitution was revamped along liberal lines. That's when I picked up interest, for the newspaper editor was included as a non-voting member of the Council. Some extremists who object to "foreign controls" might disapprove of the non-student voices occasionally heard, for instance, changes can be introduced by petition of 10 percent of the faculty, but we recognize their equal status in our community and would name faculty and administration as ultimate sources of our power.

We enjoy the full cooperation of the administration in spirit as well as in deed and that's what counts. Above and beyond the overworked student apathy situation, this is one problem the most independent editor or Council member won't ignore. There is reciprocal reliance on each other at Rosary; students are welcomed in administration offices not on a patronizing but on an official level. Misunderstandings do arise, e.g. unendorsed representation of the college by students, but relations are excellent thanks in part to a responsible Student Government Association.

Every issue of the paper carries several stories which hark back to the Student Council for their origin. It is, of course, the supreme organization on campus. Rosary's membership in NSA and NFCCS is by virtue of Student Council consent.... The Council has taken on the responsibility of maintaining the regional seat of the NFCCS Student Government Commission. Rosary edits the NSA regional newsletter and was recent host to the Midwest Student Government Conference of Catholic Women's Colleges. All this makes good news copy, good publicity for the school and opportunities for leadership beyond the average college calling.

On the minus side, it is obvious Student Government has several defects. The best laid plans and constitutions "gang oft awry" due to fluctuating leadership. Continuity is nearly impossible to achieve when so much depends on the individual .... Our club coordination board keeps the college calendar of functions straight but has done nothing to reorganize what appears to be ... a badly muddled club set-up—they are too numerous and too languishing. There is often disparity between paper plans and those projects that materialize, e.g. constitutional requirements for open Student Council meetings and Faculty-Student Senate meetings were unfulfilled this last term. Lastly, relationships between the Student Council and the newspaper are not the best. It is somewhat traditional that a news organ acts as a protagonist. This is not so much the case at Rosary as is the simple lack of integration. No Student Council can complain of apathy until they have availed themselves of every opportunity for publicity and learned that it pays to advertise.

Tim Bornstein

Co-Editor, 1953, The Cardinal, *University of Louisville,*

Although I am profoundly impressed with the great influence which student governments could exercise for the general betterment of American students, I have been disappointed—even disillusioned—to observe that they are too frequently dedicated to small purposes.

Student government, it seems to me, should represent the idealistic determination of American youth. It should be representative of the aspirations, the fears, the successes and the misfortunes of college students. It should reflect the serious attitude which is becoming to the true student, and it should be alert to improve the overall status of students.

In these basic undertakings, most student legislatures have been woefully negligent. The pattern is for student government to place its greatest emphasis upon the light and the immediate, and to avoid the serious and the distant. Positions on social committees are still more anxiously sought after than positions on curricula committees; debates on athletic policies are still more enthusiastically met than debates on academic regulations. In campus elections, organizational affiliations are still more important factors than platforms and ideas.

These, of course, are all highly generalized criticisms. From campus to campus their validity varies a good bit. Nevertheless, I think that it is fair to assert that most student governments are not viewed very seriously by the student bodies, faculty members, administrators, and frequently even by the student legislators themselves ....

I have discovered that one good guide to the capacity and maturity of any particular student legislature is its manner of approaching the question of racial discrimination in higher education. It is a good guide because discrimination is an inevitable question, and, despite the answer which a student government may give, it is frequently bound to give some answer. Unfortunately, however, there are many student governments which categorically refuse even to discuss the question .... The University of Louisville admits Negroes to all of its schools on a fully equal basis, but the University Student Council is literally frightened to investigate an area of campus activity which might be in conflict with the University's official policy.

By way of gaining experience in republican practices and procedures, student government serves a very excellent purpose to those who are active participants. I am not convinced, however, that this experience is enough in itself to justify student government. When the subject matter of a book is frivolous, the beauty of the cover and of the binding cannot compensate the serious reader. This analogy is too often true of student legislatures....

The inevitable test of whether a student government is fulfilling its obligations is whether its judgments are sought after by responsible administrators. When a student government is not consulted in the determination of administrative policy, it is usually a clear indication that the government is not to be trusted in serious matters.

As a college newspaper editor it is my obligation primarily to inform and secondly to criticize. In this capacity it has been a source of dismay to note that student representatives are not the first to recognize and to act upon their own problems, the problems of students.

In this era of international tension, the American college student is burdened with many heavy obligations. If his student government is an accurate reflection of the manner in which he proposes to meet these obligations, I am then convinced that there are sad days ahead. The stereotype of carefree college youth is very much obsolete today, but many student governments still attempt to retain the pattern of that sterotype. If student government in coming years does not reverse that pattern, if it does not accept its role with a seriousness and maturity which are demanded by the problems of our age, then student government will be hard pressed to justify its existence.

SECTION 5

Women and NSA

CONTENTS

Women played an important role in NSA in its formative years. White male domination of leadership prevailed, but there was a strong tradition of active engagement by women in student government that carried over to NSA.

NSA's informal "balanced ticket" practice at its annual conventions assured at least one woman among its five or six elected officers in five of the six years covered by this book (1949-50 was the exception).

On the regional level, women participated actively and emerged as Chairs and National Executive Committee members. Nonetheless, the distribution of elected positions was far short of the 35 percent of graduating college students made up of women in 1948.*

Gender roles and women's colleges

Four early NSA women leaders explore women's issues and NSA, and the role of women's colleges in their experience.

Janis Dowd (Rockford College, IL) and Mildred Wurf (University of California, Berkeley) reflect on why gender issues were not on the agenda. Gender roles were taken for granted and were deeply entrenched. At the same time, women from both co-educational and women's colleges were outspoken and achieved leadership positions and recognition on all levels.

Joan Lynch (Marylhurst College, OR) describes the significance of the NSA experience for students at Catholic women's colleges, and the impact on and contributions to NSA by Catholic women students. Catholic women's colleges affiliated with NSA in significant numbers and their delegates provided valuable energies and voices.

Shirley Neizer Tyler (Simmons College, MA) offers a brief reflection on the leadership opportunities offered at women's colleges. She notes the mentoring influence of veteran students, women as well as men. Rick Medalie (Carleton College, MN), 1949-50 Educational Affairs Vice President, offers a related vignette on his law school experience.

A listing of the women's colleges shows their range and also the large number of Catholic institutions.

*Statistical Abstract of the United States, 1953.

1946

1947

1947

1948

1950

1949

1950

1952

1951

1952

NATIONAL AND REGIONAL LEADERS in NSA's early years. From top of column, left: Janis Tremper Dowd (Rockford C. IL, *p. 60*), Joan Long Lynch (Marylhurst C.,OR, *p. 265*), Connie Curry (Agnes Scott C., GA, p. 444); center: Mimi Haskell Berlin, (Smith C., pp. 6, 87), Helen Jean Rogers Secondari (Mundelein C., IL, *p. 597*), Shirley Neizer Tyler (Simmons C., MA, *pp. 279, 832*), Cynthia Courtney Landry (Dunbarton C., DC, *p. 921*); right: Mildred Kiefer Wurf (U. of California,Berkeley, *p. 178*), Tesse Hartigan Donnelley (Fontbonne C., MO, *p. 951*), Sylvia Bacon (Vassar C., NY, *p.* 474).

A Post-War Women's Agenda Evolving

Vassar Miscellany News

Published Semi-Weekly

Gather Ye Rosebuds

Perhaps the most publicized common trait of Vassar students is that they are unanimously female. After graduation the common denominator will be increased: we will all be college graduates in a society that does not approve of women being ostentatiously educated.

The days of the violent feminists and suffragettes is over. American women now legally have a great deal of mobility. They have the right to vote, to attend academic schools and a steadily expanding variety of jobs are becoming available to them.

At the same time, it becomes increasingly evident that our social mores still rigidly dictate a pattern of behavior that is considered appropriately feminine. Much of the approved behavior and tabooed behavior of women in the upper economic brackets was expressed in this October's "Fortune."

As "Fortune" sees it, the American corporations are enchanted with the new generation of business men's wives who are happily acclimating themselves to their proper role in life: keeping the home and "stabilizing their husbands." "Nurturing the male ego, they seem to feel, is not only a pretty good fulfillment of their own ego but a form of therapy made increasingly necessary by the corporation way of life. . . . It is not so important for the wife, they say, to have gone to college: but it is very important not to have **not** gone to college. If she hasn't, corporation people warn, she is prey to an inferiority complex that makes it difficult for her to achieve real poise. Some corporations, accordingly, make it their business to find out whether or not the wife has a degree."

In a hundred different ways the way for women to become passive homemakers is pointed out. Because women are biologically the child bearers, it is commonly inferred that they are biologically wedded to everything the conception of the American housewife includes. "A serious career can easily be dismissed: there is almost universal agreement among wives, husbands and corporations on this score. Work before marriage, however, is generally approved of."

Succumbing to this idea of the proper role of the American housewife, the President of Mills College has recently criticized Vassar and the other eastern women's colleges. Instead of making the Mills' curriculum what President Lynn White scornfully calls an imitation of men's education, a "Family Studies" major was set up "which concerned itself not only with keeping house and raising children but with attitudes—'a vision of the family and the rewards it offers to those who devote themselves to it'."

No wonder the corporations are so pleased at the compliant group of college graduates: they are being made to order. Far from scoffing at the joys of home, motherhood, etc. the Misc is extremely doubtful as to the value of this type of education either for motherhood or for citizenship. Being a competent mother and wife involves much more than can be gleaned from a specifically tailored course. But more important than this is the notion that possessing female sex organs somehow adles the brain and limits women to a rigidly defined type of existence.

(Excerpted)

CALIFORNIA BRUIN

U C L A

Vol. XXVI No. 19 | Full United Press Wire Service | Monday, April 9, 1945

Women Dominate Campus Life

Bruins Air Vote Issue

A.W.S. Launches 'Hey-Making' Week with Spur Sponsored Box Luncheon

PRICE 10 CENTS

Dean Urges Women Assume Responsibility

Deplores Lack of Interest in Education; Urges Barnard to Meet Teaching Need

Mrs. Millicent Carey McIntosh was formally installed as Dean of Barnard at a ceremony in the gymnasium of Barnard Hall at 2:30 P.M. Friday, October 24. Mrs. Ogden Reid, Vice-Chairman of the Barnard Board of Trustees presented Mrs. McIntosh to Acting President of Columbia, Frank D. Fackenthal, who inducted her into office.

In the address following the installation the new Dean criticized women for not having made effectual use of their position in this world of conflict. "Politically most women have not taken adequate responsibility," she said. "Nationally and internationally women have been ineffectual, except in the case of rare individuals like Virginia Gildersleeve, and of rare organizations like the League of Women Voters.

"In their married life, women, along with men, seem to be ...

Seven Colleges To Confer Here On N. S. A. On Sat.

Pond, Boochever, Mather to Be Delegates at Special Meeting held at Barnard

A special meeting of the Seven College Conference will be held at Barnard next Saturday morning.

Dorms Plan Dance,

Tower Times

FRIDAY, JANUARY 17, 1947 — No. 14

SUSAN B. ANTHONY DAY COMMEMORATED AT THE U. OF R.

Joan Lane, '47, Mary Proctor, '48, Elected To Inter-Campus Council

Newly-elected representatives to the Inter-Campus

UR Alumnus Joins WHAM Staff As Supervisor

Dr. Charlotte Whitton To Be Guest Speaker At Special Luncheon

Barnard

Vol. LVI - No. 14.

Stress Woman's Role At Enlistment Rally

Three Barnard College students, who are in the Na... Corps training program, get a few recruiting pointers f... Golinken, USNR, in connection with the armed services ... was held at Barnard College last night. Left to right, at ... Headquarters, are Miss Helen Versfelt '52, Miss Marily... Golinken and Miss Patricia Drain '54.

Co-eds at Tech Would Cause Many Changes to be Made

By Buddy Flake

Upon the announcement by the State Board of Regents this week that the enrollment of women students at Tech was being considered, ...

In commenting on the proposal Dean Phil B. Narmore said, "It is my opinion that the original charter of Georgia Tech states that only men shall be admitted to the school. ... must be taken into consideration," Dean Narmore added.

Job Opportunities Increase For Secretaries, Librarians

By Beulah Sternberg

Of the two hundred forty-three graduates of the class of 1950, 28 of those seeking jobs have found employment, and 140 girls are as

SARAH LAWRENCE COLLEGE, BRONXVILLE, NEW YORK, WEDNESDAY, FEBRUARY 7, 1951

Role of Women in World Crisis

HORTON, EX-WAVE CHIEF, CALLS FOR DRAFT OF WOMEN

"Why doesn't somebody do something about drafting wom-

BOZEMAN OF SLC FAVORS COMPULSORY REGISTRATION

Representing a third, compromise viewpoint is International

COLLEGE HEADS CALL FOR VOLUNTARY REGISTRATION

Harold Taylor, president of Sarah Lawrence College, along

WOMEN DURING THE WAR attained the presence and high visibility in leadership positions men had occupied. After the war, the surge of male veterans turned the balance around once more. Women began to explore an agenda of their own which had yet to emerge (See Wurf and Dowd, this Section).

Left: Vassar College, *Vassar Miscellany News*, 10/24/51. From top above: UCLA, *Daily California Bruin*, 4/9/45; Barnard College, *Barnard Bulletin*, 10/27/47, 10/9/47; College for Women, U. of Rochester, *Tower Times*, 1/17/47; *Barnard Bulletin*, 6/8/50. Georgia Tech, *The Technique*, 5/10/47; Sarah Lawrence, *The Campus*, 2/7/51.

A Glimpse into the Past

Need for State Women's College Brings About Founding of NJC

(Material for this series of articles was taken from "The Early History of New Jersey College for Women" reprinted from the 1922 Quair.)

"Surely any state that has no college for women is sadly behind the age in which we live," wrote W. H. Faunce, president of Brown University, in a letter to Mabel Smith Douglass.

The "age" was 1914 and the letter was one of many received by Mrs. Douglass discussing the advisability of establishing a college for women in New Jersey.

The Fontbonne Frock

1927

1860's

WOMEN'S COLLEGES, independent or attached to men's universities, dominated higher education for women through the early 20th century.

Top: NJ College for Women opened in 1918, *Caellian* 11/3/49. Above from left: "The Fontbonne Frock" Fontbonne C., MO, *The Font* 11/15/27. Fashionable college wear for women at Vassar in the 1860's (*Miscellany News* Spring, 1940).

Issues in absentia

1. Women in NSA's Early Years

Janis Tremper Dowd
Rockford College, IL. NSA National Secretary, 1947-48
Mildred Kiefer Wurf
University of California, Berkeley. NSA Treasurer, 1947-48

Looking over this volume as it approached printing, our twenty-first-century sensibility saw the glaring omission of comment on the role of women in the founding of NSA. Individuals are certainly present in those very early years—Leila Anderson, Mimi Haskell, Alice Horton Tibbetts, Helen Jean Rogers Secondari, Alice Gilbert Popkin, and the two of us, Janis Tremper Dowd and Mildred Kiefer Wurf. There is no doubt we, and many other women in subsequent years, played useful, even significant, parts in the great adventure.

Janis Tremper (Dowd)

Mildred Kiefer (Wurf)

Many of the women of our NSA generation were graduates of private women's colleges who were prepared for leadership. They were not, however, prepared to assert their rights to leadership. Reviewing the list, we realized that Mildred Kiefer was the only one who attended a large, public coeducational university.

But women's issues as such were simply not on the screen. There was no women's caucus, no feminist agenda, no rallying cause of sexual harassment, date rape, equal pay, and equal representation as might be today. From our present vantage point, we recognized this omission and offer these comments as to why it was so.

Why women's issues were not "on the screen"

First, the feminist movement arrived fifteen years later. In those early days, we didn't even have the word *feminist* readily at hand. Today, it would be part of any self-description.

Second, we took some satisfaction, experienced some small but nonetheless positive feeling, about the fact that each of the first set of officers included one female, as it did one black. While this was hardly adequate recognition, it was at least a presence. Certainly, the "balanced ticket" strategy was familiar. The implicit limit was "one," and in the first two years the position was "Secretary." That we did not protest reflected our deep internalization of socially assigned roles, what we now know as sex-role stereotyping.

Finally, the immediate post–World War II period was unusual. The GI Bill brought floods of veterans, almost entirely male, to college campuses. It was widely assumed that veterans had wider experiences than we females straight from our junior or senior year of undergraduate work. Also, in the postwar period of the 1940s, society felt indebted to veterans, perhaps the last group to be so honored. The veterans were also older—two or three years older. At that age, it makes a difference.

We don't remember that the men cared more about the big issues than we did, nor were our ideas ignored if we presented them in meetings or planning sessions. But some of us gently slid those ideas in, as custom directed, rather than presenting them in the straightforward way we would now.

The fact remains that we did not present any issues that were gender specific. The issues of peace, race, and academic freedom were the important matters at hand and we agreed with those priorities. Perhaps we realized that gender issues would not be accorded the same importance, and agreed with that. We did not view the world through a gender lens.[1]

Now, some thoughts in retrospect

Even now, it has taken us a long time to protest the phrase "you-know-whats" as it appears throughout this volume. The phrase, which refers to the small Catholic colleges for women—"girls' schools"—that provided much of the organizational glue in the first years of NSA, apparently became common after our year in office. As we compiled this book, our male colleagues used it often, usually with a smile. We eventually protested, but not at first. Social conditioning dies hard.

Yet there is no question that gender—or sex—was in the air. We were "hit upon," to use today's vernacular. Sometimes we were pressured sexually when we did not wish to be, and we kept quiet about it as was expected. That code of silence would now be unacceptable, but in the late 1940s it was inescapable.

Some true romances and marriages grew from the relationships formed in those early years. Certainly, life-long important friendships were for many of us the cherished gift of our NSA experience.

Women were involved in the founding and building of NSA—some were leaders. But women's issues were not raised, nor did we even articulate those absent agenda items in any public forum.[2]

Janis Dowd was Director of Community Service and Public Affairs at Monroe Community College, Rochester, New York. She holds an A.B. from Rockford College and an A.M. from Boston University.

For extended biography, see page 66.

Mildred Kiefer Wurf is Director of the Washington Office, and Director of Public Policy, for Girls Incorporated (formerly Girls Clubs of America).

For extended biography, see page 184.

PICTURE CREDITS: *Then:* Dowd: 1947 NSA Constitutional Convention, Madison, WI (NSA photo, SHSW). Wurf: NSA Offices, 1947, Madison, WI (Schwartz). *Now:* Dowd: 1998, Rochester, NY (Schwartz). Wurf: 1999, Washington, DC (Author).

EDITOR'S NOTES

[1] In an interview with this Anthology's editor on October 29, 1998, Ken Kurtz (Swarthmore College), former Pennsylvania Regional Chair, 1950-51, observed,

> One issue that didn't explicitly come up in our day was women's rights. Certainly until Betty Friedan came out with *The Feminine Mystique*, it was not an item on the agenda and there was no women's group that brought it up at NSA. Women were certainly full participants in NSA. Women ran and were elected to national office, but not as president.
>
> Any number of them were regional chairpeople and sat on the National Executive Board. Yet I think if Helen Jean Rogers, NSA's 1948-49 Secretary Treasurer, from Mundelein College in Chicago, had announced for president of NSA, she would have gotten a hell of a lot of votes. If Sylvia Bacon, from Vassar College, who was national Vice President for Student Affairs in 1951-52, had later run for president, she might have gotten elected. Janet Welsh, NSA Vice President from Smith College in 1952-53, was also highly regarded. I can't say they would have won, but I don't think anybody would have batted an eyebrow if they ran.
>
> I think I can make a case that Al Lowenstein would not have been elected NSA president, had it not been for Helen Jean and her support for him. They made one hell of a team.

See also, Rogers (Secondari), p. 599, Bacon, p. 474, (Welsh)Brown, p. 384, and Farber, p. 591. See also Kurtz, p. 306 and p. 902.

[2] Wurf and Dowd's reflections echo the paradoxical absence of a women's issue agenda in activist student movements before World War II as well. Robert Cohen in *When the Old Left Was Young: Student Radicalism and America's First Mass Student Movement, 1929-41* (Oxford University Press, 1993), writes on pp. 270-271,

> Concern about discrimination against women also occasionally found its way into the speeches of student movement leaders. In his address before an international conference of socialist and communist students in Paris, Joseph Lash mentioned the ASU's interest in campaigns to "give greater freedom to the women students who suffer from all sorts of restrictions imposed by the university authorities" in the United States. This concern also appeared in Molly Yard's annual report to the ASU. She pointed out that "Co-eds constitute a special problem—they do not have as good athletic facilities. They live under many rules and regulations while men have none."
>
> Although such egalitarianism was both significant and radical in the context of 1930s America, it would be an exaggeration to say that the student movement gave high priority to feminist issues. Very few instances occurred where the student movement's position favoring gender equality translated into concrete action against sexual discrimination either in the schools or society. The movement's leaders sought to be nondiscriminatory in their own ranks, but did not have an extensive feminist agenda or push women's issues the way they pushed on issues of race, class, war, and peace. Thus in the Lash speech quoted above, he mentioned the issue of women's rights last: after first discussing racial discrimination and economic problems. Yard's speech was structured similarly. And in fact, after mentioning the issue of gender discrimination, Yard quickly indicated that this was not the most pressing of problems, since "women are not the worst treated group on campus. Racial groups, especially Negroes, are discriminated against at every turn."
>
> Yard's words suggest that not even the movement's leading female activists thought of women's issues as paramount. Like their male counterparts, the political agendas of these young women were set by the twin crises of Depression and war and by the larger milieu of the American Left. Generations removed from the suffragettes, women activists on campuses in the 1930s did not possess a fully developed feminist language in which to analyze gender issues. According to Molly Yard, during the Depression decade "we never thought in those days in terms of feminism. It was not a common word." But Yard and other female student activists did display at least elements of a feminist sensibility—even if they did not have a name for it—and held some notion that women should have equal access to positions of power in the movement. (This is what Yard meant when she noted that "I didn't use the word feminist at that time although I was then and have always been one.") They found their male comrades usually willing to engage in such power sharing. In short, the movement was about as open to sexual equality as the women were themselves. This openness, although not in itself the main precipitant of their politicization, made the activist community more congenial for women and helped draw them into it."

[*Note:* See McLaughlin, p. 16, Lash, p. 42, and Album, p. 46, in the Prologue, for more on Joe Lash and Molly Yard. Later in life, in 1987, Yard became head of the National Organization for Women.]

"No longer finishing schools . . . an orientation to social justice"

2. The Catholic Women's Colleges and NSA

Joan Long Lynch
Marylhurst College, Oregon. Chair, Pacific Northwest Region, 1951-52
NSA National Staff Associate, 1950-51

From the founding days of the Association, NSA provided an opportunity for young women who were students in the nation's Catholic women's colleges to take their place in the mainstream of American collegiate life. They appeared at national congresses and regional meetings in ever-increasing numbers, and became, as a group and as individuals, a significant element within the organization, even though their alma maters lacked significant name recognition or political influence.

Involvement with NSA for these young women opened avenues of understanding and tolerance for them and for the other students who came to know and work with them, despite the different views they held on some issues. For most who participated, it was a life-transforming experience. They found common cause in the great experiment that was the United States National Student Association, and the fellowship and life-long friendships that grew from their involvement enriched them, as it did all those who were lucky enough to be part of it. At the same time, something about them provoked the interest of other delegates for reasons that were never really understood. Were they somehow different from other women present? Did they perhaps carry with them in the imaginations of their peers a whiff of the cloister that set them apart? It is still a mystery.

In the beginning . . . .

The pioneer Catholic colleges for women were established in the latter part of the nineteenth century. Their first students were young women from the newly emerging Catholic middle and upper class, from families who knew the value of higher education for their sons and who wanted similar benefits for their daughters. The colleges were outgrowths of the academies and convent schools established by the various religious communities of women recruited from Europe and Canada to provide for the education, health, and welfare needs of the burgeoning Catholic population in this country. Another incentive for the foundation of religious community–owned institutions was the means they provided for the education of their members as well as other sisters at a time when it was not customary for nuns to study in secular institutions. Young teaching sisters who had been put into classrooms with only the most rudimentary training thus had the means of completing their education and obtaining necessary teaching certification.

No longer "finishing schools" where, rumor would have it, young women were taught the charming arts of china painting and embroidery, the colleges were now bona fide academic institutions, some more rigorous than others, where young Catholic women were being prepared for active participation in the academic, social, cultural and political life of the nation. As the broader American Catholic population—predominantly working-class immigrants—became more established, young women from these families joined the ranks of college women in pursuit of both intellectual development and training for careers. Although the most common role for women at the time was that of homemaker, the "socially acceptable" occupations of teaching, nursing, social work, library science, secretarial work, and music and art were the areas in which many institutions offered preparation. Religious and moral development were important in the curricula and the colleges imparted to their students a tradition of responsibility for service to others.

An "abundance of faith" and "meager financial resources"

Catholic women's colleges were established with an abundance of faith but, all too frequently, with meager financial resources. Most of them were institutions not of privilege but of opportunity. Lacking wealthy patrons, their principal endowment was the dedicated lives and labors of the remarkable women who founded and operated them. Contrary to popular belief, the "Church" did not own or support Catholic colleges unless they were established by the local diocese. Most of the women's colleges were financed by the various religious communities, which usually relied on contributions from the work of their sisters in parish schools and by the unpaid labor of the college faculty and administrators who were members of the sponsoring community. A few had some financial backing from generous friends, but for most it was a constant struggle to make ends meet. In the years before state and federal financial aid for education was available for needy students, "scholarship" help was usually in the form of reduced or free tuition. For schools with limited or no endowments, the loss of revenue from tuition added to the financial burden of the institutions. Countless Catholic women owe their education and subsequent life opportunities to the sacrifices and generosity of these women.

Single-sex education still common after World War II

Single-sex education was still very common in the post–World War II collegiate world, despite the fact that women began to be accepted in some previously all-male institutions prior to the Civil War. The Ivy League schools and many other very selective institutions were still all male. Even some state universities admitted only men to their main campuses and relegated women to other locations. With few exceptions, Catholic colleges followed this same pattern, serving either men or women.

There were about 115 Catholic women's colleges among the 250 collegiate institutions for women in the late 1940s. These schools included other church-related colleges, private, nondenominational schools, including the well-known Seven Sisters, several Southern institutions founded to educate African-American women, and a few state institutions chartered specifically for females. The number of Catholic colleges continued to grow until the early part of the 1960s, when changes in higher education related to the growth of public universities and colleges, the decline in popularity of single sex education and the downturn in religious vocations caused many women's schools to merge with other institutions, become coeducational or close their doors.[1]

The "Small You Know What's" and NSA

At the first Congress in Madison, Wisconsin in 1947, 135 delegates and alternates represented eighty-eight women's colleges. Of this number, the Catholic contingent, of 89 students representing fifty-five colleges, was the largest. Most of these schools were located in the upper Midwest, the Northeast, and along the Atlantic Seaboard, where there were large Catholic population centers. Because they were small, were not well known outside of Catholic circles (lacking as they did legendary football teams), and had names that were confusing and sometimes came in duplicate, like the "Notre Dames" of Ohio, California, and Maryland; various "Mounts"; an abundance of "Saints"; and different kinds of "Mary's," delegates from the Catholic women's schools defied easy identification. However, the affectionate nickname of "Small You Know What's" quickly attached itself to them. This came about because when queried about the location of her institution a Catholic woman student (actually, we were called "girls" then, and didn't take offense at the term) invariably started her explanation with "It's a small Catholic girl's school in. . . ." This happened so frequently that it was not long before the "Small You Know What" tag was coined for them and became part of the NSA vernacular, applied to both the colleges and the "girls" themselves.

Catholic women students brought experience in student government

While most students from Catholic women's colleges had little or no exposure to international student issues, they did come to NSA with experience in student government and an orientation to issues of social justice and "doing good," which was very compatible with the agenda of the Association. The Young Christian Student movement had cells on many of the campuses, and the Christopher Movement, with its message of lighting a candle instead of cursing the darkness, found fertile ground there as well. On their all-female campuses they were accustomed to leadership roles in school and interscholastic activities. They also had the encouragement of faculty and administrators of their colleges who tended to be among the more progressive women in the Catholic Church. Among them were a number of vibrant role models. They were not just nuns in quaint medieval garb but scholars and poets, composers and scientists, organizers and advocates. Many of these women were engaged in the renewal and reform movements in the Church in the years prior to Vatican II, and would also be on the battle lines of the civil rights and antiwar movements that were to come.[2]

It was an advantage as a woman in NSA to be from a woman's college in the early years, when males outnumbered females throughout the organization. "Girls" from all-female institutions came to congresses and regional assemblies as independent voting delegates in their own right. At that time, most delegations from coed institutions tended to be dominated, at least numerically, by men who were often older, returning war veterans. At the Michigan Congress in 1950, for example, only the large universities of Illinois, California at Berkeley, and UCLA had delegations on which there were as many females as males. Most of the rest, including Colorado, Washington, Chicago, Wayne State, and City College of New York, had more men than women. The universities of Michigan and Minnesota had no female delegates at all! On the other hand, six of the eight women who held elected or appointed posts on the National staff during the first five years were from women's colleges. Of these, three were from

Catholic institutions: Helen Jean Rogers Secondari from Mundelein, Secretary in 1947; Mary Kay Perkins, also from Mundelein, Staff Associate in 1949; and Joan Long Lynch from Marylhurst College, Staff Associate in 1950. Three were from private women's colleges: Janis Tremper Dowd, Rockford College, Secretary in 1947; Shirley Neizer Tyler, Simmons College, Executive Secretary in 1950; and Sylvia Bacon, Vassar College, Student Life Vice-President in 1951. The other two with National Staff positions were Mildred Kiefer Wurf, University of California at Berkeley, Treasurer in 1947; and Marian Andert, University of Minnesota, hired as Executive Secretary in 1951.[3]

In addition to those who served at the national level, over half of the women who served on the National Executive Committee (NEC) and held regional chairperson posts during the Association's first six years, beginning with the National Continuations Committee in 1946, were "Small You Know What's."[4] Not just mimeo-maidens or envelope stuffers, they and other young Catholic women exercised leadership as policy makers, in membership recruitment and retention, as editors of the literary magazine *Essai*, in the organization and direction of regions, as representatives at national educational forums and to international student organizations and in the coordination of various national NSA programs.[5]

As these young women participated on an equal footing with students whose life experiences, backgrounds and educational institutions were very different from their own they were able to dispel the notion that, as Catholics and women, they were somehow less capable of engagement in the larger issues of their time. They seized the opportunity that NSA gave them and became a vital force within the Association. The principles, values, energy and dedication these young women brought with them added to the growth and strength of the Association. At the same time the information, ideas and programs they brought back to their colleges enriched both student life and the institutions themselves.

Joan Long Lynch was Director of College Admissions Counseling for Immaculate Heart High School, Los Angeles, California. She holds a B.A. from Marylhurst College. (See p. 278 for an extended bio).

END NOTES

[1] There is an interesting article on the Web about women's colleges, which includes information about Catholic women's colleges. It is titled "Women's Colleges in the United States: History, Issues and Challenges." Executive Summary is available at http://www.edgov/offices/OERI/PLLI/webrept.html.

[2] Catholic women's colleges had more female presidents and tenured female faculty members than their secular counterparts. One important exception was the president of Mt. Mary's College in Milwaukee, Dr. Edward A. Fitzpatrick. He was one of only two lay presidents of Catholic colleges in the U.S. in 1946. He had a distinguished career in the government prior to his tenure at Mt. Mary, and was a supporter of NSA for many years.

[3] *Editor's note:* Among these NSA women officers appearing elsewhere in this book, see Secondari, p. 599, Perkins, p. 943, Lynch, pp. 265, 1064, Dowd, p. 60, Tyler, pp. 279, 458, Bacon, p. 474, and Wurf, pp. 128, 178. Also, 1952-53 Vice president Janet Walsh Brown, pp. 375, 1093.

[4] Patricia Groom, Maryville College, MO, and Frances Rollins, Marygrove College, MI, were elected chairmen of their respective regions and members of the NEC in December 1946. They were followed in successive years by many others, including Mary Jane Porter, Marian College, Indiana; Gloria Abiouness, Dunbarton College, DC; Joan Mauer, Marygrove, MI; Tesse Hartigan Donnelly, Fontbonne College, MO; all in 1948. The next year Mary Jane Porter was again a representative, as was Tesse Donnelly. In 1950, they were Phyllis Berezny Scannell, St. Mary's College, Notre Dame, IA; Agnes Downey, Dunbarton College, DC; Jean Anderson Holmes, Fontbonne College, MO; and Virginia Gardiner, Mount Mary College, WI. In the following year, they were Peggy Bradish, Mount St. Mary's College, CA; Joan Long Lynch, Marylhurst, OR; Eileen O'Connell, Trinity College, DC; and Ann Doyle, Mount Mary College, WI. In 1952, they were followed by Cynthia Courtney of Dunbarton College, DC (Verifying terms of office is difficult, because some regions elected their chairpersons at Congresses, while others followed different patterns.)

[5] *Editor's note:* Among these regional leaders in this book, see Donnelly, p. 951, Groom, p. 954, Gardiner, p. 934, O'Connell, p. 922, Courtney, p. 921, Bradish, p. 1043.

PICTURE CREDITS: *Then:* March 14, 1950, Marylhurst College, OR. *Now:* c. 1992 (Both from author).

November 17, 1950

The Ursuline Quill

Catholic Student Leadership Fostered at NSA Congress

By Rita McGreevy

Are Catholics outstanding leaders in the American student community? Before you attempt to answer this question, allow me to point out a few outstanding examples of such leadership which I encountered during the course of the congress of the National Student Association which I attended last August.

Approximately one-third of the membership of NSA is Catholic. From this you can see that Catholics are quite a large minority which prove acceptable to all. By working in a constructive way they have accomplished more and made wider gains than by acting destructively in such a group as a voting bloc.

Choice of President

That certain Catholic student leaders within the ranks of NSA have been considered outstanding in doing just that, can be proved from the fact that the last two presidents

September, 1952

Dunbarton Dial

Dunbarton Student Wins NSA Election

Brief reports from N.S.A. and N.F.C.C.S. senior delegates indicate that both summer Congresses were successful and to those attending, educational and stimulating.

May 22, 1947

THE SKYSCRAPER

Mundelein Aids In Drafting N.S.O. Constitution

S.A.C. Elects Delegates To Wisconsin Convention

Together with students from California, Texas, and Rhode Island, delegates Dorothy Gaughan and Mary Lou Hafner will participate in the Constitutional convention of the National Student Organization, at the University of Wisconsin, Aug. 30 to Sept. 8.

The Student Activities Council elected the representatives. Alternates are Adele Baiocchi and Helen Jean Rogers.

May 3, 1951

CENTURION

MANHATTANVILLE COLLEGE OF THE SACRED HEART, N. Y. C.

NSA Plans Region Meet

M'VILLE TO TELL OF FOREIGN STUDENTS

Art, IC Dances To Be Shown

by Mary Kay Donovan

As a grand climax of its year's activities, the Met-New York Region of NSA is planning its first annual Regional Congress at Ford-

"THEY SEIZED THE OPPORTUNITY ...and became a vital force" in NSA, Joan Lynch writes. Of some 70 Catholic women's colleges, 59 attended congresses or were members for one or more years during the period 1946-53. Clockwise from top: Ursuline C., OH; Dunbarton C., DC; Manhattanville C., NY; Mundelein C., IL.

Opportunities for Leadership at Women's Colleges

Shirley Neizer Tyler
Simmons College, MA. NSA Executive Secretary, 1950-51

Janis Dowd and Mildred Wurf in their essay are right in my judgment. Other issues had higher priorities for women, appropriate for the times. My observation is that the preponderance of small Catholic women's colleges, the Seven Sisters, and the independent women's colleges (Simmons, Agnes Scott, Mills, etc.), with their on-campus opportunities for leadership, filled the needs of women with leadership potential. Later, as single-sex colleges merged into coed institutions (Harvard/Radcliffe, Columbia/Barnard, etc.), there was some destabilization. I suspect that women's awareness of their lower status on campus and the need to assert themselves coincided with the beginnings of the civil rights and women's movements.

The women's colleges in "our day" were in one sense ahead, and in another somewhat behind the times. In my judgment the forties was a more exciting decade to have been attending women's colleges than the fifties were. (I'm not at all sure what was happening in terms of women's leadership on the major university campuses.)

Influence of the veterans

The men who were vets, at least in the Boston area, provided leadership on both the inter- and intracollegiate levels. The women vets at Simmons interacted with students and added a wonderful level of maturity to campus life. They tended not to become involved in organizations, instead focusing on their interrupted careers and making up for lost time. In an era when women were constantly being reminded that it was not healthy to start families after they reached their mid-thirties, they probably felt the pressure to finish their educations as soon as possible, and get on with their lives. How times have changed in fifty years!

(See p. 282 for extended biography.)

Gender and Diversity in Law School

Richard J. Medalie
Carleton College/U. of Minnesota, Harvard Law School '58
NSA Vice President, Educational Affairs, 1949-50

When I went to Harvard Law School in 1955-58, my class consisted of about five hundred white males, ten women, one Chinese-American, one Korean-American, and two Blacks, one of whom passed as white. Even though he was a member of my law club, I never knew he was Black until after I was out of law school. Women had only begun to be accepted into Harvard law school in 1950. That was "diversity" in those days. Almost everyone accepted the value system.

The Dean would greet the women in the first year class by saying, "Now, there are ten women in this class and I want you to know that you're taking the place of ten good men."

Women were rarely able to get jobs in law firms. I recall that Sandra Day O'Connor had to work as a secretary for a period of time. A friend of mine, in the Harvard Law School class of '53, tells the story of one of her classmates who was interviewed at one of the top law firms in Boston. The woman was absolutely terrific. The man interviewing her said, "All things being equal, you're the best of the candidates." She said, "What do you mean by, 'all things being equal?'" He said, "Unfortunately, all things aren't equal and I'm afraid we can't offer you the position."

After several years in the early 1960s as a research associate and associate research director at the Columbia Law School, Ruth Bader Ginsburg applied to become a member of the Columbia law faculty, but was not appointed. Nor did the Harvard Law School offer her a position after she spent a year there as a visiting professor. In the mid-1960s she was hired as a member of the Rutgers law faculty, becoming a full professor by 1969. Finally, she became a full professor at the Columbia Law School in 1972, a U.S. Circuit Judge in 1980, and an Associate Justice of the United States Supreme Court in 1993.

I was in the class of '58 at the law school and the class of '52 at the University of Minnesota. They were the last years of the old ways. One thing that was bothersome to me in law school was in job interviews, since my name is not obviously Jewish. I always felt compelled to inform an interviewer that I was Jewish, so that there would be no difficulties later were I to be hired by the firm. Law firms were just coming out of the "white shoe" mode; just beginning to open up, and still not to everyone.

There was a recent report about the opening of Dartmouth's archive records of their quota system. Harvard used to have one, although not in my time. In fact, substantial numbers of students at the law school were Jewish, and I would say that during my years at Harvard Law School, more than 50 percent of the student editors of the *Law Review* were Jewish, many of them from the New York City area.

(See p. 355 for extended biography.)

The U.S. Women's Colleges in 1948

*From: Richard H. Ostheimer, State College for Teachers, Albany, N.Y., The Organization of Higher Education in the United States, 1948–1949 (Columbia University Press, New York, 1951). Classifications are those used by Ostheimer. Junior Colleges in Ostheimer are not listed here. Institutions omitted by Ostheimer are followed by (§). Colleges that were NSA members or attended NSA Congresses for one or more years during 1946-1952 are shown by an *.*

UNIVERSITIES

Editor's Note: Some women's colleges attached to major universities were not listed separately by Ostheimer for statistical purposes. The following include those that appear parenthetically as attached to universities in the Ostheimer report as well as some listings (denoted by §) that were not in Ostheimer.

Public

NEW JERSEY
Rutgers University–New Jersey College for Women, New Brunswick

NORTH CAROLINA
*University of North Carolina–Women's College (§)

VIRGINIA
University of Virginia–Mary Washington College

Private, Nonsectarian

LOUISIANA
Tulane University–Newcomb College, New Orleans

MASSACHUSETTS
*Harvard University–Radcliffe College, Cambridge

NEW YORK
*Columbia University–Barnard College, New York City
*University of Rochester–The College for Women (§)

OHIO
*Western Reserve University–Flora Stone Mather, Cleveland (§)

RHODE ISLAND
*Brown University–Pembroke College, Providence (§)

SEPARATE LIBERAL ARTS COLLEGES

A. Complex

Public, Municipal
*Hunter College, New York

Private, Nonsectarian

MASSACHUSETTS
*Simmons College, Boston
*Smith College, Northampton

PENNSYLVANIA
*Bryn Mawr College, Bryn Mawr

B. Others

Public, State

ALABAMA
Alabama College, Montevallo

GEORGIA
Georgia State College for Women, Milledgeville
Georgia State Women's College, Valdosta

MISSISSIPPI
Mississippi State College for Women, Columbus

OKLAHOMA
Oklahoma State College for Women, Chikasha

SOUTH CAROLINA
Winthrop College, Rock Hill

TEXAS
Texas State College for Women, Denton

Private, Nonsectarian

CALIFORNIA
*Mills College, Oakland

CONNECTICUT
*Connecticut College for Women, New London

GEORGIA
*Agnes Scott College, Decatur
Brenau College, Gainesville

ILLINOIS
*Rockford College, Rockford

MARYLAND
Goucher College, Baltimore

MASSACHUSETTS
*Mount Holyoke College, South Hadley
*Wellesley College, Wellesley
*Wheaton College, Norton

NEW YORK
Elmira College, Elmira
*Russell Sage College, Troy
*Sarah Lawrence College, Bronxville
*Skidmore College, Saratoga Springs
*Vassar College, Poughkeepsie
Wells College, Aurora

OHIO
*Lake Erie College, Painesville

PENNSYLVANIA
*Pennsylvania College for Women, Pittsburgh

SOUTH CAROLINA
Coker College, Hartsville
Converse College, Spartansburg
Limestone College, Gafney

VERMONT
*Bennington College, Bennington
*Women's College of Middlebury (§)

VIRGINIA
*Hollins College, Hollins
*Sweet Briar College, Sweet Briar

WISCONSIN
Milwaukee-Downer College, Milwaukee

Private, Protestant

ALABAMA
Judson College, Marion

GEORGIA
Bessie Tift College, Forsyth
LaGrange College, La Grange
Shorter College, Rome
Wesleyan College, Macon

ILLINOIS
MacMurray College for Women, Jacksonville

MARYLAND
*Hood College, Frederick

MISSISSIPPI
Belhaven College, Jackson
*Blue Mountain College, Blue Mountain

NEW YORK
Keuka College, Keuka Park

NORTH CAROLINA
*Greensboro College, Greensboro
Meredith College, Raleigh
Queens College, Charlotte
Salem College, Winston-Salem
*Duke University-Women's College (§)

OHIO
*Western College, Oxford

PENNSYLVANIA
*Beaver College, Jenkintown
Cedar Crest College, Allentown
*Wilson College, Chambersburg

SOUTH CAROLINA
Columbia College, Columbia

TEXAS
Mary Hardin-Baylor College, Belton

VIRGINIA
Mary Baldwin College, Staunton
*Randolph-Macon Woman's College, Lynchburg

Private, Protestant, Negro

NORTH CAROLINA
Bennett College, Greensboro

Private, Roman Catholic

CALIFORNIA
Dominican College of San Rafael
*College of the Holy Names, Oakland
*Immaculate Heart College, Los Angeles
*Mount St. Mary's College, Los Angeles
San Francisco College for Women

COLORADO
*Loretto Heights College, Loretto

CONNECTICUT
*Albertus Magnus College, New Haven
*Saint Joseph College, West Hartford

DISTRICT OF COLUMBIA
*Dunbarton College of the Holy Cross
*Trinity College

FLORIDA
*Barry College, Miam

ILLINOIS
*Barat College of the Sacred Heart, Lake Forest
*Mundelein College, Chicago
*Rosary College, Rover Forest
*College of Saint Francis, Joliet
*Saint Francis Xavier College for Women, Chicago

INDIANA
*St. Mary-of-the-Woods College
*St. Mary's College, Notre Dame, Holy Cross

IOWA
Briar Cliff College, Sioux City
*Clarke College, Dubuque

KANSAS
*Marymount College, Salina
*Mount Saint Scholastica College, Atchison
Saint Mary College, Xavier

KENTUCKY
*Nazareth College, Louisville

MARYLAND
*College of Notre Dame of Maryland, Baltimore
*Saint Joseph's College, Emmitsburg

MASSACHUSETTS
*Emmanual College, Boston
College of our Lady of the Elms, Chicopee
*Regis College, Weston

MICHIGAN
*Marygrove College, Detroit
*Nazareth College, Nazareth
*Siena Heights College, Adrian

MINNESOTA
*College of Saint Benedict, St. Joseph
*College of Saint Catherine, St. Paul
*College of Saint Scholastica, Duluth
*College of Saint Teresa, Winona

MISSOURI
*College of Saint Teresa, Kansas City
*Fontbonne College, St. Louis (§)

NEBRASKA
*Duchesne College, Omaha

NEW HAMPSHIRE
*Mount Saint Mary's College, Hooksett

NEW JERSEY
Georgian Court College, Lakewood
*College of Saint Elizabeth, Convent Station

NEW YORK
*D'Youville College, Buffalo
*Good Counsel College, White Plains
*Manhattanville College of the Sacred Heart, New York
*Marymount College, Tarrytown
*College of Mount Saint Vincent, New York
*Nazareth College of Rochester
*College of New Rochelle
*Notre Dame College of Staten Island
Saint Joseph's College for Women, Brooklyn
*College of Saint Rose, Albany

OHIO
*Mary Manse College, Toledo
*College of Mount Saint Joseph-on-the-Ohio
*Notre Dame College, South Euclid
*College of Saint Mary of the Springs, Columbus
*Ursuline College for Women, Cleveland

OREGON
*Marylhurst College, Marylhurst

PENNSYLVANIA
*Chestnut Hill College, Philadelphia
*Immaculata College, Immaculata
*Marywood College, Scranton
*Mercyhurst College, Glenwood Hills and Erie
College Misericordia, Dallas
*Mount Mercy College, Pittsburgh
*Rosemont College, Rosemont
*Seton Hill College, Greenburg
Villa Maria College, Erie

TEXAS
Incarnate Word College, San Antonio
*Our Lady of the Lake College, San Antonio

UTAH
College of Saint Mary-of-the-Wasach, Salt Lake City

WISCONSIN
*Mount Mary College, Milwaukee

SEPARATE PROFESSIONAL SCHOOLS

A. Teachers Colleges

Public, Municipal

MASSACHUSETTS
Teachers College of the City of Boston

Public, State

MASSACHUSETTS
Massachusetts State Teachers College, Framingham

VIRGINIA
Longwood College, Farmville
Madison College, Harrisonburg

Private, Nonsectarian

ILLINOIS
National College of Education, Evanston

MASSACHUSETTS
Wheelock College, Boston

Private, Roman Catholic

OHIO
St. John College of Cleveland

WASHINGTON
Holy Names College, Spokane

WISCONSIN
Alverno College, Milwaukee

B. Medical Schools

Private, Nonsectarian

PENNSYLVANIA
Women's Medical College of Pennsylvania, Philadelphia

PART 3

International Programs: Searching for Paths to Peace

American and German students working together on a summer project rebuilding a dormitory at the University of Munich in 1948, left (Henry Halsted, see p. 659). Above, cartoon by Randy Harrison from the U. of Wisconsin *Daily Cardinal* (3/49 *NSA News*).

PART 3

International Programs: Searching for Paths to Peace

347 MADISON AVE.
NEW YORK 17, N. Y.

NSA News

of the United States National Student Association

Madison, Wisconsin — January, 1948

IUS Negotiating Team Chosen From List of Forty Applicants

To Go Abroad Next Summer

Negotiators for politically-autonomous membership of American students of the International Union of Student (IUS) were chosen by the USNSA executive committee at its December meeting.

Bill Birenbaum, University of Chicago; Don Fraser, University of Minnesota; Martin McLaughlin, Notre Dame; and Larry Jaffa, Harvard Divinity school, were elected as the four-man negotiating team.

Alternates are Milton Dobkin, Southern California, and Rob West, Yale.

More than 40 applications were received from regions all over the country. Applicants were interviewed by regional chairman. A subcommittee selected ten applicants for final consideration by the executive committee.

Procedure adopted by the committee for voting included roll call voting on each ballot, majority vote necessary to win, straight vote on each ballot for a candidate with runs-off from the balloting. Twelve votes were taken to determine the final group.

The IUS council meeting at which the negotiators will present the terms adopted by the constitutional convention, will be held next summer in Prague or Rangoon, Bur-

AN INTERNATIONAL ROLE FOR THE AMERICAN STUDENT

reports from

SOUTHEAST ASIA

STOCKHOLM

UNITED STATES

United States National Student Association

This part provides an overview of the challenges and opportunities for U.S. student leaders on the international scene during the early years of postwar reconstruction, the building of the United Nations, the evolution of the Cold War, the rise of anticolonial movements in Asia and Africa, and the entry of the United States into the Korean conflict. The evolution of NSA's international program emerges in stories of both organization and policy, as told here by its early leaders.

Relations with the International Union of Students (IUS) are reviewed. NSA failed to find a basis for collaboration with the IUS because of its Communist domination. The formation in 1952 of the non-Communist alternative, the Coordinating Secretariat of the International Student Conference (Cosec), is documented. Cosec was the outcome of groundwork laid by NSA leaders and those of other nations.

Attendance at IUS and other world student events in Europe and Latin America and travels through Asia by NSA representatives are recalled in descriptive detail.

A separate unit deals with the covert U.S. government funding of NSA's international programs, which began in 1951 and was exposed in 1967.

Student aid, travel, and exchange programs

Efforts to aid foreign students through the World Student Service Fund, and NSA's technical assistance initiatives, which presaged the later U.S. Peace Corps programs, are described.

In the period covered by this book, NSA's travel program grew to sponsorship of almost 15 percent of all U.S. student summer travel abroad. Some high times and high adventure are described in the memoirs of a number of the student leaders who were involved. Others provide a window on their experiences in work-study and exchange programs.

NSA's international program got off the ground quickly after the 1946 Chicago Conference, before the 1947 Constitutional Convention, because of a global network of service, relief, and travel organizations with prewar origins. These other pre- and postwar organizations and some of their accomplishments are described in this part.

LAYING GROUNDWORK FOR GLOBAL OUTREACH, NSA launches ultimately failed effort to find basis for membership in Communist-dominated International Union of Students (Top: *NSA News* 1/48. See p. 541). In 1951 NSA publishes its global student team reports and new efforts launched in Stockholm to start a non-communist cooperative group (Above: USNSA, Madison. see p. 527).

STUDENT SHIPS CARRY THOUSANDS to Europe in immediate post-war years (see p. 669). Photos above: students on the converted Dutch troop ship Kote Inten, 1948. (Photos: Students, Ralph Smith. Ship, Dee West.

SECTION 1

Developing the International Program

CONTENTS

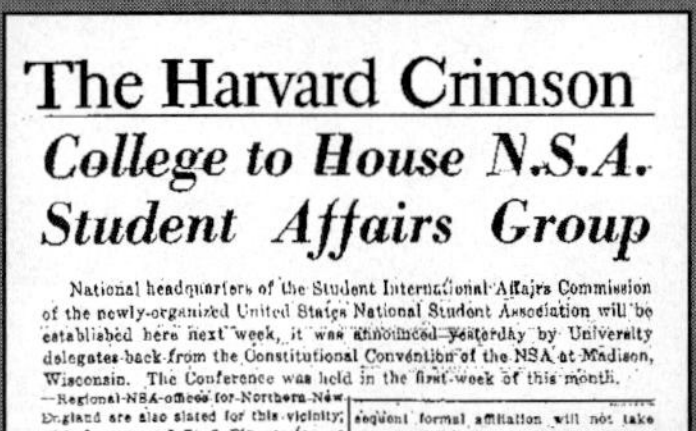

The Harvard Crimson

College to House N.S.A. Student Affairs Group

National headquarters of the Student International Affairs Commission of the newly-organized United States National Student Association will be established here next week, it was announced yesterday by University delegates back from the Constitutional Convention of the NSA at Madison, Wisconsin. The Conference was held in the first week of this month.

During its early years, NSA operated its international programs with minimal clerical staff and with volunteer student backup. Bob Smith (Yale), NSA's first international vice president, 1947-48, describes how the Cambridge office for NSA's International Commission was organized. He and his staff laid the groundwork for the work/study travel program and its popular annual guidebook, *Work, Study, Travel Abroad.*

Smith opened up the channels for coordination and program support with the World Student Service Fund, Institute for International Education, and the U.S. Commission for UNESCO, and served as NSA's first representative on the Commission. He made contact with the European national student unions and supported the staff decision to endorse Bill Ellis and Jim Smith's resignation as NSA representatives to the IUS as a result of its support for the Communist coup in Czechoslovakia (see Part 1, Section 5).

Smith also introduces us to Rob West (Yale), his 1948-49 successor, and Erskine Childers (Stanford), who followed West in 1949-50. West's and Childers' commitment to build the peace by furthering programs of international student collaboration is presented in excerpts from their writings.

Frank Fisher, Chairman of the Harvard International Committee when NSA was formed and when it moved its international office to Cambridge, tells of his experiences as traveling representative for NSA in the summers of 1950-52. He was one of a number of NSA representatives deeply interested in post-war economic and social development, whose travels in Asia, Africa and Latin America for NSA are reported in this section and elsewhere. A list of these teams and their reports is provided.

In 1950 NSA changes course with respect to the IUS

Herb Eisenberg (MIT), 1950-51 International Vice President, who later pursued a career as an architect, and Al Lowenstein, NSA President that year (See Part 1, Section 7), attended the International Student Conference in Stockholm in December 1950 in conflict with each other on how to act toward the IUS, which both agreed NSA could not join. Eisenberg lays out his approach to the issues in his memoir (See also Lynch in Part 1) and introduces us to the Students Mutual Assistance Plan he proposed, which was endorsed at Stockholm (See also Section 4 in this part).

A focus on the importance NSA placed on relations with the European and other national unions of students and on NSA's engagement with UNESCO concludes this section. The UN careers of NSA's Erskine Childers (p. 518) and the Swedish student union president, Olof Palme, illustrate the later personal alliances forged by NSA'S international program.

HARVARD HOSTED NSA'S INTERNATIONAL COMMISSION throughout the association's early years on or near Harvard Square (*Harvard Crimson*, 9/23/47). Photo of Brattle Street office staff in early 1950, from left: Helen Bryan (Sarah Lawrence), travel director (see p. 000), Opal Haynes (Oklahoma), Chris Christianson (California), Bob Delahanty (Louisville. See p. 410), Charlotte Allen (Illinois. See p. 658).

NSA Provides U.S. Student Voice in Global Forums

Varied Programs Provide Extensive Global Outreach

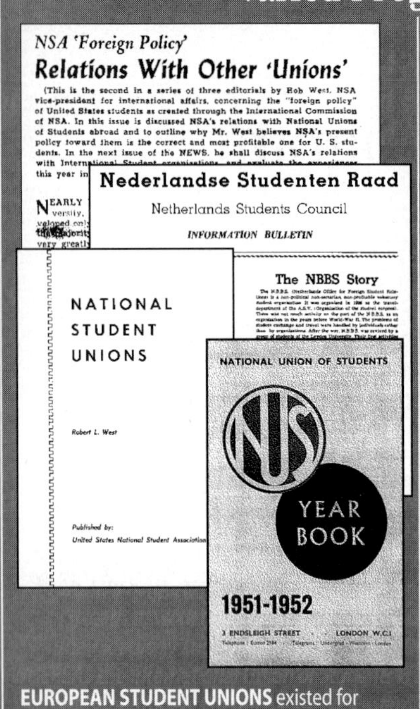

NSA 'Foreign Policy'

Relations With Other 'Unions'

(This is the second in a series of three editorials by Bob West, NSA vice-president for international affairs, concerning the "foreign policy" of United States students as created through the International Commission of NSA. In this issue is discussed NSA's relations with National Unions of Students abroad and to outline why Mr. West believes NSA's present policy toward them is the correct and most profitable one for U. S. students. In the next issue of the NEWS, he shall discuss NSA's relations with International Student organizations and evaluate the experiences this year in ...

Nederlandse Studenten Raad

Netherlands Students Council

INFORMATION BULLETIN

The NBBS Story

NATIONAL STUDENT UNIONS

Robert L. West

Published by: United States National Student Association

NATIONAL UNION OF STUDENTS

NUS

YEAR BOOK

1951-1952

3 ENDSLEIGH STREET · LONDON W.C.1

EUROPEAN STUDENT UNIONS existed for most of the 20th century and inspired the formation of NSA. The British and Dutch organizations lent early support in organizing student travel. (See pp. 529, 651) From the top: Editorial in *INSA News* 2/49; Netherlands Student Council *Bulletin*, c. 1952; Cover, "National Student Unions" by Robert L. West, USNSA 1949; British National Union of Students, London, 1951.

National Student Unions

ISS to Hold Annual Meet in New York

150 Students to Meet At Wells College July 25

Plan Orientation For Students On Volendam

NSA Sends 60 To UNESCO, Emphasizes World Awareness

Cornell Spurs Fraternities To Abolish Discrimination

international student conferences

STOCKHOLM 1950
EDINBURGH 1952
COPENHAGEN 1953
ISTANBUL 1954

From Other Lands

Report on IUS:

Pat Baker Comments in Sofia

"MUTUAL UNDERSTANDING AND FRIENDLY COLLABORATION," as stated by Cosec (see p. 576) were the goals of the many international student conferences that emerged after World War II and attracted widespread interest among American students. From the top: International Student Service, *NSA News*, 5/49 (See p. 56); U.S. Council for UNESCO, *NSA News*, 3/52 (see p. 531); Cosec report, 1954; IUS Council meeting, *NSA News*, 10/49 (see p. 580).

International Conferences

STUDENTS MUTUAL ASSISTANCE PROGRAM

ADOPTED AT STOCKHOLM, DECEMBER, 1950, AND RATIFIED AT EDINBURGH, JANUARY, 1952, AT THE STUDENT CONFERENCE WITH THE NATIONAL UNIONS OF THE FOLLOWING COUNTRIES IN ATTENDANCE:

Latin Americans Receiv... Of American Colleges ...

HOW TO RUN AN ALL-COLLEGE CONFERENCE

A REPORT ON THE NEW ENGLAND ALL-COLLEGE CONFERENCE.

"American Foreign Policy: An Evaluation"

By WILLIAM ROSEN

International Student INFORMATION BULLETIN

...ATIONAL COMMISSION ...AL STUDENT ASSOCIATION Cambridge 38, Massachusetts

INFORMATION BULLETINS AND PROGRAMS, aimed at exchange with Europe, Latin America and Asia were launched by NSA. From top: Students Mutual Assistance Program adopted by Cosec, USNSA info folder, 1951-52 (see p. 526); International News Center for Latin America managed by Atlanta, GA NSA colleges Agnes Scott, Emory, Morehouse, GA Tech, *NSA News*, 3/52 (see p. 990); New England NSA Foreign Policy Conference report, 4/52; NSA International Commission.

Information & Ideas

Cold War Conflicts Defeat Efforts at East-West Cooperation

LEADERS DISCUSS ATOM FACTS

'Citizen's role in Atom Age' to be probed at institute

CALIFORNIA *Daily Bruin*

1

THE SIMMONS NEWS

Int'l Students Day Nov. 17 First Peacetime Observance

U. S. N. S. A. and I. U. S. RELATIONS 1945 – 1955

International Commission U. S. National Student Association

2

NSA'S COLD WAR BENCHMARKS **(1)** The A-Bomb brought World War II to an end and began an atomic standoff framing the cold war conflict. (*UCLA Daily Bruin*, 5/28/47. "Mushroom Cloud," Internet.) **(2)** German troop massacre in Prague of 156 Charles U. students in 1939 was marked by International Students Day afterward. In 1946 the International Union of Students (IUS) was founded in Prague and U.S. delegates were inspired to form USNSA (Simmons C., MA *Simmons News*, 11/15/45; NSA and IUS report, 1945-1955, by Peter Jones. See p. 538). **(3)** The 1948 Czech Communist coup and IUS refusal to condemn abuse of Prague students led to NSA withdrawal from membership negotiations (see p. 540) (*Cornell Daily Sun*, 2/27/48; *NSA News*, 3/48; **(4)** In August 1950, still exploring collaboration, NSA sent 3 observers to the 2d World Student Congress (Photos to right from Dee West. Center below from left standing, NSA's Holbrook, Schwartz and West). Coinciding with U.S. Korean conflict entry, IUS roundly con-demned the U.S. (see p. 559, Report by West and Schwartz in U.S. Office of Education publication 3/15/51; Agnes Scott C.

CORNELL DAILY SUN

West Bitterly Attacks New Czech Rule

Britain, France -US Condemn It As Dictatorship

AS COMMUNISTS TAKE OVER IN PRAGUE

NSA News

the United States National Student Association

Madison, Wisconsin

Staff Supports Smith, Eli... On Repudiation of IUS

Representatives Resign as Abuse Of Prague Students Is Unprotested

3

HIGHER EDUCATION

SEMIMONTHLY PUBLICATION OF THE FEDERAL SECURITY AGENCY

The World Student Congress and International Education of American Students

By EUGENE G. SCHWARTZ and ROBERT L. WEST

THE AGNES ...WS · Wednesday, Jan. 10, 1951

North Koreans Condemn U. S. At Red-Dominated Conference

By Bill Holbrook

The North Koreans got another chance to tee off on the United States on the second day of the World Student congress.

4

News, 1/10/51). **(5)** The 1950 NSA Congress endorsed UN Korea action. In 12/50 NSA's executive committee endorsed Al Lowensteins' speech in Stockholm earlier that month (see p. 562) (*Ann Arbor News*, 8/31/50; *NSA News*, 8/51).

STOCKHOLM PLAN BACKED IN NEC VOTE

Endorse Lowenstein's Stand That Practical Action Must Face Political Reality

MOBILIZATION DEBATE

An inconclusive debate on student mobilization and full approval of the results of the Stockholm conference highlighted the December 26-31 meeting of NSA's National Executive Committee in Madison, Wisconsin.

Student Congress Upholds UN Intervention In Korea

Enthusiastic support for United Nations action in Korea was voiced yesterday by some 1,000 delegates attending the third annual National Student Congress, meeting on the ... North Korean attack a "breach of the peace" and urged the UN to establish under its supervision a unified Korean government to be determined by the free will of ...

5

Post-War Aid, Travel Link U.S. Students to the World

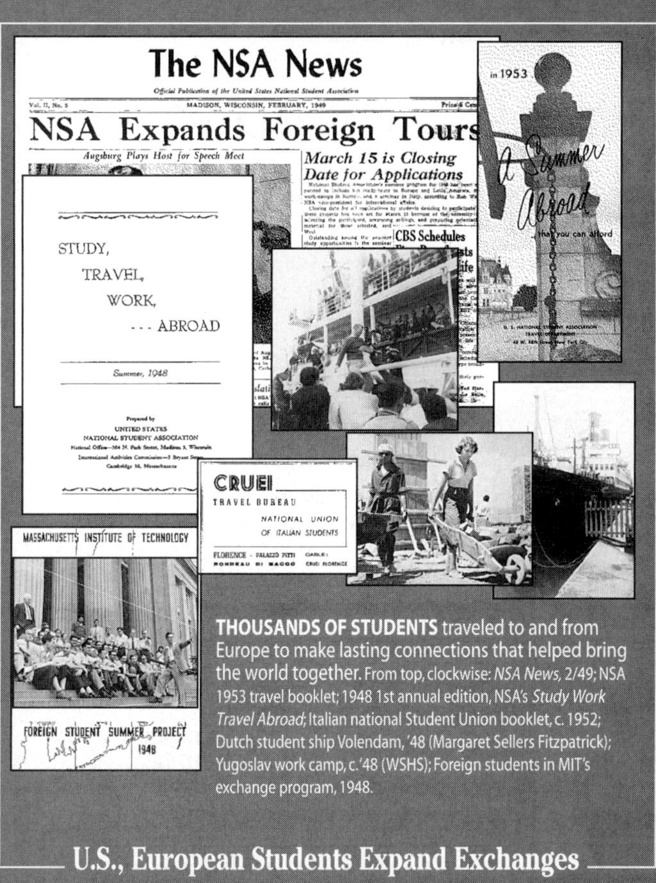

THOUSANDS OF STUDENTS traveled to and from Europe to make lasting connections that helped bring the world together. From top, clockwise: *NSA News*, 2/49; NSA 1953 travel booklet; 1948 1st annual edition, NSA's *Study Work Travel Abroad*; Italian national Student Union booklet, c. 1952; Dutch student ship Volendam, '48 (Margaret Sellers Fitzpatrick); Yugoslav work camp, c. '48 (WSHS); Foreign students in MIT's exchange program, 1948.

U.S., European Students Expand Exchanges

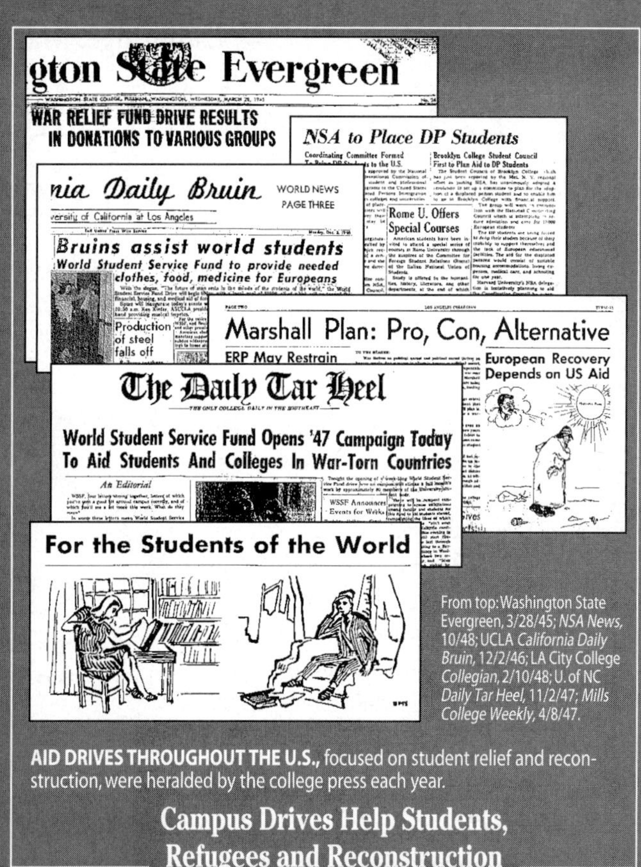

From top: Washington State Evergreen, 3/28/45; *NSA News*, 10/48; UCLA *California Daily Bruin*, 12/2/46; LA City College *Collegian*, 2/10/48; U. of NC *Daily Tar Heel*, 11/2/47; *Mills College Weekly*, 4/8/47.

AID DRIVES THROUGHOUT THE U.S., focused on student relief and reconstruction, were heralded by the college press each year.

Campus Drives Help Students, Refugees and Reconstruction

NSA Student Leaders Build a Post-War Foreign Policy

1946 World Student Congress, Prague

1946-47

(Photo details, p. 83)

William S. Ellis

Harvard. National Intercollegiate Christian Council. IUS Vice-Chair, 1946-48.

Tried to build bridge between East and West, but resigned IUS in protest over Czech coup (See pp 106, 130, 158, 188).

NSA Constitutional Convention, 1947

1947-48

(Photo details, p. 509)

Robert S. Smith

Yale. NSA V.P. Int'l. Affairs, 1947-48.

Laid groundwork for international office, student travel program, UNESCO Commission membership, global national student union relations. (See p. 504).

1950 World Student Congress, Prague.

1948-49

(Photo details, p. 558, 560)

Robert L. West

Yale. NSA V.P. Int'l. Affairs, 1948-49

Promoted strong foreign NUS relations, aid to emerging nations. Appealed for east-west dialog in behalf of peace (See pp. 515, 519, 556).

Paris. Mapping international team strategy

1949-50

(Photo details, p. 560)

Erskine B. Childers

Stanford. NSA V.P. Int'l. Affairs, 1949-50

Deployed fifteen NSA emissaries to Europe, Latin America, Asia. Stressed NSA outreach to developing nations. (See pp. 517, 609.)

14th Brazilian NUS Congress, 1951

1950-51

(Photo details, p. 527)

Herbert W. Eisenberg

MIT. NSA V.P. Int'l. Affairs, 1950-51

Developed Students Mutual Assistance Program adopted by Cosec. Furthered NSA's student exchange programs. (See pp. 520, 628).

1952 Rio Inter-American Congress

1951-53

(Photo details, p. 608)

Avrea Ingram

Greorgia Tech, Harvard. NSA V.P. Int'l. Affairs, 1951-52-53 First two-term NSA officer. Provided continuity to growing international program and served on the first Cosec Supervision Committee.

Cambridge, Massachusetts, 1947-48

1. Establishing the NSA International Affairs Office

Robert Solwin Smith
Yale University
NSA Vice President for International Affairs, 1947-48

I grew up in New York City and was educated in a liberal private school, where I was active in student government. I entered Yale in the summer of 1942, was pulled out in 1944 for active duty in the Navy, and returned in the fall of 1946 to complete my senior year. I was determined to be a serious student and make up for the time "lost" while serving in the Pacific. Yale had no student government, and we later failed in an attempt to get support for one, but there were plenty of outlets for student expression.

The founding of NSA was a direct result of the trip of a delegation of twenty-five American students to the founding congress of the International Union of Students (IUS) in Prague, Czechoslovakia, in the summer of 1946. Unfortunately, IUS fell under Communist control from the outset. This story is told in detail in several essays in this book (see Part 1, Section 1, and Part 3, Section 2).

One member of the American delegation was Curtis Farrar, a friend and schoolmate of mine from childhood, who by then was a fellow student at Yale. Curt talked to me about the IUS congress and about the forthcoming National Student Congress at the University of Chicago in December, where the founding of an American national student organization would be discussed. I volunteered to go, and was chosen as one of Yale's delegates.[1]

At the National Student Congress, we set up a National Continuations Committee (NCC) to plan for a constitutional convention for the new organization in September 1947, and set up geographic regions as the basis for preparatory activity. I was elected chair of the Southern New England Region, comprising Connecticut and Rhode Island, which held several meetings. The regional chairs and the NCC national officers became the NCC executive committee, which also held several meetings. These and subsequent NSA activities gave me a wonderful opportunity to know student leaders from around the country.

After I graduated in June 1947, I led a two-month student tour of Denmark and Czechoslovakia. We crossed the Atlantic on the *Marine Tiger*, a converted cargo ship, and went by train from Paris to Aarhus, Denmark, where we attended the annual conference of International Student Service,[2] which later became World University Service. From that conference grew lifelong friendships with a Dane and a Norwegian.[3] We then went to Prague and toured the country. A few of us returned to Prague to attend IUS's first annual meeting in August. (Another friend from that trip, Dick Heggie, became a national officer on the second NSA staff.) I flew back from Europe just in time to drive out to Madison, Wisconsin, for the exciting prospect of attending the NSA Constitutional Convention, August 30 to September 7.

Becoming NSA's international vice president

I do not remember much about the Madison conference, except that there was a lot of discussion about joining IUS, and discussion of a number of ideas for international programs for American students. Because of IUS, some students were very suspicious of the motives of the founders of NSA, fearing communist involvement. One even proudly told me that he had talked to the FBI in his home city before coming to Madison, just to be sure he'd not be getting into trouble! Others, including me, talked about ways to meet students from other nations and build on the opportunities engendered by the winning of World War II. We agreed to pursue membership in the IUS under carefully specified terms that protected our autonomy, and also endorsed the creation of opportunities for American students to travel abroad. Many of us worked hard to keep the NSA out of political or sectarian hands, by deciding that only student governments would be members of NSA.

Having just come from the meetings in Europe, and speaking at Madison about conditions there, I turned out to be the sole nominee for vice president for international student activities, and was duly elected.

Locating the international office in Cambridge

It was not logic that determined that the international office would be located in Cambridge, Massachusetts, far from Madison, Wisconsin, site of the national headquarters. Rather, it came about as a result of my personal circumstances, and, with the exception of the year 1950-1951, continued until 1960.[4]

Unfortunately, my election, which I had not even contemplated prior to going to Madison, created a serious dilemma for me. It was a tremendous honor to be elected. I looked forward to the work and I wasn't keen to be separated from the other officers. However, I had been admitted to Harvard for graduate work in international relations. My Yale degree had been based on only seven semesters, during five of which one course had been Naval ROTC. I really didn't feel I had had enough education. I was twenty-three and wanted to get on with my studies.

At the end of the NSA convention I sat down with my fellow officers, Bill Welsh, Ralph Dungan, Janis Tremper, and Lee Jones, and discussed my situation. It was agreed that I could start at Harvard half time and open the international office there. I agreed to attend all executive committee meetings during the year, to remain at the meeting sites for additional work as required, and to spend most of the following summer in Madison, helping prepare for the First NSA Congress.

I drove back East with Ralph Dungan and Ted Harris,[5] who had been chosen to head the Pennsylvania region for the coming year. I dropped them off in Philadelphia and continued home to New York City. We shared the driving and didn't stop overnight. Of course, we stopped for meals. I vividly remember a diner in Indiana that refused to serve two whites and a black traveling together. It was a bitter taste of reality in the wake of the euphoria of the Madison convention.

Getting established in Cambridge

I found office space for the first year in a couple of upstairs back rooms in the Hillel Foundation, the campus Jewish organization, in Cambridge. We had enough space for a secretary and myself, and were welcome to use the meeting rooms and mimeograph machine downstairs when necessary. We had a telephone, a couple of typewriters, and a mailing address. I was part time; the secretary, the wife of another Harvard graduate student, was part time; and we had a lot of Harvard, Radcliffe, MIT and Wellesley volunteers. It was crowded. It was hectic. It was exciting!

I took two courses three times a week, and spent the rest of the day in the NSA office. After a quick supper, I went to Widener Library, sat down at a table, put my head on my books, and napped for twenty minutes before beginning to study. I had developed this habit in the Navy when we had on-and-off watches. It came in handy in grad school—and for the rest of my life.

As agreed, I attended the several executive committee meetings in Madison and spent part of the summer of 1948 there. The other officers and I developed close and harmonious relationships, despite my being in Cambridge most of the time. We co-opted Mildred Kiefer as assistant treasurer. She became an integral part of the team. The others were Bill Welsh, of the intense demeanor, whose faith in what we were doing was intense and clear; Ralph Dungan, a warm Irishman with the quick and inquiring Jesuitical mind; and Jan Tremper, whose charms are unforgettable and whose convictions were strong. They made up a wonderful group of colleagues, better than any other group with which I have ever worked.[6]

The international programs

During the international office's first year, in addition to carrying out an enormous amount of correspondence with American students and with student organizations abroad, we published a booklet on work, study and travel opportunities abroad, sponsored a European tour for American students, and made arrangements for a student ship to cross the Atlantic in June and return in September.

The booklet, *Study, Travel, Work Abroad—Summer 1948* (the "work" was mostly nonpaying work camps) was based on an enormous research effort by a group of faithful volunteers in the Cambridge office. We wanted a small, free publication that could be circulated widely to campuses around the country. Our volunteers read and clipped, wrote off for materials, and gathered information in every imaginable way. We published the booklet in the early spring and sent it all over the country. Nothing else like it was then available, and it was an immense success. We felt very proud.[7]

The European Tri-Nation Tour was a low-cost trip that took ninety students to France, the Netherlands, and England for almost two months. We organized it jointly with the national student unions in those three countries, led by the Dutch. The trip was announced in the *NSA News* and in campus papers. We received many more than ninety applications. A selection committee of students and faculty in the Boston area chose the participants. We contracted with a local travel agency to handle ticketing, and used their offices for a lot of the work.

The plans were not without their complications. I continued to joke with Pat Blair, whose mother phoned me that spring to be sure the trip would be safe for her highly embarrassed Wellesley daughter. Pat survived not only that trip but many more interesting international experiences, both as a development professional and as the wife of a National Geographic Society photographer.[8]

The group traveled to Paris, Normandy, and Grenoble in France; studied industry and government in Holland, learned about the Benelux structure, and sailed through the canals of Friesland; then crossed the Channel to England, visited London, Oxford, and Cambridge, and worked in a student harvest camp. A letter that Ralph Lee Smith of Swarthmore wrote to the NSA office read in part:

> In the brief week that I was in Paris I spoke with the following students at the Cité Universitaire: 1) a student from French Indo-China, himself French, whose father owns a coffee plantation; 2) a former Luftwaffe pilot; 3) a student who participated in the student demonstration in Prague at the time of the Czech Communist coup [February 1948], and who subsequently fled from Czechoslovakia after numerous adventures; 4) two boys and a girl who had fought with the Communist EAM forces in Greece; 5) a student who was in both a German concentration camp and an American DP camp; and 6) many students who had worked in the French underground.

Our third major project was to arrange through the Dutch National Student Union for the use of the Dutch ship *Volendam* to take American students, including our Tri-Nation tour group, to Europe and back. About 1,500 students went to and from Europe on the *Volendam* in the summer of 1948. It was a wonderful example of what students can do when they put their minds to a constructive program.[9]

Membership in National Commission for UNESCO

Thanks to some early groundwork by Jim Smith, NCC's President, and Ralph Dungan while he was chair of the Pennsylvania region of the NCC, we had applied for one of the one hundred seats on the U.S. National Commission for UNESCO, a statutory body that planned the means for initiating and carrying out UNESCO programs in the United States.[10] This was a distinguished body, chaired by Milton S. Eisenhower, the President's brother and president of Kansas State University. Its members included prominent members from letters, education, and the arts, as diverse as Archibald MacLeish and Myrna Loy.

It was a great honor for NSA, which had only been established at the beginning of September, to be selected later that same month, at the Commission's meeting in Chicago, for one of its three "youth" seats. As international vice president, I attended the Chicago meeting as an observer. After we were officially selected, I was designated to fill the seat. A year later, I was elected by the Commission to be a member of its executive committee, still representing NSA.

In a report to the NSA executive committee after that first meeting,[11] I said that, prior to NSA's election to the Commission:

> I had been painfully sitting on my hands and keeping a gag in my mouth. That morning they discussed the topic of education for international understanding. I, as a "guest," had no right to talk, but when one of the gentlemen proposed that the program in that field be restricted to text book revision, adult education and professional conferences, I rose. The chairlady recognized me long enough for me to give my name and organization. Someone from the State Department reiterated the rule that guests were not to speak, but the group chose to waive the rule.
>
> I talked to them about the importance of student exchange, travel tours, etc., to the achievement of international understanding. Not only did I get cheers, but was asked to prepare a brief report of several specific projects.
>
> In this report I asked for dissemination of UNESCO information through student and other youth groups, for full information on study opportunities for students from all countries, for student ships between the hemispheres, for travel and study tours, for work camps, seminars and study centers, and for direct exchange with Germany and Japan. They seemed to like my suggestions and agreed to consider them.

We had a fruitful relationship with the National Commission, and our membership added greatly to our prestige among college and university presidents. I was able to promote NSA and UNESCO by speaking to about sixty audiences in a two-year period. During 1949, UNESCO sponsored, and the Carnegie Endowment for International Peace financed, a short publication entitled *Youth and UNESCO*. I had the privilege of being one of its three authors. Rob West succeeded me on the National Commission after two years.

NSA and IUS

A number of essays in this book discuss our relationships with the International Union of Students. The story reflects the early postwar era in world affairs. We were just beginning to face the full implications of the "Iron Curtain" and Stalin's duplicity. In addition, it was heady stuff for students to be "negotiating with the communists."

My involvement was small compared to the roles of Bill Ellis and Jim Smith. It's fun to recall a few vignettes, nonetheless.

In Prague in the summer of 1947, I remember being frightened by the intensity of the Indian delegation on the occasion of the declaration of India's independence from Britain in mid-August. A wild-eyed leader named Dang leapt, danced, and chanted. He later became the head of India's Communist Party.

Also in Prague, I participated in a small negotiating session with Soviet student leaders, dealing with a resolution on U.S.-Soviet student relations. One of them was the Soviet vice president of the IUS, Aleksandr Shelepin, who later became head of the KGB.

And that summer in Prague I met Bill Ellis, who had been named American Vice President in hopes that this would encourage U.S. involvement. He had been part of the 1946 group of twenty-five. He was—and still is—a tremendously thoughtful and impressive person. We have been good friends ever since.

Bill Welsh, Clif Wharton, and I met in Washington in the fall of 1947, a couple of months after the NSA founding congress. Clif, who is black and was the son of a career foreign service officer who later became the first black American career ambassador, was not allowed upstairs at the old Willard Hotel, where Bill was staying. I'm sure Clif remembered that incident many years later when he became Deputy Secretary of State in the first William Clinton administration!

We had an appointment with two State Department officials, who "put us through the wringer" with regard to IUS. They tried emphatically to dissuade NSA from joining. They spoke of the threat of communism, of the naiveté of American students who thought they could stand up to the communists, and of what this would do to NSA's reputation around the country. As I recall, we held our ground, insisting that we weren't naive, and asserting that we were going into this with our eyes open, that we were going to begin by exploring membership and reporting to our next congress before taking any formal action. NSA had further decided that not only would the congress have to approve our membership, but so would at least two-thirds of our member student bodies.

The meeting did shake us a bit.

Then came February 1948, and the Communist coup in Prague. The IUS endorsed the coup, notwithstanding a student demonstration against it. The next day, Jim Smith, serving in Prague in Bill Ellis's place while Bill was recuperating from tuberculosis in Switzerland, called Ellis, who sent a cable to Bill Welsh urging that we condemn the IUS's role and break off relations. Bill issued a press release saying that, under the circumstances, NSA was breaking off all relations with IUS. In what Bill felt to be the urgent necessity to act, he did not consult with me or with the executive committee. I recall feeling that we should have discussed it first, but Bill's judgment was good. We would have been hurt if we had not acted quickly. Many of our constituent colleges would have been shaken if we had waited.[12]

While an investigating team went to Prague the following summer, NSA never joined IUS. We continued our international programs and our activities with individual national student unions and other organizations.

Three years later, an alternative, pro-Western student organization, the International Student Conference, was founded at a conference in Stockholm. I attended as an observer for World University Service. The times had definitely changed. Al Lowenstein, NSA's President that year, gave a ringing anticommunist speech, somewhat "preaching to the choir" and not sounding at all like the protégé he was of Senator Frank Graham, former President of the University of North Carolina and a strong liberal.[13]

Rob West and Erskine Childers, international vice presidents, 1948–1949 and 1949–1950

I cannot possibly do justice to the work that my immediate successors in office did for NSA. But I cannot let this opportunity go by without saluting their memories. Rob West, who succeeded me, died in 1991, and Erskine Childers, who succeeded Rob, died in the summer of 1996. They both began prominent careers as international activities vice presidents of NSA.

Rob and I were at Yale together, where he was also a delegate to NSA conventions and became chair of the Southern New England Region after me. Born in Nebraska, he was a brilliant student and later professor of international economics. He served as U.S. foreign aid mission director and Economic Counselor of the Embassy in the Belgian Congo right after its independence. His dry humor, quick mind, and matter-of-fact way of speaking won him friends everywhere and were immense assets to NSA in the tension-filled international arena in which he served the Association.[14]

Erskine came to NSA from Stanford. He carried the prestige—and the burden—of being the grandson of a famous Englishman of the same name who fought on the side of the Irish against the British in 1916, and the son of yet another Erskine Childers, who was a president of the Irish Republic. Young Erskine was more a dreamer than a revolutionary, but his energy and drive led him to great success with NSA and an illustrious career with the United Nations Development Program. As a touch of fate that linked us, Erskine died giving his maiden speech to the World Federation of United Nations Associations (WFUNA), which had just appointed him Secretary-General. I had served as Acting and Deputy Secretary-General of WFUNA, forty years earlier.[15]

Where NSA led me

A favorite family friend of my parents and grandparents once saw me playing with lead soldiers as a child of about ten. Her father had been the founder of the first international agricultural institute in Rome after World War I, which later became the Food and Agricultural Organization of the United Nations. She said: "Robert, I want you to be a soldier of peace, not of war." I never forgot those words. Notwithstanding my service in World War II, I set out to become a soldier of peace. NSA provided my first opportunity.

From my NSA days forward, the experience of those three years became an integral part of my life. I stayed at Harvard for my master's degree and the coursework on my doctorate. I then went to Geneva for a year with World University Service. While there, I was invited to join the Permanent U.S. Delegation to UNESCO in Paris, a direct result of having served two years as the NSA representative on the U.S. National Commission.

Ten years later, when John F. Kennedy was elected President and Ralph Dungan worked on his White House staff, Ralph helped me get the position I sought with the U.S. Agency for International Development. That, in turn, led to a number of positions in the State Department and eventually to my becoming Ambassador to the Ivory Coast. An NSA delegate named Stanley Greenfield[16] always said that I'd become an ambassador, and he joked about the Robert S. Smith Homburg Fund, for me to have the proper hat to wear when the time came. I never got the homburg—and who wears hats anymore?

My relationship to NSA produced two negative occurrences, neither one NSA's fault. They were "*The China Digest* matter" and the "CIA Connection."

When my tour at UNESCO ended in 1953 due to the U.S. government's first "reduction in force," my first wife and I set out around the world for a year, while I gathered material for my Ph.D. thesis. UNESCO offered me a modest contract to interview returning UNESCO Fellows who had studied abroad. Due to American hysteria about communism, it was required of UNESCO that all Americans being offered contracts of any sort had to have security clearance. Mine never came through, despite the fact that I had just completed a full-time assignment with the U.S. government.

When I returned to the United States in mid-1954, I learned why my clearance hadn't arrived. It seems that, commencing in 1950, after the communists took over Mainland China, they published an English-language monthly entitled *The China Digest* and sent it, unsolicited, to many addressees. One of these was the Cambridge office of NSA. They were so out-of-date that the name they had was mine, even though I had completed my term with NSA in 1948. The FBI had a record of this subscription and so withheld my security clearance until I had an opportunity to confront them and explain.

The second matter involved the CIA's secret funding of NSA, which began after my time with the Association.[17] After the story appeared in the March 1967 issue of *Ramparts* magazine, it was picked up by the national press and served as the subject of a column by James Reston in the February 15, 1967, issue of the *New York Times*. Reston named a number of "former student association officials now with the Government," including Ralph Dungan and me, as having been involved.

Thanks to some quick letter writing to Reston, he published a retraction in the *Times* on March 8, stating:

> I regret that I included in this list Ralph A. Dungan, present U.S. Ambassador to Chile, and Robert S. Smith, special assistant to the Director of the Agency for International Development. This was inaccurate. Both men were NSA officials, not during the CIA's connection with the NSA, but before the intelligence agency provided any funds for the NSA.

Although Ralph took a lot of vituperative criticism from the Chilean communist press, which was anxious to make a case against the then-President of Chile, the teapot tempest died down. I respect James Reston for his retraction.

It was not just coincidence that many good things happened to me after my stint with NSA. The experience, the reputation of NSA in its founding days, the connections, and most of all the inspiration and the dreams we shared, led inexorably in those directions. And I thank God for his spiritual guidance, particularly in my later years, but also when I was barely aware of His existence and His role in my life.

It is a very different world today but, if I had it to do over again, I would still take the path I took then. And I would not hesitate to recommend it to any young person growing up at this time. My studies were important to me. I am glad I have the degrees I earned. But the life-lessons came from the so-called extracurricular activities, NSA, the travel experiences, and the people I met. Thank you, group of twenty-five who went to Prague in the summer of 1946. You helped set my life on a critical path.

Robert Solwin Smith was Ambassador to the Ivory Coast, Senior Staffer for Africa and United Nations Affairs at the National Security Council, and Vice President of the Overseas Private Investment Corporation.

END NOTES

[1] *Editor's note:* In the absence of a student government, the three-man delegation was selected from among student applicants by a Board consisting of Rev. Luther Tucker, Prof. Ralph Turner, Wallace F. Doerr, and Curtis Farrar (*Yale News,* December 10, 1946).

[2] *Editor's note:* See pp. 50, 56 for more on the ISS. In addition to Smith and Heggie (UC Berkeley), a number of other students who figured prominently in NSA's founding were in attendance, including Douglas Cater and Francis Fisher, both of Harvard.

[3] Knut Sverre, the Norwegian, became President of the Norwegian NUS and attended the 1950 Stockholm Conference. He later entered the Norwegian diplomatic service and served as DCM in Washington as well as Ambassador to Iran and Belgium. Christian Maersk, the Dane, became a UN intern the year after Aarhus and spent the whole summer in the States.

SMITH COLLEGE SCAN ASSOCIATED NEWS

Bob Smith Gives Cause For NSA Withdrawal from IUS

"International Union of Students should be limited to strict student activity without political tendencies; at present the whole trend is towards partisan political lines," states Bob Smith, Vice-President of NSA, in charge of international affairs.

On his recent visit to Smith to speak to the students who are going abroad this year, Mr. Smith was questioned on the thorny problem of NSA's recent withdrawal of negotiations for affiliations with IUS, and upheld the action of NSA saying that they were thoroughly justified in their action because the behaviour of the IUS secretariat conflicted so flatly with NSA's principles against political affiliation. He declared that "a large majority of the executive committee of IUS is communist, most particularly the members from Great Britain, Czechoslovakia, and the eastern European countries. The final example of their biased point of view was in Prague when IUS supported the action committees that disbanded the Prague and Czech Unions of Students. They failed to condemn academic discrimination in the first clear instance in which that discrimination was practiced by the left wing, where in past instances they had taken action against discrimination stemming from the right wing.

Mr. Smith suggested that students remember that NSA was never actually affiliated with IUS, but had only begun negotiations for affiliations. When questioned about the future recommencement of negotiations, he said that they might be begun again "provided there was a change in the international situation and in the executive committee membership." He believed that any connection between the two organizations now would only add to the tension between them, and hinder NSA's original purpose of bringing foreign and American students closer together.

4/23/48

IUS AFFILIATION ISSUE STIMULATED WIDE DEBATE ON US CAMPUSES. Top: Bob Smith (right front) debates affiliation during a break at NSA's 1947 Constitutional Convention. To his right is Bill Welsh (Berea College), soon to be elected NSA's first President. The 4/23/48 issue of Smith College (MA) *Scan* reports on Smith's campus visit when he explained NSA's decision to suspend affiliation efforts after the Communist coup in Czechoslovakia early that year. (NSA photo courtesy Clif Wharton)

[4] *Editor's note::* During the 1950-1951 year, the international office was moved to the national offices in Madison, Wisconsin. See Eisenberg, p. 521, for a review of the 1950-1951 year. The international office remained in Cambridge until 1960, when it was consolidated with the national office in Philadelphia. NSA's travel office was moved to New York City in 1951, where it was incorporated as Educational Travel, Inc. See Garland, p. 641, and Callahan, p. 673.

[5] Ted Harris, a Black student at LaSalle College in Philadelphia, was elected as President of NSA the following year.

[6] See essays by Janis Tremper (Dowd), Bill Welsh and Mildred Kiefer (Wurf) and interviews with Ralph Dungan and Lee Jones elsewhere in this book.

[7] *Editor's note:* This booklet was published in annual editions for many years after it first appeared and remained one of NSA's best-selling and most popular publications. See p. 676.

[8] See comments by Pat Wohlgemuth Blair, p. 650.

[9] *Editor's note:* This travel program, which was first established in NSA's Cambridge office, became one of NSA's most popular offerings and eventually led to the formation of a separately incorporated travel office in New York City. See Section 2 following.

[10] Since the U.S. government withdrew from UNESCO some years ago, the National Commission has ceased to exist.

[11] *NSA News,* 11/48, see p. 510.

[12] See Welsh essay, p. 170.

[13] See Eisenberg essay, p. 522, Stockholm story, p. 527, and Lowenstein speech, p. 562.

[14] See additional West biography, p. 516.

[15] See additional Childers biography, p. 519.

[16] See Greenfield essay, p. 155.

[17] *Editor's note:* See Welsh et al., p. 565, for a discussion of the CIA's covert Cold War funding of NSA's international program (which began in early 1952), and the international programs of other American nongovernment agencies.

PICTURE CREDITS: *Then:* NSA Constitutional Convention, University of Wisconsin, September, 1947 (*NSA Photo,* Wharton). Now: c. 2000 (Author).

ROBERT SOLWIN SMITH

Early Background and Military Service: Raised in New York City. Commissioned officer, U.S. Navy, Pacific Theater, 1943-46.

Education: A.B., Yale University, 1947, International Relations. M.A., Harvard University, 1949, Government. Ph.D., Harvard University, 1956, Government.

Career highlights: 1990-93: President, Washington National Cathedral Association. 1979-91: President, Robert Solwin Smith Associates, consulting on Africa. 1977-79: Vice President for Development, U.S. Overseas Private Investment Corporation (OPIC). 1976-77: Senior Staff Member for African and UN Affairs, National Security Council. 1974-76: U.S. Ambassador to Ivory Coast. 1969-74: Deputy Assistant Secretary for African Affairs, U.S. State Department. 1967-69: Deputy (and Acting) Assistant Administrator for Africa, U.S. Agency for International Development (USAID). 1961-67: Various positions in USAID and U.S. State Department. 1956-61: Deputy (and Acting) Secretary-General, World Federation of United Nations Associations, Geneva, Switzerland. 1951-53: Deputy U.S. Permanent Representative to UNESCO, Paris, France.

Awards: Phi Beta Kappa, Yale, 1947. Superior Honor Award, USAID, 1969. Grand Officier de l'Ordre National, Ivory Coast, 1976.

Family: Formerly married to Sally L. Smith. Married since 1973 to Anne Lee Smith. Children: Randall Alan (b. 1956), Nicholas Lee (b. 1957), Gary Gordon (b. 1960).

"In the Minds of Men the Defenses of Peace Must be Constructed"

Preamble *to the* CONSTITUTION *of the* UNITED NATIONS EDUCATIONAL, SCIENTIFIC and CULTURAL Organization

THE GOVERNMENTS OF THE STATES PARTIES TO THIS CONSTITUTION ON BEHALF OF THEIR PEOPLES DECLARE

that since wars begin in the minds of men, it is in the minds of men that the defences of peace must be constructed;

that ignorance of each other's ways and lives has been a common cause, throughout the history of mankind, of that suspicion and mistrust between the peoples of the world through which their differences have all too often broken into war;

that the great and terrible war which has now ended was a war made possible by the denial of the democratic principles of the dignity, equality and mutual respect of men, and by the propagation, in their place, through ignorance and prejudice, of the doctrine of the inequality of men and races;

that the wide diffusion of culture, and the education of humanity for justice and liberty and peace are indispensable to the dignity of man and constitute a sacred duty which all the nations must fulfill in a spirit of mutual assistance and concern;

that a peace based exclusively upon the political and economic arrangements of governments would not be a peace which could secure the unanimous, lasting and sincere support of the peoples of the world, and that the peace must therefore be founded, if it is not to fail, upon the intellectual and moral solidarity of mankind.

STUDENT PARTICIPATION IN UNESCO'S RELIEF ASSISTANCE PROGRAM is the subject at this meeting in Florence, Italy, in May 1950. From left: UNESCO's Bernard Drzewieski, Ernest Howell, member of U.S. Delegation; Robert Smith, former NSA Int'l V.P., '47-48; and Edric Weld (Harvard '48) (Hoover Institution Archives)

The Harvard Crimson 4/23/48

NSA Sends Grad Student To UNESCO Parley Today

When the 100-man United States Commission for UNESCO (U.N. Educational, Scientific and Cultural Organization) begins its annual session today in the Copley Plaza Hotel, Robert Smith 2G will take part on a full voting basis as the representative of the National Student Association.

Smith won the commission seat one year ago at the time of his election to an NSA vice-presidency. Last month the NSA Madison Convention renamed him for the coming UNESCO term and the commission's nominating committee promptly

NSA News 11/48

Smith Begins First of a Series

UNESCO Program Effective

(Note—This is the first in a series of reports on the activities of the National Commission for UNESCO which will be written by Robert S. Smith, the NSA representative on that body. Mr. Smith was elected, during the recent commission meeting in Boston, to serve on the Executive Committee, a signal honor for the commission's youngest member.)

By Robert S. Smith

The recent meeting of the U. S. National Commission for UNESCO, held in Boston in late September, seemed to me to be significantly better than the previous meetings which I had attended. I left it with a definite feeling that UNESCO is really beginning to roll, and is carrying out an effective program.

Much of UNESCO's program has a direct bearing on the work that NSA is doing. I have picked out a number of items, both from the recommendations for the international program, and from the recommendations for activities in the U. S., that show this interrelationship.

BEIRUT CONFERENCE

First, some of the recommendations that will be considered at the General Conference in Beirut, Lebanon, this month and next.

1. Approval of UNESCO's emphasis on the "stimulation, coordination, evaluation, and dissemination of information about (international voluntary) work camps."

2. Encouraging the UNESCO to act as a stimulator of fellowships through the determination of needs and resources; and reemphasizing UNESCO's role in developing "means for overcoming the barriers to interchange."

3. Recommendation that UNESCO "initiate a study of the most effective short term projects of interchange, such as summer schools, seminars, study tours, work camps, etc."

4. Praising the seminar method education, and encouraging UNESCO to plan for more for the coming years (including one on and of youth leaders).

5. Approving of the progress in the study of tensions affecting international understanding, and encouraging UNESCO to make full use of the resources of the universities in this work.

NSA'S CONTRIBUTIONS

Here are several of the U. S. program activities in which NSA is making, and can continue to make, a decisive contribution.

1. "That the National Commission again go on record as giving Reconstruction first priority among UNESCO projects in the U. S." (This is important to stress in WSSF campaigns this fall.)

2. Gratitude for work organizations have done this past year in educational reconstruction, and urging that "these projects be continued and expanded during the coming year." Besides material aid, "particular emphasis should be given to fellowships and study grants —work camps and seminars."

3. "The National Commission notes with hearty approval the promising new approaches to reconstruction being developed by local and national organizations, such as the suggestion of the NSA that a Friendship Train for Educational Reconstruction be organized . . . " (This will be implemented if enough support can be obtained from other organizations.)

4. "That the National Commission call attention to the close relationship between practical reconstruction projects and the development of international understanding by affording an opportunity for direct participation in international activities by millions of Americans in all walks of life." (WSSF.)

5. Attention called "to the need for cheap and adequate transportation in order to facilitate programs for interchange, and urging that this be made the subject of investigation by the government."

6. An inventory is to be made of all organizations, and the various types of interchange of persons, with which they work.

7. To work with the Advisory Committee on the Smith-Mundt Act for educational exchange.

8. To get the U. S. Government to "examine its policy regarding the . . . obstacles preventing foreign students from coming to the U. S."

9. To publicize, as well as endorse, projects carried on by voluntary organizations, which are in accordance with the principles of UNESCO, and are considered to be particularly meritorious. (Here is a big opportunity for NSA!)

10. To stimulate the projects of cultural interchange—such as Art Exhibits, etc.

11. "That cooperating volunteer agencies make concrete and practical their relationship to the **social tensions projects** by examining the functioning of their own programs with regard to group tensions in the U. S."

12. "The (Commission) approves with hearty appreciation the Foreign Students Summer Project at MIT, as carrying out the objectives of UNESCO, and recommends that other institutions carry on similar projects."

YOUTH PARTICIPATION

Reference to the importance of the participation of youth in the program of UNESCO was continually made during the course of the meetings. An indication of the seriousness of the National Commission, in encouraging the participation of youth, was my election to the Executive Committee.

The most effective work that NSA can do to support the program of UNESCO is a continuation and expansion of projects and activities in the international field — relief, exchanges of students, exchanges of exhibits, publications, and correspondence, and the encouragement of education for international understanding in the classroom and clubroom.

DISCRIMINATION AND ACADEMIC FREEDOM

NSA can also contribute significantly to the easing of tensions by continued work in the fields of discrimination and academic freedom. To quote Archibald MacLeish (in a formal report on "UNESCO in a Divided World"): **"UNESCO in executing its program should direct its energies as fully and as immediately as possible toward the restoration of that sense of common humanity, of a common human experience, which makes it possible for men who differ to regard each other, still, as men."** NSA's endorsement and carrying out of work along those lines will be the best way of contributing to the work of UNESCO.

9/29/47

Robert Smith, 1947, To Represent NSA In United States Commission

On September 12, the United States Commission for UNESCO approved the application of the National Student Association for one of the three seats reserved on the Commission for student organizations.

The NSA, which recently adjourned its constitutional convention, is expected to be represented on UNESCO by Robert Smith, 1947, newly elected vice president in charge of international activities.

Approximately 96 student groups throughout the country applied for seats at the United States Commission meeting held in Chicago from September 11 through 13. Approval by the Commission was subject to ratification by the State Department and the American Delegation to the UN.

Addresses Group

Besides his presentation of the NSA platform and program to the subcommission in charge of the allocation of the three seats to student groups, Smith received special recognition at plenary session of the entire Commission in order that he might report the condition of students abroad. Having just returned from Europe, where he attended the annual International Student Service convention, Smith spoke at length on the needs of students attending colleges and universities on the continent.

Early Years of UNESCO Helped NSA Focus Global Programs

UNESCO's vision of a world in harmony appealed to U.S. students' idealism. National Commission membership provided NSA a forum through which it was able to advance the programs of student exchange, relief and technical assistance which it supported.

The Harvard Student Council International Activities Committee (1946-1952)

2. NSA's "State Department"

Francis D. Fisher
Harvard University
Chairman, International Activities Committee
Harvard University Student Council, 1947

When I returned to Harvard in September 1946 after two years in the Navy, the University was optimistic and international in outlook. A great coalition of nations had just won the war. Together with our partners, America was helping rebuild a devastated Europe. American students were sending food and books to foreign universities.

It was therefore natural for the Harvard Student Council to have an International Activities Committee. I was its chairman. We were the center of the Harvard foreign student relief effort, and we sought ways for American students to go to Europe. In 1947, when the University would not officially support the establishment in Salzburg of a program of American studies for European students intellectually isolated by war, the Harvard Salzburg Seminar was legitimized as a Student Council project (to the irritation of the administration).

Our committee worked closely with Douglass Cater, the Harvard student who had been one of the twenty-five American students attending the International Union of Students (IUS) Congress in the summer of 1946. In the fall, when Doug could not attend the follow-on meeting of the "Prague 25" in New York to consider how American students might better organize themselves, I went as substitute and passed on information we had collected.[1]

At the Chicago Student Conference in December 1946, student delegates made arrangements to convene a constitutional convention in the fall of 1947 for the organization that would become NSA. The Conference designated the Harvard Student Council to act in the interim as a clearinghouse of information on international student activities. In that capacity, we published several issues of a *Students International Activities Bulletin,*[2] reporting on foreign student relief efforts, foreign travel possibilities, and the developing U.S. role in world student affairs, which we distributed widely to American campuses.[3]

The Harvard students engaged in these activities acquired significant expertise in them and established an effective network of communication with international organizations and foreign student groups. Some fifteen to twenty Harvard students made international student activities their major extracurricular activity, many of them continuing in the international field for many years. This Harvard-based resource was so useful that for many years after NSA established its headquarters in Madison, Wisconsin, NSA's Vice Presidents for International Affairs, Bob Smith, Rob West, Erskine Childers, and Herb Eisenberg, had their office in Cambridge and relied on the continuing cadre of Harvard volunteers.[4]

When NSA established a Student Travel Program, it became part of the Cambridge-based operation. NSA organized student tours abroad and participation in student work camps operated by foreign student organizations. The NSA travel office worked with the Netherlands Office for Foreign Student Relations (NBBS) to charter the Dutch ship *Volendam* from the Holland America Line, for student travel. In 1950, the NBBS representative, Jos Vos, worked out of the NSA Cambridge office for six months, sharing a house with some of our group.[5]

NSA, IUS, and the Third World

NSA at its outset sought ways to establish relationships with the International Union of Students (IUS).[6] The IUS, although initiated largely by Communist-inclined student movements, had its headquarters in Czechoslovakia, at that time still a democracy. At that time noncommunist student movements, such as the NSA, were free to express themselves. Bill Ellis, the first NSA representative to the IUS, was a graduate student at Harvard, and we provided him his home base.[7]

After the 1948 Soviet coup in Czechoslovakia and the heightening of East-West tensions, as shown by the Iron Curtain and the Berlin blockade, the IUS increasingly became simply a tool of Soviet foreign policy. Using the rallying cry of "antifascism" as an umbrella under which to gather students of the world, IUS particularly targeted the small, but important, student movements that were springing to life in the newly independent countries of Asia and Africa.

Many of us who were concerned with international student relations believed that NSA should develop direct contacts with these student groups of the Third World. Our Harvard-NSA office undertook an active program of correspondence with such groups and their leaders. However, it was difficult at a distance to identify student organizations accurately, and even more difficult at a distance to assess them and their leaders.[8]

NSA traveling representatives

In the summer of 1950, James Grant, then a Harvard law student and one of our group (later, and for many years, head of UNICEF), was given a summer job in Taiwan in agricultural development. At the end of his summer job, he was able to spend a few weeks visiting student groups in Indonesia, Burma, Indochina, Burma, Hong Kong, Malaya, and Thailand.

That same summer, I traveled to Europe on the *Volendam*, helping run the orientation program for the 1,400 students aboard. In Europe, I spent the summer on behalf of NSA in Yugoslavia, which had just broken from the Soviet-dominated Cominform. With the help of the National Union of Yugoslav Students, I visited all the universities and eased the way for NSA touring and work camp groups that passed through Yugoslavia.

In 1951, a Harvard graduate student, Melvin Conant, continued the visits to Southeast Asia. In 1952, I spent six months there traveling from university to university, from Manila to Kabul, talking to student leaders, appraising student conditions, and laying plans for cooperation.

Notes from my traveler's journal

In some countries I visited, we knew nothing of student conditions, for instance, in East Pakistan. Arriving at Dacca with my packsack and rolled-up mosquito net and no information, I hopped into a pedicab and asked for the "university," not knowing where it might be. I was taken there, and in a cafe I easily fell into conversation with students. I essentially asked them to "take me to your leader." After explaining to the head of the student union my NSA status and mission, housing was arranged in one of the dorms for the several days of my stay.

In Indonesia, through the groundwork laid by Grant and Conant and our follow-up letters, we knew the student groups and their leaders. I spent most of a month sharing the dormitory room of Subroto, then President of the PPMI, the Indonesian national union of students. (Subroto became Indonesia's Minister of Petroleum and later Executive Director of OPEC.)

Here are some excerpts from my final report to NSA on the 1952 trip to Southeast Asia, which indicate the sort of information we were collecting:

> *Indonesia*
>
> After five weeks in Indonesia I am glad that I can report that in my opinion the NSA has been following the best possible program in relation to the Indonesian student movement. The ease with which I moved into the student community (physically for the last three weeks) is a sign of the success of the two previous visits of NSA representatives and the good handling of our relations with the PPMI (correspondence, the *Bulletin* and the trip of Dahlan to Edinburgh). Dick Hafner's period of study in Jogja has contributed to the general good relations between American student organizations and those of Indonesia. Today, the student leaders, especially of the PPMI, have had personal experience of a pleasant sort with American student leaders. Assistance has been accepted from the NSA without unpleasant results. NSA is looked to as an active friend, much interested in the life and problems of students in Indonesia.
>
> *University of Malay, Singapore*
>
> The student body of the University is drawn from the upper middle class and the upper class, predominately Chinese and Indian groups. Students who come from Singapore live at home, while the dormitories are occupied by the students from "up-country." The feeling of belonging to the university community is stronger among this latter group and extracurricular activities are engaged in more actively by them. A strong Student Union governs student life, administers the sports program, and concerns itself with the welfare of students. Its annual budget currently runs at about $12,000, of which students pay two-thirds and the university one-third.
>
> *India—The National Union of Students*
>
> NUS of India is not a dying organization. It has not been active nationally and failed last year to hold its annual congress, but it has firm roots in the Bombay area, including Poona and Baroda, and good friends among the student leaders in the U.P. universities: Lucknow, Allahabad and Benares. The President, A. Shelat, has just toured these centers as well as Delhi and Agra. He is now about to set out on a tour of Mysore, Hyderabad and Madras, where NUS does not have much hold. The present method of operation is that unions join each year. No tradition is established yet, so tremendous energy must constantly be exerted to maintain the present membership.

The letters I sent back to Cambridge often asked for specific follow-up on promises I had made of information or contacts. We had a workshop/conference in the planning stage, to be held in Southeast Asia, at which students would share their experiences in meeting their problems through student initiatives. While we did not succeed in bringing that to pass, we were able to fund at least one trip for Dahlan, an Indonesian student leader, to visit Europe. NSA also sent representatives to the Middle East and to Central and South America.

These NSA bilateral contacts with foreign student movements were compatible with a new international non-IUS effort to be in touch with students throughout the world. Under the leadership of Olof Palme, then head of the Swedish National Union of Students (later the martyred Prime Minister of Sweden), a Student Mutual Assistance Program was formed, not to be in direct opposition to IUS, but to achieve practical forms of international student cooperation that IUS did not address. Former NSA President Bill Dentzer was designated in 1952 to work with this Program. The two of us conferred briefly in the Netherlands as I was returning from Southeast Asia. The decision to send Bill on this job represented an NSA policy conclusion that the Cambridge-based foreign activities had been on track.[9]

With so many different sorts of student organizations active throughout the world, knowing about them involved learning things that American students generally did not know. To help NSA leaders understand the international student world, the NSA International Office conducted a summer training program in Cambridge for a number of years to provide NSA leaders with information on foreign students and student organizations.

Funding the Harvard/NSA International Program

The Harvard Student Council was accustomed to raising funds for its activities. The Harvard Salzburg Seminar was funded by contributions from many sources. The Rockefeller Foundation funded a seminar for German student leaders that was arranged by the Harvard Student Council and held in Germany during several summers in the early 1950s. The Rockefeller Foundation also funded trips by student representatives to the Near East and elsewhere and, I believe, paid for Melvin Conant's trip.

My own trip was supported by money that came through George Franklin of the Council on Foreign Relations. The funds for the later summer training program held in Cambridge to provide NSA leaders with information on foreign student movements were mostly provided by the Foundation for Youth and Student Affairs. When I asked John Simons, an early participant in NSA who ran the Foundation, where its money came from, he told me it came mostly from two enlightened Catholic families, the Graces and the Cavanaughs. This was plausible. John had been a leading Catholic student leader, and I had understood that some such source had supported some of the delegates to IUS in 1946.[10]

Imagine my surprise in 1967 when I read accounts published, first in *Ramparts* magazine, then in the *New York Times*, and eventually everywhere, revealing that much of the funding for NSA's international program had, for many years, originated with the Central Intelligence Agency![11]

To this day I am not sure whether or not that source indirectly provided any of the funding for my trip to Southeast Asia. Three things strike me about the "CIA connection": that the CIA shared NSA's view that student groups in the Third World were important; that no effort was made to influence NSA in its policies; and that the CIA foolishly continued this program on so large a scale, for so long, that secrecy would inevitably be compromised. My view up to 1967 was that the CIA was competent, but reactionary. As it turned out, however, I had it backward.

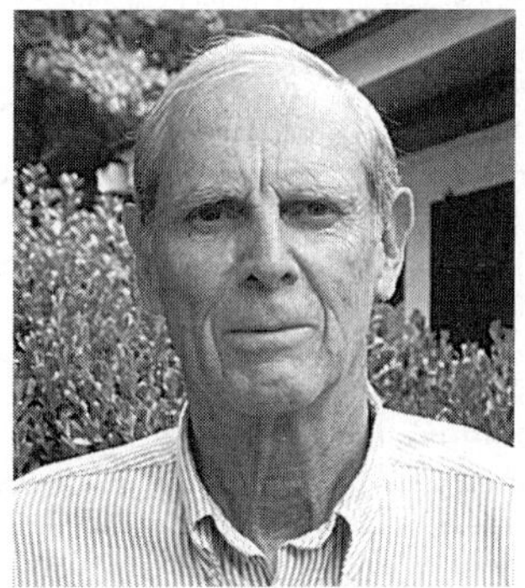

Francis Dummer Fisher is a Senior Research Fellow at the LBJ School of Public Affairs, University of Texas. He has been Assistant General Counsel at the U.S. Agency for International Development, a Fellow at the JFK School of Government, and Senior Fellow and Director, Education and Technology at the Urban Institute.

END NOTES

[1] See references to Douglass Cater in the unit on the Prague delegation, Part I, Section 1, and his role at the 1946 Chicago Student Conference, p. 113. See also, Cater, *Collapse of Youth's One World*, p. 535.

[2] See p. 118.

[3] See Rice, p. 836.

[4] Smith (1947-48) and West (1948-49) were from Yale University, Childers (1949-50) was from Stanford University and Eisenberg (1950-51) was from MIT. See Smith essay, p. 504, and Eisenberg essay, p. 520.

[5] See NSA's travel programs, p. 639, including the essay by Jos Vos, p. 651. The *Volendam* was first chartered in summer 1948. NSA's first summer tour groups (in 1947) traveled on the Holland America Line's *Kote Inten*. See "The Ships," p. 669.

[6] See Part I, Section 1. See also p. 538 for the IUS story.

[7] See more on Bill Ellis, pp. 106, 130, 158, 188.

[8] In addition to the initiatives sponsored by the Harvard Committee, the NSA in the summer of 1950, under NSA International Vice President Erskine Childers and President Robert Kelly also initiated an unusually broad-based and valuable program of international representation. The latter team, as well as Fisher, Grant, Conant, and, later, Herbert Eisenberg and Helen Jean Rogers, issued reports on their travels that offer a rare record of, and insight into, postwar student conditions and student organi-

zations in Asia, Africa, Europe, and Latin America. For a description of these reports, see p. 609, in this Section. Record copies can be found in the NSA archives at the Hoover Institution. Frank Fisher has contributed another set for this project, which will be held in the NSA archives at the Wisconsin State Historical Society.

[9] See discussions of the development of SMAP and the formation of Cosec in the essays by Joan Long Lynch, p. 273, Herbert Eisenberg, pp. 522, 526, 635, and William Dentzer, p. 301.

[10] Regarding the Catholic delegates to the 1946 World Student Congress, see "Operation University," p. 739, Kirchner, p. 76, and McLaughlin, p. 84.

FRANK FISHER IN ASIA

Frank Fisher, NSA representative, with three leaders of the PPMI (National Union of Students of Indonesia) photographed here in Jakharta, Indonesia, during Mr. Fisher's trip (*NSA News* 3/53).

[11] See "Covert U.S. Government Funding of NSA International Programs," p. 565.

PICTURE CREDITS: *Then:* c. 1948 *Now:* c. 2000 (Both by author).

FRANCIS DUMMER FISHER

Background, Military Service, and Education: Born in Winnetka, Illinois, 1926. Military service, U.S. Navy, 1944-46. Education, A.B., Harvard College, 1947. J.D., Harvard Law School, 1951.

Career: 1952-62: General practice of law, Chicago. 1962-66: U.S. Agency for International Development (USAID), Assistant General Counsel for Far East (1962-65). Deputy Director of Mission, Bogota, Colombia (1965-66). 1967-71: U.S. Department of Housing and Urban Development (HUD), Regional Director, Midwest, Chicago (1967-70); Special Assistant to Secretary of HUD (1971). 1972-77: Harvard University, Fellow, Institute of Politics, JFK School of Government (1972). 1972–77: Director, Office of Career Services and Off-Campus Learning. 1977-83: Haverford College: Henry R. Luce Professor of Ethics and the Professions. 1984-86: The Urban Institute: Senior Fellow and Director, Education and Technology. 1991–Present: University of Texas, LBJ School of Public Affairs: Visiting Scholar (1991–93); Senior Research Fellow (1993–present). Principal interests: public policies pertaining to electronic telecommunications.

Editor's note: In a letter to this editor correcting my misspelling of his middle name, Frank Fisher noted: "Dummer is an old New England name. Three Dummers graduated from Harvard before 1700."

The NSA News — March, 1953

Asian Students Emphasize Social Welfare Programs

By FRANK FISHER

The Rural Service League at Madras Christian College is one of many student welfare groups which are springing up at the colleges and universities of India and Pakistan. These groups are proving that students can take a direct and active part in doing something about their country's problems. Students can go into the villages and work on the great problems of health, illiteracy, and agricultural development.

A group of students from the University of California at Los Angeles during their visit to India, summer, 1952, worked with Indian students on one of these projects. The Americans were living with Indian students at Madras Christian College and expected to stay one week. Then some students at the college who had formed Rural Service League showed the UCLA students the village nearby which the Indian students had adopted.

In this village the Rural Service League had built a school and had arranged for a teacher to come and teach the children who were without any school.

Students at St. Xavier's College in Calcutta have formed a Student Relief Society, which works on the distribution of grains in famine-struck villages of Bengal.

In Karachi, there is a Students Welfare Organization with hundreds of members. This group recently ran a Book Collection Week, collecting from graduating students and members of the community over 2,000 books for distribution to needy students.

In Madras there are a number of colleges with student welfare organizations. One of the oldest is that at Queen Mary's College which has an active improvement program operating in a nearby slum area. Schools and vocational training courses are provided for the children and youth of the slum. So many colleges in Madras are active in welfare work that a movement is underway to form a Madras Student Welfare League, to which each of the organizations would belong and which could work on certain city-wide social problems.

Student groups in India and Pakistan have in the past been mainly the student division of one of the political parties or Unions. Now there are developing these students welfare groups which have a constructive program in which students actually contribute their time and energies toward solving some of their problems and the problems of the community in which they live.

The NSA News — April, 1953

Frank Fisher, Student Representative, Discusses Language Problems Faced by South Asian Institutions

By FRANK FISHER

When I tell people that I have just returned from visiting with the university students of South and Southeast Asia, I am frequently asked, "How did you talk to the students; what language did you use?" The answer of course is that I used English. English is the language of instruction at most colleges and universities in Pakistan, India, Burma, Malaya, and the Philippines. In general it is much easier for the English-speaking person to travel in Asia than in Europe. At the same time the people of Asia are able to communicate among themselves. At meetings of the United Nations commissions for Asia and the Far East no interpreters are needed. In what way then is there any "language problem."

The problem is that mass education must be in the native language of the people. A child can not learn well at school if his education is isolated within the school house, if he can not talk to his par- [illegible] school.

The colonization of Asia brought about a rapid development of education, but the language used in the schools was that of the imperial power, and education was seperated from the common man. With independence there is naturally a strong desire to use the native language as the medium of instruction.

But which language? There is no one national language in Pakistan, India, Malaya, Philippines, or Indonesia. Burmese is a literary language and needs much development before it can transmit the ideas of modern science and technology. The designation of national languages is being attempted in Pakistan (Urdu), India (Hindi) and the Philippines (Tagalog). But there is usually opposition to the idea of making one language (Bahasa Indonesia), different in some ways from any of the country's natural languages, is being successfully synthesized. Already instruction at one of the two [illegible] being carried on in this medium.

(Frank Fisher visited Indonesia, Burma, India, Pakistan, the Philippines and other countries of Asia during 1952 as a representative of the National Student Association. In these countries he was in contact with a wide variety of student groups and especially with National Unions of students.

The above article is the second of a series for the NSA News.)

But these national languages will also be "foreign" to many students in the countries in which they are to be used. UNESCO experts state that the language used in the first few years of school should be the language of the child's home. The first four years of education will probably be in the vernacular rather than the national language and English as foreign languages.

Why English? English not only plays an enormous role in unifying countries made up of diverse language groups (a role which can only gradually be assumed by national languages), but is also the language of foreign relations and international business. But most important to the students, English is a language needed by all students who will study past the first years of college. Just as technical students at the time of the first World War needed German, so today students of the technical sciences need English. Translation is not a realistic alternative to learning the language. The vast production of current technical journals in such fields as medicine, engineering, anthropology, appearing in English can not be translated into different languages within the forseeable future. This is a problem which exists as much for the student at Copenhagen as it does for the student at Delhi or Rangoon.

For the educator in Asia this situation presents a complicated problem. At the very time when he is increasing the use of native languages, and is developing a national language, he must make sure that the students reaching graduate levels of study command a good knowledge of English.

We must, and we shall, bring these people out of the concentration camps of Germany.

3. Robert L. West: A Special Responsibility

Yale University
Chair, Connecticut-Rhode Island Region, 1947-48. Vice President, International Affairs, 1948-49

Editor's note: He was a gunnery and demolition officer who returned from the Navy profoundly moved in conscience by his World War II experiences. Building on the professionalism and sensitivity in approaching foreign affairs established by his predecessor, Bob Smith, as a requisite to holding an NSA international vice-presidency, Rob West added the integrity of his own passionate stamp in the puruit of international understanding and the eradication of intolerance.

In an address to the Metropolitan New York Region's city-wide International Students Day commemoration at CCNY on November 19, 1948, which West entitled "Vive en Pace," he broached "the awful urgency with which we face the question of international student cooperation today . . . provided by consideration of the terrifying position in which the United States finds itself today. The United States may no longer be considered a balanced or balancing power in the scale of world politics, but exists as one of two great protagonists. . . ."

Bob Meagher (then a Met NY Region officer from CCNY), his colleague at Tufts University and a friend for 45 years, remembered West for his "imposing presence, deep well modulated voice, and his reputation for rigorous scholarship" who was also a "public international citizen, a warm, wise and understanding human being who dedicated his life to making this a more humane world." (See Meagher, Section 5.)

His was a voice heard and listened to during his years of leadership in NSA. Following are excerpts from two of his editorials in NSA News *during his service on the national staff.*

For Displaced Persons: A New Home and a New Hope in America

Originally entitled "A Realistic DP Program," NSA News 11/48

The fight against Nazism among the students of the World must go on for the eradication of all traces of the Hitler philosophy.

In Germany, American students must meet a special responsibility in redirecting the educational processes away from a system created by Hitler, and in assisting the German students to find their way back into the society of respectable and respected nations.

Also in Germany as in Austria and Italy, American students must lead the way in eliminating another legacy of Hitler . . . the existence of students living in Displaced Persons camps.

In the forefront directing American students toward the assumption of these responsibilities will be the NSA committees. Through their international activities, NSA colleges can now act to meet these responsibilities.

Judged in the simplest terms of humanity, the job of salvaging the human lives which stood condemned by Hitler, the job of restoring hope and health and opportunity to those students who have suffered the extreme measures of degradation to which Nazism was capable of dragging its human victims, the job of restoring the DP students into homes and schools is one which commends itself with the strongest moral and intellectual compulsion. We only may regret that the present DP Act, Public Law 774, appears to discriminate against the entry of many victims.

This is not a project which NSA can take or leave alone; we **must** help these students by placing them again in the educational community of which we are a part, or the wastage of human life and the despoiling of the human mind which is the heritage of Hitler will lie as our responsibility as well.

WE MUST, AND WE SHALL, bring these people out of the concentration camps of Germany in which they still exist, and give them a new home and a new hope in America.

NSA's 'Foreign Policy' — *NSA News* 1/49

To Defeat Intolerance and Dogmatism

IN THE REPORT OF THE UNESCO General Conference . . . the recently elected Director General of UNESCO Sr. Torres Bodet identifies intolerance as the deadly threat to the fundamental principles of human civilization and calls on men of good will to fight against intolerance in order to defeat enmity and discord, the legacies of war. Sr. Torres Bodet's message has, I believe, a specific relevance to the "foreign policy" of the [NSA].

THREATS TO HUMAN CIVILIZATION are often identified as bacteriological warfare, the explosive release of atomic energy, V2 rockets and so on, but none, in my opinion, compare with the awful and corrosive threat of dogmatism in men's thinking, intolerance in human relations, and the messianic complex which drives little men and great nations into crusades for the conversion of civilization into the pattern of their peculiar prejudices. Intolerance, prejudice and dogmatism, whether cast in the terms of a race, religion, or a political dogma constitute the great and final threat to the full and peaceful development of a community of man, and to our very lives.

ON THE CAMPUS, too often, intolerance and dogmatism are reflected in patterns of political intolerance and racial or religious discrimination. In the international affairs of students, intolerance and dogmatism find outlets in the search for the single, "simple solution," with the messianic aggressiveness, implying divine clairvoyance, which threatens the basic principles of international student cooperation and understanding.

THE SINGLE PRINCIPLE on which the "foreign policy" of NSA is based is "to promote international understanding and fellowship" among all the students of the world. It implies a faith in the belief that the decisions of good and evil, and of war and peace, are made in the minds of men: that it is only through understanding, and through the unceasing, tolerant, and objective search for understanding, that a community of man can be achieved and the hope of peace rekindled. It assures that students who are most involved in that development of understanding which is education can contribute to the building of a community of man through cooperation with all other students of the world on common problems and common projects. It assumes that, though the world is fragmented by nationalism, though students come from many races and practice many religions, even though the world is divided on the political level, there remain those levels of common concern on which all students can cooperate and on which the search for understanding must proceed.

THE INTOLERANT STUDENT may ridicule the search for understanding; he may argue that political difference destroys the possibility of cooperation. The dogmatic student may assert his plan for a simple, single solution to our relations abroad, based on a single race, religion or belief. The messianic student may conscript those who lack in understanding into a crusade to narrow the horizons of cooperation, to close the doors of exchange, and to substitute ideological conformity for the search for understanding. Despite the machinations and intrigues of such as these, the students of the United States will not hesitate, I firmly believe, to continue their efforts to achieve a greater measure of understanding, to cherish diversity and universality above conformity and isolation, to work through all channels which may lead to the fullest meaning of international student cooperation.

IT IS TO DEFEAT INTOLERANCE and dogmatism, and to promote understanding by cooperation with all the students of the world, that the "foreign policy" of the NSA is directed.

Yale News 4/22/48

Yale Committee Sends Delegates To NSA Meeting

Foreign Travel, CARE Among Topics Discussed In Regional Conference

Participating in the first Southern New England Regional Assembly of the National Student Association, the Yale committee sent three delegates and three observers to the University of Connecticut to discuss and consider problems and projects common to the colleges of the area.

Robert West, 1947M, chairman of the region, presided over the convention in which Brown, Connecticut College, New Haven YMCA College, Bridgeport Teachers College, New Britain State Teachers College, Trinity, Wesleyan, Pembroke, St. Joseph's College, and Albertus Magnus sent delegates.

Delegates Discuss Problems

Dividing up into two groups, national and international, the 32 delegates and 14 observers worked to prepare a set of resolutions and suggestions for future procedure.

West was an early leader in NSA's Southern New England Region, serving as its Chair in 1947-48; 32 delegates and 14 observers from 10 colleges attended its April, 1948 assembly. (More on Yale and NSA, p. 838.)

PICTURE CREDITS: *Then:* c. First National Student Congress, U. of Wisconsin, August, 1948 *(NSA News Service,* Schwartz). *Now:* June, 1984 in the USSR at a meeting of American and Russian scholars (Dee West).

Robert L. West was a professor of international economic relations at the Tufts University Fletcher School from 1966 until his death in 1991. Earlier he worked for CARE, as an economist for the Federal Reserve Bank of N.Y and the Rockefeller Foundation. He dedicated most of his life to researching and aiding the economies of Third World nations in Africa.

ROBERT L. WEST

In the words of his colleague and friend of 45 years, Bob Meagher, Rob West was "a public international citizen, warm, wise and sensitive, who dedicated his life to making this a more humane world." The following is an adaptation of an obituary written by Leigh Hurwitz, staff writer for The Tab, Newton, MA, on July 19, 1991, which also served West's home town of Wayland, MA. Some additional career highlights are added.

Town officials of Wayland, MA, are mourning the death of Robert West, the Finance Committee member who died July 17 after a six month battle with cancer. He was 65.

West, who lived in Wayland for 20 years, served on the Finance Committee for five years, including two years as chairman. Town Accountant Bob Hilliard remembers West as a brilliant and devoted man. "He showed tremendous leadership qualities and was very generous with his time," Hilliard said. "He was a big supporter of the schools and other town services."

Committee member Bob Salsburg said West was a role model. "I really looked up to him," Salsburg said. "I was always impressed by his professionalism. He gave a great deal of himself to the town. He was as fine a gentleman as you'd ever want to meet."

West was born in North Platt, N.D., and grew up in Fort Collins, Colo. He received his bachelor's, master's and doctoral degrees in economics at Yale University. He served in the U.S. Navy from 1944 to 1946.

West dedicated most of his life to researching and aiding the economies of Third World nations. For the last 26 years he was professor of international economic relations at the Fletcher School of Law and Diplomacy at Tufts University, where he focused on economic development in the world's poorest countries, especially in Africa. He is the author of more than 40 scholarly articles and coauthor of two books, *Comparative Development Perspectives* and *Defense, Security and Development.*

West served as a researcher and consultant in many African governments, including Zaire, Tanzania, Nigeria, Kenya, Gambia, Ethiopia, and Cameroon. Also for the governments of Thailand and China. He was Economic Counselor and USAID Mission Director in Leopoldville in 1962-63.

According to the *Boston Globe* he "virtually ran the Congolese economy in 1960 when he was in what is now Zaire with the African economic and political development project of [MIT's] Center for International Studies."

He also worked as an economist for the Federal Reserve Bank of New York and was assistant director of the Rockefeller Foundation's Social Sciences Program.

He was married to Eleanora deAntonio West. They have two sons, Roy E. West (married to Carolyn West) of Berkeley, Calif., and David M. West of Boston, and a grandson, Robert L. West, III.

"American student relief must carry a clear message... the simple offer of friendship and cooperation."

4. Erskine Childers: They Want to Trust Us

Stanford University
Chair, California, Nevada, Hawaii Region, 1948-49. Vice President, International Affairs, 1949-50

Editor's note: He came into NSA from Stanford University in California, a Western link in 1949-50 in the chain of Eastern Yale-Harvard-MIT International Vice Presidents who provided American students through NSA with a credible and effective voice on the international scene during its first five years. As the third, Erskine Childers, he brought a keen conscience and sense of history rooted in forebears who played a significant role in Irish history (see page after next). Childers presided over NSA's international program on strong foundations laid by Yale's Bob Smith and Rob West – a network of relationships with European and Asian student leaders, a carefully balanced strategy aimed at avoiding a Cold War disconnect with Eastern European students, a burgeoning travel program. His was a year which saw an explosion in student travel that strained NSA's financial capacity to manage it (see Lynch, Part 1, Section 8), exacerbated by the "Svalbard Incident" which stranded 800 NSA student tourists in New York for a week (See Section 5), U.S. entry in the Korean Conflict, the IUS second World Student Congress, and the mounting of NSA's International Team — twelve students dispatched on various missions to Europe, Asia and the West Indies. Coming out of California, Childers had a personal interest in Latin America, voiced in a 1948 report, a portion of which appears on the next page.

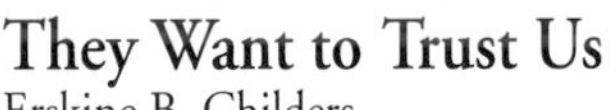

They Want to Trust Us

Erskine B. Childers
Chairman, Calif.-Nev.- Hawaii Region

American student relief must carry a clear message from its donors, the simple offer of friendship and cooperation from the American student community, the unattached aid in the reconstruction of those physical and intellectual conditions in which students of the world may make their own political decisions, may draw inspiration and information from others without fear of political strings or power-political pressurizing.

NSA's role in this matter is enormous and vital. We practice charity in its finest sense in helping students abroad, but NSA should make it clear to its campus communities that those students have something and want to give something in exchange for our assistance—a reciprocal program of international understanding through every means at their disposal.

This can be accomplished only through community-to-community relationships. This means a call from NSA to every campus relief committee to get under way a program of full personal and inter-university relations with a specifically "sponsored" student community in need of their aid. It means relief packages accompanied by letters or by requests for correspondence from individual students to individual students. It means exchange of information about each other's activities and studies. If possible exchange of students between cooperating campuses. . . .

They are looking to us, they want to place trust and confidence in our integrity of intention and constancy of objective. Ours is the responsibility; ours will be the tragic blame if we fail - and this, like so many other problems should not be left to already burdened governmental agencies.

STUDENT LEADER AT STANFORD

THE STANFORD DAILY

NSA Remains By Unanimous Excom Vote

Continued membership in the National Student Association was unanimously passed by Excom at last night's meeting.

A motion was also made and passed to delegate to the local NSA the task of finding methods of formulating and representing student opinion on national issues on which the national NSA takes a stand.

Erskine Childers, regional NSA chairman, stated that Stanford should be represented at the regional convention on such issues as academic freedom and federal aid to education.

Excom felt, however, they were not qualified to speak for the student body as a whole and that a letter should be sent to the conference stating that Stanford did not wish to be quoted on these issues at this time.

May 5, 1949

NSA Chooses Stanford Men

Erskine Childers, Stanford international relations student, was elected national vice-president in charge of international affairs at the NSA convention held during August on the University of Illinois campus. Dick Kelton, IIR president, was chosen by a regional caucus at the same meeting to replace Childers as chairman of the California, Hawaii, and Nevada region.

Childers has been active in the National Student Association since its inception two years ago, and has served as president of the Institute of International Relations at Stanford. For the past year he has served as regional NSA chairman, and has been a member of the national executive committee.

September 28, 1949

CHILDERS CHAMPIONED ACTIVE ENGAGEMENT to a reluctant student government which also questioned the value of membership to a large University and, eventually, for that reason, disaffiliated in 1950 for several years. (More on Stanford and NSA, p. 776, 1047.)

Inter-American Student Relations and NSA

Erskine B. Childers, *Chairman,*
California-Nevada-Hawaii
Regional International Commission

Editor's note: Childers represented NSA on a trip to South America in August of 1948 while he was International Commission chair of the California region. This undated report was located among the Welsh papers at the Berea College Archives.

Note: The term "American" is used here, and is understood in Latin America to encompass the entire hemisphere, and not USA alone.

At the Constitutional Convention of USNSA in 1947 attention was drawn to a proposed Congress of American Students, scheduled for October of that year, and designed to create the intra-hemispherical machinery for closer student relations. . . .

In continuation of [the] effort to convene this American Congress, a small organizational committee was established at the University of San Marcos, Lima, Peru, whose composition included both representatives of the Peruvian NSA and various students from other Latin-American countries. Full plans were laid for the hosting of the Congress in Lima on April 25th, 1948, and an agenda and proposed rules of procedure were drawn up. Invitations were sent out to every National Student Union or Association in the hemisphere, and replies indicated that the representation would be almost 100%, only one or two NSA's indicating inability to send delegations — for internal political or financial reasons.

On April 14th , 1948, the Minister of Education of the Peruvian Government called the members of the organizational committee into his office and stated that the Congress could not be held. No adequate reason was given for this arbitrary governmental cancellation; indeed, various forms of threats were used to deter the students from going ahead with their plans, including a warning that the non-Peruvian students on the committee would be requested to leave the country if they persisted in their efforts. The committee had no recourse but . . . to abandon temporarily their hopes for convening the Congress.

* * * *

Current Peruvian politics, very briefly, reveal a bitter struggle between two main opposing forces: those of the numerically small but powerful conservative and reactionary landholders and industrial capitalists, descendants of the feudal Conquistador regime, and a new popular alliance of intellectual and manual labour groups, known as the APRA, or People's Party.

[Childers goes on to describe the emergence of a popular boycott against the government, elected with APRA support, as a consequence of then government's abandonment of its platform] . . .The result of this boycott has been rule by decree . . . and various other arbitrary assumptions of power, not the least of which has been the prohibition of the American Congress of Students.

Almost every student in Peru and the majority of politically active faculty members are APRA supporters. . .

The Peruvian NSA will hold its annual National Congress in September, 1948, at which time consideration will be given to another attempt to convene the American Congress at Lima, probably towards the end of November. At the time of my leaving Peru (August 15th) no governmental statement of attitude towards this renewed effort had been received. . . .

Why is all this important to the USNSA, to students of the United States? . . . There is now no machinery which might aid in student exchange, in informational exchange, in the cementing of any kind of relationship between American students.

Latin America is undoubtedly one of the most misunderstood and poorly represented economic and cultural areas in world, and particularly from the standpoint of the US student. In spite of the fact that Latin America becomes more important economically and strategically to the US with every day that passes, the current myth persists in the USA of countries seething with puppet revolutions and dictators, sleepy peasants in permanent siesta, and a general atmosphere of complete backwardness. Yet to the Latin-American student the United States is recognized as of supreme importance in the very destinies of the countries south of the Rio Grande; and I have found, wherever I have gone, a very profound desire to know about the USA, to meet US students, to bring the two vast areas closer together in every way.

Recognized authorities speak more and more of the importance, on a reciprocal basis, of closer coordination of effort and general international understanding within this hemisphere. In the political and economic scene the groundwork has been laid, through the various Inter-American Conferences, for close cooperation under the United Nations regional provisions. There remains a great void in intercultural relations, in exchange of persons, ideas, and specific information. The US student should not allow the myth to continue that Latin America has nothing but economic and strategic value to offer the United States; there is as much to be gained from an understanding of Latin-American peoples as from an understanding of European or Asian peoples.

The void, interculturally, is there, and for this reason the proposed American Congress and Confederation of Students is of vital importance in the interests of international understanding and security. The role of USNSA in such an organization would be absolutely vital, and cannot be over-emphasized. I have it on first-hand information that the students of Latin America are looking to USNSA for support, material and inspirational, in creating this organization.

HOPES DASHED FOR INTERAMERICAN CONGRESS

Peru Tanks Eject Striking Students From Lima College

By ROB WEST

United States news-wire services reported on October 26 from Lima, Peru, that police had just rammed two Army tanks through the doors of the old Colonial Building at San Marcos University to eject eighty-three students who had barricaded themselves inside the building.

The report continued by identifying the students as members of the Peruvian Student Federation, dominated by student-members of the recently outlawed Aprista party. The students were arrested without bloodshed, as were their fellow-students of Guadalupe High School, the largest male national school in Peru, who went on strike a day earlier and had been ousted from the buildings they occupied.

NSA News, January, 1949

CLOSURE OF PERUVIAN UNIVERSITIES for the year dashed hopes for a 1948 Inter-American Congress in Lima, which never materialized. Robert West, NSA's 1948-49 International Vice President, reports in the 1/49 *NSA News* that the Student Federation of Uruguay had invited hemisphere national student unions to meet that summer in Montevideo. It wasn't until January, 1952 that the First Inter-American Student Congress was held in Rio de Janairo (see Farber, Part 3, Sec. 3).

AT CLEVELAND COLLEGE, OH. Childers (left) leaving an April 2, 1949, National Executive Committee meeting with with Dick Heggie (NSA Student Life V.P.), Bob Delahanty (KY-TN Chair) and Rob West (NSA Int'l. V.P.).

ADDRESSING THE THIRD NATIONAL STUDENT CONGRESS (left) at the University of Michigan, August 1950. Right: Seated at dais (center) with fellow 1949-50 officers Rick Medalie (left, Educational Problems V.P.) and Ted Perry (Student Life V.P.). Picture credits: *Above:* (l. to r.): Schwartz, SHSW, Marie Kelly. *Then:* NSA Staff Photo (SHSW)

THE INDEPENDENT • THURSDAY 29 AUGUST 1996

Erskine Childers

Erskine Childers succumbed to a heart attack during the 50th anniversary congress of the World Federation of United Nations Associations, of which he was Secretary-General. It is perhaps fitting for so totally dedicated a man that he died giving all of his energy and ingenuity to an international organisation that he was trying desperately to revitalise.

Childers was a most unusual person by any count. His great grandfather, Robert Childers, was a distinguished Victorian oriental scholar. His grandfather, Erskine, wrote the classic international thriller *The Riddle of the Sands*. He also fought as a trooper in the South African war and served in the First World War in the naval air service and the Royal Air Force, among other things doing much of the original aerial mapping of Palestine. After the war he returned to Ireland and joined the Republicans when they took up arms. He was executed for treason by the British in 1922 after being tried for having an automatic pistol without the proper authority. His son, also Erskine, much later on became president of Ireland.*

The third Erskine Childers, not surprisingly with such a dramatic family history, grew up with an innate distrust of great powers and of established authority. He was passionately interested in the endless quest for justice, equity and fairness in international affairs. His championing of the Palestinian cause resulted in his first book, *Common Sense about the Arab World* (1960), which he followed up in 1962 with *The Road to Suez: a study in Western-Arab relations*.

Starting his career as a writer, lecturer and broadcaster, Childers joined the UN Secretariat in 1967. His special field was economic development, and by the time he retired in 1989, he had worked with virtually all of the organisations of the UN system in all the regions of the world. His last UN position was Senior Adviser to the UN Director for Development and International Economic Cooperation.

Erskine Childers and I came together in 1989 after he had reviewed my memoirs and echoed a remark of mine deploring the slipshod way in which governments and especially permanent members of the Security Council, select the Secretary-General of the UN. We both felt that this question deserved more attention than it had received, and we worked together on a short book, *A World in Need of Leadership: tomorrow's United Nations*, which was published by the Dag Hammarskjold Foundation and the Ford Foundation in 1990. This subject is once again very much in the news, and it is sad that a new edition of this book, with a number of fresh ideas from Childers, will be published this very week, on 30 August.

Our leadership study received an encouraging reception in 1990, and over the intervening years we produced three more works on UN reform – on reorganising the secretariat, on strengthening international response to humanitarian emergencies, and on renewing the UN system. I was increasingly impressed with Childer's imagination, his vast fund of knowledge and experience, his powers of analysis and his enormous capacity for hard intellectual work. He never tired of his subject or lost his youthful zeal for pursuing it, and the best ideas in our joint works were almost always his.

He was a wonderful person to work with. His enthusiasm was constantly boosted by his passionate convictions, his loathing of anything that smacked of bullying or condescension, and his indignation at the current fashion to denigrate and downgrade international organisations, especially in the United States.

Childers knew as well as anyone how much these organisations needed improvement and strengthening – in fact he had devoted his later years to this cause – but he was outraged at the ignorance, prejudice, xenophobia and petty malice of much of the current onslaught on the UN. His indignation was intensified by the perennial failure of the United States to pay its full dues to the world organisation.

Childers: a champion of the oppressed and the less fortunate

His biting humour and his strong opinions were splendidly stimulating to those he worked with. There is no doubt however that, in the cautious world of the UN secretariat, they also diminished his prospects of advancement. More than one effort to put him in a post which would have given full scope to his great talents was effectively blocked by mumbling and unspecific reservations. I don't think Erskine Childers cared all that much. He was more interested in getting it right and keeping his principles undiluted.

He was, by nature and by inheritance, a champion of the oppressed and the less fortunate. He stood up for the developing countries and their peoples. He fought for their place on the international scene and for the programmes and activities that would help them attain it. To his last day he was indefatigable in writing, researching and addressing meetings all over the world on this subject.

Childers was also an outspoken champion of the United Nations and its mission. In *Renewing the United Nations System* he wrote, "The only hope of effectively dealing with the world's major problems in the interest of all humankind is through the progressive development of a working world community". That is what Erskine Childers devoted his life to.

Brian Urquhart

Erskine Childers, international civil servant and activist: born March 1929; twice married; died Luxembourg 25 August 1996.

**Editor's note:* In a posting to the Anthology editor, Margaret Childers, sister of the most recent Erskine, notes that Robert Erskine Childers was in fact executed by the Irish Free State for possession of an automatic firearm—not by the British and not for treason.

The international office moves back to Madison

5. NSA's 1950-1951 International Program

Herbert W. Eisenberg
Massachusetts Institute of Technology
NSA Vice President for International Affairs, 1950-51

The Foreign Student Summer Project

I was a World War II veteran in my sophomore year at MIT in the spring of 1948 when I first encountered NSA. I was wandering through the basement of Walker Memorial, the MIT student union, looking for something to do, when I saw a notice on the door of one of the student activity offices describing the Foreign Student Summer Project (FSSP).[1] This program began as an activity of the MIT NSA Committee. The relationship never changed, but FSSP soon became a much bigger activity than NSA on the MIT campus. In the program, foreign engineering and science students from all over the world would come to MIT during the summer to experience American technology. The students would attend summer school classes and then tour the country, visiting companies that were retooling after the war and incorporating new inventions developed during wartime research into the production of domestic goods. The program was the brainchild of Earl Eames and Lloyd Haynes, who had attended the NSA Constitutional Convention. They had brought NSA to the campus, securing the backing of both the student government and the MIT administration. Everett Baker, the Dean of Students, had joined the NSA Advisory Board in 1948 and was a key supporter of FSSP.[2]

Initially, I was not much interested in NSA, because I became deeply involved with FSSP, ending up as chairman for the 1949–1950 program. Everything, including a massive fund raising effort, was run by students. I realize now that our fund-raising was assisted by MIT President James Killian, who allowed us to approach large MIT contributors such as Alfred Sloan of General Motors and gave us lots of support without interfering with our activities. The faculty was equally supportive, allowing extra students into their classes and labs.

The Second NSA Congress, University of Illinois, 1949

Except for a few local meetings, I do not recall knowing much about NSA until I attended the Second NSA Congress in Urbana in 1949. Harrison White was the chairman of the NSA/FSSP committee that year. The two of us represented the MIT student government, although neither of us was an elected member of the Institute Committee, MIT's student government body. We already had some knowledge of the NSA international program through contact with the NSA International Office in Cambridge. However, domestic issues had not been high on our agenda, and we were fascinated by the scope of the problems and politics involved in the issues being dealt with by the Congress. We came to know the colleges that were represented, from the small Catholic colleges to the big Ivy League institutions—and, of course, the CCNY delegation—plus the communist student groups.

One of the first people I recall meeting was Galen Martin (Berea College, Kentucky),[3] a southerner and probably the purest liberal I have ever met, then and now. From Ken Kurtz, a West Virginia–born student from Swarthmore,[4] I learned to take an extreme position if your real position is in the middle, so you have maneuvering room to get where you want to go. Helen Jean Rogers explained the intricacies of the founding of NSA. Rollo O'Hare (University of Michigan) initiated us into the mysteries of Midwest student politics. And, of course, Allard Lowenstein explained to us the glories of the University of North Carolina Tarheels.[5] I learned the lion hunt, and used it later at several international meetings.[6] And I became totally hooked on the idea of a national student movement, run by students, with the great potential to be a positive force for world improvement.

Harrison and the oranges

Harrison C. White was asked to run for International Vice President. He was reluctant to give up a year to NSA. I had pressured him to run because I knew he would do a good job. However, during a meeting in one of the classrooms, oranges from the box lunches were used as ammunition in a friendly fire fight. Security came and took the names of the participants, including Harrison. He was embarrassed, and didn't want it to be brought up during the election, so he decided to withdraw his name! I should add that Harrison went on to get a Ph.D. in physics from MIT and then, with a Ford grant, a Ph.D. in sociology from Princeton. He taught at Harvard for many years and is now at Columbia. He is known internationally as the father of mathematical sociology. No one has mentioned the oranges for a long, long time.

The FSSP program in 1949–1950

The FSSP program took a great deal of my time during the 1949-1950 academic year and the following summer. The committee was responsible for reviewing applications from engineering and science students from many countries, sending out acceptance letters, raising money—always a major, difficult task—and arranging for accommodations, transportation, and hospitality for the thirty-plus visitors who arrived in Cambridge at the end of June.

At the end of their stay, the students took a two-week tour, visiting various manufacturing facilities, such as the Ford plants in Detroit, historic sites, and Niagara Falls. I accompanied the group, driving some of the students in my Studebaker, which was new in 1949 but well used by 1950. At the end of the 1950 tour, I drove to Michigan for the Third Congress, tired but pretty much determined that I would run for international vice president. I felt sure of the support of the New England Region, and confident that my work with FSSP had given me adequate experience and a good track record. I had visited the NSA International Office in Cambridge a number of times, but did not become well acquainted with Erskine Childers (1949-50 NSA International Vice President), though we had a cordial relationship. I was too absorbed with FSSP to give much thought to the budget and personnel problems at the International Office, and I was not aware of the *Svalbard* matter until I read about it in the newspapers.[7]

The Third Congress, University of Michigan, 1950

I do not remember much about the issues at the Third Congress. I was pretty much worn out with driving and with the FSSP activities. I knew that the travel program was in deep trouble financially and that there had been serious problems regarding the operation of the program. During one session, and after some debate, the procommunist observer from the Labor Youth League (LYL) was granted speaking privileges. In his speech, the spokesman stated that South Korea had invaded North Korea and that U.S. involvement was unjustified. The silence that followed his speech was memorable.[8]

By that time I was focusing on the elections and had gathered a lot of support. I was also in the middle of the fight for a resolution concerning "Authority within the Staff," which I believed was essential for the international program to function properly. The final compromise declared that the President should, in relation to those outside the organization, be chief spokesman for NSA; within the staff he should be first among equals. It stated that each Vice President bore primary responsibility for programs assigned to that person, with the President not having control over, or setting the agenda for, these programs. This would become a critical issue in the events occurring before, during, and after the International Student Conference of twenty-one national student unions held in Stockholm in December 1950.[9]

Just before the elections began, it was announced that Dean Baker had died in a plane crash in the Middle East. A moment of silence was requested in his memory. Dean Baker had been the most important influence on, and supporter of, the FSSP program. I had to leave the auditorium to be alone. I was sitting on a curb in the back of the building when someone came to tell me that I had been nominated for international vice president and was expected to speak very shortly. Lowenstein was elected President by a large majority, and I was supported by all states except that of my opponent, Stan Matthews from UCLA. Elmer Paul Brock, Herb Goldsmith, and Shirley Neizer completed the slate.[10] It was agreed that the office of the International Vice President would move to Madison but the travel office would remain in Cambridge until a full-time travel director could be hired. In November, the staff chose Tom Callahan for the post, and I was to find him capable and easy to work with during the significant repairs the travel program was in need of.[11]

Getting started

I drove back to Boston, loaded up the 1948 Studebaker with the international nontravel material, and headed to Madison. I asked Char Agnew, who had been working for Erskine, and Mary Saunders, a young Englishwoman who had been working for FSSP, to help me with the packing and to come to Madison for a short time to help set up the international office. The staff agreed that there was not enough money for me to stay permanently in Madison. Consequently, it was arranged that I would commute between the Cambridge and Madison offices at two- or three-month intervals. Among the most lasting memories of my year in office are the trips back and forth, involving continuous driving with stops at service areas for food and naps in the car.

Up until the discussions surrounding the Stockholm meeting, the staff got along fine. Al was on the road all the time. It became evident that Al would be out of the office most of the time and Elmer, Joan, and later, Shirley as well, kept him up to date on office activities and matters of which he needed to be aware.

Stockholm—The preliminaries

There was enough money in the budget to pay the fare for one person to attend the International Student Conference in Stockholm. I was adamant that, in accordance with the primary responsibility that each vice president held for programs and activities in his area, I should go. Al felt that the "first among equals" principle meant that he should go. He also stated that he should go because he had been elected by acclamation. Without laboring what I believed to be an irrelevance, I noted that I had been right up with him in terms of votes cast.[12]

The staff reached a compromise. Al would attend if he could find the funding for his trip. If he came, he would be the delegate, and I would be the "technical expert." Actually, we both acted as delegates. The term *technical* referred to the agreement, reached after several acrimonious staff meetings, that Al would not propose any new initiatives without clearing them with me. In any event, Al did not honor this agreement.[13]

There was an important set of matters for us to consider. The Stockholm Conference was organized as a meeting of official representatives of national student unions. The task assigned to the Conference by the participating student unions was to develop plans for international student programs and activities and to work on the technical aspects of carrying out the programs. They wished to develop a program of cooperation with all other student unions, particularly those in the underdeveloped countries. The Conference organizers wished to avoid participating in, or contributing to, East-West ideological tensions at the student level. Among other things, they did not wish to discuss the creation of a Western-oriented international student union to compete with the Communist-dominated International Union of Students, which had been established in Prague in 1946.

These constituted the ground rules of the Conference, which participants were expected to observe and respect. Al and I discussed this matter, and our relation to it, in detail. We agreed that program and policy proposals that we might make would be in accord with the principles and purposes of the Conference. If Al should find himself wishing to make proposals that might be at odds with the ground rules, he would discuss it with me and we would reach an agreement.

The World University Service meeting

Al and I agreed that, if he could make it, we would meet in London about December 15 and travel to Stockholm together. Early in December, I left for Geneva for a World University Service (WUS) meeting.[14] The trip was my first overseas flight. The minister in the seat next to me was very gracious in reassuring me about the safety of planes every time we hit a little turbulence. We missed our connecting flight on British Air when we got to London, and were rerouted through Paris on Air France. It was noon when we took off. We found ourselves on the "gourmet flight," which took an extra half hour to land at Orly so passengers could finish their meals. It was a fabulous, multicourse repast that included champagne to start, wine during the meal, and Grand Marnier after dessert. I was a bit worried when the attendant came up the aisle with a basket of wine bottles and disappeared into the cockpit for some time. The minister did not drink alcohol, so I had double drinks throughout the meal and staggered off the plane still thinking I was in the air.

In Geneva, I was informed that Al had not been able to secure funds for the trip and would not be in Stockholm.

I do not recall much about the WUS meeting other than that I was elected a vice president. When I asked what I was supposed to do, I was told not to worry, they simply needed an American in the post and I happened to be there. I was one of two persons from North America who were elected as vice-presidents. The other was Pierre Trudeau, who was to become Prime Minister of Canada. When I was reading *Parade* magazine one Sunday in the early 1960s, I saw an article about the world's three most admired politicians under the age of forty. They were Al Lowenstein; Olof Palme, whom I was soon to meet in Stockholm; and Pierre Trudeau! My wife and I had just had our fifth child, and I was quietly practicing architecture in Boston. I experienced a feeling of envy and some regret that I had not continued to work in the international arena.

After the WUS Conference, on my way to Stockholm, I stopped in Paris and Holland to discuss summer travel plans with the student travel groups, in anticipation of the 1951 program.

The Stockholm Conference

I had been thinking about the purposes of the Stockholm meeting for some time. I agreed with them. My experience with FSSP was directly relevant. During the flight to London, I had composed a draft plan for a Student Mutual Assistance Program (SMAP), for presentation as a working paper at Stockholm.[15] Features of the program included student exchange, seminars and conferences, and information exchange among participating student unions. When I arrived in Stockholm, I met Olof Palme (years later, he became Prime Minister of Sweden), my opposite number in the Swedish Student Union. He helped me get the proposal printed and distributed for discussion.

Al was there. He told me that he had decided to use his personal funds to come. Bob Smith was there representing the World University Service, and Marianne Schmidt was representing a student group that was not known to me. She was a graduate student in Europe who had attended a 1947 International Student Service conference in Switzerland as an undergraduate at New Jersey College for Women, and represented NSA at UNESCO in Paris in the summer of 1950.

I was much gratified that SMAP became one of the major resolutions to emerge from the Conference. The statement of purpose was rewritten and changed into a lengthier preamble, but the technical programs I had proposed were adopted intact.

Al's speech and its aftermath

Al and I approached European sensibilities from different poles. The Student Mutual Assistance Program had been very well received and was the topic of major discussion. For whatever reason, Al delivered a strident anticommunist speech, which violated both the ground rules of the conference and his explicit agreement with me. He did not discuss the speech with me before giving it because he knew that I would not approve. Very shortly after giving the speech, he left Stockholm.[16]

The delegates from other nations were angered by the apparent indifference of the Americans to the conference rules, to the problems of other countries (many Western nations represented at the Conference had sizable Communist student and youth groups), and to their clearly stated wishes. They passed a resolution censuring both Al and USNSA for violating the ground rules of the Conference.[17]

I believe that Al left before the motion for censure was proposed and passed and did not know of it until much later. No word of it had reached the Madison office until I returned and made my displeasure known to whomever would listen. Al was on the road, and I did not get to talk directly to him. Elmer, who administered Al's affairs in the office, did not believe me. Thus began a schism in the staff, with Elmer and Joan on one side, Herb Goldsmith and me on the other, and Shirley trying to moderate the disputes to the best of her ability.

I wrote to Olof Palme, requesting a copy of the Conference minutes to confirm the vote of censure. My letter was not very diplomatic. It expressed my anger at Al's actions and my frustration at not being believed back home. When the minutes arrived, they confirmed the censure.

Brazil

In March, I received a phone call from Helen Jean Rogers, saying that a student leader from Brazil, Paulo Egydio Martins, Secretary for International Affairs for the Brazilian Student Union (UNE), was at Harvard and had spoken to the Harvard NSA committee about establishing contact with UNE in Rio de Janeiro. I called Avrea Ingram, who was the student in charge of the Harvard office,[18] and then wrote a letter to Mr. Martins. This resulted in an invitation for NSA to send delegates to the next Brazilian student congress, in Rio de Janeiro in July 1951.

Helen Jean, who possessed substantial knowledge of Spanish, was designated as a delegate along with me, and we began the search for money for the trip. Helen Jean and I solicited funds from various foundations, but with little success. Then Helen Jean wrote to Braniff Airlines. They sent us two free round-trip tickets, which, when added to $1,300 from other sources, enabled us to attend the Congress.[19] Helen Jean was also able to stay in South America after the Congress to visit other student unions.[20]

The results of our visit and Helen Jean's extended trip are summarized in a document entitled, "Report of Latin America Team, United States National Student Association, Summer 1951," which was submitted to the staff and the International Commission in October 1951. Although I am listed as coauthor, this excellent report is entirely Helen Jean's work.[21] I can add a few personal sidelights to the story, however.

The report describes armed mayhem that occurred at a meeting on nationalization of the oil industry that took place a day or two prior to our meeting in the student union auditorium. We were shown bullet holes in the walls and ceiling early in the afternoon of our arrival. At the opening ceremony that night, we were marching down the main aisle to our seats at the front when I heard popping noises. I turned around very nervously, looking for an exit, but Paulo Egydios whispered to me that I was simply hearing fireworks in celebration of the opening of the Congress. In my speech, I discussed relations and cooperation among students throughout the Americas, and I quoted Franklin D. Roosevelt's famous dictum, "We have nothing to fear but fear itself." It produced a five-minute standing ovation.

The IUS delegate, Giovanni Berlinguer, was very cordial, and we had several polite discussions with him. He struck me as being very bright, and was obviously an experienced diplomat. His speech to the Congress was skillful and well received. At the time his brother was the director of the Italian Communist Party, and I believe Giovanni, too, became well known in Italy.

UNE and IUS

One of the main issues before the Congress was whether UNE should continue its affiliation with IUS. The Report notes that the anti-IUS students were split, with some wishing to remain in the IUS and fight to democratize it, and others advocating immediate disaffiliation. A major issue that the anti-IUS students reported to me was that UNE's current delegates to IUS were actually no longer members of the UNE and were not appointed or delegated by the UNE to be its representatives.

The day before the resolution on IUS was to be introduced, I was invited to a private caucus of the "anti" group. All were agreed that a motion to leave IUS now would probably fail and would cause a serious split in UNE. The discussion therefore focused on the wording of a stay-in-and-fight resolution. I suggested that they list their grievances with IUS as part of the motion, with the main grievance being the representation issue, and give the IUS one year to correct the problems. I knew that the IUS would not allow the democratic leadership of UNE to be represented and that failure of IUS to meet the conditions of UNE would almost certainly result in disaffiliation.

The final resolution, including the list of grievances, passed with only three dissenting votes. I suspect that resistance to the resolution was low because the pro-IUS forces were geared up for a disaffiliation fight and were disarmed by the moderate and reasonable tone of the resolution. In July 1952, I heard that UNE officially left IUS because of its failure to address the grievances that had been listed, most especially the issue of representation.

When we arrived in Rio, we left a message at the American embassy that we were representing NSA at the UNE Congress and would appreciate any help they could give us. I expected that the Ambassador would meet with us, but no invitation came. I had been told by Paulo that he could get an appointment to meet Brazilian President Vargas with one hour's notice, and I thought it strange that the Ambassador chose not to greet us. Subsequent events suggest that the Ambassador was told not to meet with us so as to avoid any appearance that we were U.S. government employees, which was certainly an impression that might have been created. The embassy did assign a press secretary to assist us, and they funded a cocktail party that Helen Jean and I gave for the student leaders from the various countries, including communist members. We had an excellent turnout, and many of the delegates who attended were clearly delighted to have been included. Berlinguer was invited but did not attend.

Subsequent events

UNE delegates attended the fourth USNSA Congress and maybe the fifth, but I do not recall any further development of direct relations with UNE. NSA's energies were focused on the Coordinating Secretariat of National Unions of Students (Cosec), which had been formed at the Second International Student conference in January 1952.[22] I stayed in touch with Paulo Egydios and, in fact, applied for a job with the family-owned company for which he worked. The company worked in fields such as heating and air conditioning, but was also developing land in the Matto Grosso for farming and mining. They declined to hire me because of their past experience with U.S. employees who came to work for several years, then returned home just when they were adequately trained to be useful. I think it would have been a great experience, although I surely would not have been a permanent expatriate.

From the spring of 1951 to the NSA Fourth Congress, University of Minnesota

Going back to the spring of 1951, relations in the office were especially strained. Al was never in Madison that I remember; if he was, I was probably in Cambridge. He did not communicate with me. Shirley Neizer did her best to reduce the problems, and she was the intermediary between Elmer and Joan, on one hand, and the two Herbs, on the other. Somehow, she managed to remain friends with both sides through it all. I was spending more time in Cambridge and New York, helping Tom Callahan with the travel program, and do not remember much happening other than making preparations for the Brazil trip.

After Brazil, I went to Europe on the *Volendam* with the travel staff, and on to Paris for meetings with the French student travel office and the International Association for the Exchange of Students for Technical Experience (IAESTE) representative from Britain. From there I returned to Holland to meet with the Dutch student travel office, returning in time for the Fourth Congress in Minnesota.

Except for one meeting at which the staff met with interested delegates to report on the past year, I do not have any outstanding memories of the Congress. The staff presentation was generally well received. Tom Callahan gave a glowing report on the success of the travel program, which was good by any standards but outstanding when compared to past performances. There was one question concerning the expenditure of NSA money for the Brazilian trip. It was easy to answer—no NSA money had been spent. The trip was unquestionably the most important NSA international activity, next to Stockholm. There were two delegates from UNE at Minnesota, and they were well received. Reading the records of the Congress shows that the struggle related to Al's Stockholm speech was not over, as he and his cohorts fought for acceptance of a resolution supporting the formation of a new international student organization. I was equally adamant that this should not take place, and it was defeated by a narrow vote, apparently because the delegates believed that the other Western student unions would not give it their support.

I had been urging Avrea Ingram to run for International Vice President. He did, and was elected without difficulty after Helen Jean refused to accept the nomination. The last time I saw Avrea remains in my mind. Helen Jean was at Harvard, and Avrea was on his way to Europe for a Cosec meeting. We had dinner together before his flight. Avrea was a formal person, and he dressed formally. It had been raining that day, and he was carrying an umbrella. After dinner, we took him to the airport. He was wearing a dark overcoat and a dark felt hat. As he turned to leave us in the terminal, carrying the umbrella like a cane, he looked like Alfred Hitchcock at the end of one of his movies, striding off into the unknown. I remember thinking that was probably the last time that I would ever see him. Tragically, it was. Avrea committed suicide in 1957, at age thirty. This was a great shock to those of us who knew and had worked with him. He was highly regarded for his excellent work as NSA International Vice President, and later as director of Cosec.[23]

After My NSA year

Getting back to the books was no mean feat, but it had to be done. I had little contact with NSA during the ensuing academic year. New people were running FSSP. They were not as interested in NSA as earlier committees had been. I remember attending an organizational meeting in New York for the founding of the International Development Placement Association (IDPA), but cannot recall much further involvement.[24]

The last official thing I remember doing is attending a World Assembly of Youth (WAY) meeting in Dakar, but I do not recall if I was representing NSA or World University Service. It was an interesting meeting, in an incredibly interesting place. We toured West Africa after the meeting, but I cannot recall any tangible results from the many resolutions that were discussed and passed at the plenary sessions. I went to a meeting at the University of Michigan to report on the WAY Conference.[25] That concluded my involvement with student and youth affairs, until I attended the 1997 meeting in Madison to celebrate NSA's fiftieth anniversary.

Recall

As I read through the documents, I am reminded that we thought we were going to make a difference, and in many ways I believe we did. Over the years, I have recalled the NSA days as really important in terms of my own growth and maturity, the significance of my wartime experience notwithstanding. Retelling the story has made it come alive again. For all the disappointments, there were many more rewards, especially the people we met and worked with, the intensity of our convictions, and the joy of thinking that we were doing something of real worth in the larger scheme of things.

Herbert Eisenberg is an architect, consultant, and expert witness in matters related to building construction, codes and standards, and life safety in the built environment.

EDITOR'S END NOTES

[1] See FSSP, p. 634.

[2] See Everett Baker, p. 841.

[3] See Galen Martin, p. 983.

[4] See Kurtz, p. 306, and p. 902.

[5] See Lowenstein, p. 283, and Murphy on NSA and North Carolina, p. 973.

[6] See Wharton, p. 145, for the original Lion Hunt script. Also see Joy Picus in Zimbabwe, p. 928, and Lee Jones in *LIFE* magazine, p. 295.

[7] See Meagher, p. 665, on the "*Svalbard* incident," concerning the NSA student summer tour ship that was stranded in New York harbor in June of 1950.

[8] For more detail on this event, see Lynch, p. 266; Fogel, p. 289; and "Life Goes to a Collegiate Convention," p. 295.

[9] See Lynch, p. 268.

[10] See Lynch, p. 269, for more detail on the national staff for 1950-1951. See also Neizer, p. 279.

[11] See Callahan, p. 673 on the travel program.

[12] The minutes of the Third Annual National Student Congress (p. 23) show the following election outcomes on August 31:

For President:	
S. Steinhauser (Long Island University)	46
R. Romer (University of Colorado	48
A. Lowenstein (University of North Carolina)	254
For Vice President, International Affairs:	
H. Eisenberg (Mass. Institute of Technology)	250
S. Mathews (UCLA)	70

[13] See Lynch, p. 273, for more on this incident.

[14] See World University Service (WUS), p. 622.

[15] See Students Mutual Assistance Program (SMAP), pp. 526, 638.

[16] See excerpts from an address by Allard K. Lowenstein to the International Student Conference, December 1950, p. 562.

[17] Robert Smith, NSA's first international vice president, 1947-1948 (see his essay, p. 507), reports in an October 23, 1998 letter to this editor:

> I was also at the Stockholm Conference in December, 1950, observing on behalf of World University Service. I, too, was struck by Al Lowenstein's vigorously anti-Communist speech—hardly necessary in that setting—which left a negative impression with many of the Europeans. In 1997, I had occasion to recall that event with an old friend, who had been in Stockholm in 1950 as president of one of the Western European NUS's, who still had negative feelings about that speech.

See also Lynch, p. 273, 8/51 *NSA News*, p. 527.

Concerning ISC "regrets" about Lowenstein speech, in its report on the Stockholm Conference, the August 1951 convention issue of *NSA News* (p. 6), notes:

> Reaction to the Stockholm speech was varied. By a vote of 12 to one with two abstentions, the conference voiced its regret that Lowenstein had given such a speech, largely on the grounds that it exceeded the terms of the Scandinavian invitation. Eisenberg called the speech a serious tactical error.
>
> The French delegate thought it was "lamentable...a great danger...purely political, a pure declaration of the foreign policy of the U.S.A." World Student News, official publication of the I.U.S., said it represented a policy of division between socialist and capitalist nations that was rejected by the honest people of the whole world.

NSA's National Executive Committee unanimously endorsed the speech. The Canadian delegate, while criticizing the timing, said he personally agreed with every word Lowenstein had said and that every student in Canada would vehemently support Lowenstein's strong stand in the matter.

[18] See Avrea Ingram, p. 575.

[19] The August, 1951 convention issue of *NSA News* (pg. 10), notes: "Thomas E. Braniff, president of Braniff International Airways, provided transportation for NSA's student ambassadors from Havana to Rio and back. Brainiff has taken a personal interest in furthering inter-American student relations and has in the past provided travel scholarships both for South American and U.S. students."

[20] See Helen Jean (Rogers) Secondari's report on this trip in her memoir on p. 597, written shortly before she died on March 28, 1998.

[21] A complete copy of this report is in the NSA archives at the State Historical Society of Wisconsin.

[22] For more on Cosec see Dentzer, p. 301, Almanac, p. 1129.

[23] See Barry Farber on Avery Ingram, p. 575.

[24] See International Development Placement Association (IDPA), p. 627. Herb Eisenberg was Vice Chairman and a member of the Board in 1953.

[25] See World Assembly of Youth (WAY), p. 778.

HERBERT W. EISENBERG

Early years and military service. Born in Boston in 1926. Mother was first generation from Russia and father emigrated to USA in 1913. Grew up in Chelsea until age 12, then Brookline until entering the U.S. Navy in 1944. Honorably discharged in 1946 after service at sea in the Pacific.

Education. Educated at Brookline High School, Thayer Academy and Massachusetts Institute of Technology. Bachelor of Science in 1952 in Engineering and Business Administration. Returned to MIT and Boston Architectural Center for design course and became a registered architect in 1961.

Career Highlights. After graduation I worked for a construction company for five years and then joined my father's architectural firm. In 1964 he passed away and I continued the firm until selling to partners in 1987, when I started a consulting firm specializing in building codes and standards. I am still providing consulting services in building codes and standards, and building construction, and serve as an expert witness in fields related to safety in the built environment. Lecturer at seminars on building codes, masonry veneers, building construction, life safety and fire protection.

Memberships and publications. Among my professional memberships are the American Institute of Architects, American Society of Safety Engineers, New England Building Association (Past President), Society of Fire Protection Engineers.

I am co-author of several publications including Revised City of Boston Building Code—Adopted 1970, Town of Watertown Building Code—Adopted 1972, and One Code: A Program for Building Regulatory Reform, AIA Task Force on Building Regulation—1975.

Family. Married Melissa Lees in 1956 (passed away in 1985) and have 6 children from that marriage and now 7 grandchildren. Subsequently married and recently divorced and living in Boston's North End. Lived in Lexington and Brookline, Massachusetts, since leaving college.

PICTURE CREDITS: *Then:* The MIT *Technique*, 1952 (MIT Museum). *Now:* 1998 (Author).

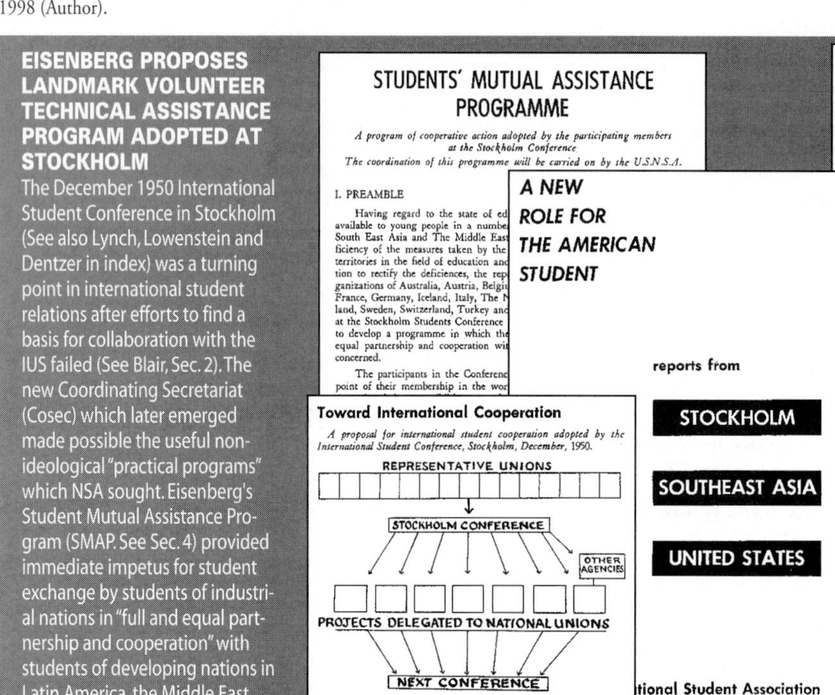

EISENBERG PROPOSES LANDMARK VOLUNTEER TECHNICAL ASSISTANCE PROGRAM ADOPTED AT STOCKHOLM

The December 1950 International Student Conference in Stockholm (See also Lynch, Lowenstein and Dentzer in index) was a turning point in international student relations after efforts to find a basis for collaboration with the IUS failed (See Blair, Sec. 2). The new Coordinating Secretariat (Cosec) which later emerged made possible the useful non-ideological "practical programs" which NSA sought. Eisenberg's Student Mutual Assistance Program (SMAP. See Sec. 4) provided immediate impetus for student exchange by students of industrial nations in "full and equal partnership and cooperation" with students of developing nations in Latin America, the Middle East, Africa and Asia.

STUDENTS' MUTUAL ASSISTANCE PROGRAMME

A program of cooperative action adopted by the participating members at the Stockholm Conference
The coordination of this programme will be carried on by the U.S.N.S.A.

I. PREAMBLE

Having regard to the state of ed
available to young people in a numbe
South East Asia and The Middle East
ficiency of the measures taken by the
territories in the field of education and
tion to rectify the deficiences, the rep
ganizations of Australia, Austria, Belgi
France, Germany, Iceland, Italy, The N
land, Sweden, Switzerland, Turkey and
at the Stockholm Students Conference
to develop a programme in which the
equal partnership and cooperation wi
concerned.

The participants in the Conferenc
point of their membership in the wor

A NEW ROLE FOR THE AMERICAN STUDENT

reports from

STOCKHOLM

SOUTHEAST ASIA

UNITED STATES

...tional Student Association

Toward International Cooperation

A proposal for international student cooperation adopted by the International Student Conference, Stockholm, December, 1950.

The above chart represents the structure with which the 21 student unions meeting at Stockholm plan to stimulate multilateral cooperation. Special projects were assigned to various of the unions, and a similar conference will be held within a year.

THE TECH — CAMBRIDGE, MASS. TUESDAY, SEPT. 26, 1950 — PRICE FIVE CENTS — VOL. LXX NO. 32 — THE OFFICIAL NEWSPAPER OF THE M.I.T. UNDERGRADUATES

Herb Eisenberg '51 Elected Vice-Pres. Of NSA Congress

Herbert W. Eisenberg, '51, was elected International Vice President of the National Student Congress at their recent meeting held on the University of Michigan campus. Elected last spring to the chairmanship of the MIT NSA, Eisenberg will be unable to serve. As International Vice President, he will spend this year at NSO headquarters in Madison, Wisconsin, as a full-time worker with a salary of approximately $2,000 per year.

As chairman of the 1950 Foreign Student Summer Project, Eisenberg brought Tech and himself into national leadership in the field of international student and educational affairs.

The NSA News

SPECIAL CONGRESS EDITION August, 1951

Korean Conflict Creates Uncertainty, Fear Among U.S. Students; Freedom Threatened

DRAFT, UMT AMONG ISSUES TO FACE FOURTH NATIONAL STUDENT GATHERING

Northrop Memorial Auditorium, University of Minnesota, where delegates gather the opening night of the Fourth National Student Congress. Harold Stassen is to give the keynote address. The Congress is expected to attract well over 500 students from all parts of the country.

New Generation Assumes Leadership As Veterans Leave Campus

Present Emergency Becomes Chief Topic of Discussion For Conferences of Educators and Students; Great Variety of Recommendations Indicate Varying Approaches.

ADULT RESPECT FOR STUDENT VIEW SEEN RISING

By MERRILL FREED

The Korean war cast its grim shadow across the college campus as American students struggled to understand and to fulfill their role in the troubled world of 1950-51.

Even adults in this mid-century year were at least at times confused and fearful. And students, who are usually sensitive to general community attitudes despite all the talk of college being an ivory tower, shared in the feeling of confusion and fear.

Indeed, the student, by virtue of his youth and his occupation, had reason to be even more concerned over the current crisis than were his elders.

Students Face Draft

He had realized that he was a young person in an age when young people are needed to fight. He had accepted the fact that any day an envelope marked "U. S. Government—Official Business" might appear in his mailbox. He knew that, in terms of his own future, discussions on campus were overshadowed by the discussions at Kaesong.

To deal with such an environment, the student of 1950 was virtually compelled to acquaint himself with a host of puzzling and complicated subjects. The draft, universal military training, ROTC, acceleration, manpower policy, student deferments--these vied with sports military training, ROTC, acceleration, manpower policy, student deferments--these vied with sports and sex as the favorite topics of conversation and thought.

And the occupation of the student — acquiring special knowledge and skills and developing the ability of independent and critical thinking necessary for good citizenship in a democratic society—placed him in an especially vulnerable position.

Incentive to Study Weakened

In the face of uncertainty as to what even the immediate future might hold, students found it hard to spend long hours in the law library or the chemistry lab. A manpower policy based in part on class standing helped to supply some of the incentive that doubt and confusion had destroyed. But it was a partial solution at best.

As Helen Jean Rogers (Catholic University), former officer of the National Student Association and one of the year's outstanding student leaders, phrased it in a speech to the American Council on Education: "All at once collegians are realizing that they may never finish school and suddenly, for some students, there is a fierce fondness for education and a deep desire to learn quickly; for others, the reaction is a different one—an attitude of 'they're going to get me for atomic fodder anyway, what do I care?' And the women students catch this uncertainty like measles from the men, and they too, are uncertain and concerned."

(To page 528, col. 1)

New Co-operation Rises in Non-Reds Of Student World

Stockholm Conference Lays Foundation for Practical, Efficient Programming

Swift-moving developments in the international student field during 1950-51 marked what many observers called the beginnings of a new and positive trend of cooperation among the non-Communist students of the world.

Among these developments were the Stockholm conference, the formation of World University Service

Among these developments were the Stockholm conference, the formation of World University Service (see page 9), the WAY assembly (see column two) and the widening of American student relations, through NSA, with Latin America (see page 10) and southeast Asia (see page 11).

For the first time in five years, an international student conference rejected the International Union of Students as a channel of cooperation and then took the next step by deciding upon a new basis of cooperation among the National Unions of Students who were dissatisfied with the IUS.

The Stockholm conference was held December 17-21 to discuss methods of promoting an efficient and practical international student cooperation. It was not meant to serve "as a platform for general political discussions" nor was it called "with the purpose of the setting up of a new international student organization."

Delegates were in attendance from the NUS'S of 19 countries, including Australia, Austria, Belgium, Canada, Denmark, Great Britain, Finland, France, Germany, Iceland, Italy, Netherlands, New Zealand, Norway, Scotland, Sweden, Switzerland, Turkey and the U. S.

Attending as guests were the NUS's of South Africa and Yugoslavia.

President Al Lowenstein represented NSA at Stockholm. Vice president Herb Eisenberg attended as a technical expert.

(To page 528, col. 2)

Pan-American Solidarity Promoted By NSA Visits to Brazil, Paraguay

A recent trip "south of the border" by two American students marked an important step toward better Pan-American student relations.

Helen Jean Rogers, former NSA national secretary, and Herbert Eisenberg, international affairs vice president, left New York on July 16 via Braniff Airlines bound for Rio de Janeiro, Brazil. There they attended the 14th national congress of the Uniao Nacional des Estudantes, the Brazilian union of students.

From Brazil they will visit neighboring countries, meeting with student leaders and gathering information about student life in South America.

The United States was the only foreign country to be represented at the Brazilian congress, which began July 26. At that meeting plans were made for a proposed Pan American student conference. The result of such a conference, it is hoped, will be the establishment of cooperative programs for the promotion of inter-American student cultural relations.

Prior to her attendance at the Brazilian meeting, Miss Rogers was the guest at the annual congress of the Seccion Especialiazada Estudiantil de Accion Catolica of Paraguay. The group, similar in nature to the Young Christian Student movement in this country, is a powerful force in the student life of Paraguay.

Herb Eisenberg, NSA vice president for international affairs, shakes hands with Paulo Egydio Martins, president of the Uniao Metropolitana dos Estudantes and secretary of the Brazilian national union of students. Eisenberg and Helen Jean Rogers attended the 14th national congress of the Brazilian organization.

Miss Rogers addressed the group in Spanish, conveying to them the good wishes of NSA. She was hardly able to conclude her speech, since there was cheering after almost every sentence. And at the finish, reported Miss Rogers, the Paraguaian students put on "a real demonstration, which indicated only the greatest friendship and respect for the U. S."

Thomas E. Braniff, president of Braniff International Airways, provided transportation for NSA's student ambassadors from Havana to Rio and back. Braniff has taken a personal interest in furthering inter-American student relations and has in the past provided travel scholarships for both South American and U. S. students.

NSA News Reports on the 1950-51 Year. These pages are a composite of articles, reassembled from their original locations throughout a special August, 1951, 10-page edition of *NSA News* prepared for the 4th National Student Congress by Merrill Freed (University of Chicago), Chair of the Illinois Region.

NSA Offered Co-ordination of SMAP at Stockholm

[From page 527, col. 5]

STUDENT LEADERS OF NON-COMMUNIST NATIONS PLAN POSITIVE CO-OPERATION

The Stockholm Speech

Speaking under point three of the agenda, titled "International Student Cooperation: Agencies, Means and Methods," Lowenstein gave a speech that aroused considerable controversy. Practical projects, he said, "would be meaningless if they were divorced from the political reality of the international situation in which these projects would have to be carried out."

Lowenstein called it "a false notion that peace can be attained by continuing to pretend that elements of great power and great wickedness do not exist." He blasted the IUS as "Soviet agents," "armed with unscrupulous deceit and with unflagging zeal," who have, "with foresight and cunning . . . laid a pattern to twist and undermine the legitimate aspirations of peoples long craving freedom."

Lowenstein pictured the student awakening to the real nature of IUS as a part of the effort "to avoid Soviet imperialism" and to win world peace.

What we want, said Lowenstein, is a committee, "set up by this conference, responsible to a future conference, to investigate the need and desirability, the financial possibility and the structural form of a new international union."

Opposes New Union Now

Lowenstein continued: "We are opposed to setting up a new union here, because first we must know that a basis exists in southeast Asia and that adequate financing is available . . . We are further opposed to setting up a new union here because we here are representatives of only 21 nations; and it is our conviction that it would be a major fallacy to have any part in the creation of a western union."

Reaction to the Stockholm speech was varied. By a vote of 12 to one with two abstensions, the conference stated its regret that Lowenstein had given such a speech, largely on the ground that it exceeded the terms of the Scandinavian invitation. Eisenberg called the speech a serious tactical error.

The French delegate thought it was "lamentable . . . a great danger . . . purely political, a pure declaration of the foreign policy of the U.S.A." World Student News, official publication of the IUS, said it represented a policy of division and fostering of non-cooperation between socialist and capitalist nations that was "rejected by the honest people of the whole world."

NSA's national executive committee unanimously endorsed the speech. The Canadian delegate, while criticizing the timing, said he personally agreed with every word Lowenstein had said and stated that every student in Canada would vehemently support his strong stand on the matter.

Plans Made for Cooperation

The Stockholm conference resolved that further cooperation between the attending NUS's would be based on the principle of delegating responsibility for the carrying out of specified projects directly from the conference to NUS's or groups of NUS's.

NUS's undertaking projects were also to undertake administrative and financial responsibility for the project.

Delegates weigh sober thoughts at the Stockholm conference, December 17-21 in Sweden. The meeting was called when it became apparent that practical projects could not be implemented through the IUS. Conferees sought another channel of co-operation in the form of delegation of projects to specific national unions of students. Planning is now under way for another assembly, this time of more than Western students, to take place in Canada later on this year. An NSA sub-commission in the New York State Region is cooperating with the Canadians.

The methods of cooperation were to be studied to see if they could be made more effective. The National Federation of Canadian University Students assumed this task. The Canadians also undertook the planning of a conference in 1951 similar to Stockholm but more broadly representative.

The conference recommended support of World University Service, considered setting up an international sports control commission, called for a survey of the structure and functions of NUS's, recommended that NUS's support equal educational opportunities for exiled students, and urged that text-book prices be reduced by setting up co-operatives.

The Belgian NUS was entrusted with the task of publishing a regular bulletin that would collect and disseminate international student news. Facilitation of study abroad became the concern of the Turkish NUS, which agreed to investigate entrance restrictions, services to students, facilities and lodging.

NSA Gets SMAP

Perhaps the most important project adopted at Stockholm was the Students Mutual Assistance Program, the coordination of which was offered to NSA. The program was designed to aid students in colonial and underdeveloped areas.

Britain and Scotland undertook, as part of the program, to examine the possibility of preparing a team to visit one of the British colonial areas in 1951. Norway promised to invite Asiatic student leaders to study in Norway for at least one year.

NSA undertook (1) the sending of highly qualified students as assistants on the technical missions of the intergovernmental agencies, and (2) the sending to under-developed areas of advanced students in technical fields on an international or national team basis.

Reaction to the results of the Stockholm conference was, again, varied. The IUS executive, meeting in Peking April 24-28, called the Stockholm program a "paternalistic" one "of interfering in the internal affairs of the colonial students" and splitting student unity.

Internation Program Implemented

The NEC in December voted to offer the Canadian NUS assistance with its projects, to endorse SMAP and to cooperate with the Belgian bulletin. Subsequently, several national sub-commissions were set up an informational sub-commission, to implement the international program.

The California-Nevada-Hawaii region voted to accept a sub-commission to investigate the wisdom of setting up a new world union of students. The New York State region was granted . . .

Conferences, Surveys Seek Solutions To Issues Created by Current Crisis

[From page 527, col. 4]

Academic Freedom Threatened

Perhaps even more critical was what seemed to be a steady weakening of traditional attitudes of freedom of thought that in the past had been a hallmark of American higher education.

A soberingly large number of abridgments of the liberties of students and professors occurred this year. Some of them are listed elsewhere in this issue.

Of course, this was not the first time that uncertainty and fear had faced U. S. students. But the mature and experienced veteran leadership of the previous four years had largely departed from the campus by 1950. Thus it was a new and younger student generation that had to face up to the problems of a troubled year.

Conferences Suggest Solutions

The types of solutions attempted were indicated by the many student conferences held or planned for this year.

In Des Moines, Iowa, June 21-4, 100 members of the student division of United World Federalists suggested that a long-range educational program aimed at shaping one-world attitudes be combined with a drive for Congressional approval of the principle that the United Nations should be developed into a world government. Student Federalists wanted a world organization capable of enacting, interpreting and enforcing world laws to maintain peace and prevent aggression.

Some 400 Newman Club members will join with leading members of the Heirarchy, educators and club chaplains to discuss "Courageous Catholocism: Its Role in Secular Universities." The convention of the 37-year old organization will be held September 6-9 at Wentworth-by-the-Sea Hotel, Portsmouth, N. H.

Another 400 students are expected to attend the eighth annual congress of the National Federation of Catholic College Students at the College of St. Thomas, St. Paul, Minn., August 26 to September 1. Participants will consider the relation of the Catholic college student to the Church's basic functioning unit—the parish.

Addressing the conclave for the first time will be Canadian Claude MacDonald (University of Toronto), president of Pax Romana, an international movement of Catholic students.

And right next door, in Minneapolis, the fourth National Student Congress of NSA will deal squarely with "The Role of the Student in the World Community."

West Offers New Plan on UNESCO

UNESCO's world program on technical assistance to underdeveloped areas directly parallels NSA interest in the students of these areas.

NSA Must Prove Itself

He suggested that the NSA Congress develop a three-point program if it wishes to collaborate effectively with UNESCO in its work in the underdeveloped areas:

1. NSA must develop with its allied national student unions a minimum international organization, with consultative status to UNESCO and the U. N. economic and social council.

NSA UNESCO DELEGATE

Robert West

2. NSA must be able to show, by maintaining a high level of responsibility and effectiveness in its projects and by financing these projects on a self-sustaining basis, that it can make an important contribution to UNESCO's aims.

3. NSA must build strong, direct ties with the students and the mass-membership representative student organizations in the underdeveloped areas; NSA must be able to show that its program will enjoy the support of both students and governments in these areas.

West recommended that NSA urge UNESCO to give top priority to pilot projects in fundamental education, technical assistance, development of student self-government, and combatting student poverty, disease and poor living conditions in the countries of Asia, Africa and South America.

West's term on the U. S. national commission is expiring this year. Alice Gilbert (Yale, Radcliffe), former chairman of NNER, was nominated by the president and international vice president of NSA to fill the position. Miss Gilbert has, however, declined the nomination.

Present Emergency Discussed

As articles elsewhere in this paper indicate, many conferences of students, educators and other groups this year were preoccupied with the present emergency. NSA participants at meetings of the American Council on Education, Pacific Student Presidents Association, White House Conference, International Association of Women Students and Students for Democratic Action all reported that the current crisis was a major topic of discussion.

The National Student Unions

"Understanding by NSA of the NUS means understanding the students and people of that nation"

NSA 'Foreign Policy'

Relations With Other 'Unions'

(This is the second in a series of three editorials by Rob West, NSA vice-president for international affairs, concerning the "foreign policy" of United States students as created through the International Commission of NSA. In this issue is discussed NSA's relations with National Unions of Students abroad and to outline why Mr. West believes NSA's present policy toward them is the correct and most profitable one for U. S. students. In the next issue of the NEWS, he shall discuss NSA's relations with International Student organizations, and evaluate the experiences this year in the light of its present policy toward them.)

NEARLY EVERY COUNTRY IN THE WORLD which includes a university, and it is well to remember that many countries have developed only one university, contains a student organization incorporating the majority of the students in that nation. These organizations, which vary greatly in scope, organization and program, we group loosely into the category of National Unions of Students. In the United States, NSA acts as the National Union of this country.

The present policy of NSA is to develop the strongest possible ties between itself and each of these (sixty-odd) NUS's abroad. NSA's exchange programs, such as the summer programs described on page one of this issue, are developed through their cooperation, and most of its other programs abroad are carried on with their assistance and cooperation. Since they represent, almost without exception, the closest ties to the students of their countries, we conceive of contacting the students abroad directly through the medium of the NUS's.

PROBABLY THE MOST IMPORTANT FACTOR to bear in mind is that no two National Unions are even closely similar. Their structures are as different as the universities they serve, and their programs, while often very similar in statement to that of NSA, vary with the difference in emphasis allotted to each section.

Most NUS's are relatively weak; some few, primarily in Western Europe, are more strongly developed than NSA. Only those in Western Europe can carry on large-scale programs with ease. Some, it should be said, are primarily organs by which the government indicates its will to the student.

Despite the variations among them, I strongly believe that the present policy of bi-lateral contact with the NUS's is the correct one for NSA. In almost all cases they can, and do, speak directly for the students in their country and NSA's goal of developing international understanding and friendships can most directly be advanced through the medium of this directly-representative body in each country..

PARTICULARLY IN THE ASIATIC COUNTRIES, where the program and policies of the NUS's are far more of political content than in NSA, the NUS speaks for the demands of its member-students; only through this medium can we reach directly to the students of those countries and propose cooperative plans which will have a meaning and a recognition among these students. Only through bi-lateral cooperation with these NUS's can we reach to the students of an area far too long neglected by NSA, and hope to have our proposals, our wish for understanding and friendship, recognized.

It is far more than coincidence which results in the close parallel between the National Union of Students of a country and the existing social pattern of that nation. This parallel so consistently appears, and is so striking, that it can safely be said that the NUS must draw its organization and program out of the existing social structure of its nation.

THIS IS BOTH A STRENGTH AND A WEAKNESS for the NUS; for NSA, it means that adjustment must in each case be made to the existing social order of that country. But the greatest strength of this phenomenon for NSA is that understanding of and by the NUS means, almost without exception, understanding of and by the students and the peoples of that nation. This understanding is the basis of NSA foreign policy; it may most successfully be achieved through strong bi-lateral ties with all the NUS's abroad. No semi-professional or semi-governmental agency offers this to NSA.

The final consideration of this policy which I should like to point out is that quite frequently it is only through the NUS that NSA can make contact with the students of a country. Since the NUS's are supported and exist solely through the efforts of the students, our cooperation to strengthen and expand the program of the NUS brings us into direct contact with the students, and earns for us the confidence and friendship of the students of each country.

—ROB WEST

NSA News 2/49

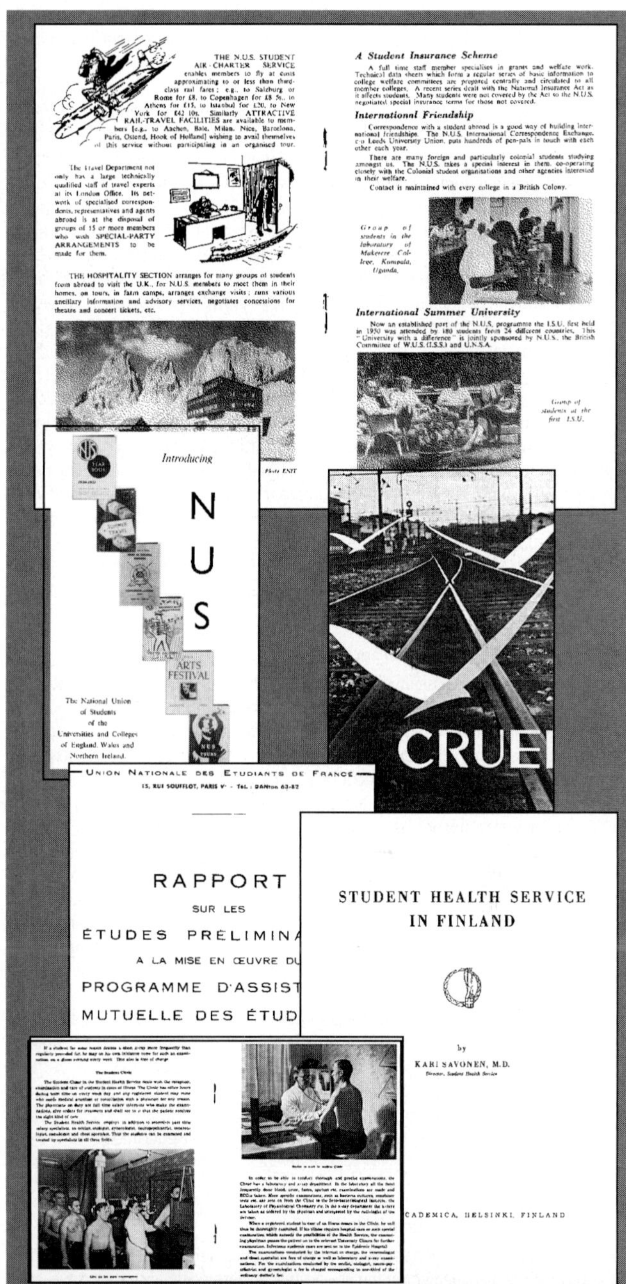

WIDE RANGE OF INTERESTS SERVED by European student unions. From top: The National Union of Students of the Universities and Colleges of England, Wales and Northern Ireland (British National Union) in its information booklet (c.1950). Picture spread features air charter service, student insurance plan, international exchange, international summer university. CRUEI, The National Union of Italian Students Travel Bureau tour booklet (c.1950). The National Union of Students of France issued a working paper for the International Student Conference in 1953 detailing applications of the NSA proposed Student Mutual Assistance Program (SMAP), adopted in Stockholm in 1951 (See p.000). The National Union of Students of Finland describes the National Student Health Service it founded in 1946 (1953 booklet).

The role of students in France and the U.S.

The Student Ideal

Pierre C. Trouvat

President, French National Union of Students, 1946-49

Excerpts from "The student Ideal," NSA Student Government Bulletin, January 1955. At the time, Trouvat was a teaching fellow and graduate student in government at Harvard University.

It seems to me that very seldom is enough emphasis put on the fact that French students—and European students in general—have a higher sense of duty toward their community and conceive of their role in the university in a manner very different from that of the American students I happen to know.

In general, the American student goes to college to study, to learn or get something he will be able to use in his future career: manners, education, a certain sense of values, a certain amount of technical knowledge, a degree which will be the Sesame which will open the door to better jobs, to a better society, or at least will confirm the position of its holder in the milieu in which he was born. The basic characteristic of this attitude is to look above all towards the future, to consider the student not as the actual human being he is today, but as the physician, the business man, the mayor, the teacher, or the taxpayer he will be in a few years.....

The student, as a result, has very seldom the feeling that he exists as such, that the student body has a special position in the community, that the part of being a student implies rights and duties toward the university community or toward the nation. Student government is limited to practical problems: organizing dances, getting new telephone booths in the dorms, deciding the kind of ice cream or soft drinks in the automatic machines. Even when problems of a higher level are discussed, the discussion always shows a strange feeling of inferiority vis-à-vis the university, a lack of consciousness of duties toward the student community, a lack of belief in a role to be played by the student either in the university or in the community....

French Student Conscious of Social Role

In contrast, the position of the French student looks rather peculiar. Of course, when he goes to the university, he is primarily interested in getting the degree without which all interesting careers would be closed to him. Without any doubt, he considers the years he will spend at the University as a transitory period between life with his parents and an independent life as a responsible citizen. But this transitory period has a character of its own and the student is conscious that he has a role to perform in society, not only as a future professional but also as a student.

First of all, he has the feeling of being a privileged person. In France, as everywhere in Europe, getting a university education is a luxury: out of a population about 1/4 that of the U. S., we have less than 150,000 students. The United States with over 3,000,000 college students, has about five times as many students per thousand population as does France. (Incidentally, figures for Germany are about the same, and figures for England show a lower ratio of students per inhabitant.)

The immediate result is that the students have the feeling of constituting an elite, and they understand the necessity of acting so as to deserve this privileged position. It implies not only that the student has a duty as such to try to set the best possible preparation for his future career, but also that he has a duty to maintain this character of elite by ensuring

a) that the university really provides the best possible education;

b) that the university is accessible to the best students, to all who deserve to become the elite of the nation.

Responsibilities of the French Student "Elite"

This explains why the students have claimed and obtained a direct responsibility in the management of the university at all levels: administration, services, program of education, discipline.

This explains also why French students under the leadership of their National Union, representing all the students in the country, discuss continuously with the government and the university authorities all problems connected with the general question of access to the university: reform of the structure of our system of education, freedom of the university, economic measures to ensure to everyone who deserves it, regardless of his social or economic situation, the possibility of going to the university....

Students Active During German Occupation

This is the reason why the stand taken by the students during the German occupation was so important.... More than any other group in France, the students participated in the underground resistance, sometimes with their faculty, more often without or even against their masters, sometimes leading their professors or persuading them to join the fight against Nazism and oppression.

Formation of the French National Union of Students

In April, 1946, we reorganized the National Union of Students, and at the Congress of Grenoble where I had the honor to be elected President of the Union, we adopted a "Charter of the Student" in which the students stated clearly what they understood to be their rights as well as their duties.

The first lines of the Preamble read:

"We, students of France, faithful to the memory of the best among us—who died to express their ideals as Frenchmen and members of the university community, In order to perpetuate the memory of their courage and of their sense of responsibility toward the community,

We have accepted this charter, which lists the rights we claim and the duties we swear to face... .

This text expresses much better than longer elaboration this consciousness of the student community, which is a very important feature of the French university.

PIERRE C. TROUVAT, French NUS President, 1946-49, in photos with Allard K. Lowenstein (right), 1950-51 NSA President in Madison, WI (Joan Lynch). **JEAN SARVONAT** (photo right), French NUS President, 1952, with his French translator at the U. Minnesota 4th National Student Congress (*NSA News*, 5/52).

U.S.-CANADIAN STUDENT EXCHANGE

Committee
for
United States - Canadian Student Exchange

CO-ORDINATED BY

U. S. NATIONAL STUDENT ASSOCIATION
INTERNATIONAL ACTIVITIES COMMISSION
5 BRYANT STREET
CAMBRIDGE 38, MASSACHUSETTS, U. S. A.

NATIONAL FEDERATION OF CANADIAN UNIVERSITY STUDENTS
U. S. - CANADIAN EXCHANGE COMMITTEE
29 QUEEN'S PARK, TORONTO, CANADA

December 8, 1947

President E. F. Dolan
Flora Stone Mather College
Cleveland, Ohio

Dear Sir:

At the
tion held i
Conference
October 12
tically end

Despit
national le
program ap
Canadian-U.
these two g
which such
graduate le
that betwee
be cited.

NATIONAL FEDERATION OF
CANADIAN UNIVERSITY STUDENTS

Headquarters: Mr. D. G. Seldon, NFCUS, McMaster Univ., Hamilton, Ontario.

Officers:
Hon. Pres.: Dr. F. Cyril James, Principal, McGill Univ.
President: Gordon Gwynne-Timothy
Vice-Presidents: Jerry Macdonald
Eugene Lavigne
Gilles Trahan
Ross B. Hamilton
Sec'y-Treas.: D. G. Seldon

Conferences: "Conferences held annually, in September or December, at one of the member universities, preferably in Central Canada for reasons of economy. Each member university entitled to send 2 delegates, 2 observers, and any number of unofficial observers."

Membership: "About 20 universities representing 60,000 students are members. A university is defined as a chartered institution granting degrees subsequent to matriculation."

A PROGRAM OF UNDERGRADUATE EXCHANGES was proposed by NSA and the National Federation of Canadian University Students (NFCUS) in 1947. Bob Smith, NSA International V.P, wrote about it (above) to all U.S. college presidents (Case Western Reserve University Archives). Smith recalls Maurice Sauve, 1947 NFCUS President, later a Canadian minister, attended the NSA Congress in Madison that year. The exchange program is cited in the NFCUS listing in NSA's 1949 directory "National Student Unions," a portion of which is shown above.

The UN and UNESCO Inspire Post-War Hopes

Editor's Note: Many of the memoirs in this anthology provide reminders that students and veterans placed high hopes for post-war peace and reconstruction in the adoption of the United Nations charter in 1945 in San Francisco, the first UN Assembly in London in the summer of 1946 and the first General Assembly of UNESCO in December (e.g., See Meyer, "A Service Man Looks at the Peace," Pt. 4, S.1, Hunt; "The Conference of Southern Students and the 1945 San Francisco Conference," Pt. 6, S.6; and Robert Smith, this section). NSA's election for one of the three youth seats on the U.S. National Commission in 1947 just after NSA's formation, "was a great honor," as Smith writes. NSA's first representative for a three year term to the commission, he was appointed to its Executive Committee. Smith was followed in 1949 by 1948-49 International V.P. Rob West, and by NSA 1951-52 President Dick Murphy in 1952. The Commission provided an early forum for NSA to voice its ideas for developing and strengthening international educational, social and cultural programs among college students (see pp. 317, 510 and 528).

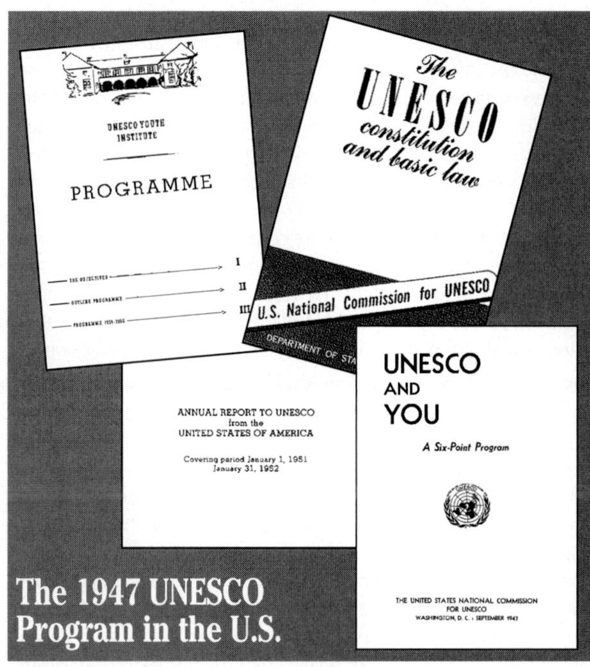

The 1947 UNESCO Program in the U.S.

Point One:
How Can You Aid in Rebuilding the World's War-Devastated Schools and Libraries?

Point Two:
How Can You Make Your Personal Opinion Felt on the Side of Peace?

Point Three:
What Can You Do to Help Dramatize UNESCO's Aims, Principles, and Projects in Your Community?

Point Four:
How Can You Help Train the Younger Generation in the Ways of Peace?

Point Five:
How Can You Personally Take Part in UNESCO's Continuing Adventure of Adult Education?

Point Six:
How Can You Help Promote Understanding Among the Racial and Religious Groups in Your Community?

Source, "UNESCO AND YOU," Dept. of State, 9/47

NSA to Plan Student Section For UNESCO Conference

Member Schools Get Invitations

Responsibility for the planning of the college and university students section of the Second National Conference on UNESCO, which will be held in Cleveland, March 31 to April 2, has been delegated by UNESCO Relations Staff to Rob West, NSA vice-president for international affairs, and Robert Smith, NSA's representative on UNESCO.

In addition to West and Smith, NSA will be represented at the Conference by Richard Heggie, vice-president for student life, and William Vobach, international affairs chairman for the Ohio Region.

Invitations have been sent to NSA Committees at all member schools asking them to send from one to three delegates.

Student Section Agenda

It will be West's and Smith's responsibility to propose an agenda and discussion topics for the student section. They will also help the group develop workable recommendations for further action in UNESCO activities.

West and Smith will be assisted by a number of students who have carried out activities in the fields of educational reconstruction, interchange of persons, education for international understanding, etc.

NSA will also participate in an exhibit prepared by the participating organizations at the Conference. The exhibit, covering 10,000 square feet of wall space in the Cleveland Auditorium, is to consist of panels and three-dimensional presentations of activities related to UNESCO's program.

Students Prepare Exhibit

A committee of students from Harvard, MIT, Wellesley, Radcliffe,

Berlin University Receives Aid

NEARLY THREE TONS of clothing, shoes, and books are being sent by Stanford students to the Free University of Berlin—a group of German students and professors who fled from Russian-controlled territory to organise a university clear of political control. Here Stanford co-eds do last-minute work on the relief shipment, collected and packed in duffel bags by students. The girls are (l. to r.) Sigrid Leube of Heidelberg, Germany, at Stanford on a student-supported foreign scholarship; Margaret Andrus of Bronxville, N. Y., university UNESCO chairman; and Gretchen Blaesing of Portland, Oreg., Stanford International Relief Organization chairman.

Canadians Seek Coc

Miss Helen Bryan of NSA's International Commission attended the Conference of the National Federation of Canadian University Students in Montreal, Dec. 28 to 31, representing the National Student Association.

Miss Bryan presented the greetings of American students and urged

liaison with the NSA such as the tually to an expanded liaison embracing other national student unions in Central and South America with which a similar community of interest exist, Therefore be it resolved that the NFCUS Executive write to the Executive of NSA informing them of their desire of

NSA News 2/49

To Bring Men and Ideas Together

The People of the world must learn to live together. The evils of ignorance must be countered by knowledge; suspicion must be offset by trust, and jealousy, by mutual respect.

The aim of UNESCO is to bring men and ideas together, but its success will depend largely on individuals, members of various organizations believing in UNESCO, who take an active part in this campaign to resolve the misunderstandings, the fears and suspicions now so prevalent among the peoples of the world.

George C. Marshall, Secretary of State

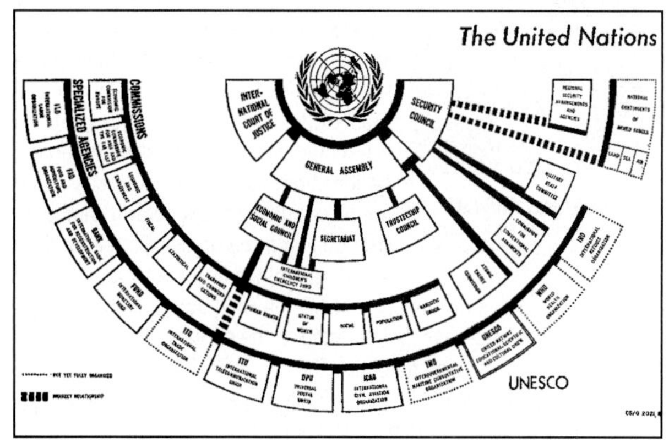

Paths to the United Nations: Erskine Childers and Olof Palme

Helen Bryan Garland
Sarah Lawrence College
Manager, NSA Student Travel Program, 1948-50
(See p. 649 for author biography)

In June 1972, the first UN Conference on the Human Environment was convened in Stockholm. It was the culmination of efforts over a period of years by the Prime Minister of Sweden, Olof Palme, a former President of the Swedish National Union of Students in 1952, and UN Secretariat staff member Erskine Childers, former NSA International Vice President for International Affairs in 1949-50, as well as many others with whom they collaborated.

While it laid the foundation for continuing international environmental initiatives (such as the Rio conference in 1992, and the Earth Council in Stockholm in 1997), it also was a stage behind which invisible forces sought to control the environmental program, so that it would not impede global commercial energy interests.

Childers and Palme were on the visible, and positive side of that story. As I was a first-handed observer of events at the time, there are two threads of the student leadership story that this event enables me to bring together and that I would like to recall in this brief commemoration of Childers and Palme. It also enables me to raise a question, as yet not fully explored, of what was going on behind the scenes.

The UN provided a career path for young internationalists

The first is that young idealistic internationalists in the years after World War II could find each other and develop their interests as student leaders, eventually pursuing careers aimed at perfecting the United Nations as a way of bettering conditions of living throughout the world.

The second is that another cohort of contemporary student leaders were building networks of influence intended to by-pass the goals of the former in order to protect global commercial interests.

Childers and Palme are good archetypes of the first mentioned, as I got to know them both through NSA, and built lifetime friendships that lasted until Palme's mysterious and still unsolved assassination in Stockholm in 1986 at the age of 59, while he was Prime Minister of Sweden, and until Childers' death of a heart attack in 1996 at the age of 69. Erskine had just delivered a speech in Luxembourg to the World Federation of United Nations Associations, of which he was Secretary General, a position he took a few years after his retirement from the United Nations Secretariat in 1990.

Erskine Childers, champion for justice within the UN

Erskine B. Childers
Stanford U., NSA International Vice President, 1949-50

Erskine was NSA Vice President when he was a student at Stanford University. He had the same name as his father, who became President of Ireland in 1973, and his grandfather, who wrote the classic spy novel *Riddle in the Sands*, and was a martyr in the Irish rebellion in 1922. Erskine had a strong interest in, and wrote about the Arab world, and was a champion of the Palestinian cause. He worked for the United Nations from 1967 to 1990. He was noted for his studies on UN reform aimed at strengthening the organization and diluting the grip of the major powers.

His collaborator in some of his reform studies, Brian Urquhart wrote, "He was passionately interested in the endless quest for justice, equity and fairness in international affairs.... More than one effort to put him in a post that would have given full scope to his great talents was effectively blocked by mumbling and unspecific reservations."

Olof Palme, champion for global social democracy

Olof Palme
Kenyon College, OH, 1947. 1951-52, President, Swedish National Union of Students

Olof graduated high school at age 17, and after completing military service his travels took him to the U.S. where he completed his undergraduate degree in 1947 at Kenyon College in Ohio. Before returning to Sweden, he hitchhiked across the U.S. to Mexico and established a bond with this country and its people of which our friendship was one expression.

In 1951 he received his law degree at Stockholm University and became the President of the Swedish National Union of Students. As President of the Swedish NUS he worked with NSA leaders of that era. This experience also launched him on a political career in Sweden in the Social Democratic Party and on the international scene. He opposed the Soviet invasion of Czechoslovakia and was a strong opponent of the US war in Vietnam.

As both Erskine and Olof rose in prominence, they found congruent interests in promoting strong environmental initiatives. By the time of the 1972 conference, however, one could find hardly a mention that these two men had helped to spearhead the environmental cause within the UN. I was intimately familiar with the events leading to the conference because of my work over a period of years with Margaret Mead as her "eyes and ears" at the UN and because of her great interest in the event.

How Childers and Palme were eclipsed in its historic annals, and how Childers fought a losing battle for reform within the UN is the second thread in my recall, a story that needs to be told in detail in another book. Suffice it to say here that not all the students of their generation who pursued careers in international affairs took the road of idealism.

The story of commercial and political interests, as yet untold

Childers and Palme were of the same generation as later prominent world figures such as George Bush, Sr. (Yale) and Henry Kissinger (Harvard) for whom geopolitical strategies and control over the levers of power were the means to attainment of their world view. Through the kind of influence the latter had built, I can see now how the staff leadership and control of the Stockholm event passed into hands that made sure its outcomes would not stand in the way of the powerful commercial and political interests that Erskine and Olof were concerned about.

The NSA story during its early years was an irreplaceably enriching experience for me. But, looking back more than 50 years later, I realize that in my naiveté I missed an equally big if not a bigger story that was unfolding around us, even while at college, being developed by other student leaders with a different agenda. It is a story of intrigue, which I hope will yet be told by others of us who were there.

Erskine B. Childers
Secretary General, World Federation of Unites Nations Associations, c. 1995

Olof Palme
Prime Minister of Sweden c. 1985

SECTION 2

NSA in the Cold War

CONTENTS

In the days of hope and promise following World War II, the U.S. students who journeyed to the Prague World Student Congress in August 1946 believed that "it would settle outstanding international problems," as U.S. delegate Douglass Cater (Harvard) wrote in his August 1949 reflections on the "Collapse of Youth's One World."

By spring 1948, the unbridgeable ideological gap created by Communist leaders controlling the International Union of Students found its decisive expression in the IUS resolution following the Czech coup. Cater described the resolution as "endorsing to the hilt, the actions of the Communists" against Czech students with its statement, "We do not defend the rights of undemocratic students."

The history of NSA's efforts to define some relationship with IUS, and then to build an international collaboration with non-Communist student unions are described in a digest of a report by Peter Jones (Yale), prepared by Pat Wohlgemuth Blair (Wellesley College), who had been a staff associate in NSA's international office in 1947–48.

During each of the years through 1950, NSA had representatives or observers in Europe at various IUS and related international events. University of Wisconsin student leaders Royal Voegeli and Norman Holmes each tell of their adventurous 1948 journey through Europe, finding their way briefly into Poland and then representing NSA President Bill Welsh at the IUS Council in Brussels.

Robert L. West's (Yale) plea to the 1950 World Student Congress on behalf of American students is reproduced, as are portions of Bill Holbrook's (University of Minnesota) reports, which were syndicated in various college newspapers. Holbrook describes vividly the drama of the Congress.

The Lowenstein address at the December 1950 International Student Conference at Stockholm is reproduced. It voices a hope for democratic political systems as one of the outcomes of technical assistance programs to developing countries.

The U.S. government gets involved—secretly

In the early years of the Cold War, the U.S. government was concerned that American nongovernment organizations have adequate financing to provide effective U.S. voices on the international stage. The government's choice to secretly fund the international programs of some of these organizations through the CIA has been hotly debated since it was exposed in 1967. NSA was one of the organizations that received this funding. In a unit devoted to the matter, the editors of this book have endeavored to bring to light whatever they could about the early origins of this program, which began in 1951.

This section closes with two poignant pieces. One is devoted to the tragically short life of Avrea Ingram, NSA's fifth international vice president. The other is a report on the final years of Josef Grohman, the first president of the IUS.

NSA Seeks Ways to Raise the Iron Curtain

The students of the United States have a responsibility in the world student community
—1947 Constitutional Convention

Unsuccessful efforts to find common ground with the Communist-dominated International Union of Students (IUS) focused NSA's 'foreign policy' goals in its first five years.

THE 1947 CONSTITUTIONAL CONVENTION
Affiliation Recommended

WHEREAS the International Union of Students, established at the Prague World Student Congress of 1946, is the most widely representative student organization in the world-and

WHEREAS study and observation of the IUS by National Continuations Committee members during the past eight months have revealed that its program of cultural and educational activities in the international field can be important in the furthering of international understanding-and

WHEREAS the students of the United States, in view of the leading role being played by this nation in world affairs, have a similar responsibility in the world student community, specifically to (1) learn more about the world at large, (2) teach the rest of the world more about the USA, and (3) learn to work together with people who do not necessarily share their ideology and political philosophies and

WHEREAS the International Union of Students is the only point of contact with the students of the nations of Eastern Europe . . .

THEREFORE BE IT RESOLVED: that the Constitutional Convention of USNSA, desirous of wholehearted and fullest cooperation with students throughout the world, while recognizing that American students, participating in IUS through the USNSA, do not intend to become involved in political issues of a partisan nature, and although at present there are fundamental differences between USNSA on the one hand and the IUS and some of its member-organizations on the other hand, nevertheless, recommends affiliation as soon as possible with the IUS, subject to the procedure stated in "Agreement on IUS Affiliation."

THE 1948 FIRST NSA CONGRESS
Negotiations are Suspended

"The Congress of the USNSA affirms the position taken by the National Executive Committee in its statement of April 11, 1948, concerning relations with the International Union of Students, and confirms that negotiations for affiliation with that body are suspended.

The USNSA will not now participate inthe formation of a Western Union or any other competitive international student union."

The April 11, 1948, statement of the NSA not only suspended affiliation negotiations with the IUS, but stated as follows, in part:

"In recognition of thepossible implications of our action, we wish to make it clearly known that the NSA shall continue in the implementation of its international program THROUGH EVERY AVAILABLE MEANS . . . It shall remain our hope that the NSA program of international student activities will contribute to an arresting of that deterioration of relations between nations which at the present time constitutes a serious threat to the peace of the world."

THE 1950 THIRD NSA CONGRESS
Global Consultations for Alternative

The USNSA will consult with the student organizations of the world in order to determine whether there exists the basis for formation of an international organization open to all students, which would embrace the characteristics of an international organization enumerated above. [NSA listed 12 requirements for non-political inclusiveness]

We stand opposed, however, to the establishment of any international organic framework for cooperation that could not enjoy the support of students in the countries of Asia, Latin America, the Middle East, Africa, and Europe who would be willing to subordinate ideological differences in common service to the above stated objectives.

IUS WAS LAUNCHED IN 1946 WITH HIGH HOPES FOR THE SOLIDARITY OF STUDENTS AROUND THE WORLD

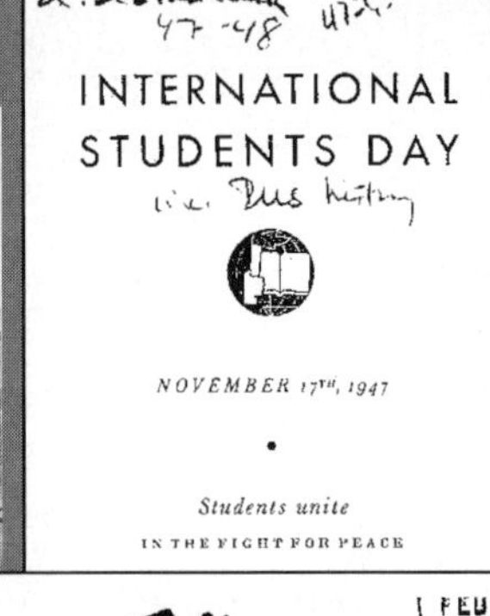

ly Sun

RY 26, 1948 — PRICE FIVE CENTS

Communists Gain Full Control Of Czech Government Reins As Gottwald Ousts Opposition

New Regime Draws Student Criticism In Mass Protests

Prague, Feb. 25 — (AP) — Communists won control of Czechoslovakia today.

CORNELL DAILY SUN

NSA Officials in Europe Resign Over Czech Anti-Student Action

Two interim representatives of the National Student ... to the International U... dents in Europe ha... their positions, pro... failure of the IUS s... censure the present Czechoslova-

ST. JOSEPH'S COLLEGE, PHILADELPHIA 31, PA.

Reds' Violence to Students Brings NSA Break with IUS

NSA Requests Official Protest Over Killing of Czechoslovakian Student by Red Police Forces; IUS Refuses To Act

...fficial ties with the ...Students for failure ...ing and injuring of ...Red's occupation of ...

...n by any government ...munist controlled. In

IUS FAILURE TO ACT DISILLUSIONED NSA

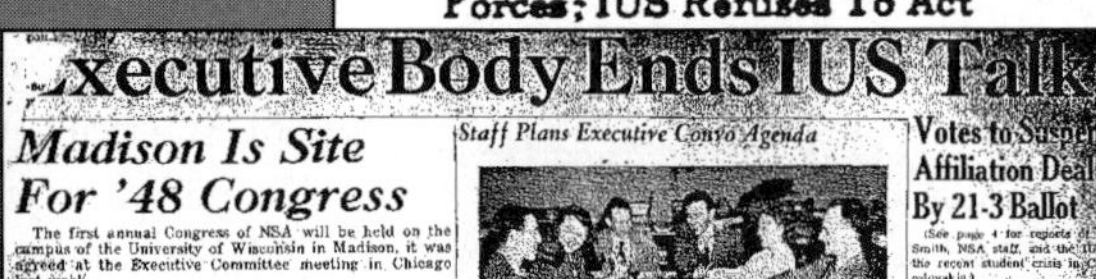

Executive Body Ends IUS Talks

Madison Is Site For '48 Congress

The first annual Congress of NSA will be held on the campus of the University of Wisconsin in Madison, it was agreed at the Executive Committee meeting in Chicago last week.

Madison was also the site of the constitutional convention of the association last summer.

Staff Plans Executive Convo Agenda

Votes to Suspend Affiliation Deal By 21-3 Ballot

The Executive Committee of NSA voted 21 to 3 to suspend negotiations for affiliation with the IUS.

Regional NSA Group Hits Move to Cut IUS Relations

A vehement protest against the recent resolution by the National Student Association's staff committee to sever relations with the International Union of Students was registered last night by Lawrence M. Jaffa 2D, chairman of the NSA's Northern New England Regional Division, and a member of the four-man board appointed in December to consider NSA-IUS affiliation.

The staff committee's resolution came early this month, following the resigna-

NSA To 'Cooperate On Specific Projects With International Union Of Students

1. It should be broadly representative of the students of the world and should not exclude students on the basis of color, creed, or political belief.

2. Full membership in the organization should be on the basis of representative national union of students alone, with a scale representing the number of registered college and university students in each union.

3. Provisional membership in those countries without a national union should be granted to repre-

...oulder, Colorado, March, 1952 — Price 5 Cen...

Conference Plans Secretariat For Worldwide Student Unity

Delegates from 23 countries voted unanimously at the Edinburgh International Student conference Jan. 3-10 to create a Coordinating Secretariat to strengthen international student cooperation.

Resolving not to form a western union of students, the conference ensured that the Secretariat would not have executive powers or extensive scope, stating:

"The Secretariat shall be the administrative agency to ensure

Meeting in the cold Scottish winter at the University of Edinburgh and the Grosvenor hotel where the conference participants were housed, the conferees also voted to place the calling of the next International Student confer-

A MEETING IN COPENHAGEN of the Consec-sponsored International Student Conference in 1953. NSA representatives: Sylvia Bacon, left. From right, Helen Jean Rogers, Avrea Ingram (Hoover Institute Archives).

AN ALTERNATIVE ORGANIZATION WA FORMED IN 1952.

NSA's leadership in 1946 believed stron ly that it would be possible for students themselves to override east-west ideolc ical conflicts through non-political mut al collaboration (see "Call to the World Student Congress" pp. 79-80). But the ga seemed unbridgeable (see Ellis, p. 106; Cater, p. 535). In a response to their frustration, NSA and other non-Communist Western student unions formed Cosec (See Lowenstein, p. 562; Dentzer, p. 301)

From the top: IUS publications (Hoover Institute Archives). *Cornell Daily Sun*, 1/26/46; 3/24/48; St. Joseph's College *Hawk*, 4/1/48, *NSA News*, 4/48; "Regional NSA," Harvard *Crimson*, 3/13/48; U. of Colorado *The Silver and Gold*, 10/5/49; *NSA New* 3/52.

The second war generation in its turn has had to learn the sad lesson of disillusionment from the implacable "our way or none" dialecticians

1. Collapse of Youth's One World

Douglass Cater
Harvard University
Member, U.S. Delegation to the 1946 Prague World Student Congress
Reprinted from The Reporter *magazine, August 30, 1949*

Editor's note: This article was written three years after Cater returned from the 1946 World Student Congress in Prague. See Cater and the Prague delegation, pp. 92, 94.

If Congressman Nixon of the Un-American Activities Committee has a dossier on me, he knows that I have journeyed halfway around the world three times since the war to confer with Russians, Bulgarians, Poles, and subversive people of several other nationalities. He has read that speakers at the conferences I attended attacked Anglo-American imperialism, encouraged the revolutionaries of Southeast Asia, condemned the actions of Chiang Kai-shek, and lauded the "people's democracies" of eastern Europe. If Nixon ever levels his sights on me I'll probably be done for.

My suspicious connection with the East began in the spring of 1946, when the Harvard Student Council chose me as delegate to the World Student Congress to be held in Prague that summer. My chief qualification was that I had a smattering of Russian, which I had picked up in my O.S.S. days. No one knew much about the conference except that a committee of prominent persons in New York was sponsoring the American delegation. Incredible as it may seem today, three years ago we were not in the habit of inquiring into the hidden motives of prominent persons. Without much ado, the student council appropriated funds to buy my passage.

Twenty-five of us from all over the country made up the American delegation. It is difficult now to describe how we felt about our mission. Europe was no longer a vast battleground for young people; Prague had become the meeting place between East and West. Our student congress was a big thing: More than 350 students from thirty-eight countries were to attend.

We passed through Paris, where the Peace Conference was about to begin, and we believed, along with many diplomats, that it would settle outstanding international problems.

Above everything else, we were eager to get to know and to work with the Russians, who flew into Prague in a swift Soviet transport plane a day or two after we had arrived in a crowded third-class railway coach. There were twenty-five of them, as there were of us. We were the two largest delegations. The morning the Russians first walked into the dining room, our Texas delegate looked up and drawled to himself: "By golly, we don't have to look under the bed any longer. There's some real live Reds standing up!" His words summed up the contempt we all felt for hysterical anti-Communism. We were going to break down ideological barriers.

To get off to a good start, we scraped together all the wine and food we could find and invited the Russians to a party. They came, bearing bottles of vodka, which they had brought along in their plane. We all drank heartily, and, in the fashion of so many diplomatic gatherings during the war, Americans and Russians mistook the warmth of alcohol for the warmth of friendship. We sang and danced together. In mock seriousness I begged a pretty blonde from the Ukraine to come with me to my native Alabama directly after the Congress. She proposed that we flee to Kiev.

Besides the Russians and ourselves, there were Cubans and Danes, Australians and Inner Mongolians, British and Viet-Namese in the thirty-eight delegations. We lived at Masaryk Kolej, a student dormitory out past Hradcany Castle. For ten days we spent all our waking hours together—meetings in the daytime, parties at night.

Our theme was "The Student's Role in the Postwar World." We were well aware of the heroic wartime roles played by students. Our meeting place had been the scene of a student uprising against the Nazis; its walls were scarred by German machine-gun fire.

In ten days, we established an organization, the International Union of Students, which "democratic" groups from every country were invited to join; we passed a flood of resolutions and laid out an extensive program. Student exchange, work camps, travel tours, an international student magazine, sanatoriums for tubercular students—all these were our projects.

The word "democratic" caused a little trouble. In attempting to define it, the Russians put forward a resolution that there could be "no discrimination because of race, creed, color, economic circumstance...." We Americans proposed "free speech, elections, minority reports," etc. The congress obligingly passed both resolutions.

All went well until it came time for the drafting commission to put the resolutions into finished shape. Then Tamara Ersheva, a Soviet delegate, who—unlike my dance partner—was deadly serious, insisted that the American resolution be dropped. I answered rather heatedly. Thereupon she turned and put me in my place with a delightful non sequitur.

"It's not us I'm thinking about," she said almost tearfully. "It's the poor Negroes in your South!"

Looking back, I can remember two or three such instances, petty and almost laughable at the time, but indicative of troubles to come. A few members of our delegation expressed concern then, but the rest of us insisted that we must give this thing a fair chance.

The congress ended in a burst of good spirits. Students seized Prime Minister [Klement] Gottwald, who had shown up for the closing celebration, and threw him high into the air. The stocky Communist boss sailed again and again over the cheering crowd, untroubled by fears of capitalist chicanery.

Still enthusiastic in spite of a few small doubts, we elected one of our delegation to remain in Prague as American vice-president. The rest of us returned to the United States. During Christmas vacation, we held a conference in Chicago. Students from two hundred or so colleges came and decided that they would establish a national student organization the following September.

Five of us went back to Prague in the summer of 1947 to attend a meeting of the governing council of the IUS. The Marshall Plan was in preparation. Russia had just put the screws on Czechoslovakia to keep it from participating in the American scheme. Someone had put the screws on the IUS, too. The meeting got underway with a fiery attack by Royko Tomavitch, a young Yugoslav who had been one of Tito's Partisans, on Britain's treatment of India. A lovely Egyptian girl harangued us about British "fascist imperialism" in Egypt. An Indonesian plopped on the table a resolution condemning the Dutch, the British, and the Americans.

One of the American delegates turned pleasantly to a new Chinese delegate sitting next to him and introduced himself. Equally pleasantly, the Chinese replied that he represented the "Anti-U.S. Atrocity League," which, it seemed, was a large and thriving student organization in his country.

I roomed next door to a little Viet-Namese named Do Dai, who used to wake me up every morning singing "My Darling Clementine" in a loud, nasal voice. "Cardboard boxes without topses served as shoes for Clementine, oh, my darling oh, my darling, oh, my..." I would hurl a shoe to halt the chorus. We were close friends, but that did not make his attacks on Viet-Nam's enemies any less ferocious. Upset by the thread of truth running through his accusations, we protested that problems such as the colonial one were not in the province of a student organization.

"What do you mean, not a student problem?" shouted Do Dai shrilly. "I cannot study because I must all the time shoot at the French. It is most certainly a student problem!"

Throughout the colonials' campaign, the Soviet delegates sat impassively. They voted to back all the colonial demands, no matter how extreme. To be sure, these were only paper resolutions being passed by little more than a paper organization. But by centering on issues which divided the world student community, they were helping to destroy the organization. No one could object to allowing the IUS to serve as a forum for student grievances; but we could not agree that it should dwell lopsidedly on the evils of the non-Soviet world.

The Russians' reports on student conditions in their own country were undiluted hymns of praise, with never a word of complaint. The implications of the Soviet system now became clear to me. Its student organization, like its labor groups, church, and press, was a company union—thc company being a government run by a tightly knit party. The independence and daring that have characterized student movements throughout history were crushed.

Royko Tomavitch, the Yugoslav, often talked with me about how to avoid a split in the IUS. He agreed that it was unwise to concentrate on irreconcilable issues. Yet not once did he side against the Russians when it came to a vote. Probably he would have [done so] at the next year's council meeting, but he was not there, nor was I.

I left Prague that August with a feeling of failure, and flew back to Madison, Wisconsin, to report to the National Student Congress. At the University of Wisconsin, more than a thousand students had gathered from all over the country to found the National Student Association. They were very much occupied with the task at hand and had little time to consider the IUS. Moreover, because of reports of its Communist leanings, they were extremely wary of having anything to do with it.

They listened to our report, though, and our recommendation that they get in and try to right the balance in the IUS. After drawing up a lengthy statement defining their reservations, they agreed.

This was a notable milestone for those of us who had been connected with the enterprise from the beginning. At last, American students were ready to participate directly in the international field. As far as working with the IUS was concerned, however, the end was approaching. Five months later, the well-known "February Events" finished democracy in Czechoslovakia.

Like all other independent organizations, the Czech Student Union was seized by a Communist "action" committee. Czech students who paraded in protest against the coup were forcibly dispersed and certain leaders [were] arrested. Our American student representative in Prague, an eyewitness, called on the IUS secretariat to protest. Instead, that body adopted a resolution endorsing, to the hilt, the action of the Communists: "We do not defend the rights of undemocratic students."

In ten days the work of two and a half years was nullified. Our representative resigned, and the U.S. National Student Association gave up its affiliation proceedings. One by one, student organizations from other non-Communist countries have been doing the same thing.

Last summer, I visited Prague for a few days to find out what happened to the IUS. Its leaders were still carrying on with the same outward enthusiasm, but a change was apparent. The Soviets, now that the organization had become a straight party "front," seemed to have lost interest. From what I could gather, the IUS was stranded, looking eagerly but vainly to Moscow for guidance.

Silas Douglass Cater, Jr. was President of Washington College in Maryland. Earlier he was a journalist with The Reporter, *and later Vice Chairman of England's* Observer. *Author of five books, he was also Special Assistant to President Lyndon Johnson and taught at Princeton, Wesleyan, Stanford, and the University of California (**see p. 93* *for extended bio).*

PICTURE CREDITS: *Then:* Masaryk Coleg, Prague, August, 1946. *Now:* c. 1967 with President Lyndon Johnson at the White House (Both courtesy Libby Cater Halaby)

CATER'S EARLY EFFORTS AS HONEST BROKER

The Harvard Crimson

Cater Hits European 'War Is Here' Attitude, Calls for Student Exchange to Keep Peace

In his first appearance before the student body of the College since his return from Prague, Douglass Cater '46 outlined the results of the Prague conference and pleaded for international coöperation on the student level at an open forum in the Lowell House Junior Common Room last night.

Coincidentally, Cater announced that the Student Council Comittee on International Student Affairs, which he heads, has made tentative plans to bring Carl Grube, Austrian Foreign Minister presently in this country, before a College audience some time this fall. Grube's talk would be the first in a possible series of forums on international relations

Citing as an example the New York Times correspondent in Prague, who told him that "the war is already on, we are

Cater, Dinet, Wharton Win Chicago Delegate Positions

..., and CLIFTON R. WHARTON, ...ty delegates to the National Stu... ...et, Jr. '44, who is in Chicago.

...r '46, Eugene A. Dinet, Jr. '44, ...the University delegates to the ... to the tabulation of yesterday's

Elliott's Charges Scored By Conference Delegate

DOUGLASS CATER '46

Cater Denies Kremlin Control Of Student Representatives At International Conference

CALLS SOURCES BIASED

Nominee Challenges Naivete In Spreading 'Misstatements' Based on Isolated Report

Specifically denying the allegations of Professor William Y. Elliott as to Communist domination of the International Student Congress, Douglass Cater '46, Harvard delegate to last summer's Prague meeting of the group, last night charged that the Government professor's information came from just one biased source.

In a statem... Elliott's slaps ... Cater traced ... one Henry Bri...

From Top: *Harvard Crimson* 10/25/46, 12/18/46, 12/20/46

CATER PROVIDED LEADERSHIP IN VOICING THE U.S. DELEGATION'S HOPES. On his return from Prague in September, 1946, Cater wrote a detailed five installment report for the Harvard *Crimson* in which he hailed the work of 37 delegations "actively working for peace" (See p. 92). He also reported on the looming conflicts with the Soviet and allied delegations, as he notes in this article. In the early months he and other returning delegates confronted concerns over Communist control of the World Student Congress (See *Crimson* article above) with a defense of its potential as a constructive open forum and spnsor of useful student exchanges. Photos clockwise above (1) On the way to Prague. Cater is on the right. (2) Standing, addressing the U.S. delegation in Prague. In the foreground from the left, Jean Casson (Unitarian Youth), Walter Wallace (Youthbuilders), Russel Austin (U. of Chicago), Curt Farrar (Student Federalists). (3) The Russian delegation at a Congress session (4) The U.S. delegation, from right: Cater, Al Houghton (U. of Wisconsin), Joyce Roberts (Pembroke C., NICC). Jewel Lubin (Delegation Secretary). Above (5) With newly elected IUS officers, from left: Joseph Grohman, President, Cater, Tom Madden (England), Secretary, unidentified. (6) Cater's Congress delegate card. (2 & 3, Joyce Roberts Harrison, 1,4,5 & 6 Libby Cater Hallaby).

2. NSA's Relations with the International Union of Students

This chronology is an abridgement of "U.S.N.S.A. and I.U.S. Relations: 1945–1955," *by Peter T. Jones (based on research by Linda Simmons), published by the International Commission of USNSA, Cambridge, MA, 1955 (mimeo).*

Written in 1955 by **Peter T. Jones**
Yale '51, Harvard Law School
Abridged and edited by **Pat Wohlgemuth Blair**
Wellesley '50, Haverford '52. NSA International Office, 1947-48

London and Washington were headquarters for international student groups working for the Allied cause throughout the Second World War. In March of 1945, the British National Union of Students called a meeting of twenty-four Allied students then in London to plan a new international student federation as soon as possible after the war's end. . . . The London Committee soon learned that Czech students under the guidance of their government were also planning a meeting to establish a new student union. . . . Neither was to be an official international student convention, as it was agreed there was insufficient time to convoke a properly mandated and truly representative assembly. . . . In spite of their agreement that the London and Prague meetings would be unofficial, however, Czech Communist students first tried to take advantage of the large Communist majority present by converting the Czech meeting into a legislative assembly. This move would have officially established a Communist-controlled federation, but it was blocked. . . .

The London meeting set up a twelve-country International Preparatory Committee to convene a constitutional convention in the summer of 1946, and "to take any action in the interest of students."[1] It was controlled by a disciplined majority which invariably voted in support of the policies which the Russian delegate initiated or endorsed. The US, which did not yet have a national student organization, was not represented after the first meeting . . . but in the ensuing months, a Preparatory Committee of nine American youth organizations put together a twenty-four-man delegation to represent the United States at the Prague constitutional convention in the summer of '46.[2]

The Prague Congress of 1946 forms the IUS

During the spring of 1946 the International Preparatory Committee for the IUS Congress had sent each delegation a copy of the proposed Congress agenda. But the day before the first working session of the Congress, the delegates were handed a new agenda. It was evident that the first part of the Congress was to be devoted to discussion of matters such as "The Tasks of Students in the Elimination of Fascism," which would involve controversial political and ideological issues and would be likely to give a political tone to the entire Congress. . . .

Pat Blair

Peter T. Jones

On the first working day of the Congress, U.S. delegate Bill Ellis [a student at Harvard and representative of the National Intercollegiate Christian Council] moved that the agenda be changed so that the more ideological matters would be discussed toward the end of the Congress. Shevstov, the head of the Soviet delegation, then rose to say, "the change of dates is impossible, move the agenda be accepted." And it was, but not before the vote revealed that Ellis's motion had strong support from the Swiss, Dutch, Chinese, Scandinavians, and the Dominions, and some support in the British and French delegations.

Most of the International Preparatory Committee's draft constitution was adopted by the plenary without much struggle. The hospitality and facilities in Prague convinced most of the delegates of the city's suitability as a headquarters so that there was no difficulty in its being adopted as the permanent site of the IUS.

A Congress of delegates from all member countries to meet every three years was adopted as the highest governing body. . . . The Communists also wanted the seventeen-man Executive Committee, which was to run the entire organization with the help of the permanent staff, to be a third governing body with policy-making powers. However, several Americans were able to win an acceptance of their amendment that the Executive Committee not be a governing body but only an administrative arm, without policy-making powers.

The second constitutional battle was over a clause requiring member organizations to carry into practice all decisions of the Governing Bodies. An American, Henry Briefs [a National Catholic Youth Conference representative], delivered a plea for the rights of member organizations. . . . The Soviets immediately spoke against it. The Dutch . . . stated they would be forced to leave if Briefs's motion was not adopted since the clause as it stood might well require them to violate their own constitution. . . .

The first vote was a show of hands. . . . It was announced that the American amendment was defeated 135 to 67, but it was noted that for the first time, the Finns and Poles had voted against the Soviets. Henry Briefs had made his own count and thought 95 had voted for the amendment, so he demanded a recount. But this time the vote was taken by delegations, one at a time. The count: 160 against, 71 for, 13 abstentions. The Finns, Poles, and a number of others had changed their vote. The Finns later stated that they had to change their vote for fear of losing their jobs when they returned home. The Dutch were true to their word that they would have to withdraw. . . .

When it came time for the Council to elect the Executive Committee, the proposed procedure was to elect the seven officers by a show of hands and the ten ordinary members by secret ballot. Tom Madden, the British chairman of the International Preparatory Committee, objected that this was unnecessary, saying that good friends could show their confidence in each other only by voting against the motion for a secret ballot. The Soviets also opposed. One of the Americans declared that it was universal procedure that if one person desired a secret ballot, then automatically there would be a secret ballot. To this the leader of the Soviets replied that it might be normal procedure in some countries, but that it was not the normal procedure in all countries. The Cuban then inquired, "In which countries do you not have a secret ballot for elections?" To this there was no reply, and after a heated debate the matter was put to a vote. The count was 44–44. The chairman broke the tie in favor of Madden's motion. Josa Grohman of Czechoslovakia was elected President of the IUS, and Tom Madden, General Secretary. The four vice presidencies went to France, China, Russia, and the United States. Bill Ellis was elected vice-president from the United States on the recommendation of the Americans on the Council. . . .

After the Congress, many of the non-Communist delegates reported to their home organizations that, in spite of weaknesses and dangers observed at the Congress, the IUS offered real opportunities for understanding and cooperation if it could be steered away from its political course. The American delegation unanimously agreed it should work with the IUS. Most of the Americans felt that it would be necessary to define the conditions under which the proposed United States national student organization would be willing to become a member of the IUS, but they all felt sincerely that such conditions could be acceptable to the IUS. . . .

The 1946 Chicago Student Conference debates IUS membership

The Chicago Conference also debated the question of membership in the IUS. Because they realized the importance of the emerging international student community, a large majority favored some kind of affiliation. But Churchill's Fulton, Missouri, speech; bitter exchanges at the Foreign Ministers' Conferences; and other events had revealed a rapidly widening gulf between the Soviet Union and the West. Thus, a number of students, influenced by this trend of events, were wary of an unconditional, undefined affiliation with the IUS, which they regarded as Communist dominated. Some of them felt that by attaching certain conditions to American membership, they might be able to bring about a shift away from some of the politics of the IUS which they regarded as partisan political, or at least assure that American students would not be identified with them. A number of other students planked for unconditional affiliation, maintaining that American students had helped create the IUS as it was and that they should not now demand for themselves special consideration which other countries had not asked for.

The resolution that emerged from this debate left the question open, in effect. It instructed the National Continuations Committee to "consider reports of this conference with a view to ascertaining under what specific condition the NSO should affiliate with the IUS"; to send the American vice president (Bill Ellis) to Prague, using the Conference's surplus funds; and to take proper steps to insure that American students were well represented in the IUS. . . .[3]

Developments in Prague find U.S. vice president a minority

In February of '47, the IUS leadership announced the creation of a Secretariat composed of the President (Grohman) and Secretary (Madden) and other members of the Executive Committee [who were] resident in Prague or in charge of departmental work, to have the power "in the absence of the Executive Committee for the development of all policies." It was to have authority in all matters and to be supported by a twenty-man administrative staff. Later in the spring, Bill Ellis was asked to be on the reviewing stand for a parade of the

Communist Youth of Czechoslovakia. As he stood on the platform watching the Communist members parade, person after person working in the Secretariat waved to him as they marched by. Almost the entire staff was there. The prediction . . . that the location of the IUS in Prague would result in the permanent staff being manned by Communists had come true. . . .

At the May meeting, Ellis felt a plan for IUS to co-sponsor a Calcutta conference in February 1949 with the World Federation of Democratic Youth (WFDY) unwise . . . .

At the summer Council meeting, tensions continued to rise....The resolutions passed by the Council stepped up the attack on colonialism everywhere, called on the World Federation of Trade Unions to end the colonial war in Indochina, and accepted "the principle that bad conditions exist among the student of Latin America because of the presence of Imperialist forces."...

NSA's Constitutional Convention, Madison 1947, proposes negotiations

At the Constitutional Convention in September 1947, the six American delegates from the IUS Council meeting recommended that the new U.S. National Student Association should proceed toward affiliation with the IUS. Although the vast majority present accepted the principle of affiliation, a few opposed. Doctrinaire socialists, for example, objected on grounds of political principle. The Minnesota Region wanted to put off affiliation for one year to enable USNSA to become firmly established at home first. Students from some of the state universities in the South and Midwest opposed affiliation because they had been told by their deans that their schools would not be permitted to join NSA if it became a member of the IUS.

But this complete opposition to membership in IUS represented a very small minority of the students. The big battle concerned the kind of membership. Doug Cater and George Fisher, just returned from Prague, introduced a resolution favoring a relationship whereby USNSA would participate in world student affairs without compromising its principles and without fear that its name would be used for partisan ends. It added the further conditions that the affiliation provide for autonomy and independence nationally and internationally, easy and effective disaffiliation, and a reduction in dues compatible with NSA's modest budget. The resolution also set forth a lengthy process for ratification, requiring approval by two-thirds of the member schools and then approval by the next NSA Congress.

The resolution also strongly emphasized the importance of the NSAs becoming a member of IUS—the fact that it was the most widely representative student organization in the world and that its program of cultural and educational activities could be important in furthering international understanding. It also [stated] that contact with Eastern European students in the IUS might "lead to an arresting of the deterioration of relations between our nation and those countries, which at the present time constitutes a serious threat to the peace of the world," and stressed the responsibilities of leadership resting on American students.

The resolution was discussed and debated in plenary, commission, subcommission, and back to the final plenary of the Congress before it was finally accepted in its original form by a vote of 429 to 35. The major opposition had been from a small group that wanted immediate and unconditional affiliation. But it seemed clear that only the strict conditions attached to affiliation made it possible for such an overwhelming majority to support membership in the IUS. . . .[4]

Deteriorating relations before and after the 1948 Czech coup

During the fall and winter after the convention, the new NSA international vice president, Robert Smith of Yale, sought to participate in IUS activities by suggesting Americans for IUS commissions going to Greece and Germany to investigate student conditions and by trying to sell the IUS monthly publication, *World Student News*, to American students.[5] IUS officers asked NSA to organize a special relief drive for the benefit of IUS relief projects, but Smith reaffirmed the fact that NSA was obligated to send all its relief funds directly to World Student Relief. The IUS would not accept this. Bob Smith called it "a rather bitter exchange of letters. . . ."

NSA made no attempt to publicize IUS political resolutions, feeling them to be one-sided and poorly documented and apt to damage the growth of NSA because of their increasingly partisan character. President William Welsh was meeting stiffening opposition to membership in the IUS, not only from students and educators but also from members of the general community, which reflected the growing opposition to communism in this country as well as the feeling that a student organization should confine itself to problems that directly concerned students as students.[6]

After the Communist takeover of Czechoslovakia on Friday, February 19, 1948, Jim Smith [who had replaced the ailing Bill Ellis][7] presented four proposals to the IUS secretariat protesting the suppression of student demonstrations, the arrest of students and the forcible dissolution of the non-Communist student organization. At the end of the meeting, finding no response, Smith resigned. . . . Bill Ellis also resigned. Then he sent . . . NSA and other U.S. student organizations the following cable:

CZECH STUDENT DEMONSTRATION FIRED ON STOP ALL STUDENT GROUPS AND NATIONAL STUDENT UNION DISSOLVED BY ACTION COMMITTEES STOP ALL ALLEGED REACTIONARY PROFESSORS STUDENTS BANNED FROM UNIVERSITY STOP EVERY DEMOCRATIC PRINCIPLE VIOLATED STOP SMITH RESIGNED STOP I RESIGNED STOP IUS SECRETARIAT REFUSED TO CONDEMN ACTION STOP ASK CONFIRMATION OF OUR ACTION BY IMMEDIATE PUBLIC CONDEMNATION OF AND DISAFFILIATION FROM IUS STOP WIRE TO SMITH AND ME ANSWER WHICH BE EITHER CONFIRM OR DO NOT CONFIRM.

NSA's staff received this message on March first. . . . They felt that an immediate response was required. . . . Knowing that both Ellis and Smith had been deeply committed to affiliation with IUS if at all possible, the Staff felt certain that neither would have resigned unless they felt IUS reaction to the coup spelled a deep and irrevocable commitment to political policies in direct conflict with all that NSA stood for. Thus, the next day President Welsh cabled Ellis "NSA CONFIRMS.". . . Shortly afterward, Bill Ellis submitted his letter of formal resignation to the IUS, writing, in part, "American students are finished with the IUS. They condemn your former omissions and your final betrayal.". . .[8]

A three-man NSA team spent much time in Prague in the summer of 1948 making its own investigation.[9] It concluded in a lengthy report that the charges leveled by Smith and Ellis were substantially correct and reported so to the 1948 NSA Congress, which overwhelmingly approved the action by the Staff and the National Executive Committee.

1948 Congress approves Staff suspension of IUS negotiations

Once the Congress had disposed of the question of affiliation, it still faced the question of future relations with the IUS. One group wanted NSA to put its major effort into supporting Western European members of IUS in their effort to win fundamental reforms at the IUS's coming Paris Council meeting. A larger group stressed the importance of continuing practical cooperation with IUS. And a small minority raised, for the first time, the question of a new international student organization, feeling that IUS had shown itself to be unreformable. . . .

The Congress finally adopted a position which put the greatest emphasis on practical cooperation. It also accepted the analysis of the investigatory team when it declared that NSA would not participate in the formation of a Western union of students or any other international student organization competitive to IUS. And, in fact, it voted to send observers to IUS meetings whenever possible. . . .[10]

No concessions were made on the issue of the coup at the IUS Council meeting in Paris, and its pronouncements stepped up the attack on the West. . . . The Council's "Appeal to the Students of the World" made the IUS position still more explicit:

> Students of the world: Rally around IUS and participate fully in its activities. . . . Be confident that if the youth demand and fight for peace, no war-mongering scheme led by the Anglo-American monopolists can succeed.

. . . The two NSA observers at the Council[11] reported that many present saw the Paris Council as the end of an era in the international student world. No organization that was wholly committed to one side of the ideological battle could be world-wide or representative of students everywhere. After the Czech revolution, the Danes had suspended membership in IUS, the Swedes had disaffiliated, and the Swiss had made a final decision not to join. The Irish Student Association had disaffiliated just before the events of February. The Dutch, who had never joined, began to put out feelers for a "new, strictly non-political very loosely federated" union. The American observers told of considerable discussion of the possibility and desirability of a new international student organization and predicted that several countries would move in that direction, with or without the USA. . . .

During the fall of 1948, International Vice-President Robert West began to implement NSA's policy of practical projects in cooperation with IUS. He publicized IUS projects offering opportunities for American participation and began plans for a sizable exchange of students the following summer. . . . By late spring, however, it was clear that, because of administrative and other difficulties between NSA and IUS, there would be no groups of American students traveling in Eastern Europe that summer. . . . NSA still planned to send some of these students to represent the United States at the Budapest Youth Festival, but the IUS instead wanted NSA to be on a coordinating committee with the Committee for International Student Cooperation, which would form the U.S. delegation. NSA refused, on grounds similar to the IUS principle enunciated at the 1946 World Student Congress that, "where a National Union exists which has a justifiable claim...to represent the vast majority of student of that country, it should call together the delegation."

While this was occurring, the IUS also stepped up its attack against the United States. . . . The IUS Executive Committee, meeting in the winter of 1949 . . . charged that the origin of the students' struggles was not only the wars of the colonial powers but also the continuance of the war policy of "the militarists and financiers of the US and their satellites."

NSA Congress of 1949 pledges cooperation but no affiliation

At the Second National Student Congress, in 1949, those who had called for a complete break with IUS at the last Congress cited the year's record of unsuccessful projects with the IUS as evidence that the policy of practical cooperation was a failure. This group—including those who simply wanted nothing to do with the IUS and those who wanted also to establish a new, non-partisan international body—had grown in strength. In the International Affairs Commission, they put up a determined fight against reaffirmation of the policy of practical cooperation. But a majority of students maintained that NSA must continue to make the effort to work through the IUS, to demonstrate the fact that NSA really wanted contact with it, and because there was no other instrument by which NSA could participate in international student affairs. . . .

Thus, by a smaller majority than the year before, the Commission and the plenary adopted a policy of continued cooperation "on specific projects of a non-political nature through all available channels, including the IUS and its member national unions of students.". . . Another resolution reaffirmed NSA's IUS policy, stating that since the IUS did not embrace the nine characteristics of a workable world-wide student organization, NSA did not now desire negotiations for affiliation. The same statement also directed the National Executive Committee to take no action before the next Congress for affiliation with any international student organization. . . . These pronouncements served as the majority's answer to the few who still advocated membership in IUS and to the new group, still very much a minority, which wanted NSA to join a new organization, should one be formed. . . .[12]

Ideological cross-currents at the 1950 Congress

Two of the members of the NSA team of observers to the IUS Congress in 1950 returned immediately to the Third NSA Congress. They recommended that it would be impractical for NSA to continue attempting to initiate projects with IUS. At the same time, they came away from Prague with deep convictions that NSA would have to work harder to fulfill its own responsibilities to the international student community. They noted the strength of IUS, its appeal to the legitimate aspirations of the underdeveloped areas, and the zealousness and sincerity of the Communists, who were firmly committed to their system.[13] But because of the intransigence of this system, and the specific criticisms the team had of IUS policy and practice, and because of world tensions, the Congress, after two years of little success, dropped its policy of practical cooperation.[14]

At the same time, it refused to adopt a resolution calling for NSA support of a new organization which could serve as a rallying point for non-Communist students. . . . That the members were sharply divided over this question was shown in the election of Allard Lowenstein (North Carolina) as President and Herbert Eisenberg (MIT) as International Vice-President. Lowenstein favored the formation of a new international federation, Eisenberg maintained student sentiment elsewhere would not support such a move at this time. . . . The effect of having a President and International Vice-President who disagreed fundamentally on NSA's overseas policy (and on whether the President should have the final decision in disputes or just be another member of the Staff) was most unhappy. It seriously weakened NSA's ability to live up to its responsibilities abroad.[15]

Faced with a more organized group of critics than ever before, the IUS Executive Committee, at its January 1951 meeting, shifted its attitude somewhat. The *World Student News* also reflected the beginning of a shift away from its hostile attitude toward a theme of cooperation on a mutually acceptable basis. . . . The same issue, however, attacked Dwight Eisenhower as a "war monger.". . .

The NSA Congress of 1951 endorses an alternate cooperating group

The central issue of the NSA Congress of 1951 was again whether a new international student organization should be established. Those in favor, headed by Lowenstein, argued that the IUS was an unreformable, totalitarian organization and that an organic framework was necessary for practical cooperation and to rally non-Communist students.[16] A leaflet by Eisenberg entitled "So the Congress May Know . . ." explained that others present opposed a new organization because the great majority of students in Europe and Asia would regard such a move as a final break with the IUS and would not, therefore, support it. After a heated debate, the Congress decided, by a close vote, against a "Western Union of Students" on the ground that it opposed any organic framework that would not receive the support of students in Asia, Africa, Latin America, the Middle East, Western Europe, and North America.

The Congress also approved the results of the International Student Conference in Stockholm and recommended the establishment of an instrumentality that would not be formally organized but would serve to coordinate the tasks of the mutual assistance program delegated to individual unions. This policy statement became the basis of NSA support for the establishment of the Co-ordinating Secretariat (Cosec) of the International Student Conference at the Edinburgh Conference the following winter. . . .[17]

IUS reacted swiftly to the Edinburgh Conference. In 1952, the *World Student News* violently attacked the Conference—and particularly NSA President Bill Dentzer and International Vice President Avrea Ingram—by cartoon, editorial, and slogan. Cosec was pictured as a guise for a Western student bloc, Dentzer and Ingram as Wall Streeters trying to split East and West.[18]

At the same time, Ingram wrote the IUS that NSA would be delighted to accept its earlier invitation to participate in some IUS-sponsored projects. . . .

The final breakup with IUS at the 1952 Congress

A major question to be determined by NSA's fifth annual Congress, in 1952, was whether to send a delegation to the upcoming IUS Unity Meeting in Bucharest, Rumania. . . . By this time, all but four Western unions—including the British and the Australians, who had originally supported the Unity Meeting—had declined the IUS invitation on the grounds that it could not be a real unity meeting since the IUS had excluded the breakaway Communist state of Yugoslavia. . . .

The final action by the 1952 Congress involving IUS was its resolution on "International Student Union Relationship," which concluded "that the present character of the IUS makes impossible the consideration of affiliation at this time." The Congress also warmly endorsed the work of the International Student Congress at Edinburgh and directed Avrea Ingram, who was reelected International Vice President, to "take such actions as will ensure our maximum participation in COSEC.". . .

Throughout the spring and summer of 1953, the IUS tried to get NSA to attend its Third Congress. It proposed a pre-Congress meeting to discuss the differences. NSA's Avrea Ingram replied that this would be acceptable if the meeting were open to all Western unions that might be interested in a discussion of differences. IUS replied that this would be impractical because it had already talked with some of the other unions, and because technical problems would interfere. Cables flew back and forth, but the two organizations could not come to any agreement, and NSA did not attend. . . . A resolution of the NSA Congress of 1953 said of cooperation with the IUS:

> . . . the USNSA is aware of its responsibility to continue to observe carefully the activities and policies of the IUS for any change that provides the opportunity for cooperation which would promote wider international understanding. Such cooperation must be initiated under conditions which give a reasonable guarantee of equality of expression, equitable representation and just and impartial administration and supervision. . . .

Subsequent attempts by IUS to broaden its appeal failed, and by 1954 only five representative national unions outside the Iron Curtain still belonged to the IUS. The NSA Congress of 1954 passed a resolution stating:

> USNSA observes that the International Union of Students has maintained its partisan political orientation, and grown increasingly unrepresentative of the students of the world, being composed largely of splinter groups....For this reason, the USNSA believes that at the present time, IUS does not constitute an appropriate instrumentality of student cooperation.

Editor's epilogue: By this time, NSA officials—unbeknownst to the student membership—had begun accepting money from the U.S. Central Intelligence Agency. These funds supported NSA's participation in rival non-Communist international groups such as Cosec and the World Assembly of Youth.[19] The question of cooperation with IUS was never again considered seriously. —Pat Blair

Pat Wohlgemuth Blair was an international development consultant, writer and editor, who contributed significantly to the development of this anthology before she died in November, 2000.

Peter Jones was general counsel to Montgomery Ward (1971-76) and Levi Strauss (1977-85). After four years in the Kennedy Commerce Department, he spent over six years in South America for W.R. Grace. Later, he taught at the U.C. Berkeley Business School. His IUS report was also published in 1956 by the Foreign Policy Research Institute at the University of Pennsylvania.

END NOTES

[1] See Tibbetts, p. 68.

[2] See listing of U.S. delegation on p. 103. See also Bellush, p. 73.

[3] See Wharton, p. 114.

[4] See Wharton, p. 145, and Allaway, p. 614.

[5] See Robert Smith, p. 506.

[6] See Welsh, p. 170.

[7] *Editor's note:* The October 1947 issue of *NSA News* reported:

> Until the negotiating team arrives in Prague next summer, NSA has elected an interim representative to the IUS Council. Bill Ellis, who has been in Prague this past year as American Vice-President of the IUS was

elected by the NSA convention. Ellis is seriously ill and wired NSA to suggest a proxy. At its meeting on September 9, the executive council recommended Jim Smith, past president of the NSA constitution [*sic*] committee. [Smith was national Continuations Committee president]. Ellis appointed Smith, who will sail from New York to Europe Nov. 18.

The Ellis relationship to NSA and IUS, and his appointment of Smith, was complicated by the fact that Ellis was also representing the National Intercollegiate Christian Council (NICC), under whose aegis he attended the World Student Congress and was elected. See NICC, Bill Ellis, and the IUS, p. 158.

[8] See the excerpts from the Ellis and Smith statements, p. 185, and the IUS response, p. 190.

[9] The members of this team were Bill Birenbaum (University of Chicago), Larry Jaffa (Harvard Divinity), and Rob West (Yale University). See Birenbaum, p. 583.

[10] See p. 534.

[11] See Voegeli, p. 548, and Holmes, pp. 553, 555.

[12] See Schwartz, p. 238.

[13] See Holbrook reports excerpts, p. 559.

[14] See Lynch, p. 268.

[15] See Eisenberg, p. 522, Lynch, p. 273.

[16] See Lowenstein's Stockholm speech excerpts, p. 562.

[17] See Dentzer, p. 301. Also, see Almanac, p. 1129

[18] *Editor's note:* Phillip C. Altbach writes on p. 4 in *The Student Internationals* (The Scarecrow Press, 1973), "Indeed, the history of the IUS and the ISC is, in microcosm, a history of the Cold War" (p. 4). On p. 6, he notes, ". . . there were valuable functions which each performed, and in a sense both the IUS and the ISC represented their constituencies' attitudes, despite covert official funding. Probably most American and Western European students during the period of ISC influence, roughly 1953 to 1965, were by and large anti-Communist and at the same time internationally-minded. Similarly, most students in the Communist bloc at this time were probably anti-imperialist and sympathetic to most of the policy positions of the IUS."

[19] See Dentzer, p. 302, and Welsh et al., p. 565. See World Assembly of Youth, p. 778

PICTURE CREDITS: *Then:* Blair: March 30, 1956, Bronx, NY at Robert F. Meagher wedding dinner (Pat Blair). Jones: c. 1951. 50th Anniversary Classbook, Yale Class of '51. *Now:* Blair: c. 1998, Washington, D.C. (*Jim Blair*). Jones: 1987 (Elizabeth Jones).

PETER TAYLOR JONES

Adapted from the Yale Class of '51 Class Book, 50th reunion class book and notes from Elizabeth Jones.

Early years. Born December 25, 1929, in New York City. Prepared at Pelham (N. Y.) Memorial High School.

Education. Majored in American studies, Yale '51. J.D. Active in the Glee Club. Harvard Law School, 1957. His report on the IUS and NSA was written during his final summer at law school.

Career highlights. Work as a researcher for Chester Bowles and in his succesful campaign for Congress ('60) led to four years in the Kennedy Commerce Department. A collaboration with Peter Grace, who chaired the Commerce Department Alliance for Progress Committee, led to 6-1/2 years with W.R. Grace in Peru and thence to Chile and Argentina. During that time he went back to Washington in behalf of Peru's sugar quota, took on the management of a fishmeal factory there, and helped in development of cooperatives and a small industrial park north of Lima. As overall Andean manager for ITT phone factories ('69-'71) he became concerned about its activities in Peru, and returned to a job in Chicago where he served 6 years as General Council to Montgomery Ward.

In 1977 he accepted an opportunity with Levi Strauss & Co. to develop their in-house legal department. While there, he was appointed by President Carter as Chairman of the InterAmerican Foundation, working autonomously in a number of South American and Caribbean nations. Funded by Congress, it gave self-help development grants to indigenous projects.

Early retirement from Levi Strauss & Company in 1985 led to an adjunct professorship at University of California, Berkeley, Business School. The Dean wrote: ". . . He was one of our most popular teachers and he brought a world of experience to Berkeley from both business and government."

Family. He was married to Elizabeth Mitchell; they have one son and two daughters. His widow writes: "He loved his family, the out-of-doors, involvement in politics and, always, singing. Sadly, his belief that he could handle most any situation led him to risk once too often on a horseback fishing trip above Aspen, Colorado. He lost in a confrontation with two horses. Somehow we always expected he would die with his boots on."

PATRICIA WOHLGEMUTH BLAIR

Early years and education. Pat was born in New York City, on November 5, 1929, to Benjamin and Helene Wohlgemuth and grew up on Long Island with her sister Jane. She graduated from high school at sixteen, entering Wellesly College, where she received her bachelor's degree with honors in 1950. She obtained a master's in the then new field of development economics at Haverford College in 1952. During this period, she was active in the National Student Association.

Career highlights. She began a lifetime of travel around the world with her voyage to Europe on a student ship. She returned to New York to her first publishing job with *The Reporter*. She began her international career in India in 1953 where she was one of the first female officers sent abroad by the United States Agency for International Development. From 1955 to 1963 she worked in New York at the Carnegie Endowment for International Peace, where she was a senior editor.

In 1964, while traveling through Ethiopia on the way home from India, she met her future husband, Jim Blair, a photographer who was on assignment for the *National Geographic*. In 1966, they moved to Washington, D.C. and bought a home in Georgetown. Pat had an active professional life as writer and editor for topics on international economic development. From 1966 to 1970, she was editor of the *Development Digest* for the National Planning Association. In 1969, she sat on the Pearson Commission board to reorganize international development policies at the World Bank. From 1970 until her retirement in 1997 she was an independent consultant, writing, editing and publishing for the World Bank, World Resources Institute, National Academy of Sciences, Asia Society and the World Affairs Council, among others. Her greatest professional concern was for the health of impoverished people in developing countries. She wrote a series of reports on Child Survival, whose success turned the program from a one-year to a ten-year allocation from Congress.

Family: She died of cancer at home on November 29, 2000. She is buried in East Middlebury, Vermont, near the second home where she spent her last eight summers. She is survived by her loving husband, Jim, her son Matthew of Colombia, South America, and her son and daughter-in-law, David and Lizanne, of San Francisco, California.

(Adapted from the December 13, 2000, memorial service program)

Observations and adventures

3. The IUS and Travels in Europe, Summer 1948

Royal J. Voegeli
University of Wisconsin
NSA Observer, IUS and Europe, 1948

The history of NSA's relationships with IUS is set forth in full detail in a number of essays in this volume. The following is a brief summary of where things stood just prior to my experiences in Europe in the summer of 1948.

At the Constitutional Convention in Madison in September 1947, the newly created NSA voted to seek membership in the IUS, but only under terms that would assure that NSA retained basic autonomy. Bill Ellis was designated as NSA's interim representative to IUS. He went to Prague, but soon become ill and journeyed to Switzerland for treatment. NSA sent Jim Smith to Prague to take his place.

In February 1948, Smith and Ellis both resigned after the Czech communist coup. In his cable to NSA informing them of his resignation, Ellis cited the IUS Secretariat's ". . . refusal to condemn the brutal and undemocratic treatment of Czech students by their government during the week of Feb. 22, 1947 . . ." and asked for ". . . confirmation of our action by immediate public condemnation of and disaffiliation from IUS.". . . NSA President William B. Welsh cabled Ellis the next day confirming his action and issued a press release stating that any relationship between NSA and IUS had been terminated. Shortly thereafter, the NSA Executive Committee voted 20–1 in support of Bill's action.[1]

The fact-finding mission and the IUS Council meeting

The Executive Committee also voted to send a three-man team to go to Prague on a fact-finding mission. The team, consisting of William Birenbaum,[2] Lawrence Jaffa, and Rob West, was to return from Prague in time to report to the NSA Convention in Madison in August 1948. This required the team to return to the United States before the IUS Council meeting in Paris in September. At that meeting the full IUS membership would consider and act upon, among other things, the Secretariat's handling of the Czech coup.

Because of the importance of having someone from NSA at the IUS Council meeting, Bill asked me to attend as his personal representative, and I readily agreed. I had been a delegate to the Chicago meeting, and as President of the Student Board at the University of Wisconsin, had been active in bringing the Constitutional Convention to Madison.[3] After the NSA office had been established in Madison, I had worked closely with the newly elected officers. I was familiar with both the background and NSA's current thinking regarding IUS.

A meeting of Western youth organizations was scheduled to be held in London in August, and Bill asked me to act as his representative at that meeting as well. Shortly after, I proposed that Norman Holmes attend the meetings with me, and Bill agreed. Norman and I spoke German and he also spoke French. We had become close friends through his work on the Wisconsin Student Board's NSA Domestic Committee.

Bill's Letter of Credentials read:

> Mr. Royal J. Voegeli and Mr. Leonard Norman Holmes are traveling in Europe for the U.S. National Student Association. Mr. Voegeli is the official representative of the President of the U.S. National Student Association and Mr. Holmes is traveling with him as an administrative aide. They will be attending the London Youth Conference for the USNSA and also the Council meeting of the International Union of Students. They will also be collecting information on various student and youth organizations in Europe, and in some ways continuing the work carried on in the earlier part of the summer by the three International Representatives sent abroad by the Executive Committee of the USNSA. . . .

The International Youth Conference, London

Our first stop was London and the International Youth Conference.[4] A distinction then existed between "youth organizations" such as the World Federation of Democratic Youth

(WFDY) and the organizations represented at the International Youth Conference, on one hand, and "student" organizations such as NSA and IUS, on the other. Youth organizations represented a broader constituency that included youth members of such groups as labor unions, trade unions, and teacher's and women's organizations, as well as student organizations.

The International Youth Conference had been called to discuss the relationship of youth organizations in the western democracies to WFDY, which was widely perceived to be Communist-dominated, and which was scheduled to meet a few weeks later in Otwock, Poland. At the London meeting, some groups that were members of WFDY favored staying in the organization, at least for the time being, while establishing a Western coordinating group that could help them to deal more effectively with WFDY's political activities and tactics. Others were prepared to give up on WFDY and establish a new international youth organization. Discussions were far reaching and often intense. In the end, no new organization emerged at that time.[5]

The WFDY meeting in Poland

There had been speculation at the London conference about what action WFDY would take at its upcoming meeting in Otwock, particularly how it would react to the London Conference. The WFDY meeting was scheduled to begin on August 21. Since the IUS meeting was not scheduled to begin until September 8, I thought it would be a good idea to attend the WFDY meeting, both as a follow-up to the London meeting, and as preparation for the IUS meeting. It also offered a great chance to travel to Eastern Europe to see what the conditions were like there.

Because of the shortage of time, I telephoned Bill Welsh to tell him about what I wanted to do, and he said he would take it up with NSA International Vice President Bob Smith and the others. A few days later, Bill called and explained that they were concerned that WFDY might try to exploit the presence of an official observer from NSA, and so they could not authorize us to go as NSA representatives.

I understood their concern, but by then I had really warmed to the idea of making the trip. After considering several alternatives, we decided to attend the meeting, not as NSA representatives, but as the representatives of another organization—an organization that we then proceeded to create out of whole cloth.

No checks or inquires were ever made. We had the letterhead printed in London, and typed out a "To Whom It May Concern" letter of introduction from the "President" for Norman and myself. The Polish embassy accepted it without question and issued a visa the following day. Once we had the Polish visa, it was a simple matter to get a transit visa from the Czech embassy. It was good for two weeks, which was ample time for our purposes.

The trip to Poland, and ominous occurrences

We left our hotel early on the morning of August 20 in a taxi for the London airport. We did not tell any of the other delegates we had been staying with that we were on our way to the WFDY meeting, since it would have led to unwanted questions about who we would be representing. At the airport, we left on a DC-3 on a direct flight to Prague. The low-level flight over Europe gave us our first views of the extensive destruction that the war had caused, particularly to the cities.

In Prague, we bought tickets for the next day for the train trip to Warsaw. To get to Otwock we would have to travel east from Warsaw, but we were told it would be best to make those arrangements in Warsaw. We had a choice of first class, second class, or third class tickets. We chose second class. It turned out to be an unlucky choice.

When we boarded the train the next morning, we learned that the second-class seats had been overbooked and that all the available second-class seats were already occupied. Because there were no more second-class seats available, it meant that we would either have to be seated in the first-class car, which was very comfortable and virtually empty, or in one of the third-class cars, which had hard wooden benches and were very crowded.

Since the overbooking had been done by the railroad and was no fault of ours, it seemed only fair that we should be allowed to move to first class and not be downgraded to the discomfort of third class. Our German-speaking conductor, however, insisted that, regardless of the overbooking and the many empty first-class seats, he could only allow passengers with "erste klass" (first class) tickets to occupy those seats, and so we would have to move back to "dritte klass" (third class). After several generally respectful but emphatic exchanges, during which it became obvious that the conductor was a man with a very hot temper, we finally relented and moved to a third-class car.

The train trip from Prague to Warsaw was like a trip back in time. As we crossed the border into Poland, we immediately noticed the scarcity of cars and trucks and the wide use of horse-drawn wagons and carts. Everything about the country seemed to have a century-ago quality. We also noticed the large number of soldiers and police, all of whom carried menacing-looking sub-machine guns. They seemed to be everywhere, not only in the towns and cities but in the countryside as well.

By the time we arrived in Warsaw around 4:00 P.M., after a bone-jarring ride in third class, we assumed that our earlier encounter with the conductor was behind us. We knew that if we had been confronted by a similar situation back in the United States, our protests would undoubtedly have been much stronger. To us, therefore, our exchanges with the conductor about being sent back to third class had been, if anything, restrained.

It was soon apparent, however, that the conductor was not through with us. As we got off the train, he was pointing us out to the station police, all of whom were armed with the same submachine guns we had seen throughout our trip through Poland. They took us to a room in the basement of the station and asked for our passports. It was, believe me, a very tense time.

As they were checking our passports, we realized that a few of them spoke some English, and as we talked, the atmosphere gradually began to change and everyone began to relax. After about thirty minutes, the ordeal ended when they returned our passports, telling us that everything was in order and that we were free to leave.

Checking in at the embassy

Although we were now free to proceed on to Otwock, it was clear that our first priority should be to go to the U.S. embassy and at least let them know we were there. We knew we would be traveling behind the Iron Curtain, in a country with a repressive Communist government that was known for its holy-war distrust of Western "imperialists." Despite that, the trip had seemed very manageable and worth taking in order to attend the WFDY meeting. It was still manageable, but the bloom was beginning to fade a bit on whether it was really worth it. We had just learned how easy it was to run afoul of the authorities, and it did not bode well for venturing even farther into Poland. In any case, the first order of business now was to get to the embassy. The rest could be decided later.

We got directions to the embassy, which, fortunately, was within walking distance. The walk to the embassy was unbelievably eerie and depressing. The heart of Warsaw, and in fact most of Warsaw, had been almost totally destroyed. The streets were mere paths through the rubble of the fallen buildings, and for long stretches, it was utterly silent. The only sounds came from an occasional intersection where the rubble had been cleared and a few people still lived in cave-like rooms dug out on the ground floor of the collapsed buildings.

When we reached the embassy, it was past business hours, but there were still lights shining from the first floor windows. After several minutes of knocking, the door opened and a man gazed out at the two of us, standing there with our luggage, not really believing what he was seeing. For my part, he was not the most confidence-inspiring sight, either. He was wearing a European-style suit, so I immediately assumed he was Polish, probably just a night watchman, and certainly not someone we were about to confide in about how we came to be there.

We found, however, that he was an American, a career foreign service officer named Ralph Jones. After several minutes of hedging, we told him how we had made the trip, including the origins of our "progressive youth" credentials. He made us feel very welcome and arranged for us to stay at the Hotel Polonia, one of the few structures still standing in Warsaw.

Change of plans

The next morning we did not proceed on to Otwock, but returned to the embassy. It was obvious that we could have an interesting experience if we stayed where we were. We were comfortably settled at the Hotel Polonia, and the embassy staff, which led rather isolated lives, were happy to have some new faces around. In a short time, they had arranged for us to meet some very interesting Poles, both in government and education, and we even went by the Polish Youth Committee office at Mokotowska 3. At night, some of the staff would host evening parties, including a farewell party that Ralph Jones gave for us at the Ambassador's residence, where Jones was living while the Ambassador was back in Washington.[6]

After five days, we left Warsaw for Prague, taking with us unforgettable memories of destruction, fear, and political suppression and vivid firsthand accounts of how Poland's Communist government had been brutally imposed on the nation by the Soviet army. Despite the heavy anti-American propaganda to which they were constantly being subjected, the prevailing private sentiment we encountered was surprisingly favorable to the United States, and particularly to individual Americans. Everyone, it seemed, had a relative somewhere in the United States, and that also helped.

In Prague, we contacted George Fisher, an old friend from the University of Wisconsin who was studying in Prague. We also went by the IUS office at Vojtesska 12, and met briefly with Josef Grohman and Tom Madden, respectively IUS President and Secretary, both of whom had just returned from the WFDY meeting. It was little more than a courtesy call, and nothing of substance was, or indeed, could have been discussed. In a few days we left for Switzerland and a meeting with Bill Ellis at the sanitarium at Leysin where he was slowly recovering, and then on to Brussels for a pre-IUS meeting of Western student unions.

The Brussels meeting of Western student organizations

When we arrived in Brussels, a long letter was waiting for us from Rob West, who had been a member of the three-man fact-finding team, and who had just been elected International Vice President at the August NSA Convention in Madison. He informed us that the Convention had voted against affiliation with the IUS but for cooperation on specific projects, such as tours and exchange of students. He also gave us detailed and helpful insights into the various western national student unions and their leaders that he had gained while in Europe with the three-man team. There were also several specific tasks he wanted us to undertake on his behalf.

The Brussels meeting, which was held at the Maison des Étudiants, began on September 3. Many of the Western student unions were represented, and the meeting was in some ways a replay of the meeting in London. The overriding question was what attitude to adopt and what action to take in reference to IUS, particularly the Secretariat's handling of the Czech coup. The Belgian NUS, which sponsored the meeting, was in a sense in the forefront, but it was the strong views of the Canadians that were most widely discussed. On the eve of the IUS Council meeting, the Canadians and Belgians were the most outspoken in opposition to IUS. The Swedes and Danes had already disaffiliated or suspended their membership, the Dutch and Swiss were on record that they would not join, and the British and French indicated that they would remain in IUS, at least until the IUS Council meeting. It was hardly a united front, but I do not think anyone expected that any real unity could be achieved at that point.

The IUS Council meeting

The IUS Council meeting was held at the Maison Internationale at Cité Université in Paris, beginning on September 8, with representatives from fifty-two countries in attendance. The tone that was to prevail throughout the Council sessions was set the first day by Josef Grohman when he presented the Executive Committee Report. It began with the standard litany of the wretched conditions in the western "imperialist" countries as opposed to the crowning achievements of the "democratic" countries. Then came an attack on the Marshall Plan. I had fully expected just such a presentation, but even I was not prepared for the violent, hateful denunciation he then delivered against Bill Ellis. Ellis was a man who had truly tried to work for understanding and cooperation with the IUS, and now he was being vilified as, among other things, "one of the greatest enemies of the IUS"; "to read his letter of resignation . . . is almost physically repulsive."[7]

Of interest as a follow-up to the Brussels meeting, the Belgium NUS delegation was granted voting rights at the Council meeting, despite their having hosted the Brussels meeting, while Canada was denied a seat on the Council. The action of Sweden and Denmark in disaffiliating and suspending membership was the subject of a long, acrimonious debate.

Then came the long awaited debate on the Secretariat's handling of the Czech coup. Two resolutions were introduced, one by Tom Madden of England and the other by Denmark. The Danish resolution was a mild one, which did not go into the Czech case by name. It simply called on the IUS to recognize that there were two conceptions of democracy in the world and to conduct their activities and adopt stands realizing and respecting that fact.

The English resolution, on the other hand, specifically addressed the Secretariat's handling of the Czech coup. It was a lengthy, seven-paragraph resolution, which concluded that, although the Secretariat should have been more forthcoming with information so as to avoid unnecessary misunderstandings, their action in not adopting any attitude toward the coup was the correct one. In effect, the resolution said that the Secretariat's action was correct, and that, if they had just explained themselves more fully at the time, everyone would have agreed with what they had done and there would have been no "misunderstandings."

After a day-long debate, the vote for the English resolution was fifty for, ten against, and ten abstaining, and the vote for the Danish resolution was just the opposite—fifty against, ten for, and ten abstaining. In reviewing my notes and materials, I tried to find a record of which countries made up the ten for, ten against, and the ten abstaining, but could not find it. In any case, that ended the issue of the Czech coup, at least as far as the IUS Council was concerned.

One of the most dramatic events at the meeting involved a prolonged and frenzied floor demonstration in support of a delegate from French Indochina. He was carried on the delegates' shoulders as they chanted, raised clenched-fist salutes, and circled around the huge meeting hall. Norman and I and several other Western delegates scattered throughout the hall did not take part, and instead remained quietly seated.[8]

The demonstrators had tolerated our remaining seated, but then Norman raised his feet and rested them, Ottoman-style, on a nearby empty chair seat. One of the Czech delegates came over and angrily knocked his feet off the chair. Norman jumped to his feet and, as he recalls (and I do not doubt), I held him back saying; "For God's sake, Norman, sit down. We're outnumbered." We were indeed outnumbered, and by some very emotionally charged people. In a moment, though, the incident passed and the demonstration continued unabated.

Aleksandr Shelepin, then and later

Not all the interesting events took place at the Council meetings. I recall a personal experience that involved Aleksandr Shelepin, who was head of the delegation from the Soviet Union. I chanced to meet him at a sidewalk cafe near the

Council meeting site, and he asked me to join him at his table. There were several other people in his group, and the conversation was polite and relaxed.

When it came time for me to leave, I gestured to the waiter for my check. Shelepin was away from the table at the time, having left to go to the men's room. I had already paid my check, which was for a very small amount, when he returned. He immediately protested about my having paid the check, and tried to hand me a French franc note for far more than my check. When I resisted, he said, "No, I know how poor you American students are. You need this, and I want you to have it"—and he was telling me that with an absolutely straight face!

I was never able to decide whether he said that because he honestly believed the communist propaganda line about the "plight and poverty" of the "downtrodden" American students, or whether he knew better and was simply putting on an act. The question of whether he was being honest or deceptive takes on added interest in light of what is now known about him.

At the time when Shelepin was in Paris as head of the Soviet "student" delegation, he was thirty years old and not a student, having graduated from the Moscow Institute of History, Philosophy and Literature in 1940. He was, in fact, second secretary (i.e., second in command) of the powerful communist youth organization, Komsomol, and even then was known as a Stalin protégé who had played a role in Stalin's purges of young communists. He continued to act as head of the Soviet "student" delegations to IUS Council meetings until at least 1950.

In 1952, Shelepin became first secretary of the Komsomol, and he went on from there to become head of the KGB under Nikita Khrushchev. As head of the KGB, he signed the indictment of the downed U-2 pilot, Francis Gary Powers, and was believed to have ordered the killing of a Ukrainian nationalist leader, Stepan Bandera, in Germany in 1959. Mikhail Gorbachev, in his book, *Memoirs*, claims that he had seen a paper written and signed in Shelepin's own hand as head of the KGB proposing the destruction of all documents connected with the NKVD's action in "one of the most heinous crimes of Stalinism," the elimination of the Polish army officers in the Katyn Forest massacres.

By 1964, Shelepin had become one of the prime movers for the ouster of Khrushchev, and when the ouster succeeded, he was awarded a seat on the Politburo. Distrusted by Leonid Brezhnev, who considered him an ambitious pro-Stalinist and a serious rival, Shelepin was gradually outmaneuvered until he had been reduced to head of the trade unions. In 1975, while leading a Soviet trade union delegation to London, he was met by huge crowds of protesting Ukrainians, who were reacting in part to documents that had just been published in the English press relating to his activities as head of the KGB. It was widely assumed that the documents had been leaked to the English press by Brezhnev's supporters to coincide with Shelepin's visit to London. Upon his return to Moscow, the protests were then used as the pretext for forcing his retirement. He died in 1994, at the age of seventy-six.[9]

Closing notes

We stayed on in Paris for another month, thoroughly enjoying that wonderful city, and then sailed for home. The summer had been an unforgettable learning experience that had also included some wonderfully happy times and memorable adventures.

On the trip home we ran into a storm that was headlined in the October 26 edition of the *New York Times*, "Raging Sea, Gales Batter Atlantic," and was described as having "gales raging at times up to seventy miles an hour." To add to the excitement, the ship we were on was a World War II Kaiser Liberty Ship. As a recent Navy line officer, I knew that those ships had a nasty habit of breaking in half in heavy seas from what was known as "brittle steel keel failure." After the heavy waves broke off about twenty feet of our bow railing, there was heightened concern about what might be coming next. Nothing more happened, however, and after a ten day crossing we docked in New York on October 31. The crossing had been a fittingly dramatic end to an eventful summer.

At home, our remaining task was to file a report on our observations, which was published in the November 1948 issue of the *NSA News*. It was a factually accurate report, I thought, but the next December issue of the *NSA News* carried an article written by an observer from Sarah Lawrence College which was captioned, "Observer Criticizes Voegeli IUS Article." The two articles represented differing but not totally opposing viewpoints. We had been far more critical of the IUS's action at the Council meeting than the writer of the December article. Our differing views represented part of the ongoing debate about the NSA/IUS issue. For the short term, the issue of NSA's relationship with the IUS had been decided at the NSA Convention in August. The long-term issue of that relationship would be the subject of continuing debate for some time to come. Hopefully, the two articles in the *NSA News* made a constructive contribution to the debate.

Finally, I must note that by returning home just in time for the November presidential election, I was able to do something that I am still proud of having done—I voted for Harry Truman.

Royal J. Voegeli was an attorney in private practice in Wisconsin and Washington, D.C., and served on the legal staff of the U.S. Nuclear Regulatory Commission. He was actively engaged in the development of this Anthology when he passed away in February 2001. (Extended biography on p. 153)

END NOTES

[1] See Welsh, p. 170.

[2] See Bill Birenbaum, p. 583.

[3] See Roy Voegeli, p. 150.

4 For the record, both Norman and I were personally responsible for all expenses associated with the trip.

[5] *Editor's note:* The World Assembly of Youth (WAY), formed in London in 1949, became such an alternative. See p. 778.

[6] On August 24, 1948, the embassy sent a classified report to the State Department in Washington, with copies to Paris and London, which reported that "On August 21, two representatives of the United States National Student Association arrived in Warsaw for the purpose of attending and/or gathering information concerning the WFDY Council meeting. They were Royal J. Voegeli and Norman Leonard Holmes....They visited the Chancery within an hour after their arrival in Warsaw (From London via Prague)...After making apparently thorough, but discreet, inquiries about the Council's sessions and composition at Otwock, Voegeli and Holmes decided that it would not be wise to endeavor to gain admission to them." It also reported that we had "impressed the embassy very favorably" and that our "conduct and alertness while in Warsaw was highly commendable and a credit to the organization which they represent."

[7] See Ellis and Smith resignations, p. 188.

[8] *Editor's note:* See the Holbrook report, p. 559, of a similar demonstration in support of a North Korean delegate during the 1950 World Student Congress.

[9] Michel Tatu, *Power in the Kremlin* (Viking Press, 1967), pp. 197-200, 477, 503-508. Fedor Burlatsky, *Khrushchev* (Charles Scribner, 1988), p. 239. *New York Times*, October 25, 1994. Mikhail Gorbachev, *Memoirs* (Doubleday, 1995), p. 481.

PICTURE CREDITS: *Then:* September, 1947, Constitutional Convention, University of Wisconsin. *Now:* c. 1999, Washington, D.C. (Both courtesy author)

U.W. STUDENT BOARD SENDS VOEGELI TO BUDAPEST IN 1949

FESTIVAL
Budapest, 1949 VIII. 14–28
ПИЩЕВЫЕ ТАЛОНЫ.
MEAL TICKETS
TICKET DE REPAS

MANAGING A DIPLOMATIC MISSION FOR NSA IN 1948

JULY 12. Letter of Credentials. William B. Welsh, NSA President, designates Royal Voegeli as "official representative" and Norman Holmes as "administrative aide. They will be attending the London Youth Conference for the USNSA and also the Council meeting" of the IUS. They will also be collecting information on various student and youth organizations in Europe."

AUG. 6. Letter to London. Outgoing International V.P., Robert S. Smith, provides 3 pages of guidance for the London Youth Conference and outlines detailed considerations regarding plans being floated by National Social Welfare Assembly (NSWA) personnel representing the U.S. to form a rival organization to the Communist controlled World Federation of Democratic Youth (WFDY). On the forthcoming IUS Council meeting he notes IUS correspondence voicing concern that NSA might send observers not likely to "make any positive step toward cooperation."

AUG. 25. U.S. Embassy, Warsaw. Foreign Service 3 pg. report on the 8/8-8/18 WFDY Annual Council meeting, for which Voegeli and Holmes made a side trip, as reported in their memoirs in this section (See footnote 6 above).

AUG. 31. Letter to Brussels. Incoming NSA International V.P. Robert L. West provides a 2 pg. update of Congress action against IUS affiliation "at this time" (See p. 534) and lists travel and exchange items to be raised informally at IUS Council meeting with NUS representatives from Denmark, Holland, England, Sweden, Finland, Belgium, Canada and others. He asks for information about the new IUS student travel identity card (See sidebar left).

PIERCING THE PAPER CURTAIN. Left: Attending 1948 World Youth Festival. From top: Meal tickets; general turnout in festival stadium; IUS student identity card; Rail ticket from Paris to Budapest. Voegeli and unidentified attendee; occupation army permit to cross border to get to Vienna (all from Royal Voegeli).

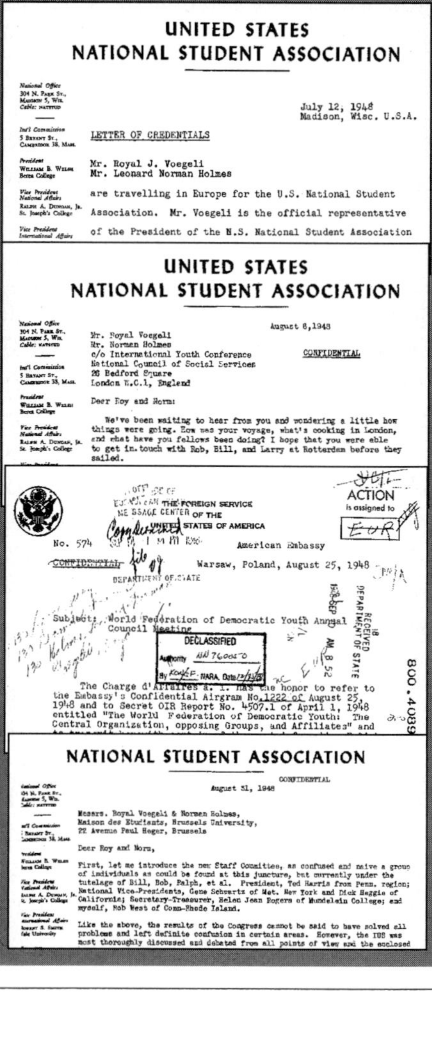

UNITED STATES
NATIONAL STUDENT ASSOCIATION

July 12, 1948
Madison, Wisc. U.S.A.

LETTER OF CREDENTIALS

Mr. Royal J. Voegeli
Mr. Leonard Norman Holmes

are travelling in Europe for the U.S. National Student Association. Mr. Voegeli is the official representative of the President of the N.S. National Student Association

UNITED STATES
NATIONAL STUDENT ASSOCIATION

August 6, 1948

Mr. Royal Voegeli
Mr. Norman Holmes
c/o International Youth Conference
National Council of Social Services
26 Bedford Square
London W.C.1, England

CONFIDENTIAL

Dear Roy and Norm:

We've been waiting to hear from you and wondering a little how things were going. How was your voyage, what's cooking in London, and what have you fellows been doing? I hope that you were able to get in touch with Rob, Bill, and Larry at Rotterdam before they sailed.

THE FOREIGN SERVICE OF THE UNITED STATES OF AMERICA

ACTION is assigned to EUR

No. 574

American Embassy

CONFIDENTIAL

Warsaw, Poland, August 25, 1948

DEPARTMENT OF STATE

Subject: World Federation of Democratic Youth Annual Council Meeting

DECLASSIFIED
Authority NN 760050

RECEIVED DEPARTMENT OF STATE

800.4089

The Charge d'Affaires a. i. has the honor to refer to the Embassy's Confidential Airgram No. 1222 of August 25, 1948 and to Secret OIR Report No. 4507.1 of April 1, 1948 entitled "The World Federation of Democratic Youth: The Central Organization, opposing Groups, and Affiliates" and

NATIONAL STUDENT ASSOCIATION

CONFIDENTIAL

August 31, 1948

Messrs. Royal Voegeli & Norman Holmes,
Maison des Etudiants, Brussels University,
22 Avenue Paul Heger, Brussels

Dear Roy and Norm,

First, let me introduce the new Staff Committee, as confused and naive a group of individuals as could be found at this juncture, but currently under the tutelage of Bill, Bob, Ralph, et al. President, Ted Harris from Penn. region; National Vice-Presidents, Gene Schwartz of Met. New York and Dick Heggie of California; Secretary-Treasurer, Helen Jean Rogers of Mundelein College; and myself, Rob West of Conn-Rhode Island.

Like the above, the results of the Congress cannot be said to have solved all problems and left definite confusion in certain areas. However, the IUS was most thoroughly discussed and debated from all points of view and the enclosed

Aftermath of the war in Cold War Europe

4. Innocence Abroad

Norman L. Holmes
University of Wisconsin
NSA Observer, IUS and Europe, 1948
Chair, Wisconsin Region

In the beginning

The pine-lined shores of Lake Mendota, a sparkling scarf of blue water, define and adorn the campus of the University of Wisconsin. On its shores in the summer of 1947, in the great theater of the Wisconsin Student Union, the founding convention of the National Student Association was held. A constant stream of student delegates from all over the country flowed in and out of the theater, occupying the lawns, the flagstone steps, and the outdoor terrace from early morning into the evening, to discuss and resolve the issues involved in the creation of this unique organization.

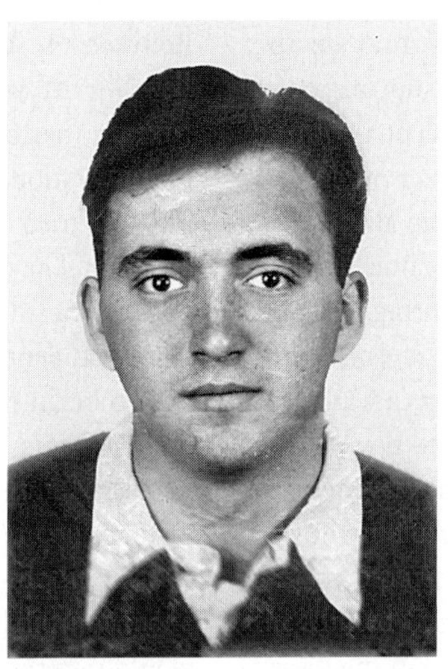

Attending summer classes, I sat in on some of the convention's plenary sessions. The maturity and relevance of the debates impressed me. Young veterans back from World War II provided an idealism and seriousness of purpose that was not to be denied. The newly elected officers of the association reflected that aspect of the convention. Bill Welsh, NSA's first President, was an infantry veteran in the Battle for Europe, and Ralph Dungan, Vice President for Domestic Affairs, had been a Navy flier.

It was not difficult to want to become involved in this future-looking student organization. At first I worked at the headquarters office on Park Street, just off University Avenue, stuffing envelopes and cranking the mimeograph machine, doing anything to give strength to the new voice of the American student. Student government was to become an engine for democracy through the exercise of responsibility by students, and I wanted to be part of it.

However, hardly had the first breath been gasped and the first shaky steps taken when forces arose to smother the organization and deny it life. Misinformed groups, traditional college and university administrators, and economic coalitions responding to the new tensions of the Cold War, sought to defeat our effort. Yet we prevailed. Meeting with students, administrators, and faculty in Milwaukee, LaCrosse, Green Bay, and Beloit, we were ultimately successful in creating a meaningful Wisconsin regional organization for NSA. We were on our way.

An assignment from Bill Welsh

The Czech coup of February 1948 and the immediately ensuing termination of NSA's relationships with the International Union of Students (IUS) are described in a number of papers in this book. The Czech National Union of Students headquarters had been physically taken over by the Communists, and the democratically elected student leaders had been ousted and in some cases arrested. IUS was perceived as a front organization of the Soviet Union, little more than a propaganda arm of Moscow. Despite this stigma, there remained interest in the idealistic vision of an international student organization conducting at least some activities that would transcend the Cold War, and perhaps provide an oasis of continuing East-West communication.

Two conferences were scheduled in Europe in the summer of 1948 that were of substantial interest to NSA. At one, a World Assembly of Youth (WAY) conference in London, national student unions and other youth groups of Western Europe and Canada were scheduled to meet and discuss their relationships to IUS in the wake of the Czech coup. The other was a meeting of the IUS Council, to take place in Paris. To provide himself and NSA with direct reports on both events, NSA President Bill Welsh appointed Royal J. Voegeli, University of Wisconsin Student Board president, as his emissary to attend the meetings, to observe, and to report. I had worked closely with Royal on the Wisconsin Region's affiliation with NSA, and Royal asked me if I would join him. With Bill's approval, I accepted the invitation, and with my trusty portable typewriter, I played Boswell to Royal's Dr. Johnson.[1]

Late in June 1948, Royal and I met with Bob Smith, NSA International Vice President, at Bob's home on Long Island, New York. After Bob's briefing, we felt prepared to confront the intrigues of international student politics.

As neither of us had traveled to Europe before, we had a sense of great adventure and excitement, coupled with a strong feeling for the seriousness of our task. Less than three years after the end of World War II, the war to rid the world of totalitarian tyranny, there was an ominous foreboding that world peace was again in jeopardy. However improbable it might seem, we were imbued with the concept that what we did might affect that fragile balance.

The Atlantic voyage and England

Early in July, Royal and I set sail from New York on the *Marine Jumper*, a converted troopship.. The ship was overflowing with young people, most of whom slept in bunks stacked four high in dank, airless decks below. Royal and I were fortunate to be booked in what had been an above-deck officers' cabin that slept four. We shared the cabin with an alcoholic English actor in his fifties who was retiring to Golders Green because he could no longer play the juvenile leads that had been his cachet. The other occupant was a Canadian businessman who, proud of his strength, boasted how he had once broken his wife's ribs when he hugged her upon returning home from a business trip. I was in mortal fear of our Canadian friend, who liked to shake hands with you to demonstrate how he could break your fingers, as a friendly gesture of course. We did not spend much time in the cabin. Our young compatriots were more intriguing; they were off on grand tours and study projects. and some were going to fight for the creation of Israel.

Arriving in London several days before the WAY conference, Royal and I explored London and hitchhiked up the Great North Road to Edinburgh. England was still in its post-war austerity period. Many items, including gasoline and food staples, were rationed. We were issued ration books, which we had to use for restaurant dining. Despite these hardships, we found the English cheerful, open, and generous. A boost was provided by the 1948 Olympic Games, which were held in London. All the hotels were fully booked.

One night on the road to Edinburgh, we were unable to find lodging and were bemoaning our fate in a pub. One of the patrons took us home. When we arrived at his modest house, he told his wife, who came to the door with toddlers clinging to her skirt, "Annie, these lads need a bed and something to eat." Whereupon, we were fed and bedded. In the morning, we were given a country breakfast of eggs, bacon, kippers, toast and jam, and tea—seemingly the family's ration for a week. Payment was refused. When we finally wrenched ourselves away, we were handed a large sack of sandwiches, because "it's too hard to find anything to eat on the road."

Back in London, the British government provided a royal reception for the WAY delegates. The conference introduced us to the Western European student factions, as well as to the non-student youth groups. Some, including the Canadians, wanted to set up rival groups as foils to IUS and the World Federation of Democratic Youth (WFDY), another group that was under communist control. No consensus emerged from the conference, but hope for an international student organization that bridged East-West tensions was clearly diminishing.[2]

Journey to Poland

Between the WAY Conference and the IUS Council meeting, WFDY was scheduled to hold a conference in Poland. Hoping that our attendance would provide us with insights in preparation for our attendance at the IUS Council Meeting, we tried to make arrangements to attend the WFDY meeting. The Polish Embassy in London would not grant us visas to the conference unless we had a letter from a "democratic" student group in the United States. As the conference was to begin in a few days, there was no time to make such arrangements.

Exercising our derring-do initiative, we had a letterhead printed for "Wisconsin Youth for Democracy." I typed a "To whom it may concern" letter on my little Hermes portable. Royal and I flipped a coin to determine which one of us would sign the letter. I can't remember now whether I won or lost the toss. Using a fictitious name, I signed the letter. We took it to the embassy and got our visas. It was probably one of the most foolish things I have ever done.

We flew from London to Prague, and continued on to Warsaw the next day by rail. There was no railroad station left in Warsaw, only rubble. We stayed at the Hotel Polonia, one of a few buildings left standing in the center of the city. It had been the Gestapo headquarters, which may account for its survival. In front of the hotel were two Polish soldiers in ill-fitting uniforms, made all the more conspicuous by their shiny new Thompson machine guns. In the subsequent days we were to see their counterparts in front of every standing building.

Across the street from the Polonia was a two-story-high rubble pile. Standing atop this pile, one could turn in a 270-degree arc and not see a single standing building; just rubble, the detritus of war. On virtually every pile there had been placed a small galvanized tin plaque, painted black, with five to ten names painted in silver of those who lay buried on the spot.

Before they left, the Nazis systematically shelled the city to bits with their tanks. When the Russians reached the outskirts of Warsaw, Colonel Bor, a Polish army officer and anti-Nazi partisan, started an uprising in the city. Not wishing to permit the creation of a Polish hero, the Soviets refused to help Colonel Bor. They also refused to permit American and British planes to land in Soviet space after flying supply and bombing missions from England, forcing the planes to fly round trips and thereby lessening their effectiveness. Only after the Bor forces had been destroyed by the Nazis did the Russians enter the city and drive the Germans out. It was many years later that we learned of the Russian massacre of Polish officers in Katyn Forest.

Wherever we went, there were squads of armed Polish soldiers, in the same ill-fitting, sometimes tattered uniforms that we had already seen, patrolling the streets day and night. In the night, one could hear the echoing thud of their pace across the cobblestones. Russian officers and soldiers were everywhere, and, by contrast with the Polish soldiers, wore shiny boots and polished insignia.

Food was plentiful in the hotel restaurant. The evening crowd was entertained by a small band that would periodically break into song with the lyrics of a local favorite, "Oh, Johnny, Oh, Johnny, How You Can Love." No evening was complete without several choruses of this borrowed piece of American culture.

Prague and Switzerland

The armed camp atmosphere of Warsaw was unnerving. In addition, our presence in Warsaw was based on the false document that we had created in London. We decided not to press our luck. To put it simply, we were scared. We regarded our efforts to get into the WFDY conference as having failed. After spending several days in Warsaw, we left and returned to Prague, where we met with Josef Grohman and Dr. Tom Madden, respectively president and vice president of IUS.

While IUS had previously resisted the entreaties of Bob Smith to permit us to attend the IUS Council meeting in Paris, our charm won the day, and it was agreed that we could attend the September 7 IUS Council meeting as observers. Our discussions with Grohman and Madden were superficial, touching only upon student travel and exchange programs.

The communist coup hung over Prague like a shroud. Fear was palpable. George Fisher was in Prague at the time, and he introduced us to people and took us on a tour of the beautiful old city long caressed by the Moldau. People were extremely reluctant to discuss the communist takeover. If you were lucky enough to find someone willing to talk about what had happened, the conversation was conducted in whispers, with repeated over-the-shoulder glances to insure that no one was listening. Every substantive discussion created the air of conspiracy.

In addition to political repression, there was austerity. Again we had ration books for restaurant dining. I remember a dinner that consisted of two three-quarter-inch meatballs, a boiled potato, and a chunk of bread, on a very large, mostly empty plate. However, unlike England, there were no smiles, no joy, no sense of hope. Unused to the grimness of repression, we left Prague saddened, chastened, and perhaps a little frightened by our new insight into the fragility of freedom.

Our meeting with the IUS leaders concluded, we made a brief visit to Bill Ellis at the clinic in Leysin, Switzerland. Bill had been U.S. vice president of IUS before the coup. Having become ill, he had gone to Switzerland for treatment, and was there when the Czech coup occurred. Bill resigned his IUS post when the IUS failed to defend the Czech National Union of Students or protest the ouster of its officers.[3] Bill felt betrayed and discouraged by what had occurred. After our visit, we left him and, with trepidation, proceeded to Paris for the IUS Council meeting.

The IUS Council meeting

To be in Paris for the first time at the age of twenty should happen to everyone. Like the British, the French government hosted events for the delegates to the meeting, including an evening tour of the Louvre. By chance I found myself walking with Tom Madden, IUS Vice President and an avowed communist. Overwhelmed by my first viewing of the extraordinary collection, I extolled its opulence and beauty. Madden grunted, "Perhaps, but it's decadent and imperialistic." I thought it unfortunate that he had to view everything through such jaded lenses.

The IUS Conference was held at the Cité Université on the outskirts of Paris, an extended complex comprised of a combination of open space and gardens and a series of multistory dormitories and apartments, some of which were designed by the French architect Corbusier. The meeting hall had a proscenium stage, packed with rows of long tables at which the delegates sat. Around the perimeter of the hall were more long, narrow tables for the observers, including Royal and me. Gray, unyielding metal folding chairs surrounded the tables. Hundreds of delegates were present from every corner of the world.

The official U.S. delegation consisted of representatives from organizations such as American Youth for Democracy, the Young Communist League, and the Association of Internes and Medical Students. Their expressed vision of the United States was of a country living in poverty, where working people were oppressed and there was a black person hanging from every lamp post. Delegates from various western European student groups asked us to address this calculated misinformation. However, as we had been admitted only as observers, we had no standing to do so, and the unanswered diatribes continued.

The former president of the Czech National Union of Students was present, with some of his colleagues from Prague. They had fled Czechoslovakia and were refugees in Paris. We listened to their stories of oppression, beatings, and arrest.

Toward the middle of the week, I received word that there was someone outside the hall who wanted to see me. There was an attractive young lady waiting for me, who explained that she was from the U.S. embassy; a representative of the CIA; intrigue beyond my dreams of conspiracy! We had a nice conversation, and she invited me to meet her at the embassy for lunch. A day or two later, I went to the embassy. I had lunch with her, and met with her once again before leaving Paris.

One afternoon, the hall erupted into chanting and shouting as a "hero" of the French-Indochina war was carried into the hall on the shoulders of delegates. With the exception of some of the western delegates and us, the hall was in turmoil, as delegates bearing the "hero" tramped up and down the aisles, shouting. As I sat in my chair with my legs resting on an adjacent chair, one member of the Czech delegation came over and slapped my legs off the chair. Hot-blooded and brainless, I lept to my feet to do battle. Royal, on the other side of the table, sprang across, grabbed my belt, and pleaded: "For God's sake, Norman, sit down! We're outnumbered." Restrained, I succumbed to discretion.

The speeches were endless. The three languages of the conference were English, French, and Russian. Every speech was translated seriatim into the two other languages. At one session, late in the day, after an hour-long speech in English, Royal said to me: "I can't sit through two hours of translation. I'm going across the street for a beer."

When he returned, he told me that when he entered the café, he saw a familiar face, the leader of the Russian delegation, a man of about thirty-five named Aleksandr Shelepin. He invited Royal to sit down. They sat together for some time, drinking and talking. When they decided to return to the hall, Shelepin went off to the men's room. Royal paid the bill for the two of them. Beer was about 50 francs, and the full bill came to about 200 francs, with 350 francs to the dollar. When Shelepin returned, he was upset to find that Royal had paid the tab, and insisted on giving Royal 10,000 francs, "I understand how tough it is for you students in the United States." Royal was always convinced of his sincerity. A few years later, the *New York Times* carried a picture and story of the new head of NKVD, the Soviet secret police. It was our old friend, Aleksandr Shelepin.

The August NSA Conference affirmed the suspension of negotiations for affiliation with IUS, and determined not to participate in the formation of a competing international student group. NSA agreed to cooperate with IUS on specific programs of educational and cultural exchange if such cooperation should prove possible.

Back home

With the IUS conference ended, Royal and I sailed home on the *Marine Tiger*. Not as lucky in our accommodations as we had been on the voyage over, we were down on "D" deck. We were hit by a hurricane, and our homeward voyage took more than ten days. We lost twenty feet of steel railing off the port bow. The fetid atmosphere below kept us topside, where I encountered one of the AIMS delegates leaning over the rail bemoaning his *mal de mer*. No longer a silent observer, I was finally able to confront him. Alas, he had no stomach for political debate, or anything else.

Returning to the Wisconsin campus in the fall, Royal and I slipped back into our academic pursuits. Late in October, before 8:00 A.M. on a Sunday morning, I was awakened by a knock on the door. A middle-aged man showed me his identification card. He was Craig Colgate of the CIA. He wanted to talk with me.[4]

Two organizations came into being in 1947. One was the U.S. National Student Association. The other was the Central Intelligence Agency.

Norman Holmes is in private practice of law in Washington, D.C. and is a member of the International Trade Advisory Committee, U.S. State Department. He served as Assistant to Vice President Hubert Humphrey and as an attorney with the Federal Trade Commission.

END NOTES

[1] For the record, Royal and I were personally responsible for all expenses associated with the trip.

[2] *Editor's note:* See background on WFDY, p. 778 and p. 546, IUS, p. 535, WAY, p. 778.

[3] See Ellis's IUS resignation, p. 188.

[4] Royal and I were debriefed by Mr. Colgate in Madison, and thereafter were invited to Chicago for further debriefings. See also "Covert U.S. Funding of NSA International Programs," p. 565.

PICTURE CREDITS: *Then:* July, 1948, passport photo. *Now:* c. 1998, U.S. Courts i.d. (Both courtesy author)

NORMAN L. HOLMES

Early Years and Military Service. Born in New York City. Attended Forest Hills High School, New York City. U.S. Army, 1951-53. 2nd Lt.. Infantry.

Education. B.S., Economics, University of Wisconsin, 1949; LL.B., Columbia University School of Law, 1957; L.L.M., International Law, Georgetown University Law Center, 1960.

Career. 1998–present, private practice of law; member, International Trade Advisory Committee, U.S. State Department. 1981-97, Blank, Rome, Comiskey & McCauley. 1981, chair, International Practices Group. Admitted to Partnership. 1981, 1979-81, General Counsel, U.S. Agency for International Development (USAID). 1970, Campaign Aide, Hubert H. Humphrey Senate Campaign Committee. 1969-70, President, International Study Project, Inc. 1967-69, Assistant, Vice President Hubert H. Humphrey. 1965-67, Counsel, Banking and Currency Committee, U.S. House of Representatives. 1961-65, Attorney, Federal Trade Commission, Division of Mergers, Bureau of Restraint of Trade, and Division of Appeals, Office of the General Counsel. 1958-61, Attorney, Department of Labor, Office of the Solicitor. 1961, Assistant to the Special Counsel, President's Committee on Equal Opportunity. 1957-58, Research Assistant, Professor Walter Gellhorn, Columbia University School of Law. 1950-51, Administrative Assistant, U.S. Economic Cooperation Administration (ECA), Labor Division, Paris, France; Field Representative, World Student Relief (WSR), Munich, Germany.

Awards. Federal Trade Commission Certificate of Commendation, 1963; Federal Trade Commission Superior Service Award, 1963.

Family. Married to Kim. Four children: Katherine, Jessica, Leah, and Margaret.

1

2

3

HOLMES IN EUROPE Clockwise from top: (1) Aboard the *Marine Jumper, a* converted troopship assigned for student travel (See Section 5 and 6); (2) The National Art Museum in Edinburgh, Scotland (3); A view from Edinburgh Castle. (Photos from Roy Voegeli).

Right: From *NSA News* 11/49 (Excerpted)

Voegeli, Holmes Report On IUS Council Meeting

By ROYAL VOEGELI and NORMAN HOLMES

(This report was written for the NSA NEWS by Royal Voegeli, law student at the University of Wisconsin, who attended the Paris Council meeting of the IUS as an observer; representing the president of the National Student Association.

The 1948 meeting of the IUS Council was opened at noon on Sept. 8 at Maison de Internationale at Cite Universite in Paris, France. With 52 nations present, all speeches and comments were translated into English, French, and Russian.

The first day's business meeting was taken up by the reading of the executive committee's report. Generally the report was a survey of the difficult conditions of students in "non-democratic" countries as compared to the educational programs of the "new democracies"; the struggle "democratic" students must wage against the reactionary forces of the world; a condemnation of the Marshall Plan as a program to enslave Europe; an attack on Bill Ellis (former vice-president of the IUS) as a disrupter of student unity; and a general survey of the work IUS has done in the past year and what must be done to accomplish its program of the next year.

COMMEND EXEC COMMITTEE

The next several days were devoted to comments of the Report by the various national delegations. By and large they assumed the same pattern.

Each delegate, with the exception of most of the Western countries, would commend the executive committee on the wonderful report they had prepared, and then would go into a general description of the conditions in their respective countries, and of their fight against the forces of reaction.

The minority of Western countries who disagreed with the executive committee report were attacked by the majority for "attempting to destroy student unity.

CREDENTIALS DISPUTE

After all the countries had commented on the report the question of credentials was brought up. There were several disputes on who should be the recognized representative group. After much discussion these were resolved, usually in favor of the smaller "democratic" group.

Canada, after much debate, was not granted a seat on the Council because of its actions in organizing the Brussels meeting. Belgium, though its case was very similar, was granted voting rights and was accepted as the accredited delegation from Belgium.

MEMBERSHIP REPORT

Following the credentials question came the membership report given by Dr. Madden of England. In it he pointed out the gains IUS has made in the past year, both as to increased membership and as to increased prestige and power which it now enjoys. This, he added, was in spite of the influences that the reactionary students were trying to bring to bear on the IUS and its members.

CZECHOSLOVAKIAN CASE

The Czechoslovakian case was decided after a one day debate. There were two motions presented to the body. One was the Danish motion which was a mild proposal calling on the IUS to recognize that there are two conceptions on democracy in the world and to conduct their activities and stands realizing and respecting this.

It did not go into the Czech case by name, but simply pointed out that certain incidents in the past have brought to light the fact that not all the members of IUS have the conception of democracy, and that if it is to remain a world-wide truly representative organization in which all students can participate, the Secretariat must conduct itself so as to give respect and acknowledgment to both these points of view.

ENGLISH MOTION PASSED

The resolution finally adopted was the English motion as follows:

With regard to the suspended membership of the Danish and Swedish national organizations and their stated reasons for this suspension, the Council declared that:

1. Though we acknowledge that some Council members hold the opinion that the actions of the Executive secretariat in connection with the recent events in Czechoslovakia were incorrect and not impartial and would like to protest about this, the majority of the Council considers that the actions of the Secretariat were correct and it thanks the Secretariat for the considerable information concerning the events which was sent out by it to the member organizations.

It considers that the Secretariat acted correctly in not adopting any attitude or making any immediate protests without first conducting full and careful inquiries.

There was surprisingly little debate on the question. The final vote was (approximately):

Danish resolution:
50 against, 10 for, 10 absianing
English resolution:
50 for, 10 against, 10 abstaining.

The business meetings were much too detailed to cover in a summary report. The Council planned sports meets for the coming year, travel and exchange conferences, student needs conferences, distributing more relief to colonial countries, etc.

CLOSED ELECTIONS

Elections were held in a closed meeting open only to the delegates. The elections resulted in the re-election of almost all of the officers who had been in before the Council meeting. In no case was there more than one man up for any office.

We speak to you in moderation...

American Students Act in the Oldest and Most Honored Traditions of Their Nation

Excerpts from August, 1950 "Statement to the Second World Student Congress by the Observer-Delegation of the U.S. National Student Association"

Robert L. West
Yale University
NSA Vice President, International Affairs, 1948-49

On behalf of the observer-delegation of the United States National Student Association, I wish to express my appreciation for the courtesy this Congress extends to us in permitting us to present this statement on behalf of American students. At this first opportunity I should also like to extend our warmest gratitude to the unions of Czech youth and students whose hospitality and assistance has contributed so much to our visit to Prague.

I have requested the permission of this body to address myself to a number of questions, directed to the student leadership in the United States and elsewhere, posed in your Executive Report. I speak in behalf and for the U.S. National Student Association and its membership of over 800,000 American students, the student bodies of over 310 colleges and universities, represented through their democratically elected student governing organs. That these opinions reflect these of the majority of American students is attested by the growing support which NSA is finding throughout the United States, and by the growing membership of NSA during its three years of existence.

Greetings from American students for student unity

From these students I extend greetings. I carry with me their sincere and heartfelt desire, in these urgent times, to search out with you those common grounds of concern of all students of the world whereon the unity of the world student movement may be based, and their desire that American students, through their representative national union, may work with you for the achievement of the aims of the IUS Constitution. For them, the NSA delegation declares its convictions that:

- American students support and endorse the principles of the IUS Constitution and the aims of that Constitution;
- American students share your concern for the threat to peace. They dedicate themselves to work for peace. They join you in your slogan: We want peace.
- American students reaffirm their support and solidarity with all students emerging from colonialism. We condemn colonialism. We stand with all students in their struggle to emancipate themselves from foreign domination and in their struggle for freedom.
- American students share in the struggle for a democratic education. They assert and defend the rights of students. They oppose and condemn on principle all segregation and discrimination against students on the basis of race, creed, color, national origin, political conviction or economic circumstance.
- American students reaffirm their desire to achieve, on the basis of these great principles, the unity of all the students of the world within a progressive and democratic international union of students. We are here in a hope that we may report back to our National Student Congress, meeting in Ann Arbor, Michigan, from the 24th to the 31st of August, that the World Student Congress of IUS has taken a course which will enable American students once again to identify themselves with the IUS, and to work with its member organizations towards the achievement of the Aims of its Constitution.

- While on these Aims we are in unity with you, it is my duty to search out and report to you on those matters which divide us. It is not with these Aims of IUS that American students disagree; in the summer of 1947 at NSA's Constitutional Convention, the student representatives voted overwhelmingy to favor NSA's negotiation for affiliation with the IUS, on the basis of certain clarifications of the IUS constitution—none of which questions the substance or the Aims of that Constitution.

Framework for American students are "inalienable rights of man"

It is rather, I believe, disagreement concerning the method by which these Aims are pursued. This is not to imply that the disagreements are of an insignificant character; for Americans, the means employed are equally important as the ends pursued—improper means can, in our view, transform the ends.

I must attempt to convey to you an understanding of the frame of reference within which the American students view IUS. For American students, born and educated to an allegiance to the principles of liberal democracy, their traditional framework of methodology in the solution of social problems differs in many basic aspects from the framework which a majority of you accept. For example, many of you analyze society from the viewpoint of Marxism-Leninism. This is not the conviction of the overwhelming number of American students. They subscribe, rather, to tenets of democracy based on the inalienable rights of man and analyze society from the viewpoint of humanistic liberalism.

It was from this viewpoint that, in April of 1948, and later endorsed by an overwhelming majority of the representatives of student governing bodies assembled in the National Student Congress, American students decided to suspend their negotiations for affiliation with the IUS. American students then stated that it was their belief that the IUS was acting more in support of the political convictions of its leaders than in support of the needs and rights of all students. For example, American students subscribed to the indictment that IUS had acted to condemn repression of students by all reactionary groups—and the NSA representatives supported the condemnations of the Franco and Kuomintang regimes and others—but the IUS had never acted to condemn the same injustices when committed by left-wing groups or regimes. For American students the principle of students' rights and needs was more important than the political orientation of those who acted against the students.

IUS must concentrate on questions wherein "widest degree of student unity may be found"

Let me be clear on one point. I do not endorse the proposition that IUS should be apolitical or nonpolitical, but that IUS must subordinate political considerations to a defense of the rights of all students and in devotion to the service of the common needs of all students. IUS must concentrate on those questions wherein the widest degree of student unity may be found. This is the core conviction of American students and the criteria by which they will judge a representative international organization of the world student community.

It would be dishonest of me not to indicate to you that American students, utilizing this criteria and their deeply held convictions concerning the proper framework of social analysis, will endorse many of the substantive criticisms of IUS methods set forth from this platform on behalf of the British National Union of Students. They will not find the Executive Report acceptable. The analysis set forth in the Executive Report will contradict, on many points, the understanding and beliefs of the vast majority of American students.

* * *

Defense of student democratic rights is "in the oldest and most honored tradition of our nation"

When IUS acts in defense of the democratic rights of students it acts in defense of peace—for peace can never be finally secured until all men enjoy equal political and social rights. These rights must include the rights to freedom of expression and belief, including political belief, the right to act in support of these beliefs, to assemble, to form parties and organizations, to publish and disseminate their views.

Such rights must include the right to self-government, for students and for nations. American students welcome all fellow-students emerging from colonialism. We welcome the emergence into self-government of the peoples of the Phillipines and Puerto Rico. The delegation has viewed with enthusiasm the accord reached by French and Viet-Nam students at this Congress. We will carry back to American students this encouraging aspect of the Viet-Nam students' fight for freedom. We have already brought before this body our proposal leading to a free and independent Korea.

In this, American students act in the oldest and most honored tradition of our nation. The United States was born out of the struggle of our people against colonialism. Our Declaration of Independence is a historic call to all men to fight forward to freedom. Woodrow Wilson's enunciation of the right of all people to self-determination is in that tradition. President Franklin D. Roosevelt's insistence that equality for all peoples be written into the Atlantic Charter is also in that tradition.

NSA expresses solidarity with colonial students seeking "self-rule"

As an expression of solidarity with colonial students, American students have insisted that funds and educational equipment distributed for relief to war-devastated areas should be used for the construction of new and enlarged facilities where most needed, as well as for reconstruction, and that the increasing proportion of American subscriptions should assist students of Asia. The NSA has worked for better relations between students from colonial and dependent areas, and students of American universities where the former 10,000 strong pursue their studies [have] worked for more scholarships and fellowships to be made available to these students. We have thrown our strongest efforts, for example, into the successful fight to provide Federal funds for impoverished students from these areas who study in our country, as for Chinese students last year.

NSA expresses its agreement with those delegates who have stated that the right to equality of educational opportunities will only be realized when colonial peoples have achieved self-rule. We oppose colonialism, imperialist penetration and dominion over subject peoples wherever such occur—in the Americas, in Asia, in Africa or in Europe—and regardless of the identity of the imperialist or the content of the ideology he may serve.

In our country the struggle of students toward a better and more democratic education continues. As the representative organization, NSA has been involved in this endeavor. We endorse the tenor of Dr. Spitzer's address before this Congress. We endorse his view that a renewed and more vigorous defense of our cornerstone of the expansion of student prerogatives and introduction of student representation on administrative and academic bodies....

* * *

NSA acts in defense of student rights, against segregation in education

Both in defense of students' rights and academic freedom the worldwide tension has created increasing burdens. NSA, in April 1949, spoke out vigorously against "the present tendency...toward the negation of long-established principles of academic freedom because of hysterical emergency conditions." Today our cause is being joined by more and more students, professors, education administrators and others. We pledge to you and to American students that this fight will go on; our successes will be expanded and our defeats will be rectified.

NSA has, since its inception, been on record as opposing all segregation in education and has worked constantly toward the elimination of all forms of discrimination. Through this forthright position, NSA has, no doubt, lost membership within the universities of the South. We have, nevertheless, succeeded in conducting many programs and demonstrations in that area directed towards the elimination of segregation and discrimination. Our human relations seminars and clinics have trained student leaders in all sections of the United States....

* * *

The "desperate urgency" in the defense of peace brings NSA before the World Student Congress

The Congress and Executive of NSA, speaking as the democratic, representative union of our students, has sent their delegation to the

World Student Congress and has presented this report, that you may know of the work and aims of American students. We return to the governing bodies of the IUS after a silence of two years in recognition of the desperate urgency that attends the defense of peace today. All men of good will must now lend their strength to the task of researching the area of possible unity. We must, in all sincerity and mutual good faith, probe for that common ground on which we may meet—to build there an example of collaboration that may contribute to a lessening of the awful tensions that divide the world.

We speak to you in moderation, omitting references to American students' opinions which, among them and among you, will only incite emotion and passionate demonstration in this time. But I must not, in searching for grounds of agreement, leave the impression that our students vacillate in their conviction or lack strength in their sincerity....

Rob West puts the question: "Will IUS be willing to forge policies which non-Marxist students can accept?"

The transcendent responsibility of our delegation is to report back to American students, assembled in the National Student Congress, what evidence we observe of the willingness of the IUS to receive diverse opinions with respect. In our political tradition we count the diversity of opinion as a strength and not a weakness. We endeavor to pursue the aims of the IUS Constitution with vigor and validity. But the American student movement of today is not Marxist.

Bluntly, the question we ask is whether the majority within the IUS is still willing to forge policies which non-Marxist students can accept....

We have faith that all students can and should be united in a single organization. We have faith in the contribution that such unity, respecting diversity, can make to peace and a better future. This is the faith held by our late President, Franklin Delano Roosevelt, in his last, undelivered address:

"Today as we move against the terrible scourge of war—as we go forward toward the greatest contribution that any generation of human beings can make in the world—the contribution of lasting peace, I ask you to keep up your faith...and to all who dedicate themselves with us to the making of an abiding peace, I say:

The only limit to our realization of tomorrow will be our doubts of today. Let us move forward with strong and active faith.

Robert West
Eugene Schwartz
William Holbrook

Delivered by Robert West
August 19, 1950

Robert L. West was a professor of international economic relations at the Tufts University Fletcher School from 1966 until his death in 1991. Earlier he worked for CARE, as an economist for the Federal Reserve Bank of N.Y and the Rockefeller Foundation. He dedicated most of his life to researching and aiding the economies of Third World nations in Africa.

PICTURE CREDITS: *Then:* August, 1950, addressing the World Student Congress in Prague, Czechoslovakia (*IUS photo*). *Now:* Lome, Togo, Africa, February, 1987, at a UN sponsored inter-African meeting (both courtesy Dee West).

A Long History of Contact

(Excerpted)

Robert L. West, From *NSA News* March, 1949

NSA HAS HAD A LONG HISTORY OF CONTACT with the International Union of Students; the founders of NSA were the students who attended the meeting in Prague in 1946 which established IUS, and who returned to develop a national student organization similar to those which have become IUS members in some fifth nations.

Although never affiliated with IUS, the 1947 Constitutional Convention of NSA outlined conditions for such affiliation and instructed that negotiations should be undertaken.

During the period from September 1947 to February 1948, NSA watched with growing apprehension the progressively partisan activities of IUS, and following the IUS Secretariat's refusal to act upon the dismissal of students and professors in Prague during the Czechoslovakia Revolution of February 1948, NSA suspended its negotiations for affiliation and accepted the resignation of its representative to IUS headquarters.

AT THE SAME TIME, IN SUSPENDING negotiations for affiliation the NSA Executive Committee reiterated the intention of NSA to carry out its program of international student activities through all channels, and sent three students to Prague and other parts of Europe during the summer of 1948.

The reports of this International Team were considered by the last National Student Congress, and that legislative body of NSA confirmed the Executive Committee action which suspended negotiations for affiliation.

The Congress also indicated NSA would not now participate in the formation of any competitive international organization based on representative student unions; and in workshops outlined a number of projects for the International Commission, notably in the exchange of students fields, requiring cooperation with the operating departments established by IUS. Since September, several other National Unions of Students have requested similar status toward IUS.

DURING THE PAST YEAR the International Commission has proposed cooperation on these practical projects to the IUS secretariat, and to the working departments, notably the Central Travel and Exchange Department.

The results, while not uniformly successful, demonstrated the practical utility of this solution to the problem of relations toward IUS, I believe.

By divorcing itself from the partisan political activities of IUS, and by careful administration of the projects it conducts in cooperation with that organization, NSA protects itself adequately from deleterious reprecussions at home. At the same time, by selecting with care the areas of cooperation, NSA serves concrete notice of its intention to carry through its program of exchanges of ideas and of students with all parts of the world.

Insofar as the member-nations of IUS channel their exchanges through the departments in Prague, and this is unquestionably true of the National Unions of Students in Eastern Europe and large areas of Asia, a continuation of our present policy appears to be, in my opinion, the correct and most advantageous one for NSA.

Western delegates, NSA's observers at 1950 World Congress fail to sway Communists.

Koreans Shout Defiance at NSA Reps in Prague

NSA Representative Report On Arrival at IUS Conferenc

(This summer students from countries all over the wor journeyed behind the Iron Curtain to attend the Secor World Student Congress. Among the Americans who atten ed this meeting was a three-man observer team representi the United States National Students association.

This is the first in a series of articles written by a memb of that team describing the congress in Prague.)

By Bill Holbrook

In December of 1949 the National Executive committee the National Student association decided to send an observ delegation to the International Union of Students sponsor convention in Prague.

For two years NSA had been rejecting IUS affiliati because of that group's close adherence to the Communist party line.

However, as 1950 approached, NSA chiefs decided they should send some people behind the Iron Curtain to act as spokesmen for the United States "to present an accurate picture of the American educational system and to refute the distorted allegations concerning American education and student life."

NSA Picks Leader

Picked to head the delegation was Erskine Childers, international vice-president of NSA. Other members were Eugene Schwartz, former NSA vice president for educational problems; Robert West, former NSA vice president for international affairs; and myself, a recent graduate of the University of Minnesota law school.

Schwartz took over as head of the delegation when Childers could not attend the Prague congress because, as international vice president, he had other duties to fulfill.

In order to keep from going into the congress cold, we met in New York and again in Paris to discuss our presentations. While in Paris visa trouble split up the delegation. Due to difficulties with IUS and the Czech government, Schwartz and I didn't get our visas until the first day of the congress. West's travel papers came through a few days earlier, and so he left for Prague before we did.

Exciting Flight

Schwartz and I got our visas from the Czech embassy on the morning of August 14. By rushing we just managed to catch the morning flight from Paris to Prague by way of Zurich, Switzerland. The flight was filled with excitement and anticipation. It was like an excursion into recent history as the plane flew over Southern Germany, where we could see the pock marks left by the bombs of the Second Wo War. And as the plane flew ov Czechoslovakia, signs of harv time were apparent.

When we landed in Prague were met by an extremely c genial and very friendly you Czech. It wasn't until later learned that he had mistaken for members of an organizati called the Defenders of Peace. T Defenders, who issued the Sto holm Appeal, were meeting Prague during the Second Wo Student congress. After lugg had cleared customs, our stud driver drove us into Prague wh we registered and were assig quarters in the Kolegi Masa a student dormitory.

Impressive Displays

In Prague the symbolism d played in flags and tremend pictures of Stalin and Gotvold w impressive if not terrifying. Soviet flag as well as Stalin's ture were being displayed pro ently. Also very much in evide was the picture of a peace d symbolizing the significance of Stockholm appeal. Pictures of lesser known Communist lea of the various people's repu of Eastern Europe and New C were also displayed.

The dormitory in which we s ed was completely filled with orful posters and slogans in m languages describing the them the congress as well as lau the peace appeal. The unif symbols of the Communist s provided the setting for the Se World Student congress.

These excerpts were published in the October 25, December 6, 1950 and January 10 and 17, 1951 issues of the Agnes Scott News, Decautur, GA.

Students at Prague Conference Cheer Idea of 'Hands off Korea'

(This is the second in a series of articles about the Communist dominated Second World Student Congress which was held in Prague this summer. The author of this first-hand account was a member of the three-man observer team representing the United States National Students Association at that meeting.)

By Bill Holbrook

From the beginning of the Second World Student Congress it became apparent that the meeting would be dominated by the thinking of the Soviet world. The first real example of this came during the reading of the executive committee report by Congress President Joseph Gorman.

The first reference to the war in Korea set off a huge demonstration. At the mention of the North Koreans the Congress delegates—most of whom considered the United States and South Korea as aggressors — broke out into clapping and rushed to the members of the Korean delegation, lifted them on their shoulders, and handed them bouquets of roses. After the clapping the majority of the Congress started chanting "Korea" and the name of the President of the North Korean People's republic.

At that point the entire North Korean delegation, armed with roses, were carried on the shoulders of the students through the convention hall amidst chanting and the play of floodlights. This part of the demonstration lasted some 10 and a half minutes.

Koreans Shout Defiance

As the Koreans — some of whom were in uniform — passed the desk where Robert West of the NSA observer delegation was sitting, they shouted slogans of defiance at him. According to West's description, "The faces of the Koreans as they passed had changed from smiles to a distorted sort of frenzy." After sixteen and a half minutes the chair requested that delegates take their seats, but this was entirely ignored as the demonstration continued unabated. It was only after about 20 minutes of demonstration that the delegates returned quietly to their seats, and Gorman was able to go on with his report. At the end of the next paragraph of the executive report the President said, "Hands off Korea." Immediately the majority picked up the phrase and chanted it in unison for four minutes.

The Scotch, who were dressed in their red academic robes, remained seated throughout this demonstration, and could be seen through the confusion of students.

Perhaps this would be a good time to pause and explain who attended the meeting. The International Union of Students stated in its official report that a total of 1,036 delegates, observers, and visitors were accredited. These represented 135 student organizations from 78 nations.

"Democratic, Progressive"

The official American delegation was composed of people picked by the Committee for International Student Cooperation (CISC). They were granted 12 voting delegate positions and should be distinguished from the NSA observer delegation. The CISC was founded by a small group of IUS proponents after the suspension of IUS-NSA negotiations. This organization has acted as the distribution center for IUS literature and has served as the nucleus of the "American Sponsoring Committee for the Second World Student Congress." From the speeches made by the official American delegation, the NSA group would observe that the delegation was composed of "democratic, progressive" students.

Similar left-wing organizations were also present from Great Britain, Canada, and the Union of South Africa.

North Koreans Condemn U. S. At Red-Dominated Conference

By Bill Holbrook

The North Koreans got another chance to tee off on the United States on the second day of the World Student congress.

Immediately after President Groman finished reading the executive report, the chairman of the Korean delegation was recognized. He cited the fact that the 15th of August was the fifth anniversary of the liberation of Korea by the Red army.

He offered thanks to the "glorious Soviet Union and to the great father and teacher, Stalin," and then launched into an attack on the United States — charging America with preparation for war and with armed intervention in Korea. He then proceeded to discuss alleged atrocities.

At the end of this speech, the whole congress — with the exception of the western delegation and the NSA observer delegation — moved slowly forward, keeping in unison and shouting.

As he stood at the rostrum, the leader of the Korean delegation was presented with flowers, medals were pinned on his chest and gifts presented to him. At the end of 18 minutes of demonstration, he was carried from the rostrum on the shoulders of shouting students who paraded around the meeting hall for five minutes more.

At this point, I would like to make some comments on the physical layout of the congress and the procedure used during the deliberations. The physical layout of the congress was impressive. The meetings took place in the old Exhibition grounds. Its buildings were decked with the slogans of the International Union of Students calling for peace, national independence and a democratic integration.

The Czech Youth Organization provided hundreds of messengers, interpreters, monitors, waiters, and guides who assisted the delegates during the formal session, at their meals, and their dormitories. In addition, the main interventions, or speeches, of the delegates were available in English, French, Spanish, Russian, and Czech through individual interpreters.

As far as the legislative procedure was concerned, little attention was paid to parliamentary procedure.

Then, too, there was a very real problem in a meeting of this sort to engage in thorough floor discussions of issues facing the body. The many technical difficulties of translation and parliamentary procedure would have made a thorough-going legislative process in this type of meeting extremely difficult.

ECHOES OF PRAGUE, 1946 in these 1950 photos of the Second World Student Congress (See Part 1, Section 2). *Previous page:* plenary session in the great hall of the old Exhibition grounds in Prague.
Photos: Dee West. Prev. pg. (2), (3) and (4), *IUS Photos.* (1) *Schwartz.*

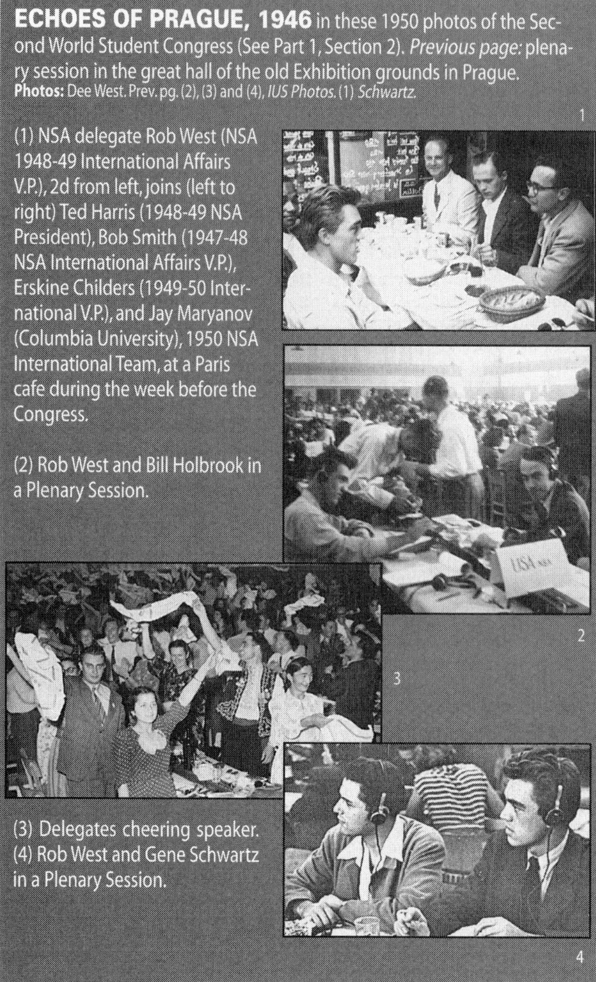

(1) NSA delegate Rob West (NSA 1948-49 International Affairs V.P.), 2d from left, joins (left to right) Ted Harris (1948-49 NSA President), Bob Smith (1947-48 NSA International Affairs V.P.), Erskine Childers (1949-50 International V.P.), and Jay Maryanov (Columbia University), 1950 NSA International Team, at a Paris cafe during the week before the Congress.

(2) Rob West and Bill Holbrook in a Plenary Session.

(3) Delegates cheering speaker.
(4) Rob West and Gene Schwartz in a Plenary Session.

William Holbrook
University of Minnesota
NSA Observer to the World Student Congress

Picture credit: 1950, in Prague (Dee West)

Editor's note: These excerpts were distributed by NSA and appeared in some college newspapers around the U.S. Holbrook's two delegation associates, Robert L. West (Yale) and Eugene G. Schwartz (City College of New York) also published a report, "The World Student Congress and International Education of American Students," which appeared in the March 15, 1951 issue of Higher Education, *published by the U.S. Office of Education.*

Western Bloc Fails to Reform Communist-Dominated I. U. S.

(This is the last in a series of articles about the Communist-dominated Second World Student Congress which was held in Prague last summer. The author of this firsthand account was a member of the three-man observer team representing the United States National Students Association at the meeting.)

By Bill Holbrook

Representatives from Western countries tried to reform the Communist-dominated International Union of Students — but failed miserably.

The strategy of the eastern bloc seemed to be to show that they had compromised on substantive issues. Western parliamentarians who questioned the precedure, however, were branded as obstructionists.

So, in effect, there were no compromises.

Western delegates realized that the IUS leadership wanted to keep at least one Western country in the organization. By doing this, the heads of IUS seemed to feel that they could keep their group from being branded as a world organization of Communist Students.

In order to accomplish this end, the IUS leadership tried to split the French delegation. They were successful in luring the leadership away from the delegation, and contributed to the ineffectiveness of the French delegation.

Thus, the attempts to reform the IUS by the Western nations failed. Like every Communist dominated organization on the international scene in the post-war world, it has been impossible to deal with them in good faith without being stepped on and being used.

Consequently the Western organizations who are perhaps disillusioned, but nevertheless more experienced, have moved away from the IUS and are now searching for some other organiaztion to fill the vacuum left by a fallen ideal.

United States
National Student Association

Address all correspondence to:

International Commission	National Offices and Publications Bureau	Public Relations Bureau
96 Winthrop Street	304 N. Park Street	c/o Swarthmore College
Cambridge, Massachusetts	Madison 5, Wisconsin	Swarthmore, Pa.
Cable: INSTUD		

President
Robert A. Kelly
St. Peter's College
Vice President
Student Life
Theodore Perry
Temple University
Vice President
Educational Problems
Richard J. Medalie
Carleton College
Vice President
International Affairs
Erskine B. Childers

May 18, 1950

Dear Student Government President:

The U. S. National Student Association---through its National Executive Committee---has decided after careful deliberation to champion the views of NSA-member student bodies and of the American student community, at the World Student Congress, Aug. 14-28, in Prague, Czechoslovakia.

HIGHER EDUCATION

SEMIMONTHLY PUBLICATION OF THE FEDERAL SECURITY AGENCY
Office of Education, Higher Education Division

VOL. VII, NO. 14 WASHINGTON, D. C. MARCH 15, 1951

The World Student Congress and International Education of American Students

By EUGENE G. SCHWARTZ and ROBERT L. WEST *

THE UNITED STATES National Student Association (NSA), representing over 800,000 students at 310 American colleges and universities, sent 3 student observers to attend the Second World Student Congress held in Prague, Czechoslovakia, last August. The Congress was sponsored by the to the Congress Secretariat, the young people represented close to 6,000,000 organized college and university students.

The Congress was a climax in the 4-year postwar evolution of relations between the university student organizations of the West and those in sympathy

No. 1 November 1, 1951 Vol. I

HISTORY OF RANGOON UNIVERSITY STUDENTS' UNION
By Robert Sun Khar
(External Affairs Officer, Rangoon University Students' Union)

The Bulletin will regularly publish a history of a student organization in each edition.

1920-1951

Rangoon, Burma--Rangoon University Students' Union was in existence long before 1920 and it was more or less an organization for social activities. It was used by certain students desiring popularity in social activities and also functioned as an organization backing the University games.

1920

However, the situation changed in 1920. The students organized themselves and boycotted, on the basis of principle, the University Act. The students felt that they needed a change in the educational system. This was the beginning of the war between the University students and the Administrative body which continued until the attainment of national freedom.

INTERNATIONAL STUDENT BULLETIN STARTS PUBLICATION

Appearance of the International Student Information Bulletin marks the beginning of a new venture in cooperation among student groups in widely-separated areas of the world. Success of the venture will depend largely upon a general understanding of the Bulletin's background and aims for the future.

These aims are actually unspectacular. The premises underlying this new publication are truisms: that students everywhere share numerous non-political problems and that the solutions of these problems will make for better education, citizenship, and personal well-being.

Student Problems

"Student problems" may pertain, among other things to self-government, housing, food, student health, textbooks and supplies, cooperatives, and part-time employment. They may involve counselling systems, student influence on curriculum and teaching methods, questions of minority groups or academic freedom.

They may revolve around the students' responsibilities to the community--particularly in

NSA MAINTAINS A PRESENCE

Although NSA suspended negotiations for membership in the IUS after the February 1948 Communist coup in Czechoslovakia it attempted to keep the lines of communication open and to avoid widening the East-West split. In his May 18,1950 letter to student government presidents above, NSA President Bob Kelly notes that "NSA's National Executive Committee feels that by sending an official American observer-delegation to this congress we can present the real views of American students" (see West, p. 556). On their return, West and Schwartz, two of the NSA observers who accompanied Holbrook, prepared a report published in *Higher Education* by the Office of Education in March, 1951. They noted the need for better training of U.S. students in foreign languages, political issues and geography. NSA also participated in the formation of the 19-student union sponsored International Student Information Service (see Dentzer, Part 1, Section 9), which on 11/1/51 announced the first issue of its *Information Bulletin* to be printed at Harvard University by the International Activities Committee of the Harvard Student Council (see Fisher in Section 1).

(Sources: Kelly Letter, U. of Colorado archives. *ISI Bulletin*, U. of Buffalo archives. *Higher Education*, Schwartz)

ACHIEVEMENTS OF THE IUS
Important dates in International Student History.
April 1946 — IUS FOUNDED AT F
IN PRAGUE.
January 1947 — VIIth World Universi
July—August 1947 — World Youth
August 1947 — 2nd Annual IUS Co
September 1947 — IXth World Univ
February 1948 — South-East Asia C
rican Conference in Mexico City
July 1948 — IUS Students Internati
September 1948 — 3rd Annual IUS
January—February 1949 — VIIIth W
lerův Mlýn, Czechoslovakia.
April 1949 — IUS Architectural St
August 1949 — World Youth and S
by the WFDY and IUS.
August 1949 — Xth World Universit
September 1949 — 4th Annual IUS
August 1950 — SECOND IUS WORL
February 1951 — IXth World Univers
April 1951 — International Student
August 1951 — THIRD WORLD FES
FOR PEACE, AND XIth WOR
IN BERLIN.
THE IUS CONSTITUTION

IUS IN ITS FIFTH YEAR
Claiming a voice for 5 million students in 74 countries, world university festivals, games, health conferences.

William I. Holbrook founded American Youth Abroad in 1949 and Americans Abroad in 1970. After receiving a law degree in 1950 he became active in Minnesota Republican politics. More recently, he has been a Board member of the Aliveness Project concerned with persons living with AIDS.

Picture credit: 1994, *Dante Graphics* (Holbrook)

WILLIAM IRVING HOLBROOK.

Early years. Born May 26, 1925 in Minneapolis, MN. Attended Marshall High School. Military service - 96th Infantry Division with service in Leyte, Philippine Islands. **Education** - BS in Law, Dr. of Scientific Jurisprudence, University of Minnesota Law School, 1950. **Career & volunteer activities.** In 1950 I was busy running the travel business. I had started in law school. In 1952 I ran the Presidential Primary for Eisenhower in Minnesota. We were a rump group since the National Eisenhower organization had made a deal with local Republican organization and Eisenhower was not as yet a candidate. We mustered 100,000 write-in votes which was partially instrumental in getting Eisenhower to run. It was known as the Minnesota Miracle. Total campaign cost $5,000. Founder of American Youth Abroad (1949) and Americans Abroad (1970) involving student and teacher tours primarily to Europe. Retired in 1986 to follow other interests. Elected at large member of the Minneapolis Park & Recreation Board 1967-1980. Mentor and Board Member during the period 1987-1992 of the Aliveness Project, a self-empowerment organization of persons living with AIDS. **Family.** Married Jane Brown, East Haven, CT, 1954. 3 children.

Stockholm: A turning point—"Lest we fail those peoples whom we represent"

This Conference Must Make a Contribution to Peace in the World

The most "practical" of technical programs . . . would be meaningless if they were divorced from the political reality of the international situation.

Allard K. Lowenstein
University of North Carolina
President, U.S. National Student Association, 1950-51

Excerpts from an address by Allard K. Lowenstein, to the International Student Conference, Stockholm, December 1950. From An International Role for the American Student, *published in 1951 by the United States National Student Association.*

Uppermost in the minds of all the delegates who are meeting together here is the crisis in the world and the uncertainty and confusion into which this generation was born. I think it is time that we tried to relate our deliberations here to the conditions which comprise the background for, and the setting of, those decisions at which we will arrive this week.

This is a "practical" conference, dedicated to working out ways of increasing cooperation among the students of the world, and through the students, of increasing good will and understanding among the peoples of the earth. Our "practical" projects are practical, as we know, only insofar as they may be of meaning and of use in the uphill quest of the human race for a fuller opportunity to live a life of dignity, in surroundings of decency, and in a world at peace. It follows, therefore, that the most "practical" of technical programs that might be evolved here would be meaningless if they were divorced from the political reality of the international situation in which these projects would have to be carried out.

The nations here represented are peace-loving nations, whose highest aspirations cannot lie fulfilled in a world at war. Nothing could be more natural, then, than that the foremost consideration dominating our thoughts and our discussions should be that this conference must make a contribution to peace in the world lest we fail those peoples whom we represent. We know, however, equally, that "peace" of itself is not enough. There is the peace that comes with the abandonment, in the face of force, of man's most cherished dreams, a peace we know to be as illusory as it is destructive of those values which make life worth living. And there is the peace of constant tensions and continuing ill-will—a peace which at best means the mere absence of the more violent forms of war.

Because we know the falseness of a peace based on a surrender of all we hold dearest in our lives, we must and we have, as free peoples, rejected the course of surrender to those who would pervert the highest hopes of decent men and in so doing would forge the weapons with which to destroy the progress of the ages and the heartfelt desires of human beings everywhere. And we can accept a world filled with tensions and ill-will, not as an adequate or permanent peace, but only because we reject from the bottom of our hearts what seems at the moment to be the only alternative.

We cannot pretend that elements of great power and great wickedness do not exist.

What we seek then to do is to help strengthen the forces and create the environment in which the present absence of war can be converted into the sort of international amity and individual dignity that is connoted to us when we speak of peace. It is a false notion that peace can be attained by continuing to pretend that elements of great power and great wickedness do not exist—elements which would prey on the yearning of free men for the opportunity to live their lives out without further strife, and to make of this yearning an insidious agent of surrender. When the Communists say they want peace we know too well what peace they want, and why; and it is about time that in our deliberations we took stock and faced facts.

We will not be contributing to the attainment of the peace we so earnestly crave if in our deliberations we confine ourselves to a discussion of techniques designed to effectuate increased student exchange or better travel programs, in a world pushed to the brink of tragedy by the willful scheming of evil men bent on world domination for one nation. Neither will we be contributing to the attainment of peace if we continue to surrender our international "political" prerogatives and responsibilities to a student group which has, since its inception, demonstrated time and time again that its only reason for existence is the furtherance of the will of these same evil men.

* * *

We are four years behind in those areas of the earth where ...the IUS has laid a pattern to twist and undermine the legitimate aspirations of people long craving freedom.

The USNSA has for four years tried in good faith, the good faith which is characteristic of free men and which is evidently inconceivable to apostles of tyranny, to submerge national or partisan differences to the overall student unity of which the International Union of Students, by its constitution and by its original composition, was to have been an instrument. We have watched while the IUS created a world structure cleverly designed to give to it a monopoly on programs for international student cooperation. We have generally abstained from contesting the distortions which have been the sum and substance of the IUS "information program" for the students of the world.

We are, as a result of our good faith and of the earnestness of our desire for one united student community, four years behind. Among students here represented these four years have produced no notably bad results, for understanding and good will among our students and peoples are based on beliefs and goals we share together, and need no bickering or bargaining to be maintained. Among other students, however, we are also four years behind. We are four years behind in those areas of the earth where communication is harder, democracy newer, and governments poorer, and where, with foresight and cunning, the IUS has laid a pattern to twist and undermine the legitimate aspirations of peoples long craving freedom. The very liberty of these people is now endangered by the confusion which has been produced by four years of virtually uncontested untruths.

Those of us who live in free lands know that the long-time colonial nations of the world will not find freedom through the slavery of Soviet rule. We know that the aspirations of these peoples seeking freedom and the opportunity for a better life are our aspirations, and we know that our freedom is inextricably bound up with their freedom.

We are aware more than ever before of the common goals and shared heritage of all free men.

We know too that we are dedicated to the strengthening of those institutions which would make possible a fuller realization of the timeless hopes of human beings of every religion and of every race and from every part of the world. We believe in democracy because it is our faith that democracy is that means of governing which makes those aspirations most easily attainable. We are aware more than ever before of the common goals and shared heritage of all free men and of all men seeking freedom, be they in Southeast Asia, in the Western Hemisphere, or behind the iron wall built by the Soviet Union and forced on its unhappy allies of Eastern Europe.

And we also now know that it is not enough for the understanding and realization of these truths to be confined to the twenty-one nations here represented. We know that the International Union of Students has used our reluctance to appear to compete, even in the market place of ideas, to usurp the words and concepts for which we know we stand; and to use these words and concepts against us among people who are our friends and who must be our allies if ever there is to be international student cooperation and genuine peace. The IUS has not been, and is not now, primarily concerned with the feelings of Western European or American students for the IUS knows that in the atmosphere of freedom which exists in our homelands there is no possibility of fear and dishonesty emerging triumphant in a contest with progress and decency. But while we have contented ourselves in this sense of security, the IUS has gone forth, armed with unscrupulous deceit and with unflagging zeal, to turn against freedom the very parts of the world where today freedom is most sought after.

* * *

Negotiations have been "doomed to failure because in the Soviet world words do not have the same meaning that they have to free men."

In their hope of continuing to immobilize free students all over the earth, the Communists continue to proclaim that those who would fight lies and would seek international good will are "splitting the student community," or are "contributing to the gulf between East and West." Every once in a while, when it seems that we may at last be awakening to the realization of the significance of this long-range stall technique, the Communists say, "Let us negotiate."...

These negotiations have been doomed to failure in every case. They have been doomed to failure because we are obliged to negotiate with students who are not free agents, as we are, but who are Soviet agents. They are doomed to failure because in the Soviet world words do not have the same meaning that they have to free men, and the process of seeking agreement in such a context can but lead to frustration and to increased ill-will...because the primary interest of the Soviet Union in its determination of IUS policies has been precisely the neutralization of the resources and convictions of the students of those nations meeting here, so that the Soviet Union might enjoy continued unchallenged sway in the areas where student opinion is so much more crucial, where nationalism is so much more intense, and where the determination of the national destiny is still to be settled. They can't let negotiations succeed because to do so would challenge their sway....

What we face today is not primarily an obnoxious political ideology, nor an unacceptable economic theory, nor an unruly Soviet nationalism. What we face—and let us face it—is the greatest menace to civilization, to the timeless truths preached by all religions, to the universities and libraries, to the art and the literature, to the games and to the homes which have evolved over the centuries. To seek to preserve these institutions is to invite the "student unity" of the one-party state, and of the untimely grave.

* * *

...Nothing would mean more to us than an indication that the foreign policy of the Soviet Union was to be changed. But we know it will not change as long as it succeeds; and we know IUS policy will not change as long as Soviet foreign policy does not change. We know too that the peoples of the Soviet Union, of China, and of the typically misnamed "peoples' democracies" are human beings. They are creatures of the same Lord, subject to the same limitations, and bearers of the same hopes as are we. We know it is crucial that we do all we can to make them aware of our love for them as human beings and of our concern for them as our brothers and our friends.

...We know that in four years of a great deal of talk about "practical cooperation" with Eastern Europe through the IUS, there has been no practical cooperation, because the last thing the IUS in the present Russian scheme of things wants is the personal interchange and understanding between our peoples and their peoples that such practical cooperation would generate....We know the crucial role which an adequate education and an educated citizenry must play if democracy is to be protected and improved. And we know too that we will not have long to improve this democracy unless we protect it, and that we cannot long protect it except as we improve it.

* * *

We are opposed to setting up a new union here, but we need to investigate the desirability, financial possibility and structural form of a new international union.

So it is that the United States calls on this conference to work out technical programs that will have meaning, but to realize the unprecedented significance which our "political" decisions will have on these technical programs as we seek to carry them out.

I think that before I conclude my written statement, I will interpolate very briefly a comment on such specific technical programs as may have been presented so far....What we do want in addition to the technical program is a continuing committee or continuing committees set up by this conference, responsible to a future conference, to investigate the need and desirability, the financial possibility, and the structural form of a new international union.

We are opposed to setting up a new union here, because first we must know that a basis exists in Southeast Asia and that adequate financing is available. We will never know these things until we create the committees to investigate and report back. We are further opposed to setting up a new union here because we here are representatives of only twenty-one nations; and it is our conviction that it would be a major fallacy to have any part in the creation of a Western union.

We are aware of the fact that anything we do here will be denounced and distorted and misrepresented by the IUS to those parts of the world which are our primary concern, so that unless we prepare ourselves to compete ideologically not against anybody, but for what we are trying to do our technical programs will lose their meaning. They will be denounced as imperialism by Dutch or American, or whoever is here, imperialists and can have no meaning in those areas we seek to reach. So it is, we say, that we cannot detach the technical from the "political."

None of us came to Stockholm on a lark; many of us came great distances to meet in this great citadel of peace and freedom whose very name has been used as an instrument for undermining peace and freedom. We speak as the mandated representatives of the students of our lands, and we cannot do aught but speak as members of a generation which faces the greatest challenge and greatest opportunity in history. Our technical know-how and our scientific achievements surpass the imagination, and it is up to us in our education to instill those values into our lives that will put this know-how and these achievements to work once and for all as weapons for the bettering, and ingredients for the enriching, of lives of human beings everywhere.

Continued cooperation on technical projects is dependent on continued peace

... In the student community we can do much really to effect peace in the world. We can undertake now to meet terror with honor, malicious attacks with facts and force with the weapons of truth. It is precisely because peace is uppermost in our minds that this conference cannot afford to divorce its technical consideration from the facts of strife. Continued cooperation on technical projects is dependent on continued peace, and we must leave no stone unturned to make whatever small contribution we are privileged to make to the sustenance and extension of the values and of the spiritual quality upon which we rest our hopes and prayers for a better world.

Editor's note: The following is the original credit note appearing in the published version of the address. Allard K. Lowenstein is President of the National Student Association for the 1950-51 academic year. A graduate of the University of North Carolina, he is twenty-one years old. In December 1950 he represented the NSA at the International Student Conference held in Stockholm, Sweden, with the student unions of twenty-one nations. As President of NSA he speaks as representative for over 900,000 American college and university students.

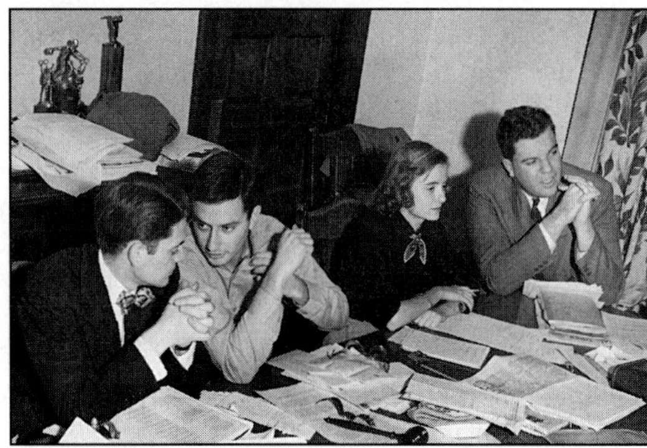

NSA National Executive Committee, Dec. 27-31, 1950, shortly after Al Lowenstein's appearance in Stockholm. From left: Elmer Paul Brock, V.P. Student Affairs; Lowenstein; Harriet Tyson (Carleton C., MN), recording secretary for NEC; Frederick D. Houghteling (Harvard), Treasurer. Sigma Alpha Epsilon House at U. of Wisconsin. (Dick Murphy, *John Mitchell, Madison*)

The Outcome of the Stockholm Meeting: International Student Conference and Cosec

John V. Delaney
Fordham '54, NSA Executive Committee
Excerpted from "World Students Organize for Freedom," America, *10/2/54.*

As the natural result of IUS activity since 1948, the democratic student unions knew for certain that future cooperation with it on practical student problems was an idle dream. They would have to find new working methods. As a first step, the democratic student unions began to disaffiliate from the IUS. This trend was heightened by the extremism of the second World Student Congress in 1950.[1]

To provide a workable instrument for cooperation, a few of the democratic student unions, particularly the Swedish and American (the U. S. National Student Association called the first meeting of the International Student Conference in Stockholm in 1950. Subsequent annual conferences have been held in Edinburgh, Copenhagen and Istanbul.[2]

The first conference, realizing its responsibilities to students in the "growth potential" areas, formulated a student mutual assistance program [SMAP], sometimes called the students' Point Four.[3] This program aims at bettering educational facilities and developing democratic student organizations and activities in these areas of the world. Its operation has been delegated to the U. S. National Student Association.

As a first step, student teams were sent to collect information about conditions in the universities in those areas. These teams have surveyed the Middle East, South America, Southeast Asia and West Africa. At the present time, technical assistance teams are being sent to these areas to work with the students. Their work is bound to bear fruit, because the best exchange of student problem-solving techniques occurs when students can talk face to face.

A technical assistance journal for student leaders is distributed to the student unions in the Middle East and Southeast Asia. Information is given on such things as the development of effective student governments, organization of cooperatives of different types, operation of textbook mimeograph centers, etc. As a logical outgrowth of the journal, a library has been established. In addition, a great amount of work has been done in arranging seminars and exchange of students. Apart from the student Point Four program, a spontaneous flow of information on student problems and policies passes back and forth between the various groups.

Through the students' Point Four, student leaders in former colonial areas learn that programs like the exchange of students and building of textbook mimeograph centers help their countries to solve basic problems of too much ignorance, too few schools and too little money. In the process they begin to realize that harangues on the evils of colonialism, though frequently justified, are not enough to meet the demands of progress toward a better life.

The ISC coordinates the activities of the national student unions through a permanent administrative agency, the Coordinating Secretariat located in Leyden, the Netherlands. Recently, for example, the secretariat organized an international meeting of representatives of the travel bureaus operated by most of the student unions. It also provides an opportunity for representatives of students in all parts of the world to formulate policy and exert influence on public opinion.

[1] See Holbrook, reporting the 1950 World Student Congress, p. 559.

[2] See Almanac, p. 1128.

[3] See pp. 526, 638 for the origins of SMAP, developed by NSA, an early application of the concept of technical assistance to developing nations. Dick Murphy on p. 630 notes, "'Point Four' was related to President Truman's inaugural address of 1949 in which he outlined an aid program for underdeveloped nations of the world to which the United States should contribute."

Revelations in 1967 reach back to the early years of the Cold War

5. Covert U.S. Government Funding of NSA International Programs

Contributors to this report, prepared specifically for this anthology, include: William Welsh, NSA President 1947-48; William Dentzer, Jr., NSA President 1951-52; Norman Holmes, Chairman, NSA Wisconsin Region 1949; Richard J. Medalie, NSA Vice President, Educational Affairs, 1949-50; and Richard G. Heggie, NSA Vice President Student Affairs 1948-49. See index for their extended biography page citations.

While this anthology considers NSA's founding and early years from 1946 to 1952, events occurred in 1967 that reflect back upon those early years.

Revelations in 1967

In February 1967, *Ramparts* magazine published an article revealing that the Central Intelligence Agency secretly had been providing funds for NSA's international program since the early 1950s and that senior NSA officers over the years had been aware of this funding. Following this revelation, which led to the disclosure of additional CIA funding of other private U.S. organizations, 1966-67 NSA President Eugene Groves acknowledged the existence of such CIA support to the Association and NSA's decision to terminate it permanently.

Some contributors to the article believe that since NSA was a private domestic association the CIA's funding of NSA's international programs was illegal and an abuse of power. Other contributors justify such funding as a necessity given the realities of the times. However, few would question that the revelations of secret subsidies and the apparent use of the NSA as an instrument of U.S. foreign policy brought about its loss of credibility in the student community.

Since reportage on this subject typically dates the beginning of the CIA-NSA relationship as "the early 1950s," the editors of this anthology deemed it necessary to attempt to identify what occurred with respect to initiation of secret CIA funding during the period covered by the anthology—1946-1952—and to report it here. After extensive investigation and contact with former NSA officers, the results of this research are described here.

This chronology should be read within the national security context of the early years of the Cold War. Government agencies utilized many private organizations in addition to student and youth groups as conduits for projecting pro-democratic messages and organizational skills to counter the Soviet threats. The extent of this in labor, literary, artistic, religious, and business organizations is well documented.

The 1946-1949 period

Because of U.S. student participation in the founding Congress of the International Union of Students (IUS) in Prague in 1946 and NSA's attempt thereafter to determine whether acceptable relations with the IUS were possible, the Association's international programs were of interest to the Department of State, the Federal Bureau of Investigation, and the Central Intelligence Agency and its predecessors. Through the common government practice at the time, involving briefings, debriefings, surveillance of meetings and review of passport applications, there was little of international importance in the programs of major private U.S. organizations that was not known by some government office.

There are, for example, several reported instances involving NSA representatives who had traveled abroad to attend IUS and other international meetings, and who upon returning were then contacted by the CIA and interviewed on the meetings they attended. In each case, the CIA's interest appears to have been on the foreign information aspects of their activity and not on NSA itself.[1] There was an instance of an approach for an interview while the person was still abroad.

There was also a reported instance a year later when the same person, then a delegate to the 1949 NSA Congress, was invited to a room away from the Congress, and then urged to take a strong anti-IUS stance at the Congress. There were indications at the time that persons doing so were government agents, but the delegate was not able to remember whether they were identified as FBI or CIA.

While it is conceivable the U.S. government during the 1946-49 period gave travel grants to American student delegates without their knowing the source, there is presently no evidence of this. It can be stated with certainty that there was no CIA financial aid to the NSA itself or to its officers in those years.

The 1950–1952 period

The first identifiable instance of CIA funding to NSA occurred in 1950. It was mentioned in a *Los Angeles Times* news story in February 1967 following exposure of the CIA's relationship to NSA. That article reported that CIA representatives secretly had told Frederick Delano Houghteling, NSA Executive Director in 1949-1950, while a Harvard undergraduate, that the $10,000–$12,000 needed to send an NSA observer delegation to the IUS Congress in Prague that summer would be supplied by the CIA through two attorneys, whom he could describe as philanthropists. In articles written in 1967 and 1997, Craig Wilson, a fellow NSA staff member with Houghteling, wrote that, in spring 1950, he and Houghteling visited law offices in Chicago and Wilmington, Delaware, and subsequently received a $6,000 check from each. NSA records[2] exist identifying those grants. In his account, Wilson added, "If it was Central Intelligence Agency money we [the NSA staff, presumably other than Houghteling, who is now deceased] didn't know it."[3] Neither did the NSA delegates who traveled on those grants.[4]

Of special interest concerning CIA views regarding NSA in this period is a February 1951 Agency memo declassified in 1994. In it, a CIA officer comments on a proposal from Harvard University government professor and CIA consultant William Y. Elliott to Agency Director Allen Dulles that CIA subsidize NSA. The memo states, "The National Student Association is not receptive to accepting governmental subsidy, because it considers such a course of action would run contrary to its basic principle of independent thought and action and would in a sense reduce it to the position of being a tool of its government." Therefore, the author writes, "I do not feel that such a subsidy is feasible, practicable, or desirable."

The author of that memo goes on to state, however, that, since anti-IUS NSA President Allard Lowenstein was about to be drafted into the Army, covert arrangements had been made for his deferment, "although Lowenstein is completely unaware of this fact."

The memorandum sets forth the CIA's willingness to utilize the "aegis" of the NSA, as differentiated from direct organizational subsidies, "where conditions are such that the use of this aegis can be obtained through the penetration which we have made into the National Student Association...[identity deleted by censorship], then we stand prepared to subsidize such individual projects by careful use of such means as will not offend or arouse the suspicion of the National Student Association." As an illustration of such a project, the writer cites current (February 1951) plans "being prepared jointly by this office and the Far East Division to convene a regional students seminar in Southeast Asia during the coming summer."[5]

In fact some students active in NSA's international program at Harvard were hoping to organize a meeting in Southeast Asia with student leaders there and NSA representatives. (Although the NSA international office officially had been moved from Cambridge to Madison in September of 1950, a group of graduate students involved in the program remained in Harvard.) When the IUS limited the NSA observer delegation to the 1950 IUS Congress in Prague to three instead of the projected twelve members, the Association used much of the $12,000 channeled through Fred Houghteling to send teams to Europe, Africa, the Middle East, and Southeast Asia to meet with student organizations there.[6] The two attorneys who were the conduits for this CIA funding received reports from the NSA national office, according to NSA records[7] on these teams' plans, progress, financial accounting and final reports to the 1950 NSA Congress.

James Grant, a Harvard University law student, made the Southeast Asia portion of these trips during the month of September 1950. Following his visit, NSA sent a second representative, Melvin A. Conant, Jr., a graduate student at Harvard, to visit Asian student groups in the spring of 1951 with a view toward the organization of a seminar in Southeast Asia. In June 1951, a letter from Grant informed the NSA office in Madison that $10,000 had been obtained for the seminar. The seminar never took place, however, and nothing more is known about the reported grant and its source. Unfortunately, James Grant died in 1995 after serving as Executive Director of UNICEF since 1980.[8]

As indicated below, it is possible in some cases and certain in others that, without the knowledge of NSA officers and representatives involved at the time, the CIA channeled additional funds to support foreign trips by NSA representatives in this period. One such trip may have been that of NSA International Vice President Herbert Eisenberg and former Secretary-Treasurer Helen Jean Rogers to attend the mid-1951 Congress of the Brazilian national student union in Rio de Janeiro. Rogers has written that airline tickets were supplied gratis by the head of Braniff Airlines in response to her letter as a fellow Catholic University alumnus.[9] However, Herb Eisenberg reports that Rogers asked him to meet with John Simons in Washington, D.C., some time before their trip. It is possible that Simons facilitated the underwriting of the Braniff tickets before the Foundation for Youth and Student Affairs existence.[10]

Simons, while a Fordham University student, served as Treasurer of the National Continuations Committee that prepared for the founding 1947 convention of NSA, and he became assistant director of the newly established Foundation for Youth and Student Affairs late in 1951. This foundation made the grants that allowed NSA delegations headed by NSA 1951–52 President William Dentzer to attend the Second International Student Conference, at Edinburgh, Scotland, in January 1952 and the First Inter-American Student Congress in Brazil the following month. The foundation was identified in the 1967 disclosures as the major conduit of CIA funds to NSA, as well as numerous other youth and student organizations. The wealth of some of this foundation's board members effectively disguised the true source of its funding for many years.

Dentzer has written that, shortly after the end of his term in August 1952 and prior to leaving for Holland to join the staff of the Coordinating Secretariat of National Unions of Students (Cosec), he was contacted by the CIA, informed that the funds raised from sources during his presidency for foreign travel of NSA representatives were CIA funds covertly channeled through these sources, and invited to consult with CIA representatives about future funding for NSA and Cosec plans. He states he later learned that it was in the latter part of 1951 that CIA began its sustained financial support of NSA's international program. He attributes the immediate impetus for this funding to U.S. government reaction to the Berlin Youth Festival in the summer of 1951 sponsored by the IUS and the World Federation of Democratic Youth. This reaction would explain why the Agency changed its posture toward NSA from that stated in the February 1951 CIA memorandum. Moreover, a National Security Council directive would change its posture in October of that year by assigning CIA responsibility for covertly countering international Communist front efforts.[11]

With the exception of Houghteling as reported above, Dentzer states that no NSA officers during their terms of office from the inception of NSA through his 1951–52 term—the period covered by this anthology—were aware of CIA funding to the Association. Dentzer asserts that NSA International Affairs Vice President Avrea Ingram was not made aware of this funding until early in Ingram's second term in that office—1952–53—and that he was the only NSA officer holding office during that term to have such knowledge.

Concluding thought

Whatever the national security justification for the contacts and travel subsidies by the CIA in NSA's initial years, this governmental actions should be viewed as the early steps in a sustained program of covert government engagement, which potentially influenced a voluntary democratic organization.

It is not possible at this time to make a historic analysis of the scope of any influence because extensive CIA documents remain classified. Within a very few years of the public disclosure of this covert relationship and the resulting loss of NSA's credibility, a successor student organization replaced the USNSA. This new association, the USSA, was different in both structure and mission from the USNSA.

Historical notes

On March 24, 1967, Under-Secretary of State Nicholas Katzenbach transmitted to President Johnson a report of the committee that he chaired at the direction of the President to review the relationship between government agencies, notably the CIA and educational and private voluntary organizations that operated abroad. In addition to this report, numerous classified notes were attached. Among the still-classified notes is a description of the approval mechanism from 1947 to 1967, "Coordination and Policy Approval of Covert Operations," prepared by the CIA for this Committee's use. This document is presently being reviewed for declassification.

Also attached to the Kalzenbach report and subsequently declassified was an account prepared by the Special Assistant for Youth, Department of State, "American Students in Post-War International Affairs." Excerpts from that document following this report in Attachment 2.[12]

In the early 1980s, the successor organization to the USNSA, the United States Student Association, filed a Freedom of Information request for all government documents related to the USNSA. The CIA was the least forthcoming and resulted in a lawsuit, the USSA v. CIA in the United States Court for the District of Columbia, Civil Action No. 82-1286. The case produced a Vaughn Index detailing documents that the CIA said are in its possession, along with the reasons why it was unwilling to declassify each document. Some of the referenced documents are undated. However, there are twenty-nine documents identified between the period of May 4, 1949, and December 12, 1952. The judge reviewed sample documents from the list and agreed with the CIA that they should not be released.

END NOTES

[1] See Holmes, p. 554.

[2] At the Hoover Institution NSA Archives.

[3] See Craig Wilson, p. 250.

[4] The three NSA observers at the IUS Congress were William Holbrook (University of Minnesota), Eugene Schwartz (City College of New York), and Robert West (Yale). Schwartz states they were unaware of the source of the funds and that he first learned of it while preparing the material for this book in 1996. West is quoted in the *Los Angeles Times* on February 19, 1967, stating, "The CIA funds undermined our whole position. I certainly would not have gone to Prague if I knew there was anything surreptitious." Ironically, Schwartz reports that on their return from Prague, the FBI, after debriefing them, lifted all of their passports. While West and Holbrook received theirs back shortly, it took Schwartz six months, the assistance of the State Department, and an interview with the Passport Bureau director before his was returned.

[5] Attachment I. Memorandum, Milton W. Buffington to CSP (Lewis S. Thompson), "United States Student Association," 17 February 1951.

Included in *CIA Cold War Records—The CIA under Harry Truman*, edited by Michael Warner. See p. 569.

[6] The NSA International Team, in its Preliminary Report to the Michigan Congress in August 1950, noted that "it was the original intention of the NEC that 12 representatives attend the second World Student Congress of the International Union of Students. This objective was frustrated by the refusal of the IUS to invite more than three representatives....Erskine B. Childers, NSA Vice President for International Affairs and team chairman, made area assignments." [See p. 609 for a complete list.]

[7] At the Hoover Institution NSA Archives.

[8] Earlier, Grant had been Assistant Administrator of AID and President of the Overseas Development Council. Conant, the other representative to visit Asia, was later on the faculty of the U.S. National War College as Professor of International Security and was the founder and editor of *Geopolitics of Energy*.

[9] See Helen Jean Rogers Secondari, p. 597.

[10] Eisenberg writes, "I used all my own money except for the airline tickets. Our hotel and meals were paid for by UNE [the Brazilian student group] as I recall," or else, he notes, by a wealthy Brazilian student officer of UNE.

[11] Cord Meyer writing in *Facing Reality: From World Federalism to the CIA* (New York: Harper and Row, 1980), pp. 101–102, discusses this early period of CIA-NSA contacts after joining the agency in the fall of 1951. William Dentzer, a contributor to this article, believes that Meyer's brief commentary about this period may be misunderstood because of its compression of events occurring over several years. Dentzer also disputes the timing of CIA's contacts with NSA in the 1950–52 period, as indicated by the information reported by him in this article.

[12] Attachment 2. Report accompanying Letter from Nicholas Katzenbach to the President, 03/24/67, C.F. Oversize Attach, Cater, US Govt. & Pvt. Vol. Organ. Box 193, LBJ Library (excerpts). See p. 570.

EDITOR'S NOTE ON SOURCING THE COVERT FUNDING STORY

Early in the eight years that this work has been in preparation, we asked the contributors to the unit on Covert Funding to provide for this Anthology a distillation of whatever we as a generation "present at the creation" of NSA (as Karl Meyer first entitled his piece, in Part 1), could find that would shed light on the presence and influence of covert U.S. government funding through the CIA and otherwise during the organization's early years.

At this writing Karen Paget, a political scientist, writer and Contributing Editor to *The American Prospect*, who was the wife of an NSA international staffer in 1965-66, is completing a study of the CIA's covert relationship with NSA. In her book proposal, she wrote, "Surprisingly, no student has written about his experience. Former Agency officials Tom Braden and Cord Meyer have written cursorily about the tie. Beyond the *Ramparts* exposé, and the press coverage at the time, no history of the relationship exists." Although this anthology has no connection with her work, I am hopeful that she will deal comprehensively with the events and issues raised by the 15-year relationship between the CIA and NSA. Meanwhile, she has written "From Stockholm to Leiden: The CIA's role in the Formation of the International Student Conference," *Intelligence and National Security*, Vol. 18, No. 2, Summer 2003, p. 134, concentrating on the 1949-52 period. It is also my hope that the generation of NSA leaders who followed us will write their own story as we have here written ours.

In the interim, some fragmentary documentation, reporting and discussion are now available outside of government files, notably in the Hoover Institution NSA archives at Stanford University, as well as some at the Wisconsin State Historical Society Archives, the LBJ Library at the University of Texas and some of the other NSA archives listed in the back of this book. These are far from a comprehensive resource on the subject, many U.S. government files having not yet been released. Also, the Bibliography of this book contains a short list, by no means complete, of additional references on the subject which were acquired during the course of this project, including some of the extensive news coverage following the *Ramparts* 1967 expose.

In the absence of published research and fully disclosed government documentation, we hope we have helped lay the groundwork for full disclosure in the future. In return we have exercised a self-imposed editorial constraint, limiting ourselves to what we have learned from our first-hand experiences and researches.

Eugene G. Schwartz, Editor

Ramparts

CORRESPONDENCE 2

ESSAYS

SPECIAL REPORTS

NSA and the CIA 29

LITERATURE 52

Apologia

Ramparts, March, 1967

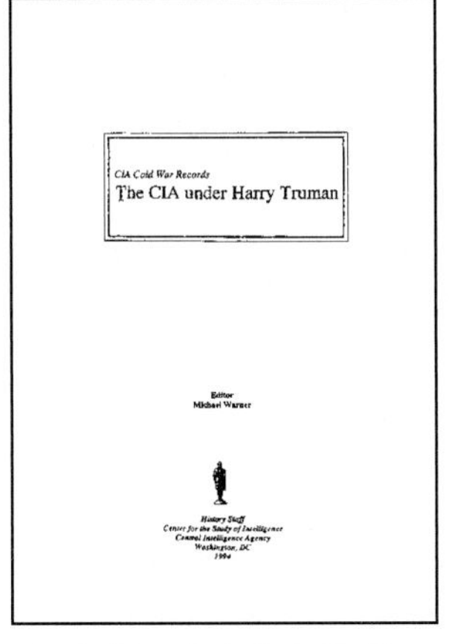

CIA Cold War Records

The CIA under Harry Truman

Editor

Michael Warner

History Staff

Center for the Study of Intelligence

Central Intelligence Agency

Washington, DC

1994

History Staff, Center for the Study of Intelligence, Central Intelligence Agency, Washington, D.C., 1994

Attachment 1: THE CIA CONSIDERS NSA IN 1951

"The National Student Association is not receptive to accepting government subsidy..."

This document was obtained from archives at the University of Texas, entitled "Cold War Records: The CIA under Harry Truman," edited by Michael Warner, published by the History Staff, Center for the Study of Intelligence, Central Intelligence Agency, Washington, D.C., 1994.

Milton W. Buffington to CSP (Lewis S. Thompson), "United States National Student Association," 7 February 1951
(carbon copy)

7 February 1951
MEMORANDUM FOR: CSP

SUBJECT: United States National Student Association

1. Reference is made to our conversation of yesterday wherein we discussed certain aspects of a conference recently held by Dr. William Elliot and Mr. Allan Dulles concerning the National Student Association.

2. The National Student Association is financed principally through dues paid in by the student unions of the colleges and universities of this county. It does, however, appeal from time to time to various outside sources, such as the Rockefeller Foundation, for funds for specific international projects which it undertakes. For example, at the present time there is pending before the foundation a request by the National Student Association for financial assistance in the amount of $60,000 for the consideration of projects for the International Student Information Service and for regional university student seminars in Germany, Southeast Asia and the Middle East.

3. The National Student Association is not receptive to accepting government subsidy, because it considers that such a course of action would run contrary to its basic principle of independent thought and action, and would in a sense reduce it to the position of being a tool of its government. This situation must be borne in mind in considering any relationship which this office might have with the National Student Association as such. It means that such relation as is maintained is an extremely delicate one, particularly with reference to the laying on of any plans involving the passing of funds.

4. There is another important factor which must be considered in connection with our relation with the NSA and that is the matter of personal differences currently rife in its high command. There is a schism between its president, Mr. Allard K. Lowenstein, and its vice president in charge of international affairs, Mr. Herbert Eisenberg, which does not make for harmony in the working of the organization as a whole at the present time.[1] Mr. Lowenstein favors a forthright stand on the part of the organization concerning communism as a political and military menace to our society. This is manifested in a speech made by Mr. Lowenstein at the Stockholm Conference called in late December by the Swedish National Student Union to discuss methods of international student cooperation outside of the communist dominated International Union of Students.[2] Mr. Eisenberg on the other hand, favors what purports to be a more idealistic, less militant stand on the subject in deference to the principle of the National Student Association, which requires it to address itself to matters of student interest and general welfare, rather than to questions of international politics. Currently Mr. Lowenstein is faced with being drafted into the Army, in view of which fact we have undertaken covertly and through the proper channels to get him deferred, although he is completely unaware of this fact. We consider this undertaking to be in order in view of the fact that we have considerable evidence that the National Executive Committee of the National Student Association supports Mr. Lowenstein.

5. Speaking specifically to the question raised by Dr. Elliot as to subsidizing the National Student Association as such, I do not feel that such subsidy is feasible, practicable, or desirable, in view of the facts hereinabove expressed. However, as individual projects arise which require the use of the aegis of the National Student Association, and where conditions are such that the use of this aegis can be obtained through the penetration which we have made into the National Student Association [*1-1/4 lines blacked out*],[3] then we stand prepared to subsidize such individual projects by careful use of such means as will not offend or arouse the suspicion of the National Student Association that the government is at all interested. An illustration of this type of activity is found in the project currently being prepared jointly by this office and the Far East Division to convene a regional students seminar in Southeast Asia during this coming summer.

6. As matters stand, it is my recommendation that we continue to operate [as] hereinabove expressed.

Milton W. Buffington

EDITOR'S END NOTES

[1] See Eisenberg, p. 522, Lynch, p. 273.

[2] See Lowenstein, p. 562, *NSA News,* p. 527.

[3] *Editors note:* Despite persistent efforts, the contributors to this Anthology have been unable to ascertain to whom the blacked-out reference refers.

Attachment 2: AMERICAN STUDENTS IN POSTWAR INTERNATIONAL AFFAIRS

"The NSA leaders steadily developed into the top specialists—in or out of government—on international student affairs."

This document was obtained from archives at the University of Texas. It is one of the declassified attachments to the report from Nicholas Katzenbach to the President regarding the relationship between government agencies, notably the CIA, and private voluntary organizations that operated abroad (03/24/67, C.F. Oversize Attach, Cater, US Govt. & Pvt. Vol. Organ. Box 193, LBJ Library).

Across a narrow table at the student union building in Prague in the spring of 1947, student representatives of East and West argued a program detail: Would an upcoming Calcutta conference, scheduled for February of the following year, be limited to university students, or would it embrace other youth as well? Would it be sponsored solely by the International Union of Students? Or would it be a joint venture of IUS and the World Federation of Democratic Youth?

For close to three hours the debate was pressed, one side led by the Soviets' Aleksandr Shelepin—subsequently to become head of the Soviet Security Ministry, the KGB—the other by the young American just out of college who was serving as interim representative of U.S. students.

At stake, it seemed clear to the American, was the degree of Communist influence that would be exerted at Calcutta on the university students of Southeast Asia, recognized by both sides as the future leaders of their countries. The West still had some say in the IUS, but in any joint effort with the World Federation of Democratic Youth, Soviet influence would overwhelm the democratic elements. The American's side lost.

The resulting "Conference of Youth and Students of Southeast Asia Fighting for Freedom and Independence"—one of three in Calcutta that spring—was of more than casual interest. Some observers have suggested that participants at the three conferences were used by Moscow to transmit its views regarding Communist insurrections in Burma, Malaya and Indonesia. While it is quite probable that orders, if they existed, were passed through a more direct channel, nevertheless the guidance, exhortations and aid given by the IUS and WFDY conference leaders to Communist youth groups from these countries doubtless provided significant support.

It was into this tough, tense world of political maneuvering that the U.S. National Student Association entered when it was organized six months later. When the original officers came to the State Department early in 1948 to discuss their plan to send observers to the IUS, they were dismissed with a lecture on their youthful naivete.[1]

Without coaching and without briefing, responsible student leaders came to recognize the nature of the struggle they were involved in. They assessed the situation and decided—again, by themselves—that action was required. And notwithstanding the unconventional funding eventually resorted to, the students pursued the conflict on their own terms.

Theirs was not the only American private association to find itself engaged with elements that were old hands at the use of organizations as weapons in the struggle for power. Trade unionists, journalists, veterans groups, intellectuals—all felt the pressure.

Democratic unions pulled out of the Communist-dominated World Federation of Trade Unions in 1949 and formed the rival International Confederation of Free Trade Unions. Since then, through training schools and travel grants, scholarships and conferences, a bitter, costly confrontation has been underway in villages and towns all over the globe.

Journalists of East and West met together in the International Organization of Journalists when it was formed, just after the Second World War, but from their key posts Communists gradually transformed it into what its first president called a "branch office of the Cominform." Non-Communist groups abandoned the IOJ and in 1952 set up the International Federation of Journalists.

Women were organized into the Women's International Democratic Federation, scientists into the World Federation of Scientific Workers, veterans into the Federation Internationale des Resistants. All were Communist-controlled, and all aimed to reach and influence the relevant professions and trades in the West and the developing areas.

The struggle, to be sure, was taking place on an international level. There is no way, however, to play a role in international federations except through a national affiliate, and thus the domestic organizations in the U.S. found themselves with the ball.

The history of the times probably is illuminated best by the experience of the American students and their national organization.

The International is founded

The founding congress of the International Union of Students, held in Prague in the summer of 1946, foreshadowed the troubles that lay ahead.

Many non-Communist countries were represented, the U.S. by a group of 25 delegates—khaki-shirted young World War II veterans in large part, then in college under the GI Bill and eager to take a hand in shaping a better world. They later became known as the Prague 25.[2] For them, an international student federation would be a kind of United Nations at the student level, an instrument for peace and understanding.

But conflict began with the work of the Credentials Committee. In ruling on official delegates, the committee selected the Communist student group of India to organize that delegation; and it cut the Italian delegation, on which Communists were a small minority, from twenty to ten (the Italian non-Communists walked out). All twenty-four of the USSR delegates were admitted, however, and business began with a clear Communist majority in place. Next, the agenda that had been prepared and circulated four months earlier by the International Preparatory Committee was discarded, and a new twenty-five-page substitute passed out.

In a vain effort to resist the majority, some of the Americans caucused with moderate elements in the Western delegations, and in a nearby beer hall Catholics on the American delegation and Catholics from Hungary, Czechoslovakia and Poland put their heads together. Before the conference was over, the Dutch had withdrawn from the IUS, charging lack of respect for the rights of minority opinions.[3]

And then NSA

Despite misgivings about the IUS, the American delegates returned from Prague convinced that this country needed a strong national student organization to hold its own in the international arena. Unquestionably any student association would have important national concerns as well; but the twenty five Americans who had observed the international give and take at Prague, the strength, effectiveness and recognition of the bodies represented there wished primarily to see an American organization that could affiliate with the federation and make the weight of its opinions felt in world student affairs.

The twenty five took the initiative. With other representatives from universities and colleges across the land, they helped form, in 1947, the U.S. National Student Association.[4] Headlines were telling of guerrilla warfare in Greece and the Truman Doctrine; the Berlin blockade was still months off. While favoring some links with the IUS, many student leaders were wary of that Communist-dominated federation.

The rupture

Before even a conditional affiliation could be worked out, events brought a rupture to NSA-IUS negotiations. The Czech coup d'état of February 1948 was decisive. Prague student demonstrations in behalf of the parliamentary form of government were suppressed, and more than 100 students were arrested. An NSA observer who had been present as the students moved up the hill to Hradcany Castle asked for an IUS protest. When the IUS sided with the Communists against the students, rejecting the appeal for a protest, NSA announced that relationships were terminated, and the American vice-president of IUS resigned.[5]

The Czech coup was not the only evidence that IUS had become simply a Soviet front. When Stalin expelled Tito from the Cominform, the Yugoslav Union of Students suddenly found itself expelled from IUS, in violation of the constitution, on grounds that it supported the "fascist oppression" of Tito's government.

Then in 1950, two months after the start of the Korean war, the second IUS congress assembled. The first session saw a frenzied demonstration. As NSA observers looked on, delegates hoisted the North Korean representatives to their shoulders and marched around the hall amid cheering and singing.[6]

For American student leaders, this was a turning point; any lingering thoughts of possible cooperation were abandoned. East and West went their separate ways.

After the Czech coup, the IUS was ruled from Moscow. Its resolutions mirrored Soviet foreign policy, its officials for the most part have been Communists, and its funds have been donated by the governments of Eastern Europe.

The Soviets also had firm control of the World Federation of Democratic Youth, a catch-all front for people defined as "youth" by the elastic Communist calendar.

The Youth Festivals

By 1947, WFDY and IUS were so tightly organized and controlled that they were able to stage the first of eight lavishly produced and financed spectaculars: the World Youth Festival. At that first Festival, held in Prague and attended by 20,000 of the world's students and youth, handsome exhibits portrayed the glories of life in the East European peoples' democracies. The American exhibit is chiefly remembered for a large poster showing a Negro hanging from a tree; the caption said 70 Negroes had been lynched in the U.S. since V-J Day. An American student representative in Prague recalls that repeated attempts to enlist the American Embassy's help in getting a representative U.S. delegation to the Festival ran into a blank wall.

The Festival in Prague in 1947 was followed by one in Budapest in 1949, in East Berlin in 1951—that one brought the West awake—in Bucharest in 1953, Warsaw 1955, and the big Sixth World Youth Festival in Moscow in 1957. With 34,000 participants and travel grants to provide, it is estimated that the Moscow production cost the sponsors many tens of millions of dollars.

By 1959, the Soviets were ready to risk staging the seventh Festival outside the Iron Curtain, in Vienna. Here was terrain in which to operate. The earlier U.S. Government position discouraging attendance was changed to permit the first real American confrontation with the Communist fronts at the popular level.

The American delegation this time was large and more nearly representative. Thousands of participants visited the American information center, set up under the auspices of the Independent Research Service; and while Vienna newspapers adhered to their decision to print no word about the Festival, a Western-operated press turned out a special daily in four languages with an accurate account of proceedings—from the West's point of view—and news of upcoming events.

The eighth Festival was brought off with some difficulty in Helsinki in 1962. Once again, a Western-edited daily became the chief source of Festival information, including the news of dissident members of an East German delegation detained aboard a ship. A "Young America Presents" exhibit with jazz bands, poetry readings, records and books was accompanied by half a hundred university students ready to exchange ideas with anyone. As at Vienna, the organized American effort was coordinated by the Independent Research Service.

Although the Festivals drew the big headlines, probably the year-in, year-out work of the fronts was at least as important for communism's expansive purposes. The annual operating budget for the IUS, exclusive of Festivals, is estimated to be in the neighborhood of $1,000,000. The money finances a variety of publications, scholarships for study in Communist countries, travel of individuals and delegations to conferences and seminars, and staff travel for on-the-spot guidance to student movements in the regions of greatest interest.

The new nations drawn in

The Communist-front IUS was strong, and it was attractive to students of the developing nations whom it encouraged in their aspirations for political freedom and social justice. These students of the Third World were eager for international contact; they wanted support for their national movements, and they wanted the give and take of an international forum. An alternative to the Communist front group, however, did not exist.

It was not American newspapers or American foundations—and certainly not the U.S. Government—that first spotted the problem and saw its significance. In this country few forces have been so little understood or so vastly underrated as the world's organized students and youth. Virtually alone among Americans, the leaders of the National Student Association recognized their significance and analyzed the problem.[7]

NSA observers back from the 1950 Prague meeting that had lionized the North Koreans were convinced that a special effort was needed if NSA were to meet its responsibilities to the international student community.

"We knew that it was going to be two worlds for awhile," recalls a former NSA member, a veteran of IUS negotiating sessions, "and that we were in for a vicious fight. At that point the chips were down."

An alternative to the Communist Front

At Christmastime in 1950, the NSA president, borrowing money for his passage, left with other American representatives for Stockholm to meet with delegates of 20 other national student groups. Murmurings had been heard earlier that year when West European and American student leaders participated in a summer seminar in Germany. Some at the seminar had serious misgivings about the West's role in the IUS and spoke openly of a rival organization. Some were going on to the IUS session; they would wait and see how things went at Prague. The Stockholm meeting was the result.[8]

NSA was by no means of one mind about a rival organization. The classic question of whether to work for change from inside or outside an entity had been argued within the association; the NSA Congress had turned aside one proposal for a new anti-Communist organization earlier in the year.

At Stockholm, an "alternative," though not a rival "organization," was shaped. It became the International Student Conference. NSA support for the move was important, but the leading or inspiring force came mainly from the Swedes.

The new grouping was to eschew controversial political questions and concentrate on practical cooperation with student unions of the developing nations. To attract Asians, Africans and Latin Americans, it was necessary that it not be mistaken as another Cold War instrument; most student leaders from the developing areas had little inclination to choose sides and become a part of the East-West struggle.

A year later, in January 1952, the Stockholm group decided to set up a Coordinating Secretariat in Leiden, the Netherlands. By 1953 they had delegated 26 projects to participating unions, planned increased support for the Student Mutual Assistance Program, and made plans to send an international team to visit educational centers in Africa.

African and Asian student unions responded, and by 1954 there were 42 participants in the International Student Conference. Now only five nationally representative student unions outside the Iron Curtain remained with IUS. New projects were planned by the ISC: an exchange of information and technical teams, seminars and work camps, a student press conference. There were publications, good-will delegations and regional conferences to come. Grants from the Foundation for Youth and Student Affairs in New York were helping to make them possible.[9]

At home, assault from the Right

With a new international student organization free from Communist control coming to life, the Americans considered it important to develop effective relations with these democratic student unions now loosely banded together.

But in the face of the challenge, the NSA of the early Fifties felt itself seriously handicapped.

Clearly, for an American body to establish relationships with the new student groups springing up around the southern half of the globe, it would be necessary to understand their revolutionary point of view and to speak to it.

But at home the United States was about to enter an era of blacklists, gray lists, suspicion and restriction. There was fear of Communist penetration of American institutions. Student and youth organizations, some of which had in fact been heavily penetrated in the depression days, were considered particularly susceptible—and hence particularly suspect.[10]

Far from being encouraged to make common cause with the anti-colonial, socialistic young elites of the emerging nations, NSA instead was defending itself against assault from the Right. The experience at an Illinois college—a false report on campus that the House Un-American Affairs Committee had declared NSA Communist, then news headlines, a referendum, and withdrawal of membership—was typical of the times. An NSA officer's denunciation of the Berkeley loyalty oath brought a flood of protests charging communism. A packaged TV student forum program with NSA participants fought for its life on station after station.[11]

Attempts to finance a program

Then there was the problem of money. NSA had begun on a shoestring. Later, a Philadelphia department store gave free office space in its building, and a newspaper friend coached the young officers in the art of writing proposals to foundations. Occasional grants of

$1500 or $2000 for specific projects materialized. No one, however, had much time to devote to fund-raising.

And there was no answer to the problem of funding administrative costs—the supplies, salaries and publications, the travel of staff or of a fraternal delegation to other countries—that constitute the great bulk of the budget and that do not fit the "project" concept usually looked for by potential private donors.

Foundations were cautious about grants in the political field; in any case, they, like the government, knew little of IUS and its potential.

At some point in the first half of the 1950s, an informal memo went to the Ford Foundation from one of the NSA founders, proposing the creation of a new fund similar to the Fund for the Republic. The money, it was suggested, could meet an important need by helping religious and secular organizations to do their job abroad. The figure of $1,500,000 was mentioned. No action resulted.

NSA was without the means even to send representatives to other national student unions' annual meetings—standard practice among the European unions.

It was scarcely a position from which to challenge international communism.

NSA and USG: A coming together

Interested observers, looking back, recall that individual student leaders had visited the State Department early in the Fifties. They were groping. To the low-level officials who received them, they explained their concern about IUS and its dangers for the future leadership of the emerging countries. Some of the students indicated financial assistance would be necessary. What did the Department think could be done?

Any notion that the foreign affairs agencies of the U.S. Government should be concerned with students as a force in international events had yet to take root in any agency of government. The pretensions of these young students could hardly be taken seriously. Certainly most officers in either State or CIA had never heard of the IUS.

Nevertheless, the students' growing conviction that IUS was a dangerous mechanism of Communist activity was followed by what has been described as a slow recognition within government, primarily within the CIA, of the same fact, and a financial relationship began.

NSA's international affairs office was situated for years in Cambridge, Mass., separate from the association's headquarters.[12] Beginning with a small sum for support of the international effort—supplies, travel for the international affairs vice-president and for delegations to ISC meetings—the agency's subsidy grew gradually as NSA adopted for itself the kind of operation that had long been standard among European student unions.

Fraternal delegations had to be sent abroad to maintain contact with counterpart unions. There were delegations to ISC meetings, then to ISC sub-group meetings. When the French or British students held their annual sessions, an American representative had to attend. Then bigger delegations were needed when such meetings attracted both East Europeans and uncommitted student leaders and became, in effect, a point of confrontation. With almost all other student unions more than 3000 miles distant, the cost was heavy.

Encouraged to exercise freedom of judgment and of action, and with the new mobility afforded them by their increased resources, the NSA leaders steadily developed into the top specialists—in or out of government—on international student political affairs. Their expertise did not go unrecognized. Confidence in their judgment grew. Indeed, their interpretation of events may frequently have nudged the Government into positions that might not otherwise have been considered.

Throughout, the object of the agency's relationship with NSA leaders was never intelligence—one reason why old pros at CIA discounted it as a serious venture.

The object was more dynamic. It was to provide the means to build a relationship between American students and those of the developing world in circumstances free from Communist influence or control, and thereby help prevent the capture of legitimate revolutionary movements.

EDITOR'S END NOTES

Because this narrative so closely follows the documented events of the times, the Anthology editor has furnished cross-references to a number of the key events referred to.

[1] See Smith, p. 507, for a report of this meeting.

[2] See Tibbetts, p. 68 and Bellush, p. 73 for a description of the U.S. delegation and how it was formed.

[3] See Blair and Jones, p. 538, for a history of NSA/IUS relations. See Ellis and Roberts, p. 106 for their report on the world Stdent Congress.

[4] See Wharton, pp. 112, 144, on the founding NSA conventions.

[5] See Ellis and Smith, p. 188, for statements on the coup and their resignations.

[6] See West, p. 556, for the NSA statement to the Congress, and Holbrook, p. 559, for a description of the Congress demonstrations.

[7] For examples of these observations see Fisher, p. 511, Childers, p. 518, West, p. 557, Lowenstein, p. 562, Rogers, p. 598. Also, on technical assistance, p. 632

[8] See Lowenstein, p. 562, for his statement to the Conference, and Eisenberg, p. 522, and Lynch, p. 273, for additional background on NSA's role and policy.

[9] See p. 565 on covert funding.

[10] This experience is treated in many of the memoirs throughout the book. For examples, see Brown, pp. 379, 785, Welsch, p. 168, Pope, p. 390, Dentzer, p. 310, and Buckley, Evans, Munger and Schodde in Pt. 4, Sec. 4.

[11] See Meyer, p. 141, for a list of some of these many attacks.

[12] For the story of the founding and operations of NSA's international office, see Smith, p. 505.

FROM THE PHILADELPHIA BULLETIN IN 1967

Editor's note: NSA had its national headquarters in Philadelphia from September of 1952 until the fall of 1965 when it moved to Washington, D.C. These editorial comments from the Philadelphia Bulletin, *which regularly reported on Association activities, are included as a sampler of press comment in 1967 when* Ramparts *magazine published its revelations about covert CIA funding of international programs sponsored by NSA and other U.S. non-government organizations.*

CIA and Students: Ends and Means

FEB 16 1967

Disclosure by a sensational West Coast magazine of hidden Central Intelligence Agency subsidies over 14 years to the nation's largest student organization—the National Student Association—has brought new embarrassment to the intelligence agency and to the American academic world. The President has ordered CIA to end all secret aid programs to student groups, and called for a review of all programs to fight Communist activities in private organizations. But once again CIA fat is in the fire.

What can be said in justification of the arrangement to use CIA funds, channeled through go-between foundations to NSA to send representatives to student congresses abroad and to further student exchanges?

That there was, and is, a problem in countering Communist propaganda among the students of many nations. That an independent American student voice needed to be heard in opposition. That the NSA lacked private funds to finance trips to international gatherings. That the American government, in coming to the financial assistance of NSA, had to do so secretly to prevent this liberal student group, which often took positions counter to Administration policy, from being labeled a bought tool.

But even if it is conceded that a legitimate national interest was involved—countering Communist-financed and manipulated student activity—the secret collaboration between a few NSA leaders and the CIA, with the knowledge of high levels in government, was a mistake. It is another instance in which the persistent Cold War mentality — any means and methods to fight communism—produced a strange blindness as to the importance of honesty, in fact and appearance, in the American scheme of things.

There would not now be all this concern about the grave injury to the reputation of American student representatives abroad, and the possible threat to the survival of the National Student Association as an organization, if the mere existence of a tie with the CIA were not enough to raise suspicions of a kind of collaboration inconsistent with independent, democratic conduct of open private organizations in our society, especially academic organizations.

Against this reaction, the protestations of a worthy aim and of innocent behavior—an NSA leader asserted that the organization never served any intelligence function or provided information of a sensitive nature to any government agency—will avail little.

Apart from the fundamental impropriety of involving CIA with the student association, the episode again calls into question the judgment of the CIA, from a practical viewpoint, in permitting itself to be so linked. Despite all precautions, it seems that sooner or later CIA dealings with students and professors and universities become matters of public knowledge and controversy.

Congress needs to ask pointed questions about CIA involvement with American universities, student groups, foundations, magazines, books, and what-have-you. It needs to review the extent to which the CIA, whose prime responsibility is intelligence, is chartered to act in countering Communist propaganda.

Students Break With CIA

AUG 15 1967

Without doubt the Congress of the National Student Association meeting at the University of Maryland will support the proposal to abandon its activities abroad. This seems assured in view of the furor caused by last February's revelation that the CIA had secretly supplied the money for the association's work abroad.

This will be a distinct loss to the country. The need for an organized student voice representing American ideals may not be as great as it was in the 1950s but it should not be supposed that the need has entirely ceased to exist. The association in past years was quite effective in countering anti-American propaganda of Communist-organized youth festivals and university groups.

The pity is that association leaders had to turn to help from the CIA for funds to carry on this laudable work. And it is an even greater pity that the CIA went overboard, as it so often does, and practically made the association a CIA adjunct by moving its headquarters from Philadelphia to a rent free building in Washington.

There is no evidence that the CIA dictated the line the students were to take abroad, but the taint was there nevertheless. The contemplated complete break with the CIA seems to have left the association's officers in a somewhat confused state of mind for they have sought grants from the State Department and the Office of Economic Opportunity. This hardly frees the association from all governmental ties. Why a private foundation has not seen fit to supply funds is an enigma.

Reproduced from the *Philadelphia Bulletin*, February 16 and August 15, 1967

Avrea Ingram was our "Secretary of State"...elected at the Minnesota Congress

6. Remembering Avrea Ingram

Barry Farber
University of North Carolina
Chair, NSA Virginia-Carolinas Region, 1951-52
NSA Delegate to 1951 Zagreb Peace Conference,
1952 Rio Inter-American Conference

For NSAers Avrea Ingram was a high official whose "suicide" required thick quotation marks on either side.

Avrea Ingram was our "Secretary of State," International Vice President, elected at the Minnesota Congress in the summer of 1950.

Shame to say, I don't know the exact date, but I believe it was a few years after his term. The news rocketed across the NSA universe that Avrea had committed suicide. Against the backdrop of shock and sadness we exchanged the usual cliches about how little we sometimes know about those we think we know well.

Avrea was one of those perpetually middle-aged men, mature beyond his years and earnest beyond your typical member of any president's cabinet. I remember envying Avrea's many international travels, but I remember being annoyed that he probably never allowed himself any time to enjoy them.

Avrea wasn't particularly friendly. He wasn't unfriendly; just business-like. It was hard to imagine him saying yes to a beer party in his home town of Talledega, Alabama. The one and only time I recall Avrea hauling off and being one of the boys, he was the life of the party. He came through the crowd around the piano and led us in the best performance of "I'm A Rambling Wreck from Georgia Tech" I'd ever heard. Then he immediately went back to being Avrea again.

For years I had no reason to question Avrea's suicide. It was no problem for me to go along with the ostensible theory that, being so intense and introverted, Avrea simply had no ways and means to jettison tension and let in the daylight.

In 1968 the news broke that certain of NSA's international activities in the early 1950s had been paid for by the CIA.

The political correctness of that day demanded that all those involved with NSA throw themselves on the floor and protest the rape of the good name of our authentic American student movement by the oleaginous creeps of the Cold War.

I went on the air on my WOR Radio show that night and congratulated the CIA for being the only branch of the United States government to recognize the importance of the NSA in fighting Moscow's effort to recruit and preempt student movements in non-communist countries. "See above" how we struck out with Gen. Omar Bradley and all other government biggies who could never get over their notion that we students were mere beer-drinkers, football-game-goers, and panty-raiders.

I must admit that for quite some time my subconscious mind successfully blocked the realization that our International Vice President "committed suicide" at precisely the period when the CIA was busy visiting its assistance upon us!

Avrea Ingram in 1953

The mind rejects untoward thoughts even more abruptly than the stomach rejects untoward food. I never gave Avrea's "suicide" another thought—until 1985!

In that year I peeled away from my radio show in New York to host "Crossfire" on CNN for a week.

Helen Jean Rogers Secondari raises a question

The enfabled Helen Jean Rogers invited me to lunch in her exquisite apartment in Georgetown overlooking the Potomac River, northern Virginia, and seemingly northern parts of North Carolina. I brought up Avrea's name along with all the other dear people we worked with and Helen Jean said something which, had it been a movie, would have occasioned a quick change of mood music.

Help me rekindle the mood I'm trying to invoke! No Russian official today when asked about the Korean War would tell you what Pravda told the communist world in June, 1950; namely, that "South Korea launched an attack upon North Korea; but the peace-loving peasants of North Korea quick rallied and 'transferred the scene of operations southward!'" He'd tell you Stalin encouraged the North to attack the South.

No American official when asked about the "Gulf of Tonkin Incident" today would tell you the North Vietnamese attacked American shipping requiring new and more permissive rules of engagement. He'd tell you the Johnson Administration rigged a pretext to take a more aggressive approach to the North Vietnamese. And each would speak devoid of any angst of confession due to the passage of quite huge hunks of time

In that same manner, Helen Jean airily dismissed any notion of Avrea's death having been self-inflicted.

"I was with him just a few hours earlier," she told me. "He was fine. He was discussing plans like the good old Avrea we all knew. Avrea Ingram did not commit suicide."

Self-censorship can be as damnable as the government kind. I didn't lace into Helen Jean and explore alternative explanations. Instead I found somebody else to reminisce about.

If there's going to be a half-century scrapbook compiled about the NSA, there should be a chapter about the death of Avrea Ingram.

The inside-the-skull "nuclear power plant" of youthful idealism that powered the NSA activists should make us feel incomplete until we've hammered the question mark around Avery's death into an exclamation point.

Editor's note: According to the Los Angeles Times, February 6, 1967, Ingram was found dead in his New York City hotel room on February 5, 1957. The article states that "The New York Medical Examiner called the death 'asphyxia by hanging' and said the indications were suicide. Some of his friends and relatives were unable to accept the finding." Bill Dentzer, NSA president during Ingram's first term, in 1950-51, writes that "I didn't think it was suicide either, until I investigated this suicide on the spot in New York."

Dick Murphy, with whom he served in his second term, 1951-52, writes, "Barry is absolutely right in his description of Avrea. My description of Avrea would accord with his as a serious, brilliant, dedicated, patriotic, orderly, calm and a little hard to know, but with a loving heart and a warm gift of friendship." Bill Dentzer, of course, knew him best. "I also recall that my region (Virginia-Carolinas) was so opposed to continuing any relationship with the IUS, that we voted unanimously to oppose Avrea's candidacy for International V.P. in 1951. A year later, he was elected Vice President and he served under me in that capacity. I grew to respect him as the wonderful person he was, especially during the six months that he served as the only other full time NSA officer (January–June 1952). I would be careful about speculating on his death because of the many unknown factors which may have gone into it."

Ingram received his BS in Industrial Management at Georgia Tech in 1947. He attended Harvard from 1949-1951, receiving an MA in foreign affairs. He was a Harvard Graduate School delegate to the 1951 NSA Congress at the University of Minnesota where he was elected to his first term as NSA's international vice president.

No attempt was made to establish anything that approximated a new international student union

Ingram reports on the 1952 Edinburgh and Rio Conferences

Editor's note: the following excerpts are from Avrea Ingram's August 19, 1952, Plenary Section report, as it appeared in the Summary Minutes of the Fifth Annual National Student Congress at the University of Minnesota.[i]

The Edinburgh conference, follow-up to the 1950 Stockholm conference, was attended by twenty-five student unions, representing 1,800,000 students. No attempt was made to establish anything that approximated a new student union. Strict adherence was paid to the Fourth National Student Congress mandate to establish an organization whose only purpose would be the coordination of the work of the national unions in practical programs.

The conference had a highly political orientation. However, the general feeling of the participants was that the purpose of the meeting was to formulate a medium to carry out such practical projects as (a) student teams studying such problems as health and technical assistance; (b) teams of specialists to work with students on such activities as the recent conference of the Phillipines National Student Council on the role of the student in the national literacy campaign; (c) expansion of scholarship and fellowship opportunities; (d) regional meetings of students such as the Inter-American conference where mutual problems can be worked out through mutual cooperation;, and (e) expansion of the exchange of technical information; e.g., ISIS [International Student Information Service] and the SMAP [Students Mutual Assistance Program] Library.

The participants then made the decision to set up a Coordinating Secretariat. . . . Jarl Tranaeus, President of the Swedish National Union of I Students, and William T. Dentzer, former President of the USNSA (1950-51), were appointed General Secretary and Assistant, respectively, of the Coordinating Secretariat.

The Inter-American conference, originally scheduled for October 1951, actually convened January 25, 1952, in Rio de Janiero. As of this date, no minutes of the proceedings have been received. The USNSA delegation included William T. Dentzer, President of USNSA; Avrea Ingram,Vice President of International Affairs, USNSA; Helen Jean Rogers, former Secretary-Treasurer of USNSA, Herbert Wright, Youth Secretary of the National Association for the Advancement of Colored People; and Barry Farber, Chairman of the Virginia-Carolina Region of the Association.

Parliamentary procedure often times bowed to extensive emotional debate. The agenda's topics covered a wide range of subjects: capitalism, communism, freedom of the rivers, discrimination. . . . The attendance was highly heterogeneous, including the entire range from extreme right to left. The group was pretty well divided —with the moderates usually in a majority, the vote usually split 26-25 in the moderates' favor. Generally, the position of the assembage was that of the "reformista."

From the USA viewpoint, the conference represented a limited success including the additional following achievements—contacts established with Latin-American students, new and enlarged hemispheric programs, and emergence of the Latin-American unions on the world student scene.

END NOTE

[i] For more on Ingram, see Dentzer, p. 301, Eisenberg, p. 524, Murphy, p. 1075.

COPENHAGEN, JANUARY 1953 International Student Conference (See Murphy, Part 6): Left: Sylvia Bacon, NSA Student Affairs Vice President (1951-52). Right and second from right: Helen Jean Rogers, former NSA 1948-49 Secretary Treasurer, and Avrea Ingram, NSA International Vice President (U.S. National Student Collection, Hoover Institution Archives).

Forty-five years later, Jim Smith and Joza Grohman rekindle an old connection.

An Epilogue to the IUS

Fifty years later Janis Dowd finds the faded and abandoned office of the IUS in Prague.

Editor's note: When Eastern Europe was once more free for travel and exchange, after the Cold War, Jim Smith was able to contact Joza Grohman for whom, clearly, he had retained an affectionate regard. Jim, Douglass Cater, and some other IUS "alumni" sought each other out to take stock of what had happened after those stormy early years. In this section, the flavor of Jim's outreach is reflected in his letters to Grohman. The sad passing of Grohman—and an era—is reprised in a letter from Grohman's friend, Jarmila Marsalkova (All three letters were furnished by Jim's sons, Michael and Philip Smith). Janis Dowd, on a summer trip in 1997, sought out the offices of the IUS, which, remarkably, although abandoned, remained intact with its name plate on the building wall. She poignantly describes the experience.

Our generation was full of ideas for a better future...but the reality was different

In the 1990s, Jim Smith Hears from Prague Once More

I still believe that one day the world must be better.

United Steelworkers of America
AFL-CIO-CLC
FIVE GATEWAY CENTER, PITTSBURGH, PA. 15222
April 9,1990

Mr. Josef Grohman
Dear Joza,

If you will permit me, I am coming to see you next month. I want to know everything that has happened to you since 1948, so we will have a long visit, I hope.

Joza, we thought so many times of you, and of Jarmila Marsalkova, and of Otik, and others we knew at the IUS. But, we feared that any effort to contact you could only cause you harm, so we did not try to do so. I have had no reason to travel to Europe until recently, and even then I feared to come to Prague and look for you, for the same reason. Until December, 1989. Now I feel I can come without hurting you. I plan to be in Prague on May 20, 1990, for a week to 10 days. Officially, our Union is sending me to Poland next week to meet with steelworkers in Solidarity. They have asked for our Union's help to learn more about wage and salary structures in the North American steel industry, and also to learn about employee ownership of steel companies in the United States.

Thereafter, I am going to Hungary and Romania, and finally to Czechoslovakia. In Prague, I hope to meet with Mr. Igor Pleskot, the President of the Czechoslovakian Metalworkers' Foundation, and/or other leaders of that organization. My purpose would be to learn how we may be able to provide information to his union about developments in metals industry unions in North America, which might be helpful in the transition to a market economy....

* * *

Please write to say that we can come to see you...With warmest personal regards, I am

Sincerely
James W. Smith
Assistant to the President

JIM SMITH
9322 Knoll Crest Loop
Austin, TX 78759
September 29, 1992

Dear Joza,
We are very excited by the news that you and Kveta are coming to the States next year. Tom is very kind to make such an invitation.

We wish to invite you and Kveta to be our guests in traveling from Chicago to Texas to spend some time with us, while you are in the U. S. It would be a great pleasure for us to have you come to visit. From Austin we could easily drive to any location in the Southwestern U. S. that interests you, from New Orleans to the Rocky Mountains of Colorado and New Mexico.

Between Austin and Houston there are several small towns which were settled more than 100 years ago by immigrants from Bohemia and Moravia. In some of them the Czech language is still spoken by most of the people. You might wish to go and see such a town....

* * *

Please send us any information you have about when you plan to come to Chicago, and also Tom Madden's address (and telephone number if you have it) . Then we will correspond with Tom to arrange a possible trip to Texas, if you and Kveta will come.

Please decide to say yes, as we are really anxious to see you both, and also to show you our part of the United States....[1]

With best personal wishes,
Jim Smith

Horole Zecka 74
10200 Praha 10
Czech Republic Prague 13.3.1995

Dear Jim,

A very bad news. Joza died on 10th March at noon. He was examined in the hospital for a suspicion of TBC (he had after the war), but it was discovered being lung cancer....

The life of an honest, good and optimistic life ended. Our generation was full of ideas for a better future of people, but the reality was quite different. But I still believe (and so Joza did), that one day, the world must be better, just for all, not only for a small upper class (we, too, have millionaires in our country again).

I heard from Ben and Tom that you plan a meeting of the "old boys" of the IUS. I wrote already to Ben that the "old boys" shouldn't forget the "old IUS girls," like me, Carmel, Jeanne and maybe we shall discover Diana, Lorraine, etc.

The lives of all of us was not easy, once up, several times down, Again up, but in spite of all of this I wouldn't change it for another one.

I am sure you are aware of the complicated situation in our country. It is not so "pink" as it seems, hearing the statements of our Prime Minister. You are in contact with the trade union people so that you know exactly what is going on here in the social sphere.

Take care, I wish you and Anna good health and I am looking forward to seeing you both in Prague this year.

Love—

Jamila

"I found the street, finally the building...the dusty room obviously had been unoccupied for some time."

The IUS Revisited in 1997

"It was hard to reconcile this abandoned place with the energetic organization that had been the subject of so many fiery discussions within NSA."

When I arranged a trip to Prague in 1997, I looked forward to finding the IUS, if it still operated there, and determining its current status. Sandy England, formerly on the staff of USSA, helped me track down an address and some telephone numbers. She reported having met an IUS representative four years earlier in Cuba, the most recent indication that the organization existed. Although I was unable to reach the IUS offices when I telephoned, there were some busy signals that I thought might indicate that they were still alive. Full of hope as ever, I wrote to the last IUS address I could locate with dates of my visit to Prague.

Shortly after we arrived in Prague several of my friends and I were mugged in a subway station. This made me hesitant, but I set off the next day, changing trains in the same unpleasant station. I emerged near the old Jewish quarter with its Old New Synagogue and Old Cemetery. The nearby House of Ceremonies, a museum exhibiting the pictures children had drawn while they were awaiting deportation in the holding camp at Terezin, was a poignant link to our early dreams for the IUS.

I found the street, and, finally, the building. There was the bronze plaque naming the IUS. Through the window I could see furniture in the casual disarray of many student organizations. But the dusty room obviously had been unoccupied for some time.

Later I learned from our embassy that the IUS had been dissolved several years earlier. The IUS had had "some difficulty with the government, problems paying the bills. The government closed the office." No one seemed to know when or where the organization had gone, or anyone who would know.

It was hard to reconcile this abandoned place with the energetic organization that had been the subject of so many fiery discussions within NSA, or with the hopes for international communication that had inspired so many of us 50 years earlier. It seemed, instead, consistent with the decision of USSA, successor to NSA, to attend to domestic issues only. I felt very sad.

Janis Tremper Dowd
Rockford College, NSA National Secretary, 1948-49

EDITOR'S END NOTE

[1] *Editor's note:* Michael Smith, one of Jim's two sons, in a December 31, 2000, letter to the editor writes:

...In 1990...Jim renewed contact with Joza Grohman, the Czech student elected to preside at the 1948 Prague session. Grohman was imprisoned for five years by the Communist authorities for his role in student demonstrations, then again in the 1960s, for a total of fifteen years. When freed at last, Joza published a Czech encyclopedia and authored several children's books. Jim's letters are being forwarded to you; unfortunately, we cannot locate Grohman's at this date. They met up in Europe, but for health reasons Joza never came to Texas.

Coda: IUS in 2002

Editor's note: A March, 1997 Circular Letter of the IUS Executive Secretariat on the IUS Web site, reports that "for over two years [it] has been going through its most difficult period organizationally and financially," and "since 1992 most member unions have failed to pay their dues." In its November 11, 2002 update, the Web site notes the following: "Today, more than 50 years later the IUS goes through its deepest crisis in history. Financially and organizationally the IUS nearly ceases to exist." Its Web site is www.stud.uni-hannover.de/gruppen/ius. An IUS archive exists at the International Institute of Social History (www.iisg.nl) in Amsterdam. The archive note states, "The main part of the documents were found in the papers of the International Student Conference (Coordinating Secretariat),[1] the western opponent of the IUS, that ceased its work at the end of March 1969 and transferred its archives and library to the International Institute of Social History.

[1] See Dentzer, p. 301.

SECTION 3

Reaching Out to the World

CONTENTS

EMORY UNIVERSITY, GEORGIA

NSA Recognizes Necessity For International Cooperation

(Emory's Student Council for some time has been a member of the National Student Association, although many students still do not know anything about NSA, what it attempts to do for member schools or what some of its ultimate aims are. The following editorial from the Daily Texan explains some things Emory students should

FROM FESTIVALS TO FORUMS. Following war's end, U.S. students traveled around the world to link with others. From top: 1946 World Student Congress (Bellush); Emory Wheel 12/9/47; International Student Conference, Copenhagen, 1/53 (see p. 578, Hoover Institute).

Several student leaders who traveled abroad representing NSA record here their impressions of college student life and aspirations in other countries.

Bill Birenbaum (University of Chicago) went to Europe in the summer of 1948 as part of a team representing NSA. His recollections of "thousands of gymnasts" assembling for the Sokol Slet at the Polytechnic Institute in Prague remained with him in his later career as an educator and as President of Antioch College.

Mary Kay Perkins, a twenty-year-old student at Rosary College, Ill., traveled under the aegis of NSA in the summer of 1951 to a small town south of Munich, Germany, to take part in a summer conference concerned with the democratization of German students. Now the Diocesan Superintendent of Schools in Bend, Oregon, she recalls that "I've carried the memory of it with me all my life. Most important is knowing that not only did I benefit immeasurably, but I was able to help others as well."

First Inter-American contacts

Barry Farber (University of North Carolina), NSA Virginia-Carolinas regional chair in 1951-52, was tapped by NSA President Bill Dentzer to fly to Zagreb, Yugoslavia, where he represented NSA and met with student leaders in the Soviet Bloc breakaway Communist nation. Farber, who spoke Croatian, further honed the skills he employed later as a linguist, author, and radio commentator. Equally fluent in Spanish and Portuguese, he also reports on his 1952 trip to Rio De Janeiro as an NSA representative to the Inter-American Student Congress.

Helen Jean (Rogers) Secondari (Mundelein College and Catholic University), whose popularity and leadership in NSA was acknowledged in an ovation at the 1951 Minnesota Congress, which Farber describes, led NSA's first delegation with Herb Eisenberg (MIT) to South America, representing the Association at the 1951 Brazilian Union of Students National Congress. She later traveled throughout the world as an award-winning TV documentary producer.

These memoirs also deal with political, educational, and social issues and events, on the campus, regional, and national levels of NSA.

U.S. Students Link to the Rest of the World

International Students Day

NORTHAMPTON, MASS.

Campus Clubs To Sponsor International Students' Day

Students Mark Czech Massacre

W. Ellis To Talk In Chapel On Student Conferences

EXHIBITION IN LIBRARY

CORNELL DAILY SUN

National Students Association Plans International Students Day Program

ISLAND UNIVERSITY

NSA Student Day Conference Discusses Foreign Good Will

Open Letter

November 17, 1948

For Us the Living

International Students Day Recalls Martyred Czechs

Today is International Students Day.

Nine years ago today, 147 students died in Czechoslovakia. They were killed as part of the Nazis' attempt to stifle the resistance movement in the country they had so recently occupied.

WRTI LOG

WORLDWIDE COMMEMORATION of November 17,1939 to mark the killing of 147 Czechoslovak students by Nazis when they occupied the country and closed the universities. (From top: Smith C. *SCAN* 11/6/46; *Cornell Daily Sun* 11/10/47; LIU *Seawanhaka*, 12/7/49; *Temple U. News*, 11/17/48).

Information Exchanges

NSA Group Establishes International Info Service

Canadian Students Push Education Aid, UNESCO

NSA-Sponsored News Center To Meet in AMB Tonight

Persons desiring to aid in organizing the International News center on the Emory campus are asked to meet in the student council room of the Alumni Memorial building tonight at 8:30, William T. Kennedy, executive director of the organization said.

Former Dutch Underground Member To Address WSSF

NSA Hears Indian Visitor

By NORMA JEAN RIDGWAY

REPORT ON RUSSIA:

Soviet Union Has 830 Colleges, More Than One Million Students

BULLETINS LAUNCHED BY NSA in 1951 circulated student news within the U.S. (International Student Information Service at Harvard) and abroad (International News Center at Emory U.) (From top: 11/1/51 *Bulletin*; 5/52 *NSA News*; "AMB." 1/31/51 *Emory Wheel*; "Dutch" 4/15/47 *Daily Pennsylvanian*; "Indian" 10/14/49 U. of Louisville *Cardinal*; "Report on Russia" - 2/20 *NSA News*).

International Representatives

Patricia Baker Is Observer To IUS Meet

Patricia Baker, NSA representative-at-large in Europe, is attending the International Union of Students Council meeting in Sofia as a non-speaking observer.

Baker

Stockowski

Report on IUS:

Pat Baker Comments in Sofia

WORLD TOUR REPORT:

Pakistani Youth Pioneering

Filipinos Friendly to Visitors

WORLD TOUR REPORT:

Freedom brings Changes to Japanese Life

Symphony Plan In Twin Cities

Representive Reports On World Tour

NSA OBSERVERS were given foreign assignments. Above, reports from Patricia Baker, Chicago State Teachers College graduate, and Sadja Stockowski (Radcliff College junior) on their summer 1949 travels (Left: *NSA News*, 10/49. Right from top: *NSA News*, 10/49,11/49,12/49,2/50).

UN and World Affairs Forums

HOW TO RUN A CAMPUS INTERNATIONAL PROGRAM

PAGE TWO — FRIDAY, APRIL 4, 1947

NSO Policy Stresses Foreign Cooperation

To broaden the channels of exchange of ideas, students, and relief between the youth of other countries and the United States, the NSO devoted one of its four panels at the Chicago convention to forming a program for international action.

FORD DAILY

World Affairs Club Organized; I.S.C. Receives 30 Applications

Transcript, Activities, Essay Needed For European Trips; Deadline Feb. 3

Group Proposes Student Institute; Many Campus Clubs Interested

UN Intercollegiate Institute Meets June 15-21 In NYC

N. Week and Fordham Men

Internationalists Will Lead UN Week; Program Decided

Noontime Forums Scheduled Daily

Warburg To Start Conference Talks

Better Understanding

Emory IRC Studies History In The Making

By Reese Cleghorn

CAMPUS INTERNATIONAL PROGRAMS, widespread and encouraged by NSA. (From top clockwise: NSA International Commission guide, 1954; *Stanford Daily*, 4/947, 1/21/47; *NSA News*, 5/52; Fordham U. *The Ram*, 10/51; U. Colorado *Silver and Gold*, 4/8/49; *Emory Wheel*, 3/25/48.

Official Delegations

NSA To Present Student Views At IUS Congress

The National Student Association has decided to champion the views of more than 800,000 American students at the World Student Congress Aug. 14-28 in Prague, Czechoslovakia.

The Congress is sponsored by the Communist-dominated International Union of Students (IUS), which operates from Prague.

Childers Will Attend London Conference

Swedish - U. S. Research Team to Visit Germany

Pan-American Solidarity Promoted By NSA Visits to Brazil' Paraguay

NEWS AND FE

NSA Represents All International Student Interests

By Toni Barron

Attention Of NSA Claimed By International Meetings

Discussion At Edinburgh Conference Centers On International Cooperation

USNSA Delegates Attend Congress At R

First Inter-American Meeting Of Students Aims For Better Hemisphere Relations

Three NSA Representatives Visit Celebration In Mexico

U.S. STUDENTS WERE SPOKEN FOR by NSA delegations to many events.

(From left, clockwise: 1950 World Student Congress, *NSA News*, 4/50; 12/50 Western student union consultations in London, *NSA News*, 11/49; German student government project sponsored by the Military Government, *NSA News*, 5/49; 1951 14th Brazilian student union conference, *NSA News*, 8/51; "Represents" - *The Carletonian*, MN, 10/7/50; "Attention," U. of NC *Daily Tar Heel*, 1/10/52; "Rio," "Edinburgh," "Mexico," *NSA News*, 11/51).

Births and rebirths

1. From the University of Chicago to Prague's Polytech

William M. Birenbaum
University of Chicago
Chair, Constitution Committee, 1947 NSA Constitutional Convention
1948 NSA IUS Observer Team
NSA National Advisory Council, 1949-52. Chairman, 1952-53

Editor's note: This unit has been adapted from portions of William Birenbaum's book, Something for Everybody Is Not Enough: An Educator's Search for His Education *(New York: Random House, 1971).*

Prologue

I was born in Macomb, Illinois, in 1923 and grew up in Waterloo, Iowa. After service in Greenland in World War II, I attended the University of Chicago, where I received a doctorate in law, as my first and only earned degree, and where I later served as a faculty member and administrator.

In this reminiscence, based on portions of my book, *Something for Everybody Is Not Enough*, written in 1971, I had occasion to reflect on my involvement in the formative years of the National Student Association while I was at the University.

After World War II, the GI Bill paid for my own "higher" education at the University of Chicago, where my professional career began under Robert M. Hutchins, during the Age of McCarthy (Joseph) and the Korean War. Since then, I have worked almost everywhere in the university world—as teacher and administrator, board member and parent, in adult and graduate education, from the urban to the international field, in public and private institutions, large and small. Where I have worked there have always been too many students and not enough money, threats to academic freedom and assaults upon faculty democracy, excessive teaching loads and inadequate parking space.

I enjoyed being a college president. Bernard Shaw once wrote Winston Churchill: "Dear Winnie, I have a new play opening in London next week. Enclosed are two tickets to the first night. Please come, and bring a friend—*if you have one.*" Sir Winston replied: "Dear Bernie, I can't make it to the opening night of your new play. But I'll come the second night—*if there is one.*" As a college president I learned who my friends were—i.e. the non-friends identified themselves. And my various productions have gotten through opening night, though the duration of the runs were sometimes problematical.

My experiences during the founding years of the National Student Association helped to sharpen the life-long interest in the quality of student life and the proper functioning of an institution of higher education—an interest I was fortunate to be able to express through the positions I enjoyed during my years in academia.

Births: A student at the university

During the war the University of Chicago must have been a place for the very young and the very old, and of course, for the girls. At least it seemed that way when we arrived on the Midway. The girls were glad to see us back—that was our impression. For the very young and the very old, our arrival must have been a very mixed bag, indeed.

But old Mother Midway, waiting patiently in her squat, graying manner for a new love affair late in life, merrily took us in, whatever her ulterior motives. Soon the seminal juices of our new altruism impregnated the campus and led to the birth of a whole new family of organizations, causes and movements. For those who were trying to keep the campus cool, our new offspring must have seemed like a noisy bunch of bastards. And by the time Congressman William Jenner and United States Senator Joseph McCarthy were attracted by the uproar, there was plenty around to look into.

The American Veterans Committee was born, and the Labor Youth League, the Lawyers Guild and CORE, the National Student Association, the *Bulletin of the Atomic Scientists,* the United World Federalists, the Henry Wallace student movement, and more. Competing literary journals, ribald and obscene, reactionary and leftish, rose and fell with regularity. The *Maroon*, rejuvenated and rambunctious, got its editors suspended and reinstalled, and did its very best to keep the deans, the faculty, and our enemies in the world at large upset. Elaine May, Mike Nichols, and others were putting together the stage for their kind of new theater. Philip Roth was in and out, preparing his complaints.

All of these happenings announced more than new births. They were really rebirths. Each embodied not only hopes for something new in the future but also intense critiques of something old from the past. It was not just that the American Legion and the Veterans of Foreign Wars were old; they stood for things that the American Veterans Committee was aggressively, specifically against. We knew even before the San Francisco Conference was over that the United Nations was a cause stillborn, so that it could not even be lost. When Adlai Stevenson sat in one of the dormitory lounges and patiently explained to us that "The United Nations will never make the peace, but only keep the peace that the national governments decide to make," he only confirmed our deep conviction that we had to federalize the world in the morning.

Twenty-five of us cooked up the National Student Association.[1] Student government then, like now, was strictly Mickey Mouse. We were grown-up men with global matters to set in order. No time to quibble about jukeboxes in the cafeteria or whether the fraternities should be allowed to serve beer. Counterparts abroad, sometimes friends we had met in foreign armies, had gone home to leadership in national student unions, European, Asian, and African, whose proclamations commanded the ears of cabinet ministers and whose manifestoes shook entire governments. But here in the States, with so many things to say, we had yet to find a voice. And then there was the peace to make, the peace we would make, our peace, whole cities to rebuild, entire nations to restore, and newly freed people who reached out their hands, we thought, to us—or to the Russians. There were the Russians, our gallant allies, already becoming former, whose wartime braveries and massive postwar armies and diplomatic coups inspired and captured the imaginations of some of my best friends. There was the deepening understanding of Hiroshima's meaning even as we occasionally kicked the soccer ball around the field where its explosion first echoed.

The campus was instantaneously politicized, and master political parties, cutting across several organizations, formed. Even the Greeks broke into right, left, and center. And when hundreds of the American Veterans Committee's members assembled every two weeks for their meetings in the lecture hall of the chemistry building, the left caucus automatically preempted the left side of the hall, the right, the right, and the centrists, the middle.

The corner tavern on Fifty-Fifth Street became the headquarters for staging the new world order. When the libraries closed at eleven, a significant part of the campus came to life and things began to get done—or so we thought.

Red Power/White Power and Black

The Maoists of that time were more numerous than now, though like young socialists at any time or place, they broke into as many factions among themselves as the Slavs in the Balkans or practicing psychologists in New York. But for many, Stalin's wartime leadership was the inspiration, and the heroic performance of the Russian people at Stalingrad was freely confused with the merit of postwar Stalinist prescriptions for the liberated people everywhere.

The Labor Youth League flourished, and its influence, or versions of it, was felt everywhere—in AVC, NSA, student government, and of course, in the support of Henry Wallace as an alternative to Messrs. Truman or Dewey in 1948. Young Communists presented a formidable and unique challenge to the rest of us. Though always a minority wherever we confronted them, they had a powerful capacity to paralyze our own machinery. And yet, to exclude them presented a painful American issue. Senator McCarthy confused the issue, for he had a loud and clear solution to the problem—a solution none of us could accept then, because it was based on the separation of one kind of American from another. It was a time when there were heated debates about whether a member of the Communist party should be allowed to teach at the university. And when the investigating committees entered the picture, the Fifth Amendment was the respectable assertion for almost everyone—Communists and anti-Communists, students and teachers alike.

Our Communist foes compelled most of us for the first time seriously to study their ideologies. It was the only way to contend with them in free and open debate. The best way to beat an enemy is to know his strategies and tactic at least as well as he. This is as true for the pages of Roberts's *Rules of Order* as it is for the wrestling mat. We organized informal seminars, and for the first time many of us read Marx; we even began to study (not for credit) the structure of Soviet government and law. And, strangely, the deeper we got into all that, the deeper went our probes into the meaning of our own beliefs and values, the structure of our own system and traditions. These were not abstract drills. Sometimes they were like cram courses, studies urgently pursued to get us ready for the test of the next night's meeting, debate, and resolution.

One of the most promising invitations I've received lately came from a group of blacks in Brooklyn who wanted me to teach a course on White Power in a street "college" they were organizing. This was to be a part of a three-course sequence they planned—Black Power, White Power and Power . . .

The prerequisite for Thinking Black is probably an introductory course on How to Think White. And until we get over this color thing, we probably ought to organize our undergraduate curriculum to include this sequence. This would be a modest first step in a voluntary transfer, in the revelation of what must be revealed.

We did everything in our power at the University of Chicago to resist our opponents' invitations to force them underground. Our forms of participatory democracy allowed for *their* participation, and we fought it out on those terms. The price of this strategy was often dear, but probably not as expensive as the alternatives they sometimes dangled before us so temptingly. Not only that, playing it this way compelled us to work out our own internal differences before we entered the larger arenas. It was often the only hope for winning.

NSA's Constitutional Convention

In 1947 at the University of Wisconsin's campus in Madison, American students for the first time drew up a constitution for themselves. It was a remarkable achievement, at least as remarkable as Woodstock, which the students did not make for themselves, or the Moratorium March on Washington, which has yet to reveal an enduring political meaning beyond the fact that it happened.

The Constitutional Convention of the United States National Student Association (USNSA) brought together the representatives of more than 350 colleges and universities, some 750 students. They came from everywhere—from the Southern state universities and from parochial colleges, from the great private urban universities and the large Middle-Western public ones, from the West coast and the East; Catholics and Communists, right wings and left, racists and civil righters, isolationists recoiling from the war, and One Worlders pursuing in their own way its consequences. They had about ten days together, and in spite of their very substantial differences, they made a constitution, wrote it down and for many years thereafter more or less lived by it.

NSA's constitution regulated its affairs through its lean years (none have been fat), through the assaults from the left in the late forties and from the right during McCarthy, through the Silence of the Eisenhower years, and the tumult of the Year of Dallas and all that has followed, including the monstrous CIA connection.[2]

At Madison I presided over the constitution-making committee.[3] After that, no faculty meeting could really upset my balance. My chairmanship catapulted me into a race for the first presidency of USNSA. But when the ballots were finally counted, a bright young history major from Berea College in Kentucky—Bill Welsh—was elected. He went on to an interesting political career, which has taken him in and out of Washington at the most exciting times. In fact, when I first visited Washington after John Kennedy took over, I was impressed by the number of young men and women there who had been delegates at the Madison Convention, who had joined JFK's team in the crucial second, third, and fourth level positions, where the programs really get shaped up, the speeches actually written, the research done, and the patronage transacted. Those who were a part of NSA's creation and its struggles during those first years never seemed to quite get over it.

NSA began its life with a student constituency on the campuses of more than a million. Two overriding purposes compelled the leaders of this constituency to make themselves a constitution and find themselves a voice at Madison, and then, to speak.

The first was to confirm the legitimacy of the constituency itself, to remark upon its existence—something almost everyone else had done except the students themselves—and to assert, because of its existence, its possession of a right to pursue its own interests, the interests of students in the United States. Campus-level self-government was a primary goal. And the first American Bill of Student Rights was issued. That bill spoke of the student as a citizen, not only with rights, but with responsibilities to pursue his causes on campus and off, into the national and then the international arenas, wherever his versions of his future might take him.

The second purpose was to demonstrate to student friends and foes abroad that America's students had grown up during the war, at least an inch. When they spoke to us now, no deans of students, learned societies or Washington bureaucrats need now respond for us. We would reply for ourselves, and in due course, hopefully, we would enter upon our obligations on the larger scene where young men and women, our age or only a few years beyond, were already Presidents and prime ministers, leading new nations and building new worlds.

Representing NSA in Europe in 1948

The National Student Association had commissioned three of us to represent its interests in Europe in the summer of 1948—Rob West, a student at Yale in international studies, Larry Jaffa, a divinity student at Harvard, and me.

NSA's interests were complicated. There were the student communities in the countries we had conquered. Our occupation armies and provisional governments still ruled in Germany and Austria, and the educational systems of those nations, devastated by the war, were our responsibility. Many of their universities had been closed. The simplest tools for learning were in short supply or utterly lacking.

Students in the newer countries of the world, in Africa, Asia, and South America especially, were left impoverished after the war, without money or jobs to sustain themselves as students, without books, often without food. The international student relief agencies, centered in the European nations, had lost touch with the traditional sources of their support. The American student body, disorganized, well-intentioned, and unaccustomed to leadership, suddenly found itself strategically the richest student community left, but without means or direction in the mobilization and implementation of its wealth, the capacity to focus its strength upon extremely urgent targets.[4]

All of the normal lines of communication in the international student community had been severed during the war. All of the exchanges of materials and people had stopped. All of the summer work and study programs had come to an end. The restoration of the "community" itself was the challenge, and this challenge turned upon the solution of some very hard, nitty-gritty problems. Who would organize and re-establish the programs at home and abroad? Who would provide the ships to transport the students during the summers? About this problem, our own country, which had produced the largest supply fleet in the world during the war, had quickly either decommissioned or given away almost all of our ships. NSA finally negotiated contracts with the Dutch National Union of Students, which had persuaded its government to allocate three or four ships in order to restore international student exchange beginning in 1949 and 1950. The Dutch students turned out to be, in my estimate, among the earth's shrewdest businessmen, whose negotiations were always conducted in an atmosphere of great levity and good humor, until you sobered up enough to find out what they had persuaded you to sign.[5]

Finally, there was the pervasive problem of how to cope with the East European, Communist-controlled national student unions. Many students in the United States and the West European countries felt it was imperative, as a step to counter the rapidly cooling relationships between the West and the Soviet Union, to enter upon a series of specific treaties with the International Union of Students. The trouble was that the IUS was a severe taskmaster, insisting upon strict control of the programs to be mounted in their countries for Western students, and even a dominant voice in the structure of programs we would plan in the United States for their countrymen. And, of course, they were most interested in the propaganda value of everything they did and said, especially with regard to the youth of the new countries in Asia, Africa, and throughout Latin America.

But many students in the West felt that no relationship with the Communists should be established until the European and American students had constructed an international federation of their own to counter the great influence of the IUS. The situation was polarizing, and the position of the two main camps was becoming clear. Integrate or separate. Everyone was being asked to choose sides.

Laughter and flags in Prague

We had barely checked into the hotel reserved for foreign visitors in the middle of Prague when the underground made its contact. The lobby was loaded with official "tourist guides" and plainclothesmen who, we thought, were keeping their eyes on us. But after we checked in and unpacked, I went down to the bar for a warm beer, and while sitting there, a young Yugoslav sailor, offering me one of his cigarettes and asking me for an American one in return, slipped me a piece of paper containing the number of a room at the Polytechnic Institute, and the hour—10 o'clock that night. We had been alerted before arriving in Prague during that summer of 1948. Nonetheless, the classic, bizarre efficiency of the contact was rather impressive. A Yugoslav sailor, yet!

One of the great public landmarks at the University of Chicago, down the Midway toward the lake near the International House, is the stony grandeur of the senior Masaryk, the great patriot-founder of the democracy of the Czechs and the Slovaks. The base of his statue is one of the places to sit on the Midway, to rest and to think.

I have always been proud of my university's employment of Eduard Benes, the Czech President-patriot, during his exile after the German annexation of the Sudetenland. Benes was gone when I arrived on the Midway, but his scholarship remained—the papers and books in which he never allowed the brilliance of his mind to dampen his passion for man's freedom, a passion which seeped through every page.

In April of 1948, but a few months before we came to Prague, the younger Masaryk had met his tragic death, crushed on the cobblestones beneath his window in the Presidential Palace. The official description of that fall: a suicide leap. But the Czechoslovakians knew then, as they know now, that Masaryk was pushed, and that with his fall their chance for independence fell too. It was a short scene in the drama of the Communist takeover under Gottwald. On the night that Masaryk died and for some days thereafter, the university students of Prague, from the venerable Charles and from the Polytechnic Institute, took to the streets of the city in behalf of freedom's law and order and their dying democracy's due processes. Some joined their leader there, in death. In Prague that year, the fall and winter came in the spring, and the season of rebirth was one of death.

But now, in 1948, it was early July; and summer, outwardly, was transforming the ancient city, its hills and arcades, its grand, tree-shaded central avenue. The beauty of the city itself denied the intrigue and the anguish, the life risks seething behind the know-nothing looks on the shopkeepers' faces—the chapel-like hush in the crowded main streets.

The nation, exhausted by the war and sickened by its most recent catastrophe, was preparing to restore one moment of its past happiness. Sokol Slet is one of the great occasions for the Czech people—the time when they, with some of the best athletes in the country and from all over the world, periodically celebrate an ancient Greek inheritance in a uniquely Central and East European style. In a massive demonstration, thousands of gymnasts assemble in a giant stadium, and with extraordinary precision mobilize individual powers into a collective dramatization of the beauty of human physical possibilities. In each city and town, each hamlet and district, clubs of athletes prepare assiduously for the Sokol, to compete in the capital for the pennants and banners, the prizes awarded, not to individuals, but to communities, to cities which honor their youth for the good of the country. Sokol had been a casualty of the war, but Gottwald, disclosing the shrewdness he was to demonstrate for years to come, had decided early in his regime to restore Sokol to the people, and to unite the deep sources of peoplehood-pride with the nation's first Red Army Day. It was a bold maneuver—Masaryk had hardly been lowered into his grave. The people would get their circus—painted red.

The rendezvous at Polytech was the night before the Sokol parade. People from all over the country converged on Prague for the spectacle.

The Czech students meant the return of Sokol to mark a popular outpouring of opposition to Gottwald. By plan, the youth of Pilsen, whose Sokol teams were second in number only to those of Prague, and whose city traditionally marched second in the day-long parade, were to provide the signal to the people of Czechoslovakia for the denunciation of their new tyrant. Our flag, the flag of the United States, was to be the symbol of defiance. The American flag in 1948 was to represent for these people and for their Red masters the freedom that had been lost and for which they were prepared to risk everything to restore. Pilsen was to carry the banners. . . . (To honor its liberation, American battalion and regimental flags had been awarded to ancient Pilsen and were housed in a hall of honor in the center of that city.)

Rumors of the plot had swept the city, and that night, as we made our way secretly to the Polytech, we saw the notices the government had hastily pasted on the lampposts prohibiting, as an act of treason, the display of foreign banners by any Czechoslovak delegation in the Sokol.

We were the official guests in Czechoslovakia of the International Union of Students (IUS), whose headquarters was there. The IUS—the federation of the Communist East European national student unions, had arranged for the official American NSA delegation of observers, the three of us, to sit in President Gottwald's reviewing stand to observe the parade. A few rows beneath him, we assembled early the next morning, and the parade began. At the head of the march came the proud athletes of Prague, and behind them the large visiting team from the Soviet Union. The Russian delegation stretched for almost three city blocks, and at their head, for almost a third of their length, a sea of the red flags of their country. The people watched in an electric silence as the handsome Russians, some contingent of their military, marched by. The people, by doing nothing, visibly upset the President.

Then came Pilsen, more than a thousand strong, American war banners at their head, each athlete carrying or wearing some version of the Stars and Stripes, paper U.S. flags pinned to their tunics, front and back. The crowds went berserk. The police cordons broke. Red, white and blue streamers suddenly filled the air. Among the masses along the streets for as far as the eye could see, small American flags appeared from nowhere. And the air filled with the shouts of the people: "Freedom!" "Masaryk!" "Russians Go Home!" President Gottwald, at least for that time, left his place of honor, and disappeared.

Everywhere I turned, the people were crying on that occasion. And, I remember well, I cried too. It is remarkable how few times I can remember crying in those years in behalf of public events in my country. There was the time when Franklin Roosevelt's cortege marched down Pennsylvania Avenue—the hours after that when I walked around and around the Washington Zoo—when all seemed lost. And that unforgettable afternoon, November 22, 1963, when I saw the young cry on Eleventh Street in front of the New School in Greenwich Village for their dead President. But they did not cry with pride, because of what we were, but because of what we weren't. And then there were the moments in front of the television screen when Jacqueline Kennedy and my country needed tears.

Blood for ink

In the basement room at the Polytech in Prague, the smell of mimeograph ink was everywhere. The students were grinding out their pamphlets to be distributed, against the law, on the streets the next day. They were to brief us before our formal negotiations with the International Union of Students, and to present to us *their* position, the reasons why we should do no business whatsoever with the Communist student unions in the East. It was a bitter-sweet situation: bitter with the gravity of their plight—sweet in the spirit of their conviction, the intensity of their beliefs, the risks they were prepared to take and were taking. *They were brave and honorable lawbreakers.*

The issue finally was an old one: *What do you do with your enemies, especially when you know who they are?* It is an issue I discussed at great length then with so many of my black friends, and with my student friends who swore by Mao's little Red Book too.

The Ph.D. language requirement in court

When we returned from Prague we brought with us a message to the American students from Josef Grohman, the president of the International Union of Students. Grohman was a professional student, blond and intense, in his late twenties or early thirties, Moscow-trained, a personal history obscure to us. He was one of the ablest and most devoted negotiators with whom I've ever dealt—the sort of man you wished were on your side. Unfortunately, he was not devoted to ours. He wrote:

> The students who love peace and work for the maintenance of peace, for the increase of democracy in all parts of the world, are working for the IUS. The students who must fight for national independence and against oppression by external or internal forces are also working for the IUS. For them national independence is basic not only to the attainment of the right to education but of the right to live in dignity as free men in a free society. Their struggles are in the interests of students in all parts of the world, for peace can only be maintained between free and democratic communities. All students who fight for democracy in their own scholastic institutions and for the extension of educational opportunities to every strata of society are carrying out the aims and ideals of the IUS.

Grohman knew what he was talking about. He had read the source texts of his ideology and the memoranda he must have received regularly from headquarters several hundred miles to the east of Prague. (He told me he had even studied our Federalist Papers!) In these respects he had an advantage over many of our Maoist students today who have never read Mao or Marx (let alone the Federal Constitution), and over many of our right-wing student activists who seem, sometimes, never to have read anything.

Grohman invited me to attend with him a session of the People's Court in Prague, where university students who had been a part of the resistance—who had disrupted the coup—were brought before a bar of justice to explain why they had broken the law, created disorder and violated the due processes of the People's Democracy of Czechoslovakia.[6]

At the session I attended there were three judges on the bench—a factory worker, a student member of the party attending Charles University, and a third person who was identified vaguely as a functionary in the new government. I heard one case, a Ph.D. candidate at Charles who was accused of participating in an illicit street demonstration and distributing prohibited literature. The student appeared without counsel. He confessed that he had indeed been a part of the action on the street, but he denied having passed out the leaflets.

He was asked if he was sorry for what he had done. He was. He was asked if he would sign, then and there, an oath of loyalty, pledging to uphold the constitution of the People's Democracy of Czechoslovakia. He said he would. . . . Then he was asked if he was prepared to substitute Russian for English as his Ph.D. qualifying language? He said he knew no Russian, and the court rejoined that this was his problem. He would simply have to begin now the study of Russian. The student argued that he did not wish to do this, since his field did not require Russian, and that it would be a waste of time.

The defendant left the room and the court deliberated briefly. Its decision was in parts: the student was prohibited indefinitely from further work at the university, and the award of his degree was indefinitely suspended; he was ordered to work in a factory in Prague for a period of not less than ninety days where he was also to attend some seminars under the political supervision of the factory's Workers Committee; he was to think very hard about whether he was prepared to substitute Russian for English, and about his capacity to identify cohorts in the demonstration; and after ninety days the court would review his situation and then determine further the disposition of his case.

The first NSA Congress

We brought our recommendations on IUS relations and other matters to the First Congress of the National Student Association in the late summer of 1948 (The second held in Madison, following the 1947 Constitutional Convention). There were no CIA subsidies for NSA then. Such a relationship would have been unthinkable for NSA and for the CIA. Our proposals were the framework of the principal debates during that meeting, and out of that Congress, among other things, came the beginnings of NSA's international study and travel agency, which for more than twenty years was one of the main instruments for the promotion of student study and travel abroad.[7]

But how we solved our problems then is not the point now. It is the quality and the complexity of the issues which should be noted, and the seriousness of purpose American student leaders brought to these difficulties. Whatever official and empowered student leadership there was on the principal campuses of the nation, NSA brought together. And when they convened, their debates were intense, their aspirations far-reaching, and the connections between the global issues and the campuses were, for a while, more than tenuous. The IUS problem had its counterpart in the growing domestic Communist youth movement. Poverty in India reached directly into the pockets of students at Iowa State. The re-establishment of international study programs touched upon a student's credit-hour planning at Georgia Tech. Campus debates instructed delegates to national NSA meetings and were meant to guide their conduct in the decisive votes. The student leaders thought then that what they did might really make a difference. Thinking that they could make a difference, however misguided they may have been, made a difference for them.

Return to Chicago and loyalty oaths

I returned to the University of Chicago late that summer, exhausted and depressed. I had seen in the German cities through which I passed, in parts of France and in London, the chaotic devastation of the war, streets in the central cities still clogged by the bombs' debris, long lines of people waiting for their weekly allowances of meat and bread, transportation systems still being pulled back together. Only in Rotterdam had the people piled the rubble into neat pyramids and planted flowers on them.

But I was eager to see my student friends on the Midway, to tell them about what I had seen, about my day in court and with President Gottwald, and how I felt. But by the time school reconvened that September, I had grown less certain about what there was to tell. Lawyers in my state were being asked to take their loyalty oaths as a condition for admission to practice. Teachers were signing their oaths to uphold the constitutions of the nation and of the state, and certifying that they didn't belong to any subversive organization. At some places teachers were being asked to renounce their rights under the Fifth Amendment as a condition of employment. And soon students, to get their federal fellowship grants, would also be asked to pledge allegiance once again. It all seemed quite mad and very sad. It had been a horrible war in which millions had died demonstrating loyalty to something, to noble causes, to personal notions of integrity, to cowardice. But apparently the war, which had tried the soul of our civilization so deeply, had left men compulsively needing to know afresh what they could be loyal to.

In Prague, more than once, I was the most loyal American on earth. But back in Chicago, new questions arose, and some of them, even now, remain unanswered in my mind.

Vassar

One twilight when I was in Greenland, I came across an old and wrinkled Eskimo sitting in front of his hut in Sondrestromfjord carving a walrus tusk. "What are you making?" I asked him. "It is already made," he said, "it is there, inside the tusk, waiting for me to find it. You wait, and I will find it, and then you will see what it is." And two or three days later, what was already there he had found—an exquisitely wise little witch doctor who looked in many ways like the wrinkled old man who had found him.

At Madison the students carved into the nature of their situation. It was to discover what was already there, a part of the eternal human search for the nature of themselves,

A few years later, as if to reassure the American people after *Time* magazine's discovery of the silent young, *Newsweek* (November 2, 1953) ran its rebuttal through the cover story, entitled "U.S. Campus Kids—Unkiddable and Unbeatable." *Newsweek* said:

> Shrewder, more mature than their grandparents, more cautious than their fathers, they worked harder and were more likely to think things through. Socially, economically, politically, emotionally and philosophically, they wanted to conform, they were thoroughly and solidly American....Most of all, they were young and wanted to make a million dollars. And some of them would.

A Princeton senior, pictured sipping his beer in a small bar, was quoted as saying: "The world doesn't owe me a living, but it does owe me a job."

A Northwestern coed, speaking from the back seat of a cream-colored convertible, said: "You want to be popular, so naturally you don't express any screwy ideas. To be popular you have to conform."

A Vassar girl, sitting cross-legged on the floor of her dormitory lounge in Bermuda shorts, put it this way: "We're a cautious generation. We aren't buying any ideas we're not sure of."

Some years later, the students at Vassar asked me to give a lecture. We met first in some great Gothic hall, where we politely exchanged pleasantries, had a cocktail, and then dinner. I talked in the chapel where the chairman of the board of trustees introduced me. Young President Alan Simpson—a former colleague at the University of Chicago College—was still in bed recuperating from his heart attack, but the president's wife was a gracious hostess and even sat through my talk.

Afterward a delightful young student, dressed in blue jeans and a sweater, invited me back with some others to her dorm "to rap." It was a cold autumn night. The comfortable lounge was warm. She turned the lamps up. From her pocket she offered me a joint, and from beneath the leather cushion on a couch she produced a pint of good Scotch, half gone, from which she poured me a stiff one in a used paper cup. From her notebook, with obvious pride, she handed me a diamond-shaped chart she had drawn, diagramming a new theory of history, from Plato to Einstein, which she herself had created in a brilliant flash of senior insight. She told me what it meant, what it proved, and it meant and proved many things. It proved, among other things, naturally, that technology—apparently the central heating in the dorm and the electrical system which provided the lamps she had turned on—was destroying man's capacity to love, to know his nature, to be himself. And then she said, "Our purposes here at Vassar are now clear. We must reduce this college to the purest form of its absurdity, and when it is there, flat on its back, exposed, we must move on to the other American institutions, whose absurdities must be laid bare on the floor."

I found all this very reassuring, having had tenure, as I did then. I felt the disruptions would pass. They were meaningless fevers, and the panty raids would return, even as they did in the spring of 1969 at Columbia next to Harlem. Legal reasoning was still the most supreme—even at Vassar. Or so it seemed.

* * *

Being on my own—and after Hutchins

By 1957 1 had been in Chicago a dozen years—more than a third of my life—the most strategic first part of being on my own. I had crossed the magic line, joined the faculty team, become one of that special breed who taught, taught in the College whose degree I never earned. But the city itself was the real test of being on my own. It forced my eyes open so that the things that came into view—on the campus, in the life of my growing family, on the streets and from the world—began to take a different turn.

My administrative assignments had taken me far afield from the practice of law, sometimes, so it seemed, into lawless fields. In the office of dean of students, I had mastered the landlord's view of dormitory life, management's methods, usually conservative and often reactionary, for containing the most vital extracurricular interests of the corporation's clients. At one point Mr. Hutchins asked me to cultivate the university's international educational programs, and I learned a bit about grantsmanship, the exchange of students and teachers, and the ins and outs of the foreign educational scene.[8]

The end of twenty Hutchins years at the university was the end of an epoch in American higher education, the finale to an experiment that almost worked, which even in its failure put the future researchers one small step ahead. The few years that followed on the Midway seemed less like the beginning of a renewal than like a retrenchment—an impression perhaps more reflective of my own state of mind than of the realities. For me it was the end of a stage in my own struggle to learn. I grew restless, eager for the unfamiliar, for the changed scene, the proper place to test what I thought I had learned. A dozen years is a long time in one place in America. In the academic world, a dozen years is almost a commitment, usually more to a place than to a process or to an idea.

After the fall of Hutchins, I found myself working in the university's evening and adult education center on La Salle Street in the financial and commercial heart of the city's Loop. But, strangely, though it was an educational place at the center of the city, educationally it was regarded as a remote outpost of the university's empire. Though its four or five thousand part-time "students" were grown-up people—first-class citizens actually operationally responsible for the transaction of important business in the city, men and women often of powerful affairs—in the university's value structure they were really second-class citizens. The university, diverted from its main purposes with the younger, was doing the older a favor, giving them a second chance, extending to them, as a matter of rare privilege, an opportunity to retool, to learn later what, presumably, they should have learned sooner.

Under Hutchins, with the invention of Great Books, Great Discussions and Great Ideas—one hundred more or less of each—"Learning for Life" or "Lifelong Learning" enjoyed for a while a high priority on the agenda. While the university was not yet prepared to reach out physically and materially into its own neighborhoods, it was eager to reach out into human minds, even adult ones, wherever they were. Some of its most distinguished scholars preferred to teach the businessmen, housewives, plumbers and lawyers at night in the Loop rather than suffer with undergraduates on the Midway during the day. Avery Craven, the great American historian, was one of these, and Bob Hutchins himself was another. But just at the time when I was learning about all this excitement downtown, headquarters, back on the Southside, was deciding that downtown really wasn't very exciting.

Events conspired to persuade me that it was time for a change—at least of place. Within the university, an academic return to normalcy reflected accurately the Eisenhower mood. The long-overdue confrontation of the University's development needs with its immediate ghetto community was provocative. But, I thought then—and still do—it takes two to confront. What provoked me most was the attempt to reshape communities in spite of themselves.

The search for a place to go next took time, but finally, Wayne State University in the middle of Detroit emerged—rough and new, apparently uninstructed and unhampered by deep tradition, eager to discover for itself fresh answers to these same problems. At the moment of truth, leaving the Midway was far more painful than arriving in Detroit. But, a curious thing: after we moved to Detroit and the years passed, the university stood second in the march of my recollections, and the Second City, first. Chicago, the city, was an incredible education; and the university, an essential, indispensable, fascinating course in the city's degree program.

Epilogue

Looking back among lessons learned, it seems even more true today that we have come to emphasize the life of our institutions more than the quality of the life of the people they are supposed to serve. Instead of the institution more accurately representing the thrust and needs of individuals, individuals are expected, more and more, to represent the thrust and needs of the institution.

Because education is such a personal thing, this juxtaposition of emphases on the school versus its citizens is not only dangerous but potentially fatal: fatal to the proper balance and harmony between being ourselves and establishing a more perfect public life; fatal to a decent relationship between the younger and the older; fatal to the voluntary acceptance of the authority of reason and wisdom, to the only kind of relationship between the teacher and the student through which education can proceed.

In the preface to his *Education,* Henry Adams says:

> Most educators of the nineteenth century have declined to show themselves before their scholars as objects more vile or contemptible than necessary, and even the humblest teacher hides, if possible, the faults with which nature has generously embellished us all. . . . As an unfortunate result the twentieth century finds few recent guides to avoid, or to follow. American literature offers scarcely one working model for high education. . . . Except in the abandoned sphere of the dead languages, no one has discussed what part of education has, in his personal experience, turned out to be useful, and what not.

"In his personal experience" is the deadly phrase, a usage now almost abandoned, for the personal experience—combining, as it always does, a man's thoughts with his actions—contains the authenticity of the man. When I wrote this in 1971, and now, that authenticity is the issue.

Everyone with whom I shared the experiences I have written of during my NSA years taught me something, as did everyone with whom I have shared my life experience. I am deeply grateful to them all, but especially to Helen, my wife, and to my children, Susan, Lauren, and Chuck. They are the most personal part of my experience, and in many ways have taught me what is most valuable.

William M. Birenbaum has been President of Antioch College and of Staten Island Community College. He was also Vice President of Long Island University and Dean of the New School for Social Research. He is currently an educational consultant.

EDITOR'S END NOTES

[1] The original twenty-five 1946 Prague delegates who organized the Chicago Student Conference in December. See p. 103.

[2] *Editor's note:* Although the current USSA constitution rests on the foundation of NSA's original 1946 document, it bears little resemblance in its content.

[3] Martin McLaughlin (Notre Dame U.), in a letter dated February 4, 1997, wrote to the editor:

> I acted as secretary to the constitution committee in Madison while Bill Birenbaum reported its deliberations to the plenary sessions. One item that seemed to us a major issue at the time was what we called the D&D problem: Some delegates, generally from large universities with multiple sessions, divided campuses, and many left-leaning or communist students, wanted to have representation from all campuses, disciplines, and time slots (morning, afternoon, evening, Saturday, etc.). This became D&D—discontinuous sessions and discontiguous campuses! The constitution committee opposed this, because it promised to overrepresent a particularly well-organized minority; but because it was disputed in the committee, the question had to be reported to the committee. Eventually we won the D&D debate, but the argument became as emotional in the process as it is arcane in the retelling.

As it turns out, common sense recognition was given to membership by day and night schools, uptown and downtown campuses, men's and women's colleges, divinity, graduate and undergraduate schools where distinct student government bodies in the same institution existed. These included CCNY, NYU, Fordham, Yale, Harvard, University of Rochester, Rutgers, St. Peter's, University of California, and others.

[4] U.S. students did contribute widely to World Student Relief during the war, and afterward to the World Student Service Fund (WSSF). NSA was a sponsor and active supporter of WSSF. It also encouraged and sponsored work-study tours during the postwar summers for students to take part in reconstruction work camps. See Sections 4 and 5.

[5] See Section 5 on NSA's summer travel programs, p. 639, and the essay on p. 651 by Jos Vos, the former Dutch student union representative to the United States.

[6] See Jim Smith's notes regarding Grohman, p. 577.

[7] See p. 673 for the story of NSA's travel office. Also, Album, p. 1103.

[8] Under the auspices of the National Student Association, and as an extension of the author's experiences in Europe in 1948, in the summer of 1949 he arranged with Chancellor Hutchins for the University to furnish housing and host seminars for three weeks for a group of forty-six visiting European students—one of the first such postwar intercollegiate cultural exchange programs. In addition to Bill Birenbaum, NSA advisors included Phil Stoddard (University of Illinois; see Stoddard, p. 655), and Martin McLaughlin (De Paul University; see McLaughlin, p. 84). Nine Chicago-area college Presidents joined in sponsoring the program. The student government at Mundelein College furnished the administration for the project under the chairmanship of Patricia A. Troy. See album, p. 664.

PICTURE CREDITS: *Then:* Visiting Rockford College, IL, 1947 (*NSA photo.* SHSW). *Now:* May, 1992 (Author).

WILLIAM M. BIRENBAUM

I was born in Macomb, Illinois, in 1923 and grew up in Waterloo, Iowa. After service in Greenland in World War II, I attended the University of Chicago, where I received a doctorate in law, as my first and only earned degree, and where I later served as a faculty member and administrator. In 1957 I moved to Wayne State University in Detroit, and four years later I became Dean of the New School for Social Research in New York. From 1964 to 1967 I was Vice President and Provost of Long Island University in Brooklyn, a position from which I was dismissed.

After my controversial dismissal from LIU, I assisted the late Senator Robert F. Kennedy with the educational planning for a project the senator was starting in the Bedford-Stuyvesant area of Brooklyn. Shortly after Senator Kennedy's assassination, I was appointed President of Staten Island Community College of the City University of New York.

While there, I helped to design and implement open admissions at the City University. Early in 1973, after Messrs. Kissinger and Nixon restored relations with the PRC, I led the first American mission to China, having persuaded their ambassador at the United Nations that Staten Island was a "peoples' college."

In 1976 I went to Antioch University, where I served as President and professor for almost a decade. At that time I did not realize that Antioch had been the first school to join NSA.

Since Antioch, I have taught and consulted and have served on several boards—corporate, academic, and nonprofit.

I am married to the former Helen Bloch, and we have three children.

Launching a lifetime of Educational Innovation. ***A Bill Birenbaum NSA Scrapbook***

"YOU MAY GRAB DEMOCRACY FROM THE CLOUDS - AND PLACE IT IN YOUR SPIRIT"

—Bill Birenbaum, keynote speech, NSA 6th National Student Congress, August, 1953, Ohio State University

Birenbaum Back From Student Mission to Europe; Reports Czechs Tense in New Regime

By ROS JENSEN
Courier Staff Writer

Somebody recently expressed the opinion that today's college and university students are not having as much fun as the students of his day—the era of the battered jalopies and bootleg liquor.

Generally the present day collegian is more interested in current problems and their solution than were many students of previous decades, others answer.

Birenbaum

Kass vs. Birenbaum on Czechs

By BEA KASS

(Bea Kass is chairman of the NSA committee of the Student Assembly. Due to space limitations, both letters have been severely cut.)

The actions of the NSA officers in severing all relations with the IUS is a serious disservice to American students, international student cooperation, and the cause of peace. It is totally outside the scope of the officers' constitutional rights.

By accepting and using press and other distortions of fact concerning recent political events in Czechoslovakia, these student "leaders" have completely missed the true significance of these events. What are the real facts about Czechoslovakia?

Czech political program

Since its liberation in May, 1945, Czechoslovakia has been governed by a coalition led by National Socialists, Catholic People's Party, Social Democrats, and Communists. Their joint program stressed nationalization of key industries, division of landed estates among ... popular approval in May, 1946. In an election free even to American correspondents, the Communist Party emerged as the leading party with 38 per cent of the vote.

Obviously neither the program nor the leadership of the new Czechoslovakia sat well with the once powerful landowners and industrialists, a group repudiated by their collaborationist war record. Encouraged from abroad, particularly by the U. S. State Dept.'s anti-Communist, "free enterprise" crusade, they attempted to sneak back into power via the conservative parties ... Communists or against the Communists." Said President Benes: "Should there be any attempts from any side to force (the Communists) out of the government, I would not give my consent to it. For me there can be no government without the Communists."

Gottwald urges resignation acceptance

Premier Gottwald appealed for support to the nation. He urged that the resignation of the 12 ministers be accepted, since they had deserted the program of the National Front. On Feb. 22, 8000 delegates to a conference of the Works Councils of all Czechoslo...

By WILLIAM BIRENBAUM

(Bill Birenbaum is head of Student Forum and is a member of the four-man negotiating team elected by NSA to IUS.)

The resignations of James Smith and William Ellis as interim representatives of the National Student Association to the International Union of Students, and the subsequent severing of relations, comes as a tragic shock to American students who sincerely desired to create an effective and democratic world student community.

The shooting and imprisonment of Czech students, and the arbitrary dissolution of the Czech National Union of Students by Communist Action Committees are condemnable components of the imposition of a Communist Government on the Czech people by an undemocratic minority. This fact, and other facts like it, are parts of the world of reality in which we exist.

The failure of a Communist-dominated IUS Secretariat to condemn an incident arising out of a Communist coup should surprise no one. Such condemnation was a political impossibility. We must assume either that the American representatives did not recognize this impossibility or that, recognizing it, they had predetermined the desirability of the ensuing results. This implies the decision by ...

CHICAGO MAROON

University of Chicago, September 18, 1953 31

UC'ers attend NSA confab Birenbaum gives keynote

Ten UC students were among the almost 700 delegates to the Sixth National Congress of the US National Student Association held at Ohio State University. The Congress was held from August 24 to September 2.

The keynote speech of the Congress was given by William Birenbaum, director of student activ-

Lawrence Buttenweiser and Joe Josephson both chaired plenary sessions. Buttenweiser was nominated for president of NSA, but declined to run while Josephson was defeated for post of vice president of international affairs. At a Collegiate Editor's Conference held under the sponsorship of NSA, the MAROON was repre-

Exchange program fails

There was lengthy debate over a proposal to investigate the possibilities of student exchange with the Soviet Union and other Eastern European nations. The exchange program was rejected by the plenary session by a seven vote margin after being presented as a minority report from the In-

FOR MORE THAN TWENTY YEARS, as a U. of Chicago delegate, member and chair of NSA's National Advisory Committee and as a Congress keynote speaker and resource person, Bill Birenbaum was an inspiring and challenging figure in NSA's development. In his keynote to the 6th Congress, Birenbaum asked, "And what is democracy if not an unshakeable belief in your ability to think, a faith in the worth, the integrity and the truth - not of the masses, not of the common-man, not of transient power, illusive respectability or tenuous security - but a faith in the worth, the integrity and the truth of the individual human being, of yourself?" (From top: *Waterloo Daily Courier*, IA, 9/12/48; *Chicago Maroon* 3/12/48, 9/18/53).

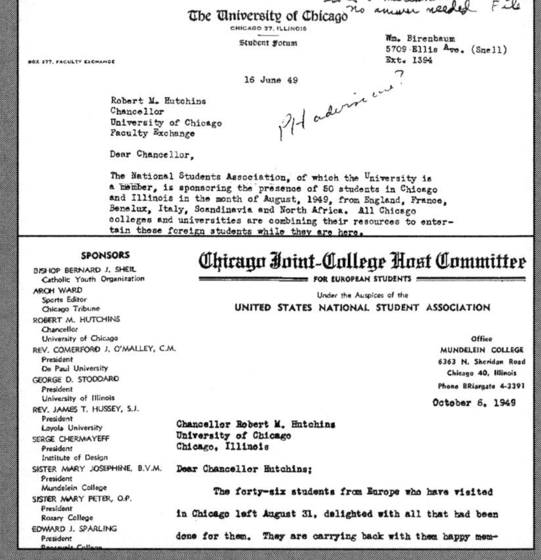

The University of Chicago
CHICAGO 37, ILLINOIS
Student Forum

BOX 277, FACULTY EXCHANGE

Wm. Birenbaum
5709 Ellis Ave. (Snell)
Ext. 1394

16 June 49

Robert M. Hutchins
Chancellor
University of Chicago
Faculty Exchange

Dear Chancellor,

The National Students Association, of which the University is a member, is sponsoring the presence of 50 students in Chicago and Illinois in the month of August, 1949, from England, France, Benelux, Italy, Scandinavia and North Africa. All Chicago colleges and universities are combining their resources to entertain these foreign students while they are here.

Chicago Joint-College Host Committee
FOR EUROPEAN STUDENTS
Under the Auspices of the
UNITED STATES NATIONAL STUDENT ASSOCIATION

SPONSORS
BISHOP BERNARD J. SHEIL, Catholic Youth Organization
ARCH WARD, Sports Editor, Chicago Tribune
ROBERT M. HUTCHINS, Chancellor, University of Chicago
REV. COMERFORD J. O'MALLEY, C.M., President, De Paul University
GEORGE D. STODDARD, President, University of Illinois
REV. JAMES T. HUSSEY, S.J., President, Loyola University
SERGE CHERMAYEFF, President, Institute of Design
SISTER MARY JOSEPHINE, B.V.M., President, Mundelein College
SISTER MARY PETER, O.P., President, Rosary College
EDWARD J. SPARLING, President, Roosevelt College

Office
MUNDELEIN COLLEGE
6363 N. Sheridan Road
Chicago 40, Illinois
Phone BRiargate 4-3391

October 6, 1949

Chancellor Robert M. Hutchins
University of Chicago
Chicago, Illinois

Dear Chancellor Hutchins;

The forty-six students from Europe who have visited in Chicago left August 31, delighted with all that had been done for them. They are carrying back with them happy mem-

BIRENBAUM ENLISTS U.C. CHANCELOR HUTCHINS to provide support for the NSA tour of 46 foreign students in the summer of 1949 (Top, 6/16/49). Together with Martin McLaughlin (DePaul) and Philip Stoddard (U. of Ill.) he served as advisor to the Joint Host Committee (10/6/49. See Bodecker, p. 660).

DISCUSSING RELIEF WORK AT ROCKFORD COLLEGE, IL, following a WSSF rally. L. to r. Maryjo Domino, Chair, IL Region; Dolores Sheslo, Rockford NSA; Mary Latino, Pres., student gov't.; William Birenbaum, U. of Chicago, member NSA Advisory Council, speaker; Francis Sprague, Rockford WSSF chairman; Mary Ashby Cheek, President, Rockford C.; Patricia Safford, Co-Chair, NSA sub-com. on Human Relations. (*NSA News* 12/49).

What NSA did for freedom—and for me!

2. Travels to Zagreb, 1951

Barry Farber
University of North Carolina
Chair, NSA Virginia-Carolinas Region, 1951-52
NSA Delegate to 1951 Zagreb Peace Conference

When Dick Murphy told me, in the spring of 1951 on the campus of the University of North Carolina, that I'd been selected to be a delegate to the NSA Congress in Minneapolis late in the summer, my first thought was. "Which girls are going along?"

Can you blame me? "Student politics" to me meant sandbox politics: toy politics. Every year the honor students from all the colleges in central North Carolina would converge on the State Capitol in Raleigh, sit in the very chairs of the state legislators and "debate," exchange parliamentary jargon, and "pass bills." I figured NSA had to be something like that on a national level; so, even if the girl roster on our Carolina delegation proved lackluster, no big deal. There'd be a whole *nationful* of girls in Minneapolis.

The 1951 NSA Congress at Minnesota

To buttress my impression of NSA as trivia for student aristocrats, I recalled *Life Magazine's* condescending coverage of the previous NSA congress: the most memorable feature of which was our schoolmate and NSA President Al Lowenstein participating in something called a "Lion Hunt!"[1] The bus ride from North Carolina to Minnesota was uneventful. But a life-lifting kind of hell broke loose when I landed inside the real NSA and had those insulting impressions I'd gathered eliminated like a blow-torch eliminates cobwebs from the upper corners of a barn.

The venerable Harold Stassen, once-upon-a-time boy governor of Minnesota and persistent presidential aspirant, was the keynote speaker.[2]

The delegates from all those hundreds of colleges and universities were serious, relentless, idealistic, purposeful, and utterly focused on things I'd never really thought about: like academic freedom, students' rights, noncensorship of student publications, fair treatment of minorities on campus (those campuses that had minorities—down South, ours didn't!), and a galaxy of other issues you don't meet sitting in the seats of the real state legislators or on a fantasy lion hunt.

The international front interested me so much that, like a drunk trying to pass himself off as sober, I had to fake interest in those domestic issues which, though I recognized as important, put my feet to sleep up to the hips. I was already fairly fluent in a dozen languages, had served in the Norwegian Merchant Marine, and attended the University of Oslo summer school. When I learned that the NSA was actively fighting the Moscow-sponsored International Union of Students I hungered to mount the free-world student ramparts with a broken bourbon bottle and join the fight.

Social Security? Unions? Medical Care? Women's issues? As they say in Little Italy, "Forgeddaboutit!" Foil those egg-sucking Commie dogs, and we can work out all that other stuff nonviolently later on.

Helen Jean Rogers declines nomination for international post

The energy level at that NSA Congress was something new and praiseworthy to me. I'd never before met young people who could earnestly pursue the rescue of civilization all day and wage beer parties literally all night. I honestly remember thinking the girls from the Catholic colleges somehow gained a stamina denied to the rest of us by virtue of obligatory attendance all their lives at early mass.[3]

There was one incident that struck me as mysterious during that Congress. During the nominations and election of national officers somebody nominated a woman I'd never heard of, Helen Jean Rogers, as International Vice President. There was a rip-roar of huzzahs from the crowd and this tall, earnest-looking young woman took the stage and thanked her supporters but declined the nomination. The crowd would not be so easily denied. They roared their importunings that she accept the nomination and the office, which obviously would have been hers by acclamation.

Helen Jean just stood there for what seemed a parliamentary eternity—ten or twelve minutes—crying. She wasn't "weeping." She was crying, while the mob urged her to accept this high honor and office.[4]

She never did. She stood there and thanked everybody and cried and declined. The nomination and the office went to Avrea Ingram of Alabama, whose mysterious "suicide" a few years later to this day remains a blot on an otherwise beautiful NSA portrait, which I address elsewhere in this anthology.[5]

Our North Carolina delegation caucused at the conclusion of the Congress and elected me regional chairman. I accepted with silent wondering as to how I could fake enough interest in my "wife," the domestic student issues, while sating my lust for my "mistress," the fighting of the student Cold War in the realm of the International.

Things broke my way!

Dentzer asks me to go to Zagreb—in 48 hours!

In October 1951, I was in Byrd Stadium on the campus of the University of Maryland at College Park. Our Tar Heel football team was playing the University of Maryland on a beautiful Saturday afternoon. Princess Elizabeth was a guest at the game. At halftime I went to the hot dog stand and to my stomp-down amazement ran into our NSA National President Bill Dentzer.

"Bill!" "Barry!"

He said he'd been trying to reach me for several days. I explained this was our big senior out-of-town football weekend and asked him why he was trying to reach me.

"The National Union of Students of Yugoslavia has invited us to send an NSA delegate to the Zagreb Peace Conference," Bill explained. "But I guess it's too late because the plane leaves Monday."[6]

"Bill," I said. "It's just Saturday. I'll go!"

"It's Saturday afternoon," Bill explained. "The State Department is closed so there's no way we could get you a passport."

In those days people didn't *have* passports. People *got* passports when they wanted to travel. I told Bill I *had* a passport left over from my summer at the University of Oslo the year before.

"Well," said Dentzer. "That means, if you want to go, you'll have to go back to North Carolina and get your clothes and passport and somehow get back up to New York in time for a Monday departure."

From JFK to Paris to Zurich to Yugoslavia

I was the host and driver that weekend of a carful of Carolina students who'd driven up from Chapel Hill together and planned to go back together leisurely after a long sleep-off Sunday afternoon. They all joined the spirit of the occasion and rallied extra early Sunday morning so we could race back to Chapel Hill where I gathered my passport and some clothes, sped over to Greensboro where I lived to pick up the suitcases my parents were good enough to pack, raced down to the train station to catch the train that would unload me in New York the next morning in time to get to the Yugoslav Consulate to get my visa to enter Tito's tantalizing Yugoslavia.

It all worked. Later that day I was at Idlewild Airport, later JFK, on a TWA plane headed to Paris and Zurich.[7]

Understand, please, that this was Yugoslavia in October 1951.

Tito and Stalin had split in March 1948. The general impression was that the courageous Tito had defied Joe Stalin and dared him to come invade Yugoslavia which, while remaining steadfastly communist, had decided to pursue an independent course and reorient its politics and economy to the West.

In truth, Stalin had kicked the contentious Tito out of the Cominform, the international communist club, and Tito had spent the ensuing six months trying to get back in. Only then had Tito spun it around to look like he was "defying" Stalin.

The Zagreb Peace Conference

The Zagreb Peace Conference I was to attend was a "Y'all Come" rally of every noncommunist and anticommunist leftist from Western Europe and the United States. Milovan Djilas, Tito's most trusted wartime lieutenant and later his most famous political prisoner, was the conference's official governmental host. Pastor Martin Niemoeller of Germany was there, a church-state celebrity who is credited with the oft-stolen-and-otherwise-misattributed quote:

> When the Nazis came after the Jews. I wasn't Jewish, so I did nothing. When they came after the trade unionists, I wasn't a trade unionist, so I did nothing. When they came after the communists, I wasn't a communist, so I did nothing. When they came after Catholic clergy, I wasn't Catholic clergy, so I did nothing.
>
> And when they came after me, there was nobody left to do anything!

Vladimir Dedijer, Tito's biographer and wartime lieutenant, was the official host to the American delegation. (Twenty-seven years later, he had defected to the West and appeared as a guest on my radio show! I had too much culture to remind him on the air that as a twerpy little kid back in Zagreb twenty-five years earlier I had told him all the fallacies of communism that he now so solemnly admitted in his weighty book.)

Obviously, the Zagreb Peace Conference was Tito's clumsy attempt to win allies in the West now that he had to redirect his entire nation in the opposite direction since he was no longer a Soviet satellite state. It was odd, much more than odd, to be in a classic dull, drab, gray, unsmiling, depressed, poor, and terrified communist country—*on our side.*

President Harry Truman, when reminded that America's newest ally and aid recipient Tito was a son-of-a-bitch, responded with, "Yeah, but he's *our* son-of-a-bitch!" Even though Tito's Yugoslavia depended totally on us; even though there were border incidents every single night along one or more of the Cominform state borders with Hungary, Romania, Bulgaria, and Albania; even though Yugoslavia was a deer dangling over a cliff with its tail tied to a daisy, their urge to evangelize communism ground ever onward.

They might have had a slightly better chance if they'd somehow been able to shuttle Western delegates directly from the hotels (luxurious) to the meeting at the Sabor (the old Croatian Parliament house) and then over to special occasions, such as a reception at the home of the mayor of Zagreb, allowing no sights, sounds, or human contacts in between. They couldn't manage it.

The barriers of social restrictions

First of all, they were defeated by the thundering drab. We couldn't escape the impression that if all the neon lightsmiths of Times Square with unlimited budget were unleashed upon the center of town to emblazon their handiwork at midnight, the Leninist Leprechauns would have drabbed everything down again by dawn.

Then, too, all the anticommunist clichés paraded themselves before us. Even though our young communist interpreters and escorts taught us how to say, "May I have this dance"*(Molim, zaples!),* the young ladies of Zagreb were afraid to dance with us. Oh. sure, they knew that Americans were now officially okay with the Tito regime at the moment. But who knew what the party line would be tomorrow, the day after, or Wednesday after next?

Let's not gloss over that one too quickly. I'm telling you at this late date that the young girls of Zagreb indeed refused to dance with American guests of honor in October, 1951, solely because they were sufficiently communist-street-smart to realize that someday—one political switch later—they could face dire punishment for "having consorted with the capitalist intruder, probably with fantasies of marrying him and leaving the workers' paradise for the gross materialism of the running dogs of the Wall Street oligarchy of atomic plunderers!"

One night at the Gradska Kavana, a major mid-town restaurant–night club on the main square. I excused myself from my young-communist escorters just long enough to go to the men's room. Inside, some English-speaking Yugoslav students warned me not to listen to what my "friends" were telling me. They told me how wretched things were in Yugoslavia and how deeply and desperately they wished they were democratic, capitalist, and free, like America.

When I returned to the table, one of the young communists who had seen those students enter the men's room after me and had accurately surmised the nature of the dialogue said, "Don't listen to them. They are bad boys. Bad boys."

History shows the bad boys were right.

Yugoslavian student Communists defend their independence

I guess the experience with Mitka bothered me the most. After the Zagreb conference concluded, the *Savez Studenata Yugoslavija* (Yugoslav Union of Students) took me and the British student representative John Clews on to Belgrade (Serbia) and Ljubljana (Slovenia). Mitka was our interpreter-escort in Belgrade. His English was excellent, and his energy was epic. "Aren't you afraid of the Hungarians and Romanians, and Bulgarians?" I once asked him regarding his neighbors who provoked one or more border incidents every single night. He clenched up his historic Macedonian face and said: "Hell, no. We'll chase the Romanians and Bulgarians into Russia. We'll chase the Hungarians into Czechoslovakia. We'll chase the Albanians into the Adriatic Sea."

John Clews was out of my class. I was twenty-one. He was in his thirties: what the British call a "professional student." Yugoslavia was the first communist country I'd ever visited. John had been in every single communist country except Albania. And this was 1951, before detente, perestroika, or any of the plastic surgeries of later eras.

John Clews, incidentally, told me he'd been in a meeting of Czech communist students who didn't think he could understand Czech (he did!) shortly after the Czech Communist coup, during which they decided to frame and arrest American AP correspondent Bill Oatis instead of UP correspondent Russ Jones, on grounds that Jones was physically tougher and might be harder to get a "confession" from. Oatis was the major victim of the early Soviet effort to show America, and their communist empire, that America didn't run the world; America didn't run Europe; and America couldn't even get one of their newsmen out of a Czech prison.

John Clews and Mitka Chalovsky got into a discussion of theoretical Marxism and Tito communism that, I'm forced to admit with some shame, I didn't even begin to understand. All I know is that later, at our hotel, John jubilated about the "concession" he had rhetorically wrested from Mitka. Unfortunately some of Mitka's young communist colleagues had also heard the "concession."

The next day, Mitka didn't show up. One of our communist handlers said he was ill. Another said his relatives unexpectedly decided to come up to Belgrade from Macedonia. John read it all clearly and instantaneously.

"Mitka's not ill." he said. "He's so healthy, if he were to sneeze he'd cure somebody. And in Yugoslavia, relatives don't just unexpectedly decide to come up to Belgrade from Macedonia. Mitka's in deep trouble because of what he told me last night."

John and I were scheduled to leave Belgrade for Ljubljana the next day. We demanded Mitka. He'd done so much for us. We virtually refused to leave without saying goodbye to our beloved Mitka.

Leaving Belgrade

At the last possible moment, Mitka was brought to us. Television was only four years old at that time; "Saturday Night Live" was not yet thought of. Mitka's "goodbye" to us, however, looked like a "Saturday Night Live" spoof on how communism brings non-people back from purgatory temporaily to please Westerners who are persnikity about things like the freedom not to disappear just because you agreed with one of the hyperintellectual political observations of John Clews.

He was brought into the train station to say goodbye to us like the ball carrier in early football's "flying wedge" formation. Surrounding him were too many communist jerseys to count. A quick handshake, a quick goodbye, no opportunity for conversation and, according to Yugoslav communist calculations at the time, John and I were thereby expected to leave Belgrade supposing our friend Mitka was okay.

"He's in trouble," said John. "I hope it's not permanent."

It wasn't!

A few years later I was visiting New York from North Carolina and happened to be driving thought the Cloisters, a monastery-like complex in upper Manhattan. My eyes fixated upon the face of a man walking—I can see it and could indicate precisely the spot even though I haven't visited the Cloisters since—and I did one of those "takes," causing me to reflect upon that face. Had I ever seen it before?

Dismissed in New York by a former Yugoslavian friend

The jury might find my story weak here, but later in the 1950s I somehow heard that Mitka was stationed with the Yugoslav Legation in New York. I do not recall how I knew. I cannot name the person who told me. "Hey. Mitka Chalovsky's in New York." Never mind. I picked up the phone in Greensboro, North Carolina, and called the Yugoslav Consulate in New York and asked for Mitka Chalovsky.

He came on in a voice-tone befitting a Swiss bank officer who didn't really remember you and whose promotion to a higher rank depended on keeping it that way.

"Mitka," I fairly shouted. "It's Barry. How are you?"

Don't forget. Mitka had interpreted all our speeches and all speeches made to us during our entire time in the Serbian part of Yugoslavia. When his student organization's plans failed and he and John Clews and I were starving at noon, walking through the city of Novi Sad with no plan for lunch, Mitka bought salami and bread from a passing gypsy, pulled out a pocket knife, and treated us to the best lunch I had in 1951. Mitka took us to the opera *Faust* with his Muslim wife in Belgrade. Mitka had exposed himself to real communist danger by telling John Clews whatever-in-hell he told him that was so heretical.

Mitka and I were friends, I thought. Mitka and I were bonded.

He spoke to me as though we'd never met.

"Oh, hello, Mr. Farber," he said.

Mr. Farber! My daddy was Mr. Farber.

"Mitka," I shouted. "It's Barry. How are you? What a joy that you're in America. I get to New York fairly often. Can we meet?"

Mitka treated that suggestion like a Hollywood sex symbol might treat a similar suggestion from a fan who happened to be an overweight pipe-fitter. NASA has no equipment sensitive enough to detect any enthusiasm in Mitka's response. It simply wasn't there.

Then Mitka finished me off.

"Mr. Farber," he said. "I saw you a few months ago driving through the Cloisters in Manhattan."

He knew my address in North Carolina. Why in hell hadn't Mitka yelled or waved when he saw me driving through the Cloisters? He had my home number. Why hadn't he called me after he saw me? In fact, why hadn't he called me before he saw me at the Cloisters'? Why hadn't he called me as soon as he got to America? I'll never blame Mitka. But I'll never quit blaming communism.

A public relations disaster for Communist Yugoslavia

There's no school for dictators, anymore than there are seeds for weeds, but if there were, you can be sure they'd teach them early in the first trimester to avoid what the Tito people did with me. My trip back to the United States was a public relations disaster for Communist Yugoslavia.

No that it mattered much at that point. Seeing the country in 1951 and having even limited contact with non-official people did the job nobly for any fair-minded, sentient American, but the trip home turned the Tito effort to impress a young American student with the virtues of Yugoslav communism into, not just one skit like the "Mitka Farewell," but fourteen solid days of "Saturday Night Live."

Their limited resources prevented the Yugoslav Union of Students from sending me home by air, which would have been a Western airline on the leg after Zagreb. Instead they arranged passage on a Yugoslav freighter out of Rijeka in the northern Adriatic. All the other passengers had been recently released from Yugoslav jails as a result of the Stalin-Tito split in March, 1948, which caused a musical-cells rearrangement in the population of all Yugoslav political prisons.

Those who'd been imprisoned for having contacts with the democratic West were excused while those with contacts to the previously desirable Cominform communist bloc abruptly took their cell-space.

On a two-week ocean voyage in 1951 on a freighter without a spa or computer game room gave me a lot of time to talk with the other passengers about their lives in Yugoslavia. My cabin-mate was Rudy Cusich, slightly younger than I and from New Jersey, who had spent almost a year with his relatives on Otok Sres, an island in the north Adriatic, and spoke fluent Serbo-Croatian.

A Yugoslav (in those days we didn't know from Serb, Croat, Bosnian, Macedonian, Montenegran, Slovenian, Hungarian, and Albanian—they were all "Yugoslavs") married to a Panamanian woman who was at the time in Panama, he had been released from prison to rejoin his wife. He had his two small sons with him who spoke no Spanish, only Serbo-Croatian, because they'd been separated from their mother for so long. Thanks to the rearrangement of the jail population he was free and allowed to go.

Testimonials on a "freedom boat" to America

To simplify things and avoid going through the political and prison life story of every single passenger on that "freedom boat" to America, just pretend that you had sought out and found the most hysterical anticommunist writer on the *Reader's Digest* masthead or in Henry Luce's Time-Life organization, and urged him to write the most lurid anti-communist scenarios his imagination could produce. In that case the resultant testimonies of those leaving Yugoslavia by virtue of the Stalin-Tito split would probably have landed slightly to the right of that rabid anticommunist's imagination.

Most of the crew had never been to America before. Never will I forget sailing into our berth in Brooklyn that sunny day in late 1951 and watching the faces of the Yugoslav crew looking at the parking lots near the pier, jammed with the cars of the longshoremen. They'd been told they were the luckiest workers in the world. They couldn't figure out who all those cars belonged to. They might well have suspected that the U.S. Congress had decided to come down to the Brooklyn pier to welcome them. At that point I was too tired to try to convince them that every American longshoreman owned a car.

At the NSA Christmas meeting of the NEC in Chicago I was criticized for writing a rather flippant report of the Zagreb Peace Conference that some felt aimed more for laughs than for any keen understanding of the current realities of Yugoslav political life.

Sorry.

The Zagreb Peace Conference got exactly what it deserved. It was nothing more than a seductive spray-deoderant for a totalitarian communist regime that had gotten itself expelled from the Moscow Cominform for uppity behavior and now desperately needed friends and allies in the West.

Don't forget. Tito did not "split" from Moscow. Tito was "kicked" out of the Stalinist fraternity, and spent the next half year trying to suck his way back in.

Remembering Elmer Paul Brock

It's time to remember Elmer Paul Brock, whose energy on stage at the 1951 NSA Minneapolis Congress won my heart. Elmer developed terminal cancer at a catastrophically early age and, as an official of the Post Office, had a trenchant last request. He wanted to meet President John F. Kennedy. *Esquire Magazine* ran a touching account of their meeting. As he entered the Oval Office, JFK walked over to him smiling, with outstretched hand, and said, "I understand you have a problem."[8]

Elmer was at our national headquarters in Philadelphia in 1952 when a member of the Union of Yugoslav Students happened to be in town. Coincidentally, I was in town, too, so Elmer paired us up for lunch and we had some pleasant reminiscences of Zagreb.

Afterwards Elmer asked how it had gone.

"I was embarrassed," I said. "I spent my time in Yugoslavia telling them how happy workers were in America, and on our way back to NSA Headquarters after lunch we passed a picket line with a lot of workers on strike."

"You got it backwards," Elmer fairly shouted. "If there'd been no picket line for him to see, the CIA should have staged one for him. He's sure-as-hell never going to see a picket line in Tito Yugoslavia!"[9]

Barry Farber is a national sydicated talk radio host. He has edited a daily newspaper, been a foreign correspondent, and writes a nationally syndicated general interest newspaper column. He speaks sixteen languages.

END NOTES

[1] See "*Life* Goes to a Collegiate Convention," p. 294. See also Wharton, p. 145 for the original "Lion Hunt."

[2] See Stassen, p. 917.

[3] *Editor's note:* Catholic women's colleges were well represented in NSA and provided many of the Association's leaders in the various regions. See Lynch, 493, Des Marais, p. 734, Perkins, p. 943, and Donnelley, p. 951. Also, Mason-Dixon, p. 921.

[4] See Secondari (Rogers), p. 599.

[5] See Avrea Ingram, p. 575.

[6] See Dentzer, p. 299.

[7] *Editor's note:* Dick Murphy, in comments written August 17, 1998, writes:

> Bill Dentzer and I were holding an NSA NIC [National Interim Committee] meeting in Washington, after which we went to the UNC-ND game. Upon returning to Chapel Hill, I was given the task (by Barry) of explaining to Dean Weaver why Barry would be absent from Chapel Hill for the next two weeks, a story about which the Dean, even though an NSA supporter, remained very skeptical !

[8] See Elmer Brock, p. 358.

[9] *Editor's note:* Dick Murphy (see note 7) writes:

> Barry's comments on Elmer Paul are right on target. Elmer was an extraordinary individual, who was the son of a letter carrier who later became Deputy Assistant Postmaster General (my deputy) at the time of his death. He served on Al Lowenstein's staff, and as such, represented Al in the Madison office [see Lynch, p. 270] while he was on the road. Recalled to active duty during the Korean conflict (war!), he represented NSA in Japan while in the Navy. In 1953, he returned to Philadelphia (his home), where he served NSA as a volunteer in the office, after Len Wilcox's departure for the Navy [see Murphy, p. 000], leaving myself and Avrea Ingram (in Cambridge) as the only full-time officers left to run the Association. See p. 1075 for additional remarks by Murphy about Brock.

BARRY FARBER

Early Years: Born 1930 in Baltimore. Graduated Greensboro High School in North Carolina. I graduated University of North Carolina in 1952. Before leaving college I was editor of a daily newspaper, a boxer, a wrestler, a steel-worker, a representative of American college students in Yugoslavia and Brazil, and an interpreter for units of the Chinese Nationalist Navy—and a Phi Beta Kappa student.

Career highlights: Since the age of twenty-one I have edited a daily newspaper and been a foreign correspondent, special assignments writer, and street reporter. My news coverage has taken me in and out of trouble spots around the world. I led Hungarians across the border after their revolution, and sped to Cuba after the fall of Batista, beating Fidel Castro to Havana by five days! I was reporting on the repression of Soviet Jews from the Moscow synagogue as early as 1956.

My nationally syndicated radio program, heard for three hours daily coast-to-coast over the Talk America Radio Network, won me the title of "Talk Host of the Year" in 1991.

My articles have appeared in *The New York Times, Readers Digest, The Washington Post, Saturday Review* and many other publications. I am a member of the Brotherhood Synagogue in New York and was twice elected to the board of the Greater New York Conference on Soviet Jewry.

I ran for Mayor of New York City, bucking a liberal tide, and tallied a 40 percent–plus primary vote.

I discovered early on the power of language to get a story, and I speak Spanish, French, German, Italian, Portuguese, Dutch, Norwegian, Danish, Swedish, Russian, SerboCroatian, Indonesian, Hungarian, Finnish, Yiddish, and two dialects of Chinese.

Family: I am married and have two children.

PICTURE CREDITS: *Then:* Inter-American Student Congress, Rio de Janeiro, Brazil, February, 1952. *Now:* c. 1980s, syndicated radio talk show host (Both by author).

FARBER REPORTS TO NORTH CAROLINA ON HIS GLOBAL TRAVELS

The Daily Tar Heel

NSA Meet To Be Held Here Soon

(Special to The Daily Tar Heel)

RIO DE JANERIO, Jan. 25 National Students Association will hold its winter regional assembly on the UNC campus, February 29 and March 1 Barry Farber, regional chairman, announced today.

Integral phases of the assembly will be forums with leaders from other campuses, and workships for student body presidents, vice-presidents, and publication editors.

Discussions will be carried on in such areas as: planning campus international programs, meeting student economic needs, planning leadership training programs, and orientation techniques.

Reports from international student conferences in Yugoslavia and Brazil will be given by regional chairman Farber, and the report from the Virginia-Carolina delegation to the American Commission of UNESCO will be presented.

Featured on the agenda will be a special performance by the Austrian God Will Tour, which will be on the campus at this time. The group is made up of 20 Austrian students now touring America with a varied routine of zither playing, dancing, and folk music.

Also highlighting the list of distinguished guests will be Bill Dintenzer, national president of NSA.

January 25, 1952

CHAPEL HILL, N. C. SATURDAY, MARCH 1, 1952

NSA Delegates From 3 States To Gather Here

Delegates from 20 different schools in North Carolina, South Carolina and Virginia began arriving in Chapel Hill yesterday afternoon to attend the regional assembly of the National Student Association being held here.

Approximately 100 delegates are expected to be here for the assembly, Barry Farber, regional chairman, said yesterday.

The delegates will hear reports from national President Bill Dentzer, Muskigum College, Ohio and Dick Murphy, Carolina. Dentzer will report on the recent student congress held in Rio De Janerio and Murphy will give one on UNESCO (United Nations Educational, Social and Cultural Organization.)

Every meeting will be held in the faculty lounge of the Planetarium and is open to the general public.

Five workshops dealing with student government, publications, and campus-international relations will take up most of the week-end regional meet.

The Austrian Goodwill troupe that performed in Memorial hall last night was part of the week-end activities of the National Student Association conference.

A MAINSTAY OF NSA's VIRGINIA-CAROLINA REGION, U. of North Carolina hosted a regional meeting in March of 1952 at which Farber, then regional chairman, reported on his trip to Zagreb to some 100 delegates from 20 colleges in the area. The *Tar Heel* gave extensive coverage to NSA campus and regional activities. (See Part 5, Sec. 6). (Above, 1/26/52, 3/1/52).

Travels of a novice roving ambassador for NSA

4. Travels to South America, 1951-1952

Helen Jean (Rogers) Secondari
Mundelein College, Chicago. NSA Secretary-Treasurer, 1948-49
NSA Latin American Observer, 1951-52

The first real contacts NSA made with national unions of students in Latin America grew out of a visit to the United States in March 1951 by Paulo Egydio Martins, the Secretary for International Affairs of the national union of students of Brazil (Uniao Nacional dos Estudantes, or UNE). After expressing interest initially to the NSA Committee at Harvard University, including Avrea Ingram and me, in cooperative programs between UNE and NSA, NSA International Vice President Herb Eisenberg wrote a response conveying NSA's desire for mutual cooperation. This led to an invitation for him and another NSA representative to attend as observers the Fourteenth UNE Congress during July in Rio de Janeiro.

I was chosen as the other NSA observer, partly because I could speak Spanish, which is similar to the Portugese language. A graduate student in international relations at Harvard at the time, I had been graduated from the Catholic University of America after serving as NSA Executive Secretary in 1948–49.

Braniff Airlines furnishes the tickets

UNE offered to pay for our stay in Rio, but our problem was to find the money to get us there. After fruitless efforts with several foundations and corporations, I thought of Thomas E. Braniff, President of Braniff Airlines, who also was a graduate of the Catholic University of America. Brazenly I wrote him and back came two tickets for our trip, with notice that he would advise Braniff branch managers in the region to help us if help was needed. Imagine their desire to help!

Relations with IUS dominates Rio agenda

The issue of UNE's future relation with the Communist-dominated International Union of Students (IUS) was a major issue at the Congress and the reason why the anti-IUS Martins wanted NSA observers present. The IUS was represented by staff member Giovanni Berlinguer, an Italian whose brother was head of the Communist Party of Italy. Congress sessions invariably convened late and continued into the wee hours of the morning. In one such session, the Congress decided overwhelmingly to specify a list of objective and unobjectionable criteria—such as non-partisan IUS secretariat activity—that the IUS should meet during the coming year, with failure to do so resulting in UNE's disaffiliation from the IUS at the next UNE Congress. This represented a compromise between those favoring immediate disaffiliation, but fearing to split UNE, and those who were pro-IUS or hopeful of reforming it, but also fearful of splitting UNE.

The UNE Congress also called for a Pan-American Student Congress to be held in October in Rio do Janeiro and for a Pan-American Union of Students to grow out of that Congress as a continuing organization. Little did I realize then that I would later be an NSA representative to that meeting, which was delayed until February of 1952, or that the continuing organization that was called for to follow up that conference would not come into being.

Return to Paraguay

After the UNE Congress, I returned to Paraguay, which I had visited just prior to that Congress. I had been received warmly then by the Student Section of Catholic Action and invited back when the National University of Paraguay—the country's only university—was in session. That group was similar to Young Christian Students in the United States at the time. The totalitarian government of Paraguay had banned the student governments that made up the national student union, but the Student Section of Catholic Action was tolerated even though it opposed this action by the government. Indeed it was the only major university student organization then in existence. When I addressed its Congress in Spanish just prior to my departure, there was cheering after almost every sentence—evidence of their gratitude for NSA's presence and their respect for the United States.

Visits to Cuba and Mexico

Cuba and Mexico were the other countries I visited in an effort to determine whether national unions of students existed there with which NSA could establish contact. These visits followed similar NSA attempts in Europe, Southeast Asia, Africa, and the Middle East.

The official student organization of Cuba was the Federacion Estudiantil Universitaria (FEU), which represented the 15,000 students of the University of Havana but not the other two, smaller universities in Cuba—FEU was anti-communist, antigovernment, anti-dictatorship, anti-vested interests, and highly nationalistic. It had a reputation as being a stepping stone toward higher political positions in Cuba, as an ex-FEU leader named Fidel Castro was to confirm later in that decade. While highly political, I found FEU willing and eager for contact with NSA.

In Mexico, the Confederacion Estudiantil Universitaria, representing all the university students of the country, apparently was not very active, due partly to financial difficulties. Since the National Autonomous University of Mexico is the largest and most important university in Mexico, the Federacion Estudiantil Universitario (FEU) there seemed the most influential group in the nation. While recent FEU elections were highly political and influenced by national politics, FEU leaders indicated more interest in cultural activities, including student exchange programs, than in political action. I recommended further exchange of persons and information between NSA and FEU and attendance of NSA representatives at the 400th anniversary of the founding of the National University in September. NSA reacted favorably to those recommendations and as NSA's budding expert on Latin America, I was an NSA representative at that anniversary celebration.

Editor's note: Unfortunately, Helen Jean Rogers Secondari died on March 28,1998, and was unable to expand upon her initial draft of this article. Among her many contributions to the National Student Association was her opening up of NSA relations with Latin American student unions.

PICTURE CREDITS: *Then:* c. 1951-52 (Murphy). *Now:* c. 1980s (Author).

Helen Jean Secondari was a five-time Emmy award–winning documentary producer. She traveled worldwide for the ABC television network. In later years she produced a newsletter, Bellissima Italia, *celebrating her love of Italian cuisine and travel. (See p. 600 for extended biography.)*

We can win practically a whole continent of friends. . . .

LATIN AMERICAN TEAM REPORT -1951

Editor's note: Quoted below is the Conclusion to the 66-page report prepared by team members Herbert W. Eisenberg and Helen Jean Rogers. For more on NSA's early Latin American initiatives see Barry Farber this Section, Eisenberg, Section 1 and Dentzer, Pt.1, S. 9.

The U.S. National Student Association has just begun to enter into cooperation with the students of Latin America. In this new venture there will be many difficulties, for we are without experience in this field, and dealing with Latin Americans will be considerably different than dealing with Europeans, the group with which the USNSA has had the most association in the past.

In working with Latin Americans, it might be particularly helpful to note some of the following impressions:

1. The Latin American students are intensely nationalistic, with an intense feeling for their country that students in the United States and in Europe too for the most part do not have, or really understand. [It] is most important that American students understand [this nationalism], and recognize it when it shows itself in strong statements and strong feelings against the United States. Part of this feeling is based on a very sharp sensitivity, and perhaps a sense of inferiority; part of it is based on actual unfortunate practices of American economic groups and businesses in Latin America.

Because this sensitivity exists the USNSA must always be particularly careful to give proper credit to the cultural and historical traditions of each country, and must give proper recognition to the works of the students.

In addition, it will be necessary for the USNSA representatives to face squarely what is good about American economic activity in Latin America, and equally squarely, admit what is bad. Only in this way can the USNSA be sure to win friends in this part of the world.

2. The political character of the Latin American student groups is much more intensely political than in this country. For this reason we must recognize that although programming is always important, we must realize that it is in the political arena too that friends will be made for us in the South.

For these reasons the Inter-American Student Conference is a challenge, and an opportunity; if we act wisely and with a real understanding and appreciation of the Latin Americans we can win practically a whole continent of friends for the USNSA.

The Conference, and the possibility that such a conference would create a permanent body in the form of a Pan-American Student Union, presents some long range values that might be briefly listed here.

1. It provides an opportunity for American students to express the real thinking of American students, thus destroying the many distortions now rampant in South America. Thus increasing the realization of students in the Americas of the many important beliefs they hold in common.

2. It will enable the students of the Americas to develop cultural and educational programs of exchanges that will assist the students of each country, and increase friendship...

3. It presents an instrument for the expression of the students of the Americas before the world clarifying much misinformation about their attitude.

4. It provides an opportunity for creating a solidarity among American students which may later lead to the participation of all the Americas in a world student organization.

The USNSA delegation feels that their mission was worthwhile, and that some lasting gains towards the goal of international understanding have been made.

With the Inter-American Conference, and its ramifications, it is hoped that the U.S. National Student Association will continue its work in the South Americas, and that relations among the students of the Americas will become better and better in the future.

It was the excitement she brought to the subject

4. Helen Jean Rogers Secondari: A Natural Leader

Mundelein College, Illinois. NSA Secretary-Treasurer, 1948-49

"NSA can give the small college . . . a voice in the national picture"

Editor's note: When Helen Jean Rogers, a sophomore at Mundelein College in Chicago, connected with NSA as campus chair in 1948, she found a medium through which she could eventually put to work on a global stage her substantial leadership and organizing energies and her high level of intellect and scholarship. Rogers in many ways epitomized what Ralph Dungan, NSA's 1947-48 Student Affairs Vice President, termed the many "smart women" at Catholic women's colleges and the influence NSA had in broadening the involvement of Catholic college women students (See Dungan in Part 6 and Lynch in Part 2). Highlights of her service were as an elected national officer in 1948-49, as first editor of the Student News Service published by the National Federaton of Catholic College Students 1950-51, as a multi-lingual NSA international representative in Europe and Latin America in 1951-52, and as an emerging television journalist on the College News Service in 1952-53. Ken Kurtz in Part 6 mentions the strong and critical support which she mustered for Al Lowenstein's Presidential candidacy in 1950.[1] Barry Farber in this Section writes of the fifteen minute standing ovation she received at the Fourth National Student Congress at the University of Minnesota when she declined the nomination as international affairs vice president. Helen Jean Rogers had become a legend in her own day.[2]

NSA News, 2/49

(cut courtesy Tech Collegian)

MISS HELEN JEAN ROGERS (center), secretary-treasurer of the National Student Association, spoke to representatives of the student councils of Beckley college, Concord college and West Virginia Tech last Monday (Feb. 7) in the Tech cafeteria lounge. Pictured from l. to r. are: Charles Forbes, president of the student council at Concord; Tom Crossan, president of the West Virginia State Federation of Colleges; Paul Settle, president of the Tech student council; Miss Rogers; Lewis McManus, president of the student council at Beckley; and Stanley Myers, publicity director of the State Federation of Colleges.

Agnes Scott News, Decatur, GA, 2/16/49

NSA Gives National Voice to Small Colleges Says Helen Jean Rogers, National Secretary

"NSA can give the small college, among other things, a voice in the national picture," stated Helen Jean Rogers, national secretary-treasurer of the National Students' association.

In an interview this week-end, Helen Jean told about NSA and of her tour of the southern regions. She stayed at Agnes Scott while she attended the Georgia-Alabama-Florida regional assembly held at Emory university Saturday and Sunday.

For the rest of the month she will be visiting and speaking at colleges and universities in this region, the Virginia-Carolina region, and also in Tennessee.

Helen Jean is the only woman officer of NSA. She attends a small Christian college for women in Chicago, Mundelain college. Mundelain is a liberal arts college and has an enrollment of less than a thousand students. She says she feels that only through NSA can the opinion of small colleges be heard above the voice of large universities.

Helen Jean was first sent as a delegate to NSA two years ago when she was a freshman. Hear-

believes students can get a picture of the various problems which will confront them when they leave college, and more important, she adds that NSA gives them a chance to learn to cope with such situations.

Helen Jean was elected to a regional office in charge of cultural activities. She then became director of the NSA art exhibit. This exhibit of outstanding student art is touring the colleges and universities of the United States and will later be on display in Prague.

After holding the position of president of the Illinois region, Helen Jean was elected to the national post. All the national officers are full-time workers. She

Rogers Speaks To Honor Society

Helen Jean Rogers, NSA national secretary - treasurer, addressed the convention of the Alpha Kappa Mu Honor Society on Feb. 11, at Morris Brown College, Atlanta, Ga.

Deans and students from 30 colleges and universities heard Miss Rogers call NSA the "voice of American students." "During its formative period it is most important that NSA have the cooperation of colleges and universities throughout the United States. NSA can provide many services for each campus but only if the campuses are willing to place their faith in the organization," said Miss Rogers.

Alpha Kappa Mu is an honorary scholastic society composed of top ranking students from 32 Negro colleges and universities. Dr. R. O. Johnson, member of the NSA Nation Advisory Council, is one of the leaders of the organization.

NSA NEWS 2/49

Rogers to Speak At College Forum

Helen Jean Rogers, secretary-treasurer of NSA, will address MADEMOISELLE's Sixth Annual College Forum, on **Freedom and Security**, Saturday, April 30, at the Hotel Commodore in New York City.

One of 55 outstanding co-eds from leading American colleges, who will be brought to New York by MADEMOISELLE for the all-day conference with educators, newspapermen, and other authorities, Miss Rogers will talk on NSA and academic freedom.

She will be one of three student speakers presenting reports on the role of the undergraduate in dealing with problems of freedom and security.

ROGERS

June Louin of the University of Southern California will report on what the undergraduate can do about civil liberties, and Gladys Chang, president of the student government at Sarah Lawrence College, will talk on freedom and responsibility in student government.

Last year Robert Smith, NSA's

NSA NEWS 4/49

AS A NATIONAL OFFICER, Rogers traveled on organizing assignments and for speaking engagements. Photos (above left and clockwise) show her: with Illinois Region steering committee, right, in 1947-48 (SHSW), meeting with Michigan Region Chair, Harvey Weisberg, and New Jersey Region chair, Bob Kelly at the 1948 NSA Congress, U. of Illinois (Schwartz); College News Conference, 1953-54, standing from left: Ken Kurtz (NSA Pennsylvania Regional Chair, 1949-50), Elmer Brock, 1950-51 Student Affairs VP, Helen Jean Rogers (NSA Secretary-Treasurer, 1948-49); Herb Wright (Youth Secretary, NAACP). Seated: Ruth Hagy (Brod), moderator; Krishna Menon, Prime Minister of India. (Brod)

It Changed my Life Forever

The following recollections are from an unpublished memoir by Helen Jean Secondari.

In 1948-49 I moved to Madison, Wisconsin to work with NSA for a year. I do not know why, to this day, my parents let me go into what they must have considered a very strange atmosphere with all of these different people, but I think the nuns convinced them that it would be a great honor for Mundelein, if I were an officer. In any event, they let me go and it changed my life. I never thought about the fact that I was the only female and all the other officers were men. That made no difference among us.

Traveling around the country, making speeches, doing my best to help run an organization, struggling against racial segregation in schools, and working for academic freedom changed my life and ideas forever. . . .

I went to Harvard/Radcliffe for graduate school and became a Teaching Fellow at Harvard, where there were almost no women on the faculty. I had no idea how I was doing as a teacher but some time later, one of my students wrote a long article about life at Harvard and mentioned me:

> Helen Jean Rogers was a terrific teacher. I do not think the fact that she was female, only a few years older than us, and very attractive too,were the main reasons for her success. It was the excitement that she brought to the subject. Political theory from Plato to Marx can be dull, but she made it contemporary and fascinating.

Loyalty Oaths Will Not Achieve the Purpose

May 17, 1951
The Editor, *Times Herald*
Washington, DC

It was with profound shock that I read in your May 16th issue the article, entitled:"Communist Rule at 10 Colleges in Illinois Charged," presenting a statement of Representative Velde(R. Ill.) in which he charged the Illinois Region of the United States National Student Association is Communist dominated.[3]

During the early days of NSA great efforts were made and parliamentary battles fought to assure that the organization would be free from domination by communist elements....

From the article it appears that Representative Velde recognizes the evils of Sovietism and that he feels the best way is to use loyalty oaths and similar types of legislation to weed out Communists.The delegates from the University of Chicago and the other representatives of Illinois schools. too, have a deep recognition of the evils of Sovietism.... However, they apparently disagree with Representative Velde as to the best method of achieving the goals.They apparently believe that special loyalty oaths for teachers and similar legislation will not achieve the purpose for which they are established and will, moreover, endanger the traditional freedoms of our educational institutions; freedom so necessary in a democratic society.

Representative Velde's statement seems to indicate that he believes these students are Communists simply because they disagree with Representative Velde on this question of *methods* of protecting our democracy....

The Communists have an insidious trick of labeling all those who oppose them on any point as Fascists.We will have reached a tragic juncture in our democracy if leaders of our country, in turn, will begin to say that all those who disagree with them are Communists.

Sincerely yours, Helen Jean Rogers

HELEN JEAN ROGERS SECONDARI

Helen Secondari was born in Fond Du Lac, Wisconsin, and grew up as Helen Jean Rogers in Chicago, the only child of William Martin and Helen O'Grady Rogers.

She attended Mundelein College for two years and then went on to Catholic University in Washington, D.C., where she graduated magna cum laude and Phi Beta Kappa.

While at Harvard/Radcliffe graduate school, she became one of the first woman teaching fellows on the faculty. After returning to Washington, she became associate producer of ABC's *College News Conference*, and later producer of *Open Hearing*, a show similar to *Meet the Press*. That is where she met her husband, John H. Secondari, who was a widower with a young son, and was then head of the Washington bureau of the network. He had already achieved some fame as author of *Three Coins in the Fountain* while working in Europe after the war.

She worked on various news programs, and became the first woman director of a film for TV news when she was sent to Havana to cover Castro's victorious arrival in Havana. After that she was sent to Africa by John Charles Daly, head of ABC News in New York, where she produced the critically acclaimed film *The Dark and the Light*, about Blacks and Whites in South Africa, Tanzania and Kenya.

In the years following, she and John Secondari became a team and, mostly together, they made more than 100 TV films all over the world. They included subjects as diverse as *The Awesome Servants* (about the computer revolution), *1492* (the discovery of America), *1776* (The independence of the U.S.), the Golden Age of the Automobile, *Troubled Land* (peasant problems in Latin America), *Custer to the Little Big Horn*, *Benjamin Franklin* and various other films including many on civil rights, race relations, and labor management questions.

They received five Emmys, two Peabodys, the National Education School Bell Award, the Marconi Prize, the Overseas Press Club Best Foreign Reporting Award, and many others. Helen Secondari was twice voted Director of the Year by the TV Critics of America.

After John Secondari died, Helen was left with their nine-year-old daughter. She continued to work in television and eventually moved from New York City back to Washington, D.C. Because of frequent travel to Italy, Helen launched a monthly publication, *Bellissima Italia*, for people who love Italy and things Italian.

In 1988, she was working on two films in addition to her publication. In September, she entered the hospital for the "minor surgical procedure" which crippled her for life. In the later years before her death, she assiduously dictated and edited, but was unable to complete, an autobiographical manuscript, which she had entitled "Malpractice," dealing with her heroic efforts to recover from the near crippling physical and sensory effects of a surgical procedure gone awry, which was initially covered up by medical personnel.

She died on March 28, 1998. She was survived by a son, John Gerry Secondari of Washington, a daughter, Linda Helen Black of New York, and, more recently, a grandson, Luca Black.

EDITOR'S NOTES

[1] Their alliance grew into a strong affectionate and good-natured bond for a period of time. While researching the Lowenstein papers at the University of North Carolina, I came across this undated typewritten note which, in context, is probably c. 1951, and reads in part, "Your second letter just came and I can't tell you how good it was to hear from you. Things are really in a mess [probably referring to the "red scare" politics in and outside of NSA at the time] and I need you so much. Please read all of the enclosed and tell me what you think about everything. Gee, I wish you were here. In things like this we can make such a good team—you know what to do and I can just sort of be charming. . . ."

[2] Helen Jean and I served on the national staff togetherr. We became dear friends and reconnected later in life. Some of our NSA staff experiences are recounted by Dick Heggie and Allan Ostar in Part 1, Sec. 6.

[3] See Alexander Pope's recollection of this controversy on p. 390.

A program that would be universal in appeal and yet practical in application

We, the Students

Helen Jean Rogers
Mundelein College, Illinois. Delegate to the NSA Constitutional Convention, 1947
NSA Secretary-Treasurer, 1948-49

Editor's note: Excerpt from an article in the Mundelein College Review, *November, 1947. In this recounting of NSA's formation and the arguments for remaining non-political and non-sectarian, Helen Jean Rogers introduces to an urban Catholic girls school its necessary connection to the "new-found consciousness" of students throughout the nation. The article also spells out the detailed form of organization which the Illinois Region built its program (see Part 6, Sec. 5). During the years after her election as NSA Secretary-Treasurer for 1948-49, Rogers became one of NSA's visible and popular national leaders, later representing it at various Latin American and European international student conferences.*

"It has been moved and seconded that we join the National Student Association; all in favor ?" A moment of tense, expectant silence; then a thousand voices united in a positive, assured aye! We have voted unanimously to join the United States National Student Association. By joining an organization representative of every type of student we have reflected our realization of the individual collegian's responsibility to the student community. The step we have taken marks the beginning of a new era of Catholic student action.

We are not alone in our new-found consciousness. Students all over the United States are stirring, are awakening from their complacent slumber to realize that through an organized effort the collegians of our country can make a worthwhile contribution to the betterment of the student world.

The collegians of the United States have not been aroused suddenly. The awakening has been a slow process which received its impetus sixteen months ago, when twenty-five American students representing ten universities and fifteen youth organizations were sent to a world youth festival at Prague[1]....

* * *

Impressed by need of immediate constructive action, the delegates on their return from Prague called a conference of American collegians at the University of Chicago on December 28, 1946. They described the students whom they had seen abroad and explained the work that student unions in foreign countries are doing to promote student welfare. Four delegates from Mundelein attended this meeting....

The conferees were soon convinced that a national federation representative of students of every social, political, economic, and religious segment of our society would be an asset to the students of the United States....Accordingly, they formulated the principles on which they believed that such an association should be based and elected a National Continuations Committee (NCC) to prepare a draft constitution and make arrangements for the constitutional convention.

As a result of the efforts of the NCC, seven hundred delegates representing more than one and a quarter million students in three hundred and fifty-six colleges and universities gathered at the University of Wisconsin on August 30, 1947, for the constitutional convention of the proposed United States National Student Association (USNSA). Four delegates, including the present writer, represented Mundelein at this meeting.

All of the delegates at Madison grasped from the first the complexity of our problems: to mold ideas of every type of student into a form that would be acceptable to all, to adopt a long and technical constitution, and to plan a program for the coming year that would be universal in appeal and yet practical in application. Nevertheless, we were determined to create a strong association which would be truly representative of American student opinion and would promote student welfare by every legitimate means.

Through the eight days of tedious discussion and endless debate the representatives approached each new problem with mature judgment and unwavering fortitude. Despite the proximity of the inviting waters of Lake Mendota, few delegates played truant from the sessions. One committee worked for forty-two hours with time out only for quick snacks. Each representative seemed to realize the importance of his ideas, suggestions, and vote.

Issues that divided the Constitutional Convention

During the convention three issues developed which were the subject of bitter debate and threatened to disrupt the meeting. The first of these was the membership of youth organizations such as the National Intercollegiate Christian Council, American Youth for Democracy, Newman Club Federation, and Young Progressive Citizens of America in the National Student Association. Some delegates argued that these organizations could supply USNSA with funds and experienced leadership; that it would be "undemocratic" to exclude them from membership. Others, including almost all of the Catholic delegates, answered that the National Student Association would be a lasting federation only if it concerned itself strictly with student problems, avoiding partisan political or sectarian religious affairs. How could USNSA escape these complications, we asked, if among the members were organizations whose avowed purposes were political or religious?

The latter viewpoint carried the day, for the majority voted to exclude organizations from membership in the USNSA and to admit only student bodies of recognized institutions of higher learning.

The second major problem facing the group was affiliation with the International Union of Students (I.U.S.). This federation was born at the Prague festival the previous summer. I.U.S. is at present Communist-dominated and its program is permeated with pro-Russian political activities. Most of the delegates, however, realized that the International Union of Students is the only medium for cooperation between students of the West and those behind the iron curtain. Moreover, we were eager to take advantage of the low-cost student tours and exchange scholarships which I.U.S. offers its members. Nevertheless, we believed that American students wanted no part in an international political organization with a definite red tinge.

Although a small radical group urged immediate affiliation despite these complications, the majority concurred with a plan presented by two prominent Catholics: the USNSA would join I.U.S. if its autonomy on all matters would be recognized, and it would participate only in the educational, non-political activities of the Union. A negotiating team will carry these provisions to I.U.S.

The third major problem, probably the most controversial question before the body, was the racial issue. Most Northerners demanded that USNSA take an unequivocal stand against segregated educational institutions as well as discriminatory educational practices in general, such as the quota systems for Jews and Negroes in many schools. The persuasive Southerners pleaded that although they themselves realized the necessity of the abolition of discriminatory practices and would work through USNSA toward this end, they would be unable to accept a constitution which contained statements diametrically opposed to their state laws. We of the North, they claimed, do not understand the complexity of their problem. Let the South work out its own difficulties, and the end result would be far more satisfactory....

The Negro delegates gained the admiration of all during this period of tension....

Jim Smith, president of the NCC, offered a compromise: the preamble to the constitution would contain a statement that the NSA would aid in securing equal educational rights for all.

The by-laws would include the additional provision that the Association would investigate minority discrimination with the aim of its eventual elimination, being cognizant of the legal limitations imposed at present. The motion was passed without a dissenting vote...[2]

* * *

The structure of NSA

The structure of the NSA as designed by the delegates and embodied in the constitution is fairly simple. There are three levels of activity: national, regional, and local. On the national level the legislative body is the National Student Congress, which meets once each year and is composed of delegates from each affiliated unit. This is the chief policy-making group of the association. The executive power is in the hands of the national officers and the executive committee, which consists of representatives of each region. This committee is empowered to shape emergency policies and to fill positions subject to the approval of the National Student Congress.

The nation is divided into twenty-six regions, each of which is autonomous. In the region the legislative body is the regional assembly composed of the campus delegates. This group will plan regional programs of activity and elect regional officers.

On the local level the student body is the legislative group which decides methods of implementing the programs of the national and regional organizations, elects delegates, and approves any constitutional amendments. Through the Commission system each Mundelein girl will have the opportunity to take part in the regional activities of the Association. To carry out the proposed program of USNSA for the coming year, three commissions on cultural, national, and international affairs have been set up within the Illinois region. Corresponding subcommissions may be organized on the campuses.

Since the greatest force militating against the development of an organized student community is the lack of contact among students, the commission on cultural activities will work toward the elimination of this major difficulty. The commission tentatively plans to initiate departmental meetings at schools in Illinois. Each member institution would be responsible for one department and would plan at least one activity during the coming year to which the students of other colleges would be invited. Thus Mundelein might be hostess to a writers' forum for all of the college journalists in Illinois, while the drama students might go to Northwestern for a play festival and the physicists to the University of Chicago for a lecture. The commission will publicize plays and lectures which are open to the public at the various schools and will make vocational information available to the students.

The Commission on National Affairs will investigate student government, book prices, and student health, and will make recommendations to member schools on how to alleviate difficulties in these areas. It will also collect information on racial discrimination, teaching methods, and curriculum reforms for the use of member colleges.

The International Affairs Commission will make available to students information on low-cost student tours and foreign exchange scholarships, and will attempt to familiarize collegians with UNESCO, IUS and WSR. It will endeavor to create on the part of the students in Illinois a better understanding of their fellow students in other countries.

These are the plans of our Illinois Region for this year. They have one aim—to aid the college student by every legitimate means to attain his student goal, the development of his intellect.

The National Student Association will be successful only if each student puts his best effort and full cooperation into it. USNSA is entirely a student project: we will not be able to depend on some long-suffering faculty member to bear the burden of our endeavor.

The students of the world need us

Because we recognized our responsibility to all students, because we knew that the students of the world need us, need our Christian philosophy and ideals now, we voted to join USNSA. The chairman might just as well have said, "It has been moved and seconded that the Students of Mundelein get out of their ivory tower and bring God into the student world through USNSA."

Each of us must have realized our obligation, we must be willing to do our utmost to carry Christ to the collegians of the world, for all of us answered, positively, assuredly, Aye!

END NOTES

[1] *Editor's note:* The original article states that the delegates were "sent by the United States government at the invitation of the Czechoslovakian Union of Students to a world youth festival at Prague." This was clearly an inadvertent error as the delegation was not sponsored or funded by the U.S. government. Tibbetts, p. 68 and Bellush, p. 73.

[2] Rogers' complete retelling of the proceedings has been condensed here. For a more full accounting of the floor debate on the discrimination and other issues, see Wharton, p. 146.

PICTURE CREDIT: c.1947-49 (SHSW)

Our participation was directed by NSA.

5. The German Summer Project, 1951

Mary Kay Perkins
Mundelein and Rosary Colleges, Illinois
NSA National Office Staff, 1949-50
NSA Delegate, Second International Student Seminar, 1951

I entered Rosary College in River Forest, Illinois, in 1950 as a junior after having served for a year as a staff associate with the NSA national staff in 1948–49. I did my first two years at Mundelein College.

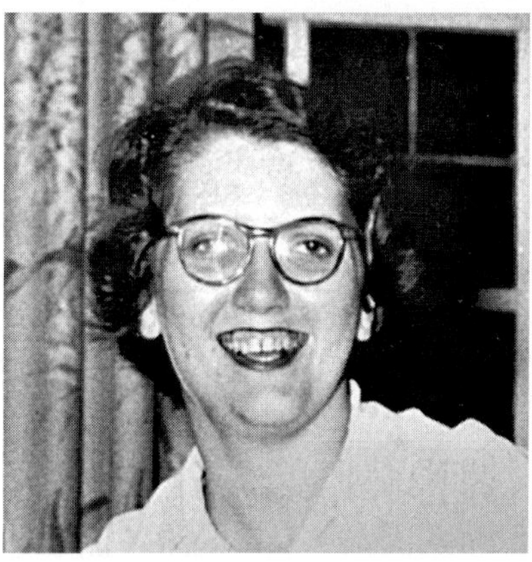

In my senior year I was one of the officers of student government. Rosary belonged to NSA,[1] and I participated in an NSA-sponsored summer conference in Germany in 1951. It was concerned with the democratization of the German University students.

There were six Americans who were representatives to the Conference, and there were two American students who took care of us. The two were from Harvard. One was Carl Safers, and I can't remember who the other one was. We were the only Americans, and the other delegates were Frank Kracovec from the University of Colorado, Bernie Siegel from Temple, Bill West from Ohio University, Sue Hobson from Sweet Briar College (VA), and a Black fellow whose name I can't remember, also a Catholic and from the University of Kansas. Frank and the fellow from Kansas were veterans and graduates.

The city was on one of the finger lakes that are south of Munich, and the name of the town is Seeshaupt Sternberger See. There was a hotel there that was owned by the University of Munich. As I recall, we slept in bunk beds, and the room I was in had, probably, six of us.

Our participation was directed by NSA. It was financed by the American military government and the Ford Foundation.

Traveling to Europe

This ship we came over on had 1,100 passengers, of whom about 1,000 were students, and the others were going to various programs. It was a Dutch ship. It was slow, and it took us ten days. But what was really nice was that they offered classes in conversational everything—in almost any language any of us would be using. What can you learn in ten days? Well, not a lot. But when you're going into a country whose language you don't know, it's nice to be able to ask directions and ask prices. So it was a very practical orientation.

In order that the Americans would not be totally ignorant when we got there, we started by spending three to five days at several German Universities. First we went to Hamburg, and then we went to Gottingen, Heidelberg, Frankfurt, Berlin, and Munich. Sometimes we stayed on campus. Sometimes we stayed with families, and some of those experiences are the experiences I'll never forget. When we got to Berlin, Sue Hobson from Sweet Briar College and I stayed with a family there.

Conference attendance and format

The conference lasted three weeks. We had spent about four weeks prior to it, visiting the German universities. We did this all in preparation so that we would have some understanding of what the German university student was like. We went in June and didn't get back until September. I got back on a Friday and had to start school on Monday. It was late into September.

The other students were from sixteen Western European countries and the United States—including Great Britain, Spain, France, Switzerland, Italy. Fifty percent were German University students and 50 percent were all the rest of us. Six delegates from one country was the most there were. I would say most of them had two or three. Altogether there were about one hundred of us. Generally, the Germans were a few years older than the rest of us—perhaps twenty-three or twenty-four.

The sessions were all in English, and we met all morning and in the evening. In the afternoon, we were free to socialize with one another. This was a good part of the benefit of the whole event, because we were very isolated. Seeshaupt is a very small community, and we were way out of town. But it was on the lake, and it was beautiful.

Passing through Berlin during the Cold War

When we were going to Berlin, the only way you could get in—at this point it's after the airlift and before the Wall—was by trains that had to go through the Russian sector. Two trains went every day. They started at the same time at night, and they passed each other. They were all run by the American army.

When we got on the train, we knew that we had the eight compartments. We went down to the dining car, because nobody wanted to sit in their compartment. We had just gotten there when we were told, "Go on back, you've been assigned specific compartments and we have to have the right people in the right compartment so that if anything happens we know whose compartment is whose." So we had to go back and reassort ourselves, after which we returned to the dining car, had dinner, and stayed there and talked.

When we got back into our individual compartments, brown wool covers had been zipped over all the windows, and we were given very strict instructions that we were never to look outside because we were going through the Russian part of Germany. So in the middle of the night, when we stopped, I woke up and took the zipper down and there were two Russian soldiers standing right outside my window—fortunately looking the other way.

"Thank you, Mr. Care"

Another time, we stayed in a building that had been a dormitory for theology students. The woman who was the house mother had been there during the war. She was Polish, and told us some of the stories of how horrible it was for them. First the Germans came and trampled them, and then the Russians came and trampled them, and then the worst of all was when the Polish Communists took over.

She had been a woman of some means, and she lost everything. She lost her family, she lost any money that she had had. After the war, when things were so bad, she said: "We would get these CARE packages and we would all open them together because it would be our way of surviving and we wanted to share the enjoyment of opening each package. This one student, who was a wonderful artist, would draw pictures of how our faces would be." And then she said, "Would you please thank Mr. Care when you go home and tell him how much we appreciated it." That kind of experience was just mind-boggling for us.

Meeting the German students

The students at Seeshaupt were all from different German Universities. The German students were older because almost all of them had either been in the army or simply had their lives interrupted by the war. I remember this one fellow so well because I knew about what he told us, and suddenly he gave it a face. He lived in Hamburg, and he described for us what had happened when the Americans, British, and French gathered together and did saturation bombing for some seventy-two hours because of the city's industrial value. He and his mother lived out in the suburbs, and there was just ash all over—the whole earth was covered with ash. And some of them had been in Russian concentration camps, so they had lived lives that certainly I couldn't have imagined.

I also recall a really very dynamic woman, her name was Evelyn Elbogen. She was someone whom I very specifically expected to see become the Director of Health and Welfare, somebody very important in German government, and she may have done so. I remember one fellow from the Free University of Berlin, who had stayed with us when we were visiting the universities.

There was an almost universal dislike of the three Swiss students. It was a combination, first, of feeling that the Swiss had taken advantage of all of us and made money off of all of us during the war, and second, my recollection is that they were unpleasant individuals in their own right. But the afternoons were wonderful—we'd go out hiking or swimming. It was a marvelous opportunity for three weeks to come to know, not on a political level, but in a deeper way than you usually would have an opportunity to, people who were very different from you and yet for whom you had responsibilities.

The European student organizations

Almost everyone had been selected through the specific student union that existed in his or her country, and all of them were people who were active in student governments. We discussed the practical responsibilities of student governments and the degrees of supervision and of financing that are needed, and how you get from point A to point B.

The German university students had just the beginnings of student governments, and they were trying to open up to what the possibilities were. Of course, from each country the student government organizations were different, and even within the United States there were differences. In some of the countries, there seemed to be much greater political involve-

Mary Kay Perkins, O.P., is Superintendent of Schools, Vicar for the Religious and Director of Adult Faith Development for the Diocese of Baker in Central and Eastern Oregon.

(See p. 946 for extended bio)

ment than there was in the United States at the time. Also, we Americans were undoubtably the youngest people there.

The role of professional staff in the European student organizations seemed important. I think they wondered how we survived with a yearly changeover of elected staff. It really was a challenge in NSA, because with the yearly changeover, and particularly with a total changeover, there are some things you had to learn again and again. Yet I feel that sometimes when you have only one person who is the holdover, that puts an undue burden on him or her to be the transmitter and it's very difficult to be that person—and, as we found out in NSA is wasn't easy to make it work.[2]

The conference was a marvelous experience for a twenty-year-old girl. I've carried the memory of it with me all of my life. Most important is knowing, that not only did I benefit immeasurably, but I was able to help others as well.

German Seminar Now In Progress

NSA Receives $10,000 Grant to Run Similar Seminar In Southeast Asia

NSA's seminar score was one down and one to go as the fourth annual Congress began in Minneapolis.

At Seeshaupt auf Starnberger See in Bavaria, eight U.S. students chosen by NSA were discussing the importance of student self-government in a democratic education with some 30 students from the nations of western Europe, largely Germany.

And Jim Grant (Harvard) announced that NSA had been donated $10,000 for a Southeast Asia seminar that will help to establish contacts with that crucial area.

American participants in the German seminar are Carl Sapers, Harvard; Mary Kay Perkins, Rosary College, Illinois; Susan Hobson, Sweet Briar College, Virginia; Bernard Segal, Temple; LeRoy Everett, Pittsburg State Teachers College, Kansas; Bill West, Ohio Wesleyan; Bill Sandler, Harvard; and Frank Krasavec, University of Colorado.

"RE-ESTABLISHING AND EXTENDING STUDENT SELF GOVERNMENT in German universities" was the objective of the student seminars. (Above: *NSA News* 8/51), German seminar students at a break (WSHS). Right: from a 1952 NSA brochure, "NSA: Strengthening the Forces of Freedom."

ENDNOTES

[1] Rosary delegates to Michigan, 1950: Jacqueline R. Kane, Jean M. McSweeny. Rosary delegates to Minnesota, 1951: Betty L. Courtney, Mary Skaff.

[2] Editor's note: NSA experimented in its third and fourth years with staggered terms for an elected Executive Secretary. Bob Delahanty of the University of Louisville filled the position for the first half of the 1949–1950 year, and Fred Houghteling of Harvard for the next calendar year. After Houghteling's term, it was dropped. During the fourth and fifth years, under Bill Dentzer and Dick Murphy, an appointed Executive Secretary, Marian Andert, a University of Minnesota graduate, served a two-year term.

PICTURE CREDITS: *Then:* c. 1949-50, Madison, WI (*NSA photo*, SHSW). *Now:* c. 1998, Bend, OR (Author)

UNITED STATES HIGH COMMISSIONER FOR GERMANY
APO 757-A Frankfort

Feb. 21, 1951

Mr. Robert L. Fischelis, Phillips Brooks House,
Harvard University, Cambridge 38, Mass.

My dear Mr. Fischelis:

I wish to thank you for your letter of January 24th. As you know, I have been interested in the Koenigstein Seminar....

The strategic place held by students of higher learning in any nation makes any attempt to stimulate democratic attitudes and practices of more than passing interest. It is true that many of the future leaders of any civilized society will come from the universities and similar institutions. What these future leaders study during their university days is important, but probably of more importance to their future leadership and influence are their self-initiated projects of self-government. For these reasons, I want to take this means of expressing my appreciation to you and the other student leaders for initiating and sponsoring the Koenigstein Seminar. I understand the sponsoring organization to be the National Student Association of the United States of America.

From what I have learned about the Seminar, the German student leaders were stimulated to continue their efforts in re-establishing and extending self-government in German universities and technical schools. They have made and are making a significant contribution in the areas of student welfare, self-government, and student-faculty relationships. In the opinion of some of my colleagues, the German students have made greater strides in reorientation than any other groups concerned with higher education....

Sincerely yours, JOHN J. McCLOY

PURPOSE OF THE GERMAN SEMINARS PROPOSED BY NSA

Excerpts from the Preface to The Report of the Third International Student Seminar, Norderney/North Sea, Germany, 1952.

The aim at the 1st Student Seminar in Konigstein/Taunus in 1950 was to lead the German Student Body out of its isolation. Therefore more than half of the participants were German students. The theme "The Student Self-Government and Self-Help" was of particular importance to the German Student Body in post-war Germany although the discussion of these problems was of general interest. The Seminar was suggested by the United States National Student Association and carried out under the sponsorship of the American High Commission in Germany. The success of the Seminar induced the participants to elect a Continuation Committee which should set up plans for another Seminar in the following year.

The 2nd International Student Seminar in Seeshaupt/Upper Bavaria in 1951 dealt with the "Role and Responsibility of Students in University and Society." The Continuation Committee outlined the programme and prepared the organisation and then sent the plans to the sponsoring National Unions. The aim of this Seminar was not so particular as that of the 1st Seminar because it should serve generally the exchange of ideas and make the participants acquainted with the problems of various countries. However, Germany was chosen again as the place to hold this Seminar, because it was felt that here especially many problems were of particular urgency and thus the host country itself stressed the importance of the question raised. In this regard too this Seminar served the particular aim to break down the isolation of the German Student Body.

At the Edinburgh Student Conference in January 1952 it was decided because of the great success of the former two Seminars to make them a permanent institution, and the Verband Deutscher Studentenschaften was charged again to run the 3rd International Student Seminar. The Continuation Committee which consisted of 7 representatives of the sponsoring National Unions met in March 1952 in Konigswinter near Bonn in order to draw up plans and to discuss technical details.

As the title for the Seminar was chosen: "The Rights and Duties of the Student in the National and International Life."

To achieve a comprehensive treatment of the theme three commissions were formed which dealt with

A) "Student Government and its Area of Competence"
B) "Economic and Social Needs of Students"
C) "The Student as a Citizen of the World."

Hopes dashed for an Inter-American student movement

6. The Rio Conference, 1952

Barry Farber
University of North Carolina
Chair, NSA Virginia-Carolinas Region, 1951-52
NSA Delegate to 1952 InterAmerican Congress

In January 1952, Bill Dentzer, NSA's president, roused me from my studies and told me to pack up and get down to Miami where a Braniff Air Line ticket would be waiting for me to Rio de Janeiro.

The Brazilian Union of Students was hosting the Inter-American Congress of Students, and Bill wanted me for my ability to speak Spanish and Portuguese.

My instructions were to show up at the airline office at a certain time and meet up with Herb Wright, who would also serve on our NSA delegation. After we met and got our tickets, we walked out upon Biscayne Boulevard to look for a place to grab a sandwich before heading for the airport.

They refused to serve us at any of the coffee shops and short-order counters because Herb was black.

We did succeed in finding a cab driver willing to take us both to the airport. He made sure we knew what a big favor he was doing for us and all the dire consequences facing him if he should get caught taking a "mixed load" of passengers. We were too hungry to waste a lot of energy thanking him and praising him for his courage, but we did cluck a few gratitudinous murmurs.

A long flight to meet Bill Dentzer, Avrea Ingram, and Helen Jean Rogers

In those days, before the passenger jets, the trip from Miami to Rio was no meal, nap, and magazine hop. The first stop was Havana, Cuba; followed by Panama; Guayaquil, Ecuador; Lima, Peru; and then the world's longest overland flight from Lima to São Paulo, Brazil. Rio was a short flight, from there.

We flew over Lake Titicaca on the border of Peru and Bolivia, which was almost as high up as we were. Then came the Mata Grosso jungle, for many, many flying hours. Bill Dentzer and International Vice President Avrea Ingram were already in Rio, Bill having flown down from the United States and Avrea having come from some NSA business in Africa.[1]

The final member of our delegation was Helen Jean Rogers, who had stubbornly turned down the job of International Vice President at the Minneapolis Congress the previous summer, even though the entire auditorium rocked and roared with the demand that she accept their appointment.[2]

The meetings were to be held in the beachfront headquarters of the Brazilian Student Union, at 132 Prahia do Flamingo, which looked exactly like the embassy of some important country. It had been. That building had been the prewar German embassy, and the surrounding history was a pretty good indication of the way things worked among our sister republics of the Americas.

Remember how correctly German and Japanese diplomats in Washington were treated when World War II broke out? Well, in 1941 when Brazil declared war on Germany the students of Brazil broke into the embassy, smashed and burned the furniture and the files, and took over the building for themselves.

That status simply continued throughout the war and crystallized into permanence thereafter!

The opening session of the congress provided our next living lesson in applied pan-Americanism. There was none! There was no opening session.

Our Brazilian hosts thought it would be a good idea to get things started with a gala reception with the ambassadors of all the countries represented—almost all of the countries south of the border. Most of the student delegates thought it was a miserable idea. Don't forget: the only democracies in the entire Western Hemisphere in 1952 were Canada, the United States, and Costa Rica. All the rest were dictatorships, some less repressive than others.

A conference of "dissidents" and "gobernistas"

Those delegates who had no problem with their home governments (read "strong man") were called "gobernistas," pawns of their governments. They had no problem lifting glasses with their country's ambassadors, because they were all on the same side. They saw themselves as junior caudillos and generalissimos, and they came to Rio, not so much to found a coherent inter-American student movement, but to act as living spray deodorants for their despotic regimes.

By far the majority, however, were what we would now call "dissidents." So far as I know, no Latin American freedom fighter has ever criticized the United States for not even caring enough about them to think up a word for them. But they should! Why is it we waited for the courageous anticommunists before we came up with the term "dissident"? We let our south-of-the-border antifascists languish all those decades there with no descriptive term for them except "those against the government"!

By far most of the delegations were composed of dissidents. Many of them had done time in political prisons and even torture chambers. The Argentine delegation risked their lives to flee Juan Peron's Argentina. The Peruvians were no better off under dictator Manuel Odria. The Cuban delegate was a communist who opposed his government. We in our delegation were the five Americans who were the least surprised when Fidel Castro seven years later handed the island over to Moscow.

Delegates snub the ambassadors

Back to the opening night that never was: when the delegates heard they were supposed to socialize with the ambassadors of all those illegitimate regimes, they said to hell with it and walked out. The bewildered ambassadors showed up and sheepishly lolly-gagged around the empty ballroom.

I felt terrible that anybody as important as an ambassador had to be publicly snubbed by students from his country. And there was a whole room full of them! My Brazilian hosts, who were, after all, the ones being most directly rebuffed by the walkout, just shrugged and said: "Forget about it. Stuff like this happens all the time around here."

When the formal sessions got underway the next day, we got another education in the internal workings of our sister republics of the Americas. The rhetoric was overheated and never-ending. We Americans sat there feeling like ice cubes in a volcano, nursing our feeble notions of resolutions, proposals, motions, parliamentary procedures, points of order, and the like. The notion of our dealing together with issues that affected "students—students," as our leader Bill Dentzer kept framing our mandate, remained, as Winston Churchill said about Sovietized Eastern Europe, "unbroken even by a star of hope."

Latin American dictatorships denounced

The written agenda of the various delegations looked well crafted: illiteracy, students' rights, academic freedom, freedom of the press for student newspapers, release of faculty members and students from political prison, protection of "huelgas estudiantiles" (student strikes) against brutal police oppression, and always, of course, "el anti-imperialismo yanqui," which meant "anti-Yankee imperialism."' That meant us. In practice, however, the Rio Conference was nothing but one hands-and-glands speaker after another, denouncing his and all the other Latin American dictatorships and demanding "la justicia—justice!"

One Argentinian delegate—his name was Tonelli—got so impassioned describing his imprisonment and torture that he simply lost it, went into a cataleptic fit, and had to be carried off the rostrum by his fellow Argentine veterans of Peron's prisons.

The gobernistas were game enough, but they were drowning in a pool of contempt from the freedom-loving dissidents. It became increasingly uncomfortable as an American delegate to sit there knowing that all the Latin American dissidents viewed us as either mostly or partially responsible for their people's plight—as well we, or at least our elders, were.

The Nicaraguan delegate, a gobernista from the time of Anastasio Somoza, stood up and tried to persuade the enraged assembly that "working from the inside" was the better way to bring down dictators. He came up with some kind of analogy about a huge tree that nobody can chop down right away, but "if enough people keep chopping and chopping. . . ."

Gradualism meets cold reception

It was the gradualist approach, or, as an accommodationist political scientist might say, "constructive engagement." That young man was lucky to get out without getting his neck wrung.

The Latin Americans were astounded to see our prepared agenda and materials totally devoid of any references to student strikes. They thought we and the Canadians were wimps when we tried to explain we didn't need them.

Only in Japan would an executive write in a report, "Sorry. At this point I got drunk."

I must admit, however, that, while not drunk, I got meaningfully distracted by Carneval, which was raging at the time, and the heat and the fatigue and the surreal, Fellini-film texture of it all. Even though I knew there were problems with their attitudes about the United States and its dominance in this hemisphere, I wasn't ready for the depth or intensity of the anti-American feeling. Bill Dentzer fired one of our interpreters when we caught him translating "Soviet satellite states" as "Democracias Populares," or "People's Democracies."

The last act of the 1952 Inter-American Congress of Students in Rio was to vote on the location of a "permanent secretariat" where the valiant labors of our two weeks would be continued toward the ultimate betterment of student life throughout the Western Hemisphere.

It's no secret that when husbands and wives pretend to be arguing about things like salt-shakers and toothpaste caps, they're really seizing upon those ostensible surrogate issues to unleash the hostilities that lace through their marriage. Likewise, pretending to argue about the location of a permanent secretariat was really nothing but a surrogate fight over who wins this thing; the anticommunist democracies of the United States and Canada and our corrupt gobernista allies, or the Marxist "justice" bloc.

Communists win the day

It was close, but the communists won and we lost.
It was decided that the Permanent Secretariat would be in Cuba.

I'm still willing to wager that if, at that instant, the U.S. State Department had been informed that the Inter-American Congress of Students in Rio had voted to locate their Permanent Secretariat in Havana, Cuba, they'd have all said, "Great. Now we can watch it and control it."

Wrong. This was a communist victory long before anybody heard the name Fidel Castro. With all the levers and buttons located in Cuba, there was nothing the truly democratic forces could do.

The last line in the movie *The Longest Night*, which was the 1960s treatment of the sinking of the *Titanic*, was, "The *Titanic* has been stricken from the British registry."

With the triumph of the anti-American, procommunist forces in Rio, the whole notion of a student movement linking the Americas was stricken from the NSA registry.

Was it a calamity? We felt like it at the time; but at that time the only democracy south of the border was Costa Rica.

Today, the only dictatorship is Cuba!

Ruth Hagy Brod and NSA

Ruth Hagy Brod, the patron saint of NSA, produced the enfabled "College News Conference"[3] on the ABC Network in those years and, shortly after the Rio Conference, managed to book General Omar Bradley on the show. He'd been a teacher at one time, and Ruth figured he'd pick up on our experiences in Rio and put them to work on behalf of the United States.

Ruth made sure I, as a member of the Rio delegation, was on that particular edition of the show.

I had just been inducted into the Army, and I was sufficiently Army-broken to be awfully uncomfortable sitting there on TV in the uniform of a buck private inquisitioning General Omar Bradley. The show went well.

What happened afterward went nowhere.

Ruth knew that we NSA students were in earnest. Alas, the popular impression of American students was that of a ribald band of beer-drinking, football-watching, panty-raiding young rowdies.

The communists were shrewdly aware that, in the Third World, the graduating class would instantly become one-third of the literate population.

We pleaded with General Bradley to help us contact the makers and shapers of the American government to take note and get behind what we students were trying to do.

He didn't get it.

But the Soviet Union collapsed anyway!

Barry Farber is a national sydicated talk radio host. He has edited a daily newspaper, been a foreign correspondent, and writes a nationally syndicated general interest newspaper column. He speaks sixteen languages. (See p. 596 for extended biography.)

END NOTES

[1] See Dentzer, p. 315, and Ingram, p. 576.

[2] See Secondari (Rogers), p. 599.

[3] See Ruth Geri Hagy and "College News Conference," p. 1084.

PICTURE CREDITS: *Then:* c. 1953-54, College News Conference (Richard Murphy). *Now:* c. 1980s, syndicated radio talk show host (Author).

NSA DELEGATES AT THE 1952 RIO CONFERENCE. From left: Barry Farber (U. of North Carolina); Brazilian translator; Bill Dentzer (Muskingum C., OH), NSA President; Avrea Ingram (Harvard), NSA International V.P.; Herb Wright (NAACP Youth Division). Helen Jean Rogers (Catholic U.) was absent when the photo was taken. (Dick Murphy)

NSA European, Asian and Latin American Teams, 1950-51

NSA's international representatives initiated in the summer of 1950

During the summer, thirteen NSA observers and representatives were sent on various missions to Europe, and one each was sent to Southeast Asia and the West Indies. Commissioned with detailed instructions and limitations, a team of ambassadors was appointed by the staff to visit and report on the student unions and student life. They were:

- British Isles—Billie Wright, Fisk University
- Scandinavia—James Garst, UCLA
- Benelux and Germany—Claude Salomon, Colorado A&M
- Italy and Switzerland—Hector Corral, Loyola of Los Angeles
- Yugoslavia and Austria—Gerald Maryanov, Columbia University
- Middle East—William Polk, Harvard
- Africa—William Strasburg, Ohio Wesleyan
- South East Asia—James Grant, Harvard
- West Indies—Fred Flach, Cornell

Maryanov's assignment was diverted to the task of opening a Paris office for NSA, and he didn't make the trip to Yugoslavia and Austria. The trip to Yugoslavia was subsequently undertaken by Frank Fisher of Harvard. Grant and Flach were technically not part of the team, which included, in addition to those listed above, an executive group consisting of Erskine Childers, Bill Ellis, Bill Holbrook, Rob West, and Gene Schwartz.

Preliminary reports published at the Third National Student Congress at the University of Michigan, August 23, 1950

- James D. Garst, *Report on Scandinavia.* Covers universities and national student unions in Denmark, Finland, and Norway. 16 pages.
- Claude Salomon, *Report on France.* Universities and national unions of students. 12 pages.
- Gerald S. Maryanov, *Report. NSA Office in Paris.* 6 pages.
- William E. Strasburg, *Report on Africa.* Nigeria. 7 pages.
- Fred Flach, *Carribbean Report.* Puerto Rico, Dominican Republic, Haiti, Jamaica, Cuba. 3 pages.
- Billie M. Wright, *Report, United Kingdom.* 6 pages.
- James P. Grant. *Southeast Asia.* Indonesia, Burma, Indo-China, Hong Kong, Malaya, Siam. 8 pages.
- William Holbrook (U of Minnesota), Eugene G. Schwartz (CCNY), Robert L. West (Yale). *Report on the Second World Student Congress, August, 1950.* Statement to the Congress and appendices.
- *Instrument, NSA European Team, Summer 1950.* 8 pages.

Mimeographed and bound reports of Harvard International Commission/NSA representatives

- Francis D. Fisher. *Students in Yugoslavia, 1950.* Covers student organizations, universities and student conditions. USNSA, August 31, 1951.
- Francis D. Fisher. *General Report on Students in South and Southeast Asia.* United States National Student Association, International Commission, Cambridge, Mass. Covers universities and student conditions in the Philippines, Indonesia, Malaya, Burma, India, and Afghanistan.
- James P. Grant. *The Student in Southeast Asia.* October 1950. International Student Information Service, International Activities Committee, Harvard Student Council. Covers student movements and conditions in Indonesia, Burma, Indochina, Hong Kong, Malaya, and Siam. (See p. 512.)
- Melvin A. Conant, Jr. *Report on Southeast and Southern Asia.* U.S. National Student Association and Harvard International Activities Committee, July 29, 1951. Covers student activities in Burma, Thailand, Singapore, Malaya, Hong Kong, the Philippines, Indonesia, India, Pakistan, and Ceylon; also, student participation in developmental programs and the ISS presence in Asia.

Mimeographed report of NSA Latin American Team

- Herbert Eisenberg and Helen Jean Rogers. *Report of Latin American Team, United States National Student Association, Summer 1951.* U.S. National Student Association, October 1951. Covers Latin American student organizations in Brazil, Cuba, Mexico, and Paraguay; also Catholic student organizations. (See p. 598.)

Second World Student Congress Observers—Published Reports

- Robert L. West and Eugene G. Schwartz, "The World Student Congress and International Education of American Students," *Higher Education,* U.S. Office of Education, March 15, 1951.
- William Holbrook, reports to the World Student Congress appearing in the *Agnes Scott News,* Agnes Scott College, Atlanta, GA, October 25 and December 6, 1950; January 10 and 17, 1951. (See p. 559.)

Editor's note: Anthology project copies of the reports listed here will be deposited in the NSA archives at the State Historical Society of Wisconsin and at the Hoover Institute. The editors of the Anthology have been unable to uncover a complete accounting of NSA's funding sources for these teams. For what is known, see Fisher, p. 511, Wilson, p. 248, and "Covert U.S. Government Funding of NSA International Programs," p. 565.

THE FIRST INTER-AMERICAN STUDENT CONGRESS IN1952

Jan. 25-Feb. 5, Rio de Janeiro. NSA delegates include International V.P. Avrea Ingram and Barry Farber (U. of NC), seated 4th and 5th from left in 1st row; Herb Wright of the NAACP Youth Division, far right in 1st row, and Bill Dentzer, Pres. Helen Jean Rogers (Catholic U.) was absent at time of the picture. (*NSA News* March, 1952).

ORGANIZING A GLOBAL INTERNATIONAL STUDENT TEAM

Editor's note: After it was decided to send an international team of thirteen students to individually represent the NSA in various parts of the world and to observe the Second World Student Congress in the summer of 1950, and more later in 1951, more than twenty students had been given such assignments. The 1950 staff committee, under the leadership of Bob Kelly, NSA President, and Erskine Childers, International Affairs Vice President, developed a detailed eight-page "Instrument. NSA European Team, Summer 1950" to formalize in writing their "objectives, organization, and mode of operation"; also an orientation plan and bibliography for preparatory reference. Accompanying these were a "Fact Sheet" that served as an overview of their job description. The Objectives as stated in the Instrument and The Fact Sheet are reproduced below.

Objectives

The basic objective of the NSA European Team has been stated by the Staff as follows:"To participate in the non-partisan activities of the world student community, in order to promote international understanding and fellowship among the students of the world."

From this derive four main objectives:

(1) To attend the World Student Congress, sponsored by the International Union of Students, as observers and as spokesman for the students of the United States.

(2) To present an accurate picture of life in the United States and of the American educational system, and to refute distorted allegations concerning American education and student life.

(3) To gauge the reactions of the various National Unions of Students that can be contacted, and of individual student leaders, to the declarations of the Second National Student Congress concerning the ideal international student organization, and to obtain ideas and suggestions concerning the means of achieving this ideal.

(4) To gather data and information leading to programs of practical activities between the NSA and the students and student organizations of the rest of the world.

NUS Liaison Representative Fact Sheet

I. Who Is Who

a. British Isles - Billie Wright of Fisk University
b. Scandinavia - James Garst of UCLA
c. France & North Africa - William Kennedy of Georgia
d. Italy & Switzerland - Hector Corral of Loyola of Los Angeles
e. The Low Countries - Claude Salomon of Colorado A & M
f. Yugoslavia & Austria - Gerald Maryanov of Columbia University
g. Middle East - William Polk of Harvard
h. Africa - William Strasburg of Ohio Wesleyan
i. South East Asia - James Grant of Harvard
j. West Indies - Frederic Flach of Cornell

II. What Is to Be Done

a. Gather information on NUS program and services
b. Observe NUS structure, finance and administration
c. Obtain information on other national student and youth groups
d. Gauge reactions to the Illinois Congress resolutions on international relationships

III. How It Can Be Done

Your job is to gather information in line with the objectives and to provide information about NSA and the United States when this is necessary. There seem three sources of information available to you: 1) Statements, resolutions, and other written documents, 2) Personal observation of conditions and 3) Direct conversations with informed persons. Utilize all three sources in your work.

The Orientation Plan contains a general outline of specific information to obtain. Do not restrict yourself to this outline; it is merely suggestive and any information you can obtain will be valuable to NSA. Before you provide information, make sure it is accurate. The extensive bibliography noted in the orientation plan will provide a valuable reference file. Don't hesitate to draw on your personal experience but by all means read and master the material provided.

IV. Chain of Command

You have been selected by the National Staff to serve as an NSA International Representative this summer. Because the Secretariat of the IUS invited NSA to send only three or four representatives to the World Student Congress, you will not definitely be going to Prague. As a result, there will be two classes of International Representatives—yourselves, the NUS Representatives and the WSC Observer-Delegation who will visit various places in Europe as a unit prior to their departure for Prague.

Your immediate superior will be Erskine Childers, who is chairman of the Observer-Delegation. He is empowered to direct your day-to-day activities and arrange your itinerary in the geographic area assigned to you, whenever he deems it necessary. In the absence of instructions from him, you will be on your own.

V. Your Obligations

1. Keep a daily diary noting the places and persons visited, materials gathered and your personal observations.
2. Conduct yourself always as a responsible representatives of the American student community.
3. Make weekly reports of your activities and your proposed itinerary for the week ahead to the Paris office of the Association.
4. Keep a running itemized account of all your expenditures.
5. Clear all your a public statements with the Chairman of the Observer-Delegation.
6. Observe the limits of your personal tour budget.
7. Prepare a thorough written report of your activities and findings together with a compilation of the materials you have gathered at the conclusion of your tour and before October 10, 1950.

VI. Your Expenses

NSA will provide you with:

1. Eastbound transatlantic passage by air or ship to the Netherlands and westbound passage by ship to New York.
2. An allowance to cover food and lodging computed at four dollars per diem while abroad.
3. A travel allotment for use in getting to and within the geographic area assigned to you.

Total amounts will vary in each case but under no circumstances should your budget be exceeded. Shape your activities and mode of living to conform to the budget.

VII. Places to Visit and People to See

1. NUS [National Union of Students] headquarters and Officers of the countries in your area.
2. The Ministry of Education in each country.
3. Headquarters and officers of student and youth groups in your area. Youthserving groups should be included.
4. The U.S. Embassy, Consulate or Information Service in the area.
5. Leading campuses and student government offices.

SECTION 4

Student Aid and Relief Programs

CONTENTS

Wellesley College News

SERVICE FUND ISSUE, NOVEMBER 3, 1947

SHARE YOUR GOOD FORTUNE

AN OUTPOURING OF GENEROSITY on U.S. campuses is typified by this headline (11/3/47)

Wartime and postwar college students brought to campus America's long tradition of voluntary assistance programs through the charitable works of community chests, and religious and other agencies. They also responded to programs for young Americans to go abroad and offer practical assistance for agricultural, technical and other training needs in less developed nations.

Many student leaders went on to work for these organizations, the government, and the United Nations.

The prominence of the World Student Service Fund (WSSF), on many campuses and nationally, is highlighted by Bill Allaway (University of Illinois), who was 1948–49 Vice Chairman for International Affairs of the Illinois Region, later to direct the Universoty of California EducationAbroad program He was drawn into the postwar student relief programs through his experiences in the Student Christian movement and the World Student Christian Federation. His story is one of a number illustrating how NSA provided student Christian movement leaders a vehicle by which to broaden their outreach (see also Bill Ellis, Part 1, and Bill Miller, Part 4).

WSSF, the U.S. affiliate of World University Service (WUS), began to operate in the United States as WUS in 1951. Jane (Wilder) Jacqz, who was a leader in NSA at the University of California at Los Angeles (UCLA) in 1947–48, joined the staff of World University Service. She was later a senior advisor to the UN development program. In 1953 she wrote about how the funds raised by WUS on more than 700 U.S. campuses went "to help students to help themselves" around the world. WSSF, and then WUS, had the endorsement and active support of NSA from the time of the Chicago Student Conference in 1946.

From student mutual assistance in 1950 to the Peace Corps in 1961

In 1948, President Truman's inaugural address advanced as "Point Four" a proposal to pool the world's technical know-how to strengthen economic and social improvement in underdeveloped areas of the world.

Dick Murphy (University of North Carolina), 1952–53 NSA President, connects a 1950 NSA proposal for a Truman-inspired Point Four Youth Corps to the day in October 1960 when the concept emerged as Kennedy's popular Peace Corps proposal in a midnight speech at the University of Michigan. George Carter (Harvard and WAY)., who led the first overseas Peace Corps project, is remembered.

U.S. students also sought to meet such challenges independently. In one such effort, the International Development Placement Association (IDPA) was launched in 1952 by a group of former NSA, Students for Democratic Action and Student Federalist leaders, and soon gained the support of NSA. Its founder, Douglas Kelley (Berea College), tells about this unique Peace Corps predecessor. Peter Weiss (St. John's, MD), later to found a leading trade mark firm, was its Executive Director and shares some recollections, as does Tom Hughes (Carleton), who later became President of the Carnegie Endowment for International Peace.

Building Bonds of Friendship Through Relief and Aid

NSA Puts Weight Behind WSSF Plans

Students INTERNATIONAL ACTIVITIES Bulletin

Campuses Rally for Overseas Relief

Five Sections Proposed for NSO in U. S.

Money-Raising Campaigns Reported Leading Drives For Foreign Student Aid

'Junior Year Abroad' Programs Feature Study in French, Swiss, Italian and Mexican Universities

Daily Bruin

WORLD NEWS PAGE THREE

Bruins assist world students

World Student Service Fund to provide needed clothes, food, medicine for Europeans

The Daily Reveille

Kitchen Emphasizes Benefits of WSSF

WSSF Backed By LSU Staff

Faculty Show Tomorrow at 7

Wellesley College News

SERVICE FUND LAUNCHES DRIVE TO BUILD WORLD OF TOMORROW

Pix from World Student Service Fund Show Poverty of Italian Students

THE CAMPUS CHEST AS EDUCATOR...

Fans Contribute Over $3,000 To WSSF at Georgia Game

The Tech

Money-Raising Carnival Planned By NSA To Aid War-Torn Universities

Military Formal To Be Held In Walker

THE TOOLS OF GIVING

A Handbook for Student Fund Raisers

UNITED STATES NATIONAL STUDENT ASSOCIATION

RELIEF TO STUDENTS IN NEED was a central fund-raising theme on U.S. campuses before, during and after the war. It was an era during which significant sums of foreign aid flowed from religious, fraternal and charitable organizations in the U.S. NSA lent formal support to the World Student Service Fund, U.S. arm of World Student Relief and principal channel for student aid (See p. 622), which distributed funds throughout Europe, South America, Asia and Africa. (From the top, clockwise: *NSA News* 11/49; *Bulletin* of the NSO 4/15/47; *Daily Reveille*, LSU, 3/11/47; *Daily Bruin*, UCLA 12/2/46; *Wellesley College News* 11/4/46; "Italian Students," *Temple U. News* 11/14/47; "Campus Chest," NSA *Student Government Bulletin* 11/1/52; *The Technique*, GA Tech 12/10/48: *The Tech*, MIT 3/18/52, "Tools," NSA handbook, 1953.

Campus Chests and World Student Service Fund

idpa

TRAINED PERSONNEL for TECHNICAL ASSISTANCE WORK

Here is a program of human assistance for the underdeveloped areas

European Students Help Reconstruct

INTERNATIONAL ACTIVITIES

Places Open for Seminar, Workcamps in Europe

The Role of American Students in the Students Mutual Assistance Program

NSA to Place DP Students

50 Colleges Adopt Purchase Card Plan

Area Committees Increased to Six

An Experiment

Groups Establish Secretariat

NSA Opens Drive for DP Scholarships Today

Phi Beta Kappas Pick Sixteen New College Members

Daily Pennsylvanian

I - F Council Approves Bowdoin Plan For Assistance To Foreign Students

Students From Europe and U.S. Exchange Jobs

100 From Institute Go Abroad Next Summer; Interviews Start Mon.

Technology NSA Commended For Foreign Student Summer Plan at Madison Convention

Baker Named To National Advisory Board

BAKER BATS, WROBLEWSKI CATCHES

LENDING A FRATERNAL HAND to the rebuilding of Europe and third world countries emerging from colonialism inspired many college students. By going abroad to work camps and traveling to Asia, Africa and Latin American countries where they could help share technology and craft, they learned about other cultures while building good will. Top: The International Development Placement Association (IDPA, p. 627) and, above right, Students Mutual Assistant Program (SMAP, p. 635) were two student-run agencies founded in the early fifties. Left: "Workcamps," *NSA News* 3/49; "Reconstruct," *Daily Californian*, UC Berkeley, 10/1/47. Placement and exchange programs brought foreign students to the U.S. From top: 1948 Displaced Persons Act opened doors for refugee placement, *NSA News* 11/48; *Harvard Crimson* 11/7/48; *Daily Pennsylvanian* 3/16/49. Bottom: *The Tech*, MIT 11/28/50, 10/1/48.

Experiences in Student Exchange, Training and Technical Assistance

My introduction to a career in international education

1. The World Student Service Fund and NSA

William H. Allaway
University of Illinois
Vice-Chairman for International Affairs, NSA Illinois Region 1948–49

In the fall of 1942 I began my studies at the University of Illinois, although I was already slated for military service. I had an introduction to Henry Wilson, longtime general secretary of the University of Illinois YMCA, and I soon made my activities base there. The following March I left for the army and served for thirty-five months, wasting my time in technical training for which I was unqualified and contributing little to the war effort. I returned to the university frustrated at the way in which war wastes human lives, even though I had been fortunate in not being put in danger.

I get the international virus

In the summer of 1946, I returned to the Illinois School of Commerce, scarcely realizing that other fields existed, but I soon changed to international relations. I also returned to activities at the Y. In the fall, I was asked to help raise funds for the World Student Service Fund (later World University Service). I met Bill Kitchen, WSSF's executive secretary and longtime leader in the New England Student Christian Movement, who inspired me to believe that there was a constructive contribution I could make after three wasted years. He asked if I would travel for WSSF for a semester, and I agreed if he could find a way for me to get to Europe to see student conditions at first hand.[1]

Thus, in the summer of 1947, I became a delegate to the World Conference of Christian Youth in Oslo and the conference of the World Student Christian Federation in Lundsberg Skola, Sweden. I traveled to Europe on the *Marine Jumper* and back on the *Marine Tiger.* On the ships, I met Bob Smith, who in September became NSA's first international vice president, Charley Boggs, who became a fellow traveler raising funds for WSSF, and, on the return voyage, a host of others who had been to the International Student Service conference in Denmark and/or the World Student Festival in Prague. In Europe, in addition to attending the meetings in Norway and Sweden, I visited student medical facilities in Leysin, Switzerland, and Combloux, France, with the help of World Student Relief. We all had extraordinary opportunities to see both the need and the opportunities to serve that were presented by the postwar student world.

Back home, some students from the *Jumper* were planning to attend the NSA Constitutional Convention in Madison. It turned out that meetings of the executive committee were scheduled during Christmas vacation at International House at the University of Chicago, my backyard. I attended some of the meetings, and Bob Smith got me interested in NSA's international program. Meanwhile, in the fall, I took my experiences to colleges and universities in the Midwest, Southwest, and California, during several months in which I familiarized myself with Greyhound schedules and learned how to raise money from students for WSSF. Returning to University of Illinois in January, I was put on the University's delegation to the NSA Illinois Region conference, where I was elected international vice chairman. We set up an international travel office in the Illini Union, and I was able to get Phil Stoddard,[2] who was developing an interest in international activities, involved in the office and NSA. We had problems because the student senate had no budget and the dean of students was opposed to NSA. We had to go directly to the president to get the money to pay NSA dues!

I was elected to the student senate in the spring of 1948 and was named a delegate to the 1948 NSA Congress in Madison. I was also appointed chairman of the campus chest for 1948–49, and organized a small group to go to a Netherlands Student Travel Bureau (NBBS) work camp that summer. Phil Stoddard and I both went to the work camp and afterwards went to Utrecht, where his father, George D. Stoddard, president of the University of Illinois, was giving the keynote address at a UNESCO-sponsored conference. Dr. Stoddard later became chairman of the U.S. National Commission for UNESCO and chairman of the Executive Board of UNESCO.

The First National Student Congress, Madison, 1948

The Czech coup had occurred early in 1948 and had received the support of the International Union of Students (IUS). NSA had responded by suspending relations with IUS. While there were still those at the 1948 Congress who thought that NSA should affiliate with IUS, at this stage they were marginalized.[3]

A vignette that I recall from the 1948 Congress concerns the attractive young folk singer Robin Roberts, who was a delegate from Sarah Lawrence. She charmed us all in the evenings on the campus with her singing and playing.

In the elections for the 1948–49 staff, Ted Harris was elected president, and Dick Heggie, Gene Schwartz, and Rob West were elected vice presidents. Al Lowenstein, an able but unknown sophomore from the University of North Carolina, had been nominated for secretary. At that point, one of the more liberal delegates from New York City put Robin Roberts's name in nomination. Confusion ensued, because she was sure to beat Al! There was a conspicuous period of stalling. Someone then came up the aisle to me and asked if I would give a seconding speech for Helen Jean Rogers from Mundelein College, who had helped to organize the Congress. I was delighted to support her, as we had worked together in the Illinois Region, so she was duly nominated and seconded. Al Lowenstein withdrew in her favor, and she was elected.[4]

Campus chests

Rob West and I hit it off well, and when he and Bill Kitchen of WSSF asked me to write a handbook for NSA on campus chests, I agreed to do so. The handbook, entitled *Relief Efforts in the University Community*, was published toward the end of 1949.

For a variety of reasons, campus chests became popular in the late 1940s. Student governments were experiencing growing requests for assistance from local, national, and international causes. Community chests saw money being raised by students and thought they should have their share. Also, new organizations with real needs, like the United Negro College Fund, appeared on the scene.

WSSF had initiated the pattern of giving on many campuses and wasn't particularly pleased by being submerged in a campus chest. However, if one was developed, it was forced to participate. The University of Illinois led the way in giving priority to student concerns in allocating campus chest funds, which meant that WSSF didn't lose out at Illinois.

Many institutions were starting campus chests and needed both a philosophy and practical assistance. I thought that it was an excellent type of information for NSA to provide. The handbook set forth the rationale for student giving, proposed priorities for student-related organizations to support, and described ways to raise money. One reason that this was important for NSA was that it was urging assistance to students who were displaced persons (DPs), and who needed guarantees of university placement and scholarship assistance before they could leave refugee camps in Europe.

We had a strong campus chest at Illinois, with 50 percent of the funds going to WSSF. The university president set up a university committee on DP students, chaired by the director of admissions. This group made provision for at least ten DP students during the first year, with the board of trustees providing tuition scholarships and housing groups taking responsibility for room and board. In addition, a large number of Chinese students was unable to return to China after the Communist victory. The campus chest cooperated with the dean of foreign students in setting up an emergency fund of $1,000. Many of these activities were inspired and carried out through the close cooperation between NSA and WSSF.[5]

The Second National Student Congress

I am not quite sure how it happened, but the University of Illinois student senate found itself hosting the second National Student Congress, from August 23 to September 3. We had built considerable support for NSA in the senate and had a good crew of volunteers to help with the logistics. By then, Phil Stoddard was chairman of the Illinois Region's international affairs commission, which was helpful in recruiting assistance from the region.

There were 389 delegates, 117 alternates, and 44 observers at the Congress. Work was done through four commissions, administration and finance, educational problems, international affairs, and student life. These broke down into roundtables and committees.[6]

At the opening session of the international affairs commission, in which I was most active, three roundtables were created: interchange of persons, educational reconstruction and relief, and interchange of information and ideas. In the afternoon, the full commission received information on "students in today's world" and NSA's channels for international student cooperation. This included UNESCO, International Student Service, International Union of Students, and information from representatives of nine National Unions of Students. With this background, we moved to the roundtables and then on to policy issues.

While the issue of the IUS had been resolved earlier with regard to membership, there was still the issue of whether there should be any form of communication and/or cooperation between NSA and IUS. There was a strong bloc against it, which included many Catholics, and a strong bloc for, which included most of the liberals. As a result of an impasse in the National Executive Committee (NEC) over who should chair the session of the international commission dealing with the IUS issue, I won the dubious distinction.

I called the meeting to order at 1:10 P.M., called for a ten-minute break at 4:30 P.M. for the rewriting of a resolution, and adjourned at 7:15 P.M., just in time for the delegates to get supper at the cafeteria. It was quite a day!

My records contain three resolutions with indications of their disposition. The first was as follows:

> Re: Criteria for an International Student Organization
>
> Whereas the USNSA desires to promote international understanding and fellowship, and
>
> Whereas attempts to establish a truly representative international organization of world students are directed toward that end,
>
> Be it resolved that the USNSA will always regard with interest and favor, and will continue to investigate any attempts directed toward the eventual establishment of a representative international organization of the world student community which the USNSA believes should include the following characteristics:
>
> 1. It should be broadly representative of the students of the world and not merely those of one area, and should not exclude students on the basis of color, creed or political belief.
> 2. Full membership in the organization should be on the basis of representative NUS's alone with a university applicable membership scale representing the number of registered college and university students in each NUS.
> 3. Provisional membership in those countries with an absence of an NUS would be granted to representative coordinating committees for a specified time only.
> 4. Questions of accreditation should be determined by a representative credentials committee, the composition of which had been approved by a majority of voting delegates.
> 5. It should be non-partisan, subordinating ideological differences in its devotion to the service of the common needs of the students of the world.
> 6. It should maintain an autonomous character in any relationship with other international organizations.
> 7. Constitutional autonomy should be guaranteed to each constituent member organization.
> 8. It should maintain internal procedures in which the will of the majority would prevail, but the rights of the minorities would be fully preserved, both before and after the reaching of decisions.
> 9. There should be publicity broadly representative of member sentiment and administered through an internationally representative secretariat.

Commission action: passed unanimously.

Next was a resolution on relations with IUS:

> Whereas the IUS does not at present incorporate the characteristics of a representative international organization of the world student community, which characteristics the USNSA believes should include: [This was followed by a listing of the nine points cited in the first resolution]
>
> Therefore Be It Resolved that the USNSA, regretting that the IUS does not now incorporate these desired characteristics, does not desire affiliation with the IUS at this time, and
>
> Be It Further Resolved that in accordance with Article 9, Section A, Paragraph 1, of the Constitution, the National Executive Committee be instructed to take no action on any official affiliation with any international student organization prior to the Third National Student Congress, nor any action clearly committing the association to affiliation.

Commission action: passed unanimously with two abstentions.

The real battle was joined in resolution 3D/104, which was presented with a majority report, 3D/104A and a minority report, 3D/104M. Resolution 104A read as follows:

> Whereas the USNSA desires to promote international understanding and fellowship,
>
> [I have the following handwritten as a second Whereas:] Whereas the IUS is one of the channels open to students in Eastern Europe:
>
> Be it resolved: that the USNSA will continue its efforts of cooperation on specific projects of a non-political nature through all available channels, <u>including the IUS and its member NUS's,</u> to implement any international policy and program of NSA which is designed to meet the needs of the American and world student community and is consonant with the stated aims of the Association.

Commission action: Vote: Aye—47; Nay—10.

Resolution 104M read:

> Be it resolved: That the USNSA will continue its efforts of cooperation on specific projects of a non-political nature through all available channels, <u>excluding the IUS because the policies and programs of the IUS are not consonant with the policies and programs of the NSA,</u> to implement any international policy and program of NSA which is designed to meet the needs of the American and world student community and is consonant with the stated aims of the Association.

Commission action: Motion by Holmes (Wisc.) Seconded. To amend d./104A by deleting underlined phrase in d./104A

and adding underlined phrase in d./104M.
Vote: Aye—23; Nay—37.

In spite of the mandate to explore areas of cooperation and efforts to have an NSA presence at IUS meetings during the next few years, I know of no concrete results flowing from these resolutions other than the exchange of some information. However, it seemed important at the time to not close the door to possible communication and cooperation if we were to get past the current antagonisms between the East and the West.[7]

Another memorable event of the Congress was convincing Erskine Childers to run for international vice president. We were successful in twisting his arm, but I am sure that he regretted it when he was confronted with the impact of the *Svalbard* incident. Bill Ellis helped to rescue the stranded students by finding them space on a gymnasium floor at City College of New York.[8]

Years later, when I went to Stanford as assistant dean of men, Erskine's major adviser scolded me for my part in getting Erskine to run, because Erskine never returned to finish his degree! While Erskine may have regretted his failure to complete his degree, it did not prevent him from making a distinguished career in the United Nations, and making significant contributions to reform in the UN through his writings in collaboration with a colleague, Sir Brian Urquhart.[9]

Postscript

My experience in the YMCA, WSSF, and NSA set me on a path toward a career in cultural exchange. In the fall of 1949, President Stoddard was named chairman of the U.S. National Commission for UNESCO. He asked me to be his assistant until the State Department could appoint someone to the post. This I did, partly in Urbana and partly at the Chicago Council on Foreign Relations, until I started a master's degree in education at Illinois in January.

In June, I had an opportunity to prepare a report for a travel organization on study opportunities for American students in France. I went to France and stayed for awhile, finishing my thesis there. Phil Stoddard and I joined a team from the U.S. National Commission for UNESCO that included Rob West and Ernie Howell, which looked into youth activities (or the lack thereof) in UNESCO. I'll let Phil tell that story.[10]

During that summer, I attended the ISS conference near Rotterdam while Bob Smith and Ted Harris were on the ISS Geneva staff. In December, I represented ISS at the Nice conference, which was the first General Conference of the International Association of Universities (IAU). I later became active in IAU through my work at the University of California. I am currently a deputy member of IAU's administrative board, and helped celebrate IAU's fiftieth anniversary at their meeting in the year 2000 in Durban, South Africa.

Although no jobs opened up in Europe, I did spend some time working with refugee students in Austria on behalf of World Student Relief. When I saw Dr. Stoddard in Paris in June, he persuaded me to finish my master's degree in the summer of 1951, so home I went. In the fall, I began to work in the newly created Chicago office of the Institute of International Education, which ultimately led to a doctorate and to my designing and implementing the University of California's Education Abroad Program.

None of this would have happened if it had not been for the vitality and selfless devotion of students in the postwar era, who did what they could to put the world to rights again. I took constant inspiration from friends in NSA, WSSF, the YMCA,[11] and mentors at the University of Illinois. I hope that the current generation of students who are following in our footsteps through the United States Student Association will derive the same rich benefits we did in creating USNSA and working with it during its early years. The search for peace and international understanding still goes on.

William H. Allaway was the founding Director of the University of California Education Abroad Program and has had a lifetime career devoted to international educational exchange, working with many agencies and universities. He has also held various positions with the International Association of Universities, most recently as University of California delegate to various of its General and Mid-Term Conferences, and currently Chairman of its Task Force on the Internationalization of Higher Education.

ENDNOTES

[1] For background on WSSF, see p. 622.

[2] See Stoddard, p. 655.

[3] See background on the IUS, p. 538. Also see "NSA Breaks with the IUS," p. 188, and Birenbaum, p. 583.

[4] For more on the First Congress, see Heggie, p. 200.

[5] *Editor's note:* Another organization (formed in 1948) that NSA supported strongly, the National Scholarship Service and Fund for Negro Students (NSSFNS), relied heavily on campus chest support. See p. 463.

[6] For more on the Second Congress, see Schwartz, p. 235.

[7] *Editor's note:* This policy was to become the subject of considerable debate, and eventual revision, during the Third Congress and the year following under the presidency of Al Lowenstein. By keeping NSA actively engaged in the oversight of international student developments, it led NSA to send observers to the August 1950 IUS World Student Congress (see p. 559), and

later to initiate the Students Mutual Assistance Program (SMAP) in Stockholm, in December 1950, and to take part in the formation of an active West European student union cooperative group (Cosec) in 1951. See Lynch, p. 273, Eisenberg, p. 526, and Dentzer, p. 301. See also Almanac, p. 1129.

[8] For more on the *Svalbard* incident, see Meagher, p. 665, and album, p. 667.

[9] See Childers, p. 517. [10] See Stoddard, p. 656.

[11] *Editor's note:* See Miller, p. 717, on the Student Christian Movement. For the significant role of the YM/YWCA in the formation of the U.S. delegation to the Prague Congress in August 1946, and the Chicago Student Congress, see pp. 68, 159. Also Allaway, p. 729, "NICC Leadership," p. 733.

PICTURE CREDITS: *Then:* c. 1953-54, College News Conference (Richard Murphy). *Now:* c. 1980s, syndicated radio talk show host (Author).

THE SPIRIT OF WSSF AS SEEN ON THE U.S. CAMPUS

Los Angeles City College, *Collegian* 4/5/48 (Excerpts)

World Students Join For Financial Relief

European and Asian recovery depends not only upon the rebuilding of industry and agriculture but also upon the rebuilding of educational institutions. And, more vitally important, the physical and moral rehabilitation of students.

The American organization devoted to rebuilding the lives of students and restoring educational opportunities wherever needed is the World Student Service Fund. It is the American over-all student relief organization, sponsored by the National Intercollegiate Christian Council, University Commission of the Council of Church Boards of Education, B'nai B'rith Hillel Foundations at American Universities, the National Students Association, and many others.

International Agency

All funds raised by W.S.S.F. are administered by the World Student Relief Fund, an international agency with headquarters in Geneva, Switzerland. One of the basic principles of the agencies is "impartial service to all students and professors in need, irrespective of race, religion, or country."

The job of rebuilding shattered universities began with the end of World War II. The project is one which will require millions of dollars and years of time. Buildings and libraries must be restored and laboratory equipment furnished.

University of North Carolina, *Tar Heel*, 11/2/47 (Excerpts)

An Editorial

WSSF, four letters strung together, letters of which you've seen a good bit around campus recently, and of which you'll see a lot more this week. What do they mean?

In words these letters mean World Student Service Fund— a unique relief organization of American students and professors for the assistance of students and professors in war-devastated countries.

To many thousands of European and Asiatic students, striving in the face of almost insurmountable odds to gain the education they must have if they are to lead their nations and the world to peace, these four letters mean life and hope, the opportunity to gain the knowledge for which they've been thirsting during the long years of war, the chance to live long enough to use that knowledge.

And to us here at Carolina—What do these four letters mean to us? Is this merely another "worthy cause" to which we'll contribute if we get around to it? Or is this appeal from our fellow students and professors something about which each of us should be deeply concerned, something we should support with our whole beings rather than with a half-hearted contribution?

WILLIAM H. ALLAWAY

Early Background and Military Service. I was born in 1924 in Oak Park, Illinois, and served for almost three years in the army during World War II.

Education. I completed my B.S. and M.A. in education degrees at the University of Illinois, and a Ph.D. at the University of Denver. I have been awarded honorary degrees from the University of Bergen, the University of Bordeaux, the University of Stirling, and the University of Sussex. I also received the Silver Medal of the University of Lund and the gold Medal of Honor of the Complutense University of Madrid.

Career. My career has been primarily in international educational exchange, with brief periods with the World Student Service Fund, the U.S. National Commission for UNESCO, World University Service, the Institute of International Education, the University of Kansas, and Stanford University. I became the founding director, in 1961, of the University of California Education Abroad Program. By the time of my retirement from the Directorship in 1989, approximately 1,200 students were studying annually in one hundred universities in thirty-five countries, in a program noted for its academic distinction.

I have been active professionally in many organizations, including the American Center for Students and Artists in Paris, European Association for International Education and NAFSA: Association of International Educators. I was Chairman of the Board (1978-83) of the Council on International Education Exchange and member of the Executive Committee of the Inter-University Centre of Post Graduate Studies in Dubrovnik.

My experience with the International Association of Universities began when I represented the International Student Service at the Constitutional meeting in Nice in 1950. Since then I have represented the University of California at five General Conferences and two Mid-Term Conferences. In 1993, I served as editor of the issue of *Higher Education Policy* devoted to academic mobility. (I am currently a deputy member of the Administrative Board and Chairman of the Task Force on the Internationalization of Higher Education.) Peace issues are a major concern of mine, and I am a member of Pax 2100 and the International Peace Research Association.

Family. In 1952, I married Olivia W. Foster, and we have two sons and a daughter.

*NAFSA was founded in 1948 as the National Association of Foreign Student Advisors. In 1963 it changed "Advisors" to "Affairs" and in 1990 was renamed as NAFSA: Association of International Educators. (See www.nafsa.org; also *IIE News Bulletin*, 4/1/48 and 10/1/48.)

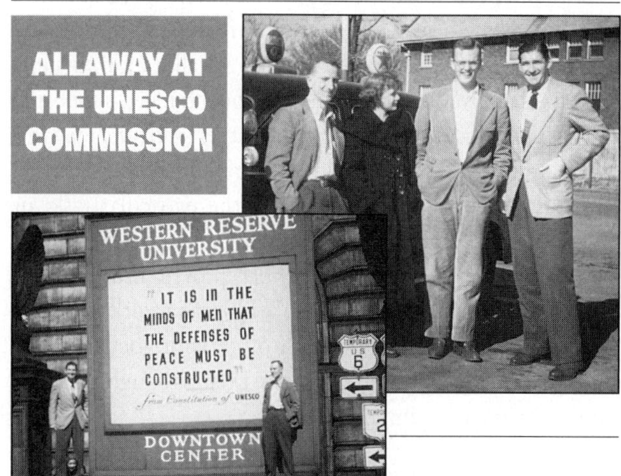

1948 UNIVERSITY OF ILLINOIS International Commission members in Cincinnati for a US Commission for Unesco meeting. Top, from left, Ralph Hartshorn, Charlotte Allen (See p. 658), Philip Stoddard (See p. 655), Bill Allaway. Bottom, from left: Bill Allaway, Ralph Hartshorn.

Contributions to WUS may mean the difference between success and failure

2. Students in Need Are Helping Themselves

Jane Wilder Jacqz
UCLA. Delegate, NSA 1947 Constitutional Convention
World University Service (Formerly WSSF) Field Staff

Editor's note: This article first appeared in NSA's Student Government Bulletin and Report, *Vol. 2, No. 2, November 1953.*

Every year students on more than 700 American campuses are urged to contribute to World University Service (formerly World Student Service Fund, Inc.) in order to help students at universities in countries impoverished by war or natural disaster.

It is natural that many American students in giving to WUS want to know not only what they're giving for but also what these students whom they're helping are doing to help themselves. Contributions to WUS's international program are often made at considerable personal sacrifice—giving comes hard these days—and the question is a valid one.

What are students in Asia and other parts of the world doing to help themselves?

The answer is "almost everything!" World University Service raises funds for just that purpose—*to help students help themselves*. Students who get help through WUS in their efforts to secure a higher education and improved living conditions don't count on WUS to do the whole job, but only a part of it. Nonetheless, gifts to WUS are important for many reasons—and often they are essential. An allocation to some Asian project from the WUS international budget, supported by contributions from American and other students, may initiate a project and stimulate local efforts to raise supplementary funds or materials to complete the particular task; or international allocations may complete a project where work has been begun, but where local efforts proved insufficient to do the job. Moreover, within the WUS framework, students in needy countries also help each other with goods-in-kind and services, not only through cash gifts, although these, of course, are the most important.

How students help themselves

Students in need help themselves in a variety of ways, which is testimony not only to the terrible handicaps they must surmount to carry on their studies but also to their ingenuity and perseverance.

Even in the area of mutual education the efforts of students to help themselves have been most rewarding. Conferences like the conference of experts on student health problems held in Singapore have borne great fruit. Others are valuable for planning or for breaking down the barriers between groups and peoples.

Students raise funds

Students help themselves in more ways than by organizing services. In many needy countries substantial funds have been raised through appeals to students and professors. Some of the projects supported by local student contributions, like the Japanese sanatorium, the Gauhati student center, and the Tambaram sanatorium, have been described above. Others worth noting include a student ward in the Patna hospital for which funds are being sought locally. In Indonesia the WUS group sold more than 200,000 postcards showing university scenes to raise money for the local program. At the Affiliated College for Women in Karachi, where there are five hundred students, funds were raised through a concert. In Bombay, university students gave more than $500 for the WUS international program as a sign of their sincere interest in helping others as they in turn were helped. After Mr. Aitken's visit to Delhi students at the seven colleges of the University of Delhi, acting at the request of the college principals, in one week raised $700 for the WUS program; among the colleges giving $100 was the Refugee Camp College where students are in desperate need.

More often, WUS international allocations fulfill a "pump priming" function—they enable local groups of students and professors to turn to their governments or to the university authorities for supplementary aid which will ensure completion of a worthwhile project in the field of student welfare. The government of India has given land for the Delhi student center, as has the government of Pakistan for the proposed Karachi hostel. In Turkey the government contributed $2,500 towards the cost of construction of a student sanatorium, supported in part by WUS. $2,500 has just been granted by the government of Pakistan to support a national conference of students and professors planned by WUS.

Among the best examples of this kind of aid is the Bombay hostel which accommodates 150 graduate students. Three years ago it did not exist. World University Service made an initial grant of $3,750—a beginning, but not enough to finance a major undertaking like this one. Prompted by the WUS offer, the government took interest in the project and completed the hostel with such a generous grant that it proved possible to use the initial WUS allocation to stock a special library of books chosen by professors of graduate courses in the Bombay area. At many university centers in Asia, health services were formed by university and government authorities only after WUS initiated work in this field. In many places WUS cooperates with government bureaus to maintain a project like the student ward at the Reed Chest Hospital in Shillong, the student ward at Tambaram in South India, the French refugee scholarship program, and the international rest center at Combloux, France, where 700 students a year receive rest and medical care. In Munich, Germany, this year the WUS committee will administer a hostel for refugee students built by a $17,500 grant from the Ford Foundation to the U.N. High Commissioner for Refugees.

That students not only help themselves but help each other is another essential aspect of the WUS idea. Within countries, groups aid each other. In Greece, students have formed a Sanatorium Visiting Committee to cheer student patients; in Japan, a team of 35 students spent twelve days at hard labor to help clean and restore Kurume University's Medical Faculty, devastated by the June floods.

Students in one country help students in another

Among the donor countries the United States is foremost, of course, but cash contributions are also forthcoming from Britain, Australia, New Zealand, the Scandinavian countries, Switzerland, and several others. Many of these cash gifts are given at great personal sacrifice—at Central College in Pella, Iowa, a Lithuanian refugee student contributed $10 to aid the Japanese university community because of the help WUS had given in bringing him to America. Hospitality is a form of giving which must not be overlooked. America sponsored a DP student resettlement plan; so did Canada. Japanese students offered two scholarships last year to students from Southeast Asia. In Norway and Sweden student groups have offered similar foreign student scholarships and resettlement possibilities. Finally, goods-in-kind are exchanged. Prefabricated houses for student centers in Israel and Egypt have been supplied by students in Finland where wood is easier to export than cash. And in Japan funds were raised to send a microscope to Rangoon, Burma, which has contributed three times to help build a student sanatorium! In Indonesia, Frank Fisher, traveller on behalf of NSA, witnessed many students working part-time and full-time to earn enough to live. One typical university student, in addition to his studies, a position in the national student union, and various responsibilities in organized labor, teaches eight high school civics classes a week and corrects his students' papers and examinations. More than 80 percent of Indonesia's high school teachers are university students! Many colleges in Pakistan, India, and other Asian countries operate on two shifts so that students may study at night and work by day.

It is the lucky students who find jobs. . . .

Organized self-help efforts

What are student needs in the impoverished and wartorn areas of the world? Stated simply, they include the need for medical attention and care, the need for housing, the need for food and clothing, funds to pay university fees and the costs of room and board, the need for educational equipment, and the need to know that someone, somewhere, cares.

Students working together are doing much to meet these needs. In the field of student health, for example, are efforts like these: Japanese students, encouraged by a grant from the international budget of World University Service, have worked for three years to build a student sanatorium at Inada-Noborito outside Tokyo. This sanatorium—now well under way—will be the first of its kind in a country where between three and six percent of the university students suffer from TB! During the summer of 1952 and 1953 teams of students worked to clear the ground on which the sanatorium is being raised. And at universities throughout Japan students and professors, despite their own great personal needs, contributed funds to help build the sanatorium. In India students in the Madras area sold blood donations to raise funds for the WUS student ward at the tuberculosis sanatorium at Tambaram.

Student efforts to improve health conditions

But perhaps the most significant development in recent years among student efforts to improve health conditions has been the initiation and expansion by WUS groups of student health services. Following an experts conference on student health held at Singapore, Malaya, in 1951, students urged as a priority requirement the development of student health services at university centers. Since then, largely through WUS efforts, medical facilities for examination and minor treatment have been initiated or supplemented at Rangoon, Burma; Aligarh, Bombay, Calcutta, Delhi, Madras and Santiniketan, India; Djakarta, Djokjakarta, and Surabay, Indonesia; and Dacca and Karachi, Pakistan. In almost every center students receive an X-ray and a physical examination at little or no cost to themselves. Local efforts are almost entirely responsible for the successful operation of these services, although contributions from the WUS international budget have gone to purchase X-ray equipment and medical supplies.

In the field of student housing, a good bit has been done through self-help efforts, although considerable capital investment is required to build student hostel accommodations in great demand throughout Asia. In Calcutta WUS supports a hostel which accommodates one hundred students, many of them refugees, without charge of lodging. Meals have been organized by the students accommodated on a cooperative basis so that they cost but a few rupees per month. In Delhi, local efforts have won a grant of land from the Indian government on which an international student center is to be raised, including accommodations for Indian and foreign students, common rooms, and a library. In Assam the WUS group has almost completed construction of a student center—for which more than $1,000 was raised through contributions from local students. A business man contributed the wood for the doors, windows and shelves in the Center, and an electrical firm installed the wiring and fixtures at half cost. In Karachi plans have been completed for a student center to be built on land contributed by the Pakistan government.

Food and clothing are also supplied in many instances of self-help activity. Cooperative canteens where meals can be purchased at low cost have been organized in Greece and elsewhere. Students at Djakarta in Indonesia purchase supplies from a cooperative store, and students in Gauhati, Assam, buy snacks at a converted military hut.

Grants to help pay living costs and university fees meet an urgent need. In Karachi students raised nearly $400 at two benefit film showings and turned the money over to a committee awarding refugee students scholarships. In France more than 300 refugee students a year depend upon WUS (with funds supplied in part by the French government) for grants to pay their university fees.

Educational equipment and books in Europe and Asia

Throughout parts of Europe and Asia, *educational equipment* is scarce and hard to get. Books are more precious than food to many students seeking to complete their education— a meal can be skipped; a textbook is essential. At the University of Athens and the University of Salonika in Greece, students, using equipment contributed through World University Service, mimeograph hundreds of sets of lecture notes each year. In Djakarta and other Indonesian university centers thousands of texts have been reproduced by WUS groups and sold to students at just enough cost to pay for fresh supplies of paper and ink. Many of these "books" are fine examples of craftsmanship with complicated diagrams and illustrations one would not expect to find in mimeographed materials.

In India at Delhi, Aligarh, and Calcutta extensive lending libraries of textbooks have been organized by student groups so that books can be made available without charge and returned for use by others.

The average Asian student, for example, is not a member of an organization or particular group which receives aid from an institution. Nor are his parents wealthy enough so that financial difficulties do not trouble him. How does he get by—? How does he pay for his room and board, university and examination fees, or buy his books?

Life is hard throughout Asia and these vital questions are not easily answered. In Japan, for example, a student cannot possibly live and study on less than 10,000 yen or about $30.00 per month. This seems little to us, but it must be remembered that board and "lodging" (a mat on which to sleep) in a private lodging house costs at least 6,000 yen per month; there are almost no university accommodations available, although the few which do exist are less expensive. Fees range from 7,200 to 10,000 yen per year in government schools and are twice that in a private institution. Some government loans are available, but the competition even for admission to the university is unbelievably stiff, when one recognizes that of the 2,200,000 students now graduating from high school at least 500,000 will want to go to college or a university while the largest number which can be accepted is 126,000! Many students take college entrance examinations a dozen or more times before being admitted to study in an institution of higher learning.

In South Korea, where $1.00 is officially valued at 60 hwan, tuition alone at colleges like Suk Myung Women's College—a cluster of shacks on a campus-in-exile in Pusan—is 12,000 hwan a year. Not many Korean girls can afford to go to college! And many who do go are without lunch or a decent place to sleep.

Throughout Asia the story is the same. The costs of living are high, accommodations and materials are scarce, and income is low.

Students in need—like their American counterparts—find jobs. In Japan more than 300,000 students must work in order to stay in school; of this number more than 50,000

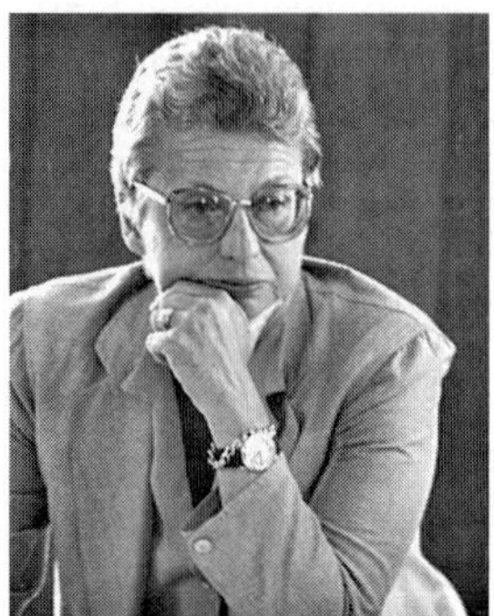

Jane Wilder Jacqz was an adviser to the United Nations who was instrumental in setting up community programs in Africa and Latin America to protect the environment and advance development.

must earn enough to cover all expenses. One typical Japanese student works five hours a day every day in a snack bar and earns 7,000 yen per month. Another may find employment as a milk delivery man, in a printing company, or selling fountain pens on the street. A third, who must also support her family, has been fortunate enough to find work as a proof-reader on an English-language paper—she attends a college where laboratory equipment was desperately needed.

This is the picture. These are the efforts. Do they pay off? The answer is thousands of times over "yes." Asian students are not only the leaders of tomorrow—they are the leaders of today. So urgent is the need for trained leadership in countries which have suffered from hundreds of years of domination and economic deprivation, no effort to forward that leadership can be considered too great. Let us always keep in mind notes such as this one—within two years, from among a graduating class of two hundred at the University of Calcutta, two students were full professors and a third a Deputy Magistrate!

Contributions to WUS may mean the difference between success and failure to students' efforts to help themselves!

PICTURE CREDITS: *Then:* c. 1948-50. *Now:* Aspen, c.1981, China c. 1993 (Margot Jacqz)

February 23, 1949 — TEMPLE UNIVERSITY NEWS

WSSF Official to Describe Plight Of Students in Europe and Asia

Dr. Wilmer J. Kitchen, executive secretary of the World Student Service Fund, will speak at a dinner tonight in Mitten Hall Clubroom at 6 P. M. Students may obtain tickets at the Dean of Students office.

Dr. Kitchen has just returned from a tour of student projects in Asia and Europe supported by the WSSF. Director of the Fund for the past two years, Dr. Kitchen has reinforced his deep interest and concern for students

Movies Will Im... 'Brotherhood'

Wilmer J. Kitchen
Executive Secretary, WSSF

BILL KITCHEN traveled widely on college campuses across the country during his tenure as WSSF Executive Secretary, and worked closely with NSA. The Temple University News article above (2/23/49) reports, "Dr. Kitchen has just returned from a tour of student projects in Asia and Europe supported by the WSSF. Director of the Fund for the past two years,Dr., Kitchen has reinforced his deep interest and concern for students abroad by first hand knowledge of student problems gained on his trip.

"A graduate of Penn State College and Union Theological Seminary, Dr. Kitchen has been active in college work throughout his professional career, having served as Chaplain of Penn State College, National Student Service Secretary for the YMCA in New England, and the first Executive Secretary of the New England United Student Christian Movement.

"During World War I, Dr. Kitchen was attached to the Army Medical Department. In the more recent global conflict, Dr. Kitchen headed a special mission to American-born Japanese in Relocation Centers."

CALIFORNIA BRUIN
UCLA

California NSA Delegates Steer Meet to Success

California played a major part in determining the future policies and organization of the newly-established National Student Association at the Madison constitutional convention, which UCLA

Six weeks

Six weeks preparation for the convention paid off as California secured the adoption of their draft preamble to the constitution, inclusion in the constitution of their faculty-advisory council plan, a provision for proportional representation on the executive committee, and a general endorsement by the whole convention of the California stand on almost every controversial issue.

California's two representatives on the constitutional committee were Jane Wilder of UCLA and Milt Dobkin from USC. New California-Neveda-Hawaii regional cochairmen are UCLA's Dick Hough and Cal's Dick Heggie, with Hans

(Continued on page 13)

Campus Rallies to World Student Aid

Wilder Quits 'Rep' Post; Vacancy Creates Problem

The question of whether a special election will be held or a presidential appointment made to fill the vacancy was unanswered at a late hour yesterday, following disclosure of the resignation of representative-at-large Jane Wilder from her Student Executive Council post.

Miss Wilder's resignation, laid yesterday afternoon on the desk of ASUCLA President Ken Gallagher, came as a complete surprise to student government officials. Miss Wilder disclosed that she is leaving her post in order to accept the position of National Field Secretary of the Students for Democratic Action.

Offers No Clue

An examination of the ASUCLA constitution offered no clue as to how the vacancy can be filled. Section 2, para. 3 of the document provides that in the event of a vacancy in an elective office, it "shall be filled in accordance with the provisions of the by-laws."

The by-laws are vague on the subject.

Miss Wilder, elected representative-at-large last spring, previously served as Welfare Board chairman. She was also chairman of the Constitutional Committee, which drew up the present ASUCLA document, and was a delegate to the recent NSA convention at Madison, Wis.

FOUNDATIONS FOR A CAREER in international organization began for Jane Wilder at UCLA with leadership in student government, NSA, Students for Democratic Action (SDA) and World Student Service Fund. *Daily Bruin* (4/6/45) banners interest in war-time/post-war student relief; UCLA initiatives in NSA (9/15/47) and Wilder move to take job as Executive Secretary of SDA (10/21/47)

JANE WILDER JACQZ

Early years: Born in Rindge, N.H., Mrs. Jacqz attended the Westlake School for Girls in Los Angeles. Her mother, Margaret Buell Wilder, wrote the book *Since You Went Away,* the basis for the 1944 film of the same name, a World War II drama that takes place on the home front. She received an Associate of Arts degree from the University of California at Los Angeles. Mrs. Jacqz suspended her studies in 1947 to become executive secretary of Students for Democratic Action, an arm of Americans for Democratic Action. She moved to Geneva in 1949 to work for the World University Service.

Career highlights: Jane Wilder Jacqz was an adviser to the United Nations who was instrumental in setting up community programs in Africa and Latin America to protect the environment and advance development. Mrs. Jacqz dedicated much of her career to strengthening nongovernmental organizations, or NGO's. Randall Curtis, director of conservation finance and policy at the Nature Conservancy, called her "the godmother of the environmental fund movement," which brings community groups to the table in countries where they often have no role.

After retiring from the United Nations in 1999, Mrs. Jacqz worked with the conservancy and others to strengthen the Global Environment Facility, a multilateral body that finances projects aimed at protecting natural resources.

"She made a great and enduring contribution to improving the human condition," said Maurice F. Strong, an adviser to the secretary general of the United Nations. Mr. Strong was the secretary general of the 1992 Rio Earth Summit.

Before joining the United Nations as a senior adviser in 1985, Mrs. Jacqz was a vice president of the African-American Institute and a consultant to the Ford Foundation and the Rockefeller Foundation. She was the executive director and vice president of the Aspen Institute for Humanistic Studies from 1979 to 1983.

Family: In addition to a daughter, Margot Jacqz, she is survived by a son, Christian Jacqz, of Watertown, Mass., a sister, Abigail Foss, of Carmel, Calif., and three grandchildren.

Mrs. Jacqz was the widow of Henri Georges Francois Jacqz. She died in New York on March 24, 2002. She was 74.

[Note: Photos of Jane Jacqz, and material for this biography, were provided by her daughter, Margot Jacqz.]

Two World Wars Inspired Student Aid Efforts

Relief

Continuing the work of relief which it has conducted since 1920, ISS has, since 1939, through the European Student Relief Fund, and since 1943, through World Student Relief, undertaken a large-scale relief action for

Student victims of the war

Ruins of Warsaw University.

Books - Study Materials - Medical Supplies
Foods - Scholarships

have been given to thousand of

PRISONERS OF WAR • REFUGEES • INTERNEES
STUDENTS OF THE OCCUPIED COUNTRIES

Today WSR continues its action; its efforts are now chiefly concentrated on Eastern Europe and the Far East:

$1,500,000 were spent in 1945-1946
$2,125,000 are needed this year

ISS needs your support • Help it to act!

1920-1946

IT'S YOUR CHANCE
TO GIVE THEM A CHANCE

In 1949 ONE HUNDRED colleges and universities in the U.S.A. gave TWO HUNDRED student D.P.'s a chance to finish their education. To date, mutual satisfaction in the experience has been reported.

From the President of a sponsoring college:
"We are delighted with our D.P. student and the way in which he has made himself at home in this community. The Governor (of the State) delivered our Commencement address last June and heard me announce that through a student initiated and student conducted effort, we would have a D.P. in our student body. The Governor returned his honorarium to be applied to the expenses of the student. When the D.P. arrived he met the Governor. We are giving this as much publicity as we can because we have an interest in the D.P. problem."

From a Student D.P.:
"It is impossible to describe in words the feelings of gratitude which I would like to convey to you for the new life I have found here. My reception in the faternity house was friendly and I feel like a member of a great family and nothing reminds me that I have been an alien. I am using every hour to get along and catch up with the class as I arrived late. Soon I hope to be completely 'on the ball.'"

In 1950 HUNDREDS of colleges and universities in the U.S.A. can give HUNDREDS of Student D.P.'s a chance to begin a new life in a new land.

1950

Woodcut by Frans Masreel

WORLD UNIVERSITY SERVICE

PROGRAM APPEAL

1954-1955

"All races, peoples, and classes today demand a share in power and wealth." This, says Arnold Toynbee, is the major problem of our time. Poverty, disease, ignorance, and despair—which haunt the vast populations of South Asia, Africa, and the Far East—must be conquered. The most powerful weapon in this fight is educated leadership.

World University Service believes that in helping students to help themselves, we not only help them but we help ourselves. For their future is our future—and educated leadership is the cornerstone of the future for all peoples.

1954

AN UNBROKEN LINE OF AID PROGRAMS. Top left: International Student Service (ISS) for World Student Relief (WSR), 1946. Top right: World Student Service Fund (WSSF) for displaced persons, 1950. In 1951 ISS, WSR and WSSF merged into the World University Service (WUS). Above: WUS 1954 U.S. appeal brochure on 700 college campuses.

WUS and WSSF

From *The Intercollegian,* April, 1951

World University Service is a relatively new international organization formed by the merging of International Student Service and World Student Relief last January.The headquarters offices of the new organization are at Rue Calvin, Geneva, Switzerland..

WUS is the international body with which the World Student Service Fund of the USA is affiliated. WSSF works with and through WUS in programs devised to aid needy students and strengthen the sense of a community of university men and women in all parts of the world, wherever friendly international contacts are still possible. Last year American students and friends contributed $528,767 to this work of aiding our fellow students in other countries. . . .

The new organization enjoys the sponsorship of the leading international student organizations: Pax Romana, World Student Christian Federation, World Union of Jewish Students, and many national unions of students. R.H. Edwin Espy, Executive of the National Student Council of YMCA, is treasurer of WUS. . . .

There is too much suffering in the world—too many wounded and dead, too much hatred and chaos. Hostilities can only increase this intolerable burden. Americans can participate in a world-wide ministry of healing and encouragement in our universities through our contributions this academic year to the World Student Service Fund.

Wilmer J. Kitchen
Executive Secretary, WSSF

3. Student Leaders Form IDPA: Peace Corps Predecessor

Douglas Kelley, Berea College, KY
Founder and Acting Chair,
International Development Placement Association, Fall 1951

Even if you feel twenty years younger, when you hit your seventies you occasionally consider how quickly generations of men and women slip away and are forgotten. And if you've made some efforts to make things better, you hope some contribution or two you've made will turn out to have lasting merit. For me the matter concerns one of the origins of the Peace Corps. Two or more histories of the Peace Corps cite as a forerunner of the 1961 Kennedy creation the "International Development Placement Association," a national organization which I put together in the fall of 1951, after my wife, Mary, and I graduated from Berea College, "where the mountains meet the Blue Grass," in Kentucky.[1]

Here is the story, including the connecting links to the Peace Corps.

During my senior year at Berea College, while serving as national chair of Students for Democratic Action (the student division of Hubert Humphrey's Americans for Democratic Action [ADA]), I corresponded with University of Michigan graduate George Shepherd, then studying for a doctorate at the London School of Economics, and with students Julius Kiano (from Kenya) and Nelson Jonnes [sic] at Antioch College, Ohio. The four of us, and Berea classmate Galen Martin,[2] agreed there ought to be a program that would place people in modestly paid jobs with indigenous organizations and governments in Africa, Asia, and Latin America.

Looking for a zeal for humanitarian service

The people placed, we proposed, would be idealists with a zeal for humanitarian service but without the ethnocentric, holier-than-thou attitudes that for decades had characterized all too many Americans and Europeans in their contacts with the darker-skinned two-thirds of humanity. We had had experiences in Quaker-sponsored voluntary work camps where students contributed their labor to inner-city community improvement projects, but now we were thinking of entry-level jobs for teachers, nurses, agricultural extension and community development workers, and cooperative organizers—people who would live and work closely with their host country coworkers.

My exploratory efforts began with a June 12, 1951, three-page, mimeographed letter sent from my home address in Lansing, Michigan, to some sixty-five youth and student leaders in many states. The letter focused on the need for skilled, motivated people to work in Africa, but in a few weeks we were including Asia and Latin America as well.

While I pondered a choice between a post-BA year at Oxford (where I'd been accepted by Ruskin College, a British trade union institution) and a tentative offer of a very challenging job managing an African farmers' marketing cooperative in Uganda, my draft board informed me that since I hadn't yet served Uncle Sam, I couldn't pick either of those options—I was told not to leave the country.

Seeking board members and funds in the fall of 1951

So the fall of 1951 found me living at Pendle Hill, a Quaker adult education center in Wallingford, outside Philadelphia. It became my congenial three-month home base while I proposed—and sought board members, endorsements, and funding for—a new organization. After first using the name International Development Association, we concluded it should be called the International Development Placement Association (IDPA). It would be a non-profit agency, to recruit highly motivated applicants with entry-level skills needed in widely assorted jobs with indigenous organizations and governments in developing nations. IDPA would recommend carefully selected applicants to those institutions and government agencies. Accustomed to the tight budgets of nonprofit organizations, we did not anticipate being able to have IDPA itself employ, transport, or pay medical or other expenses of the recruits—as Peace Corps would later do.

As potential IDPA board members I sought primarily experienced leaders of U.S. youth and student organizations; several of us had been involved in the 1947 formation (at a national convention in Madison, Wisconsin) of the National Student Association, whose first president, Bill Welsh, was from Berea College.

Two highly important recruits for the IDPA leadership were Harris Wofford (the first president of Student World Federalists,[3] in later years a JFK staff member and Peace Corps Associate Director; college and university president; U.S. Senator from Pennsylvania; and in the 1990s, CEO of the Corporation for National Service) and Frank Wallick (my predecessor as chairman of the student division of ADA; in later years, editor of the United Auto Workers' very effective Washington newsletter).

Foundation for World Government provides initial grants

Harris Wofford landed urgently needed foundation grants (from Stringfellow Barr's Foundation for World Government), to get us started. Frank Wallick was soon an assistant to Congressman Henry Reuss (D., Wisconsin), who was to play a crucial role in the procession toward the 1961 triumph of the idea. I felt Frank Wallick's two-year experience as a Brethren Service Committee volunteer working at subsistence pay in pre-Communist China would be valuable on the IDPA board; most of us then had very limited overseas experience.

In an effort to gain widespread support for the IDPA concept, I sought and, to my great satisfaction, received ringing endorsements from Supreme Court Justice William O. Douglas, TVA's former Chairman David Lilienthal, and International League for the Rights of Man (and American Civil Liberties Union) founder Roger Baldwin. Justice Douglas's statement appears with this unit.

I regret not having had a tape recorder along when I appeared for a fall 1951 New York appointment with a Ford Foundation program officer, whom I hoped would be supportive of a major grant that could greatly enlarge our tiny beginnings. My twenty-two-year-old's impassioned pitch was listened to respectfully, but at the end of something like forty-five minutes, the program officer's unforgettable exact words were: "There simply aren't enough young Americans wanting to do that kind of thing." He was a middle-aged white male, whose name I failed to record. Over 163,000 Americans have now served in the Peace Corps.

I thought of myself as an organizer, not a potential IDPA administrator, and had decided to begin graduate study of economic development planning in January, 1952 at the University of Chicago (in the Planning Program headed by Rex Tugwell and Harvey Perloff). Thus I was pleased that Barrington Dunbar, who had been a UN Children's Fund representative in Haiti, was available to serve as IDPA's first executive secretary. After I left for Chicago, Clifford Dancer was elected board chair at a December 1951 IDPA board meeting, and attorney Peter Weiss was soon chosen as IDPA's executive director, based in a new office in New York, which then moved to the Carnegie Endowment International Center, two blocks from the United Nations.[4] IDPA seemed to be on its way; my only remaining role was to serve in 1953 as an IDPA advance "scout" in Gandhi's chosen central India village, Sevagram, after a hitchhiking-to-India adventure. Harris and Clare Wofford's book *India Afire* had inspired my interest in Sevagram, where Gandhi and his Nai Talimi Sangh (New Education Organization) had established a training center for teachers and rural development workers.

By 1954, 502 potential volunteers and eighteen pioneering placements

By the time IDPA began folding, in 1954, for lack of major financial support,[5] office files held applications from 502 potential volunteers. Eighteen pioneering men and women, most of them under thirty, had been placed in a wide variety of teaching and social service positions in India, Nigeria, Indonesia, Uganda, and elsewhere. Government agencies, nonprofit organizations, and universities in several additional countries were requesting applicants. In his 1980 book *Of Kennedys and Kings: Making Sense of the Sixties,* Harris Wofford noted (p. 253) that "I.D.P.A. proved that the assignments were waiting and young Americans were ready, but that placement and recruiting was unduly costly when done on a small scale."

But as the reader knows, that was not the end of the story. In 1955 IDPA board member Frank Wallick and his wife, Ruth, joined the staff of Congressman Henry Reuss (D., Wisconsin). Frank Wallick encouraged Reuss's interest in international volunteerism, and assisted in promoting the "Point Four Youth Corps" bill, which Reuss introduced in the U.S. House of Representatives. Reuss and Senator Hubert Humphrey, with his U.S. Senate "Peace Corps" bill—using that name for the first time—proposed that resources of the federal government should make possible what major foundations had been unwilling to risk doing.

In the 1960 Wisconsin and West Virginia Democratic presidential primary campaigns, Hubert H. Humphrey advocated the establishment of a Peace Corps. In his 1976 book *The Education of a Public Man,* Humphrey recounted how (p. 229), after losing the crucial West Virginia primary to the Kennedy forces, "since I was not to get the presidential nomination, I was determined that Kennedy adopt as many of my proposals as possible." Humphrey "set out to influence his decisions, particularly in the areas in which I could make my greatest contributions: agricultural policies, civil rights, economic development, arms control, and the Peace Corps."

Presidential candidate Kennedy sparks public support for Peace Corps idea

Kennedy staff members also recommended the idea to the nominee.[6] After Kennedy briefly spoke of the possibility—never using the words *Peace Corps*—in a huge rally on the front steps of the University of Michigan Union at 2 A.M. on October 14, public support, especially among young people, was soon widespread and became impressive even to hard-nosed politicians.[7]

"For me," recalls Harris Wofford:

> it was also an old dream coming true. In the late 1940's, I had joined a group of Student World Federalists in proposing a peace force of volunteers to serve overseas in community development projects. In the early 1950's I had collaborated with Douglas Kelley in organizing the International Development Placement Association. (*Of Kennedys and Kings*, p. 253)

Wofford was soon one of newly appointed Director Sargent Shriver's close colleagues in establishing the Peace Corps administration. Sixteen months after I received a most welcome February 18, 1961, come-to-Washington-Monday telegram from Shriver, I left my political science graduate studies at Harvard to be the Peace Corps's first community relations director. In that role I proposed and organized Peace Corps recruiting and support groups ("Peace Corps Service Organizations") in twenty-five U.S. cities and provided Peace Corps staff and volunteer speakers with periodic compilations of talking points and overseas volunteers' human interest stories.

Organizing a crafts-marketing cooperative in West Cameroon

But Washington, D.C., lacked the appeal of serving in the Third World. After I read in the new regulations that Peace Corps "Volunteer Leaders" (unlike "Volunteers") could take dependents with them, my family and I signed up for two years in West Cameroon, south of Nigeria. Based near Bamenda, two hundred miles in from the coast, I proposed and organized a 1,300-member crafts-marketing cooperative, which soon doubled the monthly income of many of its woodcarver, pottery, and basket-maker members. The "Cameroon Handwork Cooperative" at first had its sales shop in a two-room mud-brick house that I rented for $5 a month. A month later, we moved it to a $10 per month, four-room house, and started trying to export; the first order from the UN Gift Shop was a major thrill. At last report the Cameroon Handwork Cooperative is still going strong, in larger quarters, nearly forty years later.

HELPING PEOPLE HELP THEMSELVES

The International Development Placement Association is rendering a significant service in our foreign relations. We of the West have too long and too often gone to the East with a domineering, ruthless, and exploitive attitude. If we are to become partners with the Asians in the works of peace, we must learn to go to Asia with humility and understanding. The International Development Placement Association is one of the agencies that meets this high standard. The men and women whom it sends to Asia will work in the villages, helping people there to help themselves. These emissaries will do more to build understanding between these two worlds than all the wealth and all the military might America can muster.

—William O. Douglas, Washington, D.C., December 6, 1951

Back in New York after the two Cameroon years, one day I noticed a gift counter in Lincoln Center's Philharmonic Hall. Crafts and other items relating to the performing arts were being displayed and sold. I asked the clerk to hand me a pair of basketry-covered musical shakers—which make a tchh-tchh-tchh sound to accompany African drumming. They still bore a Cameroon Handwork Co-op label with the member's name in my handwriting.

The maker of the shakers had been a beggar in a remote village prior to formation of the co-op. But to each monthly meeting in his village he was now bringing a big burlap sackful of his shakers, and receiving payment at a rate twice what any of them could be sold for in his own area. I mailed him a Philharmonic Hall photo postcard—perhaps the first mail he would ever have received. A schoolboy would read it to him: "Your shakers are being sold in THIS BUILDING in New York City. . . ."

Douglas Kelley retired as Director of Extension and Continuing Education for the University of Michigan–Flint. He and his wife, Mary Corsi Kelley, live in Ann Arbor, where he is a Democratic activist and collector/curator of "The Democratic Archive," his private museum of Democratic Presidential campaigns from 1800 to the present.

That elderly villager now had a regular source of income beyond his dreams—and nine successive American presidents, Democrats and Republicans, have proudly supported the Peace Corps idea. Sometimes a good idea works out.

END NOTES

[1] Mary Corsi had already helped me produce a twenty-two-page pamphlet entitled "Bread, Butter, and Brotherhood: Job Opportunities for College Graduates in the Trade Union and Cooperative Movements." See also album, p. 987.

[2] See Martin, p. 983.

[3] See Jonas, p. 761. Also p. 773 on the founding of IDPA.

[4] See Weiss, p. 637.

[5] *Editor's note:* Peter Weiss (see p. 637), IDPA Executive Director, writes in a 2/22/02 letter, "At that time, the tax-exempt section of the Treasury was run by two notoriously right-wing Southern ladies, who decided that IDPA was "just an employment agency" and, as such, not entitled to tax exempt status. That decision became final in 1954 and made it impossible to raise any more funds from foundations.

[6] See Murphy, p. 630.

[7] *Editor's note:* Kelley's observation that Kennedy did not use the term "Peace Corps" in his October 14, 1960 speech serves to point up Kennedy's almost off-hand adoption of the long-nurtured postwar concept for aid to underdeveloped countries—appearing initially as a tactical measure in his evolving presidential campaign—although later he clearly embraced it wholeheartedly in the ramp-up to his administration, and the term was also used in his October 5 "Message to New Voters." The transposition of "Youth Corps" to "Peace Corps" took place in the legislation sponsored by Senator Humphrey the previous June, and was echoed by Congressman Reuss in the House. Humphrey's substantative initiative voiced his understanding that the underlying appeal of such a program went beyond the goal of economic development to a broader yearning of the young people at the time (see p. 632). This yearning was expressed by the NSA's Executive Committee, elaborating on the 1953 NSA Congress endorsement of IDPA, that technical assistance programs were "one of the most important ways of increasing international understanding, cooperation and well-being." Involved World War II veterans and the post-war student world sought practical measures to help secure the peace for which the war was fought. Dick Murphy on p. 630 tells how the idea was kept alive.

PICTURE CREDITS: *Then:* 1951. *Now:* c. 2000 (Both from author).

DOUGLAS C. KELLEY

Education: B.A. in History and Political Science, Berea College, Kentucky; master's degree in journalism from Michigan State and in public administration from Harvard; Ph.D. (Adult and Continuing Education), University of Michigan. Fellowships at Harvard from Ford Foundation, Fund for Adult Education, and Harvard University.

Career Highlights: Retired as Director of Extension and Continuing Education, University of Michigan–Flint, after a forty-year career in public affairs and education, working for the Peace Corps, nonprofit organizations (Ohio Farm Bureau, and the Encampment for Citizenship, Inc.), community colleges and universities in northern New York and in Michigan, a Democratic Member of Congress (Don Hayworth, Mich.), and for two years as Adminstrative Assistant to Lt. Gov. Philip A. Hart. Served in the Kennedy administration as the U.S. Peace Corps's first national Community Relations Director (1962–63), and then as a Peace Corps Volunteer Leader in West Cameroon (1963–65). Also served as U.S. Army medic and news reporter, 1953–55.

Current activities: (1) Serving as campaign manager for State Representative John Hansen in his race for the state senate; and as Secretary of "Educators for Tobacco-Free Investments," seeking to end the huge investments by universities and the TIAA-CREF pension plan in the lethal tobacco industry. (2) Further developing (and finding an appropriate permanent home for) my huge collection of two hundred years of Democratic presidential campaign memorabilia. Portions of the collection, now displayed in "The Democratic Archive," a large building behind the Kelleys' house, have been displayed in university and public libraries and museums in Detroit, Ann Arbor, and Flint, MI; Charlottesville, Staunton and Richmond, VA; and Washington, D.C. (3) Active in American Political Items Collectors (APIC) and was Secretary/Editor of the Carter Political Items Collectors' committee, assisting the National Park Service to create the Carter 1976 Campaign museum.

Family: Married to Mary Corsi Kelley, a Berea College classmate and retired school social worker. (First proposed to her, 1951; asked again successfully, 1978.) Son Peter Kelley is Vice-President for Communications, American Rivers, a nonprofit organization in Washington, D.C. Grandson: Miles Nicholas Kelley, age eight.

SCIENCE MONITOR, BOSTON, MONDAY, APRIL 28, 1952 3

New Development Organization Makes Use of Youthful Talent

By Robert C. Cowen
Natural Science Correspondent of The Christian Science Monitor

New York

Half hidden by the publicity for official programs of aid to underdeveloped areas, a private organization, which may prove an important supplement to the gvernment agencies in this field, has quietly come into being.

Known as the International Development Placement Association, it is manned by a small group of students and young professionals who would rather work in a field where social conscience and world vision are needed than to concentrate only on technical careers.

Help for Uganda

The primary purpose of the new association is the placing of qualified young Americans in technical assistance work. To this end it has the good wishes and endorsement of such leading Americans as United States Supreme Court Justice William O. Douglas: Stringfellow Barr, former president of St. John's College and now president of the Foundation for World Government; and Norman Cousins, Editor of The Saturday Review.

Although it has been in existence for less than a year, IDPA has already begun to attract notice by placing two young experts in assistance work. The first of these, George Shepard, who holds a PhD. from the London School of Economics, was also the first chairman of the board of directors of IDPA. Now, at the request of the Federation of Partnerships of Uganda African Farmers, Dr. Shepard is in Uganda, Africa, putting his knowledge and enthusiasm directly into the assistance work.

* * *

The possibilities for this country are tremendous, explains Dr. Shepard in describing his work, even though the hampering effects of a restrictive colonial policy are still strongly felt. Writing in the IDPA news letter "World Report" he says:

"Almost nowhere else in the world can a little aid go as far as here in East Africa. Restrictions, discrimination, and suppression of African development hem in the African on all sides.

"This discrimination cannot long withstand intelligently directed attack, making any well-qualified assistance to help the Africans overcome barriers to progress in education, economic, and political development go a long way."

Realistic Outlook

The second IDPA placement is Patricia McMahon from Michigan State College, who has gone to India at the request of the Indian Peasant Movement. There she will live for a time in a typical Indian village and by gradually developed friendship and understanding, and by example, help the villagers meet their problems in a way that will be effective and have meaning in their own terms.

* * *

Behind the efforts of the IDPA group is a drive born of the conviction that they can fill a vital and needed function in the world today.

* * *

"The International Development Placement Association is rendering a significant service in our foreign relations," says Justice Douglas in evaluating the work of this new group.

"The men and women whom it sends to Asia will work in the villages, helping the people there to help themselves. These emissaries will do more to build understanding between these two worlds than all the wealth and all the military might America can muster."

Excerpted: *Christian Science Monitor* 4/28/52

1952: IDPA Sends Development Recruits to Asia and Africa

NOVEMBER - DECEMBER, 1952

George Shepherd on Progress in Uganda

George Shepherd, the camera-shy gent on the left, with John Stonehouse and officers of the Federation

varied membership is anxious to initiate, that this capital is only a very small part of what is needed, though at least we have some trucks and stores with which to make a beginning. The inefficiency problem is also still with us, but we have made a start through training programs to educate the officers of the Federation on elementary cooperative principles and practices. The level from which they have

VOLUME 1, NUMBER 1

IDPA BULLETIN

OCTOBER, 1952

Rashtra Seva Dal: An American in India

by Pat McMahon

About ten years ago Rashtra Seva Dal had its beginnings as a volunteer organization with a social service and secular outlook. It began in Maharashtra, and was mainly composed of Indian students who wished to encourage collective social service.

Activities of the group are limited to Maharashtra and Marathi-speaking areas, and are broken up into four overlapping parts: the Shakhas (branches), the Camp, the Sane Guruji Pathak, and the Cultural Squad.

Shakhas operate in cities and villages all over Maharashtra. They hold programs each evening, including game periods and practical training for the younger group, and

VOLUME 1, NUMBER 4

IDPA BULLETIN

OCTOBER, 1953

New Worker for Sevagram

A MONTHLY PUBLICATION OF THE INTERNATIONAL DEVELOPMENT PLACEMENT ASSOCIATION, INC. • 345 EAST 46TH STREET, NEW YORK 17, N. Y. • OXFORD 7-1590

VOLUME 1, NUMBER 3

IDPA BULLETIN

SEPTEMBER, 1953

M. I. T. Graduate Off To Ijebu-Igbo

This month IDPA's first placee in West Africa will begin a two-year teaching stint at Molusi College in Nigeria. How IDPA got M.I.T.-trained Donald Eberly together with three hundred young students in Ijebu-Igbo (Ijebu-in-the-Bush) is a story that might best be told in the order in which it happened.

At the end of January, 1953, a British journal carried an ad for a science teacher and vice-principal at Molusi College,

about to take off for foreign parts. Don got his passport renewal; his visa; his smallpox, typhoid, yellow fever, and tetanus shots. He made arrangements to take his car, a valuable item in this isolated coastal community; he spent the summer studying the area into which he was going, and received helpful letters about Ijebu-Igbo from the principal of Molusi and his English wife. "Conditions are improving at the college," wrote the principal's wife; ". . . no water or electricity available as yet, but underground tanks to store rainwater are the answer to the first, and kerosene and wood for cooking are the answer to the second. But there is the comfort of living in fresh air and solitude amidst surroundings which I, personally, have come to like very much."

". . . And what about the college and the work? The work is the best and the worst—worst because it is never-ending, and the best part of life because it is varied, and because the boys are so eager to learn.

". . . I hope when you come you like the place and the boys and us. Certainly if you want to see Africa without too thick a coating of Europeanisation, you could find it here. And as a teacher you will have the complete satisfaction of knowing you are badly needed—and appreciated."

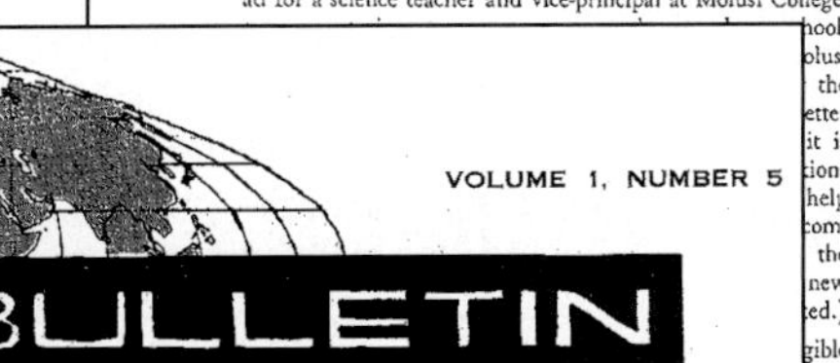

VOLUME 1, NUMBER 5

IDPA BULLETIN

NOVEMBER, 1953

Four to be Selected for Cooperative Training

Special Arrangements Have Been Made with the Extension Department of St. Francis Xavier University at Antigonish, Nova Scotia, to enable four young men selected by IDPA to receive free tuition, board, and room, in a five months program of training and practical experience in cooperative work in the Maritime Provinces of Canada. Upon successful completion of the course, which begins January 10 with one month at the University followed by four months of field work in gram is under the direction of Rev. M. J. MacKinnon, head of the Extension Department of the University, who was a member of the Canadian Government Mission sent out earlier this year to India, Pakistan, and Ceylon to study the cooperative movement as an instrument of economic development in Asia.

The adult education program of the Extension Department began in 1928 when the fishing, farming, and manufacturing industries of the Maritime Provinces were in depression. Today

HIGHLIGHTING ITS ACTIVE PLACEMENT PROGRAM, IDPA published a monthly bulletin during the 3 years until it was denied IRS tax exemption and was unable to raise further foundation grants. From the top: George Shepherd (former U. of Michigan, London School of Economics), working with Federation of Uganda African Farmers (12/52); Patricia McMahon (former U of Michigan) with the Indian Peasant Movement (10/52); Ralph Blackwood (former Ohio State U.) at Sevagram, Ghandi's Basic Education Center in India (10/53); Donald Eberley (former MIT), at Molusi College, Nigeria (10/53); 11/53 announcement of four openings for cooperative work training by St. Francis Xavier U in Nova Scotia to be applied in underdeveloped areas for at least 2 years.

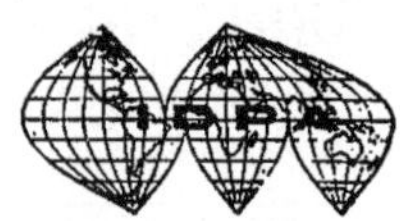

FIRST ANNUAL REPORT

August 1, 1952 — July 31, 1953

International Development Placement Association, Inc.

CARNEGIE ENDOWMENT INTERNATIONAL CENTER
345 East 46th Street New York 17, N.Y.

OFFICERS AND BOARD MEMBERS

As of July 31, 1953

OFFICERS

Clifford C. Dancer, *Chairman* Albert C. Ettinger, *Secretary*
Herbert Eisenberg, *Vice-Chairman* Eugene G. Schwartz, *Treasurer*
Ellen Cammnitzer, *Canadian Representative*

STAFF

Peter Weiss, *Executive Director* Ann Morrissett, *Staff Associate*
Elizabeth Gerson, *Secretary and Office Manager*

BOARD OF DIRECTORS

Stringfellow Barr
Thomas D. Callahan
Ellen Cammnitzer
Clifford C. Dancer
Earl W. Eames, Jr.
Herbert Eisenberg
Albert C. Ettinger
Jonathan Chukwuka Ezenekwe
James Farmer
Murray Frank
William Friedlander
Douglas Kelley
Sanford Kravitz
Kenneth Kurtz
Lewis Mumford
Robert R. Nathan
George W. Overton
Frank L. Parker
Arthur Pratt
Eugene G. Schwartz
Peter Weiss
Robert L. West

ADVISORY BOARD

Roger Baldwin
Scott Buchanan
Dr. Frank G. Boudreau
Rev. Donald Harrington
Mordecai Johnson
Reinhold Niebuhr
Jerry Voorhis
Gilbert F. White

EXECUTIVE COMMITTEE

Clifford C. Dancer
Earl W. Eames, Jr.
Herbert Eisenberg
Albert C. Ettinger
Murray Frank
Eugene G. Schwartz
Peter Weiss
Robert L. West

COUNSEL

Hatch, Root, Barrett, Cohen and Knapp
Peter Weiss

AUDITOR

Seymour S. Zucker, CPA

TO HELP YOUNG PERSONS FIND THEIR PROPER ROLES IN TECHNICAL ASSISTANCE & ECONOMIC DEVELOPMENT PROGRAMS

(From the Preface to the IDPA First Annual Report)

The International Development Placement Association was incorporated on July 31,1952.... IDPA was established to help young persons find their proper roles in programs of economic and social development in the underdeveloped areas. It came into being because no other organization filled this need and because the United States Government and the United Nations would generally not employ young persons in their programs of technical assistance and economic development.

The founders of IDPA made several assumptions about how the organization might carry out such a program. IDPA would announce the program to interested persons and organizations, receive and process applications, screen applicants, refer those approved to organizations which needed them abroad, and let organizations and applicants make their own arrangements for employment, transportation, etc.

It was also originally assumed that it would be best to concentrate the attention of the staff on finding job placement opportunities with local organizations, at the local wage and under local living conditions....

We have found the program vastly more complicated and difficult to execute than was indicated by these early assumptions. Some of these difficulties will be dealt with in the ensuing pages of this report.

We have been using the words IDPA 'recruits' to describe the people we place abroad. Ordinary placement agencies do not use such terminology. It reflects a responsibility which has crept up on us and is slowly changing the outlook for our organization.

We need to do a great deal of research into the conditions which prevail in the countries and localities where we send people. We must communicate frequently, and in detail, with our supporters and potential recruits to maintain their interest. Many of the jobs we turn up do not provide for round trip transportation costs and consequently we are helping the persons concerned raise these funds and are contributing a growing proportion of our own funds towards these expenses. This In turn has involved us in community organizational efforts throughout the country.

It is becoming apparent that IDPA ought to provide some form of training or orientation for the personnel it sends abroad, and steps in that direction are being taken. This also reflects our growing sense of responsibility to the persons being recruited and to the organizations which have asked for them....

During its first full year of operation as IDPA, Inc., the Association has made progress in defining its functions and purposes, located itself in its permanent headquarters, developed procedures and contacts for placement and recruitment and made its first actual placements.... Future reports will tell the story of the men and women at work in Asia, Africa, and Latin America....

CLIFFORD C. DANCER *Chairman*
PETER WEISS *Executive Director*
September, 1953

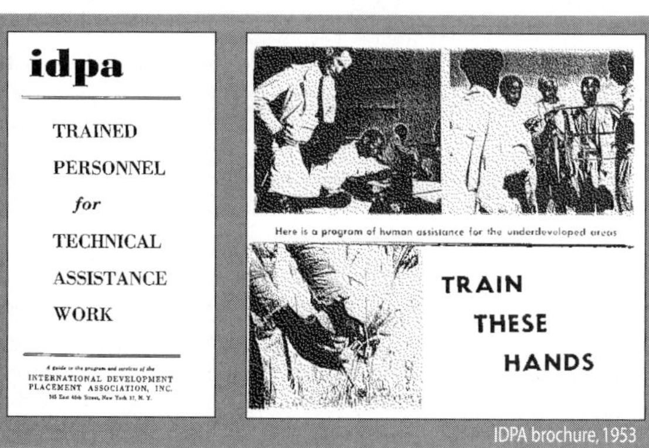

IDPA brochure, 1953

Occupational Breakdown of IDPA Applicants as of June 30, 1954

Occupational Title	No..	Occupational Title	No.
Accountants	2	Librarians and Archivists	5
Agronomists	14		
Animal Scientists	3	Machinists	3
Anthropologists	7	Midwives and Non professional Nurses	2
Architects	10		
Artists	3	Nurses	20
Bacteriologists	2	Personnel Mgrs.	5
Biologists	16	Pharmacists	2
Business Executives		Physicians and Surgeons	16
Chemists	15	Physicists	11
Community Development Workers	19	Political Scientists	10
		Psychologists	8
Conservationists	1	Public Health Workers	4
Cooperative Mgrs.	4	Public Relations Mgrs.	3
Deck Officers	1	School Principals	1
Dentists	4	Social Workers	13
Draftsmen	2	Sociologists	11
Economists	26	Soil Scientists	2
Electricians	1	Stenographers	9
Engineers		Teachers	
Misc.	7	Primary Level	16
Chemical	9	Secondary Level 9	
Civil	8	Misc.8	
Electrical	16	Arts and Crafts 6	
Mechanical	12	Language 12	
Farmers		Music	
Livestock	2	Phys. Ed 2	
Poultry	1	Science I	41
Farm Machinery		Social Sc.	9
Operators	3	Vocational Ag	3
Foresters	8	Vocational Ind	3
Foundrymen	1	of the Handicapped	4
Geographers	5	Adult Education	15
Geologists	5	Therapy Technicians	8
Govt. Executive's	4	Town Planners	4
Historians	5	Veterinarians	4
Journalists	4	Zoologists	3
		Total	501

*Approximately 5% of applicants are listed under more than one field.

Some Institutions which have asked for IDPA help in finding personnel

ASIA

India
Gandhian Constructive Workers
Indian Cooperative Union
Hislop College
Udaipur College
Benares Hindu University

Indonesia
University of Indonesia

Burma
Ministry of National Planning

Pakistan
Forman College Extension Service

Lebanon
Village School

Iraq
Women's Temperance and Social Welfare-Society

AFRICA

Gold Coast
Various Government Departments
Kumasi College of Technology
Council of Tribal Chiefs of the Kingdom of Ashanti
The University College of the Gold Coast

Nigeria
Various Central and Regional Government Departments
Lagos Town Council,
Egbado College
Molusi College
Eko Boys' High School, Lagos

Sierra Leone
Various Government Departments
Various Mission Bodies
Fourah Bay College
Union Teachers' College
Albert Academy
Harford School,
United Brethren of Africa

Liberia
Various Government Departments
The University of Liberia
Booker Washington A & M Institute
Cuttington College

From Clifford Dancer, "A Report on the Program of the International Development Placement Association" (mimeo. Probably 1954)

A vision kept alive by American college students

4. NSA, Point Four, and the Peace Corps

Richard J. Murphy
University of North Carolina
Chair, NSA Virginia–Carolinas Region, 1950–51. NSA President, 1952-53

From its inception, NSA had advocated support for technical assistance programs that would enroll students in efforts to work with people on a local level in developing countries to help build their agricultural, commercial, and industrial skills.[1]

Concept emerged after World War II

In the early years of the 1950s, the NSA International Commission in Cambridge, MA, developed a concept for what they called a Point Four Youth Corps. "Point Four" was related to President Truman's inaugural address of 1949, in which he outlined an aid program for underdeveloped nations of the world to which the United States should contribute. This NSA program was designed to be the youth part of that proposal. It was also an application of the many independent work programs around the world for American students that emerged after World War II.

The NSA International Commission was the Harvard/MIT-based unit for which the NSA had an elected vice-president who was its principal officer. When I became NSA's sixth president in 1952, we had just moved to Philadelphia. Avrea Ingram was our international vice president at Cambridge, having been re-elected at the Indiana Congress to his second term. He carried forward the policy recommendations of previous NSA Congresses, as well as his predecessor NSA vice presidents and NSA's representatives to the U.S. National Commission for UNESCO. I was NSA's third representative to the Commission, following Bob Smith and Rob West (NSA's first and second year international vice presidents, respectively). Both of them had proposed youth-based technical assistance programs to UNESCO in Paris.

The concept of a Point Four Youth Corps (which was later dubbed the Peace Corps by Senator Hubert Humphrey), was outlined in some detail in Jim Scott's NSA white paper of November 1960. It was developed even before Jim was elected the 1960-1961 international vice-president. Interestingly, the program favored by the NSA staff and its advisers at that time was one that would be privately run, with limited government financial support.[2]

Introduced in Congress in the late 1950s

The concept (for a government-run program) was taken in the late 1950s to Congress by NSA representatives and was introduced in the House by Congressman Henry Reuss of Milwaukee, Wisconsin, and by Senator Hubert Humphrey of Minnesota in the Senate. Reuss asked for a one-year test, while Humphrey proposed immediate formation of the Peace Corps. At the time it was considered by many to be a highly idealistic program that was thought to be impractical by foreign affairs experts. That especially was the view of the State Department and of the CIA and other professional organizations that were in this area dealing in international affairs.

When it was first proposed by Senator John F. Kennedy, it was denounced by President Dwight D. Eisenhower and by then Vice President Richard Nixon, who was running for president, as a "kiddie-corps" and derided as a highly impractical idea. Now, how did it get from a bill (going nowhere) introduced in the Senate by Humphrey and in the House by Henry Reuss to a proposal made by Senator Kennedy, who was then running for president—bearing in mind also that Senator Kennedy, during the time that he was in the Senate, did not sign on as a cosponsor of this bill with Senator Humphrey?

Here is the story.

How it got into a campaign message from Senator John F. Kennedy

In 1960 I was the executive director of the Democratic Platform Committee hearings. We ran the ten advance platform hearings around the country and the final platform hearings at the convention itself. I had invited the NSA to testify before the platform committee in the hopes that we could get a Peace Corps proposal written into the platform. I also wanted the students to have some input into the Democratic Platform at the time, not only about a Point Four Youth Corps idea, but other ideas relating to education. NSA did testify in Los Angeles. The people that appeared were Lenore Gauss, who was the NSA coordinator of Immaculate Heart College in Los Angeles, California, and Sue Welsh. They urged the committee to adopt a Point Four Youth Corps idea and to call for a study of it. Unfortunately, it was not included in the final platform draft.

This was in July 1960 in Los Angeles, just before the beginning of the Democratic National Convention. One month later I became the head of the young voters section of Senator Kennedy's campaign. I worked with Chuck Manatt, who was the college program director of the Democratic National Committee and a former NSA delegate from Iowa State College.

One of the things that I did at that time was to draft a message for Senator Kennedy to issue to the nation's young first-time voters (at that time you had to be twenty-one in order to vote). This message was drafted to open a nationwide new voter's month on September 1. In this message I had included a promise to look into the feasibility of creating a Peace Corps—using the name Senator Humphrey had given it.

It took one month to get the speech cleared through the speechwriters and a series of people that were involved in the organization, including Ralph Dungan's group (Ralph, NSA's 1947-48 vice president for domestic affairs, was then an assistant to Larry O'Brien, later Postmaster General); Dick Donohue, an assistant manager, who later became head of the Massachusetts Bar Association and head of Nike Corporation; Larry O'Brien, who was the campaign director at the time; and Robert Kennedy. The final and chief speechwriter was Archibald Cox, then a Harvard Law professor and later Watergate special prosecutor. When it came back to me from Archibald Cox, it had been cleared and the idea of a feasibility study of the Point Four Youth Program, now called Peace Corps, was approved.[3]

Another proposal that I had written into the speech and that I tried to get Senator Kennedy to endorse at the same time was a peacetime GI Bill. But in Archibald Cox's handwriting, it was written, "Senator is opposed."

Students' enthusiastic response inspires a new program

We released the message from Senator Kennedy on October 5, shortly after the end of new voter's month rather than at the beginning. When it came out, the *Evening Star*, which was then the evening newspaper in Washington (it no longer exists), and the Baltimore *Evening Sun* both ran the statement on the front page. The reaction was so terrific—people were coming in off the street the next morning saying that they had heard that Senator Kennedy had proposed a Peace Corps and they wanted to know how they could get involved in the campaign—that we then flashed Larry O'Brien and the Kennedy airplane in transit. We told them that we were getting these walk-ins off the street because of this Peace Corps proposal, and we suggested that Senator Kennedy mention this himself since the message was in his name.

As a result, when Senator Kennedy got to the University of Michigan after midnight on October 14, outside the Michigan Student Union, he spoke to the students extemporaneously and, among other things brought up the issue of the Peace Corps and asked, "How many of you would be willing to devote some years of your life to go to an underdeveloped country to help young students in a Peace Corps program?" There was a tremendously positive reaction from the students. On the basis of that reaction, it was then decided to have a major speech made by Kennedy on the subject before the fast approaching end of the campaign.

Fred Dutton was assigned to write the full speech, which was then given by John Kennedy in the Cow Palace in San Francisco just before the end of the campaign (see p. 633). Dutton was then the assistant to Governor Pat Brown of California (the senior Brown), and was working in the campaign for Whizzer White (later, Mr. Justice White), who headed the volunteer citizens for Kennedy.

So, when Senator Kennedy was elected the first week of November, the Peace Corps consisted of a nationwide message to new voters, the speech in the Cow Palace, and the extemporaneous remarks he had made at the University of Michigan.

Now he had to find someone to give this wonderful idea to—an idea that most experts thought was utterly impractical and was bound to fail. He decided, thankfully, to give it to his courageous brother-in-law. And out of Sargent Shriver's humane mind was created the Peace Corps, a program based on a proposal that began as a campaign promise during the 1960 campaign, and which was kept alive by generations of volunteer students and by NSA since the war's end, and also by NSA leaders, who lobbied for the concept when the time came.[4]

END NOTES

[1] See "The Role of Students and NSA in Developing Technical Assistance Programs," p. 632.

[2] See excerpt from the proposal on p. 638.

[3] See Weiss, Hughes, and Rice, p. 637.

[4] *Time* Magazine in 1976 declared the founding of the Peace Corps to be one of the 100 greatest events in American history! More than 40 years later, the Peace Corps is stronger than ever, operating in over 100 countries, some of which have established Peace Corps of their own.

Richard J. Murphy was Deputy Postmaster General during the John Kennedy and Lyndon Johnson administrations. He was for 23 years the Washington, D.C.-based Director of Government Affairs for Unisys. (See p. 786 for extended bio.)

PICTURE CREDITS: *Then:* University of Minnesota, August 1952. *Now:* 1995, Grace Lutheran Church, Washington, D.C. (Both from author).

The Role of Students and NSA in Technical Assistance Programs, 1946–1960

The only kind of war we seek is the good old fight against man's ancient enemies—poverty, disease, hunger, and illiteracy.
—President Harry S. Truman, describing his Point Four program of economic aid and technical assistance to the less developed areas of Asia, Africa, and Latin America.

Editor's Note: The founders of the U.S. National Student Association in 1946 were determined to take part in the rebuilding of a wartorn world and to contribute an active American student presence in support of the dismantling of colonial empires and for assistance to the economic development of "Third World" countries emerging from colonial status. U.S. students also expected to have a seat at the table where decisions were made.

A tradition of helping others

"The idea of young people voluntarily helping others less fortunate than themselves is as old as the human race," Roy Hoopes wrote in a 1961 Peace Corps guide.[1] He notes that the historic roots behind the generations of young Americans who went out into the far reaches of the globe to do good works flowed from the work of Christian missionaries, on the one hand, to the idea advanced by William James at the Universal Peace Congress in 1904. In order to "invent new outlets for heroic energy" he proposed the conscription of "a 'peace army' that would not only be of great help to the less fortunate of the world but would at the same time be very enlightening and inspiring to those who took part."[2]

Hoopes traces the entry of the U.S. government into such efforts from the "Thomasite" teacher corps in the Philippines in 1901, to the domestic Civilian Conservation Corps and National Youth Administration during the Depression in the 1930s. The missionary tradition found some 33,000 Protestant and Catholic young people overseas in 1960, according to Hoopes. The American Friends Service Committee war relief and community development projects since 1917 and the International Voluntary Service, formed in 1953, and considered by Hoopes a prototype of the Peace Corps, were of this tradition.

The technical assistance concept

The concept of "technical assistance" arose out of this tradition and the postwar circumstance. And while NSA was one of many groups committed to this effort, its singular contribution was to channel the energies of a new postwar generation of student leaders who were outside of the missionary and professional foreign aid establishments. These students advocated and worked to develop programs at their own initiatives through the new channel of student government and intercollegiate representation NSA was developing, and through its "seat at the table" at UNESCO and other educational and governmental forums.

Dick Murphy, a former NSA president (1952–53), in the accompanying account of his alertness to the political opportunity afforded by the Kennedy campaign to bring the Peace Corps into being, drew on his network of then current, as well as past, NSA leaders and their already researched and documented efforts to mount technical assistance programs that they had sponsored, urged, and engaged in since 1946.

Following are some benchmark highlights:

* * *

The 1946 Chicago Student Conference

At the recent Chicago Conference, representatives of a million students made plain their keen desire for closer ties to students abroad....When in the past, projects were considered for study exchanges, travel schemes or assistance to foreign students, the task of carrying through such projects remained solely with private organizations, governments, or college administrations. The delegates at Chicago demonstrated the American students' wish to participate in forming and executing such plans, and to work more closely with existing organizations for increasing the numbers of such projects.

—Jim Smith, President of the National Continuations Committee, in an editorial in the March 1, 1947, issue of the Student International Activities Bulletin, *published for the NCC by the International Activities Committee of the Harvard Student Council.*

NSA Delegates to the U.S. National Commission for UNESCO, 1948–1951

I am going to Washington for a meeting of the Executive Committee of the National Commission....there is an item on the agenda concerning "point four" of President Truman's inaugural address.

This point deals with the pooling of the world's technical and scientific "know-how," in order to make it possible for economic and social improvement in the "backward" areas of the world. UNESCO is already doing a considerable amount of work in this field, and I am hoping the Executive committee will recommend that the U.S. direct some of its activities through UNESCO.

—Robert S. Smith, NSA UNESCO Representative for 1948–49, writing in NSA News, *February 1949.*

NSA must be able to show, by maintaining a high level of responsibility and effectiveness in its projects, and by financing these projects on a self-sustaining basis that it can make an important contribution to UNESCO's aims. NSA must build strong, direct ties with the student organizations in the underdeveloped areas. NSA must be able to show that its programs will enjoy the support of both students and governments in those areas.

West recommended that NSA urge UNESCO to give top priority to pilot projects in fundamental education, technical assistance, development of student self-government, and combating student poverty, disease and poor living conditions in the countries of Asia, Africa and South America.

—NSA News, *Summer 1951, quoting Robert L. West, NSA UNESCO Representative for 1950–51.*

Third Annual National Student Congress, August 1950

There are several interesting ideas for the coming year. It is suggested that NSA might initiate and sponsor a program of student technical assistance teams to work in the underdeveloped areas for 8 to 12 months.

—*Herbert Eisenberg, NSA International Vice President writing in the* Congress Report.

Students' Mutual Assistance Program, December 1950

On December 17, 1950, student leaders from 21 nations met in Stockholm, Sweden, to discuss ways of drawing the students of the world closer together. They were concerned especially with effecting closer contacts with students of Asia, Africa, South America, and the Middle East. Most of those present had found it difficult or impossible to work toward those ends through the Communist-dominated International Union of Students. . . . Stockholm was the turning point—the birth of a new plan for international student cooperation.[3]

—A New Role for the American Student, *USNSA, 1951.*

A program of cooperative action adopted by the participating members at the Stockholm Conference. The coordination of this program will be carried on by the USNSA. . . . The sending out to underdeveloped areas of advanced students in technical fields, e.g. education, medicine, engineering, agriculture, administration, social work, etc., to work with students in these fields.

—*Extract from two-page SMAP program description, 1951.*

The International Development Placement Association, 1951

The young men and women who organized the International Development Placement Association in 1951 knew that there were plenty of young Americans willing to help make the world a decent place to live in.[4] They recognized the absence of a central agency to counsel applicants and to locate work for them. It was to meet those needs that the IDPA was founded. . . . IDPA started out to find jobs for these people. It found them in Asia and Africa. . . . The first chairman of IDPA is working in Uganda as business manager of the Federation of Partnerships of Uganda African Farmers.

—*IDPA information brochure.*

Fifth NSA National Student Congress, August 1952

One of the most important ways of increasing international understanding, cooperation, and well-being is through the technical assistance program aiding underdeveloped countries. . . . USNSA endorses the present principles and programs of IDPA. It directs the Vice President in charge of International Affairs to contact the IDPA in order to establish fuller cooperation between NSA and IDPA.

—*Minutes of the Post-Congress National Executive Committee, August 29, 1952.*

Introduction into the U.S. Congress, 1957–1960

I saw a team of four young American school teachers who were going from village to village setting up the elementary schools that the French had neglected to provide in a hundred years of colonialism. The villagers and the young Americans loved each other, and I could only regret that there were four, rather than 40, or 400, Americans working on the project.

—*Representative Henry S. Reuss, Wisconsin, in 1957*

There is a great body of idealistic and talented young men in this country. . . . The Peace Corps would tap these vital resources. There is nothing which will build greater people-to-people and government-to-government relationships than to have fine young American men helping the people of the emerging countries to help themselves. They will not only act as instructors but also will show that they are not afraid to dirty their hands in their common endeavors.

—*Senator Hubert Humphrey of Minnesota, 1960.*

NSA Lobbies for the "Point Four Youth Corps" or "Peace Corps," 1960

Since last year, before any bills were introduced into Congress, NSA has been active in drawing up testimony to be submitted to Congress to the end of authorizing a study. The concept of a Point Four Youth Corps has come a great distance since NSA has been actively involved and, if we may be permitted to insert a small boast, we feel partially responsible for its progress. Not only have NSA officers submitted testimony, but they have talked at length with Congressmen and Senators about the "Corps" and its prospects. NSA's activity centers around three goals: campus information about the "Corps," campus action in the "Corps," and political pressure for its implementation corresponding to the consensus of informed student opinion.

—*Jim Scott, NSA International Affairs Vice President, 1960–61, in a November 28, 1960, letter to student body presidents and campus newspaper editors.*

The Peace Corps Enters the Presidential Campaign in 1960

How many of you who are doctors are willing to spend your days in Ghana as technicians or engineers, how many of you are willing to work in the foreign service and spend your lives traveling around the world? On your willingness to do that, not merely to serve one or two years in the service, but on your willingness to contribute part of your life to this country, I think, will depend the answer whether we as a free society can compete.

—*Senator John F. Kennedy, early in the morning of October 14, 1960, before a large crowd of students at the University of Michigan—estimated at ten thousand.*

The activities of the NSA and the Young Democrats were, to a very considerable extent, responsible for the "spontaneous" enthusiasm which greeted candidate Kennedy's proposal in the Presidential Campaign of 1960.

—*Roy Hoopes,* The Complete Peace Corps Guide, *page 24.*

The Peace Corps Established, 1961

The purpose of the Peace Corps is to permit America to participate directly, personally and effectively in this struggle for human dignity. A world community is struggling to be born. America must be present at that birth, helping to make it successful.

—*Sargent Shriver, Director of the Peace Corps, in an address at Notre Dame University, June 4, 1961.*

The Peace Corps had captured the public imagination as no other single act of the Kennedy administration.

—Time *magazine, March 10, 1961.*

ENDNOTES

[1] Roy Hoopes, *The Complete Peace Corps Guide* (New York: Dial Press, 1961), p. 8. The Kennedy, Humphrey and Reuss quotes are from this same book.

[2] Hoopes, *The Complete Peace Corps Guide*, p. 8. See also the early work of the Student Volunteer Movement from 1890–1920, on p. 688.

[3] See "New Co-operation," p. 527, Eisenberg, p. 526.

[4] Roy Hoopes writes (p. 17):

> Another plan to send Americans abroad to work was originated by Doug Kelly, a former President of the Students for Democratic Action. In 1951, with the assistance of the Foundation for World Government, Kelly formed the International Development Placement Association, a recruiting center and employment agency for American students who wanted to work in the underdeveloped countries for local wages. Although a small organization with limited funds, the IDPA did valuable pioneer work in recruiting workers for underdeveloped countries and demonstrated the role such an organization could play. In 1954 lack of funds forced IDPA to disband, but the eighteen pioneer "peace corpsmen" who went abroad helped to prove that young, educated Americans working at the community level in the underdeveloped countries could make a unique contribution not only to our foreign aid program, but also to the cause of better understanding.

Among the founding board members were former NSA international vice presidents Robert L. West (1948–49) and Herbert Eisenberg (1950–51) and former educational problems vice president Eugene Schwartz (1948–49). The IDPA Executive Director was Peter Weiss. Peter Weiss himself elaborates on the founding impetus for IDPA through Clifford Dancer, Stringfellow Barr, and himself while working at the Foundation. See Kelley, p. 623, Weiss, p. 637, Jonas, p. 773.

MIT's Foreign Student Summer Project (FSSP)

The Tech 12/10/48, MIT

NSA To Conduct Second FSSP Next Summer

80 European, Asiatic Grads To Be Given Free Summer Course

Earl W. Eames, Jr., '49, yesterday announced plans for the second annual Foreign Student Summer Project, a plan which last year brought 62 foreign graduate students from 15 European countries together at Technology for the three month summer term. There is no cost to the participating students.

One of the most notable changes occurred when it was decided after several committee meetings to include five Far Eastern and three Near Eastern countries in next summer's invitations, although the emphasis will still remain with Europe.

Selection in April

Another change to be instituted this year will be the priority to be given to graduate students and young instructors with specific research problems. Selection of students is set for April. As was the case last year, final selection will again be made by the FSSP committee.

Since the participating students listed the fraternity living groups as one of the most valuable aspects of the FSSP, it is hoped to continue these living arrangements.

FSSP National Subcommittee

Presently at work on the FSSP committee, now a subcommittee of the national as well as the local National Student Association, are Eames, Haynes, Harrison C. White, '50; Donald J. Eberly, '50; Fred Borromeo, '50; Al Baird, '50; Robert Kandall, '50; Jens Knudson, G; Donald Gillespie, '49; Stephen Rosendaal, '49; Herbert Eisenberg, '51; Robert Arbuckle, '52; Maurice Hodaya, '51; John M. Birmingham, '51; Morris L. Wasserstein, '50, and Ferd Mikel, '49.

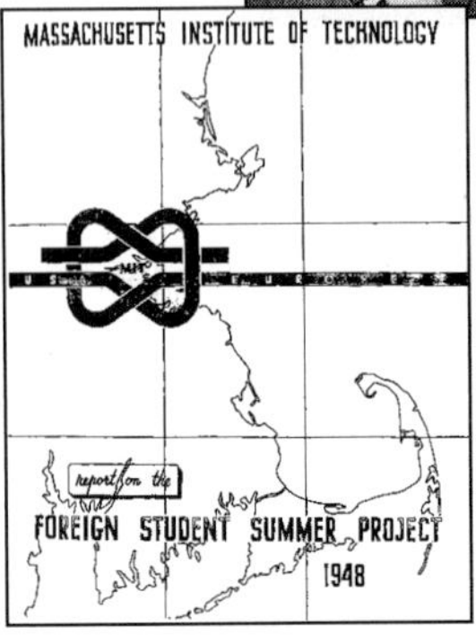

Dr. Karl Taylor Compton, President of MIT, with FSSP students at a reception sponsored by the McGraw Hill Book Company, June 16, 1948. Left, cover of the project report (Berea College, KY archives)

IIE Bulletin 1/1/52, Institute for International Education

MIT Foreign Student Summer Project

Earl W. Eames, Jr.

BEGINNING as an idea that students should be able to play their part in the educational reconstruction of Europe after the war, the MIT Foreign Student Summer Project has developed into a program far exceeding its original goals.

Back in 1948, when Lloyd Haynes and the writer helped work out details of the first project, sixty-two students from fourteen European countries took part in a summer of classroom studies and laboratory work at Massachusetts Institute of Technology. At the fourth FSSP this past summer, thirty nations from around the globe were represented by seventy-seven participants. These young men and women carried on advanced research in sixty-five fields; many of the projects were concerned with increasing and utilizing natural resources and improving living standards in the underdeveloped countries of the world.

Some FSSP participants gather at MIT

FSSP continues to be administered and sponsored by students of MIT as a voluntary effort of the student government. The necessary funds, which this year amounted to over $63,000, are raised from American sources including foundations, corporations, individuals, and the Government. MIT waives tuition for the participants, and foreign institutions provide the necessary ocean travel costs.

Highlight of this past summer was the NAM Foreign Student Motorcade, which again this year took the participants on an excellent tour of midwest manufacturing plants. A weekend conference at a camp in New Hampshire on the general topic "Social Progress through Technology" proved an outstanding addition to the regular program.

The "alumni" of the project, now numbering 289, have recently started a quarterly, *FSSP Journal*, which enables us to keep in touch with one another on both social and technical matters. We hope this international community will continue to grow in size and in strength. The present student committee is even now making thorough preparations for FSSP 1952, and we are looking forward to another good year.

EARL W. EAMES, JR. was a co-founder of FSSP.

"AWARE OF THEIR OBLIGATIONS." FSSP, one of the earliest of such programs, was a practical expression of student concerns. In its first annual report Lloyd A. Haynes, Chair of the NSA Committee, and Earl W. Eames, Jr., Chair of the FSSP Committee, wrote of its origin, "In May, 1947, we students active in the National Student Association Committee at MIT, most of whom had seen and participated in the destruction of Europe in World War II, ,and all of whom were aware of their obligation to students in the war-torn countries, decided that we would attempt to invite science and engineering students for a course during the summer of 1948."

Technical Assistance through SMAP and WAY

SMAP: Students Mutual Assistance Program. WAY: World Assembly of Youth

Herbert Eisenberg
Massachusetts Institute of Technology
NSA International Vice President, 1950-51

Editor's Note: The International Union of Students, formed at the Prague World Student Congress in 1946, was intended by its organizers to be the voice of students throughout the world and the coordinating body for international exchanges and projects. The IUS failed to fulfill this goal by becoming an instrument of Communist control and Soviet foreign policy, as Herbert Eisenberg, NSA International Vice President in 1950-1951, noted in an unpublished paper written in October 1951. This became irrefutably clear, he notes, as a result of their support of the Czech coup d'état in 1948 and the later expulsion from IUS of the Yugoslav student organization.

Eisenberg goes on to write in 1951:

After the second IUS World Student Congress in 1950, the opposition unions decided to take some collective action. A meeting of twenty-one student unions in Stockholm was called to discuss concrete means of cooperation among these unions,[1] and not to form any new organization. It was a response to the fact that the IUS was no longer an international body that worked for the good of students regardless of their political ideology. From the discussions about the establishment of contact with student organizations in other parts of the world came the Students Mutual Assistance Program (SMAP) and the recognition by student leaders of their responsibility to participate in technical assistance programs.

In contrast to the smaller gathering of student leaders in Stockholm, the World Assembly of Youth (WAY)[2] gathered five hundred and fifty youth and student leaders from sixty-five countries for its first assembly at Cornell University in Ithaca, New York. Prior to the Assembly, one hundred delegates from thirty-six countries met at a technical assistance seminar and heard from United Nations experts about problems of underdeveloped areas. It was from proposals developed at the seminar that the World Assembly of Youth adopted its community development program. Enthusiasm for the program permeated the Assembly and the Council meetings.

WAY created a special commission on technical assistance to handle and develop the proposals that resulted from the Assembly. The plans include an international community center of young people who will work especially in the fields of "handicrafts, communal responsibility, personal health, and modern methods of cultivation." It further stated that WAY will pay particular attention to respecting and developing the traditional cultures of the participating countries.

The resolution further expressed the wholehearted support of the World Assembly of Youth for the important work being carried out by the Technical Assistance Board of the United Nations. The resolution is a milestone in the activities of youth, since it is the first time that an international youth organization recorded its willingness to tackle the problems of raising the living standards of people throughout the world. WAY will operate their programs through their international secretariat, and will cooperate with their national committees in the areas where programs are to be put into operation.[3]

The Students Mutual Assistance Program (SMAP) on the other hand, does not have an international secretariat,[4] and it was delegated to each individual national union of students to implement the program as best it could. The preamble to SMAP clearly states the NUS's wish to work in mutual cooperation with student unions in other parts of the world to solve common problems. The SMAP program for action was proposed to serve as a basis for discussion, and to indicate some of the types of projects that the conference members felt were feasible for an individual union to carry out.

Among the projects mentioned were the sending of technically trained students to work with the technical students in the area on community projects; the exchange of information through newspapers and bulletins; the exchange of students in technical and other fields; and an increase of scholarships in all countries to be available to foreign students. The conference members also noted the importance of the work of the United Nations and referred specifically to the work of the fundamental education division of UNESCO.

END NOTES

[1] The programs adopted at this meeting were ratified at a conference in Edinburgh, Scotland, in January 1952, attended by the national unions of the following countries: Australia, Austria, Belgium, Brazil, Canada, Denmark, Eire, England, Finland, France, Germany, Indonesia, Israel, Italy, Netherlands, Norway, Saar [sic], Scotland, Sweden, Switzerland, South Africa, United States, Yugoslavia.

[2] The U.S. affiliate of WAY was the Young Adult Council (p. 778), a unit of the National Social Welfare Assembly, of which Mrs. Douglas Horton was president, William H. Bulkeley was chairman of the Executive Committee and Robert E. Bondy was director. Bernice Bridges was director of YAC, which was formed in 1948. It sponsored periodic summer events of discussions and workshops, attended by about one thousand young people. Each event was called the United States Assembly of Youth (USAY).

The first USAY was held at the University of Michigan, September 3–8, 1953. The second was at Oberlin College, September 8-13, 1955. USNSA was an affiliated organization, along with sixteen others. Among them were the National YMCA and YWCA, the Youth Division of the NAACP, the Student Division of the United World Federalists, National Catholic Youth Council, National Jewish Youth Conference, American Youth Hostels, Collegiate Council for the UN, Students for Democratic Action, Rural Youth of the USA, and the North American Student Cooperative League.

[3] WAY was headquartered in Brussels, Belgium. See p. 778 for a description of WAY and its origins.

[4] SMAP as an umbrella for programming soon gave way to the formation, in August 1952, as an outgrowth of the Edinburgh Conference (see note 1 above), of a full-time staff to maintain a Coordinating Secretariat (Cosec) in Leiden, Holland. See Dentzer, p. 301, Eisenberg, p. 526.

(Source: WAY and YAC documents in the Library of Congress manuscript files for Ruby Hurley, NAACP Youth Director, 1940s, and NSA archives, SHSW).

The Student Christian Movement, the World Assembly of Youth, and beyond

5. George Carter and the Peace Corps: From Student Leader to Business Leader

George Carter was born in Germantown, Philadelphia, to a family of little means, and went to college because of the GI Bill (Lincoln and Harvard). Coincidentally, it was the same neighborhood in which Ted Harris (LaSalle and Princeton. See p. 219), NSA President in 1948-49, was also born. Both pioneered as Black "firsts" in the corporate world after working abroad. Deeply religious (Carter Protestant, Harris Catholic), each brought a profound spiritual sensibility and glorious wit to his mission. From a line of influential Black clergy, Carter was torn between a pastoral calling and the man of action he became.

George Carter met Ernie Howell (See p. 838) at Harvard through the Student Christian Movement, in which Howell was prominent. There they became roommates and lifetime friends. Carter later went on a tour of Africa with Ruth Schachter (Morgenthau), Walter Carrington, Immanual Wallerstein and Murray Frank as an outcome of his involvement in the Young Adult Council and World Assembly of Youth (WAY).[1] He later became WAY's Asian Secretary.

He led the first overseas Peace Corps project (It became known as Ghana 1), and rose to become a regional director. In 1966 he joined IBM at the invitation of Tom Watson as its first Black management executive. After retiring from IBM he became president of Crossroads Africa, joined Benjamin Hooks at the NAACP in a reorganization effort, and involved himself in global as well as community programs serving children and the poor until his passing.

As recalled at his memorial service by his children, stepchildren and grandchildren, fellow Peace Corps and Johnson administration associates (Bill Moyers led the list. Sergeant Shriver was represented by a recollection in writing), fellow staffers at IBM (the President of Lotus was there) and community leaders in Westchester—George filled a room with his presence, his stories and his wide range of interests. Their memories were celebrations of joy and a tribute to a man who relished his capacity for leadership and shared it with all in his path.

George's compass found its map through his post-war student and youth activity—and as a result of many such stories as his a "Civic Generation" emerged across the land. George was an exemplar of that "Civic Generation"—(the depression/World War II generation of students that political scientist Robert Putnam so designated)—the more so because the barriers of race to be overcome were for him walls to be joyously scaled.

PHOTOS: *Then:* c.1950s. *Now:* c.1990s (Margaret Griesmer)

CARTER IN AFRICA

In 1952 Carter traveled to North Africa with the U.S. delegation to the World Assembly of Youth meeting in Dakar. Shown here with him are Immanuel Wallerstein (Columbia) and Ruth Schachter (Barnard). Below he is shown with Peace Corps volunteers in Ghana, c. 1961-63 (Margaret Griesmer)

George Carter and Sargent Shriver, Peace Corps director in the 1960s, left. Below in the late 1990s. (Margaret Griesmer)

George Carter, Citizen, built a full life and helped raise a loving and admiring family with no doubt about his purpose. George died of cancer at 76 on November 28, 2001. He is survived by his wife Margaret Griesmer Carter, his two sons, Laurent and Stephen, and 5 grandchildren. His son Edouard predeceased him. Through his second marriage he leaves Stephen, Gretchen, Martin and Rosemarie Griesmer and 8 grandchildren.

Eugene G. Schwartz, CCNY

NSA Educational Problems Vice President, 1948-49

(Editor's note: Observations about Carter's life adapted from the programs and testimonials at his memorial service, December 8, 2001 in Cortlandt Manor, NY)

[1] See Jonas, p. 771, for more on WAY, Frank and Wallerstein.

Generations of Student Federalist and NSA leaders pursued lifetime roles in international development

From Point 4 to Peace Corps: A Global Vision Kept Alive

In his 1961 book, The Complete Peace Corps Guide, *Roy Hoopes writes:*

"Although a small organization with limited funds, the IDPA did valuable pioneer work in recruiting workers for underdeveloped countries and demonstrated the role such an organization could play. In 1954, lack of funds forced IDPA to disband, but the eighteen pioneer 'peace corpsmen' who went abroad under this program helped prove that young, educated Americans working at the community level in the underdeveloped countries could make a unique contribution not only to our foreign aid program but also to the cause of better understanding."*

*See this section, pp. 623-636; also Jonas, p. 773.

Truman's Fourth Point in 1949

Peter Weiss, *IDPA Executive Director, in two letters to the Anthology editor (7/14/98 and 8/14/99) writes:*

IDPA was a project of the Foundation for World Government, then headed by Stringfellow Barr, the former President of St. John's College. Cliff Dancer and I had both worked for the Foundation. We conceived the idea of sending a study group to Israel in 1950 to examine the relevance of Israeli cooperative and collective institutions to the third world and the IDPA idea grew out of that project, promoted by Cliff and myself and financed entirely by the Foundation.

I was indeed the Executive Director of IDPA from my graduation from law school in 1952 to the latter part of 1954, when, thanks to the two right wing Southern ladies in the IRS who tried to put every progressive non-profit out of business, IDPA was finally refused tax exemption on the ground that it was an employment agency. At which point I was reluctantly forced to take up the practice of law.

My recollection, such as it feebly is, is that IDPA's links with USNSA were more personal than institutional, principally through yourself, Rob West, Murray Frank, Sandy Kravitz, Herb Eisenberg and Mildred Kiefer. (See Kelley, p. 624.)

I think it is fair to say that IDPA was one of the principal precursors of the Peace Corps, in spirit as well as operation. Roy Hoopes has that right in his Peace Corps Guide, except that IDPA's recruitment activities were not aimed so much at students as at young professionals and technicians. (We sent at least one Ph.D. to Indonesia, and an experienced town planner to Ghana).

An even earlier link was between the Point Four program and the Foundation for World Government, with which I was connected pre-IDPA and which was IDPA's principal funder. In 1948 the Foundation ran a seminar in Philadelphia with James Warburg, to discuss a series of ten or so pamphlets prepared by Dewey Anderson's Public Affairs Institute in Washington, on the role of technical assistance in economic development. I was always under the impression that this series led directly to the incorporation of the fourth point in Truman's 1949 inaugural address, but I'd be hard put to prove it. Too many of the actors involved—Winkie Barr, Dewey Anderson, Jim Warburg, Palmer Weber—are dead.

Shaping Kennedy's Platform in 1960

Thomas Hughes, *President of the Student Federalists in 1944, writes on March 25, 2000 to the Anthology editor:*

In reading the material you sent about the Peace Corps and its origins, I was impressed by the interrelationships and reappearances of personnel. Here are a few examples.

IDPA. Peter Weiss' letter to you refers to the Foundation for World Government. The Foundation itself was nearly a direct outgrowth of the early Student Federalist movement. Both Stringfellow Barr and Scott Buchanan (St. John's, Annapolis) were close adult advisers of Student Federalists. Harris Wofford', the first SF President, was on the board of IDPA as well.

The study group sent to Israel in 1950 to work on the kibbutzim was almost a pioneer Peace Corps Group itself. All three of the first national presidents of Student Federalists were part of the group in Israel - Harris Wofford, Clare Lindgren (already Mrs. Wofford), and myself. We sent reports to Barr on our experiences that summer. Harris himself wrote a 900-page history of the Foundation (unpublished). Charles A. Nelson is currently writing a book-length account of the friendship and partnership of Stringfellow Barr and Scott Buchanan that covers the unhappy odyssey of the foundation and its involvement with Henry Wallace.

So there was a seminal Student Federalist influence (1943-48) in stimulating the FWG, starting the project in Israel, and creating the IDPA. (See Jonas, p. 773.)

DEMOCRATS and the Peace Corps. From 1955-58 I was legislative counsel to Senator Hubert Humphrey who introduced the Peace Corps bill. Al Lowenstein succeeded me in that office in 1959 and may have been instrumental in drafting the Reuss-Humphrey legislation. In 1959-60 I was Administrative Assistant to Representative Chester Bowles in the House, and he also introduced legislation.

Bowles was chairman of the Democratic Platform Committee at the Democratic National Convention at Los Angeles, 1960. I was the executive director of the platform committee staff. Dick Murphy, as he writes, was executive director of the platform committee hearings. Harris Wofford was also involved. Naturally Bowles, Humphrey, Wofford, Murphy and I all wanted an explicit reference to the Peace Corps in the platform. It is my distinct impression that this was vetoed by the Kennedy entourage. Bobby didn't like the name Peace Corps which had been patented by Humphrey. And of course the State Department types (Nitze, Fosdick, et al.) were contemptuous. This, despite the fact that Ralph Dungan and Archie Cox would have been favorable.

So we ended up with the following platform language: "American foreign policy in all its aspects must be attuned to our world of change. We will recruit officials whose experiences, humanity, and dedication fit them for the task of effectively representing America abroad. . . . We must find ways to show the people of the world that we share the same goals - dignity, health, freedom, schools for children, a place in the sun - and that we will work together to achieve them. Our program of visits between Americans and other nations will be expanded, with special emphasis on students and other leaders. We will encourage study of foreign languages. . . ."

Dick Murphy mentions that it took a month to get Kennedy's Peace Corps speech cleared after the convention. This helps explain it. Incidentally, Bill Welsh, another early NSA pioneer, was also active in the Bowles platform committee staff. The 1960 Democratic Platform was itself entitled "The Rights of Man" and of course was highly controversial in the South because of its strong and explicit civil rights section.

Providing Background for the Peace Corps

Andrew Rice, *Harvard delegate to the Chicago Student Conference in 1946, writes to the Anthology editor on March 7, 2000:*

About the Peace Corps: Dick Murphy's account (See p. 630) gives a good sense of how Kennedy became committed. I was involved on a totally separate track, as one of three co-authors of a government-financed study of the "advisability and practicality" of what was then called the "Point Four Youth Corps." Congressman Henry Reuss and Senator Richard Neuberger had been able to insert a provision in the Mutual Security Act of 1960 calling for such a study under the auspices of the U.S. foreign aid agency (then called the International Cooperation Administration) and ICA contracted the study to the Colorado State University Research Foundation in Fort Collins. I was hired as the Washington-based member of the research team. Our report which came out in early 1961 (and was later published commercially under the title New Frontiers for American Youth*) provided a great deal of useful material to Sergeant Shriver and his team when the Peace Corps was created by Executive Order in March 1961. (Although ours was the "official" study, there were two or three other private studies that Shriver also used.)

*Maurice L. Albertson, Andrew E. Rice and Pauline E. Birky, *New Frontiers for American Youth: Perspectives on the Peace Corps*, Washington, D.C., Public Affairs Press, 1961

Peter Weiss, a graduate of Yale Law School, is Vice President of the Center for Constitutional Rights, and has lectured and written widely on the international law of war and peace, nuclear weapons and human rights. He was a founder and partner of Weiss Dawid Fross Zelnick & Lehrman, a leading trademark firm. He received his BA '49 from St. John's College in Annapolis, served in the Army and the US military government in Germany (1944-47). He is founder and President of the American Committee on Africa and is a member of the Arab-Jewish Peace Group in New York. He was born in Vienna and came to the U.S. in 1941.

Thomas L. Hughes is President Emeritus, Carnegie Endowment for International Peace (President, 1971-91). He graduated Carleton College, MN in 1947, was Rhodes Scholar at Oxford U., and received his JD at Yale Law School. He served in the Air Force, 1952-54 (Lt.-Major). In 1944 he was elected President of the Student Federalists, following Harris Wofford (See p. 762). He was Deputy Asst. Sec'y. ('61-63) and Asst. Sec'y, Department of State, 1963-69. He was Minister, US Embassy, London, 1969-70, and remains a trustee of several academic and NGO boards in the US and abroad.

Andrew Rice is an independent consultant and editor. He helped found and was with the Society for International Development for 18 years, becoming Executive Director. Earlier he worked as Special Assistant to Undersecretary of State Chester Bowles. He received his BA and MA from Harvard in Far East regional studies, and Ph.D. in American Government at Syracuse U. He was a Harvard delegate to the 1946 Chicago Student Conference (Rice, p. 836) and was active in the American Veterans Committee (See p. 707). He served in the signal corps during WWII and in the occupation of Japan. For a time he was a partner in Seven Locks Press, and was President of the Cabin John, MD Citizens Association.

NSA'S 1960 POINT FOUR YOUTH CORPS PROPOSALS

Excerpts from an eight-page paper circulated prior to Congressional testimony by NSA International Vice President James C. Scott on 11/10/60

Selection Process and Particular Skills

The Point Four Youth Corps must be essentially qualitative rather than quantitative. If selected individuals cannot adequately perform their assigned tasks, the program will not be a success.

Aside from the organizational framework that would grow from the Program, a well-qualified selection board would be needed to insure careful matching of skills with available positions...Is it really necessary that only college graduates be included in a Point Four Youth Corps, or are there skills in demand which could be filled by Americans who had not attended universities or colleges? Skilled carpenters, machinists, draftsmen, etc., are all needed in many of the nations that would be recipients of a Point Four Youth Corps. USNSA is convinced that places could well be available to graduates of trade and industrial arts schools....

Some Conclusions

Although not final conclusions, the following are provisional ideas reached after careful consideration by NSA staff and our International Advisory Board.

a) A Point Four Youth Corps should be privately directed with indirect government support rather than established as a separate government agency.

b) In a Point Four Youth Corps, qualitative selection is essential as the participants will be individually tested over a long period and must be able to perform competently.

c) The Selection Commission should be a private body including academicians, persons with experience in overseas work, area specialists, government representatives, individuals capable of judging work skills, and representatives of organizations engaged in related work.

d) Possible projects indicate that a Point Four Youth Corps should not be restricted to male college graduates but should also be open to non-graduates and women with requisite skills and qualifications.

e) As a beginning, the project should be highly selective, start with a small number of participants, and within a limited geographical context.

f) Co-operation should be sought between private organizations, with particular attention given to universities in the United States which have a well-developed area program and experience in work along these lines.

g) Participants in the program of the Corps should be exempted from the draft but would be "draftable" in case of a national emergency. Appropriate safeguards would be included to insure that those dismissed for disciplinary reasons would be subject to the draft. The rigorous conditions under which one would serve should be ample protection against "draft dodgers."

h) The orientation period, given the nature of the Point Four Youth Corps, should cover 6 months to one year, depending upon the assigned area. Intensive language training would be a part of this orientation. Part of the period would be spent in the U.S., and part in the country where the individual will be stationed.

PICTURE CREDITS: **Weiss:** *Then:* c. 1950s. *Now:* c. 1999 (Schwartz). **Hughes:** *Then:* c. Late 1940s (Jonas); *Now:* c. 2002 (Author). **Rice:** (Both from author), *Then:* c. 1951; *Now:* October, 1997.

PART 3. INTERNATIONAL PROGRAMS

SECTION 5

NSA Student Travel and Exchange Programs

CONTENTS

Thousands of college students traveled abroad in NSA-operated work, study, and travel programs, and many more used its popular annual, *Work, Study, Travel Abroad*, as a sourcebook for information on summer travel programs.

Just as the National Student Federation of America in the 1920s (see Prologue) launched its own international programs with the assistance of the more experienced British National Union of Students, so NSA was helped to launch its travel programs with the help and support of a Dutch student group, the Netherlands Office for Foreign Student Relations (NBBS), and their connections with the Holland America Line.

Helen Bryan Garland (Sarah Lawrence) moved easily from her job with the American Field Service to NSA's Harvard Square office, where she managed most of the first three year's of NSA's travel programs and which she describes here. Pat (Wohlgemuth) Blair (Wellesley), who was a staff volunteer in the Cambridge Office, provides a vignette of her experience.

Jos Vos, the NBBS student representative who came to Cambridge as a liaison—and who stayed and married in this country—provides a glimpse of his wartime experience during the Nazi occupation as well as what it was like setting up shop and working in the United States.

Phil Stoddard (University of Illinois) provides recollection of work camp experiences in Holland in 1948, and his 1950 experience lobbying UNESCO in Paris on behalf of youth programs.

Mary Ann (Weld) Bodecker (Smith College) and two classmates tell of an NSA tour of foreign students in this country in 1949 in collaboration with intercollegiate committees in five cities.

Student ships, a crisis and a new travel office

An album of photos and memorabilia highlights the flavor of shipboard experience. The most memorable, "The *Svalbard* Incident," found 550 students stranded in New York City when the Coast Guard kept their ship from debarking. Bob Meagher (City College of New York), who was on hand for the emergency operation set up by NSA, tells the story, as does Garland in her memoir. The event took place the week before the United States entered the Korean war.

The unanticipated expense of the *Svalbard* matter resulted in a deficit that nearly sank the Association. In summer 1951, NSA appointed Tom Callahan (St. Francis College, NY) as its first full-time Travel Director, in charge of an incorporated travel office in New York City. A digest is provided of Callahan's detailed history and description of the operation, written in 1953 for NSA's *Student Government Bulletin.* The cost of round-trip ship or air fares was $300-$385, and a 63-day tour was offered for as low as $550.

1947

International Student News

Delegates From Canada, U.S. Discuss Student Exchange

U.S. Study Abroad Planned by NSA

Foreign Orientation Will Be Developed by

NSA to Organize European Tours

Hungary Invites Students to Hold Summer Seminar

NSA ENCOURAGED TRAVEL ABROAD and student exchange as centerpieces to its mission to further international understanding. (From top: *NSA News* 10/47; U. of Louisville, *Cardinal*, 2/14/52.)

NSA Becomes a Major Sponsor of Student Travel Abroad

Fly . . .

KLM Skymaster

NSA LEADS THE WAY—

once again by offering you the "budget" chance of a lifetime to fly to Europe this summer at the lowest possible cost. KLM, the Royal Dutch Airlines, has been chartered by NSA for scheduled flights for economy-minded students and faculty members. In addition to the regular flights, we have planned late-summer flights for students entering European colleges in the fall. Our flight space is limited, so to be sure of your reservation fill out the enclosed application and send your deposit immediately. The European trip you have always dreamed of *can* become a reality!

NSA HAS CHARTERED 54-passenger KLM *Skymasters*. These top-notch planes, piloted and operated by employees of one of the finest companies in the flight field, provide fast, safe transportation on comfortable, well-serviced ships. For students who want to spend most of their time in Europe, with little time devoted to crossing—this is the lowest cost air transportation offered by any agency or airline. Included in the cost of the flight are three meals while traveling (and a handy overnight bag!), courtesy of KLM.

Eastbound Departures

June 17, 23, 24, 27, 28, 29, July 7 (from New York to London and Amsterdam)

September 3, 11, October 1 (from New York to London and Amsterdam)

Westbound Departures

August 23, 26, 31; September 1, 6, 7, 14 (from London and Amsterdam to New York)

Additional flight dates will be available later.

Prices

Exact prices will be furnished on request.

NOTE: These low cost student charter planes and ships available only to bona fide students and faculty members.

Sail . . .

Courtesy Holland-America Line — *S.S. Groote Beer*

NSA LEADS THE WAY—

in low-cost sailings to Europe with accommodations on four great student ships: three Dutch Government ships, which we use for our own tour groups, plus the Italian ship *Castel Felice*. The *Castel Felice* boasts a swimming pool, fun deck for tennis and shuffleboard, a cocktail lounge and other "luxury" features. All four ships have complete medical staffs and offer professionally staffed orientation programs. In addition . . . there will be lots of other activity such as square dancing, folk singing and motion pictures.

ITALIAN STUDENT SHIP

Eastbound Departures

S.S. Castel Felice—June 30 (from New York to Southampton, Le Havre and Bremerhaven); June 4 (from Quebec to Southampton, Le Havre and Bremerhaven)

Westbound Departures

S.S. Castel Felice—August 22, 23 (from Le Havre and Southampton to New York); August 4, 6 (from Bremerhaven and Southampton to Quebec)

Prices

Round-trip—$280 (dormitory); $300 and up (cabin)
One-way—$140 (dormitory); $150 and up (cabin)

DUTCH STUDENT SHIPS

Eastbound Departures

S.S. Waterman—June 21 (from New York to Rotterdam)

S.S. Zuiderkruis—June 28 (from New York to Rotterdam)

Westbound Departures

S.S. Waterman—August 25 (from Rotterdam to New York)

S.S. Groote Beer—September 2 (from Rotterdam to New York)

Prices

Round-trip—$300 (dormitory); $320 and up (cabin)
One-way—$150 (dormitory); $160 and up (cabin)

Other NSA Travel Services

Low Cost Student Tours

EDUCATIONAL TRAVEL, INC., operated by the United States National Student Association, administers its own travel program for students who wish to participate in a planned group-tour. NSA tours concentrate on high educational standards and feature rock bottom prices. Divided into several interest areas, NSA tours include an Arts group, a Music Festival group, an International group (emphasis on general sightseeing), a Sociology study group, an Economics and Politics group, and several Work Camp projects. Students taking these tours have the benefit of traveling under the auspices of a recognized organization with official contacts in all of the nations visited. The tour itineraries cover virtually every country in Western Europe. The average cost, including transportation, food and accommodations, is from $600-$800 per tour.

Travel Advisory Service

ON MANY CAMPUSES NSA Travel Committees act as clearing houses for general information on travel abroad. In addition, Educational Travel, Inc., maintains two offices—one in New York, and one in Paris (during the summer) where trained personnel are available to help any student with his travel problems.

'Work, Study, Travel Abroad'

NSA'S ANNUAL TRAVEL GUIDE "Work, Study, Travel Abroad" (64-pp. last year) is considered to be the only complete catalogue of information gathered from every agency or organization in the student travel field. In addition, the booklet contains valuable information on passports, visas, arrangements in Europe, currency, planning a trip, and living costs. The price is 35¢ per copy—order your 1954 edition now!

•

For information, write—

NSA EDUCATIONAL TRAVEL, INC.
48 WEST 48th STREET
NEW YORK CITY 19, NEW YORK

347

NSA CHARTERED FLIGHTS AND SPACE ON STUDENT SHIPS, becoming a major provider of low-cost tour programs as well as space for individual travel. 75-day Tri-Nation tours averaged $865. The scope of its programs are featured above in a 1953 brochure announcing its 1954 summer season (See p. 668 for 1950 report).

NSA hosts 13% of student travel in 1950

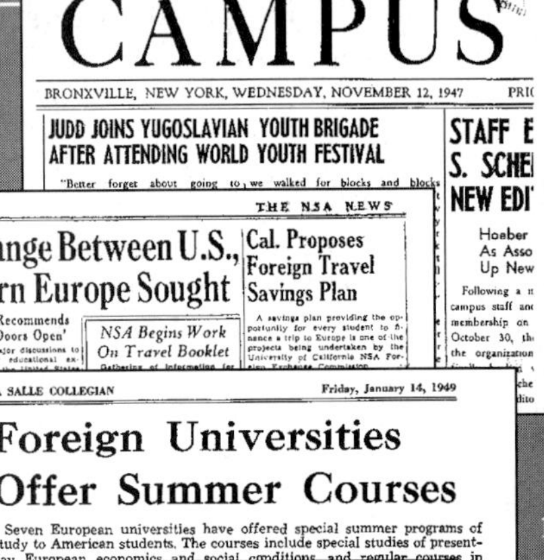

CAMPUS

BRONXVILLE, NEW YORK, WEDNESDAY, NOVEMBER 12, 1947

JUDD JOINS YUGOSLAVIAN YOUTH BRIGADE AFTER ATTENDING WORLD YOUTH FESTIVAL

STAFF E... S. SCHE... NEW EDI...

1947

Page 4 — THE NSA NEWS

Exchange Between U.S., Eastern Europe Sought

Commission Recommends 'U. S. Keep Doors Open'

Cal. Proposes Foreign Travel Savings Plan

NSA Begins Work On Travel Booklet

1948

LA SALLE COLLEGIAN — Friday, January 14, 1949

Foreign Universities Offer Summer Courses

Seven European universities have offered special summer programs of study to American students. The courses include special studies of present-day European economics and social conditions and regular course in...

1949

Weekly Publication Of The Berea College Student Association

The Wallpaper

"God Hath Made of One Blood All Nations of Men"

Vol. 17 — Berea, Ky., Saturday, April 8, 1950 — No. 23

Whitney Will Conduct Philharmonic In Two Concerts On Saturday

Next Saturday, the Louisville Philharmonic, conducted by Robert Whitney, will make its annual...

Elizabeth Hutchison Is Selected To Attend NSA European Work Camp

1950

...ENIX — Wednesday, March 14, 1951

NSA Sets April 1 Deadline For Work, Study, Travel, Tour

The deadline for applying for "work, study and travel tours" of the National Student Association this summer has been extended to April... gram in South and Central America. All of these tours were organized by and designed for students, by the NSA in co-operation with the...

1951

INDEPENDENT NEWSPAPER
...ssociated Students of the University of Colorado
...er, Colorado, Thursday, August 7, 1952 — Vol. LXI, No. 254

NSA-Sponsored Students Impressed By U.S. Sights

Fifteen students from Swiss universities arrive in Boulder today for a five day stay in Colorado. They are here under the auspices of the National Student Association.

These students, who include 11 Swiss, 3 Italians, and one German are currently in the United States on a two month study tour. The purpose of the study tour is to give these students a good general picture of life...

1952

TRAVEL TO EUROPE IN THE SUMMER OF 1948. From top: NSA Tri-Nation Tour pauses at fountain in Ghent, Belgium (*J. R. Hersleven*. Marianne Bodecker, See p. 000). U.S. students repairing a bicycle path in Walkeheren, The Netherlands (William Allaway. See p. 000). Students waiting to debark a Holland America Line student ship, c. 1950 (SHSW).

COLLEGE PRESS FEATURES EXCHANGE PROGRAMS. Left, from top: Sarah Lawrence C., *The Campus*, 11/12/47; *NSA News*, 11/48; *La Salle Collegian*, 1/14/49; Berea C., *The Wallpaper*, 3/18/50; Swarthmore C., *The Phoenix*, 3/14/51; U. of Colorado, *Silver and Gold*, 8/7/52.

Summer travel and exchange programs have campus appeal

The student ships of 1948-1951

1. Managing NSA's International Student Travel Operations

Helen Bryan Garland
Student Body President, Sarah Lawrence College 1947
Manager, NSA Student Travel Program, 1948-1950

When Rob West succeeded Bob Smith as NSA's International Vice President in 1948, the MIT students who had been working on foreign student seminars suggested that I move from the American Field Service (AFS)[1] Office to the Harvard Square NSA office, where I would be working with students, free from adult supervision. This fit precisely with my recent context at Sarah Lawrence College, from which I had graduated in 1947, which encouraged students to avoid textbooks and/or the acceptance of "isms" before they could develop fresh insights of their own. Sarah Lawrence President Harold Taylor articulated this for us in 1947.[2]

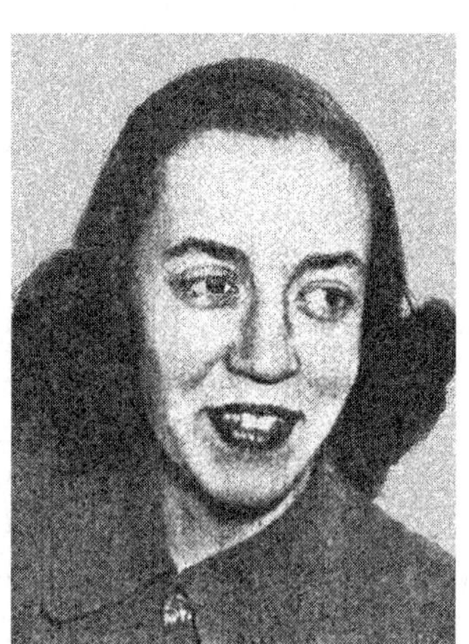

The choice was made easier because the AFS had decided to move its office to New York. My parents' home was on Acacia Street, two minutes from Harvard Square, which would allow me to live on the $50 a week salary which typified the salary offered to college women graduates in 1947.

My credentials couldn't have been better. I had attended the 1946 Chicago Conference as president of the Sarah Lawrence student government. I had been born in India, traveled and lived abroad, and spoke French. My father's cousin, Julien Bryan, a well-known documentary photographer, had served in the American Field Service in World War I. My Princeton-educated father was a Presbyterian chaplain who had just returned from the war in Europe. Helen Bryan, the aunt for whom I was named, was honoring family traditions by defying the House Un-American Activities Committee. I could claim both liberal and conservative—veritably Founding Fathers—roots! And I could type.

My first assignment from Rob was to write to every country and every organization in the world for information and publish the second volume of *Study, Travel, Work Abroad* for American students. The first edition had been put together by volunteers during Bob Smith's term the year before.[3] Rob and Mildred Kiefer and I discussed the order for the title of the blue, white, and green book and decided that "study" should be retained as the lead word. I can't remember why "work" was considered less than "travel."

My first experience with the famous "cool wrath of Rob West" came when he learned of the delay caused by a typist having mailed out to the entire world a letter saying, "Dear Minister of Education, Please let us know what opportunities exist for students to study, travel or work in Afghanistan." The typist had changed the address for each recipient, but not the name of the country in the body of the letter! At first I was mortified as we received our scolding. But then we began to receive humorous letters from such places as Canada, Switzerland, and Holland, declaring that they did not have too much information on opportunities in Afghanistan! Gradually, even Rob turned it into an ongoing joke, often inserting it into otherwise deadly serious dictation or debate.

The response to *Study, Travel, Work Abroad* swamped our office, as did the deluge of applications. I recall that we could only accept around 1,200 students for the *Volendam* that year, although we could have filled three such ships.

In June, Rob declared that once the *Volendam* sailed, our Cambridge office would be empty, and "we could all go to Crane's Beach" to celebrate—which is where the MIT students took their foreign guests!

A sudden decision to sail to Europe

Driving up to Canada to meet the *Volendam* with Linda Cabot in her family limo, we were stopped, but we were not given a ticket for speeding to meet the incoming students for Meg Weld's seminar.[4] The *Volendam* docked in Wolfe's Cove in Canada as the passengers were primarily immigrants to Canada from Holland. The outbound sailing was delayed for three hours because a bus bringing Experiment in International Living students had broken down en route.[5]

I have photos of Ed Wolfe and Wim Heyneker manning the NSA office on the dock, along with all the Canadian and

Dutch officials, who were enjoying the excitement and frivolity of such an unusual group of passengers! For most of the students, it was a first experience with the better-than-hotel features of the ship's lounges. Somewhere, the decision had been made to permit Heineken's beer to be sold from a variety of bars on board! Dinner in the main dining room before departure with Captain Casey Snellman reminded me of the many times I had sailed between India, Scotland, and the United States with my parents. At the end of the dinner, the Captain remarked that I should be sailing on this voyage.

I had booked all my friends from Sarah Lawrence and Harvard Square. Rob had said there wouldn't be much to do at the office. It dawned on me that of course I should go, to observe all our tours, work camps, and trips, and to visit the offices of the national students unions that had planned and coordinated everything with us!

After dinner, I found Rob on deck. He had unexpectedly flown up—after all, Ed Wolfe was his roommate! And wasn't Ed's sister sailing with us?

I convinced Rob of the logic and value of my plan. I had expanded my idea to include coverage of my job at the office by Wim Heyneker, the NBBS representative who had worked on arrangements for the *Volendam,* and who would be staying with his new American wife in Cambridge. I told Rob that with Wim's knowledge and her typing and English skills, they could earn my $50 a week and take over my new apartment on Chauncey Street, just a few minutes' walk from the office!

Everything was perfect! My parents wouldn't be shocked. In 1947, we had sailed on the *Queen Mary* to spend the summer in Scotland with my grandmother and my mother's whole family. I sent a message saying I would go straight to Scotland to visit before taking off to review the NSA programs. I knew that would delight my parents, and it probably would justify my asking them, in a phone call to be made by Wim, to "send cash—I have already sailed for Europe."

However, Wim and his wife forgot to phone the message until they actually got to my apartment. Meanwhile, I had "packed" with nothing but a pocketbook and a tiny suitcase, for a summer of study, travel, work, sports, and dancing in Europe.

My quick decision involved other complications. In the immediate postwar years, it was forbidden to take money out of the Western European countries. This meant that, without some sort of special dispensation, I would not be able to leave England or Holland with more money than I had when I entered, which would be the situation when my parents sent me money—Also, although I had my passport with me, it had expired. Being trained to honesty, I knew that I could not lie about it, and I also knew that my statement, "born in India," was an invitation to be asked to produce proof of citizenship.

The U.S. and Canadian officials on the dock had become friendly with Wim, Ed, and the NSA entourage. They simply "charged my ticket" to me! In a humorous flourish, I waved the expired passport in front of the Canadian officials. They had no interest, since I was American, not Canadian. I was aboard! On the ship, Stephanie Scheiffer, my Sarah Lawrence roommate, and my best friend, Betsy Augustus of Cleveland, loaned me some cash and a pair of jeans.

On board the *Volendam*

Jos Vos, who would later work in our Cambridge office, was on board the *Volendam* to help run the NBBS/NSA office. John Reurs, the son of the passenger manager of the Holland America Line, was also on board, returning to Holland after graduating from Harvard. For me, he was probably a helpful contact. When the ship docked in Rotterdam, instead of having to wait in line to go through the formalities of customs and entry, I was whisked away in a consular limousine with American flags waving on the front fenders, to have my passport renewed by the consul, who was delighted to hear news from home. "Home" was literally accurate—he had been raised in Cambridge, Massachusetts, and enjoyed having a first-hand account of the NSA Travel Office and the Student Ship Program that operated from Cambridge. His name was Duffield—after all these years, it suddenly came back to me!

I took the channel boat from Hock van Holland to England. An uncle met the boat. The *Volendam* had taken thirteen days to cross the Atlantic—plenty of time for my parents to telegraph my grandmother and arrange to make funds available to me. Unbeknownst to me or my parents, my grandmother had decided it was time to make up for all the wartime birthdays and Christmases on which she hadn't been able to send gifts since 1938. She sent a huge bunch of British bills as big as table napkins. I had no idea what the exchange rate was, but I knew it was more money than I'd dream of spending.

Harry Baum of the British National Union of Students Travel Office wrote an officious "Please allow Miss Bryan to withdraw whatever sums she requires," for every other student union office in Europe! I don't know how this must have impressed everyone, including Harry Baum! But I fulfilled each responsibility. I covered any loss to the smooth running of the office, "repaid" my parents by using only a small portion of my grandmother's gift, and did not have to account for my cash supply at every border. NSA benefited as I paid for the cost of my own training program.

Erskine Childers and the International Office

The official and personal visits that I made in England, Scotland, Holland, France, Switzerland, and Italy greatly increased my knowledge of the current condition of these nations and of the student scene. However, Rob West had flown on ahead instead of going free on the *Volendam*. And Rob West fired me!

The newly reelected Erskine Childers rehired me. When Erskine took over the International Office, we moved from the University Travel Company office, which was across from the subway kiosk in Harvard Square, to a little, old house owned by the glamorous wife of a Harvard architecture professor, which was jammed in among huge buildings across from the Pi Eta Club. We rented the second floor over her new French restaurant. We immediately abandoned our Howard Johnson lunches for incredible 99-cent lunches in the French restaurant—salads, pommes frites, breads, everything avec champignons and an array of desserts! The French lady presumably saw us as her steadies while she attracted more affluent customers!

Jos Vos had arrived to be the NBBS representative, and to coordinate Holland America Line and NSA booking of the *Volendam*. We learned that his family had been "marked" by the Nazis during the war and had gone into hiding to escape the death camps. Jos had been hidden in the home of a Protestant carpenter, who had put an axe in front of his bedroom door and said, "They'll have to get me before they get you." Before we heard this story, we thought that he was much in need of our guidance!

Jos was sending the family that had sheltered him, as well as his own, food, medicine, and treats. He was also making up for some lost time with his own diet. No one in his right mind ordinarily orders orange juice three time a day with his meals at Howard Johnson's, or has ice cream for breakfast! Erskine took particular delight in teaching Jos the finer points of American student culture. He explained dating, including sandwich dates, double dates, and much more, I'm sure.[6] Frank Fisher, who had been involved with NSA's international program, both as a Harvard undergraduate and as a student in Harvard Law School, virtually adopted Jos and made all the housing and other arrangements for and with him.[7]

Rob West had gone back to Yale for study in the Graduate School of Economics. Mildred Kiefer had gone to Madison. Our new staff included Mary Clemens Mayhew Smith, the wife of a Harvard law student, who was known as Spinney. She was a Mount Holyoke graduate, and contributed both "married woman stability" and a wonderful sense of humor. Erskine and Jos both persisted in hiring secretaries who could not type. I hired Charlotte Agnew, a Phi Beta Kappa graduate of Stanford, later the wife of Frank Fisher's brother Gerard. Erskine added an office manager—her name was Char Allen.[8] Bob Delehanty came to work with us. MITs Lloyd Haynes's fiancée, Opal, came from Oklahoma to join our staff; her skills were as great as those of Charlotte Agnew.

Erskine was one of the most dedicated and focused persons I had ever met. He did, however, seem to have a problem of occasionally trusting the wrong people! He hired a treasurer who simply did not fit. He was last seen driving off to tour Europe on a motorcycle. He disappeared as soon as the *Ballou* docked in Europe, saying he could not make sense out of the books.

Erskine got busy on air charters for student groups, beginning with Flying Tigers. As previously noted, I was responsible for producing the publication *Study, Travel, Work Abroad.* This publication more than paid for itself and for the price of the tickets to pay for transportation ($285 round trip for the *Volendam*, $310 for the *Svalbard*). The price for each tour and work camp was set by the combination of student unions that managed them. Most of their administrative work was done by student volunteers. The Dutch were outstanding in this respect, and the British were organized and "professional."

The French part was run by the Office du Tourisme Universitaire (OTU), which was elegantly and very professionally run by two Countesses, Mlle. Aviet and Mme. De Beaulieu. My AFS connections strengthened this relationship, since that office had also been involved with the first seven AFS scholars, all of them outstanding, with whom I had worked before joining the AFS office.

The *Svalbard*

Harry Baum of the British National Union of Students, the Dutch students of the Netherlands Office for Foreign Student Relations (NBBS), Kaj Pitzner-Jorgensen of Denmark, and Olof Palme of Sweden[9] (the latter two both being officials of the Scandinavian Student Union), all knew that I had been asking if the Holland-America Line could find us another ship. It was Kaj who called the Cambridge Office to tell me that they knew that the Norwegians had a wonderful "wessel" available, called the *Svalbard*. It had been built by the Germans in 1938 and given to Norway after the war as reparations. The *Svalbard* had been transporting refugees from place to place in Europe and elsewhere, but had never been to the United States.

Frank Fisher offered to introduce me to one of his law professors, Mark deWolfe Howe, who, Frank said, could explain what would be involved in chartering a ship. Through Professor Howe, we obtained legal counsel from a New York law firm specializing in admiralty law. A lawyer with this firm wrote what was called a "charter party." I learned that these matters were governed by the Geneva Convention for the Safety of Lives on the Seas, which had been promulgated in 1913. As might be expected of a Norwegian navy–owned ship, the *Svalbard* met all of the Convention's requirements.

We also knew that no ship could leave a U.S. port without clearance by the U.S. Coast Guard. As Erskine reported to the Michigan Congress in August 1948, NSA's International Commission:

> requested the Oslo authorities to make a formal diplomatic request through Washington for U.S. Coast Guard authorization of an inspection according to U.S. laws while she lay in the Oslo harbor....Despite the clearly reiterated notices to the Norwegian government that port clearance was the owner's responsibility, the Commission was compelled to engage in extensive negotiations and research into these problems to assist the Norwegian government.

These negotiations dragged on until the ship left Oslo bound for New York. The report continues: "The New York Coast Guard stated from the first . . . that they could not give a definitive ruling until the vessel was presented at the Port of New York for entrance and clearance with passengers." Additional foot-dragging while the ship rested in New York harbor for ten days, resulted in a last-day inspection, which denied the *Svalbard* permits to sail and resulted in the high drama that followed.[10]

In retrospect, I wonder who among us should have been hounding the Coast Guard for this inspection. As far as we could see and understand, there could be no reason for the Coast Guard to deny this courtesy to Norway, our courageous wartime ally. It may be that part of our problem lay in an inevitable, but unfortunate, division of responsibilities, with Erskine and the lawyers involved in paperwork and financial arrangements and me involved with individual student needs, lost tickets, supplying of the ship, and innumerable other matters. In addition, we simply did not dream that U.S. authorities would subsequently deny port clearance to a ship that was scrupulously operated by one of the world's most important and experienced shipping nations, that met all international requirements, that was involved in a mission that was strongly supported by numerous U.S. government agencies in the fields of education and international affairs, and that made both commercial and common sense as part of postwar goodwill!

Trip to Oslo

It was agreed that Erskine was too busy and that his presence in Cambridge was too essential to his projects, and I was therefore assigned to handle the next phases of the *Svalbard* arrangements. For me, it was a continuation of our dealings with Professor Howe and the officials of the Holland America Line. I found it exasperating that Jos would not involve himself in matters relating to the *Svalbard*, which meant that I had to do all the work! Naturally, he would have been instructed that he was not being paid to help the competition, but would not want to tell me so.

Early in May 1950, armed with a copy of the Geneva Convention and the actual plans for the *Svalbard*, I took the subway from Harvard Square to Logan Airport, where temporary buildings in a sea of mud provided inelegant access to a propeller-driven plane that took seventeen hours to fly to Amsterdam. On arrival, I was met by NBBS representatives whom I had gotten to know the previous summer. We had an airport conference during the stopover. They wanted to know how things were shaping up for their tours, travel programs, and work camps. For them, it was essential for this ship charter to work, or else their programs would be five hundred students short!

When I arrived in Oslo, no one came forward to meet me. I hopped off the plane in a green linen suit, with a tiny suitcase/attache case and a portable typewriter. I am wearing that same suit in a photo taken aboard the *Volendam* a few weeks later, showing me being greeted by Prince Bernhard of the Netherlands.

It dawned on me that a nearby group of men in naval uniforms was talking about how they knew for certain that the U.S. representative was to have been on that flight. Realizing that they thought that the "U.S. representative" would be a businessman, I had to step forward and try to ignore their dismay that the representative was an un-uniformed "girl" of twenty-four!

I recall the name of the Norwegian commander in charge as being Hostvedt. Four men took me to meet the broker and to drop off my suitcase at a hotel before proceeding to the ship. And all this was with no proper sleep for well over thirty hours!

Captain Andreassen of the *Svalbard* had been clued in on the indignity of the United States sending such a preposterous representative, and they were all enjoying what they thought was a private joke. I knew what was happening, and underneath I was angry and impatient with them. I didn't have much time as the sailing date was about six weeks off! I had already counted the heads (latrines) and had figured out as much as I could about the requirements of the Geneva Convention as they applied to the *Svalbard*.

As the tour of the ship began, they realized that I meant business, but they could not resist taking me even beyond the engine rooms to see the propeller shaft. I didn't know what to say—"Oh, what a marvelous and shiny shaft!" or, "Yes, it looks OK." So instead, I instinctively said the right thing: "I've seen the engine rooms of both the Queens and the

Europa." They were also startled that I knew so much about charter parties and Geneva Convention requirements.

However, they could not resist a final dig. In discussing the provisioning of the "wessel," I was able to tell them what the *Volendam* and the *Veendam* offered the students in the shops and dining areas. But when they asked what I would recommend as an adequate supply of condoms, they finally scored. I was dumbstruck! No adult in my life had ever mentioned the word or alluded to the concept. Years later, I learned that there had been many jokes about hiding in the *Volendam*'s lifeboats, and so on, but, frankly, those student ships did not allow for any privacy that I could see!

Once having settled this matter of injured dignity their way, by giving them the last word, I must say that everyone involved joined in our contagious NSA good spirits. They were humorous, adventurous, and ingenious. In the short time before the ship set sail for New York, they added paneling for card rooms and made the ship more generally appealing than it had been for refugees. Handwork and decorative art were everywhere, and a typical Scandinavian menu was to be provided. And the ship was new and precision built!

Symbols of healing, recovery, and energy

On my return flight from Oslo to Amsterdam, engine trouble forced the plane to land at the nearest airport, which was Christianstad. It was dramatic to look down and see ambulances and fire equipment below us on the ground. Happily, we landed without incident, and we sat in the sunshine actually watching the engine being removed and replaced. I put my portable typewriter on my lap and wrote up my report.

During the Amsterdam stopover, I again met with the NBBS representatives and also met with the passenger manager of the Holland America Line (HAL). He showed not a flicker of surprise at my conviction that HAL would berth the competitive student ship! Yes, it brought activity to Holland's waterfront. But more than that, I believe that he and most of the Europeans we dealt with were simply happy and invigorated by the infectious enthusiasm of the U.S. students and of NSA. He knew Jos Vos, and (as already mentioned), his son John had been on the *Volendam* with us the year before. John's father would naturally be pleased to witness the joyful "normal" scene of the ship coming in with 1,200 "normal" students, to a country still drab and still staggering to recover. We had seen the rubble that had been Hamburg and were told that Rotterdam looked the same before it had been "tidied up." Our ships were symbols of healing, recovery, and wonderful energy. NSA was doing the right job at the right time and in the right way!

Our docking arrangements were therefore secured by the highest official in charge of such matters. And years later, in 1970, I married John Reurs. He and Jos then headed the Holland America Line offices in New York.

The crisis looms

Back in the United States, Erskine and I shuttled back and forth from Boston to New York, he working mostly on the air charters and I with the admiralty lawyers and the Norwegian America Line. In retrospect, I know I startled every one of those old-line shipping types, who were affronted by my age and gender. I can still see the face of Mr. Wiersma in the Holland America Line's New York Office! But they all realized quickly that it was the subject at hand that mattered.

The first negative reaction that I encountered was from the head of the American Society of Travel Agents (ASTA). He was not amused, pleased, or inclined to share in our effort, even though I had come to inform him that we would be paying the usual 6 percent commission. He had a gun on his desk, which he had to pick up and toy with so he could watch my curiosity or apprehension. He postponed pulling the trigger; when he finally did, it produced a flame to light his cigar. To this day, I do not know what reason he may have had to oppose our plans, but he made it clear that he did.

When the *Svalbard* crisis erupted, we were working out of a hotel suite in the Woodstock Hotel—the cheapest hotel in Times Square. My sister lived in the city, so with her hospitality, I never had to charge for food, phone, or hotel accommodations for myself. Many volunteers from NSA colleges in New York were also pitching in.

All seemed to be going so well that we were not alarmed that the inspection issue had not yet been resolved between the Norwegian Government and the U.S. Coast Guard.

It was exciting to stand on the dock at the lower Manhattan pier in New York and actually watch the *Svalbard* arrive on June 12. On the morning of the scheduled departure, June 22, with hundreds of students on the dock, I had my first shock. A man in charge of admeasuring[11] said to me, "Miss Bryan, there are only seven admeasurers in the whole of the United States, and today four of them are on board your ship!"

The silence and delay had been warnings, and it was an ominous sign that the Commandant of the Coast Guard in New York, whose name was Fleming, personally escorted his men onto the *Svalbard*, after delaying the inspection until the very morning the students were ready to embark. We had to make the students wait, sitting on their suitcases on the dock. Captain Andreassen, our lawyer, and I were sitting in his office/cabin, while the Captain mildly protested that this was a terrible time to make his crew go on double duty—preparing for departure and assisting in the inspection—when the inspection could have been done on any of the past ten days while the *Svalbard* had been in port.

Throughout the day, I kept asking him how we were doing. He finally gave me a big grin, as though he had only been teasing, and said, "Looks good."

In the Captain's cabin, we celebrated with wonderful food and, I suppose, drinks, although I had never liked beer or even wine. The HAL people had informed the captain that it was "the custom" to be very liberal with bottled gifts for absolutely everyone who came aboard on business of any kind—suppliers, Coast Guard, Port Authority, Customs, and unions. It was amazing to witness the avalanche of business that was dumped on poor Captain Andreassen. He had become a real friend, like Captain Casey Snellman of the *Volendam*, who, in 1948, had stopped and turned his ship around in a busy shipping lane to rescue a student who had fallen overboard.

The ship is declared "Unsuitable"

About noon, one of Fleming's officers arrived to say that Fleming requested the Captain and Miss Bryan join him on the deck. The normal procedure would have been for them to come to the Captain's cabin. One part of the deck was surrounded by a higher level of deck, which provided access to the bridge, some of the lifeboats, and other equipment. It was lined with crew members—male and female, I was happy to see—all putting things back in place after the inspection. They could hear, and watched in amazement, as Fleming declared their lovely ship "unsuitable to clear the port of New York." For some reason, I remember that he had a hearing aid, and he was as grumpy-looking as McGrath of ASTA.

I looked at him in disbelief and said, "You're kidding!"

He replied, "This is no joking matter, young lady."

I then asked, "What must be changed? What is wrong?"

He replied that the combination of certain bunks being nineteen instead of twenty-one inches apart, and one bulkhead being too close to a wooden ladder (staircase) meant that the ship would not clear Coast Guard inspection.

I was told later that, if we had sufficient notice, we could have gone to a Bethlehem Steel Yard just across the Hudson River to make the required modifications. But when I asked Fleming how we could make the necessary changes, he replied, "I'm afraid that's *your* problem, young lady." So, with all the crew and the Captain watching and listening, I said, "Sir, I respect your rules, but I have no respect for you as a human being!" And I burst into tears.

Suddenly, I felt the lawyer's hand on my elbow as he whispered in my ear, "Let's go powder your nose. . . ." What he meant was, "Get out of here before he slaps you with penalties or a lawsuit or something terrible."

Erskine would not arrive until close to what was to be sailing time, so it was up to me to go to the NAL offices on the dock, which were empty because they were only used when there was a sailing and all the men were on the ship. I picked up a phone and called our hotel office, the broker, and anyone else I could think of who could help us decide what to do. Moments later, a too-handsome guy with what we used to call "Yale White Shoes" came into the office and, without permission, picked up another phone. I asked him who he was, and he said, "Associated Press." The wire services and all the New York papers had sent photographers and writers to get stories from the departing students. As he phoned the Coast Guard offices, I told him that the entire Coast Guard was on board the ship, but he got hold of someone who had nothing to do with the inspection and had absolutely no authority or knowledge, but who must have said, "It's probably a firetrap."

When I realized he was going to phone in that story, I told him that it was absolutely false and that there were only two minor requirements, but he interrupted me and said, "It's a good story." I didn't bother to tell him about my lack of respect for him, but I immediately worried about all the parents that would be needlessly scared to death now. Somehow I did learn that he was a Yale man!

Solving the problems

When I had put out all the necessary feelers for solving the problem, I went down to the dock where the students were waiting. To my astonishment, although Erskine had not yet materialized, Rob West had! He had had nothing to do with our office business since the previous fall. He was climbing up on one of those frame platforms used for scrubbing and painting. A hush fell over the crowd of students, and I cringed as I heard Rob announce, "There has been a slight delay." The students sensed that it was a half-truth and jumped to the logical fear that NSA had gone off with their money or that there had been some other kind of swindle. They began shouting at Rob.

I can't remember how things were resolved at that moment, but a while later it was announced that student dormitories were available: NYU, CCNY, and Columbia NSA reps had gone into action. Luckily, people such as Bob Meagher of CCNY were on the dock, ready to sail with such programs as the Seminar in Higher Education in Germany, and they instantly knew what to do![12] It was wonderful to see the crisis turn into something so full of adventure and goodwill. Restaurants, hotels, and theaters began swamping the office with offers of free or bargain-rate meals.

Imagine my outrage as I saw, from the dock, the ship *Roma* heading out to sea. Built in 1908, it was crammed with Catholic students, who were not sharing their facilities and were unobstructed by the Coast Guard!

On the way back to the office, I was appalled to see the ticker-tape–like lights around the Times Square building proclaiming, "Ship Declared Fire Trap 500 Students Stranded." The lobby of the hotel was jammed with photographers and newsmen who took to following us up and down in the elevators and eavesdropping behind potted palms. I even found one going through our files. A picture of me appeared in the afternoon *Daily News* or *Post*, with a caption indicating that I was dealing with worried parents. I was actually talking to my sister about whether I would be back for dinner. A most able group of student volunteers was handling all the parent calls. The Woodstock Hotel had never had such celebrity!

On the dock, there were photos of students who had been told to pose as though they were dejected. Frank Fisher's brother Gerry was prominent in one photo. He wasn't even sailing on the ship, having showed up to see friends off.

Erskine finally arrived at the hotel. For some reason he gave a blanket order: "No more talking to the press." At just that moment, a woman reporter from the *New York Times* named Laurie Johnson came up to me and said, "I'm not leaving here until I get the straight story." Instinct told me that this was not the time to obey orders. I nodded in the direction of one of the bedrooms, and we went in and shut the door. She sat on one bed and I sat on the other.

I told her of our early request for Coast Guard inspection and of the strange and purposeful delay on the part of the Coast Guard. I told her exactly what the costs were and what the students were paying, and described the entire postwar significance of the project. I explained that the ship was in no way a firetrap, but that the bunks had to be moved two inches and certain combinations of wooden stairs and bulkheads had to be changed. She got it! Out of the entire press corps, she was *the* best.

To my great satisfaction (and I never gloated over this with Erskine), the next morning, the upper corner of page one of the *New York Times* let the whole world, and our parents, know exactly what was going on. So much for Mr. Yaley White Shoes!

It began dawning on me that I should not be hating the press because without the news coverage, we would have been slow to find alternative solutions. Sure enough, that same day a call came through from the White House! An adviser to President Truman for maritime affairs called and said that if we worded a telegram diplomatically and respectfully, requesting him to release a U.S. marine transport, we could expect one to be released within three days!

Erskine and I dispatched a diplomatically worded telegram, and within hours we knew that the *General Ballou* was on its way. We informed the students that they would sail in three days. They were delighted with the bonus of three days in New York and three days less on the sea. The *Ballou* would make the crossing in eight days, instead of the eleven that the *Svalbard* estimated and the thirteen that the *Volendam* required.[13]

The *Volendam* sails again

I would have preferred to remain in New York for the sailing of the *Ballou,* but I was assigned to travel by train to Quebec to organize the sailing of the *Volendam* on June 26, again from Wolfe's Cove, and to be the NSA representative on board.

Despite the excitement, again, of 1,200 students, Captain Casey, and Jos Vos and Frank Fisher and their orientation program all preparing to sail on the *Volendam,* I could hardly figure out what source of outrage to focus on. Almost fifty years later, I can still only guess that there was some explanation for what was so unnatural, stupid and *wrong*, leading to the displacement of what was so *right* in the joint venture with Norway, HAL, and NSA. Or is it just the fact that I sensed manipulation? I still do not know.

About five days out into the Atlantic, I was given a radiogram. It was from Captain Andreassen and the crew of the *Svalbard,* wishing me bon voyage and all best wishes. It still brings tears to my eyes to visualize that ship sailing back empty to Norway. Captain Snellman knew how dreadful I felt about this, and he was both tactful and diverting. He allowed us to use his cabin, and each evening he arranged a reception with alternating officers and leaders of the various groups sailing with us.

On about the eleventh day at sea, Captain Snellman told us that the *Ballou* had steamed ahead of us so fast that the HAL office had radioed for instructions on how to deal with the fact that the Royal Arrival Ceremonies, complete with Prince Bernhard of the Netherlands, might greet the wrong ship! It was supposed to be the HAL/Dutch *Volendam* that the press would first sight coming in with yet another joyful load of students and linkings to the wonders of the USA! It wasn't supposed to be "The Competition"!

NBBS representatives, led by Jos Vos, responded ingeniously. A radio instruction was dispatched to the captain of the *Ballou* to allow the *Volendam* to precede the *Ballou* to the dock. The instruction was graciously received and complied with. We felt a pang when we saw all our friends lining the railings of the *Ballou* as it sat in the harbor while we proceeded to the pier, but they were having fun.

The accompanying photo, showing me, Jos Vos, and Fritz Schneider of NBBS talking with Prince Bernhard proves that all ended as it should! Frank and Jos and some others had prepared a hand-painted T-shirt for presentation to the prince, to mark our gratitude to Holland for its leadership role in postwar student ships and student travel.

Helen Bryan Garland, shown here with her husband, journalist and author Joe Garland, has been concerned with, and active through, the United Nations and in her Gloucester, MA, community in global peace, maritime and environmental preservation. She collaborated for many years with Margaret Mead in her United Nations initiatives and is working on Mead's biography.

Again, I was, and still am, so proud of the energy and ingenuity of the students!

After a summer of checking on NSA programs and visiting national student union offices, I returned to the United States on the *Volendam*. There I learned that either at or after the NSA Convention, it was decided to move the NSA Travel Office to New York. Erskine was soon to leave for England. My job as travel organizer was finished.

I moved, in some magic way, to a job at Phillips Brooks House and on to other jobs. Erskine and Spinney (Mary Clemens Mayhew Smith) and Frank Fisher arranged an engagement party in Cambridge, in cooperation with Erskine's aunt and my aunt, Mrs. George Bryan. In June, 1951, I was to marry Bob Carlson, a Harvard Law School student. He and Bob Fischelis and Don Trautman were Harvard roommates.

Erskine and Rob remained forever friends. Erskine stayed in my Hastings-on-Hudson house when he first came to the United Nations. Dreamer though he may have been, his vision for the role of NSA and the United Nations is one that we all shared.

Regrettably, I think our work has not been finished, and I do not think our World War II has been fully ended. Yet, without NSA, how "on earth" would we have been able, otherwise, to be in touch with every student in the world?

END NOTES

[1] The American Field Service (AFS) was an organization founded after World War I, which continued to sponsor international exchange programs among American and foreign students. See AFS, p. 684.

[2] *Editor's note:* Harold Taylor was also an active supporter of NSA. He delivered the keynote address at its Second National Student Congress at the University of Illinois in August 1948. See p. 888. He also served on its national Advisory Council in 1949-1950 and and from 1951 to 1953.

[3] See Robert Smith, p. 505. *Editor's Note:* In 1950 the title was changed to the more familiar *Work, Study, Travel Abroad.*

[4] See Mary Ann Weld Bodecker, p. 660.

[5] The *Volendam* sailed from Quebac for Rotterdam late in June 1948. See also p. 683.

[6] See Vos essay, p. 651. [7] See Fisher essay, p. 511.

[8] *Editor's note:* Charlotte Allen was on the University of Illinois delegation and also on the organizing staff for the Second National Student Congress in 1948 at Urbana. See Stoddard, p. 655, Album, p. 658.

[9] Olof Palme maintained lifetime friendships with many former NSA people, and later became the Prime Minister of Sweden. See p. 532.

[10] *Editor's note*: Helen Garland furnished a clipping from the May 1950 edition of the *Christian Science Monitor* in which she is quoted after her return from Oslo: "In New York, I had to see the Norwegian-American Lines who will be agents for the Norwegian Government in provisioning the ship here, and of course see the Norwegian consul. He will see that the ship is properly fitted and run according to the contract."

[11] Admeasure: To measure the dimensions and capacity of a vessel, as for official registration.

[12] See Meagher, p. 665.

[13] The *General Ballou* left New York on June 27, the same day headlines proclaimed President Truman's decision to send U.S. troops into Korea and also announced the UN endorsement of the action.

PICTURE CREDITS: *Then:* Sarah Lawrence College, *The Campus*, Nov. 17, 1946, p.1 (Sarah Lawrence Library). *Now:* c. *Boston Globe*, Feb. 21, 1999 (*Staff photo, Bill Greene*).

BRONXVILLE TO CAMBRIDGE: HELEN BRYAN MOVES TO THE TRAVEL OFFICE

Bryan Replaces Martha Rockwell

"Helen Bryan, formerly vice-president of Student Council, is now president by decision of the council," announced Martha Rockwell, resigning president after last week's council meeting. Mopsie explained the council's decision for the procedure to be followed in the event of the resignation of the president. The vice-president shall succeed the president, and a new vice-president shall be elected by the entire student body in the same way that the president is elected in the Spring. Voting will soon be held.

Having no precedent to follow, council has formulated this decision as a rule of procedure to be entered into the by-laws of the organization. The council bases its decision on the fact that the vice-president is always the student who polls the next largest vote to the president in the elections for the office held the previous Spring. Therefore the vice-president is elected by popular choice. Also she is considered qualified by her experience in working with Council to effect a smooth transition in the change of officers.

Helen Bryan is well-known to the student body, especially for her work as acting president for the first six weeks of this year when Martha was unable to return from Europe. Helen had been designated by Council to take charge of investigating the work of organizations other than the Campus with which Student Council may cooperate. Together with the investigation of such organizations the council is conducting the investigation of the establishment of a cooperative college store. Helen has been active in the athletic association since she came to college.

The Campus, Sarah Lawrence C., 11/27/46

SCENES FROM CAMBRIDGE. From top, Harvard Square, Acacia St., c. winter '48-49, left to right:: Helen Bryan; Frank Fisher (Harvard. See p. 511); Harold Taylor, Pres. Sarah Lawrence C., NSA adviser; Rob West (Yale), NSA Int'l. V.P., '48-49 (See p. 515); Helen's father, Rev. A.R. Bryan; Leila Anderson, YWCA and aunt Helen Bryan; Pat Wohlgemuth (Wellesley), Int'l office (See p. 650). (All photos, Helen Bryan Garland.)

Rooted in Scots Presbyterian traditions

Born to a Lifetime of Service and Global Outreach

Helen Bryan Garland
Sarah Lawrence College '47
Student body President. Manager, NSA Student Travel Program, 1947-51

Early background and influences

I was born in India to a Scottish mother. My father was linked inextricably to Woodrow Wilson's family via Staunton, Virginia; Davidson College; the Princeton Class of 1914; the Scots Presbyterian traditions—including separation of Church and State (and the primacy of individual conscience, which had culminated in the writing of the Declaration of Independence). My father and Frank Fisher's[1] father attended Chicago Latin School together and remained friends for their next ninety years, despite Walter's choosing Harvard over Princeton. I grew up in Livingston on Hudson, N.Y.

Our cousin, Julien Bryan, was playing a large role on the postwar scene through his experience in World War I with the American Field Service, which led to the founding of the AFS Scholarship Program in 1946–47 and to Julien's film foundation, which was designed to find what, on earth, could link us all to common causes other than war. My link with Julien would have been sufficient for the elected leaders of NSA's International Office to instruct me, simply, "to work with every student organization in the world."

Some lifetime highlights

Following service as student government president and 1946 Chicago Student Conference delegate for Sarah Lawrence College, I graduated in 1947, with a B.S. degree. I went to work for the American Field Service in Cambridge, Mass., and then on to the International Affairs office of NSA in Harvard Square, where I strengthened my friendship with Frank Fisher and his brother and met and worked with Bob Smith, Rob West, and Erskine Childers—NSA's first three international vice presidents. Also prominent were Olof Palme, then a foreign student at Carleton College, and my lifetime friend, Jos Vos, Dutch student union (NBBS) representative to NSA.

My father was by then a postwar, and former wartime, chaplain at Harvard and MIT, preaching also in the Episcopal Theological Seminary, where he officiated at many weddings. Janis Tremper and Frank Dowd were married by my father in the home shared by my college roommate, Mildred Kiefer, and Janis. Opal and Lloyd Haynes were married at our Acacia Street home.[2]

I have photos of Rob West and Leila Anderson, who will be remembered by those who traveled with her to Europe in 1946 and were part of her Y role in Chicago. Leila was a little girl in Georgia when my Aunt Helen saw her promise in a program Helen's Wellesley College promoted—I think to encourage some of the early race relations in the south. For years, Helen had been Leila's mentor. She was our family guest on many occasions. Aunt Helen did not stay with the Y, but moved on to work with Ralph Bunche on the Swarthmore Race Relations Institute. That must have been between 1925 and 1930. It was she who arranged for me to meet Dr. Bunche and have free access to the files at the United Nations when Rob West asked me, in the 1950s, to do a study for the Brookings Institute, which I titled, "Civilian Operations in the Congo."

Even though I had four children born between 1953 and 1957, I stayed in touch with as many of the NSA people as possible, which was made easier because our home in Hastings-on-Hudson in New York was exactly twenty-four miles from the United Nations. Without leaving the children, I could be involved by phone and by reading a lot of UN documents and having people stay for extended periods of time.

Dr. Margaret Mead had been part of the NSA shipboard orientation programs and knew what I was doing at the United Nations. I worked with Dr. Mead through the years on matters concerning congressional legislation and United Nations programs dealing with improvements in the human environment—a thread also connected to Olof Palme's worldwide efforts in this regard. On May 3–5, 1972, for example, I appeared (as Mrs. Riers) with Dr. Mead in testimony before the Senate Foreign Relations Committee

Olof Palme projected what he had learned and been involved in through his own life in Sweden and with NSA. He was the UN negotiator between Iran and Iraq at one time. While he was prime minister of Sweden he wrote to me in 1967 because he knew I had been among those who, with a wide range of persons such as Dr. Margaret Mead, Roger Fisher, and Prime Minister Pandit Nehru, had initiated the UN effort to step up international cooperation in all areas of life concerns. We had also been able to hold a White House conference with the influence of Doug Cater[3] as Kennedy's education adviser in the White House.

Throughout the years many NSA-connected people showed up to visit us: Ted Harris, Ernie Howell, the Fishers, Jos Vos, Mildred (Kiefer) and Jerry Wurf, Rob West and Erskine Childers. Allard Lowenstein and I were happily and mutually involved when he became a U.S. Ambassador at the United Nations.[4]

Erskine and his Thailand-born wife, Mallica Vajnarath, stayed with us for a month after he had written his second classic, *The Road to Suez.* He continued to visit, and our families became irrevocably interrelated, from the time when he embarked on the first of many missions for the United Nations, until our final conversation just before he died, in 1996.

END NOTES

[1] See Fisher, p. 511.

[2] See Janis Dowd, p. 60, and Mildred Kiefer Wurf, p. 178, Frank Dowd, p. 886.

[3] See Cater, p. 92.

[4] See Harris, p. 219, Fisher, p. 511, Vos, p. 651, Childers, p. 517, and Lowenstein, p. 283.

In Europe, signs of war were still everywhere

2. The *Kota Inten* and a Summer in Europe

Pat Wohlgemuth Blair
Wellesley College
NSA International Office, Cambridge, MA 1947-48

Thank goodness Bob Smith didn't tell me about my mother's oversolicitous phone call until a few years ago. It would have been a much less amusing story at the time.[1] I was eighteen, and embarking on the kind of life-changing adventure every teenager should have.

I believe our converted Dutch troop ship, the *Kota Inten*, was the first student ship to sail to Europe after World War II.[2] There were about 800 of us—from NSA, American Youth Hostels, Experiment in International Living,[3] and so on. We slept in five-tiered bunks, with one hold for the women, one for the men, and one for eating and socializing. The voyage took thirteen days, so there was plenty of time for the latter.[4]

In Europe, signs of war were still everywhere: rubble-filled streets in London; a patchwork of empty squares in Amsterdam, the stained glass windows of Chartres still under repair; wounded veterans; food-rationing. One of the boys in our group got sick on whole milk and chocolate the day we arrived in Geneva—he had grown unused to all that fat.

Still, it was a glorious summer. And most impressive were the student leaders we met with at every stop. I had been volunteering in the international office in Cambridge,[5] so I was already in awe of the people around NSA, most of whom were not only older than I but far more purposeful and sure of themselves. The Europeans seemed even more so. Despite the hardships of the war, they had managed to acquire the sophistication that comes from a good classical education. For the first time in my life I was exposed to people, Americans and Europeans, who intended to put their ideals into practice—and who had the smarts to do it.

Inspired by Truman's Point Four speech

After that summer, I stopped taking college for granted. Inspired by Truman's Point Four speech the following year, I rearranged my classes to focus on what was then called technical assistance, a field so new that we had no textbooks to work from.[6] At Haverford for graduate studies, I joined the Board of the International Development Placement Association, a precursor of the Peace Corps, which was started by a group of student leaders, including several NSAers (including the Editorial Director of this volume);[7] we placed several people in India before I left the Board and went myself to India, working for the American aid program. That started a life of working and traveling in the Third World, which never would have happened without those early days in NSA.

END NOTES

[1] *Editor's note:* Bob Smith writes about this incident in his essay, p. 505.

[2] See Vos, p. 651.

[3] See Halsted, p. 679, and Experiment in International Living, p. 682.

[4] I was also on the orientation staff of the *Volendam* in 1952, courtesy of Tom Callahan, who was then director of NSA's travel office (see Callahan, p. 673). I have since remained good friends with Virginia Gardner, who had been Chair of the NSA Wisconsin region and was married to Tom at the time (Album, p. 934).

[5] I had been volunteering in the International Office with Bob Smith in 1947-48 and Rob West in the first half of 1948 (see Garland, p. 643, and Smith, p. 505.)

[6] See Section 4 on Point Four and the Peace Corps.

[7] *Editor's note:* See Douglas Kelley, the founder of IDPA, p. 623. Kelley invited student leaders from several organizations to join his original board. Pat Wohlgemuth Blair wrote extensively on the Peace Corps and what was known as "technical assistance." See Wohlgemuth [Blair], p. 544.

PICTURE CREDITS: *Then:* March 30, 1956, Bronx, NY (Author). *Now:* October, 1998, Middlebury, VT (Schwartz)

Pat Wohlgemuth Blair, with her husband, National Geographic photographer Jim Blair, with whom she traveled widely. Pat was an international development consultant, writer, and editor, who contributed significantly to the development of this anthology before she died, in November 2000. (For an extended biography, see p. 544.)

Holland America Line ships provide the cornerstone for NSA's travel programs.

3. The Dutch Student Union Helps NSA Organize Its Tours

Joseph Vos
University of Leiden, Holland
Dutch student (NBBS) liaison to NSA (Travel Office), 1949-1952

As is clear from other sources, the SS *Volendam* played a very important role in the beginning years of the Travel Department of NSA. It is indeed an outstanding example of free spirit (academia) coupled with free enterprise (business) on an international level, starting in 1948, three years after the end of World War II.[1]

Origin of the Dutch student ships

What was the origin of all this? Well, I could say it was Dutch gin, but that sounds a little too flippant. The truth is that a couple of students studying law at the University of Leiden in the Netherlands were sipping the good stuff one evening in October 1947 at the Leiden Student Club. They talked to some of their friends, who had worked during summer vacation as "kitchen patrol" on-board vessels carrying Dutch emigrants to Canada. The Dutch government operated these passenger vessels, which included the *Tabinta*, the *Kota Inten* and the *Volendam*, all of which had been converted to troop carriers during World War II. They were used to carry Dutch emigrants to Canada and Australia. These vessels were not properly outfitted for the regular passenger trade, and thus they made their homeward voyages empty. We thought that it might be a splendid idea to bring U.S. students to Europe, particularly those studying under the provisions of the GI Bill of Rights. And so, those of us who worked with the Netherlands Office for Foreign Student Relations (NBBS)—a student organization involved in student travel—went to see the management of the Holland-America Line (HAL), which had been appointed by the Dutch government as operator of the vessels.

Student life in Holland

Student life in Holland up to the 1960s was basically organized along social lines, not along field of study. Men and women had their own separate clubs and associations. Some were confessional. Some were rather elitist. There were practically no working students, and students were supposed to have fun, in this their last fling of youth before becoming "pillars of society." After the war, an attempt was made to organize a more structured student life with general appeal, called the Civitas Academica, but it failed. The Dutch Student Union was a loosely knit umbrella organization and the NBBS was the travel branch—created to provide Dutch students with low-price travel opportunities. It was run by volunteers (men) and some paid secretaries (girls), and its headquarters were in Leiden. I decided to give the organization some of my time, starting in the spring of 1948.

I was born in the old, fortified city of Coevorden in the northeastern part of Holland, where my grandfather had started a dry goods store, which my father took over and continued. In the mid-1930s, we moved from Coevorden to Scheveningen, a seaside resort, near The Hague. My father and a partner expanded a textile factory (knitted ladies' and gentlemen's upper- and underwear, as they say in Dutch), and life was good. Then, in May 1940, the Germans invaded Holland and things started to deteriorate rapidly. Being Jewish, my life became more and more restricted. We were no longer allowed in cafes, restaurants, public transportation, public school, and so on. My father's business was confiscated—and the list goes on. In 1942, when the Germans started deporting Jews, we decided to go into hiding, my father and mother one way, I another, and we did not see each other again until after the war ended, in May 1945. During the war I educated myself (Latin, Greek, English. French—NO German—Mathematics, and History). I learned quite successfully, as it turned out, and in September of 1946 1 went to the University of Leiden to study law.

Holland America Line (HAL) sponsors student travel

HAL was no stranger to student travel. In the early 1920s it initiated the Student Third Class Association (STCA) and provided U.S. students with cheap third-class accommodations on their passenger vessels. STCA also published a guide of Europe, *Hand-Me-Down*, which was created from the comments of students about hotels, restaurants, and tourist services. It was one of the first consumer-oriented guides, and no establishment could buy its way into it. Student travel was well known to HAL and used, not so much for profit, but as a way to develop future repeat customers. Therefore, the idea of arranging student travel was quite familiar, and a bunch of young Dutchmen turned into a bunch of entrepreneurs, motivated, not only by idealism, but also by a desire to produce U.S. dollars for the Dutch government to buy grain and other necessities. After listening to NBBS, the Dutch government, as owner, and HAL, as operator, agreed to schedule a student sailing to Europe in June and back to the United States in September under the auspices of NBBS.

The first HAL student sailings in 1948

The first student sailings in the summer of 1948 on the *Kota Inten*[2] and the *Tabinta* were rather successful, but they showed that administratively, we had to improve. The record keeping was messy. In the ship's dorms, girls were sometimes assigned to men's quarters, and, biggest nightmare of all, it was discovered after departure that practically nobody had visas to visit or transit any country in Western Europe. This became my first major challenge. I resolved it by convincing the various consular services in Holland to send representatives to HAL upon arrival, to set up shop in the arrival hall to issue visas on the spot. We dispatched photographers on a tugboat to meet the vessel at Hook of Holland so that the students would have passport pictures. Miraculously, it worked. Talk about stress!

In the summer of 1949, things went a lot more smoothly. We used one vessel, the *Volendam*, with a capacity of about 1,300 passengers. We convinced the Dutch Railways to have a special train to Paris ready at dockside—the first since World War II—and we surrounded the train with Dutch barrel organs and herring stalls. Talk about having fun. But then, how could we have known that Americans had no taste for raw fish? We ran a Tri-Nations Tour—visiting Holland, Belgium, and France—with NSA, as our first joint venture. The NBBS treasurer and I took Helen Bryan, NSA's travel organizer and a minister's daughter, to the Folies Bergeres in Paris. Helen was a very good sport about it. She was one of the first American girls I met, and we became close friends and remain so to this very day. As a matter of fact it was her father, in her home in 1957, who married me and the Dutch lady of my heart.[3]

In the fall of 1949 1 decided to leave NBBS and go back to my law studies. By late November I received a call from Frits Schneiders, a good friend and the president of NBBS, to tell me that I had been selected to represent NBBS in the United States. Just like that: NBBS needed someone on the other side of the ocean to ensure that only students were booked by HAL, to coordinate our tours with NSA, and to set up a shipboard Orientation Program with NSA. All these items needed to be better organized. I said I would do it, but that I needed to talk to my parents and the dean of the faculty to obtain an extension of my finals. It all worked out, except that by the time I got my visa, there was no ship until after Christmas. On December 18 I boarded a Constellation instead, and landed in New York 22 hours later.

Encounters with the Immigration Service

Unbeknownst to most of the world, New York was experiencing a water shortage. Buses were not washed. Everything looked grimy, and the day I arrived was "no-shave day." Also, I ran into trouble with the Immigration—a serious Catch 22. The unshaven faces of the immigration inspectors in some sort of Quonset hut looked far from friendly, and they expressed their opinion that I was one of those Europeans who would marry one of their fine, innocent, red-blooded American girls, in order to stay in the United States. I told them that I had credentials and all I had to do was to get them from my suitcase, which was at Customs. The immigration inspector took great pleasure in informing me that Customs was a separate service and that I could not get to my suitcase until I had passed Immigration, which seemed unlikely. My salvation was a Polish rabbi who was on the same flight (he had eaten nothing but oranges, since there was no kosher food on the plane) and did not speak a single word of English. I pretended to be able to speak Yiddish and schmoozed with the rabbi. He was admitted. So was I.

Working with NSA—Doing something about improving the world

I could go on about my first experiences in this country, which were in the realm of culture shock, but that's not the point of this story. I moved to Cambridge, where the NSA Travel Office was headquartered. HAL had a branch office in Boston, where I would make sure that the passengers being booked were indeed bona fide students. Helen introduced me to Frank Fisher, with whom I developed a Shipboard Orientation Program, which for many years remained the standard.

What a dream world! I lived in a room near Harvard Square. The Travel Office was over a French restaurant, and for the first time that I could remember, I had warm feet twenty-four hours a day. What was really impressive, though, was the seriousness of all the people around me in setting out to really DO something about improving the world—something I personally had become quite disillusioned with after World War II. As I mentioned, being a Jew my war experience in occupied Holland consisted of almost three years of hiding from the Germans. As an adolescent, I grew up without having any young people around. Being alone with my books and the couple who saved my life made me feel out of touch. Some of my experiences after the war were truly awful as well.

Now I was exposed to, and working with, American students in the United States, who maybe were somewhat naive, but were convinced they could make a difference by doing the right thing. We all worked hard. And we had a lot of fun.

A Dutchman in America

As a Dutchman, I found the American dating ritual somewhat incomprehensible. Young men (and women) in Holland are much more casual about these things. So I was "taught" about heavy dates, blind dates, double dates, whatever. I could not get very enthused about it, except that I tried a couple of blind dates that worked out fine, until I once ended up with a young lady about a head taller than I with her leg in a cast.

Frank and I organized a checklist of items we felt should be covered, and we were particularly interested in preparing a presailing information booklet. We wanted students to be well prepared for their visit and tell them, not only about passports, visas and inoculations, but also what to expect and what to read. We worked out a plan for the Orientation Program and started the difficult process of selecting lecturers. We planned a shipboard newspaper and really tried to think through what was required. Though our financial resources were limited, our imagination was endless. Each day brought a new challenge.

Our student sailing in the summer of 1950 was very successful. The orientation program worked quite well and provided for some intercultural exchanges. Although there was no language barrier, a Dutch member of Parliament who was on the lecturers' staff provoked quite a bit of hilarity when, at the end of his last session, he thanked all the students for the "pleasant intercourse"! Through our resources, we were able to arrange for the Dutch Prince Consort to officially welcome the Volendam upon arrival in Rotterdam. As a gift from the U.S. students, Prince Bernard received a T-shirt from Frank Fisher.[4] A student had embellished it by drawing pennants of all the schools on-board. The gift was presented with the caveat "Wear it, but don't wash it."

I returned to the United States and was the NBBS representative until the summer of 1952. 1 attended NSA's National Congress as the representative of the Dutch Student Union and visited all major, and some not so major universities in the country; taught Dutch to U.S. students who were going to study medicine in Holland; and made a transcontinental trip by train. But none of this left me with the same overwhelming feeling as those first months in Cambridge. They shaped my future, determined my career, and persuaded me to settle in this country. Not for economic reasons, not for a red blooded American girl, but as a matter of my own free choice.

Joseph Vos enjoyed a lifetime career in international travel planning, organization and marketing for major cruise lines and providers. He held marketing positions with Renaissance, Windstar Sail, Regency, and Sun Line Cruises and managed sales and marketing for Holland America Cruises from 1952 to 1973.

END NOTES

[1] See Album, "The Ships," p. 669.

[2] See Blair, p. 650, on the *Kota Inten.*

[3] See Helen Bryan Garland, p. 649.

[4] See Frank Fisher, p. 511.

PICTURE CREDITS: *Then:* June, 1950, on board *Volendam* (Courtesy Helen Bryan Garland). *Now:* c. 1990s (Author)

JOSEPH VOS

Early years: Born January 11, 1926, in Coeverden, The Netherlands. Immigrated to the United States in October 1956.

Education: Graduate of University of Leiden Law School, The Netherlands. Majored in Civil Law, Private International Law, and Maritime Law.

Career highlights: Lifetime career in international travel planning, organization, and marketing for major cruise lines and providers. Directed charters and incentives at Renaissance Cruises, Inc. (1989-93), Windstar Sale Cruises (1985-1989); Vice President, Planning and Administration, Ocean Cruise Lines (1984), Sun Line Cruises (1976-83); Vice President, Arthur Frommer International (1975-76), Exprinter International (1973-74). From 1952-73, Manager, Sales Planning to Manager, Sales Marketing, Holland America Cruises. 1948-1952, Netherlands Office for Foreign Student Relations: as a student, developed and directed on-board orientation programs for student sailings, which brought 6,000 U.S. and Canadian students to Europe.

Family: Widowed, two adult children. **Died** June, 2001.

Note: The editors thank Kratos Vos, Jos Vos' son, for his cooperation providing background on his father.

The NBBS Story

The N.B.B.S. (Netherlands Office for Foreign Student Relations) is a non-political non-sectarian, non-profitable volontary student organisation. It was organised in 1926 as the travel-department of the A.S.V. (Organisation of the student corpora). There was not much activity on the part of the N.B.B.S. as an organisation in the years before World-War II. The problems of student exchange and travel were handled by individuals rather than by organisations. After the war. N.B.B.S. was revived by a group of students of the Leyden University. Their first activities were in the field of student exchange. Because of the strict currency regulations, which then existed, other plans were made impossible. Since this beginning, the organisation expanded until it now includes workcamps, study tours, recreation camps, art courses, sailing-camps, and the sailing of student ships between the Netherlands and North-America. Today N.B.B.S. is relatively independent of the Netherlands Student Council. There are local committees in all the 10 University-towns, each with their own local appointed representative. The central office is in Leyden. Shipping was for the first time considered in 1947 by N.B.B.S. It was learned that immigrant ships taking farmers to Canada were returning to the Netherlands empty. N.B.B.S. approached the Department of Transportation of the Netherlands Government, to see if these partially converted troopships could be used as student ships. When this was found practicable the „Kota Inten" and „Tabinta" were signed up and made their first sailings as studentships in the summer of 1948. These ships carried only 100 NSA Tri-Nation Tour students, compared with 600 on NSA tours in 1949. However, these two small ships were not capable to provide the facilities for sailings desired by N.B.B.S., so negotiations were started for the use of the „Volendam" (15000 tons). Agreements were finally made in the summer of 1948 and the ship made its first sailing with students in September of that year between Rotterdam and New York. The last two years N.B.B.S. had at its disposal the two emigrantships „Waterman" and „Zuiderkruis" or „Groote Beer", old Victory ships, beautifully rebuilt for civilian use. Last summer 1600 American students were transported between the 2 continents. The staff on those ships consists of professors, who also give lectures on various international and national subjects; students who form the first (when the students return, the last) contact with Europe and finally journalists who also give lectures. International cooperation at student level makes these tours possible. The common belief of student travel organisations is that world-wide understanding can best be achieved through international contact among students. For any information in this field apply to N.B.B.S. Rapenburg 6, Leiden.

INSTITUTE OF INTERNATIONAL EDUCATION

NBBS — Magic Letters in Student Travel

Ralph Lee Smith

"As soon as I can, I want to come back and study in Europe."

This is heard from at least half the American students who go to Europe on summer tours. It indicates how important guided summer tours for students have become in contributing to interest in educational exchange. And these days, all-student summer tours to Europe have become almost inseparable from the four magic letters "NBBS."

Few Americans can pronounce the fifty-three letter Dutch name for which NBBS stands. In English it means "Netherlands Office for Foreign Student Relations." Rejuvenated and expanded after the war by a group of students from the University of Leiden, NBBS has become the miracle-worker of European and American student organizations, moving governmental and other mountains to create facilities for low-cost student travel, work, and study programs in Europe.

Dutch Enterprise

NBBS represents a practical Dutch approach to the world's problems. Not long ago I sat in the NBBS Student Summer Center in Amsterdam and talked with several Dutch students who had worked with NBBS from the beginning of their university days. "After the war," one of them explained, "all of us were looking for real ways to win the peace. We knew there had been an NBBS before the war, and we decided to start it again — this time with a much bigger program. The idea was to bring the student youth of the world together, as much as possible, on a student-to-student basis. We believed this would create understanding on both sides, and build a better foundation for the future."

On the Friesland canals, Holland

A small organization in a small, war-devastated country, NBBS had assigned itself an ambitious task. It set to work with no fanfare but with plenty of resourcefulness.

Student Ships

United States students were the largest single group who could travel after the war. America's increasingly vital role in world affairs made it doubly important, from NBBS's point of view, for American
travel in
NBBS in
on the pr

RALPH LEE SMITH helped to organize the U. S. National Student Association in 1947, while a student at Swarthmore College. NSA and NBBS appointed him to serve on the Orientation Staff of the student ship *Volendam* during its 1951 summer sailings to and from Europe.

NBBS PROVIDED STRONG SUPPORT TO NSA as an experienced partner in its organization of tour programs; also facilitating links to the Holland America Line and KLM Airlines for transport. In 1949, Jos Vos was appointed full time NBBS representative to work out of the NSA Travel Office in Cambridge (see Vos, Garland, this section). Column left is from a 1952 NBBS newsletter. Above, an article by Ralph Lee Smith in the 11/1/51 issue of the *IIE Bulletin*. To right, NBBS brochure, c. early 1950s.

See the Old World
in a New Way
NBBS
RAPENBURG 6 · LEIDEN · NETHERLANDS

On the *Volendam*, June 1950, from left, Helen Bryan, Fritz Schneider and Jos Vos explaining the tour program to Prince Barnhard of the Netherlands. (Helen Bryan)

Tom Herbschleb, NBBS representative, visiting Madison, WI in 1950 (Joan Lynch)

CONFERENCE ON STUDENT TRAVEL ABROAD

Speakers:

PETER ZUNTZ Danish International Union of Students	JOHN HARRISON British National Union of Students
JOS VOS Netherlands Representative for Foreign Students	ROBERT TESDALE Council on Student Travel

Movies will be shown

Thursday, May 3, ~~7:30~~ 8:00 P.M. — Leverett House Junior Common Room

ADMISSION FREE

Travel conference notice, Cambridge, MA, c. 1950. Speakers include British National Union of Students representative and Council on Student Travel (See p. 694. Kratos Vos.)

NSA as inspiration and instigator

4. A Summer's Work Camp and Aftermath

Philip H. Stoddard
University of Illinois
Chairman, International Affairs, Illinois Region, NSA, 1949-50

On June 18, 1948, a small group of students from the University of Illinois set out from Quebec to Rotterdam with seven hundred students from other colleges. A converted freighter of the Holland America Line, the *Kota Inten*, took our group to a student work camp in the Netherlands. We saw ourselves as part of the first postwar wave of American students heading abroad. Others had preceded us, of course, but in far fewer numbers. Bill Allaway, for example, had attended two youth conferences in Europe the previous summer, and I had been on a study tour in Europe in 1946. How did this current adventure come about?

Bill Allaway played a key role. As he notes in his contribution to this volume,[1] he had attended the regional conference in Chicago, at which he was elected international vice chairman, and he had also set up a travel office at the University. The establishment of the office reflected the conviction of many of us that student exchanges and educational travel would help foster international understanding and new relationships between Americans and students from other countries. The Champaign/Urbana area was not a hotbed of internationally minded students, but we were determined to increase their number. We publicized the opportunities available by activities that included disseminating the UN publication, *Study Abroad*, and the NSA guide, *Study, Travel, Work Abroad—Summer 1948.*[2]

As a member of the student senate, Bill had worked out arrangements with the Dutch National Student Union (NBBS) for a group to participate in an international student work camp in Holland.[3] Lining up participation became the centerpiece of our efforts. In the end, we followed our advice to other students and signed up for the work camp ourselves. By that time, I was chairman of the student senate's NSA subcommittee on international affairs. Lloyd Ireland, a member of the senate, chaired the NSA subcommittee on student government. Bill Allaway was deeply involved in the senate and in his new responsibility as head of the campus chest fund drive.[4] Charlotte Allen (Charters) headed the subcommittee on cultural and social affairs. The four of us, plus Rex Keel, Craig Johnson, and Joyce Nicolai, made up the group bound for the work camp. Several other groups of university students were also headed for summer programs in Europe.

The work camp experience

The *Kota Inten* docked in Rotterdam on June 29, nearly two weeks before the work camp was scheduled to begin.[5] We went to Antwerp and Brussels, and then to Paris. My father was there for meetings and to revisit old haunts from his year at the Sorbonne in the early 1920s. He managed to keep us very well fed. Bill and Lloyd hitch-hiked to Geneva for meetings with officials of the World Student Relief, which was represented in the United States by the World Student Service Fund (WSSF).

There were actually two work camps, one for men and one for women, and there were two sessions of each camp, each session being one month long. The work camp for men was in the tiny village of Biggekerke, near the beach and the village of Westkappela on the island of Walcheren. The island was liberally studded with massive German-built block houses and tank traps, and it had suffered terribly during the winter of 1944–45. The Allies had bombed the dikes and flooded much of the island after direct assaults had failed to dislodge the German defenders, who controlled access to Antwerp, then in Allied hands. Fighting was heavy, and damage to the villages was great. The men's task was to build an asphalt bike path, 3.3 kilometers long, connecting two villages on the island. We finished about half the project, leaving the rest for the second session in August.

The 125 male students were housed in dike workers' barracks and lived on workers' rations. Each group of twelve occupied two fifteen-by-fifteen-foot rooms—one for sleeping on our straw mattresses and the other for sitting, eating, and storing our gear. My room contained four Americans—Lloyd, Rex, Craig, and myself—and two each of Finns, Norwegians, and Swiss, plus one Dane and one Dutchman. We had a canteen, and we had hot water once a week. We had Wednesdays, Sundays, and Saturday afternoons off.[6]

The women's work camp was at Texel, near the village of Wilhelmina in Zeeland, some distance from Walcheren. It was a "fruit harvest" camp; that is, the forty-eight women spent four weeks laboriously picking currants and digging potatoes. They lived under truly spartan conditions in an old barn.

Our schedule allowed for trips to the mainland, mostly to the Texel camp. These visits and an occasional dance—liberally supplied with Dutch gin, beer, and raspberry soda—made up much of what the camp leaders called "opportunities for joint social and cultural events." Getting to Texel, however, was a cumbersome process and generally slow. Few of us had bikes, though some managed, on one occasion, to borrow the camp's aged BMW motorcycle.

The 180 students from twelve countries who were in both camps had much to discuss. We compared our universities. The Americans received a close-up view of the problems facing college-age young people in war-ravaged Europe and learned about the daily life of the local Dutch during this difficult period of rationing and shortages. We explored each other's values, customs, and concerns. We talked about international politics, and about the great need for massive moral and material reconstruction. Many of the European students were worried about possible Soviet aggression and another war, a concern heightened by the Berlin blockade.

After the work camp

The first session of the camp ended on August 3. The next day, Bill, Char, Lloyd, and I went to Utrecht where my father, then a member of the U.S. National Commission for UNESCO and of the executive board, was giving the keynote address at the first UNESCO universities conference. Bill and Lloyd sailed on the *Kota Inten* on August 11 to attend the NSA National Congress.

Char Allen and I traveled to France, and then spent the last two weeks of August with Char's cousin, Rufus Z. Smith (later an ambassador and assistant secretary of state), who was then serving in his first Foreign Service post in the Consulate General in Amsterdam. Our visit coincided with the colorful jubilee celebrations for Queen Wilhelmina's fifty years on the throne, her abdication, and the inauguration of Queen Juliana.[7]

The *Volendam* sailed from Rotterdam to New York on September 1, packed with 1,500 students, and made the crossing in ten days. It was vastly more comfortable than the cramped *Kota Inten*. I recall only one incident. On the last day, Bill Danielson, a University of Illinois student who had been in Europe for a study tour, fell overboard while taking a photo from atop a railing. With alarms blaring and whistles blowing, the engines were reversed, ballast was shifted, a lifeboat was lowered, and Bill was rescued after fifteen minutes in the chilly water! He was sheepish and philosophical, but the ship's officers were greatly displeased and issued a stern warning to us passengers to watch our step. If Bill had fallen only five minutes later, they declared, the fog bank rolling in would have prevented any attempt to rescue him in the busy shipping lane so close to New York.

Summer 1949

The University of Illinois hosted NSA's Second National Student Congress. I had succeeded Bill Allaway as the chairman of international affairs for the Illinois region and was both a delegate and the head of the local arrangements committee—a dubious honor indeed. My familial connection[8] and the university president's "slush fund" came to our rescue by paying many of the conference bills. The administration's support also smoothed out obstacles created by elements of the university bureaucracy.

The Congress—my first—was exciting, although I missed most of the sessions and much of the excitement because I was usually preoccupied with conference details.

UNESCO and the director general

Bill and I were both in France in the summer of 1950. He was working on his master's thesis and studying opportunities for American students in France. I graduated in June, spent several weeks in Grenoble in a French immersion program, and traveled to Paris to attend lectures at the Institute for Near Eastern Studies, before beginning graduate work at Princeton in the fall.

In Paris, Bill and I joined a small team, including Ernie Howell and Rob West, from the U.S. National Commission for UNESCO, to lobby UNESCO to place greater emphasis on youth activities. Our appointments with UNESCO officials were arranged by the secretary to Arthur A. Compton, Jr., the senior officer in the American embassy in charge of UNESCO matters and a close associate of my father. Art's secretary tried to get us an appointment with the director of the Education Department, Lionel Elvin, but he turned her down. I then telephoned the secretary of Dr. Jaime Torres-Bodet, the director general. I did some shameless name dropping, and we got an appointment with Dr. Torres-Bodet.

Our purpose was to follow up the UNESCO/Carnegie Endowment publication by Bob Smith and others, entitled *Youth and UNESCO*. We were convinced that very little was going on in UNESCO with respect to young people, and we had a list of suggestions and recommendations, including one for a youth festival—and not in Prague! We also wanted UNESCO to hire some enthusiastic person to carry out our suggestions.

We had a forty-five-minute session with the director general, with his secretary serving as interpreter. Dr. Torres-Bodet listened carefully to our pitch and asked pertinent questions. A year later, William Welling became the first full-time point-of-action person in UNESCO on youth affairs. We like to think that our visit had something to do with his appointment.

NSA's impact

My work in NSA on international issues of concern to students persuaded me to change my college program. At the end of my second year, I abandoned prelaw and switched to a major in international affairs, which had been newly organized as an interdisciplinary field. I am happy to have been among the first Illini to receive a degree in that major.

I wrote my honors thesis on the Azerbaijan crisis of 1946 and moved into Middle East area studies, then a new field with few graduate programs, other than ancient history and archeology, in American universities. I was accepted by Princeton's department of Oriental Studies and eventually specialized in Ottoman history.

My graduate program was interrupted by service in the Marines during the Korean War and by extended tours for research in Turkey and Egypt. With my doctorate finally finished, I joined the Department of State's Bureau of Intelligence and Research in 1963 as an analyst of Turkish affairs and have been involved in Middle East issues ever since. After retiring from State, I served as executive director of the private, nonprofit Middle East Institute in Washington, D.C., and later, in various full- and part-time capacities, as a consultant to government agencies until my "definitive" retirement in November 1997.

Philip H. Stoddard is a specialist on Middle Eastern and Islamic affairs, and has been Deputy Assistant Secretary for Current Analysis in the Department of State's Bureau of Intelligence and Research. He has also served as Executive Director of the Middle East Institute in Washington, D.C., and as Director of the Analytic Group in the National Intelligence Council.

END NOTES

[1] See William Allaway, p. 613.

[2] See Robert Smith, p. 505, and Helen Bryan Garland, p. 641. In 1950, the title *Study, Travel, Work Abroad* was changed to *Work, Study, Travel Abroad.*

[3] See NBBS, p. 654.

[4] The Illinois campus chest raised $26,000 in 1948-1949, thanks to Bill Allaway's outstanding leadership. Half went to WSSF.

[5] I am indebted to some of the articles that Char Allen was commissioned to write for the Champaign *News Gazette* ("Champaign Girl in Europe") during that summer to supplement my faulty memory of those far-off days. See Album, p. 658.

[6] When I visited Walcheren in 1957, I discovered that "our" bike path had been destroyed by the enormous floods of 1953.

[7] Dutch sovereigns are "inaugurated," not crowned.

[8] *Editor's note:* George D. Stoddard, President, University of Illinois, 1946-53.

PICTURE CREDITS: *Then:* August, 1949, University of Illinois (Program of the Second National Student Congress). *Now:* c. 1990s (Author)

PHILIP H. STODDARD

Early Background and Military Service: I was born in 1929 in Iowa City, Iowa, and attended Milne High School in Albany, New York. I served in the U.S. Marine Corps from 1951 to 1953.

Education: I completed my B.S. degree at the University of Illinois and my M.A. and Ph.D. degrees at Princeton University.

Career: In 1955-1957, I was a Ford Foundation fellow at Ankara University in Turkey. I taught Turkish and Middle Eastern History at Princeton for a year and was an assistant professor of international relations at the State University College at New Paltz, New York, 1958-1960. After two years as a visiting fellow at the Institute for Higher Arab Studies in Cairo, I joined the Department of State in 1963 as an analyst for Turkish affairs.

During my State Department career, from 1975 to 1983, I served as Director of the Office of Research and Analysis for the Near East and South Asia in the Bureau of Intelligence and Research, a State Department Fellow at the Council on Foreign Relations in New York City (1979–80), and Deputy Assistant Secretary for Current Analysis. I received the Department of State's Meritorious and Superior Honor Awards, as well as the presidential rank of Distinguished Executive in 1982 and the U.S. National Intelligence Distinguished Service Medal in 1983.

I retired from the Department of State in 1983 to become Executive Director of the Middle East Institute in Washington, D.C. I was an independent consultant to government agencies and private industry on Middle Eastern and Islamic Affairs from 1987 to 1990, when I returned to full-time government service as Director of the National Intelligence Council's Analytic Group. I retired in 1994 and returned to government service in 1996-1997 as a member of the Director of Central Intelligence's Senior Review Panel.

My publications include articles on the Muslim world, the Arab-Israeli conflict and Middle Eastern security dynamics, as well as *Change in the Muslim World* (1981), of which I was principal editor. My translation of an Ottoman officer's memoirs, 1916-1917, was published in a Turkish edition in 1997 and an English edition in 1998. Also published in a Turkish edition was my study of Enver Pasha's "Special Force," entitled *The Ottoman Government and the Arabs, 1911-1918: A Preliminary Study of the Teskilat-I-Mahsusa* (Istanbul, 1993).

Family: I married Doris M. Stoddard in 1960, and we have two children, Leah and Evan. I have three children by a previous marriage, Michele, Christopher, and Eric.

University of Illinois work camp group reports on tours of Holland and France

1948 in Europe: New War Fears Still in the Air

September 12, 1948 Champaign News Gazette

Champaign Girl In Europe

Many Reminders Of World War II In Amsterdam

By CHARLOTTE ALLEN

AMSTERDAM, August 29 (By Mail—Delayed)—One of the most interesting cities of the world is in the province of North Holland in The Netherlands. One of the first things you must do to appreciate Amsterdam is to look it up in your atlas or your National Geographic magazine map of Western Europe. By doing this, you can understand why the people are eternally afraid of wars—they live in a port which is a vital part of all Dutch import and export trade and is a good place for the disembarkation of troops. Take a minute or two off and look up Amsterdam on your map, and we'll go on from there.

MISS ALLEN

The city is built on a maze of canals which slice it up and make it look as though most of the streets are built on the banks of narrow rivers. The canal waters move sluggishly in the parts where the glass-enclosed touring boats don't churn up waves. The waters are green and dark and the banks are fringed with flowers, weeping willows with green moss on their trunks. The canal waters sometimes freeze in the wintertime. During the war the Dutch underground was very thankful when the canals didn't freeze over—they provided a silent, lightening-fast way of disposing of German sentries and patrols. It was very simple to do—you just used the right hold on a German's throat and slipped him noiselessly in the icy water, and he drowned. An ex-member of the underground told me that it was a dangerous (because of the penalty of death if you were caught out after dark) but dependable way of decreasing the number of patroling Germans—and one of the most demoralizing to the German occupation forces here.

Old And New Sections

Amsterdam has its old and new sections. The new buildings look a lot like our modern ones in architecture except for the typically Dutch features—the orange tile roofs and the stone or concrete walls and the little chimneys and balconies. The old section has the very narrow streets and the eerie courtyards and alleys and the distinguishing little notches in the front at the roof tops. It was in the intricately built old section where a great many of the fugitive Jewish people and hunted underground headquarters were hidden during the German occupation.

Only A Small Bombed Area

Actually Amsterdam was not bombed except in a very small area. The Jewish section of the city looks bombed though. When the occupants of that section were either deported and disposed of, or in hiding in other parts of the city, their homes were gradually and stealthily picked apart down to the frames so that the other Dutch might have enough firewood to live during the practically fuelless winters of the occupation.

Also in the city you find mounds of grass and flowers with little plaques or monuments or crosses. These are the places where hostages and Dutch prisoners were shot by German firing squads. The sites of the shootings were well-remembered because any Dutch people passing at the time were made to stop and witness the executions.

Another interesting part of the city is the street called the Kalverstraat. It is near the Dam Square and it is a shopping district for everything in one street. There are shops of all kinds on both sides of the street and the street itself is about fifteen yards wide. Every time of the day I have passed that street on one of Amsterdam's discouragingly slow tram cars, it has been so packed with milling shoppers that a car cannot drive down through it.

(excerpted)

Sunday, Sept. 12, 1948

Students Home From Holland; Tell War Fear

What William Allaway, general chairman of the 1949 Campus Chest at the University of Illinois, terms "a very profitable summer" of working with 180 students from 12 countries in the reconstruction of the Netherlands has ended for seven U. of I. students.

Four of the students—Allaway, Lloyd Ireland, Rex Keel and Craig Johnson—have returned to the campus and the other three—Philip H. Stoddard, Charlotte Allen and Joyce Nicoll—are expected to arrive here in a few days.

The five young men worked with 125 other men students in building a bicycle path connecting two coastal villages on the Dutch island of Walcheren, on which the dikes were bombed in 1944 to flood out the occupying Germans.

THE TWO GIRLS worked with 48 others on the Dutch mainland at a fruit harvest camp in the province of Zeeland, 23 miles from the boys' camp. They got together for joint social and cultural events.

Living on the rations of a Dutch worker and joining in informal discussions with youths from France, Italy, Austria, Finland, Norway, Switzerland and a half dozen other nations gave Allaway and the others a new appreciation of the problems facing college-age youths in other lands.

European students "are very worried about the possibility of another war, and of possible aggressive action by Russia," Allaway noted. This concern was heightened by the Berlin crisis and the U. S. war scare, he said.

Allaway also talked with some refugee Czechoslovakian students who contended that "the United States should go to war immediately and liberate Eastern Europe."

There were about 40 of these Czech refugees in another camp, all of whom are being allowed to attend Dutch universities.

WHILE TALKING and worrying about the possibilities of another war the students were pitching in to clear up the debris of the last one, and observing other reconstruction, which Allaway said seems to be progressing well in Belgium, Holland and France at least, although material supplies are slowing up some work.

The U. of I. group visited Rotterdam, Antwerp, Brussels and Paris before going to the work camp, and Allaway and Ireland hitch-hiked from Paris to Geneva to meet with officials of the World Student Relief.

They talked also with students who have benefited from W.S.R., represented in the U. S. by the World Student Service Fund, which received 50 per cent of the $26,000 collected in last spring's Campus Chest drive, and will receive about the same percentage from the second Chest drive next spring.

After the camp ended, the students visited in Holland for a week, and attended the U.N.E.S.C.O. conference on universities at Utrecht at which President George D. Stoddard — Philip's father — was the main speaker. They had dinner with the president in Utrecht and, earlier, in Paris.

Stoddard is chairman of the U. of I. student senate committee's international activities committee, Miss Allen is chairman of the student's social and cultural committee, and Ireland is chairman of the student government clinic. These three serve as a liaison group between the student senate here and the National Student Association.

Editor's note: Charlotte Allen wrote a series of columns about her travels to Europe. She was a student leader on the U. of Illinois International Relations Committee, and helped organize NSA's Second National Congress at the University in the summer of 1949. The following year she went to Cambridge, MA where she worked in the NSA International Office (see photos on pp. 246, 501). Phil Stoddard (page 655), who provided copies of her columns, remembers her as a "bright star." She later married W.W. "Sandy" Charters and and they settled in Eugene, Oregon, where they raised a family.

Summer Work Camps: Building Friendship, Rebuilding Europe

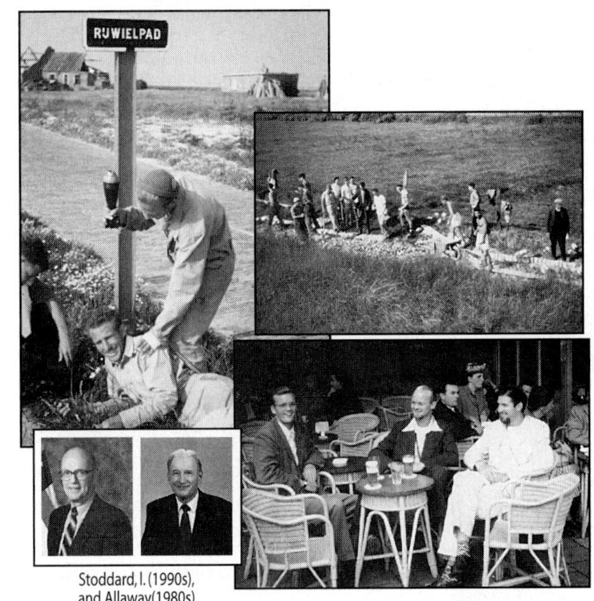

Stoddard, l. (1990s), and Allaway(1980s)

PHIL STODDARD AND BILL ALLAWAY, l. and r. above with Lloyd Ireland at a café in Utrecht, all from the U. of Illinois, relaxing after stint helping to restore a bicycle path in Wilkeheren (See pp. 613 and 655). Five U. of Illinois students took part in this work group, including Charlotte Allen (see p. 658) at another site (Photos, Bill Allaway.)

Walkeheren, The Netherlands-1948

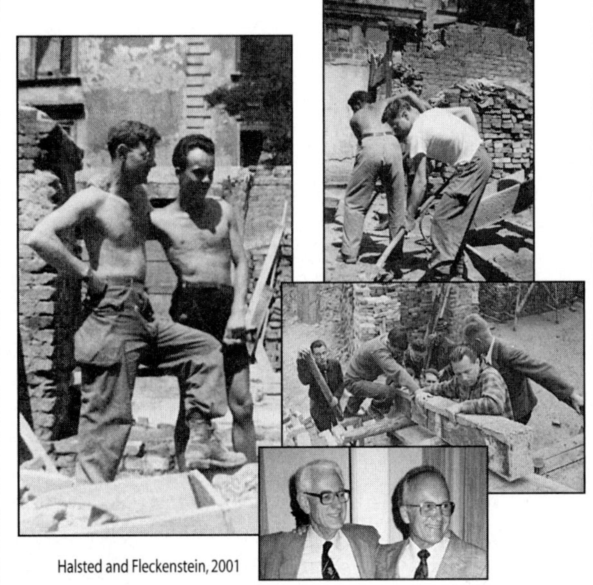

Halsted and Fleckenstein, 2001

HENRY HALSTED (Williams C., MA) returned to Germany to help rebuild the University of Munich four years after "wading ashore at Omaha Beach on D+98" (See p. 679). Working with an Experiment in International Living group he formed lifetime friendships and shaped his career interest in international exchange. (Clockwise: Halsted and Kurt Fleckenstein; Halsted and-Justin Simon. Foreground, Experiment group leader Gustav Weber holding the beam.)

Munich, Germany-1948

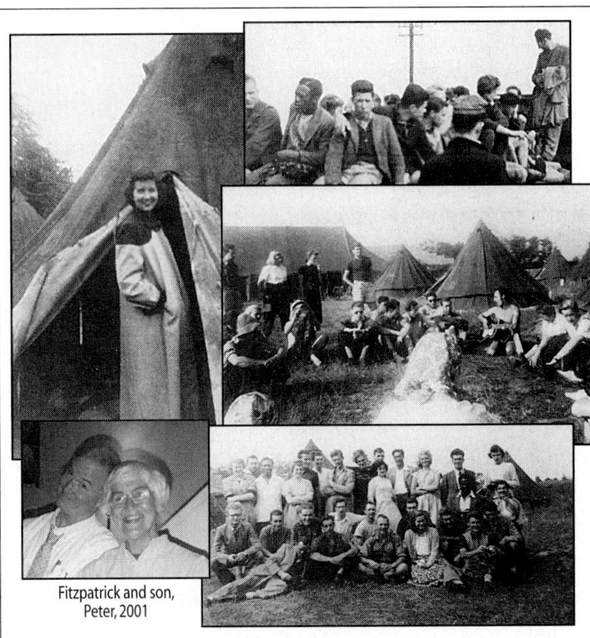

Fitzpatrick and son, Peter, 2001

MARGARET SELLERS FITZPATRICK (Regis C., MA) writes, "We were billeted in a displaced persons camp. By day we worked the farmers' lands and by night we socialized with people from the camp. Our own camp was made up of students from all over the world, even Israel, which had just become a state." (L. Sellers. From top: heading for work; songfest; the camp group.)

Kirkby, England - 1949

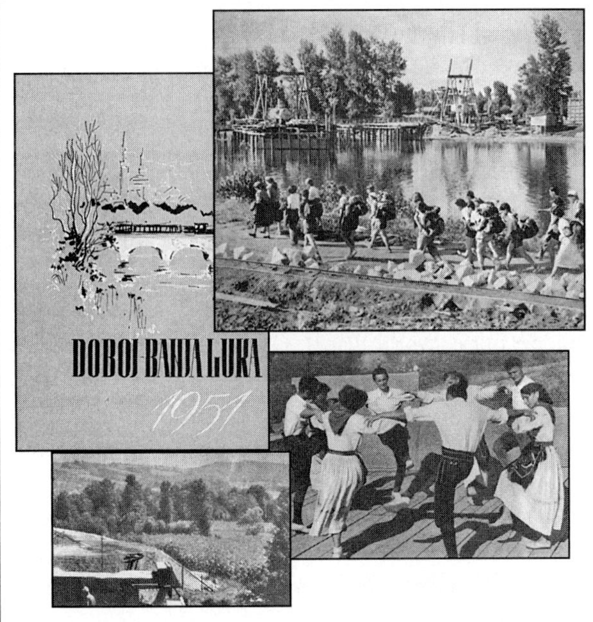

THE PEOPLE'S YOUTH OF YUGOSLAVIA organized 649 youth from 15 countries (32 from "America"), into 22 brigades with "tens of thousands" of Yugoslav youth to build the Doboj-Banja Luka railway. A Communist nation, Yugoslavia broke from the Soviet orbit and was expelled from the International Union of Students (see pp. 543, 591. People's Youth Brochure).

Rudanka - Yugoslavia - 1951

The wonderful summer of 1949

5. The NSA Foreign Student Tour of the United States

Mary Anne (Weld) Bodecker
Smith College
Chairperson, 1949 NSA Foreign Student Tour

Among my personal mementos is a faded envelope containing three or four letters and articles that reflect the year of hard work and passionate commitment that went into the planning and realization of the first and only NSA tour of foreign students to this country, which took place in the summer of 1949. "Bringing Europe to the United States this summer is one of NSA's biggest international projects and the Smith NSA has full responsibility for the plan," proclaimed a lead article in an issue of the Smith College newspaper. Fortunately, I have kept in contact with two of the women who not only helped with the planning but also accompanied the students on much of the tour. Together, Edith Arnold Sisson, Biz Storer Paynter, and I will try to resurrect some of the experiences of that year.

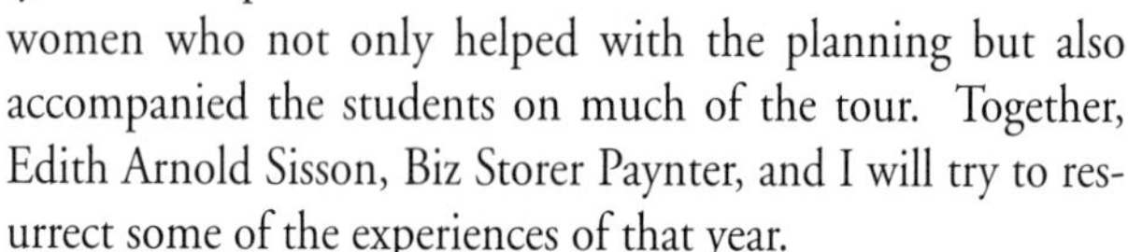

My background

From an early age, I was made aware of international events. My brother, Edric Weld, Jr. (who also became involved with NSA), and I grew up on a school campus and routinely heard discussions of current affairs. My memory stretches back to the Sino-Japanese conflict, the wars in Spain and Finland, and, of course, World War II. During the latter, two English cousins came to live with us for five years. For lesser periods of time, my family hosted refugees from Germany, Austria, Poland, and Czechoslovakia. Some of these people became lifelong friends. My father also invited two Japanese-American boys, whose families were interned in a camp in California, to become students at the school. All of these relationships opened my heart and mind to the complexities of the larger world.

At the end of the war, at age fifteen, I became an enthusiastic member of the Student Federalists, spearheaded by Harris Wofford, whose book, *It's Up to Us*, served as my manifesto. For several years, I worked hard to promote the idea of world government.[1] But, increasingly, I longed for an opportunity to go abroad. That opportunity arrived when NSA organized its first student summer tour to Europe in 1948. In my diary, written aboard the *Kota Inten* as she pulled out of Quebec, I wrote: "I didn't know whether to be serious, like a student seeking to promote international friendship, or to let myself be flooded with a prewar spirit of gaiety." Certainly, I experienced both, and out of that wonderful summer came my determination to reciprocate whenever the occasion might arise. It presented itself almost immediately when I was asked to chair the Smith NSA committee that brought "Europe to the United States" in the summer of 1949.

Planning the tour

It is not clear to me how I came to be chosen to chair the foreign student tour. Aside from my interest in international affairs and participation in the 1948 summer tour in Europe, I had no credentials for the job. At some point along the way, I came to know Bob Smith, who, as NSA's vice-president for international student activities, had an office in Harvard Square at the time.[2] Perhaps it was through him or through his connection with my brother, Edric, that I came to the job. In any case, when asked, I was torn between a desire to realize a dream and my absolute terror of how to go about doing it. To make matters worse, I was to report to Rob West, whose basement-deep voice and obvious competence left me totally unraveled at times. In retrospect, and as I came to know him better in later years, I realized that this gruffness covered a deep compassion and a determined commitment to all that he did.[3]

Our European tour had been largely cultural. However, per the restrictions of the time, students wishing to visit the United States could not obtain visas unless their trip had a specific purpose. It was decided that the purpose of the tour would be to study the U.S. government and its related agencies. The task became to organize the trip around this theme. The Cambridge staff would recruit the students and take care of finances and travel arrangements. My team would provide the itinerary, study outline, and substance of the tour.

It is appropriate here for me to refer to the dedication and creativity of the "special sub-committee of the Unity committee," as our team was called. Although we were all neophytes, we made up for our lack of experience with a determination to see that the goals were met. "The single most important feature of the tour is to create for the Europeans a durable 'sub-stratum' impression of the United States," the Smith article quotes me as saying.

To do that, we enlisted the collaboration of a number of student organizations at other colleges and universities. We approached many, by mail—we had no budget for long-distance phone calls! We worked with those that responded with enthusiasm equal to ours. These included: LaSalle University in Quebec, Colby College in Maine, William and Mary College in Virginia, the University of Kentucky in Louisville, and, for the final seminar on American Government, Mundelein College in Chicago.[4] The itinerary was established largely on the basis of these responses. Fortunately, it covered a sizable portion of the eastern United States.

We fleshed out the tour by enlisting private families as hosts for the students in Boston, through the efforts of the Smith committee, and in Washington, D.C., through the International Student House. I don't recall where they stayed in New York at the end of the summer, just before sailing home. But I do know that a few of our visitors used the final week of "free time" to go all the way to the West Coast and back!

In retrospect, it seems remarkable that we pulled off the arrangements for this trip in a way that appeared to provide a memorable summer for our forty visitors. They came from nine nations—Algiers, Morocco, England, France, Holland, Italy, Sweden, Switzerland, and the Vatican. During the planning stages, we never met any of our student counterparts. Moreover, although we were given nearly carte blanche by the Cambridge office to deal with details, we had to dovetail these with such matters as the group's composition, travel arrangements, and financial issues, all of which were being handled by Rob West and his staff. I don't recall even being asked to keep detailed records, though I do remember becoming well acquainted with the stuffy little office off Harvard Square and its delightful, hard-working occupants.

Because I was to sail to Europe once more in the autumn of 1949 for my junior year abroad in Paris and Geneva, my parents decided that I should spend the summer of the tour at home. Regretfully, but with the utmost confidence in their ability to shepherd our guests, I turned the responsibility for getting the group underway over to my colleagues, Biz and Edith. They were the brave souls who drove up the concrete slabs of highway to Quebec City, where the *Volendam* landed.[5] They were the first to greet the students and were the ones who accompanied them for a good part of the way.

As it turned out, a second group of students materialized some weeks later, and I was asked to meet them, which I did. Only one, Philippe Bongue, whose family I later visited several times in France, had a tour ticket. Many had only foreign checks. With the help of the LaSalle students and much calling back and forth to the Cambridge office, we finally boarded an overnight bus to Boston. Almost no one spoke English, but the day was saved by one student, the son of the Italian ambassador to the Vatican, who spoke several languages and served as my interpreter at the border and for other delicate transactions! In a letter of thanks to me, someone at the Cambridge office wrote, "For all we know, some of these people of whom we never heard may not be on the tour at all—but this I doubt because they got U.S. visas." Luckily, it all worked out!

Edith and Biz remember

Edith and Biz have dug into their scrapbooks and memories to provide the following picture of the tour.

We were the lucky ones chosen to do most of the day-to-day planning, and some of the accompanying, of this first postwar group visit of European students to the United States. Certainly, we lacked skills that might be required by a present-day travel bureau, but our zeal for the cause, perhaps, compensated.

As school kids, World War II had dominated our lives in many ways. Our teachers fostered the idea that individuals could make a difference, and our peers shared our ideas, idealism, and, especially, concerns about nations living together. Mary Anne, Biz, and myself went on student trips to Europe in the summer of 1948. We brought back indelible memories of the efforts, care, concern, and friendly times shared with many European students. When Mary Anne asked Biz and myself if we could help organize a reverse kind of trip, our response was, of course, YES!

As part of our responsibilities, we took on tasks of finding housing with families, arranging meetings with political figures, planning tours, finding means of travel between destinations, and having to rely on unknown, but probably equally enthusiastic, fellow students in other areas to make arrangements.

A special memory is the creation of the budget—after many insistent calls from Rob West. As I recall, Mary Anne and I sat on the bed in my dorm room and made some bold decisions: for instance, we asked ourselves: "How much per day for public transportation during the Boston stay?" and, then, authoritatively listed "20 cents." Similar calculations were made for lunches in Williamsburg, free time in Chicago, sightseeing in New York, and so on. We turned in this budget, never dreaming that it would turn out to be accurate within cents per student, which it was!

As we reminisced about the trip, a few specific impressions came to mind: staying with host families, which gave a deeper dimension to the tour; the "audience" with Boston Mayor James Curley, who then sent us, at taxpayers' expense, to have lunch in a fancy Cambridge restaurant; the politeness of the students when a guide at the Massachusetts State House proudly showed the "foreigners" the pillars of "English Italian [pronounced EYEtalian] marble from Australia"; our surprise at the frequent comments by students about materialism in America; a student's comment, in New York, upon seeing a bomb shelter: 'A bomb shelter? What do you Americans know about war?!' These events were among the many personal, funny, loving times that served to remind us that we are, indeed, part of one world.

The tour was covered by the news media in most of the areas that the students visited. One article, in a Rutland, Vermont, newspaper, chronicled the impressions of two of the female English students. The article said:

> Although there seemed to be nothing American which the Britishers really disliked, they felt that the advertising on the radio was rather annoying. "Advertisements don't always break in at the middle of plays or music do they?" they asked, and were relieved to hear that sometimes symphonies broadcast uninterruptedly.

From the perspective of about fifty years, we believe that this first postwar group visit of European students to the United States was a memorable accomplishment, both for the European students who were willing to come and for us as American students. We had wanted to make their visit, not only a study of the U.S. government, as their visas required, but also to extend it into the intangible: positive relationships between the students of the nationalities involved, including communication based on the sharing of experiences together at all levels. We believe that we accomplished this. As an indication of our mission accomplished, here is a letter which was sent to the Cambridge office by a student, speaking for the group, on August 1:

> Dear Sir,
>
> I am enclosing a cheque for $23 which I understand will cover the cost of a week's holiday for an underprivileged child. This money has been subscribed by a party of European students who are on a two month study tour of the United States. The tour is under the auspices of the National Students' Association but was largely organized by a group from Smith College.
>
> We feel this is the best way that we have of showing members of Smith how much we appreciate the amount of hard work which has obviously gone into this tour, and we would be grateful if any acknowledgment that you make be sent to the National Students' Association Branch at Smith College.
>
> Yours faithfully,

* * *

Afterword

In addition to this kind communication from our student guests, an invitation came to me from James T. Harris to attend the Second National Student Congress at the University of Illinois. "We would very much like to have you lead the discussion concerning: U.S. Tours for foreign students," the letter read. Alas! This became another missed opportunity as I was leaving shortly for Europe. My connection with NSA mostly faded away after that.

Years later, when I became involved with Reform Democratic politics in New York City, I ran into Allard Lowenstein at a fund-raiser. He kindly remembered my early contribution to the international efforts of the young NSA, and he and I became friends in a new context. Peripherally, I also kept up with the doings of Rob West, thanks to his family's friendship with my brother, Edric, and his (then) wife, Ellen Weld. We shared a weekend in New Hampshire in the late 1970s, which was filled with stories and memories of Rob's adventures in Africa and elsewhere. And then, suddenly, he was dead. Edric and I both attended the memorial service, which paid tribute to his continued dedication to the problems of internationalism as well as his devotion to his family and friends. Late and soon, it seemed, this was a man who knew where he was going.[6]

The Cambridge office is long gone as well. But sometimes as I walk through Harvard Square, I think of those "glory days," when I was full of inexhaustible energy and a great sense of purpose. I wonder what has happened to all those whose lives touched mine that year. "The students' most rewarding experience will be secured through the friends they make here," I declared in the Smith interview. Did it happen? Did it last? Did the summer of 1949 change the direction of their lives forever? Perhaps, a little, but we will never know for sure.

For reasons that I do not know, NSA decided not to continue with this experiment. The thrust of its international efforts remained overseas. But I shall hang on to the faded envelope and, from time to time, examine its contents with a renewed sense of pride. For me and my Smith colleagues, the NSA foreign student tour in the summer of 1949 will always be remembered as a great success!

Mary Anne Bodecker is a clinical social worker who is currently working with the Cambridge Hospital Multidisciplinary AIDS Program. Earlier, she was a preschool teacher.

EDITH AND BIZ

Editor's note: Edith Arnold Sisson, who lives in Concord, MA, and Biz Storer Paynter, who lives in Weston, MA, collaborated with Mary Anne Bodecker in the preparation of this recollection and contributed the following updates on themselves.

Edith Arnold Sisson: *Now, at seventy-three years of age, I am an educator/naturalist, teacher, author, and farmer as well as mom and grandma. My idealism and international concerns of the post–World War II era? They are part of the fundamentals for my concerns for the environment, my passion for teaching (in person or through writing), my love of nature and the "simple" life, and, especially, my compassion for all peoples of our world.*

Elizabeth S. Paynter: *Since graduation in 1951, I worked in personnel at a chain of restaurants in San Francisco, a hospital in Boston, and the Museum of Science. Marriage brought a change to free-lancing as a photographer/photo journalist at a local newspaper and to indulging my love of nature and children as teacher/tour guide at a local Audubon sanctuary. Wife, mother of two and volunteerism filled my life until the present.*

END NOTES

1 See Gilbert Jonas, "The Student Federalist Movement," p. 761 for the story of the Student Federalists.

2 See Robert Smith, p. 504.

3 See Robert West, p. 515, and Helen Garland, p. 641 and p. 642.

4 See Birenbaum, album on the Chicago Joint-College Host Committee, p. 590, and Album p. 665.

5 See Album, p. 664, and "The Ships," p. 669.

6 West died July 17, 1991. See p. 516.

PICTURE CREDITS. Bodecker—*Then:* 1946, high school senior photo. *Now:* March, 1997, National AIDS Memorial Grove, San Francisco (Both from author). **Painter (Storer)**—*Then:* Summer, 1948 aboard the *Volendam*. *Now:* March, 1999 (Both from Paynter). **Sisson (Arnold)**—Then: 1948. *Now:* 2000 (Both from Sisson).

MARY ANNE (WELD) BODECKER

Early Background: Born in 1929 at Saranac Lake, New York. My father was an educator, and I grew up on a school campus.

Education: B.A., Smith College, 1951. Sophia Smith Scholar Award. M.A., Goddard-Cambridge College, 1977. M.S.W., Boston University School of Social Work, 1981. Certificate Program, Family Institute of Cambridge, 1983. Certificate, Women's Theological Center, Cambridge, MA, 1988. Certificate Program, The Episcopal Divinity School, Cambridge, MA 1999-2001.

Career highlights: Preschool teacher. Data collector, Roxbury Court Clinic, Roxbury, MA, 1976-78. Clinical Social Worker, McLean Hospital, Belmont, MA, 1982-1983, 1986-1987. Marlborough Hospital Mental Health Unit, Marlborough, MA, 1983-1986. Social Justice for Women (MCI-Framingham, MA), 1988-1990. Cambridge Hospital Multidisciplinary AIDS Program, 1993-1999.

Over the years, I have been involved in a variety of educational, political, and community activities. I was involved in the Reform Democratic movement in New York City in the late 1950s, and was elected to a term on the New York County Committee. In the 1970s, I became involved in volunteer work in Massachusetts prisons. In 1988, I was hired by Social Justice for Women to create the case management program for incarcerated women with HIV/AIDS at MCI Framingham. This was the first program of its kind in the country. More recently, I helped to found Ruah-Breath-of-Life Inc., a home for homeless women with HIV/AIDS in Cambridge.

I am constantly involved in educational programs to enhance my professional competence. As I move toward retirement, I am working to incorporate these skills into my personal "retirement plan," which will include some private practice, work with support groups for caretakers and the bereaved in the AIDS field, and theological studies. My interests include reading, writing, walking, cross-country skiing, Buddhist studies and meditation, and travel. I have a fondness for cold climates. In 1995, I participated in a week of dog sledding on the frozen tundra of Baffin Island in the Arctic. In 1998, I spent two weeks in Antarctica.

Family: I married Niels Mogens Bodecker in 1952. We were divorced in 1962, and he died in 1988. Children: Alexander Weld Bodecker, born 1953; Torsten Weld Bodecker, born 1955, died 1992; Niels Weld Bodecker, born 1957.

The NSA 1949 Foreign Student Tour

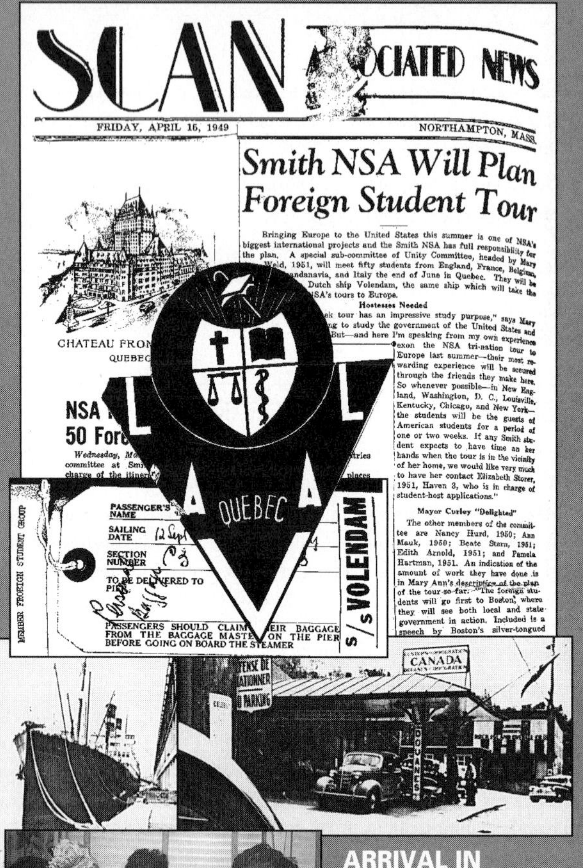

SCAN ASSOCIATED NEWS

FRIDAY, APRIL 16, 1949 NORTHAMPTON, MASS.

Smith NSA Will Plan Foreign Student Tour

Bringing Europe to the United States this summer is one of NSA's biggest international projects and the Smith NSA has full responsibility for the plan. A special sub-committee of Unity Committee, headed by Mary ... Weld, 1951, will meet fifty students from England, France, Belgium, ...andanavia, and Italy the end of June in Quebec. They will be ... Dutch ship Volendam, the same ship which will take the ...SA's tours to Europe.

Hostesses Needed

...ek tour has an impressive study purpose," says Mary ...ng to study the government of the United States and ... But—and here I'm speaking from my own experience ...exon the NSA tri-nation tour to Europe last summer—their most rewarding experience will be secured through the friends they make here. So whenever possible—in New England, Washington, D. C., Louisville, Kentucky, Chicago, and New York—the students will be the guests of American students for a period of one or two weeks. If any Smith student expects to have time an her hands when the tour is in the vicinity of her home, we would like very much to have her contact Elizabeth Storer, 1951, Haven 3, who is in charge of student-host applications."

Mayor Curley "Delighted"

The other members of the committee are Nancy Hurd, 1950; Ann Mauk, 1950; Beate Stern, 1951; Edith Arnold, 1951; and Pamela Hartman, 1951. An indication of the amount of work they have done is in Mary Ann's description of the plan of the tour so far. "The foreign students will go first to Boston, where they will see both local and state government in action. Included is a speech by Boston's silver-tongued

ARRIVAL IN QUEBEC, AND THROUGH CANADIAN CUSTOMS. From top: Smith C. *SCAN*, 4/15/49; Laval College emblem; S/S Volendam luggage ticket; Volendam in Quebec. Canadian customs crossing point. (All from Mary Anne [Weld] Bodecker.)

TOUR GROUP WELCOMED AT COLBY. From left: Prof. John F. McCoy, director of Colby-Swarthmore Summer School of Languages; Elizabeth (Biz) Storer; Simone Loufrani, French Algiers; Edith Sisson. Sisson and Storer were tour organizers at Smith (See pp. 661, 663).

31 Foreign Students In Waterville Visit

Attend French Bastille Day Social At Colby College Summer School

Colby College became an international crossroads Thursday night when 31 students from four countries in Europe and North Africa landed on campus.

More of the group from left, standing: Hugo Peterson, Sweden; John Crassley, York, England; Stan Josephs, Manchester, England; Svante Thurquist and Arne Jonson, Sweden; Jules Enneking and Jan Roben, Netherlands; Paul Dubois, Sweden. Seated, Smith's Elizabeth Storer and Edith Arnold. (*Waterville Morning Sentinel*, 7/15/49. Photos by Tobey).

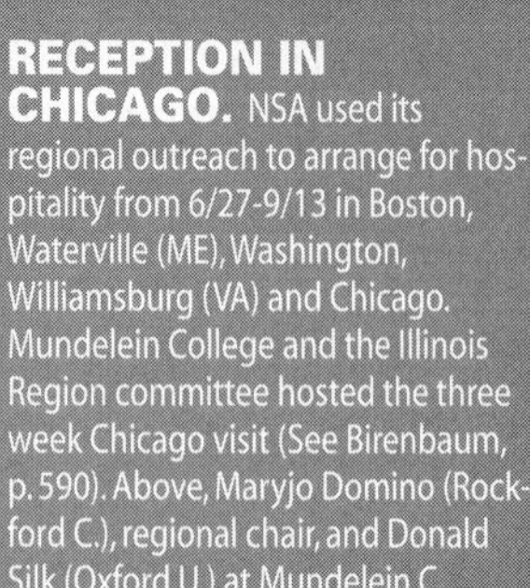

RECEPTION IN CHICAGO. NSA used its regional outreach to arrange for hospitality from 6/27-9/13 in Boston, Waterville (ME), Washington, Williamsburg (VA) and Chicago. Mundelein College and the Illinois Region committee hosted the three week Chicago visit (See Birenbaum, p. 590). Above, Maryjo Domino (Rockford C.), regional chair, and Donald Silk (Oxford U.) at Mundelein C. reception 8/49. (Photo from Marie Kelly.)

STUDENTS FROM NINE COUNTRIES. Some of the 46 students, above, who came to Chicago were from Algiers, Morocco, England, France, Holland, Italy, Sweden, Switzerland and the Vatican. Smith committee members shown in top row from left are Mary Ann Weld (third), and Elizabeth Paynter (sixth).

Sad faces turning happy

6. The *Svalbard* and the *Ballou*

Robert F. Meagher

City College of New York

Executive Secretary, NSA Metropolitan New York Region, 1947

Editor's note: In June 1950, NSA's program of student study, travel, and work abroad for US students experienced a major, though short-lived, crisis when the U.S. Coast Guard refused to allow the Norwegian ship Svalbard, *which had been chartered by NSA for its student groups and which met all safety requirements of the Geneva Convention, to clear the port of New York. This essay and the earlier essay by Helen Bryan Garland, NSA's Travel Director when the event occurred, provide information on this occurrence. The Coast Guard's action, taken when students were waiting on the pier to go aboard, after the ship had been available for inspection in New York for ten days, and weeks after the authorities had ignored NSA's request for inspection of the ship at Bremerhaven before it crossed the Atlantic, remains distressing and deeply puzzling. —Ralph Smith*

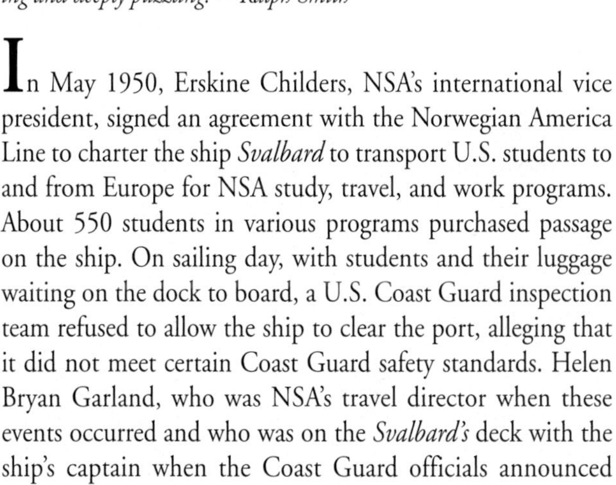

In May 1950, Erskine Childers, NSA's international vice president, signed an agreement with the Norwegian America Line to charter the ship *Svalbard* to transport U.S. students to and from Europe for NSA study, travel, and work programs. About 550 students in various programs purchased passage on the ship. On sailing day, with students and their luggage waiting on the dock to board, a U.S. Coast Guard inspection team refused to allow the ship to clear the port, alleging that it did not meet certain Coast Guard safety standards. Helen Bryan Garland, who was NSA's travel director when these events occurred and who was on the *Svalbard's* deck with the ship's captain when the Coast Guard officials announced their ruling, provides greater detail in [her] essay.[1]

The Coast Guard's action created immediate and drastic problems. Could another ship be found? What should be done with the students who were waiting to board the ship? NSA set up an emergency center in the Woodstock Hotel on West 44th Street in Manhattan. Most of the students were traveling on tight budgets, and the first priority was to find a place for them to stay.

Jay Maryanov, a Columbia University student who was active in NSA, spoke with Columbia officials. Commencement had just taken place, and there was room in Johnson Hall to house female students. Columbia said yes. I am a graduate of City College of New York (CCNY) and was at that time at Yale Law School. I spoke to CCNY officials. They made room for 120 students in Army Hall, a facility created during the war to house trainees in the Army Special Training Program (ASTP). Students who lived in the New York area took other students home. A group of twenty-five American Youth Hostelers went to the Long Island home of one of their number and slept in the back yard!

Newspapers provide major coverage

New York newspapers provided major coverage of the event. In those days, the New York Times Building in Times Square reported news by the use of moving lights which wound around the building. The students' problems were flashed for all to see. The students promptly learned that New Yorkers were neither cold nor impersonal. Offers of help from the entire metropolitan area immediately began to pour in to the NSA office in the Woodstock. Restaurants offered meals at radically reduced prices. Radio stations, concert halls, Rockefeller Center, theaters, museums, the Bronx Zoo, the New York Botanical Gardens, and other institutions invited students to visit, in most cases free of charge. In addition, it was June, the weather was warm, and many migrated to the beaches.

At the Woodstock, NSA staffers were fielding immense numbers of calls from concerned parents. The next day, at the prompting of a White House official, Erskine crafted a telegram to the White House, seeking help. It brought swift results. A U.S. government troopship, the *General Ballou*, had just arrived in the United States and was returning to Europe empty. That is, it was returning empty until Erskine's telegram arrived. It sailed on June 27, three days later, with the students aboard!

Happy faces

Margot Dunckel of Antioch chaired and coordinated an instantly created Social Activities Committee for the stranded students. When the good news of the *Ballou* was received, she and the Committee planned and organized a dance at

Columbia University's International House for the evening of June 26. The next day, the tired but happy students boarded the ship, which sailed at 3:10 P.M. In addition to members of NSA groups and the twenty-five Youth Hostelers, there were members of many other groups, including a Canadian group on its way to a conference in Pontigny, France; U.S. observers going to a meeting of the International Union of Students; and a group going to Koenigstein im Taunus to attend the first postwar international conference to include German students.[2]

Aboard the *Ballou*, there were excellent facilities, including a theater for lectures and documentary movies, a ballroom, three pianos, and deck space for sports. NSA had prepared a program of study and language groups, diverse lectures, and social activities.

It would be hard to find a better illustration of the old adage, all's well that ends well.

Robert F. Meagher is Legal Adviser to the India Interest Group and Professor Emeritus of International Law at the Fletcher School of Law and Diplomacy, Tufts University. He is a lifetime specialist on India.

PICTURE CREDITS. *Then:* 1946, on return to CCNY after army service (Author). *Now:* March, 1998, Wayland, MA (Schwartz).

END NOTES

[1] See Garland, p. 641. [2] See Perkins, p. 603, for a recollection of the 1951 German Seminar project.

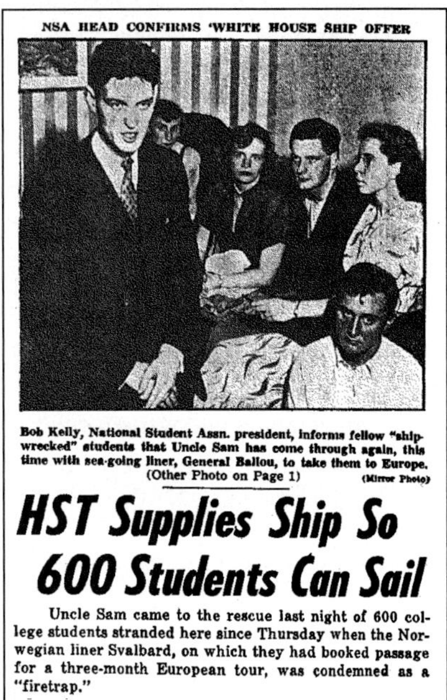

NSA HEAD CONFIRMS 'WHITE HOUSE SHIP OFFER

Bob Kelly, National Student Assn. president, informs fellow "shipwrecked" students that Uncle Sam has come through again, this time with sea-going liner, General Ballou, to take them to Europe. (Other Photo on Page 1) (Mirror Photo)

HST Supplies Ship So 600 Students Can Sail

Uncle Sam came to the rescue last night of 600 college students stranded here since Thursday when the Norwegian liner Svalbard, on which they had booked passage for a three-month European tour, was condemned as a "firetrap."

"TIRED BUT HAPPY," Bob Meagher (Above, lower right), listens to NSA President Kelly announce their "rescue" by "Uncle Sam." (*Daily Mirror*, NY, 6/25/50. See p. 667.)

ROBERT F. MEAGHER

Early Background: Born in New York City. Attended De Witt Clinton High School.

Education: City College of New York, B.S.S., January 1949; Yale University Law School, JD, June 1952; Bombay School of Economics (Fulbright student), 1952-53.

Career highlights: Legal Adviser to the India Interest Group, 1993–present; Consultant on International Economic Law, 1960–present; Professor Emeritus of International Law, Fletcher School of Law and Diplomacy, Tufts University; Professor of International Law, Fletcher School of Law and Diplomacy, Tufts University, 1967-1992; Visiting Professor of Law at various times: Harvard Law School, Indian Law Institute in New Delhi, and Melbourne and Monash Universities in Australia; Adjunct Professor of Law, Columbia University School of Law, 1972-75; Assistant Director, Public International Development Finance Project, Columbia University School of Law, 1961-1965; Legal Officer, UNWRA, Beirut, Lebanon, 1958–59; Lawyer, Winthrop Stimson Putnam and Roberts, New York City, 1954-1958; Specialist on India, visiting there once or twice a year since 1952.

Specialist on Oil and Natural Resources, lecturing over a thirty-year period throughout Asia, Africa, and the Middle East; Specialist on Law and Social Change.

Active member of numerous professional organizations, including African Law Association in America, American Society for International Law, Law and Society Association, Association of Asian Studies, American Society of Comparative Law, Association of the Bar of the City of New York, Council on Foreign Relations, International Law Association, Society for International Development, World Peace through Law Center.

Bob Meagher, Innovator and Leader Guides Freshmen and Seniors Alike

From *The Campus*, CCNY 12/2/48
By Norman Zukowsky (excerpts)

The Campus

"Transforming Freshman Misery"

No one has ever accused Bob Meagher '49 of sorcery, but five cycles of College students would gladly testify that the president of the senior class is omnipresent. The names of the organizations which have listed him in membership constitute a top level College directory. Meagher, whose smiling face and natty bow tie are better public relations than money can buy, has spent five years trying to transform his term of freshman misery into an object lesson for a kinder, happier College.

As chairman of the Big Brother Committee, Meagher—it's pronounced "Mar"—instituted a personal interview system of freshman orien-ta-tion. He had discovered that a freshman whose guidance is left to chance might never get into the scholastic and extra-curricular swing...

Meagher, never at a loss for words, is one of the few college orators who can command an audience larger than his immediate circle of intimates. His denunciation at the September Lincoln Corridor sit-down [see p. 852] commanded more attention than Dean John J. Theobold's less vehement pleas to the actionist group....

A constant spectator at all sporting events, Meagher led a student movement last term for a better deal in basketball ticket distribution.

He spent two years with the army in Europe, where he suffered an arm injury, which terminated a brilliant swimming career begun in De Witt Clinton High School and continued at the College.

A member of Delta Alpha, he commented on the current racial con-troversy among fraternities with a statement typical of his straightforward manner, "I meet every man as an individual and treat him as such."

The *Svalbard* Incident

U.S. Weather Forecast
FAIR—WARMER
(Details on Page 2)

Daily  Mirror

4c In Suburbs
5c Elsewhere

3¢

Vol. 26. No. 313. NEW YORK 17, N. Y., FRIDAY, JUNE 23, 1950 BQ FINAL EDITION ★★★★

'FIRETRAP' SHIP STRANDS 600

Coast Guard Condemns Student Liner

Story on Page 2

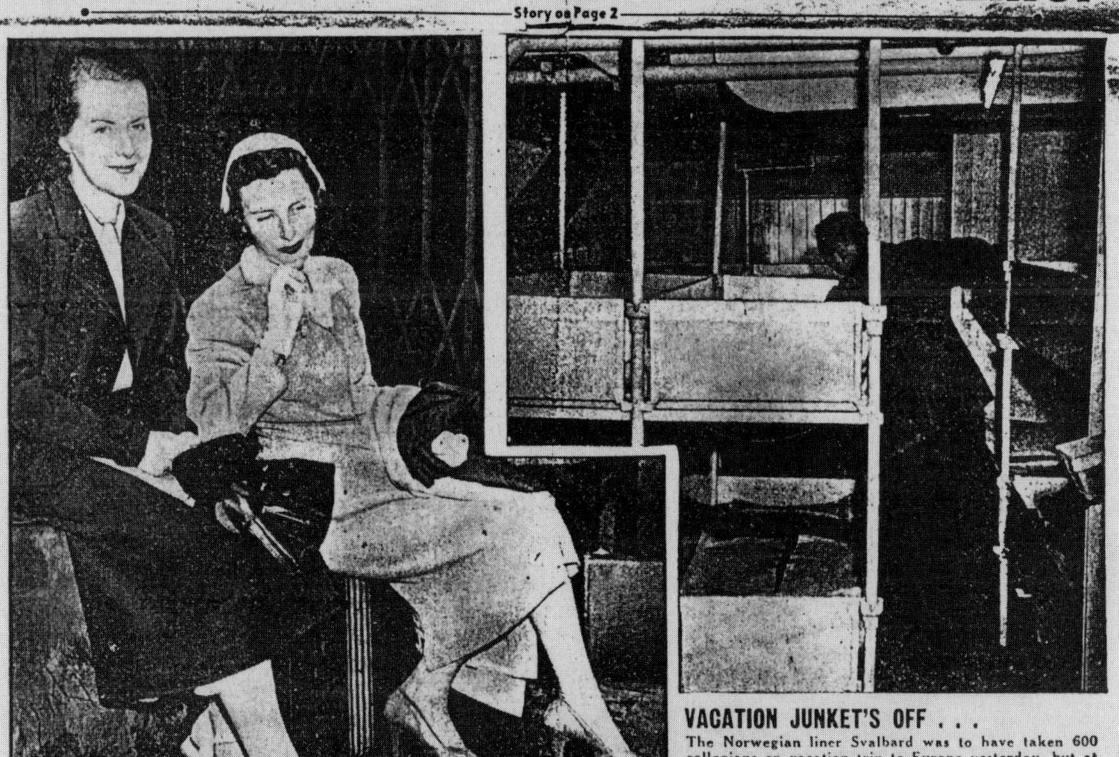

VACATION JUNKET'S OFF . . .
The Norwegian liner Svalbard was to have taken 600 collegians on vacation trip to Europe yesterday, but at last minute, the Coast Guard called it off. Double-deck, close-packed bunks above were among conditions which caused ship to be branded a "firetrap." In photo at left, Joan Gladwin (left), of Ottawa, and Joyce Mueller, Kansas City, Mo., bear up under the blow.

(Mirror Photos by Dick [illegible])

(Story and Other Photo on Page 2)

TWO DAYS BEFORE NORTH KOREAN INVASION OF SOUTH KOREA, U.S. Coast Guard refusal to clear NSA's charter ship, the Norwegian liner *Svalbard,* dominated headlines (See Garland p. 641 and Meagher, p. 665.)

Daily Mirror, NY 6/23/50

Ship a 'Firetrap,' Ban Ocean Trip By 600 Students

The laughing excitement of 600 American college students waiting on the pier with bag and baggage to embark on a vacation trip to Europe turned to sullen disappointment yesterday when the Coast Guard branded their chartered liner a "firetrap" and refused to allow it to sail.

The 6,800-ton Norwegian liner Svalbard, built by the Germans in 1938 and used by them in the invasion of Norway, was condemned two hours before she was to sail from Pier 42, North River and Morton St., at 4 p. m.

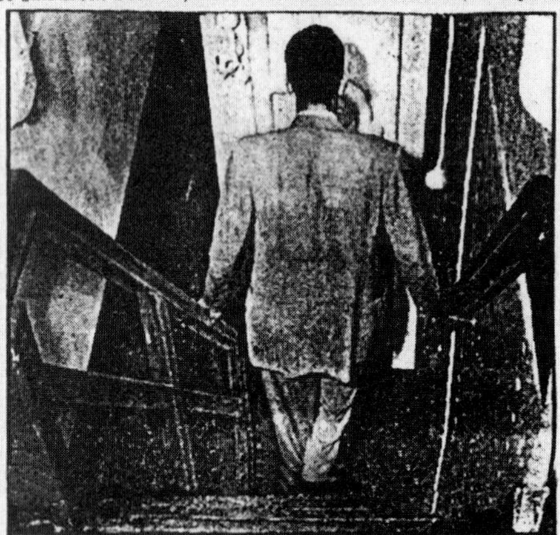

Svalbard's stairways were claimed unsafe by U. S. Coast Guard because they are too narrow and would be dangerous in emergency.
(Other Photos on Page 1) (Mirror Photo)

with college men and women from all parts of the United States.

"This ship will not be allowed to clear this port with American passengers," the Coast Guard's Marine Inspection Department announced.

When the announcement was relayed to the students, a loud moan went up. Girls wept on each other's shoulders and one husky college lad, in his anger, kicked a small bag into the water.

A Coast Guard spokesman explained that the liner, chartered by the National Student Assn. for $200,000 to carry the students to Rotterdam and back, was "generally unsuitable and did not comply with regulations for the transportation of passengers."

To Miss Helen Bryan, 24, a Sarah Lawrence College student and travel organizer for the NSA, the Coast Guard inspectors explained that the ship's stairways were too narrow and that the wooden bunks did not conform to safety regulations, also that the ship lacked an automatic fire alarm.

The Svalbard, never in New York before, was known as the Togo when used by the Germans. Later it was acquired by the United States and sold to the Norwegian government.

The Coast Guard said the vessel could clear port at any time with its crew and not more than 12 passengers. Erskine Childers, 21, vice-president of the NSA, said the organization would try to charter another ship.

The students' emergency headquarters, set up in the Hotel Woodstock, 127 W. 43d St., found billets for all stranded voyagers for the night. The girls went to Johnson Hall, on the Columbia University campus, and the men to Army Hall at CCNY, at 138th St. and Amsterdam Ave.

Miss Nancy Lee Roth, 21, of Los Angeles, just graduated from the University of California, wasn't at all down-hearted about the delay.

"I'm grateful for this chance to see some of the wonderful sights of New York," she said. "I can wait for England, France, Italy, Switzerland and Holland."

The Svalbard was due to arrive in Rotterdam July 3 and leave there Aug. 31 for the return trip.

The Coast Guard said its inspection of the vessel had not been completed and probably would require several days more.

Childers, in explaining the development to the students, said that though the Svalbard was under charter to the student association, the Norwegian American Line bears full responsibility for clearing the port of New York under U. S. regulations.

5-DAY WEATHER CHART
By Dr. Selby Maxwell

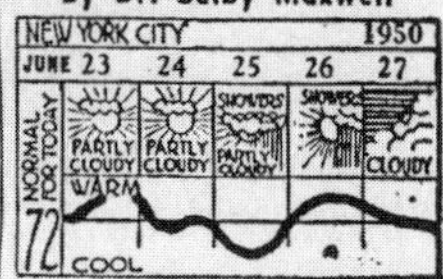

Each day Dr. Maxwell, famous meteorologist, predicts weather for the New York area for the next five days. See Sunday's Mirror for week's predictions covering adjacent areas.

New York Herald Tribune, 6/26/50

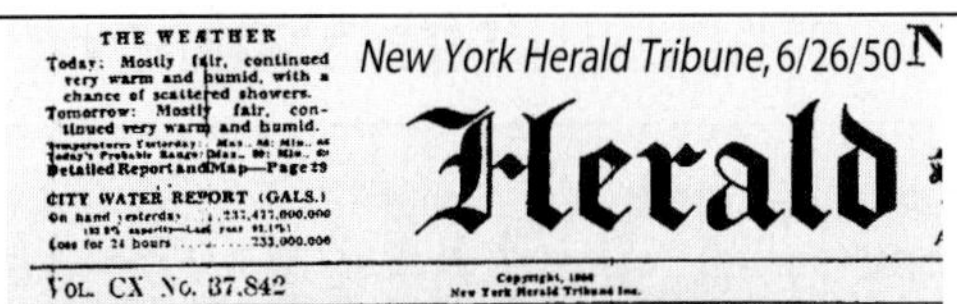

THE WEATHER
Herald
Vol. CX No. 37,842

Korea Reds Open Attack On South Korea, War On; U. S. Takes Case to U. N.

Army Base 40 Miles From Seoul Seized

Troops Cross the Border in Heavy Rain; Coastal Highway Reported Cut

BULLETIN

WASHINGTON, Sunday, June 25, (UP).—The United States early today asked the United Nations Security Council to hold an emergency session later today on the invasion of South Korea by the Communist-dominated North Korean forces.

Invasion Launched
By The United Press

SEOUL, Sunday, June 25.—Forces of Communist North Korea launched a series of attacks into the American-sponsored South Korean Republic today, and the Northern Pyongyang radio said that war had been declared formally, effective at 11 a. m. (9 p.m. Eastern daylight saving time, Saturday).

550 Students Get Money Back, Will Go to Europe on Transport

Norway Cancels Charter of Ship Called Unsafe, Returns $87,500 to Vacation Group

By Don Ross

The way was paved yesterday for the 550 stranded college students of this country and Canada to leave for Europe on Tuesday aboard the General C. C. Ballou. The Navy operated transport was offered for the students' trip following the intercession on Friday night of President Truman.

The offering hinged on cancellation of the contract between the National Student Association, of which the men and women students are members, and the Norwegian government for the charter of the motorship Svalbard, which the Coast Guard rejected for sailing as a fire hazard. A second provision was that the students' money be refunded.

Yesterday, both these points were met when the Norwegian government and the N. S. A. announced in an amicable joint statement the cancellation of the $175,000 contract for the charter of the 6,800-ton vessel and the return to the association by the government of its $87,500 deposit.

U. S. Will Hold Russia to Blame For Korea War

But State Dept. Is Silent on Direct Military Action in Defense of the South

By The United Press

WASHINGTON Sunday, June 25 State Department officials said last night the United States will hold Russia responsible for the Communist North Korean war against the independent South Korean Republic, which this country and the United Nations

NSA 1950 Tour Program

As reported to the Third National Student Congress (excerpted)

Of the 10,000 students from the United States who went abroad this summer NSA was directly responsible for sending 1,300 In other words, NSA sent 13% of the American students abroad this summer.

In regard to actual NSA tours, the International Commission ar-ranged for 600 students to go abroad on the Volendam in its 18 pro-grams. Nine of these were study tours, three seminars, and six work camps. The International Commission also arranged for the transporta-tion of 104 students to and from Europe by Chartered KLM Royal Dutch Airlines planes. In addition, NSA sent approximately 600 students abroad on the chartered ship, the General Ballou, obtained from the United States Government. The International Commission also brought foreign students to this country and planned orientation on the Volendam and General Ballou.

The Commission secured 600 berths on the SS Volendam, Dutch studentship. on which NSA cooperated with the Dutch Office for Foreign Student Relations.

In addition to these plans, in early June, the Staff authorized the chartering of the Norwegian ship "M/S Svalbard" by NSA for $175,000. This was done to provide low-cost education travel at a time when regular facilities were severely strained by an unprecedented demand for space. The Association assumed responsibility for ticketing and berthing the vessel at a roundtrip passage rate of $310, while all other responsibilities were assumed by the Norwegian government, as owners. Although the ship had never before entered an American port, it possessed an International Safety Certificate in accord with the 1929 International Convention.

Some 550 passages were sold and a preliminary deposit of $87,500 was made by NSA when a Coast Guard inspection disclosed that the ship was unsafe and would not be permitted to sail....

Direct representations to the White House were made under the advice and direction of helpful friends of NSA. In response to these requests the President made available the 13,000 ton transport "SS General Ballou," to be operated "at no cost to the government." A total expense of $160,000 is anticipated for accomodations quite superior to the Svalbard. The "General Ballou" sailed on June 28th for Rotterdam and arrived on July 6th with 550 student travelers. The total delay was three days.

"An atmosphere of excitement, enthusiasm and dedication to causes"

Life Aboard the Student Ships

Editor's note: This summary was contributed by Henry Halsted (Williams College, Massachusetts), a delegate to the NSA Constitutional Convention in 1947. Halsted took part in several visits to Europe with the Experiment in International Living, traveling on the student ships (see Halsted, p. 679). The unpublished Ellis paper referred to is in the Anthology project archives.

Writing about the student ships used, some of which were former troopships, Russ Ellis, in his "Memoir of The Early Days of Donald Watt and The Experiment in International Living," (an unpublished paper) notes:

> Before World War II most groups traveled tourist class on the luxury liners of the Cunard, French, Holland American, and North German Lloyd lines. Some alumni enjoy relating how regularly, nevertheless, they frequented the luxurious lounges of first class. In that age, however, traveling in a group sponsored by an organization such as the Experiment was the exception; most young people traveled with parents or sometimes young ladies with chaperones. The volume of student groups was not large enough to encourage shipping lines to offer sailings exclusively for an all-student passenger list.
>
> After World War II many organizations, with humanitarian or educational missions, began to sponsor student groups and the demand for inexpensive, austere transoceanic transportation was born.
>
> Few comforts had been added for the students. There were large dormitories with three-tiered bunks, gang latrines for the males, no air conditioning, cold, salt water showers, and meals served cafeteria style to long lines of hungry youngsters. The spirit of an all-student population excited by its first trans-oceanic crossing offset, nevertheless, the austerity of the accommodations.
>
> This leisurely crossing (10–12 days) provided the perfect ambience in which ten perfect strangers and a leader soon recognized themselves as a group. As the small ships gently rolled, the leaders conducted "orientation," initiating "group discussion" on the culture of the country of destination, and introducing the pronunciation of critical words of the foreign language to be encountered. Even while traveling at 12 knots there was little boredom; the evening was devoted to socializing and recreation with singing often initiated to accompany student guitars.

Youth Argosy [See Part 3, Section 6 following in this part], which sponsored the student ships, stated in its orientation material to passengers:

> If your attitude is critical and lacking in appreciation you will not enjoy it. Similarly, you will dislike the austerity of the ships, and previous to your return voyage you will be annoyed by delayed trains, downpours of rain, hot sun, cold mountains, strange food, languages and customs. Certain hardships are undoubtedly common to all travel and are more evident in the lowly sort than in the deluxe trips. But lowly travel brings with it a greater richness in human values. With an eye for drama and a heart alert to people you will find your experience valuable, enjoyable, tremendous!

These ships, restricted mainly to students, each carried 1,500 or more passengers back and forth across the Atlantic from 1947 until 1958, when charter air flights began to provide a cheaper quicker way for groups to travel to Europe. On board the ships were members of many idealistic and religious youth and student organizations and their leaders. There were Mennonite, YMCA, Quaker and World Council of Churches work camp groups going to Europe to help in building refugee housing and rebuilding churches and youth centers.

Each ship had an educational faculty team whose members gave lectures and led workshops. For example, the team on the returning *Samaria* in 1949 was made up of: Dr. Ira Reid, chairman of the sociology department of Haverford College; Dr. and Mrs. Morris Mitchel, educational directors of the Southern Cooperative Movement; the Rev. and Mrs. Alexander Stewart of the World Council of Churches; Nancy Garoutte, educational director of *Mademoiselle* magazine; and Dr. Curt Bondy, head of the psychology department at the Richmond Professional Institute of the College of William and Mary.

The atmosphere was one of excitement, enthusiasm, and dedication to causes. Student World Federalists groups, for example, were actively advocating their view and distributing literature pointing out that it had taken two world wars, fought largely on European soil, to bring the world to the point of believing that some kind of political or economic union in Europe was not only desirable, but politically possible and necessary. It was also the time of Gary Davis, the young American flyer who renounced his American citizenship to dramatize the need for world government.

THE S/S *VOLENDAM.* Introduced by the Holland-America Line for the return voyage of September, 1948, the 1,300 passenger *Volendam* became a major student tour carrier between the U.S. and Europe, and NSA tours and bookings filled the vessel in the next few years. Clockwise from top: The 1949 eastbound voyage recorded by Margaret Sellers (Fitzpatrick), of Regis C., Mass., in the first 5 photos. The last 3 are from the 1950 eastbound voyage recorded by Herb Hessler, and provided by Karl Meyer, both of the U. of Wisconsin, who traveled together (see p. 142).

800 Students Sail for Rotterdam On The *Kota Inten* in 1948

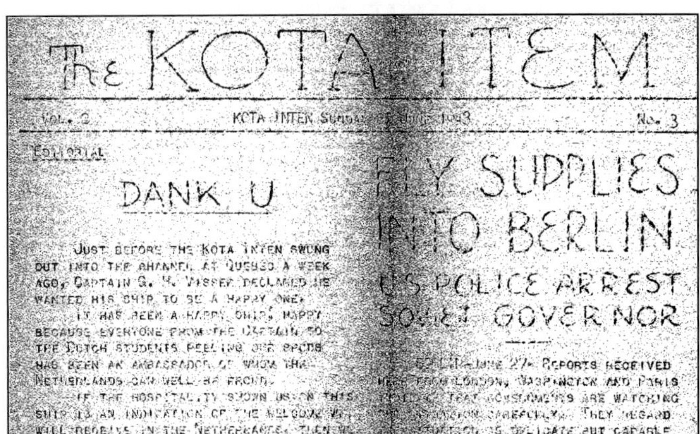

The KOTA ITEM

Vol. 2 — KOTA INTEN Sunday [illegible] June 1948 — No. 3

EDITORIAL

DANK U

Just before the Kota Inten swung out into the channel at Quebec a week ago, Captain G. H. Visser declared he wanted his ship to be a happy one.

It has been a happy ship; happy because everyone from the Captain to the Dutch students peeling our spuds has been an ambassador of whom the Netherlands can well be proud.

If the hospitality shown us on this ship is an indication of the welcome we will receive in the Netherlands, then we [...]

FLY SUPPLIES INTO BERLIN

US POLICE ARREST SOVIET GOVERNOR

[...] June 27 — Reports received here from London, Washington and Paris [...] that [...] are watching the situation carefully. They regard [...] delicate but capable [...]

Carleton C., MN, *The Carletonian* 3/20/48

N S A Sponsors Tour Of Western Europe

Nine Week Trip Costs Students About $550

A TOUR of England, France and the Netherlands has been organized for the U.S. National Student Association by the N[...]

NSA'S 1948 TRI-NATION TOUR GROUP, bound for nine weeks in Holland, Belgium, France and England, gathered on deck of Holland-America Line's *Kota Inten* in June. Other student ships that summer included HAL's *Tabita* and *Volendam* (introduced for the September return trip.) The U.S. Maritime Commission provided the *Marine Jumper* and *Marine Tiger.* The student ship program that summer was administered by the Institute for International Education. Shipboard orientation programs were provided by the American Friends Service Committee. Among those identified in this photo by Pat Wolgemuth Blair (p. 650), Meg Weld Bodecker (p. 660), 5th from R. in 4th row, and Ralph Smith, dark jacket upper right: Seated rear from left: Al and Jenny Houghton (U. of Wisc.), 3d and 4th; Fran and David McLachren, 5th and 6th; Ann Crowell, 4th fr R, 4th row; Blakie Forsythe, 5th fr R, 3rd row; and Bob Gaudino, 3d fr L, 2d row.

Vassar *Miscellany News*, 10/13/48

E. Kraft Describes Tri-nation Tour As Successful USNSA Enterprise

by Ellen Kraft '50

"But tell me really about America. Not only politics, but about your own life. What do you do there?" It was a Dutch girl who asked me this question, in a small town in Friesland, the northern part of Holland. The question, however, reflects the genuine curiosity about American life which I found among students throughout Europe this summer.

I was travelling on a tour arranged by the United States National Students Association of France, Belgium, The Netherlands and England. There were ninety of us, representing almost every state in the union, and presenting a good cross-section of American thought.

The students, our hosts in each country, were wonderful to us: they were patient as we grappled with then language and geography, and anxious to tell us everything we wished to know.

It is hard to come away with anything but a superficial impression after spending only a month in each country, and I can speak only of attitudes I felt were dominant in each country. The particular French people whom I met seemed preoccupied with the past war and with a fear of Germany's rebuilding. They were depressed about their government, the value of the franc, the shortages of food and material and the problems of rebuilding France. On the other hand, they have learned to accept much. They barely remember the days when bread was white, and clothes were plentiful. And they have rather mixed opinions of America. They respect us and yet are slightly disapproving — "You Americans seem to have no ideas about how to live," "If you live in a democracy, why is that you cannot do more if you disapprove of your government?, How can you explain your Negro problem?"

The situation in Belgium was radically different from that in France. The Belgians refer to their country as "the America of Europe," for you find there none of the shortages so common in other countries. They are riding on a crest right now, and did not wish to speak of what may happen six months from now. They preferred to tell us of their life as students of their parties and festivals and to show us the carnivals which are to be found on almost every street corner.

I found Holland to be perhaps the most hopeful of all the places I visited. In a country where all rations, and food in particular, are extremely meager, we were overwhelmed and at times embarrassed by generous hospitality. In Amsterdam we each stayed in the home of a student, during the week that we were there. My hostess insisted that I stay to dinner on Sunday — "But of course you must stay. It is the one day in the week when we are able to serve meat." And you learn not to argue, because they enjoy giving and are grateful for whatever you can give them in return.

Excerpted

SHIPBOARD NEWS The *Kota Item,* produced on each of the 13 days trip by an intercollegiate staff (Provided by Dee West).

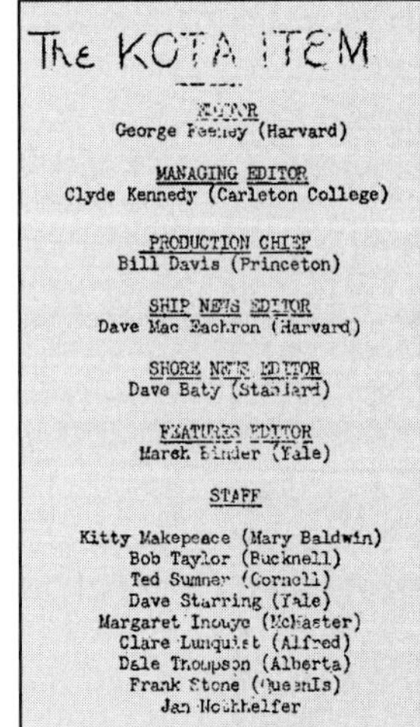

The KOTA ITEM

EDITOR
George Feeney (Harvard)

MANAGING EDITOR
Clyde Kennedy (Carleton College)

PRODUCTION CHIEF
Bill Davis (Princeton)

SHIP NEWS EDITOR
Dave Mac Eachron (Harvard)

SHORE NEWS EDITOR
Dave Baty (Stanford)

FEATURES EDITOR
Marsh Binder (Yale)

STAFF

Kitty Makepeace (Mary Baldwin)
Bob Taylor (Bucknell)
Ted Sumner (Cornell)
Dave Starring (Yale)
Margaret Inouye (McMaster)
Clare Lunquist (Alfred)
Dale Thompson (Alberta)
Frank Stone (Queens)
Jan Hochhelfer

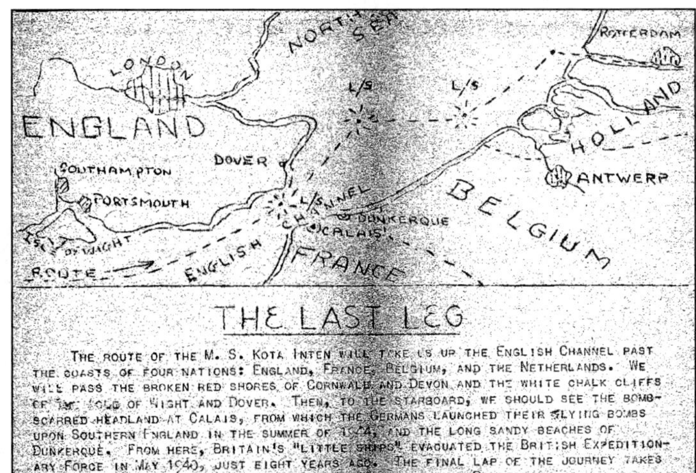

THE LAST LEG

The route of the M. S. Kota Inten will take us up the English Channel past the coasts of four nations: England, France, Belgium, and the Netherlands. We will pass the broken red shores of Cornwall and Devon and the white chalk cliffs of the Isle of Wight and Dover. Then, to the starboard, we should see the bomb-scarred headland at Calais, from which the Germans launched their flying bombs upon Southern England in the summer of 1944, and the long sandy beaches of Dunkerque. From here, Britain's "little ships" evacuated the British Expeditionary Force in May 1940, just eight years ago. The final lap of the journey takes us twenty miles up the dyked river Mass to the docks at Rotterdam.

1949 *Volendam* Voyage Marks Expansion of Student Travel

October, 1949 THE NSA NEWS

Volendam Summer Abroad Ends for NSAers

BY RALPH SMITH
Public Relations Director

HOBOKEN, N. J.—On a bright Sunday morning, at exactly 8:30, the Dutch student ship S.S. Volendam berthed here.

More than 1,500 American students who had spent their summer in countries throughout Europe hurried down the gang plank.

• • •

OF THE GROUP, more than 600 had gone abroad on seven NSA tours and seen Europe from top to bottom—Norway to Italy.

Success of the NSA travel program brought renewed support from member schools of the Association and plans are unfolding for more than 800 students to go to Europe through NSA next year.

Loaded down with wooden shoes and other souvenirs of their visit abroad, the students thronged the pier in their eagerness to get through the necessary customs inspections.

• • •

BY COMPARISON with interminably long lines that faced the students disembarking from the Volendam last year, this year's customs inspection was a pleasant, expeditious surprise.

In accordance with suggestions made by NSA to representatives of the Holland-American line, inspection was rearranged. There was no single long line for the approval of forms and passports.

The Volendam arrived at 8:30, and by 11:30 there was not a student left at the pier.

• • •

THE VOLENDAM receive da royal welcome from thousands of parents and friends, who crowded around the temporary barriers and fences to catch a first glimpse of their sons and daughters disembarking from the ship.

Shouted greetings were exchanged, and the first news of new developments at home conveyed over the din of the crowd. For their part, many of the students returned wearing numerous varieties of national costumes, and some of the men were sporting beards, so that

VOLENDAM — Joy Newberger, political science student at the University of Wisconsin, totes a life saver on the Volendam returning to the United States from the NSA Tri-Nation Tour. Summer was "worth two college years," she said.

Representative

HOLLAND-AMERICA LINE — DIRECT SERVICE BETWEEN NEW YORK AND ROTTERDAM

T.S.S. VOLENDAM. 15434 TONS REGISTER — 25620 TONS DISPLACEMENT.

"WORTH TWO COLLEGE YEARS." That estimate by Joy Newberger (Picus) (U. of Wisconsin) of her summer experience (See p. 928) reflected the feelings of many student travelers. Above: The *Volendam* as pictured on a Holland-America postcard, and on a photo provided by Mary Ann Bodecker (Smith C., p. 660), Ralph Smith (Swarthmore C.), NSA's 1949-50 Public Relations Director (see p. 897) writes of the *Volendam's* return voyage in the 10/49 issue of *NSA News*

"NO EXPERIENCE MORE WORTHWHILE"
—Smith College *SCAN* 2/13/48 editorial on student ships

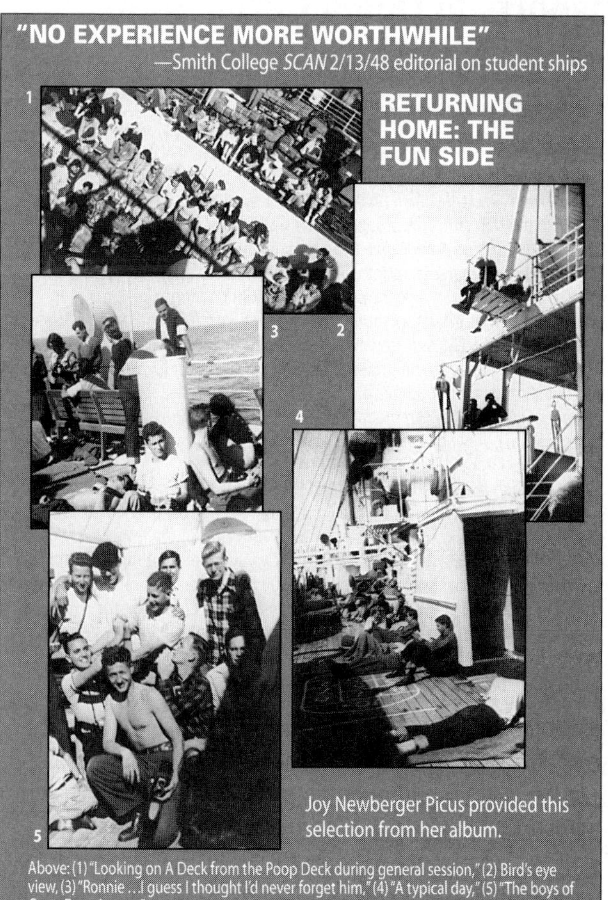

RETURNING HOME: THE FUN SIDE

Joy Newberger Picus provided this selection from her album.

Above: (1) "Looking on A Deck from the Poop Deck during general session," (2) Bird's eye view, (3) "Ronnie ... I guess I thought I'd never forget him," (4) "A typical day," (5) "The boys of Goup B cutting up."

The NSA News

Official Publication of the United States National Student Association

MADISON, WISCONSIN, FEBRUARY, 1949

NSA Expands Foreign Tours

Augsburg Plays Host for Speech Meet

March 15 is Closing Date for Applications

CBS Schedules

NSA Plans Student Tour Through Puerto Rico Jan. 27

The Metropolitan New York Region of the National Student Association is plannin... prices of 10% to 30% to students buying at stores which have sign-

NSA MEXICO STUDY TOUR IS EXTENSIVE

Three Student Tours Slated In Mexico For Next Summer

"Operation Amigos," an extensive study and travel program in Mexico, has been planned by NSA for next summer.

Students planning to attend the summer session at the National University of Mexico will go to Mexico City for six weeks of classes starting June 25. Courses are offered in both Spanish and English and include history, art, literature, economics and scrape weaving.

Student Ships

During the post-war era no activity on the student level has been more vital, no experience has proved more worth-while, than the opportunity provided for many American undergraduates to spend a summer travelling, studying, and working in Europe, to return to their colleges in the Fall with real understanding of their fellow-students abroad. The program of the National Student Association depends on this understanding and the cooperation which results.

If the practice of sending large groups of students abroad is to continue, it is essential that boats providing adequate space at low cost to students be available. If the Maritime Commission is not given congressional authority either to operate the "c-4" ships which have carried American students to Europe in previous years, or to arrange for their operation by a private line, then many people will be deprived of a valuable and important experience. Travel costs are high, and available space on commercial lines is insufficient to accommodate large numbers of students.

Bills which recommend the continuation of the student shipping services are now before the House Merchant Marine and Fisheries Committee and the Senate Interstate and Foreign Service Committee. The names of Congressmen on these committees are printed on the first page of tonight's issue. We urge you to discuss this question with the N.S.A. representative in your house and to aid Unity Committee's program by writing immediately to your own Congressmen.

M.R.P.

EXPANDED PROGRAMS

From top: *NSA News* 2/49; LIU *Seewanhaka* 1/13/49; Western Washington *Evergreen* 3/10/49; Smith College *SCAN* 2/13/48.

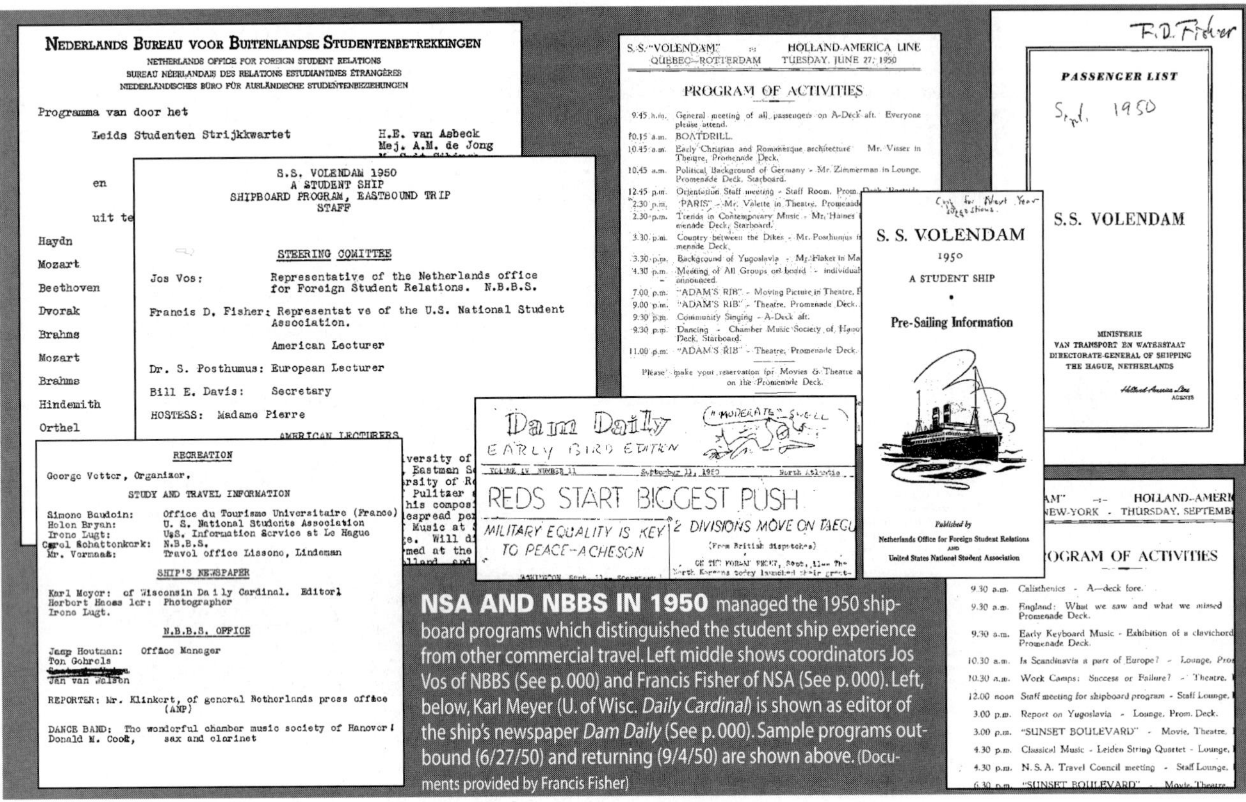

NEDERLANDS BUREAU VOOR BUITENLANDSE STUDENTENBETREKKINGEN
NETHERLANDS OFFICE FOR FOREIGN STUDENT RELATIONS
BUREAU NÉERLANDAIS DES RELATIONS ESTUDIANTINES ÉTRANGÈRES
NIEDERLÄNDISCHES BÜRO FÜR AUSLÄNDISCHE STUDENTENBEZIEHUNGEN

Programma van door het

Leids Studenten Strijkkwartet — H.E. van Asbeck, Mej. A.M. de Jong

en

uit te

Haydn
Mozart
Beethoven
Dvorak
Brahms
Mozart
Brahms
Hindemith
Orthel

S.S. VOLENDAM 1950
A STUDENT SHIP
SHIPBOARD PROGRAM, EASTBOUND TRIP
STAFF

STEERING COMITTEE

Jos Vos: Representative of the Netherlands office for Foreign Student Relations. N.B.B.S.

Francis D. Fisher: Representat ve of the U.S. National Student Association.

American Lecturer

Dr. S. Posthumus: European Lecturer

Bill E. Davis: Secretary

HOSTESS: Madame Pierre

AMERICAN LECTURERS

RECREATION

George Vetter, Organizer.

STUDY AND TRAVEL INFORMATION

Simone Baudoin: Office du Tourisme Universitaire (France)
Helen Bryan: U. S. National Students Association
Irene Lugt: U.S. Information Service at Le Hague
Carol Schattenkerk: N.B.B.S.
Mr. Vermaat: Travel office Lissone, Lindeman

SHIP'S NEWSPAPER

Karl Meyer: of Wisconsin Daily Cardinal. Editor
Herbert Haessler: Photographer
Irene Lugt.

N.B.B.S. OFFICE

Jaap Houtman: Office Manager
Ton Gehrels
Jan van Walsen

REPORTER: Mr. Klinkert, of general Netherlands press office (ANP)

DANCE BAND: The wonderful chamber music society of Hanover!
Donald M. Cook, sax and clarinet

S.S. "VOLENDAM" :: HOLLAND-AMERICA LINE
QUEBEC—ROTTERDAM TUESDAY, JUNE 27, 1950

PROGRAM OF ACTIVITIES

9.45 a.m. General meeting of all passengers on A-Deck aft. Everyone please attend.
10.15 a.m. BOATDRILL.
10.45 a.m. Early Christian and Romanesque architecture Mr. Visser in Theatre, Promenade Deck.
10.45 a.m. Political Background of Germany - Mr. Zimmerman in Lounge, Promenade Deck, Starboard.
12.45 p.m. Orientation Staff meeting - Staff Room, Prom.
2.30 p.m. "PARIS" - Mr. Valette in Theatre, Promenade
2.30 p.m. Trends in Contemporary Music - Mr. Haines menade Deck, Starboard.
3.30 p.m. Country between the Dikes - Mr. Posthumus menade Deck.
3.30 p.m. Background of Yugoslavia - Mr. Flaker in Ma
4.30 p.m. Meeting of All Groups on board - individual announced.
7.00 p.m. "ADAM'S RIB" - Moving Picture in Theatre,
9.00 p.m. "ADAM'S RIB" - Theatre, Promenade Deck.
9.30 p.m. Community Singing - A-Deck aft.
9.30 p.m. Dancing - Chamber Music Society of Hano Deck, Starboard.
11.00 p.m. "ADAM'S RIB" - Theatre, Promenade Deck.

Please make your reservation for Movies & Theatre on the Promenade Deck.

Dam Daily
EARLY BIRD EDITION
("MODERATE" SWELL)
VOLUME IV NUMBER 11 September 11, 1950 North Atlantic
REDS START BIGGEST PUSH
MILITARY EQUALITY IS KEY TO PEACE—ACHESON
2 DIVISIONS MOVE ON TAEGU
(From British dispatches)

S. S. VOLENDAM
1950
A STUDENT SHIP
Pre-Sailing Information
Published by
Netherlands Office for Foreign Student Relations
AND
United States National Student Association

PASSENGER LIST
S.S. VOLENDAM
MINISTERIE VAN TRANSPORT EN WATERSTAAT
DIRECTORATE-GENERAL OF SHIPPING
THE HAGUE, NETHERLANDS
Holland-America Line
AGENTS

"...AM" -:- HOLLAND-AMERI...
...NEW-YORK - THURSDAY, SEPTEMB...

PROGRAM OF ACTIVITIES

9.30 a.m. Calisthenics - A—deck fore.
9.30 a.m. England: What we saw and what we missed Promenade Deck.
9.30 a.m. Early Keyboard Music - Exhibition of a clavichord Promenade Deck.
10.30 a.m. Is Scandinavia a part of Europe? - Lounge, Pro
10.30 a.m. Work Camps: Success or Failure? - Theatre,
12.00 noon Staff meeting for shipboard program - Staff Lounge,
3.00 p.m. Report on Yugoslavia - Lounge, Prom. Deck.
3.00 p.m. "SUNSET BOULEVARD" - Movie, Theatre,
4.30 p.m. Classical Music - Leiden String Quartet - Lounge,
4.30 p.m. N. S. A. Travel Council meeting - Staff Lounge,
6.30 p.m. "SUNSET BOULEVARD" - Movie, Theatre,

NSA AND NBBS IN 1950 managed the 1950 shipboard programs which distinguished the student ship experience from other commercial travel. Left middle shows coordinators Jos Vos of NBBS (See p. 000) and Francis Fisher of NSA (See p. 000). Left, below, Karl Meyer (U. of Wisc. *Daily Cardinal*) is shown as editor of the ship's newspaper *Dam Daily* (See p. 000). Sample programs outbound (6/27/50) and returning (9/4/50) are shown above. (Documents provided by Francis Fisher)

From Converted U.S. Troop Transports to Dutch Cargo Ships

Editor's note: Excerpts below describe the organization of the student ship programs in 1947 and 1948. With U.S. government support, former troop ships were made available in 1947 for student travel, coordinated by the Institute for International Education (IIE) (See p. 693). In 1948, the Dutch National Union of Students through its travel unit, NBBS (See p. 654), arranged for the Holland-America Line to provide special student ship accommodations. Also in 1948 administration of the program passed to the Council on Student Travel (CST). The CST (See p. 694) consisted of 32 organizations interested in student travel, originally formed into an executive committee by the IIE. Lawrence Duggan, IIE Director, was among the first members of the NSA National Advisory Council (See p. 693). A detailed account of CST history appears on the Web site of the Council on International Educational Exchange (www.CIEE.com).

Excerpt from the 28th Annual Report of the Director, IIE, 10/1/47.

Last spring it became apparent that many groups of students who were planning to go to Europe for summer study, conferences, and reconstruction projects would be unable to find sufficient transportation on regular carriers. Early in May, as a result of the combined appeals of dozens of organizations and the endorsement of the Department of State, the United States Maritime Commission provided two partially converted troop-ships for the emergency. At the request of the State Department, the Institute agreed to coordinate transportation arrangements. It formed an Executive Committee representative of the sponsored groups, and it also sent an officer to Paris to provide information and to coordinate westbound passages.

Approximately 4,400 students and teachers, American and foreign, were served by the ships, the Marine Jumper and Marine Tiger, between June 6 and October 6. Over 2,000 were members of the 35 sponsored groups, and close to 1,500 were unsponsored students and teachers whose inquiries and applications were handled entirely by the Institute.

Excerpt from the IIE Bulletin, 3/1/48. (edited)

More than fifty organizations are planning student academic, cultural or reconstruction projects in Europe, and hundreds of unsponsored students and teachers wish to study abroad during the coming summer. Present estimates indicate transportation needed for between 8,000 and 10,000 students and teachers. In order to fill this great demand, the Negotiating Committee intends to ask the Maritime Commission, as soon as Congress has acted, to allocate three C-4 type transports as student ships from June to October 1948.

Excerpt from "Student Ships--1948," the IIE Bulletin, 4/1/48.

United States Maritime Commission, for the second year, has made two ships available for carrying American and foreign students and teachers to and from Europe during the summer months. The American ships, the Marine Jumper and the Marine Tiger, are C-4 type transports with accommodations for 600 passengers each. They will make four round trips each between June and October. These ships will call at English and French ports and on two sailings will also call at Oslo. They will be operated by the United States Lines and Moore McCormack Lines. The two ships, former troop transports, have a limited number of staterooms. The balance of passenger accommodations are in dormitories and open areas. Passage rates vary, depending on the class of accommodation and port of destination in Europe, from $140 to $200 one way.

Through the initiative of the Dutch Office for Foreign Student Relations, two Dutch transports, the *Kota Inten* and *Tabinta,* have been assigned to carry students from Quebec to Rotterdam on June 18th and July Ist respectively. Each ship, with a carrying capacity of 750, will make one east-bound trip. Early in September, the Volendam, with a capacity of 1500 passengers, will sail from Rotterdam to New York to bring back the students who go to Europe on the two small transports. Accommodations on these former cargo vessels, which have been converted into transports in order to bring Dutch farmers and their families for settlement in Canada, while not luxurious, will be adequately comfortable. Round trip tickets, at a cost of $280, will be issued for the Dutch ships. These transports will be operated by Netherlands steamship lines, under the auspices of the Dutch Office for Foreign Student Relations.

Editor's note: Russell W. Ellis (See p. 669) reports that "In 1949 the Groote Beer *and* Zuiderkruis *replaced the* Kota Inten *and the* Tabinta, *somewhat more comfortable, but not to be confused with luxury liners."*

NSA sets up independently managed Travel Department in 1950

7. NSA's Travel Department

The first program sent students to Europe in 1948. In 1950-51, 450 students participated. In 1951-52, 400 went by ship and 400 went by air.

Thomas Callahan
St. Francis College, Brooklyn, NY. NSA Travel Director, 1950-53
Mary O'Dea, Assistant Travel Director, 1951-53

Excerpted from an article in the January 1953 issue of NSA's Student Government Bulletin and Report.

*Editor's note: From its inception, the sponsorship of student travel abroad was a leading feature of NSA's interest in connecting college students to the rest of the world. The early organization and development of the program are detailed in Section 1 of this Part by Bob Smith (Yale), NSA's first international vice president in 1947–48, and in this section by Helen Bryan Garland (Sarah Lawrence), who managed the programs through the summer of 1950. The rapid expansion of the program stretched thin the resources of the Association, exacerbated by the "*Svalbard *Incident," described earlier, which beached NSA's original tour ship for that summer and resulted in a substantial loss of as much as $25,000 which took several years to liquidate.*

As a consequence, the Association set up a separate Travel Department in New York City, engaging Tom Callahan (St. Francis College) as its first director. According to the financial report submitted by its accountants to Ted Perry, former 1949-1950 Student Affairs Vice President, who was employed as its treasurer, the program booked revenues of over $170,000 for the 1950-51 year.

By the time it was incorporated as Educational Travel, Inc., in the fall of 1953, it is reported to have surpassed $250,000 in revenues, primarily from tour program fees. In order to provide fiduciary and management oversight, NSA had created a Travel Advisory Board composed of faculty and former NSA officers. The post-1953 Congress NSA Executive Committee voted to "commend Mr. Callahan for his work in the Travel Department of USNSA." Tom was replaced by C. Edwin Lacks.

A surprising number of American students travel in Europe, Latin America, and the Far East each summer. Estimates of bona fide student travel have ranged as high as five hundred thousand students a year since the end of World War II. Therefore, in most instances, services having to do with travel are a valid and legitimate area of interest for student governments.

Relationship of the Travel Department to USNSA

According to the USNSA Constitution (Revised, Congress 1952), Article V, Section 3:

> The Association shall maintain a Travel Department which shall: (a) Organize, publicize, and administer a program of tours and work camps as a service to the American student community, (b) Make such arrangements for transportation facilities as may be necessary to the tours or to the individual student, (c) Undertake such other activities as may be necessary to the efficient operation of the Travel Program. (1) The operation of the Travel Department shall be under the direction of a professional or semi-professional person whose title shall be TRAVEL DIRECTOR and who shall be responsible for the operation of the Department, subject to the policy decision of the Congress and the National Executive Committee, (a) The National Executive Committee shall appoint the Director who in turn shall select such professional and clerical staff as may be necessary to the efficient operation of the Department.

Background: Interest in travel

The Student Government Association of any college or university is primarily concerned with the welfare of its student constituents. It exists and operates solely to meet the needs and desires of students, to represent, uphold and enlighten its body. It is based upon the firm belief in the ability of young people to cater to their own interests and needs with responsibility, justice and idealism.

The Association of student government bodies is based upon that same premise. USNSA is that Student Government Association here in the United States. It is as strong on campus as the sight of its student is long on the base. An association of students represents and attempts to realize, uphold and enlighten the needs and desires of all the students. So USNSA matches these elements—and through the unity (without uniformity) existing in this larger group—it tries to bring all such programs throughout all its campuses into harmony. It gains greater strength through this cooperation, encourages participation by large numbers of individual students, so that aims may be realized sooner and with greater effectiveness and advantage to the individual student, and the community of students.

Because of the similarity of interests, needs and problems, and experience, the student community may be said to be a microcosmic edition of the non-academic world. As with the larger society, students for decades have been proposing practical projects designed to benefit the individual student and the rest of the student groups. It is hoped that what will benefit one group may be made available to all.

It is a normal desire of any person to travel and see the other side of the fence, to meet people in strange and new places, to come to understand and appreciate their attitudes, "gripes," and hopes. Because this often meant a great expense to the student, without the full assurance that the informal probing into the real Europe would even then be realized, this wish was not easily grasped.

NSA launches first program in 1948

So one of the first things which the USNSA did was to set up a Travel Department which was to investigate the possibilities of providing the average student with inexpensive, purposeful, stimulating, interesting, unusual travel opportunities and to set up programs accordingly.

Because of the union of one campus with another through the National Unions of Students [NUS] and their travel bureaux, European students had been provided with just such opportunities, on excellent standards, for decades.

The first [NSA] program sent students to Europe in 1948.

Five years ago USNSA undertook the operation of a program designed to provide students, interested in studying in Europe for the summer, with low-cost transportation and with similar benefits to their purses while they studied, and then traveled around Europe. Ninety students participated in a program which took them to Europe, had them at a University in France for a session, and then permitted them to do some traveling under the most austere conditions throughout Europe. It was an amazing success. The hardy veterans returned thrilled and pleased. USNSA had sought and found the student unions' travel offices and had had them provide our ninety with students to act as contacts and summer friends. The costs were low and acceptance of the ideas was such as to allow USNSA to consider running an even larger operation the next year.

The USNSA International Veep turned again to the NUS Travel Offices for assistance. Other tours were organized which allowed for study and travel, study while traveling, and traveling with the educational values high. The accommodations were better, and, in general, the service was made to be of a higher standard. The prices were still amazingly lower than what the field offered. The students had many student friends at the close of the summer, and they had seen Europe, and the student community through the eyes of their leaders, their student contacts, the Europeans in all walks of life who assisted the NUS Travel Offices in the presentation of full programs to our students. It was another wonderful summer.

Travel office organized in winter of 1950

Nineteen fifty was the last year that saw the International Veep undertaking the workings of the travel office. There was too much to be done now. The demand was terrific and the program needed handling by an expert. So that year, after the summer, USNSA asked Tom Callahan to undertake the responsibilities of setting up the Travel Office as an operation apart from the National Office, and of establishing the program over a broader field of interests so as to better service the great demand.

Tom set up his office here in New York in the winter of 1950. That year the Netherlands Office for Foreign Student Relations (the Travel Office for the Dutch Student Union) had secured ship space from the Government of The Netherlands. This space came in the form of a ship, the *Volendam,* which the Government gave over to the students to have filled with American student travellers, in groups, coming to Europe. (They used the sailings from Rotterdam to the States to bring over the large numbers of Dutch emigrants coming to Canada).

The management of the technical aspects of the sailing, the berthing and the crew management and general shipboard facilities were given to the Holland-America Line. The Dutch Student group had to find American Groups to fill the ships and had to provide them with an Orientation program which would fit the groups for Europe and the new lives they would have there for the summer. The NBBS (this student group) came into the New York office with Tom. They knew USNSA programs, having arranged portions of them previously. They gave USNSA space on the sailings of the *Volendam,* and they asked USNSA to help them with the Orientation program, The Dutch students were very much interested in seeing us have a strong program. They, therefore, gave us as much help as they could at the time.

Over 450 take part in 1950-51

Tom received the plans for the itineraries for the next year's programs and he set the budgets and had the brochures printed and had *Work, Study, Travel Abroad* prepared. We had over 450 participants that year, 1950-1951. Last year we operated the program again to the satisfaction of nearly 800 students. We provided them with ship transportation on the student sailings again (the *Volendam* had been scrapped and two new ships took her place). We presented the Orientation program, toured them around, placed them in work camps, and gave them the contacts at the Universities, flew them throughout Europe, bussed them through Italy, and gave them the services of two of our staff in Europe all summer in addition to the services of the travel bureaux.

Last year, well over 400 went on the tours, and nearly 400 took to the planes. The students were able to go everywhere in Western Europe, even into Yugoslavia and Berlin, and they were able to do it at a reasonable cost.

TRAVEL DEPARTMENT SERVICES

I. TRANSPORTATION

A. SHIP: ACCOMMODATION ON STUDENT SAILINGS

June/July to Europe. September from Europe

Netherlands Government Ships—*Waterman* and *Groote Beer,* New York–Rotterdam–9 days .

One class ships—supplied by the Netherlands Government, to the Netherlands Office for Foreign Student Relations (The Dutch Students' Travel Department) for use by American collegians, in cooperation with the National Student Association, under the technical supervision of The Holland-America Line.

Programs on board are designed by the students' travel staffs, and operated by these, and interested students during the trip. Recreation, eleven language tutoring and assistance, discussions with well-known figures in the educational, business, and international field, complement recreational activities.

$300 45 spaces in each of two dorms are available on the ships for student participants.
$320 710 plus, completing capacity, are cabin spaces—with two, four, five, six and seven in a cabin. Mostly outside cabins.

B. AIR:

FLIGHTS TO AND FROM EUROPE for USNSA'ers, professors, administrators. Using scheduled airline equipment, and service, on charter flights New York and Continental points. Regular, on-time departures and arrivals. Major savings in time and money, and additional opportunity . . . to spend as much time in Europe as possible.
$385 N.Y./E/N.Y.
FLIGHTS WITHIN EUROPE for USNSA'ers, from city to city, aboard top quality craft, at rates equivalent, and often lower than, Third Class Rail. Operating through the summer, May to October.

C. BUS Via Volksvogen—Amsterdam—Paris—Amsterdam. Copenhagen—Paris—Copenhagen

Every Weekend, May–October

II. ORGANIZED PROGRAMS

A. Study Tours: 9 days free, 85 total.

For students who wish to combine a summer in Europe with a summer of productive study in their field of interest, NSA provides this exceptional opportunity to get the best Europe has to offer in several important fields.
Economics and Politics: $760 June 20th–September 12th—England, Holland, Germany, France, Yugoslavia, Switzerland.
Sociology Study Tour: $760 June 20th–September 12th—Holland, Sweden, Denmark, Norway, England, Germany, France.
B. Arts Tours: 12 days free, 85 total:—Sculpture and Painting programs are a must for serious art students, and art lovers. Unique opportunities are provided to observe the new and old treasures of Europe.
Sculpture and Painting: 73 Days $790 June 20th–Sept. 12th—Holland, Belgium, France, Switzerland, Italy, Austria.
Music Festival Tour: 74 Days $825 Salzburg Festival–Austria; Holland; Lucerne Festival–Switzerland; Wagner Festival; Edinburgh Festival–Scotland.

C. International Tours:

For the sightseer with no specific study goal, but with a desire to learn something about each of the countries visited, this program fills the bill. July 1st–September 14th.

Tri-Nations:

England, France, Italy	64 day tour, $725
France, Switzerland, Italy	$730
England, France, Austria	$725
Benelux, France, Italy	12 days free, $725
	76 days total
East-West	67 days, $765

England, Germany, Austria, France, Holland, Switzerland

North-South:	67 days, $740

Denmark, Sweden, Norway, Germany, Switzerland, Italy

D. Hospitality Tour: 13 days free, 76 Total.

The best way to come to understand a country and its people is through direct and continued contact with its people—on their own ground. This tour is a wonderful adventure in international understanding. It makes it possible for students to live with families in ENGLAND, HOLLAND, and GERMANY.
63 days $550

E. Work Camp Programs: To harvest, to re-build, road-build, help out in archaeological excavations, work in factories, in forests, in mountain and lake country in an international atmosphere is an exciting thing to do. Working side by side with students from all over the world, you can spend a constructive summer at the lowest possible cost, and attain the perhaps greatest possible personal enlightenment.

Scandinavia:
Norway/Sweden.
Road Building in the Mountains and near their cities. Forestry in forest camps, with students from all over the world.
Rail Building
Denmark: Archaeological Work—Working under the expert supervision of specialists from the Royal Museum in Copenhagen, students assist in the work of excavation of Viking ruins on the Island of Bjornholm.
England: Strawberry and potato harvesting all summer long—at farms throughout the country.
France: Information available First of April.
Germany: Forestry work in Northwest Germany where innumerable young trees have been planted in the woods and mountains during the last few years.
Youth Hostel Construction Niedersachesen area. Construction and repair of damaged youth hostels.
Switzerland: Clearing and road building in two or three camps.

F. **Study Sessions:** France, England, Holland—Summer school and two week tour at close. Further information available WSTA '153 and Tour Brochure.

III. PUBLICATIONS

WORK, STUDY, TRAVEL ABROAD—an annual, outlining comprehensively, the opportunities open to students in these fields for the summer months. The *Who's Who* of the student travel field, a copy should be on display, and well-used at campus libraries and activity sponsors' desks. Available Feb. 10th.
PRICE: $.25 per copy. $.15 per copy—bulk orders—USNSA schools.
TRAVEL TIDINGS—Information bulletins duplicated at the office and forwarded to all interested, these list interesting, new points of interest, and explain travel red tape.

Editor's note: Other services described include travel to campuses to explain the programs, coordinating and training campus travel committees, and liaison with foreign student organization travel bureaus.

PICTURE CREDITS. *Then:* National Executive Committee meeting, Wayne State, MI, December, 1952 (*NSA photo.* Murphy).

NSA Organizes a Long-Term Travel Business

NSA'S EDUCATIONAL TRAVEL, INC. was incorporated in 1954, culminating its transition to independent management with projected revenues of over $400,000 as reported in July (see below right). Actually, it booked a little over $300,000 for the year (later 1954 report), over twice its $139,139 revenues in 1951 (below left), when Tom Callahan (St Francis C.) became director. NSA hosted 13% of student travelers using charters in 1950 (see p 668). The cover designs of its annual travel booklet from 1948 to 1954 reflect its growing marketing focus. (Left, fr top clockwise: *Milwaukee Journal* 11/12/50 [Callahan, right, later married Virginia Gardiner, left; Elmer Brock is between the two]; *NSA News* 11/51; NSA's annual *Work, Study, Travel Abroad* directories for 1948, 1950 and 1954. Below are financial summaries taken from mimeographed reports to the 1952-53 [left] and 1953-54 National Student Congresses.)

Sunday, November 12, 1950

—Journal Staff

Students from 12 Wisconsin colleges and universities attended a meeting of the Wisconsin chapter of the National Student association Saturday at Mount Mary college. From left are Virginia Gardiner, 5017 N. Lake dr., Whitefish Bay, a Mount Mary student; Elmer Brock, Philadelphia, vice-president of the association and Thomas D. Callahan, Brooklyn, N. Y., national travel director of the NSA, who spoke at a workshop session.

Callahan Prepares More Expansive Travel Program

Tom Callahan, travel director of USNSA, is in New York arranging a more expansive travel program again this year.

Callahan recently returned from Europe, where he and his wife, Ginny Gardiner, attended many travel meetings, including the international travel conference in Copenhagen, Denmark.

Mr. and Mrs. Callahan were married in mid-September. She was chairman of the Wisconsin region of NSA last year.

Callahan looks forward to expanded opportunities for American students to work, study, and travel abroad this summer. Preliminary information will reach the campus NSA Chairman before Christmas, while the 1952 edition of Work, Study, Travel Abroad will be off the presses in January.

STUDY,
TRAVEL,
WORK,
. . . ABROAD

Summer, 1948

Prepared by
UNITED STATES
NATIONAL STUDENT ASSOCIATION
National Office—304 N. Park Street, Madison 5, Wisconsin
International Activities Commission—5 Bryant Street,
Cambridge 38, Massachusetts

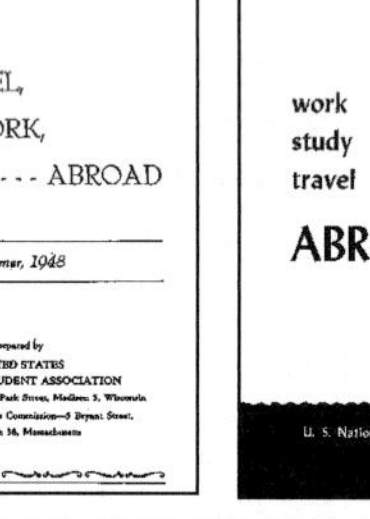

work
study
travel
ABROAD
. . . 1950
U. S. National Student Association

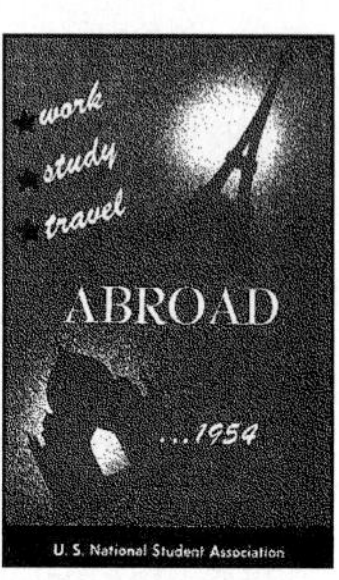

work
study
travel
ABROAD
. . . 1954
U. S. National Student Association

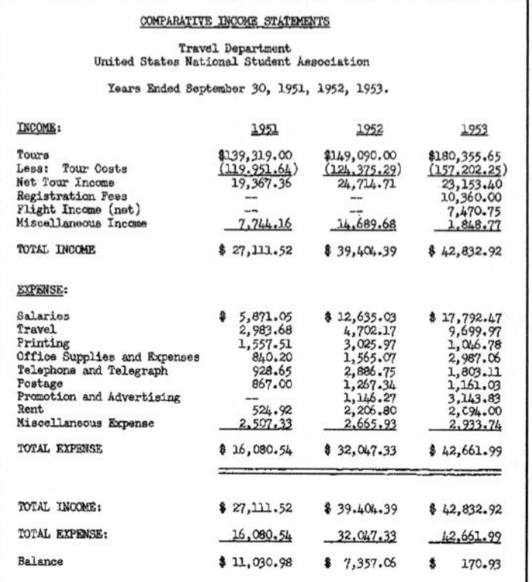

COMPARATIVE INCOME STATEMENTS

Travel Department
United States National Student Association

Years Ended September 30, 1951, 1952, 1953.

INCOME:	1951	1952	1953
Tours	$139,319.00	$149,090.00	$180,355.65
Less: Tour Costs	(119,951.64)	(124,375.29)	(157,202.25)
Net Tour Income	19,367.36	24,714.71	23,153.40
Registration Fees	--	--	10,360.00
Flight Income (net)	--	--	7,470.75
Miscellaneous Income	7,744.16	14,689.68	1,848.77
TOTAL INCOME	$ 27,111.52	$ 39,404.39	$ 42,832.92
EXPENSE:			
Salaries	$ 5,871.05	$ 12,635.03	$ 17,792.47
Travel	2,983.68	4,702.17	9,699.97
Printing	1,557.51	3,025.97	1,046.78
Office Supplies and Expenses	840.20	1,565.07	2,987.06
Telephone and Telegraph	928.65	2,886.75	1,803.11
Postage	867.00	1,267.34	1,161.03
Promotion and Advertising	--	1,146.27	3,143.83
Rent	524.92	2,206.80	2,094.00
Miscellaneous Expense	2,507.33	2,665.93	2,933.74
TOTAL EXPENSE	$ 16,080.54	$ 32,047.33	$ 42,661.99
TOTAL INCOME:	$ 27,111.52	$ 39.404.39	$ 42,832.92
TOTAL EXPENSE:	16,080.54	32,047.33	42,661.99
Balance	$ 11,030.98	$ 7,357.06	$ 170.93

TRIAL INCOME AND EXPENSE STATEMENT

TRAVEL DEPARTMENT

10/1/53 — 7/31/54

INCOME	
Tours and Flights	$ 407,814.19
Return of Loans	194.10
NSTA —Advertisements	1,280.50
TOTAL	409,238.79
EXPENSES	
Salaries	16,108.45
Payments to Student Unions	150,987.44
Travel	3,939.27
Promotion	3,754.65
Office Supplies and Equipment	4,395.72
Publications and Printing	5,781.53
Telephone and Telegraph	2,232.88
Postage	1,240.89
Ships and Flights	144,986.72
Tour Expenses	4,264.48
Insurance	189.72
Automobile Expense	2,566.50
Professional Services	1,800.07
Rent	2,217.00
TOTAL	$ 344,465.32

Editor's note: NSA's travel program was born in 1947-48, its first year, in fulfillment of the International Student Activities Panel recommendation at the Constitutional Convention that it promote the travel of American students abroad. The story of its first years are told by Bob Smith, NSA 1947-48 International Vice President (p. 504), Helen Bryan Garland, its first full-time manager working out of the International office with NSA's next two International Vice Presidents, Rob West and Erskine Childers, in Cambridge, MA, from1948-50 (p. 515, p. 517), and in the preceding article by Tom Callahan, its first full-time Director working out of a separate travel office in New York City from 1951-53 (he was appointed in November of 1950).

*As can be seen by its experience in the "*Svalbard *Incident" (p. 665), the program had its perils and liabilities. There were those within and outside NSA who questioned whether it should be in the travel business at all. Gordon Klopf (p. 329), Chairman of the national Advisory Committee at the time, addressed the issue in the 7/8/50* Advisory Council Newsletter, *shortly after the crisis created by the Coast Guard's refusal to certify the* Svalbard *was resolved:*

"It is the opinion of the Chairman of the Advisory Council that NSA should not go into the travel business, at least not to the extent that they have this year. Travel is too highly a,competitive and risky financial procedure for untrained, unexperienced and changing leadership. The purpose of serving student travel needs is a good one, but the management problem is, in the observation of the Chairman, beyond their ability and experience.

"The chairman has been quite concerned that more has not been done by the International Commission in terms of other types of international program. The entire efforts of the International Office, and a good portion of the National Office during the past months has been on travel arrangements. . . . Travel abroad is a very important aspect of the program but it is only one means, and a very limited means in terms of the American student population, of education for international understanding."

NSA's response was to unburden the international commission and begin a process of creating an independent management for the program. In August, 1952, the Congress amended the Constitution to provide for a standing Travel Advisory Board of five members to provide continuing oversight and monthly review of travel operations. Before Tom Callahan resigned his position in 1953, steps had already been taken to incorporate the operation. C. Edwin Lacks, the new director, was able to report to the National Executive Committee in August, 1954:

"This year your Travel Department became incorporated under the Membership Corporations Law of the State of New York, and was renamed United States National Student Association Educational Travel, Inc. This action was deemed advisable by the National Officers, Travel Staff, and Travel Advisory Board for the following reasons;

"1. To provide a direct and efficient control of the department and its activities by the association.

"2. To offer a sounder business basis for the department.

"3. To limit the financial responsibilities of the association and the department.

"It should be pointed out that when an officer of the association is elected he automatically becomes an officer of the corporation. This is obviously a guarantee that there is direct control of the association's travel activity. Further supervision of travel operations is rendered by the Travel Advisory Board. The Travel Office learned with satisfaction recently that the corporation has become a tax exempt organization under the provisions of section 101 (6) of the Internal Revenue Code."

According to its organizing brochure in 1977, the Association continued to provide a travel service until its merger with the National Student Lobby in 1977, when it became the United States Student Association.

SECTION 6

Other Student Travel and Exchange Programs

CONTENTS

From the time of the Chicago Student Conference in 1946 and the Constitutional Convention in 1947, NSA embraced working relationships with "all existing organizations in facilitating student tours and travel," as well as in academic exchange and relations with foreign students on U.S. campuses.

NSA also developed and carried out a major program of education and travel abroad for U.S. students (Section 5).

During the first half of the 20th century, numerous adult mentors took an interest in providing international experience for American students. Three are remembered in this section: John R. Mott, founder of the CRF; Donald Watt, founder of the Experiment; and Stephen Duggan, founder of the IIE.

Henry Halsted (Williams College, MA), an NSA Constitutional Convention delegate, joined an Experiment in International Living program in 1948 that took him back to Germany where, while in the U.S. infantry, he fought and took part in V-E day.

Halsted also provides an excerpt on his travels through Munich in 1948, which are reminiscent in their impact on him to those of Alice Horton (Part 1), three years earlier, in Russia. His overview of the history of the Experiment in International Living, founded in 1932, is included as an example of the role that nongovernment volunteer organizations played and what inspired them.

Ruth (Haines) Purkaple (University of Denver) provides a link to the significant pre- and postwar role of the YWCA and YMCA intercollegiate organizations. She moved from YWCA staff positions in Kansas and Washington State in the 1930s, to the United Service Organizations (USO) during the war, and in 1947 became program director of the Committee on Friendly Relations Among Foreign Students (CFR) in New York City, a post she held for ten years.

Purkaple describes some of the "bridge-building" challenges and values of her activities. A companion excerpt from a history of the CFR takes us back to the formation of the Student Volunteer Movement by John R. Mott (Cornell) in 1890, from which grew a global network of U.S. voluntary engagement in foreign student exchange.

A history of global U.S. student exchange

A rich tradition of both providing and coordinating such outreach already existed before the war, and these functions were resumed by organizations such as the Institute for International Education, the International Student Service through the World Student Service Fund, and the Committee on Friendly Relations, as well as new groups such as the Council on Student Travel. This section records some of their accomplishments.

A closing album highlights the historic role of the Institute for International Education and the post-war Council on Student Travel and Youth Agency.

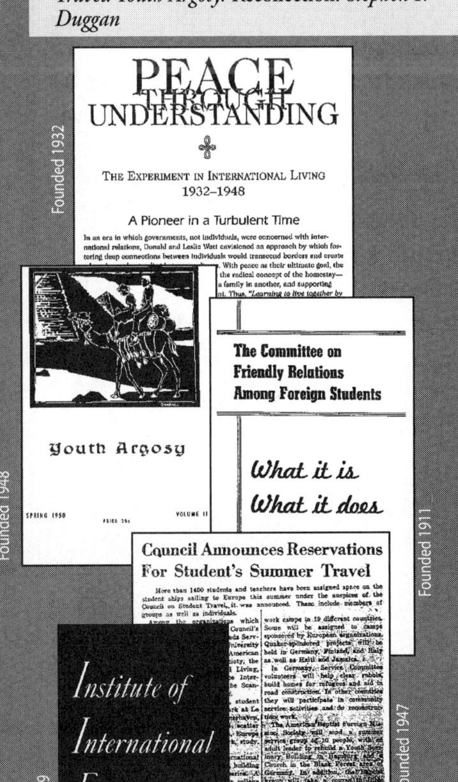

STUDENT EXCHANGE ORGANIZATIONS. From top: Experiment in International Living (Experiment Brochure). Youth Argosy (*Argosy Magazine*, Spring 1950); Committee on Friendly Relations among Foreign Students (CFR folder. C.1950); Council on Student Travel, (*The Technique*, GA Tech, 5/15/51); Institute of International Education (Annual Report 10/1/47).

A Rich Tradition of Support for U.S. Student Exchange and Travel

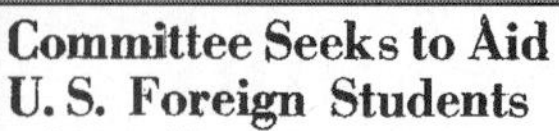

Committee Seeks to Aid U. S. Foreign Students

Needy foreign students at Columbia and other American universities and colleges may soon get a better break under federal laws concerning them if the efforts of a committee of leading educators and foreign student advisors meeting today in Washington, D. C., with

TWENTY-NINTH ANNUAL REPORT OF THE PRESIDENT

CONFERENCE ON INTERNATIONAL STUDENT EXCHANGES

The Institute took the initiative in calling the fourth in a series of national conferences on problems of student interchange, and arranged for a group of over two hundred university and college administrators, foreign student advisers, and representatives of public and private agencies interested in the subject to meet at the University of Michigan, May 10 to 12, 1948. The excellent facilities provided by the university and the great

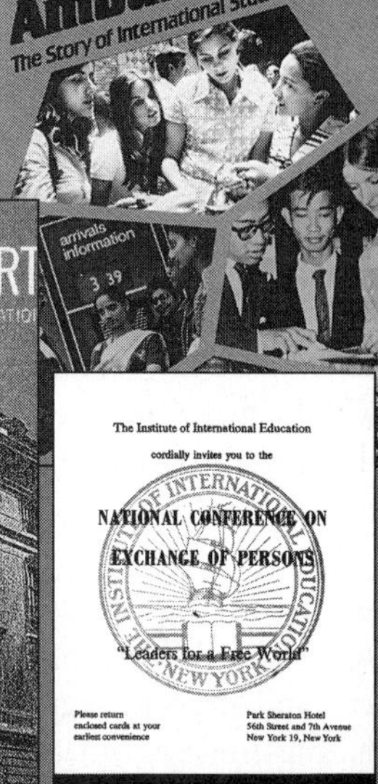

The Institute of International Education cordially invites you to the

NATIONAL CONFERENCE ON EXCHANGE OF PERSONS

"Leaders for a Free World"

Please return enclosed cards at your earliest convenience

Park Sheraton Hotel, 56th Street and 7th Avenue, New York 19, New York

February 23, 24, 25, 1955

The Committee on Friendly Relations ("Unofficial Ambassadors," see p. 688) since 1911 welcomed foreign students in the U.S. (top). The IIE administered programs of exchange for students and faculty since 1919. See p. 693 (Top left, *Columbia Spectator* 2/3/49).

Education, administration, support

"...Not by Might, Nor by Power, But by My Spirit..."

The world is aghast at the dread prospect of the United States and Russia competing for military supremacy.

This need not be, this must not be. War, or militarism to forestall war, means ultimate ruin for all. The American Friends Service Committee believes peaceful relations are possible between the United States and Russia. We do not minimize the issues that now exist between the two countries, but neither do we believe that war would settle these issues. It would only intensify them. We call for a faith that other means can be found which could lift us to a new level of life in which war is outmoded.

Here are three steps which we believe are a beginning in this new direction:

1. BEGIN PEACE TALKS NOW. Let a group of leading American citizens meet this spring to formulate proposals for a general settlement of outstanding issues between the United States and the Soviet Union. Let these proposals be widely debated and then laid before the American and Russian heads of government, urging that they meet again in new faith and with a fresh spirit.

AMERICAN FRIENDS SERVICE COMMITTEE
PHILADELPHIA, PENNSYLVANIA

The American Friends Service Committee was organized in 1917. Its first volunteer work camp was in Appalachia in 1934 (see also p. 1037). Above: photos of Quaker International Volunteers in 1952. Many church-related groups had such programs. (Swarthmore College *Bulletin*, 9/98. Top: Ad in *Mills College Weekly*, CA 5/14/48).

Helping to rebuild communities

A Lifetime of International Exchange

Although she had to cut short her '39 Experiment in France at the urging of her worried parents, Barbara (Baer) de Gomez went on to be hailed by The Experiment for "the longest period of continuous effective service."

A group leader for the first Experiment to the French-speaking community of Watertown, Nova Scotia, de Gomez shared a small house with a miner's family of 18 children. She went on to serve as U.S. cultural attaché in Chile and Bolivia, as well as official interpreter for the president of Mexico. In 1952, Donald Watt invited her to be the national director of the Mexican Experiment. "Why don't you do it for a while," he said to me." Now, nearly 50 years later, she chuckles, "So, I'm doing it for a while!"

In 1980, de Gomez received Mexico's *Aztec Eagle Award* in recognition of her contribution to the development of Mexico.

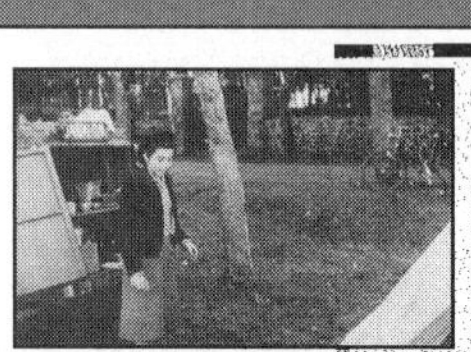

At night, the truck that Donald Watt bought for camping trips and Experiment outings became a huge tent, with ten cots placed beneath canvas covers.

1945–1948: An Instrument for Peace

As the devastating war came to an end, the work of rebuilding what had been destroyed, including understanding between adversaries, lay ahead.

Packages of Hope

The Experiment worked to relieve the catastrophic effects of war by sending food and clothing to Experiment host families all over Europe. This package campaign helped save the health, if not the lives, of numerous European partners. It was also a way to help those who had helped the organization before the war in its mission to create understanding. "The Experiment way was the right way," says one package recipient, Austrian host mother Otti H. Rollins. "People could get along with one another and forget their differences once they had felt respect and love for each other."

The Experiment in International Living since 1932 sent U.S. students to live with families abroad for the summer. "The Experiment worked to relieve the catastrophic effects of war." See p. 683. *(Experiment brochure).*

Living with families in other lands

Round the World Flight

Formed in 1948 Youth Argosy in three years booked low-cost passage for almost 25,000 students by sea and air. Its explosive growth reflected the pent-up interest in global travel. A change in air charter regulations effectively put it out of business in 1951. See p. 694 (1951 program brochure).

Learning through travel

The Experiment in International Living brought adversaries together.

1. Revisiting and Rebuilding a Shattered Europe

Henry M. Halsted III
Williams College, Massachusetts
Delegate to the NSA Constitutional Convention, 1947

In June of 1943, I graduated from secondary school in Massachusetts (Deerfield Academy) and had my eighteenth birthday. I immediately entered the summer session at college (Williams College) to get at least a start before being drafted. After six weeks of college I received greetings from President Roosevelt and a call to report for duty. I was drafted into the infantry, went to Fort Benning for basic training, and then was assigned to ASTP[1] at Carnegie Tech in Pittsburgh. A few months later that training was terminated and I was sent to the 95th Infantry Division at Indiantown Gap, Pa. I was assigned as a rifleman to E Company, 2nd Battalion, 377th Regiment.

I remember well the reaction of the "Old Timers'" to the new young ASTP smarties. At first, every time we had a ten-minute break, we ASTP guys would pull out our paperback books and start reading while the old timers smoked and cussed. After a while the noncoms in charge, annoyed by us, forbade us to read during breaks. This rather offended our sense of our First Amendment rights. But in the long run, we got assimilated and became welcome additions, especially when it came to combat.

From Omaha Beach to Williams College

The story from there—maneuvers in West Virginia; embarkation to England on August 6, 1944; staging near Winchester; wading onto Omaha Beach on D+98; joining Patton's Third Army for the assault on Metz; followed by 151 days of combat. I was in Dortmund on the day the war ended. I began in E Company, but was transferred to the I & R (Intelligence and Reconnaissance) Section in Headquarters Company, 2nd Battalion. This shift probably saved my life, though I did have a number of close calls. Many of my buddies in E Company were killed.

As I like to put it, when the army recruiters looked at my credentials and saw that I was near-sighted, they decided to put me way up front so that I could see. I ended up in the lowest level of intelligence in the infantry, namely, a battalion intelligence section, which meant patrols and operating observation posts up front. There are Intelligence units at the Supreme Headquarters, Army, Division, Regiment, and Battalion levels. We would joke about there being no intelligence below battalion level. We were, therefore, at the lowest level of intelligence.

I had some high school and college French and German, and enjoyed using those languages with the locals. I enjoyed music. Not that I am a musician, but I did carry my harmonica with me and played it on many occasions, and I still enjoy barbershop harmony. I spent many an evening on barracks steps and in billets here and there, singing and playing the old songs.

Shortly after V-E Day, the 95th was shipped back to the States to Camp Shelby, Mississippi, to train for invading Japan. With the dropping of the A-bombs in August 1945, the war with Japan ended. I got a 30-day "recuperation" leave.

With the need for an invasion of Japan removed, I was reasonably sure I would be discharged directly following my leave. I took a gamble and hastened back to college. Although the summer term had already begun and I was still in the army, I was allowed to enroll and go to classes. My gamble paid off. After 30 days of classes, I returned to Camp Shelby and was discharged. I hustled back to college. I think I missed only a week or so of classes. This move, plus the GI Bill and doing a summer term the next year, allowed me to graduate in 1948, only one year later than I otherwise would have had there been no war. A nice coincidence was that the corporal who handed me my discharge papers at Camp Shelby, Corporal Pellegrino, was the fearsome corporal who had given us bayonet training at Fort Benning two years earlier. He had remained in the States, and in 1945 I outranked him, had more points, and got out of the army sooner than he.

Searching for an understanding of the war

In my senior year at college (1947-48, following the NSA Constitutional Convention in Madison), I began looking for a way to get back to Germany. I wanted to get a handle on how World War II had come about and somehow to understand better the enemy I had faced in the war. During the war, the only Germans I had seen were soldiers seen through my binoculars or the sights of my M-1 rifle, from an observation post or while I was on patrol, or had observed with their hands over their heads surrendering, or civilians looking out of houses from which they had draped white flags. Returning at war's end so quickly to the United States, I had the opportunity to serve in the Occupation only briefly, not long enough to get a picture of the people and nation that had sought to terrorize and dominate the world. At college I had read about the rise and fall of Nazi Germany. I wanted to get back there and see more for myself.

While exploring opportunities for students to go to Germany I came across the Experiment in International Living exchange organization headquartered in Putney, Vermont. It was, I believe, one of the first such organizations to be granted approval to conduct a student program in postwar Germany. The program was seen as part of the so-called de-Nazification, or reeducation, program established in the American zone. The Experiment program provided a way for American college students to spend the summer of 1948 living and working with German students in Munich, Stuttgart, and Freiburg. The program seemed to offer an ideal way to get to know Germans at first hand in the context of that wartorn land. This was exactly what I wanted, so I jumped at it, even though it meant departing immediately after exams and missing graduation, at which I would have heard General Dwight D. Eisenhower give the commencement address.

Munich in 1948

I joined a group going to Munich. After orientation at Putney, Vermont, my group of eight, all male, flew to Switzerland and proceeded by train to Munich. The program was to spend the first two weeks living with a German family. The remainder of the summer was spent living at the university with German students and working with them on the reconstruction of a dormitory. To enroll in the university, German students had first to put in a period of three to six months' work on reconstruction. The skilled laborers, carpenters, and bricklayers were not students. They worked for the construction firms hired to restore the buildings. We students did the unskilled work, piling bricks to dry out, hauling cement, removing rubble. The girls cleaned old mortar off bricks with hammers. We spent days at the construction site, and evenings and weekends with our German counterparts, experiencing the daily life in Munich at that time and talking together about the war, the Nazi regime, and how to build a better world.

Our counterparts had been in Hitler's army, in the Wehrmacht on both the eastern and western fronts. One was the son of German Field Marshal William Ritter Von Leeb (noted for his role in initiating the 900-day siege of Leningrad), who was tried and convicted in the War Crimes trials in Nuremburg. Another was the son of a member of Hitler's cabinet. Discussing Nazi Germany, the war, and its aftermath with them was an intense and immensely interesting experience. My counterpart, Kurt, like many others, said that his father was anti-Nazi but couldn't protest or he would go to a concentration camp. He himself was too young, he said, to understand what was going on—seven when Hitler came to power. He stressed conditions in German history as an explanation for Hitler and the Nazi regime. He and his fellow students were not eager to talk politics. They were disillusioned by politics because, as they saw it, politics had brought their country down. Their focus was on survival and building a new life out of the rubble. In retrospect, our exchanges could be characterized as "mingling our innocence and hopes with their scars and fears." Together, we rebuilt a gutted dormitory.

Getting to Vienna through the Russian sector

That program ended for the American group with a visit to Salzburg, Austria. There we attended a performance of the Salzburg Music Festival, the first, I believe, following the war.[2] It was a performance of Mozart's *The Marriage of Figaro*. I was in the peanut gallery. At intermission I looked down into the ground floor of the theater, and there, to my amazement, I saw Colonel Fred Gaillard, my regimental commander in the 377th Regiment of the 95th Division, a tall, commanding figure with the head of an eagle, who was easy to pick out in a crowd. I went down to the lobby of the theater, looked for him, and introduced myself. As a member of the intelligence section of the Second Battalion, I had seen him on many occasions during the war, as I often went from battalion to Regimental HQ with information. He remembered me and immediately told me that my battalion commanding officer, Colonel Robert Walton, was then in Vienna overseeing displaced person (DP) camps. "Why don't you go to Vienna and look him up? I know he would be delighted to see you," Gaillard said to me.

That sounded great to me, so I asked how to do that. Gaillard said he would arrange a "gray pass" (I still have it) so I could go there through the Russian Sector, and would tell Colonel Walton to expect me. "Stop by my office tomorrow and I'll give you the pass," he said. I got the gray pass and then went off.

I remember how the Russians stopped the train in Linz and how terrified of them the Austrians were. I remember the

Russian soldiers getting in our compartment with us, and the problem of talking to them. I think I only knew about three words in Russian.

Visiting displaced person camps

In Vienna, where we arrived late at night, I somehow found Walton and spent the next couple of days following him around the DP camps and spending the evenings sitting around with him reminiscing about the war. He had been wounded in the assault on Metz—the first of three of the battalion's commanders to be wounded—but eventually returned to his command, near the end of the war. He savored the memories of the men under his command in combat, comparing them with the green troops he now commanded in the peacetime army of occupation, with whom he was experiencing increasing discipline and morale problems. We sat up late into the night, drinking and telling stories. It was a memorable experience for me, who had been a lowly private, and later staff sergeant, under his command during the war, to reminisce with him about the siege of Metz and the latter days of the war in the Ruhr, and also to hear his accounts of the four-power occupation of Vienna, as well as to visit the DP camps for which he was responsible.

Return in 1989

I have kept in touch with five of the German participants in the 1948 Munich project and had a reunion with them at Octoberfest in Munich in 1989. Three were still in Munich. One came from Cologne, and one from a small town in the Bavarian Alps. At the reunion, we talked about our recollections of the summer of 1948. All five talked about how important that summer project had been in redirecting their lives coming out of the war.

France in 1949-1950

In 1949 and in 1950, following the Munich project, I led groups for the Experiment in International Living to ruined France. Later, a French participant wrote:

> In 1950 France was in ruins. I saw only a world marked by war, by destruction, by the shadow of war, and by fear. I believed that it was not finished, that there would be a next war. I did not think it would be possible to build a life, to have a family. Then came the group of young Americans, attractive, idealistic, optimistic, protected, believing and acting as though anything was possible. It was a transforming experience for me.

The 1958 Soviet—U.S. Exchange

In 1958 I helped program the visit by the first Soviet youth exchange group to visit the United States under the Lacy-Zarubin Agreement, a program sponsored in part by the Experiment in International Living.[3] That was a sobering experience putting naive U.S. college students face-to-face with a highly selected group of so-called Soviet "youth" in the depth of the Cold War. It brought me in touch with yet another youth perspective coming out of World War II—the Soviet perspective.

As is often the case with searches for answers, these experiences from 1943 to 1958 raised as many questions for me as they answered, and I am still pondering.

Henry Halsted was Vice President of the Johnson Foundation at Wingspread, its Frank Lloyd Wright Conference Center in Racine, Wisconsin. He was also Vice President of the Associated Colleges of the Midwest and of the Kansas City Regional Council for Higher Education.

END NOTES

[1] The Army Specialized Training Program (ASTP) sent more than 200,000 soldiers who had completed their basic training to more than two hundred colleges and universities to study engineering, foreign languages, personnel psychology, dentistry, and medicine. Selected for their high IQs and previous educational experience, these young men believed they would eventually be assigned to technical duties requiring such training. Many expected to become officers.

When the program was abruptly curtailed in the spring of 1944, more than 100,000 trainees—excluding those in medical and dental schools—were reassigned to infantry, armored, and airborne divisions and to other army units destined for quick shipment overseas. None were in college for more than nine months, none were made officers in the program; indeed, most remained privates until the mounting casualties in their units found them stepping into leadership roles as corporals and sergeants, and occasionally through battlefield commissions, as officers. These young men (18–19-year-olds), "scholars in foxholes," became combat soldiers and suffered heavy losses in killed, wounded, and captured. See *Scholars in Foxholes* by Louis E. Keefer (Reston, VA: COTU Publishing, 1988).

[2] *Editor's note:* Allan Ostar, whose recollections appear on p. 209, writes about the "many interesting parallels" with Halsted in his own experiences:

> We both went into the army about the same time, had the basic training, went into ASTP, and ended up in the infantry. What is particularly uncanny is that we both attended the first performance of the Salzburg Music Festival after the war. Hitler had shut it down. General Mark Clark, commander of the occupation forces in Austria, thought it would be good public relations with the Austrian people to reestablish Mozart and to demonstrate that Americans really weren't cultural barbarians. One of the men in my company was assigned to be "Festspielhaus" Manager. He sneaked some of us through the back door for the first performance.

[3] See letter to President Truman (and related footnote) from Jimmy Wallace, 1946 U.S. Prague delegation representative from the University of North Carolina, p. 105.

PICTURE CREDITS. *Then:* 1945, staff sergeant, U.S. Army. *Now:* 1989 (Both from author)

A VISIT TO MUNICH IN 1948

Excerpt from an article, "Three Years After," written by Henry Halsted in 1949

Munich was an extremely busy city. The streets lined with empty walls and ruined structures were almost cleared of debris, but trucks and specially constructed railways were still carrying away the rubble from the carcasses of buildings. Trams and buses were crowded beyond capacity as people hurried back and forth. One always wondered where they came from and where they were going, and above all where they were now living. Housing was hopelessly crowded. Barracks were used where they existed, and one even saw families putting out the wash by their railroad car homes on sidings around the city. Many had found places among the rubble where they came and went like rats at the city dump.

The people seemed to be working hard and enduring. Many could be seen with missing limbs or otherwise disfigured. Many children went barefoot, and in the homes shoes would be removed to be replaced by house slippers to save the leather for months ahead. And clothing was mostly military, both Allied and German, dyed and re-cut.

The business of living: a gloomy struggle

Under these circumstances conversations and interest were limited almost entirely to the business of everyday living, food, rationing, money, rather than the future or politics. Fresh from the States, one would look first for evidence of German policy or aspiration. But one trip to the dump outside the city where the rubble had been piled in a steady stream since 1945, and is still being piled, is the quickest way to comprehend the gloomy struggle that makes the business of living vastly more important than a new constitution or machinery of government.

But life in Germany is not all so gray. I had a sharp introduction to the kind of contrasts one soon gets accustomed to. After a week living with a simple Bavarian family in a crowded apartment on the outskirts of Munich, I received an invitation to attend the Fourth of July Tea at the castle residence of the American Consul General on Sternberger See, about twenty miles from Munich.

At four o'clock I was picked up by a new Ford with a German chauffeur, and we proceeded towards our destination through a magnificent forest. It was a lovely Sunday afternoon, and many Germans were to be seen out on their bicycles. One was even taking the air on his bicycle even though he had only one leg. Many GIs went speeding by in their American cars with girls at their sides.

Presently we came to Starnberg, today a recreation area for U.S. personnel. There we saw a beautiful lake surrounded by lovely pine woods, a golf course and a yacht club for officers. On the lake some thirty sailboats were having a regatta.

At last we saw the castle on a high point overlooking Starnberger See....A hundred and fifty guests, mostly U.S. officialdom and their families, were entertained here in the castle and on arbored promenades that looked down on the lake.

The contrast with the life of the tailor and her son that I had shared for a week was jarring, and I tried to adjust to it as I was driven back to Munich through the lovely countryside, past men taking the air on crutches and in wheel chairs, past barefoot children and old women dragging home wood from the forest to serve as fuel for the coming week.

During the first few weeks we were always with our German companions, learning our way about, the language and the customs. I remember clearly the first time I was separated from Kurt. Alone in the city, I felt independent and quite enjoyed wandering around without being noticed. I was brought up short, however, when I saw two GIs drinking cokes on the steps of their mess hall. I walked in past them and found that with my passport and occupation money I could buy a coke and what's more, have a meal for fifty cents. The temptation was too great. I stayed and was served by German waiters to a meal of white bread and butter, meat, salad, mashed potatoes, cole slaw, beets, tomatoes, apple pie and coffee.

Better times seemed far away

It was then that I had my first realization of the Germans' life. I began to see why the people's faces on the streets and in the trams were so dead, why there were few signs of hope or interest. I hadn't thought the food and work really tough until the moment after I had gobbled down that meal. When better times seem so far away, it can be hard to do more than endure. When one sees only rubble, material things can take the center of interest, and meals take on a bitter earnestness. I didn't mind the German food and work, but if it was to be forever?

Our work was to rebuild a dormitory at the University. It was a girls' dormitory constructed with American funds some years ago. One could still see on the doors that remained the inscriptions: "This Room donated by Vassar College," "This Room donated by Wellesley College," "This Room donated by Mrs. X of New York City."

Much of the rubble had been removed when we arrived so that construction could begin immediately and when we left there would be something to show for our efforts.

The work was undertaken by a German contractor who supplied the foreman and such skilled laborers as bricklayers and carpenters. German students and the Americans did the unskilled work. Every German student at the University must put in a period on reconstruction before he may study. The girls work too, cleaning the mortar off old bricks that must be used again, and cooking for the boys. We piled bricks, mixed and hauled cement and removed rubble. This we did for German wages, working nine hours a day for five weeks.

From the beginning people would stop on the street and watch us work. They would lean out of windows across the way to see, and stand in amazement—because we were singing. We sang college and popular songs while we worked, and the Germans hadn't heard singing by workers since early in the war.

See author's note on p. 684.

Establishing extraordinary international lifetime connections

The Experiment in International Living

Henry M. Halsted III
Williams College, Massachusetts.
Delegate to the NSA Constitutional Convention, 1947

[Editor's note: The Experiment in International Living was among the first programs listed in NSA's popular and best-selling handbook, Study, Travel, Work Abroad, *first published in the summer of 1948. (In 1950 the title was changed to the more familiar* Work, Study, Travel Abroad.*) It was introduced as follows: "This organization is designed to take students to Europe and Latin America for an experience somewhat different from most student groups. Planned as neither a sightseeing tour or a vacation....its purpose is to create in different countries a group of people mutually aware of each other's personalities, problems, way of life, and thoughts....to learn their languages, songs and customs, and to make new friends of people whose backgrounds were different from their own."*

Donald Watt's goal when he founded the Experiment in International Living in 1932 was to seek ways to overcome the psychological barriers that separate different cultures and lead to violence and war. "The purpose of the Experiment," he wrote, "is to build up in various countries groups of people who are interested in promoting mutual understanding and respect between their own and other countries". The method, which evolved over several years, began with the idea of young individuals from different countries learning to live together by living together, learning to live and think with the "other" group. The summer "homestay" in a family in another society for each participant soon became the core element of Experiment programs.

Other program refinements came to include careful participant selection, small coeducational groups of ten college-age students, trained leaders, group discussion as a learning process using methods coming out of the field of group dynamics, and the addition to the homestay of a binational camping trip. During the first half of the summer program, the "Experimenter" attempts to adjust to the life of his host family; in the second half he widens his circle of friends when his Experiment group and their young hosts travel together about the country.

As stated in the 1950 Experiment publication *Crossroads*:

> ...if one person can be trained to understand and to work with the people of other countries, the world, by this single relationship, is an infinitesimal step closer to a state of peace....Living successfully with a foreign family is for each member of every group an "Experiment" which calls for all the intelligence, enthusiasm, tolerance and tact that the best of us possess.

This approach to international understanding was a radical step from the prevailing view that international understanding could be produced only by academic study of international relations. Donald Watt believed that it was more important to learn how to create an atmosphere of mutual confidence in which representatives of different nations could work toward common goals than it was to acquire facts about the political state of the world.

Dedicated to building the peace

The Experiment's magazine *World Odyssey*, spring 2000, in a special issue focusing on the years 1932-1948, includes the following paragraphs:

> With peace as their ultimate goal, the Watts [Donald Watt and his wife Leslie] developed an organization based on the radical concept of the homestay—sending people of one culture to live with a family in another, and supporting them in this dramatic learning environment.
>
> As one participant put it:
>
> "...It was by listening to various viewpoints and confronting assumptions in ourselves that we learned things one can never get from a textbook or a tour. Sharing daily life with host families, facing the challenges, and treasuring the joys was an amazing way to learn the intimate effects of culture and conflict on the lives of people."
>
> As world war swept over Europe in the mid-1930s the Experiment was active in Austria, Denmark, France, Germany, Italy, the Netherlands, Norway, Sweden, Switzerland, and the United Kingdom. In the final weeks of August 1939, Experiment groups found themselves scrambling to bring their Experimenters home as Europe descended into conflict and Holocaust.

Again from *World Odyssey*, spring 2000:

> No sooner was the war over than Donald Watt's Experimenters returned to Europe to do their part in the physical and emotional reconstruction. In the summer of 1946, close to 100 Experimenters helped rebuild devastated countries—both Allied and Axis....With the permission of the U.S. State Department [in 1948] the Experiment took American college students to Munich, Stuttgart, and Freiburg to live and work side by side with German students on reconstruction....Experimenters paid their own way to travel to nations in ruins and live with host families who, only months before, had been "the enemy."

I was just such an Experimenter. Having fought in Germany under General Patton, I returned in 1948 to help rebuild a dormitory at the University of Munich. In 1997, almost 50 years later, one of the German participants in the program with whom I have kept in touch over the years, sent me a Christmas card on which he wrote: "I think often of our meetings and mutual ideals. Indeed, the 1948 program and everything connected with it was the most important, decisive event for me. Influenced me deeply!"

In the decades following the war, The Experiment grew in order to address its mission more broadly. It established the School for International Training in Brattleboro, Vermont, and its Washington, D.C.-based Projects in International Development and Training, and it developed, among hundreds of initiatives, the first training programs for the U.S. Peace Corps. In 1993 the U.S. Experiment in International Living changed its name to World Learning.

THE STUDENT SHIP "NELLY." A converted warship, Henry Halsted crossed the Atlantic to France on it in the summer of 1952. Halsted writes, "Among groups on board were: International Relations Clubs, International Farm Youth Exchange, the Colgate Glee Club and the Experiment. I was hired by the Experiment and going to Europe to meet a group of Austrian Fulbright Students, to escort them from Paris to New York, and to provide shipboard orientation to prepare them for their coming year as exchange students in the U.S. *(Photo: Halsted)*

MENTOR

DONALD WATT

Donald Watt spent time in the Middle East with the British Indian Army during World War I. He was personnel director at Syracuse University when he founded the Experiment in 1932.

Photo: Karsh of Ottawa, 1976

Editor's note: The following is abstracted from information Henry Halsted contributed on the early experiences that moved Donald Watt, who died in 1977 at the age of eighty-four, to found the Experiment:

Donald Watt was of Scottish and German descent and grew up in Lancaster, PA. One of six children of a well-to-do family, he chose to devote his life to the field of human relations. He went to the Lawrenceville School and Princeton. The Sunday before commencement, he heard a talk by Edward C. Carter, American director of the YMCA work in India, who extended an invitation to Princeton students to serve in the British Indian Army in Mesopotamia (now Iraq) as YMCA secretaries. He was one of the Princetonians who accepted.

With the United States not yet in World War I, the feeling was that the time had come to join the British, who had been fighting for a year and a half. Watt saw a great deal of the Middle East, and after the war pursued graduate study in psychology at the University of Pennsylvania and at Yale. He was personnel director at Syracuse University when he founded the Experiment in International Living in 1932. As his *New York Times* obituary noted, earlier he had attended "an international summer school set up by the League of Nations in Geneva. The program failed because the students remained among their own national groups, Dr. Watt said, and there were insufficient social relations between the groups. 'International understanding can be best achieved in a family unit,' he said."

He was the author of two books, *Intelligence Is Not Enough* and *Letters to the Founder.*

AUTHOR'S NOTE: VISIT TO MUNICH, p. 680

Readers may question this article's apparent empathy for the plight of the German people and ask why it does not refer to the onus of the German nation and Hitler for bringing about the destruction the German and American students were working to repair. By this omission it demonstrates how quickly the focus of the American student volunteers in 1948 had turned from defeating Nazi Germany, fascist Italy, and imperial Japan, to building out of the rubble a peaceful world, one in which destruction, such as that which they were witnessing, could not again occur.

A NOTE ON THE AMERICAN FIELD SERVICE (AFS)

The American Field Service (AFS) began shortly after the outbreak of World War I, when a group of 15 Americans living in Paris volunteered to drive ambulances for the American Hospital there. This group's mission was to transport wounded French soldiers from the front lines to mobile medical units. By the end of the war, their number had grown to 2,500 volunteer ambulance drivers, serving on many fronts. They did not bear arms. Theirs was a mission of compassion, not conflict.

During World War II, the American Field Service's all-civilian volunteer force of ambulance drivers and medical back-up personnel, was stationed in Europe, Syria, North Africa, India, and Burma. When the war ended in 1945, AFS began an exchange program. Today more than 290,000 participants have taken part in cultural exchanges offered through AFS's programs. Born from the ashes of war, AFS today has offices in 52 countries - *Henry Halsted (Adapted from AFS web site].*

HENRY M. HALSTED III

Early years: Born 1925 of American parents in Antwerp, Belgium. There until age 7. Grew up mainly in New Jersey and Massachusetts. My father was in international business.

Military: 95th Infantry Division 1943-45, European Theater.

Education: Williams College (MA) Phi Beta Kappa '48 (Williams delegate to NSA Constitutional Convention 1947); Yale Law School 1948-49; Teachers College Columbia University (MA 1957, Ed.D. 1960).

Career Highlights: (1957-60) Washington, D.C., National Education Association Educational Policies Commission; issues worked on included NEA response to Soviet challenge to American education, school desegregation, and the impacts of mass communications on education; (1960-68) Chicago, VP Associated Colleges of the Midwest, designing and organizing cooperative on and off-campus programs and services for member institutions (Coe, Cornell, Grinnell, Knox, Monmouth, Ripon, Beloit, Lawrence, Carleton, St. Olaf); (1968-72) Kansas City, VP Kansas City Regional Council for Higher Education (Avila, Baker Univ., Central Missouri State College, Donnelly, Graceland, Kansas City Art Institute, Metropolitan Junior College, Missouri Valley College, Mt. St. Scholastica, Ottawa University, Park, Rockhurst, Saint Benedict's, Saint Mary, Tarkio, University of Missouri, William Jewell); Fulbright and Ford Foundation grantee for education projects in Africa and India; officer, National Council of Associations for International Studies; (1972-88) VP The Johnson Foundation (Racine, WI).

At Wingspread, the Frank Lloyd Wright designed home converted into The Johnson Foundation conference center, as well as in Mexico and Canada, managed and assisted in carrying out some 500 regional, national and international conferences. Developed award-winning (Peabody and Ohio State awards) weekly educational radio series "Conversations from Wingspread," that aired for many years on over 200 radio stations around the country.

If asked if I could cite one experience I wouldn't have missed for anything, it would be a 1970 trip overland by car from Switzerland to India with my son and three college students, through Austria, Yugoslavia, Bulgaria, Turkey, Iran, Afghanistan, Pakistan and the Kyber Pass, a great adventure.

I am retired now and enjoying reading about and exploring topics that have piqued my curiosity over the years but which I never until now had time to pursue.

Family: Married to Mary Ann Peterson, a piano teacher and church organist. Have a son and two daughters by a previous marriage. Son is a news director with Wisconsin Public Radio based in Madison. Daughters, a social services worker and a psychotherapist, live in Kalamazoo (MI) and Brooklyn (NY).

Saturday night socials, Sunday evening suppers, and lasting "friendly relations"

2. Bridging Student Gaps: North and South, East and West

Ruth Haines Purkaple
University of Denver
Student YWCA Executive, University of Washington, 1934-1939
Program Director, Committee on Friendly Relations, 1947-1957

From 1927 to 1933 I attended the University of Denver, where I was active in the YWCA, attending the regional conference at Estes from my freshman year on. At the time there was not an "International Affairs" major, but I participated in the International Seminar program my last two years, and was always interested in foreign events and foreign students.

From student YWCA executive to YWCA-USO staff

In 1938, I went to the World Student Christian Federation meeting in Bievre, France. From 1934-1939, I was the student YWCA secretary at Kansas State College, in Manhattan; and from 1939-1944, I was executive of the Student YWCA at the University of Washington, Seattle.

From there I went to New York as part of the YWCA-USO staff, working with campuses helping to cope with the presence of military training units stationed there. In the summer of 1946, as the USO was closing down, I became the executive for the Student Assembly of the YMCA-YWCA[1] to be held at the University of Illinois that Christmas. Bill Miller was the Student chair of the Assembly.[2]

Signing on to the CFR

At that time, Everett Stowe asked me if I'd be the program director for the Committee on Friendly Relations. They didn't know that I was interested in international affairs, but thought to utilize my USO experience. I was intrigued with the idea, so I said I'd take the job for six months—and stayed with them eleven years, before becoming the executive for the Greater New York Council for Foreign Students.[3]

From 1947 to 1950 I was deeply immersed in developing programs for the CFR. One recollection out of many was the development of the Saturday night socials in Times Square. We organized a group called "The International Student Council," made up of representative foreign students from a number of the institutions in the Greater New York area. The first chairman was an Egyptian from Columbia University, and one of the other prime movers was an Indian from Brooklyn Poly. About fifteen students made up "the cabinet." They were planning the 1948 Labor Day Week End outing at Camp Pratt on Staten Island, for which over one hundred students, primarily foreign, but including some American girls, had signed up.

How to host our first boatload of German students

A couple of weeks before, I had been notified that I would have to meet a load of German students coming in on a government boat, also docking on Staten Island on Saturday morning of the weekend. "The cabinet" was meeting and I asked them what they thought about inviting as many German students as wanted to spend the balance of the weekend with them. (Many of the German students were to remain in New York until Monday.) I remember full well the discussion that ensued. The European students all faced the situation honestly. Finally, a Hungarian girl said: "This is the hardest thing I've ever done, but if we are ever to have peace we must try to accept the Germans." A Danish man spoke up and said, "I agree, I second the motion to invite them." About twenty-five or thirty German students did go to camp, and the relationship was very strained for some, but it resulted in a permanent bonding of the entire group that has more or less continued to this day, especially for those who remained in, or returned to, the States.

This event demonstrates the mood of students at the time: trying to look ahead and plan for a better world.

From 1949 on my job also included visiting campuses around the country to ascertain how well the foreign students were being accepted and what type of social experiences were available for them. (Many of the men on the campuses were on the GI Bill and were interested in getting on with their lives, and not in any type of extracurricular activity.)

My initial entree to the campus was a combination of the foreign student adviser and the student Christian groups, essentially the "Y's." Segregation was still well entrenched in the South, but the efforts being made by student groups to bridge the gap were encouraging to this Yankee. I remember at the University of Alabama in Tuscaloosa that a church group (possibly Episcopal, though I am not sure) made a point of having Sunday evening suppers with some of the students from the neighboring Black university. They met after dark in private homes so that the neighbors would not know what was going on. Important in that culture—they ATE together! This group became interested in some of the African students in the Black institution, which was my major reason for getting involved.

Providing port services for foreign students

The major contribution of the CFR during the 1950s and 1960s was its port services.[4] In about 1948 Ben Schmoker asked the Foreign Student Advisers what they felt was the major problem, and they indicated that helping students through their entry in the United States and on to the colleges was a big concern. We set up the program with the blessing of the Immigration Service. At this time, the majority of students came by ship, and we had both staff and volunteers, who would board the ships along with the pilot and then meet the students in the Immigration Lounge as soon as they had been cleared.

Involvement in the summer travel programs

By the mid-1950s we were also involved in the summer travel programs, especially for students who were already here and wanted to "see America." We set up the VISIT program, giving them introductions into communities where they wished to stop. First, nearly everyone traveled by bus, but gradually students would pool resources and get a car to drive, many having their own contacts along the way. The CFR also set up the Camp Counselor Program, which the YMCA continues to sponsor.

The CFR started the foreign student census, and conducted it from about 1919 to 1950. However, we lacked the resources to continue, and it was turned over to the Institute of International Education to carry on (even then, they already had access to computer capabilities).

Role of denominational colleges

During the 1950s and 1960s, the denominational colleges were active in attempting to serve students from the areas where their mission programs were based. For instance, Bucknell University had an annual gathering for all Burmese students. Bucknell was sponsored by the American Baptists, and under international missionary agreements, Burma was the area for the Baptists. Similarly, Lafayette College in Easton, PA, which was a Presbyterian-sponsored institution, had an annual gathering of Iranians, as Alborz College in Iran was run by the Presbyterians.

Other colleges picked up the graduates of the Near East colleges: American University of Beirut, American University of Cairo, Roberts College in Turkey (and a couple of other colleges that I'm not sure about), which were all under the aegis of the "American Board of Commissioners" of the Congregational Church (now the United Church of Christ). Lincoln College in Pennsylvania and Bethune Cookman in Florida each ran programs for groups of African students. Because of our access to the statistical records, the CFR helped these colleges get in touch with students. In some instances members of our staff (Ben or I) would participate. These were all usually weekend events.

With the increase in the numbers of foreign students and with the change in federal policy requiring colleges to sever their denominational ties, these programs were eliminated.

Way back "when"

One more memory flashed back to me about the long tradition of foreign student hospitality in the United States—and this is about the "Cosmopolitan Clubs." During the 1920s and 1930s, many of the universities had these clubs, which brought together American and foreign students. In the Rocky Mountain region, I recall, the student YMCAs and YWCAs lent backing to them. They were essentially social, and provided happy opportunities for American and foreign students to get to know one another across cultures.[5]

CFR, in its long history of building "friendly relations" among foreign students, also helped nurture on campuses and communities all over America an experience of direct connection with the rest of the world. Moreover, it imparted to the visiting students a personal experience in this country, which transcended ideologies and politics and which they took back with them to help form the large reservoir of goodwill this country enjoyed through the years in many distant lands.

Ruth Haines Purkaple built a lifetime career around providing services to students through the YWCA, the Student Christian Movement, and in international student travel and exchange. She now lives in Denver, Colorado.

END NOTES

[1] During this time, I became acquainted with the executives of the YWCA and YMCA, Eleanor French and Bruce Maguire. I also worked with Fern Babcock and Harold (Pete) Ingalls, who were the program secretaries for the two organizations. They edited the *Intercollegian* and had a good working relationship. Looking back, and painting in broad strokes, the YWCA staff at the time was somewhat more overly idealistic and impatient, wanting to build a better society NOW, and felt that the YMCA was just too conservative—probably shaped by the YMCA's much larger investments everywhere. The YMCA folks, on the other hand, seemed to feel that the YWCA's too liberal ideas threatened to undo much of their work. *(Editor's note:* The YWCA and YMCA, through the National Intercollegiate Christian Council (NICC), played a central role in the formative events that shaped NSA in 1946 and 1947. See Part 1, Sections 1 and 2, and Part 4, Section 3).

[2] See Miller, p. 721.

[3] I concluded my work career at the University of Colorado as director of study abroad and assistant director of international education from 1968 to 1978. I'm still involved with international education at the University of Denver, and serve on a few boards as a volunteer.

[4] *Editor's note:* The NSA postcongress National Executive Committee (NEC) adopted a resolution in 1953 that stated, "The facilities for the reception and hospitality for foreign students at the port of entry and in the United States and on the campus are inadequate." It went on to direct the vice president of international affairs "to investigate programs of reception and hospitality for foreign students on their arrival at the United States port of entry, and on campus, to make recommendations to member student bodies to improve such programs, and to establish foreign student reception centers, if these prove to be necessary."

Prior to this resolution, there are no indications in the minutes of earlier Congresses or in random searches of NSA bulletins during the period 1946-1952 that the Association addressed in any special way issues or programs concerning matriculated foreign students enrolled on American college campuses. NSA programs were focused on foreign student postwar relief, American student travel abroad, UNESCO student programs, international student exchange, foreign student leadership programs, displaced person student conditions in Europe after the war, and immigration policy barriers to foreign students. NSA did support and publicize, early on, the Bowdoin Plan, a program initiated at Bowdoin College, Maine, to find ways to fund foreign student study in the United States (see p. 839).

[5] *Editor's note:* The Cosmopolitan Clubs are an interesting footnote to twentieth-century student movement history. According to Phillip G. Altbach, in *Student Politics in America* (New Brunswick, NJ, Transaction Publishers, 1997) (p. 28):

> Cosmopolitan Clubs (CC)...[were] concerned with promoting international understanding and good will. The CC began in 1903, when an International Club was organized at the University of Wisconsin. In 1907, a National Association of Cosmopolitan Clubs was founded; by 1911 it had a national membership of 2,000 from sixty countries. The organization published a monthly journal, the *Cosmopolitan Student,* which informed members of activities around the world. The Cosmopolitan Clubs were one of the first American student organizations to affiliate with an international group when they joined the Federation Internationale des Etudiants.

He notes earlier (p. 9) that "The Cosmopolitan Club movement around 1910 had improved racial and international relations among students as its major aim..."

PICTURE CREDITS. *Then:* 1948, Camp Pratt. *Now:* 1998 (Both from author)

GREATER NEW YORK COUNCIL
FOR FOREIGN STUDENTS, INC.
500 Riverside Drive, New York 27, N. Y.
Telephone: UNiversity 4-7180

The Greater New York Council for Foreign Students was organized in 1948 by a representative group of educational institutions, agencies and individuals who were in close touch with students from other countries and who wanted to serve them more effectively. They formed the Council to assist them in developing a unified program of services and activities which would more adequately meet the day-to-day needs of foreign students and advance the long range objectives of educational exchange programs.

OFFICERS

Honorary President: DR. FRANK D. FACKENTHAL
President: FATHER GEORGE B. FORD, Corpus Christi Church
1st Vice-President: DEAN RAYMOND KIRK, Polytechnic Institute of Brooklyn
2nd Vice-President: MISS THELMA MILLS, YWCA of the City of New York
Secretary: MR. PAUL GERHART, RCA Institutes, Inc.
Treasurer: MR. MARK L. PEISCH, Columbia University

Executive Director: CELESTINE G. MOTT

MEMBER ORGANIZATIONS

Academy of Aeronautics
American Friends of the Middle East
American-Scandinavian Foundation
Asia Foundation
Barnard College
Belgian-American Educational Foundation
China Institute in America
Columbia University
Committee on Friendly Relations Among Foreign Students
Corpus Christi Catholic Church
English-Speaking Union
Fordham University
Grail International
Hadassah
Institute of International Education
International House
International Research Fund
Japan Society, Inc.
Juilliard School of Music
Long Island University
Manhattan College
Manhattanville College of the Sacred Heart
National Council of Churches, Department of Ecumenical Relations
National Council of Jewish Women
Near East College Association
New School for Social Research
New York Friends Center Association
New York School of Social Work
New York University
Pace College
Parsons School of Design
Phelps-Stokes Fund
Polytechnic Institute of Brooklyn
Pratt Institute
Queens College
RCA Institutes, Inc.
Riverside Church
Rutgers University
St. John's University
Teachers College, Columbia University
Union Theological Seminary
YMCA of the City of New York

COORDINATING 26 AGENCIES IN NEW YORK CITY. Mary Thompson (see p. 688) writes in *Unofficial Ambassadors* p. 87, "Under the direction of Ruth Haines Purkaple, CFR opened a mid-town center in New York. Here students from all parts of the world and from many colleges and universities in the Greater New York area would gather for recreation and to meet and talk with one another." [c.1948 - ed.] (Above: page from program of 2/15/56 Regional Conference on Foreign Students. One of the featured speakers was James T. Harris, Jr., 1948-49 NSA President (see p. 219).

RUTH HAINES PURKAPLE

Early years and education: I was born in Denver in 1911, and attended Denver public schools, graduated from South Denver High. I attended the University of Denver where I was active in the student YWCA, attending the regional conferences from my freshman year on. At the time there was not an "International Affairs major," but I participated in the "International Seminar" program in my last two years, and was always interested in foreign events and students. I received a B.A. and an M.A.

Career highlights: In 1938 I went to the World Student Christian Federation meeting in Bievre, France. From 1934 to 1939, I was the Student YWCA Secretary at Kansas State College, in Manhattan; and from 1939 to 1944, I was Executive of the Student YWCA at the University of Washington, Seattle. After the work described in this article, for the YWCA-USO, the CFR, and the Greater New York Council for Foreign Students, I concluded my work career at the University of Colorado as director of study abroad and assistant director of international education from 1968 to 1978, when I retired. I'm still active in international education at Denver University and on a couple of boards—but as a volunteer!

Family: I first met my husband, William R. Purkaple, when I was working in Kansas, but we didn't get together until after World War II in New York. He taught political science. He died in 1964, after which I returned to Colorado to be near my elderly parents. My father, an attorney, lived to be 105 and was "with it" to the end.

A global outreach maintaining the foundations for international student exchange

The Committee on Friendly Relations among Foreign Students

Editor's note: The story of the Committee on Friendly Relations (CFR) begins with the Student Volunteer Movement (SVM) in 1890 and an idea brought into being in 1911 by John R. Mott. Collaborating with the YMCAs and the Student Christian Movement, and later with the YWCAs, CFR established a tradition of engagement with foreign students in the United States, and with similar programs through their overseas home-based Christian Associations that began at the end of the nineteenth century.

As a result of its outreach and active engagement with the Student Volunteer Movement, CFR created a network of fraternal relationships, which were firmly in place after World War II and which provided global expertise and perspectives that helped inspire the design of campus student exchange programs. It also built a global network that provided some of the relationships abroad and connections in the nonprofit world at home, which the staff and leaders of the YMCA and YWCA (which formed the National Intercollegiate Christian Council [NICC]) were able to draw upon as they took part in the building of postwar international student programs, of which the formation of NSA was a significant adjunct. The NICC's key role in the founding of NSA is described in Part 1 and Part 4 of this volume.

The vitality of the CFR story is highlighted by setting it in the context of the turbulent world events that surrounded it, as detailed in Unofficial Ambassadors, *edited by Mary A. Thompson, and published in New York by the International Student Service in 1982. (CFR changed its name to ISS in 1965, and is unrelated to the International Student Service, which was active through World War II in Europe and the United States.)*

Following are excerpts and condensations drawn from the book.

The idea of establishing an organization to help foreign students in the United States had been in the mind of John R. Mott for a long time. Mott was a religious traditionalist and tireless world traveler who, among other things, envisioned a world federation of Christian students that would establish a "telegraph of the mind in things spiritual and would give to groups of students in each country the benefit of the experience of similar societies in all other lands."

As the undergraduate president of the Christian Association at Cornell University in 1886, Mott attended the first international student Christian conference ever held in the United States. The conference, held at Mount Hermon, Massachusetts, under the direction of nationally famous evangelist Dwight L Moody, attracted 251 men from eighty-nine colleges and universities in America and Canada, as well as a small group from Germany, Norway, Japan, Armenia, Siam, india, Persia, and China.

MARY A. THOMPSON
Director, CFR/ISS, 1975-79
Joined staff in 1954

The work of the Student Volunteer Movement

It was undoubtedly out of this conference that the idea of a student volunteer organization to assist foreign students in the United States grew in the minds of Mott and his colleague, C. K. Ober, the national student secretary of the Intercollegiate YMCA. But it was not to come to fruition for more than twenty-five years. Meanwhile, upon graduation from Cornell in 1886, Mott joined Ober as a national secretary of the Intercollegiate YMCA, responsible for traveling among colleges to develop Christian student programs.

Mott assumed the task of gearing the student Christian movement into the life of the YMCA as a whole. He set up a simple organization with a small committee composed of official representatives of the Intercollegiate YMCA of the United States and Canada and the Interseminary Missionary Alliance. The organization became known as the Executive Committee of the Student Volunteer Movement (SVM), and Mott was made its chairman.

Mott stressed that the Student Volunteer Movement (SVM) was not an organization of missionaries. It was a movement of American and Canadian students to serve others in less developed lands. These student volunteers lived and worked in rural areas as teachers in government and secondary schools, with the general aim of developing native student movements.

During the [early years] of the Student Volunteer Movement's existence, from 1890 to 1920, more than 8,000 American and Canadian students spread out across the world. Eight hundred sixty-seven went to Africa, 2,525 to China, and 1,570 to India, Burma, and Ceylon. Scores of others went to Arabia, South America, Central America, the Philippines, the West Indies, Turkey, and other places. At the [1920] convention of the Student Volunteer Movement...John Mott summed up SVM's accomplishments by pointing to the "highly multiplying influence that has been exerted by students who have gone out to these foreign lands to serve as teachers."[1]

SVM influence on the YMCA

Perhaps most important, many new leaders who came out of the Student Volunteer Movement went on to become executives of urban United States YMCA's and were instrumental in making those city associations missionary in outlook. This strengthened the Y's international work, including the sending of North American Y directors overseas to help in the development of overseas YMCA's. Under Mott's leadership, the number of these fraternal secretaries overseas rose from some ten secretaries in Asia, Europe, and Latin America to more than three hundred by the time Mott resigned in 1915.

To John Mott's mind there was no more important work on earth than influencing students. Mott set out to spread his message on a larger scale. One day in April, 1911, Mott was meeting with Cleveland Dodge, chairman of the International Committee of the YMCA, in New York. At that time student migrations were creating a worldwide need. Mott talked of the need to make this situation known to individuals who were in a position to help. Andrew Carnegie was mentioned. Mott said that he had never met Mr. Carnegie.

"I will take you up to Andy now," said Dodge.

Founding the new CFR

Mott outlined his scheme to locate capable men at universities all over the world where there were large numbers of foreign students. These men would provide the students with opportunities to be exposed to the best instead of the worst sides of civilization as well as for good comradeship and stimulating ideals.

He ended by hoping that Carnegie might make a gift of $10,000 a year for at least two or three years to make possible the carrying out of his plan. Carnegie at once said that if Cleveland Dodge would give such a sum, he would do so, too. Dodge immediately accepted the challenge.

During two days Mott, meeting with others such as George Perkins and William Sloan, secured practically the entire amount necessary for starting the work, and on the following day the Committee on Friendly Relations among Foreign Students was launched.

Although financial support came through the initial gifts secured by the efforts of Mott and through supplementary funds from the YMCA's International Committee, from its founding the Committee on Friendly Relations (CFR) functioned as an independent agency, with no official relationship to the International Committee of the YMCA.

* * *

The years during and following World War I

The spread of war through Europe and China complicated the Committee's services to overseas students and proved particularly disruptive for those students in the States who had become alienated from their homelands. In New York City during the spring of 1915, there were a series of meetings among faculty and administrative offices of colleges and universities, staff executives of the Protestant, Catholic, and Jewish national offices, Red Cross officials, CFR members, and others to discuss the special problems faced by foreign students in time of war. Minutes of the meeting referred to "a growth of nationalism prevalent throughout the world." It was disturbing to notice this trend on college campuses, where the tendency to promote national rather than international ideas and loyalties sometimes provoked open hostilities.

Against this background of world unrest, Charles Hurrey, the executive secretary of CFR, called for special attention and services for students coming to the United States from an increasing number of countries. He called for the extension of established programs for the students of China to meet their growing needs. He also recommended the establishment of similar programs for students from Japan, the Philippines, and Latin America.

Perhaps more important, Hurrey was able to share his vision of the values in international education so that other individuals, organizations, colleges and universities, religious denominations, and community agencies were motivated to launch programs and services beyond the expertise and financial resources of the Committee itself. CFR's ability to motivate others was among its most important contributions to international student work at that time.

For example, one CFR Board member, Stephen Duggan, was instrumental in founding the Institute of International Education in 1919.[2]

* * *

The Depression and pre-World War II years

The decade of the 1930s was one of chaotic, worldwide upheaval. Japan invaded Manchuria in September 1931, a time when the United States and Great Britain were preoccupied with economic crises. By January 1932, Japanese troops were near Shanghai; there was famine in large parts of China; and thousands were uprooted from their homes.

The news of the Japanese invasion of Manchuria, and the growing influence of communism, resulted in division and dissension among all Chinese student organizations, including the Chinese Student Christian Association. The American people were, in general, eager to see the United States assume moral leadership, but nothing more, against the aggression. They supported international disarmament, but not policing.

On January 30, 1933, Adolf Hitler was named chancellor of Germany, and his militaristic Nazi movement was winning new converts daily. Worldwide depression had toppled about half of the regimes in Latin America. In the United States, banks in Michigan began to collapse on February 14, 1933, and were quickly followed by banks all across the nation. There were fifteen million jobless in America when, in March, the newly inaugurated president, Franklin Roosevelt, ordered a nationwide bank holiday as his first presidential act.

But in spite of global depression, unfavorable exchange rates, floods, revolution, and threat of war, total enrollment of foreign students in the United States in the academic year 1931 remained stable, with 10,187 students. China still led in numbers with 1,004 students, The majority were coming for graduate degees, with engineering and business most in demand.

The strain and anxiety that so many foreign students had to endure because of the unsettled conditions in their homelands sparked a renewed emphasis on home hospitality with American families.

* * *

The World War II years

Wars in Asia and Europe continued to disrupt the economy, shatter hopes and plans, and alter the course of millions of lives in the early 1940s. In China, war with Japan was at a stalemate. Manchuria, northern China, and coastal areas of the fertile Yangtze Valley were under Japanese control. In this chaos, the better organized Chinese Communists under the leadership of Mao Tse-Tung were beginning to have the upper hand in the internal conflicts with the nationalists under Chiang Kai-shek. Paris was occupied by German troops, and France capitulated. The "battle of the skies" for Great Britain began. Japanese troops swiftly occupied all of Indo-China. The attack on Pearl Harbor would soon follow. The decade of the forties was to be one of great trials and tribulations.

Yet activities on behalf of students continued to increase. The first conference on Latin American relations in the interest of education was held in Washington, D.C., in 1940. The call came from the Assistant Secretary of State for Cultural Relations. There were eighty colleges and universities represented. Also present were representatives from CFR, International Houses, and foreign student advisers of colleges and universities. A continuation committee was charged with reviewing general problems facing foreign students, such as course choice, orientation, social and religious adjustment, as well as studying methods of improving the services of institutions to the foreign students and compiling a master list of persons currently interested in helping foreign students.

In 1940, the number of foreign students coming to the United States increased by 373 over the preceding year, reaching a total of 8,275. The absence of students from countries at war was offset by an increase in the number of those from nonwarring areas in general, as well as of those from nonwarring areas who had been attending European universities and who, due to war, had transferred to the United States. There was an influx of Latin American students because the United States was close at hand and its facilities were available to them. In the early forties, CFR increased the fund, programs, and staff directed toward Latin American students in an effort to meet new needs in this area. Port-of-arrival services, publication production, home hospitality, and field work of personnel were the main program areas that needed expansion.

Needs of students at war

The needs of students from countries at war were recognized as being serious and difficult. "Wars in Asia and Europe have seriously affected the plans of all students from abroad, present and prospective," Anson Phelps

Stokes, Jr., chairman of the Administrative Board of CFR, pointed out in 1940. "In the past, government scholarship aid has played an important part in encouraging students to come to this country. Now such aid is curtailed in many countries, and entirely cut off in others." Without funding, many foreign students were left in a precarious position.

An American student volunteer working with refugees provides a sympathetic view of their plight. He wrote to CFR:

> While I waited for my instructions in the camp, I began to wonder what I would do if I were suddenly put into a refugee camp like this....I would make up my mind at the outset to keep mentally busy....And yet the more I talk to myself in this place, the less I seem able to think constructively. A panic seizes me and I want to run away as fast as I can.

A letter received by the CFR office from Miss Kikue Oshima, a student from Japan, specifically describes the feelings of one Japanese student while at the same time [it] portrays the confusion of many foreign students. It also provides a good idea of the difficulties faced by CFR in dealing with foreign students. She wrote:

> I have had an irresistible desire to grasp the truth and stand by it, because I could not understand the real cause of war. It's caused within me a bitter struggle between the reason and emotion and between nationalism and humanism.
>
> My coming to America meant, in one sense an escape from this inner struggle and skepticism. I wanted to see truth from a third persons point of view. Yet, since I've come to this country, I've become conscious of my burning patriotism. The more the people condemn the invasion of China, the more firmly I cling to the ultimate righteousness of Japan....
>
> And then I began to see the real disasters of the War. We are suffering and making enormous sacrifices for this war, but it is those Chinese people who are suffering the greater calamity. It is the hardest thing for human beings to see their country defeated, their cities burned, and to be driven out of their home for life....Can we blame them if they burn in the desire for life-long revenge?

* * *

The post-World War II years

By 1945, all the world was anxiously awaiting the end of the fighting, the establishment of a permanent global peace, and the restoration of normality. It was not to be that simple. As all wars, World War II was to leave great problems in its wake. Those who could braced themselves in advance. In the United States, a nation not directly devastated, preparation for the future was in an advanced state in 1945. Because of its geographical location, the United States had some perspective on the aftermath of war. It mobilized, opening its arms to refugees, doling out aid, trying to reconstruct a strong, modern, peaceful world.

CFR was doing its share. Its forecast of a tremendous post-war influx of foreign students to the United States had become a reality. In 1945, there were 7,772 foreign students in the United States; by 1947, there were 14,956. All signs told of more to come.

Many nations had programs at this time which called for increased student migration to the United States. This was understandable in light of the destruction of facilities abroad.

The year 1947 was one of significant change affecting the entire student exchange program not only for CFR but for all agencies and movements concerned with international students. Private financing of student exchanges was a general policy prior to the war. Now the Fulbnght Act involved the United States Government in student exchange agreements with eighteen countries. Student exchange was in the international spotlight. UNESCO meetings in London and Paris recommended a clearinghouse to provide information on scholarships, fellowships, standards for selection, orientation, language study, student visas, evaluation of credits, and handbooks listing available opportunities in given countries.[3]

* * *

Schmoker and Haines lead CFR in 1947

In May 1947, the responsibility for leading CFR in defining its specialized role and partnership with other foreign student service organizations fell to John Benjamin Schmoker. Schmoker came to CFR with a background of educational, religious, and community work in Minneapolis and a charismatic personality.

Earlier in 1947 Ruth Haines (later Ruth Haines Purkaple) had joined the staff as program director. These two—Schmoker and Haines—shared enthusiasm, imagination, and commitment...traits which were to revitalize CFR in the next decade.

In June 1948, a new statement of CFR policy was laid out at an administrative board meeting. That statement openly acknowledged CFR's particular and specialized functions for those foreign students with a Christian background. The statement also acknowledged that CFR's major concern was with individual foreign students whose needs were conditioned by their cultural background; that understanding and friendly cooperating relationships would be encouraged with Catholic and Jewish leaders in the United States; and that CFR reception, orientation, hospitality, and other general programs would operate without regard to the religious affiliation of students.

* * *

CFR brings together foreign student agencies

As the new Schmoker administration got under way, CFR began to face up to the realities of a new age as outlined at the 1944 Bronxville Consultation. The Committee sought to meet the challenge put forth in 1945 in the Preamble to the Constitution of UNESCO: "Since wars begin in the minds of men, it is in the minds of men that the defense of peace must be constructed." Responding to this challenge, Schmoker declared: "Open wide the doors...there is no obscurity about the responsibility. Those spared and those able shall work."

The purpose and goal of CFR was presented in 1949 as: "Education for international amity is a two-way process. We need to learn from our guest students and they from us. Our task is to be a part of a concerted effort to create a condition of mutual humility and respect." In this new climate of resolve and hope, a variety of programs sprang up.

An expanded port-of-arrival service was introduced, including new air services. An agreement was concluded by CFR and the Washington bureau of IIE to share responsibility for the annual census. The New Haven Students in Industry opened, providing a program of seminars

JOHN BENJAMIN SCHMOKER, CFR/ISS General Secretary/Director, 1947-1969, was also Secretary of the National Association of Foreign Student Advisors and a member of the NSA International Activities Control Board.

with leaders from the university, from industry, and from labor organizations. The National Association of Foreign Student Advisers (NAFSA) was formed. Its prime concern was to be the formulation of a national coordinated plan for foreign student programs.

The Greater New York Council for Foreign Students (GNYCFS) was organized, coordinating twenty-six agencies in the Greater New York City area engaged in program services to the foreign student.[4] Under the direction of Ruth Haines Purkaple, CFR opened a midtown center in New York. Here students from all parts of the world and from many colleges and universities in the Greater New York area would gather for recreation and to meet and talk with one another.

* * *

In 1950, more than 25,000 students at 1,081 colleges and universities

By 1950, the world was, for the moment at least, relatively peaceful, and reconstruction was well under way...[and] the United States was the educational center of the world. Its arms were open, generously offering educational aid to all foreigners who would come. And they came.

In 1950, there were 25,823 foreign students: 19,842 men and 5,981 women, in 1,081 colleges and universities in the U.S. This figure more than tripled that of 1945. It was still substantially below the 33,796—25,788 men and 8,008 women—who would arrive just three years later. The fifties were a busy time for foreign student service organizations as they mobilized to meet burgeoning student growth. The prediction at the 1944 Bronxville Consultation, that foreign student service would become big business, was now a reality. As a result, organizational specialization and cooperation were needed as never before.

For forty years, CFR had pioneered and somehow managed to perform more functions and assume more responsibilities than could logically be expected of it. Now there were local, national, and international agencies and associations with specialized services which could take over full control of some services CFR had provided, leaving CFR to specialize in what it did best—its "bread and butter" programs.

What John R. Mott, Cleveland H. Dodge, George W. Perkins, Andrew Carnegie, John W. Foster, Andrew D. White, William Sloane, and Gilbert Beaver had set out to do thirty-eight years before had, in some measure, been accomplished. CFR had been told to pioneer. It had....sparking a host of private agencies, institutions, and community groups interested in the welfare of the guest students. It had successfully demonstrated the power of cooperation. And it had proved that a single agency could stimulate new resources, encourage the development of new skills, and discover new leaders.

EDITOR'S NOTES

[1] The bracketed phrases in this paragraph were inserted in order to compensate for an apparent historical oversight in the original text, noted by Ruth Purkaple in a letter to the Anthology editor in 2001. The text suggested that the SVM, which existed until well past the 1950s, had its last meeting in 1920. The original phrases in that paragraph read (words deleted are italicized), "During the *course of* the Student Volunteer Movement's existence, from 1890 to 1920....At the *last* convention of the Student Volunteer Movement *in 1920*, John Mott summed up SVM's accomplishments."

[2] NSA worked closely with the IIE in the post–World War II era in developing its travel and exchange programs.

[3] NSA was actively engaged in developing and supporting UNESCO student programs. See pp. 510, 531.

[4] Ruth Purkaple also notes that "Mrs. Celestine Mott, John R. Mott's daughter-in-law, was the prime organizer."

PICTURE SOURCES: c. Schmoker and Thompson, c. 1960 (*Unofficial Ambassadors*, ISS, 1982). Thompson, c. 1979 (YMCA 12/7/79 dinner program)

MARY A. THOMPSON

The following biographical note is excerpted from the program for the Recognition Dinner given by the YMCA International at the Roosevelt Hotel in New York City on December 7, 1979.

Mary A. Thompson has spent the major part of her working life furthering the aims of international education. Since 1977, she has worn two hats—serving as Executive of the YMCA International Program Services Unit and as Director of International Student Service, the unit primarily responsible for providing international experiences for local YMCA members. She also has directly supervised the many services for international students, including Arrival, VISIT and Educational Group Travel.

Mary began her YMCA career in 1954 when she joined the staff of International Student Service (known then as the Committee on Friendly Relations among Foreign Students) as Director of Port Services.

In 1954, Port Services provided arrival help to 2,500 incoming international students. In 1979, the Arrival program has met over 15,000 students and includes services for four national refugee resettlement agencies. The VISIT Program which began with 25 communities hosting international students on vacation travel now includes 160 communities and more than 30,000 volunteers. More than 60 groups from overseas have had educational travel programs in the USA this year.

Mary was born in Mount Vernon, Washington and began her career as a teacher in the public school system of the State of Washington. In 1946, she came to New York City for graduate study at Teachers College, Columbia University, receiving a Master's Degree. From 1947-1951 she was a member of the Program Staff of International House in New York City.

From 1951-54, she served as Foreign Student Adviser and Director of the International Student Center at Fisk University in Nashville, Tennessee. She helped to make Fisk the interracial and international cultural center of all Nashville. She motivated many of her students to become involved in international affairs.

During her years in the field of international education, Mary has traveled extensively both here and abroad. She has participated in innumerable national and international conferences and worked closely with many organizations in the field. She has carried officer and board responsibility in the National Association for Foreign Student Affairs (NAFSA), the National Council for Community Services to International Visitors (COSERV), and the Council on International Education Exchange (CIEE). In 1972-73, she served as NAFSA's president. Her contacts with government officials both here and abroad have had a large impact on the growth of ISS programs.

[Since her 1979 retirement, she has served for nine years on the Board of Morningside Heights Housing Corporation in Manhattan, four years as President, and has been active in the Riverside Church and Morningside community, and with several international organizations.]

*Mary A. Thompson was Director of the International Student Service (former Committee on Friendly Relations), 1975-79. She was President of the National Association of Foreign Student Advisors. In 1951-54 she was Director of the Fisk University International Center in Nashville.**

**see "The Story of Fisk," p. 970*

"Pioneer of world-wide Christian movements, ceaseless worker in behalf of world peace"

John Raleigh Mott: World Citizen

Editor's note: Cornell graduate John R. Mott, founder of the Committee on Friendly Relations in 1911, is most noted as a founder of the Student Volunteer Movement in 1886 and the World Student Christian Federation in 1895. Following is an excerpt from his December 13, 1946, Nobel Peace Prize lecture:

Trustworthy Leadership

The most trustworthy leader is one who adopts and applies guiding principles. He trusts them like the North Star. He follows his principles no matter how many oppose him and no matter how few go with him. This has been the real secret of the wonderful leadership of Mahatma Gandhi. In the midst of the most bewildering conditions he has followed, cost what it might, the guiding principles of non-violence, religious unity, removal of untouchability, and economic independence. . . .

Let me emphasize the all-important point that Jesus Christ summed up, the outstanding, unfailing and abiding secret of all truly great and enduring leadership in the Word: "He who would be the greatest among you shall be the servant of all." He himself emobodied this truth and became "the Prince Leader of the Faith," that is, the leader of leaders.

JOHN RALEIGH MOTT

John Raleigh Mott (May 25, 1865-January 31, 1955) was born of pioneer stock in Livingston Manor, New York, the third child and only son among four children. His parents, John and Elmira (Dodge) Mott, moved to Postville, Iowa, where his father became a lumber merchant and was elected the first mayor of the town.

At sixteen, Mott enrolled at Upper Iowa University, a small Methodist preparatory school and college in Fayette. He was an enthusiastic student of history and literature there and a prizewinner in debating and oratory, but transferred to Cornell University in 1885. . . .

In the summer of 1886, Mott represented Cornell University's Y.M.C.A., at the first international, interdenominational student Christian conference ever held. At that conference, which gathered 251 men from eighty-nine colleges and universities, one hundred men, including Mott, pledged themselves to work in foreign missions. From this, two years later, sprang the Student Volunteer Movement for Foreign Missions.

During Mott's remaining two years at Cornell, as president of the Y.M.C.A. he increased the membership threefold and raised the money for a university Y.M.C.A. building. He was graduated in 1888, a member of Phi Beta Kappa, with a bachelor's degree in philosophy and history. In September of 1888 he began a service of twenty-seven years as national secretary of the Intercollegiate Y.M.C.A. of the U.S.A. and Canada, a position requiring visits to colleges to address students concerning Christian activities.

During this period, he was also chairman of the executive committee of the Student Volunteer Movement for Foreign Missions, presiding officer of the World Missionary Conference in Edinburgh in 1910, chairman of the International Missionary Council. With Karl Fries of Sweden, he organized the World's Student Christian Federation in 1895 and as its general secretary went on a two-year world tour, during which he organized national student movements in India, China, Japan, Australia, New Zealand, parts of Europe and the North East. In 1912 and 1913, he toured the Far East, holding twenty-one regional missionary conferences in India, China, Japan, and Korea.

From 1915 to 1928, Mott was general-secretary of the International Committee of the Y.M.C.A. and from 1926 to 1937 president of the Y.M.C.A.'s World Committee. During World War I, when the Y.M.C.A. offered its services to President Wilson, Mott became general secretary of the National War Work Council, receiving the Distinguished Service Medal for his work. For the Y.M.C.A. he kept up international contacts as circumstances allowed and helped to conduct relief work for prisoners of war in various countries. He had already declined President Wilson's offer of the ambassadorship to China, but he served in 1916 as a member of the Mexican Commission, and in 1917 as a member of the Special Diplomatic Mission to Russia.

The sum of Mott's work makes an impressive record: He wrote sixteen books in his chosen field; crossed the Atlantic over one hundred times and the Pacific fourteen times, averaging thirty-four days on the ocean per year for fifty years; delivered thousands of speeches; chaired innumerable conferences.

He was awarded the Nobel Peace Prize in 1946.

Dr. Mott married Leila Ada White of Wooster, Ohio, in 1891; they had four children, two sons and two daughters. He died at his home in Orlando, Florida, at the age of eighty-nine.

(Source: Kautz Family YMCA Archives, Anderson Library, U. of Minnesota)

Above: Mott in his youth, undated. Left: receiving a citation from Harry E. Smith, 1949-50 Chairman of the YMCA National Student Council at the 6/21-24/51 Centennial International Convention "for his inspiring leadership and devotion to youth of the colleges and universities of America."

(Documents and photos courtesy Kautz Family YMCA Archives, Anderson Library, U. of Minnesota).

Providing for Travel and Exchange: IIE, CST, and Youth Argosy

Editor's note: This unit concerns itself with the two organizations which provided the forums, developed the standards, and furnished administrative services for low-cost student ship travel after the war, the Institute of International Education (IIE) and Council on Student Travel (CST) – and with one group that attempted, successfully for several years, to aggregate and offer bare bones travel prices –often at 50% of what were already low-cost rates, Youth Argosy (YA).

The U.S. State Department and Maritime Commission cooperated with the various travel groups. Youth Argosy, which also enjoyed the support of the many non-profit travel organizers, focused heavily on discounted charter flights as well as discounted charter ship travel. Because of the opposition of commercial carriers and the Civil Aereonautics Board it was effectively put out of business in 1951.

In 1947, IIE organized an Executive Committee to coordinate and administer allocation of low-cost student ship travel on vessels provided by the U.S. Maritime Commission to the State Department. This government support was critical in making affordable travel possible for thousands of students after the war. For the summer of 1948, IIE transferred this function to a new group, formed by over 50 of the organizations who had an interest in foreign student travel, the Council on Student Travel. Both the IIE and CST have survived and grown to this day, the CST now known as the Council on International Education Exchange (CIEE).

The Institute of International Education

Editor's note: In the year 1948-49, IIE reported 25,464 foreign students studying in the U.S. and had a staff of 85. For the year 2001-2002 this number was 582,996. The IIE has also grown in size and scope as it has played a central role in international student exchange, responsible also for administrating the Fulbright program since 1946, sending students studying abroad (www.iie.org).

In 1947, at the birth of NSA, IIE lent its full support to the new organization. During NSA's first 5 years, 1948 through 1952, IIE's Directors, Lawrence Duggan, Donald Shank and Kenneth Holland successively served on the NSA National Advisory Council. A comprehensive and detailed history of both the IIE and the history of student exchange programs is presented in Stephen Mark Halpern's doctoral thesis for Columbia University in 1969. It is available on demand from University Microfilms in Ann Arbor, Michigan. Prepared with the cooperation of Kenneth Holland, then IIE President, Halpern provides an illuminating narrative as well as insights into the strengths and weaknesses of the IIE. Below are brief excerpts from pages 7-9 and pages 230-232 of the 266-page work:

The origins and development of educational travel in America may best be understood by studying the history of the Institute of International Education. Founded in 1919 as the first general administrative agency to organize and develop programs in international academic exchange, it grew from a small, inadequately financed organization into the largest educational exchange institution in the world. Its founder, Stephen Duggan, was a university professor with a deep commitment to the cause of peace and international understanding and from this commitment his conception of the meaning and value of educational exchange was shaped. Throughout the years that he directed his organization, he attempted to awaken the American people to the need for intercultural understanding and to introduce his contemporaries to the neglected field of cultural relations....

[Halpern traces how Stephen Duggan, after World War I, convinced that American "ignorance of international relations" needed to be addressed by "a central agency" to promote international understanding, won the support of Nicholas Murray Butler, then President of Columbia University and a director of the Carnegie Endowment for International Peace. The IIE was founded in 1919 by a grant from the Carnegie Endowment. The only other organization concerned with exchange, the Committee on Friendly Relations among Foreign Students (See p. 688) "had no interest in promoting academic exchanges".]

During the two decades following World War II, the Institute of International Education confronted new opportunities and new challenges. With the return to peacetime conditions, with the demand for exchange opportunities for foreign and American students intensifying each year, and with the birth of hundreds of new programs and scores of new organizations in international education, the Institute found itself no longer virtually alone in proclaiming the value of educational exchange. Under its new directors, and with greatly increased financial resources, it attempted to respond to the need for leadership and administrative competence so sorely needed....

STEPHEN PIERCE DUGGAN

As a professor at City College of New York before and during World War I, Stephen Duggan saw a desperate need in the U.S. for accurate information on international relations and a wider understanding by the American public of the world around them. He believed these goals could be fostered by academic exchanges among professors and students. In 1919 persuaded the Carnegie Endowment to fund the IIE. He died in 1955, leaving as a legacy an effective non-government infrastructure for the administration of international exchange

IIE's FIRST FOUR DIRECTORS. From l. Stephen Duggan (1919-46) and his son, Lawrence Duggan (1946-48), Donald Shank, acting director (1948-49), and Kenneth Holland (1950-1972), right, shown with Senator Fulbright. Duggan, Sr., doggedly pursued his international vision and passed along to his successors the platform on which they built the organization that grew to what it is today. Lawrence Duggan, Shank and Holland all served, successively on NSA's National Advisory Council from 1948-53.

During the 1950's it launched and accepted new programs, it expanded its organization to handle thousands of new students and it made serious attempts to increase both the kind and volume of information available to institutions and organizations interested in the exchange of persons.... By the 1960's it was still the largest and most experienced organization active in the field of educational exchange, but more and more it found itself having to share this field vith other important organizations....

Council on Student Travel

The following excerpts are from the Web site of the Council on International Educational Exchange (www.CIEE.org), the name to which the Council on Student Travel was changed in 1967. Also drawn upon were research by Henry Halsted and reports of the Experiment in International Living and the Institute of International Education.

The Council on Student Travel is best remembered for making possible immediately following World War II low-cost travel to Europe for thousands of students, teachers, youth and religious groups, and, with its orientation programs on board ship in which the American Friends Service Committee played a leading role, for making those crossings in both directions exciting educational experiences.

Immediately following the war a number of U.S. educational and religious groups became interested in re-establishing study, work and travel programs that had been suspended in 1939, and in making contacts with youth abroad to help rebuild a war-torn world.

Beginning in 1946 and 1947 a contingent of these groups began negotiations with the U.S. Government for student ships, and arrangements were made for the allocation of space and administration of orientation programs under a special Executive Committee on Student Travel. This committee had administrative help from the Institute for International Education until late in 1948 when it reorganized as the Council on Student Travel (CST), with a definite membership list, membership fees, and an executive committee for the administrative functions of the group.

In 1948 45 U.S., Western European, and international organizations formed an ad hoc group called the Committee for the Correlation of International Educational Enterprises (later renamed the Committee on Student Ships) to coordinate educational travel and allotment of student shipping space. This group merged with CST in 1950. From that time on CST took over handling all negotiations for chartering of student ships and continued this responsibility until the end of student ships in 1968.

During the summers of 1947, 1948, and 1949, the CST handled transportation and orientation programs on former C-4 troopships (the *Marine Jumper* and *Marine Tiger*), and other ships operated by the U.S. Maritime Commission and the United States Lines. Dutch ships were placed in service through the cooperation of the Dutch government and the Holland-America Line.

In 1949, CST consisted of 57 non-profit groups with travel programs totaling over 8,000 individuals. Honorary memberships were held by a number of U.S. and foreign government agencies concerned with cultural activities. The director in 1949 was John Rosengrant. Douglas E. Heilbrun followed as director in 1950.

In the nineteen sixties,under the leadership of John Bowman, John Trostle and Jack Eagle, the membership of CST expanded by including more schools and colleges. It broadened the scope of its operation beyond ship and air by offering program services to its member institutions. To reflect this new reach of its activities CST in 1967 changed its name to the Council on International Educational Exchange (CIEE). Today CIEE offers study abroad opportunities in 29 countries.

"For worthy young people of slender means."

Youth Argosy

Editor's note: Youth Argosy was yet another expression of one man's vision. It was to "build a youth generous, knowing and sympathetic who are living components of the one good world, essential today."

Argosy was founded by Monroe Smith, a former Boy Scout executive who, together with his wife Isabel, had also founded the American Youth Hostels in 1934. Its purpose, as outlined by Smith in an 8/19/49 report, was to "provide travel opportunities for worthy young people of slender means that they may enjoy the benefits of foreign study and travel, that they may engage in reconstruction work and other helpful projects and that they may make worldwide friendships regardless of race, color and creed."

Smith's support on his Board and Council reads like a Who's Who of executives from almost all the major players in the field of international student travel, exchange and education. Yet, as the American Youth Hostel Web site (www.gatewayhiayh.org) reports, "Youth Argosy did quite well but unfortunate circumstances caused the organization to go bankrupt in 1951. How well, was cited in its intended 1952 program brochure :

"[In the summer of 1948] it provided eight hundred passages for its members to or from Europe by air at a price of $170 per seat... Between May, 1948 and October, 1951 accumulative air passages provided by Youth Argosy have aggregated 16,300, those by ship have totaled 8,500."

What did them in? In a letter to members on 4/23/51, Monroe Smith wrote:

"On March 22nd the Civil Aeronautics Board announced its policy for 1951 on trans-Atlantic charter flights....The policy statement and new charter regulations deal a severe blow to international student travel in general and international student travel by air in particular.....The CAB ruling [on a loading procedure technicality-ed.] hits hardest the indiviual American...who is not a member of a group large enough to charter an aircraft for its exclusive use."

(Youth Argosy documents provided by Henry Halsted. See also pictorial, p. 678)

BILL WELSH APPEARS FOR NSA AT 1948 IIE-SPONSORED STUDENT CONFERENCE

THE SEPTEMBER STUDENT CONFERENCE

At the time when ground was being broken for the cornerstone of the buildings for the permanent home of the United Nations in New York City, just a few blocks away students were congregating at Town Hall for the annual September Student Conference, which was held under the auspices of IIE September 14, 15, 16 in cooperation with Town Hall and the Greater New York Council for Foreign Students.

Harry H. Pierson, director of program of the Institute, presided at the first session of the conference and the president, Laurence Duggan, welcomed the students from the various countries who were beginning their period of study in the United States. Following the speech of the first day more than 400 students attended a party at International House.

The main speakers at the three auditorium sessions were Edward R. Murrow, chairman of the Board of Trustees of IIE; Harold Taylor, president of Sarah Lawrence College; and Donald J. Shank, vice-president of IIE, who emphasized the broad variety of educational opportunities in this country.

A vital ·spect of the conference was the active partiicipation of American students. William R. Welsh, first president of the National Student Association, and other members of NSA conducted a forum on the American student's views of education in this country.

Inter-cultural emphasis was manifest in the hospitality extended to the students by the China Institute, the English-Speaking Union, the Kosciuszko Foundation, International House and several individuals.

EvaDean Kemp.

From *IIE News Bulletin*, 10/1/48

EDWARD R. MURROW, a former student leader of the 1930's (See Prologue, Section 2), prominent war-time radio journalist, Chairman of the Board of Trustees of IIE, also addressed the student leaders. Welsh had just completed his 1947-48 term as President of NSA (See Part 1, Section 5).

PART

4

Student Voices Influencing NSA

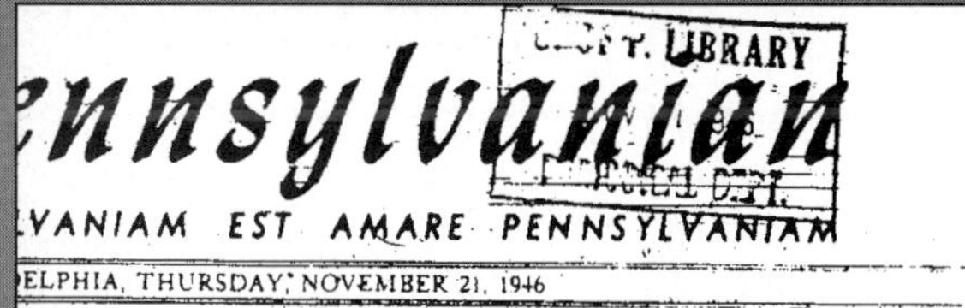

ennsylvanian

LVANIAM EST AMARE PENNSYLVANIAM

ELPHIA, THURSDAY, NOVEMBER 21, 1946 No. 31

Veteran Organizations Of The University Open Subsistance Increase Drive Today; Bolte, National AVC Head, To Aid Drive

Charles G. Bolte, national chairman of | Sponsored by the University chapter of

Agnes Scott N

AGNES SCOTT COLLEGE, WED. FEB. 12, 1947

Christianity Fundamentals Topic of Religious Week

Dr. Miller Leads Dorm Forums; Chapel Topics Student-Suggested

Centering around a practical inquiry into the fundamentals of Christianity, Agnes Scott's first post-war Religious Emphasis week will begin Monday under leadership of Dr.

rgreen

ON STATE COLLEGE, PULLMAN, WASHINGTON FRIDAY, APRIL 12, 1946

REED COLLEGE CONFERENCE FAVORS WORLD GOVERNMENT

Delegates From Northwest Campuses Vote For

and GOLD

NT NEWSPAPER

Students of the University of Colorado

Friday, May 23, 1947

New ASUC Constitution Ratified Despite Greek Combine Opposition

ASUC Commission Holds Final Meeting Of Quarter

Expressions of appreciation and miscellaneous business occupied the short meeting Wednesday night in which the 1946-47 ASUC commission wound up its activities.

Incoming president Lou Rovira announced that seven of the new commissioners will be on the campus this summer, enough to do business. First summer meeting will be June 15.

Outstanding Senior

By Kenneth Whitaker

In a heavier-than-expected vote, University students Wednesday approved a new constitution for the ASUC by a margin of 175 ballots. For the new constitution there were 837 ballots, against were 662, with six ballots voided.

Clockwise, from top: *The Daily Pennsylvanian*, 11/21/46; *The Agnes Scott News*, GA, 2/12/47; *The Washington State Evergreen*, 4/12/46; *The Silver and Gold*, U. of Colorado, 5/23/47.

PART 4

Student Voices Influencing NSA

NSA undertook to be a nonpartisan and nonsectarian voice for U.S. college and university students. It established its credibility by resting its membership on elected student governments or, where they did not exist, on a vote of the student body. Other national student groups saw in NSA a forum in which to advance their agendas or an opportunity to collaborate in programs of mutual interest.

This part provides an overview of national student organizations whose programs and interests intersected with NSA's, linked to personal stories where possible. In many instances, these organizations provided or shared student leadership locally and nationally; in others, they opposed its policies.

A section on the veterans reviews the creative and transforming impact of these students in the years during which they were a major presence on campus.

Probably no two major student movements had a greater impact on the formation of NSA than the national- and campus-level Protestant and Catholic student groups, whose influence and history are recalled.

Fraternity and sorority influence on many campuses was pervasive. NSA maintained staff-level communication with the National Interfraternity Council throughout its early years (see Part 2); although its opposition to fraternity/sorority discrimination was voiced from the start, there was little pronounced NSA activity in this area. Many of NSA's early campus champions were also fraternity members and leaders, as were some of its outspoken adversaries.

Much of the story of student activism in the Twentieth Century has as its backdrop the ideological and political challenge of communism prior to, during and following World War II. When NSA was formed in 1947, there was already present on the national scene a group of experienced and active liberal and radical left organizations, both communist and noncommunist. These organizations included the Student Federalists, Students for Democratic Action and American Youth for Democracy. Many of their liberal leaders who were active and held leadership positions within NSA are cited. The story of the Student Federalists is a highlight of post-war student idealism in action.

Organized conservative voices challenge liberals in the 1950s

While "Red Scare" anticommunist forces and reactionary fringes existed on the right both on and off campus even before the war (see Prologue and Part 2), effective mainstream voices for organized conservative and libertarian political and social agendas did not appear until the 1950s. These groups included Students for America, Young Republicans and the Intercollegiate Society of Individualists. Young Americans for Freedom were not formed until 1960 (see p.1094).

This part concludes with an overview of NSA and student activism before the 1960's, a chart showing the historic evolution and connections of major U.S. student-related religious, political, social and service organizations, and a review of formal and informal factions within NSA.

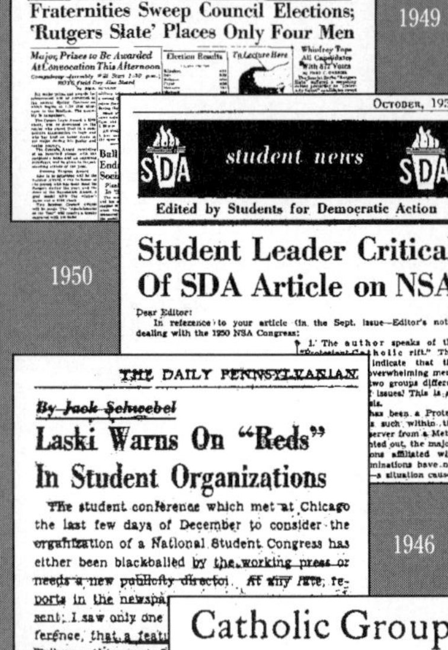

The TARGUM

Fraternities Sweep Council Elections; 'Rutgers Slate' Places Only Four Men

Major Prizes to Be Awarded At Convocation This Afternoon

1949

OCTOBER, 1950

SDA student news SDA

Edited by Students for Democratic Action

Student Leader Critical Of SDA Article on NSA

Dear Editor:

In reference to your article (in the Sept. issue—Editor's note) dealing with the 1950 NSA Congress:

1. The author speaks of the ...

1950

THE DAILY PENNSYLVANIAN

By Jack Schoebel

Laski Warns On "Reds" In Student Organizations

The student conference which met at Chicago the last few days of December to consider the organization of a National Student Congress has either been blackballed by the working press or needs a new publicity director. At any rate, reports in the newspa...

1946

Catholic Group Sways N.S.A.

National Student Association Congress Finds Organized Bloc Able to Influence Moves as Unit

CHAMPAIGN, ILL., Sept. 6.—At the National Student Association Congress held at the University of Illinois here Aug. 24-Sept. 3, only one sizable group among the 800 students in attendance knew what it wanted and was organized to get it. That was the "joint committee for student action" which drew together the 200 or so Catholic students at the congress, which consists of elected representatives from 350 ...

1949

NSA Is a Challenge

The National Student Association formed in September is really a country-wide organization of campus governments. All votes are by campuses, none by national organizations or agencies. Elected officers must quit college for a semester and work for a salary in Madison, Wisconsin, during their term. Thus in a new way, the Protestant student movement—by far the largest organized intercollegiate force—takes its place in an over-all student picture.

A notable fact at the NSA organization was Roman Catholic solidarity, backed up with a letter by Archbishop

1947

COMPETING INTERESTS saw NSA's emergence as an opportunity to provide a neutral forum from which U.S. students could be spoken for as well as a potential threat to their own agendas. From top: Fraternities on campus often elected slates which controlled the student government. NSA, being student government grounded, found opposition as well as support from within the fraternity community (See Part 2, Sec. 2) (*Targum*, Rutgers U. 5/13/49). The Students for Democratic Action (SDA), a wing of the adult ADA, took an active interest in NSA and provided a number of its leaders (See p. 781) (*ADA World*, 10/50). Concern over possible Communist influence in NSA prompted much commentary (Harold Laski in the *Daily Pennsylvanian*, 1/7/46). It also figured in the strategies of the two most significant influences in NSA's formation, the Catholic (*Christian Century*, 9/49) and Protestant student movements (*Intercollegian*, 11/47).

SECTION 1

The Veterans

CONTENTS

"THE GI BILL turned loose forces that quietly but dramatically transformed America. The GI Bill made modern America because of the ambition, maturity and energy of ordinary Americans who used the GI Bill to make their dreams come true."

—From *When Dreams Come True: The GI Bill and the Making of America* (Brassey's, Washington, 1996), by Michael J. Bennett. In the words of James MacGregor Burns of Williams College, the bill was "one of the most momentous World War II measures [that] passed Congress by mustering one of the most remarkable coalitions in this century."

Initiated to avoid the veteran neglect following World War I, the GI Bill emerged in 1944, supplanting an administration bill, after a six-month legislative battle led by the American Legion and enlisting the active support of the Hearst newspaper chain. It contained the then revolutionary provisions providing 52 weeks of financial aid as well as full tuition payments to public as well as private colleges, making up to 16 million veterans eligible regardless of race.

"The GI Bill was approved in the Senate on June 12, 1944, and in the House on June 13, and signed into law by President Roosevelt on June 22.

"By 1947, total enrollment was 2,338,226, with 1,150,000 veterans accounting for 49.2%. . . . The World War II bill, unlike the subsequent Korea, Vietnam and cold war bills, paid full tuition up to $500 a year, and Harvard and other top schools were charging $400 when the war ended. . . By 1950 more than $10 billion had been spent on education alone."

79TH CONGRESS 1ST SESSION **S. 1176**

A BILL

To amend the Servicemen's Readjustment Act of 1944, with respect to the education and training of veterans.

By Mr. PEPPER

JUNE 20 (legislative day, JUNE 4), 1945
Read twice and referred to the Committee on Finance

Possibly no college student generation before or since experienced the swift growth and culture change than did the generation following World War II, which saw its size more than double as over 2 million veterans returned to its campuses on the GI Bill.

In this section, the shared sensibilities of the veterans are seen through the memoirs of Otis Pease (Yale) delivered to his Class of '49; the still unsettling and challenging reprise of Cord Meyer's (Yale) then widely circulated 1945 *Atlantic Monthly* article, "A Service Man Looks at the Peace"; and the discussion by Bernard Bellush (CCNY and Columbia) of the activist American Veterans Committee campus presence. Ralph Smith (Swarthmore) provides a gentle epilogue to the veteran generation's aspirations and influence as he examines the generation immediately following, in the 1950s, among whom were "young people who found little about it to love."

Lasting effects and ephemeral passing

Although it was certainly lasting in many of its effects, there was also an ephemeral quality to the veteran impact on campus consciousness. Pease, whose essay provides moving examples of the war's impact in broadening the outlook and deepening the interests of the members of his class, also cites Student Federalist and 1946 World Student Congress delegate Curt Farrar's (Yale) 1949 yearbook assessment of the slow decline of political interest on campus. (See Farrar, Part 5, Sec. 1.)

The ideals that fueled much of the veteran college student engagement in that era were voiced by Cord Meyer when he wrote: "To my mind, there is only one purpose in terms of which the war is justifiable and which is at all commensurate with what is daily and irretrievably lost. . . . By our victory we gain the opportunity to construct by intelligent and radical reform a more equitable society and a peaceful world."

Veterans on the G.I. Bill Change Forever the U.S. College Landscape

Veterans flock to nation's colleges

Public Law GI Bill draw 2,600,000

WEBB LEAVES VETERANS' POST SUCCESSOR NOT YET ANNOUNCED

GI's told to avoid unapproved courses

THE CAMPUS

Undergraduate Newspaper of The City College

Enrollment Hits All-Time High; Revamp Student Life Department

Brophy Heads Administration

Alumni Fete

Swamps Registration, Forces Two Day Holiday

Cornell Daily Sun

9600 REGISTER FOR FALL TERM

Big Red Starts 60th Year With James as New Coach

News Shorts

Enrollment At All-Time High, 1946-47 Total Topped By 400

'51 Orientation Ends

THE HAWK

RECORD-BREAKING FROSH CLASS ENROLLED

Student Forum At Univ. of Pa.

Ex G.I.s Swell Ranks

Business and Science Courses Given Preference

Student Council Guides Activity

Thursday, April 4, 1946

Vets Return To W. U. But These Are Women

Nine Thousand Veterans Desiring To Enter University This Fall Already Turned Away

Enrollment Figure Approaches 4000 Mark As Registration of Men Students Doubles

Los Angeles Collegian

Admissions, Records Office Expects More To Register Before Deadline Thursday

AS President Max W. Fine Calls Initial Council Meet

Faculty Increases to 115 Many Old Instructors Return

RECORD ENROLLMENTS "swamped" some (CCNY) and found others "ready and waiting" (Cornell). From the top: *California Daily Bruin*, UCLA 5/19/47; *The Campus*, CCNY 9/23/46; *Cornell Daily Sun*, 9/27/47; The Hawk, St. Joseph's C., PA, 2/6/46; *Student Life*, Washington U., MO, 4/4/46; *The Daiily Tar Heel*, U. of NC, 6/15/46; *Los Angeles Collegian*, LACC, 9/11/45.

Expanded Enrollments

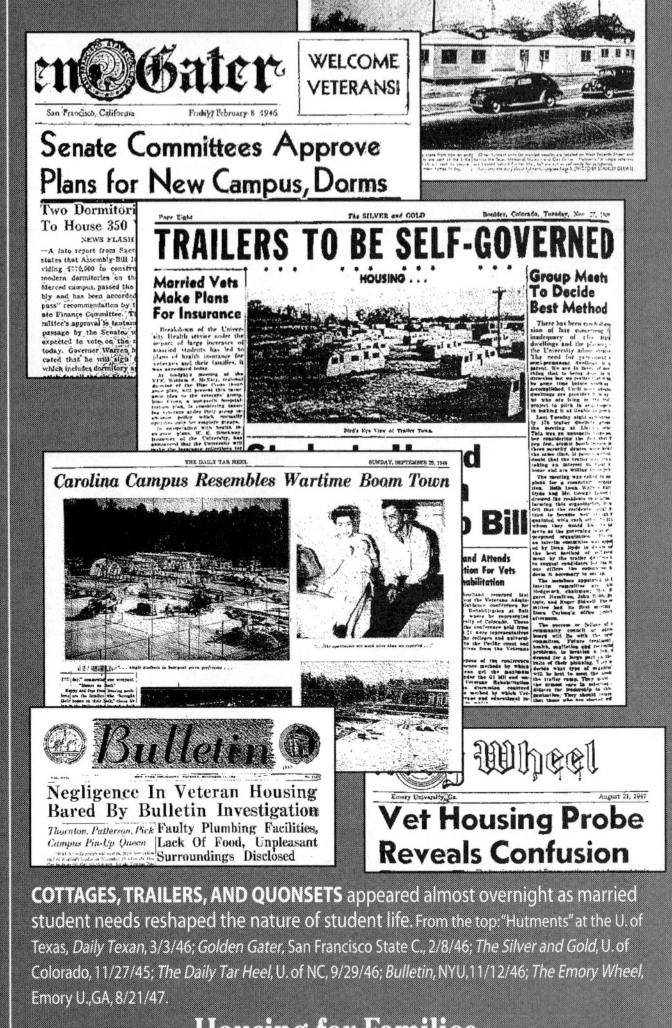

Golden Gater

WELCOME VETERANS!

San Francisco, California — Friday, February 8, 1946

Senate Committees Approve Plans for New Campus, Dorms

Two Dormitories To House 350

TRAILERS TO BE SELF-GOVERNED

Married Vets Make Plans For Insurance

Housing . . .

Group Meets To Decide Best Method

Carolina Campus Resembles Wartime Boom Town

Bulletin

Negligence In Veteran Housing Bared By Bulletin Investigation

Faulty Plumbing Facilities, Lack Of Food, Unpleasant Surroundings Disclosed

Emory Wheel

Vet Housing Probe Reveals Confusion

COTTAGES, TRAILERS, AND QUONSETS appeared almost overnight as married student needs reshaped the nature of student life. From the top: "Hutments" at the U. of Texas, *Daily Texan*, 3/3/46; *Golden Gater*, San Francisco State C., 2/8/46; *The Silver and Gold*, U. of Colorado, 11/27/45; *The Daily Tar Heel*, U. of NC, 9/29/46; *Bulletin*, NYU, 11/12/46; *The Emory Wheel*, Emory U., GA, 8/21/47.

Housing for Families

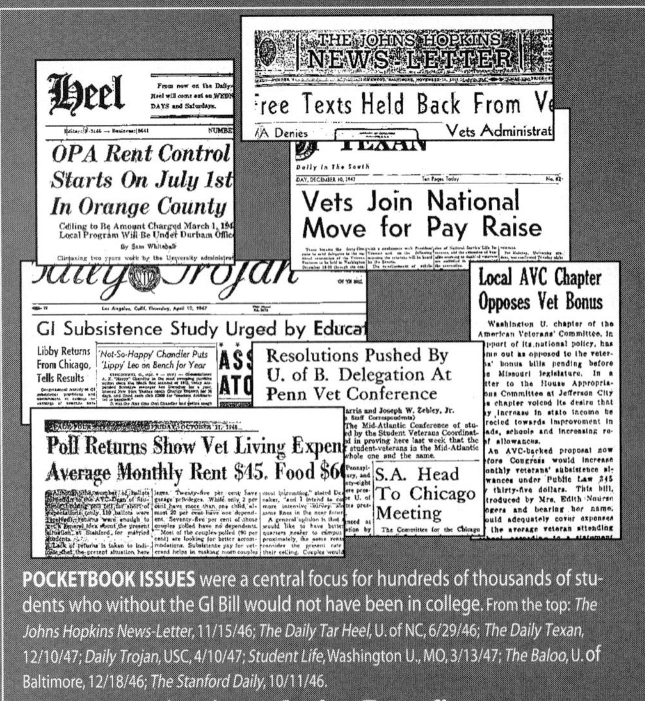

THE JOHNS HOPKINS NEWS-LETTER

Free Texts Held Back From Vets

VA Denies — Vets Administration

Tar Heel

OPA Rent Control Starts On July 1st In Orange County

Ceiling to Be Amount Charged March 1, 1946

Daily Texan

Vets Join National Move for Pay Raise

Daily Trojan

GI Subsistence Study Urged by Educators

Local AVC Chapter Opposes Vet Bonus

Resolutions Pushed By U. of B. Delegation At Penn Vet Conference

Poll Returns Show Vet Living Expenses Average Monthly Rent $45, Food $60

S.A. Head To Chicago Meeting

POCKETBOOK ISSUES were a central focus for hundreds of thousands of students who without the GI Bill would not have been in college. From the top: *The Johns Hopkins News-Letter*, 11/15/46; *The Daily Tar Heel*, U. of NC, 6/29/46; *The Daily Texan*, 12/10/47; *Daily Trojan*, USC, 4/10/47; *Student Life*, Washington U., MO, 3/13/47; *The Baloo*, U. of Baltimore, 12/18/46; *The Stanford Daily*, 10/11/46.

An Agenda for Benefits

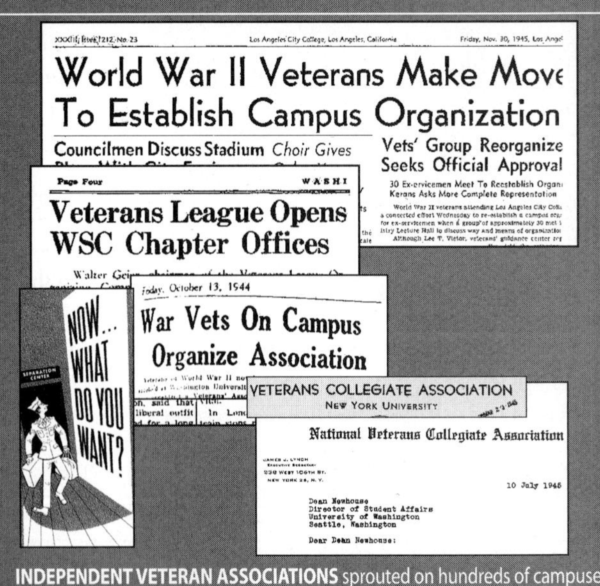

Los Angeles City College, Los Angeles, California — Friday, Nov. 30, 1945

World War II Veterans Make Move To Establish Campus Organization

Councilmen Discuss Stadium

Vets' Group Reorganizes Seeks Official Approval

Veterans League Opens WSC Chapter Offices

Friday, October 13, 1944

War Vets On Campus Organize Association

NOW... WHAT DO YOU WANT?

VETERANS COLLEGIATE ASSOCIATION

NEW YORK UNIVERSITY

National Veterans Collegiate Association

10 July 1946

Dean Newhouse
Director of Student Affairs
University of Washington
Seattle, Washington

Dear Dean Newhouse:

INDEPENDENT VETERAN ASSOCIATIONS sprouted on hundreds of campuses, as new WWII-focused national groups emerged, the most notable being the American Veterans Committee. From top: *Los Angeles Collegian*, LACC, 11/30/45; *Washington Square Bulletin*, NYU 5/14/46; *Student Life*, Washington U., MO, 10/13/44; *The Daily Tar Heel*, U. of NC, 1/18/48; from U. of Washington Archives: letterheads, National Veterans Collegiate Association.

Organizing to a Purpose

A permanent reshaping of campus culture

1. The Yale Class of 1949 and the World War II Veterans

Otis Pease

Yale '49

Adapted from a talk delivered May 28, 1999, at the fiftieth reunion of the class of 1949.

I want to share with you some thoughts about the heritage that shaped us as Yale students at the end of the 1940s, one of the three or four most significant and transformative decades in our national history.

Many ingredients of our heritage seemed predictable simply from knowing what Yale students, and others in the Ivy League, were like before 1941: entirely male; mostly WASP; raised in two-parent families well above the national norm in income and education, and residing mainly in southern New England, the Middle Atlantic, and the old industrial Midwest; educated mainly in private schools; and, for these reasons, mainly insulated from the worst blows of the nearly decade-long Great Depression. But in 1941 World War II shook and soon engulfed the nation. By the fall of 1946 the Yale classes of '48, '49, and '50 were breaking out of traditional channels and were substantially reshaping the university's cultural landscape.

Historians often speak of a "generation" gap cutting across the 1960s. Surely the gap separating those three Yale classes from their prewar brethren was no less dramatic and fateful. Postwar Yale was much less obviously WASP; only one out of five of us came from New England while Far Westerners rose to one out of eight; two out of every five in our class now hailed from public schools; one-third of our fathers and one-half of our mothers had not themselves gone to college; and our families were more likely, on average, to have felt the effects of the Depression. The average Yale senior in the years 1948 to 1950 was two years older than his counterpart in the 1930s. For these older seniors, courses and learning in general, were, relatively, much more important, fraternities much less so.

The typical prewar class

Our Yale was still a college for men, and its numbers had dramatically increased. The typical prewar class numbered 800; our class graduated nearly 1,300, and so did the following class. Our 1949 Classbook listed 1,284 seniors, if you exclude Clarence Benjamin Hiple, whose biography and picture seemed real enough at the time but who might now be more analogously described as the "Kilroy" of our class (the brainchild of Bill Swire, our good editor both then and now, and a few other nefarious war veterans), were it not that our class actually included three brothers whose *real* names were Kilroy.

Why was our class so large? Mainly because very many Yale enrollees who in normal times would have graduated in 1946 and 1947 served in the war for two to three years and were reclassified to 1948, 1949, and 1950. There were, in addition, some servicemen whom the armed forces assigned to Yale in 1943 to 1945 for special training programs, who in prewar years (for financial, social, or educational reasons) might never have applied for admission but who at war's end accepted Yale's special invitation to enroll as regular, full-time undergraduates.

All of these factors were to transform the cultural mix of the postwar student body. Even the influence of gender underwent a subtle change, as that part of the substantially "veteran" male population with wives and children lived in new Quonset-hut communities at the university's perimeter. Memorably, the GI Bill helped many in our class achieve a Yale education, which they had not previously considered within their financial reach. Nor is it insignificant that the 60 percent increase in enrollment, plus the G.I. Bill, provided the university with an unprecedented, but stable and reliable, source of income at relatively small additional expense.

Veterans bring new attitudes to the campus

But veterans at postwar Yale brought to the campus more than themselves and their tuition. Perhaps as many as two out of three embodied, even magnified, new attitudes that had begun to transform the nation. There is some evidence to suggest that for every American GI who declared on returning from overseas that he wanted never to leave the country again, there was another who brought home a new interest in the people and cultures he or she had encountered; and over 80,000 American servicemen and -women married spouses from other nations. Having rejected the League of Nations in 1919, the American public now supported the United Nations and offered it a permanent home in the United States. Japanese bombs at Pearl Harbor had virtually destroyed American isolationism, not least at universities like Yale, and four years later, two U.S. Air Force bombers over two Japanese cities made it starkly clear that henceforth, the only alternative to *no* world was *one* world and that Americans had better help preserve it.

These were some of the convictions that returning veterans brought to the campus, and the classes they took and the studies they pursued probably reinforced these convictions. I may be exaggerating the point. In a penetrating essay for our Classbook in 1949, Curtis Farrar assessed the campus political climate as one of slow decline, from an immediate postwar activism and idealistic concern for global problems to a kind of privatism, a more subdued preoccupation with our immediate social environment and our own place in it—a decline reversed only temporarily during the 1948 national election.[1]

Curt's evidence of a decline is persuasive, yet equally to be noticed was the class's continuing commitment toward a new internationalism in the world and a reinvigorated democracy at home, a commitment that Irving Murphy, class orator, would celebrate at our graduation. Our idealism may well have lessened at Yale, but I believe that it remained high, and very likely higher than had been characteristic of Yale's prewar students. It was a mindset tested by an experience of the world and of human nature perhaps unique in the history of American undergraduates. If that mindset was distinctive among those who had been in war, still it could not help but affect those in the class who had not been in war. It bore fruit, finally, within the new mixture of students that we had all become—more mature and democratic than our predecessors, and in time it contributed to a permanent reshaping of the culture of Yale itself.

The impact of the culture of war

Much of this may seem familiar, even obvious, to anyone who has read the essays and the class survey in our fiftieth reunion book.[2] But what is less obvious and calls for a deeper explanation is what I see as the centerpiece of the experience of our class. Five out of every six members of Yale '49 had been caught up in the armed forces for terms of service that averaged over two years. What did that experience with the culture of war do to us, to our life at Yale, to our resources in dealing with our subsequent careers? I confess to having reached few answers even after some years of looking, professionally, at these questions, but I also confess to a strong belief that addressing them is crucially important to an understanding of our generation.

Several years ago I undertook a survey of my class of '43 at Exeter Academy, on the occasion of our fiftieth reunion. The survey centered on our experience in the armed forces, in which 93 percent of us served, and what it revealed is pertinent, I think, to most Yale '49ers here today, a few of whom are also Exeter '43. The survey ended by asking, "Today, looking back, how do you view the impact on your own life of your experience during World War II?" "Profoundly and fundamentally," answered a significant number. "The single most revealing and affecting social experience of my life," remembered one. Another: "It showed that I could operate, compete, get involved, on my own in any situation." And this: "The complexity and immensity of war taught me to be fatalistic about life but yet to do the best you can to accept the hand that is dealt you." Many sensed that they had had their own early rendezvous with history. To be engaged in a "national life-and-death struggle," declared one, "gave us a perspective on life missing in recent generations." A few spoke of the opportunity to understand a little of war itself in a century that was to bring the threat of war to virtually every person's door. And one classmate identified a not uncommon reaction in a uniquely memorable image:

> Fighting for my country was simply a marvelous opportunity. If you're 19 years old, have a submachine gun in your hands with a bunch of concussion grenades hanging all over your body, and are assaulting a German town house to house, and you live to tell about it—that's living, believe me!

Some respondents offered a different opinion. The war "merely delayed my life," said one. Others regretted that their time in service left them as immature as they had been at school. "I wasted two years," was how another put it; "[I] learned bad habits, mainly how to goldbrick. The war was no test of character for me." "The notion that war can somehow be enriching and maturing seems to me utter garbage," wrote one of my classmates, but then he suggested how important to him had been his combat experience and how hard it was to accept a later generation's indifference to his efforts to write a play about what it had meant to him.[3]

These comments remind us of an important truth, but one frequently overlooked when observing our wartime generation. Along with positive memories about service to the nation, we carry with us at least as many negative ones. The armed forces—in which a total of 16 million persons served, and (after 1942) never less than 9 million at any one time—formed the largest bureaucracy within the United States. At their best they helped us believe in what we were doing at a crucial juncture in world history. At their worst the armed forces easily convinced most of us that there were no upper limits to the foolishness of human beings.

Who among American veterans does not remember some of the ways we put the point to ourselves? "Salute anything that moves. If it doesn't move, paint it. If it can't be painted, dig a hole and bury it." Who can forget the long lines of males awaiting physical inspection totally naked, a reasonable enough requirement, but somehow arranged to make as many men as possible—stripped of every defense—feel anxious and unsure of themselves? One GI in the First Division later recalled his first physical in the army as making some men so scared that they couldn't even piss when asked to. Never mind. "Others were so full of beer they flowed like rivers. This one guy helped about ten men fill up their bottles."[4] That is the army every veteran holds firm in memory.

Some of the powerful memories of war

But I want to return us to other memories. Let me quote from two Yale undergraduates from the 1940s, our decade.

One is Townsend Hoopes, class of '44 and varsity football captain, who wrote home about his feelings as a Marine lieutenant during the invasion of Iwo Jima. On D-plus-4 Hoopes was thrown into major combat. A twenty-minute mortar barrage struck into the middle of his battalion command unit. When he tried desperately to keep contact with his non-coms, he found his sergeant killed, his corporal wounded, two others unhurt but frozen with fear. For the next two hours he did what he could to pull his unit together.

> I was a thoroughly frightened person, badly upset and somehow convinced the battalion was doomed to decimation. I had only one thought—to get out safely and quickly—and the most fantastic ideas whirled in my head. I must get knicked by a sniper or break my ankle—anything to get off that island. It was the mental process of a coward, but the idea persisted that it was better to be a live dog than a dead lion. But when I saw my kids again—scared and rather lost—one of them weeping, I got hold of myself and realized they needed leadership. My courage returned and I determined to see the damn thing through.[5]

Hoopes's battalion of a thousand men suffered 800 killed or wounded that day, including nineteen out of twenty-one front-line officers. It would be impossible not to imagine that for the rest of his life he would be affected by what he experienced—and thought—that day. Some members of our class could tell a story like that, and surely the Yale student community of our years was affected by the presence of such men.

Hoopes's experience was in no way ordinary. Very few of us were Marine lieutenants. They were a special breed, their mindset and training unusual, fitting with what they were called on to do. We remind ourselves that four out of five persons in the American armed services in 1944 served in roles that did not expose them to combat. Most of us were ordinary veterans, whose letters, journals, and fifty-five-year-old memories recall few actions beyond the call of duty but, rather, contributions to the war not particularly heroic, or maybe merely a record of survival.

I want to round out this commentary by bringing to your attention a powerful memoir by one of our classmates, Tuck Orbison, who would be the first to assert that, despite a more-than-ordinary flair for exploring the meaning of war, he experienced indeed the war of an ordinary G1.[6] Tuck was one of my roommates in Trumbull College in the summer of 1943 and, like me, joined the army in November. Trained in mortars in an infantry company, he arrived in Europe in March 1945 with the 86th Division and entered combat for the final six weeks of the European war.

At the end of his memoir Tuck identifies two aspects of war that had particular meaning. One was the way that combat internalized a sense of responsibility toward one's comrades.

> Surviving, we were told, meant relying on each other, and my experience in Germany made me see that these were not meaningless words. Selfishness, cowardice, thoughtlessness always prejudiced the safety of the group. I don't see how I could have learned this in any other way. When crossing a street that was under fire, for example, we had to learn to cross not singly, but in rushes together. Otherwise the sniper had a chance of picking us off, one by one. . . . Playing football or ice hockey gives one team spirit, all right, but in combat solidarity becomes a matter of life and death.[7]

The other aspect of his experience that he found particularly meaningful was simply the fact of his being there.

> As an infantry private, I played an infinitesimal part in the war, yet . . . a role, however small, on such a grand stage gave me a distinct feeling that my life had meaning, that it mattered, and I was there. In the face of the great preponderance of the absurd, the irrelevant, and the inconsequential, to believe that one's life possesses significance gives one a sense of optimism and solidity, attitudes new to me at the time. The struggle against the evil of Hitler . . . is worth the effort and, win or lose, makes you feel good. I had never had that feeling before. "Do you want to live forever?" Well, yes, I do, but I also wanted to believe that my life was significant.[8]

The veterans' classes: a hard-won maturity

The veterans of 1949, along with those in the classes of 1947, 1948, and 1950, in one way or another had encountered these meanings, or others very like them, even before plunging back into the center of their college life. They had—we had—in effect experienced them at a time in our lives that allowed us to apply the immense resources of a university to the amorphous but stimulating task of trying to make sense of them. A perverse conceit tells us that a college education is too valuable to waste on the young. In the late 1940s, most veterans at Yale were, in reality, no longer "young."[9] A hard-won maturity freed us to make the most of the ambience of the university—its teachers and scholars, its community of discourse, argument, intellect, and passion—to begin to try to figure out the meaning of what it was that we had done in those great and terrible years of global conflict.

By the time of graduation this maturity, it seems to me, was no small thing to have woven into our heritage.

Otis Pease was Professor of History and Department Head at the University of Washington. He has served as Vice President of the American Historical Association and as a member of the Stanford University Board of Trustees. He has also authored a number of works on American cultural and political history.

END NOTES

[1] Curtis Farrar, representing the Student Federalists, was one of the twenty-five U.S. student delegates to the August 1946 World Student Congress in Prague, Czechoslovakia. See Part I, Section 1, and Jonas, p. 761. See also Farrar, "Postwar Student Politics and Joining NSA at Yale," p. 829.

[2] William H. Swire, editor, *Yale University Class of 1949: The American Century, Our Half: 50th Reunion, 1999* (New Haven, CT: Yale University, 1998), pp. 11–21.

[3] The quotations and summary in these three paragraphs are from material in the author's possession. See also, *Exeter 1943: Fifty Years, 1993* (Exeter, NH: Exeter, 1993), pp. 215–216.

[4] 1st Division Papers, Military History Institute, Carlisle, PA.

[5] Letter published in the *Yale Alumni Magazine*, June 1945.

[6] *Private Lessons: A Memoir of World War II* (Privately printed, 1999).

[7] Ibid., p. 151.

[8] Ibid., p. 150.

[9] *Editor's note:* Yale contributed a number of NSA leaders during its founding years, including two Vice Presidents for International Affairs: Robert S. Smith, 1947-1948, and Robert L. West, 1948-1949 (see Smith, p. 504). Graduating Yale's Law School after serving as NSA leaders in their undergraduate years were Alice Brandeis Gilbert (Radcliffe), New England Region Chair, 1948-1949; Robert F. Meagher (CCNY), Metropolitan New York Region Executive Secretary, 1947-1948; Tom Garrity (St. Peter's, New Jersey), Metropolitan New York Regional Chair, 1948-1949; and Allard K. Lowenstein (University of North Carolina), NSA President, 1950-1951. See also footnote 1 above.

PICTURE CREDITS: *Then:* July, 1948, Cornwall, UK. *Now:* Summer, 1999, Seattle, WA (Both from author).

OTIS PEASE

Background: Born in 1925. Grew up in Western Massachusetts, parents comfortably well-off in business and social work. Attended Phillips Exeter Academy, excelling in English, Latin, math, classical piano, choral singing, and chopping firewood for the war effort; merely surviving in physics and soccer. Graduated 1943. Attended Yale University briefly. Willing to serve in the war; limited by eyesight to the infantry. Survived a month of combat as replacement rifleman in the Ninth Division on the German border, late 1944, before wounds and trench foot led to a hospital in the United Kingdom and a desk job on a B-17 bomber base until the end of the war.

Education: Returned to Yale in early 1946. Gravitated to literature, history, economics, anthropology, and choral singing. Won a fellowship, 1948, for summer study at Oxford. Received a B.A. at Yale, 1949, with high honors in American Studies. Earned a Ph.D. in the same field in 1954 and won the university's dissertation prize.

Career: In 1953, began a lifelong profession as a teacher and scholar in United States history and culture: University of Texas, two years; Stanford University, ten years, earning tenure and an endowed chair; University of Washington, thirty years, five of them as Department Head. Retired in 1995. National Phi Beta Kappa Visiting Scholar to several institutions, 1968–1969. Member, Stanford University Board of Trustees, 1969-1985. Vice President, American Historical Association, 1978–1980. Published and authored works on American cultural and political history, 1870-2000, mainly on the historian Francis Parkman, American advertising, the Gilded Age, the Progressive era, cultural institutions of the Pacific Coast, and GIs in World War II and in postwar universities.

Family: Four children by first marriage (1949–1987): Jonathan Pease, college professor, Portland, Oregon; Catherine Barnhart, college professor, Bellingham, Washington; Martha Tobias, fabric designer, Sedona, Arizona; Emily Daniel, registered nurse and midwife, Montclair, New Jersey. Eight grandchildren. Married Donna McCampbell, 1988, systems analyst in the University of Washington School of Medicine.

YALE NEWS DIGEST

Yale Has Largest Combined Enrollment In History

1500 Naval V-12 Students Register For First Stay At Yale In Uniform

Half Of Those Registered From Other Universities; Under Strict Discipline

Yale Population Reaches All Time High of 7,100

Rev. E. B. O'Brien Yale '31, Named Catholic Chaplain

Over 7,000 Men Will Be Quartered On Campuses, Including Air Corps

President Seymour Issues Statement Of Welcome; University Assembly Tomorrow In Woolsey Hall

A.S.T.P. Activated At Yale June 10; Program Of Studies Starts On July 12

Trainees, All Enlisted Men, Are Quartered In South Berkeley, Calhoun

Simplicity Marks Commencement

262 Are Awarded Degrees In Ceremonies on June 6

University's Expanded Population Includes 1,375 Civilian Students

BEFORE THE VETERANS—THE MILITARY. In this 7/3/43 issue, the *Yale News Digest** reports that of 7,000 students, only 1,375 were civilians. As on many major campuses, the balance were in military training programs such as the Naval V-12 and Army ASTP to train commissioned and non-commissioned officers and specialized enlisted men.

*Most major university newspapers responded to newsprint rationing by reducing size, page count and frequency of their pubilcations, sometimes modifying the name, e.g., the *Yale News Digest* was the wartime replacement for the *Yale Daily News*, and *The Princeton Bulletin* for *The Daily Princetonian* (p. 893), and *Rutgers Cannon* for *The Targum* (p. 894).

"By our victory we gain the opportunity to construct by intelligent and radical reform a more equitable society and a peaceful world."

2. A Service Man Looks at the Peace

Cord Meyer, Jr.
Yale University, '43
Staff aide to Commander Harold Stassen at the 1945 San Fransisco Conference to found the United Nations
Excerpted from the Atlantic Monthly, *Volume 176, Number 3 (September, 1945), pp. 43-48.*

A great many people, since the war began, have tried to define the soldier's point of view and have pretended that what they have said represents the common outlook of the men who fight. There are as many different reactions to the experience of war as there are individuals engaged in it, and the average soldier is as insubstantial a figure of the imagination as the average man.

But there is one reaction common to all who have by chance or volition found themselves one day in the front line of modern battle with the brutally simple choice of killing or being killed. I do not refer to the leaders who decide war is necessary, or to generals who conduct it from a distance, or to staff personnel and service troops, or to the vast majority of those who write about it. I speak of those who, frankly, are the only ones who know what it is and who have no illusions about it, the members of the assault battalions, the front-line fighters.

"It is the men in the front line who must kill . . ."

It is the men in the front line who must kill and then discover on the still-warm body letters and pictures much like those they own themselves, the disturbing proof of a mutual humanity. They live every day with death as their closest companion, and with a growing sense of the inconsequence and futility of human life as they see the best and bravest of their friends destroyed by the casual indifference of a bursting shell or the chance precision of a sniper's bullet.

The first reaction to such an experience is universal and understandable. When one's first battle is done, when the inexhaustibly patient wounded have been cared for and those past caring have been buried, one feels no exaltation in the victory. Rather, there is no one who does not ask himself what beneath the sun could possibly be worth it. How and why has life, which once seemed so full of promise and possibility, come to this misery and degradation? Then the half-truths and shabby explanations of the war which once were adequate are so no more.

It is to men in this position that I address myself to myself as I once was before forgetfulness and the spectacle of a prosperous and uncomprehending country blurred the memory, and to all those almost without hope who today must feel as I did. If the San Francisco Conference is to be viewed in its true perspective, its achievement must be seen through the eyes of these who alone know the true cost of the opportunity presented to the delegates.

"Why and to what purpose . . ."

The comparatively small percentage of our population which daily pays the real price of victory has the undeniable right to ask why and to what purpose. To that quite understandable question, it is remarkable how many spurious and evasive answers have been given and how few honest and adequate ones. The common explanation of the war has been the necessity of defense. We were treacherously attacked at Pearl Harbor, and if we had not fought, we, as a people, should have been conquered and subjugated.

The explanation is good as far as it goes, but it does not go far enough. It neither defines the underlying conditions which made the attack inevitable nor explains how those conditions are to be changed in the future. Its inadequacy is shown by the

---

[*The following is the original author identification that appeared in the September, 1945 issue of the* Atlantic Monthly]

A graduate of Yale, Class of 1943, Cord Meyer, Jr., served as the leader of a machine-gun platoon in the 22nd Marine Regiment during our capture of Eniwetok and Guam. He was severely wounded, was decorated with the Bronze Star, and after his convalescence returned to this country. He was one of the two aides to Commander Stassen at the San Francisco Conference.[4]

fact that the same explanation was given the preceding generation for its sacrifices twenty-five years ago. One wonders if the same admission of a failure to use the opportunity of victory will have to be given the next generation as a reason for its decimation. Defense is not a sufficient explanation of the cause of the war and is an utterly inadequate positive purpose. It envisions a return to a past with which we cannot be satisfied, because it produced the present.

"By our victory . . . to construct . . . a more equitable society and a peaceful world."

To my mind, there is only one purpose in terms of which the war is justifiable and which is at all commensurate with what is daily and irretrievably lost. In the victory of our enemies we should have had absolutely no hope for the future. By our victory we gain the opportunity to construct by intelligent and radical reform a more equitable society and a peaceful world. In the light of that purpose alone do the deaths of our friends have dignity and our own misfortunes significance. If we do not employ the opportunity with honesty and foresight, then our approaching triumph is only an illusion.

Certainly, in view of what has been sacrificed for this chance, we are under the deepest obligation to use it well. But the practical necessity is as strong as the moral one. A third world war, if it occurs, will dwarf in its catastrophic proportions both its predecessors. No country will be secure from the devastation of its cities or from the possibility of invasion from sea and air.

This lesson has been driven home, with the force of actual experience, everywhere except in the Western Hemisphere, where men have been able for the last time to profit from the ever-diminishing advantage of geographical distance. Scientific progress has given us not only the power of unparalleled self-destruction but, for the first time, the technical means by which the world can be ordered as an entity. The Conference was the beginning of an attempt to make the choice between these two alternatives, and men turned toward San Francisco in the hope that the delegates there could save them from themselves.

San Francisco: facing "the central problem of our time"

At San Francisco the representatives of the fifty nations faced what seems to me the central problem of our time.[1] How far they went toward meeting it can be judged only if the problem itself is clearly understood. It is far more complex and profound than it is believed to be by those who find a full explanation of this war in German or Japanese militarism, and who believe that peace will be assured if only we can liquidate the German General Staff or eliminate the Japanese militarists. Those who propose general disarmament are similarly misguided. Mistaking effect for cause, they attempt to cure the symptoms without first diagnosing the disease.

The death of more than sixty million men and women in two wars within a single generation is the concrete result of basic conditions in international society that must be changed if we are not to see the experience repeated on a larger scale. Any brief attempt to define those conditions must necessarily be oversimplified, but the point can and must be made. Our present world is composed of more than fifty separate sovereign and independent nations. Each one of them jealously guards its twofold sovereignty, through which it proclaims itself free from any interference by others in its internal affairs and equally free in its external affairs to make any decisions that it wishes.

* * *

I for one firmly believe that if this war is not to be as abortive as the last, and if peace is to be at all possible, we must change the basic relationship of national states. Let us admit the truth that, throughout history, groups of men residing in separate communities have been able to live continuously at peace together only by subjecting themselves to a sovereign law and by creating a government that can administer, change, and enforce that law.

. . . . [T]he people living within the nations of the world must delegate to a higher government the power to decide those issues that are international.

If I have stated fairly the dilemma with which we are faced, and have indicated the way out with any degree of accuracy, it must be immediately obvious that the United Nations Charter does not pretend to make the changes that appear to be necessary.

The limits of the San Francisco accomplishment: the veto power

The limits of what was accomplished in San Francisco are evident in the veto power. . . .

These voting provisions define the essential nature of the Organization. Decided upon at Yalta and incorporated into the finished Charter at San Fransisco, the veto power is incontrovertible evidence that the major nations will retain intact their complete sovereign independence within the new Organization. . . .

Every other provision of the Charter serves to emphasize the original implications of the voting rule within the Security Council. . . .

* * *

I have been talking as though the creation of genuine government above the nations were an objective and a possibility at San Francisco. Certainly it should have been, but obviously it was not. The conference was called by the four sponsoring powers simply to gain the consent and adherence of the smaller nations to the decisions made at Dunbarton Oaks and Yalta. In this they succeeded: the final Charter was signed by all the fifty nations present. There were improvements and clarifications, but the framework of the International Organization remained unchanged from the original conception of Roosevelt, Churchill, and Stalin.

* * *

No machinery for colonial political freedom

There is no machinery or guarantee in the Charter through which the restless inhabitants of the colonial areas can find their way to freedom. Their future rests, as before, in the hands of their masters, who are not likely to surrender voluntarily so large a source of economic power. . . .

I should add that the position of the United States delegation on this question was much misunderstood by the press and public. Russia, who has no colonies and is hardly satisfied with the status quo in Asia, was able to take an immaculate moral stand for independence and employed to the full the propaganda value of her position.[2] The United States, as so often, had to play the part of mediator in order to assure the success of the Conference, and endeavored to find a compromise acceptable to Russia and the colonial powers. The declaration I have mentioned is the best that could be obtained, though it must be small consolation to those who fought on our side in Asia in the belief that victory would mean freedom.[3]

* * *

"What assurance can be given the mortally wounded . . . ?"

So I return to my beginning. What can be said of the Charter with honesty to those who have fought this war, endured its hardships, and faced its dangers with courage, in the belief that through victory we might find the way to a good society and a peaceful future? What assurance can be given the mortally wounded that the death they are about to die is not merely the pitiful by-product of a colossal struggle for power, but a meaningful sacrifice in a good cause? What consolation for the past and what hope for the future does San Francisco provide?

* * *

There is a bitter lesson here for all who have fought for a victory that they hoped might bring with it deep and necessary change. There are two prerequisites if government on a world level is to become an abiding reality for the many. First, there must be a clear comprehension that the continuation of national egotisms is at the root of our misfortunes. Second, there must be wide agreement on the general principles and values upon which this government on a world level is to be based.

Neither of these two essential conditions exists today. The war has intensified the most extreme national loyalties in many parts of Europe, Asia, and this country. The instrument of war with which we sought to cure the social body has caused it to spread. Experience is not the teacher that we thought she was, and we who are young must learn the old, unhappy truth that men are moved not so much by clear necessity and the gift of reason as by inherited patterns of thought and behavior.

No "unifying supranatural belief today"

Workable constitutions rest upon the consent of the people and grow from a community of belief and the whole ethos of a society. There is no such unifying supranational belief today. The weakness of the Charter is the historically determined result of these conditions. We live in a tragic age where the moral and intellectual resources of our time do not seem adequate to meet either our problems or our obligations.

To my companions of the past, living and dead, to those who look backward over their shoulders to San Francisco in search of the courage of hope as they prepare for the final assault on Japan, I have given what I believe to be an honest answer, but I do not pretend that it is an adequate one. The discrepancy between what we shall win by this war and what we have lost can never be adequately justified.

"No excuse for inaction or despair"

But the realization that the prospect for the immediate future is not a happy one is no excuse for inaction or despair. There is a clear course of action for those of us who are lucky enough to have survived the war and who have fought for something more than military victory. We must support the Charter to the limit as the maximum that is possible today. We must do so not with any spirit of complacency, but with the determination to see it change and grow until its impotent instruments take on flesh and blood to become the strong arms of just government for all men.

Even in this country our opponents will be many. There are, first, the old isolationists, who believe that the United States has an exclusive monopoly on all this is good, and who remain convinced, in spite of all evidence to the contrary, that we in this country can still find a unique salvation while the rest of humanity proceeds toward the purgatory that in their opinion it deserves.

Their more modern friends are the regionalists, who believe that if the United States can no longer find security within its own borders, it can still build the hemisphere into a self-sufficient system that can be defended. Not only is the construction of autonomous regional blocks that must inevitably compete and conflict a good way of promoting another war, but on the lowest level of power politics it is hardly to the advantage of the United States to foster regionalism when the systems of possible opponents are potentially far more powerful than ours.

Finally, there is the unholy alliance of the jingoists and the profiteers. The former, with easy access to certain portions of the press, will attempt to lay the emotional basis for the next war by flattering every ignorant prejudice and making every possible appeal to mass hysteria, while the latter will believe war worthwhile if there is promise of sufficient monetary return on the investment in human life. They both see another war as a necessary prelude to the dawning of the American century and the unrestrained expansion of American power. These will support the Charter as a harmless sop to be thrown to present public opinion while they go about the serious business of preparing the country for the next war.

"The Charter . . . is all that we shall have won from the war"

For those of us who have fought, not for power, but because we believe in the possibility of peace, the Charter is more than a series of harmless platitudes. Weak and inadequate as it stands today, it is all that we shall have won from the war. By our effort, it may yet become the symbol and instrument of a just order among men. No matter how remote our chances or how distant our success, we have in simple honesty no alternative but the attempt to make it that. As I have suggested, it is possible that we shall fail, and that the death agony of nationalism will be prolonged beyond our lifetime. But eventually, if the civilization of the West is not to disintegrate completely, others who believe as we do will succeed. If this hope is naïve, then it is naïve to hope.

Cord Meyer was an articulate veteran who championed a just and enduring peace. He was President of the United World Federalists, 1947-49, and spoke widely on U.S. campuses after the war. (See Jonas, p. 764.) He joined the CIA in 1951 where he was put in charge of what he described as the "limited program of covert assistance to the NSA leadership for their international activities" (p. 103, Facing Reality*). See "Covert Funding of NSA International Programs," p 565.*

EDITOR'S END NOTES

[1] See Douglass Hunt,University of North Carolina, on the Conference of Southern Students, representing 54 colleges in thirteen states, which sent two observers to the San Francisco Conference, p. 963.

[2] See Allard K. Lowenstein, 1950 International Student Conference Stockholm address, p. 562.

[3] In a part of this article not reproduced here Meyer writes: "Some provision had to be made for the vast number of colonial subjects. That provision takes the form of a mere declaration by the colonial powers that they will further the 'free institutions' of their colonial people."

[4] Harold Stassen, former governor of Minnesota (1939-43), became President of the University of Pennsylvania in 1948 and was a member of the NSA National Advisory Council from 1951 to 1959 (see Stassen, p. 719).

CORD MEYER, JR.

Early years and education: Born November 10, 1920 in New York City. Attended St. Paul's School, Concord, New Hampshire. Yale University, BA, Summa Cum Laude, 1943. Harvard University, Society of Fellows, 1946-47 and 1949-51.

Military service: US. Marine Corps, 1942-45. Retired with rank of Captain after being severely wounded at Guam. Bronze Star, Purple Heart, Presidential Unit Citation.

Government Service: Central Intelligence Agency, 1951-77: Assistant Deputy Director for Plans, 1967-73; Chief of Station, London, 1973-76; three times awarded the Distinguished Intelligence Medal; Trailblazer Award, 1997.

Private Sector: Special Assistant to Harold Stassen as member of U.S. Delegation to Founding Conference of U.N., San Francisco, April-June 1945. Active in formative years of American Veterans Committee. President, United World Federalists, 1947-49. National Weekly Syndicated Columnist 1978-1998. Lecturer, Georgetown University, 1982-88.

Publications: "Waves of Darkness," O. Henry Prize story, *Atlantic Monthly,* 1946. *Peace or Anarchy,* Little, Brown, 1947. *Facing Reality,* Harper and Row, 1980.

Family: Married to Mary Pinchot, widowed, and remarried to Starke Meyer. Three children and one stepchild. Twin brother, Quentin, killed in World War II. Died March 13, 2001.

PICTURE CREDITS. *Then:* c. 1942. *Now:* c. 1990 (Both, Starke Meyer).

ADVOCATE FOR PEACE & WORLD GOVERNMENT

Cord Meyer traveled extensively, addressing students on the threat of global warfare and the need for a stronger United Nations. At the same time he did not favor immediate disarmanent as "under present conditions [it] would be tantamount to rational suicide," as reported by the *Buffalo Bee.* The *Princetonian* rated him as "one of today's foremost young Americans."

From the top: *The Johns Hopkins News-Letter,* 12/3/48; Smith College *SCAN,* 3/2/48; *Buffalo Bee,* U. of Buffalo, 10/24/47; *Daily Princetonian,* 12/4/47.

PRICE FIVE CENTS

Cord Meyer To Discuss Choice Of Law Or War Monday In Levering

VOL. XLII. NO. 29

WORLD FEDERALIST PRESIDENT TO LECTURE, LEAD DISCUSSIONS

Friday, October 24, 1947

Cord Meyer Suggests Fear Basic In U.S., Russian Dispute

C. Meyer Asserts That U. N. Is Not An Effective Means Of Preventing Wars But Exists As A League Of Heavily Armed States

At five o'clock Sunday last, a group of citizens interested in the ...ited World Federalist movement ...thered in the Mary Seaton Room ... Kleinhans Music Hall to hear ... address by the organization's ...tional president, Mr. Cord Meyer ...

Among the guests seated at the ...eakers table was David Sprague, ...airman of the University Chap...r of the U. W. F. and Mr. Foster ...rmelee, Chairman of the Niag...a Frontier chapter of U. W. F., ...der whose auspices Mr. Meyer ...oke.

Mr. Meyer initiated his disgres...on by outlining the possible ef...ct of a global war in the near ...ture and pointed out the effects ... radioactive and biochemical dis...veries in modern warfare, with ...e additional advancements in long ...nge bombers and V-2 develop...ent. The speaker suggested that ...though the United States holds ... possible monopoly in modern des...uctive agents, within the near ...ture other nations will no doubt ...ave duplicated them or developed ...ewer methods. Since the only re-

TABLE TALK

...TONIAN

...RSDAY, DECEMBER 4, 1947 — PRICE 5c

Meyer, World Federalists' President, To Speak in Alexander Hall Tonight

Dean Godolphin, Prof. Ebenstein Support Petition Advocating Federation of World

The following statements were made yesterday by members of the Princeton faculty concerning the Princeton Petition which will be sent to the President, and to congressmen in both the federal and state legislatures. The petition calls for the strengthening of the U. N. into a world government with power adequate "to protect mankind against the mass annihilation of war."

"I am thoroughly in accord with the Princeton Petition for Peace which has been issued to mark World Unity Day Sunday, December 7. The spirit which animates this call to action seems to me to be worthy of the whole-hearted support of every citizen concerned with our future.

FRANCIS R. B. GODOLPHIN
Dean of the College

Cord Meyer
To Present Plan for Peace

AVC/Potentate and Former Aide To Stassen Will Blueprint Revamped UN at 8:30

By THOMAS P. WOLF '48

Cord Meyer Jr., national president of the United World Federalists, the principal American proponents of world government, will speak at an open meeting in Alexander Hall at 8:30 tonight.

The speech this evening is being sponsored by the same local groups which are planning to obtain some 6,000 signatures during the coming week for a petition to President Truman advocating world peace by means of world government. The World Federalists are also sponsoring the celebration of this Sunday as World Unity Day.

Mr. Meyer, whose activities rate him as one of today's foremost young Americans, was graduated from Yale in 1943 as a member of Phi Beta

A vibrant history of seminal contributions to America

3. The American Veterans Committee

Bernard Bellush

City College of New York and Columbia University
AVC Member 1944, Member AVC National Board

Throughout American history, each major war has been followed by the birth of a primarily self-serving veterans organization. They generally were extremely nationalistic, if not isolationist, in foreign policy and sought, in the process, to secure land, financial or other benefits for these veterans, even if it was detrimental to the rest of the nation. With the passage of time, they became major factors in local and national politics, each using the "soldier vote" to win measures, both good and bad, from forgetful civilian publics and administrations. World War II, however, turned out to be different on a number of scores.

Founded in 1943 for the "new veteran"

In 1943, in the midst of this worldwide conflict, three GIs and two officers rejected the old-line, tradition-bound veteran's organizations and founded the American Veterans Committee (AVC). They felt that the chasm between generations within the old veteran's organizations was too great to be bridged and that their policies and preoccupations did not respond to the hopes, needs, and aims of the new veteran. These founders of AVC wanted to keep the potential influence of these new veteran leaders on the side of "a more democratic and prosperous America and a more stable world." They wanted to break with these nationalistic organizations, feeling that only a movement like AVC could speak for those new veterans who were committed to an international organization of nations to keep the postwar peace, as well as to an international organization for veterans worldwide.[1]

The slogan these founders adopted, "Citizens First, Veterans Second," immediately indicated their sharp break with traditional veteran's organizations. AVC and its interim president, tall, dignified Charles (Chuck) Bolté, who had lost a leg while fighting with the British at El Alamein, quickly forced themselves upon the national consciousness by the breadth and vigor of their convictions and the originality of their goals, as expressed through their news releases and the organization's Statement of Intentions. They had a keen sense of what was the American soldier's greatest ambition—to become a working civilian, successfully integrated into a nonmilitary society.

Hundreds of college campus chapters formed, new leaders join

AVC grew rapidly from a membership of 900 in 1944 to over 20,000 by the end of the war, less than a year later. Each time there was a news story about it in the civilian or military newspapers, inquiries and memberships poured into its New York office. By February 1946, some 2,500 new members were streaming into the organization weekly. Moreover, 133 regional chapters were spread across the country and active college and university chapters were blossoming on hundreds of campuses everywhere. By the summer of 1946, over 60,000 veterans had joined. And still, the new members rolled in.

Like other GIs around the world, I first read about, and joined, AVC shortly after I had landed on Omaha Beach on D-day, in 1944. With the passing weeks and months, this organization attracted many who would become noted political, social, labor, and intellectual leaders of our nation, including Bill Mauldin; Franklin D. Roosevelt, Jr.; Oren Root, Jr.; Harold Stassen; Will Rogers, Jr.; Harris Wofford, Jr.; Melvyn Douglas; Ralph Bellamy; Thornton Wilder; Irving Howe; Burgess Meredith; Orville Freeman; Richard Bolling; Franklin H. Williams; Gus Tyler; Michael Straight; Cord Meyer; Gil Harrison; Meyer Bernstein; and even a youthful actor named Ronald Reagan. Reagan eventually discovered, however, that he was in the wrong pew.

In the meantime, a grateful Congress had, unknowingly, insured a number of revolutionary changes in American society, particularly through higher education. With its passage of the GI Bill of Rights, it soon obliged colleges and universities to open wide their doors to hundreds of thousands of returning veterans, by providing them with a minimum living subsistence and payment of their college tuition fees. Before the war, only a small minority of high school graduates went on to college (primarily white Anglo-Saxon Protestants of the middle and upper classes). Within months after the war's end, veterans from every economic, social, religious, and ethnic group in the nation were streaming onto campuses everywhere. And this insured educational, economic and political revolutions of great magnitude.

Returning veterans challenge minority quota systems

Like Dartmouth College in New Hampshire, for example, most private colleges had maintained rigid quota systems for the admission of students throughout the prewar years. This policy fell harshly upon blacks, Jews, Native Americans, and other racial and religious minorities. With increasing pressure from an aroused public, educated by the war against Nazism, Fascism, and Hitler's Aryan theories, it became unpopular, unwelcome, and politically indefensible for colleges and universities to maintain quota systems against minorities in the postwar years. These restrictive collegiate walls came tumbling down amid tidal waves of returning veterans, who swamped almost every campus in the nation.

By July 1, 1946, over 600,000 returning veterans—who were generally far more mature and far more serious in their commitment to college work than the average entering freshman just out of high school—had marched onto campuses, converting once quiet colleges into centers of active engagement. In classrooms where the professor, in particular, adhered to the Socratic method, veterans tended to insure heated discussion and debate and challenged the beliefs and opinions of other students, including the instructor. These veterans turned students also ensured a healthy ferment in student governments, radically changing their patterns and level of debate. Great numbers of these new student government leaders went on, after graduation, to become local, state, and national legislators. This was an exciting time to be on campus.

Typical of campus newspapers reporting some of these dramatic changes was a September 1946 issue of the City College of New York's *Campus.* Its front-page headline shouted, "Enrollment Hits All Time High." One result was a total revamping of its Student Life Department. That same month, the University of North Carolina *Tar Heel* headline proclaimed that its "Campus Resembles Wartime Boom Town." Dartmouth College speedily put up prefabricated housing for veterans with families, calling that area Sachem Village. And those houses are standing to this day, although moved to a new site off-campus.

Barriers to Jewish students eroded

In the process, Dartmouth College, headed by a new, more worldly president, like so many other institutions of higher learning not only dropped its prewar quota system for students but also, during the next few years, opened its doors wide to new young instructors with Ph.D.s from other Ivy League institutions. Hiring new staff was absolutely necessary in order to meet the needs of a burgeoning and changing student body. As a result, for example, some graduates from the City Colleges of New York, often called "the proletarian Harvard"—Queens, Brooklyn, Hunter, or City—who had gone on to get their Ph.D.s from Columbia, Yale, Harvard, Princeton, and other universities, soon were teaching at Dartmouth. And among them was a disproportionate number of instructors from Jewish, working-class families. Within one generation they had made a historic leap up the ladder of mobility.

Some Dartmouth College alumni and visiting research scholars recall a faculty with one known Jewish instructor in the math department, and another, less open, Jewish faculty member in economics. That situation also underwent revolutionary changes for, within two decades after the war, Jewish faculty members were becoming chairpersons of departments, deans of divisions, the provost, and, eventually, president of the institution. Other minorities were making similar inroads elsewhere.[2]

AVC focuses on housing shortages, GI Bill of Rights flaws

By May 1, 1946, only three months after veterans started streaming onto campuses, AVC had active chapters on fifty-six of them, with members at over fifty other universities seeking charters. The work of the college chapters became twofold: locally, they dealt with the extremely serious housing shortage and the inadequacies of the GI Bill of Rights; nationally, they focused on congressional and international issues. For some four years following the end of the war, this generation of student veterans proved to be one of the more fertile fields for the growth of AVC and for the development of leaders for the organization and for the nation.

AVC quickly surpassed all other campus veteran organizations in membership and activities. The Cornell University chapter received plaudits from university officials for its work in helping the Office of Price Administration (OPA) maintain ceilings on local housing rentals. The president of Columbia University congratulated the campus AVC for its work on a variety of local problems and for its support of the United Nations Relief and Rehabilitation Administration (UNRRA). The Washington State College chapter initiated a successful tutoring program for all veteran students, in cooperation with professors and graduate teaching assistants.

The AVC chapter at the University of Texas at Austin led the campaign for an increase in subsistence allowances under the GI Bill of Rights and removal of restrictions on the earning power of a veteran while in college. At a meeting on the same campus of the National Association for the Advancement of Colored People (NAACP), some AVCers came to hear a professor from a neighboring black university point out: "There are glaring differences in facilities offered for white students and those for Negro students in Texas. This is apparently true for lower education, but it is even more evident in higher education." AVC members knew there was much work to be done and were ready to join the struggle for full equality and integration in education.

Strong support for world government and UN relief

Because of their international commitments, there was spontaneous support among AVC campus chapters for a system of world government and UNRRA. Many of the college chapters followed Columbia's lead in supporting UNRRA by making a can of food a member's admission ticket to chapter meetings. Swarthmore College's AVC chapter ran a postcard booth outside the college dining hall for two days as part of its campaign, and that of the national organization, to "Save OPA" [Office of Price Administration]. About five hundred students responded and sent postcards to members of Congress and the White House. On the campus at Boulder, Colorado, AVCers urged students to write Congress in support of international control of atomic energy and of atomic weapons.

At the Constitutional Convention of AVC, held in Des Moines, Iowa, in mid-June 1946, some 850 delegates, including fifty women veterans and scores from campus chapters, were present. Without interruption for seventy-two hours, they discussed, debated, and voted upon an endless set of proposed resolutions. By the time these bleary-eyed delegates left for their homes, they had produced a constitution, a wide-ranging, innovative platform, and elected officers for the next year.

AVC advanced wide-ranging problem-solving agenda

Unlike other veterans' organizations, these serious, no-nonsense delegates did not even take time off to go to local bars. They sought to solve almost every major problem in the nation and the world. In the process, they proved to be far in advance of their times. They urged, for example, increased benefits under the GI Bill of Rights, extension of price controls, a commission to curtail discrimination in the workplace, abolition of poll taxes (which greatly restricted Negro voting in the South), congressional enactment of comprehensive national health insurance for all, channeling of building materials into low-cost housing and early enactment of a bill to dramatically ease the housing crisis confronting the nation.

They supported the principle of collective bargaining in the workplace and opposed the use of armed forces in labor disputes as proposed by President Harry S. Truman, and they favored full employment with a guaranteed annual minimum wage and extension of federal unemployment compensation and social security. They favored the abolition of all racial discriminatory laws and governmental action to safeguard civil liberties. And, to the dismay of old-line veterans' organizations, they voted against the adoption of a veteran's bonus by national or state governments.

As veterans, these delegates knew that without world peace and understanding, they could not achieve their domestic goals. Therefore, they supported a strong United Nations Organization and believed in the development of world government through the UN. They supported measures such as UN control of atomic energy and all weapons of mass destruction, opposed fascist governments like that of Spain, supported the endeavors of colonial peoples for independence, upheld entry into Palestine for displaced Jews, backed universal lowering of immigration barriers to all displaced persons, and urged the implementation of extensive famine relief measures abroad with an immediate restoration of food rationing at home.

Standing up for Japanese American rights

AVC recognized, far in advance of most other organizations and institutions in the nation, the terrible injustices our nation had inflicted upon Japanese Americans immediately after the Pearl Harbor attack. Thus, convention delegates urged that citizenship be given to all eligible Japanese Americans, along with indemnification for losses sustained by reason of their arbitrary evacuation from the West Coast in the spring of 1942, and that laws of a discriminatory nature against Japanese Americans be abolished.

Finally, in response to an invitation from President Truman, the AVC Convention sent a corps of its members to the San Francisco Conference of the UN to act as advisers to the American delegation.[3] A group also went to the White House to urge the president to pressure Congress to adopt much needed housing legislation. As a veteran of World War I and a developing liberal on the domestic scene, Truman welcomed them warmly. But in spite of his personal wishes, he was unsuccessful in pushing through the Congress any meaningful housing reform.

Steve Lowell and Bernard Bellush, Omaha Beach, France, winter 1944-45.

The Cold War spawns an internal AVC "civil war"

Seeking to dominate, or unduly influence, the world about them, a Cold War had erupted between the Soviet Union and the United States. Unfortunately, this conflict came to AVC with a vengeance, clouding its bright future. Within months after the Constitutional Convention, AVC became increasingly engaged in a full-blown civil war.

In some ways, this was the beginning of the end for a number of campus chapters and for many of its members. They tired of what often became an unending, internecine conflict at too many chapter meetings. Campus members, one must recall, were full-time students, who often labored at outside jobs in order to defray normal living expenses. And when they attended meetings or participated in AVC activities on or off campus, they were sacrificing what little time they could spare from family or academic responsibilities.

Failing to make successful inroads into the American Legion, as part of their popular front policy, American Communist leadership then decided to send their most seasoned and knowledgeable corps of veteran followers into growing AVC chapters around the country. They would bore from within in order to gain control of individual chapters and then the national organization. If successful, they planned to use AVC to support Soviet foreign policy and oppose Washington's endorsement of the North Atlantic Treaty Organization and the Marshall Plan.[4]

Communist strategy inspires three caucuses

These sophisticated and experienced communists and their fellow travelers, who were also masters of parliamentary procedure, would delay meetings until a late hour, by which time tired liberals would leave. At that moment, these communists would then push through their resolutions and elect their delegates to state and national conventions. Through these methods and their consistent participation as activist leaders, they gained considerable control within this basically liberal organization. Before long, they came uncomfortably close to taking over the national organization. However, thanks largely to labor leader Gus Tyler, the guru of the anticommunist faction, this did not occur.[5]

Those members who remained to carry on this internal strife divided into two, and then three caucuses—the Progressive caucus, of communists, fellow travelers and those independents who were willing to continue to work with them; the Independent Progressive caucus, composed of those opposed to a communist takeover, which included almost everyone from independent, anticommunist liberals and supporters of organized labor to Norman Thomas socialists; and the Build AVC caucus, which largely adopted a policy of "a plague on both your houses."

Conflict debilitating, some Communists expelled

Unfortunately, too much of the invaluable and scarce energies of AVC members and leaders were devoted to this debilitating conflict. Finally, by 1948, the majority anticommunist caucus decided that the time had come to push through a resolution stating: "We reject the notion that the Communist Party possesses the key to the magic formula whereby the betterment of human welfare can be achieved. We spurn the insincere cooperation of a minority group unquestioningly obeying leaders whose objectives, including a totalitarian dictatorship of the extreme left, are irreconcilable with our own." The next logical step was the adoption of a policy by the national board stating that communist members would not be accepted into AVC and that those already in the organization would have to be expelled.

During the months that followed, a small, symbolic number of alleged communists were expelled by the national organization. By the mid-1950s, other leaders of the Progressive caucus had simply left the organization when they realized they could no longer gain control.

The wave of veterans moves on to help build America

By this time as well, the overwhelming bulk of student veterans who had streamed onto the campus immediately after the war had graduated and were making their way into the business and professional worlds. They were no longer college students or members of campus chapters. All that was now part of a vibrant history, which had made seminal contributions to American education and would now do likewise toward creating "a more democratic and prosperous America."

Bernard Bellush marching in July 4, 2001, parade in Brownsville, VT, wearing his original Army jacket.

Bernard Bellush is Professor Emeritus of American History at City College. He earned a Master of Arts degree (1942) and a Ph.D. (1951) at Columbia University. His books include Franklin D. Roosevelt as Governor of New York; Union Power and New York, *written with his wife, Jewel Bellush;* The Failure of the NRA, *and* He Walked Alone: A Biography of John G. Winant. *He is a contributing editor of the newspaper* The Forward. *Bernard has received the Walter P. Reuther Award, served as Fulbright Professor at the University of Utrecht in the Netherlands, and was named Professor of the Year at CCNY (1965). He and his wife, Jewel, live in Valhalla, New York. They have two daughters, Geraldine and Deborah.* *(See Jewel Bellush, p. 73.)*

PICTURE CREDITS: *Then:* c. 1941. CCNY *Microcosm* (CCNY Archives). *Now: Windsor Chronicle, 7/12/2001* (Author).

END NOTES

[1] See Cord Meyer, "A Serviceman Looks at the Peace," p. 703.

[2] See Alfred McClung Lee, *Fraternities without Brotherhood*, p. 745.

[3] See Meyer, p. 703, Hunt, p. 963, Proctor, p. 968, Jonas, p. 763.

[4] *Editor's note:* See Joseph Lash (p. 42), whose story of a similar conflict within the American Student Union before World War II was repeated within the AVC and other U.S. student organizations after the war.

[5] *Editor's note:* See Kirchner, p. 76, for the story of how Catholic delegates to the World Student Congress in 1946 were taught how to deal with these tactics.

AVC Grew Rapidly on U.S. Campuses after War's End

The AVC Bulletin

AMERICAN VETERANS COMMITTEE, INC.

Vol. 1 No. 11 • To achieve a more democratic and prosperous America and a more stable world • July 15, 1946

Dallas Members Support Fellow Vet

AVC Fights Hard for Price Control Return

Taft Attempt to Smear AVC in Senate Speech Balked by Barkley

WASHINGTON.—Dramatic proof of the effectiveness of AVC's all-out drive to save price control came on the Senate floor, Tuesday, July 9, when Senator Robert Taft (R., O.) spent almost a half-hour analyzing a letter written by Alex Efthim, chairman of the AVC Price Control Fight Committee, briefing chapters on techniques to be used in opposing Taft and other "kill OPA" Congressmen.

Senator Taft, who has been sharply attacked by AVC for his opposition to OPA, attempted to smear AVC, but was called up short by Majority Leader Alben Barkley, who said that AVC . . . has as much right to appear before committees of Congress and to make its views known as any other group of American citizens.

"In view of the propaganda which has been disseminated on both sides of the question by all kinds of organizations, it seems to me . . . unfair to pick out one veterans' organization and denounce it because it has sought

VFW Officer Brands AVC 'Red Front'

National Vice Commander of the Veterans of Foreign Wars

U. of North Carolina *Daily Tar Heel* 12/5/46

AVC Disowns Principles Of Fascist, Red Parties

Local Chapter Votes Not to Accept Men Who Are Members of Communist Movements

In a lengthy special session Tuesday night, 65 members of the local AVC chapter reconsidered and passed the AVC National Planning Committee's resolutions disowning the principles of, and membership in fascist organzations, and the Communist Party.

The main objection to the resolution condemning Communism as sent down from New York as given by several AVC members was that it contained too much superfluous and contradictory material. They added that they agreed with the principle of the resolution, but would rather approve of one drawn up in a "more logical manner." After much debate and two defeated tabling motions, the resolution was finally passed by a close vote.

Text of Resolution

The resolution said in part "as veterans who believe firmly in the democratic ideals which we have endorsed, ... ment of human welfare can be achieved. We spurn the insincere cooperation of a minority group unquestioningly obeying leaders whose objectives, including a totalitarian dictatorship of the extreme left, are irreconcilable with our own."

Following the adoption of the national resolution, a bill was brought up stating simply that as the aims of AVC and the Communist Party are irreconcilable, all members of the Communist Party will not be accepted as AVC members and any in would have to resign. This resolution was approved by a large majority.

Taking up the first part of the meeting, the resolution on fascism was

10 QUESTIONS and ANSWERS ON AVC

1. *Why Should I Join AVC?*

You don't like the typical "veterans" organization. You're a civilian or want to be one and you don't care for funny hats or going through ceremonial hocus-pocus at a weekly meeting of the local veterans post. But . . . *you know that 12,000,000 men and women who were in uniform have tremendous potential influence.*

AVC recuiting brochure, c. 1946

STUDENT LIFE

VOLUME 71 WASHINGTON UNIVERSITY, ST. LOUIS, THURSDAY, JANUARY 9, 1947 NUMBER 12

A.V.C. HEAD TO SPEAK HERE

450 Delegates Favor W. U. Athletic Policy

World Peace Possible, Says Compton After UNESCO Conference

An opportunity to achieve per-

CHARLES BOLTE

Charles Bolte Will Discuss Problems Of Student Veteran

Charles G. Bolte, organizer and national chairman of the American Veterans' Committee, will address all Washington U. students and members of the AVC Monday, January 13 in Brown Hall at 1:30 p.m. The title of his speech has not been announced, but Herb Soule, chairman of the Washington U. AVC chapter has announced that the current problems of the student veterans will probably be discussed.

AVC Bulletin September 1, 1946

647 Chapters Are Now on AVC Roster

With chapters recruiting in Hawaii, the Virgin Islands, Mexico, Japan, Germany, Bulgaria and forty-six states of the Union, there is scarcely a veteran or serviceman or woman on the face of the globe who cannot be reached directly by AVC.

Chapters now total 647, almost double the number for last March. Among the latest to have their charters approved by the National Planning Committee are Corpus Christi No. 1, Texas; Binghamton No. 1, N. Y.; Haverhill No. 1, Mass., and Redlands No. 1, Calif.

Although organizational growth is still concentrated chiefly around large population areas, AVC has made considerable progress in small towns and rural areas. Almost thirty new chapters have sprung up in the South.

Fifty College Chapters

Of the 631 active chapters in the continental U. S., approximately fifty function on college and university campuses, ten are professional groups such as New York's Musicians' and Theatre Chapters, and three are on military posts.

Among the states, chapter representation is somewhat proportionate to population. New York, the most populous state, leads with 151 chapters, 124 of which are in Greater New York City. California boasts 79, Illinois 43, Pennsylvania 41, New Jersey, Massachusetts and Michigan, 40, 36, and 30, respectively. The two states without a single AVC office are Vermont and Nevada.

Chapters operate in Hoechst, Berlin, Munich, Sofia, Bulgaria, Irumagawa and Tokyo, Japan; and Ascom City and Coseoul, Korea. Territorially, there are four in Hawaii and one in St. Thomas, Virgin Islands.

American veterans enrolled at the University of Mexico in Mexico City have formed AVC's first civilian chapter on foreign soil.

New Chapters

CALIFORNIA

Berkeley Chapter No. 2 (Ch. 563): Gilbert Morell, Chrmn., 1007-C Ninth St., Berkeley 2, Calif. **Modesto Chapter (Ch. 564):** Joseph Sardo, Chrmn., P. O. Box 451, Modesto, Calif. **Redlands Chapter (Ch. 616):** Kristo Sugich, Chrmn., 321 Normandie Village, Redlands, Calif. **San Francisco Area Coun-**

"THE BREADTH AND VIGOR OF ITS CONVICTIONS . . . forced itself on the national consciousness," the *New York Herald Tribune* wrote of the AVC in a review of AVC President Charles Bolte's book, *The New Veteran.* Many WWII veterans found that the two major old line veterans organizations, the American Legion (which led the fight for the GI Bill) and the Veterans of Foreign Wars, dating from the 1918 World War I and the Spanish War of 1889, respectively, presented a chasm between generations "too great to be bridged."

TEMPLE UNIVERSITY NEWS October 24, 1947

AVC Grows in Prominence In Short Time on Campus

LA SALLE COLLEGIAN October 1946

AMERICAN VETERANS COMMITTEE

La Salle Needs Veteran Society

Since the close of World War II, we have seen a rapid increase in Veteran's Organizations. Many of these groups are sincerely interested in the problems of the ex-"G.I.", and their programs are honestly constructive. The usual social type of organization is also very popular. It has been suggested by many members of the student body that La Salle should have a veteran's society wherein the two ideas of sociological and social could be combined. Perhaps our school should be represented in inter-collegiate veteran circles.

Exclusive Veteran Society Would Fail

The formation of a veteran's organization is not a new idea at this school, for, during the last spring term, such an endeavor was undertaken and failed. It failed because it was exclusive by name and nature. Exclusive societies have no place on this campus. We are aware of the fact that certain clubs already on the campus are exclusive, becuse their very nature does not invite universal participation in their respective programs. These clubs do not, however, preclude intentionally any member of the school from their membership. The afore-mentioned veteran society did; it limited its membership, at first, to those veterans who were members of the school before entering the service. Shortly after its birth the post extended the privilege of membership to all veterans. Yet something was still lacking, for sixty members of the college, the non-veterans, were excluded from any activities that this club sponsored. True, it was a veteran's club, so what right did the non-veterans have to demand membership to the organization? But what right did anyone have to form an exclusive soceity in this school?

AVC Admits All Students

On almost every campus in the country, veterans and non-veterans are binding themselves together in collegiate posts of the American Veteran Committee. The success of the AVC on the college level has been responsible to its liberal membership policy. Guided by its motto, "Citizens first, veterans second", the AVC has opened its doors to all students who are interested in building a better post-war America.

The AVC is the one soicety that combines the sociological and social ideas, and it is the only society of the veteran type that has a place in college life. In colleges it has placed but one restriction on its non-veteran members; they are given no vote. And such a restriction is justified, for most of the problems that the AVC ertends its assistance are of interest to veterans alone. The social aspects of the organization would be open to all members of the school.

La Salle Should Have AVC Chapter

Yes, such a society would be desirable on this campus. It would give La Salle a voice in inter-collegiate veteran activities and a society in which every member of the student body could participate.

Different times, different dreams

4. Aftermath of the Veterans' Generation

Ralph Lee Smith
Swarthmore College, '51
NSA Public Relations Director, 1949–50

The ethos of the veterans generation was shaped by childhood memories of the Depression, of wonderfully brave parents who somehow got themselves and their children through it, and of personal participation in a great war before we were 20.

As early as 1950, I think that things were struggling to be born in America that were not contemplated in the philosophy and ethos of the GI Bill/veterans' generation that produced NSA. For the most part, these things did not initially manifest themselves prominently on college campuses, and therefore did not contribute directly to the decline of interest in NSA. By the end of the decade, however, they were poised to affect everything, everywhere.

After college, the veterans' generation set about to realize its dreams—the kinds of dreams that children of depression and war would naturally dream. They included: a good, secure job; a nice home; a car; family financial safety; a portfolio of stocks and insurance that guaranteed our wives' security for life without working if they should outlive us; and opportunity for our children.

Many of our kids, it seems, were not thrilled.

Actually, we didn't have to wait for our kids to find young people who saw little about it to love. A young person named Ellen Sander, who was a few years younger than we, attended high school in the warm, cozy 1950s that our early professional labors created. The first sentence of her wonderful personal memoir, *Trips: Rock Life in the Sixties*, reads, "Coming of age in the Fifties was pure pain." Pure pain? How could an ex-GI from a poor Depression family, and with a Purple Heart, take it seriously? How could people of the kind that created NSA understand it?

NSA—A Bridge to the New Scene

For me, NSA actually served as a bridge to the evolving scene. Music was the path. Three kinds of music were related to the changing times. The Beats loved jazz. Teenagers secretly listened behind the closed doors of their rooms to the new music called rock. An array of other persons, including some members of the veterans' generation, participated in the experience that became the urban folk revival.

My interests took me down this latter road, and NSA and the *Volendam* played a role. Robin Roberts, the lovely folk singer of the early folk revival, was seriously considered for NSA national office at the 1948 Congress. Union songs, Spanish Civil War songs, and other 1930s and 40s folk song favorites were sung at impromptu sessions at the congresses. Left-wingers treated us to such funny stuff as "Pity the Downtrodden Landlord" and "God Bless Free Enterprise," while others of us never tired of Burl Ives and "The Blue-Tailed Fly."

The professional folk singer Shep Ginandes was on either the *Kota Inten* or the *Volendam*—I don't remember which. "He does it for money!" someone whispered to me. I was impressed—maybe awed is the right word!

In June 1951, after debarking from the *Volendam*, I represented the student division of United World Federalists at the World Student Federalist Congress in Copenhagen. I ended up in Paris, and in the evenings went to Gordon Heath's folksinging cabaret near St. German des Pres. Gordon was a black American émigré with a wonderful voice. After about a week of it, I was hooked.[1]

Musicians of the folk revival voice a new ethos

In the later 1950s, I moved to Greenwich Village. Persons I met included Allan Block, a World War II veteran who had been a student at the University of Wisconsin just before the war. However, his feelings and interests lay with the emerging new ethos. He arrived in Greenwich Village, slept on Pete Seeger's floor until he could get an apartment, and set himself up as a sandalmaker in a storefront on West 4th Street. His sandal shop became one of the gathering places for musicians of the folk revival.

When a skinny kid named Bob Dylan showed up in the folksinging jams in the sandal shop, Allan taught him some guitar chords. Did you know that, in addition to giving NSA a mighty boost, the University of Wisconsin student body produced someone who gave Bob Dylan a boost on his way to his Grammys and his Kennedy Center honors?

In the Village, I met the Kentucky folk singer Jean Ritchie and became familiar with the instrument she played, the Appalachian dulcimer. I loved this instrument, bought one for thirty dollars, and played it with the old-timey string bands in the Village during the 1960s, while making a living as a freelance writer in consumer matters and public affairs.[2]

The veterans create room for new dreams

I believe that members of the veterans' generation who were most able to relate to the emerging new ethos were those who were fortunate enough to have been raised in families that were free from want during the Depression. Allan's family did not suffer, and neither did mine.

I think that, as soon as young people came along who did not have a personal memory of the Depression or of participation in war and who had the safety margin that the veterans' generation had already created by the 1950s, the thing happened that was bound to happen. *The counterculture was created by the achievement by an increasing number of families of the first two of the Four Freedoms—Freedom from Want and Freedom from Fear.*

As different as the 1940s, 1950s, and 1960s were from each other, they shared something important. Young people in each of the decades had dreams, however different the dreams may have been, and they acted to bring them about. The various dreams were all directed toward fostering change along the frontiers of American society and culture. In time, the changes that each generation sought, including greater recognition of student rights, progress in the struggle against racial discrimination, acceptance of greater freedom of choice in personal living, rediscovery of neglected musical forms, and creation of new kinds of music—moved from the frontiers of society to the mainstream.

Ralph Lee Smith is Account Executive for the Connection Newspapers of Northern Virginia and Maryland. He is also a historian of, and a performer on, the Appalachian dulcimer. A description of Ralph's folk-singing days in Greenwich Village appears in his book, When Everything Was New: Folk Songs of Greenwich Village in the 1950's and 1960's, *published by Mel Bay Music Publishers in 2005. (See p. 900 for extended biography).*

PICTURE CREDITS: *Then:* c. 1950 (Author); *Now:* 1993 (Brunner Studio, Berea, KY. Author)

END NOTES

[1] *Editor's note:* Seymour Reisen (see p. 781) writes, "I, too, spent evenings at Gordon Heath's cabaret, L'Abbaye, listening to him and his partner Lee Payant sing. Did so in 1952 while on military furlough, and again in subsequent years."

[2] In the 1970s, I became increasingly interested in the dulcimer's history and made a number of field trips to the southern Appalachians in search of dulcimer lore and folk music history. This eventually resulted in four books, *The Story of the Dulcimer, Appalachian Dulcimer Traditions, Songs and Tunes of the Wilderness Road,* and *Folk Songs of Old Kentucky.*

A New Society Was Being Created

Editor's note: Following are excerpts from When Dreams Came True: The GI Bill and the Making of Modern America *by Michael J. Bennett (Washington: Brassey's, 1996). In 336 pages, Bennett captures the origins and the sweep of the GI Bill and its empowerment of the veteran generation. (See also caption on GI Bill, page 697)*

"The mature student body which filled our colleges in 1946 and 1947 was a delight to all who were then teaching undergraduates," James Conant of Harvard recalled almost a quarter of a century later in his 1970 autobiography, *My Several Lives,* subtitled *Memoir of a Social Inventor.* The GI Bill, which Conant had warned could flood the college campuses with the least capable of the war generation, had, instead, raised college performance levels. The bill had also overcome what Conant had described in 1940 as the greatest defect in the nation's educational system. The system was, he said, "in spite of universal schooling, perpetuating, more than we realize, a *hereditary class* [emphasis Conant's] of highly educated people." The bill he had denigrated had been the greatest social invention of the century, enabling many outside that hereditary class to obtain high-quality education (pp. 240-241).

* * * *

The founding fathers believed in pursuing happiness, but many Americans after World War II had good reason to think they could make it or buy it.

The feeling wasn't new, but never before had it been so widely shared. A new society was being created while everyone thought he was just going about his business. An entire generation of entrepreneurs took advantage of a vastly expanded market created by the GI Bill of Rights, government-insured investment capital, mass-production economies, and local service outlets to create new ways of living, working, and shopping. We call it "suburbia," but that word is so familiar now its very use obscures the fact that it refers to living, school, working, and social arrangements that were virtually unknown a half century ago.... (p.277)

* * * *

Over the years, the GI Bill subtly has worked to change the face of America. The influence of this omnibus bill, put in place largely by a middle-of-the-road coalition, produced a middle-class nation. By giving veterans the wherewithal to make their dreams come true, the GI Bill of Rights was built upon a rock-solid philosophy whose enactment has had a ripple effect throughout the lives of millions of Americans. Education became a necessity; mortgage lending was altered to the point that home ownership is a national goal—not just a benefit for the monied few. As suburbs sprang up, so did an interconnecting highway system, and a different way of working, shopping, and living. The ground was laid for a high-technology information age and for blacks, hardened by the war and educated by the GI Bill, to demand equal treatment under the law... (pp. 315-316).

American life is still a struggle in a society filled with conflict and sometimes with injustice. But it's also life in a society in which liberties and opportunities have expanded dramatically over the past fifty years, in large part because of the GI Bill. These liberties and opportunities should expand further. The nation where the American Legion was formed in 1918 to combat the rule of the classes or the masses is now an overwhelmingly middle-class nation that can hope that becoming an almost exclusively middle-class nation is not a wild-eyed dream (p. 317).

Veterans on Campus

Editorial, *The Targum*, Rutgers U., New Brunswick, 1/16/46

No Campus Veterans Group

This is a frank talk to the veterans on campus, and, since we belong to that group, we feel we have every right to make it.

We understand that a meeting was held in the student union recently to attempt to organize a veteran's organization here. From reports which we received we understand, also, that the majority of the dozen-odd men who attended were in favor of such organization.

Well, we are not....

We believe that we veterans should forget that title as soon as we possibly can. We should stop feeling different from the rest of the undergraduates just because we wear that duck on our lapels. In our minds the classification of men as either veterans or as civilians is absurd. A man discharged from the armed services is a civilian just as much as he was before he went into the service, and the sooner he realizes it, the better off he is....

We hope that this attempt to organize a veteran's club is given up; we hope that the veterans on campus will hop to and fall into civilian ranks. America and Rutgers are going to need capable civilians who walk with their eyes to the front; America and Rutgers can find little help from those who walk with their eyes to the rear. *[Excerpted]*

Editorial, *The Tulane Hullabaloo*, New Orleans, 12/19/46

Veterans Didn't Fight to Perpetuate the Beer Party

The application of the American Veterans Committee for official recognition is before the University Senate this week following endorsement by the Student Council.

There appears to be no valid reasons why the application should not be accepted. Of the two arguments heard against acceptance, neither is convincing. One says that the number of vet organizations should be limited, and that the limit for Tulane's needs has been reached with the admission of the TVA (Tulane Veterans Association] and the American Legion....

Other opinions favor exclusion of the AVC on the grounds that "it is a political and not a social organization." This is as wet a statement as ever came out of a college group. How unfair that the AVC in its veteran's program trespasses on matters of government and foreign pol-icy, unaware that the vets fought World War II to perpetuate the beer party!

We look forward to a thriving AVC chapter and urge the Senate to pass upon its admittance. *[Excerpted]*

Editorial, *The Denver Clarion*, U. of Denver, 4/18/47

We Offer an Apology

Sunday afternoon, members of the AVC found ... all their literature had been ripped from [their bulletin] board. Posters had been torn up and defaced. The literature in the stacks below the bulletin board was destroyed and had been strewn over the floor of the library....

The history of the AVC on campus has not reflected tranquility. The organization was given the royal runaround by the Administration for many months before its request for a charter was approved. Once it was certified as an organization, the AVC continued to act like Peck's bad boy. They embarrassed the University by selling apples, picketing at the drop of a hat, petitioning various city fathers in the name of the University, and other acts which were designed to give more than adequate publicity to their liberal views.

It was even whispered by those "in the know" that the DU AVC was communist led, inspired or controlled, or all three. This was never proved....

In the past few months, the AVC has shown signs of being the mature, sensible, yet progressive organization many veterans have been looking for. From all indications, a thorough interior house-cleaning has taken place, and the more radical have taken a back seat. The fellow travelers have also been less in evidence at AVC meetings, and signs indicate that they have deserted the AVC for organizations of a pinker hue....

No organization, regardless of its members or its political affiliation deserves such treatment.... The political fascist who believes in any method to destroy the opposition is much more dangerous....

The Clarion wishes to apologize to the AVC for certain irresponsible elements in the student body. *[Excerpted]*

"Veterans Roundup," *The Hilltop*, Howard U., Wash. DC, 10/8/47

We Must Unite Against the Forces of Fascism

Every day, we Negro Veterans are beginning to realize that we must unite against the forces of fascism. Many of us had a chance to go overseas to Europe and, and we saw the deprivations, the miseries, the unsanitary living conditions of a destitute population under the throes of Nazi fascism. We are not yet through fighting this menace to true democracy.

We, as Negro Veterans, are at the forefront of this fight. First, we must realize that we have a special problem, which is, as history has told us down through ages, different from the problems of other veterans. When we unite to solve our problems, we will not only be solving our problems, but eventually the problems of all Negroes, and all minority groups, who have been persecuted because of their race, creed or color. We must not, and cannot, fail in this worthy cause. And the best way we can fight is to become members of a truly progressive veterans organization, which will allow us to voice our opinions, our ideas on these problems, and how we think they can best be solved. We have much in common, and it is only through an organization that we can find we have much in common....

At present the only veterans organization on campus is the American Veterans Committee....

It is hoped through this column, you veterans will become aware of the condition which surrounds you, not only as students, but as businessmen of the future, and the chance you will have for success upon graduation. *[Excerpted]*

Editorial, *The Baloo*, U. of Baltimore, 11/9/51

Vets' Influence Lessens

There was a more than gratifying response on the campus to the elections held last week. It reaffirms the fact that far from interest dying in school activities, it is growing as the influence of the University of Baltimore is growing in the collegiate world and in the business world....

A lot of this school spirit died when the veterans returned to the campus. The veteran returned with an attitude of getting to work to acquire an education, and then getting out into the world to earn that living which was denied him during his tenure in service.

Therefore there was not the customary respect paid to the old campus traditions that had flourished in pre-war times....

Now the average student is not a veteran, and is coming from the campus of High School.... His viewpoint is that of a younger man enthused with the spirit of the young.

This is reflected in our last election, and perhaps it means that a little bit of life and fun is returning to the campus. A little bit of that intangible spirit that is needed to prolong the life and reputation of an institution.

SECTION 2

The Protestant and Catholic Student Organizations

CONTENTS

The Pax Romana Congress

Gérard Pelletier

Pax Romana, international secretariat of Catholic university students, held its XXth Congress in Fribourg, Switzerland, in the first days of September. Last in the long series of international gatherings which took place this summer, both the Pax Romana Study Week and Congress were attended by a very large and representative group. Delegations from 41 different nations participated and 22 new federations affiliated.

First, in … limited deleg… the fundame… before the gr… Thus Pax Ro… up a new co…

The Summer Meetings of the W. S. C. F.

The General Committee of the World's Student Christian Federation

A. J. Coleman

The General Committee of the World's Student Christian Federation, which is its governing body, was held at the Chateau de Bossey, near Geneva, from August 10th to August 20th. It was, perhaps, the most representative committee the Federation has ever had, consisting as it did of 120 delegates and observers from 28 countries. Addresses were given on the central beliefs and responsibilities of the Christian by Prof. Högsbrö, of Denmark, Reinhold von Thadden of Germany, Rev. Pierre Maury of France and Prof. John Bennett of the U.S.A. Holy Communion was celebrated according to the usage of the Swedish, the Lutheran, the Anglican, the Orthodox, and the Reformed Churches. Martin Niemoller was unexpectedly able to be present one evening and gave a few impromptu remarks … Christian … er of the … what it … and utter

Congressus Studiosorum Orbis Terrarum

Prague 1946

Malcolm Adiseshiah

To the World Student Congress at Prague, which began on August 17th 1946, came by land, sea and air more than 300 student delegates mandated by 2,700,000 students from 40 countries of Europe, Asia, North and South America, Africa and Australasia.

In the bringing together of this vast Congress, the Czechoslovak Government, people and the National Union of Students had given of their best in time, energy, organization, administration and money. The composition of the Congress was a reflection of the student world. There was a good and large delegation of students from Soviet Russia; there was a full and enthusiastic participation of student delegations from all the countries of Eastern Europe. This certainly was one significant difference between all other international student conferences and the Prague Congress. There were strong national unions represented from the United Kingdom, Sweden, Denmark, France, Switzerland, Holland, Belgium and other countries. The East was fully represented by the large delegation from the three student movements in India, the delegation from Mongolia, the big delegation from China, and the small but important representation from Egypt, Iran and Indonesia. From the Americas, the delegation from the United States was carefully chosen to represent the important student organizations and universities on a regional basis.

Above: From *ISS Bulletin,* September, 1946

The formal and informal leadership provided in NSA by both undergraduates and professional staff of the Protestant and Catholic student movements played a critical role in NSA's formation and its survival in its early years.

In this section two key student leaders of the time provide contrasting insights into aspects of their personal experience and the interest of their movements in NSA.

Bill Miller (U. of Nebraska, Yale Divinity School) was cochair of the National Intercollegiate Christian Council (NICC), the coordinating group of the student YW- and YMCAs, in 1946, when students Bill Ellis (Harvard) and Joyce Roberts (Pembroke) and staff members Leila Anderson (YWCA) and Hoyt Palmer (YMCA) represented the NICC at the World Student Congress. He reflects on his own involvement in the Student Christian Movement and the issues that engaged him and other students (including pacifism, isolationism, race relations, and Japanese American relocation).

Miller attended the World Student Christian Federation conference in Switzerland that summer. He illuminates some of the national attitudes and interests and the theological undercurrents that animated such events.

Catholic student organizations form a caucus within NSA

Phil Des Marais (University of Minnesota) was chairman of the Joint Committee for Student Action (JCSA), which was set up to provide a caucus to coordinate the involvement of the Catholic College student representatives to NSA as well as those members of the National Newman Club Federation (NNCF) on secular campuses who had been elected as NSA delegates.

Encouraged by the Church hierarchy through the Youth Department of the National Catholic Welfare Conference, JCSA was disbanded in 1948 when it became clear that Catholic student delegates to NSA could maintain whatever liaison they wanted through the National Federation of Catholic College Students (NFCCS) and NNCF. Des Marais notes here, and other former Catholic school student leaders note elsewhere in this anthology (see Dungan, Donnelley, Perkins, and Lynch), how NSA's history was enriched by the influence of Catholic colleges and NSA on each other.

Catholic and Protestant publications followed international student developments closely. Two such articles are included in this section. (Note that, for different reasons, by the mid-1960s the NICC, NFCCS, and NNCF all had been dissolved.)

THE SUMMER OF 1946 saw 1945's summer planning bear fruit as international student and youth conferences convened across Europe (see p.58). Foremost were the renewed World Student Christian Federation in Geneva and Pax Romana in Fribourg, and the formation of the International Union of Students at the World Student Congress in Prague. The latter was a focal point of the agendas and the contrasting strategies toward affiliation by the Protestant and Catholic student groups. These two agendas contested with each other at the 1946 Chicago Student Conference and 1947 NSA Constitutional Convention (see Part 1).

Protestant & Catholic Student Groups Set NSA Outlook

Protestant Student Movement

NSA is a challenge

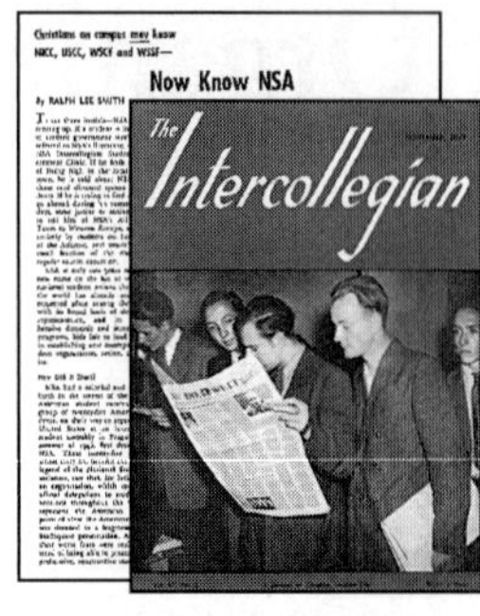

The National Student Association formed in September is really a country-wide organization of campus governments. All votes are by campuses, none by national organizations or agencies. Elected officers must quit college for a semester and work for a salary in Madison, Wisconsin, during their term. Thus, in a new way, the Protestant student movement—by far the largest organized intercollegiate force—takes its place in an over-all student picture.

A notable fact at the NSA organization was Roman Catholic solidarity, backed up with a letter by Archbishop Cushing in *Newman Club News,* which demands complete clearance by the Church hierarchy of any action by Roman Catholic students. This unity of purpose was influential, of course, in minimizing Communist effectiveness—such as that which "took over" previous national student organizations. As NSA may itself soon be related to IUS, this may again become an issue. Criticism of the new Roman Catholic "bloc" process drew the logical reply that Protestants too are free to organize just as tightly. Shall we? We may have played too long in a league where ours was the only team!

From The Intercollegian, *November, 1947. Illustration above, two years later, from November, 1949 issue of* The Intercollegian.

National Intercollegiate Christian Council (NICC) - November 1947

A Subcommittee on NICC Relationships with the National Student Association, consisting of John Casteel, Muriel Jacobson, Hoyt Palmer, Joyce Roberts (See p. 108) and Jimmie Woodward, was formed. Below are excerpts from their report to the NICC:

The committee held one meeting on November 19, 1947, to consider NICC's relationship to NSA, in the light of the action taken at NSA"s constitutional convention which eliminated sectional or interest-based national student organizations from any official connection with NSA.

The committee discussed NICC's relationship to NSA nationally as well as the implications for NICC's affiliation with IUS, in the light of NSA's position that it [NSA] should be the sole affiliating body when it shall represent a majority of American students.

The Subcommittee recommends:

that NICC establish cordial relations with NSA looking to cooperation on projects of common concern; that NICC interpret to its local Associations the functioning of NSA on the local campus and encourage support of local projects which are consistent with NICC's program and policy;

that NICC stand for the retention of two seats in the IUS Council for American national student organizations other than NSA which are affiliated directly with IUS;

that the NICC-NSA Subcommittee make this point of view known to other national student organizations which are affiliated directly with IUS...

that if the recommendation is supported this Subcommittee recommend that NICC negotiate an affiliation fee with IUS, of not less than $500.00, and assume such obligations for the support of representation in the IUS Council as may be necessary;

that Ernest Howell be responsible for interpreting this Subcommittee's recommendation to Robert Smith for use at the NSA December Council meeting....

Catholic College Students

A Major Step

A major step in the direction of organizing the American student community was taken the last week in December, 1946, when about 650 American college students gathered in the Reynolds Club and Mandel Hall, on the campus of the University of Chicago, to discuss plans for the establishment of a national student organization in the United States. Among the 475 delegates and 175 observers from 295 colleges and 19 national student organizations were a substantial group of approximately 150 Catholic students who contributed a large share to keeping this conference intellectual and non-political, controlled by students, and devoted to attempts to solve problems in a constructive way.

The Chicago students' conference marked the first time that Catholic college students in any number have taken an active part in non-sectarian student affairs in this country. The cause of this participation is to be found in an awakening interest in affairs studential, stimulated mainly by the reports of Catholic delegates who have recently returned from several student congresses held in Europe during the past summer.

From "Operation University," Joint Committee for Student Action, 1947. Illustration above from cover.

Joint Committee for Student Action (JCSA) - September 1947

Philip Des Marais, Chairman of the JCSA (See p. 734) prepared an 11-page report on the NSA Constitutional Convention in September, 1947 for the JCSA and the Youth Department of the National Catholic Welfare Conference (NCWC), which contained the following recommendations in favor of Catholic participation in NSA:

1. The NSA is an organization that will develop the vital American unity needed in these critical times, in this instance beginning with the student community. It is an organization for the common good of all students.
2. Catholic students have a responsibility to be interested in the common problems of all students.
3. It is an outlet for Charity and a form of the Apostolate.
4. It serves as an opportunity for Catholic student leaders to meet their future fellow citizens, in politics, social and economic life....
6. Serves as a preview of future American leadership.
7. Develops Catholic leaders....
8. Catholic participation prevents wrong leadership.
9. There is the whole problem of Catholic and American representation on the international student scene where Soviet Russia is making a great effort to mobilize the youth of the world....
10. Concrete NSA program of student relief, exchange, cultural, and regional unity.

...it was the unanimous opinion of the delegates from the two Catholic federations and the JCSA desk chairmen, from all sections of the country, that the Madison convention was one of the most valuable experiences of their whole college careers. The vision of the opportunity for the exercise of genuine student responsibility, of the development of formed and apostolic leadership, of the participation with their fellow American students in a vital program for the good of all was one that captured the imagination of so many of the delegates to the NSA constitutional convention at Madison, Wisconsin.

An innocent's odyssey abroad and prelude to NSA

1. Coming of Age in the Student Christian Movement

William Lee Miller

University of Nebraska; Co-chair National Intercollegiate Christian Council, 1946-47
NSA Delegate, Yale Divinity School, 1948 National Student Congress

I went to college, at the University of Nebraska, smack in the middle of World War II, in the fall of 1943. My father was a Presbyterian minister; I had (not surprisingly) been a member of Presbyterian churches he served, in Wyoming, Kansas, and Nebraska, and active in their youth groups. I became an active participant in the Presbyterian student house at the University, holding various offices both in that student fellowship and in interdenominational collaborations. From my diary it appears that I was always going to conferences. I went to a gathering of the United Student Christian Council (USCC), the new unified pan-Protestant student movement at Denison in Ohio, one Christmas, and of the Student Volunteer Movement (SVM, of course), the older missionary-recruiting organization, now rethinking "missions" in Wooster in Ohio another Christmas. And, many more.[1]

Later I also joined the student YMCA. Would it be too flippant to say I did so because the latter had an accessible ping-pong table? Yes, as it turns out from my coffee-stained notes, it would be. A friend named Bill Sakayama persuaded me to go to a regional conference of the YM-YWCA. The meeting of the Nebraska YM to which I was to give a report on the conference turned out to be the night they were to elect officers, and—such was the shortage of males—I was elected president.

There came to be a congenial small group of us (to repeat: the supply of males depleted by the war) in the student Y—taking it over, really—more raffish and "intellectual" than the Presbyterians, and perhaps more consistently liberal in our political and social opinions (which is not to say that the Presbyterian student group was consistently conservative—no mainline student religious group would be, in those different days—just less political and more mixed in point of view). A symbol of our politics at the Nebraska student Y was this altogether unlikely fact: somehow we came to subscribe to the New York City newspaper *PM*, which was the left-liberal tabloid (against those who "push people around") that you read on the subway in the evening in New York, sports starting from the back, your favorite liberal columnists in the middle, and the most recent outrage in huge headlines on the cover. We read about those outrages, not on the subway, but two days later, gathered around the ping-pong table in Lincoln, Nebraska.

The YMCA and the Student Christian Movement

When the YMCA began, after the Civil War, it was indeed a pious, "Christian," organization, as its name states, one of those pan-Protestant efforts that crossed denominational lines to try to do what the participants at least regarded as good things—to "evangelize the world in our generation," to cite one not particularly modest objective.[1] But by the time the student YMCA gathered in some rooms in a building near the campus of the University of Nebraska in 1944, the piety had been somewhat superseded and had mostly been replaced by camaraderie and social action. We did not sing hymns. Even though none of us had the slightest connection with the labor union movement, we sang, to the tune of the "Battle Hymn of the Republic," "Solidarity Forever" often enough that I believe I can now write out the words, from memory, fifty-five years later:

> It is we who plowed the prairies
> Built the cities where they trade;
> Dug the mines and built the workshops,
> Endless miles of railroad laid;
> Yet we stand outside and starving
> Mid the wonders we have made—
> But the Union makes us strong.
> Solidarity Forever,
> Solidarity Forever,
> Solidarity Forever,
> But the Union makes us strong.

Our identification with the labor union movement was, of course, temporary and naïve.[2]

These were the components—the mainline denominations (joined in the USCC) and the two Y's (joined in the National Intercollegiate Christian Council) (NICC—sorry about all these initials)—of the "Student Christian Movement" (or Student Christian Association Movement) of that time. In New England and in New York State there was a formal unified movement with that name,[3] and elsewhere there were close collaborations that came almost to the same thing.

An unwary reader from a later time and a different ideology may need to have it said that the word "Christian" did not then mean political conservatism. The "Christian right" and the "Christian Coalition" and all of that is a much later, and a much different, development.

Pacifism between World War I and World War II

Speaking of student movements, my father had been a college student, just deciding to go into the ministry, at the time of World War I—"The Great War," as it then was known. He was required while a student at Indiana University to belong to the then equivalent of the Reserve Officers' Training Corps (ROTC) (with different initials) and in that role required, under silent protest, to take a course, taught by an army officer, called "War Aims"—in which he got his only low grade, a D. In seminary and as a young pastor he partook of that strong reaction against World War I, that disillusionment with the contrast between Wilsonian idealism and the grim realities of trench warfare, and with the wartime propaganda about the "Hun" chopping off the hands of Belgian children that, fused with a long-time Protestant antiwar theme, led to a rejection of all war. This reaction was particularly strong in the Middle West and the Rocky Mountain West, and also in the "mainline" Protestant churches. It was not the same as the historic, long established, systematic pacifism—opposition to war as such—of the Quakers; it was, rather, a pacifistic inclination grounded partly in the reaction against the Great War and partly in the romantic-sentimental-idealistic inclination of liberal Protestantism, particularly in the United States. It was strong enough to be reflected in world affairs at the end of the 1920s in the Kellogg-Briand Pact, "renouncing all war."

Speaking again of student movements, it was strong enough to be reflected in the "Oxford Pledge"—a movement among students, beginning in England, to pledge oneself (in the old Protestant, individualistic, deontological manner) never to participate in another war.[4] My father, as a young pastor, preached an antiwar sermon in the church he then served, in Laramie, Wyoming, in the early 1930s, in which he asked every member of the congregation who would never participate in another war to indicate that pledge by standing. This was a dramatic enough event to have been picked up by the Associated Press, denounced by the state head of the American Legion, and discussed in furious letters to editors. The Laramie superintendent of schools was indignant enough to cross the street rather than speak to my father. I, however (then aged six or seven), was proud enough of him to make my own little counterprotest by discovering the address of the Legion commander's house and walking indignantly in front of it.

As the events of the 1930s moved toward World War II, therefore, with the rise of Hitler and with Mussolini's invasion of Ethiopia and the rest, the interpretive atmosphere in my parents' home would still be colored by this antiwar sentiment, which functioned in the political debate of those years as isolationism. Once, years later in a Fund for the Republic group in California, three of us, of the same generation, neatly distributed across the three religious groupings, were talking about our respective responses, at nine or ten or eleven, to the Spanish Civil War. Bill Clancy, the Catholic, from Detroit, where his parents listened to Father Coughlin, had been a strong supporter of Franco. Arthur Cohen, the Jew, from New York City, had been a strong supporter of the Anti-Franco Loyalists and the Abraham Lincoln Brigade, in that first fight against fascism. And I, the Protestant from the hinterland? I had been shooting baskets in the hoop attached to the garage at our house in Kansas, unaware that there was a Spanish Civil War.

My eighteenth birthday, making me eligible for the draft, came six weeks before D-day in 1944, after two and a half years of American participation in the war, and more than four years of the war in Europe. I had begun to change my mind, under the influence of events and of college professors, but not so much as to prevent me from registering as a conscientious objector. The influences that led me to do that came, not only from my parents, but also, and now more, from the Student Christian Movement. There were considerable influences in the SCM of various Quaker leaders and Methodist pacifists, of members of the worldwide pacifist organization, the Fellowship of Reconciliation; and, in general, of an antiwar sentiment that was strong in liberal Protestantism, especially, as I have implied, in the hinterland.

But it was also the Student Christian Movement, along with college courses and the newspapers, that introduced into my mind a counterargument. The argument then going on in American Protestant circles can be symbolized—oversimplifying a little—by this event. One day, I took down from my father's shelf of religious books Reinhold Niebuhr's *Moral Man and Immoral Society*, and began to read. Then I felt, more or less, like some watcher of the skies when a new planet swims into his ken. Niebuhr's Christian "realism" began to puncture the sentimental idealism of Midwestern Protestantism and of the Student Christian Movement as I had encountered it.

The Great Debate: Internationalism versus Isolationism

The great isolationist-interventionist debate of 1937–1941, (particularly 1939–1941) was, perhaps, the last in a long sequence back through American history, in which the argument within the Protestant churches was of central importance to the nation as a whole. (Slavery, of course, was the big one.) The outlook that my father had held, and by which I had been influenced, was powerful within the churches, particularly the "free" churches in the hinterland. An antiwar pacifist-isolationist outlook permeated the pages of the Chicago-based interdenominational journal *The Christian Century,* which came every week into our home as into thousands of religious homes in the Middle West. The great opponent of all this within American Protestantism, and the leading interventionist—much reviled for it by many older liberals—was, of course, Reinhold Niebuhr. I had been too young (or too out of it) to absorb that debate as it happened in 1939–1941, but by the crunch time of my own decision I recaptured it retroactively and came to side with Niebuhr.

Through the spring of 1944 I had an argument with myself—in the language of the time, it was an "existential" moment. What was in my mind? I am sure, as I think back, that I did not—in general we did not, in that place and situation—know about the Holocaust, although we had some superficial awareness of Nazi anti-Semitism. We knew, of course, that Hitler and Mussolini were moral monsters, but from our perspective, they were rather distant ones.

But in a turmoil of decisions, I came to see it differently. In the end, I decided that I was not a conscientious objector (CO), and I notified the draft board. The secretary of the draft board—I remember her looking at me as she asked, or proposed this—suggested that I might want to expunge my earlier registration as a CO, but I said that I did not feel it necessary to do that. (Ted Sorensen, another Nebraskan—neither one of us quite fits the term "Cornhusker"—also registered as CO, and didn't change his mind. That came back to haunt him many years and a thought world away, in the Senate hearings on the President-elect Jimmy Carter's abortive effort to name him director of the CIA.)

So I was now eligible for the draft. A scruffy gaggle of adolescent civilians, we gathered in the Lincoln railroad station in the early summer of 1944 and were escorted by train to Fort Leavenworth for our physical. Take your clothes off. Stand in line. Then came the tremendous anticlimax. We were told to jog in place, and the medical person with a stethoscope came down the lines listening to the beating hearts, and when he came to me he listened only briefly and then took his list and made a big, black X on my name. He heard "leakage" in the heart valve.

So instead of being drafted into the army and being shipped to Europe or the Pacific—most likely to be a part of the enormous number of men it was being said would be required for the invasion of the Japanese islands—I would go back to college. Needless to say, perhaps, this was at once a tremendous relief and a tremendous letdown.

The SCM and race: The salient social-political issue

If my (and our) ignorance about, and avoidance of, the overwhelming issues of the war and world affairs in those war years is, in retrospect, naïve and embarrassing, and our identification with labor not sullied by any knowledge or experience, our attitude and action on race was, I would like to believe, a little better than that—at least for its time and place. Race was, by all means, the most salient social-political issue for me, and for the student Christian movement as I encountered it, both locally and nationally. The link between the American student (Protestant) Christians and the attempt to overcome America's "One Huge Wrong" (Lyndon Johnson) stretches all the way back through American history. We could count ourselves as standing in the heritage of the greatest of all American student gatherings, the Lane debates, for 18 days, in 1833 in Cincinnati, under the direction of the great abolitionist Theodore Weld, at which the whole company was converted to abolitionism (the seminary president's daughter Harriet Beecher—later, Harriet Beecher Stowe—sitting in the gallery listening. And out of which would come the great company of seventy abolitionist agents, who toured the North, having tomatoes and rocks thrown at them and being run out of town, yet making converts all the same. The Student Christian Movement—the student section of the great denominations—and the YMCA and YWCA have a long and deep history that would not characterize the general national student movement in the United States, and that history included a continuing role on the subject of race, ahead of the churches as well as the society in general.[5]

People who visited from Chicago laughed at the notion that there was any problem of race in little, old, white bread Lincoln, Nebraska—but there was one, or more than one. As a state Christian Youth Council president, I was on panels on "brotherhood," often with Marie Yamashita, a Nisei, as well as various black persons, and made talks in churches and religious youth groups, to all-white audiences, in the question period of which some fellow in the back row (of course) would ask whether I would want my daughter (implicit: when I was old enough to have a daughter) to "marry one."

We came home from the regional SCM conference in Estes Park in the summer of 1944 eager to do something on race more substantial than these speeches, and we gathered interracial groups—a smaller one, and then a larger one, both meeting in the Presbyterian House—and undertook as our first project protest against Nebraska's acquiescence in racial segregation in the Big Six (as it then was) college athletic conference. The Universities of Oklahoma and of Missouri were in the Big Six, and they insisted on racial segregation, and so Nebraska and the others complied—so we were told by Nebraska authorities. (For those who know anything about college football in later years, it must be hard to picture an all-white Nebraska team—but that's what it was.)

Then, in the summer of 1945, just as the war in the Pacific was drawing to its close, I went to a "students-in-industry" project in Chicago sponsored by the SCM: we would live in the dorms of George Williams College on Chicago's South Side, get jobs in Chicago industries—not hard in wartime—and have seminars and speakers on labor and race and the city in the evenings and weekends. Each day I would take the Cottage Grove streetcar through the burgeoning black world—block after block after block, the population swollen by the wartime influx—of Chicago's South Side, to my job in a little shop that reconditioned used automobile water pumps. It was not exactly what one thinks of as "industry," but, still, working there, I knew I was not in Kansas anymore. (I would learn both about the dropping of the atomic bomb on Hiroshima—which means learning that there was such a thing as an atomic bomb—and also about the end of the war in the Pacific by reading my morning *Chicago Sun* while riding through the black South Side of Chicago on the Cottage Grove streetcar.) Almost all of my handful of coworkers were "African Americans" (as we now say—not then) and the shop was small enough that I got to know them on the job—one, a reader both of the *Chicago Defender* (the leading Negro—as we then said—newspaper) and the *Chicago Tribune*, would seem to alter his politics according to which paper he had read.

Reconciliation (FOR) and equality (CORE)

In the after-work seminars we had presentations by leaders of the Committee on Racial Equality of the Fellowship of Reconciliation (CORE), which would become known, separated from the Fellowship, in the later days of the civil rights movement. We learned from leaders of CORE about nonviolent direct action techniques they had already developed and used—including the sit-in, to become famous in 1960 with its use by students in Greensboro, North Carolina. We participated in one of those techniques, picketing a Chicago private housing project that was discriminating.

I brought back to Lincoln a little blue and gray booklet describing these devices and their philosophy, and we tried, in our way, to employ some of them: going as an interracial group to the local roller skating-rink, being turned away, protesting under the (old, unenforced) state civil rights law; eating successfully together in many eating places, including the Cornhusker Hotel (this was the North, after all, although it was the conservative North); continuing the protest against racial exclusion in the Big Six with student council resolutions, visits to administrators, letters to editors and deans, and answers to their answers (one of the best letters by Ted Sorensen); the most successful venture, a fifty-person visit to the city council to end segregation in the municipal swimming pool; and—the most ambitious—an effort to pass a state FEPC law, with a group of us testifying, for a memorable afternoon, before a committee of the Nebraska unicameral legislature in the Capitol. The most outrageous of the testimonials on the other side (by Mr. Cushman, who made Cushman motor scooters,) said that God had been trying for two thousand years to eliminate prejudice, so how could one expect the Nebraska legislature to do it? And then he lost his temper at this attempt to make the races mingle, while his son was being shot at by the "Japs."

The Japanese-American relocation

That last reference has particular resonance in that time and place. The student Christian movement in general was particularly sympathetic to the college-age Japanese Americans, whose lives had been abruptly interrupted by that most egregious of wartime national sins, the Japanese-American relocation.[6]

And the University of Nebraska, I am proud to say, distinguished itself among universities by making it easy for Nisei students to come—if a university would accept them, then they could get out of the "Relocation Centers," and many did come to Nebraska, especially from the Relocation Center in Heart Mountain, Wyoming. To say that Nebraska welcomed them certainly does not mean that all parts of the university, let alone the state, did so; the dormitories were a problem, so that many of them were housed in the denominational student centers, and Marie Yamashita in the Westminster Foundation. My college days were therefore filled (rather surprisingly, given the geography) with the names of Nisei friends: Marie and her sister, June Yamashita; Pete Ida, who would marry June; Bill Sakayama; Joe Ishikawa; and Joe Uemura, my friend, not at Nebraska but in Denver. We may not have (or I might not have) thought very clearly about world politics at that time, but the evil of the Japanese-American relocation—and the evil of racial segregation—were the sort of things we could understand.

From Nebraska to the NICC in New York

So instead of being a soldier on the beaches of Normandy or wherever, I was a college student beside the ping-pong table in Nebraska and was available for participation in the Student Christian Movement.

Given the paucity of males, my rise was vertiginous. One evening in 1945, a paltry dozen or so in the Nebraska student YMCA elected me president and delegate to the regional conference in Colorado. At the regional conference, I was elected delegate to the National Council in Riverdale, New York. At the National Council meeting I was elected chairman of the National Student YMCA, which meant also cochairman, with the YWCA chairman, of the National Intercollegiate Christian Council (NICC).

After serving for the year 1945-46, I was chosen again to serve the next year—which meant on into the quite different scene of the postwar years, with all of the ex-soldiers returning now to college, and the whole atmosphere abruptly increasing in maturity. It also meant that I would be cochairman of the NICC-sponsored National Student Assembly in Champaign-Urbana in December 1946, to which the NICC delegates to Prague would report.

In passing I mentioned that summer conference in Colorado. If you want to understand the American Christian student movement, you must get a sense of those conferences. Estes Park, Colorado; Geneva Glen, Southwest of Denver ("Geneva, our lives have been bettered by you," in which farewell sign every year someone thoughtfully altered the first "e" to an "a" in the word "bettered"); Lake Geneva, Wisconsin; Asilomar, California. Lakes, mountains, the ocean: some pleasant scene. Cabins filled with students from many colleges, getting acquainted fast. Morning devotions reflecting a rather romantic version of Christianity. A morning program loaded with idealism. Singing together songs and hymns like "We would be building, temples still undone," to the tune of "Finlandia."

Sentimental songs around the campfire at night. Humorous songs around the tables at mealtimes. To be sure, the primary attraction of these romantic-idealistic-sentimental gatherings was that they brought together, in one conveniently confined and naturally beautiful place, a wide selection, from other campuses as well as your own, of members of the opposite sex. Youthful sexual attraction, social idealism, religious sentimentalism, and natural beauty fused together in a rosy glow of happy times. There was no harm in it, I guess—except that when one spends a fortnight in such a setting while others your own age are being shot at in the mud, one feels a certain guilt and embarrassment.

The business meetings of the student YM-YW (the NICC) did not have such a rosy glow. That first trip to Riverdale, just outside New York City, was my first visit to the city that was for me, as for so many young writers in the hinterland, the city of dreams and aspirations. So, the first time I crammed in all of New York that I could, around the edges of the business meeting: I saw *Oklahoma*, ate in the Automat, rode the subway, heard Woody Herman's band at the Paramount on Times Square, rode the Staten Island ferry, and saw the great radio comedian Fred Allen himself, who was a hero of mine, taking his own tray through the cafeteria line at the Westside YMCA.

However, the content of the business meetings themselves, which were dominated by the paid professional adults, tended to be bureaucratic and jargon-ridden.

Late at night in the Lincoln (Nebraska) station, I would take the Burlington Zephyr to Chicago, sit up in a reserved coach seat, sleep if I could, transfer blurry-eyed to the New York Central Pacemaker, and do the same a second night, to wake up as the train came down from the tracks along the Hudson into Grand Central Station, which was always a bit of a thrill.

The larger world of the Student Christian Movement

In those national conventions, I learned more about the larger world of the Student Christian Movement, which I knew well enough in its local manifestations.[7] I learned in New York about the national level of the Student Christian Movement, including the new pan-Protestant organization, the United Student Christian Council (USCC).[8] And then I was chosen to be an NICC delegate to the first postwar meeting of the general committee of the World's Student Christian Federation, where I would learn about its worldwide manifestation.

In late July of 1946 the S.S. *Washington*—before the war, the flagship of American ocean liners—pulled out of New York harbor, a day late because of a dispute with the National Maritime Union (NMU). One student who would be a passenger had dealings with the NMU sufficient to provide knowledge of that union's reveille: "Arise and shine with the Maritime!" So the twenty-eight of us students in the layers of bunks on deck D-1 proceeded to rouse ourselves with that cry each morning.

The S.S. *Washington* had been refitted to carry troops—hence the bunks—but, as a great prewar ocean liner, had once had the luxury that passengers on such a ship would expect, some remnants which remained: a sun (or hurricane) deck; a boat deck; and—most important—a promenade deck, with a little library, a lounge, and so on, and with seatings at dinner, with attentive waiters. The postwar passenger list—people going to Europe in the first summer after the war—included a panorama of nationalities, featuring especially the Irish. The list also included a clutch or bevy of us going to the World Student Christian Federation in Switzerland, and at least nine who were going to the World Student Congress in Prague. The interchanges between these two sets of students would be interesting to recapture, if only my notes were better. Among the Prague delegation, I see in my notes from the time, there was a "Unitarian from Antioch" (so I described her in my notes) who had what I infer must have been a wary conversation with me, in which she expressed (I say in my notes) "much anti-church feeling."[9] There was also, according to those notes, "Jimmy Wallace of North Carolina, a pipe-smoker," and, my memory tells me, Doug Cater of Harvard, both of whom would be leaders in the new American student organization. (If Doug was not on the S.S. *Washington,* I met him somewhere else that summer.) Doug Cater—it is necessary now to say the late Doug Cater—would, in 1953, become a lifelong friend of mine, beginning when we were both on the staff of *The Reporter* magazine, Doug in Washington and I in New York City.[10]

One of Doug's first articles, in one of the first issues—in August of 1949—of the new, postwar "magazine of facts and ideas," *The Reporter*, would be a retrospective report on Prague, the (WFDY) and the International Union of Students (IUS), entitled "Collapse of Youth's One World"—giving his account of the Communist takeover of those organizations, after the hopeful anticipations of the summer of 1946 had collapsed.

Four years after that, in the Dwight D. Eisenhower summer of 1953, I would send my first proposed article, unsolicited, not to the editorial offices in New York, but to Doug in Washington, and he became the enthusiastic sponsor of my connection with that now forgotten but in its day important, liberal, anti-McCarthy, but also anticommunist magazine.

In the rosy-fingered dawn of 1946—needless to say—we did not anticipate any of this.

In that summer, Doug represented a larger world of political understanding than I was acquainted with; although he came from Montgomery, Alabama, he had been to Exeter as well as Harvard, had served in the Office of Strategic Services (OSS), and could converse knowledgeably about matters that they talked about, in a sophisticated manner, back there in what I still thought of, partly in disparagement and partly in envy, as "the East."

There was also, among those who I thought were going to Prague, a delegate from New York City, who was a sophisticated Marxist, with whom I had conversations that were intriguing, at least to me. The primary question about the Prague conference in the circles I moved in, as I remember, was already whether, or to what degree, it was Soviet or Communist dominated or controlled. Although this was 1946, before the full development of the Cold War, as the reader knows, there were already the beginnings.

I had been NICC co-chairman when our NICC delegation to Prague was chosen, and would be again when Bill Ellis and Joyce Roberts, the two students we chose, gave their report. The others in the NICC delegation to Prague characteristically were not students, but paid professional staff members, Hoyt Palmer of the YMCA and Leila Anderson of the YWCA.[11]

Characteristics of the Protestant student movements

The student YWCA and YMCA and the student movements within the major Protestant denominations (those that we now call "mainline," just as they've ceased to be the main line)[12] all were rooted in the long-standing adult institutions, which furnished continuing facilities on college campuses—buildings like the Westminster Foundation at Nebraska, Wesley Foundation, Baptist Centers—with paid professional leaders—campus pastors and YM and YW secretaries. (My father, for example, had been Presbyterian pastor to students successively at Indiana University, the University of Wisconsin, and—in combination with the downtown church—the University of Wyoming.) And then there would be, in each case, a larger structure—regional perhaps, and national, each with its full-time, paid adult staff.

On the S.S. *Washington* there were Hiel Bollinger, the head National Methodist Student staff person; Newt Fetter, the same for the Baptists; Ralph Hyslop, the same for the Congregational church; and Max Adams—a Presbyterian minister who knew my father—the same for Presbyterians. (Should it be recorded that on the second night in Paris three of us—Bollinger, Fetter, and I—went to the Folies Bergèrés, just like the most banal cliché of American tourists? The adult leaders of the Methodists and the Baptists—men in their thirties at least, maybe forties, and one student, aged twenty—who had not been the one to instigate this venture—pursued their edification.) There was also a phalanx of adult professionals with the student YMCA and student YWCA, led by Ed Espy and Eleanor Smith, respectively. These American student religious entities were the student branch of a larger, longtime, nonstudent institution, and were thus different from most true student movements elsewhere, which were less rooted in permanent adult institutions, more "voluntary" and temporary, and (perhaps) student led.

This was my impression at the time of the contrast between us Americans and those from most other countries. We were younger and much less experienced than our counterparts from elsewhere in the world—certainly that was true of me, but I think it was true, with exceptions, of American students in general, especially those from the religious movements. Most of us Americans were undergraduates; I was between my junior and senior years, just turned twenty.

Many of those from other countries had had wartime interruptions and were students in graduate, professional, and technical schools, in their late twenties or in their thirties, and some were "students" only in name. A year later, as the American veterans returned, or came to, the campuses under the GI Bill, many—perhaps most—of us American students had had no direct experience of the war, as was certainly true in my case; European students, by contrast, had almost all had direct wartime experience of some kind. And the students from elsewhere in the world tended to be an elite; much smaller percentages (generally speaking) of their population would attend college and thus acquire the romantic identity of "student" than was true (even then before the GI Bill) of the American population, which had, generally speaking, a larger middle-class component and more of that middle class attending college than elsewhere. Put these together—especially the different experiences of the war—and you have yet another version of that often repeated story about Americans in relation to Europe and the world: Innocents Abroad. Certainly that was true in my own case, but I felt it applied to many of the other Americans as well.

The World Student Christian Federation and the war's aftermath

The S.S. *Washington* landed at Le Havre. Train to Paris, three days in Paris, train to Switzerland, arriving late at night. (I remember Max Adams, the Presbyterian staff person, an able person whom I particularly respected, saying, with heavy irony, "Oh, yes, the noble Swiss," which caused me to reconsider any residual admiration for Swiss neutrality during the war). Bossey, a chateau near Lake Leman, was the scene of the first meeting of the general committee of the World's Student Christian Federation after the war. In the opening words by the chairman (no "student" he, but an imperious Dutch adult), he mentioned the names of Czech student leaders killed during the war, and the group stood in silence.

That was the first emotionally potent reminder of the war just past.

There would be many others. We toured the world horizon telling what happened to the Student Christian Movement members during the war—sort of a survey of world affairs from a student and a religious perspective, which was enormously illuminating to me.

Here is a summary I wrote at the time for an article for *Intercollegian*, the NICC magazine, that the editors of this book unearthed (I had forgotten I had written it):

> . . . in England the students are apathetic to politics, but . . . the Chileans play the game in place of football. In Czechoslovakia the SCM is an anti-nationalist force; in Indonesia the obsession is Indonesian nationalism. In Australia the pressing problem is secularism; in Finland the Inter-varsity Fellowship (conservative-fundamentalist) is strong. In Czechoslovakia there is no impenetrable barrier between Roman Catholic and Protestant; in Italy there is. In Hungary the SCM members who refuse to join the Communist Party are persecuted; in China those who sympathize with the Communists are subject to governmental pressure. In Germany and in Argentina SCM members were thrown in prison by arbitrary regimes; in many countries the SCM had had to operate secretly: in France, Holland, Hungary, SCM members were integral parts of the resistance movement. The two USAs . . . have terrific race problems to solve. The girl from Nigeria saw her first lion in the London Zoo.

It is not easy for me to convey the profundity of the impact on the mind of an inexperienced American of the still raw wounds of the terrible war and of the Nazi regime, encountered now in the immediate aftermath.[13]

We learned about the work of CIMADE, the interfaith rescue operation that saved many from the Nazi horror. We learned about André Trocme, the pastor at the little village of Le Chambon, where the church-led effort had rescued many Jewish children. (Trocme would become an official of the Fellowship of Reconciliation, the pacifist organization; by contrast, Phillipe Maury, the French SCM leader, had been an ace during the war.)

The most powerful reminders of the war just past would be the appearance of two Germans: Pastor Martin Niemoller and a man named Reinhold Von Thadden.

Niemoller was a German pastor famous in the war years and afterwards for a certain opposition to the Nazis; we did not know yet—at least, I did not—about the more thoroughgoing and consequential German Christian opponent of Hitler, Dietrich Bonhoffer. Niemoller spoke only briefly; my notes record that he said, in addition to a couple of devotional phrases, just, "Germany is a mess. . . . Go build a better world than we did. God bless you."

Von Thadden was another, longer story. He was vice chairman of the Federation (although a man in his fifties at least) and spoke both at the committee meeting at Bossey and at a later conference at Gwatt, also in Switzerland. Although he had been imprisoned by the Nazis for a time for opposing their church policy, he later served in the German (which is to say, the Nazi) army. Dutch and Czech delegates, their memories of the Occupation and the war still fresh, could scarcely bear to listen to him. Part of it was just the language—the sound of it. To hear the guttural sounds of German, spoken by a commanding male figure—von Thadden rather fit the stereotype of a German army officer—was almost more than they could bear. The Dutch chairman and presiding officer defended von Thadden by telling us that while in the German army, he was the commandant of an occupied Belgian town—the only such German officer, according to the chairman, who, after the war, would be asked to come back to the town by the townspeople. It then developed that one of the Dutch young men in the conference had been a worker in the Dutch underground smuggling Jews out of danger, and that one of the best places to do that had been this Belgian town, of which von Thadden had been Commandant. We were further informed that when the Russians occupied East Germany, his estate was taken away, his wife narrowly avoided being put in a house for Russian soldiers, and he was imprisoned for a time in Russia. So there were various extenuations for this SCM officer who had served in the German (Nazi) army. Still, one of the Federation officers reported to some of us in private that he had talked with von Thadden back in 1937 and (according to my notes from the time) "it was amazing how he could rationalize the things that were happening." Von Thadden himself reported (as part of the systematic round of reports from all the National Student Christian movements) that from 1933 to 1937, they were pretty well taken in: "the older, revivalist people were sentimental about Nazism, and the young people were Nazis." In 1937, when the church itself began to be persecuted, some began to change and join the (secretly anti-Nazi) confessional church.

Joyce Roberts, who would be, later in the summer, one of the NICC delegates to Prague, asked von Thadden point-blank the question we all harbored: how could he serve in the Nazi army? Von Thadden took it well, I see in my notes, but did not give a very satisfactory answer. There is no such thing as conscientious objection in Germany, he said, and the church (including, implicitly, student Christians) has always fallen in with, and abetted, obedience to the state. It had always been a question with him, he said, how far one should go for one's fatherland.

I got to know one of the other two (younger—but still much older than me) German delegates, a man named Jan Hermalink, who had served in the Nazi troops in the same part of northern Italy in which a Canadian delegate had served, in the Canadian army, on the other side. Jan had become a Christian after the war and his service in the German army. My summary of his position in my conversations has an element of sarcasm, about a position with which I was very familiar back home: "The Christian is a citizen of another world who must spend his time not trying to correct this world, but staying right with God."

That sort of other-worldly quietism was not characteristic of the student Christian movements from most countries.

After the WSCF general committee meeting in Bossey, most of us went to the World Student Christian Conference in Gwatt, also in Switzerland, from August 22 to August 30. For a day in between, a number of us visited sanitariums operated by World Student Relief—for which we had raised money during the war—in Leysin. I accompanied fellow American conference-goer Mimi Gowan to the room of two Polish women who knew a professor of hers. One of the women had a number branded on her arm—the first real-life reminder of that sort that I had seen. A serious awareness of the Holocaust was very slow in coming to us Americans.

The World Student Christian Federation honors a long history

The World Student Christian Federation (WSCF) was quite different from the World Federation of Democratic Youth and the International Union of Students (IUS), which came out of the Prague conference. Of course it differed in the first place in that it had an explicit doctrinal foundation—a shared religious commitment, however variously expressed.

We could sing the same hymns, with a doctrinal consent (better hymns, generally speaking, then we did in American SCM gatherings—"A Toi la Gloire" was a particular favorite) and participate in shared worship services, at least up to a point. I remember the little Orthodox priest Father Ambrose (the organization was not entirely Protestant; as in the World Council of Churches, there was an Orthodox presence) intoning before an altar "maintenant et toujours et tous les siècles des siècles," a little mysterious, but memorable. But as on politics and culture, so on theology: We Americans (many of us—me at least) were not well acquainted with the great, deep currents of Western civilization. I remember an Orthodox student (older, of course, by some years than me) asking whether in my religious world we believed in "transubstantiation in the mass." I knew we did not have a "mass"—"communion," yes—and although I did not know what "transubstantiation" meant, I was pretty sure we did not believe in it.

The WSCF was an existing organization with a long history arising out of organizations—churches—with even longer histories; it was, in other words, not something new, just being formed in the postwar world. The SCM in the United States stood in the same contrast to the new NSA. The WSCF members meeting at Bossey in Switzerland in the summer of 1946 stood in contrast to the almost simultaneous gathering of students in Prague, therefore, in this regard: the WSCF meeting was a coming back together, a reuniting, of national movements that had been joined and, in many cases, of individuals who had known each other, after a wartime interruption of eight years. (The war, as the world knew it, began, not in December of 1941, with Pearl Harbor and the American entrance into the conflict, but in September of 1939, with the Nazi invasion of Poland.)

The WSCF gatherings had looming over them, therefore, not only the huge prospective political reality that dominated Prague—Communism and the coming Cold War—but also, even more, the retrospective reality of the war. If these other student postwar ventures were oriented to the future, and to hope, much of the WSCF was oriented to the past, to memory, and to reconciliation. I wrote at the time: "SCM leaders from France, Germany, Finland, Hungary, Sweden, England, stood silently and reverently as the names of the martyred Czech secretaries were read." I wrote also that "the movements in Nigeria, the Gold Coast, and Argentina sent delegates to the meeting for the first time in many years."

As to the parallel activities in Prague, the WSCF committee's Politics Commission—much emphasized by the American delegation—enacted, not only a resolution recommending the Birmingham Students-in-Industry project, like the one I had attended in Chicago, but, more important, as its first provision, that "national movements be encouraged to participate in the World Federation of Democratic Youth and the International Union of Students, being at the same time cognizant and watchful of the strong Communist influence therein."[14]

A journey back with remembered wartime enmities

The S.S. *Ernie Pyle* was one of Henry Kaiser's ninety-day wonders—ships built with American wartime efficiency to carry troops and materiel. Unlike the S.S. *Washington*, it had never been anything but a troop ship, was still outfitted as one, and had no provisions for luxury. The name would indicate its newness: Ernie Pyle was the most famous war correspondent of that same war, who was killed while reporting it. The eight hundred passengers crowded onto it in troop-ship layers of hammocks were so diversified by nationality, politics, language, and relationship to the war, and so under the war's shadow, that when Katherine Anne Porter published *Ship of Fools*, one was reminded of that voyage on the *Ernie Pyle*. The journey was a special one—so we were told—undertaken at the request of the State Department, to bring expatriate American citizens home from Europe so that they could retain their citizenship. Some of these (perhaps rather nominal or technical) "Americans" had been detained in Europe—so my notes say—not by the Second, but by the First World War. But the electricity in the ship's atmosphere came from the varying relationships of passengers to Germany, to the other Axis partners, and to the war just ended, one year earlier. The clash of remembered enmities— the tense moments and stares of disapproval and avoidance—was much more intense than at the WSCF in Bossey, and it was unmitigated by any commonality except a shared troop ship.

I had had earlier passage on another ship, but "sacrificed" my place on it to an NICC staff person who had work she needed to do in the States—and thus bought myself two happy, carefree weeks in Paris while waiting for the *Ernie Pyle*. It departed on September 22 and took eight days in the crossing—but I had already agreed to take the fall semester off (the fall semester of my senior year—I would have enough credits to graduate with my class in the spring of 1947 without fall classes) and to tour student Christian centers in the East, both reporting on the WSCF meeting and anticipating the Student Assembly in Urbana at Christmastime.[15] That tour is, perhaps, another story. I was not the only student left behind on the *Ernie Pyle*; there were three women students, nicely distributed across denominations—one Episcopalian, one Lutheran, one Disciple of Christ—and one evening (I note), as respite from the discussion of the war and world affairs, they debated free-churchism versus liturgical churchism, with the representatives of each position upholding, not their own, but the other side.

But we all knew (from all the voices around us) that, although forms of church government had been a large issue in London in 1644, this was not a primary issue in the world of September 1946.

I came to know, because our bunks were adjacent, a young (but much older than me) Frenchman named Jean Ordner, who had been in the Maquis—the armed underground resistance, which (I patiently explain to myself in my notes) was mostly Communist but included many Protestants and Catholics. Jean said he was not proud of his compatriots (the general population) in the war. He was coming to the United States to study at the New School for Social Research in New York. After we landed, my idea of showing him New York City, other than walking among tall buildings ("*Formidable!*"), was to take him to Radio City Music Hall, where he tactfully said he was impressed by the fact that they could follow Wagner with "Doin' What Comes Naturally!"

I wish I had the time and the talent to create a novel out of the 1946 voyage back to the United States from Europe on the *Ernie Pyle*.

Bringing home the promise of WSCF and IUS

My NICC-sponsored touring in the fall and winter of 1946 featured, mostly, reporting on the WSCF gathering in Switzerland—to a (USCC) meeting in Racine, Wisconsin; to various stops in New York State—Syracuse, Union College, Colgate, Oswego, Rochester; to the New England Student Christian Movement in (my first time in) Boston; to various stops in Ohio—Ohio State, fraternity-laden Ohio Weselyan, Cincinnati, Oberlin, Cleveland. In the midst of all this traveling and speaking, I attended the meeting of the administrative committee of the National Student YMCA in New York City, at which Bill Ellis reported on Prague, recommending that the student YM be represented in the new International Union of Students, a recommendation on which the committee postponed action.[16] I learn this from mimeographed records. What I learn from my own notes is something quite different. It seems (I learn from my young self) that I was to speak to "the metropolitan Y representatives" one evening, and was on my way "home" (wherever home was) to prepare my speech when I passed the Alvin Theater just as the matinee had started, saw that it was Jose Ferrer in *Cyrano de Bergerac*, made the instant decision to buy a ticket and see the play, and went to my speech that evening "unprepared but happy."

The open but tentative attitude toward the IUS on the part of the student Y applied that fall and winter, I believe, to the Student Christian Movement in general, and to the response at the National Student Christian Assembly in Urbana after Christmas, at which I was one of the two presiders. I don't see anything specifically about that in my notes, nor can I find anything in my memory. Mark Twain said that when he was young he could remember everything, both what happened and what didn't happen—but now that he was old, he could only remember the latter.

At least from my perspective, Prague, the IUS, and the budding USNSA were, although interesting and perhaps important, still marginal. We had our own considerable student movement, with its own complexities.

And as for me personally, I wanted to give up on being a "student"—I once calculated that I had attended in my teenage years, sixteen week-long summer student or youth conferences; if shorter regional gatherings were included, the number would have been much higher. And in the apparatus of the Student Christian Association movement, one would be sitting at a table at 600 Lexington Avenue or 347 Madison Avenue or wherever, surrounded by adult professors, and there would come a moment when the chairman would say, looking at you, "And now let's hear what students [or young people] think of this."

A brief passage through NSA on my way to a vocation

I wanted to buckle down to my own education. I did, however—I don't remember how this came about—attend the First Congress of the USNSA in Madison in August of 1948, representing Yale Divinity School. By that time, the political atmosphere was a good deal different than it had been in the still hopeful summer of 1946. The blunt Communist takeover of Czechoslovakia in February of 1948 had been yet another, and a particularly stark, lesson. A preoccupation at Madison—mine, at least, to judge from ancient jottings in a journal—was to avoid becoming a "front," as the old American Youth Congress (AYC) had become, and the IUS was becoming (see Cater's article).[17] In spite of my sympathy with that purpose, I see that I seem to have had dealings mostly with what I described as a "small, disorganized, Wallace-pin-wearing 'left' group, which came [I wrote] singly from California and Colorado, and in a group—the most vocal—from Metropolitan New York." "Wallace-pin-wearing" refers, of course, to Henry Wallace of the Progressive Party—to its critics, including, by that time, me, a "fellow-traveling" or even "front" party—in the presidential election coming in November. I wrote that the combination of noncommunist liberals with "the Catholic bloc" would route the Wallace-pin wearers and keep this organization from becoming a front. I wrote, about changes in "youth" groups over time, that whereas in 1939 at the AYC, Joe Lash, the New Deal anticommunist liberal had been booed for harsh words about the Soviet Union, (where did I get this?), here at the NSA in 1948 Wallace-pin-wearing Wally Wallace was booed before he spoke, simply because he was student director of the Progressive Party (Can this be? All I know is what I read in my notes.)[18]

Apparently I was not in sympathy with either booing, and, my developing anticommunism not withstanding, I had some common purpose on particular items and some intriguing personal relationships with this Wallace-pin, left-wing group. They represented yet another world that I had not known. I see that I "refused to nominate the Colorado AYD student, whom I like, for president, and refused to be nominated [myself—presumably by this group] for regional chairman." I remember this Colorado "left" person, whom I liked but did not altogether support, taking the floor yet another time and, explaining, plaintively and humorously, that if more people would defend the point of view he was defending, he would not have to speak so often. I also remember him saying to me, toward the end of the Congress, that if he were going to be a "Christian," I was the kind of Christian he would be. I further remember one of the Metropolitan New York group (the things one remembers are not necessarily the large points of history) saying that a certain young woman—pointing to her—was his "mistress." I had not seen a "mistress" before.

I wrote back then that I was pleased to see "a real student-led student organization of strength and significance and a non-propagandistic base." I added, perhaps unfairly, that: "this is what the NICC could never be." And I added, "I like the NSA."

Nevertheless I knew I was through with it. I now had other fish to fry, trying to educate myself to be a political and social ethicist and writer, a vocation the remarkable, hopeful student summer of 1946 had helped to define.

William Lee Miller is the Miller Center Scholar in Ethics and Institutions at the University of Virginia. He is the author of several books and numerous articles published in magazines and journals. He has also been Director of the Program in Political and Social Thought, Professor of Religious Studies, and Chairman of the Department of Communications Studies at University of Virginia, and has been on the faculty at Indiana University, Yale University and Smith College.

AUTHOR AND EDITOR NOTES

[1] *Editor:* The location of some useful archives and a brief bibliography of works relating to the history of the YMCA-YWCA and the Student Christian movement will be found in the Reference section, on p. 1121.

[2] *Editor:* Tesse Hartigan Donnelly (p. 951) recalled in a conversation with the editor how a group of students at the 1948 NSA Congress embraced traditional labor anthems.

[3] *Editor:* Extensive records of the activities of the Student Christian Movement in New England (for the period 1934-1957) can be found in the Yale Divinity School archives. Wilmer (Bill) J. Kitchen, then Secretary of the SCM in New England (and later to become Director of the World Student Service Fund), announces "the first big news" in the SCM newsletter of February 23, 1946, that Joyce Roberts, of Pembroke College, was selected as a delegate to the General Committee of the World Student Christian Federation, to be held in Geneva, Switzerland, that summer. Roberts was later selected to be one of the four NICC delegates on the American delegation to the World Student Congress that August.

[4] *Editor:* The January 13, 1937, issue of the *Vassar Miscellany News*, reporting on the second annual convention of the American Student Union, headlined, "OXFORD OATH UPHELD." Phillip C. Altbach on page 66 of *Student Politics in America*, writes:

> The Oxford Pledge originated in February of 1933, when the Oxford University Student Union in England voted by a large majority that it would under no circumstances fight for king and country. . . the student newspaper at Brown University as well as other campus groups adapted the pledge to American circumstances by rewording it to read that the signer would refuse to "support the United States in any war it may conduct."

See Berlin, p. 10, and American Student Union, p. 47.

[5] *Editor:* It is generally conceded by historians, as Philip G. Altbach notes in *Student Politics in America* (p. 12. Transaction Publishers, New Brunswick, 1997), that "relatively little [student] activism of an organized nature occurred prior to 1900" in America. There was really no "student movement" in the United States, outside of the churches, until after World War I, when the National Student Federation of America was formed (see p. 30). According to the April 1947 NICC student YM/YWCA membership booklet, "the first Student YMCA was formed at the University of Virginia in 1858, and first campus YWCA at Illinois Normal University in 1873." Altbach notes that "the campus Christian movement at this period . . . was one of the few agencies functioning in large numbers of colleges which fostered some kind of social concern."

[6] *Editor:* Direct experiences with the relocation program are also noted in Wurf (Berkeley), p. 179; Suzuki (Los Angeles City College), p. 1031; see also Albums, pp. 1024, 1037 and 1052.

[7] *Author:* To be sure, we did not look upon ourselves as provincial, and certainly not as peripheral. To our minds (most of the time) we saw ourselves (not explicitly, perhaps unconsciously) as standing in the center of American history. By "we" I mean mainline Protestants, especially in the great broad center of the country. In the Southwest Kansas Council of the Boy Scouts of America, we used to sing (rather incongruously to the tune of "My Wild Irish Rose") a bragging regional song that began "The Great Central West; The region that's the best. . . ." Perhaps we didn't have much to brag about except geographical centrality. There would have been a time, in American history, when "student movement" would have meant the Student Christian Movement; up to and until just after World War II, it would have been, by all odds, the largest American national student movement.

[8] *Editor:* Leonard Clough, writing in the *Journal of Ecumenical Studies*, 32:3 (Summer 1995): 319, traces the genesis of the USCC and the student Christian movement on U.S. college campuses:

> In 1870, Luther Wishard gathered representatives of twenty-one colleges that had established volunteer student Christian fellowships. Thus began the Intercollegiate Young Men's Christian Association. Soon after that, John R. Mott and others launched an intercollegiate student Christian movement under the auspices of the YMCA and YWCA.
>
> In the early 1900s, several Protestant denominations began to look upon college campuses as mission fields. "Student workers" were employed, and student centers were built on or near many of the larger campuses. Before long, denominational intercollegiate student movements appeared alongside the Student YM-YWCAs, which had formed the National Intercollegiate Christian Council, I remember well the sense of competition and the lack of trust that denominational student workers felt toward the Y programs—and vice versa.
>
> Some people felt it was quite symbolic that it was during a violent storm in New York City that the United Student Christian Council was born, in September 1944. Certain Student Y leaders and a few denominational executives and students who served as an informal council for the World ["World" after 1960] Student Christian Federation adopted a constitution that created a federation of twelve sCm's [sic] and nine church departments of student work.
>
> Tensions between the Ys and the churches surfaced again in 1952, when the USCC became a "related body" of the National Council of the Churches of Christ in the United States. Some called it selling out to the church bureaucracy, while others complained that it was a refusal to become fully related to the churches. Nevertheless, two important things were accomplished: "student work," the financing and staffing of campus ministries, was lodged in the NCCC Department of Higher Education; and "student movements" cooperated through the USCC. By 1959, two other historical sCm's with specialized interests, the Student Volunteer Movement and the Interseminary Movement, joined the USCC, which then became the National Student Christian Federation.

[9] *Editor:* This was probably Jean Casson of the American Unitarian Youth.

[10] *Editor:* See more about Doug Cater, Jimmy Wallace, and the Prague delegation in Part 1, Section 1, p. 92. See also Cater, "The Collapse of Youth's One World," p. 535.

[11] *Editor:* See Prague delegate report, p. 806, Ellis, p. 158.

[12] *Author:* The mainline Protestant denominations are: the church of the mother country—the Episcopalian Church (Anglican); the bigger denominations that sprang from the Puritan revolt from Anglicanism in England, Presbyterians and Congregationalists (these three dominated the American colonies at first); the sectarian-revivalist churches of the common man that pulled away later—Baptists, both out of a wing of Puritanism and from the Continent, and the Methodists, out of the Anglican-Episcopal Churches (these two appeal to the frontier and the common man and passed the first ones in numbers by the time of the Civil War); the largest indigenous growth in the American West, claiming to be a movement and not a denomination—the Disciples of Christ; and the largest Protestant body from the later immigrations from Europe. Unitarians and Quakers are much smaller in number, important as they are otherwise, and may not be either mainline or Protestant.

[13] *Editor:* See Alice Horton Tibbett's notes on her visit to the Soviet Union in 1945, p. 71.

[14] *Editor:* See "Operation University," p. 739, and its expression of the Catholic Church's view on this same issue of participating in the newly emerged WFDY and IUS.

[15] *Editor:* George Todd, who was president of the Baptist Students Christian Association in 1948-1949, explained to me that for many years it was customary to rotate the use of Christmas and summer seasons for the various Christian group assemblies, for example, Year 1—The National YM- and YWCAs; Year 2, the various denominations; Year 3, the USCC; and Year 4, the Student Volunteer Movement. It was through Todd's suggestion that I was able to locate Bill Miller, author of this memoir. The attendance at these events was impressive. The January 12, 1938, issue of the *Vassar Miscellany News* headlines, "2,000 Assemble for Christian Students' Annual Conference." The January 4, 1947, issue of *The Daily Pennsylvanian* headlines, "1,400 Students of 900 Schools Attend National Student Assembly," referring to the Urbana SCM Assembly to which the author also refers.

[16] *Editor:* See Elllis and Roberts on the World Student Congress, p. 106.

[17] *Editor:* See p. 535 (Douglass Cater, "Collapse of Youth's One World," *The Reporter*, August 30, 1949).

[18] *Editor:* The reactions to Joseph Lash and Walter Wallace that Miller picks up from his notes and questions are consistent with the settings in which both spoke—Lash confronting a strong cohort of Communists and fellow travelers in the ASU (see Joseph Lash, p. 42) and Wallace appearing before an NSA Congress likely to be suspicious of the left (see note 5, p. 851); also Wallace, p. 865.

PICTURE CREDITS: *Then:* c. 1947 (*Intercollegian*, 11/47. Kautz). *Now:* c. 2002 (Miller Center, U. of Virginia).

THE STUDENT CHRISTIAN MOVEMENT ON THE U.S. CAMPUS

USCC DRIVES DEEP

At the fourth annual meeting of the United Student Christian Council, earnest words were recorded for all parts of our student movement: YM, YW, and the church-related programs as well. We share the sense of immediacy with which USCC added this introductory statement to its more explicit platform of belief and action.

WE CALL THE AMERICAN STUDENT CHRISTIAN MOVEMENT to study the role of the SCM in the secular world. We have felt here that the existence and growth of secular student agencies is asking deep and disturbing questions of the SCM. These questions test our understanding of the Christian concern for the secular world. We believe that our answers to these questions, and in a larger sense, our action in such respects as politics, the university, race, economics could take on new realism with a surer understanding of our responsibility for the sin and crisis of our time, our hope in the power of God to manifest his victory over personal and social evil, and our privilege to witness to his victory individually and corporately in worship, study and actio[...]

TO FIND SUCH A WITNESS, we feel that Christian students must examine at least the following kinds of witness among others:

1. The social relevance of the Church's primary witness in preaching the Word and administering the sacraments.
2. The witness of withdrawal from the social struggle into religious communities, brotherhoods and similar efforts.
3. The witness in society through called individuals (e.g., the Christian politician).
4. The witness in society through activities which mould

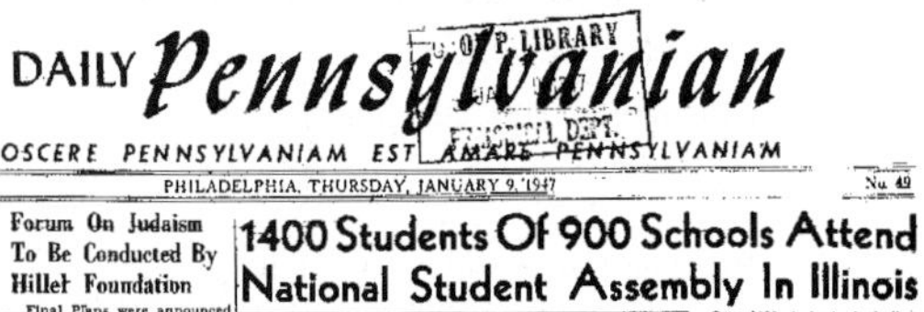

DAILY *Pennsylvanian*

OSCERE PENNSYLVANIAM EST AMARE PENNSYLVANIAM

PHILADELPHIA, THURSDAY, JANUARY 9, 1947 — No. 49

Forum On Judaism To Be Conducted By Hillel Foundation

1400 Students Of 900 Schools Attend National Student Assembly In Illinois

Over 1400 students, including 20 from the University of Pennsylvania, represented the CA...

Student Delegates Report To YMCA Tomorrow Evening

Tomorrow evening at 7 o'clock the five UNC delegates to the national convention of the Student Christian Movement will make a report to the members of the Y at a joint meeting to be held in the Roland Parker lounge of Graham Memorial. A report on the

PUBLISHED DURING THE COLLEGE

VOL. XXIII

Spelman Students Attend National Assembly of the Student Christian Movement

ALMA POWELL, '47

"It seems only yesterday that we sat here in chapel," began Bettye Washington, one of the Spelman students that attended the National Assembly of the Student Christian Association movement

SCM Conference Will Feature Outstanding U. S. Churchmen

This evening marks the opening of a state-wide conference on "The Church, The Churches and You" being held in Cutler Union this weekend. Sponsored by the N.Y. State Student Christian Movement the conference will concern itself with the present status of the Christian Church in the U.S. and in the relation of the stu-

VASSAR MISCELLANY NEWS

CHURCH PLAYS VITAL ROLE IN V.C. HISTORY

Prexy Expands Interpretation Of Church As First Presented By Matthew Vassar

Founders Envisage 'Community Church' As Flexible Channel

McCormick Expresses Views On Religious Educational Philosophy

Defines Church Concept In Address To Faculty

From top: *Intercollegian*, 12/47; *Daily Pennsylvanian*, 1/9/47; *Daily Tar Heel*, U. of NC, 1/47; *Campus Mirror*, Spelman C., Atlanta, 2/47; *The Campus*, U. of Rochester, 4/13/51; *Vassar Miscellany News*, 12/1/48

WILLIAM LEE MILLER

Early years: Born in Bloomington, Indiana on April 21, 1926. Went to school in Laramie, WY, Hutchinson, KS, and Lincoln, NE.

Education: Ph.D., Religious Social Ethics, Yale University, 1958. B.D., Summa Cum Laude, Yale University, 1950. B.A. with honors, University of Nebraska, 1947.

Career highlights: The University of Virginia, Miller Center Scholar in Ethics and Institutions, 1999-present; Thomas C. Sorensen Professor of Political and Social Thought, Director of the Program in Political and Social Thought, 1991-1999; White Burkett Miller Center Professor of Ethics and Institutions, 1987-1992; Chairman, Department of Rhetoric and Communication Studies, 1982-1990; Professor of Religious Studies, 1982-present. Indiana University, Professor of Political Science and Professor of Religious Studies, 1969-1982; Founding Director of the Poynter Center on American Institutions, 1972-1982. New Haven Board of Aldermen, Member, 1963-1969. Yale University, Associate Professor of Social Ethics, 1962-1969; Assistant Professor of Social Ethics, 1958-1962; Instructor in Social Ethics, 1951-1953; Assistant in Instruction, Philosophy, 1949-1951. *Reporter* magazine, Staff Writer and Editor, 1955-1958 (regular contributor, 1953-1965). Smith College, Assistant Professor of Religion, 1953-1955.

Publications: *Lincoln's Virtues* (Alfred A. Knopf, 2002); *Arguing about Slavery: The Great Debate in the United States Congress* (Alfred A. Knopf, 1996). *The Business of May Next: James Madison and the Founding* (University Press of Virginia, 1992). Author of six other books and numerous articles in magazines and journals, including the *New York Times Magazine*, the *Reporter*, the *Yale Review*, the *New Republic*, and *Commonweal.*

"A POTENT INFLUENCE" characterized the YMCA as the backbone of the Student Christian Movement through and directly after World War II (University of Texas 1926 YMCA development brochure, right). Shown above is Bill Miller, YMCA President, and Betty Lou Horton '47, YWCA Vice President, standing before the University of Nebraska Presbyterian House, campus home for one of the 14 "mainstream" Protestant denominations that could be found on U.S. campuses. These denominational groups, together with Student Christian Associations and the YMCA and YWCA, made up the United Student Christian Council (See next page). More than 900 colleges (see left) attended the first postwar Student Christian Movement Assembly in December 1946 at the U. of Illinois.

A Potent Influence

Extract From the Minutes of the Board of Regents, March 16, 1926

Whereas, The Board of Regents of the University of Texas feels that the University Young Men's Christian Association during the thirty-six years of its service, has grown to be one of the most efficient and constructive forces engaged in the building up and maintaining of wholesome activities and ideals among the students on the University campus, and

Whereas, For the purpose of guaranteeing the continuance of this valuable work, the Young Men's Christian Association of the University has initiated and is carrying forward a campaign for raising an endowment fund; now therefore,

Be It Resolved by the Board of Regents of the University of Texas:

1. That this program and campaign of the University Young Men's Christian Association be heartily endorsed and approved by the said Board; and

2. That copies of this resolution be sent to the President of the University Y. M. C. A., and the Chairman of its Board of Directors, together with an expression of well-wishing and the hope that the campaign may culminate in success.

A true copy.

C. D. SIMMONS, Secretary, Board of Regents.

Sources: Center for American History, U. of Texas. Photo, Miller and Horton, U. of Nebraska Cornhusker, 1946 yearbook (Love Library)

The Student Christian Movement and International Student Activity

The Protestant Christian youth and student movement was probably the driving force in motivating participation in international student activities after the war. Certainly, the New England SCM was pivotal and the YMCA and YWCA furnished important opportunities for students to act on their concerns before the student government became involved through NSA. The World Student Service Fund (WSSF), with its strong roots in the Student Christian Movement, played an important role in giving concrete action projects to the Ys and to denominational groups seeking to make a contribution after the war.[1]

As a student traveler for WSSF, my key contacts on the campus were often in the Ys and campus denominational groups because they were motivated to do something at the international level. Also, the major conferences the Ys held every four years always included outstanding speakers from overseas, and WSSF was accorded an important role. These same groups were also the ones that took an active interest in supporting refugee students who came to the campus and helped develop services for all international students at a time when there were very few foreign student advisers.

Now there are about seven thousand members of the NAFSA: Association of International Educators. I think it is clear that the campus Protestant groups helped to train a great many of the students who were later in leadership roles in student government and NSA. That was certainly the pattern at Illinois.

William H. Allaway
NSA Illinois Regional Vice Chairman for International Affairs, 1948-49

END NOTE

[1] See Allaway, p. 613, and WSSF, p. 622.

WSCF Charts Course: "That The Post-War World May Not Be Built on Hatred"

Excerpts from "Minutes of the Meeting of the General Committee of the World's Student Christian Federation," Commission on SCM Members and Political Aims, Chateau de Bossey, Céligny, Switzerland, August 9th to 20th, 1946.

A. General Recommendations.

(I) We recommend exchange of questions and answers between movements whose nations find themselves on different sides of an issue....

4) We recommend the establishment of a continuing Political Commission of the W.S.C.F. This Commission should give immediate attention to the problem of Power Politics and the Establishment of the Peace, and early attention to the relation of Christianity And Communism....

B. World Federation of Democratic Youth and International Union of Students.

In view of the fact that the W. F. D. Y. is but recently formed and that the I.U.S. has yet to be formed, we recommend that:

1) the General Committee approve the action of the General Secretary in sending observers to the preparatory meetings of the I.U.S. in Prague, in November 1945, and August 1946....

3) National movements, or their individual members, should consider seriously their participation as far as possible in these organisations;

C. World Order.

The Federation believes that international anarchy is incompatible with the Christian view of man. Therefore, we recommend that the Federation Political Commission undertake to investigate the fundamental issues involved in World Order and that similar thinking be carried out by the national movements, paying special attention to the following points: (a)The formal organization of U. N. 0.; (b) The functional international organs attached to U. N. 0. and their relation to the growing international community; (c) The relation of power politics to U. N. 0., especially as seen in the Security Council.

Regarding these problems we suggest that serious consideration be given to Natural Law, the theory of the State under God, Christian Hope and the Church Community in the planned state.

D. Resolution on Religious Freedom.

Remembering the presence in our Federation of movements in countries where full religious liberty is not practiced, we affirm our devotion to the principles of freedom of worship, of evangelisation and of expression of opinion in religious matters.

E. Resolution on the Relationship between Victorious and Defeated Nations.

The national-socialist and fascist dictatorships with their system of violence, violation of pledges, atrocities, bestial cruelties, racial arrogance and claims to the hegemony of one people over its neighbours have brought immeasurable suffering to the nations, deprived countless individuals and families of their freedom, possessions and life, destroyed peaceful work and economic prosperity, and by these means radically undermined confidence and trust between the nations.

On all sides these facts have raised a vast tide of hatred, revulsion and indignation....

On the other hand it must not be forgottten that other nations also shared in the responsibility for the growth and terrible consequences of the totalitarian systems....

The Federation urges all its members to do the utmost in their power that the post-war world may not be built on hatred....

F. Resolution on Imperialism.

We affirm that the political exploitation or economic enslavement of one nation by another is completely incompatible with the Christian understanding of the relations which should prevail among mankind.. that policies of such forcible subjection should be renounced forthwith.... We rejoice, for example, that India is on the eve of obtaining independence....

Finally, no Christian student in a nation involved can morally avoid making the attempt to transcend national interest in understanding the issues involved. The Will of God among present alternatives for the nation must be sought.

THE STUDENT CHRISTIAN MOVEMENT IN 1947

United Student Christian Council-The National Student Council of YMCA's joins with the National Student Council of YWCA's and twelve national denominational church foundations as members of the United Student Christian Council. The USCC coordinates many activities in which all the above named groups are interested, and which can best be accomplished by cooperation. The USCC is the United States section of the World's Student Christian Federation.

World's Student Christian Federation-Since 1895 the World's student Christian Federation has been the international expression of Student Christian life (See p.000). National student Christian movements in 14 countries are its members. Its staff and General Committee are international. Its headquarters is in Geneva, Switzerland. Local student YMCA's in the United States are among the many contributors to the financial support of the WSCF.

The Student Christian Association-an Alternate Plan-On some campuses it appears better to include the men and women students of the college in a Student Christian Association which serves to provide a united approach to campus religious work. The essential structure and program of the SCA are similar to the descriptions of a student YMCA found elsewhere in this booklet. Any local campus group which feels that this plan offers a better answer to their college religious work is invited to seek additional counsel from the Regional YMCA office and from the Regional YWCA office.

From "Organization of Student YMCA's and Student Christian Associations," YMCA Publishing House, Association Press, NYC, undated, c. 1947 (Yale Divinity School Archives).

What Can We Say to Europe's Students?

by MURIEL W. JACOBSON

IN THE OPEN courtyard of a Czech university residence which had been prison, torture chamber and execution place for professors and students, we stood with our hosts in the penetrating cold through a memorial service to their colleagues and friends. The black banners whipping in the wind made the only sound while the wreaths were being laid on the spot where hundreds of men and women had died in November, 1939. Where in this ravaged nation could vitality be found for the tasks of peace?

We found our answers in many places. Students were crowding into the university, which was without heat or glass for the windows, without chairs or notebooks, and only a few text books in the library. Intent on getting the education demanded of them by virtue of their citizenship in a strategic nation in a troubled world, they were taking lectures on scraps of paper, standing, from faculty members who had survived the occupation. The faculty were teaching, gladly, many hours in excess of any normal schedule.

In the YMCA we attended the first meeting in the reorganization of the Student Christian Movement. Invited to speak, we tried to express the hope that they would be able to count on our more fortunate students sharing a little of the costs of their struggle with them. We could not share fully in the explicit knowledge out of which they sang—

A safe stronghold our God is still,
A trusty shield and weapon. . . .
And though they take our life,
Goods, honor, children, wife—
These things shall vanish all,
The city of God remaineth.

Top:
Prague throngs in Wenceslas Square gather to cheer the Student Congress and what it symbolizes.

Center:
LIKE NICC is the opening session of the Student Congress.

Left:
STUDENT MEMORIAL in the Prague Cathedral recognizing martyrdom of thousands of undergraduates for truth.

(Reproduced from *The Intercollegian*, May, 1946. *The Intercollegian* was the publication of the student YMCA, Student YWCA and Student Volunteer Movement.)

¶ This summer USA student Christians will be represented at two continental world student conclaves. One is the World's Student Christian Federation, August 9-20, at Geneva. The other is the International Student Federation in Prague, August 17-30.

¶ Early this year in Prague there was a Planning Conference for this latter (ISF) Assembly. Here is an account of it by our admirable representative, MURIEL JACOBSON, of the National YW Student Staff.

¶ Are we ready—spiritually and politically—to make our American contribution in an atmosphere like this? It will take planning and prayer!

Grim, Glorious Record

As the conference opened, the agenda included statements of student activities during the war, damage to universities, student relief and post-war student cooperation:

"The University of Leyden was closed in 1940 because of a student strike against the German anti-Jewish measures." "In Yugoslavia 70% of the colleges and institutes were destroyed." "In the USSR the invaders, having destroyed the Korolenko Library at Kharkov, paved the streets with books and drove their cars over them." "For Chinese educators the slogan is 'war or no war, education must go on' and in the hinterland the universities have found temporary quarters." "About 30% of the Italian students are affected with T.B." "85% of Dutch students, actively engaged in the resistance movement, refused to sign a declaration of loyalty demanded by the Germans, though they realized they were declaring open war against the Nazis and attempts were made to deport those who did not sign." "During the last few weeks of the war student groups in Austria were able to save valuable scientific equipment." "In Norway in 1943 as a result of proposed regulations for admission to Oslo University which violated the basic principles of academic liberty faculty members protested and threatened to resign: Nine professors and 68 students were arrested. All faculties and 2,200 students protested in writing demanding their release."

"In Poland 13 centers of higher learning were organized underground and were at work during the war with secret lectures, to not more than 10 people at a time moving always from place to place to avoid arrest."

And now that the war is past, the students need a means of facilitating manifold student exchanges—through cultural and sports activities, travel and work projects. But before giving a report on the Congress debate on postwar student cooperation, it is necessary to sketch briefly the background of the Congress.

World Organization Plan

This Prague gathering, of students who had been delegates at the London World Youth Conference last November, was called for "preliminary report and exchange of ideas" on student organization and activities. It in turn set up a Preparatory Committee from 12 nations to prepare a fully delegated international student conference for this summer.

Here the aim is to set up a world structure serving student needs, in which all types of student organization may participate. A tentative draft of the constitution has already been sent out. Here decisions regarding relationships with other world student and youth organizations will be made.

NOT A STRAUSS WALTZ: Hawaiian student and his Prague interpreter.

At Prague the struggle to make findings "recommendations" and not legislation, was the real issue in the Congress. This was necessary because of unequal representation: for example, Yugoslavia had 20 votes, America one! Some of us delegates, too, had only the power of referral to our national organizations. The US-USSR-Britain bloc did succeed in limiting Congress action to "recommendation."

While there was a strong Communist and radical group in the Congress, there was an almost equally strong non-Communist group, including the Christian organizations and representatives of many of the European and the Chinese student Christian movements.

NICC delegates will go to the legislative Prague conference of the proposed International Students' Federation in August, 1946. Our participation in the ISF means we must know our way around in an organization where the struggle for control will be chiefly along political lines dictated by the most politically conscious groups. It means working with many groups unlike those with which we traditionally are associated in our international student relationships. It means fidelity to our central religious purpose. It means clear understanding of the relevance of our faith in the affairs of the political and economic international world.

Our problem is the same at the student level as that faced by the United Nations: to find ways of working together. All of us are convinced that the vast common concerns of the student world may be best served through unity in aims, even amid diverse opinions and convictions.

Editor's note: Muriel Jacobson had traveled to Europe in the summer of 1945, attending the London World Youth Conference, the Prague preparatory conference for the 1946 World Student Congress, and then on a tour of the Soviet Union. Alice Horton Tibbetts was a United States Student Assembly delegate to London, and accompanied Jacobson and others to Prague and then to the Soviet Union. Tibbetts writes of these travels in her memoir on p. 71 (including photos of Jacobson), and of Jacobson's subsequent help in setting up the U.S. delegation to the World Student Congress.

The Protestant Student Groups: The Ys, NICC, SCM, WSCF

OUR NATIONAL AND WORLD RELATIONSHIPS

When you join the YMCA and YWCA you become a part of an amazing fellowship which reaches back in time to 1844 and reaches around the world! The first YMCA was founded in London in 1844, followed by the London YWCA in 1855. The first Student YMCA was formed at the University of Virginia in 1858 and the first campus YWCA at Illinois Normal University in 1873. The YMCA on this campus began in ____ and the YWCA in ____.

The YMCA and YWCA are pioneering organizations. Many features of campus life had humble origins in the "Ys". Among them are student employment bureaus; student counselling; campus cooperatives; student government; freshman orientation; summer camps and conferences; and use of the discussion method. A unique contribution to church life has been the training of students who now in their adult life are leading the movement toward church unity in communities and in the World Council of Churches. But the greatest contribution of the "Ys" is the awakening of the minds and spirits of students who later become leaders in the social, political and religious movements of small communities and of the world.

Our YMCA and YWCA are a part of the Central-Geneva Region. Each June we send representatives to the Lake Geneva Conference where we meet students from one hundred other colleges in this region. Representatives are elected from the Geneva Region to the National Student Councils of the YMCA and YWCA, which meet for a week in September. Every three or four years delegates attend the National Assembly of the Student Christian Association Movement. Every three years representatives of student and community YMCAs and YWCAs meet in the National Council of the YMCA and the National Convention of the YWCA. The National Student Councils of the YMCA and YWCA cooperate with other national student Christian organizations through the United Student Christian Council.

When you join the YMCA or YWCA, you become a part of three world organizations: The World Alliance of YMCAs or the World's YWCA with offices in the old Secretariat Building of the League of Nations in Geneva, Switzerland; the newly formed International Union of Students with its headquarters at Charles University in Prague, Czechoslovakia; and the historic World's Student Christian Federation, with its office in Geneva, Switzerland.

FAMILY TREE

YMCAs in 1500 cities and towns | 303 Student YMCAs | SCAs 189 | 422 Student YWCAs | YWCAs in 840 cities and towns

Twelve areas of the Community YMCA | Nine regional councils of the student YMCA and YWCA or SCM | Four regions of the Community YWCA

National Council of the YMCA
National Council meets annually
National Board meets three times yearly

YWCAs of the USA
National Convention meets triennially
National Board meets semi-annually

NATIONAL ASSEMBLY OF THE STUDENT CHRISTIAN ASSOCIATION MOVEMENT
Meets every three or four years

National Student Council, YMCA | National Student Council, YWCA

National Intercollegiate Christian Council
composed of the National Student Councils of YMCA and YWCA
meets annually

United Student Christian Council of U.S.A.
to facilitate cooperation among the National Student Councils of the YMCA and YWCA and national student groups related to Protestant Churches

World's YMCA
Geneva, Switzerland | World's Student Christian Federation
Geneva, Switzerland | World's YWCA
Geneva, Switzerland

FIFTY-TWO YEARS OF WITNESS

1 9 4 7

The general secretaries:*
R. C. Mackie, W. A. Visser t' Hooft, H. L. Henriod, J. R. Mott

. . . in 1895 the WSCF was founded in a mediaeval castle at Vadstena, Sweden by representatives of American and European student Christian movements and Dr. Mott set out on his epoch-making journeys. By 1897 the Federation had spread to the Far East, India and South Africa. In 1911, at Constantinople the first effective contact was made with the Orthodox world.

. . . in 1920 H.-Ls. Henriod came into office as the Federation plunged into a vast relief effort out of which, in 1925, International Student Service arose.

. . . in 1932, in the midst of the great depression, W. A. Visser 't Hooft became general secretary and, together with the Chairman Francis P. Miller, led the discussion by which the Federation sought to reformulate its message in the light of more serious Bible study and the pressing needs of the world. At the Committee in Java, 1934, and at Mills College, California, 1936, attention was directed to the Pacific Area and its problems.

. . . in 1938 during the tension of the Munich crisis, Robert Mackie undertook the task of guiding the WSCF and preparing it to participate in the conference at Amsterdam, August, 1939 of 1500 Christian youth from seventy countries. During the war many movements in occupied countries went underground and some lost their leaders in concentration camps.

. . . in 1947 the first General Committee in eight years has been held, fellowship with the German and Japanese movements renewed and the Federation goes forward into God's future declaring "The Lord has done great things for us already, whereof we rejoice."

"ROOTED IN ADULT INSTITUTIONS," because of its church-related origins, as Bill Miller observes (p. 722), the Student Christian Movement was supported by a well-staffed professional infrastructure. John R. Mott (Cornell, 1888), in photo above right, founder of the Student Volunteer Movement in 1886, was the U.S. and World movement's inspiring early leader (See p. 692). (Top and left, from "Making Membership Meaningful," NICC, April 1947. Above: USSC brochure, 1947. Source: Yale Divinity archives).

The Student Christian Movement in a Time of Change

Editor's note: The story of the Student Christian Movement in the U.S., as represented by the YM and YWCA's on campus, the Student Volunteer Movement, the Student Christian Associations, and the various denominational student ministries, provides, until the early 1950's, the main thread of mainstream student social conscience as it was expressed on college campuses. By virtue of alumni funding and professional staffing, the SCM's component groups provided student facilities and services on a community, national and international level. The Protestant Church commitment to general education and its influence on the early organization of the U.S. higher education system shaped its future (Frederick Rudoph, "The American College and University," U. of Georgia Press, 1990). Its student movements on campus, facilitated by professional staff, maintained strong groundings in its spiritual mission. These groundings began to erode as the activism of the sixties and seventies intensified its self-questioning and led to the complete restructuring and eventual dissolution of the University Christian Movement in 1969. What follows are brief excerpts which reflect its earlier origins and the winds of change. A comprehensive effort to capture that period of change will be found in the Summer and Fall 1995 issues of The Journal of Ecumenical Studies *(Temple University). It is no coincidence, as Phil Des Marais writes on p. 736, that the Vatican had the national offices of the National Federation of Catholic College Students and the Newman Club Federation closed during that same period.*

The New Frontier for the Student YMCA and YWCA

A.L. Kershaw

Excerpts from a 14-page pamphlet based on two addresses delivered by the Reverend A. L. Kershaw to the. National Student Council of the YMCA and YWCA in August, 1955. They were background for an inquiry into the role of the Campus YMCA and YWCA. A. L. Kershaw was minister of the Holy Trinity Episcopal Church of Oxford, Ohio, and taught on occasion at Miami University. He was one of the most popular conference leaders in the Geneva region.

All too often the campus Y is anything but a provocative jolt in the social slumbers of the usual campus. This is due to several causes. Chief among them is that the members of many Y cabinets and commissions have so little understanding of the meaning of the Christian faith that there is no vital religious reference that can provide a real cutting edge, intellectually or spiritually, by which the complexities of life and thought can be grappled with. Thus some cabinet and commission meetings resemble a kind of innocuous postgraduate Sunday School class.... Beyond this, much ineptness in providing leadership intellectually on the campus derives from the difficulty of understanding the complexity of the college world itself....

Changing patterns on campus

Once the Y's carried on the major part of all Christian work on the campus. The Y's were the arm of the churches in this strategic market place of ideas and decisions, and at least morally were supported by them.

The change from the past is drastic. After many years the churches—hemselves in transition from parish-house activities and social service emphasis to a new concern for a more rigorous theological grounding adequate to interpret the crises of the wars, depression, and social breakdowns of the 1920's and 30's—began to move to the edge of the campus with foundations and chapels, with a new concern for the religious education and worship experience of students. The presence of various foundations all ministering to the same student body inevitably nourished the organization of Student Religious Councils, and in the growing complexity of student religious activities, many universities have hired staff persons to integrate the work. Often such councils were organized by the Y's. Subcommittees of such councils began cooperative work in social action and recreation, and began to focus the ecumenical concerns. Since the Hillel Foundations, the Newman Clubs, and Christian Scientists, among others, were also included in such religious councils, the ecumenical thrusts, transported from the Y's, faced complex frustrations. So Protestant Councils have also developed, that ... could facilitate greater cooperative thought, worship and activity.

Two other developments must also be mentioned as affecting the present situation wherein the role of the Y's is questioned. One is the rapid growth of the Student Union Movement, where recreation and spare time needs of the students can be.organized and provided for, with personnel trained in student recreational programs. The other is the widespread growth of student counseling facilities, the University expanding its student responsibility, to offer help on perplexing questions faced by students, as well as in situations of disturbed behavior.

Does the Y have a continuing role?

So the inevitable question comes from many sides: What about the Y's? What can they do that can't be, or isn't being, done better by some other more adequately equipped agency?

The lines between Y and church have been further blurred by the unusually high level of professional leadership in the Y, where many are as well, if not better, theologically educated than some of the campus clergy, and who share with the church, in the thrust of recent theological thought, a sense of the urgency for the Christian community. If the church is concerned with a revitalized Christian community, where love and acceptance are offered to men's needs, and the Y's also have this concern, where are they in purpose essentially different? Is the Church Sunday and liturgical, while the Y is weekdays and informal? But isn't this quibbling?

There is in the Y's a leadership of a stature which can recognize that thinking chiefly of the Y's existence as it has been can be a form of self-worship and idolatry. They live within a rich heritage whose primary devotion is to Christ and His kingdom. It is within this loyalty to the person of Christ that the role of the Student Y in a new university situation can be faced with the expectancy of loyal adventure, rather than with fear. They know that the Y is a lay movement, not an institution held by boundaries of tradition, canon, or rubric. Like the church, the underlying purpose of the Y's is to make Christ known to all people; but unlike the church, as laymen in a movement, it is free, under the guidance of the Holy Spirit, to make Christ known in fresh and startling ways appropriate to the time and the people who live in it., While nourished by the old and the traditional, the free spirits who make up a movement are not bound by the traditional. The essential thrust of a movement is to make history, not to worship it.

NICC 1947-48 LEADERSHIP GUIDES RELATIONS WITH NSA AND IUS

Photos: Intercollegian, 9/48 (Courtesy Kautz Archives)

After formation of the International Union of Students (IUS) in August 1946 (which inspired the Chicago Student Conference and the founding of NSA (see Part 1), Bill Ellis (Harvard), an NICC delegate, was elected U.S. Vice President, and the NICC initiated IUS membership (See p. 158). When Ellis took ill in 1947, he chose NSA's Jim Smith (U. of Texas) as his proxy. Both resigned in March 1948 after the Czech Communist coup (see p. 188). From top: Edwin Espy and Leila Anderson, national executives, respectively of the YMCA and YWCA, and Ernie Howell (Harvard), NICC 1947-48 Co-Chair, drafted a letter to Ellis on the proxy issue (p.158). Bottom, from left: Fred Coots, Lulla Hansen, 1948-49 NICC Co-chairman, Barbara Deitz (Ursinus) and Howell, 1947-1948 Co-Chairs. Anderson and Harold B. Ingalls, YMCA executive, Ellis's contact during his illness.

The Newman Clubs, National Federation of Catholic College Students (NFCCS), and Joint Committee for Student Action (JCSA)

2. Catholic Student Participation in NSA, 1946–1965

Philip Des Marais
University of Minnesota; Chair, NSA Minnesota Region, 1946-47
Chair, Joint Committee for Student Action, 1947-1948
NSA National Advisory Board Member, 1954-63; Chair, 1963-65

In this review of Catholic students and institutions of higher education participation in NSA, I will focus on three aspects:

1. My own participation at the Founding Congresses and subsequent activity that lasted more or less until 1965;
2. The role of Catholic delegates and student leaders at the founding meetings in 1946 and 1947;
3. Issues of special interest to Catholic participants during the following years and the development of Catholic student leaders.

Delegates to the Chicago Student Conference—1946

I first heard about NSA in 1946, when I was a graduate student in journalism and political science (under the GI Bill) at the University of Minnesota (U of M). Joan Keaveny, a neighbor in South Minneapolis and fellow alumnus of Washburn High School, was president of the All University Council. I was vice president of the Newman Club, the largest organized student group on campus, and a staff member at the *Minneapolis Tribune*. The University campus in Minneapolis was politically charged. (There were also a significant number of left-wing communists.) Irwin S. Kirkpatrick (late husband of Jeane Kirkpatrick) was my adviser and professor of political thought. He attracted over two hundred graduate students to his lectures, where he was regularly heckled by members of American Youth for Democracy (AYD) from the rear of the hall.

Joan Keaveny stopped me at Newman Hall one day saying that she wanted to nominate me for U of M delegate to a student conference to be held at the University of Chicago in December. She had learned that the Communist group would be active at the conference and that our delegation should be alert to this situation. Another delegate would be Don Fraser from the School of Law. Although Don was a staunch DFL Democrat, he was also a strong anti-Marxist. He was to become a member of the U.S. House of Representatives and four-term mayor of Minneapolis.

On December 27 our delegation arrived in Chicago, where we were housed in a very comfortable, twelve-story building, which was a dorm for foreign students.[1] At the Reynolds Club (the student union) that evening, I was approached by Martin McLaughlin, a delegate from Notre Dame and a member of the conference sponsor's committee.[2] We went over to 57th Street for a beer with Ralph Dungan[3] and Jim Dougherty, both from Philadelphia. Jim was president of the National Federation of Catholic College Students. Henry Briefs of Georgetown was also there. We were all combat veterans of World War II, and Dungan was wearing a leather navy pilot's jacket. They asked me, as an officer of the largest Newman Club in the nation, to join them in an informal group to monitor the conference on behalf of the many Catholic student participants. Out of 307 participating colleges, 80 were Catholic, plus representatives of the NFCCS and the Newman Club Federations. I did not have to be informed about the various delegates from Communist sponsored groups, namely, AYD, Young Communist League, and other subgroups. We had them all at Minnesota.

We had three principal objectives:

1 Encourage Catholic student participation in discussions and debates;
2. Work for a constitution that would be student-council based and democratic;

3. Prevent any takeover of organizational structure by the communist groups.

We were successful in all of these efforts. Elections were held for the National Continuations Committee (NCC), which would hold a Constitutional Convention in September 1947. John Simons,[4] of Fordham, was elected treasurer of the continuations committee. Five Catholic delegates, including Ralph Dungan and myself, were elected to the National Executive Committee (NEC) by virtue of being chairmen of our respective NCC regional delegations.

Formation of the Joint Committee for Student Action (JSCA) and preparation for the Constitutional Convention

Sometime during the early spring of 1947, 1 received a phone call from Msgr. Charles Bermingham, director of the Youth Department of the National Catholic Welfare Conference (NCWC) in Washington, D.C. He wanted me to meet him in Chicago to discuss a job offer. I had been recommended by Martin McLaughlin and Henry Briefs as a good prospect to direct an organized effort to promote Catholic student participation in the emerging national student movement. I would be officed in the youth department and would work with the executive secretary of NFCCS and the Newman Club Federation. This proposal had the endorsement of Archbishop Richard Cushing, Chairman of the Youth Department, and Rev. John Murray, S.J., a principal consultant in these matters.[5]

Somewhat bored with my graduate course at the U of M (large sections, etc.), I agreed to go to Washington at the end of the spring semester.

Arriving by train in Washington, I was met at the station by Charlie Schultz[6] from Georgetown and driven out to Chevy Chase, the home of Henry Briefs, where I was to stay for the summer. Henry's father was Goetz Briefs, an economics professor at Georgetown. The spacious home was a focal point for a group of graduate students from Georgetown and Catholic University. Every weekend there was a big party, but during weekdays we worked on the setup of the JCSA, which had officially been established by the boards of NFCCS and the NCF. Jim Dougherty and Ralph Dungan were frequently down from Philadelphia. They were both seniors at St. Joseph's College.[7]

A JCSA executive committee was selected, including representatives from key college centers in Boston, New York, Philadelphia, and Washington. I represented the Midwest. Our primary goal was to encourage Catholic participation at the August 1947 National Student Congress from student governments at Catholic colleges and Newman Club members at major state universities, all of which had large Newman Clubs.[8]

I proposed publishing a newsletter which I would write and mail out since I had extensive journalism experience as editor of my high school and college weeklies. Orientation meetings for Catholic delegates were organized by JCSA in the aforementioned cities.

One day, the assistant director of the NCWC, Msgr. Paul Tanner, called me into his office to show me a letter from the head of the Congregation for Catholic Education in Rome. It warned of possible NSA developing membership in the International Union of Students (IUS) and suggested that maybe Catholic colleges should not attend the Constitutional Convention. I was asked to draft a response for the signature of Archbishop McNichols, chairman of the NCWC. My letter argued the importance of Catholic College participation in this significant new development of a U.S. student movement for several reasons, and pointed out that all the Catholic student leaders were war veterans, and so forth, and would not be inclined to heed such advice from the Vatican. We never heard from them again.

Constitutional Convention

The effort to promote Catholic student attendance was very successful, with 142 voting delegates, out of approximately 600, being from Catholic institutions. All JCSA committee members kept in daily touch. But there was no Catholic student caucus.[9]

At the elections, Ralph Dungan was elected a vice president. At the subsequent Congresses (1948–1950) student leaders from the Catholic colleges continued to be elected to national offices.[10] I proposed Fr. Vincent Flynn, president of the College of St. Thomas, as a member of the new National Advisory Council of NSA, where he served from 1948 until 1953.

In the fall of 1948, 1 took over the position of executive secretary of the National Newman Club Federation and John Simons was appointed executive secretary of the NFCCS. The JCSA was discontinued[11] and national student leadership was promoted through the NFCCS and NCF, where we had representation at over 650 campuses, far more than the NSA ever had.[12]

In the meantime, I continued my graduate studies at Georgetown, as did Henry Briefs and Charles Schultz. Jim Daugherty began work at the University of Pennsylvania (Penn), where he was later to be professor and director of the Foreign Policy Research Institute.

Finishing my graduate studies at Georgetown, I returned to my undergraduate alma mater, St. Thomas, as student activities adviser and instructor in government.

Connections with NSA during the 1950s and beyond

I continued to promote NSA, with students from St. Thomas elected to the NEC and national office until 1952. After my appointment as executive vice president of the Dominican College in New Orleans in 1955, I was appointed to the new NSA national advisory board[13] that same year, along with Jim Daugherty as chairman. I served until 1965.

I subsequently became a deputy assistant and assistant secretary of the U.S. Department of Health, Education and Welfare, in Washington, D.C., and of course was available to NSA as a contact in the highest circles of the federal government. I was frequently asked by the State Department, the White House, and the CIA about NSA activities. I was usually able to clarify any doubts or confusion. My former graduate adviser, Irwin S. Kirkpatrick, was now director of the Bureau of Research Intelligence at the State Department, and we exchanged information about international student activities.

In 1958–1959, Robert Kiley of the University of Notre Dame was vice president and then president of NSA. He was from my home neighborhood in Minneapolis and a graduate of St. Thomas Military Academy. He was politically adept and a natural leader. He consulted me often and sought my help in getting Robert Kennedy to address Kiley's presidential congress at the University of Illinois in August 1959.

I was already a member of an informal national Kennedy for President committee from Louisiana. I phoned Bob Kennedy at the Senate Labor Rackets committee in Washington. He was delighted to come, and his address to the student body packed the theater at the campus, and was the highlight of the congress. He commented on his work uncovering corruption in the Teamsters Union.

Standing with me in the back of the hall was Jim Lewis, vice president for student affairs at Michigan and a member of NSA's national advisory board. At the end of Kennedy's speech, we went over to the Illinois Union. Jim called Walter Reuther on the phone, told him about Kennedy's remarks, and assured him that the Auto Workers had no reason to fear the Kennedys and the Rackets Committee, of which Sen. Kennedy was a member, in its investigation.

Of course, I told Bob Kennedy about the phone call and he was obviously pleased. This further cemented my relationship with the Kennedys and, along with Ralph Dungan's efforts (he was now a member of Senator Kennedy's Senate staff), resulted in my employment as a full-time staff member in the presidential campaign. I took a leave of absence and undertook intensive efforts to organize the presidential campaign in Louisiana and Missouri. John F. Kennedy carried both states, which were essential to his election.

After the election, Ralph Dungan called me to Washington, and I was offered a job in the new administration. So, in a real sense, my participation in NSA played an important role in my subsequent appointment in Washington.

NSA's impact, and an epilogue to the NFCCS and NCF

The influence of the NSA on the development of student governments was greatest in Jesuit institutions (e.g., Fordham and St. Josephs).[14] Student governments were long established at many Catholic institutions. After all, the NFCCS was also a federation of student governments.[15]

There was no special liaison with Protestant groups. They were perceived as rather weak, but there was congressional liaison and cooperation between Catholic student leaders and student leadership at all the Big Ten universities—all of which had significant Catholic student enrollments and large Newman Clubs—often with Catholic student centers and chapels on campus.

During 1963–66, the National Catholic Welfare Conference was supplanted—as was the Youth Department—and the national offices of the NFCCS and Newman Club Federation were closed. The reorganized United States Catholic Conference (USCC), following guidelines from Vatican II, put more emphasis on ecclesiastical matters. The NFCCS and NCF declined in significance and influence as a result of this change.

I believe that NSA was viewed as an opportunity for Catholic student contact with the wider educational community. But it must be emphasized that Catholic student leaders at the time—mostly war veterans—were focused on graduate and professional schools, jobs, and marriage.[16]

Philip H. Des Marais was Director of Government and Community Relations at College of St. Thomas, MN (1983-86), Director of Research Services, Fordham University (1969-79), Deputy Assistant Secretary at the U.S. Dept. of Health, Education and Welfare (1955-66), and administrator and faculty member at Dominican College, LA (1950-60).

END NOTES

[1] See "Chicago Student Conference" in Wharton, p. 112.

[2] See McLaughlin essay, p. 84, and extracts from doctoral thesis, pp. 818.

[3] See Dungan, p. 909.

[4] *Editor's note:* John Simons was an outspoken leader of the fledgling organization, speaking and writing on its behalf. See p. 124.

[5] *Editor's note:* Rev. John Courtney Murray, then the religion editor of *America* magazine, and Rev. Charles E. Bermingham, director of the Youth Department of the NCWC, appear in retrospect, as shown in published arti-

cles and correspondence in the archives at Catholic University to have furnished much of the energy and interest that guided the church hierarchy in its encouragement of Catholic student participation, first as members of the American delegation to the Prague World Student Congress in August 1946, and then as active participants in the Chicago Student Conference that December and in the formation of NSA at Wisconsin the following summer. It was Father Murray who articulated their mission in "Operation University," which appeared in *America* on April 13, 1946 (see p. 739). Murray counseled that "it is evident that the youth of the world is on the move . . . [and] there is no doubt that Moscow understands the power of youth." He urged the preparation and engagement of Catholic students in this movement. Writing to the Most Rev. Richard J. Cushing on July 15, 1946, that his was a "one man department" with limited resources, Father Bermingham appealed for assistance (which was later forthcoming), citing the "potentially strong threat to the interests of Catholic and American Youth in the future" presented by the newly proposed World Federation of Democratic Youth (the counterpart to the proposed International Union of Students).

[6] Schultz later became chairman of the Council of Economic Advisors, and head of the Office of Management and Budget in the Jimmy Carter administration. He is currently an economist with the Brookings Institution.

[7] *Editor's note*: Formation of a "Joint Operating Committee" to coordinate student relief and foreign student relations, and "for the proper training of Catholic students from both Federations in the December meeting that is endeavoring to form a National Union of Students" was first proposed and adopted on October 13, 1946, according to minutes of a joint meeting of NFFCS and NCF representatives held at the NCWC offices.

[8] *Editor's note:* Writing in "Report on Operation University" in the *Jesuit Education Quarterly for 1948*, Norman Weyand, S.J., presents an excellent contemporary narrative describing in detail the events, issues and key personalities relating to the NFCCS, JCSA and NSA involvements with one another. He discusses the differences of opinion among Catholic college students regarding the value of involvement with NSA, citing questions raised at his own university, Loyola, but he concludes that with "N.S.A. at its formative state, Catholic student leaders have the opportunity to help chart its path along the proper course."

[9] *Editor's note:* In a report Des Marais prepared for the NCWC and the JCSA at the time, he wrote:

> All during the convention the JCSA maintained an exhibit and literature desk in the auditorium lobby at which 200 copies of Operation University were sold and 1,000 issues of the JCSA newsletter were distributed free of charge. Henry Briefs, Georgetown University, editor of the newsletter, was informed many times by various non-Catholic leaders that the JCSA material was the most authoritative available on current student movements, and the fact that officers of practically every student organization represented at Madison secured paid subscriptions seems proof of this fact. No Catholic student caucuses were held at Madison . . . however the JCSA itself . . . for a total of never more than fifteen persons met nightly, after all sessions and caucuses were finished, to discuss the problems and issues for the succeeding day.

This was in contrast to the Chicago Student Conference when, as Martin McLaughlin wrote in his doctoral thesis, "each night after the regular sessions some kind of Catholic caucus was held to plan strategy and achieve a measure of cohesion." See McLaughlin, p. 818.

[10] Elected or appointed (where noted) national staff from Catholic colleges and Newman Club affiliations in the founding years were: 1946, John Simons, Treasurer, NCC (Fordham College); 1947, Ralph Dungan, Vice President, Domestic Affairs (St. Joseph's, Philadelphia); 1948, James T. Harris, Jr., President (LaSalle, Philadelphia), and Helen Jean Rogers, Secretary (Mundelein, Chicago); 1949, Robert Kelly, President (St. Peter's, New Jersey), and Mary Kay Perkins (appointed), Staff Associate (Mundelein, Chicago); 1950, Robert Delahanty, Executive Secretary (Univ. of Louisville), and Joan Long (appointed), Staff Associate (Marylhurst, Oregon); 1951, Marian Andert (appointed), Staff Associate (Univ. of Minnesota).

[11] *Editor's note:* In a letter from Helen Jean Rogers to Eugene Schwartz dated January 15, 1949, she writes "Last night the JCSA breathed its last. At 12:01 P.M. in the living room of the home of Miss Nancy Collins. . . ."

[12] *Editor's note:* Each year, NSA published a list of member schools, along with observers, attending the national congresses. Gordon Klopf, Dennis Trueblood, Bob Sollen, and other administrator authors also cited membership and attendance at various Congresses in their annual reports published in *School and Society* for each of the years covered by this volume. This combined historical record shows the following college attendance counts: Chicago (December 1946), 393 plus 28 national student organizations; Madison I (August 1947), 351; and the following membership counts at convention time: Madison 2 (August 1948), 251 and 44 observers; Illinois (August 1949), 280 plus 32 observers; Michigan (August 1950), 205 plus 27 observers; Minnesota (August 1951), 225; and Indiana (August 1952), 275.

[13] *Editor's note:* At its inception, NSA formed a National Advisory Council, which began functioning in 1948-1949. Stephen Schodde, in his unpublished thesis on NSA (see endnote 1, p. 339), notes that "This group after 1954-1955 became largely honorary and its duties were assumed by the National Advisory Board." In 1959, NSA discontinued the National Advisory Council and, in addition to the National Advisory Board, replaced it with another category of "National Advisors," prominent individuals who lent their names in support of the organization.

[14] See Dungan (St. Josephs), p. 909, and Di Legge (Fordham), p. 890.

[15] In the NFCCS 1951-52 Yearbook and Directory, it is described as

> a federation of student bodies of almost 200 Catholic colleges and universities in the United States. The NFCCS was founded by students in 1937 and has for its purposes to acquaint Catholic college students with their responsibility to the student community, to contribute to the development of Catholic lay leadership, to promote American Catholic student solidarity, to represent its members in the national and international scene, to act as a center of information on student affairs, and to promote democratically elected and operated student governments.

Editor's note: Norman Francis, President of Xavier University in New Orleans, a traditional black coeducational Catholic College, writes of his combined NFCCS and NSA delegate experience in the early 1950s in his essay on p. 000.

[16] *Editor's note:* Readers interested in more detail about the Catholic student movement during the years covered by this work will find extensive coverage in *America: The Jesuit Educational Quarterly, Concord Magazine* (A Catholic college student magazine no longer in print, which was edited by Vincent Giese); *Catholic Action*, and *The Catholic School Journal.* Also, see the archives at Catholic University and Georgetown, as well as at the various orders that operated many of the Catholic women's colleges at the time.

PICTURE CREDITS: *Then:* "NFCCS Yearbook and Directory," 1951-52, p. 27, Eighth National Congress (Joan Lynch). *Now:* February, 1999 (Schwartz).

REFERENCES TO CATHOLIC STUDENT LEADERS, CATHOLIC COLLEGES AND NSA

Editor's note: Following is a compilation of major references and memoirs relating to NSA and Catholic students, colleges, and mentors: Des Marais (St. Thomas, U. Minnesota), "Catholic Student Participation in NSA," p. 734; "Operation University," p. 739; "The Catholic Student Groups," p. 741; Dungan (St. Joseph's), "The Catholic Students in NSA," p. 909; Roster, "The Catholic Colleges," p. 914; Lynch (Marylhurst), "The Catholic Women's Colleges and NSA," p. 493; Kirchner (Ohio State), "Preparing the Catholic Delegation," p. 76; McLaughlin (Notre Dame), "Factions in NSA," p. 818; "Concord Magazine," p. 259. Individual leaders: John Simons (Fordham), p. 124; Ted Harris (LaSalle), p. 219, Robert Kelly (St. Peter's), p. 252. Helen Jean (Rogers) Secondari (Mundelein), p. 599; Norman Francis (Xavier), p. 429; William Buckley (Yale), p. 797; "Women's College Leadership in Mason-Dixon," p. 921; Tom Garrity (CCNY, St. Peters), p. 892; Michael DiLegge (Fordham) p. 890; Michael Rubino (Catholic U.), p. 920; Tesse Hardigan Donnelly (Fontbonne), p. 951; Mary Kay Perkins, O.P. (Mundelein), p. 943; Joan Long Lynch (Marylhurst), p. 265. Mentors: Father J.C. Murray (Woodstock), p. 740. Mother Eleanor O'Byrne (Manhattanville), p. 862; Robert I. Gannon, SJ (Fordham), p. 890; Rev. Vincent J. Flynn (St. Thomas), p. 942; Helen C. White (U. Wisconsin), p. 933.

PHILIP H. DES MARAIS

Early years: Born, Minneapolis, MN, May 29, 1920. Attended public and parochial schools of Minneapolis.

Education: College of St. Thomas, B.A., 1942. Georgetown University, M.A. (American Government), 1951; University of Minnesota, Graduate School, 1951-52. University of Iowa, Falk Foundation Fellow, 1953.

Career Highlights: Director of Government and Community Relations (1983-86), Associate Director of Development (1980-83), College of St. Thomas, MN; Director, Office of Research Services, Fordham University, NY (1969-1980); Deputy Asst. Secretary (Education and Legislation), U.S. Dept. of Health, Education and Welfare, Washington, D.C. (1960-69); Administrator and faculty member (Political Science), Dominican College, New Orleans; College of St. Thomas, MN (1950-60); Visiting professor or lecturer: Loyola U., New Orleans; Fairleigh Dickinson U., New Jersey; Washington Theological College; Bayaman Central U., Puerto Rico; New School for Social Research, NY; Adelphi U., NY.

Author, *How to Get Government Grants* (New York: Public Service Materials Center, 1975; reprint, 1980). Citation for "outstanding contribution over a period of eight years," Secretary of Health, Education and Welfare, December, 1968.

Professional, government, and community activities including Treasurer, Greater New Orleans Educational TV Foundation; Board of Advisors, Georgetown Visitation Preparatory School; Treasurer (1972-75) and President (1975-78), American Graduate and Professional Commission; Executive Secretary, White House Task Force on Urban Educational Opportunities (1967-68), Liason Officer, National Advisory Committee on Education of the Deaf (1966-69).

CATHOLIC STUDENTS SEE NSA AS OPPORTUNITY, CHALLENGE

Loyola University, Los Angeles, 5/2/47

The Loyolan

AN OFFICIAL STUDENT NEWSPAPER

WORLD LEADERSHIP NEEDED

Within a decade the world will inevitably call upon many of us to take over the reins of government. The question which presents itself is one which is deserving of much thought on the part of students throughout the nation, especially Catholic students. To what extent are we prepared to meet the vital issues which will be thrust upon us?

Here at Loyola we have a problem which plagues nearly every campus throughout the country; one which will contribute greatly to the general disintegration of our American Democratic System, if it is not recognized and checked. Whereas we have been given the opportunity to absorb true Christian principles, we, as students, have utterly failed to appreciate them to such an extent as to go forth and spread them throughout our society. We are conducting ourselves along the sad lines sad lines of complacency and indifference. Ours is the disgraceful spirit of apathy—the attitude of Nero and his "Roman fiddle."

"We need the interest in the NSO. . . for that interest will develop the type of leadership which is sorely needed in the world today."

Fontbonne College, St. Louis, 10/15/47

The Font

Student Newspaper of Fontbonne College

The Voice

With the formation of the National Student Association, the American college student has been given unprecedented voice in the educational world. He must prove whether or not he will waste that voice in emotional harangue or exercise it in making meaningful statements.

"To an extent we need the NSA, but the NSA needs us to a greater extent."

Loyola University, Chicago, 1/16/47

THE LOYOLA NEWS

VOLUME XXVI JANUARY 16, 1947 No. 16

This Concerns You

This issue of the LOYOLA NEWS contains two articles on the recent Chicago Student Conference held at University of Chicago. The acts of this conference, and the national student organization that will grow out of it, are matters affecting every man in Loyola University. Whether their final effect will be for good or ill depends on the interest and attention paid them by every student in the United States. It was due to the apathy of the students in free democracies the world over that

"Whether [they] will be another 'front' organization . . . will be determined by the general attitude of the American student body."

The Aquin

PUBLISHED BY THE COLLEGE OF ST. THOMAS

Vol. XXXIII St. Paul, Minnesota, Sunday, August 26, 1951 Extra

Philip Des Marais Guides NFCCS-NSA on Campus

By Gene Foley

Probably the man most responsible for putting NFCCS and NSA into the campus spotlight is Mr. Phil Des Marais, instructor of economics in the College.

As moderator of the NFCCS organization on campus, Mr. Des Marais is supervising the work of the National Congress committee and orienting St. Thomas NFCCS delegates in the various commissions.

After his graduation from St. Thomas in 1942, Mr. Des Marias spent three and one-half years in the Army, earning three battle stars in the European Theatre of Operations.

In 1946 he became interested in intercollegiate organizations and became one of the founders of the National Student Association, representing the University of Minnesota. He was the first Minnesota NSA chairman.

Since that time Mr. Des Marias has attended all five national student congresses of the NSA as well as all five post war NFCCS national congresses.

From 1946 to 1949 Mr. Des Marias worked in the Youth Department of National Catholic Welfare Conference in Washington, D. C. He served first as chairman of the Joint Committee for Student Action and then as executive secretary for the Newman Club Federation.

It was while working in Washington that Mr. Des Marias met his wife, Louise, who was also working for the NCWC as secretary of the Bureau of Confraternity of Christian Doctrine.

Mr. Des Marias joined the St. Thomas faculty in 1950 and was soon assigned the additional responsibilities of faculty moderator for the NFCCS and NSA.

Mr. Des Marias

DES MARAIS LAUNCHES LIFETIME CAREER IN CATHOLIC HIGHER EDUCATION. A leader in the NSA Minnesota Region (See p. 734), Des Marais was chosen to head JCSA, the Newman Club and NFCCS coordinating group set up during NSA's early years, from 1946-1948. (*The Aquin*, College of St. Thomas, St.. Paul, 8/26/51)

GEORGETOWN'S PRESIDENT DECLINES NSA observer Arthur F. McGovern's recommendation that "Georgetown's affiliation is advisable." The Very Rev. HunterGuthrie, S.J., in a 3/2/51 memorandum to Dean McGrath, follows the tradition of St. Ignatius [founder of the Jesuits] in "the Paris system of education" and chooses to "not seek membership" in NSA. (Archives, Georgetown U.)

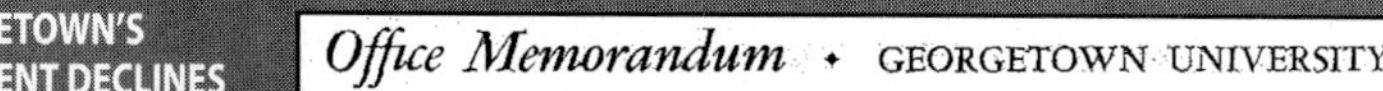

Office Memorandum • GEORGETOWN UNIVERSITY

TO : Rev. Brian A. McGrath, S. J.
Dean, College.
FROM : Very Rev. Hunter Guthrie, S. J.
President
SUBJECT: National Student Association.
DATE: 2 March 1951

This begins to look like a recurrence of the "Italian System of Education" as opposed to the "Paris System of Education", both extant in the time of St. Ignatius. When St. Ignatius founded his first college at Messina, even though it was in the Italian sphere of influence, he choose the "Paris System of Education" not only for Messina but for all the other colleges that were started during his lifetime. His successors have continued that policy. I think I shall go along with that tradition; hence, we will not seek membership in the National Student Association.

Hunter Guthrie, S. J.

Dunbarton Dial

NFCCS Regional Meeting Attracts IRC Members; AAUN Holds Third Convention at Shoreham Hotel

TEMPLE UNIVERSITY NEWS

Newman Club Furthers Religious, Social Welfare

With the strains from Norman Black's orchestra faded but not forgotten, another Shamrock Ball joins the line of former

THE HAWK

Nation's Catholic Colleges Moving Into City for NFCCS Convention

Newman Club Speaker Discusses Timely and Controversial Subject

Speaking to an overflow audience of over one hundred, Father John Merklinger, Catholic chaplain at Strong Memorial hospital, addressed the Newman Club last Tuesday

UNIVERSITY NEWS

Second Article In Series Tells How JCSA Primed Catholic Students For Convention

NEWS-LETTER

Newman Club Seen Strong Spontaneity Its Character, Father Gouch Its Pusher

NFCCS AND NEWMAN CLUBS provided a vigorous student leadership outlet and enjoyed strong Church support during the postwar decades. In 1948, Des Marais writes. They had a presence on 650 U.S. campuses.

From top and left to right: *Dunbarton Dial*, Dunbarton C., DC, Jan-Feb, 1953; *Temple University News*, 3/19/48; *The Hawk*, St. Joseph's C., 4/16/48; *Tower Times*, U. of Rochester, 2/20/48; *University News*, St. Louis U., 9/26/47; *The Johns Hopkins News-Letter*, 10/19/51.

"OPERATION UNIVERSITY"

JOHN COURTNEY MURRAY

IN THE PRESS for March 31 we had news of "Operation Nursery," mounted to crush what was described as "the first major attempt to revive nazi ideologies." What I emphasize here is the significant fact that all the leaders of this attempt were men trained to leadership in the *Hitlerjugend*.

We read, too, that the reopened German universities are crowded with students, a large group of whom talk earnestly of a "strong" Germany, and dislike professors with democratic ideas. Their own ideas were learned in the *Hitlerjugend*, and are still alive and compelling within them.

Last fall there took place in London a huge World Youth Congress. It was dominated by communist forces, embodied in a well trained delegation of youth leaders. (So strong was communist influence that the English bishops, notably the present Cardinal Griffin, were deeply concerned.) As a result of this Congress, a World Federation of Democratic Youth with headquarters in Paris, will be set up this summer. Soon, therefore, we shall see operating a sort of "Youth International."

Youth Looks to Organization

After the London Congress a committee of seven nationalities met and decided to bring into existence a new International Student Federation. A preparatory committee is now doing the organizing. It wishes to obtain the widest possible representation, from all kinds of student organizations, at an immense international gathering in Prague this summer, August 17 to 31. Catholic student groups are being invited.

Last November there also took place a big International Student Congress (600 delegates from 51 nations) in Prague. The city and the national government played the host munificently, at a cost of some five to seven million Czecho-Slovak crowns. Communist influence was again well defined and effective, if perhaps less dominant than at London. Afterwards, some of the delegates, including some Americans, were invited to visit Russia by the Soviet Youth Anti-Fascist Committee. The few American representatives at Prague were mostly left-wing.

Again, this coming summer the World Student Christian Federation will assemble in its first real postwar congress. International Student Service will likewise hold another summer session.

Finally, it has been noted that three out of four of "the public" that sought admission to the UNO sessions at Hunter College have been under twenty years of age. They did not come for entertainment; they symbolized the fact that youth is vitally interested in the movement for world organization.

Taken together, all these facts most certainly point to some conclusions. First, it is evident that the youth of the world is on the move. More than that, it is being gathered into movements—organized, inspired by ideas, self-conscious, able to utter corporate views and take collective action. These youth movements are going to help move the world, in one direction or another. Yesterday's youth movements (as in Germany) helped to create many of the problems of today. Today's youth movements will either solve these problems, or aggravate them, or create new ones.

Second, youth has discovered its own international community. Youth is youth, no matter what language it speaks. And it is determined to express its natural community in organizations, wherein international cooperation on student problems may be realized. The future leaders of international society will be trained in these organizations.

Third, there is no doubt that Moscow understands the power of youth. It is consciously enlisting the aid of youth in furthering its own purposes, whose sinister character is ably concealed beneath the aura of idealism that youth finds so seductive. The World Federation of Democratic Youth will be an agency of communist penetration. And communist forces have already signified their determination to influence the new International Student Federation, launched at London and Prague. Leaders of various international youth organizations whose inspiration is Christian, or at least humanist, are aware of this problem. They do not view with indifference the prospect of Moscow capturing the world student and youth movement. And they are taking steps to meet the problem.

The problem is also put squarely to Catholic youth, its leaders and moderators. In general, the problem is how Catholic youth can be put on the move, in the international field, in a solidly organized movement, with a truly conquering spirit, that will carry through a positive program and also combat communist influence. More concretely, the question is how *Pax Romana* can be made in living fact what it is on paper—the agency of Catholic international university student solidarity, and the Catholic representative in the world youth movement.

American Catholic Students Lag

Curiously enough, Catholic students were the slowest in realizing their need of international cooperation; among all the international student organizations *Pax Romana*, born in 1921, was the latest in the field. And it is still the weakest, at the very moment when the world situation demands that it be strongest. After World War I it performed an effective work of reconciliation, on the student plane, between the nations that had fought each other. As part of this work, it brought into fruitful affiliation all the European student federations; and in 1939 it made its ill-fated venture into the New World, holding its XIXth World Congress in New York and Washington. World War II broke out while the Congress was in session. During the war its mission was largely one of relief to students, carried on under shattering difficulties.

These phases of its work—reconciliation and relief—are not ended. But the Holy See has already indicated that a new phase must begin. The indication is in a long letter from Cardinal Pizzardo to the Second Inter-American Assembly of *Pax Romana*, held March 10-19 in Lima, Peru (at which, incidentally and significantly, there was no official United States student representation). The letter makes it quite clear that Pius XII wants the Catholic international student movement to be a strong ally in the mission upon which he has focused the eyes of the universal Church—that of creating a new spiritual unity among nations. Its special work is to be the intellectual penetration of the university milieu—the winning of the universities, professors and students, for the ideas that underlie peace and Christian world order. *Pax Romana's* old mission of fraternal union must be developed into the field of intellectual charity—the creation of that *société d'esprits* without which there can be no society of nations. In effect, what the Holy See wants is the mounting of "Operation University."

This is an immense task, of incomparable difficulty. But it is no more immense and difficult than the task to which the dynamic leftist student movement has set itself. We cannot admit that it is impossible, if only for the reason that it is imperative. The Interfederal Assembly of *Pax Romana* will address itself to the task at its meeting in Fribourg this coming August. But what I want to emphasize is the fact that the building of a strong Catholic international student movement, able to carry out the Holy Father's wishes, is the common and collective responsibility of educators, youth directors, and youth itself, everywhere.

And in this respect the United States finds itself in a peculiarly embarrassing position. On the one hand, no other country in the world is so isolationist, so backward in the matter of international student cooperation; on the other hand, no other nation has so great a responsibility in the matter. We have immense potential student leadership; but it is quite undeveloped. For instance, whatever the merits or defects of our undergraduate student organizations (and the defects are many), we have no formal university student organization. (And the university student is the proper agent of international collaboration.) In their maturity, when their capacity for leadership is readiest, our Catholic students are, for all practical purposes, cast adrift.

This problem, I think, will be the special responsibility of the National Catholic Educational Association. Taking over a private initiative, it is about to form a graduate association that will undertake the work of Catholic international intellectual cooperation. The promotion of the international student movement must necessarily be a function of this association. So, too, will be the promotion of student and professor exchange, and the foundation of a badly needed Catholic International House that will be the center of the Catholic movement for intellectual cooperation.

Beginnings are always small and difficult. But they may as well be bold. I would suggest this beginning for United States participation in the world student movement: that a group of twelve students be selected, carefully and intensively trained, and sent over to the Prague meeting of the International Student Federation in August, with the quite sober and entirely feasible intent of "taking it over." They could do it. They would not be without allies among European Catholic students. But, of course, someone would have to pay their way.

Operation University

Editor's note: Martin McLaughlin (Notre Dame) has provided invaluable suggestions and recollections in the assembly of this Anthology, including a rare copy of the 42 pg. booklet, "Operation University," which he and Henry Briefs (Georgetown) prepared for the Joint Committee for Student Action in 1947. The excerpt below underscores the ultimate significance of Father Murray's influence on the course of U.S. student organization after World War II.

An Archbishop Replies

These words were widely read in Catholic circles throughout the United States; many students and educators wrote commendatory letters to the AMERICA magazine and to the author. But most important of all, the Most Reverend Richard J. Cushing, D.D., Archbishop of Boston, and Episcopal Chairman of the Youth Department of the National Catholic Welfare Conference with the assistance of Father Charles E. Bermingham, Director of the Youth Department, determined to take action. In a letter to Father Murray, dated May 1, 1946 Archbishop Cushing wrote:

"I am forwarding to you a very concrete proposal . . . that you recruit, prepare and lead to Europe a group of student representatives to participate in the several student congresses or conferences about which we have been informed at the NCWC. It is a large order, and I realize the many problems involved. However, the needs of the times and the opportunity which this summer presents, possibly never to be duplicated again, call for extraordinary actions....

"If you are able to carry through this proposal, I designate you and those associated with you as the extraordinary representatives of the College and University Section of the National Catholic Youth Council."

Father Murray's article and Archbishop Cushing's reply were the dynamic beginnings of a campaign of student action which is still developing and expanding. The Archbishop's commission to Father Murray was accepted. After a month and a half of voluminous letter writing, weighing the qualities of unknown eligibles, and the thousand-and-one administrative and technical tasks of collecting such a group, Father Murray and his associates assembled a necessarily random and heterogeneous collection of university students at Ridgely Manor, in upstate New York, for the intensive training recommended. During the ten-day training period from June 6 to 16 the following students participated for all or part of the time: Sally Cassidy, Neil Hurley, and John Simons, of Fordham University; Joseph Matasovsky, Henry Briefs and John Lebkicher, of Georgetown University; Vincent Hogan and Martin McLaughlin, of Notre Dame University; Gerald Marron and Francis McQuade, of Catholic University; Eleanor Podkrivacky, of Barat College; Marthe Lavallée, of Columbia University; and Edward Kirchner, former president of Pax Romana and director of its North American Secretariat

John Courtney Murray, S.J. (1904-1967)

"Part of the inner architecture of the American ideal of freedom has been the profound conviction that only a virtuous people can be free."

So wrote John Courtney Murray, S. J., in his seminal work of public theology, *We Hold these Truths* (1960).

Father Murray, born in New York City in 1904, entered the Society of Jesus in 1920. He was trained in Massachusetts, Maryland, and Rome under the traditional Jesuit program of study, which, in his case, included three years teaching in the Philippines. Ordained a priest in 1933, he returned to Maryland in 1937, to the Jesuit theologate at Woodstock, where he remained a professor of theology until his death in 1967.

Murray's professional specialities were in the theology of grace and the Trinity, but his major contributions were in public theology, the area he called "religion and society." His writings in this area, however, led to much apprehension among his ecclesiastical superiors, who throughout the 1950s restricted his freedom to write and lecture on issues of church and state. But Murray's work was vindicated by his invitation from the conservative Cardinal Spellman to serve at the Second Vatican Council as a theological expert, as well as by his major authorship of the Council's "Decree on Religious Liberty." Thus, Murray became a hero and an inspiration to a whole new generation of public theologians.

Murray's major insight was into the reconcilability of the American constitutional order and the Catholic natural law tradition; or rather, he perceived that these two systems flow from a common source. "But the Bill of Rights was an effective instrument for the delimitation of government authority and social power, not because it was written on paper in 1789 or 1791, but because the rights it proclaims had already been engraved by history on the conscience of a people. The American Bill of Rights is not a piece of eighteenth-century rationalist theory; it is far more the product of Christian history. Behind it one can see, not the philosophy of the Enlightenment but the older philosophy that had been the matrix of the common law. The 'man' whose rights are guaranteed in the face of law and government is, whether he knows it or not, the Christian man, who has learned to know his own personal dignity in the school of Christian faith."

(From www.acton.org, The Acton Institute, 2/24/02. The papers of John Courtney Murray belong to the Archives of Woodstock College, Special Collections Division of the Lautinger Library, Georgetown U.)

J.C. MURRAY in the early 1950's *(Bachrach)* (Woodstock Archives, Special Collections, Lautinger Library, Georgetown U.)

The Catholic Student Groups: NCF, NFCCS, Pax Romana

(Newman Club Federation, National Federation of Catholic College Students)

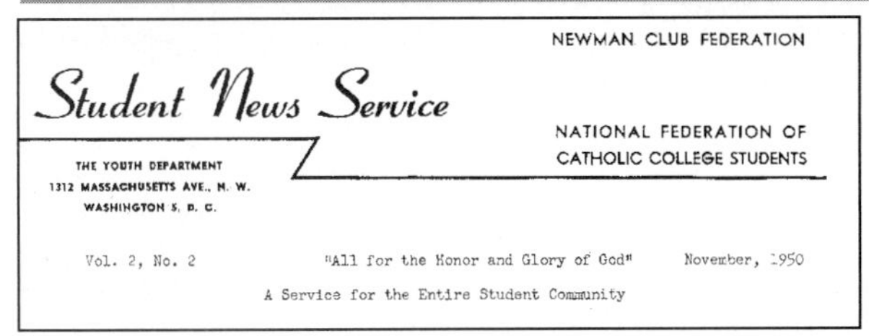
NEWMAN CLUB FEDERATION

Student News Service

NATIONAL FEDERATION OF CATHOLIC COLLEGE STUDENTS

THE YOUTH DEPARTMENT
1312 MASSACHUSETTS AVE., N. W.
WASHINGTON 5, D. C.

Vol. 2, No. 2 "All for the Honor and Glory of God" November, 1950

A Service for the Entire Student Community

Editor's note: In March, 1950, after the Joint Committee for Student Action (JCSA) had been dissolved for more than a year, a group of Catholic students in the D.C. area, led by Helen Jean Rogers, former 1948-49 NSA Secretary Treasurer, launched a newsletter sponsored by the Newman Club Federation and NFCCS; published, as stated in the first issue, "because these organizations believe that a student news service can provide collegians with much information about the university world—information that will help them to make more effective contributions as leaders in our society." Its dedication, "All for the Honor and Glory of God. A Service for the Entire Student Community."

In contrast to the Protestant's Student Christian Movement in the U.S., which had been founded earlier and engaged actively in secular initiatives, the U.S. Catholic student movement emerged somewhat later and did not commit to full participation in general student movements till after World War II.[1]

(*Daily Pennsylvanian* 10/1/47)

Newman Club Founded Here Now Includes 350 Branches

Members of the Newman Club of the University of Pennsylvania must be excused if they take exceptional pride in their organization, for it was here that Timothy Harrington asnd a small group of Catholic students founded the first Newman Club in 1892.

Harrington, a student in Medical School who had spent his undergraduate days at the University of Wisconsin, recognized the need for a Catholic discussion group at a secular college, and soon had several other students interested in his plan.

...Selection of a suitable name for the club was the next problem. The newly elected President had a special reverence for the English Cardinal John Henry Newman...

In October 1913, the Rev. John W. Keogh, A.M., was appointed Chaplain. . . .While Penn's club continued to grow, similar groups took root at Yale, Harvard and Michigan. By 1907 the Universities of Wisconsin and California had full-time chaplains. Today there are more than 350 Newman Clubs in secular schools of Hawaii, Puerto Rico, China and the United States. . . .

(*Highland University Candle*, NM, 9/3/48)

Annual Newman Meeting at Minnesota This Week

Nearly 800 priest chaplains and student delegates from over 500 Newman Clubs throughout the United States and its possessions will meet at the University of Minnesota, September 3-5, for the annual national convention. ...

The convention will have as its theme "The Social Responsibilities of the Catholic Student." The activities and plans of the various Newman Clubs will be discussed. . . .Delegates are expected from every Newman Club in America and her possessions, and prominent representatives from Canada, England, Hawaii, Switzerland, Pax Romana, Mexico and Japan.

The program includes panel sessions on "Social Action," "Religion in Higher Education," "Club Programming" . . . including discussion and resolutions on Pax Romana, Joint Committee for Student Action and World Student Service Fund (WSSF) . . . .

The National Federation of Catholic College Students

From "Report on Operation University" by Norman Weyand, S.J., Jesuit Educational Quarterly, *for January 1952.*

Archbishop Cushing, at the J.E.A. banquest at Boston last April, fervently urged us to develop student leadership in our Jesuit colleges and universities. He has repeatedly pointed out that the NFCCS provides students with an excellent opportunity to develop and evidence qualities of true leadership. And just last April the Archbishop manifested his estimation of the importance of NFCCS by personally attending the national congress of the organization at Toledo and addressing the assembled delegates from some 130 Catholic institutions. It is interesting to note that of the forty colleges represented on the list for officers and committees of the congress, the names of but five Jesuit schools appeared.

What, in short, is the nature, and what are the aims of the NFCCS? As part of the National Catholic Welfare Conference, the NFCCS is in general a coordinating agency. It is not a new and distinct campus organization with members, officers, et cetera. It can work through any existing campus organization, preferably the strongest. These may be, for example: the student council, the international relations club, or the sodality - excellent for this purpose. It may be remarked that the last national chaplain of the NFCCS, Father Berminghamof the Brooklyn diocese, was very favorable to sodality participation. Each member school has a senior and a junior delegate (not necessarily a junior and a senior in academic standing).

That the chief aims of the NFCCS are to mould a national solidarity and unity among the student bodies of the two hundred Catholic colleges and universities in the United States and to develop Catholic lay leadership can be seen from the following statement of purposes in the NFCCS Constitution (Article II):

1. To acquaint Catholic college students with their responsibility in the student community and to the post-college community.

2. To contribute to Catholic lay leadership by providing an opportunity . . . for that leadership among Catholic college students.

3. To promote solidarity and unity among Catholic colleges and universities.

4. To represent its members in national and international affairs.

5. To act as a center for information and as a medium of exchange on student affairs and other matters of interest to students.

6. To assist in the development of democratically elected student councils or their equivalents in Catholic institutions of higher learning in the United States.

Altnough the organization was formed by ten New York colleges in 1937, its growth has been slow—partially because of the recent war years and their effect on men's colleges. At present, about three fourths of the two hundred Catholic colleges and universities in the country are members [See roster of Catholic colleges, p. 000]. It now appears that before long all the Catholic institutions of higher learning will be represented in the organization.

At the national congress held in Toledo last April, students from Jesuit schools took a very active part, with the result that of five national officers elected, three were from Jesuit schools as follows: James Dougherty, St.Joseph's College, Philadelphia, president; Cornelius Scanlon, Boston College, first vice-president; and John Cunningham, Loyola,

Los Angeles, treasurer. This fact gives promise of active participation by Jesuit students in the future. Such participation is especially important today because of the relationship between the NFCCS and other organizations which have developed in the past year *[nb: JCSA and NSA]*

The Pax Romana Congress, 1946

From a report by Gerard Peletier in the September, 1946 ISS Bulletin

Pax Romana, international secretariat of Catholic university students, held its XXth Congress in Fribourg, Switzerland, in the first days of September. Last in the long series of international gatherings which took place this summer, both the Pax Romana Study Week and Congress were attended by a very large and representative group. Delegations from 41 different nations participated and 22 new federations affiliated.

First, in Estavayer-le-Lac, a small, medieval town on the Lake of Neuchatel, limited delegations of five delegates from each country met for five days to discuss the fundamentals of Pax Romana and its reorganization programme. Two days before the graduates had met and formed a special branch for Catholic intellectuals. Thus Pax Romana had two different branches, and the main problem was to set up a new constitution.

The Study Week also had to deal with the main issues that appeared in almost every international meeting this year: relief programme, international education, etc. The main decisions were - continuation in W.S.R.,[2] help to German and Japanese students, mobilization of all possible Catholic student resources for relief actions in all needy countries.

After these five days in Estavayer (27th August to 1st September), all delegations met in Fribourg for the Congress, which lasted four days and involved 700-800 people. The theme of the Congress, "Christianity in our Time and our Universities" was introduced by four speakers, and then discussed in smaller commissions....

At the end of the Congress, Pax Romana had to accept the resignations of its General Secretary, M. l'abbe Gremaud, and its Administrative Secretary, M. Salat. No definite appointments have been made yet....

Summary of Pax Romana[3]

Excerpts from "Operation University," 1947, published by the JCSA

a) Bearing in mind the great stress being put on international organizations, and especially in view of the foundation of an International Union of Students in Prague, it appears of the greatest importance that a very serious effort be made in every country toward the effective organization of Catholic students on a worldwide basis. This is particularly applicable to the United States because of its political leadership.

b) Up to, now Pax Romana has been merely an international secretariat, which loosely united students of various countries. It is hoped that the reorganization to be approved at Rome during Easter season, 1947, will bring into being a more closely united and more efficiently operating organization.... The United States is expected to take a leading role in the direction of the organization; our participation as a group so far has been too meager and haphazard.

c) Along lines of student relief much has been accomplished, thanks to the considerable contribution of NCWC, which not only permitted Pax Romana to participate on terms of equality with other student representatives in World Student Relief, but which to a great extent saved the whole organization of Pax Romana from collapsing during the war years. Aside from continuous Swiss help, it was the only source of relief. It is hoped that this work will continue ....

d) In order that the United States student groups be adequately and effectively represented at Pax Romana, it is necessary that some permanent or semi-permanent committee be established.... This committee must have enough financial backing to be able to send representatives to the sessions of the executive committee of Pax Romana, the Interfederal Assembly, and the Congresses (to be held now only once in every three years). It is suggested that this committee, for the sake of continuity and efficient administration, be composed of several permanent members selected from the NFCCS and the Newman Club Federation....

A Voice from the Trenches

Fr. Bermingham
(*LaSalle Collegian* 12/19/46)

Editor's note: Among the summer 1946 international meetings Father Murray and Cardinal Cushing were concerned with (p. 740) was the founding meeting of the World Federation of Democratic Youth (WFDY). In a four-page letter dated 7/13/46, Rev. Charles E. Bermingham, national chaplain of the Youth Department of the National Catholic Welfare Conference, who had been tracking postwar global student movement developments, voices his concerns in a way that helps explain the U.S. Church's decision to enter the secular student organization arena. Portions of the opening and closing paragraphs appear below (From Catholic University NCYC archives):

"1. This proposed organization [WFDY] presents a potentially strong threat to the interests of Catholic and American youth in the future.

"2. This Department and Catholic groups generally are in the weakest possible condition to meet this impending threat....

"The World Federation of Youth is a front organization. It is a spearhead of Communist propaganda and infiltration among the youth of the world.

"...Consequently, tactics call for the procurement of a capable leader with time and money at his disposal, who will select and train a combat team, will coordinate Catholic forces toward this objective and will go in and beat the enemy at his own game! That is what is being attempted at Prague [World Student Congress], a positive force against a positive force.

"The solution in the present order of things is beyond me... Some genius might be found to be all things to all men in different places at the same time.... In the present case, I am not able to do this job in New York in view of the work already cut out in other directions...."

END NOTES

[1] *Editor's note:* On 11/6/98, William John Shepard, Assistant Archivist at Catholic University wrote in an e-mail to the Anthology editor: "The National Federation of Catholic College Students and the National Newman Club Federation were both formed earlier in the century and joined with the Diocesan Catholic Youth Organizations under the aegis of the NCWC's (National Catholic Welfare Conference) Youth Department in 1941. This framework broke down in the 1960's, partly as a result of Vatican II, and the Youth Department was downsized and absorbed into the Education Department in 1968. Material relating to both the Youth and Education departments, especially annual reports for each, exist in the . . . records of the General Secretary and cover the period of 1941-1966."

[2] *Editor's note:* World Student Relief (WSR) was a partnership with the World Student Christian Federation and the International Student Service (See p. 622)

[3] *Editor's note:* Now known as the International Catholic Movement for International and Cultural Affairs. The President Emeritus of the U.S. federation, CMICA, is Ed Kirchner, a member of the U.S. delegation to the World Student Congress in 1946 (See p. 76). The following appeared on www.Paxromana.org, 6/13/03: "Pax Romana-ICMICA was founded in April 1947 at its first Plenary Assembly held in Rome, Italy. However its historical roots can be traced back to 1921 when Pax Romana was created as an international body of Catholic students with a secretariat in Fribourg, Switzerland. Since 1947 when the two movements, ICMICA and the International Movement of Catholic Students (IMCS), were established, they have been operating independently through their respective international secretariats and regional structures while sharing the common name Pax Romana and sharing a common international representation at the United Nations and UNESCO."

SECTION 3

The Fraternities and Sororities

CONTENTS

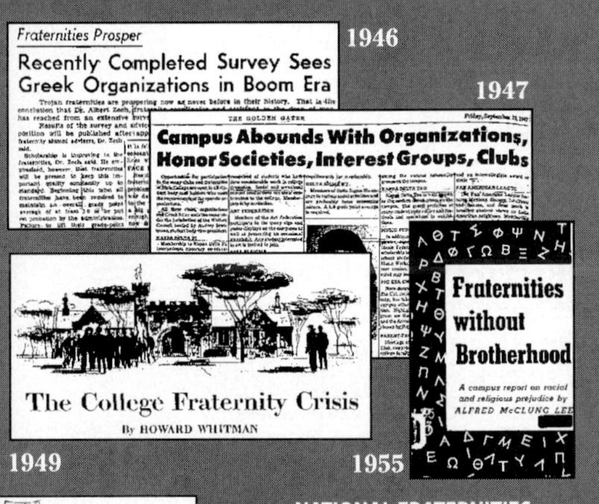

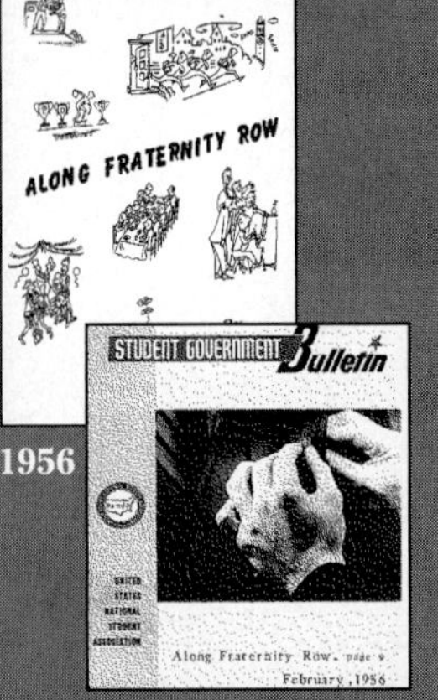

NATIONAL FRATERNITIES GREW RAPIDLY IN NUMBER, reaching 500 campuses by 1954 (Lee p. 745), providing students with social opportunities as well as policy challenges because of traditional discriminatory practices. NSA opposed those practices, while maintaining a liaison with the NIC during its early years (See Pt. 2 Sec. 2). Fraternity leaders often provided opposition to NSA as well as support.
From the top: USC *Daily Trojan*, 6/11/46; SF State C. *The Golden Gater*, 9/26/47; *Colliers Magazine*, 1/8/49; *Fraternities without Brotherhood* cover (See p. 801); "Along Fraternity Row," *NSA Student Government Bulletin*, 2/56).

In January 1949, *Collier's Magazine* ran a two- part series on "The College Fraternity Crisis," leading with the statement that "After two wars in which we fought for democracy, discrimination is still rampant on our college campuses." Excerpts from this series follow excerpts from Alfred McLung Lee's 1955 book, *Fraternities without Brotherhood.* Lee traces the history of "Aryanism" underlying exclusionary clauses and practices in college fraternities and sororities, directed at Catholics, Jews and Negroes.

Although the National Interfraternity Conference adopted a resolution in November 1949 recommending (without mandating) the elimination of such clauses, the practice was widespread throughout the 1940s and 1950s.

Lee provides examples of both the practice and efforts to alter it, noting that the practice was even more entrenched, and less documented, in sororities. He also cites NSA's policy declarations opposing restrictive membership on the basis of "race, color, religion or national origin" adopted at Congresses from 1947 to 1954.

Fraternities often decisive in NSA affiliation contests

Fraternity influence in student governments and on student life on many campuses was often decisive in initiatives for NSA affiliation (see Part 5), and frequently on the campus level was the primary source of opposition, although many NSA leaders were also fraternity and sorority members (see Part 2).

Leonard Wilcox, Jr., NSA 1953-53 National Affairs Vice President and also a member of Psi Kappa Tau, writes about these issues in "NSA and Fraternity-Sorority Discrimination" on p. 398, in Part 2. Relations between NSA and the NIC and the Pan-Hellenic Conference are also reviewed on pp. 401-409.

Bill Graham, University of Illinois Student Senate President and Sigma Pi member, addressed fraternity influence in the February 1956 issue of NSA's *Student Government Bulletin.* Referring to an NSA study, he reported that 84 percent of top student government leaders had fraternity affiliations. Graham outlines some of the issues affecting a responsible cocurricular role for fraternities at the time.

This section concludes with a recollection of Penn State's 1919-1949 Dean of Men, Arthur Ray Warnock, who was the revered Chairman of the NIC in 1950-51 and a prominent champion of the fraternity system.

A Strong Fraternity/Sorority Influence on Many Student Governments

1944
STUDENT LIFE
WASHINGTON UNIVERSITY, ST. LOUIS, FRIDAY, OCTOBER 13, 1944
SORORITIES PLEDGE 180
32 JOIN FRATERNITIES
DEAN'S HONOR ROLL
Formal Rush Week Ends As Fraternities Pledge

1945
THE SILVER AND GOLD
Official Publication Of The Associated Students Of The University of Colorado
Plans Are Started For CU Homecoming Celebration
'Beat Utah' To Be Theme Of First Major Post-War Event On Campus
Independent Students State Plans For Future Activities
Young Demos Favor Senate
Bandwagon Rental Profits Will Be Contributed To Student Union Fund

1947
WELLESLEY COLLEGE NEWS, OCTOBER 2, 1947
SOCIETIES REMAIN FAITHFULLY YOURS
Societies Offer Many Advantages To Whole College Community and To Respective Members as Well
Pins, Paint, Patches and Wallpaper Highlight Traditional Fall Program In All Redecorated Society Houses

1948
THE TECHNIQUE, ATLANTA
Independent Students Organize League at Univ. of Chattanooga

1945
Temple University News
PHILADELPHIA, FRIDAY, APRIL 27, 1945
Sixth Annual Greek Weekend Begins Today
Astron Elects Officers, Inducts New Members
Dozen Sororities and Fraternities To Participate in Greek Sing
Hobo Carnival

1948
Greek Negro Organization Plans House

Hullabaloo
NEW ORLEANS, LA., THURSDAY, MAY 13, 1948
Senate, Pan-Hel Council Ratify New Fraternity Rulings Effective In Fall
Choral Groups Concert Set For Tonight

1948

1949
EMORY WHEEL
EMORY UNIVERSITY, GEORGIA — Thursday, October 6, 1949
Fraternities Pledge Record 292 Men

DENVER CLARION
University of Denver
Independents Reorganize; All Non-Greeks Members

1949
MATHER RECORD
WESTERN RESERVE UNIVERSITY
New Activity Center Plan Inaugurated
Mather Girls Participate In Greek Week Musical

1950

THE OUTREACH OF FRATERNITIES grew from 2,500 national chapters in 1945 to 4,200 in 1954 with 400,000 members (See Lee, p. 802). Pledge weeks and campus-wide interfraternity events captured attention. The National Independent Students' Association, formed in 1938 to provide a social balance and identity for non-frat students, became more active during this period (see Pt. 5, Sec. 7), particularly in the midwest and southwest.

From top: Washington U. in St. Louis, *Student Life*, 10/13/44; U. of Colo. *Silver and Gold*, 9/14/45; *Wellesley College News*, 10/2/47; Georgia Tech. *The Technique*, 11/23/48; *Temple U. News*, 4/27/45; Denver U. *Chronicle*, 4/23/48; Tulane U. *Hullabaloo*, 5/13/48; *Emory Wheel*, 10/6/49; Denver U. *Chronicle*, 11/16/49; Flora Stone Mather C., *Mather Record*, 3/10/50.

1941
University of Washington Daily
GREEKS SWEEP FROSH
Blackstock, Pomeroy, Cl In Record B

1947
NEW MEXICO LOBO
GREEKS SWEEP ALL MAJOR OFFICES
Discrimination-Boycott Measure Carried 3 to 1
Record Turnout Sees Over 2000 Votes Cast
Spring Convocation to Start at 1:30 p.m. in Stadium

The TARGUM
Fraternities Sweep Council Elections; 'Rutgers Slate' Places Only Four Men

1949

NSA Congress Here March 28, 29
HILL TOP
GREEK POLITICAL TRUST SMASHED

1953

CAMPUS POLITICAL PARTIES on many large campuses were organized around fraternities, frequently opposed by independent coalitions. Vigorous campaigns against NSA affiliation were led by fraternity votes at LSU (p. 454) and U. of Texas (p. 995) in 1948. Howard U. independents displaced years of fraternity control in 1953. The independents at U. of NC swept the council in 1946.

Above: *U. of Washington Daily*, 10/23/41; *New Mexico Lobo*, 10/24/47; Rutgers U. *Targum*, 5/13/49; Howard U. *Hilltop*, 5/17/53.

1945
PRICE 3 CENTS
Campus Forum to Discuss Sororities and Fraternities
Morton Gould Speaker At Music Ed. Luncheon

1946
THE MATHER RECORD
National Sororities Endanger Unity, Says Student

President Says Frat Not Aware of Clause Banning Jewish Men

Fraternity Conference Debate Discrimination

1948

IFC DELEGATES VISIT NEW YORK CONFLAB THANKSGIVING WEEK

National Blue Key Group Removes Race Restrictions
Kureishi Leads Movement At Honorary's Convention

1948

1947

THE CARDINAL, LOUISVILLE, KENTUCKY
No Discrimination Allowed In New Mexico Fraternities

1949

1949

NIC Urges Fraternities To Remove Restrictions
Anti-Discrimination Issue Pressed By Undergrads
Lee Says NIC Stresses Fraternity Responsibility

1950

NYU Frat May Quit National Body Over Grand Council Order Banning Chapter That Admitted Negroes

1949

Discrimination Review
Student Voters Blast Bias At Dartmouth

1952

RESTRICTIVE MEMBERSHIP CLAUSES AND PRACTICES provoked sharp controversy which often overshadowed the equally controversial issues arising out of "rush week" pressures in selection and rejection of pledges. Alfred McLung Lee's 1955 landmark work, *Fraternities without Brotherhood* (see p. 745) provides a thoroughly documented analysis of the history and impact of fraternity practices.

From top: *Temple U. News*, 5/7/45; Flora Stone Mather C. *Mather Record*, 5/21/46; *U. of Washington Daily*, 11/16/48; Washington State College *Evergreen*, 11/24/47; *Temple U. News*, 12/31/48; USC *Trojan*, 1/5/49; U. of Louisville *Cardinal*, 3/4/49; *Middlebury Campus*, 12/1/49; NYU *Square Bulletin*, 12/10/50; U. of Colorado *Silver and Gold*, 2/11/52.

"On a national scale, the NSA between 1947 and 1954 adopted a series of policies on fair educational practices."

1. Fraternities without Brotherhood

Alfred McClung Lee

Chairman, Dept. of Sociology, Brooklyn College, 1951-57.

Excerpted from Chapters 1 and 4 of Fraternities without Brotherhood *by Alfred McClung Lee. © 1955, Beacon Press*

Will Fraternities Avoid Self Destruction?

The crucial problem facing men's and women's fraternities is not scholarship or hazing or wild parties but self-segregation—segregation on the basis of race, ethnic origin, and religion. Although fraternities have taken positive steps to deal with scholarship, hazing, and parties, only a very few have seen the need to combat and eliminate self-segregation.

When Phi Delta Theta suspended its Williams and Amherst chapters in 1953 for pledging "non-Aryans," the action aroused widespread concern about the damaging consequences of the fraternity system. In 1954 the Phi Delts changed their constitutional requirement for admission from "full Aryan blood" to "socially acceptable"; but they demonstrated their real policy by sustaining the suspension of the Amherst and Williams chapters.

The Past Grand Consul (president) of the Sigma Chi fraternity, L. G. Balfour, a leading manufacturer of jewelry for fraternities, in 1954 discussed the function of fraternities in a communication to a conference of undergraduate Sigma Chi officers. "The college," Balfour asserted, "can educate no one. At best, it can only give to the individual an opportunity to educate himself, and potentially at least, the fraternity is the best medium of self-education which has yet been devised on the American campus."

This contention is typical among fraternity leaders. They see the fraternity as an intimate and dynamic laboratory in human relations. As Balfour told his young fraternity brothers, "The avowed object of a fraternity is to promote the art of effective living with our brothers—the development of the individual in all his relations with society."

This view pictures the social fraternity as what it *can be:* a valuable social experience for young men and women on our college campuses, an approach to problems of human relations different from that of the classroom and other noncurricular campus activities. But the problem this study examines is not what that experience sometimes *can be* but what it usually is.

Reactions of fraternity leaders to criticism

How do fraternity leaders react to the growing criticism? At the November 28, 1947, meeting of the National Interfraternity Conference in New York, its current chairman, David A. Embury, insisted that people should "stop shivering at the word discrimination. . . . I love the discriminating tongue, the discriminating eye, the discriminating ear, and, above all, the discriminating mind and . . . soul. The person for whom I can find no love and no respect is the indiscriminate person. To be indiscriminate is to be common, to be vulgar."

In 1954 Balfour criticized discussion of the evils of discrimination as a means of leading fraternities "involuntarily into regimentation and control." This danger, he said, is all the more real because "college youth has always been generous, idealistic, and very democratic." (Balfour's large fraternity officially restricts its membership to white male Christians.)

For a while, certain fraternity leaders experimented with a "red-scare" technique to counteract widespread opposition to self-segregative practices. For example, Professor William Henry Shideler of Miami University at Oxford, Ohio, stated in the December 1951 issue of the Phi Kappa Tau Laurel:

> The drive to "liberalize" fraternities is one that has no fundamental basis for action. Yet all over the U.S., too simultaneously to be accidental and affecting too many campuses where there has never been a problem to be spontaneous, we find a very similar pattern of attack upon fraternities by deans of men, directors of student affairs and professors of sociology, government, and psychology. The pattern has been so nearly identical that one cannot avoid the conclusion that it all came from an original source.

It was his "personal idea," Shideler said, "that this is just another case where some well-intentioned, but misguided, people have been sucked into a deal initiated by the Communists." The wide distribution of such views has confused some Americans. But in general, responsible leaders, whether committed to discrimination or not, have not stooped to such propagandistic name-calling.

Racial and religious discrimination not limited

Racial and religious discrimination is not limited to a small group of organizations. The executive committee of the National Interfraternity Conference (NIC), which represents the sixty-one most prominent men's "nationals," met in Balfour's home at Attleboro, Massachusetts, in July 1954, to record in its minutes its *unanimous* concern about pressure from the colleges against fraternity discrimination. The executive committee complained that "various institutions apparently contemplate restricting the traditional freedom of fraternities to choose their own members." It *unanimously* resolved that "more unified action, such as the withdrawal of all charters at an institution, may be necessary or desirable as a means of self-preservation."

But four months later *The Teke*, published by one of the NIC's largest members, Tau Kappa Epsilon, strongly protested against the use of such a boycott: "For the NIC fraternities now to boycott colleges frowning on discriminatory clauses could have only one result—suicide of the fraternities participating in such action. It is hoped that the pitfalls of such unwise procedure will be recognized before it is too late."

The December 1954 convention of the National Interfraternity Conference failed to support the executive committee's proposal to boycott certain colleges. An official summary of the minutes states that "delegates said, problems in specific cases should be worked out by the procedure of direct and friendly negotiation with the authorities concerned, rather than by threats of boycott or by recourse to the courts."

The NIC's opposite number, the National Panhellenic Conference of thirty-two women's social fraternities, rarely refers to such matters in its official minutes. Very quietly—and, in all but one case, without written statements of policy—sororities segregate themselves even more effectively than the fraternities do.

* * *

400,000 members on more than 500 campuses

There are now about 400,000 undergraduate fraternity members in chapters of nationals and in locals. (The members of professional and honorary societies are not included in this figure.) More than a hundred large nationals are represented by chapters on more than five hundred campuses. The number of national chapters has expanded from about 2,500 to over 4,200 in the decade since World War II—largely through absorption of existing independent locals. One men's fraternity, Tau Kappa Epsilon, has added sixty-five new chapters; twenty men's nationals have added fifteen or more chapters each. Between 1949 and 1953 alone, TKE added 46 chapters, while three other men's nationals each accepted 23 to 38 chapters. Incidentally, TKE is not only the fastest-growing fraternity but also . . . one of those most strongly opposed to racial and religious discrimination.

While the college population has increased roughly 50 percent between 1940 and 1954, the fraternity and sorority population has more than doubled.

Less than one-fifth of all college students join the social fraternity system; but it should be realized that many denominational colleges, with combined enrollments of over 400,000, do not encourage fraternities. At large metropolitan institutions, the undergraduate campus residents constitute only a small proportion of the total student body; and fraternal groups are much more likely to enroll resident students than commuters and part-time students. At Columbia University, for example, about one-third of the students in the men's college are fraternity members; but nine-tenths of the university's undergraduates are enrolled in its other colleges—and very few of these are members. The women's college at Columbia (Barnard) bans sororities.

At residential colleges where fraternities exist, frequently one-fourth to more than one-half of the students are members, and these to a large extent include those students who are more likely to succeed in careers calling for sociable and actionist abilities.

* * *

Origins of social fraternities

The present type of college social fraternity traces its lineage most directly back to 1825 and Union College at Schenectady, New York, the "mother" of such organizations. In the three early nationals originated at Union, ritualistic mysticism and secrecy were combined with social activities.

For the next half-century, college social fraternities progressed slowly. College administrators looked with suspicion upon their secrecy and pranks and considered them a diverting influence. Most institutions banned them. Some even went so far as to require each student to promise that he would not join such a society. Most fraternities led an underground existence until after the Civil War.

Then, with the spread of industry and the expansion of higher education, fraternities came more into the open and began to win recognition. In the 1870's, they were joined by the women's fraternities, sometimes called "sororities." Pi Beta Phi, at first known as I.C. Sorosis, dates from 1867 at Monmouth College, in Illinois, where Kappa Kappa Gamma was also founded in 1870. Another of the early women's fraternities, Kappa Alpha Theta, was formed in 1870 at Indiana Asbury (now DePauw University).

This expanded role and recognition of men's and women's fraternities in many ways was a result of the increased use of higher education as a prestige requirement for technicians, engineers, and other specialists in a business society. Those seeking a college diploma for such purposes were invading what had been training schools for teachers and clerics or finishing schools for the leisurely wealthy. The social fraternities helped to modify the traditional liberal arts education to meet demands of a less intellectual striving for status.

* * *

By 1880 social fraternities had acquired such influence that they were able to bring about the dismissal of the president of Purdue University, who had promulgated a policy of requiring students to disavow intentions of affiliation with a fraternity. This date marks the approximate turning point in the history of social fraternities. Earlier, chapters were often established sub rosa, and fraternities had difficulty in fighting restrictive measures and legislation. After this date, their influence in political, business, and hence educational circles had increasingly to be reckoned with.

Thus it might be said that American colleges first embraced the social fraternity system in the early 1880s after a half-century of haphazard growth. Shortly thereafter, the issue of racial and religious restrictions on membership selection began to arise. As long as student bodies were rather homogeneous, most fraternities had no expressed policy on the subject because none was needed. Practices of exclusion were observed without their being formally specified.

* * *

Origins of antiminority agitation

Anti-minority agitation and propaganda had swept back and forth across this country for a century. From the 1830s anti-Catholic organization had taken many forms, political and social. In 1852, this movement spawned the Know-Nothings, an aggressive anti-Catholic fraternal order under the name of the Order of the Star-Spangled Banner. Everett R. Clinchy notes in his *All in the Name of God* (1934):

> Within a few years of its organization, the group hysteria fostered by the Know-Nothings spread its contagion across the country like an epidemic of infantile paralysis. Among the activities with which it is credited are the shattering of Catholic crosses, the raiding of Catholic homes and institutions, the burning of Catholic property and the murder of Catholic citizens.

One offshoot of the fraternity system in the South just after the Civil War has made fraternity historians unhappy. A group of former Confederate army officers, who were all fraternity men, in 1866 formed a convivial society to which they gave the name of Kuklos, the Greek word for circle. For alliterative purposes, the word Klan was added, and Kuklos became Kuklux or Ku Klux. The organization shortly began to emphasize "patriotism" and white supremacy. It originated in the desire to keep alive the horseplay, hazing, and camaraderie of the truncated college days of the members; but these impulses were shortly twisted and magnified to extensive terrorist proportions.

The rise of Aryanism

The very secret American Protective Association came into being in 1887 and played continuously upon anti-papal sentiments. In the 1890s, this fraternal group had about a million members, chiefly in the Midwest; its official spokesmen claimed it had overturned the political machinery of a number of states and elected more than a hundred members to Congress pledged to support the association's program.

As a part of this general interracial and interreligious unrest, stimulated by migrations and the pains of industrialization, a pseudo-scholarly propaganda of racism also came into vogue. This propaganda stemmed primarily from confused writings about the Sanskrit-speaking people who invaded India, and certain ancient inhabitants of Airyana or Iran, both known as Aryas. The term Aryan also was extended to substitute for "Indo-European" or "Indo-German" as a label for a family of languages. And then, confusedly and eventually with disastrous consequences, the label got shifted to the peoples or "race" who spoke Aryan tongues. Actually those who speak or have spoken the Aryan languages have no racial characteristics in common more specific than that they are members of the human race.

The development of Aryanism as a racist doctrine was stimulated by Count Arthur de Gobineau, author of a lengthy *Essai sur l'inegalite des races humaines* ("Essay on the Inequality of the Human Races"), originally published in 1853-1855 at Paris. Gobineau considered the culture of the old Teutonic aristocracy to be superior to that of other "races." Ancient Greek civilization presumably justified his claim of Aryan superiority, and he asserted that European history dated from the Teutonic invasion. Anti-Jewish and generally anti-foreign ideas were supported by Gobineau and the rest of this school.

Too many Americans echoed such ideas—notably Alfred P. Schultz in his *Race or Mongrel* (1908) and Madison Grant in his *The Passing of the Great Race, or the Racial Basis of European History* (1916, revised 1918). World War I brought not only a postwar backwash of even more such writings but also a vast revival of the Ku Klux Klan.

The Klan is said to have enrolled six million members by 1925.

Racist propaganda reaches fraternities and sororities

The tide of racist propaganda found its reflection in college fraternities and sororities—for instance, Phi Delta Theta. It had been organized at Ohio's Miami University in 1848. By 1910 it had seventy-eight chapters, most of which had been established during the preceding thirty-five years. As a result of actions at consecutive conventions in 1910 and 1912, the society wrote into its constitution: "Only such persons as are contemplated in the Bond of the Phi Delta Theta may be admitted, and only male, white persons of full Aryan blood not less than sixteen years of age, shall be eligible." Since a three-fourths vote at two consecutive conventions is required to change this fraternity's constitution, the policy was deeply imbedded.

The writing of such clauses into fraternal constitutions was not only a reaction to the increasing cosmopolitanism of college student bodies but also an effort by elders to restrict the democratic fraternizing of undergraduates. By 1928, more than half of the national college fraternities and sororities had specific written rules requiring exclusion along racial and religious lines. Others had the same policy but did not find it necessary or in good taste to say so formally.

On some campuses, the process had gone even further: only "white Christian" fraternities and sororities were admitted to campus interfratemity and Panhellenic councils and their social activities.

The divisive character of fraternities and sororities in American college life in the 1920s only occasionally aroused protests. In 1928 President William Herbert Perry Faunce of Brown University stated his strong conviction that separate fraternities for Jewish or other students were wrong in principle and harmful to the objectives of the university. For this reason, he refused to sanction the establishment of a Jewish fraternity at Brown. But he failed to take additional steps to solve the problem that had provided the demand for a Jewish group—the general exclusion of Jewish students from fraternities at Brown.

Returning veterans resisted self-segregation

When veterans returned to American campuses after World War II—a war many of them realized had been precipitated by warlords with an Aryan philosophy—they were confronted by the substantial residue of the long tradition of self-segregation. They faced it with a sense of resistance and with a degree of responsibility not shown by previous generations of students.

Substantial numbers of veterans joined fraternities. But many of them, although attracted, felt that exclusionary policies were undermining the kind of world Americans ought to be trying to build. To them "brotherhood" had to be a more inclusive conception. Returning veterans provided mature leadership in the fight against discrimination.

As a result of crowded postwar housing conditions, a problem aggravated by rising marriage rates and birthrates, most colleges provided family living quarters for the ex-G.I's. But many of the married veterans joined fraternities. It was not unusual to see a baby carriage being wheeled by a student wearing both a service discharge emblem and a pledge button.

At Vermont's Middlebury College, the Alpha Sigma Phi fraternity chapter was reactivated in the fall term of 1945. Some of the members who re-established it had been students in 1941, who had taken time out for war. These members recalled that in 1941 they had wanted to initiate a Jewish student, who was a football star. Their national officers had said it could not be done.

1946 Middlebury College Jewish student initiation

In the spring of 1946, this Middlebury chapter of Alpha Sigma Phi initiated a Jewish student who had worked in the underground in France against the Hitler occupation forces. At college, he was gaining recognition as a varsity tennis player. The national organization either did not identify his name as Jewish or permitted it to pass through without comment.

Then in the fall of 1946, three Jewish students were among the Alpha Sigma Phi pledges. For a time, the house members felt secure in their course, both because of the preceding case and because their constitution and bylaws as well as the ritual known to them did not contain any statement concerning racial or religious qualifications.

Middlebury's Alpha Sigma Phi faced its emergency on a January day in 1947. In the mail from the national was a copy of the ritual which specified an exclusionary policy based on race and religion. One member, a former Navy pilot, pointedly declared that the purposes of the war in which they had fought were being frustrated by such practices in college fraternities. The chapter very quickly decided unanimously to attempt to get the national fraternity to change the policy. If the attempt failed, the chapter would withdraw.

The chapter, interestingly enough, was housed in a building whose two cellars had been used during the Civil War as a way-station on the Underground Railway to help slaves escape to freedom in Canada.

The Middlebury chapter obtained support for its stand from fellow chapters. But the controlling votes were held by the remote and unresponsive hierarchy of national officials. The hierarchy refused to agree. The Middlebury chapter therefore withdrew from the national fraternity and organized a new local, Alpha Sigma Psi. In its constitution was a clause that eliminated criteria of race, religion, and ethnic origin in the selection of new members.

* * *

Deadlines for democracy

As the return of the veterans from World War II created a ferment in the fraternity world, student groups both inside and outside the fraternity system began to seek reform. College newspapers featured the problems of self-segregation and group rejection. Many chapters began to quarrel with their nationals over restrictive clauses.

As we have seen, a Roper poll in 1949 indicated, on the basis of a student sample covering members and nonmembers of fraternal groups from all sections of the country, that four-fifths opposed exclusion by fraternities on the basis of race and religion. Of the total, about three-fifths wanted no biased restrictions at all; about one-fifth favored limiting out-group members to 10 percent. Only one-fifth still wanted to maintain barriers of color and religion. In discussing the results of this poll, Elmo Roper said:

> First, let me say that we found no substantial differences between the upper and lower classmen. There was surprising unanimity among both those freshmen who might seek to join a fraternity or sorority and those seniors who would in all probability make the selection of new fraternity members.
>
> [Three in five wanted] a fraternity that freely admitted desirable members of all religions and races and that usually contained a considerable number of each. . . . They argue that all persons should be judged on individual merit—that it is silly and prejudiced to judge people on preconceived notions about their race or religion. Many of them might argue that it is not only undemocratic to draw the color or religion line, but also that an individual's personality becomes warped and slanted when be holds such views. . . .
>
> We found that men students felt slightly stronger about this than did women students. And we also found that students in the Far West had a more liberal attitude than students in any other part of the country. But, significantly, there wasn't a single section of the country, including the South, where a majority of students wanted fraternities restricted. In every case, a majority wanted an end to this particular form of discrimination. . . .
>
> [The] acid test in our survey came among those students who are now members of fraternities, many of which do place race and religious restrictions on membership. These students, in most cases, are practicing this form of discrimination, whether consciously or unconsciously. Yet even among them, the results indicate that the largest single group favors membership in a fraternity restricted only by their judgment of the individual worth of the person. . . .
>
> It isn't that . . . college students who were for ending discrimination want actively to purge from themselves all forms of prejudice. They aren't missionaries. It is more that they want to judge their fellow classmates as individuals and accept or reject them without any preconceived notions interfering.

Those who foster Aryanism often contend that minority groups "like" and "want" segregated organizations of their own. Like many other investigators, Roper found just the opposite. He discovered, for example, that four out of five Jewish students "wanted a fraternity which was open to all religions, where potential members were judged as individual personalities."

Opposition to discrimination increasing

Surveys, votes, and other activity at various colleges suggest that opposition to discrimination is increasing. For instance, in 1938 the interfraternity council at the University of Minnesota invited the Jewish and Negro fraternities to take part in its social program. Six years later, the Jewish and Negro fraternities became full members of the council. A summary of events thus describes the situation in 1947:

> Many fraternity and sorority members started discussing clause removal. A meeting of several hundred Greeks was called to air the problem. The Interfraternity Council and Panhellenic Association set up committees on human relations. Letters were sent out to national offices and other chapters across the nation. Discussions were started in the chapter houses. Replies from nationals were discouraging.

The interfraternity and Panhellenic organizations at Minnesota discovered in 1948 that 58 percent of all fraternity men and women favored the removal of racial and religious membership restrictions. Following further campus discussion of such rules, the councils reported the next year that the number of fraternity men in favor of this change had risen to 74 percent. The same percentage of fraternity women were "willing for Panhellenic to take a stand in recommending that all persons be rushed on their own merits, regardless of race or religion." Among members of sixteen sororities without restrictive provisions, 91 per cent said all men's and women's "fraternity groups should get rid of their restrictive clauses."

To judge from the 1949 Minnesota polls, even members of chapters bound by racial and religious restrictions asked that such rules be removed. Among male fraternity members presumably so bound, 70 percent said they "should get rid" of them. At the same time, four women's fraternities still had such clauses, and 56 percent of their members stated they "should get rid of restrictive clauses."

In 1950 the proportion of fraternity men at Minnesota opposing clauses reached 80 percent, and in 1951 it stood at 81 percent. In the latter year, 89 percent of those without and 73 percent of those with clauses opposed such restrictions.

Opposition at Cornell, Dartmouth, and Vermont

At Cornell University in 1951-52 the interfraternity council learned that nineteen men's lodges had written restrictive regulations. In only two did the undergraduate members approve of the clauses. In two others there was a sharp division of opinion. In fifteen of the nineteen, there was strong support for removal of nationally imposed restrictions.

In a 1949 student newspaper poll at Dartmouth, 74 percent of all students and 72 percent of the fraternity men said to eliminate racial and religious restrictions. Only 16 percent of the total and 18 percent of the fraternity men opposed change. The rest among the four in five participating students were undecided.

Dartmouth students frequently debated this subject during the next five years, and in 1954 the student council learned from a referendum that only 12 percent of those who voted asked that "all campus wide organized efforts to eliminate nationally-imposed written and unwritten fraternity discrimination clauses shall cease." All the rest, 88 percent, wanted some change: 37 percent wished to continue the mild form of coercion to change then in force upon fraternities, and 52 percent agreed to a program requiring discriminatory fraternities to modify their practices or to withdraw from the campus. . . .

At the University of Vermont, the student union in February 1955 conducted a ballot to determine the extent of support for an end to fraternity restrictions within seven years. Five out of six students voted; 86 percent answered "yes." The faculty and trustees immediately took action.

Position of the National Student Association

On a national scale, the United States National Student Association (NSA)—representing college student governments—between 1947 and 1954 adopted a series of policies on fair educational practices. These relate to race, color, national origin, sex, creed, political belief, and economic circumstance. In September 1949, the NSA urged the National Interfraternity Conference and the National Panhellenic Conference to call upon their member organizations to eliminate discriminatory practices, and it asked the same of all national, professional, honorary, social, and service societies.

In 1954, at the instruction of the annual NSA congress, Bernard S. Yudowitz of Cornell University, the association's vice-president for educational affairs, codified this series of actions for its national executive committee. This is the section of the code dealing with student organizations:

> Clauses that restrict membership on the basis of race, color, religion or national origin in student organizations in institutions of higher education are contrary to and inconsistent with democratic principles. Groups set up for specifically avowed religious purposes, however, can require their members to accept certain religious tenets.
>
> No incoming group should be allowed on campus which contains in its constitution and/or by-laws and/or ritual discriminatory clauses with regard to race, color, religion, creed, or national origin.
>
> Student bodies should set a specific time limit for the elimination of discriminatory clauses in constitutions, by-laws and rituals of officially recognized campus organizations. On their failure to remove these clauses, official campus recognition should be withdrawn. However, if it is evidenced that the organization is making a conscientious effort to eliminate the clauses, it should be granted one year's extension.
>
> During the interim period, the appropriate body should require conclusive evidence that continuous and positive efforts are being made by these organizations to remove their clauses.
>
> Student bodies should correlate with this legislative activity a continuous educational program in human relations whereby all concerned campus organizations may work together toward the idea of equality.
>
> It should be requested that each campus organization upon recruiting an individual enlighten that individual fully as to the admittance requirements of the constitution and by-laws, and the limitations of rituals with regard to race, color, religion, creed or national origin.

Such indications of student opinion and action help to belie the claim that nationally imposed patterns of group rejection in social fraternities express student mores and help to protect student "freedom" of membership selection. Opinions of both fraternity and nonfraternity students in all sections of the country appear to sustain the view that the number of students wishing to retain restrictions within the college community is a steadily diminishing minority.

* * *

Procedures for democratizing fraternities

In the democratizing of fraternities, many procedures can be useful. The first of these, the elimination of formal clauses, is now being achieved. Eldon H. Reiley, chairman of a nation-wide conference of deans and students at Massachusetts Institute of Technology in March 1955, summed the matter up:

> Perhaps the most significant aspect of the M.I.T. conference was the near unanimous agreement by the delegates that written restrictive clauses in college organizations are unwarranted

Alfred McClung Lee was a noted sociologist, author and social advocate. He taught at Brooklyn College from 1941-71, becoming Chairman of the Sociology and Anthropology Department. He was President of the American Sociological Association (1976-1977).

discriminatory practices and that from a long range viewpoint the removal of these clauses would be a step forward and is probably the first step to be taken in meeting discrimination in colleges. At no time were the old arguments that written clauses protect an individual's right to choose his own friends seriously advanced. If the M.I.T. conference is any indication of the national feeling, this once popular argument would seem to have succumbed to stronger logic.

Other helpful procedures are campus "deadlines for democracy," first to eliminate restrictive clauses and then to eliminate restrictive practices; integrated rushing; possible one-hundred-percent membership in fraternities for all eligible students; the de-emphasis of conspicuous differences among fraternity facilities; and many others discussed or suggested in this book.

The introduction of real brotherhood into fraternities has begun on some campuses. The process should be permitted to spread to more and more campuses. American college students more than ever before see the challenge of world leadership and wish to be equipped intellectually and emotionally to accept it. They realize that organizations on college campuses must not be reminiscent of those in totalitarian nations. These organizations must be American and therefore democratic.

Editor's note: This excerpt is reproduced with the permission of the author's son, Dr. Briant Hamor Lee, professor emeritus, Bowling Green State University.

ALFRED McCLUNG LEE

Alfred McClung Lee (1907-1992), noted sociologist, author and social advocate, was born in Oakmont, Pennsylvania, and married Elizabeth Riley Briant, a sociologist and writer, in 1927. They had two children.

After attaining a B.A. at the University of Pittsburgh and a Ph.D. at Yale University, Alfred McClung Lee began a long career of university teaching and scholarship.

Lee was a professor at the University of Kansas from 1934-1938, then became a lecturer and professor at New York University from 1938-42. The next university at which he taught was Wayne University (1942-1949), where Lee was the Chairman of the Sociology and Anthropology departments (1942-1947). Lee then left Wayne University to become a professor at Brooklyn College of the City University of New York from 1941-1971. He was Chairman of the Sociology and Anthropology department at Brooklyn College from 1951-1957, and in 1971 the college honored this distinguished professor by making him Professor Emeritus. He was also a Visiting Scholar at Drew University until his passing.

He was also a very active member and leader in a large number of sociological, journalistic, and humanitarian organizations both public and private. His activities included being executive director for the Institute for Propaganda Analysis (1940-1942), research consultant for the FCC (1941) and the Department of Justice (1943-1944), member of the board of directors of the ACLU in New York (1949-1956), and president and cofounder of the Society for the Study of Social Problems (1953-1954). Most notable is Lee's presidency of the American Sociological Association (1976-1977) and his founding and presidency of the Association for Humanist Sociology (1976-1977). In addition, Lee was very active in local church and community organizations including the Unitarian Universalist Association as well as the fight for academic freedom.

Lee was a prolific writer on subjects pertaining to the fields of sociology and journalism. Some of his books include *The Daily Newspaper in America* (1937), *The Fine Art of Propaganda* (1939), *Race Riot* (1943), *Principles of Sociology* (1946), *Social Problems in America* (1955), *How to Understand Propaganda* (1952), *Fraternities without Brotherhood* (1955), *Marriage and the Family* (1970), and *Terrorism in Northern Ireland* (1983).

(Editor's note: Adapted from *"The Papers of Alfred McClung Lee, Accession No. 94-001, Biographical Note,"* Brooklyn College Archives and Special Collections.)

PICTURE CREDITS: Then: c.1950 (Bryant Hamer Lee); Now c.1990 (Drew University Archives)

We've got to live democracy, not just talk democracy.

The College Fraternity Crisis in 1949

Howard Whitman
Excerpts from "The College Fraternity Crisis," *Collier's Magazine*, January 8 and January 15, 1949.

Part 1: Bigotry on the Campus

The dawn of 1949 sees the worst college fraternity crisis since 1875, when President McCosh drove fraternities out of Princeton. Today fraternities are "on probation" at some colleges. Cries for abolition are resounding at others. Many educators feel like the Middle West dean who said to me, "We'll either have good fraternities—or no fraternities."

The secret clauses, upon which the battle pinpoints, may jolt many Americans.

"Members must be of the Aryan race and not of the black, Malayan or Semitic race"-this from the constitution of one national fraternity.

Another states: Candidates for pledge-ship "must not be of Mongolian, Malaysian, Negro or Jewish blood."

The words "white Caucasian" are frequently used as an "adjustable" yardstick of discrimination. It of course rules out Negroes. It has been interpreted to rule out Jews. It has been broadened to rule out, or to put a quota upon, Catholics.

One secret clause, which sounds as if it had been lifted out of *Mein Kampf*, limits fraternity membership to "white persons of full Aryan blood."

* * *

Indexed by Race and Creed

Every year thousands of freshmen, accustomed to being regarded simply as Americans, enter college to discover that they are sorted out by fraternities into pigeonholes labeled Protestant, Catholic, Jew; then cross-filed as white, black, yellow or brown.

"Now—just a minute!" objected a fraternity man when this subject came up at the Alpha Delta Phi house at Amherst. "What about your golf clubs, your business clubs, your country clubs—aren't they doing the very same thing?"

I jotted his words in my notebook and tossed them a few days later to the president of Amherst College, Dr. Charles Woolsey Cole.

President Cole replied, "Institutions of learning ought to pick and choose the best parts of our culture, not the worst. College students ought to set the pace. If they make enough headway with the democratic idea, the country clubs and the business clubs will come along later."

Setting atop the college fraternity structure is the National Interfraternity Conference comprising 58 national fraternities. At its 40th annual meeting in New York recently, the N.I.C. abortively battled over the discrimination issue and finally put it on ice for another year.

However, some of the N.I.C.'s leaders have not hesitated to present what they call the "other side" of the discrimination picture. At one meeting, a top N.I.C. officer appealed to Americans to "stop shivering at the word 'discrimination.'"

He said, "I love the discriminating tongue, the discriminating eye, and the discriminating ear, and above all, the discriminating mind and soul. The person for whom I can find no love and no respect is the indiscriminate person. To be indiscriminate is to be common, to be vulgar."

One N.I.C. spokesman insists, "There is nothing arbitrary or capricious or unnatural about fraternity membership restrictions based on race, creed or color. College and university administrators who attempt to prevent forcibly the nation's fraternities from exercising racial and religious restrictions in choosing members are violating the tenets of democracy!"

"No discrimination: just a restrictive clause"

With softer pedal, the executive secretary of a national fraternity said to me, "I wouldn't say we discriminate. All we have is a 'restrictive clause.' You simply have to get the consent of every official of the national organization if you want to take in somebody of a different race or religion."

At Williams College, a committee on postwar extracurricular activities while stanchly [sic] defending fraternities, made this curious statement:

"It is a truism that fraternities are undemocratic. Any social or caste system is undemocratic. There is no use denying the facts of life merely because one does not like them."

That an undemocratic caste system should be a "fact of life" in American institutions of higher learning is repugnant to a good many people. Some critics insist that colleges, being tax-free, have no right to harbor such a system. They decry the fact that in 12 states even the houses owned by discriminatory fraternities are freed from taxes.

Between the extremes of the National Interfraternity Conference and those who would abolish fraternities entirely is a middle ground which is all but obscured by flying fur. Many educators feel that the fraternity system, given—as one of them put it—"a transfusion of free American blood," could get up from its sickbed and walk with a truly democratic stride.

The transfusion had better be given soon. As President John Sloan Dickey, of Dartmouth, said to me, "Our colleges cannot for long be indifferent to an influence on their campuses which tends to fashion men's attitudes in a prejudicial way. . . . We must find a solution in the not-too-distant future."

I spoke with Eric Johnston just after his recent trip to Russia. Johnston is a Theta Delta Chi, University of Washington, '17. He earnestly declared, "Our fraternities must be democratized. We're competing with another ideology in this world and the competition is likely to go on for a long time. We've got to show them and the rest of the world, that 'democracy' is more than a word over here. We've got to live democracy, not just talk democracy."

Part 2. Democracy in Action

Seventy-five young men from eleven colleges sweated out a hectic weekend in Chicago last May to launch a new national fraternity. They worked night and day. They wrote by-laws, preambles, articles, amendments and resolutions. They tore up pages, rewrote pages. Finally they came up with the constitution of Beta Sigma Tau, a fraternity which opens its arms alike to Christian and Jew, to white and Negro, to rich and to poor.

Beta Sigma Tau, which formally calls itself an "intercultural fraternity," is a dramatic outgrowth of the bare-fist battle over discrimination which is being fought on American campuses. This fraternity draws heavily upon the One World philosophy of Wendell Willkie and has attracted scores of college men to whom fraternities for "white Caucasians" or "full-blooded Aryans" are a little nauseating in this day.

By the opening of the fall term, Beta Sigma Tau—without benefit of trumpets' blare—had amassed seven full-fledged chapters, at Ohio State, the University of California at Santa Barbara, the University of Buffalo, Hobart College, Roosevelt College, Baldwin-Wallace and Ohio Wesleyan. In addition to these, four more chapters were busily forming. November saw the launching of chapters at Stanford, the University of California at Berkeley, the University of Southern California and the University of California at Los Angeles—all within the month.

While most of Beta Sigma Tau's membership is white Protestant, as is the population of the U.S., it includes Catholics, Jews, Mohammedans, Negroes, Chinese and Nisei. . . .[1]

* * *

Looking for new ways to evaluate members

The University of Wisconsin has a new interracial group—Sigma Delta Phi. Bowdoin has a new fraternity which calls itself "ARU," meaning "All Races United." The antidiscrimination movement is hopping from campus to campus.

Sobered by a war which turned out to be a young men's proposition, thousands of students are wondering whether young men shouldn't take a bigger part in running the world. They are unwilling to follow hand-me-down systems. They squirm unhappily in the long flannels of fixed ideas. They want to think for themselves.

The "wrong-side-of-the-railroad-tracks" notion is thoroughly repugnant to them. They believe no man should be evaluated by his father's bank roll, his father's clubs, or by the Social Register. No man should be excluded from a fraternity because he isn't a "smoothie" or a hot dresser, or doesn't drive a convertible.

Dr. Max McConn, formerly of Lehigh, has listed the "values" on which old-line Greek-letter cliques judge new freshmen: 1) Money. 2) Family connections. 3) Type of preparatory school attended. 4) "Personality."

* * *

At Amherst, storm center of the college fraternity crisis, the Amherst College alumni committee on postwar education reports: "The 'unwanted man' psychology plays a real role with too many students. . . . The competitive status of membership among the fraternities gives rise to a good deal of heartache and insidious comparison of social status."

Wrote Amherst's subcommittee on student activities, four fifths of whom were fraternity men themselves: "The sense of exclusiveness and social preferment . . . is hurtful to the young men who are in the fraternities because it gives them a false and undemocratic sense of superiority. And it hurts the students who are outside the fraternities by giving them a wholly unwarranted sense of being inferior and of being social outcasts."

The committee pointedly recalled that "each year in the last decade a number of otherwise thoroughly desirable young men have left college at the end of the freshman year primarily for the reason that they have failed to be elected to a fraternity."

* * *

Alternate plans at Harvard and Princeton

To demands for abolition of the fraternity system, many observers complain, "You can't leave students in a void. If you abolish fraternities, you must have a substitute plan."

Two substitute plans are now functioning with notable success: the House Plan at Harvard, and the Club Plan at Princeton. When a freshman comes to Harvard he looks over the seven "houses"—large clubhouse residences, where students live, eat and hold their parties. He applies for admission to one of them. He may prefer Lowell House. He may prefer Adams or Dunster.

The important point is: The man chooses the house—unlike the fraternity system in which the house chooses the man. The houses are interracial, nonsectarian, and conscious of neither bluebooks nor bankbooks. Harvard hangs no labels on the men it is educating for democracy.

Princeton, a foe of fraternities since Civil War days, centers its social life in seventeen "eating clubs" which are similarly democratic. Vernon Geddy, chairman of the Undergraduate Inter-Club Committee, earnestly told me, "The thing we're proudest of is that there is no racial, religious or social segregation. We take a man on his merits."

Along Prospect Street, along which the club mansions are lined in elm-shaded elegance, there is a free and wholesome tang. There is neither restriction nor exclusion. Harold Yerkes, president of the Quadrangle Club, remarked, "The club system is for everybody. Clubs aren't 'something special.' They're part of the whole college experience."

Thoughtful fraternity men know that in the Harvard and Princeton plans the fraternity system is up against a stern rival. Since the war, many fraternities, perceiving the neon handwriting on the wall, have tried to mend their ways. Most of them have tossed hazing and hell week into the ash can.

Many observers take heart from what Dan Byrd, until recently president of Alpha Tau Omega at Ohio State, called "the more mature outlook which fraternities are evincing."

END NOTES

[1] *Editor's note:* The following excerpt, on the Founding of Beta Tau Sigma, appeared on its Web site in February of 2002:

Beta Sigma Tau was founded in 1948 upon the beliefs that any man should have the opportunity to become a member of a Greek organization, regardless of his race, religion, nationality, or wealth. During the 12 years that followed, many young men at universities across the nation embraced the ideals of the Beta Sigs and joined the fraternity. Beta Sigma Tau grew rapidly with the founding of many new chapters, yet in 1960, the National Officers decided to merge with Pi Lamdba Phi, a fraternity with similar ideals, in order to form a much larger and stronger fraternity. Almost forty years later, seventeen students at The University of Toledo decided to start their own fraternity in an effort to exemplify the true attitude and meaning behind a social fraternity. These men researched the history and values of many fraternities in an effort to find one that shared their ideals. Even though it had been absorbed by Pi Lambda Phi, Beta Sigma Tau fit perfectly and was chosen. Three main reasons: hazing, exhausting dues, and uniformity, inspired these men to diverge from the existing Greek system at the University of Toledo.

Despite the University's "No-Hazing Law," nearly all of the fraternities put their pledges through degrading rituals generally treating them as lower class citizens. The founders believed that the student period should be filled with constructive activities designed to strengthen and unify the group of potential members. These men are brothers and deserve the respect of equality.

Diversity, the embrace of culture, racial, and social differences, is something missing in today's world. Everybody talks about it, but usually no action is ever taken to remove the barriers that have been erected in the past and have caused the divisions of mankind for too long. Fraternities seemed to be mostly white, all black, or all Hispanic. In addition, these groups never seemed to participate in events together in order to get to know each other and level barriers between the two. This new chapter of Beta Sigma Tau was being founded in an effort to attract an extremely diverse group of men of all races, religions, and nationalities. Also, we would strive to participate in events with as many diverse campus organizations as possible.

(*Reprinted with permission*)

In 1954, 84 percent of the top student government leaders have fraternity affiliations.

2. Student Government and Fraternity Row

Bill Graham
Sigma Pi
President, Student Senate, University of Illinois

Reprinted from Student Government Bulletin, *NSA, February 1956*

Editor's note: At the time this was written, in 1956, considerable progress had been made in addressing restrictive membership clauses in national fraternities. As described in Part 2, Section 5, NSA nationally had maintained a collaborative dialogue with the National Interfraternity Council from 1947, its first year, while at the same time supporting efforts to eliminate discriminatory membership policies through its policy pronouncements and human relations workshops. The equal interest of the Association in the influence of campus fraternities in student governments and their relationship is reflected in this article.

The statistics regarding fraternity affiliation and student government leadership contained in the recent USNSA study of *Student Government, Student Leaders, and the American College* (USNSA, 1955) merit careful consideration by those interested in the future outlook for the fraternity system or student governing organizations. This study revealed that 84 percent of the top student government leaders have fraternity affiliations. Although only slightly over 30 percent of these student leaders actually reside in fraternity housing, the frequent existence of deep-seated loyalties to the fraternity system among its members suggests a strong fraternity influence in student governing bodies.

That such a high percentage of student leaders have fraternity affiliations on those campuses where fraternities exist does not seem too surprising in itself. The process of selection channels the student leader to the fraternity. The student leader often selects a fraternity because he is a "joiner" and sees the fraternity as a means of augmenting his talents while associating with individuals of similar interests. The fraternity selects the leader largely because leadership potential is valuable to his organization: internally for continued success, and externally for prestige purposes. The real significance of the statistics lies in the cause and effect of fraternity control or influence in student government and the resultant relationships.

Fraternities act as political units on many campuses

The question naturally arises as to what constitutes the ideal fraternity–student government relationship. Ideally, the student government would give a fair representation to the fraternity viewpoint while formulating objective policy to best provide for the total student welfare. It would also provide educational programs and services to the student body. The fraternities would reciprocate by providing mature and sensitive leaders for student government, and by supporting and encouraging its programs.

Unfortunately, however, this sort of favorable relationship has not always prevailed. On many campuses, fraternities acting as political units have manipulated the operation of student government in such a selfish manner as to incur the continued wrath of the remainder of the student body and the college personnel. Vivid examples of this sort of irresponsible conduct include the purposeful creation of "greek-independent" splits through political parties to achieve election victories. This is particularly unfortunate inasmuch as it is rare indeed that a student government issue can be divided along such lines.

Some fraternities attempt to maintain control of the influential offices of student government for prestige purposes. On other campuses, there is a negligent disregard for total student welfare in the formulation of student government policy by a strong fraternity bloc. Equally unfortunate have been the hostile or reactionary attitudes when student governments have attempted to make progress in such areas as discrimination and selectivity, although the fraternities have not always been to blame for conflicts arising here.

Surely those individuals who are responsible for the creation of all such practices are cognizant of the detrimental effects upon the fraternity system, as a whole. That they are allowed to persist in such practices does irreparable harm while bringing only the most petty benefits.

No justification for student government–fraternity rivalry

Basically, there should be little justification for a continued rivalry or conflict between the fraternities and the student government. There seems to be nothing inherent in the philosophies of the organizations to set them at odds. These student organizations have as their basic purpose the fulfillment of a co-curricular role in supplementing the classroom education. This common reason for existing, similar desires for a degree of autonomy in areas of their own activities, and a desire for recognition as responsible and respectable organizations should engender cooperation. Finally, and most important, both are engaged in a process of governing. This would imply a degree of overlap, but in a mature society the end result would be cooperation, not conflict.

Although such a mature society does not universally exist, as a generalization it seems safe to say there is a promising tendency in that direction. Recent developments seem to bear out this hypothesis. For example, fraternities are tending away from hazing, "hell weeks," and rowdiness, tending towards developing interfraternity councils and other governing boards, and becoming more aware of their need to supplement the educational process by offering something more than just social benefits to members.

Similarly, that student governments collectively have established and sustained a national student organization of substantial import would seem to verify that they, too, have matured. This fact is further attested by the realization that student governments are evolving a philosophy of partnership and full responsibility in an educational community to supercede a philosophy of being merely outspoken pressure groups. It is important to note here that if the statistics concerning fraternity influence in student government hold true on a given campus, a direct correlation might well be drawn between the maturity of the fraternity system and the importance of student government at that school. This again emphasizes the need for fraternities to produce capable leaders.

Motives for fraternity involvement in student government activity

Of late, fraternities seem to be finding it generally to their advantage to participate in the areas of student government activity. However, it is necessary to examine the motives involved to get a clear perspective of the situation. Let us first examine those motives which are least desirable. In some instances participating in student government activity has been nothing more than a hypocritical subterfuge to justify the existence of fraternities which have brought the displeasure of public opinion upon themselves. In other instances it has grown solely from the realization of a dependency on student government. The same USNSA study previously mentioned found that on 50 percent of college campuses fraternities are subordinate to the student governments. It is to be suspected that student government also has a strong voice in determining fraternity policy on the remainder of our campuses. This would suggest an involuntary defensive participation in student government.

It is not infrequent that the fraternities acquiesce and "tolerate" student government because of a realization that they are a decided minority of the student population and must be careful not to inflict an excess of indignities on their fellow students. The knowledge that the college can abolish a fraternity with virtually no impact on the campus as a whole is a sobering consideration indeed.

A more desirable and morally justifiable motivation for fraternity participation in student government activity emanates from a recognition that a fraternity is a segment of the student body that can best achieve its ends through a united front and democratic presentation of majority opinion. A second and related reason would be that fraternities are accepting the responsibilities vital to the growth of the individual or organization that exists in an academic sphere. It is certainly to be hoped that the trend is toward participation on grounds such as these.

Fraternities can contribute to co-curricular values

However, fraternities generally must become more cognizant of their responsibilities to the educational community. Fraternities are frequently granted privileges not permitted other student organizations, but they must remember that they have no inherent rights above those held by other student organizations. If fraternities do not make proportionate contributions of co-curricular values to the educational process in comparison with other student groups, it will become increasingly difficult to justify their own existence. Fraternities should soon realize, if they have not already, that one of the best channels for attaining co-curricular values lies in participation, contribution, and encouragement to effective student self-government. The formalized, representative and democratic all-campus student government is thus ideal.

Fraternities and student governments can point with pride to that increasing number of campuses where a mutually profitable relationship between their organizations exists. If some of the bad relationships suggested previously prevail, however, an intensive reassessment of goals should be initiated immediately. Only in this way can the dynamic potential of these groups be realized and effective contributions made to education and individual development.

PICTURE CREDIT: c.1956 (University Archives, University of Illinois)
Note: The editors have been unable to obtain any career highlight data on Bill Graham.

A belief that fraternities "helped give shape and character to the very life of this country"

Arthur Ray Warnock: "Champion of Responsible Student Self-Government"

Dean of Men, Pennsylvania State College, 1919-1949
Chairman, National Interfraternity Conference, 1950-51

Editor's note: The Interfraternity Research and Advisory Council in its December 14, 1951, bulletin published a memorial to Dean Warnock, (portions excerpted below), which also encapsulates the positive visions advanced by fraternity system leaders. Allan Ostar (See p. 209) was editor of the Penn State Daily Collegian *while Warnock was Dean. "I knew Warnock quite well," he recalls, "Although we tangled on a number of issues when I was editor of the Daily Collegian, when I graduated in 1948 he sent me a very complimentary letter. He was very supportive of the fraternities and sororities at Penn State and of the IFC. During his 30 years as dean, campus politics were dominated by the Greeks. That began to change after the war. Also, it was not long after the war until universities did away with the positions of 'deans of men' and 'deans of women' whose primary job was to enforce rules and regulations. They were replaced by deans or vice presidents of student affairs with much broader responsibilities. Warnock was among the last of the earlier breed. The prewar concept of* in loco parentis, *watched over by those earlier deans, did not survive postwar changes. At the same time, Warnock deserves credit for not trying to discourage our participation in NSA, unlike some other traditional deans around the country."*

Ray Warnock viewed life with admirable serenity and perspective, winnowing important things from the trivial, and formulating a philosophy about student life and fraternities that was sound, inspiring, and fundamentally American. When death came to him quietly, at his home last month, Ray's friends and neighbors, those who loved him and mourned his passing, were truly legion. They were located along a road that stretched to Maine and to California, from the Deep South to the provinces of Canada, and far beyond.

A "wise counselor" for 30 years as Penn State Dean of Men

They were not alone his brothers in Beta Theta A and Phi Delta Phi to whom he gave generously of his time and affection. They included the thousands of students he had so wisely counseled at his own Alma Mater, the University of Illinois, and also during his thirty years as Dean of Men at Penn State. They also included men and women in scores of fraternities and societies across the land. As Educational Adviser and later as Chairman of the National Interfraternity Conference, as Editor of this Bulletin and as contributor to many popular and scholarly publications, as a speaker to Interfraternity gatherings in many states and on many campuses. and as the fine, friendly man that he was, Ray had won many hearts. They grieved for him because, as one in New England wrote,"He stood knowing."

Ray Warnock's life, with its ever-widening circle of friendships and of influences for good, itself exemplified one of his deep convictions about Greek-letter organizations. He saw them as agencies that helped to overcome provincialism and narrowness of viewpoint. He felt that membership in them did not restrict one's friendships, but rather multiplied a person's potential for growth in understanding and in service to the wider community.

Fraternities are "uniquely American"

He repeatedly pointed out that fraternities were "uniquely American." He believed they helped give shape and character not to student bodies alone, but to the very life of this country. It was his notion that the many organizations that Americans join, including student societies. service clubs, and the lodges of adult life, had a lot to do with the success of the democratic experiment on this continent. He saw them providing the means for "a lot of people to get into the act," to practice unselfishness and concern for others in their daily living. Because they provided such opportunities, he thought of fraternities as a part of the fabric that gave strength, richness and meaning to institutions of a free people. . . .

Ray Warnock died at 68. He was born in Illinois. He attended that state's University at Champaign-Urbana, earning membership in Phi Beta Kappa and both a bachelor's and a law degree. He was an instructor in English there from 1905 to 1907, and then became an apprentice and assistant to America's first Dean of Men, the late Thomas Arkle Clark. From this work he was called to Penn State in 1919. He remained to see the Institution grow from an enrollment of 2,400 to one of more than 12,000 students. His retirement, with emeritus rank, on August 31, 1949 came thirty years, to the day, after his appointment as Dean of Men.

Dean Warnock devoted himself enthusiastically to the promotion of good relations between town and gown. . . .

He will also be remembered as a champion of responsible student self-government at Penn State and as a chief architect and builder of its fine fraternity system. . . .

From his election as its Chairman in 1950, he gave vigorous leadership to the National Interfraternity Conference. Much of the planning for the 1951 interfraternity conferences at Virginia, commemorating the 175th anniversary of the birth of the Greek-letter idea was his responsibility. . . .

PICTURE CREDIT: c. 1944 (University of Illinois Archives).

College Press Frames the Fraternity Debate

PAGE TWO LOS ANGELES COLLEGIAN Friday Morning, October 31, 1947

National Sororities, Fraternities — Yes or No?

Social Organizations Bring High Cost, Discrimination

Snobbiness, cliques, high cost, selective discrimination, these are some of the outstanding qualities which sororities and fraternities bring to the campus.

Fraternities and sororities are beating a hasty retreat, and with the retreat come the petty excuses for which these organizations are noted. Their good fellowship cry sounds a little stale, and their feeble arguments are being stampeded by the mature outlooks of the returning veteran.

A recent survey conducted by an eastern university disclosed that the only reason fraternities and sororities have been able to exist is that they have changed. That is, the ones with intelligent leadership have changed.

Paddle-whacking days are becoming a thing of the past, and other infantile actions, so long a trade mark of these little people with big traditions, are fading into oblivion, where they belong. However, as mentioned before, the disease of hazing is not the only nauseating feature of these organizations.

The mundane ways of fraternities and sororities, sometimes referred to by astute individuals as snobbishness, continues to prevail. This cleverly concealed feeling, subtly camouflaged by actions disturbingly similar to campaign promises, is strangely parallel to the narrow philosophical outlook of a small midwestern community.

Whenever any section of our social structure has been in operation for a prolonged period of time, it tends to set up certain conventions and rules, commonly lumped together under the imposing title of traditions.

No single factor is more suffocating to progress and adaptation to the fluidity of social reform, than these much-flaunted traditions. No single factor retards the inevitable elimination of all forms of

Students Favor Social Organizations, Decline To Live in Chapter Lodgings

Social Organizations Foster Mature Social Adjustment

There is definitely a place, need, and desire for national Gr letter fraternities at Los Angeles City College should the school b come a state-supervised four-year institution.

Those persons most opposed to fraternities at City College vi the topic through immature eyes. The basis of society is one o gregarious nature. A highly self-centered person content only w himself can deny that successful adjustment to life is more portant than a single item gained by college attendance.

The desire of students to have fraternities and sororities their college campus is forcefully indicated on a national scale the results of polls conducted by Harold C. Hand, whose vol "Campus Activities" is most extensive and authoritative book intramural and intermural activities.

"The importance of the fraternity-sororities system is atte by the fact that nearly 60 per cent of all women and over 70 cent of all men are reported as preferring this type of living rangement. Since these figures include campuses with requ dormitory life as well as some colleges with no fraternity ho the actual figure is undoubtedly even higher."

Clyde C. Johnson, assistant dean of undergraduates at ne U.C.L.A., recently polled 59 national Greek letter organization what factors create a favorable environment for a college frate system. His answer may serve as a guidepost for City College.

"1. Cooperative and constructive attitudes on the part o college administration, making the fraternity system 'an int part of college life'."

"2. Strict scholastic requirements."

City College has one of the highest rated academic prog for the first two college years in California. No national organiz

"3. Maintenance of housing facilities for fraternity me and special interests in small group housing."

Many houses can be readily made available to serve as

RACIAL, RELIGIOUS AND ETHNIC BARRIERS to fraternity membership, held to be a matter of private choice, came under increasing attack as unacceptable public policy. NSA supported efforts to prohibit recognition of societies with restrictive policies (see Lee, p.806, Wilcox, p. 398).

Page Two
Monday, Oct. 3, 1949 Daily Trojan

Southern California DAILY TROJAN

★ In Defense of the Row

The much maligned Row organizations have had little opportunity to offer rebuttals to the accusation that they are undemocratic.

This accusation has been, in the majority of cases, bantered around by students who are unfamiliar with the real purpose or actual conduct of fraternities and sororities. They voice no specific objection, but are vague and dogmatic.

* * * *

Probably the big reason Row members are branded undemocratic is their supposedly exclusiveness. Here again is an unjust charge.

For the approximately 15,000 students that roam the campus, some center of activity is needed. Fraternities and sororities supply this center. They make it possible for students to make more friends than could be possible by casual campus conversation.

As a result the Row as a whole is much more gregarious than the unorganized segment of the campus. And like any other social group, if they like you, you're always welcome.

"They monopolize student government" is another grievance that some non-orgs add to their charge that the Row is undemocratic. Fraternity and sorority members pack campus offices because they are willing to spend valuable time and energy to assure the proper funtioning of student government. It takes organized groups to erect any sort of system.

Bob Padgett's victory proves that non-orgs can also fill student offices if they are willing to spend the necessary time and energy.

The charge that democracy does not prevail along 28th street sounds a little rare, a little flat. That is, when we know that the students who comprise the Row are sincere and enthusiastic in their desires to improve campus life and to make the most of their four years in it.—Bob Thatcher.

New Mexico Highlands University, 1/14/49

The Highands' Candle

Established September, 1923

FRATERNITITY DISCRIMINATION

In the last two issues of Colliers Magazine, the fraternity system of the American universities has been under attack. Fraternities which started out to be merely social organizations have become campus political machines. On some campuses there is an understanding that certain fraternities will handle certain affairs. Lawrence Deutch has often told us the story of the fraternity at one of his previous schools which considered itself the fraternity that would run the paper; other fraternities on the campus backed them in return for certain concessions.

Outside of politics, fraternities run the social events on the campuses of the nation. * * *

There are eight Greek organizations on the campus. Each of them is the possessor of a constitution which in glowing words explains the high-minded reasons for its formation. Most have no provisions for barring any particular race or creed, but how many of them have "gentlemen's agreements." The weaseling reasons for non-acceptance of certain people are cowardly. If you are going to bar a person because of his color or religion, at least be brave enough to announce it and defend yourself. Stop skulking in corners like rats.

This editorial was written by Stanley Sachs, Candle *editor. He succeeded Donald Martinez, whose memoir of the post-war Chicano Student Movement at Highlands appears on* *page 1012.*

THE DIAMONDBACK Friday, May 13, 1949

Eisenhauer's Speech University of Maryland, 5/13/49

Campus Anti-Semitism Blasted

Excerpts from a speech delivered by the student body president.

The most important single decision that confronted the Executive Council this year was the motion to join the National Student Association. There isn't time to air the arguments presented. Next year's council, I hope, will review the entire situation. However, it was not the defeat of the motion to affiliate that was discouraging: it was the reasons advanced against joining that were. For example: we know that Harvard, Yale, Chicago, and California belong to the NSA. But we also know that they are liberal schools and consequently we shouldn't have anything to do with them . . . In Madison, Wisconsin, last summer at the NSA Congress, a colored man was elected president (by acclamation, incidentally); what are they trying to prove? . . . the organization was at one time harboring Communists as members . . . a long time ago but still . . . believe it or not, on a college campus on the floor of its highest student deliberative assembly these arguments were advanced. The question we should ask ourselves is: Just what are we trying to prove — and to whom?

Anti-Semitism—Real Force

Last fall I heard there was concern being expressed because I had appointed several Jewish students to head my committees. Later in the year the Infraternity Council by secret ballot once more rejected the application of two Jewish fraternities for membership. And in the recent SGA elections every Jewish candidate save one was defeated, regardless of the ticket he ran on. I have tried to understand why many people, including many able Jewish leaders, insist that this sort of issue should never be dragged in to the limelight. They reason that throwing a glare on racial or religious prejudices interferes with the sincere efforts of the tolerant people working for harmony. I disagree somewhat. Anti-Semitism, or "hate the Jews," is a very real and ugly force on this campus, and to the people who are working for harmony, I say that your efforts must be redoubled.

Georgia Tech, 1/14/48

THE TECHNIQUE, ATLANTA, GEORGIA

WHAT FRATERNITY CRISIS?

A discussion of fraternities and their apparent changes.

In the January 15 edition of Collier's Magazine there appeared an article by Howard Whitman on "The College Fraternity Crisis."... We believe Mr. Whitman, in his comments, was trying to prove a point on which he had already decided. The general idea of his article is to define fraternities as blood brothers of the Klan, as the core of discrimination against Catholic, Jews, Negroes and foreigners....

* * *

We believe in addition there is a silent change coming about in fraternity structure. This change is an outgrowth of our change of standards ... plus one more fact that needs bringing out.

When most of our present day fraternities were organized, immigration was a big issue. Some ignorant foreigners were scraping enough money together to send their sons to college. These men, by their character, interests and personalities, were not regarded as desirable associates by the generally wealthy college men. Negroes were still in dense ignorance. Then it falls into a logical pattern that these new societies would include clauses of restriction in their charters. We do not try to judge here whether this was right or wrong; we merely are trying to give the background - something our friend in Colliers conveniently left out.

A change is coming, it seems. And the new type of organization will be one based on present day ideas.... --- T.A.C.

Page Two
Thursday, Oct. 14, 1948

Southern California DAILY TROJAN

Greeks

•Row Economy

"Millionaires! Playboys!" These two words are hurled contemptiously at fraternity men by some nonorgs. We do not think those nonorgs know the facts about fraternity costs.

It is not our purpose to recount the advantages of being affiliated with a fraternity. Rather we would like to show why a man of normal means can afford to be a fraternity man.

Figures released by the dean of men's office for the spring semester gave a total House dues averaged $6.65, while $5 was directed to social assessments. The latter figure usually covered one or two fraternity parties a week. Most parties were held away from the Row. Men who live on the Row also claim other savings; such as the economy of living near school.

Costs are scaled accordingly for those men who do not live in the house.

Playboys? Maybe so. But, the latest figures released, covering the fall semester of 1947, listed the all-fraternity average as being 1.295. The grade point for nonorgs was slightly lower, being 1.287.

U. of North Carolina, 10/46

Page Four THE DAILY TAR HEEL

Interfraternity Council Visiting Agreement

The privilege of entertaining unchaperoned women student visitors in fraternity houses is based upon the acceptance of certain basic standards. This acceptance is made in the form of a pledge to uphold these standards, and the pledge is binding on the fraternity that gives it and on every individual member of that fraternity.

An interfraternal problem, such as a program of visiting, comes within the purisdiction of the Interfraternity Counoil. Therefore, it devolves upon the Interfraternity Council to assume the responsibility for the program of unchaperoned visiting and guarantee the enviroment of a gracious home for women student visitotrs.

The Interfraternity Council accepts the responsibility for the entire visiting program and with that responsibility it takes upon itself the duty to administer and enforce the agreement that all fraternities have pledged to uphold. The assumption of responsibility is not taken lightly by this Council and the following agreement will be administered and enforced in such a manmer as to fulfill the obligations we have accepted.

The Cornell Daily Sun

Below are highlights from a series of four in-depth columns, written by Edward Hanpeter in April, 1950.

CORNELL DAILY SUN April 26, 1950 EDITORIAL PAGE

Secret Societies . . .

Far Above Cayuga's Waters Fraternity Ups and Downs

No sooner had Cornell University begun its first academic year in1868 than fraternities appeared in the village of Ithaca. Altogether some seven "secret societies," as they were then known, established chapters at the young institution during that first year. But no sooner had fraternities made their appearance than independent students organized in opposition, declaring that fraternities introduced a distinction among students of the same university, possessed no claim to existence from literary and cultural values imparted, and were nothing but dissipation societies.

A meeting of independent students on December 11, 1868, was the beginning of a fight between fraternity and non-fraternity men which has plagued the campus occasionally and every other institution in the nation where the fraternity has come into existence....

* * *

Last fall the Interfraternity Council voted unanimously for self-government, thereby receiving initial jurisdiction over all member houses and the power of determining all policies affecting fraternities....

On April 19,1945, an Interfraternity Alumni Association was formed to provide proper guidance of fraternity financial and administrative matters.

Fraternities thus appear to have reached a peak in their history on campus. Nevertheless the fraternity system has a long way to go before its past performance will be readily condoned....

CORNELL DAILY SUN April 27, 1950 EDITORIAL PAGE

Two Major Accomplishments . . .

Self-Government, IC-IFC Cooperation Mark Post-War Fraternity Scene

Two major achievements have emerged from the post-war years of the Cornell fraternity system. One is self-government, the other cordial cooperation with independent students through the Independent Council....

CORNELL DAILY SUN April 28, 1950 EDITORIAL PAGE

More Than Talk . . .

Issue of Discrimination Looms As Most Important Criticism of Fraternities

Looming as the most important change against the fraternity system in the postwar era, the issue of discrimination rapidly developed from more criticism into active attempts to remove restrictive clauses from fratenity charters. Much agitation was begun by fraternities themselves.

At Cornell in the spring of 1948 discussion was begun among fraternities to consider the problem of discrimination....

CORNELL DAILY SUN April 29, 1950 EDITORIAL PAGE

Looking Ahead . . .

Fraternity System Must Reform Or Face Ultimate Dissolution

.... The ability of the fraternity to combine with its bretheren and effect such healthy changes is the ability of the fraternity to survive. It must either accept the reality of complete dissolution and strict regimentation in the future, or reform its notorious behavior and erase discrimination from its charters - even at the expense of bucking national headquarters. American society, especially as expressed in its revered institutions of learning and liberal education, cannot tolerate brotherhood which is irresponsible and undemocratic.

PART 4. STUDENT VOICES INFLUENCING NSA

SECTION 4

The Political Movements

CONTENTS

In his history of the Student Federalist movement's ten-year life from 1941 to 1951, Gilbert Jonas (Stanford U.) captures its appeal on college campuses throughout the country, as well as the support world government enjoyed among many college faculty and U.S. leaders (voiced passionately by Cord Meyer in Section 1) as a necessary precondition to the transformation of the United Nations to a "new world sovereignty." It was a leading activist force during its lifetime.

Jonas's history shows how the U.S. national student movements were connected to the World Assembly of Youth (WAY) through its U.S. affiliate, the Young Adult Council (YAC), of which NSA was a member. WAY was the non-Communist counterforce to the Communist-controlled World Federation of Democratic Youth (WFDY).

Seymour Reisin (CCNY) provides an overview of Students for Democratic Action (SDA), which grew out of the wartime United States Student Assembly (USSA; see Prologue) and the newly formed Americans for Democratic Action in spring 1948. SDA was also influential in providing leadership for NSA (See Ken Kurtz, Swarthmore College, 1949-1950 Pennsylvania Regional Chair, in Part 5).

Reisin, who had been a member of the American Youth for Democracy (AYD) before joining the SDA, also provides some insights into the nature and appeal of the AYD and its historical context. As noted in Part 2, the effort to ban the AYD on college campuses for its Communist connections was a recurring issue on NSA's student rights agenda.

Dick Murphy (University of North Carolina), 1952-53 NSA president, provides a brief retrospective on the Young Democrats.

Emergence of a "conservative student revival"

While the center and left of organized student opinion were well represented on campus, it was the appearance of William Buckley's *God and Man at Yale* in 1951 that inspired a serious conservative philosophical and political agenda both on campus and in Young Republican Clubs (YRCs). Buckley and the YRC's saw NSA as an ideological adversary.

M. Stanton Evans's *Revolt on Campus* tells of the struggle for control of the YRC by conservative students and of their opposition to NSA as a "conduit" for political ideas that Evans saw as "very liberal indeed." Robert F. Munger's transformation of Students for MacArthur in 1952 into the Students for America focused attacks against NSA for advancing an allegedly subversive agenda.

Stephen Schodde, in his 1965 doctoral thesis on NSA, provides a vignette on the emergence in 1952 of sharp attacks on NSA from the political right. The section closes with an overview of student activism during the Cold War and before the 1960's.

Misc Investigates Political Action Groups

CAMPUS POLITICAL GROUPS IN 1949 cooled down after a 1948 campaign that saw Truman defeat Dewey in a field that included Henry Wallace's Progressive Party and Strom Thurmond's Dixiecrats. As noted by Dick Murphy (p. 773), Young Democrats were not a strong year-round presence. This Vassar survey notes that "there has never been a Young Democrats Club at Vassar," and that the Young Republican Women's Club "flourished for a few exciting pre-election months before the election," after which "the excitement died." *(Vassar Miscellany News 4/6/49)*

World Peace, Domestic Liberties Engage Activist Students

Internationalists and Federalists

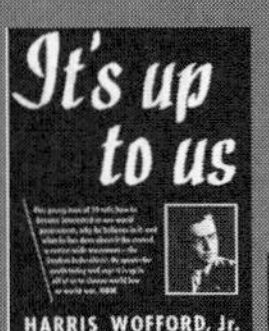
It's up to us
HARRIS WOFFORD, Jr.

1946

2,307 Students Sign UWF Petitions For World Gov't

1949

1948

Better Understanding

Emory IRC Studies History In The Making

By Reese Cleghorn

Emory has one department that studies history while it is being made, rather than after it has been made. The International Relations club has been doing this since 1922 and ...

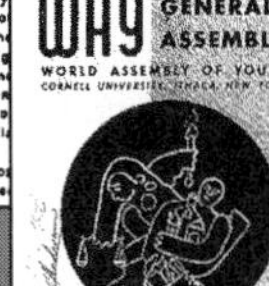
WAY
FIRST TRIENNIAL GENERAL ASSEMBLY
WORLD ASSEMBLY OF YOUTH
YOUTH AND HUMAN RIGHTS

Cosmopolitan Club Hears Chakravarty On India

One hundred and sixty-five students representing 23 countries attended the first meeting of the Cosmopolitan Club Saturday night when Dr Amiya Chakravarty spoke in the Great Hall of Levering. ... He put stress on India's friendly relations with the United States as well as her relations with the Soviet Union, stating that India was attempting to stay out of the squabble.

1951

1948

Harris Wofford, Jr.
Scarsdale H.S., NY
Student Federalist founder

Cord Meyer, Jr.
Yale U. '43
World government champion

Immanuel Wallerstein
Columbia U. '51
Chair, U.S. affiliate to WAY

STUDENT FEDERALISTS for 10 years led internationalist activism on college campuses. (Jonas, p. 761) Pre-war international relations and Cosmopolitan discussion clubs flourished. (From top left: Wofford's 1946 book on the need for Federalism; U. of Colo. *Silver and Gold* 7/1/49; *Emory Wheel* 3/25/48; Johns Hopkins *News-Letter* 10/29/48; 1951 World Assembly of Youth program cover)

Liberals and Democrats

Young Demos Favor Senate Ousting Bilbo

By Larry Small

LIBERALS! JOIN UP!

THE STUDENT Progressive
THE NATIONAL STUDENT ORGANIZATION

SDA Includes Wellesley USSA Representatives

Miriam Ernst Feder '47 and two other official delegates from the Wellesley USSA will go to Washington to attend the first national convention of the newly formed Students for Democratic Action to be held March 28-30. At this initial meeting, the group will set up a program and organization for independent lib...

WASHINGTON, D. C. FEBRUARY 16, 1949

[S]DA Begins Mid-West [O]rganizing Drive

Concentrated Campaign To Be Made In Nine ...

Students Form Campus SDA Group To Fight All Totalitarianism Forms

Alice Horton (Tibbetts)
Wellesley C. '45
USSA President, 1945

Walter "Fritz" Mondale
Macalaster C., MN '49
SDA Exec. Sec'y. 1949

Allard K. Lowenstein
U. of North Carolina '49
NSA President, 1950-51

LIBERAL LEADERSHIP provided by Students for Democratic Action after war-time U.S. Student Assembly (p. 34) became SDA in 1947. There was little presence of Young Democrats (Reisin, p. 781; Murphy, p. 785) (From top left: U.Colo *Silver and Gold*, 9/14/45; *Wellesley C. News*, 2/27/47, ad and cover from 9/47 Harvard Liberal *Union Progressive*; *ADA World* 2/16/49; L.A.CC *Collegian* 1/8/52)

Progressives and Communists

AYD FIGHTS JIM CROW

End Discrimination in the Armed Forces

AMERICAN YOUTH FOR DEMOCRACY

THE HARVARD CRIMSON

Academic Freedom—A Crimson Report

Michigan State College Expels Member of AYD

Zarichny First Put on Disciplinary Probation for Two Year Period

Ohio State U Disowns Wallaceites

Wayne University

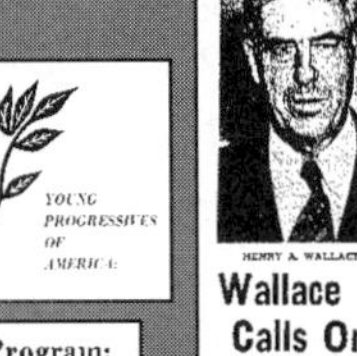
YOUNG PROGRESSIVES OF AMERICA

HENRY A. WALLACE

Wallace Calls On U.S. Faith

New foundations
A STUDENT QUARTERLY
UNITE FOR DEMOCRACY
SUMMER 1949 VOLUME TWO NUMBER FOUR

Young Progressives Outline Program; To Oppose Draft, School Quota Systems

"We will continue to fight the draft, and support Henry Wallace and the Progressive Party," declared Seymour Kestenbaum, a spokesman for the Young Progressives of America, in an interview ... sistence for student vets and other causes which will aid students and people as a whole, he continued. "The Young Progressives will continue to fight discrimination in schools and colleges, and the quota system in graduate schools ..."

Molly Lieber
Vice-Chairman, AYD
1946-47

Walter Wallace
Columbia U. '48
Sec'y, YPA Student Div. 1948

Robert W. Fogel
Cornell U. '48
Labor Youth League Leader, '50

FEAR OF U.S. COLD WAR INTENTIONS set Progressives apart from Liberals. Communist influences and collaboration (Reisin, p. 787) echoed the pre-war ASU experience (Lash, p. 42). High profile "red scare" loyalty controversies were seen to threaten student rights (Brown, p. 378). Top l. clockwise: AYD 1944 literature; *Harvard Crimson*, 5/27/49; Marxist *New Foundations*, Summer 1949; U. of Louisville *Cardinal*, 12/5/47; YPA 1948 Brochure; LIU *Seewanhaka*, 10/7/48

Conservatives and Republicans

God and Man at Yale
The Superstitions of "Academic Freedom"
by
William F. Buckley, Jr.
INTRODUCTION BY JOHN CHAMBERLAIN

Buckley To Head New College Club

William F. Buckley, author of the controversial *God and Man at Yale*, has become first president of a new "right wing" organization of college men and women, The Intercollegiate Society of Individualists. ...

Young GOP League Backs Dewey Slate; To Work With Local Group, NY Colleges

Speech Exemption

Young GOP Group Announces Essay Contest for First Voters

The Young Republican National Federation today announced an essay contest on the subject "A First Voter Looks at the Republican Party," with an all-expense trip to the GOP national convention or a $100 war bond as first prize. ...

Call To Republicans

REVOLT ON THE CAMPUS
by M. Stanton Evans

Congressional Record
PROCEEDINGS AND DEBATES OF THE 83d CONGRESS, FIRST SESSION

Students for America

Robert Munger
Pepperdine C., 51-52
Natl. Dir. Students for America

William F. Buckley, Jr.
Yale '50. Author,
God and Man at Yale, *1951*

M. Stanton Evans
Yale '55, 1954-55 conservative student movement leader

THE CONSERVATIVE STUDENT MOVEMENT emerged as an intellectual force in 1951 (ISI, p. 800, Evans p. 801). It also continued the organized attacks on NSA initiated by Students for America (p. 793). The party's "liberal" wing dominated YRC's on campus in the '40s. Top l. clockwise: *God and Man at Yale*, 1951; *Wellesley C. News*, 9/15/52; LIU *Seewanhaka*, 10/7/48; *Princeton Bulletin*, 3/13/44; *Vassar Miscellany News*, 10/16/46; *Cong. Record*, 2/23/53; *Revolt on Campus*, 1961

Note: See index for references to memoirs, recollections or career highlights of student leaders featured on this page. Credits for portrait photos appear with their use elsewhere in the Anthology.

One shining moment: The influence of Student Federalists on NSA, YAC, WAY, and IDPA

1. The Student Federalist Movement

Gilbert Jonas

1950-51 Stanford University NSA delegate

1952-53 Chair, WORLD; 1961 Peace Corps Acting Director, Far East

Editor's note: The ideal of world government was one of the many themes that animated campus political life and debate in the immediate postwar years. Prompted by our request for a memoir, Gil Jonas has written an exhaustive history of the Student Federalist movement, which has been published in book form. In this essay, we have prepared a digest of his work, which highlights the main events and issues that concerned the Federalist movement and the peripheral links to NSA through shared student leadership and joint engagement in some of the international student and youth events of the period. The complete work, One Shining Moment, *was published in 2000 by iUniverse. Pat Wohlgemuth Blair contributed extensively to preparing and editing this digest.*

The years immediately following World War II saw the rise of an American democratic student movement which remains unique in American history. Before the war, relatively few students went to college, and youth organizations were comparably few. After the war, students began to want to participate—indeed, to lead—in the shaping of their world. Of the many groups that started up in this period, two of the most successful were the Student Federalists and the U.S. National Student Association, the former embodying the idealism unleashed by the successful fight against fascism and the latter, the institution-building instincts of war veterans returning to college campuses.

The New Yorker's essayist and social critic E. B. White wrote in the years following World War II that foreign policy was the "top hat" of domestic policy. On a parallel plane, the Student Federalist movement for world government was the postwar "top hat" of the American democratic student movement, of which the U.S. National Student Association comprised the closest thing to a mass student movement in the nation.

As a postwar student activist who bridged both movements (and several others) during the period, I was presented with an interesting and singular perspective during the years which form the ideological cusp that introduced the decline of one movement and the irresistible growth of the other. The "cusp" years to which I refer are 1949 through 1951, but before coming to them I want to turn the clock back to late 1942—a year in which the United States and its dwindling allies had suffered massive military and territorial losses in Europe (especially in the Soviet Union) and the Pacific (where Japanese forces had conquered all of the European and American colonial territories east of India and north of Australia, after destroying most of the American fleet at Pearl Harbor).

The British Isles, under a stubborn Winston Churchill, were fighting off total collapse under the most destructive air assault theretofore known to human kind as the Luftwaffe pounded civilian and military targets indiscriminately. Only the dauntless Royal Air Force (RAF) stood between Britain and Nazi victory. The year 1942 was the grimmest of the war and quite possibly the grimmest of the century for America's prospects.

So it was, that on a wintry Saturday night early in that frightful year, in a demonstration of adolescent virtuosity, a sixteen-year-old Scarsdale, New York, boy was having his bath, reading his Latin lesson and listening to the radio. In a sudden luminous moment, his attention was captured by the speaker, Clarence Streit (or, as some maintain, Clare Booth Luce), who was expanding on his notion of an Atlantic union of democratic nations federated along lines similar to those which bound the American states—a notion he had introduced, to considerable applause, as far back as 1939. The boy's name was Harris Wofford, and in that very dark hour of American fortunes, he determined to organize his young peers across the land to support Streit's very grand and luminous concept.

The Student Federalist idea is born: 1942

The plan, however, gestated in Wofford's mind before he decided to bicycle thoroughout Scarsdale, persuading some of his close friends and fellow students at Scarsdale High to join him in what he would later envision as a crusade. In this way (or something similar, if not quite identical), the Student Federalist idea was born in the United States. Those of us who would later come under Wofford's charismatic spell for this and other causes know full well how hard it must have been for his peers to resist him. By April, he had persuaded six other Scarsdale High students to join him in forming the first chapter of the Student Federalists (SF). In September, the Scarsdale chapter members participated in the Shawnee Leadership Institute and signed up fifty new members from twenty schools. Over the next four months, new chapters were formed in New Rochelle and Roosevelt, NY, Chatham NJ, and Concord, MA. Students from throughout New York City formed a Metropolitan Council. Wofford then reached out to "affiliate" the Student Federalists with Streit's adult organization, Federal Union (FU), but since he didn't seek financial assistance (in fact, a portion of the students' dues went to support FU's national office), he preserved the students' independence in terms of both policy and program.

By the first half of 1943, word was reaching the hinterlands. The SF Council minutes note the receipt of a letter from Tom Hughes, of Minnesota, regarding his advocacy of the federalist idea at the National Forensic League. Hughes had organized the Mankato, MN, chapter, the first in the Midwest. This was quickly followed by the South St. Paul High School chapter, organized by Emmy Lou Lindgren, Hughes's frequent debating opponent. These three—Wofford, Hughes and Lindgren—were to dominate Student Federalist leadership until 1946, when Wofford and Lindgren (now known as Clare) were married and Hughes went off to Oxford as a Rhodes scholar.

In retrospect, it is not surprising that the idealism unleashed by World War II—that epic fight against evil—held sway over so many young and impressionable minds. It should be noted, however, that idealism in those days did not take much account of the real world that lay beyond the privileged suburbs. The initial wave of high school participants in SF was exclusively white, very Protestant, and upper-middle to upper class. These students had not yet discovered that the majority of the earth's people were not white, not Protestant, and mostly very poor. Nor were they much troubled by the fact that almost two-thirds of the human race lived under some form of despotism and could not have given a fig for the imperatives of democracy. Perhaps that is why they found such philosophical comfort in Clarence Streit's notion of an Atlantic democratic federation encompassing Britain, Canada, France, and the Benelux countries—hardly the critical mass of humanity. Even our other vitally important allies, the Soviet Union and China, were matters of indifference to them.

During the summer of 1943, the SF Council launched its first fund-raising campaign, with a goal of $500. The Council provided each chapter with a fund-raising kit, while announcing that the following year the Council expected to organize a model "World Constitutional Convention to dramatize the problems of world government." The campaign flyer listed two other objectives: garnering 5,000 signatures on a student petition "to the voting people of our country," and printing—as opposed to mimeographing—the organization's newsletter. The first issue of the newsletter had come out in April 1943, with a circulation of 500; by September, circulation had jumped to 2,000.

The petition is a most compelling document when one remembers it was drafted and adopted essentially by high school students. It calls for "complete victory by the forces of freedom" because "man cannot exist half slave, half free." It describes the then current state of affairs between nations as "anarchy," making it inevitable that "ever-recurring disputes will always lead to war." To remedy this anarchic state, the world requires "international government," specifically "Democratic World Government, securing decency and freedom for all peoples." To avoid a global despotism, the government's form must be federal. "The federal form is the only form which holds power democratically, the only form which can unite the differences in race, language and nationality that exist in the world." Thus, as early as 1943, the high school students comprising the nascent organization had developed the verbal formula that would become their objective—a universal world federal government open to every country. During late 1943 and 1944, this student petition was widely circulated, in part as the SF's first effort to influence the national election of November 1944.

Part of the campaign's proceeds were used to cover the cost of sending two SF delegates to the Federal Union convention in Peoria, IL, in November. To everyone's surprise, thirty SF delegates ended up attending the Peoria convention, during which the Student Federalists formed their own national organization and affiliated with the Federal Union. The founding delegates elected Wofford as their first president, and Hughes as vice president.

Meanwhile, the SF was growing apace. A SF campaign bulletin in August acknowledged a new chapter in Sarasota, Florida. By year-end, at the SF board meeting in Scarsdale in December, it was announced that there were twenty-five chapters in eight states. Eleven of the fifteen board members were present at this meeting, including representatives from Yale, University of North Carolina, and Queens College. Board members emerged from the four-day (and night) meeting with the basic outline of the Student Federalist apparatus for the remainder of its independent existence. They established a structure, regional divisions and a headquarters operation for the Student Federalists, which was about to go national.

As will be demonstrated, reliance on and belief in education were the bedrock of the Student Federalist organizational strategy. The plan to hold world constitutional conventions was one example. A second was the bibliography of Federalist literature approved by the board in December 1943, the first of a long and ever-growing list of books, articles, speeches, papers periodicals, reprints, and films on the subject. Yet another was the essay contests proposed by the Board for high school students on a variety of related Federalist subjects, with monetary prizes. Another key educational tool, the newsletter, had grown exponentially, reaching 5,000 by the winter of 1944. Each of Federal Union's 45,000 members also received a copy. Major publicity appeared in *Newsweek*, *PM*, and the *New York Herald Tribune*.

The most difficult aspect of the new organization's first major board meeting was grappling with finances. High school students in 1943, even relatively affluent ones, had very little access to cash. Although the finance committee determined that a sum of $5,000 was required to accomplish all of the SF's 1944 objectives, it drew up a more realistic budget of $3,000 to $3,500 to cover the costs of the first national convention, as well as part of the delegates' expenses; speaking expenses, including Wofford's national tour; literature; a poll; mailings; the petition; contest promotion; and secretarial help.

The first Student Federalist Convention: 1944

SF's first national convention met at Columbia University, in New York City, during Easter break (March 31–April 2, 1944). In all, there were 102 delegates from 75 chapters in sixteen out of the then forty-eight states. Tom Hughes, Wofford's choice to succeed him as president, presided over the three open business sessions of the delegates and over the "world constitutional convention." Wofford, about to become an Air Force cadet, and Clarence Streit, together with Representative Howard McMurray, provided the inspirational speeches. The convention decided to move SF headquarters to Washington, DC, sharing a new office with the Federal Union. In addition to the Scarsdale and Sarasota offices, it also voted to establish ten new regional offices, each manned by an activist leader, usually a board member.

More than half the delegates pledged to devote the entire summer vacation to advocacy work for the Student Federalists. An eminent journalist, Emmet Crozier of the *New York Herald Tribune*, wrote in June: "It is doubtful whether any other teen-age generation has ever thought so deeply or argued so vehemently about world affairs as the high-school youngsters represented in the Student Federalist movement." That passion and commitment was to remain for the rest of the decade, as thousands of new recruits joined the young movement. According to an organizing folder issued the following year, at the close of 1944 the Student Federalists could boast of one hundred chapters and "several thousand members," an achievement of considerable weight for a group of teenagers and a budget of a few thousand dollars. In a new development, the Student Federalists had begun to capture the imagination of college students as well.

The second SF convention was held in Chicago from September 28 to October 1, 1944. It followed the Dumbarton Oaks meeting (in Washington, DC), which prepared the structure and power arrangements of the forthcoming United Nations Organization. The global scope of the United Nations produced a permanent change in most of the Student Federalists, causing them to abandon the idea of partial federations and groupings and to emphasize the need for a government that encompassed every nation. The SF delegates realized that the strategy of relying on an Atlantic federation of democracies was no longer viable or relevant. Accordingly, as their November newsletter noted, they voted to "shift the emphasis of the organization from the immediate uninclusive federation of democracies to an eventual Federal World Democracy."

The concept of world federalism received a major boost when the November 14 issue of *Look* magazine supported the evolution of the United Nations into a world federation that would control the peaceful decentralization of Germany. Actress Ingrid Bergman was recruited as a federalist by the South St. Paul chapter. On the other hand, the autumn also brought the first congressional investigation of the Student Federalists, when Rhode Island's Senator Green presided over an inquiry into campaign spending and sought to determine whether the SF was supporting any candidate in the November elections.

The year 1945 opened auspiciously, with Supreme Court Justice Owen Roberts addressing an SF rally in Washington and scores of veterans publicly declaring their support for the objective. The SF leadership urged members who were veterans to join the American Veterans Committee and begin forming alliances with returning veterans and their groups. Meanwhile, in April, the organizing conference of the United Nations had begun in San Francisco. Several Federalists attended the historic meetings, including Wofford, Hughes, and SF Veterans Committee chairman Cord Meyer, Jr., the latter as an aide to Minnesota Governor Harold Stassen.

As the European conflict ended in May with the surrender of the Nazis, the SF issued its call for a third national convention in Washington, DC, in August. Wofford, by then on active duty, persuaded the delegates by mail and proxies to adopt as its objective a world federation and to discard the Atlantic Union concept.

The historic Concord Charter for world community

Much of the second half of 1945 was invested in planning the single most important meeting in the history of the Student Federalists—the four-day conference held in Concord, MA, to revisit and review the basic Federalist positions and to align them with the new postwar realities. Invited were representatives of both Student Federalist chapters and like-minded student organizations interested in world law and order. Eighty-five delegates from thirty-five colleges and twenty-five high schools participated in this gathering, which met from February 8 to 11, 1946. The most important result was the unanimous agreement on the ultimate objective: the formation of a world federal government—the universalist position—either by amending the UN charter or by other means. The Concord Charter called for the destruction of irresponsible nationalism while preserving national identity by transforming the UN into a "new world sovereignty." The charter recognized "frankly that the United States and the Soviet Union are the two chief obstacles to such action" and to overcome these obstacles, "we must make world citizenship a political fact." The delegates also "strongly urge[d] the unification of all adult federalist groups in a common movement for federal world government with a minimum of doctrinal conflict."

Two leading war veterans spoke movingly to the attending delegates—Cord Meyer, Jr., who had recently published an article in *Atlantic Monthly* entitled, "A Serviceman Looks to the Peace,"[1] and his successor as SF Veterans Committee Chairman, Steve Chadwick, who described in vivid detail his front-line experiences against the Nazis. As convener and temporary chairman, Wofford opened the gathering by drawing analogies between the Minutemen of Concord in 1775 and those attending the 1946 Concord meeting. He began with ringing words:

> We are here to proclaim a world people's sovereignty. We assert our citizenship in the world. . . . We are here to plan our part in the long, hard fight to achieve the birth of a democratic world civilization, protected and promoted by a federal world government . . . and to unite in a common student movement for world federation with an effective program to carry to our generation and to the people of the world.

That spring, a group of American leaders from science, business, religion, labor and government met at Rollins College, FL, from March 11 to 16 to discuss world government and control of atomic energy. The conference issued a ringing statement, declaring that the discovery of atomic fission had placed the survival of the world in grave jeopardy and that the only rational way out was to transform the United Nations into a world federal government, with a representative legislature and the power to control weapons of mass destruction. The world federalist idea was no longer the possession of a group of zealous, but innocent, teenagers venting their understandable idealism. At Rollins, some of the country's most important movers and shakers were calling for the most radical political transformation in modern times. The fallout could only help to boost the stock of the Student Federalists.

The June SF board meeting authorized both a $100,000 expansion budget, over five years, and the transfer of SF's New York headquarters to a "whole floor in a new World Government House" at 31 East 74th St., in Manhattan. The international dimension of SF took a major step forward when two delegates—Richard Shapiro, of Yale, and Foster Parmalee, of Princeton—were selected to attend the International Conference of Christians and Jews in Oxford, England, that summer. Of even greater significance for the future, two SF delegates—Curt Farrar of Yale and Eleanor Schneider of Mount Holyoke—were selected to attend the World Student Congress in Prague in mid-August, a meeting that would have long-term significance for both USNSA and SF.

During the rest of 1946, the Student Federalist leadership launched initiatives that resulted in a merger of the various adult and student world government groups, and the Concord Charter was amended. The final text, which became the "Student Federalist Charter," inserted in the opening sentence the concept of "world community" as a prerequisite for world citizenship. Support for the United Nations and its gradual transformation was affirmed. "To make world citizenship a political fact," the students maintained, "we must work to create a world government dedicated to human rights and justice under law." They called for "new world sovereignty based on the principles of federalism" which would "effectually attack the economic and social problems whose solution is essential to the creation of a world community." The addition of this clause was to have preeminent meaning for student federalists in the remaining years of its existence. It reflected a left-of-center influence by those who supported either democratic socialism or the general New Deal–Fair Deal approach to government. More important, it illuminated the vision of the preponderance of the students on two levels. First, it underlined their long-term commitment to eradicating colonialism, racism, the great disparities in wealth between the haves and have-nots, and the arms race, which sucked up so much of America's "surplus" wealth and kept it from ameliorating poverty and ignorance at home and abroad. Second, it suggested ways to approach the more immediate issues and controversies facing American foreign (and occasionally domestic) policy.

As the students were to learn, the movement's adults

found neither approach attractive or necessary. In a major sense, this division shaped the vision each held for the ultimate federal government and the powers it would have.

Moving Federalism from the campus to the political arena: 1946

The 1946 SF convention, held in Chicago, was the largest up to that time, with 160 delegates from ninety-two different colleges and secondary schools. Between the working business of the convention and attending lectures and seminars, the delegates were putting in eighteen-hour days. To save time in vote-counting, a *Life* reporter suggested the use of finger counting, wherein a person in each delegation raised the appropriate number of fingers for each vote, rather than having each delegate recorded individually. This process was reported to have injected a needed degree of humor into the otherwise serious proceedings.

The Chicago delegates received a report on the Prague meeting of the World Student Congress, which had established the International Union of Students (IUS) and voted to collaborate with the World Federation of Democratic Youth (WFDY). Curt Farrar had been instrumental in securing passage, with Soviet support, of a "Recommendation: that the students support the United Nations" and take steps to strengthen it by working for "the establishment of a democratic world system of government . . . preserv[ing] the identity of member nations while introducing the concepts of world law and world citizenship." The resolution had passed by 90 to 35, with 4 abstentions. Farrar's report on the Congress, published in the October SF newsletter, is a glaring example of wishful thinking which would make the most zealous of today's idealists cringe. However, it was written fifty-two years ago, when we had a great deal to learn both as a nation and as Federalists, and it illustrates how the Soviets exploited the idealism of American and other students, while moving covertly, as it later turned out, to control the IUS and WFDY on behalf of Kremlin interests.

Colgate "Coke" Prentice was elected SF President at the Chicago convention. A Swarthmore junior and Air Force combat veteran, he embarked on a 5,000 mile, three-month national speaking tour, appearing before an estimated 24,000 students in a dozen colleges and 16 secondary schools. Between these engagements were scores of newspaper and radio interviews, in what was probably the warmest media reception for a student federalist leader to date.

Sensing the rise in public awareness, the SF Board adopted, at its November 17–18 meeting, a resolution to make world government a political issue. This resolution effectively moved the SF units out of the isolation of the academy and squarely into the rough-and-tumble world of politics. The new stance enabled the SF and its chapters to seek to persuade state legislatures to support the "Humber resolution" calling for world federation, which fourteen states had already adopted. In addition, it allowed units to work to place world government resolutions on state ballots, to write world federation planks into each party's 1948 platform, and to support federalists for political office.

Of longer-term significance was another board resolution for the SF to act on behalf of "non-controversial, non-political, international projects furthering the world community (i.e., UNESCO, U.N. Social and Economic Council)." In a few years, student federalists would be devising imaginative implementations of this decision. The board took one other action which readers of this book will find relevant: it chose Curt Farrar as one of two representatives (Eleanor Schneider was later named the other) to be its delegates at the founding meeting of the National Student Organization in Chicago, December 27–29.[2]

Students, four adult groups, merge in 1947 to form the United World Federalists

On the weekend of Washington's Birthday, 1947, in Asheville, NC, a merger was effected of the five most important world government groups in the US: Americans United for World Government; Massachusetts Committee for World Federation; World Citizens of Georgia; World Federalists, U.S.A. (the largest delegation); and the Student Federalists (the second largest). The first organizing folder of the new entity—named the United World Federalists (UWF)—claimed that, as a result of the merger, the new organization consisted of more than 200 chapters (quite probable, considering that SF alone had 111). It also claimed that "active adherents . . . topped the hundred thousand mark" (a substantial exaggeration if "adherents" meant "members").

As many as 500 delegates and member/observers from thirty-three states attended the Asheville meeting. The policy statement they adopted, which had been worked out in advance, emphasized the minimalist position:

- Statement of beliefs: We believe that peace is not merely the absence of war, but the presence of justice, of law, of order—in short, of government and the institutions of government; that world peace can be created and maintained only under world law, universal and strong enough to prevent armed conflict among nations.
- Statement of purposes: Therefore, while endorsing the efforts of the United Nations to bring about a world community favorable to peace, we will work primarily to strengthen the United Nations into a world government of limited powers adequate to prevent war and

having direct jurisdiction over the individual in those matter within its competence.

Most of the eighty to ninety Student Federalists at the Asheville meeting, of whom twenty-nine were voting delegates, advocated a world government with powers broader than that proposed by the minimalists. But they felt compelled to swallow this position in the interests of unity. They were heartened by the inclusion of the phrase "peace is not merely the absence of war, but the presence of justice," which had come to mean, in Federalist code, economic and social advancement, human rights, and the eradication of colonialism and racism.

The membership of the Student Federalists, as well as student chapters of other merging groups, became the Student Division of the United World Federalists, whose governing body was designated the National Student Council (NSC). For the time being, a wide degree of autonomy was permitted the Student Division and its local chapters. However, the burden of financing its activities fell largely on the students themselves. Chapter organizing continued apace. In March, the Student Division announced the formation of 28 chapters, the highest single-month total, raising the overall number to 143 units. Among the major colleges affiliating were chapters from Princeton, Duke, Iowa State, Texas Christian, Texas Tech, DePauw, and the Universities of Connecticut, Michigan, and Virginia, as well as new chapters at thirteen secondary schools.

Student chapters were alerted to the fact that delegates to the first meeting of the new National Student Organization (USNSA), scheduled for Madison, WI, in early September, were being elected on campuses throughout the country. Federalists were encouraged to get themselves elected and to participate in the drafting of the NSA constitution. Meanwhile, Federalists were also being urged to take part in the World Youth Festival, scheduled for Prague from July 20 to August 17, 1947, to help provide a democratic (even Federalist) balance to the event. They were also invited by the European Union of Federalists to discuss Federalist ideas and ideals at the first of several planned international centers scheduled to open that summer at Heyst sur Mer, near Bruges, Belgium.

In June, both the Executive Council of UWF and the National Student Council held meetings. The Executive Council hired both a paid Executive Director and a paid president. The latter was Cord Meyer, Jr., a former combat marine in the Pacific and a graduate of Yale, who had also served at the Student Federalist veterans' chairman for several years. An articular speaker and seasoned writer, Meyer served as Governor Stassen's aide at the founding United Nations Conference in San Francisco and played a major role in the affairs of the American Veterans' Committee. Upshur Evans, an oil company executive who had served as a "combat intelligence officer" in Southeast Asia during World War II (most probably with the OSS), was named executive director.

The Student Council launched a nationwide membership drive. CCNY chapter president Abe Bargman was commissioned to write a report for Cord Meyer on student political action. The growth of the summer institutes had been so rapid that the Council recommended the hiring of a full-time education secretary (Eleanor Schneider), who would also organize the institutes. A Mount Holyoke graduate with an MA in international affairs, the Vienna-born Schneider and her family had fled from Austria after the Nazi Anschluss in 1938. Schneider and newly elected Student Division chairman Colgate Prentice were appointed to represent the Council at the USNSA constitutional meeting in Madison.

The crest of the federalist wave: 1947–48

Although policy conflicts between the student and adult sections of UWF continued, the Student Federalists ended 1947 with their greatest growth, outreach, and presence, both nationally and internationally. Some 150 local chapters dotted the American landscape. There were so many secondary-school chapters that the Student Council felt compelled to authorize formation of a Secondary School National Council under its jurisdiction. At the 1947 St. Louis convention, eight students were elected to the UWF Executive Council and, for the first time, none of the original founders were chosen. Among the new generation of leaders were Shane Riorden of Harvard, Larry Fuchs of New York University, and Fritjof Thygeson, about to enter Stanford, who had, in September, embarked on a four-month speaking tour of secondary schools across the United States.

In February 1948, the Student Federalist newsletter published, for the first time, an up-to-date list of active student chapters. The list totaled 149 units in thirty-one states and the District of Columbia. Seventy-seven were college and university chapters. Sixty-eight were secondary school units, of which 36 were in private prep schools and 32 in public high schools. Four were mixed. New York State, with 27, had the most chapters. Massachusetts was second, with 16. By April, the chapter total reached 201.

Meanwhile—even as the Cold War deepened—the world government issue had become so thoroughly imbued in the culture that the 1948 Scholastic Aptitude Test (SAT) exam carried a question about it. In Cleveland, more than 200,000 citizens signed petitions pledging to bring about world government; the petition drive was sponsored by the three local newspapers, the governor and his predecessor, the mayor, the local police force and trade unions, as well as leaders of the three major religious denominations. Close to 7,000 residents of Philadelphia's Main Line, a community of influence and wealth, signed a similar petition, specifically endorsing the Federalist resolutions then before both houses of Congress. Harold E. Stassen, by then a Republican presidential candidate, urged his party to support a UN Charter revision conference along with steps to strengthen Western economies and armed forces and to combat Soviet propaganda.

The year-old Americans for Democratic Action, the new anticommunist haven for the country's liberals, voted in convention to endorse world federal government, but only after passage of the Marshall Plan by Congress. Former Vice President Henry Wallace also supported the creation of a world government, without any provision for a legislature, but only after the West made fundamental compromises with the Soviets. In March, a Princeton Federalist delegation, including four students, visited President Truman with a petition calling for the immediate establishment of world government, with or without the Soviet Union. Although Truman rejected this proposal, stating that it would exacerbate the East-West power struggle, he did endorse a strengthened United Nations, blaming the Soviets for obstructing such a move.

By the end of 1948, a broad-based coalition of national organizations had endorsed world federal government. They included the American Veteran's Committee, American Education Fellowship, Americans for Democratic Action, Association of American Colleges, Committee on Public Affairs, Council for Democracy, Catholic Association for International Peace, Emergency Committee of Atomic Scientists, Evangelical Church of the Brethren, Friends of Democracy, Fellowship of Reconciliation National Council, Methodist Church Commission on World Peace, Moravian Church (Southern Province), National Association for the Advancement of Colored People (NAACP), National Education Association, Protestant Episcopal Church, Religious Society of Friends Peace Board, Southern Baptists, Synagogue Council of America, U.S. Junior Chamber of Commerce, and World Citizenship Movement. Granted that most of these organizations were liberal to begin with; nevertheless, they represented a sizable grass-roots following.

If there were any doubts about the intensive field work by the fifteen volunteer organizers, coupled with the extensive programs conducted under Abe Bargman's direction, those doubts vanished at the second Student Division convention, held November 12–14, 1948, in Minneapolis. Field Director Natalie Rogers reported that between January 1 and November 12, membership had risen from about 5,500 to 9,500, while the number of chapters increased from 149 to 272 in forty states and the District of Columbia.

At this date, the Student Federalists were probably the largest secular student organization in the country. It may be argued that the new National Student Association represented far more students, but only if the entire student body on any given campus were counted as "members." In reality, the number of truly active individuals working on behalf of USNSA was often only four or five, smaller than the chapter membership of the campus Federalist group, which often comprised many, if not most, of the student activists in Federalist and compatible organizations. Among the collaborating student and youth groups during this period were the Student League for Industrial Democracy (SLID), the Youth Division of the NAACP, the United Student Christian Council, Students for Democratic Action (SDA), Collegiate Council for the United Nations (CCUN), YMCA, YWCA, B'nai B'rith Youth Organization, World Republic, and USNSA.

The delegates to the Minneapolis convention elected Duke University junior (and navy veteran) Ralph Fleming Jr. as their new chairman. NYU's Murray Frank was elected vice chairman. Along with several long-time leaders, a new crop of Federalists was elected to the National Student Council, of whom the most important for the future of the organization was Immanuel Wallerstein, an emerging leader from Columbia University. William Holbrook, of Minnesota, who was active in the NSA Minnesota region and was later to be one of NSA's three observers to the 1950 World Student Congress, was also elected, as was the future U.S. Ambassador to the Soviet Union, Jack Matlock, of Duke.

The convention delegates voted to increase ties to other student federalist groups, including increased financial support for the international body, the World Student Federalists. They agreed to hold a mock UN Charter-revision convention among students and to study its results as a guide to future conferences. Individual chapters were urged to stage their own mock charter revisions to enact and enforce world law. The most original idea was a proposal to invite representatives of other youth and student groups to join with the Student Division in organizing world government caravans. The delegates did, however, accept the decision of the adult-dominated UWF that chapters should refrain from endorsing or opposing political candidates, even though they did endorse greater political action. On the subject of the draft, which President Truman had recommended renewing, the students were divided between support for and opposition to both conscription and universal military training.

Notwithstanding all the sanguine signs, a decline in student membership began in the first month of 1949, no doubt propelled in part by Cold War disenchantment with international cooperation of any sort. By the end of January, membership dropped from a peak of 9,500 in November 1948 to 7,600 and 221 chapters. By January 1950, the Student Division had lost 109 chapters, and student rumblings were emerging in chapters throughout the country. The decline in membership produced a concomitant decline in income, relegating the students to the position of "poor relative" vis-à-vis the UWF. In the summer, Cord Meyer resigned the presidency of UWF (to undertake graduate studies at Harvard before joining the CIA, where he played a significant role in providing support to a sizable array of private organizations within the democratic spectrum, both at home and abroad including YAC, WAY and the international programs of USNSA).[3] He was replaced by another veteran and writer, Alan Cranston of Los Altos, CA, who was later to chair the state's Democratic Party and then to serve four terms as U.S. senator for California.

Student Federalists join the struggle against racism while caught in the red scare cross-fire: 1949

In a money-saving effort, it was arranged for the Student Division to hold its 1949 assembly concurrently with the UWF convention in Cleveland, October 28-30. This move did not sit well with the students, whose executive committee met to urge planning for a separate convention the following year. The students at both meetings dealt with three recommendations to improve relations between student chapters and the adult chapters at the state level. They also adopted plans to make the student council more representative of, and receptive to, chapters in the field.

Despite the decline in membership and income from dues, special fund-raising drives among the various leaders and their friends bore significant results. In addition to salaries for the students' key headquarters positions—National Chairman Murray Frank, Student Director Natalie Rogers, and student, chapter and student-projects directors—the Student Division was able to add two other paid positions.

When the student Executive Committee met in early December 1949, its leaders determined to face up to the question of racial discrimination. Student allies, especially USNSA and SDA, and, of course, the NAACP, were dealing with the race issue head-on. Religious youth and student organizations, including the YM- and YWCA, were facing the same issue. The Student Federalists, who were already involved in starting a global anti-Communist democratic youth movement, felt there was no place for racial discrimination in their home base.

At the Cleveland assembly earlier in the year, the students had passed a resolution calling for revocation of the charter of any chapter found by the National Student Council to be barring membership to any person because of color, creed or nationality and urging the UWF to follow the same policy among adult branches. When the student Executive Committee tried to follow up on this resolution, the UWF Executive Board deflected their recommendation, suggesting that all acts of discrimination be presented to the National Executive Council, which would "take the necessary steps to correct the situation."

Clearly troubled by the refusal of the adults to act, Murray Frank drew up a four-page paper outlining the UWF bylaws that barred discrimination and the political, social and moral wisdom of expelling discriminatory chapters and state councils. He pointed out the incompatibility of seeking Third World support for world government while at the same time tolerating racial discrimination within the organization.

Apparently, the UWF adult leaders never resolved this issue, believing the most pragmatic way to gain American support for world government was to not enforce their own bylaws. Most of the students came to an entirely different conclusion. They felt the issue could not be sidestepped without harming the moral strength, and ultimately the political validity, of the world government cause. Another major bone of contention had been raised between UWF and the students.

The argument was not theoretical, as our experiences in California showed. At Stanford, which had never before admitted a Negro undergraduate student, Federalist and USNSA leaders started the university's first NAACP student chapter in late 1949, with the avowed goal of compelling the university to admit its first Negro student. After a visit from Roy Wilkins, then administrative assistant to Walter White, we demanded that the university remove the photograph from the admissions application. It complied, much more swiftly that we could have imagined. By the spring of 1950, Stanford announced that the first black undergraduate had been admitted for the fall of 1950. He was a Compton College transfer, reputedly straight A, and a four-letter athlete named Ed Tucker. After that, the racial bar disappeared rapidly.

The major programmatic focus for the students in 1950 was the organization of a publicity-generating world government caravan. On June 15, six Federalists joined the Western Caravan at the War Memorial Opera House in San Francisco and departed in three autos after a press conference. In a sign of the growing hysteria produced by Cold War anticommunism, the caravaneers experienced being taken into custody by state police and local cops along the way. A second leg of the caravan, beginning in New York City, made stops in Iowa and Illinois before joining the others in St. Louis for the National Student Council meeting, a lengthy parade through the city, and numerous radio appearances. Then the caravan, now six cars long with twenty-seven riders, left St. Louis for Washington, arriving on June 29 to be greeted by UWF president Alan Cranston at International House. The next day, they presented the petitions gathered along the transcontinental route to the Secretary of the Senate before the press and a stellar array of senators and representatives, as well as spokespersons from veterans and farmers groups. Almost forty Student Federalists had participated at various stages of the trek.

At the St. Louis meeting, Council members were apprised of a continuing decline in membership—by June it had dropped to 4,665, with 221 chapters of uneven strength and effectiveness, despite efforts to fashion close relationships with like-minded student groups. Bill Friedlander, California student chairman, reported that right-wing opposition had reached such a pitch that Federalist chapters were being asked to leave campuses and had contributed to the state legislature's rescission of a world government resolution. The Council also held a lengthy discussion about the organization of the Young Adult Council (YAC), a division of the National Social Welfare Assembly, in which Chairman Frank and several of his Council colleagues were playing important roles. YAC was to be the American member of the World Assembly of Youth (WAY), a new alternative to the Communist-dominated WFDY. Organizing meetings of WAY had been taking place in Britain and Europe since late 1949, with American representation by YAC's parent organization. The remainder of the meeting was devoted to further discussions of the relationship between the students and UWF, the shortcomings and requirements of the current structure and programs, and the strategies for impacting on the UWF convention scheduled for October in Washington, DC. The Student Council concluded just as the Korean "Police Action" had begun.

At home, it seemed nothing would stem the growing hysteria produced by Cold War anticommunism. Before Senator Joe McCarthy launched his own witch hunt, the ground had been well prepared by a group of opportunistic political figures and self-appointed watchdogs. One of the earliest of these was California's State Senator Jack Tenney, who led a state legislative assault on alleged Communist infiltration into the unions in the state, including those in the movie business. When these efforts were eclipsed by those of the House Un-American Activities Committee, he shifted his attack to other targets, including the world government movement. As a result, the California Student Federalists, of whom I was one, met with virulent opposition in town after town, including the cancellation of auditoriums for speeches and meetings. It was just such pressure that impelled the principal of Palo Alto High School to force the local Federalist chapter to remove itself from the school.

Student Federalist units in California, especially at Berkeley and Stanford, chose to fight back. We protested the Palo Alto decision. On a few occasions, we were threatened with violence in smaller towns after showing up to conduct meetings at public halls which had withdrawn permission at the last minute. We undertook the research necessary to connect the attacks to Far Right demagogues, and gave the material to a young Los Angeles newscaster by the name of Chet Huntley, himself affiliated with the California UWF. Drawing from the Student Federalists' research, Huntley attacked these critics of world government with some well-chosen editorial comments on the local NBC television station. When Huntley and the students were sued for libel, the NBC station handled the suit. Needless to say, the court upheld Huntley.

I advocate for NSA and political debate on campus—And the veteran students tip the scales

Meanwhile, the University of California at Berkeley, under pressure from an increasingly conservative legislature, imposed a loyalty oath on the faculty. In May 1950, I decided to run for off-campus representative to the Stanford Student Council. Since most of the off-campus students were World War II veterans, I fashioned a "shocking" four-plank platform calculated to totally disrupt Stanford's "pre-natal equilibrium." The first plank called for restitution of Stanford's membership in USNSA. The second urged the Stanford student body to declare support for the University of California professors who had been dismissed for refusing to sign the newly imposed loyalty oath. Third, I asked the Stanford students to send a delegate to represent them at the Rome Congress for World Government. Finally, I called for permission to debate political issues on campus.

The majority of students deeply resented my intrusion of "outside" issues on the isolated campus. Since I had no real expectation of winning, I was not dismayed by the overwhelming consensus that I would come in dead last. My main goal was to use the election as an education process. However, a number of unexpected developments arose, the most important of which being the resonance of the message with the returned veterans. They were largely very serious about their education and the reasons why they had risked their lives a few years earlier. The more I was vilified, the more they declared for our campaign. Even then, in a four-way race, I won on the third ballot with third-place votes by a slim margin.

As a member of the Stanford student government, I took the lead in getting campus Federalists, and then the entire student body, to condemn the oath and support those professors who refused to sign. It was becoming clear to Student Federalists across the nation (and to student activists in general) that the protection of civil liberties at home was a sine qua non of any sane debate over the merits of the world federalist cause. To the alliance with the NAACP, we were adding a collaboration with the American Civil Liberties Union and other liberal and internationalist movements.

Challenging the status quo: the Wallerstein memorandum

Into this simmering organizational stew a pungent element had been introduced by Immanuel Wallerstein, the students' most intellectually gifted leader, who was himself a member of the UWF National Executive Council. Since the latter part of 1949, Wallerstein had been engaged in correspondence with UWF and student leaders over the future ideological direction of the organization. A Columbia University student and later graduate student in sociology who specialized in African studies, the multilingual Wallerstein had formulated pointedly what so many of the students had sensed, even felt. Wallerstein's premise was that the majority of the world's peoples, then under colonial rule, were determined to achieve not only political independence but also to determine their own economic future and cultural rebirth. To oppose this movement "is unwise, unjust, and dangerous," Wallerstein said, "and any national policy which does not foster this revolution for freedom is doomed to failure."

Over the next year, Wallerstein urged acceptance by the UWF students of the following statement:

> that the significance of the world revolution for freedom must be brought to the attention of the American youth community; and
>
> that we must place into perspective the power struggle between the United States and the Soviet Union; and
>
> that we must support the just struggle of two-thirds of the people of the world to achieve freedom; and
>
> that we must depose from any leadership in this movement for freedom the Communists whose methods would destroy freedom; and
>
> that we must preserve and expand freedom at home, combatting tendencies to limit traditional liberties in times of crisis; and
>
> that we must support the United Nations and its specialized agencies and to seek the development of the UN into a world federal government.

Attached to a later version of this credo was a four-point action program, in which the UWF and the student federalists would work for

> an expanded, multilateral program of technical assistance and world development; the elimination of racial and religious discrimination throughout the world; negotiating of differences between nations through the UN, combining compromise with devotion to fundamental principles, while recognizing the limitations of negotiations in a lawless world; and a wider understanding of the need for a world federal government.

Matters came to a head at the October 12–15, 1950, UWF convention in Washington, DC, during which the students held a parallel convention while attending UWF's plenary sessions. A total of 530 delegates attended, including 68 student delegates. Not only did the adults summarily dismiss the Wallerstein memorandum; they went several steps beyond that ideological rejection by virtually wiping out the student division in all but name.

Over 150 students attended the four-day convention in the segregated nation's capital. This was the first time most of them had experienced America's system of Jim Crow first-hand, and the experience impacted heavily on most of them. Refusing to succumb to institutionalized segregation, the students held their convention at the interracial Inspiration House, where they also slept and took most of their meals.

The influence of the Wallerstein memorandum was felt in a number of postconvention actions relating to the Third World that were taken by the Student Federalists. Among other things, they prepared a package on the struggles of colonial peoples which was mailed to sixty-five student and youth organizations; they decided to hold a leadership training institute to help build a core of Federalists with more profound knowledge of Federalist principles and how major world issues related to them; they agreed to organize seminars throughout the country to expose student and youth leaders from other organizations to the Federalist concept and its relationship to the burgeoning world revolution; they approved a resolution to spur the interchange of ideas between U.S. Federalist units and Federalist units abroad; and they approved a project by Cooperative for American Relief to Everywhere (CARE) to raise funds for books to be distributed in the Third World by the UN Educational, Scientific, and Cultural Organization (UNESCO). (USNSA leader Rob West served as college director for CARE on the book project; he addressed a number of UWF chapters to gain support.) Another dimension of the Wallerstein memo was the decision by the board to name Abe Bargman, Curt Farrar, and James Roberts (World Student Federalist Chairman) as delegates from the UWF Student Division to the World Congress for World Government in Rome in April 1951.

In a close vote, the students elected another Navy veteran —twenty-five-year-old Thomas "Duke" Robertson, a moderate from the University of Colorado—as student chairman over Immanuel Wallerstein.

Dealing with adversity—The student membership continues to plunge in 1951

Despite all this activity among the Student Federalist leaders and despite intensive efforts to promote membership, the organization itself was clearly fading. In January 1951, UWF's year-end figures showed that paid student membership had declined to 4,377, roughly half the total at the end of 1948. With the Korean conflict heating up, by April 16, membership had plummeted to 1,758. The student proportion of UWF's membership had gone from about 20 percent in 1947 to less than 11 percent.[4] After transmitting the sum pledged to the World Student Federalists, the Student Volunteer Fund was left with only $535. Within a month, UWF management notified the student staff that all but one employee would have to be dismissed by June 30. In less than three years after merging with the four adult organizations and losing its independence as a student organization, the single most successful component within the American world government movement had risen, peaked and rapidly declined.

On February 23, in a letter to UWF Board Chairman C. M. Stanley, Immanuel Wallerstein resigned from the National Executive Council. With carbon copies to Alan Cranston and Duke Robertson, Wallerstein wrote that he was resigning because of his conviction that UWF, as then constituted, was not doing "any effective work to achieve its goals." Wallerstein's letter, which was shared with many student leaders, had a major impact. His concluding paragraph was quoted in several places. It began by saying, "I have lost faith in UWF, because UWF has lost faith in itself and its idea," and went on to describe UWF's activities as "ineffective." Wallerstein accused UWF of a "serious error of omission" in avoiding the Third World's struggles for freedom and justice, and he called for the structure, premises and membership of UWF to be "radically altered."

A number of student chapters were attracting attention by focusing on the April Congress of the World Movement for World Government. The University of Chicago chapter was stimulating debate over the structure of a world federal government. At Stanford, my proposal that Stanford send its own delegate to Rome was approved, despite right-wing opposition. As the prime mover, I was told in no uncertain terms to remove myself from consideration. A subcommittee of the student council then selected a moderate, well-spoken international relations specialist named Derek Bok (later president of Harvard) to attend the congress during our spring break. In the event of illness, Bok was to inform the alternate choice to attend in his stead. The Stanford administration and board were angry and alarmed by this unexpected development. Claiming illness, Bok never used the ticket. Nevertheless, we had won the fight for the minds of the students—at least temporarily.

Rejected by UWF's adults, students walk out and form the Interim Committee of American Federalist Youth (ICAFY)

The foundering marriage between the Student Federalists and UWF finally came to an end at the June 23–25 UWF 1951 convention in Des Moines after it became obvious that further negotiations and joint committee meetings with UWF would prove fruitless. The students passed an umbrella resolution declaring that "the present status of the Student Division within UWF, Inc., cannot be continued at this time." They then formed the Interim Committee of American Federalist Youth (ICAFY), comprised of twenty-one students representative of regional and ideological diversity, most of whom had chapter constituencies. Richard Pierson of Princeton, an ideological moderate with views closer to those of the UWF adult majority, was elected chairman. ICAFY was charged with drafting detailed proposals for policy, program, structure and finances, to be presented to a founding convention before January 10, 1952. Interested groups of Federalists would be invited to discuss the problems a new organization would face. Most important, the resolution directed that the interim committee be guided by Wallerstein's credo statement. Meanwhile, Pierson drafted a letter from ICAFY to all of UWF's Executive Council members, anticipating that the UWF Executive Council would reject the student's demands. In that event, Pierson proposed a "fraternal" relationship between the new student organization and UWF. The proposal was rejected by a large majority of the UWF Executive Council when it met in Columbus that September.

Over the summer of 1951, the ICAFY members met frequently to produce a call for the founding convention of a new world government organization that would appeal to both students and youth under thirty. They envisioned an organization which would have "a broader policy than any American world government organization to date" with a program emphasizing education, field work and the training of leaders; greater chapter autonomy (than that granted by UWF); and a magazine which would "help to build in the United States strong, creative public opinion in favor of measures necessary to create a free, just and prosperous world community." Voting representation at the convention would be by invited individuals who pledged to work within the organization, with a maximum of ten from any single school, college or community, except that delegates traveling one thousand miles would receive two votes and those traveling two thousand miles, three votes. The audience invited were both present and former youth members of the student federalist movement and selected student and youth leaders who shared the overall philosophy of the convention callers. Those most encouraged to attend were leaders from SDA, USNSA, SLID, YPSL, NAACP Youth, the Quakers, and some other religious groups. The call and subsequent discussions made it clear that the founders were not looking for large numbers but, somewhat patterned after Britain's Fabian Society, able and effective leaders and communicators.

Extending the Federalist outreach internationally: the World Assembly of Youth (WAY) and the Young Adult Council (YAC)

Perhaps the most extensive manifestation of Wallerstein's memorandum was the major role taken by student federalists in the work of the noncommunist youth groups YAC and WAY, which were just beginning to mount substantive programs. Wallerstein himself was chairman of YAC's International Affairs Committee, and Herb Weiss was a member of its Executive Committee. YAC was a coordinating committee of representatives of internationalist and socially conscious youth and student groups.[5] Its first project, in early 1951, was to hold conferences for study and action in Denver, Palo Alto, Madison, Richmond and Boston—each of which was a stronghold of student federalists, USNSA and/or SDA—relating to the Role of American Youth in Point Four.[6] Murray Frank was appointed chairman for these conferences.

At UWF Student Council meetings in 1950-51, Wallerstein reported that he and other federalists were becoming involved in shaping the international federation, WAY, of which YAC was the American representative. WAY had held a major leadership meeting in Ankara, Turkey, in 1950 and several others in Europe. Now it was scheduled to hold its first full Congress of noncommunist world youth in August of 1951 at Cornell University. YAC and UWF leaders were urging USNSA to cooperate in planning the congress. As the American representative, YAC would be entitled to about twenty-five delegates, and Wallerstein noted the federalists were doing everything possible to maximize the number of world government supporters in that delegation. Wallerstein also reported on confidential meetings held among leaders of USNSA, UWF and YAC to evaluate the 1950 Congresses held by the rival, Communist-dominated IUS and WFDY.

In the event, the American delegation to the WAY Congress included federalists Mary Coleman (University of Chicago), Wallerstein and Herb Weiss, as well as such friends as Al Lowenstein, USNSA; Ruth Schachter, Collegiate Council for the United Nations (CCUN); Toby Osos, YWCA; Ernie Howell, YMCA; Walter Carrington and Eleanor Landy, NAACP Youth Council; and later, Ted Weiss, of the Student Federalists. Federalists Elaine Klein and Bill Friedlander were among the twenty alternates. Under Howell's direction, Murray Frank, Bill Friedlander and I worked on the Congress staff, with Gene Schwartz, of USNSA, handling some of its publicity chores. (Except for myself, all had earlier worked full time for YAC planning and organizing the Congress.)

The four hundred delegates and observers attending the 1951 WAY Congress came from more than fifty nations. They met in plenaries, workshops, caucuses and hearings to fashion policy and programs appropriate to a global non-Communist youth organization. With two exceptions, the American delegation consisted of students and youth under thirty. The exceptions were Bernice Bridges, Executive Director of the National Social Welfare Assembly, sponsor of YAC, and David Davis, who listed his affiliation as the American Association for the United Nations but who was, to the knowledge of all of us, a government figure (who most of us believed to be connected with the State Department, but who, in retrospect, was probably with the CIA). We were also aware that government funds were paying for all or most of the Congress, including the staff, the lodging and the food. As the Congress progressed, we learned from a number of delegations that their travel had also been paid by an American source, presumably the US government.

The British, French, Belgian and Dutch delegations were led by much older men and women, many of them government bureaucrats or operatives. It was rumored that M. Jousselin, of the French delegation, was himself a high-ranking officer of the Duexieme Bureau. As the younger and more idealistic Americans reached out to establish relationships with delegates from colonial areas, the reaction of the West Europeans became quite apparent. Their job was, in large measure, to keep the colonial delegates, mostly hand-picked, from bolting the colonialist discipline, in the same way as they were being "protected" from Communist subversion.[7] As we gradually encouraged delegates from such remote places as Upper Volta, Chad, Ubangi Chari and Dahomey to take some tentative steps toward independence from their colonial rulers, the colonialists began to play hardball, taking their toll on the families of the delegates back in the colonies and making the delegates aware of the price. The Americans clearly had much to learn.

On the other hand, articulate delegates like Wallerstein, Lowenstein, the two Weisses, Howell and Schachter were pretty much the match of any delegates, regardless of age. The WAY Congress also proved a propitious place for the members of ICAFY to discuss the merits of a new student/youth organization with global interests and to encourage attendance at the founding meeting in October. Following the conclusion of the Congress, Friedlander and I, among others, led tours of delegates throughout the Midwest, Northeast and Washington, DC, during which "liberal" Europeans tested the racial attitudes of the Americans as far west as Detroit and Pittsburgh and, most especially, in the capital of the nation, where blacks could eat with whites only at one government cafeteria.

Too little and too late: The birth of World Order Realized through Law and Democracy (WORLD)

In retrospect, forces were converging in 1951 and 1952 which mitigated against the kind of student movement represented by the Federalists. For one thing, the leadership ranks were thinning. The heady experiences with WAY through the Young Adult Council lured a number of Federalists away. At the same time, many of the World War II veterans were reaching thirty, getting married, and settling down to careers and families. Even more costly to the leadership of the student movement was the call of the military draft. Virtually all those who had been too young for World War II were drafted into the armed services between 1951 and 1954. Among the first was Wallerstein, who later managed to persuade the U.S. Army to grant him leave from his station in Panama to attend the 1953 WAY Council meeting in Dakar.

International and domestic political affairs did not help. The war in Korea was extremely bloody and protracted. Soon the Chinese Communists would intervene. The French were facing violent setbacks in North Africa and Indochina. The Dutch, still hoping to retain control over what was to become Indonesia, were using armed forces against the rebels. The Soviets were consolidating their control over Eastern Europe and political deviationists at home. In the United States, the McCarthy era was reaching its peak, and progress to eliminate racism appeared to be stalled in the courts. Only the Attlee government in Britain was systematically (and peacefully) liquidating its colonial holdings on the Indian Subcontinent and in West Africa.

Against this backdrop, eighty delegates met at the Chestnut Street YWCA in Philadelphia, October 19-21, 1951, to answer ICAFY's call for a new federalist youth organization. They included several USNSA leaders, including outgoing president Allard Lowenstein, and others representing long-time federalist allies. Ideologically, they ranged from Fair Deal Democrats to socialists and pacifists, and almost all were adherents of world federalism. To the disappointment of some—and especially to me, as the convention chairman—very little new in the way of policy or program ideas emerged from the lengthy debates. The final policy statement embodied the liberal principles of the day: nuclear disarmament; Third World economic development; eradication of racial bigotry; the need to stand up to censorship, loyalty oaths and witch hunters; liberation of legitimate nations from Western colonialism and Soviet imperialism; establishment of world law and enforcement and interpretive institutions as well as a world legislative mechanism; a universal world organization of independent nations which could freely delegate their sovereignty to a strengthened United Nations or other world government; and a system of representation that did not totally negate the one-man, one-vote ideal. The most difficult debate was over the name: the compromise was an acronym spelling WORLD—World Order Realized through Law and Democracy. Not exactly elegant, but workable.

To demonstrate that the Student Federalists were determined to share power with sister youth and student groups, Ken Kurtz, who had narrowly lost the vote for president of USNSA a few weeks earlier, was persuaded to accept the paid chairmanship of WORLD and to work in New York City, where he was to attend Columbia's graduate school. The Federalist leaders tried as well to persuade representatives from other student and youth groups to accept board positions, but only Doug Kelley, of SDA and IDPA, and Dick Carter, of World Republic, agreed. Ken Kurtz immediately met with the UWF executive staff to outline WORLD's plans and seek UWF cooperation. WORLD members were urged to retain their UWF memberships.

The new organization was committed to promoting social and technical assistance programs, including support for Point Four, as well as urging individuals to serve in development projects abroad with IDPA (see the next section). WORLD promised to help create a closer world community by persuading Americans to register as world citizens. Finally, WORLD pledged to fight all forms of discrimination and to support academic freedom and student rights, as well as the freedoms of speech, thought, conscience, and association, and to extend these principles to the Universal Declaration of Human Rights.

At the board meeting immediately following the founding convention, a six-member executive committee composed of long-time Federalists was elected, and plans for a national advisory committee of prominent people were drawn up. Harry Lustig announced that World Republic's board had met recently and approved passing on their monthly grant of $1,000 to WORLD for one year with no strings attached, after which it would decide whether to continue. The World Republic grant was used in part for hiring a second staff member (Virginia Riorden). Programmatically, the board unanimously approved Ted Weiss's proposal that WORLD should arrange for an American community to adopt a town or village in the Third World, with WORLD helping to provide resources and facilitate exchanges of correspondence. And, after a long discussion, the board approved a plan to publish a quarterly journal of thought and opinion, with a budget of $1,400, not including payment to a managing editor.

Student precursor to the Peace Corps: The International Development Placement Association (IDPA)

The WORLD board worked closely with the International Development Placement Association (IDPA), which had been founded in the spring of 1951 by a number of Student Federalists, SDAers and NSAers—many of them inspired by the Wallerstein memorandum—and which had three WORLD members on its Board. IDPA was an independent, private nonprofit agency to promote youth and student participation in technical assistance programs in the Third World—in short, a nongovernmental Point Four program. Its first executive director was Peter Weiss.[8] The officers were Clifford Dancer, chairman; Herbert Alexander (former international vice president of USNSA), vice chairman; Al Ettinger (former executive director of SDA), secretary; and Gene Schwartz (a leader in USNSA, SF and YAC), treasurer. The board included St. John's College president Stringfellow Barr (who, in June, had made the keynote address to the annual ADA convention, after which the delegates voted for a resolution supporting world government); James Farmer, soon to become program director of NAACP and later president of the Congress of Radical Equality (CORE); and ADA founder and development expert Robert R. Nathan, one of Franklin D. Roosevelt's noted Brain Trusters.

IDPA's mission was to promote the idea of service to developing nations by Americans who could provide technical assistance and know-how while living at local wage levels as employees of government or non-profit agencies. The Association worked with potential employers abroad, who spelled out their technical assistance requirements, after which IDPA recruited and trained individuals possessing the appropriate skills, temperament and commitment for practical work in social and economic development for a minimum of a year. IDPA returnees were expected to make their work experience available through educational programs to the American people. In its first year, IDPA provided a highly qualified physicist to the faculty of the University of Indonesia; a group of social workers, as well as a nurse and a farmer, to the Gandhian basic education center at Sevagram, India, to assist with village development programs; a graduate of a leading school of technology to Nigeria to initiate a science program for a secondary school; enrollment of two Americans, a Jamaican, and a Canadian in six-month courses on the administration of cooperatives in Nova Scotia, Canada, after which each would be assigned abroad.

The example of IDPA helped to inspire such major political figures as Senator Hubert Humphrey, who called for a government-sponsored technical assistance program during the 1960 presidential race,[9] and John F. Kennedy, who co-opted the idea and actually brought it into being as the Peace Corps after he was elected. Student activists were also inspired. Among the many who later served in the Peace Corps were Harris Wofford, Murray Frank, George Carter, Walter Carrington, Gloria Gaston, and myself.

WORLD and the lasting legacy of the Student Federalists

WORLD proved short-lived. In February 1952, the UWF Executive Committee decided that membership of any of its national, state or chapter officers on the board of a group "with conflicting views" was unacceptable—a resolution clearly aimed at WORLD. The World Republic grant was withdrawn in March, despite appeals to its sponsors. From this point forward, the organization was operating on an ever-diminishing shoestring. Nevertheless, the organization possessed the talent to produce four issues of a thoughtful journal entitled World Frontiers, under Shane Riorden's direction as editor. Alas, the fourth issue coincided with the realization that the organization could not function alone much longer.

The tenacious manner in which the Europeans clung to their colonial empires had become a major preoccupation for the student leadership of WORLD. Wallerstein, Herb Weiss, Frank, and their YAC associates had been expanding anticolonial initiatives within the World Assembly of Youth and the World Student Federalists, telling the British, French, Belgians and Dutch that they too needed to adopt a world view: "We are world citizens first," a proposed policy statement from WORLD said to the other Student Federalists.

> "WSF should do everything in its power," the statement read, "to aid in the elimination of colonialism. WSF should assert the right of every area to realize its potential through development programs, land reform and reclamation projects made possible by the aid of more fortunate peoples . . . . WSF should support the right of colonial peoples, such as the Tunisians, to a hearing before the UN . . . and should condemn racial discrimination, whether it be found in South Africa, the United States, colonial areas or elsewhere. WSF should equally condemn the mass enslavement found in totalitarian countries."

This anticolonial commitment proved to be a hard sell in Europe, even among Federalists.

As the Executive Committee prepared for WORLD's second annual convention, in 1952, they voted to reduce their overhead by moving from New York. Harry Lustig was appointed to make the convention arrangements at his home campus—the University of Illinois, in Urbana, where he was a faculty member. Held between September 18 and 21, the convention attracted twenty-one delegates and less than a dozen observers. It focused mostly on program direction. I was elected chair of both the board and executive committee, and authorized to receive twenty dollars a week toward living expenses, plus travel costs for fieldwork.

In November, while I was taking graduate Chinese studies at Columbia, I organized a meeting for Professor Rom Landau, a spokesman for Moroccan independence. Afterward, I prepared a brief supporting the Moroccans, which was sent to each chapter and to allied student and youth groups. The exercise provided the Student Federalists as an organization with their first concrete struggle against functioning colonialism. It also opened the door to support for the Tunisians, and later the Algerians.[10]

WORLD's National Board on December 20, 1952,

adopted resolutions demanding repeal of the McCarran-Walter Immigration Act and the McCarran Internal Security Act, both of which were extensions of the McCarthyite hysteria against "Red" infiltration. The same Board voted overwhelmingly to call for the end of Senate Standing Rule 22, which required a two-thirds vote to limit debate (i.e., cloture) and had enabled Southern bigots to filibuster against any civil rights measure. The board voted against urging President Harry Truman to commute the death sentences of the Rosenbergs, who were convicted of handing atomic secrets to the Soviets, and against overhauling the Electoral College.

This board meeting, the first since I had replaced Kurtz, delved in-depth into the declining state of the organization. I lamented to the board the lack of involvement or support from most of the past student federalist leadership. With only nine functioning chapters and a membership of less than two hundred, I said, there was simply not enough of an underpinning to sustain a national organization. Shortly afterward, I initiated a series of meetings with SDA National Chair Sandy Levin (now a long-term U.S. Representative to Congress from Detroit) about the possibility of merging WORLD with SDA. Then, in mid-March 1953, I notified my draft board that I no longer sought conscientious objector status. Within days, the board ordered my immediate conscription.

Levin came to the June 14 WORLD board meeting in Chicago to argue for merger. However, at WORLD's third annual convention, in September 1953, in Philadelphia, the overwhelming sentiment of the remaining WORLD members was to carry on and not to merge with SDA. What was left of the Student Federalist legacy were a few dozen diehards, many of them long-term veterans, who were still convinced—in the face of overwhelming evidence to the contrary—that the American people, especially the youth, could be persuaded to rally around the world government banner. Most of them had never been much enamored of the student leadership's insistence on taking strong stands on foreign policy issues, and even fewer felt compelled to declare themselves on either race or civil liberties. Ultimately, their views were not very different from those of the same UWF from which they had parted two years earlier. Eventually, those that remained active rejoined UWF and its successor, allowing WORLD to expire in early 1954, quietly and alone, without any fanfare.

The quest for peace and justice—not for the want of trying

Many of the Student Federalists remained thoroughly committed to the same values and principles for which they had fought from 1943 to 1953. Placing the quest for freedom and justice over that for peace, over a dozen segued into the world youth movement through the Young Adult Council, with lasting impact on their fellow American youth leaders and on those who attended WAY meetings (many of whom would become leading political figures in their own countries). The former student leaders participated in American political life, either as candidates themselves or on behalf of candidates who represented the same commitment—internationalist, anticolonial, antiracist, pro-economic development, and for measures that would reduce the danger of nuclear holocaust. They continued to support UN charter revision and multilateral approaches to aid and peace. A sizable number became authoritative academics, either with regional expertise or with specialization in international organization and institutions. Several were executives in USAID and its predecessors, administering developmental aid to the Third World.[11]

Their likes among activist students were never to be seen again in the 20th century. Their combination of intelligence, commitment, idealism, and pragmatism would have been impossible to replicate, as so much of it stemmed from the experiences of the Great Depression, World War II, the explosion of the first atomic bombs, and the founding of the United Nations. The simplistic antiwar protests of the 1960s hardly compared to the complexities encountered by the student federalists in our earlier and less sophisticated age. The effects of the Cold War and the rise of anticommunist hysteria, along with the persistence of colonialism and racism here and abroad, proved too powerful to overcome, but not for want of trying.

Gilbert Jonas has been actively involved in the human rights and peace movements for half a century. He directed his own public relations and fund-raising firm specializing in these areas. He also represented the National Association for the Advancement of Colored People (NAACP) for thirty years.

END NOTES

[1] See Meyer, p. 703.

[2] See Chicago Student Conference, p. 109.

[3] *Editor's note:* See "Covert U.S. Funding of NSA International Programs," p. 565. This secret funding through dummy foundations began in late 1951 and was made known only to a few NSA officers each year until the practice was made public by an article in *Ramparts* magazine in 1967.

[4] Adult membership, at 23,000, was also down by almost 17,000 since the beginning of 1951.

[5] In 1951, the YAC members were American Red Cross (College Units), American Youth Hostels, Collegiate Council for the United Nations,

NAACP Youth Division, National Federation of Settlements, USNSA, United World Federalists, and religious groups representing youth and student divisions of the YM- and YWCA, Catholics, Jews, Unitarians, Universalists, and the United Christian Youth Movement. In future years, some of these groups would disappear, while YAC added the Association of International Relations Clubs and the Student League for Industrial Democracy (SLID). *Editor's note:* YAC was formed in 1948 as a transformation from a series of two war-time and postwar youth organization coordinating councils sponored by the National Social Welfare Assembly (NSWA). In 1962 YAC became the United States Youth Council (USYC), continuing U.S. representation to WAY. WAY continues until this day. (For more on YAC, USYC, WAY and NSWA see an unpublished 9/16/2005 memorandum to the editor by Karen Paget in the anthology archives.)

[6] Point Four was the first postwar government technical assistance program that encompassed Third World countries. It was proposed by President Truman as the fourth point of his 1948 inaugural address and became the predecessor of a long line of American aid agencies.

[7] From WAY's early days, the American position was that each colony would be regarded as a state, with voting privileges. Thus, even Puerto Rico was accorded "independent" status, and when her delegates rose to demand national independence from the United States, the American delegation also rose to its feet in enthusiastic and vociferous support.

[8] Weiss's connection to IDPA resulted from his friendship with Stringfellow Barr at Johns Hopkins University. See IDPA, p. 627, Weiss, p. 637.

[9] See Murphy, p. 630.

[10] At about this time, I also served as voluntary public relations staff for the Istiqual (Independence) Party of Morocco, which supported Moroccan independence and the ascension of Sultan Mohammed V to the throne as Moroccan king. Its representatives, Mr. El Fassi and Mr. Balafrej, were struggling (without any real resources) to make their case known to the UN.

PICTURE CREDITS: *Then:* c. 1950, *Now:* c. 1999 (Both, author)

GILBERT JONAS

Early years: I was born in Brooklyn, NY, in 1930 and attended Lafayette High School in Brooklyn.

Career highlights: I have been actively involved in the human rights and world peace movements for more than half a century. I graduated from Stanford in 1951 with a B.A. in Journalism and Social Sciences and obtained a graduate degree in Chinese Studies from Columbia's East Asian Institute in 1953 and an M.A. in International Affairs from Columbia's School of International Affairs in 1955. I directed my own public relations and fund-raising firm specializing in these areas, as well as representing labor unions, anticolonial movements, and Third World governments for almost forty years. I was the Peace Corps' first Acting Director for the Far East in 1961, following stints as chief executive of the American Medical Center for Burma and the American Friends of Vietnam. I represented the NAACP for thirty years. I was also the last elected chairman of the Student World Federalists, then known as WORLD, in 1952-1953.

Family: I was married in 1953 to Barbara Selby, an English teacher in the public school system. She had earned a B.A. and an M.A. from NYU. Our daughter, Susan, received her B.A. from Princeton and her Ph.D. from Yale School of Drama. Barbara died in 1981. I have been married to Joyce Theise since 1964. Joyce is a renowned antique jewelry expert and appears on television's *Antiques Road Show.* We have two daughters, Stephanie, who has degrees from Emerson and New York University and teaches musical theater, and Jillian, who graduated from Hunter College and earned her M.A. from NYU, in television journalism and public affairs. In October 2000, Stephanie gave birth to our first grandchild, Charles Kimute. He favors his father, Peter Stone, a venture capital specialist.

JONAS RUNS ON AN NSA PLATFORM AT STANFORD UNIVERSITY

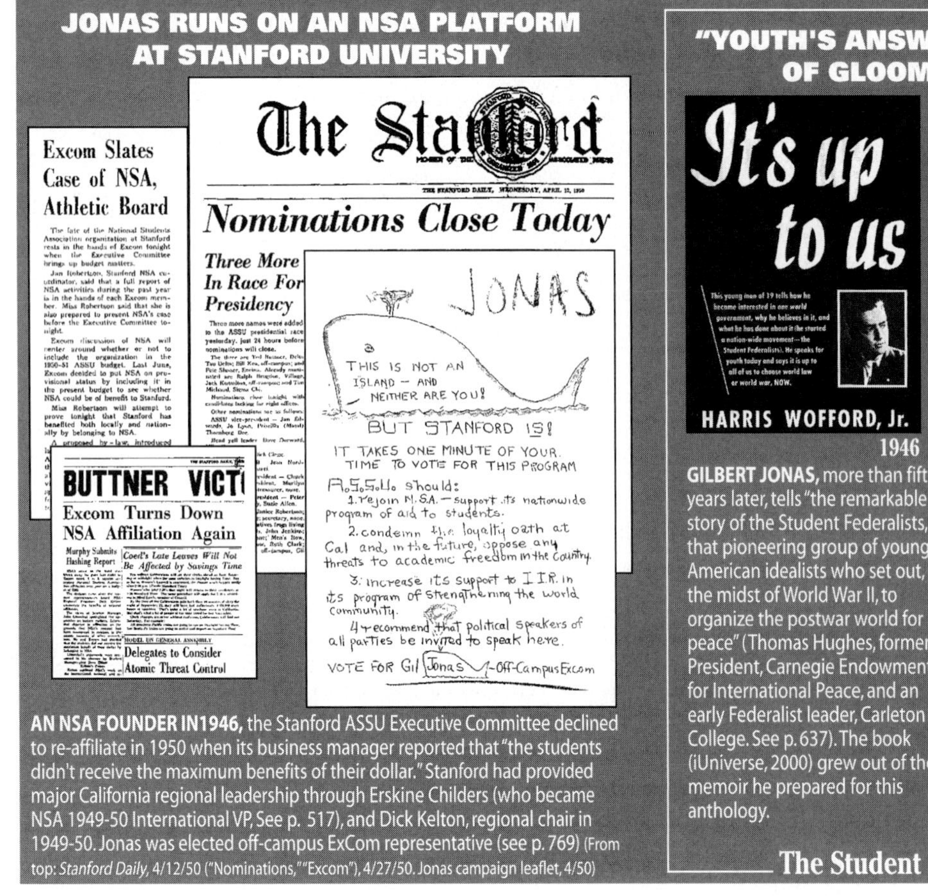

AN NSA FOUNDER IN1946, the Stanford ASSU Executive Committee declined to re-affiliate in 1950 when its business manager reported that "the students didn't receive the maximum benefits of their dollar." Stanford had provided major California regional leadership through Erskine Childers (who became NSA 1949-50 International VP, See p. 517), and Dick Kelton, regional chair in 1949-50. Jonas was elected off-campus ExCom representative (see p.769) (From top: *Stanford Daily,* 4/12/50 ("Nominations," "Excom"), 4/27/50. Jonas campaign leaflet, 4/50)

"YOUTH'S ANSWER TO THE COUNSELS OF GLOOM AND DESPAIR"

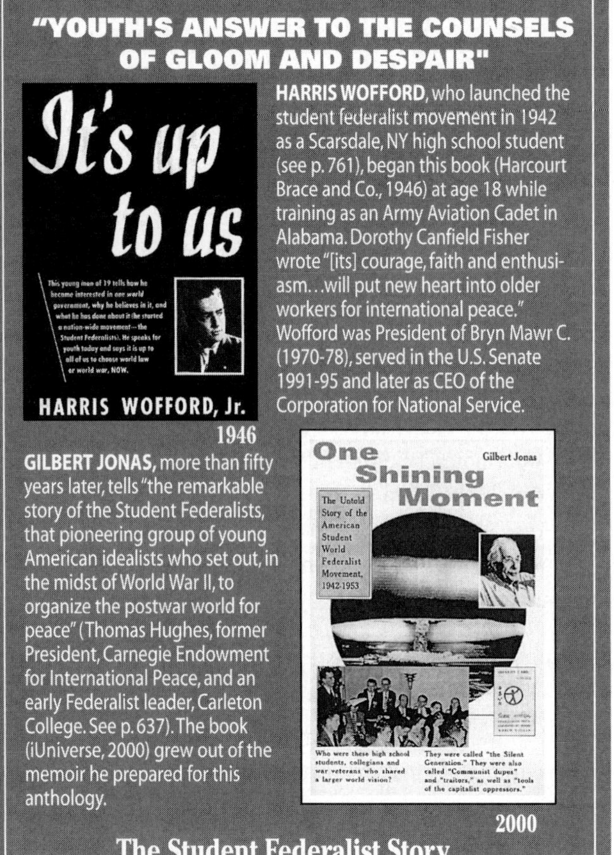

HARRIS WOFFORD, who launched the student federalist movement in 1942 as a Scarsdale, NY high school student (see p. 761), began this book (Harcourt Brace and Co., 1946) at age 18 while training as an Army Aviation Cadet in Alabama. Dorothy Canfield Fisher wrote "[its] courage, faith and enthusiasm...will put new heart into older workers for international peace." Wofford was President of Bryn Mawr C. (1970-78), served in the U.S. Senate 1991-95 and later as CEO of the Corporation for National Service.

GILBERT JONAS, more than fifty years later, tells "the remarkable story of the Student Federalists, that pioneering group of young American idealists who set out, in the midst of World War II, to organize the postwar world for peace" (Thomas Hughes, former President, Carnegie Endowment for International Peace, and an early Federalist leader, Carleton College. See p. 637). The book (iUniverse, 2000) grew out of the memoir he prepared for this anthology.

"We must make world citizenship a political fact" - The Concord Charter, 1946

1945

Wednesday, December 5, 1945

Students Work For World Government

The purpose of the Student Federalist organization and its chapters is "to develop dynamic public opinion working in the direction of world government" stated Sue Ervin '48 at a meeting last Wednesday to consider the possibility of Vassar joining this nationwide organization. A group such as this would be primarily educational: concentrating on educating themselves first in the principles of world government.

For World Government

The foremost function of such a group on campus would be to put to use the feeling that there should be an effective world organization in the event of a world crisis. The ultimate aim of the Student Federalists is a world government that acts directly on individuals. Although there is no particular platform as to how this world government should be achieved, the main efforts of the organization are to build up public opinion in favor of world government. This is done by several means: starting groups in schools and other countries,

Vassar Miscellany News 12/5/45, NY

1946

WELLESLEY

SF Activities Most Vital During 1946

Colgate S. Prentice

By Colgate S. Prentice, Pres.
1946 was certainly the most eventful period to date in the

Wellesley College News 11/11/46, MA

1947

ills College Weel

one world?

NOT WITH A BANG

Mills College Weekly 10/10/47, CA

Friday, November 14, 1947

Nash Says Federation Of World Now Possible

It isn't necessary to convince people of the necessity for world government, it is only necessary to get them to think about it, said Vernon Nash in a recent talk in Brown Hall. "We are ready to have the case made against the idea of world federation as well as for it," he stated, explaining that the arguments against world federation are so weak that they tend to sell the very idea that they attack.

VICE-PRESIDENT OF U.W.F.

Nash, journalist and news analyst, is now vice-president of the

Thyrsus Blowout

The Denver Clarion

University of Denver — Denver, Colorado

224 FORENSIC STUDENTS HERE FOR COLLEGE MEET

"Resolved That Federal World Government Should Be Established," Is Discussion Topic Of Speakers

From top: *Student Life* 11/14/47, Washington U., St Louis; *The Denver Clarion* 11/7/47

1948

SWARTHMOR

Cord Meyer Addresses AVC: Federal UN or Certain Wa

No Complete AB Defense: UWF Seeks Means to Make Future Wars Impossible

Cord Meyer, Jr., President of the United World Fedralists, delivered a powerful and convincing speech to the meeting of the Swarthmore Chapter of the American Veterans Committee on Tuesday evening, February 3, in the Friends Meeting House. Summarizing the terrible possibilities of new and improved death-dealing agents, he ridiculed the possibility of peace through "balance of power," and proposed some form of world government as the only alternative to a war which would destroy probably half, and perhaps all, of the human race. The speech was broadcast over

, MARYLAND, JANUARY 16, 1

Federalists Organization Established

A month or so ago Mr. Flickinger, instructor in Political Science and Current Affairs, asked of the Administration and was granted permission to organize a student chapter of the United World Federalists. The World Federalists members in the school to date number 25 to 30 charter members who have subscribed by remitting the required one dollar annual dues for student members. Mr. Flickinger is still in the process of organizing the chapter. It is still open for membership to any who are interested. The charter has already been sent for

From top: *Swarthmore Phoenix* 2/13/48, PA; *The Balou* 1/16/48, U. of Baltimore

1949

Official Publication of the Associated Student

Boulder, Colorado, Tuesday, May 17,

Poll Shows Majority Of Faculty In Favor Of World Government

Frank, UWF Head, Expresses UN Belief

one of six student leaders in the U.S. to take a leave of absence from school to work as a full time

NFCCS Considers World Federal Government

Fifteen Trinity girls arrived in rented cars or busses for the annual congress of the Baltimore-Washington region of the National Federation of Catholic College Students. The Congress was held at St. Joseph's College in Emmitsburg, Maryland, and was under the general

From top: *Silver and Gold* 5/17/49, U.of CO; *Bulletin* 10/28/49, NYU; *The Trinity Times* 4/49, DC

1950

Friday, April 21, 1950

United World Federalists Junket Through N. Y. In Blue Bus Caravan

by ANNE KING, '31

The United World Federalists are now traveling by caravan. On this campus Trudy Stephens and Jim Stuber, of the U. of R. student chapter are still talking about the fun they had trotting all over New York in a state-wide "Caravan" in which students and adult members from various colleges and cities joined to tour from Rochester through Seneca Falls, Syracuse, Utica, and proclaiming World Federalism to the citizenry at large. They also took over the busiest corner, handing out literature and cir-

Tower Times 4/21/50, U. of Rochester

1951

Cranston Calls For World Government As 'Only Hope'

"Communism cannot be defeated by destroying the Soviet Union," said Alan Cranston, president of United World Federalists, Friday night in Macky auditorium.

"The only hope is to inaugurate a program which is advocated by such prominent men as Winston Churchill and Nehru: that is, to work for a world government which has the power to enforce disarmament."

Cranston said he have a "sterile sovereignty" when Russia can

UWF, "the fig leaf of American imperialism.")

'Long, Tedious'

"The road would be long and tedious, but if we pursue this course we would put pressure on

Silver and Gold 4/17/51, U. of CO.

1952

WORLD Supports World Government, Studies Problems of Foreign Affairs

Silver and Gold 2/7/52, U. of CO.

IDENTITY CARD

Nº 16361

世界公民

विश्व-नागरिक

ГРАЖДАНИН МИРА

CIUDADANO DEL MUNDO

WORLD CITIZEN

"THEIR LIKES AMONG ACTIVIST STUDENTS WERE NEVER TO BE SEEN AGAIN THIS CENTURY," writes Gil Jonas in his preceding narrative of the "shining moment," the ten golden years which reached a high point of some 10,000 members and 300 high school and college chapters. Many continued on as civic and political leaders and authoritative academics and administrators with expertise in international affairs.

SOME NATIONAL STUDENT FEDERALIST LEADERS

Harris Wofford, Jr.
Scarsdale H.S.
SF Founder, 1942
Pres. Bryn Mawr C., U.S. Senator

Thomas Hughes
Carleton C., MN
1944 SF President
Pres., Carnegie Endowment

Virginia (Lastayo) Riorden
New York
1946 Chapter Secretary
Teacher, art inst. administrator

Eleanor (Schneider) Farrar
Mount Holyoke C.
1947 Chapter Secretary
VP, Joint Center Political Studies

Clare (Lindgren) Wofford
U. of Minnesota
1946 SF President

Helen (Ball) Sirkin
Wheaton C., MA
1946 SF Chairman
International Affairs, Teacher

Murray Frank
NYU
1949 SF President
Professor, Rutgers, U. Mass

Immanuel Wallerstein
Columbia U.
1949 UWF NEC
Dist.Prof.Sociology, Binghamton U.

Student Federalist

CONCORD CHARTER

In historic Concord, Mass., Feb. 8-11, 1946, eighty students, including many young veterans, met to plan the part they could play in building a federal world government. They came from 33 colleges and 20 high schools, from 25 states, and represented all the major youth groups working for world federation. They united on a common policy and program of action. They unanimously joined in an enlarged Student Federalist movement based on the following Concord Charter:

We must make world citizenship a political fact.

Existing governments have demonstrated that they are incapable of preserving peace and protecting human rights in an interdependent world. The atomic bomb blasts forever the illusion that power-politics can give us peace.

Only a new world sovereignty based on the principles of federalism can destroy the irresponsibility of nationalism while preserving national identity.

The United Nations Organization is not a federal government. It has no authority over individuals; it can only make recommendations to, or negotiate treaties with member nations; and it cannot prevent the secession of any nation. It will not be adequate unless it is capable of making, interpreting, and enforcing world law.

THE CONCORD CHARTER rallied young people "united in our determination to achieve world government in our time."

Photo sources: all from Gil Jonas, except Eleanor Farrar, courtesy The Mount Holyoke Archives and Special Collections.

The Young Adult Council (YAC) and World Assembly of Youth (WAY)

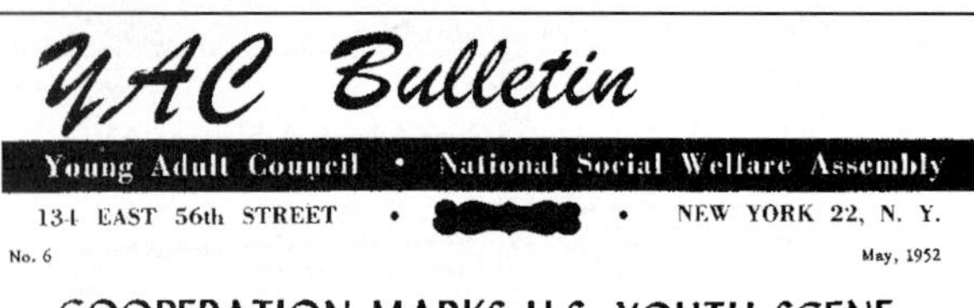
YAC Bulletin
Young Adult Council • National Social Welfare Assembly
134 EAST 56th STREET • NEW YORK 22, N. Y.
No. 6 May, 1952
COOPERATION MARKS U.S. YOUTH SCENE

The excerpts below are from YAC Bulletin, May, 1952

THE YOUNG ADULT COUNCIL

Since 1948 the Young Adult Council of the National Social Welfare Assembly has enabled urban and rural young worker and student organizations to cooperate on local, national, and international affairs. Its achievements show that YAC is already a major force in American youth life. It is the central planning body of 70 directly and indirectly associated national youth movements which serve the 18-30 age group. The national movements work together through YAC to realize common goals.

These common goals are reflected by the major areas in which YAC has worked: 1) to realize in practice the principles embodied in the Universal Declaration of Human Rights, 2) to extend programs for world social and economic development, 3) to create a world community, universal civic education, and support for the United Nations, 4) to gain youth participation in and influence upon the activities of leading national and international bodies.

* * *

The members of the Young Adult Council are 16 national young adult organizations, each represented on the Council by a delegation. The delegates are youth leaders between 18 and 30, national, regional officers or committee members of affiliated organizations. Each delegation is assisted by a staff consultant [from] the youth program of the national organization.

The Young Adult Council is an integral part of the National Social Welfare Assembly, the central planning body for national social welfare organizations in the United States. YAC operates as the planning body for young adult organizations within the general policy and procedures of the NSWA.

YAC is affiliated with the World Assembly of Youth, which unites 42 such national councils of youth organizations. Through WAY, YAC works with the world's youth leaders toward the goals stated above.

WHOM DOES YAC REPRESENT?

YAC is broadly representative of religious, student, worker, and rural youth groups. Persons from many racial and ethnic backgrounds participate in YAC and its member organizations.

Three of YAC's 16 members are themselves coordinating councils. **The United Christian Youth Movement** is composed of 32 major Protestant denominations of the United States, 37 Christian Youth Councils and 18 national youth-serving agencies representing 90 percent of the Protestant Youth of America. UCYM is administered through the Division of Christian Education of the National Council of Churches of Christ in the U.S.A.

Catholic youth are associated through the **Youth Department of the National Catholic Welfare Conference** under whose aegis are the **National Federation of Diocesan Catholic Youth Councils**; the **National Federation of Catholic College Students** with 200,000 members in 220 Catholic colleges; the **National Newman Club Federation**, an organization of 100,000 Catholic students in 550 clubs on non-Catholic campuses; and the National Catholic Youth Council, which coordinates their work. About six million Catholic youth are reached by the Youth Department of the NCWC.

The **National Jewish Youth Conference** coordinates eleven national Jewish youth organizations and more than 300 local and regional Jewish youth and young adult councils. The NJYC is sponsored by the National Jewish Welfare Board, with which are affiliated 331 Jewish community centers, and **Young Men's and Young Women's Hebrew Associations** with an aggregate membership of 502,000 persons at all age levels.

Another coordinating council of student Christian movements—the **United Student Christian Council**—has observer status in YAC. The **American Unitarian Youth** and the **Universalist Youth Fellowship**, also religious groups, are affiliated directly to YAC.

College students are represented in YAC by several organizations. **The Student Division of the United World Federalists** supports the United Nations and its evolution into a world federal government with limited powers. **The Students for Democratic Action** has a liberal nonpartisan political educational program, The Collegiate Council for the United Nations stimulates understanding of the United Nations and voices student opinion on UN issues. The North American Student Cooperative League develops and improves student cooperatives.

The United States National Student Association (NSA)—a federation of college student bodies through 300 student governments—voices the opinions and needs of students; strengthens democratic student governments; strives to maintain and to improve the free and equal educational system in the United States; and enables students to play an effective role in international student affairs.

The National Student Council of the YMCA and YWCA (now NSCY, formerly NICC) are affiliated to YAC through the National Council of the YMCA and the National Board of the YWCA.

Three associated groups are primarily of young workers and employees. They are the **YMCA National Young Adult Council** and the **YWCA's National Councils of Industrial and Agricultural Women** and **of Business and Professional Women**.

The **National Federation of Settlements and Neighborhood Houses** working with youth in 302 centers, strives for improved living standards, housing, education, health and recreation.

The **Youth Division of the National Association for the Advancement of Colored People**, uniting 310 youth councils and 85 college chapters with over 16,000 persons of all races and creeds, fights discrimination and promotes the betterment of colored people.

Farm workers and rural youth are represented in YAC by the **Rural Youth of the United States of America Conference**. *Rural Youth, U.S.A.*, serves as a coordinating force for the **Grange** youth program, the **4-H Clubs**, the **Future Farmers and Future Homemakers of America**, and the **National Junior Vegetable Growers Association**.

The American Youth Hostels represents a cross-section of youth united by the enjoyment of recreation and education found in simple modes of travel. In the United States are 200 hostels, open to youth of many organizations.

* * *

Chairman: Murray Frank

Address: 134 East 56th Street, New York 22, New York

WAY AND WFDY

The excerpt below is from The Student Internationals *by Philip G. Altbach and Norman T. Uphoff, pp. 110-111. (The Scarecrow Press, Metuchen, NJ, 1973.)*

The World Federation of Democratic Youth (WFDY) was the first international organization to appeal to youth on a world-wide and ostensibly non-political basis. Some student groups were affiliated to the WFDY, but after the founding of the IUS [See p.538], the WFDY's membership was generally limited to non-student youth. The WFDY was founded at an international conference in London in 1945 and, from the start, it was dominated by Communists. Within a year most of the non-Communist youth organizations withdrew and in 1949 the World Assembly of Youth (WAY) was founded at a meeting of more than 100 representatives of youth organizations from 37 countries.

As of 1964, WAY had representatives from 109 countries at its Assembly. WFDY and WAY function in similar manners. Both publish periodicals and sponsor various regional and international conferences. WAY has tried to keep clear of partisan politics more than WFDY has, but it is clear that both are tied to the respective sides in the Cold War, just as the international student organizations are. Both WFDY and WAY are larger than either of the student internationals [Cosec and IUS - Ed.] and include a wide range of organizations, from young farmers' groups to artists' organizations, as members. WAY is composed of national committees which represent a range of youth organizations within a particular country, while WFDY accepts affiliations from specific national youth organizations. The U. S. Youth Council is the American affiliate of WAY. There is no American member in WFDY.

Editor's note: The WFDY London Conference in 1945 was the springboard for Welleseley College's Alice Horton's later decision to form the organizing committee for the American delegation to the World Student Congress in 1946 (see pp. 68, 72).

WORLD ASSEMBLY OF YOUTH

International Organisation

In 1948 a meeting was held in London of young people from youth organisations grouped in consultative or co-ordinating bodies in the member countries of the United Nations, or where such co-ordinating bodies did not exist, the most important organisations.

The theme of the conference : The position and responsibility of young people at work and leisure » was intended to offer plenty of scope for the discussion of the general practical problems of interest to young people of every country which was to take place in ten different commissions.

At this conference the desirability of following up and intensifying the work already done was shown and the need to continue to seek adequate solutions to the problems raised in co-operation with the organisations of the United Nations. The conference decided on the creation of the World Assembly of Youth (WAY).

A meeting of the provisional Council, elected in London, was held at Ashridge in February 1949. At this meeting the Charter was drafted and arrangements were made for the definite establishment of the World Assembly of Youth.

The first proper meeting of the Council took place in Brussels from August Ist to 9th, 1949. The theme of this conference was « Young people at work : working conditions, wages, unemployment, Trade Unions, etc ». 29 countries ratified the Charter of WAY and became ordinary members. Officers and the Executive Committee were elected and four working commissions were set up.

The second meeting of the Council was held in Istanbul from August 13th to 20th, 1950. The conference dealt mainly with the problems of democratic education and illiteracy.

Who are its members ?

The members of WAY are co-ordinating committees composed of the youth organisations of various tendencies in the different countries, since successful co-operation on the international level depends on the extent to which the youth organisations have learned to work together for the benefit of all the young people of their own country.

Youth movements which wish to participate in the work of WAY must first organise themselves on the national level. A National Committee thus created may apply for admission to WAY. The Council considers the question as to whether this committee fulfils the conditions laid down in the Charter, and accepts or rejects the committee's application. Colonies or mandated territories are accepted as members of WAY on the same footing as independent countries.

Ad hoc "Young Painters USA," organized by YAC for the 1951 WAY Assembly.

WAY was the response of non-Communist youth groups in the West to provide a forum through which youth leaders could gather from emerging third world countries in Asia and Africa, as well as from Central and Latin America, and find support for their aspirations. (Above: excerpts from *WAY Forum*, June, 1951)

WORLD ASSEMBLY of YOUTH

CORNELL UNIVERSITY 1951 ITHACA, NEW YORK

Cornell Daily Sun

TUESDAY, APRIL 24, 1951

Mrs. Roosevelt to Speak Here For World Assembly of Youth

TO SPEAK HERE

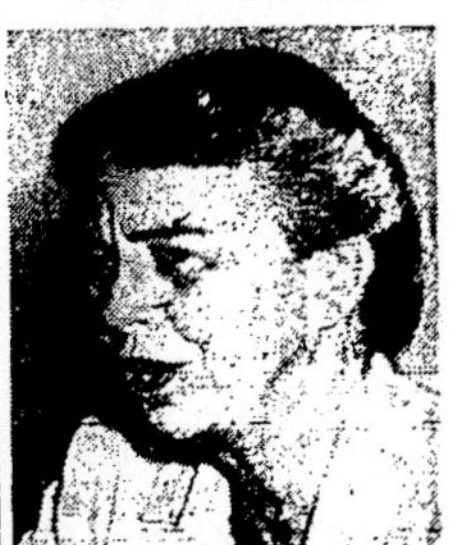

Mrs. Eleanor Roosevelt will address the 1951 General Assembly of the World Assembly of Youth to be held at Cornell Aug. 5 to 6, the Ithaca Council of Social Agencies Citizens Committee has announced.

Emphasizing the role of young people in putting into practice the principles of the United Nations Declaration of Human Rights, 500 delegates from 40 nations will gather to discuss "Youth and Human Rights."

The Young Adult Council of the National Social Welfare Assembly, representing 13 national youth organizations, is the American host to the meeting. Ithaca Council, led by Mrs. J. M. Sher-

1951 WAY ASSEMBLY ATTENDANCE

Among the sixty nations represented were the following members of WAY:

Algeria	Belgium	British Guiana	Camaroon
Canada	Dahomey	Denmark	France
Gaboon	Guinea	Gold Coast	Haute Volta
Ireland	Italy	Lebanon	Madagascar
Malta	Malaya	Martinique	Netherlands
Northern Rhodesia	Senegal	Sierra Leone	Singapore
Southern Rhodesia	Surinam	Sweden	Trinidad
Turkey	United Kingdom	United States	Union of South Africa
			Viet Nam

Additional nations included:

Alaska	India	Pakistan	Switzerland
Austria	Israel	Philippines	West Germany
Hawaii	Japan	Puerto Rico	South American Republics

Source: Young Adult Council Memorandum on the WAY General Assembly, August 1951

WAY Assembly Considers Position on Human Rights

NSA News 8/51

The student element of the American delegation to the World Assembly of Youth at Cornell University, Ithaca, N. Y., Aug. 5-17 joined with leaders of the British and French national student unions in urging that WAY take action on current problems of youth and human rights regardless of political overtones.

At the world conference on the theme "Youth and Human Rights," attended by 500 youth leaders representing 60 countries, they pushed for establishment of a precedent which they felt would at least make it possible for student groups to consider affiliation with WAY.

Against opposition from adult youth leaders, this younger faction representative of the American, British and French student unions, backed a resolution protesting the recent refusals of some Western governments to grant visas to youth wishing to attend the Berlin festival.

Purpose Achieved

Although finally the assembly adopted a milder generalized statement against infringements on student rights "in incidents of the summer", U. S. delegate Al Lowenstein (U. of North Carolina) said, "We felt we had achieved our purpose in bringing the subject to the floor for open discussion. At a conference on human rights, we cannot close our eyes to denials of student rights within our own countries.

"Even this much accomplished, offers the hope of a stronger human rights program through WAY in the future."

The 1951 assembly of WAY was the most representative gathering of officials of youth organizations in the United States since World War II. Delegates and observers in-

U.S., BRITISH AND FRENCH DELEGATES PUSHED FOR A HUMAN RIGHTS STAND. NSA's Al Lowenstein urged WAY not to soft-pedal criticism of Western visa bans to Berlin Festival.

BAILEY HALL AT CORNELL. Delegates gather informally outside the hall, and meet in formal sessions in the auditorium, August 5-17, 1951. (Photos courtesy Gil Jonas)

Program First General Assembly 1951

Youth and Human Rights . . .

The theme chosen for this First General Assembly of WAY is "Youth and Human Rights". The delegates and observers will divide into 12 workshops, each dealing with one of the subjects listed below. Under each of the workshop-titles are listed some of the problems to be discussed. Each workshop-title corresponds to one or several articles of the Universal Declaration of Human Rights, adopted and proclaimed December 10, 1948 by the General Assembly of the United Nations, and will be discussed from the point of view of the rights and duties of youth.

Human Rights Workshops

(The figures alongside the title of the workshop are the numbers of the Articles of the Universal Declaration of Human Rights to which the workshop-titles relate.)

1. Discrimination (3, 4, 5, 6, 7)
(a) Racial discrimination
(b) Slavery
(c) Status of women

2. Juvenile Delinquency (8, 9, 10, 11, 12)
(a) Legal protection
(b) Juvenile delinquency
(c) Re-education

3. Freedom of Movement (13, 14, 15, 17)
(a) Compulsory accommodation
(b) Granting of passports and visas
(c) Problems of refugees and D.P.'s

4. Family Life (16)
(a) Freedom to choose one's spouse
(b) Economic difficulties
(c) Family allowances
(d) Loans to young couples

5. Freedom of Youth Organizations (18, 19, 20)
(a) Freedom of youth movements
(b) Conditions for their existence and development

6. Citizenship (21)
(a) Citizenship rights and responsibilities for youth
(b) Education for citizenship

7. Social Security (22, 25)
(a) Housing
(b) Unemployment
(c) Social security

8. Conditions of Work (23)
(a) Conditions of work
(b) Fair wages
(c) Women's wages
(d) Participation in trade unions

9. Leisure Time (24)
(a) Holidays with pay
(b) Limitation of working hours
(c) Inclusion in working hours of the time needed for training

10. Education (26, 27)
(a) Fundamental education
(b) Democratic education
(c) Vocational training

11. World Citizenship (28)
(a) Respect for international order guaranteeing freedom and justice in all circumstances
(b) Education for peace

12. Duties and Responsibilities of Youth (29)
(a) Family, local, national and international duties
(b) Educating youth as to their rights and responsibilities

WAY Council Program—August 17-21

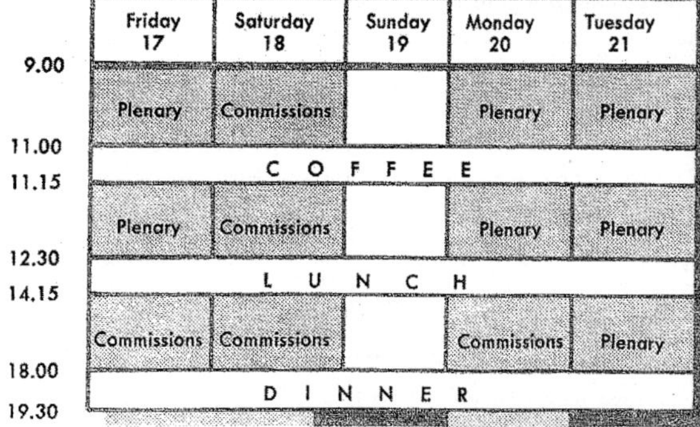

	Friday 17	Saturday 18	Sunday 19	Monday 20	Tuesday 21
9.00–11.00	Plenary	Commissions		Plenary	Plenary
11.00–11.15	C O F F E E				
11.15–12.30	Plenary	Commissions		Plenary	Plenary
12.30–14.15	L U N C H				
14.15–18.00	Commissions	Commissions		Commissions	Plenary
18.00–19.30	D I N N E R				
22.00				Plenary	

Shaded = Working Sessions
Blank = Free Time

Plenary sessions: Memorial Room, Willard Straight Hall. Commissions: Rooms to be announced.

WAY
WORLD ASSEMBLY OF YOUTH
ASSEMBLEE MONDIALE de la JEUNESSE
15, rue d'Arlon, Brussels, Belgium. Cable address: WAYOUTH, Brussels

OFFICERS
of the World Assembly of Youth 1950-1951

Chairman:	*Maurice Sauvé, Canada*
Vice-Chairman:	*T. C. Cuu, Viet Nam*
Vice-Chairman:	*G. Kreveld, Belgium*
Treasurer:	*John Frankenburg, United Kingdom*
Secretary General:	*F. P. Mercereau*
Assistant Secretary General:	*Helen Dale*

Executive Committee:
J. Annan (Gold Coast), A. Areski (Algeria), Mlle. E. Arnould (Belgium), Mlle. M. Carosi (Italy), D. Evans (Canada), E. M. Howell (U.S.A.), J. Joussellin (France), P. Keegan (United Kingdom), J. Larsen (Denmark), A. Lawrence (Guinea), R. Montagne (France), M. Tascioglu (Turkey), Miss M. Vendrik (Netherlands).

WAY Charter, Article II: Aims

a) WAY is established in order that Youth itself may study and focus attention on its needs and responsibilities. WAY is dedicated to the service of youth everywhere, and, as a democratic organization, to work through national voluntary youth organizations for the true satisfaction of youth's needs and for the fulfillment of youth's responsibilities.

b) WAY recognizes the Universal Declaration of Human Rights as the basis of its action and of its services.

c) In the achievement of its aims, WAY shall seek:

1. to increase inter-racial respect and to foster international understanding and co-operation;
2. to facilitate the collection of information about the needs and problems of Youth;
3. to disseminate information about the methods, techniques and activities of Youth Organizations;
4. to promote the interchange of ideas between Youth of all countries;
5. to assist in the development of Youth activities and to promote, by mutual aid, the extension of the work of the Voluntary Youth Organizations;
6. to encourage young people to take a full measure of responsibility, both in their own organizations and in the life of the Society as a whole;
7. to establish and maintain relations with international organizations, both voluntary and governmental;
8. to co-operate in the development of National Consultative Committees of Voluntary Youth Organizations.

Excerpted from the program booklet, "First Triennial General Assembly, World Assembly of Youth, Cornell University, Ithaca, N.Y." (Source: Library of Congress. See Almanac, p. 1128, for other assemblies.)

A postwar major political force and source of leadership

2. The SDA-NSA Connection

Seymour Reisin
City College of New York
Executive Secretary, Students for Democratic Action, 1950–51

While reviewing my files as a prelude to writing this article, I uncovered a folder issued to each registered delegate at the first annual convention of Americans for Democratic Action, held in Philadelphia in February of 1948. Following the pattern of many entranced teenagers then and now I, too, engaged in the sport of snaring "name" autographs. Though the ink on the folder has faded in the past half century, I can still identify the autographs of Eleanor Roosevelt, Arthur Schlesinger, Jr., Walter Reuther, David Dubinsky, Clarence Streit, and Elmer Davis. These were just a handful of the hundreds of Roosevelt "New Dealers," labor union luminaries, academics, religious figures, elected officials, community leaders, and high school and college students—representing the Students for Democratic Action, the student affiliate of Americans for Democratic Action (ADA)—who had gathered to carry forth the torch of progress initiated by Franklin Delano Roosevelt in 1932.

Serving as a student delegate from the City College of New York at the 1948 ADA convention represented for me the culmination of a difficult journey through the nether world of left-wing ideology. Raised by a mother whose teenage years were spent toiling in the clothing manufacturing sweatshops of New York, whose political outlook had been molded by the 1911 Triangle Shirt Waist Company fire and the "Bread and Roses" strike held in 1912 by 10,000 textile workers in Lawrence, Massachusetts, it is no surprise that my political inculcation included the sanctification of the Marxist-Leninist theory and practice ordained by Stalinist Russia.

When I entered City College in February of 1946, it was as one in an unusual freshman cohort, consisting of seventeen-year-olds and veterans returning with the experiences of the just-concluded World War II. My exposure to this group and to the famed political sophisticates of the CCNY cafeteria alcoves—brilliantly evoked by Joseph Dorman's recent prize-winning film, *Arguing the World*—led to a painful, yearlong reconsideration of political tenets that viewed Western democracy as a tool for the suppression of vast populations by a capitalist cabal and an insistence upon centralized political control as a precursor for any societal improvement. With this background I entered a world basically devoid of cant and infused with reason. Such was my personal history as I arrived as a delegate to the 1948 ADA convention.

SDA born at ADA convention of 1948

Students participated in the activities of the Convention with their leaders, Don Willner, national chairman of SDA, and William Leuchtenburg, executive secretary of SDA, moving confidently among the array of star personalities. From the initial establishment of ADA and SDA, the mutual relationship was one wherein students, while functioning with their own independent National Board, were also allocated seats on the parent ADA National Board and the SDA Executive Secretary attended and participated in all meetings of the ADA National Executive Committee. With SDA dues at a nominal level, funding for student staff, literature, and operational expenses were absorbed completely by ADA. Sharing of space in the national office in Washington and the regional office in New York made available to the SDA leadership the skills of the ADA lobbyists, public relations experts, and research staff. Rarely, if ever, did a conflict over fundamental policy develop between ADA and its student affiliate, SDA.

Why did ADA/SDA become a major political force during the postwar period when Harry Truman held the presidency from 1945 to 1953? Practically all ADA/SDA adherents were at least nominally affiliated with the Democratic Party. What outlooks or viewpoints did these people share that could not be realized through the Democratic Party? During that period, power in both houses of Congress resided with conservative southern Democrats and isolationist Midwest Republicans. With voting in the South restricted to whites only, a Southern Democrat, once elected to Congress, could look forward to decades of tenure and seniority on major congressional committees. Such a setting did not augur well for the labor-liberal alliance that had developed during the Truman years.

The programmatic goals of this alliance, developed at the founding of ADA/SDA, included an aggressive foreign policy that recognized the emerging Soviet threat, with full support given to the Marshall Plan and The Truman Doctrine; the organizing of political and social forces to end the racial discrimination and segregation that characterized many regions and activities in the United States; the completion of a successful drive to eliminate the vestiges of communist and "fellow traveler" activity, which had hobbled many liberal causes, organizations, and unions; support for the emerging United Nations; the development of state, local, and collegiate chapters to galvanize political action and education; and an aggressive response to a spreading national pattern of loyalty oaths and the phenomenon that came to be known as McCarthyism.

SDA interacts with and provides leaders for NSA

Though SDAers were attracted to ADA's commitment to national social and political issues, this did not result in a rejection of, or lack of interest in a companion development, the emergence of the National Student Association. NSA and SDA, respectively, went through planning stages in 1946-1947, culminating in first annual conventions by both organizations in 1948. In mid-1947, the national chairman of SDA, Don Willner, in an article widely distributed at NSA's founding convention in Madison, listed a series of issues for consideration by NSA, including full participation by minority groups; refusing to become a sounding board for sectarian philosophies; the development of creative curriculum patterns at colleges in response to the needs of the postwar age; international student cooperation; academic freedom; an organizational structure composed of a confederation of local student councils combined with balanced geographic representation; and the avoidance of domination by any political, religious or social groups. These were all worthy issues for consideration. Whether these issues were accepted as goals and subsequently realized is a question that undoubtedly will be addressed by other articles in this anthology.

Both organizations—NSA and SDA—served as vessels for the maturation of individuals who, in subsequent years, held positions of significant responsibility in politics, education, law, public service, and industry. It was a group distinctive because of its age range and life experience, with many having served in World War II but others barely emerging from their teens. While interacting with one another, this unique population provided leadership, not only for NSA and SDA, but also for the Student World Federalists, the American Veterans Committee, and Catholic student groups entering the national arena for the first time. As a precursor of a revolution that did not emerge until the 1960s, both NSA and SDA had significant female and African American leadership, a development in sharp contrast to the pre–World War II student groups.[1]

Examining SDA leaders who went on to prominence

An examination of the leadership that emerged from SDA is worthy of consideration and may provide an impetus for the current generation of college students. Besides Willner, whose writings impacted upon the early planning days of NSA, SDA staff and senior officers included William Leuchtenburg, an eminent Roosevelt scholar and past president of the American Historical Association; Charles Sellers, a recognized historian of the James Polk presidency; Albert Churchill Ettinger, a World War I historian; Matthew Holden, Jr., professor of government and foreign affairs and president-elect (at this writing) of the American Political Science Association; Doug Kelley, who formulated the philosophical underpinnings of the International Development Placement Association, a precursor of the Peace Corps[2]; Steven Muller, president emeritus at the Paul H. Nitze School, Johns Hopkins University; Walter "Fritz" Mondale, former vice president of the United States; William Shore, head of the New York–New Jersey Regional Planning Association; Franklin Wallick of the United Automobile Workers; Jane Wilder Jacqz of the United Nations; Kenneth Kurtz and Robert Trentlyon, both in public information, the former a radio news director, the latter a publisher of community weeklies; Alex Pope, the director of the California Citizens Budget Commission; Marvin Rich, the key administrator of the Congress of Racial Equality; Congressman Sander Levin and Senator Carl Levin; Allard Lowenstein, president of NSA and later the national chair of ADA; Dick Murphy, president of NSA and assistant postmaster general; Walter Carrington, former American ambassador to Nigeria; Michael Dukakis, former governor of Massachusetts and Democratic Party presidential nominee; Galen Martin, the publisher of the *National Fair Housing Advocate* and the executive director of the Kentucky Fair Housing Council; and Evelyn Jones Rich, currently executive director of the Rubin Foundation and formerly a dean at Hunter College.[3]

Leadership reveals itself not only within the parameters of organizational goals, policies and activities; leadership may emerge singularly when organizational response is lethargic or inadequate. From the perspective of hindsight, it appears the responses of NSA and ADA/SDA to loyalty oaths and McCarthyism were inadequate.[4] Here, the actions of individuals were crucial, in particular, the television broadcasts of

Edward R. Murrow who, in his collegiate days, had served as president of the National Student Federation of America,[5] and the forceful, graceful comments of attorney Joseph Welch at the congressional McCarthy hearings. Among students, the actions of Lloyd McAulay, then the SDA representative to the ADA National Board and the chair of the civil liberties panel at the 1950 NSA convention in Ann Arbor, Michigan, provided a sense of direction for others. McAulay, now an attorney in New York, whose four-year grueling and successful struggle to reverse his discharge for security reasons by the U.S. Navy Department—an incident that impacted upon a subsequent Supreme Court decision— served as a warning to government bureaucrats and as emotional support for those in the midst of contemplating a similar counterattack to the emergence of government-led actions to limit the civil liberties and civil rights of the citizenry.

Readers will recognize many of the individuals mentioned above, a significant number of whom participated simultaneously in positioning SDA and NSA as primary vehicles for different forms of students advocacy during the decade following World War II, which was a time of unique challenge for American students. Today, these former student leaders continue to serve.

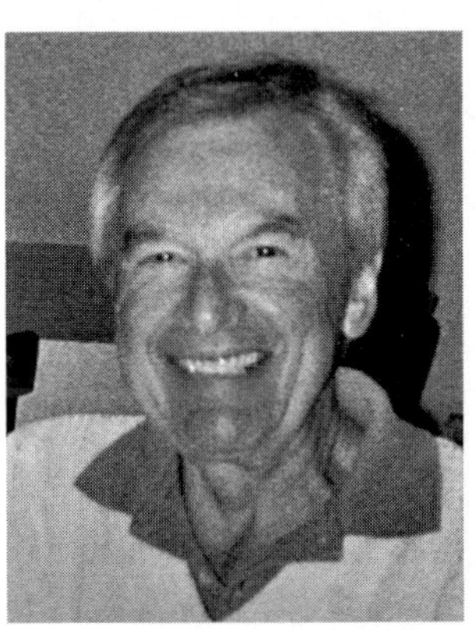

Seymour Reisin served as Executive Secretary of Students for Democratic Action in 1950, during which time he participated as an observer at the NSA convention in Ann Arbor, Michigan. In 1965, while serving as Acting National Secretary of American Friends of Vietnam, he participated once again as an observer at the NSA convention in Madison, Wisconsin. During the decades of the 1970s and 1980s, while serving as Dean of Continuing Education, Grants and Development at the Bronx Community College of the City University of New York, Reisin brought the college to national recognition as a creative developer of community-based manpower training programs centered in minority and poverty-afflicted geographic areas. Currently, he serves as a board member of the American Festival for the Arts in Houston, Texas, and the Rosen Scholars Fund in New York. He lives in the Yorkville area of New York City with his wife, Joan Wooters, an actress and film editor. His three children, now adults, also live in New York City.

END NOTES

[1] See "Women and NSA," p. 489, and "The South, Civil Rights and Segregation," p. 419.

[2] See Kelley, p. 623.

[3] *Editor's note:* A number of the leaders mentioned here appear in this work. See Jacqz, p. 618, Kurtz, pp. 306 and 902, Pope, p. 390, Rich, p. 461, Lowenstein, p. 283, Murphy, pp. 785, 973 and 1080, and Martin, p, 983. Murphy also observes, "Among the leading ADA influences on NSA were Eleanor Roosevelt and Frank Graham [former University of North Carolina president], both of whom were longtime active NSA Advisory Board members." See Roosevelt, p. 40, and Graham, p. 979.

[4] *Editor's note:* See also Brown, p. 381. In a note to the anthology editor, Dick Murphy, 1951-52 NSA President, contributed the following additional observation:

> While NSA's response to loyalty oaths and McCarthyism might have been "inadequate," as Reisin says, it certainly was not because the effort wasn't made. Al Lowenstein [1950-51 NSA president], Bill Dentzer [1951-52 NSA President], and myself spoke out consistently and frequently against McCarthy and loyalty oaths over the 1950-1953 period (e.g., my speech before the *Philadelphia Bulletin* Forum and my front page article in the *Daily Tar Heel* at UNC, copies of which are in the archives). We made enough of a noise to attract the attacks of national radio commentator Fulton Lewis, Jr., and Martha Roundtree (of Meet the Press fame), and Students for America president Robert Munger [see Munger, p. 805], not to mention Senator Willis Smith (D-NC), a former president of the American Bar Association, who reported to the State Department that I was the head of the Communist Party in Chapel Hill (while I was serving on the U.S. National Commission for UNESCO).

Murphy continues, "NSA stood virtually alone in supporting AAUP's stand on academic freedom, against loyalty oaths, and defending the right of Communists to teach if otherwise academically qualified."

[5] See Murrow, p. 26.

PICTURE CREDITS: *Then:* c. 1950, (Author). *Now:* October, 1997, New York City (Schwartz)

From *ADA World*, 2/16/49 (excerpts)

Mondale New Staff Chief

WASHINGTON- Bill Shore, National Chairman, announced the appointment of Fritz Mondale of Macalaster College, St. Paul, as Executive Secretary of SDA, to fill the vacancy left by the resignation of Jane Wilder.[1]

At 21, Fritz assumes his office as Executive Secretary with considerable expertise in politics, both on the student level and in actual campaigning. He has been in SDA since its founding in Washington in 1947.

After organizing the Macalaster College chapter he helped set up the Minnesota SDA Region, of which he was Chairman at the time of his appointment. He was one of the leaders in the student group which helped oust the extremist groups from control of the Democratic Farmer-Labor Party, and during the last campaign also managed the DFL efforts in the 2d District.

A Junior at Macalaster,[2] majoring in Poitical Science, he has been selected as a member of Student Project for Amity Among Nations[3] and will go to England this summer to study the Labour Party. At the time of his appointment, Fritz headed the Minnesota Student Lobby Group which marked an entirely new approach to student activity in state legislatures.

Jane Wilder is returning to school after a year and a half as Field Secretary and Executive Secretary...Jane has held the position as Executive Secretary since Bill Leuchtenburg resigned to take a position with the Massachusetts ADA.

[1] See Wilder (Jacqz), p. 618.

[2] *Editor's note:* Walter "Fritz" Mondale received his B.A. degree in 1951 from the U. of Minnesota, served in the U.S. Army, graduated U. of Minnesota Law School in 1958 and served as Minnesota Attorney General from 1960-1964. He was then appointed Senator to replace Hubert Humphrey, who was elected Vice President. He was returned to the Senate in 1966 and 1972. In 1976 he was elected Vice President under Jimmy Carter, serving one term. He ran against Ronald Reagan for President in 1984. He later served as U.S. Ambassador to Japan.

[3] SPAN was launched at Carleton College. See Medalie, p. 935.

Students for Democratic Action (SDA)

PROVIDING A FOCUS FOR ANTI-COMMUNIST LIBERALS

Students to Meet In Washington

The first national convention of the newly-formed Students for Democratic Action will be held in Washington March 28-30 to set up a program and organization for independent liberal college students throughout the nation.

SDA, an ... United States ... is setting up ... conformity wi... Americans for ... which is head... Leon Henders... Wyatt.

Both ADA ... cated to the ta... nation's progr... lation, protect... and extending ...

VASSAR MISCELLANY NEWS

S.D.A. Formulates Progressive Platform To Reach Goals Of Full Employment, International Cooperation, And Civil Liberty

The Vassar chapter of Students for Democratic Action has issued its platform for 1948. It is divided into four sections: campus, community, national and international. On the campus SDA wants to work for federal aid in college education, abolition of racial and religious quotas in admission, support of NSA, Student Cooperati... right of ... ning for full employment, a tax program based on ability to pay, a national health program, the maintenance of rights of labor and repeal of the Taft-Hartley Act, extension of Social Security, establishment of Fair Employment Practices Commission, voluntary recruiting instead of compulsory military training, a nat...

Tonight at 7:30 there will be a meeting of SDA in the Hoot under the leadership of Nini Almy '49, President. There will be a discussion of the Marshall Plan and a new co-op booth on the campus.

Hearts, Flowers . . .

SDA GROUP IS ORGANIZED

"To fulfill the need for political action by liberal students, aware of their responsibility to participate actively in their government, Liberal Association, a new political group on campus has been organized this spring by fifteen students," ... Fischler, 1949, president. ... Shaw, 1948, has been elec...

Practical Politics Discussed By SDA

A round table discussion on "Practical Politics" was sponsored by the Students for Democratic Action on Friday, December 16, uptown. Mr. Walpin, of the Soc... of the Republican county of Westchester. Dr. Davis, a Democrat, said that his party "hasn't won anything in Westchester in thirty years." He spoke lightly of the "mass rallies" he attended, say...

SDA Backs Liberal Action

A chapter of Students for Democratic Action has been organized on the campus of Western Reserve University and a charter has been granted to the local organization by the national group. Students for Democratic Action is an affiliate of Americans for Democratic Action, a group whose membership includes such well-known liberals as Senator Paul Douglas, Walter Reuther, Mrs. Eleanor Roosevelt, Hubert Humphrey, Chester Bowles, and Reinhold Niebuhr. ... ganized with the following purposes in mind:

1. To provide responsible liberals on the WRU campus with an opportunity for political expression and political activity.

SDA Plans Initial Meeting Today In Todd Library Lounge

Students for Democratic Action, Rochester Chapter, will meet to organize in the second-floor lounge of Todd Union this afternoon, November 5, at 4:45.

SDA is affiliated with Americans for Democratic Action, of which Arth... historian an... in Cutler U... co-founder.

All who ... dom and eco... unwilling t... ism or rea... to attend t...

SDA Makes Plans For Future

The Hopkins chapter of the Students for Democratic Action plans to get under way in the near future, executive secretary Robert Blunno announced this week.

(Above, from top left: Lobo, U. of New Mexico, 2/4/47; "Formulates," Vassar *Miscellany News*, 2/11/48; "Group," Smith C. *SCAN* 4/25/47; "Practical," *Hunter Arrow*, 1/6/50; "Plans," U. of Rochester *Campus*, 11/5/48; "Liberal," Cleveland, Case Western *Reserve Tribune*, 2/17/50; "Future," Johns Hopkins *News-Letter*, 11/12/48

The wartime US Student Assembly (See p. 34) affiliated with the newly formed Americans for Democratic Action in March 1947 and changed its name to SDA. SDA launched an aggressive organizing campaign across the country. William Leuchtenburg (Cornell. See p. 50) first SDA Exec Sec'y, carried over from the USSA, and attended NSA's Constitutional Convention.

SDA LEADERSHIP LINKS

Staff Plans Organizing Tour

WALTER MONDALE (Macalaster C. MN), 1949 SDA Exec. Sec'y with Field Sec'y Norma Dinnerstein. (See p.771).

Hold Staff Discussion

SEYMOUR REISIN (CCNY), 1950 SDA Exec. Sec'y. with Field Organizer Ralph Dummit. (See p. 769).

Two national NSA presidents were active SDA members. Al Lowenstein, '51-52 (See p. 283), and Dick Murphy '52-53 (See p. 1075), both from U. of NC. Also a number of regional Chairs, including Merrill Freed (U. of Chicago, IL), Galen Martin (Berea, KY. See p. 983), and Ken Kurtz (Swarthmore, PA. See p. 902.). Douglas Kelley (Berea), '50-51 National SDA Chair, was the founder of IDPA (see p. 623)

Al Lowenstein of SDA Is New NSA President

(By a Prominent Midwestern SDA Member)

ANN ARBOR, Mich.—The results of this year's National Student Association Congress at the University of Michigan look good to liberals. The new officers, with SDAer Al Lowenstein as President, and to a lesser extent the policy for 1950-51, are left of center.

Four out of the five new officers might be classed as liberals in the ADA sense of the word. Joining Senator Graham's former secretary, Al Lowenstein, who was elected by a margin of about 6-1, are Herbert Eisenberg of M. I. T. as International Vice-President, Harold Goldsmith, U. of Wisconsin, as Educational Problems Vice-President, and Shirley Neizer, Simmons College, Mass., as Executive Secretary. A more conservative note is struck by the new Student-Life Vice-President, Elmer Brock of LaSalle College, Penn. This group of officers should be able to provide NSA with liberal leadership.

In the policy field liberals won a rather hollow victory by retaining the present Student Bill of Rights, mainly due to the fact that the agenda was too crowded to allow a vote on a substitute that had been prepared. There was a strong drive at the Congress to head the Bill with a preamble setting forth a "natural rights" basis for the existence of students'

Murphy Elected President of SDA

Dick Murphy, rising senior from Baltimore, Maryland, was elected President of the Students For Democratic Action Tuesday night. Murphy succeeds Bob Lindsay as chairman of the junior ADA group on the campus.

Other officers elected to the slate for the coming year include Dewey Hinkle, vice-president; Nat Magruder, Secretary and John Harris, Treasurer.

The members elected at large to the steering committee were Bob Hennessee, Jack McCall, and Harry Sherrill.

Above: From left, *ADA World*, 2/16/49, 10/50; *Daily Tar Heel*, 5/19/49.

NSA as Seen by SDA in 1947: In Hope

By Don S. Willner, *National Chairman, S.D.A., 1947* (Excerpts from *The Student Progressive*, 9/47, Harvard)

A National Student Association of the United States is a great dream which has been only glimpsed by students for many years. But dreams have a tendency to get blurred. In the long nine-day session facing us here at Madison, let us try to keep clearly in mind just what we want to accomplish and what sort of NSA we want to bring into being. Here are some ideas which may merit consideration:

I. The National Student Association must include all students of the United States, regardless of race, religion, sex, section of the country, or political and economic belief…

II. The NSA must be a non-partisan service organization, not a political group….the NSA must decidedly not become a group with a viewpoint. Instead of uniting fewer students under a broad area of agreement, the NSA should unite all students under a narrow area of agreement …The NSA must not become a sounding board for a [philosophy].

III. The NSA must encourage full international student cooperation. This means student exchange, student travel, student relief, and working together with students to solve common problems…

IV. The NSA…must fight for academic freedom, for student rights, and for the goal of ending discrimination…

V. The NSA must be built squarely on the foundation of the local student council….

VI. The NSA must be internally democratic….

VII. The NSA must remain representative of the students of the nation.

SDA as Seen by NSA in 1951: In Crisis

Report by Merril Freed, U. of Chicago, NSA Observer at the 4th Annual Convention, SDA, Berea, KY (Excerpts)

Merril Freed
U. of Chicago
NSA IL Chair, 49-50
(Photo: c. 1951, Lynch)

SDA, as a liberal student organization on a national level, faces many of the same problems as does NSA. Its answers, however, are not always the same. Thus a motion to institute the penny rule was defeated 18-15 despite a vigorous speech in its favor by Frank Logan (U. of Chicago).

SDA, as NSA, may be close to collapse.[1] The small size of the convention is perhaps symptomatic. But no Bill Birenbaum rose to voice stern criticism or sober warning. And I heard fear expressed by only a very few delegates. It is difficult to account for this optimism. Perhaps SDA is counting on a revival come the '52 campaign. Perhaps it feels secure in the knowledge that it is connected with a strong adult group—ADA.

The convention itself was quite good, and the caliber of leadership elected fairly high. Berea was a perfect location for a conference—the delegates were thrown together for the entire four days, and group dynamics ran rampant.[2] There was more preoccupation with organizational problems than usual. Some delegates were worried about the use of the word "progressive" in the SDA constitution. But despite all these drawbacks, I left with the pleased feeling that SDA was still a liberal organization (at least as far as domestic affairs of academic import are concerned).

[1] See Dentzer, p. 299. *Editor's note:* That summer NSA slashed its budget and moved to Colorado for free rent.

[2] See Berea, p. 987 *Editor's note:* Group Dynamics was the alternative to parliamentary procedure NSA introduced in 1947. See pp. 335, 344.

The NSA Connection

The Young Democratic Clubs of America, 1932-60

Richard J. Murphy
University of North Carolina, NSA President 1952-53
Executive Secretary, Young Democratic Clubs of America, 1955-60

TThe Young Democratic Clubs of America (YDCA) claims to be the oldest political youth organization in America. It was recognized as the "official youth organization of the Democratic Party" by Democratic National Chairman James A. Farley, who was Franklin D. Roosevelt's campaign chairman, at the Chicago Democratic National Convention in June, 1932. The founding dinner was addressed by Dr. Robert Hutchins, youthful President of the University of Chicago; Admiral Richard Byrd, Antarctic explorer, and Will Rogers, renowned American humorist. F.D.R., Jr. was chosen as the first national treasurer, with Tyre Taylor of North Carolina as first president. Throughout the thirties and forties the Young Democrats, primarily an organization of young adults 21 to 39 years of age, met with and was addressed frequently by Presidents Roosevelt and Truman, whose programs and policies were strongly supported by the national Y.D. organization.

The YDCA, which nationally was even more liberal than the senior Democratic Party, nonetheless had several conservative state organizations and comparatively few college clubs until the late 1950s. YDCA claimed a membership of 600,000 persons and held 12 biennial national conventions from 1932 to 1959, which were addressed by the top national Democratic leaders of that period. During World War II, national conventions were not held, and a young woman, Dorothy Vredenburg (later Bush) of Alabama, who became the longest-serving national officer of any political party (48 years as national secretary of the Democratic National Committee), served as national YDCA president.

While Young Democrats were active at the state, college and local levels supporting Democratic candidates for local, state and national office, no permanent national office existed for the direction and coordination of Y.D. efforts until Democratic National Chairman Paul M. Butler established the Young Democratic division of the National Committee in 1955, of which the Y.D.C.A. was to become an integral part. I was named by Paul Butler as executive director of the division and was also designated by Y.D.C.A. President David A. Bunn (a delegate to the 1946 Chicago founding conference of NSA from Texas Christian University) as National Executive Secretary of the Y.D.C.A. Butler had first met me in 1954, while appearing as a guest on Ruth Hagy's A.B.C. College News conference, produced in conjunction with N.S.A.

Former NSA Presidents join National Democratic Committee staffs.

This was not the only time an N.S.A. national officer had played a prominent role in the Democratic National Committee. Allard K. Lowenstein, N.S.A. president in 1950-51, was brought into the National Committee headquarters for the presidential campaign of 1952 as National Chairman of Students for Stevenson, of which I was vice chairman. Later, in 1957-58, Bill Welsh, NSA's first President in 1947-48, served the National Democractic Committee as Research Director in 1957-58, and as Executive Director from 1965-71.

During the late 1950s, Young Democratic activities greatly accelerated, with the YDCA national president addressing the 1956 Democratic National Convention, providing testimony before the Democratic Platform Committee and traveling with the Stevenson presidential campaign of that year throughout the nation.

In 1957, the 25th Anniversary YDCA dinner at the Washington Mayflower Hotel honored Speaker Sam Rayburn and featured as speakers, Senators Hubert Humphrey (MN), Henry Jackson (WA) and Russell Long (LA) as well as Chairman Butler.

In 1958, the Young Democrats, led by President Nelson Lancione of Ohio, joined forces with the Young Republican National Federation in an unprecedented action, journeying to Paris to form, in conjunction with young political leaders from several European nations, the Atlantic Conference of Political Youth Leaders as part of the North Atlantic Treaty Organization. This was followed by a tour of several NATO capitals and many subsequent NATO political youth meetings in Europe and America in later years.

The 1959 YDCA national convention in Toledo, Ohio featured addresses by Senator Hubert Humphrey (MN) and Governor G. Mennen Williams of Michigan, both Y.D. favorites, a parade through downtown Toledo and a final memorable "Give-Em-Hell" address by former President Harry S. Truman before 2000 enthusiastic Young Democratic diners at the Sports Arena.

YDCA Officers become national leaders

A number of YDCA officers were elected during the fifties who later became well-known Democratic Party leaders, including Neal Smith (Cong. IA.), Phillip Burton (Cong. CA.), Patsy Mink (Cong. HI), Allan Howe (Cong. Utah), Dave Bunn (Assistant to President Johnson), Frank Church (Senator, Idaho), Maurice Gravel (Senator, Alaska) and Joseph Tydings (Senator, MD.).

In 1959, a National Student Chairman, Chuck Manatt, a former N.S.A. delegate from Iowa State, was selected to expand Y.D. college and high school activities in preparation for the upcoming 1960 campaign (over 200 new college chapters were established in 1959-60). Manatt (who many years later was to become National Democratic Chairman and U.S. ambassador) in 1960 became Acting Director of the Young Democrats Division, temporarily replacing me, when I was designated by Chairman Butler as Director of Democratic Platform Hearings for the 1960 National Convention in Los Angeles. In 1961, Manatt was succeeded as National College chairman by Jim Hunt of N.C. State University, who was later to become the longest-serving governor of North Carolina (16 years).

In the last half of the 1950s the Young Democrats gave strong support to Chairman Paul Butler and the creation of the Democratic Advisory Council, which played such an important role in drafting the 1960 Democratic platform, which in turn became the basis of the New Frontier program of President John F. Kennedy. Young Democrats played a major role in the presidential campaign of Senator John F. Kennedy, who carried young voters overwhelmingly in 1960, and gave strong support to the cause of civil rights long before that became the official policy of the Democratic Party.

The Young Democrats Young Voters Division of the 1960 Kennedy campaign also pressed for inclusion in his campaign of the original Kennedy proposal for the creation of a "Peace Corps", also championed by the N.S.A. (See Part 3, Section 4).

Finally in the late 1950s, the Y.D.C.A. boasted that the Democratic Party had elected the 19 youngest U.S. senators, the 12 youngest congressmen and 9 of the 12 youngest governors. Astonishingly, 4 of them, Hollings of SC; Byrd of W.VA.; Dingell of Mich.; and Mink of HI, are still in public office.

Richard J. Murphy has been an active participant in the Washington scene for over 45 years as an assistant cabinet officer, corporate executive and political leader. He was Deputy Postmaster General during the Kennedy and Johnson administrations. He recently retired as the Washington, D.C.–based Legislative Representative for Unisys.

Weakness on campus of Young Democrats and Young Republicans in the thirties and forties

Looking back one wonders why the Y.D.C.A. (as well as the Young Republicans) were so relatively weak on campuses (with a few notable exceptions) in the thirties and forties as compared to other political organizations (such as the S.D.A., Federalists or Y.A.F.) in the post WWII era. I believe that there are several reasons:

1. Most college students could not vote because of age (under 21).
2. Many college campuses prohibited partisan political speakers and activities (speaker's bans).
3. Many college students saw little or no connection between political parties and their interests in issues of war and peace, federal aid to education, housing and civil rights until the late forties, when they formed organizations dedicated or opposed largely to specific, as opposed to general, political interests and issues (C.C.U.N.; World Federalists, N.A.A.C.P.; S.D.A.; Y.A.F.; C.O.R.E.; S.F.A.; AMVETS, etc.)
4. All too often both senior Democratic and Republican officials, as well as their young adult groups (the Y.D.C.A. and the Y.R.N.F.) did not encourage the formation of college chapters, because of their "unsettling" and transient effects on local party organizations and issues. College Y.D. and Y.R. groups tended in most cases to exist only in presidential campaign years and then go out of business.

The nineteen fifties saw a big change in almost all these matters, energized earlier by the returning veterans, singed by the war experience and financed by the G.I. bill.

Editor's note: Sylvia Bacon, 1951-52 NSA Vice President for Student Affairs, recalls in 7/29/02 letter, "In 1949-52 there were very vigorous Young Dems and Young Repubs. As I recall the national conventions of each party in this era, both had big youth contingents. . . . Indeed I took issue with Time *magazine's identification of me and my fellow students as "The Silent Generation." It occurs to me that some student leaders may not have been as deep into party politics as I was because on some campuses a political party affiliation like a sorority or fraternity affiliation may have affected student body president election results. However, at Vassar, which colors my recollections of the pertinent years, we had a League of Women Voters posture. Young Dems and Young Repubs had little to do with student government elections or other student issues. Party political clubs had about the same relationship to student government as the stamp club or the swim club." (See Bacon, p. 474; caption, p. 759).*

RICHARD J. MURPHY

Early years and education. Dick Murphy was born on October 15, 1929, in Baltimore, MD, and attended high school at Baltimore City College. A Phi Beta Kappa graduate of the University of North Carolina at Chapel Hill, he was a member of the Golden Fleece (the highest honorary society) and President of the North Carolina State Student Legislature. In 1952, he was elected national president of the United States National Student Association.

Career highlights and government service. Dick Murphy has been an active participant in the Washington scene for over 45 years as an Assistant Cabinet Officer, corporate executive and political leader. During that time he has held public office under four Presidents of the United States, attended 17 national political conventions; participated in seven national presidential campaigns, authored the original Peace Corps proposal of President John F. Kennedy (See Pt3S4); ended segregation in the U.S. Post Office; served as a key leader in the establishment of collective negotiations for employees in the Federal government; gave the opening testimony before Congress for the creation of the U.S. Postal Service as a government corporation; was among the first to help secure public financing of national political conventions and presidential campaigns; and served as a target of attack for the Watergate conspirators in 1972.

Additionally, he has served on a number of presidential, cabinet, bipartisan and non-governmental committees and commissions; chaired or served on several American delegations to foreign conferences in Europe, Canada and South America. He holds the Benjamin Franklin (highest) award of the U.S. Post Office Department and numerous other awards and honors.

In government, Mr. Murphy served as a public member of the U.S. National Commission for UNESCO in the State Department under Presidents Truman and Eisenhower. From 1961-69 he was U.S. Assistant Postmaster General under Presidents Kennedy and Johnson, serving as one of two principal officials running the day-to-day operations of 45,000 local post offices with over 700,000 employees.

Politics. In politics, Mr. Murphy was the first Director of the Young Democrats division and Assistant to the Chairman of the Democratic National Committee; an Associate Editor of the Democratic Digest; Director of Platform Committee Hearings of the 1960 Democratic National Convention and National Coordinator for Young Voters of the Kennedy-Johnson Presidential Campaign. From 1970-73 he served as a member of the Democratic Policy Council and in 1972 was elected Director of Convention Activities (now Chief Executive Officer) of the 1972 Democratic National Convention in Miami Beach. In 1975-76 he was National Campaign Manager of the Presidential campaign of Ambassador Sargent Shriver.

Mr. Murphy has attended every Democratic National Convention since 1952 and has known, with two exceptions, every Democratic national chairman since Jim Farley, President Roosevelt's campaign manager. He has met every President since Harry Truman, and knew Eleanor Roosevelt well. He headed the Democratic Observer Delegation to three Republican National Conventions.

Business: In business, Mr. Murphy has been Executive Consultant to Harbridge House, a Boston-based think tank, where he co-authored and edited a book on public employee labor relations, has served as Vice President of Warner Cable (TV) Corporation and for almost 23 years was Director of Government or Legislative Affairs for Unisys and its predecessor companies, Sperry Univac and Sperry Corporation, where he specialized in the federal budget and its relationship to state and local governments. He has also served as a corporate fellow of the National Governors Association.

Editor's note: The following are additional essays by Dick Murphy in this Anthology: "NSA, Point 4 and the Peace Corps," p. 630; "North Carolina Leading NSA in the Region," p. 952; "From Boulder to Philadelphia," p. 1075; "In the Name of Freedom," p. 1080; "Strengthening the Forces of Freedom," p. 1082.

A link in the chain of efforts to enlist student support for Communist political aims

3. American Youth for Democracy and Its Genesis

Seymour Reisin
City College of New York
Executive Secretary, Students for Democratic Action, 1950

Editor's note: In this review and memoir, the author traces the efforts of the Communist Party in the U.S., and through it the apparatus of international communism, to control or influence the agenda of U.S. student organizations before and after World War II. During NSA's founding years, the American Youth for Democracy, while actually small in numbers of chapters and membership, was vigorously opposed by both students and administrations on many campuses and, as a consequence, frequently denied charters, thus becoming a disproportionate but emblematic subject of student rights and academic freedom campaigns nationally and on various campuses. The author explores the basis for the appeal of the Communist left for so many talented student leaders of that era. He draws on his own experience as an AYD member during his high school years, extensive research in preparation for this piece (see author's Afterword), and the documentation assembled by the NSA Anthology Project.

On May15, 1943, several months after the Soviet Union's triumph at Stalingrad, subsequently recognized as the pivotal moment of World War II, Joseph Stalin, the Soviet dictator, ordered the dissolution of the Comintern,[1] the structure composed of the communist parties of all nations. Its stated purpose, the promotion of world revolution, did not, for the moment, justify Stalin's needs. Soviet human losses at the Battle of Stalingrad alone exceeded all American losses in World War II. Stalin needed American tanks, trucks, heavy weaponry, food and a second front to relieve the pressure upon his troops. Certainly, the Comintern, which served as a reminder to America and England of the ultimate goals of communism, could be temporarily sacrificed. Within months the Communist Party of the United States responded to Stalin's decision by reconstituting itself as the Communist Political Association; and its junior division, the Young Communist League, dissolved itself on October 16, 1943. The following day, those who had dissolved the Young Communist League met again and reestablished themselves as the American Youth for Democracy.[2]

AYD is born in 1943

In a preamble to a six-page statement of intentions, AYD promised "allegiance to our country and to the cause of liberty and justice for all." Having established a position of rectitude, the writers of the statement of intentions returned to the peculiar use of language associated with the totalitarian left. "Fascism" or "fascist," clue words of political credentials, appear 18 times, rising in a crescendo to "smashing fascism" or, "We will resolutely combat the treacherous conspiracies of the fascists, defeatists and their 5th column," and "fascism is also promoted by and serves the reactionary imperialistic interests of a small clique of economic royalists in our country." The words "communist" and "communism" do not appear, with only cursory references to the Soviet Union, one of which notes the commonality of the United States and the Soviet Union as "these two most powerful democracies in the world."[3]

Young Communist League (YCL): Predecessor to AYD

Before reviewing the short and tumultuous history of AYD, it behooves us to provide a summary of tactics and strategies employed by its predecessor in the 1930s and early 40's, a period that is considered in greater detail by other contributors to this Anthology. Following its founding in 1922 the Young Communist League developed into an authoritarian, well-organized, disciplined cadre operating within and behind supposedly "progressive" organizations, either establishing these organizations or infiltrating existing ones. Political activity by the YCL at colleges remained minimal until the 1930s when, with the Nazi threat looming, the Comintern ordered the establishment of a political format that came to be known as the "Popular Front." In response YCL placed its adherents in organizations such as the American League Against War and Fascism, the Southern Negro Youth Congress, the American Youth Congress, and its collegiate affiliate, the American Student Union, an approach providing the

YCL, small numerically, with a multiplier impact of influence—however, not without incessant political struggle between those who adhered to the interests of the Soviet Union and those drawn to the political arena by faith in the social democratic ethos or the tenets of pacifism.[4]

YCL and the "Popular Front" before World War II

These two disparate elements of the Popular Front were able to function in relative unison as long as divergence in viewpoint was kept minimal. Both groups favored an anti-war pacifist position until Soviet concern about Nazi aims emerged. The Spanish Civil War of 1936 resulted in the first fissure, YCL cadres aligning themselves behind the Spanish Loyalist forces, demanding immediate military aid to the Loyalist government, while the pacifist faction, sympathetic to the Loyalists, was simultaneously opposing any steps which could widen the scope of the war. Simultaneously, the pacifist-liberal group became aware of Soviet steps to wrest control of the Loyalist government. This unusual alliance was held together by a joint concern about Nazi aggression, inspired by the Spanish Civil War, and enhanced by the German-Austrian Anschluss and opposition to the Munich Pact, which resulted first in the dismemberment of Czechoslovakia and shortly thereafter, the total occupation of that country. The alliance finally collapsed with the Hitler-Stalin peace pact of August 1939, the joint attack upon and occupation of Poland in September 1939 by Germany and the Soviet Union and the Russian attack upon Finland later that autumn.

Collapse of the Popular Front was immediate, including the demise of the American Student Union. From the start of World War II in September 1939 until the Nazi invasion of the Soviet Union in June of 1941, the schism on the political left grew ever wider, the communists insisting the war represented a struggle between competing capitalist and fascist nations, while the democratic left was split between those students adhering to the pacifism of the Oxford pledge and those who followed the strategy of President Franklin Roosevelt, which called for all possible aid to the beleaguered British, short of military entry into the conflict. Within days of the Nazi attack upon the Soviet Union, the Young Communist League was calling for all-out aid to the Soviet Union in its struggle against "fascism." The war was now a "peoples war," and the communist bureaucracy started the process to reestablish the Popular Front, its campus presence to be represented by the American Youth for Democracy.

The AYD environment

AYD represented a tactical approach at sharp variance to the format developed by the communists during the previous decade. Instead of a cluster of "front" organizations influenced by assigned YCL cadres, now the YCL membership was ordered into the AYD mold where they had to adapt to a social environment of patriotic unity during a period of world war. Who were the leaders of the newly constituted AYD? The initial publication issued by AYD, outlining procedures for membership—$1 to charter a group or club of ten; $1 for individual members; 50 cents for high school students—also provided photographs of the six smiling senior officers: Robert Thompson and Naomi Ellison as co-chairmen; John Gallo and Winifred Norman as vice-chairmen; Wm. Robert McCarthy as secretary-treasurer; and Carl Ross as executive secretary—all appearing somewhat older than students.[5] During the four- to five-year history of AYD a variety of names appeared and disappeared. Biographical information was scant and aliases—a common practice in communist circles—may have been used.

Two of the names noted above appeared frequently then and in subsequent years: Robert Thompson and Carl Ross. Robert Thompson, a World War II veteran and holder of the Distinguished Service Cross, moved in 1945 from his position as co-chairman of AYD to membership in one of the four-person leadership secretariat established by the reconstituted Communist Party of America. In 1948 Thompson was indicted under provisions of the Smith Act, sentenced to three years of imprisonment, eluding federal authorities until 1953, when he was apprehended in a California mountain hideout. While in custody he was severly injured by an anticommunist fellow prisoner. Thompson appeared again on the political spectrum in 1965 as the Communist Party representative at a Vietnam Peace Parade held in New York City. Carl Ross, the AYD Executive Secretary, had previously served as Chairman of the New York State Committee of the Young Communist League. In 1948, as head of the Minnesota Communist Party, he played a significant role in the Henry Wallace campaign for the presidency.

During the organizing period in early 1944, I, a 15-year-old high school student, joined a large AYD teen chapter in the Bronx, one that had its own "clubhouse" replete with a jukebox, plenty of 78 rpm dance records, and indirect lighting to enhance the social Friday and Saturday evening co-ed environment. Who paid the rent? I do not know. Obligations were minimal: Attend periodic meetings addressed by "war heroes" who reminded us of the need for universal military training after the war ended[6]; march in the May Day workers parade; participate in "win-the-war" rallies; organize scrap-metal collection drives for the war effort; and distribute election-day political literature at polling places. But we had our "Max." James Wechsler, the famed editor of the New York Post, described the "Max" conundrum in his "Age of Suspicion," set in the 1930s at Columbia University, where

Wechsler was the Young Communist League functionary assigned to the American Student Union:

> And there was "Max." One always uttered his name with quotation marks. I never knew him by any other name; I learned quickly that one did not ask about it, or about him. He was just there. When we faced any ideological quandary, he laid down the law. It was indicated—but never explicitly stated—that "Max" was the representative of the Young Communist International and, from the behavior of the others, one might have deduced that Stalin himself was in our presence. No one ever quarreled with "Max."[7]

In my AYD club our "Max" was a trio of older, at least two years older, teenagers who ran the "Executive Committee," planned our programs, supervised the content of the mimeographed newsletter, and never attended the Friday/Saturday night bashes. It did not take long for tension to arise between these elders and the rank-and-file younger members. Frivolity was my undoing. A short sojourn as "Membership Director" ended when in a moment of gaiety, I stamped a roll of toilet paper, sheet by sheet, with the club rubber stamp. What followed was a star-chamber "Executive Committee" hearing and a listing by the "Max" trio of my lack of social and political responsibility. The outcome? Expulsion as membership director and a return to the rank and file. In all fairness, it must have been difficult for the "Max" trio, accustomed to the discipline of the YCL environment. What can one do with recalcitrant, politically immature teenagers? A meeting was called, addressed by a senior AYD official, Claudia Jones, who reviewed the valiant efforts of "progressive" student leaders in history and, while referring to the "Max" trio as the essential nucleus of the AYD chapter, was interrupted by a quick-witted teen-ager, shouting, "Nucleus, No! Cancer, Yes!" The problem was tabled, pending completion of the war! As best as I can remember I remained with my neighborhood AYD group until I entered the City College of New York in February of 1946, choosing not to affliate with the college's AYD chapter. I needed a breather.[8]

Finding clarity on the appeal of Communism

How can one describe the college environment of February, 1946 through the eyes of a 17-year-old, observing the return of the veterans of World War II? One incident will suffice to describe the impact. It occurred during the first week of classes in an introductory course in economics. The door opened. In walked a veteran, still in uniform, officers bars removed from his shoulders, a faded patch on his shirt where a flight pin had been, dropping his duffle bag in a corner, handing his admission card to the instructor, seating himself in the first row, opening a notebook, reaching into his pocket for a pen. Silence. The instructor coughed nervously and resumed his lecture.

In the history, political science and philosophy classes, issues were illuminated by the presence of instructors who questioned and critiqued, presenting shades of grey rather than the absolutes of black and white. And, unique to CCNY, the presence of a small band of politically mature students, who constantly challenged the reasoning of those students and the occasional instructor who accepted a double standard for the totalitarian left as opposed to the totalitarian right. These challenges resulted (for me and for others) in a painful intellectual process leading to the questioning of beliefs and presumed certainties, first shedding the intellectual residue of discomfort with the absolutist environment of AYD, followed by a move to Young Progressive Citizens of America, where one found fellow students who shared the same concerns.

Within YPCA a constant enervating struggle took place between the true believers and those who questioned. Finally, clarity: a withdrawal from YPCA, recorded officially in a letter, signed by a dozen of us, appearing in *The Campus*, the college newspaper. At times I am asked, why did it take so long? Why the ability to recognize the reality of fascism, the inability to recognize the reality of communism? Let us try another quotation—the thought credited to Dr. Reinhold Niebuhr—from James Wechsler, who traveled the same route:

> . . . the communists have appealed to men's loftiest instincts, while the fascists frankly addressed themselves to men's cruelest impulses. The communists raised the banner of liberty, fraternity and equality, and then pitilessly perverted these symbols; the fascists said openly that they stood for conquest and subjugation and, eventually, for the triumph of "superior races." The communists preached an internationalism as old as the simple credo of the brotherhood of man; the facists invoked no such pretense.[9]

Campus reaction to AYD's hardline approach

In the waning days of World War II, as the Soviet Army triumphantly entered Berlin, an article appeared in the April 1945 edition of the French-published "Cahiers du Communisme," written by Jacques Duclos, head of the French Communist Party, proclaiming the end of collaboration between the communist world and the democracies. Within the following weeks hard-liners took over of the communist movement in the United States, abolishing the Communist Political Association and reestablishing the Communist Party of America. AYD did not undergo a change in name, but its popular front veneer evaporated. Nationally the political climate changed, moving rightward rather than to the left, with

Congress conducting investigations of alleged communists, including AYD leaders, followed by trials under provisions of the Smith Act—a law the communists had lauded when it had initially been applied to their arch enemy of the left, the Trotskyite faction of international communism.

As the AYD pro-Soviet position became apparent, many colleges took steps to decertify AYD chapters and expel AYD members. On the East Coast AYD chapters were barred at Brooklyn College, Queens College, and Temple University; at Harvard, the university barred the AYD publication from using the name "Harvard" as part of its publication masthead. AYD's successor group, the Young Progressives of America, was suspended at both campuses of CCNY. Syracuse University expelled a YPA member who in a street speech had referred to President Truman as a "drunken bum." In the Midwest, AYD was banned at Wayne University; another successor AYD group, Students for Wallace, was banned at Ohio State University. Michigan State University, which had not granted AYD official recognition, expelled one member of the off-campus AYD chapter for supposed violation of leaflet distribution and placed other members of the AYD on probation.

In the Rocky Mountain area, AYD was banned at the University of Colorado, where the President stated, "AYD . . . is in its underlying purpose what is known as a 'communist front.'" Continuing, the president stated the banning of AYD was prompted because "a university must guard unwary and impressionable young people by requiring forthright and frank statements of purpose" by such organizations. On the West Coast, the Seattle *Post-Intelligencer* launched an editorial-page assault on AYD noting the existence of AYD units at two high schools in Seattle and at the University of Washington and referring to AYD as "Red Fascist in origin and purpose, no less under its present phony title than it was when it openly and correctly called itself the Young Communist League."[10]

To what extent did the general student population respond aggressively to campus restrictions upon AYD? An examination of student publication articles and editorials of the time indicates complete reporting of the restrictive patterns, but limited questioning as to whether such restrictions were appropriate in a democratic society. No actions were taken by the ACLU to challenge the legality of the restrictions, nor did the expulsions of AYD chapters result in significant or sustained student reponses such as protest meetings, letters to the editors of student publications or manifestos. Almost all information uncovered indicates that protests were limited primarily to actions by AYD units or the AYD national office. Why this was so is not clear, for one can not invade the minds of students of the time, a half century ago. One can conjecture possibilities such as fear of consequences because of actions taken by Congress and the FBI; the presence of older students—veterans of World War II—who would not factor political issues into their efforts to recapture lost time; the lack of concern by liberal groups and labor unions, both in the final stages of crushing the vestiges of communism in their ranks; and the political-military expansion of the Soviet Union, replete with frightening totalitarian outcomes.

In 1948 AYD metamorphosed into the Young Progressive Citizens of America, which, in turn, became the Young Progressives of America on some campuses and Students for Wallace on other campuses, but not before AYD attempted to place its imprimatur upon the National Student Association.

AYD and the National Student Association

For AYD the establishment of the National Student Association represented an opportunity to dominate again or strongly influence the goals and program of a major student entity, as their predecessor, the Young Communist League, had accomplished in the 1930s with the American Student Union. But, AYD encountered a series of developments and realities that precluded a repetition of the 1930s, the least of which was the philosophical and tactical rigidity of the AYD leadership.

Three factors precluding success stood out in a climate not only inhospitable to the goals of AYD but, even worse from the AYD perspective, the brushing aside of AYD as inconsequential by all political, religious and social spectrums participating in the development of NSA. First was the presence of veterans, older by several years than those NSA delegates who had not experienced warfare, bringing to the 1947 Madison Constitutional Convention and the 1948 first Congress in Madison a degree of maturity not yet developed in teenagers.

Second was the development of political clarity within the non-communist left, as exemplified by the establishment of Americans for Democratic Action and its affiliate, Students for Democratic Action, the latter rising quickly to become the largest student political organization in the United States. Both ADA and SDA, heavily funded by the American labor movement, which had just completed the process of removing communists from leadership of several of the largest unions in the country, had adopted membership application and membership card statements that specifically excluded communists from membership. For Students for Democratic Action this approach was not new, since the initial leadership of the organization had come from the independent predecessor group, the United States Student Assembly, which had adopted a similar membership clause in 1943.[11]

Third, and possibly the most important factor in the checkmating of any influence by AYD, was the entry of Catholic college student groups into the national political arena, a step initiated in 1946 by the distinguished theologian and an editor of the Jesuit magazine *America,* Father John Courtney Murray, who in a seminal article stated, "Beginnings are always small and difficult. But they may as well be bold."[12] Father Murray was proposing the takeover of the forthcoming Prague meeting of the communist-controlled International Student Federation. Of course his efforts did not succeed, but his pronouncements led to the establishment of a Joint Committee for Student Action, consisting of leaders from the Newman Club College Federation and the National Federation of Catholic College Students. Though the Catholic group and the liberal group did not agree on a number of issues, they most certainly agreed upon steps to block AYD from leadership in NSA.[13]

AYD's efforts for influence within NSA, revolving around an effort to establish a formal, constitutional relationship within NSA for national student organizations such as AYD, failed. AYD found itself relegated to a role of outsider, observing what was taking place and offering critique in its publications, particularly in *The New Student,*[14] where lengthy polemics moved initially from mild criticism of the liberal and the Catholic organizations to extreme attacks upon the Catholic groups active in NSA.

By 1950, the successor group to AYD, the Labor Youth League, was positioning its attacks upon NSA directly. At the Third Annual NSA Congress, held at Ann Arbor, Michigan, a representative of the Labor Youth League, Robert Fogel, was permitted to make a statement to the Congress. Later that year, November, 1950, in a published letter, Fogel stated "this Congress showed that the NSA in its higher levels is a reactionary and dangerous organization."[15]

The last organized efforts to reestablish the "Popular Front"

In February of 1946 the Communist Party decided to establish a third political party—an "anti-monopoly, anti-imperialist party." Within a year two communist-front organizations were merged and renamed the Progressive Citizens of America, which became the root stock of the Progressive Party, positioned for a 1948 presidential election with Henry Wallace, the former Vice-President of the United States, as its presidential candidate. From the perspective of the Communist Party, AYD did not serve as an entity to enhance the third-party effort. Those AYDers wishing to remain active politically enrolled in the Young Progressive Citizens of America, where the immediate goal was to guarantee the future of the fledgling third party by realizing a goal of 10 million votes in the 1948 presidential election.[16] With this goal came another change of name to Young Progressives of America. The November 1948 election results for the Progressive Party and its progenitor, the Communist Party, were a shattering defeat. Wallace came in fourth with 1,380,000 votes or 2.3% of the total vote, polling fewer votes nationally than the Dixiecrat States Rights Party, whose voting base was limited to the Deep South.[17]

Formation of the Labor Youth League

In 1949, as it regrouped from the Wallace presidential disaster, the Communist Party established the Labor Youth League, which functioned marginally until it was disbanded in 1957. LYL and its adherents launched one major effort to reestablish a base on campuses, namely, a Conference on Democracy in Education to consider academic freedom, discrimination in education and economic problems confronting college students—the conference to be an opportunity to reestablish the Popular Front environment. Pre-conference planning meetings were held during the fall of 1949, with the Conference scheduled for December at a New York City campus. Coupled with refusals by Columbia University and New York University to provide space was press awareness of the conference plan. In a series of articles in the *New York World-Telegram* the conference was labeled as a communist-front effort, the outcome being an indefinite postponement of the conference.

In January 1950, the New York State Regional Board of Students for Democratic Action, concerned about the impact of a Popular Front renewal, organized a caucus consisting of members of SDA, the American Veterans Committee, the Young People's Socialist League, the Student League for Industrial Democracy and college groups affiliated with the Democratic Party. Plans were launched to elect a new executive conference-planning committee and, to test their numerical strength, to submit a statement of principles that condemned the lack of civil liberties both in Franco Spain and the Soviet Union. At a five-hour planning session attended by approximately 100 students, the liberal caucus defeated the Labor Youth League bloc on each vote.[18]

Liberals and Catholics collaborate to outvote the Labor Youth League

In March 1950 the two-day weekend Conference on Democracy in Education attended by 400 students, presumably representing 150 student organizations, opened at Brooklyn College with speeches by Roger Baldwin, the legendary ACLU leader, and Dr. Harold Taylor, the President of Sarah Lawrence College. For the balance of the first day a battle for control of the Conference ensued, with a tilt developing in favor of the Labor Youth League bloc. During the day parliamentary steps were taken by the liberal bloc to assure reconsideration of motions passed by the LYL bloc. Not known to the LYL was the existence of an off-campus meeting between SDA national office staff and leaders of local campus Newman clubs and the National Federation of Catholic College Students to consider the wording of program goals. Following a satisfactory completion of these discussions between the liberal group and the Catholic student groups, telephone calls went out to campus Catholic groups advising participation in the events of the second Conference day. LYL motions were reconsidered, defeated and replaced by motions agreed upon by the liberal and Catholic blocs. In the midst of these changes LYL adherents charged to the stage in anger, bedlam ensued, and the Conference unraveled, thus closing the last significant effort of the totalitarian left to control student political activity.[19]

For the balance of the 1950s political events and literature imploded upon the totalitarian left: Khruschev's 1956 speech, which exposed the brutality of the Stalin period; the Hungarian Revolution of 1956 with its valiant student leadership; Milovan Djilas's *The New Class*; Richard Crossman's *The God That Failed*; and Vladimir Dudintsev's *Not By Bread Alone.* Looming ahead for students was the Civil Rights movement, the Vietnam war, a worker-led revolution in Poland, students dancing on the crumbling Berlin wall, and the collapse of the Soviet Union.

Viewed in retrospect, AYD was a link in the chain of communist efforts to bend the U.S. student movement to the service of Soviet global stategy. Students of the mid-20th century who challenged AYD in the forums of debate as well as in college parliamentary struggles can look back on a mission well accomplished. Those who stood by the AYD and its antecedents and committed themselves to totalitarian solutions for social and economic problems were defeated by the strength of democratic ideals and by those who stood for them.

AFTERWORD

For those who seek a broader and more intensive examination of the period referred to in this essay, I would suggest the chronology, notes and references, and bibliographic essay which form the closing section of *The American Communist Movement: Storming Heaven Itself* by Harvey Klehr and John Earl Haynes (Maxwell Macmillan International, 1992) and notes, notes to pages, and the bibliographical essay which form the closing section of *Earl Browder: The Failure of American Communism* by James G. Ryan (University of Alabama Press: Tuscaloosa and London, 1997).

Research for this essay was facilitated by Marvin Lieberman, Ph.D., adjunct associate professor at the Robert F. Wagner Graduate School of Public Service, New York University, and Peter Filardo, archivist, the Tamiment Library and Robert F. Wagner Labor Archive, the Elmer Holmes Bobst Library, New York University. My thanks to both of them!

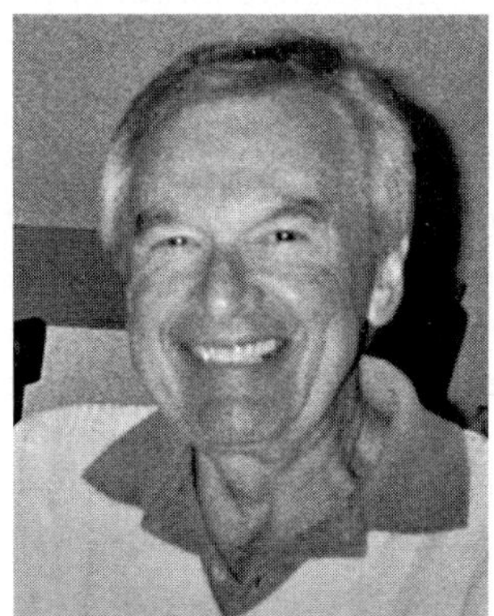

During the decades of the 70's and 80's, Seymour Reisin was Dean of Continuing Education, Grants and Development at the Bronx Community College of the City University of New York. Currently he serves as a board member of the American Festival for the Arts in Houston, Texas, and the Rosen Scholars Fund in New York.

(See p. 783 for extended biography).

END NOTES

[1] The Comintern, also called the "Communist International" or the "Third International," was formed in 1919 by the communist regime in Moscow. Communist parties of many nations joined and were expected to expel moderate socialists and pacifist from their ranks. Until its dissolution in 1943 it was the administrative entity that exercised control over communist movements throughout the world. The term "Third International" distinguished the Comintern from the "Second International" or "Socialist International" which, functioning between 1889-1914, loosely consisted of socialist political parties and trade unions. It supported parliamentary democracy. The "First International," 1864-1872, founded by British and French labor union leaders, became a verbal-philosophical battleground for factions within the socialist spectrum..

[2] *Editor's note:* In its March 15, 1947, "Report of Action Taken Regarding the Tom Paine Chapter of the American Youth for Democracy at the University of Colorado," prepared for President Robert L. Stearns, by the Special Investigation Committee, the Communist Party's newspaper *Daily Worker* is quoted as follows:

> Saturday, October 16, 1943: "Over 5,000 young Americans, many coming from various parts of the nation, packed two halls at Manhattan Center last night . . . as the Young Communist League opened its historical national convention to consider its own dissolution and the building of a new national anti-fascist organization of youth. . . ."
>
> Monday, October 18, 1943: "A new American anti-fascist youth organization was born at Mecca Temple yesterday as 332 delegates representing 190 community clubs, and 150 guests and observers ended an organizing convention initiated by the Young Communist League and by several score non-Communist youth leaders.
>
> "The convention was called into session Saturday evening immediately following the decision of a special national convention of the Young Communist League to dissolve that body.
>
> "Yesterday the new convention decided to make the new organization 'American Youth for Democracy,' and to place it 'on the side of all that is democratic, just and progressive.' It also proposed to join hands with all youth in opposing everything that is reactionary and oppressive. . . ."

The Special Investigating Committee concluded, "We have used the expression 'Communist Front'. By this expression we mean the AYD was Communist in its origin, has Communist sponsorship, and, we are convinced is used for the purpose of furthering certain objectives of the Communist Party."

[3] AYD brochure, undated, probably issued during the last months of 1943. It included the organizational program adopted October 17, 1943, and photographs of the six senior national officers.

[4] See Berlin, p. 10, McLaughlin, p. 16, Joseph Lash, p. 42, American Student Union, p. 47.

[5] Op. cit., footnote 2.

[6] Universal Military Training and the draft were issues hotly debated in NSA after the U.S. entered the Korean conflict in 1950. The 1951 Congress voted for UMT, and the 1952 Congress opposed it. See p. 370.

[7] James A. Wechsler, *The Age of Suspicion,* Andre Deutsch, London, 1954, p. 95. Confirmation of "Max" as a Comintern official who came to the United States as a representative of the Young Communist International, confirmed by documents in Soviet archives. See Klehr, Haynes and Firsov, *The Secret World of American Communism,* Yale University Press, New Haven, 1955.

[8] By February of 1946, when I entered CCNY, I was no longer active in AYD, but I had not reached the point where I could say that Communists had no place in any joint or cooperative efforts with groups adhering to democratic tenets. As a young boy, my mother sent me to the Jewish schools run by the IWO (International Workers Order). By age 11 I had my first doubts, when I questioned in class whether any validity existed for the Soviet attack on Finland. I just could not see how a tiny nation would attack the Soviet Union. I was told the revolution would take place without me! At age 13, when I graduated, the ceremony took place in the joint ALP (American Labor Party)/Communist Party headquarters on Allerton Avenue in the Bronx. A hot, muggy evening, a torture listening to the speeches about the imperialist/capitalist war in Europe, staggering out at 11 p.m., walking to the newsstand under the IRT elevated station and the *Daily News* headline,"Germany attacks Russia." A week later we were assembled for a speech about our new patriotic responsibilities in the "Peoples War."

[9] Op. cit., footnote 7.

[10] *Seattle Post-Intelligencer,* Editorial Page, April 27, 1947; *Harvard Crimson,* May 27, 1949; *Temple University News,* April 25, 1947; News Bureau, University of Colorado, "Report of Action Taken Regarding the Tom Paine Chapter of the American Youth for Democracy," March 15, 1947; Press report by United Press, March 15, 1947.

[11] *New York Times,* "Student Unit Bars Reds and Fascists," May 10, 1943.

[12] John Courtney Murray, S. J., "Operation University," *America,* April 13, 1946, p. 28.

[13] *Editor's note:* Student leadership awareness of the Catholic initiatives and of the AYD, as well as campus tolerance of the AYD, is illustrated in the following items from the Smith College student newspaper, the *Smith College Associated News, SCAN.*

In the December 10, 1946, issue, prior to the Chicago Student Conference later that month, 12 Smith College undergraduates signed a letter to the editor, a portion of which stated,

> ". . . There are at least two groups outside our Smith community which would like to dominate the [Chicago] conference: the Communist Party and the Catholic student organizations.
>
> "The chief instrument through which the communist party hopes to gain control is the national AYD.
>
> "Not all members of the AYD are communist. Many are moved by genuine idealism. But there has been no time when the AYD has disagreed with a major point of communist policy, or when it has criticised any important policy of the USSR.
>
> "We must recognize too that another disciplined influence will be present. Catholic student groups and Catholic colleges will be committed to a program which will be unrepresentative of the majority of the students in the country.
>
> "Several of our [Chicago Student Conference delegate] nominees are AYD members. Let us be sure that the delegates we send are representative of our own campus rather than outside groups."

The May 16, 1947, issue presenting AYD in its own words on page 1, reports "Explaining the formation of AYD in October 1943, Lee Marsh, Intercollegiate Director of AYD, speaking under the auspices of the Academic Freedom Committee, stated that prior to its voluntary disbanding, the Young Communist League requested various youth groups to meet to form a new organization with the broadest possible membership. American Youth for Democracy resulted.

> Its aim was not to continue YCL policies under a different name. That was unnecessary, for existing groups could do that. Rather AYD was to be a youth group run completely by young people with adults acting in advisory capacity only when requested. On the intercollegiate level it concerns itself with student problems.

The article concludes noting that it is "part of the Academic Freedom Committee's program of giving every organization an opportunity to explain its beliefs and policies, particularly when under attack."

[14] Marsh, Lee, "NSA," *The New Student,* December, 1947, p. 1, and "Polemic," April, 1948, p. 12.

[15] Fogel, Robert, *New Foundations,* November, 1950, "A Letter on NSA," p. 17. In a mimeographed publication issued by the National Student Association, dated March 11, 1963, entitled "History and Development of the United States National Student Association," edited by Edward R. Garvey, Robert Fogel was identified as executive secretary of the Labor Youth League, the successor organization to AYD. In *New Foundations,* summer 1949, Robert Fogel was identified as "an organizational secretary for the Student Division of the New York Communist Party." (See Fogel, p. 289.)

[16] *Editor's note:* Henry Wallace had become a popular speaker on U.S. campuses throughout the country, bringing out large crowds and inspiring considerable editorial comment. This laid the groundwork for the positive reception Students for Wallace got on many campuses. It is typified by the following editorial on January 9, 1948, in the Denver Clarion (University of Denver, see p. 796):

> Believing that Henry Wallace answers their need of a proponent of the concept that peace, prosperity and security are available at this time, groups of students in the East, the Far West, the Middle West and the South have organized "Students for Wallace" groups on their campuses.
>
> There is a group at Harvard University, another one composed of students from Yale, Brown, and New Hampshire universities, another at the University of California. In two days an "Ohio Citizens for Wallace" meeting will be held in Columbus. . . .Reports say that 30,000 students packed school auditoriums and baseball fields in nine southern colleges to hear Wallace in his southern tour. DU's chapel was filled to overflowing when Wallace spoke here last May 22. . . .
>
> Wallace's stand is for complete academic freedom, and it is evident that he has a large backing from students – many of whom are potential voters.
>
> We welcome "Students for Wallace" organizations on the campus. It is only through interest and study of all party candidates that we will wisely utilize our vote in this year's election.

[17] Henry Wallace had been my hero. I was devastated when the Democrats removed him from the ticket in 1944. It was hard for me to come to terms with his naivete where the Communists were concerned. Certainly the true believers assembled just as I did when I was a child and marched in the May Day parades. It was considered an honor to take the subway uptown and march down again and, if you did it a third time, the order of Lenin!!! When the smoke cleared 2 out of a hundred voters cast their ballots for Wallace, possibly a slightly higher percentage among student voters.

[18] *ADA World,* February 18, 1950, "Commies Lose; Leave Freedom Conference," p. 8.

[19] Sherris, Ted, "Popular Front Flops at N.Y. Conference," *Campus World,* April 1950, p.17.

PICTURE CREDITS: *Then:* c. 1946, High School (Author). *Now:* October, 1997, New York City (Schwartz)

1943-48: AYD Challenges and Polarizes Liberal Students

"A NEW AMERICAN ANTI-FASCIST YOUTH ORGANIZATION was born at Mecca Temple yesterday as 332 delegates, representing 190 community clubs, and 150 guests and observers, ended an organizing convention initiated by the Young Communist League and several-score non-communist youth leaders.... Immediately following the decision of a special national convention of the Young Communist League to dissolve that body ... the new convention decided to name the new organization 'American Youth for Democracy' and to place it on the side of all that is democratic, just and progressive"---

The Daily Worker, Monday, 10/1/43.

AMERICAN YOUTH FOR DEMOCRACY

· National Headquarters ·

150 NASSAU STREET, ROOM 412 • NEW YORK 7, N. Y. • PHONE: WORTH 2-3863

OFFICERS

Co-Chairmen:
WINIFRED NORMAN
VINCE PIERI

Vice-Chairmen:
LOU BURNHAM
MAYER FRIEDEN
JOHN GALLO
FRANCES GULLOTA
RUTH JETT
MOLLY LIEBER

Executive Secretary
HERBERT SIGNER

Educational—Teen-Age Director
VIVIAN LEVIN

Inter-Collegiate Director
LEE MARSH

January 7, 1947

Dear Fellow-Students:

We are sending you a copy of our latest pamphlet, The Big Squeeze...Crisis on the Campus. Written by Jo Allen, a student, this pamphlet deals with the things that today's campuses are discussing.

How to improve our educational system...how to bring education to all young Americans seeking it, without regard to race, national origin, or economic position... how to improve the democratic content of our education... how to teach democracy by practicing it on the campus through full student self-government...how to defend education against any "scarcity" program...how to meet the problem of fruitful employment in our selected fields after graduation...these are some aspects of the Crisis in Education that AYD attempts to discuss with the students and the public by means of this pamphlet.

We present this pamphlet with the hope that it will serve as a contribution to the student movement that is now growing up to meet the many needs that confront us today. The conference just concluded in Chicago, to set up a national student organization uniting all sections of campus opinion, was a high mark in this growing student movement.

As leaders of student opinion, and as participants in this new movement, your thoughts and comments on the enclosed pamphlet, and on the ideas contained in it, are most welcome. The freest discussion of these problems and the widest participation of the students in working them out, will bring us nearer to our common goal.

Fraternally yours,

Lee Marsh

AYD proposes . . .

Here is the program which AYD proposes to alleviate the educational crisis:

1. Subsistence allowances for G.I. Students raised to $100 for single vets, $25 for each dependent. Cost of living down. Reinstitution of price ceilings.
2. A ceiling on tuition fees and dormitory rents. Prices reduced to 1942 levels.
3. Substantial increases in the amount of federal and state funds for emergency and long-range housing. Build more dormitories.
4. 100,000 federal scholarships for young men and women from low income families. Stipends for students in need of financial assistance.
5. The construction of new free state universities and city colleges.
6. Federal loans and subsidies to colleges to permit the construction of more classroom and library space, well-equipped laboratories and gymnasiums.
7. An end to the quota system. Federal subsidies should be withheld from colleges which discriminate. The states should deprive colleges which employ a quota system of their tax exemption.
8. Substantial raises in faculty salaries to make pay for teachers commensurate with their role in our society.
9. Full academic freedom. The right of expression in the classroom and the right of organization on the campus.

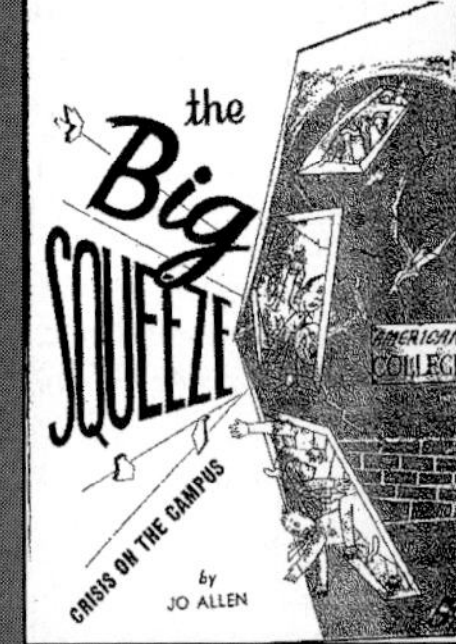

the new student 2 april 1948

PUBLISHED IN CAMBRIDGE, MASSACHUSETTS BY MEMBERS OF THE INTERCOLLEGIATE DIVISION OF AMERICAN YOUTH FOR DEMOCRACY

EDITOR LEO KAMIN
FORMAT JEAN LE CORBEILLER
STAFF GEOFF WHITE
SYD JAMES
TEX CAULFIELD

CONTENTS

Please address all communications to: THE NEW STUDENT, 12 Grove St., Boston 14, Mass.

From top: 1/7/47 Letter to student governments from Lee Marsh, Intercollegiate Director; two pages from Membership booklet. Title page, *The New Student* magazine, 4/48. (Source: U. of Washington Archives. *Editor's note:* Alice Tibbetts writes about Molly Lieber, whose name appears on the AYD letterhead as a Vice Chairman. See footnote 7, p. 72, and photo in pictorial on p. 744.)

NYU 11/43

R. 4, 1943 No. 10

AYD Recognized By A Single Vote In Heated Session

Jerry Jacobson's appointment as Student Comptroller by Day Organization President Mona Rhoda Tauber was approved unanimously by Student Council in a meeting last Monday, which also saw the passage of a resolution pertaining to club registration with the Division Coordinator as well as a blazing controversy which finally led to the recognition of "American ... for Democracy" as an ... organization.

UCLA 12/47

AYD DENIED RECOGNITION

By Irv Pearlberg

AYD's chances for campus recognition, feeble from the start, were dealt a death blow yesterday afternoon, when Organizations Control Board voted unanimously to withhold use of campus facilities from the group.

The decision came after the reading of a letter from Acting Dean of Undergraduates Clyde S. Johnson, in which it was stated that the functions of the American Youth for Democracy are largely political, and hence cannot be reconciled with University regulations.

Only a month after AYD's 10/43 formation, NYU's chapter was born in the controversy over its Communist origins that was to follow it across the country. At Temple, AYD was banned because of "falsification of its aims" by denying any affiliation with the Communist Party. UCLA barred AYD because it was "political" and not "educational" as claimed. U. of Colorado recognized AYD "for the time being," appointing a committee to investigate it more fully. From top: NYU *Bulletin*, 11/4/43; UCLA *Daily Bruin*, 12./12/47; Harvard *Crimson*. 10/4/46; U. of Colorado *Silver and Gold*, 2/18/47; *Temple University News*, 4/25/47.

...vard Crimson

...., MASS., FRIDAY, OCTOBER 4, 1946. PRICE FIVE CENTS.

Communist-Led Bloc Beaten as HLU Cleans House, Votes New Executives

Liberal Union Stages Surprise Coup to Oust Alleged Reds In Heated Four-Hour Session

BOZMAN NAMED PRESIDENT

AYD Assailed as Soviet Front In America, Tactics Exposed To Capture Liberal Groups

By Shane E. Riorden '46

After four hours of turbulent dispute in which the question of Communist-influenced candidates was fully threshed out and alleged Communistic members re-...

The SILVER and GOLD

AN INDEPENDENT NEWSPAPER

Official Publication of the Associated Students of the University of Colorado

AYD Granted Full Recognition

February 27 Deadline For CU King-Queen Entrants

Campus Groups Compile Accurate CU Alumni List

TEMPLE UNIVERSITY NEWS

VOL. XXVI—No. 66 PHILADELPHIA, FRIDAY, APRIL 25, 1947 PRICE 3 CENTS

AYD Chapter Barred from Campus

Committee of 14 Finds Group Violated Petition Statements

Constitution Adopted by Commission

Sunday Musical Slated by Hillel

House Committee, Hoover Reports Read In Support of Red Charge

Committee Statement on AYD

The following statement with respect to the matter of the American Youth for Democracy and its status on the Temple University campus was adopted unanimously by the University Committee on Controversial Affairs at its meeting on April 23, 1947. This statement is designed to cover the following points: (1) A brief summary of the history of AYD at Temple University; (2) A clarification of the point at issue; (3) A summary of the Committee's action; and (4) a re-affirmation by the Committee of the positive aspects of the University's policy on Controversial Affairs.

1. The History of AYD at Temple University.

"WHAT OF THE NSA BILL OF RIGHTS?," an editorial in the 4/48 issue of AYD's *The New Student* asks as it challenges a ban by Harvard against the magazine's use of the university's name on its masthead. "Since [the NSA constitutonal convention] violations of student rights have been mounting like uncollected garbage. The NSA Bill of Rights has not even been publicized, far less enforced.... If it can be so easily violated was it worth establishing in the first place? We think it was. We appeal the ban...as a violation of that Bill." (See Janet Brown on NSA and the Student Bll of Rights in Part 2).

"AYD will not give up its fight because it has been linked with a non-existent red international."
--President, Temple U. AYD Club

AYD: Influence Somewhat Exaggerated

Editor's note: Collier's Magazine, *a major general interest magazine of the era, regularly covered student and youth organizations and activity (see "The College Fraternity Crisis in 1949," p. 752) as did* Mademoiselle, Time, Newsweek, Life *and others excerpted in this Anthology. Below is an excerpt on the AYD written by reporter Dickson Hartwell, from a wide-ranging article which begins, "All over the country students are organizing into dozens of political clubs. . . . Spark-plugged by student veterans wise far beyond their years, undergraduates want the score on Europe, on China and on inflation," "When they find out, they want action." The article appeared, with permission, in the 2/48 edition of the NICC monthly,* The Intercollegian.

American Youth for Democracy—AYD—stimulates most of the charges of collegiate Communism. This is partly because the AYD objectives and program are no thorn in the side of the Communist Party and partly because AYD earlier this year was publicly described by the House Committee on Un-American Activities as a Communist front, formed in 1943 with the same ideology and much the same personnel as the Young Communist League. It was organized within 24 hours after YCL was dissolved to conform with shifts in Communist policy.

I put this question to an AYD member who admitted to me that he was a Communist:"How many AYD students are Communists?" About 15 to 20 per cent, he told me, on the basis of his intimate knowledge of AYD college clubs. It wasn't necessary to ask whether they controlled the organization. He had already observed that, in student groups as among others,"10 per cent of the members did most of the work and really ran the show."

Both the influence and size of AYD college groups have been somewhat exaggerated. Two-thirds of AYD members are not in college. There are less than 4,000 members in the 65 college chapters. Of these, 25 clubs have been banned from campuses and at least ten have not received recognition. To be banned is a serious handicap. Inability to use bulletin boards, the newspaper, meeting rooms and other facilities weakens any club almost to impotence.

At Ohio State, for example, the banishcd AYD meets across High Street from the campus in a Unitarian church of which Reverend Frank G. Ricker is pastor. At a recent meeting of this group only eight students showed up."After I heard that," a student told me,"I stopped worrying."

Most politically active students condemn the banishment of AYD even more emphatically than they condemn AYD itself. An undergraduate told me,"A university that is afraid of a few radicals can't have much faith in itself. We want to hear all kinds of opinions." Said another, "We'll run into Commies in adult life, won't we? The sooner we learn how to handle them, the better."

Although colleges vary widely in student political attitudes—usually reflecting the opinion of parents—on no major campus that I visited does any considerable Communist or radical group exist. Nor has there been any alarming increase. At some schools it is actually diminishing. Two years ago an AYD group was started at Missouri. There wasn't enough interest to keep it alive; this fall no application to renew its charter. Extremes of intolerance and radical thinking are as rare today as the Joe College of the goldfish-swallowing era. There is still plenty of college spirit, but, inside, it has crystallized the new idea expressed by one student:"So little effort, so few changes, would make such tremendous improvements in this world. It seems we all ought to try to do something."

NYU: Communists Use AYD as Front

From the NYU Washington Square Bulletin *11/17/45*

BULLETIN does not object to the existence of Communism, nor must this article be construed as an attack upon the Union of Soviet Socialist Republics. What BULLETIN does object to is the desire of American Communists to overthrow the United States government and set up another in its place that will call itself a democracy while operating as a totalitarinism (sic).

BULLETIN, therefore, will demonstrate as follows: (1) That the Communists are using AYD as a front to further their own aims. (2) That this constitutes a grave danger because of the nature of the aims of the Party leaders. (3) That the Washington Square College AYD fits into the general pattern of youth front organizations.

I. On October 16, 1943, the Young Communist League met at a Special National Convention (see *New York Times* and *Daily Worker* of same date), dissolved, and immediately reconstituted itself as the American Youth for Democracy. One of the leaders of the YCL wrote,"The proposal to change the program and name of the YCL . . . has its origin in what had been a basic policy of the [YCL] for many years."

II. William Z. Foster, leader of the Communist Party in the United States says "The American Soviet government will be the dictatorship of the proletariat. . . .all the capitalist parties—Republican, Democratic, Progressive, Socialist, etc. - will be liquidated, the Communist Party functioning alone as the party of the toiling masses."

III. [The BULLETIN Editor was asked to consult a non-student AYD writer who had represented himself as a disinterested student.] . . . an example of the surreptitious polictics AYD is capable of.

AYD: Judge Us by What We Do

From the Temple University News *4/18/47*

We proudly subscribe to full and equal citizenship of Communists with all democrats. Our country cannot afford to pussyfoot about the rights of Communists, or the floodgates of fascism will be opened here, just as they were In Germany after the Reichstag fire.

Judge us by what we do. Here at Temple the AYD club has been active in a campaign to raise veterans' subsistence; we have been active in participation of student government - the AYD was the only organization that was interested enough in student government to send a speaker to the ralley that was held in Mitten Hall a few weeks ago.

It was the AYD members who were active in creating interest in the Chicago Conference of Students held last December. It was then that one of the largest votes was turned out on the Temple campus. It was the AYD that was the only organization on campus that participated in the Crusade to Washington to End Lynching, held last September, such distinguished persons as Paul Robeson being the organizers.

These are just a few of the activities the AYD members have participated in - as members of the Temple AYD club, as well as members of the AYD of Eastern Penna.

AYD will not give up its fight because it has been linked with a non-existent red international. It will battle for the rights of all people to live peaceably, free from persecutions and witch hunts.

RHODA KUTNER, Arts '47,
President, Temple AYD club.

"Communists appealed to men's loftiest instincts, Fascists to their cruelest impulses."
--Rheinhold Neibuhr quoted by James Wechsler

Campus Communists Persevere in Efforts to Influence Nationwide Student Agendas

Editor's note: Communists and socialists fought over the legacy of Marxism throughout the middle part of the twentieth century. Before World War II the National Student League (communist) and Student League for Industrial Democracy (socialist) emerged, joining briefly to form the American Student Union (See Berlin, p. 9, McLaughlin, p. 15). This "united front" ultimately collapsed on the issue of communist control of its agenda in favor of Soviet aims (See Lash, p. 42). Conflict over (and mostly rejection of) extending recognition to the Young Communist League, the youth and student wing of the Communist Party centered on some version of "secrecy of the organization's membership and its political nature," the reason given in the close 5-4 January 1938 vote at Johns Hopkins (See headline below). The acknowledged hand of Communist influence in forming the AYD in 1943 (see previous page), whose leaders morphed into the Students for Wallace and Young Progressives of America in 1948 and more formally in 1950 into the Labor Youth League (See Reisin, p. 790) challenged First Amendment defenders of student rights, such as NSA, in a clash between loyalty to liberty and rejection of deception. Until NSA's break with the International Union of Students after the 1948 Communist coup in Czechoslovakia (see Ellis and Smith, p. 188), NSA was welcomed enthusiastically by the Communist Party. In "Student America Convenes!," by its student club Chairman, Marvin Shaw (Political Affairs, *10/47) NSA's founding is hailed as one "that can well become of decisive importance in both the American and international youth fields." By 1950, Robert Fogel wrote that the NSA Congress, at which he was permitted to speak for the Labor Youth League (see p. 289), "showed that the NSA in its higher levels is a reactionary and dangerous organization."*

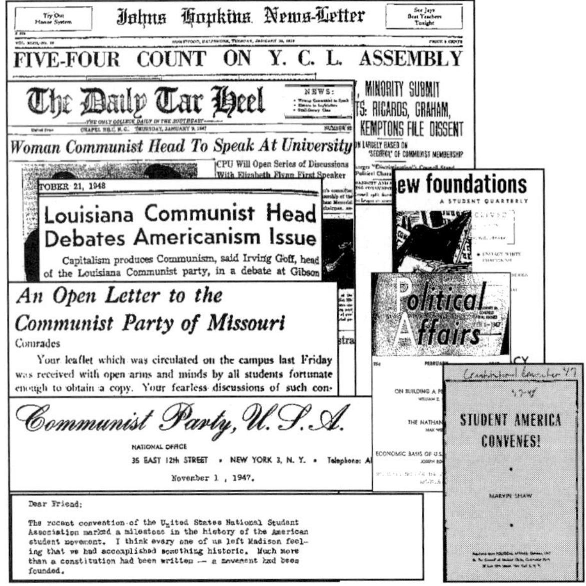
Johns Hopkins News-Letter

FIVE-FOUR COUNT ON Y. C. L. ASSEMBLY

The Daily Tar Heel

Woman Communist Head To Speak At University

CPU Will Open Series of Discussions With Elizabeth Flynn First Speaker

..., MINORITY SUBMIT ...TS: RICARDS, GRAHAM, KEMPTONS FILE DISSENT

...N LARGELY BASED ON "SECRECY" OF COMMUNIST MEMBERSHIP

...TOBER 21, 1948

Louisiana Communist Head Debates Americanism Issue

Capitalism produces Communism, said Irving Goff, head of the Louisiana Communist party, in a debate at Gibson

An Open Letter to the Communist Party of Missouri

Comrades

Your leaflet which was circulated on the campus last Friday was received with open arms and minds by all students fortunate enough to obtain a copy. Your fearless discussions of such con-

...ew foundations

A STUDENT QUARTERLY

Political Affairs

STUDENT AMERICA CONVENES!

Communist Party, U.S.A.

NATIONAL OFFICE
35 EAST 12th STREET • NEW YORK 3, N. Y. • Telephone: A...

November 1, 1947.

Dear Friend:

The recent convention of the United States National Student Association marked a milestone in the history of the American student movement. I think every one of us left Madison feeling that we had accomplished something historic. Much more than a constitution had been written — a movement had been founded.

THE COMMUNIST PARTY ON CAMPUS: Many were open to Communist Party officials through the late forties (U. of NC *Daily Tar Heel,* 1/9/47; Tulane *Hullabaloo,* 10/12/48). Washington U., St. Louis, *Student Life* edtiorial lampoons Communist Party agenda (3/20/47). By the fifties speaker restrictions were commonplace (see Brown p. 380).

Above: 11/1/47 CPUSA letter to NSA delegates enclosing a copy of Marvin Shaw's article on the Constitutional Convention (see text top of page). Above right, cover pages of Marxist student quarterly *New Foundations,* Summer '49; the monthly *Political Affairs* and reprint handout from its 10/47 issue. Top: Johns Hopkins News-Letter, 1/25/38 (see text above).

Students for Wallace Galvanize Progressives in 1948 Election. Wallace Draws Campus Crowds

Wallace Talk Draws 1000 Students

THE BEE — UNIVERSITY OF BUFFALO

THE JOHNS HOPKINS NEWS-LETTER

Wallace Addresses College Students

Speaks From University Bowl — Attacks U S "Warmong...

SC Proposes Constitution Amendments

Wellesley College News

Wallace Urges Dynamic Peace

The Denver Clarion

The Denver Clarion is published weekly by and for the students of the University of Denver. The only news policy of The Clarion is objectivity and impartiality. The Clarion is subject to censor only by ...

Students Back Wallace

Believing that Henry Wallace answers their need of a proponent of the concept that peace, prosperity and security are available at this time, groups of students in the East, the Far West, the Middle West and the South have organized "Students for Wallace" groups on their campuses.

Wallace Grou... To Dissolve; Organize YP...

Wallace Group Selects Officers; Will Hold Peace Dance On April...

STUDENT LIFE

ENGINEERS' DAY FRID...

Y.P.C.A. VOTED OFF OF CAMP...

THE A-BOMB AND COLD WAR FUELED CAMPAIGN YEAR CONTEST. From the top: U. Buffalo *Bee,* 12/12/47; Johns Hopkins *News-Letter,* 10/17/47; Rutgers *Targum,* 10/26/48; *Wellesley College News,* 5/1/47; Denver U. *Clarion,* 1/9/48; r. col: *Daily Pennsylvanian,* 4/26/48; Washington U., St. Louis *Student Life,* 3/26/48.

WAR AND PEACE WAS IN THE AIR. 1948 NSA Congress delegates were welcomed back to the U. of Wisconsin Students for Wallace with this assessment:

"Last year, when some of you and many others met here, you formed a non-partisan organization pledged to fight for the rights and needs of American students. Since that time, an organization so dedicated has become even more necessary because the shadow of another (the Last) war has been cast across our futures.

"Congress and the administration now spend as much money per day for war armaments as was spent by all nations for the UN during the whole of 1947. They still subsidize the corrupt governments of Greece and China. They have sold out millions of homeless Jews by their refusal to support partition in Palestine. They have passed Public Law 759 - the Draft Law. The skeletal form of a police-state in America has been erected. Our freedoms of conscience, expression and organization have been under concentrated attack."

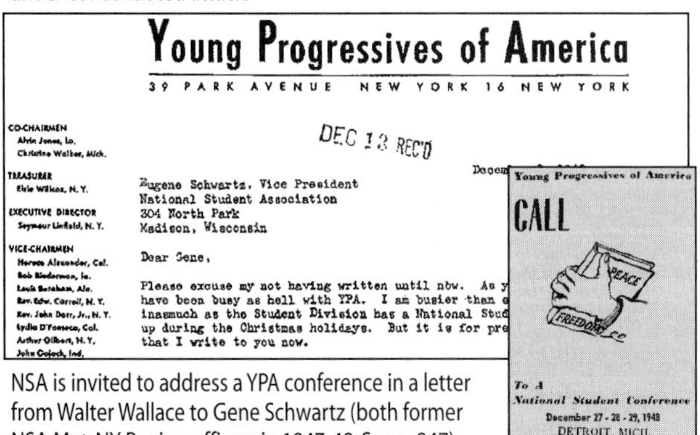
Young Progressives of America

39 PARK AVENUE NEW YORK 16 NEW YORK

CO-CHAIRMEN: Alvin Jones, La.; Christine Walker, Mich.
TREASURER: Elsie Wilkox, N. Y.
EXECUTIVE DIRECTOR: Seymour Linfield, N. Y.
VICE-CHAIRMEN: Horace Alexander, Cal.; Bob Biederman, Ia.; Louis Burnham, Ala.; Rev. Edw. Carroll, N. Y.; Rev. John Darr, Jr., N. Y.; Lydia D'Fonseca, Cal.; Arthur Gilbert, N. Y.; John Gojack, Ind.

DEC 13 REC'D

Decem...

Eugene Schwartz, Vice President
National Student Association
304 North Park
Madison, Wisconsin

Dear Gene,

Please excuse my not having written until now. As y... have been busy as hell with YPA. I am busier than ... inasmuch as the Student Division has a National Stud... up during the Christmas holidays. But it is for pre... that I write to you now.

Young Progressives of America

CALL

To A National Student Conference

December 27 - 28 - 29, 1948

DETROIT, MICH.

To launch national campaigns to

NSA is invited to address a YPA conference in a letter from Walter Wallace to Gene Schwartz (both former NSA Met. NY Region officers in 1947-48. See p. 847)

NSA is "a fairly inconspicuous organization which operates at Yale."

4. Individualism at Yale

William F. Buckley, Jr.
Yale University. 1950 Chairman of the Board, Yale Daily News

During the years 1946 to 1950, I was an undergraduate at Yale University. I arrived in New Haven fresh from a two-year stint in the army, and I brought with me a firm belief in Christianity and a profound respect for American institutions and traditions. I had always been taught, and experience had fortified the teachings, that an active faith in God and a rigid adherence to Christian principles are the most powerful influences to the good life. I also believed, with only a scanty knowledge of economics, that free enterprise and limited government had served this country well and would probably continue to do so in the future.

These two attitudes were basic to my general outlook. One concerned the role of man in the universe; the other, in all its implications, the role of man in his society. I knew, of course, of the existence of many persons who had no faith in God and even less in the individual's capacity to work out his own destiny without recourse to the state. I therefore looked eagerly to Yale University for allies against secularism and collectivism.

I am one of a small group of students who fought, during undergraduate days, in the columns of the newspaper, in the Political Union, in debates and seminars, against those who seek to subvert religion and individualism. The fight we waged continues even though little headway was made. The struggle was never more bitter than when the issue concerned educational policy.

As opportunity afforded, some of us advanced the viewpoint that the faculty of Yale is morally and constitutionally responsible to the trustees of Yale, who are in turn responsible to the alumni, and thus duty bound to transmit to their students the wisdom, insight, and value judgments which in the trustees' opinion will enable the American citizen to make the optimum adjustment to the community and to the world. I contended that the trustees of Yale, along with the vast majority of the alumni, are committed to the desirability of fostering both a belief in God and a recognition of the merits of our economic system. I therefore concluded that as our educational overseers, it was the clear responsibility of the trustees to guide the teaching at Yale toward those ends.

The reaction to this point of view has been violent. A number of persons affiliated with the University, all the way from President-emeritus Charles Seymour to a host of students, have upheld what they call "academic freedom," by which they mean the freedom of the faculty member to teach what he sees fit as he see fit – provided, of course, he is "honest" and "professionally competent." Here the argument rested when I left Yale. . . .[1]

* * *

EVIDENCES OF COLLECTIVISM IN EXTRACURRICULAR LIFE

It is interesting to note that the dominant ideological attitudes of the Department of Economics, and other departments also, bear some fruit even in undergraduate extracurricular life. Though a brief survey of those activities that lend themselves to student expression of ideas is relevant and significant, rigid generalizations about student opinion are impossible, as the great majority of Yale undergraduates do not take part in organizations of this kind. At the same time, it is likely that those who are articulate as undergraduates will also be articulate as citizens and thus their attitudes are of some interest.

The Yale Daily News

The Yale Daily News, the oldest college daily in America, is unquestionably the most influential student organization at Yale. As such, it commands an almost 100 percent reading audience, and active reader participation through its "Communications" column.

The editorial policy of the *News* is created by the chairman of the board (whose duties are also those of editor in chief). In the circumstances, the editorial page is an exact impression of the chairman's philosophies, which, as those of one man, are not important except for the fact that they elicit in the communications column campus-wide reactions to his editorials on international, national, and community issues.

The chairmen of the 1948 and 1949 Boards of the *News* were, roughly speaking, noncommittal neoconservatives. As chairman of the 1950 board, I was classified as a good number of things, the most charitable being "conservative." The chairman of the 1951 board, Garrison Ellis, is a pronounced, emphatic, undeviating, left-winger.

With recourse to these extremes, then, some generalizations as to the political temperament of the articulate members of the student body can be made by comparing reader sentiment to my year of editorial writing with that during Ellis' year. For Ellis (as also his successor) sits, broadly speaking, as far to the left of "center" as I do to the right. We are, in a manner of speaking, roughly equivalent. That is to say, if we should single out a dozen or more controversial figures or issues that serve, generally, to separate the "conservative" from the "left-winger," a fairly clear line would divide Ellis and me. Where he sympathized with Truman, Acheson, Hiss, Humphrey, and Bowles, I condemned [sic] them. Where I backed the McCarran Act, the Taft-Hartley Law, the Committee on Un-American Activities, the autonomy of private clubs and associations, and restriction of government activity, he deplored them. On the issues of a Fair Employment and Fair Educational Practices Laws, of the Brannan plan, and on the Labor government in England, we again parted company.

Now: for every letter that appeared in the Communications column of the *Yale News* berating Ellis, I was excoriated many times. And the attacks directed at me were far more splenetic. To a score of correspondents I was a "black reactionary." To one professor, I was possessed of "twisted morality." Not so with Ellis. No one—and rightly so—called him a Communist. "Idiot" was about as far as anyone went. In a word, Ellis' collectivism elicited far less protest than my individualism.

This is of some importance, it strikes me. For where public criticism is vocal and intense, it is because *the minority has offended the majority*. Even discounting the disproportionate addiction of the collectivists to propagandize their doctrines at every opportunity, I am forced to conclude from my experience with the *Yale Daily News* through several years, and from other evidence also, that at least at this college level, the great transformation has actually taken place. The conservatives, as a minority, are the new radicals. The evidence is overwhelming.[2]

* * *

The National Student Association

A fairly inconspicuous organization which operates at Yale, as it does in 289 American colleges and universities, is not an inconspicuous case in point. The National Student Association was founded in the summer of 1947 largely as a "service organization for all college students."

Primarily, it promised such services as would facilitate exchange students, curriculum comparisons, textbook-discount plans, foreign travel at reduced rates, and the like. Its highly political constitution was given little publicity, and a last-minute effort on the part of a few students to alert the Yale campus to the full implications of this body was of no avail. Yale joined up with it in December 1947, after a close, campus-wide vote.[3] Even today, the vast majority of Yale students are unaware that they are being spoken for as constituent members of the NSA by an alert pressure group and on behalf of leftist policies.

I reprint here a communication received by the *Yale News* in May 1949, which inquired into the political machinations of the NSA:

> To the Chairman of the NEWS:
>
> A letter in last week's *News* referring to the NSA as "non-political" has revived a question that has been bothering me for a couple of weeks.
>
> The *Daily Worker* of April 5 included an article saying: "The executive committee of the National Students Association yesterday took a firm stand against the dismissal of college professors for alleged membership in the Communist Party.
>
> "The Committee, representing 730,000 students in 289 American colleges, empowered its national staff to investigate . . . (three cases of dismissal or expulsion listed)."
>
> Granted, the *Daily Worker* is not above editorializing, but the statement seems to imply that the NSA is political in nature, and that Yale students are among those "represented" as upholding this point of view.
>
> I would appreciate it if someone would clarify the political stand of the NSA, since I, for one, have no desire to be represented politically by a group which I did not personally desire to join.
>
> GORDON MILLIKEN, 1949E

Mr. Milliken's concern is well founded. Early in its career, the NSA set up a subcommission on legislation which is bent on applying political pressure for the furtherance of NSA "goals." Because these goals are so loosely described in the NSA Constitution, the National Executive Committee has been able to pass resolutions, and press for legislation—always, of course, in the name of 730,000 students, a figure which includes every student of every member college—which have little or no relevance to the "service functions" of the organization. For example, as of 1949, the NSA had, to mention a few of its stands, (1) supported the entire Merchant Marine Bill (because a minor provision of the multi-million-dollar bill would have allocated several ships for student travel to Europe), (2) called for the repeal of the DP [displaced person] immigration bill on the grounds that it was discriminatory against Catholics and Jews (no apparent connection with students), (3) opposed pending state bills forbidding the hiring by state educational institutions of Communist teachers, (4) advocated Fair Educational Practices Laws, (5) pleaded for passage of the Federal Aid to Education Bill, and more besides.

My prediction is that it will be a long time before the Yale student body disaffiliates from the National Students Association. We have, again, testimony either to a majority sanction of left-wing national policies, or else evidence of deft left-wing manipulation of an insensate and tractable student body. Either spells the same thing: the predominance of leftism in undergraduate Yale.[4]

William F. Buckley, Jr., is a noted conservative columnist, speaker, author, host for 33 years of "Firing Line" on PBS TV and founder of The National Review.

PICTURE CREDITS: *Then:* c: 1950 Class Book Yale U., Manuscripts and Archives, Yale U. Library. *Now:* Painting, c. 2000 (National Review)

EDITOR'S NOTES

[1] From Buckley, Introduction, pp. xiii–xiv.

[2] From Buckley, pp. 104–107. [3] See Farrar, p. 829.

[4] From Buckley, pp. 110–112. *Editor's note:* The absence of a citation for NSA in his index seems to reinforce Buckley's disdain.

WILLIAM F. BUCKLEY, JR.

Early years and education: William F. Buckley was born in New York City in 1925 and raised in Sharon, Conn. After a two-year stint in the army he entered Yale University in 1946 and graduated with honors in 1950. He has taught and studied at Yale, the University of Mexico and the New School for Social Research.

Career highlights: After working briefly for the CIA, in 1955 Buckley founded the conservative journal *National Review.* In 1962 be began his syndicated column, On the Right. Today [2002] it appears three times a week in over 300 newspapers in the U.S. and abroad. In 1967 he was named Best Columnist of the Year, and he is a winner of the Distinguished Achievement Award in Journalism.

William Buckley began hosting his weekly television show "Firing Line" in 1966. By 1971 the program was carried coast to coast on the Public Broadcasting System. When the show ended in December 1999, it was the longest-running television program in the U. S. featuring the same host. Virtually every political and intellectual leader throughout the world has been a guest on "Firing Line." He has won an Emmy Award for program achievement and the *TV Guide* Award for the Best Television Interviewer.

In 1965 he ran for mayor of New York City, and he has been a presidential appointee to the U.S. Information Agency, the United Nations, and the National Security Council (1987).

Buckley has made four transoceanic sailing voyages, journeyed to the South Pole and written such bestsellers as *Atlantic High* and *Airborne* based on his travel experiences. He has also written a number of novels and non-fiction works including *God and Man at Yale* (1951), *Buckley: The Right Word* (1996), *Nearer My God: An Autobiography of Faith* (1997), and *The Red Hunter* (1999).

He has been awarded over 35 honorary degrees and was the recipient of the Presidential Medal of Freedom in November of 1991. Occasionally he plays the harpsichord with symphony orchestras.

Family: He has been married to his wife, Pat, for over fifty years. They have one son, Christopher, and two grandchildren.

Adapted from Keppler Associates, Inc. (www.kepplerassociates.com)

BUCKLEY'S CHARGES EVOKE VIGOROUS RESPONSE AND HOT DEBATE

Editor's note: God and Man at Yale *created a firestorm of controversy. Yale formed a committee to report on "the intellectual and spiritual welfare" of its community.Excerpts, below, were published on 2/20/52 in Sarah Lawrence College's* The Campus. *The issues Buckley raised helped inspire a conservative student movement and continue to be debated.*

Report By Yale Alumni Committee Restates Policy On Academic Freedom

Taking a stand similar to that at Sarah Lawrence on the question of academic freedom, an official Yale University committee of eight alumni answered Monday, in a report to A. Whitney Griswold, Yale president, charges that the university is indoctrinating its students with collectivist theories and promoting irreligious attitudes.

These charges were made in the controversial book, "God and Man at Yale," by William F. Buckley, Jr., who was graduated from Yale in 1950.

The committee was appointed by President Griswold in the summer of 1951 to survey "the intellectual and spiritual welfare of the university, its students and its faculty."

Indoctrination of Students

On the subject of indoctrination of students, the committee report stated: "During recent years an impression has spread in this country that the students in American schools, colleges and universities are being indoctrinated or unduly influenced by teaching of a Communistic or subversive character. Yale has not escaped charges of this kind...

No Communists on Faculty

"In the conviction that membership in the Communist party is incompatible with the intellectual and moral standards of the teaching profession, Yale does not knowingly appoint members of the Communist party to its faculty. We approve this policy. The administration of the university, which in our opinion is the group best qualified to pass judgement in the matter, knows of no Communist on the faculty at the present time. Furthermore, it knows of no member of the faculty who is trying to undermine or destroy our society, or our democratic form of government, or to indoctrinate students at Yale with subversive theories. Our inquiries confirm the accuracy of the judgement of the administration and of the University Council.

Meaning of Academic Freedom

"Much of the confused thinking that exists today has arisen from a misunderstanding of the nature of academic freedom. Perhaps this is a natural consequence of the turbulence of the present time. Academic freedom means the right, long accepted in the academic world, to study, discuss and write about facts and ideas without restrictions, other than those imposed by conscience and morality. We believe that this privilege should be enjoyed by all teachers, except those who use it to destroy individual liberty or to overthrow by violence our democratic form of government. The teaching profession recognizes principles of competence and moral conduct which forbid the use of classrooms as political platforms.

* * *

Academic Freedom & Democracy

"Whenever national affairs are at a crisis, the ancient rights and privileges that free men have fought for through the ages are in jeopardy.

* * *

In supporting academic freedom we are merely reaffirming our belief in a democratic society."

Charges of Irreligion

The committee report, in defending the university against charges of irreligion, said: "As a consequence of its examination, the committee believes that religious life at Yale is deeper and stronger than in most places outside the university. The charge that Yale is encouraging irreligion or atheism is without foundation. That religious life at Yale may become even stronger is the hope of the corporation, the university officers and this committee."

[Excerpted]

A Conservative emulation of Jack London's Intercollegiate Socialist Society in 1905

Intercollegiate Society of Individualists founded in 1953

Editor's note: M. Stanton Evans in Revolt on Campus *suggests "1953 might in a number of respects be considered the watershed year for the rise of conservatism among students. It was in that year that Russell Kirk published* The Conservative Mind, *which burst upon the nation's intelligentsia as an embarrassing and perplexing challenge." It was also the year that Frank Chodorov, "a veteran journalist and activist in the cause of freedom" formed the Intercollegiate Society of Individualists "to distribute literature to college students - to get into their hands the theories and the information being marshaled by the new [conservative] intellectual community." Evans notes that Chodorov modeled his strategy on the successes of the Intercollegiate Socialist Society, founded in 1905 by the novelist Jack London (See McLaughlin, p.15; also Album, p.49). Its purposes, "to awaken an interest in Socialism among the educated men and women of the country." Chodorov saw ISI as an antidote to "the transmutation of American character from individualist to collectivist."*

William Buckley, at a memorial to Chodorov following his passing in 1966, recalled that they first met when he spoke at Yale while Buckley was an undergraduate. "I was the ISI's first president, but I was purely a figurehead, as I was soon reminded." Chodorov felt he could more successfully raise money if he were President. "You can be V.P.," he wrote (www.cooperative-individualism.org).

Wellesley College News 9/15/52

Buckley To Head New College Club

William F. Buckley, author of the controversial *God and Man at Yale*, has become first president of a new "right wing" organization of college men and women, The Intercollegiate Society of Individualists.

The organization has just been formed and incorporated under the laws of the District of Columbia, and has opened its executive offices at 1136 18th Street, Washington 6, D. C. Its objectives, according to its constitution, are "to promote among college students, and the public generally, an understanding and appreciation of the basic principles of the American constitution, *laissez faire* economics and the philosophy of individualism."

Members Are Students

Membership in the society is limited to college students and to those who have been in college within five years. The society plans to contact students interested in the individualist approach to social problems, for the purpose of organizing discussion groups and study cells. Current trends and the government's foreign and domestic policies will be discussed. Textbooks used in college curricula will be subjected to discussion and analysis.

THE INDIVIDUALIST

DECEMBER, 1954

Published by the

Intercollegiate Society of Individualists — 30 South Broadway, Irvington-on-Hudson, New York

Masthead of the ISI periodical in 1954 in which the excerpt below appeared.

I·S·I
Founded 1953
INTERCOLLEGIATE SOCIETY OF INDIVIDUALISTS, INC.
"To Educate for Liberty"

The Intercollegiate Society of Individualists is dedicated to developing among college students and professors an understanding of the conservative philosophy of individual liberty, limited government, free-market economics, the right of private property, and the spiritual and moral underpinnings of this philosophy.

I S I believes:

- that man's activities are guided by moral law, founded in eternal principles;
- that these principles include the right of human beings to be free from the arbitrary rule of others;
- that political and economic freedom are indivisible; that the destruction of one will necessarily lead to the destruction of the other.

I S I places primary emphasis on the distribution of literature encompassing such fields as economics, sociology, history, moral philosophy, education, and political science. I S I publishes *The Individualist,* a newspaper of essays by professors and students; *Campus Report*, a newsletter on I S I activities; *Under 30,* a digest of the best articles from conservative campus publications; and essays.

In addition to its publications programs, I S I

- assists the formation of student discussion groups and I S I-associated clubs;
- encourages student organizations to publish newsletters or magazines;
- arranges lecture tours;
- sponsors conferences where students meet with prominent scholars;
- conducts annual summer schools.

I S I is a non-profit, non-partisan, educational organization, not connected with, nor a part of, any other organization or publication. I S I's program is financed entirely by voluntary contributions from individuals, business firms, and educational foundations.

Above: From ISI membership brochure distributed in the delegates packet at NSA's 17th Congress at Indiana University. Also included from the ISI Essay Series was "Popular Government," by Sir Henry S. Maine, and a pamphlet, "The Communist Mind," by Gerhart Niemeyer (Source: Schodde).

Editor's note: The ISI also provided a new and lasting platform for campus critics of NSA, following Buckley's 1951 attack, and that of the Students for America (see p. 810), The Young Americans for Freedom, formed in September 1960 at a conference at the family home of William Buckley (see "Revolt on Campus") developed an organized program of opposition to and of supporting disaffiliation from NSA (See Schodde, p. 809).

From the ISI frame of reference, NSA's definitions of student rights and academic freedom as applied to communist organizations and its programs supporting various forms of federal aid reflected its indifference to, if not support of, collectivism and the infusion of communist ideas on the American campus. In addition, NSA was felt not to be representative of U.S. students.

A lengthy article, which appeared in the 12/54 issue of The Individualist, *laid out the line of attack, which was reiterated in a similar vein on campuses throughout the country by YAF. The opening and closing paragraphs are excerpted below.*

WHITHER GOEST THE NSA?

By Thomas Kelleghan

College of Law, 1955

University of Notre Dame

The United States National Students Association, an organization remarkable for its devious use of the English language in disguising its dishonorable designs on American college students, is rapidly gaining an unwarranted prestige on the national level. However, its highly inflated balloon of respectability can easily be punctured and by so doing, the NSA will be readily identified for what it really is.

* * * *

Perhaps the most interesting feature of the NSA is its methods of ffiliating within a school. A brohure entitled "USNSA — Citizenhip — Scholarship — Fellowship" lefines NSA as "a confederation of student governments *which represents college student bodies* (emphasis added) through their own democratically elected student governments." NSA therefore claims to represent *all* students of the various member campuses. It would seem appropriate that the students be consulted on the subject of representation by a left wing organization. This was never done at Notre Dame, the audacious initiative being taken by a small group of "liberal" thinking students constituting the Student Senate who voted to affiliate with NSA last year without so much as a wink at a student referendum. To this date the students at Notre Dame have not been invited to express their will in regard to this highly questionable organization. Nor has there been any attempt to inform them of NSA's sinister policies. This is indeed a strange concept of 'democratic' government.

The time has come to halt NSA's increasing ascendancy over American campus life. Only an informed student opinion can effect a reversal.

ORGANIZATION

ISI neither advocates nor discourages the organization of groups on the campus. If students, on their own initiative, organize chapters of ISI, that is their doing. It is hoped that where this is done, the students do not forget that the purpose of ISI is to keep alive the American tradition of individualism, and will not be diverted from this purpose by action programs or political adventures . . . There are organizations of all kinds on every campus, and those interested in ISI might do better by joining such organizations for the purpose of spreading the ideas of individualism.

Historically, NSA has been very liberal indeed—Well to the left of, say, the majority of the Democratic Party in America.

5. The Young Republicans

M. Stanton Evans
Yale University 1951-55

Individualism is dying at Yale, and without a fight." That was Bill Buckley's somber conclusion in his 1951 bestseller, *God and Man at Yale.* And I can testify that, as of that year, it was depressingly correct.

I was a bewildered New Haven freshman when "Bill's book" fell upon a startled campus and exploded it into controversy. Indeed, I had hardly had time to become acquainted with the world of Yale before I found myself confronted with, and partially engaged in, a furious dialogue on its virtues and demerits.

The dispute which unfolded around *God and Man* was an education in itself. The Yale of 1951 was a community in which Liberalism, among faculty and undergraduates alike, ruled virtually without challenge. I had begun to sense this fact on my own, but the response to Bill's book vastly accelerated my understanding of it. For it established that Yale's fidelity to "free inquiry" was peculiarly selective—that it did not extend to conservative inquiries about the political impact of the Yale curriculum.[1]

* * *

Such was the Yale of the early 1950s. It was a world in which a student of conservative inclination found himself badly in need of help, counsel, and information. By chance encounter, early in my sojourn at Yale, I came upon sources which were to supply all three.

Late in my freshman year I wandered into Liggett's drugstore on the corner of York and Elm. Browsing at the newsstand, I came across a magazine called *The Freeman.* From its format, the magazine looked like any of a number of "little" periodicals, and I assumed it was yet another Liberal publication. To my amazement, I found it was strongly anti-Communist, and an eloquent proponent of free market economics. It was some thing of a landmark—the first time I had ever laid eyes on a conservative periodical of any sort.

A second encounter followed a philosophy class, in which I had engaged in a mild colloquy with Professor Paul Weiss, on the subject of states' rights. Afterward, a student came up to me and handed me a card. It contained two notations: "Intercollegiate Society of Individualists" [ISI] and "Foundation for Economic Education" [FEE]. "These groups think along lines like yours," he said. "You might want to get on their mailing list."

From these three organizations—*The Freeman*, ISI, and FEE—I was able to gather information useful to me in my groping attempt to weigh the significance of events, to assess the impact of course material. *The Freeman* carried a number of articles on raging national controversies—particularly the smouldering question of internal security. Through ISI, I received books by Frederic Bastiat, Frank Chodorov, and F. A. Harper—explaining the principles of the free market; the Washington newsletter, *Human Events*; and booklets from FEE. I became aware of the existence of conservative publishers—Henry Regnery and Devin-Adair. With a little effort, I found books from each at the Yale Co-op—Charles Callan Tansill's *Back Door to War*, and Frank Chodorov's *One Is a Crowd.*

This literature offered welcome information—but it was more than that. From the perspective of 1961, the slight quantity of materials then available to a conservative student may not seem impressive. But to me, it was a discovery beyond price; for it meant that I was no longer alone. Here were men of reputation—scholars, journalists, publishers—who shared my uneasiness, and who brought factual support and theoretical subtlety to the conservative cause.

It was on such foundations that the semblance of a conservative movement was launched at Yale. By the time I reached my junior year, we had gathered together a little nucleus of conservative-minded students. . . .[2]

* * *

This history of undergraduate politics offers, I believe, a paradigm of the young conservative movement throughout the country. What in 1951 had been only the inkling of disagreement, sensed by a few scattered individuals, and in 1953 had been merely a faltering effort to pose an alternative to the Liberal orthodoxy, has now become a full-blooded and purposeful movement. By common report, conservatism among American young people is on the upswing. The sudden volteface of the young, indeed, has become topic A among those who watch over American campuses, and has spurred a considerable amount of speculation and controversy. No one seems quite to know what it is all about, what has caused it, or where it is going.

This book has been written to shed some light on these matters. . . . Throughout this essay, I have used the words "conservative" and "Liberal" to identify the rebels and those against whom they are rebelling.[3]

* * *

The Young Republicans

That so many officers of Young Americans for Freedom (YAF) are also leaders in the Young Republican (YR) movement is neither conspiracy nor accident. Over the past decade, and particularly over the last five years, the YRs have become a strongly conservative organization. In fact, stirrings of conservative sentiment appeared in the Young GOP well before they were evident elsewhere. When it came time for the launching of YAF, several of these conservative Young Republicans threw in with the program, seeing it as a parallel venture to their work in the YRs.

The Young Republican organization has not always displayed so independent, or so conservative, a spirit. During its early years, it tended simply to reflect dominant Republican policy—partially because it was not fully recognized as an autonomous element within the party, partially because ideology seemed less important in those days. But as the YRs grew into an active, cohesive force, and as young people became more sensitive to issues, things began to change. Today, the YRs are an autonomous, and conservative, force in Republican and national politics.

YR predispositions, and the senior party's sensitivity to them, are suggested by New York Governor Nelson Rockefeller's failure to show up at the last Young GOP convention. As *Time* magazine put it, "Rockefeller prudently refused an invitation to share the stage with Nixon and Goldwater at a National Young Republican conference this summer—a rally where every hemidemisemiquaver of applause will be carefully measured." And, at Young Republican national gatherings, hemidemisemiquavers for Rockefeller are few and far between.

This now potent movement, with more than half-a-million members, has a continuous active history of only fifteen years or so, most of it conservative. The official beginnings date to June of 1931, when a National Conference of Young Republicans assembled in Washington's Willard Hotel. Approximately three hundred young people from all parts of the country, including the late Senator Robert A. Taft, were in attendance. This meeting was succeeded by the National Young Republican Organizations for Hoover, which created YR cadres in forty-five states, and led to the formation of a Young Republican National Committee. That group, late in 1935, launched what is now known as the Young Republican National Federation. J. Kenneth Bradley of Connecticut was elected permanent chairman—first of many important GOP names to emerge from YR politics.

The YRNF held its first convention in June, 1936.The meeting was addressed by a Young Republican named Styles Bridges, who also happened to be Governor of New Hampshire, and who went on to become a United States Senator. Bradley was elected to the chairmanship over a YR from Minnesota, Harold Stassen, who had been nominated by Walter J. Mahoney, now majority leader of the New York State Senate. Stassen himself had nominated Gordon Allott of Colorado, currently the senior United States Senator from that state. On that occasion Allott withdrew; later, in 1941, he was elected to the chairmanship.

The federation had hardly gotten into motion when World War II intervened and brought domestic politics to a virtual standstill. It was in 1946, at the first post-war convention in Charleston, W. Va., that the YRNF began its career as a force in American politics, and that the story of its present conservatism really begins. It was in that year that the Republican National Committee officially recognized the group as the agency through which it would work with young people, and allocated office space to it in Republican headquarters. Ralph Becker of New York was elected chairman at a special convention in May, 1946, and re-elected to a full two-year term the following year. He was succeeded, in June 1949, by John Tope of Michigan. Both were to figure in the skirmishing which grew into a full-fledged ideological battle within the organization.

The Dewey defeat of 1948, and the Taft-Eisenhower battle of 1952, introduced a Liberal-Conservative rift in YR ranks which has yet to be fully resolved. As the 1951 YR convention approached, the group was split between adherents of Taft and Dewey. In preparation for the Republican convention of 1952, the Deweyites had begun moving toward General Eisenhower. The YR gathering was a test of strength between the two factions—and, as it developed, provided an accurate forecast of the senior convention which followed. . . .[4]

With the lines thus drawn, the convention wrangled through five ballots to elect Warburton chairman, 246 to

215. The Dewey-Eisenhower wing was in control, and the YRs assumed a mildly "modernist" coloration. The same faction remained dominant through the 1953 and 1955 conventions, when Sullivan Barnes of South Dakota and Charles McWhorter of New York, respectively, succeeded to the chairmanship.

* * *

The battle against NSA

No survey of campus politics can be complete, or even relatively accurate, without some discussion of a group known as the United States National Student Association. NSA, as it is more familiarly known, is frequently considered to be the "voice" of American students. As such its political complexion and its credentials of representation have considerable bearing on the present discussion.

NSA, founded in 1947 at the University of Wisconsin, is an agglomeration of student government organizations. It claims affiliations with anywhere from three hundred to four hundred campuses, and a "membership" of 1.3 million students. Its principal concern—according to its constitution and various utterances from its officials—is with the internal problems of the academic community. Its constitution stipulates that NSA is not supposed to range into matters of politics. Section A, Article 10, of that document states: "No body acting on behalf of USNSA shall participate in sectarian religious activities or partisan political activities; they shall not take part in activity which does not affect students in their role as students." Section B of the same article says: "No substantial part of the activities of the national and regional bodies of USNSA shall be devoted to carrying on propaganda or otherwise attempting to influence legislation."

Nevertheless, NSA spends a large part of its time participating in just those prohibited activities. The group has increasingly insinuated itself into political controversies—covering everything from nuclear testing to "colonialism in Mozambique"—striking off jargonistic policy statements in the name of "American students." NSA leaders apparently look upon the college years as an apprenticeship in politics and group manipulation, rather than a time for training the intellect (a fact which shows up rather prominently in NSA's literary efforts).* This course is dictated, in the NSA view, by the canons of "interrelatedness"—meaning the relevance of everything to everything else, and thus the relevance to students of national and international affairs. Since classroom instruction does not always contribute to "intelligent citizenship," as one NSA president conceived it, "it seems all the more urgent that student government devote prime efforts toward the creation of an atmosphere conducive to developing student awareness and understanding of national and world situations."

If this policy meant simply a campaign to encourage "awareness" in general, criticism of NSA might be somewhat less vehement. But as a conduit for political ideas, the group has made it abundantly clear that to be Aware, one must also be Liberal. This fact, and the further fact that NSA claims to speak for all American students, must be measured against the signs of a conservative revival on the campus. Is NSA in fact Liberal? And if so, how representative is it of student sentiment throughout the country?

The answer is that, historically, NSA has been very Liberal indeed—well to the left of, say, the majority of the Democratic Party in America.[5]

*It is perhaps unfair to demand perfect literacy of any publication, or of any writer. But NSA's record in this respect is so unusually bad that it warrants further comment. NSA pamphlets are clogged with awkward, indistinct terms—"community-structured unit" is an example—which betray indistinct ideas. A good deal of this jargon is borrowed from the graceless vocabulary of the social scientists. Parts of some NSA publications are well-written, but the usual style is elephantine obscurity. For example, one passage from the *National Student News* reads: "Uncritical acceptance of majority positions or goals totally divorced from any feeling of personal commitment for their support or achievement and semi-fatalistic writing off of such commitment as useless characterizes many if not most campuses and students."

As for grammar, there are few infinitives so tightly constructed that NSA cannot split them. A 1956 NSA working paper argues the need for a special subcommission "to, under the supervision of the National Office, revise and bring up to date" an NSA brochure called, of all things, *Course Evaluation.* The January 1958 issue of the *News* tells us "student government control, responsibility and programming" are sometimes "non-existent," which might be viewed as a typographical error, had not the previous month's *News* disclosed that low-cost housing near UCLA was also "non-existent." The January issue also states, in a discussion of "Who's Who in American Colleges": "Rather significant is the criteria used by colleges in selecting candidates for "Who's Who." A working paper put together in 1957 similarly notes that "ours is a privileged society, with a hollow criteria of success." Misspellings are also common. . . . Such errors would not have particular significance, if it were not for the fact that NSA, in addition to its total immersion in politics, has also proposed to take a hand in the shaping of the college curriculum.

M. Stanton Evans is Director of the National Journalism Institute in Washington, D.C. He has been a nationally syndicated columnist and Radio and TV commentator. He became Chief Editorial Writer for the Indianapolis News in 1959.

END NOTES

[1] From Evans, p. 1.
[2] Ibid., pp. 5-6.
[3] Ibid., pp. 9-11.
[4] Ibid., pp. 125-128.
[5] Ibid., pp. 145-147.

PICTURE CREDITS: *Then:* c. 1955 Class Book Yale U., Manuscripts and Archives, Yale U. Library. *Now:* c. 2002 (Author).

M. STANTON EVANS

Early years and education. Born July 20, 1934, in Kingsville, Texas. Prepared at Oak Ridge (Tenn.) and Mt. Rainier (Md.) High schools and Bullis School, Silver Spring, Md. He graduated from Yale University in 1955 with a BA in English, and did graduate work in economics at New York University under Ludwig von Mises.

Career Highlights. M. Stanton Evans is currently director of the National Journalism Center, chairman of the Education and Research Institute in Washington, D.C., and publisher of *Consumer's Research Magazine.*

Evans broke into journalism with *The Freeman* and *National Review,* and then as managing editor of *Human Events,* where he is still a contributing editor and columnist. At the age of 26, he became the nation's youngest editor of a major metropolitan daily, when Eugene C. Pulliam named him to run the editorial page of *The Indianapolis News,* a position he held until 1974.

In 1971, Evans became a commentator for the CBS Television and Radio Networks. In 1973, he became a columnist for the Los Angeles Times Syndicate. In 1980, he became a commentator for National Public Radio, and in 1982, for the Voice of America, Radio America and WGMS-FM in Washington, D.C.

He has authored seven books, *Revolt on Campus, The Liberal Establishment, The Politics of Surrender, The Future of Conservatism, The Lawbreakers, Clear and Present Dangers* and *The Theme Is Freedom.* He is working on his eighth book, about Senator Joseph McCarthy.

A plaintiff in Federal "freedom of information" and First Amendment cases, Stan holds honorary doctor of laws degrees from Syracuse University and John Marshall Law School, plus honorary degrees from Grove City College and Francisco Marroquin University.

Family. Married May 1, 1951, in Rossville, Ga., to Elizabeth Scarlett Rostand.*(Compiled from Young America's Foundation [www.yaf.org-/staff] and the 1955 Yale Classbook)*

Conservative and Young Republican Clubs Emerge on U.S. Campuses

1946

Campus Conservatives Form Charter for New Campus Club

Mintz Says Applications Being Accepted For Membership; Founders Plan Meeting

Announcement was made today of a new organization being formed on the campus. It will be called the Carolina Conservative Club, and listed among its founders are Paul Mullinax, B. L. Sherrill, Elwood Mintz, Fountain Dawson and Mark Buchanan.

The charter of the organization reads as follows:

"We, members of the Carolina Conservative Club, are associating ourselves for the purpose of preserving the principles of reason, sound economy, basic human rights, just and equitable government based on sound American doctrines of free enterprise in a capitalistic democracy." The charter further states that the organization is specifically opposed to:

a. "Pressure politics and political action seeking gains for a minority

adequate military forces which are scientifically equipped.

d. "International forces to put an

1947

CORNELL DAILY SUN

Cornell Young Republican Club Has Second Meeting; Decides on Program

Holding its second meeting of the year, the Cornell Young Republican Club met last night to formulate plans for the creation of a working organization on the campus representing the Republican point of view.

lers, have been formed on the campuses throughout the country. The Club's chief interest will be in the presentation of educational information on practical politics and of Republican viewpoints.

1948

PHILADELPHIA, WEDNES

Young Republican Club, Republican Open Forum Officers Merge Groups

Morgan, Mathis Have Approval Of Stassen And Becker In Joining Forces

ELECTIONS NEXT WEEK

The University Chapters of the Young Republican Club and the Republican Open Forum have merged, according to a joint an-

I C Committee Elects Leaders

At the Independent Council Membership meeting held yesterday, 2 members were selected as chairmen. Those elected were

1949

WU Republicans To Hear Claude Bakewell Thursday

By DON HOWARD And MICHEL DEE SILVA

Former Congressman Claude Bakewell will address the Young Republican Club at a "Coffee Hour" Thursday at 3:30 in the Student Center, beginning the group's semester program.

Bakewell's address will mark his second appearance on the WU . During the campaign the politician addressed d Congressman Walter urray Thompson. l-Western Federation of oung Republicans. Ed e-president of the WU epublicans Club and a

Republicans To Organize

BY LEE HARTLEY

What the South needs is a two-party political system, says David R. Kivlat, instructor in the Fine Arts department.

Mr. Kivlat, a Republican, says he wants to help establish a Young Republican club at Emory University.

"Our appeal is not only to Republicans but to Democrats who are interested in a healthy two-party system for the South," he said.

Mr. Kivlat said he had been in touch with Bill Folsom, president of the Federation of Young Republican clubs in Georgia, and Cecil Hartness, one of the two Republican national committeemen from Georgia.

These men, along with many other Georgians, are interested in building up a Republican organiza-

will be granted a charter by the state federation, he said. Its activities would include meetings, discussions and other group participation programs.

1951

1952

1952 Number 22

Young Republicans Gather For A Mock Convention

Tomorrow night at 8:15 in the Aula, The Young Republicans will hold a Mock Convention. Ordinarily a Convention is a large and turbulent affair, and they hope to create some of the same stir and excitement here.

As the college is not fully represented by the 48 states, the delegates will represent their houses. Anyone who wants to can be a delegate. The Houses will not have proportional representation and therefore each delegate will cast a vote for her candidate. In the interests of time, they will dispense with some of the formalities. There will be a Keynote ad-

CAMPUS YRC'S FORMED STEADILY after World War II, devoted both to party politics and issues education. Unlike the Young Democrats, who seemed in that era to have ceded the college field to the SDA (Murphy, p. 785), a College Service Committee was formed in 1949 by the National YRC to focus on year-round campus organization (Evans, p. 802). As at North Carolina in 1946 (left), some independent ideologically based campus conservative clubs also formed prior to the 1951 emergence of a national Conservative movement (See ISI, p. 800). From top: Cover, NYRC 1971 history booklet; U. of NC *Tar Heel,* 8/10/46; *Cornell Daily Sun,* 12/21/47; *Daily Pennsylvanian,* 3/10/48; Washington U., St Louis, *Student Life,* 10/11/49; Emory U. *Wheel,* 3/27/51; *Vassar Miscellany News,* 4/30/52.

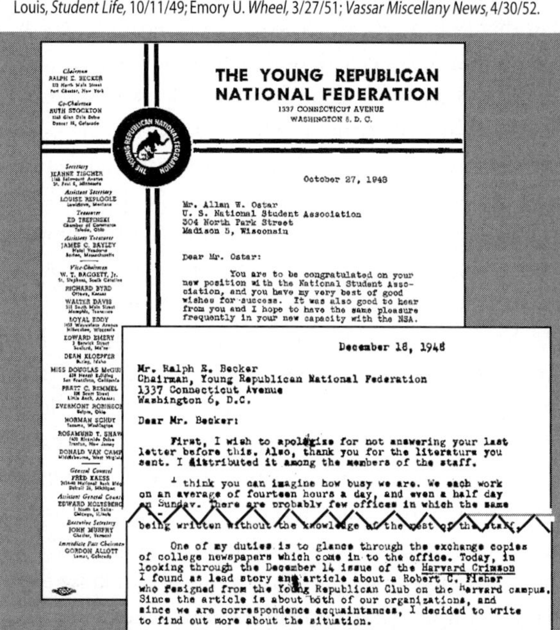

THE YOUNG REPUBLICAN NATIONAL FEDERATION
1337 CONNECTICUT AVENUE
WASHINGTON 6, D. C.

Chairman RALPH E. BECKER · Co-Chairman RUTH STOCKTON · Secretary JEANNE TISCHER · Assistant Secretary LOUISE REPLOGLE · Treasurer ED TREPINSKI · Assistant Treasurer JAMES C. BAYLEY · Vice-Chairmen W. T. BAGGETT, Jr., RICHARD BYRD, WALTER DAVIS, LOYAL EDDY, EDWARD EMERY

October 27, 1948

Mr. Allan W. Ostar
U. S. National Student Association
304 North Park Street
Madison 5, Wisconsin

Dear Mr. Ostar:

You are to be congratulated on your new position with the National Student Association, and you have my very best of good wishes for success. It was also good to hear from you and I hope to have the same pleasure frequently in your new capacity with the NSA.

December 18, 1948

Mr. Ralph E. Becker
Chairman, Young Republican National Federation
1337 Connecticut Avenue
Washington 6, D.C.

Dear Mr. Becker:

First, I wish to apologize for not answering your last letter before this. Also, thank you for the literature you sent. I distributed it among the members of the staff.

I think you can imagine how busy we are. We each work on an average of fourteen hours a day, and even a half day on Sunday. There are probably few offices in which the same

being written without the knowledge of the rest of the staff.

One of my duties is to glance through the exchange copies of college newspapers which come in to the office. Today, in looking through the December 14 issue of the Harvard Crimson I found as lead story an article about a Robert C. Fisher who resigned from the Young Republican Club on the Harvard campus. Since the article is about both of our organizations, and since we are correspondence acquaintances, I decided to write to find out more about the situation.

NSA/YRC FLAP AT HARVARD. *Editor's note: NSA and the YRNF made brief informal contact in correspondence between Ralph Becker (10/27/48), Co-Chair of the YRNF, and Allan Ostar (12/18/48), NSA Public Relations director. Ostar raises a question - a response to which has not been found - about news in the 12/14/48* Harvard Crimson *of a confidential 300-page report on NSA prepared by a Harvard YRC member and delegate to NSA's 1948 Congress at the request of National YRF President Ralph Becker and "submitted to Becker, The House Un-American Activities Committee" and the Senate's special investigating committee. Ultimately the student resigned from the YRC and was removed from the NSA delegation, protesting the abuse of his intention to "stop criticism of NSA." (See issues of the* Crimson *of that period).*

NSA is the most dangerous of the many left-wing political pressure groups on campus.

6. Robert Munger and the Students for America

Editor's note: Bob Munger emerged as a student leader at Los Angeles City College (LACC) in 1950 and 1951. He was freshman class president, a prize-winning member of the LACC debate team, and served on the student Executive Council. He was defeated for Associated Student presidency by Tom Suzuki, whose memoir appears in Part 5, Section 8. He was a member of the LACC delegation to the California regional meeting at Berkeley in November 1950. On his return he sponsored a resolution to investigate NSA, which was adopted by the Executive Council. The December 8 issue of the Los Angeles Collegian *reported "bitter discussion" over the delegation's NSA reports. After graduating the two-year college, Munger enrolled in Pepperdine College and founded the National Collegiate MacArthur Club in October 1951. In 1952 the Club changed its name to Students For America.*

In December 1952 SFA issued a six-page report entitled "National Student Association . . . An Insidious Leftist Pressure Group." Munger also appeared at various events repeating the charges. His speech on the subject at the National Interfraternity Conference in November 1952 (see NSA and the fraternities, Part 2, Section 2) was answered by NSA President Dick Murphy. Following are excerpts from various sources at the time.

From the Los Angeles Collegian, *December 8, 1950.*

Former Campus Politico Still at It

Bob Munger, who only a year ago was in the midst of the local political scene, is still at it—only now it's on a nationwide basis.

The one time City College Executive Councilman and now a student at Pepperdine College is the founder of the National Collegiate MacArthur Club. In fact, he is the director of the nationwide club.

Douglas MacArthur was the US. General who was ousted by President Truman in early February and caused one of the most controversial periods in American history. MacArthur was voted "The Top Personality of 1951" by the newspaper editors of America. . . .

Munger said Wednesday that the National Collegiate MacArthur Club is shooting for "100 chapters by '52."

"You might call that our New Year's resolution," he said.

Presently there are 22 chapters throughout the United States. Ten are in Southern California, including City and State Colleges, Pepperdine, Pasadena, Occidental, UCLA, USC, Loyola, Long Beach, and Valley.

In those 22 chapters there are about 1,000 members, most of whom are students. Munger said. Locally, there are 50 MacArthur Club members on this campus. . . .

Munger wanted it understood that the MacArthur Clubs were founded to combat Communism and Socialism and not for the purpose of promoting MacArthur to the presidency of the United States.

"A lot of students won't join because they think we are just trying to get MacArthur into the White House," Munger said. "We aren't. We're out to fight Communism and Socialism."

The club is open both to Democrats and Republicans. In fact, its slogan is: "It is no longer a question of being a Democrat or a Republican but a question of being an American." The slogan came from a MacArthur speech.

Munger says the club is open to any student in the country. . . . It costs 25 cents to become a member. The membership fee is to cover printing, postage and other organizational expenses.

The first official publication of the organization came out this week and was distributed to students all over the Southland. A monthly, it is called the *American Student* and is edited by Miss Florence McCarthy, a local student.

Most of the articles in the four page, four column tabloid were written by local students. The lead feature was written by Bob Andelson, a former Collegian staff member, now a student at the University of Chicago. Benedict Ray, assistant dean in charge of men's activities, also wrote an article.

Many people on campus think that a lot of clubs of this type will spring up all over the country in the nation's colleges and universities this year, an election year.

Plans are presently being made here on campus to start a Democratic Club.

Munger thinks this is a good thing— "whether it be a Democratic or a Republican club."

"It will create interest on the American political scene, and this is a good thing," Munger said.

Munger has appeared on several television panels during the past few months. He was on the debate team when be was a student here.

From the archival clipping, circa 1952.

MacArthur's SFA Repudiates NSA

The National Collegiate MacArthur Clubs has now become Students For America and after receiving plugs from Walter Winchell and Paul Harvey report a membership of 1,800 members on over 65 campuses.

SFA with General MacArthur as its Honorary President has launched a bitter attack on the National Student Association.

SFA which says it stands for "Truth, Loyalty, and Honor," in December used their official publication *The American Student* to make a lengthy and detailed attack on NSA for its stand for federal scholarships, academic freedom and its opposition to discrimination.

SFA quoted the NSA constitution "to guarantee all people equal rights and possibilities for . . . higher education . . . regardless of economic circumstances." The SFA article goes on to say, "If this isn't the Welfare State philosophy then nothing is. The NSA philosophy followed to its logical conclusion could only mean socialization of higher education since obviously everyone cannot afford to go to college."

NSA has in the short six years of its existence come to be recognized as the spokesman for American students to educational organizations, to governmental agencies and to students of the world. NSA holds a seat on the U.S. Commission for UNESCO and is a member of the American Council on Education.

The article's headline calls NSA "an insidious leftist pressure group" and challenges NSA stands on the student's right to organizations of his own choice, on academic freedom and on fraternity discrimination clauses which NSA opposes.

Bob Munger, who is National Director of SFA, was a speaker at both the undergraduate and senior conferences of the 44th Annual National Interfraternity Conference, which didn't adopt a liberal position on bias clauses.

The American Student article did not agree with NSA's cooperation with the American Civil Liberties Union, and repeated attacks on the ACLU for defending the civil liberties of communists.

A side-swipe was given SDA in a sentence reading, "In view of the foregoing evidence it is easy to see why the Students for Democratic Action (student branch of the infamous Americans for Democratic Action—ADA) urges its members to 'support the National Student Association (NSA), and work for school affiliation with NSA.'"

The SFA membership leaflet printed in glowing red, white and blue states that they are for the constitution, religious principles, free enterprise, economy, and strong foreign policy, while they are against immorality, subversive elements, socialistic expansion, appeasement and waste in government.

One of the SFA leaflets stated, "We are sick and tired of hearing our colleges and universities referred to as 'little RED schoolhouses.'"

The SFA has a membership questionnaire which asks quite interesting questions including the following: "Are you in favor of World Government at the present time? Are you in favor of loyalty oaths? Are you in favor of FEPC [Fair Employment Practices Commission]? Do you feel that Senator Joe McCarthy has done a good job? Do you feel that the House Un-American Activity [sic] Committee has done a good job?

Anyone desiring further information should write Students for America, P.O. Box 2124, Hollywood 28, California.

From The American Student, *Vol. 2, No. 3, March 1953.*

NSA Evades Documents Charges Poll Exposes Misrepresentation

Students For America Research Bureau

In the December 1952 issue of the *American Student* we exposed the National Student Association as the most dangerous of all the many left wing pressure groups now operating on American campuses. We showed that the NSA had achieved this somewhat dubious distinction as a result of the official status which it enjoys at schools affiliated in this loose confederation of student governments.

NSA claims to be unbiased and non-political, yet NSA advocates letting avowed Communists teach.

Basic Policy Declaration IV Academic Freedom (p. 11, USNSA Constitution) upholds the privilege of Communists and members of listed subversive organizations to teach by declaring: "The teacher has the right to join organizations . . . provided that these organizations are not illegal under civil statutes. . . . The basis for employment of faculty shall be *only* their ability to fulfill the requirements of the position." It is to be noted in this regard that the Communist Party, as well as all other fronts for the Kremlin in America, "are not illegal under civil statutes."

. . . [NSA] is claiming to be the only truly representative voice of American college students. One would gather from this then, that most American college students are in favor of letting avowed Communists teach. This simply is not true!

POLL SHOWS NSA MISREPRESENTATION

During the month of February 1953 the Associated Collegiate Press conducted a nationwide poll of student opinion in which this question was asked: "Do you think avowed Communist Party members should be allowed on college faculties?" The results were as follows:

YES 9%
NO 85%
NO OPINION 4%
OTHER 2%

Thus we can clearly see one more instance in which the NSA has taken a position in diametric opposition to the overwhelming number of students whom it claims to represent! How can the National Student Association be democratic or truly representative when it so flagrantly disregards the opinions of the great majority of students whom it claims to represent? Surely no one will deny that letting Communists teach is an important issue. Is it intellectually honest for an organization to claim to represent hundreds of thousands of students who have never even heard of that organization and who would probably disagree with that organization if they had? Is this NSA's concept of "Academic Freedom"? Bear in mind that the largest single portion of the $37,790.00 yearly NSA budget comes indirectly out of the pockets of students who are ignorant of the very existence of NSA. This money comes from student activity fees, in most cases.

DOCUMENTED CONCLUSIONS

The fully documented report by the Students for America Research Bureau came to the following conclusions:

1. NSA is milking thousands of dollars every year out of students who are ignorant of the very existence of NSA and who benefit nothing in return.
2. NSA has appointed itself as the sole representative of American college students, without their knowledge or consent.
3. NSA advocates letting Communists teach.
4. NSA condemns school authorities who eliminate Communist sympathizers from positions of trust.
5. NSA wants to allow subversive groups to function on campuses and use campus facilities.
6. NSA wants to eliminate fraternities which do not conform to its desires.
7. NSA advocates Welfare State principles as the solution to economic problems in the field of education.
8. NSA refuses to ban admitted Communists from being officers of NSA.
9. NSA does not hesitate to go against the will of the majority of students whom it claims to represent.

These nine points have been thoroughly substantiated by first hand investigation, and by official NSA documents.

It should be stated that it is not the policy of the Students For America to eliminate the freedom of expression of any person or legally operating organization, including NSA. If NSA desires to pursue a policy beneficial to communists and socialists that is their prerogative. However, if in so doing they persist in claiming to represent students who have never even heard of them and in using the money of these students as well, we feel it only reasonable that appropriate action be taken to end such injustices.

(Free copy of the complete report referred to will be mailed upon request.) See Vol. I No. 10, American Student, *Dec. 1952.*

* * *

From The Washington Post, *December 20, 1953.*

Vigilante Charge Embroils Campus

By Lawrence Laurent
Post Reporter

A West Coast students' organization attempted to gain an eastern foothold by establishing a chapter at the University of Virginia this fall, and stirred up a 10-day tempest in Charlottesville's "Academic Village."

Students who opposed the organization branded it a group of "self-appointed vigilantes."

The organization, Students for America, applied to the University's Student Council for a charter and was turned down unanimously. The resulting controversy ran to thousands of words in editorials, petitions and letters to the student newspaper, the *Cavalier Daily*. Now the Virginia leader of Students For America hopes to change some of the organization's national regulations and plans to apply for a charter again next year.

* * *

It was said that the Council felt "that to allow such an organization to use the university's name would not be in the best interests of the school, or in accord with the traditions on which the university was founded. . ."

The morning after the Council's action, the *Cavalier Daily* carried an editorial headlined, "Kindergarten Ku Klux Klan," which said that "there is a group of students here—largely first-year men—who desire to establish a chapter of Students for America at this university. The avowed purpose of these self appointed vigilantes is to search out and expose any leftists, Marxists, fellow-travelers, etc., among the students and faculty of the university. These first year men take it upon themselves to determine who is and who is not "un-American" through their own junior grade imitation of McCarthyism. We feel that this sort of kindergarten Ku Klux Klan is out of place at this university."

* * *

[The editor of the *Cavalier Daily*] says most of his objections were based on material in [SFA's] Handbook. Listed in the handbook as supporters of SFA are such persons as Gen. Douglas MacArthur, Fulton Lewis, Jr., Sen. Karl E. Mundt (R-SD), and radio commentators John T. Flynn and Walter Winchell. . . . The SFA handbook says the organization has 2500 members from more than 120 schools. . . .

* * *

The handbook lists organizations cited by the Government for subversive activity which deal with students or educational institutions. There is detailed information on "How to identify a Communist Front," "Pink Professors," "Left Wing Literature," "Phony Peace Drives," "Communist Smear Techniques," and "The Anti-Communist Hysteria."

* * *

"The method of dealing with the pink professor is of particular interest. SFA members are urged to take notes and to have the notes verified by a fellow member.

"When the information has been compiled, it should be sent to both national headquarters and regional vice director for suggestions or instructions. For obvious reasons we can't be more specific in this handbook. However, you may rest assured that many possibilities of appropriate action are always available, depending on the particular situation involved."

From the Roosevelt College Torch, *Chicago, February 16, 1953.*

USNSA president denies charge of subversion

The United States National Student Association, of which RC is a member, has replied to charges that it is "subversive" and "an insidious leftist group."

The charges had been leveled at NSA by an organization called Students For America through its publication *The American Student* and in a speech delivered by its President before the National Interfraternity Conference in New York City in November, 1952.

Prexy issues rebuttal

Richard J. Murphy, President of NSA, issued the rebuttal early this month. Part of it follows:

"USNSA takes no exception to the right of any group or individual to criticize its program, policies and activities. USNSA, however, will not stand by and allow its reputation to be damaged by irresponsible and unfounded charges such as those that have been recently made.

"Positively non-communist"

"USNSA is positively non-communist and participates in absolutely no political activity whatsoever. USNSA cooperates with no subversive organizations. USNSA is not listed on any of the so-called subversive organization listings, and it has not been cited by any of the security agencies for disloyal activities. Such charges are baseless and libelous.

"Nowhere does USNSA demand conformity to any policies, and no policy calls for the destruction of the fraternity system. Many outstanding leaders in USNSA at present and in the past have been fraternity members. USNSA does stand for the eventual elimination of discrimination in all student organizations, a policy that has been adopted as recommended to student governments.

"USNSA claims to be the most representative student organization in the United States today by virtue of the active membership of 300 student governments widely diverse in type of school and geographical location whose jurisdictions extend to over 800,000 American college students.

"Abroad, USNSA is successfully waging a campaign for the extension of democratic student life in the face of strenuous Communist propaganda efforts to win student support. Through the International Student Conference USNSA works with 35 other democratic national student associations in promotion of mutual projects of assistance. At the present time more student associations are cooperating in this effort than ever participated in Communist-inspired programs of the past.

"USNSA is proud to have the active participation of an advisory group including such outstanding Americans as Harold E. Stassen, Mrs. Eleanor Roosevelt, Very Reverend Vincent J. Flynn, Dean Althea Kratz Hottel, and Reverend Celestine Steiner, S.J. Such Americans would not be actively associated with any organization of questionable loyalty."

ROBERT F. MUNGER

Editor's note: The anthology editor and project personnel have been unable to acquire any information about Robert Munger's subsequent career highlights or early years. Confidentiality rules at Los Angeles City College and Pepperdine University have limited archivists in providing any unpublished biographical information, if there is any. However, both archives cooperated in document searches on Munger and SFA, as well as referrals to professors of the era still alive. They had no recollection of SFA. The MacArthur Library reports no material on the Students for MacArthur. We have been unable to trace any additional documents on Robert Munger or the Students for America through keyword searches in library networks and searches for the project at the Library of Congress by Roy Voegeli. There is a two-page entry on SFA by Senator Mundt in the 2/23/53 Congressional Record *(There is an unrelated SFA that was formed in 1984). The documentation for this unit is largely from NSA files at the State Historical Society of Wisconsin, the archives at the University of Texas, private papers of Dick Murphy, issues of the* Los Angeles City College Collegian, *and some brief notices in* The GraPhiC, *the Pepperdine student newspaper. Munger was a member of the debate teams at both institutions. (See also Suzuki, Pt. 5, Sec. 8, pp. 1032, 1034.)*

They argue that "the Association is not representative of the American student"

Student Critics of NSA on the Campus

Stephen Clements Schodde
Teachers College, Columbia University, 1965

Editor's note: This is an excerpt from Stephen Schodde's 1965 thesis for his degree of Doctor of Education at Teachers College, Columbia University.[1]

Among the most severe critics of the NSA are other students, particularly the student political right wing. The political right, using as a basis for criticism the Association's toleration for all shades of opinion including Communist observers at their Congresses and the generally liberal legislative resolutions emerging from the plenary floor, have sharply attacked the Association.[2] These attacks date from 1952. In November of that year, Robert Munger, president of an organization known as "Students for America" (SFA), formerly the "National Collegians for MacArthur Club," attacked the Association at the annual meeting of the National Interfraternity Conference in New York City. Although copies of Munger's speech were not available to the Association, the tenor of his remarks, which allegedly called NSA "the most dangerous of all the many left-wing political pressure groups now operating on the American campuses," was reported to the Association by friends of NSA who attended the fraternity meeting.

Deeply concerned about this news and another assault on the Association which appeared in the December issue of *The American Student,* the official publication for the Students for America, Richard Murphy, Association President, prepared a response intended to answer the SFA's attack. The mimeographed reply, approved by the National Executive Committee and distributed to all member schools as well as to those non-member schools which were considering affiliation, dissected the Munger charges of leftist extremism and broadly defended the Association's acceptability in the mainstream of American student thinking.[3]

According to Mrs. Christine Conaway, Dean of Women at Ohio State University, it was at least partly because of the Association's difficulties with the right wing that the three national professional student personnel groups issued a joint statement in the spring of 1953 lauding the Association as the "most representative American student group currently operating as a constructive force for improving student government on the campus."[4] In recent years, the Young Americans for Freedom (YAF), a conservative student group whose political idol is Barry Goldwater, has severely criticized the NSA. They argue that "the Association is not representative of the American student, is frequently partisan and political in its conduct, and ignores minority rights in its legislative process at the annual Congress."[5]

YAF attacks NSA by encouraging the disaffiliation of the campus student government from the Association. This is done either by electing student government members opposed to NSA or more often, at large schools, by requesting an all school referendum on continuing membership.[6]

Stephen Schodde is a professional mediator working in such areas as family law and neighborhood conflict. For most of his career until early retirement in 1977, he was a student personnel administrator at Drake University in Des Moines. Dr. Shodde's 1965 doctoral thesis (See footnote 1) is a primary reference for NSA history. Additional excerpts appear in Part 2.
(Photo from author, c. 2000.)

END NOTES

[1] *Editor's note:* Stephen Clements Schodde, "Certain Foci of the United States National Student Association, and Their Implications for Student Personnel Administrators." (Unpublished doctoral thesis, Teachers College, Columbia University, 1965.) A complete copy, with the permission of the author, has been made and will reside in the USNSA/USSA archives at both the Wisconsin Historical Society and the Hoover Institution. This document is more than just an excellent professional thesis, it's a very readable narrative. Those interested in the history of student life will find it a helpful resource as it takes NSA from 1946 through to the year 1965 and covers topics such as: Origins, Structure, Finances and Selected Programs, NSA, Academic Freedom and Student Rights, NSA and Desegregation, NSA and the Campus, and Trends and Implications. Appendices include a roster of national officers, advisory board and advisory council members and a bibliography. Schodde retired at 61 as Dean of Students at Drake University, Iowa. He also served in 1996 as Director of Student Development Services.

[2] The Association's opposition to the McCarran Act and the House Un-American Activities Committee have not endeared it to the rightists. See, in particular, Young Americans for Freedom, "National Student Association Report" (Washington: Young Americans for Freedom, 1963).

[3] Richard J. Murphy, Statement in Answer to the Students for America (Philadelphia: The Association, January, 1953).

[4] Conversation with Dean Conaway, a former national advisor to the Association and Dean of Women at Ohio University, Columbus, Ohio, September 1, 1963.

[5] Young Americans for Freedom, "National Student Association Report" (Washington: Young Americans for Freedom, 1963).

[6] Actually the referendum is the most effective weapon against NSA. It was used at the University of Indiana in 1963 just prior to the holding of the annual Congress on that campus. Although the referendum was successful, the Congress was held as scheduled. *Editor's note:* See Shaffer, p. 328, pictorial, p. 1074, for more on Indiana University and NSA.

Trying to do too much?

Editor's note: While there was general support for NSA from the left in its early years (see pp. 149, 796), early skepticism in an 8/47 article in The New Leader *(just before NSO became NSA) was voiced by John Roche, a Cornell University Student League for Industrial Democracy leader. He writes:*

There is a new federation of student governments and organizations known as the National Students Organization. In theory it is a nationwide, liberal outflt to which all American College students will belong. Few would oppose the theory, but in practice the NSO will have to choose between being nationwide or liberal. If it is nationwide it would be unable to take a position on racial segregation without losing its membership in states where that practice is the law. Similarly, it could not favor Federal subsidization of higher education without losing its Catholic membership. If the NSO is to succeed on an all-inclusive scale it will have to limit itself to opposing measles and cannibalism.

Is there a solution? Basic changes in our political and economic framework predicate a full solution. For example, the only effective way to eliminate post-war cynicism is to eliminate war.... Resolutions are no substitute for work.

STEPHEN CLEMENTS SCHODDE

Early years and education. I was born February 6, 1936, and graduated from St. Louis Park High School, Minnesota, in 1954. My undergraduate degree was from the College of Education in 1958. A masters degree followed in 1959 from Columbia Teachers College, New York, in 1959. In this I owe a great deal to my mentor Dr. Gordon Klopf as he was my advisor and helped me obtain my first job in Guidance and Student Personnel Administration at what was then Buffalo State Teachers College, Buffalo, New York. Work on my Ed. D. followed, and I obtained the degree in 1965.

Career highlights. There was a brief tour as a consultant on a fraternity study for a very fine liberal arts college, St. Lawrence University in Canton, New York, and then it was on to Drake University, Des Moines, Iowa, where I was fortunate to work for Dr. Arthur Casebeer for several years. After Dean Casebeer left, I stayed on at Drake and held a number of student personnel administrative positions and also managed to complete a law degree at Drake. I pursued the law degree during the "troubles" in the seventies as administrators were falling left and right over conflicts with student "rights" and presidents who wanted a peaceful campus.

While at Drake, I helped design a new student orientation program, a student-to-student tutoring program, a student judicial program and even a short lived group dynamics "sensitivity training" experience. The group dynamics approach, which was intended as a leadership training experience, was successful for awhile, but we ran out of sensitivity and new challenges came on the scene. At the time of my early retirement in 1997, I had administrative responsibilities for health, study skills, counseling and tutoring.

Today I am a professional mediator working in such areas as family law (custody and visitation issues), debtor/creditor conflicts, neighborhood disputes, victim/offender matters, truancy issues and perhaps most interestingly, animal producers and feeders and their concerned neighbors. "Not in my back yard" sorts of conflicts. The latter are the most intractable . . . a real challenge!

Family. Married to my wife Ann some 40 years now and we are proud of our children, Greg 38, Geoff 35 and Stephanie 31. Greg (a patent law attorney) and his wife, Holly, have presented us with the opportunity to grandparent three kids. Geoff, a musician, and Stephanie, an actress, both are single and loving it in Minneapolis.

ALBUM

Students for America Mount Full Court Assault on NSA in 1952-53

"NSA IS USING THE MONEY OF THOUSANDS OF STUDENTS WHO ARE IGNORANT OF THE VERY EXISTENCE OF NSA." This SFA assertion is grounded in the wide indifference to student government on major college campuses. NSA's defense of student rights, support of civil liberties and opposition to fraternity discrimination became proof to SFA of NSA's subversive sympathies. (From top: *Congresssional Record,* 2/23/53; SFA Report 12/52; *American Student,* 3/53; *Emory Wheel,* 2/5/53; Roosevelt College *Torch,* 2/16/53; U. of Va. *Cavalier Daily* headlines in a *Washington Post* montage 12/20/53.)

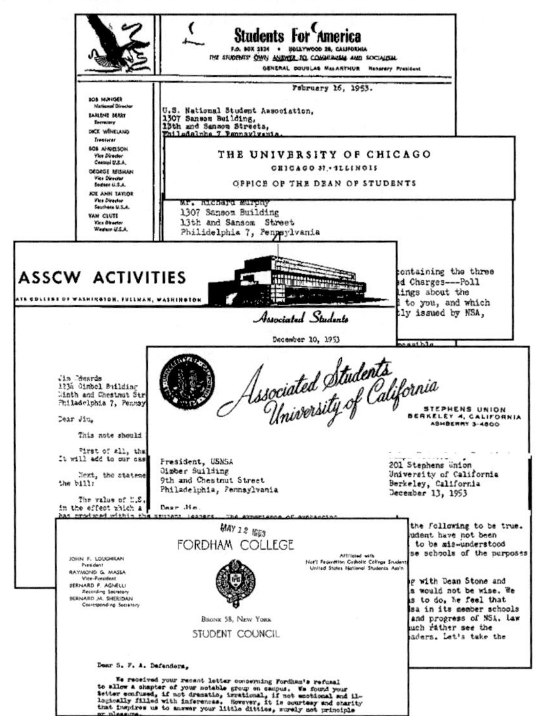

DURING A THREE-YEAR BLITZ, from 1952 through 1954, Robert Munger through Students for America created national publicity, was a featured speaker at the annual meeting of the National Interfraternity Conference in 1952 (p. 404), generated a lot of correspondence in NSA circles, and helped inspire support for NSA from a number of higher education student personnel professional associations (see fn 2, p. 328). Above from top: Munger writes NSA on 2/16/53 acknowledging receipt of a response to SFA charges from NSA VP Janet Welsh, noting "We have not yet received Mr. Murphy's answer. If, indeed an adequate answer to our charges exists." Following are three letters in refutation of SFA's charges and support of NSA (3/23/53 U. of Chicago Director of Student Activities, and student body presidents of Washington State College (12/10/53) and UC Berkeley (12/13/53). Fordham College Student Council President John F. Loughran (5/12/53) in a bitterly sarcastic letter explains why an SFA Chapter was disallowed at Fordham, paralleling a U. of Virginia choice (p. 807) that "to allow SFA use of the university's name would not be in the best interests of the school."

Communism as an ideal and a movement challenged mid-20th-century U.S. student leaders

7. How Its Own Cold War Influenced Liberal Student Activism

Barry Keating

Swarthmore College, NSA participant, 1951-54. Young Adult Council Delegate, 1953-58
International Vice-President, Students for Democratic Action, 1953-57

Editor's note: This essay by Barry Keating is part memoir and part analysis of that period in U.S. student organization history when several generations of college student leaders cut their eye teeth in pre- and post-World War II ideological battles. The worldview they shared was shaped by these battles as they moved into the political and cultural "establishment" of the latter part of the 20th century.

One theme that emerges was the omnipresent threat that Communism as an ideology and a movement, through its home-grown and passionate U.S. student champions and sympathizers, could hijack broader student organizations and movements in the service of a Soviet-inspired agenda of world conquest and subversion. Fascism, bigotry and "red scares" provided equally threatening antidotes. Students and their adult mentors responded in different ways—ranging from the collaborative "united front" thinking in the mid-thirties (See Berlin, p. 10; Lash, p. 42), to the attacks by conservatives on NSA as a dangerous hotbed of collectivist ideas and Communist sympathizers (See Schodde, p. 809).

In this monograph Barry Keating, an author of several informally published histories of the U.S. student movement, helps connect to their common cause many of the Cold War experiences reported in the previous sections of this Part; in Part 3, Section 2; and in the Prologue.

This is a short memoir about some of my own experiences in and evaluations of the student movement of the 1940's and 1950's, particularly concerning the running conflicts between student liberals and student Communists during those years, and the highly controversial role of secret U.S. government funding of student international programs.[1]

I am a social psychologist. One reason I decided to specialize in social psychology in graduate school was because of my many experiences in student movements through the years 1946-1958 while attending Garden City High School, NY; Swarthmore College, PA; and New York University. I participated in student governments from when I was a freshman in high school until I was in graduate school. I participated in the student Christian movement, student newspapers, and Americans for Democratic Action's Students for Democratic Action during those years.[2] I was a delegate to the Young Adult Council of the National Social Welfare Assembly, 1953-1958.[3] I wrote two long histories of student and youth movements for ADA (Keating, 1953 and 1956).[4]

I entered Swarthmore College in the fall of 1950, and was elected President of my freshman class. I first heard about the United States National Student Association when I went to a student council meeting. I attended the next Pennsylvania-West Virginia Regional Convention of USNSA at the University of Pennsylvania,[5] the next national convention of USNSA at the University of Minnesota,[6] and five more regional and national USNSA conventions while I was at Swarthmore.

The Swarthmore SDA

In 1950-1951, my first year in college, the Swarthmore Chapter of SDA worked on two major projects besides sponsoring liberal speakers. The first project was supporting the Clark and Dilworth political reform movement in Philadelphia. The old Philadelphia political machine ruled that city by controlling the votes from the inner city river wards. Some reform workers who had ventured into those wards had been badly beaten. Local SDA chapters sent large teams of students to work door to door in the river wards, always in groups. None of our students were attacked, but on Election Day voting at many river ward polling places was openly rigged, sometimes with violence.

The second project was fighting the local Young Progressive of America chapter for control of the Swarthmore Race Relations Committee. The issue that year was the Swarthmore town barbershop, where the barber refused to cut the hair of African-American students. YPA wanted to organize mass picketing of the town barbershop; SDA wanted the college and the local churches to convince the barber not to discriminate.[7]

The Conflict Between American Liberals and Communists

I was a student delegate to the ADA National Board for three or four years, until the mid-1950's. Every adult member of that Board seemed to have bitter personal memories of the Communists' betrayal of the liberals in 1939 after the Soviet-Nazi Pact. These were men and women who had come up out of the street level organizing and campaigning in the 1930's student movements, labor unions, civil rights groups, and New Deal politics. By the early 1950's they were congressmen, lawyers, scholars, theologians, businessmen, city council members, and labor union officers. But they all remembered 1939. Their hostility to the Communists was not, first, about the new Cold War. It dated from bitter events in the 1930's. That earlier history cast a long shadow over what happened in the 1950's.[8]

Pre-World War II Origins of ADA and SDA

As Seymour Reisin notes in his memoir (Reisin, p. 781), the Americans for Democratic Action legally began at the 1948 convention. However, that convention was only a chapter in a much longer series of often bitter events. I think this longer sequence of dramas has haunted liberals ever since.

Both ADA and SDA were essentially expansions of organizations set up in the early 1940's by liberals who had just gone through the grim experience of having their laboriously constructed progressive student organizations, cause organizations, and unions of the 1930's effectively disorganized or destroyed by internal fighting between communists and liberals (Prologue).

In 1939 American Communists suddenly switched sides because of the Stalin-Nazi Pact and, in effect, lent support to Hitler's Nazis. The Soviet Union's invasion of Finland showed more of the Communists' true priorities. The American Communists put supporting Stalin's foreign policies ahead of all the social reform programs so dear to the hearts of American liberals.

The resulting fights for leadership between liberals and Communists wrecked, or almost wrecked, many of the major reform organizations of the 1930's. Two casualties were the American Student Union and the American Youth Congress.[9]

Liberals came away from these disasters with deeply held convictions that the Communists had betrayed them and their progressive and New Deal goals, and that the Communists were really totalitarians akin to the Nazis and the Ku Klux Klan.[10]

In 1948, the ADA was an expansion of the Union for Democratic Action, organized by Reinhold Niebuhr[11] and other liberals in the early 1940's both to oppose the communists and to continue working for traditional liberal goals like human rights, social justice, labor unions, and the defeat of Old World tyrannies. The Students for Democratic Action was a change of name and a new affiliation for the United States Student Assembly, organized in 1943 by the student liberals. These were veterans of their own conflicts with the Communists (Munts, p. 34), which had just wrecked the American Student Union and the American Youth Congress (Lash, p 42).

Older Liberals Understood the Dangers of Communism

Therefore, most older liberals of the sort that participated in the new ADA considered themselves "experts" on the dangers of Communism, both domestic and foreign, before the Cold War began in the late 1940's. They readily supported basic programs of President Truman like the Marshall Plan and, later in the Eisenhower era, NATO. They reacted with fury to charges from Joseph McCarthy-type conservative reactionaries that liberals were "soft" on communism; they knew they were the ones who had fought the Communists in labor unions and student organizations.[12]

Seymour Reisin in his memoir is correct that some students in SDA came from families with Marxist orientations, and some had families with conservative political views. However, most of the SDA-ers were from New Deal, liberal-oriented families. Most student liberals of the 1950's, including myself, shared their families' ideals for social reforms and their families' memories of the 1939 Communist betrayal of those hopes.[13]

Covert U.S. Funding by the CIA for NSA and YAC

I now believe that the basic decision concerning all United States government Cold War financing of foreign and international non-government organizations (NGOs)—political parties, religious organizations, labor unions, scholarly groups, student and youth organizations—was a Truman administration National Security Council directive of October, 1951 (NSC 10/2) designating the CIA to be the secret conduit of all such funds. This decision had to be cleared with the appropriate Democratic and Republican leaders on the necessary congressional funding committees, and was followed through by both Democratic and Republican administrations from 1951 until the late 1960's. The student and youth parts of the funding became largely public by accident in 1967. Most of the rest of this almost two decades of United States government NGO funding remains secret today (Paget, 2003,135-136; and see Welsh et al., p. 567).[14]

The basic 1951 NSC decision to use CIA as the secret funds conduit to NGOs was made on broader considerations than concerns for student groups. However, our student leaders quickly discovered that "no effective international student organization has been able to function without outside financial support of some kind" (Altbach and Uphoff, 1973, p. 124). The only reliable source of funding for ISC/COSEC and WAY proved to be the United States government, disguised as the (CIA's) Foundation for Youth and Student Affairs. Our opponents, IUS and WFDY, were financed through the government of the USSR.[15]

To the best of my knowledge neither SDA nor ADA received secret funds from CIA. However both NSA and YAC (Young Adult Council of the National Social Welfare Assembly) did receive such secret funding for international student and youth programs, and there were direct connections between YAC and SDA.[16]

SDA delegates consistently advocated aggressive pro-democracy, pro-human rights and therefore anti-Communist international student and youth programs, such as strengthening the International Student Conferences/Coordinating Secretariat (ISC/COSEC) as an anti-Communist international student organization building democratic local student governments all over the world.[17] Such large international programs were only made possible by secret U.S. government funding. SDA delegates generally did not know these were from our government through the CIA, but it was always obvious that these funds were from "secret sources" in close agreement with our government. SDA also consistently supported such expensive pro-Democracy, anti-Communist international programs in YAC and WAY.

At NSA national conventions, voting on both programs and elections often were influenced by late night caucusing.[18] Almost always there was a "liberal caucus" in which SDA was influential. The majority or plurality of delegates at all seven NSA conventions I attended were Eisenhower Republicans. For example, Eisenhower defeated Stevenson by a 2 to 1 margin in the straw poll taken at the 1952 NSA national convention at the University of Indiana (Keating, 1953, p. 33).[19] However, the liberals at NSA conventions often had strong leaders and clear program ideas, and often won election and program votes.

In YAC, both NSA and SDA were voting members.[20] At YAC meetings the majority of voting delegates actually in attendance were usually from the many national Protestant, Catholic and Jewish religious organizations. Voting on programs and elections generally involved caucusing, and SDA often was influential. We had good leaders, excellent program ideas, and members in various delegations besides our own.[21]

My great-uncle, Edward Keating, was my most accurate source of information about secret CIA funding during the 1950's. He was really my beloved "grandfather." (My real grandfather died before I was born.) Edward Keating had been a congressman from Colorado, and was editor of the largest AF of L newspaper, *Labor*, from the 1920's through the 1950's. With his background information I could view all the organizations in which I was active from a better perspective.[22]

How did the ADA National Board view secret CIA financing? When I was on the board I only recall this discussed once, in the context of covert government funding of the International Confederation of Free Trade Unions (ICFTU). Representatives of the United Auto Workers (UAW) and International Ladies Garment Workers Union (ILGWU) were important members of the ADA board, and sometimes reported on the successful union organizing drives through the ICFTU in the third world. The covert government funding meant third world labor unions in ICFTU now could count on protection from the U.S. government. The Cold War was a worldwide conflict between the democracies and totalitarians, which free peoples needed to win without atomic war.

Several ADA board members had been in OSS during World War II. CIA in the early 1950's resembled a continuation of OSS and CIA had not yet received its present controversial reputation.

Setting the Stage for Post-War International Student Organization Conflict

In the mid-1940's, as the Second World War ended, the pre-war international student and youth organizations were reconstituted with strong support from Western governments. The pre-war CIE (Confederation Internationale des Etudients) was revived in the form of the International Union of Students (IUS). The pre-war Committee of International Student Organizations (CISO) of the League of Nations was replaced by the World Federation of Democratic Youth (WFDY). (The pre-war United States student government organization, NSFA, was a member of CIE, and also in CISO through the CIE).[23]

Both IUS and WFDY were quickly seized by the Communists, often using police state tactics when their international meetings and secretariats were in Eastern Europe. Further, the Communists began using their enormous financial and human resources to try to systematically gain control of student and youth organization in Asia, Africa, and South America.[24]

SDA through most of the 1940's was called the United States Student Assembly (USSA). Formed in 1943, USSA was one of the few United States student organizations that sent delegations to Europe in the 1940's (e.g., Alice Horton, p. 68) to show support to various European political and religious groups who were fighting losing battles against the Communist takeovers of IUS and WFDY. NSA was not yet organized.[25]

The free world student and youth organizations opposed the international Communist drive to control young adult groups by organizing the Coordinating Secretariat of Student Unions (Cosec) to oppose the IUS, and the World Assembly of Youth (WAY) to oppose WFDY. Both of these international organizations were made financially possible through the new programs of CIA-channeled U.S. government secret funding.[26]

In the United States, the Associated Youth Serving Organizations (AYSO), primarily composed of all the large national religious organizations of young adults, was expanded to become the Young Adult Council (YAC) of the new National Social Welfare Assembly (NSWA). This became WAY's United States affiliate. NSA, SDA, the Student Federalists,[27] and the NAACP Youth Division were all added to YAC's mostly religious organizational membership. Voting in YAC was by elected delegates from member national organizations.[28]

Tragedy came in the late 1960's with the Vietnam War. Taking secret money from CIA for international young adult programs would not be accepted by the new generation of students, either in this nation or abroad. YAC, Cosec and WAY were wrecked. NSA was wounded, and eventually reconstituted itself as the United States Student Association when it merged with the national Student Lobby in 1977.[29]

An Evaluation from the 21st Century

It seems to me that Janet Welsh Brown's essay in this volume, on "Student Rights, Academic Freedom, and NSA" (p. 375), is a beautifully clear statement about NSA's goals and why these were (and are) central to American democracy. NSA opposed the Communists leading IUS and WFDY because these Communists strongly opposed these three basic goals in America and around the world: democratic student governments, academic freedom, and student rights. NSA supported these three ideals because these ideals all concerned "students as students."[30]

I believe that both NSA and ISC/COSEC were effective in spreading the ideals of democratic student governments, academic freedom, and student rights across America and around the world from the late 1940's to the late 1960's.

Therefore, I strongly disagree with the much more pessimistic evaluations in Altbach and Uphoff's very valuable 1973 study. These authors seem to me to evaluate NSA and ISC/COSEC primarily by whether these organizations supported the "New Left" student political movements of the late 1960's, and the neutralist, anti-Cold War ideals of the Student Peace Union of the early 1960's. Neither "New Left" nor pacifist goals primarily affected "students as students"; and neither ever were capable of winning large numbers of student government elections across the United States.

I wish that international student and youth organizations supporting freedom could be created again. In political democracies each new generation can best train for citizenship responsibilities through such student and youth movements as NSA.

END NOTES

[1] See Welsh et al., p. 565.

[2] The Students for Democratic Action changed its name to Campus ADA after 1960, and then to the ADA Youth Caucus after Al Lowenstein became President of Americans for Democratic Action in 1972. See Rich, Evie; Shull, Leon; and Vollinger, Ellen. *A Brief History of ADA's Student/Youth Organization,* Washington, DC: Americans for Democratic Action. Al Lowenstein was President of NSA in 1950-51. See p. 263.

[3] See background on Student Christian Movement, p. 732, Students for Democratic Action, p. 784., and Young Adult Council, p. 778.

[4] Keating, B., 1953, *A History of the Student Government Movement in America,* Washington, DC: Americans for Democratic Action. Keating, B.,

1956, *The International Youth Movement: A Short History*, Washington, DC: Americans for Democratic Action.

[5] See Smith, "Swarthmore College and NSA," p. 897, and Kurtz, p. 902, on the Pennsylvania Region.

[6] See Pt. 1, Sec. 9, p.297

[7] *Editor's note:* Opposition to barber shop discrimination against African-Americans in college communities during the years immediately after the war was taken up on many campuses. For examples, see Ostar, p. 211, Rovira, p. 1006. For more on YPA, see Reisin, p. 790, and also p. 796.

[8] *Editor's note:* See Berlin, p. 10. Kendrick on Murrow, p. 26, Munts, p. 35, Cohen on Lash, p. 43, and Lash, p. 46; also Bellush on the AVC, p. 710.

[9] *Editor s note:* See p. 16 for Martin McLaughlin's 1948 narrative on the dissolution of the American Student Union . Also see Keating, 1953, pages 14-20, and the corrections page of that 1950 history.

[10] *Editor's note:* A strong vein of idealism powered efforts of many U.S. student leaders after World War II in their quest to build bridges of understanding with students in the Communist world. They came up against an agenda on the Communist side that also led to the disillusionment Keating refers to. See for, examples, Ellis and Roberts, p. 107, Ellis and Smith, p. 188, Holbrook, p. 559, Lowenstein, p. 563, and Birenbaum, p. 585.

[11] *Editor's note:* See Miller on the influence of Niebuhr, p. 718. Niehbur served on the NSA National Advisory Committee in 1957-58

[12] *Editor's note:* The terms "conservative" and "liberal" as used in this essay and throughout the anthology should be viewed in their historic setting. The student conservative movement of the late 20th and early 21st century was only just emerging in the early 1950's (See pp. 800, 804). The current subcategories of economic, social and foreign policy conservatives had not yet become fully defined; nor had distinctions been made both among them and with turn-back-the-clock-reactionaries and pure ethnic, religious and racial bigots. The libertarian and "pro-life" movements were also just taking shape. Within NSA's leadership then, its "conservatives" might be considered by some to be liberal today. See Kurtz, pp. 307 and 308n5.

[13]Here Freud and Stanley G. Hall are wrong about any "universal adolescent rebellion." Research clearly shows that most adolescents and young adults agree with their parents on most belief and value issues.

[14]This subject is treated at length on page 565 in Welsh et al., "Covert U.S. Government Funding of NSA International Programs." Also note Karen Paget, 2003, "From Stockholm to Leiden: The CIA's Role in the Formation of the International Student Conference," *Intelligence and National Security* 18, 134-167.

[15]See Welsh et al., note 14; Keating, 1956; Altbach and Uphoff, 1973.

[16]*Editor's note:* In a 10/11/03 e-mail to the editor, Seymour Reisin, SDA's 1950-51 Executive Secretary (See p. 781) writes, "During my year on the ADA/SDA payroll, I never became aware of any covert funding. Heavy labor union funding, most certainly!"

[17]See Paget, 2003; Altbach and Uphoff, 1973, *The Student Internationals*, The Scarecrow Press; and Dentzer on Cosec, pp. 301 and 315.

[18] See Welsh, p.171n3, McLaughlin, p. 819.

[19]*Editor's note:* See Sylvia Bacon, p. 474; Young Republicans, p. 804, Eisenhower, p. 1083.

[20] See p. 778 for list of YAC members. [21] See Reisin, p. 782, Kurtz, p. 905.

[22] Edward Keating: Classroom and Archived Papers. The Norton Library, University of Colorado, Boulder, Colorado. Keating, E., 1964, *The Gentleman from Colorado: A Memoir*, Denver: Sage.

[22] *Editor's note:* See Altbach, cited in note 17 above, p. 51: "No international student organization has ever been able to finance itself. . . . both the IUS and ISC [Cosec] received almost 90% of their funding from non-student sources. . . . the bulk of the IUS's large budget came from the Soviet government or other Eastern European sources."

[23] *Editor's note:* On NSFA and the CIE, see Kerr, p. 22, and Kendrick on Murrow, p. 26 and p. 28.

[24] See Fisher, p. 511, and Lowenstein, p. 562. [25] Keating, 1956, pp. 7-16.

[26] I think Paget's 2003 revelations about NSA and early Cold War financing strongly suggest that NSA officers could not have long avoided taking secret U.S. government money in any event. The basic problem for the future was that the funds were *secret*. United States student governments are financed through local student activity fees. Virtually all local and national student governments in the world, from Great Britain and Sweden to Russia and China were and are partly or entirely financed openly through their national departments of education. In the 1950's there was no U.S. Department of Education, only an Office of Education in the Federal Security Agency.

[27]*Editor's note:* In 1951 the Student Federalists split from UWF, leaving a student division without most of the leadership that had formed and defined the Student Federalist movement since 1942. Nonetheless Student Federalists provided key organization and leadership for the 1951 World Assembly of Youth meeting at Cornell (See Jonas, p. 773).

[28] Keating, 1956.

[29] Paget, 2003; Altbach and Uphoff, 1973. By the late 1960s, IUS and WFDY also were nearing their ends, due at least in part to bitter internal fighting between Communists supporting Moscow, or China, or the Japanese Zingakuren.

[30] *Editor's note:* NSA's founders overcame affiliation concerns over political influences within NSA by emphasizing the organization's commitment to "students as students." See John Simons, p. 125, and Jim Smith p. 127.

PICTURE CREDITS: *Then:* c. 1950 *Now:* c. 1990 (Both, author).

BARRY KEATING

Barry Keating earned his Ph.D. from New York University and taught psychology and sociology at Illinois College, University of Wisconsin—Manitowoc and the City University of New York. He is currently Adjunct Professor at the New York City College of Technology—City University of New York.

Barry Keating was bom in 1932 in Denver, Colorado, of parents active in the Democratic Party. His mother's family were farmers and Western Populists. His father's family included many men employed on the railroads and active in the railroad unions, His great-uncle, Edward Keating, was first elected to congress from Denver in the 1912 Wilson landslide. Barry's father moved to Washington, D.C., with the early Roosevelt administration; then to New York City to practice law, Barry grew up in Garden City, NY, and graduated from the public schools there.

Barry attended Swarthmore College in Pennsylvania (1950-1954), majoring in psychology. He received his M.A. in Psychology from the University of Connecticut (1955), and his Ph.D. in Psychology from New York University (1973). His doctoral dissertation was a multivariate analysis of political and religious belief systems in national opinion surveys, using the neuropsychological theories of cell assemblies of Donald Hebb.

Barry has been employed in the Research Department of the National Council of Churches; in market research, in the college teaching of psychology and the social sciences at Illinois College, the U. of Wisconsin—Manitowoc, Georgetown College (Kentucky), and the City University of New York, He is now semi-retired, and an Adjunct Professor at the New York City College of Technology—City University of New York.

In June 2000, Barry received a Service Award "in recognition of the extraordinary time, energy and service contributed to the New York State Psychological Association." He has also been active in the United Church of Christ for decades, as well as in his local congregation and in the New York City association and New York State Conference.

Barry lives in Floral Park, New York. His hobbies include writing children's stories and kite flying.

"NSA had no mass base . . . but its efforts to strengthen student government made other organizing possible."

NSA and Post-War Student Activism before 1960

By J. Angus Johnston
State University of New York at Binghamton
Secretary, United States Student Association, 1990-92

Editor's note: Following is an excerpt from Student Activism in the United States Before 1960: An Overview, *a chapter in the anthology,* Student Protest: The Sixties and After, *Edited by Gerald J. DeGroot (©Addison Wesley Longman Limited, 1998. With permission). In his chapter, Johnston traces activism from the seventeenth century. This excerpt begins with Pearl Harbor in 1941 and helps to provide a setting for the units in this section. Pre-war student activism is discussed by Miriam Berlin (p. 6) and Martin McLaughlin (p. 15) in the Prologue to this Anthology; also by Barry Keating in this section on p. 811.*

Campus-based activism virtually disappeared after Pearl Harbor. The college population dropped by nearly a third as the nation's male students went off to fight. Wartime rationing severely restricted the travel necessary for regional or national coordination, and home front work occupied time and energy which might otherwise have been devoted to political organizing. Perhaps most important, the national climate was a barren one for dissent. Conscientious objection to military service was negligible in the United States during the Second World War, and opposition to the war's aims was, if anything, even less in evidence.

The campuses were depopulated, quiet, and focused on the task at hand. To the extent that American students were engaged in organizing, it was through groups like the patriotic, pro-Allied Student Defenders of Democracy or in war relief efforts coordinated by campus religious organizations and student war councils. A few efforts were made to begin building a national, even intemational. student movement (as when a 1942 gathering called by SLID alumni and Eleanor Roosevelt brought together student veterans from more than fifty countries), but they achieved little. In 1943, students from several dozen campuses met to form the United States Student Assembly (USSA)[1], but the founding convention was marred by infighting, as the new group's leadership barred communists in an attempt to prevent an ASU-style takeover. With or without the left, USSA was never able to establish itself as a serious activist force.

The university transformed after the war

The end of the war brought with it a surge in enrollment which transformed the university forever. Youths who had put their education on hold during the war returned to campus, joined by others for whom the doors to higher education were opened by military service. The GI Bill, passed in 1944, granted unprecedented federal financial support to veterans seeking to pursue post-secondary education. By 1947, 2.3 million Americans were enrolled in college—a 50 per cent advance over the last pre-war numbers. One million of these students, nearly half the student population, were veterans of the Second World War.

Veterans tended to be older than their classmates, and many had family responsibilities.... Administrators welcomed veteran participation in student activities and governance, and ceded new responsibilities to this older, more mature cohort.

One of the most widespread interests among American veterans was international student outreach. At the war's end, several international student meetings were held in Europe, culminating in a 1946 world conference in Prague which established the International Union of Students (IUS), a left-leaning, ostensibly independent body. The American delegation to Prague, an ideologically diverse group representing ten campuses and a similar number of student and youth organizations, returned convinced of the need for a new union of American students, and set to work organizing one. The following summer students from more than 350 colleges and universities participated in the constitutional convention of the United States National Student Association (NSA).[2]

Factions in the founding of NSA

The founding meetings of the new group took place in an environment of deep factional division. Alumni and adult advisers cautioned students about their experience with communist infiltration in the thirties, while anticommunist students engaged in an intense organizing campaign to ensure their side was strongly represented.

Communist delegates, perhaps 10 per cent of the total, were embattled, but the students of NSA did not ban communist participation, as USSA's founders had four years earlier. Instead they adopted the student-government-based membership structure of the moribund NSFA and, in a closely fought vote, barred all national organizations from membership. They thus left their doors open to students of all political persuasions, but set an ideologically neutral hurdle to participation—election or appointment through student government that was bound to keep communist membership low.

In the substantive debates that followed, NSA passed a Student Bill of Rights which set down an expansive conception of student civil liberties and academic freedom, and which declared that the rights it enumerated should not be abridged on the basis of race, religion, or political views.[3] Although the delegates made clear that efforts to achieve an end to racial discrimination in higher education should proceed with sensitivity to regional differences, the association's stand—much closer to ASU's than to NSFA's—was strong enough to drive most white Southern schools away.[4]

International relations and conflict over the IUS

Many students at NSA's founding convention were hostile to IUS's geopolitical orientation, but a majority was interested in pursuing the possibility of membership. An affiliation resolution with a variety of conditions attached passed overwhelmingly in 1947, but when IUS endorsed the Soviet-backed coup in Czechoslovakia the following year, antipathy between the two groups was confirmed [5]. In the years after the split, NSA moved toward a more binary Cold War posture, helping to create a pro-Western IUS alternative in the early fifties while articulating a steadily more emphatic anticommunist world-view.[6]

At about the same time the association, in severe financial difficulty, entered into a clandestine relationship with the United States government, accepting secret financial support from the Central Intelligence Agency. The CIA relationship, which was unknown to all but the association's top officers, provided more than half of the association's budget and continued for fifteen years. Although the relationship was for more than a decade regarded as symbiotic by those few students in the know, it became increasingly untenable as the country's political climate changed. When the secret funding was exposed in 1967, it sparked bitter criticism from across the political spectrum.[7]

The McCarthy Era

Beyond NSA, there was little national student organizing during the McCarthy era. The communists had a few organizing victories in the late forties, but political repression and uninspiring policies led to a near-total loss of influence in the fifties. Organizations of the non-communist left, including the liberal Students for Democratic Action (SDA) and a variety of socialist student groups, suffered similarly. When national groups did gather a substantial following, it was most frequently as organizers of a popular local campaign, as when Columbia University's SDA chapter fought fraternity discrimination in the early fifties.

NSA's influence is harder to measure. It had no mass base on campus, but its efforts to strengthen local student government made other organizing possible. Student leaders were exposed to a wide spectrum of political and social views at the association's National Student Congresses, which attracted many hundreds of participants each year. And debates over affiliation or disaffiliation with the association frequently served as a context for the airing of important political questions on campus at a time when there was otherwise little dialogue.[8]

The Late Fifties

In the late fifties, in the wake of the Sputnik humiliation, the United States lavished money and attention on its higher education system. The first Americans to come of age in the youth culture of the rock and roll era headed off to college, and their younger siblings, the baby boom generation, would provide a tremendous in-flux of new students. College enrolment would nearly treble in the sixties. In this climate of expectancy, new groups and causes began to revitalize the campus scene.

A student peace movement arose in the east and mid-west, giving birth to the Student Peace Union, the Campus Peace Union, and Student SANE (an affiliate of the National Committee for a Sane Nuclear Policy). SPU emerged as the dominant campus peace organization after 1960, but for a while all three were active in campus organizing against nuclear testing and encroaching milit arism. At the same time, students at black colleges began experimenting with anti-segregation sit-ins in a wave of actions that, while tentative, suggested a new willingness to act on the part of students who had often been dismissed as conservative and unin-volved. In 1958 NSA, a bellwether of mainstream student liberalism, came out against nuclear testing and launched a project to train Southern students to prepare their campuses and communities for desegregation.

The year 1960 was an extraordinary one for American students. In January the venerable Student League for Industrial Democracy became the Students for a Democratic Society (SDS). In February, students in North Carolina staged a sit-in at a segregated lunch counter that sparked a wave of protests across the South. (NSA helped get. the word out through its new Atlanta race relations of-fice, openedjust a month earlier.) In April, veterans of the lunch-counter sit-ins met in Raleigh to form the Student Nonviolent Coordinating Committee (SNC)[9]. In May, students from the University of California at Berkeley were beaten by police while demonstrating outside a closed meeting of the House Un-American Activities Committee, and in September students from more than forty colleges gathered at William F. Buckley"s Connecticut estate to form Young Americans for Freedom (YAF), an association of conservative students.[10]

"The Age of Complacency is ending," the sociologist C. Wright Mills wrote that summer. "We are beginning to move again." He was right. Within a few years, SDS would be the institutional heart of the New Left. SNCC would be the other pillar of the movement.... Berkeley would be the epicentre of the decade's activism, a powerful force and symbol. And YAF would be the most important conservative student group in American history.... the Sixties had arrived.

Angus Johnston was Secretary in 1990-92 of the United States Student Association, the 1977 successor to NSA. He is a doctoral student at the City University of New York, and has written and lectured on a variety of topics in American student history.

PHOTO: 2004 (Johnston)

EDITOR'S NOTES

[1] See Munts, p. 34, on founding the USSA. [2] See Part 1, Sections 1-3.

[3] See Janet Brown, p. 378, and Robert H. Shaffer, p. 327, for discussions of NSA's Student Bill of Rights.

[4] See Prologue, Section 2 for commentaries on the American Student Union and National Student Federation of America. See Part 2, Sections 2 and 3 on Discrimination and Segregation.

[5] NSA's relations with the IUS are a central thread in the story of its founding years, treated throughout Part 1. See in particular, Cater, p. 535, and Jones, p. 538, in Part 3.

[6] The organization was Cosec (Coordinating Secretariat). See Dentzer, p. 301, Eisenberg, pp. 522, 524, and Lowenstein, p. 562.

[7] See "Covert Funding of NSA International Programs," p. 565.

[8] The McCarthy era had a major impact on NSA. See Reisin, Munger and Keating in this section, Dentzer, p. 310, and Murphy, p. 1076.

[9] See Constance Curry, p. 444, on NSA's civil rights initiatives.

[10] See Buckley, p. 797, Evans, p. 801, on the conservative movement.

J. ANGUS JOHNSTON

Angus Johnston was born in New York City in 1968. He attended Hunter High School in New York and the State University of New York at Binghamton. He served as the secretary of the United States Student Association, NSA's successor organization, from 1990 to 1992. He is presently a doctoral candidate in American History at the City University of New York, where he is nearing completion of a dissertation on the role of of NSA in American student organizing. He has served as an adviser to a number of activist and student government groups, and has written and lectured on a variety of topics in American student history. He lives in Brooklyn with his wife and daughter, and can be reached at angus@fecko.com.

A Time Line of U.S. Student and Youth Groups and the USNSA

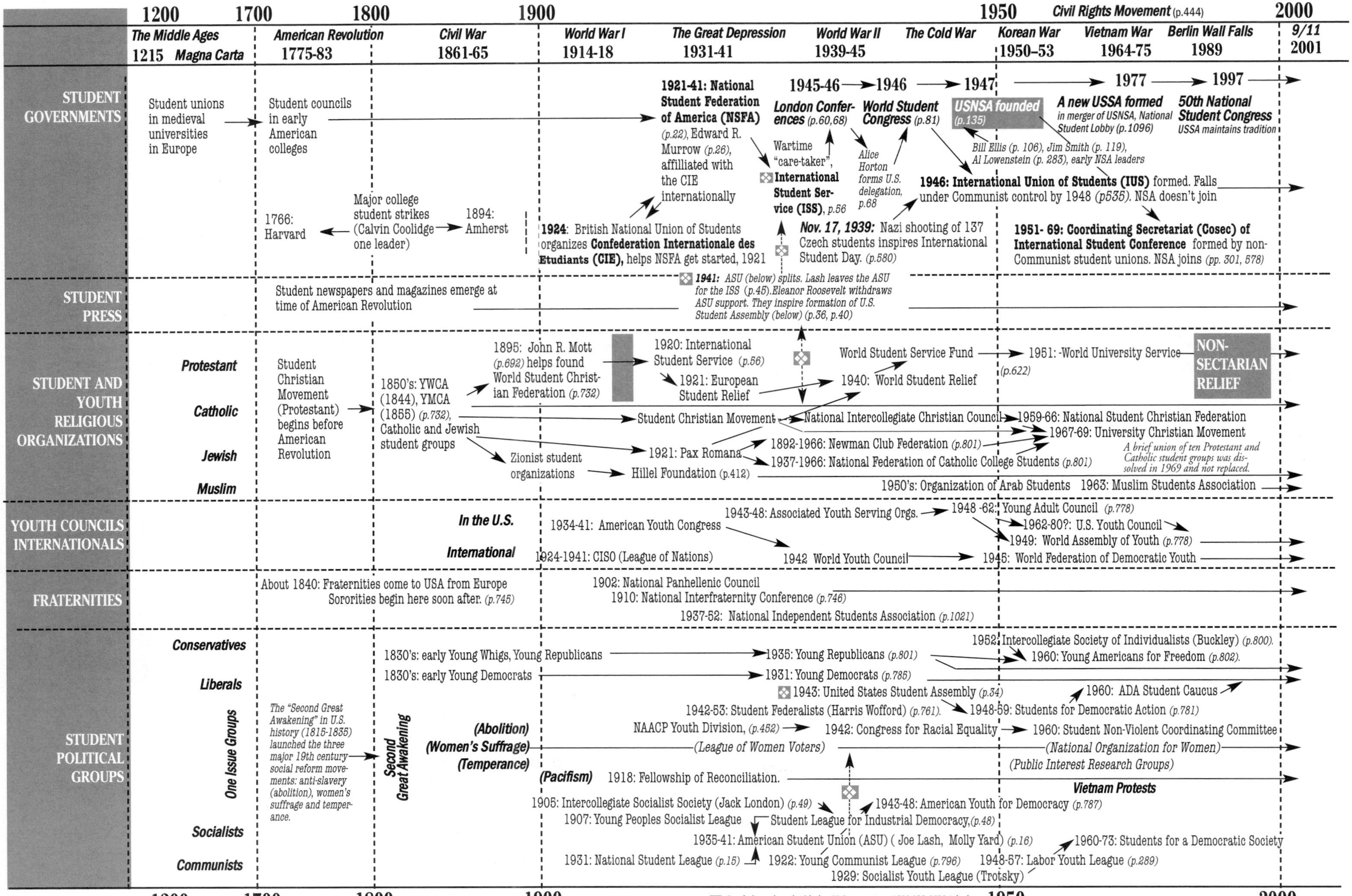

1200 · 1700 · 1800 · 1900 · 1950 · 2000

The Middle Ages 1215 Magna Carta · American Revolution 1775-83 · Civil War 1861-65 · World War I 1914-18 · The Great Depression 1931-41 · World War II 1939-45 · The Cold War · Korean War 1950–53 · Civil Rights Movement (p.444) · Vietnam War 1964-75 · Berlin Wall Falls 1989 · 9/11 2001

STUDENT GOVERNMENTS

Student unions in medieval universities in Europe → Student councils in early American colleges → 1921-41: **National Student Federation of America (NSFA)** *(p.22)*, Edward R. Murrow *(p.26)*, affiliated with the CIE internationally

1766: Harvard ← Major college student strikes (Calvin Coolidge one leader) → 1894: Amherst

1924: British National Union of Students organizes **Confederation Internationale des Etudiants (CIE),** helps NSFA get started, 1921

1945-46 → 1946 → 1947 → 1977 → 1997 →

London Conferences *(p.60,68)*

Wartime "care-taker", **International Student Service (ISS)**, *p.56*

Alice Horton forms U.S. delegation, p.68

World Student Congress *(p.81)*

USNSA founded *(p.135)*

Bill Ellis (p. 106), Jim Smith (p. 119), Al Lowenstein (p. 283), early NSA leaders

A new USSA formed *in merger of USNSA, National Student Lobby (p.1096)*

50th National Student Congress *USSA maintains tradition*

1946: International Union of Students (IUS) formed. Falls under Communist control by 1948 *(p535)*. NSA doesn't join →

Nov. 17, 1939: Nazi shooting of 137 Czech students inspires International Student Day. *(p.580)*

1951- 69: Coordinating Secretariat (Cosec) of International Student Conference formed by non-Communist student unions. NSA joins *(pp. 301, 578)*

STUDENT PRESS

Student newspapers and magazines emerge at time of American Revolution →

1941: *ASU (below) splits. Lash leaves the ASU for the ISS (p.45).Eleanor Roosevelt withdraws ASU support. They inspire formation of U.S. Student Assembly (below) (p.36, p.40)*

STUDENT AND YOUTH RELIGIOUS ORGANIZATIONS

Protestant · **Catholic** · **Jewish** · **Muslim**

Student Christian Movement (Protestant) begins before American Revolution → 1850's: YWCA (1844), YMCA (1855) *(p.732)*, Catholic and Jewish student groups

1895: John R. Mott *(p.692)* helps found World Student Christian Federation *(p.732)* → 1920: International Student Service *(p.56)* → 1921: European Student Relief → 1940: World Student Relief

World Student Service Fund → 1951: -World University Service → NON-SECTARIAN RELIEF *(p.622)*

Student Christian Movement → National Intercollegiate Christian Council → 1959-66: National Student Christian Federation → 1967-69: University Christian Movement

A brief union of ten Protestant and Catholic student groups was dissolved in 1969 and not replaced.

1921: Pax Romana → 1892-1966: Newman Club Federation *(p.801)* · 1937-1966: National Federation of Catholic College Students *(p.801)*

Zionist student organizations → Hillel Foundation (p.412) →

1950's: Organization of Arab Students · 1963: Muslim Students Association →

YOUTH COUNCILS INTERNATIONALS

In the U.S.

1934-41: American Youth Congress → 1942 World Youth Council

1943-48: Associated Youth Serving Orgs. → 1948 -62: Young Adult Council *(p.778)* → 1962-80?: U.S. Youth Council

International

1924-1941: CISO (League of Nations)

1942 World Youth Council → 1945: World Federation of Democratic Youth →

1949: World Assembly of Youth *(p.778)* →

FRATERNITIES

About 1840: Fraternities come to USA from Europe. Sororities begin here soon after. *(p.745)*

1902: National Panhellenic Council

1910: National Interfraternity Conference *(p.746)* →

1937-52: National Independent Students Association *(p.1021)*

STUDENT POLITICAL GROUPS

Conservatives · **Liberals** · **One Issue Groups** · **Socialists** · **Communists**

1830's: early Young Whigs, Young Republicans → 1935: Young Republicans *(p.801)* → 1960: Young Americans for Freedom *(p.802)*.

1952: Intercollegiate Society of Individualists (Buckley) *(p.800)*.

1830's: early Young Democrats → 1931: Young Democrats *(p.785)* →

1943: United States Student Assembly *(p.34)*

1942-53: Student Federalists (Harris Wofford) *(p.761)*. → 1948-59: Students for Democratic Action *(p.781)* → 1960: ADA Student Caucus

The "Second Great Awakening" in U.S. history (1815-1835) launched the three major 19th century social reform movements: anti-slavery (abolition), women's suffrage and temperance. → **Second Great Awakening**

(Abolition) NAACP Youth Division, *(p.452)* → 1942: Congress for Racial Equality → 1960: Student Non-Violent Coordinating Committee

(Women's Suffrage) —*(League of Women Voters)* — *(National Organization for Women)* →

(Temperance) *(Public Interest Research Groups)*

(Pacifism) 1918: Fellowship of Reconciliation. → **Vietnam Protests**

1905: Intercollegiate Socialist Society (Jack London) *(p.49)* → 1943-48: American Youth for Democracy *(p.787)*

1907: Young Peoples Socialist League · Student League for Industrial Democracy,*(p.48)*

1935-41: American Student Union (ASU) (Joe Lash, Molly Yard) *(p.16)* → 1960-73: Students for a Democratic Society

1931: National Student League *(p.15)* · 1922: Young Communist League *(p.796)* · 1948-57: Labor Youth League *(p.289)*

1929: Socialist Youth League (Trotsky)

1200 · 1700 · 1800 · 1900 · 1950 · 2000

Symbol on chart highlights U.S. war-time ASU-ISS-USSA links

Adapted by Eugene G. Schwartz from a chart developed by Barry Keating.

From "American Students Organize," p.817. See index for additional organization citations.

Catholics, liberals, and the left wing provide major group alignments

Factions in NSA

Martin McLaughlin
University of Notre Dame
Member, U.S. Delegation to the 1946 World Student Congress

This essay with its footnotes originally appeared as a portion of Chapter VI in Political Processes in American National Student Organization, *by Martin McLaughlin, April 1948, in his doctoral dissertation submitted to Notre Dame University. Some editor's notes have been added for this anthology.*

Prior to the Prague Congress—during the course of which the foundations for the present groupings in the U.S. were laid—any organizational opposition which developed in an American student group against the extreme-Left orientation and direction had been forced to withdraw.[1] The additional tensions in the new Association—such as they have been—are due to the fact that whereas previous American student organizations had been generally orientated toward the Left (or even the extreme Left), this one includes Catholic delegates who refuse to accept such leadership. Thus different alignments are established; and the old, one-sided decisions seem to have been relegated to the past.

The remote preparations for the Prague group, however, gave the same indications as in the past; although the National Catholic Youth Council was invited to send a proportionate number of delegates, the invitation was not accepted until an article in the magazine *America*[2] focused attention on the coming summer conference. At the last moment the Catholic Council selected its representatives, gave them an intensive ten days of training,[3] and then sent them to join the rest of the American delegation.[4]

At the latter group's preliminary meeting in New York City the cleavages became clear:

> This delegation could be characterized by the term "liberal" in the widest political sense. There were no members who were not left of center, but the degree of "leftness" varied from the four Catholics who were close to the center to the two known Communists at the extreme.... Two groups had definite programs and a systematic approach—the Communists and the Catholics; the rest were sure mainly that they were liberal.[5]

The tension continued throughout the Prague conference; Catholics formed an unpopular minority within the American delegation and an even more unpopular minority in the Congress itself.[6]

In American delegation meetings, however, there was unanimous agreement on the necessity for forming a national student organization in the United States. Various motives for this unanimity could be ascertained: Communists were interested in a new front to replace the American Student Union, which had not survived the war; Catholics were interested in checkmating the Communists and in making their own contribution to such an organization as the National Student Association—especially in view of the fact that they had never done so before.[7] The liberals, too (i.e., the noncommunist left)—many of whom returned from Prague with a more realistic appraisal of the political orientation—began a third alignment whose real form is more and more discernible.

This, then, is the general picture: One recognizable group, however small, is the Communists—always the tightly knit, rigidly disciplined, organized, and militant reflection of a political party properly so-called; they have real strength of internal organization.[8] Another group is formed by the Catholics, who constitute an inevitable "ideological" bloc, very loosely organized, united mainly in unswerving and not always reasoned opposition to the Communists. Between these two "extremes" is the independent majority, generally oriented at least mildly toward the Left—whose votes are the unpredictable, but finally controlling, factor. Moreover, where there are representatives of existing national student organizations of a political or sectarian nature (as there have been at these previous conventions), a group of some kind tends to form around them. It is not observed that there are Democrats and Republicans; the grouping seems to find the students banding together on the basis of beliefs and ideals shared, rather than traditional political allegiances. The main element of division now is communism.

Current group alignments began to take shape after the middle of October, 1946, which saw the last delegate back from Europe; already then the preparations for the Chicago conference were being made. The support of all "liberals" was readily available for the project; Communists following the recommendations of their delegates at Prague were also making specific preparations; and the Catholics, too, began to urge Catholic-college students to participate in the Chicago conference:

The Joint Committee for Student Action (JCCSA)—an agency of both of the existing Catholic student federations[9]—was established; its first project was to stimulate Catholic participation in the Chicago conference.[10] Letters apprising the students of the meaning, background, and importance of the event went out; the stress was laid on the positive contribution that should be made to the growing student community in the United States,[11] but the potentialities for capture of the new organization by those who had controlled previous ones [were] not minimized.

Between the Chicago conference and the Madison convention publications and correspondence continued to carry the story and the speculations; while the National Continuations Committee carried out its official work of preparation for the constitutional convention, various "information services" were busily engaged in casting as much light as possible on the background and future potentialities of the proposed National Student Association. Most prominent in the field has been the *JCSA Newsletter*[12] which had (and still has) a wide circulation among all types of delegates. Prior to the Madison meeting all student organizations urged attendance and had optimistic statements to make about the proposed organization.

The Madison Convention

Just before the convention the group alignments were analyzed by one observer in the following broad threefold arrangement:[13]

(a) Left-wing—by which he meant Communists and their sympathizers—who were aware that they had not contributed as much as they could have at Chicago and were prepared to be more effective (a comparatively small minority);

(b) The Catholics—varying from extreme right to slightly left of center—better organized and more experienced than at Chicago, united temporarily on some issues, especially elections, by "an abhorrence of communism and a common religious faith."[14]

(c) Liberals—loosely and informally allied in the past, distrustful of both the pro-Communist and the "rightist" policies, but now possessed of perhaps more than the balance of power.

At the Madison convention these three more or less organized groups could be observed—plus a sizable number of independents. Although the *Catholics* did not repeat their mistake of the previous year (i.e., no mass meetings of Catholic delegates), there was a regular evening caucus of about a dozen top leaders who planned a certain minimum strategy for utilizing the weight of the thirty-seven percent of votes represented by Catholic delegates. The pro-*Communist* faction, greatly outnumbered, arrived some ten days before the convention and presented a notable organizational effort, caucusing even more frequently than the Catholic group. The *Liberals*, too, employed the informal-caucus technique—in some cases in conjunction with Catholic leaders, sometimes with independents, and frequently with the organizational representatives.[15]

One of the five major issues presented the first day for consideration was whether to allow these existing national student organizations[16] to belong to the National Student Association; the argument for excluding them altogether, which ultimately carried, was that by inviting their direct participation as constituent members the Association was asking for elements of division—it being clear that blocs of one kind or another would form around their leaders.

An *organizational caucus* was in regular session throughout the congress and exercised considerable influence on major issues and in elections. Each region had regularly scheduled times for its *regional caucus* to meet; and in addition, for particular issues (especially the question of racial discrimination in education) there were such occasional groupings as a *Negro caucus*, a *Southern* (*white*) *caucus*, and some sectional ones—like the informal link among Big Ten universities.

"Spontaneous" Alignments

It will be readily observed that none of these "parties" came together as a direct result of the National Student Association itself, but always because of some interest other than the Association—e.g., religious, political, national organization, etc. Yet at the Madison convention itself, for the electoral campaign, two groups—almost equivalent to the beginnings of parties in the strict sense—did come into being for a very brief period. They grew up around the two major policy committees—the steering committee (formerly National Continuations Committee) and the constitution committee.

The steering committee consisted of the regional chairmen and the four national officers elected at the Chicago conference;[17] they had planned the Madison convention, had been in some sort of contact for about eight months, as a group knew far more of the background and future projection of the National Student Association than anyone else, and were able to agree on a good number of principles and candidates for office. The steering committee directed the convention: its selections for officers are the present Staff Committee, and several of its members remain on the new Executive Committee. This is not to say that the group determined the outcome of the election, but their experience and teamwork did have a very influential role there and in policy decisions as well.

The constitution committee, on the other hand, which had the task of revising the draft constitution and presenting the results clause by clause for final decision by the Congress, had never been together until the convention itself.[18] Delegates spoke of it as the place to which regional delegations sent their theorists, retaining their tacticians for parliamentary action in panel and other sessions. Whatever the cause, the constitution committee did develop a certain cohesion as a group of persons united—to some extent—in the task of producing a certain work, the constitution of the National Student Association. Their deliberations were remarkably free from the bickering of special interest groups, and most of their recommendations were later accepted with little debate. They were concerned, too, that the steering committee was becoming too powerful: and this feeling was strengthened by an apparent infringement by the steering committee on the area of responsibility properly belonging to the constitution committee.[19] More or less spontaneously, therefore, the latter group put up candidates for two of the offices—president and secretary; both were defeated, but the size of the vote cast in each case—about thirty-five percent of the total—indicated that a continuing organization could have made a powerful force of this spontaneous association.[20]

Until April, 1948, the chief divisive issue was the question of affiliation of the National Student Association with the International Union of Students, for It is a well-recognized fact that this organization is Soviet-controlled; the question was whether the United States group, by affiliation with it, would be able to modify its policies and orientation by its presence. Proponents argued that the National Student Association must join in order not to remain isolated, in order not to permit the rest of the world's student population to fall under Soviet control, or because the United States students have a duty to the world not to abandon this "last hope of peace"; they argued further that the provisions of the statement issued by the Madison convention[21] would adequately safeguard the autonomy of the American organization and provide at least the beginning of a strong check on the present course of the International Union. Opponents of affiliation also fell back upon the Madison statement, but contended that the International Union of Students could not accept it with its present leadership and that even if it did, the influence of the Association within this international organization would remain negligible compared to the added prestige that would accrue to the latter on account of the United States National Student Association's presence within it.[22]

The Current Scene

A quick survey of the present scene reveals that a certain remnant of the Catholic "party" organization still remains, linked by personal correspondence and by the *JCSA Newsletter*. The pro-Communist group, too, remains intact—its hard core more solid than ever, its periphery contracting under pressures having no direct connection with the student milieu. The Liberals are generally involved in several other organizations—chiefly Students for Democratic Action—and do not concentrate their strength operationally within the National Student Association. Most of the political maneuvering now takes place within the regions and the regional assemblies; the next national congress may develop an entirely different alignment.[23]

In this connection it should be noted, too, that a large influence has been exerted on the Association by certain forces[24] and events[25] outside the Association itself; all of these external agencies—churches, political parties, economic groups—claim, with more or less honesty, that their interest is based on a genuine concern for the Association, or more generally for higher education in the United States.

Insofar as the history of American student organizations has indicated that in the last analysis it was outside forces which destroyed them, the Executive and Staff Committees in the present situation have adopted an extremely cautious attitude toward these pressures.[26] To this extent at least, the outside groups are having a bearing on policy that is commensurate with, but quite different from, their effect on the legislation of the United States Congress. In Washington, the lobbyists are all members of the society they want to influence—i.e., the nation; acting as agents for various pressure groups, they are in a position to bring their weight to bear upon legislators or administrators by appealing either to ambition or to greed, to persuade them to sponsor legislation or to administer public law in a way favorable to the special interest they represent. Similar tactics employed by outside groups on the Staff Committee of the National Student Association have, on the contrary, produced a reaction against the pressure exerted.

END NOTES

[1] In July, 1939, the so-called right wing bolted the American Youth Congress over the refusal of the latter to act favorably on a resolution condemning communism. In December, 1939, Joseph Lash and the minority group left the American Student Union over the Union's refusal to brand the Soviet Union the aggressor in the War with Finland. In January, 1941, the National Student Federation of America disaffiliated from the American Youth Congress on the ground that the Congress was no longer capable of fulfilling its legitimate goals.

[2] J. C. Murray, S.J., "Operation University," *America*, April 13, 1946. See p. 739.

[3] See Kirschner, p. 76.

[4] *Operation University*, National Catholic Youth Council, pp. 2-4.

[5] Ibid., pp. 4-5.

[6] M. Shaw, "The Reawakening of the American Student Movement," *Political Affairs*, February, 1947.

[7] Scattered individual Catholic college students had taken part in the past conventions of the American Student Union and the National Student Federation of America, but cooperation on any scale was discouraged.

[8] At the World Student Congress in Prague these features were, as could be expected, more clearly discernible. The actual leader of the entire Congress was the chairman of the delegation from the USSR; nothing he favored was defeated; nothing he opposed was passed. Delegations from all countries east of the "iron curtain" voted solidly on every issue; Communists in the delegations of all other nations did likewise. On every issue they commanded a majority.

[9] *Operation University*, 40 ff.

[10] See Des Marais, p. 734.

[11] It is undeniably true, however, that the biggest attraction for the Catholics, despite all efforts to deemphasize it, was the opportunity offered to fight against Communists on a new battleground. At Chicago, therefore, Catholic students attended to the number of about one hundred and fifty; they appeared to others to be a solid bloc, voting docilely on all issues and elections. Across the street from the auditorium in which sessions ware held stands the Catholic club of the University of Chicago (Calvert Club)—which became, willy-nilly, the "party" headquarters. Catholic delegates (and others, too, no doubt) made use of its facilities; and each night after the regular sessions some kind of Catholic caucus was held to plan strategy and achieve a measure of cohesion. These are standard political tactics, used by all groups who wish to act together, but the Catholic lack of circumspection made them an easy target for the critics of tactics. (c. Marvin Shaw, loc. cit.; also J. C. Farrar, "American Students Talk It Over," *Nation*, January 13, 1947.)

[12] The *Newsletter*'s orientation has varied; beginning as a service to delegates of all political convictions, it became more prone to identify personalities by the organizations they lead or sponsor and to establish an anticommunist trend among its readers; since March, 1948, however, without abandoning its complete opposition to communism, it has adopted a more positive and objective tone in dealing with the problems of students.

[13] A. Lund, "The Intelligent Student's Guide to the Madison Student Conference," *Plain Talk*, August, 1947.

[14] Ibid.

[15] At the Chicago conference, existing national student organizations were granted ten percent representation on the National Continuations Committee and the same percentage of delegates at the Constitutional convention (cf. Chicago report, p. 12).

[16] A partial list: American Unitarian Youth; American Youth for Democracy; Association of Interns and Medical Students; Congregational Christian Student Fellowship; Council of Student Clubs, Communist Party; Intercollegiate Association of Women Students; Lutheran Student Association of America; National Association for the Advancement of the [sic] Colored People: National Federation of Catholic College Students; National Intercollegiate Christian Council; Newman Club Federation; Student League for Industrial Democracy; Students for Democratic Action; United World Federalists (Student Division); Young People's Socialist League; Young Progressive Citizens of America.

[17] See listing on p. 132.

[18] *Editor's note:* The Constitution Committee was headed by William Birenbaum, then a University of Chicago delegate (see Birenbaum, p. 583). Prior to the Convention, the Chicago Conference elected a Staff Committee, which met several times before the Constitutional Convention to prepare a draft constitution for consideration. The members of this committee were William McDermod (DePaul University, IL), Al Houghton (University of Wisconsin), Tom Farr (University of Chicago), and Janis Tremper (Rockford College, IL). See Dowd (Tremper), p. 60. Royal Voegeli of the University of Wisconsin later joined this group. See Voegeli, p. 150.

[19] The controversy concerned the racial issue. The constitution committee had debated and passed (25–13) a clause in the proposed preamble which pledged the Association to "work for the eventual elimination of all discriminatory educational practices." After this vote the committee proceeded with other business, and the results of the debate were carried immediately to the steering committee, which began to fear a walkout by the Southern white delegates. Five hours later a delegation from the steering committee came to the constitution committee with a compromise measure to which the Southerners had agreed. The effect of the compromise was simply to transfer the same clause from the prominent place it held as part of the preamble, to the by-laws. The steering committee's request was that the constitution committee permit the clause to be presented on the floor of the general assembly first as a by-law: if it failed of passage, then the original decision of the constitution committee would be presented. It was clear that the steering committee was already sure of passage of the clause as a by-law. The question was debated at length; at the end of the all-night session, the constitution committee, with steering committee members voting proxies on the issue, accepted the steering committee's proposal 24–14. It was almost unanimously accepted by the plenary session later on, but the steering committee's action created a great deal of resentment that did not die.

[20] *Editor's note:* The defeated candidates for president and secretary were, respectively, William Birenbaum, University of Chicago, and Jane Wilder (now Jane Jacqz), UCLA. See Wharton, p. 147, and Birenbaum, p. 583.

[21] *Program*, 34 ff: a sample of the views: "We recognize that the majority of the present leadership of IUS and many of the member organizations are far to the left of American students and that within that majority, Communists exercise influence far out of proportion to Communists within the world student community."

[22] The fact that the International Union of Students, after protesting vehemently about violations of students' rights by the Greek government, the Spanish government, and the colonial powers, maintained a studious silence in the face of similar infringements by the new Gottwald government in Czechoslovakia, has weakened the argument for affiliation almost beyond recall. In April, 1948, the Executive Committee voted to suspend negotiations for affiliation with the International Union of Students (*New York Times*, April 12, 1948).

[23] The recent action of the Staff Committee in withdrawing its negotiating team from the Prague meeting of 1948 and severing relations with the International Union of Students appears to be the issue upon which the groups will align at the next meetings of the Association.

[24] The Economic Club of Detroit [see p. 191], the Communist Party, the National Catholic Welfare Conference, and others.

[25] Particularly the Communist coup d'état in Czechoslovakia (cf. also H. W. Briefs, "Needed: a Foreign Policy for Students," *America*, April 17, 1948).

[26] That this is a salutary effect cannot be denied; yet the organization now runs the risk of refusing to work with other organizations and becoming abnormally conservative in its political and economic tendencies.

PART 5

NSA's Regions: Creating Intercollegiate Networks

825 Section 1. New England

Alice Brandeis [Gilbert] Popkin
Radcliffe College, p. 825
New England Chair, 1947-48

Curtis Farrar
Yale University, p. 829
1946 World Student Congress

Shirley Neizer Tyler
Simmons College, p. 832
NSA Exec. Secy., 1950-51

Michael Iovenko
Dartmouth College, p. 841
New England Chair, 1950-51

913 Section 5. The Midwest

Joy Newberger Picus
University of Wisconsin, p. 927
Delegate, 1950 NSA Congress

Richard J. Medalie
Carleton College, p. 935
NSA Vice President, 1949-50

Mary K. Perkins, O.P.
Mundelein College, p. 943
NSA Staff Associate, 1949-50

Tesse Hartigan Donnelley
Fontbonne College, p. 951
Missouri Chair, 1949-50

845 Section 2. Metropolitan New York

Eugene G. Schwartz
City College of N.Y., p. 847
NSA Vice-President, 1948-49

Sheldon Steinhauser
Long Iskand U., p. 852
Met. NY Chair, 1949-50

Gladys Chang Hardy-Brazil
Sarah Lawrence College, p. 858
Student Body Pres., 1948-49

Walter Wallace
Columbia University, p. 865
Met. NY Chair, 1947-48

941 Section 6. The South

Richard J. Murphy
U. of North Carolina, p. 973
NSA President, 1951-52

Galen Martin
Berea College, p. 983
KY-TN Chair, 1950-51

John Hunsinger
Georgis Tech, p. 989
NSA delegate, 1951-52

Barefoot Sanders
University of Texas, p. 995
Student Body Pres., 1947

867 Section 3. New York State & New Jersey

Leeland Jones
University of Buffalo, p.875
NSA Treasurer 1947-48

Frank Dowd
U. of Rochester, p. 885
NY State Chair, 1947-48

Thomas Garrity
St. Peter's College, p. 892
New Jersey Chair, 1948-49

John Yewell
Rutgers University, p.894
New Jersey Chair, 1947-48

973 Section 7. The Rocky Mountains & Southwest

Leonard Perlmutter
U. of Colorado p. 999
Rocky Mt. Chair, 1947-48

Luis D. Rovira
U. of Colorado, p. 1006
Student Body Pres., 1947-48

Roy Romer
U. of Colorado, p. 1007
Rocky Mt. Chair, 1950-51

Donald A. Martinez
New Mexico Highlands C., p. 1012
1946,47 NSA delegate

895 Section 4. Pennsylvania/Mid-Atlantic

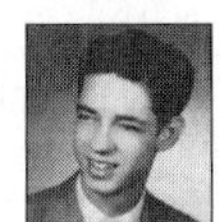
Kenneth R. Kurtz
Swarthmore College, p. 902
Pennsylvania Chair, 1950-51

Ralph Dungan
St. Joseph's College, p. 909
NSA Vice President, 1947-48

Michael J. Rubino
Catholic University, p. 920
Mason-Dixon Chair., 1948-49

Joseph W. Zebley
U. of Baltimore, p. 921
MD-DE-DC Chair, 1947-48

989 Section 8. California

Milton Dobkin
U. of Southern Calif., p. 1025
NSA So. CA Chair, 1947-48

Tom Suzuki
L.A. City College, p. 1031
Student Body Pres., 1947-48

Nancy Lee Roth Arnheim
UCLA, p. 1038
NSA Voc Guid Com Chair. 1947-48

Sally Holt Smit
U.C. Berkeley, p. 1044
NSA Reg'l. Secy 1947-48

1014 Section 9. The Northwest

William H. Gates, Sr.
U. of Washington, p. 1053
Pacific NW Chair, 1949-50

Helen Knudsen Pulsifer
U. of Washington, p. 1053
Pacific NW Secy. 1949-50

Joan Long Lynch
Marylhurst College, p. 1064
Pacific NW Chair, 1951-52

Marvin Jagnels
University of Idaho, p. 1068
Eastern Dist. V.P., 1950-51

Photo credits appear in units page referenced above

PART 5

NSA's Regions: Creating Intercollegiate Networks

The regional structure of NSA in its early years provided national communication links to and from member colleges and created local intercollegiate networks.

The regions also provided a leadership training experience for the several hundred regional officers and committee chairs elected each year by regional assemblies. Regional chairs were also members of the National Executive Committee, which met twice yearly between congresses. The number of regions declined from twenty-six in 1947–48 to twenty in 1951–1952, as NSA's more isolated members in the Southern and Rocky Mountain/Great Plains states were consolidated.

As demonstrated by the stories and albums collected in this part, the regions developed their own programs as well as adopting existing national programs. Individual campuses had direct contact with both the national staff and the regional organization, and campus students could also choose the national and regional programs in which they wanted to participate.

Active regions energized by core campuses

The most active regional groups were those with large clusters of colleges in metropolitan areas: Northern New England (Boston), Metropolitan New York, Pennsylvania (Philadelphia), Mason-Dixon (Washington, DC), Georgia—later the Great Southeast—(Atlanta), Illinois (Chicago), Michigan (Detroit and Ann Arbor), Minnesota (Minneapolis/St. Paul), Missouri (St. Louis), California (Los Angeles and San Francisco).

Other active regions were energized by a strong major university, sometimes in collaboration with a smaller active campus, such as the Great Northwest (University of Washington and Marylhurst, OR), Kentucky-Tennessee (University of Louisville and Berea College), Rocky Mountain (University of Colorado and Loretto Heights), Virginia-Carolinas (University of North Carolina and Virginia State), Wisconsin (University of Wisconsin and Mt. Mary).

College representation at regional meetings often exceeded the area's NSA enrolled membership. One-, two-, or three-day regional assemblies, leadership workshops and intercollegiate cultural events would, on occasion, attract hundreds of student leaders. At any given time, up to as many as a score of metropolitan areas, large and small, operated Purchase Card and Student Discount Service programs.

At their best, these events provided a singular experience for the students involved. While leadership changed each year and levels of activity rose and fell, there was enough continuity to provide significant volunteer presence and energy for the organization, with key educator support, and without field or professional staff.

The NSA News

Regional Notes
Regions Active Coast to Coast

Varied Progress Reported
Eighteen Regions Plan Structure at Meetings

Regions Schedule Winter Assemblies

1947-48

Northern New England Holds Human Relations Institute

Pennsylvania
Festival Features 650 Performers

Labor Relations Forum In Met N.Y.

NNER Holds Mammoth Fete

Michigan Sets Two Statewide Student Meetings

Illinois To Oppose Broyles Bills In Legislature

Rocky Mountain
Variety Show Highlights Year

Ky.-Tenn.
Region Sponsors Radio Series

California Plans Student Exhibit

AUTONOMOUS REGIONAL ORGANIZATIONS enabled student leaders to accommodate local interests and resources. During the first two years, regional constitutions were adopted and a diverse range of initiatives undertaken. They were reported nationally in *NSA News* (above) and on each campus through the college press (below).

BOSTON NSA TO MEET HERE

OPEN MEETINGS' SUCCESS QUESTIONED AT MEETING

FORTY-SIX COLLEGES WILL BE REPRESENTED FRIDAY

NSA Pres. Bob Kelly Stresses Leader Training, Program Aspect, In Talk To Met. N.Y. Region

Milholland Greets Student Delegates Representing Pennsylvania Colleges

Ga.-Ala. Student Organization Elects Meadows Secretary

Sixteen representatives of Georgia and Alabama colleges

Inter-Racial Regional Meet Discusses NSC Calls for Equal Educational Opportunities

Regional NSA Starts Action

Individual Academic Freedom Discussed By The Rocky Mountain N S A

National Students Organization Will Hold California Regional Convention at University

Northwest NSA Delegates Converging for Conference

Delegates from some 40 schools in the Northwest are

Photos. From left: New Jersey delegation at 1950 Congress. Virginia-Carolinas Responsibilty Project, c.1950 *(SWHS)*

Clips. From top: *Simmons News* 2/26/48 *The Centurion* 12/49 *Daily Collegian* 12/19/47 *Agnes Scott News* 2/26/47 Daily Reveille 4/22/47 *Student Life* 10/31/47 *Highlands Candle* 4/20/51 *Daily Californian* 2/20/47 *Washington Daily* 12/2/49

PART 5. NSA's REGIONS
CREATING INTERCOLLEGIATE NETWORKS

SECTION 1

New England

CONTENTS

The Greater Boston and Cambridge area's reach to New England's North and West drew NSA participation from among some 50 four-year colleges and universities in 1946. Connecticut and Rhode Island to the South added another 25. They counted some of America's most historic and prestigious colleges, including most of the Ivy League and Seven Women's Colleges.

They also enjoyed a tradition of student leadership and activism, and student interest in world affairs had been nurtured for almost one hundred years by the time the 1946 Prague World Student Congress attracted the U.S. delegation whose story is told in Part 1. Because colleges were separated by relatively short distances and connected by convenient rail and bus transport, it was economical to convene well-attended assemblies.

Out of this setting came young women such as Alice Horton of Wellesley (See Tibbetts, p. 68), Mimi Haskell of Smith (See Berlin, pp. 6, 87), and Alice Brandeis Gilbert of Radcliffe (See Popkin, p. 825); and young men such as Bill Ellis (pp. 106, 130, 158), Doug Cater (pp. 92, 535), Clif Wharton (pp. 112, 144), and Frank Fisher of Harvard (p. 511); Earl Eames of MIT (p. 634); Curtis Farrar (p. 829), Bob Smith (p. 504), and Rob West (pp. 515, 556), all of Yale. They took the lead working with students from all over the country to build a new national student organization: the Prague delegation was formed (Pt. 1, Sec. 1), the Chicago Conference was organized (Pt. 1, Sec. 3), and the NSA International Office of NSA was launched in Cambridge (Pt. 3, Sec. 1).

The region also benefited from the infrastructure of an active Student Christian Movement organization with a long tradition of international engagement (See Pt. 4, Sec. 1 and Pt. 3, Sec. 5.).

Organizing the Region

In this section Alice Brandeis [Gilbert] Popkin of Radcliffe looks back on her compromise election as Regional Chair. Curt Farrar describes how formation of a student government was defeated and how the vote to affiliate with NSA at Yale was won (referred to also by William Buckley on p. 785). Andrew Rice of Harvard and Henry Halsted of Williams College describe 1946-47 regional organizing efforts, and Shirley Neizer Tyler of Simmons College, who became 1950-51 NSA Executive Secretary (see also pp. 279, 458, 496), looks back on racism, politics and NSA programs.

Recollections are included of Mike Iovenko (Dartmouth), 1950-51 regional chair, and educator/mentors Dean Everett Baker of MIT ("freedom cannot come as a gift") and President Mildred McAfee Horton of Wellesley ("world order doesn't depend primarily on "students organized into intercollegiate associations").

The region provided an important cohort of African American student leaders, including the already mentioned Bill Ellis, Clif Wharton and Shirley Neizer, as well as Ernie Howell (pp. 158, 737) and George Carter (p. 636), both also of Harvard.

SMITH PLAYED ACTIVE ROLE IN NSA FROM BEGINNING; NORTHERN NEW ENGLAND REGION FORMED

Smith has played an active role in the United States National Student Association since the idea was first conceived at the World Students' Congress in Prague last year. Al-

Continuations Committee, a temporary organi... divided into ... men of whi... committee. K...

Smith College *SCAN* 10/21/47

NSA-Sponsored Symphony Includes College Choral Group

Late permissions have been obtained for freshmen and sophomores attending the NSA Symphony Forum at Rindge Technical High School on Wednesday, November 30. Girls in groups of three or more will be able to sign out till 11:45 p.m. for the concert, which begins at 8:00.

The program for the concert will include the Overture to Orpheus by Offenbach; Siegfried Idyll by Wagner, Andante Cantabile by Tchaikowsky, the Carmen Suite by Bizet, Slavonic

Simmons News 11/17/49

Vol. LXVIII, No. 153

Delegates Meet In New London To Discuss NSO

National Student Group Plans Fall Convention To Write Constitution

Four Yale delegates, Robert S. Smith, 1947, William C. Blair, 1949, Richard C. Dunn, 1947M, and Jona-

Yale Daly News 4/28/47

NEW ENGLAND COLLEGES form northern (MA, VT, NH, ME) and southern (CT, RI) regional groups in 1947. The region launched its Symphony Forum program in 1949 (see p. 368).

New England NSA Regional Highlights

1946-47

Miriam Haskell Of Smith College Discusses I.S.U.

25 Delegates Make Plans in Meeting Here

Issues of Chicago Conference Analyzed by Representatives Of 16 New England Colleges

Longley Attends Meeting In Chicago; Delegates Found Students Organization To Promote American Education

400 Colleges Represented

NSO Group To Hold Regional Assembly

Delegates Meet In New London To Discuss NSO

Students to Meet Thursday To Debate Prague Proposal

A REGIONAL VOICE IS BORN. Prague delegates return (see p. 103). Mimi Haskell (Smith) traveled the region to promote attendance at the Chicago Conference and afterward as Mass. Region Chairman (See p. 87). Conn.-RI Chair was Robert Smith (Yale, p. 504). From top l., cw: *MC* 12/5/48; *HC* 12/21/46; *BO* 1/15/47; *SC* 2/14/47; *HC* 7/30/46; *YN* 4/28/47. In photo, New England state regional chairs, fr. top: Smith (Conn.-RI), Peter Mallett (U. of Vt., VT), Haskell (Mass.), Dick Brodenberg (Dartmouth, NH).

1947-48

Bowdoin Sends Delegates To NSA Parley at Holyoke

NSA Region Head States Position On UMT As Individual

Letter To John Shiffert Explains Apparent Error

Yale Committee Sends Delegates To NSA Meeting

Foreign Travel, CARE Among Topics Discussed In Regional Conference

NSA Adopts Bowdoin Plan At Boston Conference

BOSTON NSA TO MEET HERE

FORTY-SIX COLLEGES WILL BE REPRESENTED FRIDAY

BUILDING A LASTING FOUNDATION. Massachusetts regional meetings at Holyoke (30 colleges), Simmons (46 colleges) and Conn.-RI at U. Conn (10) and others turned out hundreds of delegates to create regional structure and programming. Bowdoin's foreign student hospitality plan (See p. 000) was adopted by NSA. Larry Jaffa (Harvard Divinity), Mass. Region's active president, created controversy voicing political positions, as did Met NY's Walter Wallace (Columbia. See p. 000), that might be confused as NSA's, prompting consideration of how to balance NSA's non-partisan status and the legitimate political interests of its leaders. Conn.-RI Chair was Robert L. West (Yale, p. 515). From top: *BO* 10/29/47; *Daily Pennsylvanian* 2/35/48 reported on both Jaffa and Wallace controversies; *YN* 4/22/48; BO 2/18/48; SN 2/16/48.

1948-49

Middlebury N.S.A. To Head Culturale

NSA Gathers At Radcliffe

Group Hopes To Join Purchase Card Plan

Leaders Attend NSA Conference

N.S.A. Sponsors B.U. Conference

Human Relations Talks To Spotlight Meeting

Technology NSA Commended For Foreign Student Summer Plan at Madison Convention

Regisites Aid NSA In April Festival

NSA Starts Drive to Sell Purchase Cards

NSA Regional Meeting Held In Amherst; Plots Projects In International Fields

Baker Named To National Advisory Board

CONSOLIDATING MEMBERSHIP. A regrouped Northern New England (NNER) now embraced Maine, New Hampshire and Vermont; Chair: Alice Gilbert (Radcliffe, p. 825). A renamed SNER included Conn. and RI. Chair: Chris Par (U. of Bridgeport). Programs: NSA's Purchase Card system initiated (see p. 366), Spring festival at Regis, Emerson and MIT; DP student sponsorship; Student Govt. Clinic at Simmons; Human Relations Institute at Boston U., including NSA President Ted Harris (p. 219), and SCM leader Ernest Howell (p. 838). MIT's Foreign Student Summer Plan (FSSP) endorsed (p. 634). From top: *MC* 9/30/48; *HC* 10/20/48; *TT* 3/8/49; "Drive" *HC* 3/12/49; "Education" *HC* 3/12/49; *RH* 3/15/49; *WC* 5/19/49; *TT* 10/1/48.

1950-52

150 Delegates Here for NSA Northern New England Meet

Commissions Weigh Issues On Academic Hot Potatoes

Lowenstein On the Air

Send Men of 40 Colleges

Cynthia Brezniak

Parvin Saidi

Janet Welch

NSA Elects New Chiefs; C. Brezniak Plans Work With P. Saidi, J. Welch

NSA OPENS WIDE NORTHEAST AREA

NSA Leaders Meet, Urge Cooperation

Dagmar Halbauer (Simmons), Boston Area Chairman

W.S.S.F. Carnival Success Deans And Cars Raffled

STAYING THE COURSE. Regional leaders continued active foreign student aid and exchange programs, a reorganized Student Discount System, and policy initiatives regarding the draft, academic freedom and discrimination. Chairs were: '50-51 NNER, Mike Iovenko (Dartmouth, p. 840), and SNER: Stanford Somers (Yale Divinity); a consolidated New England, 51-52, Janet Welch (Smith, p. 375, p. 1093). From top: *TD* 11/3/50 with l to r photos of campus chair, David H. Neiditz, NSA President Al Lowenstein and Asst Dean Charles Camp; *SC* 2/27/51; *TT* 4/15/52; *SN* 10/26/50; "Halbauer," *SC* 12/27/51; "WSSF," *RH* 2/15/52.

1949-50

Navy to Give Reply on NSA Loyalty Query

Charge That Loyalty Oaths at Other Colleges Differ from Harvard's Draws Navy Check

NSA On Trial

NSA Adds Stores To Purchase Card Discount Plan List

Student Projects Thrashed Out At NSA Convention

Dance and Discussion Of Student Bill of Rights Featured By The N.S.A.

Regional N.S.A. to Give Dates As Prizes in Dance Tonight

Navy Strikes Out 'Informer Clause' from Loyalty Check

EXTENDING NSA PROGRAMMING. The Purchase Card discount plan was expanded to 63 stores in the Boston area. The region expanded its program of dinner dances accompanying regional events. 32 colleges took part in the 11/49 NNER convention at Newton College of the Sacred Heart and laid out the year's schedule of student government and human relations clinics and foreign student programs. Harvard's NSA challenged the Naval ROTC loyalty oath "informer clause" and succeeded in its deletion. From top: "Navy," *HC* 1/6, 3/6/50; "Trial," *HC* 10/6/40 challenges Harvard's NSA delegation to deliver promised benefits; "Dance," *TT* 3/7/50; "Adds," *TT* 9/30/49; "Projects," *TT* 1/1/49; 'Regional,': *TT* 10/21/49.

KEY TO COLLEGE NEWSPAPER CITATIONS IN THIS SECTION

- BO-*Bowdoin Orient* — THE BOWDOIN ORIENT
- HC-*Harvard Crimson* — The Harvard Crimson
- MC-*iMiddlebury Campus* — Middlebury Campus
- RH-*Regis Herald* — REGIS HERALD
- RN-*Radcliffe News* — The Radcliffe News
- SC- Smith College *SCAN* — Smith College SCAN
- SN-*The Simmons News* — The Simmons News
- TD-*The Dartmouth* — The Dartmouth
- TT-MIT *The Tech* — THE TECH
- WC-*The Wellesley College News* — Wellesley College News
- WR- *Williams Record* — The Williams Record
- YN- *Yale Daily News* — Yale News

Building lifetime relationships

1. New England, Radcliffe, and Harvard

Alice Brandeis (Gilbert) Popkin

Radcliffe College

NSA Northern New England Regional Chair, 1948–49

Of all the many facets of my NSA experience, what stands out most was the lasting relationships we formed. For a great many of the people for whom NSA mattered in a variety of ways, it was more meaningful than any other college experience. For me it nurtured many lifetime friendships and provided an opportunity for me to develop qualities of social and political expression that stood me in good stead throughout my life.

The causes for which we worked—building the peace after World War II, breaking down discriminatory barriers to educational opportunity, and strengthening student government—laid the groundwork for my later interest in public policy and international affairs, on the one hand, and working within the local community, on the other.

Radcliffe and Harvard at the center of NSA

After I graduated Horace Mann High School in 1945 (then one of the last all-girl high schools in New York City), I entered Radcliffe College in the fall of 1945, preparing to follow a career in the law, as had so many members of my family.[1] Radcliffe was also an all-girls school, and I profoundly believe that girls ought to go to a girls' school at some point in their lives. Today, of course, I have no chance of convincing my daughters—all of them have turned out well just the same—but it still seems to me the right thing to do.

NSA was just being formed in 1946-47, and I recall learning about it through my contacts with students at Harvard as a result of becoming active in the Radcliffe student government. Radcliffe was the women's college attached to Harvard—a relationship common among many Eastern universities at the time (such as Pembroke College at Brown and the New Jersey College for Women at Rutgers).

Harvard was at the center of NSA's organization in New England, and because of a strong interest in international relations through the Harvard Student Council International Relations Committee, it became the seat of NSA's International Affairs Commission office.[2] With an office on Bryant Street, NSA's international program was heavily staffed by Harvard and Radcliffe volunteers.[3]

It was there that I met Frank Fisher, one of the student leaders active in international affairs on campus. I remember Frank very well, and many of my early recollections of NSA relate to connections at Harvard with Frank Fisher.[4]

Early NSA Leaders

Looking through the research that the editors of this book prepared, I was reminded that Harvard was home to a number of early NSA leaders and initiatives. Doug Cater and Bill Ellis had been on the original delegation of U.S. students to the Prague Student Congress in 1946 and took part in planning the Chicago Student Conference.[5] Ellis went on to join the staff of the newly formed International Union of Students as an American vice president. He resigned in protest at the Communists' coup in Czechoslovakia in the spring of 1948 and their seizure of the Czech Union of Students.

Cater, who went on to a distinguished career in journalism and government and as president of Washington College in Maryland, wrote a number of stirring articles in the *Crimson* reporting on the Prague Student Congress and its hopes for the future. They are referenced in Part 1 of this anthology. Later, writing for the magazine *The Reporter* in August 1949, he reflected on the disappointments and disillusion over the 1948 events, in an article entitled, "Collapse of Youth's One World," which is reprinted in this book.[6]

Andrew Rice, Doug Cater, and Clifton Wharton were Harvard delegates at the Chicago Student Conference, and Clif was elected as secretary to the National Continuations Committee (NCC).[7] Both he and Ernie Howell (who represented the YMCA) provided leadership at the Constitutional Convention, as did Doug Cater. I clearly recall Doug Cater and Frank Fisher returning from Madison. They were impressive and well-spoken young men.

During the spring of 1947, it was the International Activities Committee of the Harvard Student Council that published the two issues of the NCC newspaper-sized *Student International Activities Bulletin,* circulated nationally, which reported on European study, travel, and postwar relief activities open to American students.

Involving myself in NSA

By the time of the Constitutional Convention in Madison in August of 1947, I was eager to become directly involved in NSA. Although I was painfully shy, I mustered up the courage to run for the position of Radcliffe delegate. I did second best, as a runner-up to Winifred Libbon, and so joined her as an alternate. We had both been members of the NSO "chapter" (according to the *Radcliffe News* of April 1947), which was "formed under the leadership of Betty Fitzgerald and Mary Bruchholz, Delegates to the Chicago conference."

My aunt, Elizabeth B. Raushenbush, had a home in Madison, Wisconsin, and was a professor at the university, so I had a place to visit when we got there. A year later, when I was a delegate to the First Congress in Madison (in 1948), I met Norman Holmes, who was then a Wisconsin delegate.[8] Not knowing our relationship, he showed me her house, saying to me, "This is Professor Raushenbush's home, you know—a lot of her students loved her."

Radcliffe and Harvard affiliate with NSA

Affiliation with NSA at both Harvard and Radcliffe had a lot of support, and the campaigns to join began in the fall of 1947 and culminated in heavy favorable votes in the spring of 1948. The October 14, 1947, edition of the *Crimson* reported:

> International Students Day on November 17 will mark the beginning of a week-long drive to win Radcliffe ratification of the new National Student Association constitution, delegates to Sunday's Barnard conference of women's college NSA leaders has announced.
>
> Susanne Ehrenthell '48 and Alice Gilbert '49 told the eight-school meeting that they already have a group of 46 working for NSA projects here. On the basis of this they advocated the superimposing of NSA activities on the student government structure through the creation of another vice presidency.
>
> Bombshell at the Barnard sessions was the warning of Communists sent to college presidents and newspapers by one Allan Crow.[9]

On November 28, the *Crimson* headlined that "N.S.A. Charter Gains Record Radcliffe Vote." It then wrote that "In the largest vote ever cast in the history of the Annex, 802 undergraduates—approximately 83% of the student body—marked affirmative ballots. Thirty six voters dissented." The article went on to report on the progress with two major Radcliffe-sponsored NSA projects: collection of funds and books for the "decimated library of the Charles University in Prague," and "supply and management of a camp for French, Swiss and Austrian children in a Swiss chalet for two months this summer."

Harvard was also running its own affiliation campaign, and *The Harvard Crimson* ran an editorial on November 19, 1947, which read in part:

> Put it all together, and you have something that costs each individual little and that might become America's first vital national student organization. In the origin of NSA, Harvard delegates have been notable for their leadership. At this point, it would neither be consistent nor sensible to fail to support NSA.

The November 21, 1947, edition of the *Crimson* headlined, "College Votes for NSA Affiliation; Student Ballot Shows 1382 Majority." There were a total of 1,957 votes, with 575 opposed. In the spring of 1948, 2,405 Harvard students took part in electing their NSA delegation, which included Fred Houghteling (who was subsequently Regional chair and then national executive secretary in 1949), Robert Fishelis, Robert C. Fisher, Frederick Deane, and Alfred M. Goodloe.

Becoming New England regional chair

From 1947 through 1951, New England was split into two regions, Northern (Massachusetts, Maine, New Hampshire, Vermont) and Southern (Connecticut, Rhode Island). In 1952, they were consolidated into one New England Region.[10] The first Northern New England chair was Larry Jaffa of Harvard.[11] He followed Mimi Haskell of Smith, who had chaired the earlier Massachusetts Region prior to the Constitutional Convention.

Despite my natural reluctance to step into the crossfire, I agreed to run for regional chair as a compromise candidate after the First National Student Congress concluded in September of 1948 at the University of Wisconsin. As was the case throughout the Association, various factions naturally arose in the different regions according to the makeup of their various college delegations. Since we were student government–based, these differences tended to reflect the leanings of the elected student leadership on the different campuses.

New England was no exception, and going back into the press clippings, I think the write-up of my election in the September 28, 1948, issue of *The Harvard Crimson* does a pretty good job of recreating some of the dynamics within the region:

> Alice B. Gilbert, Radcliffe '49, is the new Northern New England Chairman of the National Student Association—

probably. . . . her election, along with that of the new Vice-Chairman, Fred Houghteling '50, must be confirmed at the regional assembly some time in October.

Miss Gilbert's election came as a surprise after a tumultuous all night session that started Friday midnight had placed three other names in nomination for the chairmanship. Much of the furor in the pre-dawn conclave was the outgrowth of a regional split that had been threatening all year.

Northern New England opinion had polarized around Lawrence Jaffa, 3Dv., on the one hand, and Earl Eames of M.I.T. on the other. Jaffa was the regional chairman last year and at the time of that election had the support of a coalition in NSA including the Students for Democratic Action and leading Catholic schools.

Eames's opposition started a year ago when the person elected regional vice president at the national convention was not confirmed at the regional assembly, largely because of the opposition of Jaffa and Houghteling.

Friday's stormy caucus evidently brought the split to the head. The sun was already shining over Lake Mendota, literally if not figuratively, when the session reported out the nominations of Paul L. Wright '49, Houghteling and William Tracy of Springfield College. . . . Jaffa's subsequent defeat in the national election rendered him eligible for regional office. . . . This factor set off an intricate chain of events. . . .

Jaffa was nominated for regional chairman and accepted. The other three candidates withdrew.

Miss Gilbert was nominated as the other possible candidate that was independent of both "factions." Jaffa withdrew.

Houghteling decided to run against Miss Gilbert.

Miss Gilbert defeated Houghteling. [Houghteling was elected Vice-Chairman.]

I'm sure that there must have been high tension in the air—although all these years later I remember little of the detail.

New England was an active and energetic region, before, during, and after my year as chair, and elsewhere in this section a chronology lists many of the major events that characterized the region.

Although I had already graduated in the spring of 1949 and I was no longer representing Radcliffe, I went to the Champaign-Urbana meeting that summer to close out the Northern New England regional year. I mainly remember Urbana as a riotous occasion in addition to all the serious business—it was the innocence of youth in those days. I do seem to remember we did something we shouldn't have done, for which we were chastised.

One thing I remember learning from Father Hesburgh, president of Notre Dame, at one of the NSA events stayed with me all these years.[12] I once heard him say that as many important things go on outside of meetings as in the meetings. He gave me what seemed an incredible idea at the time —that you could leave a meeting and talk to people and that you would probably accomplish more than you would by going to the meeting itself.

Forming lifetime friendships

Looking back, I can truthfully say that the two people out of NSA that I remained closest to my entire life were Mildred [Kiefer] Wurf and Al Lowenstein. The first time I nominated Al for office (for educational affairs vice president) was when I was chairman of Northern New England, at the 1948 Madison convention. Everybody came up and said they all knew me but they didn't know Al, and they asked, "Who is that kook from North Carolina?" It was definitely a last-minute thought, and nobody expected him to run. He withdraw in favor of Gene Schwartz, who was then elected. Of course, Al was later elected NSA president at the Michigan Congress in 1950.

A number of us had migrated to Washington, D.C., after completing college and graduate school. Cynthia Courtney later also became one of my closest friends, as did Helen Jean Rogers.[13] Cynthia had been at Dunbarton College in D.C. and became NSA vice president for educational affairs in 1952-53. Helen Jean, who was NSA secretary-treasurer in 1948-49, went from Mundelein in Chicago to Catholic University and then on to Harvard, where she did further graduate work and taught for a while. Through the years, Mildred, Cynthia, Helen Jean, and I continued to have some quasi-reunions from time to time.

The connections that I made in NSA were somehow very profound in their influence. I'd been raised to believe that the individual made a difference. The people in NSA showed me that if you believed in something, you could do something about it, and they pointed the way. It is only in recent years that I ever questioned for a moment that we could make that difference, as events on the national and global scene appeared to be slipping from our grasp. Yet recent events have convinced me, more and more, that it's your relationships in the community you're in that counts—and that you can always make a difference there. And it was all those people that I knew in NSA that reinforced that for me.

I remember my friends coming up to me and saying when I graduated, "Alice, we just want to tell you we're very glad that somebody who did something worthwhile was one of our friends." And I can say now that I am very glad that many who were worthwhile were, and are, my friends.

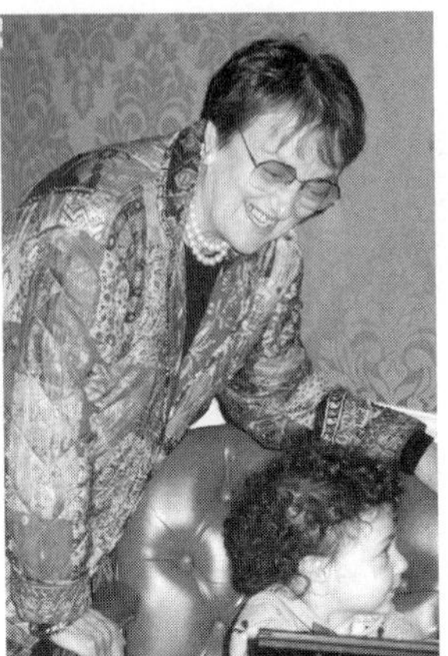

Alice Brandeis Popkin is an attorney in Chatham, MA, specializing in trusts, estate planning, and probate. Earlier, she was Associate Administrator, Office of International Activities of the U.S. Environmental Protection Agency. She was also Director of International Programs for the Peace Corps. She has taught and practiced both corporate and juvenile law. She is a member of the bar in six jurisdictions, including the Supreme Court. She is shown here with her granddaughter, Allison B. Cahn.

END NOTES

[1] My father was an attorney. My mother was an attorney. And, of course, my grandfather, Justice Louis D. Brandeis, was also. One brother completed law school and works for historic preservation, and my cousin teaches law.

[2] The New England region furnished four of the first five international affairs vice presidents. The five were: Robert S. Smith (Yale), Robert L. West (Yale), Erskine Childers (Stanford), Herbert Eisenberg (MIT), and Avery Ingram (Harvard).

[3] See Robert S. Smith, p. 504, on the formation of the International Office.

[4] Frank is also the son of Walter Fisher, and Walter Fisher and my aunt were close friends. Walter was at Harvard when my aunt was at Radcliffe. See Fisher, p. 511.

[5] See Part 1, Section 1; Cater, p. 92, and Ellis, p. 130.

[6] See Cater, p. 535.

[7] See Wharton, p. 112.

[8] See Holmes, p. 551.

[9] *Editor's note:* Allen Crow, President of the Economic Club of Detroit, circulated a ten-page memorandum/questionnaire to college presidents throughout the country, raising questions about NSA's vulnerability to communist influence and control and, as a consequence, undermining acceptance of NSA. Responding to the questions he raised occupied considerable attention of the first year's staff. See Welsh, p. 168, and Economic Club of Detroit, p. 191.

[10] *Editor's note:* At the Chicago Conference, and going into the Constitutional Convention, the region had been divided into four units: Maine and Vermont, Massachusetts, New Hampshire, and Connecticut and Rhode Island. Massachusetts, by far the largest, was then led by Miriam Haskell of Smith College. See (Haskell) Berlin, pp. 6 and 87.

[11] *Editor's note:* Larry Jaffa made news when both he and Walter Wallace, then Chair of the Metropolitan New York Region, were criticized in other college papers for lending their names as NSA regional officers to political causes—the Students for Democratic Action, in the case of Jaffa, and the Harvard Committee for Henry Wallace, in the case of Walter Wallace. See p. 851 n.5, pp. 865, 915.

[12] Father Hesburgh became a member of the NSA National Advisory Committee in 1957-1958.

[13] See Courtney Landry, p. 921, Rogers Secondari, p. 599.

ALICE BRANDEIS (GILBERT) POPKIN

Early years: Born in New York City and attended high school at Horace Mann High School for Girls.

Education: Radcliffe College, A.B. 1949, Magna Cum Laude, Phi Beta Kappa. Yale Law School, LL.B. 1953. Member of the Board of the *Yale Law Journal.*

Career highlights: 1987-present: Toabe & Riley, of Counsel, concentrating in trusts, estate planning, and probate administration, Chatham, MA. 1981-87: practicing attorney in Washington, DC. 1979-81: Consultant on international environmental issues, juvenile justice, and political organization. 1977-79: Environmental Protection Agency (EPA), Associate Administrator, Office of International Activities. Managed a staff of 33 in the administration and coordination of EPA's international programs. Represented EPA in international negotiations and conferences such as U.S. Delegation to London Ocean Dumping Convention. 1974-77: Antioch School of Law, Attorney/Professor. 1972-74: Senate Subcommittee to Investigate Juvenile Delinquency, Special Counsel. 1967-72: Georgetown Institute of Criminal Law and Procedure, Project Co-Director for research projects on "Law, Mental Disorders and the Juvenile Process." 1964-66: Representative of the Experiment in International Living while living in Morocco. 1953-61. Cahill Gordon & Reindel (New York, NY), Associate. General corporate practice, including litigation of copyright and antitrust cases.

Bar membership: Commonwealth of Massachusetts, 1978; State of New York, 1953; U.S. District Court for the District of Columbia, 1964; U.S. District Court for the Southern District of New York, 1956; U.S. Court of Appeals for the Second Circuit, 1959; U.S. Supreme Court, 1962.

Peace Corps: 1961-63: Peace Corps, Director of International Programs: coordinated and negotiated agreements with host governments and international organizations for volunteer programs. Peace Corps, Acting Chief of Private Agency Relations; Member of the original staff that set up the Peace Corps, with responsibility for private agency volunteer programs.

Family: Married to Jordan J. Popkin. We have three daughters, Susan, Anne, and Louisa, and one granddaughter, Allison B. Cahn.

PICTURE CREDITS: *Then:* 1947 groundbreaking at Brandeis University. *Now:* 2001, with granddaughter Allison B. Cahn (both provided by author).

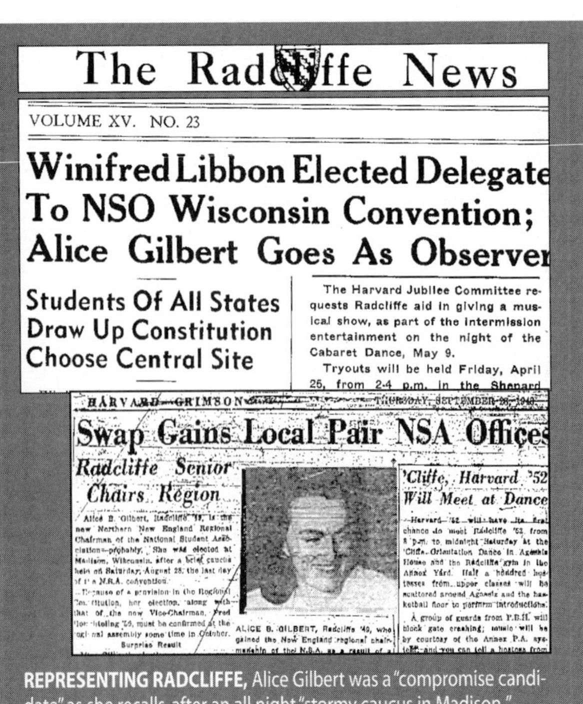

The Radcliffe News

VOLUME XV. NO. 23

Winifred Libbon Elected Delegate To NSO Wisconsin Convention; Alice Gilbert Goes As Observer

Students Of All States Draw Up Constitution Choose Central Site

The Harvard Jubilee Committee requests Radcliffe aid in giving a musical show, as part of the intermission entertainment on the night of the Cabaret Dance, May 9.

Tryouts will be held Friday, April 25, from 2-4 p.m. in the Shepard

HARVARD CRIMSON

Swap Gains Local Pair NSA Offices

Radcliffe Senior Chairs Region

Alice B. Gilbert, Radcliffe '49, is the new Northern New England Regional Chairman of the National Student Association—probably. She was elected at Madison, Wisconsin, after a brief caucus held on Saturday, August 28, the last day of the N.S.A. convention.

'Cliffe, Harvard '52 Will Meet at Dance

Harvard '52 will have its first chance to meet Radcliffe '52 from 8 p.m. to midnight Saturday at the 'Cliffe Orientation Dance in Agassiz House and the Radcliffe gym in the Annex Yard. Half a hundred hostesses from upper classes will be scattered around Agassiz and the basketball floor to perform introductions.

ALICE B. GILBERT, Radcliffe '49, who gained the New England regional chairmanship of the N.S.A.

REPRESENTING RADCLIFFE, Alice Gilbert was a "compromise candidate" as she recalls, after an all night "stormy caucus in Madison."

(For more on Harvard see Cater, pp. 94-95; Wharton, pp. 113, 118, 148).

Yale turns down student government in 1947.

2. Postwar Student Politics and Joining NSA at Yale

Curtis Farrar
Yale University
Member, U.S. Delegation, Prague, 1946 World Student Congress
Delegate, NSA Constitutional Convention, 1947

Excerpts from Class History, Part 1, *The Yale 1949 Class Book*

Author's Note: Searching for some jottings made at the time that might be relevant to the founding of the NSA, I found nothing to recommend. Then my Yale classmate, Otis Pease, mentioned my history of the Yale Class of 1949 in his reminiscence about the role of veterans at postwar Yale. Eugene Schwartz tracked it down and suggested using an excerpt, which is indeed relevant to the subject. The piece from which the following is taken was controversial at the time, and was supplemented in the Class Book, *for purposes of balance, by a second, more conventional class history. With hindsight, I would change the word "which" to "that" in one or two places, but otherwise stand by my observations. As before, I expect that some balance will be provided by other contributors.*

* * *

It is very interesting to notice how our own attitude, or, more accurately, the attitude of the undergraduate body as a whole has changed as far as active participation in politics is concerned. Think back to the fall of 1946 and the size and strength of the AVC chapter on the Yale campus.[1] The American Veterans Committee [AVC] was the largest campus organization, and its influence was very large indeed. Its internal battles to avoid left wing control were of general interest. Its program to get out the vote for congressional elections, find jobs for veterans and their wives, [and] study the financial conditions of veterans at Yale, received a great deal of attention and was highly effective.

The AVC came and went

Why is it that this organization, which had both a national program and a local one, which dealt with questions which affect us all, is completely defunct on the campus at the present moment? Of course part of the story is found in the graduation of many veterans. Many of AVC's leaders moved on to distant law schools or jobs in the State Department, and that had its effect. But there are still many veterans on campus, they still have housing and economic problems, there are still those among them easily capable of leading a group like AVC, most of them are still interested in what happens on the national scene. Yet there is no AVC.

Perhaps it was just bad tactics, poor leadership. Perhaps the veterans who returned just after the war were more liberal than those who are here now. All of these are possible explanations. But on the other hand, could it be possible that this marks a resurgence of a standard Yale attitude towards the world, one which eschews political action for bold thought and social participation? Could it be that the Ferris wheel of Yale has gotten going now so that it operates more efficiently? Perhaps the younger veterans, entering college later, are less set in their ways and knuckle under more easily to the set of social values they find neatly laid out for them. There is no proof, of course, either way, but the question is certainly worth asking.

The AYD and PCA yield to the SDA

Back in the days of '46–'47 when the American Youth for Democracy (AYD) was run off the campus on a rail, the Progressive Citizens of America [PCA] founded a chapter. The John Reed Club formed and listened to editors of the *New Masses* and other revolutionary figures. Both persisted through last year with a certain amount of activity and now seem to have gone the way of all flesh. More recently a chapter of Students for Democratic Action, an anti-communist liberal group, was formed. These lads agitated for [William O.] Douglas for President a bit, but still hold their meetings in somebody's living room. Hardly a big-time operation.

Now, of course, Yale is a conservative place, and it would be foolish to expect otherwise, but the almost total disappearance of liberal and leftist groups would seem to indicate a decisive shift of opinion in a very short time.[2]

The Federalists

The one organization with a political program which has shown any sustaining power on the campus has been the United World Federalists [UWF]. Even so, the quality of its effort has decreased considerably in the past few years. And of course, from the beginning, UWF had a definitely Yale touch. Remember the day in March of 1947 when several thousand undergraduates received live turtles through the mail? Each was inscribed, "Work for World Federation!" The hue and cry from the Society for the Prevention of Cruelty to Animals was immediate and deafening. It caused our favorite *News* columnists, those Jabberwocky people, to get off one of their better remarks: "It is amazing how many people there are who will rise in defense of a few small terrapin, but don't seem to give a damn about the fate of the human race." That stunt did have imagination, if it nearly landed its perpetrator in jail. At present, UWF is reduced to the level of recruiting members from nearby women's colleges and having them down for weekend conferences.[3]

* * *

Failed effort to organize a student council

Back in 1946-47 a group of students . . . stirred up some interest in the possibility of a Student Council at Yale. Dean DeVane, the *News*, Dwight Hall, everybody who was anybody, seemed to be behind it, and as a result there was a poll. The count was overwhelmingly in favor of such a council. So in the spring a group of students were elected to draw up a constitution for submission to the student body. The group worked hard, under careful scrutiny from the *News*. But as their document neared completion, it became apparent that all would not be clear sailing. The *News* itself stayed technically on the fence, although its editorials on the subject were of the bucket of cold water variety.

The cry was "either the Council will have no power, in which case why bother, or it will have the powers of government, which we don't want." More important, from a psychological point of view, the cry was "Student Government for Middle Western universities, but never for Yale." Then there was that half-page ad in the *News* on the morning of the election signed by, among many others, a future Budget drive head and instigated by a future chairman of the *News*. As everybody remembers, the constitution was "overwhelmingly defeated" by a vote of 2,199 for to 1,851 against. Proponents of the Council kicked themselves for having made the required vote two thirds and went around muttering about the powers that be wanting to keep all the reins in their own hands.

It is interesting, in retrospect, to remember that the margin of defeat came almost entirely from those harbingers of a future peacetime Yale, the Freshman population of the old campus. They voted two-to-one against the constitution. Next fall they will be Seniors. Is it a new Yale a'coming, or an Old Yale a'coming back?

Joining NSA—A lesson learned

The next winter the same group which had promoted the Student Council succeeded in a less ambitious enterprise and persuaded Yale to join the newly-founded National Student Association. These students, whose main revolutionary tenet is that Yale isn't so different as it pretends to be, had learned a lot from their unfortunate experience with the unratified constitution. The organization they were supporting had been attacked from various quarters as being Communist-dominated, but this view was manifestly untrue.

A Yale graduate of considerable respectability was elected as one of the officers of NSA, but that was hardly enough to put the organization over on the campus. NSA was, after all, mainly operated through local student governments on various campuses. Was this to be Student Council by a back door? NSA's supporters hoped so, eventually, but like all good politicians they denied it stoutly in public.

The tactics of this campaign were smart. The *News* was wooed and at least temporarily won. NSA's appeal was to be based on Yale's own good opinion of itself. Yale has everything. Therefore, NSA cannot do anything for Yale. But on the other hand, Yale can do a great deal for NSA. It is therefore Yale's duty to join NSA and spread blessings throughout the land. Sounds a bit silly, now, does it not? Well, it was smart. The vote was 1,331 in favor, 1,124 against, about the same proportion as on the Council Constitution. But NSA was "overwhelmingly endorsed," not defeated. Its supporters had also learned that requiring a two-thirds vote is suicide. NSA was in on a straight majority basis.

Since then, NSA at Yale has grown well, though not spectacularly.[4] In its search for funds it has put on two wonderful shows under the doubtful title of jamboriety, proving that black shoes can be just as amusing as white. Also, it has cagily confined itself to problems which affect the student directly, such as plans for summer travel, possible discounts with local merchants, student typing services, and so forth. What will happen to NSA at Yale is a very interesting question. Is there any time limit on paradoxical existence? But that is another question for Yale's succeeding and more normal generations, and not any more, for us.[5]

Yale students and self-government

If the students of Yale have not been convinced that they should take a hand in the way the University is run, they have in some cases done good work within the colleges. Several of the residential colleges have college councils which work closely with the Master and the aides to make the life of the college as close as possible to the optimum foreseen at the initiation of the College System. While the various colleges are still much more like dormitories than Oxford-type colleges, they have grown a great deal under the pressure of the post-war years. The crowding in of twice as many students as the buildings were designed to hold has made impossible the ideal, which was never realized even in those luxurious days before the war, of establishing a real and productive relationship between the Fellows of a college and the undergraduate members. Friendly interest is easily available to the rare student who seeks social and intellectual contact with faculty members outside of class, but the effectiveness of the college unit in promoting this kind of contact has been reduced almost to zero by the mere pressure of numbers.

Curtis Farrar worked with the Asia Foundation, the Agency for International Development and the World Bank. He is presently working on a history of the International Food Policy Research Institute.

YALE REJECTS STUDENT GOVERNMENT, ACCEPTS NSA

Yale Undergraduate Body Rejects Proposed Constitution 2,199-1,851

Freshmen Class, Silliman Voters Head The Field Of Yale College, School Of Engineering Balloters

Farrar Discusses Student Congress

Board to Pick Delegates To Chicago Conference

Discussing the forthcoming meeting of the Chicago Student Conference during Christmas vacation, John C. Farrar, 1947, asked that various University organizations nominate candidates from which the Yale delegation will be chosen at a meeting in Dwight Hall yesterday afternoon.

Nominations are due by Wednesday morning, and a board composed of the Rev. Luther Tucker, Professor Ralph Turner, Wallace F. Doerr, and Farrar will select three delegates with full voting privileges and three official observers from among them.

Prague Conference

New Committee Begins Meetings To Discuss NSA

National Student Group Has Non-Political View; Faces Racial Question

Holding the first of a series of scheduled meetings to consider possible Yale affiliation with the National Student Association, the Review Committee discussed the major issues arising at the constitution convention in Madison, Wisconsin during the first week of September...

After an outline of the history of the new organization, which was described as an effort to unite students

THE Nation

Atomic Bombs or Atomic Plenty?

Students Map the Future

BY CURTIS FARRAR

Campus Organizations Plan Forum To Discuss Academic Freedoms

Arthur Garfield Hayes To Be Principal Speaker: Meeting Will Highlight U. S. Civil Liberty Failures

CURT FARRAR was a major NSA advocate at Yale, having attended the 1946 World Student Congress and the Chicago Student Conference (see Part 1). Farrar was also a leader in the Student Federalists and UWF (see p. 745). (From top left, counterclockwise: *Yale Daily News* 5/28/47, 12/10/46, 11/21/47, 11/47. *The Nation* 9/20/47 featured an article by Farrar on the NSA Constitutional Convention). For more on Yale, see Buckley, p. 785, 787.

END NOTES

[1] See "The Veterans," p. 697.

[2] See Reisin on SDA, p. 781 and AYD, p. 787.

[3] See Jonas, on the Student Federalists, p. 761. *Editor's note:* Curtis Farrar was a member of the U.S. delegation to the 1946 World Student Congress in Prague, representing the Student Federalists.

[4] NSA's first two Vice Presidents for International Affairs, Robert S. Smith (1947-48) and Robert L. West (1948-49) were both Yale undergraduates. They ran their programs out of NSA's international office in Cambridge, MA. See Smith, p. 504.

[5] See excerpt on NSA at Yale from William Buckley's 1951 book, *God and Man at Yale,* p. 797.

PICTURE CREDITS: *Then:* 1946, Naval ROTC. *Now:* 1999 (Both from author). Interior photos: Scenes of student life at Yale with credits not provided (Yale 1949 *Classbook*).

CURTIS FARRAR

Curtis Farrar was born in New York City in 1927, the son of publisher John Farrar, and crossword puzzle editor Margaret Petherbridge Farrar. He graduated from Philips Academy, Andover (1944) and Yale (1949) and has a PhD in Economics from the London School of Economics (1952). He attended the World Student Congress in Prague in 1946 as a representative of Student Federalists, and was actively involved in the creation of the USNSA at Chicago and Madison.

Farrar's marriage to Eleanor Schneider in 1948 ended in divorce. He has been married to Carol Lancaster since 1980. He has five children and seven grandchildren.

Farrar worked with the Asia Foundation from 1954 to 1963, at the San Francisco headquarters, and as a field representative in Pakistan and Cambodia. From 1963 to 1982 he was with the Agency for International Development in Washington DC, moving to the World Bank in that year as Executive Secretary to the Consultative Group on International Agricultural Research. After retirement from the Bank in 1989 he became associated with the International Food Policy Research Institute. He is presently working on a history of that institute.

An African-American in Boston during the 1940s

3. Simmons College and the Northern New England Region

Shirley Neizer Tyler
Simmons College, 1946-50
Northern New England Region, USNSA Project
USNSA Executive Board, Third National Student Congress, 1950

My education at Simmons College in Boston, Massachusetts, where I concentrated on early childhood education and psychology, and later my experiences with NSA and the National Scholarship Service and Fund for Negro Students (NSSFNS), gave me resources I have drawn on throughout my career in retail personnel work and in education.[1] They provided the foundation for rewarding volunteer work over the years: School Board in Alexandria, Virginia, serving two years each as chair and vice chair (nine years of change as the schools were desegregated and enrollment increased to its highest point and then began to decline); health clinic and family service boards; hospital board committees; working with community service and focus groups; service on a regional Episcopal Schools Board; and so forth.

Racism in the 1940s

Racism was present at Simmons and rampant in Boston during the 1940s. Generally, only two African Americans were admitted to the college each year. Our one African American faculty member was seen on the main campus only once in the four years I attended! Few students knew he existed. He worked with our School of Nursing and Harvard's Medical College, or so it was rumored. Because we commuted, the other Negro classmate and I were spared some of the problems faced by the women in the class two years ahead of us, both of whom lived on campus.[2] Racial issues often confronted them as they moved around the city. I had a difficult time with a professor and an instructor my freshman year. They were no longer with the College when classes reopened my sophomore year. Fortunately Simmons has changed dramatically since then, with African Americans welcomed as students, faculty, and administrators.

Student government at Simmons was relatively well organized. We had an established, respected, student-administered honor code, unlike many schools in other parts of the country. The presence of women veterans brought us a level of maturity students may not have experienced during the 1950s. It was an exciting time to attend college. As news of USNSA's founding and productive first year came from Madison and the international office at Harvard, our student government made a commitment to be represented at the 1948 Congress at the University of Wisconsin and at the University of Illinois the following summer. I was asked to be one of our two delegates.[3] The experiences enriched my life immeasurably.

Introducing the Purchase Card System

As a commuter, my extracurricular time was limited. (Commuting from Salem took three or more hours per day!) An activist by nature, I participated in several college groups and in NSA projects to the extent possible. Simmons helped establish the Northern New England Region's Student Purchase Card Plan. To the best of my recollection, participating stores included apparel shops, restaurants, bookstores, and other small stores located near college campuses. Because students in the Boston area had the benefit of Filene's Basement, the pioneer of a unique progressive price-discounting system for merchandise purchased from a number of the country's best department stores and exclusive retailers, Boston's department, apparel, and specialty shops declined to enroll. An executive of a major store informed another committee member and me that participation would be counterproductive. I have often wondered how long Boston's Purchase Card Plan survived.[4]

Occasionally I visited NSA's international office. What an exciting climate! Housed at Harvard and guided by knowledgeable international vice chairmen with insight into the operations of the national unions of students overseas, the roles American students were playing abroad, and the ways to build American student participation in international student programs, the level of sophistication and competence within the staff was impressive.

Preelection involvement in the 1948 election

While I was at Simmons, Henry Wallace became a candidate for president. A small group of us was involved in a very loosely organized campus branch of the Young Progressives of America (YPA). At one point, we were invited to send representatives to a meeting in downtown Boston, which theoretically was to plan strategies related to various organizations participating in the campaign. Having no classes to attend that afternoon, I volunteered to represent our group. I vaguely remember that the attendees were assigned to a number of subgroups. The climate, starting from the time I arrived, changed from one where there appeared to be a great deal of informal conferencing to an uneasy quiet with few people talking. Participants waited for meetings to begin. Finally, word spread through the building that activities were canceled.

I was the only Negro (African American) present, as near as I could tell. I will never know the truth, but suspect that race was on the agenda. Whatever was being planned must have been negative. I reported my concerns to my colleagues at Simmons. We decided to withdraw from participation in the YPA, since our primary interest was in Mr. Wallace, the man, rather than YPA and related organizations. Our assessment was that if racial issues were a negative factor, Mr. Wallace's campaign was not involved. The group at Simmons was not interested in negative activities, nor in working with groups that appeared to be controlled by the Communist Party. YPA at Simmons gradually faded away. The women at Simmons were independent thinkers—unwilling to conform to groups with negative messages. I suspect that support for Wallace was as strong as ever. Each of us went down our own paths to lend that support. While Mr. Wallace lost, the country engaged in a healthy debate on national issues and priorities. That in itself was positive as the nation continued its transition from war to peace.

The Simmons College Archives

During a visit to the Simmons College campus, the editor of this book persuaded the college archivist to copy those pages in the 1940-1952 issues of the *Simmons News* that included articles about local, regional and national activities of USNSA and its affiliates. Coverage of the American Student Union (ASU) and the 1946 Chicago Student Conference and campus support for the World Student Service Fund (WSSF) and the National Scholarship Service and Fund for Negro Students (NSSFNS) are included as well.[5]

The intensity of Simmons's early involvement in intercollegiate activities has been a pleasant revelation. Two students, Esther Maletz ('49) and Patricia Murphy ('48) attended NSA's Constitutional Convention in 1946. In addition, issues of the *Simmons News* from 1948 to 1952 included relatively comprehensive reports of meetings of the Northern New England region, USNSA Congresses, and summaries of National Executive Committee meetings, as well as stories about NSA's international office. Campus activities included active participation in the Boston area's NSA-sponsored Student Purchase Plan, regional cultural activities, teas and programs featuring national and regional officers, workshops on student government and student exchange programs, sponsorship of displaced students (from 1949 to 1951), and promotion of NSA's travel program.[6]

Articles also indicate that in the early 1950s Simmons representatives Dagmar Hallbauer, Roberta Schuette, and Carol Steinberg helped lead a movement among Boston-area colleges to encourage the attendance of student-body presidents at NSA's national congresses, as well as better integration on campuses of related student government and NSA activities. These young women were all involved with the NSA committee in 1948-1950, a period when Marion Malis, Frances Hoffman, Dagmar Hallbauer, and other activists were assisting Esther Maletz and me with intercollegiate activities.[7]

Shirley Neizer Tyler recently retired as Head of School, Grace Episcopal School, in Alexandria, Virginia. (See p. 282 for an extended bio.)

END NOTES

[1] See Tyler, pp. 458 and 496.

[2] In the late 1940s, "Negro" was the politically correct term for African American.

[3] My co-delegates were Esther Maletz, in 1948, and Marion Malis and Frances Hoffman, in 1949.

[4] *Editor's note:* The Purchase Card System, launched nationally in 1948-1949 as a community-based program, continued in various forms, first as the Student Discount Service (restructured in 1950-1951) and later as the American Discount Card, as reported in the Twenty-first Congress Report.

There are few specific regional records of activity during its early years through 1952 beyond reports in student newspapers and to the National Executive Committee. See Medalie, p. 348. Simmons Student Government officially withdrew in 1952 (Simmons archives).

[5] See ASU, p. 47, WSSF, p. 613, NSSFNS, p. 463, and Chicago Student Conference, p. 109.

[6] Displaced students were young men and women who had escaped from persecution by the Nazis before and during World War II. Various organizations and colleges sponsored individual students who found placement in colleges throughout our country.

[7] Simmons College attendees at NSA-related national events included:

1946 Chicago Student Conference
Majorie Klein, '48, Mary Kerr '48

1947 Constitutional Convention
Esther Maletz '49, Patricia Murphy '48

1948 National Student Congress, University of Wisconsin
Esther Maletz, Shirley Neizer, '50

1949 National Student Congress, University of Illinois
Shirley Neizer, Marion Malis '51, Frances Hoffman '51

1950 National Student Congress, University of Michigan
Dagmar Hallbauer, Roberta Schuette, Carol Steinberg '51

1951 National Student Congress, University of Minnesota
Janet Bloom '51, Honey Bloom

Over the years between 1948 and 1952, other Simmons College NSA activists included: Adele Klein '51, Constance Marshall '47, Betty Burgess '49, Eleanor Law '50, Kay Bernard '50, Muzza Rosenstein '51, Virginia Bown '50, Alice Hershey '50, and members of the Student Government Council (Stu-G), among others. Some of the women were actively involved in regional projects, as well as those on campus (e.g., workshops on the role of Student Government, a tour of New England).

ALBUM

A College in BostonTown

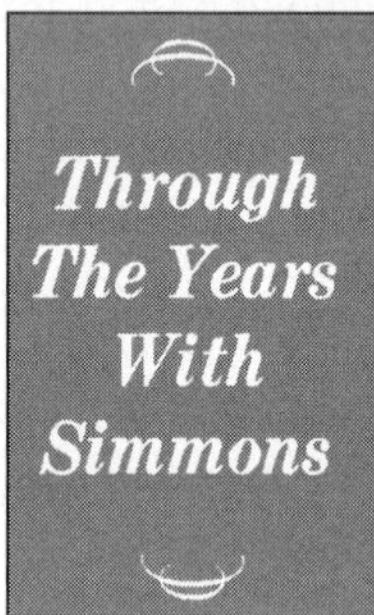
Through The Years With Simmons

Founder John Simmons and Sarah Louise Arnold, first Dean.

Illustrations and captions from *Simmons News* 4/27/39.

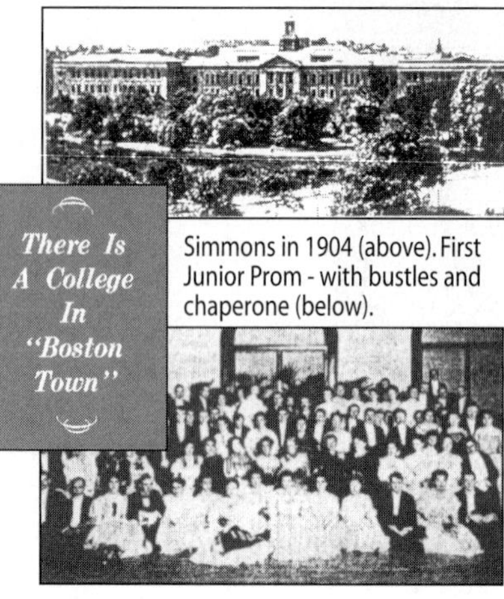
There Is A College In "Boston Town"

Simmons in 1904 (above). First Junior Prom - with bustles and chaperone (below).

INCORPORATED IN 1899, after being delayed by the great fire of Boston in 1872, the college was endowed in 1870 by clothing mfr. John Simmons, a friend of Matthew Vassar (Vassar C., 1861), as "Simmons Female College for the purpose of teaching medicine, drawing, music, telegraphy and other branches of arts, science and industry best calculated to enable the scholars to acquire an independent livelihood." *(Simmons News 1/10/52)*

Simmons: Connected to the World, 1931-1946

REPORT ON N. S. F. A. — Simmons News — REVISION OF CODE

N. S. F. A. NEWS

"FEMININITY NO HANDICAP IN WORLD OF BUSINESS"

Says Only Woman President of Public Utility

New York, N. Y.—A woman is not handicapped in business by her sex, according to Miss Mary E. Dillon, president of the Brooklyn Borough Gas Company. This opinion was given recently to a report of the Princetonian in an interview with the only woman president of a public utility.

Miss Dillon, who has been married for nine years and has, in her own words, "a very complete home-life," but still prefers to use her maiden name in business, entered the gas

1/14/32

VIRGINIA GIFFORD REPORTS ON N. S. F. A. CONGRESS

During the Christmas recess Virginia Gifford, President of Student Government, attended the Seventh Annual Congress of the National Student Federation of America, this year held at Toledo, Ohio. In her report to the Council, she stressed mainly the happenings which should prove pertinent to all college women: the honor system, international relations, Freshman orientation, smoking, busyness of Student life, and the aim of Student Government.

5/19/32

RUSSIAN STUDENTS EXTEND INVITATION TO AMERICAN GROUP

N. S. F. A. Group Sails July 6th to Study Russia as Guests of the Universities

New York, N. Y. (NSFA)—The success of the American student trip to Russia in 1932 has prompted students of the Russian universities to renew their invitation again this year through the National Student Federation to college students in the United States.

In addition to the more formal entertainment afforded by teas and dinners, the group will have an opportunity in every city they visit to meet and talk, not only to students, but to experts in the fields in which they are particularly interested.

4/27/33

N.S.F.A. RADIO PROGRAMS INAUGURATE SERIES OF TALKS ON TECHNOCRACY

New York, N. Y. (NSFA)—The four programs on the National Student Federation hour during January are on the subject of Technocracy. The first three speakers authorized to describe this new movement in the field of economics are Dr. Walter Rautenstrauch, head of the Department of Industrial Engineering at Columbia University, Dr. Earl T. Engle, Professor of Biochemistry at the College of Physicians and Surgeons, and Langdon Post, former New York Assemblyman.

Dr. Rautenstrauch, in opening the series on January 9th, spoke on "The Message of Technocracy." He said in part, "The enterprise of Technocracy is concerned with an examination of the physical basis of our society, that is, (1) determining what resources we have in terms of iron, coal, copper,

1/26/33

SIMMONS STUDENTS ENGAGED ACTIVELY in the three major prewar and wartime student organizations: National Student Federation of America (p. 30), American Student Union (p. 47) and U.S. Student Assembly (p. 34).

1938 DECEMBER 1938

SUN	MON	TUES	WED	THU	FRI	SAT
				1	2	3
4	5	6	7	8	9	10
11	12	13	14	15	16	17
18	19	20	21	22	23	24
25	26	27	28	29	30	31

Forecast

Thursday, Dec. 8
Newman Tea
A. S. U. Discussion Grou[p]
Friday, Dec. 9
Competitives
"Y" International Tea
Saturday, Dec. 10
Student House Dance
Sunday, Dec. 11
Glee Club Concert
Monday, Dec. 12
Ellen Richards' Party
Tuesday, Dec. 13
Faculty Party
Wednesday, Dec. 14
Unity-"Y" Tea
Thursday, Dec. 15
020 Tea

12/8/38

LET FREEDOM RING

NAZI persecution, recently reaching its logical climax in an org[y] of savagery, has raised voices of protest the world over. America[n] youth, however, has decided that *actions* speak louder tha[n] [wo]rds. Spontaneously, in colleges all over the country, groups are bein[g] [fo]rmed to show that the younger generation has no sympathy wit[h] [Ap]pquenindian barbarism.

At Simmons, a Refugee Committee has just been formed, condemnin[g] [th]e Nazi practice of substituting concentration camps for universitie[s]. [Th]is committee plans to rescue foreign students who have already achieve[d] [hi]gh honors in their field, or who show potentialities of doing so, and wh[o] [ha]ve been forced to discontinue their education.

Simmons Group To Aid Nazi Refugee Students

Corporation Will Give Tuition For Student

Simmons Student Refugee Commit-

ATTENTION SENIORS!!

There are only 2 more paydays for MIC before Christmas vacation: Wednesday, Dec. 7 and Wednesday, Dec. 14. After Christmas, MIC goes up 35c—so pay up your subscription NOW!!!

From top: 12/5/38, 12/8/38

THE SIMMONS NEWS

A.S.U. Convention Proposes Human Rights Roll Call

Over 1000 college students from 50 colleges in the United States went as delegates to the Fourth Annual Convention of the American Student Union, held at the City College of New York from Dec. 26 to Dec. 30. Simmons delegates to the convention were Barbara Johnson, Evelyn Sternberg, Esther Soddeck, Josephine Cluck, and Janet Phillips.

The most important accomplishment of the convention was the adoption of a Human Rights Rollcall, a petition urging study and action towards meeting human needs and developing and extending democracy at home. The American Student Union hopes to have this petition signed by 210,000 or more students and faculty.

On the question of peace, last year's program of collective security was retained. The convention gave support to President Roosevelt's student pilot plan under the N.Y.A. with the condition that these pilots be kept under civilian control.

1/12/39

The Simmons News

Eleanor Roosevelt Speaks Oct. 27 — 10/5/44

RESTRAINT MARKS V-E DAY — 5/10/45

Pres. Beatley Announces Retirements, Promotions — Students Return to Cl[asses] After Hearing News

WAR FUND DRIVE OPENS MONDAY — 9/27/45

FIRST MALE VETERANS ENROLL — 10/11/45

A-Bomb Pro-Con Faculty Opinions — SIMMONS JOINS U.S. STUDENT[S] IN CONCERN OVER BOMB ISSU[E] — 11/29/45

FRANCE TODAY ASSEMBLY TALK — Progress Halted On A-Bomb Problem — Stu-G Urges College Stud[y]

THE MARCH TO WAR AND THE PEACE THAT FOLLOWED were central to the interest of generations of Simmons students and were covered extensively by the *Simmons News* and in campus forums. Fund drives centered on aid to pre- and postwar refugee students (see Part 3, Sec. 4, p. 611).

USSA Nat'l Delegate Describes Meetings In London, Prague

(The following letter was written by Alice Horton of Wellesley, USSA delegate to the international students conferences in London and in Prague. Simmons USSA is a member of the national organization.)

"We sailed from New York October 19th aboard the Queen Mary and although she is a converted troop ship, the magnificence of the boat is still evident—with a swimming pool, several dining rooms and all of the glamorous trimmings. There are 2 of us in the American delegation, and we were joined by the Cuban, Ecuadorian, Canadian and part of the Chinese delegations. Time on board not spent planning for the conference.

The New England Region: Open for Business

Andrew Rice
Harvard University
1946 Chicago Student Conference
1947-48 Cochair, New England Region

Editor's note: Andrew Rice was one of the leaders, along with Mimi Haskell (Smith College), Henry Halsted (Williams College), Lawrence Jaffa (Yale Divinity), Alice Gilbert and Winifred Libbon (Radcliffe), Earl Eames (MIT), and many others, who helped launch the New England Region in its first year after the 1947 NSA Constitutional Convention. Following are excerpts from some documents he furnished. He writes that organizing the New England Region was complicated by "the split between the far left and the more moderates." This resulted in rotating chairs and "a lot of caucusing among us moderates to make sure certain items came up on the agenda when I was in the chair." Rice was also national vice president of the American Unitarian Youth, and an excerpt also appears here of an article he wrote for their national magazine.

Report on Accomplishments of the International Activities Committee, Harvard Student Council, January–August 1947, *Presented by the Massachusetts Region*

Last December at the Chicago Conference, the International Activities Committee of the Harvard Student Council was appointed to undertake, on a temporary basis, a program of coordination and information concerning international student activities for the NCC. Later it was agreed that the funds for its work would be the NCC regional dues of the Massachusetts region.

What has the International Activities Committee at Harvard done to carry out this assignment?

Working jointly with Radcliffe, it has, on a purely volunteer basis among all its members including its chairman:

(l) Published and distributed widely nearly 10,000 copies of the Student International Activities Bulletin. The Bulletin provided the only nearly complete compendium of information on (a) educational opportunities for American students abroad, for the summer and for the whole year; (b) travel conditions for American students abroad; (c) summer reconstruction projects; (d) methods and channels for relief activities of American students.

The Bulletin was sent to all schools represented at Chicago (and to many others), to all college newspapers, to all foreign unions of students, to interested youth and student organizations, and to other publicity sources.

(2) Established contact with a great number of agencies concerned with relief, rehabilitation, exchange and travel. Sent official representatives to meetings of the joint Travel Committee (organized to promote student ships), the Transportation Committee (organized to operate student ships), the Junior-Year-Abroad Committee of the Institute of International Education, the ad hoc committee to discuss coordination of activities of ISS and WSSF. Directors of UNESCO, the Commission for International Educational Reconstruction of the U.S. Council of Education, WSSF, IIE, WFDY, etc., conferred with the committee in Cambridge. A sound basis for future cooperation has been established if desired.

(3) Handled a considerable volume of direct request mail from students all over the country on international student activities.

(4) Undertook on an experimental scale a metropolitan Boston student-faculty meeting on the American student's relationship to UNESCO. Fourteen colleges sent representatives. This may set a pattern for regional Commission activity.

— Andrew E. Rice

* * *

UNITED STATES NATIONAL STUDENT ASSOCIATION

November 7, 1947

Dean Payson S. Wild
Graduate School of Arts and Sciences
Harvard University
24 Quincy Street
Cambridge 38, Massachusetts

Dear Dean Wild:

Two months ago on September 7, 700 student representatives meeting in constitutional convention at the University of Wisconsin created the United States National Student Association. As delegates to that convention, elected by and representing our student governing bodies, we were proud to participate in the formation of this new organization.

It comes as a particular pleasure to us that, although the national headquarters of the USNSA have been established in Madison, Wisconsin, the office of NSA's Commission on International Affairs has been set up in Cambridge. It is in charge of Robert S.Smith, one of the two national vice-presidents of the NSA, and under his direction a comprehensive activities program is being developed.

We who have worked closely towards the establishment of the NSA are glad therefore that we have now a special opportunity to acquaint you directly with the present operations and future plans of NSA. For this purpose, we are sponsoring a "Welcome to Cambridge" luncheon for Bob Smith, to be held on Monday, November 24, at one o'clock, at the Oxford Grille, 28 Church Street, off Harvard Square. To this luncheon we are inviting administration and student leaders from Radcliffe, Harvard and MIT. A representative of each school will speak briefly and Mr. Smith will respond. The proceedings will be over not later than 2:30 P.M.

We hope you can be with us at this welcoming luncheon. Reservations, at $1.25 a plate, should be made with Andrew E. Rice, 64 Kirkland Street, Cambridge 38, not later than Friday November 21.

Sincerely yours,

Winifred Libbon, for the Radcliffe delegation
Andrew E. Rice, for the Harvard delegation
Earl Eames, for the MIT delegation

For more on the early Cambridge office, see p. 501, Smith, p. 505, Garland, p. 648, and Wurf, p. 182.

STUDENTS INTERNATIONAL ACTIVITIES BULLETIN

NATIONAL CONSTITUTION DRAFTED BY NCC

Students INTERNATIONAL ACTIVITIES *Bulletin*

Campuses Rally for Overseas Relief

Five Sections Proposed for NSO in U.S.

Money-Raising Campaigns Reported Leading Drives

Students INTERNATIONAL ACTIVITIES *Bulletin*

VOL. 1, NO. 1 — MARCH 1, 1947

Food and Clothing Drives Lead Campus Campaigns To Help Rehabilitation

Bulletin Makes Its Debut To Exchange Information On Study, Travel and Relief

Plans for New Student Group Set at Chicago

New Legislation Assists Study in Colleges Abroad

New Aid Sought As World Relief Needs Increase

The Harvard International Activities Committee produced this bulletin for the National Continuations Committee in the spring of 1947, prior to the Constitutional Convention of NSA. It was circulated to colleges throughout the country. Andrew Rice was treasurer of the Committee, and delivered the following Final Financial Statement to the NCC:

February-August, 1947. Summary.

RECEIPTS		
Massachusetts Regional NCC (NCC Dues)	$518.25	
Massachusetts Regional NCC (Loan)	125.00	
World Student Service Fund Donation	100.00	
Miscellaneous contributions	1.21	
Sale of BULLETINS	10.10	
Sale of excess office equipment	1.50	
	$756.06	$756.06
EXPENDITURES		
Printing	$578.00	
Postage	99.32	
Telegraph	3.14	
Travel	5.82	
Office supplies	43.04	
Secretarial help	5.75	
Engraving	1.05	
Overtime use of office	1.41	
	$737.53	$737.53
Balance on hand, September 1, 1947		18.53
Bills Payable		
Loan from Massachusetts Regional NCC	$125.00	
Bills Receivable		
Sales of BULLETINS to:		
National Association of Internes and Medical Students	6.24	
Student Christian Assoc. Trinity Univ., San Antonio, Tex.	1.25	

Andrew E. Rice, Treasurer
Int'l Activities Committee

Weekend at Chicago

Editor's note: Events at the Chicago Student Conference are described in detail by Clif Wharton and others in Part 1, Section 3. Below are digests of opening and closing portions of Andrew Rice's report as it appeared in the American Unitarian Youth magazine, The Young Liberal, *in February 1947:*

At a quarter of one in the early morning of December 30, 1946 a momentous event took place in a crowded hall on the snow-covered campus of the University of Chicago: by unanimous vote of the assembled delegates the report of Panel I [on organization and functions] as amended by the plenary sessions was adopted. The NCC was born.

What is the NCC? What was Panel I, and what kind of a group was it that filled Mandel Hall that decisive night?...You will remember reading in the last two issues of *The Young Liberal,* the letters of Jean Casson, the AUY delegate to the World Student Congress at Prague in August, 1946. When the twenty-five American delegates returned from Europe after the Congress, they felt strongly the need for a national student organization to carry out on a national level the program of the International Union of Students (IUS) which was formed at Prague.... [see Pt. 1, Sec. 2].

So the delegates, together with the organizations which had originally sponsored their journey to Prague (including the AUY's) determined to call a national student conference to be held at Chicago during the Christmas vacation...."

The response was magnificent: "enthusiastic," as Russell Austin, who had served as chairman of the Chicago conference preparatory committee, said in his keynote address, "beyond our most wishful thought."

The delegates came from every part of the country; they were Catholics, Protestants, Jews, Negroes, whites, undergraduates, graduate students, normal school students....

The conference had one primary purpose: to discuss the advisability of the formation of a national student organization and to consider the form of such an organization and its aims and activities.

* * *

Through all the debate and parliamentary maneuvering there shone a spirit of good will and a determination to build the basis of an organization whch can truly work for and speak for the students of the United States on the problems which directly concern them. The compromises that were made on more than one issue helped forge a unity. No one group could be said to have dominated the conference; no prepared program was forced down its throat willy-nilly. The Chicago conference was a milestone for every one of America's 2,000,000 university students.

ANDREW E. RICE

Based on a "People of Cabin John" column by Barbara Martin in the Village News, *Cabin John, MD, October 1993.*

Andy Rice grew up in Wisconsin. His father was a professor of law at the U. of Wisconsin, and his mother "an energetic lady who was always helping someone." One year the family lived in Geneva, Switzerland, where his father served as the first U.S. permanent representative to the International Labor Organization. Andy attended the International School.

At Harvard, he studied political science, ran cross-country, and played cello in the orchestra. During World War II, Andy was in the Signal Corps, given training in Japanese and stationed in Washington where he translated intercepted radio messages from the enemy. With war's end, he was sent to Tokyo with the Occupation.

On the GI Bill, Andy earned a Master's degree at Harvard in Far East regional studies. He was active in the American Veterans Committee and International Activities Committee. Over the next dozen years, he had several jobs with the Federal Government and public policy organizations. In 1960, he was co-author of one of the feasibility studies that led to the formation of the Peace Corps (See p. 638—ed.).

After earning a Ph.D. in American government at Syracuse, he joined the Kennedy Administration as Special Assistant to Undersecretary of State Chester Bowles. He next worked for the Society for International Development, an organization he had helped to found 5 years earlier. He stayed for 18 years, becoming Executive Secretary.

When he retired from SID, Andy joined Seven Locks Press, a book publishing company. Andy was editor of the *Village News* for 10 years. Now he is an independent consultant and editor. He is also a very active volunteer.

Andy's wife, Connie Bergfors, is a sculptor who teaches at the Corcoran School of Art. They have twin sons, Brandt and Stefan. Brandt is a microbiologist. Stefan is a composer and pianist living in Paris.

Important Things Were Happening

Henry Halsted
Williams College
1947 Constitutional Convention

Editor's note: Henry Halsted chronicled the events during and following the NSA Constitutional Convention. He writes that his notes "were used in reports to the Williams College student government (the U.C., or Undergraduate Council), and other campus groups and for articles in publications. They provide a glimpse of the launching of NSA on one campus, of the vision delegates brought back to their campuses and tried to pass to their fellow students...." Following are brief excerpts from the material he provided (see also his essays in Part 3, Section 6 on the Experiment in International Living).

NSA at Williams

A Williams NSA council will soon be set up with representation through the social units. This council will maintain liaison with the regional headquarters and other campuses regarding NSA programs. Forums will be held and guest speakers sponsored to discuss student concerns and NSA. It is hoped that wide student interest may be aroused by speakers on UNESCO, movies about the International Union of Students, and discussions of NSA policies and programs.

Since its inception here on campus the NSA Committee has concerned itself with transmitting to Williams students information on student affairs elsewhere in NSA and in keeping NSA informed of activities here. Files are being kept on summer study, travel and work opportunities abroad. Students can keep up with the latest NSA news by consulting the NSA bulletin board in Hopkins Hall.

In addition NSA has assumed the task of producing the newsletter for the Northern New England Region. Reports from the colleges in the region will be sent to the Williams Committee which will assemble and publish them in mimeograph form for distribution to the colleges.

* * *

Members of the NSA committee are elected by the social units. This puts the NSA Committee in the unique position of being the only organization on campus with the exception of the U.C. [Undergraduate Council] which is based on social unit representation. That is why NSA was asked to handle the Marshall Plan petitions last term.

* * *

Within the regions the various colleges take different tasks. Some are studying curricula, others student exchange, others discrimination in colleges. Williams is handling the regional publication. Some examples of the fruits of these labors can be found in the excellent NSA booklet on student government and the one on foreign study, travel and work that have just been published.

What Other Campuses Are Doing about NSA.

M.I.T. is setting up a student government clinic to study existing student governments in the region and work on model governments geared to various campus situations.

Wellesley is studying the problems of the foreign students in American colleges and plans some international week-ends.

Smith is studying the curriculums in New England colleges looking to improve by student action standards and methods of instruction.

Mt. Holyoke will examine the extent of discrimination in colleges in the region.

Harvard is the national headquarters for NSA's international activities. The NSA seat on UNESCO will be occupied by the NSA Vice President in charge of International Activities, Bob Smith, a junior at **Yale.**

The **Radcliffe** Idler Club, the dramatics group on campus, has designated opening night of their spring production as benefit night for a summer camp for undernourished French city children. The Radcliffe NSA Committee is sponsoring the camp.

An NSA-sponsored institute on college radio techniques will be held in Springfield, Mass. under the direction of an announcer on the Chicopee, Mass., radio station and the Smith College NSA committee.

Williams is publishing and circulating the regional newsletter.

The Bowdoin Plan

From a letter by Henry Halsted to a faculty member about the Bowdoin plan to bring foreign students to American campuses:

Problems of taking care of these students has been turned over to the college NSA Committee now under Jim Finke with you as faculty advisor. The problems will include:

1) Orientation -- Jim Finke will be back freshman week in the fall and should contact you.

2) Working out a practicable schedule to rotate the students for meals among the social units, spreading more or less equally the cost as well as getting the students around.

3) Responsibility for the collection of the student tax which is to pay the room rents.

4) Making the foreign students at home and their stay as valuable as possible for both them and Williams

I hope all these matters can be worked out satisfactorily. I feel sure however that your influence and guidance will be very important in getting the NSA Committee to carry this plan through.
Best regards,
Henry Halsted, NSA Committee

The Williams Class of 1948

(From a letter to the Anthology editor, 9/14/98)

The 1948 Williams College Yearbook indicates that the entering freshman class that year numbered 278, bringing enrollment to a new peak of 1,107 and lowered the percentage of veterans in the student body to 53%.

Recent research on the Williams Class of 1948 shows that the class was made up of men who because of the war had entered the college at a variety of times from as early as 1942. Many had had their college experience interrupted for military service. With the then accelerated programs and three commencements a year, there were seven commencements between September 1946 and October 1948. Students had the problem of deciding with which class they would identify, the one with which they entered, the one with which they graduated, or the one with which they had spent the most time or in which they had the most friends. Of those who came to identify themselves as the Williams Class of 1948, one-third had had some "in harms way" war experience.

Another item in the 1948 yearbook. Following some commentary on student play productions, the yearbook states: "Important things were happening in the non-dramatic world, too. A majority of the undergraduates voted to ratify the constitution of the National Student Association, thus making Williams one of the first New England colleges to back the organization."

Postscript to Madison

From a letter to Seth Bidwell, his Williams College delegate colleague, who left the Constitutional Convention a day before it concluded:
Much of interest transpired after you left fair Madison. Most important were the elections. Second most important was consideration of IUS.

The election began Saturday afternoon. Jim Smith got up and said that the steering committee had appointed him chairman for the elections. This seemed the obvious decision. Jim was largely responsible for NSA, yet he was not going to accept any office. Thus he was the top leader not a possible candidate and would make a dignified chairman at the important meeting. But Jim gave a tearjerky speech explaining that it would be too much of a strain for his already shattered body and soul. He declined. Bob West of Yale was elected chairman of the session. It was soon apparent why Smith had declined. As chairman, he could have made no nominating or seconding speech.

He left the stage for a seat, and at the crucial moment gave a moving speech that put his prestige behind his candidate Bill Welsh who, as you know, was elected.... [See p. 147, p. 165.]

When the elections ended Jim Smith jumped on the stage and took the chair's mike and gave a speech praising the candidates who would soon be hailed at the banquet.... Much singing, speeches from officers and representatives of foreign student organizations --Sweden, Italy, Canada, Argentina, Peru. Jim Smith was made 1st honorary National Chair. The foreigners made it clear how much they banked on NSA to be a leading force in the world and impressed on us the different approach of foreign students to their position. They stressed their privileged position as students, and emphasized their sense of responsibility to their nations and the world.

Issue no. 2 **NNER BULLETIN [EXCERPTS]** March 10, 1948

Published twice each month by the Public Relations Office of the Northern New England Region of the National Student Association
Co-Chairman: Irene Tinker, 15 Walker St., Cambridge, Mass.
Stan Greenfield, McCulloch, C-33, Soldiers Field, Mass.
Mimeographed and circulated by Williams College, Williamstown, Mass.

NEW PUBLIC RELATIONS PROGRAM

In an attempt to provide the region with information and to serve as a general clearing house for all regional activities, the Public Relations Co-chairman Irene Tinker and Stan Greenfield have set up a public relations committee composed of stud-ents from most of the greater Boston colleges. Six members of the committee will conduct personal correspondence with the public relations men on each campus in the region. From this correspondence will come the news included in the news letter as well as ideas for further publicizing activities of the NSA

CHILDREN'S CAMP IN FRANCE

The Harvard and Radcliffe committees of the NSA are organizing for this summer a camp for undernourished French city children.... The camp is to be staffed by [volunteer] councilors chosen by the Harvard and Radcliff student bodies and by French university students.

NSA PLANS EASTER TOURS

The International Activities commissions of Northern and Southern New England regions are planning automobile tours for foreign students to many points of interest in New England during the Easter vacation. The local NSA will play host to the students while they are stopping en route. Factories, historical sites, town meetings and city halls will be visited and the students will be able to talk with mayors, governors and everyday Americans.

Henry Halsted was Vice President of The Johnson Foundation at Wingspread, its Frank Lloyd Wright conference center in Racine, Wisconsin. He was also Vice President of the Associated Colleges of the Midwest and of the Kansas City Regional Council for Higher Education.

(See extended bio on p. 684.)

WILLIAMS AMONG THE FIRST TO JOIN NSA

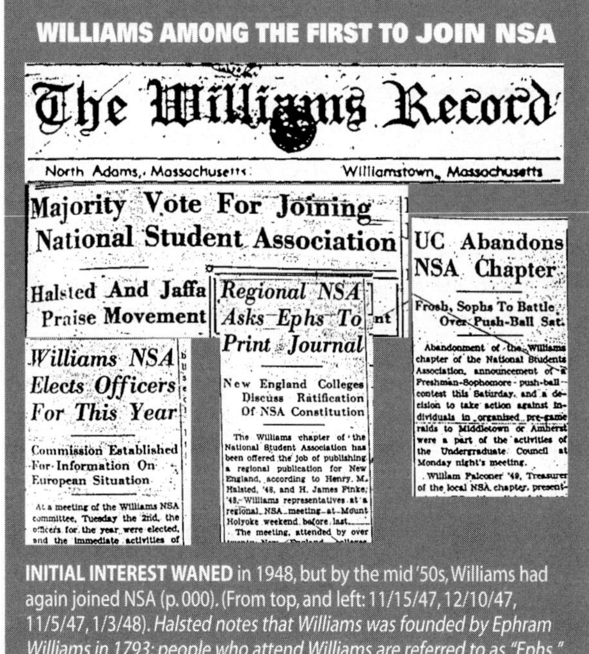

The Williams Record
North Adams, Massachusetts Williamstown, Massachusetts

Majority Vote For Joining National Student Association

Halsted And Jaffa Praise Movement

Williams NSA Elects Officers For This Year

Commission Established For Information On European Situation

At a meeting of the Williams NSA committee, Tuesday the 2nd, the officers for the year were elected, and the immediate activities of

Regional NSA Asks Ephs To Print Journal

New England Colleges Discuss Ratification Of NSA Constitution

The Williams chapter of the National Student Association has been offered the job of publishing a regional publication for New England, according to Henry M. Halsted, '48, and H. James Finke, '48, Williams representatives at a regional NSA meeting at Mount Holyoke weekend before last.

The meeting, attended by over

UC Abandons NSA Chapter

Frosh, Sophs To Battle Over Push-Ball Sat.

Abandonment of the Williams chapter of the National Students Association, announcement of a Freshman-Sophomore push-ball contest this Saturday, and a decision to take action against individuals in organized pre-game raids to Middletown or Amherst were a part of the activities of the Undergraduate Council at Monday night's meeting.

William Falconer '49, Treasurer of the local NSA chapter, present-

INITIAL INTEREST WANED in 1948, but by the mid '50s, Williams had again joined NSA (p. 000). (From top, and left: 11/15/47, 12/10/47, 11/5/47, 1/3/48). *Halsted notes that Williams was founded by Ephram Williams in 1793; people who attend Williams are referred to as "Ephs."*

ERNEST M. HOWELL

Editor's note: Ernie Howell was one of the group of Harvard veterans and student leaders who helped shape the postwar Student Christian Movement, the National Student Association and the Young Adult Council's involvement in the World Assembly of Youth. He was 1947 Co-Chair of the NICC (pp. 158, 737), member of the U.S. delegation to the 1951 World Assembly of Youth (p. 767), and on the 1953 U.S. Assembly of Youth Staff. He was appointed to the U.S. delegation to UNESCO in 1950 (p. 510).

Following service in the Corps of Engineers, and after graduating Harvard College, he entered the Russian Studies program at Harvard University. From 1952 to 1969 he was with the Asia Foundation in Pakistan, Bangladesh, Sri Lanka, Malaysia, Singapore and Vietnam. Later he was on the staff of the Carnegie Endowment for International Peace. He is currently an investment executive with Salomon Smith Barney.

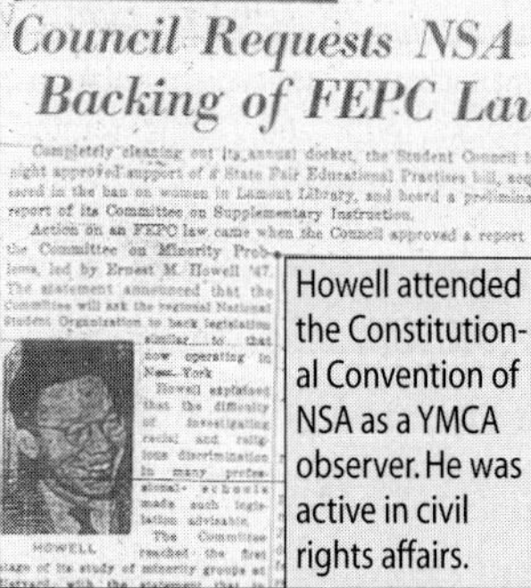

An Old Council Makes Way for a New

Council Requests NSA Backing of FEPC Law

HOWELL

Howell attended the Constitutional Convention of NSA as a YMCA observer. He was active in civil rights affairs.

(Crimson 5/11/48)

The Pros and Cons of NSA at Bowdoin

NSA Presents Many Advantages; Bowdoin Might Profit By Joining

The student body of Bowdoin will shortly be called upon to decide whether or not it wishes to join the National Student Association. It is of the utmost importance that this decision be made by the students only after the fullest possible understanding of the organization, methods, and aims of the NSA.

We firmly believe that this organization of undergraduates on a national scale would enable Bowdoin students to take a very real part in the bettering of their own college and in contributing to the welfare of other colleges and to international good will and understanding.

Bowdoin has already played a very important part in the establishment and early conduct of the NSA. Delegates were in attendance at the initial Chicago conference and at the national constitutional conference at Madison this past summer. The Bowdoin delegates to the regional conference held recently at Mt. Holyoke played a leading part in the organization of the Northern New England Region which comprises Massachusetts, Vermont, New Hampshire and Maine. Our foreign student plan received much praise. One of the Student Council members is now Vice-Chairman of the State of Maine Area for this region and is responsible for the affiliation of colleges in this state with the NSA.

The question at once arises as to what the NSA has to offer to the Bowdoin student body. The organization intends to work on a regional level through the individual student councils. Requests will be made for orientation courses for freshmen, improvement of student unions, and the better organization of social life on the campus. Part-time employment and placement services, problems of housing, and the improvement of student newspapers will also come under consideration.

The NSA will also emphasize scholarships for the needy, and holding the line on tution fees if possible. The problem of discrimination in colleges will also receive attention. NSA will press for the establishment of student-faculty committees on curricular reform. Especially it hopes to press for the study and eventual initiation of courses in the so-called "great issues".

* * * * *

Bowdoin has three sound reasons for joining this organization. First, it can help us have a better, more effective student council, and in turn a better college. Second, we will be able to help to raise the educational standards and opportunities in the nation as a whole. Third, we will be able to contribute to international understanding.

We cannot recommend too highly that Bowdoin students join this truly progressive organization.

11/12/47

NSA Congress Approves Bowdoin Plan, Study Review

The widely publicized Bowdoin Plan for foreign students and the Bowdoin Course Critique were introduced by the Bowdoin delegates to the first Congress of the National Students Association held in August at the University of Wisconsin. Both programs received the approval of the Congress.

The Bowdoin representatives, Malcolm S. Stevenson '50, Richard M. Van Orden '51 delegates, and David M. Berwind '50, alternates, were among the 700 students representing 220 colleges and universities from all over the country.

One of the highlights of the Congressional sessions was the decision against affiliation of N.S.A. with the International Union of Students whose headquarters are at Prague. This decision resulted both from material presented by members of an international visiting team and from debates conducted by the delegates at the plenary sessions.

The business of the Congress was accomplished through workshop discussions, plenary sessions, and regional caucuses. Topics relative to problems of education, student government, travel and reconstruction abroad, and foreign students were assigned to workshops which discussed and debated the issues involved. The workshops submitted their reports to the delegates in plenary session for approval.

As president for the coming year the Congress elected Ted Harris by acclamation. Harris, Phi Beta Kappa, is a negro veteran of World War II.

When the six-day Congress was over, concrete proposals had been made on such important subjects as world-wide student exchange, Student-Faculty Relations, Curricular Evaluation and Change, and Discriminatory Practices in Education. Some delegates felt that even more had been accomplished as evidenced by Stevenson's statement to the Bangor Daily News: "...It was through democratic processes that the organization survived to carry on this coming year".

9/29/48

NSA Projects Few But Worthy; Bowdoin Plan Real Contribution

By Richard M. Van Orden '51

Roughly one year ago the student body of Bowdoin College voted to ratify the constitution of the National Students Association and thereby became an affiliated member of the NSA. In April of last year, the Student Council selected a campus chairman and NSA became a reality on the Bowdoin campus.

With only three months of working time last year, the list of achievements of the Bowdoin campus unit of NSA is understandably of short proportions. While few in number, however, the achievements were notable and of considerable worth to the students.

One of the major achievements of the NSA group was the Bowdoin Plan. Granting that the Bowdoin Plan was pre-NSA, credit must be given to NSA for taking it into its custody and nursing it to the national collegiate recognition that it now enjoys.

Another NSA project was the introduction of the Bowdoin Student Council to the idea of a course critique or curriculum poll. The idea transmitted from Harvard and Yale via NSA was quickly approved and inaugurated last year on the Bowdoin campus.

Bowdoin College also took the leadership among New England colleges in providing a hospitality group for the foreign students on its campus. This NSA group, which last year took the foreign students on three trips to nearby manufacturing plants, state institutions, and military installations, is a vital contribution on Bowdoin's part to international student relations. Hospitality, once the foreign students are on the campus, has now been incorporated into the Bowdoin Plan and colleges as far west as Carleton College in Minnesota and as far south as Emory College in Georgia are basing their setups on what the students at Bowdoin did.

Bowdoin may also claim a probable first in establishing a travel bureau for students wishing to go abroad. Developed through NSA, this unit, on the mailing list of all related sources, councfled and provided expedient aid for all students who wished it.

Already one of the projects being instigated this fall by the Student Council came via NSA. Through research by the Bowdoin NSA delegates at the NSA congress this summer came the proposals for the new class election system now being adopted. The need for such a new system had long been recognized, but no one did the necessary needling.

On a national scale last year NSA carried out an extensive program to be expanded even more this year. Student Government Clinics were held throughout the country and as a result an excellent booklet on leadership and development of student government is now in the hands of the Bowdoin Student Council. Had there been no NSA there would have been no student ships enabling students to travel cheaply this past summer. The tri-nation tour of France, England, and Holland was another product of NSA. These tours of a summer's duration, and a cost of $500 as compared to $1200 charged by the University Tours, were excellently received and greatly enlarged the number of American students who got a chance to travel abroad.

These are only a sample of the concrete benefits of NSA to the students of America. While many of her accomplishments are felt only indirectly by the students, many are of a direct nature.

What the value of these ideas and projects in dollars and cents is to Bowdoin is hard to say. That kind of value is always hard to determine, for ideas need time to make their real worth felt. Those who have been overly quick to criticize the NSA should remember that NSA is young and growing, her first year was of necessity devoted largely to matters of policy and principle. However, now that her foundation is laid she can start to build with concrete projects.

10/20/48

Support Of NSA During Trial Year Voted By Council

The Student Council gave a vote of confidence to the NSA Committee on campus and to its chairman, Richard M. Van Orden '51 at its weekly meeting yesterday.

Van Orden requested Student Council assurance that NSA would not be terminated before its original year of testing, which was voted last fall, ran out. He stated that the recent campus pressure which culminated in a petition for its removal and a fiery ... day with an NSA ... had made any actio... pus committee extr... He asked either for ... fidence or removal ... tee.

Student Council ... colm S. Stevenson ... the Council had agr... a year, and that h... reason for abolishin... tion at Bowdoin bef...

3/16/49

West Defends NSA As Student Fire Hits Local Group

At an open meeting in the Moulton Union lounge on Monday night, the Student Council in conjunction with the N.S.A. presented Robert L. West, Yale '47, National Vice-president in charge of International Student Affairs for the U.S.N.S.A., in a discussion of N.S.A. problems and policies as they affect...

3/16/49

General Aims of NSA Nebulous, Audience Conduct in Bad Taste

On the corner of Hyde Hall nearest the library there is a fire alarm. At the time when snowballs are most easily made this alarm bell is a target for every person going from Hubbard Hall to the Union. Almost as big a target, this winter, has been the National Student Association. What was thrown at the ... Monday night was not snow.

Two weeks ago the ORIENT took a stand for the abolition of the NSA chapter on the Bowdoin Campus. The ORIENT, after hearing the arguments set forth by NSA Vice-president Robert West, does not change that stand. We still feel that NSA is a waste of the students' money. We feel that the aims of the NSA are far too nebulous ever to be of value to Bowdoin. This was rather conclusively proved by Mr. West's evasive answers.

But the treatment Mr. West received from at least two Bowdoin students when he spoke Monday night was shameful. The calibre of questions asked him by the general audience was poor. One student asked him why he had come to Bowdoin. Mr. West replied, naturally, that if he was unwelcome he was sorry he had answered the invitation to speak here. The trouble with the evening in general was that the students attending had come to tell, not to ask. The tone was destructive, not constructive.

Mr. West, we feel, must now know far more about Bowdoin than the Student Body now knows about NSA. He can see, if he is observant, that the term "far left of a Bowdoin student" may still refer to a Taft Republican. He may see that Bowdoin students, once they have made up their minds that something is bad, want to hear, and will listen to, nothing good about it. He may see that many Bowdoin students have little consideration for the guests who come to explain things of importance to them.

Culpable as the audience was, we still advocate the removal of the NSA chapter. We have said that Mr. West took away more ideas about Bowdoin than he left about NSA. He did not leave many ideas behind. His answers, even to the few good questions, were far from satisfactory.

As we see it, the questions asked by the students were mostly of a material nature. Mr. West's phrase, "tinsel-wrapped packages", is an excellent treatment of the necessary NSA view of these material projects — projects which are the answer for those who are not willing to wait for what the NSA considers its ultimate goals. In spite of our natural desire for something concrete, we would advocate patience with the NSA in regard to these projects if this were the only trouble with the NSA.

One cannot stop finding fault with the NSA, however, in its projects. The "ultimate goals", we feel, are either too nebulous to reach any concretion, or wrong in emphasis. We feel that the idea of national exchange of student ideas is fine, but that it will lead us nowhere. We feel that there is too little meeting ground between a university of 30,000 and a college of 1,000 to achieve any satisfactory results. We feel that the emphasis placed upon the separation of students from the rest of humanity, purely upon the basis of being students is completely wrong.

BOWDOIN'S DEBATE OVER NSA was echoed on many campuses with varying outcomes. New generations of student leaders and editors provided a continuing test of the organization's value. Bowdoin, then a strong fraternity-based men's college, was an early New England region booster. It was a participant from 1946 to 1949. Its major contribution was the Bowdoin Plan under which fraternities organized hospitality and financial support for foreign students.

Developing organizations and building blocks for the future

4. Mike Iovenko: Student Leader to Juvenile Advocate

Dartmouth College
Chairman, Northern New England Region, 1950-51

Editor's note: As chair of the Northern New England Region, Michael Iovenko was elected a member of NSA's National Executive Committee for the 1950-51 academic year at the Michigan Congress in 1950. He also attended the Minnesota Congress in 1951, where he presented the majority reports of the Organization Affairs Commission which were adopted over strong opposition, and which fully consolidated the authority of the NSA president as chief spokesman and operating officer. The Congress also voted to consolidate Southern and Northern New England into a single New England Region.

After graduation from Columbia University Law School in 1954, Mike joined the staff of World University Service (WUS) in Geneva, Switzerland. WUS is an international student relief and aid organization whose U.S. affiliate, the World Student Service Fund, was actively supported by NSA from its inception (see Allaway, Part 3, Section 4). Earlier, in 1951, at its formation combining the relief activities of the International Student Service and World Student Relief, former 1948-49 NSA President Ted Harris had been Associate General Secretary of WUS for several years.Returning to the U.S. to practice law in New York City, Iovenko was appointed Deputy Superintendent and General Counsel of the N.Y. State Banking Department in 1970 by Banking Superintendent and former NSA President Bill Dentzer, reprising their service together on NSA's Executive Committee twenty years earlier. His private law practice thereafter was interspersed with other public service posts including President of the Legal Aid Society of New York City, President of the French-American Foundation (awarded Chevalier, Ordre National de Merit, Nov. 2001, by the French Consul General), and membership on various advisory committees appointed by the governor and mayor on youth services and juvenile justice. He died unexpectedly of a heart attack on December 1, 2001, at age 71. He was survived by his wife, Nancy Newhouse Iovenko, his sons Christopher and William and his stepson Barry.

Iovenko's "sound judgement and tremendous sense of humor" and the devotion to sound organizing principles (which he brought to NSA as a student leader) were eulogized by the officers of the Legal Aid Society who remembered "the changes brought under his leadership and the support he provided thereafter have been important building blocks for the future [and] earned him our highest honor: The Society's Servant of Justice Award in 2000."

PICTURE CREDITS: *Then:* Dartmouth *Aegis,* 1951 (Dartmouth College LIbrary); *Now:* c.1990s (Nancy Iovenko)

IOVENKO LED 1950-51 REGIONAL GROWTH

The Dartmouth
The Oldest College Newspaper in America

9/29/50

Iovenko New Chairman for Regional NSA

Outlines Future Plans of Group In New England, Remarks on Convention

As a result of elections held at the recent National Student Association Congress in Ann Arbor, Mich., Michael Iovenko '51 was voted chairman of the regional group.

In this capacity, Iovenko will help direct activities for NSA in the greater New England area.

A delegate at the convention this past summer, Iovenko was "highly impressed by the goings-on of the congress" and said that he "expected much from the NSA at Dartmouth."

Largest Regional Group

The newly-elected chairman further stated that "the New England regional group is growing rapidly in size" and is the "largest and most solvent of all the NSA regional groups."

11/3/50

NSA Opens Regional Assembly Here Today

40 Northern New England Schools Send 150 Delegates

Some 150 students from an expected total of 40 colleges and universities arrive in Hanover tonight for the Northern New England Regional Assembly of the National Student Association, Michael Iovenko '51, regional chairman, disclosed last night.

Allard K. Lowenstein, national president, currently touring New England schools, stops here tonight to speak over WDBS at 9:30. Following the broadcast, he will address the delegates in Dartmouth House on present NSA policies and related topics.

Most of the Regional Assembly's business is to be transacted tomorrow. At the closing plenary session Sunday morning, delegates vote on all resolutions that pass the committee stage.

Work begins with the opening plenary session tomorrow morning at 9 in 105 Dartmouth. Assistant Dean Charles F. Camp, Undergraduate Council President Berl I. Bernhard '51 and Dartmouth NSA Council Chairman David H. Neiditz '52 welcome the delegates.

At 10:30, the delegates split into four commissions for instructions, then into subcommissions for discussion of problems concerning student life, education, international affairs on the student level, and student government. These sessions meet in Dartmouth, Thornton and Wentworth Hall classrooms.

The sub-commissions reconvene after lunch to draft resolutions. At 2:30 the sub-commissions reform into commissions to draw up the proposals to be put before Sunday's plenary session.

Elect New Advisors

On the agenda for the Saturday night plenary session at 7 in 105 Dartmouth are the election of three new advisers to the Regional Advisory Committee and the possible merging with the smaller Southern New England region.

At 8:30, the three areas of the Northern New England Region—

(Continued on Page 4)

MICHAEL IOVENKO '51 is chairman of the NSA Northern New England Region, which is meeting in Hanover this week end.

Local NSA Shows Record Of Service to Students

Problems and projects ranging from the NROTC Loyalty Oath to sacks for the Green rooters at Harvard last week end have occupied the Dartmouth NSA Council in its first two years of life.

Dartmouth joined the National Student Association following a referendum of the student body in May 1949. The local body is set up as a committee of the Undergraduate Council with three of its 10 members drawn from the UGC.

So far this year, the local NSA Council set up a Smith-Dartmouth Freshman Week End in October, arranged for rooms at Harvard

IT WAS THE LARGEST CONFERENCE the Northern New England Region ever held, Iovenko reported. NSA President Al Lowenstein "seemed a man with a mission, vigorously insisting that the student of today realize his own strength," *The Dartmouth* wrote.

WAY Leader Is Y-Wednesday Guest Feb. 18

Mr. Michael Iovenko will speak on "International Student Exchange Builds A Bridge of Understanding" at the Y—Wednesday luncheon on Feb. 18 at 12:15 p.m. Mrs. C. J. McDonnal will preside at the affair to be held in the Ann St. YWCA.

A graduate of Dartmouth and Columbia University Law School, Mr. Iovenko worked in Geneva, Switzerland, for three years at the international headquarters of World University Service. W.U.S. is an international organization working in 35 countries with a

IN GENEVA FOR THREE YEARS after graduating Columbia Law, Iovenko worked with World University Service (See p. 622) and was an elected Vice President of the World Assembly of Youth (See p. 766).(*Courant,* Hartford,CT 2/12/58)

Mike Iovenko was devoted to developing community services for children and also a passionate lifelong Francophile. He was Counsel and Deputy Superintendent, New York State Banking Department, President of the Legal Aid Society and a partner, LeBoeuf, Lamb, Greene and MacRae.

The modern undergraduate has a higher sense of social responsibility

Everett M. Baker: A Resolute Protagonist for Students

Dean of Students, Massachusetts Institute of Technology, 1947–50
Member, NSA National Advisory Committee, 1948–49

Dean Baker (1901-1950) was known throughout the country as an outstanding educator, administrator and theologian, ...[and] as a speaker at student conferences and Institutes. On August 11, 1950, he had flown to Bombay, India, to address the annual conference of the International Student Service of which he was chairman. This organization with the cooperation of the American World Student Service Fund (see p. 618) was instrumental in bringing foreign students to the United States for study in institutions of higher learning. He died on August 31, near Cairo, Egypt, when his plane crashed on the return flight.

Dean Baker was born August 28, 1901, in Newtonville, Massachusetts. A graduate of Phillips Exeter Academy and Dartmouth College, class of 1924, Dean Baker completed his graduate studies at Harvard Divinity School in 1929. In 1937, he was elected Vice-President of the American Unitarian Association, following a period of active church work throughout New England.

Before coming to MIT in 1947, Dean Baker was minister of the First Unitarian Church of Cleveland, Ohio. While Chairman of the Unitarian War Service he edited and published a book of readings entitled "Think on These Things"; three million copies of the book were distributed to men and women in the armed forces.

Under Dean Baker's guidance the Office of the Dean of Students expanded its authority and responsibility in all aspects of student welfare, the athletic program and the system of student government.

In the summer of 1949, he chaired the annual International Student Service Assembly held at Wells College in Aurora, New York. *(Editor: This conference was attended by many NSA leaders at the time. See p. 57.) He was elected ISS Chairman in March, 1950.*

--Adapted from The Tech *Baker Memorial Issue, October 1, 1950*

The Modern Undergraduate and Social Responsibilty

"I believe the modern undergraduate has a higher sense of social responsibility, a more deeply rooted concern for the commonweal than the adults who sometimes criticize his care-free playboy conduct.

"The difficulty in our undergraduate educational system at the present time is that we who are university administrators are far too hesitant to allow opportunities for for student responsibilities. Freedom cannot come as a gift. It cannot be bestowed. Freedom must be earned—dearly purchased. And the price is responsibility."

—From an address to Harvard Divinity School, April, 1950, quoted in The Tech, *10/1/50.*

The vital position of NSA Plans

Dean Everett M. Baker emphasized... the need for NSA in the fields of relief and of contact with foreign students, promoting domestic student reforms, and generally crystallizing student opinion on vital issues. "If the organization can be made strong enough to expound to hundreds and hundreds of foreign students those ideals that are so precious to us, that are the fundamental ideas of our system, and that are so necessary to world peace, its primary purpose will be fulfilled."

— From an address to an NSA meeting at MIT, as reported in The Tech *10/3/47.*

PICTURE CREDIT: c. 1949 (MIT Museum).

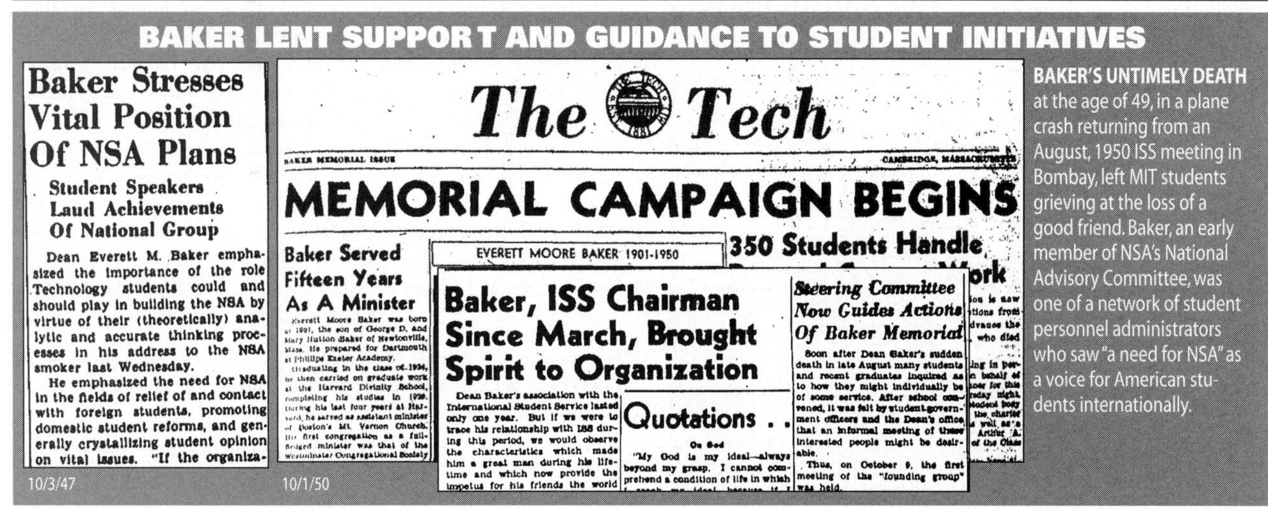

BAKER LENT SUPPORT AND GUIDANCE TO STUDENT INITIATIVES

Baker Stresses Vital Position Of NSA Plans

Student Speakers Laud Achievements Of National Group

Dean Everett M. Baker emphasized the importance of the role Technology students could and should play in building the NSA by virtue of their (theoretically) analytic and accurate thinking processes in his address to the NSA smoker last Wednesday.

He emphasized the need for NSA in the fields of relief of and contact with foreign students, promoting domestic student reforms, and generally crystallizing student opinion on vital issues. "If the organiza-

10/3/47

The Tech

BAKER MEMORIAL ISSUE — CAMBRIDGE, MASSACHUSETTS

MEMORIAL CAMPAIGN BEGINS

Baker Served Fifteen Years As A Minister

Everett Moore Baker was born in 1901, the son of George D. and Mary Hutton Baker of Newtonville, Mass. He prepared for Dartmouth at Phillips Exeter Academy.

Graduating in the class of 1924, he then carried on graduate work at the Harvard Divinity School, completing his studies in 1929. During his last four years at Harvard, he served as assistant minister of Boston's Mt. Vernon Church. His first congregation as a full-fledged minister was that of the Westminster Congregational Society

EVERETT MOORE BAKER 1901-1950

350 Students Handle ... ork

Baker, ISS Chairman Since March, Brought Spirit to Organization

Dean Baker's association with the International Student Service lasted only one year. But if we were to trace his relationship with ISS during this period, we would observe the characteristics which made him a great man during his lifetime and which now provide the impetus for his friends the world

Quotations . .

On God

"My God is my ideal—always beyond my grasp. I cannot comprehend a condition of life in which

Steering Committee Now Guides Actions Of Baker Memorial

Soon after Dean Baker's sudden death in late August many students and recent graduates inquired as to how they might individually be of some service. After school convened, it was felt by student government officers and the Dean's office that an informal meeting of these interested people might be desirable.

Thus, on October 9, the first meeting of the "founding group" was held.

10/1/50

BAKER'S UNTIMELY DEATH at the age of 49, in a plane crash returning from an August, 1950 ISS meeting in Bombay, left MIT students grieving at the loss of a good friend. Baker, an early member of NSA's National Advisory Committee, was one of a network of student personnel administrators who saw "a need for NSA" as a voice for American students internationally.

Students should be counted on to examine new propositions fearlessly and carefully.

Mildred McAfee Horton: Inspiration to a Generation

President, Wellesley College, MA
Captain, U.S. Navy, and first Director, WAVES, 1942-1945

Editor's note: As an educator as well as a spiritual leader, Mildred Horton had a strong commitment to the liberties and responsibilities of individuals commensurate with their role in society. She was skeptical of group thought, and of organizations with top-down programs intended to be replicated on all campuses. Her remarks on the role of intercollegiate organization below reflect this caution.

The Limits of Intercollegiate Association

From a talk to an NSA meeting at Simmons College, MA, on February 16, 1957 (Wellesley College Archives)

It always seems fair to me to express one's prejudices before an audience which is not acquainted with the speaker. In this instance my particular prejudice concerns the role of intercollegiate student associations. I am for them because I believe in the stimulus of contacts between colleges in a free system of higher education. I am for them as a means of communication, a place for the meeting of minds, the exchange of ideas. I am not excited by them as either the hope or the dread of American education. I do not believe that the future of national or world order depends primarily upon students organized in intercollegiate associations. Perhaps I should add that I do not believe the future depends on students any more than it depends upon statesmen, teachers, preachers, business men, all the rest of the citizenry of the nation. . . .

* * *

Believing as I do in the integrity of the individual institution I think of the role of the intercollegiate body as that of stimulating people to do a better job in their own institutions. I believe the intercollegiate organization functions best as a place to which people go for ideas which they then adapt to their own situation. I am not enthusiastic about intercollegiate bodies going on to a local campus to establish its program. My prejudice is against having an NSA project which all colleges are urged to foster, though I think it excellent for students to cone together and let each other know what is being tried in one place, what might be smart ideas to try out, what students in other parts of the world need from students in America,

Another way of saying this is that I see no particular virtue in having American students as students try to act together in the name of their status as students. You might want to discuss this sometime.

I feel so strongly that as students you are involved in the whole process of education. That ought to be your concern, because students have no different interests of a fundamental sort in education from those of college presidents.

WELLESLEY, MASS., NOVEMBER 11, 1946

Students are citizens with or without voting rights. As such they can do what any citizen can do to participate in decisions about foreign policy and practice. As students they have a special responsibility to bring more understanding to bear than they could do if they were uneducated.

This involves understanding causes of war, understanding people of other nations, understanding ourselves. The understanding needs to be genuine, not the idealistic notion of the sentimentalist but the factual comprehension of the scholar.

Students should be an element in the population which is unprejudiced in its judgments of events in the world scene, fair in its appraisal of ourselves and other nations. They are sufficiently free from the responsibilities which go with authority so that they can adventure with ideas. They should therefore be counted upon to examine new propositions fearlessly and carefully. They can point directions more convincingly than plan strategy for achieving goals but should not be excluded from either area.

Students can do much if they will, but it takes time, effort, and concern. I hope Wellesley students are willing to contribute all three in generous measure.

Mildred McAfee Horton,
President Wellesley College.

Mrs. Horton Addresses University Convocation

Mrs. Mildred McAfee Horton, wartime commander of the Waves, discussed "The Art of Living Convictions," at the second all-University convocation, yesterday in Baptist Temple.

The University Religious Council sponsored the convocation,

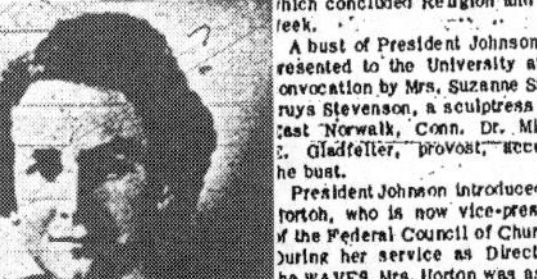

hich concluded Religion and Life eek.

A bust of President Johnson was resented to the University at the onvocation by Mrs. Suzanne Silver ruys Stevenson, a sculptress from ast Norwalk, Conn. Dr. Millard E. Gladfelter, provost, accepted he bust.

President Johnson introduced Mrs. orton, who is now vice-president of the Federal Council of Churches. During her service as Director of he WAVES, Mrs. Horton was associated with Dean Gertrude E. Peabody.

She was the only officer to out-

HORTON INSPIRED STUDENTS as an educator, spiritual leader (she was the first woman vice president of the then Federal Council of Churches), and as a trailblazer of women's "firsts" (including Director positions with NBC, RCA and New York Life). She advocated strongly for student responsibility. (Above: Temple U. *News* 11/17/50).

Opening Doors for a New Generation

Excerpted from a talk, June 10, 1995, by Diana Chapman Walsh, President, Wellesley College, at a memorial service for Mildred McAfee Horton.

One of Wellesley's truly great presidents, Mildred McAfee Horton was an inspiration to a whole generation, at the College, in the WAVES, and in an astounding array of leadership roles she played throughout her life, first in higher education, subsequently as a lay Christian leader of ecumenical institutions. ". . . She opened new doors for a whole generation of young women. A woman who enjoyed and lived life to the brim, her secret—which she now leaves us . . . was to live, always, in the present and to work, always, for the future.

Mildred McAfee Horton (1900-1994)

Mildred Helen McAfee was born in Parkville, Missouri, on 12 May 1900. She graduated from Vassar College in 1920 and received the degree of Master of Arts from the University of Chicago in 1928. She became President of Wellesley College in 1936. Taking a leave, she became the Navy's first female line officer on August 3, 1942. Commissioned a Lieutenant Commander in the Naval Reserve, she undertook the demanding task of Director of the Navy's newly established Women's Reserve. In November 1943, she was promoted to the rank of Captain. As its first Director, Captain McAfee guided the growth of the WAVES ("Women Accepted for Volunteer Emergency Service") to a force of more 80,000 Navy women in a variety of occupational specialties. Following her marriage to the Reverend Dr. Douglas Horton in August 1945, Horton continued on active duty until February 1946, when she returned to the Presidency of Wellesley College. Captain Mildred McAfee Horton died on September 1994.

--From Naval Historical Center Online Library

Editor's note: Alice Horton Tibbetts, who organized the U.S. delegation to the 1946 World Student Congress, recalls in her memoir her father's marriage to Mildred McAfee (see p. 68).

PICTURE CREDIT: 1946 (Wellesley College Archives, Margaret Clapp Library). *Title quote:* Nardi Reeder Campion, quoted by Diana Chapman Walsh, Wellesley College President, June 10,1995

A 1950 New England Regional Assembly

The Dartmouth 11/6/50

Region NSA Decides On Draft, Foreign Aid

'Conference Successful' - Iovenko; Neiditz Promises Report on Grading

By JOHN A. BALLARD

Meeting in an aura of general cooperation marred only by procedural wrangles, the regional assembly of the NSA finished its business in 105 Dartmouth yesterday, adopting resolutions on the investigation of grading and honor systems, on dissemination of draft information, and on increased liaison with foreign students.

"It was the largest conference the Northern New England Region NSA has ever held, and from most reports the most successful," stated Michael Iovenko '51, regional chairman. "Everyone was impressed with Hanover and Dartmouth, except for the weather."

"Immediate results for Dartmouth," added David H. Neiditz, campus NSA chairman, "will include a report on grading and honor systems to the UGC based on a questionnaire sent to most of the schools in the region and the release of pertinent information on the draft to the entire region channeled through Dartmouth from the national organization.

Procedural Troubles

Yesterday's plenary session voted on resolutions offered by four commissions and their sub-commissions which met Saturday to discuss various points and programs on the agenda. Most of these were passed with little opposition, but discriminatory clauses, draft deferment of national NSA officers and the regional budget led to arguments and procedural difficulties.

A special order of business introduced in relation to resolutions on the draft called for classification of national NSA officers as students during their term in office. This was made on the grounds that they have relinquished their status as students to become a necessary part of the NSA program which includes representation on the State Department's Foreign Policy Commission and on a special commission to advise the director of Selective Service.

International Aid

Many of the original resolutions introduced during the meeting were those dealing with the international aspect of NSA. According to Iovenko, this was due largely to the presence of three Harvard graduates who spent the summer working with students in Europe, Asia and the Middle East.

Proposed and passed were resolutions endorsing and planning for other seminars, spring vacation tours for foreign students already in the U.S. and a regional conference on student conditions in underdeveloped countries to be held in Boston this spring.

MIT *The Tech* 11/1/50

NSA Has Meeting At Dartmouth; Plans Foreign Students' Tours

Six delegates from the Institute attended the National Student Association's Northern New England Regional Assembly at Dartmouth College on November 4 and 5. Over 70 delegates from the New England colleges participating in NSA activities were present.

The Assembly passed a resolution establishing a series of spring vacation tours for foreign students. It is planned to have a group of thirty students visit the important cities and colleges in New England. They will be housed on their trip by the various colleges participating with the NSA. The Institute has volunteered to take a few foreign students on tours of the Niagara and T.V.A.

The Simmons News 11/9/50

Hallbauer Declaration Carried At NSA Regional Conference

Participating in the NSA Northern New England Regional Conference held at Dartmouth College, November 3-5 were five Simmons students including Dagmar Hallbauer, chairman of Boston area NSA.

Conference delegates carried a declaration introduced by Miss Hallbauer to improve the integration of the NSA campus committee with the student government.

Lowenstein--Student Must Know His Own National, International Struggle

By ROLAND M. GLASSER

Allard K. Lowenstein, president of the National Student Association, seemed a man with a mission, vigorously insisting that the student of today realize his own strength, both nationally and internationally.

"It is in the East especially that the student has extreme importance," Lowenstein stated. Indonesia's U.N. delegate and two recent Burma prime ministers were men just a couple of years out of school.

"These and other eastern nations in which the status of the student is so magnified are at present being highly propagandized by Communists. We *must* fight Communism, and only students can reach students."

Combat IUS

Lowenstein explained that the NSA is now attempting to combat the influence of the Communist-dominated International Union of Students in Asia and Africa.

"We are doing this by sponsoring student seminars in many parts of the world and by sending Americans abroad to Asia, Africa and Europe for the purpose of publicizing student life in this country."

Nationally, the college man's influence has been recognized by the government in two main areas. The NSA president pointed out that on both the Foreign Policy Committee and a special board of consultants on the draft problem, students are represented by the NSA.

"Every student in the country is being spoken for in these issues, yet a great many of them are not NSA members," Lowenstein said. "A non-member is just as dead if shot as a member."

Regarding the battle against the spectre of Communism on the home front, Lowenstein proffered a uniquely optimistic and idealist theory. He wondered why we attemp to bottle up the leftist element in the country.

"Democracy has more to offer by far than does Communism, and freedom of expression for both will prove as much. I would rather risk having a handful of Communists teaching than see investigations that often persecute the innocent while battering at the traditional freedom of education."

MICHAEL IOVENKO '51, regional chairman of NSA, directed this week end's conference and termed it "highly successful and the largest ever held in the area."

ALLARD K. LOWENSTEIN, president of the National Student Association, urges all students to realize their own national and international importance.

THE NSA COMMISSION CONCEPT provided the organizing structure for NSA regional assemblies. The four commissions that formed the conference workshops at Dartmouth were Student Life, Education and Educational Problems, International Affairs, and Administration and Finance.

Individual delegations focused on programs of greatest interest on their campuses. MIT's active international program and Simmons's interests in student government are reflected in their campus newspaper reports (above) of the conference.

Among the highlights of this event were issues pertaining to the military draft because of the Korean conflict, the appearance of NSA President Al Lowenstein (left. See p. 283), and reports from some of NSA's international team who traveled to Europe and Asia to meet with foreign student leaders that summer, including Frank Fisher of Harvard (See p. 511, p. 609).

M.I.T. NSA Takes the International Initiative

A Merry Christmas

The Tech

Technology NSA Commended For Foreign Student Summer Plan at Madison Convention

10/1/48

Editor's note: Student leaders at MIT "most of whom had seen and participated in the destruction of Europe" wanted "to play their part in its educational reconstruction and rehabilitation." (1948 FSSP Report from Lloyd Haynes, NSA Chairman and Earl W. Eames, Jr, FSSP Project Chair. See also p. 634). Through a plan which received NSA endorsement (above) and MIT administration facilities and resource support, 80 or so graduate students were brought to MIT for two months free intensive course work. FSSP was the centerpiece of an active international program which included a summer job exchange program, IAESTE, and information exchanges with technical institutes in emerging nations. MIT, with a 1948 enrollment of 5,303, was founded in 1861 by William Barton Rogers, "a distinguished natural scientist, to establish a new kind of independent educational institution relevant to an increasingly industrialized America." Women were first admitted in 1871 (web.mit.edu).

FOREIGN STUDENT SERVICE PROJECT. Some of the 80 foreign graduate students at MIT for intensive summer study in 1948 (photos: MIT Museum).

Foreign Grads To Come Here Next Summer

NSA Program Gets Under Way To Raise $21,000 for New Plan

Under a program inaugurated this fall by the National Student Association, 80 graduates of foreign universities will be able to study at the Institute for a two-month period during the summer of 1948. The Foreign Student Service Program was made public following its presentation to the faculty by President Karl T. Compton on Wednesday afternoon.

Norman Beecher, G, in charge of the FSSP for NSA, reported in a recent interview that $21,000 will be needed to defray the costs incurred by the students for food and transportation during their participation in the program. The Institute Corporation, sitting in executive session, has approved the FSSP and has agreed to make no tuition charge for these students.

The students are to be housed in some of the Technology fraternity houses, homes of greater Boston residents, and the school dormitories if necessary. Beecher said that the fraternities have already voted to support the FSSP, and

12/19/47

NSA To Conduct Second FSSP Next Summer

80 European, Asiatic Grads To Be Given Free Summer Course

Earl W. Eames, Jr., '49, yesterday announced plans for the second annual Foreign Student Summer Project, a plan which last year brought 82 foreign graduate students from 15 European countries together at Technology for the three month summer term. There is no cost to the participating students.

One of the most notable changes occurred when it was decided after several committee meetings to include five Far Eastern and three Near Eastern countries in next summer's invitations, although the emphasis will still remain with Europe.

Selection in April

Another change to be instituted this year will be the priority to be given to graduate students and young instructors with specific research problems. Selection of students is set for April. As was the case last year, final selection will again be made by the FSSP com-

12/10/48

NSA PIONEERS WITH FSSP

Since The Tech will not be published during the summer term, this being the last issue of the school year, we want to take this opportunity to extend congratulations to the NSA Committee for its work in carrying out the M.I.T. Foreign Student Summer Project and also to welcome to Technology the 80 foreign graduate students who have been invited to take part in this program of educational reconstruction.

The Tech has followed closely and with great interest the progress of the planning for this summer project, from the initial article on December 19 which announced "Foreign Grads To Come Here Next Summer," to the most recent article of last Tuesday which announced that 52 of the 80 students had already been notified of their selection.

Partly because of the fundamental worth of the plan, partly because of its uniqueness (for this is the first project of its nature ever to be held in the United States), leading educators, writers, and officials throughout the country have praised M.I.T. students for their farsightedness and initiative in successfully carrying out such a plan.

A project of such magnitude as this (the initial budget was nearly $100,000 in goods and services) could not, of course, be carried out without the fullest cooperation from everyone concerned. The Institute Committee furnished operating funds for initiating the project, Dr. Compton gave his utmost support and assistance in many ways, the M.I.T. Corporation waived tuition fees for the students, and individual members of the Corporation, the Dean of Students, and many members of the Faculty have been most helpful. In addition, most of the students are to be housed in the fraternities remaining open this summer free of charge, and many of the alumni and friends of M.I.T. have helped to make the program a success financially. M.I.T. can be justly proud of this concrete contribution to international understanding and good will.

5/21/48

2/19/52

FSSP Reaches Around The World Aiding European Reconstruction

Special for THE TECH by
Rudolf E. Kalman
Member FSSP Committee

Among the miriads of extracurricular activities that help to keep the FSSP committee busy, few operate outside of Boston or perhaps the Commonwealth of Massachusetts. But FSSP, one unconfined to narrow limits, has as its hunting ground the entire world.

Has Biggest Budget

FSSP as a campus activity is undoubtedly the largest in budget ($65,000) and scope. The name is formidable: Foreign Student Summer Project; the abbreviation should come somewhat easier: FSSP.

People who like to be exact usually designate an MTA subway car as the place of birth of FSSP. This is not at all unreasonable: the founders, Earl Eames and Lloyd Haynes, MIT juniors and veterans,

N. S. A. Initiates Affiliation With The Delhi Polytechnique

In a bid to win the friendship of an organized group of Indian students, the M.I.T. National Student Association has evolved a program of information exchange and aid with the Delhi Polytechnique, of India. The high points of the program at Tech will include large-scale publicity of the information received from Delhi, a school-wide convocation with a prominent speaker on India, and a drive for money and equipment.

Information Exchange

The basis of the project, as [illegible] by its chairman, Herbert J. [illegible]

of the program in an attempt to reach every student and staff member at Tech. They are John Copenhefer and Phil Schirm, '52, co-chairmen of the Solicitation Committee; Alex Gutwurcel, '53, Information Committee; Mike Goldman, '52, Treasurer; and Martin Greenfield, '51, Convocation Committee. Publicizing of the information received from India should begin by April 2, and the convocation and drive are slated for the middle of April.

2/20/51

F.S.S.P. Aids Point 4 Program; 5 Continents To Be Represented

The Foreign Student Summer Project of the NSA will be host to 80 scientists and engineers of 35 countries. The aim of the FSSP is to join in the drive to further better international understanding and to stimulate technological development of war devastated and underdeveloped areas by giving their technologists a short and intensive course at the Institute. This objective has been referred to by the State Department as the first positive implementation of Point Four.

For the first time in four years all five continents are represented. All of the participants must possess a degree and two years' experience. The project is designed as an intensive "packaged" program. Every attempt is made to give them a balanced view of American life.

Program Includes Industrial Tours

The program is divided into three parts. First is an intensive 12-week course of study on special research projects of interest to their own countries. Then the participants will be taken on an industrial tour of New England by the National Association of Manufacturers. Later, opportunity is provided for a few weeks of individual industrial visits.

12/18/51

Extension of FSSP to underdeveloped nations led to State Dept designation as "first positive implementation of Point 4." (See p. 632 for more on Point 4.)

Students From Europe and U.S. Exchange Jobs

100 From Institute Go Abroad Next Summer; Interviews Start Mon.

The International Association for the Exchange of Students for Technical experience is, for the second year, attempting to arrange European summer jobs for American students, and in return, obtain jobs in the United States for European students.

Last summer 37 American Junior and Senior technical students, including 29 from Technology, worked in European companies for about eight weeks, gaining industrial and cultural experience.

Main features of the program are as follows: The European associates of I.A.E.S.T.E. obtain jobs in technical industries for Ameri-

11/28/50

PART 5. NSA's REGIONS
CREATING INTERCOLLEGIATE NETWORKS

SECTION 2

CONTENTS

National Student Org Rally Today To State Delegate Rules, Explain Method, Aims Of Group

Wallace, Regional Chairman, Williams To Address Meeting

NYU Bulletin 4/6/47

Columbia to Review Case of NSA In Preparation for Council Action

Special Spectator Issue, College Forum To Highlight USNSA Information Week

NSA History Reveals Work Of 3 Parleys

Local USNSA Group Acts On Schultz Amendment, Art

The Spectator, Columbia U. 12/1/47

NSA Pres. Bob Kelly Stresses Leader Training, Program Aspect, In Talk To Met. N.Y. Region

by M. K. Donovan

The Centurion
Manhattanville C., 12/49

Metropolitan New York

Pressed into 350 square miles, some 40 New York City area colleges and universities (plus ten more qualifying separate night schools and satellite campuses), and another half-dozen institutions in their Hudson Valley orbit (such as Vassar, Sarah Lawrence and Bard) arguably provided NSA with its most colorful membership base, with ideologies ranging from conservative to radical, as well as a wide range of religious and ethnic interests.

In this section Gene Schwartz (CCNY), 1947-48 regional Vice-Chairman, recalls the region's formative years, its factional conflicts, the leadership of Walter Wallace (Columbia), its first Chairman, and the CCNY-Manhattanville connection. Sheldon Steinhauser (LIU), 1949-50 Regional Chairman, reflects on the region's movement beyond polarized positions. CCNY and LIU albums spotlight some of the student-administration conflicts, which roiled both campuses.

Bernard Schwartz (CCNY School of Business), later Chairman and CEO of the Loral Corporation, recalls how his NSA experience formed the foundation of "a lifetime of idealism." Gladys Chang Hardy-Brazil, Sarah Lawrence student body President in 1948-49, recalls intense student interest in issues of discrimination and social justice. She also reflects on the Asian-American experience.

Three college administrators are recalled for their influence and support of student interests: Mother Eleanor O'Byrne, President of Manhattanville College (located next door to CCNY, she provided the headquarters office for the region); Millicent Cary McIntosh, President of Barnard and advocate for women's education; and Harry Carman, Dean of Columbia College, who was a leader in efforts to liberalize curriculum and expand educational opportunity.

The Region provided a stage for NSA accomplishments and conflicts

With a mix of Catholic institutions, such as Fordham, Manhattan, St. Francis, and Manhattanville, and schools nationally known for student activism, such as Columbia, City College and New York University, the region provided a stage for many of NSA's student rights, academic freedom and Cold War battles, some of which are highlighted in this section's albums. It also demonstrated that opposite factions could be brought together through the unifying interests of that period.

The concentration of colleges also made possible a steady outpouring of regional programs each year, such as "culturales," intercollegiate debates and discussion forums, leadership workshops, Purchase Card and student discount plan initiatives, and foreign student hospitality.

The region provided NSA with some of its early national leaders, such as Walter Wallace (Columbia), John Simons (Fordham. See p. 124), and Enid Kass (Hunter. See p 94), all of whom were on the 1946 U.S. delegation to the World Student Congress (Part 1, Sec 2). Gene Schwartz of City College of New York (CCNY) and Sylvia Bacon of Vassar (p. 474), both served as national vice presidents, respectively in 1948-49 and 1951-52. The section closes with an album of events and leaders at Columbia, Barnard and Fordham.

THE NEW ORGANIZATION was greeted with high expectations on campuses in 1947. By 1949, Manhattanville College was able to report on national NSA President Bob Kelly's talk to "November's remarkable regional meeting at which all business was completed in the scheduled four hours."

Metropolitan New York NSA Highlights

1946-47

Enid Kass, Hunter Delegate, Urges Formation of Union

Plan Permanent N. S. O. At Chicago Meetings

Unity Among Students From 300 Colleges Notable at Largest Student Gathering of Kind

To Explain NFCCS, NSO in Talk Today

Duffy, Gallagher Report On Toledo Catholic Conference

Give National Teacher Exams

N S O Protests Abuse Of Academic Liberty

NSO Adopts Equal College Vote Policy

NSA Inter-Collegiate Hop Set For Friday

Stars Of Opera, Night Clubs Will Sing; 24 Universities Participate In Affair

A REGIONAL VOICE IS BORN. Proportional voting for larger campuses as well as for the region itself (the largest in NSA) was a major issue. Catholic colleges, already organized into the NFCCS (see p. 741) added a new affiliation. (From top l, cw: HB 10/8/46- Enid Kass was one of 10 college reps of the 25 students who attended the 1946 World Student Congress (p.81); BB 1/9/47; FR 4/25/47; NB 5/6/47- Reps of 24 colleges heard Jan Peerce, Richard Dyer-Bennett and others at the City Center Casino dance; NB 2/11/47; NB 3/21/47-The region protested, after "heated debate," AYD bans at Queens C. (NYC) and Michigan State C. (p. 779).

1947-48

Shultz Amendment Opposed by NSA Regional Group

NSA To Coordinate Regional Activities

To Write Region Constitution Dec. 6; Plan Show; International Summer Tours

NSA Announces "Culturale"

Freshman Learn Of Greek Games At Class Meeting

NSA Holds Meeting In Keating Hall

Draws Up Initial Draft Of N. Y. Constitution

NSA Meet Hails Freedom of Thought

Metropolitan NSA Forms Council of Science Students

New York NSA Favors IUS Negotiation

BUILDING A LASTING FOUNDATION. The region undertook a broad range of activities, relying on ease of travel for its frequent events. From top l., cw: FR 10/24/47 - Meeting at Manhattanville, Mother O'Byrne (p. 862) offered the region an office at the college. The region registered opposition to a proposed Board of Higher Education by-law on disloyalty; BB 11/17/47; "Coordinate" NB 1/8/48; "Culturale" plan for summer of '48, BB 12/15/47; FR 1/18/48, region completes draft of its constitution; NN 3/48 photo of Walter Wallace chairing regional meet at NYU; "IUS" CC 4/6/48, Region favored continued IUS negotiation despite Czech coup (p.188); "Science Students" CC 3/5/48; "Freedom", NB 2/6/48.

1948-49

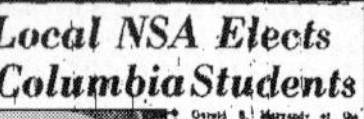

Local NSA Elects Columbia Students

A Fordham Delegate's Report On NSA Summer Congress

NSA Will Offer Student Discount

NY NSA Raps Bias in DP Bill

NSA Plans Student Tour Through Puerto Rico Jan. 27

NSA Reports New Additions To Its Projects

NSA Conducts Weekend Meet

CONSOLIDATING MEMBERSHIP. CCNY evening session's Tom Garrity, also a St. Peters day student (NJ. p. 892), was elected Chair, and Columbia's Jay Maryanov (p. 866), Vice-chair. From top l., cw: Photo: CCNY delegates at 1948 U. of Wisconsin Congress (Fr. l.: Gene Schwartz, Main; Alan Aaronson, Business) CS 9/30/48; FR 10/7/48 - Tom Gassert reported on the First Congress and the Manhattanville regional meeting; OP 11/9/48 - The region launched the discount Purchase Card System (p.366); "Weekend", CS 5/5/49 - announcing Student Rights Conference at Sarah Lawrence College; CS 2/10/49 -focus on tour programs; "Puerto Rico", LS 1/13/49; "DP", OP 11/9/48.

1949-50

N. S. A. Metropolitan Regional Assembly Asks Repeal Of Feinberg Law, 41 To 1

NSA Considers Anti-Bias Move

Local Stores To Aid NSA Purchase Plan

'Democracy In Education' Conference Arouses Metropolitan Student Groups

NSA Pres. Bob Kelly Stresses Leader Training, Program Aspect, In Talk To Met. N.Y. Region

NSA Student Day Conference Discusses Foreign Good Will

Resolution To Lift Ban on "The Nation", Passed at NSA Regional Meeting at CCNY

NSA To Hold Conference; Will Discuss Discrimination In Campus Organizations

EXTENDING NSA PROGRAMS: Conferences on discrimination, science and philosophy, expansion of the Purchase Card System, foreign student aid fundrives. From top l., cw: LS 10/26/49 - Sheldon Steinhauser of LIU elected regional President. Region supported repeal of state law requiring a state list of subversive organizations, members of which would not be permitted to teach; "Kelly", MC 12/49; International "Student Day" observance (p. 580) brought 350 students to Adelphi; "Nation", MC 3/50; "Local", CS 11/28/49 - 30 colleges to take part in student government clinic; "Anti-Bias", FR 2/9/50; "Democracy", SC 3/22/50; "Discrimination," LS 4/19/50.

1950-52

Regional NSA Chief Garfinkle Clarifies Organization's Stand

Met. NSA to Hold Philosophy Forum At Fordham Feb. 24

NSA Plans Region Meet

M'VILLE TO TELL OF FOREIGN STUDENTS

NSA 'Delegate' Launches Its First Edition

Campus Press Censorship Frowned on at NSA Forum

Voykovich Elected NSA Veep for N.Y.

'Students World Crisis Role' Is NSA Conference Theme

STAYING THE COURSE. Regional conferences focused on broad themes, "The Student Futurama" (5/12/51) at Fordham, "Press Censorship" at its first Intercollegiate Press Conference (3/22/52) at Fordham, "The Student's Role in World Crisis" (4/26-27/52) at CCNY. Regional Chairs were Norton Garfinkle (Columbia), 50-51, and James Murphy (Manhattan), 51-52. From top l., cw: BB 2/26/51; FR 2/16/51; MC 5/3/51; "Press", FR 4/3/52; "Delegate" HA 3/3/52; "Veep" FR 5/8/52; "Crisis" BB 4/21/52.

KEY TO COLLEGE NEWSPAPER CITATIONS IN THIS SECTION

BB-*Barnard Bulletin*

CC-CCNY, *The Campus*

CS-Columbia, *The Spectator*

FR-Fordham, *The Ram*

HA-*The Hunter Arrow*

HB-*The Hunter Bulletin*

LS-LIU, *Seawanhaka*

MC-Manhattanville, *The Centurion*

NN-*NSA News*

NB-NYU *Bulletin*

OP-CCNY, *Observation Post*

SC-Sarah Lawrence, *The Campus*

Collegiate neighbors discover each other in new ways while navigating factional conflicts

1. CCNY and the Metropolitan New York Region in 1947-49

Eugene G. Schwartz
City College of New York
Vice-Chairman, NSA Metropolitan New York Region, 1947-48

Editor's note: My more spontaneous and personal recollections of my postwar student, CCNY and NSA experiences are expressed in the memoir I wrote when I started on this project in 1996 (see p. 214). It is now 2003 as I complete this work and realize that a picture of NSA's early years would be incomplete without some recounting of its largest region in membership, Met New York's growing pains and pleasures, and the dedicated efforts of its leaders. As none of the other surviving actors of this period I have reached felt able to take on the task, I here provide what I can.

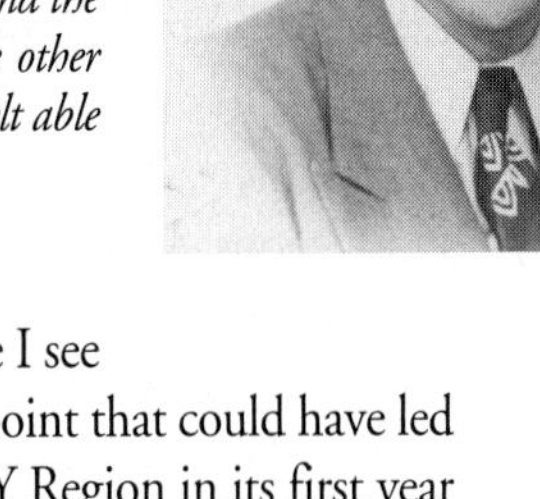

I begin with a story of discord because I see now in retrospect that it was a turning point that could have led to an unhappy break-up of the Met. NY Region in its first year of existence. Instead it tested the mettle of the organization, and the Region remained a vital force within the Association.

In its October, 1948 issue, *The Centurion,* Manhattanville College's student newspaper headlined a story about the Met. NY region's wrap-up that summer of its 1947-48 year: "NSA Completes Probe, Prepares for Congress." About "the investigation initiated last spring," it observed that "the Metropolitan New York Regional Assembly reached a decision satisfactory to the majority."

Just what that "satisfactory" decision was remains maddeningly obscure these fifty-five years since. Its principal targets were Walter Wallace (Columbia University), the region's dynamic leader[1] and one of the 25 original members of the Prague World Student Congress U.S. delegation (see Pt. 1, Sec. 1), elected as Chair both at the 1946 Chicago Student Conference and the 1947 Constitutional Convention, and myself; also our own countercharges against our accusers.

I was Vice Chairman of the region at the time. Phyllis Carbone, Manhattanville College delegate, arrived at the April National Executive Committee (NEC) meeting in Chicago, without prior notice, to press the charges against us initiated by the Hunter College (Evening) delegation. The petition was supported by the delegations of 9 of the region's 25 to 30 members.[2] Walter and I were charged with "undemocratic procedures" and failing to provide timely information to the region about the Bill Ellis letter of resignation from the IUS.[3]

The Region confronts its first major factional conflict

The NEC asked that the matter first be adjudicated within the region. Later, a five-member investigating commission was appointed. Three of its members who appear in this anthology, Bob Meagher (CCNY), Michael DiLegge (Fordham) and Sheldon Steinhauser (LIU),[4] do not recall the final resolution reached on the issue! Nor do I or Walter Wallace, who wondered, when I met him five years ago at Princeton for the first time in fifty years, whether I recalled the outcome.

At that time I had even forgotten the investigation itself, despite the fact that it was the result of at least eight hours of NEC meeting time over a period of three days.

What could have led to an exodus of some or all of the Catholic delegations from the region was somehow resolved. Cooler heads on the National Executive Committee that April, and among regional leaders later, seem to have prevailed. Something equitable from everyone's standpoint must have taken place (as the *Centurion* suggested). I could find no stories in any of the college press suggesting a scandalous turn. I myself arrived at the first Congress in Madison as temporary Chair of the region. It is conceivable that Walter had become so busily engaged in the Students for Wallace (Henry, that is) campaign for President,[5] in which he had become very active, that he welcomed turning his attention elsewhere.

A diverse community of colleges find each other

In no NSA region was there so high a geographic concentration of colleges and universities, with as large an NSA contingent of Catholic delegations,[6] as in the New York City area. Chicago, St. Louis, Philadelphia, Boston and the District of Columbia areas also provided high Catholic college numbers, but for a variety of reasons, including New York's history as a base for radical "left-wing," socialist and communist causes, the region was the most restive and combustible.

It was a continuing challenge to NSA's objective of providing a fully integrated forum for a broad base of the U.S. college student population – regionally and philosophically.[7] The entry of Catholic College students into a secular organization for the first time provided additional fuel for the fire in New York City.

The matter of multiple campuses

With multiple day, night, uptown, downtown and sometimes law or education school representation from the same university, tracking the profile of membership was confusing. At the time of the regional investigation of the charges against Wallace and myself, there were four such delegations from CCNY (32,500 students), two from Fordham (9,900), two from Hunter (11,800), then a women's college, and three from NYU (47,600). If one looked at student body populations, that left Columbia University (29,200), including Barnard, with one delegation, comparatively underrepresented in numbers.[8]

Among the many able leaders from the foregoing colleges that I recall were Bill Mishkin and Al Spelling of NYU, Walter Wallace, Russell Dunbar, and Jay Maryanov of Columbia, Margaret Mather of Barnard, Enid Kass of Hunter, Bob Meagher (Main, Day), Tom Garrity (Main, Evening) of CCNY, and Ed Cook, Mike DiLegge and Tom Gassert of Fordham.[9]

There were in 1947-48, counting the two from Fordham, nine Catholic college delegations, including College of New Rochelle, Mt. St. Vincent (Kay Shaker), Marymount, Good Counsel (Oona Burke), Manhattan, Manhattanville (Phyllis Carbone), and St. Francis (Tom Callahan).[10] There were respectively a total of 25, 22 and 30 member delegations listed at the 1947, 1948 and 1949 NSA Congresses.

It was a common experience shared by members of multiple delegations that they would likely never have met each other had it not been for regional meetings. Certainly I would never have met Tom Garrity of the CCNY evening session, for whom I had developed a fast affection and an admiration for his debating skills and passion for justice.

New York City college student governments generally welcomed NSA, and their newspapers followed NSA developments both on campus and regionally – and not without a critical as well as supportive eye.

The Veterans Association sends me to the Student Council

My own migration to NSA national office began almost accidentally when the CCNY Veterans Association chose me to represent them on the Student Council (Uptown, Day) in 1946, and I was elected by Council as one of a three-man delegation to go to Chicago that December.

On the national stage, the idea of multiple delegations was greeted with skepticism. As reported in the 1/6/47 issue of *The Campus*:

> When the combined delegation of ten students representing the Day and Evening Sessions of both centers of the College arrived at Chicago, two of their votes were challenged on the grounds that the two centers of the College were considered as one school in representation. Surprised at this, the delegates sought advice from Dr. John L. Bergstresser, former Dean of Students at the College, who is now with the University of Chicago.

The upshot was that we relinquished two of our votes, one of which was mine. "We could have brought the matter to the floor, but we didn't want to waste the limited time of the group," I am quoted as saying. "While Ascher Katz '48, and Irving Landa '47, retained theirs . . . his lack of a vote didn't prevent Schwartz from actively participating . . . [but] he was disqualified from nomination as Chairman of the Metropolitan Committee when the New York University representative challenged him on these grounds."

No New York area college representative worth his or her salt would not have already been schooled in the fine points of Roberts Rules, and blocking by procedure was a fine art unabashedly practiced when needed.

Campus political contests every six months at CCNY

Our weekly student council meetings, lasting often into the wee hours, were fields of combat for competing ideologies and factions, as well as trial heats in debating and parliamentary procedure. My interests early on were in organization and management, and in trying to find ways to reconcile the irreconcilable. Although I always felt uncomfortable in an ideological role, and I never joined any of the student political organizations (e.g., SDA, AYD, UWF, YPA), I did have political sympathies. I was allied with the more leftward factions which assembled slates at election time.

I was handily defeated in several elections running for Secretary and then President of the Student Council. I was opposed editorially by *The Campus* because, in one election, the Beaver Party on whose slate I ran "is represented by a disproportionate number of AYD members."

It is hard to believe that we ran full-bore elections for all offices every six months. That was the May, 1947 ballot at which a very bright, capable and good-natured Ascher Katz, who headed the Student Liberal Committee slate, trounced me. Bob Meagher, later to become a lifetime friend, was elected Treasurer on the SLC slate.

60-strong Met NY delegation makes its mark at Madison

In an irony of fate, Ascher was stricken by a cerebral hemmorhage in June (from which he later fully recovered and was able to carry out his office) and was unable to attend the NSA Constitutional Convention.[11] As I wrote my father that August 14th:

> As you know, having been defeated in last term's election, I had resigned myself to leading a normal life with little extra-curricular activity. With Ascher Katz' illness, it was necessary to select a replacement, and I was selected. Now it seems that the Chairman of our Regional Committee in New York [Walter Wallace] will not have returned from a youth conference he is attend-

ing in Paris in time to attend the Executive meeting of regional chairmen before the convention. Since our vice-Chairman is no longer a student [who that was I cannot remember] and will not attend the convention, the job fell to me. Having thus been boosted into a strategic political position, representing the 60 New York City delegates (approximately 100,000 students),[12] I am beginning to discover that the politics I experienced at City College were child's play compared to the experience I am now having (By this I mean . . . that it is more complex). Of particular interest are the major problems we are faced with in the organization of the NSO. . . discrimination in the South and North; participation in international student activities, and the like.

Clif Wharton and Bill Welsh in Part 1 have described the many debates and resolutions which shaped the new organization's policies, one of which concerning "equal rights and opportunities" in the Constitution was so vexing, I wrote my father on September 10, that "About midweek it almost seemed as though the USNSA might be formed without any of the Southern colleges, both Negro and white." Referring then to the debate in the Constitutional Committee:

> There was some strenuous opposition from the New England delegates to any compromise. Myself and the two other Met. NY reps on the Committee were committed to our regional decision to support any compromise which both the Negro and White Southern delegates agreed to, and fought strenuously to report the resolutions to the plenary session. The skillful handling of the entire problem by Jim Smith of Texas, president of the interim committee running the convention, remains one of the most impressive experiences of the convention.[13]

The role of the Metropolitan New York Region, despite its contentious reputation, was in reality a well-managed and constructive one, I thought. In that same letter I wrote,

> Metropolitan New York, with its 62 votes out of 650-700 represented a decisive force on many questions, and although we made a determined effort not to dominate convention debate by having two or three floor leaders (of which I was one), nevertheless when the roll call of regions was reported there was always a hush of anticpation before the Met NY vote was announced, followed by lusty cheers. Usually the region went by 50 votes or better for all questions, with a minority never larger than 17. Because of this we became particularly endeared to delegations from the South, the Colorado-New Mexico area, California and New England. . . . I arrived with a personal pledge to erase as much as possible biased attitudes towards those "New York radicals," and particularly toward City College. I'm proud to say we accomplished that aim to a great extent.

"I'm afraid that delegate from CCNY isn't taking the convention seriously."

NSA Bulletin, Wednesday 9/3/47, Madison, WI. Published by the Convention Public Relations Staff.

After the Convention, the Region goes to work

With Walter Wallace elected as Chairman for 1947-48, I was elected as Vice-Chairman and one of our two representatives to the National Executive Committee.

The CCNY Student Council was quick to adopt the NSA Constitution in September after the Constitutional Convention. The following Spring, I ran again for Council President, this time against Alan Rosenwasser, who had been a CCNY delegate to NSA and Editor of *The Campus,* and by whom I was once again defeated handily. By then *The Campus* mustered an even more vigorous front-page editorial in support of Rosenwasser and in opposition to me in its 5/13/48 issue.

Despite my disheartening political posture in the press, I was selected again to represent the college at the First Congress in 1948. There, I was mercifully removed from the local scene by election to national office—as part of a "balanced slate" on which I was the leftward member.

Tom Garrity faces off a challenge

Meantime, factional wariness in the region remained close to the surface. Suspicion over Catholic control motives by students on the left surfaced in the evening-session Council meeting after the 1948 convention. Tom Garrity, who was elected at the Congress as Chairman of the region, was brought up on written charges by Israel Levine, one of his co-delegates (with whom he had run on a slate), for allegedly having been a part of a Catholic caucus at the convention. There, Catholics were elected as NSA President (Ted Harris of LaSalle, Philadelphia) and Secretary-Treasurer (Helen Jean Rogers of Mundelein, Chicago) (see Pt.1 Sec. 6).

Tom was a gifted debater, a brilliant scholar, quick on his feet and an indefatiguable worker. He was attending the evening session of CCNY and taking day classes at St. Peter's College in Newark simultaneously.[14] An able match for his accusers, he was acquitted in the middle of the night with about fifty people in the room, as he once told me, "with the split votes of people from the left and right." In that setting the right wing was the Students for Democratic Action.[14] Had he been removed as a delegate, his legitimacy as regional Chairman would have been in question.[15]

During the year Tom Garrity was Chairman, some of the founding "old guard" had moved on, and took with them the animosities which had arisen in the early years.

Regional events flourish despite conflicts

Mike DiLegge wrote in a "Mid-Year Report" on NSA in the Fordham *Ram* in January, 1949 that

> The Region is still torn between the excesses of the left wing group, and the fossilizing effects of the right. The New York Met-

ropolitan Region has its unique problems and thus far has tried to solve them in a mature and equitable manner. With recent changes in several delegations, and the subsequent election of new members to the Regional Executive Committee, it is hoped that the cooperative leadership will develop to unite the region away from issues with political connotations, and towards projects that deal with strictly student interests. During the Spring semester, in addition to the PCS [Purchase Card discounts] system, the region plans intercollegiate conferences on student government.

In addition to special events, the region aimed for monthly meetings during the school year. These were never dull and generally attracted 50 to 100 delegates. The most contentious issues were those which dealt with the IUS and with student rights, academic freedom and freedom of the college press. The region generally rose above the fray on local campus issues – such as the 1949 City College student strike—but sunk its teeth into opposition, by large majorities of primarily non-Catholic delegates, to such proposals as the 1947 revocation of the AYD charter at Queens College and the 1949 NY State Feinberg Bill, authorizing the NY State Regents to remove or disqualify from teaching any members of "subversive organizations."

Some typical events of these first three years:

- The *Washington Square Bulletin* of 2/11/47 reports that "at a lively meeting held on February 8 and interrupted frequently by verbal clashes on the floor," the regional assembly drew up "detailed organizational plans for the continuation of its successful work in the New York District."
- On 12/18/47, the *Barnard Bulletin* reported that "Cultural plans, projected campaigns to evaluate college student governments[17] and to popularize the NSA Bill of Rights, and plans for a forum on democracy" highlighted the regional meeting on December 6 at Manhattanville College. The symposium was to be held at Fordham on 12/19, sponsored by the region's Newman Clubs. The region's International Commission was holding a festival at City College's 23d Street center on 12/29, and a regional concert was being held at the Juilliard concert hall on 12/18 – admission 75 cents.
- In its April, 1949 issue, Manhattanville's *Centurion* headlined, "M'ville Orators Victors in NSA Met. Debate; Receive Trophy At Regional Meeting, March 26." The winners were scheduled for a playoff debate with the NSA New Jersey Region at St. Peter's College "under the auspices of their Cultural Commission."

CCNY and Manhattanville College as neighbors

Two other notable slices of history come to mind. The first is the relationship between the CCNY Main Center and Manhattanville College, which had been literally next door neighbors on Convent Avenue for over forty years.[18] I doubt that any of us had any idea of what went on behind its cloistered walls. The President, Mother O'Byrne, was an active booster of NSA and provided a regional office on the ground floor of one of the dormitories.[19] A succession of CCNY regional delegates and officers, including Bob Meagher, Tom Garrity and me, enjoyed the benefits of this arrangement, as did the Manhattanville young women who, through Mother O'Byrne's insights, were introduced to more of the world around them.[20]

The 1949 CCNY Student Strike

The other memorable event was the CCNY student strike in the Spring of 1949, organized out of frustration by student leaders who were campaigning for the discharge of a professor accused of anti-Semitism in his classes and an instructor in charge of Army Hall for racial discrimination in the veteran's dormitory.

At CCNY in the Spring of 1949, as reported in the May 1949 *NSA News,* students at CCNY Main Center Day voted 2,797 to 1,885 to strike in order to force the ouster of the professor and instructor. It did come up at the region as a regional matter. It appears that there was a motion brought up, almost as a matter of courtesy, to say the region endorses the action of the student government at CCNY.

The CCNY NSA delegation did ask NSA for its backing. NSA President Ted Harris's reply is instructive in its caution, declaring that "the 'right to strike' cannot be inferred from the NSA Constitution," while offering NSA's services "to mediate the specific grievance."[21]

I recall our national staff discussions on the matter. After the huge outcry the previous year when the 1947-48 national staff under Bill Welsh was accused of acting without authority in supporting the Bill Ellis resignation from the IUS,[22] prudence overcame passion. We felt we could not assert new policy in a staff decision without Congress approval.

The Region finds its way

I think it is fair to say that the New York Metropolitan Region successfully tested the mettle of its radicals, moderates and conservatives and of its principled Catholic delegates,

Eugene G. Schwartz is a publishing and business consultant and Editor-at-Large for ForeWord Magazine. He has served as a production executive for several major publishers. After completing graduate course work in public administration at NYU in 1953, he worked as a union organizer and was in the printing business. He holds a B.S. in civil engineering from the City College of New York.

PICTURE CREDITS: *Then:* 1947 at CCNY. *Now:* 1998 (Both, author)

Marxists and secularists—to find ways to work around their conflicts and to create the opportunities for mutual understanding and collaboration here at home that NSA's leaders were struggling to make happen internationally.

For myself, fifty-five years later, I marvel at the commitment and energy student leaders and delegates poured into making NSA a viable organization. I can also admire the patience, forbearance and mentoring we enjoyed from the many administrators who trusted us. We all believed in what we were doing – for personal as well as principled reasons. We provided for each other irreplaceable and unforgettably valuable experiences, and perhaps on occasion enriched the quality of student life.

END NOTES

[1] See Wallace on pp. 000, 000.

[2] The delegations that petitioned the NEC were Brooklyn College, Fordham College, Good Counsel College,Hunter Evening, Hunter Day, Manhattan College, College of Mt. St. Vincent, Marymount College and Manhattanville College. NSA membership lists, in the larger regions especially, are not always consistent as they appear in college newspaper accounts or meeting minutes. Complete lists of the recorded membership of the region for the years 1947-48 and 1948-49 appear on pages 161 and 231.

[3] The ailing Bill Ellis and his NSA proxy, Jim Smith, resigned from the Executive Committee of the International Union of Students after the February 1948 Czech Communist coup in Prague. See p. 188.

[4] See Meagher, p. 665, Steinhauser, p. 853, and DiLegge, p. 891. According to the 4/22/48 issue of the CCNY *Campus,* the other members were Ernie Kahn, also of CCNY, and Ed Cook of Fordham's School of Education. (Cook went on to become president of C.W. Post College at LIU.)

[5] The New England Students for Wallace newsletter had named Walter Wallace as NSA Regional President in reporting a meeting with Henry Wallace. Wallace's accusers cited this as evidence of his abuse of his position, although the Chairman of the New England group sent a letter of apology. Wallace himself, in rebutting the charge, also confronted the "Catch 22" of NSA's position on partisan politics when he said, "Because I oppose discrimination against Black people, against Jews, against Catholics, and against foreign-born individuals, and because I fight for these things in all ways possible including in organizations other than NSA, I've been charged with making NSA a political organization. I have stated time and time again that I was among the individuals that first began this NSA on the basis that it would be a *non-partisan organization,* in the assumption [however] that it must be a *political* organization because all organizations and all individuals are by their very nature in society political. But what we can do is keep this organization from being a partisan political organization, except in the sense that it will be partisan in the interests of students alone." (Minutes, National Executive Committee, International House, University of Chicago, April 9-11, 1948). Italics, mine.

[6] I refer to "delegations" rather than institutions since, as noted by Martin McLaughlin (p. 818) and Phil DesMarais (p. 735), the Catholic heierarchy openly encouraged formation of the Joint Committee for Student Action (JCSA) from 1946-1949 to provide liaison and coordination for Catholic College delegations (through the NFCCS) and secular college Catholic delegates (through the Newman Club Federation).

[7] Among the factors that come to mind are logistic and historic. Boston, Chicago and Philadelphia colleges were members of strong statewide regions, while New York State north of Westchester County was in a separate region. The Mason-Dixon region (MD, DC) had a predominantly Catholic College membership to begin with. It is difficult in today's context to understand the issues as well as ideologies that divided the student conscience at the time. Martin McLaughlin (pp. 15, 88), Seymour Reisin (p. 781), Bill Miller (p. 717), Barry Keating (p. 811) and Ralph Dungan (pp. 174, 909) present useful and varied perspectives.

[8] Rounded student body population figures are from *School and Society,* 12/18/48.

[9] Walter Wallace became a Professor of Sociology at Princeton, where he still teaches and writes prolifically. Tom Garrity graduated Yale Law School and joined the firm of Donovan Leisure. He now lives in Denver. Bob Meagher is Professor Emeritus at the Fletcher School of Law and Diplomacy at Tufts (See Meagher, p. 665).

[10] Congress attendance records show St. John's University and Notre Dame College (Staten Island) joining in 1949.

[11] Ascher Katz became an attorney, a municipal judge in Westchester County, and active in Democratic politics.

[12] This figure of 100,000 now clearly seems to be understated by about 50,000. It was, of course, something of a conceit to designate the size of our constituency by direct enrollment, since not all colleges joined by student body referendum as against a student government vote, and often the majority of students did not vote in elections.

[13] See Clif Wharton's description of Jim Smith's role on p. 146, and Henry Halsted's sidelight on Smith's parliamentary skills on p. 839

[14] See Tom Garrity, Bob Kelly and St. Peters College on p. 892.

[15] The event was recorded in the minutes and reported in *Main Events,* the evening session paper. Tom had driven back from the Congress with Al Lowenstein, who attended that particular meeting,

[16] A similar recall effort from the "right" at Cornell the previous year, succeeded in removing Jack Minkoff as a delegate and hence as Chair of the New York State Region. This event, part of NSA's oral history, is not covered in any college press or archival documentation I was able to find.

[17] This plan resulted in the 1949 publication by NSA of the Met. New York region's detailed "Student Government Survey" on self-government practices, prepared by Oona Burke, Midge Dunn and Dorothy Weiss, based on responses from 158 member colleges throughout the country: 59 private, 39 public and 60 church related

[18] Manhattanville, founded in 1841, moved to its uptown site in 1847. CCNY, founded in 1847, broke ground on the neighboring property in 1907.

[19] See Mother O'Byrne, p. 862.

[20] Manhattanville moved to Purchase, NY in 1952, having sold its campus to the city for use by CCNY in expanding its own growing facility.

[21] Here is the complete letter:

April 14, 1949
SPECIAL DELIVERY, AIR MAIL

USNSA Delegation
City College of New York
New York, 31, New York

Dear Fellow Students:

In answer to your telegram of April 12th, requesting support for the "student's right to strike," I would like to state, on behalf of the staff,[21] that, in our opinion, the "right to strike" cannot be inferred from the USNSA Constitution and By-Laws. We feel, also, that the whole question of the extent to which students can, in justice and order, enforce their claims on the university community should be decided by the highest legislative authority of the United States National Student Association—the National Congress.

We hope that you will appreciate our judgement and that your representatives will be prepared to give your views at the coming congress. We offer our services to attempt to mediate the specific grievance, and help preserve the integrity of the academic community for students, administrators, and faculty.

Very sincerely,
James T. Harris, Jr.
President, USNSA

Cc: President, CCNY Student Council
Mr. Gerald Maryanov, Mr. Thomas Garrity
Strike Committee

[22] See Welsh, p.170.

CCNY and Manhattanville College

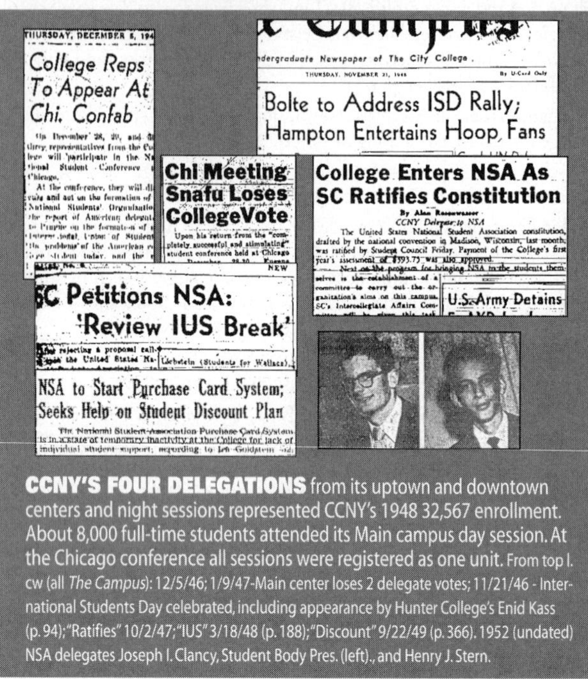

THURSDAY, DECEMBER 5, 194

College Reps To Appear At Chi. Confab

Undergraduate Newspaper of The City College

Bolte to Address ISD Rally; Hampton Entertains Hoop Fans

Chi Meeting Snafu Loses CollegeVote

Upon his return from the "completely successful and stimulating" student conference held at Chicago

College Enters NSA As SC Ratifies Constitution

CCNY Delegate to NSA

The United States National Student Association constitution, drafted by the national convention in Madison, Wisconsin, last month, was ratified by Student Council Friday. Payment of the College's first year's assessment of $193.75 was also approved.

SC Petitions NSA: 'Review IUS Break'

U.S. Army Detains

NSA to Start Purchase Card System; Seeks Help on Student Discount Plan

CCNY'S FOUR DELEGATIONS from its uptown and downtown centers and night sessions represented CCNY's 1948 32,567 enrollment. About 8,000 full-time students attended its Main campus day session. At the Chicago conference all sessions were registered as one unit. From top l. cw (all *The Campus*): 12/5/46; 1/9/47-Main center loses 2 delegate votes; 11/21/46 - International Students Day celebrated, including appearance by Hunter College's Enid Kass (p. 94); "Ratifies" 10/2/47; "IUS" 3/18/48 (p. 188); "Discount" 9/22/49 (p. 366). 1952 (undated) NSA delegates Joseph I. Clancy, Student Body Pres. (left)., and Henry J. Stern.

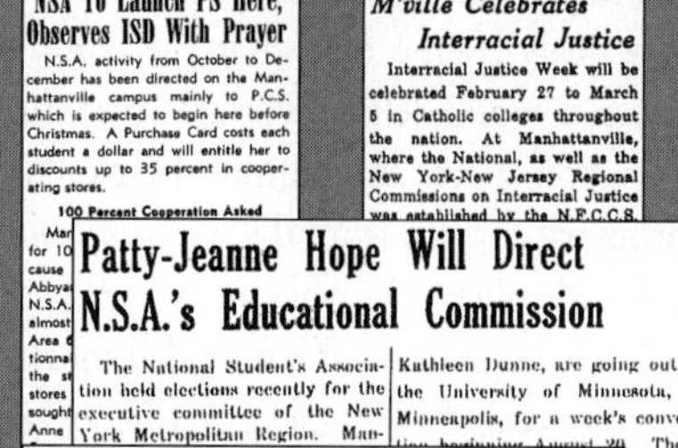

NSA To Launch PS Here; Observes ISD With Prayer

N.S.A. activity from October to December has been directed on the Manhattanville campus mainly to P.C.S. which is expected to begin here before Christmas. A Purchase Card costs each student a dollar and will entitle her to discounts up to 35 percent in cooperating stores.

100 Percent Cooperation Asked

M'ville Celebrates Interracial Justice

Interracial Justice Week will be celebrated February 27 to March 5 in Catholic colleges throughout the nation. At Manhattanville, where the National, as well as the New York-New Jersey Regional Commissions on Interracial Justice was established by the N.F.C.C.S.

NSA Provides Field For Catholic Action

by Abbyann Day

Patty-Jeanne Hope Will Direct N.S.A.'s Educational Commission

The National Student's Association held elections recently for the executive committee of the New York Metropolitan Region. Kathleen Dunne, are going out to the University of Minnesota, in Minneapolis, for a week's convention

M'ville Orators Victors In NSA Met. Debate; Receive Trophy At Regional Meeting, March 26

and Mary Kay Donovan. Debating in the final round against Michael Pantileano and John Brandt of Fordham, Mary Kay and Frannie upheld the resolution that:

The British system of socialized medicine should be enacted in the United States by Federal Legislation.

NSA Delegates Meet On Campus

by M. K. Donovan

An air of excitement pervaded Manhattanville's campus on February 4. The cause of the stir was the first 1950 regional meeting of N. Y. Met. NSA held alternately in the Blue Room, the Tea House, and classrooms of Founder's Hall.

One of the highlights of the meeting was a first-hand report on the December 27-31 session of the National Executive Committee in Madison, Wisconsin, by Bill Burke of Fordham, vice-president, and Sheldon Steinhauser of Long Is-

MANHATTANVILLE PROVIDES AN OFFICE NEXT DOOR. With an all Catholic women population of 568, the college provided a regional office and made a connection with its largely male Jewish neighboring student body. Early leaders included Phyllis Carbone, Abbyann Day, Midge Dunn, Mary Kay Donovan. From top, l. cw (all *The Centurion*): 12/48 - ISD was "well-attended in spite of withdrawal" from "ill-prepared" regional program; 2/49, national Catholic college Interracial Justice Week; "Catholic Action" 3/49; 2/50; "Hope" 5/29/51; "Orators," 4/49.

Negro, Union Discrimination Charged To Davis, Army Hall Administration

Deans Brophy, Theobald, Crawley Investigate Latest Accusations; Labor Dispute Arbitrated

Wright Permits 38 Students to Shift, SC Calls Sitdown Ballot Today at 11

Council Sets 4,000 Minimum For Referendum on 5 Points

Job Requests Drop Sharply

President Bars Disciplinary Action Against Walkout Class

Judge Delaney Blasts Wright, Quits Alumni Bias Probe Body

Tubridy Appointed As Football Coach

Claims Davis Lacks Tenure, Asks Knickerbocker Demotion

TENACIOUS PROTESTS mounted against faculty insensitivity on matters of race and religion. The Chairman of the Romance Languages Department for years accused of anti-semitism, and the newly appointed administrator of the veterans dormitory charged with "Negro segregation." From top (*The Campus*) 10/2/47, 10/8/48, 3/29/49.

STUDENTS VOTED 2,797-1,887 TO STRIKE on 4/11/49 receiving wide regional attention. College President Dr. Harry N. Wright was the focus of their anger. The 5-day strike was supported by the evening session but opposed by the downtown business school. It won a state hearing. Both faculty members were eventually reassigned. Below from l., *NSA News* 4/49; 5/20/49 letter from Hal Orbach of the evening session updating NSA on the strike; *Columbia Spectator* 9/30/48 on a 1 day strike the year before. Bottom l, *The Campus* 4/19/49. The editor-in-chief, Robert Zuckerkandle, resigned in opposition to the paper's support of the strike.

CCNY Students Strike to Oust Profs

Main Events

Columbia

Student Strike At City Protests Bias

Maintain Position; SC Strike Committee Confident of Victory, Organizes Classes

Additional Funds For 1950 Budget Seen As Unlikely

ARREST CCNY RIOTERS! Striking Students Battle Police

Authorities Refuse Action on Demands

'Campus' Editor, Protesting Support of Strike, Resigns

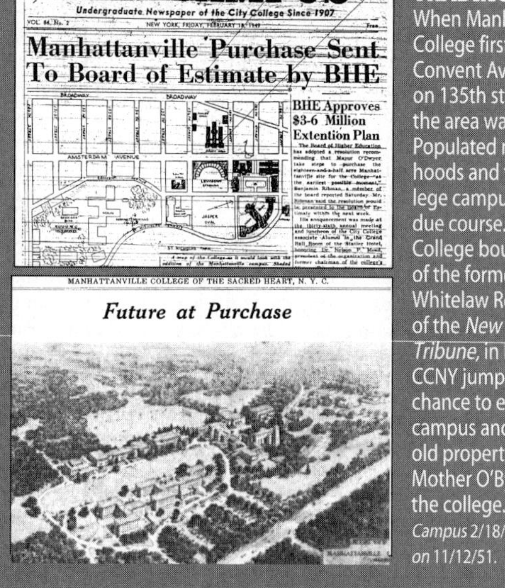

THE CAMPUS

Undergraduate Newspaper of the City College Since 1907

NEW YORK, FRIDAY, FEBRUARY 18, 1949

Manhattanville Purchase Sent To Board of Estimate by BHE

BHE Approves $3-6 Million Extention Plan

MANHATTANVILLE COLLEGE OF THE SACRED HEART, N. Y. C.

Future at Purchase

TRADING PLACES. When Manhattanville College first moved to its Convent Avenue location on 135th street in 1847, the area was rural then. Populated neighborhoods and the City College campus arrived in due course. In 1949 the College bought 250 acres of the former estate of Whitelaw Reid, Publisher of the *New York Herald Tribune*, in Purchase, NY. CCNY jumped at the chance to expand its campus and bought the old property. In 1952 Mother O'Byrne moved the college. From top: *The Campus* 2/18/49; *The Centurion* 11/12/51.

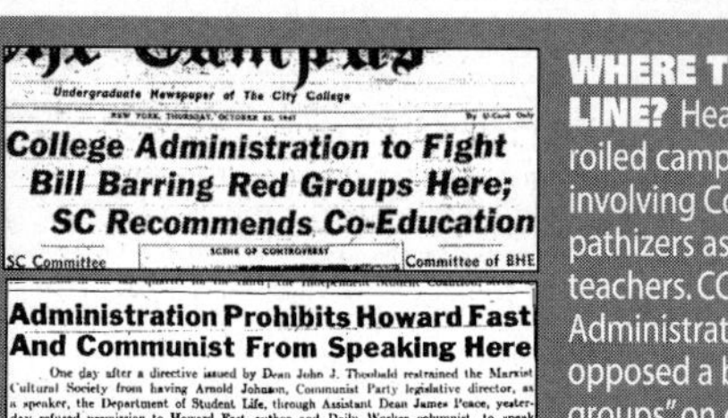

The Campus

Undergraduate Newspaper of The City College

NEW YORK, THURSDAY, OCTOBER 23, 1947

College Administration to Fight Bill Barring Red Groups Here; SC Recommends Co-Education

Administration Prohibits Howard Fast And Communist From Speaking Here

One day after a directive issued by Dean John J. Theobald restrained the Marxist Cultural Society from having Arnold Johnson, Communist Party legislative director, as a speaker, the Department of Student Life, through Assistant Dean James Peace, yesterday refused permission to Howard Fast, author and Daily Worker columnist, to speak before the College chapter of the Progressive Citizens of America.

Debate On UN

2,000 View Coronation Of New Campus Queen

WHERE TO DRAW THE LINE? Heated controversies roiled campuses on issues involving Communists and sympathizers as clubs, speakers and teachers. CCNY's Dean of Administration John Theobold opposed a ban on "subversive groups" on campus (10/23/47) and upheld a ban on speakers "identified" with them (12/1/47).

Lessons learned for a career in human relations

2. The Metropolitan New York Region in Transition

Sheldon Steinhauser
Long Island University
Chairman, Metropolitan New York Region, 1949-50

I was an idealistic "kid" of sixteen when I entered Long Island University, thanks to the New York City school system of "skipping"—a kid who began blossoming into student activities only in the last two years of high school. It was that sixteen-year-old who attended his first Long Island University Student Government meeting in the spring of 1947 and wound up being asked to serve as delegate to NSA.

Most of the male students at LIU were returned veterans. I was so inexperienced, but trying to grow from every experience. It was a pressure cooker for this "youngster," but one in which the constant talk was of the lessons learned from the experience of war and the need to move forward with a sense of idealism rooted in the soil of American ideals. It was a time of universalism matched with the resistance to change found in every generation, but it seemed that there were so many of "us" trying to craft a better world, a better nation.

Learning from the NSA Constitutional Convention in 1947

So, just having turned seventeen, off I went to my first NSA Congress—the Constitutional Convention in 1947—a mind-expanding experience. Formal sessions and all-night caucuses and conversations, from which I learned so much. Parliamentary procedure, still somewhat foreign to me—I remember tying up the International Affairs Committee by a motion—more with enthusiasm than with knowledge—to adopt the report on affiliation with IUS in a manner that precluded amendments. It took awhile to get that untangled! I vowed I would never let that happen again—and promptly came back to studying and mastering Robert's Rules of Order as thoroughly as I could.

Thanks to NSA, I really expanded my organizational skills beyond my preliminary experiences in my junior and senior years in high school and came to better understand the leverage of organization. What I learned was to ultimately carry me into a new, satisfying, life-long career as an advocate, agency executive, and consultant on human rights and diversity issues. With all of its tempering by political, social, and economic realities—and they were certainly a part of the landscape—NSA reminded me of humanity's inherent need to live the finest of its ideals.

There were so many people I looked up to in NSA for their courage, oratorical skills, the sharpness and vibrance of their thinking on major issues, their ability as parliamentary leaders, their personal warmth to me—too many to risk excluding anyone by setting forth a list of names. Many were my heroes, my models, teachers and mentors even without ever seeking to play that role. They were "right" and "left," Catholic and non-Catholic, conservative and liberal, southerner and easterner, wise beyond their years, drawing upon their intellect and their life experience. I listened, learned, understood, and appreciated so much better where people were coming from, why they were attempting to shape policies in one direction or another, explaining and protecting the existing order from more substantial change, builders of bridges and coalitions. It was all there—they were all there—the most talented, dedicated group of people I had ever encountered or ever again would encounter, and I soaked up every bit of it that I could.

Long Island University—A "Subway School"

As a relatively smaller "subway school," LIU did not have a base of leadership that was willing to spend a great deal of time on these issues. Most veterans were there to make up for time "lost" in the war. Especially at a commuter school, most people tended to go home after classes. I became a big fish in a relatively smaller pond because I was willing to grab onto responsibilities and because the students who were active were willing to afford me the chance—and I will be forever grateful to my LIU experience for providing that opportunity

As all this evolved, I became more and more conscious of the efforts in NSA to move beyond polarized positions, to seek common ground on some of the most contentious issues, whether involving NSA's role in international student affairs, its concern for student rights and academic freedom, or equality of opportunity in campus admissions and organizations. As a result, I began to see myself as a bridge builder, one who didn't want to be put into a box (though many chose to see anyone from the New York region in that vein), even though the NSA student world at that time constantly put people into boxes or, more to the point, blocs (e.g., the liberal bloc, the Southern bloc, the Catholic bloc, the "Communist" bloc).

One of my very special moments was being asked to run for president of the New York region while I was sick from hay fever and asthma at the tail end of the 1949 NSA convention and had to leave before the New York Region held its election for officers there. I agreed to it, but only if it were clear that there was widespread support. As it turned out, I was nominated by a "liberal" and the nomination was seconded by a Catholic college student—which made me feel very good.

The Metropolitan New York Region in 1949-50

That next year was an incredible one. The region became very visible in sponsoring a number of conferences concerned with discrimination in campus organizations, relief efforts to assist colleges and universities bombed out during the war, and so on. In point of fact, it was my involvement with a region-wide conference on discrimination in campus organizations that brought me into contact with a number of human relations agencies as resources, including the Anti-Defamation League of B'nai B'rith (ADL), which ultimately was to shape my personal and professional destiny.

LIU took pride in my election, as it also gave it visibility among New York colleges. I took great pride in the support of students at the Brooklyn campus and throughout the region. But we were also aware that battles for students' rights and academic freedom were becoming commonplace at many campuses throughout the nation, and we in New York were certainly not immune.

Later, when a "liberal" was elected president of LIU's student government, the administration invalidated the election. I protested and, when the election results were not reinstated, I felt, as a matter of principle, that I needed to resign as an LIU delegate (still being able to retain my regional presidency).[1] This was to come back to haunt me when I asked for permission to leave summer school early to attend the 1950 Congress. I was told that since I chose to resign as a delegate because of the election results, the school felt no obligation to assist me at that time. It was one of those "you made your bed, go lie in it," scenarios. Nevertheless, I went. Incidentally, I have warm feelings for my LIU experience, particularly the opportunity and openness for my extracurricular experiences in NSA, the International Relations Club, the Outdoor Club (can you believe?), the American Association for the United Nations (AAUN), and elsewhere.

The 1950 Convention: a lesson in outreach and silence

The 1950 convention was an admixture, exhilarating and then traumatic. I was greatly encouraged by my liberal friends and delegates in the region to run for national president. I am not sure I ever fully understood what I was doing, but I spent a lot of time listening to my friends—too much time, as it turned out, though I doubt that anything would have changed the final outcome. They were, in fact, a loving, dedicated, but relatively small group within the total national spectrum!

The big lesson gleaned from both that experience and the total NSA experience—on issues you truly care about, you need to reach out to those who are not in your corner, something I really did not work at very hard. As I said, that was a life-long learning experience.

The other area was thinking that no issue, however trivial, could be acted upon without my racing to the microphone and saying something. No, the world was not waiting for Steinhauser to suggest taking a bathroom break or arguing a point of trivia. So, I am sure it was hard to get the delegates focused on what I thought was really important. That, too, gave me some life-long lessons—such as to save yourself for the "big picture," so that people are more inclined to listen to you and to take you seriously when you do speak out.

Al Lowenstein and Roy Romer

Al Lowenstein was the symbol of a generation of students who came of age determined to make a difference in our society: he was a mesmerizing speaker, a brilliant and master statesman-politician who seemed to slip back and forth between the two roles, arousing passionate support and passionate opposition.[2] In the election for national president, Roy Romer and I had a pact—we would not withdraw from the race against Lowenstein even if we got clobbered in the vote—and did we ever get clobbered! It was one of the very few elections in his life that Roy did not win. After that happened, I was nominated for a vice presidency, and it appeared that I might actually get elected. The forces backing Lowenstein were able to get the session adjourned for lunch, during which they rounded up votes (there were rumors that I was a

"Communist from New York," etc.) and after lunch the outcome became clear—I had lost.[3]

The long hours finally got to me; a friend drove me around while, utterly exhausted, I cried and then tried to get my act together so I could go to the final reception and "face the world" —not an easy task, but I did it. And it taught me that, allowing for grieving over loss, one then had to move on in one's life. And so I did, even though I went back to at least one National Student Congress—maybe two—as an ADL representative. Another "move on" lesson had been learned—when it's over, it's over. When you leave a position of influence, it is important to move out and not try to hang on to the past as though it would be the same as when you were actively involved and had a leadership position. It is then time for others. I applied that lesson throughout my subsequent career, and it worked well for me.

Moving on to a career in human relations

After LIU, I knew I was destined to work in some field where I could give expression to my passion for human rights and give something back to the society. I tried for a position with the World Student Service Fund to help re-build bombed out colleges and universities in Europe—but there were no paid positions available. I went, also, to ADL, which fortunately had kept a record of my involvements with them as a student. They were willing to take a chance and the rest is history—a 35-year career in Columbus and primarily in Denver with a host of local, regional and national responsibilities, the opportunity early on to confront college quota systems and discrimination in fraternities and sororities, assaulting anti-Semitism but also barriers that held back so many others because of race, religion, ethnicity, gender—all such efforts would not have been possible without the knowledge and skills gleaned from my NSA years.

NSA was a defining period in my life. It brought me abundant joy, a new vision of self and, yes, the pain by which one is compelled to move quickly in crafting one's life towards maturity. NSA changed my direction from half-heartedly following a pre-medical road to one of wanting to counter prejudice and hate and re-build what had been torn down in the war. It enabled me to "grow up" into a visionary new world of hope and aspirations and ideals and to experience the joy of learning what it is to have a higher sense of self and the absolute blessing of contributing back to others. Away went the road to medical school; the science courses became the least interesting to me; classes in the humanities attracted me the most, but my real learning came through my campus and NSA activities outside the classroom.

I retired from ADL to head the Allied Jewish Federation here, then retired from that position after six years to continue teaching social issues (and now, also, aging issues) and to become a consultant on diversity, including more recently age diversity, in the workplace. And I never, ever take for granted the role NSA played in all this. I do owe so much to my NSA experience and what it did to seed and to fuel my life. For all this, NSA will always rank at the top, and will have a special place in my memories. I will be forever grateful.

Currently a college teacher, consultant on diversity issues and non-profit development executive, from 1950 to 1985 Sheldon Steinhauser held national, regional and local positions with the Anti-Defamation League. From 1985 to 1991, he was Executive Vice President of the Allied Jewish Federation of Denver.

END NOTES

[1] In its 9/22/49 edition, the *Seewanhaka* headlined the reversal of the student vote "Election Declared Void," while in the same issue it reports, "NSA Elects LIU Student NY President". On 10/26/49 it bannered the final dissolution of the student government for that year, "Council Disbanded."

[2] See Kurtz, p. 307, and Lynch, p. 370, on Lowenstein.

[3] The minutes of the 1950 Convention at the University of Michigan show that elections were held on August 31. It reported the outcomes in the following manner:

Nominations for President, USNSA

Nominee	*Nominator*	*Result*
S. Steinhauser (Met. Region)	A. Landy (New Jersey Region)	46
R. Romer (Rocky Mt.)	Raleigh Brooks (Rocky Mt.)	48
T. Walsh (Michigan)	L. Wilcox (Michigan)	declined
E. Brock (Pennsylvania)	D. Cadigan (Mason-Dixon)	declined
A. Lowenstein (Va.-Car.)		elected—254

Nominations for Vice President, Educational Affairs

S. Steinhauser (Met. N.Y.)		Vote—S—139
R. Treanor (Minn.)		declined G—180
H. Goldsmith (Wisconsin)		elected

PICTURE CREDITS: *Then:* Long Island University, *Seawanhaka,* Sept. 22, 1949, p. 4. *Now:* Denver, Oct. 22, 1999 (Schwartz)

SHELDON STEINHAUSER

Early years: A native of New York City, he attended De Witt Clinton High School. Entered Long Island University in 1946. Received a Bachelor of Science degree in 1963.

Current: President of Sheldon Steinhauser & Associates, offering professional services to assist businesses, organizations, and the public sector on diversity issues, including religion, ethnicity, race, gender, sexual harassment, sexual orientation, and the escalating age fifty–plus population. At the Metropolitan State College of Denver, holds a tenured rank of Associate Professor of Sociology, teaches classes in social issues and on the impact of the "age wave," and supervises internship students tackling community problems.

Career highlights: From 1950 to 1985, national, regional, and local executive positions with the Anti-Defamation League of B'nai B'rith. While an Anti-Defamation League official, he was a consultant on religious discrimination in employment to Western regional offices of the Equal Employment Opportunity Commission (EEOC). During his ADL tenure, he was often called on to mediate disputes in community life and served on the Rocky Mountain Advisory Council of the American Arbitration Association. He participated in the Colorado delegation in the march from Selma to Montgomery led by Dr. Martin Luther King, Jr., and visited "refuseniks" in the former Soviet Union cities of Moscow, Kiev, and Leningrad to increase public support for religious freedom. From 1985 to 1991, was Executive Vice President of the Allied Jewish Federation of Denver. Overseas travel has included numerous study visits to Europe and eight special study programs and missions to Israel, exploring social service, aging policy, and intergroup relations needs.

Citations and honors: Degree of Doctor of Public Service (Hon.), Regis University, Denver, May 1994; first annual Human Relations Award presented by the Colorado Civil Rights Commission, Martin Luther King, Jr., Humanitarian Award of the Colorado King Holiday Commission; the Colorado Civil Rights Meritorious Achievement Award; and Annual Civil Rights Achievement Award, ADL. Editorially praised as "The Gentle Lion" by the *Denver Post* in 1985, on retirement from the ADL to head the Allied Jewish Federation of Denver, for his long career in the fight against anti-Semitism and discrimination.

Membership, board or officer positions: Founding board member, Latin American Research and Service Agency (LARASA), the Denver Anti-Crime Council (by appointment of the mayor), and the Community Education Council (monitoring Denver's school desegregation program) at the behest of the Federal District Court. Past president of the Adult Education Council of Metropolitan Denver, past member of Metropolitan Denver Urban Coalition and Fair Housing Center. Appointed a delegate to the 1995 White House Conference on Aging by then U.S. Senator Hank Brown of Colorado. Member of the American Sociological Association, American Society on Aging, Western Social Science Association, and Association of Jewish Community Organization Personnel.

Publications and presentations: Presentations and materials published by the University of North Texas, 1995, by the Section on Aging of the American Sociological Association in 1996 and 2000, and *HR Magazine*, July 1998. Editorial Board member of "Sustainable Communities Review," Center for Public Service, University of North Texas. Frequently called upon as motivational speaker, moderator, and guest on radio and television programs, has written or been quoted in newspapers, including articles on age discrimination in the workplace and successfully managing an age-diverse workforce.

Family: He and his wife, Janice, a sculptor, have five children and seven grandchildren.

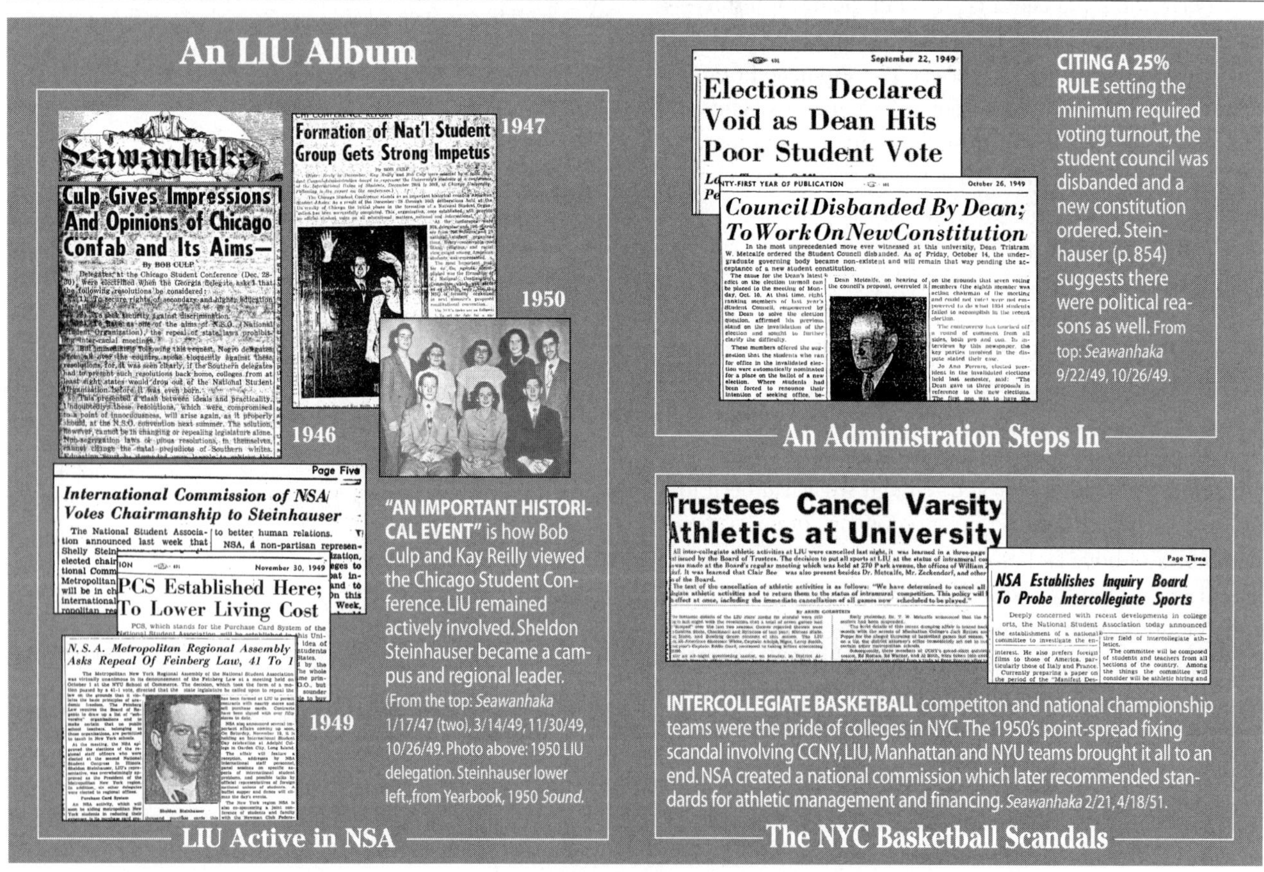

An LIU Album
Seawanhaka
Culp Gives Impressions And Opinions of Chicago Confab and Its Aims—
1946
Formation of Nat'l Student Group Gets Strong Impetus
1947
1950
International Commission of NSA Votes Chairmanship to Steinhauser
PCS Established Here; To Lower Living Cost
N. S. A. Metropolitan Regional Assembly Asks Repeal Of Feinberg Law, 41 To 1
1949
LIU Active in NSA
Elections Declared Void as Dean Hits Poor Student Vote
Council Disbanded By Dean; To Work On New Constitution
An Administration Steps In
Trustees Cancel Varsity Athletics at University
NSA Establishes Inquiry Board To Probe Intercollegiate Sports
The NYC Basketball Scandals

"AN IMPORTANT HISTORICAL EVENT" is how Bob Culp and Kay Reilly viewed the Chicago Student Conference. LIU remained actively involved. Sheldon Steinhauser became a campus and regional leader. (From the top: *Seawanhaka* 1/17/47 (two), 3/14/49, 11/30/49, 10/26/49. Photo above: 1950 LIU delegation. Steinhauser lower left, from Yearbook, 1950 *Sound*.

CITING A 25% RULE setting the minimum required voting turnout, the student council was disbanded and a new constitution ordered. Steinhauser (p. 854) suggests there were political reasons as well. From top: *Seawanhaka* 9/22/49, 10/26/49.

INTERCOLLEGIATE BASKETBALL competiton and national championship teams were the pride of colleges in NYC. The 1950's point-spread fixing scandal involving CCNY, LIU, Manhattan and NYU teams brought it all to an end. NSA created a national commission which later recommended standards for athletic management and financing. *Seawanhaka* 2/21, 4/18/51.

Experiencing first-time national politics and political "atom splitting"

3. Finding the Right Path

Bernard L. Schwartz
City College of New York, School of Business
Delegate to the Chicago Student Conference, 1946
NSA Constitutional Convention, 1947

Looking back to 1946 revives vivid memories of a period of tumultuous growth for me. I had only just returned to my college studies at City College of New York after two years in the army. Desperate to participate in the new world, to expand my citizen-horizon to wider landscapes, above all to make my contribution, I found myself at Chicago and Wisconsin sharing hopes, dreams, all-night strategy sessions, mimeographing and distributing massive proclamations. This was my first experience at national politics, at political "atom splitting" between the well-funded right and the well-mannered left, my firsthand knowledge of agenda-driven ideologues. How innocent most of us were, realizing finally and with much pain that good will was not enough. We had to develop smarts to find the right path. In the birthing of NSA, the right path was progressive and centrist. It worked, and NSA lasted for generations of students.

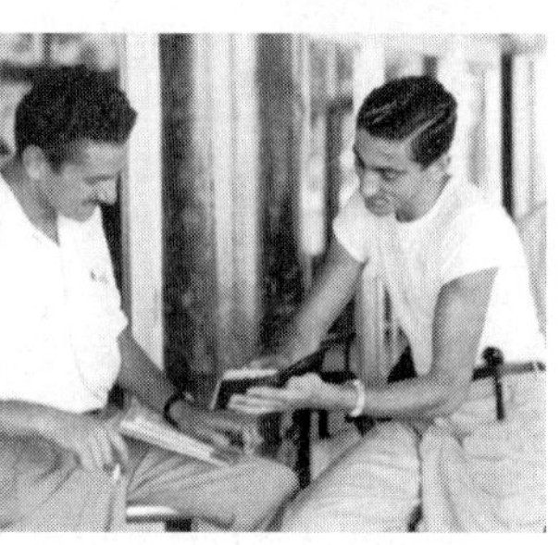

DOWNTOWN MEETS UPTOWN. Representing the "downtown" CCNY School of Business at the 1947 Constitutional convention in Madison (Pt. 1, Sec. 4), Bernard Schwartz and "uptown" CCNY's School of Engineering Gene Schwartz (not related to each other) meet for the first time and exchange notes. CCNY had 4 delegations (see p. 161).

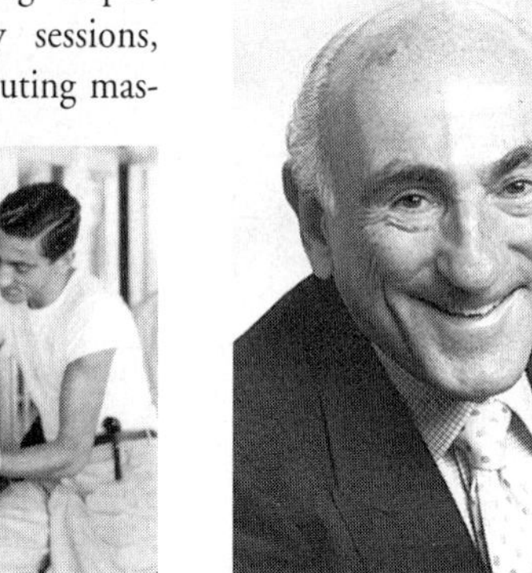

How grateful I am for the experience—it formed the foundation for a lifetime of idealism and the knowledge that "paying back" is its own reward.

Bernard L. Schwartz is Chairman of the Board and Chief Executive Officer of Loral Space Communications Ltd.

BERNARD L. SCHWARTZ

Career highlights: Chairman of the Board and Chief Executive Officer of Loral Space & Communications Ltd., a global, high-technology company headquartered in New York City. The company, created in 1996, is today one of the world's largest manufacturers of commercial satellites. It is also a leader in satellite-based services. Prior to 1996, he served for twenty-four years as Chairman of Loral Corporation, directing the company through a successful strategy of acquisition and internal development.

Over the years, he has gained significant recognition for his views and counsel on matters ranging from economic growth and industrial policy to technology and national security, which he has provided through speeches, white papers, and testimony to private research institutions, educators, and congressional committees.

Civic activity and philanthropy: He has supported a wide range of programs in medicine, education and the arts. In 2000, he established the Bernard Schwartz Chair in Political Economy at the Paul H. Nitze School of Advanced International Studies (SAIS) at Johns Hopkins University, where he serves as a member of the Advisory Council. In 1997, he established a distinguished chair in urologic oncology within the School of Medicine at Johns Hopkins.

Also in 1997, he founded the Bernard L. Schwartz Communication Institute at Baruch College. He is also a Trustee of the Baruch College Fund. At City College of New York, he established a scholarship fund program in microelectronics. He serves as a trustee of Mount Sinai–NYU Medical Center and Health System, and in 1985 funded the establishment of a structural biology program at this institute. Since 1986, he has supported a humanistic medicine program at Mount Sinai–NYU established in his name.

Recently he launched the Bernard L. Schwartz Distinguished Speakers Series and the Bernard L. Schwartz Friday Night at the Movies Film Series for the New York Historical Society. He serves as Vice Chairman of the New York Film Society and is a trustee of Thirteen/WNET Educational Broadcasting Corporation. He is also a trustee of the Democratic Leadership Council and Chair of the Board of Advisors of Blueprint, a journal of policy and politics that examines the key issues facing the nation.

Awards: He is a recipient of many awards, including the 1999 Baruch College Distinguished Alumnus Tribute Award, 1995 Man of the Year award of the Weitzmann Institute of Science, the Townsend Harris Medal for civic achievement, the Stephen S. Wise leadership award, "Man of the Year" by the America-Israel Chamber of Commerce and Industry, the American Defense Preparedness Association's industry leadership award, and the Eisenhower Award from Business Executives for National Security.

Education and Family: Bernard Schwartz graduated from City College of New York with a B.S. degree in finance. He received an honorary Doctorate of Science from City College of New York. He and his wife live in New York City and have two daughters, three granddaughters, and one grandson.

PICTURE CREDITS: *Then:* c. 1945. *Now:* c. 1990's (Both, author)

A lifetime in pursuit of equity through actions. The rise of Asian-American activism

4. Sarah Lawrence College Provides Early NSA Leadership

Gladys Chang Hardy-Brazil
Sarah Lawrence College, New York
Student Body President, 1948-49. NSA Delegate, 1948

It has been written that "Inequality appears at the very center of the major issues of our time."[1] True today, but even more so 55 years ago when college students began to organize and founded the National Student Association. As president of student government at Sarah Lawrence College in 1948-49, I was a delegate to the fledgling NSA's first annual Congress in the fall of 1948, in Madison, Wisconsin. World War II had ended and women's colleges admitted men to meet the needs of men and women veterans applying to college on the G.I. Bill. The 5/26/48 issue of our college newspaper, *The Campus,* reporting on the upcoming graduation ceremony, headlined on page one, "Largest Graduating Class From SLC Includes Six Men."[2] Men were admitted to Sarah Lawrence for the first time during the 1946-47 school year.[3]

Social Justice, civil liberties, civil rights are key issues

It was a time when students returning from war or who had grown up in a world at war were concerned and involved with social issues in the world beyond their campuses. Social justice, civil liberties and civil rights were the key issues, both on and off campus, motivating the dialogue and actions of student leaders across the nation and at the NSA Congress.[4]

The environment of the nation was poisoned by witch hunts of the House Un-American Activities Committee and later Senator McCarthy,[5] by discriminatory practices in college admissions prior to the Civil Rights Act of 1966, and by the injustice of the internment of Japanese-Americans during the war.[6]

At the founding convention NSA moved to eliminate racial segregation in all colleges, and the student bill of rights defined the conception of academic freedom for students and faculty at a time when some were under attack by Washington for their views.[7]

Sarah Lawrence sponsors Conference on Discrimination in Education, supports desegregation case

The student government of Sarah Lawrence College, with the help of a grant from NSA and in cooperation with the New York State Committee for Equality in Education held a conference on February 8, 1948 for NSA delegates from colleges in the region to push an anti-discrimination bill before the NY State legislature.

Going back to issues of *The Campus* of that period provided by the editors of the Anthology, I am reminded of how intensely we followed the issues of discrimination and segregation. At the time a celebrated case (Heman Sweatt, a Negro, was denied admission to the University of Texas Law School) was on the way to the Supreme Court. In the 12/10/47 issue, *The Campus* reports under a banner headline, "In a meeting of the entire student body here at Sarah Lawrence, the group declared itself in favor of supporting Heman Marion Sweatt . . . by a 201-11 vote, 30 abstaining." An educational program to help stimulate national support was proposed and *The Campus* was asked to act as a medium for publishing information to be sent out to colleges and universities throughout the country to accomplish this end.

In the same issue there is a lengthy front-page article by Robin Roberts, who was reporting the NSA stand on discrimination. Discussing the compromises that were made in order to retain a white Southern college membership, she concludes, "groups such as our Sarah Lawrence student body can demonstrate its principles on a more militant basis until the NSA is strong enough to exert a positive presence on our American education system" (see p. 861). I knew Robin well. She was an active leader on campus in support of civil rights and civil liberties causes, as well as a leader in the Metropolitan New York region at the time, strongly advocating for affiliation with the International Union of Students.

NSA's break with the IUS is opposed

Not always in agreement with NSA leaders, Sarah Lawrence College was in the minority in voting against breaking off negotiations for affiliation with the International Union of Students, the largest and only international student organization, in the belief that NSA participation in IUS would result in their members developing a better understanding of the U.S.[8] The NSA chose not to affiliate with IUS because it was viewed as too strongly influenced by the communist countries of Eastern Europe. It broke off negotiations in the spring of 1948 after the Communist coup in Czechoslovakia. How time changes relationships.

The Campus in its 12/15/48 issue reported adoption of a resolution by a vote of 171-11, 20 abstaining, at an All-Student meeting which directed that a letter be sent to NSA which explained its position, stating "171 students at Sarah Lawrence College urge the NSA to work for immediate affiliation with IUS [and to select] a delegation to the IUS who are vitally interested in international cooperation and will be willing to work continuously, despite discouragements, to achieve these ends."

On January 26, 1949, *The Campus* published a letter from Robert L. West, NSA International Affairs Vice President, addressed to me as student body president, in which he explained the NSA position as confirmed in a resolution of its National Executive Committee that December.

The Sarah Lawrence interest in international contact was expressed early on, my copies of *The Campus* reveal. Rita Judd, another campus NSA leader elected to the Regional organizing committee after the Chicago Student Conference, is quoted in the 2/12/47 issue as saying, "I would like to see more emphasis on the close affiliation of the N.S.O. with an international student organization."

College faculty and peers provide inspiration

The student body at Sarah Lawrence benefited from President Harold Taylor's active support and involvement with NSA. He was elected at the second annual Congress to the Advisory Council. As president of student government I was fortunate to have his interest in our delegation's role in NSA's development.[9] I was further blessed by having as my Don (faculty advisor) and mentor Professor Helen Merrell Lynd, whose friendship and counsel shaped my life. Then a peer mentor, Dr. Jean Baker Miller, founder and director of the Jean Baker Miller Training Institute in Wellesley, MA, and author of "Toward a New Psychology of Women" was two classes ahead of me. Her encouragement for me to be involved in student government and her editorial in the 4/16/47 issue of *The Campus* pointing out the necessity of a student grassroots movement for the emerging NSA for it to be effective, helped make our role as delegates purposeful, a year later.

Echoes and lessons of the past in today's events

The environment today echoes some of the issues and events of half a century ago. Government actions and proposed regulations following the tragedy of September 11, 2001, resulting in the "war" on terrorism, has led to the curtailment of civil liberties for some individuals; questions and concerns about erosion of constitutional rights; views that expressions of dissent are unpatriotic; and increased racial profiling not only of people who look Middle Eastern, but other people of color.

Thinking back to my student days, I am encouraged by the awakening of activism among the young, following the decades of the "silent generation," the "me" and "x" generations. Yet also in those decades past, I recall the involvement of students in the civil rights movement, the Freedom Schools, the Vietnam protest, and campus unrest with African-American student demands for equity and attention to their needs. Again, today I sense and can taste the emerging activism of students across the country on social and public policy issues.

In the summer of 1998, the United Students Against Sweatshops was founded. Nationwide protests have been held on more than 100 campuses demanding that their institutions stop colluding with corporate interests to the detriment of workers' health and rights here and abroad. Chapters of USAS have been insisting that their colleges hold corporations which supply university-licensed apparel to higher labor and social standards. These protests have been joined by some labor and religious organizations.

Perhaps the most dramatic example of student activism is the anti-globalization movement, begun in November 1999 in Seattle, then in Quebec and Genoa, Italy, in the spring and summer of 2001, with students and workers from many different countries, demonstrating for economic democracy and income equity, social justice, educational opportunity, health and human rights. More recently, the Hip Hop generation of young people spoke out and sang protests against the dearth of funding in urban schools, as for example the demonstration in front of City Hall in New York City by a coalition including the Hip Hop Action Network. This generation of students is exhibiting once again social consciousness and activism for social change and in the idealism of youth, hopefully will pursue their activist dreams with integrity.

Rise of Asian-American activism

A few days before the August 2002 recess of Congress, I received a call from the Asian-American Education and Legal Defense Fund asking me to telephone Senator Dodd regarding the pending legislation on electoral reform. Certain requirements in the proposed legislation could deter new immigrant citizens from registering to vote or voting and are discriminatory towards limited English speaking citizens. I was pleased with this request to call my Senator, not only for the significance of the issue, but it reflected an important change in the attitude and political involvement of Asian-Americans for their welfare and role in our multiracial society.

When I entered college more than fifty years ago, Chinese-American students I knew in colleges throughout the northeast tended to eschew political activism and more often than not were unlikely to be involved in campus extracurricular activities. "Cultural reluctance" to be involved in social and political issues was the description to explain this insular behavior. Most Asian-Americans seemed to avoid politics as an activity because they felt it might affect them negatively due to perceived prejudice and sense of inequality in mainstream America.

A tragic event twenty years ago changed the Asian-American community's apathy. On June 19, Vincent Chin, a Chinese American, was beaten to death by two autoworkers in Detroit. The ensuing outrage led to widespread protests and to a broadening of laws and attitudes regarding civil rights and hate crimes. The Asian-American political movement begun on campuses in the 1960's expanded into a grass roots movement, sparked by this heinous crime. The founding of the American Citizens for Justice, a response to the Chin killing, is another example of Asian-American activism.

Like African Americans and Latinos, Asian-Americans are recognizing the imperative of political action to achieve equality of resources.

NSA fostered collective action for social change

Fifty years ago, the excitement of common purpose and goals in the formation of the National Student Association influenced the lives of many of its participants. We learned the value and benefits of collective political action, if we were to effect social change.

I left China at the age of twelve in 1940, with my mother and five siblings, because of the Sino-Japanese War. We went first to Honolulu, Hawaii; then, after the attack on Pearl Harbor, we moved to Southern California. My father, an official in the government, remained in China. I had planned to return to China after completing my education, to participate in rebuilding the country after the devastation of a decade of war.

With the change of government in 1949 in China, it became impossible for me, as an American citizen, to pursue my plans for public service there. (I returned there after 39 years, in 1979, as a part of Secretary Joseph Califano's Department of Health, Education and Welfare ["HEW"] delegation, representing "E", to the Peoples Republic of China, shortly after President Carter recognized the PRC and established diplomatic relations).

Early influences of parents, teachers and college mates led me to a professional life of fifty years in education and broadcasting as an executive in Federal and State government, private and public universities, commercial and public broadcasting and philanthropic foundations in support of education and the arts.

The guiding principle of my work in these areas has been the pursuit of equity through actions, decisions or funding support for achieving equality of resources in the full meaning of the word "resources," be it in education, health, economic welfare, social justice or political voice and power for minorities and women. Equity of opportunity is inadequate when resources are not available.

While much has been accomplished, much more remains to be done. As noted in an American Assembly report, "Continuing and embedded prejudice prevents the vast majority of people of color from overcoming poverty, receiving fairness in the criminal justice system, attaining equal access to resources, and building political power. It would be premature to declare victory over racism and inequality."[10]

This conclusion can be applied to the rest of the world, reflecting the inequities between north and south, rich and poor. It is the challenge that still faces the students of today, even as it did fifty years ago when we launched the NSA.

Gladys Chang Hardy-Brazil is an education professional who has been a Ford Foundation officer, Presidential appointee as a senior executive in the U.S. Department of Education, Commonwealth of Massachusetts Undersecretary of Education and senior executive and consultant to public and private universities and public broadcasting.

END NOTES

[1] Daniel Singer, *Whose Millennium? Theirs or Ours?* New York: Monthly Review, 1999.

[2] *The Campus* also reported "An important part of the commencement program will be the gavel ceremony. Sally Hillman, 1947-48 president of student council, will formally turn over her duties to her successor, Gladys Chang, 1948-49 student council head. . . . *Editor's note:* Helen Bryan (Garland), later NSA's travel director, preceded Hillman as student body president for 1946-47. See Garland, p. 641.

[3] The 10/9/46 issue of *The Campus,* headlining "Men In College For First Time," reports "When Sarah Lawrence officially opened to its nineteenth year on September 26, resuming a peacetime schedule on a 3-term plan, it was with the largest enrollment in the college's history [a total registration of 344 students]. New were the 36 men veterans, who under the emergency educational program, have been accepted by the college, and who have

taken their place side by side with women in classes, in the dining room, and in group activities."

[4] See Part 2, Sections 2 and 3 on NSA and civil liberties and civil rights.

[5] *Editor's note:* In October, 1951, Sarah Lawrence College was the object of a widely publicized attack by the local American Legion, and a vigorous response by the college, arising out of its appearance in the American Legion magazine on a list of colleges under suspicion of "harboring subversives" on its campus. NSA's president at the time, Bill Dentzer, editorialized on the event as an example of McCarthyism in the March 1952 issue of *NSA News.* It is presented in detail in Part 1 on page 311.

[6] *Editor's note:* See the Tom Suzuki (Los Angeles City College) account of his experience, p. 1031.

[7] See Brown, "Student Rights, Academic Freedom and NSA," pp. 378, 381.

[8] See International Union of Students, p. 538.

[9] See Harold Taylor, p. 888.

[10] Angela Glover Blackwell, Stewart Kwoh, Manuel Pastor, *Searching for the Uncommon Common Ground,* The American Assembly. New York: W.W. Norton, 2002.

GLADYS CHANG HARDY-BRAZIL

Early years. I was born in Shanghai, China, and attended Claremont High School in California, graduating from Girl's Collegiate School.

Education. B.A., Sarah Lawrence College, 1950. Ford Foundation Foreign Area Fellow, 1954-57 (in Southeast Asia).

Career highlights. I am now retired, after a professional career of 50 years. Highlights of my career in education include: restructuring and refocusing the higher education and arts programs of the Ford Foundation in the early 80's, as Director of the Education and Culture Program; Presidential appointee as Deputy Director of the National Institute of Education in the U.S. Department of Education in President Carter's administration, with the opportunity to reorganize the agency and influence the direction of federal research in education from kindergarten through graduate school; in President Johnson's administration, I was Director of Policy, Planning and Analysis and Chief of Staff to the founding Chairman of the National Endowment for the Humanities after the act of Congress establishing NEH (and NEA), in 1966.

In Massachusetts I was appointed in 1970 by Governor Sargent as Undersecretary of Education to the first Cabinet Office for Education in the Commonwealth; then I founded the Public-Private Higher Education Forum for presidents of state and private institutions of higher education; followed by four years as Corporate Secretary of the University of Massachusetts System. Prior to that, having become an expert in long-range academic and institutional planning through grants to private universities and liberal arts colleges during my first stint at the Ford Foundation in the early 60's, I became Director of the Office of Institutional Planning and Research at Boston University. In the last decade and a half of my career I became a free-lance consultant and senior advisor for educational policy and long-range institutional planning to the presidents of Teachers College (Columbia University), The College Board, the Children's Defense Fund and the American Association of University Women (AAUW).

The highlight of my early career in broadcasting was to be a writer and Associate Producer for an Edward R. Murrow radio show. My work in broadcasting, the arts and documentary film productions continued in my subsequent foundation work through grant making, as well as being a member of Boards of Directors of public radio, aesthetic education and public television organizations.

Family: I am married to Percy Brazil, M.D. I have two children, Brian and Kathryn, whose father was the late David Keith Hardy, former professor at Brandeis University, documentary film producer-director and foreign correspondent. I also have 3 grandsons.

PICTURE CREDITS: *Then:* c. 1950. *Now:* c. 2000 (Both, author)

SARAH LAWRENCE (SLC) BROUGHT VIGOROUS ENGAGEMENT TO NSA

THE CAMPUS

VOL. XVIII · No. 5 SARAH LAWRENCE COLLEGE, BRONXVILLE, NEW YORK, WEDNESDAY, DECEMBER 10, 1947 PRICE: TEN CENTS

Sarah Lawrence Aids Sweatt In Test Case

Member Relates Stand Of NSA On Discrimination

By Robin Roberts

WALTER WHITE, NAACP DISCUSSES COVENANTS

Sweatt Case In Council

STUDENTS ASK

12/10/47

One-Half Of U. S. Colleges Aim To Create Effective NSO

Delegates from 330 of the country's colleges and universities, about one-half of the total number, met at the University of Chicago, December 28 to 30, registered strong support ...

... and the drawing up of proposals concerning purpose and make-up of the suggested NSO, representative of the wishes of the delegates and guaranteeing that all would maintain support.

However, after prolonged debate over procedure of the Conference itself, and particularly on the matters of allowing national student organizations (such as USSA, Newman Clubs, AYD) to have representation on the NCC, and of retaining panel resolutions recommending active opposition to race discrimination in all phases of student life, the Conference in a tense final session, overcame the last

(Continued on Page Three)

1/15/47

Student Council Supports NSA Move For Student Ships

By Rita Judd

Last Tuesday Student Council voted unanimously to take action on a suggestion sent to all member colleges by the NSA National Office in regard to the continuation of the student ship project of last summer.

Before the Maritime Commission can allot the ships for student use, two ...

copy of a radio broadcast made by two members of the minority group within the American Delegation to the Festival. It was strongly felt that publicity of a viewpoint that was held by eight people out of a delegation of two hundred ...

1/21/48

Council To Hold NSA Conference

The Student Council, in cooperation with the New York State Committee for Equality in Education, is holding a conference February 8 on the subject of discrimination in education as it relates to a bill to be proposed to the New York State legislature. The conference was called ...

1/28/48

Sarah Lawrence Approves Motion Urging NSA's Participation In IUS Activities

Recommends Further Student Effort For World Cooperation

By Ann Roller

Sarah Lawrence students voted in favor of a motion supporting affiliation of the NSA with the IUS at the All-Student meeting December 7. This decision was reached by the group after a discussion of the merits of the action.

... duct. One student was shot in the leg. The IUS did not take any action: it was due to this lack of action that Jim Smith resigned.

However, it was pointed out that as the IUS had not given its sanction to the demonstration it may have been justified in not defending the students.

U. S. Understanding Needed

12/15/48

"BECAUSE WE HAVE MUCH TO GAIN from experience with other students throughout the country," Babette de Bary, Editor-in-Chief, wrote in the 1/15/47 *Campus,* "because we in this college have a great deal to contribute, and because NSO can be a potent, valuable organ of and support for student democracy, surely we will . . . continue to take part creatively in the building of the National Student Organization." SLC was particularly engaged in NSA's international and civil rights programs, strongly supported maintaining relations with the IUS (see Part 3, Sec 2) and raised money for and sponsored anti-discrimination programs. (Re "Sweatt" case above, See p. 420 and p. 973).

ROBIN ROBERTS: ardent AYD champion, "a progressive, left wing organization which welcomes anyone willing to fight for its program," she wrote (4/10/46 *Campus*); also a gifted folk singer who attained wide notice in the late forties. As SLC rep to "Madison 1" and the Met NY region she lent her talents to energetic NSA program and organization building (e.g. providing "feature billing" at Yale's 5/7/48 NSA Jamboree) (*Yale News*).

HAROLD TAYLOR, SLC President, greets some of the 36 first time ever '46-'47 male students (out of its 19th year record 344 enrollment), "emergency program" veterans, at registration. Taylor (see profile, p. 888), installed in 1945, became a national spokesman in defense of academic freedom, a champion for NSA, and member of its National Advisory Committee.

EARLY SLC NSA LEADERS

HELEN BRYAN (left): 1946-47 Student Body President, attended Chicago Student Conference; was 1947-1950 NSA national travel director (see p. 641). **BABETTE de BARRY:** 1946 Campus editor, SLC rep. to Chicago Student Conference. **RITA JUDD:** 1947 Met NY regional del. **GLADYS CHANG:** 1948-49 Student Body President, 1948 National Student Congress del. (p. 854). (Photos: Bryan, deBarry, Judd, *The Campus*; Chang, *Milwaukee Journal*).

Photo sources: Roberts - Yearbook, SLC Archives; Chang-self; Others - *The Campus*

The truth will make you free.

Mother Eleanor M. O'Byrne: In Pursuit of Truth

President, Manhattanville College of the Sacred Heart
Member, NSA National Advisory Committee, 1954-57

Editor's note: Manhattanville College was founded by the Religious of the Sacred Heart in 1841 in New York City as a Catholic boarding school for girls. From 1847 to 1952 (when it moved to Purchase, NY in Westchester County) it was located between 130th and 135th streets on Convent Avenue in Manhattan, just south of the CCNY campus, which had located there in 1907.(It became co-educational in 1969, and non-denominational in its governance in 1971.) Mother O'Byrne strongly supported student government and Manhattanville's membership in NSA, and provided a ground-floor office for the Met NY Region in one of the dormitories. At the time word was that she was being discussed in Catholic circles as the "Catholic Eleanor Roosevelt."

"The Truth Will Make You Free"

Editor's note: As a spiritual leader and educator, Mother O'Byrne's task was to effectively link the latter to the former. The following is from The Centurion *reporting on her opening address to the college on 9/22/48:*

"Continue My word . . . And you shall know the truth and the truth will make you free" (John 7:31-31). . . . Steady work and disciplined enthusiasm in the quest of truth will lead to the attainment of "the perfect law of liberty," and make each Manhattanville student a "doer of the work" (James 1:25). . . .There will be a blending of many cultures, a challenging variety of defended and defensible opinions, a respect of valid differences in outlook." Also at Manhattanville the student has the opportunity to learn and study the democratic process, both in theory and practice, and to prepare herself for "fully responsible citizenship" grounded on Christian Brotherhood.

enturion

COLLEGE OF THE SACRED HEART OF NEW YORK

Manhattanville Opens Sept. 22nd With Chapel Mass; Mother O'Byrne's Address Stresses Truth, Freedom

Liberating the Liberal Arts Student

Editor's note: These are brief excerpts from a 2,500-word paper presented at the annual meeting of the Association of American Colleges, Hotel Statler, Washington, D.C., on January 12, 1955 by Mother O'Byrne.

Each September we stand in reception rooms of administration buildings, or mount rostra in auditoriums to welcome the Freshmen. These promising, personable young people are grateful to the devoted teachers in the secondary schools who have instructed them. . . . We and our faculty realize our goodly heritage and set out seriously and joyously to help these newcomers proceed prosperously in the course of liberal education on which we have just launched them.

They will sail charted and uncharted seas, make trial-runs and know the pleasures and perils of shake-down cruises. They and we hope that there will be other formal ceremonies four years from now, in which the successful "mariners" will be launched as masters on life's high seas. They and we have challenges to meet, if this second happy ceremony is to take place: they to broaden and deepen their knowledge and culture, to fashion themselves to the pattern of Aristotle's Magnanimous Man (who then and now can be identified as the liberal arts graduate), we to foster this growth in knowledge and this personal development. The two go hand in hand.

* * *

But, one wonders if we lag somewhat in fostering personal development. The truly Magnanimous Man is no mere academician. He is a well-rounded person (and "he" also signifies "she" for those who work with women). To the degree in which he is integrated, he lives the good life, the full life of knowing and giving.

* * *

There is a science of man: psychology. Let it be taught adequately and completely on our campuses. There is a science of God. Let theology have its place with other subjects, and be presented in competent and scholarly courses. One knows that there are organizational problems included in such a proposal. But men of good will and intelligence can find a way to give today's students the preparation for life which will make their knowledge fruitful and will transform them into Magnanimous Men.

ELEANOR M. O'BYRNE, R.S.C.J.

September 17, 1896-October 4, 1987

Early years: Born to Michael A. and Marie McDonough O'Byrne in Savannah, GA, she joined the Society of the Sacred Heart in 1916 and took her final vows in 1924.

Education: Received her BA degree in History from the Academy of the Sacred Heart at Manhattanville, New York City, in 1921—one of the first undergraduate degrees granted by the college. Earned a Master's Degree from Fordham; later earned a BA and MA from Oxford University.

Lifetime highlights: Returned to Manhattanville in 1933 as Associate Professor of History and Warden of Freshmen, and later became Dean and Professor of History, then President in 1945. She served as President of Manhattanville College until 1966, presiding over the move to Purchase in Westchester County in 1952. She was President of Sacred Heart College in Santurce, Puerto Rico, from 1967 until 1970. Sister O'Byrne spent her final years at the Kenwood Convent of the Sacred Heart in Albany.

This biography and other documentation courtesy Claire Gabriel, Special Collections Librarian, Manhattanville College.

PICTURE SOURCE: c. 1950s (Photo by Veronica. Manhattanville College)

A close relationship between faculty and students: an important element for effective education

Millicent Cary McIntosh: Staunch Advocate for Women's Education

Dean of Students, 1942-52, and President, 1952-62, Barnard College, New York
Member, NSA National Advisory Committee, 1949-50

Editor's note: Dean McIntosh's installation address on October 24, 1947, succeeding Dean Virginia Gildersleeve, was reported in the Barnard Bulletin *on 10/27/47. She was introduced by Frank D. Fackenthal, acting President of Columbia, who inducted her into office (Fackenthal served from October 1, 1945, when Nicholas Murray Butler retired, until Dwight D. Eisenhower was installed on October 12, 1948). The paper reported that "the new dean criticized women for not having made effectual use of their position in this world of conflict." The excerpts below are from the* Bulletin*:*

A Curriculum for Women's Colleges

"In their married life, women, along with men, seem to be overwhelmed by complexities, which too often end in the divorce court or the psychiatrist's office. As mothers, they are too often failures, having reared a generation which is producing its own new set of problems, for the solution of which authority is lacking, in the home, or church, or in educational institutions."

In suggesting certain general principles regarding curriculum for women's colleges to follow in the years ahead, Mrs. McIntosh included: Opportunity for gifted individuals to specialize, an education which will provide the tools of learning, a synthesis of knowledge along the lines of of the student's own interests and proper vocational guidance.

MILLICENT CARY McINTOSH

November 3, 1898- January 3, 2001

Millicent C. McIntosh, Barnard College's fourth Dean and its first President, was a vital force in women's education in the United States for over 40 years.

A staunch advocate of liberal arts education for women, her appointment as Dean in 1947 was a ground-breaking event in the history of women's colleges. Up to that time, none of the Seven Sisters had selected a married woman to head a college, and no women's college in the nation at that time had a mother for its leader. Mrs. McIntosh's experience validated her strongly held belief that women could successfully combine marriage and career. She had raised five children and had for 17 years been head of the Brearley School, an independent all-girls school in New York City. (Up until 1952, . . . dean was the highest office at Barnard College.)

During her five years as dean and the subsequent ten years as president, Barnard flourished in large part because of Mrs. McIntosh's innovations. . . . She had extraordinary energy, a trait that was captured by a *Christian Science Monitor* reporter who wrote: "Excepting Mrs. Franklin D. Roosevelt, there is probably not a busier American woman than Mrs. McIntosh."

The daughter of two Quaker ministers, she was born in Baltimore in 1898 and received a bachelor's degree from Byrn Mawr College and a Ph.D. in English from Columbia University. In recognition of her outstanding work in education during her long career, Mrs. McIntosh was awarded honorary degrees from 11 colleges and universities, including Princeton, Johns Hopkins, Mount Holyoke, Smith, and NYU. She appeared on the cover of *Newsweek* magazine in 1952.

Mrs. McIntosh was married to Dr. Rustin McIntosh, head of Babies Hospital at Columbia Presbyterian Hospital.

Excerpted from a 6/10/97 tribute by Herb Katz provided by the Barnard Archives.

Remembering Mrs. McIntosh

I knew Millicent McIntosh from 1938, the year I began my education at Brearly, until 1952, the year I was graduated from Barnard. . . . McIntosh was certainly the most remarkable—not character but flesh and blood woman—I have ever met, and I'm surprised no one has written her biography. Like a book that trims your sails if you're lucky enough to read it at the right moment, McIntosh did for me what my parents, worried that I was not quite up to snuff, could not. She gave me—and I'm sure countless others—the courage to use my head.

-- *Quoted from a tribute by novelist Ann Bernays in* The Chronicle of Higher Education, *2/9/2001.*

SOURCE: Bio, documents, photo (c. 1947), Barnard College Archives.

The Hunter Arrow, 3/24/49

'Student Govt.' Topic of First NYNSA Forum

The first Student Government Forum of the Metropolitan region of the U. S. National Student Association will be held at Adelphi College, Garden City, N. Y., on Sunday, April 3. Dean Millicent C. McIntosh of Barnard College will be the main speaker.

Barnard Bulletin, 10/27/47

Assume Responsibility

Deplores Lack of Interest in Education; Urges Barnard to Meet Teaching Need

Mrs. Millicent Carey McIntosh was formally installed as Dean of Barnard at a ceremony in the gymnasium of Barnard Hall at 2:30 P.M. Friday, October 24. Mrs. Ogden Reid, Vice-Chairman of the Barnard Board of Trustees presented Mrs. McIntosh to Acting President of Columbia, Frank D. Fackenthal, who inducted her into office.

In the address following the installation the new Dean criticized women for not having made effectual use of their position in this world of conflict. "Politically most women have not taken adequate responsibility," she said. "Nationally and internationally women have been ineffectual, except in the case of rare individuals like Virginia Gildersleeve, and of rare organizations like the League of Women Voters.

"In their married life, women, along with men, seem to be overwhelmed by complexities, which too often end in the divorce court or the psychiatrist's office. As mothers, they are too often fail-

"MORE THAN 200 STUDENTS from 30 colleges" attended NSA's Met. NY 4/3/49 student government forum at which Dean McIntosh declared that "a close relationship between the faculty and the students in a college is one of the most important elements in making education effective." (As reported in *NSA News* 5/49).

Our main problem is promoting wider participation in extracurricular activities.

Harry J. Carman: Advocate of Inspired Teaching

Dean, Columbia College
Chairman, National Scholarship Service and Fund for Negro Students

Editor's note: Harry Carman started farming and teaching when he was a boy, and never stopped doing either. He was an uncommon educator and administrator who was widely admired and loved by students. As Chairman of the NSA-supported National Scholarship Service and Fund for Negro Students, he lent active support to early efforts to roll back de facto segregation in the North (aee NSSFNS, p. 463).

The College: A Liberative Institution

Excerpted from "Reminiscences of Thirty Years," by Harry J. Carman, Journal of Higher Education, *March, 1951.*

When the author of this article went to Columbia in the fall of 1917, we were in the midst of the First World War. . . . At the close of the war a small group of young men from the philosophy and social-science departments asked themselves if the time was not overdue for the College to define its objectives in terms of students' needs and to devise better curricular machinery than we then had for realizing these objectives. . . .We came to the conclusion the college should be a liberative institution in the sense that it frees the mind from ignorance, fear, prejudice, and superstition and enables one to search for and contemplate truth. The college, we agreed, should be concerned with education for effective citizenship in a democratic society: citizens with broad perspective and a critical and constructive approach to life, who are concerned about values in terms of integrity of character, motives, attitudes, excellence of behavior; citizens who have the ability to think, to communicate, to make intelligent and wise judgments, to evaluate moral situations, and to work effectively to good ends with others. Columbia College, we further insisted, should provide well-balanced education for its students, thus enabling them not only to develop a philosophy of life, but also an educational foundation for whatever career or vocation each might enter upon. . . . We then asked ourselves whether the existing curriculum with its multiplicity of often unrelated departmental courses was adequate for the realization of these purposes. We decided unanimously that it was entirely unsuited. . . .

HARRY J. CARMAN

(January 22, 1884-December 26, 1964)

Born January 22, 1884, in Greenfield, N.Y., Carman was educated there in a one-room school. He taught in rural schoolhouses of New York before graduation from Syracuse University 1909, and later served as a principal of a high school in Rhinebeck, N.Y. He lectured in political science at Syracuse. Carman taught at all levels, from grade to graduate school, and in addition was a member of the Board of Higher Education of the City of New York and a trustee of six colleges.

He joined Columbia as instructor of history in 1918, reaching the rank of full professor in 1931. In 1939 he was named to the Moore Chair in American History; four years later he was appointed Dean of Columbia College. He retired in 1950 and became Dean Emeritus.

The *Spectator* in a 4/22/49 editorial cited Carman as "a man of uncommon stature. In a way he has been more than the official head of Columbia College; he has embodied its spirit."

Among Dr. Carman's works are the standard biography of *Jesse Buel, Agricultural Reformer,* a two-volume *History of the American People,* a book on Abraham Lincoln, and many articles in historical and scholarly journals.

He was awarded the Medal of the City of New York and received numerous honors in the U.S. and abroad. Carman's first wife died in 1943, and he remarried in 1953.

Compiled from a 4/25/55 Trinity College (CT) release, a New York Times *12/27/64 obituary, and the* Columbia Spectator.

SOURCES: Syracuse University Archives, Columbia University Archives and Columbiana Library. Photo: 12/12/48 *Columbia Spectator.* Portrait by Lester Merton Chase, Jr., '50, presented to Carman by the editors of the Columbian. Title quotation from 9/19/47 letter by Carman to Frank D. Fackenthal, President of Columbia University.

LIFE CYCLE OF A NATURAL BORN TEACHER

FOUNDED 1877

NEW YORK, WEDNESDAY, APRIL 21, 1937.

As We Don't See Them

HARRY J. CARMAN

Who Taught Farmers' Sons and Daughters in a One Room School Before Going to College

By JAMES J. KENNEDY

DAY, APRIL 19, 1949 — 5 Cents

Trustees Pass Retirement Plan; Dean Carman to Relinquish Pos

DEAN CARMAN

Automatic Retirement Ruling Will Affe

Preserve World Peace With Interfaith Movement: Carman

VOL. XCV.

Former Dean Carman Gets Hamilton Award

Retire Trustees Too!

The announcement that Harry J. Carman must retire from his post as Dean of Columbia College in June 1950 raises some mixed feelings in us. Obviously, the new regulation is aimed at injecting new blood into the administrative and academic staffs with the assumption that such acton will give incentive to the younger men whose talents might otherwise be lost.

The rules strikes us as being too ironclad. If the retirement age was established to bring in new blood just for the sake of new blood, the invaluable assets of such men as Dean Carman, Professor Zanetti, Dr. Pegram, Dean Finch, and the many other valuable leaders of Columbia who have reached the retirement age will be wasted.

FORCED TO RETIRE as Dean when Trustees in 1949 adopted automatic retirement ages, Carman returned to his role as a popular history teacher; his retirement also triggered a 4/19/49 *Spectator* editorial wondering if the rules were too "ironclad"; if it was "just to bring in new blood just for the sake of new blood, the invaluable assets of . . . the many other valuable leaders of Columbia who have reached the retirement age will be wasted." Reporting on Carman's Hamilton Award on 2/13/51, he was cited as "an especially ardent advocate of inspired teaching."

(From the top: *Columbia Spectator* 4/21/37, 4/19/49, 2/8/51, 2/13/51, 4/19/49)

NSA at Columbia/Barnard and at Fordham

Editor's note: Following the pattern of many universities, both Columbia and Fordham after the war presented to their student bodies proposals to create formal university-wide student councils which would include the various schools and class organizations that made up the campus. The simultaneous emergence of NSA provided an information source as well as moral support to the student leaders advancing the vision of student government. An ironic outcome at Columbia was the disaffiliation by the broad-based CUSC, leading both the Columbia College and Barnard College councils to re-affilliate separately. See index for more on Columbia and for more on Fordham.

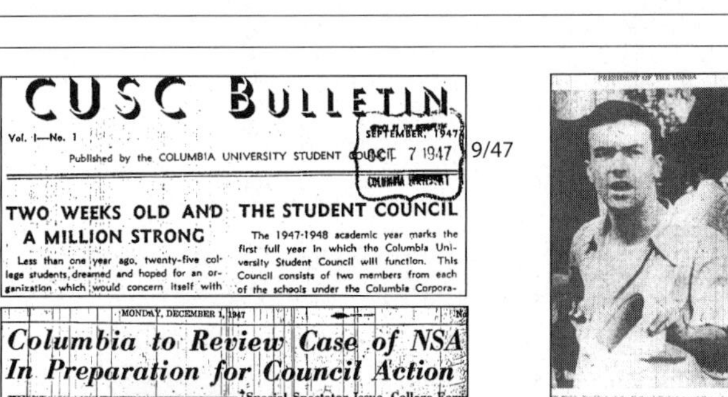

CUSC BULLETIN

Vol. I—No. 1 Published by the COLUMBIA UNIVERSITY STUDENT COUNCIL

TWO WEEKS OLD AND A MILLION STRONG

THE STUDENT COUNCIL

The 1947-1948 academic year marks the first full year in which the Columbia University Student Council will function. This Council consists of two members from each of the schools under the Columbia Corpora-

9/47

MONDAY, DECEMBER 1, 1947

Columbia to Review Case of NSA In Preparation for Council Action

Special Spectator Issue, College Forum To Highlight USNSA Information Week

NSA History Reveals Work

12/1/47

THE NEW NSA and its President, Bill Welsh, are welcomed.

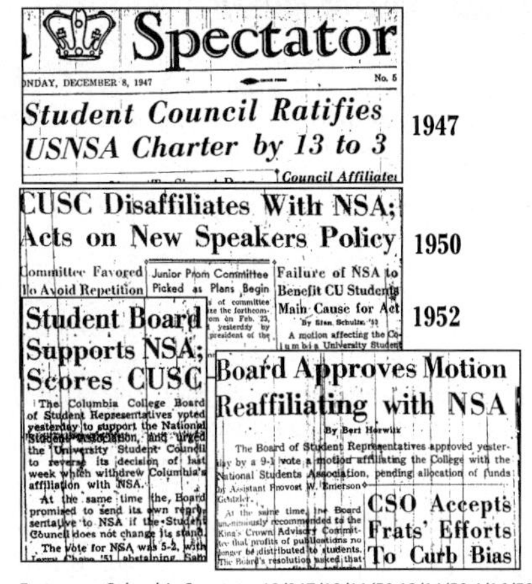

Spectator

MONDAY, DECEMBER 8, 1947

Student Council Ratifies USNSA Charter by 13 to 3

1947

CUSC Disaffiliates With NSA; Acts on New Speakers Policy

1950

Student Board Supports NSA; Scores CUSC

1952

Board Approves Motion Reaffiliating with NSA

CSO Accepts Frats' Efforts To Curb Bias

From top: *Columbia Spectator* 12/847/12/11/50,12/14/50,4/16/52

INDEPENDENT STUDENT BODY JURISDICTIONS at first enabled all of the University schools to combine into one delegation in 1947 through the new university-wide Student Council (CUSC). When CUSC decided to disaffiliate in 12/50 after CUSC Chairman Charles Lazarus "bitterly and furiously denounced the NSA," Barnard on 2/8/51 and Columbia College on 4/16/52 re-affiliated independently (see editorials from *Spectator* and *Barnard Bulletin* on next page).

Barnard Bulletin

National Student Association Fosters Campus Activities, Foreign Study Plans, Guards Rights

College Plans Special Implementation Committee

Women's Colleges Hold Conference

Barnard Plans Activities To Further Aims of NSA

Barnard Affiliates with NSA By Rep Assembly Decision

1951

LOIS BOOCHEVER AND MARGARET MATHER (left) reported on the 1947 Constitutional Convention (Above left, *Barnard Bulletin* 10/30/47). After the CUSC disaffiliated (See above), Barnard affiliated on its own (*Bulletin* 2/8/51).

Walter Wallace: Regional Founder

A KEY FIGURE AT THE FOUNDING EVENTS. From top: Wallace on left, leaving for the World Student Congress (*Daily Mirror* 7/10/46. See p. 94); At 12/46 Chicago St. Conf., from l. Ralph Dungan (St. Joseph), John Yewell (Rutgers), unknown, Jack Minkoff (Cornell), Wallace (See p.118); With Columbia delegation to Constitutional Convention, from l. Michael Kaplan, Meg Mather (Barnard), Russell Dunbar (Law), Wallace, William Hochman (Grad. Faculty (*Lion Ledger*, 2/48); At 1947 Const. Conv. at U. of Wisc, from left: John Simon (Fordham), Jim Smith (U. Texas), Bill Welsh (Berea), Alan Aaronson (CCNY), Wallace, Dungan, Gene Schwartz (CCNY).

Delegates to Chicago Set For Duties

Smith Tells Spec His Mind Is Open; Wallace Is on Speaking Trip

Chicago Conference Decides on New National Student Association

Wallace Plays Big Role At Chicago Convention

Walter Wallace and Stan Smith, Prague, Czechoslovakia, last sum

FRIDAY, MAY 9, 1947

Wallace, Mascott, Foster Victors in All-College Race; 1300 Votes Cast

PROMINENT 1946-47 CAMPUS LEADER. From top (All *Columbia Spectator*): Wallace, after his return from Prague in September, on a speaking tour in North Carolina before leaving for Chicago (12/18/46); "Overwhelmingly elected Chairman" of the Met. NY Region, he played an important role on the convention floor" (both 1/7/47); elected to the Student Board (5/9/47).

STUDENTS ADOPT SUPPORT OF NSO AT RECENT MEET

By Skippy Katz

Wallace To Speak At SPA Meeting On Student Union

Walter Wallace, Regional NSO Head, At Town Meeting Tomorrow At 4

N. ELMENDORF

SPEAKING FOR THE NEW "NSO" TO COLLEGES ACROSS THE REGION. From above left: Sarah Lawrence College (SLC) (*The Campus* 1/9/47); NYU (*Washington Square Bulletin*, 2/7/47); Barnard (*Barnard Bulletin* 3/24/47). Wallace evoked interest by citing the origins of International Students Day. "The National Student Organization began wherever there were progressive students, but really in Prague in 1939," he told the SLC students, when the Gestapo raided student dormitories and shot 150 students (See p. 580). Several international conferences later, "Fifteen American student groups worked well together" at the 1946 World Student Congress and arranged to hold the Chicago Student Conference at which the NSO was proposed (See also Berlin, p. 6 for more on origins).

Jay Maryanov: Working to Make It Work

APPLYING THE STUDENT BILL OF RIGHTS

Digest from a report (c. May, 1948) by Gerald S. Maryanov, Chairman, Columbia Delegation, to the Met NY Region, on a widely headlined "Student Bill of Rights infraction," in which he took pride in students and administration for the manner in which the situation was resolved," resulting in the change of a University regulation.

On December 12, 1947, the Columbia University chapter of the Progressive Citizens of America scheduled a meeting at which Howard Fast, noted novelist, was to speak. He was barred from doing so on the grounds "that no person who is under sentence may be accorded the privilege of University faciltities." A campus-wide Academic Freedom committee was formed; the Student Council requested reconsideration on the grounds that denial of access "for the purpose of exercising the right of free speech cannot be justified." The Student Council was granted representation on a university committee to study the matter and a new policy adopted requiring consultation with the Council. Howard Fast spoke on the Columbia campus on April 16, 1948.

(*Photos.* from top: Schwartz, SHSW, Dee West)

From top: Maryanov (c) at 4/48 NEC meeting with Fred Houghteling (NNER) and Ben Labaree (SNER); right, with Tom Garrity, MNY Regl. Pres., and Gene Schwartz, Natl V.P.; In Paris 8/50 (r) with Bob Smith, 47-48 Int'l. V.P., and Erskine Childers, 49-50 Int'l. V.P.

Spectator

Local NSA Elects Columbia Students

NSA to Institute Purchase Cards

Schools Will Name All CUSC Proxies

NSA Chairman Hits Olivet College Student, Prof Ouster

Benitez, Puerto Rico University Prexy, Discusses Education

World Students Day Will Be Observed on Campus Friday

MANAGING NSA'S PRESENCE AT COLUMBIA in 1948-49, from top (all *Columbia Spectator*): Maryanov and Vera Hurst (Grad. Faculty) elected Regional Vice Pres. and Sec'y. (9/30/48); supporting a Michigan Region protest over expulsion of Olivet students (See p. 389) (10/14/48); Student Council authorizes NSA Purchase Card Plan (See p. 366) (11/22/48); Noon assembly celebrating International Students Day (11/16/48).

Fordham OK's NSA's and Its Own Charters

RAM

S CONVENTION

Disputed Council Balloting Slows Constitution Passage

Gaels to Hold Leprechaun Ball In Dealy Nov. 21

Michael DiLegge

THE RAM

Students Ratify New Constitution

Debaters Win 5th Straight

Council Approves Set Of Election By-Laws

RAM

Council O.K.'s NSA Constitution

Gallagher's Backing Results in Support For Student Group

MICHAEL DiLEGGE, WARREN GALLAGHER, AND THOMAS GASSERT, NSA delegates, argued that NSA was representative and that Catholic students can take up points where NSA presents the "wrong ideas." The oppposition claimed it was "little known and little supported" and "denies authority" (*Ram* 3/12/48). DiLegge also chaired the campus Convention at which Fordham's new Student Council charter was adopted after "fierce" debate, and then ratified by student referendum (*Ram* 11/11/48, 3/24/49).

The Met. NY Region Keeps in Touch

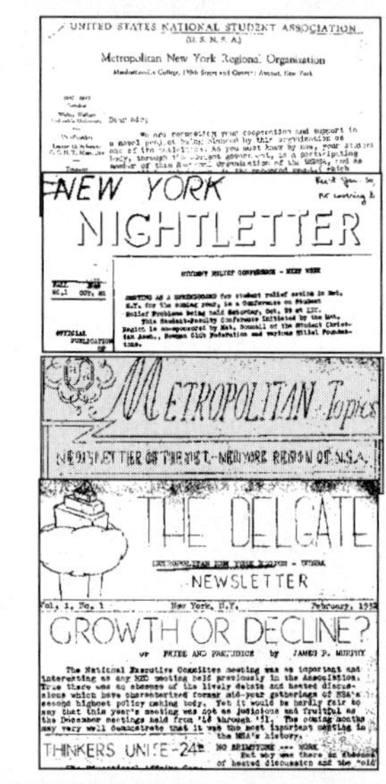

United States National Student Association

Metropolitan New York Regional Organization

NEW YORK NIGHTLETTER

METROPOLITAN Topics

NEWSLETTER OF THE MET. NEW YORK REGION OF N.S.A.

THE DELEGATE

NEWSLETTER

GROWTH OR DECLINE?

THINKERS UNITE-24

WITHOUT FAX, XEROX OR E-MAIL, the written word went out via mail (1947-48 letterhead, top), an mimeographing: 10/21/48 *Nightletter* announces student-faculty relief conference; 12/17/50 *Metropolitan Topics* discusses regional International Commission program; 2/52 *The Delegate* on arangements for the forthcoming regional Philosophy Conference.

FIRST INTERCOLLEGIATE CONCERT

March 19, 1948, Hunter College

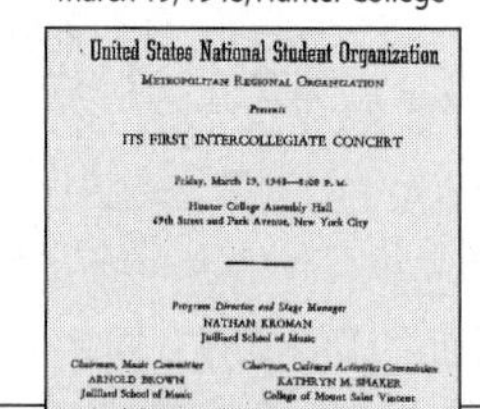

United States National Student Organization

Metropolitan Regional Organization

Presents

Its First Intercollegiate Concert

NSA from Different Angles

THE RAM

THE STUDENT VOICE

The Student Council has taken a significant stride forward in the recent reorganization of its assembly. Previously classed by some as merely a Senior class sounding-board, the clique tag now falls by the wayside. For with the addition of the entire executive panels of the four undergraduate years, the Council presents a truer cross-section of college opinion. This integration of class leaders will also lend itself to more coordinated action in the activities sponsored by the Council. Already this new impetus is evident in the plans for the Council's War Memorial Fund Night.

In another farsighted move the Council has sanctioned the formation of a National Student Association Committee. A glance at the preamble of the NSA constitution will show the extensive field of operations that this organization has carved out for itself. Dealing, as it does, with the fields of racial discrimination, academic freedom, and students' rights, an NSA meeting room can become a trap for the unwary delegate. Our present delegation has taken an important part in the formation of the NSA and, therefore, has an intimate knowledge of the inner workings of the organization; but future delegates would be handicapped by a lack of experience. To avoid this pitfall, the committee will groom the delegates in the procedure and aims of the NSA, and thus enable them to fill their roles competently. This move rates a salute for the Student Council.—J. V.

10/24/47

Barnard Bulletin

NSA

Barnard's student body has taken on a new responsibility in the realm of government. This is our first full year as members of the United States National Student Association. Few of us are acutely aware of this association, its aims or accomplishments. Bulletin presents the case for affiliation with NSA (see stories page 1, 3).

Bulletin supports NSA and urges active participation by our representatives in the affairs of NSA which now are our concern. We decry the attitude of, "What can NSA do for us?" Rather we ask how can we work within NSA so that this one great national student organization can make itself felt in national and international affairs. This is an opportunity, recently given, for students to speak as one on issues that concern them. We hear of newspapers and magazines conducting surveys to feel the pulse of the American student. NSA can be this pulse if those affiliated with it and those who are representatives to it have the broad outlook.

11/12/51

Columbia Spectator

Thursday, March 27, 1952.

NSA

It's good news to hear that the College Board of Student Representatives is considering joining the National Students' Association. Columbia's name has been absent from the NSA rolls for over a year now, ever since the University Student Council voted to disaffiliate. This has been rather regrettable in view of Columbia's preeminent status among the nation's colleges and universities.

CUSC left NSA because the council members felt that Columbia was not getting its money's worth. But the reason for the limited appeal that NSA had to this campus may lie a little deeper than that. It was probably due to the diverse nature of CUSC, the sponsoring group of NSA at Columbia. The council tried to spread NSA too thinly here.

Therefore, it is felt that if the College Board supervises a new Columbia membership in NSA, there will be an appeal to a smaller, more homogeneous group of students.

3/27/52

SECTION 3

New York State/New Jersey

CONTENTS

Weekend NSA Conference Here; Conisders Educational Needs

NJC and Rutgers Theaters Announce Student Players

Easton, Landy Will Speak At Meetings

New Jersey College for Women, 3/25/48

VOL. 1. APRIL

NY Regional Convention of NSA To Convene Here; 100 Expected

The first convention of the New York Region of NSA will be held at Norton Union this week-end, April 17 and 18, and will be attended by an estimated 75-100 delegates, coming from colleges and universities from all over the state except from the metropolitan New York area.

University of Buffalo, 4/12/48

Both the New York State and New Jersey regions held several well-attended regional assemblies annually, with attendance of up to 25 colleges in New Jersey and up to 55 colleges in New York.

New York State has large numbers of colleges spread out over long distances. Like California, it organized itself into two subregions in order to span its jurisdiction from Poughkeepsie, where Vassar switched to and from Metropolitan New York, to Buffalo, home of NSA's first national treasurer, Leeland Jones (University of Buffalo). Jones took what was known as "The New Jersey Plan" for a student discount program and successfully tested it in the Buffalo area.

New Jersey, to the south, was more compactly clustered, with two nodes—one at the Rutgers/New Jersey Women's College campus in New Brunswick, and the other in the Newark/Jersey City/Bergen County area across the Hudson from the Metropolitan New York region. John Yewell of Rutgers, an outstanding leader who served as regional chair after Chicago and during NSA's first year, attended the Constitutional Convention with Bob Kelly (St. Peters, Jersey City), who was elected NSA president in 1949-1950.

This section opens with interviews in which Lee Jones recalls his student leadership and his experience as an African-American who surmounted racial barriers in college football, in the army and on the Buffalo Common Council.

Albums on Rutgers and Princeton (which rejected membership in NSA) are presented. Tom Garrity (who had also been Chair of the Met. NY Region) and Bob Kelly, regional student leaders at St. Peter's College, are also highlighted.

Marianne Schmidt, a New Jersey College for Women student leader interested in international relations, attended several ISS summer events for her college and was in attendance with Herb Eisenberg and Al Lowenstein at the Stockholm International Student Conference in 1950.

Regions attracted steady levels of participation

Both State regions attracted larger numbers of colleges to their regional events than were listed on NSA's membership rolls and also ran successful intercollegiate leadership conferences. Upstate New York colleges generally welcomed NSA participation. Albums are included featuring the April, 1950 regional convention at Rochester Institute of Technology, and NSA at the University of Rochester and Cornell University.

Jack Minkoff of Cornell, lately retired as a Pratt Institute dean, was New York State's first regional chair. He was followed by Frank Dowd of the University of Rochester, who later became Vice President of Lincoln University and then Vice President for Student Activities at Rochester. Cornell was also home to Robert Fogel, Labor Youth League observer to NSA's Congress (see p. 289) and head of Cornell's Marxist discussion group, who later became a Nobel Laureate in Economics.

New York State and New Jersey NSA Highlights

New York

1946-47

'NationalStudents' Nominate Minkoff As Region Leader

TUESDAY, MAY 20, 1947

Proposals for Constitutional Changes Offered at Cornell NSO Conference

Jack Minkoff

18 UPSTATE NY COLLEGES launched the NY State region, electing Jack Minkoff of Cornell (above) as its Chair. He was followed by Frank Dowd, U. of Rochester (below) in 1947-48 (above fr left CS 1/7/47, 5/20/47. Photo: NSA (see p. 118).

1947-48

(Below, cw: *CS* 10/22/47, *RC* 12/12/47, 4/16/48.)

Subcommittees to Increase Efficiency in NSA Program

University of Buffalo Host To NSA Regional Assembly Saturday, Sunday

Constitutional Convention Of NSA To Convene At Eastman School

Frank Dowd

1948-49

NSA Seeks Solutions To Campus Problems

NSA Works To Protect Rights Of Students; Aims At Broader International Cooperation

Vassar NSA Reviews Contributions Of Last Year

NATIONAL STUDENTS ASSOCIATION NEWS

NSA Sponsored Inter-Collegiate Dance Features Two Bands in Memorial Aud.

NSA—Representing American Students

Offers Program of Regional, Campus Activities Projects

ANNUAL CONVENTION IN ACTION

At Cornell . . .

NSA PROGRAM BENEFITS were headlined and regular regional meetings and galas led organization- building. (Fr top cw: *VM* 10/5/49, *TB* 10/12/48; *BB* 10/15/48, *CS* 12/6/48)

1949-50

NSA's President To Visit Campus

National Students Assn. Will Convene At R.I.T. With Contests & Forum

SPRIT

186 Representatives Register at Conference

NSA . . . What Is It? What Are Its Goals?

State Conference, RIT, 3/31/50 (Photo: SHSW)

NSA Presidents Al Lowenstein (50-51, above l.) and Bill Dentzer (51-52, below r.) addressed regional events.

1950-52

Prince Street, River Campus Host For NSA Conference

State-Regional Conference Held By NSA This Weekend

Democratic N.S.A. To Meet In Albany For Regional Conference

55 COLLEGES attended the 4/51 Regional Assembly at U. of Buffalo (left). Federal aid, Canadian relations and draft laws were among topics for Western and Eastern district meetings.

(1949-50, 1950-52 clip credits. Fr top, cw: BB 11/11/49, RC 3/5/50, RS 4/1/50, BS 10/?/51,"Weekend" BS 4/27/51, RC 11/17/50).

New Jersey

1947-48

N. J. Region of NSO Meeting Held Here; 22,500 Represented

SA To Go To Princeton

Wardle, Yewell Win Leading Posts In New Jersey Region of NSA

Student Delegates Visit NJC for April Sessions

John Yewell

(Fr. top, cw: *TT* 2/18/47, *CN* 11/13/47, *PB* 2/24/47.)

17 NJ COLLEGES met at Rutgers after Chicago and elected John Yewell their first Chair; re-electing him for 47-48. 30 colleges gathered that Spring. Bob Kelly ('48-49, St. Peter's, see p. 252) was elected NSA President for 49-50 (see Pt 1, Sec 7). (Fr top: CA 12/4/47, 3/25/48). Photo: NSA (See p. 118).

1949-50

Ariel Landy Elected Chairman Of NSA's New Jersey Region

Regional Conference of NSA To Be Held Nov. 5, 6 At NJC

NSA Names Study Group On Education

Regional NSA Convenes Here

Fr. bot. left, cw: TT 11/11/49, 9/16/49, 10/11/49, CA 5/11/50.)

NJ delegation att the 1950 National StudentCongress (NSA photo)

1951-52

NSA Holds Congress In New Brunswick

RUTGERS AND ST. PETER'S alternated as sites for the 15 to 25 colleges attending its regional events. Ariel Landy, 49-50 (Rutgers) and Rosemary Honecker, 50-51 (NJ College for Women) were regional chairs. College newspapers, student government, student exchange and student rights were major themes.

(Fr. l. PW 11/10/50, 2/27/51)

KEY TO COLLEGE NEWSPAPER CITATIONS IN THIS SECTION

AF - Alfred U., *Fiat Lux*

BA - U. of Buffalo *Argus*

BB - U. of Buffalo - *The Bee*

BS - U. of Buffalo, *The Spectrum*

CA - NJ C. for Women *The Caellian*

CN - NJ C. for Women (Pre-war) *Campus News*

CS - *Cornell Daily Sun*

PB - *The Princeton Bulletin (Wartime)*

PD - *The Daily Princetonian*

PW - St. Peter's College *Pauw Wow*

RC - U. of Rochester, College for Men, *The Campus*

RT - U. of Rochester, College for Women, *Tower Times*

RS - *SPRIT*, RIT

TB - *The Bardian*

TT - Rutgers, *The Targum*

VM - *Vassar Miscellany News*

A lot of soldiers coming back weren't ready to accept the old status

1. The University of Buffalo and NSA

Leeland Jones, Jr.
University of Buffalo
NSA Treasurer, 1947-48

This recollection is based on interviews with Leeland Jones by Janis Tremper Dowd, Rockford College, IL, NSA Secretary, 1947-48; and Gene Schwartz, NSA Vice President, Educational Problems, 1948-49, in Buffalo, NY March 13 and June 19, 1998.

"The Buffalo Plan" and NSA

Gene: How did you come to be on the U. of Buffalo delegation to the NSA Constitutional Convention in 1947?

Lee: I had gone to the Chicago conference in 1946. When the Constitutional Convention came up before our student council, I was the president of the Norton Union, and therefore of the student council. We picked a delegation and decided to go. We didn't have enough money voted to send all the delegates. We went over to Lois Chasin's house. Her mother had a nice spread for all the delegates. I got them to agree that all the delegates in our quota should go. We figured out that by cutting down on our expenses and each person paying a little bit more, we could make it. So we loaded up and got to Wisconsin with everybody we were supposed to have.

We found ourselves having quite a problem with the various student organizations that came to the Wisconsin meeting, many to the left and some to the right. In Prague there had been no U.S. organization to represent all the students of the United States. Various proposals came up on how a U.S. NSA should be set up. At first the Convention seemed a little radical to some of us. There were many who thought there should be representatives from each of the student organizations. To us that didn't represent the nation we came from. Others said no, it's got to be in some other way. My suggestion became known as the Buffalo Plan, that we do it in a more democratic manner and follow the way the United States does things, that is, through representation of the individuals from the various schools comparable to representation from the various states. It was also the Buffalo Plan that the organization be called the United States National Student Association, so that it would not be related in any way to any other country.

Janis: So that was the Buffalo Plan? Tell us now about the Purchase Card System.

Lee: After my election at the Convention as Treasurer of NSA, I called home to my wife Carlita and told her, "It means living in Madison for a year." She said, "Nope." She had spent four years as a student there—some of which she wasn't quite happy about as far as living in dormitories was concerned. And we had a child to be concerned about. So we made arrangements to have the Treasurer's salary used to hire someone to handle NSA's financial affairs in Madison. I would be moving from campus to campus and do what I could and keep up with what was going on financially. But then I said, I have got to do more than this. So I devised the Purchase Card System. We started it in Buffalo. I saw it was working pretty well, so when I got to one of our NSA meetings I proposed it as a national plan, and it was accepted.

Janis: So the Purchase Card Plan was a brand new idea. What was the plan?

Lee: By being a student at a member school of NSA, you would get an NSA purchase card for a fee. We got several large businesses to make discounts. It was really a discount card, a card made out of cardboard because that was before the celluloids came in. In any case, businesses were quite happy to come in because they wanted student business. That was the way it happened.

Janis: So then you had to recruit the businesses to agree to be part of this?

Lee: Right.

Janis: What you were proposing was a plan that you would develop in Buffalo that would be a model available to any NSA member school to copy.

Lee: Buffalo was a sample.

Gene: Do you remember how it was that you got picked to run as treasurer? I ask everyone how they got selected. Very few seem to remember.

Lee: And I'm going to fit into that category, I'm afraid. I do know that we had a lot of activity going on and that I would lead singing groups in the evening. And there was a group of people, there must have been five or six, who got together and came to me one night and asked if I would run for treasurer. That's all I can remember.

Gene: Do you happen to remember who they were?

Lee: One was from Michigan. I'd have to do some thinking on that one.

Gene: So, in other words, a group of delegates who were putting together a slate.

Lee: It could have been that. I believe that was it. They didn't mention that there were other people on a slate, as I recall. They didn't say, "Will you run for treasurer?" They asked me if I would run for one of the offices, for an office. That's what it was.

Janis: Did you have any of the skills to be a treasurer?

Lee: My first three years were in economics, and then law school. And since then I've been on the board handling finances for the university, which is the biggest business we've got around here, and working on the finances of AAA, the City Council, and the county legislature.

Janis: I asked that because nobody asked me whether I had any skills as a secretary.

Lee: You acquired those after the fact, too?

Janis: Not very much. But everybody pitched in and did what they could.

Gene: So you didn't spend any time in residence in Madison. You went back to Buffalo and then attended the Executive Committee meetings. I got the impression that you were a fairly well formed individual when you came on the scene at NSA and you may have had more of an influence on NSA than NSA had on you.

Lee: Oh, we had some good times together. But keep in mind that I was coming out of the Service, a little older than some of the others.

Gene: Well, you're four years older than I am. You were born in '21. I was born in '25. So we both might have come out of the Service at the same time, but we were certainly in a different generation.

New York State Region

Gene: Do you recall being in the New York State Region, what the NSA did to bring some of the region's colleges together?

Lee: It is true that the Purchase Card Plan brought colleges together. Ryan—I can't recall his full name—he talked with me for years. He was a representative from Canisius College who went to Wisconsin. Canisius, I think, had only two delegates, but they were with UB so much of the time while we were in Wisconsin. We really should have called it the UB/Canisius Plan, the way we worked together on it.

Janis: What about Medaille College in Rochester?

Lee: I can't remember who the delegates were from there. State College had delegates. Cornell, of course, was there, and Rochester Institute of Technology. Yes, definitely, RIT.

Janis: This Purchase Card Plan then brought together not only the Buffalo institutions, but also the state institutions.

Lee: Yes. I'd sure like to know which schools that are now in SUNY [State University of New York] joined NSA at that time.

Janis: In 1947? I guess very few. Wouldn't you?

Lee: They are so strong now it makes me feel funny that they were not active then.

Janis: I know. What a transformation of the SUNY system there has been over these fifty years!

Lee: Many of these colleges, just like the University of Buffalo, were active then. That doesn't say that they were all that big and powerful. I don't know how it was done to get information to all those colleges about the convention.

Janis: Well, we did a lot of that from the national office. Even when we had the Chicago meeting, somehow we got hold of directories of the colleges, all of the colleges and universities that existed. And we had practically no money to do it. But how we got all those lists—Russ Austin would have been the person, and then Jim Smith who did that work. They probably had a lot of help from the University of Chicago.

Lee: That could be. I know that from Chicago we came home and somehow didn't seem to have any problems getting money to go to Madison—we'd never sent anybody out of town to anything until then, except for football or basketball teams.

University of Buffalo Student Government

Janis: There was a new mood on the campus, wasn't there?

Lee: That's true. A lot of soldiers coming back who just wanted things to do, and they weren't ready to accept the old status school.

Janis: That's right.

Lee: I do know that when I came back, I switched from economics to sociology and anthropology as a result of my terrible experiences in the Army with discrimination. I came back fighting like it was out of style, and the University was easy to work in because of our chancellor, Chancellor Kapen. We called them Chancellors at that time, and not presidents as they are now. Chancellor Kapen was quite a liberal person, insisting that students had rights. When we had a strike at the University of Buffalo campus and I was the leader, Chancellor Kapen made arrangements for me to meet with him once a month just to help bring about adjustments.

The students were dissatisfied with the way the tuition and monies were handled at the University. We had a controller, much the same as the City of Buffalo did. Today I'm on the City of Buffalo's Commission to change the charter of the city, and this year we're proposing to get rid of the controller. I just laughed remembering that back in 1947 or 1948, whenever it was, the students were striking to get rid of the University controller.

Janis: The controller was the conservative.

Lee: Yes, stop the money! And so we came out and fought and won. I raised cain about the controller of the University. We had a mass meeting at Norton Union, where everything took place out on the front steps, those huge beautiful steps! I was at law school downtown at the time. Near the courts is where the law school was, not out on campus. I took the bus back to the campus, but couldn't get in the front door for the meeting I'd called. People were packed in there. So I had to go through a back window to get in. Got in, and told the people what we needed to do. Get a bonfire ready—that was the way we used to do things at that time. Then the evening news came out saying, "About sixty people showed up." I thought to myself how could they misrepresent like that?

I'm chairman now of a committee to stop lies. That's a hard way to put it, but it's the ethics committee of the Buffalo charter revision commission, which is trying to find out how to stop misrepresentations in journals and elsewhere, particularly relating to people in government, government officials and codes that come out of the city. Once again I am back to my experiences of those NSA times.

Janis: Yes, we learned a lot, didn't we?

Gene: The UB Student Council was in a pretty strong position at the time. I recall your telling me what kind of relationship it had had with the administration in those years. Who dominated the Council? The frats? The athletes?

Lee: The Council definitely was dominated by fraternities and sororities. Peculiarly enough, there were no houses on campus as such, but on the periphery of the campus there were fraternity houses. I was president of the independents. Later I joined Beta Sigma Tau, which was an interracial fraternity. Although the fraternities and sororities dominated the council and student life generally speaking, the student newspaper, student government, and other organizations were in Norton Union, our student union. Dottie Haas, who was director of the student union, went to Chicago with me. She is passed now, but she was a tremendous person.

Janis: Right. She had good sense, good judgment.

Lee: Even though I say fraternities and sororities dominated what was going on on campus, their national organizations had little effect on Buffalo because it was an extremely liberal university and had been known as such nationwide. We had a nice working relationship all over the campus. The athletes we were bringing in brought a rejuvenation of football and basketball at the time I entered the university in 1941. My freshman numerals read 1944, but of course the Army interrupted everything. We had a good football team when we entered. All of us were on football scholarship.

The Norton Union

Gene: How did the students feel about the Council? Was it typical student apathy until Council elections?

Lee: Norton Union was so dynamic, and the sole place where people came together. Everybody was in everything. If you wanted anything to do in extracurricular activities, you went to the Union. Not like it is now. Now they have many facilities. The union is just part of it.

They do have at the university now a very strong student union, even as we had then, but theirs is entirely different. They've got millions of dollars in their treasury and things of that nature. I don't say there was apathy. I was chairman of the Convocation Committee and brought in several national artists. As a matter of fact, I brought in Duke Ellington for a Junior Prom. Just before he came I went into the Army. I had to go AWOL to get to the Prom where I was tapped for the honorary society.

I hadn't even thought of going, although I was junior class president. I went to the commanding officer and said, "The school is just a few miles from here, from Fort Niagara to Buffalo, at the Hotel Statler. Can I make arrangements to go, sir?" "No. What do you think you're in? You're in the Army now." But one of my buddies, Bob Ghent, who is now a pharmacist in L.A., came to get me.

He took me through a graveyard and over a hill. We got to the Hotel Statler, and were having a good time when the time came to be tapped for Bison Head. I didn't know I was going to be tapped. That's quite an honor. And they didn't know I was going to be there. In any case, we marched down the aisle to be tapped, and all the people were applauding, all of them in black tie. Of course, I was in uniform—and there

Lee Jones on UB's 1941 football team. According to the UB *Reporter*, February 15, 1946, "when Jones took the field for a 1941 game at Johns Hopkins University in Baltimore . . . [he] became the first African-American . . . to set foot on a field south of the Mason-Dixon line" (University of Buffalo archives).

was an officer from Fort Niagara. Sweat came down me like it was going out of style.

They tapped me. Gave me the honors. The officer didn't know who I was and I did not know who he was, but I do know I came down from the stage, got right into the car, and had Bob take me right back to the graveyard.

Janis: And you got away with it.

Lee: I got away with it.

Years in the Army

Gene: What were the years you were in the Army?

Lee: I went into the service in late 1942, the early part of 1943, and I came out in 1946. I went back to Buffalo as a junior and then I was back on the football team.

Gene: They kept you in trim while you were in the service?

Lee: I had the opportunity in the service to play football. You've probably heard about the 99th Pursuit Squad that was all Black flyers that trained at Tuskegee and then went overseas. I did not join them until after they came back. I was a Signal Officer and asked to be transferred to this group because they were to go back overseas as a combat group.

They had fighter planes at first, but light bombers after that. The most fun I had was playing some football there. I was a cryptographic security officer, and probably the only Black one they had in the Service.

I had finished top of my class in Signal Corps training, so I could pick whatever branch, part of the Signal Corps, I wanted to go into. I took cryptography. They checked out everything! They were interviewing people all over Buffalo, anybody I'd ever known, because it was top-secret stuff. This was the beginning of our computers and scanners. We actually had scanners in World War II—drum-looking things.

Gene: And you were converting documents digitally?

Lee: Exactly right. Just minor documents. We could send modified pictures but very good road maps and things of that nature. Physical maps.

Janis: What wonderful calisthenics for your brain.

Lee: It really kept me going.

There is one story that I want to tell you. Carlita and I met in college-type fashion. In Maryland they would not allow Blacks to go to certain colleges of the State University. So her father, Dr. Carl Murphy, who was treasurer then of the Board of Trustees at Morgan College, sent her to Wisconsin. She had three sisters in journalism because he had a newspaper, one of the Afro-American newspapers. She had graduated and was back home and the University of Buffalo was playing Johns Hopkins in football. It was the first time they had an interracial game in the South.

I was playing that night, and after that game, when we got to Baltimore, they wouldn't allow me to stay in the hotels. At one hotel they said, "No, no, can't have you here. We'll call this other hotel, an African-American hotel, and maybe you can stay there." So I went over there.

Mike, the assistant coach, wanted to go with me, and I said, Oh, no, and I went over alone. When I got there I called the Afro-American newspaper.

Rejection by Annapolis on account of race

But, to digress, I had been appointed by a black congressman from Illinois, William A. Dawson, to the Naval Academy, and they wouldn't let me in because of race. First I was appointed to West Point. West Point accepted me and I'm on my way to go. The congressman from Buffalo came to my father's undertaking parlor and asked my father how he felt about my being transferred over to Annapolis along with another person he had picked. "These two fellows, their grades are good and they're both athletes, I think that together they can go through it."

Gene: You mean no Black person had ever graduated from Annapolis?

Lee: Right. I had been trained to be an Army officer. And my father said: "Well, you'll have to talk to him. That's entirely up to him." My father had been a Service man himself. So, I thought about it and said: "Okay, I'll go." But when Annapolis said no, I couldn't then go back to the West Point appointment.

Gene: They rejected both of you?

Lee: Yes. He went on to get his commission in the Navy and I got my commission in the Army. Had things gone right, I would have been in West Point in 1939. The Navy said, "You've got physical problems," which I didn't have. The Army had not found a problem. I wanted to get into the Air Corps. Finally, I did get into the Signal Corps.

Gene: Did they have Black congressmen then?

Lee: Oh, yes. There was Adam Clayton Powell in New York City, Dawson, Mitchell, Oscar in Illinois. Those were the only ones at that time, but you've got to remember right after the Civil War there were Black congressmen and senators.

But back to the hotel in Baltimore. I called the *Afro-American* newspapers and they said to me: "You can't stay there. You just got back from the Olympics. It is not good for you to be staying there." I said, "Then what do I do?" They sent a car and took me to a beautiful house up in Morgan Park near Morgan College. We got out, and they had good-looking girl butlers at the door. So I married one of them and brought her back to Buffalo, two years later. My wife and I have been married now going on fifty-three years. Our wedding was a huge, black-tie wedding.

Gene: I see it right here in the May 12, 1945, *Philadelphia Afro-American.*

Lee: This is the newspaper Carlita's niece runs. She is the editor of the *Baltimore Afro-American,* and her mother is the editor of the *Afro-American* in Washington, D.C.

Janis: You know, Lee, that Frank and I spent the 1960s at Lincoln University. We were near Oxford in Pennsylvania, and I spent a fair amount of time in Baltimore. And Frank was a vice president at Lincoln University. We lived in the village.

Lee: That was a school I liked very much.

Recruiting Black colleges for NSA

Lee: Visiting colleges in the South was one of the biggest experiences that I had with NSA. I remember my not being able to join the NSA staff in Madison because my lady was heavy with child at that time. I went back and worked out of Norton Union, where I was president of the student body.

Our arrangement was that I would recruit southern colleges for NSA. I hit many of them that I happened to know about because in the Service I had played football against some of these colleges with our Army team, and I had met people such as Clem Hodges's group, and Dr. Dabney at Talladega. They were living under squalid conditions—four and five guys to a very small room—you wouldn't believe it. I had come from the University of Buffalo with everything gorgeous. It is amazing that they came out of those situations and became brilliant men and did wonderful things.

They're naming a new school after Clem Hodges, a former NSAer. Clem was a tremendous person. He was from Talladega College. We were in the same fraternity, the Blue League.

Janis: Talladega was coeducational, wasn't it?

Lee: Right.

Janis: I went to Rockford, a women's college in Illinois, ninety miles northwest of Chicago.

Lee: Did you? And wasn't there an associate school for men nearby?

Janis: Yes, when it was founded—Beloit College in Wisconsin, about three miles away. It was supposed to be the companion school, I think, but in fact, I never went to Beloit. I had no idea about that campus. This was during the war and the way I got my dates was that a friend of mine who had been a premed student at Indiana University with a bunch of other premeds got transferred to Camp Grant, which is four miles outside Rockford. This was in my freshman year. So he called and said, "I have some friends who want to meet girls," and here I was in a woman's college that was starved for men. So we set up a dating bureau. And would you guess who was elected president of the freshman class as a result of that?

Lee: Go girl!

Janis: Can you imagine anyone more popular than the one who could introduce you to a premed student? It was wonderful.

Lee: Our football team had a training camp in Canada given to us by wealthy alumni. We had sailboats—everything! A story goes with that, too.

When I got to Canada I arrived late because I was really kind of a star of the team. When I came into the training camp a boy by the name of Ray Whalen who had transferred I believe from LSU to Buffalo, said, "Who's that?" They were all going hello to me. They said, "That's Leeland Jones, he's the quarterback." "Well," he says, "I don't think I can play because my father would not be happy about this." They all joked and laughed all over the place. He couldn't take that so we battled on the field and became the very best friends.

Then one Christmas, it must have been about twenty years ago, we were sitting in the living room and had gifts all around and the Christmas tree all lit up. A phone call comes. It was Dixie Whalen! He said: "Leeland, I've been blind. Not socially blind, physically blind for many years, and I just got my sight back, and the first person I wanted to call was you." Ray Whalen had become dean of a school for Black students.

Janis: That's going right from LSU and those attitudes and those stereotypes to dean of a Black college.

Lee: It was an amazing experience to have that phone call. He talked with me a couple of times after that, but at our fiftieth reunion we couldn't get in touch with him. I don't know what happened.

Janis: You were the link, you were the reason, you were the experience that made it possible for him.

Lee: I'm certain of it.

Gene: I was talking to Norman Francis who is president of Xavier University. He was part of the Xavier, New Orleans, delegation to NSA in 1950. He subsequently became presi-

Leeland Jones is a civic leader in the City of Buffalo, New York, and was President Pro Tem of the Buffalo Common Council.

dent of the university. He told me a similar story. He befriended a fellow who was going to Loyola, who was white. NSA was the first organization to bring the Black and the white colleges together. This fellow became mayor of New Orleans. They keep telling each other, "You know, we've got to write our story." I'm sure there were lots of relationships that were developed, that resulted from those contacts—in NSA as well as on football fields. (See Norman Francis, p. 429.)

END NOTE

[1] The program for the Constitutional Convention in Madison lists thirty-five preregistered delegates from twenty-five colleges in the New York State region.

PICTURE CREDITS: *Then:* 1947 NSA staff photo, Constitutional Convention *NSA News.* October 1947. *Now:* 1996 (Author).

LEELAND N. JONES, JR.

Early years and family: Leeland Newton Jones, Jr., is the oldest of three children born to Leeland N. Jones, Sr., and Julia Anthony Jones. He has two sisters. Leeland married Carlita Murphy of Baltimore, Maryland, on May 5, 1945. They have three children, Dr. Leeland Anthony Murphy Jones, Dr. Johnaaron Murphy Jones, and Carlita Candace Murphy Jones Perkins.

Leeland graduated from Public School 32 and from the old Technical High School, where he was Student Body President, Captain of the football and debate teams, and President of the freshman and junior classes. He was appointed to West Point in 1939 by Congressman William A. Dawson of Chicago and was accepted at the Naval Academy but barred from entry due to race.

He attended the University of Buffalo, was President of freshman and junior classes, Captain of the debate team, President of Norton Union, Captain of the football team, first Black quarterback on the football team, Law School Council Representative, President of Delta Chi, and a member of Kappa Sigma Phi Honor Society.

Military: He graduated first in his class as a second lieutenant Signal Corps, and became the first African-American Cryptographic Officer, and taught cryptography until called into the reorganized 99th Pursuit Squadron in charge of Signal Communications. While in the service he was licensed to preach at Bethel AME Church in 1944.

Career highlights and elected public service: Prior to being elected to public office, Leeland worked in service positions at the local YMCA and American Legion post, with the New York State Education Department Bureau of Adult Education as a Young Adults Specialist, and as a teacher of English at Burgard Vocational School and Grover Cleveland School. He was elected to the Board of Supervisors of Erie County (now the Erie County Legislature) in 1950-52 representing the Fifth Ward; he was also Chairman of the Citizens' Committee to Combat Drug Addiction.

Leeland was the first Black elected to the Buffalo Common Council, January 1952 to December 1956, representing the Ellicott District, and served as President Pro Tempore.

Following his term in elected office, he worked with the New York State Commission Against Discrimination (now known as Human Rights Commission) as a field representative, making him the first Black to be employed in the Buffalo Office of that agency; the Buffalo Urban League, Inc., as Associate Director for Job Development and Employment; and the State University of New York (SUNY) Central Office as Research Project Director. He directed the Buffalo Urban Center, a postsecondary educational institution specializing in remedial and special education.

When he retired Leeland became assistant to the President and Vice President for Erie Community College City Campus.

Civic organizations: Among the organizations Leeland has worked with are: Buffalo and Erie County Planning Association; Campfire Girls of Erie County; IBPOE of W; Elite Lodge Buffalo and State Director of Economics; NAACP Buffalo Chairman Housing Committee; Cochairman of the United Negro College Fund; Disabled American Veterans (DAV); AMVETS; Odd Fellows; Masons (Prince Hall) 32 and Shrine; YMCA Business and Professional Men's Club; Bethel AME Church; Mary Crosby Chappell Education and Black History Foundation; Niagara Frontier Afro-American Historical Association.

Awards and recognition: Leeland has received many awards during his years of public service. Among them are: Gold Key Man of the Year—Jr. Chamber of Commerce; Athlos Fraternity Sportsmanship Award; first NYS Civil Liberties Award, IBPOE of W; AME Church Race Relations Award; Lions Club Speakers Award; All-High Football Award; Hall of Fame, University of Buffalo Athletics, Man of the Year, 1988—Mayor Griffin.

UNIVERSITY OF BUFFALO, NSA AND THE N.Y. STATE REGION

VOL. 1 SEPTEMBER 2nd, 1947, BUFFALO, NEW YORK NUMBER 1

"BUFFALO PLAN" GOES TO WISCONSIN

BUFFALO PLAN SOLVES PROBLEM OF THE N. S. A.

U. B. Representatives Solve Hot Issue At Conference

Jones, Lutz, Chassin and Quinn Answer Big Problem at University of Wisconsin

A thousand American students gathered on the University of Wisconsin campus last week in the most representative student conference ever held in the United States. A million college and university students were represented by delegates elected from about 400 campuses, and every conceivable sort of student organization, including nation - wide groups in behalf of such diverse causes as world federalism, student co-ops, Catholicism, student self-government, Methodism, Communism, industrial democracy, and Zionism participated.

The purpose of the meeting was to set up officially a new and all-inclusive national student organization, to better the lot of the student by promoting increased and equalized educational opportunities, the extension of democratic student government and of student-faculty cooperation, the betterment of student living conditions, and the facilitation of inter-national student relief and exchange.

Buffalo Delegates to N. S. A. Conclave

LEELAND N. JONES, Jr. (Senior Man) — CAROLYN A. LUTZ (Senior Woman)

JOHN P. QUINN (Junior Man) — LOIS M. CHASSIN (Junior Woman)

Jones, Lutz, Chassin, Quinn Leave To Attend National Meeting at U. of Wisconsin

Doctors Nathaniel Cantor, Harold G. Hewitt, and Reginald H. Pegrum are to be nominated to N.S.O. Faculty Advisory Board. Chancellor Capen fully endorses "Buffalo Plan."

The "Buffalo Plan" will be placed before the convention of the National Student Organization when that body meets at the University of Wisconsin Aug. 30 through Sept. 9.

Fundamentally the plan is this: the National Student Organization is to be thought of as a completely representative body for all the students attending colleges and universities throughout the country. To do this effectively, those in the organization should be only those who have been elected to offices in the student government of their own alma mater. Representatives from other student organizations, such as the A. Y. D., Y. M. C. A, and others, important as their activities are on the campus level, have not been elected by the general.

NSA IS NOT EXCLUSIVE; STUDENTS MUST PARTICIPATE

You as a UB student are a member of the National Student Association. You probably did not know that you belonged to this organization and you may know little if anything about it.

The NSA is an organization which consists of representatives from most of the colleges and universities in this country. They have sectional conventions and an annual national convention.

Your logical reaction to this is probably "So what!" Well, the NSA is a congress of the students of the United States and is accepted by the public in general as the voice of the American college student.

At the last national convention in the early part of September the NSA passed resolutions concerning academic freedom, discrimination in student organizations, and international student organizations. Were you in agreement with the decisions reached by the NSA? You probably have no idea what decisions were reached and yet these decisions received publicity and were interpreted by the American public as an expression of your beliefs.

As a college student you should actively participate in the formation of the NSA decisions which are subscribed to you. You can demand greater publicity from the campus publications on the actions of the NSA, but you can only insure your agreement with these actions by participating in their formation. You can do this by being present at NSA committee meetings and by joining that committee.

Delegates Chosen To N. S. A. Convention At Rochester U.

The controversial International Union of Students will be chief topic of discussion at a regional conference of the National Students' Association to be held this weekend in Rochester University, it was declared by John P. Quinn, one of six University of Buffalo delegates.

The international organization, with headquarters in Prague, Czeckoslavakia, was discussed at length during a convention of the national NSA held last September at University of Wisconsin, Mr. Quinn brought out. Opponents declared it might give the NSA a communistic tinge through adverse publicity throughout the nation. Proponents, taking an opposite tack, said American students should be leaders in a student organization as the United States was in forming the United Nations.

Prior to discussions, the group will elect officers and select executive and program committee members. They also will adopt a constitution for the New York State Regional Body.

NSA MEMBERSHIP BASED ON STUDENT GOVERNMENTS was the core of the "Buffalo PLan," which the Buffalo delegation advocated effectively at the Constitutional Convention. Excluding other student organizations from any role within the association was a major goal of NSA's founders. (See Wharton, p. 144, "NIICC," p. 159). (From top: *Argus* 9/2/47, *Bee* 12/12/47).

ACTIVE PARTICIPATION IN NSA by its near 10,000 students was encouraged by student leaders and editorial writers (Above l. *Argus* 9/26/49; *Bee* 12/12/47).

N. S. A. Regional Constitution Under Study By N. U. Board

Last Thursday evening the Board of Managers officially ratified the constitution of the new United States National Students' Association. The Board is at present considering the State Regional Constitution for ratification which will then make the University of Buffalo an official member of the N.S.A.

The National Students' Association is an organization of college and University students throughout the nation. It represents approximately one million five hundred thousand college students in over five hundred colleges.

At present a committee, headed by John P. Quinn, is organizing the next New York State regional convention which will be held here at the University of Buffalo in April. The invitation to the New York

Norton Host To 100 Delegates For N. S. A. Convention April 17

Norton Union will act as host to approximately 100 student - delegates who will assemble here on April 17 and 18 for the National Student Association's regional convention.

A banquet for all delegates and attending observers is to be held in Norton Union at 6 P.M. on Saturday, April 18th.

Included on the convention's agenda are items such as the confirmation of regional appointments by the state executive board, reports from domestic commission on local and national affairs, and reports from the international activities commission on world student concerns.

Reports from the Alfred convention on housing, a discussion of financial programs with a report from the treasurer, Robert J. Evans, a report on the University of Buffalo privilege card plan, and a general discussion of regional

ADOPTING A REGIONAL CONSTITUTION under NSA's decentralized structure (see Appendix, p. 0000) was the first order of business, in addition to laying out a local intercollegiate agenda. (From top: *Bee* 1/16/48, 3/19/48)

Surveying the hundreds of text books turned-in for resale by students, Kenneth Helfrich, chairman of the National Student's Association, prepares for the daily rush on the new Used-book Store.

Students Profit As NSA Bookstore Sales Mount

The Used-book Store which opened on this campus last Monday came as the culmination of over a year's preparation on the part of the National Student Association. It is the first successful venture undertaken at UB to reduce the high cost of text books to the student body.

Offering to sell texts at two-thirds their list price, the book store has been deluged since the beginning of the last exam period with books from students wishing to regain a part of the cost of their texts. On last Monday the NSA book store opened its doors to lines of students eager to save on this semester's book bill. In the first three days of operation over $1,600 was taken in in the sale of used text books.

Helfrich, Chairman of NSA, "and it has been demonstrated that students are overwhelmingly in favor of the project. We are extremely grateful to the faculty who have aided us in securing book lists and have immeasurably assisted us in publicizing our enterprise."

Mr. Helfrich added, "The NSA plans continuance and enlargement of the Used-book Store in order to offer the fullest service possible to the students of the University of Buffalo."

(*Spectrum* 2/9/51)

N.S.A. Spring Show Tonight, Gala Revue is Planned

The Spring Talent Show will be presented by the National Students Association of U. B. in Norton Auditorium tonight at 8:00 P.M., and at that time the curtain will go up on what promises to be an evening of stellar entertainment. For 60 cents per person those attending will see a diversified program presenting everything from "Figaro" to clever impersonations. Tickets to the show will be on sale in Norton lobby all day today and at the door tonight.

In addition to the U. B. Thespian efforts acts have been entered from Niagara University, St. Bonaventure College, and Buffalo State Teachers College. An impressive array of prizes is being offered to the most talented entertainers. For first place winners there will be 15 dollars and a trophy, which is being given by Sigma Kappa Sorority. Second prize will be 10 dollars, and the third place award is 5 dollars. Competing for these prizes are v

N.S.A. Announces Discount Cards To Be Sold Now

One of the National Student Association's most worthy activities will begin to bear fruit on Monday, March 15, when privilege cards granting discounts at a number of local stores and service organizations will be placed on sale through the local Privilege Card Committee members.

Buffalo has been selected by the national NSA as the trial area for this discount plan which will afford savings of from 5 to 30% on student purchases of goods and services. Leeland Jones has been appointed by the Executive Committee of N. S. NSA as the Director of the national privilege card system. These discount cards will be accepted at stores throughout the country when the plan is fully implemented. Other areas

PRACTICAL SERVICE PROGRAMS and fall and spring fund-raising entertainments highlighted UB's NSA activity. Led by Lee Jones, UB pioneered NSA's successful test of the Purchase Card System in Buffalo (see Medalie, p. 349, Album, p. 366). (From top: *Bee* 4/28/50, 3/12/48)

It all began in grammar school

NSA: A Link in a Lifetime of Service in Buffalo, New York

Leeland Jones
University of Buffalo
NSA Treasurer, 1947-48

In interviews with Janis Tremper Dowd, Rockford College, IL, NSA Secretary, 1947-48, and Gene Schwartz, City College of New York, NSA Vice President, Educational Problems, 1948-49. Conducted March 13 and June 19, 1998, in Buffalo, NY.

Buffalo in the 1940s

Gene: Back in your college days in the forties, was there a large African-American population in Buffalo in those years?

Lee: In the city proper, there may have been about 13,000 out of a population at that time of about 450,000. The university had maybe a dozen Black students. That was it. When I say a dozen, I mean graduate and undergraduate school.

I Loved My Politics

Janis: It's really outstanding that you were the president of the Student Body.

Lee: I had been president of my Student Body in high school and we had about the same proportion of people. I loved my politics.

Janis: But you were also president of the Junior class. Were you president of your Freshman and Sophomore classes also?

Lee: I was vice-president and on the Council of those. Then I got on the Council at the University of Wisconsin years later when I went back to law school there. I took labor law and contracts. They had a brilliant teacher, Dr. Paige, at the Wisconsin Law School. Everybody wanted to be under him. He had just settled that steel strike they had. And, so I got under him. But while I was there, I said, oh my, I don't see some things going so good here, so I ran for the summer school Student Council at Wisconsin.

Janis: And then you were on the Buffalo City Council, weren't you?

Lee: Yes, but before that I got on the Board of Trustees of the University of Buffalo as a graduate. At that time it was a private university and a certain proportion of the membership on the board had to be graduates of the university. The fellows in law school were saying, "Leeland, why don't you run? You can get some of the things adjusted around here." I said, "Listen, I want to get myself finished and out of here just like you do." But they encouraged me, so I ran and votes came in from all over the world.

Gene: Was it one of those formerly church-related schools that went private?

Lee: Yes, I guess most of the schools were.

Janis: The University of Rochester was—It may have been Baptist. We're talking well over 100 years ago, aren't we?

Lee: At the time that happened, Grover Cleveland was the president of the University of Buffalo—Chancellor, as we called it then.

Gene: Was there an attitude problem in Buffalo toward Blacks in those years?

Lee: Oh definitely! There was an attitude all over the country.

Gene: Were you able to go to restaurants or public places?

Lee: Yes, but there were some places where you didn't get treated properly. When I was on the Common Council, they decided to change the center square in downtown Buffalo, a part of the city that I represented. The businessmen would use me as much as the people that I tried to represent in the community. They wanted the square changed in such a manner that the traffic would flow smoothly and still have the people taken care of. Everything went along nicely and I said, "Looky here, you've got a men's toilet over here and a women's toilet over there that you have to go down under the ground to get to. The reason that they kept those things going, was to keep Negroes from going into the department stores downtown to use their places. Well, I said, "This is a part of history that I want to save, so when I had the contracts made for tearing down all the property and redoing the landscaping, I said, 'I want this done in a way that in later years people will know what has happened.'"

Gene: So you had a personal history of having a leadership impulse when you were in school and you got involved in student activities in high school. By the time you got to college, you were the kind of a kid who went where the action was, so to speak.

It started off in grammar school

Lee: It started off in grammar school—Public School 32. I got elected Secretary of our graduating class in 1935 and won the city-wide speaking contest.

Gene: And you competed interracially.

Lee: Yes, definitely. The year before that, a fellow by the name of James Holmes, who is now a retired U.S. Army General, had become one of the winners of the local contest and then he went on to the city championship and came in second. So Mrs. Brock, our assistant principal of the school, trained and worked with him, because she was determined that Public School 32 have itself a winner this next year. She had him all trained and ready. Then came the contest.

Mrs. Richmond, my English teacher in the fifth and sixth grades, encouraged me to go out for it. I wasn't all that interested because that would take away from my fun in sports. I did go out for it though, and I won the local championship. Mrs. Brock said, "No, no. We can't have that. We'll have the teachers judge this time instead of the students." So the teachers judged the second time, and they picked me. My topic was Toussaint L'Ouverture.

Gene: The Haitian revolutionary.

Lee: Right. And I went on from there. The school followed me as though it were a football game that they were going to cheer. They went across the street to Technical High School for the local event, and to Hutchinson High School for the city championship. My school just poured in there on buses. So that gave me the spirit.

Janis: Plus you came from a background with your father as an undertaker. He was a leading person in the community.

Up from slavery after the Civil War

Lee: Right, my father and my uncle. Oh, my grandfather—that's another story that must be told. He got on the school board in Waverly, NY, even though he was a slave when he came. Right after the Civil War he followed the troops going back to Pennsylvania. They picked him up and took him along as one of theirs. A local family raised him and he got a plot of land there and married a woman whose family had been free. We keep in communication with that family—the Molineaux family.

Gene: This is in Waverly?

Lee: Powell, PA—and Waverly's right across the line. My grandmother, whom I never met, died before I was born. She did not like the Pennsylvania school system. So she said, "I want to raise my kids in New York." So they crossed the borderline and raised everybody in Waverly, NY. My grandfather was taught to read and write. He was a very dynamic person. He came to Buffalo and opened a dairy and did a very good business here. Always working. All his kids went on to school. My aunt went to Temple and Houghton. My Uncle Martin went, too. Then came my father, who is a very strong person. He insisted that we were going to have an education.

I had two sisters. I was the oldest, each of us four years behind the other. My sister Esther died about four years ago. She was the historian of the family. My sister Eunice is a CPA. My mother, incidentally, was a school teacher in Waverly. My father met her in the service in Louisville, KY and he brought her to Buffalo.

Training in public speaking and coaching in football

My father would train me in public speaking. After I had won the city championship, he thought, my goodness, the Elks have a scholarship that they give out, a Chancellor's scholarship, four years at the college that you chose. It was in a lump sum as I recall. My father would take us into the funeral parlor, set up the chairs and have all my buddies come in. They didn't want to come, and I didn't want to do this thing. He said he would coach us in football if they would sit down and listen to me speak. I'd go over and over the speech. At that time my speech was "The Negro and The Constitution." Afterwards he would take us in the backyard and coach us in football. I never got to use the oratorical contest scholarship, even though I won the national championship. But all those buddies of mine, that he had sit down and listen to me, got football scholarships.

Gene: Because of that training and coaching.

Lee: Yes. Years later when I decided to run for office, I was going down the street and these guys came up saying, "Hey, Leeland, how about coaching us in football?" I said, "Geez, guys, I'd like to, but I'm going to law school and trying to do these other things. I think it would be a little bit too much." I got halfway down the street and I thought to myself, "Hey, 22 guys, and they've got girlfriends," so I ran back and talked to them. The person that had asked me to do this was George Arthur. He just retired as president of the Common Council of the city.

Janis: So you did coaching in a lot of things, didn't you?

Lee: I coached for a while and then I turned it over to Dr. Eskines. He had just finished dental school and he was going back into the Service. At that time, they would let you finish school and then you had to take up your Army card.

I did not graduate from law school. I graduated from undergraduate school. I resigned from law school. I had to go in the hospital for surgery. So, I never got a law degree. I'm sorry that I didn't take the time to do it. I completed all the work that was necessary to go for my bar reading. I only had about one-half year of reading to do, fortunately with Bill Mahoney, probably one of the greatest criminal lawyers in the country.

An heirloom reaching back to the emancipation era

Gene: So what line of work did you go into?

Lee: Education. I retired as Assistant Vice-President of the community college here, assistant to the president. There's another story. A fellow by the name of Molineaux was assistant to the president of Buffalo State Teachers College. He was a retired Colonel and I at that time was assistant to the president of Erie Community College. One day he called and said, "Are you any kin to the Henry Jones of Waverly, NY?" I said, "Oh, yes" and we had a talk and became very close. I would go out to his place and go horseback riding. I still stay in contact with his whole family.

He gave me, and I have it in our garage now, a bedstead head and foot that my grandfather carved shortly after emancipation—that he had carved using a new turner's lathe. Molineaux' wife refinished furniture so she had taken that old bedstead and brought it back into good-looking shape, and now I'm giving it, of course, to my grandchildren.

Janis: You know I was at Monroe Community College. I was Director of Community Service, then Director of Public Affairs, so we were in the same system. I retired about eight years ago. I guess '75 is when I started.

Lee: My retirement was before that. I'm retired now 10 years.

Janis: Back when Frank and I were at Lincoln University there was only one hotel. And so I got to know a lot of distinguished men and women as our houseguests. That was, in every respect, a wonderful experience for us. It was during the 60s. Horace Mann Bond had been the president before we went down. It was a fine college and it had a wonderful history.

What was most useful for me was how much I was able to learn because we were then the minority, the white minority. It was predominantly Black there, and it was very useful to learn something about how it feels to be in the minority. In addition, we were urban people in a rural community and there is a lot that you don't know when you come from a city about how to do everything in a rural community—how to burn your trash outdoors and what the firepile [?] is used for and all that. So there were an awful lot of situations where we were clearly the klutzes, the outsiders, because we hadn't had rural experience.

And then the third thing was that my child was ill and had seizures and had to wear helmets.

Lee: What was the helmet, the purpose of the helmet?

Janis: Because if he would fall, he might be cut in the head. But, in a small town, that's pretty suspect. I made a colorful helmet, bright orange, yellow/orange, marigold colored terry cloth, a big decoration on it, because I thought, "This is a child who likes color. Let's make it a wonderful hat." And I overheard people say, "How could a mother do that?" You learn a lot in that situation.

Gene: Getting back to your early years at the University—what changes do you see in the fifty-five years since then?

From University of Buffalo to State University

Lee: It's not the University of Buffalo any longer, it's the State University of New York at Buffalo. So it's U at B now, not U of B. The campus has been set up so that people won't just drive all through it from one main street to the other, as they had been doing for years. Now we have to take circuitous routes to get places. Hayes Hall was the flag building of the campus. The buildings now in the back are all "new" stuff. The Quonsets came on campus shortly after the war. Seems as though they keep them up anyway.

Janis: They were to be temporary buildings, weren't they, and they're going to last a lifetime.

Lee: They've just decided to spend several millions of dollars to refurbish and fix the campus up. The only thing that they do with the south campus now is use it for health sciences: med school, dental school, nursing school and all of that. I'm talking about graduate school. We have actually now a Dean of Health Sciences, which takes in all of these.

The Student Union has gone out to the other campuses. They've got a big beautiful building on the old campus, too. The students themselves got that building because they wanted the Union in a building just like the Faculty Association. The faculty has no building as such. They thought that's what they would do with the students, but the students fought it like mad and got their own building.

There are also dormitories. They were not here when I was going to school. There was what we called the polo ground, where we would practice football. But now it's all dormitories.

Janis: Is there a hospital here?

Lee: The VA hospital is across the street. Buffalo has a very unique program. There are five hospitals all associated with the university, many of them in their own particular fields. Public health is all in one place. I went over there recently to be on a research group where they checked me over and then sent all of my records across the street, over to the VA hospital.

As I said, we have these five hospitals where the consortium works with the university. They have a huge setup in each one of them and in the VA hospital here. My son took his degree here, did most of his work over here at the VA, and then with the other four hospitals before going out of town.

Janis: And what is his specialty, Lee?

Lee: He's a psychiatrist now. He was in internal medicine and it got to him, the business of people coming to him all chopped up and beaten up. He's heavy in his religious activities, too, he's a pastor.

Janis: And is he also a Leeland?

Lee: He is. He's the third. He has a son that is out in the world. He finished his work in Massachusetts. Funny thing about our family. They go back to school and get what they're after, but late. My daughter is working on her doctorate now, she's been married 25 years.

Gene: How many children have you got?

Lee: Three. One's a lawyer in Hawaii, got there on football scholarship, just as my son got through school here on football scholarship.

Janis: And what is your daughter's degree going to be in?

Lee: Well, she took her bachelor's and master's here and at Buffalo State in education. It's exceptional child education that she got her master's in. She is now on the faculty at one of the universities in the Maryland/Virginia area.

In my time, if people wanted to live on campus, they lived in frat houses. There were no dormitories then. With the state coming in, they put up more dormitories than they did student houses.

Janis: You have a very impressive gym.

Lee: That's what we call now the little campus. The huge $16 million edifice is now where the music building once was. My wife and I held our 50th wedding anniversary there a couple of years ago. It is one gorgeous thing. Our president is pretty sharp. Incidentally, we've been very lucky on presidents at the university.

One of our presidents was a civil engineer, and his idea was building edifices. He was good at that. Another came along and his concept was unifying the school so that you had programs that overlapped. If you were in engineering, you were going to make sure that you got a whole lot of sociology and medicine and whatnot along with your field. So all the disciplines were interwoven. Now we're talking about the university not just being the flagship of the state program but being in research, a regular university.

Janis: I know that within the huge state university system there are very special needs that go along with different colleges. What is it in Buffalo?

Lee: Being a university. Making sure that all of the colleges have their opportunities to do things at the highest level.

Janis: Buffalo also has streets that changed their names, one side to the other.

Lee: Main Street was at one time the boundary line. When you were on one side of the street, that had a name. No two sides of a street had the same name except Virginia Street, the street that I was raised on. I also had the pleasure of naming streets when I was on the Council.

Janis: Which ones did you name?

Lee: Nash Street. Reverend Nash, who was an underground railroad minister, church minister, of the Michigan Avenue Baptist Church, lived on the street right behind the church. When I was on the Common Council we were changing the names of streets that might be Post Office problems, and I made sure that one was named Nash Street.

NSA provided a model for collaboration

Gene: Lee, when you look back at your NSA experience, is there anything that stands out as having had a strong influence on you?

Lee: The idea of universities coming together from all over played a very important part in my thinking of what you can do with nations—but as you know I'm truly a local government person. Seeing different areas come together helped me quite a bit. The County Board of Supervisors is made up of a lot of towns from all over. Ours, at one time, had no executive branch. We had a supervisor from each village or town, and they came together and did the executive as well as the legislative work. Now we've got a County Executive that handles a huge program.

Getting them into a oneness of thinking to get things going is something that actually I picked up as basic from NSA. They didn't know me, I didn't know them, we had come from different communities, different influences, and yet we were able in a short period of time to get something going that lasted this long. And so it is with the Board of Supervisors. All of these villages and towns, they had no idea what my problems were in the inner city and I didn't know what theirs were. So, we were finding out that we could get together, put our heads together and come out with solutions that would be for the benefit of this area—Erie County.

Lee Jones and Janis Dowd in 1998. (For extended biographies see Jones, p. 874, and Dowd, p. 66.)

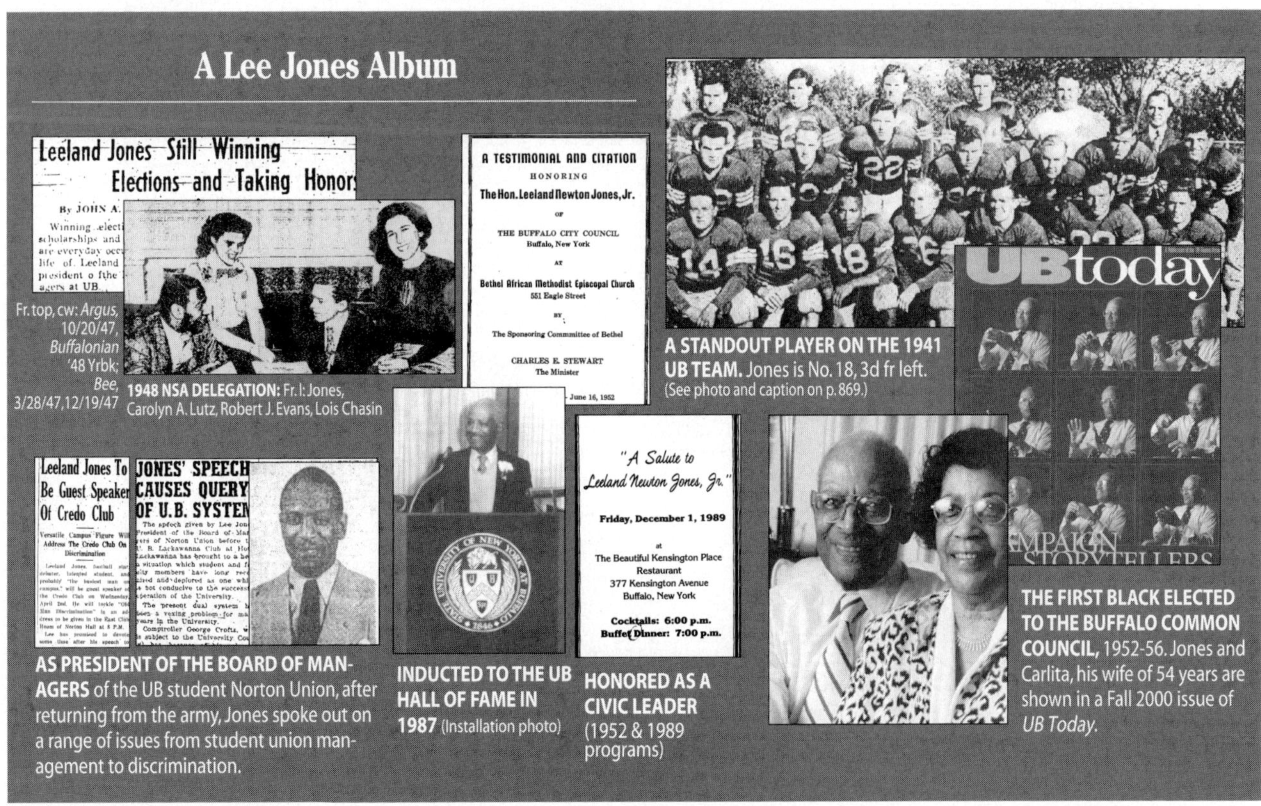

A Lee Jones Album
Leeland Jones Still Winning Elections and Taking Honors
A TESTIMONIAL AND CITATION
HONORING
The Hon. Leeland Newton Jones, Jr.
OF
THE BUFFALO CITY COUNCIL
Buffalo, New York
AT
Bethel African Methodist Episcopal Church
551 Eagle Street
BY
The Sponsoring Commmittee of Bethel
CHARLES E. STEWART
The Minister
June 16, 1952
Leeland Jones To Be Guest Speaker Of Credo Club
JONES' SPEECH CAUSES QUERY OF U.B. SYSTEM
"A Salute to Leeland Newton Jones, Jr."
Friday, December 1, 1989
at
The Beautiful Kensington Place Restaurant
377 Kensington Avenue
Buffalo, New York
Cocktails: 6:00 p.m.
Buffet Dinner: 7:00 p.m.
UBtoday

Fr. top, cw: *Argus*, 10/20/47, *Buffalonian* '48 Yrbk; *Bee*, 3/28/47, 12/19/47

1948 NSA DELEGATION: Fr. l: Jones, Carolyn A. Lutz, Robert J. Evans, Lois Chasin

A STANDOUT PLAYER ON THE 1941 UB TEAM. Jones is No. 18, 3d fr left. (See photo and caption on p. 869.)

AS PRESIDENT OF THE BOARD OF MANAGERS of the UB student Norton Union, after returning from the army, Jones spoke out on a range of issues from student union management to discrimination.

INDUCTED TO THE UB HALL OF FAME IN 1987 (Installation photo)

HONORED AS A CIVIC LEADER (1952 & 1989 programs)

THE FIRST BLACK ELECTED TO THE BUFFALO COMMON COUNCIL, 1952-56. Jones and Carlita, his wife of 54 years are shown in a Fall 2000 issue of *UB Today*.

A New York State Regional Convention

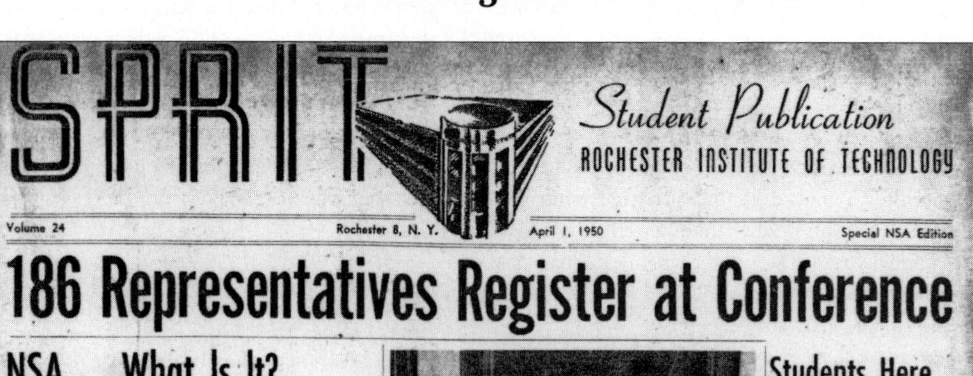

SPRIT Student Publication

ROCHESTER INSTITUTE OF TECHNOLOGY

Volume 24 | Rochester 8, N. Y. | April 1, 1950 | Special NSA Edition

186 Representatives Register at Conference

NSA . . . What Is It? What Are Its Goals?

The National Student Association (NSA), is an organization of college student bodies, represented through their student governments. It was created to serve the long-existing need for a representative intercollegiate unit to serve the American student community, and to promote student interests and welfare.

Formed in 1946

NSA was formed in 1946 by a group of American students who had just returned from attending a students' conference in Europe. These Americans conceived the idea of forming a national student union and were the nucleus of the NSA's first student congress which was held in the summer of 1947 in Wisconsin. The organization expanded so fast that today more than 300 institutions of higher learning throughout the country are bona fide members.

Membership in the NSA is open to all colleges and similar schools, providing these institutions ratify the NSA constitution and, of course, pay the necessary dues. [illegible] dues is the main element of finance in the organization. Some Some additional revenue is obtained through the sale of periodicals published by NSA.

Some of NSA's aims include: improved student governments, promotion of international understanding, maintenance of academic freedom and development of better educational standards.

NSA Policy

Policy for NSA is determined by the National Student Congress held each year. However, no college or university must abide by any policy decision reached at the congress. These policies are the goals that NSA is striving for, but always subject to modifications necessitated by the individual school.

Each member college of the NSA belongs to one of 27 geographical regions. Each region has its own constitution and executive officers. Regional headquarters is the main link that any member school has with the national staff and is the agency primarily responsible for the activities of NSA.

All national officers are elected at the congress, and under no circumstances may hold office for more than two years. No "professional" students or administrative officers are allowed to develop within the association.

Advisory Council

Through its National Advisory Council, consisting of nine prominent educators serving staggered terms, continuity is maintained. Continuity is also assured through the development of regional officers who often assume student national roles.

Milton S. Eisenhower, chairman, U. S. National Commission for UNESCO, and president of Kansas State College, has this to say about NSA:

"I am glad to endorse the excellent work which the NSA is doing in the field of education for international understanding . . . such projects deserve the fullest support of the American college student body."

Local Musicians Provide Free Dance Music

Through the courtesy of the Rochester Musicians' association, students attending the dance at the Hotel Rochester following the banquet will trip the light fantastic to the music of Charles Kellogg and his Orchestra—with no cost to NYSNSA.

Mr. Kellogg and his music-makers were made available through the Recording and Transcription fund of the American Federation of Musicians by the office of James C. Petrillo, president. The necessary funds were allocated to the Rochester Musicians' association through this fund.

Judah Eliezer clarifies a point at a NYSNSA Regional Conference Committee meeting. L. to r., Claudia Symonds, Eliezer, Joan Harlan and Gene Penler, chairman. Committee members absent are Edgar Posner and William Lapp.

Art and Photo Exhibitions Viewed by Delegates

Student artists and photographers from colleges in upstate New York who entered the NYSNSA Art Exhibition and Photo salon had their work viewed by the numerous representatives attending the regional conference.

A total of 79 paintings were entered in the art contest, chiefly water colors. At the close of the Photo salon, 105 entries had been submitted, the majority of them in the non-amateur section.

Monetary prizes for the Art exhibition were contributed by the Student Council and Sigma Kappa Delta sorority of Rochester Institute of Technology. Prize money for the Photo salon was made available by the regional treasury.

Chairman of the Art exhibition, Claudia Symonds, stated that some of the entries appeared to be of a professional nature. She said the first college to send in an entry was University of Rochester

Edgar Posner, chairman of the Photo Salon committee, arranged for the various college groups attending the conference to be photographed while in business sessions. This was made possible through the cooperation of the RIT Department of Photographic Technology and was instituted in order that these photos might be reproduced in the various college newspapers showing their representatives in action.

Student Delegates Enjoy Get-to-gether Friday Night

Doing their best to prove that a better inter-collegiate feeling of friendship will result in more successful business sessions, student representatives last night cashed in on self-introductions to make the first social affair of the conference a huge success. The second, and major social event of the three-day assembly, will be the dance in the ballroom of the Hotel Rochester tonight.

"Ye Olde College Inn" was the theme of the informal get-together. The motif was especially evident with the lanterns placed about, and the numerous college pennants utilized for decorations. The slogan of the conference, "Build NSA", was driven home with the pennants reading 'Academic Freedom', 'Bill of Rights', 'Purchase Card System', 'Travel Tours', etc.

Student - faculty relationships were furthered with the constant mingling of student representatives with faculty observers.

Throughout the evening, students were observed talking semi-business affairs with fellow-delegates—much to the satisfaction of the conference officials who felt that the outcome of the assembly would be that much more successful.

Students and faculty members of Rochester Tech's Art department cooperated to make the pennants constituting the decorations for "Ye Olde College Inn." Claudia Symonds, chairman of the Art exhibition, was in charge of decorating the lounge. She was assisted by Joan Harlan and other Tech students.

Students Here From 35 Schools In Upstate Area

Dr. L. L. Jarvie Principle Speaker

At press time for this special issue of SPRIT, approximately 186 students, representing more than 35 institutions of higher learning in upstate New York, had registered for the 1950 spring conference, of the New York State Region of the United States National Student Association. These figures include the students who have registered for the editor's forum which is being held in conjunction with the regular NYNSA meeting.

Schools Attending

At the close of the official registration period on Mar. 24, students from the following institutions had indicated they would attend:

Canisius college, College of St. Rose, Cornell university, D'Youville college, Le Moyne college, Niagara university, Rochester Institute of Technology, Russell Sage college, St. Lawrence university, Siena college, Syracuse university, University of Rochester College for Women, University of Rochester School of Nursing, William Smith College and Colgate university.

Also, Nazareth college, Union college, Champlain college, Hobart college, Brockport S. T. C., Fredonia S. T. C., Potsdam S. T. C., N. Y. S. Institute of Agriculture and Technology in Morrisville, Paul Smiths college, N. Y. S. Institute of Applied Arts and Sciences in Binghamton and Tri-Cities college.

Other colleges getting in under the wire of the closing date are: Buffalo S. T. C., N. Y. S. Agriculture and Technical Institute in Delhi, Hamilton college, Bard college, N. Y. S. Institute of Applied Arts and Sciences in Utica University of Rochester College for Men.

The executive committee notified the regional conference committee to accept registrations after the deadline. Though the late registrants are not listed here, that policy was put into effect.

All work and no play makes Johnny a dull boy. Students attending this conference don't intend to be placed in a similar situation. Delegates above are enjoying the Get-to-gether.

Students attending the Regional Conference are shown as they registered in their individual capacities. As of 3:30 p.m. on Friday, more than 175 representatives had signed.

Reproduced from *SPRIT*, Student Publication of the Rochester Institute of Technology, April 1, 1950, with permission from the University News Services, Rochester Institute of Technology, RIT. No longer published, a letter accompanying the permission noted that "This publication has evolved over the years, and we now have a weekly student magazine."

EDITORIAL

Welcome

The administration, faculty and students of Rochester Institute of Technology eagerly welcome the representatives of sister educational institutions to the Regional Conference. We hope that the time you spend here will be most profitable, and that you will find it enjoyable as well.

Though Tech has not the spacious campus and magnificent edifices that often go with institutions of higher learning, it is not lacking in sincerity, good student-faculty relationships, hospitality and other old-fashioned qualities which go to make a school more than just a dispenser of knowledge. In its primary endeavor—to train men and women in certain technological fields—it has been and continues to be successful. RIT may be a street-car college, but its favorable characteristics would make up a train endless in length.

We hope that you will breathe deeply of the friendly air, and that all your accomplishments at the conference will be made in true amiability.

Regional Conference

From points as far west as Niagara Falls and as far east as Albany, students representing numerous institutions of higher learning are attending this spring conference of the New York State Region of the United States National Student Association. You have come here for the primary purpose of obtaining media which will prove of a beneficial nature to your college—keep that foremost in your mind.

Any discussion will yield results which are directly proportional to the contributions made to it. Therefore, when the panel or commission leaders start the ball rolling, do your best to keep it rolling. Contribute anything which you feel might benefit the others in your discussion group. And when a speaker has completed his talk and asks for questions, don't hesitate—or your question may go unanswered. In other words, take an *active* part.

Introduce yourself to other students at your dinner table or at the dance. Much can be done on your free time to promote a better inter-collegiate feeling. Through such a better feeling, accomplishments will be greater. Remember, your fellow students are making your trip to the conference possible. You owe it to them to make a maximum effort in getting the most out of this three-day session.

If, during the conference, there is a suggestion you wish to make to some responsible person, seek out a member of the Executive Committee or Regional Conference Committee. He will give your idea serious consideration and will act accordingly.

The conduct of you, as an individual, can't help but reflect on your college and on this conference. Let's live up to the ladies and gentlemen that our associates know we are.

Build NSA

"Building NSA" is the theme of this conference. Representatives from NSA-member colleges in the upstate New York area should be aware of this at all times. By our conduct and application let us try to exemplify true NSAers. We want to make this region stronger, and we can do just that by bringing new schools into the fold. However, other colleges and universities will not join unless they are sold on our actions. Let's not give them reason for *not* joining.

STUDENT PUBLICATION
Rochester Institute of Technology

Vol. 24 April 1, 1950 Special

Harold C. Garfinkle, Editor-in-chief
William M. Runyan, Student Publisher

Gene Penler .... Managing Editor
Robert Entwistle .... City Editor
Eli Gordon .... Photo Editor
Francis Vendetti .... Production Manager
George Rosenberg .... Business Manager
Joseph Sarr, Jr. .... Advertising Manager
Richard Metzler .... Circulation Manager

WRITERS—Phyllis Garver, Myron Klineberg, David Milbauer, Richard Obrecht, Mimi Rauber, Rosemary Rauber, Pat Ryan, Roger Stabley, Anne Taylor, Janice Wirtner, Joan Gubert, June Stoner, Natalie Gitelman, Marcia Adamy, Shelly Heald, Norton Carson.

EDITORIAL ASSISTANTS—Dave Bischof, Frank Comparato, Ken Chase, R. F. Garty

STAFF PHOTOGRAPHERS—Randall Houck, John Murray, Larry Cornell, Jerry Kunin, Morrie Miller, Harvey Samuels, Gil Stark.

CARTOONISTS—Ernie Ferrone, Glen Zulauf, Dick Kane.

PRODUCTION ASSISTANTS—Stanley Egert, Vince Vitolo, Richard Landes, Bennett Shaffer, Joe Murrelle, Gerald Tuthill, Tom Stofer, Richard Arnold, Bob Snyder, Nanson Caldwell, Vincent O'Toole, John Leonard, Bill Wemyss, Judah Eliezer, Ken Albrecht, Leslie Prinse.

ADVERTISING ASSISTANT—Bob Johnson.

MANAGERIAL ASSISTANT—Arnold Terreri.

CIRCULATION ASSISTANTS—Patricia Donaldson, Richard Peters, George Schriever.

Introducing

HY NISSENBAUM
President of NYSNSA

Unassuming and efficient, NYSNSA's president is Hy Nissenbaum, a 22 year old senior at Syracuse university. Long active in NSA affairs, Hy took the helm of this region's sinking ship when he was elected to the presidency at a regional meeting last Fall. Since that time he has guided us in a firm, progressive manner, and under his capable leadership, NYNSA is destined to regain its rightful place on the national level.

Hy attended Brooklyn college in his own home town for two years before he was called upon to serve 19 months in the Army. It was after he was discharged that he enrolled at Syracuse university.

Since high school days Prexy Nissenbaum has always been keen toward student organizations. At Syracuse, he has served as a Men's Student Government assemblyman and at present is a Public Relations director.

Upon graduation in June, Hy intends to do graduate work in public administration.

DICK APPEL
Chairman, Genesee District

The active chairman of the up-and-coming Genesee District of the NYSNSA is friendly Dick Appel, 22, and a junior at the University of Rochester.

A native of Portland, Oregon, Dick is studying chemical engineering. He has been a member of the university's NSA committee since his freshman year. Last summer he represented his college at the Second National Student Congress at the University of Illinois. He was elected to his present position as district chairman last spring.

Thirteen months were spent in the Army by Dick. This may, in part, account for his obvious maturity and leadership ability. As the only non-senior on the Executive committee, NYSNSA will have to depend on Dick Appel for guidance during the coming year.

Dick is assistant circulation manager of his university's student publication and a member of Theta Delta Chi fraternity. His spare time during the winter months is spent skiing, and during the warmer weather he can usually be located on one of the many nearby golf courses.

MARY MORAN
Secretary of NYSNSA

Attractive, energetic Mary Moran of the College of St. Rose, Albany, is the capable secretary for the New York State Region of the National Student Association.

A senior at 21, Mary was graduated from the Academy of the Holy Names in her native Albany before entering St. Rose where she is majoring in both English and French.

Last summer she represented her college at the Second National Student Congress. Mary is serving her second consecutive year as regional secretary. Her extraordinary efficiency in that office has lessened considerably the work of the individual members of the Executive committee and NSAers throughout the region have benefited by her diligence.

A member of the Student Senate for her four college years, she was elected to its presidency in her fourth year. Swimming is her favorite sport and dramatics her pet hobby. She conducts a weekly radio program, "Patterns in Poetry," over an Albany station.

WILLIAM E. KOTARY
Vice-President of NYSNSA

The University of Rochester's splendid contribution toward NSA is handsome William "Bill" Kotary, vice president of the New York State Region. A senior who's major is business administration, Bill is serving his second consecutive term in the vice-presidency.

The 'veep' graduated from Boonville, N. Y. high school and soon entered the University of Rochester. Bill took time out from his studies to serve five years in the U. S. Army. He participated in four campaigns and earned his 'tracks'—captain's bars—before being discharged.

Bill's NSA activities include: past chairman of the Genesee district of the NYSNSA, present chairman of the U. of R. NSA committee, delegate to UNESCO conference in Cleveland last year and university delegate to the first NSA Congress in 1947.

All types of sports are enjoyed by Bill. Incidentally, he has been a member of the varsity soccer team for his past three college years. He was president of his sophmore class and is a member of Theta Delta Chi fraternity.

Academic Freedom and Student Rights....

Academic freedom and *student rights* are perhaps NSA's two foremost matters of policy.

The National Student association believes that certain conditions and guarantees should exist on the college campus to insure the freedom of inquiry, research and opinion essential to the educational progress in a democracy.

These guarantees, outlined in the association's by-laws, are not presented as absolute standards required of each of NSA's members, but as goals to be striven for and as criteria to be followed in the judgment of individual appeals brought before NSA. NSA believes that the ability of a man to teach and the qualification of a student to learn, should be based primarily upon the character and qualities of the individual.

By its constitution, NSA is prohibited from participating in "partisan political activity" in all levels of the association. Some activities of the association, however, such as its legislative program and academic freedom program, may be construed as "political."

Such programs are based upon the broad aims of the association and are not geared to the support of a particular political party or doctrine. NSA does stand opposed to any political doctrine which would stifle free and democratic education in the United States.

along educational lines—seeks to influence the attitudes of communities rather than to coerce them, and provides for the development of programs on the local and regional level "to implement its stated principles with regard to the legal limitations involved." (At the last New York state conference, the national policy on discrimination was reaffirmed by regional members.)

NSA does not set itself up above student governments on the campus, but rather seeks to "stimulate and improve" democratic student government.

The National Student association has no organizational ties with any religious, political, social and professional student groups throughout the country. It does consult with them, however, on projects of mutual concern.

It has been the policy of the association to cooperate with all international student groups in the implementation of its exchange of persons and information programs.

RIT Student Council Endorses Resolution On Scholarships

On Mar. 6, the student government of R I T endorsed a resolution favoring a Federal program of scholarships—the first school in NSA to initiate such action.

This is the text of the resolution adopted:

Whereas, the National Student Association Committee of Rochester Institute of Technology is in accord with the basic principles of a federal program of scholarships and fellowships as adopted by the American Council of Education at its meeting on December 12, and 13, 1949, and

Whereas, the National Student Association was represented at such a meeting and was in general agreement with these basic principles whereby necessary financial aid would be made available to qualifying student applicants regardless of race, religion or national origin, and

Whereas, the NSA committee of RIT feels such a program for federal aid is of immediate concern to the educational welfare of the country as a whole, therefore

Be It Resolved, that the Student Council of Rochester Institute of Technology, Rochester, New York, duly elected by and for the Student Association of over 1,600 members hereby endorses the American Council of Education's program for federal scholarships, and

Be It Further Resolved, that said

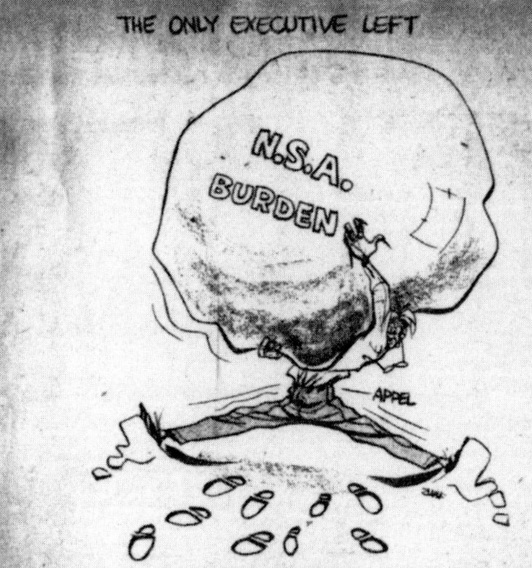

BUILD NSA

Occupational Pattern Shown in Tech History

By NORTON CARSON

Paralleling the growth of its home city, the Rochester Institute of Technology has developed along with the industries here that are world-renowned for their technical perfection and high qualities of production control.

The history of the Institute dates back to 1829. It was in that year that a group of persons in the old frontier village of Rochester banded together to form the Athenæum to promote the cultural interests of the community.

Mechanics Institute Founded

The need for trained technical workers in the rapidly expanding industries of the city resulted in the founding in 1885 of the Rochester Mechanics Institute.

This new educational venture was largely the result of the efforts of Captain Henry Lomb, a local industrialist, who not only contributed to and supported the venture, but also interested other leaders in the community to do likewise.

Merging of the Schools

Expanding rapidly, the school pioneered in an increasing number of areas of practical education. Six years later, in 1891, the Mechanics Institute and Athenæum were merged, uniting the objectives of technical training and the cultural needs of the well-rounded individual.

For many years the institution bore the name of the Rochester Athenæum and Mechanics Institute but in 1945 this was changed to the Rochester Institute of Technology to beter express the school's characteristics and objectives.

Expansion With Industry

The parallel expansion of the Institute with the Rochester industries has been apparent in the registration data of the school. Last year, for example, while 79 per cent of the students came from New York state, 21 per cent represented 37 different states other than New York, and nine foreign countries.

Development of the Institute has been characterized by the formation of departments as new areas of training have been added. These have always enjoyed considerable freedom in the development of procedures and techniques to suit their own needs.

Large Grants Given

Other large industrialists, such as the Gleasons and George Eastman, gave large grants to the Institute without which it would not have developed as it has.

The idea of cooperative education also came into its own at this time, that is, to send a student to classrooms for a period of time and then out into industry for an equal period for practical application of theory. This system is still used in all but the Applied Art, Photographic Technology, and Publishing and Printing departments.

Representative Student Body

Students at the Institute come from all over the world to take full advantage of the technical opportunities that are afforded at this school. Also, graduates are serving not only the immediate community here, but throughout the country and the world.

It is also well to bear in mind that the Institute is not merely a technical school where graduates are turned out on a production basis, but a center where the individual student can assimilate technical competence with living and getting along with the various adjustments in modern life.

Management Courses Offered

Serving the industries in another educational capacity, the Institute also has management courses in the night school division that are attended by several thousand persons from business and industry.

These subjects have helped advance hundreds of people in the Rochester area each year. Also, there are special short courses that are continually being offered in the various mechanical fields, such as screw machine technology.

NYSNSA's Record Commendable Over Three Year Period; Sets National Pace

NSA Notes

Discounts of five to twenty-five percent on things students buy are secured through the U.S. National Student Association Purchase Card System, which may be used by any institution of higher education in the United States.

* * *

The U.S. National Student Association is the "trouble-shooter" for the individual student governments.

* * *

The Association compiles information and projects ideas of value to all sizes and types of institutions.

(Continued on Page 4)

BMOR

Wilbur "Jack" Bradigan, a senior at the University of Buffalo, has been selected as Big Man of the Region.

Jack has done outstanding work during the past year as chairman of the commission on the Purchase Card System. A connoiseur of fast women and slow horses, he is usually seen wearing the latest in Canadian sportswear (i. e. blazer jackets.)

An asset to all who know him, Jack is sure to be a success in his chosen vocation.

FRANK J. DOWD
University of Rochester, '48

Perhaps the most dominant theme running through the discussions of those who created the National Student Association was that this organization must be democratic in nature. The regional structure which was adopted was an attempt to insure this characteristic. Far too often past student associations had failed because their national offices had lost contact with the very students they were supposed to represent. It was this warning which prompted the organizing of N.S.A. on a regional basis. Such a regional breakdown would not only serve to inform both the national and campus components of N.S.A. as to what the other was thinking and doing, but it would also make possible a student organization within the national body which could attack and solve problems of a local nature.

Actually, New York State as a regional organization goes back farther than the N. S. A. constitutional convention. It was at the Chicago Student Conference in December of 1946 that the region was first organized under the energetic leadership of Jack Minkoff of Cornell University. The following summer New York State took its place as one of the official regional organizations of the N.S.A.

Constitutional Convention

Regional officers were first elected in the summer of 1947 in Madison, Wisconsin. However, the region did not begin to function in a legal sense until its own constitutional convention which was held at the Eastman School of Music, University of Rochester in November. This meeting was particularly noteworthy for three reasons: the recognition of the many educational problems in this area which students might profitably explore; a recognition of the semantic difficulties involved in the actual formulation of a constitution; and the significant remarks of our guests, Harold Taylor of Sarah Lawrence and Howard Hanson of the Eastman School.

In its first year of existance the job of the New York State Region was two-fold. On the one hand, it had to work toward ratification among the colleges of the state while on the other hand, a workable program had to be formulated. Despite the concern and downright despair of many loyal students we surprised even ourselves by discovering that by the summer of 1948 this region was the third largest in voting power.

Noteworthy Projects

In regard to program, a number of projects deserve particular note. At the Christmas meeting of the National Executive Committee the Buffalo area was chosen as the local area for the initiation of the student "purchase card plan". Under the direct leaderstip of Lee Jones, national treasurer, and Nancy Glancy of the University of Buffalo this area of the region bent every effort to prove the practicality of the plan to reduce student living costs. Locally the project proved to be a complete success and the plan was adopted as part of the national program.

A student government clinic held at Alfred University in the Spring of 1948 indicated the value of student give and take in this all important field of student activity. For the first time in recent years the student leaders of this state were able to find out the progress of various colleges in developing their student governments.

As mandated by the representatives attending the Regional Constitutional Convention, the regional officers spent a great deal of time collecting information on the questions of discrimination and the advisability of a state university

(Continued on Page 4)

This is a photograph of the new 4-color web-fed offset press to be installed at Rochester Institute of Technology.

New Web Offset Press Due to Arrive at RIT

Establishment of a $250,000 laboratory for experimentation and training for four-color web offset press operation at Rochester Institute of Technology, has been announced by Dr. Mark Ellingson, president.

The laboratory, which will be an additional division of RIT's Publishing and Printing department under Byron G. Culver, is to be set up in collaboration with the American Type Founders and more then 20 printing and supply industries.

Focal point will be a four-color Webendorfer offset press, provided by American Type Founders. Capable of delivering a complete 16-page full size newspaper, printing both sides simultaneously, the 42-ton press operates on a 30-horsepower motor. The laboratory, in full operation, would utilize approximately one-third the power which now operates the entire Institute.

Building Completed Feb. 1

Building of the press was completed Feb. 1 followed by a six-week test run in Elizabeth, N. J., under direction of the ATF, the Institute, and Readers' Digest. It then was dismantled and shipped to RIT in units.

Dr. Ellingson predicted that several months will be required to set the press up and get it in operation. It is expected to be ready for use here by the opening of the fall semester in September. Although all details for the education program have not been completed as yet, it is expected that students may enroll in the fall, for specialized work in this area.

Located in Clark Building

The laboratory will be located in the basement of the Clark building, which also houses the Publishing and Printing department on the second floor. Masons have already lowered a 30-inch pit in the basement floor to make room for the 10-foot high machine. The press is nearly 52 feet long and 12 feet wide.

In addition to the offset unit, the laboratory will include complete platemaking, facilities, camera room, paper storage area, shipping and sample room. These, plus auxiliary equipment for the laboratory, have a value of approximately $250,000, and are provided by interested industries.

Result of Conference

The laboratory will be the only one of its kind in operation. The project grew out of a conference on problems of education and training for the offset web-fed field held December, 1948, at RIT at which representatives of major industries and printing companies concerned were present. The Lithotech foundation collaborated with the Institute in arranging the conference

"SPRIT," student newspaper at RIT, which is edited and published entirely by the students, will be used as a "guinea pig" for experiments in photo-typesetting, deadline studies and materials testing. There are some 50 web

NYSNSA History . . .

(*Continued from Page 3*)

in New York. The regional officers met frequently with state educational officials and others working on this problem. Looking to the future, committees were organized to lay plans for a regional cultural festival and traveling art exibits.

The bulk of activity in the international field consisted of passing information on foreign travel to member schools, tentatively formulating a speaker's bureau, and distributing information questionnaires which would be of value for any future action in the international student field.

International Program

Both the international and the domestic programs as well as the ratification campaign were aided by publicity campaigns under the able direction of Charles Warner of the Eastman School. In the course of the school year 1947—48 a series of newsletters, a booklet describing the national and regional beginings of N.S.A. and specific news releases were distributed by the regional public relations office.

By the time of the first official congress of the region, which was held at the University of Buffalo in the Spring of 1948, it was evident that a further area breakdown was necessary in order for the region to fuction properly. Many of the projects that the region wished to work on required frequent meetings which were impossible in an area the size of this state. As a result much of the time of the delegates to the Buffalo meeting was spent formulating a sub-regional breakdown. Undoubtedly this discussion detracted from many important programing decisions that should have been made. However, the five area regional breakdown that was finally arranged made possible many cooperative programs that would have been otherwise impossible. It is interesting to note that the "area" arrangement that was drafted at Buffalo has been the model that several other regions have followed.

Responsible Students

It is difficult for one who has profited as much as this writer from his experiences in N.S.A. affairs to objectively evaluate the worth of the early work done in this region. Of course there were many things we hoped to do that were not done. On many campuses N.S.A. work was restricted to a very few people. However, I think it can be said that if the students of this rgion more fully appreciate their role in education and are

NSA's Leaders Give Proof of Youth's Ability

Five college students, with an average age of 21½ years, head the national staff of the National Student Association.

They are: Robert A. Kelly, president; Theodore Perry, vice-president for student life; Richard J. Medalie, vice-president for educational problems; Erskine B. Childers, vice-president for international affairs; and Fred Houghteling, executive secretary.

Their terms, Houghteling excepted, began following the August NSA Congress.

KELLY, 20, of Jersey City, N. J., is a senior in history at St. Peter's College, N. J., and has been active in the Association since its first beginnings.

He attended the Constitutional Convention held in Madison, Wis., in August, 1947. He became an original member of the New Jersey Regional Executive Committee, and was later elected its vice-chairman and finally chairman.

Outside NSA, he distinguished himself as national champion in the American Legion Oratorical Contest, 1945.

PERRY, 25, of Philadelphia, Pa., is a senior in accounting at Temple University, and has been active in NSA since its first Congress.

He was chairman of the Philadelphia sub-region of Pennsylvania and chairman of a regional sub-commission on academic freedom.

Perry was the first student to gain a high position in the National Association for the Advancement of Colored People, when he was appointed to the board of directors of the Philadelphia branch of NAACP.

(Perry is representing the national staff at this regional conference.)

NSA-CONSCIOUS Carelton College, Minn., formerly had Medalie, 20, of Minneapolis, Minn., pre-med junior, for its campus chairman.

He was also co-chairman of the NSA western area headquarters sub-commission, on educational practices and human relations.

Medalie has also been active in the Minnesota SPAN (Student Project for Amity among Nations) Association and Carelton student government.

CHILDERS, 20, a junior studying international relations at Stanford, was born in Ireland. His father was a high official in the last De Valera government and his grandfather a famed patriot.

In the short two years he has spent in this country, he has assisted in the founding of a secondary school designed to promote international understanding and citizenship, in Arizona, and been active in Stanford student government.

For NSA, he supervised Latin American relations as U. S. representative in Lima, Peru, and was co-chairman of the California, Nevada, Hawaii region.

Fred Houghteling, 22, of Harvard, recently replaced Robert Delahanty as executive secretary of NSA. Houghteling's present duties include setting up the 1950 national Congress which will be hel at the University of Michigan. This summer, Fred plans to go on a travel scholarship to Europe.

TECH SPEAKS

By CAROLYN AUYER

What is your opinion of the NSA conference?

Joan Henry
AA Senior

To unite student government throughout the country is one of the goals brought closer to reality through the NSA conference at RIT.

Mrs. Kelly
P & P Staff

I share RIT's enthusiasm for NSA and believe it can be a powerful and constructive force if its energies are properly handled.

Patricia Barry
Pub. Dir.

The conference, with editors' forum, art contest, and discussion of student affairs, is a good sign of the broad interests of NSA.

Steve Andras
P&P Senior

A few of the issues already executed through NSA along with proposed plans for the future, indicate sucess and a long stay at RIT. Congratulations!

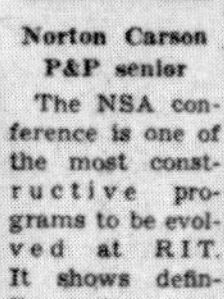

Norton Carson
P&P senior

The NSA conference is one of the most constructive programs to be evolved at RIT. It shows definite mature progress.

Jody Thompson
AA Frosh

It will facilitate the interchange of ideas among schools. NSA should keep in mind that it serves the individual student.

Convention Speakers Represent Broad Educational Background

The New York State Region of the NSA is fortunate in having as its guest speakers the persons listed below. They represent a broad cross-section of individuals familiar on the educational scene in the State of New York and on the national level as well.

Wesley I. Clark. A graduate of Marietta college, Ohio, Prof. Wesley Clark received his Doctor of Philosophy degree from the University of Pennsylvania. He served in the capacity as assistant to the Secretary of the Interior and worked with Harold L. Ickes in Washington after he had resigned that position.

Prof. Clark taught government at the Wharton School, University of Pennsylvania, and was a newspaper reporter with the Philadelphia Evening Bulletin and other newspapers for ten years.

At present, he is acting dean of the Syracuse University School of Journalism.

Donald W. White. A major in advertising when he was graduated from Louisiana State university, Donald M. White served three years in the field artillery in the recent war. Soon after his discharge, he came to Rochester Tech to study the technical aspects in newspaper production.

While at RIT, he served as assistant to Byron G. Culver, supervisor of the Publishing and Printing department and as an instructor in subjects related to printing, such as report writing advertising, etc.

Last fall Mr. White became managing editor of the Post-Herald corporation and in November was elected secretary of the Western New York Newspaper Publishers association.

Lawrence L. Jarvie. A graduate of Ohio State university where he later received his Ph.D., Dr. Lawrence L. Jarvie has led an active life in the field of education.

A native of Scotland, Dr. Jarvie has served in various educational capacities in Wyoming, Ohio, Washington, D. C., Illinois and New York. From 1937 to 1942 he was director of research at Rochester Institute of Technology.

During World War II, Dean Jarvie was chief of training for the Command and General Staff school. In 1946 he returned to the New York State Department of Education. A member of Phi Delta Kappa fraternity, Dr. Jarvie has served as advisor editor to Harper Bros., publishers.

Elizabeth B. Emlen. As regional

in aiding students the world over.

Mrs. Emlen first became interested in student work when she served with the National Japanese-American Relocation council, resettling Nisei students. At the end of the war, she joined her husband as a representative of the American Friends Service committee and spent 15 months in Europe.

Convinced by her experience that the personal element in WSSF is the organization's most important aspect, Mrs. Emlen brings to the Regional Confrence a quiet but persuasive personality, experience and faith in students as a vital force for peace.

Byron G. Culver. When the Department of Publishing and Printing was organized in 1937 at RIT, Byron G. Culver, painter, designer and typographer was selected to head it.

Mr. Culver has done considerable free lance work in commercial and industrial design and in illustration, and once was commissioned to do special work for the Munsell Color company.

In 1946 and 1947, he was elected president of the National Graphic Arts Educational association. The Rochester Club of Printing House Craftsmen elected him its president for two years commencing in 1944.

Leo F. Smith. A member of Phi Beta Kappa fraternity, Dr. Leo Smith received both his master and doctor's degree from the University of Chicago. Sometime earlier, he had received his A. B. from Occidental college.

At present, Dr. Smith is in charge of the research department and counseling center at Rochester Institute of Technology. In conjunction with Dr. Jarvie and a third person, Dr. Smith wrote "How to Read in Science and Technology" which was published by Harper Bros.

In demand as a speaker, he has authored many articles which have been published in various educational publications.

NSA Notes . . . .

(*Continued from Page 3*)

NSA Conference in Action
Photos by Harvey Samuels,
Jerry Kunin
N·Y·S·N·S·A
REGIONAL
CONFERENCE
N·Y·S·N·S·A
REGIONAL
CONFERENCE

Rochester Institute of Technology Organizes the Regional Assembly

CONFERENCE CHAIR GENE PENLER REPORTS

1950 RIT Yearbook, Wallace Library, RIT

More than 200 persons, representing 40 schools in upstate New York, attended the annual spring conference of the New York State Region of the U. S. National Student Association. The three-day assembly was held at Rochester Institute of Technology on March 31, April 1 and 2, 1950.

Highlight of the conference was an editors' forum which was held in conjunction with the regular sessions. Visiting editors had the opportunity to examine thoroughly Rochester Tech's Department of Publishing and Printing, which has reproduction equipment valued in excess of $700,000. A special NSA issue of RIT's student publication, *Sprit*, was published at the conference for the benefit of the representatives.

Panels and commissions included Bill of Rights, Student Unions, Role of the College Newspaper, Student Government Structure and Finances, Student-Faculty Relationships and Leadership.

NSA Vice President Ted Perry: "The best conference"

Principal speakers at the conference were Lawrence Jarvie, executive dean of the State University of New York; Wesley Clark, Syracuse University School of Journalism; Leo Smith, Director of Research at Rochester Institute of Technology; and Ted Perry, NSA Vice-president. According to Perry, the NYSNSA regional conference was the best he had witnessed in the history of USNSA.

Cultural aspects of the assembly were art and photo contests. Students from numerous upstate colleges responded to make both exhibitions successful. Social events included a dinner in the RIT cafeteria on Friday night which was later followed by an informal mixer in "Ye Olde College Inn." Saturday night a highly successful banquet was held in the Hotel Rochester.

Rochester Tech's NSA Committee constituted the Regional Conference Committee. Members were Claudia Symonds, Edgar Posner, Judah Eliezer, Joan Harlan, William Lapp, Don Tarleton and Gene Penler chairman. Harold Garfinkle, editor of *Sprit*, led the editors forum.

Photographs, posters, cartoons and literature prepared for and during the conference will be on display at the Third Annual Congress, which will be held August 23-31 at the University of Michigan.

CONFERENCE REGISTRATION LIST

Bard College
Brockport S.T.C.
Buffalo State Teachers College
Canisius College
Champlain College
Colgate University
College of St. Rose
Cornell University
D'Youville College
Fredonia S.T.C.
Hartwick College
Hobart College
Houghton College
Lemoyne College
N.Y. State Ag. and Mech. Inst. - Morrisville
N.Y. State Ag. and Tech. Inst. - Delhi
N.Y. State Ag. and Tech. Inst. - Canton
N.Y. State Inst. of Applied Arts & Sciences - Binghamton
N.Y. State Inst. of Applied Arts & Sciences - Buffalo
Nazareth College
Niagara University
Paul Smith's College
Potsdam S.T.C.
Rochester Business Institute
Rochester Institute of Technology
Rosary Hill College
Russell Sage College
Siena College
St. Bonaventure College
St. Lawrence University
Syracuse University
Triple-Cities College
Union College
University of Buffalo
University of Rochester - Men
University of Rochester - Nursing
University of Rochester - Women
Utica Tech
Wells College
William Smith College

Conference report and document source: Archives, Rochester Institute of Technology

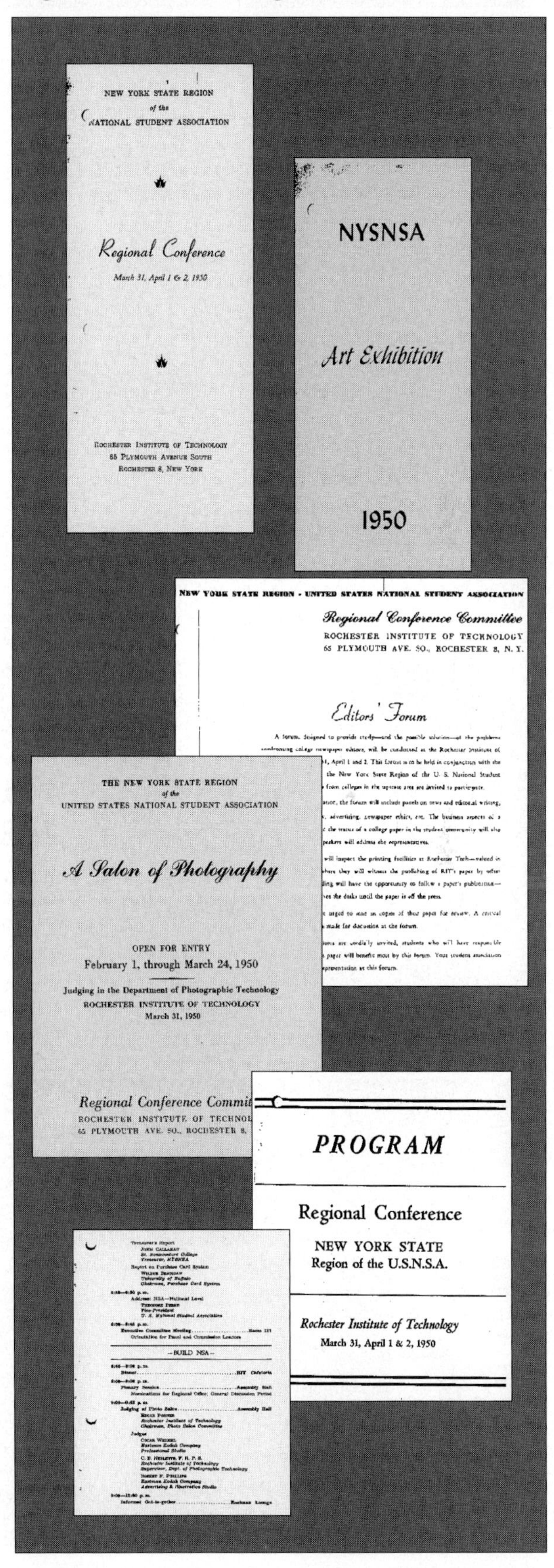

NEW YORK STATE REGION of the NATIONAL STUDENT ASSOCIATION

Regional Conference

March 31, April 1 & 2, 1950

Rochester Institute of Technology
65 Plymouth Avenue South
Rochester 8, New York

NYSNSA

Art Exhibition

1950

NEW YORK STATE REGION • UNITED STATES NATIONAL STUDENT ASSOCIATION

Regional Conference Committee

ROCHESTER INSTITUTE OF TECHNOLOGY
65 PLYMOUTH AVE. SO., ROCHESTER 8, N. Y.

Editors' Forum

THE NEW YORK STATE REGION of the UNITED STATES NATIONAL STUDENT ASSOCIATION

A Salon of Photography

OPEN FOR ENTRY
February 1, through March 24, 1950

Judging in the Department of Photographic Technology
ROCHESTER INSTITUTE OF TECHNOLOGY
March 31, 1950

Regional Conference Commit
ROCHESTER INSTITUTE OF TECHNOL
65 PLYMOUTH AVE. SO., ROCHESTER 8,

PROGRAM

Regional Conference

NEW YORK STATE
Region of the U.S.N.S.A.

Rochester Institute of Technology
March 31, April 1 & 2, 1950

—BUILD NSA—

University of Rochester/College for Men/College for Women

THE CAMPUS

Editor's note: All four divisions of UR—Men's, Women's, Nursing, Eastman School of Music—maintained active NSA membership during its early years. Noted composer Howard Hansen, Eastman's director, addressing the 1947 Regional Assembly, "warned the students of impetuous action. . . . Claiming it was the youth that wore the black, brown, and red shirts, he cautioned American youth against alien ideologies."(The Campus *12/19/47*)

Rochester Delegates At NSA Convention

The six University of Rochester delegates to the constitutional convention of the National Student's Association prepared this week to report to their various student governments concerning the program and actions of this new student movement. From August 7 to September 8 the Rochester aggregation representing Eastman, The Nursing School, and the Men's and Women's colleges met at the University of Wisconsin with 700 other delegates representing 351 leading colleges and universities throughout the United States to write the NSA constitution and plan a program of activities to improve education and to promote friendship and understanding among students both at home and abroad.

Representing the four divisions of the University were: Paul Abel and Chuck Warner from Eastman, Kay Sanney from Prince Street, Ann McCaffery from the School of Nursing, and Frank Dowd from the River Campus.

The Campus 10/3/47

Tower Times

Published Weekly by the College for Women of the University of Rochester

VOL. XVII—Z 514 ROCHESTER, N. Y., DECEMBER 12, 1941 No. 11

UR Head Issues War Statement

President Alan Valentine Advises Students About Crisis

"OUR COUNTRY IS NOW COMPLETELY INVOLVED in an all-out war ... there has been disagreement as to the wisdom of the policies ... which have brought us to this crisis. But the crisis has arrived, and such differences of opinion must now become past history." President Valentine's statement following Pearl Harbor in 1941 echoed Fordham President Father Gannon's (p. 888), setting the tone of resolve on campuses across the country.

Rochester Host To NSA At Weekend Convention

International affairs, human relations, and student life are among the subjects to be aired by students from 25 colleges who will come to the River Campus, University of Rochester, this Saturday and Sunday, March 26 and 27.

The occasion will be the New York State Regional Convention of the U. S. National Student Association, to which the University of Rochester branch will be host. Arrangements are in charge of William Kotary, Paul Bourgeois, and Richard Appel of the U of R Men's College.

Colleges which will be represented at the convention include Cornell, Syracuse, Champlain, Bard, Skidmore, Vassar, Siena, Wells, Houghton, Nazareth, Rochester Institute of Technology, D'Youville, University of Buffalo, Clarkson, St. Rose, Niagara, Buffalo State Teachers, Buffalo Technical Institute, William Smith College, St. Bonaventure, Canisius, Alfred, and Rosary Hill.

Purposes of NSA

The NSA, according to Kotary, is pledged among other things "to maintain academic freedom and student rights, to stimulate and improve democratic student governments, to develop better educational standards, facilities, and teaching methods, to improve student cultural, social and physical welfare, to promote international understanding and fellowship, to guarantee to all people, because

Bill Ryan, President of the Student Association

The Campus 3/25/49

UR Observers Report 'Pink' Hue Of N. S. O. Unfounded

The perversities of parliamentary procedure plus a blizzard in the best Windy City manner could not dull the perspicacity nor dampen the enthusiasm of the three Rochesterians sent to observe the national student conference held during Christmas vacation at the Uni-

Constitutional Convention of NSA Discussed in Assembly Wednesday

A new term, "NSA" seeped into the college vocabulary of the Women's Campus as a result of Wednesday's assembly. Students were informed of the principles and the constitution of a National Students' Association as conceived this year at the constitutional

NSA Sponsors Student Govt. Clinic To Be Held March 12 At Syracuse

Al Lowenstein To Speak On Policies of NSA At Demitasse Tonight

The Prince Street Campus will be hostess tonight at one of the most exciting and interesting events on the calendar. Al Lowenstein, National President of the United States National Students' Association, arrives in Rochester today and will be featured at a dinner held in his honor tonight at Cutler Union.

Al is twenty-one years old, a graduate of the University of North Carolina. On the basis of

NSA To Combine Campus Talent In Variety Show

The NSA will reign supreme Saturday night, January 6, in Cutler Union with a Variety Show featuring entertainment from the local colleges. The admission price of sixty cents, covers both the show itself and a dance, sponsored by the SA's of both campuses which will follow the program. The proceeds from the evening will go to the World Student Service Fund.

Program features will include a modern tap dancing demonstration by students from

"THE NSA COMMITTEE ON CAMPUS SHOULD BE AN ARM OF THE STUDENT GOVERNMENT" (Claire King, 1950 Campus NSA Rep., in the *Tower Times*, 10/7/49). Active collaboration marked UR's membership. (Fr. top, *Tower Times*: l., 1/10/47, 12/12/47, 3/4/49; r., 10/27/50, 12/15/50)

Historical note: UR was founded in 1850 as a Baptist-sponsored institution; women were first admitted in 1900, due in large part to the efforts of Susan B. Anthony. The school of music was named after George Eastman, founder of Eastman Kodak, a major donor (www.rochester.edu). Enrollment in 1948 was around 5,000 (School and Society, *12/18/48).*

Frank J. Dowd: Campus and Regional Leader

The Campus 4/25/47

An honors student in history ('48), campus leader and member, Board of Control.

Editor's note: Recalling the day in November of 1944 when a German 88mm shell struck his jeep, Dowd wrote in 1987, "Like all young men, I was certain I could not die. I continued this belief through the severing of my jugular vein and other adventures. This is not to say I wasn't scared—often." Dowd married Janis Tremper (See p. 60, also Jones, p. 874), NSA's 1947-48 Secretary-Treasurer. They had three children. He was Vice President at Lincoln University (PA), and retired as Vice President for Student Affairs at the University of Rochester.

Frank Dowd Re-elected President of State NSA at Regional Convention

by Dave Parker

Frank Dowd, senior and member of the board of control, was reelected president of the New York State National Students Association at the regional convention held at Rochester last week-end. After demonstrating his executive ability by skillfully chairing the difficult constitutional convention, Dowd was able to win the election by a large majority over his one opposing candidate.

He had previously been chosen to head the regional organization at the national convention held at Madison, Wisconsin in Septem-

Dowd laid a foundation for the N.Y. State Region. The Regional Assembly favored formation of a state university in N.Y. (*Campus* 12/19/47).

Cornell University

Editor's note: The Cornell Student Council and Cornell Daily Sun *provided vigorous support for NSA in its founding years. For a period in 1950-51, the Council disafilliated by close and hotly contested margins (see right). In August, 1951, the campus was host to the World Assembly of Youth (see p. 767). Jack Minkoff '48 (later to become Dean at Pratt Institute) was the first Chair of the NY State Region. Robert Fogel '48, Labor Youth League leader (later a Nobel Laureate in economics), appeared in opposition to the Korean War at the 1950 National Student Congress (see p. 289). Bob Beyers, 1952-53 editor in chief of the Cornell Daily Sun (later a renowned educational journalist), became NSA Public Information Director in 1954-55 (see p. 481).*

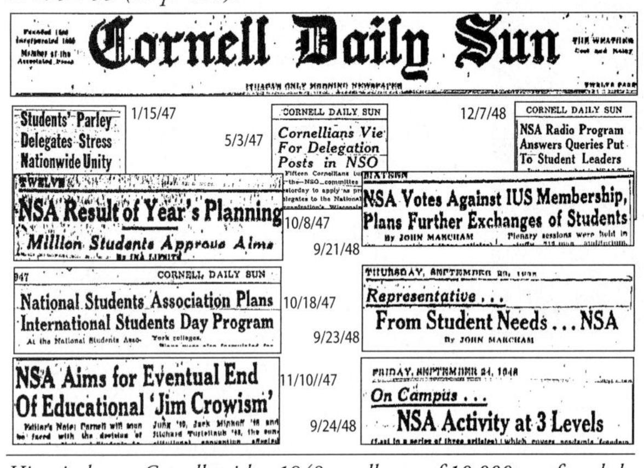

Cornell Daily Sun

Students' Parley Delegates Stress Nationwide Unity — 1/15/47

CORNELL DAILY SUN — Cornellians Vie For Delegation Posts in NSO — 5/3/47

CORNELL DAILY SUN — NSA Radio Program Answers Queries Put To Student Leaders — 12/7/48

NSA Result of Year's Planning — Million Students Approve Aims — 10/8/47

NSA Votes Against IUS Membership, Plans Further Exchanges of Students — By JOHN MARCHAM — 9/21/48

CORNELL DAILY SUN — National Students Association Plans International Students Day Program — 10/18/47

Representative . . . From Student Needs . . . NSA — By JOHN MARCHAM — 9/23/48

NSA Aims for Eventual End Of Educational 'Jim Crowism' — 11/10//47

FRIDAY, SEPTEMBER 24, 1948 — On Campus . . . NSA Activity at 3 Levels — 9/24/48

Historical note: Cornell, with a 1948 enrollment of 10,000 was founded in 1865 by Ezra Cornell, contributing funds and his Ithaca farm for the new land-grant university (www.cals.cornell.edu).

Cornell: "Not an Island Unto Itself"

Cornell Daily Sun 5/8/50

INITIAL SUPPORT FOR NSA WAS BREECHED in 1950 when the Student Council suspended membership. An aggressive campaign led by Nancy Helm, '53, Council Vice President resulted in a 23-4 vote to rejoin in 11/51.

Council Ratifies New Constitution of NSA

Campus Linked With National Student Group

Cornell became one of the first universities officially connected with the National Student Association as the Student Council voted last night to ratify the NSA constitution and affiliate with its national organization.

10/31/47

NSA—Representing American Students

Offers Program of Regional, Campus Activities Projects

ANNUAL CONVENTION IN ACTION

At Cornell . . .

12/6/48

Council Rejects NSA by 1 Vote; Takes Action after Long Debate

Membership Not Worth Expense, Council Decides

11/17/50

Council Passes NSA Affiliation By Heavy Vote

Coming as the climax to four weeks' discussion, deliberation, and debate, Student Council last night approved a resolution to rejoin the National Student Association by a decisive 23-4 vote.

10/17/51

Cornell and the NSA

Should Cornell be a member of the National Student Association?

Is the Student Council justified in spending over $200 of the students' money each year to have Cornell included in NSA?

What can Cornell give to the NSA, and what can the NSA give to Cornell?

These are the questions the Student Council will be considering tonight as it tries to determine the future of NSA on this campus.

We think Cornell would be shirking its responsibility as a university if it failed to rejoin NSA. We think the Council should act promptly to see that Cornell becomes again a part of the only organization which represents American students on a nation-wide scale.

Just what will NSA do here in Ithaca for Cornell students? Not much; a local NSA council is primarily a service organization which handles the work of fund-raising drives, special contests, and similar activities. At Cornell this work is done by the Student Council or by other organizations; an additional Council would be superfluous.

The value of the NSA to Cornell will be less concrete, but not less genuine. NSA is the only organization which can meet the Communist "International Union of Students" on its own terms to tell the students of other countries the truth about America and her schools. NSA is the only organization which can represent American students—all American students—in the United Nations commissions, in the State Department, with the officials of the Selective Service organization. These are all functions which the NSA has taken up in the three short years of its existence. There will be additions, and important additions, to the work of the National Student Association.

Cornell should have a part in this work. Cornell should be a member of the NSA.

11/9/50

Alfred University

Fiat Lux 3/30/48

Student Representatives To Air Common Problems In Government, Activities

Confab Sponsored Jointly By Alfred Student Groups And New York State NSA; Colleges' Response Encouraging

About 25 upstate New York colleges and universities already have accepted an invitation to the NSA-Alfred Student Conference, April 9-10, to air common problems in their campus and women's governments, student union and campus newspaper.

Included in this number are representatives from Bard, Brockport, Buffalo State, Champlain, Colgate, Cornell, Eastman School of Music, Elmira, Hartwick, Hobart, LeMoyne, Rochester Busines Institute, Russell Sage, St. Lawrence, Siena, Union, University of Buffalo and William Smith.

Sponsored jointly by Alfred student groups and the New York State National Student Association, the conference will provide delegates with an opportunity to discuss such vital problems as the relationships between the college administration and the

Editor Explains ... In Fiat ... l Staff

... of the Fiat Lux ... suggested by Editor ... e Robarts '48, last ... at the regular staff ... zation of responsi-

1949 Kanakadea Yearbook (Herrick Memorial Library)

INGRAM PAPERNY, '49, was 1947-48 NY State Vice-Chair and organizer of the 4/48 conferences attended by 25 colleges.

Editor's note: After dropping out of NSA, Alfred re-affiliatd in 1955. In "The History of the Student Senate," Michael J. Pellicotti (Class of 2000) writes (p. 28), regarding NSA's civil rights programs, "in its ten years on campus, the NSA had a major impact." (See Curry, p. 444.) Alfred, in Alfred, NY, was founded in 1836 by the Seventh Day Baptists "and has always been non-sectarian and co-educational" (www.herr.alfred.edu). Its enrollment was 1,177 in 1948.

Colgate University

COLGATE UNIVERSITY
HAMILTON, NEW YORK

Philosophy and Religion

15 March 1952

The National Student Association
Madison, Wisconsin

Dear Sirs:

As one who has had a good deal of respect for the N.S.A., I was distressed to read the lead editorial in this week's "Colgate Maroon". Were I a student instead of an instructor here, I should wish to write a letter of protest myself, but in my present capacity, and without the specific facts to make a hard-hitting rebuttal, I guess the best I can do is to give you the opportunity (if you have not already had it) to speak for yourselves. The paper is published on Wednesday afternoon's, so if you intend a reply, I hope you can do it while the iron is hot.

State Historical Society of Wisconsin

The Colgate Maroon 3/12/52 [excerpted]

Colgate Maroon

FOUNDED 1868

COLGATE UNIVERSITY, Hamilton, N. Y., MARCH 12, 1952

N. S. A ? NO THANKS

Student Senators should consider carefully the proposal to affiliate with the National Student Association. There seems to be very little of value in the N. S. A. for Colgate, or much that Colgate would want to cooperate with.

Two years after our brothers and friends started dying in Korea the N. S. A. — which wants us to join — still cannot make up its mind wether to become a full-fledged member of the IUS, or withdraw completely from it! Should there then be any question whether or not Colgate joins?

The MAROON insists that Colgate not affiliate with the N. S. A. for the following three reasons:

1) Their on-campus program is of no interest or value to us.

2) Colgate rejects the basic N. S. A. supposition that American students need to organize to protect their rights.

3) We disagree with their approach toward domestic policy-making, international affairs and communism.

Colgate students, then, should understand what the N. S. A. means for them, weigh the $35 annual dues and $75 initiation fee, and then instruct their senators to turn thumbs down on the N. S. A.!!

ALERTED BY A COLGATE INSTRUCTOR, who wrote "I doubt that your cause would be favored by mentioning how you happened to hear about this lamentable editorial," Bill Dentzer, NSA President (p. 305), wrote a comprehensive letter on 3/31/32 *(SHSW)* to the Editor of the Maroon in which he noted "NSA has constantly refused joining [IUS] because of the political connections of IUS." He termed the editorial "unfair," although "written in all sincerity . . . mistatement and misinterpretation of the facts have been the greatest barrier to a just judgement of the association."

Editor's note: Colgate was founded in 1819 by the Baptist Education Society, and located in Hamilton, NY. It was named in 1890 after the Colgate family, and became co-educational in 1970 (www.colgate.edu). Its enrollment in 1948 was 1,517.

Higher education reform holds too little reference to the student and his place in contemporary life.

Harold Taylor: "To Make of Each College a Model Society"

President, Sarah Lawrence College, Bronxville, NY
Member, NSA National Advisory Committee, 1949-50, 1951-53, 1957-58

Editor's note: Harold Taylor was a fresh and innovative voice on the education scene. He spoke out forcefully on acadmic freedom issues (See p.000) and was a strong supporter of student involvement in the entire education process. An active supporter of NSA, he served on its National Advisory Committee and appeared at national and regional NSA conferences as a speaker and resource person. Below are excerpts from the keynote address he delivered at the Second National Student Congress at the University of Illinois on August 24, 1949.

In the past ten years, the American college student has shown that he is a responsible person. He has handled his own affairs. He has chosen a career. He has worked his way through college. As a student, he has edited newspapers, run businesses, fought a war, chosen a wife, married her, supported a family, voted for a president. But during these years, while young men and women in college have been doing all of the things which adults do, they have been treated, for the most part, as intellectual children. The student has been given very little responsibility for his own education. It has been organized for him by trustees, Boards of Regents, faculty committees, alumni committees, legislatures, businessmen, newspaper publishers, college presidents, parents, and educators. Almost everyone in America, including the Communist Party and the American Legion, now wants to help in organizing college education.

A whole host of the uninformed have accordingly risen to form themselves as an over-all American Committee dedicated to protecting American college students from themselves and to preventing lively growth in their political and social maturity. It has become a national conviction that ability to function as an executive in any branch of business, industry, banking, newspaper, or political life equips a person to reform education. All those who have thus interested themselves in the sanctity of the American college have lined up together with one great handicap in carrying out their enterprise. They are, for the most part, unaware of the interests, talents, capacities, and maturity of the present American student.

Students are ready to take responsibility

This lack of awareness is, in some degree, shared by educators and faculty members who are responsible for the formal organization of the college program. It is because of the lack of close relationship between all the planners, academic and non-academic, and the acting, thinking, learning student in each college that the student has not been given the responsibility he is ready to take. He is presented with education already systematically organized into credits, units, grades, majors, courses, curricula, lectures, tests, mimeographed sheets, grade-point averages, and other educational preventatives. The American student is accordingly over-organized.

The story of student life in America is one of gradual emancipation from the intellectual and social controls of the educational system and from economic circumstances which have prevented the wider spread of higher education for all. From an informal look at the history of students in America, I would say that on most social questions and on most educational questions, the students have been ahead of the educators in suggesting liberal reforms which eventually have been proved wise in adoption.

The National Student Association: full of good ideas

Now you have been through the war, and the years after, and are all more serious and stronger because of the severity of your social and military education. I can see in this generation of college students, young people who are interested in politics, civil rights, social reform, and education. Students now want more responsibility as adults to run their own affairs. They have shown themselves capable of doing so on every campus where they have been given the opportunity.

I think I am betraying no secret when I say that now they are setting about the task of educating the older generation, and the first people to get the benefit will be their professors. The National Student Association is strong, good, liberal, responsible, and full of new ideas, some of which may curl the hair of the academic profession. The students in this country are taking responsible leadership. . . .

* * *

Too few colleges and universities have grasped the essential truth stated by the President's Commission on Higher Education, that the total development of the individual is the primary concern of the college. The present plans for the reform of higher education have been made with too little reference to the individual student and his place in contemporary life. They have been conceived by members of the academic community, meeting in committee, isolated from the student's world, and accordingly have been conceived in conventionally academic terms,

The regular materials of the old college curriculum have now been rearranged in a form which guarantees that every student will be treated to the same intellectual discipline and will be provided with a set of reports, digests, and surveys of knowledge. This eliminates the individual aptitudes, interests, and needs of the students. . . .

In the absence of a dynamic philosophy, other than the natural cohesion of similar subjects, it has been assumed that the welfare of each department in the college should be the central concern of the planning, and accordingly, representatives of various groups within the faculty have been assembled into committees on curriculum. . . .

Committees on curriculum: A "cartel system"

Throughout the country, this forms something in the nature of a cartel system, with only a few businesses, like Sarah Lawrence and Bennington, able to continue in operation outside the monopoly. The students comprise an increasingly large body of consumers, with the difference, as between them and other consumers, that no attention is paid to their individual wants and no market research is considered necessary. The fact that the new curriculum is now in operation from Los Angeles to Boston is a tribute to the seriousness and purpose, ingenuity, diligence, and sound business sense of the American academic community. It preserves intact the heritage of the past, the departmental system, and the authority of the faculty mind over the American student.

* * *

Students do know about their university. They can tell anyone who is interested which are the bad teachers, which are the entertainers, which are good teachers, which are soft-hearted, which are left or right wing, which are dull, which ones care about students, and which ones they consider useless. . . .

Students and faculty should plan curriculum together

All [the] sources of educational thought should be tapped for the use of the university. The most important single reform we could undertake to aid the student is to give him responsibility, and greater freedom to carry it out. His courses should be planned by research and discussion with students and faculty together. There should be a recognized student curriculum committee with power to share in the actual construction of the curriculum. In the absence of a recognized student curriculum committee, the students themselves can take the responsibility for forming one and can help to improve the quality of instruction without waiting to be asked. . . . The student and teacher, in their true roles, are actually two students working together, one of whom knows more than the other. . . .

The modern citizen needs to be secure enough about his own judgment to face any idea or situation with a confidence that he can form his own conclusion. He needs discipline enough in his emotional response to enjoy life at its best and to sustain himself at its worst. He needs an aim in life towards which his future is directed and which his education is helping him to fulfill. He needs teachers, deans, and administrators who realize that universities and colleges exist to help him achieve these qualities by whatever means can be devised. He needs all these things because his world today is confused, overpowering, and tense, and he and his friends, in our anxious age, can help to put it right.

HAROLD TAYLOR
(1914-1993)

Harold Taylor, who first came to national prominence in 1945 when at the age of thirty he was appointed as the third president of Sarah Lawrence College, is known as one of the most provocative and original thinkers in the field of American education.

Taylor received the B.A. and M.A. degrees in 1935 and 1936 for honors work in philosophy and literature at the University of Toronto, where funding for his graduate work was awarded through the university's Moss Scholarship for accomplishments as an athlete, musician, writer, and student. From 1936 to 1939, Taylor attended the University of London in England, where he received his Ph.D. in philosophy in 1938.

In 1939, Dr. Taylor joined the philosophy faculty at the University of Wisconsin, for a period of six years, with a leave of ab-sence for war service in psychological research for the National Defense Research Council.

As the president of Sarah Lawrence College, he continued his scholarly interests and taught philosophy both at the New School for Social Research and at Sarah Lawrence College. The author of *Art and Intellect* (1960), *On Education and Freedom* (1953), and *Essays in Teaching* (1952), and of more than 300 articles on philosophy and education published from 1945 to 1962 in journals and magazines, Dr. Taylor developed theories for the radical reform of education.

Following his retirement from Sarah Lawrence College in 1959, Dr. Taylor continued writing and lecturing and traveled extensively in the United States, the Soviet Union, Asia, the Middle East, Europe, and Australia. In the 1960s, Taylor served as founder and chairman of the Committee on Peace Research and co-founded the Peace Research Institute. In the 1970s, Taylor founded and chaired the United States Committee for the United Nations University

Adapted from "Biographical Note," Harold Taylor Papers, Sarah Lawrence College Archives

PICTURE CREDIT: c. 1949 (Sarah Lawrence Archives)

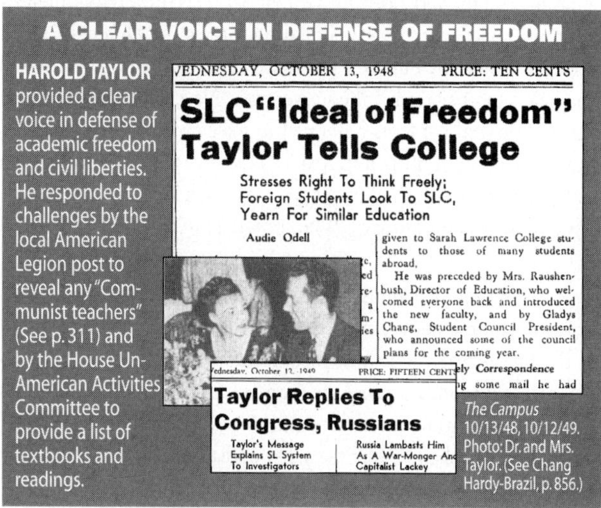

A CLEAR VOICE IN DEFENSE OF FREEDOM
HAROLD TAYLOR provided a clear voice in defense of academic freedom and civil liberties. He responded to challenges by the local American Legion post to reveal any "Communist teachers" (See p. 311) and by the House Un-American Activities Committee to provide a list of textbooks and readings.
WEDNESDAY, OCTOBER 13, 1948
PRICE: TEN CENTS
SLC "Ideal of Freedom" Taylor Tells College
Stresses Right To Think Freely; Foreign Students Look To SLC, Yearn For Similar Education
Audie Odell
given to Sarah Lawrence College students to those of many students abroad.
He was preceded by Mrs. Raushenbush, Director of Education, who welcomed everyone back and introduced the new faculty, and by Gladys Chang, Student Council President, who announced some of the council plans for the coming year.
Correspondence
some mail he had
PRICE: FIFTEEN CENTS
Taylor Replies To Congress, Russians
Taylor's Message Explains SL System To Investigators
Russia Lambasts Him As A War-Monger
Capitalist Lackey
The Campus 10/13/48, 10/12/49. Photo: Dr. and Mrs. Taylor. (See Chang Hardy-Brazil, p. 856.)

The new St. Peter's College would teach only intelligent and ambitious students.

Robert I. Gannon, S.J.: Champion of the Traditional Liberal Arts

President, St. Peters College, Newark, NJ, 1930-36
President, Fordham University, The Bronx, New York City, 1936-60

Editor's note: Robert I. Gannon, S.J., provided leadership to two colleges, prominent in NSA's formative years, which shaped the quality of their student bodies and the organizing talents, debaters, and tacticians among leaders who emerged from them in the New Jersey and Metropolitan New York Regions. In New Jersey it was prewar St. Peter's College that later contributed to NSA its leaders Bob Kelly and Tom Garrity.[1] In New York, it was wartime and postwar Fordham University that provided John Simons, Warren Gallagher, John Duffy, and Michael Di Legge.[2]

Who should go to college?

When Father Gannon was assigned to revive St. Peter's College in 1930, he wrote of himself in the third person as "the dean, young and inexperienced and not too intelligent; the sort of man with a strong back and a head full of convictions," and of the opportunity to bring into being his vision for an urban college in Jersey City (from The Poor Old Liberal Arts *[New York: Farrar, Straus and Cudahy, 1961]):*

There were no bad habits to overcome, no intrenched interests, no tired, disillusioned teachers, no students organized to passive resistance. So then and there it was determined, sitting on the roof looking at the linoleum factory, and in full smell of Colgate's down the street, that the new Saint Peter's College would be a novelty in American education. It would offer a first-class liberal arts course and teach only intelligent and ambitious students. In other words, it would give what it ought to give only to those who ought to get it—an almost unheard-of procedure. That meant that the dean would announce on the very opening day that Saint Peter's was not interested in numbers or in display. It had no interest in athletic or social prestige. When the question was asked on every hand: "When will you field a football team?" the answer was, "Never." When asked how many thousand students he hoped to have eventually, the answer was, "A maximum of six hundred." Thus, thirty years ago, the little college in the slums acted on a question which is still making headlines in the papers of today: "Who should go to college?"

* * *

Beginning work on the sixteenth of August [1930], it was possible to open the doors a month later with 70 freshmen. At the end of the first quarter, 3-4 of them were dropped. It was not as cold-blooded as it sounds because the dean was planning a February class where the promising ones who had misjudged the situation could have a second chance, but the news spread fast and the students who survived learned what was expected of them.

What the dean himself learned over the next six years was that educators in general do not realize the potentiality for work that exists in every pleasure-loving American boy with brains enough to deserve a college education. He may groan and weep and exercise ingenuity worthy of a better cause to avoid exerting himself. But if from the start he knows that the faculty means business and if the pressure is turned on a little at a time without ever being relaxed again, he ends up by taking twice as much education (nobody can give him an education!) as one would expect in the average institution. Or he transfers to more congenial surroundings, which is a splendid idea.

And so it happened at Saint Peter's. Real students came eventually from a radius of 50 miles precisely because they heard that there was a premium on hard work and brains, or because they wanted to study under a particular professor, or because it was said that top-flight medical schools would welcome any pre-med recommended by the little college on Newark Avenue.

"It was our war from the first."

Editor's note: On the occasion of Fr. Gannon's retirement, The Ram *(1/13/49) recalled "With the outbreak of war in 1941 . . .to insure that as many as possible could graduate before leaving . . . he announced a three-year accelerated course." In* The Poor Old Liberal Arts *(p. 156, op. cit.) Fr. Gannon quoted his 1942 academic year opening address to Fordham students in which he forecast that the accelerated course concept might have a peacetime use as well.*

"We have learned at last," he said to the student body assembled on the Edwards Parade, "that we can rely on no more barriers of time or place; that isolationism is as dead as the A.P.A. Only a year ago there were loyal Americans, and I was one of them, who felt that this was not our war, that if we kept to ourselves, no one would dare to attack us. We used to say that if the Soviet were wiped off the face of the earth it would be good riddance and that the feeble and guilty old British Empire was not worth one American life. We protested violently when we saw our president, as we used to put it, 'spoiling for a fight,' dragging us step by step into an endless and dreadful war which no enemy wanted to declare. Today it is humiliating, but many of us are ready to stand up in meeting and confess that we were wrong and he was right. It was our war from the first. If he had listened to us, China, Russia and Great Britain would now be prostrate and we should be facing our zero hour alone and unprepared. As it is, our strangely assorted allies are far from prostrate and their immense courage, backed up at last by the full power of the United States, will make this a long war with good news at the end.

"Of course, the longer the war, the longer the convalescence. Policing tasks that will face us for years to come will take as great an army as any offensive campaign, and cleaning up the wreckage, physical, financial and moral, at home and abroad, will require a large armed force for at least another generation. We shall have to reserve a year out of our crowded young American lives for military service."

Recollections of Father Gannon at Fordham

Michael Di Legge
Fordham College
Treasurer, Metropolitan New York Region, 1948-49
Chairman, Student Government Constitution Committee

I first came to know Father Gannon while I was a freshman at CCNY [City College of New York] trying to get as many credits [as possible] under my belt before being drafted into the Army. Ironically at the time while Father Gannon was overwhelming audiences with speeches on the values of "tradition," I was studying the philosophy of John Dewey at CCNY under Professor Ratner, which, of course, was espousing the opposite point of view. When I once told this to Father Gannon he was amused and said that a good scholar examines both sides of any issue before coming to a conclusion, adding that he was pleased to see that I [had] selected Fordham to resume my undergraduate studies.

As a Fordham delegate to the NSA I served the [Metropolitan New York] Region as treasurer, chairman of the Student Rights Conference (I prepared a long report on this issue), organized a Labor-Relations Work Shop Conference for Union Leaders in the Bronx, and after graduation chaired the NSA Finance-Administration Committee which made recommendation for reorganizing the national office. However, my main task and focus was to revamp the Student Government structure at Fordham. I was asked by our Student Council to chair the Student Government Constitutional Committee. This is where I devoted most of my time and energies during my Junior and Senior Years.

Encouraging a new student government at Fordham

While Father Gannon encouraged and supported our efforts in NSA, my dealings with him were as Chairman of the Student Constitutional Committee, which was charged with drafting a new Student Government Constitution based on the principles of participatory democracy.

Father Gannon was then in his last year of his long tenure as President of Fordham University. He had established a world reputation as an educator, speaker on an array of subjects and preacher on theology and Catholic Doctrine. On campus he was known to demand academic excellence, and while encouraging sports he did not support football as a major endeavor of the University. He was, above all, a priest in the tradition of the Society of Jesus—a Jesuit.

He encouraged and supported our proposals to reform student government at Fordham College and raised no objection to using the phrase "student rights" in the document—a phrase which was considered anathema by some traditional Jesuit educators. The Constitution was approved by a student convention and student referendum. For a Jesuit College it was somewhat revolutionary. Father Gannon had expressed the view that student government activities (and NSA) were a good training ground for student leaders and students in general in preparing themselves for their future civic responsibilities and in strengthening the nation's democratic institutions. I was very much impressed with his liberal views in this context.

In other matters: his Faith, the primacy of the liberal arts, he was a traditionalist, as expressed in his speeches and his writings, and, above all, he had a delicious sense of humor.

Michael Di Legge was with the U.S. Foreign Service, U.S. Department of State and Agency for International Development.

END NOTES

[1] Tom Garrity was president of the Metropolitan New York Region in 1948-1949. He attended St. Peter's in New Jersey and City College of New York evening sessions in New York simultaneously. He was also a St. Peter's delegate to the New Jersey Region. Bob Kelly was president of the New Jersey Region in 1948-1949 and NSA president in 1949-1950.

[2] John Duffy and Warren Gallagher were Fordham University delegates to the Chicago Student Conference. John Simons represented Fordham Law School and was elected treasurer of the National Continuations Committee. See Simons, p. 124.

PICTURE CREDITS: *Gannon:* c. 1940's. *DiLegge Then:* 1949 Maroon Yearbook (Both, Fordham U. Archives, Bronx, NY). *DiLegge Now:* c. 1990's (Author).

Fr. Gannon Lashes Truman Report

By LEONARD BAKER

Attacking the "present campaign for educational inflation," the Rev. Robert I. Gannon, S.J., President of Fordham University, denounced as a "fraud" the current report of the President's Committee on Higher Education. He then went on to say that "one-third of the so-called (college) students are in the way, cluttering up the place and interfering with other people's intellectual progress."

Father Gannon delivered his address before 1,000 former students at the 94th annual alumni dinner, held on Feb. 9 at the Hotel Commodore. His Eminence, Francis Cardinal Spellman, '11, presided, and Mr. Walter J. Black, President of the Fordham University Alumni Association, was toastmaster.

"The fraud in the present campaign . . . consists in swelling the number of incompetents in American colleges and calling it 'equality of opportunity,'" said the Fordham president. He attacked the report, which calls for an increase to over four million students in higher education by 1960, on the grounds that "small effort has been made to enumerate or analyze our present startling failures at the high school and college level, and also that college training will become inferior if flooded with students." He stated that, on the basis of fifty years' experience, he knows no educator with high ideals who would admit we had half that number ready to attend college.

Fr. Gannon

The board's approval of the proceedings of the Hart Committee, a fact-finding group in the New York Council, was also condemned by the Jesuit educator: "If you want your American blood to run cold, read the record and learn the methods and principles that were involved when a small but powerful political group had one of the world's greatest universities on the rack and was turning the screws."

Denying that he was the sponsor of any of the anti-discrimination bills now under consideration at Albany, which he said had been reported in the press, Father Gannon stated that one of these bills was sure to be adopted in New York, although such legislation is not needed.

His speech was not entirely one of denunciation, for he praised sections of the report as "admirable enough, though commonplace of today's academic discussions.

As to the unwanted one-third of the student body, Father Gannon went on to point out that "If we need more room to take care of the boom in 1960, let us create a good part of it by clearing out the useless lumber that we have already on our campuses. That will be like adding one new institution to every two in existence. Then by making it more and more difficult to get into college, we can raise the whole tone of our higher education to the point where we can someday produce a few much-needed national leaders."

"BY MAKING IT MORE DIFFICULT TO GET INTO COLLEGE, WE CAN RAISE THE WHOLE TONE OF OUR HIGHER EDUCATION." Gannon attacked the President's Committee on Higher Education report as a "fraud ... swelling the number of incompetents in American colleges and calling it 'equality of opportunity'" (*The Ram* 2/20/48). Resolutely defending his 1930 vision, voiced at St. Peter's, to "teach only intelligent and ambitious students," (above) he told the 94th annual alumni dinner that "small effort has been made to enumerate or analyze our startling failures at the high school and college level."

2. Tom Garrity, Bob Kelly and NSA at St. Peter's

Editor's note: Tom Garrity, raised in Manhattan, and Bob Kelly, in Jersey City, met at St. Peter's, where they became good friends and debating team adversaries. Garrity, who for three years simultaneously attended the CCNY evening session and St. Peter's during the day, was Met. NY Regional Chair in 1948-49, while Kelly was New Jersey Regional Chair. The following year (1949-50), Kelly became NSA president (See Part 1). Returning to St. Peter's in the fall of 1951, both he and Garrity became national debating champions, continuing activity in NSA. Both went on to law school and legal careers: Kelly at Harvard and with Dewey Ballentine, Garrity at Yale and with Donovan Leisure.

NSA Holds Congress In New Brunswick

Pauw Wow To Attend Paper Panel; Garrity Leads Petrean Groups

The New Jersey Region of the National Students Association will begin this evening a New Jersey Student Congress at New Jersey College for Women, New Brunswick, N. J. The Congress will continue tomorrow and Sunday, holding numerous panels to discuss various facets of student affairs. All member and non-NSA schools and colleges in the state have been invited to participate.

Tom Garrity

A note of particular interest in this Congress is the general invitation that has been extended to student leaders to attend. Special panels will be held for the heads

Regional Campus Newspaper Clinic. The *Pauw Wow* editors, seriously concerned with strengthening their collegiate newspaper relations, will attend. A Student Government Panel will discuss special problems not considered elsewhere in the Congress.

The purpose behind the Congress is the urgent need to introduce New Jersey student leaders to each other and to NSA, to create an understanding of the purposes of the Educational Community and an awareness of its problems, and to adapt programs commensurate with student needs. The program of the Congress is planned to achieve these aims.

The session this evening will open with two addresses, one, by Rosemary Honecker, President NJ-NSA and the other by Allard Lowenstein, President US-NSA. Following these addresses, the group will then break up into three panel discussions which will carry on to Saturday evening.

The first panel will discuss The American Student and the Students of the World, which will include aid in relief and reconstruction to foreign students of war-torn countries; improvement in exchange of persons, information and ideas, and a fostering of closer relations and better understanding on individual campuses of

The second panel will deal with The Student and His Role Toward Expanding Educational Opportunities. This discussion will dwell on formulating a positive program to fight against discrimination and segregation

on campus; improving relations between the student and school government, including administration; methods of easing and implementing the economic situation of the student; and the role of NSA in sponsoring and initiating legislative action in behalf of the student.

The third panel will discuss The Student and His Role in Preserving and Extending the Democratic Values of American Education which will have as its central topics the rights of students, academic freedom, and strengthening student governments as a means of exercising and defending those rights.

Fr. O'Connell, Garrity To Plan Pavan

The policy of the *Pavan*, the Literary Quarterly of St. Peter's, as announced by its editor Tom Garrity, will be modified this year to place greater emphasis on articles of sociological and philosophical topics.

The new moderator of the *Pavan* is Fr. Thomas G. V. O'Connell, S.J. Fr. O'Connell said of the policy of the

cultural, while its touchstone of quality is literary. If an idea is expressed vividly and interestingly, whether philosophic, historical, or sociological, the Quarterly will want to give it circulation among the students as of cultural importance. Articles must be pleasant to read and

Essays, stories, poems, et al, are now being accepted in preparation for the next issue of the *Pavan*, due in Novem-

GARRITY LED THE ST PETER'S DELEGATION to the11/10/50 NJ Regional Congress at NJ College for Women at which expanding educational opportunities was a key theme. NSA President Al Lowenstein addressed the meeting (Pauw Wow 11/10/50). **BOB KELLY'S 1949-50 NSA PRESIDENCY** was launched after he nominated NSA VP Gene Schwatrz for the position and was in turn prevailed on to run against Schwartz (See Part 1, Sec. 7). Below: Kelly is congratulated by Jersey City Mayor John V. Kenney while college officials look on (*Pauw Wow* 10/6/49).

Robert Kelly N.S.A. National President Draft-Elected Over Man He Nominated

When the St. Peter's seniors returned this fall for their last year, one well known face was missing. Robert A. Kelly was not with them. This past August, at its National Congress, Bob had been elected President of the National Student Association. Consequently, he had to withdraw from school to devote himself entirely to this important, national organization. But these few sentences hide much of the drama that surrounded the election.

In late August, more than 500 delegates, representing almost a million students, assembled on the campus of the University of Illinois for the Second National Congress of the

Historical note: St. Peter's is a Jesuit College founded in 1872, closed in 1918 after WWI and re-opened in 1930 (See Gannon, p. 885). In 1948 it had an enrollment of 1,712. It became co-educational in 1966 (www.spc.edu).

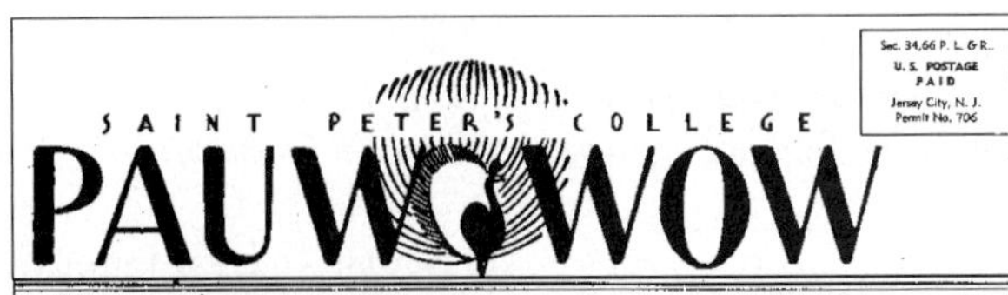

Y CITY, N. J., FEBRUARY 27, 1951 No. 8

Bellarmine Wins Championship As All-Senior Team Shines

Left to Right: Joe Ryan, Tom Garrity, Bob Kelly, Jim Mulvaney.

The Bellarmine Debating Society received top honors in winning the trophy in the National Debating Tournament sponsored by the National Federation of Catholic College Students. Ten Catholic Colleges participated in debating the national topic: "Resolved, that the non-communist nations should form a new international organization." The trophy, which will be in St. Peter's possession for one year, may be retained after three successive victories.

The victorious Petreans are all members of the Senior Class. Bob Kelly and Jim Mulvaney formed the affirmative team while Joe Ryan and Tom Garrity made up the negative.

Debaters In West Point Finals

Kelly and Garrity, "One-Two Punch" Place In District With Four Others

St. Peter's Bellarmine Debating Society took one giant step to advance within striking distance of the Nation's most coveted debating championship by qualifying for the fianls of the National Invitation Debate Tournament with a deadlock-breaking victory against Penn State in the Regional Preliminaries held at Penn State College April 6 and 7.

Tom Garrity and Bob Kelly, debating alternately both sides of the national topic, "Resolved that the non-Communist nations of the world should form a new international or-

tinued its most successful season. The N. F. C. C. was addec Champions debating t al topic de runoff last

On Apr tionals we James Evr affirmative Jack Saue placed thi Tourname Philadelph

GARRITY AND KELLY sharpened leadership skills on the Bellarmine debate team (*Pauw Wow* 2/27/51, 4/13/51) Garrity's work as editor of the literary quarterly (l. *Pauw Wow*, 9/29/50) suggests that Father Gannon's vision for St. Peter's as a "first class liberal arts" school "with a premium on hard work and brains" was much alive (See p. 885). Garrity also provides the rationale for continued student support for NSA. (R. *Pauw Wow* 10/13/50)

N.S.A. Convention Held At Michigan

By Tom Garrity

Conclusion. Two items have been made very evident by the Third National Student Congress:

1. The NSA and the American student movement are with us to stay. The NSA is strong and growing. It has been widely accepted by educational organizations and government as the spokesman for American college students, and it is beginning to effect qualitative changes in an often lackadaisical U. S. student community.
2. The conflict between freedom and totalitarianism has laid new responsibilities upon the NSA to make democracy more meaningful-and hence more magnetic and dynamic, in the educational community, nationally and internationally.

It would be difficult to impress upon St. Peter's students too strongly the import of what NSA is doing. The NSA Committee presents the following as a preliminary recommendations to the St. Peter's Student Council:

1. The activation of student service projects which meet the major needs of our students.
2. Increased study of the matters covered at the Congress, especially discrimination, federal aid to education and the NSA international program through lectures and study sessions. Especially important is the Crisis Study Program recommended by the Congress, for the examination of the roots of the present world situation and what students can do for peace and the preservation of the Judaeo-Christian tradition of Western civilization.
3. The establishment of student-faculty committees to cover such matters as curricular reform and to enlarge student participation in campus life.
4. Active support for the forthcoming New Jersey Student Congress, being prepared in large part under St. Peter's NSA sponsorship, which will review methods by which New Jersey colleges can implement the decisions of the National Student Congress.

Bob Kelly (l) and Tom Garrity at the 4/49 NSA National Executive Committee Meeting in Cleveland. (*Photos: Schwartz*)

Princeton University: "No Grounds for Joining"

1947: YES

THE NATIONAL STUDENTS ORGANIZATION

International Student Community

At the Chicago Conference it was stated that American students "have recognized the existence of an International student community" and, accordingly, "it should be the aim of the NSO to make the greatest possible American contribution to that community." The premise, couched in language characteristic of student groups, is extremely idealistic and abstract, if not false. It all depends on one's conception of the word "community." But the panel which phrased this thought followed through with some concrete suggestions which would go a long way in creating such an "international community." We believe that their plans will greatly interest Princetonians. They include an integration of existing student travel agencies and a central agency for the dissemination of information concerning student exchanges, travel and relief. For the present, it was recommended that the Harvard Student Council on international activities be used as the functioning committee. For those undergraduates who want to study in foreign universities and who want to make inexpensive trips to Europe and other continents, the establishment of such a clearing-house of information will greatly facilitate such plans. Reciprocal agreements with other countries would also increase the number of foreign students studying in this country.

We believe that Princeton should support the work of the NSO. The group has gotten off to an auspicious beginning and Princeton now has a chance to pioneer and contribute to its development.

Excerpted

NSO Delegate Tells Of Political Success Despite Lack of Cash

Describes to Undergraduate Council Convention Held in Wisconsin

Princeton's two-man delegation to the convention of the National Students Organization held in Madison, Wisconsin this summer was politically successful, but was hampered by a lack of authorized funds, according to a report which Boris Sokoloff '49 turned over to the Undergraduate Council last night.

Sokoloff, who went to Madison with Arnold Wettstein '49, told the Council that expenses run up by two of them at the week-long convention totalled $177., of which only $90 had been supplied them by the Council.

The financial plight of the Princeton delegation was so severe that they were obliged to hitch-hike back to their home communities.

In the political sphere, Princeton's delegates fared better. Wettstein was selected a sub-panel head and introduced a measure which won the support of the convention. He was proposed for the regional constitutional committee and also as treasurer for the New Jersey region.

1948: NO

No Grounds for Joining

NSA SHOWDOWN. During the past term we have consistently opposed the movement which is under way to push Princeton into active membership in the National Student Association. Tonight representatives of the Undergraduate Council will conduct a dorm-to-dorm vote on this question. Because the NSA has failed to convince us that it is an organization which merits Princeton's participation, we urge undergraduates to vote against joining.

SHADY PERFORMANCE. The origins of NSA have never been sufficiently clarified. The aims of the organization are lofty, vague and general. So far its accomplishments have been negligible. Many of the problems which the NSA hopes to solve do not exist at Princeton. Furthermore, we are more acutely conscious of and more anxious to resolve our own peculiar problems than any impersonal bund of students from other schools can hope to be.

For these reasons, and because the NSA has not assured us that it can perform a single constructive service that Princeton organizations cannot handle by themselves, we feel that the proposal to join the NSA should be decisively voted down.

MOVING FROM SUPPORT TO OPPOSITION, *The Princetonian* (4/8/48) urged that "NSA should be decisively voted down," because it "has not assured us that it can perform a single constructive service that Princeton organizations cannot handle themselves." On 2/18/47 it counseled that "the group has gotten off to an auspicious beginning." (Top r. 10/10/47)

VICTORY IN1945

The Princeton Bulletin

Wartime Successor to THE DAILY PRINCETONIAN

Vol. III PRINCETON, N. J., WEDNESDAY, AUGUST 15, 1945 No. 74

PRINCETON GOES WILD AT VICTORY ANNOUNCEMENT

"Henry IV, Part I" To Be Given by Cast Of Undergraduates

Princeton Team to Enter Intercollegiate Debate

A two-man debate team from

Nassau Hall Bell Tolls Three Hours, Bonfire Consumes Tojo Effigy

Following the Japanese surrender on VJ, Day August 14, "excitement swelled to a fever pitch with guns cracking, bands playing and mobs milling all over confetti-strewn Nassau Street."

Affiliation Defeated 620-429

THE DAILY PRINCETONIAN

DEI SUB NUMINE VIGET

NSA Vote Set For Tomorrow Council Rejects Postponement

By HARRY HEHER JR '49

An undergraduate vote on the NS question will go through as planne the Undergraduate Council annou ced last night as a last-minute mov ment toward postponement amon the members came to no a ail. The balloting, said Dav W. Romig '48, Chairman, w be conducted on a dormitory-to-dorm itory basis tomorrow night, with v ters being able to register any " sues too vague" opinion and not restricted—by a definite affirmati or negative choice. It was furth decided that 65 per cent quorum the entire undergraduate body wou suffice to make the election vali and that a majority of this numb would determine the result. Every e fort will be made, it was emphasiz to reach as many as possible.

Wettstein Prompts Decision

The discussion of postponement w prompted by a letter from Arno Wettstein '49, regional public agent for NSA, to Romig, which w read at the beginning of the me ing. "As it stands now," said We stein, "NSA will be defeated Princeton," because of a lack of pr per publicity explaining the organi tion. It is pretty obvious," he ad ed, "that our policy will be one splendid isolation—the students ju don't know enough about it."

His suggestion that the vote

Door-to-Door Balloting Will Decide NSA Issue

Support of Princeton membership in the NSA by 65% of the undergradu ates will be necessary to decide the University officially in favor of joinin the organization, it was announced last night by David W. R. Romig '48 President of the Undergraduate Council. The balloting will be conducte on a door-to-door basis on Wednesday April 7, with the platform of th association printed on the revers side of the referendum.

At latest count the Undergraduat body remains split on the value o NSA to Princeton, with oppositio resting on the fear that the nation wide student group may pass unde communist control. Leading support ers of Princeton membership ar Romig, Boris Sokoloff '49, and Owe W. Roberts '46, who foresee great ad vantages in having organized studen representatives both in Washingto and in UNESCO. The accomplish ments thus far obtained, they poin out, include the preparation of European travel encyclopedia and ac tive participation in securing the re cent G.I. allotment increase in Con gress.

NSA Intentions Outlined

The groups stated intentions are non political, non-partisan and are aime principally at providing a nationa bargaining agent for students. It ha twice resisted, said Sokoloff, powe ful attempts by communists to gai control of the governing board. Pres ent members include Vassar, section of Yale and Harvard and Smith.

NSA PARTICAPATION TO BE DECIDED TODAY IN CAMPUS-WIDE POLL

Princeton decides tonight whether or not it will be part of the NSA. Starting at 8:30, the Undergraduate Council will make a door-to-door Campus survey to see if a majority of students wish to join this nation-wide group.

The constitution of the NSA appears on page 2 of this issue. Students who are not familiar with the group's program are urged to read this declaration of its aims.

David W. Romig '48, Council chairman, last night encouraged all men to cast their ballots on this question. "Unless enough people vote," he declared, "tonight's polling will be invalid."

Three Alternatives Offered

He announced the very simple procedure for taking the vote. Members of the Council will leave copies of the mimeographed ballot at every door about 8:30 and will collect them again about an hour later. Students need only check one of the three alternatives offered on the ballot.

Vol. LXXII, No. 81

NSA Doomed In-Campus Poll Idea Hits First Major Setback

Princeton Rejects NSA, Returns From Seven Dorms Ind

On the basis of early but complete returns from seven random dormitories, NSA appears doomed at Princeton for the present. A bare 30 per cent of the 530 ballots tallied in the preliminary check were marked affirmatively. Approximately half of those polled opposed the issue, while the rest indicated that they did not know enough about NSA to feel qualified to vote.

Dormitories included in the early check last night were Little, 1903, 1879, West, Witherspoon and Walker. Undergraduate Council Chairman David W. Romig '48 said complete returns would be announced Monday in the DAILY PRINCETONIAN.

Council Members Distribute Ballots

Ballots were distributed after 8:30 last night by Council members despite a last-minute effort in the Council's Tuesday meeting to postpone the vote. The group voted to go ahead as planned, but added a third alternate choice to the ballot which provided an opportunity to register no opinion.

Voters who registered no opinion appear to have assured the defeat of NSA. The 20 per cent in that category represent the marginal votes which might conceivably have turned the tide in favor of the national student group. Despite liberal publicity on both sides of the question in the PRINCETONIAN, an unusually large number of undergraduates baffled by the issues at stake.

Should the issue finally as predicted, Princeton w become the first major university to specifically NSA constitution. Yale, H Smith are among the members of the organizat

Romig urged undergr turn in ballots that were n last night to 205 Nassau

"Princeton is thus the first major Eastern university to have decided against joining the NSA. Yale, Harvard, Smith and more than a score of other colleges in the area have affiliated with the organization," *The Princetonian* reported 4/12/48. (From top: *Princetonian* 4/7/48, 4/12/48, 4/8/48, 4/12/48, 4/9/48.)

Historical note: Originally named the College of New Jersey, Princeton, like Rutgers, has colonial roots, having been chartered in 1746 to a group of Presbyterian trustees as "the fourth college to be established in British North America, after Harvard, William and Mary, and Yale, in that order." Undergraduate coeducation was initiated in 1969 (www.princeton.edu).

Rutgers University, NJCW, and the New Jersey Region

In Memoriam

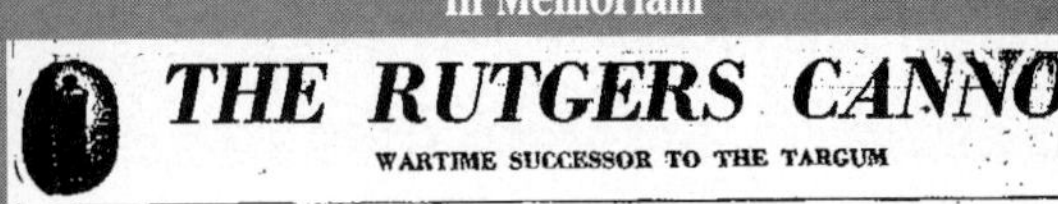

THE RUTGERS CANNON

WARTIME SUCCESSOR TO THE TARGUM

...me 1 New Brunswick, N. J., June 1, 1945 No. 6

Chapel Service Honors 180 Rutgers Dead

After VE Day on May 8, 1945, the names of undergraduates and alumni who "died on the field of honor" were read at a Kirkpatrick Chapel Ceremony.

(*The Rutgers Cannon*, wartime successor to *The Targum*, 6/1/45)

*Editor's note: The NSA Student Bill of Rights provided many student governments for the first time a comprehensive definition of rights. Considerable debate among students and administrators resulted. (See Brown, p. 338, and Klopf, p. 332). For many, the notion was too radical and impeded affiliation. Others adopted it in their affiliation vote without formal attachment to their constitutions. Rutgers was one among many which moved to add provisions to its constitution and to balance its support of NSA while dropping "provisions that are removed from the Rutgers campus . . . expressly designed to oppose less liberal universities." (*The Targum *1/18/48).*

Exploring the Right Campus Role for NSA

Mahoney Is New NSA Chairman

Ed Mahoney, Student Council ... man as chairman of Rutgers chapter of the National Student Association in accordance with an NSA recommendation that the chairman of the group be a member of Council.

Formerly the NSA committee, as distinct from Council's standing NSA group, had chosen its own chairman, but the new move emanates from a mutual desire to unify the group into one effective committee.

Members of the student body are still eligible to work on the NSA committee. The present outside committee has been merged into the Council NSA group.

In order to make NSA files more accessible to members of the group, Council moved at last Tuesday's meeting to purchase a filing cabinet for sole use of NSA records. The records will be kept in the Council chambers.

Council established a committee to meet with Chaplain Abernethy and attempt to derive a satisfactory charity fund-raising plan on campus.

The possibility of running buses to the Ag Farm, similar to the transportation system to the Heights, will be checked by Coun-

NSA Can Become Council's 'Good Right Arm,' Says Kahn

By WALT JOYCE

"The National Student Association can become the good right arm of Student Council," said John Kahn at last week's Student Council meeting in Student Union. Kahn had been invited to address Council concerning NSA by Counsellor Mike Nagle, chairman of the NSA committee.

He outlined the ways in which NSA could be of value to Council. "NSA is the only undergraduate organization which can speak for students on a national basis.

Information Exchange

"It can serve as the right arm of Council through inter-school information exchange and can put programs of Council into action, thus relieving it of much time-consuming leg work."

He suggested that Council designate a group of students as an NSA committee and have this group work closely with Council. Student Council sends three representatives to the NSA committee, one Council member from each class. One of those men serves as vice chairman of the committee.

Council Appointees

Joe Ambrose of the junior class and Norm Driscoll of the class of '54 were appointed to assist Nagle, who is vice-chairman of Student Affairs.

Dave Davis, another member of the '50-51 Council, presented the final report of the Faculty Rating committee at this Council meeting.

He recommended that Charles Moreno, an NSA member who worked on the Faculty Rating committee this year, be appointed to head next year's program. Moreno was approved for the post by Council.

Davis offered seven suggestions which he felt would aid the Faculty Rating group in their work, and help "avoid the mistakes made by this year's committee, and consequently make the job more efficient and satisfactory."

He recommended that the program be put on a permanent basis, but restricted to the Colleges of Arts and Sciences as it is now. He cited this as a job which could be handled by NSA which would be responsible to Council, and further suggested that it be undertaken later in the year.

editor-in-chief of the publication, announced yesterday. The handbook has a revamped format.

The 64-page booklet which covers the important aspects of college life will be sent during the Summer to all incoming students.

The NSA Committee was seen as a Student Council information channel to the intercollegiate scene as well as in managing NSA campus programs, such as the Faculty Rating program (see p. 372). (From left: *The Targum* 10/17/50, 5/15/51)

Student Council Adapts NSA Student Bill of Rights to Its Constitution Revision

Revisionists Incorporate Five Articles of NSA Bill of Rights

Decide On This Course at Tuesday Meeting; Nine Were Presented for Scrutiny

The Constitutional Revision committee of the Student Council last Tuesday approved five articles of the Bill of Rights of the National Student Association, for inclusion into the revised constitution.

Meeting in regular session at the Student Union, the committee ratified the points after discussing six articles of the Students' Rights section of the constitution. ... others were discussed at a ... meeting.

The articles approved were:

1. The right of every student to exercise his full rights as a citizen in forming and participating in local, national, or international organizations for intellectual, religious, social, political, economic or cultural purposes, and to publish and distribute their views ...

More Articles

2. The right of recognized student organizations to use the institution's name, subject ...

3. The right to invite and hear speakers of their choice on subjects of their choice.

4. The right of students to engage freely in off-campus activities provided they do not claim to represent the institution, exercising their rights as citizens of community, state and nation.

5. The right to establish and issue regular publications free of ...

A BETTER PLAN OF ACTION

Acting with the thoughtful deliberation that has characterized their work during the past semester, the members of the Student Council Constitution Revision committee voted down Tuesday the proposal that the Bill of Rights from the by-laws of the National Student Association be included verbatim in the new constitution.

Revision Committee Voted in Favor Of a Wiser Plan

It was felt that rather than accept the generalizations of the NSA bill, a more pertinent list might be composed—a list that would stand for more because its precepts would be made to apply here at Rutgers.

As we have maintained in the past, the Bill of Rights, as listed in the NSA by-laws, deals almost exclusively with ideals. In spirit these ideas might be all well and good. In theory they are fine. In practice, however, we feel that they would indeed prove cumbersome because of their complete generalities.

(From left: *Targum* 2/6/48, 1/18/48 (both excerpted).

Historical note: Officially the State University of New Jersey (by legislation in 1945 and 1956), Rutgers was founded as Queen's College by a group of Dutch ministers who were granted a charter by Governor William Franklin (Ben Franklin's son) in 1766. It was the 8th colonially chartered college. Rutgers became co-educational in 1970 (www. libraries.rutgers.edu).

New Jersey College for Women (NJCW)

GA President Roessler and Margaret Crooke Represent NJC At Chicago Student Conference

Discussed Setting Up National Student Organization in U. S.

By BERNICE ROESSLER '47

[illegible]

Marianne Schmidt

Schmidt ('48) represented NSA at UNESCO in Paris in the summer of 1950, and was on the delegation with Herb Eisenberg and Al Lowenstein at the 1950 Stockholm Conference (see p. 519). She atttended the 1947 ISS conference for NJCW (see p. 56) (Photo: *Caellian* 4/16/47).

Historical note: The New Jersey College for Women was founded by Rutgers in 1918. It remains a women's college, renamed in 1955 after its first dean, Mabel Smith Douglass. Rutgers became co-educational in 1970 (www.Rutgers.edu). NJCW was independently affiliated with NSA.

The Targum Provides NSA Background

RUTGERS AND NJCW provided active leadership in the New Jersey Region. In three issues of *The Targum* (9/16, 9/20 and 9/23/49) Ariel Landy, Regional Chair, discusses the issues and results at the 1949 2d National Student Congress at the University of Illinois (Part 1, Sec. 6).

Second NSA Congress Airs Federal Aid and Discrimination

Nearly 350 Schools Represented at Talks Held Last Month on University of Illinois Campus

By ARIEL LANDY

NSA Attempts to Clarify Local Authority of Campus Committee

Administration Commission Studies Organization Problems Concerning Member Campuses

By ARIEL LANDY

A Mature NSA Shows Desire To Cooperate With IUS Group

Resolution Passed by Student Congress—Would Renew Efforts in International Projects

By ARIEL LANDY

John Yewell

Elect Yewell President Of New Student Council

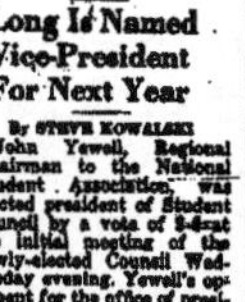

Long Is Named Vice-President For Next Year

By STEVE KOWALSKI

John Yewell, Regional Chairman to the National Student Association, was elected president of Student Council by a vote of 8-4 at the initial meeting of the newly-elected Council Wednesday evening. Yewell's opponent for the office of president was Harry Brown.

Frank Long, ...

NSA REGIONAL CHAIR following Chicago and the Constitutional Convention, Yewell was elected student body president in 1948 under the newly revised student council constitution (*Targum* 5/21/48).

SECTION 4

Pennsylvania/Mid-Atlantic

CONTENTS

Penn State, *The Daily Collegian* 1/1/5/48

Educational Objectives...
NSA Endorses GI Subsidies, More Professor Ratings

Delegates Form NSA Constitution In 3-Day Session at State College

Temple University News 1/7/48

U. of Baltimore, *The Baloo* 10/28/49

U of B Host to Forthcoming NSA Mason-Dixon Meeting

Students to Fight High Prices With N.S.A. P.C.S. Cards

This section begins with a commentary by Ralph Smith on the strengths and weaknesses of NSA on the Swarthmore College campus. Smith was NSA's Public Relations Director in 1949-50. Swarthmore's tradition of providing national student leaders since the 1930's is highlighted in an album. Ken Kurtz, also from Swarthmore, 1950-51 Pennsylvania regional chair, writes about student leadership in NSA from the Students for Democratic Action and the Student Federalists, and of their interactions with Catholic college student leaders. He adds insights and anecdotes about NSA Presidents Ted Harris, 1948-49 (LaSalle College, p. 249), and Al Lowenstein, 1950-51 (University of North Carolina, p. 283).

Pennsylvania's 107 colleges provided a broad base for membership, as well as for attendence at its regional events, often attracting one or two hundred delegates from 40 to 50 colleges. Many of NSA's national leaders came from its ranks. Among them, Ralph Dungan (St. Joseph's College), later to become New Jersey's first Chancellor of Higher Education, was NSA's 1947-48 Vice President for Student Affairs. His memoir explores the dynamics of Catholic college student governments and the influence of Catholic college students and NSA on each other (see also Dungan, p. 174). A roster of Catholic colleges in 1948 is provided. See also NSA Vice Presidents Ted Perry, 1949-50 (Temple University, p. 356), Elmer Brock, 1950-51 (La Salle College, p. 358), NSA 1948-44 Public Relations Director Allan Ostar (Pennsylvania State College, p. 209) and 1946 World Student Congress delegate Frank K. Mayers (University of Pennsylvania, p. 94).

Two mentors are featured: Harold Stassen, President of the University of Pennsylvania, and Althea Kratz Hottel, Penn's Dean of Women, both members of NSA's National Advisory Committee and strong supporters of the Association. A chronicle of regional events is included, drawn from college newspapers at La Salle College, St. Joseph's College, Pennsylvania State College, Temple University, and the University of Pennsylvania.

Mason-Dixon Region centered on smaller area colleges

Michael Rubino (Catholic University), 1948-49 Regional Chair, cites the significance of CU's decision to join NSA in drawing in other area colleges. Nonetheless, four of the major area universities did not join NSA: American, Georgetown, George Washington and Maryland. Maryland did host a major regional meeting in 1950 and attended the early national and regional conferences. Emmet Hurley of Georgetown was the region's first Chair after Chicago, followed by Joe Zebley of the University of Baltimore. Johns Hopkins provided significant early leadership through Stanley Greenfield (see p. 155), and Howard University remained an active member, hosting several regional conventions.

The region offered a forum for student leaders of area colleges. Some of these leaders, debates and events are highlighted in pictorials featuring Baltimore, Dunbarton, Trinity, Howard, Temple, LaSalle, and Maryland.

AREA COLLEGES FORM TWO REGIONS, meeting several times annually, with active interest in domestic programs. Key national leaders emerge from both regions (see above).

Pennyslvania/Mid-Atlantic NSA Highlights

Pennsylvania

1946-47

Mayers Delivers Prague Students Conference Talk

Select Delegates
Men, Women To Send One Each To Chicago

NSA Goals to Be Discussed at Convocation

NSA Delegate Election Friday

FRANK K. MAYERS, PENN DELEGATE to the 1946 World Student Congress (p. 94) helped set the stage for the Chicago Student Conference (p. 109) at which the region was launched. Ralph Dungan (St. Joseph's, p. 000), its first chair, is shown with the regional delegation (front l. above) at the 1947 NSA Constitutional Convention (p. 129). (Fr. l, *DP* 10/20/46, 12/6/46; *TN* 12/10/47)

National Conference Names Dungan State Chairman of Regional NCC

Milholland Greets Student Delegates Representing Pennsylvania Colleges

200 Delegates Will Attend NSA Sessions Tomorrow

1947-48

(Fr. l, top: *HJ* 1/24/47; *TN* 11/12/48; *DC* 12/19/47; Photos (Ostar), fr. l: Regional delegation at Penn State 6/48; Regional Exec. Committee, 4/48, at Bloomsburg State Teachers C., Fr. l: Louis Ieradi (Rittenhouse C.), Frank Mihalin (Duquesne), Ted Harris (47-48 Chair, La Salle), Karen Knaplund (Bryn Mawr), Ralph Smith (Swarthmore), and Harry Reitz (Bloomsburg).

FROM 40 TO 90 COLLEGES attended regional meetings. The 12/47 event at Penn State (top, r.) featured a state-wide student government clinic. The 11/48 event (Top, ctr.) was chaired by Ted Perry (Temple).

Pennsylvania Festival Features 650 Performers

an Intercollegiate Music Festival

Meet Elmer Brock

NSA Convention Will Be Held At Beaver Coll.

Swarthmore NSA Host For Week's Conclave Of Exec. Committee

Ieradi is Delegate At Education Confab

Malin Talks to NSA About Civil Liberty At Regional Banquet

Students to Attend NSA Conerence on Student Government

Students from 9 Colleges Attend NSA's Weekend Peace Program

1949-51

THE 1949 CULTURALE AND MUSIC FESITVAL featured 650 performers from 18 colleges in three different programs and was the largest such NSA effort (See p. 368). Elmer Brock (LaSalle, p. 358) was 1949-50 chair. Civil liberties and peace issues emerged during the McCarthy and Korean War era. Fr. l., top: *NSA News* 5/49; Culturale circular 4/49; *LC* 10/7/49; *SP* 11/16/49; bot: *SP* 3/1/50; *TN* 12/15/50, 4/13/51 (photo); *TN* 5/9/51: U. Penn, CCNY, Fordham, Swarthmore, Antioch, Brooklyn, Cheney and Lincoln were represented; "Malin," a former Swarthmore professor *SP* 12/13/50, *SP* 4/18/51.

Temple University NEWS

Rally will Oppose Loyalty Oath

Pitt Students, Faculty Fight Oath; State Paper Opposes It Editorially

Dignitaries will Speak On Bill in Stouffer Hall

LOYALTY OATH INITIATIVES AND STRONG OPPOSITION in many states (p. 381, 388) were echoed by the Pechan senate bill. The *News* editorialized, "loyaty oaths cannot make men loyal." Fr. top: *TN* 4/18/, 5/7/51.

Pennsylvania Area Tries Faculty Rating, Calls for De-Emphasis Of Intercollegiate Athletics

NSA Chooses Phila. For New Headquarters

NSA MOVED from Boulder in 1952 (p. 000). The region was outspoken on college governance issues. *SP* 4/33/52; TN 10/3/52.

1952

Additional excerpts *not in this section:* LaSalle C., pp. 221, 224, 359); Penn State, p. 213; St. Joseph's, p. 176; Temple U., pp. 41, 59, 357; U. of Pennsylvania, p. 48, p. 95)

Md.-Del.-DC

Catholic U. Participates In National Union Project

NFCCS Delegates Will Elect Representatives to JSCA

Washington Area Schools Meet In Copley Lounge

Students, Professors

National Student Union Forms In Chicago; Hopkinsmen Attend

Zebley To Head NSO Regional Meeting Here

Students Approve Hopkins' Joining NCC, 514 - 325

Delegates To Be Chosen By Student Council

Preamble Adopted By NSA At Regional Meeting In DC

BALTIMORE AND D.C. COLLEGES anchored the new Mason-Dixon region. Catholic U. and Georgetown helped launch national coordination of Catholic college NSA participation and leadership (pp. 78, 738, 920). Stanley Greenfield at Johns Hopkins brought PR skills to NSA regionally and nationally (p. 155).

(Fr. top, cw: *CT* 12/6/46; *TH* 11/22/46; *JH* 1/10/47, 3/31/47, 10/17/47. Bot. l.: *TB* 3/14/47)

1946-47

U. BALTIMORE hosted regional meeting after Chicago. (Above. See p. 921.)

1948-53

Helen Jean Rogers addresses 1950 regional meeting (p. 000).

NSA Regional Meeting Held In Washington, D. C.

U of B Host to Forthcoming NSA Mason-Dixon Meeting

Students to Fight High Prices With N.S.A. P.C.S. Cards

NSA Arranges for Regional Congress; Planning Group Meets at Hood College

Senior to Preside Over NSA Session

NSA Agenda Lists Congress, Press Conference for Region

General Hershey Speaks to Mason-Dixon

Dunbarton Student Wins NSA Election

Cynthia Courtney (3d fr rt) and regional officers at 1952 National Student Congress (p. 000)

Diamondback

STUDENTS VOTE 'NO' TO NSA

WOMEN'S COLLEGES IN D.C. followed veteran chairs Emmet Hurley (Georgetown), Joe Zebley (U. Baltimore), Mike Rubino (Catholic U.) and Richard Cadigan (Loyola) with Dunbarton's Gloria Abiouness (1950) and Agnes Downey (1950-51), Trinity's Eileen O'Connell (1951-52) and Dunbarton's Cynthia Courtney (1952-53); Courtney in 1953-54 became national Vice President for Educational Affairs. Regional meetings rotated between Baltimore and DC campuses. Students at U. Maryland turned down membership after four years of vigorous debates on affiliation (p. 924). Georgetown's President vetoed student recommended membership (p. 742). Fr. top, l to r: "Regional," *TB* 3/18/49; "Host"; PCS," *TB* 10/28/49; "Arranges," *TB* 3/14/52; "Senior," *TT* 10/19/51; "Hershey," *NSA News* 8/51; "Dunbarton," *DD* 9/52; "No," *DB* 1/19/51).

Additional excerpts *not in this section:* Johns Hopkins, p. 157; Catholic U. and Georgetown, pp. 78, 742

KEY TO COLLEGE NEWSPAPER CITATIONS IN THIS SECTION

CT-Catholic U. *The Tower*

DB-U. of Maryland *Diamondback*

DC-Penn. State C. *Daily Collegian*

DD-*Dunbarton Dial*

DP-*Daily Pennsylvanian*

HH- Howard U. *Hilltop*

HJ-St. Joseph *The Hawk*

JH-*Johns Hopkins News-Letter*

LC-*La Salle Collegian*

SP-*Swarthmore Phoenix*

TB-U. of Baltimore *The Baloo*

TH-Georgetown U. *The Hoya*

TN-*Temple University News*

TT- *The Trinity Times*

TG-*The Greyhound*

Successes and problems

1. Swarthmore College and NSA

Ralph Lee Smith
Swarthmore College 1951
NSA Public Relations Director, 1949-50

NSA at Swarthmore, 1947-51

There is a brief paragraph in the minutes of the Swarthmore College Student Council meeting for December 14, 1947, that reads as follows: "Gordon reported that Bobbie Darrow would be unable to go to the N.S.A. Regional Conference and that it would be necessary to choose someone to replace her. The Council decided by unanimous vote to send Ralph Lee Smith in Bobbie's place."

I was a first-semester freshman at Swarthmore when this happened. The "N.S.A. Regional Conference" cited in the minutes was the constitutional convention of the Pennsylvania Region of NSA, which took place at Penn State on December 19-20, 1947, three months after NSA was formally established. I do not recall taking Bobby's place, and cannot imagine at all why the Student Council should have picked me. I have to say that it led to interesting adventures.

In the late fall of 1996, I agreed to write a piece for this book on what NSA looked like from a campus perspective at Swarthmore as events unfolded from 1947 to 1951. As a result, I spent some Saturday afternoons in the Swarthmore College library, reading minutes of the student council and back issues of the college's weekly newspaper, *The Phoenix*. I had utterly forgotten nearly everything that I found there! Bit by bit the memories came back.

Swarthmore's experiences with NSA during the approximate period 1946–1948 were characterized by great interest and substantial support. Beginning in 1948, arrangements made for creating an "NSA Committee" on campus brought about structural and other problems. During the approximate period 1949–1951, student interest in many things beyond the boundaries of the campus declined. NSA was one of many things that were affected by this decline.

Initial enthusiasm

Swarthmore was founded by the Society of Friends (Quakers) and has historically been interested in international affairs and in efforts to promote world peace. The school has also long enjoyed a reputation as one of the nation's top colleges academically. These things virtually guaranteed that the founding of NSA would engender great interest on campus. From November 1946, when it first reported on the upcoming Chicago Convention,[1] and on through the 1948 school year, *The Phoenix* carried all stories about NSA on its front page.

The student body elected Swarthmore's representatives and alternate to the Madison Convention.[2] The representatives were Bobbie Darrow and Larry Weiskrantz; the alternate, Paula Adler. All three were among the college's top students.

Returning from Madison, they wrote or contributed to exhaustive articles that were carried in three successive issues of *The Phoenix*. Any member of the Swarthmore community who was not fully up on IUS, the race compromise, and student government and student rights in higher education had only himself or herself to blame.

The regional race relations clinic

At the Pennsylvania Region Convention in December 1947, the delegates voted to establish a regional race relations clinic and domiciled it at Swarthmore under the chairmanship of Larry Weiskrantz. Larry and a small committee at Swarthmore designed an exhaustive questionnaire covering racial practices in higher education in the state and sent it to the president and student council of every Pennsylvania college and university.

When the questionnaires were returned, Larry and his committee tabulated the results and publicized them extensively. The picture they painted, although respectfully presented, left little doubt about how big the problems were. I believe that it was the first time that undergraduate students had ever taken it upon themselves to conduct and publicize such a survey in Pennsylvania, and perhaps anywhere else in America.

Relating to NSA

Swarthmore affiliated with NSA by campus-wide vote on November 21, 1947, after Madison and before the first Pennsylvania Region meeting. The Student Council took up the question of how to relate to the new organization and, specifically, whether a new committee of the council should be established to perform the task.

> Since logically the people who have already attended conferences of the NSA and hold positions in that organization ought to serve on the NSA committee, the question [of whether an NSA Committee should be established] was decided in the affirmative [the minutes of the Council's February 15, 1948 meeting state].

There was no stated requirement that any member of the Committee be a member of the student council. Nor were the questions addressed of how the committee's membership would be selected, what reporting procedures should be followed, and what the committee should do.

As it happened, the committee had no shortage of ideas. Among other things, it immersed itself in a Pennsylvania Region–sponsored artistic event called the Culturale and worked hard and successfully to bring a Displaced Person student to the campus. However, what all this had to do with either NSA or the great majority of Swarthmore students was not clear to some Student Council members.

Working with problems

At its March 14, 1949, meeting, the Council revisited the structural problem. "It was decided that next year the NSA committee on campus shall be a committee under the student council," the minutes state, which perhaps was a way of rapping knuckles. "However," they continue, "the committee will be open to all students and will choose its own officers." Anything gained by the first sentence was lost by the second.

At the April 16, 1950, meeting of the Council, the "NSA issue" broke to the surface. If there was a specific triggering occurrence, the minutes do not mention it. But the minutes state, "Joe Jones [that is not his name] requested that the Council place on the agenda for next week an evaluation of the NSA at Swarthmore."

The Campus NSA Committee

The minutes of the April 23 meeting read in part as follows:

> *NSA at Swarthmore.* Ralph Smith gave a report on the results of a recent meeting of old-timers in NSA on the reorganization of the Association. He reported that NSA was founded as an association of student governments because of the need for one organization to foster and represent the interests of a real "student community" in this country. The situation has now changed and there is little feeling on American campuses of a real community of interests among students. NSA, in response to new needs, has changed its original emphasis and become more of a service organization, rather than an association of student governments as originally projected.
>
> As NSA grew, many student governments set up standing committees to deal with all NSA work, and the "NSA Campus Committee" arose. In time, these groups took over the work and the responsibility of student governments for the NSA, and the student councils lost touch with the work of the association. The NSA evaluation group has recommended that all NSA work, information, etc., be funneled solely through student governments on each campus. If these student governments want to undertake an NSA program, they will either pass it along to one of their standing committees to handle or set up a special committee.[3]

The Swarthmore NSA Campus Committee met and discussed these proposals and, with some differences among the members, voted to accept them. The Council approved the action and abolished the NSA Campus Committee. The Committee's various activities were integrated into the work of the Council and its regular committees.

Declining interest

Meanwhile, some Council members had developed doubt about the value of NSA membership to the Swarthmore student body. The Student Council appropriated funds for the NSA committee and for travel to conventions. There were plenty of competing demands for the funds, for activities whose benefits to the student body were clear beyond doubt. Was the Council exercising proper stewardship?

Beginning about 1949, interest in NSA also declined among the college's students. From what I have been able to learn, this decline of interest was not limited to Swarthmore, but manifested itself on other campuses as well.

An item in the Student Council minutes for December 10, 1950, reads:

> *Delegates to the NSA regional convention:* Ken Kurtz [who ran for NSA president in 1951] pointed out the desirability of having someone from next semester's Student Council attend the NSA regional convention next weekend, so that the Student Council will not then know even less about NSA than it does now. The suggestion was made that if more interest is not manifested in NSA, perhaps the whole question of Swarthmore's membership in NSA and its participation in NSA should be re-evaluated.[4]

Al Lowenstein misses a date

The minutes of the January 7, 1951, council meeting state, "On the recommendation of Ken Kurtz, the Council's evaluation of the National Student Association and its activities as related to Swarthmore will be postponed until the Council can meet with Al Lowenstein, Chairman [sic] of NSA, who will be at Swarthmore on 18 January."

The minutes of the January 18 meeting state that Lowenstein couldn't make it to Swarthmore. No reasons are specified. His failure to come was unfortunate. The Student Council would have been helped if it could have talked with him at this juncture in the college's relations with NSA.[5]

The Council makes decisions

At the Student Council Meeting on January 21, Ken Kurtz, a fellow student named Frank Elliott, and I made a report to the Council in which we recommended that a new Student Council Committee be formed, called the Committee on National and International Student Affairs. This Committee, the minutes say:

> would act as liaison and dispenser of information between campus groups and not just NSA, but also organizations like the National Education Association. The Committee would keep in correspondence with these organizations outside campus which were of concern to students and make information available to interested groups on campus.

The minutes say that our suggestion was tabled, but it is clear that such a Committee existed before the Council met on May 27, 1951, during my last days as a student. At this meeting the Student Council bit the NSA bullet. It considered, in extenso, a report on NSA that had been prepared by the Committee on National and International Student Affairs. The minutes state:

> There was considerable discussion as to whether NSA is worth to Swarthmore what it costs (last year it cost $275, according to Kurtz, this including the cost of membership, publications, and part payment of expenses for delegates to the NSA regional and national conventions). It was pointed out as another reason why Swarthmore might discontinue its participation in NSA.
>
> In defense of NSA, it was argued that one cannot place a price tag on something which furthers good student government; that student apathy plagues many other worthwhile activities and should not be considered a reason for discontinuing them; and that participation in NSA gets the name of Swarthmore around in the academic world.

The outcome of the debate was that the Council approved continued participation for another year in NSA and approved the appropriation of $43 for regional and national dues, $7 for publications, and $200 for expenses of the Swarthmore delegation to the NSA Convention in the Fall. All these amounts were in accordance with the recommendations of the report.

A few days later, I graduated.

What Was Happening?

I think that contributing factors to these events included the following:

- NSA's inability to develop a domestic agenda of programs with grass-roots appeal, that student governments could clearly recognize as being worth an investment of time and money on behalf of their student bodies;
- the shift from largely veteran to largely non-veteran student bodies between 1947 and 1951;
- that students with a strong interest in NSA were, as a group, a liberal minority in a more conservative youth environment and that we often forgot it; and
- the coming of the nonpolitical ethos of the 1950s and the "silent generation."

I look back on the leaders of the veterans' generation as being the last Victorians. We believed in Progress, just like the Victorians did. We believed that it could be achieved through the application of discipline to life and rationality to human affairs. We believe that we—you and I—could help Progress along. These beliefs were headed for some historic potholes, not far down the road![6]

My role in NSA

I was born in 1927 and grew up in Cheyney, Pennsylvania, some twenty-five miles west of Philadelphia, during the Depression. My father was general manager of the Philadelphia Better Business Bureau, and commuted to his work. His job gave me two things—protection from the economic impact of the Depression and interest in work with a public service orientation. My parents were also much interested in antiques, and this interest, with its relationship to the arts, influenced my postcollege life.

After high school, at age seventeen, I entered the Navy, and as a result served exactly six weeks in World War II! Despite the fact that I did not have the direct experience of war, my worldview was very much that of the veterans.

I entered Swarthmore College in September 1947 and graduated in 1951. During those years, I served as a delegate from Swarthmore to a number of regional and national NSA conventions. At the constitutional convention of the Pennsylvania Region of NSA in December 1947, I was elected regional public relations (PR) director. I was appointed as national public relations director in 1949-1950 but served for only a few months, because I was concerned (justifiably) about my studies and decided to return to school.[7] I was on NSA's first student tour of Western Europe in 1948, and, after I graduated, was on the NSA orientation staff aboard the *Volendam* in the summer of 1951.[8]

In the fall of 1949, as national PR director, I went to Cambridge and spent some time in the international office, working with Erskine Childers in matters relating to publicizing the NSA summer travel program. From there I went to New York and visited *Reporter Magazine*, for whom Doug Cater was doing some writing.[9] They didn't want an article on NSA, but they took out a nice big half-page ad for *Reporter Magazine* in the *NSA News*!

I then stopped by the Institute of International Education (IIE), where I found that the Institute wanted to know about the NSA travel program, but from the perspective of its potential positive influence on the interest of participating students in pursuing studies abroad. I subsequently wrote two articles on the travel program for the *IIE News Bulletin,* an attractive little magazine with a substantial readership.[10]

From New York I returned to Madison, where I sought to address a communications problem that seemed to me important at the time, and in retrospect seems to me to be even more so. I established contact with most or all of the regional PR directors and encouraged them to launch a regular NSA newsletter for their regions, to be sent to the president and student council president of each member college. It would provide an information and idea exchange.

We had published such a newsletter for the Pennsylvania Region when I was PR director there, and NSA people on the campuses, who often felt isolated, liked it. Loyal members of the Swarthmore NSA committee gathered once a month to run the mimeo machine, address and seal envelopes, and sort the mailing by destination in accordance with the requirements of our third-class postal permit, of which we were immensely proud.

In the Madison office, stress emanated from Bob Kelly's tendency to isolate himself physically from the staff by going into his office and closing the door, with the clear implication that he did not wish to be disturbed. He often remained secluded until well into the night. We other staffers believed that, among other things, he was struggling with the question of just what the duties of his office might be and what steps he should take to carry them out, and perhaps with a pride that prevented him from sharing his difficulties with us.

Ralph Lee Smith is currently Marketing Consultant, The Connections Newspapers. He is also a historian of, and a performer on, the Appalachian dulcimer.

This behavior was especially disconcerting to Ted Perry, who was a happy and outgoing personality. Late one night, Ted tapped gently on Kelly's closed door. "Yes?" came the voice from behind the door. "Kelly," Ted responded, struggling to stifle his laughter, "What is truth?" Bob leaped up from his chair and flung open the door, and the two of them wrestled and laughed together.

I can't remember if Kelly answered the question![11]

END NOTES

[1] See Wharton, p. 112. [2] See Welsh, p. 165.

[3] *Editor's note:* How to position NSA relations and programs on campus without by-passing student governments remained a vexing issue. See Appendix, p. 1120, for digest of the reorganization report. Also Jim Smith, p. 127, and Rutgers U., p. 88.

[4] See Kurtz, pp. 306 and 902.

[5] *Editor's note:* Al Lowenstein was the 1950-1951 NSA president. See Lynch, p. 270.

[6] See Ralph Lee Smith, p. 712. [7] See Schwartz, p. 241.

[8] See p. 654, p. 669 on student ships, p. 671.

[9] See Cater, "Collapse of Youth's One World," p. 535.

[10] *Editors note:* See Album, p. 654, for reproduction of Smith's 1951 article.

[11] See Wilson, p. 248.

PICTURE CREDITS: *Then:* c. 1950 (Author). *Now:* 1993 (*Brunner Studio, Berea, KY,* Author

RALPH LEE SMITH

Early years. Born in Philadelphia, PA, in 1927. Attended high school at Swarthmore High School, Swarthmore, PA, and at Admiral Farragut Academy, Pine Beach, NJ, from which he graduated in 1945.

Education. B.A., English, Swarthmore College, 1951. M.Ed., Social Foundations of Education, University of Virginia, 1987.

Career in Brief: Current: 1998-2002 Director of Research, City/County Communications & Marketing Association; NAHB Research Center. Public Information Director, 1982-1996; Media General Cable of Fairfax, Institutional Network Director, 1976-1982; Telecommunications consulting, 1972-1976; Associate Professor of Journalism, Howard University, Washington, D.C., 1957-1972; freelance journalist in science and public affairs.

Journalism awards include: National Magazine Award for Public Service, Columbia University Graduate School of Journalism; University of Missouri Award for Excellence in Business and Financial Journalism, University of Missouri Graduate School of Journalism; Medical Journalism Award, American Medical Association; Distinguished Medical Writing Award, The Arthritis Foundation. 1954-57. Editor, National Better Business Bureau, New York.

Best-Known Books. *The Health Hucksters*, 1960; *The Wired Nation*, 1972; *The Story of the Dulcimer*, 1986; *American Dulcimer Traditions*, 1997; *Songs and Tunes of the Wilderness Road*, 1999.

Biographical Information: *Who's Who in America.*

Family: Married to Shizuko Maruyama of Chiba, Japan. They have one daughter, Lisa Koyuki Smith. He has two sons, David and Robert, by a previous marriage.

Student Engagement and Leadership at Swarthmore

Editor's Note: Swarthmore College, a co-educational college founded by the Religious Society of Friends in 1869, is one of three originally Quaker sponsored colleges in Eastern Pennsylvania. Haverford (1833), a men's college (now co-educational), attended the Chicago Student Conference but did not join NSA. Together with Bryn Mawr (1885), a women's college (see Rich, p. 461), Swarthmore maintained active NSA membership. Swarthmore President Frank Aydelotte, installed in 1921, is credited in "Campus Life" by Helen Horowitz with raising academic standards and transforming over a period of twenty years its highly social, athletic and fraternity-centered campus life. "He got his Board of Managers to agree that "Swarthmore was a college and not a social club." The campus provided opportunities for generations of outstanding national student leaders. 1948 enrollment was 1,035.

Swarthmore and NSA

Swarthmore PHOENIX

10/10/47

NSA Puts Stress on Action; Panel on College Gov'ment

What precisely can the National Student Association accomplish? No matter how noble the idealism upon which it is based, no matter ... government systems, for, if the NSA succeeds in developing strong and functional student governments throughout the American colleges

12/18/46

CHICAGO NOTES

4/21/49

Swarthmore Sends Choir and Maxin To NSA Culturale

10/7/48

Swarthmore Takes Lead At NSA Conventions

Delegates Champion Liberal Programs

NSA-IUS Relationship Creates Major Problem

4/22/52

NSA: Swarthmore's Link With Other Campuses

National: One-Fourth of Nation's Students Unite in Idea Exchange, Action

International Program: NSA Pays for Youth Hostels, Aids Needy and Refugee Students

Accomplishments: Act on Nationwide College 'Burning Issues' at Summer Meet

(Ostar, Ted Schreiber)

Photo: Ralph Smith addressing the 6/48 Penn. Regional Convention at Penn State.

The Swarthmore Phoenix reported extensively on NSA. Lada Hulka, one of the college's Chicago Student Conference delegates, was the USSA representative on the U.S. delegation to the 1946 World Student Congress (p. 84).

Connections to the Larger World

Swarthmore, Tuesday, October 31, 1933

We Who May Die

Students of America, the youth of the Western world are in danger! The statesmen have failed to meet the severe tests of the time of truce which has been called peace. Unless they can be prevailed upon to change their attitude, millions of young men will again be drawn into the maelstrom of war.

Less than twenty years ago men were slaying each other at the behest of their governments. Most of those who engaged in combat would have willingly risked their lives in peace time to rescue from danger any one of those who, when war was declared, automatically became their mortal enemies. When war came they fought, and millions of them died, because they had been told and they believed that in no other way could justice

1933-1939

ALL-COLLEGE VOTE ON WORLD PEACE ISSUES IS TOMORROW MORNING

Students and Faculty Get Chance to Register Sentiment on Current Problems

STUDENTS HEAD PROJECT

Peace Poll Shows Students Favor Giving Non-Military Aid to Warring Democracies

By Creighton Lacy

Recalling World War I, the peace movement (p. 10) and Oxford Peace pledge in the 1930's had strong appeal (l. to r. 10/31/33, 10/16/34, 5/16/39).

1948-1950

Seven Members of Phi Kappa Psi Resign In Protest Against National Fraternity

Wednesday, November 22, 1950

Council Opposes Loyalty Oath; Plan Referendum

The Student Council passed unanimously, last Sunday, a resolution against the special loyalty oath (imposed on the faculty of the University of California by the Board of Regents)...

Fraternity discrimination (see p. 743), academic freedom (p. 381), civil rights and the Cold War (p. 390) captured the attention of Swarthmore students in the years following World War II. (L. to r. 12/16/48, 11/22/50)

SIXTY PER CENT MAJORITY VOTE CAST FOR ABOLITION OF WOMEN'S FRATERNITIES

PRESENT NEW SOCIAL PROGRAM IN PLACE OF FRATERNITY ACTIVITIES

Curtailment Brings Increased Emphasis on College Functions

SUPPORT OF ALL NEEDED

All Four Classes Take Stand Against Organizations in W.S.G.A. Ballot

ACTION FINAL, SAYS BOARD

"Abolition" is the conclusive answer given by the women students to the question "What shall be done with fraternities on the Swarthmore campus?", registered by yesterday's vote of 168 for

Yard was a leader in displacing sororities. After WWII she became a founder of NOW.

MOLLY YARD (See p. 46)
Executive Secretary, American Student Union, 1933

Phoenix l. to r.: 10/18/32 (Photo and clip), 12/13/33.

Capacity Audience Hears First Lady; Applauds Speech On Four Freedoms

Standing Ovation In Dining Room

Rogers, Exec. Secy. of student union, shown with its President, Cy Levinthal and Mrs. Roosevelt. She later became a State of Wisconsin legislator.

Rogers Unanimously Elected USSA Head

Mary Lou Rogers, executive secretary of the SSU, was elected President of the United States Student Assembly on Sunday afternoon at the final session of USSA's first national conference, held in New York. Since there were no additional nominations from the floor, Miss Rogers, who was the only presidential candidate on the slate which had been prepared by the Presiding Committee's subcommittee on nominations, was elected by acclamation. She had previously been elected to the Presiding Committee and served as chairman of the sub-committee on

MARY LOU ROGERS MUNTS
President, U.S. Student Asssembly, 1943-44 (See p. 34)

Phoenix l. to r.: 10/18/32 (Photo and clip), 3/23/43, 5/11/43.

An air force veteran, Prentice later worked for Senator Sherman Cooper (KY), and in the State Department.

Prentice Returns to Campus Life After Heading Student Federalists

This year sees the return to the campus of Colgate Prentice, who, as national president of the Student Federalists, was absent last year. Elected head of this nation-wide organization at the Chicago National Convention, Coke felt that he could not do justice to the job unless he devoted his full time to it.

Coke first became interested in world-federation after his discharge ... in insuring world peace. He spent most of last year traveling through the country on an extended speaking tour. He addressed student groups in all parts of the country, as well as attending five summer institutes which met for the purpose of training student leadership. One of the most important conferences he went to was the

COLGATE PRENTICE (See p. 753)
President, Student Federalists, 1946-47

Photo: Wellesley *College News* 11/11/46. Above: *Phoenix* 10/24/47.

Smith Replaces Roy As Campus NSA Head; DP's May Study Here

Ralph Roy stepped out this week as chairman of the NSA DP Committee, due to the pressure of other work, and was replaced by Ralph Smith, chairman of the NSA Campus Committee. Smith will be assisted by Ellinor Ruden and Frank Solomon.

The committee, which hopes to see DP students admitted to Swarthmore

R. Smith Elected NSA Publicity Head

Ralph Lee Smith, Swarthmore's alternate to the second annual congress of the National Student Association, was elected a national officer as the interim national public relations director.

At the Congress meeting, held at the University of Illinois, the

Smith Chairs Regional Peace Conference

Student governments and student campus groups at colleges and universities throughout the Philadelphia area are planning large intercollegiate conference By What Means Peace? to be held at Temple University on the week

Smith was on staff during the 1949-50 presidency of Bob Kelly (p. 241). He has written books on folk songs in Appalachia and Greenwich Village and on the Appalachian Dulcimer.

RALPH LEE SMITH (See also p. 716)
Public Relations Director, USNSA 1949-50

Photo: *NSA News* 10/49. *Phoenix*: l. to r. 3/10/49, 10/5/49, 4/25/51.

Kurtz spoke widely at other colleges. He launched a lifetime career in broadcast journalism on the Swarthmore station and with the College News Conference.

Student Views Are Represented At State Department Conference

by Ken Kurtz

Last weekend I had the good luck to represent American college students at the annual National Conference on U. S. Foreign Policy sponsored by the Department of State in Washington. About 150 national organizations were represented through the National Student Association, which had selected me as it's delegate. Unfortunately, I can't say too much about what was said at the Conference by State Depart-

satisfaction with the present idea

K. Kurtz Discusses Role Of US's Youth

Youth's place in United States foreign policy was the subject under consideration at a meeting of Public Discussion Dec. 3. Leading the discussion was Mr. Ken Kurtz, graduate student in political science at Columbia. Mr. Kurtz is a member of NSA and the United World Federalists.

KENNETH R. KURTZ (See p. 306, p. 902)
Chair, NSA Pennsylvania Region, 1950-51

Photo: Yearbook, c. 1951. l. *Phoenix*: 5/9/51; r. Vassar *Miscellany* 12/5/51.

Keating was active in the Pennsylvania NSA region. He wrote several papers on the of student movements. He teaches at CUNY.

SDA Sees Peril to National Existence in UMT; Urges Its Defeat

Dresden, Keating Attend UNESCO Meeting in N. Y.

The State Department invited Dr. Dresden, head of the mathematics department at Swarthmore, and Barry Keating, a sophomore,

BARRY KEATING (See p. 811)
Internat'l. V.P., Students for Democratic Action, 1952-53

Photo: *Phoenix*: l. to r. 2/19/52, 3/4/52

Diary of an idealistic activist

2. Forum for Diversity and Debate: The Pennsylvania Region

Kenneth R. Kurtz
Swarthmore College
Chair, Pennsylvania Region, 1950-51

Editor's note: This essay has been prepared by the editors from transcripts of an interview conducted with Ken Kurtz in Lexington, Kentucky, in October, 1998, with the addition of material researched in Pennsylvania regional college newspapers and USNSA archives.

I was involved in student government as President of the Student Council at Weston High School in West Virginia. We had an enrollment of about 300. Weston was a little town of 8,000 in the north-central part of the state, in a county of 22,000. There was an association in West Virginia of various high school student councils, and I also attended the annual convention there. So when I got to Swarthmore, it was entirely logical to continue to be involved in student council activities.

My family was born in Virginia—[they were] Pennsylvania Dutch, which is German. They migrated into West Virginia—I don't know how many years ago. But all of the family, by the time I came along—back to the grandfathers and great grandfathers—had all been in West Virginia.

I am the son, grandson, and stepson of lawyers. My paternal grandfather was a lumber mill superintendent. [But the man could do anything in the world with his hands. He considered himself a carpenter.] My mother's father, my grandfather, was an attorney and coal mine operator. [At one point he said to me, "I am the only coal operator in West Virginia that John L. Lewis will talk to," which he took as a compliment—although the rest of the coal operators didn't look on him with much favor. And he was involved in the mine wars of the 1920s in West Virginia. But he could negotiate with John L. Lewis and the United Mine Workers, I think, because he was just as stubborn as Lewis.]

My mother's family was from Morgantown, at West Virginia University. And one of her lineal descendants was the first graduate of the law school—in 1870 or '80 something.

In return for my not leaving the local high school for a college prep school, I agreed to accept my mother's recommendation that I enroll at Swarthmore.

Swarthmore and the Quaker heritage

With that background, in the fall of 1947, I found myself at Swarthmore. I really wanted to major in journalism but discovered right off the bat there was no journalism major at Swarthmore. There was a very good student newspaper, however, and an even better student radio station. I got hooked on radio and ended up more in broadcast journalism. I read somewhere at that time that the best preparation for journalism really was a liberal arts education. Because I was interested in covering government and political news, my actual major was political science. Of course, that fit right in with student government.

I also discovered for the first time that there was something called NSA. *The Phoenix*, the Swarthmore newspaper, was running a series of articles by a male and two female students who had been to the Constitutional Convention. They came back to urge Swarthmore to join NSA. One article was totally devoted to international relations and the International Union of Students (IUS), and the rest touched on domestic policies, federal aid to education, and all the things we argued about then and argued about for a couple more decades thereafter.

As a result of their work and the articles, Swarthmore became one of the early members. It's a small campus—it was 1,000 students when I was there, and it was the largest enrollment they had had to that date. Swarthmore was founded by Quakers who believed in coeducation. There had been a big religious schism. Haverford was male, and they were the conformist Quakers. The Swarthmore Quakers were the nonconformist Quakers because they believed in the education of women. So they were coed from the word go—from about 1840 or something on that order. My own family, incidentally, had no relation to the Quakers.

Out of the ferment that was going on right after the war, there were issues of academic freedom, federal aid to education, and discrimination. Swarthmore was very active on the discrimination front. We had what we called the race relations committee. Most of these issues were covered by committees of the student government, and they recruited volunteers.

NSA committee becomes a gateway to the national scene

So when the council voted to join NSA, they set up an NSA committee. You put up a sign-up sheet on the bulletin boards: the student council has named an NSA committee, it's going to have its organizational meeting in one of the lodges at such and such a date—come one, come all! And if you came and stayed, you were on the NSA committee. A young man whom I had met there, named Ralph Smith (who later became national public relations director of NSA in 1949-1950), and I were very much interested in NSA. So we ended up on the NSA committee.[1]

I worked on many other council committees over those years, chief of which was the NSA committee. One was a committee that the council set up to oppose a religious quota system in our admissions policy, which was part of our antidiscrimination work. In my junior year, I won a one-year seat in student government.

Several of us, Ralph and I in particular, let it be know that we were interested in being delegates to the Pennsylvania regional meeting, so Swarthmore paid our way and we went to the regional meeting.[2] The following year, which would have been August of 1949, Ralph and I and some others were sent by Swarthmore to the Champaign-Urbana conference at the University of Illinois. Later, some of us went to the conventions at Michigan in 1950 and Minnesota in 1951.

Bob Kelly, whom I first met at the University of Illinois Congress in 1949, had a lot to do with my interest in parliamentary procedure because he was a master of it. In many ways he won the presidency that summer because he had conducted the general sessions so well, serving as parliamentarian and temporary chair.[3] In those years, if you were a candidate for national office, particularly for president, you were given a chance to be a chairman of a session—to test your mettle, in other words. There were people on the floor who would make certain that you really got tested—not necessarily your friends. Kelly handled all comers with aplomb and dispatch, and I think that had a lot to do with his becoming president.

Although the Second Congress at the University of Illinois is the one that Ralph Smith and I attended, I was told a story about the first conference in Madison, which I did not attend, which is very much worth the telling.

Birenbaum's dramatic nomination of Harris for NSA president

It was obvious that summer of 1948 in Madison that there were a number of exceptional candidates for president. One of them was Ted Harris (La Salle College, Philadelphia), and another was Bill Birenbaum (University of Chicago).[4] A number of people wanted Ted to run. The story I was told is that Ted was really pretty self-effacing and did not want to run. He would like to be president, he told people, but he just didn't want to get involved in the rough and tumble of an election.

In the nominating session, Bill Birenbaum was nominated to be president, and he was reported to have made an outstanding speech. He discussed his vision for NSA, where he thought the organization ought to go, its goals, where it should lay its stress, the things it ought to do, the need to build a student community. The speech was extremely well received, and the house was impressed to no end with him. Then, at the end of his talk, having laid out his vision for NSA, he paused and said something like, "Nevertheless, for personal reasons I cannot accept this nomination."

Bill walked off the stage into the wings as a thousand jaws dropped in the audience. Nobody really knew what was going on for a while. Suddenly, the door at the rear of the hall opened. Bill Birenbaum marched down the center aisle to a microphone on the floor and asked for recognition from the chair. The chair recognized him. Speaking from the floor mike, Bill said, "I would like to nominate, for president of NSA, Ted Harris."

And Ted Harris was elected. A postscript on this, which says something about Swarthmore and about NSA, is that a fairly cynical student editor of the paper later asked me, "Why didn't you all tell us that this James Ted Harris who was elected president in a day, was not only a Catholic, but a Black person?" I said, "Pete, it didn't seem to be important to us." And that was just the way Swarthmore looked at things. Pete was a veteran and he still was a little cynical, but in the eyes of Swarthmore, if Ted Harris was the best person, it didn't make a tinker's damn that he was (a) Catholic and (b) Black.

Ted Harris: an outstanding leader

Ted was a person you could not fail to like. It was just so obvious that he was a sincere person and interested in the well-being of the student community—an outstanding person. Dynamic in his own quiet way, religious in his own quiet way, he simply had a personality that won people over to him.

He was also one of the early chairmen of the Pennsylvania region during 1947-48. (I was later chairman during 1949-1950.) I first met Ted when he came to the Swarthmore campus in 1947 at a time NSA was trying to reach out to the IUS in some fashion, which was yet to be determined by the national board. NSA had announced throughout the country that it was going to take applications for students it would be selected to go and negotiate some type of understanding with IUS.

Senior people in NSA, and Ted was one of them, went to various campuses where interest was indicated. NSA had said around the country, "If you'd like to be considered to be on the team that will go abroad and negotiate an NSA/IUS relationship, let us know and we'll send somebody to your campus." Ted told me that he had about six or eight campuses throughout Pennsylvania. Something like twenty-one to twenty-two students in his region had applied to be on the team—eight were from Swarthmore, one of the smallest schools in Pennsylvania, but with this tremendous interest in International Affairs.

I was one of the eight. I had no more business being on the NSA negotiating team than the man on the moon. But it was apparent to all of us who believed in one world and hadn't been tainted by John Foster Dulles and the Cold War at that point that the students should not rupture themselves the way the adults had. As long as we had a chance for hands across the sea, we ought in our idealism to make the 110 percent effort to get along with IUS.

Well, I think Ted spent about ten minutes with me overall, during part of which he ate a sandwich because he had been on constant appointments with all of these students. Between mouthfuls he smiled and said, "That's good," and so on and so forth. But I recognized even more when the interview was over that I was totally unqualified to be on the NSA team. I thanked Ted for hearing me. He had such an engaging smile. It was the first time I met him. I became a firm friend thereafter.

The team that Ted and others had gone around screening was never formed and never sent because of the coup in Prague that spring.

Leadership and issues in the PRUSNSA Region

Pennsylvania furnished a number of outstanding early NSA leaders. Ralph Dungan (St. Joseph's College), the first regional chairman after the Chicago Conference, was NSA's first national vice president for domestic affairs, in 1947-48. Then came Ted Harris (La Salle College) as President in 1948-49. Allan Ostar of Penn State was appointed national public relations director that same year. Following Ted was Bob Troxell of Penn State. Elmer Brock (also from La Salle), another regional president, was elected vice president for student affairs in 1950-51, in the Lowenstein administration. Then I succeeded Elmer as regional president. And, of course, I ran for president in 1951 and was defeated by Bill Dentzer. I've written about that in Part 1 of this anthology.[5]

Our region also tended to be more issue oriented than leadership oriented, if I can make that distinction. At our annual regional conference, we would have workshops on a particular topic that seemed to be of interest to students. We had lots of workshops on how to have a more effective student government, as well as how to solve problems in the field of discrimination. We also always got more colleges at the regional meeting than showed up at the Congress.

Pennsylvania also had the Intercollegiate Conference on Government (ICG), which was also student government oriented. I went to that, too. It met once a year in Harrisburg and would sometimes take the form of a national party nominating convention. Sometimes it was like a small UN Assembly. But the conference always had a student government component. It was unique to Pennsylvania. A lot of student government leaders would attend that and would get to know each other there as well as through the regional NSA.

At the time I was involved, in the late 1940s and early 1950s, there were more colleges and universities in the Philadelphia metropolitan area than in any other area of the United States except Boston. Catholic schools were the biggest block. There was a plethora of small institutions of all shapes and size.

Among them were what we used to call the "small you know whats"—that meant a small Catholic girls' school.[6] There were lots of them, all over the place. To their credit, their students were not only bright, they were energetic. If you wanted to get something done, you gave it to a small you know what, and they got it done. They were the workers. We had people like Joan Gaily, and others I can think of who were sharp as a tack and who would debate academic freedom and loyalty oaths. Maybe not always from a standpoint that you agreed with, but—they were well prepared.

Then there was Lois Fitzimons from Mount Mercy in Pittsburgh, a girl who just worked tremendously hard, in the western part of the state particularly. The main Catholic college leadership came from people like Ralph Dungan, Elmer Brock, Father Thomas; also Elwood Kaiser, who later became Father Kaiser, and from whom I occasionally still get letters.

The Pennsylvania region was essentially Pittsburgh and Philadelphia. We didn't have anything around Harrisburg, which is too bad, because we could have met at the center. LaSalle and St. Joseph's were the powerhouses for the men's school in eastern Pennsylvania. There weren't really any men's schools in the west.

Mount Mercy was in Pittsburgh, although it's called Carlow College now. We had maybe half a dozen schools there. We had a small school up in Allegheny—Thiel College in Greenville, and another, Mercyhurst, up in Erie. But in the east we had Swarthmore, University of Pennsylvania, and Temple. And St. Joe, LaSalle, Beaver, Bryn Mawr, Albright—these were the schools that anchored the eastern part. Albright was a very active small school. Bryn Mawr was a powerhouse. Pennsylvania College for Women was a powerhouse in the western part of the state. (It was renamed Chatham College in 1955 after William Pitt, the first Earl of Chatham, and remains a women's college to this day.)

Accommodating and debating differences with Catholic college students

We had our differences, and we debated them vigorously. In most areas, though not all, we were able to come to an accommodation. I believe we understood each other in all areas, however, whether or not we agreed. Most of the Catholic schools were far more conservative than liberal Swarthmore. They would approach things from a different perspective. Yet in certain areas, like discrimination, it was the Catholic schools, in many ways, who pushed everybody else into a truly nondiscriminatory position. I wish that a lot of the other religiously affiliated schools had been as strong on improving race relations as the Catholic school were.

On the other hand, on loyalty oaths, academic freedom, and the Student Bill of Rights, it was another matter. Their view was far more restrictive than ours. So we would have tremendous debates on the loyalty oaths question, for example. Can you see a Quaker taking a loyalty oath? There was no way. So, we would uphold our point of view, and there were very few cases of friendships broken over these differences.

That didn't mean that we were all in lockstep on different sides. For example, I didn't mind quoting Father J.C. Murray and his view that engagement was needed on the international scene as a counterfoil to Soviet-dominated groups such as the International Union of Students.[7] When one of the Catholic students said no, we ought to pick up our marbles and walk away, my argument for staying was the same as Father Murray's.

I also learned that the Church was far from monolithic inside itself. There were the Jesuits, the Dominicans, the Christian Brothers, the Benedictines—all with a slightly different slant. They would argue with each other on theology at the drop of a hat. I used to argue that Communism was not a monolith, either. Those were the days of China, Albania, Russia—there were cracks in the monolith. We learned about these things in NSA.

World War II's aftermath ushered in the era of organized Catholic college student participation in non-Catholic groups, as the NSA experience demonstrated. The war was an eye-opening, liberating, and energizing experience for young students of all faiths. I found there was a whole group of students at Catholic colleges, many of whose goals in life were no different than those of the group I associated with on our campus at Swarthmore.

Influence of the Students for Democratic Action

We also had an extremely active SDA chapter on campus, part of which was formed originally in opposition to the American Youth for Democracy (AYD).[8] And we had one or two AYD members on campus, but there was no chapter. We had people who supported Henry Wallace and the Progressive Party in the election of 1948. Our SDA group was quite prominent within SDA and within ADA. I would say the general political persuasion of the Swarthmore student body as a whole (and it's always dangerous to generalize) would have been pretty much found in SDA— and it certainly was mine.

Paradoxically, Swarthmore also had a Jewish quota—the only quota the school had. We worked to eliminate it. (I always claim facetiously that I got in on the hillbilly quota, but any other quota I was opposed to.) It was a continuing fight throughout the time we were in college. It was the one mote in the eye of Swarthmore college.

Swarthmore also, at one time, ran roughshod over student rights, and we let the college know we were unhappy about it. So this whole area of academic freedom—reaching out to IUS, not wanting the Cold War to come down on the campus, antidiscrimination—these were issues I was very much concerned with and issues I wanted to see NSA not falter in. And I wasn't alone in that. You have Ralph Smith. You have a lot of SDA people like Galen Martin (Berea College), Alex Pope and Frank Logan (both of the University of Chicago), and a great many others who also were interested in NSA. Sometimes it was hard to tell in some NSA regional caucus whether or not you were in an SDA meeting as well. I recall Illinois being one example.

It's not hard to understand why those of us who would take the title of student activist proudly were involved in kindred groups like this. The World Student Service Fund (WSSF) was one, because after the war there were a lot of broken colleges and students who were living from hand to mouth abroad. There were things that you wanted to do to help them. Although WSSF would never say this, I'll say it. If the democracies didn't come to the aid of these students through any means possible, including WSSF, we damn well knew who would come to their aid. And that was the specter we were unwilling to accept.

So here you can have a political activist, like myself, also working in a service fund, which was about as nonpolitical as you can get in the international student community. Its strong religious orientation doesn't mean it was devoid of politics. Also, if you run down the list on many campuses—I know it was true of Swarthmore—of those who belonged to the United World Federalists, they'd also be in SDA. SDA was in NSA.[9] And some of the NSA people would later on work with the World Student Fund, extending the links.

A linking of kindred groups

NSA extended links in many ways. I don't think I ever went to an NSA Congress where some white southern student didn't tell me that he had met a black student leader for the first time and was somewhat surprised to find he liked the guy or girl and that they could get along. He wasn't sure how it was going to sell back on his campus, but NSA brought these people together, as the Ys did, as SDA did, as the Federalists, I'm sure, did—although that was not much of a component of their activity. But it was a component for NSA. I think NSA had an awful lot to do with the improvement of interracial relations in the South.

After the 1951 Congress, I went to Columbia University for two years, in New York. While in New York, I was involved in the activities of the Young Adult Council. I also had an overlapping relationship with the World Student Service Fund. While I was at Columbia, I was still assisting WSSF in some ways. At that time, part of the student division of the United World Federalists had broken off and formed an organization called WORLD. I was the first chairman of WORLD while I was at Columbia.

Gil Jonas (Stanford University) was second chairman of WORLD. So, you met the same friends Monday at the WSSF, and Tuesday at the United World Federalists meeting, and Friday at the SDA beer party. It should come as no surprise that I don't remember which group asked me to represent them on the Young Adult Council, but I did it for a portion of the two years that I was in New York.

I was also on the Board of the International Development Placement Association (IDPA). Doug Kelly of the Federalists asked me. Jim Farmer and Doug Kelly were two of the movers. Earlier, while I was at Swarthmore, I went to a Point Four conference in Washington sponsored by the State Department, where Justice William Douglas spoke on Truman's Point Four program to develop the underdeveloped world. Point Four inspired the formation of IDPA.[10]

Justice Douglas spoke on the program quite a bit. He was one of our heroes on campus—for his views from the bench as well as his ex cathedra views on other things. Especially his environmentalism, though it wasn't called that then. Here was this Supreme Court Justice off climbing mountains. Theodore Roosevelt, maybe—but a Supreme Court Judge! In 1952, I was the youngest alternate delegate at the Democratic National Convention. I was representing West Virginia. And when my delegate was absent one day and they asked me to vote, my vote was for Douglas. Fortunately, my delegate came back before the roll was called and canceled my vote.

Political issues in NSA

Although NSA's constitution required that it not engage in politics, certain issues, by the very nature of their concern to "students as students," required a political agenda. For example, Universal Military Training (UMT) was a big issue in our day. I was one of the chief debaters who favored UMT and who also supported the draft, with reservations, in a big debate at the National Presbyterian Youth Conference, which I went to between high school and college. Yet I was also a member of a small group of Swarthmore students that later went to a protest outside the Federal Court Building in Philadelphia. We gave moral support to two of our fellow students who were conscientious objectors. Both of them were Quakers. One I was fairly close to. We went to the protest and to appear in court to say by our presence, "Newt and Bill, we support you."

The two students were sentenced to a year and a day in the federal penitentiary for being conscientious objectors during the Korean War. It was almost an article of faith on our campus that you could support the draft and still believe that this guy had every right not to support it and to be a conscientious objector if he wanted to.

Ted Harris and I had a discussion one time because I had said that NSA had to get involved in partisan politics. And Ted said to me, "You mean politics, don't you? You don't mean partisan politics." I said, "Of course Ted, you're right, I misspoke." I never thought NSA should be involved in the partisan sense of backing a Democrat, Republican, Henry Wallace, or anybody else. But by the nature of the beast, NSA had to be involved in politics. And I would certainly have supported NSA's position, even if it was different from mine. NSA was made up of "draft bait" people, and for NSA not to take a position on Korea or, later, on Vietnam, would have been just unthinkable.

Debating the value of NSA

As Ralph Smith has noted in his piece, the general question at Swarthmore was, are we getting our money's worth from NSA?[11] There was a general feeling that NSA and its stand on issues mirrored, very largely, the Swarthmore standpoint. We would have liked NSA to have been a little bit more liberal, but that was no great problem. Ours was a very self-contained campus. We strongly supported NSA's position on academic freedom and on antidiscrimination. A lot of our students went abroad on the international travel program, but we could have done it on our own. But we always put the travel guides and the bulletins up on the bulletin board. We always put people in touch with the Cambridge NSA office so that they could go abroad.

We even, I think, made an abortive attempt to put in the Purchase Card System, but here you are in a small village of Swarthmore, 2,500 people, twenty-five miles west of Philadelphia. What you couldn't find in the Village, you surely could find in Philadelphia. So the discount card didn't fly very well. But we kept selling it, largely on the basis that we need to support NSA's policies: antidiscrimination, academic freedom, student rights, representation in Washington, representation in the international community, eligibility for the study/travel/work abroad programs. But, some of us would be saying, we're paying these dues and all we're doing is sending Ralph Smith and Ken Kurtz off to the conferences and paying their bills. They're getting a benefit, but what is the campus getting? Every year we had to fight that fight again.

Summing up

The veteran generation was a strong influence in our day. To a certain extent, in the early years, NSA got some of its support from college campuses and from administrators because the veterans coming back to the campus after the war were involved.

They were much more mature than the same class levels of prewar years. This presumably gave some impetus to the faculty rating systems that NSA supported. My class at Swarthmore in 1951 was the first class after the war in which there was a nonveteran majority among the males. We then became the norm for succeeding classes, even with the Korean and Vietnam conflicts on the horizon. I suspect that every class from that point on had a majority of nonveterans.

Looking back, I think one could argue that NSA represented the predominant middle of the student community. It could be center, left-center, or right-center, but it was still the middle. The veterans in the early days had a lot to do with that, and the people who took a United World Federalist or SDA point of view would contribute to that. It was before the "me generation." We were still altruistic, optimistic, and perhaps naïve: maybe a little bit more than we should have been. To an extent some of us thought Wendell Willkie's "one world" view ought to be given a chance before we just threw it into the ashcan of history. And that's why some of us tried to do something with IUS, even when it was apparent that they might not be as willing to extend a hand to us. We were still willing to take a chance for longer period than a lot of others were.

NSA was a landmark experience in my life. I would not have missed it for anything.

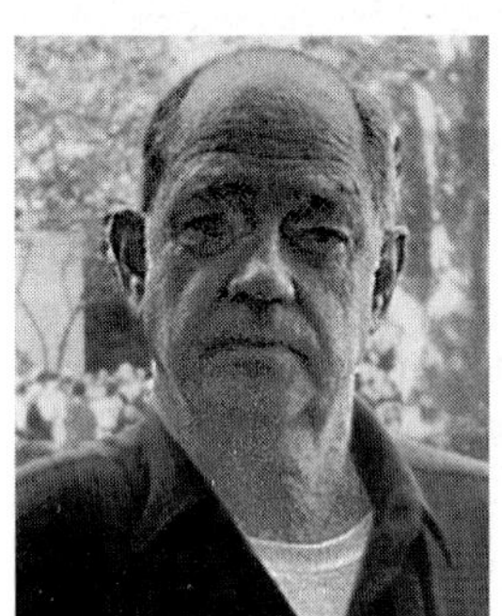

Kenneth R. Kurtz has been a radio and TV broadcast journalist since 1955, working with stations in Augusta, GA, Charleston, SC, Wayne, IN, Greensboro, NC, and Lexington, KY. He currently hosts public affairs and news shows for Kentucky PBS.

(See p. 308 for extended biography.)

WORLD FEDERALISM AT SWARTHMORE

Going back to the early years, I had a strong interest in the importance of maintaining dialog on the international level and was a supporter of the world federalist concept along with Colgate Prentiss, practically one of the founding fathers of the United World Federalists (see pp. 765, 901). He was one of the two or three students most responsible for the student division of he United World Federalists. He had been away working for the United World Federalist Student Division and was back on campus.

The Federalists were part of the general internationalist approach that the Swarthmore campus took in many things. We also had an active World Student Service Fund committee. We were active in student relief efforts, and our students would spend their summers working on American Friends Service Committee projects abroad, doing relief work—building homes and hospitals and co-ops all over the world. It was an active internationalist campus in many ways.

END NOTES

1 See Ralph Smith, p. 847.

2 See the chronology of regional meetings in this section, p. 915.

3 See Schwartz, p. 235, and Kelly, p. 252.

4 See Harris, p. 219, Dungan, p. 909, Birenbaum, p. 590, and Heggie, p. 205.

5 See Kurtz, p. 306.

6 *Editor's note:* For more on Catholic women's colleges, see Lynch, p. 493, Perkins, p. 943, and Donnelly, p. 951.

7 'See "Operation University," p. 739.

8 See Seymour Reisin on the SDA, p. 781. See American Youth for Democracy, p. 787.

9 See Jonas, p. 761.

10 See IDPA, p. 623, and Murphy, p. 630.

11 See Ralph Smith, p. 898.

PICTURE CREDITS: *Then:* c. 1951, Swarthmore College Yearbook (Swarthmore College Archives). *Now:* c. 2001 (Author).

"The door opens . . . it's Al, ready to go to the National Executive Committee meeting."

Looking back on Al Lowenstein

Ken Kurtz
Swarthmore College
Chair, Pennsylvania Region, 1949-50

Al Lowenstein: A visit to the Met NY Region and a Plane Ride to Madison, Wisconsin

Once Al walked in on a meeting of the Met New York region and one of Al's supporters got up and said, "We have a visitor here, Al Lowenstein." He wasn't president then. He was a Chapel Hill (University of North Carolina) NSA representative, but well known throughout the organization. The supporter moved that we open the floor to our guest for anything he wanted to say. Immediately somebody said, "No, no, that's out of order. This is the Met New York region and only delegates and alternates may have the floor." So for thirty minutes this argument goes back and forth—point of order, point of parliamentary privilege! Several votes are taken. Finally, by a narrow margin, the vote is carried to extend the privileges of the floor to Mr. Lowenstein for anything he has to say. Al gets up and says, "Thank you very much, but I really don't have anything to say," and sits down. And the person got up who had been opposing this all along and said: "I object. He's got to say something now."

I can recall another Al story. It occurred when I was in Madison at the winter meeting of the executive board over the Christmas holidays. It was the first time in my life I had flown commercially. I got on a DC-3 at a little airport near my house, and we had to make three stops before we got to Pittsburgh, which was only 150 miles as the crow flies away.

In Pittsburgh I was going to get on a big plane, a Northwestern Starcruiser, and fly into Madison and attend the meeting. But we can't get to Pittsburgh—we're forced down with ice on the wings. The airline puts us on a bus. We take the bus from Wheeling to Pittsburgh and we get there a couple of hours late. Nevertheless, Northwest is also late. The plane is late because it couldn't get off the icy runway at LaGuardia to fly into Pittsburgh.

The plane finally arrived after midnight. It was a non-stop Pittsburgh to Madison, as I recall. I got off the plane at the Madison airport and there's Elmer Paul Brock, who is surprised to see me, because he's expecting Al Lowenstein and I'm very definitely not Al Lowenstein. Elmer asks, "Where is Al?" I say: "What do you mean?" He says, "Well, Al is supposed to be on your plane." I say: "Well, there weren't very many people on the plane, but I sure as hell didn't see Al."

By this time, the plane has taxied off. It just literally dropped me and maybe one or two other people at Madison airport, and it's turning off to go off to Minneapolis. Elmer goes into the airport and they radio the plane to see if there's an Al Lowenstein on board. Turns out, Al had gotten on the plane in New York, dead tired from something. He had slumped down in the back seat and gone to sleep. I never saw him in Pittsburgh—he was practically down on the floor. He didn't get off at Madison.

In ten minutes, the plane is back, landing at the Madison airport. The door opens, they wheel up the stairs, and one solitary passenger, who is half asleep, gets off, comes down the stairs, and it's Al, ready to go to the National Executive Meeting.

They don't run airlines that way anymore, either.

(For more on Lowenstein, see Pt. 1, Sec. 8 and pp. 283, 562, 976, 979, and 991)

The Campus Radio Station

My number-one activity at Swarthmore was the student radio station, although I occasionally wrote some articles for the student newspaper. It was one of those small carrier stations that only broadcast to the campus through the dorm wiring. If you volunteered you got elected.

A number of us were interested in news—public affairs and sports. So I formed the special events crew for the station and we broadcast the football games and the basketball games. At Swarthmore, hardly a week would go by without a public forum or an outside speaker or lecturer, and we had wired every lecture hall on the campus. Students learned they could stay in their room and the student radio station and my special events unit would broadcast all the lectures and concerts. If they didn't want to go, they could hear it in their room. I was also station manager in my senior year.

When I got to Columbia, which had a journalism school, I found they also had a radio and television department in graduate school. Although my major was political science, and I was technically enrolled in public law and administration, what I really wanted to do was to cover government and politics. So, I also took courses in broadcasting. Then, when I gave up my academic career to go into the army, I ended up in a signal corps installation, in a public information office, doing radio and television, wire service, newspaper and magazine writing.

This was in 1953-55, just after Korea was winding down. When I came out of the service, based on my military, public information office experience, I was hired by a small radio station in Augusta, Georgia, outside of Fort Gordon—and the rest as they say is history. I was the first full-time broadcast journalist in the history of Augusta radio, and they had about a dozen stations down there. Everybody ripped and read the Associated Press wire, but nobody had a full-time reporter on the staff. So I was the one man full-time news department at my radio station. I did everything. I was it. Forty years later, I retired actively from radio and television journalism.

Ken Kurtz
Swarthmore College
Chair, Pennsylvania Region, 1949-50

Catholic colleges and NSA energize each other

3. The Catholic Students in NSA and St. Joseph's College

Ralph Dungan
St. Joseph's College, Philadelphia
Chair, Pennsylvania Region, 1946-47
NSA Vice President, Domestic Affairs, 1947-48

I grew up in Philadelphia, in Germantown and Mt. Airy, before the war. I went to a parochial elementary school and to a preparatory Jesuit high school called St. Joseph's. It was not physically connected to the St. Joseph's College at that time. It was in downtown Philadelphia. I had one brother, two years younger, who is now dead.

My father was a lawyer and my mother was a nurse. She came from the anthracite coal regions of Pennsylvania. Father was a native of Philadelphia who went to St. Joseph's College and then to University of Pennsylvania law school. My father was up to his eyeballs in politics. What I had seen of the law was not conducive to my thinking positively about it as a career. I decided I didn't want to go into law, although I would have been good at it.

We were very lucky during the Depression years. We didn't have much of a sweat economically. It was after the Depression, at the beginning of the war, that things got tough. I was very much aware of the Depression through school. There were obvious disparities in circumstance. But the area in which we lived at that time—Mt. Airy, Philadelphia—was upper-middle class. People there were not hurting really hard.

Military service influences career goals

I enlisted fairly early, when I was seventeen, in the Navy's Aviation Cadet (V-5) Program. We were given initial training in Piper Cubs and then sent off to Navy preflight school for the regular training.[1]

We were sent to Muhlenberg College and did our training at the Allentown/Bethlehem airport. That was in the middle of winter; so we couldn't do much flying. Then we went to preflight school at the University of Georgia. I did my primary flight training at Olathe, Kansas, and then advanced flight training at Pensacola, Florida. I got my wings in January of 1944, and I was sent back to Olathe as an instructor pilot.

I stayed in Olathe until the latter part of the war, I guess the spring of 1945, when I was sent up to Ottumwa, Iowa—again into the heartland—to another Navy training base.[2] Finally, we were discharged, in December of 1945, and I came back to Philadelphia.

Although family finances did not permit college enrollment before I went into the service, I did attend night school at Drexel for a couple of years, in chemical engineering. I chose chemistry then because I had gotten a job at a big steel plant in a chemical lab. When I came back, though, my whole career outlook had changed. By the end of January 1946 I was enrolled at St. Joseph's College.

During my wartime experience I used to think a lot about what I would do and what life was all about. Even though I was not in combat, I thought about all these people killed in the war, and that if people didn't get involved we would get back into another mess. I decided then to go into public service, and I pursued a regular B.A. in Political Science.

It is interesting to look back over that period and see that many people did emerge with a stronger social conscience than they ever had before the war. Yet I've never been quite sure how socially broad-minded veterans as a group were. There were individual veterans who were terrific. But the run of them were just ordinary guys. And they often didn't even respond to the leadership of those people who were on the cutting edge of external issues.

My friendship with Ted Harris

Early on I had my eye on going to the Woodrow Wilson School at Princeton, because I had heard good things about that program. As it turned out, when I finished college, I did apply and was accepted into the second graduate class. It was a pretty small class at that time.[3]

Ted Harris got to Woodrow Wilson just as I was graduating, in 1952.[4] Interestingly, Ted and I had lived very close to one another in Germantown. I knew Ted very well from way back, before NSA was even a dream in anyone's mind. I knew the house he lived in because we lived on the same street, just a block away. While I was in high school, my family moved out to a farm briefly. Then we moved back to Upsal Street in Germantown, and that's where I got to know Ted Harris.

Ours was becoming an integrated neighborhood and I think Ted's was one of the first Black families to move into such a rather haughty white neighborhood. There were a lot of big houses there, with big, expansive lands around them. His house was one of the nicest on the street, a beautiful old, Colonial-type house made of fieldstone.

Ted went to a Christian Brothers high school and then on to La Salle College. I remember Ted's father well. He was a postman, and he used to deliver mail to our house. St. Joseph's was a Jesuit school. We both went to the same parochial elementary school up through the eighth grade, however. The elementary school was operated by nuns, located in most cases near where you lived.

There was a great rivalry between La Salle and St. Joe's in Philadelphia in the football and basketball leagues. Not so much academically, although we always thought of them as not being "top drawer"—those "old Christian Brothers guys." In truth, it was a very good college and got better as time went on.

In those days we had separate men's and women's schools. The system seemed to work well. Discipline was really tight. Even the best two public schools in Philadelphia were unisex: Boys High and Girls High. They produced the high-flying kids who were very high in academic standards.

While at college, I didn't see a lot of Ted. We no longer lived in the same neighborhood. My mother had died during the war, and our household was broken up when I came back. But I did see him at intercollegiate events, such as international clubs, the kind I was active in as an undergraduate. There was a young Jesuit scholastic (Father Gerard J. Campbell, later president of Georgetown University), who taught political science and history at St. Joseph's at the time. He actively stimulated outward looking activity on the part of students in the international relations club, and he influenced students such as Jim Dougherty and me, who were political science majors.

I knew Ted Harris well enough, though, that when I became head of the Pennsylvania region during the National Continuations Committee (NCC) phase in the spring of 1947, I went to Ted to try to get him interested in NSA.

Organizing NSA in Pennsylvania

For a variety of reasons, I did not do as much traveling around the state during the spring of 1947 as I should have. A lot of the Pennsylvania Region at the Madison convention that summer was not because of any direct action of mine. We did mailings, but didn't have a lot of one-to-one meetings on campuses, except in the Philadelphia area. I felt rather guilty about that, but it turned out well and we had good representation. It was a very difficult job for all the people in the regions. You were selling an idea that wasn't there yet.[5]

Incredibly, we got a whole national convention going and a new organization started in six months while continuing a full load of academic work back at college. This really suggests that there was something intrinsic in the social environment that was impelling this thing forward. It wasn't simply due to the heroic activity of a relatively small group of people.

In fact, my whole active period with NSA, whether in the Continuations period or in the first year, was 99 percent organization. If Gordon Klopf, Janis Tremper, and Mildred Kiefer hadn't really pushed me on the student government pamphlet that we produced when I was national vice president, it would never have gotten done. It was not high among my priorities at all. I was out hoofing it.

My recollection is that, to a very large degree, I was operating in an unknown environment. Student governments weren't necessarily the initial gateway to affiliation. For example, I would attempt to go through the international relations club or some such organization. Oftentimes that's where you would find people who were politically and socially sensitive. Sometimes there wasn't yet an established student government. Oftentimes, the membership on an NSA committee was common to both.

Our major appeal was that it was important for students to band together—protecting student rights and academic freedom. Actually, these were not issues for me. Academic freedom was never discussed on a Catholic college campus, not because people didn't understand what it was or weren't concerned about it, it was not the priority that it would have been, for example, at City College of New York or any of the other big secular campuses, such as Wisconsin or California.

International issues motivated interest in NSA

In those early years I was not aware of an academic or student rights issue in the Philadelphia area at a place like Temple or the University of Pennsylvania. The latter, of course, was a fraternity dominated, typically establishment Ivy League place. You didn't have student rights issues there as major out-front, big all-campus or all-city issues. There may have been some, but I don't recall any of significance being raised in the Philadelphia area in 1947 and 1948.

Unlike, as Barefoot Sanders wrote, was the case at the University of Texas, where the biggest problem affecting students was the NSA-IUS issue, that wasn't the case in our area.[6] It was a vague feeling that the United States ought to be more outgoing and involved in the postwar world. I don't think there were very many students interested in the domestic programs, whether it would be academic freedom or student government stimulation. We got a little flicker of interest here and there—but I found we got a very good response to the business of faculty rating, particularly with veterans.

Students were very much more concerned than, I think, historically they had been with the quality of the education they were getting. They were looking for ways they might influence that. That, to me personally, was a much more important issue.

The veteran contribution

In that regard, probably the most important contribution the veterans made was that they were serious about their studies and they forced institutions to measure up to produce quality education. No faculty could ever stand up and give a lecture that was not untrue but was not the full story, and get away with it. That was probably what was behind the positive reception given to NSA's faculty-rating system. In these days it's much easier to approach department heads or senior professors and have a man-to-man with them than it was in our time. There was no tradition of this kind of conversation, particularly in the small religious institutions.

I don't recall what I thought at the time, but looking back on it, the strongest driving force toward bringing that critical mass together that became the convention in Madison was probably Alexis de Tocqueville's observation about the general American instinct for forming an organization where one didn't exist.

And the basic interest, however it was stimulated, that brought people to Madison for the Constitutional Convention didn't change significantly in the six- or seven-month period between Chicago and Madison. Basically, people were already engaged.

Attending the 1946 Chicago Student Conference

I was prompted to go to the Chicago Student Conference in December of 1946, and ultimately to involve myself in NSA, because of two good friends at St. Joseph. One was a professor, Gerry Campbell. He later became president of Georgetown. The other was my colleague and friend Jim Dougherty, who was the National Federation of Catholic College Students (NFCCS) representative and a great friend of Ed Kirschner.[7] Ed was very interested in Pax Romana. Campbell was very much in league with what Jim and I did later.

We sort of divided the turf. Jim took the NFCCS ,and I went the NSA route. Jim and I were really like the Bobbsey twins. We ran against one another for student body president. His father had been very active in Democratic politics, as was mine. He had marvelous oratorical skills. He went on to get a Ph.D. and became a distinguished professor emeritus in politics at St. Joseph's.

There wasn't much student government at Catholic schools before the war. Student government didn't have a strong presence at St. Joseph's; it had come in after the war, and they were trying to accommodate to the impact of all the veterans. It had been a flaccid place with a very low enrollment—barely keeping alive. A lot of the smaller colleges had a really tough time during the war. So, it was like an oyster, in which we could grow anything we wanted.

I was on the GI Bill. I had saved a little money during the war, and I had a little Chevy coupe. Jim lived at home. He was the idol of his mother and sisters. He was free to do anything and didn't have any obligations. Jim and I went to meetings and got things going on the campus. We were motivated to raise the consciousness of our own student body and to get the students interested in something other than their degree in Business Administration and Accounting.

Energizing changes within the Church

A lot of this activity was internal and was responding to changes pressing within the Church. I remember facing the president of my college one day, brash as hell. We marched in and told him the Church ought to be more socially conscious, and so forth. He was an old conservative Irish-Catholic priest and he said, "Sufficient for the layman to keep the commandments and say the Our Father." Laymen were not to get their noses into all this stuff, much less anything ecclesiastical and how worship services ought to be run.

But there were also individuals among the clergy who ran these schools who were delighted with what was happening. They had been in the doldrums for a long while, and they saw all these bright guys coming back full of beans and, for them, it was great. The dean of our college was a marvelous man. He used to hold private seminars in the evening when our work was done, and we would go through Plato. I'll never forget when we had a seminar on *The Republic.* We had a half dozen guys, and Jim and I were both members. There was also a girl from the office. It was a terrific session. These faculty responded to the bright young fellows who were coming along, and they tolerated a lot of expression that they never would have tolerated in my father's day.

Operation University at Catholic Colleges

John Courtney Murray, an important figure among the Jesuits, was a highly regarded major voice for this new generation of faculty. He was a great theologian at Woodstock Theological College. Woodstock was in Maryland and was the theological seminary for the Jesuits outside Washington. Murray wrote the famous *America* magazine article, "Operation University," which helped launch Catholic student involvement in the emerging postwar student movement around the world and which alerted the Church to the Cold War significance of the formation of IUS and the importance of getting Catholic students involved.[8]

Our activity in the student government at St. Joe's preceded the formation of NSA. We did a lot of new things. For instance, I worked in the bookstore part time. I didn't think of it at the time, but what I was trying to do was start a cooperative bookstore—sell your books back to the coop or to the next generation of students. But in doing so, we were also interfering with the college's new book cash flow.

Student government among Catholic colleges was really a postwar phenomenon. It's very probable also that the women's colleges, places like Mundelein and Rosary and Manhattanville, which tended to be progressive, had grown during the wartime period much more than the predominantly men's colleges. They were probably out ahead, and had some very smart women.

In any event, there emerged after the war a student government and activist leadership presence on many college campuses that wasn't fully accepted by all of the administrations. There were a lot of colleges in Pennsylvania. I was stunned, as chairman of the region, at how many colleges there were in Pennsylvania—eighty-five, as I recall. But these student governments were very much mirror images of the body politic. They had the same kinds of problems in trying to get people out to register and vote.

It was actually part of the education process, trying to get people to be more open and to expand their horizons. I suppose it went better in the immediate postwar era because there was a sufficient leaven of veterans who were keyed in and who did enjoy reading the newspaper and were interested in more and more things. I would say the run of college kids, veteran or not, could care less. I remember having violent discussions with my fellow students in terms of getting people out to vote.

On many campuses—and I would say that was true in most of the Catholic colleges—you didn't have the problems that would provoke active movements toward student government. You still had that old discipline operating. Many of the faculties and administrations in the Catholic colleges were hostile, because it meant grief to them. They were going to have to deal with these guys when they went down and asked for something. But the wiser of them saw it as an important part of the whole developing educational scene.

Changing views of student status

The old idea of in loco parentis, while still heavily prevalent in the lower schools and even some high schools, was weakening in the colleges. The advent of the war had a lot to do with the changes. None of the veteran students were buying it, and some of the younger faculty went along with the vets. I think that it died out in most places, except perhaps in the girl's colleges.

There was a man by the name of Monsignor John Cronin who was at the National Catholic Bishop's Conference. John, whom I knew, was a very divisive voice. He was cherubic and he did it in a nice way, but he was very negative. He was an opposite to John Courtney Murray or Father George Higgins, who was a junior colleague of Cronin's. Higgins was very much in the John Courtney Murray school.

I recently read an excellent book, *The American Catholic*, which traces the church back to its roots in the United States. This whole period is discussed. There was a big ferment going on in the Church. It was evolving very rapidly and a lot of the individual professors and college administrators were all going through a big transformation. At the same time the student community was going through it under the pressure of the veterans. Of course there were some negative elements—the anticommunist business—but on the whole I think it was positive. It was more along the J. C. Murray line of thinking than otherwise.

Influences of Catholic schools and NSA on each other

Returning to the impact of all of this within NSA, there were different perspectives on the goals for Catholic students. Father Murray was a great expositor of an open and pluralistic kind of involvement—you've got to get in there to be a part of what's happening.

But then you had within the Joint Committee for Student Action, the Catholic caucus in NSA, the Phil Des Marais and John Simons group, which leaned toward a much more negative anticommunist twist to the same goal. I wasn't personally involved in the JCSA.[9]

I don't think the Catholic schools, per se, had very much of an influence on NSA—although they furnished a lot of organizational energy. I do think the NSA had a big influence on many of the Catholic schools. It was primarily on individuals—although in my college that reflected itself within the college itself. The professors and administrators were always interested in what the hell was going on and would question it, not in any nefarious way, but they really were curious. And they saw what was happening to all of us. Those who were unconvinced became convinced that this was a very good idea. I think that, you could almost say, was a universal reaction on the part of professors and administrators.

One issue of great Catholic school interest in NSA policy had to do with federal aid to education.[10] If you broaden it, the issue was then, and is now, a question of individual citizen choice. I was made very sensitized to this during the time I was chancellor of Higher Education in New Jersey. While I was not directly responsible for what I call the lower schools, I met so many parents of young children, particularly up in Newark, who were desperate. They were being dumped on terribly by that public school system, as they probably are today, and all parents wanted was an opportunity to be able to put their children in an environment—it didn't matter whether it was religious or secular—where their kids would be safe and able to learn. Neither of those were options in many of the public schools.

In our era on the college level, that was all solved by the GI Bill. It was aid to the individual and he could take his bucks wherever he wanted. There was virtually no federal intervention in higher education under the GI Bill.

Ralph Dungan was Chancellor for Higher Education in the State of New Jersey. Earlier, he was Special Assistant to Presidents John F. Kennedy and Lyndon Johnson and Ambassador to Chile. He currently lives and maintains a small farm in St. John, Barbados. (See p. 177 for an extended biography.)

END NOTES

[1] We were flying primary trainers called the Yellow Peril. It was a Stearman biplane, fabric covered, with a 225-horsepower engine and two-seat dual control. The student was in the rear and the instructor up front. It a basically stable plane design meant for a lot of power-off landings, which we introduced very early to kids who were going into carriers. It was also applicable for flying aerobatics—loops, slow-mos and that kind of thing—which was what the primary instruction curriculum in the air was all about.

[2] Eventually, toward the end of the war in June or July of 1945, we were transported to Pensacola, where we were going to be trained as what they called Carrier Supply Replacement Pilots or Carriers. By then, they had more pilots than they knew what to do with. It was clear the war was over, and they gave us an opportunity to sign up with the regular Navy. If you didn't sign up, you just sat around on the beach in Pensacola. That drove me crazy, so I volunteered for other kinds of duty, like being the assistant officer at the General Headquarters—anything to keep busy.

[3] A chap by the name of Don Wallace, a Harvard economist, came back after the war to head up the place. He really saw it as a trade school for the civil service. It was aimed more broadly at journalism than anything else. It was definitely not intended to be a scholarly doctoral program, it was not in the Princeton pattern at all. However, over the years it changed, and his conception was modified. It became much more academically oriented, as the rest of Princeton is.

[4] Ted Harris, La Salle College, was elected 1948-49 president of NSA at the First National Student Congress in Madison. See Heggie, p. 205, and Harris, p. 224.

[5] Pennsylvania had forty-nine delegates and observers at the 1946 Chicago Student Conference representing twenty-six colleges: see Roster of Colleges, p. 133. At the 1947 Constitutional Convention, twenty-nine Pennsylvania colleges were represented. Five of the 1946 colleges did not attend (Haverford, Lafayette, Lehigh, Lincoln, Marywood, Westminster), but were replaced by thirteen additional colleges: Albright, Carnegie Tech, Chestnut Hill, Duquesne, Martin, Misericordia, Mt. Mercy, Rittenhouse, St. Francis, Sproul, State Teachers, Thiel, Women's Medical College. Convention rosters in subsequent years show the following college counts: 1948—15, 1949—23, 1950—19, and 1951—16. The 1957 membership roster shows thirty-one colleges in Pennsylvania–West Virginia Region, of which three were from West Virginia.

[6] See Barefoot Sanders, p. 995.

[7] See Ed Kirschner, p. 76.

[8] See "Operation University," p. 739. See also Des Marais, p. 734, and McLaughlin, p. 818.

[9] See Des Marais, p. 735, and Simons, p. 124.

[10] See p. 370.

PICTUE CREDITS: *Then:* 1947, Constitutional Convention (*NSA News*, October, 1947). *Now:* January, 1998, St. John, Barbados (Schwart).

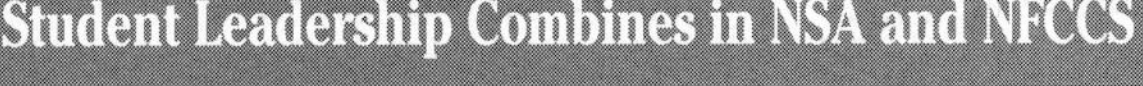

NSO To Meet Here In Regional Caucus

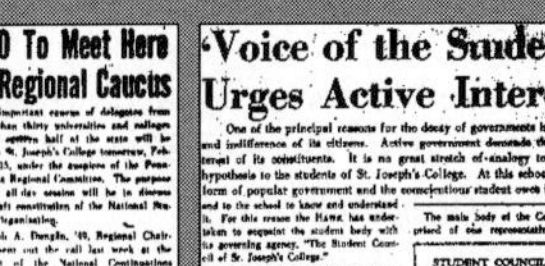

THE HAWK

Two Student Groups Appoint Ivers Regional Publicity Head

Will Edit Regional N. S. A. Publication And Lead Publicity Committee For N. F. C. C. S. Relief Campaign

National Conference Names Dungan State Chairman of Regional NCC

Treasurer's Post Goes to James E. Dougherty '50, During Chicago Meeting of National Student Conference

STATE CHAIRMAN

STATE TREASURER

JIM DOUGHERTY AND RALPH DUNGAN "divided the turf" between NFCCS and NSA, Dungan writes. St. Joseph's had installed student government in 1945 (r. above), providing a setting for student leadership in NSA and NFCCS. (See Des-Marais, p. 734). Most of the Catholic Colleges "didn't have the problems that would" provoke student movements, but there was "a sufficient leaven of veterans" who were not buying the "old discipline" to expand the horizons of student activity on many Catholic College campuses.

From top l, cw: 2/14/47 (both), 10/24/47, 1/24/47 (fr. l., Dungan, Dougherty.

St. Joseph's before and after the War

230 College Students Will Refuse War Draft

Voting Strongly Against United States Intervening in European

Faculty Confident, Students Calm; Meet War With United Front

RECORD-BREAKING FROSH CLASS ENROLLED

1851-1951

From top, *The Hawk*: 11/3/39, 12/19/41, 2/6/46, 2/5/51.

Editor's note: As on most U.S. campuses before Pearl Harbor, many students opposed U.S. military intervention although they supported aid to Britain (see Prologue, p. 10, Fordham, p. 890, Swarthmore, p. 901). Returning veterans energized the campus (Dungan, p. 911). St. Joseph's, founded by the Jesuits in 1851, in the late 1960's joined many Catholic colleges legally separating ownership from the Church. Women were admitted in 1970; in 1978 it became a University. (www.sju.edu). 1948 enrollment was 2,168.

For more on Dungan, Dougherty and St. Joseph's see Pt. 1, Sec. 5, p.176. For a list of major Anthology citations of Catholic students and colleges, see p. 737.

The U.S. Catholic Colleges in 1948

Source: Richard H. Ostheimer, State College for Teachers, Albany, N.Y., The Organization of Higher Education in the United States, 1948-1949. *Columbia University Press, New York, 1951. Classifications are those used by Ostheimer. 32 junior, and 6 teachers and professional colleges and 97 seminaries in Ostheimer are not listed here. Institutions omitted by Ostheimer are followed by (§). The 1948-49 Education Directory (Government Printing Office) reports 188 Catholic 4-year colleges and 29 Junior colleges. There were a total of 1,277 4-year colleges and 451 junior colleges.*

Members of NSA or attendees at NSA Congresses for 1 or more years from 1946-52 are shown with an *.

UNIVERSITIES

Private, Roman Catholic, both Men and Women

DISTRICT OF COLUMBIA
*Catholic University of America
*Georgetown University

ILLINOIS
*DePaul University
*Loyola University (includes West Baden College)

LOUISIANA
Loyola University

MASSACHUSETTS
*Boston College (includes Weston College of the Holy Spirit)

MICHIGAN
*University of Detroit

MISSOURI
*St. Louis University (includes St. Mary's College, St. Mary's, Kansas)

NEBRASKA
Creighton University

NEW YORK
*Fordham University
*St. John's University

PENNSYLVANIA
Duquesne University

WISCONSIN
*Marquette University

Private, Roman Catholic, Men

INDIANA
*University of Notre Dame

SEPARATE LIBERAL ARTS COLLEGES

Complex

Private, Roman Catholic, Both Men and Women

NEW YORK
*Canisius College
*Niagara University

OHIO
*University of Dayton

WASHINGTON
Seattle University

Private, Roman Catholic, Men

CALIFORNIA
*Loyola University of Los Angeles
University of San Francisco
*University of Santa Clara

NEW YORK
*Manhattan College

OREGON
University of Portland

PENNSYLVANIA
*Villanova College

WASHINGTON
Gonzaga University

Private, Roman Catholic, Negro, Both Men and Women

LOUISIANA
*Xavier University

Others

Private, Roman Catholic, Both Men and Women

IOWA
*Saint Ambrose and Marycrest Colleges

MICHIGAN
*Aquinas College

Private, Roman Catholic, Men

ALABAMA
Spring Hill College

CALIFORNIA
*Saint Mary's College

IOWA
*Loras College

KANSAS
*Saint Benedict's College

MARYLAND
*Loyola College
Mount Saint Mary's College
Woodstock College and Seminary

MASSACHUSETTS
College of the Holy Cross

MINNESOTA
*Saint Mary's College
*College of Saint Thomas

MISSOURI
Rockhurst College

MONTANA
Carroll College

NEW HAMPSHIRE
Saint Anselm's College

NEW JERSEY
*Saint Peter's College
Seton Hall College

NEW YORK
Saint Bernardine of Siena College
*Saint Bonaventure College

OHIO
*John Carroll University
Xavier University

PENNSYLVANIA
*LaSalle College
*St. Francis College
*St. Joseph's College
*St. Vincent College
*University of Scranton

RHODE ISLAND
Providence College

VERMONT
St. Michael's College

WASHINGTON
Saint Martin's College

WISCONSIN
Saint Norbert College

Private, Roman Catholic, Women

CALIFORNIA
Dominican College of San Rafael
*College of the Holy Names
*Immaculate Heart College
*Mount Saint Mary's College
San Francisco College for Women

COLORADO
*Loretto Heights College

CONNECTICUT
*Albertus Magnus College
*Saint Joseph College

DISTRICT OF COLUMBIA
*Dunbarton College of Holy Cross
*Trinity College

FLORIDA
*Barry College

ILLINOIS
*Barat College of the Sacred Heart
*Mundelein College
*Rosary College
*College of Saint Francis
*Saint Francis Xavier College for Women

INDIANA
*Saint Mary-of-the-Woods College
*Saint Mary's College, Notre Dame

IOWA
Briar Cliff College
*Clarke College

KANSAS
*Marymount College
*Mount Saint Scholastica College
*Saint Mary College

KENTUCKY
*Nazareth College

MARLYAND
College of Notre Dame of Maryland
*Mt. St. Agnes College
*Saint Joseph's College

MASSACHUSETTS
*Emmanuel College
College of Our Lady of the Elms
*Regis College

MICHIGAN
*Marygrove College
*Nazareth College
*Siena Heights College

MINNESOTA
*College of Saint Benedict
*College of Saint Catherine
*College of Saint Scholastica
*College of Saint Teresa

MISSOURI
*Fontbonne College (§)
*College of Saint Teresa

NEBRASKA
*Duchesne College

NEW HAMPSHIRE
*Mount Saint Mary College

NEW JERSEY
Georgian Court College
*College of Saint Elizabeth

NEW YORK
*D'Youville College
*Good Counsel College
*Manhattanville College of the Sacred Heart
*Marymount College
*College of Mount Saint Vincent
*Nazareth College of Rochester
*College of New Rochelle
*Notre Dame College
*Saint Joseph's College for Women
*College of Saint Rose

OHIO
*Mary Manse College
*College of Mount Saint Joseph-on-the-Ohio
*Notre Dame College
College of Saint Mary of the Springs
*Ursuline College for Women

OREGON
*Marylhurst College

PENNSYLVANIA
*Chestnut Hill College
*Immaculata College
*Marywood College
*Mercyhurst College
Misericordia College
*Mount Mercy College
*Rosemont College
*Seton Hill College
Villa Maria College

TEXAS
Incarnate Word College
*Our Lady of the Lake College

UTAH
College of Saint Mary-of-the-Wasatch

WISCONSIN
*Mount Mary College

A 1946-1952 Pennsylvania Regional Chronicle

As reported in **UP**-*Daily Pennsylvanian* **LS**-*La Salle Collegian* **PS**-Penn. State C. *Daily Collegian* **SJ**-St. Joseph *The Hawk* **TU**-*Temple University News*

SJ 3/11/39 **230 COLLEGE STUDENTS WILL REFUSE WAR DRAFT**. Voting Strongly Against United States Intervening in European War. Poll Results Startle.

SJ 12/19/41 **FACULTY CONFIDENT, STUDENTS CALM; MEET WAR WITH UNITED FRONT.**

SJ 2/6/46 **RECORD-BREAKING FROSH CLASS ENROLLED.** Ex-GI's Swell Ranks.

UP 2/6/46 **MAYERS IS ELECTED PRAGUE DELEGATE**. "Frank A. Mayers, Wharton '47, was elected as the University's representative to the forthcoming Prague conference by a plurality of 540 votes. A total of 1,845 votes were cast, with 42.7% of them in favor of Mayers. Arnold J. Friedhoff, Medical '47, received the second highest number of votes totaling 249." There were a total of 11 candidates.

UP 6/12/46 **MAYERS DELIVERS PRAGUE STUDENTS' CONFERENCE TALK**. Frank K. Mayers "will report on the parley" in Houston hall auditorium tomorrow.

UP 12/11/46 **WSGA AND UNDERGRAD COUNCIL TO SELECT DELEGATES TO NATIONAL STUDENT CONFERENCE.** Applications being accepted from interested male and women undergraduates for the Dec. 28-Dec. 30 Chicago meeting "to consider the formation of National Union of American Students."

SJ 1/24/47 **NATIONAL CONFERENCE NAMES DUNGAN STATE CHAIRMAN OF REGIONAL NCC.** Treasurer's Post Goes to James E. Dougherty '50, During Chicago Meeting of national Student Conference.

TU 4/25/47 **AYD CHAPTER BARRED FROM CAMPUS.** Committee of 14 Finds Group Violated Petition statements. Editorial: "American Youth for Democracy at Temple University is no more...let's get the issue at hand clearly understood...was the AYD taking orders from the communist Party and serving as that party's organization on college campus? ... the committee considered the statement of J. Edgar Hoover, '... that the AYD was the successor to the Young Communist League...' and found that it was and 'could do nothing but bar the AYD.' However, *The News* sees no reason why avowed communist or socialist clubs should not be allowed to be organized as discussion groups on campus."

SJ 5/9/47 **JAMES DOUGHERTY ELECTED NATIONAL PREXY OF NFCCS**. Catholic College Delegates Select St. Joseph's Freshman at Toledo Congress. "Over 500 delegates representing 135 Catholic Colleges ... also selected Thomas Harper of La Salle College, Philadelphia, as one of three vice presidents."

SJ 6/4/47 **COLLEGE SEND THREE TO N.S.O. CONVENTION.** Thomas Ivers '49, Ralph Dungan '49, and James Dougherty '50 will represent the college at the Constitutional Convention In August.

SJ 10/3/47 **DUNGAN RECEIVES VICE-PRESIDENCY OF N.S.A.** Will Head Domestic Activities Commission. "The most recent achievement toward [St. Joseph's national) college prominence was the election of Ralph A. Dungan, '49 ... in the newly formed and powerful United States National Student Association...James F. Dougherty, '50, attended the convention as President and representative of the National Federation of Catholic College Students in Madison, August 31-Sepember 9.

LS 10/24/47 **TED HARRIS PENNSYLVANIA REGIONAL HEAD OF NSA.** With Harris, a pre-law student, returning from the NSA convention in Madison, Wisconsin from August 30- September 7 "came the grueling story of the seemingly endless work that resulted in a national organization of American students. The story is one of tribute to the diligence, ingenuity and enthusiasm of American youth..."

TU 10/24/47 **AVC GROWS IN PROMINENCE IN SHORT TIME ON CAMPUS**. "To fill the need for an organization with policies formed by veterans of World War II, AVC came to Temple in April, 1946...Fast becoming an important organization on campus, AVC stuck to its policy of accepting members without regard to race, creed or color."

UP 12/16/47 **N.S.A. CONSTITUTION PASSED BY 10-2 VOTE OF COUNCIL**. "The NSA constitution will now be considered by the Committee on Student Affairs, and if approved, will mean that the University of Pennsylvania will become a member of the United States National Student Association."

PS 12/19/47 **MILHOLLAND GREETS STUDENTS REPRESENTING PENNSYLVANIA COLLEGES**. "Delegations from 90 colleges (sic) throughout the state will total 175...Temple's the largest at 14. Penn State is allotted 12. Robert Troxell, chairman of the Cabinet committee on the convention" announced that the convention will be addressed by James Milholland, Acting President of Penn State, and Ralph Dungan, national Vice President in charge of domestic affairs . . . .Ted Harris, LaSalle College undergraduate and president of the regional organization will introduce Mr. Milholand.

SJ 12/19/47 **STUDENT COUNCIL UNANIMOUSLY APPROVES NSA CONSTITUTION**. A report read by Benjamin T. Britt, chairman of the Constitutional Review committee stated in part that "the committee unanimously agrees that there were no points of major disagreement between the concept of the student's role in today's affairs as proposed by the USNSA, and that held by the students of St. Joseph's College."

UP 1/9/48 **NSA CONVENTION DRAFTS REGIONAL CONSTITUTION.** "Attended by 150 delegates representing 46 Pennsylvania colleges and universities, the convention was presided over by Ted Harris of La Salle College, NSA Regional Chairman...Among the problems considered ... were present day race relations in regional colleges... [a] study of student government constitutions... the new Taft and Fulbright laws...considerations for the selection of the four-man NSA negotiating team to be sent to [the IUS conference in Prague]...and current international student problems." The convention was held at Penn State College, December 19-21.

PS 3/12/48 **CABINET UNANIMOUSLY VOTES NSA MEMBERSHIP.** "Jane Fouracre was named chairman of the permanent NSA Committee."

TU 3117/48 **CZECHOSLOVAKIAN COUP BRINGS BREAK OF NSA WITH INTERNATIONAL GROUP.** Two NSA representatives at Prague, James Smith of the U. of Texas and William Ellis of Harvard, "resigned over failure of IUS to protest mistreatment of Czechoslovakian students during Communist coup d'etat."

TU 3/17/48 **PENNSYLVANIA TAKES ACTION IN NSA CONTROVERSY.** "Unauthorized use of the name of the New York Regional Chairman of U.S.N.S.A. in a release issued by the Harvard Committee for Wallace touched off a controversy which has resulted in a request from the Pennsylvania Region that the national chairman take action to prevent any recurrence of the incident."

UP 3/19/48 **NSA DELEGATIONS TO MEET AT PENN.** "Representatives from [25] colleges in the Eastern Region "will meet in the main lecture room of the Zoology Building." Planning for the meeting was handled by Anne Jaffe, President of the WSGA.

PS 5/11/48 **COLLEGE NAMED AS CONVENTION SITE**. "Two hundred and twenty-five delegates are expected to represent Pennsylvania's 45 member schools" at the regional convention at Penn State, June 10-13. "Topics which will be considered are student welfare and government, a Pennsylvania Culturale, election of regional officers."

PS 5/14/48 **NSA TAKES VOTE ON US POLITICS**. "Members of the (campus] NSA adopted a policy of the national and regional executive committees taking a stand on issues which directly affect students... Racial discrimination at the College was also discussed by the members in preparation for a policy to be presented to a workshop on interracial discrimination at the regional convention."

PS 5/14/48 **NSA OUTLINES STUDY ABROAD ON 'MAN IN TODAY'S WORLD.'** "[NSA] programs for foreign study and exchange include study in German universities, correspondence with foreign students and hospitality to foreign students this summer, James Bachman reported to the local chapter..."

TU 11/12/48 **200 DELEGATES WILL ATTEND NSA SESSIONS TOMORROW**. "Approximately 200 students from 42 colleges and universities will gather in Mitten hall tomorrow at a meeting of the Eastern sub-Region...Sub-regional Chairman, Theodore Perry, Teachers '49, will preside ... Six committees will formulate their reports ... cultural, purchase card, student government, domestic affairs, and the workshop analysis committee...The cultural committee will discuss the regional culturale to be held in the spring. Also under discussion will be the art seminar and plans for the national Art Exhibit in the Philadelphia area ...the student government committee will discuss the structure and functions of student government, student apathy, student rights, and faculty-student-administration relations..."

TU 1/5/49 **NSA DELEGATION ASSIGNED TO SURVEY DISCRIMINATION.** "The campus unit ... was assigned the race relations clinic for the Pennsylvania area at the regional NSA convention (at Albright College) in Reading on Dec. 12 to 19 .... the clinic will disseminate information and suggest remedies to alleviate (discriminatory practices in educational institutions] . . the 125 delegates from 36 eastern colleges and universities . . . were divided into six workshops... [purchase card plan), international affairs, student affairs, economic affairs, and cultural topics."

UP 1/17/49 **NSA GROUP PLANS STUDENT AID THROUGH LOCAL PROGRAM.** "Pennsylvania's participation in this wide and comprehensive program. but it was not until a month ago that the Executive Committee for NSA at Penn, made up of ten men and four women, was selected by a screening committee composed of members of the Undergraduate Council, the Women's Student Government Association and the University Administration."

TU 2/23/49 **WSSF OFFICIAL TO DESCRIBE PLIGHT OF STUDENTS IN EUROPE AND ASIA**. "Dr. Wilmer J. Kitchen, Executive Secretary of the World Student Service Fund has just returned from a tour of student projects in Asia and Europe supported by the WSSF."

TU 2/25/49 **NSA PRESIDENT HONORED; 110 DELEGATES AT BANQUET.** "James 'Ted' Harris, president of NSA was honored" in Mitten Hall Saturday night.

SJ 3/11/49 **NSA ANNOUNCES SUMMER TRAVEL PLANS COMPLETED.** "In all, 18 different plans for work, study and travel abroad are being offered this year in the vastly expanded travel program. Tours listed included trips to Holland, Britain, France, Italy, Belgium, Scandinavia and South America."

TU 4/8/49 **MET THEATRE TO BE SCENE OF CULTURALE, APRIL 22,23.** "Nearly 700 students from 20 Pennsylvania colleges and universities will participate at the MetTheatre, Broad and Poplar Sts." It will include an exhibition of student paintings and drawings, "vocal and instrumental solos and duets, folk dancers, collegiate bands, male and female glee clubs and several specialty numbers... "Participating schools include Albright, Allegheny, Beaver, Bloomsburg State Teachers, Bryn Mawr, Bucknell, Chestnut Hill, Drexel Institute, Franklin and Marshall, King's College, La Salle, Lehigh, Misericordia, Penn State, Pennsylvania, Rosemont, St. Joseph's, St. Vincent's, Swarthmore, and Temple.... Tickets are $1 per performance."

LS 12/16/49 **EIGHT TO ATTEND NSA CONVENTION.** Eight members of the campus NSA committee will represent La Salle at the regional convention at Albright College, Reading, Pa. "Over 150 student delegates and observers are expected to attend... and to formulate programs for the remainder of the year... workshops are: student government, human relations, regional organization, campus organization, world student service fund and displaced Persons program, foreign affairs and Purchase Card System . . . Elmer Brock '50, is President of the Pennsylvania Region... other issues [include] the forthcoming intercollegiate music festival ... Mary M. Fowler, Dean of students at Beaver college, will deliver the keynote address. She is the youngest Dean of student in the country...Ted Perry, [national NSA] vice president in charge of student life, will also address the convention... Seven schools are sending representatives of their administration..."

TU 9/29/50 **TED PERRY RELAXES HERE. TOURED NATION LAST SUMMER.** "After traveling 3,500 miles, visiting 200 colleges and meeting 2,000 people, Ted Perry is taking a rest...The recently retired NSA National Vice President...[after a] 12 month leave of absence is completing his last term at Teachers College."

LS 11/13/50 **FOUR TO ATTEND NSA CONVENTION.** "Four students will represent LaSalle at the Pennsylvania Regional Convention to be held at the University of Pennsylvania this weekend. Over 150 delegates and observers are expected to attend...Miss Althea Hottel, Dean of Women at the Univ. of Penna. will be the keynote speaker... Brother George Thomas, Dean of Freshmen, and Chairman of the Faculty Advisory Board of the region, will address the convention on the role of student government in faculty-student relationships ... Elmer Brock '50, who is national vice president of student affairs, will attend the convention ... Dr. Patrick Malin, President of the American Civil Liberties Union, will be the principal speaker at a special banquet to be held Saturday evening . . On Sunday, the third and final plenary session will elect a regional president for the remainder of the year ... Samuel Elphern from Temple University, who was elected last June, has been called to active duty. Ken Kurtz of Swarthmore has been serving as temporary President."

LS 10/4/50 **NSA BACKS U.N. KOREAN STAND; FEDERAL AID TO EDUCATION**. "The Korean war competed with campus problems for the attention of representatives of more than 300 colleges attending the Third Annual National Student Congress in August at the University of Michigan. Students ... strengthened their own stands on academic freedom, discrimination and scholarships, but did not complete work on a revised Student Bill of Rights. Federal aid to private and parochial schools as well as public institutions won support."

LS 6/2/50 **SEVEN STUDENTS WILL ATTEND NSA CONVENTION.** The regional convention at Camp Hilltop, Downingtown, Pa., from June 11 - 13. "A major address to be delivered by A. Blair Knapp, vice-president of Temple University." Elmer Brock '50, is president of the region.

LS 12/13/50 **FOUR TO ATTEND NSA CONVENTION.** "[Over 150 student delegates are expected to attend the] Regional convention to be held at the University of Pennsylvania this weekend. Miss Althea Hottel, Dean of Women at the Univ. of Penn., will be the keynote speaker..."Other speakers include "Brother George Thomas, Dean of Freshmen [La Salle) and chairman of the Faculty Advisory Board of the Region...Elmer Brock '50, national vice president of student affairs... Dr. Patrick Malin. President of the American Civil Liberties Union.

LS 1/17/51 **NSA PRESIDENT TO SPEAK ON CURRENT AFFAIRS AT SWARTHMORE TOMORROW.** "Al Lowenstein will speak on current affairs which vitally affect students today... All La Salle students have been invited to attend the meeting in the Friends Meeting House on Swarthmore campus."

TU 3/5151 **WSSF DONATION REVIEWED.** "The $2,000 donation voted the World Student Service Fund by the 1950 Senate at its final meeting Feb. 15 was reconsidered by the 1951 Senate Thursday...Louis Leradi, Arts '51, regional representative of [NSA] for WSSF, told the Senate that for some unknown reason the money had not been delivered before China's entry into the Korean war."

An inspirational appeal to the youth of America

Harold Stassen: "The Man Who Was Too Far Ahead of His Time"

President, University of Pennsylvania, 1948-53. NSA Advisory Committee, 1951-58

Editor's note: Harold Stassen is first mentioned in Part 4 of this book (p. 707), in a footnote to "A Service Man Looks at the Peace," an article by Cord Meyer, Jr. Meyer was one of his two staff assistants when Naval Commander Stassen was a member of the U.S. delegation to the founding conference of the United Nations in San Francisco in April, 1945. At that conference, Stassen was reported to have "led a losing fight to keep the veto out of the United Nations Security Council. But he initiated the provision that allows member nations to take collective action against an agressor even when such an action was vetoed." (N.Y. Times, *3/5/2001).*

Dick Murphy, NSA President in 1952-53, writes:

Harold Stassen was a tower of strength and support for N.S.A. during the nineteen fifties. As a candidate for the Republican nomination for President in 1948 and President of the University of Pennsylvania, Governor Stassen was a major figure in the city of Philadelphia when I came there in 1952 to establish the N.S.A. national headquarters in that city.[1]

Stassen was also a member of N.S.A.'s National Advisory Board, which he had joined following his appearance at our Minnesota National Congress in 1951, and he had been actively involved in inviting us to establish our national office in Philadelphia. Together with his Dean of Women at Penn, Althea Kratz Hottel, and Ruth Geri Hagy,[2] an editor of the *Philadelphia Bulletin* and producer of the College News Conference (all of whom were active in the 1952 Eisenhower presidential campaign), President Stassen anchored a trio of strong support for and defense of the N.S.A., when and where we needed it, especially from attacks from the right led by Fulton Lewis, Jr., Senator Joseph McCarthy and Martha Roundtree.

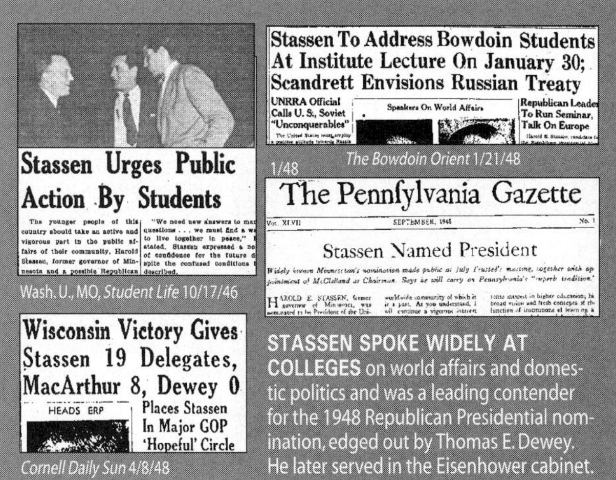

Wash. U., MO, *Student Life* 10/17/46

The Bowdoin Orient 1/21/48

1/48

Cornell Daily Sun 4/8/48

STASSEN SPOKE WIDELY AT COLLEGES on world affairs and domestic politics and was a leading contender for the 1948 Republican Presidential nomination, edged out by Thomas E. Dewey. He later served in the Eisenhower cabinet.

President Stassen took an active role on N.S.A.'s National Advisory Board, on which he served for seven years, even following his appointment to a cabinet level position in the Eisenhower administration in 1953. He was always available for help and advice whenever we called upon him and his stature and friendship with N.S.A. leaders counted mightily to our benefit at a critical time.

On Whether Communists Should Be Permitted to Teach

Excerpts from presentation to a conference of the members of the Pennsylvania Senate and House on 4/30/91 regarding the proposed loyalty oath legislation for university faculty.[3]

I am convinced that the bill pending before you would not help eliminate Communism or subversive activities, and would seriously damage education in Pennsylvania. . . . Throughout these twenty-five years of my adult life, I have consistently and alertly opposed in an effective manner Communist infiltration and subversive activities. . . .

[After listing eight reasons why the proposed legislation will not work, he continues:]

The method that should be followed is the method that your universities are now following. We cooperate closely with the Federal Bureau of Investigation and with the intelligence agencies of the Armed Services in uncovering any facts that may be relevant to activities of a subversive or Communist nature. We carefully investigate new members of our faculties, and we follow up any information pointing adversely to present members of our faculties.

Our faculty is with us in this respect. Our faculty, in their resolution opposing Senate file 27, state specifically that they do not consider that any Communist is competent to teach. I consider it clear that under existing law any proven Communist or person engaged in subversive activities can be discharged from any faculty or public position in this state. It is necessary to get the evidence against them, and that will still be necessary if you pass this bill. . . .

You are entitled to insist upon the continuing cooperation of the presidents of your universities toward this end of combatting Communism and subversion. . . . But I plead that you do not make the mistake of endeavoring to impose upon our distinguished and loyal faculties this special oath, clearly unconstitutional, clearly contrary to the basic American tradition of respect for the loyalty and law-abiding nature of our fellow citizens.

[1]See Murphy, p. 1075 on NSA's move to Philadelphia.

[2]See p. 1084 for Ruth Hagy (Brod) and the College News Conference.

[3]*Editor's note: Proposals to impose loyalty oaths on college faculty were widespread at this time. The argument that Communists are unfit to teach was used as a disqualifier that could override issues of tenure and academic freedom.* *See Brown, p. 381, Album, p. 388, University of Washington, p. 1061.*

On American Education: The Need for Teaching Moral and Ethical Values, Citizenship and Leadership

Excerpts from an address to the American Association of School Administrators, Hotel Ambassador, New Jersey, February 21, 1951 (Archives).

I do not feel that anyone can impartially appraise the developments in this nation of both a cultural and material nature in a brief space of two centuries without giving a very high mark to American education. But . . . I believe that it does have some serious deficiencies which, unless corrected, may in time cause this great nation to fail in its position of eminent world leadership; and if it thus fails, great will be the fall thereof.

I consider these three deficiencies are represented by the need:

First, for greater teaching and emphasis to the youth of the land of the moral and ethical values in human life; second for an increased stimulation and preparation of the students of today for a role as active, informed citizens of the free society of tomorrow; and third for the definite education of numbers of the most gifted and competent youth of today for top policy leadership of the nation in the half century ahead.

Some individual teachers and some school systems now do outstanding work in bringing to their pupils a deep understanding and acceptance of those underlying moral principles which are so essential if life is to reach the depth and fullness which it is intended to have. Many have been the examples in history of education without moral foundations and with a perverted sense of morals. The most recent example, of course, has been the tragic record of the German nation under Hitler.

It is my conviction that in too great a degree those in education have been tending to say that moral training is for the home and the church and not for the school. Certainly a primary responsibility does rest in the home, and another key role should be taken by the church. But these are not enough. In fact, it is always the case that a large percentage of youth are growing up in homes which are themselves deficient in their moral foundations and one-half of all the youth of the nation grow up with no contact with any church or Sunday School or definite character building institution. Thus if the society as a whole is to be firmly grounded in its moral and ethical standards through the overwhelming acceptance by its people, it is essential that the educational system should play a strong role in this field.

Whether it should be done by bringing out these lessons in the course of the teaching of literature and of language, of geography and of history, of social studies and of mathematics; or whether it should be through the direct teaching of personal conduct and ethics; or whether both methods should be used, is secondary. The need for the greater emphasis is in my mind an impelling need.

Student betrayals of trust reflect on the educational system

In recent years a surprising number of able young people have been removed from positions of trust by loyalty boards and a number of them have been convicted by juries for crimes which involve conduct of a treasonable nature. In most instances these young people have had extended contact with our educational system.

In recent days a shocking number of present students have been arrested for accepting bribes to betray their schools, their classmates, their personal bond, in deliberately losing athletic contests for the benefit of sordid gamblers (see Album, p. 850).

These dual developments have a basic interrelationship in a reflection of moral and ethical weakness. They are very serious. I submit that our American educational system cannot entirely escape some share of the responsibility for these actions.

The athletic scandals should cause our entire American educational system to take a careful look in the mirror. . . .The national betrayals of trust by young people who have had the advantage of extended education should cause some soul-searching by the educators of America.

PICTURE SOURCES: *Then:* c. 1952 (U. of Pennsylvania Archives).

TITLE QUOTE: Robert T. McCracken, quoted in the *NY Times,* July 30, 1948. *Eyebrow:* Undated interview by Maralyn Lois Polak

HAROLD STASSEN
(1907-2001)

Born April 13, 1907, in Dakota County, Minnesota. A graduate of the University of Minnesota (1927), and of its Law School (1929), Stassen had been elected Republican Governor of Minnesota in 1938 at the age of 31, the youngest governor in history, and re-elected in 1940 and in 1942. He delivered the keynote at the Republican 1940 national convention.

He was elected Vice President of the Northern Baptist Convention in 1941. He served on the staff of Admiral William F. Halsey in the Pacific Theater from July, 1943 until the end of the war, when he was discharged with the rank of Captain. He was awarded the Legion of Merit, Bronze Star and six battle stars for action in the Philippines, South China Sea and Formosa, Okinawa and Honshu.

In April in 1945, he was appointed by the President to the U.S. delegation to the San Francisco Conference.

In 1948, he withdrew in favor of Governor Dewey for the Republican nomination for President. He was elected President of the University of Pennsylvania in September, 1948. In 1953 he was put in charge of foreign aid programs by President Eisenhower, and from 1953 to 1958, he served with cabinet rank as special assistant to the President on disarmament matters.

He was married in 1929 and had two children. He practiced law in Philadelphia and was a Republican presidential primary candidate seven times. He died on March 4, 2001.

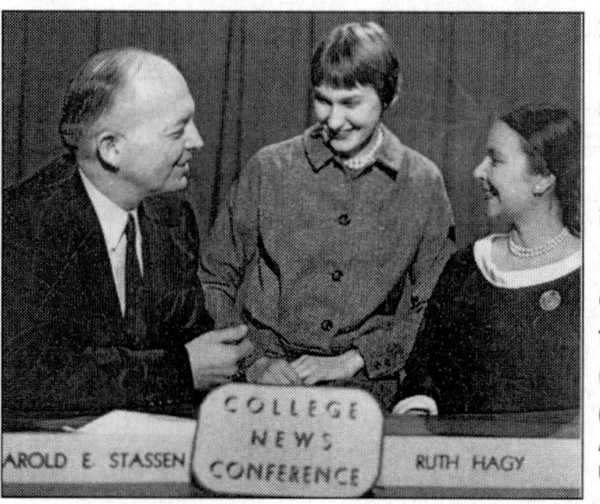

STASSEN INVITED NSA TO PHILADELPHIA in 1952. He is shown here with Ruth Hagy (r.) in 1957 on the College News Conference. Hagy was instrumental in providing a new financial footing for the organization. Both were on the NSA Advisory Committee (see Murphy, p. 1075). (Photo from U. of Pennsylvania Archives. The student, center is unidentified.)

We have an opportunity to cultivate the fruits of the spirit

Althea Kratz Hottel: A Pathbreaker for Aspiring and Talented Women

Dean of Women, University of Pennsylvania. NSA National Advisory Commitee, 1951-54

Editor's note: Dean Hottel, together with President Harold Stassen, encouraged NSA to relocate in Philadelphia and introduced NSA President Dick Murphy to Ruth Hagy, who arranged for free office space (see Pt. 6, Sec. 1).

Radically Separate Plans Are Not Needed

In educating the human mind, the task is not merely to add something to it, but to do something to it. Besides giving deeper understanding, a wider knowledge, and fine powers of response, the process must fuse new qualities into thoughts, feeling, and action. As women assume multiple responsibilities, their greatest need appears to be for a liberalizing program that teaches not only knowledge but also the interrelationships of knowledge; for one which develops an appreciation of spiritual values as well as attitudes and abilities that enable them to become useful persons capable of influencing their society and culture. Narrow educational and training programs designed in accordance with what is considered good for a particular sex would limit rather than expand their horizons. From the information thus far available to the Commission on the Education of Women, radically separate plans of education for men and women are not indicated. Both need broad and diverse opportunities for elective courses designed to stimulate and develop a wide variety of interests and abilities. . . .

The quality of a civilization depends not only on its knowledge and its ability to use that knowledge, but on the values held important by its people. Spiritual and moral principles which are basic to humanity must be taught, for religious understanding can both endow and enrich human personality.

Excerpted from the 1955 report. Dean Hottel was its author and Director of the ACE Commission on the Education of Women.

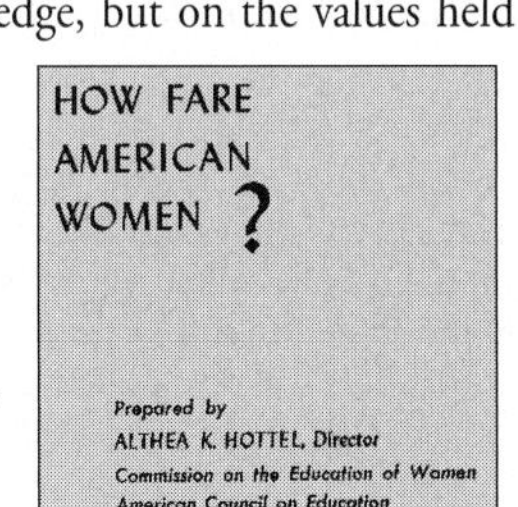
HOW FARE AMERICAN WOMEN ?

Prepared by
ALTHEA K. HOTTEL, Director
Commission on the Education of Women
American Council on Education

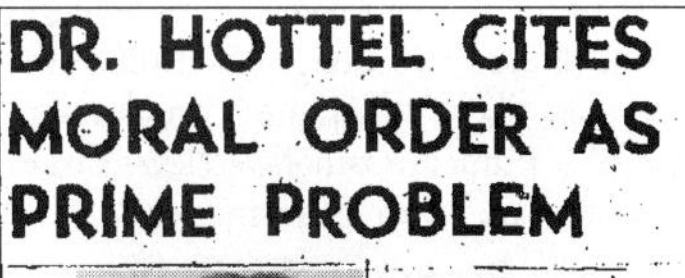
DR. HOTTEL CITES MORAL ORDER AS PRIME PROBLEM

Dean Of Women Discusses Issues During "Religion-In-Life Week" Interview

Gimbel Award Winner

"Reconstruction of our world is not primarily a problem in engineering and not primarily a problem in politics, but the underlying task is to recover a sense of a moral order," stated Dr. Althea K. Hottel, Dean of the College of Women in an interview regarding Pennsylvania's first Religion In Life Week since 1938.

Dr. Hottel who was this year's recipient of the Gimbel award for her contribution to education, went on to say that the activities of that week will present a real challenge to us. "The world today needs individuals with real depth, power and the ability to sort the wheat from the tares. During the Religion in Life Week, we have an opportunity to measure our stature for this task, to cultivate the fruits of the spirit, to harness the heroism of the war for peace making to fuse our convictions with our actions."

A CHALLENGE TO CULTIVATE THE FRUITS OF THE SPIRIT.
(*Daily Pennsylvanian* 2/25/48)

ALTHEA KRATZ HOTTEL
(1907-2000)

From a piece prepared for the June 16, 2000, memorial service by University President Judith Rodin (Archives).

Althea Kratz Hottel was 92 when she died in January, 2000. She was a pioneer in women's education and a role model for generations of women at Penn. I still remember the power her name conveyed when I was an undergraduate at Penn. It is often hard to remember that it took pathbreakers like Althea Hottel to open the doors for the younger generations of aspiring and talented women. She encouraged us, in words and by example, to reach for our personal goals. And she did it by being an extraordinary person, both in her personal warmth and intelligence and in the strength of her character and commitment.

Althea Hottel was a graduate of the Class of 1929, junior class president and president of the Women's Student Government Association. She earned her Ph.D. in Sociology in 1940, and taught in the Department of Sociology for some 20 years.

In 1936, Dr. Hottel was appointed Directress of Women. In 1943, she became Penn's first Dean of Women—and also Penn's first woman dean. It was a position she held until 1959.

On her retirement from the Deanship, the Althea K. Hottel Award was established to honor "intellectual competence, commitment to ideals and principles, and loyalty to the University of Pennsylvania." After her retirement, she was elected to the Board of Trustees, only the second women to serve as a Penn Trustee.

Dr. Hottel served as president of the American Association of University Women, where she led the fight to eliminate racial discrimination in the association. Dr. Hottel provided crucial leadership to Penn at a time when women students were taking their place, in numbers and in academic strength, next to men. She enriched Penn and stood as a beacon for women's education.

Dr. Hottel was a native of Lansdale, PA. She was married to Abram S. Hottel, Jr. She served from 1952 for six years as U.S. representative on the Social Commission of UNESCO.

PICTURE SOURCES: *Then:* c. 1957 (U. of Pennsylvania Archives).
TITLE QUOTE: Judith Rodin, above. *Eyebrow:* Excerpted from 2/25/48 *Pennsylvanian* interview, p. 1.
DOCUMENT SOURCES: U. of Penna. Archives.

DURING THE SUMMER OF 1946 Mrs. Hottel attended the British International Student Service Conference at Hoddesdon, England, and the World Student Christian Federation Conference at Gwatt, Switzerland. She observed the World Student Congress in Prague. She represented the American Association of University Women (AAUW), conferring with the Federations of University Women in England, France, Belgium, Holland, Italy and Czechoslovakia about the international study and relief grants available through the AAUW for women scholars in the areas previously occupied by the Germans. (For more on the postwar International Student Service conferences, see p. 56; on the World Student Congress, Pt. 1, Sec. 2, p. 81.)

A Greater Washington outreach

4. Founding the Mason-Dixon Region

Michael J. Rubino
Catholic University
Chair, Mason-Dixon Region, 1948-49

The Catholic University of America (CUA) was urged from several quarters to consider joining the NSA in 1946-47. I was the president of the sophomore class (1947) of over nine hundred students. Assigned by the Student Government to report on the pros and cons of NSA membership, I contacted the NSA leadership and conferred also with the existing Catholic student organizations—the National Federation of Catholic College Students (NFCCS) and the Newman Clubs. Together these had formed under the aegis of the National Catholic Welfare Conference a Joint Committee for Student Action (JCSA) in the Youth Department. Phil Des Marais was its director.[1] It was formed primarily to collaborate with Pax Romana, the international Catholic student organization headquartered in Fribourg, Switzerland.[2]

The CUA, at my urging, decided to join NSA and work actively to persuade other area colleges and universities to do the same. We succeeded in some cases, particularly in the case of smaller women's colleges such as Goucher, Hood, Trinity, Dumbarton, and perhaps St. Agnes College in Baltimore. The major area colleges and universities—Georgetown, George Washington, American, and the University of Maryland (UMD)—were largely indifferent and uncooperative.[3] (The UMD-Baltimore campus did send representation. They were pretty much a downtown, day student, separate campus.)[4]

We coined the name "Mason-Dixon Region" because it seemed proper to encompass the reality of actual and potential members in the Greater Washington area. Because the CUA had trained many Catholic educators in advanced degrees over the years, its decision to join NSA was, in large part, responsible for attracting other Catholic colleges and universities in the U.S. to participate.

The NSA as an organization never really made a significant impact in this area. The students at that time in history were largely returned veterans who had their goals set on completing their education and furthering their careers. The most frequent objection was the cost of joining and participating in regional and national meetings. More often than not, a decision to join hinged on the availability of funds, and the case for joining was never particularly compelling.

Marshall Plan Demonstration

The Mason-Dixon Region did organize a large and successful demonstration for the benefit of Congress in favor of the Marshall Plan. It drew upon students from the entire East Coast—several hundred, organized by region. It was featured prominently in *Time* during that era with an article and a photograph of the long line of students about to ascend the Capitol steps. In the Capitol, the students met with their congressional leaders and had a successful two-hour lobbying rally. The threat of communist disruption never materialized.

Michael J. Rubino is an investment adviser who served with the Central Intelligence Agency in Europe.

END NOTES

[1] See Des Marais, p. 734.

[2] See Kirchner, p. 76.

[3] In a 1/20/04 letter to the editor, Rubino elaborates on the impact of CU's membership. He writes, "The fact is that CU's decision to join NSA influenced Catholic college across the country. Consider that many, if not most, of the administrators of these colleges had received one or more advanced degrees at CU and you can imagine their positive response when CU opted to join NSA. . . . You will recall that there was a concern during the formative years of the student movement about communist activists taking control or at least exercising undue influence, particularly in the efforts seeking to affiliate with the IUS. The significant number of small Catholic colleges which followed CU's lead into NSA achieved two things: (a) it made the organization more representative and less likely to fall under the domination of a small activist faction, and (b) it brought Catholic colleges out of their protective shell and into the mainstream of student activities."

[4] Originally known as Maryland-Delaware-District of Columbia Region, it was represented at NSA's 1947 Constitutional Convention by American University, Catholic University, College of Notre Dame (MD), Dunbarton College of the Holy Cross, Georgetown University, Goucher College, Hood College, Howard University, Johns Hopkins School of Medicine, Johns Hopkins University, Loyola College, Morgan State College, Mt. St. Agnes College, Princess Anne College, Trinity College, University of Baltimore, University of Maryland and Western Maryland College.

Women's colleges provide a driving force

5. Regional Leadership in Mason-Dixon

Editor's note: Close bonds of collaboration were formed by a diverse group of active students, clustered around 15-20 participating colleges in Baltimore and Washington. Most were Catholic schools, led by two women's colleges, Dunbarton (closed in 1976) and Trinity and Catholic U., but with active participation of student leaders from the U. of Baltimore (largely a part-time urban campus), Johns Hopkins (in the early years), Hood College (women's), and the federally chartered Negro college, Howard University. Non-members Georgetown (membership vetoed by its President, See p. 742) and U. of Maryland (turned down by hotly fought Council votes almost annually, See p. 924) often had observers at regional events, and U. of Md. hosted more than 100 delegates at its 1950 Regional Congress.

EMMET HURLEY, GEORGETOWN U.

Chair, Maryland-Delaware-D.C. Region, NCC, 1947

Emmet Hurley

Georgetown is the first Jesuit and oldest Catholic university in the U.S. Founded in 1789; 1948 enrollment: 5,667.

Hurley Elected Committeeman

As an organizational measure the Chicago Conference elected four officers and 30 regional members to a National Continuations Committee, which, in conjunction with a staff committee of five, has the considerable job of writing a constitution for the proposed NSO and making arrangements for a constitutional convention at which the constitution may be approved next summer and the NSO established. Emmet Hurley of Georgetown was elected committeeman for the Maryland-Delaware-D. C. region and thus automatically became chairman of the NCC Committee in this region.

The NCC includes three delegates from national student organizations and thereby lies a story. It was originally planned that all national student organizations such as the National Federation of Catholic Colleget Students and the American Youth for Democracy would be represented on the NCC and eventually in the NSO, but an orating, drawling, long-legged delegation from the University of Texas appeared on the scene with a program which entirely excluded national student organizations and spoke loudly and well for "grass roots democracy, suh!" and the freedom from interference for the NSQ from outside forces. The Texans were primarily motivated by a desire to shake loose from youth organizations which are fronts for the Communist Party. They took a lavish suite at the Bismark Hotel in Chicago's Loop and in the best convention style invited all delegates to drop up

on the scene with a program which entir... organizations and spoke loudly and well

The Hoya 1/17/47)

JOSEPH W. ZEBLEY, U. OF BALTIMORE

Chair, Maryland-Delaware-D.C. Region, 1947-48

Joseph Zebley, Jr.

The University of Baltimore is a private institution founded in 1925 by "a group of Baltimore civic leaders who wanted to provide low-cost, part-time evening study . . . for working adults." It became a state institution in 1988. 1948 enrolled: 2,009.)

Zebley To Report On N. S. O.

According to the student newspapers of other schools, the Chicago Meeting of university and col- ... surroundings. The college students of the State of Georgia are showing at this time that a strong stand for justice on their part is playing a great role in the political scandal existing in that State at present.

The Baloo, 1/31/47

11/21/47

Zebley To Head NSO Regional Meeting Here

(Special To The Baloo)

WASHINGTON—The National Continuations Committee of the National Student Organization for the Maryland, Delaware, and D.C. regional area decided that the next regional meeting would be held at the University of Baltimore on March 22.

Emmet Harley, of Georgetown University, the regional president, will report on the Chicago meeting held March 8-9 then.

Joseph W. Zebley, president of the Student Council of the University of Baltimore, was selected president of the Baltimore, Western Shore of Maryland N. S. O. groups, and vice-president of the regional area.

Stanley Greenfield of Johns Hopkins, was elected to head publicity

Photo: *The Baloo,* 10/24/47

3/14/47

USNSA Officers

Delegates to the Maryland, Delaware, District of Columbia Regional Assembly of the U. S. National Student Association elected regional officers and chairmen at their last meeting. Joseph Zebley, Jr., returning president of the University of Baltimore Student Council was elected regional President. Eustace Seignoret, Howard University student government leader, was elected Vice-President; Mary Catherine Ostmann, of Dunbarton, Sevcretary; and Mary Jane Comerford, of Trinity College, Treasurer.

National Education week was opened in Washington last Sunday with the regional president, Zebley, and publicity chairman, Schultze, Father

RICHARD CADIGAN, LOYOLA COLLEGE

Chair, Maryland-Delaware-D.C. Region, 1949-50

Cadigan, Rodowsky Represent Evergreen At NSA Convention

Two Loyola students, Lawrence Rodowsky and Richard Cadigan, represented the college at the annual National Student Association Congress held at the University of Michigan, Ann Arbor, Michigan, August 23 to September 1.

The Association, representing the vast majority of American student opinion on the college and univer- ... dom. A discount card service is planned that would enable college students to purchase clothes, appliances, etc., at a reduced cost.

Cadigan Sponsors Bill

Cadigan Article Published

The November issue of the Student News Service, a monthly published by the Newman Club Federation in conjunction with the NFCCS, contains an article by Richard Cadigan, Loyola junior, "Are There Subversive Teachers Today?" Copies are in the library.

From left: The Greyhound 10/20/50, 12/8/50 1/18/52, 11/19/48

NSA Delegates Planning Student Buying Discount

A discount plan has been established for Loyola students in cooperation with merchants in the Govans area under a service of the National Student Association. The program has been set up by a committee headed by Lawrence F. Rodowsky, NSA delegate, aided by Jeremiah Murnane, Maurice Reeder and Charles Broomfield, in conjunction with the NSA committee of Notre Dame of Maryland.

NSA Exhibition Of Student Art Scheduled Here

A national art exhibit, featuring selected paintings of students throughout the country, and sponsored by the National Student Association, will be held in the Ever-

GREYHOUND

A Jesuit men's college, founded 1852. Women admitted when it merged with Mt. St. Agnes in 1971. 1948 enr.: 1,519.

CYNTHIA COURTNEY LANDRY: DUNBARTON COLLEGE

Chair, Mason-Dixon Region, 1952-53. NSA Vice President, Educational Affairs, 1953-54

Dunbarton Dial

Dunbarton Student Wins NSA Election

Brief reports from N.S.A. and

Cynthia Courtney, '53, was elected president of the Mason-Dixon Region at a post-Congress meeting of colleges in this area. One of Cynthia's projects this year is a campaign to recruit more colleges in the region to active membership in the N.S.A.

During an assembly in the near future, delegates will present to the student body a detailed report on both Congresses.

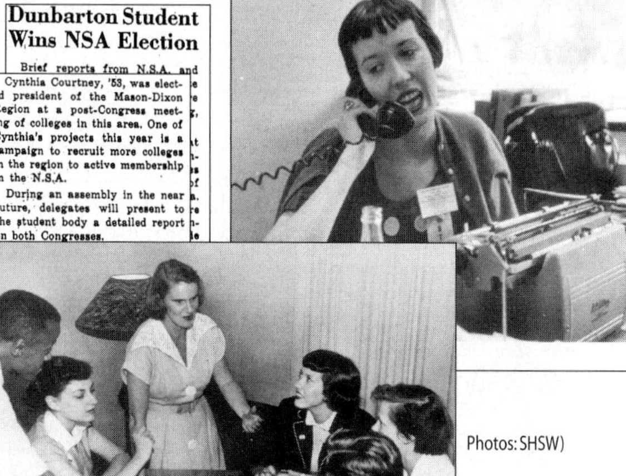

Photos: SHSW)

Cynthia Courtney, third from right, at Mason-Dixon officer's meeting, Fifth National Congress, August 1952 at Indiana University, Bloomington.
(Bottom, fr. l. Charles Johnson (Howard U.), Treasurer. Included but not identified: Nancy McCreary (Dunbarton), Secretary; Jim Gayhardt (U. of Baltimore), Vice President. *(For historical note see p. 922.)*

In her senior year, after being active in student affairs at Dunbarton College, Cynthia Courtney became Mason-Dixon chair at the Fifth congress and, later, NSA Vice President for Educational Affairs, in 1953-54.

Committed to a lifetime of public service, she taught student government to high school students, worked for Radio Free Europe and worked with Ted Harris, former NSA 1948-49 president, in the development of the American Society for African Culture. In 1961, she became Chief of Operations for the fledgling Peace Corps operations in West Africa.

Until her death in 1992, Cynthia maintained close contact with African political figures, particularly in Nigeria and Liberia. She also accompanied her husband, Commander Adelard F. Landry (USN) on his overseas assignments. On their return to the United States she resumed high school teaching, which often included student leadership training trips to Washington, D.C., where her students met and interviewed government officials.

Sylvia Bacon
Vassar College
NSA Vice President Student Affairs, 1951-52

GLORIA ABIOUNESS/AGNES DOWNEY DUNBARTON COLLEGE

Chairs, Mason-Dixon Region, 1950 (Spring); 1950-51

Gloria Abiouness

The Dunbarton Dial, fr. left: 9/4 (photo and clip), 3/50.

Delegates Attend NSA Congress

By GLORIA ABIOUNESS

More than one million students from 350 United States colleges and universities were represented at the second annual Congress of the National Students Association, held at the University of Illinois from August 24 to September 3. The Congress, which was the largest student meeting ever to convene in the United States, is regarded as the major intercollegiate student event of the year. Agnes Downey, '51, and the writer attended as delegates from Dunbarton.

The NSA Congress operated in several phases. In addition to discussing mutual problems of student government and campus life, such questions as federal aid to

Senior Named NSA Delegate

Gloria Abiouness, a resident senior, was recently appointed by the NSA as a student representative to attend the Mid-Century White House Conference on Children and Youth which will convene in Washington March 23 and 24.

As members of one of four Advisory Councils set up by the National Citizens Committee of this Mid-Century White House Conference, Gloria and other official representatives from National youth serving organizations will attend meetings of the Council at the Federal Security Building.

Functions of the Advisory Council will include: recommending means for effective youth participation in the Mid-Century White House Conference; developing principles for and methods of youth

University Is Host To Mason-Dixon, NSA Group

On Sunday, October first, the University of Baltimore was host to representatives of the Mason-Dixon Region of the United States National Student Association. Delegates were present from Dumbarton College, Georgetown University, Hood College, Howard University, Loyola College, Trinity College, Notre Dame of Maryland, Catholic University, and Mt. St. Agnes. Representing the University of Baltimore were Earl Gerding, Ruth Ellen Stansbury, and Jay Rosenberg.

Downey, president of the region, w[as] elected at the national convention [in] Ann Arbor, Michigan.

The next regular meeting will b[e]

The Baloo (U. Baltimore, 10/6/50

Dunbarton College was founded by the Sisters of the Holy Cross in 1935, and was closed in 1973. Its 1948 enrollment was 237.

Agnes M. Downey

(Photo: Joan Lynch)

University of Baltimore

The Baloo

The Baloo — JANUARY 21, 1948

USNSA TAKES STAND FOR ACADEMIC FREEDOMS

By Joseph W. Zebley, Jr.

THE PREAMBLE TO OUR NATIONAL STUDENT CONSTITUTION:

We, the students of the United States of America, desiring to maintain academic freedom and student rights, to stimulate and improve democratic student governments, to develop better educational standards, facilities, and teaching methods, to improve student cultural, social,

Henry Carp Goes To Washington

Valentine Day Dance Scheduled

Kappa Sigma Kappa

NSA Regional Meeting Held In Washington, D. C.

The Maryland, Delaware, and Washington, D. C. members of the National Students' Association held a regional meeting on Sunday, March 6, at Howard University in Washington. The various committees reported on the work accomplished the past month.

The Human Relations Committee announced that it was promoting better inter-faith, inter-racial relations through the NSA Newsletter. The Legislative Commission reported that it was in contact with all bills pending in Congress that concerned higher education.

VOLUME XVI

U of B Host to Forthcoming NSA Mason-Dixon Meeting

The University of Baltimore will be the host at the forthcoming National Student Association regional meeting of the Mason-Dixon district this Sunday, October 30. The meeting will be held in Charles Hall at 2 p.m. and the Student Body is invited to attend.

This will be the first time the

Students to Fight High Prices With N.S.A. P.C.S. Cards

Oct. 1949.—(NSA NEWS) Students will fight high prices this year with "Purchase Cards."

MARYLAND, JANUARY 13, 1950

NSA Announces 1950 Travel Plans Cost To Be Lower

Madison, Wisc.—Travel Programs of the U.S. National Student Association will provide a summer of education and adventure for more than 800 students in 1950.

Tentative prices for tours range from $340 to $625 for nine travel

NUMBER NINE

Gerding, Karson, Zahner Attend NSA Regional M-D Convention

Earle Gerding, Kit Karson, and Matt Zahner represented the University of Baltimore at the First Regional Student Congress of the Mason-Dixon region of the NSA, at College Park last Saturday and Sunday, February 25 and 26. The convention was designed to better acquaint the students with the conditions and problems of the member colleges in the region.

Gerding, well-known throughout the region for his participation in conference activities, is the regional treasurer and public relations director. Earle handles all the paper work connected with the meetings of NSA

Earle Gerding

Representative Reports On Annual N. S. A. Convention

By Ruth Stansbury

The Fourth Annual Congress of the National Student Association was held at the University of Minnesota from August 20 thru August 31. It was attended by more than five hundred students representing approximately three hundred fifty colleges and universities.

The main topics of the Congress were: revising of the national staff, consideration of a new world union of students, and a definite program of action for the coming scholastic year.

Immediately prior to the Congress, a meeting of student body presidents was held. From these

The second big issue of the Congress was whether N.S.A. should take decisive steps to form a new world union of students to be the democratic counterpart of the exist-

(Continued on Page 4)

New Council Will Meet Monday

N.S.A. Meets At Notre Dame College

On February 10, 1952, the monthly meeting of the Mason-Dixon region of the N. S. A. was held at the Notre Dame of Maryland College. Eileen O'Connell, president of the region,

RETURNING FROM THE CHICAGO STUDENT CONFERENCE in 12/46, Joe Zebley wrote in *The Baloo*, having noted heated debates and pressures, "at the end, a spirit of cooperation, the National Students Organization was formed here.... Your writer, as the U.B. delegate from U.B., left Chicago with one thought in mind: We'll be hearing much more about the near future!" Zebley became the first regional Chair (see p. 921), and laid the groundwork for active reporting and participation in NSA at UB. Earle Gerding launched the regional newsletter in 1950 (see p. 923. Photo: Joan Lynch).

(*The Baloo*, from top l., ccw: 1/30/48; 3/18/49; "Host," "PCS" 10/28/49; "Travel" 1/13/50; "Gerding" 3/3/50; "Convention" 10/5/51; "Notre Dame" 2/15/52). *(For historic note on UB, see p. 921).*

EILEEN O'CONNELL: TRINITY COLLEGE

Chair, Mason-Dixon Region, 1951-52

Senior to Preside Over NSA Session

Eileen O'Connell, '52, will preside over the first meeting of the Mason-Dixon Region of the National Students' Association to which all students are invited Sunday at 2:30 p.m. in Social Hall.

Elected chairman of the region during the Fourth National Congress of the NSA at the University of Minnesota, Eileen is the first Trinity student to hold that office. In succeeding Agnes Downey

NSA Arranges for Regional Congress; Planning Group Meets at Hood College

To complete plans for the Regional Congress, April 6, five Trinity girls will attend the Baltimore-Washington regional National Students' Association meeting, Sunday, at Hood College, Frederick, Md.

Eileen O'Connell, '52, regional

at the same time as the NSA delegates, Sunday, and will report their decisions to the assembly.

These conclusions will determine what professional journalists will be asked to address the May conference, how it is to be set up, and what it will consider.

The Trinity Times, fr. to left 10/19/51, 3/14/52, 1/30/47, 3/24/47.

Eileen M. O'Connell

(Photo: *The Trinilogue*, 1951 Yearbook

Trinity College was founded in 1897 by the Sisters of Notre Dame as a Catholic liberal arts college for women. It is located in Washington, DC, near the Catholic University campus. Its 1948 enrollment was 480.

AILEEN McGOVERN LAUDS THE CHICAGO CONFERENCE

Miss Aileen McGovern was elected to represent Trinity at the Chicago Student Conference, December 28-30. Miss McGovern was well qualified to act as a delegate because of her active participation and interest in other intercollegiate work. Other positions held by Miss McGovern include: senior delegate to the N. F. C. C. S. and council member of the Washington Desk of the Joint Committee for Student Action (J. C. S. A.).

NATIONAL CONTINUATIONS COMMITTEE OF NSO MEETS

Margaret Wade and Mary Jane Comerford represented Trinity as delegate and observer, respectively, at a meeting of the National Continuations Committee of the National Student Organization at Howard University, February 20.

The main points on the agenda were the problems of adequate publicity and fund-raising, the question of a suitable method of representa-

Howard University

HILLTOP

THE HILLTOP — FRIDAY, NOVEMBER 7, 1947

U. N. S. A. Maps Program for Year

The work of the United States National Student Association will be divided into three main programs for the coming year, namely Educational Opportunities, Student Governments, and International Activities. Panels discussing these were formed at the convention to consider proposals for the USNSA program and to set up legal machinery through which the constitution will be enforced.

The Educational Opportunities'

in proportion to the family unit to meet the high living costs. Though we at Howard are not affected by increases in tuition fees, the students of Howard will be interested to know that the USNSA's program includes action to prevent such increases without a detailed discussion between student governments and the administrations of such college affected.

Because of insufficient funds which some schools receive, the curriculum of such schools are

In cases where some students transfer from one college to another, credits and courses are often not accepted, thus causing the student to spend a longer time in college or repeat courses. To remedy this situation, the USNSA has investigated a system whereby comprehensive examinations have been given to prevent such occurences.

These are not all of the issues discussed in the panel. Other

NSA; EVERY STUDENT'S JOB

Too often a student on Howard's campus asks a classmate, "What is NSA?" It's too Often because no one on this campus should be out of the know when it comes to the operations of such an organization. Why this organization? Because you are a member of it! Howard is a member of the National Students Association which means that each individual in the Howard community is a member.

is one of the most important. On this campus is locataed the sub-commission on Legislation. It is the job of this sub-commission (committee) to follow the action in Congress and investigate all bills discussed and voted on which concern institutions of higher learning. The purpose of Howard's sub-commission is to keep the other colleges and universities abreast of all legislation brought up in Congress concerning them.

The NSA committee here pub-

DECEMBER 18, 1952 — (Excerpted

Valaida Explains NSA's Negative Stand On Eighteen Year-Old Vote

Valaida Smith last week defended her delegation's decision to vote against giving the vote to eighteen-year-olds, a matter considered at a recent meeting of the National Student Association which was held at Dunbarton College, here in Washington. Valaida was chairman of the delegation.

The Howard delegation's vote came as a surprise. Earlier in the fall, in a campus-wide mock presidential election, the question of the eighteen-year-old vote was posed and the student body voted overwhelmingly in favor of extension of the suffrage to that age group.

According to Valaida three-member delegation, also included Charles J[ohnson] and William Santos, con[sulted] with Student Council

Both groups were in agreement on a negative vote. The Student Council wanted the delegation to go mandated. Executive sessions of NSA decided otherwise. Valaida added that eighteen-year-olds were immature in general but that the eighteen-year-old college senior was a little more

Stormy NSA Levels Guns For Confab Here, On Mar[ch]

Approximately 150 delegates will converge on [the Univer]sity on March 28 and 29 when the Mason-Dixon National Student Association will hold its Regional Thirteen Member Schools, from Washington and n[earby] will be represented.

The NSA has been a controversial organization since last Fall, when Howard's delegation ignored a wide poll in favor of the eighteen-year-old vote an[d] it in a subsequent NSA meeting. The story was December 18 edition of the HILLTOP.

WELCOME

N. S. A.

Program For NSA Regional Congress March 28-29

Saturday, March 28

9:00-10:30 Registration

Interracial Meeting

A unique approach to the interracial-problem is the calling card of the local group of The Congress of Racial Equality which met in the Browsing Room of Founder's Library on October 24. The principles that groups acting to erase discrimination against Negroes must be interracial; that the main efforts in resisting Jim Crow traditions and practices must be through direct opposition, and that all violence must be avoided, are the principles of CORE, and represent the difference between CORE and other related organizations.

Lynn Seitter, Boston-born daughter of a Methodist minister, and one of the organizers of the group here, opened the discussion with a brief history of the group's activities in Washington. They began on July 1, 1947, with a meeting to representatives from 11 states and Canada, who lived cooperatively from July 1 to the 31, in a house at 918 N St., N. W. She described the planning and tactics used by the group to attack the Jim Crow Coffee Shop at the YMCA. A sit-down strike in the shop was carried out for three days after a test group including two Negroes was refused service. In the course of the three "sits", they were "gassed" with amonia fumes and ran into a door block formed by a "welcoming committee" of Y officials, police and hangers-on who were looking for trouble. Finally, they forced a meeting with a Y committee to discuss the discrimina-

SEGREGATION IN PUBLIC PLACES was common in the D.C. area after WWII. While NSA's programs were interracial, Howard students worked actively through CORE and the NAACP to challenge Jim Crow (above and see also p. 467). Howard was active in the region from its inception.

Charles Johnson — Valaida Smith

HOWARD'S 1952-53 NSA LEADERS. Smith was campus NSA head (Photos and documents courtesy Howard University Archives).

Howard University was chartered by Congress in 1867 and named after Gen. Oliver O. Howard, Civil War hero, who was a founder and Commissioner of the Freedman's Bureau. In 1928 Congress authorized an annual federal appropriation (www.howard.edu). 1948 enrollment was 5,231.

1950 MASON-DIXON REPORTS

MASON – DIXON REPORTS

No.3 Baltimore, Md. February 12, 1950

From the desk of
H. Earle Gerding (U. of Baltimore)
PR Man

WELCOME ST. MARY'S JUNIOR COLLEGE

At the last regional meeting, the delegate from St. Mary's Junior College, Miss Bette Jane Laufer, informed me that the student council had voted to affiliate with the N.S.A. on the regional level. . . .

AT THE MOUNT

Mt. St. Agnes College sponsored a benefit dance, January 21, 1950, for the D.P. student scheduled to attend the Mount next year. The Association of Student Governments of Baltimore held a meeting this weekend at the Mount. The topic: "Methods of Electing Student Government Officers."

TRAVEL PROGRAM

The U.S. National Student Association is sponsoring a "Work, Study, Travel" program this summer and from reports it shapes up to be The Best around. For more information contact your NSA delegate or write this office.

MASON DIXON REPORTS

The "Mason Dixon Reports" ever growing mailing list now includes the public relations bureaus of the following NSA regions: Great Northwest, Illinois, Indiana, Ohio, Pennsylvania, Southern New England, Wisconsin, Northern New England, Missouri, New Jersey, Minnesota, Michigan and the Kentucky-Tennessee Region. . . .

NEEDED

Ralph Smith's mule train whip may be applied to this region if I soon don't receive some word and copy for the "Reports" from certain schools in this REGION!

N.S.A. ART TOUR

Notre Dame College received the NSA Art Exhibit on March 5, 1950. The exhibit was displayed in the Fourier Art Gallery at the college from said date 'til March 10, 1950, when it was sent to Hood College in Maryland.

AND FROM HOOD COLLEGE . . . . (at last)

The Exhibit arrived at the college on March 13, 1950 and will be on display till the twentieth. It was placed in the lobby of the Administration Building which (from all reports) is the most conspicuous place on campus. . . .

Also, word is that a Faculty Rating (or more tactfully known as the Evaluation of Instruction, since improvement of the quality of instruction is its real purpose) is due to be completed about the time of spring vacation.

AT DUNBARTON COLLEGE

News is that they are to have a discussion assembly on the Student Bill of Rights, out of which a stand is to be ascertained, and this info added to the library of the Bill of Rights Committee. . . .

What do YOU know about the World Student Service Fund? For your information a sheet on WSSF INTERNATIONAL HIGHLIGHTS is enclosed with this newsletter. This is the first in a series of info sheets on the main organizations NSA is cooperating with or sponsoring.

(Excerpted from *Mason Dixon Reports*, 2/12/50)

A 1950 Regional Congress

(Excerpted from *Mason Dixon Reports*, 3/15/50)

Keynote Speaker: Dr. Francis Brown
American Council on Education

Orientation Speaker: Al Lowenstein
NSA President

Foreign Program: Helen Jean Rogers
Catholic U., NSA Secy-Treas., 1948-49

Faculty Meetings

Discrimination Round Table

Student Rights Round Table

The Diamondback

NSA Visits University For Annual Convention

Though Not Member, Maryland Is Host; SGA Committee Named To Observe

The weekend program of the National Student Association Mason - Dixon Regional Congress will get underway here Saturday at 10:30 a.m. when all visiting delegates register.

Although this University is not a member of the association, Smokey Pierce, committee chairman, Jean Askin, Gene West, Charles Kehne, Janice Lovre, Harry Ortis, and Willard Stevenson have been appointed to attend and observe the weekend program of events.

Failed Last Year

The congress is being held at this University in an attempt to settle the question of whether or not Maryland will join NSA. The Executive Council has been considering the matter for nearly three years, but heated opposition from one faction of the Council last year prevented affiliation. A vote registering a ratio of two to one defeated the proposal to join the organization last spring.

NSA was organized with the intention of joining similar student movements throughout the world, but has since concentrated on problems confronting local student governments. Approximately 300 colleges and universities are at present members of the organization.

2/21/50

Gerding, Karson, Zahner Attend NSA Regional M-D Convention

Earle Gerding, Kit Karson, and Matt Zahner represented the University of Baltimore at the First Regional Student Congress of the Mason-Dixon region of the NSA, at College Park last Saturday and Sunday, February 25 and 26. The convention was designed to better acquaint the students with the conditions and problems of the member colleges in the region.

Gerding, well-known throughout the region for his participation in conference activities, is the regional treasurer and public relations director. Earle handles all the paper work connected with the meetings of NSA Regional and publishes the monthly news-letter, entitled "Mason-Dixon Reports," which covers the various regions throughout the whole country along with matters of interest to students and college presidents in the Mason-Dixon region.

Meeting with well over one hundred representatives from member colleges, the delegates participated in the various commissions, sub-commissions, and plenary sessions. Kit Karson carried the views of the University into the debate on educational problems, which included discussion on scholarship plans, federal aid, academic freedom, and the educational community.

Honor System Drawn Up

On the Student Life Commission, delegate Matt Zahner joined with the other colleges in the planning of material on student rights, student government, and campus discrimination. Among the resolutions drawn up by this commission was one on the establishment of an honor system at member colleges.

All three delegates were very well versed on their respective topics, Kit having spent many hours specializing on educational problems while a member of the Maryland Association of Junior Colleges; Matt by being very active in U of B campus life, including publi-

3/3/50

Dunbarton Dial

NSA Regional Parley Slated for Feb. 25-26

The first Regional Congress of the Mason-Dixon Region of the National Student Association will be held February 25 and 26 at Maryland University.

Its purpose is to explain NSA and its functions, to have students exchange ideas, and to formulate definite resolutions about area problems. Sub-commissions under the Student Life Committe will consider student governments, the Student Bill of Rights, and discrimination problems. The Com-

2/50

The Johns Hopkins News-Letter

NSA Report Made To SC

Johnny Power, a Student Council representative to the National Student Association Congress held recently at the University of Maryland, gave a complete report of his weekend at a recent SC meeting.

3/17/50

The Baloo

Although not a member, U. of Maryland hosted more than 100 delegates from 14 area colleges. Joseph Tydings, student body president, gave the welcoming address.

NSA is viewed in different ways

Students Consider the Ideals and the Promise of NSA

Every Student Belongs

Delegation Approves Purchase Cards And Reports; Commends Action of NSA

Temple University NEWS

Personalities That Glitter

Ted Perry Relaxes Here; Toured Nation Last Summer

By MARTIN SALDITCH

NSA Names Dean Knapp Adviser

A. Blair Knapp, vice president in charge of student personnel services, was elected to the faculty advisory committee at the Fifth Annual Regional Conference of the National Student Association. The conference was

Our Contribution to NSA 11/12/48

Temple plays host tomorrow to some 200 students from 42 colleges and universities in eastern Pennsylvania at a sub-regional meeting of the National Students Association. It is a pleasure and an honor for TU students to welcome to our campus the representatives from nearby institutions.

Since its inception in the summer of 1945, NSA has made rapid strides. It has grown from a loose association of several schools to a national organization with the support and participation of more than 700 schools.

The scoffers have been surprised by the strength of NSA. Such an organization, loosely federated and limited by distance and a small budget, plus the additional factor of lack of continuity, could hardly be expected to thrive and grow. Yet it has done just that.

Supported by dues collected from member schools, which comes directly from the student government and the students themselves ultimately, NSA is fast becoming a nationally important, influential, responsible agency for expressing student

Since its earliest days, NSA has had the backing of Temple students. Our delegates have attended various meetings in Chicago; Madison, Wis.; Penn State, and other places. They have held important offices in local, regional and national NSA organization. A large share of Student Senate's budget is earmarked early in the term each year for NSA expenditures in dues and delegate expenses.

The meeting on our "home field" tomorrow is a tribute to the Temple students who have toiled so long and so hard in the mutual interests of NSA and Temple. It is a day of which we can all be proud — that we have become an integral part of the NSA.

Every Temple student belongs to NSA. It becomes essential for each of us to know and to take part in its activities. The framework has been constructed; the superstructure and the decorations depend upon our own contribution.

"A TRIBUTE TO THE TEMPLE STUDENTS who have toiled so hard in the interests of NSA and Temple." The *Temple News* hailed the 11/48 regional assemble held at the university. Ted Perry became an NSA Vice President in 1949-50 (p. 356). Dean Knapp was a strong NSA supporter (p. 957). *(Temple University was chartered as Temple College in 1888 by Russell H. Conwell, a Baptist minister and a renowned inspirational orator. In 1965 it became a "state-related institution" [www.temple.edu]. Enrollment in 1948 was 14,349.)*

Temple University

Progress and Prestige

Our Problem

Should We Join National Association?

By HANK SAYLOR

10/3/47 2/20/48

Diamondback

SGA Rejects Membership In NSA, 9-2

3/1/49 **SGA Will Review NSA Tonight; Region Chairman Rubino Speaks**

12/1/50 **COUNCIL VOTES 8-7 TO JOIN NSA**

12/8/50 **Petition Forces Referendum On NSA**

12/15/50 **NSA VOTE DELAYED TILL 1951**

1/10/51 **NSA Faces Student Vote Tomorrow**

Affiliation Question Gets Forum Quiz

1/19/51 **STUDENTS VOTE 'NO' TO NSA**

The Modern Esau? 3/8/49

HANK SAYLOR, President of the Men's League, and delegate to the 1947 Constitutional Convention (p. 135), recommended affiliation "with the emphasis that we…'go easy' in taking such a far-reaching step." (*Diamondback* 10/3/47). By 2/48 he was in opposition because he believed "that the summer convention was led by reds," and the $700 cost could be better spent (2/20/48). Membership was voted down 9-2 by SGA, supported only by the Independent Student Assn. and Assn. of Veterans reps (2/20/48). The issue went back and forth until its 1951 referendum defeat.

Editorial 3/8/49, excerpted.

Joining NSA Means Progress, Prestige

WOULD you like special discounts on your purchases in Washington, Baltimore, or even College Park? That is, but one of the numerous benefits that the National Student Association offers us.

As pointed out in SGA debates on the advisability of joining the NSA, the other advantages Maryland students would receive from this venture, both singly and collectively, far outweigh the cost of joining the network of nearly 300 colleges and universities.

In doing so, we would be the recipients of surveys and studies about national and international student problems. Regional and national meetings would serve as clearing houses for facts, ideas, experience, and advice among the universities.

Since the NSA is carried out on a regional basis, we would be allowed flexibility in working out the policies of the national body to fit our immediate needs. This fact clearly rules out the argument that by joining, we would be placed under a dictatorship.

THE regional setup would also give us a strong and direct voice in matters with which Maryland is specifically concerned. Due to the size of our student body, six voting delegates and an alternate for each would represent the University at the regional meeting. We would have the largest number of delegates and therefore be the most powerful group in the regional assemblies.

Make It Your Organization

La Salle COLLEGIAN

5/16/51

Brock Returns to Post As NSA Vice President

Elmer Brock '50, has returned to the post of the National Student Association. Earlier resigned his office in an unexpected move the vice-presidency two weeks ago. In his first statement since resuming his all college students to apply immediately fo

TED HARRIS TO CHAIR NSA ASSEMBLY AT PENN STATE

Four La Salle student-delegates will attend the first Assembly of the Pennsylvania Region of the United States National Students tion, adopt a 1948 budget and officers. The Regional Assembly will the highest legislative and poli

12/19/47

9/5/47, "Federation Forum," excerpted.

On August 30, delegates from student bodies in every state will gather at the University of Wisconsin to adopt a constitution and prepare a program for the proposed National Student Association. This meeting will be the most significant gathering of students in the history of United States colleges. The constitution and program which will evolve from nine days and nights of intensive discussion and study will constitute the fundamental basis for this new and original student organization. Upon ratification of the constitution, the National Student Association will be the most potent force on the student scene.

The NSA will represent the student population of this country by virtue of the fact that its legislative body will be composed of elected representatives from colleges and universities in every state in the union. The power of this organization to sway public opinion in the name of American college students, and the danger of its abuse in the wrong hands, is obvious.

To date, 89 Catholic colleges and universities will be represented at Madison. It is the general opinion among the delegates from Catholic colleges that, though there is no necessity for forming a Catholic bloc, as such, there is a need for a strong, well-principled leadership. * * * *

Inasmuch as the National Student Association will purport to represent every college student, as in all truly representative bodies, each student should scrutinize his delegate carefully.

* * * * Literally, make the NSA your organization.

THE *LA SALLE COLLEGIAN* supported and covered NSA extensively. The college provided two of NSA's prominent leaders, both of whom served as regional chairs before being elected to national office: Ted Harris (p. 219), 1948-49 President, and Elmer Brock, 1950-51 Vice President for Student Affairs (p. 358). *(La Salle College, now La Salle University and coeducational, was founded in 1863 by the De La Salle Christian Brothers [www.lasalle.edu]. Enrollment in 1948 was 2,495.)*

La Salle College

Connected to the World

9/22/39

Neutrality Poll Shows War Fear

Students Believe Nation May Enter European Conflict

On the eve of the United States' special Congressional session to revise neutrality, a poll conducted yesterday among nearly 400 members of the Maryland student body showed that fifty-eight percent of the students polled believed that America will be drawn into the European War.

The poll also revealed that sixty-six percent are in favor of the administration's plan to allow all nations to purchase American materials on a cash and carry basis. In the cross-section poll The Diamondback Terp Trotter found that only forty percent of the student body reached gave as their opinion the possibility that the United States can remain neutral. Thirty-four percent expressed confidence in the neutrality law as it stood before the special session.

5/11/45

Seventh War Bond Drive Starts Monday

Moody Crowns · Board Sponsors · *ROTC Plans* · Stamp Shack, Bridge

Share With Students Abroad In WSSF Drive
Universities Set Million Dollars For 1946 Goal
Prisoners of War Express Appreciation For Book Supplies
World Student Service Fund

1/11/46

3/28/48 Tuesday, March 23, 1948

Campus Sentiment Split On Draft-UMT Issue

4/18/50 **U. OF MD. RULED TO ADMIT NEGRO**

Diamondback

State's Highest Court Overrules Rejection Of Esther McCready

MAJOR PRE- AND POSTWAR ISSUES that occupied student attention at the U. of Maryland and elsewhere

(The U. of Md. reaches back to the privately chartered Maryland Agricultural College in 1858. It became a land grant college in 1864. It evolved to Maryland State College in 1916, when women were first admitted. [www.inform.umd.edu].) Enrollment in 1947 was 10,612.

University of Maryland

SECTION 5

CONTENTS

The Midwest

The 1946 Chicago Student Conference, the subsequent 1947 Constitutional Convention and the first four National Student Congresses were held in the Midwest (Part 1). NSA chose Madison, Wisconsin, as the site of its headquarters because its founders wanted the association to maintain a distance from the centers of special interest groups in the East.

Active leadership at other major universities in Ohio, Michigan, Illinois, Minnesota, Iowa and Missouri helped maintain a productive regional presence in the six Great Lakes states (290 4-year colleges—23% of the national total) and six Plains states (114 4-year colleges) throughout NSA's early years.

In her opening memoir, Joy Newberger Picus (later to become a five-term LA city councilwoman) tells how she was drawn into NSA at Wisconsin and the leadership training experience it provided. UW's John Patrick Hunter is remembered. Later an award-winning journalist, he was *NSA News*'s first editor. A recollection of UW's Helen C. White, a member of NSA's Advisory Committee, follows. Rick Medalie introduces Carleton College and the Minnesota region, where a successful annual international summer study program was developed. Rev. Vincent Flynn, President of St. Thomas and an advisor to NSA and to Catholic college students, is remembered.

Mary Kay Perkins, O.P., writes of her student days at Mundelein College, growing up in Chicago, and the active cluster of Illinois colleges in NSA. Mundelein hosted NSA's national art tour and was the home college of Helen Jean Rogers (Secondari), one of NSA's outstanding national leaders (p. 599).

Tesse Hartigan Donnelley's essay (Fontbonne) together with a recollection of Pat Groom (Maryville), both Missouri regional Chairs, provide insights into how many student leaders from the Catholic women's colleges found ways to harmonize their spitirual commitment with their leadership activities in the broader community.

Throughout this section, albums and pictorials highlight more than thirty colleges and their student leaders in ten of these states (after its first year, NSA had no members from the Dakotas). While the Plains states (Missouri, Iowa, Kansas, Nebraska, the Dakotas) were generally combined in two-state regions, the Lake states (Michigan, Ohio, Indiana, Illinois, Wisconsin, Minnesota) maintained single-state identity in their regions.

Indiana University, a notable holdout to membership, even after hosting NSA's Fifth Annual National Student Congress in 1952, joined later in the 1950's (see Robert H. Shaffer, later Dean of Students, p. 326).

Indiana contributed Martin McLaughlin (Notre Dame, p. 84) and Dennis Trueblood (Indiana State Teachers, p. 345), two of NSA's outstanding early national leaders.

Other regional leaders are cross-referenced in the various albums.

National Student Assn. Organizes

1,000 Students From All Regions Meet For 10-Day Conference Here

U. of Wisconsin *Daily Cardinal* 9/30/47

THE MIDWEST PREFERENCE. In order to be located away from Eastern influence and closer to the center of its membership, NSA chose Madison, Wisconsin for its headquarters, and Midwest colleges for the site of its National Student Congresses during 1946-1951.

Midwest NSA Highlights

Gov. Williams Speaks to NSA's First Human Relations Clinic

—Detroit Collegian photo

GOV. G. MENNEN WILLIAMS and NSA Pres. Ted Harris were featured speakers as 136 students gathered for a three-day NSA-sponsored Human Relations Clinic at Wayne University, Detroit. In the above picture, Governor Williams is shown between Harvey Weisberg, chairman of the Michigan region and Blanche Edwards (at left) and Mrs. Williams, Bill Pratt, co-chairman of the clinic, and Ted Harris (at extreme right).

The delegates attempted to find a realistic approach to the problem of combatting discrimination. Other speakers included Eugene Schwartz, NSA vice-president; Nicholas Paster, director of student activities at Roosevelt College, Chicago; and George House from the fellowship of reconciliation in New York.

May, 1949

Michigan

Wisconsin Officers Confer at La Crosse State Teachers

Delegates to the Wisconsin regional convention confer at LaCrosse State Teachers' College April 30 and May 1. Left to right are Jack Killian, University of Wisconsin; Lynn Giese, University of Wisconsin; Lei Gutske, LaCrosse State Teachers; Sally Green, University of Wisconsin; Gene Sleeve, Marquette University, Milwaukee; and Bud Aldrich, University of Wisconsin.—LaCrosse Tribune Photo.

May, 1949

Wisconsin

28 Colleges Map Program Plans

NANCY YERGES, OHIO REGIONAL CHAIRMAN, AND DICK PETERS, Ohio Wesleyan University student body president (seated at desk), talk with representatives of non-member schools at the Ohio Region Assembly held at Ohio State University, December 4-5. Delegates from 28 colleges and universities mapped plans for foreign student hospitality programs, PSC activity and human relations projects.

January, 1949

Ohio

Augsburg Plays Host for Speech Meet

(cut courtesy of Augsburg Echo)

AUGSBURG COLLEGE'S Arline Thorsen makes a point to interested listeners at the NSA-sponsored Speech Meet last weekend with Augsburg being the host to ten Minnesota colleges. Taking in Arline's extemporizing are Jim Rooney, St. Thomas; Merideth Foss, Augsburg; and Joan Hedeen, St. Catherine's.

February, 1949

Minnesota

Indiana Discusses Regional Activities

Pictured during a session of the "very successful" Indiana regional meeting of Jan. 11, Denny Trueblood leads a discussion of regional activities which resulted in projects on equalization of credits, student orientation, graduate study, student government clinic, foreign student hospitality, and Canadian-U.S. exchange. Ten Indiana schools attended.

January, 1948

Indiana

Bus Passes

—University of St. Louis News

SIGNING PETITION—St. Louis president, Father Patrick J. Holloran, signs NSA-sponsored petition for reduced bus fares for college students in the St. Louis, Mo., area. At left is Mary Therese Hartigan, chairman, NSA Missouri Region.

April, 1950

Missouri/Kansas

Traveling Student Art

NSA ART TOUR—Mary Kay Perkins (left) and Lucille Crews plan the second year of Mundelein College's NSA art tour. They are inspecting a water color by Joan Fritchie, Mundelein. More than 75 schools are expected to exhibit art work.

October, 1949

Illinois

All photos above reproduced from issues of *NSA News.*

KEY TO COLLEGE NEWSPAPER CITATIONS IN THIS SECTION

- **ILI** - U. of Illinois, Daily Illini — THE DAILY ILLINI
- **ILN**- *The Loyola News* — THE LOYOLA NEWS
- **ILC** - *Chicago Maroon* — MAROON
- **ILS** -Mundelein C., *The Skyscfraper* — THE SKYSCRAPER
- **ILV**-Rockford C., *The Vanguard* — THE VANGUARD
- **INS** - Indiana State. Teachrs C. *Indiana Statesman* — INDIANA STATESMAN
- **IND** - *Indiana U., Daily Student* — THE INDIANA DAILY STUDENT
- **MIM**- *The Michigan Daily* — The Michigan Daily
- **MNA**-St. Paul C., *The Aquin* — The Aquin
- **MNC**- Carleton C., *The Carletonian.* — The Carletonian
- **MND** - *Minnesota Daily* — Minnesota Daily
- **MOF**-Fontbonne C., *The Font* — The Font
- **MOS** - Washington U., *Student Life* — STUDENT LIFE
- **MOU**-St. Louis U., *University News* — University News
- **MOW**-Webster C. *The Web* — THE WEB
- **OHB**- *The Akron Buchtelite*, U. Akron — THE AKRON BUCHTELITE
- **OHC** - Ashland C., *Ashland Collegian* — ASHLAND COLLEGIAN
- **OHM** -Flora Stone Mather C. *The Mather Record* — THE MATHER RECORD
- **OHR** - Western Reserve U., *The Reserve* — Reserve Tribune
- **OHQ**- *The Ursuline Quill* — The Ursuline Quill
- **OH** - *Wooster Voice* — Wooster Voice
- **WIC**-U. Wisconsin, *Daily Cardinal* — The Daily Cardinal

A lifetime of civic engagement

1. From Student Government to City Government

Joy Newberger Picus
University of Wisconsin
NSA delegate, 1950 Congress. Volendam *tour group, 1949*

I entered the University of Wisconsin in September 1947 as a not yet 17-year-old student, and a not very sophisticated one at that. The school was larger than it had ever been (18,000), and out-of-state students were no longer welcomed, because of the crush of veterans. I was accepted in mid-August on the basis of a scholarship application (no scholarship, but admittance), if I could find a place to stay. My widowed mother was getting married at the end of August and was completely involved with arrangements, packing, moving, and obviously not in a position to be helpful. Finding a place to stay in that very full housing market was the trick—the rest was easy.

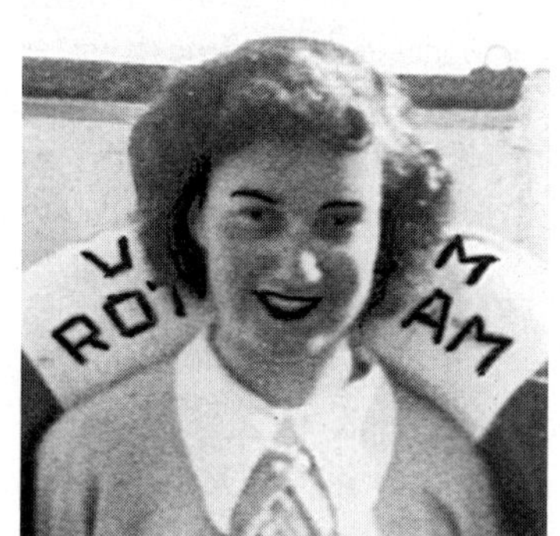

So, I took the train, by myself, from Chicago to Madison, managed to find myself a room in an Independent Women's (I bet we called them Girls') Dorm, and returned home on Cloud 9, or higher. My aunt shopped with me for clothes, my brother and sister-in-law drove me up to school with my radio alarm clock and portable typewriter. I loved the University from the minute I got there, and I still do. I chose Political Science as my major. It was not then a very popular major, least of all for female students.

My Freshman year with Hillel, the Wisconsin Players—and NSA

I was dismayed to discover that first semester students were not allowed to participate in extracurricular activities. It was an effort to protect them from too much fun and not enough studying. I found that I could participate in Hillel activities, and I did, and that a fairly new organization on campus, National Students Association, was not proscribed. So I went there and helped out. Although I remember the office on Park Street, I have very little memory of what I did there. Probably I helped send out mailings. I've always been good at that, having trained at the feet of my politically active mother. I vaguely understood the purpose and what we would now call the mission of NSA, but I am certain the bigger picture of what these bright and busy students from around the country were trying to accomplish, and the political ramifications of it all were lost on me. Or maybe I sell myself short, and it's the memory, not the perception, that's lacking.

During my first year, my major activity was with Hillel. At the end of the year I was awarded a Hillel key, customarily given to seniors, in recognition of my achievements. I have remained active in the Jewish community throughout most of my life and contribute to Hillel Foundations at many of the schools that members of my family have attended.[1]

Also, after first semester, I got involved with the Wisconsin Players and appeared in a few plays, and did behind the scenes work in others. At some point I realized that others were better at that game than I, so I found other outlets. I also realized that I liked speaking my own words and ideas better than those of other writers. But the experience was wonderful, and I remain an actress at heart. During my political career, it came in very handy, and I often thought that only Ronald Reagan "did sincere" better than I!

Student government, group dynamics and parliamentary procedure: 1948

So I turned to Student Government, and spent my sophomore, junior and senior years toiling in those vineyards. Clearly that related to the NSA experience. The biggest issues on campus were race and housing, and the two were clearly related. Human Relations was a big subject, and I know I "did" a lot of it. About this time Gordon Klopf, then student activities adviser, appeared in my life.[2] He became a major influence in my college life, and I attribute much of what I accomplished in the future to him. Group dynamics was not yet an everyday concept, but I learned about it, and about discussion leading and getting the most from a group, from Gordon, during that time. I never forgot it, either.

I chaired a number of Student Board Committees. One year I ran for Independent Student representative on Student Board and lost. Women in government weren't too popular then. We made more coffee than policy. I did serve on Student Board for at least a year, but attended meetings regularly for three years. It was my introduction to parliamentary procedure. I became an expert, and although I rarely needed the sophisticated skills I honed at Wisconsin, they were there for me when I needed them. Interestingly enough, as a member of the Los Angeles City Council, we rarely used parliamentary procedure to win our points, operating under some pretty unusual rules that gave credit to Robert's Rules, but deviated substantially. I used those skills a lot at national and state conventions of the League of Women Voters and the American Association of University Women during the 1960s and 1970s.

New friends and connections: Goldsmith and Lowenstein

My best friends in NSA were Rick Medalie, Herb Goldsmith, Al Lowenstein and Craig Wilson.[3] I loved it when Craig published a picture of me returning on the *Volendam*, from an NSA trip to Europe, on the front page of the NSA newspaper. Herb was a Wisconsin student—we had worked closely together in student government. Al was an incredible presence—I followed his career whenever I could and, like all those who knew him, mourned his untimely death.[4] There was a group of young women from Catholic schools, mainly Mundelein College in Chicago, and I was friendly with them. I recall signing out of my dorm for an "overnight" and spending a night with them, giggling and laughing, probably at the home of a relative.

Off to Europe on the *Volendam*: 1949

In 1949 1 signed up for an NSA trip to Europe. I don't believe my mother would have let me go if she had known how unchaperoned we really were. I was saved from frequent misadventures by my own naiveté. The *Volendam* left from Quebec in late June. I traveled there by coach train, with 3 or 4 other young women from Chicago, and roomed with them at a pension, as we explored Quebec for a few days. We had ten days at sea. I was in one of the better dorms. There were ninety-six of us in one room of this partially reconverted troop ship, which had started life as a luxury liner. I had a bottom bunk, near the bathroom. We had only cold water, and showers were salt water. It was fun at eighteen, and life aboard the ship was interesting, exciting, and romantic. Plays by a troop of Dutch actors, lectures on the contemporary European scene and high spirited young people enjoying each other, all coexisted.

I took daily French lessons, using a method taught to soldiers during the war. My group had two weeks in Holland, two weeks in London and two weeks in France, ending in Grenoble, after which we had ten days of free time. We were very serious—engaging other students, government officials, strangers, in deep conversations about the world, current events, governmental issues, the future of the world. In England all anyone talked about was "socialized medicine." Most thought it would be a disaster. I hitchhiked to the south of England with a female member of my group, and traveled through the south of France and into northern Italy with another one. We had many wonderful adventures, but it was safe for two innocent young American females traveling alone. We sailed home from Rotterdam to New York, went through customs, and then I took my very first plane ride to Chicago. School started in a few days. But that European trip, under NSA auspices, was one of the major highlights of my youth. I occasionally run into someone who was on the *Volendam* that year.[5]

The Michigan convention and "Going on a Lion Hunt": 1950

During the summer of 1950, I was a delegate to the NSA Convention in Ann Arbor, Michigan. Unlike Wisconsin, where two-percent beer could be purchased and consumed on campus, beer was not available on the Michigan campus, and I was appalled by the lengths people went to—to buy it and drink it. Good lesson there. My notes indicate that I was very involved, leading discussion groups and politicking to get certain resolutions approved, and people elected to office. We were generally successful.

Recently, on a photo safari in Zimbabwe, our group was walking through tall grass, looking for elephants. (If we had to look for them, plainly, they weren't around.) In my head, as we swished through the grass, came the words: "I'm going on a lion hunt." No one else seemed to know what I thought must have been a childhood game. In fact, they thought I had had too much sun. A few years later, reading materials prepared for this publication, I came upon the "lion hunt" used at the Michigan Convention![6]

Student leadership training and career choices

Working with Gordon Klopf, I was involved in two Student Leadership Conferences, one at Green Lake, WI, and the other in Kohler, WI, as guests of the Kohler Co. I know that the officers of NSA were at the Kohler Conference, which took place in September 1950. We would look at it now as good "team building," with some goal setting and idea generating. These conferences also played a significant role in my lifelong approach to problem solving and organizational operations. Green Lake was a Methodist or Baptist Conference ground, and I remember that smoking and drinking were prohibited. I don't recall that this caused any problems, however. At Kohler we toured the Kohler manufacturing plant. I have always purchased Kohler bathroom and kitchen equipment for my home whenever I had the opportunity to choose. Talk about loyalty!

I wish I could recall the details of a major brouhaha on campus regarding housing—almost certainly dealing with discrimination against minority students. The issue went to the Board of Regents, and their unfavorable decision was made public on a Saturday in late May 1951. I was called for comment by the local press, probably the *Capitol Times.* I recall my response exactly: "The students of the University of Wisconsin have been lied to and duped for two years by the Board of Regents." The nuances of what they did, or more likely, didn't do, escape me, but that opening sentence is ingrained in my memory. I was terribly proud of myself for being so outspoken; my dear mother worried for fear I would not be allowed to graduate! But this was before 1964 and the Berkeley Free Speech movement, and I suspect the regents saw me only as a minor annoyance.[7]

Just before I graduated, I had a conversation with Professor David Fellman of the Political Science Dept. who had taught several courses I particularly enjoyed. He said to me: "Why aren't you enrolled in Yale Law School?" My response sounds absurd to any present day college female, but I was shocked at the question—going to law school had never entered my mind.[8] Only three or four women had earned law degrees from Wisconsin during the years I was there, and it wasn't an option. But the Professor put the bug in my ear, and from then on, I considered law school as a possibility. When a good time for it came, many, many years later, I made a deliberate decision to continue doing what I had been doing in the community, and not to go to law school. It was the proper decision. It led to a remarkable career opportunity.

After graduation: Family and community involvement, 1951

After graduation, with honors, in June 1951, I followed the path most young women of my generation followed. I found an interesting job with the Chicago American Civil Liberties Union (it paid poorly, but I learned issues and community), got married, and became the prototype educated woman of the 1950s who stayed home with her children. When my husband, Gerry Picus, got his Ph.D. in physics from the University of Chicago in late 1953, we moved to Washington, DC, where he took his first job.

My goal was children, and I had the customary three, each one two years apart. Before they were born, however, I spent hours on Capitol Hill listening to Congressional debates, and we explored Washington's noted and hidden treasures. This was long before Kennedy, Camelot, and TV, and was a much different Washington than exists today. Still, it was a wonderful place for those of us who love government. After my children were born, I involved myself very actively in the League of Women Voters and held major leadership positions. I was fortunate to have wonderful supportive friends and neighbors right near by, but the League was my intellectual salvation.

We moved to California in December 1959 and I immersed myself in League, and added to it with AAUW and the activities that come with children—Parent-Teacher Association (PTA), Scouts, Temple, and so on. I was almost always Legislative Chair for the PTA, but did a year as president at the local Junior High. My hardest job was Cub Scout den mother, but I worked at it, and did it successfully, despite a lack of natural aptitude. We were proud of our son achieving Eagle Scout rank. I loved being president of the local branch of AAUW, and we wielded substantial community influence during the years I was active.

In January 1970, I participated in a five-day in-residence program, called Training for Leadership in Community Action, under American Association of University Women (AAUW) auspices. It was like a follow-up to Green Lake and Kohler. And it was the great "click" moment of my life. We talked about risk taking, and I knew then I could do anything I wanted to. I had served as Local Action Chair for the Los Angeles League, and at that point realized that I was tired of trying to influence the decision makers and wanted to *be* a decision maker.

From decision influencer to decision maker

I ran for the Los Angeles City Council in 1973, having no access to money or power. Women as political candidates were not yet taken seriously. I ran against a one-term incumbent (always hard to beat), but, surprising everyone, I forced him into a run-off and then lost by 500 votes— a scant 1 percent. Disappointing as the experience was, I always knew I would run again. I did, and was elected to the LA City Council in July of 1977. I served through June of 1993. Local elections in California are nonpartisan, but I owned up to being a Democrat. I always faced opposition in my reelection campaigns, and took pride in winning in a district that voted overwhelmingly time and time again for Republicans Ronald Reagan as president and George Deukmejian as governor.

LA Council members have a lot of power, in land use, budget, providing services and public policy. The city provides us with a good-sized staff, which for me averaged fifteen people, who worked at my discretion. Tip O'Neill was right when he said "all government is local," and we worked hard to be responsive to our constituents, to be creative and to be everywhere they wanted us to be. Since the infamous Proposition 13 was enacted less than a year after I took office, it often was a challenge.[9]

My major public policy achievements were in garbage, hazardous waste, child care and dependent care, and women's issues. I mentored many women locally, in California, and throughout the country, through my activities in the National League of Cities and the League of California Cities, where again, I held major leadership positions. I was president of the California Elected Women's Association for Education and Research and president of Women in Municipal Government, a national organization.

Making the world a better place. NSA and Wisconsin made the difference

Writing this memoir forced me to look through some of the daily appointment books that I kept during my college years. What I discovered is that I haven't changed very much—I am still involved in innumerable activities, usually in a leadership capacity, still concerned with making the world a better place. The Joy Newberger of 1950 is instantly recognizable as the Joy Picus of 2001. The energetic young adult of 1950 is the vigorous retiree of 2001—wiser, I hope, mellower, I know.

In retrospect, I never anticipated living through a revolution, and the intervening years, without question, witnessed a major social revolution. Feminism, the change in sexual mores, the liberation from the closet of blacks, Hispanics, gays, and more, have all had a profound effect on our society and on us. What did NSA and Wisconsin have to do with my response to these events? Just about everything.

Joy Newberger Picus served four terms (sixteen years) on the Los Angeles City Council and continues her community service on several boards including Friends of the Griffith Observatory; University of Wisconsin Foundation; and Jewish Homes for the Aging. She and her husband, physicist Gerald Picus, have two grown sons and a daughter and six grandchildren.

END NOTES

[1] For more on Hillel, see Jick, Washington University, p. 412.

[2] See Klopf, p. 329.

[3] See Medalie, pp. 347 and 935, and Wilson, p. 248.

[4] See Lowenstein, p. 283.

[5] See *Volendam*, p. 671. See also Meyer, p. 142.

[6] See Life Goes to a Collegiate Convention, p. 294. Also, see Wharton, p. 145, and Lynch, p. 266.

[7] *Editor's note:* The January 3, 1951, edition of the Wisconsin *Daily Cardinal* reports, in a banner-headlined front-page article, that:

> President Edwin B. Fred yesterday appointed a five-member student-faculty committee to work toward elimination of racial and religious discrimination against members of the university community. . . . Student members nominated by student board are Lyle Miller, law student, and Joy Newberger, senior in letters and science.
>
> The establishment of the committee . . . completed a two-year study of discimination and the adoption of a series of reports by the students, faculty and the board of regents. . . .
>
> Karl Stieghorst, student board president and chairman of the board's evenly [divided] student-faculty committee on human rights said his group would hold a meeting in the near future to decide if it would continue. The emergency committee was formed when the regents rejected the faculty approved human rights document 933.

Newberger was also a member of the emergency committee, the paper noted. The report dealt with discrimination in dormitories, private housing, and fraternities as well as principles of human relations and student responsibility,

[8] See *Women in NSA*, p. 489, Dowd, p. 491, and Medalie, p. 496.

[9] Proposition 13, approved in June 1978, amended the California Constitution by limiting local property taxes to 2 percent of assessed valuation (a huge cutback everywhere) and severely limiting their increase. Local governments then had to struggle to find funding for essential services.

PICTURE CREDITS: *Then:* 1949 on the *Volendam* to Europe. *Now:* c. 1993 as candidate for City Council of Los Angeles (both from author).

JOY NEWBERGER PICUS

Born Joy Newberger in Chicago, Illinois, in 1930, Picus attended Sullivan High School and received a B.A. in Political Science at the University of Wisconsin in 1951. Married to physicist Gerald Picus, they have two sons and a daughter, and six grandchildren.

In July 1993 Joy Picus completed four terms (sixteen years) as a member of the Los Angeles City Council, where she represented 232,000 West San Fernando Valley residents. She earned a reputation as an effective and responsive elected official who got the job done.

For eight years, Councilwoman Picus chaired the Human Resources and Labor Relations Committee, which set policy for Los Angeles' 35,000 municipal employees. Picus was successful in implementing her agenda to create a "family friendly" workplace, recognizing that many employees are also parents struggling to balance conflicting work and home responsibilities. Through her leadership, the City Council adopted a comprehensive Child Care Policy, and in July 1996, a child care center for city employees was named the Joy Picus Child Care Center, in her honor.

Picus was seen as a national leader in the area of eldercare also, recognizing that many midcareer workers are facing the additional burden of helping to care for aging parents. She was the prime mover behind an intergenerational day care center for seniors and toddlers that opened in November of 1993.

Joy Picus is known nationally for her aggressive efforts to promote opportunities for women. She was honored by *Ms.* magazine as a 1985 "Woman of the Year" for her work on Los Angeles's precedent setting pay equity agreement. She served as president of several women's organizations, and has been recognized and honored by many organizations, including the League of Women Voters, Women in Business, Jewish Business and Professional Women, and Temple Aliyah as Woman of the Year in 1994. The YWCA of Greater Los Angeles honored her with their rarely given Athena Award in 1994.

Since leaving office in July 1993, Joy Picus has been actively involved in the community, currently serving as president of the

The University of Wisconsin and NSA

Editor's Note: The university was the site of the 1947 Constitutional Convention (p. 144) and the First National Student Congress (p. 200). Roy Voegeli, 1947 student body president, writes of how he won the support of President Fred and the administration (p. 150). The association chose Madison as its headquarters for the first four years. The assignment of Gordon Klopf as liaison with NSA led to his selection as first Chair of National Advisory Committee (p. 329) and his strong influence in providing continuity for the national staff in its early years. Although NSA's office was off campus (pp. 167, 180), university facilities, volunteers and personnel were near at hand and lent important infrastructure and social support. With Madison and the university as its home base, NSA's founding became part of Wisconsin history, and its official archives are maintained by The State Historical Society of Wisconsin. In addition to Joy Picus and John Hunter in this section, other early NSA leaders from Wisconsin in this book include Karl Meyer, then editor in chief of the Daily Cardinal *(p. 138), and Norman Holmes, later NSA delegation chair, who, together with Roy Voegeli (p. 545), represented NSA in Europe in the summer of 1948 (p. 551).*

Welcoming NSA to Wisconsin

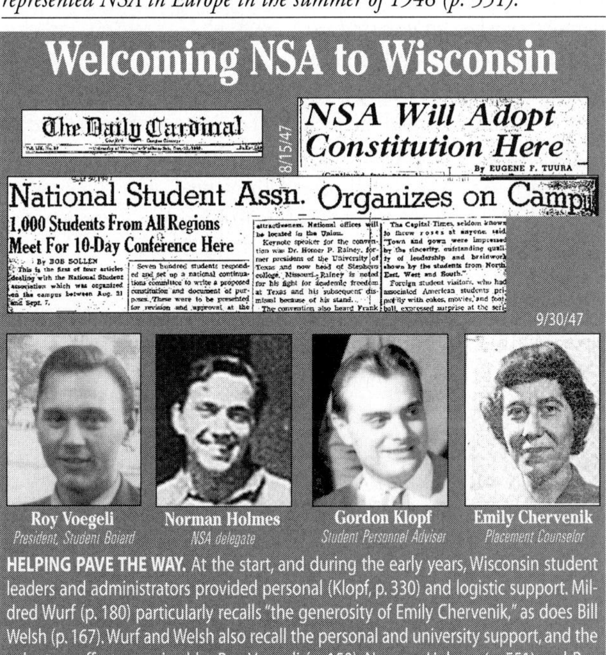

The Daily Cardinal

8/15/47

NSA Will Adopt Constitution Here

By EUGENE F. TUURA

National Student Assn. Organizes on Campu

1,000 Students From All Regions Meet For 10-Day Conference Here

By BOB SOLLEN

This is the first of four articles dealing with the National Student association which was organized on the campus between Aug. 31 and Sept. 7.

Seven hundred students responded and set up a national continuations committee to write a proposed constitution and document of purposes. These were to be presented for revision and approval at the

attractiveness. National offices will be located in the Union.

Keynote speaker for the convention was Dr. Homer P. Rainey, former president of the University of Texas and now head of Stephens college, Missouri. Rainey is noted for his fight for academic freedom at Texas and his subsequent dismissal because of his stand.

The convention also heard Frank

The Capital Times, seldom known to throw roses at anyone, said: "Town and gown were impressed by the sincerity, outstanding quality of leadership and brainwork shown by the students from North, East, West and South."

Foreign student visitors, who had associated American students primarily with cokes, movies, and football, expressed surprise at the seri

9/30/47

Roy Voegeli — *President, Student Board*
Norman Holmes — *NSA delegate*
Gordon Klopf — *Student Personnel Adviser*
Emily Chervenik — *Placement Counselor*

HELPING PAVE THE WAY. At the start, and during the early years, Wisconsin student leaders and administrators provided personal (Klopf, p. 330) and logistic support. Mildred Wurf (p. 180) particularly recalls "the generosity of Emily Chervenik," as does Bill Welsh (p. 167). Wurf and Welsh also recall the personal and university support, and the volunteer effort organized by Roy Voegeli (p. 150). Norman Holmes (p. 551) and Roy Voegeli (p. 545) furnished "eyes and ears" for Bill Welsh and the staff in their summer observer team trip to Europe in 1948. *Photos: l. to r: Voegeli and Holmes,* 1948 (Voegeli); *Klopf,* 1948 (*NSA News, LaCrosse Tribune*); Chervenek (*Capital Times* 7/3/56)

For more* Daily Cardinal *excerpts, see pp. 143, 154.

JOY NEWBURGER PICUS *(From page 930)*

Friends of the (Griffith) Observatory. She chairs the Los Angeles Committee of the University of Wisconsin Foundation. She currently chairs the Foundation's Women's Philanthropy Council and holds a seat on the Board of Directors of the Foundation. Joy is the United Way representative to the Children's Planning Council, a county agency created to coordinate and promote programs on behalf of children, a position which gives her a seat on the Board of Directors of United Way of Greater Los Angeles. Joy also serves on the Board of the Jewish Homes for the Aging and the Valley Alliance of the Jewish Federation Council.

Keeping a Watchful, Friendly Eye

"DEMOCRATIC ACTION IS OFTEN SLOW," *The Cardinal* wrote, as it assessed NSA's first year (right). Proximity to NSA's national office, as well as an active NSA delegation, provided material for continuing comment and debate. From May 24-29, 1951, in NSA's fourth year, the paper ran a four-part series of critical articles taking the Association to task for running a severe travel budget deficit (see p. 272) and for conflicts among officers (See Lynch and Neizer, Pt. 1 Sec. 8). It concluded editorially with a series of recommendations for strengthening management, capped with its "sincere desire to see the NSA play a powerful and effective role representing American students." On June 1 it printed rebuttals from three NSA officers and its travel director.

— *An Editorial* —

NSA Attacked; Can Stand On Record

Sept. 22, 1948

YESTERDAY A STUDENT BOARD member charged the National Student association with "incompetence" and "poor performance."

The charges stir interest but only in a negative way.

It was the intention of the Cardinal to answer the charges point by point. Rebuttal and countercharges, however, cannot hide the important fact that NSA's newness has worn off. The second convention, rececntly-completed, did leave the delegates disheartened and frustrated.

It is certain now that the NSA can not pave the way for a new order. Sectionalism, local sovereignty and the issue of political participation have crept into the clear, well-formulated plans. The problems that plagued national student organizations in the past exploded at the convention in Madison this year. The year of enthusiasm and expectation that surrounded National Student development was over. The sympathetic coverage of the national press was gone. Reporters hung around looking for "reds" and disunity.

BUT NOW A COMPLAINT is registered. The convention it was charged, "passed the buck, failed to live up to its obligations." What the student board member means is not clear.

Of course, the convention did not attend to everything it should have. "A few crackpots wrangling over parliamentary procedure" were not to blame. The implication that democratic procedures stand in the way of getting things done is all too clear.

This was a national convention. Delegates came from all parts of the country. Some were office-seekers; others championed programs and issues. The international situation bordered close to war. The Washington witch-hunt had stepped up its probings of the American scene.

These elements were part of every debate, every convention floor fight. NSA battled for its life. It had been hampered. A revolt of Southern schools on the issue of "educational opportunity" was buried by the President's Civil Rights program. The attempt to keep the lines open between the East ayd the West was smashed by the pressures of public opinion, membership in the International Union of Students became a sign of friendliness with the Soviet Union.

These issues had to be worked out. It took time. Democratic action is often slow.

Historical note: The University of Wisconsin was incorporated in 1848, "open alike to male and female students," the same year that Wisconsin attained statehood. The first degrees were not issued to women until 1869 due to controversies surrounding creation of separate facilities for their housing. (www.library.wisc.edu) Its 1948 enrollment of 22,356 was the fifth largest in the U.S.

The first editor of NSA News *in 1947 engages global attention in 1951*

2. John Patrick Hunter: A Matter of Conscience

Columnists battled the pros and cons . . . Pravda *editorialized . . .* Newsweek *carried a full page.*

Reporter John Hunter, First Editor of NSA Newspaper, Gains National Spotlight with Independence Day Petition Feature

From NSA News, *August 1951*

Many NSAers may have seen accounts of the Fourth of July refusals of 111 citizens in Madison, Wisconsin, to sign their names to a petition consisting solely of excerpts from the Declaration of Independence and the Bill of Rights.

But few are aware that the author of the original controversy-arousing article—mustached, outspoken John Hunter—was the organizing force and first editor of the *NSA News.*

Hunter, now reporter and editorial assistant on the Madison evening daily, *The Capital Times,* traces his history in NSA back to the very beginnings at the historic Chicago Student Conference in December, 1946. Then an undergraduate at the University of Wisconsin, Hunter offered [*sic*] Wisconsin as a site for NSA's constitutional convention in August, 1947.

His current national fame is based on the feature story he wrote on his Independence Day quest to find signers to a petition containing only excerpts from the Declaration of Independence and the Bill of Rights. He found only one signer in 112 requests.

NSA NEWS, August, 1951

Repercussions

The repercussions of the article were felt several weeks later when President Truman mentioned the results in a national address at Detroit. Truman cited them as an example of the danger posed to democracy when an unrestrained campaign of lies and smears could create such fear of signing petitions.

Columnists battled the pros and cons, *Pravda* editorialized on it, the *New York Post* obtained similar results from its own petition, and *Newsweek* carried a full page with pictures. The climax was a national TV show over CBS in New York, August 11, presenting Hunter and the lone signer.

An old battler for student rights—as a first delegate to NSA from the midwest, straight-talking John Hunter still carries his banner for freedom of thought.

John Patrick Hunter:
A matter of conscience

In the summer of 1951, a young reporter for The Capital Times in Madison was assigned a Fourth of July story. He could have written about flags or fireworks, but instead chose to compile a petition made up exclusively of excerpts from the Declaration of Independence and the U.S. Constitution.

Of 112 people he asked to sign it, 111 refused. Such was the fear of the "red scare" inspired by Wisconsin Sen. Joe McCarthy's reign of political terror. John Patrick Hunter might have won a Pulitzer for the simple heroic elegance of his story; but his boss didn't believe in entering contests.

To all of us who "grew up" in a Madison newsroom where Hunter was the dean of writers, that didn't matter. We understood that we were in the presence of an American whose conscience was as unstinting as Daniel Webster's. I never heard a word of this story from his lips; he never had any time to bend an elbow over past glories — he was always consumed by the injustices of the present day.

Whenever the state of journalism dismays me, and there are times, I comfort myself that there remain those who believe that the task of reportage is not only to inform and entertain but to witness.

Name-dropping is an unpardonable sin against good manners; but you will forgive me: John Patrick Hunter was a witness then, and in retirement, he remains one, even to those whose lives have been influenced by his work — I'm privileged to be among them — though some may never have known his name.

Jacquelyn Mitchard
Author
Madison

John Patrick Hunter was born in Richwood, W.Va., on June 4, 1916. He attended Richwood High School. From 1942 to 1945 he was a combat correspondent in the Pacific theater with the U.S. Navy SeaBees. After graduating the University of Wisconsin with a BS in 1950, his career began as a general assignment and political reporter with the Capital Times, *Madison, WI, 1951-60, later serving as editorial page editor, 1960-70, and associate editor, 1970-95. At Wisconsin he was a columnist and on the* Daily Cardinal *board from 1946 to '48. He was founding editor of* NSA News *in 1947.*

In 1989 he received the ACLU Civil Libertarian of the Year award. Winner of numerous journalism awards, he was inducted into the Milwaukee Press Club Media Hall of Fame in 1997. He lives with his wife, Merry Marx Hunter (UW '48), in Madison. They have three sons, one daughter and 7 grandchildren.

Left: from the *Milwaukee Journal Sentinel* Sunday, December 28, 1998. "People Who Shaped Our Lives from 1900–2000" (with permission, *Journal Sentinel* and Jacqueline Mitchard).

"The Purple Goddess": An intense and independent spirit

Helen C. White: Her Students Came First

Professor, College of Letters and Science, University of Wisconsin; Chair, English Department, 1955-58
NSA National Advisory Commitee, 1948-50

Editor's Note: Helen White was one of those memorable persons whose presence seemed larger than life and who became a legend in her own time. A scholar of wide-ranging accomplishments and recognition, she became a good friend to NSA and its national staff in its founding years and is well recalled in this anthology by Bill Welsh, Mildred Wurf, Ralph Dungan, Dick Heggie ("very approachable and had a certain regal air") and Allan Ostar ("someone who cared about students").

"I Have Confidence . . ."

Editor's note: On April 29, 1948 Helen White responded to a letter from Very Rev. Vincent J. Flynn, President of St. Thomas College, asking her opinion of NSA, on whose Advisory Committee he had also been asked to serve (see p. 942). Here is her response:

As regards the National Student Association, I have run into some of the fears you suggest, interestingly enough at one of the midwest state universities. I have a good deal of confidence in the young men at the head of this organization—one of them, the president, I met at the meeting of the Unesco National Commission, and he seemed to be an admirable sort from every point of view.

I have also had quite a long and frank talk with a couple of the officers here. They are not only fine and well-intentioned people, but quite intelligently aware of the problems involved in what they have undertaken. I think the action they have recently taken in regard to the International Student Organization [International Union of Students—ed.] as a result of the Czech [coup] demonstrates their alertness and good sense [p. 189], and I have heard from friends here during their conference this summer that the whole thing was managed very well.

Last Saturday I was down at Mundelein College at a conference of English and Journalism students at Illinois, which was called as part of the N.S.A. cultural program. It was an excellent job. The young president of the conference told me that some of the leftists of Chicago had wanted to present a resolution concerning the officers' action in breaking off the negotiations with the international group. She very sensibly told them that that did not belong on their agenda and so that was squelched. I think we should emphatically go on working with the youngsters. The leftists will, of course, make every effort to do all they can. I agree with you that we should give the youngsters all the help we can. It won't be bad for the youngsters to learn that the leftists can be kept from [asserting] a disproportionate influence if they are alert enough. I am so glad you are on the board. It was one of the things that encouraged me to accept, too.

With every good wish to you, I Am,
Very sincerely yours,

Helen C. White

(Document source: State Historical Society of Wisconsin)

First NSA Cultural Group To Convene Here, April 24

English and Journalism students of Illinois will gather here April 24 for the first intercollegiate conference of the NSA cultural program.

This meeting, sponsored jointly by Mundelein and the NSA Illinois region, will provide an opportunity for students to discuss their special interests and to plan inter-school projects in this field.

Helen Jean Rogers, chairman of the NSA Illinois cultural commission, will act as general chairman.

An address by Richard J. Finnegan, editor of the Chicago Sun-Times, at 9:30 a.m., will set the pace for student consideration of modern writing.

Professor Helen C. White, of the University of Wisconsin English department, will speak at the close of the conference at 3:15 p.m. Miss White is a member of the NSA Advisory council, a U. S. representative on UNESCO, and the author of several historal novels.

Ideas will be exchanged in two discussion sessions, each consisting of three panels. The morning groups will consider The Purpose and Importance of the College Newspaper, Writing Short Stories, and Leisure Time Reading, under panel chairmen Marilyn Tamburrino, Kathryn Malatesta, and Margaret Wolf.

Ruth Casey, Jeri Mangold, and Frances Wager will lead the afternoon sessions discussing The Purpose of the College Literary Magazine, Norms of Literary Criticism, and Editorial and Feature Writing.

Mundelein College, *The Skyscraper* 4/12/48

THE SKYSCRAPER

CLOSING SPEAKER. Helen White wrote Father Flynn (above) about the Illinois Region's first intercollegiate cultural conference at which she was a featured speaker. Helen Jean Rogers (p. 599), Illinois Cultural Commission Chair, presided. Rogers was elected 1948-49 national Secretary-Treasurer that summer.

Helen Constance White (1896-1967)

(Adapted from the UW College Library, General Library System Web site http://college.library.wisc.edu/geninfo/hcw).

She had an intense focus, an independent spirit, was kind and thoughtful, possessed serenity and offered physical and spiritual nourishment. These are some of the attributes used to describe Helen C. White by her colleagues, students and friends throughout her long career.

Born November 26, 1986, in New Haven, CT, Ms. White talked and read early, excelled in school and received top honors in college. She distinguished herself professionally and personally as teacher, writer, humanist and Catholic. Her scholarly works live on as classics in the field.

She graduated Radcliffe College summa cum laude and Phi Beta Kappa in 1916 and received her A.M. in English in 1917. She joined UW as an English instructor in 1919. Became the first woman full professor in the College of Letters and Science in 1936 and Chair of the English Department in 1961. She was President of the American Association of University Women (1941-47), President (and first woman head) of the American Association of University Professors, serving on scores of academic, Catholic and professional boards and recipient of numerous awards and honors. Ms. White died on June 7, 1967, in Norwood, MA.

At the beginning of her career at UW-Madison she was simultaneously an assistant professor and Ph.D. candidate. She spent every Saturday morning tutoring whoever came to her office, "almost to the neglect of my own graduate work. But I felt compelled to do what I could to get the boys (veterans of World War I) on their feet."

Her former students remember her with awe and fondness. One such personal account is found in Toni McNaron's memoir of Ms. White, "The Purple Goddess," excerpted below:

> I knew Helen C. White's work on seventeenth century metaphysical poets in England. My dissertation was to be on John Donne . . . and set about getting myself admitted to her department. My application was accepted in the fall of 1961. . . I went promptly to the English Department . . . My name was spoken in a low melodic tone, and I rose to enter my hero's chamber.
>
> The woman who welcomed me, standing several inches over six feet, had snow white hair crowning a luminous face (a trace of the faintest pink lipstick was the only visible sign of makeup) and wore a suit of the deepest purple I'd ever seen. (in the South of that time, very elderly ladies sometimes wore lavender to teas, but this was royal purple with no muting or apology.)
>
> I have no idea what either of us said during the fifteen minutes of my visit, but I left in a fog of adoration which never dissipated during the three years I was a student [and of] my exposure to Miss White, or the Purple Goddess, as she was called by English Department graduate students.

PHOTO CREDIT: c. 1950 (University of Wisconsin - Madison Archives)

NSA in the Wisconsin Region

1947-48

WISCONSIN REGIONAL LEADERS, NSA NATIONAL STAFF and Wisconsin and Illinois students met in June 1948 at the first annual Lake Forest (IL) leadership training conference sponsored by NSA and the National Conference of Christians and Jews (NCCJ); group dynamics techniques were introduced as the central process governing NSA regional and national events (See p. 333). Top row, fr. r.: Ralph Dungan, NSA V.P. National Affairs, 3rd fr. r. Norman Holmes, U. Wisconsin NSA Chair: 4th row, 6th fr. l,, Janis Dowd, NSA Secretary; 3d row r., Gordon Klopf, U. Wisconsin adviser to NSA; 2d row r. Maurice H. Terry, NCCJ Wisconsin regional director (Ward McMasters).

1948

Mikwaukee Journal 9/9/48

The lack of good campus leaders was discussed Thursday at the student leadership conference, sponsored by the Wisconsin region of the National Student association. The meeting was at the Cavern room of the Marquette university administration building. From the left are Donald Forbes, 5530 N. 31st st., representing Marquette university; Lois Gutzke, La Crosse, of La Crosse State Teachers college, and Lynn Giese, 1126 S. Layton blvd., of the University of Wisconsin, conference chairman. —Journal Staff

1950

NSA News 5/50

Teacher College Problems

SPECIALIZED EMPHASIS—Leading the way toward consideration of special-school problems, this panel at a recent Wisconsin Regional Assembly worked out an amendment to the Wisconsin NSA constitution setting up a fourth commission on teacher college problems. Left to right: Winston McDaniel, regional president, University of Wisconsin; Ashley Ellefson, LaCrosse State Teachers College, who was later elected head of the newly-formed commission; Jim VanTassel, LaCrosse; Bill Banks, Stout Institute; Doris Stensgaard, Eau Claire State Teachers College; and Craig Wilson, NSA director of publications.

1949

Mount Mary Times, undated 1949

Action in a plenary session! Winston McDaniels, Regional NSA President, calls for order during an outburst of response in a plenary session commission report.

Seated left to right in the first row are: Les Scharf, Madison, Regional Public relations Director; Craig Wilson, Director of Publications on the National NSA staff; Betty Nemec, Delegate from Mount Mary; Virginia Gardiner, Mount Mary Delegate; Nancy Walters, Delegate from Madison; and Dick Schenk, Regional International Commission Chairman from Madison.

1951

Milwaukee Journal 8/26/51 (Thayer)

The Wisconsin delegation to the National Student association convention in Minneapolis is shown in caucus Saturday before it introduced a resolution opposing "McCarthyism." The students did not mention Senator McCarthy (Rep., Wis.) by name. From left are Thomas Smith, Madison, University of Wisconsin; Robert J. Berg, Fort Atkinson, Stout institute; Rita Baer, Neenah, UW; Armond Fields, Milwaukee, UW; Anne Doyle, Wausau, Mount Mary college, and Virginia Gardiner, 5017 N. Lake dr., Whitefish Bay, also of Mount Mary college. —Acme Telephoto

WISCONSIN'S MEMBERSHIP BASE was drawn from 35 4-year colleges, with 7 attending the Chicago Student Conference and 11 joining in its first year

For more on Wisconsin not in this section: Welsh, Wurf, Meyer, Heggie, Ostar in Pt. 1, Secs. 4, 5 and 6; Voegeli, p. 150, Klopf, p. 329.

1950-51

Virginia Gardiner was elected to the top N.S.A. office in the state, the regional chairmanship, at the third annual National Student Congress held at Ann Arbor, Michigan, August 23-31. She will hold the position for one year. Bettyanne Nemec accompanied her to the convention as an alternate delegate.

Mount Mary Times, undated 1950

NSA Appoints Mount Marian To State Group

Virginia Gardiner, '52, chairman of the Wisconsin region of NSA, was recently appointed to the UNESCO State Council planning committee. The purpose of this planning committee is to set up a state council for publicity, promotion, and distribution of information for the UN.

There are between 15 and 18 such state councils in the country at present. Each council, by having members of as many state groups as can participate, will be able to contact as many people as possible and spread information about the UN.

MOUNT MARY COLLEGE in Milwaukee provided two Wisconsin regional chairs, Virginia Gardiner (Thayer) in '50-51, and Ann Doyle in '51-52. Earlier chairs had been from the University of Wisconsin: John P. Hunter ('46-47), Fred Stender ('48-49), and Winston McDaniel ('49-50); and in '47-48, George Capwell of Pioneer State Teachers College.

Mount Mary College was founded as St. Mary's Institute in 1872 by the School Sisters of Notre Dame (www.mtmary.edu). 1948 enrollment was 933.

The formative years—A strong and active region

3. Carleton College and the NSA Minnesota Region

Richard J. Medalie
Carleton College, Minnesota
NSA Vice President, Educational Affairs, 1949-50

The Minnesota Region

Carleton's Rick Medalie and Harriet Tyson, preparing for Spring 1949 Minnesota Region traveling art exhibit

Minnesota was a very active NSA region in its formative years. It had strong contingents from the University of Minnesota, as well as from the Catholic schools, such as St. Catherine's and St. Thomas. The other schools were also active, but the University and the Catholic schools were the real hub. Carleton College had a student body president at the time, David Jewel, who was very supportive of NSA. Dick Newman was the chair of the NSA Committee at Carleton at that time.

The region met several times during the school year. Meetings were quite well attended. They were usually held in the Twin Cities, where a large number of schools were concentrated. *The Carletonian* reported fifteen colleges and the University in attendance at the November 15, 1947, weekend regional meeting following the NSA Constitutional convention.[1] It was sponsored jointly at the campuses of Carleton and St. Olaf colleges. Phil Des Marais of the University of Minnesota, the first regional chairman after Chicago, was replaced by Norris Erdahl of St. Olaf for the 1947-1948 year.[2]

By and large there was agreement within the region among the college delegations on most issues of domestic policy. We did have a strong liberal bent on discrimination, academic freedom, federal aid and other such issues. Even the Republicans were quite liberal—whatever liberal meant in those days. On the other hand, there was at the time a very vocal Wallaceite faction (supporters of Henry Wallace), which furnished a minority voice on the left.

Student governments were very strong on almost all the campuses, including those at the more active Catholic colleges. In 1949, Bob Treanor, who was from St. Thomas and a prominent regional leader, became chairman.

Politics at Carleton College

Carleton is located in Northfield, Minnesota—a small town where everything was completely self-contained. You could go for months without reading a newspaper. The tuition at that time was $1,350—including room, board, and all other fees! All our social life was completely taken care of.

The college had an interesting political complexion. We had around 950 students at the time, which could be broken down into approximately 850 Republicans, 50 Democrats, and 52 Wallaceites. I had expected Carleton to be much more politically activist than I found it to be. After all, it was right after the war, and the large number of ex-GIs gave it a cosmopolitan atmosphere.

The liberal leanings of this otherwise conservative campus were expressed by such things in 1948 as the formation by the Carleton Student Association (CSA) of the Carleton Civil Rights Committee and the abolition by the College, with the approval of students, faculty, and President Laurence Gould, of the two exclusive men's social clubs on campus, the Philomathians and the Adelphics. In 1949, Marlin Smith and I became cochairmen of NSA's Western Area Headquarters of the NSA Educational Practices and Human Relations Subcommission.

St. Olaf College was on the other side of the river, and there was a great competition between the two colleges. St. Olaf was Lutheran. Other than the University of Minnesota, all of the schools had a religious affiliation more or less. McAllister College and Hamline Unversity had become more secular.

There was also a very strong internationalist outlook on those campuses. Bill Holbrook (who was one of NSA's three observers to the second World Student Congress in the summer of 1950), Louise Miller of the University of Minnesota, and Bob Treanor of St. Thomas were among the international affairs leaders. This international outlook was a tradition that actually went back to before the war in many of the Christian-affiliated schools.

A substantial portion of the political activity was inspired by Hubert Humphrey's leadership. Students for Democratic Action (SDA) was quite strong on the Minnesota campus and at some of the other schools—St. Thomas was one that I recall.

The conservatism at Carleton was typical of the small colleges in the region, although some of the Catholic schools had a peculiar brand of conservative/liberal mix. They were very violently against the International Union of Students (IUS), because IUS was Communist controlled, but they were very actively engaged in civil rights, antidiscrimination, and a number of other domestic issues.

The 1948 Truman-Dewey election campaign

The Presidential election in 1948 was a remarkable event—Truman versus Dewey—the outcome of which stunned everyone. There we were, our small band of Carleton Democrats, being hit on in all sorts of ways. The Republicans were lording it over us because Dewey was obviously going to win, and the Wallaceites were also active and vigorously challenging Truman. Then came that wonderful election, and, after it was announced that Truman had won, we broke into the bell tower of the college and started ringing the bells at 10:30 in the morning.

The dozen of us Democrats who had organized the break-in of the bell tower then went into the student union, sat at a large table in the center, and toasted Truman's election with our coffees. Everyone else gave us dirty looks.

The Federal Aid to Education controversy

Laurence M. Gould, who was president of Carleton at the time, became one of the educational leaders—if not the leader—opposing federal aid to education. He was firmly opposed because he felt it was going to undermine academic freedom. (Not that he minded that Carleton and other colleges were getting funds for the Reserve Officers' Training Corps.) In truth, there were many serious educators then who viewed all forms of federal intervention as dangerous.[3]

It soon became known that federal aid to education was one of the issues that was going to be voted on at the NSA congress in 1949. There was a mass meeting of the student body—about nine hundred or so students in the chapel—at which the vote was to be taken to instruct the NSA delegation as to what it should do. There was a debate on both sides, after which there was an overwhelming vote by the student body instructing the NSA delegation to vote against federal aid to education and to explain our opposition. Ironically, one of the NSA policies I was charged with advancing when I became educational affairs vice president was federal aid to education! I wrote several editorials in favor of federal aid in *NSA News* and represented NSA at conferences in its support.

The long road from northern Minnesota to the world

One of the reasons I decided not to go back to Carleton after my term in national office was that I had been exposed to an outside world with a broader view. I look back with fascination at the road I traveled from the sheltered and limited experiences of my youth to that wider world that my NSA experience helped open up for me.

Although I was born in Duluth, I grew up during the 1930s and 1940s in a very small town, Chisholm, Minnesota. Chisholm had a population of about 7,500–8,000 at the time. It was right in the heart of the iron ore country. Because every shovel-full of iron ore was taxed to the hilt, we had multimillion-dollar schools; our junior high school had an Olympic-sized swimming pool, as did the senior high school. We also had a concert orchestra and a high school marching band.

The Depression, however, had a serious impact on our city as elsewhere, and we were doubly affected because the mines would close down for about five to six months a year; snow fell around the first of November and lasted till the end of May, sometimes till early June.

Born a little too late for World War II, I missed it by a few years. I graduated high school in 1947. I was in college during the Korean War. In 1950, it was touch and go as to the draft; no one knew what was going to happen. A classmate of mine was secretary of the draft board, however. As a result, we all received educational deferments. My graduating class had one hundred students, and ninety of us went on to college. Education was highly revered. Most of the children had parents who were miners in the open pits, but there was a small percentage of us whose parents were business owners and professionals. My father was one of the two dental surgeons in the town. After the war, my father drew his patients from the entire Iron Range.

Interracial and interfaith experiences

While growing up, I also had no interracial experience. When I went to college there was only one Negro student—Al Tinnen.[4] He was a terrific person, and was one of the top football players at the college. He was also one of the great actors on campus. The Carleton Players was a very fine college thespian group. He played the leading part in Berthold Brecht's *Caucasian Chalk Circle*, which had its world premiere at Carleton College. Al was a wonderful vocalist as well. He sang with the college dance band. I especially recall his singing his signature closing piece at the end of every Saturday night dance—"In My Solitude."

Meeting Ted Perry, a Negro student from Temple University in Philadelphia, and being his roommate part of the time when we were both NSA vice presidents in Madison was a significant experience for me—and probably for him, too. We had become very, very close friends. We had gone to a meeting in Chicago during October, after which Ted and I went to an affair where I was one of perhaps only a half dozen whites. All the rest were black. Suddenly finding myself in a minority situation had a very transforming effect on me.

Interestingly, there were a good number of Jewish students at Carleton. Nonetheless, it was a church-affiliated school—Congregational and Episcopalian—and we all attended the religious services at the college. We had compulsory chapel three times a week: Tuesday morning, Friday morning, and Sunday vespers. One could take only four cuts per semester. Despite compulsory chapel, the college was nevertheless moving toward becoming more secular.

We all accepted the system the way it was, while working within it as the way of furthering social change. It was only when the civil rights movement later emerged that attitudes changed. Up to that time, the value system was generally accepted by everybody.

Richard J. Medalie is in law practice in Washington, D.C., and counsel to the New York law firm of Brock Partners. He is also Chair of the Appleseed Foundation, in Washington, D.C., a national nonprofit corporation, the goal of which is to organize statewide systemic, public interest law centers throughout the country.

(See p. 355 for an extended biography.)

END NOTES

[1] I owe much of the citations of names, dates and events to material furnished by my good friend and classmate George Soule, the former chairman of Carleton's English Department, who lives in Northfield. George conducted research in the Carleton College archives and copied pages from the student newspaper for this article.

[2] See regional chronology, p. 940.

[3] See extracts from Gould's letter to the *Carletonian* on federal aid, p. 938.

[4] In keeping with the custom of the time, African-Americans referred to themselves as Negroes.

PICTURE CREDITS: *Then:* 1949 Minnesota Region art exhibit (WSHS). *Now:* 1997 (Schwartz).

The Carletonian

Vol. LXVIII, No. 8 Carleton College, Northfield, Minnesota Saturday, November 6, 1948

NOV 6 1948 LIBRARY

NSA Regional Parley Continues Here Today

NSA CONVENTION committee Jerry Sonosky, Marilyn Marvel, Dick Newman, chairman, and Richard Medalle discuss problems confronting them during the first meeting held here yesterday. It was the first meeting of the eleven participating colleges since the national convention at Madison, Wisconsin, last August.

11/6/48

NSA Delegates Present Report On Congress Decisions At Madison

CARLETON NSA committee recently participated in the annual national congress held at the University of Wisconsin. The Carleton delegation, consisting of Dick Newman, Eve Perl and Rick Medalie, has submitted the following report to *The Carletonian*.

Taking unprecedented action, seven hundred delegates representing about 250 colleges and universities throughout the country, elected Ted Harris, a Negro from Pennsylvania, the new president of the National Student Association at the annual NSA congress held in Madison, Wisconsin, August 23 to 28. All personal prejudice was cast aside as the delegates accomplished what our elders, unfortunately, have not been able to accomplish: election of a man because he is qualified.

On Friday, August 27, the delegates voted not to affiliate with the Soviet-dominated, Communist-controlled International Union of Students (IUS), and at the same time rejected any notion of forming an anti-Soviet western union of students.

The IUS question, which had occupied more time in the plenary sessions than any other piece of business took many hours to solve. A small obstructionist minority represented the major barrier in the solution of the IUS question; however, these pro-affiliations showed no real strength when the final decision was made.

Civil Rights, Co-op, 'Antigone' Interest NSA Convention

ENTHUSIASTIC interest was shown in three Carleton student projects: the Civil Rights committee, the social Co-op and last year's "Antigone" road trip, by delegates to the first annual National Student Association convention at Madison, Wisconsin, this summer.

This is reported by Eve Perl, Dick Newman and Rick Medalie, Carleton's three representatives at the six-day meeting.

The Carleton Civil Rights committee plan, described in last week's Carletonian, was first aired in the Minnesota Region NSA caucas, where it met with a warm reception, according to Medalie. From there the project went on to be presented at the national convention.

Carleton College

Located in Northfield, about 30 miles south of downtown Minneapolis, Carleton College was able to furnish significant leadership in the Minnesota Region, taking on cultural, human relations and international exchange projects. Rick Medalie, who was elected 1950-51 NSA Vice President for Educational Problems (p. 347), was Co-Chair with Marlin Smith in 1949 of the NSA Sub-Commission on Human Relations. In 1948 he was Chairman of the Minnesota intercollegiate campus SPAN program of summer study abroad (see p. 941).

Founded in 1866 as a co-educational institution by the Minnesota Conference of Congregational Churches, Carleton College is autonomous and non-sectarian but continues to maintain membership in the Council for Higher Education of the United Church of Christ (www.carleton.edu). Its 1948 enrollment was 1,124.

The NSA delegation is instructed by the Student Association to vote against federal aid.

Carleton Debates Federal Aid

Carletonian "Clearing House" Reviews Federal Aid to Education

Editor's Note: A role for the federal government in financing public education was being hotly debated following World War II. The Carleton College Carletonian*'s "Clearing House" page ran a letter from college President Laurence Gould and a response from student Jerry Sonosky on May 14, 1949, which encapsulate the debate at the time. The Carleton Student Association voted to instruct its NSA delegation to the Second NSA Congress at the University of Illinois in 1950 to oppose Federal aid.*

There cannot be Federal Aid without Federal control

TO THE EDITORS:

... The present bill before Congress is highly objectionable in itself. It is the result of lobbying at the national level. In no case has there been a request for federal aid from the states that are supposed to need it so badly. No local school board, no state school board, no local chamber of commerce, no taxpayer's association, no group of any sort has requested federal aid....

I am as heartily in favor of equalizing educational opportunities as any educator in this country. The present proposals before Congress do not safeguard such equalization. An amendment proposed by Senator Lodge which would eliminate segregation and racial discrimination of all sorts was defeated...

... The present bill before Congress is deliberately phrased in such a way as to lead people to believe that every state is actually securing some subsidy. Part of the facts have been withheld. The National Education Association in its publication on March 11, 1949 gives a list of the states with the amounts each will receive. Minnesota will receive \$2,900,000. There should have been an additional column which showed what each State would pay. It would have revealed that Minnesota would pay some 6,000,000 dollars to receive 2,900,000 dollars. I insist that you do not subsidize somebody by taking two dollars away from him and giving him one in return; yet school people throughout the state are under the Illusion that they are getting 2,900,000 dollars because all of the facts have not been placed before them....

One of the greatest illusions about federal aid is the supposition that we can have federal aid without federal control. As a matter of fact, it would be dishonest, if not illegal, for the government to collect our taxes and then allocate them somewhere without exercising any control over them....

One of my friends commenting upon the bill said this: "One of the strangest features of the federal aid bills and the propaganda supporting them is the clause in the bill saying there shall be no federal control when elsewhere in the bill there are controls."...

We were once dedicated in the United States to the belief that the well being of man came through his own accession of responsibility, but ours has now become a mass age. People are living and thinking in standardized fashion. The declining importance of the individual is already widespread in political and economic thought and, sad to say, is gaining acceptance in education theory as well. In our drift toward statism we have reached a critical point in education beyond which we must not go.

—L. M. GOULD

There will be no Federal controls over policy

TO THE EDITORS:

. . . The opponents of federal aid [base their arguments] on three points: First, that the states can take care of themselves. Secondly, the danger of federal control of education. And finally, the danger to such schools as Carleton.

As to the first argument we need only look at the facts. If the 11 poorest states in the Union were to use 100 percent of their taxable income for education they still would not be able to spend as much on their school systems as the 25 richest states in the Union.... As to the second argument . . . there are two types of control: namely, financial control and policy control. The second control is what we have to worry about. Whether we know it or not, the federal government has FINANCIAL CONTROL over every activity in which federal funds are used.... Control of school policy, I admit, is the last thing this country should have.... The bill before Congress today expressly states that there will be no federal controls of policy.

. . . As to the danger of standardization and the death of liberal schools, there are but two things to say. First, we have standardization along state lines today, and yet our system is still free, but not adequate. Secondly, if schools such as Carleton must die so that millions of American children can have adequate educational opportunities, then I say, "May its soul rest in peace!"

—JERRY SONOSKY

NSA ADVOCATED FOR FEDERAL AID

NEC Adopts Legislative Goals Urges Federal Aid Support

Asks U.S. to Aid Private Colleges

Federal aid to higher education should include assistance to private colleges for capital outlay but not for operating costs, the National Executive Committee (NEC) decided at its Chicago meeting.

The NEC called upon Congress to adopt legislation for federal aid to the states for higher education, and endorsed the major provisions of the President's Commission on Higher Education report concerning the financing of public institutions and a direct individual scholarship plan.

Dissent from Report

Dissenting from the Commission's report, the NEC urged that funds for capital outlay be allocated to private as well as public institutions.

Voting 20 in favor, with one abstention, the NEC outlined the following goals which it felt would be met by federal aid to education legislation:

1. The expansion of facilities of higher education as recommended by the President's Commission.
2. The improvement and expansion of primary and secondary education through federal aid.
3. A national program of federally financed scholarships to individuals on the basis of ability and need.
4. Federal aid to the states for the operating costs of public institutions of higher education.
5. Federal aid to the states for suport of capital outlay to all institutions, regardless of source of control.

All member colleges of NSA were called upon to solicit the support of the public and their legislators for the passage of such a bill.

In its discussion of the proposals presented by the Staff the NEC centered most of its debate about the provisions concerning private institutions and aid to states maintaining segregated schools.

Concerning the private schools the NEC felt that "the balance between public and private institutions is one of the primary values of our educational system." Endorsing aid to such institutions for capital outlay in order to maintain an equity between these two types of institutions, the NEC qualified its support by stating, "no funds shall be appropriated for those personnel, services or facilities exclusively and specifically for sectarian religious purposes."

Opposes Segregation

While the body recognized the need for aiding the poorer states, many of whom in the South maintain segregated systems of education, it reiterated its opposition to such segregated systems of education and specified that federal funds should be distributed so that equal amounts would be spent on white and colored students.

Taking cognizance of the fears held by many educators, that federal aid might lead to federal controls the NEC called for safeguards to insure that the educational system in the United States be maintained "free of excessive government control."

SUPPORT FOR AID TO PRIVATE COLLEGES, limited to capital outlays, had broad support within the association. A significant number of Educators agreed with Carleton's President Gould (above), opposing aid of any kind. (See p. 370 on NSA policy.)

NSA News 1/49, excerpted

Here's The Way Carleton Does It!

ED MILLER, Hamline U., chairman of Minnesota Region, is shown leading the plenary session of the Regional assembly held here in November. Representatives from 14 Minnesota schools were in attendance.

MEETING OF CARLETON'S NSA COMMITTEE evaluating applications for the '49 National Student Congress. Left to right (around table): Gardner Soule, Dick Hausknecht, Marlin Smith, Rick Medalie, Jerry Sonosky, Harriet Tyson, Marva Robins (hidden), John Rosenheim, Eve Perl, and Mike Herbst.

'Prize-winning Student Government . . .'

NSA Story - Carleton Style

(EDITOR'S NOTE: The following article doesn't necessarily imply that the Carleton student body completely supports the legislative program of the NSA. See Vox Pop column in this issue.)

By JERRY SONOSKY

IN MARCH, 1948, the NSA Committee at Carleton College formally became a permanent standing committee of Carleton's Student Association. Since that time, the committee has served as a liaison between the student body and NSA. At the congress last August, two members of Carleton's committee, Rick Medalie and Dick Newman, were chosen regional officers.

NOVEMBER, 1948, found Carleton's NSA Committee playing host to the Fourth Minnesota NSA Regional Assembly. Soon after, a program of activity which earned for Carleton the distinction of being named one of the outstanding NSA student governments in the country.

- One of the first major achievements of the committee was the establishing of a Carleton Foreign Student Aid Committee on campus. Student funds were allocated and the committee set itself the task of aiding foreign students who wished to come to Carleton.
- On a regional basis, the committee cooperated with USNSA in its work with President Truman's Commission on Displaced Persons. Through this commission, it is planned to bring additional foreign students to all the colleges of Minnesota.

DECEMBER, 1948, Carleton was appointed as the Western Area Headquarters for the USNSA Human Relations Subcommission. Cooperating with the Carleton Civil Rights Committee, the subcommission is aiding other colleges in this area set up similar Civil Rights Committees.

- Through the initiative of Carleton's NSA Committee, a Minnesota College Art Exhibit was assembled and circulated throughout the schools of Minnesota. At the same time, the committee disseminated information on USNSA foreign travel and study programs. Through its efforts, 20 Carleton students have been aided in their attempts to study and travel abroad.
- This coming August, four Carleton students will represent the Carleton student body at the second annual National Student Congress.

DICK BREMICKER, Fran Heim, and Stan Purdham (l. to r.) are shown in a dramatic scene from the Carleton NSA-sponsored tragedy, "Antigone". The play was shown before Minnesota regional schools.

JOHN PETERSON, one of Carleton's twenty students planning to take advantage of NSA's foreign travel program, goes over final details with Gardner Soule, Eve Perl, and Dick Newman, Carleton NSA's international affairs committee.

JEAN WILSON, Bill Holmquist, Marty Larsen, officers of CSA, and Rick Medalie, NSA chairman, discuss the NSA Student Leaders' Clinic held at Hamline last March, in the studios of CSA's new radio station.

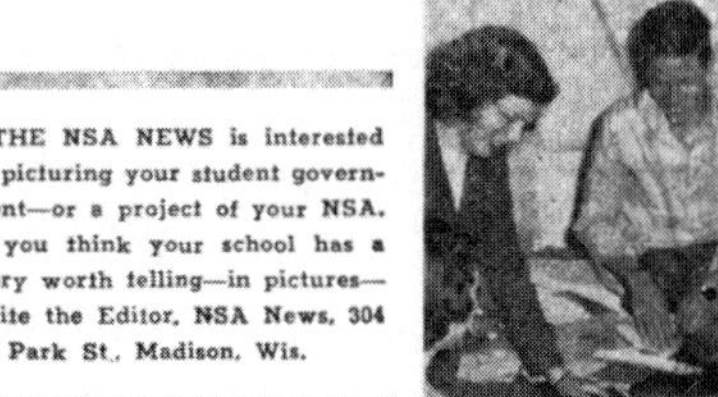

THE NSA NEWS is interested in picturing your student government—or a project of your NSA. If you think your school has a story worth telling—in pictures—write the Editor, NSA News, 304 N. Park St., Madison, Wis.

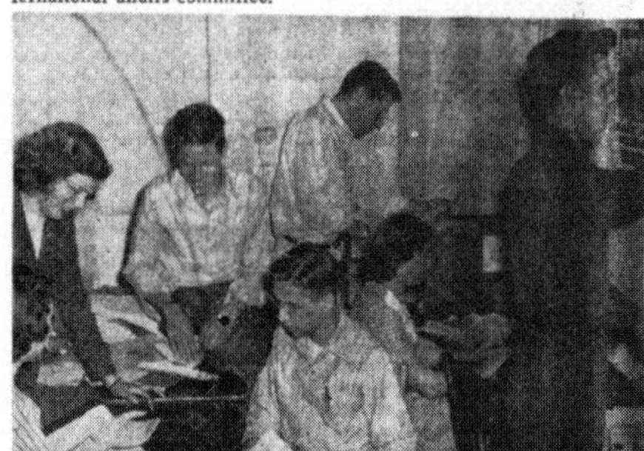

CARLETON'S Civil Rights Committee and the Carleton National Student Association preparing for the Minnesota Human Relations conference held at Macalester College, May 7.

A Minnesota Regional Chronicle

As reported in *The Carletonian,* "Official newspaper of Carleton College"

3/24/47 **MINNESOTA COLLEGE DELEGATES ESTABLISH REGIONAL COMMITTEE.** "Following a plan . . . started at a Chicago Student Conference . . . thirteen students representing the college students of Minnesota met at the University of Minnesota's Coffman Memorial Union January 24." Hank Krivetsky was the Carleton delegate . . . the machinery for the regional organization was set up under the Chairmanship of Phil Des Marais of the University of Minnesota. . . . Voting will be based on student population . . . each college [was] asked to contribute 20 dollars per authorized delegate to support the regional and national organizations temporarily.

5/10/47 **CARLETON SENDS TWO DELEGATES TO REGION MEETING AT U OF M.** Walter Crane and Hank Krivetsky are attending the second meeting of the Minnesota Region of the National Student Organization.

9/27/47 **DELEGATES FROM 350 COLLEGES FORM NSA.** Report of Constitutional Convention at the University of Wisconsin in August.

10/25/47 **RECORD SUM EXPECTED IN SERVICE FUND DRIVE.** "The World Student Service fund receives a large portion of our collection . . . Carleton-in-China will also receive a considerable amount . . . Carleton again has a representative in China. Fern Larson '47 assumed her teaching duties at Peiping during this past summer."

11/8/47 **NSA TO HOLD MINNESOTA REGIONAL CONVENTION HERE.** "Breaking all precedent, Carleton and St. Olaf colleges join forces next weekend to act as joint hosts. . . . Representatives of fifteen colleges and the U. of Minnesota are expected to arrive in Northfield next Friday afternoon."

11/15/47 **"AMERICAN STUDENTS POLITICALLY INERT," SAYS ANDERSON.** Youngest member of St. Olaf faculty addresses three-day convention of Minnesota Region. Carleton represented by Dick Newman and Hank Krivetsky; alternates Eve Perl and Mary Bry. 15 Minnesota colleges attend.

3/6/48 **NSA INAUGURATES OLE-CARL INTERMURALS.** "On Wednesday, March 8, the intramural basketball champions of St. Olaf College travel to Sayles-Hill gymnasium for the first National Student Association-sponsored interscholastic event."

4/24/48 **MEDALIE MAKES SPAN INTRODUCTION TUESDAY.** Medalie is campus SPAN chairman. The Student Project for Amity Among Nations sends students abroad for a summer program of study, work projects and community involvement. "Plans for 1949 include work projects in Puerto Rico, Venezuela, French Canada, Italy, Austria, France, Belgium, Luxembourg, The Netherlands, Sweden, Palestine and China, with Egypt, England and Germany as alternates. The University of Minnesota will send 140 students; St. Olaf 10; McAlister 10; Carleton 8; Gustavus Adolphus 8; and Augsburg 6; with ten others to be allocated according to applications received."

5/22/48 **STUDENT BODY APPROVES CIVIL RIGHTS COMMITTEE.** President Bob Henderson of the CSA presented the resolution to the House of Representatives. "The primary purpose of the committee . . . would be to 'urge people to influence their legislators, especially in the small town and rural areas where people are unaware of the civil rights problem.' " The CSA selected Carleton's NSA national congress delegates, Marva Robins and Dick Newman, and alternates, Rick Medalie and Rick Lawton.

9/18/48 **NSA VOICES STUDENT IDEAS OF DEMOCRATIC GOVERNMENTS.** Recap of NSA activity and Congresses. "Locally, NSA put the Carleton produced play, 'Antigone' on the road." "The exchange was an unprecedented activity. The play was received enthusiastically at St. Olaf College, Hamline University and St. Cloud Teachers College." . . . "NSA conducted a weekly radio program on station KDHL in Faribault."

9/25/48 **CIVIL RIGHTS, CO-OP, "ANTIGONE" INTEREST NSA CONVENTION.** Carleton delegates presented program ideas to the First NSA Congress at the University of Wisconsin. Report on convention detailed, including vote "not to affiliate with the Soviet-dominated, communist controlled IUS," and the accomplishment of the delegates:of "what our elders have, unfortunately not been able to accomplish—election of a man because he is qualified"—referring to Ted Harris (La Salle College), "a Negro from Pennsylvania" who was elected NSA President (1948-49).

11/6/48 **NSA PARLEY CONTINUES HERE TODAY.** Two-day regional meeting of Minnesota Colleges organized into four workshops: Civil Rights and Educational Practices, Cultural and International Affairs, Publc Relations and Purchase Card System. Officers: Ed Miller, Hamline University, Chairman; Louise Miller, U. of Minnesota, Vice Chairman; Dick Newman, Carleton, International Affairs Chairman; and Rick Medalie, Carleton, National Affairs Chairman.

2/5/49 **CARLETON HEADS NSA HUMAN RELATIONS WORK.** NSA Western Educational Practices and Human Relations Subcommission headquartered at Carleton. Co- Chairmen are Rick Medalie and Marlin Smith.

3/12/49 **CARLETON RECEIVES ART EXHIBIT THROUGH NSA.** Collection of student art work from eight Minnesota colleges organized by Harriet Tyson, chairman of the NSA Art Committee. The colleges circulating the exhibit are Concordia, St.Thomas, Itasca Jr. College, College of St. Scholastica, Hamline University, St. Cloud State Teachers, St. Olaf and Carleton.

4/16/49 **SEND DELEGATES TO REGIONAL, NATIONAL MEETINGS.** March regional NSA meeting voted to cooperate with Carleton in a Minnesota Civil Rights Conference in May. Also reviewed art exhibit program, plans for literary magazine under direction of College of St. Theresa. Rick Medalie, Marlin Smith, Mike Herbst and John Rosenheirn attended. Dave Birt, U. of Minnesota, and Marlin Smith were regional delegates to the April meeting of the NSA National Executive Committee in Cleveland.

9/24/49 **MEDALIE ACCEPTS NSA VEEP POST.** Medalie elected Vice President for Educational Affairs in August at University of Illinois NSA Congress. Also attending for Carleton were Bill Holmquist, Ruth Connolly and Marlin Smith.

1/21/50 **NSA TO HOLD FORUM FOR STUDENT LEADERS.** CSA to sponsor campus meeting and has also arranged for Robert Kelly (St. Peters College), national President of NSA (1949-50), to speak to Carleton students February 7 in the Great Hall. Discussion of NSA's proposed national magazine insert, "Fortnightly."

2/24/51 **NSA PRESIDENT CONDEMNS OATH.** Allard Lowenstein, NSA President (1950-51), of the U. of North Carolina, who had addressed Carleton students the previous fall, "recently stated that the University of California's loyalty oath for teachers has aided and encouraged the Communists."

5/5/51 **NSA COMMITTEE ASKS, "IS IT WORTH KEEPING?"** Pro (Margaret Schlipf) and Con (Toni Barron,John Sage, Gail Melik) presented on feature page "the second in a series of articles" to acquaint students with NSA.

5/12/51 **ON NSA.** Editorial commenting on "growing pains" and a "split" NSA committee, "Carleton didn't join NSA in a day. Let's not rush in or out in one poorly attended, hurry- for-lunch-CSA meeting after Chapel." Commenting on the national level, the editorial notes "NSA this year has been an example of ordered confusion. Partly because of an unfortunate constitutional amendment passed at the national convention last August, countless decisions have been held in deadlock with no authority to make them. . . . Yet the NSA is a young organization. These may be growing pains. . . ."

5/26/51 **NSA REQUESTS STUDENTS TO APPLY FOR CONGRESS.** Applications for membership on the delegation to the Minnesota Fourth Congress dealing with "student government, honor systems, athletics, campus organizations and student orientation."

10/27/51 **COLLINS TOURS EUROPE UNDER NSA AUSPICES.** Sally Collins reports on NSA and NBBS sponsored summer tour, sailing on the Dutch student ship *Volendam.*

12/1/51 **MINNESOTA REGIONAL ASSEMBLY CONVENES ON CARLETON CAMPUS.** Eighty students represent 11 colleges at three-day convention, scheduled to be addressed by William Dentzer (Muskingum College), President of NSA (1950-51). Colleges attending: Carleton, St. John, St. Thomas, Macalester, Hamline, Concordia, Augsburg, St. Catherine, St. Benedict, St. Theresa and St. Olaf. Panel leaders include William Birenbaum (student activities director, U. of Chicago), Louise Miller (USAF) and Robert Treanor (Secretary to Congressman Eugene McCarthy). Dentzer's plane was grounded and he couldn't make it. One college from Iowa also attended.

12/1/51 **WHY NSA?** Editorial. "The enthusiasts, in an attempt to keep students and schools interested, have diverted too much of their attention to campus projects and campus crusades. . . . Let's forget some of the talk about concert bureaus and recreational facilities and focus on some problems that pull the campus away from its isolated self- centeredness; questions of national and international importance which can be influenced by student action. This kind of organization at Carleton, and at many schools like it, could become more than a silent campus visitor."

1/19/52 **OFFICERS OF NSA ATTEND RIO STUDENT CONFERENCE.** Reports on "the first inter-American student congress at Rio de Janeiro, Brazil."

U. of Minnesota , Carleton, St. Theresa and the Region

Carleton Sends Two Delegates to Region Meeting at U. of M.

REPRESENTING the Carleton student body, Wilder Crane and Hank Krivetsky are attending the second meeting of the Minnesota region of the National Student Organization today and tomorrow in the Coffman Memorial Union of the University of Minnesota.

The regional meeting, which ends a three day Spring Conference on Student Affairs conducted by the University of Minnesota, was called to discuss the recent national executive council meeting in Chicago and make plans for the NSO's constitutional convention scheduled for this coming September. Bill Smith of the University of Texas, national president of the NSO, will address the group, which represents the majority of Minnesota college students.

Phil Des Marais

Carletonian 5/10/47

'Essai' Plans Quarterly In January

"Essai"—NSA's national literary magazine—will become a regular quarterly beginning in January.

Carol M. O'Brien, St. Theresa College, Minn., will be editor and Daniel A. McCarthy, St. Mary's College, Minn., will be business manager.

• • •

A PILOT EDITION for autumn 1949 appeared at the recent NSA Congress and won enthusiastic support from delegates.

Distribution of the 40-page magazine is through the NSA campus committees, which sell them directly to students at 25 cents each.

NSA News 10/49

Historic notes: The University of Minnesota was founded as a preparatory school in 1851, closed during the Civil War, and reopened as a land grant university with the support of John Sargent Pillsbury (www.umn.edu/twin cities). 1948 enrollment, the U.S. second largest: 32,199.

The SPAN REPORT

STUDENT PROJECT FOR AMITY AMONG NATIONS

February, 1948 Minneapolis, Minnesota Vol. I, No. I.

SPAN Promotes Foreign Seminars

★ ★ ★ ★ ★ ★ ★ ★ ★

SPAN Seeks Program Extension at Conference

EXTENSION OF SPAN'S program to Carleton and nine other Minnesota colleges is the aim of the constitution of that organization approved at the state-wide conference held at the University of Minnesota on Saturday, February 28.

With understanding and friendship among nations as its goal, the SPAN program has been approved by the house of representatives but still must be given faculty approval before Carls can go abroad in 1949 under the plan.

The conference, attended by representatives of Gustavus Adolphus, Hamline, Macalester, Mankato Teachers, St. Catherine's, St. Cloud Teachers, St. Olaf, St. Thomas and the University of Minnesota, met in discussion groups to approve the new plans. Carleton committee members were Richard

visory committee in each school according to the quota of the school.

This "Student Project for Amity among Nations" was first organized at a YMCA weekend camp in October, 1946, but until this year only students from the U of M and its Duluth branch have been participating. Last summer, forty students traveled to England, France, Spain and Sweden each to do research on a particular problem in

Carletonian 3/6/48

Chicago U To Follow SPAN Plan

50 Students to Take Part in Foreign Study Seminar Next Summer

Fifty University of Chicago students will follow the Minnesota lead this summer individually in foreign countries.

Tentatively, the Chicago SPAN plan calls for selection of qualified students who will then decide their country and subject of study. Credit for study must be arranged by the student in his own department.

Minnesota to Send 40 to 4 Countries

SPAN foreign study seminars, now fully a part of the University of Minnesota curriculum, are organized for 1948.

Forty students have been selected for study in four countries—Argentina, Czechoslovakia, England and Germany.

Selections were made from 200 applications on the basis of scholarship, proposed study topic and background for it, language ability, demonstrated interest in world affairs and community activity. Other considerations were age, year in school and ability to work with a group.

One faculty adviser for each country will be selected from applications, with consideration for skilled leadership as well as social science background in the area; ability to benefit academically and language proficiency.

Faced with financial, transportation, housing and presailing problems, the 1948 selectees began weekly business meetings Feb. 3. Officers were elected and red tape tasks apportioned to committees.

Financial arrangements will be on a new basis. A businessmen's committee represented throughout Minnesota will or-

Foreign Study Costs

The average living costs for 2½ months in Europe, according to accounts kept by 1947

TRAVEL AND STUDY FOR CREDIT joined curriculum and international understanding during the years of expanding student interest in foreign affairs and reconstruction. Initiated at a YM-YWCA camp at the University of Minnesota 1946, a separate intercollegiate group, SPAN, Inc., brought together nine other colleges in the rest of the state in 1948 to expand the program. (*The Span Report* and documentation from Center for American History, U. of Texas, Austin)

Minnesota Regional Assembly Convenes On Carleton Campus

TIN CANS & BROOMS

'Mock' NSA Congress Held at Saint Teresa

With tin cans and broom sticks, St. Teresa College, Winona, Minn., has explained NSA to every student on its campus.

A mock NSA Congress with more than 500 students being the delegates was held as a regular compulsory convocation.

• • •

VIRTUALLY EVERY student in the school attended.

The Congress lasted 45 minutes, but students considered resolutions in all phases of NSA activity.

Here are some of the resolutions they approved:

NSA News 11/49

The College of St. Teresa was founded in 1894 by the Sisters of St. Francis of the Congregation of Our Lady of Lourdes, and was closed in 1989. 1948 enrollment: 621.

See p. 937 for Carleton note.

Eighty Students Represent Eleven Colleges At Three-Day Convention

By Anne Crozier

WILLIAM DENTZER, national president of the United States National Student Association, will speak tomorrow afternoon at the final plenary session of the Minnesota Regional NSA assembly which is now being held at Carleton.

Eighty people are attending the three-day assembly. Gustavus Adolphus' delegation of 18 members is the largest at the convention; the colleges of St. John's and St. Thomas have sent 12 and 7 delegates, respectively. Other schools that will be represented are Macalester, Hamline, Concordia, Augsburg and the colleges of St. Catherine, St. Benedict, St. Theresa and St. Olaf.

Carletonian 12/1/51

MINNESOTA REGIONAL MEMBERSHIP remained steady at 13 of the 32 four-year colleges in the state. The region sponsored regular intercollegiate cultural events. St. Teresa produced NSA's literary magazine, *Essai*, in 1949-50 (see Cashen, p. 362). U. of M"s Phil DesMarais (l. above) was an early leader (see p. 738).

"Among them we can be sure will be found the Catholic leaders of tomorrow"

Rev. Vincent J. Flynn: Adviser to Catholic College Student Leaders

President, College of St. Thomas, St. Paul, MN. NSA National Advisory Council, 1947–53

Editor's Note: Vincent J. Flynn was National Chaplain of the National Federation of Catholic College Students (NFCCS) from 1948 to 1950 and was recommended as an NSA Advisory Committee member by Phil DesMarais (p. 738), Chair of the Joint Committee for Student Action (JCSA). He took a keen interest in Catholic student participation in student organization affairs.

"There is something of a row . . ."

Editor's note: On April 21, 1948, Rev. Flynn wrote to Professor Helen C. White at the University of Wisconsin, who had also joined the NSA Advisory Committee, asking her opinion about NSA and voicing some concerns about "leftist" influence, which had a great deal to do with the decision by the Church to encourage Catholic colleges to join the NSA (see John Courtney Murray, "Operation University," p. 743). Professor White's reply appears on p. 933. Rev. Flynn's query is reproduced below:

I should also be very happy if you would tell me what you think of the National Students Association. Last January I received a communication from that organization, asking me if I would be one of the adult advisors. So far as I know, you are the only other Catholic on the Board. I have been strongly in favor of our youngsters getting into the organization, but I have met some opposition on the ground that the constitution and bill of rights made membership on our part rather questionable. Besides I have been told that the New York area organization is definitely under leftist control. I know, of course, that in the Midwest it is under perfectly respectable auspices. In Catholic circles, there is something of a row going on as to whether we should go on with participating in the organization, or whether we should withdraw in high disdain. My opinion, at the moment, is that we should continue to work with the youngsters until we find a very good reason not to. I should be very happy for your comments.

Sincerely yours,

(Very Rev.) Vincent J. Flynn

AT THE 2nd NATIONAL STUDENT CONGRESS, 1949. Father Flynn, shown here with 1948-48 NSA President, Ted Harris (LaSalle College), addressed a plenary session at the U. of Illinois. He was also keynote speaker at the 4th Congress in 1951 at the U. of Minnesota.

NSA Staff photo (Schwartz)

Freedom to Study the Truth

(Excerpted from an extensive address to the XXII International Student Service Annual Conference, 1949)

I believe that academic freedom means freedon to study the truth and to proclaim it without any interference from anybody, Church or State, army, navy or air force; truth is the object of the scientist's search and no ecclesiastical organization, no political organization, has a right to interfere with that search. Now academic freedom on the other hand must not be confused with academic license. If you commit a young person to the hands of another for the training of his mind, you expect that teacher to have a sense of responsibility. You expect him not to palm off his theories as facts. You expect him to keep within the limits of truth. You do not have absolute freedom in the political sphere or in any other sphere of life. My freedom must be bounded by the rights of others. . . .

I have been opposed to unnecessary investigations of loyalty on college campuses by ill-informed and ill-advised hysterical persons, simply because I do not wish this precious prerogative of the academic profession interfered with. . . . For the very same reason I have been opposed to federal aid to education of any kind, any more, I should say, than is being given at present. I am opposed to federal aid to education either public or private because I believe that such aid carries with it the danger of federal control. . . .

REV. VINCENT JOSEPH FLYNN (1901-1956)

Born at Avoca, Minn., Father Flynn was graduated from St. Thomas Academy and received his B.A. from St. Thomas College. He was ordained a priest in 1927, when he joined the faculty of St. Thomas after preparation at St. Paul Seminary and Catholic University.

He received an M.A. from the University of Minnesota in 1929 and his Ph.D. in English from the University of Chicago in 1939. In 1944 he was installed as President of the College of St. Thomas and St. Thomas Military Academy.

Active in many organizations, he was regional chairman of the National Conference of Christians and Jews at the time of his death.

He was director of the Minnesota United Nations Association, He was president of the Association of American Colleges in 1950 and national chaplain of the National Federation of Catholic College Students (1948-50).

Father Flynn died of a heart attack July 6, 1956. Samuel Scheiner, in behalf of the Jewish Community, wrote on 7/18/56 in the *Minneapois Star,* that he "never turned a deaf ear to any cause which would make his community, state and nation a better place in which to live."
(Adapted with excerpts from the *Minneapolis Tribune* obituary, 7/8/56)

CREDITS: *Eyebrow quote:* "President's Corner," welcoming 8th Congress of the NFCCS, *The Aquin* 8/26/51. *Documents and top photo* (c.1950s): courtesy Special Collections, O'Shaignessy-Frey Library Center, University of St. Thomas.

4. Mundelein College, Chicago, and the Illinois Region

Mary Kay Perkins
Mundelein and Rosary Colleges, Illinois
NSA National Office Staff, 1949-50

In 1947 the reason I went to Mundelein was the fact that at that time my parents knew that I wanted to enter a religious community and they were very much opposed. In fact, I wanted to enter right out of high school and they said no. They wanted me to know another community of Sisters—the Sisters that my mother had had in high school. The same ones who ran Mundelein—The Sisters of the Blessed Virgin Mary (BVM's).

Going to Mundelein turned out to be the healthiest thing that ever happened to me, although it was very difficult to get there. It took me almost two hours each way, because I lived far west and I had to take the elevated train all the way to downtown, transfer, take it to 6300 North, get off at Mundelein and walk five to six blocks.

It was a gorgeous location—right on Lake Michigan, which also meant that in the wintertime the last two blocks walking to Mundelein was like walking into a hail storm made out of straight pins. It was so cold.

The buildings are still there, but Mundelein has been absorbed by Loyola University, which is right next door, and Mundelein no longer exists. But it was a wonderful school. It did a great deal for people of moderate means. Mundelein was a little bit to women what De Paul University was to men. It tried to provide for those people who couldn't afford to go away from home.

De Paul was twenty to thirty blocks almost straight south of Mundelein and was also an Urban day-hop. And, pretty much, Loyola was, too. Loyola has become co-ed, so the old Mundelein building is being used for education.

The Debating Union in Chicago

There are many, many highly educated women in Chicago who came out of Mundelein. At the college, they were much encouraged to participate in a great deal of extracurricular activity. For instance, they had a debate team. Debating was very active in Chicago. On an intercollegiate level, close to ten Chicago colleges took part, including the University of Chicago, University of Illinois, De Paul, Loyola, Lewis, Saint Xavier's, and Mundelein. And that's how I really got to know Bill Birenbaum—because he was the University of Chicago debate coach.[1]

So I joined the debate team—in fact, I would say the vast majority of the people active in NSA came out of the debate team. I'm very proud of that.[2] Mundelein also became a chapter of Delta Sigma Rho, which was the big national debating fraternity. And that was a big event, because it was national recognition of our program. I can still remember the topics for both years I was there. One was "Federal World Government," and the other was "Aid to Education." "Federal World Government" was a widely debated topic at the time.

We had a very active chapter. The Sister who directed it was quite elderly—she had taught my mother English in high school. Sister Mary of the Cross—and she was a tiny little powerhouse, and I'm probably older now than she was then, but I so much remember her dynamism in spite of her age.

If you were interested, you could have a debate every Friday night. It was as if there were a basketball game and if you wanted to play in it you were invited in. You could have a debate if you wanted to participate. And then there were, I guess you'd call them regional debates, conferences that you would go away to. I remember going up to some in Madison.

Chicago, Mundelein Meet; Debate Labor Problems

Chicago's debate team met members of the Mundelein college squad in the first scheduled debate of the year last Tuesday night to consider the question, "Should Labor have a direct share in management of industry." The debates were not judged.

William Birenbaum and Lowden Wingo, judged by Forum director Huber: Wax as one of the University's top teams, took the negative position versus Marion King and Mary Lou Hafner of Mundelein.

Outlining the successful "multiple-management" plan which is comprised of two control boards, one management and the other labor representatives, the affirm-

FUTURE NSA DELEGATES Birenbaum (Chicago) and Hafner (Mundelein) debated each other in 1946. *(Maroon* 11/22/46*)*

NSA at Mundelein

When I entered Mundelein as a freshman, the 1946 Chicago Conference had already been held and the 1947 constitutional convention in Madison was just completed.[3] Mundelein had taken part in the formation of the Illinois Region, and at the time I arrived there was a student council at Mundelein—it was a going concern.

I got involved in NSA activities through the debating team. When you weren't talking about your debating topics they would talk about this committee that was going to be formed as a part of the National Student Association. Mundelein had an NSA committee, which reported to the student government. There was no great competition for the NSA delegation. Those who were very active were chosen by the student government, and it was almost a foregone conclusion it would be those who were willing to give the time and who were interested in it. I met Helen Jean Rogers through the committee in my freshman year of 1947–1948. She was an active leader in support of NSA at Mundelein. Helen Jean was later Cultural Chairman for the region and elected national secretary-treasurer for the year 1948-1949.

The Illinois Region was pretty much the Chicago Region—although when Mary Jo Domino became chairperson in 1948-1949 she was from Rockford, straight to the West, and she was definitely not from Chicago. But still, Mary Jo was the one elected and it was because of her effective leadership and commitment.[4]

Outside of Chicago, probably the only two good-sized colleges in NSA would have been the University of Illinois, Champaign-Urbana and Rockford College.[5] There might have been a few others, but not many.[6]

My first connection with NSA as an activity was in 1948-49 either through the symphony forum or the art exhibit—both of which I was active in.

The Symphony Forum and National Art Exhibit

Among the things I worked on was providing symphony tickets through the Symphony Forum.[7] Ted Perry was very supportive of that during his term of office in 1949–1950. I recall going down and meeting with a group of people and the director of the symphony. I'll never forget the exciting opening night. We had the center box.

The intention of Symphony Forum was to allow people of very modest means to do something which was really part of education in the broader sense of not just studying, but cultural things as well.

There was also a program of discussion or orientation that usually was arranged around the concert. Sometimes you actually got to meet the conductor and some of the individual artists, which was really a very exciting part of it. Discounted tickets were offered. And then the discussions usually were in the hall where the concert was going to take place, right before the concert.

Chicago had a wonderful symphony and had some marvelous conductors—Rafael Kubelik, for example. One of the selections—I don't remember the name of it—was by a Hungarian composer, and it was very modern, and difficult to listen to. But it was wonderful and was being introduced as something new. Education doesn't always mean going with the familiar. Sometimes it opens a new door for you—and Symphony Forum opened some of those doors.

I also became national cochairman of the traveling art exhibit and that really took up as much time as I had left. It was my primary activity. The other Mundelein person I worked with was Lucille Crews. We undertook to organize the routing it would take, to be certain that all the art started off in the right kind of packing cases, so that the students' art work would be protected, and that it went to the right places. The actual network of contributing art students was handled by the NSA national office.

The 1949 National Student Congress opens a new door

I remember the Urbana Congress being incredibly well run, and the excitement of meeting with so many very different people from different parts of the country. There's nobody so provincial as somebody who is brought up in a big city. (When I taught in Chicago, there were kids who had never been downtown. "Why, what's downtown? I can go out to the shopping mall, I don't need to go downtown.") So I went to all kinds of subcommittee meetings, impressed by meeting people like Ben Jones from the University of North Carolina, and Char Allen and Phil Stoddard of the University of Illinois, who helped organize the convention. I was very impressed by Phil because his dad was the president at the University. What struck me most then was meeting people who thought very differently, but were interested in many of the same things that I was interested in.

I recall being incredibly busy, and it just seemed that you hardly got any sleep. If you weren't at a committee meeting or at a big plenary meeting you were off sharing ideas with other delegates. Also, it was the first and only time I ever remember going out to a strip joint. I don't remember who the fellow was, but he took me there. So that, too, was part of my education.

I got so involved because I thought NSA was doing such great things, and I wanted to do more. Along with others of us from Mundelein, we had already traveled up to Madison several times to help out with office projects and mailings—recruited by Helen Jean Rogers the year she was on staff. So it really captured my fancy enough at Urbana to decide to go to Madison and work on staff in 1949-50.

This caused a great uproar in my family—not in opposition to NSA, but to my taking a year off. My parents had this horrendous fear that if I stopped college I wouldn't go back. For me it was totally just taking a break for one year—I liked studying too much. But my education was also very important to my father. The only two times I ever remember my father crying was when his mother died and when I told him that I was going to quit school for a year to work for NSA.

Prejudice, diversity, and affinities

During the year I was on staff, NSA had its executive committee meeting in December 1949, at the University of Chicago. That was the first time I'd ever really experienced prejudice firsthand. A group of about ten of us went out to dinner near the campus and we were refused entrance to a restaurant because Ted Perry—an African American from Temple University who was NSA vice president for student life—was with us. Of all the places, the University of Chicago had such an international atmosphere, I couldn't believe it. I thought, that's horrible. I was up there talking to the man at the door and hearing him say, "We have no tables." I said, "What about all those empty tables?" He said, "They're all reserved." I just couldn't believe what I was hearing. It was like the difference between reading about something and being there—like when we went to Europe. You can see movies of the bombed-out buildings, but to see a real bombed-out building nearby is a completely different experience.[8]

NSA, in the best sense of the word, confronted me with diversity. Different religions, different kinds of schools, different finances, different races, which had not been within my experience. I remember when I was in high school, we took a trip to Washington and went on the boat trip down to Mt. Vernon. And there was this sign, "Black and White," and I thought that was the name of the company! I didn't realize that that was the Black waiting room and this was the white waiting room. I just had no idea of what that meant. And that was just what NSA gave me on a more personal experience of reality—you might be in a discussion group with very, very different people, people who were Orientals, people who were Black, people who were from New York City even! I didn't know anybody from New York City. I'd only been through there as a kid.

It was just a wonderfully healthy part of my growing up. It's one thing to read about people in books and it's something else to know that you sat down and shared with someone your ideas, and hopes, or stuff that you were angry about, or things that weren't working well, or things that really needed to be changed. It was a wonderful awakening.

There were a number of Catholic girls who were active in the Chicago area in the Illinois region—all having experiences similar to mine. But I don't remember particularly banding together because of our religion. It was more based on the kind of ideas we shared. Although Mary Jo Domino was Catholic, it was that I liked what she had to say and the way she said it, and that her leadership was worthy because of who she was. And I think of some of the others from other regions whom I met—Tesse Hartigan of Fontbonne College in Missouri and Gloria Abiouness of Dunbarton College in [Washington,] D.C. I didn't listen to them more because of where they were from, but because of who they were and what they had to say.

Elsewhere in this Anthology I've written about my trip to Germany and my experience as a student in Catholic schools. Bringing it all together, I would not be who I am were it not for what NSA added to my life.

Mary Kay Perkins, O.P., is Superintendent of Schools, Vicar for the Religious and Director of Adult Faith Development for the Diocese of Baker in Central and Eastern Oregon.

END NOTES

[1] See Birenbaum, p. 579. *Editor's note:* Henry Halsted in a 9/14/98 letter to the Anthology editor writes, "I was struck, but not surprised by the extent to which NSA student leaders stressed the role and importance of their college debating experience in preparing them for their leadership roles in NSA domestically as well as internationally. This led me to recall my own participation in debating at Williams, as president of the debating club, as a member of the national forensic society Delta Sigma Rho, and in 1948 hosting at Williams the Oxford debating team that included Sir Edward Boyle, later Secretary of Education in the UK, and the Honorable Anthony Wedgwood Benn, who later won fame giving up his title in order to run for Parliament in the Labour Party. The subject of that debate was 'The Nationalization of Basic Industries.' Needless to say Oxford won. The most important debate tournament for us that year, one in which more than thirty colleges and universities participated, was held at the University of Vermont. You won't be surprised that the topic was 'Resolved That a Federal World Government Should Be Established.'"

[2] See Tom Garrity and Bob Kelly, at St. Peter's College, p. 892, and Milton Dobkin at USC, p. 1029.

[3] The 1946 Mundelein delegate was Rita Stalzer. The observers were Regina Bess and Ethel Degnan. The delegates to the Constitutional Convention were Dorothy Ganghan, Mary Lou Hafner, and Helen Jean Rogers.

[4] Paul F. Kirk of De Paul University was 1947 Regional chairman for the National Continuations Committee. Subsequent chairs were Sam Golden, University of Chicago, 1947-1948; Mary Jo Domino, Rockford College, 1948-1949; Merrill A. Freed, University of Chicago, 1949-1950 and 1950-1951; Manfred Brust, University of Illinois, 1951-1952.

[5] Rockford College also provided national leadership when Janis Tremper (Dowd) was elected national NSA secretary for the year 1947-1948.

[6] The region had twenty-seven members and observers coming out of the Constitutional Convention. They were: Augustana College, Aurora College, Barat College of the Sacred Heart, Bradley University, Chicago Medical School, Chicago Teachers College, College of St. Francis, De Paul University, Evansville College, George Williams College, Illinois Institute of Technology, Illinois State College, John R. Knox College, Le Clerc College, Loyola University, Mundelein College, National College of Education, North Park College, Northwestern University, Rockford College,

Roosevelt College, Rosary College, St. Xavier College, University of Chicago, University of Illinois, University of Illinois Medical School, Wright Junior College. In addition, 20 colleges attended the First Congress in 1948; 25 in 1949; 18 in 1950; and 9 in 1951.

[7] See Medalie, p. 352.

[8] I learned this when NSA sent me to Germany in the summer of 1951. See p. 603.

MARY KAY PERKINS

Early Background: Born 1930 in Chicago. Attended Trinity High School in Lake Forest.

Education: 1947-49, Mundelein College; 1950-52, Rosary College, B.A. in French. Summer 1951, NSA representative to Institute on "The Democratization of the German University Student," Munich, Germany; 1964, Western Reserve University, Master's in Romance Languages; 1982-83, Sabbatical studying in Iowa and Texas.

Career highlights: 1953-54, entered the religious community of the Sinsinawa Dominicans, of which I am still a member; 1954-82, taught High School French in Washington, D.C.; Chicago; Greenwich, Conn.; Dubuque, Iowa; and Madison, Wisc.; 1983-89, Chief Administrator, Dominican Mother House, Sinsinawa, Wisconsin; 1989-90, work change sabbatical; 1990-93, Diocesan Director of RENEW for the Diocese of Baker in Central and Eastern, Oregon; 1993 to present, Diocesan Director of Adult Faith Development for the Diocese of Baker. Also, Vicar for Religious, and in 1996, Superintendent of Schools.

PICTURE CREDITS: *Then:* C. 1949-50 (SHSW). *Now:* c. 1998 (Author).

Loyola University and Mundelein College

Editor's note: Close neighbors on the north shore of Chicago, Mundelein (women's) and Loyola (men's) colleges provided an intercollegiate social as well as academic exchange. Located in the host city for the Chicago Student Conference at the University of Chicago in December, 1946 (Pt. 1, Sec. 3), student leaders at both colleges took an active interest in the organization from the start. Coverage of NSA in their student newspapers voiced shared Catholic college concerns over NSA's falling under Communist influence and becoming involved in political affairs.

Mundelein "can solve the problem"

10/6/47

Open Letter to the Student Body

The time for action is here. We have presented to you our report on the National Student Association as a possible and positive means for Catholic Action.

Now you must decide and vote on whether or not Mundelein will affiliate with NSA. We are sincerely convinced that the advantages of such affiliation far surpass the POTENTIAL disadvantages.

However, we would like to weigh on an intellectual basis the valid objections against affiliation, among which are:

1. The possibility of the small school losing its identity through the preponderance of larger, more powerful units.
2. The trend of the same larger units toward student domination of campus authority.
3. The danger of the infiltration of political pressure groups into the organization.
4. The association of NSA with the International Union of Students, an organization having political complexion.

We believe that member schools of Mundelein's type can solve the problem satisfactorily.

Your NSA Delegates,
Dorothy Gaughan — Mary Lou Hafner
Adele Baiocchi — Helen Jean Rogers

5/22/47

Mundelein Aids In Drafting N.S.O. Constitution

S.A.C. Elects Delegates To Wisconsin Convention

Together with students from California, Texas, and Rhode Island, delegates Dorothy Gaughan and Mary Lou Hafner will participate in the Constitutional convention of the National Student Organization, at the University of Wisconsin, Aug. 30 to Sept. 8.

The Student Activities Council elected the representatives. Alternates are Adele Baiocchi and Helen Jean Rogers.

The students will make the final decisions about the aims and activities of the NSO passed at the Chicago Conference last December. They will determine its structure, its relationships with other organizations, and the dues it will charge member student bodies. They also will elect the national and ...

THE SKYSCRAPER

12/2/46 — **December Student Congress Will Consider National Union**

10/6/47 — **Illinois Delegates Convene To Adopt NSA Constitution**

Adele Baiocchi, Dorothy Gaughan, Mary Lou Hafner, and Helen Jean ... was chairman of the International ... mittee, of which Geraldine ...

2/16/48 — **25 Students Work On NSA Program**
Attend Regional Conference At University of Illinois

10/4/48 — **Junior Delegate Elected Secretary-Treasurer of NSA**

Helen Jean Rogers ex '50, who, as a Mundelein delegate, helped to form the National Student association at Madison in 1947, was elected national secretary-treasurer of the association at the second convention, in August.

Miss Rogers, who finished her sophomore year at Mundelein in June, will devote a year away from studies to her position as a national officer.

As Cultural Commission chairman, Miss Rogers organized the Culturale for Illinois' colleges co-sponsored by NSA and Mundelein in April, and acted as chairman of the NSA Art exhibit held at the Madison convention.

11/7/49 — **President Cites Advantages of NSA Membership**

A contribution toward the establishment of a "new world order of peace security, and freedom" is, in the opinion of Sister Mary Josephine, B.V.M., President of the College, one of the benefits to be derived from the ... national activities of the National Student association.

MUNDELEIN'S PRESIDENT Sister Mary Josephine, BVM saw in NSA a contribution to a new world order of "peace, security and freedom."

3/17/52 — **NFCCS, NSA Promote Summer Tours On International Day**

Student tours will be the topic for the International Day program, March 20, sponsored by NSA with NFCCS cooperating.

HELEN JEAN ROGERS, regional Cultural Commission chairman in 1947-48, was elected 1948-49 NSA Secretary-Treasurer and became a prominent national leader (p. 599). *Mundelein college was founded in 1929 by The Sisters of Charity, BVM and was merged into Loyola U. in 1991. Enrollment in 1948: 905.*

Loyola: "the danger of indifference"

This Concerns You

This issue of the LOYOLA NEWS contains two articles on the recent Chicago Student Conference held at University of Chicago. The acts of this conference, and the national student organization that will grow out of it, are matters affecting every man in Loyola University. Whether their final effect will be for good or ill depends on the interest and attention paid them by every student in the United States. It was due to the apathy of the students in free democracies the world over that the communists were able to seize control of the International Union of Students formed at Prague last summer. There will certainly be an effort to repeat that **coup de etat** in this country. Whether they will succeed or fail, whether the prospective association of college and university students will be another "front" organization on the lines of the late and little lamented American Youth Congress, will be determined by the attitude of the general-American student body.

Thus far the preparations are promising and therefore we are in danger of falling back into indifference and leaving the field to the enemy. Let's not.

THE LOYOLA NEWS

10/2/47 — **LEFT WINGERS TRY TO WRECK USNSA MEET**

Negro, Southern White Agree to Outlaw Race Prejudice

4/15/48 — **RALPH DUNGAN GUEST SPEAKER FOR JCSA MEET**

NSA Vice-Pres. Warns of Split of East and West

At the April 5th meeting of the Joint Committee on Student Action, Mr. Ralph Dungan, active vice-president of the National Student Association, spoke on "Our Challenge in the Coming NSA Convention."

1/16/47 — ***Loyola Sends Members To Student Conference***

10/7/48 — ***Madison Meeting Shows Big Future for NSA***

9/29/49 — ***U.S. Student Organizations Move To Cut Off Commies***

United States students have set up their conditi...

9/29/49 — **NSA Congress In Dither Over NSA-IUS Cooperation**

Let's Have No More Of This 'Liberal' Nonsense

Again this week The News is carrying in its "Letters to the Editor" column a letter in defense of Vincent Giese, whose "Declaration" (Concord, November) we slammed as immature and unreal (Dec. 1). The writer of this letter reiterates the general thesis: university administrative forces (including Loyola's) are anti-democratically disregarding and violating "student rights."

Among these student rights our extra-liberal friends imply—and sometimes actually declare—the right to publish without censorship, the right to represent their university in national and international student organizations without any check by the university administration, the right to decide what teachers will be employed by the school, and the right to share in the disciplinary powers of the administration. "Rules and regulations out the window! This is a democracy" is their valiant battle cry against the insidious monster, the administration!

The Tenth Muse 2/23/50

"Rights" Get The Works

By Ted Rickard

It was my very good luck to listen in the other day to a conversation concerning "student rights." The topic was being discussed by the Union external relations committee in the form of a synopsis of the main points in all proposed "Student Bills of Rights." There were about 12 rights and four or five responsibilities mentioned in this brief. I haven't had such a hearty laugh in a very long time.

After a vice-president of the National Student association reassured me that the NSA was not contemplating an investigation of Loyola for violations of student rights and ...

On the surface, these look little like a couple things th...

SKEPTICAL ABOUT THE NSA STUDENT BILL OF RIGHTS, *Loyola News* wrote in its 1/19/50 editorial that proponents "show their lack of judgement by supposing that a university can be run effectively and prudently in a democratic fashion, students and faculty acting, as it were, on a par. The very nature of a university is against this. . . ." In 1947, the paper headlined "a big future for NSA." Brian Buckley was regional co-Chair then. Loyola remained active until it dropped out of NSA in 1951-52.

Loyola U. was founded in 1870 by the Society of Jesus (Jesuits). Enrollment in 1949 was 7,934.

The early years and later insights of an Irish-American girl

Bred in Chicago to Be a "Small You-Know-What" Activist

Mary Kay Perkins
Mundelein and Rosary Colleges, Illinois
NSA National Office Staff, 1949-50

Editor's note: A small "you-know-what" in NSA days referred to one of scores of Catholic women's colleges throughout the country that belonged to the organization and brought to it a bounty of optimism and energy (see Lynch, p. 493). This is a digest from the transcript of an interview with Sister Mary Kay Perkins, O.P., held in Bend, Oregon, July 18, 1998.

One of my memories of my late grade school–early high school years is the day that my father turned thirty-nine. When a family man turned thirty-nine he was no longer draftable. I look back now and think, thirty-nine is pretty old to be taking somebody who is the father of a family, but until that birthday, he lived under the shadow of the draft.

I enjoyed being an only child until I was eight. I was talking to adults most of the time. And then the day before my eighth birthday, my sister Peg was born. My brother Tom was born when I was twelve, sister Pat was born when I was fourteen, and brother Mike was born when I was eighteen.

Coping during the Depression

My mother was a liberated woman long before it was fashionable. She went back to work when I was about 18 months old, which women didn't do for the most part during the mid-1930s. My mother taught school in the Chicago public school system. My dad started off as an accountant in a brokerage firm.

My folks were married in April of 1929. The crash was in November, and Mary Kay was born in January. When my mother was much older and in the nursing home, I remember her saying, "And Mary, we just weren't ready." I was so hurt at the time, and yet I think now, for what are you less prepared than parenthood—even in the best of times? But to then have the whole economic system fall to pieces right when you were just beginning and when you had just about nothing to start with!

As the 1930s went on, my dad had a choice of working three weeks and taking a week off or working the four weeks but still getting only paid for three, and he worked because he wouldn't have known what to do. He stayed with that company almost all his life. He became an account executive and then he became the manager. He was in the Chicago office, then in the Oak Park office, and then, in the late 1960s he was transferred to Florida.

Starting a new life in the sixties

They had been down there for several years when he got a phone call saying, "George, don't bother coming back, we've gone bankrupt." They were stockbrokers. It was at a time when many stockbrokerage firms went belly up. He had worked for them from 1928 to 1970 and he lost his job, his pension, and his life insurance—after forty-two years of loyalty to a company that was not a huge company, with a few branch offices, and who you really thought of as personal family friends. It was just devastating.

Even though my dad was older, my youngest brother Michael was still in college and he still had big bills coming in. So, in his mid-sixties he went the rounds of brokerage firms in Florida, and he finally got into a company that liked the maturity and experience he had. And he had five or six absolutely wonderful years.

The family attitude toward education

My parents were Irish-Americans. Both of their parents were pretty poor. Three of my four grandparents were born in Ireland, so they were recently come. As is very typical of Irish-Americans, the most important thing other then their faith was their education. If my mother were alive now she'd be about ninety-one, and she had a college education. There aren't a lot of women of that age who had a college education. She loved education. Both of my parents were readers, and as a consequence we're all readers, and we're all active in promoting local libraries.

There was no issue that the guys go to college and the girls would get married. We all definitely agreed that you could do whatever you wanted to do. My brothers had to do the dishes as well as the sisters, and my brothers had to learn to cook as well as the girls. And everybody was going to college. And we all went to different colleges. Some went to private schools and some went to state schools.

Going to school on the West Side of Chicago

I grew up on the West Side of Chicago, and it was typical at that time that when people moved, everybody moved on the first of May. A lot of people who rented moved, so we lived at several places, consistently moving further west. My neighborhood was fairly homogeneously Irish-American. It was very middle class. There were no Blacks and no Asians. Nearby there were lots of Germans, lots of Italians, Polish—Western Europeans primarily.

I have lots of early memories of school and other things. Yet, you hear the stories so often you wonder if you remember the event or you've heard the story told so much. The first story I remember about myself is that I went to kindergarten for a couple of days and then I refused to go back. I lived across the street and I could see the kindergarten. I just didn't like it and I didn't go. Then I got into first grade and went to Catholic schools—four years to Saint Thomas Acquinas, and then, when we moved, I went four years to Saint Catherine of Sienna. Those early grades were coeducational, except in the eighth grade when they separated us.

Just before I started high school, we moved out of Chicago, into Oak Park, which is the first suburb west. About half of us who lived in Chicago went to Sienna High School, and the rest of us who lived in Oak Park went to Trinity High School.

I went to high school in 1943 to 1947. They were interesting years for me. The high school that I went to—Trinity in River Forest—was a good school from which just about everybody would go on to college. While I was in school there still weren't lots of choices for women. Lots of women still went into teaching. Since I loved education, and I loved to study, and I loved to read, school was fun for me.

I had had the Sisters of Mercy all through grade school, and I always felt they were really good teachers because I felt very well prepared for high school. The Sisters at Trinity in River Forest were a different kind than I had had before. They were Dominicans, and that's the group that I eventually entered.

The influence of extraordinary teachers

These Sisters changed my life because they challenged me to be more then I thought I could be. They created projects or experiences that were above and beyond. I got into translating some actual letters from French and then we translated a whole book. They were very dynamic people, but it was not only the education approach, it was the way they dealt with people. It was the way they had expectations of people, the way they believed in me and my friends, which made me really think that, yes, this would be something I'd like to do. I was also active socially. I dated, I went to proms. I never did get totally devoted to one person, but I would go out with a fellow maybe for six months, so that I had a variety of experiences.

One of the tough things about Trinity for me was that it was a pretty wealthy place and I wasn't. There were some rough economic times while I was there. Of course, we were much better off as we got into the 1940s than we had been in the 1930s.

I had an excellent language teacher, Sister Gregoire. She probably was the most significant influence on my life. My friends and I all had her in our sophomore year for English and we decided we didn't ever want to work that hard again in our whole lives. So we all decided to take Spanish because she taught French. Guess who taught Spanish that year? The same one. But she was the one who really became a great influence in my life. When I went on to college, my first two years were at Mundelein, and my last two years, after returning from the year off I took working at the NSA national office, were at Rosary College. She had moved to Rosary, so I had her for English and Spanish in high school, and then when I got to college I had her for French.

It was pretty much almost taken for granted that you would continue your education in those days. It was so on the part of the parents— the poor as well as the rich—and it was certainly so on the part of the faculty.

Working and belonging to a union while in high school

One thing that made me feel out of it a little bit at school was that as soon as I was sixteen, I started to work. I worked for the telephone company because about the only jobs that were easily available were with the telephone company or in department store sales. Since there was no way I could tell someone something looked attractive on them if I felt they looked awful in it, the telephone company was the clear choice.

It was a good place to work and was one of the few places that paid well enough. It was the first time I ran into one-parent families run by women. If a woman was divorced, or her husband was dead and she still had children, they paid a decent enough wage.

Basically I worked twenty hours a week as a switchboard operator. We still had the old cable plug-in system. And I remember when the whole board would light up. It was incredible. You just knew when something really big was happening—like the death of President Roosevelt or the end of the war—because everybody picked up their phone and the little lights went on.

As a consequence then, I wasn't free to participate in some school activities that I would have liked to. One of the hardest times I recall was when I had to work on Christmas (you would work two of the three big holidays: Thanksgiving, Christmas, and New Year's). I remember this one time because it snowed so terribly hard and I had to walk all the way from home over to the telephone company.

It was also my first experience belonging to a Union and having to picket during a strike. Because we were in the middle of a strike when I was a senior, I had to get permission from my shop steward not to picket in order to take my senior class trip.

Reflections on a teaching career and a 1970s bombing

I've recounted some of my recollections of my college years, NSA and the German Project elsewhere in this anthology. Were it not for those college and NSA years I would not be the person I am today.

After graduation I entered the order and taught high school for thirty years in Washington, D.C.; Chicago; Greenwich, Connecticut; Dubuque, Iowa; and Madison, Wisconsin. I taught French and Spanish primarily. I also taught economics and English in the earlier days. I am now in a community called the Sinsinawa Dominicans.

Because of the experiences I had, I think I'm a better teacher. I was able to open kids up to the fact that there is a life out there beyond us. And I think that that's very good.

If you draw a comparison between students closer to today (I've been a school administrator and out of teaching since 1983) as compared to students after the war during the time I was a high school student, I think we were more globally interested.

It was very interesting to teach in Madison at the time of Vietnam. I was very aware of student unrest. At the end of one school day we had an emergency faculty meeting to discuss what we were to do with our students if we were invaded by university students. The answer, essentially: stay in your room. That's all we could do.

They were protesting a lot in those years. I remember the bombing at the University of Wisconsin in the physics building.

I was awakened by that bomb. We were maybe a mile from it, but I could feel the concussion of that bomb in my bedroom. The two Armstrong brothers and another never found were thought to be responsible. A physicist who was working late, who had a wife and child, was killed.

Attitudes toward authority and discipline

When we started NSA we took authority into account by creating an advisory board and it was really important to us to be connected to them. We had as an objective to be connected to the Establishment so that we'd have a voice there, because otherwise we felt we would not have been heard.

Today, I look at authority as it would be reflected in my own classroom, and I see that it is almost totally based on my relationship to the students. I had lots of trouble with authority many times in my own life. I remember reading an article once that had an interesting distinction made. It said, "There are people who have authority and there are people who are authority. And the people who are authority have no trouble in sharing it, and the people who have authority hang onto it very tightly."

I really think that if you can participate in authority, you're much more likely to have kids buy into it. And I really felt that I never had difficulty with it within my own classroom. I always had a level of authority, but it was based on my sharing it with the students. In seeking their input I was tough, but I listened to them. My feeling is that you have to earn it as a person. And I think an institution has to also. I don't believe you can just impose it. Whereas in the past an institution could get away with just imposing it.

A commitment to social justice

Within this Diocese where I now work as school superintendent, we have three Indian reservations—but the Indians aren't where the schools are. Once a year we have a big event that I run for the adult faith program in Central and Eastern Oregon. It is an event called the Festival of Faith. It's on a Friday night, Saturday, and Sunday. It's my feeling that I have a really strong obligation to present some issues of social justice, such as those affecting the Indians.

Most recently, at this writing, I had a workshop opposing the School of the Americas. It's just entitled, "The School of the Americas, Question of Social Justice." The School of the Americas is the place where we train the armies of all the South American countries and teach them—in effect—how to torture one another. Now, that's a very one-sided reaction, but it's something I think we need to be informed about and to question.

There are some very, very conservative folks here in Eastern Oregon—there's a real isolationist streak, a very different way of looking at things—and there is great opposition to ecological progress. So, I've also had a workshop on the environment. The Bishops of this area wrote a pastoral letter on the use of the Columbia River Basin, and that's what I had the workshop on. Just to inform people. I feel that you can't let them go on in selective ignorance.

There were also primarily spiritual workshops at this event. There were workshops on Scripture. Our keynote speaker was one of our own Sisters who teaches at Catholic University, Sister Kate Dooley.

Women in the Church

The "O.P." that follows my name means Order of Preachers. The letters identify the Dominicans, and the O.P. is something that gives me great grief simply because the church says the women may not preach. So I'm a member of the Order of Preachers and women are not allowed to preach. And I always say, would you tell the Sisters of Charity they couldn't be charitable?

I am also among the women in the Church who would like to see women ordained. I would not care to be one of them myself because you'd have to be extraordinarily courageous, just like those first Episcopal women who went through very tough times. But I have really heard little girls say at the convent—this is before they could even be altar servers—"Why can't I be? My brother can be, why can't I be?"

I think if you're a member of the Church, you're a member of the Church. I remember saying to the Bishop I worked for at one time, "I sincerely believe that at some point and time when the need is great enough, they're going to find a reason to change their mind and do it." And he said, "Well, I don't think that's going to happen." I said, "Well, I do." And that's okay, we can disagree.

Chicago and NSA to the high desert in Oregon

Being here in Eastern Oregon is quite a contrast, coming out of Chicago as I do. Most of my friends can't believe I've stayed here. But I like it. It is an interesting road to have traveled from Madison, Wisconsin, and NSA to this least populous Catholic diocese in the United States.

I would be a different person if I hadn't been a part of NSA and NSA hadn't been a part of me. I could have been a much more isolated person. As it is, even at this great distance from my beginnings, I remain fully engaged.

The Illinois Region

Editor's note: The region was anchored by the U. of Illinois in Urbana and the U. of Chicago, Roosevelt and Mundelein Colleges, and the cluster of Chicago area members. It was home to some of NSA's most memorable leaders: U. of Chicago: Bill Birenbaum (p. 581), Merrill Freed, Frank Logan, Alexander Pope (p. 390); U. of Illinois: Bill Allaway (p. 613), Phil Stoddard (p. 655), Charlotte Allen (Charters) (p. 658); Rockford College: Janis Tremper (Dowd) (p.60), Mary Jo Domino (Pritz); Mundelein College: Helen Jean Rogers (Secondari) (p. 599), Mary Kay Perkins (p. 943).

MARY JO DOMINO (Rockford College), leaving 4/49 NEC meeting, led the region in its turbulent 48-49 and 49-50 years. (Photo: Schwartz)

Fighting off the "Red Scare"

The Big Witch Hunt

Communistic Activities In Colleges Probed

Ill. Senate's Communist Witchhunt Arouses Student Protest At Chicago U.

Hutchins Testified Broyles Bills Were "Unconstitutional And Un-American"

Communist Investigation Was A Means For Getting Even With Chicago School For Rowdiness Of Students Who Booed Legislators, Correspondent Reports

ACADEMIC FREEDOM *Newsletter*

Illinois NSA votes to have freedom week

Students must help

Crimson hits McCarthy queries Pusey on hiring

Above: Illinois Region *Newsletter* 12/2/53 launched during McCarthy era. Left, from top: U. Maryland *Diamondback* 3/23/49; Washington U., St. Louis, 5/13, 5/17, 5/20/49.

DAVID BRODER, Editor in Chief of the *Chicago Maroon* (later to become a renowned national political reporter) syndicated a special series of articles on the Broyles investigations of alleged communist activities at Chicago and Roosevelt (See Pope, p. 390) which appeared in *Student Life*, Washington University (St. Louis). It made headlines throughout the college press (see U. of Md. *Diamondback* above. Similar commissions appeared in New York, California and a number of other states (see Canfield Committee, U. Wash, p. 1061, and Janet Brown's review of Academic Freedom cases and NSA on p. 381 and ff.).

Building a Program

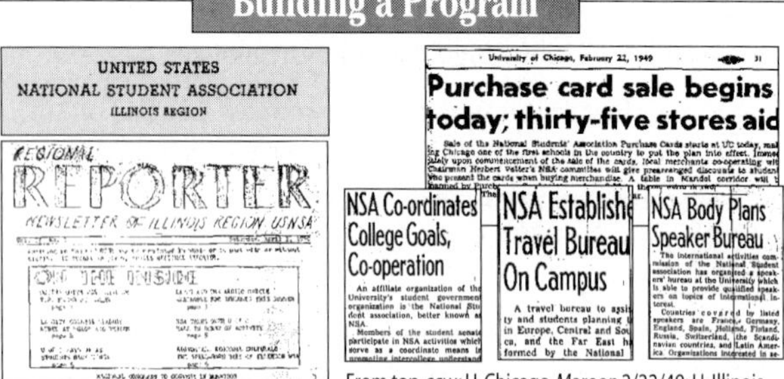

UNITED STATES NATIONAL STUDENT ASSOCIATION ILLINOIS REGION

REGIONAL REPORTER

NEWSLETTER OF ILLINOIS REGION USNSA

University of Chicago, February 22, 1949

Purchase card sale begins today; thirty-five stores aid

NSA Co-ordinates College Goals, Co-operation

NSA Establishes Travel Bureau On Campus

NSA Body Plans Speaker Bureau

From top: 1948 Lhd; 1950 Newsletter

From top, ccw: U. Chicago *Maroon* 2/22/49; U. Illinois *Daily Illini* 2/12. 3/1, 3/12/49

"IF WE HAVE ACTIVE REGIONS . . . NSA WILL NEVER DIE." In a 10/3/49 letter to Gene Schwartz, Mary Jo Domino, in her second term as Regional Chairman, expressed a belief in an imperative vision that drove its leaders around the country. Followed in 1950-51 by Merrill Freed (U. of Chicago), and in 1951-52 by Manfred Brust of the U. of Illinois, they led the region in its role as a voice for academic freedom, a channel for international student travel and exchange programs (see pp. 590, 613, 655) and a laboratory for student government clinics. It successfully hosted through Mundelein College the National Art Exhibit (pp. 369, 944)`, but failed, as did some other regions (Michigan, Nebraska) in an effort to organize a regional Culturale in 1949-50 (See p. 956), an event successfully mounted in Pennsylvania and New England (pp. 368).

For more excerpts:* Chicago Maroon, *pp. 90, 110.* Daily Illini, *p. 234. Mundelein C.* Skyscraper, *pp. 495. See Mundelein C./Loyola U. Album, p. 946.

Launching NSA

The Chicago Maroon

Austin Heads US Prague Group

DECEMBER 2, 1946 — Price 5 Cents

Many Schools Attend Student Conference To Convene At UC

"Colleges and Universities all over the country are now in the process of electing delegates to the December Chicago ..."

Friday, February 14, 1947 — THE CHICAGO MAROON

Mr. Smith Comes To Chicago

University of Chicago, February 1, 1949

Action replaces distrust as UC'ers lead NSA fight

Editorials: NSA

The opportunities the student body has of making itself known to the off-campus world are, to say the least, scarce. Principally because of its largely diversified and disparate interests, it is apt to find itself being represented to the laity often during the cource of the year by unrepresentative splinter groups rather than by a democratically elected spokesman body of the student constituency.

When this situation arises the slighted students with anguished howls protest "the damage done to our university." Yet when these people have the opportunity to choose those who will represent their university, their vitality ebbs. No all-campus election has drawn more than 1500 students to the polls. Eighty per cent of the student body does not speak when its voice would have strength.

At this time students are once again confronted with one of their few opportunities to elect a spokesman body. The elections for a National Student Association delegation on April 28 will reveal whether the UC student body is content with voicing its opinions in between elections or if it will come out to the polls and elect a slate of delegates who will represent their views before the NSA National Convention.

We believe that NSA has something material for the benefit of every student on this campus. We believe that the vast majority of students here have honest, reasoned-out opinions on the issues which will be decided on the 28th. If the student body desires to retain and to increase these benefits and to be truly represented at the convention they will vote on the 28th. They will vote for delegates who will honestly vote for issues at the NSA National Convention in accord with the directions they have received from their constituency, a group not of 1500 but of 8000.

From top: 8/2/46, 12/2/46, 2/1/47, 2/1/49. 4/22/49

FOLLOWING THE 12/46 CHICAGO STUDENT CONFERENCE, Tom Farr of the U. of Chicago was selected for the Staff Committee of four (see Dowd, p. 64) to do the first draft of the NSA Constitution and prepare for the Constitutional convention. Bill Birenbaum, later to become President of Antioch, headed the drafting committee at the convention itself (p. 583). The University provided the momentum for the launch of NSA in providing facilities for the Continuations Committee and leadership for its development. Russel Austin (p. 90) earlier headed the U.S. delegation to the 8/46 World Student Congress which called the Chicago meeting (See Pt. 1, Secs. 2 and 3).

Historical note: U. of Chicago was founded in 1890 by the American Baptist Education Society and John D. Rockefeller (www-news.uchicago.edu). 1948 enrollment: 9,519.

Maintaining Affiliation

9/15/49

THE DAILY ILLINI

National Student Association Holds 2nd Congress at UI

WGS Presidents Feel Undecided About NSA

Student Senate Opens Debate Over NSA

MIA Tables Vote To Hold Funds From NSA

Senators Urged to Remain in NSA

Phil Stoddard Charges Disinterest Cause of Failure; Group will Ask For Campus Government Study

We Need NSA, It Needs Us

From top: 1/5/50, both 1/17/50

1/12/50 1/11/50

NSA AT THE U. OF ILLINOIS enjoyed the support of university President George Stoddard (p. 656), who provided extensive facilities for NSA's Second National Student Congress in 1949. Bill Allaway (p. 613), Phil Stoddard (p. 655), Charlotte Allen (Charters) (p. 658) helped organize the convention. While U.I. maintained its membership throughout NSA's early years, it was periodically questioned as was the case in 1950 (see above). In recommending that U.I. stay in NSA (1/11/50 above) *The Daily Illini* saw the benefits of NSA in "bringing the student voice into society" and in "the exchange of ideas pertaining to student welfare . . . and between the students of this country and the students of Western Europe."

Historical note: The U. of Illinois was a Morrill Act land grant university founded in 1867 as the Illinois Industrial University (www.uiuc.edu). 1948 enrollment was sixth largest in the U.S. at 27,773.

A long way from St. Louis to A lifetime mission of service

5. The 1949 NSA Congress—And Beyond

Tesse Hartigan Donnelly
Fontbonne College, Missouri
Chair, Missouri-Kansas Region, 1949-50

On a steamy August morning in 1949 my mother and father waved their farewells from the platform at Union Station, St. Louis, as the Illinois Central carried me toward Urbana, Illinois, on my first solo journey. When I descended from that train, I found myself like Alice in another land. I was eighteen and about to begin my sophomore year at Fontbonne College, one of the hundreds of small Catholic women's colleges then dotting America's educational landscape. The student body president had appointed me the school's NSA delegate. I was undoubtedly among the least informed students then converging on Urbana.[1]

Wonderland

The people I encountered in this strange new land were different from the St. Louis types I had grown up with. The tall tanned guys from the California delegation dressed in a casual-chic fashion that suggested they were on their way to a beach barbecue. The Metropolitan New York delegation, by contrast, seemed to consist of intense sun-shunners whose Saturday-best dark trousers and white shirts—open at the neck, sleeves rolled—declared that they had absolutely no time for frivolity. There were also honey-voiced lads from the Deep South who spotted me for an innocent but failed to notice the armor with which fifteen years of Catholic schooling had suited me. Truly a girl of the times, I barely noticed the female delegates.

Pat Groom, who had been chair of the Missouri-Kansas region, left that position vacant when she became a full-time worker for the Young Christian Students (YCS). (This was a time before Pat Robertson and Ralph Reed had colonized the word "Christian.") Pat Groom knew me from my campus YCS group. She must have recommended me as her successor. Soon after arriving in Urbana, I found myself a thoroughly confused participant in late-night meetings of the National Executive Committee (NEC), which was functioning as the steering committee for the Congress.

My college had begun admitting black women as students the year I entered, but NSA afforded me my first opportunity to get to know black men. As I sat night after night at the NEC table, I grew steadily in appreciation of serious, gentle Ted Harris. His firm but patient leadership kept our meetings as nearly on course as student meetings can be. Ted Perry, like Ted Harris an African American from Pennsylvania, led my group in the Educational Affairs Commission. His extroverted, bear-hugging personality provided a contrast in styles that inoculated me against the temptation to think positive stereotyping was a desirable substitute for the negative variety. I am grateful to these two men for loosening the grip of racism on my imagination and understanding.[2]

Awakening

As, day and night, discussion followed discussion, focus on Congress issues replaced my Alice-like disorientation. Those issues and the dreams they expressed are still my issues and my dreams: a world where trust and cooperation triumph over suspicion and contention; a nation able to overcome the corrosive legacy of slavery while avoiding the politics of resentment; public schools in which quality education is the norm; schools at all levels where students are active and respected members of the learning community with rights and responsibilities that are consonant with their level of development.

While involved in the discussion process that clarified these issues, I was learning that students could aspire to the same dream while differing about both the philosophical basis establishing its legitimacy and the means for realizing it. This NSA experience taught me the fundamental importance of what Parker Palmer calls "staying at the table" with those whose philosophy and strategies disagree with yours. By "staying at the table" you can discover those steps toward the dream that all agree to take.

This lesson, clear in retrospect, emerged gradually and incompletely during the course of the 1949 Congress. During the discussions about federal aid to education, I came to the point of view that what my Roman Catholic tradition had taught me about justice required supporting federal aid even if it excluded aid to religious schools. Improving schools in poor states whose children, almost across the board, were scandalously under served outweighed in my mind the harm of denying aid to Catholic schools.

Holding this position, I found myself voting not only with those who opposed aid to Catholic schools because it violated their understanding of the separation of church and state but also with some who held Catholic educators to be the pope's puppets and "Catholic education" to be an oxymoron. On this issue, I even voted with those who held that religion was the opiate of the people and those who saw the Roman Catholic Church as the Whore of Babylon. Furthermore, I voted against many of my co-religionists, particularly those whose point of view was shaped by their experience in National Federation of Catholic College Students (NFCCS), which had a quasi-official church status.[3]

I don't want to represent myself as a brave and independent thinker. The truth is that I was part of a generation of Catholics emerging from the immigrant ghetto and awakening to political and social issues that transcended sectarian interests. The presence of a significant number of delegates from small Catholic women's colleges testified to this move of Catholics toward greater participation in secular American life. However, that presence was also the result of the conviction on the part of Catholic administrators and churchmen that Catholic students in NSA would present a Catholic point of view and would counter the putative threat of a communist takeover within the student movement.[4]

A fall from grace

The latter perspective was represented in Champaign-Urbana by the Joint Committee for Student Action (JSCA), an agency of the NFCCS and the Newman Federation. The leaders were mostly men, strongly influenced by JCSA elder statesman Phil Des Marais. They viewed the Catholic girl delegates as sorely in need of their guidance and were generously disposed to provide it to us.

I came to the attention of the JCSA because my gratuitous position as chair of the Missouri-Kansas Region suggested I might have some strategic value and serve, like Prufrock, as "one who would do to swell a progress." I was recruited to participate in an all-night caucus whose sole purpose I recall as denying the presidency to "left-wing" Gene Schwartz and securing it for Bob Kelly, reliably Catholic from a Jesuit school. (I don't remember Bob as having any part in this caucus.)

The frisson of being part of a "secret cabal" vanquished my good angel. I agreed to help with a parliamentary subterfuge that was somehow calculated to swing the election. I remember gaining the floor and delivering my lines. I remember that Bob was elected. But most painfully I recall my shame and remorse at feeling I had betrayed a process I had learned to revere.

It is common parlance to equate "loss of innocence" with one's first sexual experience. However, the etymological meaning tells us that to be innocent is "not to do harm." That day in Urbana I felt convicted by my own conscience of an action that revealed I could no longer lay claim to innocence.

From the perspective of the almost fifty years that followed, with their mistakes, missteps, and downright mischief, the qualms of that eighteen-year-old seem spectacularly overblown. Nevertheless, the experience did teach her something about the meaning and value of integrity.

Bringing NSA home

The guilt occasioned by my perceived fall from grace also contributed to the energy and determination that I brought to the challenge of organizing the Missouri region. That year NSA spearheaded a petition drive in St. Louis for a student pass on public transportation. We staged a successful regional meeting at Washington University attended by about one hundred students from the state's colleges and universities. We hosted a visit of the Austrian Goodwill Tour, finding housing and arranging a public performance by this multitalented group. This last project won me a place in the files of the Federal Bureau of Investigation. The Austrian Goodwill Tour included members of the Austrian Communist Party, which was a legal political party. It didn't take much to qualify as a subversive in those days.

Working for the region carried with it an experience of collegiality with men that was then hard to come by. I met the men of the region not as suitors, seducers, or competitors but as colleagues who did not resent my being in a position of leadership. These relationships laid a foundation for similarly rewarding collaborations later in life.

My college supported my work with NSA. Part of my tuition was paid by a work scholarship; my job was to operate the college switchboard for a few hours every week. One day, Sister Marcella, Fontbonne's president, called me to her office to tell me that she saw my duties as regional chair for NSA as service to the community that would satisfy my scholarship's requirements.

Those college administrators who sent young Catholic women to an NSA congress had in mind what their students could contribute to the student movement. I wonder if they had reckoned with everything their students might bring back to their colleges. One of the things I brought back was enthusiasm for student rights. This conceptual grandchild of the Enlightenment had been a virtual stranger at my college but received a warm welcome in the campus YCS-NSA circle.

Observe, judge, and act

The staff of our student newspaper was restive under the close control exercised by their nun-moderator. Following the YCS method of observe, judge, act, our group gathered information, formed a judgment, and finally decided that the action best calculated to achieve change was the publication of a underground newspaper laying bare this infringement of student rights.

The student who worked in an administration office and was a competent typist acted as our publisher. Another work-scholarship student, who delivered college mail, distributed *The Gusher* (our upstart rival to *The Font*, the official paper) to every faculty box. Of course, each student got a copy.

Neither the faculty nor the administration appeared amused by our clever and daring sortie in underground journalism. Though I'm sure suspension and/or expulsion crossed a few minds, the fact that the conspirators included almost every student leader had a moderating effect. We were let off with some harsh words. I seem to recall that the newspaper's staff was given a faculty advisor with a lighter touch.

If the NSA Enlightenment liberals educated those of us from small Catholic colleges in the vocabulary of rights, YCS students involved in NSA brought a firm grounding in the concepts of service and community to bear on discussions of student life. Oona Burke, YCS member and NSA delegate from the College of New Rochelle, articulated this perspective in her report on the New York Metropolitan Region's survey of student government (*Concord,* December 1949). Commenting on the view that "student government members might well be paid for all the time and energy they expend on behalf of the student community," Oona wrote:

> What would become of the concept of service so much lacking in our government today? There would always be the danger of making participation in student government a money-making venture only. That would be repugnant to the development of the student movement which needs, above all, selflessness and a strong concept of service.

Those of us whose participation in NSA was shaped by YCS formation could have taken our warrant from that same issue of *Concord.* In the words of its editors, we number ourselves "among those who believe that the historic mission of the Catholic Church is to work for [and with] all those who thirst after justice and oppose oppression and exploitation."

END NOTES

[1] See "NSA's Third Year," p. 233. [2] See Harris, p. 219 and Perry, p. 356. [3] See Des Marais, p. 734. [4] See Murray, p. 739.

PICTURE CREDITS: *Then:* c. 1948. *Now:* c. 1999 (both from author).

Historical note: Fontbonne College, now a co-educational university, was founded in 1917 as a women's college by the Sisters of St. Joseph of Carondelet (www.fontbonne.edu). Its 1948 enrollment was 539.

Tesse Donnelly followed a career path aimed at unsettling various establishments. In the early 1970s she helped to found the St. Giles Family Mass Community, an alternative, lay-governed Roman Catholic Community. She cofounded, and currently works with, Limina, an organization devoted to examining and celebrating women's life experience.

TESSE HARTIGAN DONNELLY

I was born Mary Therese Hartigan in St. Louis, Missouri, on October 20, 1930. I graduated from Christ the King School, University City, Missouri, in June 1944 and from St. Joseph's Academy, Clayton, Missouri, in June 1948. After attending Fontbonne College, Clayton, Missouri, for two years, in the fall of 1950, I went to Chicago to work full-time for two years with the headquarters team of the Young Christian Students (YCS).

I lived in what was called the Young Christian Workers (YCW) Girls' House. This was actually an apartment carved out of the first floor of a great ramshackle house predating the Chicago fire and located on LaSalle Street near North Avenue in a neighborhood of dubious character. About six women who worked for YCW or YCS lived there. Our sleeping quarters included a dining room converted to a dorm and a very small bedroom that was entered through a closet. Shirley Neizer and Joan Long were among our overnight guests, while Al Lowenstein, Elmer Brock, and Merril Freed sometimes sat at our table.

In June 1954, I graduated from the College of New Rochelle, and in the fall of that year became a graduate student in history at the University of Chicago, which awarded me an M.A. in 1956. While I was a student at Chicago, anthropologist Frank Lynch S.J. introduced me to his nephew Bill Donnelly, a fellow in hematology at Cook County Hospital.

Bill and I married in June 1957. We have five children. We have lived in Oak Park, Illinois, for thirty-five years. The only career path I can claim is that of unsettling various establishments. In the 1960s we participated in protests against real estate firms that refused to serve black buyers and supported the successful efforts that led to Oak Park's open housing ordinance. In the early 1970s, we helped found an alternative, lay-governed Roman Catholic Community known as the St. Giles Family Mass Community. We are still active with the Community, particularly in promoting adult learning experiences, such as an upcoming course entitled "Christian Reflections in a Buddhist Mirror."

Also in the 1970s, we helped establish at Oak Park and River Forest High School a four-year, alternative learning community that included students in governance, curriculum design, and teaching. Along the way, I collaborated in organizing a Candlelight March of Families protesting the bombing of Cambodia, served as president of the board of the C.G. Jung Institute of Chicago, worked the precincts for my friend Marilyn D. Clancy when she made an unsuccessful bid for Henry Hyde's seat in 1976, and, with two other friends, founded Limina, an organization that creates participatory events examining and celebrating women's life experience.

"A movement is a way of life"

6. Pat Groom: A Believer in Harmony

Maryville College, St. Louis. Chair, NSA Missouri-Kansas Region, 1946-47; Vice President, 1947-48

PATRICIA GROOM (1926-1951)

Editor's note: Pat Groom was born in Kansas City, Mo., in 1926 and graduated Maryville College in St. Louis. She was active in the Young Christian Students (Y.C.S.) and believed, as she wrote, that "The Christian must reach out to people and accept them: more, to receive them, to love them." In this sense, she typified many young Catholic student leaders for whom this mission meant an involvement with people on the very practical level of their day-to-day needs and interests. A leader on her campus, she became an early advocate for NSA after the Chicago Student Conference, where she was elected Chair of the Missouri-Kansas Region.

In 1950, she went to Paris to work at the international service headquarters of the YCS. While there, she succumbed to what Tesse Donnelley writes was thought to be "a consequence of a constitution weakened by an earlier bout with rheumatic fever" and died at the age of 25. In the 1952 Bulletin, *the editor wrote:*

"Pat was a very civilized American. With her surprisingly fine background in history and theology she retained an undeniable Missouri flavor. . . . She had sharpened her ability to appreciate what was not in her tradition. That ability for appreciation helped her in what I sometimes thought was her chosen work, translating ideas from culture to culture, tradition to tradition and person to person.

"Pat was a great believer in harmony. I imagine she would have called it unity. But as harmony or unity, she liked adjusting the parts so that they could all play together."

On this page are excerpts from some of her writings assembled in the 2/52 Memorial Issue (Vol. VI, No. 11) of the Y.C.S. Bulletin. *The* Bulletin, *put together by friends of Pat Groom, including Tesse (Hartigan) Donnelley, was provided in a file of material furnished by Joan Long Lynch (p. 493). Additional recollections and the photo above were provided by Paule Verdet, a close friend of Pat's, who also helped administer a scholarship fund established by Pat Groom.*

NSA and the YCS

The Catholic line would not admit that students had "fundamental rights," student gov't. and press being their civil rights while in school. I'm fairly sure that misplaced notions of authority are the problem with Catholic education. It's a vicious circle: the colleges need student gov't. to have NSA, and they need NSA to get decent student gov't. etc., *ad nauseam.*

How is YCS different from NSA? To me it seems that our life as Christians is the only explicit difference. YCS "formally" can't be too different from NSA. "Formal YCS" would just be another organization—but if a movement is a way of life—? It also seems that YCS must continually be buried and die, where NSA lives, grows, builds and assimilates on the surface.

Reading Danielou in the latest *Dieu Vivant* provoked some thought on the sides relative to this —the role of Christians in politics or science as prophets—or as those whose lives are charged with grace as with a current: only if Christians grasp, partake of social, political secular life can this secular life be "charged or transformed." Therefore, the Christian's obligation to participate—"temporal redemption of the Universe": The Christian as a co-creator.

Maryville College was founded by the Religious of the Sacred Heart in 1872 as an academy for young women. It became a four-year college in 1923 and a co-educational university in 1991 (http://maryville.edu). In 1948 it had an enrollment of 301.

The International Scene at Home

The foreign students in my own college! The girls from Latin America, the girls from China, the boys at the U. [St. Louis U.] from Europe—they were a curious lot, so we thought. Funny how we thought of them as a "lot." Maybe we were a little awed. They spoke English uniquely, but better than we spoke anything but our beloved Americanese. Maybe we sensed an uneasy difference in our school systems. Kids senior high school age were competing with our sophs and juniors. These kids were beavers. They worked more than some of us saw fitting—class averages were boosted. Their clothes were different. Their ideas—did we ever find out about them—or their families, or why they wanted to study here, or what they usually kept in their iceboxes. Generally we never got beyond the "What do you think of America?" stage—nor did they. They were different. We were comfortable in our sameness.

. . . We can spend years dreaming about our World Wide Student Community and we can have international study weeks, and it's all a waste of time, just nice words, unless we get to know the foreign students in our own school. The guys and gals from South America, Austria, France, China. If we can share with these kids our books, our plans, our work on projects, our families our fun, our hopes—if we can share theirs, we have begun to know people, they to know us. Then only does our attempt to love our student world become less dreamy. This love needs a flesh and blood realism. It is a love for people we know—a Person.

YCS Bulletin 2/52

Pat Groom (right) and co-worker Marie Tessier-Lavigne at the International service headquarters of YCS in Paris, "helping foreign students stranded in a strange country."

NSA in Missouri/Kansas

Editor's note: Missouri and Kansas with 53 and 44 four-year colleges each, were one region except for 1949-50, when Kansas was joined to Nebraska. Members (from 10 to 17) concentrated in St. Louis, home to St. Louis U. with 5 affiliated women's colleges (Fontbonne [See p. 000], Maryville, Webster and two junior colleges), Washington U., and branches of the U. of Missouri (Columbia) and Lincoln U. (Jefferson City), the state's Negro 4-year college. Lincoln attended Chicago in 1946 and joined in 1950-51. Kansas members dotted Route 40 west, from U. of Kansas campuses in Kansas City and Lawrence to Manhattan (Kansas State) and Salina (Marymount, Kansas Wesleyan). On the eastern Missouri border, Mt. St. Scholastica (Atchison), and Kansas State Teachers College, Pittsburg. Regional chairs: Pat Groom ('46,' 47-48, Maryville), Peggy Mason ('48-49, Webster), Tesse Hartigan ('49-50, Fontbonne), Jean Anderson ('50-51, Fontbonne).

AMONG THE LEADERS of the National Student Association meeting today through Sunday in regional conference at the University of Missouri are, from left: Janet Garbacz of Webster College; Mitzi Mazzoni of Webster College; Mary Therese Hartigan of Fontbonne College, regional chairman, and Robert Delahanty, executive secretary of the Association. 15 schools including Washington and St. Louis Universities, Harris Teachers College, Webster, Maryville and Fontbonne Colleges are represented. (*St. Louis Star-Times* 12/2/49).

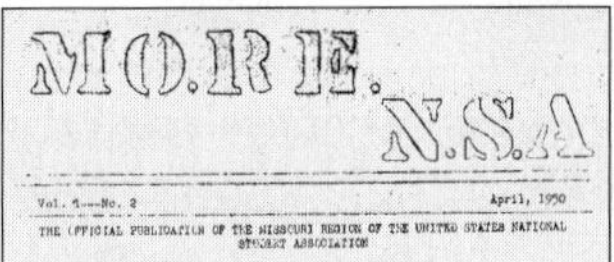
MO.RE N.S.A
Vol. 4—No. 2 April, 1950
THE OFFICIAL PUBLICATION OF THE MISSOURI REGION OF THE UNITED STATES NATIONAL STUDENT ASSOCIATION

1949-50

The Second Regional Assembly of the Missouri Region of the United States National Student Association will be held at Washington University on April 21, 22, and 23. . . .The Assembly will open with a keynote on "Is America Achieving Its Purpose." This will be followed by a talk on "NSA and Student Government," delivered by Robert A. Kelly, President of the National Student Association. (*MO.RE NSA*, 4/50)

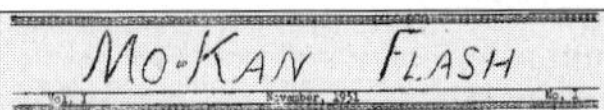
Mo-Kan Flash

1950-51

The campus of Pittsburg State Teachers College will be the setting for the Fifth Assembly of the Missouri-Kansas Region. . .on Friday, Saturday, and Sunday, November 16, 17, and 18.

Introductory and welcome talks will be given by Dr. Eugene E, Dawson, Dean of Students, and Student Council President Ronnie Roderique. Keynote speeches will be given by Dr. Alfred Farrell, Lincoln University, and Leroy Everett, KSTC Pittsburg. (*Mo-Kan Flash*, 11/51)

[11/51 *Mo-Kan Flash*]

Webster College

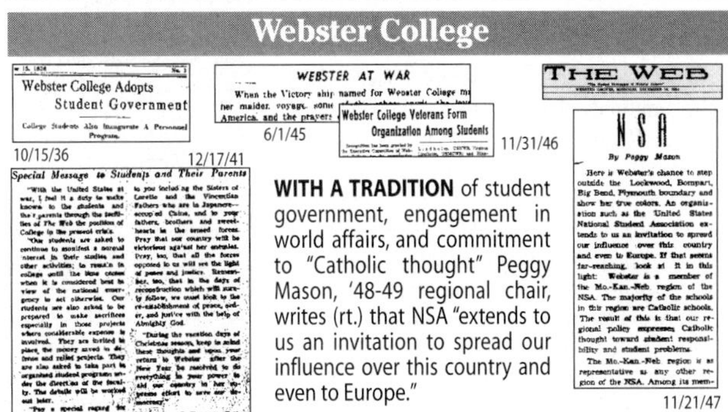
Webster College Adopts Student Government
College Students Also Inaugurate A Personnel Program
10/15/36

WEBSTER AT WAR
When the Victory ship named for Webster College m… her maiden voyage, some… America, and the prayers…
6/1/45

Webster College Veterans Form Organization Among Students
11/31/46

12/17/41
Special Message to Students and Their Parents
"With the United States at war, I feel it a duty to make known to the students and their parents through the facilities of *The Web* the position of College in the present crisis.
"Our students are asked to continue to manifest a normal interest in their studies and other activities; to remain in college until the time comes when it is considered best in view of the national emergency to act otherwise. Our students are also asked to be prepared to make sacrifices especially in those projects where considerable expense is involved. They are invited in place, the money saved in defense and relief projects. They are also asked to take part in organized student programs under the direction of the faculty. The details will be worked out later.
"Pay a special regard for those who are near and dear to you including the Sisters of Loretto and the Vincentian Fathers who are in Japanese-occupied China, and to your fathers, brothers and sweethearts in the armed forces. Pray that our country will be victorious against her enemies. Pray, too, that all the forces opposed to us will see the light of peace and justice. Remember, too, that in the days of reconstruction which will surely follow, we must look to the re-establishment of peace, order, and justice with the help of Almighty God.
"During the vacation days of Christmas season, keep in mind these thoughts and upon your return to Webster after the New Year be resolved to do everything in your power to aid our country in her supreme effort to save our democracy."
George F. Donovan, Pres.

THE WEB

NSA
By Peggy Mason
Here is Webster's chance to step outside the Lockwood, Bompart, Big Bend, Plymouth boundary and show her true colors. An organisation such as the United States National Student Association extends to us an invitation to spread our influence over this country and even to Europe. If that seems far-reaching, look at it in this light: Webster is a member of the Mo.-Kan.-Neb. region of the NSA. The majority of the schools in this region are Catholic schools. The result of this is that our regional policy expresses Catholic thought toward student responsibility and student problems.
The Mo.-Kan.-Neb. region is as representative as any other region of the NSA. Among its mem-
11/21/47

WITH A TRADITION of student government, engagement in world affairs, and commitment to "Catholic thought" Peggy Mason, '48-49 regional chair, writes (rt.) that NSA "extends to us an invitation to spread our influence over this country and even to Europe."

Historic note: Now Webster U., it was founded as Loretto College in 1915 by the Sisters of Loretto. It became co-ed in 1962 (www.webster.edu).1948 enrollment: 435.

The Font
Student Newspaper of Fontbonne College
10/3/47

The Voice
With the formation of the National Student Association, the American college student has been given unprecedented voice in the educational world. He must prove whether or not he will waste that voice in emotional harangue or exercise it in making meaningful statements.
When a million voices begin expounding theories about "securing and maintaining academic freedom and the rights of students," there should be someone nearby to see that the bounds of academic freedom are not overstepped. That's where we come in. Not Fontbonne alone, for there will be others to act as pacifiers with us. The emotional element is present in every organization and it needs a steadying agent to balance it. Without that steadying agent, a minority can sway even a clear-thinking majority.
Many of the issues to be brought before the NSA will be of a nature pertinent to us. Pertinent to us as students, as Catholic students, as Catholic students of a small school. Within nine months we must declare our intentions of accepting or rejecting membership in the National Student Association. We can take it or leave it, but consider. To an extent, we need the NSA; but the NSA needs us to an even greater extent. We should enter, and enter not so much with the idea of what we can get out of it, as what we can give to it.
10/15/47

THE UNIVERSITY NEWS
Student Newspaper of St. Louis University
ST. LOUIS, MO., OCTOBER 31, 1947

Stanton Elected NSA Region President
Hold Offices In Mo.-Neb.-Kan. Region
JACK STANTON · PAT GROOM · TOM ...
Three Of U. Delegation Win Offices In Assembly
Advantages Listed As Students Form Consumer's Co-Op
Athletic Department Says 'Plenty Seats'
WHAT IS NSA?
'Keep An Eye On Them'--America

1947-48

MANY STUDENT LEADERS AND COLLEGE ADMINISTRATORS supported NSA warmly in MIssouri, notwithstanding some concerns that NSA might lean too far leftward. Stephens College President Homer Rainey (p. 122) was a member of the NSA National Advisory Committee, 1948-1950.

Stephens College President Advocates NSA, Urges Student Participation

"The students of America should have such an organization as the National Student Association," Dr. Homer P. Rainey, member of the Advisory Council of NSA and president of Stephens College at Columbia, Mo., said last week-end in a conference with John Stanton, Arts junior and president of the Missouri-Kansas-Nebraska region of NSA.

Dr. Rainey added that no one knows when such an excellent opportunity for organization will again be presented to the American student. If colleges and universities do enter NSA in sufficient number to make it truly representative, then that student movement will have reached its ultimate goal. If they do not … political interest in people who would in turn be good for politics. For too long, Dr. Rainey said, politics has been viewed by American students as a dirty business, a business to which they should not like to lower themselves. Such an organization as NSA could be used to get the right people interested and ready to participate

5/7/48

Washington University

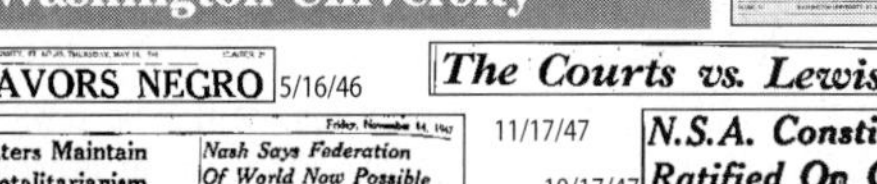
STUDENT LIFE
TREND FAVORS NEGRO 5/16/46
The Courts vs. Lewis 12/12/46
Oxford U. Debaters Maintain Socialism Not Totalitarianism
Nash Says Federation Of World Now Possible
11/17/47
N.S.A. Constitution Ratified On Campus 10/17/47
CAMPUS POLITICAL SCENE ACTIVE
Dewey Leads Campus Poll, 54%-31%; Truman Ahead In St. Louis, 47%-35% According To BCC, YRC Surveys
Hilltoppers Casting Ballots
10/29/48
Senate Orders Review Of Campus Y. P. C. A. 1/29/48
3/22/49 NEGRO POLICY LIBERALIZED
1767 Pro, 516 Con, In SCAN's Poll On Fall Negro Entrance
Committee Heads Urge Chancellor To Use Results In Reformulating University Admissions Policy
5/10/49

TWENTY COLLEGES attended the first regional assembly at WU on 2/27/47. Major issues of the day, illustrated above, surrounded the growth of NSA. Integration, the crippling United Mine Workers strike, Cold War, federalism and national politics engaged students. Membership was ratified on 10/15/47 by a vote of 927-100.

Kansas State Teachers College

Editor's note: KSTC in the Southeast corner of the state (now Pittsburg State U.) joined NSA in 1947-48, withdrew in January 1949 because it had "derived little or no benefit" from NSA (1/4/49 Student Council (SC) letter), and rejoined in 1950-51. Max Lee Minor, SC President, sent NSA President Al Lowenstein a note on 11/4/50 suggesting NSA should provide a "free student voice" working with the Voice of America. Lowenstein replied on 2/19/51 saying "it would be unwise for us to participate formally in a government program." He suggested that KSTC might want to form a committee to assist in an information program NSA was developing (p. 562). Minor wrote on 2/26/51, "Steve Blum is our NSA Chairman here. . . . We are going to try to institute that program" (SHSW NSA archives).

Max Minor

THE COLLEGIO
NSA Regional Meeting Begins Here Tomorrow
Conference Will Study Effective Student-Faculty Relationships

Historical notes: Washington U. in St. Louis was founded in 1853 as Eliot Seminary and was named Washington U. in 1857 (http://library.wustl.edu). 1948 enrollment: 13,860. ♦ U. of Missouri established in 1839. Women first admitted in 1869, 1950 first Black graduate (www.system.missouri.edu). 1948 enrollment: 13,964. ♦ Kansas State Teachers College (now Pittsburg State U.) was established as the Auxiliary Manual Training Normal School of Pittsburg in 1903. First to admit Blacks in the 1930's (www.pittstate.edu). 1948 enrollment: 1,441. ♦ St. Louis U. founded 1818. The Jesuits assumed control in 1826. Women admitted in 1908, Blacks in 1944 (www.slu.edu). 1948 enrollment: 10,015. ♦ See p. 951 for more on Fontbonne.

NSA in Iowa/Nebraska

Editor's note: NSA's presence in the plains states of Iowa, Nebraska and the Dakotas drew from a pool of 26 4-year colleges in Iowa, 18 in Nebraska, and 21 in South and North Dakota. 13 of these colleges attended in the 1947 Constitutional Convention. From '47-'48 to '49-'50 Iowa was a single-state region, ranging from 4 to 7 members. Regional Chairs, successively, were Terrence Rooney (U.of Dubuque), Dale S. Bingham (U. of Iowa), and Richard Dice (U. of Iowa). Nebraska was combined with Missouri for the first two of those years, and then with Kansas in '49-'50. In 1950-51 it was combined to become the Iowa-Nebraska Region. Regional Chair was Ross Williams (U. of Iowa); in '51-'52, Pat Donohue (Clarke).

"Selling NSA" One School at a Time

(Excerpted from Regional Report, *1950-51)*
Ross A. Williams *(State University of Iowa), Chairman*

The Iowa-Nebraska Region was created out of the old Iowa and Kansa-Nebraska Regions by the last Congress. There are at present only four member schools in the two states—Clark College in Dubuque, Marycrest College in Davenport, State University of Iowa in Iowa City and Grinnel College in Grinnell. As might be expected the regional offices are divided among the member schools—SUI, being the central and in some respects the most active member, has always held the regional chairmanship. The other three members hold down the vice-chairmanships. The regional Secretary-Treasurer and Public Relations Director are appointed by the Chairman from his school, at which the regional office is located....

The first regional assembly was held on the 7th of October. Invitations were sent to all the larger colleges and universities in Iowa and Nebraska. Five schools, including the member schools, responded by sending delegates. Although there were only a dozen people in attendance the group concentrated on two things: a new regional constitution and a bigger and better regional meeting.

As a result of hard work and good planning by the NSA committee at Grinnell College and by various people in the national office a second regional meeting was held the weekend of December lst thru 3rd at Grinnell College.... This time eleven schools, including the member schools and three schools from Nebraska, responded by sending forty-eight delegates.

The objective of the meeting was to sell NSA...by giving the delegates a view of NSA in action and by discussing in the workshops all the aspects of various NSA projects and activities.

A very important by-product of the second meeting was the strengthening of the various member schools. This reanimation can be seen in the programs each school has planned. All four schools are contemplating some sort of a leadership training program; the NSA committee at SUI has already drafted a tentative schedule for a thirty-day training program. Clarke College and Marycrest plan three-day sessions with outside schools participating. Grinnell College will shortly start work on a speakers bureau in conjunction with an international awareness program. Either Grinnell or SUI will serve as a clearinghouse for information on next summer's tour program. All this activity is encouraging and gives promise of a firm backbone on which a larger regional structure can be molded.

For more on the University of Nebraska, see William Lee Miller, p. 721.

Starting over Again

(Excerpted from Regional Report, *1951-52)*
Pat Donohue *(Clarke College), Regional Chairman*

From September until the early part of December, the Iowa Nebraska Region did not function. This was due to the fact that the State University of lowa and GrInnell College had disaffiliated from NSA, which left Wartburg, Clarke, Marycrest, Parsons and Nebraska Wesleyan as member schools.... and so in the early part of December Bill Dentzer asked Clarke College to contact as many schools as possible for a meeting to be held on December 6th.

This meeting was held at Clarke College and the following schools participated: Wartburg, St. Ambrose, Loras, U. of Iowa, U. of Dubuque and Clarke.... Since none of the member schools had enough experience in NSA to set up good programs for reorganization, it was decided that Wartburg would correspond and attend a few meetings of the Minnesota Region and Marycrest would do like-wise with the Illinois Region.... To date, the member schools in the region are: Parsons, Wartburg, Marycrest, Nebraska Wesleyan and Clarke. The interested schools in the region are: Loras College, St. Ambrose College, Luther College and the U. of Dubuque.

A Culturale Unrealized: Nebraska and Michigan

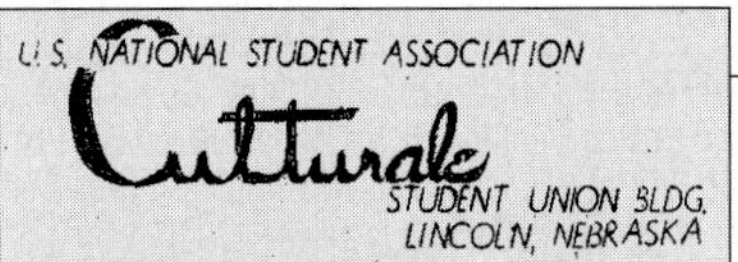

U.S. NATIONAL STUDENT ASSOCIATION
Culturale
STUDENT UNION BLDG.
LINCOLN, NEBRASKA

Dear Friend of the American College Student:...the USNSA Executive Committee is presently considering the holding of a CULTURALE during the summer of 1948 ... an attempt to bring together students from every section of the country, with divergent interests and ideas and to provide an opportunity for each student to grow through contact with other segments of the overall culture of the American student....

Eugene Berman, December 1947

"OVERWHELMING FAVORABLE RESPONSE" to a national survey (above) was reported by Eugene Berman at Nebraska, and a permanent committee was appointed at Michigan. Although a number of regionally based cultural events were successfully mounted (see p. 368), the ambitious plan for a national event never came off due to NSA's inability to raise the funds.

Detroit to Be Student Host

5,000 to Study Life in America in 1949

Detroiters will have an opportunity next year to sell democracy to representatives of a host of European and Asiatic countries teetering before the onrush of communism.

About 5,000 students from colleges and universities in 72 countries will come to Detroit in the summer of 1949 to watch an American city in action. The National Student Association (NSA) is sponsoring the mass expedition.

Weideman

The idea was born last summer following a world meeting of students at Prague in which the leading European student groups were Communist-front organizations, according to Carl Weideman, Jr., Detroit College of Law student and national committee executive of NSA.

"The delegates were given the idea that America was solely a place of Negro lynchings, race discrimination, class distinction and religious intolerance," Weideman said. "We want to present America as it is."

Detroit News 5/48

Historical notes: The U. of Iowa was founded in 1847, 59 days after Iowa statehood (www.uiowa.edu). 1948 enrollment: 10,550. ♦ The state's land grant university, the U. of Nebraska was founded in 1869 (www.unl.edu). 1948 enrollment: 10,525. ♦ Clarke College was founded in 1843 by Mary Francis Clarke, foundress of Sisters of Charity of the Blessed Virgin Mary; men first admitted 1979 (www.clarke.edu). 1948 enrollment: 446. ♦ Founded 1846 as Iowa College by "a group of transplanted New Englanders with strong Congregational and social reformer backgrounds," it later began to call itself Grinnell College after its abolitionist benefactor, Josiah Bushnell Grinnell (www.grinnell.edu). 1948 enrollment: 1,142.

As each year passed, my confidence in the leadership of NSA grew

A. Blair Knapp: Confidence in Student Leadership

Vice-President, Temple University, 1949-50. President, Denison University, Ohio, 1951-1968
NSA National Advisory Council, 1951–54

Editor's Note: A. Blair Knapp was among those postwar student personnel administrators who believed strongly in student self-government and developing student leadership. He became a Pennsylvania regional advisory committee member while student personnel vice president at Temple University, and joined the NSA National Advisory Committee after becoming President of Denison University in Ohio. In an October, 1953 article, reproduced here in full, from "at Denison," he saw NSA as "an opportunity to strengthen the concept that students are citizens of the college community and, as such, have much to contribute to the community government of the college."

Denison University in Granville, Ohio, was founded in 1831 by the Ohio Baptist Education Society, becoming known as Granville College. In 1854 it was renamed in honor of William S. Denison, a financial contributor. Shepardson College for Women was consolidated with the University in 1927 (www.denison.edu). Its 1948 enrollment was 1,371.

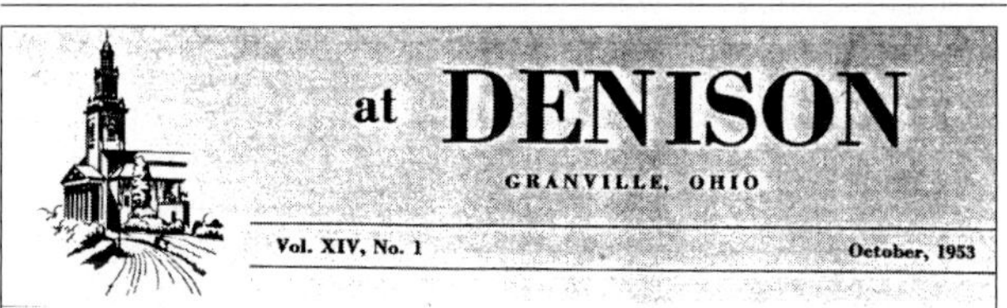

at DENISON
GRANVILLE, OHIO
Vol. XIV, No. 1
October, 1953

N.S.A., The National Student Association, has aroused as much controversy as any new aspect of American higher education. It continues to do so in some quarters today in 1953 as much as it did nearly seven years ago at the first preliminary meeting in Chicago in December 1946. The original sponsors for that meeting were, rightly or wrongly, suspect in the eyes of many. Some felt that they were too closely allied with the International Union of Students, which on more than one occasion had demonstrated its subservience to Communist control.

Early suspicions of NSA resolved

Those who were suspicious of this first meeting were quickly reassured. Many more delegates came from more colleges than had been expected. The rank and file of American students from all over the country quickly took charge. As I recall, not a single member of the sponsoring group was elected to office and none was appointed to the first important committees. Our students there representing largely veterans gave immediate proof of two facts: one, they wanted a national student association; two, they wanted no part of any Communist influence or control.

As a Dean of Students in 1946 on a campus whose leaders were from the beginning enthusiastic workers for N.S.A., I was compelled to be vitally concerned. As each year went by my confidence in the student leadership of N.S.A. continued to grow. In each of the annual congresses they have beaten down all the attempts to subvert the purposes of N.S.A. to questionable ends.

Difficulties confronting NSA

There have been difficulties, of course. Finances have been a constant problem. N.S.A. is a big enterprise. Its top leaders have been expected frequently to take a year's leave of absence and to serve the organization full time at pitifully small salaries. Often the treasury has been so low that vital publications and mailings had to be postponed or eliminated. Dues were too high in the beginning and some colleges felt it necessary to withdraw. Adequate provision for sound financing continues to be a problem. The continuity in leadership, always a major difficulty in any student enterprise, has been especially vexing in N.S.A. because of the magnitude of the enterprise. This was complicated still further as mature veter-

NSA Names Dean Knapp Adviser

A. Blair Knapp, vice president in charge of student personnel services, was elected to the faculty advisory committee at the Fifth Annual Regional Conference of the National Student Association. The conference was held Dec. 16 to 18 at Albright College in Reading with 50 colleges and universities from Pennsylvania participating.

The University sent a 10-student delegation and a faculty adviser to the conference, which was called to coordinate NSA activities on campuses in the state.

At the conference, work was divided into three commissions: administration, domestic and international. Each commission was in turn sub-divided into workshops to handle various phases of the commission's work. Two University students, Lou Ieradi, Arts '51 and Wally Johnson, Arts

Dean Knapp Promoted To Vice President Post

A. Blair Knapp, dean of students, has been elevated to the post of Vice President in Charge of Student Personnel Services, President Robert L. Johnson announced today.

A. BLAIR KNAPP
. . . to a new post

Dean Knapp Addresses NSA Group

The Human Relations Committee of National Student Association heard a reiteration of the relationship between NSA and Student Senate from University Vice-President A. Blair Knapp Monday afternoon.

"American students are represented through their student governments," said Knapp, paraphrasing the organization's constitution. "No such thing as a

From left: *Temple University News* 12/12/48, 1/6/50, 3/1/50.

an students graduated and their places of leadership were taken by younger students of more normal college age. From the beginning it was made clear that N.S.A. was to be represented on the local campuses of the country through the regularly established student governments. Top leaders nationally were never in doubt about that basic point but some regional leaders, and more particularly some students, became confused either unwittingly or by design, On many campuses the N.S.A. set themselves up as a group competitive to the established student government, in direct contradiction to one of the basic tenets of the organization. The result was confusion and friction which, particularly in the early days, did much to cause loss of prestige and status for the organization.

Other elements "went overboard" in terms of "student rights" without being equally specific and insistent upon student responsibilities. To those in education, as well as some outside who were ready to believe the worst, this was proof of a subversive intent. On occasion some leaders were perhaps too quick to set themselves up as an agency to investigate alleged violations of academic freedom on the local campuses, thereby giving the already doubting Thomases the "proof" that they desired.

NSA has been in the main a constructive force

Yet with all of these troubles, some of which will always be present in a student organization and others which can be solved as the organization matures, N.S.A. has been in the main a constructive force in American higher education. It has consistently resisted the influence and thwarted attempts to control on the part of the Communist influences. From the beginning N.S.A. has made it clear that it would have no truck with I.U.S. unless and until that group ceased to be interested primarily in being a propagandistic vehicle for Soviet Communism.

Its publications on student activities of all kinds have been by and large the most readable and best publications available anywhere in this field. Despite their youth and lack of experience the top leadership year after year has been composed of young men and young women of whom American colleges can well be proud. National meetings of educational groups of all kinds have profited from their participation in the programs. More than once have I been impressed with the realistic way in which they have presented a student point of view on educational problems which deserved and earned the respect of those who listened. In cooperation with student groups in Latin America, in the Scandinavian countries, and in the British Isles they have helped, more than we are able presently to assess, to create a leadership for the youth of the free world along lines wholly consistent with our great American democratic tradition,

A going organization

N.S.A. is a going organization. It is representative of a large segment of American college students. Isn't it time we accepted it as an opportunity to strengthen the concept that students are citizens of the college community and, as such, have much to contribute to the community government of the college? When presidents, as well as personnel workers, so view it and act accordingly, N.S.A. will fulfill its destiny.

- A. Blair Knapp

A. BLAIR KNAPP (1905-1968)

Born April 30, 1905 in Duluth, MN, Knapp grew up in Genoa, N.Y. He received his B.A. and M.A. from Syracuse University where he was Dean of Men from 1935 to 1946. After service with the U.S. Air Force in World War II he joined Temple University as Dean of Students, 1946-49, and Vice President, 1949-51. He was president of the National Association of Student Personnel Administrators, 1951-52, Ohio College Association President, 1964-65, and served on numerous higher education boards and commissions.

Presiding over the largest period of university growth and expansion, John E. F. Wood '24, writing in the July 1968 *Denison Alumnus* commented,

> The Knapp legacy which we cherish the most does not have to do with buildings or budgets, important as they are. When we say that the 17 years of Blair Knapp's presidency are a golden age in Denison's history we refer most importantly to what he did for the quality of the College and the quality of its program. . . .
> The contribution made by Blair Knapp to this process stemmed from profound convictions as to the mission of a liberal arts college and sharp insights as to the means of fulfilling that mission.
> He began with an enthusiastic belief in young men and women. He liked them. He had confidence in them. He had no greater delight than in seeing them develop their powers and free their minds. And he expected much of them.
> A corollary of his interest in students was his conception of the central importance of the teaching faculty. He wanted a strong faculty. To him a strong faculty was one gifted and accomplished in scholarship. It was also one having the will and the power, beyond scholarship, to help young men and women to bring out the best in their lives.

Knapp was married to Gertrude M. Park and had three children. He died of a heart attack on May 14, 1968.

(Adapted from documents furnished by the Denison University Archives.)

SOURCES: Photo: October, 1951, *The Alumnus,* Denison University. Documents courtesy of the Denison Univesity Archives.

NSA in Ohio and Indiana

Editor's note: Organized as two separate regions, the states were combined in 1951 into one Ohio-Indiana Region with a combined potential membership base of 104 (of which 11 were Catholic colleges), out of 1,277 nationwide. NSA National Student Congress attendance ranged from a high of 38 in 1948 to 25 in in 1951. Only two states, Pennsylvania (107) and New York (122), had larger numbers of colleges, Three prominent national leaders came from the area: Dennis Trueblood (Indiana State Teachers), who was 1948-49 Indiana region Chair and later went on to become 1951-52 Chair of the NSA Advisory Committee while at Indiana University (p. 345); and Bill Dentzer (Muskingum College), Ohio Region Chair in 1950-51, elected NSA President for 1951-52 (p. 299). Martin McLaughlin of Notre Dame attended the 1946 World Student Congress and was a prominent speaker and writer championing formation of NSA (p. 84).

Case Western and Flora Stone Mather

THE MATHER RECORD

Reserve Tribune

NSA Establishes National, Regional, Campus Programs

Adelbert Men Report On Student Meeting

Voice in Educational Matters

The Mather Record 10/15/47

"National Student Association has been established to give students throughout the country a voice in educational matters, just as Mather Students' Association gives the student body a voice in the conduct of campus affairs.

A nation-wide student government is being established to carry out the policies and programs which this responsibility calls for….

Ohio, as a region, wished to work directly through already existing clubs and organizations on campuses…"

Up to American Students

The Reserve Tribune 10/31/47

"The benefits to be derived from USNSA are more than meets the eye. In this postwar period of international bickering and power politics, students are perhaps the only individuals who can work together to promote better fellowship and understanding throughout the world. It is up to American students to begin to think in world terms and to make education an implement for better understanding and comprehension of the problems which face students today and citizens tomorrow."

Western Reserve College was founded in 1826 by David Hudson in Hudson, OH (www.hudson.oh.us). Case School of Applied Science (after a donor, Leonard Case) was founded in 1880, renamed Case Institute of Technology in 1947. Flora Stone Mather was founded in 1888 to complement Western Reserve's Adelbert College for men. All joined in 1967 as Case Western Reserve U. in Cleveland (www.cru.edu). 1948 enrollments: Western Reserve, 12,876; Case, 1,675; Mather: 760 est. (incl. in WRU).

Indiana State Teachers College

NSA Forms Student Government Clinic; Draft Constitution 10/22/47

INDIANA STATESMAN 2/26/48

STATE JOINS NATIONAL STUDENT ASSOCIATION

Council Decides In Vote. Decision Culminates Many Weeks Of Promotion And Long Discussion

For Promotion of Student Welfare

Indiana Statesman 2/26/48

Dennis Trueblood, chairman of the Indiana Region, stated that NSA is the culmination of the efforts of campus leaders throughout the United States to organize for the promotion of student welfare, regardless of political beliefs, race, religious convictions or economic conditions.

Note: Indiana University hosted the 1952 5th National Student Congress (p. 1079). Unlike Indiana State, affiliation efforts were defeated until the late 1950's.

Indiana State Normal School was founded in Terre Haute in 1865, renamed Indiana State Teachers College in 1929. Reflecting its broadened franchise it became Indiana State University in 1965 (www.indstate.edu). 1948 enrollment: 2,420.

For more on Indiana: Shaffer, p. 328, Trueblood p. 346. 5th National Student Congress, p. 1077, 1079.

Organizing the Region

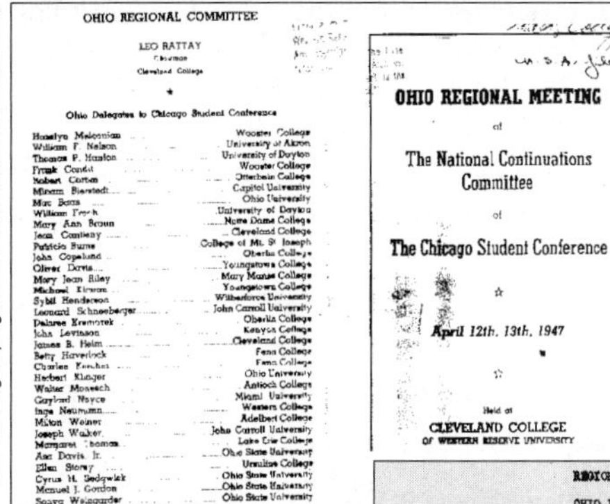

OHIO REGIONAL COMMITTEE

LEO RATTAY
Chairman
Cleveland College

Ohio Delegates to Chicago Student Conference

Hosstyn Melconian	Wooster College
William F. Nelson	University of Akron
Thomas F. Hanlon	University of Dayton
Frank Condit	Wooster College
Robert Corbin	Otterbein College
Miriam Bierstedt	Capitol University
Marc Boss	Ohio University
William Frech	University of Dayton
Mary Ann Braun	Notre Dame College
Jean Comiskey	Cleveland College
Patricia Burns	College of Mt. St. Joseph
John Copeland	Oberlin College
Oliver Davis	Youngstown College
Mary Jean Riley	Mary Manse College
Michael Kirwan	Youngstown College
Sybil Henderson	Wilberforce University
Leonard Schneeberger	John Carroll University
Delores Kremorek	Oberlin College
John Levinson	Kenyon College
James B. Helm	Cleveland College
Betty Haverlock	Fenn College
Charles Fescher	Fenn College
Herbert Klinger	Ohio University
Walter Moesch	Antioch College
Gaylord Noyce	Miami University
Inge Neumann	Western College
Milton Weiner	Adelbert College
Joseph Walker	John Carroll University
Margaret Thomas	Lake Erie College
Asa Davis, Jr.	Ohio State University
Ellen Storey	Ursuline College
Cyrus H. Sedgwick	Ohio State University
Manuel J. Gordon	Ohio State University
Sonya Weinquarder	Ohio State University

OHIO REGIONAL MEETING

of

The National Continuations Committee

of

The Chicago Student Conference

April 12th, 13th, 1947

Held at

CLEVELAND COLLEGE
OF WESTERN RESERVE UNIVERSITY

(1947 Ohio region program from Case Western Reserve archives)

25 COLLEGES gathered in April, 1947 to form the Ohio Region before the Constitutional Convention. Leo Rattay of Cleveland College was the first regional chair.

REGIONAL NEWSLETTER of OHIO-INDIANA REGION USNSA

Notre Dame joins NSA

INDIANA AND OHIO combined into one region at the 1951 Congress. Notre Dame and Ohio State rejoined NSA.

Ursuline and Akron

Catholic Student Leadership Fostered at NSA Congress
By Rita McGreevy

The Ursuline Quill

THE AKRON BUCHTELITE

Council Votes To Join NSA

Working Constructively

The Ursuline Quill 11/17/50

Catholics in…NSA have found it more practical and beneficial to take an active part in formulating resolutions on debatable issues which prove acceptable to all. By working in a constructuve way they have accomplished more and made wider gains than by acting destructively in such a group as a voting bloc.

Learning from Each Other

The Akron Buchtelite 11/11/47

We are very fortunate.…Discrimination here is almost unknown. But while we don't have discrimination, neither do we have school spirit.…By joining NSA we can help other colleges understand our ways of eliminating discrimination, while they may help us get school spirit.

Ursuline College is a women's college founded in 1871 by the Cleveland Ursulines. Still under their sponsorship, it became independent in 1968 (www.ursuline.edu). 1948 enrollment: 222. ♦ University of Akron was founded as Buchtel College in 1870 by the Ohio Universalist Convention, named after supporter John R. Buchtel. Its assets were transferred to the city of Akron in 1913 (www.uakron.edu). 1948 enrollmnent: 4,673.

Ashland and Wooster

Wooster

NSA CONFERENCE SUGGESTS CURES FOR WOOSTER MINORITY PROBLEMS

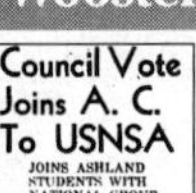

Council Vote Joins A. C. To USNSA
JOINS ASHLAND STUDENTS WITH NATIONAL GROUP

Dropping Discrimination

Wooster Voice 2/20/48

The discriminatory clause which the Board of Christian Education imposes on the college is un-Christian, undemocratic and incompatible with the tenets of liberal education. We therefore recommend a concerted protest be forwarded immediately.…

A Step toward Student Rights

Ashland Collegian 1/16/48

With the student council's ratification of the constitution of the USNSA, the students of Ashland College have made a huge step towards student rights.…*The Collegian* applauds [NSA] in leading the students of America toward a definite place in the leadership of the country

Co-educational Ashland College (now a private university) was founded in 1878 by the Brethren Church (www.ashland.edu). 1948 Enrollment: 626. ♦ Wooster College was also founded as a co-educational institution by Presbyterians in 1866 (www.wooster.edu). 1948 enrollment: 1,282.

For more on Muskingum College, Ohio, see p. 305.

NSA in the Michigan Region

Editor's note: Led by U. of Michigan, Wayne U. and Marygrove College, the region provided local and national leadership and an active program of student government workshops. From U. of Michigan: Craig Wilson, 1949-50 editor of NSA News (p. 248), Leonard Wilcox, 1952-53 National Affairs V.P. (p. 398), Phil Berry (pp. 1070, 1072), his replacement after Wilcox was drafted and Harry Lunn, 1954-55 President. From Wayne: Rollo O'Hare, 1951-52 Educational Affairs Vice President. Regional Presidents: Frances Rollins, Marygrove (1947); Harvey Weisberg, Michigan ('47-'48, '48-'49); Duane Johnson, Wayne ('49-'50, '50-'51); Leonard Wilcox, Michigan ('51-'52). UM was the site of the 3rd National Student Congress (Pt. 1, Sec. 7).

REGIONAL EXECUTIVE COMMITTEE meets in October, 1948: Seated, fr. l.: Pat Kessell (Secretary), Harvey Weisberg (President), Gene Schwartz (NSA Educational Problems Vice President), Arlynn Rosen (Secretary); Standing: Jerry Cohen (Public Relations), Joan Mauer (PCS Committee), Bob Wilder (Vice President), and Joe Hansknecht (NEC member) (NSA News, 11/48).

Michigan Daily Tracks NSA

The Michigan Daily

4/30/47 (Ann Arbor News)

Texas Student Will Address Campus Rally

Jim Smith, president of the National Student Organization's continuations committee and a student at the University of Texas, will speak on "Why We Need a National Organization" at an informational rally to be held at 8 o'clock tomorrow night at the Michigan Union.

The rally is sponsored by the University Student Legislature and the unity committee which represents 15 campus organizations. It is designed to prepare students for ...

9/23/47

NSA Elects 'U' Student Region Head

Harvey Weisberg, law student, was elected president of the Michigan Region of the National Student Association at the organization's constitutional convention held early this Fall at the University of Wisconsin.

Weisberg, who is president of the Student Legislature, was elect- ...

11/27/47

Regional NSA Meets Sunday

Will Discuss Plans For IUS Conference

Plans to send a negotiating team to the International Union of Students' conference in Prague next summer will be discussed at the Michigan Region National Student Association Meeting Sunday at the Highland Park YMCA in Detroit, Harvey Weisberg, Regional president, announced.

750,000 REPRESENTED:

NSA Congress Plans New Projects

ONE YEAR OLD—Part of the Michigan Region delegation to the NSA Congress ...

NSA Opens Three Day Leadership Conference

Weisberg Cites Delegates' Participation In Solution of College Community Problems

3/26/49

9/20/48

7/20/50

State Region Prepares for NSA Congress

Legislature Votes To Stay with NSA

10/11/51

EXECUTIVE BOARD:

'U' Students To Attend NSA Meeting at Wayne

By HARRY LUNN

Two University students will attend the semi-annual meeting of the National Executive Committee of the National Student Association when it meets from Dec. 26 to 31 at Wayne University.

Leah Marks, '55L, a Student Legislature member and NSA Public Relations Director, and Phil Berry, Grad., former SL vice-president and head of the NSA Financial Advisory Board, will participate in ...

12/13/52

For more Michigan Daily excerpts, see pp. 110 , 137, 264

In the eye of the Academic Freedom Storm

Michigan State College Expels Member of AYD

Zarichny First Put on Disciplinary Probation for Two Year Period

U of Michigan Ends Worker Education School

Sigler, Williams Fight Gubernatorial Battle Over Suspension of Service

Bloomfield College Asks No 'Red, Near-Pink' Instructors

Olivet Spawns Rebel School

Six Fired, Twelve Instructors Quit

Staff Receives Olivet Petition

No Just Reason Found To Dismiss Olivet Prof

MRNSA NEWSLETTER

Volume III, Number 4
March, 1950, Detroit, Michigan

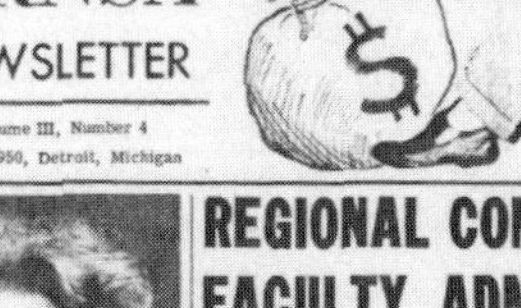

JACK BURNS
Regional Treasurer

REGIONAL CONVO DISSECTS RIGHTS; FACULTY, ADMINISTRATORS ATTEND

LORRAINE RAWLINGS
New SL and SG Veep

VISITS FIVE NON-NSA SCHOOLS

Perry Breezes Thru State

Ted Perry, USNSA vice president for student life and student government, will make a whirlwind visit to Michigan next week on his way East.

Siena Picture Absent; Tour Plans Altered

Views Vary on Import of Student Bill

SHOULD COMMUNISTS BE ALLOWED TO TEACH?

'There Are Communists, and There Are...'

By LORRAINE RAWLINGS
Aquinas College
Chairman, Student Life Commission

From top: *Harvard Crimson* 5/27/49 Academic Freedom series (p. 388); Above l. *NSA News*, "Staff" 11/48, "Reason" 1/49; Right, *MRNSA Newsletter*, 3/50, pp. 1 and 2.

ACADEMIC FREEDOM AND STUDENT RIGHTS. *Editor's note: The Michigan Region provided a microcosm of the issues and debates raised by campus anti-communist initiatives, Cold War fears of subversion, and debates among students themselves on the meaning of student rights and academic freedom and on NSA's role in their defense. Janet Brown in her review of NSA's record in its first five years notes (p. 383) that while "NSA compiled a record as a staunch defender of liberty . . . [it] never had the resources, human or financial, to conduct a really thorough investigation." National officers felt constrained from intervening directly in cases brought before them, despite the Association's clear policy positions (op. cit.), shifting responsibility for action to the regional level. As early as Spring 1947, Jim Smith, President of the National Continuations Committee (NCC), responded with caution to the Michigan Region's appeal for support in opposition to the suspension of seven students at Michigan State (p. 120), laying out a series of steps they could take for "intelligent, effective student opposition to coercive tactics by those who refuse to recognize student rights."*

Among the several threads of debate within the Association were the voices of the Catholic College students attempting to reconcile NSA's positions with the those of the Church and their faith with respect to college governance as well as the moral issues involved in granting speech and teaching rights. Illustrative is the article (left) by Lorraine Rawlings (Aquinas College), 1949-50 regional Student Life Commission Chair, in which she addresses the question of whether communists (no) or atheists (yes) should be permitted to teach.

PART 5. NSA's REGIONS:
CREATING INTERCOLLEGIATE NETWORKS

SECTION 6

CONTENTS

The South

Racism and the fear of communism ran strong on many Southern campuses after World War II, and it was easy to play on these feelings in NSA affiliation votes in the South. When the student body presidents of Louisiana State University (Gillis Long, p. 454) and the University of Texas (Barefoot Sanders, p. 995) returned from NSA's Constitutional Convention in 1947, their active campaigns for affiliation (described in this section), vigorously supported by the college newspapers, went down to resounding defeats in the face of attacks on alleged leftist influences (LSU: "Send Our Students to Moscow: Vote for NSA.").

Many returning veterans, though, white and black, were outraged and no longer willing to put up with segregation and discrimination, and NSA provided one of many channels through which efforts to dismantle the system were directed. Some early intiatives in the South are described in Pt. 2, Sec. 2 in the memoirs of Norman Francis (Xavier University, New Orleans, p. 429), John Peoples (Jackson State College, Mississippi, p. 421), Barry Farber (University of North Carolina, p. 441) and Constance Curry (Agnes Scott College, Atlanta, p. 444).

Some strong footholds in the South, despite the controversies

This Section begins with the formation of the United Nations in 1945, and Douglass Hunt's memoir of the Conference of Southern Students organized to provide observer representation at the San Francisco Conference. Charles Proctor (Fisk University), president of the Southern Conference, recalls San Francisco in an article written at the time. Fisk's leadership in race relations is presented in the mentoring role of sociologist Charles S. Johnson, its first black president.

Dick Murphy (University of North Carolina), Galen Martin (Berea College, Kentucky) and John Hunsinger (Georgia Tech), together with various albums, describe NSA's presence in North Carolina and Kentucky (University of Louisville, Berea) and in the Atlanta area (Emory, Georgia Tech, Agnes Scott, Morehouse). The mentoring role and strong support for NSA by Frank Graham, President of the University of North Carolina, is recalled.

Some of NSA's outstanding national leaders and three of its first six presidents came from the South: Bill Welsh (Berea, 1947-48, p. 165) and Al Lowenstein (1950-51, p. 283) and Dick Murphy (1952-53, p. 1075), both from the University of North Carolina. NSA's first national leader, Jim Smith, President of the National Continuations Committee, hailed from Texas (p. 119).

A number of black colleges in the South maintained membership throughout this period: Xavier, Jackson State, Morehouse, Fisk, Arkansas A&M. They contributed local and regional leadership (See also Howard, in D.C., p. 922). The section closes with a recollection by Barefoot Sanders of the hotly contested referendum at the University of Texas, at which affiliation was defeated.

With 30 percent (301) of the nation's 1948 four-year colleges (938), the twelve traditional Southern states provided only ten to twelve percent of NSA's membership during its early years.

The Daily Reveille

All-White Clause Passed In Final Conference Meet

Inter-Racial Regional Meet Discusses NSO, Calls for Equal Educational Opportunities

Curet Elected Region Prexy

Panel Three Debates Race

Daily Reveille, LSU, 4/22/47

SIMULTANEOUS INTERRACIAL AND SEGREGATED MEETINGS AT LSU in 1947 typify the dilemmas facing white and black students in Southern states as NSA and other groups laid the groundwork for integration (Pt. 2, p. 454).

NSA Regional Highlights in the South

West Virginia-Virginia-Carolinas

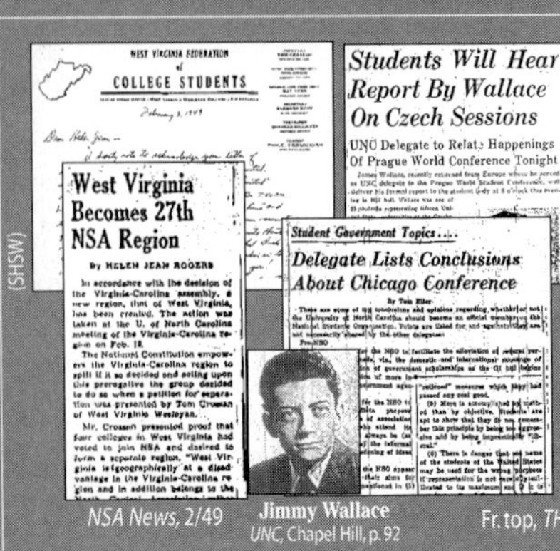

West Virginia Federation of College Students

West Virginia Becomes 27th NSA Region

By Helen Jean Rogers

Students Will Hear Report By Wallace On Czech Sessions

UNC Delegate to Relate Happenings Of Prague World Conference Tonight

Student Government Topics...

Delegate Lists Conclusions About Chicago Conference

Va.-N.C. Regional NSA Meet Gets Underway Here Today; National Officer Will Speak

Students Here To Represent 20 Schools

100 Delegates To Hold NSA Conference Here

(SHSW)

NSA News, 2/49

Jimmy Wallace
UNC, Chapel Hill, p. 92

Fr. top, *TH*, l.: 10/16/46, 1/27/47; r.: 10/21/49, 2/18/53

The University of North Carolina led the region as well as providing national NSA Presidents Al Lowenstein ('50-51, p. 283) and Dick Murphy ('52-53, p. 1075). UNC's Jimmy Wallace was one of the 10 college reps on the 1946 U.S. delegation that returned from Prague to launch the NSA (Photo: *TH* 10/16/46).

Kentucky-Tennessee

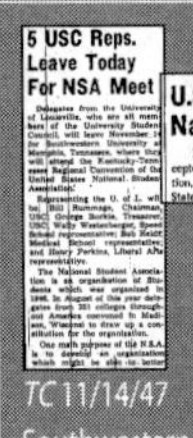

5 USC Reps. Leave Today For NSA Meet

U.S.C. Votes In Proposal To Join National Student Association, 9-3

1947-48 *TC* 3/3/48.

TC 11/14/47

Southwestern U. in Memphis hosted 11/15/47 regional event.

Bob Delahanty
U. of Louisville, (p. 410) '48-49 Regional Pres.

Natl. Student Body Costly, Idealistic–Rejected by U. of K.

TC 3/3/48.

1948-50

Purchase Card Plan Commences Oct. 24

TC 10/12/49. See p. 366

NSA To Convene At U. of K.

TC 11/12/48.

Although not a member, UK hosted 11/19/48 regional convention.

TW 12/9/50

NSA Conference Draws Students from Ky., Tenn.

USC Members Pass Faculty Rating System For A&S, Speed Schools

TC 12/6/50. See pp. 360, 372

Berea College (KY) and the University of Louisville provided the leadership and energy that maintained active memberships and regional events. Bill Welsh of Berea became NSA's first President (p. 165), and Louisville's Bob Delahanty, NSA's first Executive Secretary (p. 410). Charles Proctor of Fisk U. in Nashville was a member of the U.S. Delegation to the 1946 World Student Congress (p. 94) and President of the 1945 Conference of Southern Students (p. 968).

Georgia-Alabama-Florida

Ga.-Ala. Student Organization Elects Meadows Secretary

NSA Art Exhibit To Visit Atlanta Area In Spring

Newman Club Holds Meeting, Makes Plans

Delegates of Southern Schools Attend NSA Meeting at Emory

Purchase Card Sales Will Begin Tomorrow

Cards Will Entitle Students To Discounts on Purchases

NSA-Sponsored News Center To Meet in AMB Tonight

Maroon Tiger

Students Spearhead Civil Rights Confab at A. U.

1947-49

NSA Elects Curry Regional Chairman

1950-53

Connie Curry
Agnes Scott, Atlanta p. 444

Emory College, Georgia Tech, Agnes Scott and Morehouse Colleges in the Atlanta area and the University of Miami and Barry College for Women in Florida provided regional continuity. NSA's International News Center, launched 1951, was hosted at Georgia Tech. (p. 990). 16 Ga.-Ala. colleges attended the org-anizing meeting on 2/27/47. Florida was then a separate region. In 1953 all 3 states were combined with Louisiana, Mississippi and Texas to form the Great Southern Region.

Left fr. top: *AS* 2/26/47, *TE* 2/26/49, *MT* 2/48; Right, fr. top: *AS* 11/12/49, *TE* 2/28/50, *NSA News* 5/52, *AS* 10/7/53. Photo: Curry.

Race Relations

Integrated Southern Area YMCA, YWCA Conference Held At Berea

By Lorenzo Gunn, YMCA Delegate

The annual regional conference of the Southern Division, national student YMCA and Southern area student YMCA convened at Berea college, Berea, Kentucky this summer. This conference was a historical moment in the history of the Southern region because the YMCA and YWCA conference policy was brought into agreement when the YMCA regional council voted in December, 1947 to sponsor only integrated conferences.

The Student Christian Movement and the Y's played key roles in the desegregation buildup, sponsoring interracial events and meeting places (see John Peoples, p. 425. *MT* 10/48).

Xavierite Wins Interracial Day Speech Cup

Students Seek to End Discrimination

Catholic Committee of the South

Xavier Archives

The only Black Catholic college in the U.S. was actively engaged in interracial outreach (see Norman Francis [left in both photos above], p. 429; *Xavier Herald*, fr. top, 3/50, 2/51).

Discrimination and race relations were at the top of social action agendas after World War II. Both Protestant and Catholic student and community organizations accelerated the "low profile" interracial events they had been conducting for some years (see Peoples and Francis in Pt. 2, Sec. 3). NSA's public position in favor of desegregation, while working within the Southern State legal frameworks (see p. 451), cost it memberships, but provided additional legitimacy for student leaders and student governments who were ready to engage the issue.

Internationalism

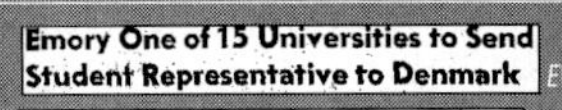

Emory One of 15 Universities to Send Student Representative to Denmark

EW 4/10/47

Executive Officer Will Open WSSF Drive

Fund Dates to China War; Promotes World Education

DR 3/8/47

NSA Recognizes Necessity For International Cooperation

EW 12/9/47

Fans Contribute Over $3,000 To WSSF at Georgia Game

TE 12/10/48

Students To Europe! NSA Sponsors Tours

TC 2/14/52

Students Attend NSA Meets In Europe, South America

AS 1/30/52

Southern colleges had a tradition of strong interest in international relations and i n support of student aid programs in Europe, Asia and Latin America. In 1945, 55 colleges from 13 states joined in the Conference of Southern Students in order to provide an observer delegation to the San Francisco Conference and to support the formation of the new United Nations Organization (p. 963).

Arkansas-Louisiana-Mississippi-Texas-Oklahoma

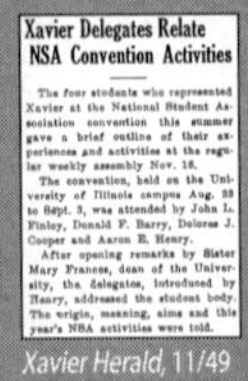

Xavier Delegates Relate NSA Convention Activities

Xavier Herald, 11/49

Affiliation With NSA Is Urged by Long, Teekell and Other Student Body Leaders

LSU Votes 'No' to NSA Affiliation by 2 to 1

By L. Gibbs Adams

Daily Reveille, LSU, 12/12/47, 2/19/48

Texas Delegation, Jim Smith Star at National Student Meet

The Daily Texan

NSA Rejected, 2,533-1,874, in Heavy Vote

Daily Texan, 9/16/47, 2/19/48

1947-49

John Peoples
Jackson State C., MS p. 421

Aaron Henry
Xavier U. New Orleans p. 456

Harry Alexander
Xavier U., New Orleans p. 454

Gillis Long
LSU, Baton Rouge p. 455

Barefoot Sanders
U. of Texas, Austin p. 0000

When 18 colleges attended the 1947 Texas-Oklahoma regional meeting there was promise for the organization, as was the case at the first La-Miss-Ark meeting. The resounding NSA affiliation defeats at LSU and Texas, despite student leader and student newspaper support, kept membership too low to maintain effective regional organization in those states after 1947-48 (see caption above).

KEY TO COLLEGE NEWSPAPER CITATIONS IN THIS SECTION

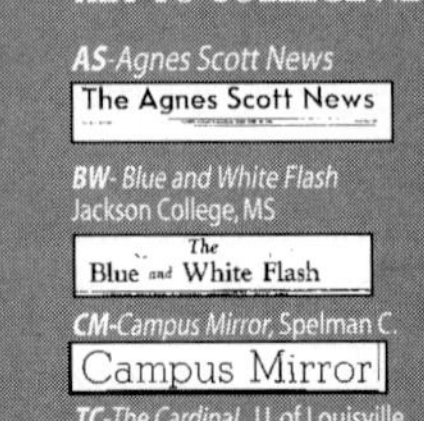

AS-Agnes Scott News — The Agnes Scott News

BW-Blue and White Flash Jackson College, MS — The Blue and White Flash

CM-Campus Mirror, Spelman C. — Campus Mirror

TC-The Cardinal, U. of Louisville — The Cardinal

DR-The Daly Reveille, LSU — The Daily Reveille

EW-The Emory Wheel — The Emory Wheel

MH-The Miami Hurricane, U. of M. — The Miami Hurricane

MT-Marron Tiger, Morehouse C. — Maroon Tiger

PW-Purple and White, Millsaps C. — Purple and White

TE-The Technique, Georgia Tech. — Technique

TH-Daily Tar Heel, U. of N.C. — The Daily Tar Heel

TU-Tulane Hullabaloo — Tulane Hullabaloo

TW-The Wallpaper, Berea C. — The Wallpaper

TX-The Daily Texan, U. of Texas — The Daily Texan

XA-The Xavier Herald — The Xavier Herald

See Part 2, Sec. 3 for more on Jackson State C., Xavier U, LSU and Southern Colleges and Civil Rights

There was an optimistic period in the country at that time

1. The Conference of Southern Students and the 1945 San Francisco Conference

Douglass Hunt
University of North Carolina
Executive Secretary, Conference of Southern Students, 1945
Speaker of the UNC Student Legislature, 1945-46

Editor's note: This essay has been prepared by the editor from the transcript of an interview conducted with Douglass Hunt, John Sanders and Ben Jones on October 28, 1998, in Chapel Hill, North Carolina.

I was born in Winston-Salem but I grew up in Greensboro, where I also went to high school. I entered the University of North Carolina in the fall of 1941—the school year my father lost everything he had. I went home and went to work expecting to be drafted, since I turned eighteen in January of 1942. I was called up, went down to Fort Bragg, was stamped as "unphysically fit," and was sent home. I worked in a radio station, sold war bonds, ran newspaper and tin can collections for the war effort, and made a lot of speeches to civic clubs and the like. And I helped my father get back on his feet. Then, in March of 1944, having been rejected for service a few more times, I had enough money put together to come back to school and finish working my way through. I went around the clock and graduated in June of 1946, by which time the military had lowered the physical standards, the war being over, and they took me for limited service.

A period of optimism in the country

As a consequence, I was at the University when the war ended. There was an optimistic period in the country at that time. I think there was a strong feeling that, by God, we had won the war, and we could do all sorts of wondrous things to keep it from happening again. There seems to have been more of a united sense of purpose in the country during and after the war than at any time we had experienced before or since. So the United Nations, the Marshall Plan, and many of the national programs of outreach and service were an expression of that feeling. So also it was that the formation of an organization like NSA has to be seen in that context, as a product of that psychology of optimism.

The San Francisco conference in the summer of 1945 at which the United Nations charter was adopted was the first major event in that postwar spirit.[1] There was a great enthusiasm among many students to be represented at that conference.

If you were going to send observers to San Francisco, they had to represent an organization. So, taking the initiative at UNC, we formed, on eight days' notice, the Conference of Southern Students, representing fifty-four southern colleges and universities, black and white, in thirteen Southern and border states from Florida north to Virginia and west to Oklahoma and Texas.

On each of these campuses, delegates were selected by a student government agency. We addressed letters to the president of the student body, and then we raised the money and paid their way to travel to get this done. And we had beds for everybody in the community, black and white. And we got contributions from prominent businesspeople, like Mr. C.C. Spaulding, the head of Mutual Life Insurance Company, the largest black-owned insurance company in the world, as well as from many other people.

Charles Proctor of Fisk elected president

We met on the third floor of Alumni Hall to hold the meeting at which the organization was formed.[2] We elected as president Charles Proctor, who also was the president of the student body at Fisk University.[3] I was chosen as executive secretary. Two observers were selected to go to the San Francisco conference and report back to the colleges. Maurice Clifford, a black sophomore medical student at Meharry Medical College in Nashville, was one of the observers, and I was the other. The son of schoolteachers from Washington, D.C., he capped his career as president of the Medical Col-

STUDENT GOVERNMENT AT THE UNIVERSITY OF NORTH CAROLINA IN 1945-46

At the time there were dozens of previous constitutions for separate organizations. There was not a comprehensive constitution of the student government when the new constitution was proposed in 1945 by the constitution committee. There had been earlier attempts made by the student legislature when Terry Sanford was its speaker and then when Bill Cochrane was its speaker.* We had a student government that prided itself on not having a constitution. In fact, it thought of itself more like the English form of a parliament grounded in some kind of Magna Carta. The student council was a judicial body by that time, and it tried only honor court cases, campus code violation cases, and the like. The student legislature was the legislative branch of student government and actually passed code laws under authority of the constitution that had been enacted in Cochrane's days.

But there was no document or structure that integrated the entire student government, including such separate entities as the co-ed senate, the interfraternity council, the student council, and the women's honor council. What this constitution committee did was to provide a comprehensive framework and charter to fit those organizations together. It provided a tripartite government due to the legislative and judicial branches. We could never have done it if it hadn't been for World War II and the perception that everything had sort of collapsed and needed to be revivified.

The student body president chaired the student council, and had done so since 1909 or thereabouts. I believe Frank Graham (later President of the University) may have been the first president of the student body to be the chair of the student government. There was a class council before that. A good story of this and my own account of it appears in *The Story of Student Government jn the University of North Carolina,* a book by Albert and Gladys Coates, for which Albert asked me to write the chapter about the coming of the constitution.

—Douglass Hunt

* *Note:* Terry Sanford later became Governor, U.S. Senator and then President of Duke University. Bill Cochrane served 30 years as a distinguished U.S. Senate staff director.

lege of Pennsylvania. William Poteat became our adviser. He was assistant secretary of the Y.[4]

The Y had staged the 8th biennial Institute of Human Relations on campus. I was co-Chairman and we had invited participation by representatives of the State Department. The theme of the Institute was "the World We Want." The State Department represenatives suggested we form a regional student organization and send observers to the San Francisco Conference of the United Nations.

Drafting the new United Nations Charter

Maurice Clifford and I went to San Francisco, and we sent back reports to all fifty-four colleges and universities (*see Background unit following*). We were housed at the University of California, Berkeley, in the International Student Center. They gave us room and board. We attended toward the end of the two-week sessions with the so-called Gray Cardholders group. They were people like Dorothy Detzer of the League of Women Voters and others who had not been selected to be observers by the State Department in the beginning. When the organizers began to take in regional organizations and national organizations of lesser size, they created an adjunct group of people, of which we were a part. The person who probably spent more time with us from the State Department than anybody else was Andrew Cordier, later the president of Columbia University, where I worked for him.[5]

The group also met with Secretary of State Stettinius, who later resigned to serve as U.S. representative to the United Nations, toward the end of the two weeks we were there. I can remember sitting at the door in his office as he came in. It was in the building across from the Fairmont Hotel, on Nob Hill. Grace Cathedral is at least a full block beyond. There was a time when I could identify the provisions of the charter that group had especially espoused (one has to do with the Trusteeship Council) and others they had not. I wrote about that in our newspaper, the *Tar Heel*, after I got back. Although I can't recall the specifics now without looking back at ancient files, it was a significant piece of work.[6]

Needed: A replacement for the American Student Union

After the conference was over and we came back and resumed normal life, I was speaker of the Student Legislature, and we were trying to get a new constitution ratified through the fall of 1945 and the spring of 1946.[7] Then, when I was invited to go to the UN Assembly in London in 1946, it seemed not to be very practical for me.[8] It was important for us to really put the Conference of Southern Students in place. We needed to replace the old American Student Union [9] and this seemed to be a start.[10] The other thing I needed to do was to see the constitution through and ratified. Finally, I was also due to graduate in June of 1946. So I passed on London and focused on the work ahead.

Douglass Hunt was Vice President for Finance at Columbia University and Special Assistant to the U.S. Secretary of the Treasury.

END NOTES

[1] *Editor's note:* See Cord Meyer, "A Serviceman Looks at the Peace," p. 707.

[2] Maurice Clifford graduated from Dunbar High School in Washington, D.C., in 1937; received an A.B. from Hamilton College in Clinton, N.Y., in 1941; and received an M.A. from the Unversity of Chicago in 1942. While a sergeant in the army, he had been assigned to the Meharry Medical College.

[3] Charles Proctor was later selected by Fisk University to be a member of the U.S. delegation to the August 1946 World Student Congress in Prague. When that delegation returned, it issued a call to the Chicago Student Conference in December of 1946, at which plans were laid for the formation of the U.S. National Student Association. See p. 000.

[4] William Poteat later became Professor of the Philosophy of Religion and Chairman of the Department of Philosophy at Duke University. He was a brilliant teacher and there are those who will tell you how profoundly he influenced their lives.

[5] I was later vice president of Columbia and then deputy to the president for finance in 1973.

[6] *Editor's note:* For an absorbing narrative of the San Francisco Conference, including the role of the "unofficial" observers, see Stephen Schlesinger, *Act of Creation: The Founding of the United Nations,* Westview Press, 2003.

[7] *Editor's note:* See sidebar, previous page.

[8] In the summer of 1946, the United Nations held its first meeting in London and elected Trygve Lie secretary-general.

[9] See American Student Union, pp. 42, 47).

[10] *Editor's note:* The following year (1947), the National Student Association was formed. See also below on the short-lived National Conference of Students (both Douglass Hunt and Al Lowenstein were among the founders) formed in the Spring of 1946 at North Carolina, before the U.S. delegation to the World Student Congress had returned to call the Chicago Student Conference the following December (Pt. 1, Secs. 1-3).

PICTURE CREDITS: *Then:* c. 1946 (Coates, *The Story of Student Government in the University of North Carolina*). *Now:* November, 1988, Chapel Hill (Schwartz).

DOUGLASS HUNT

Among the milestones in his life, Douglass Hunt cites witnessing Franklin Delano Roosevelt's inauguration to the presidency on March 4, 1933, and seeing Winston Churchill up close twice in one day in 1954. Both a student and participant in the history of his time and steeped in its events and traditions, Hunt has contributed richly to his Chapel Hill community as a student, memorialist for the many outstanding UNC alumni of his generation, Lay Reader, Vestryman and Senior Warden of the Chapel of Cross, and member since 1973 of numerous boards and committees associated with the development and well-being of the University of North Carolina, from which he received his AB in 1946. He earned a law degree from Yale in 1953. He practiced law in Washington, DC, until 1961, when he joined the U.S. Treasury Department as Special Assistant to the Under Secretary and then to the Secretary of the Treasury. From 1969-1973 he was Columbia University Vice President for Finance and then Deputy to the President. From 1973 he held various positions in administration at UNC, serving as Vice-Chancellor for Administration from 1980-1996. He married MaryJane Fairbairn Abdill. They have four children and three grandchildren. He was born in Winston-Salem in 1924 and graduated Greensboro, NC, Senior High School in 1941—*Editor*

Douglass Hunt: Speaker of the Student Legislature

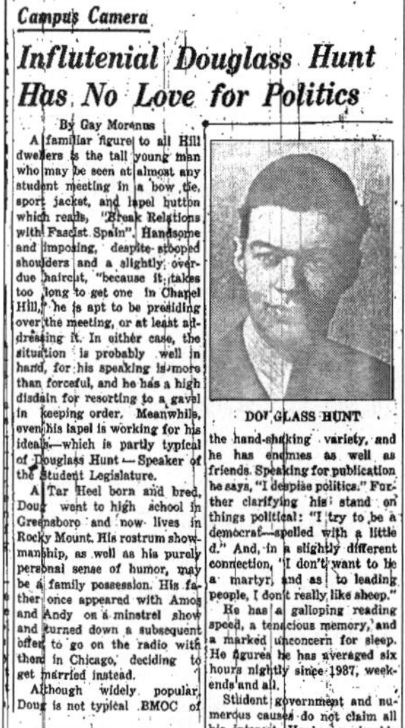

Campus Camera

Influtenial Douglass Hunt Has No Love for Politics

By Gay Morenus

A familiar figure to all Hill dwellers is the tall young man who may be seen at almost any student meeting in a bow tie, sport jacket, and lapel button which reads, "Break Relations with Fascist Spain". Handsome and imposing, despite stooped shoulders and a slightly overdue haircut, "because it takes too long to get one in Chapel Hill," he is apt to be presiding over the meeting, or at least addressing it. In either case, the situation is probably well in hand, for his speaking is more than forceful, and he has a high disdain for resorting to a gavel in keeping order. Meanwhile, even his lapel is working for his ideals—which is partly typical of Douglass Hunt — Speaker of the Student Legislature.

A Tar Heel born and bred, Doug went to high school in Greensboro and now lives in Rocky Mount. His rostrum showmanship, as well as his purely personal sense of humor, may be a family possession. His father once appeared with Amos and Andy on a minstrel show and turned down a subsequent offer to go on the radio with them in Chicago, deciding to get married instead.

Although widely popular, Doug is not typical BMOC of the hand-shaking variety, and he has enemies as well as friends. Speaking for publication he says, "I despise politics." Further clarifying his stand on things political: "I try to be a democrat—spelled with a little d." And, in a slightly different connection, "I don't want to be a martyr, and as to leading people, I don't really like sheep."

He has a galloping reading speed, a tenacious memory, and a marked unconcern for sleep. He figures he has averaged six hours nightly since 1937, weekends and all.

Student government and numerous causes do not claim all his interest.

DOUGLASS HUNT

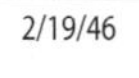

2/19/46

The Daily Tar Heel

Sesquicentenn

New Student Party

Chuck Heath Named to Head SP Activities

Implies Discipline For Top Officers

Claude Th
For May F

4/12/46

Constitution Presented To Student Legislature

Bill to Tax Students for Failure to Vote Deferred for Approval of Administration

By Trudy Walton

The long-awaited campus constitution arrived on the legislative scene Thursday night when Speaker Douglass Hunt presented the 15-page document to the Student Legislature.

Before its passage, the Constitution bill will involve lengthy sessions of debate, "two hours for each section," Hunt prophesied. It will appear in its entirety in the Tar Heel early next quarter before the special session of the Legislature is called April 1, 2, and 3 when that body will sit as a convention to examine the constitution.

Walt Brinkley, Naval ROTC who in view of his graduation this month resigned his post as chairman of the Elections Committee, will be succeeded by Jack Hester, also a Naval ROTC student.

Discussion Deferred

Discussion on the bill to tax each student one dollar for failure to vote in a campus election was deferred until South Build

3/16/46

Legislature Reverses Vote On Trial Bill

In a complete reversal, the Student Legislature voted last night by a 13-12 margin to reserve in the proposed student constitution the right of every accused man before the student council to face his accuser if he so desires.

The decision threw out the 14-10 vote of the previous evening to approve an amendment which would have left the question of accused and accuser up to the discretion of the student council.

Leader in the fight against the amendment last night, in addition to Doug Hunt and Jimmy Wallace, was Bill Crisp, CPU chairman, who charged "moral

4/18/46

Hunt, Student Party candidate for Speaker in November, 1944, introduced the bill and appointed the committee that created a written student constitution. The Coates (below left) wrote it was "the highest peak" in 150 years of student government at the University.

May, 1946

The One-World Telegram

Vol. I. No. 1. Chapel Hill, N. C. May, 1946

National Conference Of Students' Is Formed By Intercollegiate Gathering; Structure Unique

Wolfe Heads Organization Set Up To Fight Segregation

Principles Stated

Hunt, Robinson Address Meeting

NCS 'Program' Hits At Army Jim Crow, Seeks End Of Fraternity Discrimination

NCS STATEMENT OF PRINCIPLES

'Dual Society' Concept Denounced As Group Votes Indorsement Of Permanent FEPC And Backs World Government Principle

Vermont Sorority Suspended After Pledging Colored Girl

Alpha Xi Delta Chapter At UVM Placed Under Year's Ban By National Officers; Hunter College Situation Delicate

International Meet To Be Held In Prague

17 Campuses Represented In Newly-Formed Statewide Virginia Intercollegiate Council

***"STATEMENT OF PRINCIPLES:** Because we believe that the central value in human existence is human personality . . . we therefore are opposed to discrimination and segregation . . . anti-Semitism and any*

Published in 1985 by the Professor Emeritus Fund at UNC.

LAYING THE GROUNDWORK for constitutional reform in student government at the University of North Carolina, Douglass Hunt used the power of his position and his rhetorical skills to lead the reform of 150 years of proud tradition in student self-government and closely guarded custom and power centers among the social club and class structures on campus. He was instrumental in formation of the Student Party which, with the election of Bill Mackie in 1949, displaced for four years the fraternity-controlled University Party (see Murphy, p. 973). He took part in the closely contested selection of Jimmy Wallace as UNC member of the U.S. delegation to the 1946 World Student Congress (p. 968), and joined forces with Al Lowenstein in forming the short-lived National Student Conference (above right), a precursor to the Chicago Student Conference which founded the NSA.

Materials Concerning the San Francisco Conference

Berea has come to life regarding Dunbarton Oaks

A LETTER FROM BEREA COLLEGE

Most of these kids are from the mountains, few of them have money, and all of them work

On May 16, 1945, Douglass Hunt and William H. Poteat wrote a letter to delegates who had attended the Chapel Hill Conference, which included the following:

We had a letter from Dorothy Tredennick of Berea College accompanying Berea's contribution for the San Francisco Conference. We thought you might be interested in part of it:

"I don't know whether [or not] you appreciate the circumstances of the average Berea student. Most of these kids are from the mountains, few of them have money, and all of them work about two thirds of their way through school, this in spite of the fact that the tuition is only 160 dollars a year. So you can see why I was definitely depressed when the resolution was passed at our conference asking each campus to endeavor to raise $50. I also felt a little guilty because you people at Chapel Hill had made such an excellent showing when you raised money for our conference.

"At any rate, I came back to Berea fired with enthusiasm, as I think most of the people at Chapel Hill that Sunday were, and I was determined to get some money out of Berea, in spite of the tradition that Berea students were not to be solicited for anything. I am happy to say that I met with success.

"Berea has come to life regarding Dunbarton Oaks*; we have done chapel programs, newspaper articles, panel discussions, forums, etc., and this week I did my darndest in a full school chapel program in which I reported on the conference, what we accomplished and what we hoped for the future. At that time, I made a strong plea for contributions, and in the two days since that chapel, we have collected sixty-five dollars and seventy-seven cents! The deans and the president were extremely pessimistic from the start, but they are eating their words and sharing my pleasure at the outcome. . . . Berea students are definitely behind the venture, and of the five hundred solicited, it is obvious that all of them gave."

* *Editor's note:* In October, 1944, the 26 nations that had pledged not to make a separate peace with the Axis powers met at Dunbarton Oaks and drafted proposals for a United Nations Charter. The 1945 San Francisco Conference, called by President Roosevelt as a consequence, was opened on April 25 by President Truman just a few weeks after Roosevelt died on April 12. The Conference of Southern Students was held on April 15th.

COLLEGES ATTENDING THE CONFERENCE OF SOUTHERN STUDENTS

Executive Committee
Conference of Southern Students

Charles D. Proctor, Fisk University, Nashville, Tenn. *President*
Douglass Hunt, University of North Carolina, Chapel Hill, N. C. *Executive Secretary-Treasurer*

ALABAMA: Martha Nell Raines, *Alabama College*, Montevallo, Ala.
ARKANSAS: Helen Bailey, *Hendrik College*, Conway, Ala.
FLORIDA: Janet Haas, *Rollins College*, Winter Park, Fla.
GEORGIA: Bill Herring, *Emory University*, Emory, Ga.
KENTUCKY: Dorothy Tredennick, *Berea College*, Berea, Ky.
LOUISIANA: James McGovern, *Loyola University*, New Orleans, La.
MISSISSIPPI: Sam Barefield, *Millsaps College*, Jackson, Miss.
NORTH CAROLINA: Millie Blackman, *Meredith College*, Raleigh, N. C.
OKLAHOMA: Georgia Stricklen, *Oklahoma A. and M.*, Stillwater, Okla.
SOUTH CAROLINA: Francis Wallace, *South Carolina State College*, Orangeburg, S.C.
TENNESSEE: Evelyn Hail, *University of Chattanooga*, Chattanooga, Tenn.
TEXAS: Alan Myers, *Southern Methodist University*, Dallas, Tex.
VIRGINIA: James Bryant, *Virginia Union University*, Richmond, Va.

LIST OF DELEGATES AND ADDRESSES FOR THE SOUTHERN CONFERENCE OF STUDENTS

President—Charles Proctor
Executive Secretary—Douglass Hunt

Alabama

1. Miss Martha Nell Raines, Alabama College, Montevallo.
2. Miss Sadye Appleby, Tuskegee Institute, Tuskegee.
3. Miss Gloria Watson, Box 982, University of Alabama, University.

Arkansas

4. Miss Helen Bailey, Hendrix College, Conway.
5. Mr. Clifford Davis, Philander Smith College, Little Rock.

Florida

6. Mr. Horace Hill, Bethune Cookman College, Daytona Beach.
7. Miss Patricia Aiken, Box 164, Florida State College for Women, Tallahassee.
8. Miss Janet Haas, Rollins College, Winter Park.
9. Mr. Bill Colson, S.A.E. House, University of Florida, Gainesville.

Georgia

10. Mrs. Maxie Cochrane, Box 228, Atlanta University, Atlanta.
11. Mr. W. C. Herring, Emory University, Emory.
12. Mr. Guy L. Darnell, Jr., Morehouse College, Atlanta.
13. Mr. Forrest Champion, Jr., University of Georgia, Athens.

Kentucky

14. Miss Dorothy Tredennick, Berea College, Berea.
15. Miss Lucy Myer, University of Kentucky, Lexington.

Louisiana

16. Miss Stella Pecot, Dillard University, New Orleans.
17. Mr. James D. McGovern, Loyola University, Law School 6365 St. Charles Ave., New Orleans.

Mississippi

18. Mr. Sam Barefield, Box 5027 Millsaps College, Jackson.
19. Mr. Doug Stone, University of Mississippi, University.

North Carolina

20. Miss Joyce Ebley, Bennett College, Greensboro.

21. Mr. William McLaughlin, Black Mountain College, Black Mountain.
22. Mr. Robert Hollinger, Davidson College, Davidson.
23. Miss Ada Lou Allen, Eastern Carolina Teachers College, Greenville.
24. Mr. Myrlon Gatling, Duke University, Durham.
25. Mr. Raymond Wood, Guilford College, Guilford College.
26. Mr. A. T. McDaniel, Jr.,Box 661, North Carolina College for Negroes, Durham.
27. Miss Millie Blackman, Meredith College, Raleigh.
28. Mr. L. W. Gatlin, P.O. Box 3008, State College, Raleigh.
29. Mr. Douglass Hunt, Y.M.C.A., Chapel Hill, University of North Carolina.
30. Miss Zoe Swecker, Woman's College of U.N.C., Greensboro.

Oklahoma

31. Miss Georgia Stricklen, Okla. Agri. & Mech., 1207 College Ave., Stillwater.

South Carolina

32. Mr. Robert W. Touchberry, Clemson College, Clemson.
33. Mr. Frances Wallace, South Carolina State College, Orangeburg.
34. Mr. William Preston Horton, Box 1837, University of South Carolina, Columbia.
35. Mr. Clifford E. Jones, Wofford College, Spartanburg.

Tennessee

36. Mr. Charles D. Proctor, Chemistry Research Bldg., Fisk University. Nashville.
37. Miss Marinell Ross, Maryville College, Maryville.
38. Sgt. Maurice Clifford, Meharry Medical.College, Nashville.
39. ________, Scarritt College, Nashville.
40. Mr. Edward Mullins, Tennessee State College, Nashville.
41. Miss Janet Burdette, Tusculum College, Greenville.
42. Mr. John McGowan, Vanderbilt University, Nashville.
43. Miss Evelyn Hail, University of Chattanooga, Chattanooga.

Texas

44. Mr. Alan T. Myers, SAE Box, Southern Methodist University, Dallas.
45. Miss Anna Buchanan, University of Texas, Austin.

Virginia

46. Miss Alta Ayers, Westhampton College, University of Va., Richmond.
47. Mr. John M. Wilbur, Jr., University of Richmond, Richmond.
48. Miss Mary Lou Manning, Kappa Kappa Gama, William and Mary, Williamsburg.
49. Mr. Rudolph Aggrey, 406 Wigwan Ave., Hampton Institute, Hampton.
50. Mr. John E. Manahan, University of Virginia, Fairview Farms, Scottsville.
51. Mr. James H. Bryant, Virginia Union University, Richmond.
52. Mr. Joe M. Owen, Union Theological Seminary, Richmond.
53. Mr. Leonard Rex Criminale, P.O. Box 4, Washington and Lee, Lexington.
54. Miss Esther Foote Ellis, Box 82, Randolph Macon W. College, Lynchburg.
55. Mr. Robt. H. Hahn, V.P.I. Box 610, Virginia Tech. Station, Blacksburg.

Editor's note regarding the document source: When Douglass Hunt first recorded his recollection of his attendence at the San Francisco Conference, it was without the benefit of long since displaced files. A little over a year later, during a visit to the archives at the Center for American History, The University of Texas at Austin, in the Lyndon Johnson Library, I came across in the student activities correspondence files—by accident, as is so often the case—the Berea letter and an undated "News Release" containing the listings. The listings are reproduced with addresses and abbreviations as they appeared in the release. They put a human face on and bring to life in vivid simplicity Douglass Hunt's memories of those promising times.

High Hopes for the San Francisco Conference

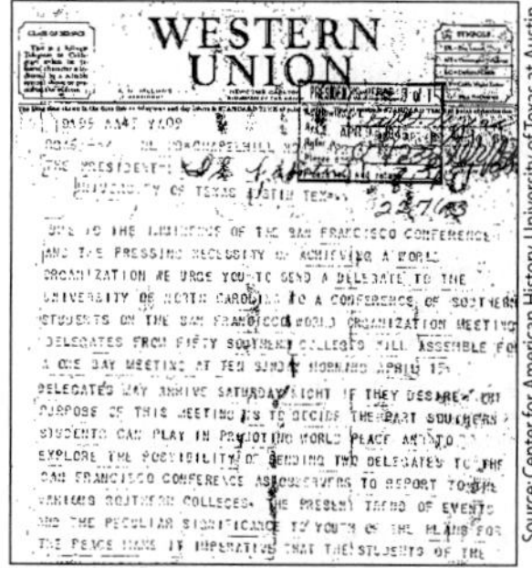

WESTERN UNION

THE SIMMONS NEWS

Is the Dumbarton Oaks Plan The Way to Lasting Peace?

WILL SAN FRANCISCO RATIFY THE CHARTER?

SF Conference Builds Machinery For Peace

Source: Center for American History, University of Texas at Austin

PROSPECTS FOR AN EFFECTIVE NEW WORLD ORGANIZATION that would replace the failed League of Nations and secure the peace led to postwar planning for a United Nations organization launched at the Dunbarton Oaks conference in 1944. Interest among students was widespread as exemplified by the Southern Student Conference about which Douglass Hunt writes, as well as among veterans groups and Federalists (see also Meyer, p. 707, and Jonas, p. 751). Above left, 4/15/45 telegram to U. of Texas (see below). From top: *The Simmons News*, Boston, 4/19/45; *The Denver Clarion*, U. of Denver 5/11/45 (see column, right).

North Carolina Invites Texas to Chapel Hill

A telegram dated April 9, 1949 (see above), from Ralph R. Glenn, chairman of arrangements, to "The President, University of Texas, Austin, Texas," reads in part:

Due to the imminence of the San Francisco Conference and the pressing necessity of achieving a world organization we urge you to send a delegate to the University of North Carolina to a conference of Southern students on the San Francisco world organization meeting . . . The purpose of this meeting is to decide the part Southern students can play in promoting world peace and to explore the possibility of sending two delegates to the San Francisco Conference as observers. . . .The present trend of events and the peculiar significance to youth of the plans for the peace make it imperative that the students of the South participate in the discussions of those plans.

Denver University Chancellor Reports on the Conference

The primary job of the international representatives now attending the San Francisco Peace conference is that of creating machinery for enforcing peace. The rest of the world problems can wait to be completed at later dates and other conferences, said Chancellor Ben M. Cherrington, Denver University chancellor, consultant to the United States delegation at the conference.

. . . . A new and rather surprising angle to the conference was the fact that there has been a rising tide of support for including in the new charter to be formed by the [Economic and Social] council, a Bill of Human Rights. Nowhere do the Dunbarton Oaks proposals refer to the Four Freedoms or to the human rights endorsed by the Atlantic Charter. Delegations from large and small nations are asking that a world Bill of Rights be drafted at the conference. . . .

Excerpt from The Denver Clarion, *May 11, 1945, University of Denver.*

A Close Call Choosing the North Carolina Delegate to Go to Prague

A group of students, chaired I believe by Bill Poteat of the Y, met in the upstairs of Graham Memorial on one afternoon in the Spring of 1946, to select a delegate from the University of North Carolina to go to Prague. The candidates were Jimmy Wallace, later the mayor of Chapel Hill, among other things, Junius Irving Scales, whose name is well known from the Smith Act case, *United States versus Scales* (I think that's the name of the case); and Sybil Goerch, who is the daughter of Carl Goerch, then editor of the State magazine.

The race really was between Wallace and Scales. Al Lowenstein, who was a member of the selection committee, was playing a game of pickup basketball down in Woollen Gym, and when we counted noses and it became fairly clear that the race was close, we sent a runner to the gym to bring Al back. He came back, and his vote made the tie, which the chairman of the selection committee then broke in favor of Wallace, and we sent Wallace to Prague.

Al tipped the scales on the Prague experience in an important way. Here is why.

I had known about Scales from our high school days, because I had grown up in Greensboro and Scales was a best friend of a good friend of mine who was a year ahead of me down here in college. So I knew that generally, his views were far to the left, as did others of us who were aware of his politics. But he had strong defenders from the faculty and from others who spoke and who put him forward as a good candidate. His public posture often took in people of a liberal view. So it really was a close call.

Later in time he became a more public figure. He was often to be seen in the Intimate Book Shop making a speech, and he had friends among other students. He was, I think, the chairman of the Communist Party in North Carolina. It was not so obvious when he was a student, so I think it's understandable that a lot of people didn't know a lot about Junius Scales. But it was a near thing, Jimmy Wallace's election, and we did the right thing.

Jimmy was a wonderful delegate. Jimmy had one of the sharpest senses of humor and the ability to phrase it of anybody I've ever known. He was the Southern delegate at the Chicago Student Conference who, while acting as parliamentarian during a critical debate, suggested, "let's separate into two parts, those with drawls and those without."* Jimmy was a Renaissance man—he even played the piano. And later, when he was a full professor at North Carolina State University for twenty-odd years, he won the outstanding teaching prize every time he was eligible for it.

Near the end of June I went into the army, and I received mail there. I remember getting some letters from Jimmy after the trip to Prague, and maybe some during the trip. And all those things that came, I sent home to my mother, who—like all mothers of our generation—carefully saved them.

—Douglass Hunt

* See Clif Wharton's account, p. 114.

Jimmy Wallace Comes Back With a Message

Editor's note: Jimmy Wallace took his wit, wisdom and parliamentary skills to a global stage when he joined the U.S. delegation to the World Student Congress. He came back with a message that left its mark not only on his fellow delegates but on many of the generation of student leaders from around the country who helped found the National Student Association at the Chicago Student Conference. He chose the community of Chapel Hill as his lifetime stage, where he became a civic leader and Mayor. For more on Jimmy Wallace and on his journey to Prague see pp. 92, 94-97, 105.

Jimmy Wallace Chosen Prague Delegate

Tar Heel Campus Camera

Jimmy Wallace; the Man Who Dislikes the Most Things Most

By Gay Morenus

It is to be hoped that Jimmy Wallace achieves some degree of extra-university fame; if for no other reason than for the challenging research problem his character would make some twenty-first century graduate student in history. In spite of all scholarly efforts, however, Jimmy would probably remain as enigmatic as he is today. Certainly no column of newsprint can hope to encompass his personality. However, there's no harm in hunting him up and seeing what we can learn.

Finding Wallace is no problem. The most likely place to look is a certain Franklin Street pastry shop where he often pounds out "The Maple Leaf Rag" on the piano, with a poker face and rolling eyes; or drinks ing pronouncements on campus politics or atomic power.

He comes from Jamesville, an Eastern Carolina town of 600 which, he modestly explains, "wasn't named for me. In Jamesville people say what they mean, and I've never gotten used

Though Jimmy's aversions are best known, his fondness for Chapel Hill and the University, for good books and bull sessions, for People in General and a few friends in particular, is just as characteristic. He also likes sports, and thinks our basketball team "magnificent."

Wallace has been active on campus since 1940, notably as Tar Heel columnist, last year's CPU president, present head of the men's Inter-Dorm Council, and one of Student Legislature's most active members. He himself is typically emphatic about the organizations to which he does not belong: Grail, Golden

Czech Capital Will Be Scene Of Conference

To Travel In Europe, Report Upon Return

By Dick Koral

Jimmy Wallace will represent the University of North Carolina at the International Student Conference this August. The UNC Preparatory Committee, representing the overwhelming majority of student organizations here elected him after a two and one-half hour session in which three candidates were thoroughly questioned and their qualifications discussed.

Sails with Others

Wallace will leave for New York a few days before the American delegation sails for Prague to participate with representatives of ten other college

From top, *Daily Tar Heel*, 5/31/46, ?/46, 10/16/46 (photo).

Students Will Hear Report By Wallace On Czech Sessions

UNC Delegate to Relate Happenings Of Prague World C

James Wallace, recently returne as UNC delegate to the Prague deliver his formal report to the st ing in Hill hall. Wallace was one of 25 students representing fifteen United States universities at the Czechoslovak-sponsored worldwide assembly, which met August 18-31. He was the only delegate from a southern school.

Discuss Recommendations, Work

In his address tonight Wallace is expected to discuss both the final recommendations of the assembly and the work and attitudes of its individual members. In addition he is to relate his own experiences as Carolina representative.

The Chapel Hill YMCA received the official invitation from the Czech government's preparatory committee May 1, and in turn set up of local preparatory body under Walt Stuart

Prague Conference Attained Major Goal, Wallace States

UNC Delegate Terms Student Meeting 'Miniature United Nations Assembly'

By Bill Sexton

Characterizing the 1946 World Student Congress at Pragu a "miniature United Nations assembly," UNC Delegate Jim Wallace last night reported to the students he represented t "the conference accomplished its major objective . . . the for tion of an International Student union."

He told how the 300 students fr 40 nations went on record for wo government, set up organization the new world student federat with headquarters in Prague, and termined to reassemble in th years.

Noted "Eternal Disagreement"

The Carolina delegate, one of representing the United States at August session, noted "eternal d agreement" between Catholic me bers from all countries and the ren

The Conference and Fascism

Most Widely Misused Word In World Defied Definition

Spain and Its Use....

Suffering of Spanish People Under Franco Was Condemned

Summing Up...

Forming of World Government Termed Essential to Survival

From top, 1946: 10/16, 10/17, 10/25, 10/27, 10/?, 10/?.

WALLACE gave an oral report on the World Student Congress and wrote six columns for the *Tar Heel*. See pp. 94-97 for some excerpts from his and other delegate reports.

Junius Irving Scales

Chapel Hill Communist Party Openly Revealed by Circular

By Raney Stanford

The presence of a local chapter of the Communist party in Chapel Hill was officially revealed yesterday, with the issuance of an information circular from the "Communist Party of Chapel Hill, Junius Scales, chairman."

On being contacted after the release of the circular, Scales explained that the organization in Chapel Hill is a "small, active, representative group" affiliated with the North and South Carolina district and national headquarters of the party in America.

or deny this, he said this accusation "should not be dignified by a reply from any one who believes in the tradition of American liberty."

But in a statement to the Daily Tar Heel yesterday Scales stated: "I have been associated with the Communist party for a number of years. I am now speaking in

DEFEATED BY ONE VOTE to be UNC delegate, as Douglass Hunt recalls (above), Scales came from a prominent North Carolina family and enjoyed fraternity support. He did not reveal his Communist Party membership until a year and a half later.

(*Daily Tar Heel* 10/30/47)

"The South's first regional step to true democracy"

Charles Proctor: "A Great Vision of the Future"

Charles Proctor

Fisk University delegate and President of the 1945 Conference of Southern Students. Member of the 1946 U.S. delegation to the World Student Congress.

Editor's note: Fisk University's archivist reports that there was no student newspaper or yearbook when Proctor was a student there. His service as a black student leader in his time is documented earlier in this section by Douglass Hunt (p. 963), and in the following article. It appeared in the April, 1945 edition of The Fisk Herald, *the student literary magazine. In turn it was a reprint from an undated issue of the University of North Carolina* Tar Heel. *His presence on the U.S. delegation to the World Student Congress was reported in the press (See p. 94). Proctor, who later went on to a career in pharmacology, opens a window on a brief moment of hope in race relations when he writes, "it seemed as if the spirit of racial prejudice had taken a holiday at Chapel Hill last April 15." The issues discussed at the Chapel Hill conference preceding San Francisco—Dunbarton Oaks, Bretton Woods, contents of the proposed charter—are discussed by Cord Meyer in "A Service Man Looks at the Peace," (p.703). See also* Act of Creation: The Founding of the United Nations *by Stephen Schlesinger (Westview Press, 2003). The original title of the article was "A Vision Comes to North Carolina University."*

"As I watched and listened, I saw a great vision of the future, when all citizens, male and female, black and white, shall sit down together and deliberate the laws of the land."

—LEE SILVERSTEIN (University of North Carolina *Tar Heel*)

Perhaps the columnist who wrote those lines has been justly prophetic in his vision, for truly the Conference of Southern Students, held recently on the campus of the University of North Carolina, has sounded a new note in intercollegiate and interracial cooperation. Assembled there were campus leaders from fifty or more colleges and universities spread all over the South, young people who had come primarily to consider the problems which center around the San Francisco World Security Conference and who went away having done this and far more. By establishing themselves as a permanent body, this group of thirty-eight Caucasian and fifteen Negro delegates deliberately took the South's first regional step to true democracy. Acting for the fifty thousand Southern students the conference unanimously adopted a resolution which has become its preamble.

The spirit of racial prejudice takes a holiday

No greater plea for action in the quest for human rights could be made than is embodied in these words: "We, the members of the Conference of Southern Students, believing that we must constantly and actively defend the ideals of human justice, freedom, and democratic action, and believing that peace can only be won by the maintenance of these practical necessities everywhere in the world, do hereby establish the Conference of Southern Students to disseminate information, inspire action, and serve as an organ of expression for the students of all southern colleges and universities who subscribe to the foregoing principles." It is no small wonder that such a preamble was adopted—it seemed as if the spirit of racial prejudice had taken a holiday at Chapel Hill last April 15th. The delegates were too busy attempting to justify the conference's stand on Dunbarton Oaks and Bretton Woods to remember the pigment proportions of the several delegates who held the floor during the discussions on these important proposals. Intellectual honesty permeated the very air!

And it is my belief that these efforts, taken in such an atmosphere, were not in vain. As Russian claims and demands, and even Russian silence on certain issues, seem to point more and more to her growing nationalistic spirit and her distrust of other powers, there are many who would say that the resolutions of Chapel Hill were unrealistic in their outlook—idealistic impossibilities which the San Francisco Conference will find impracticable. Despite this reality the Chapel Hill group took the stand that San Francisco will not be the last place that the nations of the world will hold a security meeting and that therefore the conference, representing a bloc of the opinion of American youth, should be firm in expressing what it believed to be the most desirable conditions for world peace that would be lasting.

This move was most significant in that it recognized that peace will be maintained, in the ultimate analysis, not wholly by the representatives of states and nations, but by the massed opinions of the peoples who will profit by its attainment. In order to secure these ends the conference wholeheartedly endorsed the Bretton Woods Proposals as the only plan yet presented that granted minimum economic security commensurate with peace to all of the nations and approved the Dumbarton Oaks Plan while recommending certain additions and changes to it. These changes seemed to reflect the democratic atmosphere of the conference as the resolutions called for the inclusion of a "Bill of Rights" in the world peace charter that would assure the rights of all peoples, regardless of color, race or creed, and the right of petition; as they struck out against the possibility of one of the "Big Five" making itself impervious to the charter's laws on aggression and declaration of aggression by calling for less than a unanimous vote of the five permanent members in the Security Council for the rendition of decisions concerning action against aggressor nations.

One other important resolution which allowed for political and economic advancement was passed, and read as follows: "That the agreement drawn up at San Francisco include provisions for the re-examination and revision of the machinery for international cooperation within a maximum of five years of the date of the establishment of the international organization." The discussions which led to these resolutions were remarkable: all the delegates spoke well and many sides of the issues in question were brought out.

Hopes for a permanent organization

The group proved itself no less capable or democratic in setting up the framework of its permanent organization. Providing itself with a president, secretary, treasurer and thirteen executive committeemen, one from each of the states represented, it has given vent to the foundation of long time permanency. Proof of its democracy is shown in its selection of officials. Its president is Charles D. Proctor. Douglass Hunt of the University of North Carolina is secretary-treasurer, and four of the executive committeemen are Negroes. Maurice Clifford, A.S.T.P. Sgt. from Meharry, who might as well be "our own," is one of the conference's delegates to San Francisco; Hunt is the other, while Proctor and James Monohan of the University of Virginia are first and second alternates respectively. It is significant that a Negro should be the first president of an interracial collegiate organization in the South.

Perhaps the significance is traceable to a new era: of thought penetrating the minds of southern youth that was first envisioned in a practical way in the minds of a few students like Doug Hunt, Jack Anderson, Buddy Glenn, Mary Lib Barwick and others who thought up this "harebrained" scheme less than two weeks ago when they were walking down the University of North Carolina's fraternity row "just thinking about something somebody had said in a seminar somewhere." In any event, the conference would do well to remember the words of Frank Graham, President of the Universiity of North Carolina, even as it provokes the interest of southern students in current affairs. He said, "This undertaking will take courage and I am certain that the only thing that this body need fear is fear itself!" I think that Dr. Graham was right and I believe that the students of the South know that he was.

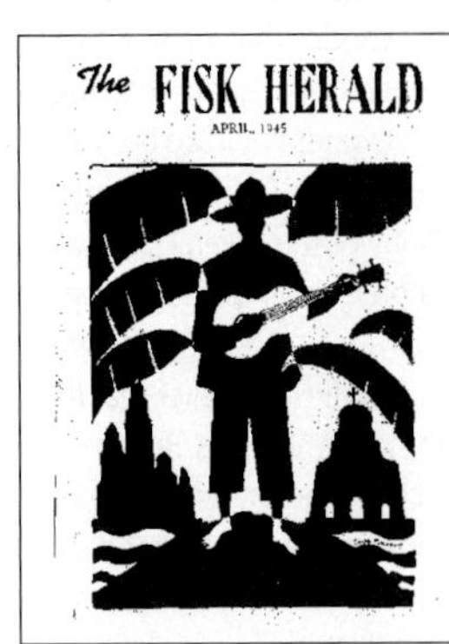

The Story of Fisk

Barely six months after the end of the Civil War, and just two years after the Emancipation Proclamation, three men—John Ogden, the Reverend Erastus Milo Cravath, and the Reverend Edward P. Smith—established the Fisk School in Nashville, named in honor of General Clinton B. Fisk of the Tennessee Freedmen's Bureau, who provided the new institution with facilities in former Union Army barracks near the present site of Nashville's Union Station. In these facilities Fisk convened its first classes on January 9, 1866. The first students ranged in age from seven to seventy, but shared common experiences of slavery and poverty—and an extraordinary thirst for learning.

The work of Fisk's founders was sponsored by the American Missionary Association—later part of the United Church of Christ, with which Fisk retains an affiliation today. Ogden, Cravath, and Smith, along with others in their movement, shared a dream of an educational institution that would be open to all, regardless of race, and that would measure itself by "the highest standards, not of Negro education, but of American education at its best." Their dream was incorporated as Fisk University on August 22, 1867.

The tradition of excellence at Fisk has developed out of a history marked by struggle and uncertainty. Fisk's world-famous Jubilee Singers originated as a group of traveling students who set out from Nashville in 1871, taking the entire contents of the University treasury with them for travel expenses, praying that through their music they could somehow raise money enough to keep open the doors of their debt-ridden school.

From its earliest days, Fisk has played a leadership role in the education of African-Americans. Fisk faculty and alumni have been among America's intellectual, artistic, and civic leaders in every generation since the University's beginnings. Among them have been such figures as W.E.B. Du Bois (Fisk class of 1888), the great social critic and co-founder of the NAACP. Booker T. Washington—the great educator who was Du Bois' famous philosophical adversary as well as the founder of Tuskegee University—served on Fisk's Board of Trustees, married a Fisk alumna, and sent his own children to Fisk. Charles Spurgeon Johnson, Fisk's first black president, helped to conceive the modern science of sociology. The distinguished artist Aaron Douglas served on the Fisk faculty for many years, and his murals decorate the walls of the University's administration building. Arna Bontemps, Sterling A. Brown, Robert Hayden, and James Weldon Johnson were among several Fisk faculty members who became major figures in American literature. The acclaimed composer-musicologists John W. Work, Sr., John W. Work, Jr., and John W. Work, III, were Fisk alumni and members of the faculty. Professor St. Elmo Brady, one of the first African-Americans to achieve eminence in chemistry, was for many years on the Fisk faculty. Probably no single institution has played so central a role as Fisk in the shaping of black learning and culture

Text [excerpted] and photo from Fisk Web site (www.fisk.edu).
1948 enrollment: 973.

Myself

Excerpted from a brief reflection appearing in The Fisk Herald *literary magazine of December, 1943. The memoir was written in 1939.*

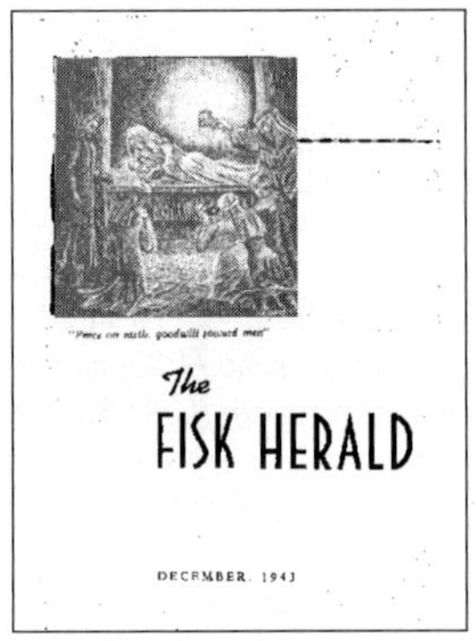

My recollections of my own individual person are entered herein.... A self is not something I was endowed with at birth. It is something I am creating as I live my daily life. Whether that self will be vapid or virile, barren or productive, a source of misery or a source of power that depends solely upon the interests I cultivate, the thoughts I permit, the ideals I reach out after, the reactions I let myself enjoy.

My present views impart to me that life's greatest achievement is the continual remaking of yourself so that at last you know how to live....

... Thus my mentality has given you my soul, gentle reader. It in itself represents naught but a mere ideal, an intangible essence. As trial comes, is tried on me, and then receives my inner self's judgment, I remember that I am not perfect. This holds true even in my regard to my conscience. My life at Fisk has given me such an experience. I struggled against odds which I knew were impossible to surmount. Finally, it took the personification of the odds herself to show me that sentimental infirmity has no place in courageous action. Sometimes I am glad that I have had and am having a trial, for I am slowly gaining a peace of mind, an understanding of people, and a genuine tolerance of others.

—Charles D. Proctor

CHARLES D. PROCTOR

Education: Fisk University: BA, 1943, MA 1946. Loyola University, Chicago, Ph. D., 1950. Florida A&M University, D.Sc.

Career: Pharmacologist/Toxicologist. Professor and Chairman, Dept. of Pharmacology, Meharry Medical College.

PICTURE CREDIT: *Then:* 1946 World Student Congress, Prague (Libby Cater).
DOCUMENTS: Courtesy, Fisk University Archives.

"The education of the American Negro has had a paradoxical character, for it passes on to him the rich cutural heritage of democratic America while denying him full participation in this heritage."

Charles S. Johnson: "Social Statesman"

President, Fisk University, 1946-56
Member, NSA National Advisory Council, 1950-53

Editor's note: Charles S. Johnson was of the generation of Negro educators who provided both scholarship and leadership in the movement toward racial integration and interracial cooperation that preceded Brown v. Board of Education and laid the groundwork for the subsequent civil rights movement.

He was the first black president of Fisk (founded in 1867) and has been called the "godfather to the Harlem Rennaissance." "With the assistance of a corps of vigorous young minds," he founded the reknowned Fisk Race Relations Institute in 1944. It was "an arena for an exchange of concepts . . . by men and women of diverse ethnic roots . . . a theater for spirited, bold, persistent, sometimes angry, often provocative voices," which drew such outstanding leaders as Thurgood Marshall and Martin Luther King to its forums (from "Charles Spurgeon Johnson Remembered," by L. M. Collins, Fisk archives).

He followed R.O. Johnson, Professor of Education at Atlanta University, as one of the Black educators who served on the NSA Advisory Council.

Education and Realism

(Excerpts from a talk delivered at Hampton Institute Convocation, September 19, 1946, provided by Fisk University Archives.)

This year, President Bridgman informs me, there are approximately fifteen hundred students at Hampton, almost twice as many as there have been before. Not only is this student body the largest in the history of the institution but it is probably the most varied as to age, background and interests. Nearly half of you are veterans, which means that you are somewhat older than you would ordinarily be coming out of high school into college, that you have seen places and done things that would not ordinarily have fallen to your lots and that your way of thinking about a number of things has probably changed.

Many of the faculty, too, are new as a natural result of the sudden expansion in size of the student body. The student often thinks of a teacher as an unchanging feature of the landscape who stays in place while students come and go, but in the classrooms in the next day or two many of you will be faced by teachers who have never been in that classroom before, who have perhaps never even faced a class before. This means that you will have to learn together how best to progress toward the goals which all of you are consciously, or unconsciously, seeking.

What are these goals? Why have you, often at considerable sacrifice to yourselves or to your parents, decided to spend a year or two, or three or four, at Hampton Institute? I should like to ask first, What is it that students feel to be most important to them? What is it that gives zest for life and such interest in education as they may have, apart from the dominant and sometimes dominating concerns of their parents in them? If these ideas were to be summarized, I should say that students, and particularly Negro students, are interested less in the abstract values of education for education's sake than in the more immediate and intimate, problems of acquiring, through the medium of education, a new cultural status. They are interested in laying the foundation for personal and economic security, and in eventually finding psychic and emotional satisfactions on the plane of living to which no stigma of inferiority attaches, of living fully in a free world.

Freedom and security are difficult for most persons to obtain, and particularly for Negro students. But I would like to emphasizee that in the world today, and regardless of race or color, if we tend to think of freedom and security as goals which we can reach merely as individuals by virtue of our own individual competitive efforts, we are doomed from the outset to defeat. America has been a land of individualism. Even those of us who have been shut out from the actual realization of the typical American success story have been affected by it to the extent that we tend to think of our success, our citizenship, our obligation to society, our morality even, in terms of individual effort. In school and college we think we have succeeded if we get high grades, keep out of trouble and earn a degree showing that we have completed the required number of hours entitling us to a certain academic or vocational status.

In the matter of earning a living we think we have succeeded if we can get and keep a better than average job which gives us either better than average income or a higher degree of social prestige. In our professional life we think that if we attend church regularly, are kind to our families and honest in our dealings with others we have fulfilled the demands of morality and good citizenship.

All these concepts are the heritage of a pioneer period when a man's life achievement was to a large extent actually the result of his own efforts. The family was the economic as well as the social unit, and responsibility to the family group was the primary responsibility. A man got his satisfaction in life out of a security which he could actually create by his own labor. His family were fed and clothed by the things which he produced, and there was a direct and vital connection between the work which he did and the satisfaction of his most basic needs.

* * * *

Over and beyond [the] need for the satisfaction of individual psychological requirements is the obligation that educated persons have to work for a society in which these satisfactions have become available to all. Those of you who are veterans were asked to serve your country in the name of the extension and protection of freedom and security. Many of you did serve without a clear definition of what freedom and security were, and without the certainty that your service was bringing you any closer to them. Your service, however, did bring you an opportunity for education which you might otherwise not have had. This education should be used to help you to learn just what these good things are which we seek, and how we can move toward them in the context of the modern world.

The Education of Negroes in the Post-War World

(Excerpts from a talk delivered in 1952, provided by Fisk University Archives)

Editor's note: In this talk Johnson highlights the cultural and social dilemmas confronting Negro educators who advocate for taking part in an American society defined "by the realities of segregation and racial subordination."

The problem of devising an education program for Negroes which will enable them to make their full contribution to American life is not accurately defined as a problem in intercultural education. The situation of the Negro in the United States is different from that of any other minority group. Memories of American Negroes of the present generation do not go back beyond their environment in this country, nor does their culture differ except in degree from that of the white population. As Langston Hughes discovered after visiting Africa, to seek a social heritage for Negroes in the United States, "I did not feel the rhythms of the primitive singing through me and so I could not live and write as though I did. I was only an American Negro—who had loved the surface of Africa and the rhythms of Africa—but I was not Africa. I was Chicago and Kansas City and Broadway and Harlem."

This is not to say that the educational needs of the Negro population are identical in every respect with those of the white population, or, indeed, that the educational needs of the white population are individually identical. The difference in stresses suggested relates itself to the past opportunities of the respective groups and as a consequence, to the disparity in levels or planes of the culture, and the unique personality difficulties engendered by these factors. All of these have a bearing upon education, present and future.

* * * *

Closely allied to the problem of understanding oneself is the problem of understanding one's relation to the community and nation. This is especially difficult in the case of Negro children, since the relationship itself is an ambiguous one, defined on the one hand by the uncompromising principles of the American creed, on the other by the realities of segregation and racial subordination. In the first edition of his book written at the close of World War I, Bogardus refers to the Negro situation in the United States, which seem to have meaning at the stage of race relations which we find at the close of World War II.

> Although the Negroes are native-born, speak the English language, and have adopted the rudimentary cultural standards of the white people, they have lived long in the land without adequate economic and educational opportunities, and they have not reached a level where they fully understand and appreciate Americanism. They have been the victims of such an extensive segregation movement, following the days of slavery and reconstruction, that a startling degree of stupid misunderstanding and blind race prejudice has been fanned, at times, to flames. The Negro problem is the leading race question in the United States today. It underlies the welfare of the nation; it demands the salutary leavening influence of an adequate Americanization spirit.

* * * *

Any program of socialized education for Negroes which had as one of its objectives teaching the Negro to be patriotic in a meaningful way would have to face the difficulties of making the ideology functional. The first problem is to find Negro teachers to whom the concept of patriotism has value and meaning, and the second is to provide an environment in the American setting in which these ideals can find expression.

An immediate problem which has to be faced now in the field of Negro education is the absorption by present educational institutions, especially the separate schools and colleges for Negroes in the South, of the Negro veterans who plan to continue their education under the G.I. Bill of Rights or in some other way. . . .

CHARLES SPURGEON JOHNSON

(1893-1956)

(Adapted from a biography provided by the Fisk University Archives)

Charles Spurgeon Johnson was born in Bristol, Virginia, on July 24, 1893, the son of a Baptist minister. He attended Wayland Academy and Virginia Union University and pursued graduate study in the field of sociology at the University of Chicago.While at Chicago, he became Director of Research and Investigations for the Chicago Urban League and in 1919 was appointed Associate Executive Secretary of Chicago's Commission on Race Relations following the race riots in that city. The volume, *The Negro in Chicago,* published by the University of Chicago Press (1922), resulted from this work.

During World War I he was in combat as Regimental Sergeant Major in the 803rd Pioneer Infantry. In 1921, he became Director of Research for the National Urban League and founded the periodical *Opportunity*, a journal of Negro life, which he edited until 1928 when he became Director of the Department of Social Sciences at Fisk University. He was elected President of Fisk in 1946.

He served on numerous national and international committees and commissions concerned with health, education and race relations appointed by Presidents Hoover, Roosevelt and Truman. He was among twenty educators sent to Japan in 1946 to advise General MacArthur on the reorganization of Japan's educational system. He was appointed by President Truman in 1946 as one of the ten U.S. delegates to the first session of UNESCO in Paris. He was on the Executive Committee of the U.S. National Committee for UNESCO.

From 1943 to 1948, he was co-director of the Race Relations Program of the Julius Rosenwald Fund and was a member of its Board. From 1944 to 1950 he was director of the Race Relations Division of the American Missionary Association of the Congregational and Christian Churches of America.

In the fall of 1955, Dr. Johnson was elected Chairman of the UNESCO Conference of experts on race and race relations in the world. On invitation of the American-Scandinavian Foundation and the universities of Stockholm, Oslo and Copenhagen, he made a lecture tour of the Scandinavian countries.

He has written extensively for national and professional journals and has received many awards and honorary degrees for his work in the field of race relations. His Harvard University award characterized him as "Educator, author and social statesman; wise in his unremitting efforts to move America forward towards our historic goals of real equality and justice."

Dr. Johnson was survived by his wife, Marie Antoinette Burgette, and three sons. He was a member of the Congregational Church and a Deacon in the Fisk Union Church.

PICTURE CREDIT AND DOCUMENTS: Courtesy of Fisk University Archives.

The "Athens of the South": Civil rights and student leadership

2. North Carolina: Leading NSA in the Region

Richard J. Murphy
Virginia-Carolina Regional Chairman, 1950-51
NSA President, 1952-53

I entered the University of North Carolina in September of 1947. That's when I first met Al Lowenstein, who was to have a significant influence on my life as he did on so many others. Al was one or two years ahead of me at the University and became a well-known and influential student leader both on campus and nationally.[1] I will write more about him later. Going through my scrapbook now, I find two major editorials I wrote for the *Daily Tar Heel*, and a speech I gave at the Philadelphia Bulletin Forum, around which I can relate some of the highlights of NSA activity at North Carolina and in the Region.

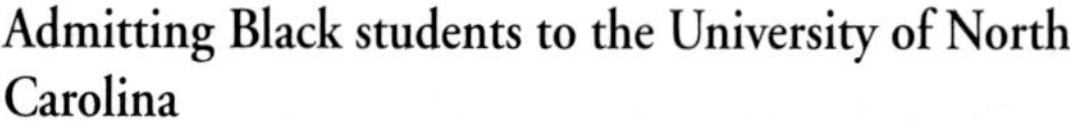

Admitting Black students to the University of North Carolina

Wiping out segregation was a galvanizing issue of our day at the University. In an editorial which I wrote in the *Tar Heel* in 1951, which related to segregation and the admission of the first Black students to the University of North Carolina at Chapel Hill, I said:

> There should be no second class student at the University of North Carolina. Any person who gains admission here is entitled to be a student first class. To admit students and then to discriminate against them because of race, religion, creed or economic circumstance is thoroughly repugnant to the cardinal principle for which this venerable citadel of democracy and freedom has long stood—equal treatment for all students, special privileges for none.

This was the climax of a long struggle in which NSA people on the campus had, for several years, agitated to get Black students admitted to the University, especially after the Sweatt case had been decided in June of 1950, involving the University of Texas and the admission of the first Black student into law school there.[2]

NSA people on campus and other student government leaders had petitioned the University, rather than wading through years of litigation, to voluntarily admit Black students, especially to the graduate schools, where the case of inequality was clear. There were no alternative schools, whether they were equal or not. The University was completely segregated at that time, as was nearly everything in the state.

By this time, Dr. Frank Graham had left the University, and there was a new president who was much more conservative than Dr. Graham. Dr. Graham believed that we really ought to have Blacks in the university. He was the president of the University of North Carolina from 1933 until 1949, when he was appointed to the U.S. Senate to fill the unexpired term of Senator J. Melville Broughton (who had just been elected and had died of a heart attack within days thereafter).

Dr. Graham's appointment to the Senate was historic because he was, at that time, the most liberal man ever appointed to the Congress from the South. He was a tremendous inspiration to students; also a longtime supporter and adviser of NSA, serving on our National Advisory Council from 1949 to 1953.

Seating Blacks at football games

Unfortunately, the University never admitted Black students voluntarily. It was forced, by court order, to admit them in the fall of 1951. When the Black students were first admitted, they were put in a dormitory separate from the rest of the students. The worst indignity of all was that at the football games, rather than being seated in the Student Section (this was the flashcard section, where we did the card tricks), they were put behind the goalpost in the end zone, separate from all the other students. Well, we exploded.

First of all, I was asked to write an editorial for the *Daily Tar Heel*, which I still think was a pretty stinging one. Secondly, Barry Farber, who was my successor as the regional chairman of NSA, got every athlete who was attending a regular meeting of the Monogram Club at the University to sign a petition, which he brought to the student legislature that evening, where I was the principal speaker supporting the position (which was adopted) that the Black students ought to be removed from the goalpost area and seated with the rest of the students. Then, Henry Bowers, the student body president and an NSA delegate, denounced the University's action and galvanized support for his position from a score of campus groups. The University administration had to completely reverse its stand within ten days, which was really historic. Nothing like that had ever happened before.

Student leaders at the University

Farber, incidentally, is now in New York as a national radio commentator. He ran for mayor on New York's Conservative party ticket. He was then, and still is, a Republican. His piece about the Kenan Stadium incident appears in Part 3 of this anthology.

The incident was also a good example of the NSA influence on campus, because all of the people providing the leadership for this campaign were the NSA people in the student government. The president of the student body, Henry Bowers, was an active NSA supporter and delegate, as was his predecessor, John Sanders, a wonderful man who later became vice president of the University and head of the Institute of Government. Bowers, a calm but steadfast leader, later became vice chancellor of North Carolina State University. Ben Jones, who was the local and regional NSA chairman before me, became one of the leading philanthropists to the University.

The Red Scare and McCarthyism

We were all very active on behalf of civil rights, and had, for a long time, been agitating for the admission of Black students. One time, at an organizing meeting in the back room of Aggie's Restaurant in 1951, we opened the meeting to anyone who wanted to come. There was a person who sat in the meeting whom none of us recognized. He was an older man who introduced himself as somebody from South Carolina who was interested in the issue of integration.

We later found out that he was a spy. He reported the event to U.S. Senator Willis Smith, a former president of the American Bar Association and the man who had beaten Dr. Graham in the dirtiest Senate race that's ever been run in North Carolina. Smith was a predecessor of Jesse Helms. In fact, Jesse Helms was his campaign manager.

Senator Smith then reported to the U.S. State Department that I was the head of the Communist Party in North Carolina because I presided over this meeting to get Black students admitted to the University! At that time I had just been appointed to the National Commission for UNESCO representing NSA, so the State Department called me to Washington to go into this matter. This was the height of the Joseph McCarthy period. In 1950 McCarthy had made his famous speech in West Virginia about the number of communists in the State Department and then held everybody in fear of his accusations for several years after that. To be identified to the government as a Communist (especially by a U.S. Senator) was then a very serious matter, and it took quite a while to clear the matter up.

I was elected by the National Executive Committee in 1951 to a three-year term on UNESCO, and I served under President Truman and into the first year of the Dwight Eisenhower administration. I followed in the footsteps of Bob Smith and Rob West, NSA's first two representatives to the Commission. I was then a senior at the University and later spent one additional year as a graduate student before I became NSA president.

Arguing for freedom of action

I wrote another long article on the subject of academic freedom for the *Daily Tar Heel* on February 22, 1952. The *Daily Tar Heel* was the principal paper in the town because it was a small town, but there was a weekly town paper as well. The *Daily Tar Heel* was one of the best completely student-run papers in the country back then. (*The Cornell Daily Sun*, *The Chicago Maroon*, *The Harvard Crimson*, *The Yale Daily News*, and *The University of Michigan Daily* were also premier papers at that time.) Barry Farber was one of the editors of the *Tar Heel* while I was there, as was Dick Jenrette, later of the investment firm Donaldson, Lufkin and Jenrette.

The paper decided to run my article as an editorial. This editorial concerned itself with:

> a creeping intellectual paralysis that has come to grip the American educational community. This paralysis finds its roots in fear and conformity generated by the nature of the cold war . . . [and] the disastrous effects of such practices as loyalty oaths, bans on speakers, the outlawing of student political groups. . . .The effect has been to stifle free thought and discussion—to make people afraid to think on their own and doubly afraid to act on their own.[3]

I especially took up the issue of two members of the Board of Trustees, the Clark brothers. They were major industrialists, and they were also white supremacists who tried to intimidate the students—especially the student body president, John Sanders—by writing letters to their hometowns, telling people that the conduct of these students at the University was disgraceful because they were favorable to admitting Blacks. I noted in the editorial that "On Tuesday morning, the Dialectic Senate received a letter from this man (John Clark) demanding the names and addresses of all those who had voted in favor of equal treatment for all students in recent resolutions."

Attending UNESCO meeting causes trouble

The editorial was written after I had returned from a four-day national meeting of UNESCO in New York City. NSA had run the youth section of the meeting, dealing with how to organize young people to support UNESCO, what projects they could participate in, and what UNESCO was doing internationally among youth.

I had picked up a lot of ideas from that conference for the editorial, which got a lot of comment around the state for the next several months. It also landed me before the Board of Trustees because the two men I was attacking were trustees, but the university administration defended our freedom of expression and made clear their disapproval of the Clark brothers' action. Naturally, the parents of the students atacked, especially in small towns, would become alarmed because the Clark Brothers equated our actions with communist activity. This was a time in which we also had an active Ku Klux Klan in the state. Those guys meant business. For people who were associated with the admission of Blacks to anything, there was a real and present danger.

When the editorial was published, in 1952, I was chairman of the National Interim Committee, a five-member body formed by the NSA Congress to advise the NSA president in between sessions of the National Executive Committee. It was formed the year before I was elected president (1952) at the University of Indiana Congress.

Makeup of the Virginia-Carolinas Region

At that time, UNC was a member of the Virginia-Carolinas Region. The region also included North Carolina State University and several Black colleges (at one of which, Jesse Jackson later became a student and active in student government). Other members included North Carolina College in Durham, Duke, Wake Forest, and Johnson T. Smith University.

We had several small Black schools, both in North Carolina and in Virginia, that were members or came to regional meetings—Virginia Union College, Virginia State, and North Carolina A & T, for example.

Among white schools in Virginia were Virginia Poly Tech., Mary Washington College, Randolph Macon Women's College, and Sweet Briar. We had a number of women's colleges, including the women's college of the University of North Carolina at Greensboro.

South Carolina was not actively represented, although as I recall, we had two Black schools from South Carolina at one regional meeting. I believe that the University of South Carolina sent an observer delegation to at least one of the conferences while I was there.[4]

Both segregation and communism were hot button issues in the South. The segregation issue was overwhelming because everything was segregated. We couldn't hold meetings in any public building if we wanted to include a sit-down dinner. We had to hold them in churches—the few that would take us!

Integrated social events held in church only

When I was regional chair, virtually the only white church in which you could hold an integrated social meeting in the whole state was in Charlie Jones's Presbyterian church in Chapel Hill. We would have our suppers there. We would have our socials there, our receptions. We could go over to the University and use the Graham Memorial Student Union or the Dialectic Senate Building for formal meetings themselves, but we couldn't have any social activities on the University campus. That was the time in which bathrooms were segregated, drinking fountains were segregated, bus stations were segregated, buses were segregated—and you had to travel by bus in North Carolina at the time, because that was the main public means of transportation. Everything was segregated. We were the only organization at that time that was having joint meetings involving Black and white students crossing state lines.

Catholic colleges or student groups were weak in the region. When I was a student at Chapel Hill, we didn't even have a Catholic church. The Catholics used to hold services in Gerard Hall. Later, there was a Catholic church built. But we just didn't have that many Catholic students. The big churches were the Baptists and the Methodists and they had huge churches. And then came the Presbyterians after that. I was a member of that church.

A third major article I have found is the full text of a speech that I was invited by Mrs. Ruth Geri Hagy to give at the annual Philadelphia Bulletin Forum. It was sponsored by the *Philadelphia Bulletin*, which was the leading newspaper in Philadelphia at that time. It was a hundred year old paper—the standard of conservative Republicanism in Philadelphia.

Mrs. Hagy, who had become our great patron when we moved our NSA office to Philadelphia, was the women's editor of the *Bulletin* as well as the head of the Bulletin Forum, a three-day meeting that presented leading public figures at the Academy of Music, home of the Philadelphia Orchestra.[5] For NSA to be invited was a great honor, especially in the McCarthy era. In the speech, I outlined the NSA International Program as of the beginning of 1953. It's about the international role of the American student, what NSA was doing about it and what it had been doing about it since

1947. The complete text of the speech was reprinted in the *Philadelphia Bulletin*, a first for NSA.

Al Lowenstein stands out as a leader

Among the student leaders at North Carolina, Al Lowenstein stood out. He was very brilliant and was absolutely the greatest orator I have ever heard, with the possible exception of Hubert Humphrey. He was a powerful speaker. Here was a Jew and a Willkie Republican from Scarsdale, New York, in the heart of Dixie, espousing the admission of Blacks to the University, academic freedom, and other such causes and who had as his greatest heroes three people: Eleanor Roosevelt, to whom he was literally like a son; Norman Thomas, a Socialist, who was a frequenter of his father's restaurant; and Frank Graham, a Liberal Democrat and president of the University of North Carolina, who did not believe in segregation but had to administer the segregation laws of the state and who was a wonderful spirit and inspiration to us all.

Not only was Al a great orator with superior intellectual power, an avid newspaper reader and collector, but he also prided himself on being a great wrestler.[6] I don't know how great a wrestler he was, but he was a fervent one. He used to have a whole group of friends called "gym friends" that he would recruit for the Student Party, of which we were both members. At that time I was chairman of the Student Party.

He was a very slight guy with poor eyesight. He was not athletic at all, but he loved wrestling. He would go down to the gym and meet people who had not a political thought in their mind, and he would bring them to Student Party meetings, where we would be talking about the political issues of the day.

The Student Party and its leaders

The Student Party was really the liberal party on the campus. It was made up of both fraternity and nonfraternity people who were strong supporters of NSA. It fought the very conservative University Party, which was heavily fraternity dominated and believed that you ought to blindly defend fraternities, with all of their discriminatory clauses. That was another of the big issues we were fighting about—to eliminate discriminatory clauses from fraternities on the campus. Much of that wasn't done until many, many years later.

The fraternities dominated the student government until the Student Party came along and elected Bill Mackie, a Phi Gamma Delta, as our first student body president. (He later became the head of the History Department at Virginia Polytechnic Institute [VPI] for many years) He was a strong NSAer. He went to the Second NSA Congress at Illinois.

John Sanders was our second strong student body president, and Henry Bowers, our third. Ken Barton, who was our candidate to succeed Bowers, was defeated, but nonetheless he was an outstanding NSA chairman on the campus. Other prominent NSAers during this period included Banks Talley, who was secretary treasurer of the student body, and later became vice chancellor of North Carolina State University, Director of the North Carolina Symphony, and Director of the National Trust for Historic Preservation. And Barry Farber, whom the Student Party elected as editor of the *Daily Tar Heel*. He was a conservative Republican as well as very progressive on social issues, very much in favor of integration of the University and very much an internationalist. His views were very similar to those of Ben Jones, another Republican who was an ardent NSAer and chairman of the Virginia-Carolinas Region.

Barry Farber became our NSA representative to the Zagreb Youth Festival. He went almost directly from the football game we were attending in Washington, D.C., when Bill Dentzer appointed him in 1951 (because he spoke Croatian) and flew to Zagreb the next day.[7] I had to go back and explain to the University why he wasn't returning for the next two weeks.[8]

When Barry was inducted into the army, he set the all-time record for the number of languages spoken by any individual. He had learned these languages up as a young person in Baltimore, by going down to the waterfront and speaking to sailors. His grammar was terrible, but his vocabulary was terrific.

Finally, there was Jimmy Wallace, one of NSA's legendary founders in 1946 (and holder of four university degrees), who had returned to graduate school and served as sort of senior adviser to our NSA group. Jimmy later became mayor of Chapel Hill.[9]

Al Lowenstein and the Korean War

Al Lowenstein will go down in history as the leader of the Dump Lyndon Johnson movement and of the Anti–Vietnam War movement in 1968. But when he came to the NSA Congress at the University of Michigan in August of 1950, he was a floor leader attempting to get the resolution passed endorsing the action of President Truman in sending American troops into Korea.

This was the beginning of the Korean War.[10] The resolution carried overwhelmingly on the floor of the NSA Congress on the basis of Al's speech, and he was subsequently elected president at that Congress. Later, he led the opposition to the Vietnam War, but he was the leader for the endorsement of President Truman's action in the Korean War.

Korea had a lot to do with the subsequent speech that Al made five months later in Stockholm.[11] He was very upset with the communist invasion of South Korea. I know that he conversed with Mrs. Roosevelt before he went to Stockholm about what stand he ought to take on the issue of affiliation with the International Union of Students (IUS). This issue was particularly difficult for people who came from the South in NSA because the South was a very tough anti-communist area of the country, as Barefoot Sanders, University of Texas student body president in 1947-48, pointed out.[12] This was a key issue for NSA affiliation among Southern schools. It was very difficult in the South to defend NSA membership in an organization that was dealing with the IUS.

The Stockholm Conference

The issue when Lowenstein went to Stockholm mostly concerned whether there ought to be a separate organization set up to counter the IUS or whether there should just be cooperation on practical projects, which is the way actually it worked out. Cosec was set up as a separate organization to cooperate on practical projects, but it was not to be anti-IUS.

Al went with a strong attack on the IUS by pointing out its communist domination and by saying that we ought to have an alternative to it, but he didn't specify what the nature of that alternative ought to be. A number of people felt that Al had gone a little bit too far in Stockholm by alienating some of the other Western student unions (many of which faced internal communist problems of their own) with such a strong stand against the IUS and its failures.

But Al had the feeling, which I know was shared by Mrs. Roosevelt at the time, that something had to be done to fight the communists. Shortly before, Mrs. Roosevelt had been instrumental in establishing the Americans for Democratic Action (ADA) to fight the Wallace Progressives, who, she was afraid, were going to take over the liberals and distort the traditions that they supported through communist influence and infiltration.

Influence of the Americans for Democratic Action

I notice in the September 1950 issue of the *ADA News,* which is headlined "Al Lowenstein of SDA Elected NSA President," that the whole thrust of the article is about a very active SDA leader who was now being recognized as a leader in the student world.[13] It is useful to note that while the ADA represented the left and was an organization of New Deal liberals led by Mrs. Roosevelt, it also had this very strong anti-Communist stand—not in the Joe McCarthy sense, but in the sense that these people had seen what the communists had done to domestic organizations in this country. These liberals were determined that they should not be working with the communists in the same organization because eventually the communists would take it over.

Ralph McGill, of the *Atlanta Constitution*, was exactly of that same kind of mind. Dr. Graham, one of the most liberal human beings you ever met, was that way. In the post-war era, he saw the danger of the communists, and he wasn't about to buy the idea that Truman was responsible for the Cold War, which was the line being voiced by the pro-Soviet left.

When we were on campus in 1948 at Chapel Hill, I was the head of the Students for Democratic Action (SDA), which was the student branch of ADA. At the same time, I was very active in the NSA. And many of the NSAers at UNC were in the SDA. We were the only group on the campus actively supporting Harry Truman's reelection. The majority of the students of the campus, and this was a heavily Democratic campus, were supporting Strom Thurmond, who was running for president, with Fielding Wright of Mississippi as vice president, on the Dixiecrat ticket.

We've come a long way since then. Just visit Chapel Hill today and ponder the fact that the most famous Tar Heel alumnus of today, Michael Jordan, would not even have been considered for admission fifty years ago!

Richard J. Murphy was Assistant Postmaster General during the Kennedy and Johnson administrations. He was for 23 years the Washington, D.C.–based Director of Government Affairs for UNISYS (for an extended biography, see p. 786).

END NOTES

[1] See the essay on Lowenstein by Joan Long Lynch, p. 283.

[2] The landmark Heman Sweatt case challenged the "separate but equal doctrine" and the right of the state of Texas to force Sweatt to attend a segregated, Negro law school. The Supreme Court ruled in favor of Sweatt. The case was filed by the Southern Conference Educational Fund, Inc., and led the way to breaking down segregation in higher education in the South. See p. 420.

[3] See Janet Brown on NSA and academic freedom issues, p. 375.

[4] The Virginia-Carolinas roster of colleges at the 1952 Fifth Annual Student Congress includes Duke University, Randolph Macon College, Sweet Briar College, Virginia State College, Virginia Polytechnic Institute, University of North Carolina, Wake Forest College and the Women's College, University of North Carolina. Two colleges from South Carolina, Limestone and Allen University, appear on the roster for the Chicago Student Conference in 1946. Clemson A&M College attended the 1950 Michigan convention. The 1957 NSA membership roster shows thirty-five colleges in the Virginia-Carolinas Region.

[5] See Ruth Hagy Brod, p. 1084.

[6] See Hunsinger, p. 991.

[7] See Farber, p. 592.

The University of North Carolina and the Virginia-Carolinas Region

Editor's note: When the University of North Carolina was invited to select a member of the U.S. Delegation to the World Student Congress in Prague in the summer of 1946 (Pt.1, Sec. 2), it became fully engaged in building the new national organization, contributing leadership at every level, including two national presidents, Al Lowenstein (1950-51, pp. 283, 562), and Dick Murphy (pp. 630, 1033). The region embraced a pool of 111 4-year colleges in North and South Carolina, Virginia, and West Virginia, of which 24 were Negro colleges. Attendance at congresses ranged from 9 to 19 (with up to 4 Negro colleges). As many as 20 or more colleges would appear at regional events. During 1946-48, Virgina/West Virginia and the Carolinas were separate regions. They consolidated in 1948-49, and then West Virginia became a separate region in 1949-50, with 7 members. In 1952-53, West Virginia was combined with Pennsylvania, accommodating the region's long-time member, West Virginia Wesleyan. After the Chicago Conference, Clemson University became the only member from South Carolina in 1950-51. Johnson C. Smith, Sweet Briar, Randolph Macon, Marshall and, later, Duke were among the other colleges contributing leaderhsip to the region.

Some Issues and Leaders

Law School Approves Negroes As Day Students

Poll Conducted by Durham Herald Reveals 59 Per Cent Favor Move

Trustees Rule Clark's Tirades Against UNC Individual View

UNC Students Protest Campaign 'Against Campus Opinion Freedom'

Board's Stand 'Very Unfair,' Clark Claims

Gray, And Textile Magnate Exchange Heated Statements

UNC STUDENTS were ready to support integration. The law school admitted its first Black students (See Farber, p. 440) in 1951 without a court order. Free speech came under attack when a prominent trustee in 1952 attacked a "red fringe" at the University for their support of integration (see Murphy, p. 1080).

From top: *Tar Heel* 5/12/48; *Durham Morning Herald* 3/1/52; *Raleigh News and Observer* 2/?/52.

AL LOWENSTEIN helped write the new UNC student constitution (See Hunt, p. 000) and rose to campus prominence before being elected 1950-51 NSA President. **DICK MURPHY'S** leadership won him the same position two years later.

Backs Lowenstein For Vice-President

Dick Murphy Chosen NSA Head

Second UNC Student So Honored

Di. Phi Schedule

Dick Murphy Now Member Of UNESCO

From top: *Tar Heel* 3/10/49, 9/24/52, 9/21/51.

Historical Note: Although chartered by the state in 1789 and opened in 1795, it was not until 1881 that the University of North Carolina received its first legislative appropriation. In 1931 it was consolidated with the Women's College at Greensboro and State College at Raleigh under a single Board of Trustees. Frank Graham (p. 979) was the first consolidated President (www.unc.edu). 1948 enrollment at Chapel Hill: 7,548.

Leading the Region

1947-48

12/9/47 — **NSA Honors Howe, Clampitt Baker, Gerns with Offices**

Herman Baker

12/10/47 All from *The Daily Tar Heel*

Bring Your NSA Back Home (Excerpted)

"In this section of the country ... indications are that NSA will become a useful organization."

1948-49

Jess Dedmond

2/19/49 **Regional NSA Convention Opens On Campus Today**

2/20/49 **Conclave Hears Rogers**

Calls Group Voice Of U.S. Students

Registration Begins at 2; Meet Tonight

HELEN JEAN ROGERS (Mundelein C., IL), NSA's 1948-49 Secretary, made a well-received organizing tour throughout the South (See pp. 226, 599)

10/21/49 **Va.-N.C. Regional NSA Meet Gets Underway Here Today; National Officer Will Speak**

Students Here To Represent 20 Schools

10/23/49 ***NSA Hears Carmichael, Delahanty, Meeting Set To Adjourn Today***

BEN JONES became a major UNC benefactor.

1949-50

Ben Jones

See Bob Delahanty (U. of Louisville, KY), NSA 1949 Exec. Secy, p. 410.

1951-52

Barry Farber

1950-51

Ann Sulzberger

10/13/50 ***NSA Leader Leaves Post***

ANN SULZBERGER replaced Hal Brown (NC State), who protested NSA's stand on academic freedom.

5/4/51 **NSA Meetings Get Underway This Afternoon**

7 Schools Attend Conference Here; Weaver To Speak

1/26/52 **NSA Meet To Be Held Here Soon**

BARRY FARBER represented NSA in Yugoslavia and Brazil (See pp. 441, 575, 591, 606).

1952-53

Ken Barton

2/18/53 **100 Delegates To Hold NSA Conference Here**

Photos: U. of North Carolina Library, *Yearbooks*

RICHARD J. MURPHY, END NOTES (Continued)

[8] See Farber, p. 591.

[9] See Wallace, pp. 92, 94-97, 105.

[10] Gene Schwartz and Rob West reported on the anti-U.S. demonstrations in Prague at the beginning of the Korean War when they attended the World Student Congress with Bill Holbrook as NSA observers. See p. 559.

[11] See Eisenberg, p. 522. Also see the Lowenstein speech at Stockholm, p. 562.

[12] See Sanders, p. 995.

[13] See Reisin, p. 781.

PICTURE CREDITS: *Then:* U. of Minnesota, August 1952. *Now:* 1955, Grace Lutheran Church, D.C. (Both, author).

No abuse of freedom should cause us to strike down freedom of speech or publication as the fresh resource of a free university, a free religion, and a free state.

Frank Porter Graham: "The Beloved 'Dr. Frank'"

President, University of North Carolina
Member, NSA National Advisory Council, 1949-1953

Editor's note: In a distinguished career extending through the early and mid-20th century, Frank Graham became a voice of the progressive South, understanding of its traditions as well as "a prophet of social change [espousing] equal rights for all men before the weight of court opinion and national law was brought to bear upon these issues," as cited by the UNC News Bureau in its 2/14/72 press release. Dick Murphy recalls Frank Graham as "a tremendous inspiration to students." He was beloved by generations of students. They were united also by a deep loyalty to the institution. In a moving tribute at the Frank Graham Jubilee Symposium, Douglass Hunt describes the relationship between Dr. Graham and Al Lowenstein, NSA's 1950-51 President, and a campus leader from the year of his arrival there in 1946 (see Lowenstein, p. 283).

Al Lowenstein and Frank Graham

(Excerpts from Frank Graham Jubilee Symposium address by Douglass Hunt, Assistant to the Chancellor (See also Hunt, p.963).

Al was the closest thing Dr. Graham had to a son. . . . Frank and Al worked together to make real the ideals they shared in behalf of the causes in which they saw those ideals at peril. From 1945, when they met, until Dr. Frank's death in 1972 they were close as affectionate collaborators and as mutually admiring friends.

When they met, Al was a 16-year-old freshman at Chapel Hill, Dr. Frank was the 59-year-old president of the University. One friend has said of that first year, "How is it that, so soon after their meeting, this freshman became the keeper of the conscience of the president of the University?" I think I would say that Dr. Graham kept his own conscience and Al kept his, but that, from the beginning, their association was no one-way street: from the beginning they powerfully influenced each other. Four years after they met, Dr. Graham became a United States Senator from North Carolina and Al became one of his advisors. Twenty-four years after they met, Al became a United States Congressman from New York, and Dr. Graham was his counselor. In between, they both worked for the United Nations and for the cause of human rights wherever they saw a chance to heal the ancient running sores of humanity.

. . . Persuaders both, Graham and Lowenstein were convinced that in the long run—sometimes the very long run—human beings could be led by reason to do right and forsake wrong. But both were patient and thought it a part of the good to wait and work until persuasion could win the victory. Neither was surprised by the folly human beings can commit or the evil they do. Thus both were able to remain clear-eyed through years of disappointment.

Interracial Student Assemblies

Editor's note: At a meeting of the racially segregated North Carolina Student Legislature in December, 1945, a hotly contested motion was adopted inviting students from North Carolina Negro colleges to attend. The event aroused state-wide controversy, including threats to cut off funding for the event, and Graham, in his capacity as President, Consolidated University of North Carolina, issued a two-page statement on 12/9/45, excerpted below:

In consideration of the motion . . . to invite representatives of the Negro colleges of this State to participate in sessions of the Student Legislature, when it was suggested to some of the students that if they voted for what was to them their honest convictions, the appropriation to their institution would therefore likely be cut, I can understand their indignation at such a reflection on our State Legislature, and such a form of attempted coercion as unworthy of a free assembly. . . .

For many years churches and civic groups have sponsored in North Carolina and other Southern States interracial meetings and conferences. . . . It is a cause for hope in this troublous world that young men and women of our colleges and universities in a youthful general assembly . . . are thoughtfully and idealistically concerned with the pros and cons of such state matters as improving our schools, in providing adequate twelve months salaries for teachers, in the veto power of the governor, and in such international matters as sharing with wise safeguards atomic knowledge and more effectively organizing the world for full production and lasting peace. It is to them anomalous sincerely to hope to organize an international assembly of the peoples of all nations, colors and creeds [the UN] and at the same time in our own State Assembly of Youth to exclude representatives of our own Negro colleges in North Carolina.

The University's Role in the New Age

(Excerpts from an address by Dr. Graham at a UNC 1945 Sesquicentennial event)

The colleges and universities have within themselves the men and resources to help mankind onward toward the new age. The University must help to make adjustments, not as lags in the social process, but as leaders, of the people in need of the truth which can come from honest and thorough research in all fields, from informed and dedicated teaching, and from clear responsible thinking, by scholars who seek the truth and who, in their own lives, are free and unafraid to find and speak the truth as they find it. The scholars and teachers, scientists and philosophers of the universities have had a vital and creative part in every major scientific, agricultural, industrial, educational, professional, social, intellectual, and spiritual development of modern times. If society should fail now more adequately to sustain the schools, colleges, and universities, then society, in failing its own high purpose, will set in motion its own downfall. The universities cannot, without their own self-destruction, fail society in this hour. . . .

The true, the beautiful and the good in the free and responsible campus democracy

The curriculum of the college, often an age behind the highest need of the age it should be highly serving, cannot afford in these times to be belated or provincial in any place on earth or any period of history to come. The curricula should vitally represent the best of all branches of human knowledge. . . . Youth in the college needs both the scientific view and the spiritual aspirations of the whole person for the true, the beautiful and the good in the free and responsible, self-governing campus democracy, through which the students may have a vital part in their own education in preparation for their part in the great society of men and nations in the high adventure of creative cooperation toward the Kingdom of God. . . .

The Need for Political and Social Mechanisms

The curriculum of the school and college is thus one of the intellectual, social, and spiritual mechanisms needed to keep the human being and human society abreast of the scientific mechanisms of an advancing technology. The scientific mechanisms carry with them the necessity for the invention of political and social mechanisms for the human mastery of their power so that the pecuniary will be subordinated to the industrial, and the industrial subordinated to the human and spiritual. . . . Immediately, the world in this potentially tragic hour needs cooperation, cooperation between nations for justice and peace, cooperation between management and labor for reconversion, full production and fair distribution, and cooperation between governments, industries, endowed institutes, agricultural and engineering experiment stations, and graduate schools of the universities for cooperative research, not only in science, agriculture, industry, business and medicine, with their humane and dramatic victories, but also in all fields of knowledge and human relations, whose economic and social tensions may compress psychological bombs of devastating power. . . .

Atomic Power and the Need for Spiritual Revolution

The atomic revolution demands an intellectual and spiritual revolution. As the home of the atomic bomb, by virtue of her geographic and economic position, international cooperation, presidential daring, business and military genius for organization and production, university leadership, the devotion of preeminent scientists of many lands and the loyalty of workers from many states, America has a great moral responsibility. America, for the sake of her own soul, must take the lead in putting the atomic bomb under the ban and control of world goverment. America must, with wise safeguards, share the knowledge and use of atomic power with all the peoples, for full production and fair distribution within the nations, and for justice and peace among the nations. Standing where cross the high road and the low road of human destiny, America, with her mechanisms and her universities, let us pray, will not, in her choice, fail mankind in this tragic hour, but will rise to the responsibility of her power and the opportunity of her greatness to give fresh hope to the stricken and fearful peoples of the earth as brothers of men and sons of God for one cooperative world in our time.

A tribute to CHAPEL HILL

BY FRANK GRAHAM PRESIDENT UNIVERSITY OF NORTH CAROLINA

IN CHAPEL HILL among a friendly folk, this old University, the first state University to open its doors, stands on a hill set in the midst of beautiful forests under the skies that give their color and their charm to the life of youth gathered here. Traditions grow here with the ivy on the historic buildings and the moss on the ancient oaks. Friendships form here for the human pilgrimage. There is music in the air of the place. To the artist's touch flowers grow beautifully from the soil and plays come simply from the life of the people. Above the traffic of the hour, church spires reach toward the life of the spirit. Into this life, with its ideals, failures, and high courage, comes youth with his body and his mind, his hopes and his dreams. Scholars muster here the intellectual and spiritual resources of the race for the development of the whole personality of the poorest boy, and would make the University of North Carolina a stronghold of liberal learning with outposts of research along all the frontiers of the world. Great teachers on this hill kindle the fires that burn for him and light up the heavens of the commonwealth with the hopes of light and liberty for all mankind.

FRANK PORTER GRAHAM

(October 14, 1886-February 16, 1972)

(Adapted from the "Dictionary of North Carolina Biography," U. of North Carolina Press)

Born in Fayetteville, N.C., Graham attended Charlotte High School and graduated University of North Carolina, Phi Beta Kappa, in 1898. He served in the Marine Corps in World War I. In 1914 as an instructor of history, he began "years of brilliant classroom teaching that were to influence the lives of countless undergraduates" at UNC from 1914 until he was appointed President in 1930, serving until 1949.

During World War II, Graham gave much of his time to public service on several defense boards. In 1946, President Harry S Truman appointed Graham to the President's Committee on Civil Rights. which in 1947 made a historic report on the nation's racial problems and proposals for their solution. He served as U.S. representative in 1947 on the UN committee on the Dutch-Indonesian dispute. He also helped organize and was the first president of the Oak Ridge Institute of Nuclear Studies (1946-49).

In 1949 he was appointed by Governor Kerr Scott to fill an unexpired term in the Senate. He was narrowly defeated in a heated Democratic re-nomination primary in which the winning side used the racial issue extensively to Graham's disadvantage. In 1951 he was appointed UN representative to mediate the dispute between India and Pakistan over Kashmir. Later he served as an assistant secretary general of the United Nations.

A deeply religious man, Graham was active in the work of the Presbyterian Church. Married to Marian Drane in 1932, they had no children.

CREDITS: All documents are from The Graham Papers, Southern Historical Collection, The Library of the U. of North Carolina at Chapel Hill. *Photo:* c.1946. *Above title quote:* Frank Graham, 12/9/45 University News Bureau release.

A riddle confronting Northern whites and Southern whites of good will as they faced each other and their prejudices

"The Mind of the South"

Editor's note: During an interview I had in October 1998 with Douglass Hunt, John Sanders, and Ben Jones, I put the question that I suspect every white Northerner faced in the first few years of the NSA experience: how to explain the striking contradictions and the deep passions that characterized race relations in the South. Not that prejudice in the North was unfamiliar to us—its de facto practice was everywhere. Throughout this anthology are poignant stories from Northern white students describing their hostile encounters when traveling or socializing in public places with their black fellow students. But these encounters were with the overtly prejudiced.

Of a different order were the encounters at NSA conferences in 1946 and 1947 of Northern white students with Southern white students of evident good will, in circumstances where issues of race were confronted in ways that Northern whites had not experienced and could not easily dismiss with simple moral judgments.

Douglass Hunt quoted Frank Graham, when he took the oath of office on Armistice Day 1931 as president of the university, that in the South there are two great races which will go up together or go down together. To understand this interdependence, he recommended, and John Sanders bought and presented me with a copy of, the groundbreaking 1941 work, The Mind of The South, *by* Charlotte News *editor W. J. Cash (reprint, New York: Alfred A. Knopf, 1971; Vintage, 1991).*

Following is a review of this book as it appeared in The Technique, *the student newspaper of Georgia Institute of Technology, on December 10, 1948. Its appearance at that time was prompted by the 1948 presidential elections in which Harry Truman defeated Thomas Dewey for the presidency, with both Henry Wallace on the Progressive ticket and Strom Thurmond on the States Rights ticket.*[1] *Thurmond's party, popularly known as the Dixiecrats and reflecting the segregationist voices of the time, received thirty-nine electoral college votes in the Southern states. Southern college student newspapers frequently editorialized on, and examined, these issues.*

From *The Technique* (Georgia Tech, Atlanta), December 10, 1948

The Mind of the South: Here is a picture of the old South, and a view of its people.

The Mind of the South, written by W. J. Cash, and reviewed by Woodie Grice

Along the southern boundary of Pennsylvania there lies a porous Iron Curtain which is known to all students of American history as the Mason and Dixon Line. This line was famous in ante bellum days for dividing the slave from the free states, and it still exists today to set off a unique portion of these United States—Dixie. To realize its existence, we have only to recall the way in which it cropped up during the recent national election.[2]

What factor has caused the people of this region to be unique? What causes certain of its citizens to dress up in bed sheets and go around scaring hell out of others? A brilliant attempt to psychoanalyze the region has been made by W. J. Cash, a late North Carolina editor, in his book, *The Mind of the South.*

This book is essentially an interpretative history of the South, with the accent on social, economic, and psychological influences. Mr. Cash places his basic character, a simple Anglo-Saxon immigrant, in a frontier land which yielded him a relatively ample livelihood with the exercise of a minimum of ingenuity. The plantation system, the cotton economy and the conflict with the "tariff gang" then lead this simple, unanalytical man into the Civil War, through reconstruction, and up the long hill toward industrialization.

Anglo-Saxon white immigrants populated the South

Mr. Cash discounts the legend of the aristocratic origin of the ruling class and avers that it arose, with the exception of a few "Virginians," from the mass of simple immigrants by a process of selection. The slave labor used by the plantation system made unnecessary the exploitation of white labor and thus created an independent class of poor whites on marginal land. This fact, coupled with the nearness in time to the frontier, the common origins of the people, and the united front of the white man against the negro, brought about a society which Mr. Cash believes to be unique in world history.

These same factors give the author's Southerner his other characteristics: a tendency towards violence, a romantic and superstitious mind, an aversion to reality, a love, a pleasure, and—most important—a high degree of individualism. These traits explain the dominance in southern religious life of the fundamentalists, doctrines of the evangelical sects and the extraordinary influence of the fire-eating demagogue.

This peculiar society found itself in the position of defending the moral wrong of its slave economy against a hostile Yankee. It was easy for the romantic Southerner to transcend reality and believe in a dream that his society was the most perfect on earth. The best of the planters developed a real feeling of noblesse oblige; all believed in the dream and fought criticism of it. The result of this was the greatest tragedy for the Southern mind—a complete intolerance of anything foreign and a resistance to the new ideas and skepticism so necessary to progress.

Post–Civil War factories employ poor whites and exclude negroes

The Civil War intensified this clannish feeling and created new economic and social problems. The old class of the completely independent poor white was robbed of its lands by the vicious cotton financing system of reconstruction. The paternalistic landholders saw the poor whites and the negroes coming into competition with each other as tenant farmers. What could be done to hold the color line and to stave off financial collapse? Factories to employ the poor whites and to exclude the negroes and to gain the riches of the Yankee were the answer. And so they sprang up, plantation-like, on the outskirts of growing Southern towns. So spontaneous was their growth that in some towns the people contributed their dimes and quarters to build the factory.

We then follow the Southern mind through the rise of Babitry [*sic*], the exploitation of cheap labor, and the ravages of a fluctuating cotton market up to 1941. Along the way Mr. Cash detects some intellectual improvement caused by the universities, but he deplores the fact that this improvement takes no real hold on the people—the "best people" included. The author concludes that the Southern mind, in spite of improvements, still has its characteristic vices: "violence, intolerance, aversion and suspicion to new ideas, an incapacity for analysis, . . .

attachment to fiction and false values, ... sentimentality and a lack of realism."

Place of the negro in the Southern pattern remains unanswered

This book is a great individual intellectual effort, but it is necessarily, because of its scope, non-authoritative. In many places, Mr. Cash has pieced his argument together with personal observations and generalities. Never does the author really come to grips with the problem of the negro's eventual place in the Southern pattern. It must be said, too, that not all of Mr. Cash's analysis and criticism is peculiar to the South, but [rather] is part of America—itself not too far removed from the frontier.

But here is a very important contribution to Southern literature which should be read by all who have any claim to enlightenment. Mr. Cash makes plain the need for competent, intelligent leadership as necessary to the eventual solution of the South's problems. If any reader feels the fires of this leadership smoldering in his being, he can find a focus in this book.

Editor's note: It is difficult, to this eye and ear, and at this point in time, not to take notice of the irony that in distilling the "Mind of the South," respectfully and thoughtfully, we are nonetheless limiting our definition of "the South" to include the European-American mind, while excluding the African-American mind, the latter being a presence and integral part of "the South" with which the former is also trying to deal.

END NOTES

[1] See Students for Wallace and Progressive Citizens of America, p. 796, and Reisin, p. 791.

[2] See also Part 3, Section 3, for other views of that period.

A 1951-52 Virginia - Carolinas Regional Assembly

NSA Delegates From 3 States To Gather Here

Delegates from 20 different schools in North Carolina, South Carolina and Virginia began arriving in Chapel Hill yesterday afternoon to attend the regional assembly of the National Student Association being held here.

Approximately 100 delegates are expected to be here for the assembly, Barry Farber, regional chairman, said yesterday.

The delegates will hear reports from national President Bill Dentzer, Muskigum College, Ohio and Dick Murphy, Carolina. Dentzer will report on the recent student congress held in Rio De Janerio and Murphy will give one on UNESCO (United Nations Educational, Social and Cultural Organization.)

Every meeting will be held in the faculty lounge of the Planetarium and is open to the general public.

Five workshops dealing with student government, publications, and campus-international relations will take up most of the week-end regional meet.

The Austrian Goodwill troupe that performed in Memorial hall last night was part of the week-end activities of the National Student Association conference.

Daily Tar Heel 3/1/52

VIRGINIA - CAROLINAS REGION
NATIONAL STUDENT ASSOCIATION
Conference, Feb. 29, March 1, 1952

MEMBER SCHOOLS

1. University of North Carolina — Chapel Hill, N. C.
   Barry Farber, Chairman, 112 "A" Dorm
   Jane Jenkins
   Dick Murphy
   Bill Carr
   Mel Stribling
   Henry Bowers
   Joel Fleishman
2. Women's College of the University of North Carolina — Greensboro, N. C.
   Martha Lohr, Chairman, New Guilford Dorm,
   Betsy Bachman
   Joann Wicker
   Mary Ann Spencer
   Ellen Strawbridge
   Sally Beaver
   Lucille Gille
   Ruth Idol
   Carolyn Haden
3. Randolph-Macon College — Lynchburg, Va.
   Mary W. McHenry, Chairman, Box 172
   Marty Edmundson
   Ann Mitinger
4. Sweet Briar College — Sweet Briar, Va.
   Edith Bell, Chairman
   Martha Legg
   Jane C. Roseberry
   Jane Collins
   Dale Hutter
   Ann Collins
   Burney Parrott
   Sally Hueber
5. Virginia State College — Petersburg, Va.
   Al Cade
   Samuel Thompson, Chairman
   George Kelsey
   Parnell Avery
6. Duke University, Women's Government — Durham, N. C.
   Jackie Lewis, Chairman
   Jane Lindsay
   Barbara Evans
   Thelma Stevens, Box 6072, College Station
7. Duke University, Men's Government — Durham, N. C.
   Al Raywid, Chairman
   Jim Chappell
   Vince Anderson
   Danta Germino

NON-MEMBER SCHOOLS

1. Sullins College — Bristol, Va.
   Nancy Peckham, Chairman
   Mart Alcott
   Carolyn McKinney
2. Lynchburg College — Lynchburg, Va.
   Charles Cumiskey, Chairman
   Gloria Layne
   Gail McMahon
   Hazel Crawford
   Thomas Jefferson
3. Virginia Tech Station, Military — Blacksburg, Va.
   Gene Sutherland, Chairman
   Kent Comegys
   Teddy Harris
4. Virginia Tech Station, Civilian — Blacksburg, Va.
   George Beamer, Chairman
   Bill Kayor
5. Montreat College — Montreat, N. C.
   Pat Williams, Chairman
   Faye Britt
   Jolene Parks
   Colleen Story
6. Atlantic Christian College — Wilson, N. C.
   Jimmy Peebles, Chairman
   Geraldine Corbett
7. Virginia Union — Richmond, Va.
   Romaine Smith, Chairman
   Ken Smith
8. Wake Forest College — Wake Forest, N. C
   Dan Fagg, Chairman, Sigma Chi Hous
   L. M. Wright
   Pat Mast, Charles Glanvill
   Richard Barnett, Nancy Morris
9. Hampton-Institute — Hampton, Va.
   Al Brown, Chairman, 246 Pierce Hal
   Lillian Robinson
10. Davidson College — Davidson, N. C.
   George Nichols, Chairman
   Larry Dagenhart
11. Longwood College — Farmville, Va.
   Lucy Page Hall, Chairman
   Nancy Driskill, Eleanor Koch
   Bobbie Obenshain, Polly Brothers
12. University of South Carolina — Columbia, S. C.
   Floyd Spence, Chairman
   Bill Novit, Fran Hagood
   Joe Pearce, Pat Davis
13. Meredith College — Raleigh, N. C.
   Marie Edwards, Chairman, Box 81
   Pat Smathers, Alstine Salte
   Venetia Stallings, Georganne Joy

(State Historical Society of Wisconsin: NSA Archives)

Historical notes: ♦ Rechartered in 1906 as the University of South Carolina, after the Civil War USC saw the closing of its predecessor, South Carolina College (founded in 1801), enrollment of Black students during Reconstruction, its closing again in 1877 and reopening as an all-white agricultural college in 1870. In 1963 the university was again integrated (http:// president.sc.edu). 1948 enrollment: 4,395. ♦ Renamed Virginia State College in 1946 (now University since 1979), it was chartered 1882 as Virginia Normal and Collegiate Institute, took over Hampton Institute's land-grant designation from private Hampton Institute in 1920, became Virginia State College for Negroes in 1930 (www.vsu.edu). 1948 enrollment: 1,900. ♦ Sweet Briar (VA) is a women's college founded in 1901 in a bequest from the widow of civic leader Elijah Fletcher, in memory of her daughter (www.sbc.edu). 1948 enrollment: 452. ♦ Co-ed Randolph Macon College (VA) was founded by Methodists in 1830 and named after two non-Methodists, John Randolph and Nathaniel Macon. Its Women's College founded 1890 continues today (www.rmc.edu). 1948 enrollment, Men's: 548; Women's: 701.

Berea College offers leadership.

3. NSA in Kentucky-Tennessee

Galen Martin
Berea College, Kentucky
Chair, Kentucky-Tennessee Region, 1950-51

When I returned to Berea College from the Navy in 1947, I brought with me an inclination to challenge authority. I had already been something of an agitator in high school. I grew up in East Rainelle, West Virginia, a small lumber town in the southeastern part of the state. The town was dominated by a nonunion company, the Meadow River Lumber Company, although the overwhelming, surrounding economy was coal; it was coal country. Clearly, I was influenced by the most dominant figures of our time in West Virginia, John L. Lewis and Franklin Delano Roosevelt. Many homes in the area had pictures of both men on their walls. My dad was a Republican—and very lonesome politically, as there were not many Republicans in East Rainelle. My mother leaned more to the Democratic Party.

Berea's historic commitment to Appalachia and to emancipation

Berea turned out to be just the right place for me. A little of its history will help explain why. Berea was founded in 1855 as a one-room school by John Gregg Fee, a vigorous antislavery preacher. Fee was given the land for the school by the first Cassius Marcellus Clay, a Kentucky emancipationist and a Yale graduate. Berea's early teachers were recruited from Oberlin College in Ohio, a strong antislavery institution. In 1869, Berea formalized its status as a college. The school maintained an almost equal black and white enrollment until 1904, when Kentucky passed the Day Law, largely directed at Berea, which prohibited interracial education.[1]

Through the years, Berea developed a set of "Great Commitments" on a foundation of Christian faith, the first of which was "to provide an educational opportunity for students from Appalachia who have great promise and limited resources." It is a residential campus, which incorporates a work program for all students intended to foster "a way of life characterized by plain living, pride in labor well done, zest for learning, high personal standards and concern for the welfare of others."[2]

My high school preparation for college was spotty, so Berea's dedication to serve the needs of underprepared students was ideal for me. I soon became active in the speech honorary society and in the Student Council. By my junior year in 1950, I was NSA campus coordinator and had mounted an unsuccessful, but instructive, run for Student Association president.[3] My main opponent was Fontaine Banks, with whom I attended the NSA Illinois Congress as a Berea delegate in 1949.

Looking back at clippings from *The Wallpaper*, the college newspaper, I see the beginnings of an attitude that has stayed with me throughout my life. Writing in behalf of my candidacy on the subject of leadership, I said: "Leadership in our association demands good sportsmanship and the absence of bitterness. All must realize that mature people can have honest differences of opinion and still be friends."

NSA's CIA funding link affronted the Berea spirit

In that spirit, I must address the linking of NSA with secret CIA funding for its international programs, which was exposed by *Ramparts* magazine in 1967. At the fiftieth NSA reunion in Madison, Wisconsin, in 1997, Craig Wilson, who was *NSA News* editor in the national office when Bob Kelly was president in 1949-50, read the part of his essay appearing in this anthology that deals with his own experience with the CIA money. Craig believes that the linkage began during his term as editor, when he and Fred Houghteling, then NSA executive secretary, made a trip east to raise money for NSA. Fred wasn't straightforward with Craig about the source of the money to finance the "international team" of observers NSA planned to send to Europe and Asia in the summer of 1950. The money ($10,000) came from secret government sources. Once the funding was established in an organized way, the annual sums grew into the six figures.[4]

Wrong to take the money, wrong to promise secrecy

I must speak about what I believe the response of Berea students and faculty would have been if they had known about the funds. Berea was very cognizant of the postwar efforts for peace, and the Fellowship of Reconciliation had a strong influence on the campus at that time. Quakers and pacifists, while a small minority, were quite vocal at Berea. They were strong leaders in many campus groups. The sociology professor Dr. Roscoe Giffin, who later got me involved in civil rights work, was one of those voices, as was Dean Widler, head of the Economics Department. Those leaders would have been shocked and totally aghast at the idea that while Berea was struggling to come up with its dues to support NSA, that organization was taking money from the CIA—and a lot of it—and that everybody at the helm of NSA was swearing to keep it a secret from the members. They would have thought this was just plain wrong, and I continue to think it was wrong.

I still believe that people can have honest differences of opinion and still be friends and work together. I am not condemning anyone or any view. I don't object to people having the view that there was nothing wrong with the CIA linkage, and I heard that view expressed at the Madison reunion. I just want the record to show that I completely disagree. I think it was wrong to take the money and doubly wrong to promise the government to keep it a secret from the NSA Board and member schools. I felt betrayed when I learned about it. As Janet Welsh Brown writes elsewhere in this book, "it was a betrayal of the integrity of our efforts."[5]

NSA fostered leadership training in human relations

The principles of honesty in your dealings and listening to one another while making clear your own point of view were embedded in one of NSA's most important programs in leadership training and human relations. I was the beneficiary of this training when I attended the 1950 College Conference at Lake Forest, Illinois, sponsored by the National Conference of Christians and Jews (NCCJ) and NSA.

I was one of the five group leaders at this conference, along with Robert McCaffrey, Joy Newburger, Dennis Trueblood, and Richard Medalie.[6] Ted Perry of Temple University, who was NSA vice president for student affairs, was cochair. Gordon Klopf, Chair of NSA's Advisory Council, was dean.[7] Participating in that conference was a wonderful, meaningful experience for me.

The conference used a workshop format and focused on group process and group leadership relating to student participation in campus activity and student government in a democratic process. The skills learned there fit into the leadership attitude I had already developed for myself, and I applied them at Berea and in the regional NSA. When I became Kentucky-Tennessee Regional Chair in September 1950 after the Michigan NSA Congress, I established the regional offices at Berea. Our first major program was a leadership training conference, held at Berea on December 9, which forty-five students from eleven Kentucky and Tennessee colleges attended. The workshops followed the Lake Forest model.[8] Bob Delahanty, former regional president and the then NSA national executive secretary, addressed the group.

The Kentucky-Tennessee Region

In the Kentucky-Tennessee region of NSA we worked hard to build a useful program of services to student government and to foster community among the colleges of the region. Berea, along with the University of Louisville, provided much of the leadership. The University of Kentucky was active for a while but voted against affiliation in March 1948, the same month Berea and Louisville voted in favor.[9]

At the time, there were eighty-five colleges and universities in the two states. Most of them were in Tennessee, but we also had significant numbers in Kentucky. We had a good mix and we worked hard to build participation in NSA. Ursuline, the Catholic women's college in Louisville, was particularly active. Other active member schools included Fisk, Southwestern at Memphis, Tennessee State, Tusculum, and Nazareth College.[10]

Although our national membership was always less than nine colleges during the first five years, we tended to have up to fifteen colleges at our regional meetings, with forty to fifty delegates. In addition to the student government and leadership workshops, several colleges launched NSA's Faculty Rating System. Louisville operated the Purchase Card Discount Program in the city for several years. There was always interest in NSA's summer travel and exchange programs, although we didn't seem to be involved much in the international affairs part of the program.

Here is the lineup of regional presidents: 1946, NCC temporary chair, Howard Bowles, University of Kentucky; spring 1947, Bill Welsh, Berea; 1947-48, James Harpster, Christian Brothers College; 1948-49, Bob Delahanty, University of Louisville; 1949-1950, Jim Bowling, University of Louisville; 1950-51, Galen Martin, Berea; 1951-52, Thomas Pfau, University of Louisville.

Race relations issues

Race relations were at the forefront at Berea and in the region, especially in Kentucky, whose history in that area was significantly different from Tennessee's. Tennessee had more race-baiting politicians. Although Kentucky was a former slave state, there was little political demagoguery of the issue. However, Kentucky did pass the Day Law about 1904, banning integrated education of the races. When the law was relaxed in 1950, Berea admitted its first two black students in almost fifty years.

One of the more memorable integration issues at the time was the Heman Sweatt case. It was a landmark case in which the "separate but equal" doctrine in Texas was challenged in the U.S. Supreme Court. Sweatt was forced by the state to attend a Negro law school. It was a college-level precursor to *Brown v. Board of Education* at the elementary and high school levels. I remember that we collected money at Berea in a lard bucket at a chapel program to give to Sweatt's legal fund. A look at the *Wallpaper* reminds me that Berea was host to a number of interracial meetings during the immediate postwar period, mostly sponsored by the YM- and YWCA and the Student Christian Movement.

Students for Democratic Action

Probably the most lasting influence on me, in terms of career as well as friendships, was the connection I made with Students for Democratic Action (SDA), an affiliate of Americans for Democratic Action. Ralph Forbes was chairman of the Berea SDA chapter, and Doug Kelley was one of our prominent members.

My first job after college was as national executive secretary of SDA. Mary Lou Allgood, who had been our regional NSA public relations director, and I married in September 1951 and moved to Madison, Wisconsin. I was a graduate student in the Department of Labor Economics, an outstanding program. Before the semester was up, Ken Kurtz and Doug Kelley sent me a telegram urging that I apply for the executive secretary vacancy at SDA, and I did. I finished the semester, and we moved to Washington, DC. In the SDA job, I followed three of the many fine leaders to emerge from SDA, Sy Reisin, Fritz Mondale, and Albert Ettinger. I stayed in the job for two years.[11]

My NSA and SDA activities dovetailed in a lot of ways. I went to four NSA congresses: Illinois (1949), Michigan (1950), and Minnesota (1951) as a Berea delegate and Indiana in 1952 as SDA executive secretary. For me, the most memorable congress by far was the one in Minnesota, when Ken Kurtz, Swarthmore College, Pennsylvania, ran against Bill Dentzer, Muskingum College, Ohio, and came within a hair's breadth of beating Dentzer. The story I remember best came out of a meeting of what we called the "liberal caucus." At one point in the meeting, someone asked why Al Lowenstein wasn't there. Isn't he a liberal, people asked? Herb Eisenberg quipped: "That has nothing to do with it.We just object to him hypnotizing everybody." To me, that fabulous comment summed up Al's appeal.

Herb had been the vice president for international affairs the previous year, when Al Lowenstein was president. That was the difficult year when NSA introduced the concept of first among equals on the national staff, which created endless conflict.

NSA, SDA, and the liberal caucus

Members of the liberal caucus met many times at the Michigan and Minnesota congresses. At the Minnesota meeting, it became my lot to challenge Helen Jean Rogers as a legitimate candidate for International Vice President.[12] The caucus asked me to make the point of order that Helen Jean was neither a delegate to the congress nor a student. This was not easy for a guy from Berea and West Virginia, but I did it and she withdrew.

As I look back on it, I think the goals of NSA and SDA were complementary and the differences were not that significant. SDA was farther to the left and had a much broader agenda. SDA had a firm anticommunist position. I think it was entirely right to maintain a strong exclusion of communists. One may argue that from a civil liberties point of view, but SDA and its parent organization, ADA, were very clear that they had no common ground with communists.

There was a lot of cross-over between NSA and SDA because of leaders who were active in both. (Sy Reisin writes about that elsewhere in this book.) I recall that Alex Pope and Frank Logan at the University of Chicago were very active in both, as were leaders in several New York colleges.[13]

But the liberal caucus, of which SDA was a leader, was not really that large or that consequential. The caucus backed Kurtz against Dentzer and Lowenstein (who was also an SDA member). SDA was not a string puller or a manipulator; we were a small group with a common interest.

NSA's influence

More than anything else, NSA gave me contacts with many people who have enriched my life. I think of people I have kept in touch with from time to time over the years. Ken Kurtz is the one I've kept up with the most. He's been a journalist in television news in South Carolina, West Virginia, Indiana, and Kentucky, where he is now. We met through NSA. Although we were both from West Virginia, he was from the northern part of the state, far from where I lived.

Another of my lasting relationships has been with Sandy Levin, now a member of the U.S. House of Representatives. (His brother, Carl, is in the Senate). I served under three SDA presidents, and to me, Sandy was clearly the best. He was outstanding. Before going to Washington, DC, Sandy was a Michigan state senator. He was the Michigan Democratic party chairman and ran unsuccessfully for governor two times.

Would I have become executive secretary of SDA without the NSA experience? Who's to say? One of my college professors, a Quaker from Iowa, said to me at one point, "Galen, you know, there is a profession for people called 'executive director.'" So he saw me in that context, even as I chaired the Kentucky-Tennessee Region of NSA, and that's all I've ever done. After my two years with SDA, I worked for public power groups for two years. Then I directed the Kentucky Council for Human Relations, a private group and one of twelve state organizations set up by the Southern Regional Council in Atlanta.

For four years, I worked for the Unitarian Service Committee in Knoxville, Tennessee, on school desegregation. I was the lone staff person, and it was not easy. When the Kentucky Legislature created the Kentucky Commission on Human Rights in 1960, I was recruited to be its first executive director, a position I held for twenty-eight years. After retiring in 1989, I was the Democratic nominee for Congress from the Fourth Congressional District for nine months in 1990. Since 1991 I have directed the Kentucky Fair Housing Council, which helps to file suits in federal and state court against housing discrimination. I'm certain that NSA was a real factor in the opportunities I had and the career choices I made.

In a broader context, I think NSA made a valuable contribution to the whole movement for student rights. NSA championed the independence of student government and student newspapers from administration control and censorship, and it raised consciousness about these important issues on campus and among administrators.

Galen Martin is Executive Director of the Fair Housing Council in Louisville, Kentucky.

END NOTES

[1] In response to the law's enactment, the trustees "raised $400,000 and endowed a new school for Black students, Lincoln Institute, located near Louisville. When the Day Law was amended in 1950 to allow integration above the high school level, Berea College again opened its doors to Black students." See *Berea College: A Brief History*, a pamphlet by Dr. Elizabeth Peck, for the inspiring story of the college's history.

[2] Peck, *Berea College*.

[3] Although Berea's academic program was founded on strong democratic principles, *The Wallpaper*, in its April 8, 1950, issue reporting on the election outcome, noted that "The first Berea College Student Association election was held on May 7, 1947. Student government had been urged for a long time, and permission was granted to have one earlier that year." One of the first and controversial exercises of its power arose when the Council adopted a bylaw requiring selection of the *Wallpaper* editor by its Publications Committee instead of by the volunteer *Wallpaper* staff, as had been the custom.

[4] See Wilson, p. 249, and Welsh et al., p. 565. Both these essays address the CIA secret funding issue.

[5] See Brown, p. 385.

[6] See Joy Newberger Picus, p. 928. Joy was a student at the University of Wisconsin. Dennis Trueblood, of Indiana State Teachers College, became chair of the NSA National Advisory Committee in later years. Rick Medalie, of Carleton College, Minn., was NSA's vice president for educational affairs at the time.

[7] See Klopf, p. 335.

[8] The colleges attending from Tennessee were Swift Memorial, Le Moyne, Fisk University, Middle Tennessee State, East Tennessee State, and Tusculum. Those from Kentucky were: Berea, Nazareth, University of Louisville, Southern Baptist Seminary, and Villa Madonna.

[9] According to the University of Louisville paper, the Student Government Association at the University of Kentucky defeated affiliation 19 to 7, as "being too costly and too idealistic." It used a secret ballot so that members could vote "without fear of reprisal from their party." Berea's Student Council voted to affiliate by a unanimous vote in March 1948, following a student poll that approved affiliation by a vote of 572 to 60. Louisville's University Student Council voted 9 to 3 to ratify the NSA Constitution that same month. We have a copy in the NSA archives of a special two-page broadside issue of the *Wallpaper* published in May 1947, for the regional National Continuations Committee following the Chicago Student Conference. It reports on the March 23–24 regional meeting held in Lexington at the University of Kentucky, at which Berea's Bill Welsh, then a junior, was elected president of the region. It also included a complete reproduction of the talk given by Charles Boggs, a junior at Kentucky, who delivered the keynote address. He had been travelling secretary for the World Student Service Fund (see p. 622), which received widespread support at Berea and other college campuses in the region during those years. The meeting was also welcomed by Leo M. Chamberlain, vice president of the University of Kentucky, and by the attorney general of the state of Kentucky.

[10] The following colleges were members or attended national congresses at various times during the period 1946–1952: Berea (46–52), Christian Brothers Junior College (48), East Tennessee State (51,52), Fisk (49–51), Kentucky State College (46), King College (46,48), Morehead (52, observer) , Murray State (52, observer) , Nazareth (46–49), Peabody (47), Southwest at Memphis (47–49), Tusculum (49,50), University of Kentucky (46,47,49), University of Louisville (48–52), University of Tennessee (52, observer), Ursuline (46,48,49), Villa Madonna (46).

[11] See Reisin, p. 787.

[12] Helen Jean Rogers had been an undergraduate at Mundelein College in Chicago and a graduate student at Catholic University. She also served as the elected NSA secretary on the 1948-49 national staff. See Secondari (Rogers), p. 599.

[13] See Pope, p. 390.

PICTURE CREDITS: *Then:* c. 1946, in Navy uniform at Berea College (Author); *Now:* 50th National Student Congress, Madison, WI, 1997 (Sylvia Bacon).

GALEN MARTIN

Early years: Born 1927 and raised in East Rainelle, West Virginia, where I attended high school.

Education: B.A. in Economics, Berea College, 1951. JD, University of Louisville Law School, 1967. Doctor of Laws, Berea College, 1970.

Career Highlights: I have worked for civil rights in the South for forty years beginning in 1956, especially to implement the *Brown v. Board of Education* decision. I was one of the attorneys for the plaintiffs that sued in 1972 for the merger of and desegregation of the Louisville and Jefferson schools. In September 1988 I was one of the attorneys who filed suit to prevent the segregation of Louisville's Central High School. From January 1991 to the present I have been Executive Director of

Berea College : "To Assert the Kinship of All People"

Editor's note: Berea College was born in 1855 out of the abolitionist movement. It was founded by anti-slavery Kentuckians, preacher John Gregg Fee and landowner Cassius Marcellus Clay, determined to bring an interracial education to a slave state, guided by a Christian ethic. It was located to serve the Appalachian region and drew its students from "African-Americans freed by the American Civil War and 'loyal' white mountaineers." Guided by a self-help goal, it developed a work program "rather than following the typical tuition model" (www.berea.edu). The college remained true to its tradition, as wrote Berea graduates Bill Welsh, NSA's first President (p. 365), and Galen Martin, 1950-51 KY-TN regional President (p. 983). NSA provided another outlet for student leaders to act on Berea's values. 1948 enrollment: 1,079.

To Serve the Appalachian Region

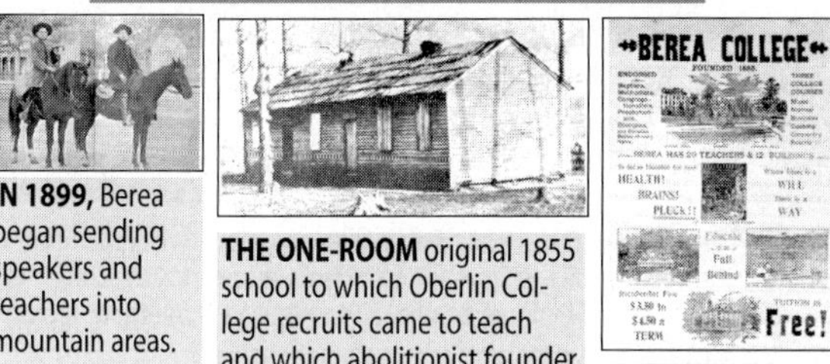

IN 1899, Berea began sending speakers and teachers into mountain areas.

(Photos and captions: Elisabeth Peck, *Berea College: A Brief History*).

THE ONE-ROOM original 1855 school to which Oberlin College recruits came to teach and which abolitionist founder John Fee hoped "would give an education to all colors, classes, cheap and thorough."

ADMISSIONS PROMOTION used in the early 1900's.

To Provide an Interracial Education

The Wallpaper, fr top, 1950: 3/18, 4/8, 4/15

Day Law Amendment Is Approved By House

Berea One Of Three Colleges Planning To Admit Negroes

Berea Will Admit Negroes Under Amended Day Law

THE DAY LAW, passed in 1904, compelled Berea to segregate. The college raised $400,000 to endow Lincoln Institute for Black students. With the law's repeal, Berea re-integrated.

A Historic Meeting

Maroon Tiger 10/48, Morehouse College, GA,

Integrated Southern Area YMCA, YWCA Conference Held At Berea

By Lorenzo Gunn, YMCA Delegate

THE SOUTHERN AREA YMCA joined the YWCA the first time in an interracial conference. This is the significant event about which John Peoples (Jackson State, MS) writes (p. 421).

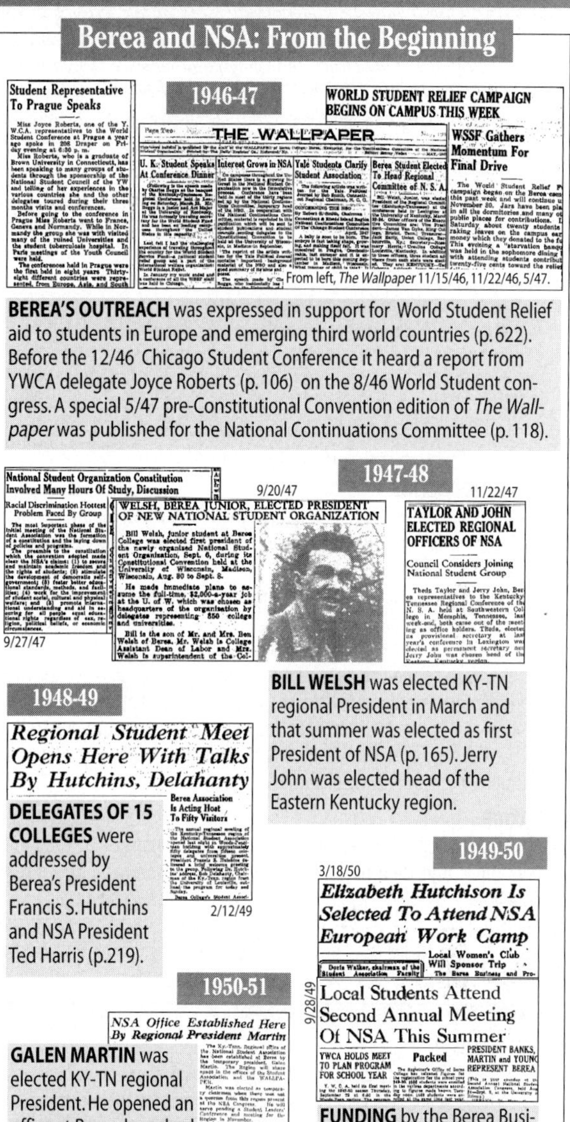

Berea and NSA: From the Beginning

1946-47

Student Representative To Prague Speaks

WORLD STUDENT RELIEF CAMPAIGN BEGINS ON CAMPUS THIS WEEK

THE WALLPAPER

WSSF Gathers Momentum For Final Drive

From left, *The Wallpaper* 11/15/46, 11/22/46, 5/47.

BEREA'S OUTREACH was expressed in support for World Student Relief aid to students in Europe and emerging third world countries (p. 622). Before the 12/46 Chicago Student Conference it heard a report from YWCA delegate Joyce Roberts (p. 106) on the 8/46 World Student congress. A special 5/47 pre-Constitutional Convention edition of *The Wallpaper* was published for the National Continuations Committee (p. 118).

1947-48

National Student Organization Constitution Involved Many Hours Of Study, Discussion

9/27/47

9/20/47

WELSH, BEREA JUNIOR, ELECTED PRESIDENT OF NEW NATIONAL STUDENT ORGANIZATION

11/22/47

TAYLOR AND JOHN ELECTED REGIONAL OFFICERS OF NSA

BILL WELSH was elected KY-TN regional President in March and that summer was elected as first President of NSA (p. 165). Jerry John was elected head of the Eastern Kentucky region.

1948-49

Regional Student Meet Opens Here With Talks By Hutchins, Delahanty

2/12/49

DELEGATES OF 15 COLLEGES were addressed by Berea's President Francis S. Hutchins and NSA President Ted Harris (p. 219).

1949-50

3/18/50

Elizabeth Hutchison Is Selected To Attend NSA European Work Camp

9/28/49

Local Students Attend Second Annual Meeting Of NSA This Summer

FUNDING by the Berea Business and Professional Women's Club sent a student to a 1950 NSA summer work camp program (p. 675).

1950-51

NSA Office Established Here By Regional President Martin

9/30/50

GALEN MARTIN was elected KY-TN regional President. He opened an office at Berea, launched a newsletter and planned a Student Leader's Conference.

GALEN MARTIN (Continued)

Kentucky's Fair Housing Council. Also Editor of *National Fair Housing Advocate*, an eight-page monthly newsletter, nearing 20,000 circulation, that reports housing discrimination case settlements. From January to November 1990, I was the Democratic nominee for Congress, campaigning for tax equity, the environment, affordable child care, unpaid family leave, campaign reform, civil rights, and an end to the savings and loan scandal.

From the time it began in 1961 to October 1969, I was Executive Director of the Kentucky Commission on Human Rights. From 1952 to 1954 I was Executive Secretary of the Students for Democratic Action. I have been admitted to law practice on all federal levels, including the Supreme Court, and have served with a number of other human relations and consumer groups. I appeared on the CBS network program *60 Minutes* in the headline story, featuring excerpts on sexual harassment from the keynote speech to the Coal Mining Women's Conference, Fall 1982.

Organizations and Awards: President, International Association of Human Rights Officials, 1983-85. President, National Association of Human Rights Workers, 1967-68; Legal Counsel, 1970-76. First Vice President, Louisville Branch, National Association for the Advancement of Colored People. Berea College Service Award, 1984, Carter G. Woodson Black History Award, 1991.

Personal and family: I have long been active in skiing, biking, and beekeeping, and have been a ski instructor at Aspen, Colorado, 1985-1991. I am married to Mary Lou Allgood. We have two sons, one daughter, and eight grandchildren.

The University of Louisville/The Kentucky-Tennessee Region

Editor's note: U. of Louisville student leaders and editors welcomed NSA and together with Berea College (p. 987) provided local and national leadership. Regional membership and Congress attendance ranged from 6 to 10, and regional conferences drew 10 to 15 of the 64 four-year colleges in the two states. King and Southwestern in Tennessee, and Nazareth and Ursuline in Kentucky added to the base. Of 9 Black colleges in the region, Fisk maintained membership from 1949 on. Its President, Charles S. Johnson, joined NSA's Advisory Committee in 1950. Fisk's Charles Proctor was Vice-Chairman of the 1946 U.S. World Student Congress delegation (p. 94) and President of the Conference of Southern Students (p. 968).

Louisville and Berea Anchor the Region

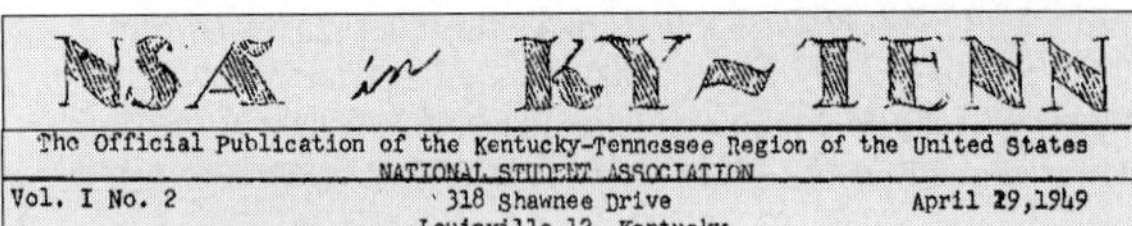

NSA in KY-TENN

The Official Publication of the Kentucky-Tennessee Region of the United States NATIONAL STUDENT ASSOCIATION

Vol. I No. 2 · 318 Shawnee Drive, Louisville 12, Kentucky · April 29,1949

ON DISCRIMINATION

In the last Newsletter I promised to give you the results of the referendum vote on discrimination taken at the University of Louisville. Here they are:

	Yes	No
Prohibiting organizations with discriminatory clauses	991	1,143
Existing organizations given 5 years to remove clauses	879	1,261
Administration petitioned: stop discriminatory policies	1,025	1,116

Of course to me the results were disappointing because all the referendums were defeated. Still, it must be remembered that just a few years ago it would have been impossible for such a vote to be taken . . .the trend in thinking of the average Southern student is changing in favor of anti-discrimination. . . .

ART TOUR

We are going to try to send the exhibit to **Memphis** for the four schools there and then back to **Louisville** to be shown at the three schools here. . . . —*Bob Delahanty*

STUDENT GOVERNMENT NEWS

Published by the Ky.-Tenn. Region of the National Student Association

Box 1999, Berea College Station, Kentucky · October 31,19

CAMPUS NEWS

Latest reports from **King College**, Bristol, Tennessee, indicate they are hard at work developing an honor system for their campus. . . . Approximately eighty-five **University of Louisville** deans and faculty members, student presidents, chairmen and council members attended a Leadership Camp on September 17. . . . At **Villa Madonna College**, Covington, Kentucky, students have organized and are operating a book exchange. . . .

PREXY TAKES A TRIP

The Regional President . . .recently made a trip to Louisville to contact Bob Delahanty, former Regional President and National Executive Secretary, as well as NSA Chairmen at **Nazareth College, Ursuline College** and the **University of Louisville**. . . . *Galen Martin*

REGIONAL ORGANIZATION BUILDERS

Bob Delahanty *U. of Louisville, 48-49*

Sam Stumbo *U. of Louisville, 49-50*

Galen Martin *Berea College, 50-51*

Ky-Tn Regional delegates at the 1949 NSA Student Congress

Photos, from left: U. of L. *Cardinal* 10/31/47, U. of L. 1950 *Thoroughbred*, Martin, U. of L. 1950 *Thoroughbred*

Bringing NSA to Louisville

USNA Head Meets Reps. On Campus

U.S.C. Votes In Proposal To Join National Student Association, 9-3

Collegiate Women Are Better Wives And Home Assets

NSA To Convene At U. of K.

Fr. top down, l. to r.: *Cardinal*, 1/23/48, 3/3/48, 11/12/48, 10/6/50, 10/9/52, 10/1/48, 10/?/49.

Affiliation

U of L Representatives Attend Student Congress

NSA Initiates Sixth Season; Activity Is National, Local

4 Students Attend Conference at IU

Vice-President Tells Association Purposes

Leadership

Leadership Camp Requests Student-Faculty Committee

Campus Leaders Meet At Camp Chelan; Faculty Representation Much Increased

Playshop Elects Nine

NSA PRESIDENT BILL WELSH (Berea, p. 165) helped lay groundwork in 1948 for U.L. membership. He joined Bob Delahanty, SB President (p. 410) at their annual leadership conference. U. of Kentucky was member, then dropped out. Delahanty was appointed NSA's first national Executive Sec'y. in 1950 (p. 234, 237).

Race Relations

MODIFICATION OF THE 1904 DAY LAW enabled Louisville and other colleges to admit Negroes, despite the fact that grade and high school segregation continued. NSA joined community groups in working for repeal.

Bro'hood Week To Be Observed By Student Panel In Discussing Racial, Religious Understanding

Charles Farnsley Will Moderate Forum Wednesday At Official Convocation In University Playhouse

Negro Admittance To Main Library Hailed By Leaders

No Easy Road To Race Relations

Policy Of Segregation Temporarily Continued By Board Of Trustees

U of L to Admit Negroes To Some Schools This Fall, All Schools In '51

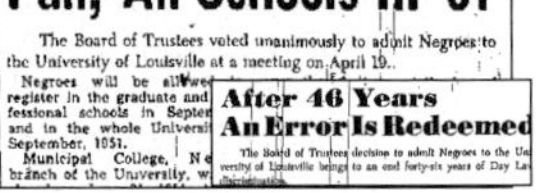

After 46 Years An Error Is Redeemed

Clockwise, fr top. l.: *Cardinal* 1/20/48, 5/20/48, 3/4/49, 11/4/49, 4/28/50, 4/28/50.

Purchase Card

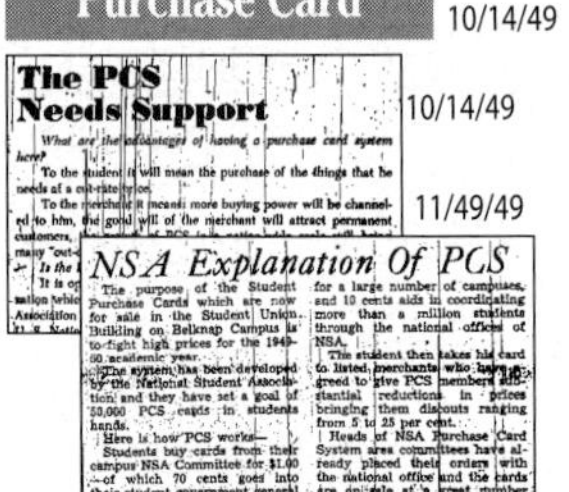

The PCS Needs Support

NSA Explanation Of PCS

10/14/49

10/14/49

11/49/49

Purchase Card Plan Commences Oct. 24

Savings Available To All Students

THE PCS DISCOUNT system (p. 366) was introduced in 1949, despite Louisville Merchant Association opposition, enrolling 30 to 40 independent stores.

Faculty Rating

INTRODUCED IN 1949, *The Cardinal* questioned usefulness of NSA's Rating System (p. 360) in 1952 (See also Klopf, p. 332).

USC Members Pass Faculty Rating System For A&S, Speed Schools

Rating System Due Here Soon

Faculty Rating Forms Distributed In A & S

Why Rate? System Is Farce

Clockwise, fr.l.: *Cardinal*, 12/6/50, 12/16/49, 1/10/52, 2/14/52

Historical note: Privately supported Jefferson Seminary (1813), Louisville Medical Institute (1837) and Louisville Collegiate Institute (1837, renamed Louisville College in 1840) combined into an under-funded University of Louisville in 1846, later financed by the city. Louisville College for Negroes was added in 1931 and dissolved with the coming of integration in 1950-51. In 1970 Louisville joined the state system (www.louisville.edu). 1948 enrollment: 7,264 (including 333, College for Negroes).

NSA brings a national and global outreach

4. NSA, Football, and Social Progress at Georgia Tech

John Hunsinger
Georgia Institute of Technology
NSA Delegate, 1951 and 1952 Congresses

In some respects I was probably typical of most Georgia Tech students of my day, both in my interests as a student and in my goals at the college. I saw college as an important stepping stone to a good job, a place to make useful connections for later in life, and an opportunity for a good education. Georgia Tech graduates made more money than those of any other college in the South. But I also had a passion for music and sports, for achievement and for community involvement. That last motive is what got me into student government, and through that, the National Student Association.

My involvement in the NSA yielded many friendships, especially those with Al Lowenstein and Connie Curry—and some memorable experiences. I would like briefly to share some reflections about them.

Having been All-State, All-South, and honorable mention All-American Fullback at Brown High School in Atlanta (I also played French horn in the high school orchestra and trumpet in a Dixieland band), I entered Georgia Tech on a football scholarship in the school year 1950-51. I earned my master's degree there in Industrial Engineering in 1955.

My connection with NSA began in 1951–52 when, as a result of coming on to the Student Council, I was also selected to be on our NSA delegation. There was an active regional group, especially in the Atlanta area. We also had a lot of intercollegiate activity with Agnes Scott College, both for social reasons—we were all men and they were all women—and because of our mutual interests in music and other programs. Connie Curry, who went to Agnes Scott and was later a Great Southern Regional Chair, became a good friend.[1]

I came from a family that had a long history of interest in both sports and music. They also believed in giving to your community, and I think that's why, throughout my life, being involved in some kind of civic activity and giving something back have always been high on my list. Today, as a businessman in Atlanta, I continue to serve on boards such as the Atlanta Symphony Orchestra, the Georgia Tech Library and Georgia Tech Alexander Tharpe Athletic Boards, and the Atlanta Union Mission Rescue Board.

Georgia Tech and social issues

One thing significant about Georgia Tech and its interest in NSA was that we never really got that actively involved in the social problems around us because if you didn't hit the books, you flunked. There's never been a "Panty Raid" at Georgia Tech—not because we weren't capable of "Panty Raids," but because we were too damn busy.

We were interested in communication with other Universities and in the swapping of ideas. Our facilities at Tech were not as up-to-date as they are today. We were interested in getting to know students in other parts of the country. I think that the national and international outreach of NSA is what attracted us. We almost laughed about the communist stuff. We thought the accusation was funny. Some people even called me a communist because of NSA.

We also had our own international program. We had a relationship with other engineering colleges in Europe. We would raise funds at Tech to send our students over to their campuses, and they would send their students to our campus. I had a roommate, Fritz Gaser, from Switzerland who was a physicist, working on his master's for a year. And we were very interested in swapping engineering ideas.

Women at Georgia Tech

The question of opening George Tech to female students is a good example of how conservative social attitudes were at Tech and how slow they were to change after World War II—

and also how I myself came to change my position and become a champion for the women when they arrived. The men at Tech were reluctant to have women enter Georgia Tech even though time many thought it would be a good thing.[2] Although the Regents first began to study the admission of women in 1947, it took until 1952 for it to happen.

The April 11, 1952, issue of the Georgia Tech paper, *The Technique,* headlined: "REGENTS APPROVE OF CO-EDS: Bitter Argument Precedes 7–5 Vote; 25 Women Will Seek Engineering Degrees." The article reported that "Regent Edgar Dunlap of Gainsville declared, 'Here is where the women get their noses under the tent. . . . We'll have home economics and dressmaking at Tech yet.'"

The fact was that most of us liked having just male students. In the Student Council, we were very opposed to women enrolling. At the time, I had gotten to know the president, Colonel Van Leer, since he had singled me out along with a number of our athletes who were good students. He'd talk about us at the Rotary Club and the Kiwanis, and then he would write us a note. He was a very gracious person.

So, here I am at Student Council, and I'm fighting against the rules being bent in order to help the women coming in, and the president's wife calls me up and says, "John, I wish you could help me," and wants to come by and see me. She had been in a sorority, and she wanted to get a chapter at Georgia Tech. One of the rules we had was that you had to have, say, fifteen or twenty members of an organization in order to be recognized on campus. Well, they didn't have enough people, since they only had ten or twelve women initially. And she wanted me to be her spokesman before the Student Council to get them to bend the rules so that if you didn't have a certain number of students, you could still get an organization. And the more she talked about it, the more I bent. So she finally convinced me, and I became her floor leader after vigorously opposing the change. I did a complete flip-flop in a matter of a couple of weeks.

Today, women are 15 or 20 percent of the population of Georgia Tech. And they are doing very well. And some of the women who enrolled at that time are major alumni leaders now. But back then it was a brand new idea, and being as conservative as we were, it took a little while for it to sink in.

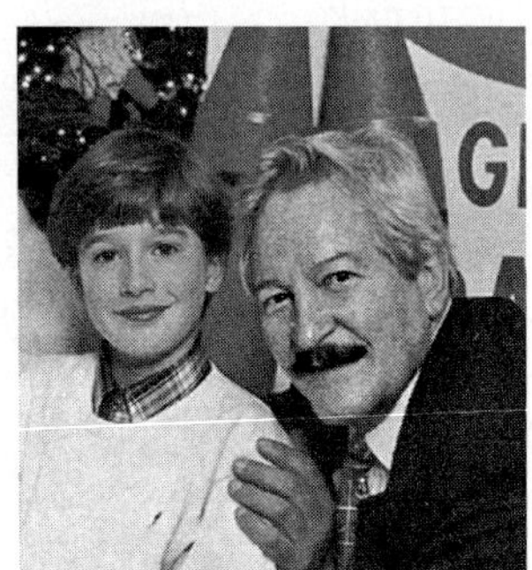

John Stewart Hunsinger, shown here with one of his two sons, Jonathan Christopher, is President of John Hunsinger & Company, and an industrial engineer, real estate broker and developer in Atlanta, Georgia. He has served as chairman of the State of Georgia's Sports Hall of Fame. He was selected to the Georgia Tech Athletic Hall of Fame and received the Distinguished Alumni Award from the School of Industrial and Systems Engineering at Georgia Tech.

Cross-Country with Al Lowenstein: Athletics and a Caring Connection

John Hunsinger
Georgia Institute of Technology
NSA Delegate, 1951 and 1952 Congresses

I first met Al Lowenstein at the Minnesota convention in August of 1951. Our delegation then consisted of myself, Randolph Sockman, John McGilleson, and William Kennedy. Al had just come off his term as NSA president, and Bill Dentzer of Muskingum College was elected to replace him, with Avrea Ingram, a former Georgia Tech graduate then at Harvard, as international vice president.[3]

We connected in an unexpected way. Because football practice began right after Labor Day, I arranged with the athletic department at Minnesota to use their facilities. Al, at the time, was prominent in NSA. I had also heard that he was doing tutorial work at North Carolina with athletes. As he was one of the NSA heroes at the convention, I was eager to meet him. We met and talked about our mutual interests. I told Al about my workout routines and that I was also on the wrestling team.[4] Al said he'd like to work out with me. So, we went off to the gym and we wrestled. Despite the fact that he was slight of build, Al was a very good athlete, but he did not like the sprints and running of laps.

We met again at the Indiana Convention in August of 1952. At that time, Ben Bishop, George Cannon, John Newberry, and I were on the Tech delegation. Tech was proud of its participation, and when the August 22, 1952, issue of *The Technique* announced our attendance, it also reported on Tech's participation in NSA:

> Throughout the world there exists an organized community of students. . . . There is a need of an organization of American students to act on their behalf in working with and assisting students in other nations, many of whom still struggle to rebuild their universities and educational facilities in an aftermath of war. To furnish a medium of free exchange of ideas and information between students on an international basis, the International News Center was established with its main office here at Georgia Tech by Bill Kennedy '52 late in September of 1951.[5]

Avrea Ingram was elected international vice president for his second term at that Congress, along with Dick Murphy as president. Al was there as a member of the NSA Advisory Board, and we did some more spare-time workouts.

Al came through Georgia at the end of my junior year. I was in Officer's Basic Camp in El Paso, Texas, in the artillery. He talked to my family, and when he came through Texas, he called me up. He asked me if I would like to travel with him on to California. He was going to California, Oregon, and Washington, and then coming back through the Rockies, to Chicago, and then to New York. I told him I couldn't make it. I had another week or two of training. And he said: "Well, I'm going on to L.A. Here is where I am going to be. Why don't you join me there?" I said, "Al, I don't have a car, but I could probably hitch hike or work my way over." Al knew a bunch of Jewish fraternities, so I got the names of the various fraternities where he would try to get a free visit.

A week or two later, when I graduated from the Reserve Officers' Training Corps (ROTC) and got my check, I found some guys who were going as far as Phoenix, Arizona. I gradually worked my way from there to Los Angeles, California, and found Al there, which, looking back on it, was very daring and lucky.[6] I finally hooked up with him in Los Angeles. He had a beat-up car and a directory, a little black or blue book, which he kept with him. When I traveled with him, I was amazed that he had names and addresses of people that lived in every state that we happened to be visiting.

So as we moved up the California coast, he would call these people and he'd say: "This is Al Lowenstein. How are you doing? It would be good to see you again." They were very impressed at getting a call from the former president of the NSA. Al was a very popular person, everybody liked him. He had no enemies. In due course, he'd have them saying, "Well, why don't you come by and grab lunch or have dinner with us?" "Oh no, I don't want to do that, that's too much," he'd say. "Oh, come ahead," they'd say. So, we never bought a meal. And generally we could get a place to sleep that night.

The West was beautiful country, and it was a fascinating trip! Al and I became fast friends. He was such a creative person. We spent most of our time arguing. He and I didn't agree on anything. He tended to be a Northern Liberal, and I tended to be a Southern Conservative. So on almost everything we talked about, we were in different camps. But it never seemed to affect our relationship. We cared for each other. He was just a wonderful, caring person.

Al tended to want to move more actively on civil rights. I tended to want to go through the course gradually. I had grown up in an area of Southwest Atlanta where we were at the center for Black education in the United States, maybe even the world. I had gotten to meet Martin Luther King, Jr., and I got to know his dad pretty well. Of course, I knew his wife, Coretta. But, we tended to believe in the gradualist approach at Georgia Tech. Although Tech was integrated in less than a day, when I was going to Tech, we tended to think more about taking the time to go through the courts, rather than going on marches.

END NOTES

[1] Curry, whose own memoir appears on p. 444, later became a civil rights attorney, the Southern Field Representative of the American Friends Service Committee and Director of the Office of Human Services in Atlanta.

[2] "The Surveyor," an editorial page column by Henry Caulkins in the March 8, 1947, issue of *The Technique,* reports that in a "Surveyor" poll, 58.1 percent of the students said yes to the question, "Do you think you're missing a substantial part of college life by attending a school that is not coeducational?" At the same time, "63.7% said they would not welcome girls on campus." The May 10, 1947, issue of *The Technique* notes that "the Education Committee [of the Board of Regents] was directed to investigate the possibility of admitting women students to Georgia Tech, the only State college now restricted to men."

[3] I remember talking to Al about when he first became president. He spent a lot of time talking about such things as stationery and office procedures, which today we call micro-management. And he was desperately trying to keep all these people together on his staff, and people had very strong opinions about these matters. It was hard for me to understand why it made any difference what color the stationery was, or the size of the type, or whatever. They spent half a day on what, at best, should have taken fifteen minutes. And I recall that it seemed very difficult for Al to hurt somebody's feelings, and I don't ever remember him hurting my feelings. We never got into any knock-down-drag-outs. He had this ability to work around conflict. I do remember that at his meetings, sometimes the good feelings seemed to be more important than action.

[4] We had so many players in 1951-52 that you had to find a place to play. Today we call them special teams. In my day we called them suicide squads—kickoff, punt returns, the high attrition areas. And you had to be 120 percent better in order to be seen. I was playing along as a left defensive end. You had to be fast and sure at tackling, and we didn't play crashing in, like the pros do for conditioning the ends. All the linemen had to go out for wrestling. I was matched up with a tackle from Pennsylvania, who was at least fifty pounds heavier than I and had no sense of humor. I told him, "Let's try to make it look good, and then you can pin me," and he just kind of growled at me. He beat the hell out of me. I though he was going to kill me. But I knew enough about wrestling, and survived. So I also wrestled Al Lowenstein.

[5] *The Technique* went on to describe the two tasks of the Center: (1) "to give other students in other countries an objective picture of our American way of life," and (2) "to better acquaint students of the United States with the ideas, problems and interests of students in other lands." To carry out its work, the paper reported:

> (1) It will publish a bi-monthly newspaper to be sent to foreign countries. . . . The first publication was published following the first Inter-American Student Conference held in Rio de Janeiro in January 1952. This paper is entitled, *The Student Life* (*La Via Estudianta*) [and] (2) it will issue press releases bi-weekly, to college newspapers across the United States.

[6] I didn't think of it at the time, but it was a kind of safe country then. You could hitchhike, and you didn't worry that the person who picked you up might do you in. And the person who picked you up didn't think that you might do him in. And it was a fun thing. You could go great distances without any money. So I would sight-see as I went. I went to the Petrified Forest, I went to the Grand Canyon. I'm sure I didn't go the quickest route!

Georgia Tech and NSA

Editor's note: Georgia Tech was one of the mainstays of NSA support in the Atlanta area. It contributed 1950-52 International VP Avrea Ingram (p. 575), and two regional Chairs (see pp. 230, 318), and provided the seat of NSA's International News Center in 1951 (See Hunsinger, p. 990).

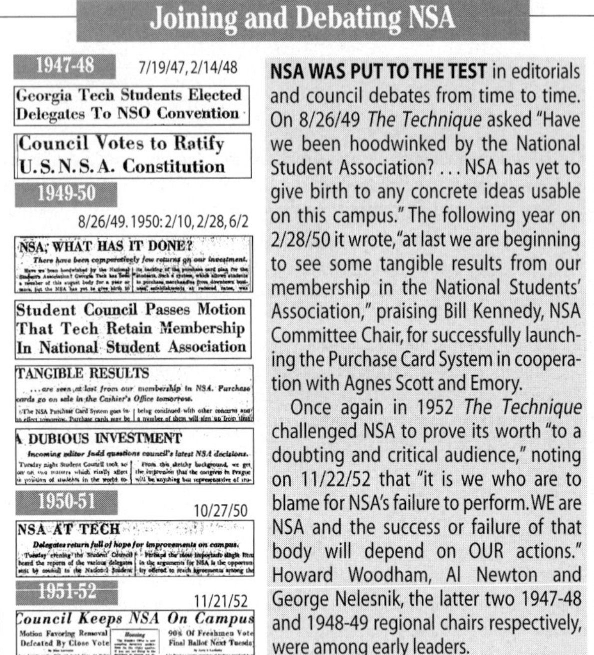

Joining and Debating NSA

1947-48 7/19/47, 2/14/48

Georgia Tech Students Elected Delegates To NSO Convention

Council Votes to Ratify U.S.N.S.A. Constitution

1949-50 8/26/49. 1950: 2/10, 2/28, 6/2

NSA; WHAT HAS IT DONE?

Student Council Passes Motion That Tech Retain Membership In National Student Association

TANGIBLE RESULTS

A DUBIOUS INVESTMENT

1950-51 10/27/50

NSA AT TECH

1951-52 11/21/52

Council Keeps NSA On Campus

NSA WAS PUT TO THE TEST in editorials and council debates from time to time. On 8/26/49 *The Technique* asked "Have we been hoodwinked by the National Student Association? . . . NSA has yet to give birth to any concrete ideas usable on this campus." The following year on 2/28/50 it wrote, "at last we are beginning to see some tangible results from our membership in the National Students' Association," praising Bill Kennedy, NSA Committee Chair, for successfully launching the Purchase Card System in cooperation with Agnes Scott and Emory.

Once again in 1952 *The Technique* challenged NSA to prove its worth "to a doubting and critical audience," noting on 11/22/52 that "it is we who are to blame for NSA's failure to perform. WE are NSA and the success or failure of that body will depend on OUR actions." Howard Woodham, Al Newton and George Nelesnik, the latter two 1947-48 and 1948-49 regional chairs respectively, were among early leaders.

Historical note: Georgia School of Technology opened in 1888. In 1948 it became Georgia Institute of Technology. It admitted women in 1952 and African Americans in 1961 (www.gatech.edu). 1948 enrollment: 5,726.

Following NSA Programs

4/24/48 N.S.A. Breaks With I.U.S. On World Crisis Attitude

2/24/50 Applications Now Ready For NSA Travel Program

8/20/48 For Academic Freedom

2/28/50 Purchase Card Sales Will Begin Tomorrow

1/14/49 Nalesnik Attends NSA Meet; Extension of GI Bill Favored

10/31/50 Third Student Congress Discusses Korean Battle

1/25/49 NSA Discusses DP Students And Federal Aid to Education

4/6/51 National Student Association Directs College Sport Probe

NATIONAL AND INTERNATIONAL ISSUES commanded headline attention in *The Technique*, as did engagement in NSA travel programs and the Purchase Card (PCS) discount system. Tech student leaders placed great weight on NSA efforts to address economic needs.

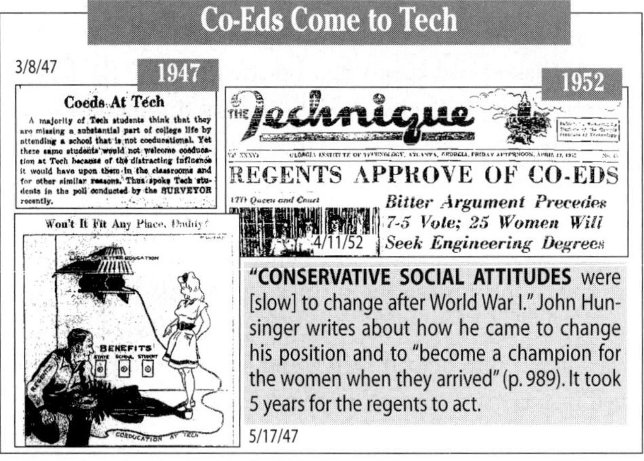

Co-Eds Come to Tech

3/8/47 1947

Coeds At Tech

A majority of Tech students think that they are missing a substantial part of college life by attending a school that is not coeducational. Yet these same students would not welcome coeducation at Tech because of the distracting influence it would have upon them in the classrooms and for other similar reasons. Thus spoke Tech students in the poll conducted by the SURVEYOR recently.

1952

The Technique

REGENTS APPROVE OF CO-EDS

Bitter Argument Precedes 7-5 Vote; 25 Women Will Seek Engineering Degrees

4/11/52

"CONSERVATIVE SOCIAL ATTITUDES were [slow] to change after World War I." John Hunsinger writes about how he came to change his position and to "become a champion for the women when they arrived" (p. 989). It took 5 years for the regents to act.

5/17/47

JOHN STEWART HUNSINGER

I was born in Columbia, South Carolina, December 2, 1930, where my Dad, a Georgia tech football player in 1928 and 1929, was coaching in a school as an assistant coach. My great uncle, "Pup" Phillips, played football at Georgia Tech (1916-1919). He was captain of coach (The Trophy Memorial Award) John Heisman's last team in 1919. "Pup" scored a TD in 1916 against Cumberland and Georgia Tech roared to a 222-0 victory.

When my folks were divorced, we moved to Atlanta and my mother and I went to live with my grandparents. Grandmother got me involved in music, and I sang and played the French horn. I also played the trumpet in the marching band, as well as doing Dixieland work and blowing taps and reveille at camp on the bugle.

I started playing football, both in my own high school, Brown, and as a "ringer" for a local Catholic school. I was president of my class, senior valedictorian, and an All-Southern, All-American football player—selected as the most valuable Back for the state of Georgia in 1949—and headed straight for Georgia Tech. Grandfather got me in the Boy Scouts, and I became an Eagle Scout.

Fascinated with physics, I started out in the physics department and moved to Industrial Engineering, graduating as Most Outstanding Senior in my class. I received my master's degree in Industrial Engineering in 1955. Along the way I continued in football, playing on the undefeated 1952 varsity team, which won the Sugar Bowl that year and a National Football Championship, as well as on the 1953 and 1954 teams, which won another Sugar Bowl and a Cotton Bowl game. This makes me a third generation football player at Georgia Tech and part of three national championships in 1917 (through my Great-uncle "Pup"), 1928 (through my dad), and 1952. I was selected for the Academic and SAE All-American teams in 1954. Other honors included Tau Beta Pi, Phi Kappa Phi, and President of ODK and ANAK.

After working for several years as an Industrial Engineer and completing two years as an officer in the U.S. Army, I joined Pope and Carter Company as a real estate salesman in 1961. I won the Million Dollar Club Award for three straight years, and rose to become President of the firm's development company. In 1969 I formed my own real estate brokerage and development firm, John Hunsinger & Company. Today, I remain active in the real estate industry as President of John Hunsinger & Company and its development arm, Hunsinger Enterprises.

In 1982, I was elected President of the Atlanta Board of Realtors. I was appointed to the Georgia Athlete Agent Regulatory Commission by the governor in 1989, and in 1992 and 2001 served as its Chairman. I have also served as a board member or officer of such organizations as the Society of Industrial Realtors, Atlanta Union Mission, Atlanta Urban League, Atlanta Chamber of Commerce, World Trade Club of Atlanta, and State of Georgia Sports Hall of Fame. I served on the Munich, Germany, Olympic Committee and on the Atlanta Olympic Committee. I continue to be active in sports and served as Chairman of the State of Georgia's Sports Hall of Fame in 1993 and 1994. I am married to the former Kathleen Blalock, and we have two sons, Jonathan (13) and Matthew (9). I also have two sons and a daughter by a previous marriage.

Agnes Scott, Emory and Morehouse in Atlanta

Editor's note: Together with Georgia Tech (p. 992), Agnes Scott, Emory and Morehouse kept the NSA vision active in the Southeast. As shown here at Emory and Agnes Scott, and at Georgia Tech, there were students who questioned NSA's value and challenged NSA advocates. Agnes Scott produced one of NSA's outstanding leaders, a leader in the civil rights movement, Connie Curry (See pp. 444, 1102).

Agnes Scott College

Debating Affiliation in 1949

News Stands Against N S A

News Says 'No' to NSA

Agnes Scott is not ready for NSA. Neither financially, psychologically, politically, nor practically.

If the money comes from Student government, campus organizations that are having to scimp already, will have to cut expenses even more. If the money comes from the students, then there will be "just one more" opportunity to "put the bite on" wallets that are very much in demand already.

Psychologically, the section, the state, and the city surrounding Agnes Scott are not ready to accept passively Agnes Scott's entrance into an organization involving inter-racial meetings and with a Negro president.

Southern patrons of Agnes Scott are not going to be interested in whether or not Agnes Scott accepts all of the ideals of NSA. The one thought that will be predominant in conservative southern minds is the fact that Agnes Scott is a member of an organization that does not believe in racial discrimination.

Coming at a crucial period in the present campaign, we will be taking a drastic chance on not reaching our goal if we join NSA.

Politically speaking, Georgia law forbids any inter-racial meetings including eating, drinking, or socializing. The state schools are not allowed to have any kind of inter-racial meetings on their campuses, and the administration feels that

AS 5/11/48

Guest Ed Talks Back

How long will we remain "campused"?

Will we remain so forever? Right now we are at a crossroads in our progress as students; our membership in NSA would be an outlet through which we could become "uncampused" and better able to face the problems that will face us as college graduates.

The arguments against our joining a national student organization have been put before the students. First, it is said, being a southern women's college we already belong to the pertinent organization, the Southern Association of Student Governments. Why, then, being Americans, should we not belong to the United States National Students Association? This body has a seat on UNESCO and is recognized as

Letters to the Editor

Dear Editor,

Now that the voting on NSA has been completed and the reports are in, it is time to congratulate the News on the fact that it took such a definite stand on the issue which was before us.

Although many of us did not agree with the News, as was evidenced by the voting, we feel that there was a concrete good in the mere statement of opinion voiced by the paper.

Many papers have tried to straddle the fence on such matters.

Dear Editor,

I want to compliment The News on taking a stand last week.

That 48-pt. headline really woke the campus up to the importance of the NSA issue. The editorial brought the objections of NSA clearly out in the open where they could be accepted or answered. Equal space was given to the arguments in favor of NSA which is more than many papers would do.

Criticism has flown freely because The News took such a strong stand on a 3 to 2 vote of the editorial staff. NSA passed

AS 5/18/49

NSA Membership was approved in a 1949 student referendum by a 2-1 ratio.

Tracking NSA

S G Delegates Will Attend N S A Meeting

Delegates from Agnes Scott plan to attend a regional convention of the National Student association slated for Friday and Saturday at Emory University.

Although Agnes Scott is not a member of the association, delegates from here have been invited to take part in the convention. The purpose of the meeting is to get student leaders together to discuss the entire association and solve problems in student govern-

2/11/48

Ten States Receive Bids To AS Tourney

Agnes Scott, playing host to the All Southern Intercollegiate Debate Tournament on Feb. 25 and 26 will furnish two teams to participate.

Jessie Hodges and B. J. Crowther will comprise the affirmative team, while Barbara Quattlebaum and Dot Medlock will debate for the negative. They will not be

2/2/49

10/5/49

Delegates Report on Activities At NSA's Congress in Urbana

By Charlotte Kay

Point of information . . . point of personal privilege . .

Foreign Universities Need Books, Student Materials

Since the W. S. S. F. is receiving 90 per cent of the Combined Charities money, background information is pertinent to the student body about this organization. Three years after the second World War, the devastated universities are being re-

11/16/49

12/6/50 (See p. 559)

Students at Prague Conference Cheer Idea of 'Hands off Korea'

(This is the second in a series of articles about the Communist dominated Second World Student Congress which was held in Prague this summer. The author of this first-hand

Students Attend NSA Meets In Europe, South America

American students were represented this month by the U. S. National Student Association (NSA) at two world student conferences of vital importance in the quest for mutual student understanding. The student meetings in Edinburgh, Scotland and Rio de Janiero, Brazil, were attended

1/30/52 (See Pt. 3, Sec. 3)

The Agnes Scott News reported extensively on NSA international programs.

Connected to the World

1933-1940

A. S. Delegates Attend Congress Of N. S. F. A.

Margaret Ridley and Charlotte Reid represented Agnes Scott at the eighth annual congress of the National Stu-

E. R. MURROW PRAISES YOUTH OF AMERICA

The United States is practically the only country in which youth is not in revolt against the existing order, it was stated by E. R. Murrow, former president of the N. S. F. A., who spoke in chapel last Wednesday on the general trends and attitudes in foreign universities.

In Europe there is a trend away

NSFA Considers World Crisis

Delegates Convene During Xmas Holidays

How can U. S. college and university students face the present world crisis?

With this question as their paramount problem, 200 National Student Federation of America delegates from all corners of the nation

1947-1951

Ideas Cross Race Lines

The interracial discussion of the Civil Rights report at Atlanta university on Feb. 27 and 28 has deep meaning for southerners, particularly southern college students.

That issues such as segregation and educational, economic and political equality could be discussed open-mindedly in the South by Negro and white is significant; that southern college students of both races could as equals exchange ideas, learning in that stimulating interchange how fundamentally similar they are in intelligence, ambitions and interests is

Is Freedom Of Speech Enough? Not In Senator McCarthy Case

By CISSIE SPIRO

The federal government must protect our right to freedom of speech; the federal government must also furnish us with

Policy Controversy Rages; General Meets Opposition

...General MacArthur's dismissal has stirred speculation from all sides and, though the positive consequences of it will not be known for some time, proponents and adversaries around the world are fighting it out with words. Last week the News published an editorial which presented the pro-MacArthur side of the story. This week the same author has interviewed a strong advocate of the policy of the State department and United Nations in Korea. The views stated are those of Cissie Spiro,

a military stalemate. Then only can we hope to come to a peaceful agreement in Korea.

From all perspectives the situation is grave. Our one consolation is that the Communists

AN ACTIVE MEMBER OF THE PRE-WAR NSFA (National Student Federation of America), a student government federation which dissolved in 1941 with the advent of World War II (p. 30), the AS News, as did much of the college press (p. 480), focused on student interest in post war issues, such as race relations, academic freedom, the Korean war and Truman's dismissal of General MacArthur (p. 258).

From top, l.: *Agonistic*, both 1/11/33; *Agnes Scott News* 1/17/49; r.: 3/3/47, 6/5/50, 5/9/51.

Historical note: Agnes Irvine arrived in Pennsylvania from Scotland in 1816. One of her sons, George Washington Scott, together with a group of Presbyterian leaders, founded the Decatur Female Seminary in 1889, chartered as Agnes Scott College in 1906. It is an independent women's college, affiliated with the Presbyterian Church (www.agnesscott.edu). 1948 enrollment: 544.

For more *Agnes Scott* and *AS News* excerpts: pp. 31, 444 (Curry), 450, 559, 599.

Historical notes for p. 994: ♦Barry College (now University), Miami Shores, was founded 1940, administered by the Adrian Dominican Sisters (www.barry.edu). 1948 enrollment: 291. ♦ The U. of Miami, privately supported, was chartered in 1925 (www.miami.edu). 1948 enrollment: 8,679. ♦U. of Alabama was founded in 1820, having enrollments of under 200 well into the 1890's. It first admittd women in 1893, Blacks in 1963 (www.ua.edu). 1948 enrollment: 9,150.

Morehouse College

Editor's note: Morehouse attended the 1946 Chicago Student Conference and every other Congress through 1952-53 except for 1947. It formed its student government in 1929, and joined the National Student Federation of America in 1930.

Top NSA Post Goes To Negro

Southern Area Job Goes To E. Wright

Ted Harris, a Negro student from La Salle University, was named national president of the National Student Association at the first annual meeting of the group held in Madison, Wisconsin. Ernest Wright, vice president of the Morehouse Student Body, was among the 800 delegates from 250 public and private schools who witnessed this unusual event.

Morehouse college is a member of this national group which is comprised of white and Negro schools all over the country. Wright, who was elected to the office of vice-president of the Alabama, Florida, Georgia region, was an official delegate from Morehouse college.

In an exclusive interview here, Wright saw the election of Harris as indicative of the anti-racism of the National Student Association. A busy campus figure, Wright holds offices in various other campus organizations including the Maroon Tiger and Alpha Phi Alpha fraternity.

Students Should Support NSA On Local, Regional And National Basis

By Ernest Wright

The first National Congress of the United States National Student Association was held at the University of Wisconsin, Madison, Wisconsin, August 23 to 28. Gathered at Madison were 750 delegates, alternates and observers, representing over 750,000 students.

Out of eleven workshops, using a "non-directive" technique free of agenda and pre-arranged planning, came project proposals for action by the NSA staff during the next year. Sectionalism reared its ugly head on such heatedly debated questions as segregation and discrimination in education and unity among students of the world.

The workshop treating discrimination in which the writer participated was characterized by violent discussions of the problems of discrimination in every phase of student life. Since matters of policy must be decided at congressional assemblies, it was necessary to take a forthright stand on this issue.

The most controversial issue at the congress was that of negotiations for affiliation with the International Union of Students. Upon recommendation of the National Executive Committee of NSA and five delegates were sent to Europe this summer

When the congress ended many delegates expressed the feeling that too much hedging had been engaged in at the conference. But when one realizes that the NSA is only one year old and [illegible] in its formative years, one recognizes that understanding, interest and desire for NSA must come as this young organization begins to approach adolescence and maturity.

NSA must be directed to students on the campuses. The basic unit of NSA is the individual student body. Through the medium of NSA, the voices of students are to be heard in community, national and international affairs so that students may contribute to national and international understanding and peace.

ERNEST WRIGHT, elected Vice-President of the G-A-F region at Madison in 1948, reported NSA to be "a group of mature men and women quite intent on improving student affairs. . . ."

Maroon Tiger 10/48. Photo: r.: *Morehouse Alumnus* 11/48.

Historical note: Morehouse College was founded by the Springfield Baptist Church as Augusta Institute in 1867. Spelman College is a historically Black college for women founded in 1881 as the Atlanta Baptist Female Seminary. In 1929-30 both Morehouse and Spelman affiliated with the Atlanta University System, which today includes Clark Atlanta University and Morris Brown College (www.morehouse.edu). 1948 Morehouse enrollment: 769.

See pp. 421, 467, 987 for *Maroon Tiger* excerpts on the College's 1948 civil rights focus.

Emory University

An Early NSA Booster . . .

Emory One of 15 Universities to Send Student Representative to Denmark

Council Issues Call For NSO Applicants

A call for applications for a third delegate to the National Student Organization was issued this week by Student

Emory Made NSA Member At SAC Meet

Emory University was approved as a member school of the National Student Association at the

Fom top: *EW* 4/10/47, 7/31/47, 4/1/48.

Al Foster, '46-'47 Regional Chair

EW 11/1/51

NSA—Students United

Among other pertinent items in its long comprehensive report on the status of the American university system today, the current issue of the New Republic has a section devoted to the National Student association. Since the NSA's news headquarters will soon be situated in Atlanta, Emory students have an especial interest in the values and policies of that student group.

The article points out that the NSA is one of the strongest attempts to date to organize college students throughout the country. Previously, problems facing students had been dealt with on a local or regional basis.

It should be obvious that with the emergence of such national issues as universal military service and loyalty oaths, these problems can no longer be handled effectively on the local level. A strong national organization is needed; and if NSA is the answer, Emory will be in a key position to provide the leadership requisite to any group desirous of shaping

AFTER ATTENDING THE CHICAGO STUDENT CONFERENCE, Emory sent a delegations to the International Student Service conference (p. 56, 59) and the NSA Constitutional Convention in the summer of 1947. *(Photo: Yearbook, xxxx).*

. . . Seeks an Alternative in 1952

EW 10/16/52

Council Committee Will Study Possibility of Leaving NSA

"THE DIFFICULTY I SEE WITH NSA is that it is an organization so entangled with declarations of policy concerning 'academic freedom' and equal rights and opportunities for education that it seems to have lost sight of the fact that its primary concern ought to be the development and enhancement of student government on the campus.

—Stell Huie, Student Body President 10/16/52.

10/15/53

Emory Univ. Leaves NSA

Council Votes 14-4 In Favor of Quitting

New Student Association Approved by Delegates

Six Southern Universities Ready Join Emory-Sired Organization

10/29/53

A Great Loss

Self-satisfaction breeds degradation . . . and Student Council this week demonstrated in action the self-satisfaction which has characterized it for the past year. In voting to quit NSA it stated its irresponsibility to national and international affairs

"IN VOTING TO QUIT NSA [the Student Council] stated its irresponsibility to national and international affairs and opinions . . . In quitting, Student Council refuses to send delegates to a national convention at which national issues affecting students are discussed, and at which there is an exchange of ideas on the purpose and operation of student government . . ."

—The Emory Wheel, editorial, 10/29/53

Historical note: Emory U. was founded in 1834 by the Georgia Methodists Conference as its Manual Labor School; it was chartered to become Emory College in 1836. It became co-educational in 1953, although women had attended courses since 1938 under an agreement with Agnes Scott. It admitted its first full-time black students in 1963 (www.emory.edu). 1948 enrollment: 3,642.

The Southeast Regions: Georgia, Alabama, Florida

Editor's note: A core of Atlanta colleges together with the U. of Miami and Barry College in Florida anchored NSA activity in the three-state area of Georgia, Alabama and Florida. Membership ranged from 6 to 9 colleges, with as many as 20 attending regionals, out of the 66 4-year colleges in the three states. The U. of Alabama followed NSA as an observer from 1946 to 1951. Morehouse (GA) and Tuskegee (AL) were two Black colleges that followed NSA. In 1953-54, NSA combined the three states into a Great Southern Region with colleges in Texas, Louisiana and Missisippi. Connie Curry of Agnes Scott (pp. 444, 1102) was its first Chair.

1946-1947

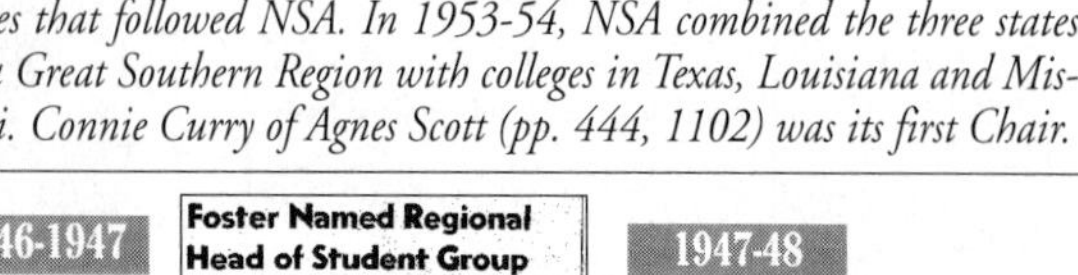

Foster Named Regional Head of Student Group

Ga.-Ala. Student Organization Elects Meadows Secretary

EW 2/27/47

AS 2/26/47

1947-48

Tech To Send Four Students To National Congress of NSA

Three Attend NSA Meeting At Emory

Ellis To Retire From U.S. Army

TE 7/30/48

AS 2/18/48

1948-49

Nalesnik and Lacy Elected Officers in Regional NSA TE 12/10/48

Nalesnik Attends NSA Meet; Extension of GI Bill Favored TE 1/14/49

NSA Regional Assembly To Hold Forums Saturday AS 2/9/49

Agnes Scott housed women delegates from Bessie Tift (GA), Alabama Poly, Florida State, Judson C. (AL) and Wesleyan C. (GA)

Regional Leaders

Al Foster
Emory U., 1946-47

George Nelesnik
Georgia Tech, 1947-48

Stuart McDonald
U. of Miami, 1950-51r

Constance Curry
Agnes Scott, 1953-54

1949-50

Delegates of Southern Schools Attend NSA Meeting at Emory TE 12/6/49

NSA Art Exhibit To Visit Atlanta Area In Spring AS 11/2/49

Woods Joins Staff Of NSA's 'Essai' AS 11/2/49

For Essai see p. 364

U. OF MIAMI success in operation of NSA's Purchase Card System (p. 367) encouraged Agnes Scott, Ga. Tech and Emory to launch the system in Atlanta. It aroused merchant controversy and ultimately failed. The NSA Art Exhibit (p. 369) showed at Agnes Scott and Emory.

1950-51

EW 4/13/51

NSA To Convene Here April 13-14 TE 5/22/51

Weekend of Planning Proves NSA Conference A Success

U. OF FLORIDA hosted May joint meeting of NSA and Florida Intercollegiate Press Association following Emory April district meet.

1951-52

NSA Holds Regional Convention Here EW 4/3/52

JOHN HALEY, Emory, 1951-52 NSA Student Government Vice President (p. 298), attended the regional event.

Regional Workshop *(SHSW)*

GEORGIA-ALABAMA-FLORIDA Regional Convention

March 28,29,30, 1952

Emory University

Prepared by Wayne Whisler, University of Miami, *Regional Vice-Chairman*

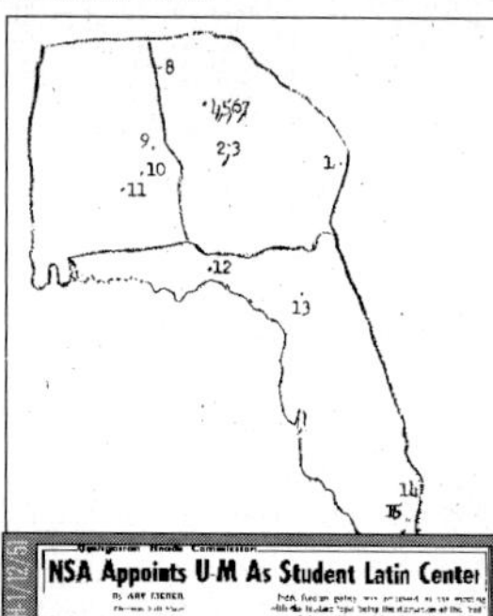

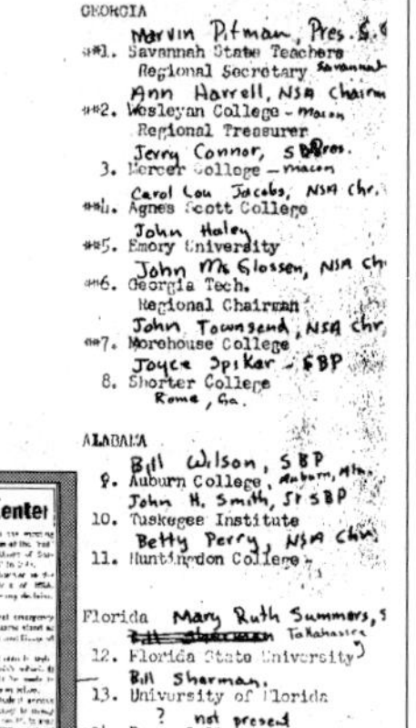
GEORGIA
1. Savannah State Teachers — Marvin Pitman, Pres. S.B.
Regional Secretary — Ann Harrell, NSA Chairm
2. Wesleyan College — Macon
Regional Treasurer — Jerry Connor, SB Pres.
3. Mercer College — Macon
4. Agnes Scott College — Carol Lou Jacobs, NSA Chr.
5. Emory University — John Haley
6. Georgia Tech. — John McGlossen, NSA Ch
Regional Chairman
7. Morehouse College — John Townsend, NSA Chr.
8. Shorter College, Rome, Ga. — Joyce Spiker, SBP
ALABAMA
9. Auburn College — Bill Wilson, SBP
10. Tuskegee Institute — John H. Smith, Sr SBP
11. Huntingdon College — Betty Perry, NSA Chm
Florida — Mary Ruth Summers
12. Florida State University
13. University of Florida — Bill Sharman
14. Barry College — Wayne Whisler

**NSA Member Schools

NSA Appoints U-M As Student Latin Center MH 1/12/51

Aram Goshgarian, former Miami student body President, heads NSA Latin American Affairs Commission.

Historical notes: see page 993

Students at Ten Georgia Colleges Help Hold at Bay a Disputed Governor

Emory Wheel 1/27/47

2000 Students March on Capitol; Protest Talmadge 'Rule By Force'

By WORTH McDOUGALD

More than 2000 students—at least half of them from Emory—marched on the Georgia capitol Tuesday afternoon and hanged Herman Talmadge in effigy.

Protesting "violence as a method of achieving public office" and demanding that Talmadge vacate the office he took over on Jan. 16, the crowd assembled at nearby Hurt park and began an orderly march through the streets of Atlanta. Denied police permission to use the middle of the streets, the students, marching four abreast, paraded down the sidewalks. Atlanta citizens joined the group as they reached the business

Final Enrollment Reaches 3504

Emory's enrollment for the Winter Quarter comes to a grand total of 3504 students. The number of students enrolled in the various

Bulletin Board Gets New Guardian

The unkept appearance of the quadrangle bulletin board will get a face lifting Monday. The surgeons of this delicate operation are the members of Alpha Phi Omega service fraternity who will be in charge of the patient's daily maintenance.

Long the target for notices of all sizes and shapes, the bulletin board will now have regulations

IN JANUARY, 1947 Herman Talmadge was selected by the legislature to replace his father, Eugene Talmadge, who died in December before taking office. Ellis Arnall, the outgoing governor believed M.E. Thompson, the newly elected lieutenant governor, should be sworn in, and refused to vacate the office till the courts decided the outcome. Meantime Herman Talmadge took the oath and proceeded to act as governor, despite widespread protests and the Secretary of State's refusal to allow the use of the State seal. The court ruled in favor of Thompson, and Talmadge was elected in 1948 to fill the balance of his father's term ("None So Deaf," *EW* 1/27/47).

Suspicions about IUS affiliation rule the day

5. A Hard-Fought Texas Affiliation Battle

Barefoot Sanders

University of Texas delegate, NSA Constitutional Convention, 1947
University of Texas Student Body President, 1948

I attended the Madison Convention of NSA in August 1947, as a member of the University of Texas (UT) delegation. One of my principal recollections of that Convention was our delegation's opposition to affiliation with the International Union of Students (IUS). Our position was strictly pragmatic; we believed, and events proved, that any kind of connection with the IUS would be harmful on the campus when we tried to affiliate with the NSA. Jim Smith felt strongly about our opposition, and we had a rather unpleasant session with him. We all had a high regard for Jim, but believed that he was out of touch with the situation on the UT campus.

Affiliation with the NSA was rejected in a campus-wide vote in winter 1948, after a hot campaign. The principal—and phony—issue was the alleged communist influence of IUS on the NSA. I was elected student president in spring 1948. Because of the adverse vote on the NSA a few months earlier, I had no involvement with the NSA as student president or thereafter.

My recollection is that a few years later, in the early 1950s the situation changed and UT once again participated in the NSA.* However, I had graduated in the summer of 1950.

**Editor's note:* The University of Texas affiliated with NSA in 1953-54.

PICTURE CREDITS: *Then:* c. 1948. *Now:* c. 1990's. (Provided by author.)

Barefoot Sanders, a former U.S. Assistant Attorney General, is currently Senior Judge of the United States District Court in the Northern District of Texas.

HAROLD BAREFOOT SANDERS

Born in Dallas, Texas, in 1925. He received his B.A. from the University of Texas in 1949, and his L.L.B. in 1950. He served in the Texas Legislature, 1952-58. United States Attorney, Northern District of Texas, 1961-65. Assistant Attorney General, Department of Justice, 1965-67. Legislative Counsel to President Johnson, 1967 to 69. Democratic candidate, U.S. Senate, 1972. Has served on as a United States District Judge since 1979 (Chief Judge, 1989-1995). Judicial Conference of the United States, 1989-1992. President, Fifth Circuit District Judges Association, 1990-92. He married May Elizabeth Forrester, and they have three daughters.

University of Texas: Leading the Way to NSA, but Passing at the Goal Line

Editor's note: Texas was selected by Alice Horton and the American Preparatory Committee to the 1946 World Student Congress (p.68) as one of ten colleges on the 25 member U.S. Delegation. The University provided major leadership for NSA's founding through Joe Malik on the Prague delegation, Jim Smith at the 1946 Chicago Student Conference and 1947 Constitutional Convention, Jack Skaggs, head of the 1947 NSA delegation, and Leo Goodman, elected the first Chair of the Texas-Oklahoma region.

1946-47

Students Asked to Contribute Funds —
Malik to Be Delegate to Prague

THE DAILY TEXAN
Jim Smith Elected National Student President

18 Colleges Send Delegates To NSA Region Conference

NSA Delegates Frame Constitution

Leo Goodman Made Regional NSA Chairman

Daily Texan, from top, l.: 6/11/46, 1/7/47; r.: 3/23/47, 9/16/47, 9/24/47.

Assembly Considers NSA Constitution

1947-48

Referendum Vote On NSA Petitioned

By CHARLES H. ROW

VOTE THE DAILY TEXAN VOTE

Students Vote on NSA Affiliation Today

New Auditor's Receipt Needed to Cast Ballot

NSA Rejected, 2,533-1,874, in Heavy Vote

Full-time Students To Get Vet Increase

BBA, Law, Engineering Go Overwhelmingly Against

Daily Texan, from top, l.: 11/14/47, 12/12/47, 2/18/48, 2/19/48.

The Pro and Con of the NSA

AGAINST

NSA has been rejected by SMU, TCU, Rice, LSU, and Texas Tech. Not one Texas school has approved it by a vote of the student body. (Stephen F. Austin Teachers College is the only Texas school affiliated with NSA.)

From the Texan's news stories, you'd think school were falling all over each other trying to join, but NSA itself doesn't officially claim but 47 members. (Note: It claims the University of Texas, somewhat prematurely.)

Those who oppose NSA have been painted as Ku Kluxers, witch-hunters, calamity-howlers. Those who support it have been pictured as red-blooded Americans going out to fight the reactionaries. It's about time to see what the situation really is.

NSA came about as a result of the formation of an international students association, which was avowedly communistic. The American delegates, knowing American students wouldn't swallow that, then formed NSA. But Stalin's soap-boxers weren't satisfied, so they worked within NSA. When the NSA constitution was written, it provided that NSA could easily affiliate with any other group! And NSA has ALREADY PASSED a resolution favoring affiliation with the VERY COMMUNISTIC ASSOCIATION which was originally opposed!

What does that sound like to you: (1) a grass-roots student organization, or (2) another "professional youth movement" which can serve as a communist-front organization? Surely not the former!

Look at it this way: If NSA formed a local chapter and solicited individual memberships, it might be a good thing. But instead, it wants a blank check to speak for every student in every member school!

NSA claims liberalism because it favors racial equality. But will agitating help or hinder solution of our racial problems?

Did you stop to think how typically left-wing this appeal on the basis of racial equality is? Don't all communist organizations paint themselves as saviours of minority rights? Then, when their philosophy triumphs, what happens to ALL rights? There's no need to answer that one.

Did you read the constitution of NSA in the Texan? You'll notice that the national group can do anything not prohibited by the constitution. AND NOTHING IS PROHIBITED. On the other hand, the local chapters can do ONLY WHAT DOES NOT CONFLICT WITH NATIONAL POLICY! In other words, New York and Chicago can tell you what you believe, and so far as your local chapter is concerned, you can't question their statement.

What do you expect to get out of the $1500 a year NSA will cost this student body? Well, what you'll actually get is a subscription to the NSA newspaper, WHICH HAS NOT EVEN BEEN DISTRIBUTED ON THIS CAMPUS BECAUSE THOSE WHO SUPPORT NSA DON'T WANT YOU TO SEE IT: IT'S THAT RADICAL.

ANTI-NSA COMMITTEE

Ed. note: This is the first in a series of three articles on the National Students Association. Both sides of the dispute for and against the University's affiliation with NSA will be presented before the special campus election to be held February 18.

FOR

At a time when a general attitude of apathy toward all forms of student organizations pervades our own campus, and others also, the project of a National Students Association seems to many to be ambitious indeed. And many pertinent questions have been raised concerning the purposes of such an organization. Those of us who have worked with the NSA in any capacity during the past year feel very strongly that we here at the University have much to gain by affiliating ourselves with the NSA and participating in its activities. For my own part, our different reasons for favoring affiliation can be summarized in three ways.

First, our participation in the NSA program will bring a great many benefits to our students and to the campus as a whole. The three phases of NSA activity are student government and welfare, educational opportunity and scholarships, and international exchange of students and student travel abroad.

By coordinating our efforts with the efforts of other colleges and universities throughout the United States through the agency of NSA, we will be able to accomplish more in these fields than we would ever be able to do alone. We should be able to bring speakers and shows to the University cheaper than before, by arranging to book them at other schools in this part of the country during the same period they are scheduled here.

We will be able to have complete information on available scholarships, here and at other schools, and publish that information. A project will be undertaken whereby complete information on vocational opportunities will be made available to graduates. The way will be open for arranging for student travel abroad, either in groups or as individuals. The path will be made much easier for those students here who desire to go to schools in foreign countries, and information on such opportunities will be compiled by the national organization of the NSA. Certainly it is obvious that those projects can be accomplished more efficiently and more fully by a nationa agency, set up by students and operated by them, than by individuals or individual schools working alone.

A second reason which should be urged in favor of affiliation arises from the fact that the NSA is largely a product of students from The University of Texas. Over a year ago UT representatives outlined and set up the organizational structure of the NSA, and established its aims. Due to their endeavors, students from all over the country consider Texas as a leader in the NSA, and the action taken on affiliation on this campus will be keenly observed by other schools.

Since the University has played a leading part in the founding and growth of NSA, and since the NSA is undertaking projects which will be of unquestioned benefits to participating students and universities, it would seem that there should be no hesitancy as to our position—and that we will vote affirmatively on affiliation. There are, however, those who, either through misinformation or honest doubt, do not favor our affiliation—and that brings us to our third and most cogent reason for advocating our affiliation with the NSA.

The plain fact is that we have everything to gain and nothing to lose by becoming a part of the organization. The NSA is a confederation, functioning on a democratic basis, with representation according to the number of students in the particular college or university. No outside groups are included; only the student governments of schools of higher education. We can withdraw from the organization at any time we please. It will function primarily as a service activity, for the benefit of its members; it is not organized for participation in national and state politics. There are, doubtless, as some claim, certain technical defects in its constitution, and that instrument is open to interpretation in some of its parts. In regard to such flaws, our attitude has been that by associating ourselves with NSA, we will be able to work toward the elimination of these minor flaws; certainly, they should constitute no basis for outright rejection of affiliation. Only those with narrow vision and finicky, legalistic minds will so maintain.

To most, the potential benefits of the National Students Association and our own position of leadership in it will be compelling arguments in favor of affiliation.

The NSA, then, is a challenge to all students, veterans and non-veterans alike. Its successful existence will be, in itself, an answer to those now objecting to it, because they believe that all college students are immature. We strongly recommend that the campus vote "yes" on the issue of affiliation with the NSA.

BAREFOOT SANDERS

Daily Texan 2/13/48. Documents and clippings from The Center for American History, UT Austin.

NSA Convention Drafts Regional Constitution

Goodman to Head Two-state Area For Second Term

Machinery for bringing the National Students Association to the local level was the chief accomplishment of the first Regional Assembly of the Texas-Oklahoma area, held on the Southern Methodist University campus in Dallas last Saturday and Sunday.

Delegates to the meeting drafted a constitution for the regional organization and elected officers for the coming year.

Leo Goodman of the Univer-

TX 12/10/47

THE TEXAS-OKLAHOMA REGION showed promise when 22 colleges met 12/6-12/7/47 at Southern Methodist U. When U. of Texas later voted down afilliation it unravelled as an organization, with five to eight colleges in both states maintaining membership each year. These included The U. of Tulsa and the U. of Oklahoma. Some others in the original region: U. of Houston, Stephen F. Austin, Rice Institute, Texas Christian, Texas A&M, Oklahoma A&M, Texas Tech, Our Lady of the Lake.

Historical note: The Congress of the Republic of Texas first ordered a site for a university in 1839. Various events intervened through statehood, secession, the Civil War and its aftermath before the university was formally opened in 1883. African Americans were first admitted in 1950 as a result of the U.S. Supreme Court decision in Sweatt v. Painter. *In 1967 the main branch of the university system was named The University of Texas at Austin (www.tsha.utexas.edu). 10th largest 1948 U.S. enrollment: 17,028.*

More on the University of Texas, Joseph Malik, Jim Smith, pp. 98, 119, 123

SECTION 7

The Rocky Mountains and Southwest

CONTENTS

University of Colorado, *Silver and Gold* 9/27/51

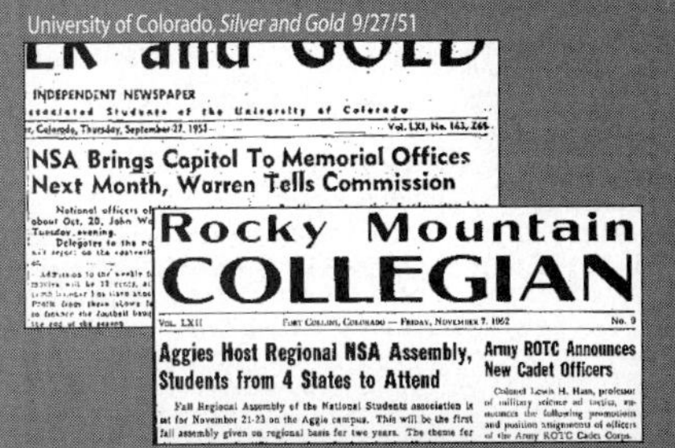

ER and GOLD

INDEPENDENT NEWSPAPER

Associated Students of the University of Colorado

Colorado, Thursday, September 27, 1951 — Vol. LXI, No. 163, 265

NSA Brings Capitol To Memorial Offices Next Month, Warren Tells Commission

National officers of ... about Oct. 20, John W... Tuesday evening.

Delegates to the ...

Rocky Mountain COLLEGIAN

Vol. LXII — Fort Collins, Colorado — Friday, November 7, 1952 — No. 9

Aggies Host Regional NSA Assembly, Students from 4 States to Attend

Fall Regional Assembly of the National Students association is set for November 21-23 on the Aggie campus. This will be the first fall assembly given on regional basis for two years. The theme for

Army ROTC Announces New Cadet Officers

Colonel Lewis H. Han, professor of military science and tactics, announces the following promotions and position assignments of officers of the Army ROTC Cadet Corps.

Colorado A&M, *Rocky Mountain Collegian* 11/7/52

Extending 1,200 miles northward and 600 miles east to west, embracing all or portions of six of the country's most sparsely populated states, NSA maintained a presence in the Rocky Mountain Region largely through the interest of six to eight colleges in Colorado and New Mexico—with the University of Colorado, Colorado A&M and New Mexico Highlands University at its core. It included Montana, Wyoming and, for brief periods in the early years, Utah and Idaho. Termed "unviable" by one regional chair, reaching the 58 four and two-year colleges in the 630,000 square mile region compared dauntingly to organizing among the 76 insitutions in 10,550 square mile Massachusetts.

New Mexico Highlands University in Las Vegas was a member and almost lone outpost for NSA in the Southwest from the time of its attendance at the Chicago Student Conference in 1946. It affiliated with the region, centered in Denver, and hosted occasional Rocky Mountain meetings. One of them, in 1949–1950, was led by Roy Romer, then regional chair and later governor of Colorado and Los Angeles superintendent of schools.

The story of the Rocky Mountain Region in its early years is told by Len Perlmutter who, working his way through the University of Colorado, spans the wartime and postwar era. His service as editor and as a columnist on the *Blue and Gold* provides a sidebar on how a major university paper was put together in those years. He later became a prominent Colorado civic leader.

Luis Rovira, then Colorado's student body president and now a retired Colorado chief justice, provides a vignette on discrimination against Blacks at that time. Rovira also initiated a proposal, then unsuccessful, to have the football Big Six (which had just become the Big Seven, with Colorado's admission) drop its Jim Crow rules. A similar initative was taken by the University of New Mexico in its conference two years later.

The Chicano Student Revolution

Unique to the region were the Chicano students in New Mexico. With a legacy of more than 300 years in the region, they were originally a non-English-speaking people whose forebears, unlike the Native Americans, were allowed to remain on their land and were given unconditional citizenship. Donald Martinez, later a District Attorney and Judge, tells the story of the Chicano student veteran generation and its efforts to overturn a century of discrimination and land ownership abuse.

Albums on the University of New Mexico, New Mexico Highlands, University of Colorado, Colorado A&M and Regis College, as well as on Southwest College Newspapers recall area college outreach.

A background unit is provided on the Independent Student Associations of the era, alternatives to the Fraternity and Sorority Conferences. Also a recollection of Dean Arnow Nowotny of the University of Texas, a major supporter of the ISA's, who was a mentor to Jim Smith, President of the National Continuations Committee, which launched the NSA (Pt. 1, Sec. 3).

Colleges in the Denver area centered the Rocky Mountain Region. In 1951-52, NSA moved its national headquarters there for a year (Pt. 1, Sec. 9).

Rocky Mountain NSA Highlights

1946-48

Student Meet in Prague in August

CU Representative Reports On Chicago Convention

D. MARTINEZ, J. WHORTON ATTEND NSO CONSTITUTIONAL CONVENTION

Academic Freedom Committee Formed

Clockwise from top l.: **LO** 5/3/46, SG 1/14/47, **HC** 1/17/47, **SG** 4/4/47

1948 REGIONAL ASSEMBLY registration at U. Colorado 2/17/48 (p. 1011) (UC at Boulder Library).

JERRY GOODMAN (U. Colo.) was the region's first president. NSA's origins were followed closely in key New Mexico and Colorado colleges. 1947-48 leadership in the region was also provided by **Jack Whorton** (NM Highlands U., p. 1018) and **Len Perlmutter** (U. Colo., p. 999). Formation of an Academic Freedom Committee at U. Colo. reflected the national and state un-American committee pressures on public university campuses in the region.

1948-50

NSA Area Convention Opens Tonight

The SILVER and GOLD

Prator And Chopman Talks Highlight Evening's Affairs

NSA Will Investigate Universities Fears Of Teachers' Radical Ideas

SG 10/21/49, 4/8/49, **SG** 4/49

JOHN OLSON (Colorado A&M), 1948-49 regional president, keynoted the 10/49 assembly, chaired by **Frank Krasovek** (U. Colo.), 1949-50 president. The 3-day event was organized into student government, student life, educational problems and international panels. The *Silver and Gold* reported NSA's Exec. Committee stand against teacher firings (See Brown, p. 381).

The Chicano Student Movement

NEW MEXICAN VETERANS "set about organizing Chicano students to redress the many wrongs we saw about us." **Donald Martinez** writes about the Chicano revolution which emerged at New Mexico Highland University (p.0000), empowering Chicano students and reversing a a campus culture in which "there wasn't one Spanish-speaking professor." Membership in NSA was linked to their "burning sense of injustice," Martinez writes. Student leaders testified before the legislature in 1951 in protest against inaction by the administration, leading to the replacement of the college president by the Regents.

Student Body Sitting Tight

THE HIGHLANDS CANDLE

"Aria da Capo", "L" Now In Production

Joe Angel, Student Body President, leads college budget crisis student strategy meeting (*HC 1/18/52*).

1951-52: NSA Moves to Colorado for a Year

In severe financial straits, NSA accepted an offer of space at the U. of Colorado. On 9/27/51, Lisle T. Ware, Director of the Student Affars Center, wrote NSA President Bill Dentzer, "We are all looking forward to your arrival ... I note you are counting on us for two large desks ... if you do have these bring them along, they seem to be at a premium on campus at present."

NSA Moves National Offices To Boulder; Headquarters Represent 195 Colleges

SG 9/21/51

HEADQUARTERED IN BOULDER after 4 years in Madison, NSA conserved resources as it weathered the Red Scare and Korean war (see p. 299).

1950-52

Romer Discusses Results Of NSA National Meeting

Individual Academic Freedom Discussed By The Rocky Mountain N S A

Clockwise from top: **SG** 1/16/51, **HC** 4/20/51, **SG** 3/25/52, **LO** 3/18/52, 3/2/51, 3/8/51

Regional NSA Group Plans Frosh Orientation Meeting

Student Urges UNM to Join National Students Association

ASUC Approves Red Probe Action

Faculty Completes Oath Of Allegiance; Signup Unanimous

ROY ROMER (U. Colo.), 1950-51 Regional President (p. 1007), later Colorado Governor, relayed NSA's Stockholm conference report of non-Communist western student unions (pp. 522, 562). Although it took part in regional events, it wasn't until 1958 that U. of New Mexico joined NSA. Issues of academic freedom occupied the regional agenda. The U. of Colorado got 100% faculty oath of allegiance signups in response to a 1950-51 Board of Regents loyalty investigation.

Dealing with Discrimination: 1947-49

Future of New Mexico Indians Is Subject of Hawley Pamphlet

Navajos Haven't Had Chance Is Verdict of Noted Author In N M Quarterly Review

LO 4/13/48, 4/6/48

NATIVE AMERICANS who had served in the army in WWI and WWII were still unable to vote in New Mexico and Arizona in 1948.

Students Seek Legal Action Against Bonnie Briar Owner

Top: **SG** 4/14/49, **DC** 2/14/47

Two DU Students Sue Tavern Owner

DISCRIMINATION in Boulder and Denver restaurants and barber shops were aggressively attacked by students by demonstrations, boycotts and in court (See Rovira, p. 1006).

Discrimination Boycott Measure Carried 3 to 1

Colored Student Refused Service

LO 10/24/47, 9/18/47

BOYCOTTS IN ALBUQUERQUE were authorized by University of New Mexico students after Black students were refused service in local and chain restaurants.

400 Attend Conference; To Discuss Civil Liberties

NSA Regional Delegates Discuss Race Problems

DC 2/18/49, **SG** 10/25/49

14 COLLEGES FROM 4 STATES attended NSA's 10/49 conference at which all questions regarding race in admissions records were opposed (p. 1010).

KEY TO COLLEGE NEWSPAPER CITATIONS IN THIS SECTION

LO-*New Mexico Lobo* 8/17/45

NEW MEXICO LOBO — WARS END BRINGS HOPE FOR PEACE

HC-*Highlands Candle* 1/17/47

The Highlands' Candle — CHICAGO DELEGATES ENDORSE N. S. O.

SG-*Silver and Gold* 9/20/46

The SILVER and GOLD — Enrollment Tops All Records With 7,500

DC-*Denver Clasrion* 5/16/47

The Denver Clarion — UNESCO Conference Draws DU Students

RM-*Rocky MountainCollegian* 11/21/52

Rocky Mountain COLLEGIAN — Ten Colleges to Attend Regional Meet

BG-*Regis Brown & Gold* 4/25/51

The REGIS BROWN & GOLD

Returning veterans and a populist region shape its character

1. NSA in Colorado and the Rocky Mountain Region

Leonard (Len) Perlmutter
University of Colorado, Editor, Silver & Gold, *1945*
Chairman, NSA Rocky Mountain Region, 1947-48

Editor's note: This essay and the unit following have been prepared by the editors from transcripts of an interview conducted with Len Perlmutter in Denver, CO on October 26, 1999, with the addition of material researched in Rocky Mountain regional college newspapers and USNSA archives.

When I enrolled at the University of Colorado in 1943, my family had already established itself in the construction business in Colorado. My father, uncles, and aunts had come over from Russia in the early 1900s, and when they got to Denver they found a big small town—now it's a small big town.

It was a place that supported a lot of individualism and populism, people pulling themselves up by their bootstraps and with an attitude that everyone counts. Everyone is important. Don't let the government run your life, but the government is also important. We've come a long way since then in creating bonds of community, but that spirit is still in the air.

Of course, the University in Boulder was always a more socially conscious place, and while the city was very conservative when I was there, the college campus, which was the major activity in the community, was relatively open and progressive.

When I went to work as a columnist and then an editor on the *Silver and Gold* (*S&G*), I had a good perch from which to observe what was going on, on campus as well as in the world at large. I was sports editor in 1944 and editor of the paper in 1945.

In those days, we reported on general national and international news as well as the college scene, so working on the newspaper was an education as well as a job.

The end of the war and return of the veterans change campus life

The veterans started coming back after VE and VJ days in 1945, and by 1946 we had the real flood. In August of 1945, there were some really interesting issues about what they were going to provide for the veterans in the way of dormitories and housing. We already had a "trailer town," and there was talk of prefabricated housing. The area set up for veterans (mostly Quonset huts) was called Vetsville. The veterans elected their own "Mayor" and councilmen.

We had a peak enrollment in the fall of 1945 of 4,500, but in September of 1946 we reported an enrollment of 7,500, with 9,000 applications turned down. The peak for enrolled veterans according to the *S&G* was 4,671. There were a lot of new people who were not unwashed kids out of high school. These men and women were interesting characters. A lot of them had had unusual experiences in the service. A lot of them had families. That was one of the housing issues. How are you going to provide for people who come back with wives and kids or are soon to have kids? It was a transformation of the campus. Adults were going to be going to school there.

I think the veterans had a positive and maturing effect on the whole campus because they had a sense of justice and of what's fair. They had gone to war. They did understand why they had gone. Most of them recognized that it had been over a difference between a society without opportunity and a society that had promise. And their influence was felt on campus and in the community.

The end of the war was a momentous event. In the August 1945 issue of the *Silver and the Gold*, after the victory over Japan, the front page headlined, "CU Hails Peace," and we featured photos of Truman, Atlee, Stalin and Chiang Kai-shek.

Having grown up during the Depression and witnessed the hardships faced by many Americans, I was concerned about the future. I editorialized in that same issue: "At last we have won the struggle on the battlefields for the liberation of all freedom loving peoples of the world. Yet we now face a terrific struggle at home to give substance to this hard-won liberty."

I expressed concern that we address postwar economic issues firmly and asserted that if there were another Depression during the reconversion period, "the youth of the United States will be sorely pressed." I concluded:

> We need a strong student youth movement to carry through and carry the banner for a strong American youth as a whole. We should be the leaders, for we supposedly have the advantages of higher education. In order to use these advantages we must solidify and make ourselves felt in the coming struggle against reaction.

I get involved in NSA and student politics

Here was the groundwork for my enthusiasm over the formation of the National Student Association in 1947. Colorado was at the Chicago Student Conference in December 1946, represented by Jerry Goodman. According to the records, the only other Rocky Mountain colleges there were Colorado College, out of Colorado Springs, and New Mexico Highlands University, out of Las Vegas. Jerry Goodman became the first regional chair after the Chicago Conference. Bill Malkovich and I were at Madison for the University, and I was elected regional chair for 1947-48.

I also attended the First Congress in Madison the next summer, in 1948. By then I had finished my B.A., distributed in chemistry, mathematics, German and political science and gone on to graduate school.

During this time, I also got involved in campus politics. A mix of major issues was beginning to arise—such as university expansion plans before the state legislature, the University's entry into the Big Six basketball conference, racial discrimination by tradesmen off campus, and granting full recognition of a charter for the American Youth for Democracy (AYD)—which was accused of being a communist-front organization.

As a result of the AYD controversy, I became part of an organizing group that decided to form an Academic Freedom Committee to build up a body of background on academic freedom issues and be available to deal with any future issues. Vice chair of the committee was Robert Loper, who became head of the Department of Drama at Stanford. He went from there to the University of Washington.[1] The *S&G* noted that the Committee's formation received the "blessings" of CU President Robert L. Stearns, who had presided over that entire postwar period of growth and development on the campus.

One recurring contest on campus surfaced each year with the election of ASUC members and officers. There were always two major slates, one fielded by the Independent Students Association (ISA) and the other by the fraternities and sororities through the Interfraternity Conference (IFC). While the fraternity-sorority group was always a powerful force on campus, the Independents always had a strong voice as well. This was due to the makeup of the student body itself.

Strength of the "Independents" on campus

Colorado is a public university, and it had a tremendous number of out of state students. It was a wonderful place to go to school. The ambiance—the physical setting—is just superb. A lot of people came there because it was going to be their last real joyous vacation and their parents could afford to send them. But there were a lot of people who, like me, came from the public school system in the State and from all over the Midwest and Western United States.

The public universities were the premier universities. We didn't have the Yales and the Harvards. Denver University (DU) and Colorado College were the closest things, but they were not the premier schools in the state. Plus, while the tuition was $4,000 at DU, it was $250 at Boulder. So we had a lot of students there from all over the state of Colorado. Particularly with the GI bill, we suddenly started to get students from everywhere who had not necessarily intended to go to college.

If you worked in the construction industry, as I did, you would know that two-thirds of the people working in it were brilliant, but they grew up in the Depression. The job superintendents could all have been Ph.D.'s in a different setting, a postwar setting, but instead they had to go to work. They went to work building things and doing things—they were just gifted people. But the educational opportunities were not the way they were from World War II on. So, a lot of the people on campus after the war were these kinds of people, and they tended to be independents.

Well, some of us wanted to offer an alternative between the two factions, and so we formed the con-FUSION Party, and fielded a slate in 1947 and 1948. My running mate was Byron Lipman the first time, and there were three of us the second time. I was elected on both occasions, largely due to the proportional representation system of elections we had, which prevented any one group from completely controlling the outcome. The second time around, John Barnhill joined our slate. He was a fraternity man who eventually became state district judge. In the *Silver and Gold* issue of April 15, 1947, our somewhat tongue-in-cheek announcement was quoted:

> Realizing fully well that the world stands or falls on this ASUC election, as it has so many times in the past, we the con-FUSION Party in the person of Len Perlmutter and By Lipman, are convinced that the student government must be as

representative as possible in order to continue the tradition of masterly achievement of our ruling bodies in the long history of the University.

We have neither political nor social affiliation nor have vested financial interests but are instead sincerely committed to better student government operated by the near extinct common man.

The ASUC and Luis Rovira

As it turned out, the Greek slate candidate, Luis Rovira, who was elected ASUC president by a vote of 1,890 to 1,539, proved to be a spirited and progressive leader. He and I became lifetime friends. Eventually, he became chief justice of the Colorado State Supreme Court.

Lou was out front on the early racial discrimination issues that we confronted in those years as we battered away at traditional barriers. With our school having been admitted to the Big Six—making it the Big Seven —Lou Rovira attacked the Big Six Jim Crow Rule, which prohibited mixed races in the game. He was quoted at their Lincoln, Nebraska, meeting in December of 1947, as stating, "I am adamant in my opposition to racial segregation . . . [rather than participate], I would prefer a complete withdrawal." Although the Big Seven coaches voted five to two to retain the rule that January (Colorado and Nebraska voted against), it was Colorado through Rovira that first challenged the practice.[2] The January 20 issue of the *S&G* reported:

> **Jim Crow Restrictions Stay in Effect after Big Seven Meeting**
>
> A Missouri Valley Athletic Association ruling which permits members to exercise "Jim Crow" restrictions upon guest athletic teams remains unchanged, as all effort failed to secure its reversal at last month's meeting of faculty representatives at Kansas City.[3]
>
> Professor Walter B. Franklin, Colorado's representative presented the motion . . . after several hours of heated debate the motion was tabled by a vote of five to two. The Universities of Colorado and Nebraska opposed the tabling resolution. . . .
>
> Meanwhile a poll taken at the university of Oklahoma showed that the students themselves, by a ratio of two to one, opposed the existing "Jim Crow" statutes of Oklahoma's athletic program. This followed the success of the action taken by Southern Methodist University, which formerly adhered to such rulings, in playing Penn State, which had two Negro members on its team, in the New Year's Cotton Bowl classic. . . .
>
> According to Rovira, existing "Jim Crow" rulings have evolved from the improper interpretation of state laws in Oklahoma and Missouri prohibiting the entry of Negro students in "white" state universities. He explained, however, there was no legislation prohibiting the appearance of Negro athletes at athletic events in the affected states.

Launching NSA at the University of Colorado

Turning back to the beginnings of NSA at Colorado and in the region, my memory has been helped considerably by looking back at the reports in the *Silver and Gold* and by the research done by the editors of this Anthology.

The January 14, 1947, issue of the *S&G* has an article by Jerry Goodman reporting on the December 1946 Chicago Student Conference, in which he states that:

> a regional meeting of all schools in the Colorado–New Mexico region must be held in order to map out a program of activity in this region and for the formulation of regional plans for the [constitutional] convention. As chairman of this region I have called for representatives of all national student organizations on campus to meet for the purpose of formulating student opinion on our own campus and holding the regional meeting at CU.

The Chicago Conference and the Constitutional Convention were greeted by very little press comment at Colorado, probably, in retrospect, because there was also very little dissent and our region was a sparsely populated one. Bill Malkovich and I were chosen to go the Constitutional Convention in Madison, and issued a report that appeared in the October 24 *S&G*:

> The groundwork for NSA was laid at the Chicago Students Conference last Christmas when 700 students representing 800,000 students from 300 colleges and universities saw clearly a real need for a functioning national student organization. . . .
>
> Much can be accomplished by U.S. students through this organization and nothing will be sacrificed in the three level plan of the organization which preserves the autonomy of the student government on the individual campuses. . . .Campus-wide activities will be coordinated on a regional level, however . . . the entire emphasis of the program is on the individual campus and its rights and privileges combined with the power and experience of other college and student groups.

Following the Madison convention, we organized ourselves to introduce NSA on campus and build a regional program. In December, the ASUC formed an NSA committee with myself as chair, plus Frank Garland, Ed McNulty, Peter V. Bessol, Sherman Finesilver, and Bobbie Folley.

Our immediate campus program focused on supporting the student relief drive of the World Student Service Fund, promoting NSA's summer travel programs, and actively sponsoring the week-long Brotherhood Week programs on campus.

A brief burst of controversy wasn't long in coming when Dick Mulhern generated an eight-column headline in the *S&G*, "Commission Orders Local NSA Committee Probe," as a consequence of his charge that "the CU delegation voted questionably at the NSA Assembly in Madison." He went further to allege that "tinted CU personalities were regional leaders" and supported this with our vote to support negotiations for affiliation with the International Union of Students.[4]

There was a swift response, with the *S&G* itself editorializing on January 27, "It is regrettable that the word 'probe' was ill-advisedly used in the headline on the story. . . . It also would have been better to mention Perlmutter's denials in the story," and by January 30, the *S&G* was headlining that "ASUC Vindicated NSA Group: Gives Vote of Confidence." It reported that an audience of nearly one hundred interested students attended the meeting, noting that

> Mulhern stated that he received his information on the NSA convention in a letter from Phil Demaret [*sic*], Chairman of the Minnesota Region of the NSA, who characterized his views in writing, "I might be very prejudiced, but I feel that CU students should know what others think. . . ." Mulhern then read excerpts from a letter he received from Bill Murray, a Colorado College delegate to NSA.

The letter was favorable to the UC delegation and their actions. Meanwhile, Luis Rovira had checked with Denver University (Mulhern had earlier stated that DU had withdrawn from NSA)—and determined that in fact they had not yet voted on NSA. Rovira denounced "the libel and smear campaign." Mulhern was unable to withdraw his motion for an investigation, and it was unanimously defeated. Finesilver was also quoted as saying that NSA was not representative of the student body.

In the same issue, the *S&G* editorialized:

> The campus NSA group has been completely vindicated of the charges leveled against it. . . .There can be no doubt that the basic theories of the NSA are sound. . . . For the most part, it is a group of thinking Americans who will be the nation's leaders of tomorrow. It is only right that there be a national organization through which the ideas and aims of controlling citizenry can be transmitted to the present-day legislators, businessmen and teachers.
>
> But it cannot be denied that control of such an organization as NSA could be a powerful weapon in the hands of the wrong elements. How valuable such control would be to such elements is indicated in the reports emanating from the Madison, Wisconsin convention of NSA, which stated that a determined attempt to gain control of the convention was made by left-wing groups. . . .
>
> From this point it is hoped that other schools in the area will follow the Colorado leadership in joining the national student group.

On February 3, the *S&G* ran my response, "Perlmutter Answers to Charges Against NSA group," in which I noted:

> To be perfectly honest, these should never have been charges, they should have been questions. As charges they were absurd. As questions they might have been legitimate. . . . Unfortunately, the NSA and the University have been burdened by a stigma by virtue of the entire episode. I sincerely hope that this stigma can be washed away as easily as the charges.

Organizing the Rocky Mountain Region

In September of 1947, the region had not yet been named Rocky Mountain, having been renamed shortly thereafter, and coming out of the Constitutional Convention it was called Utah, Wyoming, SE Idaho, No. Colo. I was elected chair. A separate region, Arizona, New Mexico, Southern Colorado, was designated, with Jack Wharton of New Mexico Highlands as the chair. New Mexico Highlands eventually attached itself to the Rocky Mountain Region.

We set about organizing our first regional meeting in February, at which twenty-six representatives from eleven colleges attended.[5] The *S&G* reports:

> It was the hope of University NSA leaders that through this convention schools in the area might become more acquainted with the association, thus facilitating the affiliation of these colleges with the NSA. . . .
>
> Representatives from various colleges [pointed out] that benefits possible through NSA would accrue to small and large schools alike. The representative from Colorado State College of Education stated that affiliation with NSA will necessitate active participation in and understanding of democratic government by students and will tend to give all students a better knowledge of international relations.
>
> Other benefits included the achievement of student faculty cooperation in doing NSA work together; work on a national basis to eliminate discrimination in educational institutions; increased financial aid to students throughout the world; and, locally, investigation of problems on campus through grievance and domestic affairs committees.

Elsewhere in this section, the editors have prepared a chronology of regional activity during the next few years. Looking at the clippings of that era, it is satisfying to see that the organization kept going a lively forum, through which colleges in the area were able to address issues such as academic freedom and discrimination, conduct student government and human relations workshops, and sponsor intercollegiate cultural and social programs.

For one year, during 1950-51, NSA maintained its national offices at the University in Boulder, while it was regrouping from serious budget problems. Bill Dentzer, NSA's president that year, got as much *S&G* coverage as any local personality, and the University community was very supportive of the group's presence.

It was also during that year that Roy Romer was chairman of the Region. Roy went on to become governor of the state, head of the Democratic National Committee, and, at this writing, has just started a new career as Superintendent of Schools in Los Angeles.

NSA in Colorado during its formative years helped to incubate a fair number of state and national leaders in government, journalism, and business. It added to my start on a lifetime that has always included some form of service to the community. There is always some kind of uplifting you can do for people. I was always politically active, because it was something that you had to do. And it was enjoyable. When NSA came along, it was also something I had to do—and I enjoyed doing it.

END NOTES

[1] His brother and I were roommates at college. We became good friends, and he became my business partner for forty-five years.

[2] See Rovira, p. 1006.

[3] The University of Missouri student body had passed a resolution opposing the existing rule and proposing a change. It was this proposed change that was supported by five of the Big Seven student representatives at their meeting, and the next month opposed by five of the seven faculty representatives.

[4] See NSA/IUS history, p. 538, and Part I, Section 1.

[5] The colleges included: Loretto Heights, Regis, Denver University, Colorado A&M, Iliff School of Theology, Colorado Women's College of Education, Weber College (Ogden, Utah), and the University of Colorado.

PICTURE CREDITS: *Then:* 1945-46 U. Colorado Yearbook (Rovira). *Now:* 1999, Denver (Schwartz).

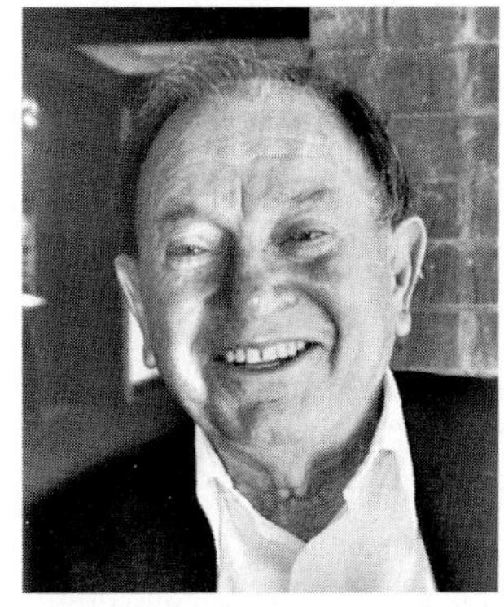

Len Perlmutter is a construction industry executive and a civic leader in Denver, Colorado.

LEONARD PERLMUTTER

Early years: Born in Denver, October 16, 1925, and attended West Denver High School.

Education: B.A. University of Colorado, 1948. Post-graduate, 1948-1950.

Career highlights: Partner, Perlmutter & Sons, Denver, 1947-1958; Vice President, Prestressed Concrete of Colorado, Denver, 1952-1960; Stanley Structures, Inc., Denver, President, 1960-1983; Chairman of the Board, 1983-87; Director, Colorado Natural Bankshares, Inc., 1976-93; Adjunct Professor, Graduate School of Public Affairs, University of Colorado, 1987-89; Chief Executive Officer, Economic Development, Governor's Office State of Colorado, 1987-88; Chairman of the Board, Colorado Open Lands, 1989; Chairman of the Board, 1981-82, Life Trustee University of Colorado Foundation, Boulder; Director, Santa Fe Opera Association, New Mexico, 1976-1985; National Jewish Research and Medical Center Denver: Trustee and Emeritus, 1971—, Chmn. Bd., 1981-83, President and CEO, 1991-93; President, Denver Symphony Association, 1983-84; Chairman of the Board, 1985; Recipient, Humanitarian American Jewish Committee, 1981; Prestressed Concrete Institution: Pres. 1977, Director, 1973-74, Fellow, 1994-); President, LAP, Inc., 1985-.

Family: Married Alice Love Bristow. Children: Edwin George, Joseph, Kent, and Cassandra Love.

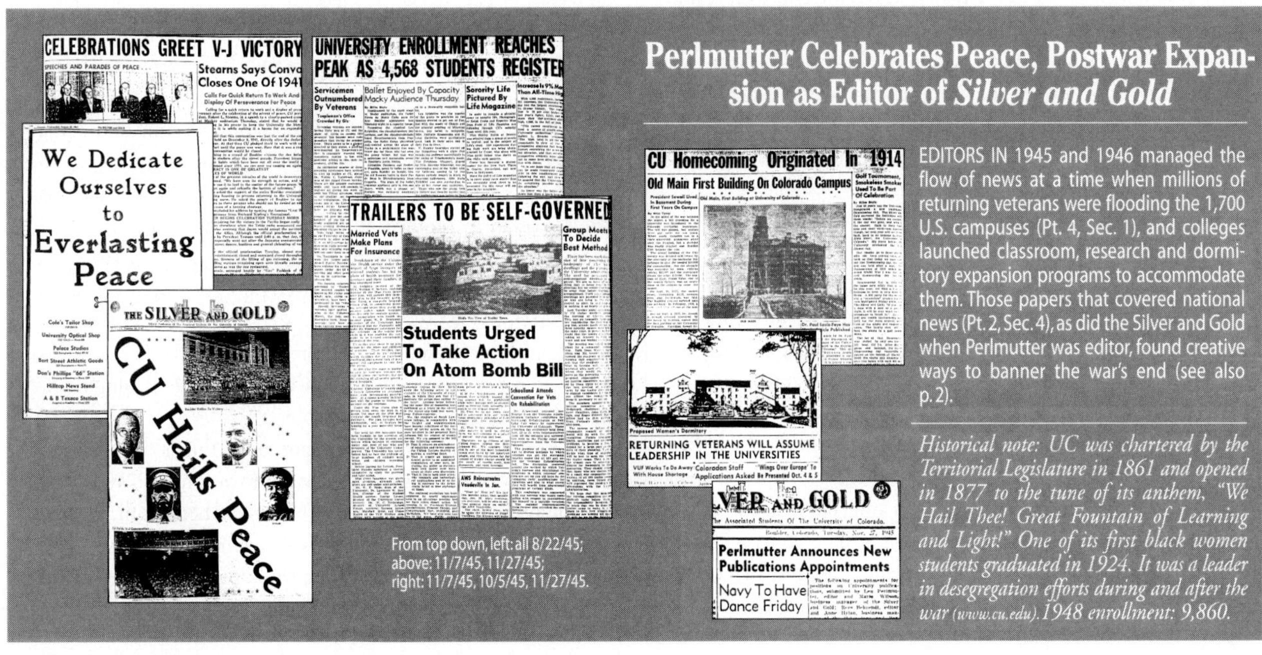

From top down, left: all 8/22/45; above: 11/7/45, 11/27/45; right: 11/7/45, 10/5/45, 11/27/45.

Perlmutter Celebrates Peace, Postwar Expansion as Editor of *Silver and Gold*

EDITORS IN 1945 and 1946 managed the flow of news at a time when millions of returning veterans were flooding the 1,700 U.S. campuses (Pt. 4, Sec. 1), and colleges launched classroom, research and dormitory expansion programs to accommodate them. Those papers that covered national news (Pt. 2, Sec. 4), as did the Silver and Gold when Perlmutter was editor, found creative ways to banner the war's end (see also p. 2).

Historical note: UC was chartered by the Territorial Legislature in 1861 and opened in 1877 to the tune of its anthem, "We Hail Thee! Great Fountain of Learning and Light!" One of its first black women students graduated in 1924. It was a leader in desegregation efforts during and after the war (www.cu.edu). 1948 enrollment: 9,860.

Lifetime lessons learned while working my way through college

Running a College Newspaper and Other College Work Assignments

Len Perlmutter
Editor, Silver and Gold, *University of Colorado, 1945*

The *Silver and Gold* was described on its masthead as "An Independent Newspaper" and the "Official Publication of the Associated Students of the University of Colorado."

We were publishing the *Silver and Gold* twice a week and the *Boulder Daily Camera,* a newspaper in town, set the type and printed it. Twice a week we'd carry the manuscript to the printer for typesetting and running galleys. I'd have to go down with my editorials last, while they were setting up the type and pages, and then I'd proofread. The whole paper—writing, editing, proofreading, makeup—was put together by the students. We'd do all of the paste makeup at our little offices that we had down in the basement of the Memorial Building.

There was a level of social concern and maturity on the campus that was remarkable. These weren't unscrubbed kids. And it was reflected in the scope of our newspaper coverage. They really had an exceptional journalism department at the University. The head of it was Ralph Crossman. I think he came from the University of Missouri, but he had also been in the newspaper business. And then there was Gayle Waldrop, who succeeded him but had been on the faculty for a long time. These men were there for many years.

A lot of the people on the paper were either journalism majors or minors who were interested in journalism. The university had a good business school, too, and a lot of people doing the selling of the ads were all pretty bright, competent students who wanted a business career. And the business office was right there too, side by side with editorial. Plus, it was fun.

One student, Harry O. Lawson, who wanted to write, came back from the service in 1945. A native of New York, he enrolled as a journalism major and became sports editor shortly thereafter. He succeeded to editor in chief later in his undergraduate career. He eventually became chief administrator for the court system in the state of Colorado. He's retired now, and he teaches law at the University of Denver part time.

How the paper was put together

We'd come in after class or in the evening and staff would sit down and do their stories on the old, standard ribbon typewriters. As editor, I didn't pass on every story. We had a news editor, a city editor, a sports editor, a society editor, and a crew of reporters for each. And we all talked. We'd have a meeting to review what was happening and what was going in the paper. But we'd also have a format of how much space generally we were going to give for various kinds of news and columns. For example, the sports editor knew he had to at least fill up the back page.

My job was to set a general policy and make sure that everyone else was on the job. The system sort of ran itself. The *Camera* was an afternoon paper, so we would go down after they finished their day and we had access to their paste-up room.

The Board of Publications, consisting of faculty and students chosen by the ASUC, appointed the key staff on the paper and approved staff recommendations of the editor. The university business department furnished the business management and accounting.

People would start on the paper because they had an interest in it at the time, so they'd get a job as a reporter or in the business office selling ads. There was on-the-job training, and they were there for three or four years and built up some good experience. Meanwhile, the Journalism Department and the whole English Department were available to them. They were always interacting with these advisers, so they got continually critiqued for what they did, technically as well as socially and philosophically.

Everybody was paid a little bit. I was paid around $40 a month. The sports editor got $15 or $20 a month. That was money in those days, when the stipend for Vets was $50 a month. I'd help sell some of the advertising too, so I'd get commission on that.

Lessons learned at work

And I also worked at other jobs. I was the guy in charge of the coat check stand at all the major dances. In fact, working my way through college taught me a lot of useful lessons. It was my business training. I took one class, and that was at the sorority house at Kappa Kappa Gamma where I hashed. It was a very important lesson. When I started there, there were five of us working, forty-two girls, and one cook. When I left there were nine of us, a cook and a helper, and new equipment, and there were forty-four girls.

The only thing that changed was that each time they had a rush week, some of the alumni would complain that they had to wait too long for a meal or for some other thing. As I had acquired seniority on the staff, the housemother came to me and asked, "What should we do?" I said we obviously needed more help—but that wasn't the only answer. So I got myself a place as a supervisor, where I was working hard doing nothing and giving advice and getting paid for it. Afterward, I reflected on how this change transpired so easily. The answer was the most important lesson I ever had in business.

The lesson was, when you've got to get things done, understand what it is that you're really trying to accomplish and every step you need to get there. But don't overstep, because hiring a lot of people to meet a crisis simply diverts your best people to train them, and by then the crisis is over. My subsequent career was in cyclic construction and related manufacturing. We kept staffing for one crisis at a time instead of managing how to deal with the crisis with the people we had.

Before I had retired, we had grown to 1,500 +/- employees. In my last message to the managers I reminded them that in a time of reducing business demand, the least gut-wrenching people to lay off were those you hadn't hired. The other maxim I repeated regularly was: in times of increased demand the customer won't be able to receive before we are not able to deliver!

NEW MEXICO LOBO

Semi-Weekly Publication of the Associated Students of the University of New Mexico

Student Delegation Approaches Governor

Advisers on Tap Between Jan. 7 And the 21st

Hispanic Series Presents Talk On Early Days

DEMPSEY AGREES TO CONFERENCE

THE SOUTHWEST COLLEGE PRESS IN THE LATE 1940'S AND 1950'S

College papers emulated the general press in their complex layouts and coverage. They produced multiple issues weekly, demanding considerable skill and professionalism.

From top, descending: U.of New Mexico 12/17/46; U of Colorado 4/23/47; U. of Denver 5/8/47; New Mexico Highlands College 3/12/48. The U of Colorado 9/21/51 *Silver and Gold* features location of NSA as national headquarters at the University in 1951-52.

Alleviated one step at a time by many people

2. Chipping Away at Raw Racism

Luis D. Rovira

University of Colorado, Student Body President, 1947-48

The racism that existed in Boulder, on the campus, in the state, and in the nation after the war was "raw" and could only be alleviated one step at a time by many people.

The Big Seven issue was but a drop in the bucket. [See Perlmutter, p. 1001.] However, when added together with what was going on in the other universities, it made a difference.

Another fight I engaged in was in my third year of law school. I was a proctor in the men's dormitory. One of the men who lived there was black. He told me one day that he was going to Denver, thirty-five miles away, to have his hair cut. When I asked him why, he told me that no barbershop in Boulder would cut his hair. I was both surprised and shocked.

I started to research the Colorado statutes and found a long forgotten statute that prohibited racial discrimination in theaters and barbershops. With this law in hand, I asked the black student to go back to the barbershop and ask for service. I had two of my friends in the shop, and when he was refused service, they were witnesses to the event.

I brought suit against the barber, obtained lots of publicity in the school and city newspapers, and helped to support a student boycott of all barbershops, which finally got them to change their policies. In the court case we had a hung jury, but achieved our goal.

Luis Rovira was Chief Justice of the Colorado Supreme Court and is an active Colorado civic leader.

It was a learning experience for a young lawyer that was to stand me in good stead over the years.

LUIS D. ROVIRA

Luis Rovira was born in San Juan, Puerto Rico, in 1923. He served in the U.S. Army Infantry from 1943 to 1946 in the European Theater, and in the U.S. Air Force from 1946 to 1951. He received his B.A. (1948) and L.L.B. (1950) at the University of Colorado. Chief Justice of the Colorado Supreme Court from 1990 to 1995, he is currently Senior Judge of the Judicial Arbiter Group. He served as a Justice of the Supreme Court from 1979 to 1995 and as a District Court Judge from 1976 to 1979. From 1950 to 1976 he was in private practice.

Judge Rovira served as Chairman of the Colorado State Health Facilities Council, President and Chairman of the Board of the Mile High United Fund, Chairman of the Board of the Metropolitan Assn. for Retarded Children, and on many other boards and committees concerned with children, youth, and health. He is currently on the Boards of the Children's Hospital and the Denver Foundation.

He is married to Lois Ann Rovira, and they have two children, Dr. Douglas K. Rovira and Ms. Merilyn Rovira.

Rovira Attacks Racial Barriers

Lou Rovira Elected President Of ASUC

The SILVER and GOLD

AN INDEPENDENT NEWSPAPER

University of Colorado Enters Big Six

3/4/47

4/23/47

THE BIG 6 BECAME THE BIG 7 when Colorado entered in 1947. As Len Perlmutter writes (p. 1001) "it was Colorado through Rovira" that first challenged the rule that prohibited mixed races in football games when Rovira attended the 12/47 Conference meeting. In 1949, while in law school Rovira brought suit against a local barber in behalf of a Black dormitory mate who was refused service. While keeping its letters column open to the shop owner, the *Silver and Gold* (right) refused to take shop advertising.

Because Bigotry Exists . . .

4/6/49

Because two students wanted a cup of coffee early Sunday morning ...

THE SILVER AND GOLD

Editorial And Opinion

Page 2 — Wednesday, April 26, 1950

4/26/49

Barber Shop Bigotry

Edward E. Johnson, a graduate student in psychology at the University, is a Negro.

Because he is a Negro, Johnson was flatly refused service on two occasions at the Buff Barber shop, 1317 College avenue.

Because Fred Hall, proprietor of the Buff Barber shop, feels that "mixing trade" will hurt his business, Hall told Johnson twice during the month of March that "we don't serve colored people" and turned Johnson away.

Hall admitted in justice of the peace court here Monday that Johnson's charges were true.

The fact that the jury deadlocked at 3-3 on the question ...

. . . .

... Johnson's attorney filed suit for individual damages of $300, while the law provides a less severe minimum penalty under criminal misdemeanor proceedings as an alternate remedy.

Nevertheless, racial discrimination by barber shops violates the spirit and letter of the Colorado Civil Rights statute. The statute states:

"All persons within the jurisdiction of said state (Colorado) shall be entitled to the full and equal enjoyment of the accommodations, advantages, facilities and privileges of inns, restaurants, eating houses, barber shops, public conveyances on land or water, theatres, and all other places of public accommodation and amusement, subject only to the conditions and

I treasure the experiences and friendships.

3. Students: A Real Voice in World Affairs

Roy Romer
Colorado A&M, University of Colorado Law School
President, Rocky Mountain Region, 1950-51

My involvement with NSA began during my senior year at Colorado A&M, now Colorado State, when I was student government president. After graduation and prior to my first year at University of Colorado Law School, I attended the Third NSA Student Congress at the University of Michigan in August 1950, as president of NSA's Rocky Mountain Region. During the academic year that followed, I continued as regional president in that large, six-state area. Our fall regional convention at Fort Collins, Colorado, and the spring convention at New Mexico Highlands University in Las Vegas, New Mexico, covered a wide range of topics, including student government services, potential regional cultural activities, international education programs, and challenges to academic freedom. Indeed, the theme of the spring meeting was "Preserving Individual and Academic Freedom in the Present Crisis." I treasure the experiences and friendships provided by those years.

From The Silver and Gold *(University of Colorado), January 16, 1951.*

Romer Discusses Results of NSA Meeting

Roy Romer, freshman law student at Colorado and regional president of NSA, has just returned from a meeting in Madison, Wis., of the 23 regional presidents of NSA. . . .

The conference was held to discuss the results of the recent meeting of the leaders of the students of the western union held in Stockholm. . . . One of the main points brought out at this meeting was that next year there should be another meeting held in the Western Hemisphere with representation from all of the countries of the world rather than just the Western nations. . . .

The real issue next year will be whether it will be composed of the representatives of all nations of the world or just of a western bloc.

"Whether students know it or not they have a real voice in world affairs, and the student world is the last door open for a universal understanding," said Roy Romer.

NSA was also given a project at the meeting in Stockholm, which was to give technical aid to Southeast Asia. The next meeting of NSA . . . will be held this summer, and it will be decided there exactly what aid the U.S. is in a position to offer.

PICTURE CREDITS: *Then:* 1949-50 Colorado State A&M Student Body President *(Yearbook). Now:* c. 2000 (Author).

Roy Romer, Superintendent of Schools, Los Angeles Unified School District, is a former three-term Governor of Colorado and General Chairman of the Democratic National Committee.

ROY ROMER

Roy Romer's career has spanned the private sector, the world of politics and the field of education. Romer was named Superintendent of Schools of the Los Angeles Unified School District by the Los Angeles City Board of Education on June 6, 2000.

Romer was Governor of Colorado for three terms, from 1986 to 1998, and was the general chairman of the Democratic National Committee from 1997 to 2000. He has long been an advocate and an activist for educational issues at the state and national levels. He was vice chair of the Democratic Leadership Council, an information-age think tank that examines a variety of issues and where he studied effective educational strategies and school reform initiatives. He served as chair of the Educational Commission of the States and chair of the National Education Goals Panel. He helped develop the first national education "report card" in the early 1990s, and in 1996 he was awarded the prestigious Harold W. McGraw Jr. Prize in Education.

Romer grew up in southeastern Colorado. He and his wife, Bea, have seven children and 18 grandchildren. Romer holds a bachelor's degree in agricultural economics from Colorado State University (1950), earned a law degree from the University of Colorado (1952), studied ethics at Yale University and was a legal officer in the U.S. Air Force. He also practiced law in Denver in the 1950s and 1960s. He has been involved in family-owned businesses in agriculture and agricultural equipment for many years, helped develop Colorado's Centennial Airport, ran a flying school and owned and operated a ski area.

Silver and Gold 1/16/51

Romer Discusses Results Of NSA National Meeting

Roy Romer, freshman law student at Colorado and regional president of NSA, has just returned from a meeting in Madison, Wis., of the 23 regional presidents of NSA representing 325 universities and colleges throughout the U.S. The approximate total of the students represented is 800,000.

The conference was held to dis-

Highlands Candle 4/20/51

Individual Academic Freedom Discussed By The Rocky Mountain N S A

New Mexico Highlands University was the scene last weekend for the Rocky Mountain Regional Meeting of the National Students Association where some 50 delegates from a six state area were on hand.

Delegates registered late Friday afternoon and early evening at the student lounge. Nick Taylor, state chairman for the organization, was Highlands student in charge of the convention.

The meeting got underway Saturday morning with a general session presided over by Roy Roamer, president of the region-

bers that educators of an iron-handed land stress what to think rather than how to think. Unlike our country, controversial issues are not taught or spoken of in dictatorial regimes, for, to their way of thinking, it cracks social solidarity.

Dr. Baylon warned: "To fight opponents, we must study negative data. We must 'know our enemy'."

"We must be open-minded at all times, we must be tolerant. In this way, we can reach conclusions, though they may be only tentative."

ACADEMIC FREEDOM AND INTERNATIONAL RELATIONS highlighted the region's agenda. The region sponsored visiting foreign students in the summer of 1951. Romer presided over regional assemblies at Colorado College and New Mexico Highlands (above right).

Administrators Look at the University of Colorado and NSA

Editor's note: College administrations around the country saw in NSA opportunities and threats, uncertainties and possibilities (See Shaffer, p. 326). Examples of various levels of concern, some overcome and others not, abound in this anthology: e.g., U. of Chicago (p. 193), U. of Southern California (p. 1030), College of St. Thomas (p. 942) and Georgetown U. (p. 742). Many administrations saw opportunities in NSA for furthering student self-government (Klopf, pp. 334, 336), and NSA strongly encouraged student-educator collaboration. The excerpts below of correspondence and memos by U. of Colorado administrators typify the levels of consideration and, in this case, the positive outlook of a college administration.

[Documents from University of Colorado Archives]

Bringing Democracy to the Campus

From a two-page letter on the subject of NSA and student rights by Clifford Houston, Dean of Students, to President Robert L. Stearns, April 27, 1948.

Dear President Stearns:

Thank you for the file of correspondence concerning the N.S.A. Student "Bill of Rights" which was sent to you by Dean Darley: I am very much interested in this matter.

While I was attending the meetings of the American College Personnel Association, in late March, I heard Bill Welsh, President of the National Students Association, plead for giving students some real and final authority for something (newspaper, or social affairs, etc,) while they are in college.* His plea was well conceived and well said and was based on the thesis that (1) college graduates do not take an active part in community affairs generally (many Doctors and Engineers are the worst offenders), apparently because they did not do so in high school or college, (2) we talk about Democracy a great deal in college but we don't do much about it, in most institutions.

The more I attend national meetings and visit college campuses the more convinced I become that most colleges and universities are not very democratic institutions; I never cease to be impressed, however, and to be grateful that the University of Colorado is so democratic. There really is little Democracy in the administration of many colleges. Comparatively few have a real faculty Senate; few have or really use an Executive Council for policy determination; comparatively few have a functioning committee system. In many of them there exists a real feud between a very busy and harrassed administration and a faculty that cannot or will not understand administrative problems. Too frequently, however, this gulf exists because the administration cannot or will not take the time to establish two-way communication with the faculty....

In the college field, students, as well as the faculty, are affected by such a condition. The students characteristically adopt one of two extreme attitudes: (1) a "radical" or "labor-union-negotiation" idea that "management" must be wrestled with, in order to gain "rights" or (2) a "don't give a damn" feeling—because the faculty and administration "won't let us do anything."

In talking to the regional convention of N.S.A. last week I put the issue squarely up to the student delegates from seven colleges and universities.... I stated emphatically that it is our responsibility to help students develop student-body organizations which are capable of governing many of their activities, with a mininum amount of faculty and administrative "control."

I scored, however, a belligerent or "labor-union-negotiation" student approach to the faculty and administration. I deplored the tendency to emphasize "rights."... I reminded them that the public and boards of control (properly) hold us responsible for what happens and that the extent to which we are willing to relinquish much of our control is in direct proportion to our confidence in students and their methods of operation.

*Note: See Welsh speech, "Democracy Through Student Government," delivered to ACPA, p. 185.

University Community Should Take an Interest

From a two-page letter on the status of NSA on campus, by Harry Carlson, Dean of Men, to Dean W.F. Dyde, university Vice President, June 15, 1948.

Dear Professor Dyde:

... Our ASUC has appointed six student delegates; namely, Leonard Perlmutter, Bill Eaton, Joe Holden, Pete Bessol, Bob Foley [Barbara Folley], and Bill Maikovich to attend the National Congress.... These are representative University students whom we can trust to use good judgment.

In my opinion the USNSA can be a constructive organization representing the most important youth group in the United States. It is of vital importance that this youth movement receive the benefits of mature and wise counsel.... We spend thousands of dollars from student fees each year on dances, banquets, student publications, forensics, music, sports, and freshman orientation. I believe that we are justified in spending $1,000 of the non-athletic ASUC budget, on an experimental basis, in order to help further the very worthy aims of the USNSA.... all members of a University community should take an active interest in such matters in order to insure democratic representation and wise guidance of idealistic and enthusiastic youth.

It Is Filling a Real Need and We Can Profit by It

From a one-page letter by Clifford Houston, Dean of Students, to Vice President W.F. Dyde on an issue raised by a UC Regent, dated November 4, 1948.

Dear Professor Dyde:

You will recall that one of our Regents was not favorably disposed toward approval of an A.S.U.C. budget item which provided for travel expense for delegates to the N.S.A. convention.... those delegates reported to the A.S.U.C. last night that... the convention was profitable for those who attended it. The major items discussed dealt with the status of higher education, student life on the campus, improvement of student government and international relations.

The young man who made the report... was Pete Bessol, a young Catholic who is a leader in the Newman Club.... During the discussion last night Len Perlmutter... and other student leaders urged that the President and Commissioners of the A.S.U.C. attend Regional and National meetings of N.S.A. hereafter and the "program" of the N.S.A. become the program of A.S.U.C....

Mrs. Simmons and I are encouraging the A.S.U.C. Commission to adopt the policy of sending the newly-elected student body officers to to the N.S.A. as a means of broadening their horizons.... I am not worried at all about the present political complexion of the N.S.A. During the convention this year there was no evidence of radicalism. I sincerely believe that it is filling a real need and that we can profit by it.

A Group to Experiment with Group Action

From a one-page letter about her attendance at the Michigan NSA Congress, by Lorraine Miller, Assistant to the Director of Student Activities, to Gordon Klopf at the U. of Wisconsin, NSA's Advisory Committee Chairman, April 3, 1950.

Dear Gordon:

... Mr. Ware, the director of Student Activities here, has decided that the return from having a representative at the congress might increase with repetition, consequently I am eagerly looking forward to being in Michigan this summer. One of the NSA advisers here, Dr. Jack R. Gibb has been doing a great deal of work in group dynamics* (the participative group is his preferred term) and is planning to attend the congress this summer too, as he is convinced that NSA is the logical group to experiment with this type of group action. He is quite a dynamic person himself, one you will enjoy meeting.

*Note: NSA played a major role in the introduction of this alternative to parliamentary procedure in managing meetings. See pp. 335, 344.

"The Great Desert, Plains and Mountain Region"

Editor's note: With a four-state (plus pieces of two others) unwieldy territory stretching 1,200 miles north and 600 miles wide, in May, 1954 Bob Hunter (U. Colorado), Rocky Mountain regional president, looked back on the early years of the region in his report and suggested "the problem of geographical distance is and I believe always will be an insoluble problem." He suggested the region be named "The Great Desert, Plains, and Mountain Region of the Central United States." Of the 39 four-year colleges in Colorado, New Mexico, Wyoming and Montana, the region's membership was concentrated in Colorado and New Mexico, enrolling 7 to 9 colleges and up to twice as many at regional events. The U. of Colorado provided the region's energy center and most of its Presidents: Jerry Goodman ('46-47), Len Perlmutter ('47-48), Frank Krasovek ('49-50) and Roy Romer ('50-51). Others were John Olson, Colo. A&M ('48-49) and Patrick Eagan, Regis C. ('51-52). At first the region was split between North and South, the North including Idaho, which went to the Great Northwest, and the South including Utah, later its own region. Southern region chairs were Jack Whorton ('47-48) and Winfield Meadows ('48-49), both from NM Highlands U. [For chronological regional highlights see pictorial, p. 998]

Issue No.3 [*Digest from the original*] March 28, 1950

NSA PRESIDENT BOB KELLY VISITS THE REGION

The national president, Bob Kelly from St. Peters College in New Jersey, was in the Rocky Mountain Region March 3-7. Wherever he went he was a big hit. Bob Atkinson, Student Body Prexy of Trinidad JC, said the faculty was particularly impressed with the high calibre of NSA officers. If they could have, Denver U. would have kept Bob there all day and then some. Colorado College forWomen wouldnt have minded that either—all he had to do was pick a Queen and crown her. Regis and Loretto put on a feed for the fellow. Took notes on Bob's speech for two hours and he had so much to say I still have writer's cramp. Aggies (A&M) went all out for Bob—he received a royal welcome and was able to hook a ride up to Laramie. Bob also made an impressive stop at Colorado U. and CSCE. Being national prexy and only twenty is quite an accomplishment.

International Interests

World Student Service Fund Opens All-University Campaign May 12

Miss Judith Austin, who is travelling for the World Student Service Fund regional office in St. Louis, was on campus Wednesday to promote a WSSF campaign which begins at DU Monday, May 12. Collections will be handled through organization presidents.

... working with student centers there. "WSSF funds are used well and reach the people who really benefit by them," she said. The money goes through direct channels to the students abroad who need aid.

OPENS MONDAY

The drive at the University will extend from May 12 through May 17. WSSF extends the hope that every DU student will contribute one dollar or more to the ...

Aid For Students Request Of WSSF In Urgent Drive

Colleges and Universities In Foreign Countries Need

...ical Party; ... of Policy

NSA-Sponsored Students Impressed By U.S. Sights

Fifteen students from Swiss universities arrive in Boulder today for a five day stay in Colorado. They are here under the auspices of the National Student Association.

World Peace Is Goal Of N S A International Affairs Program

By Claude Salomon

"The entire International Affairs program of the National Student Association is just a means to an end. The means is anything we can figure out, and the end is World Peace." This wa...

POSTWAR EUROPEAN RECONSTRUCTION inspired World Student Service Fund and campus chests drives (pp. 613-622). NSA's summer travel programs (p. 639) were popular, and regional colleges sponsored foreign student visitors (p. 660). Jack Reich of U Colo chaired a DP (Displaced Persons) student sponsorship committee which brought 3 European students a year to the campus for study.

From top: *Denver Clarion* 5/9/47, *New Mexico Lobo* 12/2/47, *Silver and Gold* 8/752, *Rocky Mountain Collegian* 9/23/49

Regional Leaders

Jerry Goodman — *U. Colorado., 1946-47*

Jack Whorton — *NM Highlands U., 1947-48*

John Olson — *Colo. A&M, 1948-49*

Patrick Eagan — *Regis C., 1951-52*

See also **Roy Romer**, p. 1003. Photos: Goodman: 1947 Yearbook (*Coloradan*, Archives). Whorton: 1948-49 Yearbook (*Southwest Wind*, Archives). Olson. 1948 Yearbook (Archives). Eagan: 1951 Yearbook (*The Ranger*, Archives).

Denver Drops Out

AFTER 6 MONTHS of membership in 1951, Denver withdrew. It continued to attend regional events. The *Silver and Gold* comments, providing one more anecdote on the engaging powers of NSA's 1950-51 president, Al Lowenstein (see pp. 908, 991).

Denver University Drops From NSA After Unanimous Student Senate Vote

The University of Denver student senate voted unanimously Tuesday night to sever all relations with the National Student association. They felt that NSA had little to offer the student body.

Last spring the Denver university voted to join NSA on a temporary basis until December of this year so that first-hand information on the inner workings of NSA could be gathered.

Students Attended Meeting

Five Denver students were sent to the fourth annual NSA convention at the University of Minnesota during August. Following the report of this delegation, the senate decided to cut off membership in NSA.

The delegation pointed out that Denver students already had 14 of the 17 points listed in the NSA Bill of Rights.

Statement Expected

Bill Dentzer, president of NSA, was expected to issue a statement regarding this withdrawal when he returns to Boulder tomorrow.

Dentzer, who is planning a tour of the Rocky Mountain NSA schools in two weeks, will probably go to Denver before that time for a conference with the Denver university ...

The Price Of A Free Ride

The delegates from Denver university to the National Student congress in Minneapolis during August said they were going to quit NSA, and last week the student senate voted unanimously to drop out.

Under the pursuasive and enlightened tutelage of Al Lowenstein, last year's NSA president, the Denver student body, through the senate, voted to join NSA on a temporary basis until first-hand information could be gathered to "further inform members as to the inner workings of the organization."

Lowenstein is a baggy-kneed, friendly guy, whose ingenuousness is matched only by his ability to make his listeners understand in simple terms what a less adroit speaker would have to frame in nine syllable jaw-breakers.

Warren Tasset, one of the DU representatives to the August convention, tells of how Lowenstein arrived in Denver via airline with only a laundry box for luggage. The greeting delegation recognized him only because no one else getting off the plane could match, within a dozen years, the age of the man they were waiting for.

Understandably the DU student senate could have been so impressed with his sincerity and easy manner that they gave NSA a try. They should not, however, have forgot so quickly the principles and goals of NSA which Lowenstein undoubt...

From top: 11/6/51, 11/7/51

Historical note: DU was founded by Territorial Governor John Evans in 1864 as co-ed Colorado Seminary with close ties to the Methodist Church. Name was changed to the University of Denver in 1880 (Curator of Archives). *1948 enrollment: 11,299.*

Student Discounts

Local Stores Join NSA Discount Plan

NSA, Chamber Plan Meeting To Revamp Discount System

NSA officials and the chamber of commerce are working out difficulties today which arose in the application of the Student Discount service in Boulder, Campus NSA Chief George Christiansen said today.

At a meeting yesterday morning the merchants committee of the chamber of commerce ...

1,000 Students Hold Discount Cards; Four Merchants Give Lower Rates

About five hundred students signed up for the Student Discount service at registration Monday and Tuesday. Total sales of SDS cards to date are just under 1,000.

SDS, sponsored by the National Student association, is a plan to ...

... cities where the service is in effect are: Berkeley, Calif.; Bridgeport, Conn.; Washington, D.C.; Miami, Fla.; Atlanta, Ga.; Chicago, Ill.; Detroit, Mich.; Minneapolis, Minn.; Buffalo, N. Y.; Athens, Ohio, and Bethlehem, Pa.

NSA'S STUDENT DISCOUNT SYSTEM was successfully mounted in the Denver area after its reorganization to provide for more local flexibility and control (p. 366). Local merchants at first objected (as sometime happened in other regions), but differences were resolved. The cards were honored nationally by participating stores.

From top: *Silver and Gold* 12/6/50, 1/5/51, 2/8/52

Roots: Douglass Cater Visits

ROCKY MOUNTAIN REGION of the NATIONAL STUDENT ASSOCIATION

REGIONAL ASSEMBLY

April 30 - May 1

University of Colorado
Boulder, Colorado

Douglass Cater: Guest Speaker

The Rocky Mountain Region of National Student Association is fortunate to have, as guest speaker, one of the founders of NSA, Mr. Douglass Cater. Mr. Cater will deliver his address at the opening banquet of the Spring Assembly.

Mr. Cater, who is the Washington Editor of **Reporter Magazine**, received his A.B. and M. A. at Harvard. While in school, Cater was the delegate to the International Students Congress in the summer of 1946. In 1947 he was on the committee which founded the Salzburg-Harvard Seminar in American Studies.

Born in Montgomery, Alabama, Mr. Cater served with O.S.S. during World War II, has traveled extensively, and is one of the outstanding figures on the Washington scene.

1954 Assembly Announcement (Stephen Schodde)

REACHING BACK TO EARLIER NSA LEADERSHIP, the spring 1954 regional assembly featured 1951-52 past-NSA President Bill Dentzer (p. 299) and Douglass Cater, then Washington Editor of the *Reporter Magazine* (see Cater, p. 92, p. 535). Cater was on the U.S. delegation to the World Student Congress in 1946 and a leader on the Harvard delegation at the Chicago Student Conference (p. 113).

Colorado A&M/Regis College

A Means to an End: World Peace

Rocky Mountain COLLEGIAN

1949

Aggies Well Represented at National Students' Association Convention at University of Illinois

The United States National Students Association held its annual convention August 23 to September 3 at the University of Illinois with the participation of 750 delegates representing 275 schools and a million students throughout the United States.

Four delegates from Colorado A & M, who had been chosen last spring ... convention representing Aggies. Roy Romer, student body president; ... vice president of NSA; Claude Salomon, local NSA chairman; and Raleigh ...

CAMPUS LEADERS HEADED NSA DELEGATIONS to national and regional events, lending strong support to NSA's international programs.

World Peace Is Goal Of N S A International Affairs Program

By Claude Salomon

"The entire International Affairs program of the National Student Association is just a means to an end. The means is anything we can figure out, and the end is World Peace." This was the concensus of opinion of the delegates attending the Second National Student Congress at the University of Illinois, and more specifically of the people interested in International Affairs.

The exchange of students, or "Ambassadors of Good Will," to, and from the United States was recommended as the best approach to solve a great many of the differences existing in the world today ...

... sponsored by NSA gives European students who have been displaced from their homes a chance to come to the United States, get an education and then go back to their ...

Fourteen Delegates To Attend Regional N S A Convention To Be Held This Weekend

Fourteen delegates from Aggies will attend the regional N.S.A. convention to be held at the University of Colorado starting the evening and lasting until Sunday evening.

The main purpose of this convention of 15 Rocky Mountain ...

Top and middle: 9/23/49. Bottom: 10/21/49

Student Union Expansion, NSA, Displaced Persons Discussed By Student Council

The meeting was called to order by the president, Roy Romer. Roll was taken and the minutes of the previous meeting were read and approved.

... of the Lyceum was a big success, with a total of $128.20 ... only about $13, the fact that the showing did not run ...

OUR CONCERN

By ROY ROMER

DP STUDENTS. The student council advocated bringing two DP students to A&M under NSA-sponsored program (p. 612).

1950

From top: 1/20/50, 2/10/50. Right: 2/10/50

Aggies Present Skit At Greeley

NSA TALENT EXCHANGES. A&M performers (Claude Salomon on left) took part in the popular regional intercollegiate program.

Problems Discussed

Aggie N S A Delegates Will Attend Annual Spring Convention

4/21/50

Aggies Host Regional NSA Assembly, Students from 4 States to Attend

Fall Regional Assembly of the National Students association is set for November 21-23 on the Aggie campus. This will be the first fall assembly given on regional basis for two years. The theme for this year is to be "The American Student in the National and International Crisis."

NSA hosted fraternity, sorority and independent reps from 10 colleges. 11/7/52

1951-52

11/2/51

Editorial

NSA is under sharp fire from a number of students on the campus. They seem to feel that too much of the money is spent off-campus and the students are not deriving sufficient good from the money appropriated by student council. These students are correct in the belief that a large part of NSA money is spent off-campus, but this does not mean that it is wasted.

We don't wish to minimize the importance of NSA activities on the campus, but we do believe that these people are very short-sighted if they don't consider the national and international activities of NSA. Students are one of the most significant forces in the ideological battle now being waged between East and West. They will be the leaders of tomorrow, and now, while their thought patterns are being formed, is the ideal time to convince them of the superiority of our way of life.

The Communists realize that and have organized their students militantly. The Berlin Youth Festival last summer with its one million participants is ample evidence of that. The Collegian office receives regular publicity releases from a number of Communist student organizations, most of them being mailed directly here from behind the Iron Curtain.

It is time we in the United States took advantage of the tremendous intellectual force our students can exert on other students the world over. The best means now at our disposal is NSA's international program. We can't afford to junk it.

Regional Leaders

John Olson
Rocky Mt Regional Pres, 1948-49

Roy Romer
Rocky Mt Regional Pres, 1950-51

Claude Salomon
NSA International Team, 1950

JOHN OLSEN was an agronomy major who went on to become an Arizona rancher and founder of four Olsen's Feed Stores. **ROY ROMER** became Governor of Colorado (See p. 1003). **CLAUDE SALOMON** represented NSA to France in the summer of 1950 (p. 609). At the age of 4 he had escaped with his family to Mexico from Nazi Germany. A 1951 graduate in economics, he went on to a 41-year international career with Procter & Gamble, culminating as president and general director of P&G's Mexican operations.

Photos: *Silver Spruce* yearbook

Colorado A&M

Understanding Student Government

The REGIS BROWN & GOLD

Dedicated To A Greater "Regis of the Rockies"

Vol. XXXV, No. 8 REGIS COLLEGE — DENVER, COLORADO APRIL 25, 1951

Pat Eagan Elected Regional Chairman at NSA Convention

The Rocky Mountain Region of the National Student Association elected Patrick Eagan, Regis junior, to the position of regional chairman at its convention in Las Vegas, New Mexico, April 14-15.

Mr. Eagan was delegated to represent Regis by the Student Council as a result of the critical view of NSA taken by Mr. Eagen in an article which appeared in the last issue of the **Regis Brown and Gold.** The Student Council was impressed by the objective approach to NSA manifested by Mr. Eagen in his article and decided that his presence in the delegation would assure them of an accurate report.

Patrick Eagan

At the convention Eagan quickly won the respect of the other delegates by his constructive suggestions and thorough understanding of student government problems. His competence and interest were so clearly shown that he was elected to the chairmanship by a unanimous vote.

Eagan Active on Campus

A native of Grand Junction, Colorado, Eagan is majoring in history at Regis and has been active in such organizations as Aquinas Academy and the Variety Club.

"Preserving Individual and Academic Freedom" was the theme of the convention. The delegates were privileged to hear an address on the far-reaching implications of their theme by the National President of NSA, Mr. Al Lowenstein. Mr. Lowenstein pointed out how communist propaganda is always focused on students. He described the efforts which NSA is making to counteract the effects of such propaganda. A special concern was expressed over the situation in South-east Asia where the native population has long been exploited by British and Dutch imperialism. Mr. Lowenstein pointed out that free education is the most cherished hope of these peoples. The communists tell them that Americans wish only to perpetuate the evils of imperialism. The speaker held that the most effective way to discredit the communists is for American students to speak to the student populations of such countries through the agencies of NSA. "If the students of South-east Asia could be given a true picture of American education," he said, "Communism would be a lost cause in those areas."

Regis Government Active

Regis was also represented at the convention by John Spradley, acting campus chairman of the Regis NSA; the Reverend William B. Faherty, S.J., Faculty Moderator; and two alternate delegates, Dan Hartnett and Rudy Brada. After attending a commission which took up the problems of student governments in the region, Father Faherty observed that the Regis student government seems to have more extensive powers than others in this area.

1951

Editorial staff, *Brown and Gold. The Ranger,* 1951 Regis Yearbook.

A CHAMPION FOR NSA AT REGIS, Patrick Eagan was also on staff and a columnist on *The Regis Brown and Gold.* In the photo above, he is third from left in the rear shown working with editorial staff. The 1951 Regis Yearbook, *The Ranger,* wrote about the paper that "A definite achievement coming from this year's efforts was the interest created in the national Student Association as a result of Pat Eagan's series of editorials on the decline of the organization at Regis.""

Regis College

Historical note: A&M was a Land Grant college which opened in 1879 as the Agricultural College of Colorado. Women students numbered 44 of the 179 in 1892. In 1935 it became the Colorado State College of Agriculture and Mechanic Arts and in 1957 Colorado State University (www.colostate.edu). 1948 enrollment: 3,783.

Historical note: Regis was started as Las Vegas College in 1877 in Las Vegas, NM, by a group of exiled Italian Jesuits. It moved to Morrison, CO in 1884 as College of the Sacred Heart; became Regis College in 1921. It became co-ed evenings in 1945, full time in 1968. When Loretto Heights College closed in 1988 it absorbed some of its programs. It became Regis U. in 1991(www.regis.edu). 1948 enrollment: 580.

A University of Colorado/Rocky Mountain Regional Chronicle

As reported in the *Silver and Gold*, 1947-1949

7/29/47 **MUST THE CHILDREN DIE.** Editorial. Two Negro boys in Mississippi await execution (Quoted from the *Daily Worker*)

10/24/47 **STUDENTS PLAN NATIONAL ASSOCIATION.** Report on NSA Constitutional Convention in Madison, Wisconsin. Pix of Len Perlmutter and Bill Malkovich

12/2/47 **DELEGATES DECRY BIG SIX JIM CROW RULE.** ASUC President Lou Rovira meeting in Lincoln, Nebr previous Saturday, "I am adamant in my opposition to racial segregation . . . (rather than participate) I would much prefer a complete withdrawal."

1/20/48 **ASUC (PICKS) NSA HEADS** Len Perlmutter, Committee Chair. Frank Garland, Ed McNulty, Peter Bessol, Sherman Finesliver, Bobbie Folley.

1/23/48 **JIM CROW RESTRICTIONS STAY IN EFFECT AFTER BIG 7 MEETING.** (Formerly the Big 6). Vote by coaches 5-2 (Colorado and Nebraska against).

1/23/48 **COMMISSION ORDERS LOCAL NSA COMMITTEE PROBE.** "Leftist Jibes Hurled. Seek Full Report on Group Actions." 8 column headline. Dick Mullhern, "The CU delegation voted questionably at the NSA Assembly in Madison." "Tinted CU personalities were regional leaders." 3 voted yes to allow national organizations to join NSA, and for NSA to affiliate with the IUS. Perlmutter, Commissioner of Education and Culture on the ASUC, "denied the charges."

1/23/48 **ROVIRA, MCFARLANE DISCUSS CHEATING VS. HONOR SYSTEM.** Rovira urges its establishment.

1/27/48 Full page devoted to Editorial (supporting the 1/23 front page article) and three letters criticizing the coverage as out of proportion to what actually transpired at the meeting.

1/30/48 **ASUC VINDICATES NSA GROUP: GIVES VOTE OF CONFIDENCE.** Audience of nearly 100 interested [Des Marais] students attend meeting. Mulhern stated that he received his information on the NSA convention in a letter from Phil Demaret (sic) [Des Marais], Chairman of the Minnesota Region of the NSA, who characterized his views in writing, "I might be very prejudiced, but I feel that CU students should know what others think." "Mulhern then read excerpts from a letter he received from Bill Murray, a Colorado College delegate to NSA," favorable to the UC delegation and their actions.

Rovira had checked with Denver Unliversity—Mulhern had earlier stated that DU withdrew from NSA—and determined that in fact they had not yet voted on NSA. Rovira denounced "the libel and smear campaign." Mulhern was unable to withdraw his motion for an investigation and it was unanimously defeated.

Finesilver was quoted as saying that NSA was not representative of the student body.

EDITORIAL: NSA MOVES AHEAD.

2/3/48 **PERLMUTTER ANSWERS TO CHARGES AGAINST NSA GROUP.**

EDITORIAL: Apology for the paper's original coverage.

2/17/48 **NSA MEETING DRAWS 11 COLLEGES** (Last Saturday). Loretto Heights, Regis, Denver U., Colorado A&M, Iliff School of Theology, Colo. Woman's College of Education, Weber College (Ogden, Utah), Univ. of Colo. 26 Reps. Meeting was led by Perlmutter.

2/20/48 **NSA OUTLINES INTER-CAMPUS WORK, COOPERATION PLANS.** Article about World Student Service Fund (WSSF) and summer travel and study programs.

2/24/48 **BROTHERHOOD WEEK OPENS ON CAMPUS.**

Lou Rovira sets aside week for campus activities.

EDITORIAL: Supports Brotherhood Week and NSA sponsorship.

3/9/48 **NSA SPLITS FROM IUS OVER CZECHS.** Response to street violence and closing down student organizations.

EDITORIAL: NSA MEETS THE TEST. NSA proves independence.

4/30/48 **GREEKS, INDEPENDENTS EACH WIN 6 ASUC SEATS.** Joe Reynolds, President.

Len Perlmutter wins 13th Chair, "Successful 3d Party Bid for Second Straight Year."

5/11/48 [ASUC Favors Seat on Regents]

5/21/48 **REGIONAL ASSEMBLY PLANS DISCUSSION AT NSA MEET.**

11/12/48 **ASUC HEARS NSA DELEGATES.** Reports on Regional Conference at Ft. Collins the prior weekend. Pete Bessoll leads UC delegation of 10.

3/9/49 **NSA VARIETY SHOW APRIL 10 FEATURES SKITS FROM 10 NEIGHBORING SCHOOLS.**

Mildred Pottebaum, Program Chairman. Univ of Colo, Colo State College of Ed, Colo College, Colo College for Women, Regis, Pueblo Jr. College, Trinidad State Jr. College, Weber Jr. College (Utah), Idaho State College.

NSA News 4/49

Rocky M'tn Region Plans Convention

MEMBERS OF THE ROCKY MOUNTAIN Region executive committee meet at the student union on the Colorado State (Greeley) campus to plan the Spring Convention at Colorado College, Colorado Springs. They are (l. to r.) Bill Murray, public relations officer, Colorado College; Barbara Folley, secretary, Colorado University; John Olsen, president, Colorado A&M; Jamie McClendon, domestic affairs chairman, Colorado State (Greeley) and Pete Bessols, foreign affairs chairman, Colorado University. –Photo by C. W. Holmes, CSCE Mirror

3/31/49 **TICKETS FOR NSA VARIETY SHOW HERE SATURDAY NIGHT ARE AVAILABLE.** Date changed to April 2.

4/5/49 **LETTER TO EDITOR.** Decries Negro comic interpretation by UC group singing spirituals at the Variety Show. (A later letter from someone who attended disputed the charge.)

"We must lift our eyes beyond the narrow confines of our own campus"

4. The Chicano Student Movement and NSA at New Mexico Highlands

Donald A. Martinez

New Mexico Highlands University. Editor, The Highlands Candle, *1947-48*
Delegate, 1946 Chicago Student Conference, 1947 NSA Constitutional Convention

Author's note: This memoir is an annotated digest of an interview I had with the Anthology editor on February 15, 2003, in Santa Fe, New Mexico.

When New Mexico veterans returned to college after World War II, many under the GI Bill, we set about organizing Chicano students to redress the many wrongs we saw about us.

In order to understand this student activism at Highlands after World War II, and how I became involved in student government and in NSA, it is necessary to set it in the context of New Mexico history, and its takeover by the Americans—as despicable an act of aggression as has been committed anywhere. Known in this country as the U.S.-Mexican War, it was really an invasion of Mexico in 1846. It was concluded by the Treaty of Guadalupe Hidalgo on May 10, 1848.[1]

The Chicano student movement, which began at Highlands, is a product of this history, which set the pattern of discrimination and appropriation of lands that followed.

Historic land grants plant seeds of conflict

The story begins with most of the New Mexico settlers who were already here on land grants. Las Vegas, where New Mexico Highlands University is located, was a land grant. North of it was the Mora land grant. South of it was the Tecolote land grant. The whole territory was parceled out in this manner before the Americans came. The older grants were from the Spanish days. The Las Vegas grant was one of the last ones. The others were from the Mexican regime. They were of doubtful authenticity, however, because Mexico after independence from three centuries of Spanish rule in 1823 had never gotten itself completely together.

When the Americans took over, they generally adopted the prior existing laws, whether or not there had been the authority or structure to give land grants. When the U.S. Congress sent William Pelham out in 1854 as Surveyor General to pass on the titles, he did an excellent job of looking into them, considering he was one man by himself and he had this whole territory, which then included Utah, Colorado, Arizona, and parts of Nevada.

After several years, he made a report to Congress and he recommended as many land grants as he could look into for their approval, which they did. However, it gave rise to a very peculiar sort of title situation. Many of the land promoters who came in those early territorial days fabricated or claimed deeds with wording that should not have been there. So, to make a long story short, the Las Vegas grant was not approved by Congress, because it was in conflict with a subsequent Mexican grant. What Congress did was approve the subsequent grant, and grant the original grantees an equal number of acres all over the state.

Las Vegas was the place where the American invasion first took place. Thirty-two years later, the Santa Fe Railroad came through in the 1880's. Las Vegas was the center of the main line. It was bigger than Albuquerque or Santa Fe. There was always jostling and hustling for land within the community. The smart lawyers went to court and got the district courts under its "equity" powers to appoint a Board of Trustees for the land grants. They appointed four Anglos and three Hispanics, so the Anglos took over the grant from there on. One of the things that the Anglos did was to start a new municipality east of the old pueblo. They called it City of Las Vegas.

In the meantime, the town (the old Pueblo) was growing up toward the new railroad facilities. But when they incorporated the city, they incorporated it separate and apart from the town. So, we had a schism here. We had the City of Las Vegas, an incorporated municipality in the late 1800's. And we had the Town of Las Vegas, which continued the old pueblo, and never incorporated until 1924. Throughout this period of time, people would settle here and file their claims and there was a tremendous amount of conflict.

World War I and World War II veterans come home to discrimination

Many of the local residents had already been with Teddy Roosevelt's troops in Cuba in 1898 during the Spanish American War. They came back and they were all proud and they were recognized and they had parades carrying them all around the town. So, when World War I broke out, there was a tremendous reaction of patriotic fervor. All of the local people went in, and they served, and they came back, and they found they were still being discriminated against by the establishment in New Mexico.

Just before World War II came along, they had taken our National Guard units in Las Vegas to the Philippines. After Pearl Harbor in 1941, many of the boys were killed in the death march on Battan. Our district judge's older son was captured in the death march, and for years they didn't know what had happened to him, because the Japanese had him in the death camp.

So, in our community there was a lot of sentiment for the war, not because of patriotism, but because of what had happened to the boys that had been taken to Japan, and for the rest of the national guard in New Mexico that were going to Europe. Then it came down to the same experience the boys in World War I had. Gung ho loyal Americans returned after the war and encountered the same terrible discrimination and prejudice that followed World War I. It mostly had to do with stealing your property. If you had a piece of property and an Anglo took you to court, your lawyer would say, "Don't bother. You don't want to defend yourself. Because you're not going to win."

In my own experience, I volunteered the day after Pearl Harbor. Enlistments were frozen, and they swore us in on January 2nd. Initially I was with the Southeast Training Command of the United States Air Force before it became the Air Corps. For some reason they thought I was mechanically inclined, and they sent me to more mechanic schools than you could shake a stick at. I went to school from one end of the country to the other.

Later I did service in Guam. I was in a B-20 unit. They brought us back from Guam to the Philippines in a flat-bottomed LST (Landing Ship Tank). There were about 600 of us aboard.

When I returned in 1945 and entered Highlands, you would be hard put to find a single Hispanic name mentioned as a student leader, athlete, or homecoming queen in *The Highlands Candle*—nothing. The same if you go through the *New Mexico Lobo,* the University of New Mexico college newspaper.

Chicanos had learned to be quiet and behave themselves. But when the veterans came back from World War II, we cured that. The University of New Mexico was a lot more of a monolithic institution, and it took a lot more to get students to go there. So, most of the Hispanic students preferred to go to Highlands. That's why we had such a strong student group at Highlands. You had to go through all sorts of high jinks to get into UNM, and when you did get in you had to be quiet and well behaved, and not stir up the waters. So, we started going over there from Highlands and meeting with those students, trying to get them to stand up and speak for themselves.

The Chicano identity

The situation at Highlands was such at that time that in the whole university there was only one Spanish-speaking professor. We thought that wasn't right and we organized ourselves into a Chicano movement to deal with it.

Once we started our activity in Las Vegas, others were encouraged throughout the state. At UNM they were very slow and very timid, but they eventually got going and they accomplished a good deal. On the other hand, we never could get a foothold in the Eastern Military University. A lot of our people went to school in "Little Texas" down south at the school of agriculture [New Mexico College of Agriculture and Mechanic Arts] in Las Cruces to take engineering and agriculture and they were pretty much quiet there as well.[2]

People wonder how we came to identify ourselves as Chicanos instead of, say, Spanish-Americans, Hispanics or Latinos. We have always been Chicanos. We go back long before that term became popular. In New Mexico we had a stereotype that comes from old lower Mexico of being big with big hats and big walrus moustaches—the big garrulous figures, aggressive and warlike—called Chicanotes, which means "big" Chicanos. And so we distinguished ourselves from that as Chicanos—chicanitos, the diminutive. Chico is the prefix for small.

Gaining control of student government

At Highlands, there was one member in the student senate, as they called it, from each class, and one from each Greek organization. There were quite a number of Greek organizations among the Anglos, so we organized a Greek organization in order to get enough people on the student Senate to make a difference. It was called Alpha Zeta Iota—AZI. And we formed a girl's fraternity also. It was Phi Lambda Kappa.

We were also politically active all over the state. We would go into those areas where there was a lot of discrimination, and campaign against one side or the other in the primaries—in those days they were all Democrats. Students from Highlands in those areas would advise us that something was going on and we would go down there. We walked the picket lines in Silver City for the unions, and we'd go down and take food and clothing and blankets.

Maurilio E. Vigil, a political science professor at NMHU, writes in his history of the university:[3]

> Following World War II, many Hispanics had returned—matured in age and sobered by the realities of war—as students to Highlands. These students were no longer intimidated, as they had been before the war, by the "white establishment" and were not willing to abide the type of discrimination and prejudice they had experienced in the past. Most felt they had "paid their dues" in the war effort. They were now prepared to take on the establishment."[4]

Some other student leaders

One name that always comes to mind is a guy by the name of Gilbert B. Sanchez.[5] He was the most intellectual, the most well read, the most philosophical among us. He's the one who turned me on to that great work of literature, in many ways a parable of our times, *Cien Años de Soledad—One Hundred Years of Solitude*—by Gabriel Garcia Marquez, and many other things. He was kind of an artist, and very much taken with Diego Rivera.

Some other student leaders I recall include Frankie Varella, who was student body president, and his brother, Richard. There was a good athlete by the name of Betran Sedillo. Also, Max Valdez, Arthur Gonzales and Max Sanchez, who became state Treasurer. They all belonged to AZI. Others in later years also held public office.[6]

The National Student Association

My recollection of the National Student Association is that there were people in that organization who were speaking out against discrimination—speaking out against continuation of segregation. We were looking for ways to express our opposition to practices such as segregation in the South, anti-union activities and pro-militaristic programs. All of these things were in the picture as well as the whole swing towards liberalism.

NSA offered one way for us to express our feelings about such broad issues in a national forum. That was why I became involved and went to the Chicago Student Conference in December of 1946 with Trammel B. Ford. Despite the fact that we felt we weren't as well prepared as we could have been by the conference leaders, and there were only one school each represented from what was then the New Mexico and Colorado Region,[7] we recommended, as reported in the 1/17/97 issue of *The Highlands Candle,* that "It will be up to HIGHLANDS to propagate the NSA here in New Mexico and to the Colorado school to start things moving in Colorado . . . we should decide to participate fully in all activities of the NSO."[8]

That spring, Jack Whorton and I, both of us juniors and on the *Candle* staff, were selected to represent NMHU at the Constitutional Convention of NSA in August of 1947. On our return, I became editor of T*he Candle* and wrote recommending affiliation in an editorial on 12/5/47:

> While this organization is still in its infancy it has, nevertheless produced a program of activities which show a maturity and a deep concern with the vital problems of Western Civilization that few people have been inclined to credit to the American student. With its feet planted firmly on the solid ground the association has set out, not to redeem the world, but to do all within the practical limits of its sphere of activities toward bettering the conditions of the American student and improving the overall picture of world relations.

Jack Whorton, a fine arts major at the time, was elected NSA Rocky Mountain Regional Chairman at the convention.[9] He was a brilliant Highlands student who stands out as a leader. Jack had a good perception of what issues affected us and what was important. He was a driving force.

He went on to law school, practiced law in Alamogordo, stayed there for years and finally got fed up. They were extremely conservative down there, and he dropped out from practicing law and went to Louisiana. That's the last I heard of him.

NSA and the Fight against Injustice

We had a burning resentment against injustice from the beginning. That's why we were at the National Student Association convention. That's why we were down there in Mississippi. That's why we went to Kent State. That's why we went to California to help the National Farm Workers Union when they were doing their bit. That's why we went to Silver City and walked with the pickets down there.

It's not an engagement that you can pick and choose. If you're going to fight injustice, you've got to fight it at all levels. For instance, because of my experience in journalism and printing, I would help some of the other students with their papers. Once I wrote, in essence, the same papers for two students—one Anglo and the other a Chicano. The Anglo got an A and the Chicano got an F. So we raised hell with them.

Another teacher—who was the drama teacher—wouldn't let any of the Chicanos take parts in the school presentations and plays unless they were the maids or the servants or the sweepers. There were several professors we really had to do battle with and made it so hard for them that they had to leave. We raised hell with the Governors about the people that they were appointing to the Board of Regents. It probably wasn't until the late sixties that we finally got a group of Chicanos on the Board with sufficient gumption and the strength to hire the first Hispanic president of the university. That was Dr. Francisco Angel in August 1971. He was followed by John Aragon. And subsequent to that we had one by the name of Sanchez. Today we have a lady, Sharon Caballero, who is an Anglo but married to a man with a Spanish name.[10]

There were local issues involving discrimination in the community against Negro students. In a 1/14/49 editorial then *Candle* editor Stanley Sachs wrote regarding a local incident, "Last week, at La Cantina, there occurred another of the all too frequent demonstrations that freedom is a restricted commodity . . . the saddest part of the of the whole affair is that has been reported that the protest about the presence of a Negro was entered by another student. . . ."

Editorials also appeared in *The Highlands Candle* about the treatment and the lack of attention being paid to the welfare of Native Americans, although there weren't many of them in school at Highlands. The nearest ones were in Santa Fe, mostly from the Navajo reservation. On 12/5/47 in an editorial on the occasion of the Brotherhood Caravan, I wrote:

> The plight of the Navajo Indian has finally been brought forcibly to the attention of New Mexico's citizens. Even in Las Vegas, the usually smug, inert residents have opened their eyes and decided to take action. . . . Meanwhile, we should not forget that the American Indian is the responsibility of the entire nation. . . .

We tried to encourage them to come to Highlands. We can't get away from the fact that we are cousins. There was such a mixture between the Spanish people and the natives.

Here is an example of the type of thing we encountered. After having been District Attorney, I got to be District Judge in Las Vegas. During those 22 years, Las Vegas was the location of the state insane asylum (they don't call it that now, but that's what it was). After the United States Supreme Court laid down some rules and regulations about treating those with mental illness with respect, I'd go in there because it was in Las Vegas and find that the doctors couldn't talk to the Indians. They didn't speak their language, and they'd come in there and give this horrible diagnosis of what they thought the problem was with them. So, we made the hospital start bringing in an interpreter.

As I look back, the spirit of my engagement in these issues at the time is summed up in the closing words of my 12/15/47 editorial on the National Student Association:

"If we are to have any say so in the era of our own generation then we must lift our eyes beyond the narrow horizons of our own campus and participate today!"

Donald A. Martinez practices law in Las Vegas, NM. He was a San Miguel County District Attorney and District Judge.

DONALD A. MARTINEZ

I was born in 1923 in Boulder, Colorado, and although I was raised in Santa Fe, Albuquerque and then Las Vegas, my family goes far back in Las Vegas history. My grandfather was governor of New Mexico in 1917. He was a man who was elected to office and died in less than 60 days, of pernicious anemia. My mother baptized the battleship *New Mexico.* My Dad was from Colorado. He was in printing and publishing newspapers. He became the editor of the Spanish edition of the Santa Fe *New Mexican.* My grandfather was also the publisher of a newspaper, *La Voz del Pueblo.* So I spent a lot of time in my very young days in the print shops. I used to be able to run a linotype machine. This was good preparation for service on the staff and then as editor of *The Highlands Candle.*

When I went to school, we had a lot of Jesuit training and a lot of that community commitment. In grade school, it was the brothers at St. Michael's in Santa Fe. Then I went to three high schools. The first one was Lourdes in Albuquerque. It was a special boarding school that had been established by Archbishop Gerken of Texas. He was a Southerner, also the Archbishop of Santa Fe—a German and a liberal. And if you get a Southerner who is a liberal, you've got a real liberal. He established the boarding school as a vocational school, an academic school, and a pre-seminary. Because it was a pre-seminary, we got a lot of that religious training. We had to go through that daily. Part of that training was what goes on in the Bible, and as in any religion a dedication to the public good.

The other school that I went to was a nun's school in Las Vegas, where I spent my junior year. In my senior year, I went to the Highlands Training School, the high school that was operated by Highlands University, and I finished within the first three months. Highlands was then called the Normal School. The whole place, from high school to kindergarten, was there to train teachers in the school system of New Mexico. I finished high school in December 1941 at the time the war started.

When I got back, I started Highlands. I don't know what would have happened without the GI Bill. I got my college degree because of it, but I worked my way through law school at Georgetown University in Washington, DC. I had a job with a Senator from New Mexico, who had been a friend of my grandfather in earlier days, Senator Dennis Chavez. He was our role model and inspired me to go to law school. Of course we didn't have a law school in New Mexico. I believe the law school in New Mexico was started in 1963.

Everything I have written about in this memoir are the reasons I went to law school. All the fights about the land. Everybody being cheated out of the land. Everybody getting the short end of the deal in the Anglo—in the "Gringo" courts, if I can put it that way. There were not enough Hispanic attorneys or Chicano attorneys. After graduation, I returned to Las Vegas, practiced law, entered pubic life and politics, and was elected District Attorney and then District Judge, at which I served for 22 years. I continue to practice law, handling land grant cases.

I had two sisters and one brother. One sister is still living. I have seven children: one daughter who is an electronics engineer in Tucson; another daughter that's a teacher; another son that's a lawyer; another son that's a mechanic; another son that works in one of those laboratories in Albuquerque; another son that's with the U.S. forest service; and another son who is still trying to put it together.

The mother of my first six children died of cancer. Her name was Eloise Scott. I met her at Highlands, and she went to DC with me. My wife today is Loretta Cockrell.

PICTURE CREDITS: *Then*: *Southwind*, 1948 NMHU Yearbook. *Now*. Santa Fe, NM 2/03 (Schwartz).

EDITOR'S NOTES

[1] The following overview of New Mexico and of Highlands history draw upon three works: Ruben Salaz Marquez, *New Mexico: A Brief Multi-History*, Cosmic House, Albuquerque, NM, 1999; Maurilio E. Vigil, *Defining Our Destiny: The History of New Mexico Highlands University*, New Mexico Highlands University, Las Vegas, NM, 1993; Howard Bryan, *Wildest of the Wild West: True Tales of a Frontier Town on the Santa Fe Trail*. The history of discrimination against people of Mexican origin influenced the development of the State from its inception as a territory in 1850 after the Treaty of Guadalupe Hidalgo was signed on May 10, 1848, following the Mexican War, which New Mexicans saw as an unprovoked invasion. Based on historically debated origins of the conflict, under President James K. Polk the U.S. Congress declared war on Mexico on May 13, 1846.

In August, Brig. Gen. Stephen Kearny invaded New Mexico without resistance from New Mexican militia or dragoons. He arrived in Las Vegas on August 15, and on August 22 in Santa Fe declared all of New Mexico to be a part of the United States and "All persons are hereby considered citizens of the United States." Among the consequences of the Treaty was "[evasion] of a clear cut statement of a standard that will be used to adjudicate land grants in the newly acquired territories." This ambiguity led to a series of legislative acts and court rulings that erased protections of private property guaranteed by the treaty so that "Within a generation the Mexican Americans who had been under the ostensible protection of the treaty became a disenfranchised, poverty-stricken minority."

The problem was further exacerbated by the two earlier 1825 and 1835 Town of Las Vegas conflicting Land Grants to which Donald Martinez refers. New Mexico wasn't granted Statehood until January 1912. Marquez quotes R.W. Larson in *New Mexico's Quest for Statehood, 1846-1912,* UNM Press, 1968, ". . . the Catholic religion provoked the prejudice and dislike of a predominantly Protestant nation." It can be observed that an instinctive distrust of New Mexico's essentially Hispanic and Indian people and culture was "the last and most durable brick added to the strong wall of opposition that prevented the territory from becoming a part of the Union until 1912" Maurilio E. Vigil also writes (p.15), "The most important reason for denying Statehood to New Mexicans was the widely held assumption that New Mexicans were 'foreigners' who spoke Spanish and were reluctant to adopt the English language." Overcoming this prejudice was the chief objective of the comprehensive public school system for the territory called for in 1891 by the New Mexico Legislative Assembly.

"Territorial law mandated that any teacher in a public school must not only be able to teach in English, but also be familiar in the Spanish language if employed in a predominantly Spanish-speaking region." In 1893, the legislature approved establishing two "normal schools" in Silver City and Las Vegas. The latter institution was the New Mexico Normal School at Las Vegas, now New Mexico Highlands University.

[2] The following institutions of higher education in New Mexico are listed by Ostheimer (cited, p. 497) for 1948-49:

University of New Mexico, Albuquerque
Eastern New Mexico College, Portales (Public co-ed, Liberal Arts)
New Mexico State Teachers College, Silver City (Public, co-ed)
New Mexico Highlands University, Las Vegas (Public, co-ed)
New Mexico School of Mines, Socorro (Public technical, co-ed)
New Mexico College of Agriculture and Mechanic Arts, State College (Public technical, co-ed)
Montezuma Seminary, Montezuma (Catholic, men)
New Mexico Military Institute, Roswell (Public, men, junior college)

New Mexico population grew from 531,818 in 1940 to 681,787 in 1950. In 2000 it stood at 1,819,046 (Census Bureau). According to Vigil (cited above), p. 59, "Full-time enrollment at Highland reached an all-time high of 1,039 in 1951." In 2000, NMHU reports 3,085 undergraduate and graduate students.

[3] Maurilio E. Vigil (cited above), p. 61.

[4] Eloy Garcia in his 1997 thesis (cited in fn 6 below) writes, p. 2, "New Mexico Highlands University has had a turbulent and tumultuous past. Most of the major struggles at the university have revolved around the concept of control, or attempted control, of the university." On pp. 11-13:

"During the tenure of Edward Eyring (1938-1951), a group of Chicano students, most of whom were veterans of World War II, founded a Chicano-oriented fraternity called Alpha Zeta Iota (AZI). AZI was chartered at New Mexico Highlands University on January 29, 1946, with its primary purpose being the 'promotion of fellowship, while cultivating and striving for higher scholastic standards, and support of all school traditions and social activities.' Gilbert 'Gillie' Sánchez, a sophomore from Mora, was elected president; A.A. Martínez [No relation to Donald—ed.], a Junior from Española, was elected Vice-President; Anselmo Bernal from Chacón was named Secretary-Treasurer, Donaldo 'Tiny' Martínez, a freshman from Las Vegas, was named Student Council representative; and Beltrán Sedillo, a sophomore from Belén, was named the other charter member. . . . 'Tiny' remembers how segregated and racist Highlands University was during this era, as the division of East and West Las Vegas fostered continual racial animosity amongst servicemen returning from the war.

"AZI members recognized that the student political power structure was dominated by the numerous Greek fraternities which flourished on campus during this time. Student government was composed of a representative from each class and a member from each fraternity and sorority. Being that most members of the fraternities and the sororities were Anglos, with the majority coming from out of state, there were no Chicanos on the student senate. Consequently, they had no representation—no political voice.

"Before World War II, Highlands University had never had a large Chicano student enrollment, and therefore never been forced to face the question of perceived institutional racism. AZI's membership attempted to get the Highlands Administration to recognize their grievances and concerns. Returning Chicano servicemen were now enrolled in college, in their own home state and town, but they were soon forced to desist from speaking Spanish in the hallways or in classrooms. AZI also noticed a lack of representation in student government, and the members found themselves in constant struggle with professors over language and race issues. Chicano students wanted to know why there were not any Chicano professors or administrators working at the university. These issues were brought before Highlands administration and faculty, with little or no action taken to resolve these problems. Instead, students who raised these issues were dubbed militant and radical, and they were suspect of being communist sympathizers. As hindsight has shown, most of these issues had to do with racist attitudes directed toward the local populace of Chicanos by an all-Anglo university administration and faculty, who were transplanted in New Mexico due to their jobs at Highlands University."

[5] Donald Martinez writes further, "Sanchez would never tell us what the B. stood for. Years later as an attorney I was handling a property case and I ran across his grandmother and his grandfather's property and I saw her name was Isabel B. Sanchez. So I figured this must be her maiden name. I checked into it and it turned out to be Birenbaum. Birenbaum was a merchant that was up near Fort Union. And this man, Sanchez, from Mora married Birenbaum's daughter. So we were sitting in the bar in Las Vegas one time, and my friend Gilbert came in, and I waited till the moment was opportune, and I said, "Hey, Gilbert Birenbaum!" He was taken aback. He was just amazed.

[6] See Eloy J. Garcia, Jr., "The Chicano Student Movement at New Mexico Highlands: An Interpretive History," Master of Arts thesis in Southwest Studies, Graduate Division, College of Arts and Sciences, New Mexico Highlands University, May 17, 1997. Garcia writes (p. 21), "Many members of Alpha Zeta Iota later became leaders and supporters of the Chicano movement of the late 1960s continued into the 1990s . . . such as NMHU President John Aragon, NMHU Professor Dr. Willie Sanchez, NMHU Professor Dr. Anselmo Arellano and District Judge and Attorney Donaldo "Tiny" Martinez. . . ."

[7] The University of Colorado was represented by Jerry Goodman. There were also two observers registered from Colorado College.

[8] The new organization was referred to as the National Student Organization (NSO) prior to the Constitutional Convention.

[9] Convention attendance and post-Congress membership records for NSA in 1948 are sketchy, as there is no "official" record in the archives at the University of Wisconsin. The pre-convention program lists only Colorado College (Colorado Springs). A national office mailing list for 1947-48 in the Bill Welsh papers at the Berea College archives lists Colorado College, Arizona State College (Tempe) and Highlands University. No record has been found of the 1947-48 regional meeting. The 12/47 National Executive Committee minutes show Len Perlmutter of the University of Colorado (See p. 999) representing the Rocky Mountain Region, while Jack Whorton is seated for Arizona-New Mexico, Southern Colo. In August 1948, Colorado A&M, Regis College and Loretto Heights College joined the others. It is likely that all of these colleges formed the region during the 1947-48 year.

[10] See Eloy J. Garcia, Jr. (cited above), p. 43ff. Dr. Francisco Angel was the first Chicano to head the university, appointed in August of 1971. See also Maurilio E. Vigil (cited above), p. 85ff. Donald Martinez as District Attorney continued to work towards installation of a Chicano President. Following a highly contentious selection process in 1970, Vigil writes that Martinez, "a Highland alumnus of the 1940s and now an influential Democratic leader in San Miguel County, filed criminal misdemeanor charges in May, 1970 against three Highlands regents . . . [that they] unlawfully made a final decision 'at a secretly held meeting not open to the public.'" Warrants for their arrest, student protests and sit-ins followed. After a five-day hearing and more than 40 witnesses, the suit was dismissed in August 1970. The regents' nominee at the time withdrew, and an interim appointment eventually led to Angel's appointment.

THE 1946 NMHU CHICANO STUDENT MOVEMENT GREEK ORGANIZATIONS

Phi Delta Kappa

Eva Luna
Founding President
1946-47

Mary Espinoza
Student Senate Rep
1947-48

Emboldened by the returning veterans, Chicano women joined in the movement providing votes and collaboration in gaining a Chicano majority on the Student Senate. The sorority was organized 2/5/46 by **Eva Luna, Sophie Valdez** and **Tillie Sanchez.**

Alpha Zeta Iota

Gilbert Sanchez
Founding President
1946-47

"He was the most intellectual, the most well read, the most philosophical among us."

"We organized a Greek organization in order to gain enough people on the student Senate to make a difference," Donald Martinez recalls. The returning veterans "were not willing to abide the type of discrimination and prejudice they had experienced in the past," Professor Maurilio E. Vigil writes. The society was organized 10/20/46.

Other founding officers from the top:
A.A. Martinez
Vice President
Anselmo Bernal
Secretary-Treasurer
Donald A. Martinez
Student Senate representative

PICTURE CREDITS: *Southwest Wind*, NMHU Yearbooks, 1945-46, 46-47 and 47-48.

New Mexico Highlands University: "The Pen is Mightier . . ."

The Highlands Candle

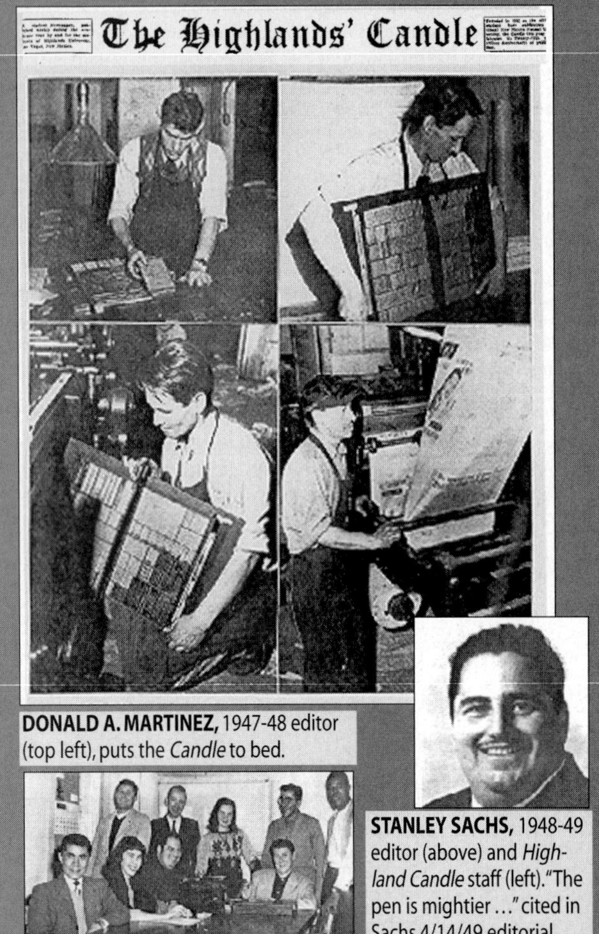

DONALD A. MARTINEZ, 1947-48 editor (top left), puts the *Candle* to bed.

STANLEY SACHS, 1948-49 editor (above) and *Highland Candle* staff (left). "The pen is mightier . . ." cited in Sachs 4/14/49 editorial. (Photos: *Southwest Wind*)

Joining NSA

T. FORD AND D. MARTINEZ ARE CHOSEN

Will Attend Chicago Student Conference; $250 Expense Allotted

Trammell B. Ford and Donald A. Martinez were chosen Wednesday night to represent Highlands University at the Chicago Students Conference, December 28 to 30, by the Student Council. Other busi-

Students Attend N.S.A. Meeting

Three Highlands University students returned to the campus yesterday after attending and taking part in the regional meeting of the National Student Association held during the past weekend at Ft. Collins, Colo.

The students and the divisions of the meeting which they attended were Nick Taylor, student affairs; Pat Wheelock, education; and John Aragon, international affairs. The three will offer a complete report on the groups' discussion during the next meeting of the Highlands student senate.

From top: 12/30/46, 11/17/50

"WE HAD A BURNING RESENTMENT AGAINST INJUSTICE . . . that's why we joined NSA," Donald Martinez writes (p. 1014). NMHU's student leaders saw membership as part of its commitment "to bettering the conditions of the Amerian student and improving . . . world relations."

Trammel Ford **Donald Martinez**

1946 Chicago Student Conference Representatives

D. MARTINEZ, J. WHORTON ATTEND NSO CONSTITUTIONAL CONVENTION

D. A. Martinez and Jack Whorton left Wednesday, August 28 for Madison, Wisconsin. At the last meeting of the summer Student senate, August 12, the two were chosen to be delegates from Highlands University to the constitutional

veteran, junior, member of the Student Senate, the Candle Staff and very active in the Young Democrat Club of New Meico, and active member of the Alpha Zeta Iota Fraternity. His home is in Las Vegas, New Mexico.

Jack Whorton — *NSA Constitutional Convention*

Frank C. Varella — *1947 Student Body President*

The Highlands' Candle

Senate Approves Affiliation With USNSA Wednesday By 7 to 1 Vote

National Students Association Prexy Issues Call For Greater Democracy In Student Government

Chicago, Ill.—(I. P.)—Debunking the idea that it is dangerous for students to have a direct means of

cy for a nation that prides itself on the capacity of its people to govern themselves."

Candle, from top: 9/5/47, 3/19/48, 9/24/48

The Southwest Wind

THE NMHU YEARBOOK, *The Southwest Wind,* from which all of the student leader photos in this unit were obtained, celebrated the region's culture in its art, and in its student organizations and student government with tasteful good humor.

"Defining Our Destiny"

(Museum of New Mexico)

Las Vegas, NM Plaza in the 1880's (F.E. Evans)

NMHU Donnelley Library, 1999 (Schwartz)

NMHU Catlog 1997

New Mexico Normal School, 1900 (www.nmhu.edu)

THE CONQUEST AND ACQUISITION OF NEW MEXICO IN 1848 created a new cohort of American citizens out of a native Spanish-speaking populaton that had settled the land for three centuries. The politcs of the statehood achieved in 1912 required schools that would train teachers for this new territory. New Mexico Normal School in Las Vegas (later Normal University in 1899 and Highlands University in 1941) was one of two created by the Territorial Legislature and opened in 1893 for this purpose. As Murilio E. Vigil wrote in "Defining Our Destiny" (see fn 1, p. 1016), overcoming prejudice against granting Statehood to a Spanish-speaking population was a primary goal (Editor's note).

University of New Mexico: "Now That The War Is Over . . ."

Editor's note: During NSA's first six years, the University of New Mexico attended and hosted occasional regional and national events, but it was not until 1958 that it is listd as a member. As with many of the colleges that did not affiliate with NSA, the student newspaper's headlines and columns of the era reflect nonetheless the strong interest of student leaders and organizations in the events and issues with which NSA was concerned. Only 120 miles south of New Mexico Highlands, the Chicano revolution of which Donald Martinez writes (p. 1013) didn't ignite the UNM campus in the same way. Hispanic names appear sparingly in the Lobo *of that period. Yet, as seen on this page, the campus was challenged by the passion for peace, civil rights and inclusion that emerged everywhere after the war.*

1945

Now that the War Is Over . . .

Tuesday, August 14th was the day for which the whole world has been waiting for six long years. For the first time in many years all nations are at peace with one another. To many of us here at the University of New Mexico, and at all other universities, it was the first day that we have attended a peace-time college.

The subconscious feeling of responsibility that we have ... was suddenly replaced by one of "The war's over, doesn't matter now!" The announcement of the acceptance of the peace brought about a period of wild jubilation, and it seemed to bring everything back to a normal college life, and the "war effort" is forgotten. Some of the students have been made older by their four years in a war-time university, but, on the other hand, the accelerated program has admitted a large group of younger students with an entirely different mental outlook. Colleges are going to be faced with one of the hardest problems they have ever had since the beginning of formal education ...

Lobo 8/17/45

Supporting Global Student Aid

1944

Contribute to the WSSF Drive February
UNM Goal---$1.00 For Every Student

NEW MEXICO LOBO

5th War Loan Drive on Campus June 9

Lieutenant Campa Writes From Somewhere in Italy — Mrs. Moonlight In Rehearsal — *Mrs. Tireman Gives Book Review June* — Student Senate Sponsors Dance

1946

WSSF Drive Ends Saturday
National Fraternities Name Pledges

1950

World Student Drive Set May 1

The World Student Service Fund will open its annual drive for funds on campus the first week of May. Often referred to ... building to house the 20,000 volumes already collected for a library. In addition, the school hopes to be able to build a properly equipped laboratory. Aside from educational equipment, WSSF also provides food for teachers and students.

1952

Here's What Happens to WSSF Money

By OLAF GRAEHL

The drive week of the world stu- ... able now to support themselves by their own means. Some of these ...

From top: 1/21/44, 5/26/44, 4/5/46, 4/11/50, 3/20/52

11/16/44

Students of the World Unite in Plans for Reform of Education

International Students' Day on Nov. 17 brought vividly to mind the ravages to students and the universities in Europe and Asia in these tragic war years. On the threshold of peace, the return of students to universities in the occupied countries is a harbinger of a great realistic reformation in education and of the development of a hopeful student unity and ... To these humanitarian and intellectual ends, the World Student Service Fund has worked since 1937 ... students of all stricken lands according to need and regardless of race, nationality, religion or politics.

INTERNATIONAL STUDENTS DAY marked the killing by Nazis in 1939 of 137 Czech students (p. 580). It focused wartime and postwar student aid and relief. The World Student Service Fund, later the World University Service (Pt. 3, Sec. 4, p. 611), was the agent for student contributions. NSA became an official sponsor of WSSF, and many of its leaders went to work for WSSF or WUS after graduation.

A Part of New Mexico History

Lobo 11/18/49

The university in 1889

Schwartz

The Zimmerman Library in 1999

UNIVERSITY OF NEW MEXICO — VITA HOMINUM LUX — 1889

Historical note: Founded by the territorial legislature in 1889 (www.unm.edu), the university played a major role in training the leadership that brought New Mexico into statehood in 1912. 1948 enrollment: 4,889.

Tracking NSA Events, But. . .

1946

Student Meet in Prague in August

On International Student Conference is to take place in Prague this summer from August 17 to 31.

The main purpose of the Conference has been stated in the appeal sent to all student organizations:

"We consider that the main problem confronting the World Student Congress will be that of establishing a representative international students' organization uniting in its ranks all the democratic student organizations of the world with the aim of ensuring a lasting and stable peace, of promoting frien...

1949

Congress Asked to Provide Federal Program Of Scholarships by National Student Group

The U. S. National Student Association has called upon Congress to enact legislation to provide a national program of federally financed scholarships for approximately 300,000 college students. The "Civilian G.I. Bill" would provide for ... were not enrolled in colleges. Some 50 per cent of this group are in families whose income is below $3,000 per annum. Average tuition and living costs at college ranging between $750 and $1,000 yearly indicate the pressing need for finan-

1949

One Million U. S. Students Discuss Academic Ideas

URBANA, Ill. More than a million students swapped ideas for ...

NSA Attacks 50 Million Grant

A $50,000,000 grant to Jefferson Military College, Washington, Miss., has been condemned by the president of the U. S. National Student Association.

President Robert A. Kelly called the gift from Judge George Armstrong of vast mineral and oil reserves, "deplorable."

From top: 5/3/46, 9/20/49, 11/18/49

1952

Student Urges UNM to Join National Students Association

Someone once said, "Never try to talk a politician into anything."

But Carol Claydon, a sophomore transfer student from the University of Colorado, isn't taking much stock in it. She's trying to talk politicos into placing a chapter of the National Students Association (NSA) on the campus.

She first approached the Student ...

NSA Constitution Due for Reconsideration by Council

By Ed Lahart

Student Council Says "No" to Joining NSA

A motion to reconsider the National Students' Association constitution and to rescind the action of last year's Student Council in passing the constitution was accepted by the Council Tuesday.

The decision was unanimous.

"We don't know what the NSA will do for UNM," said Councilwoman Joann McNay. Councilman Jo McMinn added, "UNM has nothing to gain from NSA."

The Council officially designed the Student Spirit Sing as an annual affair of Rallycom, student spirit organization.

A motion to make Joan Lewis the fifth member of the standby Ath-

Council Will Send Representatives To NSA Convention Nov. 21-23

Should UNM Go Into NSA? Council Keeping Open Mind

Religion Should Come From Heart Says Billy Graham

Five Students to Go On Fort Collins Trip Denver Finances Told

From top: 4/8/49, 3/20/52, 10/17/52, 10/17/52, 11/14/52

AMBIVALENCE TOWARD NSA was reflected in the vote not to join in October of 1952, and the decision in November to attend the regional conference. The choice not to join was unanimous. "We don't know what the NSA will do for UNM," said one councilmember.

Attacking Discrimination

Colored Student Refused Service

Service was refused to George Long, UNM sophomore, at Oklahoma Joe's Monday morning, because George is colored.

A waitress at the establishment said that George could be served if he would enter the restaurant by way of the back door and eat his ...

Oklahoma Joe Incident Closed By Committee

"Any University student is welcome at my establishment, regardless of color, nationality or religion."
(signed) Joe Frimlaur.

Walgreen Ban May Be Lifted; Report Policy Change

Senate Move Seen After Negro Test Group Is Served

Border Conference to Vote On Use of Negro Athletes

Racial Hot Potato Faces Delegates At Winter Session

UNM to Vote in Favor Of Permitting Negroes To Compete in Texas

LET'S GET THE HELL OUT

Our reaction, "Let's get the hell out of the Border Conference," is not a new one.

Once before it was prompted by the lax standards of officiating permitted by the Conference, which has developed an almost unbeatable combination of "home-town" referees.

This time it is considerably strengthened by the need that is almost certain to develop in El Paso this weekend. Certain Texas institutions have childishly insisted that they won't permit their young men to compete with Negro athletes.

It is very possible that in the near future a Negro will be playing on a UNM team. Our standards of competition will be that if a Negro is good enough to make the team, he is good enough to play in Texas or anywhere else.

As long as the Texas schools continue to display their lack of understanding of true sportsmanship, we will continue to suggest, "Let's get the hell out."

From top, above: 9/19/47, 9/23/47; right: 2/21/50, 12/13/49, 12/13/49.

LOCAL MERCHANT AND ATHLETIC CONFERENCE barriers angered students, who mounted boycotts and protested policies. The 1949 UNM effort to revoke Border Conference racial discrimination on the playing field echoed the 1947 U of Colorado action (pp. 1001, 1006).

Questioning the "Red Terror"

CALIFORNIA LOYALTY OATH

The eyes of academic America have been watching Berkeley, California with great interest for the past month or so. For an important issue is being fought there, at the University of California, and the world-famous campus has been in a continual uproar.

Twelve men, the Regents of that institution, have attempted to force a "loyalty oath" upon the instructors, making them swear that they are not and have never been Communists or Communist-sympathizers.

Reaction on the Cal campus has been overwhelmingly opposed to the oath. Our source, The Daily Californian, student newspaper, reports that the Faculty Senate has gone on record almost 100% in opposition. In addition, student groups have acted in protest meetings, and at last report, a strike was imminent.

The Daily Californian has been editorially opposed to the oath, and student opinion, as reflected in their letter column, is similarly inclined. One letter suggested the following song, to the tune of the "Battle Hymn of the Republic":

4/13/50

"THE SITUATION IS DARK," the *Lobo* editorialized, "when the irrational Red terror sweeping the country hits the college campus in such a manner. In an attempt to preserve the American way, nonthinking do-gooders lay aside all American principles of free expression and thought" (see pp. 381, 394).

The Independent Student Associations in the Southwest

Independents at Colorado

Independent Students State Plans For Future Activities

ACTIVITY BOOKS WILL BE AT MACKY NEXT WEEK

Students must call for their

Bandwagon Rental Profits Will Be Contributed To Student Union Fund

The SILVER and GOLD

AN INDEPENDENT NEWSPAPER

Official Publication of the Associated Students of the University of Colorado

ISA Candidates Reveal Qualifications For ASUC

'Confusionist' Party Enters Campus Election Race

Case Of Vetsville vs. Austin Is On Trial In Moot Court

Fraternity Slate Candidates Have High Grade Averages

New ASUC Constitution Ratified Despite Greek Combine Opposition

By Kenneth Whitaker

In a heavier-than-expected vote, University students Wednesday approved a new constitution for the ASUC by a margin of 175 ballots. For the new constitution there were 837 ballots, against were 662, with six ballots voided.

ASUC Commission Holds Final Meeting Of Quarter

Expressions of appreciation and miscellaneous business

Colorado ISA Chapter Sends Four Members To National Convention

Four members of ISA council will comprise the Colorado delegation to the National Independent Student association convention to be ... ested in information on better and different ways to hold a dance, possibilities for unusual types of decorations and different publicity

From top: *Silver and Gold* 9/14/45, 4/15/47, 5/23/47, 4/19/49.

THE INDEPENDENT

Official Publication of the Independent Students Association

VOL. I, NO. 2 — UNIVERSITY OF COLORADO, BOULDER — APRIL 14, 1948

WILLIS, STARR TO HEAD ISA TICKET

Joan Willis was chosen to fill the lead position on the Independent ticket at Monday's ISA Council meeting thus becoming one of the first women candidates for the ASUC presidency. Miss Willis, at present in California with a Speakers Congress debate team, had the highest popular vote tabulation at last week's primary election.

Chosen for the two follow-up positions were Paul Starr who, at the primaries, accumulated the largest sum of number one vote preferentials, and James Buehring, at present ISA Athletic Manager. Jack Randle, Viking Vice-President will run fourth on the Independent slate, while Kent Yowell, a Greek, also running number 10 on the Combine ticket, was picked by the council for ISA's number five position.

Twelve candidates were selected by ISA for the thirteen council positions with one vacancy on the ballot caused a recently-

Joan Willis

3rd Party Joins Election Race

With the announcement of a four-man slate of candidates, the Wallace-for-President Club broadens the ASUC election field to three parties vying for representation. The Wallace ticket, headed by Leonard Perlmutter, threatens to split the Independent vote, thus giving advantage to Greek candidates.

Service Honorary Benefits Students

by Norman Kaplan

Alpha Phi Omega is a service fraternity, having a definite program of activities in which the pledges and members direct their energies for the benefit of their tivity.

The purpose of Alpha Phi Omega, as being carried out by the chapters, is "to assemble col-

Presenting E. J. Nash...

Fifth member of the Nash family to be active on the CU campus, E.J. follows the example set by sisters in leading or taking t in many student organiza-s. All four sisters, who are n a ranch near Canon City in thern Colorado, were either in rtar Board or Hesperia and e active in ISA.

.J., the present contribution he Nash family to CU's campis president of Women's Club; ember of Hesperia, ASUC Enainment and Culture commit- and the University Memorial

A HOUSE DIVIDED

Six thousand of CU's eight thousand students are independents. There are thirteen seats on the ASUC commission. Hence it follows that at least eight of those seats should be filled by independents. Seven seats are held by Greeks, though, and representation is entirely disproportionate.

There are two reasons for the existence of this situation. One is the consistent failure of more than the equalizing two thousand to vote; Greeks always go to the polls. The other is that independent malcontents, given proof at Independent primary elections of their unpopularity, lose sight of IAS's aims and, for purely selfish reasons, split the non-Greek vote with a third party.

Such a party, has appeared again this year. It is led by the same individual who split the Independent vote last year. We shall not mention them by name, nor shall we unjustly vilify them. That would only make them martyrs. We shall, however, analyze their purposes, and show how Independents can still capture an ASUC majority.

This party admits that it intends to use its strength to foist national political interests upon the campus. Try as we may, we fail to see any justification for this action. We like to see that CU students are interested in national politics and participate fully; that is their duty as American citizens. However, CU and national politics are divorced in essence. We rebel at the thought of a small group of students attempting to use ASUC as a sounding board for national political objectives.

There is no reason for the independent student to feel discouraged, though. He can still find himself victorious when the votes are counted. The secret is organization. Organize your dorms, your rooming houses, your clubs. Come down to the polls en masse.

Whereas the Hare system of proportional representation would insure an Independent split in the case of a small vote, the third party, too, is small, but highly organized. Therefore, a large Independent vote would make the third party—a constant—and its vote, small by proportion. Its existence would have absolutely no significance.

The question remains for you, the voter, to decide. Are you, the majority, willing to be dominated by organized minority? Are you willing to see your democratic privileges trampled upon by any number of smaller than your own? The answer will be found at the polls.

A SOCIAL AND POLITICAL ALTERNATIVE TO FRATERNITIES, the ISA at CU offered a complete social and athletic program. All independents on campus were automatically members and entitled to vote in electing its class representatives and officers. ISA ran slates in elections and, although 75% of the students were independents, generally ran second to the "Greek Combine." **LEN PERLMUTTER'S "CONFUSION PARTY"** was a third party thorn in their side (see editorial, left), splitting their vote and electing him to the ASUC in 1947 (p. 996). In 1948, Perlmutter was seen to be bringing national politics to the campus when he ran on the Wallace-for-President ticket.

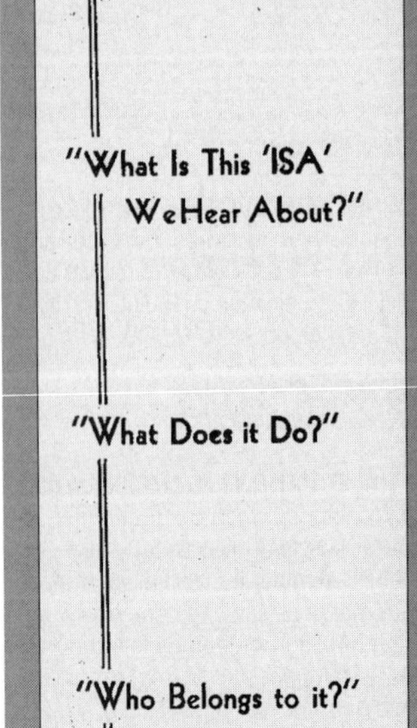
"What Is This 'ISA'
We Hear About?"
"What Does it Do?"
"Who Belongs to it?"

"WHAT IS THIS 'ISA' WE HEAR ABOUT?"

"WHAT DOES IT DO?"

"WHO BELONGS TO IT?"

Every term at the close of registration when initials "ISA" begin to appear in The Silver and Gold (the campus newspaper), these questions are asked by new students at the University. But usually no one tries to give coherent answers; consequently, the newcomers often tend to overlook the Independent Students Association.

WHAT ISA IS

Briefly, ISA is an organization which strives to co-ordinate CU for Independents for their mutual benefit, one which attempts to provide social, athletic, and political activity for all students.

WHO BELONGS

Every student who is not pledged to or a member of any social sorority or fraternity is classified as an "independent"; all independent students belong to ISA.

DUES — NONE

Because of its efficient business organization, ISA is not forced to rely upon its members for financial support in the form of dues. It cost nothing to be an Independent.

SOCIAL ACTIVITIES

The immediate and most important aim of the Association is to arrange social activities for CU students. To help do this, ISA is sponsoring the following:

a. An hour dance every Monday night in the ball room of the Memorial Student-Union Building.* The best campus bands play; admission is usually fourteen cents.

b. Two- and three- hour dances on Friday nights in the Memorial ball room; admission is twenty-five cents and up.

c. A mixer for new students at the beginning of every term. Admission is twenty cents.

d. A formal dance with the best band possible; admission is approximately $1.25.

e. A play-reading group for those interested in dramatics. This group, which has excellent coaching in histrionics, meets weekly.

f. A chorus which sings modern, popular, and classical songs. It, too, mets every week under expert direction. The time and place will be stated in The Silver and Gold.

g. Sunday suppers at 6 p.m. in the basement of Memorial; cost is thirty-five cents.

ATHLETICS

Another service rendered by the Independent Students Association is that of providing opportunity for all to take active part in intramural athletics. Before the start of every intramural tournament, the athletic director of ISA calls a meeting of Independent athletes, assigns them to teams or lets them choose their own teams, and registers the teams with the intramural sponsor.

The next intramural sport will be softball. If you want to play, scan the pages of The Silver and Gold; and when that publication announces where teams are organizing, be there!

POLITICS

Politically, ISA has failed. Every election, because of the kindness of the Greek Combine,* about three Independents are elected to positions on the ASUC Commission.* Three Independents represent 3500 students while ten Greeks represent the 1100 other students who belong to the fraternities.

Of course, there is reason for the characteristic Independent inability to get themselves elected. You, the Independents, don't support your candidates. All Independents are ever asked to do during elections is to nominate candidates and to vote for them; but most Independents are too indifferent, too selfish, or just too pre-occupied to mark an X for their own candidates who have independent interests at heart.

Think it over; for before long, ISA propagandists will be urging you to vote. And if you, the Independents, do bother to do so, you might surprise yourselves by winning an election.

* The Greek Combine is a compact organization of all the fraternities and sororities on the campus to promote their politics.

* The ASUC Commission is the governing body of the Associated Students of the University of Colorado.

REEVES

Reeves is an organization which works first to improve the University of Colorado and second to promote CU Independents. It puts on all the dances, serves the ISA suppers, handles publicity, and performs whatever duties the ISA Council (the governing body of the Independent Students Association) designates as well as co-operating with the ASUC Commission on all-school affairs.

The members of Reeves are selected from applications every term. When new members are called for in The Silver and Gold, any interested student may petition for membership

ISA COUNCIL

A council of elected and appointed officers directs the affairs of ISA. The elected five —president, vice-president, secretary, treasurer, and ASUC Representative—make all appointments and decisions of major importance while the appointed fourteen perform the duties which their titles indicate.

The present officers of ISA are:

President.....Bob Barrell
Vice-president.....Jim Abbott
Treasurer.....Warren van Metre
Secretary.....Ruth Hall
ASUC Representative.....Rachel Maddox
Dance Manager.....Oliver Swanson
Athletic Director.....Bruce Polich
Publicity Director.....John Carroll
Representative to the Senate of Associated Women Students.....Jo Murfin
Senior Women's Representative.....Mary Edith Drexel
Senior Men's Representative.....Howard Segal
Junior Women's Representative.....Charlotte Johnson
Junior Men's Representative.....Paul Glove
Sophomore Women's Representative.....Renee Morrell
Sophomore Men's Representative.....Don Orazem
Freshman Women's Representative.....Natalie Coursen
Freshman Men's Representative.....William Malkovich
Women's Dorm Representative.....Ila Allen
Men's Dorm Representative.....Milton Waxman

ISA brochure, c. 1948 (Archives, University of Colorado)

The National Independent Student Association

"Keep the organization inexpensive. Keep it democratic. Keep your old-timers to give it continuity. Boundaries should disappear. The organization should raise ordinary people above the crowd and make leaders of them."

—Dean Arnow Nowotny, University of Texas
1947 NISA Convention

Editor's note: NISA was founded on the initiative of college administrators in the mid-thirties who felt that students who were not selected by fraternities did not have equivalent organized social, service and intramural outlets (the large majority on major campuses). Unlike the issue of fraternity discrimination which roiled college campuses after World War II (See Pt. 4 Sec. 3; Pt 2, p. 398), the problems of social exclusion were dealt with by a movement to provide alternatives. Centered largely in the Midwest and West, and actively supported by networks of Deans of Men and Deans of Women, it grew to 78 members in 33 states in 1948. I have not found further documentation beyond that point, although it doubtless rests in a number of college archives. I have found no reference to NISA or the ISA movement in any of the books on college student life appearing in the bibliography to this anthology.

A Brief History of NISA

Excerpts from an undated, unsigned typescript apparently written early in 1948 from the Washington State University Libraries.

When fraternities first started, a selective process began which left certain individuals on the outside, regardless of the reasons involved. On the day that the selections were made, it is probable that some of those who were left out began to think in terms of a rival or counter-group, and as the years passed, the terms "Greeks" and "Independents" were applied to the two factions....

In looking over the student body of his school, Dr. J.F. Findlay, now president of Drury College at Springfield, Missouri, realized that fraternities reached a very small percentage of the students, and that the far larger group of unorganized students had no benefits of organiztion, representation, social programs, intramural programs, or means to be of service to the college.

It is true that these unorganized students had made feeble attempts to organize at various schools throughout the country, but Dr. Findlay conceived the idea of a national meeting of representatives of these groups to gather and discuss their problems. As a result, the first National Convention of Independent Students was held in 1938 at the University of Oklahoma, with thirteen deans or faculty sponsors, and 109 students from twenty-three colleges in atendence.

In the address of welcome, Dr. W.B. Bizzell, late President of the University of Oklahoma, stated that "the educational processes on a campus cannot go forward without the development of the right kind of intellectual atmosphere. This atmosphere can best be developed only when there is a friendly relation between students. This relationship must be developed by the students themselves. The independent organizations, therefore, have a very definite educational responsibility in this regard....The independent men's groups can promote better than anyone else true campus democracy....

NISA was to be democratic and inexpensive....This policy has been carried out consistently over the years, and under the able leadership of Dean Arno Nowatny of Texas (see next page)...NISA grew in size and numbers, until the late war forced a curtailment of activities. Even during the war years, Dr. Findlay, Dean Nowtny and Dr. Ben Galland of the University of Colorado kept the NISA alive.... Last year the national convention was once again held at the University of Oklahoma, and plans are now underway for the biggest and best ... at Iowa State on May 7-8, 1948."

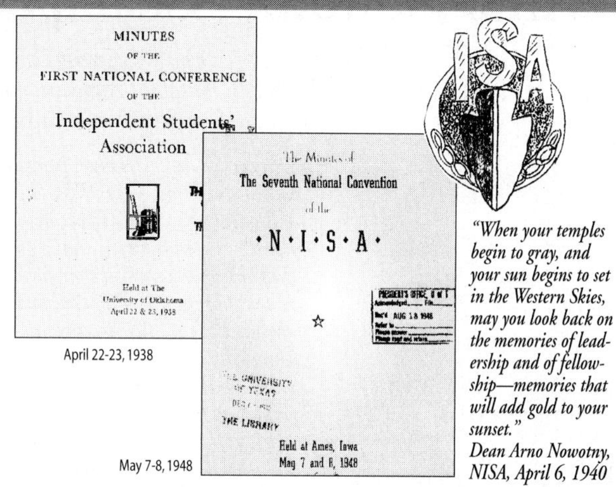

April 22-23, 1938

May 7-8, 1948

"When your temples begin to gray, and your sun begins to set in the Western Skies, may you look back on the memories of leadership and of fellowship—memories that will add gold to your sunset."
Dean Arno Nowotny, NISA, April 6, 1940

1948 NISA Membership *[As listed in the November, 1948 NISA Newsletter]*

NORTHEAST
Clarkson College
Cornell University
Pennsylvania State College
Rider College
St. Lawrence University
Syracuse University
Westminster College

SOUTHEAST
Alabama Polytechnic Institute
University of Alabama
University of Chattanooga
Emory University
University of Florida
Marshall College
Mercer University
Millsaps College
University of Tennessee
Vanderbilt University

PACIFIC COAST
University of Idaho
Oregon State College
Washington State College
University of Washington

ROCKY MOUNTAIN
University of Colorado
Colorado College
Colorado State (A&M)
Colorado State (Education)
Denver University
Montana State University
Montana State College
Utah Agricultural College
University of Wyoming

SOUTHWEST
University of Arkansas
Louisiana State University
University of New Mexico
Oklahoma City University
University of Oklahoma
Southern Methodist University
University of Texas
University of Tulsa

CENTRAL
University of Akron
Albion College
Beloit College
Butler College
DePauw University
Franklin College
Hillsdale College
University of Illinois
Indiana University
Indiana State Teachers College
Michigan State College
University of Michigan
Northwestern University
Ohio State University
Ohio University
Purdue University
Valparaiso University
Western Illinois State College
Whitewater College
University of Wisconsin

MIDWEST
Baker University
Culver-Stockton College
Drake University
Drury College
Iowa State College
State University of Iowa
Iowa Wesleyan College
Kansas City University
Kansas State College
Kansas State Teachers College
University of Kansas
University of Minnesota
University of Nebraska
North Dakota State College
Simpson College
University of South Dakota
Washburn University
Washington University
Wichita University

Note: The 7th National Convention of NISA at Iowa State, May 7-8, 1948 was attended by 231 delegates and 13 faculty from 36 colleges and universities.

Western Conference NISA Newsletter Welcomes NSA

Digest from a lengthy article in the Western Conference of Independent Organizations Newsletter, *1 April, 1948. Denver, Colo.*

Representatives from the several states of this region will meet in Boulder to draw up a constitution for the Regional National Student Association. The convention meets April 8, 1948....More than 700 delegates representing 351 leading colleges and universities met on the University of Wisconsin campus in September, 1947. These delegates wrote a constitution and formed an organization which will give the American college student unprecedented representation in the educational world. The convention formulated a vital program of activities, designed to improve education and promote friendship and understanding among the students of the world. *[There follows a digest of the NSA Constitution, Student Bill of Rights, and national and international programs].*

Is your university a member of NSA? If not, why?

SOURCES: Colorado U. ISA, Western Conference, NISA Newsletters: *Archives, University of Colorado*; Minutes, NISA, 1938-1948: *University of Texas at Austin, Library*; NISA history mss, c. 1948: *Washington State University Libraries.*

"We begin where the curriculum ends"

Arno Nowotny: Champion for Independent Students

Dean of Student Life, University of Texas, 1943-64
President, National Association of Deans and Advisers of Men, 1946-47
Executive Secretary, National Independent Students Association, 1940-49

Editor's note: Arnow Nowotny retired three times—in 1964 (Dean of Student Life), 1969 (Development Board Consultant) and 1980 (unpaid consultant)—before he died in 1982 at the age of 83. Yet, he had already built a 30-year career at the University of Texas by 1954, the era with which this Anthology is concerned. As 1946-47 President of the National Association of Deans and Advisers of Men, 1947-50 President of national service fraternity Alpha Phi Omega and 1940-49 National Executive Secretary of the National Independent Students' Association (NISA), he enjoyed a national presence as one of those energetic student personnel professionals who helped shape the quality of their college experience for so many students and student leaders.

Jim Smith, in the letter excerpted below, provides documentation of one of the countless ways in which such influence is exercised. The NISA album on the preceding pages is a tribute to Nowotny's national reach.

Thirty Years Service to UT Helps Nowotny Advise Student

By BILL ROBERTSON

Perhaps you are one of those unfortunate students who has a "big" problem, and your troubles include anything from not knowing where the next meal is coming from to a bad case of frustration at the hands of a beautiful freshman co-ed.

If so, chances are that you need to consult the "little man."

That "little man" is Dr. Arno Nowotny, Dean of Student Life. For nearly three decades this colorful personality has been ironing out social difficulties for UT students.

A visit to Dean Nowotny's small, but comfortable, office in the Main Building shows that a large share of campus business is carried on there. Yet, only seconds after meeting the congenial Dean, students are surrounded by a warm, unbusiness-like friendliness.

Dean Nowotny, known to many people as "Shorty," (he barely cracks the five-foot mark) sits at a desk to the left of his office door. The desk, covered with various papers and other items, attests to the amount of work which passes through his hands.

A long career of devoted service to the University had its start for Dr. Nowotny in 1918 when he entered as a freshman. In 1925, he received his bachelor of arts and bachelor of laws degrees and became a member of the UT faculty.

As a student, he was an active member of the Cowboys, Friars, Pi Sigma Delta, Hildebrand Law Society, YMCA Cabinet and Sigma Delta Chi.

"We begin where the curriculum ends," Dean Nowotny asserts. "Our big job concerns the student who feels he is not a part of campus life aside from his studies. We try to find those students and make them feel a sense of belonging."

It was with this idea that a blueprint for Mica was long ago conceived by the Dean. That pattern has grown into a successful, efficient organization.

Concerning students from foreign countries, Dean Nowotny says "we should make friends with foreign students and get to know them well."

Dean Nowotny was co-founder of the University chapter of Alpha Phi Omega, national service fraternity. The Student Employment Bureau is another function of the Main University which had its beginning through the efforts of this man.

The slightly-greying little man, whose enormous capacity for vigor and enthusiasm has brought him a wealth of experience, agrees that one of the most decisive periods in his life came in 1937 when he was offered a position on the faculty of Texas Technological College in Lubbock.

"It was the most difficult decision that I ever had to make," Dean Nowotny recalls. "There was an attractive salary advancement and additional prestige involved in the move but my roots were deep in the University and I had a great sense of responsibility to my friends here."

In the following years his principles and deep devotion to an institution were to be repaid.

In 1943, after serving seventeen years as an assistant to the Dean of Men, Dr. Nowotny was appointed Dean. In 1946, the Board of Regents appointed him Dean of Student Life, a post which had been vacant since the death of Dean V. I. Moore in August, 1943.

Dean Nowotny firmly believes that students of today are more serious and self-sufficient than those of the preceding generations.

"I do not believe that any school in the nation with an enrollment in the neighborhood of 16,000 students could be as healthy and operate as smoothly as the University," he says with pride.

"The young people of this age are better fed, better housed, and better governed than any before," observes Dean Nowotny.

Nowotny Elected Head of Deans

At a meeting of the National Association of Deans and Advisors of Men, held last week at Purdue University, Dean Arno Nowotny was elected president of the organization.

Other officers are Dean L. K. Neidlinger of Dartmouth College, vice-president, and Dean Fred Turner of the University of Illinois, secretary.

The topics of discussion at the three-day meeting included the housing situation, veterans' organization, and fraternities.

Those who attended the meeting from the University were Mr.

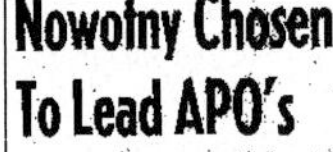

Nowotny Chosen To Lead APO's

National Convention Elects UT Dean

Eighteen University delegates wearing boots, chaps and loud shirts put on a real show at the national convention of Alpha Phi Omega in Kansas City, Mo., December 28-29, and before the last gavel sounded they had not only let everyone know that Texas' Alpha Rho chapter was present, but Dean of Student Life Arno Nowotny, co-founder and faculty advisor of the University chapter,

Daily Texan: top, 11/4/54. Above fr. left: 4/25/46, 11/7/47. Photo: UT Office of Public Affairs. *Alcalde* cover left, clippings and biographic information: Center for American History, UT Austin.

A TRIBUTE TO DEAN NOWOTNY FROM JIM SMITH

Editor's note: Jim Smith was elected President of the National Continuations Committee at the 1946 Chicago Student Conference. Upon his return he wrote an 8-page report to Dean Nowotny (see p. 119) which contained these eloquent acknowledgments of the dean's support.

STUDENTS' ASSOCIATION
THE UNIVERSITY OF TEXAS, AUSTIN

January 5, 1947

Dear Dean Nowotny,

Before I say anything I wish to thank you from the very bottom of my heart for all the things you did to make our trip to Chicago possible. The financial problems you ironed out, the advice you gave on the mechanics of fund-raising and money handling, your constructive ideas in the first meeting of our delegation, and your attitude throughout, were the basic reasons for the success of our delegation at the Conference. . . .

. . . I wish to have considerable conversation with you before leaving for Chicago in February. As I resign my office of President of the Students' Association, may I say that while we have disagreed on many points, I feel that our fundamental agreements on other basic issues have been more important possibly than the disagreements. You have been a positive force in my education and training, and therefore I believe that our relationship has been a profitable one to me. Thanks again for your cooperation in the problems of our delegation to Chicago, and thanks for all the times previous to that and all the times which lay ahead when your friendly cooperation has proven and will prove so valuable. I am sincerely, your friend, Jim Smith.

Jim Smith

"We need more experience in the democratic way of living. May we engage in such extra-curricular activities. . . for the serious experience in government, for training in leadership and followership.'"
—Address, 4/4/1940 NISA 3d Annual Convention.

Editor's note: In its September/October 1981 issue, Alcalde, *the University of Texas alumni magazine, devoted a lengthy tribute to Dean Nowotny. In 1980 the title Dean of Student Life Emeritus was conferred on him, and in 1981 he received the University's Presidential citation. The article was headlined, "Shorty Stands Up Again," declaring, "While he didn't stand tall physically, he became a towering presence on the University of Texas campus and in the community."*

SECTION 8

CONTENTS

Cultivation of NSA Aims Brings Fruit in Convention of 33 California Colleges on the Leland Stanford Farm

By Grover Heyler

After a year's period of organization, constitution and firing up spirit, concrete domestic and international projects which will bring to life the idea of a National Students Association were proposed at the Stanford regional convention last weekend.

routine work of approving a constitution seemed to be the chief interest of the larger schools, already used to the idea of an NSA through attendance at the Madison, Wis., convention this summer.

Colleges which had sent observers for the first time, however, were more concerned with getting a clear picture of the or-

excellent Institute on International Relations.

For example, the convention enthusiastically adopted its plan to push sponsorship of a seminar in Europe on American Civilization and Culture, copied from the Harvard-Rutgers-Yale project at Salzburg last summer; a time these student bodies

the work of these commissions, as planned by the convention, will appear in tomorrow's *Bruin*. Both universities will be headquarters for two years, although every college is to have groups working on the projects.

NSO Delegates To Meet At Pepperdine

An important meeting of the representatives of the colleges and universities in Southern California will be held this Saturday, April 26, at Pepperdine College in Los Angeles.

The meeting will begin at 10 a.m. and will continue throughout the entire day. Loyola will be represented by a student delegation and a faculty member authorized by the Dean of the Faculties

CALIFORNIA COLLEGES north and south convened to form the new region in 1947. (From top: *Daily Bruin* 4/23/48, *Loyolan* 4/25/47)

California

Fifteen California colleges were able to fund thirty-eight delegates to the 1947 Constitutional Convention in Wisconsin, an expensive proposition then as now. Their journey was preceded by a meeting of 106 delegates and observers from twenty-one colleges held at Berkeley and followed by a meeting of twenty-five colleges at Stanford to draft a regional constitution. Two sub-regions, North and South, were created.

California experienced problems of time and distance, and some fierce opposition to affiliation, by both those who were suspicious of possible un-American leanings and those who felt their colleges needed little in the way of help from others. The latter explains why San Francisco State dropped out in 1949–1950. The former explains why University of Southern California President Fred D. Fagg vetoed the decision of its Associated Students to join in 1948.

Despite the foregoing, strong interest and leadership came from campuses in both subregions, North (University of California at Berkeley, Mills, Stanford, Cal Arts, College of Holy Names), and South (University of California at Los Angeles, Loyola of Los Angeles, Los Angeles City College, Occidental, Mt. St. Mary's). Early leaders nationally included Berkeley's Mildred Kiefer (national treasurer, 1947-48) and Dick Heggie (student government vice president, 1948-49) and Stanford's Erskine Childers (international vice president, 1949-50). Los Angeles City College's Wally Longshore, 1950 regional vice president, later became the 1954-55 national affairs vice president when he was a student at UCLA. Albums highlighting some of these colleges appear in the section.

California: a focal point of controversy and advocacy

California was one of the states with an active legislatively sponsored teacher loyalty oath campaign, which engaged NSA opposition. It was also home to scores of thousands of Japanese Americans who had been interned during the war, some of whom returned to college afterward. Tom Suzuki, 1949-1950 Los Angeles City College (LACC) student body president and NSA delegate, shares some of his experiences in and out of the internment camps.

LACC was also the home base for Tom Munger (Part 4), the founder of Students for MacArthur and Students for America in 1951-52. Munger, a prize-winning intercollegiate debater (as was Milton Dobkin, below), was defeated by Suzuki in their student body president contest. Munger had been an LACC regional NSA delegate and became a critic of the association.

Jane Wilder Jacqz of UCLA was an active advocate for the World Student Service Fund (WSSF), whose staff she joined (see Part 3), as did Sally Holt Smit, who writes about WSSF in this Section. NSA's national Symphony Forum program was initiated by Paul Denise at San Francisco State (see Part 2 Section 1).

Milton Dobkin, NSA Southern California 1947-1948 regional chair, whose tenure spanned enrollment first at LACC and then USC, describes the politics of NSA, the impact of the veterans, and the role of fraternities at USC. Nancy (Roth) Arnheim recalls NSA at UCLA and as a gateway to both her career in vocational guidance and a lifetime of civic engagement. The section closes with a tribute to Monroe Deutsch, Vice President and Provost Emeritus at UC Berkeley during the time of his service on the NSA Advisory Committee.

California Regional NSA Highlights

California Colleges Consider the New Organization . . .

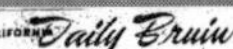

Daily Bruin

Watch for it . . .

Beginning Monday, the Bruin will print the first of a series of reports from the delegates to the National Student Association, NSA, formerly NSO, held a convention in Madison, Wisconsin, during the summer, and UCLA sent three elected and two appointed delegates. They were Hans Morkisch, Dick Hough, and Kristy Koestner. In addition, there were two appointed members from Student Executive Council, Jane Wilder, Rep-at-Large, and Ken Gallagher, ASUCLA president.

Report on NSA

STUDENT LEADERS GIVE VIEWS ON NSA

SEC VOTES 'YES' ON NSA

Hayes, Nichols Run-offs Told

THE DAILY CALIFORNIAN

ASUC Affiliates With NSA; Voted By Executives

Hap Arnold, Heggie Speak At University Meeting Today

Support the NSA

DC-11/12/47

MC-11/21/47

Board of Directors Votes Approval of NSA Proposition

O'Leary, Allen Trek South to Convention

GG-4/23/48

NSA Remains By Unanimous Excom Vote

SD-5/5/49

THE STANFORD DAILY

WILL NATION'S CAMPUSES BE UNITED?

SD-1/20/47

Loyolan

Student Council To Study N.S.O.

LC-1/5/49

MAJOR COLLEGE DAILIES provided extensive coverage of NSA's formation and its relation to existing student governments.

. . . Raise Funds to Rebuild Europe

1945

'Books for Russia' drive begin

DB-6/7/46

DB-9/17/45

To Italy

Bruins aid students in devastated nations

1946

1947

Assembly to Kickoff WSSF Campus Drive; . . . man to Speak

DT-4/18/47

To Europe

SC-Texas Battle of Dollars Will Aid Foreign Students

WSSF DRIVE IN FULL SWING

To Greece

1952

MC-2/21/52

NSA News-2/49

To Germany

1949

For more on WSSF, See p. 613

. . . Mark War's End

1945-48

V-E DAY ANNOUNCED

British declare victory in Europe is official

Emperor Issues Cease Firing Orde . . .

Pleads Surrender Time Extension

Peace Treaties Signed: Rioting Italians Protest

LOYOLA ENROLLMENT HIGHEST IN HISTORY

AVC Head Recommends Support of Baruch Plan, Compulsory Disarmament

From top: DT-5/8/45, DB-8/17/45, DT-2/11/47, LC-9/23/46, GG-1/9/48

WORLD EVENTS were followed closely by the college press during the war, an interest that remained with the return of veterans on campus (see "The Veterans," p. 697).

. . . Reflect on Japanese-American Internment

1945

California Bruin

Bloom Analyzes Nisei Resettlement in Forum

8/27/45

Mills College

It Happened Here

10/3/45

MOST OF THE 110,000 DETAINEES were California residents. Tom Suzuki recounts his experience (see pp. 1031 and 1037).

. . . Build a Regional Organization

1947

NSA Holds First Meeting, Plans Group Expansion

DB-9/26/47

DB-4/23/48

NSA Convention Commences Tomorrow

Daily Bruin

McHenry, Hahn, Gallagher To Address Student Meet

1948

NSA News 12/48

1948 REGIONAL ASSEMBLY addressed by Verne Stedman, Regional PR Director

1949

Longshore Greets Delegates At NSA Regional Conference

LA-10/21/49

1950

TO-3/17/50

NSA World Affairs Conference Gathers on Campus Tomorrow

1951

NSA Recognition Brings National Student Voice

LA-5/8/51

Photos credited in text/albums

Mildred Kiefer
Berkeley, Chair, 46-47
47-48 NSA Staff, p.178

Dick Heggie
Berkeley, Chair, 47-48
48-49, NSA VP, p.199

Erskine Childers
Stanford, Chair, 48-49
49-50, NSA Intl VP, p. 517

Jack Knox
Occidental. Co- Chair, 48-49

Peggy Bradish
Mt St Mary, Chair, 51-52

CALIFORNIA REGION BUILDERS

. . . Confront Loyalty Oaths and the 'Red Scare'

DT-2/18/48

Dean Hits Red Charge

NSA 'Commie Front'—Dr. Jacobsen; Collegian Gains Tri-Weekly Status

LA-3/48

DB-2/24/47

COLLEGE 'RED' HUNT

DC-8/4/50

Daily Californian

Oath fever is spreading

What Is Academic Freedom?

Tenney 'Red' Label Applied to UCLA

Fear of Red Infiltration Keeps SC Out of NSA

GG-5/18/50

DT-4/18/47

DT-3/16/47

FEAR OF COMMUNIST INFLUENCE in the schools was pervasive (See p. 381, 388, 394). In California: State Senator Tenney's investigations, Richard Nixon's congressional campaigns, House Un-American Hollywood investigations, and the California Regents loyalty oath initiative, among various threats.

. . . and Debate Whether to Affiliate

DT EVALUATES WORK OF NSA

DT-10/8/47

ST-4/28/49

Excom Tables NSA For Another Week

Gallagher Hits NSA Student Bill Of Rights' Provisions as 'Vague'

DB-11/7/47

NSA Constitution Shows Groundwork

DT-2/17/48

Senate Vote on NSA Unreflective—Dr. Fagg

DT-4/30/48

Senate Kills Hot NSA Issue

DT-4/18/49

NSA on Trial

Who's Guilty—NSA or the Students?

LA-9/22/51

NSA'S VALUE was examined each year as new generations of student leaders and editors took a fresh look at the level of student interest and benefit.

More Daily Californian *on UC Berkeley and Regional NSA: Wurf, p. 184, Heggie, p. 207.*

KEY TO COLLEGE NEWSPAPER CITATIONS IN THIS SECTION

DB- *California Daily Bruin, UCLA*

DC- *Daily Californian, UC Berkeley*

DT - *Daily Trojan, USC*

GG- *Golden Gater, SF State*

HL- *Humboldt Lumberjack*

LA - *Collegian, LA City College*

LC- *Loyolan, Loyola College*

MC - *Mills College Weekly*

SD- *Stanford Daily*

TO - *The Occidental*

A battle lost against the Red Scare at USC

1. Launching NSA in Southern California and at USC

Milton Dobkin
University of Southern California
Chair, Southern Section, California Region, 1947-48

I approach this task with some misgivings and some apprehension. It has been over fifty years now since most of the events on which I will comment took place.

I have participated in enough oral history over my career to know how unreliable unverified oral history is, even unverified memoirs as such.[1] And yet, I am one of the few survivors of the era, and there is little documentation other than what appears in the *Daily Trojan,* the student newspaper of the University of Southern California at that time. For example, five or six Associated Students presidents of the University that were in office during the period just prior to the formation of the NSO, and later the NSA, and who participated in one way or another in the deliberations and the decisions leading to the University of Southern California's participation through its Associated Students are no longer alive.[2] I speak of Jim Mitchell, Paul Wildman, Johnny Davis, Al Wiggins, Bob Padgett, and another whose name escapes me at the moment. Likewise, a number of my friends of that era are gone, as well as adversaries; Such people as Phil Burton, June Louin-Tapp, Pat Hillings, Joe Holt, and others who were very active during the conflict over NSA affiliation. Several who remain are in no condition to give their verifications or corrections to the things of which I am about to write.

Background to the University of Southern California

So, given the foregoing situation, I will proceed to do what I can to offer a memoir. First, it is necessary to understand, at least from my perspective, some of the things that distinguished the University of Southern California from other, similar institutions. At the time, it was the largest private university (and may still well be for that matter)—in California and in the Western states at least. It had a curious, if not unique, history. When it was founded in 1879 (and here I turn to a bit of reference material) by members of the Methodist Episcopal Conference of Southern California, the land on which it was built—which was called Western Los Angeles at the time and now is Central Los Angeles—was donated by three civic leaders. They were a Catholic, an Episcopalian, and a Jew, and they attracted broad support for their objective.

UCLA was not even a gleam in anyone's eye at this time, and no other universities or even colleges of any real repute in the area were operating in a manner meant to attract a variety of students. While I am sure there were biases at work in the recruitment of students, particularly an emphasis on students with Christian backgrounds, in many ways the University was ahead of its time. The first graduating class of about thirteen or fourteen people had a population of roughly 40 percent women—"young ladies," as they were known at that time. That was unusual in both public and private institutions of higher education. Because USC was a private institution, and probably because it was church related for a good portion of its existence (later that affiliation was severed), it was not an inexpensive college to attend. In socioeconomic terms, it attracted mostly upper-middle to upper-class students. But early on it also attracted a variety of international students. This added to the diverse composition of the student body. Color was not a bar to admission to the university, although records were kept on admission forms of the number of students of color.

Impact of World War II and the veterans

These conditions were dramatically modified—first by the start of World War II and then by its aftermath. At that point (circa 1946), for example, out of the 13,000 or so undergraduate students at the University, 9,000 were returning veterans. Many of them would never have gone to USC were it not for the GI Bill, which provided the funding that they never could have afforded themselves.

UCLA, the only other major university in the area at that time, was far out of town, almost in Santa Monica, a major distance from Los Angeles with little if any available public transportation. Its admission standards were based on the very upper level of the high school college-prep graduates. Since many veterans had not had such a record when they graduated high school, they chose USC—and their impact on the University was noticeable almost immediately.

I had gone to community college, the first member of my family to ever graduate high school. My parents were both immigrants—my father from Ukraine and my mother from a small village on the Russo-Polish border, which had changed nationality intermittently. Both of my parents were of Jewish heritage, but neither practiced Judaism. My father was a Puritan ethicist who detested organized religion and loved intellectual and cultural pursuits even though he had no formal education.

When Pearl Harbor occurred, I was Associated Students president at Los Angeles City College. It was at City College that I began to be interested in student activism, and particularly in international matters relating to peace and justice. As a consequence, when I came out of World War II with the advantages of the GI Bill, I was able to enter USC, and almost immediately I became a student activist. Because some of my background from City College was known, I was promptly elected junior class president.

When the Chicago Student Conference was announced, I was selected by the Student Senate to attend along with AWS president Anita Norcop. I was excited by the notion of getting support in the student body for participation in such organizations as the NSO, as the interim forming group for NSA was called. Because of the student body's composition, I felt it was more likely to become interested in this sort of activity than might otherwise be the case.

NSA affiliation and campus politics

During this period of time, the political scene at USC among students was in a state of vigorous competition. The fraternities and sororities (the "row") had been taken over by a group of students with special political interests and self-interests among the fraternities and sororities. Its political group was called "the Tong." This was slang for TNE, Theta Nu Epsilon, a secret society devoted to controlling student government in the interests of the row.

Most male veterans, it happened, were not interested in becoming fraternity members, and those women who had been in the service were not all that interested in joining sororities. At first the efforts of such independent students to organize in some way to be part of student government was not actively resisted by the Tong. They thought their control would never be affected. But, as veterans began to gather together in an operation called the Unity Party, they became more effective. While also an independent, I was not a member of that party, but even so, I also became more effective. The Tong's concerns began to rise.

The Tong's chief concerns were related to control. If, in fact, the Unity Party, or I in combination with the Unity Party, had been able to really operate with a majority influence in student government, that would have blocked the fraternity row's ability through TNE to control student perquisites. So these folks began to do whatever they could to see to it that they could retain control.

This is probably one of the reasons why NSA affiliation was, in the end, doomed—despite general support at the outset for sending Anita Norcop and me to Chicago, sending five of us to the August 1947 Constitutional Convention in Madison, and the hotly debated 14-11 vote to affiliate by the Student Senate in February 1948.[3]

University president vetoes NSA affiliation and keeps control

When the recently installed university President Fred D. Fagg vetoed the action of the Student Senate several months later, in April, I believe he did so for a combination of reasons. First, his was a very conservative administration, which was very nervous about a potential communist threat (the days of vigorous red baiting were already in full gear on the West Coast).[4] In addition, I believe he did it partly—although I have no real evidence of this—because of the close relationship between the administration and the fraternity and sorority row, and to avoid any loss of money the alumni were giving to the University.

Since it was to the University's interest to keep control, and this was an instance where some of their folks had broken ranks on philosophical and ideological grounds with respect to the importance of student government, the veto could be taken to show the student government that the administration was in charge of such matters. Furthermore, the row people who felt apprehensive about their loss of control over student government, and some of whom were participating in the red baiting, would then be able to regain control.

This exercise of control is made apparent in the April 18, 1948, issue of the *Daily Trojan*, when the president of the Associated Students at that time, Johnny Davis, refused to permit a discussion of reopening the NSA affiliation matter after the veto because "we have been told this body has no power to discuss NSA." This was a unique approach to the exercise of student government, which probably was not characteristic of most other colleges.

The two principal political figures in TNE (both are gone now and unable to comment on the accuracy of my statements) were Patrick Hillings and Joe Holt. Both were veterans. Joe was a former Marine. Both were extremely conservative and interested in maintaining control as well as supporting conservative causes. Pat Hillings, for example, was very active in the original Richard Nixon campaign for Congress; he was also, later on, active when Helen Gahagan Douglas ran for the Senate against Nixon. Hillings and his cohorts were very active in the latter campaign. They were not at all loath to use charges of communism in the student body elections as well.

The independents and campus personalities

Interestingly, on the other side of the fence, the independent students were coming to power through the Unity Party, which was also a tightly controlled organization through its own structure. Jesse Unruh, an independent who was to become the "big daddy" of the California State Legislature, was later honored by the same university administration that originally had worked with the row to try to see to it that the Unity Party, and Jesse Unruh in particular, would not have any serious influence.

Another part of the picture was the presence of a campus satirist and humorist who was poking fun at everyone in sight—that was Art Buchwald, who is still alive and flourishing. His presence on campus and the kinds of things he wrote were thorns in the side of all campus politicians, regardless of whether they were members of the row or independent.

Another person of that period who was part of the Unity Party, against whom I ran for Associated Students President along with the winner, Johnny Davis, was Joe Flynn. The name may not be memorable to some, but he was the Captain in the *McHale's Navy* television series, the short, flustered officer who had to rely on others to support his behavior and solve his problems.

The university forensic team

In the midst of all of this, perhaps the most active people, some on the row and some not, who took part in student government were the members of the forensic team. The forensic team was made up almost entirely, but not completely, of people who were on tuition scholarships to USC because of prizes and honors they had won in high school forensics competition. Forensics had a high standing on many campuses in those years, and intercollegiate and national competitions were popular among students.

I and my partner, "Buster" (later called "Barney") Coyle, who had also come back to USC from LA City College at the end of the war—we had debated at LA City College together—were two of perhaps only three or four individuals in the history of forensics at USC in the postwar years who were not on scholarship. We were there on the GI Bill, and because we didn't have or need scholarships, we were free to engage in a variety of other activities. Barney concentrated on law school, but we still did a lot of debating together.[5]

When Barney wasn't available, I became a kind of trainer, especially for foreign students who joined the forensics team. Among them was Omar Kureishi, who became a very prominent journalist. He was from India. His partner, Kamal Faruki, was from what was to be Pakistan later on. This lent an international flavor to the forensic team, in which was nurtured a variety of understandings and interests in international matters. So it was natural that out of that group and the people against whom they competed in regional and national argumentation competitions, there would emerge a devotion to freedom of speech and a leaning toward activism.

While a number of debaters at various campuses chose legal careers, many also went into politics. Among those who come to mind from USC are June Louin-Tapp, Al Wiggins, Ed Stegeman, and Lillian Stevens (later a judge), while at UCLA, Frank Mankiewitz was prominent.

My partner on the first trip to Chicago, Anita Norcop, was on the women's section of the debate team. A very conservative Catholic, she was very supportive of the original formation of the NSA. Among the people who later participated in debate, both in and out of forensics, were Howard Kotler, an adversary of NSA (he was one of the people involved in TNE and also a debater); Al Wiggins, who later became Associated Students president; and June Louin-Tapp, who became a faculty member at the University of Minnesota law school and also was a consultant at the University of Chicago, I believe. She was an internationalist, also. These folks were very quick to speak their minds or to raise arguments just for the sake of argument, if nothing else. In general they supported activist student government and participation in NSA as such. That's reflected by some of the stories in the *Daily Trojan* that still are available in print.

NSA participation nationally and regionally

Recalling my participation in NSA, I attended the Chicago Student Conference in 1946, and was part of the constitutional writing group at Madison in 1947. I recall the physical pain when we went for forty-eight hours without sleep in the process of hammering out an early draft of the constitution. It was an eye-opener to me, and I enjoyed the exchange with such a diverse group of students. Many of them came from institutions whose agendas had nothing to do with participation in an American version of an international student movement, which is what I anticipated NSA would become.

I also became active in what was the Southern California section of the California-Nevada-Hawaii regional organization of NSA. As a matter of fact, I served as Chair of it. My memory does not permit me to recall the specifics of these sessions, even though I know that I participated in and presided over meetings that involved students from UCLA and Loyola, I think even Pomona at one point, and certainly LA City College. But it was not effective in mobilizing support for NSA among campuses.[6]

The status of student government and activism

Student government at the university level was pretty rudimentary in those days. In fact, the student government at LA City College was far more vital and able to take positions and do more things off campus than the four-year colleges and universities seemed to be able to do.

It is hard to speculate why this was the case. Perhaps it was a combination of the pre-World War II time and the tradition of student government at LACC. Anti-war sentiment in the'30s was dominant and caused students of lower socioeconomic backgrounds to empathize with social justice causes. Unemployment was a major source of dissatisfaction with the establishment and also led to activism.

Post–World War II students at four-year colleges and universities were concerned with "catching up" for "lost time." In addition, in the 1930s, the traditional student governments at senior colleges and universities were commonly devoted to athletics and social activities. There was not much student government interest in national and international affairs.

Internationalism fostered early NSA support

It is fair to say that one of the reasons why the Chancellor of the University of Southern California who preceded President Fagg, Rufus B. Von Kleinschmidt, originally supported interest in NSA as he did, was that in spite of his political conservatism, he was also an internationalist. There was a school of international relations even at that time at USC, and Von Kleinschmidt was patron to a number of foreign students (many from privileged classes).

We had a large mixture of students who were important to the university and who came from a variety of places, such as India, Africa, the Middle East, South America, and some from Europe as well. They were important in building its reputation in international affairs, and some of them became quite prominent, if not notorious.

One of the people whom I taught to debate in the American style (he had known the English Oxford style) in later years was the prime minister of Pakistan, Zufikar Ali Bhutto (who was later executed). He was known to us as a shy, sweet-mannered, handsome young man we called Zufi. I helped him learn to debate when I was graduate manager of the University forensics team. This traditional USC background of international interest and openness to people of different colors and creeds—even before World War II—was the basis for developing interest in NSA among some faculty and administration. That interest receded when Fred Fagg took office as university President. He was an archetypal "heartland" person of strict fundamentalist religious heritage. He had his bachelor's degree from Redlands University, and he had been an administrator at Northwestern University, both private and conservative institutions. When he came to USC he brought those values and that orientation with him, and it was easy for him to make short shrift of the effort to affiliate with NSA.

On the other hand, Chancellor Von Kleinschmidt would, once in a while, take a surprisingly courageous position. For example, shortly after Pearl Harbor he asked the students of the University to be sure that they did not blame the Nisei who were in attendance at USC for what the Nation of Japan had done.[7] That was a very difficult thing to do on the West Coast in those early years. It was an act which I learned about later and was to me very surprising, because it didn't fit the general culture, which was devoted to what could only be described as "Jap baiting" in Southern California.[8]

Although this is a USC and Southern California memoir, my NSA story would not be complete without reference to the nice relations I enjoyed with Dick Heggie and with other Northern Californians, such as Mildred Kiefer, and Southern Californians such as Gene Tighe, with whom I became acquainted through NSA.[9] In closing, I remain apprehensive that I may be mischaracterizing certain individuals and events based on a memory of affairs transpiring long ago for which I have no concrete evidentiary record. If taken in that spirit, I hope this "snapshot" will help bring alive the general circumstances surrounding NSA and USC during those formative years.

Milton Dobkin is Professor of Speech Emeritus and Vice President for Academic Affairs Emeritus, Humboldt State University, California. He is a member and President of the Board of Trustees, Redwoods Community College District. He has served on the faculty and administration of Humboldt since 1955.

END NOTES

[1] *Editor's note:* Where possible, with all of the essays in this Anthology, we have tried to narrow the range of these uncertainties by two principal means: (1) peer reviews by other former student leaders who were engaged in the events of that period, and (2) reference to supporting documentation out of college archives, NSA files, and student newspapers reports, which can verify names and dates and furnish contemporaneous background.

[2] During the period December 1946–August 1947, the as yet to be formed National Student Association (NSA) was widely referred to as the National Student Organization (NSO).

[3] The delegates, in addition to myself, were John Houk, Diane Lockhart, Paul Wildman, and Pat Hillings.

[4] *Editor's note:* During this period, Alan B. Crow, president of the Detroit Economic Club, a business association, wrote hundreds of college presidents enclosing an eight-page, legal-size outline of "Challenging Questions" as a basis for "further investigation" of the organization. I found an inquiry about NSA addressed to Frank D. Fackenthal, Provost of Columbia University, by A. S. Raubenheimer, educational vice president of USC, dated March 15, 1948, in the Columbiana archives attached to the Crow questionnaire. See Detroit Economic Club and NSA, p. 191.

[5] *Editor's note:* Other debating teams within NSA were the Tom Garrity–Bob Kelley pair at St. Peter's in New Jersey (see Garrity, p. 892), and the Chicago area intercollegiate debating network (see Perkins, p. 943).

[6] 3/25/47: "Five USC representatives, Milt Dobkin, Doral Bennett, Dick Gilson, Fred Knell and student body President, Jim Mitchell, traveled north to attend the [regional] meeting . . . held in Berkeley over the weekend. . . . the two-day parley was attended by 21 colleges and universities and junior colleges. The combined groups sent a total of 53 voting delegates and 53 observers. . . . the delegates went into panel sessions to discuss additions and deletions to the proposed NSO constitution, clarification of ideals and purposes, and suggestions for the betterment of students and student life."

10/8/47: "Representatives from all the southern California universities sending delegates to the national meeting at Madison, and scattered delegations from Northern California, met at Marymount College, Sunday, July 27, to do the necessary preparatory work. . . . a master synopsis . . . was compiled and mimeographed by [Milt] Dobkin, and Jane Wilder and Dick Hough, UCLA."

10/28/47: "A regional constitution was drafted at Stanford last Sunday by representatives of 25 colleges and junior colleges of California. SC delegates were Milt Dobkin, Don Robertson, Diane Lockhart, John Houk, Bill Stevens and Dick Eshelman,... Loyola University of Los Angeles was chosen as the college to house the domestic affairs commission [Gene Tighe, Chair], while Stanford was selected as the base for the international affairs commission [Charles Martin, Chair]. . . . [Regional Cochairmen elected were] Dick Heggie, UC and Dick Hough, UCLA; and secretary, Sally Holt, UC. Bob McCoy, Fresno State was elected Treasurer. Besides [Milt] Dobkin, Virginia Titus, Stanford, and John Speers, San Mateo Junior College, were elected members-at-large [of the Executive Committee]."

[7] While their names have fled from memory, there were three Nisei men I knew at LACC, one an athlete, and two in student government. We worked and "played" together. I was shocked one day at their sudden "absence" and did not learn the reason until weeks later.

[8] *Editor's note:* While visiting Milton Dobkin in 1999 at Humboldt State University, I came upon the following notice on page one of the 12/17/41 issue of the *Humboldt Lumberjack*, "Mutsuhito Club Votes to Change Name of Group." The Club was a women's achievement organization. See also Suzuki, p. 1031, and Miller, p. 717.

[9] See Heggie, p. 199, and Wurf (Kiefer), p. 178.

MILTON DOBKIN

Early Background: I was born and raised in Los Angeles, January 31, 1922. My parents were Morris and Ida Dobkin; my father was an immigrant from Ukraine, my mother, from a village on the Polish-Russian border. I attended Hyde Park Elementary School, Horace Mann Junior High School, and Manual Arts High School. I studied classical piano.

College and Military: I entered Los Angeles City College (LACC) in September 1940. Working on and off campus, I received my A.A. degree in June 1942. I was Associated Students President (1941-42). I also earned a Civil Air Patrol pilot license. During the war I enlisted in the U.S. Navy Air Corps briefly, was discharged after waiting for training, and reenlisted in naval reserve. My active service as a petty officer and aviation instrument specialist was completed in October 1945. I was discharged at war's end as a naval air cadet. At the University of Southern California I received an A.B. in 1949 (Speech, with minors in English and Social Sciences) and an A.M. in 1950 (Speech, with honors). I did advanced graduate work in speech and was Visiting Associate Professor in Speech (1952–1967).

Career Highlights: I acquired a California General Secondary credential, and my professional career began with teaching in secondary high schools (Beverly Hills, David Starr Jordan in Watts, LA; Los Angeles High School), adult evening schools, and LACC part time. In 1955 I moved to Humboldt State College in Arcata, Calif. (now Humboldt State University) for the bulk of my academic professional career. There I have served as Assistant Professor of Speech (1955), Speech Department Coordinator (1958-1960), Language Arts Division Chairman (1960-62), and Assistant Dean for Academic Affairs (1964-66). From 1966 to 1969 1 served as State College Dean, Faculty Affairs, CUSC Chancellor's Office. I was Vice President for Academic Affairs (1969-1984) and served as Acting President during the academic year 1973-74. 1 have also served in numerous university and California system-wide academic curriculum and policy committees, as well as being active in campus and system-wide bodies involving faculty governance and in scholarly associations. During the period 1962-1968 1 held a number of visiting professorships in speech in California and Montana. From 1987 to 1992 I served as President of the California State University Emeritus and Retired Professors Association.

Family: My wife, Bette June (Mattison) Dobkin and I have been married since 1952. We have a daughter and a son and two grandchildren.

PICTURE CREDITS: *Then:* c. 1950. *Now:* c. 2000 (Both, author).

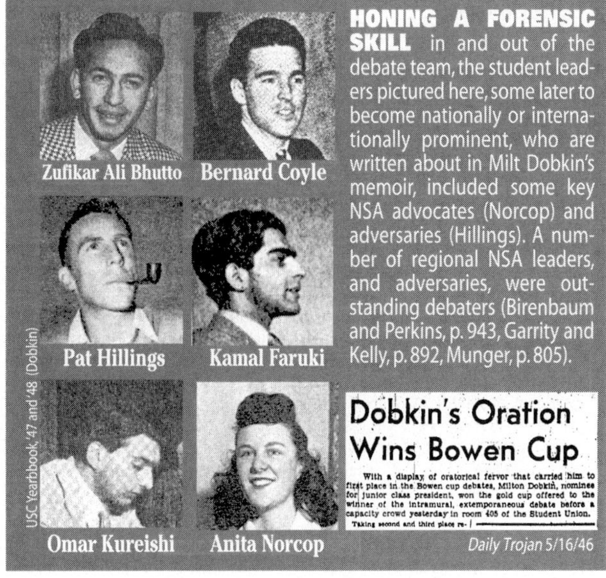

Dobkin's Oration Wins Bowen Cup

With a display of oratorical fervor that carried him to first place in the Bowen cup debates, Milton Dobkin, nominee for junior class president, won the gold cup offered to the winner of the intramural, extemporaneous debate before a capacity crowd yesterday in room 405 of the Student Union.

Taking second and third place re-

Daily Trojan 5/16/46

HONING A FORENSIC SKILL in and out of the debate team, the student leaders pictured here, some later to become nationally or internationally prominent, who are written about in Milt Dobkin's memoir, included some key NSA advocates (Norcop) and adversaries (Hillings). A number of regional NSA leaders, and adversaries, were outstanding debaters (Birenbaum and Perkins, p. 943, Garrity and Kelly, p. 892, Munger, p. 805).

Caught in the "Red Scare" Crossfire, USC Council Wary of NSA

Editor's note: USC's initial student leader and Daily Trojan *enthusiasm for NSA membership was dampened when the newly inaugurated college President in 1948, Fred Fagg, overruled a favorable affiliation vote. State legislative loyalty oath and un-American investigations, reinforced by Richard Nixon's strongly anti-subversive congressional and senate campaigns, created an intimidating atmosphere which lent more effect to the other chief opposition rationale: "the benefit isn't worth the money."*

"The Hue and Cry"

No AYD on Campus—Warren

Dean Bans Possible Troy Political Groups

TROpinion Upholds Right of Free Speech

Students Show Heavy Opposition To Henry Wallace Ban by Bowl

Dean Hits Red Charge

LA POLICE EJECT DT MANAGING EDITOR FROM TENNEY COMMITTEE RED HEARING

Are We Afraid?

Freshman Rep. Richard M. Nixon, R., Calif., would have us believe he has found the answer to communism. In a pamphlet received by the DT, sent to us by Representative Nixon, we are told that the Mundt bill, now before congress, is a panacea designed to protect us from every subversive move made in the United States by "master conspirators."

The bill makes "illegal the knowing and willful advocacy of the overthrow of the government of the United States by any means for the purpose of subverting the interest of the United States to that of a foreign Communist power . . . It is not necessary to prove advocacy of force and violence. It will only be necessary to prove knowing and willful participation in the foreign-directed Communist conspiracy . . ."

What are we afraid of, Representative Nixon? Are we afraid that our way of life cannot be defended before the onslaught of militant communism? Or are we afraid to remove the causes of communism? Are we afraid to tackle the job of combatting inflation, the job of housing, of health, and a myriad of other problems which are the very breeding ground upon which communism can take root and sprout like Jack's beanstalk?

We must be afraid of something to continue this hue and cry day after day, week after week, month after month. And Americans aren't accustomed to being afraid, Representative Nixon. We have a long, proud heritage that we are willing and able to defend against any ideology you can name. And we don't have to stuff a gag into the other fellow's mouth to do it either.

From top, clockwise: 4/18/47, 4/29/47, 2/18/48, 4/8/48. Left: 5/10/48 editorial by Jerry Maher (excerpted) concluded, "The plan offered by you and your committee is the totalitarian method."

"WHAT ARE WE AFRAID OF?," the *Trojan* asked Rep. Nixon, who advanced the Mundt bill which would make "illegal the knowing and willful advocacy of the overthrow" of the government for subversive purposes. Fear of subversive speech or membership drove restrictions and investigations (p. 380).

USC ASKS COLUMBIA FOR ADVICE ON NSA

UNIVERSITY OF SOUTHERN CALIFORNIA
LOS ANGELES 7

March 15, 1948

Dr. Frank D. Fackenthal, Columbia University
Dear Dr. Fackenthal:

We at the University of Southern California are faced with a divided student opinion as to the University's affiliation with the National Student Association.

We are informed that Columbia University is a member of the National Student Association . . . [I] am very anxious to learn what the attitude of your administration is toward the National Student Association and your experience to date with the character of its activities.

President Fagg asked me to try to get the reactions of the Columbia University administration. . . .

A.S. Raubenheimer, Educational Vice President

Columbia University
New York 27, N.Y.

March 30, 1948

Dear Dr. Raubenheimer:

. . . The Columbia University Student Council has ratified the constitution of the National Student Association on both the national and regional levels. To date, however, no dues have been paid and consequently the Columbia student body does not have actual membership in the [NSA]. The administration has been following the development of the [NSA] rather closely, but has neither recognized nor refused to recognize the organization. . . . Affiliation with the [NSA] was approved by the Council without resort to a student referendum.

. . . I will be happy to exchange information with you at a later date, however, after we have had further experience with this organization.

Albert C. Jacobs, Provost

(Source: Columbiana archives, Columbia University. See p. 865 for NSA at Columbia.)

All Politics Is Local

1945

PRESIDENT DISSOLVES SENATE

Extent of order not certain; Scott cancels nomination assembly; registration hits 1800

ADMINISTRATION LIFTS BAN ON ASSC

Spring voting plans proceed

All-U program set for Troy

Fraternities Prosper

Recently Completed Survey Sees Greek Organizations in Boom Era

BOB PADGETT WINS

Non-Orgs Push in First Student Body President in 27 Years

Fr. top: 5/14/45, 5/22/45, 6/11/46, 9/29/49

1949

EXISTENCE OF A SECRET POLITICAL FRATERNITY led long-time President Rufus B. Klensmid to suspend student government, the first such intervention in 20 years. The issue resolved, four years later the first Independent study body president in 27 years was elected (see Dobkin, p. 1025).

AS A SIDE-BAR, 1945 "ALL-U PROGRAM" (above) announced the appearance of a Danish and U.S. student in an ASSC Assembly to "discuss unity of the world" at the World Youth Conference to be held in London that summer, a predecessor event to the World Student Congress in 1946 that led to the formation of NSA (see Dowd, p. 60).

1946

Sift Politics, Dobkin Asks

Junior President Proposes Probe

Dobkin Lights Political Fires In SC Senate

Dobkin Proposes Bipartisan Senate Vet Seat Amendment

Persons Names Homecoming Contest Judges

Measure Giving Franchise Awaits Debate, Ratification

UNRUH WINS VET SEAT; SENATE OKAY

Turner to Speak At SC Assembly

Solons Discuss Written Rules For SC Groups

Dobkin Praises Prom Combo

MILTON DOBKIN stood between the two traditional student parties. A veteran himself, he supported independent representation for the 9,000 veterans as a further campus political counterforce (Dobkin, p. 1025).

Jesse Unruh (abv, left) became "the Big Daddy" of the California State Legislature.

Clockwise fr "Dobkin Lights": 10/16/46, 9/19/46, 10/31/46, 12/13/46.

1946 Fr left: 12/17/46, 3/25/47 1947

Norcop, Dobkin To Represent SC at Chicago

Dobkin Rides Again

NSO Selects Troy As Panel Location

LAS Council Plans Forum

Below: 2/20/48, 4/29/48 1948

Senate Approves NSA Affiliation After Stormy Debate

President Vetoes NSA

1950

Below: 5/12/50, 10/12/50

AL WIGGINS ELECTED

Senate Debates NSA Powder-Keg

THE STUDENT BODY PRESIDENCY changed hands again with the Wiggins election in May. His GUP party voted against NSA affiliation. Opposition was largely grounded in a feeling that NSA was "pinkish" and would add little benefit to the ASSC.

Senate Hears NSA Leader Deny Red Ties

Students May Aid

Senate Nixes NSA Votes 20-5 Against Joining Organization

5/20/50

NSA PRESIDENT BOB KELLY received a standing ovation from the ASSC Council.

Historical note: In 1879 Los Angeles Judge Robert Maclay Widney formed a board of trustees and secured a donation of 308 acres of land as both a site and an endowment from three prominent members of the community, a Protestant horticulturalist, an Irish-Catholic pharmacist and businessman and a German-Jewish banker and philanthropist. USC first opened its doors to 53 students and 10 teachers in 1880 (www.usec.edu/about). 1948 enrollment: 20,454 (12th largest in the U.S.).

Out of the internment camps and onto the campus

2. Los Angeles City College and NSA in 1949–1951

Tom Suzuki

Student Body President, Los Angeles City College 1951
Delegate to NSA Third National Student Congress, Michigan, 1950

Looking back, I have no clear recollection as to how or why I got involved in student politics at Los Angeles City College (LACC)—except perhaps as a natural expression of my enthusiasm and a certain inclination to connect with the wider world.

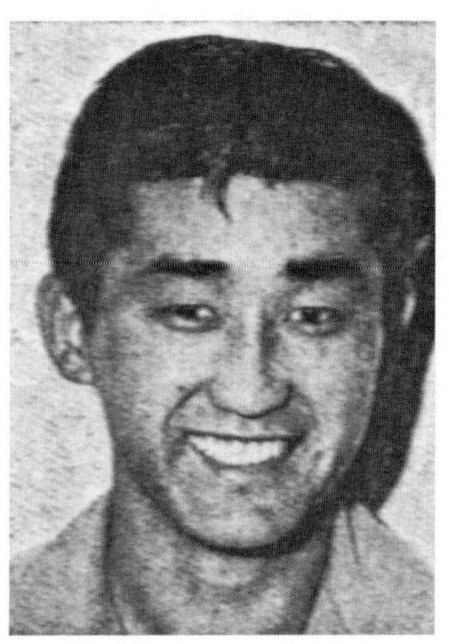

Whatever the reasons for getting involved in student politics, it's clear as I leaf through clippings from our student newspaper, the *Los Angeles Collegian*, for the school years 1949–1950 and 1951, that I was deeply involved. I served as a member of the Associated Students (AS) Executive Council, as AS vice president, as a delegate to the NSA Convention at the University of Michigan in August of 1950, and as student body president in the spring of 1951.

Detour to the internment camps

I got to LACC by way of a detour to internment camps for over three years during World War II and a move to Illinois for a year, while we were allowed to leave camp but not allowed to return to the Pacific coast.

I was the next-to-the-youngest of eight children growing up in Compton, California, on the family vegetable farm. We had moved to the farm about 1936. Like so many other families, we were recovering from the depths of the Great Depression. The farm had rich soil and good irrigation. Although the effects of the Depression were still evident everywhere, the farm was a promise of better things to come. Still, there were lots of family stories about my mother and oldest brother going to work on a larger neighboring farm for a dollar a day for work from sunup until sundown. And I remember my family packing celery heads twelve to a crate and selling them for a nickel. Twelve to a crate meant they were prize heads of celery. A loaf of bread was a nickel. So that translated into a lot of time, resources, and labor to buy one loaf of bread for a family of ten.

My parents and older siblings persevered, and by 1941 we had begun to climb out of the devastation of the Depression. We owned a car and a truck in addition to farm equipment. We were doing well enough that the family could take day trips to the beach on Saturdays in the summer—Saturdays because Sundays were picking days. The wholesale markets needed to be supplied for the Monday trade. I remember coming home from church with my younger brother on December 7, 1941, and being irritated that all the usual Sunday radio programs we were eager to listen to were being interrupted by news about an attack on a place I had never heard of called Honolulu. We finally went out to the fields to complain to my older brothers about the interruptions. I explained what little I could interpret of the news. I remember that the elders of the family then rushed to the house to hear the broadcasts for themselves. I don't remember whether my brother and I followed them or simply stayed in the field to play.

Tulare Racetrack and Gila River

In the resultant hysteria and anti-Oriental climate, President Franklin D. Roosevelt signed Executive Order 9066, which gave the War Department authority to remove people of Japanese ancestry from coastal areas. First there were curfews and travel restrictions. In the late spring of 1942, we were shipped out to camps. The notice to prepare for evacuation came with very little time to settle our affairs. One could only take what could be carried, which meant a suitcase or bundle for each adult and a smaller one for each young child. We were sent to Tulare racetrack in the San Joaquin Valley to live in horse stalls. Tulare was one of a number of Assembly Centers hurriedly converted to house the 120,000 evacuees of Japanese ancestry while more permanent internment centers were built. The camp was a prison surrounded by barbed wire with armed guards in towers.

After a summer at Tulare, our family was interned at Gila River, Arizona, on an Indian reservation in the desert outside

Phoenix. Gila River was one of ten internment camps scattered from Arizona to Arkansas. Gila River consisted of two camps. The camps consisted of blocks of sixteen tar-papered barracks each, which served as living quarters. In addition, each block had a mess hall, men's and women's toilet and shower units, a laundry room, and a recreation hall. Each barrack was typically divided into four family units. Each family unit was one, undivided room. We subdivided the area into what passed for rooms by draping sheets and blankets over ropes stretched out like clotheslines. We were given bunkbeds, mattresses, and blankets. There was no other furniture, although I remember ultimately having a table and some chairs. I don't recall whether they were store-bought or cobbled together out of scrap lumber. Probably the latter.

Outwardly, life for teenagers was typical of the time — school, sports, other leisure time activities, including Boy and Girl Scouts, clubs of one sort or another and outdoor movies when the weather permitted.

During the early years in camp, those who were of age had to swear allegiance to the United States or be deported. Having sworn allegiance to the country, anyone of age suddenly was eligible for the draft. So three of my brothers were drafted out of camp. One had been drafted before we were sent to camp. I always found it somewhat strange that we were in that place, and yet they were drafting all the young men into the Army. As naive as I was, it all seemed a little incongruous to me. As an adult, I realized how extraordinarily ironic it was.

In late 1944, we were able to leave camp but not allowed to return to the West Coast, so my younger brother and I moved to Illinois with my parents. My four older brothers were still in the service with the U.S. Army in Europe and in Japan. One sister had left camp shortly before us to work with the Internal Revenue Service in Washington, D.C., and my oldest sister was in another camp with her husband and family. In Illinois my dad had arranged a job as caretaker of a Girl Scout summer camp, Camp Cutten, about sixty miles north of Chicago, just south of Waukegan. I started my freshman year in high school at Antioch High School.

Culture shock in both directions

It turned out that my brother and I were about the only non-whites in our schools. It was a flashback to before the war, when he and I were about the only Japanese-Americans in an otherwise all-white elementary school. So we both relived the culture shock of going from a predominately all-white society to an all-Japanese one, back to an all-white culture again. But the transition was made easy by the friendly reception of everyone we met. For my part, I soon felt absolutely at home. The year we spent in Illinois before we were allowed to return to California is one of my happiest teenage memories.

When we finally returned to California, we had nothing but our personal belongings. We had no home; we owned no property. We fell on the charity of the Buddhist church of Gardena, a suburb of Los Angeles, where we lived in a hostel for several months until we could get ourselves together and rent a place to live.

We were among the fortunate. Most of our personal things had been held for safekeeping by our prewar landlord and were intact. Many others lost even their family belongings. My father went back to work in Gardena. We began to put down roots. My brothers began returning from the Army. My father acquired a little bit of property. (I have no idea where he came by the resources to buy property.) My brothers went to work. My father started a wholesale nursery, and we began the long, slow recovery from the internment.

LA City College (LACC) and NSA

I graduated from Dorsey High School in Los Angeles. My interest in student politics had its start there. I was student body vice president for boys in my senior year.

A few things stand out for me about my time at LACC. NSA was a very active presence on the campus and occasionally a subject of lively controversy. The foundation for the organization at LACC was set by K. Wallace Longshore, a popular LACC and Southern California regional student leader. Later, in 1954, he became a NSA national vice president while he was a student at the University of California at Lost Angeles (UCLA).[1]

Another personality who passed through LACC and served on the Student Council while I was there was Bob Munger. He was an LACC debate team champion who went on to become founder of the National Collegiate MacArthur Club in 1952. Munger was a leading campus critic of NSA and at one point persuaded the student council to investigate NSA as a lobbying group. He was my opponent when I was elected student body president in January of 1951.[2]

We took NSA seriously, as the *Collegian* reveals. I recall that NSA's Student Bill of Rights was a major item at the Michigan Congress and the subject of my report to the students on my return. I was student body vice president at the time. My fellow delegates, student body president George Rogers, Matt Suddleson, and Earl Wilson, reported on the other major commissions dealing with international, educational, and student affairs.

I recall, even now, being awed by the level of accomplishment and awareness of the student leaders I met at the NSA conventions, and especially in Michigan the summer of 1950. Not only by Allard Lowenstein of North Carolina, who was elected president that summer, and Bob Kelly from St. Peter's in New Jersey, who was the outgoing president, but many others.[3] They were so clearly engaged and informed about the major issues of the time. I think it was my first brush with really knowledgeable students at a high level. It made a lasting impression.

I was impressed, not only because I was coming from a City College, but because my own background had not prepared me for that level of intensity. For a long time afterward, I followed their progress as much as I could. I especially remember Lowenstein being involved in the civil rights issues of the day. NSA had an influence. LA City College was actively involved, and we believed in the value of NSA. We were not without our nay-sayers, but we remained a member and sent delegates to the regional and national meetings. NSA was our connection to the wider intercollegiate community and the student issues of the day.

Student protest leads to resignations

LACC was an urban campus near downtown LA populated largely by day-hop students and students working while putting themselves through school. They were from working-class families, so most of their energy was expended in their studies. Few students seemed interested in, or had time for, larger student issues. We had a somewhat middling sports program. We had a full-fledged newspaper and all the accoutrements of a college, but most of the students were much too busy for extracurricular activities.[4]

The concerns of the student government were parochial issues such as which social events were to take place and the rules for the conduct of such events. It had some say in the athletic program and the rights of students in campus social life. The student council approved the charters—and activities—of service clubs and other student organizations. Against that background, the reaction of the Executive Council to a prohibition against the discussion of a larger philosophical issue was a surprise to many.

While I was a Student Council member in March of 1950, the University of California Loyalty Oath issue was commanding attention everywhere, and the matter was brought before the Executive Council for debate. *The Collegian* quotes the LACC president, Dr. Howard S. McDonald, as feeling that the action of the Regents and University of California faculty was not a concern of students at LACC. Therefore, McDonald prohibited the Executive Council from discussing the issue.

Members of the Executive Council were incensed. As a result, all but one of the twelve members of the Council—and a number of other student leaders—resigned in protest. The latter included Mark Gilman, the AS president, as well as Bob Munger, rally chairman and my future opponent for the student body presidency, and Earl Wilson, NSA coordinator. *The Collegian* headline added, "AS Government Future Uncertain." The Council adopted a lengthy resolution, which said in part that "these recent policies of the administration have destroyed any real functions of the student government and have made it impossible for the student government to properly represent the student body of Los Angeles City College."

My decision was surely informed by my exposure to NSA. Although we believed fervently, the walkout wasn't precipitate: there was a lengthy debate among student leaders before the decision was taken. The walkout received widespread press coverage throughout the city.

The Collegian reports that negotiations between the administration and students began the next day, and by April 21, a month later, a settlement had been reached, with the students returning to their offices and the administration lifting its ban on discussions. President McDonald is quoted as saying, "This has brought us closer together," and both sides acknowledged that the action and reaction was perhaps too hasty.

The Korean War, the GI Bill, and graduation

After graduating LA City College with an Associate of Arts degree, I joined the Air Force and went through basic training and then waited out my cadet application. After some nine months' wait and six months of cadet training, I was commissioned a second lieutenant. I was assigned to Japan and spent two and a half years as a radar observer in all-weather jet fighters during the height of the Korean conflict. After the Korean War ended in 1954, I spent another six months in Japan before returning to the States to finish out my Air Force stint in Portland, Oregon.

With my service completed, I married Virginia Kawasaki, whom I had met when she worked in the offices of the Deans of Student Affairs at LACC. I returned to Chouinard Art Institute—now the California Institute of Fine Arts—on the GI Bill to get my B.F.A.

So my college education was spread over about eight years. Some of the most memorable were the two years at Los Angeles City College. Most of my interests in politics and public policy were nurtured there. NSA was a huge part of my political and social awakening.

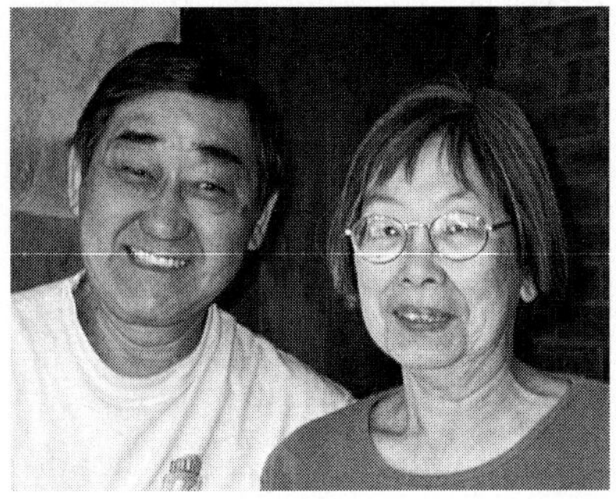

Tom Suzuki, shown here with his wife, Virginia, is on the faculty of the Stanford University Alumni Association Professional Publishing Program and runs his own design studio in Fairfax, VA. He served as art director of Time-Life Books and CRM Books.

END NOTES

[1] See Longshore, p. 1035.

[2] See Munger and Students for America, p. 805.

[3] See Kelly, p. 252, and Lowenstein, p. 283.

[4] *Editor's note:* Other "day-hop" institutions of the time that serve as the sites for memoirs in the work include City College of New York (see Schwartz, p. 847), St. Peter's, N.J. (see p. 892), St. Joseph's, Pa. (see Dungan, p. 909), Simmons College, Mass. (see Neizer, p.832), Trinity College, Washington, D.C. (see O'Connell, p. 922), University of Buffalo (See Jones, p. 862), and Mundelein College, Ill. (see Perkins, p. 942).

PICTURE CREDITS: *Then:* 1950 (Los Angeles *Collegian*, p. 4, 12/8/50. *Now:* March, 1999 (Schwartz).

THOMAS SUZUKI

Born: February 16, 1930, Brawley, California

Education: 1945, Antioch High School, Illinois. 1946, Gardena High School, California. 1947-48, Dorsey High School, Los Angeles, California. 1948-1951, Los Angeles City College, California. 1956-58, Chouinard Art Institute (now California School of Fine Arts), Los Angeles, California.

Military: 1951-56, 1st lieutenant, U.S. Air Force, Fukuoka, Japan, and Portland, Oregon.

Career Highlights: 1959-1964, Assistant Art Director, General Dynamics Astronautics, San Diego, California. 1964-1970, Suzuki and Wright, graphic design firm, San Diego, California. 1970-74, Art Director, CRM books, Del Mar, California. 1974-76, Art Director, Clareville Publishing, London, England. 1976-1982, Art Director, Time-Life Books, Alexandria, Virginia. 1982-present, Art Director, Tom Suzuki, Inc., graphic design firm, Falls Church and Fairfax, Virginia.

Family: 1956, Married to Virginia Kawasaki. 1967 and 1970, adopted two children from Japan, John David Suzuki and Mariko Suzuki.

A Tom Suzuki/Los Angeles City College Album

Editor's note: Los Angeles City College in 1948 was a two-year commuter college that also provided a gateway to later professional degrees for working students. It was the starting point for many prominent entertainment and public figures in the state. Its student newspaper and many campus leaders embraced NSA enthusiastically. A cohort of campus leaers also opposed the association for alleged communist leanings. Tom Suzuki, as a Council member and candidate for student body president, was drawn into this crossfire.

Council Consideration of 1950 Loyalty Oath Leads to Clash with Administration

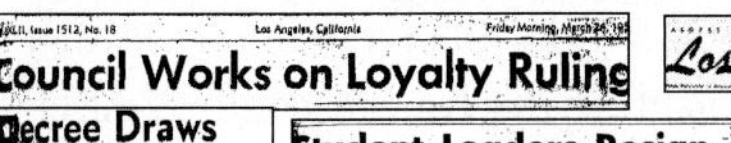

Los Angeles Collegian

Council Works on Loyalty Ruling

Decree Draws Legislative Fire

Student Leaders Resign in Protest

16 Object to Administrative Rules; A.S. Government Future Uncertain

Vets Protest Loss of Office

Above: 3/24/50, 3/27/50

THE 1950 LOYALTY OATH requirement for UC faculty provoked sympathetic debate in the Student Council. LACC at first ruled against the right of the Council to place the issue on its agenda.

Right: 3/29/50. Below: 4/21/50

Resigned Councilmen Confer With Dr. McDonald

Dr. Mc Donald Reinstates Students

Administration Accepts Council's Request As Resignees Return to Official Positions

Fr l. Howard S. McDonald, Mark Gilman.

Leaders Deny Red Leanings

Members Request Privilege Of Free Voice at Meetings

COUNCIL MEETS AGAIN

Government Resumes Business With Free Discussion Assured

MARK GILMAN, student body president, Tom Suzuki, Finance Chairman, Tom Munger, an NSA opponent, joined 13 others in resigning in protest. Students and administration later reached an agreement "as friends" with assurances of "free discussion" in Student Executive Council meetings (see loyalty oaths, p. 1046).

Delegates Report on 1950 NSA Congress

Suddleson Reports on NSA Com[...]

Students Discuss Health Welfa[...]

From left: 10/11/50, 10/18/50

Suzuki Reports NSA Action On Academic Bill of Rights

"When a student enters academic society, he acquires a right to those goods which are necessary for the attainment of the end of academic society," Suzuki explained in his report.

Council Debates Instructing Delegates

NSA Issues Cause Long Battle In Executive Council Session

Politicos Aim Fire At Delegate's Report

Exhibits Feature Native's Culture

TOM SUZUKI, A.S. vice president, presided over the committee of the whole into which the council dissolved for N.S.A. reports.

Council Erupts Over NSA Question

From left: 12/8/50, 10/27/50

Bob Munger led support for limiting LACC delegate voting freedom at regional assemblies and for an investigation of NSA.

Suzuki Goes for the Gold

Students Accept, Refuse Constitution, Forum Discusses Party Platforms

Munger, Suzuki Head Contest

Town Hall Airs Political Issues

Fr l. Tom Suzuki, Ed Barkett, Bob Munger

Above: 1/10/51. Below: 1/15/51

TOM SUZUKI, (later art director at Time-Life Books), defeated Munger and voiced "the hope that more students will take an active interest in student government." Bob Munger went on to form Students for MacArthur and the national anti-NSA movement, Students for America (see p. 805).

Suzuki Triumphs by Landslide Vote

ECA Chief Outlines Methods Toward International Peace

Student Ticket Takes Seven Council Seats

An LACC/Southern California Chronicle

As reported in the *Los Angeles Collegian*

9/16/47 Students Find Representation With National Student Association.
It would appear that City College, growing fast and furious, would benefit from representation on NSA - Editorial

12/2/47 Council Postpones Action on National Student Group

2/20/48 NSA Delay Prods Action, Investigation

3/20/48 NSA 'Commie Front'—Dr. Jacobson
Dr. Einar Jacobson, President of LACC, says there is reason to believe it so.

3/19/48 City College Assured Benefits from NSA—Editorial

4/2/48 President Gives "Green Light" to NSA Membership

4/16/48 Executive Council Slates NSA Election for June

6/2/48 Voters Approve NSA Issue in Near Record Turnout (826-343)

9/21/48 California Delegates Storm NSA Wisconsin Convention

9/28/48 NSA Meets for-Sub Regional Conference (at LACC).
LACC committee: Arnie Gordon, Gloria de la Valle, Sumner Sweet, K. Wallace Longshore, Norman Dash, Frank Cook, Russell Grigory.

11/16/48 King Reports NSA Meeting to Council.
Weekend regional at Berkeley. Delegates: Dick Docter, Betty Jo Hamilton, K. Wallace Longshore, Dorothy Andrews, Bob Docter

11/19/48 Council Votes for Increased NSA Activities.
Committees on foreign student orientation, student-faculty relations, vocational guidance, intercollegiate cultural exchange, purchase card, public relations

12/14/48 Executive Council Establishes Groundwork for NSA Group

3/25/49 NSA Formulates Low Price Plan

4/22/49 NSA Slates Travel Plan for Mexico, Summer Study

5/6/49 Council Debates NSA Issue.
AS President, Dick Docter calls special meeting to reverse LACC delegation's academic freedom stand and require instructed delegates. Defeated by 4-3 margin.

6/1/49 NSA Acts as Student Representative to National, International Organizations

10/7/49 NSA Region Debate. Longshore Officiates During Purchase Card Speech.

10/21/49 Longshore Greets Delegates at NSA Regional Conference
Newspaper Editors Gather During Weekend Meeting. Northern and Southern California colleges.

10/28/49 NSA Implementation Congress Approves New Classroom Techniques, Discussions.

11/18/49 Council Forms Student Board for Closer NSA Cooperation

3/3/50 Students Make Applications for NSA Summer Tours

3/17/50 Legislators Analyze Oath, Peace Motions. Kelly Speaks at Luncheon.
1949-50 NSA President Robert Kelly speaker at a luncheon-reception in his honor.

9/29/50 Legislators Hear Delegate Report on NSA Meet
George Rogers, AS President, Tom Suzuki, vice president, Matt Suddleson and Earl Wilson deliver Michigan Congress report

10/18/50 Suzuki Reports NSA Action on Academic Bill of Rights

10/27/50 Council Erupts Over NSA Question
Issue of whether NSA should have a vote on the Council and whether NSA delegates should be instructed how to vote at Sacramento student government conference.

1/12/51 Speakers Hit Political Issues
Tom Suzuki (Student Ticket party) and Bob Munger (College Advancement Party) vie for Presidency. Munger attacks Suzuki support for NSA.

1/15/51 Suzuki Triumphs by Landslide Vote

4/27/51 Lowenstein Explains Importance of NSA
1950-51 NSA President Al Lowenstein to Executive Council: UMT will be a big issue this summer.

9/17/51 Three Hold Key to NSA
Melba Meloy, Ralph Ybarra and Dion Morrow, delegates to the Minnesota Congress, will have to "prove that NSA can benefit the campus" or LACC might very well drop its membership.

9/25/51 NSA On Trial—Editorial
"NSA is the organization that makes us an integral part of the voice of student America"

10/5/51 NSA Sponsors "World Opinion"

LACC Provides Regional and National NSA Leaders

Milton Dobkin, 1940-42/1946

Los Angeles Collegian

12/10/41

Dobkin Calls Defense Council

An Editorial

Declaration of War Rouses Student Leader to Action; Emergency Steps Taken

Alumni Elect Committees; Plan Drive

LACC Hosts Oratory Meet

Photo: Dobkin 4/26/46

MILTON DOBKIN, student body president at LACC during Pearl Harbor. After the war, he entered USC under the GI Bill, where he became an NSA leader (see p. 1025). He returned to LACC in March 1946 to help form the new Alumni Association. He also became a statewide oratory winner, at a competition held in April at LACC.

K. Wallace Longshore, 1949-52

Longshore Greets Delegates At NSA Regional Conference

Newspaper Editors Gather During Weekend Meeting

Panel Presents European View

SOUTH OF THE BORDER

Longshore Instructs Seminar In Basic Parliamentary Law

Longshore Tells Aids to Leaders At Next Seminar

Photos, fr l. Longshore, Student Body President, Sumner Sweet, NSA Rep.

From top: 10/21/49, 12/2/49, 5/1/50

Council Votes New Policy; Motion Revises NSA Stand

Peace Session Stresses Unity

Council Attracts College Interest

Holmes Announces Requirements For Entrance Into State College

Panel Discusses Trade Benefits

Linguists Give Joint Installation

Photo: Longshore. From top: 5/9/49, 5/22/50

WALLY LONGSHORE brought wide-ranging talents to leadership roles at LACC, Cal State and then UCLA, becoming a legislative press aide, a publicist and writer in later life— unimpeded by the loss of both legs to diabetes in more recent years. As 1954 NSA National Affairs Vice President, he helped expand NSA's student government leadership programs. At LACC, Longshore established NSA as a service and advocacy organization. In May of 1949 (above), he led the LACC student council factions to unite on a resolution supporting academic freedom at the University of Washington (see p. 1061), while defining a limited basis for dismissal.

Linked to National, World Concerns, LACC Brings NSA into Its Orbit

USO Assembly Opens Final Bond Drive

Los Angeles Collegian

Navy Men Appear On Victory Program

Lt. Walter Graniki, 'I Wouldn't Stay Captured' Author, Gives Talk to Cubs on War Experiences

Look Out Vaqueros, Here We Come

Cubs Play Host to Esther Williams

Enrollment Figure Approaches 4000 Mark As Registration of Men Students Doubles

Alpha Women Crowd City College Campus

Rushing Alpha Women Find Time to Talk

Color-Wise Coeds Wear Bright Hues

President Ev... Calls AWS

Stinson Forecasts Record 10,000 Enrollment; Diehl Schedules 1325 Classes for Semester

Sacramento 'Fiddles' While Veterans 'Burn'

25 New Instructors Join CC Faculty Day Forces

School Group Investigates Veteran Housing Conditions

Hollywood Talent Launches WSSF Drive

Los Angeles Collegian

FINALS

Left: "USO": 11/6/45. "Finals": 1/15/46. "4,000": 9/11/45. "Alpha": 9/11/45. School: 2/19/46. "10,000": 2/4/47. "WSSF": 12/3/48

Move Toward Democracy Via Student Government

6/11/46

Why was there so little interest displayed by the majority of City College students in the recently postponed Associated Students elections? Is it lack of school spirit? Is it a feeling of hopelessness caused by the administration's allegedly heavy-handed control of the student government?

Taking the first point, lack of school spirit, unfortunately, implies lack of pride in City College, which comes right down to lack of pride in ourselves, for we, you and I, are City College. Without us, City College would be as lifeless as an assortment of 'empty warehouses. But it is alive, because you and I are alive. But do we act like it?

Let us look at the activities of the past few weeks. The only election of the term was postponed until next fall because

To Combat Communism, Eliminate What Causes It

1/15/46

According to numerous raucous and all-too-widely heard factions and publications in the United States, the prime problem confronting the country, even over full employment, reconversion, etc., is the everlasting fight against the "Red menace." According to them, we are missing the greatest bet of our life by not taking advantage of the atomic bomb and our superior military strength to destroy finally this vile excresence on the science of economics and the practice of government.

The trouble with those who remain so vociferously, and at times boringly, anti-Communist, is that they fail to realize the correct means of fighting communism. Their demands for forcible suppression are typically short-sighted and at great variance with a logical appraisal of the situation.

First, communism thrives on suppression. The violent measures taken in all capitalist countries to down this rising tide welded the dissident elements making up the movement

AFTER THE WAR

LACC's HOLLYWOOD LOCATION provided access to star talent for its celebrations and causes—and also served as an alma mater (Esther Williams, above) for many of those same stars. The college experienced explosive enrollment growth in the few years following the war; the dominance of women in campus life evidenced in the *Collegian's* headlines gave way to the return of veterans and male-dominated athletics.

ADVOCATING FOR STUDENT GOVERNMENT and more student participation, the *Collegian* wonders if apathy is due to "lack of school spirit" or "the administration's allegedly heavy-handed control of student government." In an earlier editorial, the paper addressed "the everlasting fight against the 'red menace,'" suggesting "they fail to realize the correct means of fighting Communism."

LACC: Engaged in National and World Affairs

From left: 4/21/48, 3/17/50, 5/16/51

Students Rout Speakers at UMT Demonstration

Council Supports Resolution Favoring International Peace

Club Debates Labor Issues

Rogers Starts Mobilization

Kismet Reveals Working Groups For Conference

Student Speaks Four Tongues, Plans To Teach

Voters View UMT At Spring Election

NSA Voices Poll Results

WAR, PEACE AND CIVIL RIGHTS (below) were among issues that engaged students. Pro-UMT students who broke up a small anti-UMT rally in 1948 "sullied a principle upon which our nation is based," the *Collegian* wrote.

USA Goes on 'Equality' Week While Crosses Burn in Georgia

3/6/51

Rally Concludes Freedom Crusade

10/2/50

Students Attend Final Program; Wanger Speaks

3/13/51

Another Frankenstein?

Historical note: Los Angeles Junior College was established in 1929 by the Los Angeles Board of Education. In 1931 it became part of a separate LA Junior College District. In 1938 its name was changed to Los Angeles City College. In 1969 the LA Community College District was separated from the LA Unified School District (www.lacitycollege.edu). 1948 enrollment: 10,038.

NSA Comes to LACC

3/48

NSA 'Commie Front'--Dr. Jacobsen; Collegian Gains Tri-Weekly Status

Budget Gets Council Okay

Paper Sets New Policy

GEORGE KAPLAN, councilman, refuted Dr. Jacobsen's comment that he believed the N.S.A. was

BOB HEIDERICH, Collegian executive editor, claims tri-weekly paper will insure adequate

CLEARANCE BY THE BOARD OF EDUCATION and California Junior College Assn. led to Presidential reversal (in contrast to the USC ban, p. 1030). *The Collegian* found "it was impossible to find a single student prepared to write against" NSA (3/19/48 below).

President Gives 'Green' Light to NSA Membership

9/28/49

3/9/48

City College Assured Benefits From N.S.A.

Despite the most diligent efforts of the editorial staff of the Collegian, it was found impossible to find a single student prepared to write against the National Student Association.

Therefore, the original plan to present a "pro" and "con" on the N.S.A. had to be abandoned. We present, instead, some of the predominant points in favor of City College joining this organization.

Since this is an issue of some importance at this time, we invite comments and suggestion from anyone who feels strongly on the subject.

THE EDITORS

Aspirants Vie For NSA Post At Conclave

LOU FRANKLIN, veteran councilman, was instrumental in obtaining Dr. Jacobsen's approval for National Students Association.

Dr. Jacobsen Delivers Okay To Council

6/1/49

5/8/51

NSA Recognition Brings National Student Voice

N.S.A.—fish or fowl?

If put to most students, this question would have little or no meaning. The problems of N.S.A. recognition by the average student have been great, with only a few realizing the extent of the workings of the organization.

The National Students Association is, first and foremost, the only composite body through which

NSA Works as Link Between Colleges

5/18/49

Operation Amigos Boosts Actual Friendships

To National, International Organizations

NSA Meets for Sub Regional Conference

4/2/48

Panel Views Aid to Britain

Group Uses Local Campus For Session

3/17/50

Legislators Analyse Oath, Peace Motions

Executive Council Tables Loyalty Inquiry Question; DaValle, Young, DeWitt, Lead Opposition Fight

4/27/51

President Speaks To Exec Council

Lowenstein Explains Importance of NSA; House Rules Committee Members Named

NSA PRESIDENTS Bob Kelly ('49-'50) and Al Lowenstein ('50-'51) both visited and addressed the LACC student council. The war in Korea, related peace movement and universal military training issues were on their agendas. NSA supported the Korean War in 1950 (pp. 265-267), and UMT in 1951; opposed UMT in 1952 (p. 371).

More albums on LACC and NSA: pp. 1034, 1035

The World War II Internment of Japanese Americans

American Refugees: The Japanese-American Relocation

Excerpted from the American Friends Service Committee Web site, www.afsc.org/hist/2002/japanam.htm. (More on AFSC, p. 679.)

Soon after the Japanese attack on Pearl Harbor in 1941, the United States government began a program of relocating people of Japanese ancestry who lived on the West Coast. Some 110,000 people—citizens and non-citizens—were interned. After the evacuation, the AFSC, under the signature of Clarence Pickett, its executive secretary, released a statement to members of the Religious Society of Friends stating, "... we should share in such ways as our limited resources permit in breaking the force of this calamity which has come upon the Japanese population."

The American Friends Service Committee's quick reaction to the internment at the beginning of World War II is not surprising. The reason lies in the history of the Service Committee and the Religious Society of Friends, and the particular interest of Clarence Pickett.

Clarence Pickett was the youngest child of a large family. His sister, Minnie Pickett, left the family farm to go to Japan as a missionary ... and later married a fellow missionary, Gilbert Bowles. She and Gilbert spent forty-five years of missionary work in Japan. Clarence Pickett was fascinated by his sister's descriptions of Japan and ... retained his interest in Japan.

Before Clarence Pickett became the AFSC executive secretary in 1929, the Service Committee was involved in trying to address the tremendous resentment caused by the Japanese exclusion clause in the Immigration Act of 1924. ... [and] missionaries from the Philadelphia Mission Board had helped establish a Quaker presence in Japan....

All of these strands created connections that produced a vigorous effort to help Japanese-Americans ... removed to camps in the interior states of the West and as far to the East as Arkansas by the end of 1942....

Two programs were established to help get people out of internment camps. The first, which started almost immediately, was an effort to find colleges and universities in Midwest and Eastern states that would be willing to receive evacuees who were already students or were eligible to enter schools of higher education. The other program was geared to the release of those who could find jobs in the same areas of the United States where college opportunities were being sought....

Approximately 4,000 students were assisted in resuming or beginning their college careers through the National Japanese American Student Relocation Council, of which the AFSC was a member agency. In addition to the help students received, hundreds of other Japanese Americans found help through the hostels projects, upon being released from the internment camps and seeking Jobs.

The end of the war terminated these programs. The AFSC then provided a considerable arnount of the material aids sent to Japan through the Licensed Agencies for Relief in Asia....

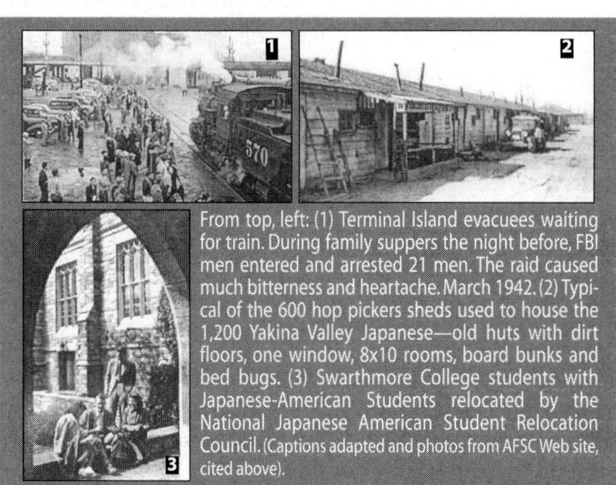

From top, left: (1) Terminal Island evacuees waiting for train. During family suppers the night before, FBI men entered and arrested 21 men. The raid caused much bitterness and heartache. March 1942. (2) Typical of the 600 hop pickers sheds used to house the 1,200 Yakina Valley Japanese—old huts with dirt floors, one window, 8x10 rooms, board bunks and bed bugs. (3) Swarthmore College students with Japanese-American Students relocated by the National Japanese American Student Relocation Council. (Captions adapted and photos from AFSC Web site, cited above).

"Don't Feel Sorry for Us"

5/4/42

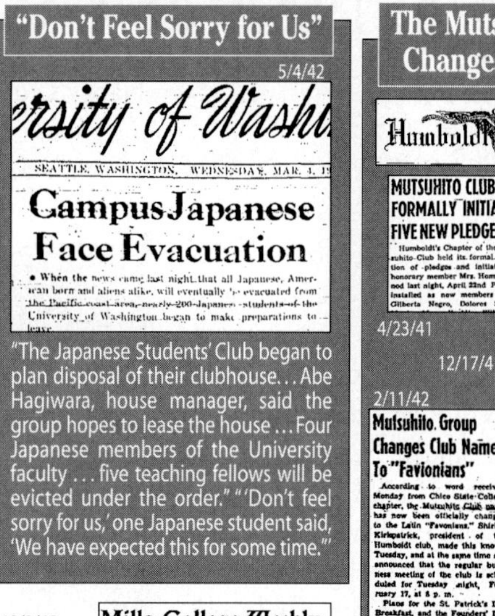
ersity of Wash

SEATTLE, WASHINGTON, WEDNESDAY, MAR. 4, 19

Campus Japanese Face Evacuation

• When the news came last night that all Japanese, American born and aliens alike, will eventually be evacuated from the Pacific coast area, nearly 200 Japanese students of the University of Washington began to make preparations to leave.

"The Japanese Students' Club began to plan disposal of their clubhouse... Abe Hagiwara, house manager, said the group hopes to lease the house ... Four Japanese members of the University faculty ... five teaching fellows will be evicted under the order." "'Don't feel sorry for us,' one Japanese student said, 'We have expected this for some time.'"

The Mutsuhito Club Changes Its Name

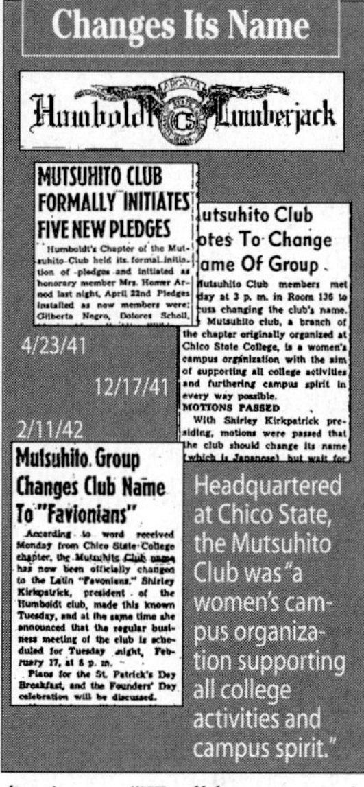
Humboldt Lumberjack

MUTSUHITO CLUB FORMALLY INITIATES FIVE NEW PLEDGES

Humboldt's Chapter of the Mutsuhito Club held its formal initiation of pledges and initiated as honorary member Mrs. Homer Arnod last night, April 22nd Pledges installed as new members were: Gilberta Negro, Dolores Scholl,

4/23/41

utsuhito Club otes To Change ame Of Group

utsuhito Club members met day at 3 p. m. in Room 136 to uss changing the club's name. Mutsuhito club, a branch of the chapter originally organized at Chico State College, is a women's campus organization with the aim of supporting all college activities and furthering campus spirit in every way possible.

MOTIONS PASSED

With Shirley Kirkpatrick presiding, motions were passed that the club should change its name (which is Japanese) but wait for

12/17/41

2/11/42

Mutsuhito Group Changes Club Name To "Favionians"

According to word received Monday from Chico State College chapter, the Mutsuhito Club name has now been officially changed to the Latin "Favonians." Shirley Kirkpatrick, president of the Humboldt club, made this known Tuesday, and at the same time she announced that the regular business meeting of the club is scheduled for Tuesday night, February 17, at 8 p. m.

Plans for the St. Patrick's Day Breakfast, and the Founders' Day celebration will be discussed.

Headquartered at Chico State, the Mutsuhito Club was "a women's campus organization supporting all college activities and campus spirit."

10/3/45 **Mills College Weekly**

It Happened Here

The return of Japanese Americans to the West Coast, has resulted in varying receptions for them. Some have returned to their truck farms only to be shot at by vengeful white neighbors. Or they have been the targets for more insidious attacks by the gossips, the strife mongers, and those who see in the Japanese features inborn traits of cruelty, slyness, and maliciousness. Some, however, have been more fortunate and have been employed at places such as Mills, where they are relatively protected by those to whom it is apparent that such characteristics are not hereditary, but are the results of long rigorous training and drilling in the beliefs that deem such qualities good. We recognize in Japanese Americans the same ideals and loyalties of any American who has grown up in an atmosphere fostering individual development and respect for the rights of individuals. May those Japanese, who, incidentally, are working alongside the Chinese here at Mills, serve as a silent reminder to us that it is possible for men to live together in cooperative peace.—J. G. '46.

Editor's note: "We all knew it wasn't good," Mildred Kiefer Wurf writes of the Japanese-American roundup she observed as a high school student. (p. 179). Tom Suzuki (p. 1026) provides personal testimony to the accommodations described in the sidebar, lower left. William Miller (p. 720) writes of bringing Nisei students from Wyoming camps to U. Nebraska and "the evil" of the relocaions.

Enrollment Discrimination against Japanese Americans during the War

Excerpted from "Race and Religion in Selective Admissions," by Robert Redfield, University of Chicago, appearing in the July, 1949 issue of the Journal of the American Association of College Registrars, *and reprinted by the Anti-Defamation League of B'nai B'rith.*

During the war, the obstacles to enrollment [of United States citizens of Japanese parentage] differed greatly from one institution to another, but not according to the location of the institution in the North or in the South. Some colleges and universities showed more courage than others in admittlng such students at a time when the Japanese-Americans were unjustly excluded as a group from participation in the national life.

Some small colleges, especially some with church leadership, were bold in admitting Japanese-Americans against opposition in their local communities. Others—and some of the largest and most independent universities were included—seemed positively eager to use the ambiguous and changing pronouncements of the War Department as to enrollment of Nisei students as cover for their own disposition to discriminate. The large institution with war contracts to carry out and military officers close at hand often offered little resistance to advices that Nisei be excluded from its campus.

Certain results were absurd—an administrative officer found himself denying admission as a student to some young Americans with Japanese parents, and perhaps on the same day signing a form appointing to the teaching faculty some Japanese alien hired to teach the Japanese language to soldiers of our army.... The problems of discrimination in education raised by the removal and dispersion of Americans of Japanese origin were nationwide, and presented to all of us in common terms the basic issues of ethnic discrimination in American education.

Launching a lifetime of interest in career counseling and promoting understanding

3. NSA at UCLA and Beyond

Nancy Lee Arnheim (Roth)
University of California, Los Angeles
NSA Delegate at Large, 1948-49; Chair, NSA Subcommission on Vocational Guidance, 1948-49

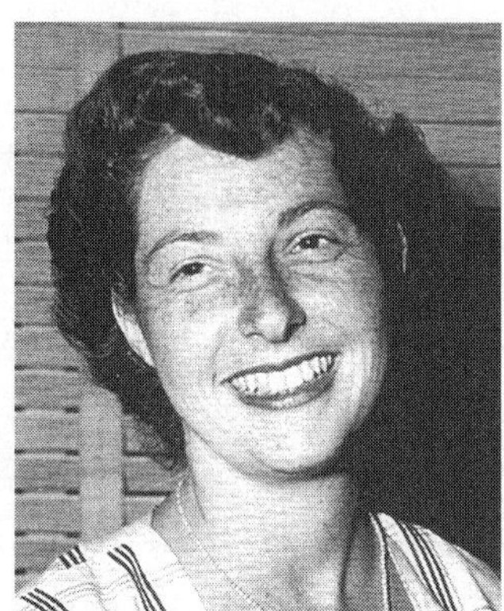

All my student years I was concerned with student rights and the ability of a student to communicate and be heard by many without prejudice. I wrote a constitution for my high school; later, a Bill of Rights for UCLA, and chaired the World Student Service Fund on campus. I helped found NSA, which incorporated the principles I believed in: uniting students from different backgrounds and locations to learn from each other and work toward common goals. It was exciting to think I could help make this happen. As I look back on those times I am reenergized by those dreams. Also, I smile because I'm still doing the same thing.

NSA enters student life at UCLA

Taking root in 1947, but really beginning in 1948, NSA entered student life on the UCLA campus and was accepted as part of a new organization to provide more student programs. In the first election of its kind, I was elected "Delegate-at-large" for NSA, which let me be an advocate for anything of general interest. We helped bring nationally known speakers to campus, had a three-day Institute on Foreign Aid Programs and arranged through the ASUCLA library to have books sent to the University of Caen, France. We held a Regional Convention to talk about student rights, foreign study and travel, discrimination and student welfare.

During that time I was one of a few students sent to San Francisco to the UNESCO Conference. It was thrilling to hear Margaret Mead speak to us about her studies and research and to challenge us to form a group that would bring peace to the nations of the world. Eleanor Roosevelt inspired us to think more about the fact that "wars begin in the minds of men, so should peace." I worked with a local congressman on student rights issues, which were included in the material printed. This experience was very important to me and later helped me obtain a job in the Department of State UNESCO Relations staff in Washington, D.C.

An interest in vocational guidance

My particular interest then, and later as a career, was to provide vocational guidance for students, start a library with vocational material and have more interaction with faculty in vocational fields. I wrote the national NSA office, and they said I would be the national and local chairman of vocational guidance. They encouraged me to go ahead with plans to survey the schools throughout the country to determine what was being done in this area and write a monograph on the subject. I did just that, and it was an eye-opening experience to learn there was so little being done in the field. Sending material to 60 universities, we laboriously compiled our findings. Of course, this was before computers, instant graphs, and email, so this was a slow process. Meanwhile, I helped organize a local convention to help educate my fellow Bruins on the workplace and how they might find a suitable vocation. The head of our UCLA placement service, Mildred Foreman, was a moving force in our conference and later was a mentor, writing a reference for me to help me find my first real job.

The 1948 NSA Congress

Because of my local involvement in NSA I was asked to attend the 1948 NSA Congress in Madison, Wisconsin. This was the first time I was to go out of California, being a second generation native. I went to work as a telephone operator to earn the necessary money so I could attend the conference. I still remember the excitement of seeing the greenery of Madison, the streams and trees and swimming in a fresh water lake. We had cheese and ice cream from the dairy on campus, and I met people that I had corresponded with and saw new faces from all over the U.S. It was exciting to talk with students who had similar thoughts and wanted to explore the same ideas that I had. It was hot! Being brought up in Southern California I did not know about humid hot summers. It was a challenge, but I still remember the talks, walks and shared thoughts that later would become programs for many of us. I presented my findings on vocational programs in the U.S. and encouraged other colleges and universities to start work on their own and to begin libraries and conferences. Many of them did.

The Washington Student Citizenship Seminar

The following summer I was accepted into the Washington Student Citizenship Seminar made up of 96 students from 28 different states. We were chosen for our differences in geography, religion, race and interests. Sponsored by the National Intercollegiate Christian Council (NICC), we were chosen primarily for our leadership positions on our respective campuses and for what we might contribute of our new-found knowledge to our schools because of our experience.

There were 42 men and 54 women and we were put into rooms with those we had nothing in common with. We worked five days a week in some governmental agency, heard speakers at night, went to a different house of worship every weekend and learned our government from the ground up. The first week we met President Truman, our congressional representatives, went to embassies, and even had a scavenger hunt where we counted the steps of the Lincoln Memorial and the columns of the Supreme Court building. It was the hottest summer in 14 years and I wrote home that my plastic rain-coat was leaking inside. There was no air conditioning at the Barksdale, but no one complained.

I was one of the lucky people to have a job that was interesting. Many had filing jobs at the VA, menial jobs in the parks and just something to keep them busy. Because of my NSA experience, I was employed as a clerk typist at the Dept. of State on the UNESCO Relations staff. I read everything that came into the department, catalogued it and sent it to the appropriate person. I took over for a man who was going on vacation. I was trained for two weeks and then on my own for the summer. If the temperature got above a certain point, they closed the non–air-conditioned office and we were free to do what we wished, with pay. I even tried the clay tennis courts and swam at Oak Creek Park.

This was a time of political unrest. Our director of the Seminar was a personal friend of Alger Hiss and attended the same church. We heard a lot of discussion about Whittaker Chambers. The Taft-Hartley was being debated in Congress. They were redecorating the Senate chambers. Our group had two black and an American Indian students who were not allowed into some restaurants in our capital. I tried to give my seat on a bus to a black lady with a child and was told I could not do this. Our group was the first whites to enter a local Baptist church, but we felt welcome. All this was a learning experience I still treasure and I brought back to UCLA.

During my senior year, I was World Student Service Chairman and united our campus with a fundraising show highlighted by Pete Matz as musical director (he later did the arranging for Carol Burnett and many marvelous programs). We organized NSA conferences, did another Occupational Conference, worked more with foreign travel and trained people to take over our jobs. Highlighting four wonderful years, I was chosen as valedictorian of my class of 1950 to speak on "A United Individual," sharing the platform with Ralph Bunche of UN fame, before leaving two days later to go on an NSA trip to Europe.

Stranded in New York on the way to Europe

When my friend and I arrived in New York we thought we would be leaving the next day on a student ship to Europe. We were to sail on the Norwegian ship *Svalbard,* but the Coast Guard declared it unsafe for travel and a firetrap. Here we were, checked out of our hotel and waiting on the dock. I knew someone in New York, so we checked back into the hotel and went out to see the city. What a time we had: going to see the Statue of Liberty, the Empire State Building, the wonderful museums and even the Rockettes at Music City. Four days later, President Truman found us an army transport ship, the *General Ballou,* and we sailed, at last. We had bunk beds, three high. We celebrated both American and Canadian Independence Day on board and finally landed in Amsterdam 7 days later.

My friend and I were on a tri-nation NSA tour of Holland, France and England, specializing in the art and industry of each country. Our first country was Holland and I was placed with a family at random. The girl who chose me thought her brother would like me. As it turned out, Inez and I became good friends, our mothers wrote each other and the next year she came to visit me. I fixed her up on a blind date, they fell in love and I was maid of honor in their Los Angeles wedding. Our children have gone to school together and we still are friends.

At that time the war in Korea was a highlight on the news and we Americans were not too comfortable being away from home. It didn't stop us from enjoying everything, meeting NSA people all over Europe but it did prevent me from applying to the UNESCO staff in Paris for full-time employment. I had corresponded with them before leaving, but with world affairs uncertain, I returned home to go into personnel work.

"A World of Friends Is a World of Peace"

Since my NSA days I have done many things, but as I read over these experiences, I realize that they made a distinct impact on my life. I was asked to speak at my UCLA class's 25th reunion and just updated my graduation speech. I believe that people really don't change; they just mature and become more of what they were. Our Student Body President became a Superior Court Judge. Our ASUCLA Vice President was the first woman head of the USC Law School. I am now President of the Los Angeles Friendship Force, a

Nancy Lee Arnheim is President of The Friendship Force of Los Angeles. She founded a career center at Culver City Junior High School and was President of the California Adult and Continuing Education Counselors Association.

non-profit organization in over 60 countries committed to promoting cross-cultural understanding between people. We stay in homes of people of different nations and host them in ours. A motto of our group is "A World of Friends Is a World of Peace." Just think, it all started with NSA.

END NOTES

[1] See p. 531 on NSA and UNESCO.

[2] See Heggie, p. 202, on NSA's subcommission system, and Medalie, p. 347, on NSA's domestic programs.

[3] See Part 1, Section 6 on the 1948 Congress.

[4] The NICC also played an important role in the founding of NSA. See p. 158, and p. 730 on NSA and the NICC.

[5] See Part 2, Section 3 on NSA and segregation and civil rights.

[6] See Allaway, p. 613, and Jacqz, p. 618 for more on NSA and WSSF. Also Smit, p. 1044, on WSSF in California.

[7] See Meagher, p. 665 on the *Svalbard-Ballou* event. Also Callahan, p. 673, on NSA's travel programs.

PICTURE CREDITS: *Then:* UCLA Yearbook, 1948. *Now:* 2001 (Author).

NANCY LEE ARNHEIM (ROTH)

Early Background: I was born in Los Angeles, California and attended Los Angeles High School.

Education: University of California at Santa Barbara and UCLA, B.S. degree in psychology in 1950. Later attended University of Washington and received M.A. from Norwich University, Vermont College, in Career Counseling.

Career highlights: After graduation, I went into personnel work before returning to UCLA to get a Psychometrist Credential. I then was a psychologist at the Triboro Hospital in New York 1954-55. Married in 1956, 1 served as Area and Public Relations Director for the League of Women Voters writing, directing and appearing on TV and Radio programs as well as representing LA at national and state conferences (1967-1973). Served on and chaired Community Advisory Councils, tutored in special projects in local junior and senior high schools, volunteered at a community career center and became a National Parliamentarian. Returning to the workplace in 1973, 1 founded a career center at Culver City Junior High and began counseling there and at the Culver City Adult School, where I served at President of the faculty. Elected President of the California Adult and Continuing Education Counselor Association. From 1989 to 1994 was a GAIN Counselor at Los Angeles Trade Technical College and taught personal development classes. Retired in 1994 to begin as a docent for the Los Angeles Conservancy, and now serve as President of The Friendship Force of Los Angeles.

Family: In 1956 I married Don Arnheim. Our two children married, and each had one child. Don passed away in 1990.

NSA Comes to UCLA

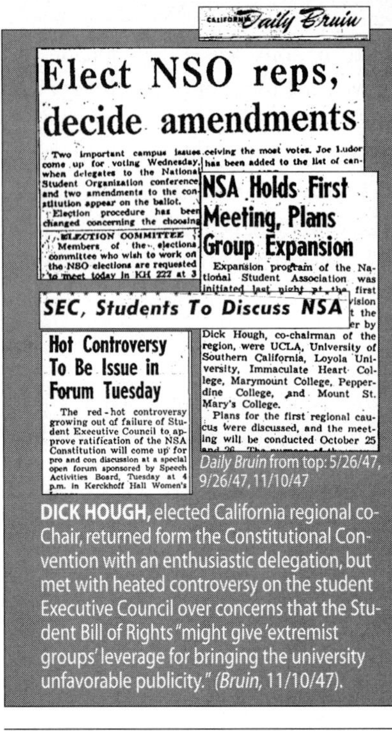

California Daily Bruin

Elect NSO reps, decide amendments

Two important campus issues come up for voting Wednesday, when delegates to the National Student Organization conference and two amendments to the constitution appear on the ballot.

Election procedure has been changed concerning the choosing ... ceiving the most votes. Joe Ludor has been added to the list of can-

ELECTION COMMITTEE

Members of the elections committee who wish to work on the NSO elections are requested to meet today in KH 222 at 3

NSA Holds First Meeting, Plans Group Expansion

Expansion program of the National Student Association was initiated last night at the first ... Dick Hough, co-chairman of the region, were UCLA, University of Southern California, Loyola University, Immaculate Heart College, Marymount College, Pepperdine College, and Mount St. Mary's College.

Plans for the first regional caucus were discussed, and the meeting will be conducted October 25

SEC, Students To Discuss NSA

Hot Controversy To Be Issue in Forum Tuesday

The red-hot controversy growing out of failure of Student Executive Council to approve ratification of the NSA Constitution will come up for pro and con discussion at a special open forum sponsored by Speech Activities Board, Tuesday at 4 p.m. in Kerckhoff Hall Women's

Daily Bruin from top: 5/26/47, 9/26/47, 11/10/47

DICK HOUGH, elected California regional co-Chair, returned form the Constitutional Convention with an enthusiastic delegation, but met with heated controversy on the student Executive Council over concerns that the Student Bill of Rights "might give 'extremist groups' leverage for bringing the university unfavorable publicity." *(Bruin, 11/10/47).*

UCLA DAILY BRUIN Friday, May 28, 1948

NSA

Current Semester's Work, Promising Future Plans, Show Worth of University's Newly-Organized National Student Association Chapter

Sub-Commissions Expected To Expand Activities; New Plans on Fire for Fall Term

New plans, ideas, and programs are scheduled for the agenda of the National Student association executive committee here when the fall semester starts.

In addition to carrying out the program already set up under the organization, most sub-commissions jobs will be expanded. Many of the ideas that were put into effect this semester, the Foreign Library drive, Speakers bureau, Audio Visual and others, were on trial and necessarily on a relatively small scale.

Results of the NSA regional conventions, the UNESCO conference, and ideas of individual Bruins have furnished additional plans to be considered and wherever possible, put into effect.

SEC SEAT

Foremost in the minds of the ...

Faculty Members See NSA Future

Views on NSA and its duties were indicated by two faculty members, Dr. Dean E. McHenry, dean of UCLA's division of social sciences, and Dr. Milton E. Hahn, dean of students, when they addressed the NSA regional convention here at UCLA.

Speaking before representatives from 19 schools, Dr. McHenry stated, "If campus branches of NSA succeed, even in small measure, in overcoming apathy among students, I have no doubt that they will find the leadership and the program to answer the challenge—to face real problems and

KRISTY KOESTNER
NSA Chairman

New NSA Officers Campus Elected

Chief of the elected officers and head of NSA next semester will be Chairman Kristy Koestner. Miss Koestner, an old hand at NSA, has served previously as a delegate to both regional and national conventions and as a member of the NSA executive board at UCLA. Assisting her through the handling of correspondence and finance will be Secretary-Treasurer Lynn Harris Hicks.

Nancy Lee Roth has been chosen as an NSA delegate-at-large. Among her duties is that of representing the NSA membership as a whole. Well known on campus, Miss Roth has served as both national and local chairman of voca-

National Student Association Meets With Great Success In Short UCLA Existence

By Dolores Spevack

In each of its projects, the National Student association, the only national organization representing American college students and serving all areas of student needs, has met with unusual success in the few months of its existence at UCLA.

What NSA has accomplished since November 13, 1947, when SEC voted to put UCLA into the association, can best be shown by the work of the various sub-commissions since that time.

Through the sponsorship of the Speaker's bureau, Matt Weinstock, noted newspaperman and author of "My L.A.," Dr. Hans Reichenbach, noted logician and professor of philosophy at UCLA, and other speakers have appeared before campus audiences this semester. Weinstock spoke on the topic, "World Journalism" at an open forum, and answered questions from the floor at the conclusion of his speech, while Dr. Reichenbach spoke on the general topic of philosophy and science at one of a series of lectures designed to acquaint Bruins with work in various fields of professional research.

FOREIGN AID

A three-day Institute on Foreign Aid programs, also sponsored by the Speaker's bureau, presented such outstanding speakers as George V. Allen, assistant secretary of state, who aired the necessity of improving our foreign relations. Student speakers gave viewpoints on foreign aid of men including President Harry Truman and Robert Taft during the Institute.

Dr. Stafford L. Warren, who is engaged in research on the topic of radiation injuries, recently showed colored pictures and spoke on Bikini experiments through the sponsorship of NSA, while Ernst Papanek, executive director of American Youth for World Youth, Inc., aired the situation of young people in Europe at another campus meet-

NSA, with the cooperation of AWS and the Bureau of Occupations, sponsored a four-day Occupational conference recently which featured such prominent speakers as Robert Aland, vice president of Roy M. McDonald and Co., publishers, and Muriel Morse, assistant general manager of the Los Angeles Civil Service commission.

BOOKS TO FRANCE

Arranged by the Foreign Library commission, an ASUCLA library is being established at the University of Caen in France. Books, procured by means of a $1000 appropriation granted by SEC, and donations of books by Bruins during a five-day drive, are currently being sent to France.

Through the Travel Tours com-

NSA Organized On Tri-Level Student Plan

NSA was established last summer, when more than 700 delegates from 300 colleges and universities held the Constitutional convention on the campus of the University of Wisconsin.

It was organized on national, regional, and local levels. On the

Daily Bruin 5/28/48

BILL STOUT, *Daily Bruin* editor in 1945 was UCLA rep on the U.S. Delegation to the Word Student Congress (pp..94, 103) [Another *Bruin* editor, **JIM GARST** was a member of the NSA International Team in in 1950 (p.609).] After its formative 1947-48 year, **KRISTY KOESTNER** (above), was elected to head the growing NSA program on campus for the 1948-49 year. Dean of Students, Dr. Milton E. Hahn (above), lent support to NSA, and also addressed its spring regional convention at UCLA.

A Student Leader's Album: Nancy Roth Arnheim

1948-49 Building NSA on Campus

Reaffirmation in Unity

When I entered the Madiso[n] convention, I entered a world o[f] student thinking, living, and act[ing]. I found there representative[s] of about three-quarters of a mil[l]ion students, all intently interest[ed] in the welfare of the America[n] student and eager to develop an[d] improve student government an[d] student life. Though they dif[fered] in every respect, they me[t] under a single National Studen[t] association with the purpose o[f] integrating their ideas into con[structive] plans for the comin[g] year.

... guidance was accepted and on the following day copies of the report were issued to each attending school. Also, plans were made to investigate infringements of student academic rights, as well as acts of unnecessary discrimination on campuses. I saw how the non-partisan, non-political, non-sectarian principles of NSA were upheld and put into working actuality.

I bring back to UCLA, as a result of my 123 hours of living NSA, a reaffirmation in my belief in the ability of students to work together in a strong unity. I bring new ideas which are a result of much national exchange, and hopes which come from my view of past successes.

I return from Madison with a strong desire to see full student participation and cooperation in order to make NSA here the working body it is on the other campuses. UCLA's NSA will contribute as much to its student welfare as each of 14,500 members contributes to its present program.

Nancy Lee Roth
UCLA-NSA delegate-at-large

From *Daily Bruin* 10/5/48, above, and other '48-'49 undated issues.

UCLA Granted NSA Special Committee

National Subcommittee on Vocational Information has again been granted to UCLA by the NSA, an organization which disseminates information on this vital interest to students in colleges throughout the country.

Last year this body was established by Nancy Lee Roth, who supervised a survey to determine the extent and effectiveness of counselling and guidance services in our schools. When completed, the findings of this subcommission will be published and sent to all NSA member-schools in the country.

Among the projects planned by this group is the establishment of a coordinating center for vocational information on the west coast. A library will be started to answer the following questions which most students ask themselves one time or another: "What shall I do after graduation? What's the future, the pay, the training needed, the opportunities for advancement?" The answers will be found in a series of up-to-date booklets in each field, comprising the library.

The regional information library will begin this year and will be at the disposal of students of all NSA schools in the vicinity.

Volunteers are required to undertake the tremendous correspondence with schools, firms and institutions necessary to carry out this project. Others are needed to help build the library.

Signups for this and other NSA subcommissions, such as those on ...

"I BRING BACK NEW IDEAS," Nancy Roth wrote after returning from the 1948 National Student Congress. Her strong interest in Vocational Guidance brought NSA's commission to UCLA. She also advocated for the Student Bill of Rights, and furthered other NSA service programs.

NSA Confab Discusses Plans

The UCLA delegation of NSA traveled to LACC Saturday afternoon for a sub-regional meeting.

Kay Longshore, sub-regional chairman, gave a brief talk and then introduced the main speaker of the day, Erskine Childers, California-Nevada-Hawaii senior co-chairman.

Childers spoke on the policies to be discussed before the National Executive council in August. A few of these policies mentioned were academic freedom, discrimination and federal aid in education.

Childers urged more inter-regional correspondence and reminded those in attendance of the purposes and aims of NSA.

The meeting then dissolved into small groups to discuss the Purchase Card plan, student government, legislative effects in government and inter-campus programs.

Roth to Keynote NSA Work Today

The workings of the National Students' Association will be explained today, from 4 to 5 p.m., in the KH men's lounge, to students interested in both student and federal governmental functions.

The general background of the organization will be discussed by NSA rep-at-large Nancy Lee Roth, while Lyn Harris Hicks and Bob Gaudin will describe the work at NSA in the fields of international, national and local enterprise.

Students, interested in bettering international student relationships, and securing domestic scholarships and financial assis-...

NSA Member Planning UCLA Bill of Rights

Coupled with this week's commemoration of Bill of Rights week, a leading member of National Students association is working on a possible UCLA counterpart of the 157-year old document safeguarding American political rights.

Nancy Lee Roth, national chairman of NSA's guidance and personnel subcommission and local NSA member-at-large is currently investigating the possibilities of enacting a bill of rights, applicable to this campus, into the ASUCLA constitution.

PRELIMINARY STAGE

At present, the work is still in a preliminary stage. Basing her work on national, state and NSA bills of rights, she is planning a great deal of necessary research into constitutions of other schools throughout the country and investigation into other aspects of the problem before concrete suggestions are presented.

In explaining the plan, Miss Roth said, "In any institution such as UCLA which is dedicated to the spirit of free inquiry and discussion, it is only natural that its student government should take the lead in safeguarding the basic rights of its members."

EXPLICIT PROVISIONS

She explained that such a document would probably include explicit provisions concerning freedom from denial of campus rights because of race, color, creed, national origin or political affiliations.

Miss Roth is accepting suggestions from any interested students. She can be contacted through the NSA office in KH dining room A.

1948-49 Electioneering

VOTE TODAY

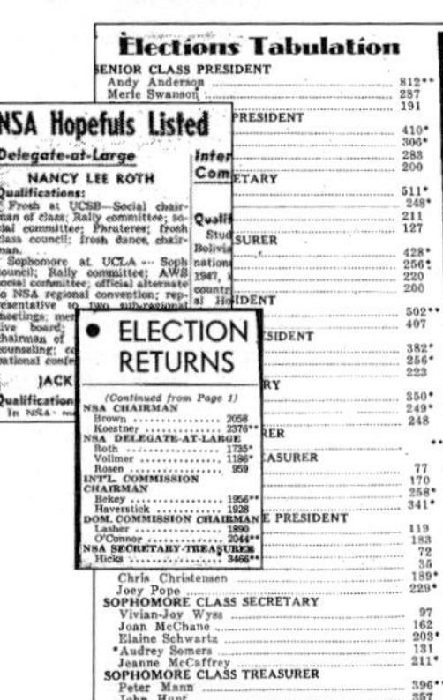
Elections Tabulation

SENIOR CLASS PRESIDENT
Andy Anderson 812**
Merle Swanson 287
..... 191

NSA Hopefuls Listed

Delegate-at-Large

NANCY LEE ROTH

Qualifications:
Frosh at UCSB—Social chairman of class; Rally committee; social committee; Phrateres; frosh class council; frosh dance chairman.
Sophomore at UCLA — Soph council; Rally committee; AWS social committee; official alternate to NSA regional convention; representative to two sub-regional meetings; ...

• ELECTION RETURNS

(Continued from Page 1)

NSA CHAIRMAN	
Brown	2058
Koestner	2376**
NSA DELEGATE-AT-LARGE	
Roth	1735*
Vollmer	1186*
Rosen	959
INT'L. COMMISSION CHAIRMAN	
Bekey	1956**
Haverstick	1928
DOM. COMMISSION CHAIRMAN	
Lasher	1890
O'Connor	2044**
NSA SECRETARY-TREASURER	
Hicks	3466**

Chris Christensen	189*
Joey Pope	229*
SOPHOMORE CLASS SECRETARY	
Vivian-Joy Wyss	97
Joan McChane	162
Elaine Schwartz	203*
*Audrey Somers	131
Jeanne McCaffrey	211*
SOPHOMORE CLASS TREASURER	
Peter Mann	396**
John Hunt	357
URA PRESIDENT	
Pat Olson	2388*
Marilyn Gee	1278
NSA COORDINATOR	
Nancy Lee Roth	1639*
Bob Gaudino	1100*
Dana Pazarowitz	896

Nancy Lee Roth

Qualifications

NSA Delegate-at-large (elected).
Chairman of National Subcommission on Vocational Guidance for 2 years.
Delegate to UNESCO and on Executive Committee for Collegiate Council for United Nations (CCUN).
Frosh, Soph and Junior Councils.
Rally Committee.
Phrateres and AWS Social Committee.
Co-chairman of Southern California WSSF Conference.
Official Delegate to National NSA Convention and Regional Convention; Representative at NSA sub regionals for 2 years.
Member of NSA Executive Board for 2 years.

Daily Bruin: Left: 5/11/48. Right: 5/13/49

1949 A Summer Seminar in the Nation's Capitol

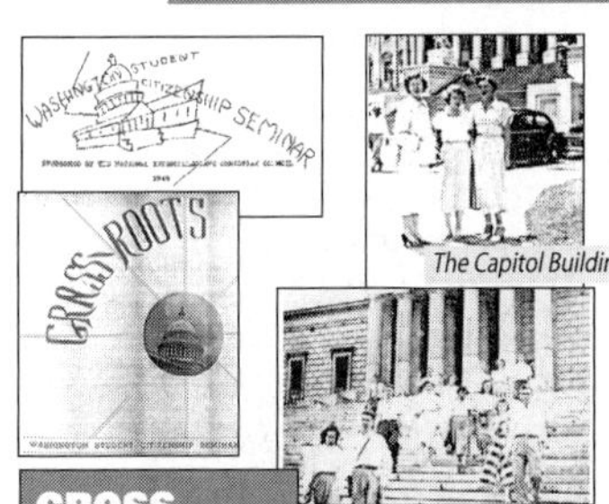

The Capitol Building

CROSS COUNTRY BY RAIL to a $9/day job with the government

WESTERN UNION

Travel the Santa Fe and B&O

Photos, memorabilia: Nancy Roth Arnheim

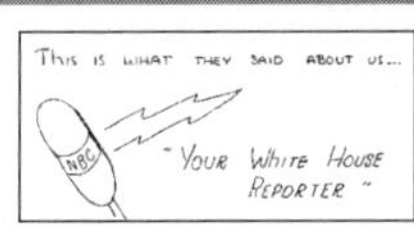

Excerpts from a broadcast, 6/29/49, Station WRC.

A group of young men and women visited President Truman today to talk about learning to become good citizens. There were 96 of them from [67] colleges and universities all over the nation and they'll work in government jobs as clerks for July and August, with evening seminars to talk over what they're learning about government.... The group is sponsored by the college division of the YMCA and YWCA [National Intercollegiate Christian Council], but there is ... no bar of sex or of religion or of race.... All are living in a small hotel here in Washington.

1948 Conventioneering

UCLA DELEGATES to the 1948 1st National Student Congress. Nancy Roth on right. Jim Garst to her left.

Bruin, 4/48

Brown, Koestner in Fight For NSA Chairmanship

Elected Officers to Attend August National Meet in Madison, Wisconsin

The door clanged shut Friday to bar any more applicants from filing for the NSA election which will be held concurrently with the general ASUCLA elections May 6 and 7.

Left to fight it out are Vince Brown and Kristy Koestner for ...

Matchbook cover, memento

Madison, Wisc., conventioneers remember the reknowned toasted Danish at Rennebohm's Drug Store.

VOCATIONAL GUIDANCE PAPER, presented to workshop by Nancy Lee Roth, proposes information service adopted by NSA and located at UCLA the following year.

Photos: Nancy Roth Arnheim

1950 Commencement at Last

NANCY LEE ROTH AND LESLIE MITTLEMAN address UCLA's largest graduating class—3,586 students—at the Hollywood Bowl on June 18, 1950. Roth's theme was "A United Individual." Principal speaker was UCLA alumnus Dr. Ralph Bunche, U.N. Trusteeship Division Director.

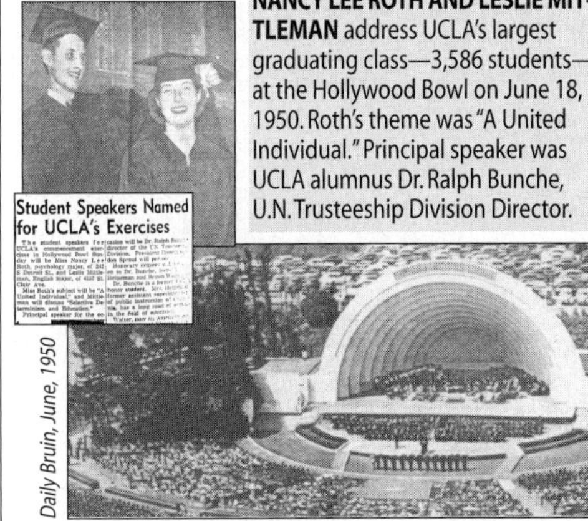

Student Speakers Named for UCLA's Exercises

The student speakers for UCLA's commencement exercises in Hollywood Bowl Sunday will be Miss Nancy Lee Roth, psychology major, of 242 S Detroit St., and Leslie Mittleman, English major, of 4137 St. Clair Ave.

Miss Roth's subject will be "A United Individual," and Mittleman will discuss "Selective Determinism and Education."

Principal speaker for the occasion will be Dr. Ralph Bunche, director of the UN Trusteeship Division. President Robert Gordon Sproul will preside.

Honorary degrees will be given to Dr. Bunche, ... Heineman and ...

Dr. Bunche is a former UCLA honor student. Mrs. Heineman, former assistant superintendent of public instruction of California, has a long record of service in the field of education.

Walter, now an American ...

Daily Bruin, June, 1950

1950 And a Summer in Europe

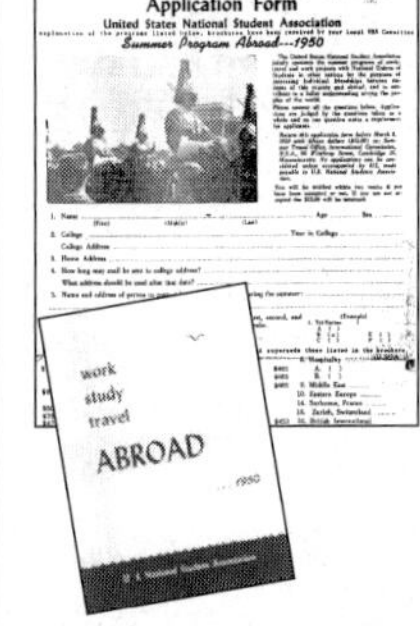

while the U.S. enters the war in Korea

"THE WAR IN KOREA WAS A HIGHLIGHT... and we Americans were not too comfortable being away ...," Arnheim writes (p. 1039). "It didn't prevent us from enjoying everything.... with world affairs uncertain, I returned home."

...with an unplanned side trip in New York City

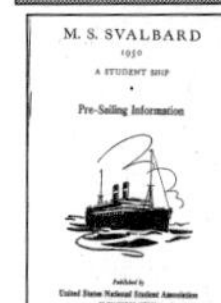

STUDENTS WERE STRANDED for 4 days in NYC until a replacement ship was provided by the U.S. (Roth, p. 1039. See also p. 665).

"CAMPED OUT" AT THE BARBIZON, Roth wired home when they were ready to leave.

WESTERN UNION

NEW YORK NY JUNE 26 1950
THE R L HALBOYS AND MRS LEO I ROTH
1317 BROWN ST MARTINEZ CALIF
DEFINITELY SAILING TUESDAY ON GOVERNMENT SHIP GENERAL B BALLOU HAVE HAD WONDERFULY DINAMIC STAY AND STILL WILL MAKE THE SAME TOUR, FLYING HOME. EARLY ANNIVERSARY WISHES
NANCY LEE

Memorabilia: Arnheim

UCLA Anchors Southern California Launch of NSA

Editor's note: UCLA provided early leadership in forming NSA., Hans Morkisch, Dick Hough, Kristy Koestner (p. 1040), Jane Wilder (later Jacqz, p. 618) and ASUC President Ken Gallagher attended the Constitutional Convention in 1947. Hough became 1947-48 regional co-Chair with Dick Heggie (p. 199). (See also Nancy Roth Arnheim, p. 1038; Bill Stout and Jim Garst, p. 1040). During the affiliation debate Gallagher initially blocked affiliation, breaking a tie, on the grounds that the Student Bill of Rights was too vague. A compromise for affiliation was later adopted.

1947

9/26/47

Watch for it . . .

Beginning Monday, the *Bruin* will print the first of a series of reports from the delegates to the National Students Association. NSA, formerly NSO, held a convention in Madison, Wisconsin, during the summer, and UCLA sent three elected and two appointed delegates. They were Hans Morkisch, Dick Hough, and Kristy Koestner. In addition, there were two appointed members from Student Executive Council, Jane Wilder, Rep-at-Large, and Ken Gallagher, ASUCLA president. As you may or may not know, these delegates met with tremendous success, and California came through as playing a major part in the forming of the NSA constitution.

Jane Wilder of this campus, and Milt Dobkin of USC are the two California representatives on the constitutional committee, and UCLA's Dick Hough, along with Cal's Dick Heggie, are regional co-chairmen for California-Nevada-Hawaii area. Hans Morkisch is now the treasurer of the same region.

California NSA Delegates Steer Meet to Success

California played a major part in determining the future policies and organization of the newly-established National Student Association at the Madison constitutional convention, which UCLA delegates termed "tremendously successful".

Crediting the maturity and leadership ability of students from every part of the United States for the far-reaching accomplishments of the convention, the UCLA delegation praised the spirit of cooperation and compromise which key-noted every convention action.

Six weeks

9/15/47

Cultivation of NSA Aims Brings Fruit in Convention of 33 California Colleges on the Leland Stanford Farm

By Grover Heyler

After a year's period of organization, constitution, and firing up spirit, concrete domestic and international projects which will bring to life the idea of a National Students Association were proposed ... routine work of approving a constitution seemed to be the chief interest of the larger schools, already used to the idea of an NSA through attendance at the Madison, Wis., convention this summer.

Colleges which had sent observers for the first time, how- ... excellent Institute on International Relations.

For example, the convention enthusiastically adopted its plan to push sponsorship of a seminar in Europe on American Civilization and Culture, copied from the Harvard-Rutgers-Yale project at ... the work of these commissions, as planned by the convention, will appear in tomorrow's *Bruin*. Both universities will be headquarters for two years, although every college is to have groups working on the projects.

Join the Parade

10/29/47

1948

NSA Convention Commences Tomorrow

UCLA *Daily Bruin*

VOL. XXXIII, No. 48 — University of California at Los Angeles — Friday, April 23, 1948

McHenry, Hahn, Gallagher To Address Student Meet

Delegates, Observers from California, Hawaii, Nevada to Discuss Problems

'NEED SOUND, CONSISTENT LIBERALISM' — MILTON HAHN

NSA Panels Report on Variety of Subjects

Rights of Student Government Aired

Foreign Study Report Given

Panel Hits

HANS MORKISCH, Convention Chairman

GLORIA HARRISON, SEC Representative

McHenry Urges 3-Point Program to Fight 'Apathy'

Dean Gives Welcoming Address

NSA Holds Regional Meeting Here

Sixty Delegates Discuss Interests

The California - Nevada - Hawaii Region of the National Student association held its semi-annual convention as 60 delegates, alternates and observers, representing 35 California colleges and universities, gathered here over the weekend.

Dr. Dean McHenry, dean of social sciences, and Erskine Childers, senior NSA regional co-chairman, opened the convention with keynote addresses.

The activities of the rest of the conference were divided into two general categories: the plenary sessions and the workshops. The plenary session considered ques-

Lee Nichols, member of the

McHenry, Childers Open NSA Regional Convention

"Interesting American students in political issues" and providing them with "a non-partisan means of expressing themselves to students throughout the world" were the overall problems which keynote speaker Dean McHenry, dean of social sciences, and Erskine Childers, NSA regional co-chairman presented to the 60 delegates and observers at Saturday morning's opening session of the NSA regional convention.

"American students don't grow up as rapidly as those in Europe or South America," declared McHenry. In spite of the "straitjacket" effects of a Regulation ... support the state and federal programs for educational scholarships. He emphasized that unless this is done, the advantages of widespread education will be lost when the GI bill runs out.

Dr. McHenry also recommended endorsing of general aid to education and the 18 year old vote. "Young people from the ages of 18 to 21 are the most alert critically," he stated.

Likening the United Nations to the Articles of Confederation, in that they enabled us to survive until we were ready for a stronger union, Dr. McHenry declared that it was possible to build a nation

INTRODUCING NSA in a series of seven articles reprinting and analyzing the NSA constitution and convention reports, the Daily Bruin wrote on 9/26/47 that "California came through as playing a major part in the forming of the NSA constitution."

Photos, from left: Hans Morkisch, Gloria Harrison

From top: 4/23/48, 4/26/48, 5/9/49

1949

Issues of the Times

1945

Regents consider disloyalty

Board acts to curb UCLA radicalism

The regents of the University, remaining in open session, devoted most of their Friday afternoon meeting on campus to a discussion of the unfavorable publicity which was recently accorded UCLA as a result of student participation in the picket line.

An oral appeal by Robert Challman, Cal-Vets president, and petitions from Bruin Service Wives and the alumni association for improved housing conditions for veterans were answered by a plain statement from Dr. Robert Gordon Sproul, president of the University, that the regents were aware of the problem and hoped to

12/17/45

COLLEGE 'RED' HUNT — only the beginning

Early this month members of the American Youth for Democracy chapter at Michigan State College distribu-

Student government??

At a later date in the semester, a concrete program of Constitution-consciousness will be conducted on campus. With an enrollment of nearly 15,000, it seems a bit difficult to comprehend that only a mere handful bother to take sufficient interest in the prime issues of student government.

A new constitution for the ASUCLA is now being

PANEL URGES RACIAL UNITY

California *Daily Bruin*

Members voice hope for equality and education

Orchestra to perform at Music Week concert

Fr. top: 2/24/47, 2/27/47, 5/6/47

1947

1949

NSA Sponsors Prof Evaluation In 47 Classes

Forty-seven classes, selected at random, are being given an opportunity by NSA during the next three days to air their opinions of

1/5/49

THE POLICY AGENDA was dominated by issues of academic freedom and inclusiveness in admissions and social organization membership (see Part 2, Sec. 2). NSA lent active support to developing programs of faculty evaluation (p.372).

Historical note: In 1881, the Los Angeles State Normal School was established. In 1919 it became the second campus, and was named the Southern Branch of the University of California; in 1927, renamed the Univesity of California at Los Angeles. Until 1929 it was located on what is now the campus of Los Angeles City College (www.library.ucla.edu). 1948 enrollmnent: 14,570.

79th CHARTER DAY

THE CALIFORNIA CAMPUS

Davis · Mt. Hamilton · San Francisco · La Jolla · Los Angeles · Riverside · Santa Barbara · Berkeley

Eight University Campuses Commemorate 79th Birthday

Charter Day Ceremonies Observed From Davis Campus to La Jolla

Scholarships

Maclise Fund Stimulates Intra-University Study

President Robert Gordon Sproul

1947

3/47

UCLA and USC face War's End and Its Aftermath

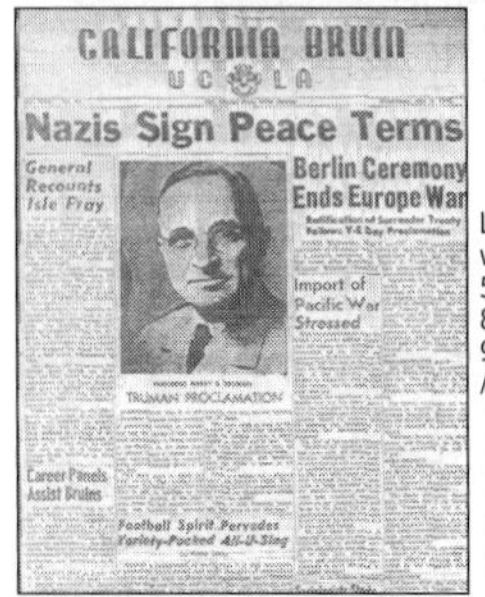

CALIFORNIA BRUIN — UCLA

Nazis Sign Peace Terms

General Recounts Isle Fray

Berlin Ceremony Ends Europe War

Import of Pacific War Stressed

TRUMAN PROCLAMATION

Career Panels Assist Bruins

Football Spirit Pervades Variety-Packed All-U-Sing

California Bruin — University of California at Los Angeles

Emperor Issues Cease Firing Order; Pleads Surrender Time Extension

President Authorizes Wage Rise

MacArthur Grants Delay as Hirohito Dispatches Envoys to Enforce Terms

Conference Investigates Difficulties of Veterans

L., clockwise: 5/9/45, 8/17/45, 9/17/454 /16/45,

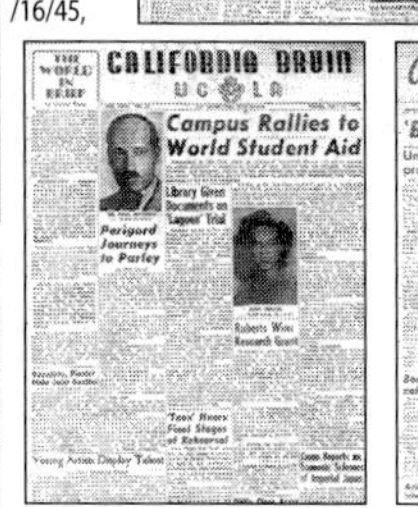

CALIFORNIA BRUIN — UCLA

Campus Rallies to World Student Aid

Library Given Documents on 'Lapan' Trial

Perigord Journeys to Parley

Roberts Wins Research Grant

Young Artists Display Talent

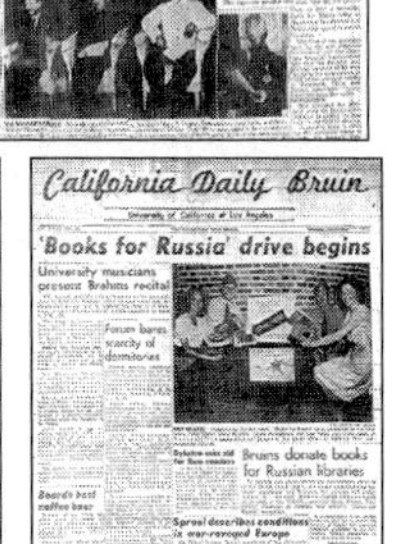

California Daily Bruin

'Books for Russia' drive begins

University musicians present Brahms recital

Forum bares scarcity of dormitories

Bruins donate books for Russian libraries

Sproul describes conditions in war-ravaged Europe

Football spirit prevails over All-U-Sing

SUPPORT FOR EUROPEAN STUDENTS, EAST AND WEST, was central to campus fund drives in the years during and following the war (p. 611).

FDR DIES AS VICTORY NE

SOUTHERN CALIFORNIA DAILY TROJAN

Truman t presiden oath of

Franklin Delano Roosevelt

Americans cross Elbe, Berlin battle begins

Britons mourn chief's passing

L., clockwise: 4/13/45, 5/8/45, 5/8/45, 9/17/47, 3/2/49

V-E DAY ANNOUNCED

Last defended Nazi fortress taken by Russians following hard 84-day siege, Reds say

British declare victory in Europe is official, statesmen broadcast

LARGEST NAZI MURDER CAMP LOCATED

Marshal Stalin

Daily Trojan

Second UN Assembly Meets in Tense Mood

Medical Tests Blanks Ready

Kyser Waxes Trojan Songs

Revolts Spread in Latin America

Political Wars Follow Pattern

Latin American Governments in Brief

Democracy May Be Losing Out In Central American State

ROOSEVELT'S PASSING just weeks to VE day and the San Francisco Conference left a nation mourning (p. 41).

SEEDS OF CONFLICT were planted, reaching fifty years and beyond.

Loyola, Mt. St. Mary and NSA

Editor's note: Loyola, Mt. St. Mary and Immaculate Heart College were steadfast Southern California NSA members from its inception. They brought along intermittently two small area junior colleges, Marymount (which consolidated with Loyola in 1973) and Notre Dame. In the Bay area, the University of Santa Clara (which dropped out in 1951-52, opposing NSA's academic freedom position) and Holy Names were the other Catholic college members.

NSA and NFCCS at Mt. St. Mary

1951-52

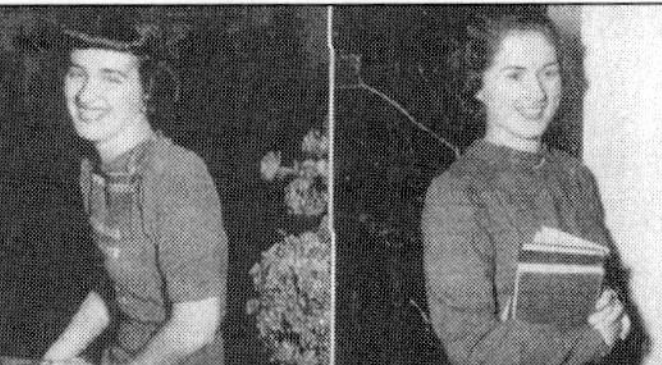

Peggy Bradish, NSA Regional President, 1951-52 — Beverly Halpin, NFCCS Regional President, 1951-52

Associated Students — Mount Saint Mary's College — Los Angeles · California

CATHOLIC WOMEN'S COLLEGES maintained an active intercollegiate regional presence in both NSA (fn 2, p. 308, Lynch, p. 493) and the National Federation of Catholic College Students (p. 741), often providing energetic leadership, as did Mt. St. Mary.

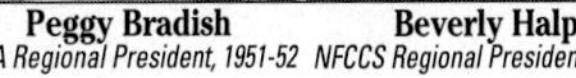

Gloria Padilla
NSA Regional Treasurer 1951-52

NSA: "Student art tour ... Purchase Card ... study/travel program ... International Affairs Conference ... ticket bureau ... leadership training at LACC ... vocational guidance." (From left (above): Gloria Padilla, Roselyn Peukart, Dorothy O'Hara, Peggy Bradish, Beverly Halpin).

NFCCS: "Overseas Service Program ... Mary's Hour ... fashion show ... carnival at Loyola ... pilgrimages to Rome ... press forum ... Europe blood bank." (Below: NFCCS Committee)

Above, NSA delegates, from left: Celine Freitas, Joan Shaw, Gloria Padilla, Alice Connors.

PEGGY BRADISH, 1951-52 California NSA regional chair, was a chemistry major. "Her ideas on students' rights and academic freedom did not go unheard at any of the congresses she attended in the East," the student yearbook observed.

Photos and citations from Mt. St. Mary yearbooks, 1949-52, courtesy Mt. St. Mary's Archives.

Historical note: Mt. St. Mary's College is a women's college founded in 1925 by the Sisters of St. Joseph of Carondelet, founders also of Fontbonne College in St Louis (www.msmc.la.edu). 1948 enrollment: 561.

Loyola: in at the Beginning

1946

LOYOLA ENROLLMENT HIGHEST IN HISTORY

Fox Loyola Theater Premiere Oct. 3

Opening Night Receipts To University

Loyolan

Los Angeles, Calif., Friday, May 24, 1946

VETERANS FRONT

by LEO MAJICH

A few months ago, Life magazine carried quite a spread on the activities of the Ku Klux Klan, describing their initiation with a lot of exclusive pictures, etc. Once again this organization has reared its head and no one seems to pay ... months when Klan activities broke loose all over the country. We saw what happened to a Fraternity down in U. S. C. and to families in our negro sections of L. A. What happened about them? Our city investigators termed them a ...

AN INFLUX OF VETERANS AND SWELLING ENROLLMENTS lifted the student population from its wartime low of only 65 to over 1,200 men, 80% of whom were veterans (9/23/46). The *Loyolan* veterans interest column (10/25/46) was echoed in many college papers. Fox West Coast Theaters opened its nearby movie house and contributed first-night receipts to the University.

CHICAGO BOUND

Bill Richards, (center), Loyola's representative to the Chicago Conference, talks over plans with Jack McCaffery and Jim Cotter. —Photo by Smurda

BILL RICHARDS returned from the Chicago Student Conference (p. 109) recommending "immediate action" to study joining the proposed NSO, providing "this institution a real means of expounding Catholic Action within an organization that will influence students of every race, creed and color throughout the country" (*Loyolan* 1/20/47).

1946-47

[R]ICHARDS TO REPRESENT [L]OYOLA AT CONFERENCE

by WALT SCARBOROUGH

Bill Richards will entrain Christmas night at 7:15 for Chi[cago] ... National Conference of College Students. He will be met ... by N.F.C.C.S. and Newmann Club officials who will ... [Ca]tholic delegates while at the conference.

12/20/46

[S]TUDENT REPORTS ON [C]HICAGO CONVENTION

... THE STUDENT BODY OF LOYOLA UNIVERSITY:

... Chicago Student Conference has laid the foundation for a work[able], recognized, and representative national organization of American [col]lege and university students. Amidst numerous factions, representing ...

... any affiliation with the International Union of Students pending a thourgh study of the motivating principles behind that organization.

5. The adoption of the constitution and the formal creation of NSO will take place next July at Chicago.

It is the opinion of the writer that Loyola University should take immediate action in studying the possibilities of joining the proposed NSO and should cooperate with the National Continuations Committee.

Such action will give to this institution a real means of expounding Catholic Action within an organization which will influence students of every race, creed, and color throughout the country.

It is the recommendation of the writer that the President of Student Body appoint a committee to investigate in detail the whole structure of the proposed organization with the idea of associating our student body with the national association.

Respectfully submitted,
WILLIAM D. RICHARDS,
Delegate to the Chicago Student Conference,
Loyola University of Los Angeles

1/20/47

Student Council To Study N.S.O.

Student Prexy Nick Papageorges announced yesterday that Loyola will attempt to take an active part in the program of the National Federation of Catholic College Students. This program is to instill Catholic principles into the newly-formed National Student Convention. With the help of Bill Richards, Loyola delegate to the recent Chicago conference of the NSO, Papageorges expects to inaugurate an active program on campus.

1/5/49

Students Leave For Berkeley

Loyola is sending Jack Cunningham and Len Hull as delegates to ...

NSO Delegates To Meet At Pepperdine

An important meeting of the representatives of the colleges and universities in Southern California will be held this Saturday, April 26, at ...

Delegates Report On Conference

Len Hull, Jack Cunningham and Jim Reilly represented Loyola last week-end at the California regional convention of the proposed National Students Organization in Berkeley. The convention was attended by delegates from 39 colleges, universities and junior colleges of the State of California. ...

Lions Take Lead In Regional NSO Meet

Ventura Junior College and San Diego State College added their names to the rapidly growing list of endorsements of the Loyola version of the preamble to the National Students' Organization constitution, at a meeting held last Saturday at George Pepperdine College. Glendale J. C., Marymount, Pasadena ...

WORLD LEADERSHIP NEEDED

Within a decade the world will inevitably call upon many of us to take over the reins of government. The question which presents itself is one which is deserving of much thought on the part of students throughout the nation, especially Catholic students. To what extent are we prepared to meet the vital issues which will be thrust upon us?

Here at Loyola we have a problem which plagues nearly every campus throughout the country; one which will contribute greatly to the general disintegration of our American Democratic System, if it is not recognized and checked. Whereas we have been given the opportunity to absorb true Christian principles, we, as students, have utterly failed to appreciate them to such an extent as to go forth and spread them throughout our society. We are conducting ourselves along the sad lines and lines of complacency and indifference. Ours is the disgraceful spirit of apathy—the attitude of Nero and his "Roman fiddle."

What can we do to combat this sinister activity sponsored by an organ- ...

From left, top to bottom: 3/21/47, 3/28/47, 4/25/47, 5/2/47. Right: 5/2/47.

REGIONAL MEETINGS, NORTH AND SOUTH, prepared California delegations for the September 1947 Constitutional Convention. California Catholic college delegates lined up behind a preamble draft prepared by Loyola delegate Jack Cunningham, which began, "In an age where Totalitarian systems of Government are spearheaded throughout the world by youth movements based on hatred and intolerance ...," and concluded, "the purpose of this organization shall be to promote the common good of all students"; declaring for "the inalienable rights of man" and the "natural rights" endowed by God, the *Loyolan* observed "there should be no room for subversive elements who would deny these fundamantal concepts" (5/2/47). Interested also in "charity and justice," Bill Richards saw in the NSO an opportunity to provide leadership and further these goals (5/2/47).

Historical note: Loyola Marymount University was formed in 1973 by Loyola University, a men's college founded by the Society of Jesus as Loyola College in 1911, and Marymount College, founded as a women's junior college by the Religious of the Sacred Heart of Mary in 1933 (www.lmu.edu). Loyola 1948 enrollment: 1,731.

Organizing for student aid abroad

3. NSA's First Year in California and Working for WSSF

Sally Holt Smit
University of California at Berkeley
Secretary, California-Nevada-Hawaii Region, 1947-48

Toward the end of my junior year at the University of California at Berkeley, I first heard of the anticipated formation of the National Student Association through my work on campus with the World Student Service Fund (WSSF). The inaugural convention of the NSA was to take place at the University of Wisconsin in Madison in the late summer of 1947. 1 was selected to attend, representing the University of California, along with Ginny Rei, Dick Heggie, Tom Tonkin, and some others. We met with delegates from universities all over the United States who were interested in setting up, and joining, a National Student Association. We had many interesting sessions with everyone present and several regional meetings. At one of the latter, Dick Heggie was selected as chairman of the Western region (California, Nevada, and Hawaii) and I as secretary. Our job in the fall and spring of 1947–48 was to hold regional meetings and visit colleges and universities within our region, help committees there to spread knowledge of the NSA, and encourage them to join, as well as working on our own campus, the University of California, which did join.

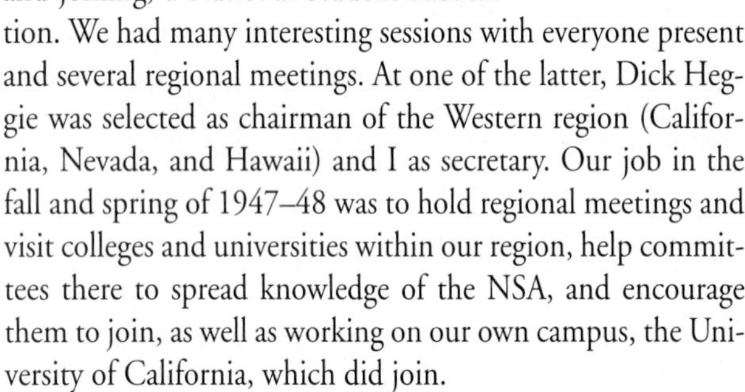

I remember well the enthusiasm for the NSA at the Madison Convention, and also the idealism, But we discovered back in our region that there were some individuals who were negative and tried to block their universities from joining the NSA, calling it political and connected with, and influenced by, left-wing student organizations in Europe, one of which was the International Union of Students (IUS). But after the 1948 coup in Czechoslovakia, negotiations that had started with the IUS were broken off. I particularly remember Pat Hillings at USC, who was vocal and active in keeping USC from joining the NSA.[1] But the majority of the students we worked with were enthusiastic and saw the benefits of learning from and sharing with other universities and supporting a national student "voice." I also remember two very effective students at Stanford with whom we often met—Ginny Titus and Erskine Childers, whose family had been prominent in the government of Ireland.[2]

By June of 1948, when I graduated, about seventeen universities in our region had joined the NSA.[3]

Working with the World Student Service Fund

During my junior and senior years at Berkeley, I had been involved with WSSF, helping with the annual drives to raise money on campus. Our student body was always responsive, and the drives went well. I worked with Dick Thomas, the regional secretary. Thus I learned about the World Student Relief (WSR) meeting to be held in Combloux in 1948. The meeting was to have been held in Burma, which attracted me even more, but things were too shaky in that part of the world.

I then spent the summer in Europe attending a two-week international conference of World Student Relief, the parent organization of the World Student Service Fund, which was supported by the NSA, with about 160 delegates from countries all over the world. There were 40 of us from the United States. There were representatives from "giving" countries, like the United States, Holland, England, and France—those who were raising money to assist students and universities damaged by World War II—and "receiving" countries, like Poland, India, Indonesia, and so on. We learned of the needs—physical and scholastic—of these latter student communities, and gathered material to use later in speaking and fundraising on our campuses.

My main purpose in going to Combloux was to meet with students from various parts of the world and hear the stories of those receiving aid and those giving aid. In addition to traveling to Scandinavia and visiting with students there, I traveled through Germany to visit the displaced students camps and to Czechoslovakia, which had just turned communist. It was a fascinating summer.

I also met my future husband, Jan Smit, at Combloux, as he was one of six delegates from Holland. Holland had turned from being a receiving country to a giving country. I visited Holland with him and saw the student Displaced Person camps there. I returned to the United States in September and was assigned to the Northwest region, to visit campuses in Washington and Oregon, help them with their WSSF drives, and be their guest speaker, talking about what I had seen and heard in Europe.

In the late spring of 1949 I returned to Holland while Jan finished his law degree in Leiden. I worked with the local WSR-ISS group while there. During 1949 and 1950, while we lived in Philadelphia, where Jan had a scholarship to study graduate economics at the University of Pennsylvania, I worked with Betty Emlen in the East-Central Region, also visiting campuses, speaking, and helping with their WSSF drives. It was very rewarding work, and I remember it all well, as though it were yesterday. Jan and I returned to Holland in 1952, and from then on I had no more contact with WSSF or WSR, but I shall always remember the dedicated people who worked for WSSF and the good job they did.

Sally Holt Smit met her future husband Jan at the 1948 World Student Relief Conference and raised a family of four children during the course of Jan's global assignments with Royal Dutch Shell over a period of thirty-five years. They now live and make wine in the Santa Inez Valley of California.

END NOTES

[1] 'See Dobkin, p. 1025.

[2] Childers was chair of the California-Nevada-Hawaii Region in 1948-49 and was elected national vice president for international affairs for 1949-50. See Childers, p. 517.

[3] California colleges attending the August 1949, Second National Student Congress at the University of Illinois, were: California College for Arts and Crafts, College of Holy Names, College of the Pacific, Mills College, Mount St. Mary, Occidental College, Stanford University, University of California at Berkeley, University of California at Lost Angeles, University of Hawaii, University of Santa Clara, University of Southern California, Loyola University, Los Angeles City College, San Francisco State College, and the College of Osteopathic Physicians and Surgeons.

PICTURE CREDITS: *Then:* c. 1947-48, NSA Board, Berkeley. *Now:* 1997 (Both, author).

SALLY HOLT SMITH

Early Years: I was born in San Francisco and attended high school at Westridge in Pasadena and the Branson School in Ross.

Lifetime highlights: I attended Vassar College for two years before transferring to the University of California at Berkeley, where I graduated in June of 1948. I attended the World Student Relief conference, along with 40 delegates from the U.S. It was held that year in Combloux, France. There I met my future husband, Jan Smit, who was a delegate from Holland. Coincidentally, he had met Dick Heggie at the same conference in Denmark the previous year. After Jan completed his law studies at Leiden University, we traveled to California, where we were married in August of 1949. Jan had received a scholarship to the Department of Economics at the University of Pennsylvania, so we spent the first three years of our married life in Philadelphia. I studied Home Economics at Drexel University and International Relations at the University of Pennsylvania.

After Jan passed his Ph.D. exams in Economics, we returned to Holland in the spring of 1952, where he joined Royal Dutch Shell, first as a lawyer and then switching to Marketing. In 1954, after the birth of our first child, we were sent to Buenos Aires, Argentina. Thus began our peregrinations of thirty-five years through South and Central America and Europe. We lived in Argentina, Colombia, Panama, Italy, Holland, and England and had three more children born in different countries. Jan's Shell career ended in London, where we lived for fifteen years. In 1985, after never having lived in the United States since 1952, we built our dream house on ten acres in the Santa Ynez Valley of California, which we had purchased in 1967. Now we enjoy visits from our four children and six grandchildren, travel extensively, grow grapes and make wine, as well as indulging in our mutual love of opera by attending many performances each year. We became an international family thanks to the WSR and the Combloux Conference.

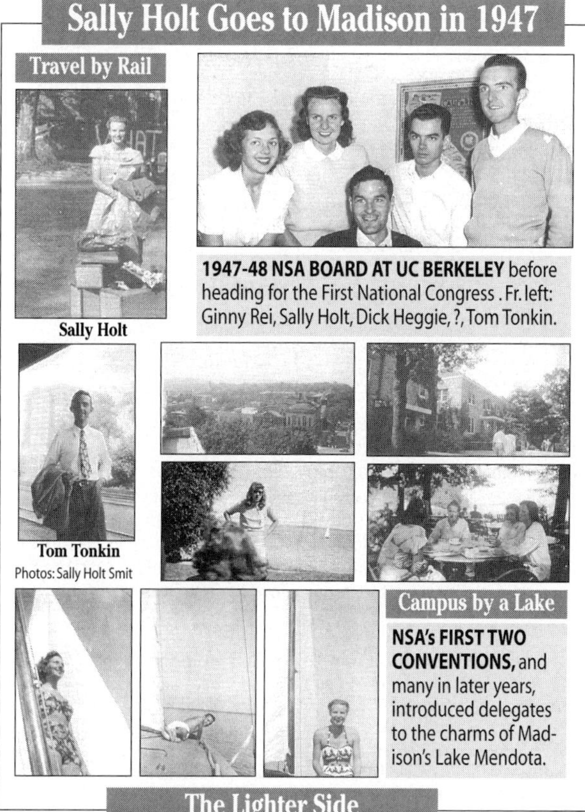

Sally Holt Goes to Madison in 1947
Travel by Rail
Sally Holt
1947-48 NSA BOARD AT UC BERKELEY before heading for the First National Congress . Fr. left: Ginny Rei, Sally Holt, Dick Heggie, ?, Tom Tonkin.
Tom Tonkin
Photos: Sally Holt Smit
Campus by a Lake
NSA's FIRST TWO CONVENTIONS, and many in later years, introduced delegates to the charms of Madison's Lake Mendota.
The Lighter Side

The University of California at Berkeley

Editor's note: UC Berkeley, with UCLA to the south, provided active anchoring for NSA in California. UC Berkeley regional chairs and co-chairs: Mildred Kiefer ('46-47), Dick Heggie ('47-48), Paul Pitner ('50-51). Kiefer (p.178) went on to serve as acting treasurer in Madison ('47-48) and then to work in the Cambridge international office ('48-49). Dick Heggie (p. 199) was elected 1948-49 NSA Vice President for Student Affairs. The loyalty oath conflict in 1950-51 was one of several major West Coast university "red scare" variants reflecting fears of subversion which challenged NSA to find a practical way to intervene (see Brown, p. 382).

Students Join Professors Opposing Loyalty Oaths

1950-51

Regents debate; fire six professors

Daily Californian

PUBLISHED WEEKLY DURING THE SUMMER

Vol. 142 Berkeley, California, Friday, August 4, 1950 No. 7

Oath fever is spreading

Regents leave 39 profs in quandary: they get no checks, no appointments

Oakland council O.K.'s city oath

From top: 7/28/50, 8/4/50

Below: 10/10/50

A resolution

Petitions embracing the following resolution will begin circulating on campus today. The resolution was adopted by Ex-committee Sept. 27. It is essentially the same as one adopted by the Academic Senate Sept. 26.

So that every student will know exactly what he is being asked to sign, we print it in toto.

PETITION TO THE BOARD OF REGENTS OF THE UNIVERSITY OF CALIFORNIA:

WHEREAS: We the undersigned students of the University of California adhere to the principle that the Academic Senate can best set standards for faculty appointment and,

WHEREAS: The principal of tenure has been violated by the arbitrary dismissal of professors who have served the University up to thirty-five (35) years and,

WHEREAS: As a consequence of said action we as students have been directly affected in that:

1. Forty-three (43) courses essential to the completion of college curricula are no longer being offered, and

2. Work toward advanced degrees formerly offered by the discharged professors can no longer be completed, and

3. Degrees received from this University may not in the future carry the same academic worth as in the past,

THEREFORE: BE IT RESOLVED THAT: We the undersigned support the Academic Senate in its expression of appreciation of the stand taken by the minority of the Regents and President Sproul in support of the recommendation of the faculty committee on Privilege and Tenure, and in its condemnation of the action on the part of the majority of the Board of Regents acting by a vote of twelve to ten.

Below: 10/22/51, 11/19/51

Regents move to end 'oath'

The Daily Californian

48 employes refuse to sign new University agreement

MONARCH OF COLLEGE DAILIES

Vol. 146 Berkeley, Calif., Monday, Nov. 19, 1951 No. 45

Board of Regents drops special loyalty 'oath'

By MARTIN SMITH

"WE THE UNDERSIGNED support the Academic Senate . . . its condemnation of the action on the part of the majority of the Board of Regents acting by a vote of twelve to ten," concluded the petition circulated by the ASUC. Regents were charged with violating tenure in the intended firing of professors who failed to sign a loyalty oath. The regents' reversal resulted from protest and eventual support by Governor Warren for reversal.

Historical note: In 1947, Berkeley was one of eight UC campuses with Davis, Mt. Hamilton, San Fransisco, La Jolla, Los Angeles, Riverside and Santa Barbara: total enrollment 39,565 (see UCLA Historical note, p. 1042). UCB, an outgrowth of the College of Caifornia founded 1855 in Oakland by once Congregational Minister Henry Durant, was chartered in 1868 in a merger with the state's land grant Agricultural, Mining & Mechanical Arts College (www.berkeley.edu). 1948 Berkeley enrollment: 23,145.

Careful Planning Leads to Orderly Affiliation

More Daily Californian *on UC Berkeley and Regional NSA: Wurf, p. 184, Heggie, p.207.*

1947-48

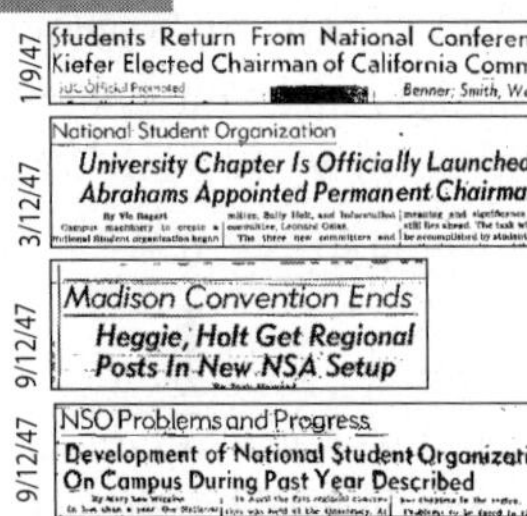

1/9/47 — Students Return From National Conference; Kiefer Elected Chairman of California Committe[e]

3/12/47 — National Student Organization: University Chapter Is Officially Launched; Abrahams Appointed Permanent Chairman

9/12/47 — Madison Convention Ends: Heggie, Holt Get Regional Posts In New NSA Setup

9/12/47 — NSO Problems and Progress: Development of National Student Organization On Campus During Past Year Described

Ginny Carpenter, ASUC Vice President, Reports on NSA's Madison Convention

11/12/47 — THE DAILY CALIFORNIAN: ASUC Affiliates With NSA;

2/20/48 — Committee Report: NSA Relations to ASUC Tentatively Recommended

HOW TO INTEGRATE ASUC AND NSA effectively was a challenge faced by member student governments throughout the country. Creating separate committees or chapters invited competitive tensions. ASUC's solution was to have an NSA subcommittee to its Executive Committee that would act as a liaison and information body, recommending programs to be assigned to existing or new ASUC committees.

GOOD WORKING RELATIONS among ASUC student government leaders and emerging NSO/NSA leaders during the stages of development from Chicago through the Constitutional Convention led to a smooth affiliation process. This was in contrast to the more conflicted experiences at USC, UCLA, Stanford and San Francisco State. ASUC President Ed Welch was one of the Chicago Student Conference delegates along with Marylin Smith, VP. Smith opened the March, 1947 organization meeting for the campus NSO committee, turning Chairmanship over to El Abrahams. For the Constitutional Convention, Sub-Chairman Tom Tonkin and Committee member Sally Holt joined Dick Heggie, Don Lang, new ASUC President, Ginny Carpenter, ASUC VP, and others on the delegation. On their return, Heggie and Holt were elected Regional co-Chair and Secretary respectively. Tom Tonkin became campus chair.

Hosting the Region's PR Office

3/15/50 Digests

NATIONAL STUDENT ASSOCIATION REGIONAL PUBLIC RELATIONS OFFICE

BULLETIN

Vol. — *California-Nevada-Hawaii Region* PAGE ONE

PCS PROGRESS IN BERKELEY—BUT NOT IN STUDENT STORE

Store Board's action clears the way for implementation of PCS [Purchase Card System] in stores off campus – in such a way that it is non-competitive with the ASUC store.

REGIONAL ASSEMBLY—STUDENT ROLE IN EDUCATIONAL WORLD

Nearly 50 delegates from California colleges and universities will attend the 7th CNH Regional Assembly in Berkeley April 1-2.

SOUTHERN DISTRICT ESSAY CONTEST ON DISCRIMINATION

Essays must relate to the general topic of discrimination in higher education – one hundred dollars in prizes will be given out.

NSA-WSSF CHORAL FESTIVAL APRIL 18 IN SAN FRANCISCO

Six college choruses will appear in the 2nd Annual Bay Area NSA-WSSF Choral Festival at the War Memorial Opera House: Mills College A Capella Choir, Stanford Medical School's Men's and Women's Choruses, Santa Clara Men's Glee Club, U. of California's Glee Club and Treble Clef.

NSA SPREAD TOO THIN, R. HEGGIE SAYS

Rather than doing nothing, NSA is doing too much, Dick Heggie, former regional chair and national VP told UC activities chairmen recently. Heggie is now with the World Affairs Council of Northern California.

Stanford University/San Francisco State College: Opt In, Drop Out

Editor's note: San Francisco State, Fresno State, San Jose State, and UC Berkeley were a Northern California state college presence during NSA's first few years. By 1951 the three state colleges had dropped out. Stanford, Mills College, California College of Arts and Crafts, the University of Santa Clara and Holy Names were the main private college members. Stanford dropped out in 1951. As shown in this album, despite an interested college press, NSA advocates at Stanford and SF State were unable to override student government leaders and faculty advisers who felt that the benefits didn't justify the costs. For more on Stanford see Childers, p. 317, Jonas, p. 776.

The Veterans

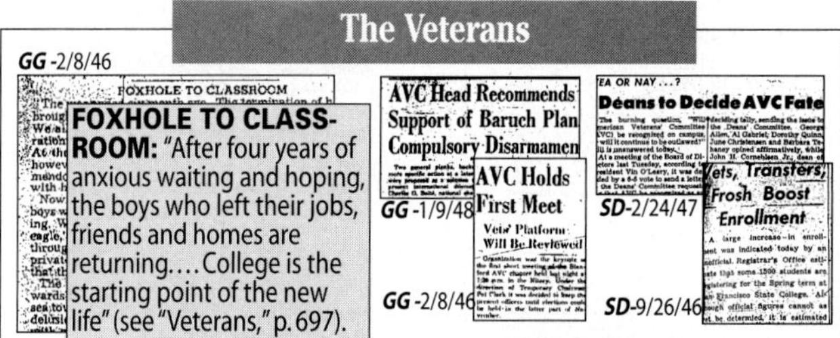

GG-2/8/46

FOXHOLE TO CLASSROOM

AVC Head Recommends Support of Baruch Plan Compulsory Disarmament

AVC Holds First Meet

Vets' Platform Will Be Reviewed

EA OR NAY . . . ? Deans to Decide AVC Fate

Vets, Transfers, Frosh Boost Enrollment

GG-1/9/48 SD-2/24/47 GG-2/8/46 SD-9/26/46

FOXHOLE TO CLASSROOM: "After four years of anxious waiting and hoping, the boys who left their jobs, friends and homes are returning.... College is the starting point of the new life" (see "Veterans," p. 697).

Student Government

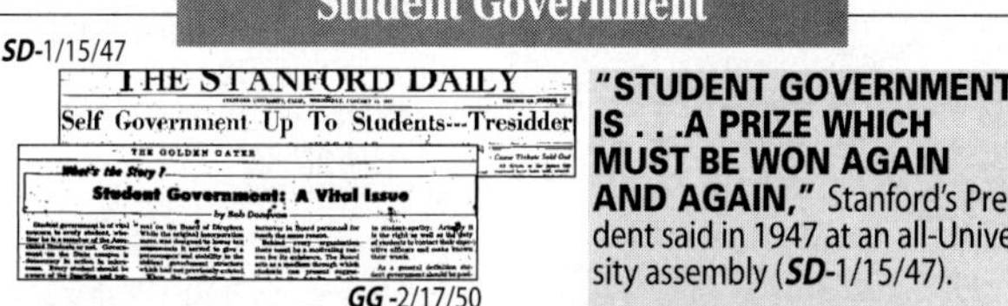

SD-1/15/47

THE STANFORD DAILY

Self Government Up To Students---Tresidder

THE GOLDEN GATER

What's the Story? Student Government: A Vital Issue

GG-2/17/50

"STUDENT GOVERNMENT IS . . . A PRIZE WHICH MUST BE WON AGAIN AND AGAIN," Stanford's President said in 1947 at an all-University assembly (***SD***-1/15/47).

"The college made its presence felt. . . ."

--Vincent O'Leary, 1947-48 SF State Student Body President, after regional assembly

Board of Directors Votes Approval of NSA Proposition

O'Leary, Allen Trek South to Convention

GG-4/23/48

State to Entertain Two Commissions Of NSA in Future

College Makes Presence Felt at Southern Meet

GG-4/30/48

Report on NSA Convention . . . Discuss International Affairs

NSA Meet Held At Heathcliff Hall

Gator President Spurs Institutions To Hitch With NSA

Chief Executive Lists Objectives of Group

Clkwise, fr top: ***GG***-10/8/48, 5/7/48, 10/7/49

Vote to Sever N.S.A. Ties

NSA Asks Reversal

Board Rejects Request

Fr top: ***GG***-12/2/48, 12/9/48

"WHO DOES AN NSA REPRESENTATIVE SPEAK FOR, AND BY WHAT RIGHT?" After initial student leader support and enthusiasm for NSA, Student Board debate (***GG***-12/2/48) centered on limited student participation and on lack of interest in NSA. Supporters countered that "NSA is not an organization, but an arm of student government," and cited its regional and national outreach. State withdrew in Spring 1949.

George Allen
NSA Committee Chair,48-49 Regl. Purchase Card Chair

Phil Ryan
Student Body Pres, 49-50 Opposed NSA

Burk Faraola
Student Body Pres, 50-51 Favored NSA affiliation

PHIL RYAN had opposed affiliation as not the best use of student funds. **GEORGE ALLEN**, Art Padilla, Jack Hurley and others led the affiliation effort. **BURK FARAOLA** won on a platform to re-affiliate, but didn't get Board votes.

Photos: ***GG***- 4/8/49, 4/22/49, 2/6/51

As reported in The Stanford Daily (SD) and the Golden Gater (GG)

THE STANFORD DAILY

Golden Gater

Postwar Student Aid

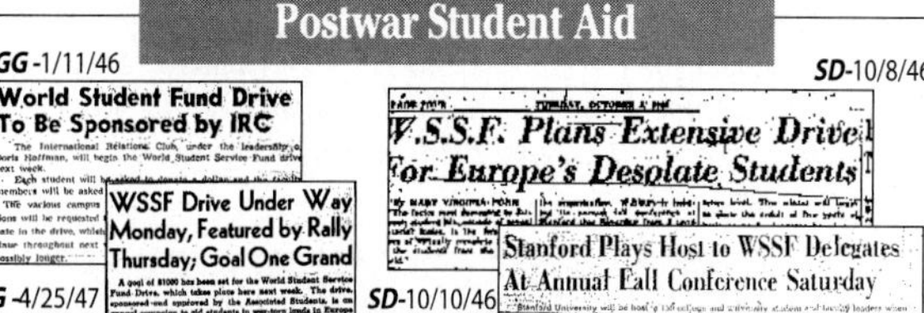

GG-1/11/46

World Student Fund Drive To Be Sponsored by IRC

WSSF Drive Under Way Monday, Featured by Rally Thursday; Goal One Grand

GG-4/25/47

SD-10/8/46

W.S.S.F. Plans Extensive Drive for Europe's Desolate Students

Stanford Plays Host to WSSF Delegates At Annual Fall Conference Saturday

SD-10/10/46

"THE EUROPEAN STUDENTS REPRESENT A GENERATION OF DESPAIR," World Student Service Fund traveling secretary and Occidental graduate Jim Glaser and Mills student Mary Ann Nichols reported after their 1946 European tour on behalf of WSSF. (***SD***- 10/8/46. See also p. 611)

Academic Freedom

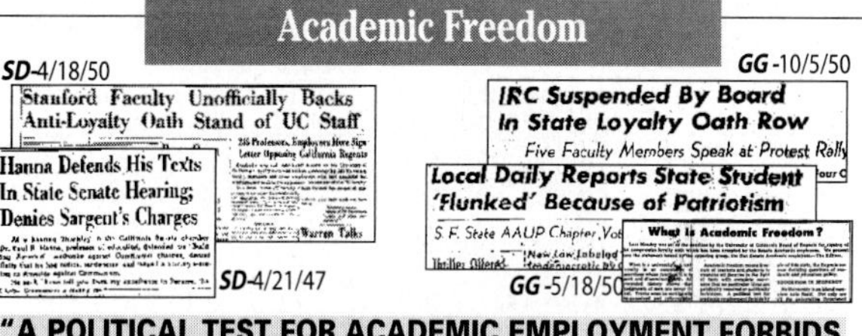

SD-4/18/50

Stanford Faculty Unofficially Backs Anti-Loyalty Oath Stand of UC Staff

Hanna Defends His Texts In State Senate Hearing; Denies Sargent's Charges

SD-4/21/47

GG-10/5/50

IRC Suspended By Board In State Loyalty Oath Row

Five Faculty Members Speak at Protest Rally

Local Daily Reports State Student 'Flunked' Because of Patriotism

What is Academic Freedom?

GG-5/18/50

"A POLITICAL TEST FOR ACADEMIC EMPLOYMENT FORBIDS BY DECREE THE REACHING OF CERTAIN CONCLUSIONS, and threatens all who question ... with loss of their jobs," proclaimed UC Berkeley non-Senate academic employees. The *Golden Gater* and *Stanford Daily* followed the thread of California academic freedom cases (See p. 375).

"One of the Most Wonderful Experiences . . ."

---Marilyn Sidwell and Nancy Allen, Stanford delegates, 1946 Chicago Conference

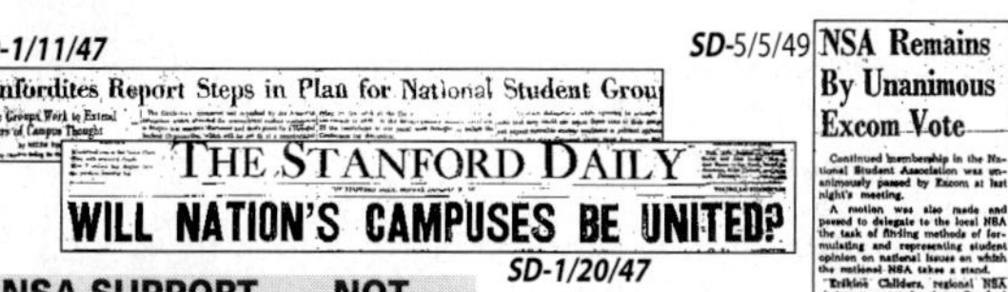

SD-1/11/47

Stanfordites Report Steps in Plan for National Student Group

THE STANFORD DAILY

WILL NATION'S CAMPUSES BE UNITED?

SD-5/5/49

NSA Remains By Unanimous Excom Vote

SD-1/20/47

Excom Vetoes NSA Affiliation

Favors Independent Local Group To Continue Similar Activities Here

Athletic Award Policy Change

NSA Grabs Chance For 2nd Review

Excom May Study Affiliation Issue Tomorrow Night

"NSA SUPPORT . . . NOT STIMULATED BY PRESSURE OF A CONCERNED STUDENT WORLD." HANK ROSIN, student body president, made the case that "NSA did a great job" in smaller colleges, but "well-established student bodies" didn't get as much benefit (***SD***- 4/13/50).

Erskine Childers
Calif. Regional Chair, 1948-49 NSA Int'l. VP, 1949-50

Richard Kelton
Calif. Regional Chair, 1949-50 Stanford IIR President

(More Childers: p. 517, p. 532) Photos: ***SD***- 5/5/49, 9/28/49

ERSKINE CHILDERS got unanimous support for NSA in 1949 (see p. 517) with caution that Excom felt they "were not qualified" to speak for Stanford students "on such issues as academic freedom and federal aid" (***SD***- 5/5/49). **DICK KELTON** lost a 1950 effort, 8-6 (***SD*** -4/13/50), to retain membership, arguing for benefits of "pooled information and action."

Historical notes: San Francisco State University (so named in 1974) is the outcome of San Francisco Normal School, created in 1899, an outgrowth of the city's first teacher training class in 1855. It gave way in 1861 to the California State Normal School, the first state-supported institution of higher learning, becoming SF State College in 1921. Men were first admitted in 1929 (www.sfu.edu). 1948 enrollment: 5,320.

◆ *Transcontinental railroad magnate and former governor Leland Stanford and his wife Jane established Stanford University in Palo Alto. It opened in 1891 on the more than 8,000 acres that had formed his trotting horse stock farm (www.stanford.edu). 1948 enrollment: 8,364.*

Regional Leadership North and South: Mills and Occidental

Editor's note: The diversity of colleges in California participating in NSA included large campuses such as USC, Stanford and UC , and smaller independent colleges such as Mills and Mt. St. Mary. Regional leadership was well distributed. Its chairs and co-chairs included: Dick Heggie, UC Berkeley and Dick Hough, UCLA ('47-48), Erskine Childers, Stanford, and John Knox, Occidental ('48-49), Dick Kelton, Stanford ('49-50), Paul Pitner, UC Berkeley ('50-51), Peggy Bradish, Mt. St. Mary ('51-52), Lowell Vye, Mills College ('52-53).

Occidental: 'A Western Pioneer'

1949-50

Global Perspective

NSA World Affairs Conference Gathers on Campus Tomorrow

"Global Perspective" will be the theme of an inter-campus conference on international affairs to be held at Occidental from 9:00 a.m. to 11:30 p.m. Saturday, March 18. The conference will be presented by International Affairs Commission, N.S.A.; the Collegiate Council for United Nations; International Relations Clubs and the World Student Service Fund. The purpose is to gather students together to discuss world events and further acquaint them with the aims and activities of various student organizations.

Key Addresses

Several noteworthy personalities will be heard: Dr. Wytze Gorter, Professor of International Economics at UCLA will speak on "Accounting for the Dollar Shortage." The Honorable David Owen, Assistant Secretary-General, Department of Economic Affairs of the United Nations will give an address the subject of which is not known. Mr. Robert Kelly, President of the National Student Association, will deliver the principle address entitled "A New International Morality."

Morning Program

The morning will be devoted to South American subjects. "New Patterns in Spanish America" will be the subject of a panel lead by South American students attending L.A.C.C. and L.A.S.C. at 9:45. A Pan-Ameri-

MR. ROBERT KELLY, President of the National Student Association will address the international affairs conference this Saturday, in Women's Lounge.

3/17/50

The Occidental

NSA Calls for Congressional Action on "Civilian G.I. Bill"

The U. S. National Student Association (NSA) has called upon Congress to enact legislation to provide a national program of federally financed scholarships for approximately 300,000 college students. The "Civilian G.I. Bill" would provide for direct support to the individual on the basis of need and ability, and would be administered by the states without discrimination as to race, creed, economic or social status.

Remove Economic Barriers

The purpose of the NSA pro-

NSA Rating Forms To Aid Faculty

The NSA (National Student Association) recently distributed faculty rating scale forms to the faculty of Occidental College.

Experts from the Psychology Department of the University of Wisconsin prepared these forms especially for the students of Oxy to enable the students to express their opinion on each instructor.

Each faculty member was asked to pass the rating scales to the student, asking the student to maturely rate the instructor, according to the scales, that were obtained by the National Student Associa-

NSA Plans New Summer Travel For Students

If you are planning to travel, study, or work abroad next summer, or interested in discussing the opportunities available come to **Alumni Chapel today at 12:15.** The NSA (National Student Association) is conducting ten study-tours and five workcamps in cooperation with the National Unions of students of the respective countries. All projects will be conducted by the students of the countries to be visited. Student-guides will conduct all travelling and studying groups, and every ef-

Fr .top: 4/22/49, 2/25/49, 3/4/49

Occidental's NSA Committee brought national programs ro the campus

The Eye of the Beholder

1948-49

KNOX CHAMPIONED NSA in the face of determined and articulate opposition led by an editor of *The Occidental*, who felt NSA had done "absolutely nothing" for the college (below). Jack Knox, Mary Lou Fife and other members of his committee mounted a spirited defense. Knox also appealed to pride in Occidental as a "western pioneer in the national intercollegiate movement."

Jack Knox
Calif. Regional Co-Chair, 1948-49
Grand National Forensic 1st Place

Yearbook photo: *La Encina*, 1949

The Challenge

5/4/49

GROWL, TIGER GROWL

Once again it seems necessary to consider **one of the greatest farces** that has ever taken place on the Oxy campus —**NSA**, the so-called National Student Association.

It is now almost two years since the **wild-eyed evangelists of NSA** first called upon this campus, bringing with them promises of exchange assemblies, purchase card systems, inter-school cooperation, and many other gaudy items. **We have spent, as a student body, several hundred dollars** for dues to this "organization" and for the trotting of delegates here and there.

* * * *

And, after two years, **what d**o we have to show for it? **Absolutely nothing.**

* * * *

The answer is, of cou[rse] clear. **NSA should be drop**

The Response

5/13/49

Those of you who have kept up with the NSA Bulletin Board and articles about NSA in previous issues are aware of progress this organization is making. Next time the **NSA News** is distributed in the post office look over a copy.

It might well be indicated that Occidental College is a western pioneer in the national intercollegiate movement. Pioneers have traditionally had to put up with discomfort and lack of progress until they begin to work together. People who are interested in the betterment of student life in this country should at least give constructive criticism and an atmosphere of encouragement even if they might lack the inclination or aptitude to actually help.

Sincerely,

JACK KNOX.

Mills: Brings Its Spirit to NSA

More from** Mills College Weekly **on pp 59, 367, 368, 485, 487, 503, 777

The NSO

1947

Harold Laski wrote an article in *The Nation* the other day which is interesting to all students because it discusses "Students in Politics," and especially important to Mills students because of their work in world relief. In his article Mr. Laski says that a students' organization has one of two fairly well-defined purposes: "It exists either to make the path of learning an easier one, or to promote a body of specific political doctrine in which its members are interested. The first type, of which the Interna-tional Stud[...] Student Se[...] sarily unco[...] provide rel[...] exchange o[...] dom . . ."

Mills is a[...] Mr. Laski's[...] Executive [...] student con[...] would have[...] on the Na[...] last Monda[...] pointed because it turned out to be definitely non-political. They thought we had not accomplished

"The NSO won't make headlines or hold mass meetings . . . but neither will it destroy itself and leave undone its quietly constructive work."

1/17/47

10/17/47

11/14/47

Mills College Weekly

CAMPUS TODAY--COMMUNITY TOMORROW

Heineman Will Speak Opening Vocational Day

11 Subjects to Be Discussed Vocational D[ay]

SOCIAL WORK GOVERNMENT SCIENCES

HEALTH WRITING PERSONNEL CHILD AID VOLUNTEERS MUSIC, DRAMA

Lorrie Eisenberg and Friends Live with Students In Turin

The trip from Paris to Turin was an interesting one. The train wound its way through the French Alps ... tered their house as strangers, completely unknown to them and they to us. But perhaps the odds were in our favor. We had a curiosity ...

Lorrie Eisenberg
Reported on her 1947 ISS trip to Europe, ASMC Secy

"We symbolized America to them . . . the first American students they had ever had the chance to meet and talk with."

Mills College Weekly

Mills Acts On A-Bomb

A. A. Hold Week Picnic Thursday

Three to Speak on War Trials at Forum

Forum Plans Mass Meeting; Truman, Congress to be Wired

1949

10/28/49

N. S. A.

by Louise Alport

Midterms and formals be-darned! MY last weekend was spent with seventy-eight other delegates at the California-Nevada-Hawaii Regional Assembly in Los Angeles. This body hears and tries to coordinate plans of the individual schools for the period between the bi-yearly regional meetings, assuming the responsibility for planning and implementing those NSA projects requiring cooperation among several campuses. Its host October 22 and 23 was Los Angeles City College.

A plea for a "responsible college press" was issued at the first general session by Mr. Harris of the Los Angeles Times. The speaker stated that the "Relation of the College Newspaper to the Campus" is a fun[...] important fu[...] as an inform[...] reader, an [...] for its staff, [...] ous opinions[...]

Louise Alport
1949-50 NSA, Mills Weekly

"Our job is to find out how to fit the policies and the idealism of the National Student Association to the peculiarities of the CNH Region."

Sally Zook
ASMC President, NSA, 1951-52

1951

Editorials

3/15/52

"Almost every other group in the country is represented on a national level by some organization . . . the student community of the United States which comprises a large part of the population is represented by only one such organization, the National Student Association."

"CAMPUS TODAY--COMMUNITY TOMORROW" (top of page) was an attitude that was reflected in the continuous and enthusiastic support of NSA by Mills student leaders.

Editorials

"The why and wherefore of the *Student Bill of Rights* is simple: the desire for an uncensored, truthful education. . . . [to] ensure for every student the opportunity to [think and act in] the 'free market of ideas.'"

3/20/52

1952

Lowell Vye
Calif. Regional Chair, ASMC

Photos: ***The Crest*** Yearbook

Historical notes: Occidental College, founded 1887 in Los Angeles by a group of Presbyterian ministers and laymen, has had no formal religious association since 1910. Its first student body was made up of 27 men and 13 women (www.oxy.edu). 1948 enrollment: 1,365 ♦ In 1865, Cyrus and Susan Mills, Christian missionaries returning from the Sandwich Islands, bought the Young Ladies Seminary, founded in 1852, from Oberlin graduate Mary Atkins. In 1889 the college granted the first BA degree to a woman west of the Mississippi. Located in Oakland, it remains a women's college, with graduate programs for men (www.mills.edu). 1948 enrollment: 766.

"Amid the welter of war, let us guard the university and freedoms which it preserves."

Monroe E. Deutsch: Inspired as a Scholar and Dean

Provost Emeritus, University of California, Berkeley
Member, NSA Advisory Council, 1948-51

Editor's note: Monroe Deutsch was among those educators who were schooled in classical traditions and who rose to prominence in the first half of the 20th century, both before and after the war. While those of his generation championed traditions and a younger generation of educators advocated for more student choice in curriculum, many of them came together and advocated for greater student empowerment and responsibility in the governance of student life. Mildred Kiefer Wurf (See p. 178), California regional chair in 1947 and a UC Berkeley student, remembers that "his practice was to have an hour each week when any student could see him about anything . . . He indeed was recognized as an exceptional educator and human being. Following are excerpts from The Letter and the Spirit, *a selection of his addresses (University of California Press, 1943).*

Preservation of the University

Editor's note: This is an excerpt from a wartime commencement address delivered at Stanford Universty on June 14, 1942. In it Deutsch "makes a plea for the studies that have no direct relation to warfare: for letters, the social sciences, pure science, art, music and philosophy."

Amid the welter of war let us guard the university and the freedoms which it preserves and embodies. It is easy to say this in the abstract; but when a concrete case occurs, when public hysteria rises, and patriotism assumes the guise of a baleful monster, then stand up for the freedom of your university—yes, of all universities.

In this period of war, colleges, like other institutions, have undergone certain alterations—external changes, I trust they are. Because technically trained men and women are desperately needed, we are all seeking to complete the basic education of physicians, chemists, engineers, physicists, and the like as rapidly as possible. And this we must of course do. We must also offer courses fitting men and women to participate in many ways in our war effort. These must include practical courses and those that seek to teach what the issues of the war really are. All this is proper and good.

But there is great danger that we may look at all university education through glasses clouded by the mist of war. After all, universities will go on living long after the struggle is over, and men and women will be educated once more, we hope, without immediate thought of preparation for war.

So I wish to make a plea for the studies that have no direct relation to warfare: for letters, the social sciences, pure science, art, music, and philosophy. I admit that each of these can be shown to be of use at the present time: the musician can write a stirring song; the poet may rouse men as Tyrtaeus the Spartan did; the historian may help by showing the roots of the struggle; the economist may aid in finance and other problems. Yet, though this is true, these studies do not exist primarily for such a purpose.

And the university must not let the temporary situation turn young men and women completely away from the pursuits that are essential in a civilized society. Let a Hitler shape all education to the uses of war; but if we imitate him, then, however the war may end, he will have won, for we will have turned not only plowshares but harps and paintbrushes into swords.

Mankind will need religion and letters, song and sculpture, law and the social sciences, long after the trumpet sounds that prayed for armistice. Think what a barren world, a desert, we should have if all these disappeared from the face of the earth.

DEUTSCH ENDORSES THE NEW NSA

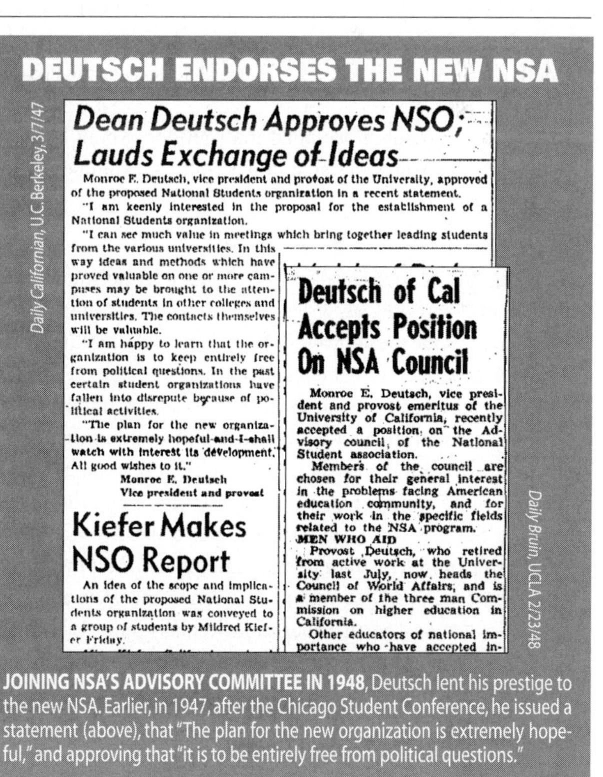

Daily Californian, U.C. Berkeley, 3/7/47

Dean Deutsch Approves NSO; Lauds Exchange of Ideas

Monroe E. Deutsch, vice president and provost of the University, approved of the proposed National Students organization in a recent statement.

"I am keenly interested in the proposal for the establishment of a National Students organization.

"I can see much value in meetings which bring together leading students from the various universities. In this way ideas and methods which have proved valuable on one or more campuses may be brought to the attention of students in other colleges and universities. The contacts themselves will be valuable.

"I am happy to learn that the organization is to keep entirely free from political questions. In the past certain student organizations have fallen into disrepute because of political activities.

"The plan for the new organization is extremely hopeful and I shall watch with interest its development. All good wishes to it."

Monroe E. Deutsch
Vice president and provost

Kiefer Makes NSO Report

An idea of the scope and implications of the proposed National Students organization was conveyed to a group of students by Mildred Kiefer Friday.

Daily Bruin, UCLA 2/23/48

Deutsch of Cal Accepts Position On NSA Council

Monroe E. Deutsch, vice president and provost emeritus of the University of California, recently accepted a position on the Advisory council of the National Student association.

Members of the council are chosen for their general interest in the problems facing American education community, and for their work in the specific fields related to the NSA program.

MEN WHO AID

Provost Deutsch, who retired from active work at the University last July, now heads the Council of World Affairs, and is a member of the three man Commission on higher education in California.

Other educators of national importance who have accepted in-

JOINING NSA'S ADVISORY COMMITTEE IN 1948, Deutsch lent his prestige to the new NSA. Earlier, in 1947, after the Chicago Student Conference, he issued a statement (above), that "The plan for the new organization is extremely hopeful," and approving that "it is to be entirely free from political questions."

University of Utopia

Editor's note: These are excerpts from an address delivered on June 6, 1941, six months before Pearl Harbor, at the annual Phi Beta Kappa-Sigma Chi meeting at the University of Washington. In it, Deutsch echos some of the themes in defense of liberal education and the need for excellence voiced by Father Gannon of Fordham University in his 1961 memoir, The Poor Old Liberal Arts *(see p. 890).*

We have all, I presume, at times allowed our imaginations free sway and built in the clouds an ideal city, an ideal state, an ideal world. And, being university men and women, we have dreamed dreams of an ideal university.

We must admit the insuperable difficulty of constructing the ideal of a single section of life. We know that an ideal university could only exist if we had an ideal society, ideal students, ideal teachers, ideal facilities, and (you will not be surprised if I add) ideal financial support. This would be taking on a large order, you will agree. It would involve the problem of finding ideal ancestry, ideal environment, ideal economic and political conditions—in fact, an ideal world.

Let us, therefore, narrow our discussion and command our imaginations to flit about within the limits of the college campus.

* * * *

. . . After our experiments with absolutely free election, with majors, and with a few units of requirements in certain large fields, we seem to me to be driven to do for the year 1941 what earlier educators did when they set up their old curriculum. Let me quickly disabuse your minds of any impression that I am a reactionary and think we can solve our problems of today merely by turning back the hands of the clock. No, we must make our curriculum in the light of the present. We must, for example, see the importance of both the natural sciences and the social sciences in our modem world.

But the curriculum we build must give our young men and women who are being educated in our colleges a common, a unified, background.

* * * *

But, after all, our University of Utopia demands more than a curriculum. There are teachers and students to be considered.

What is your—and my—ideal teacher in this ideal university of our dreams? We want men and women who themselves have both a broad education and excellent specialized training. They must have a double interest, or, rather, a double enthusiasm: on the one hand, a zest for scholarship; on the other, a keen interest in the students and a realization of the importance of the function of teaching. But this is not all; I should add to these two desiderata one which I consider also of primary importance. And this is character. After all, a university may prove a bane rather than a blessing, if a young man or woman, though intellectually trained, is morally undermined. And most important in its effect on the students is the character of the teacher.

We should seek something affirmative in our teachers—the kind of personality that shines through the man's utterances and leaves its deep imprint on his students. Some phrase of his, casually dropped, may fall like fructifying seed into the mind of the student and shape the course of his life.

* * * *

If one is only the repository of knowledge in a particular subject, and uninterested in the throbbing young people sitting before him, put him in a research institute, a museum, or a library. Let him deal with books, equipment, or machines, but not with that delicate thing, the personality of young people.

And what of the students? They should not be pampered and coddled; but neither should they be treated as automatons, subject to stringent, inflexible rules. It must be remembered that human beings are constantly meeting conditions which keep them from attaining the best of which they are capable. But as to their studies, they should be expected to meet searching standards, and in this respect the humanities and the social sciences should be no more content with slovenly work than the natural sciences.

MONROE E. DEUTSCH (1879-1955)

Editor's note: The following is adapted from the UC Berkeley Bancroft Library biographical sketch for the Deutsch papers.

Monroe Emanuel Deutsch, professor of classics and Vice-President and provost of the University of California, was born in 1879 in San Francisco. An excellent student, he graduated from Lowell High School in San Francisco, and then worked his way through the University of California, receiving his bachelor's degree in 1902 and his master's degree in 1903. He first taught for a year in the Mission High School in San Francisco, and later in the Berkeley High School where he remained until 1907, when he became an assistant in Greek at the University of California and worked for his doctorate. This he received in 1911. He attained full professorship in Latin in 1922.

In 1918 he became the first Dean of Summer Sessions at Los Angeles. He retained this position for three years, and, in the summer 1922, was appointed Dean of the College of Letters and Science at Berkeley. In 1930 he was named Vice-President and Dean of the University, serving in this capacity until his retirement in 1947, one of the longest periods of administrative service of any university official.

Deutsch, active in many extra-curricular organizations, was president of the Commonwealth Club of California in 1943 and 1944, of the board of trustees of the Rosenberg Foundation, of the San Francisco International Center, of the northern California branch of the American Association for the United Nations, of the California Chapter of Phi Beta Kappa, of the Berkeley Rotary Club and of the Berkeley Community Chest, and member of the national boards of the Association for the United Nations and the Conference of Christians and Jews. He was decorated Chevalier of the French Legion of Honor, Commander of the Chilean Order of Merit, and recipient of the Danish Christian X Medal. In 1929 he was awarded the Benjamin Ide Wheeler Medal for distinguished service to the City of Berkeley. Deutsch received honorary Doctor of Laws degrees from St. Mary's College, Santa Clara College, Occidental College and Mills College.

He edited a collection of the writings of Benjamin Ide Wheeler, and authored *The Letter and the Spirit,* 1943, a collection of his own speeches, *Our Legacy of Religious Freedom,* and *The College from Within,* 1952 and numerous articles. He died in 1955.

PICTURE CREDIT: *NSA News,* August, 1951.

PART 5. NSA's REGIONS: CREATING INTERCOLLEGIATE NETWORKS

SECTION 9

The Northwest

CONTENTS

NSA's northernmost outpost in Washington, Oregon and Idaho enjoyed a period of active leadership at the University of Washington through a succession of regional chairs who also provided a national voice on NSA's Executive Committee: Norman Israel (1947-48), Dan Pulsifer (1948-49), and William Gates (1949-50). They were followed in 1950-51 by James Seelig (Eastern Washington College of Education), in 1951-52 by Joan Long (Lynch) (Marylhurst College, OR), who had been national staff associate the previous year (see Part 1), and Kenneth Strand (Washington State College) in 1952-53.

Bill Gates, Sr. (now Co-chair and CEO of the Bill and Melinda Gates Foundation), joins Helen Knudsen Pulsifer in a reflection on their leadership years at University of Washington and NSA. Washington was another of the states with an active Un-American Affairs legislative committee, whose investigations at the University attained national prominence.

Encompassing an area some 450 miles wide and 750 miles north to south, with a census of 41 four-year colleges (six in Idaho), NSA's membership of 7 or 8 institutions, with twice as many or more attending regional events, was clustered around an inner triangle of Seattle, Portland and the neighboring cities of Pullman,WA (WashiIngton State) and Moscow, ID (University of Idaho).

Regional leaders focus on developing campus-level programs

Joan (Long) Lynch provides an overview of the region's character and history. Albums are furnished on Marylhurst, Lewis and Clark and Reed in Oregon and on Eastern Washington State and the University of Idaho/Washington State College NSA partnership across state borders.

Excerpts of reports from regional leaders highlight the sentiment of student leaders in the area that "the nature of student government in the Northwest is different from that in other areas" (Kenneth Strand, p. 1066), and that "NSA puts too much emphasis on national and international issues" (Mac McCredy, p. 1063).

The section closes with a tribute to Dean S. Newhouse, an early and enthusiastic supporter of NSA at the University of Washington, who had built a strong relationship with Gordon Klopf, NSA's first Advisory Committee Chairman. Together with others in a new generation of student personnel administrators that emerged after World War II, he championed NSA as "an experiment in self-government so significant that everyone interested in democracy should be watching it with the keenest interest."

Northwest NSA Delegates Converging for Conference

Delegates from some 40 schools in the Northwest are expected to arrive today for the NSA regional conference to be held on the campus tomorrow and Sunday.

The business session of the conference will get under way ... following welcome addresses ... breakfast by Dean Edward

University of Washington Daily

12/2/49

Reed College Acts as Host To Northwest Region Meet

Approximately 40 delegates representing seven member colleges and universities in the Great Northwest region of the National Student Association, met this past week-end at Reed college ... assembly.

Marylhurst, 12/8/51

NORTHWEST COLLEGE members anchoring NSA in the Portland area and in Eastern and Western Washington, despite their small numbers, maintained an active organization, periodically drawing up to 15 or more colleges to their assemblies.

Northwest Regional NSA Highlights

Advocating for Affiliation

Oregon Reed College. RC- 1/30/47

Delegate to National Student Conference at Chicago Urges Permanent Reed Participation in Organization

Washington U. of Washington. UW-12/5/47

Delegates To Discuss, Vote On NSA Constitution Today In Organizations Assembly

Executive Board Votes Tuesday On NSA Question

USNSA APPROVED; IC, IFC, PANHELLENIC WILL BE ORIENTED

Idaho U. of Idaho. TA- 10/8/48

Washington State C. WS-3/1/48

AFFIILATION VOTES were generally taken by student governments rather than through referendums. They tended not to spark the campus-wide controversies as did affiliation contests in California. Although the Universities of Washington and Idaho were active members, the University of Oregon, while sending delegates to occasional regional assemblies, never joined.

Maintaining an International Outlook

Farquharson Forms Student Organization To Promote Peace

Group Founded in East Spreads to West, Chase, Beard, Flynn Back New Society To Keep America Out of Foreign War

Washington State Evergreen

VICTORY BELL HERALDS SURRENDER NEWS

NORTHWEST COLLEGE CONGRESS ADOPTS PEACE RESOLUTIONS

Left, from top: *UW* 10/10/39 *WS* 5/9/45, 4/12/46

CAMPUS CHEST DRIVE STARTS TODAY

University of Washington Daily

National Student Assn. Begins Drive To Place DP's in U.S. Colleges

Great N.W. Asks Renewal Of Fulbright

Students To Hear WSSF Group Head

From top,: *UW* 11/4/47, 12/7/48. *TA*-11/9/48. Above, rt.: *NSA News* 4/50.

INTERNATIONAL AFFAIRS captured Northwest college student attention, with a tradition of interest in rhe Pacific rim. Major university papers tracked wartime events closely (pp. 834, 1060).

Japanese-American Internment

UW-12/8/41

Terminal Island evacuees, 1941 (AFSC)

5/4/42

INTERNMENT OF JAPANESE-AMERICANS troubled many students. At the same time the shock of Pearl Harbor stunned American Nisei themselves (above), many of whom fought in the armed forces while their families remained in internment camps (see Suzuki, p. 1031. Also pages 1037, 720).

Building Regional Organization

1947-48

Three Delegates to Be Sent to Portland NSA Regional Conference

1948-49

Idaho Observers Attend USNSA Meet At Pullman

From left, top: *UW*-2/8/48, *TA*-10/19/48 Middle: *UW*-12/6/49, Bottom: *TT*-4/51, *TT*-12/18/51, *EW*-1/17/51

1949-50

NSA Regional Conference Discusses Intercollegiate Activity, Course Evaluation

Music Units Join Forces For Concert

REGIONAL MEETINGS ROTATED among the four to eight member colleges, attracting two or three times their number. The Northwest region of the Pacific Student President's Association also continued a tradition of annual meetings since the 1930's, leading Henry Schmitz, UW President, after reading NSA Regional Chair Kenneth Strand's regional report (p.0000), to observe in a 3/23/53 letter to Glen Nygreen that "top student groups, like the rest of us, are becoming a little over-organized."

1950-51

Veep Reports On Confab

Reed College Acts as Host To Northwest Region Meet

Forum Attracts Interest, Youth Topic Of Debate

1951-52

Northwest meet set for February 2, 3, 4; Seelig will officiate

Woolf pens labor story

Loyalty Oaths and the Red Scare

NSA News 2/49

Washington Faculty Dismissals Arouse Nation-Wide Comment

UW-2/25/48

Students Protest Banning Politics From U Campus

NSA prexy criticizes loyalty oath

EW-1/31/51

THE UNIVERSITY OF WASHINGTON was the principal object of a state legislative anti-Communist probe in 1948, one of many throughout the country that attracted national attention (see pp. 388, 1061).

KEY TO COLLEGE NEWSPAPER CITATIONS IN THIS SECTION

- UW - *University of Washington Daily*
- SU - *Seattle University Spectator*
- PL - Lewis and Clark College (*Pioneer Log*)
- WS - *Washington State Evergreen*
- RQ - *Reed College Quest*
- TA - *The Argonaut*, U. of Idaho
- EW- Eastern Washington State (*The Journal*)
- TT - *The Tower*, Marylhurst C.

Regional Leaders

Portland area delegates: Fr. l.: Joan Long, *Marylhurst*; Lois Cook, *Reed*; Rosemary Marshall, *Marylhurst*; Tam Trotta, *Lewis and Clark*. August, 1949, at Illinois Congress (Joan Long Lynch).

John Elwood
Lewis and Clark College
Regil Chair, 1946-47

Norman Israel
University of Washington
Regil Chair, 1947-48

Dan Pulsifer
University of Washington
Regil Chair, 1948-49

William Gates
University of Washington
Regil Chair, 1949-50

James Seelig
Eastern Wash. Coll. of Ed.
Regil Chair, 1950-51

Joan Long
Marylhurst College
Regil Chair, 1951-52

1. NSA at the University of Washington and the Pacific Northwest Region

William H. Gates, Sr.
University of Washington
President, NSA Pacific Northwest Region, 1949-1951,
and
Helen Knudson Pulsifer
University of Washington
UW NSA Delegate, 1949-1950

Editor's Note: As recalled in an interview with Gene Schwartz, NSA vice president, educational problems, 1948-49, in Seattle, Washington, on July 13, 1998.

Academic Freedom and the University of Washington

Gene: We are reflecting on the Pacific Northwest Region and University of Washington back in 1948, 1949, and 1950. And also reviewing articles in some of the issues of the *University of Washington Daily* at the time.

Bill: As I recall, there were three things going on that the students—and I think it's pretty fair to say that the majority—certainly the majority of students were upset about. One was this Un-American Activities Committee that was called the Canwell Committee.

Gene: Was that a state committee?

Bill: That was a committee of the state legislature, and it was really bad. As a result of that committee's activities, there were six professors who had tenure hearings—three of whom lost their jobs. One, not so charged, resigned. And it also led to some very interesting stuff having to do with a professor by the name of Melvin Rader, whom one of the witnesses charged with being a communist, and part of it had to do with Rader having been at a meeting somewhere in the country. A fellow by the name of Ed Guthman, who is a journalist in Los Angeles today, later dug into that and was able to prove that Dr. Rader and his wife had been at a lodge in the mountains in Western Washington and couldn't possibly have been at that meeting—as well as some other, similar proofs. That was the most vivid. Rader was later completely exonerated from all of those charges, and there was a great deal of apology here, there, and everywhere.

One of the things that occurred in the midst of that had to do with Harry Bridges. He was very prominent in the news at that time, and the question of whether the Longshoreman's Union was a communist-oriented organization. Somebody wanted to give the university a professorship or a scholarship that had Harry Bridges's name connected with it, and the university refused it.

Gene: Who was the president of the university at that time?

Bill: Raymond Allen.

Gene: Where did he stand on these issues of academic freedom?

Bill: Careful. Finger in the wind sort of a guy.

Helen: Where was Canwell from?

Bill: Canwell was from Spokane, which has always been the conservative end of the state politically. That committee got formed in the legislature and it's hard to separate how much of it is just bandwagon kind of stuff. This took place in 1948–49. It preceded McCarthy's heyday, which came later, in the 1950s.

Gene: But if you were to narrow the range of your recollection and just zero in on the student government and the student body, generally, what was their attitude towards issues of this sort? It sounds as though this came down on the side of what we would call academic freedom.

Bill: Yes. Another issue, Gene, which I think is a good barometer of that was an event called the political speakers ban. Nobody who was engaged in a campaign could speak on the campus. In fact, I think it went farther than that. I think it was anybody who could be defined as a political speaker could not speak on the campus. We were up in arms about that. We had a very successful petition campaign, and it was changed, ultimately.

There isn't any question where the student body stood on that. It was clearly on the liberal side of that issue. The university came to recognize that the ban was a lot of foolishness.

Value of NSA debated

Gene: Now I want to switch a little bit. What comes up in these *Washington Daily* articles in a couple of places, and it's raised by faculty people, as well as by the interfraternity council and the associated men were the questions, "Is there any value to NSA? Is it worth our money? Are they really doing something?" There was a professor quoted as saying, "In law school we would really look at what they do and not what they claim to be doing."

Helen: I think that was an ongoing concern, wasn't it?

Bill: Yes, that was pretty much so.

Gene: In March of 1950, you're going to the Board to get the appropriation for the $1,100 membership fee. And here is Pete Mellitz, interfraternity council representative, saying "NSA has accomplished nothing that students could not have done for themselves," and Harry Cross, law school faculty member, warning in the open discussion that we should judge NSA on what it has done and not what it claims to do. Then there's Bob Anderson, of the Associated Men, who feared that NSA would, in the future, get to be too much of a crutch for student groups needing ideas.

Of course, you are in there defending the organization, explaining that NSA's position is to represent students in things in which they are interested. You may not agree with the ideas, they may be radical or not, but if students are interested in them, they have a right to discuss them and clear them up. I get the message that what energized your engagement, and I would assume by inference, the leadership on campus was the whole idea of being part of a community where it wasn't so much what you accomplished, but the fact that you got together to consider things that were of concern. Is that a fair way to characterize it?

Bill: There was value in a national organization of students. It was an added ingredient which was a clear plus. I remember arguing that interaction with people from City College of New York and St. Peter's and North Carolina, whatever, was a thing of terrific value. Not only for the people that went there, but for the student governments that they represented.

Helen: I think it's also true that for the men who went, the boys who went, they would have been primarily veterans, so they had a much broader perspective on the world and what the role of education was. I was interested in the size of the delegations we sent to the conventions.

Bill: We had a lot of people.

Pacific Northwest Region

Gene: There were about forty schools at the two regional meetings that are recorded here.

Bill: Yes. The regional meetings were very successful.

Gene: Even though NSA only had seven member schools in Washington-Oregon at the time, many more attended regional meetings.[1] And this was true of other areas, by the way. Like the Virginia-Carolinas—they may have had about seven or eight member colleges, but they'd get twenty-five or thirty colleges showing up to their regional meetings. So there was a lot more interest—there was real interest in getting together.

Bill: There was. Typical of any organization, not just a student organization, I remember also that one of the big issues was the relative rights of the member representatives and the nonmember schools as to who had a chance to speak.

Helen: Yes. The nonmembers could only speak after all of the members had spoken.

Gene: Did either of you know Dean Newhouse?

Helen: I know Dan [Pulsifer] knew him pretty well.[2]

Bill: I knew him.

Gene: Did he have any kind of an influence on campus that comes back to mind?

Bill: Yes. He was a significant person, but I think the more significant one was Glen Nygreen.

Helen: I think so. Glen Nygreen was the one who worked with Norm Israel and Gummie Johnson, the first ones in NSA. They were the representatives in 1947 to the Constitutional Convention.

Glen Nygreen, I think, was the one who really got this together. He's the one that encouraged Dan and got Dan involved.

Bill: Glen went to the regional meeting. He encouraged us a lot. He was a major factor.

Gene: It says here in the *Daily* that Glen Nygreen addressed the constitutional convention on behalf of Dean Newhouse because Dean Newhouse couldn't attend. I know that Dean Newhouse and Gordon Klopf, as student personnel professionals, carried on quite an extended correspondence on the subject of NSA during those years.

Helen: Glen was quite a mentor for Dan.

Bill: I also remember Chuck Owens.

Gene: Now the name Brock Adams comes up at the time, who I gather later on in life was elected U.S. Senator and then got into some political trouble.

Bill: He was ASUW [Associated Students of the University of Washington] President.

Organization of NSA on campus

Gene: There is mention in here about the Campus Chest. I remember the Campus Chests were really a very important vehicle for students contributing to valuable causes.

Helen: In the three years of the Washington student paper, *The Daily*, that I reviewed, the Campus Chest was mentioned frequently. This structure consolidated other drives and encouraged all the groups' supporters to contribute to the Campus Chest, which would then establish allocation ratios for the member groups

Gene: But there is one report there that the decision was taken not to combine the World Student Service Fund with the Campus Chest because, as the woman who was quoted as opposing it said, "They would set a precedent and have to start bringing in other funds."

Helen: I have no thoughts on that.

Gene: Another thing that is mentioned here is that the NSA's presence on campus was manifest through an NSA committee and that it needed to have some kind of articles or bylaws.

Bill: Yes. There was such an organization.

Gene: So there was a separate NSA committee? Was that under control of the student government?

Bill: Yes.

Gene: It says here, Bill Gates is chairman of the assembly's by-law committee and the Board of Control passed unanimously a plan of organization for the local national student association unit. I figure from this article that the local unit is the University of Washington (UW) unit. So, apparently, there was a plan of organization that had to be approved by the Board of Control, and the Board of Control was the student government.

Bill: Yes. But the kind of wild herring in this is the Organizations Assembly, which had no legislative position—no authority whatsoever— but it met with thirty or forty, occasionally fifty or sixty, people gathered in a big auditorium, and they basically raised a lot of hell without any responsibility for it. The Board of Control ran the student government. It was the student government and it was all students. There was no faculty involved.[3]

Helen: And there was formal representation by the other organization.

Gene: So it appears as though, even though you had articulate opposition, that you always had a strong vote from the Board of Control in favor of NSA.

Bill: That is correct.

Helen: Until, in 1951, it kind of fell apart, and the Control Board decided to withdraw from NSA.[4]

Gene: Here I see there was a fellow by the name of Art Degginger who was chair of the NSA committee in 1948.

Bill: I would assume so.

Gene: Then we see a regional conference in February of 1949 at UW. And Glen Nygreen is addressing the conference and expecting forty schools to be represented. That's a great turnout.

Bill: I'm surprised at that number.

Gene: You're there in order to draft a constitution for the region. That was an interesting thing, as I recall. The regions all went about having to develop their own constitutions. It was like: "Okay, here we are. We need bylaws." Now here you are, in April of 1949, Helen Knudson. You're being elected as an NSA delegate.

NSA programs and student government

Gene: Now, here's another place in the *Daily* where somebody questions whether or not NSA was worthwhile. Let's pick out some programs mentioned in the *Daily* articles. It mentions the Purchase Card System. Was that something that operated when you were active?

Helen: No. My recollection is that Dan, who was a General Studies major had to have a marketing related project. So he took on a project of interviewing the merchants in the university district to determine what their attitude would be to participating in a student Purchase Card System. I don't think it ever happened. There was mixed response on the part of the merchants.

Bill: I don't think we ever implemented that plan.

Gene: Okay. How about the faculty rating system? It was another program that was implemented by NSA, and a lot of campuses around the country introduced it. Was quality of teaching an issue at the time?

Bill: I don't know why, I'm inclined to say no. It seems to me I would remember or these articles in the *Daily* would reflect this somehow. We certainly have a faculty rating system now that's been in place for years and years.

Gene: It's in here as a subject that came up at the region, but that doesn't mean anything was done. As the UW professor says, let's look at what they did and not what they—

Bill: Intended to do or said.

Gene: There were a lot of good intentions we had in those days that couldn't turn into programs everywhere.

Gene: Did student government at UW through the Board of Control have a very significant position in campus life?

Bill: Oh, very.

Gene: —And in extracurricular activities. So the Board is something that the typical student paid attention to when elections came around?

Helen: I'm looking at one of the articles that gives a vote count in one of the elections. It will give you an idea of how many positions were slated in 1949 and 1950—and how many voted.

Bill: We had what—about 18,000 students? And we'd get 2,500 or something like that voting.

Gene: In the election reported here, the maximum vote for the presidential candidates was about 4,500.

Helen: That was pretty good.

Bill: That's a quarter of the total.

Gene: I see the Board of Control managed a budget that included athletics at the time. Did they also run the Student Store?

Bill: No. They did not. They had a representative to that board, but that board was independent.

Gene: Was UW a campus that you could say was controlled heavily by fraternities and athletics? I don't get the impression reading the paper that was the case.

Bill: Yes, actually I think it probably was.

Helen: But I think the veterans made a big difference. Certainly, before the war the fraternity system would have been much more in control. But there were a lot of independents, and the independent organizations, I think, broadened student concerns to inlude fanily housing and child care, for example.

Bill: They were very strong. I remember when it was sort of an issue—almost on a partisan basis—whether it was going to be an independent or fraternity person who was elected to an office, and particularly the presidency. Phil Palmer was an independent and then after him was a fellow by the name of Sam Stanley who was a fraternity person.

Helen: Well, he was about twenty-seven.. So he wasn't the rah-rah fraternity type.

Bill: I think that dichotomy was stronger in the earlier 1940s.

Regional organization

Gene: Do you recall at all if the presence of Catholic schools was an issue in the Northwest Region in terms of factions?

Bill: Not in our region. It was something we talked about, but I don't think there was any playing out of such a dichotomy.

Gene: The Metropolitan New York region would be the archetypical example of where there was heightened awareness of factions among college delegaions.

Helen: I don't recall any Catholic schools in the state of Washington that were involved with us.

Bill: I don't think so.

Gene: Actually, in the *Daily* article on the Constitutional Convention, it includes amongst the seven Northwest Region colleges that were to attend Reed College in Oregon, Central Washington, Seattle College, Washington State, Idaho University, and Northern Idaho Junior College.

Bill: Seattle was a Catholic school.

Gene: So Washington was not really that strong a Catholic school state.

Helen and Bill: No.

Bill: Probably more now than it was then. Seattle University has become a significant institution.

Gene: One of the things that is true about a number of the regions in the Midwest and East and middle America in general is that—we used to kid about it—the Catholic girls' schools furnished a tremendous amount of leadership energy on the regional level. A lot of them became regional chairs. Manhattanville College, which was right next door to the City College of New York, gave us an office, and I remember getting acquainted with Mother O'Byrne and the sisters there—for me that was the first time I'd ever spoken to a Catholic nun. But they opened a lot of doors to us.

Helen: I think there was more of a Protestant heritage in the West. The Scandinavians and the wheat farmers—people who had migrated from the Midwest.

Gene: You didn't have as strong a Southern European presence.

Bill: I just don't think of us as having quite the same priority on those kinds of identities, Gene. You didn't really think of people as Catholic. I haven't the slightest idea among my friends if they were Catholics or Presbyterians.

Gene: That was probably one of the great things about the Northwest. It was uncontaminated.

Bill: I think that's right. I think that is a legitimate way to put it.

Controversial issues

Gene: Here is a story about the loyalty oath within the ROTC. NSA's national organization denounced it. But it was not an issue for Washington because—according to this article—there were no complaints raised by any of the Washington ROTC people. It arrived on campus because NSA had taken a position on it in connection with Harvard. Do you recall that as being a point of contention here?

Bill: I don't recall that at all. There was a loyalty oath issue on our campus, but it had to do with the faculty.

Gene: Here's a a *Daily* reference to a Control Board meeting where you're presenting, in March of 1950, the rationale for continuing the membership in NSA, and where there was some faculty opposition. There is a paragraph about the underlying danger of radicalism that was officially entered into the discussion by Mellitz. He charged that NSA could hurt the students by radical pressure. Was that a significant point of view?

Bill: That's Pete Mellitz of the Interfraternity Council. The organization was viewed as radical—the Mellitz statement there is typical of the opposition.

Gene: I've learned in going through the college newspapers and archives that NSA in the Northwest during your era and in Dan Pulsifer's and Joan Long's eras was a fairly articulate organization.

Bill: Yes.

Gene: From your sense of the other colleges in the area, would you say that the turnout would indicate that there was similar interest among a number of other colleges in the organization?

Bill: I think that's right, at least for some of them.

Helen: Marylhurst is the one that sticks in my mind as being more active than maybe the rest of them.[5]

Bill: Oh, much so.

Helen: But I suspect that it was the personal enthusiasm and initiative of the representative that made them stand out more than some of the other schools.

Gene: So, it all depended on whether there was a person or persons on a particular campus that had a vision or conviction and pursued it.

Helen: I think that the number of articles in the *Washington Daily* indicate that it was of interest to the community as a whole. I was surprised. I was interested in finding that there was as much press coverage of NSA as there was.

Gene: I have been quite impressed in my researches for the Anthology by the coverage NSA was receiving in college papers all over the country at the time.

Bill: I'm sure that—there's no misstatement about it—I was regarded as a flaming liberal, and a lot of that and being active in the NSA were related to one another.

Helen: You said you were considered a flaming liberal?

Bill: John Ellis recalls my being referred to at the Fiji House as Red Bill.[6]

Helen: Well, I think part of the distinction was that you were a little older and you were a little more worldly than those of us who came right from high school into college, you know. Your perspective was much broader.

Reflecting on the NSA experience

Gene: If you were to look back without trying to turn yourself into a historian and somebody asked you: "Well, what do you think was the greater value of NSA at the time? What do you think was worthwhile about your experience or the presence of the organization? What are some of the things that you would pick out without trying to gild the lily?"

Helen: The attention paid to the NSA in the *Daily* broadened the perspective of the student body as a whole by raising issues that the student body normally and otherwise probably wouldn't have considered in their own niche within the university. Whether the student was an independent or within a fraternity or sorority, or whatever their activities were within the campus, they were more specifically focused on their education than their social life. These issues being raised and discussed—and even the role of the student body in making decisions of this kind—would have had, I think, a very positive impact as far as involvement in the outside community, too.

Bill: I think NSA probably was singular in giving students a sense of being a cohort, of representing a distinct, identifiable segment of society in the political sense, which I don't think they otherwise had. I don't think they thought of themselves as being politically significant.

Helen: I wonder if they do now, Bill?

Bill: I think they definitely do now. At least I hear every month from the ASUW representative and the graduate student representative at the Board of Regents, and they definitely think of themselves as being an organized entity which has an agenda. The scene has shifted—day care.

Helen: Oh, okay. That's what I was going to ask you. What do they see their agenda as today?

Bill: Getting a student on the Board of Regents, which was not dissimilar to the kind of thing we were bashing about in our days, and of course day care—but that is a new thing, a big thing. Very big.

Gene: Looking at it from a personal experience, there were really not a lot of kids actually involved in NSA, if you count the numbers. So there was a heightened individual experience for those who were.

Bill: Tremendous individual experience. I've never had more fun than those two trips to the Midwest. Seriously, I've never had more fun. It was very exciting.

Gene: Did you come out of it with more than you went in with, in terms of perspective or outlook?

Bill: Absolutely. No question about it. Very, very positive perspectives.

Gene: You know it's a leading question because I think that from a social standpoint, NSA's greatest value was what it contributed to the people who took part in it.

Bill: I would agree with that.

Gene: And you can't help but look at these headlines and articles and realize that they are replicating themselves in hundreds of student newspapers around the country for at least, perhaps, ten or fifteen years beyond our era. That's a lot of kids who went in and out of discovering each other and discovering the world. It's hard to say what kind of impact we had on the scheme of things institutionally at the time, but it certainly made a difference in terms of what people came away with who contributed to the society. That's what I'm discovering in this project.

Bill: I remember clearly sitting in the auditorium there in Champaign-Urbana, Illinois, and a sense of exhilaration seeing those kids from everywhere.

Helen: I can remember where I sat in that room.

Bill: You do?

Helen: Yes. It flashed through my mind just now.

Bill: I just don't remember Madison at all for some reason, but I have a clear recollection of Illinois.

Gene: I have fragmentary memories, and at this point in time it's hard for me to know what I remember and what has been reconstructed. But some things do come back. You may or may not have any sense of what I'm coming away from this meeting with, but in terms of what I'm trying to do with this book—rather than just simply have a collection of memoirs that, when they get stitched together, will not necessarily create the entire flavor—I figure this is the one shot we're going to have to produce a book that puts into print something you can pull off the shelf to learn about that era. And so these little bits and pieces of what people are telling me are finding their way into the book. Others can interpret as they see fit, but it represents what you're telling me, not what I'm telling somebody else. The book is our memories and our documentation of that era. I think it was a great period of time.

The University of Washington campus was liberal and active

Bill: Make no mistake about the fact that at the University of Washington, the campus was liberal, and it was active. It was aggressive on political issues. When they said, you can't have a political speaker, the students—I mean not every student, obviously—there was not any question where the student body stood on that. They basically rose up. Then, when this Canwell thing started, there was a thing called the Student Organization for Academic Rights (SOAR), and that organization gathered folks immediately and it was strongly supported. They really thought those hearings were something awful—and they were something awful. They were really bad.

Gene: Did they take place during your tenure? The hearings?

Bill: No. We've now settled the fact. It was in 1948, before my tenure. But to me one of the most exciting experiences was when Bill Gerberdring (the president of the University) made a speech apologizing to everybody involved. Somebody gave some money for a Harry Bridges Scholarship, and he used that occasion of a public announcement to apologize to the professors who had been fired, to professors who had resigned, to professors whose reputations had been massacred. It was really a significant thing. It didn't get nearly the press I thought it should.

Gene: So, in many respects, the NSA really extended an ethos that already existed on the campus?

Bill: Yes. It would be an exaggeration to give it large credit in making that state of affairs, but it was clearly a product of that state of affairs and having a national association that represented students was consistent with the general atmosphere.

NSA needed to become more than a political voice

Gene: So the value probably was really that NSA provided a vehicle for UW to extend that attitude throughout the Northwest Region to the extent that it attended regional meetings and expressed this view amongst students from other colleges?

Helen: No, I think that probably those of us involved with the NSA were more focused on some of the other activities that we've already discussed. It would have been premature for us at the time we were in school to be that aware and concerned—

Bill: The regional meetings were just housekeeping meetings. We were so sort of caught up in the—

Helen: In the process.

Bill: —and internal matters.

Gene: Getting organized? Rules? Bylaws?

Helen: Yes.

Bill: All that kind of stuff.

Helen: Yes. We weren't tilting at any windmills.

Bill: No, we really weren't. Not in those days.

Gene: I noticed that in some of your statements in the *Washington Daily,* the real hoped-for benefit of NSA would be projects that brought people together in practical activities, as opposed to making statements and expressing a point of view.

Bill: Yes.

Gene: But by having that kind of organization, you could make the statement and have the point of view and give it voice.

Bill: And of course, part of that, Gene, was that you needed to have something to talk about besides the student political voice, because if that's all you talked about, then your difficulties at home were going to be even greater than they were. In spite of the general liberality of the student body, there wouldn't be a lot of excitement about spending money on something that was just a political voice.

Helen: Agreed.

Helen Pulsifer has focused her lifetime career on volunteer management, including positions with the American Association of Retired Persons (AARP) and as Executive Director of the Seattle King County Bar Association.

Bill Gates, Sr., is currently Co-Chair and CEO of the Bill and Melinda Gates Foundation.

ENDNOTES

[1] The Third Congress at Illinois in 1949 was attended by Lewis and Clark College, Marylhurst College, Reed College, University of Idaho, University of Washington, and Washington State College. At the Fifth Congress at Minnesota in 1951, only Eastern Washington College, University of Idaho, and Washington State College were in attendance. The April 1, 1950, Northwest regional meeting at Marylhurst College, Oregon, lists seventy-five delegates representing seventeen colleges: Marylhurst, University of Idaho, Lewis and Clark, Pacific University, University of Portland, Oregon State College, University of Oregon, Reed College, St. Martin's College, College of Puget Sound, Whitworth College, Seattle University, Gonzaga University, Seattle Pacific College, Eastern Washington College of Education, University of Washington, and Washington State College. On February 2, 1949, the *Washington Daily* reported "delegates from 40 schools in the Northwest are expected to arrive today for the NSA regional conference to be held on the campus tomorrow and Sunday."

[2] Dan Pulsifer was chairman of the Great Northwest Region, as it was known in 1948-49. He later married Helen Knudson.

[3] The Organizations Assembly was a separate body at which all campus student organizations were represented.

[4] The University of Washington disaffiliated at about that time.

[5] Marylhurst College in Oregon hosted a number of regional meetings and programs. Its delegate, Joan Long, became regional chair in 1948-49 and was staff associate in the NSA national office during the year 1949-1950.

[6] Phi Gamma Delta Fraternity.

PICTURE CREDITS. Gates: *Then:* August, 1949, U. of Illinois, 2d National Student Congress (Joan Lynch). *Now:* July, 1998, Seattle (Schwartz). **Pulsifer:** *Then:* c. 1949 (Author). *Now:* July, 1998, Seattle (Schwartz).

HELEN K. (KNUDSON) PULSIFER

Early years and education: A native of Seattle, I spent my freshman year at Bryn Mawr College and received a B.A. from the University of Washington. I majored in Far East Studies, including Russian language and history.

Career highlights: My overall career focus was on volunteer management. I retired in 1996 from the AARP, where my major responsibilities were recruiting, training and enhancing effectiveness of volunteers in working with employers and with older workers: to maintain a supportive workplace for older people and to assist folks as they planned for retirement. I was spokesperson, wrote informational pieces and participated with academic, public and business groups. Prior to that I was the Executive Director of the Seattle King County Bar Association where I was responsible for the development and implementation of association goals and programs, membership growth and volunteer recruitment. I supervised a staff of 20-28, and administered the budget.

Volunteer activities: I am urrently co-managing a volunteer Guardianship Monitoring Program for the King County Superior Court. Earlier, I worked with the Seattle Board of Ethics/Fair Campaign Practices Commission and Municipal League of King County. I was Committee Chair and Trustee, Washington Literacy and League of Women Voters.

Family: I married the late Dan Pulsifer. We have four children and families all living in Seattle

WILLIAM H. GATES, SR.

Early years and education: Born in Bremerton, Washington, in 1925 and attended the Bremerton Public School System. Graduated Bremerton High School in 1943 and enlisted U. S. Army in 1944. Attended Fort Benning officer candidate school and served in the Philippine Islands and Japan. Honorably discharged as a First Lieutenant in November 1946. Received a BS in 1949 and LLB in 1950 from the University of Washington.

Career highlights: Currently Co-Chair of the Bill & Melinda Gates Foundation. Previously with Preston Gates & Ellis, Attorneys at Law, from 1964 to 1997.

Professional Activities: Admitted to the Bar of the State of Washington, 1950. Service included American Bar Association: Commission on Public Understanding about the Law, Chair, 1987-90; House of Delegates, 1975-78, 1983-93; Lawyers' Professional Liability Committee, 1974-86. Chair, 1976-79. Washington State Bar Association: Board of Governors, 1972-75; President, 1986-87. National Conference of Bar Presidents (President 1982-83); President, Seattle-King County Bar Association, 1969-70; and various other state and national law and court commissions.

Corporate Boards of Directors: SeaMED Corporation, 1995-1999; Center for Naval Analysis (CNA), 1995-1998; Washington Research Foundation, 1994-1997; Mutual of America Capital Management Corporation, 1991-1998; Intermec Corporation, 1989-1992.

(Continued on following page)

University of Washington: War Declared and Its Aftermath

U.S. Tells Japan: 'Little Chance of Agreeme

Hull Restates Stand

Nazis Battle at Moscow; British Roll On in Libya

Japan Attacks Pearl Harbor

Dive Bombers, Parachute Troops, Torpedo Planes

Strategic Military Zones in 'Pacific,' New Home of War

'Hostile Plane

Without Hate and Without Fear

"NO LONGER CAN WE SAY, 'THIS IS NOT OUR WAR,'" Bill Duncan, editor of the *UW Daily,* wrote in an editorial on 12/8/41. "From today on, the world will find we are not the weaklings they thought, that they took our reluctance for war as weakness when it was in reality a praiseworthy disgust for the idiocy of war. . . We go to war not with hate in our hearts, but with love for our style of doing things . . . with full realization of the hell before us and acknowledgment of our own guilt in the world flare-up, but with the firm conviction that we are united at last, that victory lies before us and that our sacrifices are not in vain." Pearl Harbor resolved the pro- and anti-interventionist debate that held student attention until then (see pp. 10, 32, 44, 47, 890).

From top: *UW Daily:* 11/27/41, 12/8/41, 12/9/41

'Hostile Planes' Appear Off Coast; Force San Francisco Blackout

University of Washington Daily

Students Ask Early Exams; May Enlist

Night Flashes

FR TO ASK WAR TODAY?

No Immediate Effect on ROTC Men Expected

CAMPUS GROUPS PLEDGE TOTAL WAR AID

MAY LOWER DRAFT AGE

Proposed Measure Makes 3,916 Students Eligible

CAMPUS DEFENSE COMMITTEE FORMED

From top, l.: 12/8/41, 12/10/41 2/26/42. r: 1/17/44, 4/12/45, 4/20/45

1941-42

War Chest Drive to Open Nov. 29

1942

Campus Mourns Roosevelt's Death

Here Was A Man

1944-45

"HERE WAS A MAN who chose to die in the front line of duty, a soldier to the end . . . equaled by a few, surpassed by none."

Proposals for Dumbarton Oaks World-Peace

Record Enrollment Reaches 15,309

Vets' Checks Slowed By Enrollments

Dead War Heroes Given Memorial

Parking For 2600 Cars Is Provided

Noon, Night Sessions To Handle Overflow; Faculty Numbers 952

From left: 10/2/46, 5/27/47.

1946-47

VETERANS RETURNED, swelled enrollments and broadened the agenda for student activism (see "The Veterans," p. 697).

Japanese-American and Alien Relocation

'Can't Believe It's True'—Japanese Studen

'We Will Not Shirk Our Duty,' Nipponese

1941

NW Aliens Will Be 'Removed'

Biddle Names Seven Prohibited Military Areas in Washington

WSSF Drive Will Help U Evacuees

U. Students Urge Nisei Be Retained

YM-YW Has Nisei Forum

From top: 12/8/41, 2/5/42, 3/3/42, "WSSF" 3/13/42, "YM" 4/19/45.

1942

1945

WEST COAST COLLEGES were deeply affected by Japanese-American and alien relocation policies induced by fears of subversion and coastal invasion. Students expressed remorse and provided assistance during and after the war (see p. 1037, Miller, p. 720).

Aid to Students Abroad

$5 Donation to WSSF Buys Suit for Chinese

1942

1947

CAMPUS CHEST DRIVE STARTS TODAY

University of Washington Daily

Current Year's Quota Pegged at $22,500; Caravan Opens Drive

Overseas Students Thank WSSF for Economic Aid

1949

THE WORLD STUDENT SERVICE FUND WAS THE CHANNEL for campus fundraising each year for student relief abroad. It was strongly supported by NSA and the major world and national religious organizations (p. 622).

From top: *UW Daily:* 2/5/42, 11/4/47, 2/15/49

WILLIAM H. GATES *(Continued from previous page)*

Civic activities and awards: Most recently on the Board of Regents, University of Washington, 1997-, and on the Boards of United Way of America 1999-, Seattle Symphony Foundation 1998-, and Seattle Foundation, 1995-97. Has served also with numerous civic organizations, including Oregon Shakespeare Festival Association, 1993-99; Lower Hood Canal Clean Water District Advisory Board, 1993-95; United Way of King County 1989-91; Greater Seattle Chamber of Commerce, 1986-89; Chief Seattle Council, Boy Scouts of America, 1985-90; Municipal League: 1968-74. Vice President, 1969, 1970 and 1973; Board of Trustees, Seattle Repertory Theatre, 1967-85; Board of Directors, Seattle Planned Parenthood Center, 1966-72; City of Seattle Board of Adjustment, 1959-64, Chairman, 1962-64; Recipient of Distinguished Eagle Scout Award, 1991; University of Washington Law School Distinguished Alumnus, 1991; American Judicature Society Herbert Harley Award, 1992; Washington State Bar Award of Merit, 1992; E. Donnall Thomas Medal of Achievement, Fred Hutchinson Cancer Research Center, 1995; 2000 Recognition Award, University of Washington, 2000; Doctor of Humanitarian Service (Honorary), University of Puget Sound, 2001; A.K. Guy Award, 2001.

Family: Married to Mimi Gardner Gates. Three children of deceased wife, Mary: Kristi, Bill and Libby.

Academic Freedom and Free Speech Controversies at UW

Editor's note: In his recollection (p. 1054) Bill Gates recalls the 1948 Canwell Committee un-American investigation and the campus speaker bans. These issues, along with an eruption of loyalty oath conflicts in the 1950's, were typical of academic freedom challenges at a number of major public universities around the country. NSA's Executive Committee in April, 1949 took a position reaffirming its opposition to dismissals of faculty solely for organization membership (see pp. 374, 382) and authorizing a staff inquiry into the U of Washington case. Controversy was generated within the Association both on its position and on whether the Executive Committee had the right to interpret the Association's policy.

The Canwell Committee Lights a Fire

1948

7/22/48

U Faculty Members Face Contempt Charges

University of Washington Daily

Ethel, Phillips, Eby and Gundlach To Be Cited for Refusal To Testify At Stormy Canwell Investigation

University Profs On Firing Line At Canwell Hearings

Institute Will Discuss Good Government

Commie Spy Ring Exists In U. S. Gov't

SET UP IN MARCH, 1947, by the state legislature, the Canwell Committee was to "investigate subversive persons and groups." Faculty at the University named before the commiittee in 1948 as Communists were called to testify. Those who refused to answer the question were cited for contempt. As a result complaints about their fitness were brought by the administration to the Faculty Committee on Tenure.

The Universiy Investigates and Responds

1948-49

11/19/48 "Who Is Loyal to America?" Asks Professo[r]

2/8/49 [AL]LEN SAYS NO THOUGHT CONTROL AT U

7/20/48 STUDENT POLL REVEALS: Canwell Objectives OK'd But Tactics Deplored

10/5/48 President Allen Lauds Academic Freedoms In Assembly Address

2/1/49 Pres. Allen Cites 'Severe Indictment' of Communists By Faculty Tenure Group

Raymond B. Allen
President, UW, 1946-52

PRESIDENT ALLEN stood by the University's academic freedom code, and endorsed the tenure committee's majority report that membership in the Communist Party was an issue of competence and not belief. For six months students and faculty engaged in intensive study and debate on Communism and academic freedom.

Regents Overrule Faculty on Dismissals

1949

DISMISSAL PROTEST MEETING TODAY; ASSEMBLY TO CONDUCT STUDENT POLL

Statement Protesting Dismissals Issued By 8 On Physics Faculty

Profs Used Red Tactics During Trial

Protesting Students To Meet at Unitarian Church at 4 p.m. Today

Committee Reports On Faculty Probe

Summarized here are the recommendations of the Committee on Tenure and Academic Freedom in the cases of the six faculty members charged with communist activity. Included are the recommendations made in each case by President Raymond B. Allen and the decisions of the board of regents:

Prof. Ralph H. Gundlach:
For dismissal 7
For retention 4
President Allen ..... For dismissal
Board of Regents ..... For dismissal

Prof. Herbert J. Phillips:
For dismissal 3
For retention 8
President Allen ..... For dismissal
Board of Regents ..... For dismissal

Prof. Joseph Butterworth:
For dismissal 3
For retention 8
President Allen ..... For dismissal
Board of Regents ..... For dismissal

Prof. E. Harold Eby:

THE TENURE COMMITTEE called for one dismissal and five retentions. President Allen recommended dismissal of three. The regents agreed with Allen. The *UW Daily* conducted two student polls on the issues. In July of 1948 in an informal poll, the paper headlined "Canwell Objectives OK'd But Tactics Deplored." Most students interviewed opposed the Committee's practice of not permitting witnesses to defend themselves. In January, in a survey of 1,000 students, only 33% of the undergraduates knew the names of the dismissed professors. Majorities of 40%-50% approved of the dismissals.

Events at UW Attract National Attention

Academic Freedom—Crimson Report — *Harvard Crimson 5/28/49. See p. 388*

U of Washington Leads List Of Faculty Dismissal Cases

Washington Faculty Dismissals Arouse Nation-Wide Comment — *NSA News 2/49*

UW 1/7/49

Academic Freedom Group Planning to Introduce Bills

By BILL RAY

Ghosts of the Canwell committee and its investigation of un-American activities still live to haunt the University.

UNIVERSITY OF WASHINGTON
OFFICE OF THE PRESIDENT
SEATTLE 5

March 25, 1949

"We have had hundreds of letters from persons expressing all shadings of approval or disapproval of the University's action in these cases. . . . I want parents to know that the University of Washington has engaged in no 'purge,' no book-burnings, no hunt for 'Reds.' The atmosphere of of academic freedom must surround all faculty members. . . .

Raymond B. Allen, President
In a letter to parents
(UW Libraries, Manuscripts and Archives)

The Political Speech Ban

1948

3/10/48

[De]bate Fails To Bring Any Action on Speaker

University of Washington Daily

[CO]NTROL BOARD VOTES TO CANCEL BAN

Regents Again Refuse To Lift Speaker Bar

Students Protest Banning Politics From U Campus

Group Action Taken

From top: l. 2/27/48, 3/11/48, 5/21/48, 2/25/48.

THE THREE LAYERS of student governance: Organizations Assembly, ASUW and Control Board, voted to repeal a policy prohibiting political speakers (e.g., President Truman, former VP Henry Wallace). The Regents voted to retain the ban.

Arguments on Speaker Ban

The issues in the several-weeks-old speaker-ban debate, which is bidding to become one of the hottest campus battles in recent years, need clarification.

Those who would lift the ban against political speakers make the following arguments:

1. A healthy student interest in political matters will result if political speakers are allowed to speak on campus.

2. A strictly academic approach to politics, or any subject, is self-defeating because it lacks reality.

3. Eagleson hall, just off the campus, is too small to accommodate the students who would like to hear prominent speakers.

4. College students are intelligent enough not to be unduly swayed by whatever they might hear in a campus talk.

On the other side of the fence are those who oppose lifting the ban for what they term "practical considerations." Their arguments are:

1. If political speakers, who are not approved by members of the state legislature, appear on campus, University relations with Olympia will be greatly harmed in regard to procuring appropriations for the University.

2. It is foolish to risk embarrassing University officials with Olympia just so students can see "real live" politicians on campus, when students may hear the speakers elsewhere in the city.

3. Lifting the ban would leave the Assemblies committee and the University wide open to charges of being unfair to one side or the other in regard to selection of speakers.

4. If the ban were lifted and the campus turned into a political battleground for conflicting ideologies and beliefs, it would be difficult to uphold the contention that the reason for study of un-American ideologies on the campus is to understand their line of thought.

The arguments of both sides are compelling and well taken. The case, as many would have us believe, is not completely open and shut.—DAN McDONOUGH.

Pre-War "Red Threat" Precursors

1939

University of Washington Daily

'Red Probe' Proposals Tabled by Vote During Stormy 'Drums' Session

[A]MERICA'S DRUMS' OFFICERS RESIGN

20 Members Also Withdraw; Denounce Red-Baiting Action; Substitute Society Is Planned

ASUW Induction Planned Tonight In Meany Hotel

From left: 4/26/39, 4/27/39.

LAUNCHING OF A NEW "PATRIOTIC GROUP," "America's Drums," sponsored by the Veterans of Foreign Wars, was thwarted when all its student officers and 20 members resigned. A VFW official denied membership to two members of the campus "Student Peace Council" who tried to join and were accused of being Communists.

Student Government at UW Debates the Place for NSA

Editor's note: The large-university, multi-layered structure of student government at Washington is shown in NSA's complicated acceptance by student leaders at the University. The story was told by Chuck Gerold, Washington Daily *Night Editor, who recounted, in a lengthy 2/29/49 article, "NSA Stands for World Freedom," NSA's history from the days of the 1946 World Student Congress and how, in 1948, the Organizations Assembly, under the leadership of ASUW Vice President Brock Adams, looking to revitalize itself "seized NSA with both fists, voted to join the national organization and urged the ASUW to make the move official."*

The Board of Control was pro-NSA, too. It took action to affiliate by appointing Phil Palmer a national delegate. The assembly countered by electing Art Degginger its representative. An ASUW election was held and Dan Pulsifer was named by the student body at large as the third delegate. "Dean Newhouse was behind the movement, too. . . he has been named one of nine NSA national advisory councilmen. Pulsifer is now NSA Chairman of the Great Northwest Region. . . ." "Now that we have NSA, what do we do with it?," Gerold asked. During its first four years, UW leaders gave it a run. Opponents challenged the value in relation to cost, and the ASUW withdrew in 1951. By 1957, NSA shows them as having rejoined.

1946-47: Attending the Founding Conventions

4/47

NSO Official Visits With UW Leaders

Russ Austin, vice-president of the continuations committee of the National Students Organization, visited the University yesterday to discuss the organization with student leaders.

Norman Israel
NSA Delegate
1947-48 Regional Chair

Conference Delegates To NSO Approved By Board of Control

5/29/47

UW Students Will Attend NSO Meet

Three University men will attend the constitutional convention of the National Student organization which will convene next month in Wisconsin.

7/31/47

PREPARING FOR THE CONSTITUTIONAL CONVENTION, ASUW President Gummie John- son, Norm Israel and John Huston returned from the 12/46 Chicago Confer- ence and ar-ranged for Russ Austin, Continuations Committee Vice President (p.90), to meet with UW student leaders. Israel, Jim Stuart and Brock Adams were chosen to go to Madison in 8/47.

1948-49: Getting Organized

NSA-ASUW Future Relationship Will Be Aired on Agenda Today At Organizations Assembly Meet

NSA Official Tells of Plans To Unite College Students

National Student Assn. Begins Drive To Place DP's in U.S. Colleges

From top: 10/21/48, 11/2/48, 12/7/48

NSA Plan Passed By Board
Board of Control OK's New Organization For Student Government 1/6/49

Stanley, Whitehead, Maxwell Win Other Top Student Body Offices; Knudson Is NSA Representative 4/14/49

Dan Pulsifer
Regional Chair, 48-49 1949

Helen Knudson
NSA Delegate, 49-50

Phil Palmer
ASUW President, 49-50
NSA Delegate, 1949

ASUW WAS AUTHORIZED to set up an NSA Committee as a liaison with national NSA, formed of ASUW and Organizations Assembly committee people. Proposal was presented by Bill Gates, chair of the assembly's by-laws committee. Dick Heggie, NSA VP, addressed the Organizations Assembly in November. Helen Knudson was elected NSA delegate. Phil Palmer, NSA advocate, was elected ASUW President.

1947-48: Pros and Cons of NSA Membership

Board Members Hear Varied Reports From Convention Delegates

NSA Constitution Referred To Organization Delegates For Opinions at Assembly

Nearly one hundred delegates to the Organizations Assembly yesterday became the first University group to begin the task toward ratification or rejection of the National Student Association constitution.

Benefit or Mumbo-Jumbo?...

From top, l: 10/21/47, 11/14/47, 11/18/47.
rt: 1/9/48, 3/2/48, 3/31/48

Board of Control Passes ASUW Affiliation in NSA

Acceptance of a qualified membership in the National Student association was voted Wednesday by the Board of Control. The vote was 9 for, 3 against and 3 abstentions.

NSA Representative Urges ASUW Set Up Student Affairs Study

NSA Should Be Given Time To Prove Itself, Critics Told By Delegate to Conference

Art Degginger
NSA Delegate

Brock Adams
Ch. Organizations Assem.
ASUW Vice Pres.

BROCK ADAMS AND JIM STUART, editor of the *Daily,* returned with concerns over the new constitution and the value of NSA for UW. They later resigned the delegation, leaving Norm Israel. Art Degginger became a supportive delegate, urging the ASUW to give NSA some time. NSA staff member Mildred Kiefer (p. 178) met with delegates in March.

Weighing the Benefits

1949-50

Northwest NSA Delegates Converging for Conference

Delegates from some 40 schools in the Northwest are expected to arrive today for the NSA regional conference to be held on the campus tomorrow and Sunday.

NSA Delegates Start Convocation

NSA Proposal 'Heard' By Organizations Assembly

NSA Affiliation Also Gets Nod After Two-Hour Heated Debate

From top: 12/2/49, 1/13/50, 3/2/50
Top rt: 2/1/51

1951

Control Board Decides Washington Will Drop Membership in NSA

Four years of tumultuous ASUW membership in the National Student association was climaxed yesterday when the board of control voted to withdraw from the national organization.

THE REGIONAL MEETING in December 1949 featured an address by Glen Nygreen, student affairs director on "The Student in the Educational Community." Bill Gates led the conference in panels on "student government, activities programs and education evaluation." **IN 1950,** the ASUW sent 7 delegates to the Michigan Congress (p. 263), where support for the Korean War and a report from the World Student Congress were debated. Delegates returned pleased with their experience but concerned about whether NSA was delivering on its promise (See next page).

From left: **Dean Newhouse,** *Director of Student Affairs* **Glen T. Nygreen,** *Executive Officer, Office of Student Affairs.* **Mac McCredy** *ASUW President, 50-51 NSA Delegate 1950.*

Historical note: In 1861 the territorial legislature provided for a university and Arthur A. Denny, Edward Lander and Charles C. Terry deeded the 10 acres for a campus occupied until 1894, a year after the present campus was purchased. 30 students formed the first one-room class. During the next 15 years the university was closed four times for want of funds. In 1899 Washington was adminitted as a state and the territorial university became State University (www.lib.washington.edu). 1948, eleventh largest U.S. enrollment: 16,650.

Students and Administrators at U of W Consider NSA

Editor's note: Detailed reports discussing NSA's pros and cons, by both students and administrators, can be found in college archives around the country. At some, evidence of early years of membership consist of brief discussion digests and resolutions reporting renewals or appropriations of funds in student government minutes or student activity reports (see, e.g., Swarthmore, p. 897, Xavier, p. 437, and U. of Colorado, p. 1008). In others, a key word search will come up empty, while the student newspaper will have provided extensive coverage—and vice versa. The Manuscript and Archives Division at the University of Washington preserved a good record of early NSA student reports. It covers the cycle of affiliation, execution of programs, and membership reconsideration reported in the Washington Daily. *Here are highlights from some of these documents. After withdrawing in 1951, the University rejoined several years later.*

1948: Observing "The Competence of NSA . . ."

Comments on the First National Congress

(Excerpted from a 4-pp. undated report, c. 9/48)
Dean Newhouse, *Director of Student Affairs*

Some student delegates may report back locally that the Congress was not a profitable investment for the local student body. I suspect this is true for those students too new and uninformed to participate. NSA recognition of their needs through adequate instruction in student citizenship and leadership responsibilities can correct this. While dues and travel costs are high, particularly in the eyes of students, they are not out of line with other educational costs.

The competence of NSA to handle its toughest problems at the national level cannot be questioned if one reviews its record. Its competence at the regional level varies widely from region to region. Its capacity to assist local college student government is inadequate as yet.

Every Dean of Students should have the additional opportunity to observe how competent students can be without his help.

Is a National Student Organization necessary? The answer is "yes". When we successfully work to induce student leaders to run their affairs with maturity and responsibility, we have to accept their right to work for their interests and objectives in a mature way. . . .

1947-50: History of ASUW Participation in NSA

(Excerpted from a 14-pp. report to the Board of Control, 2/15/50)
Ben Hayes, *Chairman, NSA Committee*

Attendance at regional assemblies and national congresses in 1947, 1948 and 1949. Regional Presidents: Norman Israel (1947-48), Dan Pulsifer (1948-49), William Gates (1949-50).

Past Accomplishments (Information from Art Degginger):
1) Job Placement Pamphlet. 2) College Constitution Collection. 3) Student Faculty Directory. 4) Purchase Card System Survey. 5) Displaced Persons Program. 6) International Research Seminar. 7) Distribution of NSA News. 8) Presentation of National Student Issues to the Organization Assembly.

Accomplishments of 1949-50:
1. Art Tour Display
2. Work, Study Travel Abroad Assemblies
3. National Campus Club investigation
4. Symphony Forum Organization
5. Formation of the ASUW International Committee:
   (a) Continuous Hospitality Sub-Committe, (b) International Information Sub-Committee, (c) International Program Sub-Committee
6. Reorganization of the NSA Committee

Present Projects:
1. Faculty-Rating System Evaluation
2. AMS Evaluation: Constitution, Election Procedures and Program
3. Leadership Training Conference
4. Student Faculty Directory (with Publications Committee)
5. Establishment of a Regional Educational Film Exchange
6. Establishment of a Share-the-Entertainment Group

1950: Reports on the National Student Congress

(Excerpted from a 3-pp. undated report, c. 9/50
Bob Mucklestone, *NSA Delegate*

The National Student Association I believe is a very worthwhile organization, if only for the fact that it is a national organization of college student governments providing the oppportunities for closer contact. . . .The NSA Congress is also very worthwhile as far as the individual is concerned . . .

The items voted on, I believe, were not of interest to the whole assembly, of course . . . due to the diversity in representation. On some campuses, NSA is almost solely interested in national and international politics. An example of this is CCNY or almost any of the New York schools.

. . . Talking to many of the delegates and asking them the relation NSA had to their student government, I drew the general conclusion that NSA had been pushed on to many campuses and that it did not really represent the student governments. . . .

[Mucklestone recommends that UW be represented by its ASUW officers, in a position to know their needs, that the NSA committee be limited to an information function, with projects handled through the Board of Control.]

* * * *

(Excerpted from a 2-pp. undated report, c. 9/50)
Ben Hayes, *NSA Delegate*

My attendance at the NSA Congress has furthered my conviction that NSA is a valuable organization and well worth ASUW affiliation.

I don't like everything about NSA, but I do feel that its dangers and weaknesses are more than compensated for by its unique values. . . . The ASUW will receive from its membership in NSA exactly in proportion to what it contributes. . . .

* * * *

(Excerpted from a 2-pp. undated report, c. 9/50)
Don Taylor, *NSA Delegate*

I feel my attendance [at the NSA Congress] was a rewarding experience. However, the question of importance is, are such trips rewarding to the students at large . . .? An unhesitating yes would be my answer. . . . It is impossible to measure the effect upon the student body itself when their leaders are so revitalized. . . .

* * * *

(Additional reports were submitted by **Mildred Gellerman**, *ASUW Program Supervisor (4pp),* **Mac McCredy**, *ASUW President (8pp), delegates* **Janet Crawford** *(2pp) and* **Duane Enochs** *(2pp). The reports were submitted to the ASUW and to University President Raymond B. Allen by Mac McCredy to provide "a clearer picture of the workings, thought and benefits [of NSA] and the reason for its existence.")*

1951: A Letter of Withdrawal

February 7, 1951 *[Excerpts]*

Mr. Allard K. Lowenstein, President
National Student Association

Dear Mr. Lowenstein:

This letter is to inform you of the official withdrawal of the University of Washington from membership in the National Student Association. At the meeting of our Board of Control last Wednesday, January 31, 1951, the Board voted unanimously for this action. We have withheld informing you of this action due to the request of James Seelig, our regional chairman, pending our appearance at the regional meeting this past weekend.

The reasons for our decision are as follows:

1. NSA puts too much emphasis on national and international issues.

2. . . . NSA cannot be such a spokesman because there are many large colleges and universities not represented at their national conventions.

3. In principle, NSA is fine; on practice it has failed.

4. Requested information on . . . projects have not been forthcoming.

5. East coast student governments are far behind the west coast and as such the problems are not similar.

6. There may be a moral obligation to pay any debts incurred by NSA should they discontinue.

7. Our money can be better spent in other areas.

May I say in closing that we at the University of Washington agree with you in ideal, but the functions [NSA should perform are not forthcoming].

Sincerely, **Mac McCredy**, ASUW President

It was a challenge to maintain good communications among schools.

2. Organizing the Pacific Northwest Region

Joan Long Lynch
Marylhurst College, Oregon
NSA National Staff Associate, 1950-51
Chair, Pacific Northwest Region, 1951-52

In 1950, before Microsoft, Starbucks, Nike, and Big Sky made the Pacific Northwest and the northern Rocky Mountain states "hot" destinations to visit and desirable places in which to live, the four-state area including Washington, Oregon, Idaho, and Montana was the most remote outpost of the country. (Alaska and Hawaii had not yet been admitted to statehood.) It was the same in the history of the National Student Association. What was to become the Great Northwest Region was huge—390,892 square miles of rugged mountain ranges; dense forests; lush valleys; high, arid plateaus; great rivers; and cattle ranches and rolling wheat fields that went on forever. Thinly populated, with few metropolitan areas, it was separated from the rest of the country by distance and formidable geography. The forty-one or so colleges and universities in the region were also spread from one end to the other. There were not yet any superhighways, and it was a challenge to maintain good communications between schools.

Most colleges located near the population centers

A handful of students from colleges in the area had attended the Constitutional Convention in Madison in 1947. However, organizing and sustaining the student movement in this far-flung corner of the country was always difficult. Most of the institutions of higher education were located in or near the population centers, in the Willamette Valley of Oregon, the eastern shore of Puget Sound in Western Washington, the Spokane Valley and Palouse country of Eastern Washington, and in smaller communities in Idaho and Montana. Public colleges and universities were the most numerous and enrolled the largest number of students. Seven Catholic colleges and a dozen or so Protestant-related institutions, several of which had been founded by Christian missionaries in the early nineteenth century, made up the private college roster. Only Reed College in Portland enjoyed the distinction of being an "independent," small liberal arts college of national stature. There were few junior colleges in any of the states at this time.

Membership in USNSA grew slowly until the happy coincidence of a recruiting swing through the region by 1948-49 national vice president Dick Heggie (on his way to his wedding in California) and the election of Bill Gates as regional chair in the spring of 1949.[1] Gates was a law student at the University of Washington, and under his leadership at the 1949 Congress and his influence as a member of the National Executive Committee, the region began to prosper. Many schools sent delegates to regional meetings without affiliating, and others joined the Association but could not afford to send delegates to the Congresses; nonetheless, there was a vitality and new awareness of issues affecting students beyond the local and parochial, which added to the educational experiences of countless students in the region.

Importance of student government in the Northwest

Student government was important to Northwest college students, and on some of the larger campuses, the associated students managed large budgets and owned and operated impressive facilities. The Student Union movement was strong in the region, and in time on some campuses there began to be competition between the Student Union proponents and those who supported membership in NSA, particularly when student activity fees began to decline with the dropoff in enrollment in the 1950s.

NSA had adopted the Travel Pool program in the early days of the Association in order to equalize the cost of sending delegates to the annual Congresses. The program was vital to colleges in the Great Northwest. In 1950-51 the system was failing, in part because some schools refused to pay their assessment. At the same time, the deplorable state of the National Association's financial affairs meant that many institutions were not reimbursed for their travel costs. The University of Washington was very vocal in demanding a full accounting of the organization's finances and threatened to disaffiliate if such a report was not forthcoming. The University made good on its threat when a financial statement was not produced, and began a campaign on the West Coast to encourage other schools to also disaffiliate. However, the campaign was not successful. The Great Northwest Region continued to promote the goals and objectives of USNSA to member and nonmember schools and to provide students in the region with the opportunity to participate with their peers in working for the improvement of their own educational experiences, as well as for the realization of a more just and caring society.[2]

Joan Long Lynch was Director of College Admissions Counseling for Immaculate Heart High School, Los Angeles, California. She holds a B.A. from Marylhurst College. (See p. 278 for an extended bio.)

END NOTES

[1] See Heggie, p. 226.

[2] *Editor's note:* The University of Washington reappears in NSA's 1957-58 membership list.

A Regional Meeting at Marylhurst College

SPRING ASSEMBLY - 1950

GREATER NORTHWEST REGION,

NATIONAL STUDENT ASSOCIATION

Marylhurst College, Oregon—April 28, 29, 30, 1950

Seventeen schools, as listed at the end of this report, were represented at this semi-annual meeting. Ten representatives of the University of Washington were included among the sixty (60) students comprising the conference group. Chairman of the regional group is Bill Gates of the University of Washington.

The Commission on International Student Affairs is one of the standing commissions of all NSA groups. Resolutions were presented by this group, and adopted by the Assembly, as follows:

1. Urged the expansion of Fulbright Scholarships, the creation of U.S. Government scholarships for American students to study abroad, and the promotion of reciprocal scholarships through private financial sources.

2. Urged increased emphasis on World Student Service Fund (WSSF) activities on individual campuses.

3. Asked the National group to thoroughly investigate possible U.S. student participation in the 1951 World Youth and Student Festival.

Proposed by this commission but defeated by the Asssembly was a resolution on World Government. The basis of the prevailing opposition was the feeling that this issue was one of general public interest rather than of student concern primarily. It was agreed that it was with the latter type of issue that the NSA should concern itself.

Several voting delegations were split on this issue. The majority of the University of Washington delegation voted against the World Govermmt resolution.

Little attention was given to national student issues. Much attention was given to problems of student union buildings, and to student activities generally.

Two new notes deserve special mention.

1. The group discussing student governent adopted as one of the fundamental purposes of student government the statement:

"To promote the general welfare of the school."

2. The group discussing the so-called "Student Bill of Rights" approved a new section entitled "Student Responsibilities" in which a statement of the reciprocal duties of students was attempted.

The costs to individual campuses of membership in the NSA was of great concern. Much attention was given to delimiting the functions of NSA groups on the local, regional and national levels in order to justify costs and to remove any feeling of local student governments that NSA was in competition with them.

BILL GATES (U. of Washington), Regional President, presides over assembly session at Marylhurst. *(Lynch)*

SUMMARY

1. The emphases of concern for the general welfare of the school and for student responsibilities were significant.

2. The continued strong participation of the Catholic schools is encouraging.

3. A realistic placing of limits on ambitions for the development of the organization is proceeding.

4. The USNSA is still the only United States student group which claims to speak for the majority of American college students and is so recognized by the U.S. Office of Education and the Department of State.

- Glen T. Nygreen, Executive Officer of Student Affairs [U. of Wash.]
(Member: Regional Advisory Committee)

PARTICIPATING SCHOOLS

IDAHO	University of Oregon	Seattle Pacific College
*University of Idaho	University of Portland	Seattle University
OREGON	WASHINGTON	*University of Washington
Lewis and Clark College	College of Puget Sound	
*Marylhurst College	*Eastern Washington College of Education	*Washington State College
Pacific University		
Reed College	Gonzaga College	Whitworth College
Oregon State College	St. Martins College	(*Voting member)

[Undated report by Glen Nygreen, provided by Joan Long Lynch]

Historical note: Marylhurst College was founded as St. Mary's Academy and College in 1893 by The Sisters of the Holy Names of Jesus "to serve the educational needs of Northwest women." In 1930 it was renamed Marylhurst and moved to its present location. In 1974 it became co-educational and in 1998 became Maryhurst University (www.lib.washington.edu). 1948 enrollment: 233.

Regional Leaders View Northwest Challenges

Editor's note: The Great Northwest Region posed logistical and philosophical challenges which its regional Presidents addressed in different ways. The fundamentals remained the same: (1) a huge geographic expanse with clusters of colleges widely dispersed, and (2) a feeling by some student leaders, at the larger universities in particlar, that Northwest student government interests were differerent than those of concern elsewhere. How three successive latter-day Regional Presidents saw these concerns are shown in excerpts from their reports below. Although the University of Washington withdrew in 1951 for several years, Washington State College, Eastern Washington College of Education, University of Idaho and Marylhurst College in Oregon provided continuing core membership

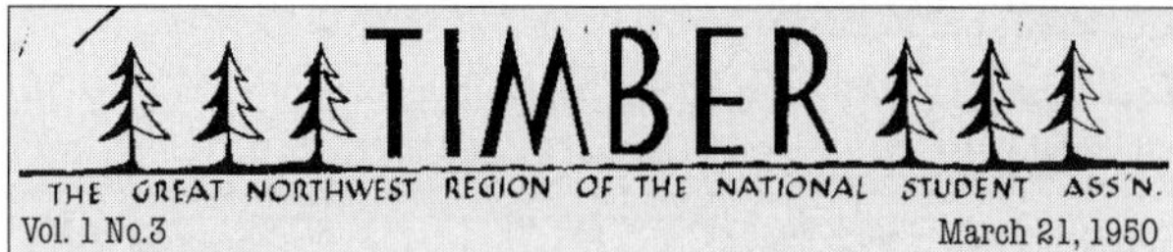

MISSION ACCOMPLISHED - Quite Naturally (1949-50)

Ever since the first meetings of NSA people from the Great Northwest have worked to take the emphasis in the Association off of the quasi-political activities and turn it in the direction of working on the problems of the student and student government in their educational and campus activities. Delegates to the national Congresses from this region have consistently been critical of the the large proportion of timc and attention devoted to the issue about IUS, Discrimination, Academic Freedom, etc.

It can clearly be reported that as NSA goes into the third full year of its operation that the emphasis has shifted in the direction that our delegates and many others have wished.

In spite of the fact that this has long been the feeling of the bulk of the Great Northwesterners we can hardly take credit for the change that has taken place. This shift of emphasis can be credited very simply to two factors.

The first of these is the change of personnel in the NSA heirarchy. Any organization at its inception is made up most largely of the pushers and idealists who see big goals and have big dreams and who, accordingly, think in terms of national legislation and world reform. Also, the founders of NSA were in large part older students, veterans already active on the national political scene with political axes to grind. Now NSA has attracted into its activities the student's student, and student government personnel whose interests and ideals, though no less commendable and ambitious than those of our founders, are centered about the immediate problems of the individual student and his student government.

The other factor which has contributed to the now accomplished shift of emphasis in NSA is the simple fact that most of the broad, heated policy issues have been disposed of, and the way is cleared for putting ourselves in to the less spectacular but equally important problems which are largely devoid of political coloration.

We now need to take care that we do not become so absorbed in these non-spectacular, "non-political" problems that we lose sight of the possibilities for NSA contributions to the determination of those quasi-political issues affecting the educational world. If we fail to keep our minds and imaginations open to this area we will take from our Association one of its unique and worthwhile functions.

Bill Gates

GREAT NORTHWEST REGIONAL REPORT (1951-52)

Member Schools. *Washington:* Washington State College, Pullman; Eastern Washington College, Cheney. *Idado:* University of Idaho, Moscow; College of Idaho, Caldwell; *Oregon:* Reed College, Portland; Marylhurst College, Marylhurst.

Interested Non-Member Schools: *Washington:* Holy Names, Spokane. *Oregon:* Eastern Oregon College, La Grande; Central Oregon College, Monmouth; Southern Oregon College, Ashland; Vanport College, Portland; University of Oregon, Eugene.

Regional Assembly: A regional assembly was held at Reed College, Portland, on December 14-16 at which the six member schools . . . and several non-member schools were present. The group considered . . . international, student government, educational affairs, and took action on many points. The region is interested in sponsoring a summer tour for foreign students in the Northwest, is establishing an art tour, and has undertaken an expansion program. At the assembly, the delegates expressed a great deal of enthusiasm for the work of the association. . . .The next assembly will be held at Washington State College some time in April, when it is hoped that Bill Dentzer [NSA President] will be able to attend.

Outside activities of the Chairman: Addressed the Oregon Federation of Collegiate Leaders, and was received very warmly . . . plans being made now for visits of the Chairman to all four states. . . . Will see about getting a speaker [at] the Pacific States Presidents Association meeting to be held in Seattle in May.

N.B. We are hampered program-wise by the vastness of the region, and the lack of sufficient funds to operate with. However, this is what we are trying to overcome, and with luck the situation in another year may be very different.

From an undated report to the National Executive Committee by Joan Long, 1951-52 Regional Chairman

Student Leaders Attend Conferences at EWCE

Officers of the Great Northwest region of the National Student association attended regional conference on the Eastern Washington College of Education campus. Left to right, they are Marvin Jagnels, University of Idaho, vice president for the eastern district; Mary Frances Cavanaugh, Marylhurst college, Oswego, Ore., vice president for the southern district; Nadine Zornes, EWCE, regional secretary-treasurer; James Seelig, EWCE, regional chairman. In the Great Northwest region are colleges in Alaska, Washington, Oregon, Idaho and Montana. The delegates discussed current student problems at sessions.

The clipping above, unidentified as to date and source, refers to 2/2/51 regional assembly at Eastern Washington College of Education (State Historical Society of Wisconsin).

A 1952-53 REPORT ON A REGIONAL TOUR

Editor's note: Kenneth Strand (Washington State College), 1952-53 Regional President, toured his tri-state region and visited 24 of the colleges. In a 3/1/53 five-page report to the Association, he analyzed the history and the organization needs and prospects for the region. He noted that three independent regional organizations also existed : The Pacific Student Body President's Association, The Evergreen Conference of Student Body Presidents (Washington) and the Oregon Federation of Collegiate Leaders. He recommended the formation of a single regional group, "a possible Northwest Federation of Student Leaders," proposing that NSA "consider an affiliation of the regional organization—not each individual school—through payment of one lump sum to cover the services received from USNSA." His "Definition of the Problem":

When [the basic needs of student government are met] the other facets of the NSA program—namely, the international activities, the concern over academic freedom and related topics, and acting as a voice for the American student to various government and educational organizations—would more readily be accepted. The schools in this area, while interested in these broader aims, will not join the organization for these reasons alone.

I am convinced that the nature of Student Government in the Northwest is sufficiently different from that in other areas . . . that it is unrealistic to expect the student in the Northwest to give active consideration to the problems which face the majority of Eastern student governments and which are not yet problems in the Northwest. This is especially true when student governments in the Northwest are . . . responsible for the successful operation of the associated student body type of government and the development of the community concept.

Lewis and Clark/Reed/Eastern Washington

Editor's note: The Eastern Washington College Journal *reported on 2/14/51 that the NSA Northwest regional conference "is not concerned with political pressures on the national level, but is interested in promoting student welfare on individual campuses." Reflecting the theme appearing elsewhere in this section, Vern Bahr, President of the Idaho student body, said, "At the national convention last summer in Ann Arbor the difference in viewpoints of eastern and western members of NSA was apparent. Students from eastern colleges seemed to think in terms of political pressure; western representatives feel the function of NSA is betterment of student government, intelligent approach to campus situations."*

Eastern Washington College of Education

Northwest meet set for February 2, 3, 4; Seelig will officiate

Crammed "between the book-ends" of Eastern activity this quarter is a National Students' association regional meeting on campus, February 2, 3, 4. Six Northwest colleges will be represented.

Marvel Washburn, NSA regional chairman on UN affairs, is one of the representatives who will arrive from the University of Idaho. Chairman on student affairs, representing Marylhurst college, Oregon, and on educational affairs, University of Washington, have also been named delegates to the Eastern convention. Delegates from Reed college in Oregon and from Washington state also plan to attend.

Chairman of the Northwest student officers' confab is Jim Seelig, ASB president and regional chairman of NSA. Seelig was named to the post at a national meeting in Ann Arbor, Michigan, last summer.

Vice president of ASB, Jack Martin, will be another of Eastern's active participators in the regional meet, acting as official host to the six guest schools. Martin traveled to Madison, Wisconsin, with Seelig during Christmas vacation to attend a national executive meet of national NSA.

On colleges and universities, the student leaders plan a review of the draft program and the effect of the draft program on NSA in the northwest.

"Although the three days of conferring are planned to use a lot of 'intellectual elbow-grease,' visiting students will take part in some social activity," Seelig said. "A banquet is tentatively scheduled in the New Dorm."

James Seelig
Regional Chair, '50-51

NSA CONCERNED WITH STUDENT WELFARE ALONE

The Great Northwest regional conference of the National Students Association is not concerned with political pressures on the national level, but is interested in promoting student welfare on individual campuses.

This opinion was expressed by leaders of the two-day conference which met recently on the Eastern Washington college campus.

Vern Bahr, president of the University of Idaho student body, said "At the national convention in Ann Arbor last summer the difference in viewpoints of eastern and western members of the NSA was apparent. Students from eastern colleges seemed to think in terms of political pressure; western representatives feel the function of the NSA is betterment of student government, intelligent approach to campus situations."

"We cleared the air concerning the University of Washington's resignation. We feel that instead of weakening the organization it has drawn us closer together. The region neither approves nor condones the action taken by the university," Seelig explained.

Officers were elected. James See-

1950-51

NSA prexy criticizes loyalty oath

The president of the National Student Association Wednesday said the University of California's loyalty oath for teachers has aided and encouraged the Communists. He called on American students to become aware of the "sinister implications" in the oath.

In a statement to the 800,000 members of NSA, Allard K. Lowenstein said that measures, like the oath "make it difficult to stand effectively against Communist attempts to depict America as a land fast losing its freedom and to picture American education as a tool of a few powerful and selfish men."

Calling the oath "one of the most unwarranted invasions of academic rights yet perpetrated," Lowenstein pointed out that none of the professors dismissed for refusing to sign the oath were even alleged to be Communists.

He said American students must combat Communism wherever it oc-

From left: *EWCE The Journal* 1/17/51, 2/14/51, 1/31/51

STUDENT BODY PRESIDENTS MEET. From left: Vern Bahr, U of Idaho; Bill Green, Washington State; James Seelig, Eastern Washington and Clarence "Mac" McCredy, U of Washington.

REGIONAL CONFERENCE BANQUET. Seated outside the table, left to right: Vern Bahr, U of Idaho; Mary Frances Cavenaugh, Marylhurst; Bill Green, WSC; Marvin Durham, UW; Ann Cavin, UW; James Seelig, ECWE; Mildred Gellerman, UW; Mac McCredy, UW; Hekmut Belser, foreign student; Carol Morgan, WSC; Lloyd Buscher, EWC. Seated l. to r., inside, are Ray Caviness, EWC; Elizabeth Wilcox, U of I; Marvin Jagels, U of I, Jack Martin, Harry Sherburne and Nadine Zornes, all of EWC.

Photos: WSCE 1951 Yearbook *Kinnikinick*

Lewis and Clark Represented at Prague, 1947

JOHN ELWOOD represented Lewis and Clark at the12/46 Chicago Student Conference, where he was elected regional chair for Oregon-Washington. Before attending the 1947 NSA Constitutional Convention he represented LC at the 1947 World Youth Festival. Elwood is shown above (standing) being introduced at an LC ceremony (1945 LC *Voyageur*).

Reed College, Oregon

REED COLLEGE QUEST

1/30/47

Delegate to National Student Conference at Chicago Urges Permanent Reed Participation in Organization

Delegations from the student governments of 350 colleges and universities in the United States met at Chicago December 28-30 and decided to form a national student organization. A constitutional convention has been scheduled for next summer; the next Conference will probably be held the following September.

The aims of the NSO, as proposed by the Chicago Student Conference, are "to promote student friendship on national and international scale, to secure for all people the rights and possibility of primary, secondary, and higher education regardless of sex, race, or religion; to secure for all students an extensive scholarship and family allowance and the provision of textbooks, supplies, and all other means to assure their independence wherever necessary; to secure the elimination of all forms of discrimination in student life; to encourage student-faculty cooperation on student problems and the extension of democratic student-controlled student governments and to establish the independence and freedom from censorship of student organizations and publications; to assure that all activity funds are controlled by the students themselves; and to foster student cultural activities and to secure the widest possible publication of advances of knowledge in social sciences, and the fine arts, and methods of circulation of these problems which would make available to all students the fullest information regarding such new developments."

Eunice Hyllested, former Reed student who attended the conference as an observer, wrote back in her report: "I *do* want to say that I think the N.S.O. is going to be powerful, important, and helpful—and I think Reed should affiliate with it, and send at least one delegate next time." In the list of resolutions which were discussed, she starred for particular notice one which read: "Whereas it is an aim of the NSO to extirpate discrimina-

1947

10/2/47

National Student Body Started, Student Says

Organizational plans and constitution for the United States National Student association have been completed, according to Judith LaFollette, official Reed delegate who attended the organization's second convention in Madison, Wisconsin, early in September. Approximately one-half the college students in the country were represented at the assembly of the group, which hopes to further opportunities for college students, and bring all colleges together, for the investigation of uniform privileges and rights.

Among issues brought before the convention was the question of segregated schools in the southern states, with an endeavor to find a policy satisfactory to both southern and northern students. Affilia-

1948

3/15/48

Meeting on NSA Here To Interest Colleges

This Saturday in the S. U. at one o'clock a meeting will be held at Reed to discuss the possibilities of national student organization through the medium of the National Student Association. Invitations have been extended to 10 colleges in the Portland area to send representatives of their student bodies to the meeting.

At the present time Reed and Lewis and Clark are the only schools in the Portland metropolitan area affiliated with the NSA and the purpose of this meeting will be to present the NSA program to representatives of Portland area student bodies for their consideration.

4/12/48

Reed Leads NSA In Local Organization

Student leaders from seven colleges in the Portland area met at Reed just before Easter vacation. They came at the invitation of the Reed College National Student Association Committee, Rip Collins, Judy LaFollette and Richard Meigs. The meeting's purpose was to discuss the program offered by the NSA.

Since Reed is the only local school affiliated with it, the Reed committee took it upon itself to call this meeting in hopes of interesting other Oregon colleges. Those represented at the meeting were Lewis & Clark, Vanport, Oregon State, the University of Oregon, the University of Portland, Marylhurst, and Reed.

"I THINK THE NSO IS GOING TO BE POWERFUL, IMPORTANT AND HELPFUL," Eunice Hillested, Reed observer to the Chicago Student Conference reported (1/30/47 above). After dropping out for a year due to "monetary difficulties," Reed rejoined citing in the *Quest,* "NSA since its founding has gradually increased in importance" (10/30/50 left).

10/30/50

New "Quest" Editor Found, Council Talks About Paper, N.S.A.

The "Quest" got a new assistant editor and was saved from oblivion last Tuesday, when the Council decided to table the question, 'Should the "Quest" be

N.S.A. Advantages Listed; National Group At Reed

During last Tuesday's Student Council meeting affiliation with the National Student Association was approved. At least once, prior to this the student council has refused affiliation because of insufficient finances.

The NSA is designed to give the college students a voice that can be heard in the local and national affairs which affect education. In addition, the NSA serves as a clearing house for information concerning the activites of colleges and college students.

Major concern of the NSA is the administration, finance of student government and national student organizations. International student problems, student life where it concerns economic and social problems, and student rights also lies within its scope.

1950 10/30/50

1951

NORTHWEST REGIONAL CONFERENCE
December 14-16, 1951, Reed College

Friday	4 pm	Registration, Eliot Hall
	6 pm	Dinner, Commons, $1.10
	8 pm	First Plenary, Student Union (Dr. Peters, Reed: Student Union)
Saturday	8:15am	Breakfast, Commons, pay by dish
	10 am	Second Plenary, Student Union
	10:30 am	Committees: (a) Student Life/Govt. (b) Educ. Affairs and Human Rels. (c) International Affiars
	12:00	Lunch, Commons, Cafeteria style
	1:30 pm	Committees
	5:30	Banquet, Coffee Shop, $1.25
	7:30	India Edwards, Natl Dem Comm.
Sunday	8:15	Breakfast, Commons, pay by dish
	11 am	Final Plenary

Historical notes: Lewis and Clark College was founded by Presbyterian pioneers as Albany Collegiate Institute in 1867. The school moved to Portland's southwest hills in 1942 and took its present name (www.lclark.edu). 1948 enrollment: 1,232 ◆ Reed College was founded in 1908 and named for Oregon pioneers Simeon and Amanda Reed, whose estate set up a board to found an institution of learning in Portland "with no limits other than an insistence on equality and secularism" (www.reed.edu). 1948 enrollment: 710 ◆ In 1890 the State Normal School opened in Cheney, WA. In 1937 the state's Normal Schools were designated as Colleges of Education, and Cheney became Eastern Washington College of Education. In 1961 it became Eastern Washington State College and in 1977 Eastern Washington University (www.wsu.edu). 1948 enrollment: 1,364.

University of Idaho/Washington State College

Editor's note: U of Idaho and Washington State College student government leaders supported NSA membership while also concerned over the emphasis on policy debates as compared to "practical projects." Four of the five WSC delegates to the 1949 Student Congress at Illinois each wrote a comprehensive report appearing in The Evergreen. *A typical judgment was expressed by Carol Morgan on 11/9/49: "In general I felt that too much time was spent on policies rather than solid programs we were able to sink our teeth into. . . . I found, however, that a very clear exchange of ideas could be had. . . . Through its collective efforts NSA can bridge the gap where there has previously been a lack of organization among colleges."*

Washington State College

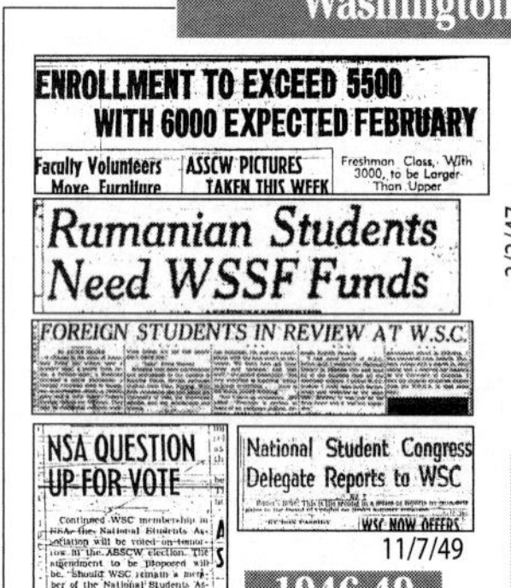

ENROLLMENT TO EXCEED 5500 WITH 6000 EXPECTED FEBRUARY

Rumanian Students Need WSSF Funds

FOREIGN STUDENTS IN REVIEW AT W.S.C.

NSA QUESTION UP FOR VOTE

National Student Congress Delegate Reports to WSC

11/7/49

1946-49

NSA Passed by Overwhelming Student Vote

From top: 101/46, 9/3/48, 1/20/47, 5/4/49, 5/6/49

EDITORIAL

Communism or Democracy—Which Shall It Be?

3/3/47

The students of America, as a whole, are failing to take enough ... interest in our governmental policies and affairs. ... We, as the future business men and women of America ... Miss Giovanni Ribet, student speaker with the World Student Service ...

CONTINUED NSA MEMBERSHIP was voted 2953 to 228 in a May, 1949 referendum. Student-faculty grading, foreign student hospitality, a travel office and student housing surveys were among programs sponsored by the NSA Committee.

Edward R. Murrow Returns

1946 5/24/46

ED MURROW, ALUM, RETURNS TO WSC FOR COMMENCEMENT

ALUM-SENIOR DAY IS SATURDAY

1942 1/30/42

Large Crowd Hears Edward R. Murrow

MURROW was a 1930 graduate who became President of the National Student Federation of America and went on to a career as a war correspondent and world renowned radio and television commenyator (p. 26).

The Cougars and the Vandals: Then and Now

Washington State Evergreen

Students Await Annual Civil War with U of Idaho

WS-10/14/49

NSA Plans Purchase Card System For Idaho And WSC

TA-8/8/49

JUST ACROSS THE BORDER, Idaho (Vandals) and WSC (Cougars) maintained continuous membership and collaborated on NSA projects.

(Left: U. of Idaho Library, UI logo. Above: Edward R. Murrow School of Communication, WSU Logo. Shown also Pullman and Moscow road maps, Rte 270 road signs. Photo: 7/2000, Schwartz).

University of Idaho

Affiliation

The Idaho Argonaut

Executive Board Votes Tuesday On NSA Question

Dave Weeks To Air NSA Information Before Final Vote

Idaho Delegation To Participate In NSA Conclave

1948-49

Dahlstrom Heads NSA Committee For Campus Work

Bob Dahlstrom

From left: 10/8/48 10/12/48, 10/15/48, 1/21/49

DAVE WEEKS, ASUI PRESIDENT, introduced NSA in a "Fireside Chat" over KUOI radio. "NSA's avowed purpose is the enhancement of student welfare [and] to contribute to the welfare of the national and international community." UI was represented at the Constitutional Convention by Boyd Hanson who reported, "NSA will give the college student unprecedented representation in the educational world" (10/8/48 above).

Policy

Southern Students, Fight Intolerance In Schools

1947-49

NSA Congress To Consider Student Government, Art

NSA Plan Calls For Student Aid, Better Teachers

Student Congress Delegates Discuss Common Problems

NSA Takes Stand Against Dismissal Profs Accused Of Communism

Students To ... With Profess ... In Borah For

From top, left: 12/16/47, 2/6/48; center: 4/12/49; rt: 5/29/49, 9/16/49

NSA CONGRESSES AND POLICIES were reported by *The Argaunaut.* Robert Moulton and Vernon Bahr represented the U of Idaho at the 1948 Congress (p. 197).

Programs

1950-51 NSA Committee

Photos: Gem of the Mountains 1951-52 Yearbooks

Marvin Jagels
NSA Regional VP

MARVIN JAGELS, 1950-51 Eastern District Regional VP was a member of the debate squad, Ag club and Student Services Council

1948-49

Students To Hear WSSF Group Head

'Operation Amigos' Is Added To NSA's Summer Program

Rating Plan Considered By Welfare Committee

Idaho Student Rating Plan Being Used By Instructors

FACULTY RATING (p. 372), summer travel, foreign student aid and freshman orientation program revision were the campus programs managed by the NSA committee.

From top: 11/9/48, 4/12/49, 2/24/48, 12/14/48

Historical notes: The University of Idaho was established by the territorial legislature in 1889, one year before Idaho's admission as a state (www.lib.uidaho.edu). 1948 enrollment: 3,634 ◆ Founded as Washington State Agricultural College and School of Science in 1890, it was named State College of Washington in 1905 until 1959, when it became Washington State University (www.wsu.edu). 1948 enrollment: 6,562.

NSA is an experiment in self-government so significant, that everyone interested in democracy should be watching it with the keenest interest.

Dean S. Newhouse: Fostering Student Government for Democracy

Director of Student Affairs, University of Washington, 1933-48
Dean of Students, Case Institute of Technology, Ohio, 1949
Member, NSA National Advisory Council, 1948-51

Editor's note: Dean S. Newhouse (first name "Dean") advocated for strong student governments and was an early supporter of NSA while at the University of Washington. He collaborated with Gordon Klopf, NSA's first Advisory Committee Chair (see correspondence next page), and spoke out for the Association during attacks upon it by the Students for America in 1951. His eloquent testimonial to NSA on the next page reflects the high hopes held for NSA by many administrators and the value they saw in it.

Student Government—Romance and/or Reality

Excerpts from an 8-page address delivered before the Constitutional Convention of the National Student Association, September 1947 [Berea College Archives]

I have yet to find a dozen persons who know what they mean when they say student government. It is one of those terms like "democracy," "liberty," "education," "sportsmanship" which has come to mean so many things to so many people that no one can be sure what the other is really talking about. Some of us have made the error of assuming that student government necessarily means democratic student government. Actually there are many cases of government by students which are anything but democratic. Some assume that it cannot be student government unless it is democratic student government which is truly representative of the entire student body. In many cases, the student governing agency fails to represent half of the students in any meaningful way.

For many students it is simply a voluntary extracurricular activity which provides them with the opportunity to obtain experience in administering enterprises. Not that such experience is not good, but it isn't necessarily student government.

For many deans and administrators, student government has appeared as an administrative device. The dean has said to himself, "I'm tired of the trouble these student problems make for me. Some of the students think they can handle them better. I'll give them a try at it. If they can't do it, at least they will then feel better about my doing it."

Romantic notions of student government

A large group of students have what appears to me to be romantic notions of student government. Never having had the opportunity to study it carefully, they yearn for self-determination, for liberation from regulations imposed by outside authorities, for a chance to try out the democratic ideals they have learned from teachers, orators and books.

I find romanticists about student government everywhere I go: not only among students but also among businessmen, among women's groups, among faculty members, and even among college administrators. They say, "Let the kids do it," or, "Youth will find a way." Even in the published literature of education there are evidences of it; I think the early nineteen-twenties might well be called the romantic period of student government. This was the time when "the honor system" swept the country; when the problem of cheating in exams was to be solved by putting uncorrupted youth "on its honor." When students said, "turn this toughest of all administrative problems; we'll handle it." When administrators and faculty members said, "These young adults are as yet uncorrupted; they have the enthusiasm, the energy, the integrity, the ambition to succeed where we have failed." In a few schools . . . the honor system did succeed and is operating successfully at this time, but in the huge majority, it bowed quietly out in a few years. Evidently enthusiasm, energy, ambition, and youthful non-corruption were not enough. . . . Judging by results, it was a romantic dream.

I am convinced that idealism, enthusiasm, energy are not enough to insure success. Self-government requires more than the desire for or the belief in self-government. Some of these requirements we have been learning from experience at the University of Washington; it has been interesting to find that student leaders in other schools, deans of students, [student] union building directors have been having some of the same learning experiences. . . .

The authority on which student government operates is not a sovereign power, but is delegated by the administration or faculty. . . . The student government must function as though it is sovereign and, at the same time, remember that it is not. . . . However, this is a reality in student government. It cannot be evaded.

I know from experience that democratic student government can function on delegated authority. It has been proved in many colleges. It becomes an administrative branch of the college

I believe student government is an effective laboratory in democracy. . . . I hope the National Student Organization can prove to be an effective force for making student government appreciated for its true significance and worth to the cause of democracy.

NSA Needs to Support Sound Student Government

Editor's note: Dean Newhouse was keenly interested in NSA's potential to help empower and strengthen student self-government. He was also concerned, as were other student personnel administrators, that it could siphon off student leaders and compete with or even dominate student governments. He forged a strong alliance with NSA's adviser, Gordon Klopf, at the University of Wisconsin (see p. 337). The following exchange of correspondence between them and with Harold E. Stewart, Assistant Dean of Student Affairs at Wayne University in Detroit, deals with the issue of NSA's relationship to student government.

One question I have had in my mind is the extent to which the Executive Committee of the U.S.N.S.A. makes use of the resource provided by its very excellent Advisory Committee. Judging from certain aspects of our local situation I would like to see the Executive Committee emphasize to the local school committees that (1) the U.S.N.S.A. was formed to work through local student government, not to dominate it; and (2) that the local U.S.N.S.A. Committee should not be thought of as a vehicle through which two or three people may attempt to dominate a local college scene or as a medium for the expression of their own biases, prejudices, ambitions and disagreements with other students and with administrative officials. I know of nothing that will discredit U.S.N.S.A. so rapidly on college campuses as failure to observe the above.

12/3/48 letter from Stewart at Wayne U to Newhouse at U Washington

I would agree with you that attempts of NSA Committee delegates to dominate their local student government could discredit NSA rapidly. I think the officers and members of the Executive Committee would agree with you, and that they would probably go further and say say that such attempts to dominate are contrary to the basic objectives of NSA. There has never been any charge of such domination on our campus, so I have not given the matter any particular thought, but I can see that such a situation could easily exist in other schools due to the character of their student government or to extraordinary ambitions and abilities on the part of NSA Committee members.

12/9/48 letter from Newhouse at U Washington to Stewart at Wayne U

Having been at Wayne, I can readily see what is happening on the campus. They prohibit all political activity and discussion, and are apparently questioning how sound this policy is. I just had a long letter from my co-worker, the Counselor of Women, asking for my suggestions and recommendations in light of our student political policies here at Wisconsin. It sounds as though the liberal element at Wayne is using the local BSA Committee as a medium of expression for their point of view. I think this is bad for NSA, but what the National, or even the Regional, can do about it is doubtful.It's a local problem and very much a part of the Wayne picture. However, I think the Executive Committee can emphasize the fact that NSA local commissions must not dominate the student government program. They must remain a part or leg of it.

12/17/48 letter from Klopf at U Wisconsin to Newhouse at U Washington

Your comments on the Wayne University situation as regards student government and local NSA influence are very interesting. They lead me to speculate that it is very possible that NSA delegates will be rebellious minorities on their own campuses where student government doesn't have established autonomy. Such rebellion will be good in many respects and may turn into constructive and successful leadership, but it may also cause some institutions to decide that NSA is a source of difficulty and insist that it be avoided. Such thinking takes me back to my original thinking about NSA, which is that it cannot exist except on the basis of sound local student government, and that therefore it is absolutely necessary that NSA consider the encouragement and development of sound student government on local campuses as its primary function.

12/22/48 letter from Newhouse at U Washington to Klopf at U Wisconsin

What I Think of N.S.A.

From *NSA News*, April, 1951

N.S.A. is an experiment in self-government so significant that everyone interested in democracy should be watching it with the keenest interest. It isn't a national organization for youth, guided by a professional staff, but one of youth, completely autonomous, which uses the advice of experience only as it sees fit. Each year since its beginning, the voice of experience has predicted it must fail —because of subversive influence, problems of race and religion, financial problems, lack of continuing leadership, and disinterest of students of the college campuses.

But N.S.A. has demonstrated that it never fails to defeat subversion by sticking faithfully to democratic methods and principles. Since its very beginning, Catholic, Jew and Protestant, negro, oriental, and white have worked together constructively and happily for their mutual welfare. Every year, idealistic students who think they must rebel to achieve their goals are won over to the responsible methods of fact finding and appraisal, education, effective communication and cooperation.

And its achievements have been significant in themselves: I think of support of World Student Service Fund, of education, of Displaced Persons in American colleges, of student tours abroad, of relations with student federations of other free countries. I think of its thoughtful guides to effective local organization of student government, of Campus Chests, of teacher-evaluation programs; I think of its relations with educational groups: associate membership in the American Council on Education and the National Education Association, its seat on the U. S. UNESCO Commission. Its major program for this year, leadership training, may be its greatest contribution.

The future of NSA cannot be predicted, cannot be guaranteed. But in five years, it has demonstrated that it can be as sound and strong and active as college students' willingness to take responsibility for the practice of their faiths.

Dean S. Newhouse, Dean of Students, Case Institute

DEAN S. NEWHOUSE (1909-1955)

Editor's note: The following is adapted from an April 14 obituary in the Seattle Times *and an April 22 obituary in the* Case Tech. *He had been Dean of Students at Case since 1949 and was appointed Director of Admissions in the fall of 1954.*

Dean Newhouse was born in Altmont, Kansas, in 1909. He studied at the University of Idaho and was graduated from the University of Washington in 1930. He took graduate work at Columbia.

Newhouse taught in Seattle area high schools before joining the University of Washington faculty in 1936, where he held the posts of Assistant Dean of Men, Registrar, Dean of Men and Director of Student Affairs. He was elected President of the Pacific Coast Collegiate Registrars Association in 1940, and served as the Vice President of the National Association of Deans of Men in 1949.

In 1949 he became Dean of Students at Case Institute of Technology in Cleveland. The *Case Tech* reported that he "soon displayed his genius for administration. He considered the student as a person, not just as a unit in an educational institution, and worked for development of the man outside the classroom. During the course of his stay, Case took the first steps in its conversion from a 'street car college' to a 'residence college.'"

Newhouse was survived by his wife, son and daughter.

PICTURE CREDIT: c. 1950 (Case Western Reserve University Archives). DOCUMENT SOURCES: Case Archives, State Historical Society of Wisconsin (Klopf papers in the NSA collection), University of Washington Libraries Archives.

PART 6

Epilogue: What Happened Later

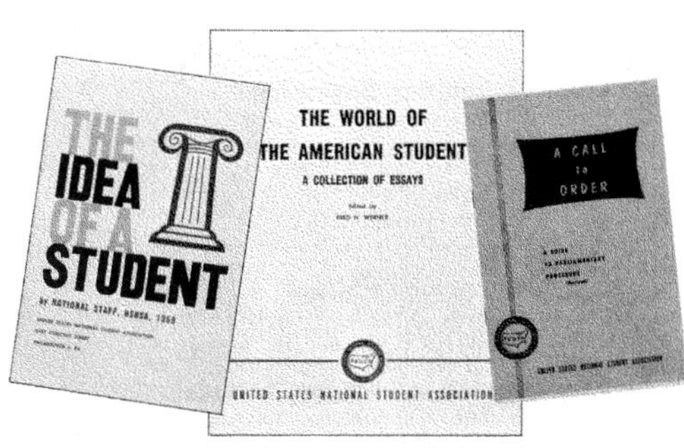

Nixon Urges Students To Take Greater Role In National Affairs

Student leadership and the degree of student concern with public issues have been cited by Vice President Richard Nixon as factors which can determine the nation's survival in the atomic age. Mr. Nixon expressed this opinion at a recent meeting in his office with USNSA President Ray Farabee.

In discussing the role of students in national affairs, the Vice President expressed the hope that college students would be "more concerned with public issues." He stated that "In our democracy, it is imperative that we develop the broadest possible understanding of the issues confronting our nation."

Vice President Nixon and Mr. Farabee also discussed the significance to students of the recently published 2nd Report of the President's Committee on Education Beyond the High School. Arrangements were made for USNSA to distribute copies of this report to student body presidents and other campus leaders in member colleges. USNSA will sponsor a nation-wide conference program on the student's role in implementing the findings of this report.

The USNSA President said that he felt that students could make a significant contribution in several of the areas in which the Committee made recommendations for immediate action. These included faculty salaries, teacher recruitment, student economic problems, and guiding and counseling services. Plans for the conferences are being drawn up by Willard Johnson, USNSA Vice President for Educational Affairs. It is expected that many of the 355 member colleges of USNSA will participate in the conferences which will be part of the Association's leadership development program.

National Student News

VOL. I — NO. 1 PHILA., PA., FRIDAY, NOV. 1, 1957

USNSA PRESIDENT IN WASHINGTON: Vice President Richard M. Nixon, left, discussed student leadership and the actions of the 10th National Student Congress with USNSA President Ray Farabee.

Sixty National Unions Join In Program Of International Student Cooperation

Delegates from sixty national unions of students participated in the seventh International Student Conference (ISC), making this the largest and most representative ... continue to collect information on student problems in Algeria and other countries where they have already begun studies. They will also attempt to enter Spain and Iran to gather material for ... dentials Committee. Later, USNSA was voted a place on the nine-nation Supervision Committee which oversees the work of the Coordinating Secretariat (COSEC), the ...

USNSA Urges Support Of Integration Efforts In Little Rock Arkansas

Urging forthright efforts toward school integration and condemning those who interfered with its peaceful achievement, USNSA wired President Eisenhower and Governor Orval Faubus to express student opinion regarding the Little Rock incident.

In telegrams sent on Sept. 12 and signed by USNSA President Ray Farabee, law student at the University of Texas, and retiring USNSA President Harold Bakken of ...

SURVIVING ITS BUDGET CRISIS AND THE DRAFT, NSA's move to Philadelphia provided stability and access to support enabling its leaders to develop program and service continuity. The Cold War, McCarthyism, the civil rights movement and internal politics provided major challenges. (Top left: NSA Report to the 11th National Student Congress. Right, above: NSA's *National Student News*, 11/1/57. Below: USNSA Annual Report, 1959-60.)

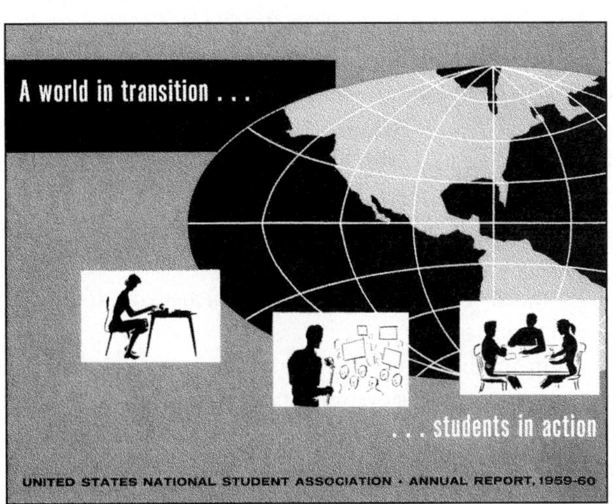

PART 6

What Happened Later

The principal goal of this anthology has been to bring alive the first five formative years of the U.S. National Student Association. The accomplishments of NSA's leaders enriched both their own experiences and the contemporary higher education scene and also laid the foundation for an organization that survived that formative period.

In 1977, a much-transformed NSA merged with another organization, the National Student Lobby, to form what became a new U.S. Student Association (its acronym, USSA, was an unrelated echo of the USSA of the 1940s). The USSA considers NSA to be a part of its organizational heritage in an unbroken line and continues to hold annual Student Congresses each summer.

As Janet (Welsh) Brown, NSA 1952-53 student affairs vice president, notes in Section 2, "the full NSA/USSA story remains untold . . . and those of us who have worked on this volume must urge our successors at NSA/USSA and other scholars to complete the task."

NSA's move to Philadelphia in 1952 marks a new era

The description of NSA's move to Philadelphia in 1952, by Dick Murphy (University of North Carolina), the association's sixth president, lays the groundwork for the full telling of that story. Ruth Hagy Brod's College News Conference, described in Section 1, enlisted the aid of former NSA leaders, and provided students with a weekly national Sunday television news presence for more than ten years—a platform from which NSA strengthened its presence as a voice for students.

Murphy's two pieces in Section 1 on strengthening freedom are testimony to NSA's vigilance in defense of academic freedom during the decades of the Cold War and the fears of communist subversion which roiled U.S. campuses and student organizations, discussed earlier in Parts 2 and 3.

Janet Brown's review of several histories and dissertations on NSA provides both a glimpse into some of the major events of the post-1952 period and a critique of these histories.

The albums at the close of Section 2 provide a glimpse of the scope during its first ten years of NSA's outreach in programs concerned with student leadership, student government, civil rights, higher education policy and student travel and exchange.

Jim Smith's call to American students, to organize to maintain strong, democratic student self-governments, which he expressed as President of NSA's founding committee in 1947 (page 127), was being realized.

Moving Day for Students Association

Officers of the United States National Student Association move furniture in their new headquarters at 1307 Sansom. From left: Avrea Ingram, vice president of international affairs; Leonard A. Wilcox, Jr., vice president for national affairs; Richard J. Murphy, president of the association, and Janet Welsh, vice president for student affairs.

National Student Association Moves Headquarters Here

Philadelphia became a center of national college student activity yesterday when the United States National Student Association opened its new headquarters at 1307 Sansom.

vice president for national affairs, and Marion Ander, executive secretary. Mrs. Ruth Geri Hagy, director of the Philadelphia Bulletin Forum, is senior staff advisor to the national officers.

FROM ITS NEW HEADQUARTERS, A NATIONAL STUDENT VOICE is provided for its student government members as the USNSA and its successor, USSA, move into fifty years of history. (Above: Philadelphia Bulletin 10/25/52. Below: From "NSA Report, 1959-60")

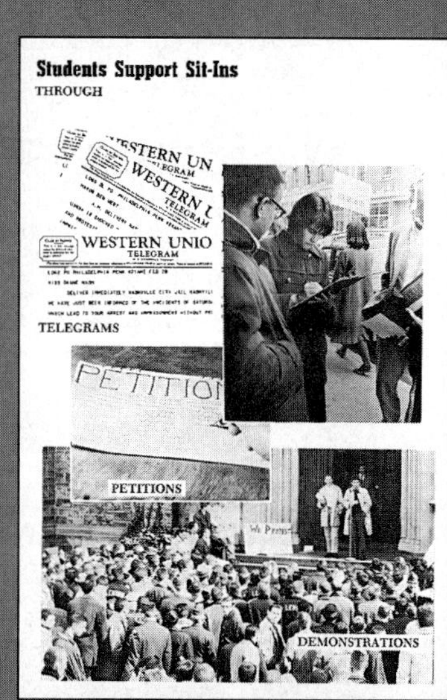

Students Support Sit-Ins
THROUGH
WESTERN UNION
TELEGRAM
TELEGRAMS
PETITION
PETITIONS
DEMONSTRATIONS

SECTION 1

Moving East

CONTENTS

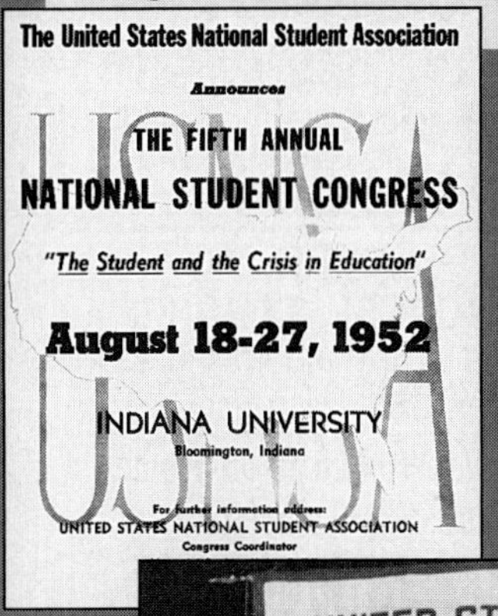

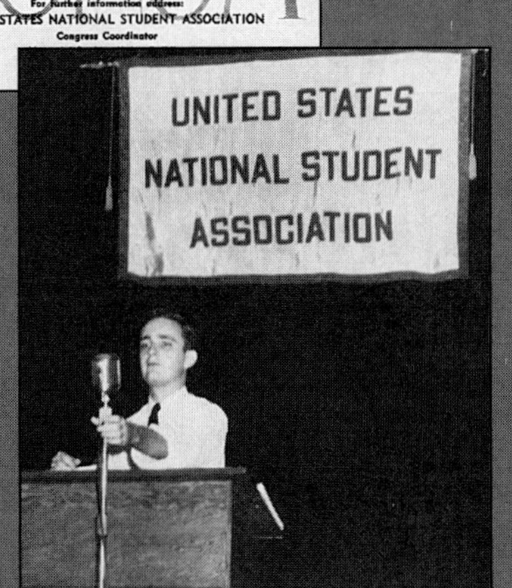

When Dick Murphy (University of North Carolina) moved NSA to Philadelphia in September 1952, NSA left behind its commitment to locate in the "middle of America," in order to be closer to the center of gravity of its membership and to other national groups located on the East Coast with which it collaborated.

The new location was also closer to likely sources of financial support, and it required less expenditure on travel and communications.

Murphy and his staff had "come up through the ranks" of NSA during the last two or three years of the period covered by this book. They brought links to its founders and founding years as grounding for the year to come.

The new officers, who were again mostly campus-based, were national affairs, student affairs, student government, and educational affairs vice presidents: respectively, Leonard Wilcox (University of Michigan), Janet Welsh (Smith College), Steve Voykovich (Fordham University), and Manfred Brust (University of Illinois). The International Vice President was a re-elected Avrea Ingram (Harvard University). While continuing to build on NSA's domestic and international programs, the staff was also coping with aggressive "Red Scare" attacks from Students for America and erosion of male staff by the draft.

NSA finds an "angel" and is repositioned on a sounder footing

In addition to describing how he was able to restart the organization while key members of the staff were being drafted, Murphy introduces us to Ruth Geri (Hagy) Brod, a television producer and journalist who took NSA under her wing. Her two main initiatives in behalf of NSA launched the association on a new and sounder footing in its new environs.

First, during the year she raised $50,000 for NSA from the Philadelphia business community—a sum equal to almost twice the average of its annual budgets in prior years—and found NSA free office space.

Second, she also used NSA talent for both production and panel appearances on her new television program, *College News Conference*, which brought the Association to the attention of a national audience and provided a springboard for future public relations.

NEWLY ELECTED PRESIDENT Dick Murphy (U. of North Carolina) addresses the Fifth National Student Congress at Indiana University. (SHSW) Top left: 1952 Congress announcement.

1952-1953 Album

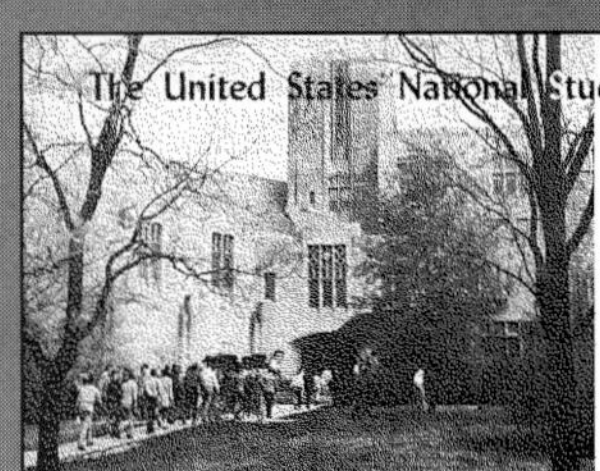

The United States National Student Association

ANNOUNCES
THE FIFTH ANNUAL
NATIONAL STUDENT CONGRESS

Indiana University
August 18-27, 1952
Bloomington, Indiana

5th NSA Congress Convenes August 18 At Indiana U.

The Fifth Annual National Student congress of the United States National Student association ... uled for Aug. 18-27 in ... ton, Ind., will feature d... on the highlights of the ... emic year.

More than 700 studen... senting approximately 30... and 800,000 students, wi... on the Indiana universit... to review student affairs... pus, national and int... levels.

NSA will celebrate the fifth an- ... dent interest as UMT, selective ...

STUDENT EDUCATION CRISIS N S A CONFERENCE SUBJECT

The Fifth Annual National Student Congress of United States National Student Association will feature highlights of the past academic year when more than 700 students representing approximately 300 colleges and 800,000 students meet to discuss student affairs on the campus, national, and international level from August 18-27 at Indiana University in

include debate on such questions of student interest as UMT, selective service policy, inter-collegiate athletics, the 18-year-old vote, and international student relations, along with the many workshops on all phases of student activity on campus. Efforts also are being made to bring back as many former NSA officers as possible.

The Congress will be preceded

From top: Fifth Congress announcement (SHSW); *NSA News* 5/52 (Murphy); *Mills College Weekly* 5/22/52

DAILY HERALD-TELEPHONE.

I.U. Host To 600 N.S.A. Delegates

Mould Opinion Of Students

Approximately 600 student delegates from 300 colleges representing 700,000 students converged on Indiana University today for the fifth annual international convention of the controversial National Student Association.

The Congress, seeking to mould student opinion on virtually all issues of the day from Universal Military Training to academic freedom, will run through August 27.

American politics will hold sway on August 23 when young political leaders of the Democrat and Republican parties debate the issues of the 1952 Presidential campaign.

Richard Nelson, administrative assistant to Governor Stevenson of Illinois, the Democrat standardbearer, and Philip Willkie, an Indiana State Representative from Rush County who has rocketed into prominence in national Republican politics, will participate.

THE OBSERVATION POST — Page Three

NSA Elects New National Officers; Delegates Opposed to UMT, Batista

By Neil Dimschitz

In a burst of spontaneous acclaimation, Richard Murphy of the University of North Carolina, was elected sixth president of the United States National Students Association at NSA's fifth annual student congress, at the University of Indiana, August 18th-27th.

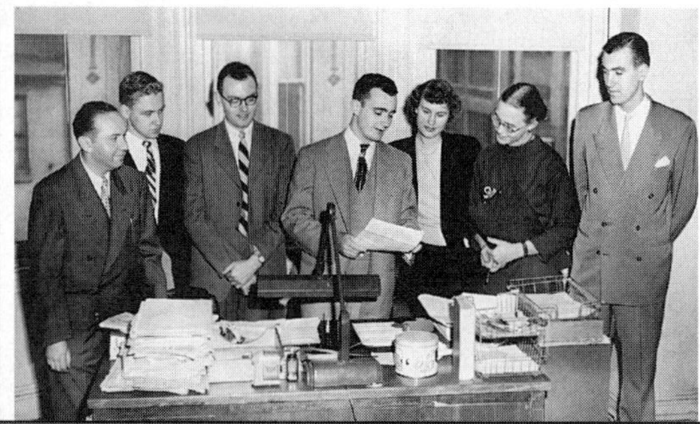

1952-53 NATIONAL STAFF From left: Manfred Brust (U. of Ill.), V.P. Educational Affairs; Leonard Wilcox (U. of Mich.), V. P. National Affairs; Avrea Ingram (Harvard U.), V.P. International Affairs; Richard Murphy (U. of N. Carolina), President; Marion Andert (U. of Minn.), Executive Secretary; Janet Welsh (Smith C.), V.P. Student Affairs; Stephen Voykovich (Fordham U.), V.P. Student Government. (Murphy, *Evening Bulletin*)

LAUNCHED FIVE YEARS EARLIER, NSA reached its Fifth Congress poised to fulfill the hopes of the 1946 Chicago Student Conference which called for its formation. (Clockwise from top: Bloomington, IN *Daily Herald Telephone*; CCNY *Observation Post* 9/22/52; Photos (SHSW), delegates at the Indiana Congress)

Temple University NEWS

NSA Chooses Phila. For New Headquarters

Philadelphia will be the center of NSA affairs when the National Student Association opens its central office Monday at 13th and Sansom sts.

The nationwide organization of college student governments is moving from its home office in Boulder, Colo. to be closer to a greater number of schools and to provide maximum service.

One-half of all of the colleges in the country are located within a 600-mile radius of Philadelphia, the Association found.

Richard J. Murphy, newly elected president of the organization, a student at the University of North Carolina, said that it was necessary for the office to be near the centers of educational activity in Washington, D.C. and New York City, and to have advice and counselling of outstanding people in the personnel field.

arrived NOV 8 - 1952 INQ.

Gimbels Donates Students Office

New headquarters of the National Student Association in the Gimbel Building will be dedicated at 4:30 P. M. tomorrow. Dr. Althea K. Hottel, dean of women at the University of Pennsylvania, will turn a gold key to open the office suite.

The headquarters offices are a gift to the students from Gimbels. Arthur C. Kaufmann, executive head of Gimbels, will present the offices to Eugene H. Keating, vice president of the association. Keating, a student at the College of St.

NSA SETTLES IN PHILADELPHIA

(Top: *Temple U. News* 103/52, *Philadelphia Bulletin* 11/8/52)

American Students: Organized

35 National Unions Attend Copenhagen Conference

Emphasize Practical Work for Equalization of Educational Opportunities Everywhere, Support University Autonomy, Oppose Discrimination, — Eastern Europeans Group Decline to Attend.

Representatives of 35 national ... Germany, Paraguay, Philippine...

NSA DELEGATION at Third International Student Conference (1/53). Left side of table: Avrea Ingram, International V.P.; Richard Murphy, President; Helen Jean Rogers, 1948-49 Secretary-Treasuer, then at Radcliffe College. Right side: David Duberman, formerly U. of Alabama, then at U. of Paris; Richard Holler, U. of California student body President; Sylvia Bacon, 1951-52 Student Life V.P., then at London School of Economics. (Hoover Institute archives)

Building New Alliances Abroad

USNSA president denies charge of subversion

Academic Freedom Week Feb. 15 - 22
Student Play 1 P M Thursday
See:

3 Deans' Groups Back Association As Student Voice

In a unanimously adopted resolution, the National Association of Deans of Women, the National Association of Student Personnel Administrators, and the American College Personnel Association stated that "the NSA is the mo[st] representative national student o[r]ganization in the United States."

At a joint-meeting recently he[ld] in Chicago, these three organiz...

VELDE DECLARES NSA WILL NOT BE STUDIED

The Un-American Activities Committee has no intention to investigate the NSA, declared Harold H. Velde, chairman of the Un-American Activities Committee, in ... by any special interest group.

Earlier Remarks Misinterpreted

Mr. Velde indicated that remarks made by him in Congress in 1951 had been "misinterpreted."

Murphy Addresses Deans of Women National Education Association

... students, educa- ...ity groups fill the ...ard Murphy, NSA ... e will address the National Associa- ... Bulletin Forum on March 16 as well as a number of speeches at various colleges and universities.

Educator Lauds Participants

Commenting on the participation of NSA officers in educational

Students Meet Experts on Network TV

JUNIOR PRESS CONFERENCE, left of ABC TV ('52): James Carey, Sec'y.-Treas. of AFL-CIO and Ruth Hagy, moderator. Standing, from left: Robert Kelly (Harvard), 1949-50 NSA President; Elmer Brock, 1950-51 NSA Educational Problems V.P.; Ruth Standsbury, U. of Baltimore; Ed Meese, Yale U. (*NSA News* 3/53)

From top: Roosevelt C., Il, *Torch* 2/16/53; "Deans," *NSA News* 4/53; "Velde," *NSA News* 3/53; "Murphy," *NSA News* 3/53

Establishing a National Voice

NSA's first year in the East launches a new era for the association.

1. From Boulder to Philadelphia

Richard J. Murphy
University of North Carolina
NSA President, 1952-53

When I came to Philadelphia I had a mandate from the Fifth National Student Congress at Indiana to move the office to the East (no city specified) from Boulder, Colorado, where Bill Dentzer had moved it the year before, after four years in Madison, Wisconsin. They had only been there one year. Even though we had free rent and support from the University,[1] we had to get out of the Far West because it was simply too expensive to operate from that location. The NSA president was normally on the road half of the time, and we couldn't afford the back and forth travel costs. But, of course, I had no money. The treasury was absolutely bare when I was elected president. We didn't have a dime.

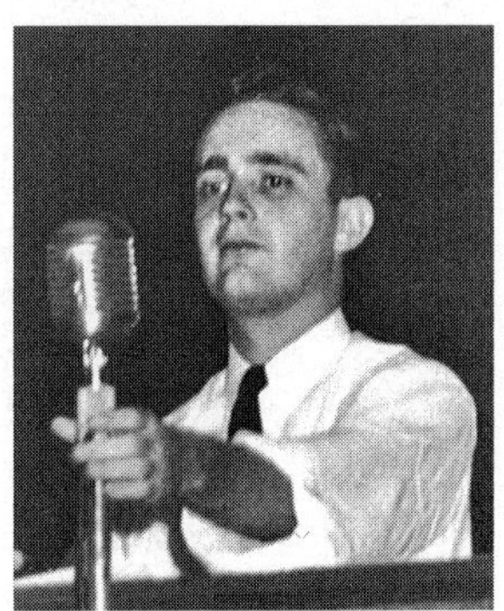

We had an office in Cambridge for the International Commission, of course, but that was separate.

Avrea Ingram, who was elected with me as international vice president, operated out of that office. He was the first officer of NSA to be reelected to a second term, having first been elected with Bill Dentzer. Avrea was a very courteous, intelligent Alabaman who had graduated from Georgia Tech, a dedicated patriot with a great sense of humor and an extensive knowledge of foreign affairs. I had initially opposed his election for his first term in 1951, but came to regard him with the highest esteem and admiration.

Welcome to Philadelphia

Shortly after my election I received a call from Marie Minnick, who was the student body president at the women's college of the University of Pennsylvania, inviting us to Philadelphia, and additional calls from the dean of women, Althea Kratz-Hottel, and from the president of the University, Harold Stassen. Both Governor Stassen and Dean Hottel had already joined NSA's National Advisory Board the year before.

Althea Kratz-Hottel at that time was also serving as the national chair of Women for Eisenhower and 1952 was the year Eisenhower was campaigning against Adlai Stevenson. Dean Hottel said that she thought we could get free office space if we were to come to Philadelphia. Well, naturally, that was a godsend to me. So I went to Philadelphia.

I remember going to Rittenhouse Square and up the stairs in this big high-rise apartment house. I knocked on the door of Ruth Geri Hagy's apartment—a woman whom I had never met, but who was a friend of Marie Minnick.

When the door suddenly flew open, a woman appeared and said, "You must be Dickie and I'm Ruthie and I'm going to raise fifty thousand dollars for the NSA," and I nearly dropped dead on the spot. That was twice the size of any annual budget we had had for the first five years.

Well, Mrs. Hagy made good on her promise, and she ultimately raised the fifty thousand dollars for us from receptions that she organized with the mayor of Philadelphia, Joe Clark, with Dick Dilworth, the district attorney, and with Walter Annenberg, who was then the owner of WFIL-Television.[2] This was the first money that NSA had ever raised for its domestic programs. She also obtained free office space from Albert Greenfield, Philadelphia's largest realtor, and later from Bernard Gimbel, in his renowned department store.

The *College News Conference* on ABC

Ruth started the *College News Conference* program (at first called "Junior Press Conference," a name we quickly insisted be changed) five weeks after I met her, with NSA providing the students for the program. It was the best public relations NSA ever had, and it went on the air as an ABC national television sustaining program every Sunday morning. It ran for ten years, with the NSA providing student body presidents and college editors to be the panelists.[3]

The original NSA producer was Elmer Paul Brock, who had just returned from Japan from Navy service in the Korean War. Elmer had been NSA vice president for student affairs in 1950-51. Helen Jean Rogers, NSA secretary-treasurer in 1948-49, also served as a producer for two years.[4] Marciarose Shestack of Philadelphia, who later became the first news anchorwoman on television, was an early permanent panelist. Another panelist in the first few months of the show was a young law student from Yale, Ed Meese, who later became U.S. attorney general, in the Reagan administration.

The office of the *College News Conference* was at the NSA headquarters for the first two years. This office was on the second floor, over a tailor's shop, in the building at 13th and Sansom Street in Philadelphia, one block from John Wannamaker's Department Store, two blocks from City Hall, and two blocks from the Union League Club, the strongest right-wing Republican club in America. And to this office over the tailor's shop, during the course of the year I was there, came General Omar Bradley, chairman of the Joint Chiefs of Staff, who was a guest on the news conference—quizzed by the students provided by NSA. Ruth brought him over to our student headquarters to show him how we were living.

The NSA staff and the Korean War draft

It had been decided at the Indiana Congress that there would be one full-time additional elected officer in Philadelphia, with the rest being campus-based officers. The City College of New York student newspaper, *The Observation Post*, reported in its September 22, 1952, issue that "The elections climaxed a ten-day 'marathon,' which resembled an international rather than a national conference of students: youths from Holland, Switzerland, West Germany, India, Iran, the Philippines, Cuba and many other nations addressed the congress and participated in the discussions. The congress was preceded by a four-day College Newspaper Editors' Conference and a similar Student Body Presidents' conference, both sponsored by NSA."

The campus-based staff included Janet Welsh, Smith College, vice president for student affairs; Steve Voykovich, Fordham College, vice president for student government; and Manfred Brust, University of Illinois, vice president for educational affairs.

Leonard Wilcox, a superb officer, who was elected to the newly established post of vice president for national affairs, had been president of the student body of the University of Michigan. He was to join us full time in Philadelphia, where he began publication of the *NSA Student Government Bulletin*. Leonard was, incidentally, vice chairman of Students for Eisenhower. I held the same position in Students for Stevenson, and we were roommates! Since Leonard was about to be drafted in December and he didn't want to go into the Army, he went down at Christmas time and enlisted in the Navy for a three-year stint. We were full-time NSA officers and the Korean War was going on. As soon as we left student status and became full-time officers, we lost our draft deferment, which we would have retained had we stayed on campus.

So in January of 1953, Leonard left us. In his place I later appointed Phillip Berry—also from the University of Michigan—to be vice president.[5] Phil came in the first part of June of that year. So from January to June we had no additional vice president, and it was just myself and Marion Andert, who was the executive secretary. In order to save money, Marion lived in a convent while she was in Philadelphia. Marion was from Minnesota. A former officer of the Newman clubs, she was a very devoutly religious and energetic worker, who had also been executive secretary under Bill Dentzer the previous year. NSA owes a tremendous debt to her.

I was on the road a good bit of this time, and at the end of January I was in Copenhagen presiding at the International Student Conference, when I opened up a telegram and found a notice that I'd been drafted. I was to report to my draft board the following Monday. I had to come back to the United States almost immediately.

General Hershey offers a draft delay

When I got back to the country I went to our office in Philadelphia, where I found another telegram stating that I was to report to General Hershey's office the next Monday morning in Washington. Hershey was national head of Selective Service. I had only been in Washington once before in my life, so it was quite an adventure. I went to General Hershey's office, where he began to quiz me about the International Student Conference (ISC) and what I was doing in Copenhagen. What was the ISC all about? What was the International Union of Students (IUS) all about? What were we doing? So I proceeded to tell him.

At the end of a twenty-minute conversation between Hershey and myself, he said to me:

> I'll tell you what I'm going to do. 1 like what you've been doing in Copenhagen and I like what NSA has been doing. I'm going to make a deal with you. I'll give you a six-month postponement of your induction, not a deferment—on the condition that you not try to go back to school again [you would get a deferment automatically again if you became a student] but you will agree to go into the Army the day that your term of office expires; you will go in as a private and you will remain as a private during the two years that you serve in the Army.

He did not want me to have officer status because he felt that that would be some kind of a privilege. He wanted me to serve as a grunt. Which I did. I ended up serving on the faculty of the Ordnance School at Aberdeen, MD, and was the post I & E man. I continued from time to time to do the *College News Conference* show, which had moved to Washington, to WMAL-TV. I used to do the show on Sunday, come back and pull KP and prison guard, teach the Ordnance School, and give the weekly Post I&E [Information and Education] briefing at the end of the week.

It is interesting how all this apparently came about. After Lenny had joined the Navy, I was the only full time elected officer left in the national headquarters. So we wrote to Mrs. Roosevelt, to Dr. Stassen, and to several of the other members of our Advisory Council. Gordon Klopf was among them, and he wrote a letter on my behalf.

I know that Dr. Stassen wrote to the Republican National Committeeman from Michigan to try to get Lenny's postponement of his induction. That failed. I think Arthur Summerfield, who later became postmaster general in Eisenhower's administration, tried to get them to work with the local draft board, and that failed. So it was somewhere between Dr. Stassen, Mrs. Roosevelt, Gordon Klopf, and the president of the American Council on Education, Dr. Frank Brown (who also intervened and wrote a letter to the local draft board pleading that I be given a postponement, not a deferment, because there would be no full-time national officer left to the association). I think Dr. Stassen played a key role because almost at that very moment he wrote the letter, he was appointed by Eisenhower to be the "secretary of peace" in his cabinet.

Highlights of the Indiana Congress and the year in Philadelphia

A few of the highlights of this year are worth retelling. Robert Kernish, in his 1965 "History of NSA," recalls:

> Due, perhaps to a more optimistic military situation in Korea, the stand in favor of Universal Military Training was reversed, Congress resolutions endorsed the 2nd ISC [International Student Conference] and opposed USNSA attendance at an IUS "unity meeting," noting IUS's record of bad faith in dealing with the Association. The Congress proposed a National Leadership Training Program, amended the student Bill of Rights, opposed commercialization and abuses of intercollegiate athletics, favored a national Fair Employment Practices Law, and directed staff to investigate long-range fund-raising programs.

After we moved into our offices, Kernish notes, "The first issues of the *Student Government Bulletin* appeared, and in printed format." This was to become NSA's major monthly medium for articles and discussion on issues relating to student life and interests:

> The 1952-53 year also saw increased cooperation with major educational organizations, as well as the start of a series of vicious attacks on USNSA from a right-wing youth group called Students for America.[6] The Association asked some of the organizations with which it was working to investigate it and prepare a public report, and a joint committee of the national Association of Deans of Women, the American Personnel and Guidance Association and the National Association of Student Personnel Administrators found USNSA to be in no danger of subversion, and to be following policies that could not be construed as subversive.[7]

As reported in the Roosevelt College (Chicago) *Torch* in its February 16, 1953, issue, "The charges had been leveled at NSA by an organization called Students for America through its publication *The American Student* and in a speech delivered by its president before the National Interfraternity Conference in New York City, November, 1952."[8] The article also reported my rebuttal, which began by stating:

> USNSA takes no exception to the right of any group or individual to criticize its program, policies and activities. USNSA, however, will not stand by and allow its reputation to be damaged by irresponsible and unfounded charges such as those that have been recently made.

On the international front, Kernish reports, among other initiatives, that "USNSA attended the third ISC in Copenhagen, a very successful meeting which expanded the Student Mutual Assistance Project,[9] endorsed the work of the COSEC [sic] staff and laid plans for an international delegation to visit educational centers in Africa." NSA's travel program was becoming financially more stable and was being managed out of New York City by Tom Callahan, during his last year as its director. The program was also incorporated late that year as United States National Student Association—Educational Travel Incorporated.

And, finally, the International Relations Student Seminar was begun in Cambridge. This was a serious attempt to educate NSA leaders as to the nature and variety of issues they would face in their dealings with foreign student leaders and the professional leaders of the communist-run IUS.

Laying the foundation for years to come

It was a busy year, with many challenges as we laid the foundation for the years to come, despite an almost empty treasury, officers being drafted for military service, and strident attacks on our loyalties from a handful of fraternities, right-wing student and business groups, and commentators such as Fulton Lewis, Jr., and Martha Roundtree. Looking back, I can appreciate how much of NSA's value and staying power we owed to the nineteen active regional organizations and the close to three hundred member colleges we began the year with—which continued to rely on the voluntary efforts of their student leaders and on their campus support to develop their programs and further the Association's goals. Nationally, we were able to:

- establish a home headquarters that lasted for many years;
- launch a nation-wide television show that brought prestige to the Association and developed student leaders for well over a decade;
- prepare the first complete NSA financial statement (due mainly to Phil Berry);

- raise the first private support for our domestic programs and a sizable increase for our international programs;
- speak out strongly for academic freedom (at the peak of McCarthyism) and against segregation and discrimination, both on and off campus; and
- rebuild an organizational structure without career professional staff, strengthened by the active support of our National Advisory Council, the Philadelphia-area NSA colleges, the business and cultural community's initial financial contributions, mobilized by Ruth Hagy, and Marion Andert's indefatigable management of our office operations.

Perhaps, to me, the most rewarding achievement of that year was the letter sent to me at the beginning of the 1953 Ohio State Congress by President Dwight Eisenhower, which said that the USNSA "was rendering a significant service to this country and to the people of the world." That letter, coming as it did in the face of charges that NSA was a "subversive" organization, was worth its weight in gold.[10] It also greatly relieved my father's fears that I was leading a "radical organization, that would get us all into difficulty"!

NSA had turned the corner from its founding years into the future with an established and resilient presence on the student, administration, and international scenes. It was my good fortune to be there and to work with some of the finest people I have ever known, many of whom have remained lifelong friends. That experience profoundly changed the course of my life and is cherished in my heart, even today.

Richard J. Murphy was Assistant Postmaster General during the Kennedy and Johnson administrations. He recently retired as the Washington, D.C.–based Director of Government Affairs for 23 years at UNISYS. (See p. 786 for extended biography.)

END NOTES

[1] Bill Dentzer and Celia shared a house there with Roy Romer and his new bride. Romer had been Chair of the Rocky Mountain Region. He later became Chairman of the Democratic National Committee and was three times Governor of Colorado.

[2] Annenberg later became the Ambassador to England under President Reagan. He was one of the wealthiest men in America.

[3] See College News Conference, p. 1084.

[4] Rogers later went on to a career as a noted ABC-TV documentary producer, traveling throughout the world in partnership with John Secondari, who became her husband. See Secondari, p. 599.

[5] Berry later became managing partner of Ernst & Ernst in Pittsburgh.

[6] See Students for America, pp. 805, 810.

[7] See footnote 2, p. 328.

[8] See Wilcox p. 398 and ff.

[9] See SMAP, pp. 526, 635.

[10] See Eisenhower, p. 1083

PICTURE CREDITS: *Then:* 5th Anniversary National Student Congress, Indiana U., August 1952. *Now:* 1995, Grace Lutheran Church (Both, author).

MURPHY: "WE LAID THE FOUNDATIONS FOR YEARS TO COME"

NATIONAL EXECUTIVE COMMITTEE meeting at Wayne U., MI, 12/52. From left, around the table, regional reps: Lois McPherson (Upsala C.), NJ; Manfred Brust, VP Educational Affairs; Henry Stern, Met. NY alternate; Hugh Schwartz (CCNY), Met. NY; Joanne Rappaport, Wisconsin; Kenneth Barton (U. of North Carolina), Va.-Carolinas; Charles Aswad (Harpur C.), N.Y.; Richard Welsh (U. of Detroit), MI; Katherine Fisher, NSA International Commission; Ron Rodrique (Pittsburgh State C.), Mo.-Kan.; Linwood Starbird (Yale), New England; Art Johnson (Wayne U.), MI; James Young (Ohio Wesleyan C.), OH.; Francis De Lucia (Temple U.), PA; Cynthia Courtney (Dunbarton C.), Mason-Dixon; Richard Murphy, President; back to camera: Kenneth Strand (Wash. State C.), Northwest; on sofa: Phil Berry, NSA National Financial Advisory Board.

Army Inducts Student Leader

[Special to The Evening Sun]

Aberdeen Proving Ground, Md., Oct. 13—The former president of the world's largest student organization is now a basic trainee here.

Richard J. Murphy, son of Mr. and Mrs. James Murphy, 710 Melville avenue, Baltimore, was inducted into the Army after completing a one-year term as president of the United States National Student Organization.

A graduate of the University of North Carolina, Private Murphy was in Sweden attending an international conference of student leaders when he received his initial notice to report for induction.

During his presidency of the N.S.A., an organization which represents 365 American colleges and universities, he traveled about 100,000 miles.

MURPHY TRAVELS. Clockwise, above: Dick Murphy and International Vice President Avrea Ingram at the 1953 Copenhagen International Student Conference. Murphy, right, and NSSFNS representative, left, with Frank Graham, NSA advisor and former U. of North Carolina president, at 1958 NSA Congress. *Baltimore Sun* (10/13/53) reports Murphy's induction, fulfilling his promise to Selective Service director Hersey, who allowed Murphy to complete his NSA term. (Photos, Murphy)

"One is impressed by the efforts . . . to retain a strong vital organization."

Fifth Annual Student Congress at Indiana, 1952

Dennis Trueblood, Indiana University *and*
Gordon Klopf, State University of New York College for Teachers, Buffalo

Excerpted from School and Society, Vol. 76, *November 1, 1952. Editor's note: At the time this was written, both authors were members of the NSA National Advisory Council and former Chairmen of the Council.*

The United States National Student Association celebrated its fifth anniversary at its annual Congress held August 8-27,1952, at Indiana University. Some 400 delegates and alternates in addition to 23 foreign students, 25 educational organization representatives, and fourteen visitors and guests deliberated for nine days. With an attendance of over one hundred delegates, a Student Government President's and an Editor's Conference were held immediately preceding the congress....

* * *

Working virtually night and day, in many instances, the delegates discussed problems ranging from the finance and structure of student government to FEPC, UMT, and the McCarran Act.

Beginning in small discussion groups, the delegates formed tentative resolutions and exchanged ideas on common problems of students and their education. The delegates then moved into commissions where resolutions were drawn up for final presentation to the total assembled delegates. The last three and a half days of the congress were spent in passing resolutions basic to the association's various policy stands and on improving the association's internal operation.

Of significant interest to the educational world was a resolution condemning UMT but urging continuation of the present national selective service act as long as there is a national emergency. The resolution was based on the assumption that UMT would institutionalize military service as a part of American life.

* * *

The Congress passed a strongly worded resolution accusing the International Union of Students, the Communist-dominated world union of students, of failing to cooperate on practical program projects.The fifth congress reaffirmed the NSA desire to cooperate with any student group, including the IUS, on practical, nonpolitical projects. As further proof of desire to co-operate in program activities in the international area, the congress fully indorsed steps being taken to set up the Coordinate Secretariat (COSEC) at Leiden, Holland. COSEC will co-ordinate and stimulate exchange of ideas and projects on an international level for student groups throughout the world.

* * *

The fifth congress dealt at some length with the domestic program of the association. Of particular interest to educators will be the proposals for leadership education programs on campuses—a series of nation-wide leadership conferences to devise methods of developing leadership on the individual campus. Such a program will require the co-operation of a number of national educational groups. Art tours, drama-exchange programs, health insurance, civilian defense programs, relations of NSA to student government, financial problems of student governments, and other domestic programs were discussed at length.

The congress again attempted to strengthen its financial status. With the reduction of its international debt of several years' standing, the delegates realized that the association's problem was one of financial control of budget as well as budget planning. A five man financial board, of whom two are educators, was created to review all financial operations of the association and will have the power to publish all information about the financial status of NSA.

The travel department of the association was also given a board of control which, in addition to financial counsel, will set policy and advise on the internal operations of the travel program. The International Commission will also have a policy board to review its fund-raising activities. All of these policy boards will be responsible to the association's executive committee.

In a move to strengthen further the association's relationship to its advisers, the congress elaborated in detail the duties of the National Advisory Council in an attempt to make the advisory system more functional.

* * *

As two persons who have followed the association since its origin, it is encouraging to observe that the delegates continue to develop the most ambitious student project in the American educational scene in this century. Founded by a mature group of American GI students immediately following World War II, NSA is now faced with adjustment problems as younger leadership comes to the helm of the association. One is impressed by the efforts that these students are making to retain a strong, vital organization, an organization which wants to serve as a responsible part of the educational community, but not subservient to any sector of the educational community.

ORGANIZATION BUILDERS

NSA'S 1952-53 LEADERS. Top: left, Avrea Ingram (Harvard), serving his second term as International VP. Right: Cynthia Courtney (Dunbarton), second from right, Chair of Mason-Dixon, with regional delegates. Above: Clockwise from top: Merrill Freed (U. of Chicago), Dick Murphy (U. of North Carolina), President; Leonard Wilcox (U. of Mich.), National Affairs VP; inset: Stephen Voykovitch (Fordham U.), Student Government VP; seated: Manfred Brust (U. of Ill.), Educational Affairs, VP; Janet Welch (Smith C.), Student Affairs, VP; Thomas Callahan (St. Francis C.), Travel Office Director; inset: Philip Berry (U. of Mich.) replaced Wilcox after he was drafted into the Navy.

A creeping intellectual paralysis grips the educational community

In the Name of Freedom

If we have no faith here, then where can faith be found?

Richard J. Murphy
University of North Carolina
NSA President, 1952-53

Adapted from a column written for *The Daily Tar Heel*, February 14, 1952. *Editor's note: Murphy became President of NSA in August 1952. In this article, written prior to his election, and the one that follows, he voices the concerns of NSA leaders about the underlying causes and effects of the anticommunist, anti-subversive "hysteria," which he characterized as having induced a "creeping intellectual paralysis on college campuses." The effects were not only substantive, but also had their impacts on NSA's own organizing efforts. A consequence was the Association's decision to focus on the meaning of freedom as a theme for the 1953 (sixth) Congress.*

For the past few years I have viewed with the greatest alarm a creeping intellectual paralysis that has come to grip the American educational community. This paralysis finds its roots in fear and conformity generated by the nature of the cold war. In our efforts to combat the grave menace posed by the actions of Soviet Russia, we have allowed ourselves to become the prisoners of a doctrine of negativism, which has led us to repudiate the historic principles for which we claim to be fighting.

Under the guise of anticommunism we have allowed professional patriots and opportunistic politicians to equate change with communism, and dissent with disloyalty. Paradoxically, this nation, which was once known because of its belief in freedom, as the country where a permanent peaceful revolution was continually taking place to extend the benefits of the "good life" to more and more, has abandoned its historic role in favor of becoming a nation in which a premium is placed upon conformity and advocacy of the status quo. No segment of American life has managed to remain untouched by the growing notion that to conform is the proper—and safe—thing to do.

Our schools and colleges have manifested the most serious case of this illness—the very place where it can be least tolerated.

Intimidation prevails

During the past few years, through my association with the U.S. National Student Association and the National Commission for UNESCO, I have seen at close range the disastrous effects of such practices as loyalty oaths, bans on speakers, the outlawing of student political groups, the prohibition of text books, the political phenomenon known as "McCarthyism," and the intimidation of students and faculty members who did not conform to the majority view.

The effect has been to stifle free thought and discussion, to make people afraid to think on their own and doubly afraid to act on their own. Political curiosity of mature men has been seriously reduced through fear of joining political organizations or of signing petitions, and we have come to parrot, as would children, the majority view.

In short, our generation has come to be known as "the generation of jelly fish" (in the *Wisconsin Cardinal),* or the "silent generation" (*Time Magazine),* or the "fearful generation" (*New York Times*).

For a long time, I used to compliment myself that the University of North Carolina, with its long-standing tradition of freedom and Tar Heel common sense, had been able to weather this storm relatively unscathed. Gradually, however, I came to see that such was not the case. On the contrary, what has been taking place here in the last few years is in many ways much more insidious than that which has been happening at other colleges—more insidious because it operates largely under-cover and in silence.

Insidious practices

I think the time has come to make public many of the insidious practices that have so cleverly laid low our once-cherished intellectual independence in the hope that we can better understand and combat these forces by first identifying them. I offer the following observations to which I have given serious thought during the last several months.

The post-war years have seen a marked and shocking decline in the political interest and consciousness of the student body. Much of this is due to what can be termed "normal" apathy, but this apathy has grown to such huge proportions that one must look elsewhere in order to understand and ascertain the significance of the decline of such organizations as the Carolina Political Union, the International Relations Club, the Collegiate Council of the United Nations, and the Students for Democratic Action.

Several national organizations have looked into this problem extensively and have found a direct correlation between the growing apathy and the tendency toward fear and conformity. Students whose views are substantially to the left of Robert A. Taft or Joe McCarthy are strongly reticent to identify themselves with organizations which may later turn up on the lists of an SBI [State Bureau of Investigation] or an FBI agent—and several non-partisan organizations have appeared on such lists. . . .

* * *

Impact of non-conformity on the faculty

If fear of non-conformity has had such results upon the students, it has been disastrous upon the faculty. When the Board of Trustees [of the University of North Carolina] attempted to administer a loyalty oath to students and faculty members, the Administration defeated the move in a courageous statement, "If We Are To Keep the University Free." Then the Administration quietly instituted their own political questionnaire for faculty members.

Only two individuals of the faculty—Phillips Russell of Journalism and Joseph Straley of Physics—dared to speak out in opposition during a faculty meeting, although the local Association of College Professors issued a formal protest to the administration. A similar questionnaire, beaten down by courageous individuals at more enlightened institutions such as Harvard and Chicago, literally tore the University of California to shreds. Not a public murmur from our faculty—only private grunts! The faculty has yet to recover from the intellectual setback created by this questionnaire.

The worst effect among the faculty members has been noticeable defensiveness and unwillingness to take stands. This is particularly striking when compared to the activity of the faculty of 1940 and the activities of the faculties of other institutions today. This trend is especially evident in the social science departments. Professors continually apologize for their views, state over and over that they aren't communists, are fearful of being reported by students as having expressed dangerous ideas, and never encourage, as they once did, students to engage in political activity.

More importantly, the professors themselves are reticent about engaging in political activities or taking a stand on such controversial issues, for instance, as segregation.

* * *

Self-appointed censors

All the above, however, are relegated to a rather insignificent role when compared to the activities of those self-appointed censors of student opinion and guardians of the faculty minds. I refer specifically to the activities of one John Clark, his brother Dave, and others of their persuasion as found on the Board of Trustees.

I cannot recall or conceive of any other institution of higher learning which has permitted a man to sit on the Board of Trustees and at the same time to use the best methods of the Gestapo to intimidate students.

In the case of John Clark, the battle over conformity finds expression in the race issue. The question here is not whether one is for or against segregation, but for the right to hold an opinion contrary to that of John Clark. In the last year this man has written letters about students to the mayors of their home towns, and to other prominent officials throughout the state in an effort to intimidate those students because of their views, which were in opposition to his own, sowing the seeds of fear and distrust, possibly of disloyalty, and causing an untold amount of mental duress to those who are the object of his attacks.

Only Tuesday morning, the Dialectic Senate received a letter from this man demanding the names and addresses of all those who had voted in favor of equal treatment for all students in recent resolutions.

These people, in all probability, face an ordeal similar to that faced last year by the President of the Student Body and the President of the YMCA, when they were concerned with a similar issue.

An even more flagrant example of the ordeal which students must undergo is found in the case of a gentleman who identified himself as a Mr. Rutledge from South Carolina. He attended a student political gathering as a guest, after which the President of the University received a letter completely distorting the facts of the meeting and naming certain students as members of a subversive group. This information has since been forwarded, in the case of at least one student, to the office of a prominent Southern senator, who is now passing along the false information in a gratuitous fashion to a number of government agencies as possible evidence of disloyalty.

As a result, this student will probably never be able to pass a security check. These are but a few of the examples with which I happen to be personally familiar. Many more ought be brought to light in the pages of the *Daily Tar Heel* soon.

Repression: The way of frightened power

Who is to blame for this situation? Certainly it would be presumptuous of us to pin the blame on any one group such as the Faculty, Administration, or Board of Trustees. And, in all fairness, it should be said that the Administration has withstood rather well, and with courage, a number of the most flagrant cases of student intimidation. Certainly it has retained its integrity better than many other institutions, but greater effort and greater courage need to be shown if we are to reverse the dangerous trend of events of the past few years.

We are today quite properly interested in frustrating Russian military and political power and in restoring peace throughout the world. However, our methods thus far used in achieving this goal indicate that we are coming uncomfortably close to the adoption and practice of many principles found in the communist lexicon.

"Repression is the way of frightened power," said a man closely connected with Chapel Hill, and "freedom is the way of enlightened faith." The duty of the University is clear, for if we have no faith here, then where can faith be found?

THE CRISIS IN EDUCATION—CALL TO THE FIFTH NATIONAL STUDENT CONGRESS

THE CRISIS . . . in education challenges the student. Do these words seem melodramatic and the situation overdone? If so, then the crisis in education truly is greater than you think.

There has surely been a great deal of nonsensical talk about a "silent generation" if there is not a crisis in education, for who is to speak out if it is not those who are in the process of being "educated." Ineffective student government, disaffected student bodies, the absence of real thinking, the lack of international awareness, over-emphasis and commercialization of athletics, widespread hysteria, paralysis of academic freedom, moral sloth, spiritual decadence, disinterest, apathy, fear, and prejudice—these things do exist.

Strong words, you say. Perhaps. No crisis in education? Think again. The existence of this crisis is both reason in itself for the existence of the United States National Student Association and cause for that National Student Association to do something about the crisis.

The Fifth National Student Congress of USNSA will convene August 18, 1952, at Indiana University, to begin discussion of what students can do to meet . . .

THE CHALLENGE . . . At no other time in this country or elsewhere, have students had the opportunities to influence national and world currents as they do now. The voice of student America, coming from the smallest discussion groups to the most tense plenary session of the Fifth National Student Congress, will be eagerly listened to by our own American and fellow students the world over. . . . [t]he Congress could have no more fitting a subject for the younger generation to consider.

Many student government bodies long have wanted to do something about the crisis in education as it manifested itself on campus in the form of student apathy, group prejudice, lack of adequate leadership, and other problems, but they first want to know HOW. At the Fifth National Student Congress, NSA hopes to spell out in clear and concrete language what role student governments should play, and specifically, HOW they play it. The place of NSA on campus and the theory and practice of student government are main objects of emphasis this year.

No better time for newly elected student leaders to tackle their problems through joint effort at the National Student Congress, [than] just before the great annual migration of American college youth back to a whirlwind year of campus activities.

As the present and future of America, let's take a good look at where we stand in this crisis, and decide what we, as student leaders are going to do about it. It is a challenge we dare not refuse.

William T. Dentzer, *President, USNSA*, 1951-52

Strengthening the Forces of Freedom

An editorial appearing in the April 1953 NSA News

Richard J. Murphy
University of North Carolina
NSA President, 1952-53

There has seldom been a time in human history when freedom was more in need of friends: friends who understand that the struggle for freedom has been one of the central themes of human history; that freedom is more than a word but a condition, a way of life, a thing of the spirit involving a set of relationships between man and man, man and God, man and himself; who understand that freedom is often more readily destroyed by some of its misguided partisans than by its avowed enemies. This is especially true today, for more people are proclaiming themselves in favor of freedom who understand the least about it than ever before, and this is the real danger to freedom—lack of deep-felt conviction and serious thought as to its implications.

If we are to be intelligent partisans and advocates of a free world for which we are often asked to die, then we must undertake a rigorous self-examination of the meaning of freedom in the modern world, and must seek to marshal all of our resources to cultivating its spirit. Where can this be better done than in the universities whose very existence is founded in the first freedom—freedom of the mind and conscience.

The Sixth NSA Congress to examine what freedom means

It is for this reason that the United States National Student Association has decided to devote its Sixth National Student Congress to the examination of what freedom means, what are the forces which threaten it, what are the factors which contribute to its growth, and what might students do to contribute to its strength.

We are living in a century in which the struggle for freedom has erupted so violently throughout the world as to cause serious repercussions in our lives as students, for it has largely been the students who have found themselves called upon during this century to take the lead in the fight for freedom and against aggressive tyranny, both in the intellectual and martial fields. Too often, however, in our effort to secure liberty for all peoples we have tended to place too little emphasis on developing certain positive resources of freedom in our own backyard and have taken certain basic sources of freedom's strength too much for granted.

The resourcefulness of the free, critical mind; the strength of a competent command of facts; the potentialities of democratic, student government; the vitality of voluntary campus organizations; the dynamic structure of our educational system; the possibilities for independent international activity on the part of students; and the existence of a strong national student movement with international counterparts are vital sources of strength to the free world, and upon their strengthening depends in a large degree the success or failure of freedom in our time.

This is a task which demands the attention and energy of every responsible student government leader in the country. This August, student leaders from over 300 colleges and universities, representing some 1,000,000 students, will convene at The Ohio State University, to meet with student leaders from all sections of the world and to hear outstanding Americans in public life, in an effort to provide concrete methods to strengthen freedom through their student governments and voluntary student action, to meet the challenge which confronts us both at home and abroad.

There is no more stimulating experience in student self-government and no more representative gathering of the elected leaders of collegiate America. It is an ideal opportunity for newly-elected student leaders to gain in knowledge and friendship through a mutual attack on the problems now facing local campuses. Don't fail to take advantage of it.

10 SF MARCH 15, 1953 THE SUNDAY BULLETIN PHILADELPHIA, PA.

A Student Leader Outlines the International Role of American Youth

Murphy Tells Of Changes Since War

Richard J. Murphy, president of the United States National Students Association, struck a blow for academic freedom in his talk at The Bulletin Forum Wednesday afternoon.

"In a democratic society," he said, "the vitality of the life of a community depends on the highest freedom of the mind and voluntary group associations."

Repression, he said, is the way of frightened power, and freedom is the way of enlightened hope.

His address follows:

The challenge of change has a peculiar significance for the American students for we, perhaps, more than any other segment in society have had our lives geared to change.

To begin with, the student community in higher education, itself, is constantly changing every four years.

Secondly, as a segment of society, specifically devoted to intellectual endeavor, we are charged by the community to gather and assimilate knowledge, to develop a critical and independent judgment, and to bring our critical faculties to bear on the re-examination of all aspects of our culture and knowledge, in order that we might be more devoted to the good in our heritage and more responsible to what needs to be improved, for it has long been a premise of the American dream that the world of tomorrow should be better and that critical judgment so necessary to intelligent progress has long been the chief concern of the citadels of higher learning.

Universities have always been the fountainhead for the injection of seeds of change into society and without their careful nurture and implantation society would deteriorate. It is for this reason that we at times seem so stubborn to protect that atmosphere conducive to the development of free enterprise and ideas which we call "academic freedom", for new ideas are often disturbing and are not always popularly received by a given generation.

No Self-Pity

Finally, there is no other segment in American life that has experienced the momentous change of the last 20 years with greater impact.

Consider if you will the economic hardships of the depression days. The student ranks were immediately hard hit and depleted. World War II meant that the greatest burden fell upon the young men of the nation, for they were the ones who gave voluntarily of their lives and services in the defense of democracy.

The readjustment of the post-war years commanded the greatest degree of flexibility, and the terror of Communist imperialism has made our student lives a day-to-day proposition.

It is in response to one particular challenge of change that my theme flows this evening, for nowhere is the student response to the challenges of the time more fruitfully demonstrated than in their developing role in international affairs.

Prior to the 1940's, there was relatively little international activity among American students.

Serious Problems

The characterization of the student generation of the '20's as a goldfish-swallowing, fur-coated juvenile dancing the Charleston and playing mahjong is past but not forgotten. The '30's saw a keen interest in more serious problems, especially, political and economic ones, and organization among students on a national level for mutual aid and contact began to grow.

The war and post-war years wrought a tremendous change in student life and left a firm impact on the student mind. The price of "going it alone" had been paid in blood, and the returning veterans who jammed the universities were deadly serious in purpose and more mature in mind.

They were determined to aid other peoples in rebuilding their shattered lives and communities and were determined to forge bonds of friendship and association with peoples of other lands to secure the hard won peace for which they had given so much.

This was the guiding spirit that led to the founding of a national student organization in the United States.

The NSA, today, has many different functions much too detailed to go into here, but which may be summed up by saying that it aims at developing better citizenship and democracy both at home and abroad through self-improvement.

In closing, let me tell you about the kind of world which I believe the majority of students desire:

A world where there are differences without hate; where men become brothers in the sight of God and in the human heart; where the least of these our brethren has the freedom to struggle for freedom. A world in which respect for the past is not called "reaction" and hope for the future is not called "revolution"; where the integrity of simple people is beyond price and the daily toil of millions is above pomp and power; where the majority is without fear, and all people have hope.

This is the world we desire . . . so . . . we pledge ourselves to stand with the freedom-loving students throughout the world in the common struggle that one day we may live together as brothers in peace and harmony.

Philadelphia Sunday Bulletin, 3/15/53 (Excerpted)

The responsibilities of students as custodians of democratic thought

A Message from President Eisenhower

The White House
Washington

August 23,1953

1953

Dear Mr. Murphy:

I very much regret that I've been unable to accept Governor Lausche's invitation to address the opening session of the Sixth National Student Congress at Ohio State University. However, I do want to extend to you on this occasion my heartiest wishes for a successful meeting.

To you, the college students of America, is given the great privilege of studying in free democratic universities where the opportunity is open to all to seek the truth in a chosen field of learning, free from the chains of totalitarian doctrine. Upon you, therefore, as custodians of democratic thought, falls the responsibility of making your belief in the values of a free and open society into a living and vital reality both at home and abroad. Those of us who today are elected to public office take comfort in the knowledge that you are preparing yourselves intellectually and spiritually to shoulder this burden.

By making possible ever greater opportunity for the exercise of democratic responsibility on the campus, and by enabling American students and students of other lands to work together toward the solution of their common problems, the United States National Student Association is rendering a significant service to the people of this country and to the world.

Sincerely,

Dwight D. Eisenhower

1948

Columbia Spectator

Eisenhower Inaugurated as 13th President of Columbia University

New President, in Exclusive Statement, Charts College's Course of Progress

"You possess cultural advantages second to none"

To the Students of Columbia College:

. . . . My special dedication to you is a persistent effort to assure you the facilities that will provide you the well-rounded environment, during your college days, essential to your greatest profit as students. In the magnificent facility headed by Dean Carman and in the intellectual wealth of Columbia traditions, you possess cultural advantages second to none in the entire academic world.

If all of us work together, . . . Columbia without question, will provide its undergraduates the best possible preparation for a useful and happy life.

—Dwight D. Eisenhower
October 12, 1948

1952

YORK Tribune

Late City Edition

FIVE-CENTS

Eisenhower Says He Supports McCarthy's Aim, Not His Method; Stevenson Invades Taft's State

Governor Calls For | *Sir Roger Makins Is Appointed* | General Declares He Would Oust Reds

1944

1954

DWIGHT D. EISENHOWER was Supreme Allied Commander in Europe during World War II, where he mounted the invasion of Normandy in 1944; President of Columbia University from 1948 to 1952; and U.S. President from 1953 to 1961. During the McCarthy era he at first equivocated but then used the power of the Executive Office to bring McCarthy to account. He sent troops to Little Rock to enforce Brown v. Board of Education in 1957. In his 1961 farewell address he urged vigilance against "ruthless" communism and warned against "the acquisition of unwarranted influence . . . by the military-industrial complex."

Sources: Dwight D. Eisenhower Library. The American Experience, www.pbs.org. *New York Herald Tribune*, 10/4/52. *Columbia Spectator* 10/12/48.

From 1952 to 1963: Bringing students and NSA into American homes

2. Ruth Hagy Brod: Evangelist for Students, NSA and the *College News Conference*

Editor's note: Ruth Hagy Brod was one of those singular individuals who takes on a mission and, by force of her energy and commitment, can cast a deciding vote in the future of her cause. She did that for NSA in 1952 as Dick Murphy, NSA's 1952-1953 president, notes below on this page.

In a 1960s New York Herald Tribune *interview, she summed up the rationale behind her mission: "One has only to consider for a moment the massive impact of youth's culture and attitudes on adult-life style to evaluate properly how important it is to maintain constant communication between the generations: look at music, fashions in dress, resistance to the Vietnam War, the unseating of President Lyndon Johnson . . . interest in religion, meditation, the occult."*

When NSA came to Philadelphia in 1952, she saw in the Association both an exemplar of her mission as well as a resource for student leadership talent that could help shape the new television program she was starting. NSA provided both panelists ands production talent for the program.

In the 1950s, after the College News Conference *was launched, there were only three national weekly television news programs:* Face the Nation *(CBS),* Meet the Press *(NBC), and* College News Conference *(ABC). As Al Brod, her husband, now recalls, "CNC often beat out the other two in making national news." The text following is a digest of material prepared for a 1962 National Educational Television prospectus for its last year, and for a 1956 "Closeup" newspaper article by Bennett Schiff.*

Ruth Hagy Brod founded the Peabody Award–winning *College News Conference* in 1952 (known then as the *Junior Press Conference*) with the belief that America's college students—the leaders of tomorrow—should have a nationally televised forum in which to ask questions about their concerns through interviews with our country's top government officials, leaders of industry and labor, and representatives of foreign governments.

Her dream became a reality in many different ways: the program attracted nationally and internationally famous guests whose deeds and words affected the welfare of millions. The responses given to the relentless probing of those students frequently made Monday morning headlines. Their candor, enthusiasm, and curiosity brought forth surprising statements, which gave the program all the drama and excitement of a major press conference.

And as she knew they would, "her students" went on to become the leaders of today. To mention only a few: Jay Rockefeller, governor of West Virginia; Al Lowenstein, former congressman from New York; Richard Murphy, former assistant postmaster general; Helen Jean Rogers, award-winning documentary producer; Barbara Rose, internationally famous art critic; Frances FitzGerald, prize-winning journalist; and TV personality Marciarose Shestak.

During those years when *College News Conference* appeared on ABC, and then later on NET, such luminaries were guests as: President John Kennedy; Secretary of State Dean Rusk; The Honorable Averell Harriman; Herman Kahn; Senators Barry Goldwater, Jacob J. Javits, Hubert H. Humphrey, John Sparkman, Henry Jackson, William Knowland, Paul Douglas, and Wayne Morse; Secretary of Labor Arthur Goldberg; Secretary of Agriculture Ezra Taft Benson; Walter Reuther; Glen Seaborg, Chairman of the Atomic Energy Commission; General Bernard Shriever; Abba Eban and Golda Meier of Israel; Krishna Menon of India; Sir Leslie Munro, President of the UN General Assembly; and many others.

College News Conference was unique in another way: over fifty national and many local educational and civic groups and over four hundred colleges and universities co-operated in the selection of

A Friend in Troubled Times

The Association owes a tremendous debt to Mrs. Hagy, who befriended us when few were willing to stick their necks out, at the height of the McCarthy miasma. Ruth was the Women's Editor of the *Philadelphia Bulletin* and Director of the *Philadelphia Bulletin* Forum, one of the top week-long public affairs events in Philadelphia, to which she invited me to speak in 1953 at the Academy of Music. All of the other speakers were prominent national and civic officials.

Ruth not only created *College News Conference,* but she became Chair of the NSA Financial Advisory Board and helped to stabilize NSA financially. Moreover, she became a sort of surrogate mother to the staff in Philadelphia, feeding us when we ran out of money (often), and playing Edith Piaf songs, which we loved to sing, on her piano (she had been a concert pianist). She also introduced scores of NSA leaders, whom she loved, to some of the top leaders of our country.

Her involvement with NSA helped to give us considerable credibility when we needed it, and she was very proud of "her kids" over the years. On many occasions in that troubled time I thanked God for a friend like Ruth Hagy.

Richard J. Murphy
University of North Carolina, NSA President, 1952-53

leading students to act as panel members, sponsored their transportation to Washington, and heavily promoted the program through local newspaper publicity and bulletins to their members. It was also an official project of the U.S. National Student Association. This widespread grass-roots organization was of tremendous benefit in promoting community pride and reaching into the heart of college campuses. In an interview Ruth Hagy Brod said:

> The quality of young people is constantly being proven by current historical events—in Hungary for example—and elsewhere where it is the college students who object to oppressive or corrupt government. . . . We try to pick panelists who have a special interest and knowledge of the subject the guest is an expert on and very often the kids know too much for the guest. . . .
>
> When young people get past the age of 17 or 18 they discover the world with unjaded eyes and all of its wonders and all of its imperfections, and they want to change it.
>
> It is the great premium time of idealism.

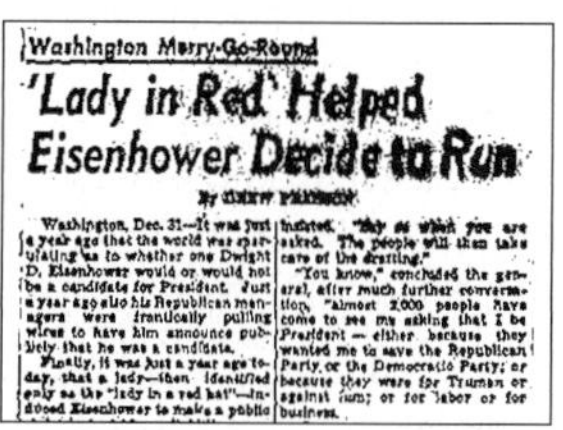

Washington Merry-Go-Round

'Lady in Red' Helped Eisenhower Decide to Run

Washington, Dec. 31—It was just a year ago that the world was speculating as to whether one Dwight D. Eisenhower would or would not be a candidate for President. Just a year ago also his Republican managers were frantically pulling wires to have him announce publicly that he was a candidate.

Finally, it was just a year ago today, that a lady—then identified only as the "lady in a red hat"—induced Eisenhower to make a public

[illegible]. "Say as which you are asked. The people will then take care of the drafting."

"You know," concluded the general, after much further conversation, "almost 2,000 people have come to see me asking that I be President — either because they wanted me to save the Republican Party, or the Democratic Party; or because they were for Truman or against him; or for labor or for business.

Ruth Hagy and President Eisenhower — and then NSA

In his 12/31/52 syndicated column, Drew Pearson wrote, "It was just a year ago today that a lady—then identified only as 'the lady in a red hat'—induced Eisenhower to make a public statement of his availability. It was 3 PM Paris time on the day before New Year's that she, the lady in a red hat, pulled up in a limousine in front of SHAPE, Eisenhower's headquarters."

In a 12/3/2003 letter, Al Brod wrote, "On New Year's day, General Omar Bradley arranged for Ruth to fly to Shape headquarters to meet with Eisenhower. Ruth explained to him that as a soldier, he was obligated to serve as called just like Ruth's son-in-law at the time had been called and went into the Army. At that meeting, Eisenhower told her that he would run for President, and then Ruth flew back to Philadelphia.

"At that time, NSA moved to Philly and was totally penniless. Ruth was able to secure an office for them and practically fed them herself. Because of her success with Ike, she raised $50,000 for NSA to continue its work."

THE FIRST SHOW: Standing from left: Dick Murphy, NSA 1952-53 President; Al Lowenstein, NSA 1949-50 President; Roger Alan Moore; Len Wilcox, NSA 1952-53 Vice President, National Affairs. Seated: Sen. Richardson Dilworth, Ruth Hagy, Sen. Hugh Scott. (Murphy)

1958 Peabody Award Winner

Television Programs for Youth: At a time when a small fraction of the younger generation is making bad headlines, it is comforting and stimulating to have *College News Conference* give our alert and thoughtful young Americans the opportunity to speak with world leaders. It also serves the unique diplomatic function of displaying a vital young America to the representatives of foreign countries. In recognition of these facts, the Peabody Award for the outstanding television program for youth goes to "College News Conference."

About the Awards: The George Foster Peabody Awards, established in 1939 and first awarded in 1940, recognize distinguished achievement and meritorious service by radio and television networks, stations, producing organizations, cable television organizations and individuals. They perpetuate the memory of the banker-philanthropist whose name they bear. The awards program is administered by the Henry W. Grady College of Journalism and Mass Communication at the University of Georgia. Selections are made by the National Advisory Board upon recommendations of special screening sessions of the faculty.

Television, 1945–1952: In 1945 there were fewer than 7,000 working TV sets in the country and only nine stations on the air in New York, Chicago, Los Angeles, Philadelphia, and Schenectady, NY. In 1946 the Joe Louis–Billy Conn heavyweight fight was viewed by 150,000 people on 5,000 sets. By January 1949 there were 98 TV stations in 58 market areas. In 1951 there were 12 million sets, only 25 of which could receive color. By year's end in 1952, there were 20 million TV households. (Source: www.high-techproductions.com.)

RUTH HAGY BROD

Early years and education: Born Ruth Fleischman, May 31, 1911, in New York City. Attended PS 40 in the Bronx (where she was editor of *Forty Winks*) and Hibbard High School in Chicago. Child pianist concert prodigy, Bachelor of Music, Chicago Musical College, 1926. Also completed three years prelaw, Crane Jr. College, Chicago, 1928. University of Chicago, 1928–29.

Career highlights: Feature writer, columnist, editor, special projects promotion: 1931-38, *Chicago Daily News*, *Chicago Daily Times*, *Fawcett*, and *Dell* magazines. 1939-1961, *Philadelphia Evening Ledger*, *Philadelphia Bulletin*. ABC-TV *College News Conference*. 1962-63, foreign correspondent in South Vietnam. 1966-74, Author, volunteer, and Poverty Program coordinator for various New York City agencies. Freedom Foundation and other awards.

Global travel: Ruth and Al Brod traveled throughout the world interviewing numerous heads of state such as the Prime Ministers of India and of Turkey. They represented the United States at the Atlantic Congress. They were also guests in Greece of King Paul and Queen Frederica.

Family: Widow of Louis Y. Hagy, III, Philadelphia newspaper executive. Wife of Albert Thomas Brod, Member of N.Y. Stock Exchange, President, A.T. Brod & Co. Daughter, Sybil Joan Buffman.

Ruth Hagy Brod died in 1980. A memorial service held on May 29 was attended by more than 600 people.

PICTURE CREDITS: *Previous page:* 1957, *College News Conference*, 5th Anniversary (Murphy). *Next page:* All except WFIL photo courtesy Al Brod (top of page photo: Edgar S. Brinker, Phila.). WFIL photo with permission Broadcast Pioneers.

"COLLEGE NEWS CONFERENCE" ON WFIL-TV IN 1954

This picture was taken sometime between October 1954 and December of that same year. The four college students standing participated in the WFIL-TV broadcast then known as *College Press Conference*. The young woman in the black dress is Marciarose Shestack (a Broadcast Pioneers member). She became a television newscaster and for many years broadcast on Channel 3, KYW-TV in Philadelphia. The other three students are (l. to r.) Pat Priest (Mt. Vernon College); Paul Sigmund (Georgetown), NSA International Vice President, 1954-55; and David Dulles (Swarthmore).

Seated are Shelly Gross and United States Congressman from Minnesota Walter H. Judd, who stayed in Congress until 1963. Shelly was filling in for Ruth Hagy Brod, the regular host, who was on vacation. From 1952 to 1960, this program aired on Sunday afternoons. However, from October 1953 to December 1954 there was also a prime-time version (Mondays, 9 P.M. to 9:30) against CBS-TV's *I Love Lucy*. This was a classic example of counter-programming. The Sunday afternoon program changed to *College Press Conference*. It used this title for only three months, from October of 1954 to the cancellation of the primetime version in December of 1954. At that time, it went back to its original name, *Junior Press Conference,* and then changed its name again to *College News Conference* on the ABC-TV network. *(Text adapted from the official archives of the Broadcast Pioneers of Philadelphia. Photo originally donated by Broadcast Pioneers member Shelly Gross. All rights reserved.)*

RUTH BROD WITH CNC GUESTS AND PANELS, 1952-54. From the top: (1) Elmer Brock (NSA 1950-51 Vice President), Brod, Dick Murphy (NSA 1952-53 President), Marie Minnick, (U. of Pennsylvania NSA). (2) Robert Kennedy, Al Brod, Ruth Brod. (3) Ruth Hagy faces off with Soviet premier Nikita Khrushchev. (4) John F. Kennedy, Brod. (5) Standing, European youth leaders from NATO countries and second from left, Helen Jean Rogers (NSA secretary-treasurer, 1948-49); seated: Paul Henry Spaak, NATO Secretary General, Ruth Brod. (6) Sen. William F. Knowland, Al Brod, unidentified, Ted Kennedy, Ruth Brod. (7) Eleanor Roosevelt, Ruth Brod.

"The State Department filed a protest . . . This was not Meet the Press. This was a bunch of college students"

NSA leaders on News Forum Panels Make News

Ken Kurtz
Swarthmore College
Chair, Pennsylvania Region, 1949-50
(see page 308 for bio)

The College News Conference

Ruth Geri Hagy ran the College News Conference out of her station in Philadelphia. She was a power in Philadelphia broadcasting and media circles, and charitable, and philanthropic and everything else. I had met her, I believe, at some forum in Philadelphia and I'd done some radio things or newspaper stuff that I think came to her attention.

This was the early day of black and white television, pre-video tape. She had diplomatic contacts anywhere and she got the Indian ambassador, V.K. Krishna Menon, a very sharp and acerbic personality, who from the Indian position of neutrality had criticized the U.S. role in Korea rather sharply for a diplomat. He was Oxford or Cambridge educated and he had that clipped British accent. Although he was smart, and he was an able diplomat, Helen Jean Rogers[1] nailed him with a couple of questions about his criticism of our government's policy in Korea, and he went further than he'd ever been before.

He said, flat out, that the U.S. had no business meddling in Korea, it's between the North and the South to settle this. So why don't you back off and let them do it. The State Department filed a formal protest of his remarks made on this television program. Helen Jean and I were sitting side by side and she asked the really sharp question that nettled him to the point that he became somewhat undiplomatic and made his comments. Now, part of what he said, I agree with, I wasn't totally convinced that some of our policies in Korea were quite what they ought to be, but it was also perfectly true that if he wanted to say this in private and express the Indian government's viewpoint, that was the channel you were supposed to use. You didn't go on national television and say these things.

I suspect it was after the Chinese went in, and I would have agreed with Mr. Menon that it was MacArthur's reckless going north of the parallel that brought them in, and that I would rather the United States had driven them back to the parallel and then quit and said, now, let's have peace. But we didn't do it that way. Anyhow, my recollection is that the State Department filed a formal protest, the first time it had ever been done on a television program. This was not *Meet the Press*. This was a bunch of college students that Ruth Geri Hagy had womped up.

There was a *Philadelphia Bulletin* reporter assigned to cover the show. After this show, he pulled Helen Jean and me, and some of the others aside and said, "I've got some great quotes of this guy. I'm going to file a story and I'm going to put it on the AP. There's going to be a ruckus," he said. And he was right.

KURTZ AND ROGERS QUESTION KRISHNA MENON at the College News Conference in 1953. Standing from left: Ken Kurtz (NSA Pennsylvania Regional Chair, 1949-50); Elmer Brock, 1950-51 Student affairs VP; Helen Jean Rogers (NSA Secretary-Treasurer, 1948-49), Herb Wright (Youth Secretary, NAACP). Seated: Ruth Hagy (Brod), moderator, V.K. Krishna Menon, Prime Minister of India. (Brod)

The *Philadelphia Bulletin* and *New York Herald Tribune* Forums

Hagy was a great friend of NSA. She had run the *Philadelphia Bulletin* Forum and had a real understanding of young people, as did another lady, Helen Hyatt Waller, who did the same thing for the *New York Herald Tribune* Forum. And we had an essentially NSA program at the Waldorf Astoria as part of Waller's forum as well. Sylvia Bacon,[2] Herb Goldsmith and I, among others, were on a panel debating whether a college student should be deferred from the draft. Taking one point of view was Lieutenant General Louis B. Hershey, head of the selective service system. Herb and Sylvia and I had some different viewpoints on it, but we also had some different viewpoints with General Hershey.

Mrs. Waller had gone to international student conferences herself. I think she'd gone to Prague once and had written a book about it before she joined the *Herald Tribune* staff. She also was a great friend of college students and college student organizations such as NSA in New York.

ENDNOTES

[1] See Rogers (Secondari), p. 599.

[2] See Bacon, p. 474.

1952-1953 National Organization

(As presented in the Fifth National Student Congress Directory)

NATIONAL OFFICERS

President
Richard J. Murphy, *University of North Carolina*
Vice-President, National Affairs
Leonard A. Wilcox, Jr., *University of Michigan*
Philip C. Berry, *University of Michigan* **[June-Aug. 1953]**
Vice-President, Student Affairs
Janet Welsh, *Smith College*
Vice-President, Educational Affairs
Manfred Brust, *University of Illinois*

Vice-President, Student Government
Stephen Voykovich, *Fordham University*
Vice-President, International Affairs
Avrea Ingram, Jr., *Harvard University*
Travel Director
Thomas Callahan, *St. Francis College*
Assistant Travel Director
Mary O'Dea
Executive Secretary
Marion Andert, *University of Minnesota*

REGIONAL REPRESENTATIVES TO THE NATIONAL EXECUTIVE COMMITTEE

California, Nev., Hawaii
Lowell Vye
Mills College

Great Southern
Roger Walker
University of Miami

Great Northwest
Kenneth Strand
Washington State College

Illinois
Larry Buttenweiser
University of Chicago

Kentucky–Tenn.
David Jones
U. of Louisville

Mason-Dixon
Cynthia Courtney
Dunbarton College

Metropolitan New York
Hugh Schwartz
CCNY Main, Evening
James R. Berry
CCNY Main, Day

Michigan
Richard Welsh
University of Detroit
Art Johnson
Wayne University

Minnesota
Gene Keating
College of St. Thomas

Missouri–Kansas
Ron Roderique
Pittsburg State College

New England
Arnold Schuchter
Harvard University
Linwood Starbird
Yale University

New Jersey
Lois MacPherson
Upsala College

New York State
Charles A. Aswad
Harpur College

Ohio–Indiana
James Young
Ohio Wesleyan College

Pennsylvania–W. Va.
Francis De Lucia
Temple University
Herman Dupre
St. Vincent's College

Rocky Mountains
Shirley DePorter
Colo. State C. of Education

Virginia, Carolinas
Kenneth Barton
Univ. of North Carolina

Wisconsin
Harley Hinrichs
Univ. of Wisconsin

NATIONAL ADVISORY COUNCIL

(From Stephen C. Schodde 1965 Doctoral thesis)

William B. Birenbaum, Chair
Director of Student Activities, University of Chicago

William T. Dentzer
NSA President, 1951-52

Very Rev. Vincent J. Flynn
President, College of St. Thomas

Frank Graham
United Nations Mediator

Kenneth Holland
Director, Institute of International Education

Althea Kratz Hottel
Dean of Women, University of Pennsylvania

Charles S. Johnson
President, Fisk University

Gordon J. Klopf
Dean of Students, Buffalo State College

A. Blair Knapp
President, Denison University

Mrs. Carl W. Meinecke
Dean, Colby Junior College

Eleanor Roosevelt
U.S. Representative, UN General Assembly

Harold Stassen
President, University of Pennsylvania

Rev. Celestine Steiner
President, University of Detroit

Harold Taylor
President, Sarah Lawrence College

Dennis L. Trueblood
Student Activities Counselor, Indiana University

1952-53 Roster of Colleges, Fifth National Student Congress

(From the Fifth National Student Congress Directory. Institutions in italics attended with visitor status.)

MEMBER COLLEGES

California-Nevada-Hawaii
College of Holy Names
Immaculate Heart College
Loyola University
Mills College
Mount St. Mary's College
University of California, Berkeley
University of California at Los Angeles

Georgia-Alabama-Florida
Agnes Scott College
Barry College
Emory University
Georgia Tech
University of Miami
Florida State University

Great Northwest
Eastern Wash. College of Education
Marylhurst College
University of Idaho
Washington State College

Gulf Coast
A&M College, Arkansas
Dillard University
Southern University
Xavier University
Mississippi State College
Southeastern Louisiana College
Southwestern University

Illinois
Chicago Teachers College
De Paul University
Lewis College
Mundelein College
Rockford College
Roosevelt College
Rosary College
St. Xavier College
University of Chicago
University of Illinois

Iowa–Nebraska
Wartburg College
Luther College
State University of Iowa
University of Dubuque

Kentucky, Tennessee
Berea College
East Tennessee State College
Fisk University
University of Louisville
Morehead State College
Murray State College
Tennessee Polytechnic Institute
University of Tennessee

Mason-Dixon
Catholic University of America
College of Notre Dame
Dunbarton College
Hood College
Howard University
Notre Dame College
Trinity College
University of Baltimore
Goucher College

Michigan
Marygrove College
University of Detroit
University of Michigan
Wayne University
Michigan State College

Minnesota
Carleton College
College of St. Benedict
College of St. Catherine
College of St. Theresa
College of St. Thomas
Gustavus Adolphus College
Hamline University
Macalester College
St. John's College
University of Minnesota

Missouri–Kansas
Fontbonne College
Kansas State College
Maryville College
Mt. St. Scholastica College
Pittsburg State Teachers College
University of Missouri
Webster College
Friends University
Lincoln University

New England
Albertus Magnus College
Bennington College
Boston College
Dartmouth College
Emmanuel College
Framingham State Teachers College
Harvard University
Harvard Graduate School, Arts & Sciences
Massachusetts Institute of Technology
Mount Holyoke College
Newton College of the Sacred Heart
Radcliffe College
Regis College
Simmons College
Smith College
St. Joseph College
University of Bridgeport
University of Massachusetts
University of Vermont
Wellesley College
Wheaton College
Yale University
Bradford Junior College

New Jersey
College of St. Elizabeth
New Jersey College for Women
Rutgers University
Upsala College

New York Metropolitan
CCNY Business Day
CCNY Business Evening
CCNY Main Day
CCNY Main Evening
College of New Rochelle
Columbia College
Fordham College
Fordham School of Education
Good Counsel College
Hunter College
Hunter College–Evening
Iona College
Manhattan College
Manhattanville College
Marymount College
New York University, University Heights
New York University, Washington Square
Notre Dame College
Queens College
Sarah Lawrence College
St. John's University
Vassar College

New York State
Buffalo State Tech Inst
College of St. Rose
Cornell University
D'Youville College
Fredonia State Teachers College
Harpur College
LeMoyne College
Niagara University
Russell Sage College
St. Bonaventure College
Siena College
Skidmore College
Syracuse University
University of Buffalo
University of Rochester–Women
University of Rochester–Nursing
Genesee State Teachers College

Ohio–Indiana
Antioch College
Baldwin-Wallace College
Capital University
College of Wooster
Fenn College
Indiana State Teachers College
Muskingum College
Ohio Wesleyan College
Saint Mary of the Woods College
University of Notre Dame
Ursuline College
Youngstown College
DePauw University
Ohio State University
Indiana University
Purdue University
St. Mary's College

Pennsylvania
Bryn Mawr College
Lehigh University
Mercyhurst College
Mount Mercy College
Pennsylvania College
Pennsylvania State College
Seton Hill College
St. Vincent College
Swarthmore College
Temple University
West Virginia Wesleyan College
University of Pittsburgh
University of Pennsylvania

Rocky Mountain
Colorado A. & M. College
Colorado Women's College
Loretto Heights College
Trinidad State Jr. College
University of Colorado

Virginia, Carolina
Duke University
Randolph-Macon College
Sweetbriar College
University of North Carolina
Virginia Polytechnic Institute
Virginia State College
Wake Forest College
Women's College, University of North Carolina

Wisconsin
Mount Mary College

NSA ENTERS ITS SIXTH YEAR—Former staffers share a birthday cake at the 1952 National Student Congress, Indiana University. Standing, from left: Al Lowenstein (U. of N. Carolina), 1950-51 President; Denny Trueblood (Indiana University), Chairman, National Advisory Council; Bill Dentzer (Muskingum C., OH), 1951-52 President; Ted Perry (Temple U.), 1949-1950 V.P. Student Life; Fred Houghteling (Harvard), 1949-1950 Executive Secretary; Ted Harris (La Salle C., PA), 1948-49 President. Seated, from left: Mary Kay Perkins (Rosary C., IL), 1949-1950 Staff Associate; Sylvia Bacon (Vassar), 1951-52 VP Student Affairs; Helen Jean Rogers (Catholic U.), 1948-49 Secretary-Treasurer. (Murphy).

Eisenhower inaugurated and Stalin dies

Wonderful Town opens and Mount Everest is scaled

Korean armistice signed. USSR explodes hydrogen bomb. Communist Pary appoints Khrushchev first secretary. Queen Elizabeth coronation. Congress creates new cabinet post of Secretary of Health, Education and Welfare. Wage and price controls remaining since the war are removed. Published: Skinner's *Science and Human Behavior;* Bellow, *The Adventures of Augie March*. Opened on Broadway: Miller's *The Crucible*; Anderson's *Tea and Sympathy*; Bernstein's *Wonderful Town*; *Kismet* based on Borodin's music. Died: playwright Eugene O'Neill, poet Dylan Thomas, composer Sergei Prokofiev. On the music charts: "Doggie in the Window," "Stranger in Paradise," "I Love Paris." Academy Award to *From Here to Eternity*. Cinemascope technology in U.S. theaters. Mt. Everest scaled for the first time by Hillary and Tenzing. Nobel prize for medicine to Selman A. Waksman, American, for discovery of streptomycin. U.S. tennis player Maureen Connolly wins women's Grand Slam. Southern California defeats Wisconsin 7-0 in Rose Bowl. Yankees win fifth consecutive World Series, 4-2, over Brooklyn.

Source: Adapted from citations in Bernard Grun, *The Timetables of History* (Simon and Schuster, 1991)

BUDGETING NSA'S MILESTONES: 1952-53

INCOME STATEMENT

NATIONAL OFFICE
United States National Student Association

Year Ending September 30, 1953

Balance, October 1, 1952				$1,545.48
INCOME:				
Fifth Congress Transfer		$ 88.27		
Educational Projects, Inc., Administrative Fee		1,133.75		
Publications		1,731.82		
Dues		10,917.50		
Contributions		5,972.49 ← First Domestic Program Money Raised. Mostly W. [illegible], Ruth Hagy		
Friends of the Association		267.50		
Miscellaneous		145.00		
TOTAL INCOME			$ 20,256.33	
EXPENSE:				
Salaries		$ 6,703.10		
Travel		1,084.77		
Supplies and Services		1,846.55		
Postage		1,953.83		
Publications and Printing		4,803.10		
Rent		1,725.00		
Telephone and Telegraph		972.59		
Legal and Accounting Fees		83.13		
Miscellaneous:				
Moving	$ 728.73			
ACE Dues	100.00			
Art Exhibit	200.00			
Commission Expenses	637.45			
Subscriptions	56.45			
Citation to Donor	50.00			
Bank Charges	34.05			
Miscellaneous	64.02	1,870.70		
TOTAL EXPENSE			$ 21,042.77	
Deficit				($ 786.44)
Balance, October 1, 1953				$ 759.04

(NOTE: The Income Statements for the Congress and the National Office must be considered as an entity, as work in the two units is actually inseparable.)

INCOME STATEMENT

International Office
United States National Student Association

September 1, 1952 - September 30, 1953

INCOME:			
Foundation for Youth and Student Affairs		$ 50,772.06	
William Smith, Houston, Texas		3,000.00	
Committee for Free Asia		164.00	
Japan Society		1,558.57	
Miscellaneous contributions		616.52	
TOTAL INCOME			$ 56,111.15
EXPENSE:			
Full-time Senior Personnel		$ 4,186.38	
Part-time Senior Personnel		103.00	
Administrative Assistance		3,276.05	
Stenographic Assistance		4,546.27	
Translations		13.50	
Auditing		150.00	
Bookkeeping		130.00	
Telephone and Telegraph		1,437.27	
Postage		1,223.35	
Stationery		235.25	
Mimeograph and Office Supplies		1,712.91	
Miscellaneous		310.78	
Rent		1,470.00	
Electricity		54.87	
Janitorial Services and Supplies		195.99	
Travel		17,212.36	
Hospitality of Foreign Student Leaders		1,311.58	
Contingencies		697.38	
Publications		2,096.23	
Social Security		180.82	
Dues and Donations		10,428.69	
TOTAL EXPENSE			$ 50,972.68
Excess of Income over Operating Expense:		$5,138.47	
Transfer to Capital Surplus:			
Purchase of Furniture and Fixtures	$2,150.97		
Payments of Prior Liabilities	1,432.09		
Unallocated Revenues	378.87		
Leadership Training Expense (not refundable)	(6.12)	$3,855.81	
Unexpended Income			

SEPARATE NATIONAL AND INTERNATIONAL OFFICE STATEMENTS appear for the first time. Dick Murphy reports they were prepared by Phil Berry, 1953 National Affairs Vice President. The $21,042 national office statement almost equals the $21,009 of 1951-52—both being the lowest of the first six years. At the same time the international office's $56,111 in revenues reflects the first year of significant Foundation for Youth and Student Affairs support ($50,000), which was revealed in 1967 to be a conduit for covert U.S. government funding (see Part 3, Section 2).

PART 6 EPILOGUE: WHAT HAPPENED LATER

SECTION 2

Nineteen Fifty-three and Beyond

CONTENTS

An Intercollegiate Newspaper

THE NSA NEWS

National Office: 1307 Sansom St. Philadelphia, Penna.

Official Publication of the United States National Student Association

6th Year, No. 2 — April, 1953 — Price 5 Cents

3 Deans' Groups Back Association As Student Voice

Ohio State Site of NSA National Congress

10 NSA Delegates Invited to Japanese Student Assembly

Mrs. Roosevelt Features Educational Assembly

NSA Leadership Training

1000 Students Eligible For USAY This August

1953

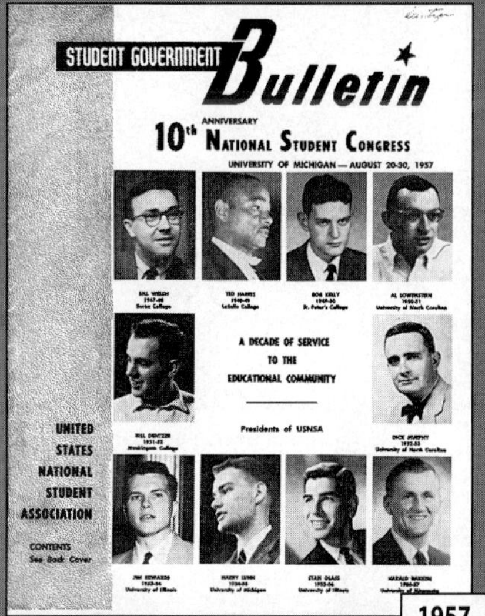

STUDENT GOVERNMENT Bulletin

ANNIVERSARY 10th NATIONAL STUDENT CONGRESS

UNIVERSITY OF MICHIGAN — AUGUST 20-30, 1957

A DECADE OF SERVICE TO THE EDUCATIONAL COMMUNITY

Presidents of USNSA

UNITED STATES NATIONAL STUDENT ASSOCIATION

CONTENTS See Back Cover

1957

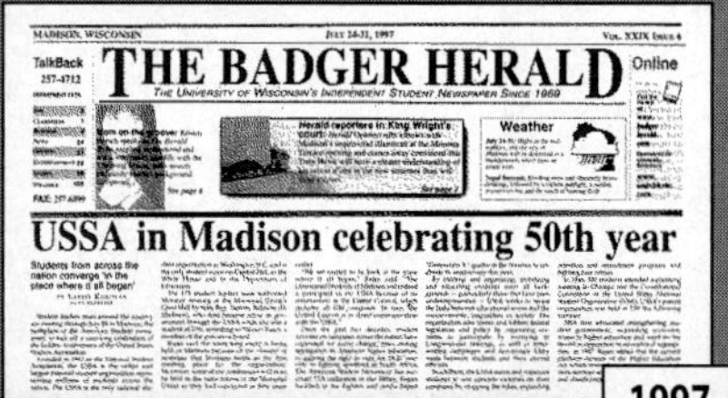

MADISON, WISCONSIN — JULY 24-31, 1997 — VOL. XXIX ISSUE 4

THE BADGER HERALD

THE UNIVERSITY OF WISCONSIN'S INDEPENDENT STUDENT NEWSPAPER SINCE 1969

TalkBack 257-4712

Online

Weather

USSA in Madison celebrating 50th year

Students from across the nation converge 'in the place where it all began'

1997

"**STRENGTHENING THE FORCES OF FREEDOM.**" The central theme of the Sixth USNSA Congress in 1953 finds a variation in the USSA's 50th Congress theme, "50 Years Closer to Freedom." From top: *NSA News* April, 1953; "Student Government Bulletin," Vol. 5, No. 4, April 1957; *Badger Herald* (U. of Wisconsin independent student newspaper), 7/24-31/57.

In this section, Janet Welsh Brown's review and critique of several histories, book chapters, monographs and doctoral theses that cover NSA's history for the period following 1952 serves also as an overview of the main themes and stages in its subsequent history.

In 1977, NSA merged with the National Student Lobby (NSL) to form a new organization, the United States Student Association (USSA), folding itself into an unbroken line of NSA's corporate standing and structure. The anthology was undertaken to mark the USSA's Fiftieth National Student Congress in 1997. It was held at the University of Wisconsin, where NSA had been founded with such high hopes and energy fifty years earlier.

As Brown notes in her review, the materials available "do not constitute, even collectively, sufficient sources on which to base a history." Nonetheless, one can lay out a general chronology, and can share her hope that "our successors at NSA/USSA and other scholars will complete the task" of bringing together an "important piece of educational and political history."

The rest of the story has yet to be told by those who appear in it.

The sponsors and editors of this book view this story as foundational for the future and as a contribution to the history of its times. We have described as best we can how and why our student generation created an American national student organization, and designed and carried out its activities and programs. Our goal was to share and record experiences that were of immense value to each of us. Hopefully, doing so will also illustrate some of the useful forms that student leadership can take, as well as some of its pitfalls, and will also be helpful in future assessments of the era.

We feel a certain satisfaction, and even wonder, that what we began has survived these many years in the hands of our children and even grandchildren. But the "rest of the story" was played out by them according to their own script. It needs to be told and celebrated in its own terms by those who followed us. In that way, they can provide their own examples of student leadership, and contribute to future assessments by detached observers and historians.

Years of Growth and Transformation: 1953-1997

Above: 6th, 1953–Ohio State U.; From right: 7th, 1954—Iowa State C.; 8th, 1955—U. of Minnesota; Below, from left: 9th, 1956—U. of Chicago; 10th, 1957—U. of Michigan; Far right: U.S. students in Europe with NSA's travel program.

The Rest of the First Ten Years

OCT 6 1960

(Not printed at Government expense)

Congressional Record

United States of America

PROCEEDINGS AND DEBATES OF THE 86th CONGRESS, SECOND SESSION

Thirteenth Anniversary of the U.S. National Student Association

EXTENSION OF REMARKS
OF
HON. JOSEPH S. CLARK
OF PENNSYLVANIA
IN THE SENATE OF THE UNITED STATES
Saturday, July 2, 1960

There being no objection, the statement was ordered to be printed in the Record, as follows:

THIRTEENTH ANNIVERSARY OF THE U.S. NATIONAL STUDENT ASSOCIATION

The U.S. National Student Association (USNSA) is a confederation of student governments ...

... on selected American campuses with reduced study loads, in order to study the structures and operation of American campus organizations. Seventeen students arriving in this country next month will bring the total number of foreign student leaders participating in this project to 75.

The Eighth International Student Rela- ...

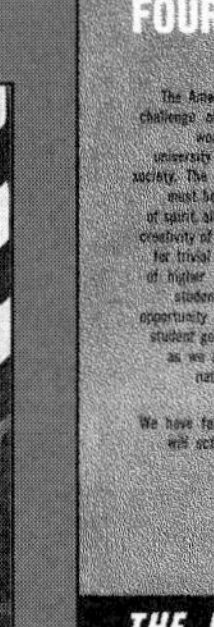

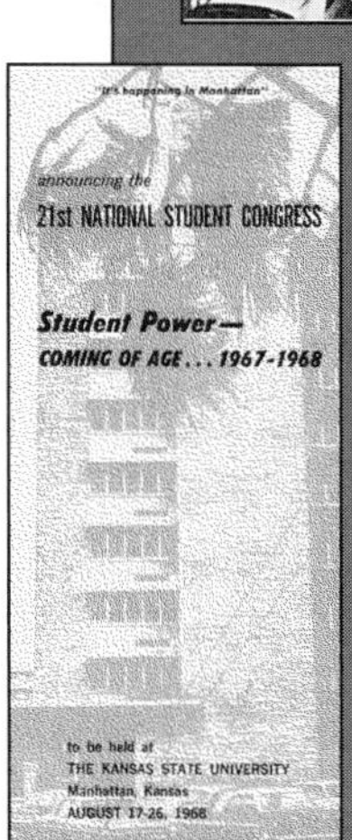

Above: 14th, 1961—U. of Wisconsin; 21st —1968, Kansas State

In 1977 NSA merged with the National Student Lobby to form a new United States Student Association

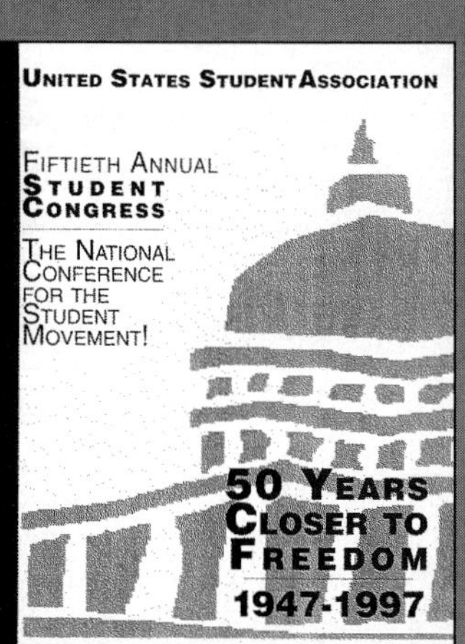

From left: NSA-NSL membership brochure, 1974-77. 50th, 1997—U. of Wisconsin.

Years of Student Forums and Changing Times

Histories of NSA reviewed

1. After the First Five Years...

Janet Welsh Brown
Smith College, New England Regional Chair, 1951-52
NSA Vice President, Student Affairs, 1952-53

Our knowledge of NSA and our understanding of the American student movement since 1953 is thin indeed. For an adequate assessment of the impact of NSA on the campus and the nation, one would need to examine (1) the continuing and new issues before the annual Congresses, and which factions in the organization stood where and why; (2) the size of the membership from year to year and the annual budgets, the allocation of funds to international, national and campus activities, and the sources of funding; (3) the structural and administrative changes that were made and in response to what forces; and (4) a thorough analysis of all of the above. Although there is something known in the readily accessible sources about each of these categories, the information is hardly adequate for creating a comprehensive picture of the organization. The following, therefore, is a review of several available accounts of NSA since 1952. As is apparent to any reader of these few documents, they do not constitute, even collectively, sufficient sources on which to base a history. There is a lot of research remaining for our younger colleagues to do.

An official record, *The History of the USNSA*, was compiled by Robert Kernish and published by NSA in 1965. It is a running summary of the major issues debated at each Congress, plus a few highlights of the following year. Some of the same issues that were controversial during the first five years turned out to be critical also to the ongoing definition of the organization. NSA policy on student rights and academic freedom was challenged and upheld by every Congress, even in the worst of the McCarthy years. Opposition to loyalty oaths and defense of the independence of the student press were regularly debated and upheld, though often by narrow margins. Racial issues became steadily more prominent as the drive for desegregation of education gained momentum after the 1954 Supreme Court decision. Financing higher education was often an issue, though it was transformed over time from a demand for federal aid to education to proposals for income tax deductions for educational expenses.

For the first time in 1958, a resolution against discrimination by campus organizations was defeated—a sign of the increasing organization of opposition to NSA in fraternities, though the Kernish history does not tell us so. The 1957 Congress repealed a long-standing policy opposing the vote for eighteen-year-olds, leaving NSA without a position on this issue until Congress endorsed the vote in 1964. There was a major NSA effort to end the universities' practice of acting in loco parentis. New national issues arose, including opposition to nuclear testing and apartheid, support for statehood for Alaska and Hawaii, and support for a Peace Corps.

And one also sees in the record a raft of new programs to serve campus interests: a press service, attention for scarce campus housing, support for student literary magazines, concerns about mental health, promotion of volunteer opportunities for students. Most years there was relatively little debate about international issues reported in this record, despite the fact that most of the budget was spent on international programs. Through ups and downs, NSA continued to operate its summer travel programs, supported Cosec as an alternative to the IUS, sent representatives to International Student Conference events, and sponsored international student exchanges. The single program that had the most far-reaching effect on the organization itself was the creation, in 1953, of the annual International Relations Student Seminar, which thereafter became the training ground and screening process through which subsequent NSA presidents and international vice presidents passed.

This official NSA history includes no real picture of the organization's financing, except for occasional mention of financial stress, deficits, or improvements and periodic receipt of grants from private foundations, usually Ford, mostly to support campus activity to encourage student involvement in policies that affect them. The reader is never told the number of member schools, the size or allocation of the budget, the number of employees, or even the names of the officers, except for the president elected each year—so one cannot tell, for instance, that during the ten years after 1954 there were only two women elected to national office.

The official Kernish history is more complete in recording structural changes. The elected vice presidents of education, student government, and student affairs remained on their campuses, perpetuating the two classes of officers (full time and campus based) until 1959, when these offices were eliminated altogether. At the same time, regional offices were set up around the country by and under the control of the national office (perhaps to offset the ineffectiveness of some regions—we are not told). In 1960 the international office was finally moved from Cambridge, Massachusetts, into the national office in Philadelphia, presumably making coordination and oversight tighter. The annual review of existing basic policies was made mandatory in 1963, which would have made amendment easier.

In 1964 a constitutional amendment was passed requiring the direct election of delegates, a move that would attenuate the influence of elected student governments in NSA and make it easier for any small, well-organized campus interest group, such as fraternities or the Young Americans for Freedom (YAF) to influence the election outcome. But by far the most important shift in power (to a handful of elected officers) resulted from the elimination in 1963 of the National Executive Committee (elected regional officers, acting with the national officers), which until then served as a check on the officers and shared considerable power with the national office. Any political scientist reading of these structural changes would sense major underlying political battles, but this record does not mention or identify the adversaries.

The YAF claimed credit for many of these changes as part of their campaign against NSA, but there is no discussion of its role in these events in the official history. That record also says that some of these proposals for structural changes were, in fact, initiated by the NSA officers, but the Kernish history gives us no clue to their reasons. Were they bending to pressure from the right because they thought the reforms good for the organization or making an effort to head off something worse? Though this official history is an important document for beginning an inquiry into NSA, it may tell us as much by what it leaves out as by what has been included. In either case, it gives the reader no real sense of the dynamics within the organization or on the nation's college campuses.

Partial answers, but only partial, may be found in a limited number of other available studies. In Stephen Clements Schodde's 1965 Ed.D. dissertation for Columbia Teachers College, there is more detailed analysis of certain issues, especially student rights and race relations, that were selected because these thorny issues were the ones most likely to cause headaches for the deans and other college administrators to which this dissertation was directed. The chapter on civil rights, for instance, charts NSA's progress on the question of racial equality from moral exhortation (1947 to 1954), to the development of a legal strategy for integration (1954 to 1960), and then to direct action (after 1960). In this study there is also a useful analysis of the struggle over the in loco parentis doctrine and a clearer picture of increased campus activism that becomes apparent in the early 1960s.

This dissertation gives us more detail on some of the structural changes, too, and Schodde sometimes shares his insight into the impetus and implications of the changes. It is a useful study, despite its selectivity, but one wishes for similar analysis of NSA international policy and financial problems. Though Schodde outlines the National Advisory Board's role in approving the budget and staff appointments, there is no analysis of the extent of consultation or who really bears the responsibility for those decisions, and the discussion of the source and allocation of funds is understandably sacrificed to the greater concern with the financial viability of the organization. The failure to take a hard look at finances and management looks a bit naive in retrospect, but many organizations had casual budgeting and record keeping in those days.

Another source of information is Philip G. Altbach's *Student Politics in America* (McGraw-Hill, 1974). Its chapters on pre–World War II student organizing experience provide historical context and reveal patterns of student activism over several generations. There is lots of information on student politics, but most of it is on the peace (antinuclear and anti–Viet Nam) and civil rights organizations, not on NSA. He provides a detailed account of the conservative YAF's campaign to weaken NSA, an effort in which they partially succeeded. But overall, the effect of the book is to discount the role that NSA played in important national issues. For instance, Altbach barely mentions NSA in his reportage on campus civil rights activity and concludes that the profound student discontent, activism, and revolt of the 1960s were not fully reflected in NSA. And the women's movement, which saw unprecedented growth in the 1960s, appears to have had no impact on NSA—a judgment shared by my own colleagues who were on campus in that decade.

One's acceptance of the book's conclusion—that students in general have not had a significant effect on major U.S. social movements, especially in comparison to students in Europe and the developing countries—must be tempered by his own analysis of significant student impact on the civil rights and antiwar movements.

Despite their ideological extremes and some inaccuracies, two studies from the political right—M. Stanton Evans'

Revolt on the Campus (Regnery, 1961) and *NSA Report*, published by the YAF in 1962—help explain the national and campus political context within which NSA worked and some of the politics within NSA itself. The authors of both publications clearly thought NSA sufficiently influential—indeed, subversive and dangerous—to justify a full-scale attack and, on YAF's part, a multiyear campaign to destroy NSA. Schodde quotes NSA President Dennis Shaul in 1963 as blaming the YAF campaign, with some help from the Young Republicans, for the unusual number of colleges disaffiliating from NSA that year. In a 1967 article, the YAF claimed credit for bringing NSA down, though the revelations that same year of Central Intelligence Agency (CIA) funding must surely share the credit. (Ironically, though the official Kernish history of the supposedly progressive NSA does not mention a single woman in the period under discussion, the Evans book identifies numerous activist women student leaders in the conservative organizations.)

One final collection of articles on NSA tells us how little the public really knows about the organization after 1952 and how much research still needs to be done. This is a collection of eighteen articles, letters, and reports put together by NSA to prepare delegates to the 1967 Congress for a discussion of the disclosures about the CIA's involvement in NSA. They reflect a wide variety of opinions and emphases: the shock and outrage of students who feel betrayed; a defense by former NSA presidents who cooperated with the CIA; speculations on the future of the organization; analyses from nonstudent critics, both liberal and conservative (neither of which defended the CIA); and questions about the extent of control and influence of the CIA on NSA and the other organizations and unions it financed.

Today some of these pieces are amusing (e.g., Strom Thurmond calling the CIA "subversive"), and some are surprisingly dismissive, even scathing, about students in general. The protestations from "witting" and "unwitting" past NSA leaders (the claim that NSA never took positions or did anything that it wouldn't have done anyway, even if it hadn't had CIA funding) sound disingenuous and/or naive. It is hard for the reader to accept that the organization was never pressured by the CIA, except maybe on NSA's opposition to the war in Viet Nam. It is difficult indeed for anyone who has raised money to keep a not-for-profit organization afloat to believe that donors, especially large donors, especially donors supplying up to 80 percent of annual expenses, have no influence on the programs or management of the organization.

Perhaps the most injurious finding in these pieces is the realization that all of NSA's top leaders from 1953 on (i.e., all the presidents and the vice presidents for international programs except one) were products of the intensive annual pre-Congress seminars where twelve or so carefully selected students were immersed over several weeks in the history and analysis of postwar international student affairs in general and NSA's role in particular. Some of these students had apparently not, prior to their selection, been very visible in NSA. The seminars were paid for by the CIA and instruction was given by outside experts and former NSA officers, some of whom were on the CIA payroll. Thus, for ten years, unknown to the congressional delegates who subsequently voted for officers nominated from this group, key officers of the organization were vetted during close scrutiny in the seminar process.

Some of the articles in this collection called for the dissolution of NSA. Most, including a piece by NSA's own National Supervisory Board, called for a detailed investigation, full disclosure, and declassification of all information relating to CIA involvement in NSA and other organizations and unions similarly funded. But the Katzenbach Committee, charged by President Johnson with investigating the whole affair, instead quickly clamped on the economy lid, recommending only that the clandestine funding of private organizations be stopped and that the government develop alternative mechanisms for openly funding private programs of interest. And there was no further investigation. To this date the public does not know which or how many organizations were thus tainted, or how controlling was the CIA support—or, indeed, whether it continues. It is, as I can testify, very difficult, if not impossible, for researchers to get facts from the CIA files, even on events that happened very long ago and even with legal assistance.

Sandy England's Indiana University master's thesis, *The Impact of Women's Leadership in the National Student Association and the United States Student Association (1946–1994)*, alleges that, as more women students achieved leadership after 1967, NSA became more proactive on progressive causes. Teasing out cause from effect in this narrative is difficult because of the many inaccuracies, imprecise language, and frequent omission of dates, but the document nevertheless makes clear that major political and structural shifts occurred following the CIA disclosures. NSA was in disarray and debt for several years. (England, alas, is as uninterested in budget and other vital organization statistics as were the other authors under review.) There was a reported $500,000 deficit in 1967, with no CIA to cover the shortfall as in previous years. In 1969 President Nixon banned all federal funds to NSA. Income shrank, and so did the organization.

Student delegates at the Congresses did become more radical in their thinking in these years. A strong Black Caucus, formed in 1969, pushed resolutions declaring that racism "must be the prime focus of the student movement," granted

$50,000 to a new African-American student organization, and subsequently required that delegations to the Congress include people of color, women, and (later) homosexuals and graduate students. Tactics also changed as NSA joined class action suits against the federal government for its failure to enforce laws to combat racial and sexual discrimination.

The first woman president of NSA was elected in 1971. She gained national attention by going to North Viet Nam at Hanoi's invitation. That same year, eighteen-year-olds were granted the vote, and a national surge of student political action was reflected also in NSA, which ever since has had a lobbying program on national issues in Washington, D.C. A competing organization, the National Student Lobby (NSL), was formed that year to advocate for student interests, and in 1974 NSA followed suit, changing its tax status to that of a 501(c)4 organization and establishing the NSA Foundation, which was able to accept tax-free contributions to work on nonpolitical campus issues and services.

Rivalry between the NSA and NSL was resolved in 1977 with a merger of the two organizations—renamed the United States Student Association (USSA) —a union that England describes as requiring NSA to move a little to the right while the NSL moved a little to the left. The merger apparently signaled a greater emphasis on "educationally related" issues, including the high cost of, and difficulty in access to, higher education, which remains a major concern of USSA to this day. Other issues included diversity in higher education and an array of new women's issues: rape on campus, sexual harassment and abuse, reproductive rights, the needs of women of color, and support for the Equal Rights Amendment. These issues were undoubtedly related to the big increase in women "participants" (not defined by England, but she probably means the officers, staff, and board members of USSA) from 31 percent in 1976 to 71 percent in 1986. On several issues over the years USSA has mounted campus campaigns and trained student activists in cooperation with organizations such as the National Abortion Rights Action League (NARAL) and the Midwest Academy. The objective, then as now, seems to be to get and keep students actively involved in issues that affect them. And the political orientation appears to be progressive or left of center.

At the turn of the century, USSA has its first African-American woman president, Kendra Fox-Davis. There is only one vice president, also a woman. Both serve full time in Washington, along with three other staff, in charge of lobbying, campus organizing, and diversity, and two part-time staff, who are shared with Jobs for Justice and Choice, two organizations with which USSA collaborates. Issues on which the students "campaign" are determined at the annual Congress.

Currently, these issues are federal financial aid (including assistance for graduate students), child care, the Supreme Court case considering whether student fees can be used for political purposes, campus hate crimes, and affirmative action. Financing comes from students, mostly from whatever amount the students vote to assess themselves in periodic campus referenda, a process that requires real voter education to succeed—and assures attention from the national officers. A Board of Directors (all students now, unlike its predecessor National Supervisory Board, which was created in 1963, and was made up of nonstudents) is made up of ten elected regional officers and twenty-two representatives of Congress-sanctioned caucuses.

Coupled with diversity requirements for the delegations, this structure assures overrepresentation at the national level of groups that were heretofore underrepresented in higher education. The Board has real power: it approves budgets, takes positions on issues, and recruits and hires staff—and its members function also as additional links between the national office and their campuses. USSA claims to reach 3.5 million students in 350 schools across the country, with their strongest campuses in Wisconsin, Oregon, and California. The national office is reluctant to give out budget or membership figures. Its political tone and decentralized power structure make the USSA in 2000 sound a bit like the feisty, struggling NSA of 1947-1952.

But the full NSA/USSA story remains untold. The sources cited in this review are inadequate for the task. Further research in the archives and interviews with the players are needed, and those of us who have worked on this volume must urge our successors at NSA/USSA and other scholars to complete the task—to tell the whole history of the organization since 1952. There is some urgency for the task: some of the participants have died, and for all of the participants, memories fade and records are discarded or otherwise mislaid—and thus, this important piece of educational and political history could be lost.

Janet Welsh Brown, shown here with her husband, Norman Brown, a physicist, was a senior associate (later fellow) at the World Resources Institute from 1985 to 2000. She was executive director of the Environmental Defense Fund from 1979 to 1984. Earlier, she taught political science at Sarah Lawrence College, Howard University, and the University of the District of Columbia. (See p. 387 for extended biography.)

The USNSA Creed

A world where there are differences without hate . . .

. . . This is the world we desire.

The USNSA Creed, 1954

Editor's note: The USNSA Creed was taken from the last two paragraphs of a speech given before the Philadelphia Bulletin Forum in March 1953 by 1952-53 NSA President Dick Murphy. Murphy recalls that it was inspired by a speech he had heard given by Frank Graham, U. of North Carolina President (1930-49). Cynthia Courtney, NSA 1953-54 Educational Affairs Vice President persuaded then NSA President Jim Edwards and the national staff to adopt it as a creed, and it began appearing in NSA literature in 1954. It is shown here as it appeared with a message from President Kennedy in an NSA information brochure, c. 1961. (See Murphy, p. 1082f, also Graham, p. 979 and Courtney, p. 921).

THE WHITE HOUSE

WASHINGTON, D.C.

The National Student Association has splendidly articulated our national ideals and reflected the vigor of our college and university young people. The NSA has behind it years of useful activity and experience. It has made generous and effective contributions in many areas of public policy—foreign affairs, civil rights, academic freedom and international student exchange.

The NSA has played a most significant role in expanding opportunities for educational assistance and exchange to the underdeveloped areas of the world. The NSA has helped to prove the worth of broader education exchange programs and to develop support both here and abroad.

Your debates, and even more your actions, have been responsible, forward-looking and affirmative. Your 1959 Congress stood in sharp contrast to the festival which had recently ended in Vienna.

I am certain that young people all over the world will find in your work and activity a confident assurance that America can yet seize the opportunities and promises of a free world.

Sincerely yours,

JOHN F. KENNEDY

PREAMBLE TO THE USNSA CONSTITUTION:

"We, the students of the United States of America,

desiring to maintain academic freedom and student rights . . . stimulate and improve democratic student governments . . .

USNSA CREED

"A world where there are differences without hate; men become brothers in the sight of God and in the human heart; where the least of these our brethren has the freedom to struggle for freedom. A world in which respect for the past is not called 'reaction' and hope for the future is not called 'revolution'; where the integrity of simple people is beyond price and the daily toil of millions is above pomp and power; where the majority is without fear, and all people have hope.

"This is the world we desire . . . we pledge ourselves to stand with the freedom loving students throughout the world in the common struggle that one day we may live together as brothers in peace and harmony."

A Message from President Kennedy 1961

"I am certain that young people all over the world will find in your work and activity a confident assurance that America can yet seize the opportunities and promises of a free world."

Source: NSA Information brochure, c. 1961.

Kennedy library.

JOHN F. KENNEDY was U.S. President from January 20, 1961, to November 21, 1963, when he was assassinated in Dallas, Texas. Kennedy is recalled in this book for his role in creating the Peace Corps, which was the culmination of postwar efforts by a number of student groups, including NSA, to send young people abroad to provide technical assistance to emerging nations. The story of NSA's role is told in Part 3, Section 4.

1957-58 National Organization Ten Years Later

NATIONAL OFFICERS, 1957-1958

(From Stephen C. Schodde, 1965 doctoral thesis)

President
Raymond Farabee, *University of Texas*
Executive Vice-President
Donald F. Clifford, *Catholic University of America*
Vice-President, Student Affairs
Reginald H. Green, *Whitman College, Washington*

Vice-President, Educational Affairs
Willard R. Johnson, *University of California, Los Angeles*
Vice-President, Student Government
Robert R. Kiley, *University of Notre Dame*
Vice-President, International Affairs
Bruce D. Larkin, *University of Chicago*

REGIONAL REPRESENTATIVES TO THE NATIONAL EXECUTIVE COMMITTEE

(From 1958 11th National Student Congress Report)

California, Nevada, Hawaii
Edward Baum
U. of Calif., Los Angeles
Willis D. Hawley
U. of Calif., Berkeley
Carolinas–Virginia
Hugh McCall Lupold
North Carolina State Coll.
Barbara Sampson
Sweet Briar College
Great Northwest
William H. Stuart
Washington State College
Great Southeast
Harvey Charles Koch, Jr.
Tulane University
Great Southwest
Joan Krenek
Southwest Texas State

Illinois–Wisconsin
Phil Stichter
Northwestern University
Matt Iverson
University of Wisconsin
Mason-Dixon
Jack Kreuter
American University
Metropolitan New York
Bernard Pucker
Columbia University
Anne Rosenbaum
Hunter College
Michigan
S. John Byington
Ferris Institute
Marne Gleason
Michigan State

Minnesota-Dakotas
Jim Banovetz
U. of Minnesota, Duluth
Margaret Platt
North Dakota State
Missouri–Kansas
Steve Lucas
St. Benedict's College
New England
George Henry
Mass. Inst. of Tech.
Charlotte Acquaviva
Radcliffe College
New Jersey
Jerry Minskoff
Newark State College
New York State
Nancy Cashimere
Alfred University
Carol N. Cordell
College of St. Rose
Ohio–Indiana
Mike Rudman
Oberlin College
Sarah Manning
Ohio State College
Pennsylvania–West Virginia
Richard J. Frankel
Drexel Institute
Rocky Mountains
Richard Scott
University of Colorado
Utah
Ray Geigle
Brigham Young University

NATIONAL ADVISORY COUNCIL, 1957-1958

(From Stephen C. Schodde, 1965 doctoral thesis)

Wallace M. Alston
President, Agnes Scott College

Harry Bullis
Chairman of the Board, General Mills

Ralph J. Bunche
Under-Secretary, United Nations

Erwin D. Canham
Editor, Christian Science Monitor

Christine Y. Conaway
Dean of Women, Ohio State University

Rev. T. M. Hesburgh, C.S.C.
President, University of Notre Dame

Reinhold Niebuhr
Vice President, Union Theological Seminary

Walter P. Reuther
President, United Automobile Workers

Eleanor Roosevelt

George N. Shuster
President, Hunter College

Harold E. Stassen

Robert M. Strozier
President, Florida State University

Edmund G. Williamson
Dean of Students, University of Minnesota

O. Meredith Wilson
President, University of Oregon

1958 NSA Membership – 11th National Student Congress

(From the 1958 11th National Student Congress Report)

MEMBER COLLEGES

California-Nevada-Hawaii

Immaculate Heart College
Los Angeles City College
Los Angeles State College
Mills College
Mount St. Mary's College
University of California, Berkeley
University of California at Los Angeles
University of Hawaii
University of Southern California
Whittier College

Carolinas–Virginia

Atlantic Christian College
Averett Jr. College
Belmont-Abbey College
Bennett College
Bridgewater College
Claflin College
Clemson Agricultural College
Columbia College
Converse College
Davidson College
Duke Univ. (Women's Student Govt.)
East Carolina College
Fayetteville State Teachers College
Flora McDonald College
Furman University
Greensboro College
Hampton Institute
Hollins College
Lenoir Rhyne College
Lynchburg College
Mary Baldwin College
Mary Washington College
North Carolina College
N.C. State Coll. of A.&E.
Queens College
Randolph-Macon Women's College
Salem College
Southern Carolina State College
Sweet Briar College
University of North Carolina
University of South Carolina
Virginia Polytechnic Institute
Virginia State College
Winthrop College
Wofford College
Women's College, Univ. of North Carolina

Great Northwest

Central Wash. College of Education
Eastern Wash. College of Education
Marylhurst College
Montana State University
Reed College
University of Alaska
University of Idaho
University of Portland
University of Washington
Washington State College

Great Southeast

Agnes Scott College
Barry College
Bishop College
Clark College
Morehouse College
Morris-Brown College
Savannah State College
Shorter College
Spring Hill Cottage
University of Miami

Great Southwest

Arkansas A.M. & N.
Arkansas A & M
Dillard University
Houston-Tillotson College
Oklahoma City University
Our Lady of the Lake College
Phillips University
Southern University
Southwest Texas Teachers College
Southwestern University
St. Mary's of the Dominican
University of Oklahoma
University of Texas
Wayland Baptist College
Xavier University

Illinois–Wisconsin

Augustana College
Barat College of the Sacred Heart
George Williams College
Lakeland College
Mt. Mary College
Mundelein College
National College of Education
North Park College
Northwestern University
Rockford College
Roosevelt College
Rosary College
Southern Illinois Univ.
University of Chicago
University of Illinois
U. of Wisc.–Madison
U. of Wisc. –Milwaukee
Wright College

Iowa–Nebraska

Briar Cliff College
Central College
Iowa State College
Simpson College
State University of Illinois
University of Dubuque
Wartburg College

Kentucky–Tennessee

Bellarmine College
Carson-Newman College
Centre Coll. of Kentucky
Fisk University
George Peabody College
Georgetown College
Kentucky State College
King College
LeMoyne College
Maryville College
Nazareth College
Pikeville College
Southwestern at Memphis
Transylvania College
University of Louisville
Vanderbilt University

Mason-Dixon

American University
Catholic University of America
College of Notre Dame of Maryland
Coppin State Teachers College
Dunbarton College of the Holy Cross
Howard University
Maryland State Teachers College–Frostberg
Maryland State Teachers College–Towson
Morgan State Teachers Coll.
Trinity College

Metropolitan New York

Barnard college
Brooklyn College
CCNY - Baruch Day
CCNY - Baruch Evening
CCNY Main Day
CCNY Main Evening
College of New Rochelle
Columbia University
Fordham College
Fordham School of Education
Good Counsel College
Hunter College - Bronx
Hunter College - Park Avenue
Long Island University - C.W. Post
Manhattan College
Manhattanville College of the Sacred Heart
Marymount College - New York City
Marymount College - Tarrytown
New York Univrsity
New York University - Washington Square
Notre Dame College of Staten Island
Pratt Institute
Queens College
St. John's University - Long Island
St. John's University College
St. Joseph's College
Sarah Lawrence College
Yeshiva College
University of Baltimore
Washington College
Wesley College

Michigan

Bay City Junior College
Central Michigan College
Flint Junior College
Ferris Institute
Hope College
Marygrove College
Mercy College
Michigan State University
Michigan College of Mining & Tech.
University of Michigan
Wayne State University

Minnesota-Dakotas

Augsburg College
Bethany College
Bethel College & Seminary
Carleton College
College of St. Benedict
College of St. Catherine
College of St. Theresa
College of St. Thomas
Concordia College
Gustavus Adolphus College
Hamline University
Huron College
Hibbing Junior College
Macalester College
North Dakota Ag. Coll.
St. John's University
Southern State Teachers Coll.
University of Minn.–Duluth
University. of Minn.–Minneapolis
Yankton College

Missouri–Kansas

Central Missouri State College
Coffeyville College
College of Emporia
Kansas State Teachers College–Pittsburgh
Marymount College
Maryville College
Mt. St. Scholastica College
Southeast Missouri State College
St. Benedict's College
University of Kansas
University of Kansas City
University of Missouri
Webster College
William Jewell College

New England

Albertus Magnus College
American International College
Babson Inst. of Business and Admin.
Bennington College
Boston College
Bradford Junior College
Brandeis University
Colby College
Dartmouth College
Eastern Nazarene College
Emmanuel College
Fisher Junior College
Garland Junior College
Harvard–Radcliffe Graduate Council
Massachusetts Institute of Technology
Mitchell College
Mount Holyoke College
Mt. St. Mary's College
Newton College of the Sacred Heart
Northeastern University
Pembroke College
Quinnipiac College
Radcliffe College
Regis College
Simmons College
Smith College
Springfield College
State Teachers College
–Bridgewater
–Castleton
–Framingham
–Keene
–Salem
–Westfield
Trinity College
University of Bridgeport
University of Maine
Univ. of Rhode Island
Wellesley College
Wheaton College
Wheelock College
Williams College
Worcester Jr. College
Yale College

New Jersey

College of St. Elizabeth
Douglass College
Drew University
Fairleigh-Dickinson College
Glassboro College
Jersey City Jr. College
Jersey City State Teachers College
Monmouth College
Newark College of Engineering
Rutgers University
Rutgers Graduate Council
Rutgers U.–South Jersey
St. Peter's College
State Teachers Coll.–Newark
Upsala College

New York State

Alfred Ag & Tech. Inst. of State University
Alfred University
Bard College
Canisius College
Clarkson Institute
College of St. Rose
Cornell University
D'Youville College
Erie County Tech Inst
Harpur College
Hartwick College
LeMoyne College
Niagara University
Oneonta State Teachers Coll.
Orange County Community College
Rochester Inst. of Tech.
Rosary Hill College
Russell Sage College
Skidmore College
State Teachers College
–Brockport
–Buffalo
–Cortland
–Fredonia
–New Paltz
–Plattsburg
–Potsdam
Union College
University of Buffalo
University of Rochester–Nursing
Vassar College

Ohio-Indiana

Antioch College
Ashland College
Baldwin-Wallace College
Capital University
College of Wooster
Defiance College
Denison University
DePauw University
Fenn College
Fenn College (Evening)
Indiana University
John Carroll University
Muskingum College
Oberlin College
Ohio State University
Otterbein College
Saint Mary's College
Taylor University
University of Notre Dame
Ursuline College
Western College for Women
Wilberforce University
Wilmington College
Youngstown College

Pennsylvania–West Virginia

Alderson-Broadus College
Allegheny College
Alliance College
Beaver College
Bethany College
Bryn Mawr College
Cedar Crest College
Chatham College
Chestnut Hill College
Dickinson College
Drexel Inst. of Tech.
Gannon College
Grove City College
Hershey Junior College
Immaculata College
Juniata College
Lincoln University
Lycoming College
Mercyhurst College
Mount Mercy College
Philadelphia Textile Inst.
Rosemont College
St. Francis College
St. Vincent College
Seton Hill College
Sheppard College
Swarthmore College
Temple University
University of Pennsylvania (WSG)
West Virginia State College
West Virginia University
West Virginia Wesleyan College

Rocky Mountain

Colorado State University
Colorado State Coll. of Ed.
Colorado Women's College
Loretto Heights College
Regis College
University of Colorado
University of New Mexico

Utah

Brigham Young University
College of Southern Utah
University of Utah
Utah State University
Weber College

1953-1961: NSA Matures, Prologue to the Sixties

USNSA EDITION

The Michigan Daily

USNSA EDITION

Sixty-Six Years of Editorial Freedom

SPECIAL ISSUE ANN ARBOR, MICHIGAN, TUESDAY, AUGUST 20, 1957 FOUR PAGES

'U' Opens Doors For Conference

West Quad To House Participants; Staff To Occupy Activities Building

Nerve center of the 10th National Student Congress will be the new million and a half dollar Student Activities Building.

USNSA staff, public relations personnel, travel office and student government displays will all occupy space in the large first floor secretariat area, regularly headquarters for the University's Student Government Council.

The Congress secretariat and the office of the coordinator will be located in the Student Publications Building.

More than 900 Congress participants will be housed and fed in West Quadrangle immediately behind the Michigan Union. University student government personnel will serve as hosts and guides for delegates and will be located on the Quadrangle's first floor concourse.

West Quad will also have a snack bar open to Congress delegates from 10 p.m. to 2 a.m. Commercial displays will be located on the second floor concourse.

Plenary sessions through Friday, August 23, will be held in Rackham Auditorium' in the Rackham Building, the center of the University's Graduate School.

Business Plenaries in Ballroom

The remaining business plenaries will be held in the ballroom of the Michigan Union.

Subcommission' sessions will take place in Mason Hall classrooms. Commission ssesions will be held in the four Angell Hall auditoriums. These rooms can be found in the new buildings immediately behind and attached to Angell Hall.

The National Executive Committee will hold its nightly meetings in the third floor conference room of the Michigan Union.

To Meet in SAB, West Quad

Regional caucuses will meet in rooms in the Sutdent Activities Building and in the basement of West Quad.

The rooms in Mason and Angell Halls will be closed at midnight. Those in the Student Activities Building at 2 a.m.

University Health Service facilities will be available for treatment of minor ailmenst every morning except Saturday and Sunday. *More sreious health problems* will be treated at the University Hospital. Delegates have been asked to indicate that they are attached to the Congress when seeking treatment.

University recreation and entertainment facilities are available as indicated in the brochure issued to each participant.

President Welcomes Congress

The University of Michigan extends a most cordial welcome to the 10th Congress of the United States National Student Association.

I have observed with more than casual interest the growth of the National Student Association from the time it was founded in 1947. Its gradual inclusion of all aspects and categories of student activity, and its development of a strong pattern of administration, are indications of intelligent leadership and wise planning.

In concluding the first decade of its life, may the National Student Association in its meetings at this University repeat the success it achieved when its Congress met with us in 1950.

—Harlan Hatcher
University President

Editors Meet To Evaluate Their Roles

Karl Mayer, editorial writer for the Washington Post and Times Herald, will keynote the first Student Editorial Affairs Conference August 17 through 20

Designated "The Press on Campus, the conference will bring together college editors from all parts of the United States to discuss the responsibilities and role of the student press in the educational community.

Sponsored by the United States National Student Association, SEAC was established by the Ninth Congress and the National Executive Committee on the recommendation of the 30 editors who participated in the Student

Problems

Congress delegates and participants having problems involving University buildings or facilities or difficulties with University or city officials should contact Congress Coordinator Gene Hartwig either at the Student Publications Building, NO 2-3241 or at the

Africa Hosts Seventh ISC Sept. 11-21

Delegates To Air Rights Violations

By DAVE BAAD
Former Daily Editor
Special to The Daily

IBADAN, Nigeria—Student representatives from 60 countries are making last minute preparations for travel to this inland city in western Nigeria for the Seventh International Student Conference.

Bringing more toan 200 delegates to Ibadan's beautiful new University College, the Conference will provide 10 days discussion from Sept. 11 to 21 on problems faced by students in all parts of the world.

Students will begin arriving here the first week in September, with some coming even before for the East, West, Central African Seminar in Achimota, Ghana, Sept. 1 to 8.

Tours Scheduled

For early arrivals not attending sessions of the Seminar, the National Union of Nigerian Students, organizers of the Conference, has scheduled tours of nearby areas of Nigeria.

The Seventh Conference will climax the most extensive programs of events and activities in ISC's seven-year history.

Many firsts dot the program mandated by the Sixth ISC in Ceylon last September. For the first time seminars have been held for students from particular regions in order to facilitate examination of educational problems in specific areas of the world.

Central American and Caribbean students convened for a Seminar, July 28 to August 5 in Mexico; a North African cultural seminar in Tunisia is presently in progress and the Seminar in nearby Ghana will take place shortly.

Seminar Held Again

The International Student Seminar, a Conference fixture since the beginning, will be held again this year, the site being Stockholm, Sweden.

The well-known international student magazine, The Student, published since April, 1956 in English, French and Spanish was recently circulated for the first time in a fourth language, Arabic, as the result of a recommendation by the sixth ISC.

In addition this past year the Conference has sponsored the first Asian Student Press Cinference, the European Student Welfare Conference, the Seventh International Student Travel Conference, a Study Tour for Asian Student Leaders, and a five-man delegation to nine countries in South America.

Helsinki Host

From Aug. 26 to 31 the Seventh International Student Press Conference will meet in Helsinki, Finland, where much discussion is ex-

Delegates To Argue Key Issues Facing Education

STUDENT ACTIVITIES BUILDING—The million and a half dollar new headquarters of student government at Michigan will house the USNSA staff, public relations center, and some of the regional caucuses.

USNSA 10th Congress To Re-Argue Federal Aid To Undergraduate Policy

With the recent defeat of the federal school aid bill, delegates to the 10th United States Student Association Congress will be re-arguing the entire question of federal scholarship and loan programs.

Passage of legislation which would provide scholarships and loans for college students is not *anticipated in either this or the* next session of Congress.

Over 50 bills proposing federal assistance to undergraduates in the form of scholarships and/or loans have been introduced during the current session.

Bills to Aid

Though differing in plans for administration and cost of the programs, the bills are all designed to aid those high school graduates who find it impossible to enter college because of financial considerations.

The President's Committee on Education Beyond the High School has estimated that ". . . in the face of shortages in almost every field, approximately 100,000 well-motivated and highly trained high school graduates fail to continue their education each year—largely

stated at its Ninth National Student Congress last summer, "USNSA believes that it is in the national interest to afford financial relief to those students unable to assume the whole cost of higher education themselves, such that no qualified student need miss the opportunity for such education."

The Association also called for the application of 30 per cent of the cost of tuition and fees to the federal income tax paid by individuals. Delegates to the Chicago Congress favored awarding stipends on the basis of need and competitive examinations.

Association To Testify

The Association has been invited to testify before the House Committee considering the proposed bills. It is expected that legislative hearings will begin in January and will be followed by "field" hearings.

In all probability the committee, after hearing testimony, will fashion its own recommendations for presentation to the full House.

Delegates to the 10th Congress will be examining the federal scholarship and loan question in the "Relations with State and Federal Government" sub-commission.

Critics of federal aid have claimed that a large number of scholarship and loan funds go unused and are proof of the lack of sufficient need for its implementation.

The President's Committee, in

TRAVEL:

ETI Tours Attract 528

Educational Travel, Inc., an affiliate of USNSA, this year was the means by which 528 American students traveled abroad.

According to Andre A. Bonard, executive director of ETI, the most popular tours this year were the rock-bottom price Hobo tour and the separate tours through Central and Southern Europe.

Equally popular was the Volks-

CCNY President To Open Congress

NSA Officers Answer Khrushchev On Long-Term Student Exchange

Delegates representing almost a million college students across the nation convene today to participate in the opening of the 10th National Student Congress.

In sharp contrast to the Communist controlled and Soviet sponsored Sixth World Festival of Youth and Students just completed in Moscow, the Congress brings together 1,000 U.S. and foreign student leaders for 10 days of vigorous discussion and democratic resolution of problems confronting the American student community.

Keynoting this 10th Congress of the United States National Student Association will be Buell G. Gallagher, president of the City College of New York, at the plenary scheduled for 7:15 p.m. today in Rackham Auditorium.

President Gallagher is American chairman of World University Service (WUS) and former assistant commissioner for higher education in the U.S. Office of Education. His speech, "The American Student — Profile and Promise," will set the theme for this year's gathering.

Delegates Argue Resolutions

Following the opening sessions delegates will begin the process of hammering out Congress resolutions and policy stands in subcommission, commission and plenary sessions.

Among the areas expected to come under consideration, are the questions of federal aid to under-

BUELL GALLAGHER

Student Body Presidents To Convene

Three hundred student body presidents from across the nation will convene Saturday, Aug. 17 for the Seventh Annual Student Body Presidents Conference.

At Saturday's opening session the campus presidents will hear Prof. Max Wise of Teacher's College, Columbia University, keynote the conference with an address on "The Student and American Higher Education."

At their banquet Monday night in the Michigan League, conference participants will be addressed by Prof. Lionel Laing of the University. Prof. Laing was chairman of the study committee out of which [illegible] Student Government Council two years ago.

Providing an opportunity for the student body president to gain knowledge and experience in areas necessary to the improvement of student government as a dynamic force in higher education, the Conference will feature discussions, workshops and special problem solving sessions.

About 250 of the presidents attending the SPBC will be from United States National Student Association member schools, and another 50 from non-member schools.

In terms of percentages, 15 per cent of the presidents will come from large universities, 15 per cent from smaller state schools, 30 per cent from Catholic schools, 15 per cent from other church supported

Above: 8/20/57 *Michigan Daily* special edition for 10th NSA Congress. Below, from left: Report, 9th National Student Congress. Report; 10th National Student Congress.

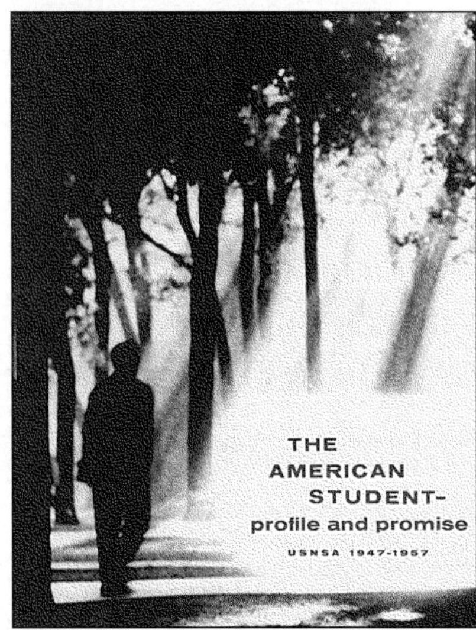

THE
AMERICAN
STUDENT-
profile and promise
USNSA 1947-1957

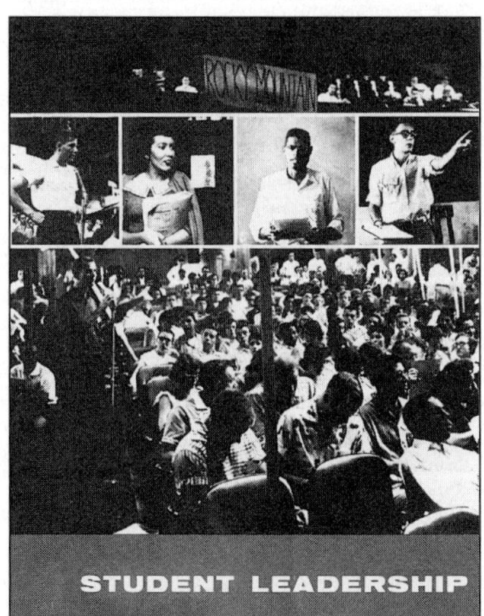

10TH YEAR AGENDA: LEADERSHIP, EDUCATION, & GLOBAL ISSUES

PROGRAMS OFFER CHALLENGES AND OPPORTUNITIES FOR LEADERSHIP

THE FOREIGN STUDENT LEADERSHIP PROJECT

STARTED BY NSA IN 1955, the Foreign Student Leadership Project (FSLP) was designed as an educational experience for American and foreign student leaders by bringing American students into close contact with a group of representative foreign students, who had previous leadership experience in student activities and organization. The overseas guest selected to participate in the Project was awarded a scholarship to live and study for one year at a prominent American college or university. Through academic studies and particularly through responsibility in planning and organizing student activities, the FSLP participant could share his or her aims and hopes with American students as well as learn about theirs. (Adapted from FSLP information brochure, c. 1960)

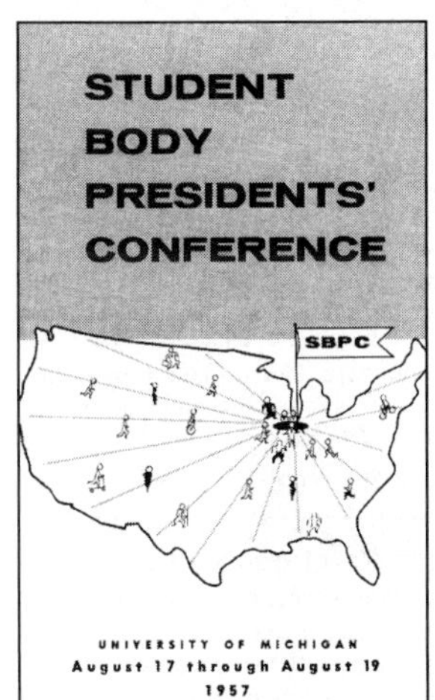

THE 1957 SEVENTH ANNUAL three-day conference program highlighted themes such as "The Student and American Higher Education," "Student Government and the Administrative Process" and "Our International Responsibilities." Open to both member and non-member schools. Room charges were $2.75/night.

(Source: Conference information brochure)

purposes of the student body president's conference

✓ 1. To confront the student body president with the problems and responsibilities which uniquely apply to him in his position.

✓ 2. To aid him in comprehending his role in the total academic community.

✓ 3. To enable him to see himself as a leader of one group responsible for developing a realistic approach toward the solution of some of the major problems facing higher education.

✓ 4. To provide an opportunity to clarify his own basic philosophies of student government, develop administrative techniques and widen his perspective and knowledge of the role of student government.

✓ 5. To make him more aware of his function in the attainment of the goals of higher education.

agenda

FRIDAY, AUGUST 16

6:00 p.m. to 12:00 midnight Registration for conference participants.

SATURDAY, AUGUST 17

9:00 a.m. to 2:00 p.m. Registration for conference participants.

2:00 p.m. Keynote Address:
"The Student and American Higher Education."
Discussion groups:
The responsibility of the university in providing leaders for society.
Student government's role in leadership development.
Developing campus leadership opportunities.
Student government leadership retreats and training programs.

7:00 p.m. Address: **"A College Atmosphere Called Freedom."**
Discussion groups:
The development of free and mature campus attitudes in academic and co-curricular affairs.
Are colleges turning out only a stereotyped "Joe College"?
Student, faculty and administration cooperation in developing the individual.
Student government programs to develop creative and challenging student attitudes.

10:00 p.m. Informal reception with foreign student leaders, advisory personnel and USNSA staff.

SUNDAY, AUGUST 18

2:00 p.m. Panel Presentation: **"Student Government and The Administrative Process of the College."**
Discussion groups:
Student government's relations with the college administration.
Factors affecting college decisions — students, alumni, community, state.
A positive approach to student-faculty relations.
Specific programs which student government can develop to improve student-administration communication, cooperation and understanding.

5:30 p.m. Dinner Session: Small group discussions according to size of school, concerning organization and internal administration of student governments.

7:30 p.m. Address: **"Student Government and The Educational Processes of The College."**
Discussion groups:
Student government as an educator: the role of students in determining the educational processes.
What are the reasons for complacency and uninformed acceptance on the college campus?
What student government programs — course evaluation, seminars, study groups — are effective?

MONDAY, AUGUST 19

9:00 a.m. Panel Presentation: **"The Adjustment of the New Student."**
Discussion groups:
The overall orientation process for the incoming student.
Analysis of attitudes, ideas and concepts of entering students.
Goals of orientation programs — adjustment to what?
Programs in high school, summer months, orientation week, and first year of college.

12:00 noon Luncheon Session: Small groups according to size of school, to discuss areas of concern to the Student Body President that are not covered in Conference sessions.

2:00 p.m. Presentation: **"Our International Responsibilities"** (Involvement of Conference on Foreign Student Affairs participant.)
Discussion groups:
Can student governments ignore international events?
Development of campus wide programs of international awareness and foreign student programming.
Problems of international student relations, importance of students internationally, concern of American students with problems of international student relations.

7:00 p.m. Closing Banquet: Banquet Address: **"Not a Thought Provoker But an Obligation."**
Conference adjournment.

THE STUDENT BODY PRESIDENTS' CONFERENCE

From NSA's founding,

AN UNBROKEN LINE OF COMMITMENT TO CIVIL RIGHTS

USNSA AND THE SIT-INS

"We pledge ourselves . . . to a world where men become brothers in the sight of God and in the human heart; and where our brethren have the freedom to struggle for freedom." USNSA CREED

On February 1, four freshmen from North Carolina Agricultural and Technical College entered the F. W. Woolworth store in downtown Greensboro, sat down at the lunch counter and ordered a snack. Refused service, they remained seated until the store closed.

Quietly, but firmly, these students had started a moral protest which was to spread throughout the South within the month and reach the conscience of the entire nation before the end of the school year. The "Greensboro Coffee Party" triggered a movement which was to be labeled "the greatest step toward desegregation since the 1954 decision."

Recognition or endorsement of the "sit-ins" was to become part of the agenda of many student, educational and human relations organizations—plus platforms of the 1960 Presidential campaign.

Students had shown the nation that an individual could effectively protest moral wrongdoing with nothing more than conscience and dedication for protection against those who would defiantly refuse him equal rights.

Dedicated as they were, the Southern students anxiously looked

to the North for support of the movement. USNSA National Affairs Vice President Curtis Gans, a resident of North Carolina, toured the South soon after the outbreak of the protest investigating the validity and spontaniety of the movement. Convinced that it had both, he reported his findings to other USNSA officers.

On February 27, after 81 Nashville students had failed to receive adequate legal protection during a sit-in demonstration, USNSA issued its first call for Northern support for the Southern students.

A telephone and wire campaign aroused nationwide student support for the non-violent sit-ins, and inside of 24 hours over 80 messages of support arrived arrived in Nashville, among them USNSA's own wire, and eight schools had held sympathy demonstrations for the Southern students.

These activities formed a basic pattern of action which continued throughout the semester. USNSA, in cooperation with other student groups, mobilized support action throughout the North and West, as students across the country took up the fight for equal rights through mass meetings, sympathy demonstrations, pickets, telegrams, resolutions and petitions.

The USNSA National Office undertook an intensive information campaign, issuing periodic reports to editors and student body presidents of member schools, keeping the student community up to date on the Protest Movement.

A Southern Student Scholarship and Defense Fund, established by USNSA at the request of member schools, provided a clearinghouse for monies already being collected on campuses. Over $7,000 poured into the National Office in the months that followed, the bulk of which was forwarded to the National Scholarship Service and Fund for Negro Students to aid students expelled from Southern schools.

In April, the Association obtained a $10,000 foundation grant for an emergency conference on the Sit-In Movement. Held in Washington, D.C., the Conference drew more than 400 college leaders anxious to learn more about the sit-ins.

From a full day's session of reports on the aims and directions of the protest movement, delegates strongly endorsed the sit-ins, condemned reprisal action by government and university officials and called for inter-regional cooperation in support of the movement.

USNSA's work in the sit-ins received strong support from delegates to the 13th National Student Congress, who adopted legislation urging continued support of the movement through messages, continued fund raising and cooperation with the Student Nonviolent Coordinating Committee.

Southern Project

Neither in his community nor in his educational experience does the Southern student have an opportunity to develop a full understanding of the complexities of Southern problems. There is a need for a learning experience which will better equip the Southern student to contribute effectively to the solution of the human relations problems which exist on his campus and which will later confront him in a Southern community.

Constance Curry
Project Director

To help meet this need, USNSA, with a $60,000 grant from the Ford Foundation, launched a two-year Southern Student Human Relations Project with offices in Atlanta, Georgia; the first student-sponsored effort of its type in the South.

Attempting to clarify the international, national and regional aspects of human relations questions, Southern Project director, Constance Curry, planned several inter-racial conferences in the Deep South and provided speakers and working materials for other such conferences.

The first year of operation for the Southern Project culminated with the Third Southern Student Human Relations Seminar (SSHRS) at the University of Minnesota in August, 1959.

Through lectures, discussions and a common living experience, sixteen students from Negro, integrated and all-white Southern colleges and universities sought to create a deeper appreciation for the needs and problems of race relations and to develop programs usable on Southern campuses and in Southern communities.

The Project office played an unforeseen but vital role when the Sit-In Movement exploded last February. Miss Curry traveled to numerous communities where demonstrations occurred to observe and report first hand accurate information on the movement, compiling and distributing a newsletter for distribution to the American student community.

During the second year of operation, Miss Curry plans to concentrate on campus and community human relations programming, working closely with allied human relations agencies in the South.

From the 1961 14th National Student Congress Report (see Curry, p. 446).

Southern Student Human Relations Seminar

Neither in his community nor in his educational experience does the Southern student have an opportunity to develop a full understanding of the complexities of the Southern problems. This is due partly to the traditional social and economic pressures exerted on the individual within a Southern community, and to the fact that the experience of integration in Southern education including the colleges and universities is, at this time, extremely limited or totally absent. There is a need for a learning experience which will better equip the Southern student to contribute effectively to the solution of the human relations problems which exist on his campus and which will later confront him in a Southern community.

To help meet this need, fifteen Southern student leaders participated in a four-week USNSA-sponsored Southern Student Human Relations Seminar at Ohio State University in August, 1958. Representing both segregated and desegregated schools, the Southern students provided a wide cross-section of opinion on the race question. . . .

Financed by a $6,000 grant from the Field Foundation, the Seminar was directed by Ray Farabee, 1957-58 President of USNSA, with Dr. Warren Ashby, professor of ethics at the Woman's College, University of North Carolina, acting as group consultant.

(Excerpted from Report of the 11th National Student Congress, 1958)

To learn about the world

NSA TOURS REACH EUROPE, ASIA, LATIN AMERICA

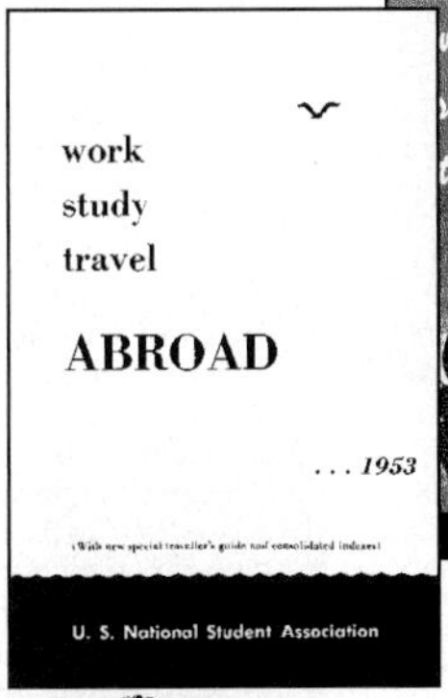

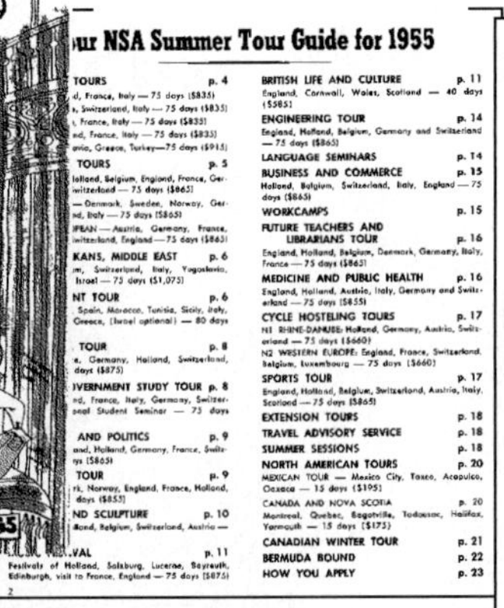

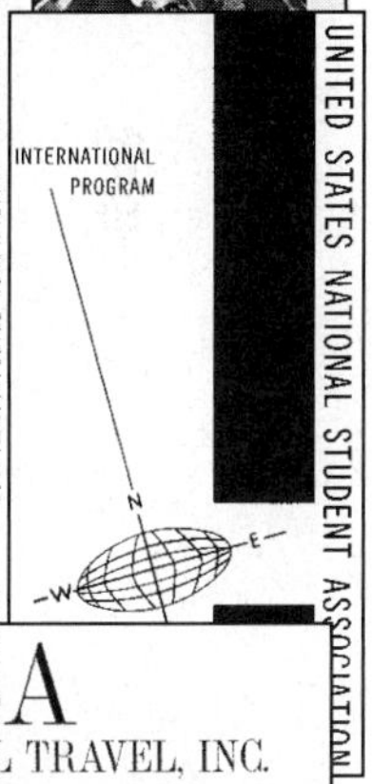

Top: Covers and pages out of NSA's annual travel directory (1948-54). Below: NSA travel and international program information brochures (1955-1964).

IN ALLIANCE WITH EUROPEAN STUDENT UNIONS, NSA built a global travel program, becoming one of the major student travel agencies. In 1961 it had thirty programs sending 900 students abroad and bringing more than 100 foreign students to the U.S. It provided information services to thousands more.

Jim Smith's 1946 Vision

NSA'S FOUNDATION: STRONG DEMOCRATIC STUDENT GOVERNMENT

STUDENT GOVERNMENT BULLETIN AND REPORT

U.S. Report on Soviet Education

Student Leaders Seek Educational Reforms; See Danger in Science Race

National Student News

Cabinet Member Urges Greater Aid for Students

USNSA Protests Rights Denial to Student Leader

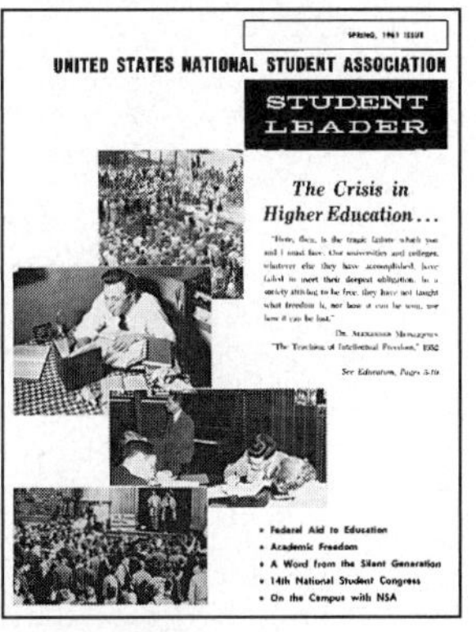

Editor's note: NSA's founders had a vision that in the United States a strong, representative national student organization could be built—strong enough to undertake effective campus initiatives, and democratic enough to elect representative national delegates to set policy (see Smith, page 127). NSA developed programs and publications to support this vision (see Part 2).

From left above: *Student Government Bulletins*, Vol. 1 #1, 10/52; Vol. 5 #1, 11/56; Summer, 1961. *The Student Leader*, Summer, 1961. *National Student News*, Vol. 1 #2, 12/1/57.

THE BEGINNING

American Students Organize after World War II

MAY 9, 1945, PULLMAN, WASHINGTON

VICTORY BELL HERALDS SURRENDER NEWS

MAY 7, 1945

V-E DAY

THE NSA CHARTER

APPENDIX

Framing a Comprehensive Vision

CONTENTS

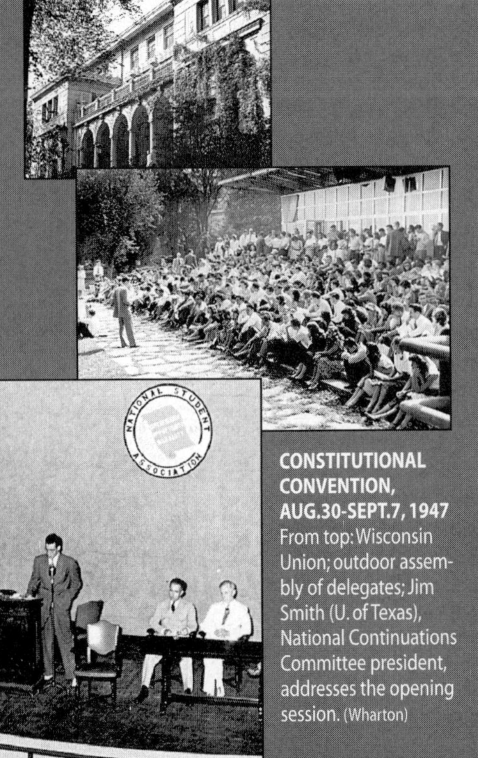

CONSTITUTIONAL CONVENTION, AUG.30-SEPT.7, 1947
From top: Wisconsin Union; outdoor assembly of delegates; Jim Smith (U. of Texas), National Continuations Committee president, addresses the opening session. (Wharton)

Harvard Crimson
Student Council Backs New N.S.A. Constitution

THE HAWK
Student Council Unanimously Approves NSA Constitution

THE Technique
Council Votes to Ratify U.S.N.S.A. Constitution

The Caellian
Assembly Adopts NSA Constitution at First Meeting of the Year

RATIFYING THE NSA CONSTITUTION, which included its preamble and Student Bill of Rights, was the action required for affiliation. Above, from top: *Harvard Crimson,* 9/30/47; *The Hawk,* 12/19/47, St. Joseph's College, PA; *The Technique,* 2/14/48, Georgia Tech; *The Caellian,* 10/23/47, New Jersey College for Women.

The student leaders who founded the Association were inspired by their traditions and their historic time and place. They expressed that inspiration in the preamble to the NSA Constitution, which begins,

> We, the students of the United States of America desiring to maintain academic freedom and student rights, to stimulate and improve democratic student governments . . .

and concludes,

> . . . and to preserve the interests and integrity of the government and Constitution of the United States of America, do hereby establish this Constitution of the United States National Student Association.

The words in between are a spirited commitment to inclusiveness, international understanding, and the betterment of student life and circumstance.

Pursuing America's Vision

The original NSA Constitution, its supporting policy statements and an overview of its form of organization follow in this Appendix.

In the spirit of that Constitution and its vision, and with the limited financial resources at hand, the founders launched the United States National Student Association.

1. Official Call
to the
National Constitutional Convention
for the
National Student Organization
to be held in
Early September
at

The University of Wisconsin

Madison, Wisconsin

Cover of official call booklet

called by

The National Continuations Committee

Of the Chicago Student Conference

University of Chicago

Reynolds Club, Room 301

5706 University Avenue

Chicago 37, Illinois

Much could be gained if American students would unite their efforts

CALL TO THE CONSTITUTIONAL CONVENTION OF THE NATIONAL STUDENT ORGANIZATION

(As it appeared in the original undated 1947 invitation booklet)

This meeting will be the most significant gathering of students in the history of United States colleges

Have you ever wondered how the students at the University of Wisconsin and the University of Texas built their Student Union Buildings? How they administer them now? How do the students at Harvard, Stanford, or Notre Dame handle their student governments? How do the academic standards of your college or university compare with those of the University of Michigan, or Chicago, or Yale?

Have you ever wished for information on opportunities for student travel in Latin America, Europe, or Asia? Have you ever felt that there should be a means for students to study at foreign universities at some reasonable expense? Have you ever had the thought that students could offer something to improve their campuses, and their society as well, if their voices could be heard?

Certainly any American college student has entertained some of these thoughts at one time or another. It has long been the idea of student leaders throughout the nation that college and university students can solve many of their own problems if only they could "get together," and work with each other to attain their common objectives. Much could be gained if American students would unite their efforts in a national organization of students.

Just such an association is in the process of formation now. Students from over the entire country are now taking steps toward the fulfillment of a basic need in student life, the formation of a student community-of-interest organization.

This summer, delegates from student bodies in every state will gather at the University of Wisconsin to adopt a constitution and prepare a program for the proposed National Student Organization. This meeting will be the most significant gathering of students in the history of United States colleges. YOUR CAMPUS SHOULD BE REPRESENTED THERE! The organization which delegates from your school can help bring into being will be for student purposes only, and will have no political, religious, or similarly partisan objectives.

The story behind the Constitutional Convention to be held this summer is a relatively simple, though an interesting one. The series of events that lead up to the coming summer meeting started at a meeting of the World Student Congress at Prague, Czechoslovakia, in August 1946. It was at this Congress that the International Union of Students was formally launched.

Present at Prague, among students from almost every nation, were twenty-five American delegates, ten elected by the student bodies from ten universities such as Fisk, Chicago, Harvard, Texas, etc., and fifteen from national student organizations such as the National Intercollegiate Christian Council (YM-YWCA), the National Federation of Catholic College Students and the Newman Club Federation, the American Youth for Democracy, Intercollegiate Division, the Student Federalists, the United States Students' Assembly, etc.

While in Europe, these American delegates were very much impressed by the work of national unions of students in England and Europe, as contrasted with the complete absence of anything comparable in the United States. When they returned to the United States, these delegates decided to call a conference of American students to sound out campus opinion on the desirability of forming a national student organization for the United States.

The conference was held at the University of Chicago, December 28-30, 1946. Here over 700 students, representing 800,000 students of 300 colleges and universities, and 20 national student organizations, discussed the aims and purposes of the proposed NSO and its organizational principles and decided to organize a "National Student Organization." Also, the Chicago Student Conference decided to form a National Continuations Committee, whose duties are to raise funds, publicize the coming Constitutional convention, and prepare a draft constitution as a basis for this summer's meeting. The Chicago Students Conference elected the officers for the NCC, the chairmen of the various geographical regions throughout the United States, and a staff committee of four to prepare material for the meeting to be held at Wisconsin.

At the present time, these jobs have been largely completed. Enclosed you will find the draft constitution and proposed program for the NSO. It is of utmost importance that you consider these carefully. These two documents will largely be the basis of discussion and consideration this summer. Further, discussion of these questions should be undertaken on a campus-wide level in order that your delegates may best be qualified to represent the student opinion on your campus.

The Convention will last from one to two weeks, between September lst and 15th. At the convention, the delegates will revise the proposed constitution to suit their liking, adopt it, and then begin discussions of the various student problems with which the organization can deal on a local, regional and national level. They will elect national and regional student officers for the first year of the new organization, and they will select a site for the central offices of the organization. Before they adjourn they will adopt a program of activities for 1947-8, such as the proposed program.

Read the proposed program and see if you don't agree that your student body can benefit from participation in these activities. If you do agree, study the enclosed sheets on "Credentials" to find out how your campus can secure representation, and go to work now to ensure attendance of your delegates, who must be chosen soon.

Further information on housing costs, travel expense reductions, and the like, will be sent to you soon. In the meantime, contact your regional chairman, whose name is on the enclosed list of officers, for more information on the background of the Convention, and begin action now to select your delegates.

We, the students of the United States of America . . .

2. The Constitution of the USNSA

Including the Student Bill of Rights

As adopted September 7, 1947

We, the students of the United States of America, desiring to maintain academic freedom and student rights, to stimulate and improve democratic student governments, to develop better educational standards, facilities, and teaching methods, to improve student cultural, social, and physical welfare, to promote international understanding and fellowship, to guarantee to all people, because of their inherent dignity as individuals, equal rights and possibilities for primary, secondary, and higher education regardless of sex, race, religion, political belief or economic circumstance, to foster the recognition of the rights and responsibilities of students to the school, the community, humanity, and God, and to preserve the interests and integrity of the government and Constitution of the United States of America, do hereby, establish this Constitution of the United States National Student Association.

ARTICLE I. NAME

A. The name of this organization shall be the United States National Student Association.

ARTICLE II. LEGISLATIVE AUTHORITY

A. The legislative body of the USNSA shall be known as the National Student Congress.
B. The Congress shall meet annually during the summer vacation.
C. The Congress shall:
   1. Accredit its own membership.
   2. Enact all laws and by-laws necessary to the proper functioning of the USNSA pursuant to this Constitution.
   3. Determine policies and programs.
   4. Assess the members of the USNSA in accordance with provisions of the by-laws. Such assessments shall be collected by the regions and forwarded to the national office.
   5. Determine and approve annual budget.
   6. Nominate and elect the Executive Officers.
   7. Create, or approve the creation of, all appointive offices.
   8. Approve all appointments made by the Executive Committee.
   9. Approve all programs to be undertaken in the name of the USNSA, except as otherwise specified in this Constitution.
   10. Impeach, suspend, or remove Executive Officers and expel or suspend member student bodies by a two-thirds majority vote, on the basis of the findings of the Executive Committee.
   11. Invalidate by a two-thirds vote all decisions of both regional and national bodies of the USNSA found to be in conflict with this Constitution.
   12. Sustain or reject impeachment actions of the Executive Committee.
   13. Exercise the final and supreme power of judicial review.
   14 Exercise all other powers not expressly prohibited to it by this Constitution.
D. Membership in the Congress shall include:
   1. Representatives elected by their entire student body.
      a. When this is not feasible, they shall be selected by the democratically constituted student government of their entire student body.
      b. All representatives prior to their election shall certify their intention to continue their studies at their respective colleges or universities in the period following the Congress.
   2. All outgoing members of the Executive Committee.

ARTICLE III. EXECUTIVE AUTHORITY

A. The Executive Committee of the USNSA.
   1. The Executive Committee shall consist of the members of the Staff Committee, without vote, and the regional representatives.
   2. The presiding officer shall be the President of the USNSA. He shall be empowered to cast one vote in the event of a tie vote.
   3. Each voting member shall cast one vote. All decisions shall be by a majority of such votes unless otherwise specified.
   4. The Executive Committee shall meet at least twice between sessions of the Congress. Special meetings may be called by a majority of its own membership, by the Staff Committee, or by its presiding officer.
   5. The Executive Committee shall:
      a. Determine the date and place of the annual session of the Congress.
      b. Supervise collection of funds on the national level in accordance with the budget.
      c. Supervise the execution of policies established by the Congress.
      d. Determine by the two-thirds vote emergency policies of the USNSA when such decisions may be required by immediate and imperative problems arising in the period between annual sessions of the Congress. Such decisions shall be reviewed by each Regional Assembly at its next meeting,
      e. Nominate by majority vote all members of the Advisory Council. The nominations shall be approved by a two-thirds vote of the Congress.
      f. Approve by a two-thirds vote all appointments made by the President to fill vacancies on the Staff Committee.
      g. Serve as the steering committee of the Congress.
      h. Suspend by a two-thirds vote Executive Officers in the period between annual sessions of the Congress.
      i. By majority vote, determine the order of succession of the vice-presidents in the event that the president is unable to fulfill the duties of his office.
   6. A quorum of the Executive Committee shall be two-thirds of the members, representing not less than one-half of the regions.
B. The Staff Committee of the USNSA.
   1. The Staff Committee shall consist of the Executive Officers and the National Editor.
   2. Each member shall be elected annually by the Congress from its own membership, with the exception of the National Editor, who shall be elected in accordance with the by-laws.
   3. Under no circumstances shall any person be elected to the Staff Committee more than twice.
   4. Each member shall be permitted to withdraw from any part or all of his course of study during his term of office without prejudice to his standing as a student under the Constitution.
   5. Each member shall be compensated for his services as specified in the annual budget.
   6. The Staff Committee shall:

a. Advise and assist Executive Officers.
b. Determine the publication policies of the USNSA in accordance with this Constitution and the decisions of the Congress.

C. The Executive Officers of the USNSA.
1. The Executive Officers shall be the President, Vice-Presidents, Secretary, and Treasurer.
a. The President shall:
(1) Be the chief executive officer of the USNSA.
(2) Officially represent the USNSA.
(3) Make all clerical appointments necessary and proper to the fulfillment of his office.
(4) Be responsible for the general execution of all decisions of the Congress and the Executive Committee.
(5) Fill any vacancies which may occur in the Staff Committee subject to the provisions of this Constitution. Any person so appointed shall act in a temporary capacity until approved by the Executive Committee.
(6) Perform such duties as specifically delegated to him by the Congress and/or by this Constitution. He shall delegate such of his powers as shall be necessary to the fulfillment of his office, subject to the disapproval of the Executive Committee.
b. The Vice-Presidents shall:
(1) Be equal in number to the number of National Commissions.
(2) Succeed the President in case of his removal, resignation, death, or inability to fulfill his office. The order of succession shall be determined by majority vote of the Executive Committee.
(3) Assist the President in the performance of his duties.
(4) Execute the program of the National Commissions in accordance with the provisions of this Constitution and the By-Laws.
c. The Secretary shall:
(1) Supervise the keeping of records and the handling of all official correspondence.
(2) Be office manager of the national offices.
(3) Send minutes of the Executive Committee meetings to all member student bodies.
d. The Treasurer shall:
(1) Prepare an annual budget, in accordance with the recommendations of the Staff Committee, to be presented to the National Student Congress.
(2) Collect members' dues and receive all other funds of the USNSA.
(3) Be the sole disbursing agent of the USNSA.
(4) Disburse funds only upon written request in accordance with the annual budget.
(5) Keep complete and accurate accounts of the receipt and disbursal of all funds.
(6) Prepare annual financial reports, which shall have been approved by a registered firm of certified public accountants, to present to the Congress, and prepare such other reports as the Executive Committee shall request.

ARTICLE IV. REGIONAL ORGANIZATION OF THE USNSA

A. The regions, as defined in the by-Laws, shall form organizations consisting of all member schools within their areas.
1. Each Regional Organization shall establish a separate Constitution which does not conflict with any part of this Constitution.

B. The legislative body of the Regional Organization shall be the Regional Assembly.
1. All representatives to the National Student Congress shall be members of the Regional Assemblies.
2. The Regional Assembly shall:
a. Determine policies within its region, provided that such policies shall not conflict with this Constitution or with the policies and programs determined by the National Student Congress.
b. Discuss proposed national policies and programs of the USNSA.
c. Promote within its region, the policies and programs adopted by the Congress.
d. Exercise all other powers and perform all other duties which may be delegated to it by other sections of this Constitution, the National Student Congress or its Regional Constitution.

C. The Regional Executive Committee shall be composed of the Regional Officers and such other members as the Regional Constitution shall provide.
1. The Regional Executive Committee shall:
a. Determine the date and place of Regional Assembly meetings.
b. Supervise the collection and expenditure of regional funds.
c. Supervise the execution of policies and programs determined by the National Student Congress and the Regional Assembly.
d. Exercise such powers and perform such other duties as are delegated to it by the Regional Constitution.

D. The Regional Officers shall be a Regional President, Vice-President, Secretary, Treasurer and such other officers as the Regional Constitution shall provide.
1. All Regional Officers shall be elected annually before the end of the National Student Congress as provided in the Regional Constitutions.
2. The Regional President shall serve as a voting member of the Executive Committee.
3. The powers and duties of the Regional Officers shall be specified in the Regional Constitution.

ARTICLE V. THE COMMISSION SYSTEM OF THE USNSA

A. The activities of the USNSA shall be executed through the commission system.
1. Each National Commission shall be administered by one of the national Vice-Presidents and such other subordinate officers or personnel as authorized in the by-Laws.
2. Each National Commission shall:
a. Initiate surveys on student problems within its jurisdiction.
b. Prepare reports for the member student bodies, the Regional Assemblies, the Executive Committee, and the National Student Congress.
c. Plan and coordinate national programs leading to the solution of student problems in accordance with this Constitution, by-Laws, and the resolutions of the National Student Congress.

B. The Regional Assemblies shall establish administrative structure necessary for the functioning of the Commissions at the regional level.

C. The member student bodies shall establish administrative structure necessary for the functioning of the Commissions at the campus level.

ARTICLE VI. MEMBERSHIP IN THE USNSA

A. Affiliation.
1. Student bodies of recognized colleges and universities or any other institution of higher learning which have been recognized by the Staff Committee and which are located within the territorial limits of the United States may affiliate with the USNSA if they ratify this Constitution and their Regional Constitutions. Adequate proof of ratification by the student body or student government of that institution must be presented to the national and regional offices of the USNSA.

B. Disaffiliation.
1. Upon notification to the national and regional offices of the USNSA, a member student body may initiate disaffiliation proceedings on its campus.

2. Disaffiliation shall be concluded upon presentation to the national and regional offices of adequate proof that the member student body desires to withdraw and resign from the USNSA.

ARTICLE VII. IMPEACHMENT OF USNSA OFFICERS AND EXPULSION AND SUSPENSION OF USNSA MEMBERS

A. Officers of the USNSA may be impeached and convicted on the following grounds:
   1. Embezzlement, fraud, or other felony.
   2. Conduct reflecting on the good name of the USNSA.
   3. Malfeasance in office.
   4. Actions contrary to, or in violation of, this Constitution.
B. Member student bodies of the USNSA may be expelled and suspended only on the following grounds:
   1. Actions contrary to, or in violation of, this Constitution.
   2. Failure to pay dues.

ARTICLE VIII. ADVISORY COUNCIL

A. The Advisory Council shall consist of nine educators and professional men selected in accordance with the provisions of this Constitution. Each shall serve a three-year term.
B. The Advisory Council shall advise and consult the National Student Congress, the Executive Officers, and the several national agencies of the USNSA at their request or upon its own volition.
C. The Advisory Council shall elect annually a chairman from its own membership.
   1. The chairman shall:
      a. Appoint all members of the Council to undertake advisory duties related to specific activities of the USNSA.
      b. Have the option of sitting on the Executive Committee ex officio, without vote. He may delegate a representative from the Council for the duty.

ARTICLE IX. MEMBERSHIP OF THE USNSA IN OTHER ORGANIZATIONS

A. Affiliation.
   1. The USNSA may affiliate with other organizations of a national or international character whose principles and policies are deemed consonant with this Constitution and the policies of the USNSA only by the following method:
      a. The Executive Committee shall consider all matters of affiliation and shall report to the National Student Congress on the desirability and possibility of such affiliation.
      b. The Congress shall consider all matters of affiliation and determine its recommendation by a two-thirds majority vote.
      c. An affirmative recommendation on the matter of affiliation shall be presented to the member student bodies of the USNSA for approval. Member student bodies shall individually ratify such recommendations by democratic elections or by approval of their democratically constituted student governments. Ratification shall be by two-thirds majority vote of the member student bodies taken within eight months of the recommendations of the Congress, provided that member bodies not voting within this time shall be counted in the affirmative.
B. Suspension of affiliation.
   1. The USNSA may suspend its affiliation in any organization by a majority vote of the National Student Congress, or by a majority vote of all the voting members of the Executive Committee.
C. Disaffiliation.
   1. The Executive Committee shall consider all matters of disaffiliation and shall report the findings to the National Student Congress.
   2. The USNSA may disaffiliate by a majority vote of the Congress.

ARTICLE X. METHOD OF RATIFICATION OF THE CONSTITUTION

A. The USNSA shall be formally constituted within thirty days after the ratification of this Constitution by a majority of the student bodies represented at the Constitutional Convention. This ratification must take place within a nine month period.
B. Ratification shall be by vote of the student body or by duly chosen representatives of the student body. In either case, ratification shall be by a majority of the votes cast.
C. This Constitution shall be provisional until it is ratified.

ARTICLE XI. METHOD OF AMENDMENT

A. All amendments to the Constitution shall be approved by two-thirds of the representatives present and voting in a regular session of the National Student Congress, subject to the following procedure:
   1. All proposed amendments must be approved by at least one-third of the members of the Executive Committee prior to consideration by the Congress.
   2. All proposed amendments shall be presented in written form to the delegates of the Congress at least three days prior to Congress action. They shall also be read to a plenary session of the Congress at least two days prior to final action.
   3. In the event that a proposed amendment receives a majority vote of the Congress but fails to receive the required two-thirds vote, it shall be submitted to the member student bodies for approval by referendum or for approval of the student governments. The amendment shall be adopted if approved within a period of eighteen months by a majority of the member student bodies comprising two-thirds of the total students enrolled in member student bodies of the USNSA.

BY-LAW I (To secure and maintain equal rights)

The USNSA will seek to secure and maintain equal rights for all people, and secure equal opportunities for education at all levels regardless of race, national origin, sex, creed, and political belief or economic circumstances; especially by securing the eventual elimination of all forms of discriminatory educational systems anywhere in the United States, since the United States National Student Association is opposed in principle to such systems.

BY-LAW II (Investigation and discussion of problems of inequality)

The United States National Student Association encourages wide investigation and discussion of the problems of inequality, which exist throughout the United States, in order to secure their elimination. However, in view of the complex nature of the problem, with its diversity throughout the United States, and the limitations imposed by present state rights, statutes, and laws, it shall be the policy of the United States National Student Association to take action on the national, regional, and campus levels through the corresponding organization of the USNSA to implement its stated principles, with regard to the legal limitations involved.

BY-LAW III. BILL OF RIGHTS

In order to preserve and extend these conditions indispensable to the full achievement of educational objectives, and with full cognizance of the responsibilities and obligations which ensue from any assertion of fundamental rights, the National Student Association holds the following rights essential to the full development of the student as an individual and to the fulfillment of his responsibilities as a citizen:

1. The right of every student to a college education.
2. The right to conduct research freely and to publish, discuss, and exchange any findings or recommendations, whether individually or in association with local, national, or international groups.
3. The right of students to a clear and concise statement, before entering college, of their contractual rights, obligations, and responsibilities pertaining to educational and extra-curricular activities.

4. The right of every student to exercise his full rights as a citizen in forming and participating in local, national, or international organizations for intellectual, religious, social, political, economic or cultural purposes, and to publish and distribute their views.
5. The right of recognized student organizations to use the institution's name subject to its regulations with respect to off-campus activities.
6. The right of students and recognized student organizations to use campus facilities, provided the facilities are used for the purpose contracted, subject only to such regulations as are required for scheduling meeting times and places.
7. The right to invite and hear speakers of their choice on subjects of their choice.
8. The right of students to engage freely in off-campus activities, provided they do not claim to represent the institution, exercising their rights as citizens of community, state, and nation.
9. The right to establish and issue regular publications free of any censorship or other pressure aimed at controlling editorial policy, with the free selection and removal of editorial staffs reserved solely to the organizations sponsoring these publications.
10. The right to establish democratic student governments with adequate democratic safeguards against abuse of their powers.
11. The right to petition through proper channels for changes in curriculum or professors.
12. The right of equal opportunity to enjoy these rights without regard to race, color, sex, national origin, religious creed, or political beliefs.

Application of the Foregoing Rights Should Be in Accordance with the Following Criteria:

1. **Recognition:** University and college administrations may properly require official recognition of student organizations as a condition for assigning them campus facilities and giving them any financial support which the college or university may make available.

(a) Where campus organizations or publications in effect enjoy a monopoly of certain college or university facilities or finances, the college or university administration may property insist on adequate safeguards for democratic terms of membership and control, and for including in publications the expression of points of view opposed to those of the editors, provided that all such safeguards are to be democratically student formulated and administered.

(b) In the case of all other organizations and publications, recognition should be qualified only by the requirement that these organizations are genuinely connected with students or faculty at that college or university and do not demonstrably interfere with the stated purposes and program of the institution itself. Recognition should not be used as a lever: 1. To control the purposes or programs of the organizations or publications; 2. To force them to merge with other organizations or publications on the campus against the wishes of their membership; or 3. To dictate their form of organization or procedure.

2. Limitations imposed by recognition: Recognition may properly limit the manner in which organizations or publications may use the name of the college or university off-campus, such as requiring them to indicate clearly that they do not represent the views of the institution. Recognition may also properly limit the manner in which organizations may employ university facilities or finances in taking action—as sharply distinguished from expressing opinion—directly affecting matters off-campus. But no disciplinary action may properly be taken against students, faculty members, or their organizations or publications for activities off-campus not purporting to represent or involve the institution, or for expressing opinions on-campus concerning matters off-campus.

3. Faculty advisors: In institutions having faculty advisors for student organizations, such advisors should be chosen or approved by the student organization itself. Student groups should not be forbidden to function because no faculty member will consent to serve as their advisor.

4. Written policies: All policies and procedures involving or affecting the rights of academic freedom, and the conditions of recognition of student and of faculty organizations and publications, should be clearly stated in writing after consultation with the groups affected. They should be formally accepted by the entire campus community. These policies and procedures should in no case be subject to change without notice under the pressure of a particular situation, and the groups affected should participate at all times in their application.

The USNSA strongly urges the acceptance of the Bill of Rights. A private institution established not only for purposes of providing liberal education, but also for specifically avowed purposes, may exercise its recognized right to set up clearly defined standards in line with those purposes. However, the student must be fully acquainted with such standards upon applying for admission, and these standards must not exempt the institution from performing those functions which are the responsibility of any college or university in a democratic society. No educational system can abrogate this obligation to prepare students for the role of citizenship.

The USNSA is in accord with the principles of academic freedom as expressed by the American Association of University Professors, in Vol. 32 #4 AAUP Bul. *Concerning academic freedom* we believe that:

1. The teacher is entitled to freedom of research, and in the publication of the results is subject only to the limitations imposed by the performance of his other academic duties; but research for pecuniary return should be based upon an understanding with the institution.
2. The teacher is entitled to freedom in the classroom in discussing his subject, but he should not introduce into his teaching controversial matter which has no relation to his subject.
3. The teacher has the right to join organizations whether religious, political, or social, provided that these organizations are not illegal under the civil statutes, without being discriminated against through economic, social, or political pressures because of such activity.
4. When the teacher speaks or writes as a citizen outside the campus he should be free from institutional censorship or discipline.
5. The basis for employment of faculty shall be only their ability to fulfill the requirements of the position.

Limitation of academic freedom because of the avowed purposes of the institution should be clearly stated in writing at the time of the appointment. Since the teacher is a man of learning and an educational officer, his profession and institution may be judged by his utterances. At all times he should be accurate, exercise appropriate restraint, and make every effort to indicate that he is not an institutional spokesman.

At the discretion of the Staff Committee a full investigation may be conducted with the report to be submitted to the NEC [National Executive Committee] and the institution concerned. Further action may be taken by the NEC with regard to the publication of the report if deemed necessary by that body.

In case of violation of the bill of rights or academic freedom, a preliminary Staff Committee investigation can be initiated at the request of the college administration, student government, or a student petition.

BY-LAW IV. ELECTION PROCEDURE

A. Nominations shall be accepted during the period from the convening of the National Student Congress until nominations are declared closed in the plenary session on elections.
   1. A nomination accepted before the plenary session on elections shall be submitted in writing to the chairman of the Executive Committee and shall contain the signature of the nominator and the signature of the nominee, in acceptance of the nomination.
   2. A nomination from the floor of the plenary session on elections must

be accepted by the nominee before the nomination is placed on the official ballot.

3. In the event that any candidate withdraws following the closing of nominations, the election procedure shall be halted immediately and nominations shall be re-opened.
4. A candidate defeated for election in one office is eligible for nomination, and can run for another office.
5. There shall be one nominating speech of five minutes for each candidate and an acceptance speech of three minutes from the nominee during the plenary session on elections.
6. In the plenary sessions on elections, the chairman shall read all written nominations for that particular office under consideration before nominations from the floor are opened.
7. The order of nominating speeches shall be determined by lot immediately after the closing of nominations.

B. Voting shall be by roll call of the regions.

C. A candidate shall be declared elected when he receives a majority of the total votes cast.

1. If a candidate has not received a majority on the first ballot, the leading candidates, receiving 75% of the votes cast, shall stand for election in a run-off.
2. Should subsequent elections be necessary, the candidate receiving the lowest number of votes shall be dropped from the ballot.

D. All delegates and alternate delegates and members of the Executive Committee shall be eligible for nomination to National Office.

BY-LAW V. THE COMMISSION SYSTEM

There shall be established two National Commissions. These Commissions shall be:

A. The National Commission on National Student Affairs.
B. The National Commission on International Student Affairs.

BY-LAW VI. REGIONAL DISTRIBUTION

1. Interpretation of the powers of Regional Assemblies.

Regional Assemblies may alter mutual regional boundaries by consent of the regions concerned, such action to become effective when notification as to the action taken is forwarded to the National Executive Committee.

2. Regional membership.

Members may change their regional membership with the consent of the regions concerned.

3. Regional representation on the National Executive Committee.

Regional representation on the National Executive Committee shall be determined on the basis of member student bodies of the region, each region having one representative with one additional representative for regions representing more than 55,000 member students.

4. Regional Organization.

The following shall constitute the regions of the USNSA:

a. Maine, New Hampshire, Massachusetts, Vermont.
b. Connecticut, Rhode Island.
c. Metropolitan New York, Puerto Rico.
d. New York State.
e. Pennsylvania.
f. New Jersey.
g. Maryland, Delaware, District of Columbia.
h. Ohio.
i. Michigan.
j. West Virginia, Virginia, North Carolina, South Carolina.
k. Georgia, Alabama, Florida.*
l. Kentucky, Tennessee.
m. Illinois.
n. Iowa.
o. Indiana.
p. Wisconsin.
q. Minnesota.
r. North Dakota, South Dakota.
s. Louisiana, Mississippi, Arkansas.
t. Texas, Oklahoma.
u. Missouri, Nebraska, Kansas.
v. Arizona, New Mexico, Southern Colorado (south of 38 degrees, 45 minutes).
w. Utah, Wyoming, Southeastern Idaho, Northern Colorado.
x. Washington, Oregon, Greater Idaho, Montana, Territory of Alaska.
y. California, Nevada, Territory of Hawaii.

*The region is empowered to divide itself into two separate regions if the Regional Assembly so decides, this decision to become effective upon notification to the National Executive Committee.

BY-LAW VII. THE NATIONAL EDITOR

A. Written applications.

1. Applicants for the position of National Editor must apply in writing to the National Executive Committee, including in their applications the following items:
   a. A statement of past experience.
   b. Samples of previous work.

B. Interviews.

1. From all applicants, the National Executive Committee shall select five to be interviewed personally during the week prior to the convening of the annual National Student Congress.

C. The National Editor shall be appointed from among the five candidates interviewed in accordance with the provisions of this Constitution.

BY-LAW VIII. REPRESENTATION IN THE NATIONAL STUDENT CONGRESS

Voting representation in the National Student Congress shall be based on the following scale:

Under 1,000	1
1,001–2,000	2
2,001–3,500	3
3,501–5,000	4
5,001–7,000	5
7,001–10,000	6
Over 10,000	7

BY-LAW IX. ASSESSMENT OF DUES

Dues shall be assessed on member bodies in proportion to their enrollment, provided that no member body shall be assessed for more than 10,000 students enrolled.

Scale of Assessment as Established by the Executive Committee, Sept. 9, 1947:

Under 300	$ 25
301–1,000	35
1,001–2,000	79
2,001–3,500	128
3,501–5,000	177
5,001–7,000	241
7,001–10,000	315
Over 10,000	369

We have a part in this organization

3. Statement of Southern Delegates Concerning Educational Discrimination in Southern States

We fervently hope that you will realize that conditions vary in different parts of the South as they do in different parts of the North, and that the program cannot be the same in all southern regions.

Editor's Note: The original Constitution together with panel reports and the following statement appear in a 44-page booklet published by USNSA, entitled United States National Student Association: 1947-1948 Madison, Wisconsin Constitutional Convention.

We, the delegates from the southern regions of the USNSA, including Tennessee, Arkansas, Georgia, Texas, Mississippi, Florida, Virginia, West Virginia, North Carolina, South Carolina, Kentucky, and Louisiana, present the following statement:

Please let it be understood:

1. That we favor equal education for all American citizens, regardless of race, color, political belief, or economic circumstance.

2. That we have been working in this direction within our own regions since the Chicago Student Conference, although we were bound in no way as schools to take any action. We believe that the following facts bear out our sincerity in this issue:

We have been holding inter-racial meetings in all southern regions, in many places against severe opposition. These meetings have been extremely difficult because of the necessity of housing colored delegates, securing permission to meet inter-racially, in many cases in direct violation of state law, securing eating facilities where white and colored delegates could be fed together. This is positive action. A number of southern regions have elected colored executives, vice-president, secretary, and treasurer. Regional inter-racial meetings have been reported in the newspapers through the efforts of the delegates and this has caused much discussion and thought in southern areas.

In sports, the southern regions have worked toward the acceptance of Negro players on a basis of their ability rather than their color. For example, in Florida a scheduled football game was canceled with Penn State because a Negro player was a member of the Penn State team. This action caused an expression of widespread disapproval among Florida students.

We have encouraged the booking of Negro entertainers by our cultural entertainment committees. At the University of Texas a two night performance of Carmen Jones did more toward creating respect and understanding for the Negro race than a year of speeches and argument possibly could have accomplished. This is positive action.

Finally, we would like to make it clear that we intend to continue work in this direction within our own regions in the manner best suited and most opportune in each region. We fervently hope that you will realize that conditions vary in different parts of the South as they do in different parts of the North, and that the program cannot be the same in all southern regions.

We have a part in this organization. We have participated in it from the beginning, and we shall continue to participate in it and work for its success. Let us work together toward a solution of this situation. That is the fervent wish of the southern delegates to this Convention.

Excerpts from the report of the Constitutional Convention

4. Highlights for a National Student Agenda

Strengthening student government, expanding educational opportunities, cooperating with students around the world

A Summary Report of the Panel on Student Government

Editor's Note: These highlights are excerpted from the booklet United States National Student Association: 1947-1948 Madison, Wisconsin, Constitutional Convention.

The section of this report that concerns itself with the compiling of basic policies to be followed by the National Student Association in regards to Student Rights and Academic Freedom of teachers is contained in the By-Laws of the Constitution. The remaining portions of this panel report are found below. The various programs that are outlined are done so with the idea that the National Student Association will be working through the local student governing bodies on campuses of member schools, helping them follow through on national programs affecting their individual campuses.

STUDENT GOVERNMENT: STRUCTURE AND FUNCTIONS

The commission of the USNSA on Student Government and Student Government Functions shall work from certain fundamental premises. The first of these is that one of the principal purposes of the new organization will be to strengthen student government systems. If the new organization succeeds in developing strong and functional student governments throughout American colleges and universities, it will help to provide the mechanism through which American students can receive a real education in democracy.

Student Governments provide the opportunity for student leader and ordinary student alike to obtain badly needed practice in such citizenship activities as intelligent voting, parliamentary procedure, responsible representation of public opinion, intelligent leadership of public action, analysis of community problems and solution of those problems.

The general purpose of student government is to aid in developing the society of any educational institution so that it may better

1. Aid in the self-education of each student through his student government.

2. Awaken the student to his rights, responsibilities, and his common interest with the rest of the college or university community.

3. Coordinate all faculty and student activities toward a common goal.

Control of the Student Society is exercised not for its own sake, but only to implement the desired transformation of the whole society of any educational institution. Any control which does not further such a transformation is unnecessary and undesirable, regardless of who imposes it.

It is recommended that the USNSA Commission further the establishment of courses, either for credit or not, on the purposes, functions, and techniques of Student Government.

THE RELATIONSHIP OF STUDENTS, FACULTIES, AND ADMINISTRATIONS

It is a primary aim of the USNSA to develop a campus community spirit based upon student, faculty, and administration understanding and friendship. This can be accomplished by periodic meetings within an institution of representatives from student, faculty and administrative groups, meeting to discuss problems that jointly affect the life of the community. Regional meetings along these same lines should also be held. The orientation program for students should include information on the specific methods used on the campus to further this community development. The Constitution of the student governing body should clearly define the authority delegated to it, and a clear channel should be established through which suggestions may flow from each group. It is further suggested that encouragement within an institution of student, faculty, and administration participation in such activities as sports, dramatics, music, dances and receptions will do much to encourage understanding and cooperation.

CONSTITUTIONS

General and specific problems exist with regard to the various structural and functional provisions of student governing body constitutions. The National Commission should work toward the solution of these problems. Among the problems are: the purposes of student governing bodies; types of student governing bodies; powers of these bodies; their functions; their relation to faculties and to other campus organizations; delegation of authority; etc. There is a very special problem with regard to where a student governing body should draw the line limiting its activities as a student governing body.

It is recommended that the National Commission promote the adoption by student governing bodies of the USNSA policy on this point which is:

> shall specifically refrain from becoming involved in partisan political affairs, sectarian considerations, or similar matters which do not directly affect students in their functions and activities as students, with the single exception that they shall stand unalterably opposed to any political doctrine which would stifle free and democratic education in the USA.

With regard to the problem of delegation of authority and related subjects, we recommend that the National Commission conduct special research on the following points:

Definition of the authority a student government must possess in order to be considered a true government; how much authority various administrations delegate to student governments; control over other campus organizations—their charters, activities, and representation; authority of faculty and students in joint boards; powers of investigation and interpretation; selections of advisors; relation of the authority of student government to the authority of the university and community; special interests; specific statement of delegated powers in the Constitution.

The National Commission shall assemble a file of the Constitutions of the student governing bodies of all member schools.

The National Commission shall conduct surveys to collect factual data on: feeling with regard to student government in general and in specific cases; reaction to, opinion of, and support for specific constitutions; structural and functional provisions of the institution (size in numbers, resident or non-resident, fraternal or non-fraternal, amount of faculty influence, political societies, strength of blocs, etc.); alignment of constitutions to the aims, purposes, programs, etc. of USNSA.

The National Commission shall compile reports that will contain the results of these surveys. It shall analyze the requirements of different types of schools and make specific recommendations as to the provisions of the constitution which would be advantageous to these different types of schools. It shall present a number of constitutional articles suitable for different student body requirements on each of the divisions of the constitution, rather than in the form of one model constitution for each type of school.

STUDENT APATHY

Student apathy is an overall self-centered approach to the role of the student (as related to the institution, the community, and the nation) which leads to a pronounced lack of interest in the affairs of the students, organizations, activities, and elections.

The USNSA Commission shall investigate the causes of student apathy, temporary and permanent, all of which are manifestations of a self-centered attitude. Among the causes to be investigated are: the inactivity of the student governments themselves; changes of values brought on by the war and varied technological developments; veteran and non-veteran groupings; over-crowded institutions and communities; commuting students; improper financial controls of student government expenditures; that kind of supervision by faculty administration groups which deprives students of much initiative; high pressuring which intimidates faculty groups into silence, and deprives the students of faculty advice and experience; and lack of adequate social opportunities and functions.

The above mentioned causes are in no way complete but are proposed to the panel as a starting point for a national commission to work toward preventative and remedial action on this vital issue.

* * *

A Summary of the Panel on Educational Opportunity

One of the three major sections of the program of activities of the National Student Association will be concerned with the problem of educational opportunity. Panel II was conducted primarily with the questions of economic barriers, educational discrimination, educational facilities, academic standards, curricula reform, and graduate study opportunity.

ECONOMIC BARRIERS

Panel II endorsed the principle of granting federal, state, and local aid to higher education. The following implementation was proposed for the USNSA: The NSA advocates a program of federal aid to the individual student who is scholastically qualified but financially unable to secure a higher education, aid which will be granted without regard to race, religion, sex, or political belief; support[s] increase in GI subsistence in proportion to the family unit; encourage[s] increased private contributions to scholarship and loan funds by organizations as well as individuals; encourage[s] individual colleges and universities to adopt more liberal scholarship policies; work[s] to prevent the increase of educational fees, and ask[s] that, when such increases are necessary, the administration discuss the problem with the local student government, especially with regard to those students for whom the raising of fees will be a hardship; encourage other legislative programs designed to alleviate economic barriers to educations. The Panel also recommends further consideration of the Privilege Card Plan and, in cooperation with the North American Student Cooperative League, investigation of the problems and promotion of student cooperatives.

EDUCATIONAL DISCRIMINATION IN SOUTHERN STATES

The Panel proposed that the USNSA, working through its regions, should survey comparative educational opportunities for Negro and white students in the South. The survey shall include state regulations concerning discrimination. On the basis of the survey there shall be direct action on the campus level, coordination of action on the regional level, and formulation of broad policy on the national level. The National Commission shall distribute the report of the survey.

EDUCATIONAL DISCRIMINATION IN NON-SOUTHERN STATES

Recognizing that only two considerations, character and academic standing, are valid in determining admission to an educational institution, the Panel decided that the following practices of discrimination on the basis of race, religion, sex, national origin, economic circumstances, or political beliefs which recognize the sovereignty of the U.S. Constitution, shall be considered unfair practices: to deny or limit the admission of, or otherwise discriminate against any person; to make, or cause to be made, any oral or written inquiry; to discriminate in the use of its facilities against any student or group of students; to announce, establish, or follow a policy of denying or limiting, through the device of a quota system or otherwise, admission of students or use of facilities. The USNSA shall consider it unfair for an educational institution to penalize any person because he has opposed, testified or participated in any proceedings in connection with the above practices or related laws.

However, the USNSA recognizes the right of an institution which has as one of its major purposes, religious instruction in a particular faith to give preference to students of that faith.

The Panel suggested that Human Relations Committees be established on the campus and regional level as part of the implementation of this program, with the further recommendation that faculty members be included in the Committee on the campus level. A program including the use of audio-visual materials shall be part of the expanded educational service of the USNSA.

The Panel also proposed that the USNSA request non-southern state legislative bodies to include stipulations in subsidy-granting legislation which will withhold subsidies and deny tax exemption to those schools which are found guilty of unfair educational practices as defined in this report. Since the matter of educational opportunity and discrimination in its broader implications is important to the nation as a whole, and since this problem, with its ramifications, is rarely limited to the area of its origin, a constructive appeal should be made on a national scale, taking into consideration local needs and financial ability to meet those needs.

EDUCATIONAL FACILITIES

Recognizing the importance of improved educational facilities in primary and secondary schools as well as in colleges and universities, Panel II resolved that the USNSA should take action nationally, regionally, and locally, in support of increased governmental grants or appropriations for educational facilities on all levels of education. In accordance with this principle the Panel proposed specifically: that federal aid should be of such a nature as to bring educational facilities in all states up to the national median as determined by the National Office of Education; that the USNSA endorse the raising of teachers salaries; that regional investigations be conducted on these and similar problems concerning educational facilities, sending the results of such investigations to the National Office for action. Students are encouraged to act in cooperation with the community on such programs. The Panel recommended also that new state and municipal institutions be established or the facilities of existing institutions similar to them be improved where necessary. Funds for this purpose shall be provided by federal loans, subsidies, and state appropriations to be distributed at the discretion of the state legislatures.

ACADEMIC STANDARDS

Recognizing that the USNSA, through regions and on the campus, shall work for the improvement of the academic standards of specific institutions, and with the general educational standards of state primary and secondary systems, Panel II proposed: that the Commission on National Student Affairs be concerned only with general academic standards on a national or regional basis and deal with academic standards in specific institutions only when student governments or administrations of these specific institutions request aid; that the USNSA undertake to have teacher evaluation grading charts made available to the administrative departments of colleges and universities; that the USNSA investigate a system of comprehensive examinations to be given to transfer students to substantiate transfer credits, when in doubt; that the USNSA collect information on student guidance and orientation programs for distribution to schools where such facilities are not available; that the USNSA concentrate on educational standards of institutions affiliated with the USNSA for the present and at a future date the National Commission shall concern itself with standards of secondary and primary institutions; that the USNSA investigate and work to prevent abuse of the privilege of tenure and the lowering of academic standards by teachers.

CURRICULA REFORM

Panel II unanimously recommended a program of curricula reform which might be undertaken successfully by the USNSA in the coming year. The program is to be carried out on the campus, in the region, and nationally through Curriculum Committees to be established within the framework of the Commission on National Student Affairs on each level. The committee on the campus level may include faculty members. It shall be specifically concerned with: initiation and direction of orientation programs for freshmen which would aid them in understanding the basic philosophy of liberal education and the outstanding points in their college curriculum; comprehensive study of the adequacy of the present curriculum; recommendation to the faculty and administration of specific courses suggested by the USNSA Commission on National Student Affairs or by the students themselves; cooperation in the conduct of whatever rating systems of faculty, courses, or departments are used in the institution; cooperation in the distribution of information concerning current educational trends; action as a clearing house for complaints and suggestions from the student body regarding academic and curricular problems.

The Panel further recommended a specific type of course to be considered by the USNSA this year. It is a synthesizing course incorporating study of the social, political, cultural, economic, and ideological problems of today. The Commission on National Student Affairs is instructed to prepare an outline for such a course, working in cooperation with existing educational associations, and compiling information on similar courses now being taught. The brochure finally issued by the Commission should include a syllabus describing the projected program and containing the suggestions of experts, and an outline of the various forms in which such a course might be offered. This outline, together with specific suggestions for implementation, should be widely distributed.

Other proposals of the panel were that all schools which are members of the USNSA must be invited to attend all USNSA conferences, regional or otherwise, and shall be asked to participate in all activities of the USNSA, in keeping with the By-Laws of the Constitution of the USNSA; and that it shall be a primary purpose of the USNSA to encourage membership in this organization of all schools which are now non-members.

It was agreed that the USNSA shall make regional surveys of all educational facilities, incorporating them into a national report which will serve as the basis for the appropriate action of the USNSA. Audio-visual aids and other programs should be introduced to form a basis for inter-racial and inter-religious understanding.

A Summary Report of the Panel on International Student Activities

Discussion in Panel III was divided into two major sections: discussion of the various organizations with which the USNSA will be interested in working, and proposed activities of the USNSA in the international field.

In order to facilitate discussion, speakers were invited to present at the beginning of the panel work a short exposition of the nature and activities of several of the organizations with which we were concerned. Lawrence Duggan, director of the International Institute of Education, and Witmer Kitchen, executive secretary of World Student Service Fund, were the principal speakers. There were also discussions of International Student Service, UNESCO, and the International Union of Students. Concerning the organizations, it was resolved: that it is the opinion of Panel III that in its recommendations on organizational relations it has considered only one affiliation, that to IUS; that it considers the relationships to UNESCO, WSSF, and ISS cannot be affiliations in the sense of the USNSA Constitution.

UNESCO

It was unanimously decided to seek representation of the USNSA on the National Commission for UNESCO. The Drafting Committee of Panel III recommends that, as part of its program of international activities, the USNSA establish, with the sanction of the National Commission for UNESCO, regional UNESCO councils of student groups with possible youth groups, and through these student UNESCO councils aid in the establishment of general regional UNESCO councils of all interested groups.

WORLD STUDENT SERVICE FUND (WSSF)

Having thoroughly discussed the technical reports of the staff members of WSSF and ISS, with particular reference to the distribution of relief on the basis of need only, having examined closely the organizational relationships and sponsorship of WSSF and ISS, being satisfied with examination of the budgets of both groups, and with the operational agreement that exists between ISS, World Student Relief, Pax Romana, World Student Christian Federation, IUS, World Organization of Jewish Students, and WSSF in the field of student assistance activities, it was resolved that the USNSA should become sponsor of WSSF, on the agreement that a unified student relief effort through an effective organization such as WSSF will result in maximum contribution and effectiveness.

INTERNATIONAL STUDENT SERVICE (ISS)

On the basis of discussion of ISS by staff members and the report from the ISS Assembly meeting in Denmark, July, 1947, that it has agreed to recognize an extended WSSF as its representative in the United States, it was resolved that USNSA, as a sponsor of WSSF, encourage and endorse expansion of WSSF activities to work toward formation of World Student Service or combination of ISS and WSSF. Until that time, the USNSA should utilize facilities of ISS, nationally and internationally, and it is considered that this is in no way in conflict with the relationship of the USNSA to IUS.

INTERNATIONAL UNION OF STUDENTS (IUS)

Resolution on USNSA Affiliation with IUS.

I. PREAMBLE

WHEREAS the International Union of Students, established at the Prague World Student Congress of 1946, is the most widely representative student organization in the world and

WHEREAS study and observation of the IUS by National Continuations Committee members during the past eight months have revealed that its program of cultural and educational activities in the international field can be important in the furthering of international understanding and

WHEREAS the students of the United States, in view of the leading role being played by this nation in world affairs, have a similar responsibility in the world student community, specifically to (1) learn more about the world at large, (2) teach the rest of the world more about the U.S.A., and (3) learn to work together with people who do not necessarily share their ideology and political philosophies and

WHEREAS the International Union of Students is the only point of contact with the students of the nations of Eastern Europe and

WHEREAS such contact may lead to an arresting of that deterioration of relations between our nation and those countries, which at the present time constitutes a serious threat to the peace of the world and

WHEREAS the National Student Association will be the largest and most representative student organization in the United States and therefore can most effectively represent US students in the international field,

THEREFORE BE IT RESOLVED: that the Constitutional Convention of USNSA, desirous of wholehearted and fullest cooperation with students throughout the world, while recognizing that American students, participating in IUS through the USNSA, do not intend to become involved in political issues of a partisan nature, and although at present there are fundamental differences between USNSA on the one hand and the IUS and some of its member organizations on the other hand, nevertheless, recommends affiliation as soon as possible with the IUS, subject to the procedure stated in "Agreement on IUS Affiliation."

II. AGREEMENT ON IUS AFFILIATION

1. Privileges of Membership.
   a. Upon the USNSA attaining the membership of the majority of US students and officially ratifying its affiliation with the IUS, the USNSA shall be the sole organization entitled to represent the students of the United States in the IUS. The present American member organizations shall withdraw from the IUS. However, American student organizations other than the USNSA may participate in the IUS, coordinating their activities through USNSA. The USNSA shall reserve the right to select all United States members on the IUS governing body and to approve all United States students who will be employed in any capacity by the IUS.
   b. The USNSA shall be authorized to act as republishing and distributing agency within the United States for all IUS publications and the Executive Committee of USNSA shall insure that such publications are made available to all students that may desire them.
   c. The USNSA shall be accorded equitable representation in the governing bodies of the IUS.
2. Political Autonomy of the USNSA.
   a. This affiliation shall not be construed in any way as constituting an endorsement of the decisions made by the IUS prior to the effective date of this affiliation.
   b. No decision of the IUS which may be specifically repudiated by the USNSA shall bind or shall be published as representing the opinions of American students.
   c. In any case where a decision is published by the IUS Congress, Council, or Executive Committee, the right of a minority to append a report with equitable access to publication shall not be denied.
   d. Affiliation of USNSA with IUS shall not be construed as constituting any official connection with the autonomous associates of the IUS.
3. Administrative Autonomy of the USNSA.
   a. On the national level the USNSA shall have complete administrative autonomy.
4. Finance.
   a. Until the next Congress of the IUS the financial obligations of the USNSA shall be determined by negotiations for a fixed sum consonant with the financial conditions of USNSA.
   b. After the next IUS Congress the financial obligations of USNSA shall be negotiated on the basis of the scale of representation.
5. Disaffiliation.
   a. This affiliation agreement may be suspended immediately upon notification of the IUS by the President of USNSA acting in accordance with procedures outlined in the constitution of USNSA; and official disaffiliation shall take place in conformity with constitutions of the USNSA and the IUS.
   b. Equal responsibility for publicizing suspension or disaffiliation shall rest upon the executives of the USNSA and the IUS.
6. Effectiveness of this Agreement and its Contingencies.
   a. Subject to the conditions herein before stated, the Constitutional Congress of the USNSA favors affiliation with the International Union of Students. This Congress therefore authorizes the Executive Committee of USNSA to undertake negotiations with the IUS and to guarantee maximum American participation in that organization during the coming year (including preparation and sending of an American negotiating delegation to the IUS Council meeting during the summer of 1948). Final ratification of any affiliation agreement reached by the USNSA Executive Committee and the IUS will be considered by the next Congress of the USNSA. Any agreement reached by the USNSA Executive Committee and the IUS shall be submitted to the next session of the National Student Congress. Ratification shall be in accordance with the Constitution of the USNSA.
   b. If any condition contained herein shall necessitate an exercise of the constituent power of the Congress of the IUS in favor of this agreement, this agreement shall be considered to be tentatively in effect until the earliest occasion on which such power may be exercised.

III. STATEMENT TO AMERICAN STUDENTS

The following statement is an attempt to present frankly and completely the views and reasoning of the Constitutional Convention of USNSA in favoring the affiliation with IUS.

In the opinion of the Constitutional Convention, the decisive considerations favoring USNSA affiliation with IUS were twofold:

1. The great and urgent need for specific and largescale means of contact and familiarization of the students of countries whose present mutual differences, suspicions, and lack of information may well lead to continuing and increasing unrest and even war throughout the world.

2. The more immediately practical advantage of affiliation with IUS—the many international projects and activities in which American students and colleges can profitably take part as a member organization of IUS.

In considering the question of affiliation, the Constitutional Convention was well aware of a number of important and quite likely controversial factors:

1. We recognize that the majority of the present leadership of IUS and many of the member organizations of IUS are far to the left of American students and that within that majority, Communists exercise influence far out of proportion to Communists within the world student community.

2. The IUS has tended to lay greater stress upon political activities and expressions of opinions than is customary or desirable in student organizations in the United States which are avowedly nonpartisan and nonsectarian. The traditions and temper of most student movements outside the U.S., the fundamental ideological conflicts in many countries, and the present leadership of IUS are at the base of this important difference.

3. The United States, through the USNSA, cannot as a member of IUS enjoy, in some instances, the support of the present majority of IUS in view

of the above considerations. For the same reasons, the USNSA may continue for some time to remain in a minority position on many major issues within IUS.

4. As a member of IUS, the USNSA will have both to exercise the strictest constant care to avoid the abuse of its prestige and backing for activities contrary to or outside its scope and program, and be prepared for possible difficulties and disappointments.

But together with the above factors, the Constitutional Convention, believing that the conditions it has adopted will protect the USNSA from possible abuse through its affiliation with IUS, considered the factors listed below, and came to the conclusion that these are as important and even decisively more so than those listed above:

1. Mutual understanding and acquaintanceship with other countries, particularly with those like the Soviet Union which, up to date has been most inaccessible to, and in frequent disagreement with the U.S., can be decisive in helping to avert ever more intensified friction which may lead to a disastrous atomic world war.

2. A minority position in an international organization, as may be that of USNSA in IUS, offers an opportunity for extensive and significant modifications of an otherwise possibly extreme orientation of the organization.

3. The practical advantages and services of IUS, already offered or in the process of development, are numerous and can be of the greatest value in furthering contact of American students with foreign students and their countries

> Educational and student exchange, national and international tours, exchange of student publications and information, world-wide sports events, student relief, reconstruction and study of educational facilities, faculty conferences and exchange, joint projects and exchanges on art, drama, dance, science, etc.

4. Membership in IUS will not preclude USNSA participation in other international organizations, such as International Student Service and World Student Relief.

5. Disaffiliation of USNSA from IUS can be achieved simply and promptly according to the USNSA Constitution in case a sizable segment of the USNSA may so desire after affiliation has taken place.

6. IUS is at present by far the largest international association of national student organizations, and includes countries such as the Soviet Union, Asiatic and colonial lands with whom far reaching cooperation and joint activities for students are difficult, if not impossible, outside of IUS today.

Basic to the consideration of affiliation by the Constitutional Convention was its attitude towards the underlying outlook of USNSA in case of affiliation with IUS. The Convention felt that it must be based on a sincere and wholehearted intention to work with IUS and other member countries in friendship and without hidden purpose.

Attempts at division into blocs with consistently differing points of view may well defeat the entire purpose of USNSA affiliation with IUS. This does not mean that USNSA may not attempt to represent and promote its point of view on every appropriate issue, nor that it should reject cooperation of other member organizations agreeing with it on particular specific issues or on overall attitudes.

The emphasis in IUS, as elsewhere throughout the world, must be on cooperation, moderation, and mutual give and take. It is in this spirit, having considered the matter at length and in all detail, that the Constitutional Convention of USNSA proposes affiliation with IUS under the procedure set forth in the "Agreement on IUS Affiliation" adopted by the Constitutional Convention of USNSA.

RESOLUTION: That the USNSA express a vote of confidence in the work of Mr. Bill Ellis as Vice President of the IUS to date; and that Bill Ellis be unanimously endorsed as the interim representative of the USNSA pending the mission of the negotiating delegation to Prague next summer.

That the present members of the IUS Council, with the exception of the American Vice President, be requested to relinquish their seats in the IUS Council in favor of the USNSA negotiating delegation; except that one American position in the Council be irrevocably reserved to represent the present student organizations affiliated with IUS until such time as the USNSA represents a majority of American students.

5. Organization and Finance

Getting Started

Editor's Note: NSA was launched with clear purposes and simple organizational outlines. The budget below, as adopted by the Constitutional Convention and reported in its minutes, and the organization chart published in the October, 1948 issue of *NSA News* reflect this optimism. The complexities of organizational development revealed themselves in due course and, as noted below, commanded serious attention in the years following.

USNSA BUDGET FOR THE YEAR 1947-1948 (adopted by the Consitutional Convention 9-7-47, and revised by NEC 12-27-27)

Budget Item	CC	NEC Revison
Officers salaries	$12,000	11,000
Secretarial help	8,500	4,400
Office rental	2,400	1,400
Travel	5,000	5,000
Postage	500	2,450
Telephone-telegraph	600	1,150
Printing	3,000	5,000
Office equipment	1,944	3,044
Magazines and periodicals	200	200
Press clipping service	200	200
Miscellaneous	500	1,000
Total	$34,844	$36,844

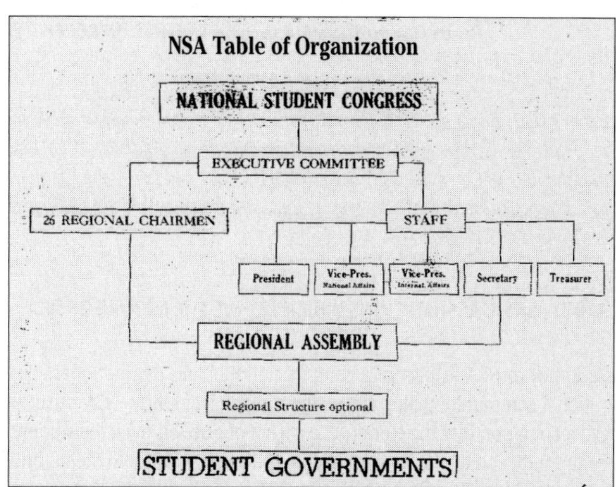

Budgets and financial notes for the years 1947-48 through 1952-53 will each be found at close of Part 1, Sections 5-9, and Part 6, Section 1. Typical annual budgets for the early years, which were expected to pay for the full-time staff salaries of five to seven people, plus office expense (exclusive of international programs) were:
1947-48: $36,884 1948-49: 25,300 1949-50: 28,002
1950-51: 26,500 1951-52: 21,009

Facing Reality

Editor's Note: NSA officers assumed that as a non-profit, non-political organization, their sole tax obligation was to withhold income taxes, which they did. Excerpts from NSA's correspondence with the Internal Revenue Service during the five years it took to clarify its tax status are revealing of both NSA's failure to anticipate the tax consequence of its annual changing of the guard, as well as of the tenacity of the IRS:

April 14, 1949
To: Collector of Internal Revenue, District of Wisconsin

Enclosed you will find filled out form 1024 "Exemption Affidavit" submitted for the United States National Student Association *[with 9 enclosures - ed.]*. . . .

Yours very truly,
James T. Harris, Jr., President

* * * *

August 31, 1949
To: United States National Student Association

Before a ruling can be made it will be necessary for you to furnish a financial statement showing a classified list of your receipts and disbursements for your last complete year of operation and your assets and liabilities as of the end of that year.

You are also requested to submit a statement sworn to by one of your principal officers setting forth the following information:

1. . . . State definetely what was done in 1948 and 1949 to carry out [the extensive activities in the 1948-49 Program]. . .

3. . . . . Whether you have actually been made a member of, or have you renewed negotiations with the International Union of Students.

4. . . . . Have you been appointed a committee of UNESCO. . .

This information should [be furnished within 30 days] and marked for the attention of IT:P:ER:CWL.

Very truly yours,
E.I, McLarney, Deputy Commissioner of Internal Revenue

* * * *

October 14, 1949
To: Mr. E.I. McLarney, Deputy Copmmisioner of Internal Revenue

In reply to IT:PER-CWL sent from your office on October 12 *[exemption not recognized—ed.]* . . . . We would ask your indulgence for any oversight which may have occurred and we would request that your office forward us directions so that we may supply the information necessary . .

Very truly yours,
Robert A. Kelly, President, U.S.N.S.A.

* * * *

July 6, 1950
To: Robert A. Kelly, United States National Student Association

. . . your organization has been granted exemption from filing income tax returns under section 101(8) of the Internal Revenue Code. . . . The extent of liability is limited . . . it is requested that you advise whether compensation has been paid to to officers or other employees for services performed . . . the amount paid to each and the date on which paid. . . .

Sincerely yours,
Collector of Internal Revenue, District of Wisconsin

* * * *

July 31, 1950
To: Collector of Internal Revenue, Milwaukee, Wisc.

[In a 3 page letter-ed.]. . . . If your request means that you want a complete itemized payroll for the last three years, showing the date and amount of each salary payment, I must report that to date this has proved beyond my capabilities. Whether an exact report of each individual payment could ever be made is uncertain, since a good part of the early financial records of the Association were lost in transit last August, before the present set of officers were elected.

Sincerely yours,
Frederick D. Houghteling, Executive Secretary, USNSA

* * * *

January 15, 1951
To: Collector of Internal Revenue, Milwaukee, Wisconsin

[NSA was advised by the IRS] it is not entitled to exemption [under 101(6)] . . . I would appreciate a further clarification of this ruling. . .

Sincerely yours,
Herbert Goldsmith, Vice President, USNSA

* * * *

April 20, 1954
To: USNSA, Gimbel Building, Philadelphia 7, Pennsylvania

It is our conclusion . . . that you are exempt from Federal income tax under the provisions of section 101 (6) of the Code, beginning with October 1, 1952. .

Very truly yours,
Chief, Exempt Organizations Branch

Editor's note: For more on NSA's tax status and its incorporation, see note 8, p. 276 and note 3, p. 281.

The "The unit of structure of NSA is the individual student body"

The Organization Review Commission—1950

"The active emphasis of [NSA] must be severely delimited to 3 or 4 major objectives at any one time"

Editor's Note: Below are the highlights of the specific recommendations made by the NSA Special Advisory Committee on Organizational Affairs (SACOA) in May, 1950. The Committe was composed of 41 current and former NSA national and regional leaders (see Schwartz, p. 242, and Lynch, p. 267 for additional background to SACOA):

PART I - BASIC ASSUMPTIONS WHICH DEFINE THE NATURE OF NSA

Referring to NSA as part of a campus, national and international educational community that exists within a civic community, "NSA exists in the recognition that the student is a citizen of both his own, the student community and the larger educational community." Student "needs and interests" arise out of this context, and it was recommended that programs and projects are valid only insofar as they connect to them. Thus, the National Student Congress and program and planning bodies should "define each program of the Association and emphasize the objective to be achieved."

"The unit of structure of NSA is the individual student body" as represented by its student government. The committee was unconditional in its conviction that a representative organization must be maintained if it is to be a credible reflection of "a student community on the national level and that it function through elected student governments." This would mean "that the National Organization would cease to recognize the existence of NSA Committees as formal units of NSA structure."

PART II - GENERAL CONSIDERATIONS DEALING WITH PROGRAM TECHNIQUES

While "the realm of NSA activity encompasses the whole gamut of student life . . . it must be realized that the active emphasis of the Association must be severely delimited to three or four major objectives at any one time." The committee then laid out some specific administrative guidelines and criteria to aid staff "in establishing and evaluating the projects that compose a program."

The committee put certain programs to a test in the light of the foregoing, for example

(1) The Purchase Card System involved major liability for a minor "end in itself" and should be dropped.

(2) The international study tours "so absorbs the time and energy of the staff that it threatens to become an end in itself." The committee recommended that the tours be "reduced to the status of tools and means."

(3) "Outside agencies and student subcommittees" should be considered to relieve the administrative burden on the vice president.

(4) The need for stronger and more focused internal public relations.

(5) NSA programs should have "high social content" and "high intellectual content."

(6) It recommended NSA regional and campus level "forums and discussions of the various disciplines that compose a college curriculum."

PART III - CONSIDERATIONS DEALING WITH STRUCTURE AND ADMINISTRATION

(1) Regions: The committee reviewed four possible scenarios for regional organization, including the possibilities of 6 or 7 large geographical areas serviced by sectional travelling secretaries. It made no recommendation but suggested seven criteria for choice, including: representation of students to other bodies, local public relations, recruitment of new colleges, carrying out activities and exchange of ideas, stimulation of campus programs.

(2) Finance: Dues should cover expenses. (Viewed in retrospect, something of a non-sequitur. This general recommendation did not really deal with the critical financial situation which was examined in detail by Mike DiLegge's subcommittee and about which they made procedural and fund-raising recommendations).[2]

(3) "The committee was unanimous in feeling that the consideration of Washington, D.C. and New York City as possible locations for the national office is highly inadvisable." They advised that NSA consider the effects of location on (1) the character of the organization, (2) effectiveness of coordination and control, and (3) economy of operation. Based on the foregoing a minority wanted to stay in the mid-west, while a majority recommended a move to the middle-Atlantic area. Consolidating with the International office was a secondary consideration they felt.

(4) A series of recommendations on delineation of commissions and selection of the Public Relations and Publications Director.

(5) "The difficulties arising from the rapid turnover of top level personnel can no longer be ignored." The committee recommended several steps to make overlap and transitions between incoming and out-going staffs possible

ENDNOTES

[1] As it turned out the Purchase Card System, which became known as the Student Discount System, remained a functioning program at least well into the late fifties or early sixties (see p. 366).

[2] Mike Di Legge recalls a trip to the Cambridge office to review the accounting systems there and the concern at the time over the need for a system that could pass audit muster when required. As he noted in a 4/23/50 letter to Helen Jean Rogers, "Administration and Finance is not a subject which lends itself to metaphysical speculation."

REFERENCE

CONTENTS

Directory, Almanac, Resources and Higher Education in 1948

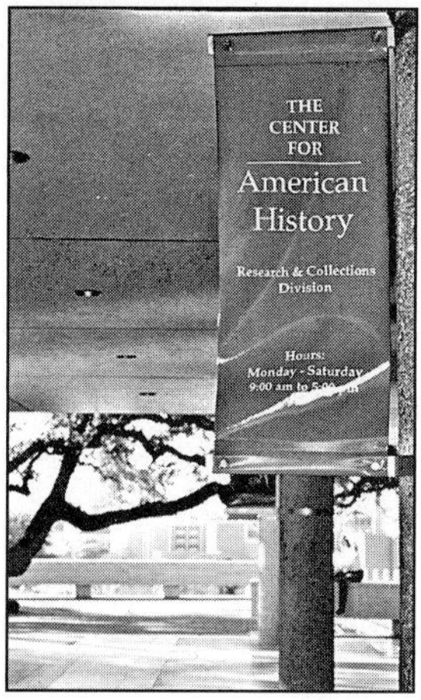

THE CENTER FOR AMERICAN HISTORY at the U. of Texas in Austin contains the University archives and Prague delegation, Chicago Student Conference and Jim Smith documents.

THE STATE HISTORICAL SOCIETY OF WISCONSIN, located near the U. of Wisconsin campus, Madison. It maintains the official archives of the NSA from its inception. (*Robert Granflaten, SHWS)*

COLLEGE AND UNIVERSITY LIBRARIES throughout the U.S. provided much of the documentation that is cited in this book. From top, clockwise, Nielson Library at Smith C., *Smith Scan;* The Hoover Institute on the Stanford U. campus, the complete NSA International Commission files through 1967; The Louis Round Wilson Library, at the U. of North Carolina, repository of the Lowenstein papers; Catholic University, repository for the National Catholic Youth Council and the NFCCS; Yale Divinity School Library, holding records of the Student YMCA and World Student Christian Federation. (Photos, including Texas [above, right], *Schwartz)*

The sponsors of this work have relied heavily on material found in college library archives of student government records, papers of presidents, deans, and student personnel administrators, yearbooks, and bound and microfilm files of college newspapers. A trove of material doubtless resides in some of these collections, yet to be explored. The orderly archiving and cataloging of student activity records seems largely to have been left to chance before the early 1950's.

For ease of reference, we have provided a summary listing of national officers and advisors, in chronological order for NSA's first ten years.

Abbreviations for the many organizations cited in the text and index are listed, as well as an almanac of major dates and events referred to in this book.

The editors have also listed the college and other libraries and archives they visited or contacted, with an indication of the scope of material to be found.

The bibliography, in addition to primary resources referenced by the editors, incorporates selected citations from some other bibliographies, largely unpublished, that can be useful. We have sought to collect as much information as possible that could lead researchers and storytellers to useful resources. These other bibliographies have led us to secondary sources that enabled us to verify names, dates, and places that rest uncertainly in memories fifty years later.

Higher Education in 1948

U.S. College enrollment in 2002-3 stood at 15,927,928, and the total number of colleges and universities at 4,168 according to the U.S. Department of Education. In 1948, the U.S. Office of Education reported enrollments and institutions at 2, 410,000 and 1,728 respectively. Veteran enrollment had already decreased to 953, 247 from its previous year's high of 1,149,933. The size and demographic profile of the college student population which nurtured the student activity recalled in this volume has transformed itself in many ways. In this section the editors have provided the metrics in tables reproduced from that earlier era.

Finally, we have separate indexes for access by: (1) name, (2) college and college newspapers, (3) subject, and (4) Anthology authors; also, additional index finding aids leading to the many rosters and to the benchmark events and key personalities cited in the book that frame the stories of NSA and of other student organizations and leaders during the pre- and post-World War II era.

1. Directory: National Officers and Advisors

OFFICERS OF THE UNITED STATES NATIONAL STUDENT ASSOCIATION, 1947–1957

Source: Stephen Clements Schodde, Certain Foci of the United States National Student Association and Their Implications for Student Personnel Administrators. *Doctoral thesis, Teachers College, Columbia University, 1965.*[1] *Schodde provides a listing of officers and advisors through 1964-65.*

The following are elected officers of the Association from 1947 to 1957. Since the Chicago Conference, all Congresses have been held approximately during the last two weeks in August. The reader will also note that titles of elected officers were occasionally changed.

1946–1947—A National Continuations Committee was established at the University of Chicago, December 30, 1946. Following are the officers of that committee:

James Smith, President, University of Texas
Russell Austin, Vice-President, University of Chicago
Clifton R. Wharton, Secretary, Harvard University
John Simons, Treasurer, Fordham University

1947–1948—Elected at the Constitutional Convention at the University of Wisconsin, Madison:

William B. Welsh, President, Berea College
Ralph A. Dungan, Jr., Vice-President, National Student Affairs, St. Joseph's College
Robert S. Smith, Vice-President, International Student Affairs, Yale University
Janis C. Tremper, Secretary, Rockford College
Leeland N. Jones, Jr., Treasurer, University of Buffalo

1948-1949—Elected at the First Congress, University of Wisconsin, Madison:

James T. Harris, Jr., President, La Salle College
Richard G. Heggie, Vice-President, Student Life, University of California
Eugene G. Schwartz, Vice-President, Educational Problems, City College of New York
Robert L. West, Vice-President, International Affairs, Yale University
Helen Jean Rogers, Secretary-Treasurer, Mundelein College

1949–1950—Elected at the Second Congress, University of Illinois, Champain-Urbana:

Robert A. Kelly, President, St. Peter's College
Theodore Perry, Vice-President, Student Life, Temple University
Richard J. Medalie, Vice-President, Educational Problems, Carleton College
Erskine B. Childers, Vice-President, International Affairs, Stanford University
Robert E. Delahanty, Executive Secretary, University of Louisville
Frederic D. Houghteling, Executive Secretary, Harvard College

1950–1951—Elected at the Third Congress, University of Michigan, Ann Arbor:

Allard K. Lowenstein, President, University of North Carolina
Elmer Paul Brock, Vice-President, Student Affairs, La Salle College
Herbert B. Goldsmith, Vice-President, Educational Affairs, University of Wisconsin
Herbert W. Eisenberg, Vice-President, International Affairs, Massachusetts Institute of Technology
Shirley V. Neizer, Executive Secretary, Simmons College

1951–1952—Elected at the Fourth Congress, University of Minnesota, Minneapolis:

William T. Dentzer, President, Muskingum College
Sylvia Bacon, Vice-President, Student Affairs, Vassar College
Rollo O'Hare, Vice-President, Educational Affairs, Wayne University
Avrea Ingram, Vice-President, International Affairs, Harvard University
John Haley, Vice-President, Student Government, Emory University

1952–1953—Elected at the Fifth Congress, Indiana University, Bloomington:

Richard J. Murphy, President, University of North Carolina
Leonard A. Wilcox, Jr., Vice-President, National Affairs, August 1952–March 1953, University of Michigan
Philip C. Berry, Acting Vice-President, National Affairs, June 1953–August 1953, University of Michigan[2]
Janet Welsh, Vice-President, Student Affairs, Smith College
Manfred Brust, Vice-President, Educational Affairs, University of Illinois
Avrea Ingram, Vice-President, International Affairs, Harvard University
Stephen Voykovich, Jr., Vice-President, Student Government, Fordham University

1953–1954—Elected at the Sixth Congress, Ohio State University, Columbus:

James M. Edwards, President, University of Illinois
Eugene H. Keating, Vice-President, National Affairs, College of St. Thomas
Leonard N. Bebchick, Vice-President, International Affairs, Cornell University
Lois MacPherson, Vice-President, Student Affairs, Upsala College
Cynthia A. Courtney, Vice-President, Educational Affairs, Dunbarton College
Amy Botsaris, Vice-President, Student Government, Pennsylvania College for Women

1954–1955—Elected at the Seventh Congress, Iowa State University:

Harry H. Lunn, Jr., President, University of Michigan
Paul E. Sigmund, Jr., International Affairs Vice-President, Georgetown University
Wallace Longshore, National Affairs Vice-President, University of California, Los Angeles
Al Nagy, Student Affairs Vice-President, Denison University
Ann Beckner, Student Affairs Vice-President, from July 21, Denison University
Bernard S. Yudowitz, Educational Affairs Vice-President, Cornell University
Maurice Blumberg, Student Government Vice-President, University of Colorado

1955–1956—Elected at the Eighth Congress, University of Minnesota:

Stanford L. Glass, President, University of Illinois
Clive S. Gray, International Affairs Vice-President, University of Chicago
Gene R. Preston, National Affairs Vice-President, University of California, Los Angeles
James R. Turner, Student Affairs Vice-President, University of North Carolina

Joel Sterns, Educational Affairs Vice-President, Northwestern University
Raymond Farabee, Student Government Vice-President, University of Texas

1956–1957—Elected at the Ninth Congress, University of Chicago:

Harold Bakken, President, University of Minnesota
Cliff Sheets, Executive Vice-President, Wayne State University
Daniel D. Idzik, Executive Vice-President, from January 1, University of Buffalo
Bruce D. Larkin, International Affairs Vice-President, University of Chicago
James Pomroy, Student Affairs Vice-President, Allegheny College
Ann Beckner, Educational Affairs Vice-President, Denison University
Robert F. Bennett, Student Government Vice-President, University of Utah

1957–1958—Elected at the Tenth Congress, University of Michigan, Ann Arbor:

Raymond Farabee, President, University of Texas
Donald F. Clifford, Executive Vice-President, Catholic University of America
Bruce D. Larkin, International Affairs Vice-President, University of Chicago
Willard R. Johnson, Educational Affairs Vice-President, University of California, Los Angeles
Robert R. Kiley, Student Government Vice-President, University of Notre Dame
Reginald H. Green, Student Affairs Vice-President, Whitman College

MEMBERS OF THE NSA NATIONAL ADVISORY COUNCIL (Later Changed to National Advisors)

This group after 1954–1955 became largely honorary, and its duties were assumed by the National Advisory Board.[3]

1948–1949

Everett Moore Baker, Dean of Students, Massachusetts Institute of Technology
Monroe E. Deutsch, Provost-Emeritus, University of California, Berkeley
Laurence Duggan, Director, Institute of International Education
Rev. Vincent J. Flynn, President, College of St. Thomas
R. O. Johnson, Assistant Director, Project for Adult Education of Negroes, United States Office of Education
Gordon J. Klopf, Student Activities Counsellor, University of Wisconsin
Dean Newhouse, Director of Student Affairs, University of Washington
Homer Rainey, President, Stephens College
Helen C. White, Professor of English, University of Wisconsin

1949–1950

Gordon J. Klopf, Chairman, Student Activities Counsellor, University of Wisconsin
William B. Birenbaum, Student Activities Advisor, University of Chicago
Monroe E. Deutsch, Provost-Emeritus, University of California, Berkeley
Very Rev. Vincent J. Flynn, President, American Association of Colleges
Frank P. Graham, Past President, University of North Carolina (U.S. Senator, North Carolina)
James T. Harris, Jr., President, 1948–1949, United States National Student Association
R. O. Johnson, Professor of Education, Atlanta University
Dean Newhouse, Dean of Students, Case Institute of Technology
Harold Taylor, President, Sarah Lawrence College
Helen C. White, United States National Commission for UNESCO
Millicent McIntosh, Dean, Barnard College
Mrs. Carl W. Meineke, Dean, Colby Junior College
Donald Shank, Director, Institute of International Education

1950–1951

Gordon J. Klopf, Chairman, Student Activities Counsellor, University of Wisconsin
William B. Birenbaum, Director of Student Activities, University of Chicago
Monroe E. Deutsch, Provost-Emeritus, University of California, Berkeley
Very Rev. Vincent J. Flynn, President, College of St.Thomas
Frank P. Graham, Past President, University of North Carolina
Kenneth Holland, Director, Institute of International Education
Charles S. Johnson, President, Fisk University
Robert A. Kelly, President, 1949–1950, United States National Student Association
Mrs. Carl W. Meineke, Dean, Colby Junior College
Dean Newhouse, Dean of Students, Case Institute of Technology

1951–1952

Dennis L. Trueblood, Chairman, Student Activities Counsellor, Indiana University
William B. Birenbaum, Director of Student Activities, University of Chicago
Very Rev. Vincent J. Flynn, President, College of St. Thomas
Frank P. Graham, United Nations Mediator
Kenneth Holland, Director, Institute of International Education
Althea Kratz Hottel, Dean of Women, University of Pennsylvania
Charles S. Johnson, President, Fisk University
Gordon J. Klopf, Student Activities Counsellor, University of Wisconsin
A. Blair Knapp, President, Denison University
Allard K. Lowenstein, President, 1950-1951, United States National Student Association
Mrs. Carl W. Meineke, Dean, Colby Junior College
Eleanor Roosevelt, United States Representative, United Nations General Assembly
Harold Stassen, President, University of Pennsylvania
Rev. Celestine Steiner, S.J., President, University of Detroit
Harold Taylor, President, Sarah Lawrence University

1952–1953

William B. Birenbaum, Chairman, Director of Student Activities, University of Chicago
William T. Dentzer, President, 1951–1952, United States National Student Association
Very Rev. Vincent J. Flynn, President, College of St. Thomas
Frank P. Graham, United Nations Mediator
Kenneth Holland, Director, Institute of International Education
Althea Kratz Hottel, Dean of Women, University of Pennsylvania
Charles S. Johnson, President, Fisk University
Gordon J. Klopf, Dean of Students, Buffalo State College
A. Blair Knapp, President, Denison University
Mrs. Carl W. Meineke, Dean, Colby Junior College
Eleanor Roosevelt, United States Representative, United Nations General Assembly
Harold Stassen, President, University of Pennsylvania
Rev. Celestine Steiner, S.J., President, University of Detroit
Harold Taylor, President, Sarah Lawrence College
Dennis L. Trueblood, Student Activities Counsellor, Indiana University

1953–1954

Lucile Allen, Dean, Pennsylvania College for Women
Wallace M. Alston, President, Agnes Scott College
Ralph J. Bunche, Director, Department of Trusteeship, United Nations
Erwin D. Canham, Editor, *Christian Science Monitor*
Christine Y. Conaway, Dean of Women, Ohio State University
Althea Kratz Hottel, Director, Commission on Education of Women, American Council on Education
Clifford Houston, Dean of Students, University of Colorado
A. Blair Knapp, President, Denison University
Eleanor Roosevelt
George N. Shuster, President, Hunter College
Harold E. Stassen, Director, Foreign Operations Administration
Rev. Celestine J. Steiner, S.J., President, University of Detroit
Hurford E. Stone, Dean of Students, University of California
Robert M. Strozier, Dean of Students, University of Chicago
Edmund G. Williamson, Dean of Students, University of Minnesota

1954–1955

Lucile Allen, Dean, Pennsylvania College for Women
Wallace M. Alston, President, Agnes Scott College
Ralph J. Bunche, Under-Secretary, United Nations
Erwin D. Canham, Editor, *Christian Science Monitor*
Christine Y. Conaway, Dean of Women, Ohio State University
Clifford Houston, Dean of Students, University of Colorado
Mother Eleanor M. O'Byrne, President, Manhattanville College of the Sacred Heart
Eleanor Roosevelt
George N. Shuster, President, Hunter College
Harold E. Stassen, Director, Foreign Operations Administration
Robert M. Strozier, Dean of Students, University of Chicago
Lynn T. White, Jr., President, Mills College
Edmund G. Williamson, Dean of Students, University of Minnesota

1955–1956

Lucile Allen, Dean, Pennsylvania College for Women
Wallace M. Alston, President, Agnes Scott College
Ralph J. Bunche, Under-Secretary, United Nations
Erwin D. Canham, Editor, *Christian Science Monitor*
Christine Y. Conaway, Dean of Women, Ohio State University
Clifford Houston, Dean of Students, University of Colorado
Mother Eleanor M. O'Byrne, President, Manhattanville College of the Sacred Heart
Eleanor Roosevelt
George N. Shuster, President, Hunter College
Harold E. Stassen, Special Assistant to the President of the United States
Robert M. Strozier, Dean of Students, University of Chicago
Lynn T. White, Jr., President, Mills College
Edmund G. Williamson, Dean of Students, University of Minnesota

1956–1957

Lucile Allen, Dean, Chatham College
Wallace M. Alston, President, Agnes Scott College
Willard W. Blaesser, Dean of Students, University of Utah
Ralph J. Bunche, Under-Secretary, United Nations
M. Porter Butts, Director, College Union, University of Wisconsin
Erwin D. Canham, Editor, *Christian Science Monitor*
Christine Y. Conaway, Dean of Women, Ohio State University
Mother Eleanor M. O'Byrne, President, Manhattanville College of the Sacred Heart
Eleanor Roosevelt
George N. Shuster, President Hunter College
Harold E. Stassen, Special Assistant to the President of the United States
Robert M. Strozier, Dean of Students, University of Chicago
Lynn T. White, Jr., President, Mills College
Edmund G. Williamson, Dean of Students, University of Minnesota

1957–1958

Wallace M. Alston, President, Agnes Scott College
Harry Bullis, Chairman of Board, General Mills
Ralph J. Bunche, Under-Secretary, United Nations
Erwin D. Canham, Editor, *Christian Science Monitor*
Christine Y. Conaway, Dean of Women, Ohio State University
Rev. T.M. Hesburgh, C.S.C., President, University of Notre Dame
Reinhold Niebuhr, Vice-President, Union Theological Seminary
Walter P. Reuther, President, United Automobile Workers
Eleanor Roosevelt
George N. Shuster, President, Hunter College
Harold E. Stassen
Robert M. Strozier, President, Florida State University
Edmund G. Williamson, Dean of Students, University of Minnesota
O. Meredith Wilson, President, University of Oregon

MEMBERS OF THE NSA NATIONAL ADVISORY BOARD[4]

March 1954–August 1954

Gordon J. Klopf, Chairman, Dean of Students, State University of New York College for Teachers at Buffalo
William B. Birenbaum, Director of Student Activities, University of Chicago
William E. Buys, Department of Forensics, Wayne University, Michigan
Ruth Geri Hagy Brod, *Philadelphia Bulletin*
Philip Jacob, Professor of Political Science, University of Pennsylvania
Marguerite Kehr, retired, former Dean of Women at Bloomsburg State College, Bloomsburg, Pennsylvania. Also former adviser to the National Student Federation of America (NSFA), which flourished prior to World War II and was then the approved national student organization.
John A. Lang, Jr., Secretary to Representative Charles B. Dean, North Carolina, United States House of Representatives. He was also a former president of the National Student Federation of America (NSFA).
Dennis L. Trueblood, Student Activities Counsellor, Indiana University

1954–1955

James Dougherty, Chairman, Instructor in Social Science, St. Joseph's College, Philadelphia
William B. Birenbaum, Director of Student Activities, University of Chicago
Elmer Paul Brock, Past NSA officer, Assistant to the President, Harcum Junior College, Pennsylvania
Ruth Geri Hagy Brod, *Philadelphia Bulletin*

Philip H. Des Marais, Executive Vice-President, St. Mary's Dominican College, Louisiana
Philip Jacob, Professor of Political Science, University of Pennsylvania
Marguerite Kehr, retired, former Dean of Women at Bloomsburg State College, Bloomsburg, Pennsylvania, and former adviser to the NSFA
Gordon J. Klopf, Dean of Students, State University of New York College for Teachers at Buffalo, Educational Consultant, United States Department of State
John A. Lang, Jr., Past President of the NFSA
Dennis L. Trueblood, Director, Office of Aids and Awards, University of Kansas

1955–1956

James Dougherty, Chairman, Instructor in Social Science, St. Joseph's College, Philadelphia
Philip C. Berry, Past "acting" NSA Vice President[5]
John C. Clevenger, Dean of Students, State College of Washington (now Washington State University)
William G. Craig, Dean of Men, Stanford University
Philip H. Des Marais, Executive Vice-President, St. Mary's Dominican College
Marguerite Kehr, retired former Dean of Women, Bloomsburg State College, Bloomsburg, Pennsylvania, and former adviser to the NSFA
Gordon J. Klopf, Dean of Students, State University of New York College for Teachers at Buffalo
John A. Lang, Jr., Past President of the NSFA
Charles W. McCracken, Dean of Students, Allegheny College
Dennis L. Trueblood, Director, Office of Aids and Awards, University of Kansas

1956–1957

James Dougherty, Chairman, Instructor in Social Science, St. Joseph's College, Philadelphia
Philip C. Berry, "acting" NSA officer
Douglas Cater, former NSA "founder," Washington Editor, The Reporter
Philip H. Des Marais, Executive Vice-President, St. Mary's Dominican College
Jack R. Gibb, Research Professor, University of Delaware
Marguerite Kehr, retired, former Dean of Women, Bloomsburg State College, Bloomsburg, Pennsylvania, and former adviser to the NSFA
Gordon J. Klopf, Dean of Students, State University of New York College for Teachers at Buffalo, Educational Consultant
John A. Lang, Jr., Past President of the NSFA
Glen A. Olds, Director, United Religious Work, Cornell University
Charles W. McCracken, Dean of Students, Allegheny College

1957–1958

James Dougherty, Chairman, Instructor in Social Science, St. Joseph's College, Philadelphia
Philip H. Des Marais, Executive Vice-President, St. Mary's Dominican College
Marguerite Kehr, retired, former Dean of Women at Bloomsburg State College, Bloomsburg, Pennsylvania, and former adviser to the NSFA
Gordon J. Klopf, Dean of Students, State University of New York College for Teachers at Buffalo
James Lewis, Vice-President for Student Affairs, University of Michigan
Paul MacMinn, Specialist for Guidance and Student Personnel Affairs, Department of Health, Education, and Welfare
Charles W. McCracken, Dean of Students, Trenton State Teachers College
Glen A. Olds, Director, United Religious Work, Cornell University
Harold Taylor, President, Sarah Lawrence College

ENDNOTES

(By Stephen Schodde)

[1] Sources: Edward R. Garvey et al. (eds.), *History and Development of USNSA* (Philadelphia: The Association, 1963); Alexander Korns, *NSA Almanac* (Philadelphia: The Association, 1964); letterheads of the Association for the time period; correspondence connected with a "Study of the Leadership of the United States National Student Association from 1946 to 1960," by Dr. Gordon J. Klopf and Dr. Dennis Trueblood. This correspondence included in the private papers of Dr. Klopf.

[2] Wilcox, with a draft notice pending, enlisted in the Navy in March of 1953. Berry was appointed to fill out the term in June of 1953.

[3] Source (Schodde): United States National Student Association headquarters in Philadelphia. Extensive use was made of NSA letterheads for the period. These may contain some inaccuracies.

[4] Source (Schodde): United States National Student Association headquarters in Philadelphia. Sources used were minutes of the National Executive Committee, letterheads, and correspondence. Some inaccuracies may exist, however, for the early years. After 1959-1960, appointments were limited to three-year terms. (This was done to prevent domination by a small group of advisers.) The first advisory board was formed toward the end of the academic year in 1954 in order to provide a closely knit group that was reasonably near Philadelphia and could meet more frequently with the national staff than was the case with the National Advisory Council.

[5] Philip C. Berry was appointed to fill out the unexpired term of Leonard A. Wilcox, Jr., vice president, national affairs, in 1952-53. In March 1953, Wilcox, with a draft notice pending, enlisted in the Navy.

ORGANIZATIONS SENDING DELEGATES TO THE 1946 CHICAGO STUDENT CONFERENCE

American Federation of Negro College Students
American Unitarian Youth
American Youth for Democracy, Intercollegiate Division
Association of Internes and Medical Students
Comgregational Christian Student Fellowship
Intercollegiate Association of Women Students
Intercollegiate Zionist Federation of America
National Association for the Advancement of Colored People
National Federation of Catholic College Students
National Intercollegiate Christian Council
National Self Government Committee
Newman Club Federation
Student Federalists
Students for Federal World Government
U.S. Student Assembly c/o Union for Democratic Action
Young Peoples Socialist League

(Continued on page 1126)

2. ABBREVIATIONS and ACRONYMS

AAUP American Association of University Professors
AAUW American Association of University Women
ACE American Council on Education
ACLU American Civil Liberties Union
ADA Americans for Democratic Action
AFS American Field Service
AFSC American Friends Service Committee
AIMS Association of Interns and Medical Students
APC American Preparatory Committee
ASU American Student Union
AUY American Unitarian Youth
AVC American Veterans Committee
AYC American Youth Congress
AYD American Youth for Democracy
AYH American Youth Hostels
AYSO Associated Youth Serving Organizations

CARE Committee for American Relief to Europe
CCUN Collegiate Council for the United Nations
CFR Committee on Friendly Relations Among Foreign Students
CIA Central Intelligence Agency
CIE Confederation Internationale des Etudiants
CIER Commission for International Educational Reconstruction
C-N-H NSA California-Nevada-Hawaii Region
Cosec Coordinating Secretariat (of the International Student Conference)
CP Communist Party
CTED Central Travel and Exchange Dept. of IUS

FSSP Foreign Student Summer Project (MIT)

IAWS Intercollegiate Association of Women Students
IF Interfraternity
IIE Institute of International Education
ISA International Student Assembly
ISI Intercollegiate Society of Individualists
ISS International Student Service
IUS International Union of Students

JCSA Joint Committee for Student Action

LID League for Industrial Democracy

NAACP National Association for the Advancement of Colored People
NBBS Netherlands Office for Foreign Student Relations
NCC National Continuations Committee (of the Chicago Student Conference)
NCCJ National Conference of Christians and Jews
NCYC National Catholic Youth Conference
NEA National Education Association
NEC National Executive Committee (of the NSA)
NFCCS National Federation of Catholic College Students
NFCUS National Federation of Canadian University Students
NIC National Interfraternity Conference
NICC National Intercollegiate Christian Council
NISA National Independent Student Association
NNER Northern New England Region (of the NSA)
NSA National Student Association (see also USNSA)
NSC National Student Congress (of the NSA)
NSFA National Student Federation of America
NSL National Student League
NSO National Student Organization (acronym used in 1946-47 before the USNSA was named)
NSSFNS National Scholarship Service and Fund for Negro Students
NSWA National Social Welfare Assembly
NUS National Union of Students (i.e., French NUS)

PCA Progressive Citizens of America
PR Pax Romana

SACOA Special Advisory Committee on Organizational Affairs (NSA-1950)
SCM Student Christian Movement
SDA Students for Democratic Action
SF Student Federalists
SHSW State Historical Society of Wisconsin
SLID Student League for Industrial Democracy
SNER Southern New England Region (of the NSA)
SSA Student Service of America
SVM Student Volunteer Movement

UNESCO United Nations Educational, Scientific, and Cultural Organization
USNSA United States National Student Association (also NSA)
USCC United States Christian Council
USSA United States Student Assembly
USYC United States Youth Council
UWF United World Federalists

WAY World Assembly of Youth
WFDY World Federation of Democratic Youth
WSCF World Student Christian Federation
WSSF World Student Service Fund

YAC Young Adult Council
YCL Young Communist League
YD Young Democrats
YDCA Young Democratic Clubs of America
YMCA Young Men's Christian Association
YPCA Young Progressive Citizens of America
YR Young Republicans
YRNF Young Republican National Federation
YWCA Young Women's Christian Association

ORGANIZATIONS SENDING OBSERVERS ONLY TO THE 1946 CHICAGO STUDENT CONFERENCE

(Continued from page 1125)

Association of Cosmopolitan Clubs
B'nai B'rith Hillel Foundation
Board of Christian Education, Presbyterian Church in the USA
Council of Student Clubs, Communist Party
Lutheran Student Association of America
Methodist Student Movement
Michigan Student Veterans Association
National American Veterans Committee
North American Student Cooperative League
Student League for Industrial Democracy
Washington Youth Council
Young Citizens Political Action Commiittee

3. NSA Almanac

Source: "NSA Almanac," *edited by Michael Schwartz and Alexander Korns. Unpublished mimeograph, USNSA, 1964, 36 pp. (available in the State of Wisconsin Historical Society archives). Note: Several factual errors have been corrected or clarified by Anthology editors.*

NSA CONGRESSES

Preparatory Convention, December 1946, University of Chicago, Chicago.
[Chicago Student Conference]
Constitutional Convention, August-September 1947, University of Wisconsin, Madison.
(Henceforth, all Congresses are in August.)

1.	1948	University of Wisconsin	Madison
2.	1949	University of Illinois	Champaign-Urbana
3.	1950	University of Michigan	Ann Arbor
4.	1951	University of Minnesota	Minneapolis
5.	1952	Indiana University	Bloomington
6.	1953	Ohio State University	Columbus
7.	1954	Iowa State University	Ames
8.	1955	University of Minnesota	Minneapolis
9.	1956	University of Chicago	Chicago
10.	1957	University of Michigan	Ann Arbor
11.	1958	Ohio Wesleyan University	Delaware
12.	1959	University of Illinois	Champaign-Urbana
13.	1960	University of Minnesota	Minneapolis
14.	1961	University of Wisconsin	Madison
15.	1962	Ohio State University	Columbus
16.	1963	Indiana University	Bloomington
17.	1964	University of Minnesota	Minneapolis

INTERNATIONAL ORGANIZATIONS

A. International Student Organizations

1. **ISC**

ISC	International Student Conference, established 1950 in Stockholm, held every year to year and a half subsequently
Cosec	Coordinating Secretariat of National Unions of Students, established 1952 as ISC's Secretariat, with limited powers. Headquarters in Leiden, the Netherlands.
SUPCOM	Supervision Committee, established in 1952 to supervise Cosec between ISCs. In 1964 included nine national unions of students (NUSs) elected by the ISC.
RIC	Research and Information Commission, established by ISC in 1954 to investigate violations of student rights. Presents reports to ISC.
IUEF	International Universities Exchange Fund, established by the ISC and related to COSEC, tries to expand exchange.
IBCA	International Bureau of Cultural Activities, an agency of COSEC.
ISTC	International Student Travel Conference, a meeting of the travel departments of NUSs, sponsored by the ISC and COSEC.
ISPC	International Student Press Conference, a meeting of national student press groups sponsored by the ISC and COSEC.
ISS	International Student Seminar, held irregularly under the sponsorship of COSEC and an NUS, for representatives of NUSs.
IB	Information Bulletin, a COSEC publication.
CIE	Conference Internationale des Etudiants, the French name for ISC.

2. **IUS**

IUS	International Union of Students, established 1946 in Prague. Headquarters in Prague.
ISR	International Student Relief, a division of IUS established 1950.
BSFAC	Bureau of Students Fighting Against Colonialism, one of the original bureaus of the IUS.
PID	Press and Information Department, also an original bureau of the IUS.
UIE	Union Internationale des Etudiants, French name for IUS.

3. **Religious**

Pax Romana	International organization of Catholic students.
WSCF	World Student Christian Federation
WUJS	World Union of Jewish Students

4. **Other**

REA	Reunion des Etudiants Allies, first international student organization, founded 1919 in Strassbourg
CIE	Confederate Internationale des Etudiants, name of REA after 1924. Secretariat was in Brussels. The group folded in 1940.
ISMUN	International Student Movement for the United Nations

B. International Youth Organizations

WAY	World Assembly of Youth, established 1948 with present headquarters in Brussels.
WFDY	World Federation of Democratic Youth, established 1945 in London. Headquarters are in Budapest.
YCI	Young Communist International, established 1919 in Berlin, disbanded together with the Communist International (CI) in 1943.
IUSY	International Union of Socialist Youth, a social democratic international.

C. International Trade Union Organizations

ICFTU	International Confederation of Free Trade Unions, formed in London in 1949, headquartered in Brussels.
IFCTU	International Federation of Christian Trade Unions, a Catholic grouping.
WFTU	World Federation of Trade Unions, established in Paris in 1945. Present headquarters in Vienna.
IFTU	International Federation of Trade Unions, or "Amsterdam International," which existed between the wars with its headquarters in Amsterdam.
Profintern	Name of trade union organization allied with Comintern between the wars.
ILO	International Labor Organization, affiliated with the United Nations, with headquarters in Geneva.

D. International Relief Groups

WUS	World University Service, established 1950, with headquarters in Geneva, includes national committees, each of which includes students and faculty.
ISR	International Student Relief, established 1950 with headquarters in Prague.
ESR	European Student Relief, established 1920, name changed to International Student Service in 1925.
ISS	International Student Service, established 1925, disbanded in 1950 when WUS was formed.
WSR	World Student Relief, established 1939 as ally of ISS, disbanded in 1950 when WUS was formed.

E. International Service Groups

FIANEI	Federation Internationale des Associations Nationales des Etudiants Ingeneaus, serving engineering students.

MEETINGS OF INTERNATIONAL ORGANIZATIONS

World Assembly of Youth

Meetings

Council	*Assembly*	*Date*	*Site*
1st	--	1949	Brussels
2nd	--	1950	Istanbul
3rd	1st	1951	Ithaca (U.S.A.)
4th	--	1952	Dakar
5th	2nd	1954	Singapore
6th	--	1956	Berlin
7th	3rd	1958	New Delhi
8th	--	1960	Accra
9th	4th	1962	Arhus (Denmark)
10th	5th	1964	Amherst

World University Service

Meetings

Mysore, India	1950
Grenoble	1952
Istanbul	1953
Oxford	1954
Helsinki	1955
Mysore	1956
Nijenrode, Netherlands	1957
Quebec	1958
Ibadan, Nigeria	1959
Tutzing, Germany	1961
Tokyo	1963

World Youth Festivals

Prague	1947
Budapest	1949
East Berlin	1951
Bucharest	1953
Warsaw	1955
Moscow	1957
Vienna	1959
Helsinki	1962

International Union of Students

List of IUS Congresses

1st World Student Congress	1946	Prague, Czechoslovakia
2nd World Student Congress	1950	Prague, Czechoslovakia
3rd World Student Congress	1953	Warsaw, Poland
4th World Student Congress	1956	Prague, Czechoslovakia
5th World Student Congress	1958	Peking, China
6th World Student Congress	1960	Baghdad, Iraq
7th World Student Congress	1962	Leningrad, USSR

International Student Conference

Conference Number and Site	*Date*
1. Stockholm	December 1950
2. Edinburgh	January 1952
3. Copenhagen	January 1953
4. Istanbul	January 1954
5. Birmingham	July 1955
6. Peradeniya, Ceylon	September 1956
7. Ibadan, Nigeria	September 1957
8. La Cantuta, Peru	February 1959
9. Klosters, Switzerland	August 1960
10. Quebec, Canada	August 1960
11. Christchurch, New Zealand	June 1964

USNSA DELEGATIONS TO THE INTERNATIONAL STUDENT CONFERENCE

1. *Stockholm [1950]*
Allard Lowenstein
Herbert Eisenberg
[Mariane Schmidt]*

2. *Edinburgh [1952]*
William Dentzer
Avrea Ingram
{John Simons}*

3. *Copenhagen [1953]*
Richard Murphy
Avrea Ingram
Helen Jean Rogers
Sylvia Bacon
[Richard Holler]*
David Duberman

4. *Istanbul [1954]*
James Edwards
Leonard Bebchick
William Dentzer
James T. Harris
William Scott Ellis

5. *Birmingham [1955]*
Harry Lunn
Paul Sigmund, Jr.
Clive Gray
James Edwards
Luigi Einaudi

6. *Ceylon [1956]*
Bruce Larkin
Clive Gray
James Edwards
Stanford Glass
Luigi Einaudi

7. *Ibadan [1957]*
Bruce Larkin
Clive Gray
Daniel Idzik
M. Crawford Young
Marian McReynolds

8. *Lima [1959]*
Robert Kiley
Williard Johnson
Bruce Larkin
Manuel Aragon
James Edwards

9. *Klosters [1960]*
Isabel Marcus
Manuel Aragon
Robert Kiley
James Edwards
Peter Eccles

10. *Quebec [1960]*
Edward Garvey
James Scott
Robert Aragon
Don Emmerson
Manuel Aragon

11. *New Zealand [1964]*
Alexander Korns
Jim Scott
Dave Spencer
Edward Garvey
Thomas Olson
Bill McClaskey

**Note:* bracketed names above were listed in the 1964 NSA Almanac as delegates, but are known by William Dentzer and others to have been self-directed observers rather than delegates.

INTERNATIONAL ORGANIZATION OFFICERS

World Assembly of Youth

1949-52

President	M. Sauve	Canada
Vice Presidents	G. Kreveld	Belgium
	T.C. Cuu	Viet Nam

1952-54

President	Guthrie Moir	Great Britain
Vice Presidents	Antoine Lawrence	Guinea
	Ruth Schachter	United States

1954-56

President	Guthrie Moir	Great Britain
Vice Presidents	Antoine Lawrence	Guinea
	Immanuel Wallerstein	United States

1956-58

President	Antoine Lawrence	Guinea
Vice Presidents	Eric Wee	Singapore
	Immanuel Wallerstein	United States

1958-60

President	Ravindra Varma	India
Vice President	Ambroise Agboton	Dahomey

1960-62

President	Ravindra Varma	India
Vice Presidents	Jose Antonelli	Argentina
	Michael Iovenko	United States

1962-64

President	Carlos Delgado	Peru
Vice Presidents	Henry Johnson	Sierra Leone
	Robert Kiley	United States
	Joseph Siow	Malaya
Treasurer	Christian Aaslund	Norway
Secretary General	David Wirmark	
Asst. Secs. Gen.	Jose Cambriella	
	George Vumi	

Cosec: 1952-64

Pre-Ceylon

Administrative Secretaries

Jarl Traneus (August 1952-January 1953)	Sweden
John Thompson (January 1953 on)	U.K.

Associate Secretaries

William Dentzer (October 1952-August 1953)	U.S.
Enrique Ibarra (March 1953-1954-??)	Paraguay
Avrea Ingram (August 1953-September 1956)	U.S.
Antonio Lopez (1954-September 1956-??)	Chile

Ceylon (September 1956-September 1957)

Administrative Secretary

John Thompson	U.K.

Associate Secretaries

Juan Barros Barros	Chile
Hans Dall	Denmark
Jim Edwards	U.S.
Isaac Omolo	Kenya

Nigeria (September 1957-February 1959)

Administrative Secretary

Hans Dall	Denmark

Associate Secretaries

Musa Bin Hitam	Malaya
Peter Hornsby	U.K. (Finance)
Mario Reyes Chavez	Bolivia
Crawford Young	U.S.
Isaac Omolo	Kenya

Peru (February 1959-August 1960)

Administrative Secretary

Hans Dall	Denmark

Associate Secretaries	
Lovemore Kutambanengwe	Southern Rhodesia
Norman Kingsbury	New Zealand
Bruce Larkin	U.S.
Mario Reyes Chavez	Bolivia
Musa Bin Hitam (resigned August 1959)	Malaya
Sylvio Mutal	Turkey (Finance)
Eustace Mendis (October 1959-August 1960) (interim appointment to replace Bin Hitam)	Ceylon

Klosters (August 1960)

Administrative Secretary	
Norman Kingsbury	New Zealand
Associate Secretaries	
Lovemore Mutambanengwe	Southern Rhodesia
Jyoti Shankar Singh	India
Patricio Fernandez	Chile
Magnus Gunther	Union of South Africa
Robert Kiley	U.S.
Sylvio Mutal	Turkey (Finance)
Administrative Secretary (replaced Kingsbury in September 1961)	
Jyoti Singh	India
Associate Secretary (replaced Singh in September 1961)	
Kenny Khaw	Malaya

NSA PRESIDENTS

(Status as compiled by NSA Almanac editors as of 1964)

1947-48—BILL WELSH—Berea College, was Director of Research for the Democratic National Committee, now is Administrative Assistant to Senator Hart of Michigan.

1948-49—TED HARRIS—LaSalle University, was Assistant Executive Director of the American Society for African Culture (AMSAC), now working in Leopoldville for Ford Foundation.

1949-50—BOB KELLY—St. Peter's College, now in Tom Dewey's Law Firm.

1950-51—ALLARD LOWENSTEIN—University of North Carolina, Yale Law School, was a Special Assistant to Senator Humphrey, then traveled to South and Southwest Africa, was a free-lance writer, now on the faculty of the University of North Carolina.

1951-52—BILL DENTZER—Muskingum College, was with Department of the Army, now with ICA. [AID]*

1952-53—DICK MURPHY—University of North Carolina, was Executive Secretary of Young Democrats, is now Assistant Postmaster General.

1953-54—JIM EDWARDS—University of Illinois, was NSA Overseas Representative, then Associate Secretary COSEC, attended Yale Law School, served as clerk to Justice Whittaker, now with a law firm in New York.

1954-55—HARRY LUNN—University of Michigan, was with COSEC Asian Delegation, now with Department of Air Force in Paris.

1955-56—STAN GLASS—University of Illinois, Harvard Law School, was Executive Director of Educational Travel, Inc., now practicing law.

1956-57—HARALD BAKKEN—University of Minnesota, Director of Foreign Student Leadership Project, 1957-59, Director of 8th and 9th ISRS, now studying American History at Harvard.

1957-58—RAY FARABEE—University of Texas, Texas Law School, now works for Senator Yarborough of Texas in Austin.

1958-59—BOB KILEY—Nortre Dame University, was Associate Secretary of COSEC, now finishing PhD at Harvard.

1959-60—DON HOFFMAN—University of Wisconsin, was NSA Overseas Representative in Paris.

1960-61—DICK RETTIG—University of Washington, was NSA Overseas Representative in Paris.

1961-62—ED GARVEY—University of Wisconsin, was NSA Overseas Representative in Paris, now with US Army.

1962-63—DENNIS SHAUL—University of Notre Dame, now in Harvard Law School.

1963-64—GREG GALLO—University of Wisconsin.

NSA INTERNATIONAL AFFAIRS VICE PRESIDENTS

(Status as compiled by NSA Almanac Editors as of 1964)

1947-48—BOB SMITH—worked in Geneva with WFUNA, now works for ICA. [AID]*

1948-49—BOB WEST—Yale, now in Congo with UN finance operations.

1949-50—ERSKINE CHILDERS—Stanford, Irish, now does free-lance work for radio and magazines.

1950-51—HERB EISENBERG—Massachusetts Institute of Technology, now an architect in Boston area.

1951-53—AVREA INGRAM—Harvard, became Associate Secretary of COSEC, deceased 1957.

1953-54—LEN BEBCHECK—Cornel University, Yale Law School, worked for Civil Aeronautics Board, now practicing law.

1954-55—PAUL SIGMUND—Georgetown University, received PhD at Harvard University, was NSA Overseas Representative in Paris, now Assistant Professor in Government at Princeton University.

1955-56—CLIVE GRAY—University of Chicago, was NSA Overseas Representative in India, received PhD in Economics at Harvard University, has gone to Nigeria with ICA, working on thesis in the U.S.

1956-58—BRUCE LARKIN—University of Chicago, was Overseas Representative in Paris, Associate Secretary of COSEC, now at Harvard in East Asian Studies.

1958-59—WILLARD JOHNSON—UCLA, then Johns Hopkins School of Advanced Studies, studying in Africa, thesis in Cameroons, will teach at MIT.

1959-60—ISABEL MARCUS—Barnard College, was at London School of Economics, living in Berkeley.

1960-61—JIM SCOTT—Williams College, NSA Overseas Representative in Burma and then Paris, now at Yale, Asian studies.

1961-62—DON EMMERSON—Princeton University, now Associate Secretary of COSEC.

1962-63—DON SMITH—University of Texas, now in Grad School, Univ. of Texas.

1963-64—ALEX KORNS—Harvard University, was Overseas NSA Representative in Paris.

**Note:* ICA was succeeded by AID in 1961.

4. Archives and Libraries

*Editor's note: The systematic practice of documenting student life and organization seems to have first widely emerged in the early 1950's. Many archives and special collections at university libraries contain rich lodes of unexpected material not otherwise catalogued. Others draw a complete blank despite yearbook and college newspaper evidence of student activity. In addition to keyeword document file searches, primary places to do manual page or folder by folder searches would be in yearbooks; annual reports; president's, dean's and student activities office papers; student government minutes; alumni publications and college newspaper bound volumes or microfilms. Significant collections bearing on the NSA story and identified by the editor are listed below. In addition, a complete list of libraries consulted by visit or mail is provided. The librarian or archivist assisting project personnel at the time of major contact during project research from 1996-2004 is listed for each. The degree of coverage of 1945-53 NSA—related events and issues, when it could be evaluated by the editor, is shown by asterisks: *—"occasional;" **—"regularly;" ***—"extensively featured."*

Primary Collections Bearing on the NSA Story

State Historical Society of Wisconsin. Madison. Library and Archives: Principal national archive of NSA publications, documents and photo collections, from its founding through 1978 to its merger with the National Student Lobby to become the USSA; USSA archives to date. NSA in its early years: college affiliation records, domestic programs, national student congresses, national executive committee, advisory council and regional organizations. *Donna Sereda, Director, Acquisitions and Collections Management.*

The Hoover Institution. Stanford, CA. Library and Archives: Principal national archive of NSA International Commission records from 1946-1968: documents, publications, photos and audio. NSA and its relations abroad and during the cold war. Also holdings for the American Council on Education, 1918, and the Asia Foundation, 1951-1968. *Elena Danielson, Director.*

Berea College, Berea, KY. *Wallpaper*** Archives, Hutchins Library: Papers of William Welsh, first NSA President, 1948-49. Economic Club of Detroit issue with NSA. *Shannon H. Wilson, College Archivist.*

Catholic University, DC. *Tower.** Archives Annex, Mullen Library: Records of the National Catholic Youth Conference, National Federation of Catholic College Students, National Newman Club Federation, Joint Committee for Student Action, internal church and Vatican memoranda on IUS and NSA. *William John Shepherd, Assistant Archivist.*

Georgetown University, DC. *Hoya.** Special Collections Division, Lauinger Library: Woodstock Archives and papers of J.C. Murray on Operation University, matters related to U.S. Catholic college student participation in post-war secular student organizations. *John Reynolds, Archivist.*

Howard University, DC. *Hill Top.*** Moorland-Spingarn Research Center: A major repository "preserving the legacy of the Black experience." Segregation. Civil Rights. Mason-Dixon Region. *Clifford Muse, University Archivist.*

Institute of International Education, New York City. Records room: IIE Annual Reports, *IIE Bulletins* and documents related to student and faculty exchange and to student travel from 1919 through to the years directly following World War II. *Daniel Greenspahn, Alumni Research Officer.*

Kautz Family YMCA Archives, MN. Records of Student YMCA, Committee on Friendly Relations Among Foreign Students, 1910-60s.(Later name change to International Student Service, 1962.) *Dagmar K. Getz, Assistant Curator.*

Library of Congress, Washington, DC. Limited collection of NSA publications.The papers of Ruby Hurley, NAACP Youth Director through 1950 contain extensive records of the Young Adult Council, World Assembly of Youth and NSA correspondence. Collections on the National Interfraternity Conference and Panhellenic Conference.

National Archives, Washington, DC. State Department files: 1946 World Student Congress in Prague (International Student Conference). Embassy cables, department correspondence with the American Preparatory Committee, internal department memos, Congress documents.

Union Theological Seminary, New York City. Burke Library: National Intercollegiate Christian Council: *The Intercollegian* on film 1878-1961. In print, 1960-67. Dept. of Student Work, Board of Education, Methodist Church: *Motive,* 1941-1972. *Seth Kasten, Reference Librarian.*

University of North Carolina, Chapel Hill. *Tar Heel.* North Carolina Collection, Wilson Library: Papers of NSA's fourth President, Allard K. Lowenstein; UNC President and member NSA Advisory Council, Frank Graham. North Carolina student government. *Bob Anthony, Curator.*

University of Texas at Austin. *Daily Texan.* The Center for American History: Pre-World War II national student organizations. Preparations for 1946 World Student Congress. American Preparatory Committee announcements. Jim Smith correspondence and documents. Chicago Student Conference, Constitutional Convention. *Ralph Elder, Assistant Director.*

Yale Divinity School, New Haven, CT. Archives: Records of the World's Student Christian Federation, Student Christian Movement work by state. International Student Service and SCM in World War I and II, National Student Council of the YMCA and YWCA, National Intercollegiate Council. *Martha Smalley, Research Services Librarian.*

Other College Libraries and Newspapers

Unless otherwise noted, resources are available in Archives, Special Collections, Media, Microforms and/or Periodicals departments. Due to resource limitations, oral history projects, with a few exceptions, were not accessed in the research for this project. This list includes only those colleges and newspapers actually contacted or accessed by the Anthology editor or staff. As a result useful highlights may be missing on some major institution libraries. Those contacted represent about 10% of the 1277 four-year higher education institutions in 1948. As indicated in the Acknowledgments, some college newspaper research (such as at Harvard and Carleton) was done for the project early on by volunteers who were not asked to search other holdings.

Agnes Scott College, GA. *Agonistic; Agnes Scott News.*** McCain Library: Constance Curry.

Alfred University, NY. *Fiat Lux. Laurie L. McFadden, University Archivist.*

Ashland College, OH. *Ashland Collegian.*

Atlanta University Center, GA. Robert W. Woodruff Library: serving Clark Atlanta U., Spelman, Morehouse and Morris Brown Colleges.

Bard College, NY. *Bardian.* Few records.

Barnard College, NY. *Barnard Bulletin**** See also Columbia University.

Bloomsburg (College) University, PA. Dean Marguerite Kehr. NSFA. *Robert Dunkleberger, University Archivist.*

Boston University, MA. John and Helen Jean (Rogers) Secondari Collection, Rogers biography mss. *Alex Rankin, Assistant Director for Manuscripts.*

Bowdoin College, ME. *Bowdoin Orient.* ***

Carleton College, MN. *Carletonian*** Richard J. Medalie, Thomas Hughes.

Case Western Reserve University, OH. *Reserve Tribune** The Mather Record.*** Combining Case, **Western Reserve** and **Flora Stone Mather.** Kelvin Smith Library. Pristine early years national NSA collection. *Tom Steman, Archivist.*

City College of New York— Day. *Campus**, Observation Post*** **Eve.-** *Main Events.*** Eugene Schwartz, Robert F. Meagher, Thomas Garrity, Seymour Reisin, Met. NY Region. Josph P. Lash. ASU. CCNY strikes. *Barbara Dunlap, Archivist.*

College of St. Teresa, MN. Original two issues of *Essai,* NSA's literary magazine. The college is closed and archives are kept by the remaining sisters. *Sister Margaret Clare Styles.*

College of St. Thomas, MN. *Aquin.* Phillip DesMarais, Rev. Vincent J. FLynn.

Colorado State University (Colorado A&M College).*Rocky Mountain Collegian.** Morgan Library: Roy Romer, John Olsen, Claude Salomon. *Patricia Van Deventer, Technician.*

Columbia University, NY. *Columbia Spectator.**** University Archives and Columbiana Library: National and Met. NY NSA, Walter Wallace, Jay Maryanov, National Scholarship Service and Fund for Negro Students, Dean Harry Carman. *David H. Hill, Assistant Director.*

Cornell University, NY. *Cornell Daily Sun**** Olin Library: Nothing on NSA in archives. Robert Fogel, Robert Beyers, Jack Minkoff. *Susan Szasz Palmer, Head of Public Services.*

Dartmouth College, NH. *Dartmouth.*** Rauner Special Collections Library: Mike Iovenko, New England Region. *Sarah Hartwell.*

Drew University, NJ. Alfred McClung Lee, A. Blair Knapp. *Jean Schoenthaler, Archivist.*

Dunbarton College, DC. *Dunbarton Dial.** College closed. Congregational Archives, Sisters of the Holy Cross, Notre Dame, Indiana: Cynthia Courtney, Gloria Abiousness. *Sister Julie McGuire.*

Eastern Washington College of Educ., WA. *Easterner* Charles V. Mutschler, Archivist.*

Eastman School of Music, NY. Charles J. Warner. *David Peter Coppen, Special Collections Librarian.*

Emory (College) University, GA. *Emory Wheel.**** Robert W. Woodruff Library: Regional and National. Al Foster. *Beverley B. Allen, Reference Archivist.*

Fisk University, TN. Charles Johnson, Charles Proctor. *Beth Howse, Special Collections Archives.*

Fontbonne College, MO. *Font.* ** Tesse Hartigan (Donnelly). *Sister Jane Hassett.*

Fordham University, NY. *Ram.**** Walsh Library: Fr. Robert Gannon, SJ, Michael DiLegge, Warren Gallagher. Little on NSA. *Patrice Kane, Archivist.*

Georgia Institute of Technology. *Technique.**** George Nelesnik, John Hunsinger.

Harvard University, MA. *Harvard Crimson.**** George Carter, Douglass Cater, William Ellis, Francis Fisher, Alice Gilbert (Radcliffe), Frederick Houghteling, Ernest Howell, Andrew Rice, Clifton Wharton, World Student Congress, New England Region, Harvard International Activities Committee.

Holy Names College, CA. NSA and NFCCS on campus. *Catriona Wendroff, Reference Librarian.*

Humbolt State (College) University, CA. *Humbolt Lumberjack.* The Mitsuhito Club. *Joan Berman, Special Collections Librarian.*

Hunter College, NY. *Hunter Arrow.* * *Hunter Bulletin.* ** Enid Cass. WSC.

Indiana (State Teachers College) State University. *Indiana Statesman.*** Dennis Trueblood, Indiana Region. *Susan Davis, University Archives.*

Indiana University. *Indiana Daily Student.* Dennis Trueblood, Robert Shaffer. Virtually nothing on NSA in paper or files. *Brad Cook, University Archives.*

Jackson State (College) University, MS. *Blue and White Flash.* John Peoples.

Johns Hopkins University, MD. *Johns Hopkins News-Letter.** Stanley Greenfield.

La Salle (College) University, PA. *La Salle Collegian.* *** Archives: Elmer Paul Brock, James T. Harris, Regional. *Brother Joseph Grabenstein, University Archivist.*

Lewis and Clark College, OR. *Pioneer Log.* John Elwood. *Doug Elwood, Archives.*

Long Island University, NY. *Seawanhaka.* ** Brooklyn Archives: Sheldon Steinhauser. *Ellen Belcher, Special Collections & Preservation Librarian.*

Los Angeles City College, CA. *Los Angeles Collegian.****Tom Suzuki, Tom Munger, K. Wallace Longshore. *The Collegian* provided extensive issues coverage and NSA news. *Barbara Vasquez, Reference Librarian.*

Louisiana State University. *Daily Reveille.* *** (1946-48). Hill Memorial Library. Segregegation and civil rights issues.

Loyola College, MD. *Greyhound.* * Loyola/Notre Dame Library. *Susan Cooperstein, User Education Librarian.*

Loyola Marymount University, CA. *Loyolan.* ** Combining Loyola U. and Marymount College in 1968. *Neil Bethke, Archives and Special Collections.*

Loyola University, IL. *Loyola News.* **

Manhattanville College, NY. *Centurion.* Mother Eleanor O'Byrne. *Betty Gallagher, Reference Librarian.*

Marylhurst College, OR. *Tower** Joan Long (Lynch).

Massachusetts Institute of Technology. *TheTech.* *** FSSP, Earl Eames, Herbert Eisenberg, Dean Everett Baker.

Middlebury College, VT. *Middlebury Campus.***

Mills College, CA. *Mills College Weekly.* *** F.W. Olin Library: Lorrie Eisenberg, Louise Alport, Sally Zook, Lowell Vye. *Janice Braun, Special Collections Curator.*

Millsaps College, MS. *Purple and White.* Methodist Student Movement.

Morehouse College, GA.(Atlanta U.) *Maroon Tiger.* **Dawn Williams, Asst. Archivist.*

Mount Holyoke College, MA. Edward R. Murrow Papers. *Juliana Kuipers, Archives Assistant.*

Mount St. Mary's College, CA. Peggy Bradish. *Claudia Reed, Archives*

Mundelein College, IL. *Skyscraper.* ** Gannon Women's Center: Sparce NSA documentation: Helen Jean Rogers (Secondari), Mary Kay Perkins. Mundelein was absorbed by Loyola. *Sister Anna Ida Gannon.*

Muskingum College, OH. William T. Dentzer, Jr. *Robin Hansen, Library Director.*

(New Jersey College for Women) Douglass College. *Campus News, Caellian*** .

New Mexico Highlands University. *Highlands Candle.* Thomas C. Donnelley Library: Jack Wharton, Donald Martinez, Chicano Student Revolution. *Kathleen M. Kroll, Head of Reference/Circulation.*

New York University. *NYU Bulletin.* ** Bobst Library. *Teresa Mora, Archivist.*

Occidental College. CA. *Occidental.* * *Jean Paule, College Archivist.*

Pennsylvania State (College) University. *Daily Collegian.**** Allan Ostar, Dean Arthur Warnock.

Pittsburg State University (Kansas State Teachers College). *The Collegio.* ** Max Lee Minor, Regional NSA. *Randy Roberts, Curator of Special Collections.*

Princeton University, NJ. *Princeton Bulletin, Daily Princetonian.* **

Radcliffe College, MA. *Radcliffe News.* Alice Gilbert, Winifred Lebon.

Reed College, OR. *Reed College Quest.* * *Gay Walker, Special Collections Librarian.*

Regis College, CO. *Regis Brown and Gold.* * Dayton Memorial Library: Patrick Eagan. *Elizabeth Happy, Archives.*

Regis College, MA. *Regis Herald.*** *Eleanor M. Deady, CSJ, Reference Librarian.*

Rochester Institute of Technology, NY. *SPRIT.**** Wallace Library: NY Region. *Jody Sidlauskas.*

Rockford College, IL. *Vanguard.* Janis Tremper (Dowd), Maryjo Domino (Pritz).

Rutgers University, NJ. *Targum.**** Alexander Library: John Yewell, Ariel Landy, NJ Region. *David Kuzma, Special Collections and Archives.*

San Fransisco State U. (College), CA. *Golden Gater.* *** *Helene Whitson, Archivist.*

Sarah Lawrence College, NY. *Campus.* *** Helen Bryan (Garland), Gladys Chang (Hardy-Brazil), Robin Roberts, Harold Taylor, Region. *Patricia Owen, Archivist.*

Seattle University, MA. *Seattle University Spectator.* No NSA records.

Simmons College, MA. *Simmons News.* *** Outstanding national, regional, campus NSA coverage. Comprehensive NSA document and publication archival collection. *Claire Goodwin, College Archivist.*

Smith College, MA. *Smith College SCAN.* *** Miriam Haskell (Berlin), Janet Welsh (Brown). Mary Ann Weld (Bodecker), New England Region.

Spelman College, GA. *Campus Mirror** (Atlanta University).

Stanford University, CA. *Stanford Daily****. Erskine Childers, Gilbert Jonas. ASSU files. *Polly Armstrong, Special Collections.*

St. Joseph's College, PA. *Hawk* .*** Drexel Library: Ralph Dungan, Jim Dougherty.

St. Louis University, MO. *University News.* *** Pius XII Memorial Library.

St Peter's College, NJ. *Pauw Wow.* ** Robert Kelly, Tom Garrity. *Alan Delozier, Archivist.*

Swarthmore College, PA. *Swarthmore Phoenix.**** McCabe Library: Molly Yard, Mary-Lou Rogers (Munts), Colgate Prentiss, Ralph Smith, Kenneth Kurtz, Barry Keating.

Temple University, PA. *Temple University News.**** Paley Library: Ted Perry.

Trinity College, DC. *Trinity Times.* ** Eileen O'Connell. *Sister Mary Hayes, Archivist.*

Tulane University, LA. *Tulane Hullabaloo.*

University of Akron, OH. *Akron Buchtelite.* **

University of Alabama. *Crimson White.* * W.S. Hoole Special Collections Library.

University of Baltimore, MD. *Baloo.* ** Langsdale Library: Earl Gerding, Joseph Zebley, Mason-Dixon Region.

University of Buffalo, NY. *Argus,*** *Bee.* ** Lee Jones, NY State Region, NSA from 1946-64, 1967 Congresses. *Rodney Gorme Obien, University Archives.*

University of California, Berkeley. *Daily Californian.* *** Mildred Kiefer (Wurf), Richard G. Heggie, Sally Holt (Smit), Calif. Region. National NSA.

University of California, Los Angeles. *Daily Bruin.* *** Jane Wilder (Jacqz), James Garth, Nancy Roth (Arnheim), Region. *Charlotte B. Brown, University Archivist.*

University of Chicago. *Chicago Maroon.* *** Joseph Regenstein Library: Extensive national and regional from 1949, William Birenbaum, Chancellor Hutchins, Dean Strozier, Chicago Student Conference. *Deborah Levine.*

University of Colorado. *Silver and Gold.* *** Len Perlmutter, Rocky Mountain Region, Academic Freedom, Civil Rights, National NSA, Discrimination, ASU, NSFA. *David Hayes, Archivist.*

University of Denver. *Denver Clarion.* ** Penrose Library. *Jennifer Thompson, Archives.*

University of Idaho. *Argonaut.* ** *Terry Abraham, Head, Special Collections.*

University of Illinois. *Daily Illini.* ** University Archives. Corr. and docs. Illinois Region. Student Life and Cultural History collection. National Interfraternity Conference. *Ellen Swain, Archivist for Student Life/Culture.*

University of Louisville. *Cardinal.*** Egstrom Library: Robert Delahanty. KY-TN Region. *Margaret Merrick, Media Dept.*

University of Maryland. *Diamondback.* ** Hornbake Library: NSFA. *Jennie A. Levine, Assistant Curator for Historical Manuscripts.*

University of Miami, FL. *Hurricane.* ** Stuart McDonald. *William Walker, Librarian.*

University of Michigan. *Michigan Daily.**** Bentley Historical Library: Harvey Weisberg, Craig Wilson, Harry H. Lunn, Leonard Wilcox, Michigan Region. *Nancy R. Bartlett, Reference Archivist.*

University of Minnesota. *Minnesota Daily.*** Archives, Walter Library: Philip Des-Marais, Willliam Holbrook, Richard J. Medalie, Marion Andert, Minnesota Region. *Penny Crosch, Archivist.*

University of New Mexico. *New Mexico Lobo.* * Zimmerman Library. *Nancy Brown-Martinez.*

University of Pennsylvania. *Daily Pennsylvanian.* *** Frank Mayers, Dean Althea Hottel, Pres. Harold Stassen. *Mark Lloyd, Director, University Archives.*

University of Rochester (C. for Women), NY. *Tower Times.**** **(C. for Men)**, *Campus.**** Frank Down. NY Region. *Amy Barnum, Special Collections.*

University of Southern California. *Trojan.****. USC Libraries, Special Collections

University of Washington. *University of Washington Daily.**** Suzzallo and Allen Libraries: Academic Freedom, AYD, Pres. Raymond Allen, Dean Newhouse, Glen Nygreen, Norman Israel, Dan Pulsifer, Helen Knudson (Pulsifer), William Gates, Sr., National, regional NSA. *John Medlin, Secretary, Special Collections.*

University of Wisconsin. *Daily Cardinal.**** Archives, Memorial Library: NSA National Office and Wisconsin Region, Norman Holmes, Joy Newberger, Karl Meyer, John Hunter, Royal Voegeli, Gordon Klopf, Emily Chervenik, Helen White. *J. Frank Cook, Director.*

Ursuline College, OH. *Ursuline Quill.*** Ralph M. Besse Library. *Sister Catherine McBride, Archivist.*

Vassar College, NY. *Vassar Miscellany News.**** Sylvia Bacon. ASU. *Nancy McKechnie, Special Collections.*

Washington State (College) University. *Washington State Evergreen.**** Edward R. Murrow, Ida Louise Anderson. *Lawrence R. Stark, Assistant Archivist.*

Washington University, MO. *Student Life.**** Olin Library. Leon Jick, National, regional. *Carol Prietto, Archivist.*

Webster (College) University, MO. *Web.*** Peggy Mason. *Kathy Gaynor, Archivist.*

Wellesley College, MA. *Wellesley College News.**** Margaret Clapp Library. Alice Horton (Tibbetts), Mildred McAfee Horton. Pat Wohlgemuth (Blair). *Wilma R. Slaight, Archivist.*

Williams College, MA. *Williams Record.** Henry Halsted, New England Region. *Sylvia Kennick Brown, College Archivist.*

Wooster College, OH. *Wooster Voice.*** College of Wooster Libraries. Special Collections.

Xavier University, LA. *Xavier Herald.**** Harry Alexander, Aaron Henry, Norman Francis. Catholic Committee of the South. *Lester Sullivan, Archivist.*

Yale University, CT. *Yale Daily News.*** William Buckley, Curtis Farrar, Robert S. Smith, Robert L. West. *William R. Massa, Jr., Public Services Archivist.*

5. Bibliography

Note: This bibliography has been assembled from Anthology Project resources, references in various of the Anthology memoirs, and resources that may be found in the archives at the State Historical Society of Wisconsin, the Hoover Institute, or by search at the college libraries listed previously. Also included are citations, followed by a bracketed reference drawn from the 1948 McLaughlin [M] and 1965 Schodde [S] dissertations, the 1956 Peter Jones IUS/NSA history [J] and the 1952 NSA publications catalog [N]. With some exceptions, NSA document and periodical citations have been limited to the first five years of NSA, and others to publication prior to the NSA tenth anniversary in 1957.

BOOKS

The Setting and Prologue

Berns, Walter. *Making Patriots.* Chicago and London: University of Chicago Press, 2001.

Cash, W.J. *The Mind of the South* New York: Vintage Books, 1991. (First published in 1941 by Alfred A. Knopf.)

Cohen, Robert. *When the Old Left Was Young: Student Radicals and America's First Mass Student Movement, 1929-1941.* New York and Oxford: Oxford University Press, 1993.

Goodwin, Doris Kearns. *No Ordinary Time: Franklin and Eleanor Roosevelt: The Home Front in World War II.* New York, London, et al.: Touchstone, 1994.

Kendrick, Alexander. *Prime Time: The Life of Edward R. Murrow.* Boston and Toronto: Little, Brown & Company, 1969.

Thompson, Mary A. *Unoffical Ambassadors: The Story of International Student Service* [The CFR]. New York: International Student Service, 1982.

Watt, Donald B. *Intelligence Is Not Enough.* Experiment Press, 1967.

Wilkins, Robert. *Jefferson's Pillow: The Founding Fathers and the Dilemma of Black Patriotism.* Boston: Beacon Press, 2001.

The GI Generation, Civil Rights and Cold War Era

Bennett, Michael J. *When Dreams Came True: The GI Bill and the Making of Modern America.* Washington, DC: Brassey's, 1996.

Brokaw, Tom. *The Greatest Generation.* New York: Random House, 1998.

Chafe, William H. *Never Stop Running: Allard Lowenstein and the Struggle to Save American Liberalism.* New York: Basic Books, 1993.

Coleman, Peter. *The Liberal Conspiracy: The Congress for Cultural Freedom and the Struggle for the Mind of Postwar Europe.* New York: The Free Press, 1989.

Curry, Constance, et. al. *Deep in Our Hearts: Nine White Women in the Freedom Movement.* Athens, GA, and London: University of Georgia Press, 2000.

Diamond, Sigmund. *Compromised Campus. The Collaboration of Universities with the Intelligence Community, 1945-55.* New York and Oxford: Oxford University Press, 1992.

Henry, Aaron, with Curry, Constance. *Aaron Henry: The Fire Ever Burning.* Jackson, MI: University Press of Mississippi, 2000.

Hoopes, Roy. *The Complete Peace Corps Guide.* New York: The Dial Press, 1961.

Keefer, Louis E. *Scholars in Foxholes.* Reston, VA: COTU Publishing, 1988.

Meyer, Cord. *Facing Reality: From World Federalism to the CIA.* Lanham, MD, and London: University Press of America, 1982, by arrangement with Harper and Row.

Saunders, Frances Storer. *The Cultural Cold War: The CIA and The World of Arts and Letters.* New York: The New Press, 1999.

Schlesinger, Stephen. *Act of Creation: The Founding of the United Nations.* Westview, 2003.

Wink, Robin W. *Cloak and Gown: Scholars in the Secret War, 1939-1961.* New York: William Morrow and Company, Inc., 1997.

Student Life, Organization and Activism

Altbach, Philip G. *Student Politics in America: A Historical Analysis.* New Brunswick, NJ, and London: Transaction Publishers, 1997. (Originally published in 1974 by McGraw-Hill, Inc.)

______, and Uphoff, Norman T. *The Student Internationals.* Metuchen, NJ: The Scarecrow Press, 1973.

DeGroot, Gerard J., ed. *Student Protest: The Sixties and After.* London and New York: Longman, 1998.

Evans, M. Stanton. *Revolt on the Campus.* Chicago: Henry Regnery Company, 1961.

Harrington, Ann M. and Moylan, Prudence, eds. *Mundelein Voices: The Women's College Experience, 1930-1991.* Chicago: Loyola Press, 2001.

Horowitz, Helen Lefkowitz. *Campus Life: Undergraduate Cultures from the End of the Eighteenth Century to the Present.* Chicago and London: The University of Chicago Press, 1987.

Jonas, Gilbert. *One Shining Moment: The Untold Story of the American Student World Federalist Movement, 1942-1953.* iUniverse.com, 2000.

Lee, Alfred McClung. *Fraternities Without Brotherhood: A Study of Prejudice on the American Campus.* Boston: The Beacon Press, 1955.

Lehtonen, Risto. *Story of a Storm: The Ecumenical Student Movement in the Turmoils of Revolution.* Grand Rapids, MI. and Cambridge, UK: William B. Eerdmans Publishing Company.

Levine, Arthur and Cureton, Jeanette S. *When Hope and Fear Collide: A Portrait of Today's College Student.* San Fransisco: Jossey-Bass Publishers, 1998.

Peters, Scott J. *The Promise of Association: A History of the Mission and Work of the YMCA at the University of Illinois, 1837-1997.* Champaign, IL: University YMCA, 1997.

Wechsler, J. A., *Revolt on the Campus.* New York: Civici-Criede Publishers, 1935. [M]

Issues of Higher Education

Birenbaum, William M. *Something for Everybody Is Not Enough: An Educator's Search for His Education.* New York: Random House, 1971.

Buckley, Jr., William F. *God and Man at Yale: The Superstitions of "Academic Freedom."* Washington, DC: Regnery Gateway, 1986.

Deutsch, Monroe E. *The Letter and the Spirit: A Selection from Addresses by Monroe E. Deutsch, Vice President and Provost.* Berkeley and Los Angeles: University of California Press,1943.

Ehrlich, Thomas. *Civic Responsibility and Higher Education.* Phoenix, AZ: American Council on Education/Oryx Press, 2000.

Gannon, Robert I., S.J. *The Poor Old Liberal Arts: A Personal Memoir of a Lifetime in Education.* New York: Farrar, Straus & Cudahy, 1961.

Kerr, Clark. *The Uses of the University.* Cambridge: Harvard University Press, 1963. [S]

Kors, Alan Charles and Silverglate, Harvey A. *The Shadow University: The Betrayal of Liberty on America's Campuses.* New York, London, Toronto and Singapore: The Free Press, 1998.

Peoples, Jr., John A. *To Survive and Thrive: The Quest for a True University.* Jackson, MS: Town Square Books, 1995.

Rudolph, Frederick. *The American College & University: A History.* Athens, GA, and London: The University of Georgia Press, 1990 (originally published, New York: A. Knopf, 1962).

DISSERTATIONS AND THESES

England, Sandy. *The Impact of Women in Leadership on the National Student Association and the United States Student Association, 1946-1994.* Dissertation for Master's Degree at Indiana University. 1996.

Garcia, Jr., Eloy J. *The Chicano Movement at New Mexico Highlands: An Interpretive History.* Las Vegas, NM: New Mexico Highlands University, 1997 [Unpublished].

Halpern, Stephen Mark. *The Institute of International Education: A History.* [Columbia University]. Ann Arbor, MI: University Microfilims, 1969.

Makuen, Donald R. *An Analysis of the Concept of Student Responsibility in Higher Education, 1950-1960.* Unpublished Ed.D. thesis, Teachers College, Columbia University, New York, 1963. [S]

McLaughlin, Martin M. *Political Processes in American National Student Organizations.* Notre Dame, IN: University of Notre Dame, 1948.

Schodde, Stephen. *Certain Foci of the United States National Student Association and Their Implications for Student Personnel Administrators.* Dissertation submitted to Teachers College, Columbia University, for the Degree of Doctor of Education. New York: 1965.

Smith, Ralph Lee. *American Relations with the International Union of Students, 1945-48: Efforts of Students from Russia, America and Other Nations to Create a World Student Organization After World War II.* Post-Master's course term paper. University of Virginia, 1988.

INFORMAL HISTORIES OF NSA

Garvey, Edward R., et al. *History and Development of USNSA.* Philadelphia: U.S. National Student Association, March 15, 1963.

Jones Peter T. *The History of the USNSA Relations with the International Union of Students, 1945-1956.* Philadelphia: Foreign Policy Research Institute, University of Pennsylvania 1956. [Also published in an edition by the USNSA] [S]

Kernish, Robert. *The History of USNSA.* Washington, DC: July, 1965.

Young Americans for Freedom. *NSA Report: A Report on the U.S. National Student Association by Young Americans for Freedom, Inc.* Washington, DC: December 15, 1962.

JOURNALS

Altbach, Philip G. "The National Student Association in the Fifties: Flawed Conscience of the Silent Generation." *Youth and Society*, Vol. 5, No. 2, December, 1973.

Medalie, Richard J., "Grading the Teachers," *Phi Beta Kappan*, January, 1950.

Riggs, Lawrence. "Report by the National Association of Student Personnel Administrators Representative to the Associated Student Governments of the United States of America," *National Association of Student Personnel Administrators Journal*, Vol. II, 1:17-18, July, 1964. [S]

Schwartz, Eugene G. and West, Robert L. "The World Student Congress and International Education of American Students," *Higher Education,* VII:14, March 15, 1951. U.S. Office of Education.

Thurber, L. Newton, guest ed. "Perspectives on Ecumenical Christian Presence in U.S. Universities and Colleges, 1960-1995: Part I. Ecumenical Student Christian Movements, 1960-95." *Journal of Ecumenical Studies*, 32:3. Summer 1995. Part II: "Student Christian Ministries and Issues, 1960-95."*Journal of Ecumenical Studies*, 32:4, Fall, 1995. [Both issues include retrospectives to earlier years.]

Welsh, William B. "United States National Student Association," *Higher Education,* V:5, November 1, 1948. U.S. Office of Education.

Weyand, Norman, S.J. "Report on Operation University," *The Jesuit Education Quarterly,* January, 1948.

School and Society journal: Reports on NSA

Fitzpatrick, Edward A., "Student Bill of Rights," August, 1948.

Klopf, Gordon. "The College Administrator Looks at the National Student Association," August 27, 1949.

Klopf, Gordon, and Trueblood, Dennis. "A Report on the 1950 NSA Congress," November 25, 1950.

______. "The USNSA: An Evaluation," August 11, 1951.

______. "The 1952 Congress of the USNSA," November 1, 1952.

Lynch, Marion and Klopf, Gordon. "A Report on the 1949 NSA Congress," December 10, 1949.

Sollen, Robert H. "Report on the National Student Association," July, 1949.

Trueblood, Dennis L., and Birenbaum, William. "Fourth National Student Association Congress," December 15, 1951.

ARTICLES AND PUBLICATIONS

International Student Service (ISS)

ISS Bulletin. Geneva: Issues of September 1946, November 1946. Containing reports of post-war international student conferences.

ISS Through the War, 1939-1946: A Report Prepared for the XXth Annual Conference. Cambridge, July 22nd-29th, 1946. Geneva: ISS, 1946.

Krauschaar, Otto F. "New Stirrings in American Colleges," *University.* Geneva: ISS, March, 1948.

The New Program of the United States Committee of International Student Service. Introduction by Eleanor Roosevelt. New York: ISS, 1941.

Pre-World War II and Wartime

"American Students Unite," *Nation,* 142 (1936) 33. [M]

Baker, L. H., The National Student Federation of the United States of America, *School and Society,* 26 (1927) 237-8. [M]

Bliven, B., "Citizens of Tomorrow: Fourth Annual Convention of American Student Union," *New Republic,* 97 (1939) 283. [M]

Clark, E., "Lo, the Poor Student," *New Republic,* 77 (1934) 277-8. [M]

Goldberg, C. L., "Southern Youth Points the Way," *New Republic,* 112 (1945) 641. [M]

"Have the Young Gone Sour? Meetings of the National Student Organizations," *New Republic,* 104 (1941) 39. [M]

"Is There a Student Movement in America?" *New Republic,* 81 (1935) 264. [M]

Kelly, J. E., "Little Red Schoolboys," *America,* 60 (1939) 344-5. [M]

Kershaw, A.L., *The New Frontier for the Student YMCA and YWCA.* New York: National Student Council of the YMCA and YWCA, 1955.

Meltzer, M., and Forrest, R., "The Students Say 'Twaddle,'" *New Masses,* January 14, 1941. [M]

"National Student League War Poll," *School and Society,* 39 (1934) 433-4. [M]

"Pink to Red," *Time,* 35 (1940) 32. [M]

Ross, I., "The Student Union and the Future," *New Republic,* 102 (1940) 48-49. [M]

Spivack, R. G. "Youth Reorganizes," *Nation* 152 (1941) 71. [M]

"Students International," *Catholic Action,* 29 (1947) 6-8. [M]

Varney, H. L., "Left Kidnaps American Youth," *American Mercury,* 44 (1938) 391-402. [M]

Wechsler, J. A., "Politics on the Campus," *Nation,* 149 (1939) 732-3. [M]

______. "Student Union Begins," *New Republic,* 85 (1936) 279. [M]

After World War II

Briefs, H. W., "Needed: a Foreign Policy for Students," *America,* 79 (1948) 24. [M]

Concord Magazine, "Editorial: Catholic Students at the National Student Association Congress. . . ," December, 1949, p. 25.

"Cooperation Gets Students Stress," article on the Birmingham International Student Conference. *Christian Science Monitor,* July 16, 1955. [J].

Farrar, John Curtis. "American Students Talk It Over," *Nation*, 164 (1947) 45. [M]

______. "Students Map the Future," *Nation*, 165 (1947) 279. [M]

______. "What About the IUS," *The Student Progressive*, published by the Harvard Liberal Union, September 1947. [J]

Giese, Vincent J. "Leadership in Action," *Concord*, October, 1949.

Jacobson, Muriel, W., "What Can We Say to Europe's Students?," *The Intercollegian*, May, 1946.

Lund, A. "Our Student Comes of Age," *Plain Talk*, 2, (1947) 10-12. [M]

______. "The Intelligent Student's Guide," *Plain Talk*, 2 (1947) 14-17. [M]

McLaughlin, Martin M. "Student Congress at Prague," *America*, 76 (1946) 291-3. [M]

______. "Conference in Chicago," *America*, 76 (1947) 711-714. [M]

______. "National Student Association," *America*, 78 (1947) 149-51. [M]

______. "Spotlight on Students," *The Catholic World*, 166 (1947) 130-7. [M]

Murray, John Courtney. "Operation University," *America*, April 13, 1946.

M. T. W., "Students, On Guard!" *Plain Talk*, 2 (1947) 4-7. [M]

Palmer, E. Hoyt, "NSA Comes Up Shouting," *The Intercollegian*, November, 1947.

Schultze, C. L., "The National Student Association: With or Without Catholic Influence?," *Catholic Action*, 29 (1947) 11. [M]

Schwartz, Eugene G. and West, Robert L, "The World Student Congress of IUS," *The Intercollegian*, January, 1951.

Shaw, M., "The Reawakening of the American Student Movement," *Political Affairs*, February, 1947. [M]

______. "Student America Convenes," *Political Affairs*, October, 1947. [M]

Simons, J. J., "Need for a National Student Group," *The New Leader*, August 23, 1947. [M]

The American Student-Profile and Promise. Philadelphia: The Association, 1957. [S]

Voegeli, Royal. "Student Rule, National Scale," Guest Editorial, *Wisconsin State Journal*, August, 1947. [S]

Willner, Donald. "For a National Student Organization," *The Student Progessive.* Harvard Liberal Union, April, 1947, pp. 18-19. [S]

After 1957

American Civil Liberties Union. *Academic Freedom and Civil Liberties of Students in Colleges and Universities.* Revised edition. New York: The Union, 1963, [S]

Conservative Study Group. *The Congress Conservative.* No. 3, August,1964. [S]

Green, Reginald H. *The College Student and the Changing South: Report of the Southwide Student Human Relations Conference.* Philadelphia: The Association, 1959. [S]

National Association of Women Deans and Counselors. *A Descriptive and Evaluative Statement Regarding the United States National Student Association.* Boston Convention of the National Association of Women Deans and Counselors, 1963. (Mimeographed.) [S]

NSA and U.S. Government Covert Funding

Fullbright, J. William, "We Must Not Fight Fire with Fire," *New York Times*, April 27, 1967.

Los Angeles Times. A series of 1967 investigative articles covering NSA as well as the entire range of non-government organizations involved, by Stuart H. Loory, Don Irwin, Vincent Burke, Joseph Kraft and others: Februatry 19, 24, 25, 26 February 26, 1967.

Paget, Karen. "From Stockholm to Leiden: The CIA's Role in the Formation of the International Student Conference," *Intelligence and National Security*, Vol. 18, No. 2, Summer 2003, p. 134,

Stern, Sol. "NSA and the CIA," *Ramparts*, March, 1967, pp. 29-39.

Werdell, Philip. *The CIA and the Kiddies: Conflicting Evaluations. What Did it Mean? What Should Be Done?* Washington, DC: U.S. National Student Association, August, 1967.

COLLEGE NEWSPAPER REPORTS

Note: See index to colleges and college newspapers on p. 1169 for additional reference to college newspaper articles cited in the Anthology.

The Agnes Scott News. Bill Holbrook (University of Minnesota) reports on his experiences at the 1950 World Student Congress in Prague as a member of the NSA Observer Team. Atlanta, GA, 1950: 10/25, 12/6; 1951: 1/10, 1/17.

Cornell Daily Sun. A series of articles by Edward Hanpeter on the history of fraternities at Cornell and issues of fraternity discrimination and reform. Ithaca, NY, 1950: 4/26, 4/27, 4/28, 4/29.

Daily Bruin. A series of reports on the NSA Constitutional Convention. University of California at Los Angeles, 1947: 9/29, 9/30, 10/1, 10/2, 10/3, 10/6, 10/7.

Daily Californian. "A series of articles exploring the functions, processes, organization and activities of the [NSA]." Variously by Vance Stadtman and Carol Noderer. University of California, Berkeley, 1948: 9/28, 10/8, 10/28, 11/11.

_______. A series on California's loyalty oath issue. University of California, Berkeley, 1950: 10/23; 1951: 2/7, 10/22, 11/19.

Daily Tar Heel. Reports by Jimmy Wallace on his experience as a U.S. delegate to the 1946 World Student Congress. University of North Carolina, Chapel Hill, 1946: 10/16 to 10/29.

The Harvard Crimson. A review of student rights and academic freedom cases around the nation, written by John G. Simon, Burton S. Glinn and David E. Lillienthal, Jr. Cambridge, 1949: 5/17, 5/25.

Temple University News. Features on the death of President Roosevelt and on VE Day. "To Us . . .The Torch," April 16, 1945. "They Died for the Freedoms Men Hold Dear," May 28, 1945.

The Phoenix. Reports by and letters from Swarthmore undergraduates serving in the U.S. Army in World War I, dealing with death, gassing, dawn of peace and return home. Swarthmore College, PA, 1918: 11/12, 11/26, 12/27; 1919: 1/14, 2/11.

Student Life. A series of reprints on the Broyles seditious activities commission in Illinois and Chancellor Hutchins' reponse from the *Chicago Maroon*, by *Maroon* staff writers Frank Woodman, June Marks and David Broder. Edited by Jack Samuel and the *Student Life* staff. Washington University in St. Louis, 1949: 5/13, 5/15, 5/17.

PUBLICATIONS—USNSA

Note: Following its move to Philadelphia in 1952, NSA published on a broad spectrum of student life and student government functions through its Student Government Bulletin and in separate booklets. Almost all of these will be found in the NSA Archives at the State Historical Society of Wisconsin and, for international publications, at the Hoover Institute.

Student Government

Bacon, Sylvia. *Student Bill of Rights: Statement and Commentary.* Denver: The Association, 1951, 8pp. (Mim.) [N]

Brock, Elmer. *A Call to Order: Guide to Parliamentary Procedure. Revised.* Philadelphia: The Association, 1952, 16pp. [N]

______. *Freshman Orientation, New Meaning.* Madison: The Association, 1951 9pp. [N] (Mim.)

Dungan, Ralph; Klopf, Gordon; and Heggie, Richard. *Student Leadership and Government in Higher Education.* Madison: The Association, 1950. [Earlier edition by Dungan and Klopf, 1948.] [N]

Freidson, Eliot. Student Government, *Student Leaders and the American College.* Phildelphia: The Association, 1955. [S]

Goldsmith, Herbert. *SDS Handbook.* [Student Discount System] Madison: The Association, 1950, (Mim.) [N]

Schwartz, Eugene G., edited by Medalie, Richard J. and Goldsmith, Herbert B. *Faculty Rating.* [Madison: The Association, 1951, 12pp. (Mim.) [Earlier editions in 1949 and 1950]

Medalie, Richard J. *Campus Co-ops.* [Madison: The Association, 1950.]

Perry, Ted. *Student Government-Administration and Techniques.* Madison: The Association, 1950, 55pp. (Mim.) [N]

Prize Winning Entries: First Annual Democratic Campus Award Contest: Sixth Annual Richard Welling Student Government Achievement Competition. Philadelphia: The Association, 1962. [S]

Sanders, John, and Brock, Elmer. *Honor System in Higher Education.* Madison: The Association, 1951, 35pp. (Mim.)

"Student Body Presidents Conference, Second Annual Meeting Report and Directory: August, 1952." Compiled in *Student Government Bulletin.*

Trueblood, Dennis and Perry, Ted. *A Continuing Leadership Program*, Madison: The Association, 1950, 19pp. (Mim.) [N]

Program Aids

Bowdoin Plan, Bowdoin College. Fraternity housing for foreign students. Madison: The Association, 1948, 8pp. (Mim.) [N]

Carleton DP Plan, Carleton College. Madison: The Association, 1949.[N]

Chervenik, Emily. *Planning a Job Opportunities Conference.* Madison: The Association, 1948.

Colorado DP Plan, National Sub-Commission on Displaced Persons (University of Colorado). Madison: The Association, 1949, 5pp. (Mim.) [N]

Colorado Graduate Travel Savings Plan, University of Colorado. Madison: The Association, 1950, 2pp. (Mim.) [N]

Harrington, James J. *Student Discount Service.* Philadelphia: The Association, 1959. [S]

International Affairs

International Student Conference In Stockholm, Swedish National Union of Students, 1951, 12pp. (Mim) [N]

Travel Department. *Work, Study, Travel Abroad.* Cambridge: The Association, 1952. 48pp. [N] [Also published in 1948, 1949, 1950 and 1951]

USNSA Staff. *An International Role for the American Student.* Cambridge: The Association. 1951, 23pp. [N]

West, Robert L. *National Student Unions.* Cambridge: USNSA, 1949.

Human Relations

Medalie, Richard J., and Klopf, Gordon. *Human Relations and the Educational Community.* Madison: The Association, 1950, 33pp. [N].

Michigan Attitudes Survey, Michigan Daily, University of Michigan. Ann Arbor: 1949, 4pp. [N]

USNSA Congresses

Report of the Constitutional Convention. University of Wisconsin. Philadelphia: The Association,, 1947. [S]

Program and Report. 1948-1949: First National Student Congress, August 23-28. University of Wisconsin. Madison: The Association, 1947.

Report on the Second Annual National Student Congress. University of Illinois. Madison: The Association, 1949. [S]

USNSA Congress Report: Third Annual National Student Congress. August 23-31,1950. University of Michigan. Madison: The Association, 1950.

Minutes, Fourth Annual National Student Congress. University of Minnesota, August 20-29, 1951.

Congress Report: Fifth National Student Congress. Indiana University. Philadelphia: The Association, 1952.[N]

Summary Report: 7th National Congress. Philadelphia: The Association, 1954. [J]

Summary Report: Eighth National Student Congress. Philadelphia: The Association, 1955. [S]

Student Leadership in American Education: Summary Report of the Ninth National Student Congress. Philadelphia: The Association, 1956. [S]

Excerpts from Resolutions of the Tenth Congress. Philadelphia: The Association, 1957. [S]

USNSA Organization

A World in Transition: Students in Action. Philadelphia: The Association, 1960. [S]

Codification of USNSA Policies: Revised, 1952. (Mim.) Philadelphia: The Association, 1952.

Liebert, Roland. *Analysis of the American Association of University Professors, Statement on Faculty Responsibility for the Academic Freedom of Students in Relation to Policies and Principles of the United States National Student Association,* Student Government Bulletin (Philadelphia: The Association, undated). pp. 5-15. [S]

Murphy, Richard J., *Statement in Answer to the Students for America.* Philadelphia: The Association, 1953. [S]

NSA - Citizenship, Scholarship, Fellowship (Revised). Denver and Philadelphia: The Association, 1952 ,10pp. folder. [N]

USNSA Constitution: Revised, 1952. Philadelphia: The Association, 1952.

Periodicals

Essai. A literary magazine. Two issues were published, in Fall, 1949, and Spring, 1950. College of St. Theresa, Minnesota.

International Student Information Bulletin. An occational newsletter. Vol. 1 No. 1 launched November 1, 1951. International Activities Committee, Harvard Student Council.

National Student News. Monthly tabloid, November through May, Vol. 1 No. 1 launched in 1957.

NSA News. Tabloid published approximately monthly during the school year from 1947-48 to 1952-53 (see p. 293 for publication history).

Student Government Bulletin. Vol. 1, No. 1 appeared October, 1952. Published monthly in 8.5 x 11 booklet format.

Students International Activities Bulletin. Two issues were published for the National Continuations Committee in March and April, 1947, by the International Activities Committee. Harvard Student Council.

United States National Student Association News. Newsletter published monthly during the school year, Vol. 1, No. 1 launched in 1953.

DOCUMENTS AND REPORTS — USNSA

Note: During NSA's first five years through 1952-53, each National Student Congress was preceded by staff reports and working papers on organization and, for each of the Commissions, on Student Government, Educational Problems, International Affairs, etc. They were followed by a directory and minutes. Minutes of the National Executive Committee meetings were also circulated, usually in December and April. Almost all of these reports are preserved and will be found in the NSA Archives. They are not listed here.

Codification of Policy: Ninth National Student Congress. Philadelphia: The Association, 1956. [S]; *Tenth National Student Congress.* Philadelphia: The Association, 1957. [S]

National Continuations Committee for National Student Organization, *Official Minutes, March 1-3, 1947.* [M]

______, *Official Minutes, August 27-30, 1947.*[M]

National Continuations Committee of the Chicago Student Conference. *Report of the Chicago Student Conference, December 28-30, 1946.* Prepared by the National Continuations Committee. [S]

______. *Suggested Program and Proposed Constitution and By-Laws for the National Student Organization.* A report prepared by the National Continuations Committee , 1947.[S]

______. *Official Call to the National Constitutional Convention for the National Student Organization.* Chicago: National Continuations Committee, 1947. [M]

National Student Association Liaison Committees of the National Association of Deans of Women, National Association of Student Personnel Administrators, and American College Personnel Association. *Report on the United States National Student Association, April 1, 1953.* [S]

______.*United States National Student Association: Evaluation and Descriptive Statement,* February 20, 1958. (Mimeographed). [S]

1947-1948 Financial Report. Philadelphia: The Association, 1948. (Mimeographed.) . [S]

Report of the Peace Corps. Philadelphia: The Association, 1961. [S]

Student Responsibility in an Age of Challenge. Philadelphia: The Association, 1959. [S]

United States National Student Association. *Report of the Constitutional Convention Including a History, the Constitution and By-Laws and Summarized Panel Reports Which Outline the Program of the USNSA.* Madison, Wisconsin: United States National Student Association, 1947. [M]

______. *Report: Student Dimensions; Education, Community, Society.* Philadelphia: The Association, 1963. [S]

International Team Reports

Note: During 1950 and 1951, NSA commissioned over a dozen students to travel to Europe, the Middle East, Africa, Asia and South America to study and contact other national student organizations. The team members and the reports these team members prepared are listed and described on page 609 of this Anthology. The countries covered in the reports received include:

Africa: Nigeria;

Asia: Afghanistan, Burma, Ceylon, Hong Kong, India, Indo-China, Indonesia, Maylaya, Pakistan, Philippines, Siam, Singapore;

Carribbean: Cuba, Dominican Republic, Haiti, Jamaica, Puerto Rico;

Europe: France, Scandinavia (Denmark, Finland, Norway), United Kingdom, Yugoslavia.

South America: Brazil, Mexico, Paraguay.

DOCUMENTS — OTHER

Domestic Affairs

American Student Union. *The Student Almanac. New York: 1939.* [M]

______. *Constitution.* New York: American Student Union, 1939. (High school Handbook). [M]

______. *Keep Democracy Working. Making It Serve Human Needs, Report of Proceedings, Fourth National Convention, American Student Union,* 1939. [M]

Brown, Francis J. and Anliot, Richard B., Editors. *Human Relations in Higher Education: A Report of a National Student Conference Held at Earlham College, March 29-31, 1951.* American Council on Education.

National Catholic Welfare Conference, *Report on the International Student Assembly.* Washington, DC: 1942. [M]

National Catholic Youth Council, *Operation University.* Washington, D.C.: 1947. [M]

National Student Federation of America, *Proceedings, Fourteenth Annual Congress, Purdue University, Lafayette, Indiana, December 27-31, 1938.* [M]

______. *Fifteen Years of Student Leadership.* Washington, DC: National Student Federation of American, 1940. [M]

International — General

British National Union of Students (BNUS). *A Meeting of Students from 38 Different Countries, 10-11 November, 1945,* p.12,17. [J]

______. *Report on a Conference of Students from Thirteen of the United Nations, Held on March 24th & 25th, 1945.* BNUS. [J]

______. *Program for the Two-Day London Meeting for Students Attending the World Youth Conference,* November 10-11, 1945. BNUS, Document #3. [J]

McLean, Catherine D.,*Report of the World Youth Congress Held in Prague, Czechoslovakia, August 18-31, 1946,* Canadian Federation of Newman Clubs, November 30, 1946. [J]

Taylor, Charles, *NFCUS Report of the Unity Meeting.* NFCUS, 1952. [J]

International — World Student Congress/IUS

Report on the Work of the Credentials Committee of the World Student Congress at Prague, August 1946 signed by Carmel Brickman, secretary of the Committee and Thonas Madden, chairman of the International Preparatory Committee. [J]

Reports and Resolutions of the IUS Executive Committee Meeting, Berlin, January 13-18, 1951. *World Student News* V:2 Supplement. [J]

British National Union of Students. *Report of the NUS Observers to the Council Meeting of the International Union of Students, Moscow, 1954.* [J]

______. *Report of the Official Observers of the (British) National Union of Students, on the Third World Student Congress, 1953.* [J]

______. *Report on the First Meeting of the World Student Congress, Prague, 1945.* [J]

Coleman, A.J. *The World Congress of Students — Prague 1946,* World Student Christian Federation observer. [J]

Danish National Union of Students. *Report on the IUS Congress, 1950.* [J]

Ellis, William S. and Roberts, Joyce. *Report of the World Student Congress* written for the National Intercollegiate Christian Council in the fall of 1946. [J]

International Congress of Students, *Invitation,* Prague, Czechoslovakia, August 20, 1945. [J]

International Union of Students, *Constitution. International Union of Students.* Prague, Czechoslovakia: 1946. [M]

______. Official Reports, Council Meeting, August, 1947. [M]

______. *Resolutions of the World Students Congress.* Prague, Czechoslovakia: 1946. [M]

______. *Members of the Executive Committee and Council.* Prague, Czechoslovakia: International Union of Students, 1946. [M]

______. *Congress Bulletin,* June 1953, July 1953. [J]

______. *Resolutions of the World Student Congress,* published by the IUS Information Department, August 1946. [J]

______. *Minutes of the IUS Executive Committee Meeting, February 1947.* IUS. [J]

______. *Report on the Executive Committee Meeting in Vienna, 1954.* [J]

______. *Minutes, World Student Congress, 1946.* [J]

Jacobson, Muriel, *Report of the World Student Congress, Prague, Czechoslovakia,* official report to the National Student YWCA-YMCA, December, 1945.

Madden, Thomas, The International Preparatory Committee, *The British Medical Students Journal,* I:1, 1946. [J]

______. *The World Student Congress in Prague, 17th November,* 1945, *The British Medical Students Journal,* I:1, 1946. [J]

World Student Congress, Complete Minutes and Panel Reports, Prague, Czechoslovakia, August 15-30, 1946. [M]

World Student News. 1946 World Student Congress edition. [J]

International — International Student Conference/Cosec

Cosec. *International Student Cooperation.* Brochure: 1953. [J]

______. *Resolutions, International Student Conferences.* Stockholm, 1950; Edinburgh, 1952; Copenhagen; 1953; Istanbul, 1954. Cosec: 1954. [J]

Proposal for International Cooperation passed by the International Student Conference, Birmingham, England, 1955. Cosec. 1955. [J]

Resolutions passed by the fifth International Student Conference, Birmingham, England, 1955. Cosec: 1955. [J]

Students' Mutual Assistance Programme, A program of cooperative action adopted by the participating members at the Stockholm Conference. Circular published by Cosec: undated, c. 1951.

6. COLLEGES AND UNIVERSITIES IN 1948

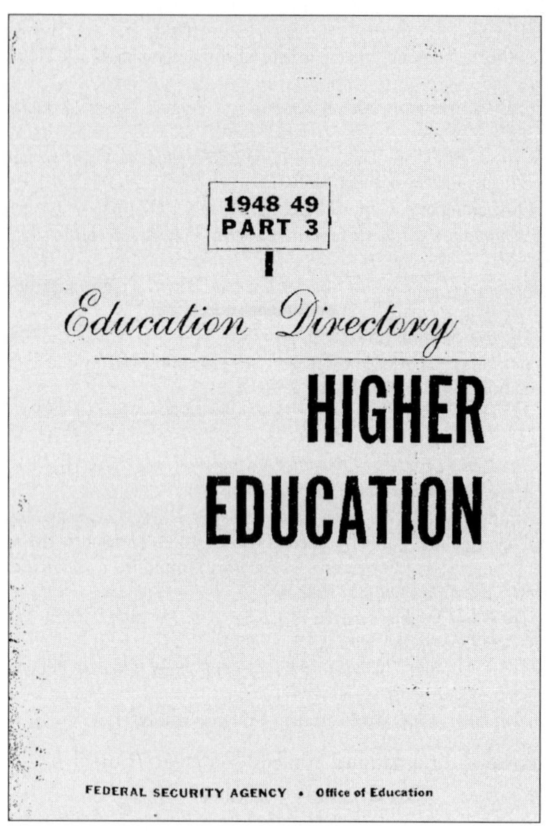

1948 49
PART 3

Education Directory

HIGHER EDUCATION

FEDERAL SECURITY AGENCY • Office of Education

PART 3
HIGHER EDUCATION

CONTENTS

INSTITUTIONS OF HIGHER EDUCATION INCLUDED IN THIS DIRECTORY

Institutions offering at least a 2-year program of college-level studies are included in this directory. Types of institutions included are as follows:

A. UNIVERSITIES, COLLEGES, AND TEACHERS COLLEGES:

1. Accredited by the following agencies.
   (a) American Association of Colleges for Teacher Education.
   (b) Association of American Universities.
   (c) Middle States Association of Colleges and Secondary Schools.
   (d) New England Association of Colleges and Secondary Schools.
   (e) North Central Association of Colleges and Secondary Schools.
   (f) Northwest Association of Secondary and Higher Schools.
   (g) Southern Association of Colleges and Secondary Schools.
   (h) State universities or State departments of education.
2. All State-supported institutions.

1

2 EDUCATION DIRECTORY, 1948–49

3. Four-year institutions which are not accredited by any agency but which enroll 100 or more resident college students in regular session, graduate at least 10 students annually, and furnish evidence that their work is accepted at full value by at least three institutions accredited by agencies listed under A-1.

B. INDEPENDENT PROFESSIONAL AND TECHNOLOGICAL SCHOOLS:

1. Accredited by professional associations or approved by State universities or State departments of education.
2. Not accredited by any agency but which enroll 25 or more resident students of college grade in regular session, graduate at least 5 students annually, and furnish evidence that their work is accepted at full value by at least three institutions accredited by agencies listed under B-1.

C. JUNIOR COLLEGES AND NORMAL SCHOOLS:

1. Accredited by the agencies listed under A-1 (above).
2. Not accredited by any agency but which require high-school graduation for entrance, offer 2 years of work of college grade, enroll 50 or more resident students of college grade in regular session, and furnish evidence that their work is accepted at full value by at least three institutions accredited by agencies listed under A-1.

CLASSIFICATION OF INSTITUTIONS

Institutions are classified according to their offerings into four types:

1. Colleges and universities offering liberal arts; 4-year; degree-granting.
2. Professional and technological schools—independently controlled.
3. Teachers colleges (4-year; degree-granting) and normal school (2- or 3-year; non-degree granting).
4 Junior colleges; 2- or 3-year; not granting baccalaureate degrees.

ISSUED ANNUALLY

The Education Directory of the Office of Education is issued annually in the following parts:

1. **Federal Government and States.**
2. **Counties and Cities.**
*3. **Higher Education.**
4. **Education Associations and Directories.**

As soon as each part is off the press copies may be purchased at nominal cost through the Superintendent of Documents, U. S. Government Printing Office, Washington 25, D. C.

***Part 3. Higher Education was prepared by Theresa B. Wilkins, Higher Education Division, Office of Education.**

FEDERAL SECURITY AGENCY – Oscar R. Ewing, Administrat[illegible]
Office of Education – – Rall I. Grigsby, Acting Commissi[illegible]

United States Government Printing Office, Washington : 19[illegible]
For sale by the Superindentent of Documents, U. S. Govern[illegible]
Printing Office, Washington 25, D. C. – – – – – – – Price [illegible]

ENROLLMENT

For each institution for which data are available, the total enrollment of regular students of college grade, excluding extension, correspondence, and subcollegiate students, in the fall of 1947 is given. Where figure is italicized, the enrollment is estimated.

Institutions of higher education in the United States

State or outlying part	Total	Colleges and universities	Professional and technological schools	Teachers colleges and normal schools	Junior colleges	Institutions for Negroes (included in columns 2-6)
1	2	3	4	5	6	7
Alabama	26	12	3	5	6	7
Arizona	6	1	1	2	2	
Arkansas	24	12	1	2	9	5
California	99	36	15		48	
Colorado	18	6	2	3	7	
Connecticut	27	8	5	6	8	
Delaware	4	2	1		1	1
District of Columbia	25	11	6	2	6	3
Florida	17	11	1		5	4
Georgia	51	23	9	2	17	11
Idaho	9	4		2	3	
Illinois	99	38	35	9	17	
Indiana	37	25	8	2	2	
Iowa	48	23	2	1	22	
Kansas	44	20	1	2	21	
Kentucky	40	14	7	4	15	1
Louisiana	18	16	1	1		5
Maine	15	6	2	4	3	
Maryland	31	15	7	5	4	3
Massachusetts	76	28	17	16	15	
Michigan	44	21	9	4	10	
Minnesota	44	16	8	8	12	
Mississippi	33	11		3	19	7
Missouri	53	17	10	7	19	8
Montana	11	4	1	3	3	
Nebraska	23	13		5	5	
Nevada	1	1				
New Hampshire	8	5		2	1	
New Jersey	33	11	10	7	5	
New Mexico	8	3	1	3	1	
New York	122	66	31	26	49	
North Carolina	52	27		6	19	12
North Dakota	13	4		5	4	
Ohio	67	47	16	2	2	2
Oklahoma	36	11	1	6	18	1
Oregon	19	12	1	5	1	
Pennsylvania	107	53	29	14	11	2
Rhode Island	11	3	5	2	1	
South Carolina	32	21	3		8	9
South Dakota	16	7	1	4	4	
Tennessee	48	28	6	5	9	8
Texas	80	33	5	7	35	11
Utah	10	5	1		4	
Vermont	12	7		3	2	
Virginia	42	20	8	2	12	6
Washington	24	12		4	8	
West Virginia	19	11		6	2	3
Wisconsin	39	15	7	13	4	
Wyoming	2	1			1	
Outlying parts of the United States						
Alaska	1	1				
Canal Zone	1				1	
Hawaii	1	1				
Puerto Rico	2	2				
Total	1,728	790	277	210	451	104

8 EDUCATION DIRECTORY, 1948–49

Control of higher education

Types of institutions	Total	State control	District or city control	Private control	Denominational control: Protestant	Roman Catholic	Jewish
1	2	3	4	5	6	7	8
College and university	722	[1] 108	14	190	254	154	2
Professional and technological school	270	[2] 21	2	153	71	20	
Teachers college and normal school	198	159	5	18	3	13	
Junior college	434	[1] 43	180	87	95	29	3
Institutions attended predominantly by Negroes							
College and university	68	22		13	32	1	
Professional and technological school	7			4	3		
Teachers college and normal school	12	9	3				
Junior college	17		2	1	14		
Total: White institutions	1,624	[3] 331	201	448	423	216	5
Total: Negro institutions	104	31	5	18	49	1	
Grand total	1,728	[3] 362	206	466	472	217	5

[1] Includes 1 under Federal control.
[2] Includes 4 under Federal control.
[3] Includes 6 under Federal control.

Student bodies in higher education

Types of institutions	Total	Institutions for men	Institutions for women	Coeducational institutions
1	2	3	4	5
College and university	722	87	155	480
Professional and technological school	270	84	9	177
Teachers college and normal school	198	1	26	171
Junior college	434	33	76	325
Institutions attended predominantly by Negroes				
College and university	68	2	3	63
Professional and technological school	7	1		6
Teachers college and normal school	12			12
Junior college	17			17
Total: White institutions	1,624	205	266	1,153
Total: Negro institutions	104	3	3	98
Grand total	1,728	208	269	1,251

DECEMBER 18, 1948 SCHOOL AND SOCIETY 419

STATISTICS OF ATTENDANCE IN AMERICAN UNIVERSITIES AND COLLEGES, 1948

By
RAYMOND WALTERS
PRESIDENT, UNIVERSITY OF CINCINNATI

A LULL in enrollment—welcomed by educators—has come to American universities and colleges. After large increases during the immediate postwar years, attendance totals this autumn are only slightly above those of the autumn of 1947, with numerous institutions recording decreases. Reports received from 726 approved universities and four-year colleges, as of November 1, 1948, show a total of 1,580,783 full-time students and a total of 351,196 part-time students, or 1,931,979 in all. These figures represent an approximate increase of only 9/10 of 1 per cent in full-time attendance and an approximate increase of 4½ per cent in part-time attendance for 1948 over 1947 (based on 674 institutions supplying exactly comparable statistics). For "substantially all of the 1,800 institutions of higher education in the United States," the Office of Education, FSA, reports enrollments, not differentiated as to full-time and part-time, of 2,410,-000 "total students" this fall, or 72,000 (3.1 per cent) more than a year ago.[1]

What maintains the current level? The answer is clear. It is the host of veteran students for whom a grateful nation, through the Veterans Administration, is paying tuition costs and subsistence allowances. The veterans account for over 40 per cent of the 1948 attendance totals.

In practically all entering classes there has been a halt in numbers. As compared with 1947, the decrease in freshmen is about 10 per cent. This decrease reflects the somewhat smaller number of pupils in the high schools of the nation, in consequence of the lower birth rate of the depression period. Accordingly, the freshman-class recession may be continued next year, possibly accelerated by the peacetime draft. Moreover, a considerable proportion of veteran students will be graduating.

This respite in the enrollment flood will be gratefully received by administrators and faculties. In order to accommodate the postwar flood of students, exceeding by more than three fourths the 1939 prewar peak, administrators have exerted to their utmost in providing classrooms, laboratories, and housing facilities, and faculties have carried teaching loads and class sizes too great for satisfactory results. These burdens they have borne cheerfully, out of appreciation for the war service of the GIs and especially in recognition of the good academic work the GIs have performed.

There is full realization in academic circles that the current and prospective lag in attendance is a breathing spell only. The present secondary-school population will shoot up when the huge number of babies born since World War II demobilization reach high-school and then college age. It is estimated that by 1956–57 there will be approximately 1,778,000 more pupils in high schools than there are in 1948–49 (8,048,000 pupils as compared with 6,270,000).[2]

Facing universities and colleges—especially tax-supported institutions which must accept additional students—are the problems that the next decade will present regarding finances, building construction, and staffing for the enlarged college population.[3]

Recession of the Veteran Tide. The attendance of veterans in "institutions of higher learning" as of

[1] Statement, November 14, 1948. Federal Security Agency, Office of Education, Federal Security Administrator Oscar R. Ewing. A table, not differentiated as to full-time and part-time enrollments, shows that an undesignated number of "universities, colleges, and professional schools" have 1,961,000 "total students," or 78,000 (4.1 per cent) more than in the fall of 1947; that an undesignated number of "teachers colleges" have 170,000 total students, or 8,000 (4.9 per cent) more than in 1947; that an undesignated number of "junior colleges" have 11,000 (5 per cent) fewer total students than in 1947; and that an undesignated number of "Negro institutions" have 3,000 (4.1 per cent) fewer total students than in 1947.

[2] U. S. Office of Education, FSA, statement quoted in SCHOOL AND SOCIETY, September 4, 1948, Vol. 68, p. 149.

[3] See "Estimates of Future College and University Enrollment" by J. Harold Goldthorpe, *Higher Education*, Vol. IV, No. 4, March 15, 1948, U. S. Office of Education. Also "Higher Education for American Democracy," Report of President's Commission on Higher Education, 1947.

TABLE I

I. UNIVERSITIES AND LARGE INSTITUTIONS OF COMPLEX ORGANIZATION

1. Under Public Control

Institution	Veterans Full-Time	Nonveterans Full-Time	Veterans and nonveterans All Resident	Full-Time Teaching Staff	Total Number Teaching Staff
Colleges of C. of N. Y. ...	6,767	21,507	62,403	1,889	3,359
Bklyn. C. ..	2,100	6,087	15,126	460	813
City C.	3,549	7,627	32,567	900	1,600
Hunter C. W	681	5,485	11,780	324	780
Queens C. ..	487	2,358	2,930	155	216
Indiana U. ...	6,731	7,688	22,042	675	975
La. State U. & A. & M. C. .	4,845	5,822	11,501	457	806
Miami U.	1,816	3,541	5,401	276	350
Mich. State C.	8,298	6,794	16,010	798	956
Mont. State U.	1,880	1,522	3,456	160	220
Municipal U. of Wichita ...	1,370	1,132	3,130	119	171
Ohio State U.	11,748	10,479	28,848	1,325*	2,075*
Ohio U.	2,768	3,154	6,401	278	855
Ore. State C. .	3,618	3,746	7,408	441	546
Pa. State C. ..	5,597	4,020	9,792	...	921
Rutgers[1]	4,686	4,425	19,189	826	1,329
State C. Wash.	3,079	3,577	6,656	428	552
U. of Akron ..	1,392	1,368	4,678	181	259
U. of Alabama	4,670	4,374	9,150	585	685
U. of Arizona.	2,304	2,763	5,673	276	385
U. of Arkansas	2,782	2,128	4,979	274	291
U. of Calif., incl.	19,737	23,681	43,418	1,912	3,638
Berkeley ..	10,872	12,278	23,145	727§	1,656§
Los Angeles	5,781	8,789	14,570	405§	885§
Other Campuses ..	3,084	2,619	5,703	821§	1,138§
U. of Cincinnati	3,614	3,808	16,096	887	907
U. of Colorado	4,380	5,185	9,860	595*	750*
U. of Conn. ..	3,927	3,195	8,271	474	658
U. of Florida .	5,395	4,608	10,003	603	649
U. of Georgia	3,709	3,202	7,087	375	408
U. of Idaho ..	1,650	1,984	3,634	210	234
U. of Illinois .	12,553	12,068	27,773	1,460†	3,249‡
U. of Iowa ...	5,058	5,492	10,550	625	1,228
U. of Kansas	5,219	4,278	9,751	436	1,088
U. of Kentucky	4,310	3,042	7,848	442	473
U. of Louisville[2]	2,510	2,175	7,264	238	613
U. of Maine ..	2,765	2,014	4,795	286	328
U. of Michigan	10,803	10,201	23,044	1,187	1,527
U. of Minn. ..	14,598	12,250	32,199	...	...
U. of Miss. ...	1,700	1,609	3,339	212	264
U. of Missouri[3]	8,216	5,175	13,964	725*	1,196*
U. of Nebraska	4,900	5,160	10,525	466	691
U. of Nevada .	839	851	1,774	117	145
U. of N. H. ..	1,805	1,754	3,594	220	271
U. of N. Mex. .	2,511	2,117	4,889	248	324
U. of N. Car. .	4,331	3,272	7,640	328	535
U. of N. Dak. .	1,384	1,181	2,661	165	180
U. of Okla. ..	6,393	5,122	12,174	465	672
U. of Oregon .	....	....	6,892	...	...
U. of S. Car. .	2,346	1,494	4,395	208	239
U. of S. Dak. .	1,009	892	1,950	135	169
U. of Tenn. ..	4,004	3,474	7,903	581	692
U. of Texas[4] .	9,330	7,698	17,028	796	1,139
U. of Toledo .	1,833	2,347	5,954	206	305
U. of Utah ..	....	....	9,034	450	675
U. of Vt[5]	1,492	1,545	3,145	199	274
U. of Va. M ..	3,084	1,838	5,015	317	705
U. of Wash. ..	9,024	7,164	16,650	648	1,677
U. of Wis. ...	11,507	10,849	24,756*	1,051	1,942
U. of Wyoming	1,689	1,474	3,293	285	310
Wayne U. ...	4,247	4,611	17,925	462	916
W. Va. U. ...	3,582	2,775	6,707	343	487
Totals	259,795	257,555	684,507	26,685	43,578

* Estimated.
† Does not include any non-salaried clinical staff.
‡ Includes 644 on non-salaried clinical staff.
§ Includes duplicates which have been deducted from grand total.
[1] Including New Jersey College for Women and the University of Newark.
[2] Including Louisville Municipal College for Negroes.
[3] Including School of Mines & Metallurgy.
[4] Including dentistry but not medical students.
[5] Including State Agricultural College.

2. Under Private Control

Institution	Veterans Full-Time	Nonveterans Full-Time	Veterans and nonveterans All Resident	Full-Time Teaching Staff	Total Number Teaching Staff
Boston C. M .	3,481	2,690	7,198	307	418
Boston U. ...	6,164	4,596	18,617	800*	1,100*
Brigham Young	1,504	3,130	4,886	200	260
Brown	(4,651)		4,651	...	...
Catholic U. of America ...	1,854	1,974	4,618	380	476
Clark U., Mass.	537	476	1,075	58	75
Columbia (Incl. Barnard C.)	9,992	11,620	29,164	...	2,568
Cornell U. ...	4,417	5,655	10,072	975	2,190
Creighton ...	1,670	1,081	2,844	144	356
Dartmouth M	1,298	1,600	2,898	241	325
De Paul	2,673	1,965	9,776	235	350
Drake	2,324	1,658	4,929	188	285
Duke	2,026	3,088	5,114	252	360
Emory	2,040	1,428	3,642	311	588
Fordham	3,860	3,281	9,944	271	484
Georget'n U. M	2,677	2,038	5,667	290	604
George Wash.	3,566*	2,530*	12,283	425*	800*
Harvard U. M	6,099	5,808	11,907	...	2,203
Howard U. ..	2,024	2,851	5,231	366	467
Johns Hopkins	1,380	1,353	6,808	617	1,198
Lehigh M	1,856	1,203	3,523	230	308
Loyola, La. ..	1,056	904	2,562	105	246
New York U. .	11,627	11,478	47,647	1,291†	3,321†
Northwestern .	5,248	5,610	23,788	550	1,769
Princeton M .	1,350	2,061	3,411	257	504
Rice Institute	446	1,115	1,561	88	155
St. John's U., N. Y.	2,464	1,798	7,187	166	225
St. Louis U. .	4,334	3,698	10,015	373	1,104
South. Meth. .	3,745	2,868	8,777	228	318
Stanford	3,739*	4,131*	8,364	471	1,089
Syracuse	8,184	9,122	19,698	...	1,518
Temple	4,686	4,464	14,349	667	1,014
Tufts	1,973	1,470	3,581	...	747
Tulane[1]	2,392	2,751	6,681	449	856
U. of Buffalo .	4,114	2,189	11,093	...	...
U. of Chicago .	3,650*	4,850*	9,519	781	900
U. of Denver .	6,284	2,800	11,299	350	675
U. of Detroit .	4,145	3,425	9,787	244	467
U. of Kansas City	1,274	844	3,544	126	240
U. of Notre Dame M ...	2,506	2,584	5,090	351	509
U. of Pa.	4,915	4,927	14,803	800	2,259
U. of Pittsburgh	7,945	6,020	19,526	504	1,513
U. of Richmond	987	1,045	3,108	85	150
U. of Rochester	1,895	2,098	5,058	365	809
U. of S. Calif.	10,487	4,221	20,454	821	1,095
Vanderbilt ...	1,693	1,961	3,709	358	485
Washington U.	3,832	3,664	13,860	454	1,264
Western Reserve	3,465	2,634	12,876	303	865
Yale M	4,052	4,634	8,686	660	1,397
Totals	173,870	159,831	474,820	17,132	40,804

* Estimated.
† For 1947–48.
[1] Including H. Sophie Newcomb Memorial College.

TABLE I—(continued)

II. COLLEGES OF ARTS AND SCIENCES

Institution	Veterans Full-Time	Nonveterans Full-Time	Veterans and nonveterans All Resident	Full-Time Teaching Staff	Total Number Teaching Staff
Adelphi	800	1,368	2,196	105	158
Agnes Scott W	4	535	544	55	57
Ala. Pub. W .	3	742	749	68	70
Albertus Magnus W	1	220	226	25	40
Albion	393	957	1,368	56	77
Albright	371	405	799	41	51
Alfred U.	437	499	1,177	79	122
Allegheny ...	358	701	1,075	76	79
Alma	274	364	648	36	39
Amer. Int. C. .	866	583	1,599	41	42
American U. .	714	479	3,898	97	239
Amherst M ..	417	797	1,217	103	...
Anderson	279	411	827	44	55
Antioch	353	767	1,167	47	88
Ark. S. C. Pub.	505	587	1,877	50	60
Asbury	227	727	956	36	38
Ashland	238	315	626	29	51
Atlanta U. ...	108	133	364	33	60
Atlantic Union	110	226	339	28	33
Augustana, Ill.	486	829	1,518	57	70
Augustana, S.D.	327	457	813	48	54
Aurora	199	203	509	29	38
Austin	259	347	625	35	40
Baker	201	464	666	36	42
Baldwin-Wallace	729	901	1,801	60	83
Barat C. of the Sacred Heart W........	0	315	315	43	43
Bard C.	73	220	295	32	40
Barry C. W ..	3	251	291	20	23
Bates	261	566	832	50	55
Baylor	2,274	2,576	5,054	165	210
Beaver W	11	577	592	51	67
Belhaven W ..	0	226	231	25	28
Beloit	303	757	1,063	77	78
Bennett W ..	0	461	463	39	40
Bennington W	6	301	307	47	53
Berea	218	830	1,079	79	95
Bessie Tift W	1	236	239	26	26
Bethany, Kans.	106	255	404	30	33
Bethany, W. Va.	228	478	719	51	51
Bethel	20	383	412	37	42
Bethune-Cookman	332	711	1,048	49	49
Birmingham-Southern ..	465	609	1,078	47	64
Blue Mountain W	0	265	266	28	28
Bowdoin M ..	467	542	1,011	63	78
Bowling Green Pub.	1,620	2,850	4,525	236	291
Bradley U. ...	2,196	1,423	4,171	142	212
Brenau C. W .	0	[illegible]	284	34	35
Briar Cliff W	5	189	305	30	32
Bridgewater .	157	345	512	23	37
Bryn Mawr W	20	697	717	70	102
Bucknell	1,167	1,209	2,411	128	135
Butler	1,875	1,752	5,114	146	211
Calvin	393	1,039	1,459	44	57
Canisius	1,079	1,060	3,457	68	119
Capital	283	845	1,179	85	105
Carleton	237	883	1,124	98	108
Carroll, Mont.	144	229	394	20	24
Carroll, Wisc.	355	439	807	44	53
Carson-Newman	234	590	888	40	41
Carthage	236	424	685	35	39
Catawba	389	441	839	53	58
Cedar Crest W	6	376	382	36	41
Centenary ...	567	505	1,712	61	88
Central, Iowa	140	367	507	33	36
Central, Mo. .	258	510	775	43	48
Centre, Ky. ..	244	366	626	41	43
Chapman	122	192	314	43	48
Chestnut Hill W	5	469	596	38	47
Chico S. C. ..	542	575	1,273	66	72
Citadel Pub. M.	910	1,044	1,954	126	126
Claflin U.	84	338	424	26	29
Clark C., Ga. .	194	652	846	38	45
Coe	333	377	899	45	63
Coker W	20	264	291	29	33
Colby	326	755	1,085	67	81
Colgate M ...	718	784	1,527	119	123
C. Misericordia W	5	435	760	31	48
C. of Charleston Pub ...	85	278	374	19	23
C. of Idaho ..	211	262	488	30	33
C. of Medical Evangelists	132	197	329	62	..
C. of Mt. St. Joseph-on-the-Ohio W ...	4	417	456	44	49
C. of Mt. St. Vincent W .	0	633	811	58	58
C. of New Rochelle W ...	2	848	852	63	67
C. of Notre Dame of Maryland W	1	403	440	36	55
C. of Our Lady of the Elms W	0	279	281	22	25
C. of Puget Sound	985	898	1,950	72	88
C. of St. Benedict W	0	225	259	36	41
C. of St. Catherine W ...	9	764	879	69	88
C. of St. Elizabeth W	5	659	664	47	53
C. of St. Francis W	3	297	397	47	52
C. of St. Mary-of-the-Wasatch W ...	0	75	75	16	18
C. of St. Rose W	12	517	869	30	64
C. of St. Scholastica W ..	7	426	483	34	40
C. of St. Teresa, Minn., W ..	4	606	621	49	54
C. of St.Teresa, Mo., W	4	163	259	19	40
C. of St. Thomas M	1,266	857	2,123	106	145
C. of the Holy Cross M ...	803	1,042	1,845	108	108
C. of the Holy Names W ..	14	316	380	26	52
C. of the Pacific	502	420	1,160	59	124
C. of William and Mary .	811	1,135	1,969	106	127
C. of Wooster	333	944	1,282	87	87
Colorado C. ..	480	776	1,283	56	62
Concordia ...	324	843	1,277	56	64
Conn. C. W ..	0	841	850	87	99
Converse W ..	7	364	383	37	44
Cornell C. of Iowa	194	578	782	54	68
Culver-Stockton	152	299	452	29	35
Dakota Wesleyan	134	241	381	33	40
Davidson M ..	272	677	949	60	61
Davis & Elkins	403	401	847	37	42
Denison	394	965	1,871	81	89
De Pauw	527	1,612	2,168	124	132
Dickinson ...	386	577	967	59	66
Dillard	137	404	561	43	49
Doane	144	312	459	29	35
Dominican C. of San Rafael W	4	302	319	30	37
Drew	138	258	404	32	43
Drury	384	459	1,150	42	64
Duchesne W .	0	236	245	19	19
Dunbarton C. of the Holy Cross W ...	0	201	237	24	37
Duquesne	2,539	1,869	5,270	146	393
D'Youville W .	5	423	428	30	33
Earlham	200	564	796	40	48
Eastern Nazarene	101	365	466	28	35

TABLE I—(*Continued*)

Institution	Veterans Full-Time	Nonveterans Full-Time	Veterans and nonveterans All Resident	Full-Time Teaching Staff	Total Number Teaching Staff
Eastern New Mexico	227	871	622	48	68
Elmhurst	221	514	750	42	49
Elmira *W*	29	389	545	42	55
Elon	412	379	791	40	40
Emmanuel *W*	2	731	738	54	68
Emmanuel Missionary	319	551	1,049	46	58
Emory & Henry	253	339	592	26	28
Erskine	172	240	412	38	34
Evansville	854	592	2,278	83	90
Fenn	1,048	510	5,060	183	289
Findlay	151	163	371	22	27
Fisk	250	702	973	57	72
Fontbonne C. *W*	2	295	539	32	45
Franklin C., Ind.	231	360	591	33	37
Franklin & Marshall *M*	782	628	1,418	80	83
Furman	585	722	1,323	70	74
Geneva	385	488	1,485	38	58
George Pepperdine	766	784	1,588	76	119
George Williams	212	122	387	19	32
Georgetown	270	457	744	50	55
Georgia S. C. for W. *Pub.*	8	999	1,006	100	101
Georgia S. Woman's C. *Pub.*	2	851	354	23	30
Georgian Court *W*	1	233	234	26	40
Gettysburg	650	610	1,264	87	98
Gonzaga *M*	899	668	1,642	66	78
Good Counsel *W*	1	383	387	24	35
Goshen	55	554	748	33	42
Goucher *W*	8	721	740	49	70
Greenville C.	141	265	430	26	32
Grove City	605	839	1,448	60	75
Guilford	268	331	608	29	33
Gustavus Adolphus	449	796	1,261	59	64
Hamilton *M*	223	388	611	59	59
Hamline U.	451	700	1,163	69	82
Hampden-Sydney *M*	130	292	422	27	27
Hanover	243	436	682	37	48
Hardin-Simmons	668	1,089	1,922	70	95
Hastings	268	492	793	50	50
Haverford *M*	189	366	555	58	67
Heidelberg	258	569	839	50	60
Hendrix	180	397	583	36	37
Hillsdale	252	424	689	40	45
Hiram	247	376	624	34	40
Hobart and Wm. Smith C.	441	777	1,221	61	71
Hofstra	989	881	2,818	96	140
Hollins *W*	0	346	356	40	44
Holy Names *W*	6	176	210	19	31
Hood *W*	1	514	524	51	55
Hope	401	763	1,181	54	65
Houghton	116	679	816	36	46
Howard C.	742	450	1,210	55	62
Huntingdon	158	547	725	39	46
Huron	128	164	308	24	28
Illinois C.	231	314	560	34	38
Illinois Wesleyan	514	754	1,288	74	88
Immaculata *W*	0	337	337	34	48
Immaculate Heart *W*	18	445	699	41	48
Incarnate Word *W*	29	381	535	62	65
Indiana Central C.	175	270	464	34	38
Iowa Wesleyan	242	338	591	51	56
James Millikin	688	748	1,703	64	96
Jamestown	132	318	456	25	29
John B. Stetson	1,103	892	2,118	81	101
John Carroll *M*	1,055	884	2,285	67	96
Johnson C. Smith	225	472	732	37	37
Juniata	253	418	687	40	45
Kalamazoo	240	397	663	49	49
Kent State	3,371	2,654	6,654	276	376
Kentucky S. C.	209	440	654	39	41
Kenyon *M*	256	374	630	48	65
Keuka *W*	4	427	454	30	40
King C.	65	155	227	14	16
Knox	274	559	838	65	68
Knoxville	67	187	259	16	17
Lafayette *M*	1,075	981	2,060	135	135
LaGrange *W*	15	129	147	21	23
Lane	139	313	537	18	23
Langston U.	234	496	742	59	68
Lake Erie *W*	0	168	194	23	31
Lake Forest	821	572	1,222	38	60
LaSalle *M*	1,215	780	2,495	90	97
LaSierra	272	415	801	40	51
Lawrence	329	703	1,036	68	76
Lebanon Valley	372	448	983	45	54
LeMoyne	241	57	316	19	24
Lenoir-Rhyne	348	425	804	40	48
Lewis & Clark	649	569	1,232	66	80
Limestone *W*	38	300	339	31	35
Lincoln Memorial U.	173	342	516	28	34
Lincoln U., Mo.	323	524	864	68	75
Lincoln U., Pa. *M*	187	310	498	33	36
Lindenwood *W*	0	435	488	48	54
Linfield	346	479	860	44	50
Livingstone	79	273	362	29	38
Loras	619	841	1,489	72	72
Loretto Heights *W*	8	419	467	36	50
Louisiana	288	694	932	47	48
Loyola C., Md. *M*	577	424	1,519	51	132
Loyola U., Cal. *M*	646	878	1,781	69	76
Luther	372	492	875	42	53
Lynchburg	319	381	722	39	49
Macalester	655	1,183	1,858	98	137
MacMurray *W*	1	681	721	61	66
Madison	78	1,157	1,806	85	94
Manchester	188	652	865	34	35
Manhattan *M*	1,476	1,135	2,611	120	145
Manhattanville C. of the Sacred Heart *W*	16	489	568	72	83
Marietta	721	456	1,223	61	71
Marshall *Pub.*	1,250	1,457	3,268	157	167
Mary Baldwin *W*	0	822	824	31	34
Marygrove *W*	4	766	770	81	91
Mary Manse *W*	3	157	335	42	42
Mary Washington *W*	44	1,456	1,574	76	81
Marylhurst *W*	6	216	238	25	37
Marymount, Kans. *W*	2	245	265	26	33
Marymount, N. Y. *W.*	(575)		575	57	60
Maryville, Mo. *W*	0	288	301	19	35
Maryville, Tenn.	199	685	886	54	58
Marywood *W*	15	555	730	45	56
McPherson	74	286	409	28	32
Mercer	647	576	1,302	76	76
Mercyhurst *W*	3	221	228	31	33
Meredith *W*	3	503	535	45	50
Middlebury	425	788	1,213	74	74
Midland	151	305	484	29	35
Miles	170	431	654	27	30
Mills *W*	20	746	766	78	98
Millsaps	277	496	807	37	45
Milwaukee-Downer *W*	17	332	376	41	47
Mississippi	428	536	964	44	103
Miss. S.C. for W. *Pub*	1	1,058	1,071	81	81
Mo. Valley	262	254	546	31	37
Monmouth	261	629	891	55	55
Moravian *M*	249	149	402	25	28
Morehouse *M*	374	395	769	36	64
Morgan S. C.	479	941	1,718	86	99
Morningside	514	516	1,154	52	71
Morris Brown	258	503	824	43	46
Mount Angel Seminary *M*	12	64	76	15	15

TABLE I—(*Continued*)

Institution	Veterans Full-Time	Nonveterans Full-Time	Veterans and nonveterans All Resident	Full-Time Teaching Staff	Total Number Teaching Staff
Mount Holyoke *W*	8	1,182	1,190	107	133
Mount Mary *W*	11	656	933	46	86
Mount Mercy *W*	5	403	625	38	43
Mount St. Mary's Cal. *W*	7	420	561	37	44
Mount St. Mary's Md. *M*	393	270	663	24	33
Mount St. Scholastica *W*	2	380	394	33	39
Mount Union	405	552	1,018	50	50
Muhlenberg *M*	754	523	1,277	95	95
Mundelein *W*	7	898	905	67	77
Municipal U. of Omaha	843	1,067	3,218	72	136
Muskingum	300	644	952	60	73
Nazareth, Ky. *W*	7	381	848	35	59
Nazareth, Mich. *W*	1	202	254	22	44
Nazareth C. of Rochester *W*	3	423	516	40	54
Nebraska Wesleyan	561	276	873	47	52
Newberry	277	265	542	31	31
N.Y.S.C. for Teachers	240	1,159	1,767	85	86
Niagara U. *M*	780	716	1,755	82	100
N. Carolina C.	210	762	972	63	66
North Central	327	588	935	44	50
Northwest Nazarene	167	395	663	32	48
Northwestern S. C. of La.	502	1,146	1,685	101	101
Norwich *M*	229	404	635	37	39
Notre Dame, Ohio *W*	1	291	292	25	35
Notre Dame of Staten Is. *W*	0	273	275	18	25
Oberlin	551	1,628	2,197	166	173
Occidental	576	707	1,365	54	91
Ohio Wesleyan	572	1,509	2,124	117	134
Oklahoma C. for W.	7	557	689	52	52
Ottawa	185	384	583	27	33
Otterbein	318	573	900	53	72
Ouachita Baptist C.	259	514	777	43	55
Our Lady of the Lake *W*	19	349	454	49	55
Pacific Union	255	568	907	41	41
Pacific U.	566	366	947	40	55
Paine	46	247	328	20	22
Park	103	417	538	45	45
Parsons	186	180	376	31	33
Pasadena	203	424	627	35	40
Pennsylvania C. for *W.*	6	498	506	45	59
Philander Smith	91	308	450	33	38
Phillips	297	695	1,107	56	68
Pomona	369	775	1,149	82	108
Prairie View A. & M. C. of Texas	464	1,539	2,015	105	115
Principia	105	350	461	30	39
Providence *M*	1,060	840	2,520	103	108
Queens *W*	25	359	448	38	46
Radcliffe *W*	29	1,236	1,265	...	...
Radford *W*	8	772	775	54	60
Randolph-Macon *M*	242	303	548	30	30
Randolph-Macon *W*	2	695	701	75	75
Reed	296	374	710	57	60
Regis *W*	2	578	580	51	60
Ripon	228	451	686	51	59
Roanoke	248	374	633	34	37
Rockford *W*	49	403	697	37	59
Rockhurst *M*	437	368	1,109	38	53
Rollins	215	409	630	62	69
Roosevelt	1,900	2,090	6,014	250	350
Rosary *W*	4	694	702	66	74
Rosemont *W*	3	321	341	28	44
Russell Sage *W*	82	590	689	60	68
St. Anselm's *M*	373	278	651	45	45
St. Augustine's	86	326	442	22	28
St. Benedict's *M*	200	329	529	45	45
St. Bonaventure *M*	1,060	753	1,966	90	95
St. Edward's Seminary *M*	21	99	120	14	14
St Francis *M*	431	312	754	27	35
St. Joseph, Conn. *W*	7	455	616	31	40
St. Joseph's, Md. *W*	1	183	184	20	36
St. Joseph's, N. Y. *W*	0	468	468	45	49
St. Joseph's, Pa. *M*	1,011	663	2,168	51	80
St. Lawerence	616	886	1,683	81	95
St. Martin's *M*	197	183	333	34	37
St. Mary, Kans. *W*	2	286	370	39	44
St. Mary of the Springs *W*	2	229	273	26	44
St. Mary of the Woods *W*	0	388	388	49	52
St. Mary's, Calif. *M*	378	510	888	56	56
St. Mary's, Minn. *M*	199	288	487	38	38
St. Mary's of Notre Dame *W*	2	508	657	34	52
St. Michael's *M*	568	469	1,082	46	56
St. Norbert *M*	350	408	761	29	51
St. Olaf	473	1,216	1,708	108	118
St. Patrick's Seminary *M*	19	137	156	12	12
St. Paul Seminary *M*	81	200	281	23	23
St. Peter's *M*	825	716	1,712	52	87
St. Vincent *M*	454	435	893	14	35
St. Xavier, Ill. *W*	6	283	522	36	39
Salem *W*	15	292	320	24	36
Samuel Huston	194	412	616	34	39
San Francisco C. for W.	(382)		416	44	48
San Francisco S. C. *Pub.*	1,206	2,090	5,320	154	195
San Jose S. C.	3,055	3,986	7,268	307	385
Sarah Lawrence *W*	28	309	842	65	78
Scarritt	6	108	132	15	18
Scripps *W*	0	246	246	26	31
Seattle U.	1,238	1,323	2,946	101	125
Seattle Pacific	221	384	631	31	40
Seton Hall	(6,086)		8,391	320	324
Seton Hill *W*	27	456	540	53	64
Shaw	207	696	907	39	52
Shorter *W*	1	212	217	27	29
Siena	1,477	687	2,652	88	107
Siena Heights *W*	1	345	406	29	29
Simmons *W*	92	1,240	1,394	92	171
Simpson	290	481	774	38	45
Skidmore *W*	28	989	981	78	87
Smith *W*	5	2,179	2,282	260	295
Southeastern Louisiana	472	726	1,241	99	99
Southwestern, Kans.	198	357	601	42	42
Southwestern, at Memphis	204	510	746	60	74
Southwest La. Inst. *Pub.*	1,421	1,917	3,370	191	229
Spelman *W*	8	382	390	33	45
Springfield	1,044	316	1,572	71	88
Spring Hill *M*	290	411	801	41	46
Susquehanna	188	319	509	37	42
Swarthmore	289	741	1,035	92	109
Sweet Briar *W*	1	451	452	52	57
Talladega	59	279	338	28	36
Tarkio	100	137	241	17	25

TABLE I—(*Continued*)

Institution	Veterans Full-Time	Nonveterans Full-Time	Veterans and nonveterans All Resident	Full-Time Teaching Staff	Total Number Teaching Staff
Taylor	148	384	527	27	33
Texas Christian	2,000	1,062	4,457	181	232
Texas	187	533	742	35	35
Texas S. C. for for W. *Pub.*	29	1,990	2,042	171	180
Thiel	285	374	666	37	43
Tillotson	145	438	615	31	36
Tougaloo	93	260	356	19	30
Transylvania .	224	294	528	29	39
Trinity, Conn. *M*	402	490	1,290	65	90
Trinity, D. C. *W*	0	477	480	61	61
Trinity U., Texas	629	575	1,414	77	101
Tusculum ...	128	207	335	24	27
Union, Ky ...	224	219	458	24	27
Union, Neb. ..	282	486	924	44	74
Union, N. Y. *M*	887	612	1,952	120	126
U. of Chattanooga	642	667	1,755	65	97
U. of Dayton	1,411	1,044	3,424	132	195
U. of Dubuque	186	494	692	40	45
U. of Miami .	4,947	3,593	8,679	390	460
U. of Portland	1,249	721	1,970	98	98
U. of Redlands	480	695	1,286	67	74
U. of San Francisco *M*	1,399	814	3,044	85	134
U. of Santa Clara *M* ...	550	588	1,138	70	82
U. of Scranton *M*	1,217	500	2,655	86	110
U. of the South *M*	263	238	501	41	44
U. of Tulsa ..	1,476	1,409	4,629	175	250
Upsala	908	565	1,500	67	105
Ursinus	384	652	1,039	52	53
Ursuline *W* ..	0	222	222	30	37
Valparaiso ...	810	1,118	1,942	95	120
Vassar *W* ...	31	1,370	1,401	156	188
Vill Maria *W*	0	204	290	27	30
Villanova *M* ..	1,319	1,257	3,581	130	140
Va. Mil. Inst. Pub. *M*	193	603	796	67	67
Va. S. C. ...	440	1,338	1,900	138	144
Va. Union U. .	273	606	922	42	55
Wabash *M* ...	234	382	616	42	47
Wagner Mem. Lutheran ..	518	460	1,462	57	64
Wake Forest .	1,080	1,023	2,111	130	181
Walla Walla .	410	667	1,184	46	65
Wartburg C. .	133	480	573	33	39
Washburn Mun. U.	880	782	2,020	77	117
Washington C.	195	294	491	30	33
Washington and Jefferson *M*	593	445	1,048	70	84
Washington and Lee *M* .	605	661	1,269	67	81
Washington Missionary .	199	333	624	47	58
Webster *W* ..	1	342	435	35	60
Wellesley *W* .	4	1,740	1,744	162	213
Wells *W*	0	304	304	48	48
Wesleyan C. *W*	14	523	577	61	67
Wesleyan U. *M*	386	584	955	84	101
Western *W* ..	0	534	534	50	56
Western Maryland	251	555	831	58	64
Westminster, Mo. *M*	278	327	608	33	39
Westminster, Pa.	460	689	1,206	66	77
W. Va. S. C. *Pub.*	594	1,002	1,608	69	71
W. Va. Wesleyan	354	436	844	32	37
Wheaton, Ill. .	422	1,072	1,581	88	113
Wheaton, Mass. *W*	0	488	488	60	67
Whitman	208	540	837	47	57
Whittier ...	547	676	1,288	47	55
Whitworth ..	265	550	815	40	50
Wiley	287	255	578	35	40
Willamette ..	509	752	1,310	67	76
William Jewell	318	439	768	36	36
Williams *M* ..	447	679	1,126	118	131
Wilmington ..	240	335	632	31	38
Wilson *W* ...	5	470	478	56	58
Winthrop *W* *Pub.*	3	1,214	1,251	109	118
Wittenberg ..	608	844	1,776	76	102
Wofford *M* ..	366	281	668	36	36
Woman's C.-U. of N. C. *Pub.*	26	2,035	2,104	179	197
Xavier U., La.	375	519	1,001	79	91
Xavier U., Ohio *M*	971	967	3,429	79	182
Yankton	140	261	416	31	35
Youngstown .	2,034	1,111	4,679	87	222
Totals	158,808	270,611	498,284	26,611	32,632

TABLE I

III. INDEPENDENT TECHNICAL INSTITUTIONS

1. Technological Institutions

Institution	Veterans Full-Time	Nonveterans Full-Time	Veterans and nonveterans All Resident	Full-Time Teaching Staff	Total Number Teaching Staff
A. & M. C. of Texas, *Pub.* *M*	4,423	3,895	8,539	500*	560
A. & T. C. of North Carolina	1,458	1,278	2,768	120	124
Alabama Poly. Inst. *Pub.* .	4,352	3,113	7,654	420	438
Alcorn A. & M. C.	191	321	512	45	57
Arkansas A. & M. C. .	243	269	542	30	30
Calif. Inst. of Tech *M* ...	730	541	1,271	200	275
Carnegie Tech.	1,460	1,899	4,649	277	312
Case Inst. of Tech. *M* ...	1,087	574	1,675	133	175
Clarkson C. of Tech. *M* ...	1,184	613	1,797	96	105
Clemson Agric. C. *M*	1,919	1,301	3,277	246	263
Colo. A. & M. C. *Pub.* .	2,150	1,622	3,788	218	240
Colo. School of Mines *Pub.*	804	414	1,218	97	101
Cooper Union	266	428	1,208	67	177
Drexel Inst. of Tech.	1,588	1,589	3,347	208	239
Florida A. & M. C.	512	1,107	1,619	125	125

TABLE I—(*Continued*)

Institution	Veterans Full-Time	Nonveterans Full-Time	Veterans and nonveterans All Resident	Full-Time Teaching Staff	Total Number Teaching Staff
Georgia Inst. of Tech *M* ...	3,256	2,120	5,726	296	338
Hampton Inst.	669	911	1,624	136	147
Illinois Inst. of Tech.	2,234	1,505	8,030	204	379
Iowa S. C. of Ag. & M. A. *Pub.*	....	....	10,064	1,045	1,232
Kans. S. C. of Ag. & Ap. Sc. *Pub.*	3,965	3,266	7,433	622	793
Louisiana Poly. Inst. *Pub.* .	1,128	1,507	2,667	169	184
Mass. Inst. of Tech.	2,250*	3,143*	5,393*	571*	772*
Mich. C. of M. & Tech. *Pub*	1,381	774	2,171	153	154
Mississippi S. C. *Pub.* .	2,347	1,215	3,571	219	252
Montana S. of Mines *Pub.* .	219	128	348	30	34
Montana S. C. *Pub.*	1,454	1,559	3,013	192	220
Newark C. of Eng'g.	962	547	2,676	136	157
N. Mex. C. of Ag. & M. A *Pub.*	890	732	1,660	125	145
N. Car. S. C. of Ag. & Eng'g. *Pub.*	3,436	1,641	5,227	408	448
N. Dakota Ag. C.	1,175	1,222	2,397	155	179
Northeastern U.	2,220	2,014	7,330	160	350
Oklahoma A. & M. *Pub.* ...	6,200	4,507	11,050	610	800
Poly. Inst. of Brooklyn *M*	1,153	818	5,770	142	409
Purdue *Pub.* .	7,899	6,608	14,674	890	1,277
Rensselaer Poly. Inst.	2,617	1,498	4,525	293	375
Rhode Island S. C. *Pub.* .	1,117	1,408	2,574	220	235
Rose Poly. Inst. *M* ...	444	122	566	40	40
S. Car. S. C. .	481	702	1,487	135	135
S. Dakota S. of Mines *Pub.*	472	220	697	48	49
S. Dakota S. C. of Ag. & M. A. *Pub.* ...	917	1,234	2,179	173	196
Southern U. *Pub.*	481	1,288	1,769	119	123
State A. & M. C. (Ala.) ..	304	566	870	40	40
Stevens Inst. of Tech. *M* ...	977	529	2,216	109	112
Tenn. A. & I. S. C.	709	1,401	2,110	170	200
Tenn. Poly. Inst.	830	828	1,827	78	85
Texas C. of A. & Ind. *Pub.*	851	988	2,100	94	117
Texas C. of Mines & Met.	833	1,002	2,075	80	103
Texas Tech. C. *Pub.*	2,733	3,284	6,106	260	318
Tuskegee Inst.	1,248	1,153	2,401	206	237
U. S. Coast Guard Acad. *M*	131	274	405	46	62
U. S. Mil. Acad. *M*	991	1,471	2,462	265	265
U. S. Naval Acad. *M* ...	(3,320)		3,320	468	468
U. of Mass. *Pub.*	2,600	1,480	4,080	260	264
Utah S. Ag. C. *Pub.*	2,264	2,000	4,352	273	290
Worcester Poly. Inst. M	546	819	892	84	95
Totals	86,751	74,898	198,596	12,501	15,295

* Estimated

TABLE I—(*Continued*)

III. INDEPENDENT TECHNICAL INSTITUTIONS

2. Teachers Colleges

Institution	Veterans Full-Time	Nonveterans Full-Time	Veterans and nonveterans All Resident	Full-Time Teaching Staff	Total Number Teaching Staff
Ala. S. T. C., Florence *Pub.*	455	768	1,233	66	74
Ala. S. T. C., Jacksonville *Pub.*	459	649	1,186	48	59
Ala. S. T. C., Livingston *Pub.*	158	277	435	30	39
Ala. S. T. C., Troy *Pub.* .	409	514	1,401	55	55
Albany S. C. Pub.	77	398	756	39	89
Appalachian S. T. C. *Pub.*	317	647	964	52	64
Arizona S. T. C. Flagstaff *Pub.*	321	339	684	45	55
Arizona S. C. Tempe *Pub.*	1,676	1,735	3,656	115	126
Austin Peay S. C.	171	280	589	29	38
Ball S.T.C. *Pub.*	958	1,768	2,970	144	159
Central State, C. Okla. *Pub.*	378	515	951	63	65
Chicago T. C. *Pub.*	59	675	950	54	58
Colo. S. C. of of Ed. *Pub.*	784	1,100	1,954	113	143
Concord C. *Pub.*	342	520	862	49	49
Conn. T. C. (N. Britain)	575	627	1,540	96	110
Delta S.T.C. *Pub.*	241	345	589	54	58
East Carolina T. C. *Pub.*	489	880	1,384	95	101
East Central State C., Okla. *Pub.* .	481	639	1,217	62	67
Eastern Montana S. N. School *Pub.*	84	214	380	27	30

TABLE I—(*Continued*)

Institution	Veterans Full-Time	Nonveterans Full-Time	Veterans and nonveterans All Resident	Full-Time Teaching Staff	Total Number Teaching Staff
Eastern Ore. C. of Ed. *Pub.*	196	337	600	28	28
Elizabeth City S.T.C. *Pub.*	48	427	475	20	25
Fairmont S. C. *Pub.*	425	522	1,178	57	61
Fayetteville S.T.C. *Pub.*	66	458	563	27	29
Fort Hays Kans. S. C. *Pub.*	358	550	976	74	92
Fort Valley S. C. *Pub.* .	141	515	1,011	47	69
George Peabody C. for T. ..	808	780	1,936	86	189
Georgia T. C. *Pub.*	239	485	724	40	44
Great Falls C. of Ed.	133	411	544	23	38
Harris T. C. *Pub.*	176	1,012	1,265	55	62
Henderson S.T. C. *Pub.* ...	254	516	897	53	54
Ill. S. U. Carbondale *Pub.*	1,165	1,655	3,010	162	240
Ill. S.C. Eastern *Pub.* ..	568	855	1,899	114	125
Ill. S.T.C. Northern *Pub.*	577	1,091	1,668	95	126
Ill. S.C. Western *Pub.* ..	416	926	1,392	96	104
Indiana S.T.C. *Pub.*	1,068	1,303	2,429	91	121
Iowa S.T.C. *Pub.*	877	2,191	3,068	256	270
Kansas S.T.C. Emporia *Pub.*	617	782	1,441	114	124
Kansas S.T.C. Pittsburg *Pub.*	801	724	1,620	120	134
Kentucky S.C. Eastern *Pub.*	514	836	1,375	81	92
Marylhurst T.C. *W*	0	67	146	25	26
Memphis State C. *Pub.*	773	1,362	2,310	102	105
Michigan C. of Ed., Central *Pub.*	989	1,275	4,244	149	151
Michigan C. of Ed., Northern *Pub.* ...	490	512	1,002	88	84
Michigan C. of Ed., Western *Pub.*	1,463	2,371	4,559	275	290
Michigan S.N.C., *Pub.*	817	1,515	2,428	218	224
Miner Teachers C. *Pub.*	80	521	551	28	31
Minn. S.T.C., Bemidji *Pub.*	246	322	578	56	56
Minn. S.T.C., Mankato *Pub.*	418	796	1,308	68	68
Minn. S.T.C., Moorhead *Pub.*	186	478	710	37	40
Minn. S.T.C., St. Cloud *Pub*	529	1,026	1,580	79	86
Minn. S.T.C., Winona *Pub.*	202	391	597	49	55
Minot State T.C. (N.D.) *Pub.*	252	529	789	46	64
Miss. Southern C. *Pub.*	876	828	1,911	102	114
Mo. S. C., Central *Pub.*	496	990	1,529	77	111
Mo. S.T.C., Northeast *Pub.*	397	483	982	74	76
Mo. S.T.C., Northwest *Pub.*	299	559	858	70	82
Mo. S.T.C., Southeast *Pub.*	555	931	1,495	63	69
Mo. S.T.C., Southwest *Pub.*	582	1,124	1,896	84	86
Mont. S.N.C. *Pub.*	80	136	219	12	22
Murray S.T.C. *Pub.*	584	751	1,427	87	88
National C. of Ed. *W*	7	359	412	38	45
Nebr. S.T.C., Chadron *Pub.*	114	249	378	49	49
Nebr. S.T.C., Kearney *Pub.*	279	541	820	51	61
Nebr. S.T.C., Peru *Pub.* .	129	246	377	37	42
Nebr. S.T.C., Wayne *Pub.*	208	543	759	49	52
N.J. S.T.C. Montclair *Pub.*	436	851	1,728	85	98
N.J. S.T.C. Trenton *Pub.*	192	707	961	71	82
N. M. Highlands U. *Pub.*	365	276	728	49	70
N. M. S.T.C. *Pub.*	174	216	505	32	42
Oregon C. of Ed. *Pub.*	184	294	484	41	46
Pacific Lutheran C.	398	454	897	42	53
Pa. S.T.C., Indiana *Pub.* .	445	1,010	1,669	101	101
Pa. S.T.C., Kutztown *Pub.* .	320	669	1,046	51	54
Pa. S.T.C., Mansfield *Pub.*	348	569	924	69	78
Pa. S.T.C., Shippensburg *Pub.*	339	398	739	54	54
Pa. S.T.C., Slippery Rock *Pub.*	325	545	896	57	62
Pa. S.T.C., West Chester *Pub.*	515	1,218	1,747	90	100
Sam Houston S.T.C., *Pub.*	876	1,198	2,252	128	187
San Diego S.C. *Pub.*	1,762	2,206	4,515	180	220
S.D.S.T.C. North, Aberdeen *Pub.* ..	268	455	748	45	50
Southern Oregon C. of Ed. *Pub.*	236	335	654	35	40
Stephen F. Austin S.T.C. *Pub.*	493	742	1,269	74	74
Stout Institute *Pub.*	461	468	929	60	69
Sul Ross S.T.C. *Pub.*	267	452	776	50	52
Tenn. S.C., Johnson City *Pub.*	516	950	1,499	67	72
Tenn. S.C., Murfreesboro *Pub.*	454	556	1,198	58	58
Texas S.T.C., East *Pub.* .	795	1,283	2,078	95	103
Texas S.T.C., North *Pub.* .	1,579	3,284	5,118	239	348
Texas S.T.C., Southwest *Pub.*	645	1,127	1,772	95	115
Texas S.T.C., West *Pub.* .	435	751	1,238	73	76

TABLE I—(*continued*)

Institution	Veterans Full-Time	Nonveterans Full-Time	Full-Time Veterans and nonveterans	All Resident Teaching Staff	Total Number Teaching Staff
Va. S.T.C., Farmville *Pub.*	17	658	680	50	54
Wash. C. of Ed., Central Ellensburg *Pub.* .	456	825	1,303	65	85
Wash. C. of Ed., Eastern Cheney *Pub.*	507	836	1,364	80	97
Wash. C. of Ed., Western Bellingham *Pub.*	494	806	1,319	92	94
West Liberty S.T.C. *Pub.*	197	323	716	30	36
Western Carolina T.C. *Pub.*	249	298	550	33	39
Western S.C. of Colorado *Pub.*	282	401	683	37	48
Wilson T.C. *Pub.*	68	392	652	45	50

Institution	Veterans Full-Time	Nonveterans Full-Time	Veterans and nonveterans All Resident	Full-Time Teaching Staff	Total Number Teaching Staff
Winston-Salem T.C.	84	388	472	28	31
Wisc. S.T.C., LaCrosse *Pub.*	343	746	1,102	76	78
Wisc. S.T.C., Milwaukee *Pub.*	439	1,265	1,715	110	116
Wisc. S.T.C., Oshkosh *Pub.*	290	558	854	58	59
Wisc. S.T.C., River Falls *Pub.*	300	528	831	54	57
Wisc. S.T.C., Superior *Pub.*	286	552	844	63	65
Wisc. S.T.C., Whitewater *Pub.*	281	467	750	61	61
Totals	45,948	78,207	135,822	7,701	8,762

October 31, 1948, is 953,247[4] under Public Law 16 or Public Law 346. On the same date a year ago there were 1,149,933 veterans.[5] This is a decrease of 17 per cent.

From constituting approximately one half of the total collegiate enrollment in 1947, the veteran attendance has receded this year to approximately 42 per cent. The decrease is largely because fewer veterans are enrolled in the freshman and sophomore years.

For 674 comparable *approved* universities and four-year colleges, the 1948 figures reveal a total of 686,368 full-time veteran students, a decrease of 11 per cent as compared with 1947. As to types of institution, analysis shows the following: 55 public universities, 255,464 full-time veterans, a 12 per cent decrease; 43 universities under private control, 154,999 full-time veterans, a decrease of 8½ per cent; 431 independent colleges of arts and science, 150,760 full-time veterans, a decrease of 11 per cent; 50 independent technological institutions, 82,531 full-time veterans, a decrease of 9½ per cent; 95 independent teachers colleges, 42,614 full-time veterans, a decrease of 12 per cent.

While the number of veteran students has decreased, as would be anticipated, their academic persistence rate is remarkable. They are sticking it out in junior- and senior-college classes and in graduate and professional schools in a measure exceeding all records of students in earlier peacetime years.

[4] Letter to present writer, November 17, 1948, from S. H. Coile, Vocational Rehabilitation and Education, Veterans Administration, Washington, D. C.

[5] Telegram November 29, 1947, from H. V. Stirling, director, Vocational Rehabilitation and Education, Veterans Administration.

Freshmen and Their Choices. Reports of 643 institutions for which data are available for both 1947 and 1948 show that, in five broad fields, there has been a decrease of 13 per cent in the number of men students in freshman classes, as compared with 1947 (which in turn for 640 comparable institutions was 23 per cent below the number entering in 1946); and a decrease of 2 per cent in the number of women students in freshman classes (which in turn for 640 comparable institutions was a decrease of 3.7 per cent as compared with the number entering in 1946). This sharp drop in the number of men students in the freshman year may be attributed to the decline in the number of veterans (predominantly men) entering college.

Inasmuch as Selective Service regulations permitted college freshmen to complete their first year, there is no reason to believe that the peacetime draft had any material effect upon the enrollment of freshmen for 1948–49. It is impossible, of course, to predict the future effect upon college and university attendance of the draft or of Universal Military Training, in the event UMT should be approved by Congress.

Table IV will afford significant material for administrators and other students of higher education as disclosing the choices freshmen have made as to entering five broad fields: liberal arts, engineering, commerce (or business administration), agriculture, and "teachers college." As these data have been supplied in this series of articles for many years, comparisons with earlier enrollments will help to show educational trends.

Prospects for the Near Future. Factors as to collegiate attendance during the next few years include,

TABLE II

GEOGRAPHICAL DIVISION SUMMARY
Full-time Students

	Division and State	Number of Insti-tutions	Number of Full-time Students
(1)	*New England*		
	Maine	4	7,696
	New Hampshire	3	7,108
	Vermont	5	6,222
	Massachusetts	25	65,402
	Rhode Island	3	9,076
	Connecticut	9	20,751
(2)	*Middle Atlantic*		
	New York	51	167,697
	New Jersey	12	28,112
	Pennsylvania	55	100,346
(3)	*East North Central*		
	Ohio	40	98,913
	Indiana	21	55,468
	Illinois	35	84,530
	Michigan	19	72,137
	Wisconsin	15	34,669
(4)	*West North Central*		
	Minnesota	19	44,528
	Iowa	15	26,097
	Missouri	25	46,465
	North Dakota	4	6,138
	South Dakota	8	7,319
	Nebraska	13	20,493
	Kansas	17	29,078
(5)	*South Atlantic*		
	Delaware	..	.....
	Maryland	11	12,264
	District of Columbia	10	22,928
	Virginia	22	24,574
	West Virginia	9	15,289
	North Carolina	26	37,971
	South Carolina	14	16,040
	Georgia	21	25,422
	Florida	7	24,078
(6)	*East South Central*		
	Kentucky	12	20,059
	Tennessee	22	28,922
	Alabama	15	28,820
	Mississippi	11	13,308
(7)	*West South Central*		
	Arkansas	7	8,978
	Louisiana	12	31,747
	Oklahoma	8	29,406
	Texas	27	75,863
(8)	*Mountain*		
	Montana	7	8,193
	Idaho	3	4,669
	Wyoming	1	3,163
	Colorado	8	27,889
	New Mexico	5	7,879
	Arizona	3	9,138
	Utah	3	8,973
	Nevada	1	1,690
(9)	*Pacific*		
	Washington	16	37,588
	Oregon	13	16,187
	California	31	101,555

on one hand, the depressive effect of national man-power demands such as Selective Service or Universal Military Training and, on the other hand, the stimulating effect of any provision which Congress may make granting Federal scholarships for students in colleges and universities.

Readers of SCHOOL AND SOCIETY are familiar with the recommendations of the President's Commission on Higher Education for a national program of Federally financed scholarships and fellowships, to start with some 300,000 undergraduate students and 10,000 fellowship students. Action to initiate such a program may be taken by Congress in 1949. There is a possibility also of the reintroduction of a bill setting up a National Research Foundation under which, as earlier proposed, 6000 four-year competitive scholarships might be awarded to high-school graduates evidencing scientific promise and 300 three-year competitive fellowships for college graduates.

Latest among scholarship proposals is the Congressional bill now being prepared under the sponsorship of the National Education Association's Department of Higher Education. As reported by the Associated Press December 13, 1948, the bill would provide 200,000 scholarships at an estimated cost to the federal government of $100,000,000 the first year and more thereafter. According to present plans, award of $400 to $500 would be made upon the basis of competition.

Attendance in Urban Universities. Although no special table is presented, a study has been made of attendance in approved institutions holding membership in the Association of Urban Universities and of attendance in all other institutions. The findings reveal that 47 AUU member institutions have total enrollments of 330,246 full-time students, or 1 per cent more than in 1947, and total enrollments of 197,018 part-time students, or 1 per cent more than a year ago. For all other approved universities and four-year colleges, the comparable figures are: Total enrollments of full-time students, 1,152,370, or .9 per cent more than in 1947; and total enrollments of part-time students, 110,423, or 11 per cent more than a year ago.

Attendance in Junior Colleges. From Jesse P. Bogue, executive secretary of the American Association of Junior Colleges, Washington, D. C., the report has been received that the enrollment for 625 junior colleges for 1947–48, as compiled for the Junior College Directory, was 505,453. For 1946–47, the enrollment in 663 junior colleges totaled 449,468.

Other Enrollment Studies. There are several other

TABLE III

1939 AND 1948 CLASSIFICATION COMPARISONS

	Classifications	1939		1948	
		Full-Time	All-Res..	Full-Time	All-Res.
55	Universities, public	272,758	321,851	490,507	586,382
49	Universities, private	175,680	265,403	337,852	474,820
432	Colleges of Arts and Sciences	236,546	265,238	413,758	465,635
49	Technological Institutions	85,721	92,385	157,151	170,909
91	Teachers Colleges	82,087	87,918	112,694	122,512
676	**Totals:**	**852,792**	**1,032,795**	**1,511,957**	**1,820,258**

valuable tabulations of collegiate attendance, especially that of the Office of Education. It may be pointed out that for certain institutions the Office of Education figures, obtained earlier in the fall, differ slightly from those in this SCHOOL AND SOCIETY article, which are reported officially by the registrars of universities and colleges at approximately Novem-

TABLE IV

FRESHMAN FULL-TIME ENROLLMENTS

In Five Fields: Liberal arts, engineering, commerce (business administration), agriculture, "teachers college"

	Classifications	Men		Women	
		1947	1948	1947	1948
47	Universities, public	66,726	58,391	24,011	24,096
86	Universities, private	38,800	35,018	8,844	8,415
427	Colleges of Arts and Sciences	80,495	69,604	53,076	51,127
47	Technological Institutions	33,275	28,891	3,582	3,398
86	Teachers Colleges	21,970	18,042	14,488	14,456
643	**Totals:**	**241,266**	**209,946**	**103,996**	**101,492**

ber 1, 1948. Moreover, this SCHOOL AND SOCIETY study calls for a differentiation between full-time and part-time students not presented in other studies. Such differentiation has been declared by educators to be useful in comparing the differing types of instructional service rendered by various institutions, particularly by the city universities where the teach-

TABLE V

LARGEST INSTITUTIONS

Institution	Students Full-time	Rank	Students All-Res.	Rank
U. of California[1]	43,418	1	43,418	2
U. of Minnesota	26,843	2	32,199	4
U. of Illinois	24,616	3	27,773	6
New York U.	23,100	4	47,647	1
U. of Wisconsin	22,356	5	24,756*	7
Ohio State U.	22,227	6	23,848	8
Columbia U.[2]	21,612	7	29,164	5
U. of Michigan	21,004	8	23,044	10
Syracuse U.	17,306	9	19,698	13
U. of Texas[3]	17,028	10	17,028	18
U. of Washington	16,188	11	16,650	19
Michigan State C. of Agriculture and Applied Science	15,092	12	16,010	21
U. of Southern California	14,658	13	20,454	12
Purdue U.	14,507	14	14,674	24
Indiana U.	14,414	15	22,042	11
U. of Pittsburgh	13,965	16	19,526	14
U. of Missouri and School of Mines and Metallurgy	13,391	17	13,964	..
Harvard U.	11,907	18	11,907	..
U. of Oklahoma	11,515	19	12,174	..
City College of New York	11,176	20	32,567	3
Northwestern U.	10,853	21	23,788	9
Boston U.	10,760	22	18,617	16
Oklahoma Agricultural and Mechanical College	10,707	23	11,050	..
Louisiana State U. and Agricultural and Mechanical C.	10,667	24	11,501	..
State U. of Iowa	10,550	25	10,550	..
Rutgers U.[4]	.....	..	19,189	15
Wayne U.	.....	..	17,925	17
U. of Cincinnati	.....	..	16,096	20
Brooklyn C.	.....	..	15,126	22
U. of Pennsylvania	.....	..	14,803	23
Temple U.	.....	..	14,349	25

* Estimated.
[1] Includes all campuses.
[2] Includes Barnard College.
[3] Includes dentistry but not medicine.
[4] Includes New Jersey College for Women and University of Newark.

ing of part-time students forms a considerable proportion of the entire program.

Basis and Definitions. This 1948 study of attendance is based on the list of institutions accredited by regional associations, as compiled by the Council on Medical Education of the American Medical Association. Incidentally, it may be said that the Association of American Universities, at its October meeting in Philadelphia, voted to discontinue accreditation.

In Table I, the classification follows recommendations made in 1932 by a committee of the Association of American Colleges, of which the present writer was chairman.

Table II assembles full-time student totals according to the standard geographical divisions of the United States.

Table III shows comparisons of full-time and grand-total enrollments for 1939 (last pre-World War II normal year) and for 1948 in classified groups.

Table IV presents comparative figures of freshman students in five major fields for 1947 and 1948, covering institutions supplying these figures for liberal arts, engineering, commerce (or business administration), agriculture, and "teachers college."

Table V lists the 25 institutions having the largest enrollments of full-time students and of totals of both full-time and part-time students, as of November 1.

It should be stated that, in Tables I, III, and V, a change is made in the coverage of grand-total enrollments. In earlier studies of this series, summer-session attendances for the preceding summer were included, but are *not* so included in the present figures. The 1939 and 1947 statistics for grand-total enrollments have been correspondingly adjusted so that all grand-total enrollments are now comparable.

In requesting data from registrars, the following definitions were given:

A full-time student is defined as a student who has completed a high-school course and is devoting substantially his full time (12 hours or more is the Veterans Administration stipulation) to study during the collegiate year. [Completed on p. 430, below]

A part-time student is one whose main time and attention are given to some other employment and who takes late afternoon, evening, or Saturday classes.

The full-time teaching staff comprises those individuals on full-time employment for the academic year, who devote at least one half of their time to giving instruction; limited to those who hold the rank of an instructor (or its equivalent) and higher ranks.

The total teaching staff includes these groups: the full-time faculty; individuals devoting less than half of their time to teaching; teaching assistants, fellows, research assistants if they do some teaching, and others who teach.

Because of the additional expense involved, the detailed study of enrollments in 30 representative universities is omitted.

ACKNOWLEDGMENTS AND AFTERWORD

Eugene G. Schwartz, Editor
City College of New York
Vice Chairman, Metropolitan New York Region, 1947-48
NSA Vice President, Educational Problems, 1948-49
[See page 247 for extended biography]

"There is something here that is bigger than both of us," Bill Welsh (Berea College, KY) wrote to Jean Justice, his fiancée, after his election as NSA's first president in September, 1947. "People came distrusting each other, afraid of new ideas, but after eight days they realized there is a system in the world by which each man is given a fair chance to be heard, where each man can work for his own ideas without being scoffed at, and then when the final decision is made, a compromise can be reached that will be fair to everyone. . . . It couldn't happen anywhere, darling, except in America."

Bill Welsh, in that letter (p. 173), expresses an underlying belief that I think we all shared. At one point we thought we might even entitle this work, "A Generation That Believed in America."

During the eight years this book has been taking shape, many persons have helped to make its publication possible. They included former student leaders and advisers within the National Student Association, and within related religious, political, veterans and internationalist student organizations—active during the early post- World War II years, as well as prior to and during the war; family members and children of former student leaders; editors, researchers and designers; book production and manufacturing professionals; office supply and photo-copy services; and archivists and librarians at universities and colleges throughout the country.

More than any others, however, I must acknowledge Clif Wharton's unflagging support and commitment to the project from its very beginning. Through his efforts, funding of the project was made possible by early grants from the Rockefeller Brothers Fund, Culpepper Foundation, Carnegie Corporation and W. K. Kellogg Foundation. Together with later grants from the Bill and Melinda Gates Foundation through the good offices of Bill Gates, Sr., they accounted for $247,000 of the more than $400,000 raised for development and production over an eight-year period.

More than 140 individuals and several other foundations contributed the balance, including significant donations from the Bernard and Irene Schwartz Foundation, Janis Tremper Dowd and Daan Zwick, Ben Jones, Leonard Perlmutter and the Shelly and Donald Rubin and Spencer Foundations. They are all listed on the last page of this book. The USSA Foundation provided valuable collaboration, sponsorship and services as a fiduciary, which enabled us to avoid establishing and maintaining an independent tax-exempt host of our own.

Fund-raising efforts on many fronts over the years have been spearheaded by Sylvia Bacon, Bill Dentzer, Stanley Greenfield, Dick Heggie, Dick Murphy, Allan Ostar, Evelyn Jones Rich, Clif Wharton and Mildred Wurf. In December 2004 the completion of our development effort was marked by a reception hosted by Jack Rosenthal, President of the New York Times Foundation. Bill Dentzer's wise counsel, in particular, has guided me through the many organizing stages of the project's development.

The former NSA leaders of nearly sixty years ago, joined together since 1996 in sponsoring, writing for, and raising money to support this project, have each been steadfast friends and advisers. All have earned my special gratitude for the quality of their commitment. Four of the original 23 have passed: Helen Jean Secondari, Pat Wohlgemuth Blair, Royal Voegeli, and my dear friend Gordon Klopf, our adviser then and generous helper until recently.

At the expense of redundancy elsewhere, and in addition to Clif Wharton, I must mention Janis Tremper Dowd, Bill Welsh, Mildred Kiefer Wurf, Allan Ostar, Dick Murphy, Sylvia Bacon, Bill Dentzer, Dick Heggie, Joan Long Lynch, Martin McLaughlin, Henry Halsted, Alice Popkin, Rick Medalie, and in very special ways, Ralph Smith for their editorial attention and support. Their yeoman efforts to get me to pare down the size of the work constrained me somewhat, but an encyclopedic treatment seemed determined to capture the soul of this book.

Of the 98 authors providing the 129 by-line pieces, 87 wrote 118 original memoirs. An additional 25 student leaders, 29 mentors (of whom 25 were educators) and four U.S. presidents are remembered in recollections and profiles.

Important to our research early on was access to the collections on NSA at the State Historical Society of Wisconsin in Madison and at the Hoover Institute in Stanford, CA. Donna Sereda, Director of Acquisitions and Collections Management at Wisconsin, was especially helpful during the course of development.

I cannot speak too highly and gratefully about the more than 130 special collections and archives librarians who helped us. They are all listed in the Archives and Librarians section on page 1131.

Those that stand out in responding to repeated inquiries and/or providing large batches of document copying include: Ralph Elder at the University of Texas Center for American History; Dagmar Getz at the Kautz Family Archives on the YMCA in Minneapolis; Elena Danielson at the Hoover Institute, Stanford; Johnathan Williams at Catholic University; John Reynolds at Georgetown; Shannon Wilson at Berea, KY; Cifford Muse at Howard University; Martha Smalley at Yale Divinity School; Daniel Greenspahn at the Institute for International Education; Bob Anthony at the University of North Carolina; Beverley Allen, Emory University, GA; Patricia Owen, Sarah Lawrence, NY; Barbara Vasquez, Los Angeles City College; David Hayes, University of Colorado; Charles Mutschler, Eastern Washington State College; Lawrence Stark, Washington State College; Terry Abraham, University of Idaho; Joseph Grabenstein, La Salle College, PA.

Members of the project committee, listed on page iv, contributed memoirs and documents, and reviewed each other's essay drafts for accuracy, completeness and footnoting. The archives to this project will have a complete collection of their commentaries.

Clif Wharton, already at work on his own autobiography, contributed adaptations which appear in Part 1 and which inspired our early authors to reach into memory. Together with Allan Ostar, who had then recently retired as President of the Association of State Colleges and Universities, Clif's standing as former President of Michigan State University and Chancellor of the State University of New York lent important credibility to the sponsorship of the project and to Allan's early success in having Stanley Ikenberry, then President of the American Council on Education, agree to publish the work when it was completed, and when we had raised the funds to deliver a first printing. In the years following, the late Jim Murray, Publications and Development Vice President at the ACE, and a former colleague of mine at Prentice Hall, was steadfast in maintaining ACE endorsement for publication of the book.

Clif's rol-o-dex, and those especially of Dick Murphy, Bill Ellis, Ernie Howell, Joan Long Lynch, Gordon Klopf and Connie Curry, led to the ever-widening network of the authors we recruited.

Thanks also to Ben Jones who, in 1998, hosted me on a three day visit to the University of North Carolina and to its extensive Southern history archives and the Al Lowenstein and Frank Graham papers. There I interviewed Douglass Hunt and John Sanders and met historian Bill Leuchtenburg, SDA's first executive secretary, who led me to Mary Lou Munts (Swarthmore) in Madison. She in turn connected me to Trude Lash and Molly Yard (Swarthmore).

Al Brod made available priceless photographs and correspondence from Ruth Hagy Brod's collection of her national television College News Conference on which NSA was featured (p. 1084).

Additional research was provided by some of our authors and contemporaries: Craig Wilson for Ohio colleges; Alice Popkin and Caldwell Titcomb at Harvard; Merrill Freed at U. of Chicago; Dolores Delahanty at U. of Louisville; George Soule at Carleton College, MN; Richard Heggie at U.C. Berkeley; and Frank Fisher at U. of Texas. For several years in midproject Gwen Tapper was engaged to provide permissions and Library of Congress research.

Ernie Howell (Harvard) led me to Len Clough, Jean Burkehardt, Ruth Purkaple (U. of Denver) and Kathy and George Todd, all of whom assisted in advice and educated me to the many aspects of the Student Christian Movement as it reinvented itself through the years since its late 19th-century founding by John Mott (p. 692). George Todd suggested I contact Bill Miller (U. of Nebraska), whose memoir (p. 717) is one of the high points of the book. It was a revelation for me as I came to understand the role of the Student Christian Movement as the major outlet for social conscience and action on U.S. college campuses through the midcentury, and its critical role in assuring NSA's independence from partisan or sectarian student organization influence (pp. 158, 732).

Martin McLaughlin's (Notre Dame, IN) invaluable 1948 doctoral thesis on student organizations, his advocacy for Catholic college student engagement with NSA, and Philip DesMarais' (Aquinas, MN) leadership in the Catholic Joint Committee for Student Action, recalled in their memoirs, provide insight into the effective execution of theologian J. C. Murray's vision for "Operation University" (p. 739). Unveiling the story of the Catholic college engagement in secular student organizations after World War II is one of the great untold stories brought to light in the anthology.

Joan Long Lynch (Marylhurst College) helped me to understand the Catholic women's college network, whose membership and energies were so valuable in NSA's growth. It was at her urging also that I belatedly contacted Bill Gates, Sr. (U. of Washington), who followed me in NSA councils by a year and whom I hadn't known at that time. In addition to a taped interview with his classmate Helen Knudson Pulsifer, he facilitated major financial support to the project from the Bill and Melinda Gates Foundation.

Bill's interview was one of nineteen I conducted, from which we prepared treatments for editing and signoff by the authors. They led me to a meeting with Ralph Dungan (St. Joseph's College) at his tropical plantation house among his goats and rabbits in St. John, Barbados, in January of 1998. It was the first of my many interview adventures, which included: a day at the racetrack with Ken Kurtz (Swarthmore) in Lexington, KY; a serene and warmly nostalgic weekend on the high desert in Bend, OR with Sister Mary Kay Perkins (Mundelein, Rosary); a drive north from New Orleans after a visit with President Norman Francis of Xavier University into the America of its deep-south past, where I met with retired President John Peoples of Jackson State in Jackson, MS; a seat at the Atlanta Symphony after a late-night meeting with developer John Hunsinger (Georgia Tech); two meetings and a tour of Buffalo with Lee Jones (U. of Buffalo) and Janis Dowd (Rockford College, IL), when she and I recorded some of the vignettes of Lee's adventurous life.

I began to do such interviews after I realized that there were a significant number of contributors who were simply not able to face down a blank page on their own. Yet, in interviews, the paragraphs and pages poured forth.

Gil Jonas, a dear friend and stalwart fund-raiser for good causes throughout his life, was not one who was thwarted by a blank page. At my request in 1998, he wrote a comprehensive history of the Student Federalist movement (p. 761), including an excursion into its leadership connections with the Young Adult Council, World Assembly of Youth and International Development Placement Association. With the help of Pat Blair, we edited its 80 pages down to 16 pages, prompting Gil to expand it to his own 280-page landmark history of the Student Federalists, *One Shining Moment,* which he published in 2000 (iUniverse). He connected me with Seymor Reisin who prepared his autobiographical pieces on the Students for Democratic Action and on American Youth for Democracy, incubators for some of the notable liberal academic, labor and political leaders of the last half of the 20th century.

With permission of Regnery Publishers, we included excerpts from the writings of William F. Buckley Jr. and M. Stanton Evans, Yale graduates and leaders of the new conservative student movement in the 1950s. Both describe the opposition to NSA from the right. Evans also traces the birth of the Young Americans for Freedom alongside the transformation the Young Republicans (pp. 797, 801).

It took considerable searching at the Library of Congress and Young Republican headquarters for Roy Voegeli to confirm why I was not able to find an organized national conservative political movement during NSA's founding years—there was none until journalist Frank Chodorov and Bill Buckley founded the Intercollegiate Society of Individualists (p. 800), patterned after Jack London's Intercollegiate Socialist Society formed 50 years earlier.

There is not enough room to relate my many memorable experiences at more than 125 campuses and their libraries, peering at microfilm and bound book archives of college newspapers, and copying off their pages of ephemera and history. It was at one of these visits to Wellesley that I discovered it was Alice Horton who organized the U.S. delegation to the Prague World Student Congress. None of the surviving delegates with whom we were in touch could quite remember her exact name. With the help of the archivist, we reached Alice Horton Tibbetts in Madison, Wisconsin. She connected us to Jewel Lubin Bellush (U. of Wisconsin), delegation secretary, both of whose memoirs (p. 68, p.73) reveal how a few dedicated individuals were able to lay the groundwork for a national movement.

Political scientist Jewel, it turns out, is married to historian Bernard (CCNY, Columbia), an early member of the American Veterans Committee. By a route that led from Andy Rice (Harvard), to former labor leader and now columnist Gus Tyler, to Lou Harris, the former pollster, I came to Bernie Bellush, ready to recreate the AVC of that era (p. 703).

The big surprise in this book—and perhaps its most distinctive contribution to the story of college student life—is the book's reliance on the college press to show the way in which NSA was perceived on college campuses, and how it helped set an agenda for debate and engagement in public policy as well as intercollegiate issues. When I started on the work I knew I wanted to reinforce each memoir with a headline or two about NSA on the author's campus—but I did not realize that I would find played out such dramas as integration efforts, the "red scare" and the internment of Japanese-American students; also the role of the religious and fraternity movements on campus, as well the extent to which general news was being covered by the college dailies. I began to realize that I could tell the entire story of world events leading to, during and following the war without any reference to the *New York Times* or other commercial newspapers (a financial blessing as well, since *New York Times* permissions fees were prohibitive.)

It would not have been possible to document the regional and campus stories in Part 5 without reference to the college press. Through their reports, for example, it is known that two, three or even four times as many colleges would attend regional events as would join the association or attend National Student Congresses during NSA's first five years. Such vigorous campus affiliation campaigns as those at Maryland, LSU, Texas, Stanford and others, and enthusiastic receptions at California, Chicago, Wellesley, Barnard and North Carolina—sometimes represented by two or three lines in the student government minutes—were extensively chronicled in the college press. (Contrariwise, student government minutes sometimes chronicled an NSA story not reported in the papers.)

In the course of excerpting the college newspapers, the book also presents a panoramic view not to be found anywhere else of what college journalism was like in the middle of the twentieth century. NSA leaders recognized the importance of the press in reaching students on the campus and cemented its relationship through the annual newspaper editors conference that accompanied each National Student Congress after 1951 (Part 2, Section 4).

Notable among those who carefully read the original manuscripts were Martin McLaughlin, Dick Heggie, Allan Ostar, Mildred Kiefer Wurf and Bill Dentzer. Small booklets could be published of their detailed comments alone. Henry Halsted, above all, gave countless hours to careful proofreading of the entire book, especially the captions and credit lines in the pictorials and albums, most of which were completed in the last two years. His unstinting and devoted attention to detail is remarkable and invaluable.

During the period through early 2003, Ralph Smith worked with me from his home in Reston, VA, as a consulting editor. He reviewed and edited many of the essay drafts in the book. His influence on the organization and tone of the work is substantial. He and Bill Dentzer read and edited all of the frontmatter, Prologue, and the seven part and 39 section openers. They introduced clarity, consistency and reasonable syntax in the narratives where they could.

Ralph has given of his time and advice in many ways, and has provided me with an additional final review of the entire book. He has also contributed two memoirs (pp. 712, 897). Ralph opened my eyes to the defining role of our Depression experience as a veterans generation bringing a new civic conscience and educational purpose to the campus, as well as to our arguably fading reach into the decades that followed. He offers his viewpoint in a short, sensitive piece on p. 712.

The reach of post-war student organizations to the Vietnam era could not survive the anger and alienation of activist students in the late sixties and early seventies. Virtually all of the student religious, social-action and political groups of the center and left were dissolved and/or replaced. At the outset of this project, as a consequence, when I got in touch with the major Protestant and Catholic youth organizations of today, no one that I first spoke to had ever heard of the National Federation of Catholic College Students or the National Intercollegiate Christian Council. And, although the present United States Student Association (USSA) considers itself in direct line to the earlier U.S. National Student Association (USNSA), of which it is the corporate heir, USSA is in fact a significantly different kind of organization, reflecting a different activist ethos from that of its predecessors. The time line chart on p. 817, Angus Johnston's piece on postwar student activism before the 1960s (p. 815), Janet Brown's important piece "After the First Five Years" on page 1087 and our unit on NSA in the Cold War (Part 3, Section 2), suggest a later student organization history that will be of a vastly different character from that in this book—one of an era of social protest and change emerging alongside a golden age of intercollegiate student government leadership.

Almost all of the original memoirs in the Prologue and Parts 1, 2, 3 and 6 of this book were written in first draft in 1996, 1997 and 1998. A number of the memoirs in Parts 4 and 5 were written in each of the years from 1999 to 2003. In such a lapse of time to publication, present tense has a way of becoming past tense, biographies have a way of changing as job descriptions change, grandchildren arrive on the scene, honorary degrees increase in number and, sadly, friends and loved ones depart. Temptingly, also, new letters, photos, clippings and other ephemera emerge—too late for inclusion, but not too late for establishing a date or name that was missing. The anthology project will deliver to the Wisconsin Historical Society a substantial archive of such materials to add to its NSA holdings.

A word on reviewing: all the original material in this book was looked at by an editorial committee of ten (see p. iv), plus Ralph and myself. Usually, several additional people with special expertise or relevant experience were sent the manuscript for review. Later in the next stage of production Henry Halsted and Bill Dentzer proofread selected units for content and style. Joan Kennedy Taylor, who joined the project as manuscript and production editor, made valuable suggestions for clarifying structure and sequence in the work.

At an early project meeting in 1996, Norman Holmes encouraged me not to be bound by a preconceived plan and to let the book grow from the material at hand. This license to follow the story led from my originally intended 400 page trade paperback, planned to appear in time for the 1997 50th National Student Congress, to the 1244-page volume you are now holding.

Three of our number, Pat Wohlgemuth Blair, Royal Voegeli and Henry Halsted, provided invaluable research and fact-checking support. Pat undertook to follow leads at Catholic University, Georgetown and the Association of Jesuit Colleges where she was able to find most of the documentation filling in the gaps and backing up the recollections of Martin McLaughlin, Ed Kirchner and Phil DesMarais on Catholic participation in the founding of NSA. Together with Janet Welsh Brown, and Janet's husband Norman, Pat assembled a wealth of material on the careers of several hundred of the people who are cited in the book. They also discovered how cold the trail can get tracking down people of our generation.

Roy Voegeli spent several years trying to get an official history of the Young Republican Clubs (which was eventually found in a carton in a store room at YRC offices in DC). He also uncovered the exceptional trove of documentation Jewel Lubin Bellush assured us we would find in U.S. Ambassador Steinhardt's files of his tenure in Prague during the 1946 World Student Congress. It took Roy three visits to the State Department Archives before they figured out the right key words—International Student Conference—to locate the files we wanted. They provided the content for the albums on pages 99-104. Roy also kept the lines open to the University of Wisconsin's special collections. The University was home for NSA during its first four years, and the Wisconsin Historical Society reasonably considers NSA to be a part of Wisconsin history.

Important original essays were researched and prepared by several of the scholars among our number, who went beyond personal memoirs and related events. I am indebted to Janet Welsh Brown for her analysis of NSA's academic freedom and student rights initiatives (Part 2) and her review of the few extant earlier NSA histories (part 6); also, historian Mimi Haskell Berlin for her opening essay (Prologue) describing the historic setting for U.S. student organization. Excerpts from Martin McLaughlin's 1948 doctoral thesis on political processes in student organizations and on NSA's formation provide an invaluable resource (pp. 15, 818).

Henry Halsted (Williams College, MA) had been engaged in student exchange programs earlier in his career, and had an invaluable collection of materials relating to the Experiment in International Living (p. 683), the short-lived Youth Argosy, his travels to Europe and the connections he had kept with German students alongside whom he worked in 1948 doing reconstruction at the University of Munich (p. 659). A veteran, Henry was also helpful in providing materials on the American Veterans Committee (AVC). He led me to Otis Pease, whose paper on the impact of military service on the Yale Class of 1949 (p. 699) provides poignant insight on the veteran war time experience. It is followed by Cord Meyer's moving (and widely hailed at the time) 1945 *Atlantic Monthly* article on "A Service Man Looks at the Peace" (p. 703).

Pease mentions a section in the Yale yearbook by Curt Farrar, which provides a picture (p. 829) of Yale's rejection of student government and its approval of entry into NSA—the latter choice roundly deplored by Bill Buckley in an excerpt from *God and Man at Yale* (p. 797).

Inclusion of the Cord Meyer piece has some irony and sentiment attached to it. Meyer was in charge of the CIA operation launched in 1951 to provide covert funding to U.S. nongovernment organizations so that they could afford to attend the many international events that were a part of the Cold War in those years. An ardent internationalist who was head of the World Federalists, his work in the CIA was, to him, an extension of his support for the cause of freedom throughout the world (Meyer, *Facing Reality*, University Press of America, 1982).

Because so many former NSA leaders felt betrayed by the undercover nature of government support through the CIA, which only two or three officers at a time knew about, Cord Meyer's legacy is colored by his CIA connection and the diminished regard with which many Americans have viewed the CIA since the Vietnam era. I came to know about Cord Meyer through development of this anthology, and to appreciate his life's mission: his passionate defense and support of the United Nations and his insistence that by our victory of World War II, as he wrote, "we gain the opportunity to construct by intelligent and radical reform a more equitable society and a peaceful world. In the light of that purpose alone do the deaths of our friends have dignity and our own misfortunes significance. If we do not employ the opportunity with honesty and foresight, then our approaching triumph is only an illusion." (Echoes of that hope resonate once again today [2005] during the war and efforts at political transformation in Iraq.)

The irony is that Meyer's place in NSA history is clouded by the covert mission he undertook to carry out. The poignant note is that we reached him through his family shortly before his death, when he gave permission for us to reproduce his *Atlantic Monthly* article, and he learned with satisfaction that he was also being remembered for his passionate idealism as a young man.

The Cold War thread of the NSA story has many dramatic and compelling aspects. The young leaders of NSA who were engaged in its international program revisit the sobering imperatives of that tense period of conflict in Parts 1 and 3—Bill Ellis, Jim Smith, Bob Smith, Frank Fisher, Rob West, Erskine Childers, Bill Holbrook, Herb Eisenberg, Helen Jean Rogers (Secondari), Mary Kay Perkins, Bill Birenbaum, Barry Farber, Avrea Ingram (who died young, mysteriously and seemingly at his own hand [p. 575]) and Helen Bryan (Garland)—to name some of the figures whose vivid stories appear in this book.

NSA's international program brought American student leaders to meet and work with many European, Asian and Latin American student leaders. The bonds with the Europeans were especially strong—the British, Dutch, French and Swedes in particular. On page 532, Helen Bryan Garland provides an insight into one of these bonds. Erskine Childers, NSA's 1950-51 international vice president, and Olof Palme, who was head of the Swedish National Union of Students and later became Sweden's Prime Minister (assassinated in 1986), met through NSA and continued their relationship when Erskine went to work for the UN.

Garland also raises questions about how and why Olof and Erskine's later initiatives at the UN were frustrated: to advance a strong global environmental program, and also to reform the UN and to take it out of the hands of global special interests.

Garland suggests that other students of the same generation, who moved out of college into positions of influence at the UN and among global corporate interests, formed an informal network to render UN influence ineffective when it stood in the way of global corporate interests. These initiatives, she asserts, began as a cadre of future civic leaders, such as Erskine and Olof, were also getting their basic training in campus student organizations and in NSA.

The members of this network, prominent on the world stage and now in their retiring years, came from among both student leaders and college administration advisers. She feels that they deceived their student colleagues while manipulating their leadership positions to advance their future career intentions.

To evaluate the truth of this view from all sides and do it total justice would require more space than this work can afford, taking us into a whole other range of issues and personalities. Because of Helen's contributions to this anthology and to NSA's early years of development, and the considerable thought she has given to the subject, I feel it important that readers know of her concerns.

The thread can be picked up by exploring the biographies of Margaret Mead, with whom Garland served for many years as an associate, of Erskine Childers and Olof Palme and of the leaders of the UN environmental programs. Garland writes in her piece on Childers and Palme (p. 532) there is also "a story of intrigue, which I hope will yet be told by others of us who were there."

Questioning the integrity of their NSA experience is voiced by some for whom covert CIA funding is the critical issue. The issue of betrayal in connection with U.S. funding channeled through the CIA is also raised in this anthology by Janet Welsh Brown (p. 386) and Galen Martin (p. 983). Going further, there is one contemporary of ours who declined to write for this book because of his feeling that the 1967 revelations (p. 565) irretrievably contaminated the story. I myself discovered that my trip to Prague in 1951 as one of three NSA observers was secretly paid for by government funds provided through two "front" attorneys (see Craig Wilson, p. 248).

The sponsors of this anthology undertook at the outset to explore what evidence they could uncover about covert government funding during "our watch." Their findings, prepared by a group headed by Bill Welsh, NSA's first president, are discussed in the unit beginning on page 565. In my editor's note to that unit, I cite Karen Paget, a former 1966-67 NSA staffer and political scientist, who has been working on a study of the origins and extent of the CIA's covert relationship with NSA. Finally, Barry Keating provides additional context in his piece, "How Its Own Cold War Influenced Liberal Student Activism," on p. 811.

Turning to domestic themes, inclusion of the memoirs by two black college presidents, Norman Francis of Xavier University and John Peoples of Jackson State Univesity, were a result of Connie Curry's introductions. In order to get their stories, I traveled to New Orleans and then to Jackson, MS, where I interviewed and taped each of them—another of the high points for me in the acquisitions stage. I also visited Louisiana State University on that trip, where I found in the *Reveille* the remarkable story of the Xavier delegate protest that led to the first integrated regional meeting and the contest at LSU before and following it (p. 454).

Most of the section on the South in Part 2 came about because Bill Welsh urged me to see if I could reach Aaron Henry (p. 456)—who, sadly, died shortly thereafter—and to connect with other former black student leaders in the South. The actions taken by many returning veterans, white and black, to reverse the traditions of exclusion and discrimination on U.S. campuses is one of the most moving and inspiring chapters in post-war student activism.

A number of other themes thread their way through the NSA story. They are of interest not only in the telling, but for the insights I believe they provide on some of the common ground that keeps together the otherwise diverse ethnic, cultural and religious strands that co-exist and collaborate within American society.

The four that come most to mind are how America's two major Christian branches found a way to bring their youth together in a secular arena; how the values of community and of civic and political engagement were blended with the pursuit of self-interest and self-development through the fostering of student leadership, faculty collaboration, democratic process and student self-government; and, as a challenging test of the first two, the way in which student leaders dealt with issues of discrimination and segregation and with communism's ideological and cold-war challenges.

A signal element, also, in NSA's outlook was its emphasis on collaboration with faculty and administration. The anthology includes 25 tributes to educators who, as "mentors," provided support to NSA and leadership in areas of student life.

NSA provided a forum for policy debate and formulation of programs that dealt with these issues. It provided channels of activity by means of which adversaries found areas of common interest and found they could work together. All this took place at the same time as factions of all kinds sought to gain political advantage and favorable outcomes in NSA's legislative process; and, in its early years, without the support of professional staff.

As a collective memoir and sourcebook, the Anthology provides narrative examples of how student leaders responded to these challenges and opportunities. They carried this experience with them throughout later life.

The role of the Student Christian Movement and their professional staff and of the Catholic student groups and church leaders appear throughout the book and are focused on especially in Part 4, Section 2, and in Part 1, Sections 1 through 4. The stories of William Miller, Bill Ellis, Ruth Purkaple, Mary Thompson, Martin McLaughlin, Ralph Dungan, Phil DesMarais, Tesse Hartigan Donnelley and Loan Long Lynch are especially illuminating.

Gordon Klopf and Janet Welsh Brown, in Part 2, Sections 1 and 2, provide an examination of NSA's strengths and weaknesses in its development of student leadership programs and advocacy for student rights (and its later extension to "rights and responsibilities"). NSA's pre-civil rights support of interracial and human relations programs are explored in Part 2, Section 3, especially in the stories by Norman Francis, Connie Curry, Barry Farber, Dick Murphy and Shirley Neizer Tyler (also in Tyler, Part 5, Section 1).

The sophisticated understanding of cold war issues and the communist challenge that postwar liberal student leaders brought to the table is especially highlighted in the stories of Seymour Reisin, Gilbert Jonas and Barry Keating in Part 4, Section 4. These understandings were informed by the history of communist efforts to gain control of student and youth organization agendas in the United States before, during and after World War II, as is brought out in the book's Prologue by Mimi Haskell Berlin, Mary Lou Rogers Munts and Martin McLaughlin, and by Bernard Bellush in the American Veterans Committee story in Part 4, Section 1.

At the same time, a vast outpouring of generosity in providing postwar reconstruction and third-world aid, and a lively and earnest interest in building bridges of understanding prompted thousands of U.S. students to travel abroad each summer. NSA developed at one point the largest U.S.-sponsored student travel program, and sent observers throughout Europe, Asia and South America to make connections with other student groups. NSA's international program and its early efforts to maintain contact with students in the communist world stand as a monument to the idealism and positive outlook of American students during the cold war era. The broad sweep of student international engagement is presented in Part 3 of the anthology. Of the many stories and recollections of unusual interest are those by Douglass Cater, William Birenbaum, Barry Farber, Mary Kay Perkins, Phil Stoddard, Mary Ann Weld Bodecker, Jos Vos, Helen Garland and Henry Halsted.

Also of historical interest are the "foreign policy" visions of NSA's leaders as expressed by Bob Smith, Frank Fisher, Rob West, Erskine Childers, Herb Eisenberg, Al Lowenstein and Bill Dentzer, among others. They attempted to mainain a balance in the defense and advocacy of human liberty throughout the world while keeping open the channels of communication to the recently defeated axis powers, and communist and colonial areas of the world. The promise of the United Nations was also a lodestar of that era.

Two significant and creative early civic initiatives by voluntary organizations are described in the stories of the National Scholarship Service and Fund for Negro Students (NSSFNS), which still exists today in a different form, and the International Development Placement Association (IDPA). NSSFNS (p. 463) is recalled in Shirley Neizer Tyler's and Evelyn Jones Rich's stories about how black students were recruited for placement in all white colleges in the North. IDPA (p. 627) was formed to provide skilled volunteers for technical assistance to emerging third world post-colonial countries. It was a Peace Corps forerunner. Elements of the story of its brief but productive life and its aftermath are told by one of its founders, Douglas Kelley, and by Dick Murphy and Peter Weiss.

In lieu of having a book ready for the 50th National Student Congress, our anthology committee prepared a commemorative envelope with facsimiles of the original Chicago Student Conference and Constitutional Convention programs and a preview booklet, "A Time for Vision," which contained Clif Wharton's NSA memoirs. The design of that preview booklet was created by Don Wright, and edited by his partner, Ronnie Shushan, of Broadview Media in Woodstock, NY. They then took on the assignment of creating a design concept for the entire work.

It was a daunting task because of the many elements in the book. When my good friend and contemporary, Joan Taylor, came on board as manuscript and then production editor, followed by Shaun Johnston as art manager, the two of them set about figuring out how to present the multiple elements coherently. Their organizing concepts, visible in such elements as pages labeled "background," "album," "vision," or "mentor," enabled us to develop design specifications to cover the 27 different style groupings that made up the three concurrent threads in the work: the narratives (part and section overviews), the memoirs and tributes, and the resource pages (background and albums.)

The key to maintaining sanity in putting this book together has been a content checklist system, flexible enough to expand and contract, whereby every text and graphic element that needs to be tracked and accounted for, both for location and for permissions, has a file number—for paper and for electronic purposes. There are more than 450 such text elements and about 4,000 images. Many of the images that show only headlines or portions of text were scanned in more complete versions which reside in the picture files of the pagemaking program, QuarkXpress—a sort of hidden graphic time capsule that can be retrieved in the future.

Along the way, the basic sequencing of the elements of the book was reshuffled to much editorial consternation. What is now the Prologue was originally intended to be in the back of the book; at one point in 2001, we considered, and repaged the book as a possible two-volume set. For fear that were we to follow that plan, volume 2 might never see the light of day, I went back to the single- volume plan.

The project committee itself also revisited the title of the book in 2002, and settled on *American Students Organize*. Prior to that, the working title was *Pursuing America's Vision*. And earlier, we tried out *A Generation That Believed in America.* In the first book plan, in early 1997, the title was *U.S. Students Organize After World War II: The Founding Years of the U.S. National Student Association, 1947-51*. In the end, we came back to a version of that.

Many members of the committee have been and remain deeply concerned that this book not be viewed as an expression of self-congratulation or triumphalism. Yet, unquestionably, we all share a sense of pride and appreciation for our efforts, even if some of those efforts were sometimes imperfect, unsuccessful and perhaps even of marginal value or irrelevant in the scheme of things.

On October 9, 2001, I delivered to Otto Barz and George Ernsberger at Publishing Synthesis in Manhattan the "manuscript" for the book. It was in simulated 2-column page format, set in Microsoft Word. The book in their hands went through copyediting in six batches, and two passes of page proofs in part and section units. Deborah Constantine has put these complex pages together in Quark.

During the time the work has been incubating they have extended both patience and credit beyond the call. Sufficient time passed so that PubSyn needed to upgrade their version of Quark last year to keep pace with the needs of their major text, reference and professional publishing clients. In order to avoid the risks in upgrading software in so large and complex a project's midstream, our book now resides on the hard drive of its original computer in its original version of Quark, retained solely for the purpose.

My appreciation and admiration also goes to the proofreader Linda Robinson; to Kay Schlembach, who did a masterful job creating the three main indexes to the book; and to Nicole Balant, who copyedited the original manuscript and served as production editor for the final pages.

Shaun Johnston did pre-paging layouts on our own Quark platform through the middle of Part 4, after which I took over when he persuaded me it would reduce time and labor considerably by eliminating the paper layouts I was handing to him. Half the album images in the book were scanned by Susanne Teizsch. Shaun scanned most of the author head shots, and I scanned the balance of Part 4 and all of Part 5. We used Hewlett-Packard desktop scanners.

Heroes and heroines in the eight years of having to make internal copies, multiple copies of college newspaper microfilm printouts, and review and preview copies of the various stages of the book worked at a succession of copy shops: Woodstock Copy Center, Staples in Ulster, Kinko's in Albany and, in the last two years Office Depot in Ulster/Kingston, NY, which has delivered superb digital copying from disk. My ability to respond promptly to the needs of previewing the entire work and various selections from it has been possible only because of the quality of workmanship, enthusiasm and support of the copying crew at Office Depot—Debbie, Chris, Robb, Samantha and Kelley who, by the time of completion were almost like family.

During the course of this project several operating systems of Windows have come and gone, the capabilities and quality of copying has improved, pdf readers have become ubiquitous, and broadband transmission of huge electronic files has collapsed turnaround times. The production of this work would probably not have been feasible were it not for the technological revolutions taking place alongside of it. And last but not least, the people of the U.S. Postal Service in Malden on Hudson and in Saugerties, NY and UPS in Kingston have expeditiously handled our mailings.

At the time of this writing we have not yet gone to press, but it is not too early to thank Bill Ralph and Jim Scarbrough of Malloy, Inc., our printers-to-be in Ann Arbor, MI for patiently providing annual updates to our manufacturing estimates as the size of the book grew and the schedule attenuated.

A word on how this book came about. Our decision in January of 1996 had incubated over the course of a year. In January of 1995, after attending Helen Jean (Rogers) Secondari's annual Twelfth Night reunion, Mildred Kiefer Wurf invited me and Anne Harris, the widow of Ted Harris, to a dinner afterward with Bill and Jean Welsh, whom I hadn't seen since the summer of 1948, when I was elected NSA Vice President for Educational Problems.

Not having followed student events in later years, I learned that NSA was still alive, albeit in a different form, and the 50th National Student Congress was coming up in the summer of 1997. Wouldn't it be nice if we did something to commemorate the event, we mused.

A year later the same conversation and the same question arose. I had also learned about the 1967 revelations regarding covert government funding of NSA and various other youth, labor and cultural organizations for their international activities during the cold war (Part 3, Section 2). It seemed that for many, when NSA was mentioned the first thought that came to mind was "the CIA connection." This would generally lead, we noted, to a discussion of college student activism after World War II, from the flower children and the silent generation to the free speech movement, the civil rights revolution, Woodstock and the Vietnam protest era.

I have to admit that I could not identify with any of these events, although I have a clear recollection of trying to put my own life, family and career together while those currents swirled about me. I wondered what happened to the vision and energy that inspired me during my post-war years from 1946 through 1951.

I had retained some close friendships with those whom I shared the adventure of 1948-49 in Madison. It was an intensely personal experience of developing new relationships and broadened outlooks, along with doing the job we were elected to do. Fifty years later, revisiting that experience, the memory of much of what had transpired was encrusted and obscured by the years in between. But what I did connect with that evening at that dinner was the sense that among my associates, the CIA revelations and turbulent years that preceded and followed them were not really our story.

I recalled especially my dear friends Rob West of Yale, then international vice president, and Ted Harris of LaSalle in Philadelphia, NSA President of our year—both departed by 1996. Rob was an international economist, for whom honesty and probity were paramount, who devoted much of his life to bettering the economies of East Africa, and whom I admired in life more than any other man. Ted was an African American possessed of good humor, quickness of mind, eloquence of expression, and devotion to his Catholic faith and his family. His own inner struggles threw him off target at times, and led him on a life's journey through business and international agency positions, a period of despair in West Africa and a return home to satisfying work with schools in Philadelphia's inner city. During our year in Madison, he confronted me with an examination of faith and set me on a lifetime journey to discover myself.

I remembered also Helen Jean Rogers (later Secondari), who came up to Madison from Mundelein College in Chicago—a "freshly scrubbed" 18-year-old who soon revealed a brilliant, tough-minded capacity for reasoning and expression and a buoyant optimism and energy that became the motor of our staff and who won my deepest affections. She later became a globe-trotting TV documentary producer with her husband, John Secondari. Helen Jean, through a mischance of medical malpractice in 1988 was functionally impaired in every way except in clarity of mind, and ten years thereafter, in 1998, died of her impairments and—possibly even more so—of her despair at the loss of her husband some years before.

I thought that these people deserve to be remembered for who they were and what they did. It was clear that if we didn't tell their story and ours, it would probably remain invisible in the archives and in college newspapers, yearbooks and ephemera of student life. So, I said, "Let's do a book. Let's tell our own story. If you help me find the authors, collaborate in reviewing the content and raise the money, I will do the book."

As a consequence I became acquainted with a diverse group of people in their youth. I believe every reader will enjoy and be enriched by meeting them. They appear here together at a time when they were ready to do big things for the sake of big ideas, as they moved on to build their lives and the society of which they were a part.

Although my more than fifty years in the printing and publishing industries should have signaled the extended effort this undertaking would entail, I see now that I had absolutely no idea in 1996 of the journey on which I was embarking. It would take me back to an age of hope and promise and to the rediscovery of a vision for a world without hate which lives on in our hearts, and in whose fulfilment we believe, without a doubt, is our destiny. Now at the project's conclusion, I do not regret a moment of it.

Malden on Hudson, NY
January 2006

INDEX

CONTENTS

1154 How to Use This Index
1155 Index to Names
1172 Index to Colleges and College Newspapers
1187 Index to Subjects
1208 Index to Authors, Student Leader Recollections and Mentor Tributes

MILESTONES IN THE NEWS

1945 World War II ends, the United Nations is born; *Animal Farm* published, *Carousel* opens on Broadway. *52*

1946 The Nuremberg Trials and the Iron Curtain; *The Iceman Cometh* and *Annie Get Your Gun* open on Broadway. *134*

1947 The Marshall plan is launched and India is declared independent; *A Streetcar Named Desire* opens; Jackie Robinson breaks the color barrier. *162*

1948 The Berlin Airlift is launched and the State of Israel is formed; *South Pacific* opens and Joe Louis retires. *196*

1949 People's Republic of China is formed; apartheid in South Africa; *1984* is published and *Death of a Salesman* opens. *232*

1950 McCarthyism and the Korean War; Cool Jazz and *Guys and Dolls.* *262*

1951 MacArthur relieved of command, Rosenbergs sentenced to death; *Catcher in the Rye* published, *The King and I* opens. *293*

1952 First Hydrogen Bomb exploded, Queen Elizabeth II is crowned; Ellison's *Invisible Man* published, *High Noon* opens. *320*

1953 Eisenhower inaugurated and Stalin dies; *Wonderful Town* opens, Mount Everest is scaled. *1084*

Highlights of the NSA Story

BENCHMARK EVENTS

8/18-8/31/46 *World Student Congress, Prague, Czechoslovakia* *81*
(300 delegates from 38 nations. 24-member U.S. delegation) *94, 103*

12/28-12/30/46 *Chicago Student Conference, University of Chicago*
(727 delegates, observers, 307 colleges, 28 national student orgs.) *109*
Jim Smith (*University of Texas*) *President*, Continuations Committee *119*

8/30-9/7/47 *Constitutional Convention, University of Wisconsin*
(750 delegates and observers, 351 colleges) *135*
William B. Welsh (*Berea College*, Kentucky), *President.* *165*
(Headquartered in Madison, Wisconsin, first four years).

8/23-8/28/48 *First Congress, University of Wisconsin*
(550 delegates and observers, 295 colleges) *199*
James T. Harris, Jr. (*LaSalle College*, Pennsylvania), *President* *219*

8/24-9/3/49 *Second Congress, University of Illinois*
(800 delegates and observers, 312 colleges) *233*
Robert F. Kelly (*St. Peters College*, New Jersey), *President* *252*

8/23-8/31/50 *Third Congress, University of Michigan*
(780 delegates and observers, 232 colleges, 100 administrators) *265*
Allard K. Lowenstein (*University of North Carolina), President* *283*

8/20-8/29/51 *Fourth Congress, University of Minnesota*
(500 delegates and observers, 225 colleges) *299*
Annual Student Body President's Conference launched *1101*
William Dentzer (*Muskingum College*, Ohio), *President* *305*
(Moved headquarters to Boulder, Colorado, one year)

8/18-8/27/52 *Fifth Congress, University of Indiana* (450 delegates and observers, 275 colleges) *1079*
First Annual College Newspaper Editor's Conference *477*
Richard Murphy, *University of North Carolina, President* *1075*
(Moved headquarters in 1952 to Philadelphia for next 15 years)
(Headquartered in Washington, DC, from 1967)

1977 Merged with the National Student Lobby to form the U.S. Student Association (USSA) *1092*

1945 p.41
1946 p.81
1947 p.135
1948 p.199
1949 p.233
1950 p.265
1951 p.299

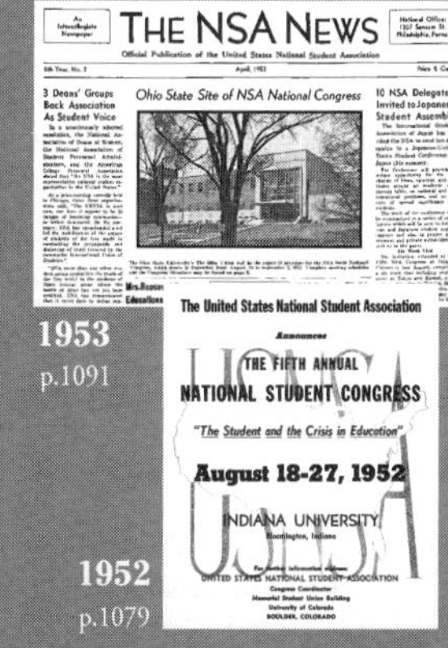

1953 p.1091
1952 p.1079

HOW TO USE THIS INDEX

Four indexes provide references by

(1) individual name
(2) college name and college newspaper
(3) subject
(4) author, student leaders, mentors

The first three listings and their subcategories offer key words useful in library, archive and internet searches.

The fourth index lists the 98 authors, 25 student leader recollections, 25 mentor tributes and 4 U.S. president tributes featured in the book, including their memoir unit titles and their biographic highlights.

Names and titles of individuals and colleges are indexed as they appeared in 1946-52, and are cross-referenced to current updates (e.g. college to university, single to married name).

Because of the numerous rosters and album pages in this anthology, each page citation in the index is coded to distinguish references in text, background, albums or end notes from those in lists. The lists' codes are detailed below:

(a) Reference and almanac
(b) U.S. Negro colleges
(c) U.S. Catholic colleges
(e) Other events
(r) NSA congress rosters
(w) Women's collegess

These lists, and those on the previous page, feature subjects, events and rosters that profile the NSA story. Other indexing conventions are described in the introductory notes to each of the four indexes.

ROSTERS

National Student Association (r)

Other Rosters (b,w,c)

Reference and Almanac (a)

Other Events and Organizations (e)

Index to Names

Note: f indicates appearance in photo, photo caption, college press headline or newspaper clipping ouside stated page range; n indicates note; **bold** locators indicate principle memoirs or commentaries; university affiliations are at the time of NSA involvement; ***italic bold*** locators indicate primary biographic reference; *italic text* indicates primary NSA positions, university and/or organization affiliation, attendance at cited event; abbreviations and acronyms are defined on p. 1126.

A

Aaronson, Alan *(City College of New York)*, 216f, 846f, 865f
Aaslund, Christian, 1129a
Abdill, MaryJane Fairbairn, 965f
Abel, Leonard, 157
Abernathy, Bradford, 967e
Abiouness, Gloria *(Dunbarton College, DC; regonal Chair, 1950)*, 351, 495n4, 896f, 922f, 945
Abrahamson, Frank, 478e
Abrams, Susan D., 355
Acquaviva, Charlotte, 1098r
Adams, Arthur S., 416
Adams, Brock, *(U. of Washington)* 187f, 1055, 1062f
Adams, Henry, 589
Adams, Max, 722, 723
Addams, Jane, 60
Adler, Paula, 897
Agatha, M., 432f, 437
Agboton, Ambroise, 1129a
Aggrey, Rudolph, 966e
Agnew, Charlotte "Char," *(Stanford U., CA)* 271, 280, 521, 643
Aiken, George D., 103e
Aiken, Patricia, 966e
Aitkin, Douglas, 57f
Albertson, Maurice L., 638
Alexander, Harry T. *(Xavier U., LA; regional Chair, 1948-49)*, 230r, 340n7, 432, 434, 435, 436f, 437, **455f**, 962f
Alexander, Herbert, 774
Allain, Charles, 437
Allaway, Olivia W. Foster, 617
Allaway, William H. "Bill" (*U. of Illinois*), 57f, 228-29, 236, 317, 611, *(WSSF)* **613-*17***, 655-57, 659f, 729, 950f
Allen, Ada Lou, 967e
Allen, Charlotte "Char" (later Charters) *(U. of Illinois)*, 225f, 236, 237, 247, 501f, 617f, 655, **658f**, 659f, 944, 950f
Allen, Fred, 721
Allen, George, 1047f
Allen, Lucile, 1124a
Allen, Nancy, 1047f
Allen, Raymond B., *President, U. of Washington)* 1053, 1061f, 1063
Allgood, Mary Lou, 985, 987
Allison, Bill, 410
Allott, Gordon, 802
Allyn, Harriet M., 103e
Alport, Louise, 1048f
Alston, Frank, 442
Alston, Wallace M., 1098r, 1124a
Altbach, Phillip G., 5, 9, 10, **14**, 47, 544n18, 687n5, 727n4-5, 778f, 814n1, 1088
Alvarez, Manuel, 115e, 132r
Andelson, Bob, 805
Anderson, Bob, 1054
Anderson, Dewey, 637
Anderson, Ida Louise *(Washington State College)*, mentor, **29**
Anderson, Jack, 970
Anderson, Jean, 291r, 955
Anderson, Leila *(YWCA. World Student Congress, Prague, 1946)*, 967e, 84, 103e, 107, 491, 648f, 649, 715, 722, 733f
Anderson, Robert O., 93
Anderson, Roy, 280
Andert, Marian *(U. of Minnesota. 1951-52, 52-53 NSA Executive Secretary)*, 281, 297, 299, 300, 304f, 305f, 318r, 399, 492n1, 1074f, 1076, 1088r
Andress, John R., 465f
Andrews, Dorothy, 1035
Angel, Francisco, 1015, 1017n10
Angel, Joe, 998f
Angell, Norman, 463
Anliot, Richard B., 416-17
Annenberg, Walter, 1075
Anthony, Susan B., 886
Antonelli, Jose, 1129a
Appel, Richard, 291r
Appleby, Sadye, 966e
Aragon, John, 1017n6
Aragon, Manuel, 1129a
Aragon, Robert, 1129a
Arellano, Anselmo, 1017n6
Arnall, Ellis, 994
Arnheim, Don, 1040
Arnheim, Nancy Lee Roth *(U. of California, Los Angeles)*. See Roth, Nancy Lee.
Arnold, Edith, later Sisson *(Smith College)*, 660, **661-663**, ***663f***, 664f
Arnold, Lewis E., 291r
Arnold, Sarah Louise, 834f
Arthur, George, 877
Ashby, Warren, 1102
Aswad, Charles A., 371, 1078f, 1088r
Atkins, Mary, 1048f
Atkinson, Bob, 1009
Augustus, Betsy, 642
Aum, Richard A., 478e
Austin, Russell *(U. of Chicago, IL)*: biographical and career highlights, 90f, ***91***; *Chicago Student Conference (1946)*, 109, 113, 120, 870; *Nat'l Continuations Committee Vice President* (1946-47), 65, 91n2, 110f, 115e, 116, 118f, 126f, 132r, 1062f; NSA *Constitutional Convention (1947)*, 150, 950f; World Student Congress, Prague (1946), 65, 73, 81, 84, **90-91**, 94, 96, 97, 103e, 537f
Aviet, Countess, 643
Aycock, William, 31e
Ayers, Alta, 966e

B

Babcock, Fern *(YWCA)*, 687n1
Bacon, Sylvia A. *(Vassar College, NY)*: academic freedom and student rights (1949), 376, 381, 383, 474-75; anthology contributing editor, iv, 1146; biographical and career highlights, 474f, 475f, ***476;*** College News Conference (TV), 1087; College Newspaper Editor's Conference (1952), 469; *Copenhagen Conference (1953)*, 22, 1074f, 1129a; female leadership, 218n11, 330, 489f, 492n1; *Int'l Student Conference (ISC, 1953)*, 534f, 576f; on C.Courtnet (Landry), 921; NSA: *Nat'l Student Congress (1952)*, 328n1, 474-76; *Vice President of Student Affairs (1951-52)*, 298f, 299-300, 318r, 376, 383, 399, 474-76, 476n5, 845, 1122. On young Democrats and Republicans, 786
Bahr, Vern, 1067f, 1068f
Bailey, Helen, 966e
Baiocchi, Adele, 946f
Baker, Ella, 447
Baker, Everett Moore (*Dean, Massachusetts Institute of Technology. NSA Advisor, 1948-49)*, 230r, 338, 520, 521, 823, **841** (mentor), 1123a
Baker, Herman, 195r, 978f
Baker, Patricia "Pat" *(Chicago Teachers College, IL)*, 240, 580f
Balant, Nicole, 1151
Bakken, Harold *(U. of Minnesota. NSA President, 1956-57)*, 1122, 1130a
Balant, Nicole, 1151
Baldwin, Roger *(ACLU)*, 624, 628r, 790
Balfour, L.G., 745
Balistrin, Catherine, 478e
Ball, Helen, later Sirkin *(Wheaton College, MA. SF)* 777f
Ballentine, Dewey, 892
Bandera, Stepan, 549
Banks, Fontaine, 983
Banovetz, Jim, 1098r
Barat, Marie, 437
Barefield, Sam, 966e
Bargman, Abe *(CCNY. SF)*, 767, 770
Barker, Lucius J., 455f
Barkett, Ed, 1034f
Barnes, Joseph, 311
Barnes, Sullivan, 803
Barr, Stringfellow "Winkie" *(President, St. Johns College, MD. UWF. IDPA)*, 624, 628e, 634n4, 637, 774
Barron, Toni, 940
Barros, Juan, 1129a
Barry, Babette de, *(Sarah Lawrence College)*, 861f
Barton, Kenneth *(U. of North Carolina. Regional chair, 1952-53)*, 404, 443n3, 976, 978f, 1078f, 1088r
Barwick, Mary Lib, 970
Barz, Otto, 1151
Basescu, Ronnie, 442
Bass, Meyer, 72f
Bastiat, Frederic, 801
Batchler, Anna, 123
Baum, Edward, 1098r
Baum, Harry, 642, 643
Bazelon, David L., 355
Beard, Charles A., 31e
Beaver, Gilbert, 691
Bebchick, Leonard N. "Len" *(Cornell U., NSA VP of International Affairs, 1953-54)*, 1122, 1129a, 1130a
Becker, Ralph *(YR)*, 802, 804f
Beckner, Ann, 1122, 1123a
Beecher, Harriet, 719
Bell, Charles, 435, 437
Bellamy, Ralph, 707
Bellush, Bernard *(City College of New York; Columbia U. AVC)*, 394f, 697, **707-11**, ***710***, 1147, 1150
Bellush, Jewel Lubin *(U. of Wisconsin; Columbia U. World Student Congress, Prague, 1946)*, 55, 69, **73-75**, ***75***, 83f, 94, 98f, 103e, 109, 168, 537f, 710, 1147, 1149
Belser, Hekmut, 1067f
Belzung, Laurie, 95, 96, 97
Bendall, Elizabeth, 249
Benedict, Harry, 49
Benes, Eduard, 11, 188, 584
Benn, Anthony Wedgwood, 945
Bennett, Doral, 1029n6
Bennett, Michael J., 697, 713
Bennett, Robert F., 1123a
Benson, Ezra Taft, 1084
Bentel, Dwight, 480, 482f
Bercey, Don, 228f
Berezny, Phyllis, later Scannell *(St. Mary's College, IN. Regional chair, 1950-51)*. 276n4, 291r
Bergfors, Connie, 836
Bergman, Ingrid, 763
Bergstresser, John L., *(dean, U. of Chicago)*, 848
Berlin, Gerald A., 13
Berlin, Larry, 955f
Berlin, Miriam Haskell "Mimi" (*Smith College, MA)*: biographical and career highlights, 6f, 12f, ***13***, 87f, 89f, 1149-50; female leadership, 330, 489f, 491; historical view of American society and student movements, 2, **6-13**; *Int'l Student Service (ISS) conference and tour (1946)*, 967e; Nat'l Continuations Committee (1946-47), 13, 88-89, 115e, 118f; NSA: *Constitutional Convention (1947)*, **87-89**; New England region (*regional chair, 1946-47)*, 6, 89, 115e, 172f, 195r, 823, 824f, 826, 835. *World Student Congress, Prague (1946)*, 51f, 81, 87-89
Berlinguer, Giovanni *(IUS)*, 523, 524, 597
Berman, Eugene *(U. of Nebraska. Regional chair, 1946-47)*, 115e, 132r, 956f
Bermingham, Charles E.*(NCYC)*, 472, 735, 736n5, 740, 741, **742**
Bernal, Anselmo, 1016n4, 1017f
Bernard, Kay, 834n7
Bernays, Ann, 863
Bernhard, Prince of the Netherlands, 644, 647, 653, 654f
Bernhill, John, 1000
Bernstein, Goldie, 296f
Bernstein, Ira J., 478e
Bernstein, Meyer, 707
Berry, James R., 1088r
Berry, Philip C. *(U. of Michigan)*: national office aide (1951), 274; *NSA advisor, financial* (1954-57), 1077, 1078f, 1090, 1125a; NSA MI region (Midwest), 291r, 318r, 960; NSA *Vice President, Nat'l Affairs (1953)*, 398, 400, 1076, 1077, 1079f, 1088r, 1122, 1125n2
Bess, Regina, 945n3
Bessol, Peter V. *(U. of Colorado)*, 1001, 1008, 1011
Bestwick, Dick, 441
Bevin, Ernest, 413
Beyers, Robert W. "Bob" *(Cornell U.; Editor-in-Chief,* Cornell Daily Sun, 1952-53; *NSA public information director, 1954-55)*, 404, **480-81**, ***481***, 487
Bhutto, Zufikar Ali, 1028, 1029f
Bidwell, Seth *(Williams College)*, 838
Bilbo, Thomas, 423
Bin Hitam, Musa, 1130a
Binder, Carroll, 143
Bingham, Dale S., 230r, 956
Birenbaum, Helen Bloch, 590
Birenbaum, William M. "Bill" (*U. of Chicago, IL)*: biographical and career highlights, 581f, 589f, ***590*** (as president of Antioch College), 1149, 1152; debate coach, 943; *IUS Coun-*

D

E

F

G

H

I

N

O

T

U

V

Y

Z

Index to Colleges and College Newspapers

Note: f indicates appearance in photo, photo caption, college press headline or newspaper clipping outside stated page range; n indicates note; cross-references to names refer to name index included in this volume; cross-references in [brackets] refer to subject index included in this volume; dates in parenthesis indicate publication dates.

A

B

C

D

E

I

J

K

N

O

P

Q

R

S

T

U

Acknowledgment of Special Permissions

Editor's note: The editors of the anthology provided information about intended use and requested permission from all of the college newspapers excerpted in this volume. We wish to thank those many newspaper editors, business managers and archivists who responded to our requests for non-exclusive permissions and a general release. Many of the college newspaper excerpts used in this volume are of sufficient brevity as to qualify for fair use and some are from college papers of fifty or more years prior to anthology use that have since been discontinued; others are of a vintage to have likely lapsed into public domain. In order to assure that we would have permissions where required, the editors contacted all of the college papers, or their college archives, excerpted in this work regardless of the extent of use. In a number of instances, despite repeated efforts, we were unable to locate or obtain responses from responsible parties. In other instances, we were requested to post specifically worded notices. These notices follow:

Permission acknowledgments for excerpts from other publications and books appear with their uses throughout this anthology.

BOOK JACKET PHOTO CREDITS. From top of cluster, counter-clockwise: (1) Robert L. West (Yale U.), NSA 1948-49 International Vice President, addressing the IUS World Student Congress in Prague, August, 1950. (2) Miriam [Haskell] Berlin (Smith College), New England Region Co-Chair and Lee Jones (U. of Buffalo), later 1947-48 NSA Treasurer, at the August, 1947, Constitutional Convention, University of Wisconsin (Madison I). (3) Convention delegates at Madison I. (4) From left to right at Madison I: Curt Farrar (Yale), Merrill Freed (U. of Chicago), and Bill Welsh (Berea C.), later to be NSA's 1947-48 President. (5) Vol. 1, No. 1, NSA News, October, 1947, (6) Jim Smith (U. of Texas), later President of the National Continuations Committee, addressing the December, 1946 Chicago Student Conference at the University of Chicago. (7) From left at the August, 1949, 2d National Student Congress, U. of Illinois: Harvey Weisberg (U. of Michigan), Chair of the Michigan Region, Robert Kelly (St. Peter's College), later 1949-50 NSA President, and Helen Jean [Rogers] Secondari (Mundelein College), 1948-49 NSA Secretary-Treasurer. (8) U. of Wisconsin Student Union, 1947.

Index to Subjects

Note: f indicates appearance in photo, photo caption, college press headline or newspaper clipping outside stated page range; n indicates note; cross-references to names refer to name index included in this volume; cross-references in [brackets] refer to college/college press index included in this volume; **bold** indicates principal reference; a,b,c,e,r and w indicate appearance in various rosters as listed on p. 1149.

A

F

G

H

I

J

N

Q

R

S

T

Y

Z

Index to Authors, Student Leader Recollections and Mentor Tributes

Note: Except as indicated, these authors have contributed original memoirs, or adaptations of already published materials, prepared expressly for this anthology. Others, shown with an (*) following their name, are excerpted with permission cited from their publishers or from themselves, or are excerpted and adapted from NSA documents. "Recollections" of student and civic leaders, and tributes to "Mentors" include excerpts from writings or speeches from various sources, and are credited where they appear in the book. Undergraduate affiliations in *italic*. Career highlights are [bracketed].

Student Leader Recollections

Mentor Tributes

U.S. Presidents

DONORS

Development and production of this book has been made possible by the generous donations of foundations, individuals and corporate funds. The statements and views expressed in this book are those of the authors only. On this page we have listed all of those to whom we are indebted.

Foundations

Carnegie Corporation of New York
Charles E. Culpepper Foundation
Bill and Melinda Gates Foundation
William H. Gates, Sr. Foundation
Joelson Foundation
W.K. Kellogg Foundation
Andrew W. Mellon Foundation
Leonard and Alice Perlmutter Foundation
Rockefeller Brothers Fund
Shelley and Donald Rubin Foundation
Bernard and Irene Schwartz Foundation
Spencer Foundation

Individuals and Corporations

Allaway, William
Arnheim, Nancy Roth
Bacon, Sylvia
Barnes, Jr., Harry G.
Barr, Martin and Rhoda
Barton, Kenneth
Batchelder, Richard L.
Bebchick, Leonard
Bellush, Bernard and Jewel Lubin
Berlin, Mimi Haskell and Gerald
Berman, Eugene B.
Berry, Philip C.
Birenbaum, William
Blair, James, P.
Blumberg, Morrie
Bodecker, Mary Anne Weld
Bonney, Dennis
Bowers, Henry
Brennan, Anne Searls
Brod, Albert
Brown, Janet Welsh and Norman L.
Brust, Manfred
Cashen, Carol O'Brien and Raymond
Clifford, Donald
Clough, Leonard
Cohen, David and Carla
Culbertson, Mary Virginia
Curry, Constance
Dentzer, Jr., William T.
DiLegge, Michael
Dobkin, Milton
Donnelly, William
Dowd, Janis Tremper and Daan Zwick
Dunbar, Ernest
Dungan, Ralph
Einaudi, Luigi and Carol
Eisenberg, Herbert W.
Ettinger, A. Churchill
Farabee, Ray
Farber, Barry
Farrar, Curtis
Farrar, Eleanor Schneider
Fege, Arnold
Fisher, Francis D.
Ford Motor Company Fund
Frank, Murray
Freed, Merrill
Frei, Adoria Brock
Garmel, Marion
Gates, William H.
Gibbs, James L.
Goldsmith, Herbert
Gray, Clive
Greenfield, Stanley
Guenter, Raymond and Doris
Halaby, Libby Cater
Harcourt, Inc.
Heggie, Richard
Hoffman, Donald A.
Holbrook, Mrs. William
Holmes, Norman and Kim
Howell, Ernest
Hunt, Douglass
Idzik, Ann B.
Idzik, Daniel
Iovenko, Michael
Jones, Ben
Jones, Leeland
Keating, Barry John
Kelley, Douglas C.
Kern, Irwin S.
Klopf, Gordon
Lancaster, Carol
Leyton, Stacey
Littlefield, Jennifer
Lofgren, James
Lucas, Herbert
Lustig, Harry
Lynch, Joan Long and Donald J.
Macy, Francis
Marple, Dorothy J.
McCaulay, Lloyd
McLaughlin, Martin M.
Meagher, Robert F.
Medalie, Richard J. and Susan
Mehl, Barbara
Michalowska, Iryna
Motsch, Carrie
Muller, Steven
Murphy, Richard
Niebuhr, Christopher
Nosse, Robert
Olson, John
O'Scannlain, Dairmuid F.
Ostar, Allan W.
Packer, Joel
Parsons, E. Spencer
Paynter, Elizabeth R.
Pease, Otis
Peoples, John
Perkins, Mary Kay
Persinger, Mildred
Picus, Joy Newberger
Pope, Alexander and Katherine
Popkin, Alice Brandeis
Price, Pamela and Robert
Pritz, Mary Jo Domino
Purkaple, Ruth
Reisin, Seymour
Rice, Andrew E.
Rich, Evelyn Jones
Roe, Richard L.
Rothman, Stanley
Rovira, Luis D.
Sanders, Harold Barefoot
Schwartz, Eugene G.
Secondari, Linda
Shaffer, Robert H.
Shakow, Alexander and Mrs. Patricia
Shinn, Ruth
Shockley, Dolores
Shore, William B.
Sigmund, Paul E.
Sims, Harold and Lana
Sisson, Edith and Thomas
SLG, Inc.
Smit, Sally Holt
Smith, Michael B.
Smith, Robert S.
Smith, Ralph Lee
Spiegel, Eleanor Durham
Steinberg, Bruce and Eve
Steinhauser, Sheldon
Stoddard, Philip
Suzuki, Tom
Sweeney, Joseph
Tenneco
Thompson, Vaughn
Tibbetts, Alice Horton
Tyler, Shirley
Tyson, Harriet
Uphoff, Norman
Voegele, Roy
Wallerstein, Immanuel
Walters, Robert
Wasch, Monte
Weiss, Peter
Welsh, William
Werdell, Philip
Wharton, Clifton
Wilcox, Leonard
Wilkins, Renate B.
Wilson, Craig
Wimer, William E.
Wurf, Mildred Kiefer
Younger, Doris Ann

"A world where there are differences without hate. . . This is our desire."
--The USNSA Creed, 1954, (p. 1091)

A National Voice for American Students is Born

Columbia Daily Spectator

NSO—Student Voice

Four months ago, at the University of Chicago, 700 observers representing 800,000 students in 300 colleges and universities in the United States, overwhelmingly passed a motion to establish a National Student Organization. The gears started turning from that day on. A continuations committee was elected to draw up a draft constitution for the approval of the members. A staff committee was appointed to pave the way for a massive, all-inclusive, constitutional convention. Publicity staffs were selected to keep the colleges in constant touch with the progress of these groups.

The draft constitution was completed this month and colleges all over the continent are receiving copies. The staff committee having made tentative arrangements for a convention at the University of Wisconsin sometime between September 1 and 15, is extending invitations to hundreds of colleges and universities.

It would seem that for the first time in history, American students will have some instrument for expressing their thoughts, revealing their needs, and satisfying their legitimate requests. With the adoption of the constitution this September 3,000,000 students will be allied in the attempt to better the educational conditions in this country.

On a regional basis, the NSO is preparing to press for equality of education in the South. Already, regional committees elected at the Chicago conference have arranged interracial meetings. In Kentucky, the NSO is ready to challenge the state law prohibiting such meetings.

On the national level, the NSO plans to investigate and improve the academic, cultural, social and physical conditions of campus life.

On the international level, the NSO hopes to gain a seat on the United Nations Educational, Scientific, and Cultural Organization. (See page 1).

On all levels, it looks as if a fine beginning has been made. The continued success of the whole organization depends upon the sustained interest of the students on every campus in the nation.

"IT LOOKS AS IF A FINE BEGINNING HAS BEEN MADE," *The Columbia Spectator* wrote on 4/22/47 (left) as colleges around the country began to debate "Yes" or "No" to affiliation (Los Angeles City College *Collegian* 5/28/48). 700 delegates from 350 colleges gathered at the University of Wisconsin to hammer out a constitution. Photos from top left: (1) "Welcome Delegates" banner outside Student Union, (2) Delegates awaiting session outside Wisconsin Union, (3) Conference break. From left: Curtis Farrar (Yale U.), Merrill Freed (U. of Chicago), Bill Welsh (Berea C., KY), Bob Smith (Yale U.), (4) Plenary session in Union Theater, (5) Jim Smith (U. of Texas), President of National Continuations Committee, addressing Plenary Session. From right, Royal Voegeli, President of WI student body and Edwin R. Fred, U. of WI President.

136

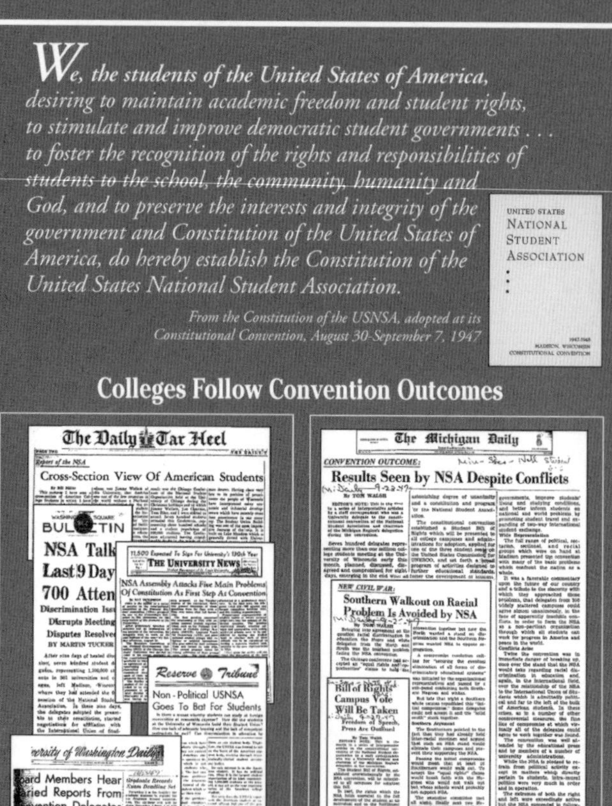

We, the students of the United States of America, desiring to maintain academic freedom and student rights, to stimulate and improve democratic student governments . . . to foster the recognition of the rights and responsibilities of students to the school, the community, humanity and God, and to preserve the interests and integrity of the government and Constitution of the United States of America, do hereby establish the Constitution of the United States National Student Association.

From the Constitution of the USNSA, adopted at its Constitutional Convention, August 30-September 7, 1947

Colleges Follow Convention Outcomes

Left, from top: U. of NC *Daily Tar Heel* 10/16/47. NYU *Washington Square Bulletin* 9/25/47. St. Louis U., MO. *The University News* 10/10/47. Western Reserve University, OH, *Reserve Tribune* 11/14/47. *University of Washington Daily* 10/23/47.

"NSA Goes to Bat for Students"

Above, from top: *Michigan Daily* 9/23/47, 9/25/47, 9/27/47

"Astonishing Degree of Unanimity"

137

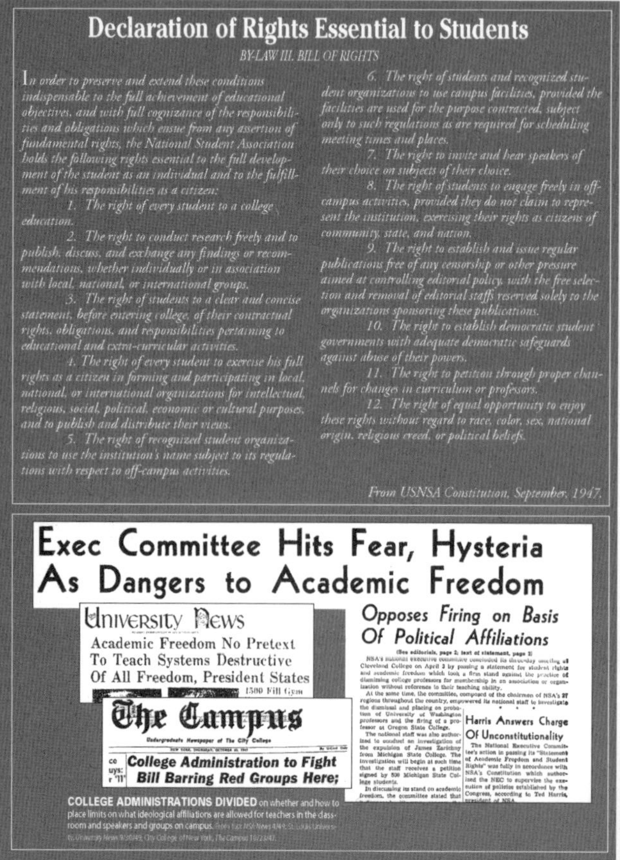

Declaration of Rights Essential to Students

BY-LAW III. BILL OF RIGHTS

In order to preserve and extend these conditions indispensable to the full achievement of educational objectives, and with full cognizance of the responsibilities and obligations which ensue from any assertion of fundamental rights, the National Student Association holds the following rights essential to the full development of the student as an individual and to the fulfillment of his responsibilities as a citizen:

1. *The right of every student to a college education.*
2. *The right to conduct research freely and to publish, discuss, and exchange any findings or recommendations, whether individually or in association with local, national, or international groups.*
3. *The right of students to a clear and concise statement, before entering college, of their contractual rights, obligations, and responsibilities pertaining to educational and extra-curricular activities.*
4. *The right of every student to exercise his full rights as a citizen in forming and participating in local, national, or international organizations for intellectual, religious, social, political, economic or cultural purposes, and to publish and distribute their views.*
5. *The right of recognized student organizations to use the institution's name subject to its regulations with respect to off-campus activities.*
6. *The right of students and recognized student organizations to use campus facilities, provided the facilities are used for the purpose contracted, subject only to such regulations as are required for scheduling meeting times and places.*
7. *The right to invite and hear speakers of their choice on subjects of their choice.*
8. *The right of students to engage freely in off-campus activities, provided they do not claim to represent the institution, exercising their rights as citizens of community, state, and nation.*
9. *The right to establish and issue regular publications free of any censorship or other pressure aimed at controlling editorial policy, with the free selection and removal of editorial staffs reserved solely to the organizations sponsoring these publications.*
10. *The right to establish democratic student governments with adequate democratic safeguards against abuse of their powers.*
11. *The right to petition through proper channels for changes in curriculum or professors.*
12. *The right of equal opportunity to enjoy these rights without regard to race, color, sex, national origin, religious creed, or political beliefs.*

From USNSA Constitution, September, 1947.

COLLEGE ADMINISTRATIONS DIVIDED on whether and how to place limits on what ideological affiliations are allowed for teachers in the classroom and speakers and groups on campus. From top: *NSA News* 4/49. St. Louis University, *University News* 9/30/49, City College of New York, *The Campus* 10/23/47.

374

Students Target Segregation, Race Relations, Quotas

Through the Courts

In Racial Practice

With Student Outreach

With Campus Drives

ELIMINATION OF SEGREGATED EDUCATION, RACIAL SCREENING AND QUOTAS became a national agenda in support of which a broad spectrum of religious, civil rights, higher education and student groups joined. During its early years NSA collaborated actively with many of them (see appendix for abbreviations): notably, the NAACP, NCCJ, NICC, NFCCS, ACLU, NSSFNS and the American Council on Education.

Left from the top: *Daily Texan*, 3/19/46; Berea College, KY *Wallpaper*, 2/6/50; Cover page, respondent's brief, Heman Sweatt photo, both Center for American Studies, U. of Texas Archives; *Maroon Tiger*, 10/48, Morehouse C., Atlanta; Los Angeles City College *Collegian*, 2/17/48, Xavier C., *LA Record*, 2/49. Right from the top: U. of MD *Diamondback*, 4/18/50; Columbia U. *Spectator*, 2/17/50; U. of Louisville *Cardinal*, 4/28/50; Temple U. 10/18/50; U. of NC *Tar Heel*, 10/18/50; U. of Buffalo *Bee*, 4/23/48; *Barnard Bulletin*, 11/19/51.

1947

The Vassar Miscellany News 12/10/47

Through Action Programs

420